ADVANCES IN NEURAL INFORMATION PROCESSING SYSTEMS 11

ADVANCES IN NEURAL INFORMATION PROCESSING SYSTEMS

Published by Morgan-Kaufmann

NIPS-1
Advances in Neural Information Processing Systems 1: Proceedings of the 1988 Conference,
David S. Touretzky, ed., 1989.

NIPS-2
Advances in Neural Information Processing Systems 2: Proceedings of the 1989 Conference,
David S. Touretzky, ed., 1990.

NIPS-3
Advances in Neural Information Processing Systems 3: Proceedings of the 1990 Conference,
Richard Lippmann, John E. Moody and David S. Touretzky, eds., 1991.

NIPS-4
Advances in Neural Information Processing Systems 4: Proceedings of the 1991 Conference,
John E. Moody, Stephen J. Hanson and Richard P. Lippmann, eds., 1992.

NIPS-5
Advances in Neural Information Processing Systems 5: Proceedings of the 1992 Conference,
Stephen J. Hanson, Jack D. Cowan and C. Lee Giles, eds., 1993.

NIPS-6
Advances in Neural Information Processing Systems 6: Proceedings of the 1993 Conference,
Jack D. Cowan, Gerald Tesauro and Joshua Alspector, eds., 1994.

Published by The MIT Press

NIPS-7
Advances in Neural Information Processing Systems 7: Proceedings of the 1994 Conference,
Gerald Tesauro, David S. Touretzky and Todd K. Leen, eds., 1995.

NIPS-8
Advances in Neural Information Processing Systems 8: Proceedings of the 1995 Conference,
David S. Touretzky, Michael C. Mozer and Michael E. Hasselmo, eds., 1996.

NIPS-9
Advances in Neural Information Processing Systems 9: Proceedings of the 1996 Conference,
Michael C. Mozer, Michael I. Jordan and Thomas Petsche, eds., 1997.

NIPS-10
Advances in Neural Information Processing Systems 10: Proceedings of the 1997 Conference,
Michael I. Jordan, Michael J. Kearns and Sara A. Solla, eds., 1998.

NIPS-11
Advances in Neural Information Processing Systems 11: Proceedings of the 1998 Conference,
Michael S. Kearns, Sara A. Solla and David A. Cohn, eds., 1999.

ADVANCES IN NEURAL INFORMATION PROCESSING SYSTEMS 11

Proceedings of the 1998 Conference

edited by
Michael S. Kearns, Sara A. Solla and David A. Cohn

A Bradford Book
The MIT Press
Cambridge, Massachusetts
London, England

© 1999 Massachusetts Institute of Technology

All rights reserved. No part of this book may be reproduced in any form by any electronic or mechanical means (including photocopying, recording or information storage and retrieval) without permission in writing from the publisher.

This book was printed and bound in the United States of America.

ISSN: 1049-5258
ISBN: 0-262-11245-0

Contents

Preface xv

NIPS Committees xvii

Reviewers xix

Part I Cognitive Science

Evidence for a Forward Dynamics Model in Human Adaptive Motor Control,
Nikhil Bhushan and Reza Shadmehr 3

Perceiving without Learning: From Spirals to Inside/Outside Relations,
Ke Chen and DeLiang L. Wang 10

A Model for Associative Multiplication,
G. Björn Christianson and Suzanna Becker 17

Facial Memory Is Kernel Density Estimation (Almost),
Matthew N. Dailey, Garrison W. Cottrell and Thomas A. Busey 24

*Multiple Paired Forward-Inverse Models for Human Motor Learning and
Control*, Masahiko Haruno, Daniel M. Wolpert and Mitsuo Kawato 31

Utilizing Time: Asynchronous Binding, Bradley C. Love 38

Mechanisms of Generalization in Perceptual Learning,
Zili Liu and Daphna Weinshall 45

A Principle for Unsupervised Hierarchical Decomposition of Visual Scenes,
Michael C. Mozer 52

Bayesian Modeling of Human Concept Learning, Joshua B. Tenenbaum 59

Part II Neuroscience

*Temporally Asymmetric Hebbian Learning, Spike Timing and Neural Response
Variability*, L. F. Abbott and Sen Song 69

*Contrast Adaptation in Simple Cells by Changing the Transmitter Release
Probability*, Peter Adorján and Klaus Obermayer 76

*Where Does the Population Vector of Motor Cortical Cells Point during
Reaching Movements?*, Pierre Baraduc, Emmanuel Guigon and Yves Burnod . . . 83

Recurrent Cortical Amplification Produces Complex Cell Responses,
Frances S. Chance, Sacha B. Nelson and L. F. Abbott 90

Neuronal Regulation Implements Efficient Synaptic Pruning,
Gal Chechik, Isaac Meilijson and Eytan Ruppin 97

Divisive Normalization, Line Attractor Networks and Ideal Observers,
Sophie Deneve, Alexandre Pouget and Peter E. Latham 104

Synergy and Redundancy among Brain Cells of Behaving Monkeys,
Itay Gat and Naftali Tishby 111

Analyzing and Visualizing Single-Trial Event-Related Potentials,
Tzyy-Ping Jung, Scott Makeig, Marissa Westerfield, Jeanne Townsend,
Eric Courchesne and Terrence J. Sejnowski 118

Spike-Based Compared to Rate-Based Hebbian Learning,
Richard Kempter, Wulfram Gerstner and J. Leo van Hemmen 125

Signal Detection in Noisy Weakly-Active Dendrites,
Amit Manwani and Christof Koch 132

The Role of Lateral Cortical Competition in Ocular Dominance Development,
Christian Piepenbrock and Klaus Obermayer 139

Multi-Electrode Spike Sorting by Clustering Transfer Functions,
Dmitry Rinberg, Hanan Davidowitz and Naftali Tishby 146

Modeling Surround Suppression in V1 Neurons with a Statistically Derived Normalization Model, Eero P. Simoncelli and Odelia Schwartz 153

Information Maximization in Single Neurons,
Martin Stemmler and Christof Koch 160

The Effect of Correlations on the Fisher Information of Population Codes,
Hyoungsoo Yoon and Haim Sompolinsky 167

Distributional Population Codes and Multiple Motion Models,
Richard S. Zemel and Peter Dayan 174

Part III Theory

Tractable Variational Structures for Approximating Graphical Models,
David Barber and Wim Wiegerinck 183

Almost Linear VC Dimension Bounds for Piecewise Polynomial Networks,
Peter L. Bartlett, Vitaly Maiorov and Ron Meir 190

Dynamics of Supervised Learning with Restricted Training Sets,
A. C. C. Coolen and David Saad 197

Dynamically Adapting Kernels in Support Vector Machines,
Nello Cristianini, Colin Campbell and John Shawe-Taylor 204

Phase Diagram and Storage Capacity of Sequence-Storing Neural Networks,
A. Düring, A. C. C. Coolen and D. Sherrington 211

Finite-Dimensional Approximation of Gaussian Processes,
Giancarlo Ferrari-Trecate, Christopher K. I. Williams and Manfred Opper 218

Linear Hinge Loss and Average Margin,
Claudio Gentile and Manfred K. Warmuth 225

Unsupervised and Supervised Clustering: The Mutual Information between Parameters and Observations, Didier Herschkowitz and Jean-Pierre Nadal 232

Convergence of the Wake-Sleep Algorithm,
Shiro Ikeda, Shun-ichi Amari and Hiroyuki Nakahara 239

The Belief in TAP, Yoshiyuki Kabashima and David Saad 246

Optimizing Classifers for Imbalanced Training Sets,
Grigoris Karakoulas and John Shawe-Taylor 253

Inference in Multilayer Networks via Large Deviation Bounds,
Michael Kearns and Lawrence Saul 260

Stationarity and Stability of Autoregressive Neural Network Processes,
Friedrich Leisch, Adrian Trapletti and Kurt Hornik 267

Computational Differences between Asymmetrical and Symmetrical Networks,
Zhaoping Li and Peter Dayan 274

A Precise Characterization of the Class of Languages Recognized by Neural Nets under Gaussian and Other Common Noise Distributions
Wolfgang Maass and Eduardo D. Sontag 281

Direct Optimization of Margins Improves Generalization in Combined Classifiers, Llew Mason, Peter L. Bartlett and Jonathan Baxter 288

On the Optimality of Incremental Neural Network Algorithms,
Ron Meir and Vitaly Maiorov 295

General Bounds on Bayes Errors for Regression with Gaussian Processes,
Manfred Opper and Francesco Vivarelli 302

Mean Field Methods for Classification with Gaussian Processes,
Manfred Opper and Ole Winther 309

On Line Learning with Restricted Training Sets: Exact Solution as Benchmark for General Theories, H. C. Rae, Peter Sollich and A. C. C. Coolen 316

Tight Bounds for the VC-Dimension of Piecewise Polynomial Networks,
Akito Sakurai 323

Shrinking the Tube: A New Support Vector Regression Algorithm,
Bernhard Schölkopf, Peter L. Bartlett, Alex J. Smola and Robert Williamson . . . 330

Discontinuous Recall Transitions Induced by Competition Between Short- and Long-Range Interactions in Recurrent Networks,
N. S. Skantzos, C. F. Beckmann and A. C. C. Coolen 337

Learning Curves for Gaussian Processes, Peter Sollich 344

A Theory of Mean Field Approximation, Toshiyuki Tanaka 351

Part IV Algorithms and Architecture

Learning a Hierarchical Belief Network of Independent Factor Analyzers,
Hagai Attias 361

Semi-Supervised Support Vector Machines, Kristin Bennett and Ayhan Demiriz . . 368

Lazy Learning Meets the Recursive Least Squares Algorithm,
Mauro Birattari, Gianluca Bontempi and Hugues Bersini 375

Bayesian PCA, Christopher M. Bishop 382

Learning Multi-Class Dynamics, Andrew Blake, Ben North and Michael Isard . . 389

Approximate Learning of Dynamic Models, Xavier Boyen and Daphne Koller . . . 396

Fisher Scoring and a Mixture of Modes Approach for Approximate Inference and Learning in Nonlinear State Space Models, Thomas Briegel and Volker Tresp . . . 403

Global Optimisation of Neural Network Models via Sequential Sampling,
João F. G. de Freitas, Mahesan Niranjan, Arnaud Doucet and Andrew H. Gee . . . 410

Efficient Bayesian Parameter Estimation in Large Discrete Domains,
Nir Friedman and Yoram Singer 417

A Randomized Algorithm for Pairwise Clustering,
Yoram Gdalyahu, Daphna Weinshall and Michael Werman 424

Learning Nonlinear Dynamical Systems Using an EM Algorithm,
Zoubin Ghahramani and Sam T. Roweis 431

Classification on Pairwise Proximity Data,
Thore Graepel, Ralf Herbrich, Peter Bollmann-Sdorra and Klaus Obermayer . . . 438

Outcomes of the Equivalence of Adaptive Ridge with Least Absolute Shrinkage,
Yves Grandvalet and Stéphane Canu 445

Visualizing Group Structure,
Marcus Held, Jan Puzicha and Joachim M. Buhmann 452

Source Separation as a By-Product of Regularization,
Sepp Hochreiter and Jürgen Schmidhuber 459

Learning from Dyadic Data,
Thomas Hofmann, Jan Puzicha and Michael I. Jordan 466

Sparse Code Shrinkage: Denoising by Nonlinear Maximum Likelihood Estimation, Aapo Hyvärinen, Patrik Hoyer and Erkki Oja 473

Restructuring Sparse High Dimensional Data for Effective Retrieval,
Charles Lee Isbell, Jr. and Paul Viola 480

Exploiting Generative Models in Discriminative Classifiers,
Tommi S. Jaakkola and David Haussler 487

Maximum Conditional Likelihood via Bound Maximization and the CEM Algorithm, Tony Jebara and Alex Pentland 494

A Polygonal Line Algorithm for Constructing Principal Curves,
Balázs Kégl, Adam Krzyżak, Tamás Linder and Kenneth Zeger 501

Unsupervised Classification with Non-Gaussian Mixture Models Using ICA,
Te-Won Lee, Michael S. Lewicki and Terrence J. Sejnowski 508

Learning a Continuous Hidden Variable Model for Binary Data,
Daniel D. Lee and Haim Sompolinsky 515

Neural Networks for Density Estimation, Malik Magdon-Ismail and Amir Atiya . . 522

Exploratory Data Analysis Using Radial Basis Function Latent Variable Models, Alan D. Marrs and Andrew R. Webb 529

Kernel PCA and De-Noising in Feature Spaces, Sebastian Mika, Bernhard Schölkopf, Alex J. Smola, Klaus-Robert Müller, Matthias Scholz and Gunnar Rätsch 536

Very Fast EM-Based Mixture Model Clustering Using Multiresolution Kd-Trees, Andrew W. Moore 543

Replicator Equations, Maximal Cliques, and Graph Isomorphism, Marcello Pelillo 550

Using Analytic QP and Sparseness to Speed Training of Support Vector Machines, John C. Platt 557

Regularizing AdaBoost, Gunnar Rätsch, Takashi Onoda and Klaus-Robert Müller . 564

Boxlets: A Fast Convolution Algorithm for Signal Processing and Neural Networks, Patrice Y. Simard, Léon Bottou, Patrick Haffner and Yann Le Cun . . . 571

Batch and On-Line Parameter Estimation of Gaussian Mixtures Based on the Joint Entropy, Yoram Singer and Manfred K. Warmuth 578

Semiparametric Support Vector and Linear Programming Machines, Alex J. Smola, Thilo T. Frieß and Bernhard Schölkopf 585

Probabilistic Visualisation of High-Dimensional Binary Data, Michael E. Tipping 592

SMEM Algorithm for Mixture Models, Naonori Ueda, Ryohei Nakano, Zoubin Ghahramani and Geoffrey E. Hinton . . . 599

Learning Mixture Hierarchies, Nuno Vasconcelos and Andrew Lippman 606

Discovering Hidden Features with Gaussian Processes Regression, Francesco Vivarelli and Christopher K. I. Williams 613

The Bias-Variance Tradeoff and the Randomized GACV, Grace Wahba, Xiwu Lin, Fangyu Gao, Dong Xiang, Ronald Klein and Barbara Klein 620

Basis Selection for Wavelet Regression, Kevin R. Wheeler and Atam P. Dhawan . . 627

DTs: Dynamic Trees, Christopher K. I. Williams and Nicholas J. Adams 634

Convergence Rates of Algorithms for Visual Search: Detecting Visual Contours, A. L. Yuille and James M. Coughlan 641

Blind Separation of Filtered Sources Using State-Space Approach, Liqing Zhang and Andrzej Cichocki 648

Part V Implementation

Analog VLSI Cellular Implementation of the Boundary Contour System, Gert Cauwenberghs and James Waskiewicz 657

Active Noise Canceling Using Analog Neuro-Chip with On-Chip Learning Capability, Jung-Wook Cho and Soo-Young Lee 664

A Micropower CMOS Adaptive Amplitude and Shift Invariant Vector Quantiser, Richard J. Coggins, Raymond J. W. Wang and Marwan A. Jabri 671

Optimizing Correlation Algorithms for Hardware-Based Transient Classification, R. Timothy Edwards, Gert Cauwenberghs and Fernando J. Pineda 678

VLSI Implementation of Motion Centroid Localization for Autonomous Navigation, Ralph Etienne-Cummings, Viktor Gruev and Mohammed Abdel Ghani 685

A Neuromorphic Monaural Sound Localizer, John G. Harris, Chiang-Jung Pu and Jose C. Principe 692

An Integrated Vision Sensor for the Computation of Optical Flow Singular Points, Charles M. Higgins and Christof Koch 699

Computation of Smooth Optical Flow in a Feedback Connected Analog Network, Alan Stocker and Rodney Douglas 706

A High Performance k-NN Classifier Using a Binary Correlation Matrix Memory, Ping Zhou, Jim Austin and John Kennedy 713

Part VI Speech, Handwriting and Signal Processing

An Entropic Estimator for Structure Discovery, Matthew Brand 723

Coding Time-Varying Signals Using Sparse, Shift-Invariant Representations, Michael S. Lewicki and Terrence J. Sejnowski 730

Controlling the Complexity of HMM Systems by Regularization, Christoph Neukirchen and Gerhard Rigoll 737

Maximum-Likelihood Continuity Mapping (MALCOM): An Alternative to HMMs, David A. Nix and John E. Hogden 744

Markov Processes on Curves for Automatic Speech Recognition, Lawrence Saul and Mazin Rahim 751

Part VII Visual Processing

A Phase Space Approach to Minimax Entropy Learning and the Minutemax Approximations, James M. Coughlan and A. L. Yuille 761

Example-Based Image Synthesis of Articulated Figures, Trevor Darrell 768

Learning to Estimate Scenes from Images, William T. Freeman and Egon C. Pasztor 775

Learning to Find Pictures of People, Sergey Ioffe and David Forsyth 782

Attentional Modulation of Human Pattern Discrimination Psychophysics Reproduced by a Quantitative Model, Laurent Itti, Jochen Braun, Dale K. Lee and Christof Koch 789

A V1 Model of Pop Out and Asymmetry in Visual Search, Zhaoping Li 796

Support Vector Machines Applied to Face Recognition, P. Jonathon Phillips 803

Learning Lie Groups for Invariant Visual Perception,
Rajesh P. N. Rao and Daniel L. Ruderman 810

General-Purpose Localization of Textured Image Regions, Ruth Rosenholtz 817

Probabilistic Image Sensor Fusion,
Ravi K. Sharma, Todd K. Leen and Misha Pavel 824

Orientation, Scale, and Discontinuity as Emergent Properties of Illusory Contour Shape, Karvel K. Thornber and Lance R. Williams 831

Classification in Non-Metric Spaces,
Daphna Weinshall, David W. Jacobs and Yoram Gdalyahu 838

Part VIII Applications

Making Templates Rotationally Invariant: An Application to Rotated Digit Recognition, Shumeet Baluja 847

Probabilistic Modeling for Face Orientation Discrimination: Learning from Labeled and Unlabeled Data, Shumeet Baluja 854

Adding Constrained Discontinuities to Gaussian Process Models of Wind Fields,
Dan Cornford, Ian T. Nabney and Christopher K. I. Williams 861

Vertex Identification in High Energy Physics Experiments,
Gideon Dror, Halina Abramowicz and David Horn 868

Familiarity Discrimination of Radar Pulses,
Eric Granger, Stephen Grossberg, Mark A. Rubin and William W. Streilein 875

Fast Neural Network Emulation of Dynamical Systems for Computer Animation,
Radek Grzeszczuk, Demetri Terzopoulos and Geoffrey E. Hinton 882

Call-Based Fraud Detection in Mobile Communication Networks Using a Hierarchical Regime-Switching Model, Jaakko Hollmén and Volker Tresp 889

Graph Matching for Shape Retrieval,
Benoit Huet, Andrew D. J. Cross and Edwin R. Hancock 896

Scheduling Straight-Line Code Using Reinforcement Learning and Rollouts,
Amy McGovern and Eliot Moss 903

Bayesian Modeling of Facial Similarity,
Baback Moghaddam, Tony Jebara and Alex Pentland 910

Reinforcement Learning for Trading, John Moody and Matthew Saffell 917

Graphical Models for Recognizing Human Interactions,
Nuria M. Oliver, Barbara Rosario and Alex Pentland 924

Independent Component Analysis of Intracellular Calcium Spike Data,
Klaus Prank, Julia Börger, Alexander von zur Mühlen, Georg Brabant and
Christof Schöfl 931

Applications of Multi-Resolution Neural Networks to Mammography,
Clay D. Spence and Paul Sajda 938

Robot Docking Using Mixtures of Gaussians,
Matthew M. Williamson, Roderick Murray-Smith and Volker Hansen 945

Using Collective Intelligence to Route Internet Traffic,
David H. Wolpert, Kagan Tumer and Jeremy Frank 952

Part IX Control, Navigation and Planning

Robust, Efficient, Globally-Optimized Reinforcement Learning with the Parti-Game Algorithm, Mohammad A. Al-Ansari and Ronald J. Williams 961

Gradient Descent for General Reinforcement Learning,
Leemon Baird and Andrew W. Moore 968

Non-Linear PI Control Inspired by Biological Control Systems,
Lyndon J. Brown, Gregory E. Gonye and James S. Schwaber 975

Optimizing Admission Control while Ensuring Quality of Service in Multimedia Networks via Reinforcement Learning,
Timothy X. Brown, Hui Tong and Satinder Singh 982

Viewing Classifier Systems as Model Free Learning in POMDPs,
Akira Hayashi and Nobuo Suematsu 989

Finite-Sample Convergence Rates for Q-Learning and Indirect Algorithms,
Michael Kearns and Satinder Singh 996

Exploring Unknown Environments with Real-Time Search or Reinforcement Learning, Sven Koenig 1003

The Effect of Eligibility Traces on Finding Optimal Memoryless Policies in Partially Observable Markov Decision Processes, John Loch 1010

Learning Instance-Independent Value Functions to Enhance Local Search,
Robert Moll, Andrew G. Barto, Theodore J. Perkins and Richard S. Sutton . . 1017

Barycentric Interpolators for Continuous Space and Time Reinforcement Learning, Rémi Munos and Andrew W. Moore 1024

Risk Sensitive Reinforcement Learning, Ralph Neuneier and Oliver Mihatsch . . 1031

Coordinate Transformation Learning of Hand Position Feedback Controller by Using Change of Position Error Norm, Eimei Oyama and Susumu Tachi 1038

Learning Macro-Actions in Reinforcement Learning, Jette Randløv 1045

Reinforcement Learning Based on On-Line EM Algorithm,
Masa-aki Sato and Shin Ishii 1052

A Reinforcement Learning Algorithm in Partially Observable Environments Using Short-Term Memory, Nobuo Suematsu and Akira Hayashi 1059

Improved Switching among Temporally Abstract Actions,
Richard S. Sutton, Satinder Singh, Doina Precup and Balaraman Ravindran . . 1066

Experimental Results on Learning Stochastic Memoryless Policies for Partially Observable Markov Decision Processes, John K. Williams and Satinder Singh . . 1073

Index of Authors 1081

Keyword Index 1085

Preface

This volume contains the papers presented at the Twelfth Annual Conference on Neural Information Processing Systems (NIPS), held in Denver, Colorado from November 30 to December 5, 1998. These papers cover a wide range of topics in neural computation, including the design and analysis of learning algorithms, learning theory, reinforcement learning, neuroscience, cognitive science, vision, speech, VLSI implementations, and applications in areas such as artificial intelligence, applied statistics, pattern recognition, signal processing, control, finance, and data analysis.

Paper selection was competitive and based on the reports of three specific referees per paper, and the global recommendations of the members of the Program Committee. This year we evaluated 474 submissions to select the 150 papers included in this volume. The NIPS acceptance ratio continues to be lower than that of many journals; many good papers are left out due to limitations imposed by the length of the Conference and the size of the Proceedings. In a clear indication of the intellectual health of the conference and the expected high quality of the accepted papers, attendance remains high at about 500 participants. In addition to loyal followers, we are glad to welcome new faces every year, as we rely on the infusion of new ideas and new approaches to maintain the sense of excitement that is the hallmark of NIPS. It is in this spirit that the NIPS Foundation provided financial support to allow many graduate students and young investigators to attend the meeting.

NIPS brings together top scientists with broadly varying backgrounds, such as statistics, mathematics, computer science, physics, electrical engineering, neuroscience, and cognitive science, unified by a common desire to understand the mechanisms for information processing in the brain, and to apply this knowledge to the design of new and efficient computational and statistical strategies. Annual gatherings with a single track format for oral sessions, complemented by very lively posters sessions, have led over the years to the development of an interdisciplinary and highly interactive community, characterized by a fruitful exchange of ideas between participants interested in theory, algorithms, applications, and implementations. The conference continues to grow and evolve in ways that reflect the changing needs and interests of its constituency. A scan of the preceding NIPS volumes provides an inspiring survey of the fast-paced development of the field over the past 12 years; NIPS both reflects and contributes to this vibrant scientific enterprise.

In addition to the strong program of contributed papers included here, the conference featured a lively schedule of invited speakers. Bernardo Huberman of Xerox PARC gave the banquet talk on "The Laws of the Web"; additional invited talks were given by Eero Simoncelli of New York University on "Cortical Normalization Models and the Statistics of Visual Images," Larry Abbott of Brandeis University on "Temporally Asymmetric Hebbian Learning, Spike Timing, and Neural Response Variability," Haim Sompolinsky of Hebrew University on "Computation by Cortical Modules," Eugene Charniak of Brown University on "Statistical Natural Language Processing: Better Living Through Floating-point Numbers," and Neil Gershenfeld of MIT on "Things That Think."

As is traditional, the main conference was followed by two days of intensive workshops on a collection of topics that reflect the diversity of NIPS, and preceded by a day of tutorials that provide a pedagogical introduction to topics of current interest. This year we heard from William Bialek of NEC Research on "Do We Understand the Neural Code?," Jean-François Cardoso of CNRS and ENST, Paris, on "Independent Component Analysis and

Blind Separation of Signals," Henry Markram of the Weizmann Institute on "Neocortical Synapses," Peter Bartlett of the Australian National University on "Learning Theory and Generalization for Neural Networks and Other Supervised Learning Techniques," Daniel Kersten of the University of Minnesota on "Computational Vision: Principles of Perceptual Inference," and Joachim Buhmann of the University of Bonn on "Exploratory Data Analysis and Data Visualization."

The continued success of NIPS is the result of the parallel and distributed effort of many devoted individuals. We extend our thanks to the members of the organizing committee, the program committee, the publicity committee and the NIPS Foundation board. Special gratitude is due to the 191 referees whose integrated efforts led to the superb conference program presented here, and to the authors who provided the high quality material upon which the program was built. Thanks to the workshop chairs Richard Zemel and Sue Becker, tutorials chair Klaus-Robert Müller, publicity chair Jon Baxter, treasurer Bartlett Mel, and local arrangements chair Arun Jagota. A special thanks to Thomas Petsche, who in his role of Publication Chair for NIPS*96 developed an excellent and comprehensive set of formatting tools for the production of both the Conference Program and the NIPS Proceedings. Finally, we are particularly grateful to Rosemary Miller and Kathie Hibbard for their stellar work with all aspects of the conference logistics, from registration and administration to dinner menus and poster arrangements; we also thank the many student volunteers who assisted them on site. Special thanks to Kathleen Burgess for her highly efficient and reliable help with the monumental task of processing the submitted papers, and to Pamela Hawkins for her invaluable assistance with the coordination of the tasks of the program committee.

We hope that the papers will provide useful and enjoyable reading, and we look forward to seeing you all at the many NIPS to come!

Michael S. Kearns, AT&T Labs – Research
Sara A. Solla, Northwestern University
David A. Cohn, Just Research

January 1999

NIPS Committees

Organizing Committee

General Chair	*Michael S. Kearns*, AT&T Labs – Research
Program Chair	*Sara A. Solla*, Northwestern University
Workshop Co-Chairs	*Richard Zemel*, University of Arizona
	Sue Becker, McMaster University
Tutorials Chair	*Klaus Mueller*, GMD FIRST
Publicity Chair	*Jonathan Baxter*, Australian National University
Publications Chair	*David A. Cohn*, Harlequin, Inc. and Just Research
Treasurer	*Bartlett Mel*, University of Southern California
Local Arrangements Chair	*Arun Jagota*, University of California, Santa Cruz
Contracts	*Scott Kirkpatrick*, IBM Watson Labs
	Gerald Tesauro, IBM Watson Labs
Web Master	*Doug Baker*, Carnegie Mellon University

Program Committee

Program Chair	*Sara A. Solla*, Northwestern University
Program Co-chairs	*Andrew Barto*, University of Massachusetts, Amherst
	Joachim Buhmann, University of Bonn
	Lars Kai Hansen, Danish Technical University
	Nathan Intrator, Tel-Aviv University
	Robert Jacobs, University of Rochester
	Esther Levin, AT&T Labs – Research
	Alexandre Pouget, Georgetown University
	David Saad, Aston University
	Lawrence Saul, AT&T Labs – Research
	Sebastian Thrun, Carnegie Mellon University
	Manfred K. Warmuth, University of California, Santa Cruz
	Yair Weiss, Massachusetts Institute of Technology

Publicity Committee

Publicity Chair *Jonathan Baxter*, Australian National University
Liaisons
Australia, Singapore and India *Marwan Jabri*, University of Sydney
Europe *Joachim Buhmann*, University of Bonn
Hong Kong, China and Taiwan *Lei Xu*, Chinese University of Hong Kong
Israel *Hava Siegelmann*, Technion
Japan *Kenji Doya*, ATR Research Laboratories
Turkey *Ethem Alpaydin*, Bogazici University
United Kingdom *Alan Murray*, Edinburgh University
South America *Andreas Meier*, Simon Bolivar University

NIPS Foundation Board Members

President *Terrence Sejnowski*, The Salk Institute
Vice President for Development *Gary Blasdel*, Harvard Medical School
Treasurer *Eric Mjolsness*, Jet Propulsion Laboratory
Secretary *Gerald Tesauro*, IBM Watson Labs
Members *Leo Breiman*, University of California, Berkeley
 Jack Cowan, University of Chicago
 Stephen J. Hanson, Rutgers University
 Michael I. Jordan, University of California, Berkeley
 Scott Kirkpatrick, IBM Watson Labs
 Richard Lippmann, MIT Lincoln Laboratory
 John Moody, Oregon Graduate Institute
 Michael Mozer, University of Colorado, Boulder
 Dave Touretzky, Carnegie Mellon University
Emeritus *Terrence Fine*, Cornell University
 Eve Marder, Brandeis University
NIPS*98 General Chair *Michael S. Kearns*, AT&T Labs – Research

Reviewers

Tulay Adali
Shunichi Amari
Chuck Anderson
James Anderson
Martin Anthony
Chris Atkeson
Andrew Back
Wyeth Bair
Leemon Baird
Pierre Baldi
Dana Ballard
Shumeet Baluja
David Barber
Peter Bartlett
Eric Baum
Jonathan Baxter
Tony Bell
Yoshua Bengio
Michael Berry
Michael Biehl
Christopher Bishop
Avrim Blum
Leon Bottou
Herve Bourlard
Craig Boutilier
Justin Boyan
Matthew Brand
Christoph Bregler
Emanuela Bricolo
Timothy Brown
Nicolas Brunel
Nader Bshouty
Christopher Burges
Neil Burgess
Matteo Carandini
Richard Caruana
Nestor Caticha
Gert Cauwenberghs
Nicolo Cesa-Bianchi
Eric Chang
Andrzej Cichocki
Ton Coolen
Corinna Cortes

Gary Cottrell
Mark Craven
Trevor Darrell
Gustavo Deco
Michael Denham
Joachim Diederich
Thomas Dietterich
Leif Finkel
Jozsef Fiser
Paolo Frasconi
William Freeman
Brendan Frey
Nir Friedman
Juergen Fritsch
Bernd Fritzke
Patrick Gallinari
Zoubin Ghahramani
C. Lee Giles
Moises Goldszmidt
Geoffrey Goodhill
Michael Gray
Edwin Hancock
John Harris
Simon Haykin
David Heckerman
John Hertz
Tom Heskes
Thomas Hofmann
David Horn
Yu Hen Hu
Michael Isard
Tommi Jaakkola
Marwan Jabri
Charles Jankowski
Nathalie Japkowicz
Thorsten Joachims
Michael Jordan
Yoshiyuki Kabashima
Leslie Kaelbling
Bert Kappen
Shigeru Katagiri
Mitsuo Kawato
Daniel Kersten

Hiroaki Kitano
Adam Kowalczyk
Stefan Kremer
John Kruschke
Tor Sverre Lande
Jan Larsen
Peter Latham
John Lazzaro
Yann LeCun
Daniel Lee
Tai-Sing Lee
Te-Won Lee
Todd Leen
Torsten Lehmann
Nick Littlestone
Michael Littman
David Lowe
Gabor Lugosi
Sridhar Mahadevan
Maja Mataric
Andrew McCallum
Ron Meir
Bartlett Mel
David Miller
Kenneth Miller
Melanie Mitchell
Tom Mitchell
Baback Moghaddam
Andrew Moore
Javier Movellan
Michael Mozer
Klaus Mueller
Paul Munro
Noboru Murata
Alan Murray
Rod Murray-Smith
Jean-Pierre Nadal
Kenny Ng
Klaus Obermayer
Erkki Oja
John Oliensis
Bruno Olshausen
Manfred Opper

Guenther Palm
Ronald Parr
Barak Pearlmutter
Fernando Pereira
Michael Perrone
Thomas Petsche
Roberto Pieraccini
Jose Principe
Mazin Rahim
Anand Rangarajan
Rajesh Rao
Carl Rasmussen
A. David Redish
Pamela Reinagel
Thomas Richardson
Tony Robinson
Dan Roth
Sam Roweis
Henry Rowley
Philip Sabes
Maneesh Sahani

Eric Saund
Stefan Schaal
Rob Schapire
Jeff Schneider
Bernhard Schölkopf
Holger Schwenk
Sebastian Seung
Jude Shavlik
John Shawe-Taylor
Patrice Simard
Eero Simoncelli
Yoram Singer
Satinder Singh
Padhraic Smyth
Peter Sollich
Michael Spivey
Richard Sutton
Csaba Szepesvari
Michiaki Taniguchi
Josh Tenenbaum

Michael Tipping
Naftali Tishby
Mike Titterington
Geoffrey Towell
Volker Tresp
Todd Troyer
Ian Underwood
Chris van den Broeck
Marc Van Hulle
Nuno Vasconcelos
Paul Viola
Vladimir Vovk
Yuedong Wang
Daphna Weinshall
Wim Wiegerinck
Christopher Williams
Ronald Williams
Laurenz Wiskott
Robin Woodburn
Richard Zemel
Kechen Zhang

Part I
Cognitive Science

Evidence for a Forward Dynamics Model in Human Adaptive Motor Control

Nikhil Bhushan and Reza Shadmehr
Dept. of Biomedical Engineering
Johns Hopkins University, Baltimore, MD 21205
Email: nbhushan@bme.jhu.edu, reza@bme.jhu.edu

Abstract

Based on computational principles, the concept of an internal model for adaptive control has been divided into a forward and an inverse model. However, there is as yet little evidence that learning control by the CNS is through adaptation of one or the other. Here we examine two adaptive control architectures, one based only on the inverse model and other based on a combination of forward and inverse models. We then show that for reaching movements of the hand in novel force fields, only the learning of the forward model results in key characteristics of performance that match the kinematics of human subjects. In contrast, the adaptive control system that relies only on the inverse model fails to produce the kinematic patterns observed in the subjects, despite the fact that it is more stable. Our results provide evidence that learning control of novel dynamics is via formation of a forward model.

1 Introduction

The concept of an internal model, a system for predicting behavior of a controlled process, is central to the current theories of motor control (Wolpert et al. 1995) and learning (Shadmehr and Mussa-Ivaldi 1994). Theoretical studies have proposed that internal models may be divided into two varieties: forward models, which simulate the causal flow of a process by predicting its state transition given a motor command, and inverse models, which estimate motor commands appropriate for a desired state transition (Miall and Wolpert, 1996). This classification is relevant for adaptive control because based on computational principles, it has been proposed that learning control of a nonlinear system might be facilitated if a forward model of the plant is learned initially, and then during an off-line period is used to train an inverse model (Jordan and Rumelhart, 1992). While there is no experimental evidence for this idea in the central nervous system, there is substantial evidence that learning control of arm movements involves formation of an internal model. For example, practicing arm movements while holding a novel dynamical system initiates an adaptation process which results in the formation of an internal model: upon sudden removal of the force field, after-effects are observed which match the expected behavior of a system that has learned to predict and compensate for the dynamics of the imposed field (Shadmehr and Brashers-Krug, 1997). However, the computational nature of this internal model, whether it be a forward or an inverse model, or a combination of both, is not known.

Here we use a computational approach to examine two adaptive control architectures: adaptive inverse model feedforward control and adaptive forward-inverse model feedback control. We show that the two systems predict different behaviors when applied to control of arm movements. While adaptation to a force field is possible with either approach, the second system with feedback control through an adaptive forward model, is far less stable and is accompanied with distinct kinematic signatures, termed "near path-discontinuities". We observe remarkably similar instability and near path-discontinuities in the kinematics of 16 subjects that learned force fields. This is behavioral evidence that learning control of novel dynamics is accomplished with an adaptive forward model of the system.

2 Adaptive Control using Internal Models

Adaptive control of a nonlinear system which has large sensory feedback delays, such as the human arm, can be accomplished by using two different internal model architectures. The first method uses only an adaptive inverse dynamics model to control the system (Shadmehr and Mussa-Ivaldi, 1994). The adaptive controller is feedforward in nature and ignores delayed feedback during the movement. The control system is stable because it relies on the equilibrium properties of the muscle and the spinal reflexes to correct for any deviations from the desired trajectory. The second method uses a rapidly adapting forward dynamics model and delayed sensory feedback in addition to an inverse dynamics model to control arm movements (Miall and Wolpert, 1996). In this case, the corrections to deviations from the desired trajectory are a result of a combination of supraspinal feedback as well as spinal/muscular feedback. Since the two methods rely on different internal model and feedback structures, they are expected to behave differently when the dynamics of the system are altered.

The Mechanical Model of the Human Arm

For the purpose of simulating arm movements with the two different control architectures, a reasonably accurate model of the human arm is required. We model the arm as a two joint revolute arm attached to six muscles that act in pairs around the two joints. The three muscle pairs correspond to elbow joint, shoulder joint and two joint muscles and are assumed to have constant moment arms. Each muscle is modeled using a Hill parametric model with nonlinear stiffness and viscosity (Soechting and Flanders, 1997). The dynamics of the muscle can be represented by a nonlinear state function f_M, such that,

$$F_t = f_M(N, x_m, \dot{x}_m) \qquad (1)$$

where, F_t is the force developed by the muscle, N is the neural activation to the muscle, and x_m, $\dot{x}_m$ are the muscle length and velocity. The passive dynamics related to the mechanics of the two-joint revolute arm can be represented by f_D, such that,

$$\ddot{x} = f_D(T, x, \dot{x}) = D^{-1}(x)[T - C(x, \dot{x})\dot{x} + J^T F_x] \qquad (2)$$

where, $\ddot{x}$ is the hand acceleration, T is the joint torque generated by the muscles, x, $\dot{x}$ are the hand position and velocity, D and C are the inertia and the coriolis matrices of the arm, J is the Jacobian for hand position and joint angle, and F_x is the external dynamic interaction force on the hand.

Under the force field environment, the external force F_x acting on the hand is equal to $B\dot{x}$, where B is a 2x2 rotational viscosity matrix. The effect of the force field is to push the hand perpendicular to the direction of movement with a force proportional to the speed of the hand. The overall forward plant dynamics of the arm is a combination of f_M and f_D and can be represented by the function f_p,

$$\ddot{x} = f_p(N, x, \dot{x}) \tag{3}$$

Adaptive Inverse Model Feedforward Control

The first control architecture uses a feedforward controller with only an adaptive inverse model. The inverse model computes the neural activation to the muscles for achieving a desired acceleration, velocity and position of the hand. It can be represented as the estimated inverse, $\hat{f}_p^{-1}$, of the forward plant dynamics, and maps the desired position x_d, velocity $\dot{x}_d$, and acceleration $\ddot{x}_d$ of the hand, into descending neural commands N_C.

$$N_C = \hat{f}_p^{-1}(\ddot{x}_d, x_d, \dot{x}_d) \tag{4}$$

Adaptation to novel external dynamics occurs by learning a new inverse model of the altered external environment. The error between desired and actual hand trajectory can be used for training the inverse model. When the inverse model is an exact inverse of the forward plant dynamics, the gain of the feedforward path is unity and the arm exactly tracks the desired trajectory. Deviations from the desired trajectory occur when the inverse model does not exactly model the external dynamics. Under that situation, the spinal reflex corrects for errors in desired $(x_{md}, \dot{x}_{md})$ and actual $(x_m, \dot{x}_m)$ muscle state, by producing a corrective neural signal N_R based on a linear feedback controller with constants K_1 and K_2.

$$N_R = K_1(x_{md} - x_m) + K_2(\dot{x}_{md} - \dot{x}_m) \tag{5}$$

Adaptive Forward-Inverse Model Feedback Control

The second architecture provides feedback control of arm movements in addition to the feedforward control described above. Delays in feedback cause instability, therefore, the system relies on a forward model to generate updated state estimates of the arm. An estimated error in hand trajectory is given by the difference in desired and estimated state, and can be used by the brain to issue corrective neural signals to the muscles while a movement is being made. The forward model, written

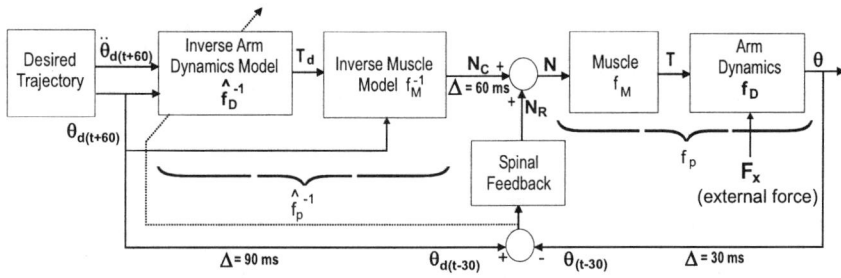

Figure 1: The adaptive inverse model feedforward control system.

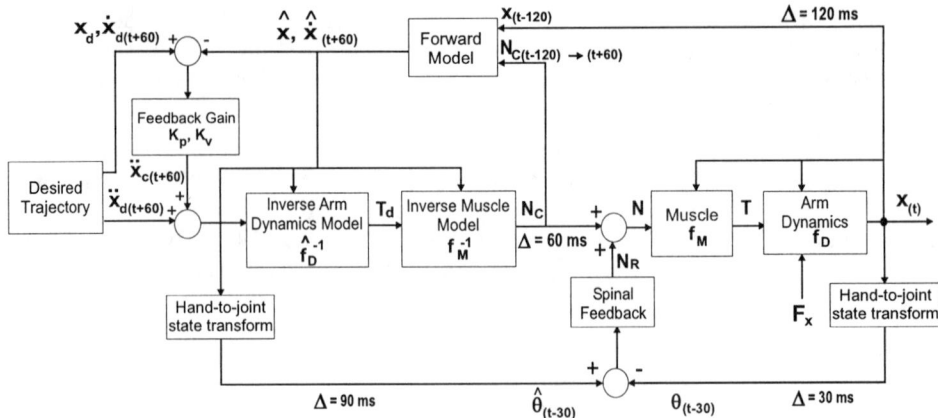

Figure 2: A control system that provides feedback control with the use of a forward and an inverse model.

as $\hat{f}_p$, mimics the forward dynamics of the plant and predicts hand acceleration $\hat{\ddot{x}}$, from neural signal N_C, and an estimate of hand state $\hat{x}$, $\hat{\dot{x}}$.

$$\hat{\ddot{x}} = \hat{f}_p(N_C, \hat{x}, \hat{\dot{x}}) \tag{6}$$

Using this equation, one can solve for $\hat{x}, \hat{\dot{x}}$ at time t, when given the estimated state at some earlier time $t - \tau$, and the descending neural commands N_C from time $t - \tau$ to t. If t is the current time and τ is the time delay in the feedback loop, then sensory feedback gives the hand state x, $\dot{x}$ at $t-\tau$. The current estimate of the hand position and velocity can be computed by assuming initial conditions $\hat{x}(t - \tau) = x(t - \tau)$ and $\hat{\dot{x}}(t - \tau) = \dot{x}(t - \tau)$, and then solving Eq. 6. For the simulations, τ has value of 200 msec, and is composed of 120 msec feedback delay, 60 msec descending neural path delay, and 20 msec muscle activation delay.

Based on the current state estimate and the estimated error in trajectory, the desired acceleration is corrected using a linear feedback controller with constants K_p and K_v. The inverse model maps the hand acceleration to appropriate neural signal for the muscles N_C. The spinal reflex provides additional corrective feedback N_R, when there is an error in the estimated and actual muscle state.

$$\ddot{x}_{new} = \ddot{x}_d + \ddot{x}_c = \ddot{x}_d + K_p(x_d - \hat{x}) + K_v(\dot{x}_d - \hat{\dot{x}}) \tag{7}$$
$$N_C = \hat{f}_p^{-1}(\ddot{x}_{new}, \hat{x}, \hat{\dot{x}}) \tag{8}$$
$$N_R = K_1(\hat{x}_m - x_m) + K_2(\hat{\dot{x}}_m d - \dot{x}_m) \tag{9}$$

When the forward model is an exact copy of the forward plant dynamics $\hat{f}_p = f_p$, and the inverse model is correct $\hat{f}_p^{-1} = f_p^{-1}$, the hand exactly tracks the desired trajectory. Errors due to an incorrect inverse model are corrected through the feedback loop. However, errors in the forward model cause deviations from the desired behavior and instability in the system due to inappropriate feedback action.

3 Simulations results and comparison to human behavior

To test the two control architectures, we compared simulations of arm movements for the two methods to experimental human results under a novel force field environment. Sixteen human subjects were trained to make rapid point-to-point reaching

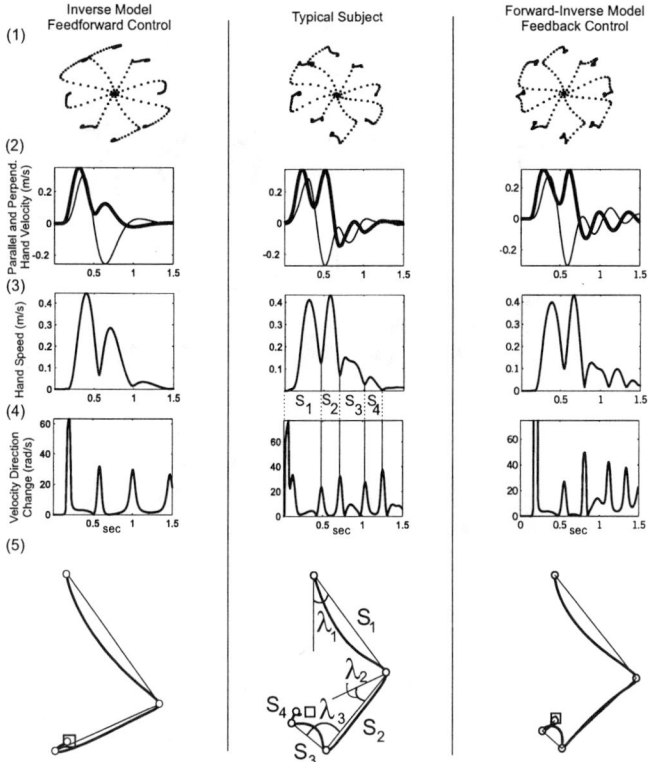

Figure 3: Performance in field B_2 after a typical subject (middle column) and each of the controllers (left and right columns) had adapted to field B_1. (1) hand paths for 8 movement directions, (2-5) hand velocity, speed, derivative of velocity direction, and segmented hand path for the $-90°$ downward movement. The segmentation in hand trajectory that is observed in our subjects is almost precisely reproduced by the controller that uses a forward model.

movements with their hand while an external force field, $F_x = B\dot{x}$, pushed on the hand. The task was to move the hand to a target position 10 cm away in 0.5 sec. The movement could be directed in any of eight equally spaced directions. The subjects made straight-path minimum-jerk movements to the targets in the absence of any force fields. The subjects were initially trained in force field B_1 with B=[0 13;-13 0], until they had completely adapted to this field and converged to the straight-path minimum-jerk movement observed before the force field was applied. Subsequently, the force field was switched to B_2 with B=[0 -13;13 0] (the new field pushed anticlockwise, instead of clockwise), and the first three movements in each direction were used for data analysis. The movements of the subjects in field B_2 showed huge deviations from the desired straight path behavior because the subjects expected clockwise force field B_1. The hand trajectories for the first movement in each of the eight directions are shown for a typical subject in Fig. 3 (middle column).

Simulations were performed for the two methods under the same conditions as the human experiment. The movements were made in force field B_2, while the internal models were assumed to be adapted to field B_1. Complete adaptation to the force field B_1 was found to occur for the two methods only when both

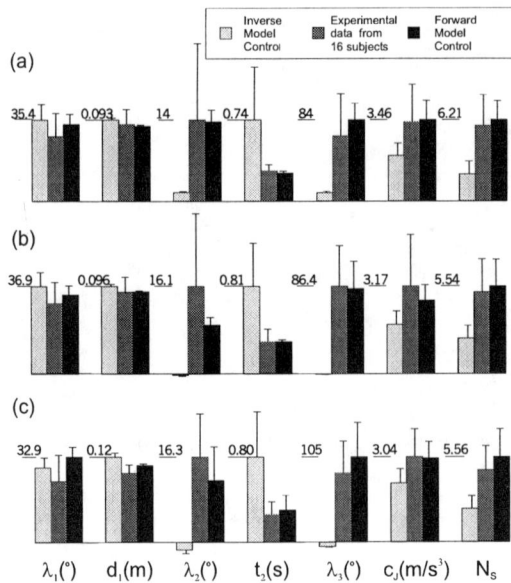

Figure 4: The mean and standard deviation for segmentation parameters for each type of controller as compared to the data from our subjects. Parameters are defined in Fig. 3: λ_i is angle about a seg. point, d_i is the distance to the i-th seg. point, t_i is time to reach the i-th seg. point, c_j is cumulative squared jerk for the entire movement, N_s is number of seg. point in the movement. Up until the first segmentation point (λ_1 and d_1), behavior of the controllers are similar and both agree with the performance of our subjects. However, as the movement progresses, only the controller that utilizes a forward model continues to agree with the movement characteristics of the subjects.

the inverse and forward models expected field B_1. Fig. 3 (left column) shows the simulation of the adaptive inverse model feedforward control for movements in field B_2 with the inverse model incorrectly expecting B_1. Fig. 3 (right column) shows the simulation of the adaptive forward-inverse model feedback control for movements in field B_2 with both the forward and the inverse model incorrectly expecting B_1. Simulations with the two methods show clear differences in stability and corrective behavior for all eight directions of movement. The simulations with the inverse model feedforward control seem to be stable, and converge to the target along a straight line after the initial deviation. The simulations with the forward-inverse model feedback control are more unstable and have a curious kinematic pattern with discontinuities in the hand path. This is especially marked for the downward movement. The subject's hand paths show the same kinematic pattern of near discontinuities and segmentation of movement as found with the forward-inverse model feedback control.

To quantify the segmentation pattern in the hand path, we identified the "near path-discontinuities" as points on the trajectory where there was a sudden change in both the derivative of hand speed and the direction of hand velocity. The hand path was segmented on the basis of these near discontinuities. Based on the first three segments in the hand trajectory we defined the following parameters: λ_1, angle between the first segment and the straight path to the target; d_1, the distance covered during the first segment; λ_2, angle between the second segment and straight path to the target from the first segmentation point; t_2, time duration of the second segment; λ_3, angle between the second and third segments; N_S, the number of segmentation points in the movement. We also calculated the cumulative jerk C_J in the movements to get a measure of the instability in the system.

The results of the movement segmentation are presented in Fig. 4 for 16 human subjects, 25 simulations of the inverse model and 20 simulations of the forward model control for three movement directions (a) $-90°$ downward, (b) $90°$ upward and (c) $135°$ upward. We performed the different simulations for the two methods by systematically varying various model parameters over a reasonable physiological range. This was done because the parameters are only approximately known and also vary from subject to subject. The parameters of the second and third segment, as represented by λ_2, t_2 and λ_3, clearly show that the forward model feedback control performs very differently from inverse model feedforward control and the behavior of human subjects is very well predicted by the former. Furthermore, this characteristic behavior could be produced by the forward-inverse model feedback control only when the forward model expected field B_1. This could be accomplished only by adaptation of the forward model during initial practice in field B_1. This provides evidence for an adaptive forward model in the control of human arm movements in novel dynamic environments.

We further tried to fit adaptation curves of simulated movement parameters (using forward-inverse model feedback control) to real data as subjects trained in field B_1. We found that the best fit was obtained for a rapidly adapting forward and inverse model (Bhushan and Shadmehr, 1999). This eliminated the possibility that the inverse model was trained offline after practice. The data, however, suggested that during learning of a force field, the rate of learning of the forward model was faster than the inverse model. This finding could be paricularly relevant if it is proven that a forward model is easier to learn than an inverse model (Narendra, 1990), and could provide a computational rationale for the existence of forward model in adaptive motor control.

References

Bhushan N, Shadmehr R (1999) Computational architecture of the adaptive controller during learning of reaching movements in force fields. *Biol Cybern*, in press.

Jordan MI, Flash T, Arnon Y (1994) A model of learning arm trajectories from spatial deviations *Journal of Cog Neur* 6:359-376.

Jordan MI, Rumelhart DE (1992) Forward model: supervised learning with a distal teacher. *Cog Sc* 16:307-354.

Miall RC, Wolpert DM (1996) Forward models for physiological motor control. *Neural Networks* 9:1265-1279.

Narendra KS (1990) Identification and control of dynamical systems using neural networks. *Neural Networks* 1:4-27.

Shadmehr R, Brashers-Krug T (1997) Functional stages in the formation of human long-term memory. *J Neurosci* 17:409-19.

Shadmehr R, Mussa-Ivaldi FA (1994) Adaptive representation of dynamics during learning of a motor task. *The Journal of Neuroscience* 14:3208-3224.

Soechting JF, Flanders M (1997) Evaluating an integrated musculoskeletal model of the human arm *J Biomech Eng* 9:93-102.

Wolpert DM, Ghahramani Z, Jordan MI (1995) An internal model for sensorimotor integration. *Science* 269:1880-82.

Perceiving without Learning: from Spirals to Inside/Outside Relations

Ke Chen* and DeLiang L. Wang
Department of Computer and Information Science and Center for Cognitive Science
The Ohio State University, Columbus, OH 43210-1277, USA
{kchen,dwang}@cis.ohio-state.edu

Abstract

As a benchmark task, the spiral problem is well known in neural networks. Unlike previous work that emphasizes learning, we approach the problem from a generic perspective that does not involve learning. We point out that the spiral problem is intrinsically connected to the inside/outside problem. A generic solution to both problems is proposed based on oscillatory correlation using a time delay network. Our simulation results are qualitatively consistent with human performance, and we interpret human limitations in terms of synchrony and time delays, both biologically plausible. As a special case, our network without time delays can always distinguish these figures regardless of shape, position, size, and orientation.

1 INTRODUCTION

The *spiral* problem refers to distinguishing between a connected single spiral and disconnected double spirals, as illustrated in Fig. 1. Since Minsky and Papert (1969) first introduced the problem in their influential book on perceptrons, it has received much attention and has become a benchmark task in neural networks. Many solutions have been attempted using different learning models since Lang and Witbrock (1988) reported that the problem could not be solved with a standard multilayer perceptron. However, resulting learning systems are only able to produce decision regions highly constrained by the spirals defined in a training set, thus specific in shape, position, size, and orientation. Moreover, no explanation is provided as to why the problem is difficult for human subjects to solve. Grossberg and Wyse (1991) proposed a biologically plausible neural network architecture for figure-ground separation and reported their network can distinguish between connected and disconnected spirals. In their paper, however, no demonstration was given to the spiral problem, and their model does not exhibit the limitations that humans do.

---

*Also with National Laboratory of Machine Perception and Center for Information Science, Peking University, Beijing 100871, China. E-mail: chen@cis.pku.edu.cn

There is a related problem in the study of visual perception, i.e., the perception of *inside/outside relations*. Considering the visual input of a single closed curve, the task of perceiving the inside/outside relation is to determine whether a specific pixel lies inside or outside the closed curve. For the human visual system, the perception of inside/outside relations often appears to be immediate and effortless (see an example in Fig. 2(a)). As illustrated in Fig. 2(b), however, the immediate perception is not available for humans when the bounding contour becomes highly convoluted (Ullman 1984). Ullman (1984) suggested the computation of spatial relation through the use of visual routines. Visual routines result in the conjecture that the inside/outside is inherently sequential. As pointed out recently by Ullman (1996), the processes underlying the perception of inside/outside relations are as yet unknown and applying visual routines is simply one alternative.

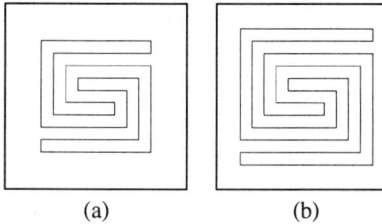 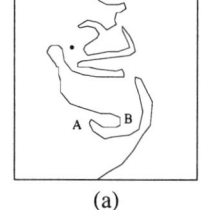 

(a) (b)   (a)   (b)

Fig. 1: The spiral problem. (a) a connected single spiral. (b) disconnected double spirals (adapted from Minsky and Papert 1969, 1988).

Fig. 2: Inside/Outside relations. (a) an example (adapted from Julesz 1995). (b) another example (adapted from Ullman 1984).

Theoretical investigations of brain functions indicate that timing of neuronal activity is a key to the construction of neuronal assemblies (Milner 1974, Malsburg 1981). In particular, the discovery of synchronous oscillations in the visual cortex (Singer & Gray 1995) has triggered much interest to develop computational models for oscillatory correlation. Recently, Terman and Wang (1995) proposed *locally excitatory globally inhibitory oscillator networks* (LEGION). They theoretically showed that LEGION can rapidly achieve both synchronization in a locally coupled oscillator group representing each object and desynchronization among a number of oscillator groups representing different objects. More recently, Campbell and Wang (1998) have studied time delays in networks of relaxation oscillators and analyzed the behavior of LEGION with time delays. Their studies show that loosely synchronous solutions can be achieved under a broad range of initial conditions and time delays. Therefore, LEGION provides a computational framework to study the process of visual perception from a standpoint of oscillatory correlation.

We explore both the spiral problem and the inside/outside relations by oscillatory correlation in this paper. We show that computation through LEGION with time delays yields a generic solution to these problems since time delays inevitably occur in information transmission of a biological system. This investigation indicates that perceptual performance would be limited if local activation cannot be rapidly propagated due to time delays. As a special case, LEGION without time delays reliably distinguishes between connected and disconnected spirals and discriminates the inside and the outside regardless of shape, position, size, and orientation. Thus, we suggest that this kind of problems may be better solved by a neural oscillator network rather than by sophisticated learning.

2 METHODOLOGY

The architecture of LEGION used in this paper is a two-dimensional network. Each oscillator is connected to its four nearest neighbors, and the global inhibitor (GI) receives excitation from each oscillator on the network and in turn inhibits each oscillator (Terman

& Wang 1995). In LEGION, a single oscillator, i, is defined as

$$\frac{dx_i}{dt} = 3x_i - x_i^3 - y_i + I_i + S_i + \rho \tag{1a}$$

$$\frac{dy_i}{dt} = \epsilon\Big(\lambda + \gamma \tanh(\beta x_i) - y_i\Big). \tag{1b}$$

Here I_i represents external stimulation to the oscillator, and S_i represents overall coupling from other oscillators and the GI in the network. The symbol ρ denotes the amplitude of a Gaussian noise. Other parameters ϵ, β, λ, and γ are chosen to control a periodic solution of the dynamic system. The periodic solution alternates between the silent and the active phases of near steady-state behavior (Terman & Wang 1995). The coupling term S_i at time t is

$$S_i = \sum_{k \in N(i)} W_{ik} S_\infty(x_k(t-\tau), \theta_x) - W_z S_\infty(z, \theta_z), \tag{2}$$

where $S_\infty(x, \theta) = 1/\big(1 + \exp[-\kappa(x-\theta)]\big)$ and the parameter κ controls the steepness of the sigmoid function. W_{ik} is a synaptic weight from oscillator k to oscillator i, and $N(i)$ is the set of its immediate neighbors. τ is a time delay in interactions (Campbell & Wang 1998), and θ_x is a threshold over which an oscillator can affect its neighbors. W_z is the positive weight used for the inhibition from the global inhibitor z, whose activity is defined as

$$\frac{dz}{dt} = \phi(\sigma_\infty - z). \tag{3}$$

where $\sigma_\infty = 0$ if $x_i < \theta_z$ for every oscillator i, and $\sigma_\infty = 1$ if $x_i(t) \geq \theta_z$ for at least one oscillator i. Here θ_z represents a threshold to determine whether the GI z sends inhibition to oscillators, and the parameter ϕ determines the rate at which the inhibitor reacts to stimulation from oscillators.

We use *pattern formation* to refer to the behavior that all the oscillators representing the same object are synchronous, while the oscillators representing different objects are desynchronous. Terman and Wang (1995) have analytically shown that such a solution can be achieved in LEGION without time delays. However, a solution may not be achieved when time delays are introduced. Although the loose synchrony concept has been introduced to describe time delay behavior (Campbell & Wang 1998), it does not indicate pattern formation in an entire network even when loose synchrony is achieved because loose synchrony is a local concept defined in terms of pairs of neighboring oscillators. Here we introduce a measure called *min-max difference* in order to examine whether pattern formation is achieved. Suppose that oscillators O_i and O_j represent two pixels in the same object, and the oscillator O_k represents a pixel in a different object. Moreover, let t^s denote the time at which oscillator O_s enters the active phase. The min-max difference measure is defined as $|t^i - t^j| < \tau_{RB}$ and $|t^i - t^k| \geq \tau_{RB}$, where τ_{RB} is the time period of an active phase. Intuitively, this measure suggests that pattern formation is achieved if any two oscillators representing two pixels in the same object have some overlap in the active phase, while any two oscillators representing two pixels belonging to different objects never stay in the active phase simultaneously. This definition of pattern formation applies to both exact synchrony in LEGION without time delays and loose synchrony with time delays.

3 SIMULATIONS

For a given image consisting of $N \times N$ pixels, a two-dimensional LEGION network with $N \times N$ oscillators is used so that each oscillator in the network corresponds to one pixel in the image. In the following simulations, the equations 1-3 were numerically solved using the fourth-order Runge-Kutta method. We illustrate stimulated oscillators with black squares. All oscillators were initialized randomly. A large number of simulations have been conducted with a broad range of parameter values and network sizes (Chen & Wang 1997). Here we report typical results using a specific set of parameter values.

3.1 THE SPIRAL PROBLEM

For simulations, the two images in Fig. 1 were sampled as two binary images with 29×29 pixels. For these images, two problems can be addressed: (1) When an image is presented, can one determine whether it contains a single spiral or double spirals? (2) Given a point on a two-dimensional plane, can one determine whether it is inside or outside a specific spiral?

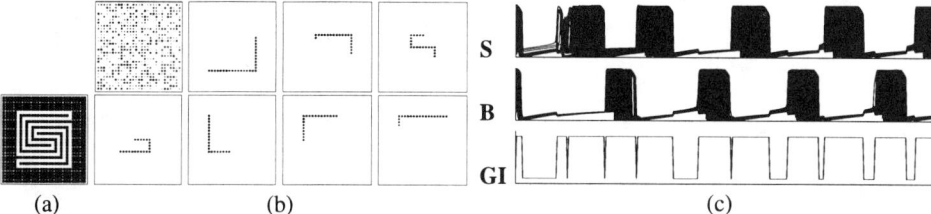

Fig. 3: Results of LEGION with a time delay $\tau = 0.002T$ (T is the period of oscillation) for the spiral problem. The parameter values used in this simulation are $\epsilon = 0.003$, $\beta = 500$, $\gamma = 24.0$, $\lambda = 21.5$, $\alpha_T = 6.0$, $\rho = 0.03$, $\kappa = 500$, $\theta_x = -0.5$, $\theta_z = 0.1$, $\phi = 3.0$, $W_z = 1.5$, $I_s = 1.0$, and $I_u = -1.0$ where I_s and I_u are external input to stimulated and unstimulated oscillators, respectively.

We first applied LEGION with time delays to the single spiral image in Fig. 1(a). Fig. 3(a) illustrates the visual stimulus, where black pixels correspond to the stimulated oscillators and white ones correspond to the unstimulated oscillators. Fig. 3(b) shows a sequence of snapshots after the network was stabilized except for the first snapshot which shows the random initial state of the network. These snapshots are arranged in temporal order first from left to right and then from top to bottom. We observe from these snapshots that an activated oscillator in the spiral propagates its activation to its two immediate neighbors with some time delay, and the process of propagation forms a traveling wave along the spiral. We emphasize that, at any time, only the oscillators corresponding to a portion of the spiral stay in the active phase together, and the entire spiral can never be in the active phase simultaneously. Thus, based on the oscillatory correlation theory, our system cannot group the whole spiral together, which indicates that our system fails to realize that the pixels in the spiral belong to the same pattern. Note that the convoluted part of the background behaves similarly. Fig. 3(c) shows the temporal trajectories of the combined x activities of the oscillators representing the spiral (S) and the background (B) as well as the temporal activity of the GI. According to the min-max difference measure, Fig. 3(c) shows that pattern formation cannot be achieved. In order to illustrate the effects of time delays, we applied LEGION without time delays to the same image. Simulation results show that pattern formation is achieved, and the single spiral can be segregated from the background by the second period (Chen & Wang 1997). Thus, LEGION without time delays can readily solve the spiral problem in this case. The failure to group the spiral in Fig. 3 is caused by time delays in the coupling of neighboring oscillators.

We also applied LEGION with time delays to the double spirals image in Fig. 1(b). Fig. 4(a) shows the visual stimulus. Fig. 4(b) shows a sequence of snapshots arranged in the same order as in Fig. 3(b). We observe from these snapshots that starting from an end of one spiral a traveling wave is formed along the spiral and the activated oscillators representing the spiral propagate their activation. Due to time delays, however, only the oscillators corresponding to a portion of the spiral stay in the active phase together, and the entire spiral is never in the active phase simultaneously. The oscillators representing the other spiral have the same behavior. The results show that the pixels in any one of double spirals cannot be grouped as the same pattern. We mention that the behavior of our system for the convoluted part of the background is similar to that for the double spirals. It is also evident from Fig. 4(c) that the pattern formation is not achieved after the network was stabilized. We also applied LEGION without time delays to the double spirals image for the same purpose as described before. Simulation results also show that anyone of spirals can be segregated from both the other spiral and the background by the second period (Chen & Wang 1997). Once again, it indicates that the failure to group the double spirals in Fig. 4 results from time delays.

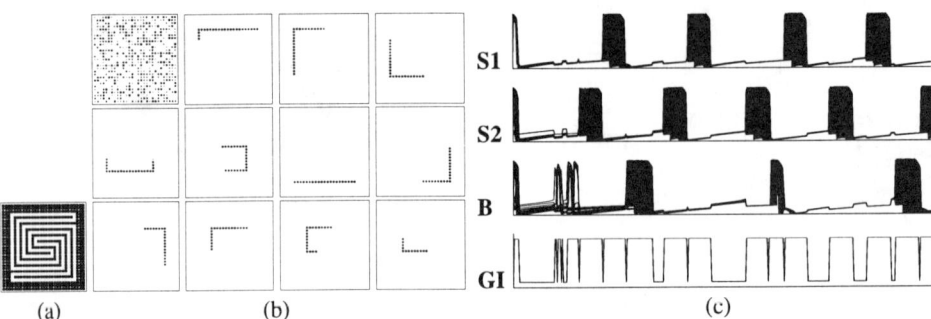

Fig. 4: Results of LEGION without time delays for the spiral problem. The parameter values used are the same as listed in the caption of Fig. 3. In (c), **S1** and **S2** represent two disconnected spirals. **B** and **GI** denote background and the global inhibitor, respectively.

For the spiral problem, pattern formation means that solutions to the two problems in question can be provided to the questions of counting the number of objects or identifying whether two pixels belong to the same spiral or not. No such solutions are available when pattern formation is not achieved. Hence, our system cannot solve the spiral problem in general. Only under the special condition of no time delay can our system solve the problem.

3.2 INSIDE/OUTSIDE RELATIONS

For simulations, the two pictures in Fig. 2 were sampled as binary images with 43×43 pixels. We first applied LEGION with time delays to the two images in Fig. 2. Figures 5(a) and 6(a) show the visual stimuli, where black pixels represent areas A and B that correspond to stimulated oscillators and white pixels represent the boundary that corresponds to unstimulated oscillators. Figures 5(b) and 6(b) illustrate a sequence of snapshots after networks were stabilized except for the first snapshot which shows the random initial states of networks. Figures 5(c) and 6(c) show temporal trajectories of the combined x activities of the oscillators representing areas A and B as well as the GI, respectively.

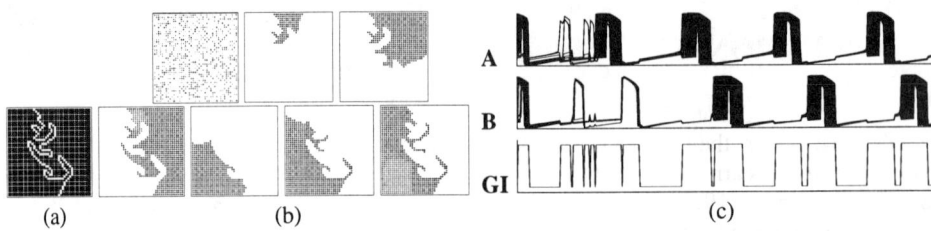

Fig. 5: Results of LEGION with a time delay $\tau = 0.002T$ for Fig. 2(a). The parameter values used in this simulation are $\epsilon = 0.004$, $\gamma = 14.0$, $\lambda = 11.5$ and the other parameter values are the same

as listed in the caption of Fig. 3. In (c), **A**, **B**, and **GI** denote areas A, B, and the global inhibitor, respectively.

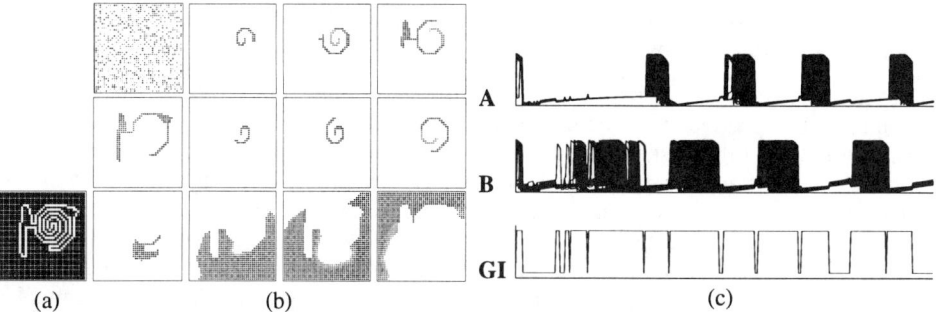

Fig. 6: Results of LEGION with a time delay $\tau = 0.002T$ for Fig. 2(b). The parameter values used and other statements are the same as listed in the caption of Fig. 5.

We observe from Fig. 5(b) that the activation of an oscillator can rapidly propagate through its neighbors to other oscillators representing the same area, and eventually all the oscillators representing the same area (A or B) stay together in the active phase simultaneously, though they generally enter the active phase at different times due to time delays. Thus, on the basis of oscillatory correlation, our system can group an entire area (A or B) together and recognize all the pixels in area A or B as elements of the same area. According to the min-max difference measure, Fig. 5(c) shows that pattern formation is achieved by the second period. In contrast, we observe from Fig. 6(b) that although an activated oscillator rapidly propagates its activation in open regions as shown in the last three snapshots, propagation is limited once the traveling wave spreads in spiral-like regions as shown in earlier snapshots. As a result, at any time, only the oscillators corresponding to a portion of either area stay in the active phase together, and the oscillators representing the whole area are never in the active phase simultaneously. Thus, on the basis of oscillatory correlation, our system cannot group the whole area, and fails to identify the pixels of one area as belonging to the same pattern. Furthermore, according to the min-max difference measure, Fig. 6(c) shows that pattern formation is not achieved after the network was stabilized. In order to illustrate the effects of time delays and show how to use an oscillator network to perceive inside/outside relations, we applied LEGION without time delays to the two images in Fig. 2. Our simulations show that LEGION without time delays readily segregates two areas in both cases by the second period (Chen & Wang 1997). Thus, the failure to group each area in Fig. 6 is also attributed to time delays in the coupling of neighboring oscillators. In general, the above simulations suggest that oscillatory correlation provides a way to address inside/outside relations by a neural network; when pattern formation is achieved, a single area segregates from other areas that appear in the same image. For a specific point on the two-dimensional plane, the inside/outside relations can be identified by examining whether the oscillator representing the point synchronizes with the oscillators representing a specific area or not.

4 DISCUSSION AND CONCLUSION

It has been reported that many neural network models can solve the spiral problem through learning. However, their solutions are subject to limitations because generalization abilities of resulting learning systems highly depend on the training set. As pointed out by Minsky and Papert (1969), solving the spiral problem is equivalent to detecting connectedness. They showed that connectedness cannot be computed by any diameter-limited or order-limited perceptrons (Minsky & Papert 1969). This limitation holds for multilayer perceptrons regardless of learning scheme (Minsky & Papert 1988, p.252). Unfortunately, few people have discussed generality of their solutions. In contrast, our simulations have shown that LEGION without time delays can always distinguish these figures regardless of shape, position, size, and orientation. We emphasize that no learning is involved in LEGION. In terms of performance, we suggest that the spiral problem may be better solved by a network of oscillators without learning.

Our system provides an alternative way to perceive inside/outside relations from a neural computation perspective. Our method is significantly distinguished from visual routines (Ullman 1984, 1996). First, the visual routine method is described as serial algorithms, while our system is an inherently parallel and distributed process although its emergent behavior reflects a degree of serial nature of the problems. Second, the visual routine method does not make a qualitative distinction between rapid effortless perception that corresponds to simple boundaries and slow effortful perception that corresponds to convoluted boundaries – the time a visual routine, e.g. the coloring method, takes varies continuously. In contrast, our system makes such a distinction: effortless perception with simple boundaries corresponds to when pattern formation is achieved, and effortful perception with convoluted boundaries corresponds to when pattern formation is not achieved. Third, perhaps more importantly conceptually, our system does not invoke high-level serial process to solve such problems like inside/outside relations; its solution involves the same mechanism as it does for parallel image segmentation (see Wang & Terman 1997).

Acknowledgments: Authors are grateful to S. Campbell for many discussions. This work was supported in part by an NSF grant (IRI-9423312), an ONR grant (N00014-93-10335), and an ONR Young Investigator Award (N00014-96-1-00676) to DLW.

References

Campbell, S. & Wang, D.L. (1998) Relaxation oscillators with time delay coupling. *Physica D* **111**:151-178.

Chen, K. & Wang, D.L. (1997) Perceiving without learning: from spirals to inside/outside relations. *Technical Report OSU-CISRC-8/97-TR38*, The Ohio State University.

Grossberg, S. & Wyse, L. (1991) A neural network architecture for figure-ground separation of connected scenic figures. *Neural Networks* **4**:723-742.

Julesz, B. (1995), *Dialogues on perception*. MIT Press.

Lang, K. & Witbrock, M. (1988) Learning to tell two spirals apart. *Proceeding of 1988 Connectionist Models Summer School*, pp. 52-59, Morgan Kaufmann.

Milner, P. (1974) A model for visual shape recognition. *Psychological Review* **81**:512-535.

Minsky, M. & Papert, R. (1969) *Perceptrons*. MIT Press.

Minsky, M. & Papert, R. (1988) *Perceptrons (extended version)*. MIT Press.

Singer, W. & Gray, C.M. (1995) Visual feature integration and the temporal correlation hypothesis. *Annual Review of Neuroscience* **18**:555-586.

Terman, D. & Wang, D.L. (1995) Global competition and local cooperation in a network of neural oscillators. *Physica D* **81**:148-176.

Ullman, S. (1984) Visual routines. *Cognition* **18**:97-159.

Ullman, S. (1996) *High-level vision*. MIT Press.

von der Malsburg, C. (1981) The correlation theory of brain function. *Internal Report 81-2*, Max-Planck-Institute for Biophysical Chemistry.

Wang, D.L. & Terman, D. (1997) Image segmentation based on oscillatory correlation. *Neural Computation* **9**:805-836.

A Model for Associative Multiplication

G. Björn Christianson*
Department of Psychology
McMaster University
Hamilton, Ont. L8S 4K1
bjorn@caltech.edu

Suzanna Becker
Department of Psychology
McMaster University
Hamilton, Ont. L8S 4K1
becker@mcmaster.ca

Abstract

Despite the fact that mental arithmetic is based on only a few hundred basic facts and some simple algorithms, humans have a difficult time mastering the subject, and even experienced individuals make mistakes. Associative multiplication, the process of doing multiplication by memory without the use of rules or algorithms, is especially problematic. Humans exhibit certain characteristic phenomena in performing associative multiplications, both in the type of error and in the error frequency. We propose a model for the process of associative multiplication, and compare its performance in both these phenomena with data from normal humans and from the model proposed by Anderson *et al* (1994).

1 INTRODUCTION

Associative multiplication is defined as multiplication done without recourse to computational algorithms, and as such is mainly concerned with recalling the basic times table. Learning up to the ten times table requires learning at most 121 facts; in fact, if we assume that normal humans use only four simple rules, the number of facts to be learned reduces to 39. In theory, associative multiplication is therefore a simple problem. In reality, school children find it difficult to learn, and even trained adults have a relatively high rate of error, especially in comparison to performance on associative addition, which is superficially a similar problem. There has been surprisingly little work done on the methods by which humans perform basic multiplication problems; an excellent review of the current literature is provided by McCloskey *et al* (1991).

If a model is to be considered plausible, it must have error characteristics similar to

---

*Author to whom correspondence should be addressed. Current address: Computation and Neural Systems, California Institute of Technology 139-74, Pasadena, CA 91125.

those of humans at the same task. In arithmetic, this entails accounting for, at a minimum, two phenomena. The first is the *problem size effect*, as noted in various studies (*e.g.* Stazyk et al, 1982), where response times and error rates increase for problems with larger operands. Secondly, humans have a characteristic distribution in the types of errors made. Specifically, errors can be classified as one of the following five types, as suggested by Campbell and Graham (1985), Siegler (1988), McCloskey et al (1991), and Girelli et al (1996): *operand*, where the given answer is correct with one of the operands replaced (*e.g.* $4 \times 7 = 21$; this category accounts for 66.4% of all errors made by normal adults); *close-miss*, where the result is within ten percent of the correct response ($4 \times 7 = 29$; 20.0%); *table*, where the result is correct for a problem with both operands replaced ($4 \times 7 = 25$; 3.9%); *non-table*, where the result is not on the times table ($4 \times 7 = 17$; 6.7%); or *operation*, where the answer would have been correct for a different arithmetic operation, such as addition ($4 \times 7 = 11$; 3.0%)[1].

It is reasonable to assume that humans use at least two distinct representations when dealing with numbers. The work by Mandler and Shebo (1982) on modeling the performance of various species (including humans, monkeys, and pigeons) on numerosity judgment tasks suggests that in such cases a coarse coding is used. On the other hand, humans are capable of dealing with numbers as abstract symbolic concepts, suggesting the use of a precise localist coding. Previous work has either used only one of these coding ideas (for example, Sokol et al, 1991) or a single representation which combined aspects of both (Anderson et al, 1994).

Warrington (1982) documented DRC, a patient who suffered dyscalculia following a stroke. DRC retained normal intelligence and a grasp of numerical and arithmetic concepts. When presented with an arithmetic problem, DRC was capable of rapidly providing an approximate answer. However, when pressed for a precise answer, he was incapable of doing so without resorting to an explicit computational algorithm such as counting. One possible interpretation of this case study is that DRC retained the ability to work with numbers in a magnitude-related fashion, but had lost the ability to treat numbers as symbolic concepts. This suggests the hypothesis that humans may use two separate, concurrent representations for numbers: both a coarse coding and a more symbolic, precise coding in the course of doing associative arithmetic in general, and multiplication in particular, and switch between the codings at various points in the process. This hypothesis will form the basis of our modeling work. To guide the placement of these transitions between representations, we assume the further constraint that the coarse coding is the preferred coding (as it is conserved across a wide variety of species) and will tend to be expressed before the precise coding.

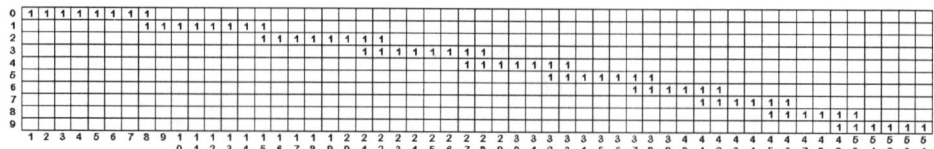

Figure 1: The coarse coding for digits. Numbers along the left are the digit; numbers along the bottom are position numbers. Blank regions in the grid represent zero activity.

---

[1]Data taken from Girelli et al (1996).

2 METHODOLOGY

Following the work of Mandler and Shebo (1982), our coarse coding consists of a 54-dimensional vector, with a sliding "bump" of ones corresponding to the magnitude of the digit represented. The size of the bump decreases and the degree of overlap increases as the magnitude of the digit increases (Figure 1). Noise in this representation is simulated by the probability that a given bit will be in the wrong state. The precise representation, intended for symbolic manipulation of numbers, consists of a 10-dimensional vector with the value of the coded digit given by the dimension of greatest activity. Both of these representations are digit-based: each vector codes only for a number between 0 and 9, with concatenations of vectors used for numbers greater than 9.

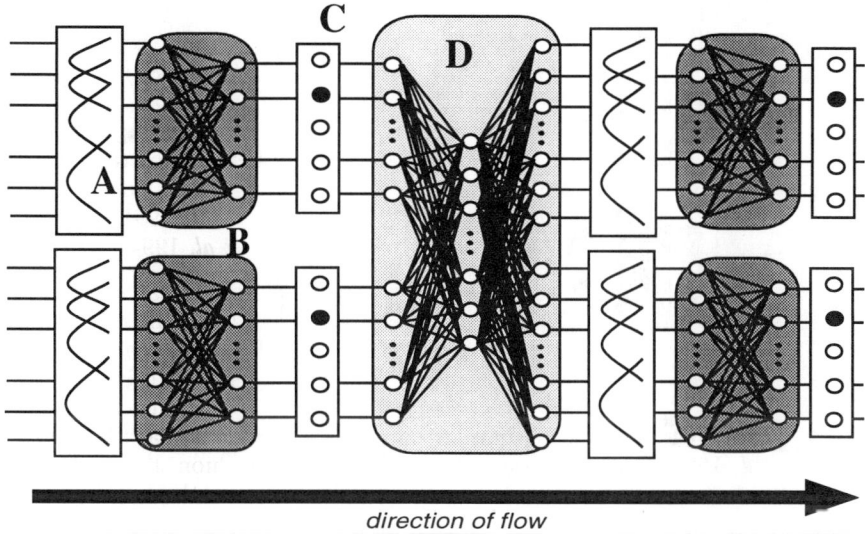

Figure 2: Schematic of the network architecture. (A) The coarse coding. (B) The winner-take-all network. (C) The precise coding. (D) The feed-forward look-up table. See text for details.

The model is trained in three distinct phases. A simple one-layer perceptron trained by a winner-take-all competitive learning algorithm is used to map the input operands from the original coarse coding into the precise representation. The network was trained for 10 epochs, each with a different set of 5 samples of noisy coarse-coded digits. At the end of training, the winner-take-all network performed at near-perfect levels. The translated operands are then presented to a two-layer feed-forward network with a logistic activation function trained by back-propagation. The number of hidden units was equal to the number of problems in the training set (in this case, 32) to force look-up table behaviour. The look-up table was trained independently for varying numbers of iterations, using a learning rate constant of 0.01. The output of the look-up table is coarse coded as in Figure 1. In the final phase, the table output is translated by the winner-take-all network to provide the final answer in the precise coding. A schematic of the network architecture is given in Figure 2. The operand vectors used for training of both networks had a noise parameter of 5%, while the vectors used in the analysis had 7.5% noise. Both the training and the testing problem set consisted of ten copies of each of the problems listed in Table 2, which are the problems used in

Anderson et al (1994). Simulations were done in MATLAB v5.1 (Mathworks, Inc., 24 Prime Park Way, Natick MA, 01760-1500).

3 RESULTS

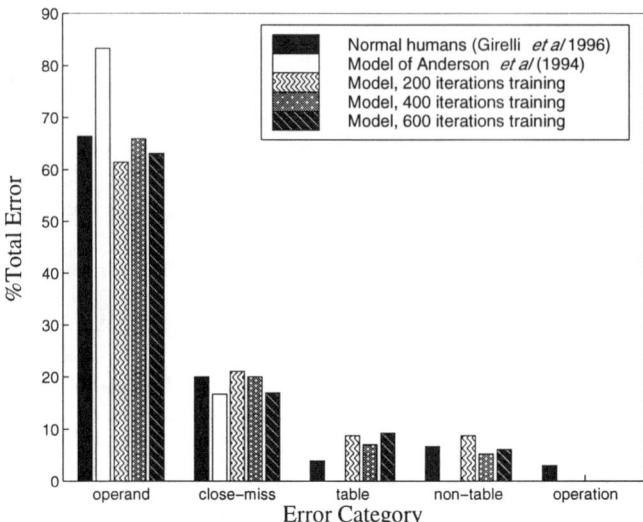

Figure 3: Error distributions for human data (Girelli et al 1996), the model of Anderson et al (1994), and our model.

Once a model has been trained, its errors on the training data can be categorized according to the error types listed in the Introduction section; a summary of the performance of our model is presented in Table 1. For comparison, we plot data generated by our model, the model of Anderson et al (1994), and human data from Girelli et al (1996) in Figure 3. In no case did the model generate an operation error. This is to be expected, as the model was only trained on multiplication, it should permit no way in which to make an operation error, other than by coincidence. A full set of results obtained from the model with 400 training iterations is presented in Table 2[2].

Table 1: Error rates generated by our model. A column for operation errors is not included, as in no instance did our model generate an operation error.

Iterations	Errors in 320 trials	Operand (%)	Close-miss (%)	Table (%)	Non-table (%)
200	114	61.4	21.0	8.8	8.8
400	85	65.9	20.0	7.1	7.1
600	65	63.7	16.9	9.2	10.8

---

[2]As in Anderson et al (1994), we have set $8 \times 9 = 67$ deliberately so that it is not the only problem with an answer greater than 70.

Table 2: Results from ten trials run with the model after 400 training iterations. Errors are marked in boldface.

Problem	\multicolumn{10}{c}{Trial}
	1	2	3	4	5	6	7	8	9	10
2 × 2	4	4	4	4	4	4	4	4	4	4
2 × 4	8	8	8	8	8	8	8	8	8	8
2 × 5	10	10	10	10	10	10	10	10	10	10
3 × 7	21	21	21	21	21	21	21	21	21	21
3 × 8	24	24	24	**64**	24	24	**21**	24	24	**21**
3 × 9	27	27	27	27	27	27	**21**	27	27	27
4 × 2	8	8	8	8	8	8	8	**10**	8	8
4 × 5	20	20	20	20	**30**	20	20	20	20	20
4 × 6	24	24	24	**20**	**20**	24	24	**20**	24	**35**
4 × 8	32	32	32	32	**22**	32	32	32	32	32
4 × 9	36	36	36	36	**27**	36	36	**30**	36	36
5 × 2	10	10	**30**	10	10	10	10	10	10	10
5 × 7	30	**42**	30	**35**	**35**	**35**	30	30	**35**	**35**
5 × 8	30	30	30	**35**	30	**34**	30	30	**40**	**34**
6 × 3	24	**18**	**18**	24	**28**	**12**	**18**	**18**	24	24
6 × 4	24	24	24	**18**	24	24	24	24	**18**	**18**
6 × 5	30	30	30	30	30	30	30	30	30	30
6 × 6	36	**42**	36	36	36	36	36	36	36	36
6 × 7	42	**32**	**49**	42	42	42	42	42	42	42
6 × 8	**64**	**49**	**42**	**49**	**44**	**44**	**64**	**48**	**40**	**44**
7 × 3	24	21	21	21	21	21	21	21	21	**24**
7 × 4	**22**	28	28	28	28	28	28	28	28	**32**
7 × 5	35	35	35	35	35	**30**	35	35	35	35
7 × 6	42	42	42	42	42	42	42	42	**49**	42
7 × 7	**29**	49	49	49	49	**52**	49	**42**	49	**42**
7 × 8	**64**	**64**	56	**64**	56	**64**	56	56	**64**	56
8 × 3	24	24	**21**	24	**34**	24	24	24	24	24
8 × 4	32	32	32	32	32	32	**64**	32	32	32
8 × 6	**44**	**49**	**49**	**44**	**44**	**46**	**42**	**49**	**44**	**56**
8 × 7	56	**52**	56	**49**	**62**	**46**	**64**	**64**	**49**	56
8 × 8	64	64	64	64	**54**	64	64	64	64	64
8 × 9	**67**	**67**	**67**	**67**	**67**	**67**	**67**	**67**	**67**	**67**

The convention in the current arithmetic literature is to test for the existence of a problem-size effect by fitting a line to the errors made versus the sum of operands in the problem. Positive slopes to such fits would demonstrate the existence of a problem size effect. The results of this analysis are shown in Figure 4. The model had a problem size effect in all instances. Note that no claims are made of the appropriateness of a linear model for the given data, nor should any conclusions be drawn from the specific parameters of the fit, especially given the sparsity of the data. The sole point of this analysis is to highlight a generally increasing trend.

4 DISCUSSION

As noted in the Results section above, our model demonstrates the problem-size effect in number of errors made (see Figure 4), though the chosen architecture does not permit a response time effect. The presence of this effect is hardly surprising, as all models which use a representation similar to our coarse coding (Mandler & Shebo, 1982; Anderson et al, 1994) display a problem-size effect.

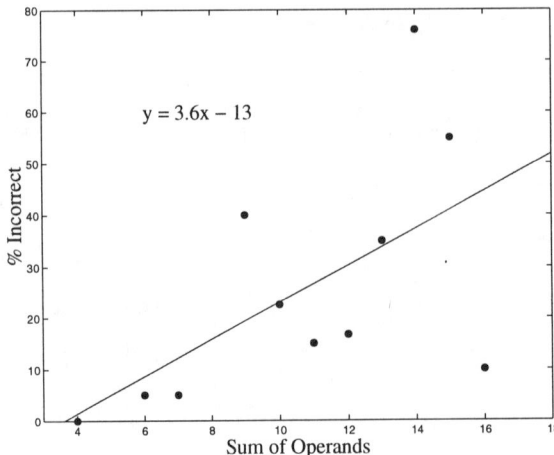

Figure 4: Demonstration of the problem size effect. The data plotted here is for the model trained for 400 iterations, as it proved the best fit to the distribution of errors in humans (Figure 3); a similar analysis gives a best-fit slope of 1.9 for 200 training iterations and 1.1 for 600 training iterations.

It has been suggested by a few researchers (*e.g.* Campbell & Graham, 1985) that the problem-size effect is simply a frequency effect, as humans encounter problems involving smaller operands more often in real life. While there is some evidence to the contrary (Hamman and Ashcraft, 1986), it remains a possibility.

It is immediately apparent from Figure 3 that our model has much the same distribution of errors as seen in normal humans, and is superior to the model of Anderson *et al* (1994) in this regard. That model, implemented as an auto-associative network using a Brain State in a Box (BSB) architecture (Anderson *et al*, 1994; Anderson 1995) generates too many operand errors, and no table, non-table or operation errors. These deficiencies can be predicted from the attractor nature of an auto-associative network. It is the process of translating between representations for digits, and the possibility for error in doing so, which we believe allows our model to produce its various categories of errors.

An interesting aspect of our model is revealed by Figure 3 and Table 1. While increased training of the look-up table improves the overall performance of the model, the error distribution remains relatively constant across the length of training studied. This suggests that in this model, the error distribution is an inherent feature of the architecture, and not a training artifact. This corresponds with data from normal humans, in which the error distribution remains relatively constant across individuals (Girelli *et al*, 1996). As noted above, the design of our model should permit the occurrence of all the various error types, save for operation errors. However, at this point, we do not have a clear understanding of the exact architectural features that generate the error distribution itself.

Defining a model for associative multiplication is only a single step towards the goal of understanding how humans perform general arithmetic. Rumelhart *et al* (1986) proposed a mechanism for multi-digit arithmetic operations given a mechanism for single-digit operations, which addresses part of the issue; this model has been implemented for addition by Cottrell and T'sung (1991). The fact that humans make operation errors suggests that there might be interactions between the mechanisms of associative multiplication and associative addition; conversely, errors on these tasks may occur on different processing levels entirely.

In summary, this model, despite several outstanding questions, shows great potential as a description of the associative multiplication process. Eventually, we expect it to form the basis for a more complete model of arithmetic in human cognition.

Acknowledgements

The first author acknowledges financial support from McMaster University and Industry Canada. The second author acknowledges financial support from the Natural Sciences and Engineering Research Council of Canada. We would like to thank J. Linden, D. Meeker, J. Pezaris, and M. Sahani for their feedback and comments on this work.

References

Anderson J.A. et al. (1994) In *Neural Networks for Knowledge Inference and Representation*, Levine D.S. & Aparicio M., Eds. (Lawrence Erlbaum Associates, Hillsdale NJ) pp. 311-335.

Anderson J.A. (1995) *An Introduction to Neural Networks*. (MIT Press/Bradford, Cambridge MA) pp. 493-544.

Campbell J.I.D. & Graham D.J. (1985) *Canadian Journal of Psychology*. **39** 338.

Cottrell G.W. & T'sung F.S. (1991) In *Advances in Connectionist and Neural Computation Theory*, Burnden J.A. & Pollack J.B., Eds. (Ablex Publishing Co., Norwood NJ) pp. 305-321.

Girelli L. et al. (1996) *Cortex*. **32** 49.

Hamman M.S. & Ashcraft M.H. (1986) *Cognition and Instruction*. **3** 173.

Mandler G. & Shebo B.J. (1982) *Journal of Experimental Psychology: General*. **111** 1.

McCloskey M. et al. (1991) *Journal of Experimental Psychology: Learning, Memory, and Cognition*. **17** 377.

Rumelhart D.E. et al. (1986) In *Parallel distributed processing: Explorations in the microstructure of cognition. Vol. 2: Psychological and biological models*, McClelland JL, Rumelhart DE, & the PDP Research Groups, Eds. (MIT Press/Bradford, Cambridge MA) pp. 7-57.

Siegler R. (1988) *Journal of Experimental Psychology: General*. **117** 258.

Stazyk E.H. et al. (1982) *Journal of Experimental Psychology: Learning, Memory, and Cognition*. **8** 355.

Warrington E.K. (1982) *Quarterly Journal of Experimental Psychology*. **34A** 31.

Facial Memory is Kernel Density Estimation (Almost)

Matthew N. Dailey   Garrison W. Cottrell
Department of Computer Science and Engineering
U.C. San Diego
La Jolla, CA 92093-0114
{mdailey,gary}@cs.ucsd.edu

Thomas A. Busey
Department of Psychology
Indiana University
Bloomington, IN 47405
busey@indiana.edu

Abstract

We compare the ability of three exemplar-based memory models, each using three different face stimulus representations, to account for the probability a human subject responded "old" in an old/new facial memory experiment. The models are 1) the Generalized Context Model, 2) SimSample, a probabilistic sampling model, and 3) MMOM, a novel model related to kernel density estimation that explicitly encodes stimulus distinctiveness. The representations are 1) positions of stimuli in MDS "face space," 2) projections of test faces onto the "eigenfaces" of the study set, and 3) a representation based on response to a grid of Gabor filter jets. Of the 9 model/representation combinations, only the distinctiveness model in MDS space predicts the observed "morph familiarity inversion" effect, in which the subjects' false alarm rate for morphs between similar faces is higher than their hit rate for many of the studied faces. This evidence is consistent with the hypothesis that human memory for faces is a kernel density estimation task, with the caveat that distinctive faces require larger kernels than do typical faces.

1 Background

Studying the errors subjects make during face recognition memory tasks aids our understanding of the mechanisms and representations underlying memory, face processing, and visual perception. One way of evoking such errors is by testing subjects' recognition of new faces created from studied faces that have been combined in some way (e.g. Solso and McCarthy, 1981; Reinitz, Lammers, and Cochran 1992). Busey and Tunnicliff (submitted) have recently examined the extent to which image-quality morphs between unfamiliar faces affect subjects' tendency to make recognition errors.

Their experiments used facial images of bald males and morphs between these images (see

Figure 1: Three normalized morphs from the database.

Figure 1) as stimuli. In one study, Busey (in press) had subjects rate the similarity of all pairs in a large set of faces and morphs, then performed a multidimensional scaling (MDS) of these similarity ratings to derive a 6-dimensional "face space" (Valentine and Endo, 1992). In another study, "Experiment 3" (Busey and Tunnicliff, submitted), 179 subjects studied 68 facial images, including 8 *similar* pairs and 8 *dissimilar pairs*, as determined in a pilot study. These pairs were included in order to study how morphs between similar faces and dissimilar faces evoke false alarms. We call the pair of images from which a morph are derived its "parents," and the morph itself as their "child." In the experiment's test phase, the subjects were asked to make new/old judgments in response to 8 of the 16 morphs, 20 completely new distractor faces, the 36 non-parent targets and one of the parents of each of the 8 morphs. The results were that, for many of the morph/parent pairs, subjects responded "old" to the unstudied morph more often than to its studied parent. However, this effect (a *morph familiarity inversion*) only occurred for the morphs with *similar* parents. It seems that the similar parents are so similar to their "child" morphs that they both contribute toward an "old" (false alarm) response to the morph.

Researchers have proposed many models to account for data from explicit memory experiments. Although we have applied other types of models to Busey and Tunnicliff's data with largely negative results (Dailey et al., 1998), in this paper, we limit discussion to *exemplar-based* models, such as the Generalized Context Model (Nosofsky, 1986) and SAM (Gillund and Shiffrin, 1984). These models rely on the assumption that subjects explicitly store representations of each of the stimuli they study. Busey and Tunnicliff applied several exemplar-based models to the Experiment 3 data, but none of these models have been able to fully account for the observed similar morph familiarity inversion without positing that the similar parents are explicitly blended in memory, producing prototypes near the morphs.

We extend Busey and Tunnicliff's (submitted) work by applying two of their exemplar models to additional image-based face stimulus representations, and we propose a novel exemplar model that accounts for the similar morphs' familiarity inversion. The results are consistent with the hypothesis that facial memory is a kernel density estimation (Bishop, 1995) task, except that *distinctive exemplars require larger kernels*. Also, on the basis of our model, we can predict that distinctiveness *with respect to the study set* is the critical factor influencing kernel size, as opposed to a context-free notion of distinctiveness. We can easily test this prediction empirically.

2 Experimental Methods

2.1 Face Stimuli and Normalization

The original images were 104 digitized 560x662 grayscale images of bald men, with consistent lighting and background and fairly consistent position. The subjects varied in race and extent of facial hair. We automatically located the left and right eyes on each face using a simple template correlation technique then translated, rotated, scaled and cropped each image so the eyes were aligned in each image. We then scaled each image to 114x143 to speed up image processing. Figure 1 shows three examples of the normalized morphs (the original images are copyrighted and cannot be published).

2.2 Representations

Positions in multidimensional face space Many researchers have used a multidimensional scaling approach to model various phenomena in face processing (e.g. Valentine and Endo, 1992). Busey (in press) had 343 subjects rate the similarity of pairs of faces in the test set and performed a multidimensional scaling on the similarity matrix for 100 of the faces (four non-parent target faces were dropped from this analysis). The process resulted in a 6-dimensional solution with $r^2 = 0.785$ and a stress of 0.13. In the MDS modeling results described below, we used the 6-dimensional vector associated with each stimulus as its representation.

Principal component projections "Eigenfaces," or the eigenvectors of the covariance matrix for a set of face images, are a common basis for face representations (e.g. Turk and Pentland, 1991). We performed a principal components analysis on the 68 face images used in the study set for Busey and Tunnicliff's experiment to get the 67 non-zero eigenvectors of their covariance matrix. We then projected each of the 104 test set images onto the 30 most significant eigenfaces to obtain a 30-dimensional vector representing each face.[1]

Gabor filter responses von der Malsburg and colleagues have made effective use of banks of Gabor filters at various orientations and spatial frequencies in face recognition systems. We used one form of their wavelet (Buhmann, Lades, and von der Malsburg, 1990) at five scales and 8 orientations in an 8x8 square grid over each normalized face image as the basis for a third face stimulus representation. However, since this representation resulted in a 2560-dimensional vector for each face stimulus, we performed a principal components analysis to reduce the dimensionality to 30, keeping this representation's dimensionality the same as the eigenface representation's. Thus we obtained a 30-dimensional vector based on Gabor filter responses to represent each test set face image.

2.3 Models

The Generalized Context Model (GCM) There are several different flavors to the GCM. We only consider a simple sum-similarity form that will lead directly to our distinctiveness-modulated density estimation model. Our version of GCM's predicted P(old), given a representation $\mathbf{y}$ of a test stimulus and representations $\mathbf{x} \in \mathbf{X}$ of the studied exemplars, is

$$pred_\mathbf{y} = \alpha + \beta \sum_{\mathbf{x} \in \mathbf{X}} e^{-c(d_{\mathbf{x},\mathbf{y}})^2}$$

where α and β linearly convert the probe's summed similarity to a probability, $\mathbf{X}$ is the set of representations of the study set stimuli; c is used to widen or narrow the width of the similarity function, and $d_{\mathbf{x},\mathbf{y}}$ is either $\|\mathbf{x} - \mathbf{y}\|$, the Euclidean distance between $\mathbf{x}$ and $\mathbf{y}$ or the weighted Euclidean distance $\sqrt{\sum_k w_k (x_k - y_k)^2}$ where the "attentional weights" w_k are constants that sum to 1. Intuitively, this model simply places a Gaussian-shaped function over each of the studied exemplars, and the predicted familiarity of a test probe is simply the summed height of each of these surfaces at the probe's location.

Recall that two of our representations, PC projection space and Gabor filter space, are 30-dimensional, whereas the other, MDS, is only 6-dimensional. Thus allowing adaptive weights for the MDS representation is reasonable, since the resulting model only uses 8 parameters to fit 100 points, but it is clearly unreasonable to allow adaptive weights in PC and Gabor space, where the resulting models would be fitting 32 parameters to 100 points. Thus, for all models, we report results in MDS space both with and without adaptive weights, but do not report adaptive weight results for models in PC and Gabor space.

SimSample Busey and Tunnicliff (submitted) proposed SimSample in an attempt to remedy the GCM's poor predictions of the human data. It is related to both GCM, in that it

---

[1] We used 30 eigenfaces because with this number, our theoretical "distinctiveness" measure was best correlated with the same measure in MDS space.

uses representations in MDS space, and SAM (Gillund and Shiffrin, 1984), in that it involves sampling exemplars. The idea behind the model is that when a subject is shown a test stimulus, instead of a summed comparison to all of the exemplars in memory, the test probe probabilistically samples a *single* exemplar in memory, and the subject responds "old" if the probe's similarity to the exemplar is above a noisy criterion. The model has a similarity scaling parameter and two parameters describing the noisy threshold function. Due to space limitations, we cannot provide the details of the model here.

Busey and Tunnicliff were able to fit the human data within the SimSample framework, but only when they introduced prototypes at the locations of the morphs in MDS space and made the probability of sampling the prototype proportional to the similarity of the parents. Here, however, we only compare with the basic version that does not blend exemplars.

Mixture Model of Memory (MMOM) In this model, we assume that subjects, at study time, implicitly create a probability density surface corresponding to the training set. The subjects' probability of responding "old" to a probe are then taken to be proportional to the height of this surface at the point corresponding to the probe. The surface must be robust in the face of the variability or noise typically encountered in face recognition (lighting changes, perspective changes, etc.) yet also provide some level of discrimination support (i.e. even when the intervals of possible representations for a single face could overlap due to noise, some rational decision boundary must still be constructed). If we assume a Gaussian mixture model, in which the density surface is built from Gaussian "blobs" centered on each studied exemplar, the task is a form of kernel density estimation (Bishop, 1995).

We can formulate the task of predicting the human subjects' P(old) in this framework, then, as optimizing the priors and widths of the kernel functions to minimize the mean squared error of the prediction. However, we also want to minimize the number of free parameters in the model — parsimonious methods for setting the priors and kernel function widths potentially lead to more useful insights into the principles underlying the human data. If the priors and widths were held constant, we would have a simple two parameter model predicting the probability a subject responds "old" to a test stimulus **y**:

$$pred_y = \sum_{x \in X} \alpha e^{-\frac{\|x-y\|^2}{2\sigma^2}}$$

where α folds together the uniform prior and normalization constants, and σ is the standard deviation of the Gaussian kernels. If we ignore the constants, however, this model is essentially the same as the version of the GCM described above. As the results section will show, this model cannot fully account for the human familiarity data in any of our representational spaces.

To improve the model, we introduce two parameters to allow the prior (kernel function height) and standard deviation (kernel function width) to vary with the *distinctiveness* of the studied exemplar. This modification has two intuitive motivations. First, when humans are asked which of two parent faces a 50% morph is most similar to, if one parent is distinctive and the other parent is typical, subjects tend to choose the more distinctive parent (Tanaka et al., submitted). Second, we hypothesize that when a human is asked to study and remember a set of faces for a recognition test, faces with few neighbors will likely have more relaxed (wider) discrimination boundaries than faces with many nearby neighbors.

Thus in each representation space, for each studied face **x**, we computed $d(\mathbf{x})$, the theoretical distinctiveness of each face, as the Z-scored average distance to the five nearest studied faces. We then allowed the height and width of each kernel function to vary with $d(\mathbf{x})$:

$$pred_y = \sum_{x \in X} \alpha(1 + c_\alpha d(\mathbf{x})) e^{-\frac{\|x-y\|^2}{2(\sigma(1+c_\sigma d(\mathbf{x})))^2}}$$

As was the case for GCM and SimSample, we report the results of using a weighted Euclidean distance between **y** and **x** in MDS space only.

Model	MDS space	MDS + weights	PC projections	Gabor jets
GCM	0.1633	0.1417	0.1745	0.1624
SimSample	0.1521	0.1404	0.1756	0.1704
MMOM	0.1601	0.1528	0.1992	0.1668

Table 1: RMSE for the three models and three representations. Quality of fit for models with adaptive attentional weights are only reported for the low-dimensional representation ("MDS + weights"). The baseline RMSE, achievable with a constant prediction, is 0.2044.

2.4 Parameter fitting and model evaluation

For each of the twelve combinations of models with face representations, we searched parameter space by simple hill climbing for the parameter settings that minimized the mean squared error between the model's predicted P(old) and the actual human P(old) data.

We rate each model's effectiveness with two criteria. First, we measure the models' global fit with RMSE over all test set points. A model's RMSE can be compared to the baseline performance of the "dumbest" model, which simply predicts the mean human P(old) of 0.5395, and achieves an RMSE of 0.2044. Second, we evaluate the extent to which a model predicts the mean human response for each of the six categories of test set stimuli: 1) non-parent targets, 2) non-morph distractors, 3) similar parents, 4) dissimilar parents, 5) similar morphs, and 6) dissimilar morphs. If a model correctly predicts the rank ordering of these category means, it obviously accounts for the similar morph familiarity inversion pattern in the human data. As long as models do an adequate job of fitting the human data overall, as measured by RMSE, we prefer models that predict the morph familiarity inversion effect as a natural consequence of minimizing RMSE.

3 Results

Table 1 shows the global fit of each model/representation pair. The SimSample model in MDS space provides the best quantitative fit. GCM generally outperforms MMOM, indicating that for a tight quantitative fit, having parameters for a linear transformation built into the model is more important than allowing the kernel function to vary with distinctiveness. Also of note is that the PC projection representation is consistently outperformed by both the Gabor jet representation and the MDS space representation.

But for our purposes, the degree to which a model predicts the mean human responses for each of the six categories of stimuli is more important, given that it is doing a reasonably good job globally. Figure 2 takes a more detailed look at how well each model predicts the human category means. Even though SimSample in MDS space has the best global fit to the human familiarity ratings, it does not predict the familiarity inversion for similar morphs. Only the mixture model in weighted MDS space correctly predicts the morph familiarity effect. All of the other models underpredict the human responses to the similar morphs.

4 Discussion

The results for the mixture model are consistent with the hypothesis that facial memory is a kernel density estimation task, with the caveat that distinctive exemplars require larger kernels. Whereas true density estimation would tend to deemphasize outliers in sparse areas of the face space, the human data show that the priors and kernel function widths for outliers should actually be increased. Two potentially significant problems with the work presented here are first, we experimented with several models before finding that MMOM was able to predict the morph familiarity inversion effect, and second, we are fitting a single

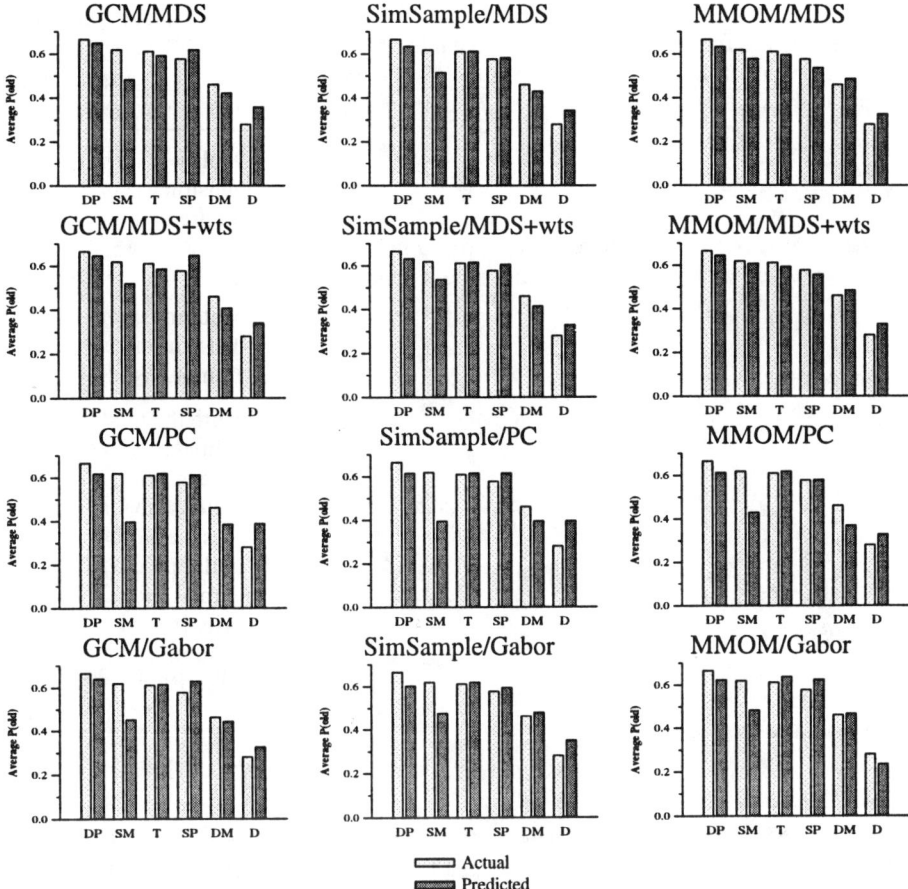

Figure 2: Average actual/predicted responses to the faces in each category. Key: DP = Dissimilar parents; SM = Similar morphs; T = Non-parent targets; SP = Similar parents; DM = Dissimilar morphs; D = Distractors.

experiment. The model thus must be carefully tested against new data, and its predictions empirically validated.

Since a theoretical distinctiveness measure based on the sparseness of face space around an exemplar was sufficient to account for the similar morphs' familiarity inversion, we predict that distinctiveness with respect to the study set is the critical factor influencing kernel size, rather than context-free human distinctiveness judgments. We can easily test this prediction by having subjects rate the distinctiveness of the stimuli without prior exposure and then determine whether their distinctiveness ratings improve or degrade the model's fit.

A somewhat disappointing (though not particularly surprising) aspect of our results is that the model requires a representation based on human similarity judgments. Ideally, we would prefer to provide an information-processing account using image-based representations like eigenface projections or Gabor filter responses. Interestingly, the efficacy of the image-based representations seems to depend on how similar they are to the MDS representations. The PC projection representation performed the worst, and distances between pairs of PC representations had a correlation of 0.388 with the distances between pairs of MDS representations. For the Gabor filter representation, which performed better, the correlation is 0.517. In future work, we plan to investigate how the MDS representation (or a representation like it) might be derived directly from the face images.

Besides providing an information-processing account of the human data, there are several other avenues for future research. These include empirical testing of our distinctiveness predictions, evaluating the applicability of the distinctiveness model in domains other than face processing, and evaluating the ability of other modeling paradigms to account for this data.

Acknowledgements

We thank Chris Vogt for comments on a previous draft, and other members of Gary's Unbelievable Research Unit (GURU) for earlier comments on this work. This research was supported in part by NIMH grant MH57075 to GWC.

References

Bishop, C. M. (1995). *Neural networks for pattern recognition*. Oxford University Press, Oxford.

Busey, T. A. (1999). Where are morphed faces in multi-dimensional face space? *Psychological Science*. In press.

Busey, T. A. and Tunnicliff, J. (submitted). Accounts of blending, distinctiveness and typicality in face recognition. *Journal of Experimental Psychology: Learning, Memory, and Cognition*.

Dailey, M. N., Cottrell, G. W., and Busey, T. A. (1998). Eigenfaces for familiarity. In *Proceedings of the Twentieth Annual Conference of the Cognitive Science Society*, pages 273–278, Mahwah, NJ. Erlbaum.

Gillund, G. and Shiffrin, R. (1984). A retrieval model for both recognition and recall. *Psychological Review*, 93(4):411–428.

J. Buhmann, M. L. and von der Malsburg, C. (1990). Size and distortion invariant object recognition by hierarchical graph matching. In *Proceedings of the IJCNN International Joint Conference on Neural Networks*, volume II, pages 411–416.

Nosofsky, R. M. (1986). Attention, similarity, and the identification-categorization relationship. *Journal of Experimental Psychology: General*, 116(1):39–57.

Reinitz, M., Lammers, W., and Cochran, B. (1992). Memory-conjunction errors: Miscombination of stored stimulus features can produce illusions of memory. *Memory & Cognition*, 20(1):1–11.

Solso, R. L. and McCarthy, J. E. (1981). Prototype formation of faces: A case of pseudomemory. *British Journal of Psychology*, 72(4):499–503.

Tanaka, J., Giles, M., Kremen, S., and Simon, V. (submitted). Mapping attractor fields in face space: The atypicality bias in face recognition.

Turk, M. and Pentland, A. (1991). Eigenfaces for recognition. *The Journal of Cognitive Neuroscience*, 3:71–86.

Valentine, T. and Endo, M. (1992). Towards an exemplar model of face processing: The effects of race and distinctiveness. *The Quarterly Journal of Experimental Psychology*, 44A(4):671–703.

Multiple Paired Forward-Inverse Models for Human Motor Learning and Control

Masahiko Haruno[*]
mharuno@hip.atr.co.jp

Daniel M. Wolpert[†]
wolpert@hera.ucl.ac.uk

Mitsuo Kawato[*◦]
kawato@hip.atr.co.jp

[*]ATR Human Information Processing Research Laboratories
2-2 Hikaridai, Seika-cho, Soraku-gun, Kyoto 619-02, Japan.
[†]Sobell Department of Neurophysiology, Institute of Neurology,
Queen Square, London WC1N 3BG, United Kingdom.
[◦]Dynamic Brain Project, ERATO, JST, Kyoto, Japan.

Abstract

Humans demonstrate a remarkable ability to generate accurate and appropriate motor behavior under many different and often uncertain environmental conditions. This paper describes a new modular approach to human motor learning and control, based on multiple pairs of inverse (controller) and forward (predictor) models. This architecture simultaneously learns the multiple inverse models necessary for control as well as how to select the inverse models appropriate for a given environment. Simulations of object manipulation demonstrates the ability to learn multiple objects, appropriate generalization to novel objects and the inappropriate activation of motor programs based on visual cues, followed by on-line correction, seen in the "size-weight illusion".

1 Introduction

Given the multitude of contexts within which we must act, there are two qualitatively distinct strategies to motor control and learning. The first is to use a single controller which would need to be highly complex to allow for all possible scenarios. If this controller were unable to encapsulate all the contexts it would need to adapt every time the context of the movement changed before it could produce appropriate motor commands—this would produce transient and possibly large performance errors. Alternatively, a modular approach can be used in which multiple controllers co-exist, with each controller suitable for one or a small set of contexts. Such a modular strategy has been introduced in the "mixture of experts" architecture for supervised learning [6]. This architecture comprises a set of expert networks and a gating network which performs classification by combining each expert's output. These networks are trained simultaneously so that the gating network splits the input space into regions in which particular experts can specialize.

To apply such a modular strategy to motor control two problems must be solved. First how are the set of inverse models (controllers) learned to cover the contexts which might be experienced—the module learning problem. Second, given a set of inverse modules (controllers) how are the correct subset selected for the current context—the module selection problem. From human psychophysical data we know that such a selection process must be driven by two distinct processes; feedforward switching based on sensory signals such as the perceived size of an object, and switching based on feedback of the outcome of a movement. For example, on picking up a object which appears heavy, feedforward switching may activate controllers responsible for generating a large motor impulse. However, feedback processes, based on contact with the object, can indicate that it is in fact light thereby switching control to inverse models appropriate for a light object.

In the context of motor control and learning, Gomi and Kawato [4] combined the feedback-error-learning [7] approach and the mixture of experts architecture to learn multiple inverse models for different manipulated objects. They used both the visual shapes of the manipulated objects and intrinsic signals, such as somatosensory feedback and efference copy of the motor command, as the inputs to the gating network. Using this architecture it was quite difficult to acquire multiple inverse models. This difficulty arose because a single gating network needed to divide up, based solely on control error, the large input space into complex regions. Furthermore, Gomi and Kawato's model could not demonstrate feedforward controller selection prior to movement execution.

Here we describe a model of human motor control which addresses these problems and can solve the module learning and selection problems in a computationally coherent manner. The basic idea of the model is that the brain contains multiple pairs (modules) of forward (predictor) and inverse (controller) models (MPFIM) [10]. Within each module, the forward and inverse models are tightly coupled both during their acquisition and use, in which the forward models determine the contribution (responsibility) of each inverse model's output to the final motor command. This architecture can simultaneously learn the multiple inverse models necessary for control as well as how to select the inverse models appropriate for a given environment in both a feedforward and a feedback manner.

2 Multiple paired forward-inverse models

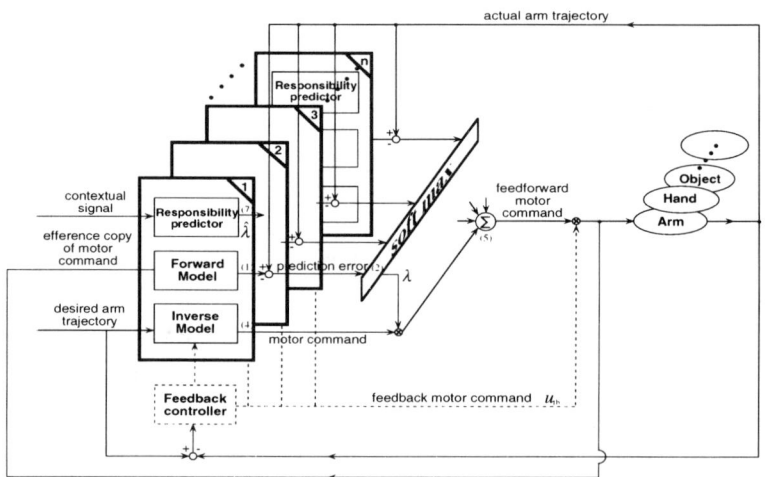

Figure 1: A schematic diagram showing how MPFIM architecture is used to control arm movement while manipulating different objects. Parenthesized numbers in the figure relate to the equations in the text.

2.1 Motor learning and feedback selection

Figure 1 illustrates how the MPFIM architecture can be used to learn and control arm movements when the hand manipulates different objects. Central to the multiple paired forward-inverse model is the notion of dividing up experience using predictive forward models. We consider n undifferentiated forward models which each receive the current state, x_t, and motor command, u_t, as input. The output of the ith forward model is $\hat{x}^i_{t+1}$, the prediction of the next state at time t

$$\hat{x}^i_{t+1} = \phi(w^i_t, x_t, u_t) \quad (1)$$

where w^i_t are the parameters of a function approximator ϕ (e.g. neural network weights) used to model the forward dynamics. These predicted next states are compared to the actual next state to provide the responsibility signal which represents the extent to which each forward model presently accounts for the behavior of the system. Based on the prediction errors of the forward models, the responsibility signal, λ^i_t, for the i-th forward-inverse model pair (module) is calculated by the soft-max function

$$\lambda^i_t = \frac{e^{-|x_t - \hat{x}^i_t|^2 / 2\sigma^2}}{\sum_{j=1}^{n} e^{-|x_t - \hat{x}^j_t|^2 / 2\sigma^2}} \quad (2)$$

where x_t is the true state of the system and σ is a scaling constant. The soft-max transforms the errors using the exponential function and then normalizes these values across the modules, so that the responsibilities lie between 0 and 1 and sum to 1 over the modules. Those forward models which capture the current behavior, and therefore produce small prediction errors, will have high responsibilities [1]. The responsibilities are then used to control the learning of the forward models in a competitive manner, with those models with high responsibilities receiving proportionally more of their error signal than modules with low responsibility. The competitive learning among forward models is similar in spirit to "annealed competition of experts" architecture [9].

$$\Delta w^i_t = \epsilon \lambda^i_t \frac{d\phi_i}{dw^i_t}(x_t - \hat{x}^i_t) = \epsilon \frac{d\hat{x}^i_t}{dw^i_t} \lambda^i_t (x_t - \hat{x}^i_t) \quad (3)$$

For each forward model there is a paired inverse model whose inputs are the desired next state x^*_{t+1} and the current state x_t. The ith inverse model produces a motor command u^i_t as output

$$u^i_t = \psi(\alpha^i_t, x^*_{t+1}, x_t) \quad (4)$$

where α^i_t are the parameters of some function approximator ψ.

The total motor command is the summation of the outputs from these inverse models using the responsibilities, λ^i_t, to weight the contributions.

$$u_t = \sum_{i=1}^{n} \lambda^i_t u^i_t = \sum_{i=1}^{n} \lambda^i_t \psi(\alpha^i_t, x^*_{t+1}, x_t) \quad (5)$$

Once again, the responsibilities are used to weight the learning of each inverse model. This ensures that inverse models learns only when their paired forward models make accurate predictions. Although for supervised learning the desired control command u^*_t is needed (but is generally not available), we can approximate $(u^*_t - u^i_t)$ with the feedback motor command signal u_{fb} [7].

---

[1] Because selecting modules can be regarded as a hidden state estimation problem, an alternative way to determine appropriate forward models is to use the EM algorithm [3].

$$\Delta \alpha_t^i = \epsilon \lambda_t^i \frac{d\psi_i}{d\alpha_t^i}(u_t^* - u_t^i) = \epsilon \frac{du_t^i}{d\alpha_t^i} \lambda_t^i (u_t^* - u_t^i) \simeq \epsilon \frac{du_t^i}{d\alpha_t^i} \lambda_t^i u_{fb} \qquad (6)$$

In summary, the responsibility signals are used in three ways—first to gate the learning of the forward models (Equation 3), second to gate the learning of the inverse models (Equation 6), and third to gate the contribution of the inverse models to the final motor command (Equation 5).

2.2 Multiple responsibility predictors: Feedforward selection

While the system described so far can learn multiple controllers and switch between them based on prediction errors, it cannot provide switching before a motor command has been generated and the consequences of this action evaluated. To allow the system to switch controllers based on contextual information, we introduce a new component, the responsibility predictor (RP). The input to this module, y_t, contains contextual sensory information (Figure 1) and each RP produces a prediction of its own module's responsibility

$$\hat{\lambda}_t^i = \eta(\gamma_t^i, y_t). \qquad (7)$$

These estimated responsibilities can then be compared to the actual responsibilities λ_t^i generated from the responsibility estimator. These error signals are used to update the weights of the RP by supervised learning.

Finally a mechanism is required to combine the responsibility estimates derived from the feedforward RP and from the forward models' prediction errors derived from feedback. We determine the final value of responsibility by using Bayes rule; multiplying the transformed feedback errors $e^{-|x_t - \hat{x}_t^i|^2/\sigma^2}$ by the feedforward responsibility $\hat{\lambda}_t^i$ and then normalizing across the modules within the responsibility estimator: $\hat{\lambda}_t^i e^{-|x_t-\hat{x}_t^i|^2/2\sigma^2} / \sum_{j=1}^n \hat{\lambda}_t^j e^{-|x_t-\hat{x}_t^j|^2/2\sigma^2}$

The estimates of the responsibilities produced by the RP can be considered as *prior* probabilities because they are computed before the movement execution based only on extrinsic signals and do not rely on knowing the consequences of the action. Once an action takes place, the forward models' errors can be calculated and this can be thought of as the *likelihood* after the movement execution based on knowledge of the result of the movement. The final responsibility which is the product of the prior and likelihood, normalized across the modules, represents the *posterior* probability. Adaptation of the RP ensures that the prior probability becomes closer to the posterior probability.

3 Simulation of arm tracking while manipulating objects

3.1 Learning and control of different objects

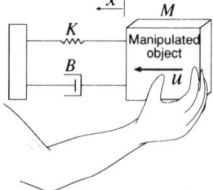

	M (Kg)	B (N m^{-1} s)	K (N m^{-1})
α	1.0	2.0	8.0
β	5.0	7.0	4.0
γ	8.0	3.0	1.0
δ	2.0	10.0	1.0

Figure 2: Schematic illustration of the simulation experiment in which the arm makes reaching movements while grasping different objects with mass M, damping B and spring K. The object properties are shown in the Table.

To examine motor learning and control we simulated a task in which the hand had to track a given trajectory (30 s shown in Fig. 3 (b)), while holding different objects (Figure 2). The manipulated object was periodically switched every 5 s between three different objects α, β and γ in this order. The physical characteristics of these objects are shown in Figure 2. The task was exactly the same as that of Gomi and Kawato [4], and simulates recent grip force-load force coupling experiments by Flanagan and Wing [2].

In the first simulation, three forward-inverse model pairs (modules) were used: the same number of modules as the number of objects. We assumed the existence of a perfect inverse dynamic model of the arm for the control of reaching movements. In each module, both forward (ϕ in (1)) and inverse (ψ in (4)) models were implemented as a linear neural network[2]. The use of linear networks allowed M, B and K to be estimated from the forward and inverse model weights. Let M_j^F, B_j^F, K_j^F be the estimates from the jth forward model and M_j^I, B_j^I, K_j^I be the estimates from the jth inverse model.

Figure 3(a) shows the evolution of the forward model estimates of M_j^F, B_j^F, K_j^F for the three modules during learning. During learning the desired trajectory (Fig. 3(b)) was repeated 200 times. The three modules started from randomly selected initial conditions (open arrows) and converged to very good approximations of the three objects (filled arrows) as shown in Table 1. Each of the three modules converged to α, β and γ objects, respectively. It is interesting to note that all the estimates of the forward models are superior to those of inverse models. This is because the inverse model learning depends on how modules are switched by the forward models.

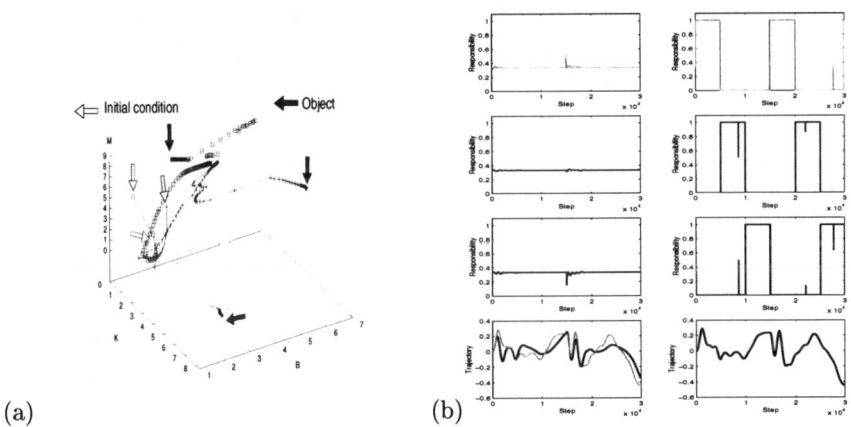

Figure 3: (a) Learning acquisition of three pairs of forward and inverse models corresponding to three objects. (b) Responsibility signals from the three modules (top 3) and tracking performance (bottom) at the beginning (left) and at the end (right) of learning.

Module	M_j^F	B_j^F	K_j^F	M_j^I	B_j^I	K_j^I
1	1.0020	2.0080	8.0000	1.0711	2.0080	8.0000
2	5.0071	7.0040	4.0000	5.0102	6.9554	4.0089
3	8.0029	3.0010	0.9999	7.8675	3.0467	0.9527

Table 1: Learned object characteristics

Figure 3(b) shows the performance of the model at the beginning (left) and end (right) of learning. The top 3 panels show the responsibility signals of α, β and γ modules in

---
[2] Any kind of architecture can be adopted instead of linear networks

this order, and the bottom panel shows the hand's actual and desired trajectories. At the start of learning, the three modules were equally poor and thus generated almost equal responsibilities (1/3) and were involved in control almost equally. As a result, the overall control performance was poor with large trajectory errors. However, at the end of learning, the three modules switched almost perfectly (only three noisy spikes were observed in the top 3 panels on the right), and no trajectory error was visible at this resolution in the bottom panel. If we compare these results with Figure 7 of Gomi and Kawato [4] for the same task, the superiority of the MPFIM compared to the gating-expert architecture is apparent. Note that the number of free parameters (synaptic weights) is smaller in the current architecture than the other. The difference in performance comes from two features of the basic architecture. First, in the gating architecture a single gating network tries to divide the space while many forward models splits the space in MPFIM. Second, in the gating architecture only a single control error is used to divide the space, but multiple prediction errors are simultaneously utilized in MPFIM.

3.2 Generalization to a novel object

A natural question regarding MPFIM architecture is how many modules need to be used. In other words, what happens if the number of objects exceeds the number of modules or an already trained MPFIM is presented with an unfamiliar object. To examine this, the MPFIM trained from 4 objects α,β,γ and δ was presented with a novel object η (its (M, B, K) is (2.02,3.23,4.47)). Because the object dynamics can be represented in a 3-dimensional parameter space and the 4 modules already acquired define 4 vertices of a tetrahedron within the 3-D space, arbitrary object dynamics contained within the tetrahedron can be decomposed into a weighted average of the existing 4 forward modules (internal division point of the 4 vertices). The theoretically calculated weights of η were (0.15,0.20,0.35,0.30). Interestingly, each module's responsibility signal averaged over trajectory was (0.14,0.24,0.37,0.26). Although the responsibility was computed in the space of accelerations prediction by soft-max and had no direct relation to the space of (M, B, K), the two vectors had very similar values. This demonstrates the flexibility of MPFIM architecture which originates from its probabilistic soft-switching mechanism. This is in sharp contrast to the hard switching of Narendra [8] for which only one controller can be selected at a time.

3.3 Feedforward selection and the size-weight illusion

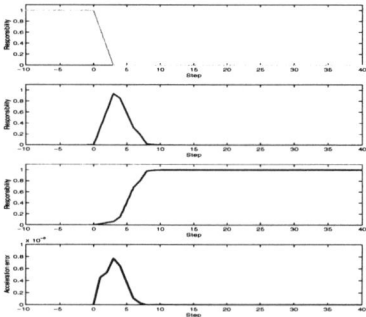

Figure 4: Responsibility predictions based on contextual information of 2-D object shapes (top 3 traces) and corresponding acceleration error of control induced by the illusion (bottom trace)

In this section, we simulated prior selection of inverse models by responsibility predictors based on contextual information, and reproduce the size-weight illusion. Each object was associated with a 2-D shape represented as a 3×3 binary matrix, which was randomly placed at one of four possible locations on a 4×4 retinal matrix (see Gomi and Kawato for more details). The retinal matrix was used as the contextual input to the RP (3-layer sigmoidal feedforward network). During the course of learning, the combination of manipulated objects and visual cues were fixed as A-α, B-β and C-γ. After 200 iterations of the trajectory, the combination A-γ was presented for the first. Figure 4 plots the responsibility signals of the three modules (top 3 traces) and corresponding acceleration error of the control induced by the illusion (bottom trace). The result replicates the size-weight illusion [1, 5] seen in the erroneous responsibility prediction of the α responsibility predictor based on the contextual signal A and its correction by the responsibility signal calculated by the forward models. Until the onset of movement (time 0), A was always associated with light α, and C was always associated with heavy γ. Prior to movement when A was associated with γ, the α module was switched on by the visual contextual information, but soon after the movement was initiated, the responsibility signal from the forward model's prediction dominated, and the γ module was properly selected. Furthermore, after a while, the responsibility predictor of the modules were re-learned to capture this new association between the objects visual shape and its dynamics.

In conclusion, the MPFIM model of human motor learning and control, like the human motor system, can learn multiple tasks, shows generalization to new tasks and an ability to switch between tasks appropriately.

Acknowledgments

We thank Zoubin Ghahramani for helpful discussions on the Bayesian formulation of this model. Partially supported by Special Coordination Funds for promoting Science and Technology at the Science and Technology Agency of Japanese govenmnent, and by HFSP grant.

References

[1] E. Brenner, B. Jeroen, and J. Smeets. Size illusion influences how we lift but not how we grasp an object. *Exp Brain Res*, 111:473–476, 1996.

[2] J.R. Flanagan and A. Wing. The role of internal models in motion planning and control: Evidence from grip force adjustments during movements of hand-held loads. *J Neurosci*, 17(4):1519–1528, 1997.

[3] A.M. Fraser and A. Dimitriadis. Forecasting probability densities by using hidden Markov models with mixed states. In A.S. Wiegand and N.A. Gershenfeld, editors, *Time series prediction: Forecasting the future and understanding the past*, pages 265–282. Addison-Wesley, 1993.

[4] H. Gomi and M. Kawato. Recognition of manipulated objects by motor learning with modular architecture networks. *Neural Networks*, 6:485–497, 1993.

[5] A. Gordon, H. Forssberg, R. Johansson, and G. Westling. Visual size cues in the programming of manipulative forces during precision grip. *Exp Brain Res*, 83:477–482, 1991.

[6] R. Jacobs, M. Jordan, S. Nowlan, and G. Hinton. Adaptive mixture of local experts. *Neural Computation*, 3:79–87, 1991.

[7] M. Kawato. Feedback-error-learning neural network for supervised learning. In R. Eckmiller, editor, *Advanced neural computers*, pages 365–372. North-Holland, 1990.

[8] K. Narendra and J. Balakrishnan. Adaptive control using multiple models. *IEEE Transaction on Automatic Control*, 42(2):171–187, 1997.

[9] K. Pawelzik, J. Kohlmorgen, and K. Müller. Annealed competition of experts for a segmentation and classification of switching dynamics. *Neural Computation*, 8:340–356, 1996.

[10] D.M. Wolpert and M. Kawato. Multiple paired forward and inverse models for motor control. *Neural Networks*, 11:1317–1329, 1998.

Utilizing Time: Asynchronous Binding

Bradley C. Love
Department of Psychology
Northwestern University
Evanston, IL 60208

Abstract

Historically, connectionist systems have not excelled at representing and manipulating complex structures. How can a system composed of simple neuron-like computing elements encode complex relations? Recently, researchers have begun to appreciate that representations can extend in both time and space. Many researchers have proposed that the synchronous firing of units can encode complex representations. I identify the limitations of this approach and present an *asynchronous* model of binding that effectively represents complex structures. The asynchronous model extends the synchronous approach. I argue that our cognitive architecture utilizes a similar mechanism.

1 Introduction

Simple connectionist models can fall prey to the "binding problem". A binding problem occurs when two different events (or objects) are represented identically. For example, representing "John hit Ted" by activating the units **JOHN**, **HIT**, and **TED** would lead to a binding problem because the same pattern of activation would also be used to represent "Ted hit John". The binding problem is ubiquitous and is a concern whenever internal representations are postulated. In addition to guarding against the binding problem, an effective binding mechanism must construct representations that assist processing. For instance, different states of the world must be represented in a manner that assists in discovering commonalities between disparate states, allowing for category formation and analogical processing.

Interestingly, new connectionist binding mechanisms [5, 9, 12] utilize time in their operation. Pollack's Recursive Auto-Associative Memory (RAAM) model combines a standard fixed-width multi-layer network architecture with a stack and a simple controller, enabling RAAM to encode hierarchical representations over multiple processing steps. RAAM requires more time to encode representations as they become more complex, but its space requirements remain constant. The clearest example of utilizing time are models that perform dynamic binding through synchronous firings of units [17, 5, 12]. Synchrony models explicitly use time to mark relations between units, distributing complex representations across multiple time steps.

Most other models neglect the time aspect of representation. Even synchrony models fail to fully utilize time (I will clarify this point in a later section). In this paper, a model is introduced (the asynchronous binding mechanism) that attempts to rectify this situation. The asynchronous approach is similar to the synchronous approach but is more effective in binding complex representations and exploiting time.

2 Utilizing time and the brain

Representational power can be greatly increased by taking advantage of the time dimension of representation. For instance, a telephone would need thousands of buttons to make a call if sequences of digits were not used. From the standpoint of a neuron, taking advantage of timing information increases processing capacity by more than a 100 fold [13]. While this suggests that the neural code might utilize both time and space resources, the neuroscience community has not yet arrived at a consensus. While it is known that the behavior of a postsynaptic neuron is affected by the location and arrival times of dendritic input [10], it is generally believed that only the rate of firing (a neuron's firing rate is akin to the activation level of a unit in a connectionist network) can code information, as opposed to the timing of spikes, since neurons are noisy devices [14]. However, findings that are taken as evidence for rate coding, like elevated firing rates in memory retention tasks [8], can often be reinterpreted as part of complex cortical events that extend through time [1]. In accord with this view, recent empirical findings suggests that the timing of spikes (e.g., firing patterns, intervals) are also part of the neural code [4, 16]. Contrary to the rate based view (which holds only that only the firing rate of a neuron encodes information), these studies suggest that the timing of spikes encodes information (e.g., when two neurons repeatedly spike together it signifies something different than when they fire out of phase, even if their firing rates are identical in both cases).

Behavioral findings also appear consistent with the idea that time is used to construct complex representations. Behavioral research in illusory conjunction phenomena [15], and sentence processing performance [11] all suggest that bindings or relations are established through time, with bindings becoming more certain as processing proceeds. In summary, early in processing humans can gauge which representational elements are relevant while remaining uncertain about how these elements are interrelated.

3 Dynamic binding through synchrony

Given the demands placed on a representational system, a system that utilizes dynamic binding through synchrony would seem to be a good candidate mental architecture (though, as we will see, limitations arise when representing complex structures). A synchronous binding account of our mental architecture is consistent (at a general level) with behavioral findings, the intuition that complex representations are distributed across time, and that neural temporal dynamics code information. Synchrony seems to offer the power to recombine a finite set of elements in a virtually unlimited number of ways (the defining characteristic of a discrete combinatorial system).

While synchrony models seem appropriate for modeling certain behaviors, dynamic binding through synchrony does not seem to be an appropriate mechanism for establishing complex recursive bindings [2]. In a synchronous dynamic binding system, the distinction between a slot and a filler is lost, since bindings are not directional (i.e., which unit is a predicate and which unit is an argument is not clear). The slot and the filler simply share the same phase. In this sense, the mechanism is more akin to a grouping mechanism than to a binding mechanism. Grouping units together indicates that the units are a part of the same representation, but does not sort out the relations among the units as binding does.

Synchrony runs into trouble when a unit has to act simultaneously as a slot and a filler. For instance, to represent embedded propositions with synchronous binding, a controller needs to be added. For instance, a structure with embedding, like **A**→**B**→**C**, could be represented with synchronous firings if **A** and **B** fired synchronously and then **B** and **C** fired synchronously. Still, synchronous binding blurs the distinction between a slot and a filler, necessitating that **A**, **B**, and **C** be marked as slots or fillers to unambiguously represent the simple **A**→**B**→**C** structure. Notice that **B** must be marked as a slot when it fires synchronously with **A**, but must be marked as filler when it synchronously fires with **C**. When representing embedded structures, the synchronous approach becomes complicated (i.e., simple connections are not sufficient to modulate firing patterns) and rigid (i.e., parallelism and flexibility are lost when a unit has to be either a slot or a filler). Ideally, units would be able to act simultaneously as slots and fillers, instead of alternating between these two structural roles.

4 The asynchronous approach

While synchrony models utilize some timing information, other valuable timing information is discarded as noise, making it difficult to represent multiple levels of structure. If **A** fired slightly before **B**, which fired slightly before **C**, asynchronous timing information (ordering information) would be available. This ordering information allows for directional binding relations and alleviates the need to label units as slots or fillers. Notice that **B** can act simultaneously as a slot and a filler. Directional bindings can unambiguously represent complex structures.

Phase locking and wave like patterns of firing need not occur during asynchronous binding. For instance, the firing pattern that encodes a structure like **A**→**B**→**C** does not need to be orderly (i.e., starting with **A** and ending with **C**). To encode **A**→**B**→**C**, unit **B**'s firing schedule must observably speed up (on average) after unit **A** fires, while **C**'s must speed up after **B** fires. For example, if we only considered the time window immediately after a unit fires, a firing sequence of **B**, **C**, no unit fires, **A**, and then **B** would provide evidence for the structure **A**→**B**→**C**. Of course, if **A**, **B**, and **C** fire periodically with stochastic schedules that are influenced by other units' firings, spurious binding evidence will accrue (e.g., occasionally, **C** will fire and **A** will fire in the next time step). Luckily, these accidents will be less frequent than events that support the intended bindings. As binding evidence is accumulated over time, binding errors will become less likely.

Interestingly, the asynchronous mechanism can also represent structures through an inhibitory process that mirrors the excitatory process described above. **A**→**B**→**C** could be represented asynchronously if **A** was less likely to fire after **B** fired and **B** was less likely to fire after **C** fired. An inhibitory (negative) connection from **B** to **A** is in some ways equivalent to an excitatory (positive) connection form **A** to **B**.

4.1 The mathematical expression of the model

The previous discussion of the asynchronous approach can be formalized. Below is a description of an asynchronous model that I have implemented.

4.1.1 The anatomy of a unit

Individual units, when unaffected by other units, will fire periodically when active:

$$\text{if } R_{t_i} \geq 1, \text{ then } O_{t_{i+1}} = 1, \text{ otherwise } O_{t_{i+1}} = 0. \quad (1)$$

where $O_{t_{i+1}}$ is the unit's output (at time $i+1$), R_{t_i} is the unit's output refractory period which is randomly set (after the unit fires) to a value drawn from the uniform distribution between 0 and 1 and is incremented at each time step by some constant (which was set to .1 in all simulations). Notice that a unit produces an output one time step after its output refractory period reaches threshold.

4.1.2 A unit's behavior in the presence of other units

A unit alters its output refractory if it receives a signal (via a connection) from a unit that has just fired (i.e., a unit with a positive output). For example, if unit **A** fires (its output is 1) and there is a connection to unit **B** of strength +.3, then **B**'s output refractory will be incremented by +.3, enabling unit **B** to fire during the next time step or at least decreasing the time until **B** fires. Alternatively, negative (inhibitory) connections lower refractory.

Two unconnected units will tend to fire independently of each other, providing little evidence for a binding relation. Again, over a small time window, two units may fire contiguously by chance, but over many firings the evidence for a binding will approach zero.

4.1.3 Interpreting firing patterns

Every time a unit fires, it creates evidence for binding hypotheses. The critical issue is how to collect and evaluate evidence for bindings. There are many possible evidence functions that interpret firing patterns in a sensible fashion. One simple function is to have evidence for two units binding decrease linearly as the time between their firings increases. Evidence is updated every time step according to the following equation:

$$\text{if } \rho \geq (t_{U_j} - t_{U_i}) \geq 1, \text{ then } \Delta E_{ij} = -(1/\rho)(t_{U_j} - t_{U_i}) + (1/\rho) + 1. \quad (2)$$

where ρ is the size of the window for considering binding evidence (i.e., if ρ is 5, then units firing 5 time steps apart still generate binding evidence), t_{U_i} is the most recent time step unit U_i fired, and ΔE_{ij} is the change in the amount of evidence for U_i binding to U_j. Of course, some evidence will be spurious. The following decision rule can be used to determine if two units share a binding relation:

$$\text{if } (E_{ij} - E_{ji}) > k, \text{ then } U_i \text{ binds to } U_j. \quad (3)$$

where k is some threshold greater than 0. This decision rule is formally equivalent to the diffusion model which is a type of random walk model [6]. Equations 2 and 3 are very simple. Other more sophisticated methods can be used for collecting and evaluating binding evidence.

4.2 Performance of the Asynchronous Mechanism

In this section, the asynchronous binding mechanism's performance characteristics are examined. In particular, the model's ability to represent tree structures of

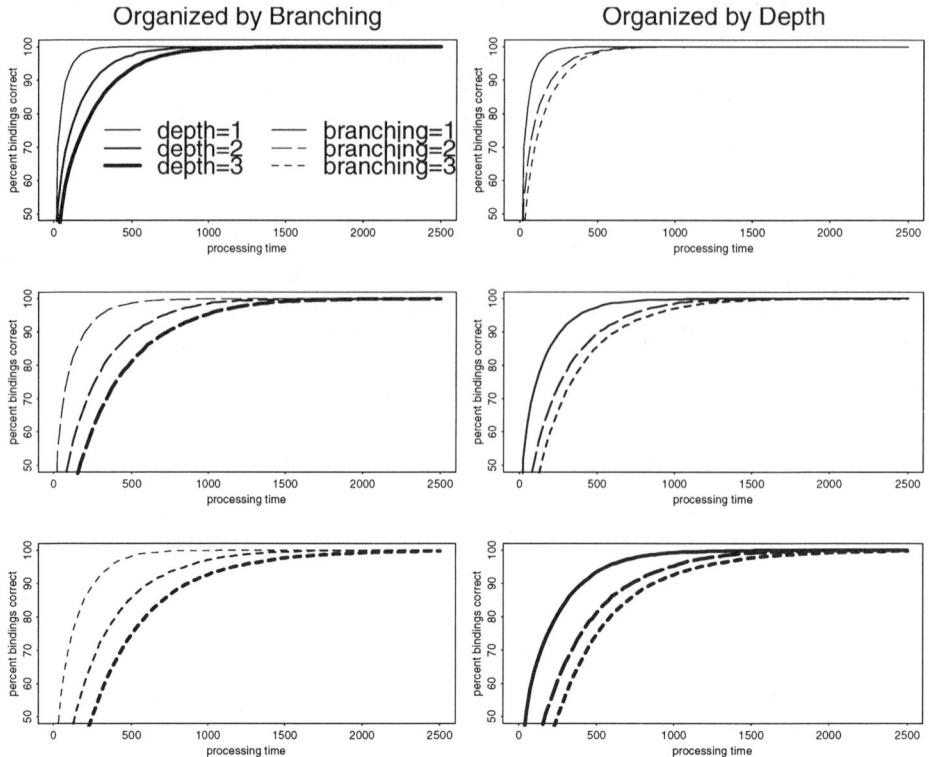

Figure 1: Performance curves for the 9 different structures are shown.

varying complexity was explored. Tree structures can be used to represent complex relational information, like the parse of a sentence. An advantage of using tree structures to measure performance is that the complexity of a tree can be easily described by two factors. Trees can vary in their depth and branching. In the simulations reported here, trees had a branching factor and depth of either 1, 2, or 3. These two factors were crossed, yielding 9 different tree structures. This design makes it possible to assess how the model processes structures of varying complexity. One sensible prediction (given our intuitions about how we process structured representations) is that trees with greater depth and branching will take longer to represent.

In the simulations reported here, both positive and negative connections were used simultaneously. For instance, in a tree structure, if **A** was intended to bind to **B**, **A**'s connection to **B** was set to +.1 and **B**'s connection to **A** was set to −.1. The combination of both connection types yields the best performance.

In these simulations both excitatory and inhibitory binding connection values were set relatively low (all binding connections were set to size .1), providing a strict test of the model's sensitivity. The low connection values prevented bound units from establishing tight couplings (characteristic of bound units in synchrony models). For example, with an excitatory connection from **A** to **B** of .1, **A**'s firing does not ensure that **B** will fire in the next time step (or the next few time steps for that matter). The lack of a tight coupling requires the model to be more sensitive to how one unit affects another unit's firing schedule. With all connections of size .1, firing patterns representing complex structures will appear chaotic and unorderly.

In all simulations, the time window for considering binding evidence was 5 time steps (i.e., Equation 2 was used with ρ set to 5).

Performance was measured by calculating the percent bindings correct. The bindings the model settled upon were determined by calculating the number of bindings in the intended structure. The model then created a structure with this number of bindings (this is equivalent to treating k like a free parameter), choosing the bindings it believed to be most likely (based on accrued evidence). The model was correct when the bindings it believed to be present corresponded to the intended bindings.

For each of the 9 structures (3 levels of depth by 3 levels of branching), hundreds of trials were run (the mechanism is stochastic) until performance curves became smooth. The model's performance was measured every 25th time step up to the 2500th time step. Performance (averaged across trials) for all structures is shown in Figure 1. Any viewable difference between performance curves is statistically significant. As predicted, there was a main effect for both branching and depth. The left panels of Figure 1 organize the data by branching factor, revealing a systematic effect of depth. The right panel is organized by depth and reveals a systematic effect of branching. As structures become more complex, they appear to take longer to represent.

5 Conclusions

The ability to effectively represent and manipulate complex knowledge structures is central to human cognition [3]. Connectionists models generally lack this ability, making it difficult to give a connectionist account of our mental architecture. The asynchronous mechanism provides a connectionist framework for representing structures in a way that is biologically, computationally, and behaviorally feasible. The mechanism establishes bindings over time using simple neuron-like computing elements. The asynchronous approach treats bindings as directional and does not blur the distinction between a slot and a filler as the synchronous approach does.

The asynchronous mechanism builds representations that can be differentiated from each other, capturing important differences between representational states. The representations that the asynchronous mechanism builds also can be easily compared and commonalities between disparate states can be extracted by analogical processes, allowing for generalization and feature discovery. In fact, an analogical (i.e., graph) matcher has been built using the asynchronous mechanism [7]. Variants of the model need to be explored. This paper only outlines the essentials of the architecture. Synchronous dynamic binding models were partly inspired from work in neuroscience. Hopefully the asynchronous dynamic binding model will now inspire neuroscience researchers. Some evidence for rate-based firing (spatially based) neural codes has been revisited and viewed as consistent with more complex temporal codes [1]; perhaps evidence for synchrony can be subjected to more sophisticated analyses and be better construed as evidence for the asynchronous mechanism.

Acknowledgments

This work was supported by the Office of Naval Research under the National Defense Science and Engineering Graduate Fellowship Program. I would like to thank John Hummel for his helpful comments.

References

[1] M. Abeles, H. Bergman, E. Margalit, and E. Vaadia. Spatiotemporal firing patterns in the frontal cortex of behaving monkeys. *Journal of Neurophysiology*, 70:1629–1638, 1993.

[2] E. Bienenstock. Composition. In A. Aertsen and V. Braitenberg, editors, *Brain Theory: Biological Basis and Computational Principles*. Elsevier, New York, 1996.

[3] D. Gentner and A. B. Markman. Analogy-watershed or waterloo? structural alignment and the development of connectionist models of analogy. In S. J. Hanson, J. D. Cowan, and C. L. Giles, editors, *Advances in Neural Information Processing Systems 5*, pages 855–862. Morgan Kaufman Publishers, San Mateo, CA, 1993.

[4] C. M. Gray and W. Singer. Stimulus specific neuronal oscillations in orientation columns of cat visual cortex. *Proceedings of the National Academy of Sciences, USA*, 86:1698–1702, 1989.

[5] J. E. Hummel and I. Biederman. Dynamic binding in a neural network for shape recognition. *Psychological Review*, 99:480–517, 1992.

[6] D.R.J. Laming. *Information theory of choice reaction time*. Oxford University Press, New York, 1968.

[7] B. C. Love. Asynchronous connectionist binding. (Under Review), 1998.

[8] Y. Miyashita and H. S. Chang. Neuronal correlate of pictorial short-term memory in primate temporal cortex. *Nature*, 331:68–70, 1988.

[9] J. Pollack. Recursive distributed representations. *Artificial Intelligence*, 46:77–105, 1990.

[10] W. Rall. Dendritic locations of synapses and possible mechanisms for the monosynaptic EPSP in motorneurons. *Journal of Neurophysiology*, 30:1169–1193, 1967.

[11] R. Ratcliff and G. McKoon. Speed and accuracy in the processing of false statements about semantic information. *Journal of Experimental Psychology: Learning, Memory, & Cognition*, 8:16–36, 1989.

[12] L. Shastri and V. Ajjanagadde. From simple associations to systematic reasoning: A connectionist representation of rules, variables, and dynamic binding using temporal synchrony. *Behavioral and Brain Sciences*, 16:417–494, 1993.

[13] W. Softky. Fine analog coding minimizes information transmission. *Neural Networks*, 9:15–24, 1996.

[14] A. C. Tang and T. J. Sejnowski. An ecological approach tp the neural code. In *Proceedings of the Nineteenth Annual Conference of the Cogntive Science Society*, page 852, Mahwah, NJ, 1996. Erlbaum.

[15] A. Treisman and H. Schmidt. Illusory conjunctions in the perception of objects. *Cognitive Psychology*, 14:107–141, 1982.

[16] E. Vaadia, I. Haalman, M. Abeles, and H. Bergman. Dynamics of neuronal interactions in monkey cortex in relation to behavioral events. *Nature*, 2373:515–518, 1995.

[17] C. von der Malsburg. The correlation theory of brain function. Technical Report 81-2, Max-Planck-Institut for Biophysical Chemistry, Göttingen, Germany, 1981.

Mechanisms of generalization in perceptual learning

Zili Liu
Rutgers University, Newark

Daphna Weinshall
Hebrew University, Israel

Abstract

The learning of many visual perceptual tasks has been shown to be specific to practiced stimuli, while new stimuli require re-learning from scratch. Here we demonstrate generalization using a novel paradigm in motion discrimination where learning has been previously shown to be specific. We trained subjects to discriminate the directions of moving dots, and verified the previous results that learning does not transfer from the trained direction to a new one. However, by tracking the subjects' performance across time in the new direction, we found that their rate of learning doubled. Therefore, learning generalized in a task previously considered too difficult for generalization. We also replicated, in the second experiment, transfer following training with "easy" stimuli.

The specificity of perceptual learning and the dichotomy between learning of "easy" vs. "difficult" tasks were hypothesized to involve different learning processes, operating at different visual cortical areas. Here we show how to interpret these results in terms of signal detection theory. With the assumption of limited computational resources, we obtain the observed phenomena — direct transfer and change of learning rate — for increasing levels of task difficulty. It appears that human generalization concurs with the expected behavior of a generic discrimination system.

1 Introduction

Learning in biological systems is of great importance. But while cognitive learning (or "problem solving") is typically abrupt and generalizes to analogous problems, perceptual skills appear to be acquired gradually and specifically: Human subjects cannot generalize a perceptual discrimination skill to solve similar problems with different attributes. For example, in a visual discrimination task (Fig. 1), a subject who is trained to discriminate motion directions between 43° and 47° cannot use this skill to discriminate 133° from 137°. Generalization has been found only when stimuli of different attributes are interleaved [7, 10], or when the task is easier [6, 1]. For example, a subject who is trained to discriminate 41° from 49° can later readily discriminate 131° from 139° [6]. The specificity of learning has been so far used to support the hypothesis that perceptual learning embodies neuronal modifications in the brain's stimulus-specific cortical areas (e.g., visual area MT) [9, 3, 2, 5, 8, 4].

In contrast to previous results of learning specificity, we show in two experiments in Section 2 that learning in motion discrimination generalizes in all cases where specificity was thought to exist, although the mode of generalization varies. (1) When the task is difficult, it is direction specific in the traditional sense; but learning in a new direction accelerates. (2) When the task is easy, it generalizes to all directions after training in only one direction. While (2) is consistent with the findings reported in [6, 1], (1) demonstrate that generalization is the rule, not an exception limited only to "easy" stimuli.

2 Perceptual learning experiments

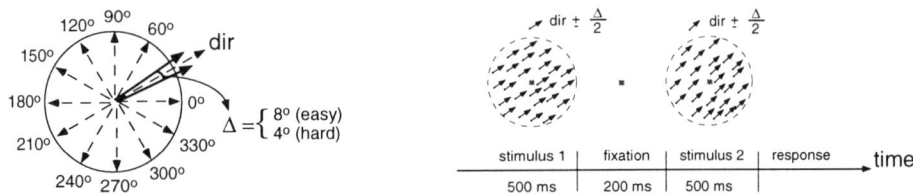

Figure 1: Schematic of one trial. **Left**: the stimulus was a random dot pattern viewed in a circular aperture, spanning 8° of visual angle, moving in a given primary direction (denoted dir). The primary direction was chosen from 12 directions, separated by 30°. **Right**: the direction of each of the two stimuli was randomly chosen from two candidate directions ($dir \pm \Delta/2$). The subject judged whether the two stimuli moved in the same or different directions. Feedback was provided.

The motion discrimination task is described in Fig. 1. In each trial, the subject was presented with two consecutive stimuli, each moving in one of two possible directions (randomly chosen from the two directions $dir + \Delta/2$ and $dir - \Delta/2$). The directional difference $|\Delta|$ between the two stimuli was 8° in the easy condition, and 4° in the difficult condition. The experiment was otherwise identical to that in [2] that used $|\Delta| = 3°$, except that our stimuli were displayed on an SGI computer monitor. $|\Delta| = 8°$ was chosen as the easy condition because most subjects found it relatively easy to learn, yet still needed substantial training.

2.1 A difficult task

We trained subjects extensively in one primary direction with a difficult motion discrimination task ($\Delta = 4°$), followed by extensive training in a second primary direction. The two primary directions were sufficiently different so direct transfer between them was not expected [2] (Fig. 2). Subjects' initial performance in both directions was comparable, replicating the classical result of stimulus specific learning (no direct transfer). However, all subjects took only half as many training sessions to make the same improvement in the second direction. All subjects had extensive practice with the task prior to this experiment, thus the acceleration cannot be simply explained by familiarity.

Our results show that although perceptual learning did not directly transfer in this difficult task, it did nevertheless generalize to the new direction. The generalization was manifested as 100% increase in the rate of learning in the second direction. It demonstrates that the generalization of learning, as manifested via direct transfer and via increase in learning rate, may be thought of as two extremes of a continuum of possibilities.

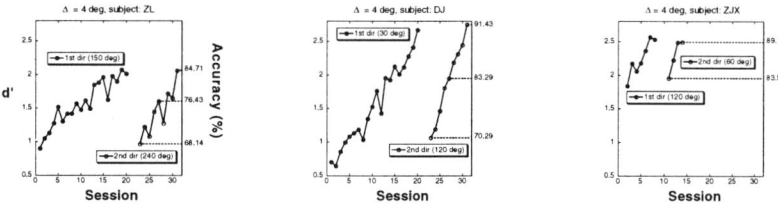

Figure 2: Subjects DJ and ZL needed 20 training sessions in the first direction, and nine in the second; subject ZJX needed seven training sessions in the first, and four in the second. The rate of learning (the amount of improvement per session) in the second direction is significantly greater than in the first ($t(2) = 13.41, p < 0.003$).

2.2 An easy task

We first measured the subjects' baseline performance in an easy task — the discrimination of motion directions 8° apart — in 12 primary directions (64 trials each, randomly interleaved). We then trained four subjects in one oblique primary direction (chosen randomly and counter-balanced among subjects) for four sessions, each with 700 trials. Finally, we measured again the subjects' performance in all directions. Every subject improved in all directions (Fig. 3). The performance of seven control subjects was measured without intermediate training; two more control subjects were added who were "trained" with similar motion stimuli but were asked to discriminate a brightness change instead. The control subjects improved as well, but significantly less ($\Delta d' = 0.09$ vs. 0.78, Fig. 3).

Our results clearly show that training with an easy task in one direction leads to immediate improvement in other directions. Hence the learned skill generalized across motion directions.

3 A computational model

We will now adopt a general framework for the analysis of perceptual learning results, using the language of signal detection theory. Our model accounts for the results in this paper by employing the constraint of limited computational resources. The model's assumptions are as follows.

1. In each trial, each of the two stimuli is represented by a population of measurements that encode all aspects of the stimulus, in particular, the output of localized direction detectors. The measurements are encoded as a vector. The decision as to whether the two stimuli are the same or not is determined by the difference of the two vectors.

2. Each component of the input measurements is characterized by its sensitivity for the discrimination task, e.g., how well the two motion directions can be discriminated apart based on this component. The entire population itself is generally divided into two sets: *informative* — measurements with significant sensitivity, and

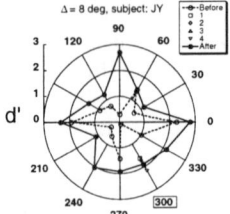 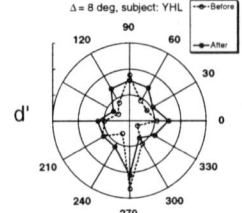 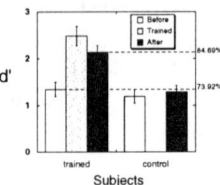

Figure 3: **Left**: Discrimination sensitivity d' of subject JY who was trained in the primary direction $300°$. **Middle**: d' of control subject YHL who had no training in between the two measurements. **Right**: Average d' (and standard error) for all subjects before and after training. **Trained**: results for the four trained subjects. Note the substantial improvement between the two measurements. For these subjects, the d' measured after training is shown separately for the trained direction (middle column) and the remaining directions (right column). **Control**: results for the nine control subjects. The control subjects improved their performance significantly less than the trained subjects ($\Delta d' = 0.09$ vs. 0.78 ; $F(1,11) = 14.79, p < 0.003$).

uninformative — measurements with null sensitivity. In addition, *informative* measurements may vary greatly in their individual sensitivity. When many have high sensitivity, the task is easy. When most have low sensitivity, the task is difficult.

We assume that sensitivity changes from one primary direction to the next, but the population of *informative* measurements remains constant. For example, in our psychophysical task localized directional signals are likely to be in the *informative* set for any motion direction, though their individual sensitivity will vary based on specific motion directions. On the other hand, local speed signals are never informative and therefore always belong to the *uninformative* set.

3. Due to limited computational capacity, the system can, at a time, only process a small number of components of the input vector. The decision in a single trial is therefore made based on the magnitude of this sub-vector, which may vary from trial to trial.

In each trial the system rates the processed components of the sub-vector according to their sensitivity for the discrimination task. After a sufficient number of trials (enough to estimate all the component sensitivities of the sub-vector), the system identifies the least sensitive component and replaces it in the next trial with a new random component from the input vector. In effect, the system is searching from the input vector a sub-vector that gives rise to the maximal discrimination sensitivity. Therefore the performance of the system is gradually improving, causing learning from session to session in the training direction.

4. After learning in one training direction, the system identifies the sets of *informative* and *uninformative* measurements and include in the *informative* set any measurement with significant (though possibly low) sensitivity. In the next training direction, only the set of *informative* measurements is searched. The search becomes more efficient, and hence the acceleration of the learning rate. This accounts for the learning between training directions.

We further assume that each stimulus generates a signal that is a vector of N measurements: $\{I_i\}_{i=1}^{N}$. We also assume that the signal for the discrimination task is the difference between two stimulus measurements: $\mathbf{x} = \{x_i\}_{i=1}^{N}$, $x_i = \Delta I_i$. The same/different discrimination task is to decide whether $\mathbf{x}$ is generated by noise — the null vector $\emptyset$, or by some distinct signal — the vector $\mathcal{S}$.

At time t a measurement vector $\mathbf{x}^t$ is obtained, which we denote $\mathbf{x}^{st}$ if it is the signal $\mathcal{S}$, and $\mathbf{x}^{nt}$ otherwise. Assume that each measurement in $\mathbf{x}^t$ is a normal random variable: $\mathbf{x}^{nt} = \{x_i^{nt}\}_{i=1}^N, x_i^{nt} \sim N(0, \sigma_i), \mathbf{x}^{st} = \{x_i^{st}\}_{i=1}^N, x_i^{st} \sim N(\mu_i, \sigma_i)$. We measure the sensitivity d' of each component. Since both the signal and noise are assumed to be normal random variables, the sensitivity of the i-th measurement in the discrimination task is $d_i' = |\mu_i|/\sigma_i$. Assuming further that the measurements are independent of each other and of time, then the combined sensitivity of M measurements is $d' = \sqrt{\sum_{i=1}^M (\mu_i/\sigma_i)^2}$.

3.1 Limited resources: an assumption

We assume that the system can simultaneously process at most $M \ll N$ of the original N measurements. Since the sensitivity d_i' of the different measurements varies, the discrimination depends on the combined sensitivity of the particular set of M measurements that are being used. Learning in the first training direction, therefore, leads to the selection of a "good" subset of the measurements, obtained by searching in the measurement space.

After searching for the best M measurements for the current training direction, the system divides the measurements into two sets: those with non-negligible sensitivity, and those with practically null sensitivity. This rating is kept for the next training direction, when only the first set is searched.

One prediction of this model is that learning rate should *not* increase with exposure only. In other words, it is necessary for subjects to be exposed to the stimulus **and** do the same discrimination task for effective inter-directional learning to take place. For example, assume that the system is given N measurements: $N/2$ motion direction signals and $N/2$ speed signals. It learns during the first training direction that the $N/2$ speed signals have null sensitivity for the direction discrimination task, whereas the directional signals have varying (but significant) sensitivity. In the second training direction, the system is given the N measurements whose sensitivity profile is different from that in the first training direction, but still with the property that only the directional signals have any significant sensitivity (Fig. 4b). Based on learning in the first training direction, the system only searches the measurements whose sensitivity in the first training direction was significant, namely, the $N/2$ directional signals. It ignores the speed signals. Now the asymptotic performance in the second direction remains unchanged because the most sensitive measurements are within the searched population — they are directional signals. The learning rate, however, doubles since the system searches a space half as large.

3.2 Simulation results

To account for the different modes of learning, we make the following assumptions. When the task is easy, many components have high sensitivity d'. When the task is difficult, only a small number of measurements have high d'. Therefore, when the task is easy, a subset of M measurements that give rise to the best performance is found relatively fast. In the extreme, when the task is very easy (e.g., all the measurements have very high sensitivity), the rate of learning is almost instantaneous and the observed outcome appears to be transfer. On the other hand, when the task is difficult, it takes a long time to find the M measurements that give rise to the best performance, and learning is slow.

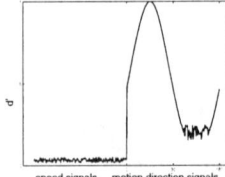 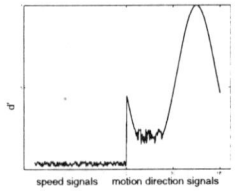

Figure 4: Hypothetical sensitivity profile for a population of measurements of speed and motion direction. **Left**: First training direction — only the motion direction measurements have significant sensitivity (d' above 0.1), with measurements around 45° having the highest d'. **Right**: Second direction — only the motion direction measurements have significant sensitivity, with measurements around 135° having the highest d'.

The detailed operations of the model are as follows. In the first training direction, the system starts with a random set of M measurements. In each trial and using feedback, the mean and standard deviation of each measurement is computed: μ_i^{st}, σ_i^{st} for the signal and μ_i^{nt}, σ_i^{nt} for the noise. In the next trial, given M measurements $\{x_i^{t+1}\}_{i=1}^M$, the system evaluates $\delta = \sum_{i=1}^M \left(\frac{x_i^{t+1}-\mu_i^{st}}{\sigma_i^{st}}\right)^2 - \left(\frac{x_i^{t+1}-\mu_i^{nt}}{\sigma_i^{nt}}\right)^2$, and classifies **x** as the signal if $\delta < 0$, and noise otherwise.

At time T, the worst measurement is identified as *argval* of $\min_i d'_i$, $d'_i = 2|\mu_i^{sT} - \mu_i^{nT}|/(\sigma_i^{st} + \sigma_i^{nt})$. It is then replaced randomly from one of the remaining $N - M$ measurements. The learning and decision making then proceed as above for another T iterations. This is repeated until the set of chosen measurements stabilizes. At the end, the decision is made based on the set of M measurements that have the highest sensitivities.

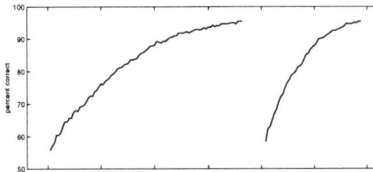 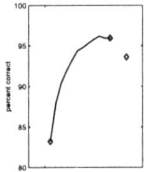

Figure 5: Simulated performance (percent correct) as function of time. **Left**: Difficult condition — the number of measurements with high d'_i is small (4 out of 150); there is no transfer from the first to the second training direction, but the learning rate is increased two-fold. This graph is qualitatively similar to the results shown in the top row of Fig. 2. **Right**: Easy condition — the number of measurements with high d'_i is large (72 out of 150); there is almost complete transfer from the first to the second training direction.

At the very beginning of training in the second direction, based on the measured d'_i in the first direction, the measurement population is labeled as *informative* — those with d'_i larger than the median value, and *uninformative* — the remaining measurements. The learning and decision making proceeds as above, while only *informative* measurements are considered during the search.

In the simulation we used $N = 150$ measurements, with $M = 4$. Half of the N measurements (the *informative* measurements) had significant d'_i. In the second training direction, the sensitivities of the measurements were randomly changed, but only the *informative* measurements had significant d'_i. By varying the number of measurements with high d'_i in the population of *informative* measurements, we get the different modes of generalization(Fig. 5).

4 Discussions

In contrast to previous results on the specificity of learning, we broadened the search for generalization beyond traditional transfer. We found that generalization is the rule, rather than an exception. Perceptual learning of motion discrimination generalizes in various forms: as acceleration of learning rate (Exp. 1), as immediate improvement in performance (Exp. 2). Thus we show that perceptual learning is more similar to cognitive learning than previously thought, with both stimulus specificity and generalization as important ingredients.

In our scheme, the assumption of the computational resource forced the discrimination system to search in the measurement space. The generalization phenomena — transfer and increased learning rate — occur due to improvement in *search sensitivity* from one training direction to the next, as the size of the search space decreases with learning. Our scheme also predicts that learning rate should *only* improve if the subject both sees the stimulus **and** does the relevant discrimination task, in agreement with the results in Exp. 1. Importantly, our scheme does not predict transfer *per se*, but instead a dramatic increase in learning rate that is *equivalent* to transfer.

Our model is qualitative and does not make any concrete quantitative predictions. We would like to emphasize that this is not a handicap of the model. Our goal is to show, qualitatively, that the various generalization phenomena should not surprise us, as they should naturally occur in a generic discrimination system with limited computational resources. Thus we argue that it may be too early to use existing perceptual learning results for the identification of the cortical location of perceptual learning, and the levels at which modifications are taking place.

References

[1] Ahissar M and Hochstein S. Task difficulty and the specificity of perceptual learning. *Nature*, 387:401–406, 1997.

[2] Ball K and Sekuler R. A specific and enduring improvement in visual motion discrimination. *Science*, 218:697–698, 1982.

[3] Fiorentini A and Berardi N. Perceptual learning specific for orientation and spatial frequency. *Nature*, 287:43–44, 1980.

[4] Gilbert C D. Early perceptual learning. *PNAS*, 91:1195–1197, 1994.

[5] Karni A and Sagi D. Where practice makes perfect in texture discrimination: Evidence for primary visual cortex plasticity. *PNAS*, 88:4966–4970, 1991.

[6] Liu Z. Learning a visual skill that generalizes. Tech. Report, NECI, 1995.

[7] Liu Z and Vaina L M. Stimulus specific learning: a consequence of stimulus-specific experiments? *Perception*, 24(supplement):21, 1995.

[8] Poggio T, Fahle M, and Edelman S. Fast perceptual learning in visual hyperacuity. *Science*, 256:1018–1021, May 1992.

[9] Ramachandran V S. Learning-like phenomena in stereopsis. *Nature*, 262:382–384, 1976.

[10] Rubin N, Nakayama K, and Shapley R. Abrupt learning and retinal size specificity in illusory-contour perception. *Current Biology*, 7:461–467, 1997.

A Principle for Unsupervised Hierarchical Decomposition of Visual Scenes

Michael C. Mozer
Dept. of Computer Science
University of Colorado
Boulder, CO 80309–0430

ABSTRACT

Structure in a visual scene can be described at many levels of granularity. At a coarse level, the scene is composed of objects; at a finer level, each object is made up of parts, and the parts of subparts. In this work, I propose a simple principle by which such hierarchical structure can be extracted from visual scenes: Regularity in the relations among different parts of an object is weaker than in the internal structure of a part. This principle can be applied recursively to define part-whole relationships among elements in a scene. The principle does not make use of object models, categories, or other sorts of higher-level knowledge; rather, part-whole relationships can be established based on the statistics of a set of sample visual scenes. I illustrate with a model that performs unsupervised decomposition of simple scenes. The model can account for the results from a human learning experiment on the ontogeny of part-whole relationships.

1 INTRODUCTION

The structure in a visual scene can be described at many levels of granularity. Consider the scene in Figure 1a. At a coarse level, the scene might be said to consist of stick man and stick dog. However, stick man and stick dog themselves can be decomposed further. One might describe stick man as having two components, a head and a body. The head in turn can be described in terms of its parts: the eyes, nose, and mouth. This sort of scene decomposition can continue recursively down to the level of the primitive visual features. Figure 1b shows a partial decomposition of the scene in Figure 1a.

A scene decomposition establishes part-whole relationships among objects. For example, the mouth (a whole) consists of two parts, the teeth and the lips. If we assume that any part can belong to only one whole, the decomposition imposes a *hierarchical* structure over the elements in the scene.

Where does this structure come from? What makes an object an object, a part a part? I propose a simple principle by which such hierarchical structure can be extracted from visual scenes and incorporate the principle in a simulation model. The principle is based on the statistics of the visual environment, not on object models or other sorts of higher-level knowledge, or on a teacher to classify objects or their parts.

2 WHAT MAKES A PART A PART?

Parts combine to form objects. Parts are combined in different ways to form different objects and different instances of an object. Consequently, the structural relations among different parts of an object are less *regular* than is the internal structure of a part. To illustrate, consider Figure 2, which depicts four instances of a box shell and lid. The components of the lid—the top and the handle—appear in a regular configuration, as do the components of the shell—the sides and base—but the relation of the lid to the shell is variable. Thus, configural regularity is an indication that components should be grouped together to form a unit. I call this the *regularity principle*. Other variants of the regularity principle have been suggested by Becker (1995) and Tenenbaum (1994).

The regularity depicted in Figure 2 is quite rigid: one component of a part always occurs in a fixed spatial position relative to another. The regularity principle can also be cast in terms of abstract relationships such as containment and encirclement. The only difference is the featural representation that subserves the regularity discovery process. In this paper, however, I address primarily regularities that are based on physical features and fixed spatial relationships. Another generalization of the regularity principle is that it can be applied recursively to suggest not only parts of wholes, but subparts of parts.

According to the regularity principle, information is implicit in the environment that can be used to establish part-whole relationships. This information comes in the form of statistical regularities among features in a visual scene. The regularity principle does not depend on explicit labeling of parts or objects.

In contrast, Schyns and Murphy (1992, 1993) have suggested a theory of part ontogeny that presupposes explicit categorization of objects. They propose a *homogeneity principle* which states that "if a fragment of a stimulus plays a consistent role in categorization, the perceptual parts composing the fragment are instantiated as a single unit in the stimulus representation in memory." Their empirical studies with human subjects find support for the homogeneity principle.

Superficially, the homogeneity and regularity principles seem quite different: while the homogeneity principle applies to *supervised* category learning (i.e., with a teacher to classify instances), the regularity principle applies to *unsupervised* discovery. But it is possible to transform one learning paradigm into the other. For example, in a category learning task, if only one category is to be learned and if the training examples are all positive instances of the category, then inducing the defining characteristics of the category is equivalent to extracting regularities in the stimulus environment. Thus, category learning in a diverse stimulus environment can be conceptualized as unsupervised regularity extraction in multiple, narrow stimulus environments (each environment being formed by taking all positive instances of a given class).

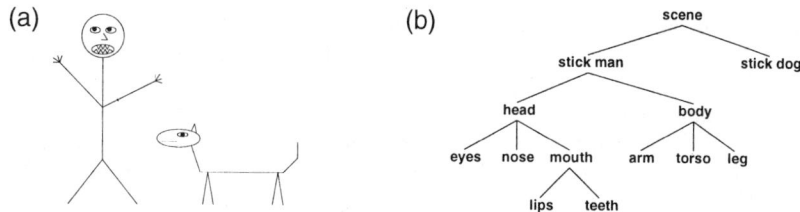

FIGURE 1. (a) A graphical depiction of stick man and his faithful companion, stick dog; (b) a partial decomposition of the scene into its parts.

FIGURE 2. Four different instances of a box with a lid

There are several other differences between the regularity principle proposed here and the homogeneity principle of Schyns and Murphy, but they are minor. Schyns and Murphy seem to interpret "fragment" more narrowly as spatially contiguous perceptual features. They also don't address the hierarchical nature of part-whole relationships. Nonetheless, the two principles share the notion of using the statistical structure of the visual environment to establish part-whole relations.

3 A FLAT REPRESENTATION OF STRUCTURE

I have incorporated the regularity principle into a neural net that discovers part-whole relations in its environment. Neural nets, having powerful learning paradigms for unsupervised discovery, are well suited for this task. However, they have a fundamental difficulty representing complex, articulated data structures of the sort necessary to encode hierarchies (but see Pollack, 1988, and Smolensky, 1990, for promising advances). I thus begin by describing a novel representation scheme for hierarchical structures that can readily be integrated into a neural net.

The tree structure in Figure 1b depicts one representation of a hierarchical decomposition. The complete tree has as its leaf nodes the primitive visual features of the scene. The tree specifies the relationships among the visual features. There is another way of capturing these relationships, more connectionist in spirit than the tree structure. The idea is to assign to each primitive feature a *tag*—a scalar in [0, 1]—such that features within a subtree have similar values. For the features of stick man, possible tags might be: **eyes** .1, **nose** .2, **lips** .28, **teeth** .32, **arm** .6, **torso** .7, **leg** .8.

Denoting the set of all features having tags in $[\alpha, \beta]$ by $S(\alpha, \beta)$, one can specify any subtree of the stick man representation. For example, $S(0,1)$ includes all features of stick man; $S(0,.5)$ includes all features in the subtree whose root is stick man's head, $S(.5,1)$ his body; $S(.25,.35)$ indicates the parts of the mouth. By a simple algorithm, tags can be assigned to the leaf nodes of any tree such that any subtree can be selected by specifying an appropriate tag range. The only requirement for this algorithm is knowledge of the maximum branching factor. There is no fixed limit to the depth of the tree that can be thus represented; however, the deeper the tree, the finer the tag resolution that will be needed.

The tags provide a "flat" way of representing hierarchical structure. Although the tree is implicit in the representation, the tags convey all information in the tree, and thus can capture complex, articulated structures. The tags in fact convey additional information. For example in the above feature list, note that **lips** is closer to **nose** than **teeth** is to **nose**. This information can easily be ignored, but it is still worth observing that the tags carry extra baggage not present in the symbolic tree structure.

It is convenient to represent the tags on a range $[0, 2\pi)$ rather than $[0,1]$. This allows the tag to be identified with a directional—or angular—value. Viewed as part of a cyclic continuum, the directional tags are homogeneous, in contrast to the linear tags where tags near 0 and 1 have special status by virtue of being at endpoints of the continuum. Homogeneity results in a more elegant model, as described below.

The directional tags also permit a neurophysiological interpretation, albeit speculative. It has been suggested that synchronized oscillatory activities in the nervous system can be used to convey information above and beyond that contained in the average firing rate of individual neurons (e.g., Eckhorn et al., 1988; Gray et al., 1989; von der Malsburg, 1981). These oscillations vary in their *phase*, the relative offset of the bursts. The directional tags could map directly to phases of oscillations, providing a means of implementing the tagging in neocortex.

4 REGULARITY DISCOVERY

Many learning paradigms allow for the discovery of regularity. I have used an autoencoder architecture (Plaut, Nowlan, & Hinton, 1986) that maps an input pattern—a representation of visual features in a scene—to an output pattern via a small layer of hidden units. The goal of this type of architecture is for the network to reproduce the input pattern over the output units. The task requires discovery of regularities because the hidden layer serves as an encoding bottleneck that limits the representational capacity of the system. Consequently, stronger regularities (the most common patterns) will be encoded over the weaker.

5 MAGIC

We now need to combine the autoencoder architecture with the notion of tags such that regularity of feature configurations in the input will increase the likelihood that the features will be assigned the same tags.

This goal can be achieved using a model we developed for segmenting an image into different objects using supervised learning. The model, *MAGIC* (Mozer, Zemel, Behrmann, & Williams, 1992), was trained on images containing several visual objects and its task was to tag features according to which object they belonged. A teacher provided the target tags. Each unit in MAGIC conveys two distinct values: a probability that a feature is present, which I will call the feature *activity*, and a tag associated with the feature. The tag is a directional (angular) value, of the sort suggested earlier. (The tag representation is in reality a complex number whose direction corresponds to the directional value and whose magnitude is related to the unit's confidence in the direction. As this latter aspect of the representation is not central to the present work, I discuss it no further.)

The architecture is a two layer recurrent net. The input or *feature* layer is set of spatiotopic arrays—in most simulations having dimensions 25×25—each array containing detectors for features of a given type: oriented line segments at 0°, 45°, 90°, and 135°. In addition, there is a layer of *hidden* units. Each hidden unit is reciprocally connected to input from a local spatial *patch* of the input array; in the current simulations, the patch has dimensions 4×4. For each patch there is a corresponding fixed-size *pool* of hidden units. To achieve a translation invariant response across the image, the pools are arranged in a spatiotopic array in which neighboring pools respond to neighboring patches and the patch-to-pool weights are constrained to be the same at all locations in the array. There are interlayer connections, but no intralayer connections.

The images presented to MAGIC consist of an arrangement of features over the input array. The feature activity is clamped on (i.e., the feature is present), and the initial directional tag of the feature is set at random. Feature unit activities and tags feed to the hidden units, which in turn feed back to the feature units. Through a relaxation process, the system settles on an assignment of tags to the feature units (as well as to the hidden units, although read out from the model concerns only the feature units). MAGIC is a mean-field approximation to a stochastic network of directional units with binary-gated outputs (Zemel, Williams, & Mozer, 1995). This means that a mean-field energy functional can be written that expresses the network state and controls the dynamics; consequently, MAGIC is guaranteed to converge to a stable pattern of tags.

Each hidden unit detects a spatially local configuration of features, and it acts to reinstate a pattern of tags over the configuration. By adjusting its incoming and outgoing weights during training, the hidden unit is made to respond to configurations that are consistently tagged in the training set. For example, if the training set contains many corner junctions where horizontal and vertical lines come to a point and if the teacher tags all features composing these lines as belonging to the same object, then a hidden unit might learn to detect this configuration, and when it does so, to force the tags of the component features to be the same.

In our earlier work, MAGIC was trained to map the feature activity pattern to a target pattern of feature tags, where there was a distinct tag for each object in the image. In the present work, the training objective is rather to impose *uniform* tags over the features. Additionally, the training objective encourages MAGIC to reinstate the feature activity

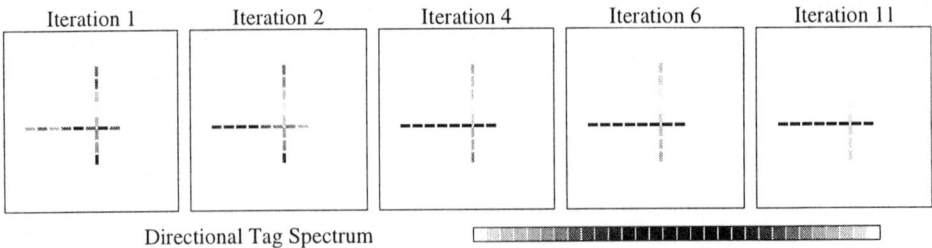

FIGURE 3. The state of MAGIC as processing proceeds for an image composed of a pair of lines made out of horizontal and vertical line segments. The coloring of a segment represents the directional tag. The segments belonging to a line are randomly tagged initially; over processing iterations, these tags are brought into alignment.

pattern over the feature units; that is, the hidden units must encode and propagate information back to the feature units that is sufficient to specify the feature activities (if the feature activities weren't clamped). With this training criterion, MAGIC becomes a type of autoencoder. The key property of MAGIC is that it can assign a feature configuration the same tag only if it learns to encode the configuration. If an arrangement is not encoded, there will be no force to align the feature tags. Further, fixed weak inhibitory connections between every pair of feature units serve to spread the tags apart if the force to align them is not strong enough.

Note that this training paradigm does not require a teacher to tag features as belonging to one part or another. MAGIC will try to tag all features as belonging to the same part, but it is able to do so only for configurations of features that it is able to encode. Consequently, highly regular and recurring configurations will be grouped together, and irregular configurations will be pulled apart. The strength of grouping will be proportional to the degree of regularity.

6 SIMULATION EXPERIMENTS

To illustrate the behavior of the model, I show a simple simulation in which MAGIC is trained on pairs of lines, one vertical and one horizontal. Each line is made up of 6 colinear line segments. The segments are primitive input features of the model. The two lines may appear in different positions relative to one another. Hence, the strongest regularity is in the segments that make up a line, not the junction between the lines. When trained with two hidden units, MAGIC has sufficient resources to encode the structure within each line, but not the relationships among the lines; because this structure is not encoded, the features of the two lines are not assigned the same tags (Figure 3).

Although each "part" is made up of features having a uniform orientation and in a colinear arrangement, the composition and structure of the parts is immaterial; MAGIC's performance depends only on the regularity of the configurations. In the next set of simulations, MAGIC discovers regularities of a more arbitrary nature.

6.1 MODELING HUMAN LEARNING OF PART-WHOLE RELATIONS

Schyns and Murphy (1992) studied the ontogeny of part-whole relationships by training human subjects on a novel class of objects and then examining how the subjects decomposed the objects into their parts. I briefly describe their experiment, followed by a simulation that accounts for their results.

In the first phase of the experiment, subjects were shown 3-D gray level "martian rocks" on a CRT screen. The rocks were constructed by deforming a sphere, resulting in various bumps or protrusions. Subjects watched the rocks rotating on the screen, allowing them to view the rock from all sides. Subjects were shown six instances, all of which were labeled "M1 rocks" and were then tested to determine whether they could distinguish M1 rocks from other rocks. Subjects continued training until they performed correctly on this task. Every M1 rock was divided into octants; the protrusions on seven of the octants were generated randomly, and the protrusions on the last octant were the same for all M1 rocks. Two groups of subjects were studied. The A group saw M1 rocks all having part A, the B group saw M1 rocks all having part B. Following training, subjects were asked to delineate the parts they thought were important on various exemplars. Subjects selected the target part from the category on which they were trained 93% of the time, and the *alternative target*—the target from the other category—only 8% of the time, indicating that the learning task made a part dramatically more salient.

To model this phase of the experiment, I generated two dimensional contours of the same flavor as Schyns and Murphy's martian rocks (Figure 4). Each rock—call it a "venusian rock" for distinction—can be divided into four quadrants or parts. Two groups of venusian rocks were generated. Rocks of category A all contained part A (left panel, Figure 4), rocks of category B contained part B (center panel, Figure 4). One network was trained on six exemplars of category A rocks, another network was trained on six exemplars of category B rocks. Then, with learning turned off, both networks were tested on five presentations each of twelve new exemplars, six each of categories A and B.

Just as the human subjects were instructed to delineate parts, we must ask MAGIC to do the same. One approach would be to run the model with a test stimulus and, once it settles, select all features having directional tags clustered tightly together as belonging to the same part. However, this requires specifying and tuning a clustering procedure. To avoid this additional step, I simply compared how tightly clustered were the tags of the target part relative to those of the alternative target. I used a directional variance measure that yields a value of 0 if all tags are identical and 1 if the tags are distributed uniformly over the directional spectrum. By this measure, the variance was .30 for the target part and .68 for the alternative target ($F(1,118) = 322.0$, $p < .001$), indicating that the grouping of features of the target part was significantly stronger. This replicates, at least qualitatively, the finding of Schyns and Murphy.

In a second phase of Schyns and Murphy's experiment, subjects were trained on category C rocks, which were formed by adjoining parts A and B and generating the remaining six octants at random. Following training, subjects were again asked to delineate parts. All subjects delineated A and B as distinct parts. In contrast, a naive group of subjects who were trained on category C alone always grouped A and B together as a single part.

To model this phase, I generated six category C venusian rocks that had both parts A and B (right panel, Figure 4). The versions of MAGIC that had been trained on category A and B rocks alone were now trained on category C rocks. As a control condition, a third version of MAGIC was trained from scratch on category C rocks alone. I compared the tightness of clustering of the combined A-B part for the first two nets to the third. Using the same variance measure as above, the nets that first received training on parts A and B alone yielded a variance of .57, and the net that was only trained on the combined A-B part yielded a variance of .47 ($F(1,88) = 7.02$, $p < .02$). One cannot directly compare the variance of the A-B part to that of the A and B parts alone, because the measure is structured such that parts with more features always yield larger variances. However, one can compare the two conditions using the relative variance of the combined A-B part to the A

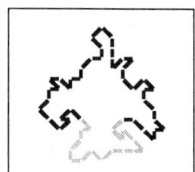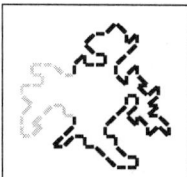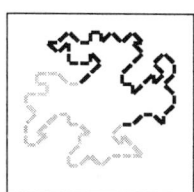

FIGURE 4. Three examples of the martian rock stimuli used to train MAGIC. From left to right, the rocks are of categories A, B, and C. The lighter regions are the contours that define rocks of a given category.

and B parts alone. This yielded the same outcome as before (.21 for the first two nets, .12 for the third net, $F(1,88) = 5.80$, $p < .02$). Thus, MAGIC is also able to account for the effects of prior learning on part ontogeny.

7 CONCLUSIONS

The regularity principle proposed in this work seems consistent with the homogeneity principle proposed earlier by Schyns and Murphy (1991, 1992). Indeed, MAGIC is able to model Schyns and Murphy's data using an unsupervised training paradigm, although Schyns and Murphy framed their experiment as a classification task.

This work is but a start at modeling the development of part-whole hierarchies based on perceptual experience. MAGIC requires further elaboration, and I am somewhat skeptical that it is sufficiently powerful in its present form to be pushed much further. The main issue restricting it is the representation of input features. The oriented-line-segment features are certainly too primitive and inflexible a representation. For example, MAGIC could not be trained to recognize the lid and shell of Figure 2 because it encodes the orientation of the features with respect to the image plane, not with respect to one another. Minimally, the representation requires some version of scale and rotation invariance.

Perhaps the most interesting computational issue raised by MAGIC is how the pattern of feature tags is mapped into an explicit part-whole decomposition. This involves clustering together the similar tags as a unit, or possibly selecting all tags in a given range. To do so requires specification of additional parameters that are external to the model (e.g., how tight the cluster should be, how broad the range should be, around what tag direction it should be centered). These parameters are deeply related to attentional issues, and a current direction of research is to explore this relationship.

8 ACKNOWLEDGEMENTS

This research was supported by NSF PYI award IRI-9058450 and grant 97-18 from the McDonnell-Pew Program in Cognitive Neuroscience.

9 REFERENCES

Becker, S. (1995). JPMAX: Learning to recognize moving objects as a model-fitting problem. In G. Tesauro, D. S. Touretzky, & T. K. Leen (Eds), *Advances in Neural Information Processing Systems 7* (pp. 933-940). Cambridge, MA: MIT Press.

Eckhorn, R., Bauer, R., Jordan, W., Brosch, M., Kruse, W., Munk, M., & Reitboek, H. J. (1988). Coherent oscillations: A mechanism of feature linking in the visual cortex? *Biological Cybernetics, 60*, 121–130.

Gray, C. M., Koenig, P., Engel, A. K., & Singer, W. (1989). Oscillatory responses in cat visual cortex exhibit intercolumnar synchronization which reflects global stimulus properties. *Nature* (London), *338*, 334–337.

Mozer, M. C., Zemel, R. S., Behrmann, M., & Williams, C. K. I. (1992). Learning to segment images using dynamic feature binding. *Neural Computation, 4*, 650–666.

Plaut, D. C., Nowlan, S., & Hinton, G. E. (1986). *Experiments on learning by back propagation* (Technical report CMU-CS-86-126). Pittsburgh, PA: Carnegie-Mellon University, Department of Computer Science.

Pollack, J. B. (1988). Recursive auto-associative memory: Devising compositional distributed representations. In *Proceedings of the Tenth Annual Conference of the Cognitive Science Society* (pp. 33–39). Hillsdale, NJ: Erlbaum.

Schyns, P. G., & Murphy, G. L. (1992). The ontogeny of units in object categories. *In Proceedings of the Fourteenth Annual Conference of the Cognitive Science Society* (pp. 197–202). Hillsdale, NJ: Erlbaum.

Schyns, P. G., & Murphy, G. L. (1993). The ontogeny of transformable part representations in object concepts. In *Proceedings of the Fifteenth Annual Conference of the Cognitive Science Society* (pp. 917–922). Hillsdale, NJ: Erlbaum.

Smolensky, P. (1990). Tensor product variable binding and the representation of symbolic structures in connectionist networks. *Artificial Intelligence, 46*, 159–216.

Tenenbaum, J. B. (1994). Functional parts. In A. Ram & K. Eiselt (Eds.), *Proceedings of the Sixteenth Annual Conference of the Cognitive Science Society* (pp. 864–869). Hillsdale, NJ: Erlbaum.

von der Malsburg, C. (1981). *The correlation theory of brain function* (Internal Report 81-2). Goettingen: Department of Neurobiology, Max Planck Institute for Biophysical Chemistry.

Zemel, R. S., Williams, C. K. I., & Mozer, M. C. (1995). Lending direction to neural networks. *Neural Networks, 8*, 503–512.

Bayesian modeling of human concept learning

Joshua B. Tenenbaum
Department of Brain and Cognitive Sciences
Massachusetts Institute of Technology, Cambridge, MA 02139
jbt@psyche.mit.edu

Abstract

I consider the problem of learning concepts from small numbers of positive examples, a feat which humans perform routinely but which computers are rarely capable of. Bridging machine learning and cognitive science perspectives, I present both theoretical analysis and an empirical study with human subjects for the simple task of learning concepts corresponding to axis-aligned rectangles in a multidimensional feature space. Existing learning models, when applied to this task, cannot explain how subjects generalize from only a few examples of the concept. I propose a principled Bayesian model based on the assumption that the examples are a random sample from the concept to be learned. The model gives precise fits to human behavior on this simple task and provides qualitative insights into more complex, realistic cases of concept learning.

1 Introduction

The ability to learn concepts from examples is one of the core capacities of human cognition. From a computational point of view, human concept learning is remarkable for the fact that very successful generalizations are often produced after experience with only a small number of positive examples of a concept (Feldman, 1997). While negative examples are no doubt useful to human learners in refining the boundaries of concepts, they are not necessary in order to make reasonable generalizations of word meanings, perceptual categories, and other natural concepts. In contrast, most machine learning algorithms require examples of both positive and negative instances of a concept in order to generalize at all, and many examples of both kinds in order to generalize successfully (Mitchell, 1997).

This paper attempts to close the gap between human and machine concept learning by developing a rigorous theory for concept learning from limited positive evidence and testing it against real behavioral data. I focus on a simple abstract task of interest to both cognitive science and machine learning: learning axis-parallel rectangles in $\Re^m$. We assume that each object x in our world can be described by its values $(x_1, \ldots, x_m)$ on m real-valued observable dimensions, and that each concept C to be learned corresponds to a conjunction of independent intervals ($min_i(C) \leq x_i \leq max_i(C)$) along each dimension

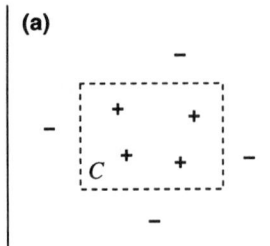 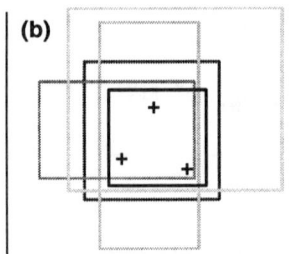 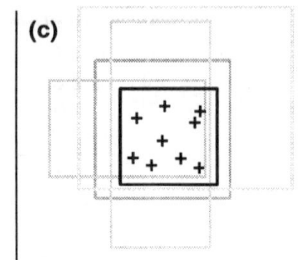

Figure 1: (a) A rectangle concept C. (b-c) The *size principle* in Bayesian concept learning: of the many hypotheses consistent with the observed positive examples, the smallest rapidly become more likely (indicated by darker lines) as more examples are observed.

i. For example, the objects might be people, the dimensions might be "cholesterol level" and "insulin level", and the concept might be "healthy levels". Suppose that "healthy levels" applies to any individual whose cholesterol and insulin levels are each greater than some minimum healthy level and less than some maximum healthy level. Then the concept "healthy levels" corresponds to a rectangle in the two-dimensional cholesterol/insulin space.

The problem of generalization in this setting is to infer, given a set of positive (+) and negative (-) examples of a concept C, which other points belong inside the rectangle corresponding to C (Fig. 1a.). This paper considers the question most relevant for cognitive modeling: how to generalize from just a few positive examples?

In machine learning, the problem of learning rectangles is a common textbook example used to illustrate models of concept learning (Mitchell, 1997). It is also the focus of state-of-the-art theoretical work and applications (Dietterich et al., 1997). The rectangle learning task is not well known in cognitive psychology, but many studies have investigated human learning in similar tasks using simple concepts defined over two perceptually separable dimensions such as size and color (Shepard, 1987). Such impoverished tasks are worth our attention because they isolate the essential inductive challenge of concept learning in a form that is analytically tractable and amenable to empirical study in human subjects.

This paper consists of two main contributions. I first present a new theoretical analysis of the rectangle learning problem based on Bayesian inference and contrast this model's predictions with standard learning frameworks (Section 2). I then describe an experiment with human subjects on the rectangle task and show that, of the models considered, the Bayesian approach provides by far the best description of how people actually generalize on this task when given only limited positive evidence (Section 3). These results suggest an explanation for some aspects of the ubiquotous human ability to learn concepts from just a few positive examples.

2 Theoretical analysis

Computational approaches to concept learning. Depending on how they model a concept, different approaches to concept learning differ in their ability to generalize meaningfully from only limited positive evidence. *Discriminative* approaches embody *no* explicit model of a concept, but only a procedure for discriminating category members from members of mutually exclusive contrast categories. Most backprop-style neural networks and exemplar-based techniques (e.g. K-nearest neighbor classification) fall into this group, along with hybrid models like ALCOVE (Kruschke, 1992). These approaches are ruled out by definition; they cannot learn to discriminate positive and negative instances if they have seen only positive examples. *Distributional* approaches model a concept as a probability distribution over some feature space and classify new instances x as members of C if their estimated probability $p(x|C)$ exceeds a threshold θ. This group includes "novelty detection" techniques based on Bayesian nets (Jaakkola et al., 1996) and, loosely, autoencoder networks (Japkowicz et al., 1995). While $p(x|C)$ can be estimated from only positive examples, novelty detection also requires negative examples for principled generalization, in order to set an appropriate threshold θ which may vary over many orders of magnitude for different concepts. For learning from positive evidence only, our best hope are algorithms that treat a new concept C as an *unknown subset* of the universe of objects and decide how to generalize C by finding "good" subsets in a hypothesis space H of possible concepts.

The Bayesian framework. For this task, the natural hypothesis space H corresponds to all rectangles in the plane. The central challenge in generalizing using the subset approach is that any small set of examples will typically be consistent with many hypotheses (Fig. 1b). This problem is not unique to learning rectangles, but is a universal dilemma when trying to generalize concepts from only limited positive data. The Bayesian solution is to embed the hypothesis space in a probabilistic model of our observations, which allows us to weight different consistent hypotheses as more or less likely to be the true concept based on the particular examples observed. Specifically, we assume that the examples are generated by *random sampling* from the true concept. This leads to the *size principle*: smaller hypotheses become more likely than larger hypotheses (Fig. 1b – darker rectangles are more likely), and they become exponentially more likely as the number of consistent examples increases (Fig. 1c). The size principle is the key to understanding how we can learn concepts from only a few positive examples.

Formal treatment. We observe n positive examples $X = \{x^{(1)}, \ldots, x^{(n)}\}$ of concept C and want to compute the *generalization function* $p(y \in C|X)$, i.e. the probability that some new object y belongs to C given the observations X. Let each rectangle hypothesis h be denoted by a quadruple (l_1, l_2, s_1, s_2), where $l_i \in [-\infty, \infty]$ is the location of h's lower-left corner and $s_i \in [0, \infty]$ is the size of h along dimension i.

Our probabilistic model consists of a prior density $p(h)$ and a likelihood function $p(X|h)$ for each hypothesis $h \in H$. The likelihood is determined by our assumption of randomly sampled positive examples. In the simplest case, each example in X is assumed to be independently sampled from a uniform density over the concept C. For n examples we then have:

$$p(X|h) = 1/|h|^n \text{ if } \forall j, x^{(j)} \in h \quad (1)$$
$$= 0 \text{ otherwise,}$$

where $|h|$ denotes the size of h. For rectangle (l_1, l_2, s_1, s_2), $|h|$ is simply $s_1 s_2$. Note that because each hypothesis must distribute one unit mass of likelihood over its volume for each example ($\int_{x \in h} p(x|h) dh = 1$), the probability density for smaller consistent hypotheses is greater than for larger hypotheses, and exponentially greater as a function of n. Figs. 1b,c illustrate this size principle for scoring hypotheses (darker rectangles are more likely).

The appropriate choice of $p(h)$ depends on our background knowledge. If we have no *a priori* reason to prefer any rectangle hypothesis over any other, we can choose the scale- and location-invariant *uninformative* prior, $p(h) = p(l_1, l_2, s_1, s_2) = 1/(s_1, s_2)$. In any realistic application, however, we will have some prior information. For example, we may know the expected size σ_i of rectangle concepts along dimension i in our domain, and then use the associated maximum entropy prior $p(l_1, l_2, s_1, s_2) = \exp\{-(s_1/\sigma_1 + s_2/\sigma_2)\}$.

The generalization function $p(y \in C|X)$ is computed by integrating the predictions of all hypotheses, weighted by their posterior probabilities $p(h|X)$:

$$p(y \in C|X) = \int_{h \in H} p(y \in C|h) \, p(h|X) \, dh, \quad (2)$$

where from Bayes' theorem $p(h|X) \propto p(X|h)p(h)$ (normalized such that $\int_{h \in H} p(h|X) dh = 1$), and $p(y \in C|h) = 1$ if $y \in h$ and 0 otherwise. Under the uninformative prior, this becomes:

$$p(y \in C|X) = \left[\frac{1}{(1+\tilde{d}_1/r_1)(1+\tilde{d}_2/r_2)}\right]^{n-1}. \tag{3}$$

Here r_i is the maximum distance between the examples in X along dimension i, and $\tilde{d}_i$ equals 0 if y falls inside the range of values spanned by X along dimension i, and otherwise equals the distance from y to the nearest example in X along dimension i. Under the expected-size prior, $p(y \in C|X)$ has no closed form solution valid for all n. However, except for very small values of n (e.g. < 3) and r_i (e.g. $< \sigma_i/10$), the following approximation holds to within 10% (and usually much less) error:

$$p(y \in C|X) \approx \frac{\exp\{-(\tilde{d}_1/\sigma_1 + \tilde{d}_2/\sigma_2)\}}{\left[(1+\tilde{d}_1/r_1)(1+\tilde{d}_2/r_2)\right]^{n-1}}. \tag{4}$$

Fig. 2 (left column) illustrates the Bayesian learner's contours of equal probability of generalization (at $p = 0.1$ intervals), for different values of n and r_i. The bold curve corresponds to $p(y \in C|X) = 0.5$, a natural boundary for generalizing the concept. Integrating over all hypotheses weighted by their size-based probabilities yields a broad gradient of generalization for small n (row 1) that rapidly sharpens up to the smallest consistent hypothesis as n increases (rows 2-3), and that extends further along the dimension with a broader range r_i of observations. This figure reflects an expected-size prior with $\sigma_1 = \sigma_2 = axis\_width/2$; using an uninformative prior produces a qualitatively similar plot.

Related work: MIN and Weak Bayes. Two existing subset approaches to concept learning can be seen as variants of this Bayesian framework. The classic MIN algorithm generalizes no further than the smallest hypothesis in H that includes all the positive examples (Bruner et al., 1956; Feldman, 1997). MIN is a PAC learning algorithm for the rectangles task, and also corresponds to the maximum likelihood estimate in the Bayesian framework (Mitchell, 1997). However, while it converges to the true concept as n becomes large (Fig. 2, row 3), it appears extremely conservative in generalizing from very limited data (Fig. 2, row 1).

An earlier approach to Bayesian concept learning, developed independently in cognitive psychology (Shepard, 1987) and machine learning (Haussler et al., 1994; Mitchell, 1997), was an important inspiration for the framework of this paper. I call the earlier approach *weak Bayes*, because it embodies a different generative model that leads to a much weaker likelihood function than Eq. 1. While Eq. 1 came from assuming examples sampled randomly from the true concept, weak Bayes assumes the examples are generated by an arbitrary process *independent* of the true concept. As a result, the size principle for scoring hypotheses does not apply; all hypotheses consistent with the examples receive a likelihood of 1, instead of the factor of $1/|h|^n$ in Eq. 1. The extent of generalization is then determined solely by the prior; for example, under the expected-size prior,

$$p(y \in C|X) = \exp\{-(\tilde{d}_1/\sigma_1 + \tilde{d}_2/\sigma_2)\}. \tag{5}$$

Weak Bayes, unlike MIN, generalizes reasonably from just a few examples (Fig. 2, row 1). However, because Eq. 5 is independent of n or r_i, weak Bayes does not converge to the true concept as the number of examples increases (Fig. 2, rows 2-3), nor does it generalize further along axes of greater variability. While weak Bayes is a natural model when the examples really are generated independently of the concept (e.g. when the learner himself or a random process chooses objects to be labeled "positive" or "negative" by a teacher), it is clearly limited as a model of learning from deliberately provided positive examples.

In sum, previous subset approaches each appear to capture a different aspect of how humans generalize concepts from positive examples. The broad similarity gradients that emerge from weak Bayes seem most applicable when only a few broadly spaced examples have been observed (Fig. 2, row 1), while the sharp boundaries of the MIN rule appear more reasonable as the number of examples increases or their range narrows (Fig. 2, rows 2-3). In contrast, the Bayesian framework guided by the size principle automatically interpolates between these two regimes of similarity-based and rule-based generalization, offering the best hope for a complete model of human concept learning.

3 Experimental data from human subjects

This section presents empirical evidence that our Bayesian model – but neither MIN nor weak Bayes – can explain human behavior on the simple rectangle learning task. Subjects were given the task of guessing 2-dimensional rectangular concepts from positive examples only, under the cover story of learning about the range of healthy levels of insulin and cholesterol, as described in Section 1. On each trial of the experiment, several dots appeared on a blank computer screen. Subjects were told that these dots were randomly chosen examples from some arbitrary rectangle of "healthy levels," and their job was to guess that rectangle as nearly as possible by clicking on-screen with the mouse. The dots were in fact randomly generated on each trial, subject to the constraints of three independent variables that were systematically varied across trials in a $(6 \times 6 \times 6)$ factorial design. The three independent variables were the horizontal range spanned by the dots (.25, .5, 1, 2, 4, 8 units in a 24-unit-wide window), vertical range spanned by the dots (same), and number of dots (2, 3, 4, 6, 10, 50). Subjects thus completed 216 trials in random order. To ensure that subjects understood the task, they first completed 24 practice trials in which they were shown, after entering their guess, the "true" rectangle that the dots were drawn from. [1]

The data from 6 subjects is shown in Fig. 3a, averaged across subjects and across the two directions (horizontal and vertical). The extent d of subjects' rectangles beyond r, the range spanned by the observed examples, is plotted as a function of r and n, the number of examples. Two patterns of generalization are apparent. First, d increases monotonically with r and decreases with n. Second, the rate of increase of d as a function of r is much slower for larger values of n.

Fig. 3b shows that neither MIN nor weak Bayes can explain these patterns. MIN always predicts zero generalization beyond the examples – a horizontal line at $d = 0$ – for all values of r and n. The predictions of weak Bayes are also independent of r and n: $d = \sigma \log 2$, assuming subjects give the tightest rectangle enclosing all points y with $p(y \in C|X) > 0.5$.

Under the same assumption, Figs. 3c,d show our Bayesian model's predicted bounds on generalization using uninformative and expected-size priors, respectively. Both versions of the model capture the qualitative dependence of d on r and n, confirming the importance of the size principle in guiding generalization independent of the choice of prior. However, the uninformative prior misses the nonlinear dependence on r for small n, because it assumes an ideal scale invariance that clearly does not hold in this experiment (due to the fixed size of the computer window in which the rectangles appeared). In contrast, the expected-size prior naturally embodies prior knowledge about typical scale in its one free parameter σ. A reasonable value of $\sigma = 5$ units (out of the 24-unit-wide window) yields an excellent fit to subjects' average generalization behavior on this task.

4 Conclusions

In developing a model of concept learning that is at once computationally principled and able to fit human behavior precisely, I hope to have shed some light on how people are able

---

[1] Because dots were drawn randomly, the "true" rectangles that subjects saw during practice were quite variable and were rarely the "correct" response according to *any* theory considered here. Thus it is unlikely that this short practice was responsible for any consistent trends in subjects' behavior.

to infer the correct extent of a concept from only a few positive examples. The Bayesian model has two key components: (1) a generalization function that results from integrating the predictions of all hypotheses weighted by their posterior probability; (2) the assumption that examples are sampled from the concept to be learned, and not independently of the concept as previous weak Bayes models have assumed. Integrating predictions over the whole hypothesis space explains why either broad gradients of generalization (Fig. 2, row 1) or sharp, rule-based generalization (Fig. 2, row 3) may emerge, depending on how peaked the posterior is. Assuming examples drawn randomly from the concept explains why learners do not weight all consistent hypotheses equally, but instead weight more specific hypotheses higher than more general ones by a factor that increases exponentially with the number of examples observed (the *size principle*).

This work is being extended in a number of directions. Negative instances, when encountered, are easily accomodated by assigning zero likelihood to any hypotheses containing them. The Bayesian formulation applies not only to learning rectangles, but to learning concepts in any measurable hypothesis space – wherever the size principle for scoring hypotheses may be applied. In Tenenbaum (1999), I show that the same principles enable learning number concepts and words for kinds of objects from only a few positive examples. [2] I also show how the size principle supports much more powerful inferences than this short paper could demonstrate: automatically detecting incorrectly labeled examples, selecting relevant features, and determining the complexity of the hypothesis space. Such inferences are likely to be necessary for learning in the complex natural settings we are ultimately interested in.

Acknowledgments

Thanks to M. Bernstein, W. Freeman, S. Ghaznavi, W. Richards, R. Shepard, and Y. Weiss for helpful discussions. The author was a Howard Hughes Medical Institute Predoctoral Fellow.

References

Bruner, J. A., Goodnow, J. S., & Austin, G. J. (1956). *A study of thinking*. New York: Wiley.

Dietterich, T., Lathrop, R., & Lozano-Perez, T. (1997). Solving the multiple-instance problem with axis-parallel rectangles. *Artificial Intelligence* **89**(1-2), 31-71.

Feldman, J. (1997). The structure of perceptual categories. *J. Math. Psych.* **41**, 145-170.

Haussler, D., Kearns, M., & Schapire, R. (1994). Bounds on the sample complexity of Bayesian learning using information theory and the VC-dimension. *Machine Learning* **14**, 83-113.

Jaakkola, T., Saul, L., & Jordan, M. (1996) Fast learning by bounding likelihoods in sigmoid type belief networks. *Advances in Neural Information Processing Systems 8*.

Japkowicz, N., Myers, C., & Gluck, M. (1995). A novelty detection approach to classification. *Proceedings of the 14th International Joint Conference on Aritifical Intelligence*.

Kruschke, J. (1992). ALCOVE: An exemplar-based connectionist model of category learning. *Psych. Rev.* **99**, 22-44.

Mitchell, T. (1997). *Machine Learning*. McGraw-Hill.

Muggleton, S. (preprint). Learning from positive data. Submitted to *Machine Learning*.

Shepard, R. (1987). Towards a universal law of generalization for psychological science. *Science* **237**, 1317-1323.

Tenenbaum, J. B. (1999). *A Bayesian Framework for Concept Learning*. Ph. D. Thesis, MIT Department of Brain and Cognitive Sciences.

---

[2]In the framework of inductive logic programming, Muggleton (preprint) has independently proposed that similar principles may allow linguistic grammars to be learned from positive data only.

Bayesian Modeling of Human Concept Learning

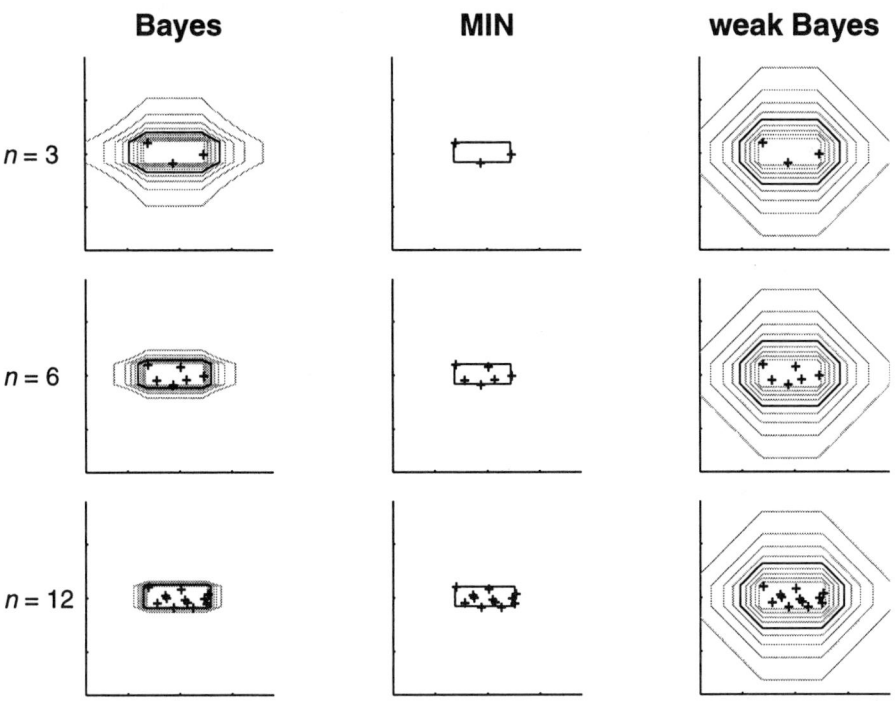

Figure 2: Performance of three concept learning algorithms on the rectangle task.

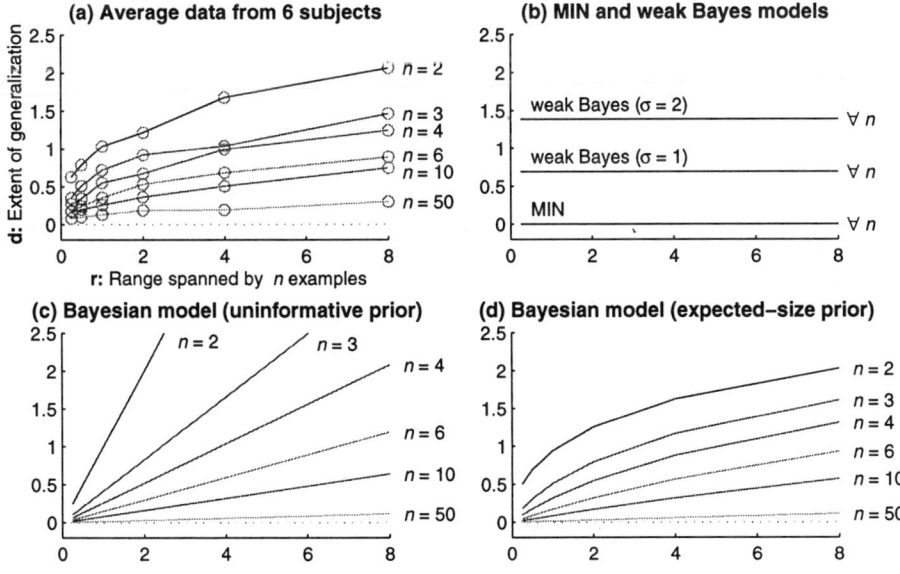

Figure 3: Data from human subjects and model predictions for the rectangle task.

Part II
Neuroscience

Temporally Asymmetric Hebbian Learning, Spike Timing and Neuronal Response Variability

L.F. Abbott and Sen Song
Volen Center and Department of Biology
Brandeis University
Waltham MA 02454

Abstract

Recent experimental data indicate that the strengthening or weakening of synaptic connections between neurons depends on the relative timing of pre- and postsynaptic action potentials. A Hebbian synaptic modification rule based on these data leads to a stable state in which the excitatory and inhibitory inputs to a neuron are balanced, producing an irregular pattern of firing. It has been proposed that neurons *in vivo* operate in such a mode.

1 Introduction

Hebbian modification of network interconnections plays a central role in the study of learning in neural networks (Rumelhart and McClelland, 1986; Hertz *et al.*, 1991). Most work on Hebbian learning involves network models in which the activities of the individual units are represented by continuous variables. A Hebbian learning rule, in this context, is specified by describing how network weights change as a function of the activities of the units that transmit and receive signals across a given network connection. While analyses of Hebbian learning along these lines have provided important results, direct application of these ideas to neuroscience is hindered by the fact that real neurons cannot be adequately described by continuous activity variables such as firing rates. Instead, the inputs and outputs of neurons are sequences of action potentials or spikes. All the information conveyed by one neuron to another over any appreciable distance is carried by the temporal patterns of action potential sequences. Rules by which synaptic connections between real neurons are modified in a Hebbian manner should properly be expressed as functions of the relative timing of the action potentials fired by the input (presynaptic) and output (postsynaptic) neurons. Until recently, little information has been available about the exact dependence of synaptic modification on pre- and postsynaptic spike timing (see however, Levy and Steward, 1983; Gustafsson *et al.*, 1987). New experimental results (Markram *et al.*, 1997; Bell *et al.*, 1997; Debanne *et al.*, 1998; Zhang *et al.*, 1998; Bi and Poo, 1999) have changed this situation dramatically, and these allow us to study Hebbian learning in a manner that is much more realistic and relevant to biological neural networks. The results may find application in artificial neural networks as well.

2 Temporally Asymmetric LTP and LTD

The biological substrate for Hebbian learning in neuroscience is provided by long-term potentiation (LTP) and long-term depression (LTD) of the synaptic connections between neurons (see for example, Malenka and Nicoll, 1993). LTP is a long-lasting strengthening of synaptic efficacy associated with paired pre- and postsynaptic activity. LTD is a long-lasting weakening of synaptic strength. In recent experiments on neocortical slices (Markram *et al.*, 1997), hippocampal cells in culture (Bi and Poo, 1999), and *in vivo* studies of tadpole tectum (Zhang *et al.*, 1998), induction of LTP required that presynaptic action potentials preceded postsynaptic firing by no more than about 20 ms. Maximal LTP occurred when presynaptic spikes preceded postsynaptic action potentials by less than a few milliseconds. If presynaptic spikes followed postsynaptic action potentials, long-term depression rather than potentiation resulted. These results are summarized schematically in Figure 1.

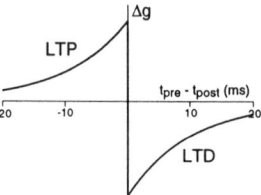

Figure 1: A model of the change in synaptic strength Δg produced by paired pre- and postsynaptic spikes occurring at times t_{pre} and t_{post} respectively. Positive changes correspond to LTP and negative to LTD. There is an abrupt transition at $t_{\text{pre}} - t_{\text{post}} = 0$. The units for Δg are arbitrary in this figure, but data indicate a maximum change of approximately 0.5 % per spike pair.

The curve in Figure 1 is a caricature used to model the weight changes arising from pairings of pre- and postsynaptic action potentials separated by various intervals of time. This curve resembles the data from all three preparations discussed above, but a couple of assumptions have been made in its construction. The data indicate that there is a rapid transition from LTP to LTD depending on whether the time difference between pre- and postsynaptic spiking is positive or negative, but the existing data cannot resolve exactly what happens at the transition point. We have assumed that there is a discontinuous jump from LTP to LTD at this point. In addition, we assume that the area under the LTP side of the curve is slightly less than the area under the LTD side. In Figure 1, this difference is imposed by making the magnitude of LTD slightly greater than the magnitude of LTP, while both sides of the curve have equal exponential fall-offs away from zero time difference. Alternately, we could have given the LTD side a slower exponential fall-off and equal amplitude. The data do not support either assumption unambiguously, nor do they indicate which area is larger. The assumption that the area under the LTD side of the curve is larger than that under the LTP side is critical if the resulting synaptic modification rule is to be stable against uncontrolled growth of synaptic strengths.

Hebb (1949) postulated that a synapse should be strengthened when the presynaptic neuron is frequently involved in making the postsynaptic neuron fire an action potential. Causality is an important element in Hebb's statement; synaptic potentiation should occur only if there is a causal relationship between the pre- and postsynaptic spiking. The LTP/LTD rule summarized in Figure 1 imposes causality through a tight timing requirement. The narrow windows for LTP and LTD seen in the data, and the abrupt transition from potentiation to depression near zero separation between pre- and postsynaptic spike times impose a strict causality condition for LTP induction.

3 Response Variability

What are the implications of the synaptic modification rule summarized in Figure 1? To address this question, we introduce another topic that has been discussed extensively within the computational neuroscience community in recent years, the origin of response variability (Softky and Koch, 1992 & 1994; Shadlen and Newsome, 1994 & 1998; Tsodyks and Sejnowski, 1995; Amit and Brunel, 1997; Troyer and Miller, 1997a & b; Bugmann et al., 1997; van Vreeswijk and Sompolinsky, 1996 & 1998). Neurons can respond to multiple synaptic inputs in two different modes of operation. Figure 2 shows membrane potentials of a model neuron receiving 1000 excitatory and 200 inhibitory synaptic inputs. Each input consists of an independent Poisson spike train driving a synaptic conductance. The integrate-and-fire model neuron used in this example integrates these synaptic conductances as a simple capacitor-resistor circuit. To generate action potentials in this model, we monitor the membrane potential and compare it to a threshold voltage. Whenever the membrane potential reaches the threshold an action potential is "pasted" onto the membrane potential trace and the membrane potential is reset to a prescribed value.

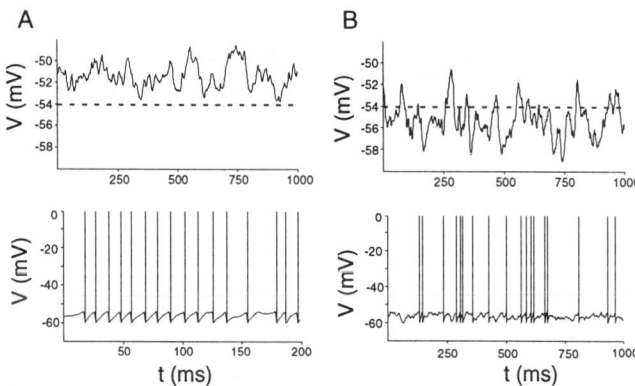

Figure 2: Regular and irregular firing modes of a model integrate-and-fire neuron. Upper panels show the model with action potentials deactivated, and the dashed lines show the action potential threshold. The lower figures show the model with action potentials activated. A) In the regular firing mode, the average membrane potential without spikes is above threshold and the firing pattern is fast and regular (note the different time scale in the lower panel). B) In the irregular firing mode, the average membrane potential without spikes is below threshold and the firing pattern is slower and irregular.

Figures 2A and 2B illustrate the two modes of operation. The upper panels of Figure 2 show the membrane potential with the action potential generation mechanism of the model turned off, and the lower panels show the membrane potential and spike sequences that result when the action potential generation is turned on. In Figure 2A, the effect of the excitatory inputs is strong enough relative to that of the inhibitory inputs so that the average membrane potential, when action potential generation is blocked, is above the spike threshold of the model. When the action potential mechanism is turned back on (lower panel of Figure 2A), this produces a fairly regular pattern of action potentials at a relatively high rate. The total synaptic input attempts to charge the neuron above the threshold, but every time the potential reaches the threshold it gets reset and starts charging again. In this regular firing mode of operation, the timing of the action potentials is determined primarily by the charging rate of the cell, which is controlled by its membrane time constant. Since this does not vary as a function of time, the firing pattern is regular despite the fact that the synaptic input is varying.

Figure 2B shows the other mode of operation that produces an irregular firing pattern. In the irregular firing mode, the average membrane is more hyperpolarized than the threshold for action potential generation (upper panel of Figure 2B). In this mode, action potentials are only generated when there is a fluctuation in the total synaptic current strong enough to make the membrane potential cross the threshold. This results in slower and more irregular firing (lower panel of Figure 2B). The irregular firing mode has a number of interesting features (Shadlen and Newsome, 1994 & 1998; Tsodyks and Sejnowski, 1995; Amit and Brunel, 1997; Troyer and Miller, 1997a & b; Bugmann et al., 1997; van Vreeswijk and Sompolinsky, 1996 & 1998). First, it generates irregular firing patterns that are far closer to the firing patterns seen *in vivo* than the patterns produced in the regular firing mode. Second, responses to changes in the synaptic input are much more rapid in this mode, being limited only by the synaptic rise time rather than the membrane time constant. Finally, the timing of action potentials in the irregular firing mode is related to the timing of fluctuations in the synaptic input rather than being determined primarily by the membrane time constant of the cell.

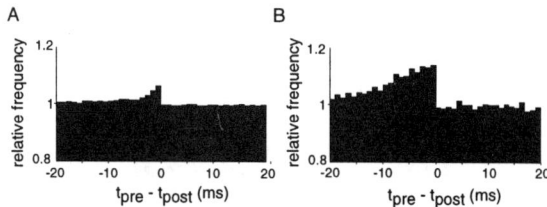

Figure 3: Histograms indicating the relative probability of finding pre- and postsynaptic spikes separated by the indicated time interval. A) Regular firing mode. The probability is essentially flat and at the chance level of one. B) Irregular firing mode. There is an excess of presynaptic spike shortly before a postsynaptic spike.

An important difference between the regular and irregular firing modes is illustrated in the cross-correlograms shown in Figure 3 (Troyer and Miller, 1997b; Bugmann et al. 1997). These indicate the probability that an action potential fired by the postsynaptic neuron is preceded or followed by an presynaptic spike separated by various intervals. The histogram has been normalized so its value for pairings that are due solely to chance is one. The histogram when the model is in the regular firing mode (Figure 3A) takes a value close to one for almost all input-output spike time differences. This is a reflection of the fact that the timing of individual action potentials in the regular firing mode is relatively independent of the timing of the presynaptic inputs. In contrast, the histogram for a model neuron in the irregular firing mode (Figure 3B) shows a much larger excess of presynaptic spikes occurring shortly before the postsynaptic neuron fires. This excess reflects the fluctuations in the total synaptic input that push the membrane potential up to the threshold and produce a spike in the irregular firing mode. It indicates that, in this mode, there is a tight temporal correlation between the timing of such fluctuations and output spikes.

For a neuron to operate in the irregular firing mode, there must be an appropriate balance between the strength of its excitatory and inhibitory inputs. The excitatory input must be weak enough, relative to the inhibitory input, so that the average membrane potential in the absence of spikes is below the action potential threshold to avoid regular firing. However, excitatory input must be sufficiently strong to keep the average potential close enough to the threshold so that fluctuations can reach it and cause the cell to fire. How is this balance achieved?

4 Asymmetric LTP/LTD Leads to an Irregular Firing State

A comparison of the LTP/LTD synaptic modification rule illustrated in Figure 1, and the presynaptic/postsynaptic timing histogram shown in Figure 3, reveals that a temporally asymmetric synaptic modification rule based on the curve in Figure 1 can automatically generate the balance of excitation and inhibition needed to produce an irregular firing state. Suppose that we start a neuron model in a regular firing mode by giving it relatively strong excitatory synaptic strengths. We then apply the LTP/LTD rule of Figure 1 to the excitatory synapse while holding the inhibitory synapse at constant values. Recall that Figure 1 has been adjusted so that the area under the LTD part of the curve is greater than that under the LTP part. This means that if there is an equal probability of a presynaptic spike to either precede or follow a postsynaptic spike the net effect will be a weakening of the excitatory synapses. This is exactly what happens in the regular firing mode, where the relationship between the timing of pre- and postsynaptic spikes is approximately random (Figure 3A). As the LTP/LTD rule weakens the excitatory synapses, the average membrane potential drops and the neuron enters the irregular firing mode. In the irregular firing mode, there is a higher probability for a presynaptic spike to precede than to follow a postsynaptic spike (Figure 3B). This compensates for the fact that the rule we use produces more LTD than LTP. Equilibrium will be reached when the asymmetry of the LTP/LTD modification curve of Figure 1 is matched by the asymmetry of the presynaptic/postsynaptic timing histogram of Figure 3B. The equilibrium state corresponds to a balanced, irregular firing mode of operation, and it is automatically produced by the temporally asymmetric learning rule.

Figure 4A shows a transition from a regular to an irregular firing state mediated by the temporally asymmetric LTP/LTD modification rule. The irregularity of the postsynaptic spike train has been quantified by plotting the coefficient of variation (CV), the standard deviation over the mean of the interspike intervals, of the model neuron as a function of time. Initially, the neuron was in a regular firing state with a low CV value. After the synaptic modification rule reached an equilibrium state, the CV took a value near one indicating that the neuron has been transformed into an irregular firing mode. The solid curve in Figure 4B shows that temporally asymmetric LTP/LTD can robustly generate irregular output firing for a wide range of input firing rates.

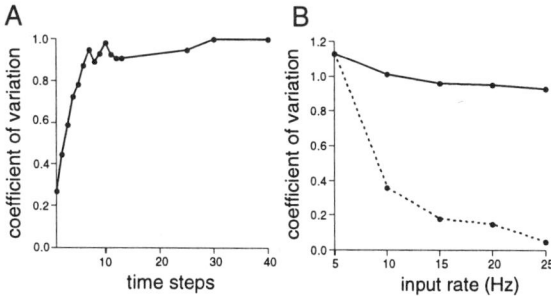

Figure 4: Coefficient of variation (CV) of the output spike train of the model neuron. A) Transition from a regular to an irregular firing state as temporally asymmetric LTP/LTD modifies synaptic strengths. The units of time in this plot are arbitrary because they depend on the magnitude of LTP and LTD used in the model. B) Equilibrium CV values as a function of the firing rates of excitatory inputs to the model neuron. The solid curve gives the results when temporally asymmetric LTP/LTD is active. The dashed curve shows the results if the synaptic strengths that arose for 5 Hz inputs are left unmodified.

5 Discussion

Temporally asymmetric LTP/LTD provides a Hebbian-type learning rule with interesting properties (Kempter et al., 1998). In the past, temporally asymmetric Hebbian learning rules have been studied and applied to problems of temporal sequence generation (Manai and Levy, 1993), navigation (Blum and Abbott, 1996; Gerstner and Abbott, 1997), motor learning (Abbott and Blum, 1996), and detection of spike synchrony (Gerstner et al., 1996). In these studies, two different LTP/LTD window sizes were assumed: either of order 100 ms (Manai and Levy, 1993; Blum and Abbott, 1996; Gerstner and Abbott, 1997; (Abbott and Blum, 1996) or around 1 ms (Gerstner et al., 1996). The new data (Markram et al., 1997; Bell et al., 1997; Zhang et al., 1998; Bi and Poo, 1999) give a window size of order 10 ms. For a 1 ms window size, temporally asymmetric LTP/LTD is sensitive to precise spike timing. When the window size is of order 100 ms, changes in stimuli or motor actions on a behavioral level become relevant for LTP and LTD. A window size of 10 ms, as supported by the recent data, suggests that LTP and LTD are sensitive to firing correlations relevant to neuronal circuitry, such as input-output correlations, which vary over this time scale.

Temporally asymmetric LTP/LTD has some interesting properties that distinguish it from Hebbian learning rules based on correlations or covariances in pre- and postsynaptic rates. We have found that the rule used here is not sensitive to input firing rates or to variability in input rates. If we split the excitatory inputs of the model into two groups and give these two input sets different rates, we see no difference in the distribution of synaptic strengths arising from the learning rule. Similarly, if one group is given a steady firing rate and the other group has firing rates that vary in time, no difference in synaptic strengths is apparent. The most effective way to induce LTP in a set of inputs is to synchronize some of their spikes. Inputs with synchronized spikes are slightly more effective at firing the neuron than unsynchronized spikes. This means that such inputs will preceded postsynaptic spikes more frequently and thus will get stronger. This suggests that spike synchrony may be a signal that marks a set of inputs for learning. Even when this synchrony has no particular functional effect, so that it has little impact on the firing pattern of the postsynaptic neuron, it can lead to dramatic shifts in synaptic strength. Thus, spike synchronization may be a mechanism for inducing LTP and LTD.

Acknowledgments

Research supported by the National Science Foundation (DMS-9503261), the Sloan Center for Theoretical Neurobiology at Brandeis University, a Howard Hughes Predoctoral Fellowship, and the W.M. Keck Foundation.

References

Abbott, LF & Blum, KI (1996) Functional significance of long-term potentiation for sequence learning and prediction. *Cerebral Cortex* **6**:406-416.

Amit, DJ & Brunel N (1997) Global spontaneous activity and local structured (learned) delay activity in cortex. *Cerebral Cortex* **7**:237-252.

Bell CC, Han VZ, Sugawara Y & Grant K (1997) Synaptic plasticity in a cerebellum-like structure depends on temporal order. *Nature* **387**:278-281.

Bi G-q & Poo M-m (1999) Activity-induced synaptic modifications in hippocampal culture: dependence on spike timing, synaptic strength and cell type. *J. Neurophysiol.* (in press).

Blum, KI & Abbott, LF (1996) A model of spatial map formation in the hippocampus of the rat. *Neural Comp.* **8**:85-93.

Bugmann, G, Christodoulou, C & and Taylor, JG (1997) Role of temporal integration and fluctuation detection in the highly irregular firing of a leaky integrator neuron model with partial reset. *Neural Compu.* **9**:985-1000.

Debanne D, Gahwiler BH, Thompson SM (1998) Long-term synaptic plasticity between pairs of individual CA3 pyramidal cells in rat hippocampal slices. *J. Physiol.* **507**:237-247.

Gerstner, W & Abbott, LF (1997) Learning navigational maps through potentiation and modulation of hippocampal place cells. *J. Computational Neurosci.* **4**:79-94.

Gerstner W, Kempter R, van Hemmen JL & Wagner, H (1996) A neural learning rule for sub-millisecond temporal coding. *Nature* **383**:76-78.

Gustafsson B, Wigstrom H, Abraham WC & Huang Y-Y (1987) Long-term potentiation in the hippocampus using depolarizing current pulses as the conditioning stimulus to single volley synaptic potentials. *J. Neurosci.* **7**:774-780.

Hebb, DO (1949) *The Organization of Behavior: A Neuropsychological Theory*. New York:Wiley.

Hertz, JA, Palmer, RG & Krogh, A (1991) *Introduction to the Theory of Neural Computation*. New York:Addison-Wesley.

Kempter R, Gerstner W & van Hemmen JL (1999) Hebbian learning and spiking neurons. (submitted).

Levy WB & Steward O (1983) Temporal contiguity requirements for long-term associative potentiation/depression in the hippocampus. *Neurosci.* **8**:791-797.

Malenka, RC & Nicoll, RA (1993) MBDA-receptor-dependent synaptic plasticity: Multiple forms and mechanisms. *Trends Neurosci.* **16**:521-527.

Minai, AA & Levy, WB (1993) Sequence learning in a single trial. *INNS World Congress on Neural Networks* **II**:505-508.

Markram H, Lubke J, Frotscher M & Sakmann B (1997) Regulation of synaptic efficacy by coincidence of postsynaptic APs and EPSPs. *Science* **275**:213-215.

Rumelhart, DE & McClelland, JL, editors (1986) *Parallel Distributed Processing: Explorations in the Microstructure of Cognition, Volumes I & II*. Cambridge, MA:MIT Press.

Shadlen, MN & Newsome, WT (1994) Noise, neural codes and cortical organization. *Current Opinion in Neurobiology* **4**:569-579.

Shadlen, MN & Newsome, WT (1998) The Variable Discharge of Cortical Neurons: Implications for Connectivity, Computation, and Information Coding. *Journal of Neuroscience* **18**:3870-3896.

Softky, WR & Koch, C (1992) Cortical cells should spike regularly but do not. *Neural Computation* **4**:643-646.

Softky, WR & Koch, C (1994) The highly irregular firing of cortical cells is inconsistent with temporal integration of random EPSPs. *Journal of Neuroscience* **13**:334-350.

Troyer, TW & Miller, KD (1997a) Physiological gain leads to high ISI variability in a simple model of a cortical regular spiking cell. *Neural Comp.* **9**:971-983.

Troyer, TW & Miller, KD (1997b) Integrate-and-fire neurons matched to physiological F-I curves yield high input sensitivity and wide dynamic range. *Computational Neuroscience, Trends in Research*. JM Boser, ed. New York:Plenum, pp. 197-201.

Tsodyks, M & Sejnowski, TJ (1995) Rapid switching in balanced cortical network models. *Network* **6**:1-14.

van Vreeswijk, C & Sompolinsky, H (1996) Chaos in neuronal networks with balanced excitatory and inhibitory activity. *Science* **274**:1724-1726.

van Vreeswijk, C & Sompolinsky, H (1998) Chaotic balanced state in a model of cortical circuits. *Neural Comp.* **10**:1321-1327.

Zhang LI, Tao, HW, Holt CE, Harris WA & Poo M-m (1998) A critical window for cooperation and competition among developing retinotectal synapses. *Nature* **395**:37-44.

Contrast adaptation in simple cells by changing the transmitter release probability

Péter Adorján   Klaus Obermayer
Dept. of Computer Science, FR2-1, Technical University Berlin
Franklinstrasse 28/29 10587 Berlin, Germany
{adp, oby}@cs.tu-berlin.de   http://www.ni.cs.tu-berlin.de

Abstract

The contrast response function (CRF) of many neurons in the primary visual cortex saturates and shifts towards higher contrast values following prolonged presentation of high contrast visual stimuli. Using a recurrent neural network of excitatory spiking neurons with adapting synapses we show that both effects could be explained by a fast and a slow component in the synaptic adaptation. (i) Fast synaptic depression leads to saturation of the CRF and phase advance in the cortical response to high contrast stimuli. (ii) Slow adaptation of the synaptic transmitter release probability is derived such that the mutual information between the input and the output of a cortical neuron is maximal. This component—given by infomax learning rule—explains contrast adaptation of the averaged membrane potential (DC component) as well as the surprising experimental result, that the stimulus modulated component (F1 component) of a cortical cell's membrane potential adapts only weakly. Based on our results, we propose a new experiment to estimate the strength of the effective excitatory feedback to a cortical neuron, and we also suggest a relatively simple experimental test to justify our hypothesized synaptic mechanism for contrast adaptation.

1 Introduction

Cells in the primary visual cortex have to encode a wide range of contrast levels, and they still need to be sensitive to small changes in the input intensities. Because the signaling capacity is limited, this paradox can be resolved only by a dynamic adaptation to changes in the input intensity distribution: the contrast response function (CRF) of many neurons in the primary visual cortex shifts towards higher contrast values following prolonged presentation of high contrast visual stimuli (Ahmed et al. 1997, Carandini & Ferster 1997).

On the one hand, recent experiments, suggest that synaptic plasticity has a major role in contrast adaptation. Because local application of GABA does not mediate adaptation (Vidyasagar 1990) and the membrane conductance does not increase significantly during adaptation (Ahmed et al. 1997, Carandini & Ferster 1997), lateral inhibition is unlikely to account for contrast adaptation. In contrast, blocking glutamate (excitatory) autoreceptors decreases the degree of adaptation (McLean & Palmer 1996). Furthermore, the adaptation is stimulus specific (e.g. Carandini et al. 1998), it is strongest if the adapting and testing stimuli are the same. On the other hand, plasticity of synaptic *weights* (e.g. Chance et al. 1998) cannot explain the weak adaptation of the stimulus driven modulations in the membrane potential (F1 component) (Carandini & Ferster 1997) and the retardation of the response phase after high contrast adaptation (Saul 1995). These experimental findings motivated us to explore how presynaptic factors, such as a long term plasticity mediated by changes in the transmitter release probability (Finlayson & Cynader 1995) affect contrast adaptation.

2 The single cell and the cortical circuit model

The cortical cells are modeled as leaky integrators with a firing threshold of -55 mV. The interspike membrane potential dynamics is described by

$$C_m \frac{\partial V_i(t)}{\partial t} = -g_{\text{leak}}(V_i(t) - E_{\text{rest}}) - \sum_j g_{ij}(t)(V_i(t) - E_{\text{syn}}) . \tag{1}$$

The postsynaptic conductance $g_{ij}(t)$ is the integral over the previous presynaptic events and is described by the alpha-function

$$g_{ij}(t) = \frac{g_{\max}}{\tau_{\text{peak}}} \sum_s^{|\text{spikes}|} p_{ij}(t_j^s) \cdot R_{ij}(t_j^s) \cdot (t - t_j^s) \cdot \exp\left(1 - \frac{t - t_j^s}{\tau_{\text{peak}}}\right), \tag{2}$$

where t_j^s is the arrival time of spike number s from neuron j. Including short term synaptic depression, the effective conductance is weighted by the portion of the synaptic resource $p_{ij}(t) \cdot R_{ij}(t)$ that targets the postsynaptic side. The model parameters are $C_m = 0.5$ nF, $g_{\text{leak}} = 31$ nS, $E_{\text{rest}} = -65$ mV, $E_{\text{syn}} = -5$ mV, $g_{\max}^{\text{exc}} = 7.8$ nS, and $\tau_{\text{peak}} = 1$ ms, and the absolute refractory period is 2 ms, and after a spike, the membrane potential is reset 1 mV below the resting potential. Following Tsodyks & Markram (1997) a synapse between neurons j and i is characterized by the relative portion of the available synaptic transmitter or resource R_{ij}. After a presynaptic event, R_{ij} decreases by $p_{ij} R_{ij}$, and recovers exponentially, where p_{ij} is the transmitter release probability. The time evolution of R_{ij} between two presynaptic spikes is then

$$R_{ij}(t) = 1 - (1 - (R_{ij}(\hat{t}) - p_{ij}(\hat{t})R_{ij}(\hat{t}))) \exp\left(\frac{-(t - \hat{t})}{\tau_{\text{rec}}}\right), \tag{3}$$

where $\hat{t}$ is the last spike time, and the recovery time constant $\tau_{\text{rec}} = 200$ ms. Assuming Poisson distributed presynaptic firing, the steady state of the expected resource is

$$R_{ij}^{\text{st}}(f_j, p_{ij}) = \frac{1}{1 + p_{ij} f_j \tau_{\text{rec}}} . \tag{4}$$

The stationary mean excitatory postsynaptic current (EPSC) $I_{ij}^\infty(f_j, p_{ij})$ is proportional to the presynaptic firing frequency f_j and the activated transmitter $p_{ij} R_{ij}^\infty(f_j, p_{ij})$

$$I_{ij}^\infty(f_j, p_{ij}) \propto f \, p_{ij} \, R_{ij}^\infty(f_j, p_{ij}) . \tag{5}$$

The mean current saturates for high input rates f_j and it also depends on the transmitter release probability p_{ij}: with a high release probability the function is steeper at low presynaptic frequencies but saturates earlier than for a low release probability.

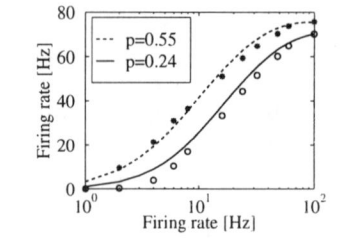 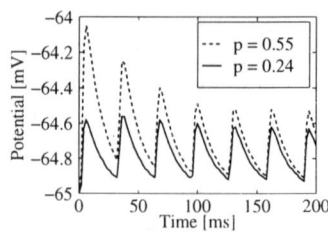

Figure 1: Short term synaptic dynamics at high and low transmitter release probability. (a) The estimated transfer function $O(f, p)$ for the cortical cells (Eq. 7) (solid and dashed lines) in comparison with data obtained by the integrate and fire model (Eq. 1, circles and asterisks). (b) EPSP trains for a series of presynaptic spikes at intervals of 31 ms (32 Hz). p=0.55 (0.24) corresponds to adaptation to 1% (50%) contrast (see Section 4).

In order to study contrast adaptation, 30 leaky-integrator neurons are connected fully via excitatory fast adapting synapses. Each "cortical" leaky integrator neuron receives its "geniculate" input through 30 synapses. The presynaptic geniculate spike-trains are independent Poisson-processes. Modeling visual stimulation with a drifting grating, their rates are modulated sinusoidally with a temporal frequency of 2 Hz. The background activity for each individual "geniculate" source is drawn from a Gaussian distribution with a mean of 20 Hz and a standard deviation of 5 Hz. In the model the mean geniculate firing rate (Fig. 2b) and the amplitude of modulation (Fig. 2a) increases with stimulus log contrast according to the experimental data (Kaplan et al. 1987). In the following simulations CRFs are determined according to the protocol of Carandini & Ferster (1997). The CRFs are calculated using an initial adaptation period of 5 s and a subsequent series of interleaved test and re-adaptation stimuli (1 s each).

3 The learning rule

We propose that contrast adaptation in a visual cortical cell is a result of its goal to maximize the amount of information the cell's output conveys about the geniculate input[1]. Following (Bell & Sejnowski 1995) we derive a learning rule for the transmitter release probability p to maximize the mutual information between a cortical cell's input and output. Let $O(f, p)$ be the average output firing rate, f the presynaptic firing rate, and p the synaptic transmitter release probability. Maximizing the mutual information is then equivalent to maximizing the entropy of a neuron's output if we assume only additive noise:

$$\begin{aligned} H\left[O(f,p)\right] &= -E\left[\ln \operatorname{Prob}(O(f,p))\right] \\ &= -E\left[\ln \frac{\operatorname{Prob}(f)}{|\partial O(f,p)/\partial f|}\right] \\ &= E\left[\ln\left|\frac{\partial O(f,p)}{\partial f}\right|\right] - E\left[\ln \operatorname{Prob}(f)\right]. \end{aligned} \quad (6)$$

(In the following all equations apply locally to a synapse between neurons j and i.)

In order to derive an analytic expression for the relation between O and f we use the fact that the EPSP amplitude converges to its steady state relatively fast compared to the modulation of the geniculate input to the visual cortex, and that the average firing rates of the

---

[1] A different approach of maximizing mutual information between input and output of a single spiking neuron has been developed by Stemmler & Koch (1999). For non-spiking neurons this strategy has been demonstrated experimentally by, e.g. Laughlin (1994).

presynaptic neurons are approximately similar. Thus we approximate the activation function by

$$O(f,p) \propto S(f)\, p\, R^\infty(f,p), \tag{7}$$

where $S(f) = \frac{f^\alpha}{f+\Theta}$ accounts for the frequency dependent summation of EPSCs. The parameters $\alpha = 1.8$ and $\Theta = 15$ Hz are determined by fitting $O(f,p)$ to the firing rate of our integrate and fire single cell model (see Fig. 1a). The objective function is then maximized by a stochastic gradient ascent learning rule for the release probability p

$$\tau_{\text{adapt}} \frac{\partial p}{\partial t} = \frac{\partial H\left[O(f,p)\right]}{\partial p} = \frac{\partial}{\partial p} \ln \left| \frac{\partial O(f,p)}{\partial f} \right|. \tag{8}$$

Evaluating the derivatives we obtain a non-Hebbian learning rule for the transmitter release probability p,

$$\tau_{\text{adapt}} \frac{\partial p}{\partial t} = -2\tau_{\text{rec}} f R + \frac{1}{p} + \frac{\tau_{\text{rec}}(fa-1)}{a + \tau_{\text{rec}} p(fa-1)}, \tag{9}$$

where $a = \frac{\alpha}{f} - \frac{1}{f+\Theta}$, and the adaptation time constant $\tau_{\text{adapt}} = 7$ s (Ohzawa et al. 1985). This is similar in spirit to the anti-Hebbian learning mechanism for the synaptic strength proposed by Barlow & Földiák (1989) to explain adaptation phenomena. Here, the first term is proportional to the presynaptic firing rate f and to the available synaptic resource R, suggesting a presynaptic mechanism for the learning. Because the amplitude of the EPSP is proportional to the available synaptic resource, we could interpret R as an output related quantity and $-2\tau_{\text{rec}} f R$ as an anti-Hebbian learning rule for the "strength of the synapse", i.e. the probability p of the transmitter release. The second term ensures that p is always larger than 0. In the current model setup for the operating range of the presynaptic geniculate cells p also stays always less than 1. The third term modulates the adaptation slightly and increases the release probability p most if the input firing rate is close to 20 Hz, i.e. the stimulus contrast is low.

Image contrast is related to the standard deviation of the luminance levels normalized by the mean. Because ganglion cells adapt to the mean luminance, contrast adaptation in the primary visual cortex requires only the estimation of the standard deviation. In a free viewing scenario with an eye saccade frequency of 2-3 Hz, the standard deviation can be estimated based on 10-20 image samples. Thus the adaptation rate can be fast ($\tau_{\text{adapt}} = 7\,s$), and it should also be fast in order to maintain good a representation whenever visual contrast changes, e.g. by changing light conditions. Higher order moments (than the standard deviation) of the statistics of the visual world express image structure and are represented by the receptive fields' profiles. The statistics of the visual environment are relatively static, thus the receptive field profiles should be determined and constrained by another less plastic synaptic parameter, such as the maximal synaptic conductance g_{max}.

4 Results

Figure 2 shows the average geniculate input, the membrane potential, the firing rate and the response phase of the modeled cortical cells as a function of stimulus contrast. The CRFs were calculated for two adapting contrasts 1% (dashed line) and 50% (solid line). The cortical CRF saturates for high contrast stimuli (Fig. 2e). This is due to the saturation of the postsynaptic current (cf. Fig. 1a) and thus induced by the short term synaptic depression. In accordance with the experimental data (e.g. Carandini et al. 1997) the delay of the cortical response (Fig. 2f) decreases towards high contrast stimuli. This is a consequence of fast synaptic depression (c.f. Chance et al. 1998). High modulation in the input firing rate leads to a fast transient rise in the EPSC followed by a rapid depression.

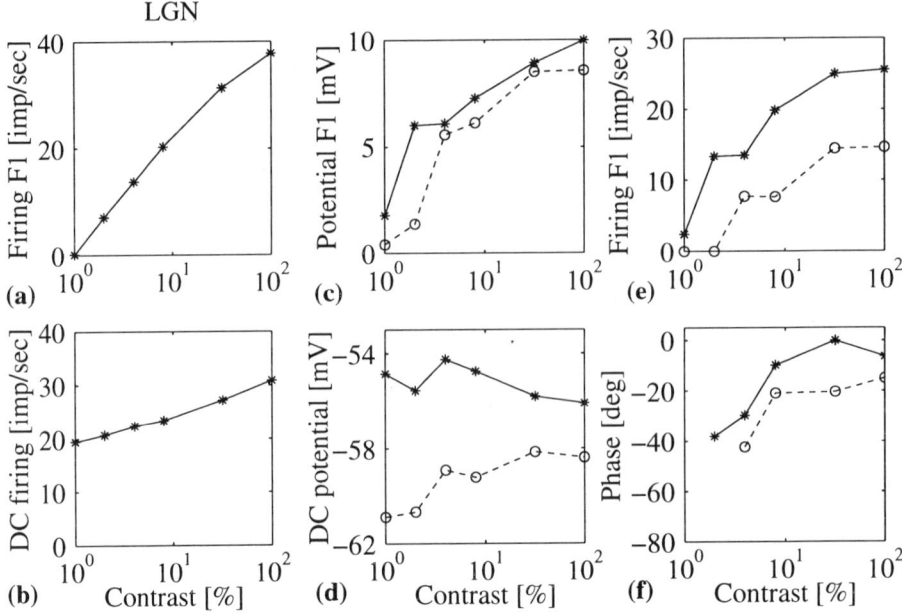

Figure 2: The DC (a) and the F1 (b) component of the geniculate input, and the response of the cortical units in the model *with* strong recurrent lateral connections and slow adaptation of the release probability on both the geniculocortical and lateral synapses. The F1 (c) and the DC (d) component of the subthreshold membrane potential of a single cortical unit, the F1 component of the firing rate (e), and the response phase (f) are plotted as a function of stimulus contrast after adaptation to 1% (solid lines) and to 50% (dashed lines) contrast stimuli. The CRF for the membrane potential (c, d) is calculated by integrating Eq. 1 without spikes and without reset after spikes. The cortical circuitry involves strong recurrent lateral connections.

The model predicts a shift of 3-5 mV in the DC component of the subthreshold membrane potential (Fig. 2d)— a smaller amount than measured by Carandini & Ferster (1997). Nevertheless, in accordance with the data the shift caused by the adaptation is larger than the change in the DC component of the membrane potential from 1% contrast to 100% contrast. The largest shift in the DC membrane potential during adaptation occurs for small contrast stimuli because an alteration in the transmitter release probability has the largest effect on the postsynaptic current if the presynaptic firing rate is close to the geniculate background activity of 20 Hz. The maximal change in the F1 component (Fig. 2c) is around 5mV and it is half of the increase in the F1 component of the membrane potential from 1% contrast to 100% contrast. The CRF for the cortical firing rate (Fig. 2e) shifts to the right and the slope decreases after adaptation to high contrast. The model predicts that the probability p for the transmitter release decreases by approximately a factor of two.

The F1 component of the cortical firing rate decreases after adaptation because after tonic decrease in the input modulated membrane potential, the over-threshold area of its F1 component decreases. The adaptation in the F1 firing rate is fed back via the recurrent excitatory connections resulting in the observable adaptation in the F1 membrane potential. Without lateral feedback (Fig. 3) the F1 component of the membrane potential is basically independent of the contrast adaptation. At high release probability a steep rise of the EPSC to a high amplitude peak is followed by rapid depression if the input is increasing. At low release probability the current increases slower to a lower amplitude, but the depression is

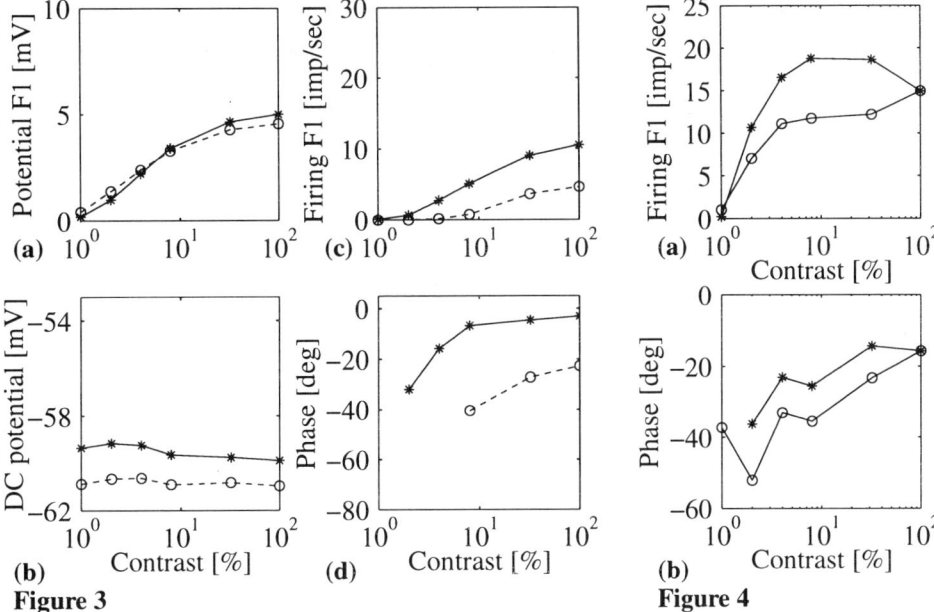

Figure 3: The membrane potential (a, b), the phase (d) of the F1 component of the firing rate, and the F1 component (c) averaged for the modeled cortical cells after adaptation to 1% (dashed lines) and 50% (solid lines) contrast. The weight of cortical connections is set to zero. The CRF for the membrane potential (a, b) is calculated by integrating Eq. 1 without spikes and without reset after spikes.

Figure 4: Hysteresis curve revealed by following the ramp method protocol (Carandini & Ferster 1997). After adaption to 1% contrast, test stimuli of 2 s duration were applied with a contrast successively increasing from 1% to 100% (asterisks), and then decreasing back to 1% (circles).

less pronounced too. As a consequence, the power at the first harmonic (F1 component) of the subthreshold membrane potential does not change if the release probability is modulated. It is modulated to a large extent by the recurrent excitatory feedback. The adaptation of the F1 component of the firing rate could therefore be used to measure the effective strength of the recurrent excitatory input to a simple cell in the primary visual cortex.

Additional simulations (data not shown) revealed that changing the transmitter release probability of the geniculocortical synapses is responsible for the adaptation in our model network. Fixing the value of p for the geniculocortical synapses abolishes contrast adaptation, while fixing the release probability p for the lateral synapses has no effect. Simulations show that increasing the release probability of the recurrent excitatory synapses leads to oscillatory activity (e.g. Senn et al. 1996) without altering the mean activity of simple cells. These results suggest an efficient functional segregation of feedforward and recurrent excitatory connections. Plasticity of the geniculocortical connections may play a key role in contrast adaptation, while—without affecting the CRF—plasticity of the recurrent excitatory synapses could could play a key role in dynamic feature binding and segregation in the visual cortex (e.g. Engel et al. 1997).

Figure 4 shows the averaged CRF of the cortical model neurons revealed by the ramp method (see figure caption) for strong recurrent feedback and adapting feedforward and recurrent synapses. We find hysteresis curves for the F1 component of the firing rate similar to the results reported by Carandini & Ferster (1997), and for the response phase.

In summary, by assuming two different dynamics for a single synapse we explain the saturation of the CRFs, the contrast adaptation, and the increase in the delay of the cortical response to low contrast stimuli. For the visual cortex of higher mammals, adaptation of release probability p as a substrate for contrast adaptation is so far only a hypothesis. This hypothesis, however, is in agreement with the currently available data, and could additionally be justified experimentally by intracellular measurements of EPSPs evoked by stimulating the geniculocortical axons. The model predicts that after adaptation to a low contrast stimulus the amplitude of the EPSPs decreases steeply from a high value, while it shows only small changes after adaptation to a high contrast stimulus (cf. Fig. 1b).

Acknowledgments The authors are grateful to Christian Piepenbrock for fruitful discussions. Funded by the German Science Foundation (Ob 102/2-1, GK120-2).

References

Ahmed, B., Allison, J. D., Douglas, R. J. & Martin, K. A. C. (1997), 'Intracellular study of the contrast-dependence of neuronal activity in cat visual cortex.', *Cerebral Cortex* **7**, 559–570.

Barlow, H. B. & Földiák, P. (1989), Adaptation and decorrelation in the cortex, *in* R. Durbin, C. Miall & C. Mitchison, eds, 'The computing neuron', Workingham: Addison-Wesley, pp. 54–72.

Bell, A. J. & Sejnowski, T. J. (1995), 'An information-maximization approach to blind sepertation and blind deconvolution', *Neur. Comput.* **7**(6), 1129–1159.

Carandini, M. & Ferster, D. (1997), 'A tonic hyperpolarization underlying contrast adaptation in cat visual cortex', *Science* **276**, 949–952.

Carandini, M., Heeger, D. J. & Movshon, J. A. (1997), 'Linearity and normalization in simple cells of the macaque primary visual cortex', *J. Neurosci.* **17**, 8621–8644.

Carandini, M., Movshon, J. A. & Ferster, D. (1998), 'Pattern adaptation and cross-orientation interactions in the primary visual cortex', *Neuropharmacology* **37**, 501–511.

Chance, F. S., Nelson, S. B. & Abbott, L. F. (1998), 'Synaptic depression and the temporal response characteristics of V1 cells', *J. Neurosci.* **18**, 4785–4799.

Engel, A. K., Roelfsema, P. R., Fries, P., Brecht, M. & Singer, W. (1997), 'Role of the temporal domain for response selection and perceptual binding', *Cerebral Cortex* **7**, 571–582.

Finlayson, P. G. & Cynader, M. S. (1995), 'Synaptic depression in visual cortex tissue slices: am in vitro model for cortical neuron adaptation', *Exp. Brain Res.* **106**, 145–155.

Kaplan, E., Purpura, K. & Shapley, R. M. (1987), 'Contrast affects the transmission of visual information through the mammalian lateral geniculate nucleus', *J. Physiol.* **391**, 267–288.

Laughlin, S. B. (1994), 'Matching coding, circuits, cells, and molecules to signals: general principles of retinal design in the fly's eye', *Prog. Ret. Eye Res.* **13**, 165–196.

McLean, J. & Palmer, L. A. (1996), 'Contrast adaptation and excitatory amino acid receptors in cat striate cortex', *Vis. Neurosci.* **13**, 1069–1087.

Ohzawa, I., Sclar, G. & Freeman, R. D. (1985), 'Contrast gain control in the cat's visual system', *J. Neurophysiol.* **54**, 651–667.

Saul, A. B. (1995), 'Adaptation in single units in visual cortex: response timing is retarted by adapting', *Vis. Neurosci.* **12**, 191–205.

Senn, W., Wyler, K., Streit, J., Larkum, M., Lüscher, H.-R., H. Mey, L. M. a. D. S., Vogt, K. & Wannier, T. (1996), 'Dynamics of a random neural network with synaptic depression', *Neural Networks* **9**, 575–588.

Stemmler, M. & Koch, C. (1999), Information maximization in single neurons, *in* 'Advances in Neural Information Processing Systems NIPS 11'. same volume.

Tsodyks, M. V. & Markram, H. (1997), 'The neural code between neocortical pyramidal neurons depends on neurotransmitter release probability', *Proc. Natl. Acad. Sci.* **94**, 719–723.

Vidyasagar, T. R. (1990), 'Pattern adaptation in cat visual cortex is a co-operative phenomenon', *Neurosci.* **36**, 175–179.

Where does the population vector of motor cortical cells point during reaching movements?

Pierre Baraduc*
pbaraduc@snv.jussieu.fr

Emmanuel Guigon
guigon@ccr.jussieu.fr

Yves Burnod
ybteam@ccr.jussieu.fr

INSERM U483, Université Pierre et Marie Curie
9 quai St Bernard, 75252 Paris cedex 05, France

Abstract

Visually-guided arm reaching movements are produced by distributed neural networks within parietal and frontal regions of the cerebral cortex. Experimental data indicate that (1) single neurons in these regions are broadly tuned to parameters of movement; (2) appropriate commands are elaborated by populations of neurons; (3) the coordinated action of neurons can be visualized using a neuronal population vector (NPV). However, the NPV provides only a rough estimate of movement parameters (direction, velocity) and may even fail to reflect the parameters of movement when arm posture is changed. We designed a model of the cortical motor command to investigate the relation between the desired direction of the movement, the actual direction of movement and the direction of the NPV in motor cortex. The model is a two-layer self-organizing neural network which combines broadly-tuned (muscular) proprioceptive and (cartesian) visual information to calculate (angular) motor commands for the initial part of the movement of a two-link arm. The network was trained by motor babbling in 5 positions. Simulations showed that (1) the network produced appropriate movement direction over a large part of the workspace; (2) small deviations of the actual trajectory from the desired trajectory existed at the extremities of the workspace; (3) these deviations were accompanied by large deviations of the NPV from both trajectories. These results suggest the NPV does not give a faithful image of cortical processing during arm reaching movements.

---

*to whom correspondence should be addressed

1 INTRODUCTION

When reaching to an object, our brain transforms a visual stimulus on the retina into a finely coordinated motor act. This complex process is subserved in part by distributed neuronal populations within parietal and frontal regions of the cerebral cortex (Kalaska and Crammond 1992). Neurons in these areas contribute to coordinate transformations by encoding target position and kinematic parameters of reaching movements in multiple frames of reference and to the elaboration of motor commands by sending directional and positional signals to the spinal cord (Georgopoulos 1996). An ubiquitous feature of cortical populations is that most neurons are broadly tuned to a preferred attribute (e.g. direction) and that tuning curves are uniformly (or regularly) distributed in the attribute space (Georgopoulos 1996). Accordingly, a powerful tool to analyse cortical populations is the NPV which describes the behavior of a whole population by a single vector (Georgopoulos 1996). Georgopoulos et al. (1986) have shown that the NPV calculated on a set of directionally tuned neurons in motor cortex points approximately (error $\sim 15°$) in the direction of movement. However, the NPV may fail to indicate the correct direction of movement when the arm is in a particular posture (Scott and Kalaska 1995). These data raise two important questions: (1) how populations of broadly tuned neurons learn to compute a correct sensorimotor transformation? Previous models (Burnod et al. 1992; Bullock et al. 1993; Salinas and Abbott 1995) provided partial solutions to this problem but we still lack a model which closely matches physiological and psychophysical data on reaching movements; (2) Are cortical processes involved in the visual guidance of arm movements readable with the NPV tool? This article provides answers to these questions through a physiologically inspired model of sensorimotor transformations.

2 MODEL OF THE VISUAL-TO-MOTOR TRANSFORMATION

2.1 ARM GEOMETRY

The arm model has voluntarily been chosen simple. It is a planar, two-link arm, with limited (160 degrees) joint excursion at shoulder and elbow. An agonist/antagonist pair is attached at each joint.

2.2 INPUT AND OUTPUT CODINGS

No cell is finely tuned to a specific input or output value to mimic the broad tunings or monotonic firing characteristics found in cortical visuomotor areas.

2.2.1 Arm position

By analogy with the role of muscle spindles, proprioceptive sensors are assumed to code muscle length. Arm position is thus represented by the population activity of $N_\tau = 20$ neurons coding for the length of each agonist or antagonist. The activity of a sensor neuron k is defined by:

$$\tau_k = \sigma_k(L_{n(k)})$$

where $L_{n(k)}$ is the length of muscle number $n(k)$, and σ_k a piecewise linear sigmoid:

$$\sigma_k(L) = \begin{cases} 0 & : L \leq \lambda_k \\ (L - \lambda_k)/(\Lambda_k - \lambda_k) & : \lambda_k < L < \Lambda_k \\ 1 & : L \geq \Lambda_k \end{cases}$$

Sensibility thresholds λ_k are uniformly distributed in $[L_{min}, L_{max}]$, and the dynamic range is $\Lambda_k - \lambda_k$ is taken constant, equal to $L_{max} - L_{min}$.

2.2.2 Desired direction

The direction **V** of the desired movement in visual space is coded by a population of $N_x = 50$ neurons with cosine tuning in cartesian space. Each visual neuron j thus fires as:

$$x_j = \mathbf{V} \cdot \mathbf{V}_j$$

$\mathbf{V}_j$ being the preferred direction of the cell. These 50 preferred directions are chosen uniformly distributed in 2-D space.

2.2.3 Motor Command

In attempt to model the existence of muscular synergies (Lemon 1988), we identified motor command with joint movement rather than with muscle contraction. A motor neuron i among $N_t = 50$ contributes to the effective movement **M** by its action on a synergy (direction in joint space) $\mathbf{M}_i$. This collective effect is formally expressed by:

$$\mathbf{M} = \sum_i t_i \mathbf{M}_i$$

where t_i is the activity of motor neuron i. The 50 directions of action $\mathbf{M}_i$ are supposed uniformly distributed in joint space.

3 NETWORK STRUCTURE AND LEARNING

3.1 STRUCTURE OF THE NETWORK

Information concerning the position of the arm and the desired direction in cartesian space

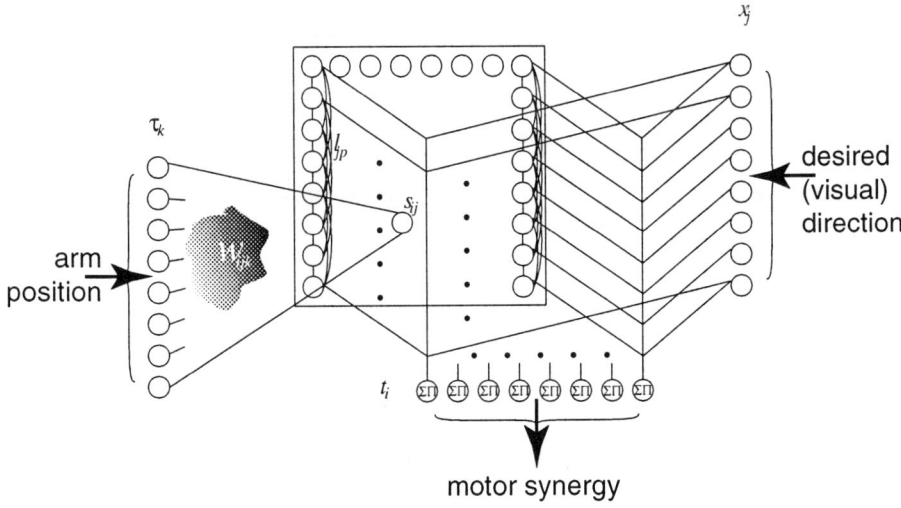

Figure 1: Network Architecture

is combined asymmetrically (Fig. 1). First, an intermediate (somatic) layer of neurons forms an internal representation of the arm position by a combination of the input from the N_τ muscle sensors and the lateral interactions inside the population. Activity in this layer is expressed by:

$$s_{ij} = \sum_k w_{ijk}\,\tau_k + \sum_p l_{jp}\,s_{ip} \qquad (1)$$

where the lateral connections are:

$$l_{jp} = \cos\left(2\pi(j-p)/N_\tau\right)$$

Equation 1 is self-referent; so calculation is done in two steps. The feed-forward input first arrives at time zero when there is no activity in the layer; iterated action of the lateral connections comes into play when this feed-forward input vanishes.

The activity in the somatic layer is then combined with the visual directional information by the output sigma-pi neurons as follows:

$$t_i = \sum_j x_j\,s_{ij}$$

3.2 WEIGHTS AND LEARNING

The only adjustable weights are the w_{ijk} linking the proprioceptive layer to the somatic layer. Connectivity is random and not complete: only 15% of the somatic neurons receive information on arm position. The visuomotor mapping is learnt by modifying the internal representation of the arm.

Motor commands issued by the network are correlated with the visual effect of the movement ("motor babbling"). More precisely, the learning algorithm is a repetition of the following cycle:

1. choice of an arm position among 5 positions (stars on Fig. 2)
2. random emission of a motor command (t_i)
3. corresponding visual reafference (x_j)
4. weight modification according to a variant of the delta rule:
   $\Delta w_{ijk} \propto (t_i x_j - s_{ij})\,\tau_k$

The random commands are gaussian distributions of activity over the output layer. 5000 learning epochs are sufficient to obtain a stabilized performance. It must be noted that the error between the ideal response of the network and the actual performance never decreases completely to zero, as the constraints of the visuomotor transformation vary over the workspace.

4 RESULTS

4.1 NETWORK PERFORMANCE

Correct learning of the mapping was tested in 21 positions in the workspace in a pointing task toward 16 uniformly distributed directions in cartesian space. Movement directions generated by the network are shown in Fig. 2 (desired direction 0 degree is shown bold). Norm of movement vectors depends on the global activity in the network which varies with arm position and movement direction.

Performance of the network is maximal near the learning positions. However, a good generalization is obtained (directional error 0.3°, SD 12.1°); a bias toward the shoulder can be observed in extreme right or left positions. A similar effect was observed in psychophysical experiments (Ghilardi et al. 1995).

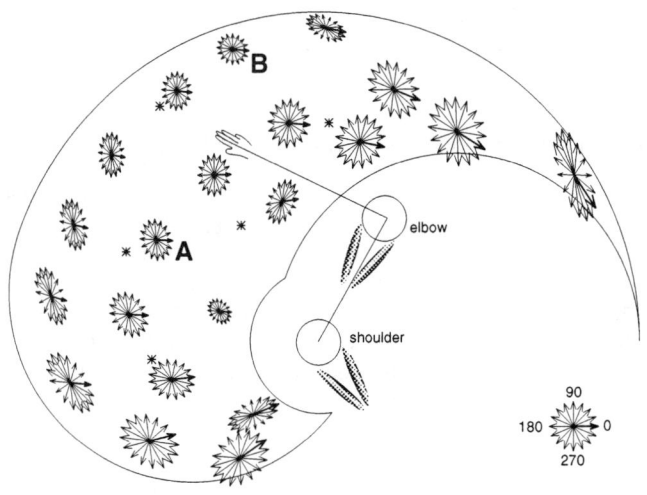

Figure 2: Performance in a pointing task

4.2 PREFERRED DIRECTIONS AND POPULATION VECTOR

4.2.1 Behavior of the population vector

Preferred directions (PD) of output units were computed using a multilinear regression; a perfect cosine tuning was found, which is a consequence of the *exact* multiplication in sigma-pi neurons. Then, the population vector, the effective movement vector, and the desired movement were compared (Fig. 3) for two different arm configurations A and B marked on Fig. 2. The movement generated by the network (dashed arrow) is close to the

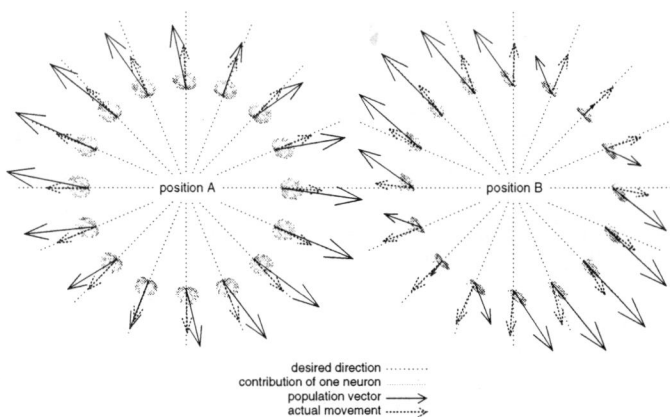

Figure 3: Actual movement and population vector in two arm positions

desired one (dotted rays) for both arm configurations. However, the population vector (solid arrow) is not always aligned with the movement. The discrepancy between movement and population vector depends both on the direction and the position of the arm: it is maximal for positions near the borders of the workspace as position B. Fig. 3 (position B) shows that the deviations of the population vector are due to the anisotropic distribution of the PDs in cartesian space for given positions.

4.2.2 Difference between direction of action and preferred direction

Marked anisotropy in the distribution of PDs is compatible with accurate performance. To see why, let us call "direction of action" (DA) the motor cell's contribution to the movement. The distribution of DAs presents an anisotropy due to the geometry of the arm. This anisotropy is canceled by the distribution of PDs. Mathematically, if $\mathbf{U}$ is a $N \times 2$ matrix of uniformly distributed 2D vectors, the PD matrix is $\mathbf{UJ}^{-1}$ whereas the DA matrix is $\mathbf{UJ}^T$, $\mathbf{J}$ being the jacobian of the angular-to-cartesian mapping. Difference between DA and PD has been plotted with concentric arcs for four representative neurons at 21 arm positions in Fig. 4. Sign and magnitude of the difference vary continuously over the workspace and

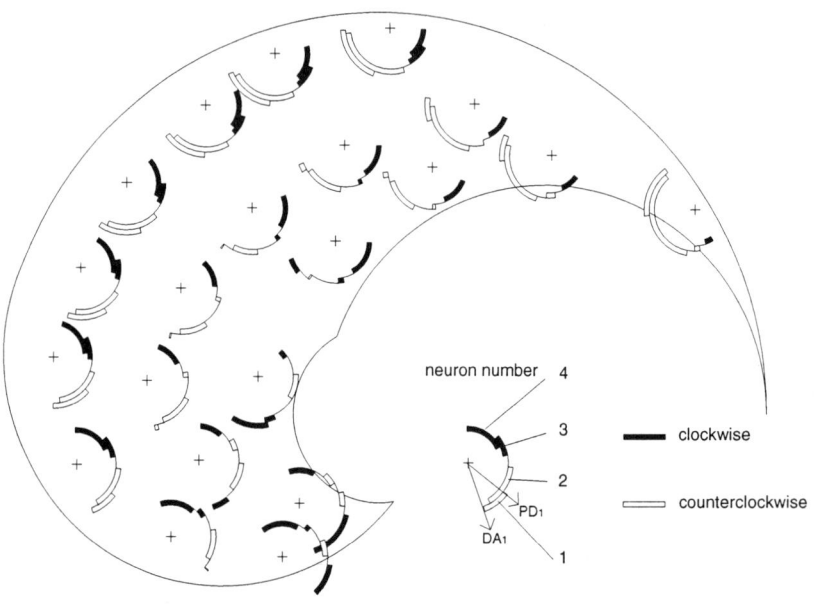

Figure 4: Difference between direction of action and preferred direction for four units.

often exceed 45 degrees. It can also be noted that preferred directions rotate with the arm as was experimentally noted by (Caminiti et al. 1991).

5 DISCUSSION

We first asked how a network of broadly tuned neurons could produce visually guided arm movements. The model proposed here produces a correct behavior over the entire workspace. Biases were observed at the extreme right and left which closely resemble experimental data in humans (Ghilardi et al. 1995). Single cells in the output layer behave as motor cortical cells do and the NPV of these cells correctly indicated the direction of movement for hand positions in the central region of the workspace (see Caminiti et al. 1991). Models of sensorimotor transformations have already been proposed. However they either considered motor synergies in cartesian coordinates (Burnod et al. 1992), or used sharply tuned units (Bullock et al. 1993), or motor effects independent of arm position (Salinas and Abbott 1995). Next, the use of the NPV to describe cortical activity was questioned. A fundamental assumption in the calculation of the NPV is that the PD of a neuron is the direction in which the arm would move if the neuron were stimulated. The model shows that the two directions DA and PD do not necessarily coincide, which is probably the case in motor cortex (Scott and Kalaska 1995). It follows that the NPV often points neither in the actual movement direction nor in the desired movement direction (target direction), especially for unusual arm configurations. A maximum-likelihood estimator does not have these flaws; it would however accurately predict the *desired* movement out of the *output* unit activities, even for a wrong actual movement. In conclusion: (1) the NPV does not provide a faithful image of cortical visuomotor processes; (2) a correct NPV should be based on the DAs, which cannot easily be determined experimentally; (3) planning of trajectories in space cannot be realized by the successive recruitment of motor neurons whose PDs sequentially describe the movement.

References

Bullock, D., S. Grossberg, and F. Guenther (1993). A self-organizing neural model of motor equivalent reaching and tool use by a multijoint arm. *J Cogn Neurosci 5*(4), 408–435.

Burnod, Y., P. Grandguillaume, I. Otto, S. Ferraina, P. Johnson, and R. Caminiti (1992). Visuomotor transformations underlying arm movements toward visual targets: a neural network model of cerebral cortical operations. *J Neurosci 12*(4), 1435–53.

Caminiti, R., P. Johnson, C. Galli, S. Ferraina, and Y. Burnod (1991). Making arm movements within different parts of space: the premotor and motor cortical representation of a coordinate system for reaching to visual targets. *J Neurosci 11*(5), 1182–97.

Georgopoulos, A. (1996). On the translation of directional motor cortical commands to activation of muscles via spinal interneuronal systems. *Brain Res Cogn Brain Res 3*(2), 151–5.

Georgopoulos, A., A. Schwartz, and R. Kettner (1986). Neuronal population coding of movement direction. *Science 233*(4771), 1416–9.

Ghilardi, M., J. Gordon, and C. Ghez (1995). Learning a visuomotor transformation in a local area of work space produces directional biases in other areas. *J Neurophysiol 73*(6), 2535–9.

Kalaska, J. and D. Crammond (1992). Cerebral cortical mechanisms of reaching movements. *Science 255*(5051), 1517–23.

Lemon, R. (1988). The output map of the primate motor cortex. *Trends Neurosci 11*(11), 501–6.

Salinas, E. and L. Abbott (1995). Transfer of coded information from sensory to motor networks. *J Neurosci 15*(10), 6461–74.

Scott, S. and J. Kalaska (1995). Changes in motor cortex activity during reaching movements with similar hand paths but different arm postures. *J Neurophysiol 73*(6), 2563–7.

Recurrent Cortical Amplification Produces Complex Cell Responses

Frances S. Chance, Sacha B. Nelson, and L. F. Abbott
Volen Center and Department of Biology
Brandeis University
Waltham, MA 02454

Abstract

Cortical amplification has been proposed as a mechanism for enhancing the selectivity of neurons in the primary visual cortex. Less appreciated is the fact that the same form of amplification can also be used to de-tune or broaden selectivity. Using a network model with recurrent cortical circuitry, we propose that the spatial phase invariance of complex cell responses arises through recurrent amplification of feedforward input. Neurons in the network respond like simple cells at low gain and complex cells at high gain. Similar recurrent mechanisms may play a role in generating invariant representations of feedforward input elsewhere in the visual processing pathway.

1 INTRODUCTION

Synaptic input to neurons in the primary visual cortex is primarily recurrent, arising from other cortical cells. The dominance of this type of connection suggests that it may play an important role in cortical information processing. Previous studies proposed that recurrent connections amplify weak feedforward input to the cortex (Douglas et al., 1995) and selectively amplify tuning for specific stimulus characteristics, such as orientation or direction of movement (Douglas et al., 1995; Ben-Yishai et al., 1995; Somers et al., 1995; Sompolinsky and Shapley, 1997). Cortical cooling and shocking experiments provide evidence that there is cortical amplification through recurrent connections, but they do not show increases in orientation or direction selectivity as a result of this amplification (Ferster et al., 1996; Chung and Ferster, 1998). Recurrent connections can also decrease neuronal selectivity through the same form of amplification, generating responses that are insensitive to certain stimulus features. Although the ability to sharpen tuning may be an important feature in cortical processing, the capacity to broaden tuning for particular stimulus attributes is also desirable.

Neurons in the primary visual cortex can be divided into two classes based on their responses to visual stimuli such as counterphase and drifting sinusoidal gratings. Simple cells show tuning for orientation, spatial frequency, and spatial phase of a grating (Movshon et al., 1978a). Complex cells exhibit orientation and spatial frequency tuning, but are insensitive to spatial phase (Movshon et al., 1978b). A counterphase grating, $s(x,t) = \cos(Kx - \Phi)\cos(\omega t)$, is one in which the spatial phase, Φ, and spatial frequency, K, are held constant but the contrast, $s(x,t)$, varies sinusoidally in time at some frequency ω. In response to a counterphase grating, the activity of a simple cell oscillates at the same frequency as the stimulus, ω. A complex cell response is modulated at twice the frequency, 2ω. To create a drifting grating of frequency ν, $s(x,t) = \cos(Kx - \nu t)$, the spatial phase and spatial frequency are held constant but the grating is moved at velocity ν/K. A simple cell response to a drifting grating is highly modulated at frequency ν, while a complex cell response to a drifting grating is elevated but relatively unmodulated. The differences between complex and simple cell responses are a direct consequence of the complex cell spatial phase insensitivity.

Previous models of complex cells generate spatial-phase invariant responses through converging sets of feedforward inputs with a wide range of spatial phase preferences but similar orientation and spatial frequency selectivities (Hubel and Wiesel, 1962; Mel et al., 1998). These models do not incorporate recurrent connections between complex cells, which are known to be particularly strong (Toyama et al., 1981). We propose that the spatial phase invariance of complex cell responses can arise from a broadening of spatial phase tuning by cortical amplification (Chance et al., 1998). The model neurons exhibit simple cell behavior when weakly coupled and complex cell behavior when strongly coupled, suggesting that the two classes of neurons in the primary visual cortex may arise from the same basic cortical circuit.

2 THE MODEL

The activity of neuron i in the model network is characterized by a firing rate r_i. Each neuron sums feedforward and recurrent input and responds as described by the standard rate-model equation

$$\tau_r \frac{dr_i}{dt} = I_i + \sum W_{ij} r_j - r_i.$$

I_i represents the feedforward input to cell i, W_{ij} is the weight of the synapse from neuron j to neuron i, and τ_r is a time constant. Previous studies have suggested that, for a neuron receiving many inputs, τ_r is small, closer to a synaptic time constant than the membrane time constant (Ben-Yishai et al., 1995; Treves, 1993). Thus we choose $\tau_r = 1$ ms.

The feedforward input describes the response of a simple cell with a Gabor receptive field

$$I_i = \left[\int dx G_i(x) \int_0^\infty dt' H(t') s(x, t-t') \right]_+ ,$$

where $s(x,t)$ represents the contrast function of the visual stimulus and the notation $[\ ]_+$ indicates rectification. The temporal response function is (Adelson and Bergen, 1985)

$$H(t') = \exp(-\alpha t') \left(\frac{(\alpha t')^5}{5!} - \frac{(\alpha t')^7}{7!} \right),$$

where we use $\alpha = 1/\text{ms}$. The spatial filter is a Gabor function,

$$G = \exp\left(-\frac{x^2}{2\sigma_i^2}\right) \cos(k_i x - \phi_i),$$

where σ_i determines the spatial extent of the receptive field, k_i is the preferred spatial frequency, and ϕ_i is the preferred spatial phase. The values of ϕ_i are equally distributed over the interval $[-180°, 180°)$. To give the neurons a realistic bandwidth, σ_i is chosen such that $k_i \sigma_i = 2.5$. Initially we consider a simplified case in which $k_i = 1$ for all cells. Later we consider the spatial frequency selectivity of neurons in the network and allow the value of k_i to range from 0 to 3.5 cycles/deg.

In this paper we assume that the model network describes one orientation column of the primary visual cortex, and thus all neurons have the same orientation tuning. All stimuli are of the optimal orientation for the network.

Spatial phase tuning is selectively broadened in the model because the strength of a recurrent connection between two neurons is independent of the spatial phase selectivities of their feedforward inputs. In the model with all $k_i = 1$, the recurrent input is determined by

$$W_{ij} = \frac{g}{(N-1)},$$

for all $i \neq j$. N is the number of cells in the network, and $0 \leq g < g_{max}$, where g_{max} is the largest value of g for which the network remains stable. In this case $g_{max} = 1$.

3 RESULTS

The steady-state solution of the rate-model equation is given by $r_i = I_i + \sum W_{ij} r_j$. To solve this equation, we express the rates and feedfoward inputs in terms of a complete set of eigenvectors ξ_i^μ of the recurrent weight matrix, $\sum W_{ij} \xi_j^\mu = \lambda_\mu \xi_i^\mu$ for $\mu = 1, 2, \ldots, N$, where λ_μ are the eigenvalues. The solution is then

$$r_i = \sum_{\mu=1}^{N} \left(\frac{\xi_i^\mu}{1 - \lambda_\mu} \sum_{j=1}^{N} I_j \xi_j^\mu \right).$$

This equation displays the phenomenon of cortical amplification if one or more of the eigenvalues is near one. If we assume only one eigenvalue, λ_1, is close to one, the factor $1 - \lambda_1$ in the denominator causes the $\mu = 1$ term to dominate and we find $r_i \approx \xi_i^1 \sum_j I_j \xi_j^1 (1 - \lambda_1)^{-1}$. The input combination $\sum_j I_j \xi_j^1$ dominates the response, determining selectivity, and this mode is amplified by a factor $1/(1 - \lambda_1)$. We refer to this amplification factor as the cortical gain.

In the case where $W_{ij} = g/(N-1)$ for $i \neq j$, the largest eigenvalue is $\lambda_1 = g$ and the corresponding eigenvector has all components equal to each other. For g near one, the recurrent input to neuron i is then proportional to $\sum_j [\cos(\Phi - \phi_j)]_+$ which, for large numbers of cells with uniformly placed preferred spatial phases ϕ_i, is approximately independent of Φ, the spatial phase of the stimulus. When g is near zero, the network is at low gain and the response of neuron i is roughly proportional to its feedforward input, $[\cos(\Phi - \phi_j)]_+$, and is sensitive to spatial phase.

The response properties of simple and complex cells to drifting and counterphase gratings are duplicated by the model neuron, as shown in figure 1. For low gain (gain = 1, top panels of figures 1A and 1B), the neuron acts as a simple cell and its activity is modulated at the same frequency as the stimulus (ω for counterphase gratings and ν for drifting gratings). At high gain (gain = 20), the neuron responds like a complex cell, exhibiting frequency doubling in the response to a counterphase grating (bottom panel of Figure 1A) and an elevated DC response to a drifting grating (bottom panel, Figure 1B). Intermediate gain (gain = 5) produces intermediate behavior (middle panels).

The basis of this model is that the amplified mode is independent of spatial phase. If the amplified mode depends on spatial frequency or orientation, neurons at high gain can be selective for these attributes. To show that the model can retain selectivity for other

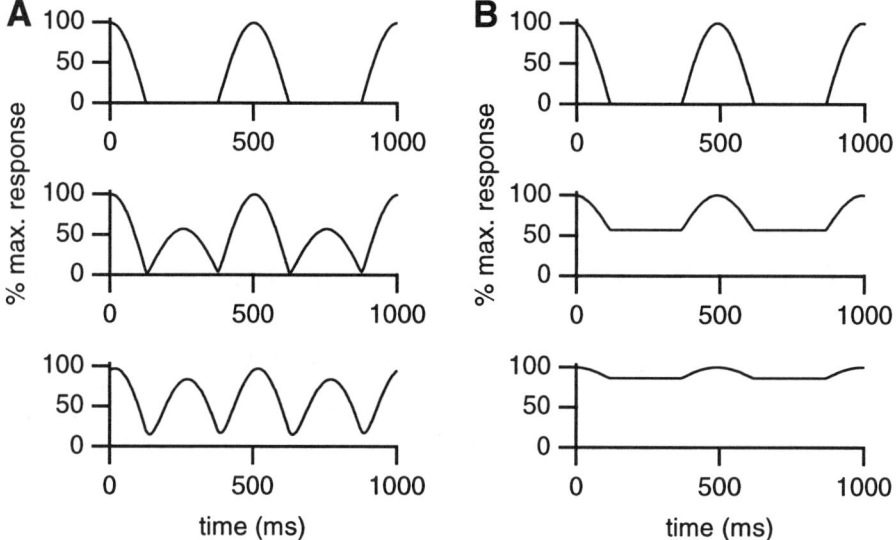

Figure 1: The effects of recurrent input on the responses of a neuron in the model network. The responses of one neuron to a 2 Hz counterphase grating (A) and to a 2 Hz drifting grating (B) are shown for different levels of network gain. From top to bottom in A and B, the gain of the network is one, five, and twenty.

stimulus characteristics while maintaining spatial phase insensitivity, we allowed the spatial frequency selectivity which each neuron receives from its feedforward input, k_i, to vary from neuron to neuron and also modified the recurrent weight matrix so that the strength of the connection between two neurons, i and j, depends on $k_i - k_j$. The dependence is modeled as a difference of Gaussians, so the recurrent weight matrix is now

$$W_{ij} = \frac{g}{(N-1)} \left[2\exp\left(-\frac{(k_i - k_j)^2}{2\sigma_c^2}\right) - \exp\left(-\frac{(k_i - k_j)^2}{2\sigma_s^2}\right) \right].$$

Thus neurons that receive feedforward input tuned for similar spatial frequencies excite each other and neurons that receive very differently tuned feedforward input inhibit each other. This produces complex cells that are tuned to a variety of spatial frequencies, but are still insensitive to spatial phase (see figure 2). The spatial frequency tuning curve width is primarily determined by $\sigma_c = 0.5$ cycle/deg and $\sigma_s = 1$ cycle/deg.

Cells within the same network do not have to exhibit the same level of gain. In previous figures, the gain of the network was determined by a parameter g that described the strength of all the connections between neurons. In figure 3, the recurrent input to cell i is determined by $W_{ij} = g_i/(N-1)$, where the values of g_i are chosen randomly within the allowed range. The gain of each neuron depends on the value of g_i for that neuron. As shown in figure 3, a range of complex and simple cell behaviors now coexist within the same network.

4 DISCUSSION

In the recurrent model we have presented, as in Hubel and Wiesel's feedforward model, the feedforward input to a complex cell arises from simple cells. Measurements by Alonso and

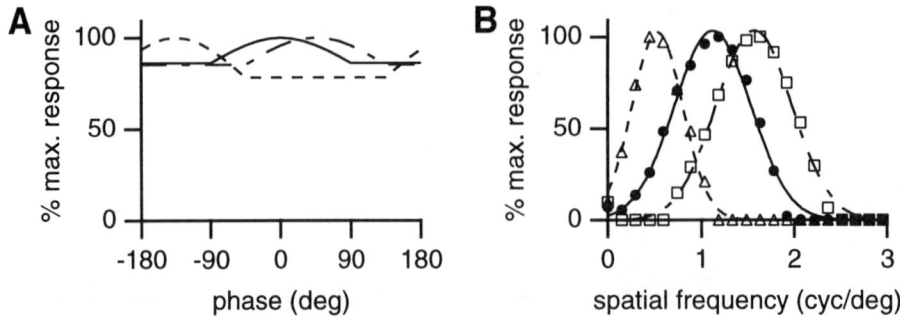

Figure 2: Neurons in a high-gain network can be selective for spatial frequency while remaining insensitive to spatial phase. Both spatial phase and spatial frequency tuning are included in the feedforward input. A) The spatial phase tuning curves of three representative neurons from a high-gain network. B) The spatial frequency tuning curves of the same three neurons as in A.

Martinez (1998) support this circuitry. However, direct excitatory input to complex cells arising from the LGN has also been reported (Hoffman and Stone, 1971; Singer et al., 1975; Ferster and Lindström, 1983). Supporting these measurements is evidence that certain stimuli can excite complex cells without strong excitation of simple cells (Hammond and Mackay, 1975, 1977; Movshon, 1975) and also that complex cells still respond when simple cells are silenced (Malpeli, 1983; Malpeli et al, 1986; Mignard and Malpeli, 1991). In accordance with this, the weak feedforward simple cell input in the recurrent model could probably be replaced by direct LGN input, as in the feedforward model of Mel et al. (1998).

The proposed model makes definite predictions about complex cell responses. If the phase-invariance of complex cell responses is due to recurrent interactions, manipulations that modify the balance between feedforward and recurrent drive should change the nature of the responses in a predictable manner. The model predicts that blocking local excitatory connections should turn complex cells into simple cells. Conversely, manipulations that increase cortical gain should make simple cells act more like complex cells. One way to increase cortical gain may be to block or partially block inhibition since this increases the influence of excitatory recurrent connections. Experiments along these lines have been performed, and blockade of inhibition does indeed cause simple cells to take on complex cell properties (Sillito, 1975; Shulz et al., 1993).

In a previous study, Hawken, Shapley, and Grosof (1996) noted that the temporal frequency tuning curves for complex cells are narrower for counterphase stimuli than for drifting stimuli. The recurrent model reproduces this result as long as the integration of synaptic inputs depends on temporal frequency. Such a dependence is provided, for example, by short-term synaptic depression (Chance et al., 1998). Hubel and Wiesel's feedforward model (1962) does not reproduce this effect, even with synaptic depression at the synapses.

We have presented a model of primary visual cortex in which complex cell response characteristics arise from recurrent amplification of simple cell responses. The complex cell responses in the high gain regime arise because recurrent connections selectively deamplify selectivity for spatial phase. Thus recurrent connections can act to generate invariant representation of input data. A similar mechanism could be used to produce responses that are independent of other stimulus attributes, such as size or orientation. Given the ubiquity of invariant representations in the visual pathway, this mechanism may have widespread use.

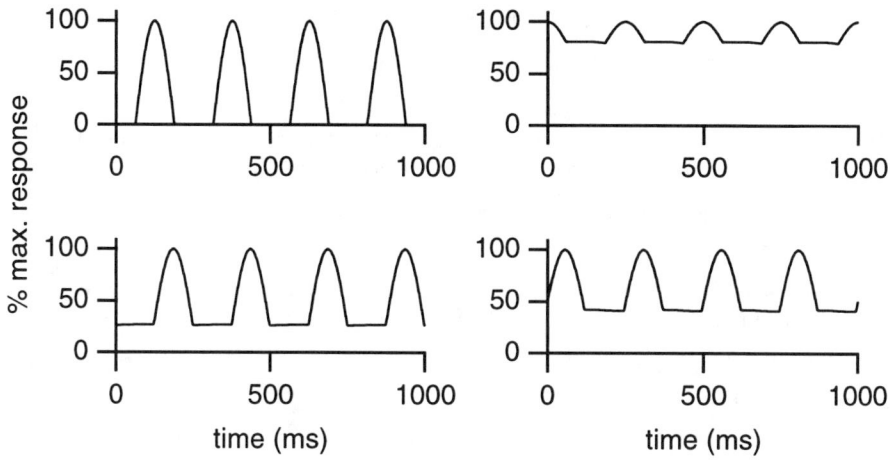

Figure 3: Responses to a 4 Hz drifting grating of four neurons from a large network consisting of a mixture of simple and complex cells. The two traces on the left represent simple cells and the two traces on the right represent complex cells.

Acknowledgements

Research supported by the Sloan Center for Theoretical Neurobiology at Brandeis University, the National Science Foundation (DMS-95-03261), the W.M. Keck Foundation, the National Eye Institute (EY-11116), and the Alfred P. Sloan Foundation.

References

Adelson, E. H. & Bergen, J. R. Spatiotemporal energy models for the perception of motion. *J. Opt. Soc. Am. A.* **2,** 284-299 (1985)

Alonso, J-M. & Martinez, L. M. Functional connectivity between simple cells and complex cells in cat striate cortex. *Nature Neuroscience* **1,** 395-403 (1998)

Ben-Yishai, R., Bar-Or, L. & Sompolinsky, H. Theory of orientation tuning in visual cortex. *Proc. Natl. Acad. Sci. USA* **92,** 3844-3848 (1995)

Chance F. S., Nelson S. B. & Abbott L. F. Complex cells as cortically amplified simple cells. *(submitted)*

Chung, S. & Ferster, D. Strength and orientation tuning of the thalamic input to simple cells revealed by electrically evoked cortical suppression. *Neuron* **20,** 1177-1189 (1998)

Douglas, R. J., Koch, C., Mahowald, M., Martin, K. A. C. & Suarez, H. H. Recurrent excitation in neocortical circuits. *Science* **269** 981-985 (1995)

Ferster, D., Chung, S. & Wheat, H. Orientation selectivity of thalamic input to simple cells of cat visual cortex. *Nature* **380,** 249-252 (1996)

Ferster, D. & Lindström, S. An intracellular analysis of geniculo-cortical connectivity in area 17 of the cat. *J. Physiol. (Lond)* **342,** 181-215 (1983)

Hammond, P. & MacKay, D. M. Differential responses of cat visual cortical cells to textured stimuli. *Exp. Brain Res.* **22,** 427-430 (1975)

Hammond, P. & MacKay, D. M. Differential responsiveness of simple and complex cells in cat striate cortex to visual texture. *Exp. Brain Res.* **30**, 275-296 (1977)

Hawken, M. J., Shapley, R. M. & Grosof, D. H. Temporal-frequency selectivity in monkey visual cortex. *Vis. Neurosci.* **13** 477-492 (1996)

Hoffman, K. P. & Stone, J. Conduction velocity of afferents of cat visual cortex: a correlation with cortical receptive field properties. *Brain Res.* **32**, 460-466 (1971)

Hubel, D. H. & Wiesel, T. N. Receptive fields, binocular interaction and functional architecture in the cat's visual cortex. *J. Physiol.* **160**, 106-154 (1962)

Malpeli, J. G. Activity of cells in area 17 of the cat in absence of input from layer A of lateral geniculate nucleus. *J. Neurophysiol.* **49**, 595-610 (1983)

Malpeli, J. G., Lee, C., Schwark, H. D. & Weyand, T. G. Cat area 17. I. Pattern of thalamic control of cortical layers. *J. Neurophysiol.* **56**, 1062-1073 (1986)

Mel, B. W., Ruderman, D. L. & Archie, K. A. Translation-invariant orientation tuning in visual complex cells could derive from intradendritic computations. *J. Neurosci.* **18** 4325-4334 (1998)

Mignard, M. & Malpeli, J. G. Paths of information flow through visual cortex. *Science* **251**, 1249-1251 (1991)

Movshon, J. A. The velocity tuning of single units in cat striate cortex. *J. Physiol.* **249**, 445-468 (1975)

Movshon, J., Thompson, I. & Tolhurst, D. Spatial summation in the receptive fields of simple cells in the cat's striate cortex. *J. Physiol. (Lond)* **283**, 53-77 (1978)

Movshon, J., Thompson, I. & Tolhurst, D. Receptive field organization of complex cells in cat's striate cortex. *J. Physiol. (Lond)* **283**, 79-99 (1978)

Shulz, D. E., Bringuier, B. & Frégnac, Y. A complex-like structure of simple visual cortical receptive fields is masked by GABA-A intracortical inhibition. *Soc. for Neurosci. Abs.* **19**, 628 (1993)

Sillito, A. M. The contribution of inhibitory mechanisms to the receptive field properties of neurones in the striate cortex of the cat. *J. Physiol. (Lond)* **250**, 305-329 (1975)

Singer, W., Tretter, F. & Cynader, M. Organization of cat striate cortex: a correlation of receptive-field properties with afferent and efferent connections. *J. Neurophysiol.* **38**, 1080-1098 (1975)

Somers, D. C., Nelson, S. B. & Sur, M. An emergent model of orientation selectivity in cat visual cortical simple cells. *J. Neurosci.* **15**, 5448-5465 (1995)

Sompolinsky, H. & Shapley, R. New perspectives on the mechanisms for orientation selectivity. *Current Opinion in Neurobiology* **7**, 514-522 (1997)

Toyama, K., Kimura, M. & Tanaka, K. Organization of cat visual cortex as investigated by cross-correlation technique. *J. Neurophysiol.* **46**, 202-214 (1981)

Treves, A. Mean-field analysis of neuronal spike dynamics. *Network* **4**, 259-284 (1993)

Neuronal Regulation Implements Efficient Synaptic Pruning

Gal Chechik and Isaac Meilijson
School of Mathematical Sciences
Tel Aviv University, Tel Aviv 69978, Israel
ggal@math.tau.ac.il   isaco@math.tau.ac.il

Eytan Ruppin
Schools of Medicine and Mathematical Sciences
Tel Aviv University, Tel Aviv 69978, Israel
ruppin@math.tau.ac.il

Abstract

Human and animal studies show that mammalian brain undergoes massive synaptic pruning during childhood, removing about half of the synapses until puberty. We have previously shown that maintaining network memory performance while synapses are deleted, requires that synapses are properly modified and pruned, removing the weaker synapses. We now show that neuronal regulation, a mechanism recently observed to maintain the average neuronal input field, results in weight-dependent synaptic modification. Under the correct range of the degradation dimension and synaptic upper bound, neuronal regulation removes the weaker synapses and judiciously modifies the remaining synapses. It implements near optimal synaptic modification, and maintains the memory performance of a network undergoing massive synaptic pruning. Thus, this paper shows that in addition to the known effects of Hebbian changes, neuronal regulation may play an important role in the self-organization of brain networks during development.

1 Introduction

This paper studies one of the fundamental puzzles in brain development: the massive synaptic pruning observed in mammals during childhood, removing more than half of the synapses until puberty (see [1] for review). This phenomenon is observed in various areas of the brain both in animal studies and human studies. How can the brain function after such massive synaptic elimination? what could be the computational advantage of such a seemingly wasteful developmental strategy? In previous work [2], we have shown that synaptic overgrowth followed by judicial pruning along development improves the performance of an associative memory network with limited synaptic resources, thus suggesting a new computational explanation for synaptic pruning in childhood. The optimal pruning strategy was found to require that synapses are deleted according to their efficacy, removing the weaker synapses first.

But is there a mechanism that can implement these theoretically-derived synaptic pruning strategies in a biologically plausible manner ? To answer this question, we focus here on studying the role of neuronal regulation (NR), a mechanism operating to maintain the homeostasis of the neuron's membrane potential. NR has been recently identified experimentally by [3], who showed that neurons both up-regulate and down-regulate the efficacy of their incoming excitatory synapses in a multiplicative manner, maintaining their membrane potential around a baseline level. Independently, [4] have studied NR theoretically, showing that it can efficiently maintain the memory performance of networks undergoing synaptic degradation. Both [3] and [4] have hypothesized that NR may lead to synaptic pruning during development.

In this paper we show that this hypothesis is both computationally feasible and biologically plausible by studying the modification of synaptic values resulting from the operation of NR. Our work thus gives a possible account for the way brain networks maintain their performance while undergoing massive synaptic pruning.

2 The Model

NR-driven synaptic modification (NRSM) results from two concomitant processes: **synaptic degradation** (which is the inevitable consequence of synaptic turnover [5]), and **neuronal regulation** (NR) operating to compensate for the degradation. We therefore model NRSM by a sequence of degradation-strengthening steps. At each time step, synaptic degradation stochastically reduces the synaptic strength W^t ($W^t > 0$) to W'^{t+1} by

$$W'^{t+1} = W^t - (W^t)^\alpha \eta^t; \quad \eta \sim N(\mu^\eta, \sigma^\eta) \quad (1)$$

where η is noise term with positive mean and the power α defines the *degradation dimension* parameter chosen in the range $[0, 1]$. Neuronal regulation is modeled by letting the post-synaptic neuron multiplicatively strengthen all its synapses by a common factor to restore its original input field

$$W^{t+1} = W'^{t+1} \frac{f_i^0}{f_i^t} . \quad (2)$$

where f_i^t is the input field of neuron i at time t. The excitatory synaptic efficacies are assumed to have a viability lower bound B^- below which a synapse degenerates and vanishes, and a soft upper bound B^+ beyond which a synapse is strongly degraded reflecting their maximal efficacy. To study of the above process in a network, a model incorporating a segregation between inhibitory and excitatory neurons (i.e. obeying Dale's law) is required. To generate this essential segregation, we modify the standard low-activity associative memory model proposed by [6] by adding a small positive term to the synaptic learning rule. In this model, M memories are stored in an excitatory N-neuron network forming attractors of the network dynamics. The synaptic efficacy W_{ij} between the jth (pre-synaptic) neuron and the ith (post-synaptic) neuron is

$$W_{ij} = \sum_{\mu=1}^{M} \left[(\xi_i^\mu - p)(\xi_j^\mu - p) + a \right], \, 1 \leq i \neq j \leq N \quad ; \quad W_{ii} = 0 \quad (3)$$

where $\{\xi^\mu\}_{\mu=1}^M$ are $\{0,1\}$ memory patterns with coding level p (fraction of firing neurons), and a is some positive constant [1]. The updating rule for the state X_i^t of the ith neuron at time t is

$$X_i^{t+1} = \theta(f_i^t), \quad f_i^t = \frac{1}{N}\sum_{j=1}^N g(W_{ij})X_j^t - \frac{\mathcal{I}}{N}\sum_{j=1}^N X_j^t - T, \quad \theta(f) = \frac{1+sign(f)}{2} \quad (4)$$

where T is the neuronal threshold, and $\mathcal{I}$ is the inhibition strength. g is a general modification function over the excitatory synapses, which is either derived explicitly (See Section 4), or determined implicitly by the operation of NRSM. If g is linear and $\mathcal{I} = Ma$ the model reduces to the original model described by [6]. The overlap m^μ (or similarity) between the network's activity pattern X and the memory ξ^μ serves to measure memory performance (retrieval acuity), and is defined as $m^\mu = \frac{1}{N}\sum_{j=1}^N (\xi_j^\mu - p)X_j$.

3 Neuronally Regulated Synaptic Modification

NRSM was studied by simulating the degradation-strengthening sequence in a network in which memory patterns were stored according to Eq.3. Figure 1a plots a typical distribution of synaptic values as traced along a sequence of degradation-strengthening steps (Eq. 1,2). As evident, the synaptic values diverge: some of the weights are strengthened and lie close to the upper synaptic bounds, while the other synapses degenerate and vanish. Using probabilistic considerations, it can be shown that the synaptic distribution converge to a meta-stable state where it remains for long waiting times. Figure 1b describes the metastable synaptic distribution as calculated for different α values.

Evolving distribution of synaptic efficacies

a. Simulation results   b. Numerical results

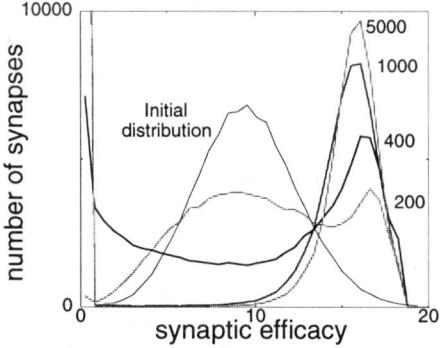
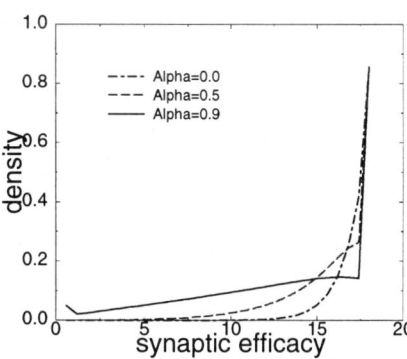

Figure 1: Distribution of synaptic strengths following a degradation-strengthening process. a) Synaptic distribution after $0, 200, 400, 1000$ and 5000 degradation-strengthening steps of a 400 neurons network with 1000 stored memory patterns. $\alpha=0.8$, $p = 0.1$, $B^- = 10^{-5}$, $B^+ = 18$ and $\eta \sim N(0.05, 0.05)$. Qualitatively similar results were obtained for a wide range of simulation parameters. b) The synaptic distribution of the remaining synapses at the meta-stable state was calculated as the main eigen vector of the transition probability matrix.

---

[1] As the weights are normally distributed with expectation $Ma > 0$ and standard deviation $O(\sqrt{M})$, the probability of a negative synapse vanishes as M goes to infinity (and is negligible already for several dozens of memories in the parameters' range used here).

a. NRSM functions at the Metastable state

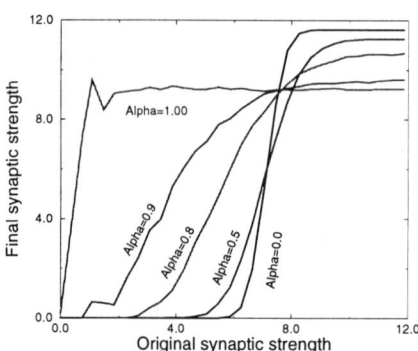

b. NRSM and random deletion

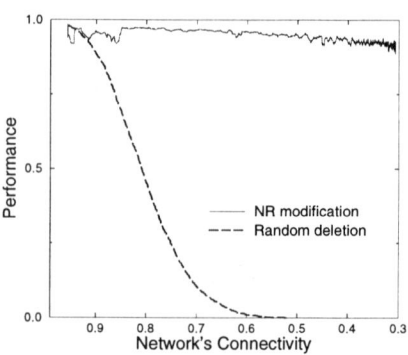

Figure 2: a) NRSM functions at the metastable state for different α values. Results were obtained in a 400-neurons network after performing 5000 degradation-strengthening steps. Parameter values are as in Figure 1, except $B^+ = 12$. b) Performance of NR modification and random deletion. The retrieval acuity of 200 memories stored in a network of 800 neurons is portrayed as a function of network connectivity, as the network undergoes continuous pruning until NR reaches the metastable state. $\alpha = 0$, $B^+ = 7.5$, $p = 0.1$, $m_0 = 0.80$, $a = 0.01$, $T = 0.35$, $B^- = 10^{-5}$ and $\eta \sim N(0.01, 0.01)$.

To further investigate which synapses are strengthened and which are pruned, we study the resulting synaptic modification function. Figure 2a plots the value of synaptic efficacy at the metastable state as a function of the initial synaptic efficacy, for different values of the degradation dimension α. As observed, a sigmoidal dependency is obtained, where the slope of the sigmoid strongly depends on the degradation dimension. In the two limit cases, additive degradation ($\alpha = 0$) results in a step function at the metastable state, while multiplicative degradation ($\alpha = 1$) results in random diffusion of the synaptic weights toward a memoryless mean value. Different values of α and B^+ result in different levels of synaptic pruning: When the synaptic upper bound B^+ is high, the surviving synapses assume high values, leading to massive pruning to maintain the neuronal input field, which in turn reduces network's performance. Low B^+ values lead to high connectivity, but limit synapses to a small set of possible values, again reducing memory performance. Our simulations show that optimal memory retrieval is obtained for B^+ values that lead to deletion levels of $40\% - 60\%$, in which NR indeed maintains the network performance. Figure 2b traces the average retrieval acuity of a network throughout the operation of NR, versus a network subject to random deletion at the same pruning levels. While the retrieval of a randomly pruned network collapses already at low deletion levels of about 20%, a network undergoing NR performs well even in high deletion levels.

4 Optimal Modification In Excitatory-Inhibitory Networks

To obtain a a comparative yardstick to evaluate the efficiency of NR as a selective pruning mechanism, we derive optimal modification functions maximizing memory performance in our excitatory-inhibitory model and compare them to the NRSM functions.

We study general synaptic modification functions, which prune some of the synapses and possibly modify the rest, while satisfying global constraints on synapses such as the number or total strength of the synapses. These constraints reflect the observation that synaptic activity is strongly correlated with energy consumption in the brain [7], and synaptic resources may hence be inherently limited in the adult brain.

We evaluate the impact of these functions on the network's retrieval performance, by deriving their effect on the signal to noise ratio (S/N) of the neuron's input field (Eqs. 3,4), known to be the primary determinant of retrieval capacity ([8]). This analysis, conducted in a similar manner to [2] yields

$$\frac{S}{N} = \frac{E(f_i|\xi_i = 1) - E(f_i|\xi_i = 0)}{\sqrt{V(f_i|\xi_i)}} = \sqrt{\frac{N}{M}} \frac{m^\mu}{\sqrt{p}} \frac{E[z\hat{g}(z)]}{\sqrt{E[\hat{g}^2(z)] - pE^2[\hat{g}(z)]}} \quad (5)$$

where $z \sim N(0,1)$ and g is the modification function of Eq. 4 but is now explicitly applied to the synapses. To derive optimal synaptic modification functions with limited synaptic resources, we consider g functions that zero all synapses except those in some set A, and keep the integral

$$\int_A g^k(z)\phi(z)dz \quad ; \quad k = 0, 1, \ldots \quad ; \quad g(z) = 0 \,\forall z \notin A \quad ; \quad \phi(z) = \frac{e^{z^2/2}}{\sqrt{2\pi}} \quad (6)$$

limited. We then maximize the S/N under this constraint using the Lagrange method. Our results show that *without any synaptic constraints* the optimal function is the identity function, that is, the original Hebbian rule is optimal. When the *number of synapses* is restricted ($k = 0$), the optimal modification function is a linear function for all the remaining synapses

$$g(W) = aW - \mu a + b \quad \text{where} \quad \begin{cases} a = \sqrt{\frac{1}{\int_A z^2 \phi(z)dz}} \\ b = \sigma a \frac{\int_A z\phi(z)dz}{(1 - \int_A \phi(z)dz)} \end{cases} \quad \begin{cases} \mu = E(W) \\ \sigma^2 = V(W) \end{cases} \quad (7)$$

for any deletion set A. To find the synapses that should be deleted, we have numerically searched for a deletion set maximizing S/N while limiting $g(W)$ to positive values (as required by the segregation between excitatory and inhibitory neurons). The results show, that **weak synapses pruning**, a modification strategy that removes the weakest synapses and modifies the rest according to Eq. 7, is optimal at deletion levels above 50%. For lower deletion levels, the above g function fails to satisfy the positivity constraint for any set A. When the positivity constraint is ignored, S/N is maximized if the weights closest to the mean are deleted and the remaining synapses are modified according to Eq 7. We name this strategy **mean synapses pruning**. Figure 3 plots the memory capacity under weak-synapses pruning (compared with random deletion and mean-synaptic pruning) showing that pruning the weak synapses performs at least near optimally for lower deletion levels as well. Even more interesting, under the correct parameter values weak-synapses pruning results in a modification function that has a similar form to the NR-driven modification function studied in the previous Section: both strategies remove the weakest synapses and linearly modify the remaining synapses in a similar manner. In the case of *limited overall synaptic strength* ($k > 0$ in Eq. 6), the optimal g satisfies

$$z - 2\gamma_1 [g(z) - E(g(z))] - \gamma_2 k g(z)^{k-1} = 0 \quad , \quad (8)$$

and thus for $k = 1$ and $k = 2$ the optimal modification function is again linear. For $k > 2$ a sublinear modification function is optimal, where g is a function of $z^{1/(k-1)}$,

Capacity of different synaptic modification functions g(w)
a. Analysis results   b. Simulations results

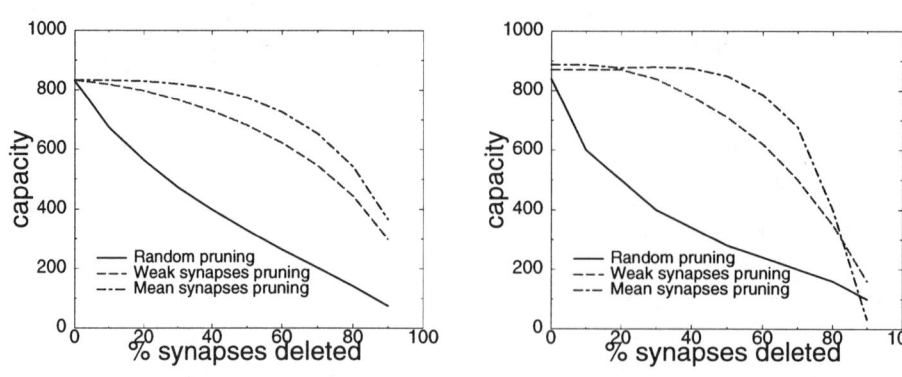

Figure 3: Comparison between performance of different modification strategies as a function of the deletion level (percentage of synapses pruned). Capacity is measured as the number of patterns that can be stored in the network ($N = 2000$) and be recalled almost correctly ($m > 0.95$) from a degraded pattern ($m_0 = 0.80$).

and is thus unbounded for all k. Therefore, in our model, bounds on the synaptic efficacies are not dictated by the optimization process. Their computational advantage arises from their effect on preserving memory capacity in face of ongoing synaptic pruning.

5 Discussion

By studying *NR-driven synaptic modification* in the framework of associative memory networks, we show that NR prunes the weaker synapses and modifies the remaining synapses in a sigmoidal manner. The critical variables that govern the pruning process are the *degradation dimension* and the *upper synaptic bound*. Our results show that **in the correct range of these parameters, NR implements a near optimal strategy, maximizing memory capacity in the sparse connectivity levels observed in the brain**.

A fundamental requirement of central nervous system development is that the system should continuously function, while undergoing major structural and functional developmental changes. It has been proposed that a major functional role of neuronal down-regulation during early infancy is to maintain neuronal activity at its baseline levels while facing continuous increase in the number and efficacy of synapses [3]. Focusing on up-regulation, our work shows that NR has another important interesting effect: that of modifying and pruning synapses in a continuously optimal manner. Neuronally regulated synaptic modifications may play the same role also in the peripheral nervous system: It was recently shown that in the neuro-muscular junction the muscle regulates its incoming synapses in a way similar to NR [9]. Our analysis suggests this process may be the underlying cause for the finding that synapses in the neuro-muscular junction are either strengthened or pruned according to their initial efficacy [10].

The significance of our work goes beyond understanding synaptic organization and remodeling in the associative memory models studied in this paper. Our analysis bears relevance to two other fundamental paradigms: Hetero Associative memory and self organizing maps, sharing the same basic synaptic structure of storing associations between sets of patterns via a Hebbian learning rule.

Combining the investigation of a biologically identified mechanism with the analytic study of performance optimization in neural network models, this paper shows the biologically plausible and beneficial role of weight dependent synaptic pruning. Thus, in addition to the known effects of Hebbian learning, neuronal regulation may play an important role in the self-organization of brain networks during development.

References

[1] G.M. Innocenti. Exuberant development of connections and its possible permissive role in cortical evolution. *Trends Neurosci*, 18:397–402, 1995.

[2] G. Chechik, I. Meilijson, and E. Ruppin. Synaptic pruning during development: A computational account. *Neural Computation. In press.*, 1998.

[3] G.G. Turrigano, K. Leslie, N. Desai, and S.B. Nelson. Activity dependent scaling of quantal amplitude in neocoritcal pyramidal neurons. *Nature*, 391(6670):892–896, 1998.

[4] D. Horn, N. Levy, and E. Ruppin. Synaptic maintenance via neuronal regulation. *Neural Computation*, 10(1):1–18, 1998.

[5] J.R. Wolff, R. Laskawi, W.B. Spatz, and M. Missler. Structural dynamics of synapses and synaptic components. *Behavioral Brain Research*, 66(1-2):13–20, 1995.

[6] M.V. Tsodyks and M. Feigel'man. Enhanced storage capacity in neural networks with low activity level. *Europhys. Lett.*, 6:101–105, 1988.

[7] Per E. Roland. *Brain Activation*. Willey-Liss, 1993.

[8] I. Meilijson and E. Ruppin. Optimal firing in sparsely-connected low-activity attractor networks. *Biological cybernetics*, 74:479–485, 1996.

[9] G.W. Davis and C.S. Goodman. Synapse-specific control of synaptic efficacy at the terminals of a single neuron. *Nature*, 392(6671):82–86, 1998.

[10] H. Colman, J. Nabekura, and J. W. Lichtman. Alterations in synaptic strength preceding axon withdrawal. *Science*, 275(5298):356–361, 1997.

Divisive Normalization, Line Attractor Networks and Ideal Observers

Sophie Deneve[1] Alexandre Pouget[1], and P.E. Latham[2]
[1]Georgetown Institute for Computational and Cognitive Sciences,
Georgetown University, Washington, DC 20007-2197
[2]Dpt of Neurobiology, UCLA, Los Angeles, CA 90095-1763, U.S.A.

Abstract

Gain control by divisive inhibition, a.k.a. divisive normalization, has been proposed to be a general mechanism throughout the visual cortex. We explore in this study the statistical properties of this normalization in the presence of noise. Using simulations, we show that divisive normalization is a close approximation to a maximum likelihood estimator, which, in the context of population coding, is the same as an ideal observer. We also demonstrate analytically that this is a general property of a large class of nonlinear recurrent networks with line attractors. Our work suggests that divisive normalization plays a critical role in noise filtering, and that every cortical layer may be an ideal observer of the activity in the preceding layer.

Information processing in the cortex is often formalized as a sequence of a linear stages followed by a nonlinearity. In the visual cortex, the nonlinearity is best described by squaring combined with a divisive pooling of local activities. The divisive part of the nonlinearity has been extensively studied by Heeger and colleagues [1], and several authors have explored the role of this normalization in the computation of high order visual features such as orientation of edges or first and second order motion[4]. We show in this paper that divisive normalization can also play a role in noise filtering. More specifically, we demonstrate through simulations that networks implementing this normalization come close to performing maximum likelihood estimation. We then demonstrate analytically that the ability to perform maximum likelihood estimation, and thus efficiently extract information from a population of noisy neurons, is a property exhibited by a large class of networks.

Maximum likelihood estimation is a framework commonly used in the theory of ideal observers. A recent example comes from the work of Itti et al., 1998, who have shown that it is possible to account for the behavior of human subjects in simple discrimination tasks. Their model comprised two *distinct* stages: 1) a network which models the noisy response of neurons with tuning curves to orientation and spatial frequency combined with divisive normalization, and 2) an ideal observer (a maximum likelihood estimator) to read out the population activity of the network.

Our work suggests that there is no need to distinguish between these two stages, since, as we will show, divisive normalization comes close to providing a maximum likelihood estimation. More generally, we propose that there may not be any part of the cortex that acts as an ideal observer for patterns of activity in sensory areas but, instead, that each cortical layer acts as an ideal observer of the activity in the preceding layer.

1 The network

Our network is a simplified model of a cortical hypercolumn for spatial frequency and orientation. It consists of a two dimensional array of units in which each unit is indexed by its preferred orientation, θ_i, and spatial frequency, λ_j.

1.1 LGN model

Units in the cortical layer are assumed to receive direct inputs from the lateral geniculate nucleus (LGN). Here we do not model explicitly the LGN, but focus instead on the pooled LGN input onto each cortical unit. The input to each unit is denoted a_{ij}. We distinguish between the *mean* pooled LGN input, $f_{ij}(\theta, \lambda)$, as a function of orientation, θ, and spatial frequency, λ, and the *noise* distribution around this mean, $P(a_{ij}|\theta, \lambda)$.

In response to a stimulus of orientation, θ, spatial frequency, λ, and contrast, C, the mean LGN input onto unit ij is a circular Gaussian with a small amount of spontaneous activity, ν:

$$f_{ij}(\theta, \lambda) = KC \exp\left(\frac{\cos(\lambda - \lambda_j) - 1}{\sigma_\lambda^2} + \frac{\cos(\theta - \theta_i) - 1}{\sigma_\theta^2}\right) + \nu, \qquad (1)$$

where K is a constant. Note that spatial frequency is treated as a periodic variable; this was done for convenience only and should have negligible effects on our results as long as we keep λ far from $2\pi n$, n an integer.

On any given trial the LGN input to cortical unit ij, a_{ij}, is sampled from a Gaussian noise distribution with variance σ_{ij}^2:

$$p(a_{ij}|\theta, \lambda) = \frac{1}{\sqrt{2\pi\sigma_{ij}^2}} \exp\left(-\frac{[a_{ij} - f_{ij}(\theta, \lambda)]^2}{2\sigma_{ij}^2}\right). \qquad (2)$$

In our simulations, the variance of the noise was either kept fixed ($\sigma_{ij}^2 = \sigma^2$) or set to the mean activity ($\sigma_{ij}^2 = f_{ij}(\theta, \lambda)$). The latter is more consistent with the noise that has been measured experimentally in the cortex. We show in figure 1-A an example of a noisy LGN pattern of activity.

1.2 Cortical Model: Divisive Normalization

Activities in the cortical layer are updated over time according to:

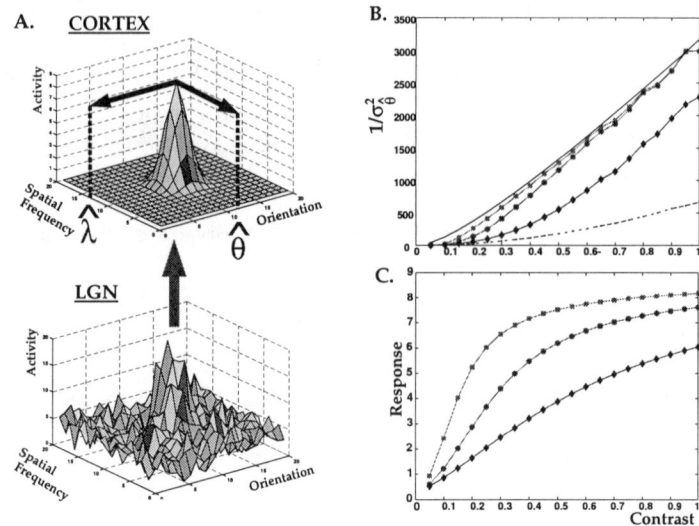

Figure 1: A- LGN input (bottom) and stable hill in the cortical network after relaxation (top). The position of the stable hill can be used to estimate orientation ($\hat{\theta}$) and spatial frequency ($\hat{\lambda}$). B- Inverse of the variance of the network estimate for orientation using Gaussian noise with variance equal to the mean as a function of contrast and number of iterations (0, dashed; 1, diamond; 2, circle; and 3, square). The continuous curve corresponds to the theoretical upper bound on the inverse of the variance (i.e. an ideal observer). C- Gain curve for contrast for the cortical units after 1, 2 and 3 iterations.

$$u_{ij}(t+1) = \sum_{kl} w_{ij,kl} o_{kl}(t), \quad o_{ij}(t+1) = \frac{u_{ij}(t+1)^2}{S + \mu \sum_{kl} u_{kl}(t+1)^2}, \quad (3)$$

where $\{w_{ij,kl}\}$ are the *filtering* weights, $o_{ij}(t)$ is the activity of unit ij at time t, S is a constant, and μ is what we call the *divisive inhibition* weight. The filtering weights implement a two dimensional Gaussian filter:

$$w_{ij,kl} = w_{i-k,j-l} = K_w \exp\left(\frac{\cos[2\pi(i-k)/P] - 1}{\sigma_{w\theta}^2} + \frac{\cos[2\pi(j-l)/P] - 1}{\sigma_{w\lambda}^2}\right) \quad (4)$$

where K_w is a constant, $\sigma_{w\theta}$ and $\sigma_{w\lambda}$ control the width of the filtering weights, and there are P^2 units.

On each iteration the activity is filtered by the weights, squared, and then normalized by the total local activity. Divisive normalization *per se* only involves the squaring and division by local activity. We have added the filtering weights to obtain a local pooling of activity between cells with similar preferred orientations and spatial frequencies. This pooling can easily be implemented with cortical lateral connections and it is reasonable to think that such a pooling takes place in the cortex.

2 Simulation Results

Our simulations consist of iterating equation 3 with initial conditions determined by the presentation orientation and spatial frequency. The initial conditions are chosen as follows: For a given presentation angle, θ_0, and spatial frequency, λ_0, determine the mean cortical activity, $f_{ij}(\theta_0, \lambda_0)$, via equation 1. Then generate the actual cortical activity, $\{a_{ij}\}$, by sampling from the distribution given in equation 2. This serves as our set of initial conditions: $o_{ij}(t=0) = a_{ij}$.

Iterating equation 3 with the above initial conditions, we found that for very low contrast the activity of all cortical units decayed to zero. Above some contrast threshold, however, the activities converged to a smooth stable hill (see figure 1-A for an example with parameters $\sigma_{w\theta} = \sigma_{w\lambda} = \sigma_\theta = \sigma_\lambda = 1/\sqrt{8}$, $K = 74$, $C = 1$, $\mu = 0.01$). The width of the hill is controlled by the width of the filtering weights. Its peak, on the other hand, depends on the orientation and spatial frequency of the LGN input, θ_0 and λ_0. The peak can thus be used to estimate these quantities (see figure 1-A). To compute the position of the final hill, we used a population vector estimator [3] although any unbiased estimator would work as well. In all cases we looked at, the network produced an unbiased estimate of θ_0 and λ_0.

In our simulations we adjusted $\sigma_{w\theta}$ and $\sigma_{w\lambda}$ so that the stable hill had the same profile as the mean LGN input (equation 1). As a result, the tuning curves of the cortical units match the tuning curves specified by the pooled LGN input. For this case, we found that the estimate obtained from the network has a variance close to the theoretical minimum, known as the Cramér-Rao bound [3]. For Gaussian noise of fixed variance, the variance of the estimate was 16.6% above this bound, compared to 3833% for the population vector applied directly to the LGN input. In a 1D network (orientation alone), these numbers go to 12.9% for the network versus 613% for population vector. For Gaussian noise with variance proportional to the mean, the network was 8.8% above the bound, compared to 722% for the population vector applied directly to the input. These numbers are respectively 9% and 108% for the 1-D network. The network is therefore a close approximation to a maximum likelihood estimator, i.e., it is close to being an ideal observer of the LGN activity with respect to orientation and spatial frequency.

As long as the contrast, C, was superthreshold, large variations in contrast did not affect our results (figure 1-B). However, the tuning of the network units to contrast after reaching the stable state was found to follow a step function whereas, for real neurons, the curves are better described by a sigmoid [2]. Improved agreement with experiment was achieved by taking only 2-3 iterations, at which point the performance of the network is close to optimal (figure 1-B) and the tuning curves to contrast are more realistic and closer to sigmoids (figure 1-C). Therefore, reaching a stable state is not required for optimal performance, and in fact leads to contrast tuning curves that are inconsistent with experiment.

3 Mathematical Analysis

We first prove that line attractor networks with sufficiently small noise are close approximations to a maximum likelihood estimator. We then show how this result applies to our simulations with divisive normalization.

3.1 General Case: Line Attractor Networks

Let $\mathbf{o}_n$ be the activity vector (denoted by bold type) at discrete time, n, for a set of P interconnected units. We consider a one dimensional network, i.e., only one feature is encoded; generalization to multidimensional networks is straightforward. A generic mapping for this network may be written

$$\mathbf{o}_{n+1} = \mathbf{H}(\mathbf{o}_n) \tag{5}$$

where $\mathbf{H}$ is a nonlinear function. We assume that this mapping admits a line attractor, which we denote $\mathbf{G}(\theta)$, for which $\mathbf{G}(\theta) = \mathbf{H}(\mathbf{G}(\theta))$ where θ is a continuous variable.[1] Let the initial state of the network be a function of the presentation parameter, θ_0, plus noise,

$$\mathbf{o}_0 = \mathbf{F}(\theta_0) + \mathbf{N} \tag{6}$$

where $\mathbf{F}(\theta_0)$ is the function used to generate the data (in our simulations this would correspond to the mean LGN input, equation 1). Iterating the mapping, equation 5, leads eventually to a point on the line attractor. Consequently, as $n \to \infty$, $\mathbf{o}_n \to \mathbf{G}(\hat{\theta})$. The parameter $\hat{\theta}$ provides an estimate of θ_0.

To determine how well the network does we need to find $\delta\theta \equiv \hat{\theta} - \theta_0$ as a function of the noise, $\mathbf{N}$, then average over the noise to compute the mean and variance of $\delta\theta$. Because the mapping, equation 5, is nonlinear, this cannot be done exactly. For small noise, however, we can take a perturbative approach and expand around a point on the attractor. For line attractors there is no general method for choosing which point on the attractor to expand around. Our approach will be to expand around an arbitrary point, $\mathbf{G}(\theta)$, and choose θ by requiring that the quadratic terms be finite. Keeping terms up to quadratic order, equation 6 may be written

$$\mathbf{o}_n = \mathbf{G}(\theta) + \delta\mathbf{o}_n. \tag{7}$$

$$\delta\mathbf{o}_n = \mathbf{J}^n \cdot \delta\mathbf{o}_0 + \frac{1}{2}\sum_{m=0}^{n-1}(\mathbf{J}^m \cdot \delta\mathbf{o}_0) \cdot \mathbf{H}'' \cdot (\mathbf{J}^m \cdot \delta\mathbf{o}_0), \tag{8}$$

where $\mathbf{J}(\theta) \equiv [\partial_{\mathbf{G}(\theta)}\mathbf{H}(\mathbf{G}(\theta))]^T$ is the Jacobian (the subscript T means transpose), $\mathbf{H}''$ is the Hessian of $\mathbf{H}$ evaluated at $\mathbf{G}(\theta)$ and a "$\cdot$" represents the standard dot product.

Because the mapping, equation 5, admits a line attractor, $\mathbf{J}$ has one eigenvalue equal to 1 and all others less than 1. Denote the eigenvector with eigenvalue 1 as $\mathbf{v}$ and its adjoint $\mathbf{v}^\dagger$: $\mathbf{J} \cdot \mathbf{v} = \mathbf{v}$ and $\mathbf{J}^T \cdot \mathbf{v}^\dagger = \mathbf{v}^\dagger$. It is not hard to show that $\mathbf{v} = \partial_\theta \mathbf{G}(\theta)$, up to a multiplicative constant. Since $\mathbf{J}$ has an eigenvalue equal to 1, to avoid the quadratic term in Eq. 8 approaching infinity as $n \to \infty$ we require that

$$\lim_{n \to \infty} \mathbf{J}^n \cdot \delta\mathbf{o}_0 = 0. \tag{9}$$

---

[1] The line attractor is, in fact, an idealization; for P units the attractors associated with equation 5 consists of P isolated points. However, for P large, the attractors are spaced closely enough that they may be considered a line.

This equations has an important consequence: it implies that, to linear order, $\lim_{n \to \infty} \delta \mathbf{o}_n = 0$ (see equation 8), which in turn implies that $\mathbf{o}_\infty = \mathbf{G}(\theta)$ which, finally, implies that $\theta = \hat{\theta}$. Consequently we can find the network estimator of θ_0, $\hat{\theta}$, by computing θ. We now turn to that task.

It is straightforward to show that $\mathbf{J}^\infty = \mathbf{v}\mathbf{v}^\dagger$. Combining this expression for $\mathbf{J}$ with equation 9, using equation 7 to express $\delta \mathbf{o}_0$ in terms of $\mathbf{o}_0$ and $\mathbf{G}(\theta)$, and, finally using equation 6 to express $\mathbf{o}_0$ in terms of the initial mean activity, $\mathbf{F}(\theta_0)$, and the noise, $\mathbf{N}$, we find that

$$\mathbf{v}^\dagger(\theta) \cdot [\mathbf{F}(\theta_0) - \mathbf{G}(\theta) + \mathbf{N}] = 0. \qquad (10)$$

Using $\theta_0 = \theta - \delta\theta$ and expanding $\mathbf{F}(\theta_0)$ to first order in $\delta\theta$ then yields

$$\delta\theta = \frac{\mathbf{v}^\dagger(\theta) \cdot [\mathbf{N} + \mathbf{F}(\theta) - \mathbf{G}(\theta)]}{\mathbf{v}^\dagger(\theta) \cdot \mathbf{F}'(\theta)}. \qquad (11)$$

As long as $\mathbf{v}^\dagger$ is orthogonal to $\mathbf{F}(\theta) - \mathbf{G}(\theta)$, $\langle \delta\theta \rangle = 0$ and the estimator is unbiased. This must be checked on a case by case basis, but for the circularly symmetric networks we considered orthogonality is satisfied.

We can now calculate the variance of the network estimate, $\langle \delta\theta \rangle^2$. Assuming $\mathbf{v}^\dagger \cdot [\mathbf{F}(\theta) - \mathbf{G}(\theta)] = 0$, equation 11 implies that

$$\langle \delta\theta \rangle^2 = \frac{\mathbf{v}^\dagger \cdot \mathbf{R} \cdot \mathbf{v}^\dagger}{[\mathbf{v}^\dagger \cdot \mathbf{F}']^2}, \qquad (12)$$

where a prime denotes a derivative with respect to θ and $\mathbf{R}$ is the covariance matrix of the noise, $\mathbf{R} = \langle \mathbf{N}\mathbf{N} \rangle$. The network is equivalent to maximum likelihood when this variance is equal to the Cramér-Rao bound [3], $\langle \delta\theta \rangle^2_{CR}$. If the noise, $\mathbf{N}$, is Gaussian with a covariance matrix independent of θ, this bound is equal to:

$$\langle \delta\theta \rangle^2_{CR} = \frac{1}{\mathbf{F}' \cdot \mathbf{R}^{-1} \cdot \mathbf{F}'}. \qquad (13)$$

For independent Gaussian noise of fixed variance, σ^2, and zero covariance, the variance of the network estimate, equation 12, becomes $\sigma^2/(|\mathbf{F}'|^2 \cos^2 \mu)$ where μ is the angle between $\mathbf{v}^\dagger$ and $\mathbf{F}'$. The Cramér-Rao bound, on the other hand, is equal to $\sigma^2/|\mathbf{F}'|^2$. These expressions differ only by $\cos^2 \mu$, which is 1 if $\mathbf{F} \propto \mathbf{v}^\dagger$. In addition, it is close to 1 for networks that have identical input and output tuning curves, $\mathbf{F}(\theta) = \mathbf{G}(\theta)$, *and* the Jacobian, $\mathbf{J}$, is nearly symmetric, so that $\mathbf{v} \approx \mathbf{v}^\dagger$ (recall that $\mathbf{v} = \mathbf{G}'$). If these last two conditions are satisfied, the network comes close to being a maximum likelihood estimator.

3.2 Application to Divisive Normalization

Divisive normalization is a particular example of the general case considered above. For simplicity, in our simulations we chose the input and output tuning curves to be equal ($\mathbf{F} = \mathbf{G}$ in the above notation), which lead to a value of 0.87 for $\cos^2 \mu$ (evaluated numerically). This predicted a variance 15% above the Cramér-Rao bound for independent Gaussian noise with fixed variance, consistent with the 16% we obtained in our simulations. The network also handles fairly well other noise distributions, such as Gaussian noise with variance proportional to the mean, as illustrated by our simulations.

4 Conclusions

We have recently shown that a subclass of line attractor networks can be used as maximum likelihood estimators[3]. This paper extend this conclusion to a much wider class of networks, namely, any network that admits a line (or, by straightforward extension of the above analysis, a higher dimensional) attractor. This is true in particular for networks using divisive normalization, a normalization which is thought to match quite closely the nonlinearity found in the primary visual cortex and MT.

Although our analysis relies on the existence of an attractor, this is not a requirement for obtaining near optimal noise filtering. As we have seen, 2-3 iterations are enough to achieve asymptotic performance (except at contrasts barely above threshold). What matters most is that our network implement a sequence of low pass filtering to filter out the noise, followed by a square nonlinearity to compensate for the widening of the tuning curve due to the low pass filter, and a normalization to weaken contrast dependence. It is likely that this process would still clean up noise efficiently in the first 2-3 iterations even if activity decayed to zero eventually, that is to say, even if the hills of activity were not stable states. This would allow us to apply our approach to other types of networks, including those lacking circular symmetry and networks with continuously clamped inputs.

To conclude, we propose that each cortical layer may read out the activity in the preceding layer in an optimal way thanks to the nonlinear pooling properties of divisive normalization, and, as a result, may behave like an ideal observer. It is therefore possible that the ability to read out neuronal codes in the sensory cortices in an optimal way may not be confined to a few areas like the parietal or frontal cortex, but may instead be a general property of every cortical layer.

References

[1] D. Heeger. Normalization of cell responses in cat striate cortex. *Visual Neuroscience*, 9:181–197, 1992.

[2] L. Itti, C. Koch, and J. Braun. A quantitative model for human spatial vision threshold on the basis of non-linear interactions among spatial filters. In R. Lippman, J. Moody, and D. Touretzky, editors, *Advances in Neural Information Processing Systems*, volume 11. Morgan-Kaufmann, San Mateo, 1998.

[3] A. Pouget, K. Zhang, S. Deneve, and P. Latham. Statistically efficient estimation using population coding. *Neural Computation*, 10:373–401, 1998.

[4] E. Simoncelli and D. Heeger. A model of neuronal responses in visual area MT. *Vision Research*, 38(5):743–761, 1998.

Synergy and redundancy among brain cells of behaving monkeys

Itay Gat *
Institute of Computer Science and
Center for Neural Computation
The Hebrew University, Jerusalem 91904, Israel

Naftali Tishby [†]
NEC Research Institute
4 Independence Way
Princeton NJ 08540

Abstract

Determining the relationship between the activity of a single nerve cell to that of an entire population is a fundamental question that bears on the basic neural computation paradigms. In this paper we apply an information theoretic approach to quantify the level of cooperative activity among cells in a behavioral context. It is possible to discriminate between synergetic activity of the cells vs. redundant activity, depending on the difference between the information they provide when measured jointly and the information they provide independently. We define a synergy value that is positive in the first case and negative in the second and show that the synergy value can be measured by detecting the behavioral mode of the animal from simultaneously recorded activity of the cells. We observe that among cortical cells positive synergy can be found, while cells from the basal ganglia, active during the same task, do not exhibit similar synergetic activity.

{itay,tishby}@cs.huji.ac.il
Permanent address: Institute of Computer Science and Center for Neural Computation, The Hebrew University, Jerusalem 91904, Israel.

1 Introduction

Measuring ways by which several neurons in the brain participate in a specific computational task can shed light on fundamental neural information processing mechanisms. While it is unlikely that complete information from any macroscopic neural tissue will ever be available, some interesting insight can be obtained from simultaneously recorded cells in the cortex of behaving animals. The question we address in this study is the level of synergy, or the level of cooperation, among brain cells, as determined by the information they provide about the observed behavior of the animal.

1.1 The experimental data

We analyze simultaneously recorded units from behaving monkeys during a delayed response behavioral experiment. The data was collected at the high brain function laboratory of the Haddassah Medical School of the Hebrew university[1, 2]. In this task the monkey had to remember the location of a visual stimulus and respond by touching that location after a delay of 1-32 sec. Correct responses were rewarded by a drop of juice. In one set of recordings six micro-electrodes were inserted simultaneously to the frontal or prefrontal cortex[1, 3]. In another set of experiments the same behavioral paradigm was used and recording were taken from the striatum - which is the first station in basal ganglia (a sub-cortical ganglia)[2]. The cells recorded in the striatum were the tonically active neurons[2], which are known to be the cholinergic inter-neurons of the striatum. These cells are known to respond to reward.

The monkeys were trained to perform the task in two alternating modes, "Go" and "No-Go"[1]. Both sets of behavioral modes can be detected from the recorded spike trains using several statistical modeling techniques that include Hidden Markov Models (HMM) and Post Stimulus Histograms (PSTH). The details of these detection methods are reported elsewhere[4, 5]. For this paper it is important to know that we can significantly detect the correct behavior, for example in the "Go" vs. the "No-Go" correct detection is achieved about 90% of the time, where the random is 50% and the monkey's average performance is 95% correct on this task.

2 Theoretical background

Our measure of synergy level among cells is information theoretic and was recently proposed by Brenner et. al.[6] for analysis of spikes generated by a single neuron. This is the first application of this measure to quantify cooperativity among neurons.

2.1 Synergy and redundancy

A fundamental quantity in information theory is the mutual information between two random variables X and Y. It is defined as the cross-entropy (Kullbak-Liebler divergence) between the joint distribution of the variables, $p(x, y)$, and the product of the marginal distributions $p(x)p(y)$. As such it measures the statistical dependence of the variables X and Y. It is symmetric in X and Y and has the following familiar relations to their entropies[7]:

$$\begin{aligned} I(X;Y) &= D_{KL}[P(X,Y)|P(X)P(Y)] = \sum_{x,y} P(x,y) \log\left(\frac{p(x,y)}{p(x)p(y)}\right) \quad (1) \\ &= H(X) + H(Y) - H(X,Y) = H(X) - H(X|Y) = H(Y) - H(Y|X). \end{aligned}$$

When given three random variables X_1, X_2 and Y, one can consider the mutual information between the joint variables (X_1, X_2) and the variable Y, $I(X_1, X_2; Y)$ (notice the position of the semicolon), as well as the mutual informations $I(X_1; Y)$ and $I(X_2; Y)$. Similarly, one can consider the mutual information between X_1 and X_2 *conditioned* on a given value of $Y = y$, $I(X_1; X_2|y) = D_{KL}[P(X_1, X_2|y)|P(X_1|y)P(X_2|y)]$, as well as its average, the conditional mutual information,

$$I(X_1; X_2|Y) = \sum_y p(y) I_y(X_1; X_2).$$

Following Brenner *et. al.*[6] we define the *synergy level* of X_1 and X_2 with respect to the variable Y as

$$Syn_Y(X_1, X_2) = I(X_1, X_2; Y) - (I(X_1; Y) + I(X_2; Y)), \quad (2)$$

with the natural generalization to more than two variables X. This expression can be rewritten in terms of entropies and conditional information as follows:

$$\begin{aligned} Syn_Y(X_1, X_2) &= \quad (3) \\ &= H(X_1, X_2) - H(X_1, X_2|Y) - ((H(X_1) - H(X_1|Y)) + (H(X_2) - H(X_2|Y))) \\ &= \underbrace{H(X_1|Y) + H(X_2|Y) - H(X_1, X_2|Y)}_{Depends\ On\ Y} + \underbrace{H(X_1, X_2) - (H(X_1) + H(X_2))}_{Independent\ of\ Y} \\ &= I(X_1; X_2|Y) - I(X_1; X_2). \end{aligned}$$

When the variables exhibit positive synergy value, with respect to the variable Y, they jointly provide more information on Y than when considered independently, as expected in *synergetic* cases. Negative synergy values correspond to *redundancy* - the variables do not provide independent information about Y. Zero synergy value is obtained when the variables are independent of Y or when there is no change in their dependence when conditioned on Y. We claim that this is a useful measure of cooperativity among neurons, in a given computational task.

It is clear from Eq.(3) that if

$$I_y(X_1; X_2) = I(X_1; X_2) \ \forall y \in Y \Rightarrow Syn_Y(X_1, X_2) = 0, \quad (4)$$

since in that case $\sum_y p(y) I_y(X_1; X_2) = I(X_1; X2)$.

In other words, the synergy value is not zero only if the statistical dependence, hence the mutual information between the variables, is affected by the value of Y. It is positive when the mutual information increase, on the average, when conditioned on Y, and negative if this conditional mutual information decrease. Notice that the value of synergy can be both positive and negative since information, unlike entropy, is not sub-additive in the X variables.

3 Synergy among neurons

Our measure of synergy among the units is based on the ability to detect the behavioral mode from the recorded activity, as we discuss bellow. As discussed above, synergy among neurons is possible only if their statistical dependence change with time. An important case where synergy is not expected is pure "population coding"[8]. In this case the cells are expected to fire independently, each with its own fixed tuning curve. Our synergy value can thus be used to test if the recorded units are indeed participating in a pure population code of this kind, as hypothesized for certain motor cortical activity.

Theoretical models of the cortex that clearly predict nonzero synergy include attractor neural networks (ANN)[9] and synfire chain models(SFC)[3]. Both these models predict changes in the collective activity patterns, as neurons move between attractors in the ANN case, or when different synfire-chains of activity are born or disappear in the SFC case. To the extent that such changes in the collective activity depend on behavior, nonzero synergy values can be detected. It remains an interesting theoretical challenge to estimate the quantitative synergy values for such models and compare it to observed quantities.

3.1 Time-dependent cross correlations

In our previous studies[4] we demonstrated, using hidden Markov models of the activity, that the pairwise cross-correlations in the same data can change significantly with time, depending on the underlying collective state of activity. These states, revealed by the hidden Markov model, in turn depend on the behavior and enable its prediction. Dramatic and fast changes in the cross-correlation of cells has also been shown by others[10]. This finding indicate directly that the statistical dependence of the neurons can change (rapidly) with time, in a way correlated to behavior. This clearly suggests that nonzero synergy should be observed among these cortical units, relative to this behavior. In the present study this theoretical hypothesis is verified.

3.2 Redundancy cases

If on the other hand the conditioned mutual information equal zero for all behavioral modes, i.e. $I_y(X_1; X_2) = 0 \ \forall y \in Y$, while $I(X_1; X_2) > 0$, we expect to get negative synergy, or redundancy among the cells, with respect to the behavior variable Y. We observed clear redundancy in another part of the brain, the basal ganglia, during the same experiment, when the behavior was the pre-reward and post-reward activity. In this case different cells provide exactly the same information, which yields negative synergy values.

4 Experimental results

4.1 Synergy measurement in practice

To evaluate the synergy value among different cells, it is necessary to estimate the conditional distribution $p(y|x)$ where y is the current behavior and x represent a single trial of spike trains of the considered cells. Estimating this probability, however, requires an underlying statistical model, or a represented of the spike trains. Otherwise there is never enough data since cortical spike trains are never exactly reproducible. In this work we choose the rate representation, which is the simplest to evaluate. The estimation of $p(y|x)$ goes as follows:

- For each of the M behavioral modes $(y_1, y_2.., y_M)$ collect spike train samples (the *training* data set).

- Using the training sample, construct a Post Stimulus Time Histogram (PSTH), i.e. the rate as function of time, for each behavioral mode.

- Given a spike train, outside of the training set, compute its probability to be result in each of the M modes.

- The spike train considered correctly classified if the most probable mode is in fact the true behavioral mode, and incorrectly otherwise.

- The fraction of correct classification, for all spike trains of a given behavioral mode y_i, is taken as the estimate of $p(y_i|x)$, and denoted P_{c_i}, where c_i is the identity of the cells used in the computation.

For the case of only two categories of behavior and for a uniform distribution of the different categories, the value of the entropy $H(Y)$ is the same for all combinations of cells, and is simply $H(Y) = -\sum_y p(y) \log_2(p(y)) = \log_2 2 = 1$. The full expression (in bits) for the synergy value can be thus written as follows:

$$\sum_x p(x) \left[-\sum_y P_{c_1,c_2} \log_2(P_{c_1,c_2}) \right] \overset{?}{>} \tag{5}$$
$$1 + \sum_x p(x) \left[-\sum_y P_{c_1} \log_2(P_{c_1}) \right] + \sum_x p(x) \left[-\sum_y P_{c_2} \log_2(P_{c_2}) \right],$$

If the first expression is larger than the second than there is (positive) synergy and vice versa for redundancy. However there is one very important caveat. As we saw the computation of the mutual information is not done exactly, and what one really computes is only a lower bound. If the bound is tighter for multiple cell calculation, the method could falsely infer positive synergy, and if the bound is tighter for the single cell computation, the method could falsely infer negative synergy. In previous works we have shown that the method we use for this estimation is quite reasonable and robust[5], therefore, we believe that we have even a conservative (i.e. less positive) estimate of synergy.

4.2 Observed synergy values

In the first set of experiments we tried to detect the behavioral mode during the delay-period of correct trials. In this case the two types of behavior were the "Go" and the "No-Go" described in the introduction. An example of this detection problem is given in figure 1A. In this figure there are 100 examples of multi-electrode recording of spike trains during the delay period. On the left is the "Go-mode" data and on the right the "No-Go mode", for two cells. On the lower part there is an example of two single spike trains that need to be classified by the mode models.

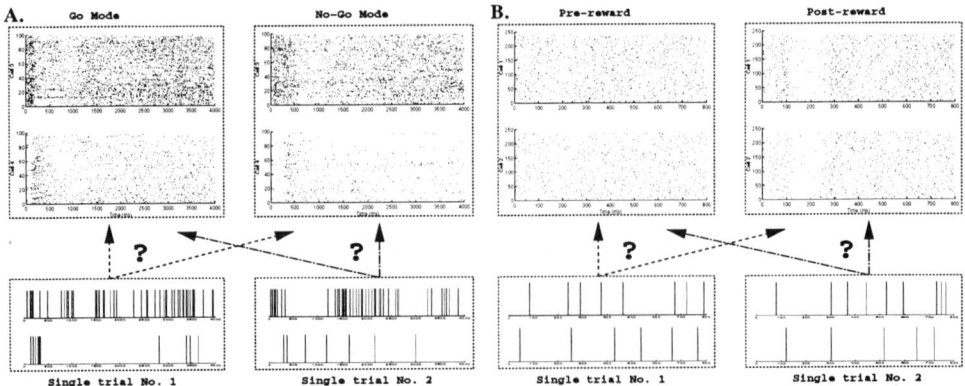

Figure 1: Raster displays of simultaneously recorded cells in the 2 different areas, in each area there were 2 behavioral modes.

Table 1 gives some examples of detection results obtained by using 2 cells independently, and by using their joint combination. It can be seen that the synergy is positive and significant. We examined 19 recording session of the same behavioral modes for two different animals and evaluated the synergy value. In 18 out of the 19 sessions there was at least one example of significant positive synergy among the cells.

For comparison we analyzed another set of experiments in which the data was recorded from the striatum in the basal ganglia. An example for this detection is shown in figure 1B. The behavioral modes were the "pre-reward" vs. the "post-reward" periods. Nine recording sessions for the two different monkeys were examined using the same detection technique. Although the detection results improve when the number of cells increase, in none of these recordings a positive synergy value was found. For most of the data the synergy value was close to zero, i.e. the mutual information among two cells jointly was close to the sum of the mutual information of the independent cells, as expected when the cells exhibit (conditionally) independent activity.

The prevailing difference between the synergy measurements in the cortex and in the TANs' of the basal ganglia is also strengthen by the different mechanisms underlying those cells. The TANs' are assumed to be globally mediators of information in the striatum, a relatively simple task, whereas the information processed in the frontal cortex in this task is believed to be much more collective and complicated. Here we suggest a first handle for quantitative detection of such different neuronal activities.

Acknowledgments

Special thanks are due to Moshe Abeles for his encouragement and support, and to William Bialek for suggesting the idea to look for the synergy among cortical cells. We would also like to thank A. Raz, Hagai Bergman, and Eilon Vaadia for sharing their data with us. The research at the Hebrew university was supported in part by a grant from the Unites States Israeli Binational Science Foundation (BSF).

Table 1: Examples of synergy among cortical neurons. For each example the mutual information of each cell separately is given together with the mutual information of the pair. In parenthesis the matching detection probability (average over $p(y|x)$) is also given. The last column gives the percentage of increase from the mutual information of the single cells to the mutual information of the pair. The table gives only those pairs for which the percentage was larger than 20% and the detection rate higher than 60%.

Session	Cells	Cell1	Cell2	Both cells	Syn (%)
bl16b	5,6	0.068 (64.84)	0.083 (66.80)	0.209 (76.17)	38
bl21b	1,4	0.201 (73.74)	0.118 (69.70)	0.497 (87.88)	56
bl21b	3,4	0.082 (66.67)	0.118 (69.70)	0.240 (77.78)	20
bl26b	0,3	0.062 (62.63)	0.077 (66.16)	0.198 (75.25)	42
bl26b	1,2	0.030 (60.10)	0.051 (63.13)	0.148 (72.22)	82
cl77b	2,3	0.054 (62.74)	0.013 (61.50)	0.081 (68.01)	20
cr38b	0,2	0.074 (65.93)	0.058 (63.19)	0.160 (73.08)	21
cr38b	0,4	0.074 (65.93)	0.042 (62.09)	0.144 (71.98)	24
cr38b	3,4	0.051 (62.09)	0.042 (62.09)	0.111 (69.23)	20
cr43b	0,1	0.070 (65.00)	0.063 (64.44)	0.181 (74.44)	36

References

[1] M. Abeles, E. Vaadia, H. Bergman, *Firing patterns of single unit in the prefrontal cortex and neural-networks models.*, Network 1 (1990).

[2] E. Raz, et al *Neuronal synchronization of tonically active neurons in the striatum of normal and parkinsonian primates*, J. Neurophysiol. 76:2083-2088 (1996).

[3] M. Abeles, *Corticonics*, (Cambridge University Press, 1991).

[4] I. Gat, N. Tishby and M. Abeles, *Hidden Markov modeling of simultaneously recorded cells in the associative cortex of behaving monkeys*, Network,8:297–322 (1997).

[5] I. Gat, N. Tishby, *Comparative study of different supervised detection methods of simultaneously recorded spike trains*, in preparation.

[6] N. Brenner, S.P. Strong, R. Koberle, W. Bialek, and R. de Ruyter van Steveninck, *The Economy of Impulses and the Stiffnes of Spike Trains*, NEC Research Institute Technical Note (1998).

[7] T.M. Cover and J.A. Thomas, *Elements of Information Theory.*, (Wiley NY, 1991).

[8] A.P. Georgopoulos, A.B. Schwartz, R.E. Kettner, *Neuronal Population Coding of Movement Direction*, Science, 233:1416-1419 (1986).

[9] D.J. Amit, *Modeling Brain Function*, (Cambridge University Press, 1989).

[10] E. Ahissar et al *Dependence of Cortical Plasticity on Correlated Activity of Single Neurons and on Behavioral Context*, Science, 257:1412-1415 (1992).

Analyzing and Visualizing Single-Trial Event-Related Potentials

Tzyy-Ping Jung[1,2], Scott Makeig[2,3], Marissa Westerfield[2]
Jeanne Townsend[2], Eric Courchesne[2], Terrence J. Sejnowski[1,2]

[1]Howard Hughes Medical Institute and Computational Neurobiology Laboratory
The Salk Institute, P.O. Box 85800, San Diego, CA 92186-5800
{jung,scott,terry}@salk.edu
[2]University of California, San Diego, La Jolla, CA 92093
[3]Naval Health Research Center, P.O. Box 85122, San Diego, CA 92186-5122

Abstract

Event-related potentials (ERPs), are portions of electroencephalographic (EEG) recordings that are both time- and phase-locked to experimental events. ERPs are usually averaged to increase their signal/noise ratio relative to non-phase locked EEG activity, regardless of the fact that response activity in single epochs may vary widely in time course and scalp distribution. This study applies a linear decomposition tool, Independent Component Analysis (ICA) [1], to multichannel single-trial EEG records to derive spatial filters that decompose single-trial EEG epochs into a sum of temporally independent and spatially fixed components arising from distinct or overlapping brain or extra-brain networks. Our results on normal and autistic subjects show that ICA can separate artifactual, stimulus-locked, response-locked, and non-event related background EEG activities into separate components, allowing (1) removal of pervasive artifacts of all types from single-trial EEG records, and (2) identification of both stimulus- and response-locked EEG components. Second, this study proposes a new visualization tool, the 'ERP image', for investigating variability in latencies and amplitudes of event-evoked responses in spontaneous EEG or MEG records. We show that sorting single-trial ERP epochs in order of reaction time and plotting the potentials in 2-D clearly reveals underlying patterns of response variability linked to performance. These analysis and visualization tools appear broadly applicable to electrophyiological research on both normal and clinical populations.

1 Introduction

Scalp-recorded *event-related potentials* (ERPs) are voltage changes in the ongoing *electroencephalogram* (EEG) that are both time- and phase-locked to some experimental events. These field potentials are usually averaged to increase their signal/noise ratio relative to artifacts and other non-phase locked EEG activity. The averaging method disregards the fact that in single epochs response activity may vary widely in both time course and scalp distribution. These differences are in part attributed to different strategies employed by subjects for processing different stimuli, to differences in expectation, attention, and arousal occurring in different trials, and/or to variations in alertness and fatigue [2, 3]. Single-trial analysis, on the other hand, can avoid problems due to time and/or phase shifts and can potentially reveal much richer information about event-related brain dynamics in endogenous ERPs, but suffers from pervasive artifacts associated with blinks, eye-movements, and muscle noise, and poor signal-to-noise ratio arising from the fact that non-phase locked background EEG activities often are larger than phase-locked response components.

We present here new methods for analyzing and visualizing multichannel unaveraged single-trial ERP records that alleviate these problems. First, multi-channel EEG epochs were analyzed using Independent Component Analysis (ICA), a signal processing technique that can decompose multichannel complex data into spatially fixed and temporally independent components. Next, a new visualization tool, the 'ERP image', is introduced for visualizing relations between single-trial ERP records and their contributions to the ERP average. To form an ERP image, the recorded potentials at one channel are plotted as parallel lines and single-trial ERP epochs are sorted in order of reaction time. ICA, applied to the single-trial EEG records from normal and autistic subjects in a visual selective attention experiment, derived components whose dynamics were affected by stimulus presentations and/or subject responses in distinct ways. We demonstrate, through analysis of two sample data sets, the power of the proposed analysis and visualization tools for increasing the amount and quality of information about event-related brain dynamics that can be derived from single-trial EEG data.

2 Independent Component Analysis of EEG data

Bell and Sejnowski [5] have proposed a simple neural network algorithm that blindly separates mixtures, $\mathbf{x}$, of independent sources, $\mathbf{s}$, using infomax. They showed that maximizing the joint entropy, $H(\mathbf{y})$, of the output of a neural processor minimizes the mutual information among the output components, $y_i = g(u_i)$, where $g(u_i)$ is an invertible bounded nonlinearity and $\mathbf{u} = \mathbf{Wx}$, a version of the original sources, $\mathbf{s}$, identical save for scaling and permutation. Lee et al. [1] generalized the infomax algorithm to perform blind source separation on linear mixtures of sources with either sub- or super-Gaussian distributions. Please see [5, 1] for details regarding the algorithms.

ICA is suitable for performing blind source separation on EEG data because: (1) it is plausible that EEG data recorded at multiple scalp sensors are linear sums of temporally independent components arising from spatially fixed, distinct or overlapping brain or extra-brain networks, and, (2) spatial smearing of EEG data by volume conduction does not involve significant time delays[1]. In single-trial EEG analysis, the rows of the input matrix $\mathbf{x}$ are the EEG signals recorded at different electrodes, while the columns are measurements recorded at different time points.

---

[1] See [4] for details regarding ICA assumptions underlying EEG analysis.

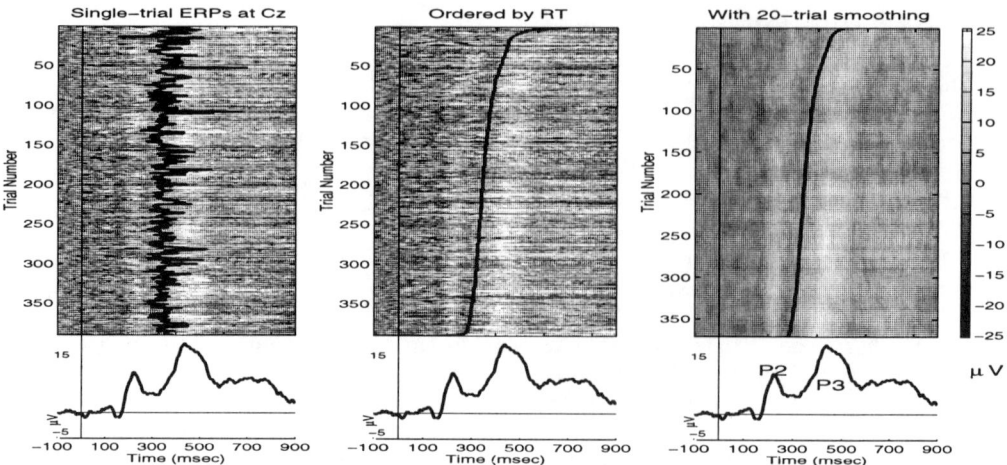

Figure 1: ERP images. *(left panel)* Single-trial ERPs recorded at a central electrode (Cz) and time-locked to onsets of visual target stimuli *(vertical left line)*, plotted with subject reaction times *(thick black line)*. *(middle panel)* The 390 single trials were then sorted (bottom to top) in order of increasing reaction time. *(right panel)* To increase signal-to-noise ratio and minimize EEG signals not both time- and phase-locked to the experimental events, the trials were averaged vertically using a 30-trial moving window advanced in one-trial increments.

The rows of the independent output data matrix $\mathbf{u} = \mathbf{Wx}$ are time courses of activation of the ICA components, and the columns of the inverse matrix, $\mathbf{W}^{-1}$, give the projection strengths of the respective components onto the scalp sensors. The scalp topographies of the components provide evidence as to their physiological origin (e.g., eye activity should project mainly to frontal sites). EEG signals of interest (e.g., event-related brain signals) can then be obtained by projecting selected ICA components back onto the scalp as $\mathbf{x}' = (\mathbf{W})^{-1}\mathbf{u}'$, where $\mathbf{u}'$ is the matrix of activation waveforms, $\mathbf{u}$, with rows representing activations of "irrelevant" sources set to zero.

3 Methods and Materials

EEG data were recorded at 29 scalp electrodes and 2 EOG placements from 2 normal and 1 autistic subjects who participated in a 2-hr visual selected attention task in which they were instructed to attend to circles flashed in random order at one of five locations laterally arrayed 0.8 cm above a central fixation point. Locations were outlined by five evenly spaced 1.6-cm blue squares displayed on a black background at visual angles of ±2.7 deg and ±5.5 deg from fixation. Attended locations were highlighted through entire 90-sec experimental blocks. Subjects were instructed to maintain fixation on the central cross and press a button each time they saw a circle in the attended location (see [6] for details).

4 Results

The ICA algorithm was applied separately to concatenated 31-channel single-trial EEG records from two normal and one autistic subjects. The derived independent components had a variety of distinct relations to task events. Some were clearly time-locked to stimuli presentations, while others were time-locked to subject responses. Still others captured spontaneous EEG activity together with blinks, eye-movements, and muscle artifacts, while others accounted for oscillatory and other background EEG phenomena.

4.1 ERP image

To investigate variability in the latencies and amplitudes of event-evoked responses in spontaneous EEG, we here introduce a new visualization tool, the ERP image. An example shown in Figure 1 (*left panel*) plots 390 single-trial ERP epochs time-locked to onsets of target stimuli (vertical left line) and recorded at a central electrode (Cz) from a normal subject. Each horizontal trace represents a 1-sec single-trial ERP record whose potential variations are plotted in different colors. The thick line plots the subject reaction times (RT) in successive trials. Note the trial-to-trial fluctuations in ERP latency and reaction time. The ERP average of these trials is plotted in the bottom of the panel. Next, the single trials were sorted in order of increasing reaction time (Fig. 1 *middle panel*), and were then smoothed with a 30-trial moving average (*right panel*). Note that, in all but the longest-RT trials, the early positive feature (P2) is time-locked to stimulus onset (i.e. is stimulus-locked), and that the P3 feature follows RT in nearly all trials (i.e. is response-locked). ERP image plots allow visualization of relations between event-related EEG trials and single-trial contributions to their ERP averaged. They disclose a tight link between the amplitudes and latencies of individual event-related responses and subject behavior.

4.2 Removing blink and eye-movement artifacts from EEG records

Autistic subjects tend to blink more frequently than normal subjects [8]. ICA, applied to this data set in which about 50% of the trials were contaminated by blinks, successfully isolated blink artifacts to a single component (Fig. 2A, *left*) whose contributions could be removed from the EEG records by subtracting out the component projection [7]. Though the subjects were instructed to fixate during each 90-sec blocks, it has been suspected, though poorly documented, that their eyes tended to drift towards target stimuli presented at peripheral locations. Here, a second ICA component accounted for these small horizontal eye-movements (Fig. 2B, *right*). Fig. 2B (*5 traces*) also shows separate ERP averages (at periocular site EOG2) of responses to targets presented at the five different attended locations. The size of the prominent eye movement-related component is proportional to the angle between the stimulus location and the fixation point. Figure 2C shows the averaged ERPs at the same site in response to stimuli presented at the five different attended locations, before (*faint traces*) and after (*solid traces*) artifact removal. After artifact correction, the averaged ERPs to stimuli presented at the five different locations were independent of stimulus location.

4.3 Extracting event-related brain activity from EEG Records

In these data, ICA also separated stimulus-locked, response-locked, and non-phase locked background EEG activities into different independent components. Numbers of components in each class varied across subjects. Figure 3A shows the projections of the subgroups of ICA components accounting primarily for (*left*) stimulus-locked, (*middle*) response-locked, and (*right*) remaining non-phase locked background EEG activity at site PO3. Notice that, (1) both the response latencies and active durations of the early stimulus-locked P1 and N1 components were very stable in nearly all trials, (2) the peak of the later P3 component covaried with reaction time, and (3) the projections of ICA components accounting for non-phase locked background EEG activity contributed very little to the averaged ERP (*right panel*, bottom

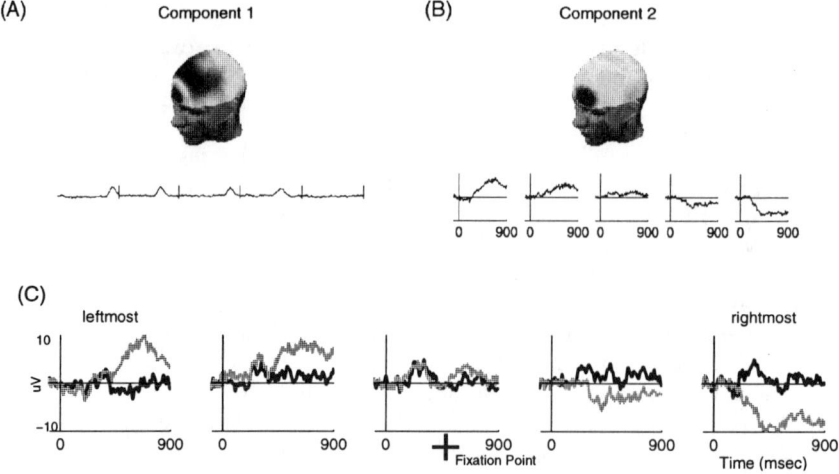

Figure 2: **(A)** (*left*) Scalp topography and 5 consecutive 1-sec epochs of the activation time course of an ICA component counting for blink artifacts in 641 single trials recorded from an adult autistic subject. **(B)** The scalp topography of a second eye-movement component and its averaged activation time courses in response to target stimuli presented at the five different attended locations. **(C)** Averaged ERPs at site EOG2 to targets presented at each of five attended locations, before (*faint traces*) and after (*solid traces*) artifact removal.

trace). These results indicate that ICA makes possible the extraction and separation of event-related brain phenomena of all types from single-trial EEG records.

4.4 Re-aligning single-trial event-related potentials

Figure 3B (*left panel*) shows the raw artifact-corrected single-trial ERP epochs (the sum of the data in Fig. 3A). Response latency fluctuations resulted in temporal smearing of the P3 feature in the averaged ERP (*bottom left*). Realigning the single-trial ERP epochs to the median reaction time sharpened the averaged P3 (*center panel*, P3'), but unfortunately made the early stimulus-locked activity out of phase and the early averaged ERP thus absent in the first 200 msec. Because ICA separated stimulus-locked and response-locked activity into different independent components, we could realign the time courses of the response-locked P3' component to the median reaction time and project the adjusted data, along with the unaligned time courses of stimulus-locked components (P1/N1), back onto the scalp sensors (*right panel*). This realignment preserved the early stimulus-locked P1/N1 while sharpening the response-locked P3. The method minimized temporal smearing in the averaged ERP arising from performance fluctuations (*left & right* panels).

4.5 Event-related oscillatory EEG activity

ICA, applied to multichannel single-trial EEG records, can also separate multiple oscillatory components even within a single frequency band. For example, Figure 3C plots scalp topographies and ERP images of activations of two ICA components accounting for alpha activity in target-response epochs from a normal subject. Note that the activity of the first component (*left panel*) was augmented following stimulation, while the activity of the second component (*middle panel*) was blocked by the subject response. When the same spatial filter was applied to EEG records from another session in which the subject was instructed to attend to but not to respond

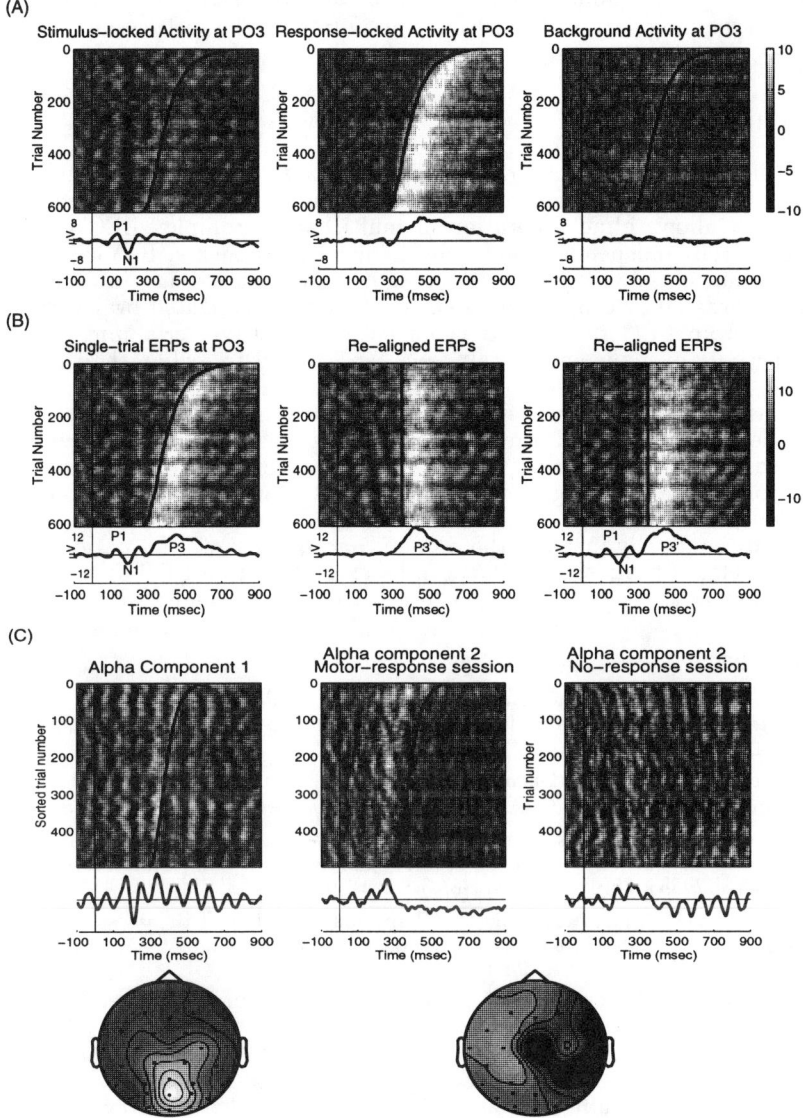

Figure 3: (A) Projections of ICA components at site PO3 accounting, respectively, for stimulus-locked (*left*), response-locked (*middle*), and non-phase locked background EEG activity (*right*) at one posterior site, PO3. (B) (*left*) Artifact-corrected single-trial ERP records time-locked to stimulus onsets (*left*), and subject responses (*center*). Note that the early ERP features (P1, N1) are not in phase in the response-locked trials, and do not appear in the response-locked average (*center bottom*). (*right*) Projections of the response-locked components were aligned to median reaction time (355 ms) and summed with stimulus-aligned component projections, forming an enhanced stimulus-aligned ERP (right bottom). (C) ERP-image plots of activations of ICA components accounting for alpha activity in EEG recorded from a normal subject. The alpha activity extracted by these components were either augmented (*left*) or blocked (*middle*) by subject responses. When the spatial filter for the second alpha component (*middle*) was applied to EEG records from another session in which the subject was asked only to 'mentally note' the occurrence of target stimuli, blocking was replaced by continued phase-locking.

to target stimuli, this alpha activity was not blocked (*right panel*). ICA identifies spatially-overlapping patterns of coherent activity over the entire scalp rather than focusing on single scalp channels or channel pairs.

5 Conclusions

We have developed analytic and visualization tools for analysis of multichannel single-trial EEG records. Single-trial ERP analysis based on Independent Component Analysis allows blind separation of multichannel complex EEG data into a sum of temporally independent and spatially fixed components. ICA can effectively remove eye and muscle artifacts without altering the underlying brain activity in the EEG records. ICA can also be used to extract event-related brain phenomena of all types from EEG records. It can identify spatially-overlapping patterns of coherent activity over the entire scalp, and can be used to realign the time courses of response-locked components to prevent temporal smearing in the average arising from performance fluctuations. ERP images make visible systematic relations between single-trial EEG or MEG records and experimental events, and their relations to averaged ERPs. ERP images can also be used to display relationships between phase, amplitude and timing of event-related EEG components time-locked to either stimuli or subject responses. The analysis and visualization tools proposed in this study dramatically increase the amount and quality of information on event- or response-related brain signals that can be extracted from ERP data. Both tools appear applicable to electrophyiological research on normal and clinical populations.

References

[1] T.W. Lee, M. Girolami and T.J. Sejnowski (1999) Independent Component Analysis using an Extended Infomax Algorithm for Mixed Sub-Gaussian and Super-Gaussian Sources, *Neural Computation*, **11**(2): 606-33.

[2] H. Yabe, F. Satio & Y. Fukushima (1993) Median Method for Detecting Endogenous Event-related Brain Potentials, *Electroencephalog. clin. Neurophysiolog.* **87**(6):403-7.

[3] H. Yabe, F. Satio & Y. Fukushima (1995) Classification of Single-trial ERP Sub-types: Application of Globally Optimal Vector Quantization Using Simulated Annealing, *Electroencephalog. clin. Neurophysiolog.* **94**(4):288-97.

[4] S. Makeig, T-P Jung, A.J. Bell, D. Ghahremani, and T.J. Sejnowski (1997) Blind Separation of Event-related Brain Responses into Independent Components, *Proc. Natl. Acad. Sci. USA*, USA, **94**:10979-84.

[5] A.J. Bell & T.J. Sejnowski (1995). An information-maximization approach to blind separation and blind deconvolution, *Neural Computation* **7**:1129-1159.

[6] S. Makeig, M. Westerfield, J. Covington, T-P Jung, J. Townsend, T.J. Sejnowski, and E. Courchesne (in press) Functionally independent components of the late positive event-related potential in a visual spatial attention paradigm, *J. Neuroscience*.

[7] Jung T-P, Humphries C, Lee TW, Makeig S, McKeown MJ, Iragui V, Sejnowski TJ (1998) Extended ICA Removes Artifacts from Electroencephalographic Data, In: *Advances in Neural Information Processing Systems* **10**, 894-900.

[8] J.G. Small (1971) Sensory Evoked Responses of Autistic Children, In: *Infantile Autism*, 224-39.

Spike-Based Compared to Rate-Based Hebbian Learning

Richard Kempter[*]
Institut für Theoretische Physik
Technische Universität München
D-85747 Garching, Germany

Wulfram Gerstner
Swiss Federal Institute of Technology
Center of Neuromimetic Systems, EPFL-DI
CH-1015 Lausanne, Switzerland

J. Leo van Hemmen
Institut für Theoretische Physik
Technische Universität München
D-85747 Garching, Germany

Abstract

A correlation-based learning rule at the spike level is formulated, mathematically analyzed, and compared to learning in a firing-rate description. A differential equation for the learning dynamics is derived under the assumption that the time scales of learning and spiking can be separated. For a linear Poissonian neuron model which receives time-dependent stochastic input we show that spike correlations on a millisecond time scale play indeed a role. Correlations between input and output *spikes* tend to stabilize structure formation, provided that the form of the *learning window* is in accordance with Hebb's principle. Conditions for an intrinsic normalization of the average synaptic weight are discussed.

1 Introduction

Most learning rules are formulated in terms of mean firing rates, viz., a continuous variable reflecting the mean activity of a neuron. For example, a 'Hebbian' (Hebb 1949) learning rule which is driven by the correlations between presynaptic and postsynaptic rates may be used to generate neuronal receptive fields (e.g., Linsker 1986, MacKay and Miller 1990, Wimbauer et al. 1997) with properties similar to those of real neurons. A rate-based description, however, neglects effects which are due to the pulse structure of neuronal signals. During recent years experimental and

---
[*]email: kempter@physik.tu-muenchen.de (corresponding author)

theoretical evidence has accumulated which suggests that temporal coincidences between spikes on a millisecond or even sub-millisecond scale play an important role in neuronal information processing (e.g., Bialek et al. 1991, Carr 1993, Abeles 1994, Gerstner et al. 1996). Moreover, changes of synaptic efficacy depend on the precise timing of postsynaptic action potentials and presynaptic input spikes (Markram et al. 1997, Zhang et al. 1998). A synaptic weight is found to *increase*, if presynaptic firing *precedes* a postsynaptic spike and decreased otherwise. In contrast to the standard *rate* models of Hebbian learning, the spike-based learning rule discussed in this paper takes these effects into account. For mathematical details and numerical simulations the reader is referred to Kempter et al. (1999).

2 Derivation of the Learning Equation

2.1 Specification of the Hebb Rule

We consider a neuron that receives input from $N \gg 1$ synapses with efficacies J_i, $1 \leq i \leq N$. We assume that changes of J_i are induced by pre- and postsynaptic spikes. The learning rule consists of three parts. (i) Let t_i^m be the time of the mth input spike arriving at synapse i. The arrival of the spike induces the weight J_i to change by an amount w^{in} which can be positive or negative. (ii) Let t^n be the nth output spike of the neuron under consideration. This event triggers the change of all N efficacies by an amount w^{out} which can also be positive or negative. (iii) Finally, time *differences* between input spikes influence the change of the efficacies. Given a time difference $s = t_i^m - t^n$ between input and output spikes, J_i is changed by an amount $W(s)$ where the *learning window* W is a real valued function (Fig. 1). The learning window can be motivated by local chemical processes at the level of the synapse (Gerstner et al. 1998, Senn et al. 1999). Here we simply assume that such a learning window exist and take some (arbitrary) functional dependence $W(s)$.

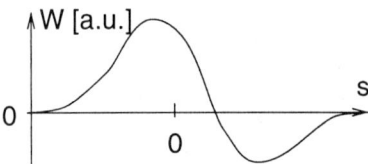

Figure 1: An example of a learning window W as a function of the delay $s = t_i^m - t^n$ between a postsynaptic firing time t^n and presynaptic spike arrival t_i^m at synapse i. Note that for $s < 0$ the presynaptic spike *precedes* postsynaptic firing.

Starting at time t with an efficacy $J_i(t)$, the total change $\Delta J_i(t) = J_i(t+\mathcal{T}) - J_i(t)$ in a time interval $\mathcal{T}$ is calculated by summing the contributions of all input and output spikes in the time interval $[t, t+\mathcal{T}]$. Describing the input spike train at synapse i by a series of δ functions, $S_i^{\text{in}}(t) = \sum_m \delta(t - t_i^m)$, and, similarly, output spikes by $S^{\text{out}}(t) = \sum_n \delta(t - t^n)$, we can formulate the rules (i)–(iii):

$$\Delta J_i(t) = \int_t^{t+\mathcal{T}} dt' \left[w^{\text{in}} S_i^{\text{in}}(t') + w^{\text{out}} S^{\text{out}}(t') + \int_t^{t+\mathcal{T}} dt'' \, W(t''-t') S_i^{\text{in}}(t'') S^{\text{out}}(t') \right] \quad (1)$$

2.2 Separation of Time Scales

The total change $\Delta J_i(t)$ is subject to noise due to stochastic spike arrival and, possibly, stochastic generation of output spikes. We therefore study the *expected* development of the weights J_i, denoted by angular brackets. We make the substitution $s = t'' - t'$ on the right-hand side of (1), divide both sides by $\mathcal{T}$, and take the expectation value:

$$\frac{\langle \Delta J_i \rangle(t)}{\mathcal{T}} = \frac{1}{\mathcal{T}} \int_t^{t+\mathcal{T}} dt' \left[w^{\text{in}} \langle S_i^{\text{in}} \rangle(t') + w^{\text{out}} \langle S^{\text{out}} \rangle(t') \right]$$
$$+ \frac{1}{\mathcal{T}} \int_t^{t+\mathcal{T}} dt' \int_{t-t'}^{t+\mathcal{T}-t'} ds\, W(s) \langle S_i^{\text{in}}(t'+s) S^{\text{out}}(t') \rangle . \quad (2)$$

We may interpret $\langle S_i^{\text{in}} \rangle(t)$ for $1 \leq i \leq N$ and $\langle S^{\text{out}} \rangle(t)$ as *instantaneous* firing rates.[1] They may vary on very short time scales – shorter, e.g., than average interspike intervals. Such a model is consistent with the idea of temporal coding, since it does not rely on temporally averaged *mean* firing rates.

We note, however, that due to the integral over time on the right-hand side of (2) temporal averaging is indeed important. If $\mathcal{T}$ is much larger than typical interspike intervals, we may define *mean* firing rates $\nu_i^{\text{in}}(t) = \overline{\langle S_i^{\text{in}} \rangle(t)}$ and $\nu^{\text{out}}(t) = \overline{\langle S^{\text{out}} \rangle(t)}$ where we have used the notation $\overline{f(t)} = \mathcal{T}^{-1} \int_t^{t+\mathcal{T}} dt'\, f(t')$. The *mean* firing rates must be distinguished from the previously defined *instantaneous* rates $\langle S_i^{\text{in}} \rangle$ and $\langle S^{\text{out}} \rangle$ which are defined as an expectation value and have a high temporal resolution. In contrast, the mean firing rates ν_i^{in} and ν^{out} vary slowly (time scale of the order of $\mathcal{T}$) as a function of time.

If the learning time $\mathcal{T}$ is much larger than the width of the learning window, the integration over s in (2) can be extended to run from $-\infty$ to ∞ without introducing a noticeable error. With the definition of a temporally averaged correlation,

$$C_i(s;t) = \overline{\langle S_i^{\text{in}}(t+s) S^{\text{out}}(t) \rangle} , \quad (3)$$

the last term on the right of (2) reduces to $\int_{-\infty}^{\infty} ds\, W(s) C_i(s;t)$. Thus, correlations between pre- and postsynaptic spikes enter spike-based Hebbian learning through C_i convolved with the learning window W. We remark that the correlation $C_i(s;t)$ may change as a function of s on a fast time scale. Note that, by definition, $s < 0$ implies that a presynaptic spike *precedes* the output spike – and this is when we expect (for excitatory synapses) a positive correlation between input and output.

As usual in the theory of Hebbian learning, we require learning to be a slow process. The correlation C_i can then be evaluated for a constant J_i and the left-hand side of (2) can be rewritten as a differential on the slow time scale of learning

$$\frac{d}{dt} J_i(t) \equiv \dot{J}_i = w^{\text{in}} \nu_i^{\text{in}}(t) + w^{\text{out}} \nu^{\text{out}}(t) + \int_{-\infty}^{\infty} ds\, W(s) C_i(s;t) . \quad (4)$$

2.3 Relation to Rate-Based Hebbian Learning

In neural network theory, the hypothesis of Hebb (Hebb 1949) is usually formulated as a learning rule where the change of a synaptic efficacy J_i depends on the correlation between the mean firing rate ν_i^{in} of the ith presynaptic and the mean firing rate ν^{out} of a postsynaptic neuron, viz.,

$$\dot{J}_i = a_0 + a_1 \nu_i^{\text{in}} + a_2 \nu^{\text{out}} + a_3 \nu_i^{\text{in}} \nu^{\text{out}} + a_4 (\nu_i^{\text{in}})^2 + a_5 (\nu^{\text{out}})^2 , \quad (5)$$

where a_0, a_1, a_2, a_3, a_4, and a_5 are proportionality constants. Apart from the decay term a_0 and the 'Hebbian' term $\nu_i^{\text{in}} \nu^{\text{out}}$ proportional to the product of input and

---

[1] An example of rapidly changing instantaneous rates can be found in the auditory system. The auditory nerve carries noisy spike trains with a stochastic intensity modulated at the frequency of the applied acoustic tone. In the barn owl, a significant modulation of the rates is seen up to a frequency of 8 kHz (e.g., Carr 1993).

output rates, there are also synaptic changes which are driven separately by the pre- and postsynaptic rates. The parameters $a_0, \ldots, a_5$ may depend on J_i. Equation (5) is a general formulation up to second order in the rates; see, e.g., (Linsker 1986).

To get (5) from (4) two approximations are necessary. First, if there are no correlations between input and output spikes apart from the correlations contained in the rates, we can approximate $\langle S_i^{\text{in}}(t+s) S^{\text{out}}(t)\rangle \approx \langle S_i^{\text{in}}\rangle(t+s) \langle S^{\text{out}}\rangle(t)$. Second, if these rates change slowly as compared to $\mathcal{T}$, then we have $C_i(s;t) \approx \nu_i^{\text{in}}(t+s) \nu^{\text{out}}(t)$. Since we have assumed that the learning time $\mathcal{T}$ is long compared to the width of the learning window, we may simplify further and set $\nu_i^{\text{in}}(t+s) \approx \nu_i^{\text{in}}(t)$, hence $\int_{-\infty}^{\infty} ds\, W(s)\, C_i(s;t) \approx \tilde{W}(0)\, \nu_i^{\text{in}}(t)\, \nu^{\text{out}}(t)$, where $\tilde{W}(0) = \int_{-\infty}^{\infty} ds\, W(s)$. We may now identify $\tilde{W}(0)$ with a_3. By further comparison of (5) with (4) we identify w^{in} with a_1 and w^{out} with a_2, and we are able to reduce (4) to (5) by setting $a_0 = a_4 = a_5 = 0$.

The above set of of assumption which is necessary to derive (5) from (4) does, however, not hold in general. According to the results of Markram et al. (1997) the width of the learning window in cortical pyramidal cells is in the range of ≈ 100 ms. A *mean* rate formulation thus requires that all changes of the activity are slow on a time scale of 100 ms. This is not necessarily the case. The existence of oscillatory activity in the cortex in the range of 50 Hz implies activity changes every 20 ms. Much faster activity changes on a time scale of 1 ms and below are found in the auditory system (e.g., Carr 1993). Furthermore, beyond the correlations between mean activities additional correlations between spikes may exist; see below. Because of all these reasons, the learning rule (5) in the simple rate formulation is insufficient. In the following we will study the full spike-based learning equation (4).

3 Stochastically Spiking Neurons

3.1 Poisson Input and Stochastic Neuron Model

To proceed with the analysis of (4) we need to determine the correlations C_i between input spikes at synapse i and output spikes. The correlations depend strongly on the neuron model under consideration. To highlight the main points of learning we study a linear inhomogeneous Poisson neuron as a toy model. Input spike trains arriving at the N synapses are statistically independent and generated by an inhomogeneous Poisson process with time-dependent intensities $\langle S_i^{\text{in}}\rangle(t) = \lambda_i^{\text{in}}(t)$, with $1 \leq i \leq N$. A spike arriving at t_i^m at synapse i, evokes a postsynaptic potential (PSP) with time course $\epsilon(t - t_i^m)$ which we assume to be excitatory (EPSP). The amplitude is given by the synaptic efficacy $J_i(t) > 0$. The membrane potential u of the neuron is the linear superposition of all contributions

$$u(t) = u_0 + \sum_{i=1}^{N} \sum_{m} J_i(t)\, \epsilon(t - t_i^m) \qquad (6)$$

where u_0 is the resting potential. Output spikes are assumed to be generated stochastically with a time dependent rate $\lambda^{\text{out}}(t)$ which depends linearly upon the membrane potential

$$\lambda^{\text{out}}(t) = \beta\, [u(t)]_+ = \nu_0 + \sum_{i=1}^{N} \sum_{m} J_i(t)\, \epsilon(t - t_i^m). \qquad (7)$$

with a linear function $\beta[u]_+ = \beta_0 + \beta_1 u$ for $u > 0$ and zero otherwise. After the second equality sign, we have formally set $\nu_0 = u_0 + \beta_0$ and $\beta_1 = 1$. $\nu_0 >$ can be interpreted as the spontaneous firing rate. For excitatory synapses a negative u is impossible and that's what we have used after the second equality sign. The sums run over all spike arrival times at all synapses. Note that the spike generation process is independent of previous output spikes. In particular, the Poisson model does not include refractoriness.

In the context of (4), we are interested in the expectation values for input and output. The expected input is $\langle S_i^{\text{in}} \rangle(t) = \lambda_i^{\text{in}}(t)$. The expected output is

$$\langle S^{\text{out}} \rangle(t) = \nu_0 + \sum_i J_i(t) \int_0^\infty ds\, \epsilon(s)\, \lambda_i^{\text{in}}(t-s) \,, \tag{8}$$

The expected output rate in (8) depends on the convolution of ϵ with the input rates. In the following we will denote the convolved rates by $\Lambda_i^{\text{in}}(t) = \int_0^\infty ds\, \epsilon(s) \lambda_i^{\text{in}}(t-s)$.

Next we consider the expected correlations between input and output, $\langle S_i^{\text{in}}(t+s) S^{\text{out}}(t) \rangle$, which we need in (3):

$$\langle S_i^{\text{in}}(t+s) S^{\text{out}}(t) \rangle = \lambda_i^{\text{in}}(t+s) [\nu_0 + J_i(t)\, \epsilon(-s) + \sum_j J_j(t)\, \Lambda_j^{\text{in}}(t)] \,. \tag{9}$$

The first term inside the square brackets is the spontaneous output rate. The second term is the specific contribution of an input spike at time $t+s$ to the output rate at t. It vanishes for $s > 0$ (Fig. 2). The sum in (9) contains the mean contributions of all synapses to an output spike at time t. Inserting (9) in (3) and assuming the weights J_j to be constant in the time interval $[t, t+\mathcal{T}]$ we obtain

$$C_i(s;t) = \sum_j J_j(t)\, \overline{\lambda_i^{\text{in}}(t+s)\, \Lambda_j^{\text{in}}(t)} + \overline{\lambda_i^{\text{in}}(t+s)} \,[\nu_0 + J_i(t)\, \epsilon(-s)] \,. \tag{10}$$

For excitatory synapses, the second term gives for $s < 0$ a positive contribution to the correlation function – as it should be. (Recall that $s < 0$ means that a presynaptic spike precedes postsynaptic firing.)

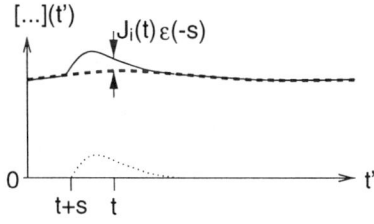

Figure 2: Interpretation of the term in square brackets in (9). The dotted line is the contribution of an input spike at time $t+s$ to the output rate as a function of t', viz., $J_i(t)\,\epsilon(t'-t-s)$. Adding this to the mean rate contribution, $\nu_0 + \sum_j J_j(t')\, \Lambda_j^{\text{in}}(t')$ (dashed line), we obtain the rate inside the square brackets of (9) (full line). At time $t' = t$ the contribution of an input spike at time $t+s$ is $J_i(t)\,\epsilon(-s)$.

3.2 Learning Equation

The assumption of identical and constant mean input rates, $\overline{\lambda_i^{\text{in}}(t)} = \nu_i^{\text{in}}(t) = \nu^{\text{in}}$ for all i, reduces the number of free parameters in (4) and eliminates all effects of rate coding. We introduce $\Gamma_i^{\text{in}}(t) := [\tilde{W}(0)]^{-1} \int_{-\infty}^\infty ds\, W(s) \lambda_i^{\text{in}}(t+s)$ and define

$$Q_{ij}(t) = \tilde{W}(0)\, \overline{[\Gamma_i^{\text{in}}(t) - \nu^{\text{in}}][\Lambda_j^{\text{in}}(t) - \nu^{\text{in}}]} \,. \tag{11}$$

Using (8), (10), (11) in (4) we find for the evolution on the slow time scale of learning

$$\dot{J}_i(t) = k_1 + \sum_j J_j(t)\, [Q_{ij}(t) + k_2 + k_3\, \delta_{ij}] \,, \quad \text{where} \tag{12}$$

$$k_1 = [w^{\text{out}} + \tilde{W}(0)\,\nu^{\text{in}}]\,\nu_0 + w^{\text{in}}\,\nu^{\text{in}} \tag{13}$$

$$k_2 = [w^{\text{out}} + \tilde{W}(0)\,\nu^{\text{in}}]\,\nu^{\text{in}} \tag{14}$$

$$k_3 = \nu^{\text{in}} \int ds\,\epsilon(-s)\,W(s)\,. \tag{15}$$

4 Discussion

Equation (12), which is the central result of our analysis, describes the expected dynamics of synaptic weights for a spike-based Hebbian learning rule (1) under the assumption of a linear inhomogeneous Poisson neuron. Linsker (1986) has derived a mathematically equivalent equation starting from (5) and a linear graded response neuron, a rate-based model. An equation of this type has been analyzed by MacKay and Miller (1990). The difference between Linsker's equation and (12) is, apart from a slightly different notation, the term $k_3\,\delta_{ij}$ and the interpretation of Q_{ij}.

4.1 Interpretation of Q_{ij}

In (12) correlations between spikes on time scales down to milliseconds or below can enter the driving term Q_{ij} for structure formation; cf. (11). In contrast to that, Linsker's ansatz is based on a firing rate description, where the term Q_{ij} contains correlations between *mean firing rates* only. In his Q_{ij} term, mean firing rates take the place of Γ_i^{in} and Λ_i^{in}. If we use a standard interpretation of rate coding, a mean firing rate corresponds to a temporally averaged quantity with an averaging window or a hundred milliseconds or more.

Formally, we could define mean rates by temporal averaging with either $\epsilon(s)$ or $W(s)$ as the averaging window. In this sense, Linsker's 'rates' have been made more precise by (11). Note, however, that (11) is asymmetric: one of the rates should be convolved with ϵ, the other one with W.

4.2 Relevance of the k_3 term

The most important difference between Linsker's rate-based learning rule and our Eq. (12) is the existence of a term $k_3 \neq 0$. We now argue that for a *causal* chain of events $k_3 \propto \int dx\,\epsilon(x)\,W(-x)$ must be positive. [We have set $x = -s$ in (15).] First, without loss of generality, the integral can be restricted to $x > 0$ since $\epsilon(x)$ is a response kernel and vanishes for $x < 0$. For excitatory synapses, $\epsilon(x)$ is positive for $x > 0$. Second, experiments on excitatory synapses show that $W(s)$ is positive for $s < 0$ (Markram et al. 1997, Zhang et al. 1998). Thus the integral $\int dx\,\epsilon(x)\,W(-x)$ is positive – and so is k_3.

There is also a more general argument for $k_3 > 0$ based on a literal interpretation of Hebb's statement (Hebb 1949). Let us recall that $s < 0$ in (15) means that a presynaptic spike *precedes* postsynaptic spiking. For excitatory synapses, a presynaptic spike which precedes postsynaptic firing may be the *cause* of the postsynaptic activity. [As Hebb puts it, it has 'contributed in firing the postsynaptic cell'.] Thus, the Hebb rule 'predicts' that for excitatory synapses $W(s)$ is positive for $s < 0$. Hence, $k_3 = \nu^{\text{in}} \int ds\,\epsilon(-s)\,W(s) > 0$ as claimed above.

A positive k_3 term in (12) gives rise to an exponential growth of weights. Thus any existing structure in the distribution of weights is enhanced. This contributes to the *stability* of weight distributions, especially when there are few and strong synapses (Gerstner et al. 1996).

4.3 Intrinsic Normalization

Let us suppose that no input synapse is special and impose the (weak) condition that $N^{-1}\sum_i Q_{ij} = Q_0 > 0$ independent of the synapse index j. We find then from (12) that the average weight $J_0 := N^{-1}\sum_i J_i$ has a fixed point $J_0 = -k_1/[Q_0 + k_2 + N^{-1}k_3]$. The fixed point is stable if $Q_0 + k_2 + N^{-1}k_3 < 0$. We have shown above that $k_3 > 0$. Furthermore, $Q_0 > 0$ according to our assumption. The only way to enforce stability is therefore a term k_2 which is sufficiently negative. Let us now turn to the definition of k_2 in (14). To achieve $k_2 < 0$, either $\tilde{W}(0)$ (the integral over W) must be sufficiently negative; this corresponds to a learning rule which is, on the average, anti-Hebbian. Or, for $\tilde{W}(0) > 0$, the linear term w^{out} in (1) must be sufficiently negative. In addition, for excitatory synapses a reasonable fixed point J_0 has to be positive. For a stable fixed point this is only possible for $k_1 > 0$, which, in turn, implies w^{in} to be sufficiently positive; cf. (13).

Intrinsic normalization of synaptic weights is an interesting property, since it allows neurons to stay at an optimal operating point even while synapses are changing. Auditory neurons may use such a mechanism to stay during learning in the regime where coincidence detection is possible (Gerstner et al. 1996, Kempter et al. 1998). Cortical neurons might use the same principles to operate in the regime of high variability (Abbott, invited NIPS talk, this volume).

4.4 Conclusions

Spike-based learning is different from simple rate-based learning rules. A spike-based learning rule can pick up correlations in the input on a millisecond time scale. Mathematically, the main difference to rate-based Hebbian learning is the existence of a k_3 term which accounts for the causal relation between input and output spikes. Correlations between input and output spikes on a millisecond time scale play a role and tend to stabilize existing strong synapses.

References

Abeles M., 1994, In Domany E. et al., editors, *Models of Neural Networks II*, pp. 121–140, New York. Springer.

Bialek W. et al., 1991, *Science*, 252:1855–1857.

Carr C. E., 1993, *Annu. Rev. Neurosci.*, 16:223–243.

Gerstner W. et al., 1996, *Nature*, 383:76–78.

Gerstner W. et al., 1998, In W. Maass and C. M. Bishop., editors, *Pulsed Neural Networks*, pp. 353–377, Cambridge. MIT-Press.

Hebb D. O., 1949, *The Organization of Behavior*. Wiley, New York.

Kempter R. et al., 1998, *Neural Comput.*, 10:1987–2017.

Kempter R. et al., 1999, *Phys. Rev. E*, In Press.

Linsker R., 1986, *Proc. Natl. Acad. Sci. USA*, 83:7508–7512.

MacKay D. J. C., Miller K. D., 1990, *Network*, 1:257–297.

Markram H. et al., 1997, *Science*, 275:213–215.

Senn W. et al., 1999, *preprint*, Univ. Bern.

Wimbauer S. et al., 1997, *Biol. Cybern.*, 77:453–461.

Zhang L.I. et al., 1998, *Nature*, 395:37–44

Signal Detection in Noisy Weakly-Active Dendrites

Amit Manwani and Christof Koch
{quixote,koch}@klab.caltech.edu
Computation and Neural Systems Program
California Institute of Technology
Pasadena, CA 91125

Abstract

Here we derive measures quantifying the information loss of a synaptic signal due to the presence of neuronal noise sources, as it electrotonically propagates along a weakly-active dendrite. We model the dendrite as an infinite linear cable, with noise sources distributed along its length. The noise sources we consider are thermal noise, channel noise arising from the stochastic nature of voltage-dependent ionic channels (K^+ and Na^+) and synaptic noise due to spontaneous background activity. We assess the efficacy of information transfer using a signal detection paradigm where the objective is to detect the presence/absence of a presynaptic spike from the post-synaptic membrane voltage. This allows us to analytically assess the role of each of these noise sources in information transfer. For our choice of parameters, we find that the synaptic noise is the dominant noise source which limits the maximum length over which information be reliably transmitted.

1 Introduction

This is a continuation of our efforts (Manwani and Koch, 1998) to understand the information capacity of a neuronal link (in terms of the specific nature of neural "hardware") by a systematic study of information processing at different biophysical stages in a model of a single neuron. Here we investigate how the presence of neuronal noise sources influences the information transmission capabilities of a simplified model of a weakly-active dendrite. The noise sources we include are, thermal noise, channel noise arising from the stochastic nature of voltage-dependent channels (K^+ and Na^+) and synaptic noise due to spontaneous background activity. We characterize the noise sources using analytical expressions of their current power spectral densities and compare their magnitudes for dendritic parameters reported in literature (Mainen and Sejnowski, 1998). To assess the role of these noise sources on dendritic integration, we consider a simplified scenario and model the dendrite as a lin-

Signal Detection in Noisy Weakly-Active Dendrites

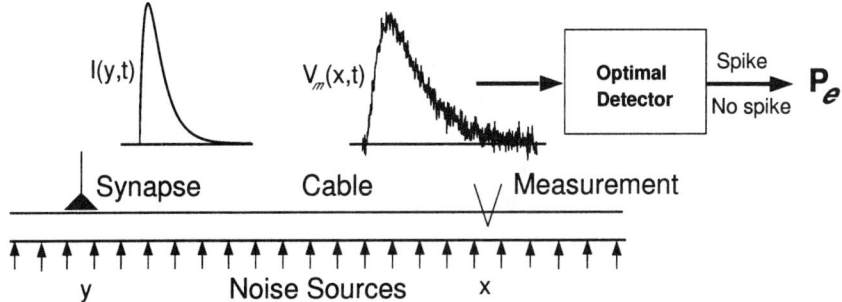

Figure 1: Schematic diagram of a simplified dendritic channel. The dendrite is modeled a weakly-active 1-D cable with noise sources distributed along its length. Loss of signal fidelity as it propagates from a synaptic location (input) y to a measurement (output) location x is studied using a signal detection task. The objective is to optimally detect the presence of the synaptic input $I(y, t)$ (in the form of a unitary synaptic event) on the basis of the noisy voltage waveform $V_m(x, t)$, filtered by the cable's Green's function and corrupted by the noise sources along the cable. The probability of error, P_e is used to quantify task performance.

ear, infinite, one-dimensional cable with distributed current noises. When the noise sources are weak so that the corresponding voltage fluctuations are small, the membrane voltage satisfies a linear stochastic differential equation satisfied. Using linear cable theory, we express the power spectral density of the voltage noise in terms of the Green's function of an infinite cable and the current noise spectra. We use these results to quantify the efficacy of information transfer under a "signal detection" paradigm[1] where the objective is to detect the presence/absence of a presynaptic spike (in the form of an epsc) from the post-synaptic membrane voltage along the dendrite. The formalism used in this paper is summarized in **Figure 1**.

2 Neuronal Noise Sources

In this section we consider some current noise sources present in nerve membranes which distort a synaptic signal as it propagates along a dendrite. An excellent treatment of membrane noise is given in DeFelice (1981) and we refer the reader to it for details. For a linear one-dimensional cable, it is convenient to express quantities in specific length units. Thus, we express all conductances in units of S/μm and current power spectra in units of A^2/Hz μm.

A. Thermal Noise
Thermal noise arises due to the random thermal agitation of electrical charges in a conductor and represents a fundamental lower limit of noise in a system. A conductor of resistance R is equivalent to a noiseless resistor R in series with a voltage noise source $V_{th}(t)$ of spectral density $S_{Vth}(f) = 2kTR$ (V^2/Hz), or a noiseless resistor R in parallel with a current noise source, $I_{th}(t)$ of spectral density $S_{Ith}(f) = 2kT/R$ (A^2/ Hz), where k is the Boltzmann constant and T is the absolute temperature of the conductor[2]. The transverse resistance r_m (units of Ω μm) of a nerve membrane is due to the combined resistance of the lipid bilayer and the resting conductances of various voltage-gated, ligand-gated and leak channels embedded in the lipid matrix. Thus, the current noise due to r_m, has power

---

[1] For sake of brevity, we do not discuss the corresponding signal estimation paradigm as in Manwani and Koch (1998).

[2] Since the power spectra of real signals are even functions of frequency, we choose the double-sided convention for all power spectral densities.

spectral density,

$$S_{Ith}(f) = \frac{2kT}{r_m} \quad (1)$$

B. Channel Noise

Neuronal membranes contain microscopic voltage-gated and ligand-gated channels which open and close randomly. These random fluctuations in the number of channels is another source of membrane noise. We restrict ourselves to voltage-gated K^+ and Na^+ channels, although the following can be used to characterize noise due to other types of ionic channels as well. In the classical Hodgkin-Huxley formalism (Koch, 1998), a K^+ channel consists of four identical two-state sub-units (denoted by n) which can either be open or closed. The K^+ channel conducts only when all the sub-units are in their open states. Since the sub-units are identical, the channel can be in one of five states; from the state in which all the sub-units are closed to the open state in which all sub-units are open. Fluctuations in the number of open channels cause a random K^+ current I_K of power spectral density (DeFelice, 1981)

$$S_{IK}(f) = \eta_K \gamma_K^2 (V_m - E_K)^2 n_\infty^4 \sum_{i=1}^{4} \binom{4}{i} (1-n_\infty)^i n_\infty^{4-i} \frac{2\theta_n/i}{1 + 4\pi^2 f^2 (\theta_n/i)^2} \cdot \quad (2)$$

where η_K, γ_K and E_K denote the K^+ channel density (per unit length), the K^+ single channel conductance and the K^+ reversal potential respectively. Here we assume that the membrane voltage has been clamped to a value V_m. n_∞ and θ_n are the steady-state open probability and relaxation time constant of a single K^+ sub-unit respectively and are in general non-linear functions of V_m (Koch, 1998). When V_m is close to the resting potential V_{rest} (usually between -70 to -65 mV), $n_\infty \ll 1$ and one can simplify $S_{IK}(f)$ as

$$S_{IK}(f) \approx \eta_K \gamma_K^2 (V_{rest} - E_K)^2 n_\infty^4 (1-n_\infty)^4 \frac{2\theta_n/4}{1 + 4\pi^2 f^2 (\theta_n/4)^2} \quad (3)$$

Similarly, the Hodgkin-Huxley Na^+ channel is characterized by three identical activation sub-units (denoted by m) and an inactivation sub-unit (denoted by h). The Na^+ channel conducts only when all the m sub-units are open and the h sub-unit is not inactivated. Thus, the Na^+ channel can be in one of eight states from the state corresponding to all m sub-units closed and the h sub-unit inactivated to the open state with all m sub-units open and the h sub-unit not inactivated. m_∞ (resp. h_∞) and θ_m (resp. θ_h) are the corresponding steady-state open probability and relaxation time constant of a single Na^+ m (resp. h) sub-unit respectively. For $V_m \approx V_{rest}$, $m_\infty \ll 1$, $h_\infty \approx 1$ and

$$S_{INa}(f) \approx \eta_{Na} \gamma_{Na}^2 (V_{rest} - E_{Na})^2 m_\infty^3 (1-m_\infty)^3 h_\infty^2 \frac{2\theta_m/3}{1 + 4\pi^2 f^2 (\theta_m/3)^2} \quad (4)$$

where η_{Na}, γ_{Na} and E_{Na} denote the Na^+ channel density, the Na^+ single channel conductance and the sodium reversal potential respectively.

C. Synaptic Noise

In addition to voltage-gated ionic channels, dendrites are also awash in ligand-gated synaptic receptors. We restrict our attention to fast voltage-independent (AMPA-like) synapses. A commonly used function to represent the postsynaptic conductance change in response to a presynaptic spike is the *alpha* function (Koch, 1998)

$$g_\alpha(t) = \frac{g_{peak} \, e}{t_{peak}} t e^{-t/t_{peak}}, \; 0 \le t < \infty \quad (5)$$

where g_{peak} denotes the peak conductance change and t_{peak} the time-to-peak of the conductance change. We shall assume that for a spike train $s(t) = \sum_j \delta(t-t_j)$, the postsynaptic conductance is given $g_{Syn}(t) = \sum_j g_\alpha(t-t_j)$. This ignores inter-spike interaction

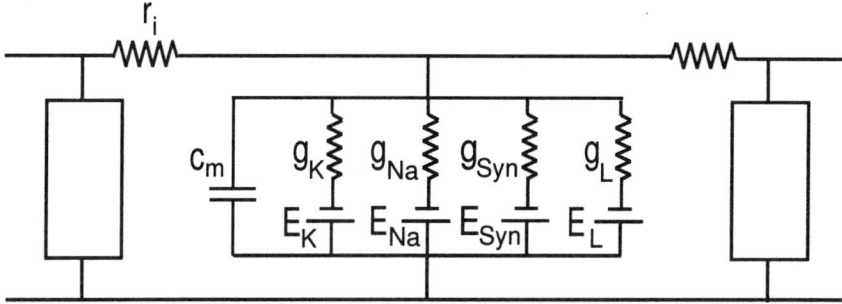

Figure 2: Schematic diagram of the equivalent electrical circuit of a linear dendritic cable. The dendrite is modeled as an infinite ladder network. r_i (units of Ω/μ m) denotes the longitudinal cytoplasmic resistance; c_m (units of F/μ m) and g_L (units of S/μ m) denote the transverse membrane capacitance and conductance (due to leak channels with reversal potential E_L) respectively. The membrane also contains active channels (K$^+$, Na$^+$) with conductances and reversal potentials denoted by (g_K, g_{Na}) and (E_K, E_{Na}) respectively, and fast voltage-independent (AMPA-like) synapses with conductance g_{Syn} and reversal potential E_{Syn}.

and synaptic saturation. The synaptic current is given by $i_{Syn}(t) = g_{Syn}(t)(V_m - E_{Syn})$ where E_{Syn} is the synaptic reversal potential. If the spike train can be modeled as a homogeneous Poisson process with mean firing rate λ_n, the power spectrum of $i_{Syn}(t)$ can be computed using Campbell's theorem (Papoulis, 1991)

$$S_{ISyn}(f) = \eta_{Syn}\lambda_n(V_m - E_{Syn})^2 \mid G_\alpha(f) \mid^2, \tag{6}$$

where η_{Syn} denotes the synaptic density and $G_\alpha(f) = \int_0^\infty g_\alpha(t)\, exp(-j2\pi ft)\, dt$ is the Fourier transform of $g_\alpha(t)$. Substituting for $g_\alpha(t)$ gives

$$S_{ISyn}(f) = \eta_{Syn}\, \lambda_n\, \frac{(e\, g_{peak} t_{peak}(V_m - E_{Syn}))^2}{(1 + 4\pi^2 f^2 t_o^2)^2} \tag{7}$$

3 Noise in Linear Cables

The linear infinite cable corresponding to a dendrite is modeled by the ladder network shown in **Figure 2**. The membrane voltage $V_m(x,t)$ satisfies the differential equation (Tuckwell, 1988),

$$\frac{\partial^2 V_m}{\partial^2 x} = r_i \left[c_m \frac{\partial V_m}{\partial t} + g_K(V_m - E_K) + g_{Na}(V_m - E_{Na}) \right.$$
$$\left. + g_{Syn}(V_m - E_{Syn}) + g_L(V_m - E_L) \right] \tag{8}$$

Since the ionic conductances are random and nonlinearly related to V_m, eq. 8 is a nonlinear stochastic differential equation. If the voltage fluctuations (denoted by V) around the resting potential V_{rest} are small, one can express the conductances as small deviations (denoted by $\tilde{g}$) from their corresponding resting values and transform eq. 8 to

$$-\lambda^2 \frac{\partial^2 V(x,t)}{\partial x^2} + \tau \frac{\partial V(x,t)}{\partial t} + (1+\delta)V(x,t) = \frac{I_n}{G} \tag{9}$$

where $\lambda^2 = 1/(r_i G)$ and $\tau = c_m/G$ denote the length and time constant of the membrane respectively. G is the passive membrane conductance and is given by the sum of the resting values of all the conductances. $\delta = \tilde{g}_K + \tilde{g}_{Na} + \tilde{g}_{Syn}/G$ represents the random changes in the membrane conductance due to synaptic and channel stochasticity; δ

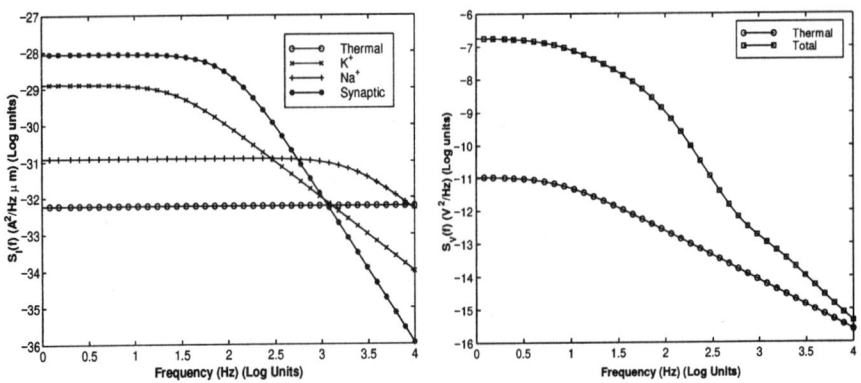

Figure 3: (a) Comparison of current spectra $S_I(f)$ of the four noise sources we consider. Synaptic noise is the most dominant source source of noise and thermal noise, the smallest. (b) Voltage noise spectrum of a 1-D infinite cable due to the current noise sources. $S_{Vth}(f)$ is also shown for comparison. Summary of the parameters used (adopted from Mainen and Sejnowski, 1998) : $R_m = 40$ kΩcm^2, $C_m = 0.75$ μF/cm^2, $r_i = 200$ Ωcm, d (dend. dia.) = 0.75 μm, $\eta_K = 2.3$ μm^{-1}, $\eta_{Na} = 3$ μm^{-1}, $\eta_{Syn} = 0.1$ μm^{-1}, $E_K = -95$ mV, $E_{Na} = 50$ mV, $E_{Syn} = 0$ mV, $E_L = V_{rest} = 70$ mV, $\gamma_K = \gamma_{Na} = 20$ pS.

$V_{rest}) + I_{th}$ denotes the total effective current noise due to the different noise sources. In order to derive analytical closed-form solutions to eq. 9, we further assume that $\delta \ll 1^3$, which reduces it to the familiar one-dimensional cable equation with noisy current input (Tuckwell, 1988). For resting initial conditions (no charge stored on the membrane at $t = 0$), V is linearly related to I_n and can be obtained by convolving I_n with the Green's function $g(x, y, t)$ of the cable for the appropriate boundary conditions. It has been shown that $V(x,t)$ is an asymptotically wide-sense stationary process (Tuckwell and Walsh, 1991) and its power spectrum $S_V(x, f)$ can be expressed in terms of the power spectrum of I_n, $S_n(f)$ as

$$S_V(x, f) = \frac{S_n(f)}{G^2} \int_{-\infty}^{\infty} |\mathcal{G}(x, x', f)|^2 \, dx' \tag{10}$$

where $\mathcal{G}(x, x', f)$ is the Fourier transform of $g(x, x', t)$. For an infinite cable

$$g(X, X', T) = \frac{e^{-T}}{\sqrt{4\pi T}} e^{\frac{-(X-X')^2}{4T}}, \quad -\infty < X, X' < \infty, \ 0 \leq T < \infty \tag{11}$$

where $X = x/\lambda$, $X' = x'/\lambda$ and $T = t/\tau$ are the corresponding dimensionless variables. Substituting for $g(x, x', t)$ we obtain

$$S_V(f) = \frac{S_n(f)}{2\lambda G^2} \frac{\sin\left(\frac{\tan^{-1}(2\pi f\tau)}{2}\right)}{2\pi f\tau \, (1 + (2\pi f\tau)^2)^{1/4}} \tag{12}$$

Since the noise sources are independent, $S_n(f) = S_{Ith}(f) + S_{IK}(f) + S_{INa}(f) + S_{ISyn}(f)$. Thus, eq. 12 allows us to compute the relative contribution of each of the noise sources to the voltage noise. The current and voltage noise spectra for biophysically relevant parameter values (Mainen and Sejnowski, 1998) are shown in **Figure 3**.

---

[3]Using self-consistency, we find the assumption to be satisfied in our case. In general, it needs verified on a case-by-case basis.

4 Signal Detection

The framework and notation used here are identical to that in Manwani and Koch (1998) and so we refer the reader to it for details. The goal in the signal detection task is to optimally decide between the two hypotheses

$$H_0 : y(t) = n(t), \quad 0 \leq t \leq T \quad \text{Noise}$$
$$H_1 : y(t) = g(t) * s(t) + n(t), \quad 0 \leq t \leq T \quad \text{Signal + Noise} \quad (13)$$

where $n(t)$, $g(t)$ and $s(t)$ denote the dendritic voltage noise, the Green's function of the cable (function of the distance between the input and measurement locations) and the epsc waveform (due to a presynaptic spike) respectively. The decision strategy which minimizes the probability of error $P_e = p_0 P_f + p_1 P_m$, where p_0 and $p_1 = (1 - p_0)$ are the prior probabilities of H_0 and H_1 respectively, is

$$\Lambda(y) \underset{H_0}{\overset{H_1}{\gtrless}} \mathcal{L}_0 \quad (14)$$

where $\Lambda(y) = P[y|H_1]/P[y|H_0]$ and $\mathcal{L}_0 = p_0/(1-p_0)$. P_f and P_m denote the false alarm and miss probability respectively. Since $n(t)$ arises due to the effect of several independent noise sources, by invoking the Central Limit theorem, we can assume that $n(t)$ is Gaussian, for which eq. 14 reduces to $r \underset{H_0}{\overset{H_1}{\gtrless}} \eta$. $r = \int_0^\infty y(t) \, h_d(-t) \, dt$ is a correlation between $y(t)$ and the *matched filter* $h_d(t)$, given in the Fourier domain as $H_d(f) = e^{-j2\pi fT} \mathcal{G}^*(f) S^*(f)/S_n(f)$. $\mathcal{G}(f)$ and $S(f)$ are Fourier transforms of $g(t)$ and $s(t)$ respectively and $S_n(f)$ is the noise power spectrum. The conditional means and variances of the Gaussian variable r under H_0 and H_1 are $\mu_0 = 0, \mu_1 = \int_{-\infty}^\infty |G(f)S(f)|^2/S_n(f) \, df$ and $\sigma_0^2 = \sigma_1^2 = \sigma^2 = \mu_1$ respectively. The error probabilities are given by $P_f = \int_\eta^\infty P[r|H_0] \, dr$ and $P_m = \int_{-\infty}^\eta P[r|H_1] \, dr$. The optimal value of the threshold η depends on σ and the prior probability p_0. For equi-probable hypotheses ($p_0 = 1 - p_0 = 0.5$), the optimal $\eta = (\mu_0 + \mu_1)/2 = \sigma^2/2$ and $P_e = 0.5 \, \text{Erfc}[\sigma/2\sqrt{2}]$. One can also regard the overall decision system as an effective binary channel. Let M and D be binary variables which take values in the set $\{H_0, H_1\}$ and denote the input and output of the dendritic channel respectively. Thus, the system performance can equivalently be assessed by computing the mutual information between M and D, $I(M;D) = \mathcal{H}(p_0 (1 - P_m) + (1 - p_0) P_f) - p_0 \mathcal{H}(P_m) - (1 - p_0) \mathcal{H}(P_f)$ (Cover and Thomas, 1991) where $\mathcal{H}(x)$ is the binary entropy function. For equi-probable hypotheses, $I(M;D) = 1 - \mathcal{H}(P_e)$ bits. It is clear from the plots for P_e and $I(M;D)$ (**Figure 4**) as a function of the distance between the synaptic (input) and the measurement (output) location that an epsc. can be detected with almost certainty at short distances, after which, there is a rapid decrease in detectability with distance. Thus, we find that membrane noise may limit the maximum length of a dendrite over which information can be transmitted reliably.

5 Conclusions

In this study we have investigated how neuronal noise sources might influence and limit the ability of one-dimensional cable structures to propagate information. When extended to realistic dendritic geometries, this approach can help address questions as, is the length of the apical dendrite in a neocortical pyramidal cell limited by considerations of signal-to-noise, which synaptic locations on a dendritic tree (if any) are better at transmitting information, what is the functional significance of active dendrites (Yuste and Tank, 1996) and so on. Given the recent interest in dendritic properties, it seems timely to apply an information-theoretic approach to study dendritic integration. In an attempt to experimentally verify

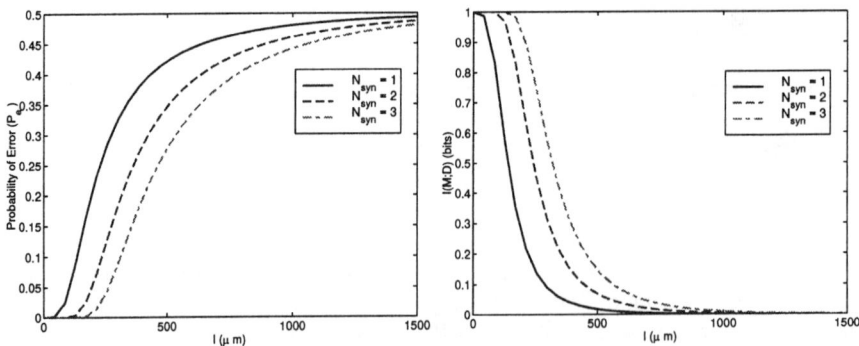

Figure 4: Information loss in signal detection. (a) Probability of Error (P_e) and (b) Mutual information ($I(M;D)$) for an infinite cable as a function of distance from the synaptic input location. Almost perfect detection occurs for small distances but performance degrades steeply over larger distances as the signal-to-noise ratio drops below some threshold. This suggests that dendritic lengths may be ultimately limited by signal-to-noise considerations. Epsc. parameters: g_{peak} = 0.1 nS, t_{peak} = 1.5 msec and E_{Syn} = 0 mV. N_{syn} is the number of synchronous synapses which activate in response to a pre-synaptic action potential.

the validity of our results, we are currently engaged in a quantitative comparison using neocortical pyramidal cells (Manwani *et al*, 1998).

Acknowledgements

This research was supported by NSF, NIMH and the Sloan Center for Theoretical Neuroscience. We thank Idan Segev, Elad Schneidman, Miki London, Yosef Yarom and Fabrizio Gabbiani for illuminating discussions.

References

DeFelice, L.J. (1981) *Membrane Noise.* New York: Plenum Press.

Cover, T.M., and Thomas, J.A. (1991) *Elements of Information Theory.* New York: Wiley.

Koch, C. (1998) *Biophysics of Computation: Information Processing in Single Neurons.* Oxford University Press.

Mainen, Z.F. and Sejnowski, T.J. (1998) "Modeling active dendritic processes in pyramidal neurons," In: *Methods in Neuronal Modeling: From Ions to Networks,* Koch, C. and Segev, I., eds., Cambridge: MIT Press.

Manwani, A. and Koch, C. (1998) "Synaptic transmission: An information-theoretic perspective," In: Kearns, M., Jordan, M. and Solla, S., eds., *Advances in Neural Information Processing Systems,* Cambridge: MIT Press.

Manwani, A., Segev, I., Yarom, Y and Koch, C. (1998) "Neuronal noise sources in membrane patches and linear cables," In: *Soc. Neurosci. Abstr.*

Papoulis, A. (1991) *Probability, Random Variables and Stochastic Processes.* New York: McGraw-Hill.

Tuckwell, H.C. (1988) *Introduction to Theoretical Neurobiology: I.* New York: Cambridge University Press.

Tuckwell, H.C. and Walsh, J.B. (1983) "Random currents through nerve membranes I. Uniform poisson or white noise current in one-dimensional cables," *Biol. Cybern.* **49**:99-110.

Yuste, R. and Tank, D.W. (1996) "Dendritic integration in mammalian neurons, a century after Cajal,"

The Role of Lateral Cortical Competition in Ocular Dominance Development

Christian Piepenbrock and Klaus Obermayer
Dept. of Computer Science, Technical University of Berlin
FR 2-1; Franklinstr. 28–29; 10587 Berlin, Germany
{piep,oby}@cs.tu-berlin.de; http://www.ni.cs.tu-berlin.de

Abstract

Lateral competition within a layer of neurons sharpens and localizes the response to an input stimulus. Here, we investigate a model for the activity dependent development of ocular dominance maps which allows to vary the degree of lateral competition. For weak competition, it resembles a correlation-based learning model and for strong competition, it becomes a self-organizing map. Thus, in the regime of weak competition the receptive fields are shaped by the second order statistics of the input patterns, whereas in the regime of strong competition, the higher moments and "features" of the individual patterns become important. When correlated localized stimuli from two eyes drive the cortical development we find (i) that a topographic map and binocular, localized receptive fields emerge when the degree of competition exceeds a critical value and (ii) that receptive fields exhibit eye dominance beyond a second critical value. For anti-correlated activity between the eyes, the second order statistics drive the system to develop ocular dominance even for weak competition, but no topography emerges. Topography is established only beyond a critical degree of competition.

1 Introduction

Several models have been proposed in the past to explain the activity depending development of ocular dominance (OD) in the visual cortex. Some models make the ansatz of linear interactions between cortical model neurons [2, 7], other approaches assume competitive winner-take-all dynamics with intracortical interactions [3, 5]. The mechanisms that lead to ocular dominance critically depend on this choice. In linear activity models, second order correlations of the input patterns determine the receptive fields. Nonlinear competitive models like the self-organizing map, however, use higher order statistics of the input stimuli and map their features. In this contribution, we introduce a general nonlinear

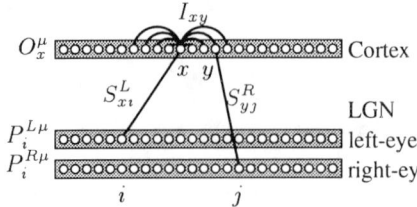

Figure 1: Model for OD development: the input patterns $P_i^{L\mu}$ and $P_i^{R\mu}$ in the LGN drive the Hebbian modification of the cortical afferent synaptic weights S_{xi}^L and S_{xi}^R. Cortical neurons are in competition and interact with effective strengths I_{xy}. Locations in the LGN are indexed i or j, cortical locations are labeled x or y.

Hebbian development rule which interpolates the degree of lateral competition and allows us to systematically study the role of non-linearity in the lateral interactions on pattern formation and the transition between two classes of models.

2 Ocular Dominance Map Development by Hebbian Learning

Figure 1 shows our basic model framework for ocular dominance development. We consider two input layers in the lateral geniculate nucleus (LGN). The input patterns $\mu = 1, \ldots, U$ on these layers originate from the two eyes and completely characterize the input statistics (the mean activity $\bar{P}$ is identical for all input neurons). The afferent synaptic connection strengths of cortical cells develop according to a generalized Hebbian learning rule with learning rate η.

$$\Delta S_{xi}^{L\mu} = \eta \sum_y I_{xy} \bar{O}_y^\mu P_i^{L\mu} \quad \text{subject to} \quad \sum_i (S_{xi}^L)^\nu + (S_{xi}^R)^\nu = \text{const.} \quad \forall x \quad (1)$$

An analogous rule is used for the connections from the right eyes S_{xi}^R. We use $\nu = 2$ in the following and rescale the length of each neurons receptive field weight vector to a constant length after a learning step. The model includes effective cortical interactions I_{xy} for the development of smooth cortical maps that spread the output activities $\bar{O}_x^\mu$ in the neighborhood of neuron x (with a mean $\bar{I} = \frac{1}{N}\sum_x I_{xy}$ for N output neurons). The cortical output signals are connectionist neurons with a nonlinear activation function $g(.)$,

$$\bar{O}_y^\mu = g(H_y^\mu) = \frac{\exp(\beta H_y^\mu)}{\sum_z \exp(\beta H_z^\mu)} \quad \text{with} \quad H_y^\mu = \sum_j (S_{yj}^L P_j^{L\mu} + S_{yj}^R P_j^{R\mu}), \quad (2)$$

which models the effect of cortical response sharpening and competition for an input stimulus. The degree of competition is determined by the parameter β. Such dynamics may result as an effect of local excitation and long range inhibition within the cortical layer [6, 1], and in the limits of weak and strong competition, we recover two known types of developmental models—the correlation based learning model and the self-organizing map.

2.1 From Linear Neurons to Winner-take-all Networks

In the limit $\beta \to 0$ of weak cortical competition, the output $\bar{O}_y^\mu$ becomes a linear function of the input. A Taylor series expansion around $\beta = 0$ yields a correlation-based-learning (CBL) rule in the average over all patterns

$$\Delta S_{ix}^L = \eta\beta \sum_{z,j} \frac{1}{N}(I_{xz} - \bar{I})(S_{zj}^L C_{ji}^{LL} + S_{zj}^R C_{ji}^{RL}) + \text{const.},$$

where $C_{ji}^{RL} = \frac{1}{U}\sum_\mu P_j^{R\mu} P_i^{L\mu}$ is the correlation function of the input patterns. Ocular dominance development under this rule requires correlated activity between inputs from

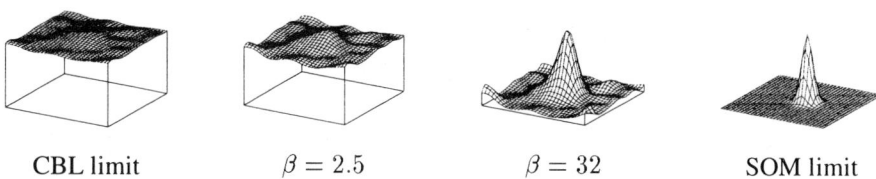

| CBL limit | $\beta = 2.5$ | $\beta = 32$ | SOM limit |

Figure 2: The network response for different degrees of cortical competition: the plots show the activity rates $\sum_y I_{xy} \bar{O}_y^\mu$ for a network of cortical output neurons (the plots are scaled to have equal maxima). Each gridpoint represents the activity of one neuron on a 16×16 grid. The interactions I_{xy} are Gaussian (variance 2.25 grid points) and all neurons are stimulated with the same Gaussian stimulus (variance 2.25). The neurons have Gaussian receptive fields (variance $\sigma^2 = 4.5$) in a topographic map with additive noise (uniformly distributed with amplitude 10 times the maximum weight value).

within one eye and anti-correlated activity (or uncorrelated activity with synaptic competition) between the two eyes [2, 4]. It is important to note, however, that CBL models cannot explain the emergence of a topographic projection. The topography has to be hard-wired from the outset of the development process which is usually implemented by an "arbor function" that forces all non-topographic synaptic weights to zero.

Strong competition with $\beta \to \infty$, on the other hand, leads to a self-organizing map [3, 5],

$$\Delta S_{ix}^{L\mu} = \eta I_{xq(\mu)} P_i^{L\mu} \quad \text{with} \quad q(\mu) = \text{argmax}_y \sum_j (S_{yj}^L P_j^{L\mu} + S_{yj}^R P_j^{R\mu}) .$$

Models of this type use the higher order statistics of the input patterns and map the important features of the input. In the SOM limit, the output activity pattern is identical in shape for all input stimuli. The input influences only the *location* of the activity on the output layer but does not affect its shape.

For intermediate values of β, the *shape* of the output activity patterns depends on the input. The activity of neurons with receptive fields that match the input stimulus better than others is amplified, whereas the activity of poorly responding neurons is further suppressed as shown in figure 2. On the one hand, the resulting output activity profiles for intermediate β may be biologically more realistic than the winner-take-all limit case. On the other hand, the difference between the linear response case (low β) and the nonlinear competition (intermediate β) is important in the Hebbian development process—it yields qualitatively different results as we show in the next section.

2.2 Simulations of Ocular Dominance Development

In the following, we study the transition from linear CBL models to winner-take-all SOM networks for intermediate values of β. We consider input patterns that are localized and show ocular dominance

$$P_i^{L\mu} = \frac{0.5 + eye^L(\mu)}{2\pi\sigma^2} \exp\left(-\frac{(i - loc(\mu))^2}{2\sigma^2}\right) \quad \text{with} \quad eye^L(\mu) = -eye^R(\mu) \quad (3)$$

Each stimulus μ is of Gaussian shape centered on a random position $loc(\mu)$ within the input layer and the neuron index i is interpreted as a two-dimensional location vector in the input layer. The parameter $eye(\mu)$ sets the eye dominance for each stimulus. $eye = 0$ produces binocular stimuli and $eye = \pm\frac{1}{2}$ results in uncorrelated left and right eye activities.

We have simulated the development of receptive fields and cortical maps according to equations 1 and 2 (see figure 3) for square grids of model neurons with periodic boundary conditions, Gaussian cortical interactions, and OD stimuli (equation 3). The learning

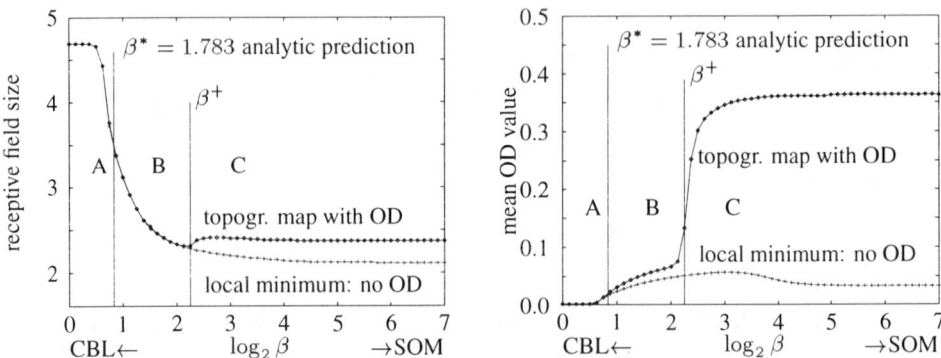

Figure 3: Simulation of ocular dominance development for a varying degree of cortical competition β in a network of 16×16 neurons in each layer. The figure shows receptive fields sizes (left) and mean OD value (right) as a function of cortical competition β. Each point in the figure represents one simulation with 30000 pattern presentations. The cortical interactions are Gaussian with a variance of $\gamma^2 = 2.25$ grid points. The Gaussian input stimuli are 5.66 times stronger in one eye than in the other (equation 3 with $\sigma^2 = 2.25$, $eye(\mu) = \pm 0.35$). The synaptic weights are intialized with a noisy topographic map (curves labeled "no OD") and additionally with ocular dominance stripes (curves labeled "with OD"). To determine the receptive field size we have applied a Gaussian fit to all receptive field profiles S_{ix}^L and S_{ix}^L and averaged the standard deviation (in grid points) over all neurons x. The mean OD value is given by $\frac{1}{N}\sum_x |\sum_i (S_{ix}^L - S_{ix}^R)/\sum_i (S_{ix}^L + S_{ix}^R)|$.

rate is set at the first stimulus presentation to change the weights of the best responding neuron by half a percent. After each learning step the weights are rescaled to enforce the constraint from equation 1.

The simulations yield the results expected in the CBL and SOM limit cases (small and large β) for initially constant synaptic weight values with 5 percent additional noise. In the CBL limit, our particular choice of input patterns does not lead to the development of ocular dominance, because the necessary conditions for the input pattern correlations are not satisfied—the pattern correlations and interactions are all positive. Instead, the learning rule has only one fixpoint with uniform synaptic weights—unstructured receptive fields that cover the whole input layer. In the SOM limit, our set of stimuli leads to the emergence of a topographic projection with localized receptive fields and ocular dominance stripes. The topographic maps often develop defects which can be avoided by an annealing scheme. Instead of annealing β or the cortical interaction range, however, we initialize the weights with a topographic projection and some additive noise. This is a common assumption in cortical development models [2], because the fibers from the LGN first innervate the visual cortex already in a coarsely topographic order.

For intermediate degrees of cortical competition, we find sharp transitions between the CBL and SOM states and distinguish three parameter regimes (see figure 3). For weak competition (A) all receptive fields are unstructured and cover the whole input layer. At some critical β^*, the receptive fields begin to form a topographic projection from the geniculate to the cortical layer. This projection (B) has no stable ocular dominance stripes, but a small degree of ocular dominance that fluctuates continuously. For yet stronger competition (C), a cortical map with stable ocular dominance stripes emerges.

The simulations, however, show that a topographic map without ocular dominance remains a stable attractor of the learning dynamics (C). For increasing competition its basin of attraction becomes smaller, and smaller learning rates are necessary in order to remain within the binocular state. On the one hand, simulations with slowly *increasing beta* lead to a to-

Role of Lateral Cortical Competition in Ocular Dominance Development 143

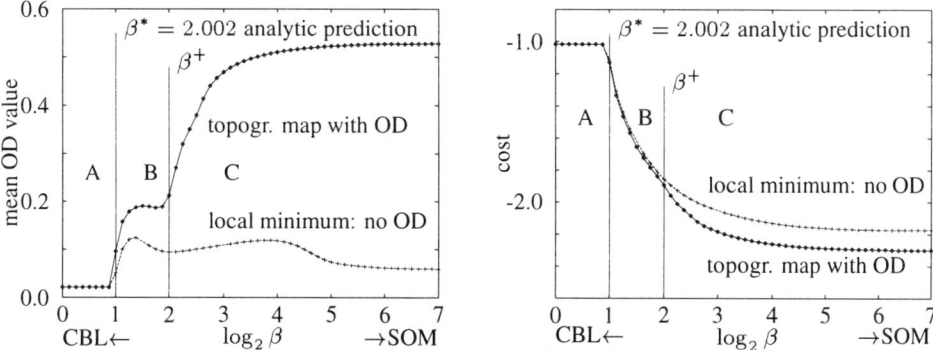

Figure 4: Simulations for the learning equation 5. The figure shows the mean ocular dominance (left) and the cost (right) as a function of β. The parameters are identical to figure 3 and $eye(\mu) = \pm 0.425$.

pographic map and ocular dominance stripes suddenly pop up somewhere in regime C—for small learning rates later than for large ones. On the other hand, in simulations with *decreasing* β and an initially topographic map with ocular dominance, we find a second critical β^+ at which the OD map becomes unstable.

To understand the system's properties better, we analytically predict the value β^*—the point where structured receptive fields emerge—and discuss the relation to cost functions to get some intuition about the value β^+ in the following paragraph.

2.3 Analysis of the Emergence of Structured Receptive Fields

For $\beta < \beta^*$ the system shows basically CBL properties—in our case constant weights and unstructured receptive fields. It is possible to study the stability of this state analytically. We consider the learning equation 1 under a hard renormalization constraint that enforces $\sum_{i=1}^{M}(S_{xi}^L)^2 + (S_{xi}^R)^2 = 2M\bar{S}^2$ by rescaling the weights after each learning step. A linear perturbation analysis of the learning rule around constant weights yields a critical degree of competition $\beta^* = (\bar{S}\lambda_{\max}^K \lambda_{\max}^I)^{-1}$ where $\bar{S}$ is the strength of the constant synaptic weights. $\lambda_{\max}^K$ is the largest eigenvalue of the input covariance matrix

$$\frac{1}{\bar{P}}\left(\begin{bmatrix} C_{ji}^{LL} & C_{ji}^{LR} \\ C_{ji}^{RL} & C_{ji}^{RR} \end{bmatrix} - \bar{P}^2\right),$$

which has to be diagonalized with respect to L and R, as well as with respect to i and j. The input correlation functions for the patterns from equation 3 are given by $C_{ji}^{LL} = C_{ji}^{RR} = (\frac{1}{2} + 2eye^2)\frac{1}{U}G(i-j, 2\sigma^2)$ and $C_{ji}^{LR} = C_{ji}^{RL} = (\frac{1}{2} - 2eye^2)\frac{1}{U}G(i-j, 2\sigma^2)$ where $G(\vec{i}, \sigma^2)$ is a two-dimensional Gaussian with variance σ^2. The eigenvalues with respect to L and R in this symmetric case are the sum and difference terms of the correlation functions $K_{ij}^{\text{sum}} = \frac{1}{\bar{P}}(C_{ji}^{LL} + C_{ji}^{LR} - \bar{P}^2)$ and $K_{ij}^{\text{diff}} = \frac{1}{\bar{P}}(C_{ji}^{LL} - C_{ji}^{LR})$. The term K_{ij}^{sum} is larger for positive input correlations and in the next step we have to find the eigenvalues of this matrix. For periodic boundary conditions and in the limit of large networks, we can approximate the eigenvalue by the fourier transform of the Gaussian and finally obtain $\lambda_{\max}^K = \exp\left(-(\sigma 2\pi/m)^2\right)$ (for a square grid of $M = m \times m$ neurons). $\lambda_{\max}^I$ is the largest eigenvalue of $(\frac{1}{NI}I_{xz} - \frac{1}{N})$ and Gaussian cortical interactions I_{xy} with variance γ^2 on $N = n \times n$ output neurons yield $\lambda_{\max}^I = \exp\left(-\frac{1}{2}(\gamma 2\pi/n)^2\right)$. Stronger competition beyond the point β^* leads to the formation of structured receptive fields. It is interesting to note, that the critical β^* does not depend on $eye(\mu)$, the strength of ocularity in the input patterns. The predicted value for β^* is plotted in figure 3 and matches the transition found in the simulations.

2.4 Hebbian Development With a Global Objective Function

The learning equation 1 does not optimize a global cost function [5]. To understand the dynamics of the OD development better and to interpret the transition at $\beta*$, we derive a learning rule very similar to equation 1 that minimizes the global cost function E,

$$E = \frac{1}{U}\sum_{\mu,x} O_x^\mu \text{cost}_x^\mu \quad \text{with} \quad \text{cost}_x^\mu = -\sum_{y,j} I_{xy}(S_{yj}^L P_j^{L\mu} + S_{yj}^R P_j^{R\mu}). \quad (4)$$

We minimize this cost function in a stochastic network of binary output neurons O_x^μ that compete for the input stimuli, i.e. one output neuron is active at any given time. The probability for a neuron y to become active in response to pattern μ depends on its advantage in cost over the currently active neuron x:

$$P(O_x^\mu = 1 \to O_y^\mu = 1) = \frac{\exp[-\beta(\text{cost}_x^\mu - \text{cost}_y^\mu)]}{\sum_z \exp[-\beta(\text{cost}_x^\mu - \text{cost}_z^\mu)]}.$$

This type of output dynamics leads to a Boltzmann probability distribution for the state of the system. We marginalize over all possible network outputs and derive a learning rule by gradient descent on the log likelihood of a particular set of synaptic connections (subject to $\sum_i (S_{xi}^L)^n + (S_{xi}^R)^n = \text{const.}$).

$$\Delta S_{xi}^L = \eta \frac{\partial}{\partial S_{xi}^L} \log \text{Prob}(\{S_{xi}^L, S_{xi}^R\}) = \frac{\partial}{\partial S_{xi}^L} \log \sum_{\{O_x^\mu\}} \frac{1}{Z} \exp(-\beta E).$$

Finally, we obtain a learning rule that contains the expectation values $\bar{O}_x^\mu$ (or mean fields) of the binary outputs,

$$\Delta S_{xi}^{L\mu} = \eta \sum_y I_{xy} \bar{O}_y^\mu P_i^{L\mu} \quad \text{with} \quad \bar{O}_x^\mu = \frac{\exp(\beta \sum_{y,j} I_{xy}(S_{yj}^L P_j^{L\mu} + S_{yj}^R P_j^{R\mu}))}{\sum_z \exp(\beta \sum_{y,j} I_{zy}(S_{yj}^L P_j^{L\mu} + S_{yj}^R P_j^{R\mu}))}. \quad (5)$$

This learning rule is almost identical to equation 1, it only contains an additional cortical interaction inside the output term $\bar{O}_x^\mu$, but it has the advantage of an underlying cost function.

Figure 4 shows the development of ocular dominance according to equation 5 and the associated cost is plotted for each state of the system. The value β^* of the first transition is calculated analogously to the previous section and $\lambda_{\max}^I$ becomes the maximum eigenvalue of the matrix $(\frac{1}{NI} \sum_y I_{xy} I_{yz} - \bar{I})$ which is $\lambda_{\max}^I = \exp\left(-(\gamma 2\pi/m)^2\right)$. Around β^+ a topographic map without ocular dominance is a stable state and it remains stable for larger β. In addition, a different minimum of the cost function equation 4 emerges at β^+: an ocular dominance map with a lower associated cost. This shows that an ocular dominance map becomes the preferred state of the system beyond β^+ although the binocular topographic map is still stable. In the SOM limit $\beta \to \infty$ the binocular topographic map becomes unstable and ocular dominance stripes develop.

The value β^+ marks the first emergence of an ocular dominance map. For the simulations in the figures 3 and 4 we have used positive correlations between the two eyes—a realistic assumption for OD map development. For weaker correlations ($eye(\mu)$ approaches $\pm\frac{1}{2}$), β^+ decreases. For anti-correlated stimuli, an ocular dominance map develops even in the CBL limit [4] (this, however, requires additional model assumptions like inhibition between the layers within the LGN). Such a map has no topographic structure (if not imposed by an arbor function) but mostly monocular receptive fields. The value β^* is not affected directly by those changes and the monocular receptive fields localize, if β^* is exceeded. Consequently, the "feature" OD emerges, if it is dominant in the relevant pattern statistics—for anti-correlated eyes around $\beta = 0$, and for positive between-eye-correlations only in the regime of higher order moments at β^+.

3 Conclusions

We have introduced a model for cortical development with a variable degree of cortical competition. For weak competition it has CBL models, for strong competition the SOM as limit cases. Localized stimuli with ocular dominance require a minimum degree of cortical competition to develop a topographic map, and a stronger degree of competition for the emergence of ocular dominance stripes. Anti-correlated activity between the two eyes lets OD emerge for weak competition and localized fields only beyond a critical degree of competition.

A Taylor series expansion of the learning equation 1 yields a CBL model that uses only second order input statistics. For increasing β the higher order terms become significant which consist of the higher moments of the input patterns. In this contribution, we have used only simple activity blobs in two eyes, but it is well known that in the winner-take-all limit features like orientation selectivity can emerge as well [3].

The soft cortical competition in our model implements a mechanism of response sharpening in which the input patterns do still influence the output pattern shape. This should relax the biologically unplausible assumption of winner-take-all dynamics of SOM models and yields similar ocular dominance maps. Cortical microcircuits—local cortical amplifiers—have been proposed as a cortical module of computation [6]. Our model suggests that such circuits may be important to sharpen the responses during the *development* and to permit the emergence of feature mapping simple cell receptive fields.

Our model shows that small changes in the degree of cortical competition may result in qualitative changes of the emerging receptive fields and cortical maps. Such changes in competition could be a result of the maturation of the intra-cortical connectivity. A slowly increasing degree of cortical competition could make the cortical neurons sensitive to more and more complex features of the input stimuli.

Acknowledgements

This work was supported by the Boehringer Ingelheim Fonds (C. Piepenbrock) and by DFG grant Ob 102/2-1.

References

[1] S. Amari. Dynamics of pattern formation in lateral-inhibition type neural fields. *Biol. Cyb.*, 27:77–87, 1977.

[2] K. D. Miller, J. B. Keller, and M. P. Stryker. Ocular dominance column development: Analysis and simulation. *Science*, 245:605–615, 1989.

[3] K. Obermayer, H. Ritter, and K. Schulten. A principle for the formation of the spatial structure of cortical feature maps. *Proc. Nat. Acad. Sci. USA*, 87:8345–49, 1990.

[4] C. Piepenbrock, H. Ritter, and K. Obermayer. The joint development of orientation and ocular dominance: Role of constraints. *Neur. Comp.*, 9:959–970, 1997.

[5] M. Riesenhuber, H.-U. Bauer, and T. Geisel. Analyzing phase transitions in high-dimensional self-organizing maps. *Biol. Cyb.*, 75:397–407, 1996.

[6] D. C. Somers, S. B. Nelson, and M. Sur. An emergent model of orientation selectivity in cat visual cortical simple cells. *J. Neurosci.*, 15:5448–5465, 1995.

[7] A. L. Yuille, J. A. Kolodny, and C. W. Lee. Dimension reduction, generalized deformable models and the development of ocularity and orientation. *Neur. Netw.*, 9:309–319, 1996.

Multi-electrode spike sorting by clustering transfer functions

Dmitry Rinberg **Hanan Davidowitz** **Naftali Tishby**[*]

NEC Research Institute
4 Independence Way
Princeton, NJ 08540
E-mail: {dima,hanan,tishby}@research.nj.nec.com
Categories: spike sorting, population coding, signal processing.

Abstract

A new paradigm is proposed for sorting spikes in multi-electrode data using ratios of transfer functions between cells and electrodes. It is assumed that for every cell and electrode there is a stable linear relation. These are dictated by the properties of the tissue, the electrodes and their relative geometries. The main advantage of the method is that it is insensitive to variations in the shape and amplitude of a spike. Spike sorting is carried out in two separate steps. First, templates describing the statistics of each spike type are generated by clustering transfer function ratios then spikes are detected in the data using the spike statistics. These techniques were applied to data generated in the escape response system of the cockroach.

1 Introduction

Simultaneous recording of activity from many neurons can greatly expand our understanding of how information is coded in neural systems[1]. Multiple electrodes are often used to measure the activity in neural tissue and have become a standard tool in neurophysiology [2, 3, 4]. Since every electrode is in a different position it will measure a different contribution from each of the different neurons. Simply stated, the problem is this: how can these complex signals be untangled to determine when each individual cell fired? This problem is difficult because, a) the objects being classified are very similar and often noisy, b) spikes coming from the same cell can

---

[*]Permanent address: Institute of Computer Science and Center for Neural Computation, The Hebrew University, Jerusalem, Israel. Email: tishby@cs.huji.ac.il

vary in both shape and amplitude, depending on the previous activity of the cell and c) spikes can overlap in time, resulting in even more complex temporal patterns.

Current approaches to spike sorting are based primarily on the presumed consistency of the spike shape and amplitude for a given cell [5, 6]. This is clearly the only possible basis for sorting using a single electrode. Multiple electrodes, however, provide additional *independent* information through the differences in the way the same neuron is detected by the different electrodes. The same spike measured on different electrodes can differ in amplitude, shape and its relative timing. These differences can depend on the specific cell, the electrode and the media between them. They can be characterized by linear transfer functions that are invariant to changes in the overall spike waveform. In this paper the importance of this information is highlighted by using *only* the differences in how signals are measured on different electrodes. It is then shown that clusters of similar *differences* correspond to the same neuron. It should be emphasized that in a full treatment this transfer function information will be combined with other cues to sort spikes.

2 Spikes, spectra and noise

The basic assumption behind the spike sorting approach described here is that the medium between each neuron-electrode pair can be characterized by a linear system that remains fixed during the course of an experiment. This assumption is justified by the approximately linear dielectric properties of the electrode and its surrounding nerve tissues.

Linear systems are described by their phase and amplitude response to pure frequencies, namely, by their complex transfer function $H(\omega) = O(\omega)/I(\omega)$, where $I(\omega)$ and $O(\omega)$ are the complex spectra (i.e. Fourier transform, henceforth called spectrum) of the input and output of the system, respectively. In the experiments described here the input signal is the spectrum of the action potential generated by cell j, denoted by $S_j(\omega)$ and the output signal is the spectrum of the voltage measured at electrode μ, denoted by $V^\mu(\omega)$. The transfer function of the system that links $S_j(\omega)$ and $V^\mu(\omega)$ is then defined as $H^\mu_j(\omega) = V^\mu(\omega)/S_j(\omega)$.

If the transfer functions are fixed in time, the ratio between the complex spectrum of any spike from cell j as detected by electrodes μ and ν, $V^\mu(\omega)$ and $V^\nu(\omega)$, is given by,

$$T^{\mu\nu}_j(\omega) \equiv \frac{V^\mu(\omega)}{V^\nu(\omega)} = \frac{H^\mu_j(\omega)S_j(\omega)}{H^\nu_j(\omega)S_j(\omega)} = \frac{H^\mu_j(\omega)}{H^\nu_j(\omega)}, \qquad (1)$$

which is independent of the cell action potential spectrum $S_j(\omega)$, provided that the spike was detected by both electrodes.

Thus, even if a spike varies in shape and amplitude, $T^{\mu\nu}_j(\omega)$ will remain a fixed complex function of frequency. This ratio is also invariant with respect to time translations of the spikes. In addition, the frequency components are asymptotically uncorrelated for stationary processes, which justifies treating the frequency components as statistically independent[7]. The idea behind the approach described here is shown in Figure 1.

In real experiments, however, noise can corrupt the invariance of $T^{\mu\nu}_j$. There are several possible sources of noise in experiments of this kind: a) fluctuations in the transfer function, b) changes in the spike shape, ς_j and c) electrical and electrochemical noise, n^μ.

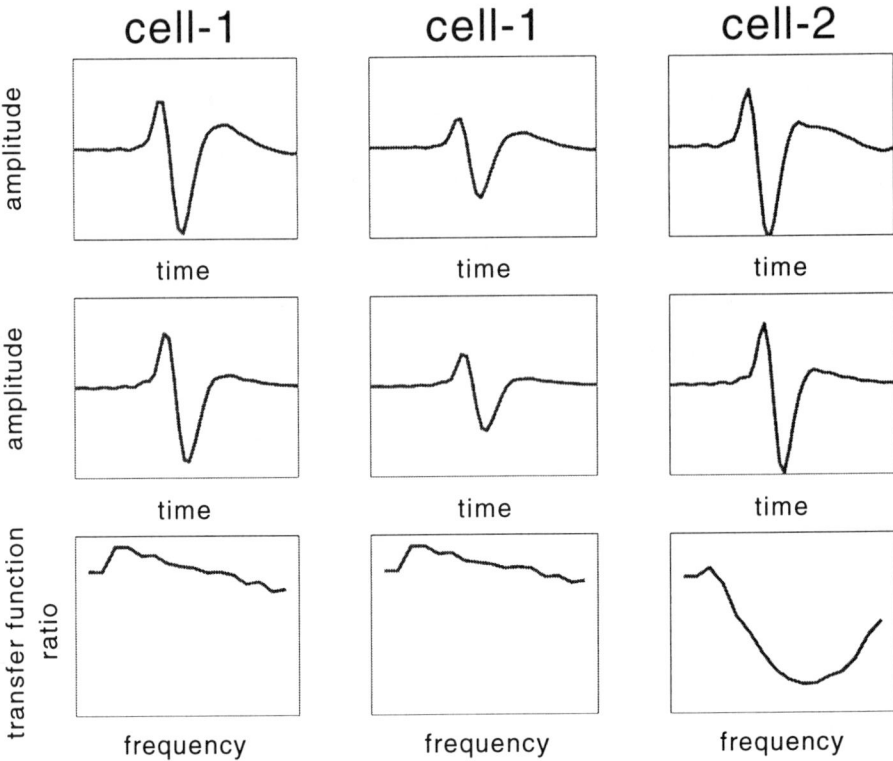

Figure 1: The idea behind spike sorting by clustering of transfer function ratios. Two spikes from the same cell (cell-1) may vary in shape/amplitude during bursting activity, for example. Although the spike shapes may differ, the transfer functions relating them to the electrodes do not change so the transfer function ratios are similar (two left columns). A different cell (cell-2) has a different transfer function ratio even though the spikes shapes themselves are similar to those of cell-1 (right column).

If H_j^μ varies slowly with time, the transfer function noise is small relative to ς_j, n^ν and n^ν. $T_j^{\mu\nu}$ can then be expanded to first order in ς_j, n^μ and n^ν as

$$T_j^{\mu\nu}(\omega,t) = \frac{H_j^\mu(S_j+\varsigma_j)+n^\mu}{H_j^\nu(S_j+\varsigma_j)+n^\nu} = \frac{H_j^\mu}{H_j^\nu}\left(1+\frac{n^\mu}{H_j^\mu S_j}-\frac{n^\nu}{H_j^\nu S_j}\right), \qquad (2)$$

which is independent of ς_j. Since the noise, n^μ, is uncorrelated with the spike signal, S_j, the variance at each frequency component can be considered to be Gaussian with equal variances on the real and imaginary axes. Thus the mean of $T_j^{\mu\nu}$ will be independent of S_j, ς_j and n^μ while its variance will be inversely proportional to S_j.

3 A model system: the escape response of the cockroach

These techniques were tested on a relatively simple neural system - the escape response system of the American cockroach. The escape behaviour, which has been studied extensively [9, 10, 11], is activated when the insect detects air currents

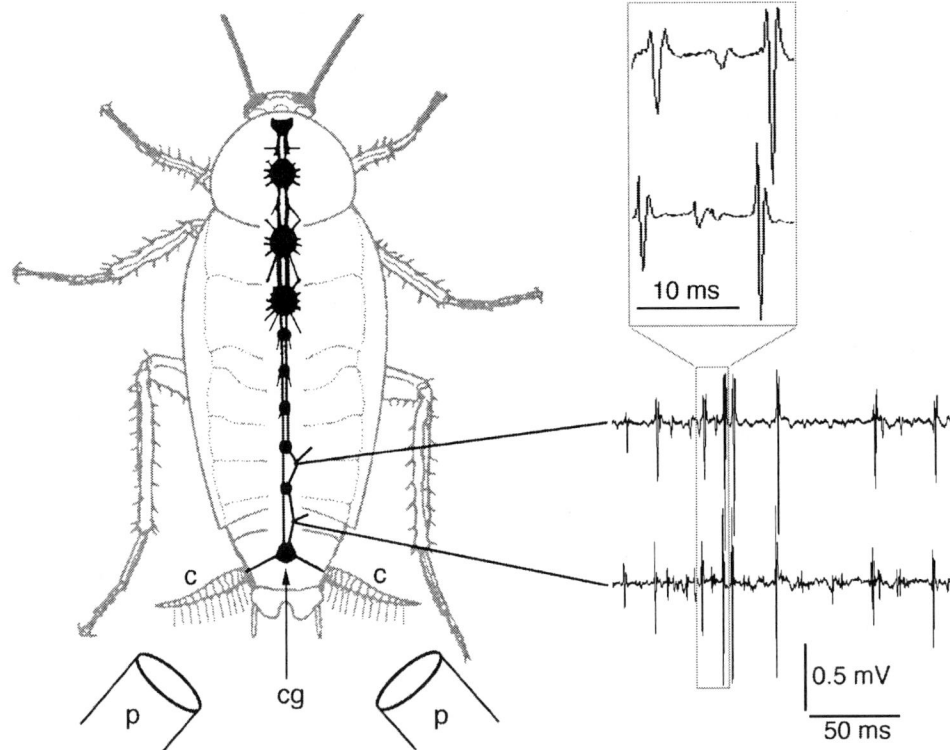

Figure 2: A schematic representation of the experiment. Typical raw data measured on two electrodes is shown at right. Relative time delays are evident in the inset, but are not a necessary condition for the sorting techniques described here. Abbreviations are: p-puffers, cg-circal ganglion, c-cerci.

produced by the movements of a predator. The insect detects the approach of a predator, determines the direction of approach and starts running in an appropriate direction. The cockroach does this by detecting the movement of several hundred fine hairs located on two appendages, called cerci, protruding from the posterior end of the animal. Each of these hairs is connected to a single neuron. Axons from these cells converge on a dense neuropil called the cercal ganglion (cg), where directional information is extracted and conveyed to the rest of the body by axons in the abdominal nerve. This is shown schematically in Figure 2.

This system proved to be well suited as a first test of the sorting technique. The system is simple enough so that it is not overwhelming (since only 7 neurons are known to contribute to the code) but complex enough to really test the approach. In addition, the nerve cords are linear in geometry, easily accessible and very stable.

Male cockroaches (*Periplaneta americana*) were dissected from the dorsal side to expose the nerve cord. The left and right cords were gently separated and two tungsten wire electrodes were hooked onto the connective about 2 mm apart, separated by abdominal ganglia. The stimulus was presented by two loudspeakers driving two miniature wind tunnels pointed at the cerci, at 90 degrees from one another as shown in Figure 2. Recordings typically lasted for several hours. Data were collected with a sampling frequency of $2 \cdot 10^4$ S/s which was sufficient to preserve the high frequency components of the spikes.

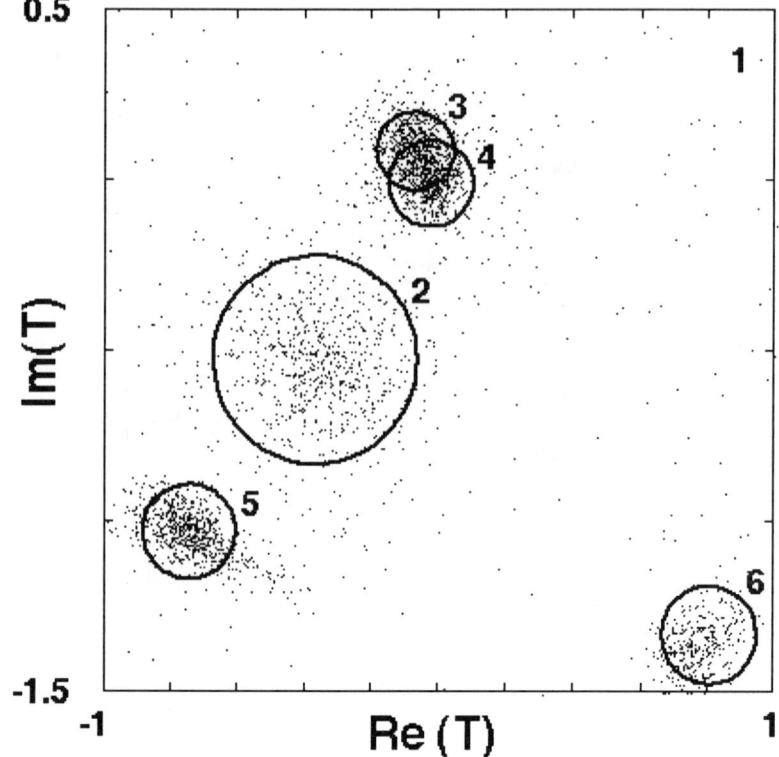

Figure 3: Real and imaginary parts of $T_j^{\mu\nu}$ a single ω. The circles have centers (radii) equal to the average (variance) of $T_j^{\mu\nu}$ at $\omega = 248.7$ rad s^{-1}. Note that while some clusters seem to overlap at this frequency they may be well seperated at others. Cluster-1 is dispersed throughout the complex plane and its variance is well beyond the range of this plot.

4 Clustering and the detection of spikes

The spike sorting algorithm described here is done is two separate stages. First, a statistical model of the individual spike types is built from "clean" examples found in the data. Only then are occurrences of these spikes detected in the multi-electrode data. This two-step arrangement allows a great deal of flexibility by disconnecting the clustering from the detection. For example, here the clustering was done on transfer function ratios while the detection was done on full complex spectra. These stages are described below in more detail.

4.1 The clustering phase

First, the multi-electrode recording is chopped into 3 ms long frames using a sliding window. Frames that have either too low total energy or too high energy at the window edges are discarded. This leaves frames that are energetic in their central 2 ms and are assumed to carry one spike. No attempt is made to find all spikes in the data. Instead, the idea is to generate a set of candidate spike types from clean frames.

Once a large collection of candidate spikes is found, $T_j^{\mu\nu}(\omega)$ is calculated for every

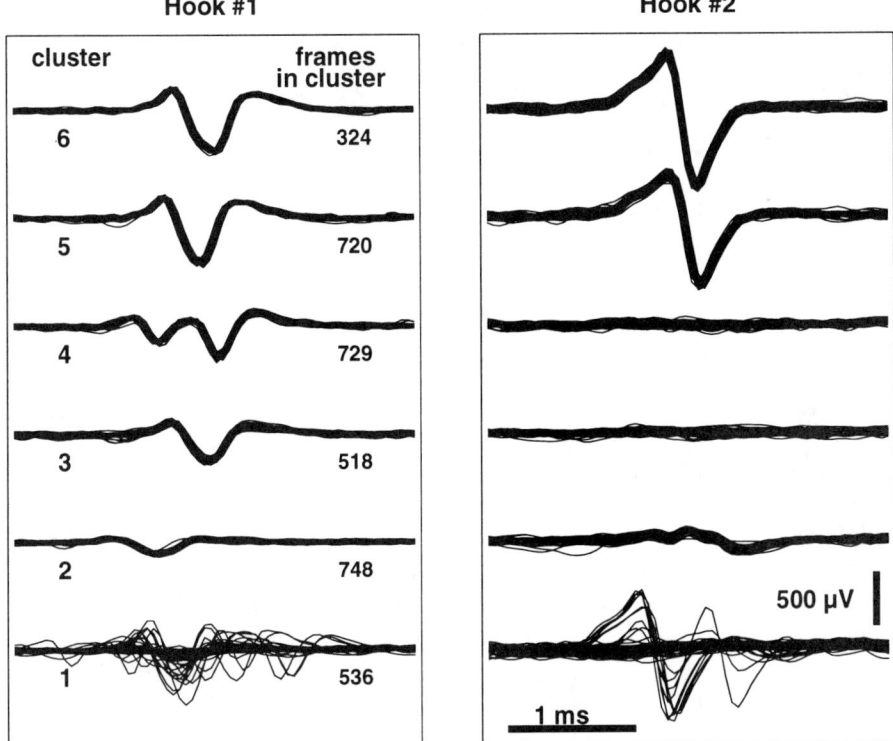

Figure 4: Results of clustering spikes using transfer function ratios. Note that although cluster-5 and cluster-6 are similarly shaped on hook-1 they are time shifted on hook-3. Cluster-1 is made up of overlaps which are dealt with in the detection phase.

spike. These are then grouped together into clusters containing similar $T_j^{\mu\nu}(\omega)$. Results of the clustering are shown in Figure 3 while the corresponding waveforms are shown in Figure 4. Full complex spectra are then used to build a statistical model of the different spike types, $\{V_j^\mu(\omega), \sigma_j^\mu(\omega)\}$, which represent each cell's action potential as it appears on each of the electrodes.

4.2 The detection phase

Once the cluster statistics are determined, an independent detection algorithm is used. The data is again broken into short frames but now the idea is to find which of the spike types (represented by the different clusters found in the previous steps) best represents the data in that frame. Each frame can contain either noise, a spike or an overlap of 2 spikes (overlaps of more than 2 spikes are not dealt with). This part is not done on transfer function ratios because dealing with overlaps is more difficult.

5 Conclusion

A new method of spike sorting using transfer function ratios has been presented. In effect the sorting is done on the properties of the tissue between the neuron and the electrode and individual spike shapes become less important. This method may be useful when dealing with bursting cells where the transfer function ratios should remain constant even though the spike amplitude can change significantly. This technique may prove to be a useful tool for analysing multi-electrode data.

Acknowledgments

We are grateful to Bill Bialek for numerous enlightening discussions and many useful suggestions.

References

[1] M. Baringa. Listening in on the brain. *Science* **280**, 376-378 (1998).

[2] M. Abeles. *Corticonics*, (Cambridge University Press, Cambridge, 1991)

[3] B.L. McNaughton, J. O'Keefe and C.A. Barnes. The stereotrode: a new technique for simultaneous isolation of several single units in the central nervous system from multiple unit records. *Journal of Neuroscience Methods*, **8**, 391-7 (1983).

[4] M.L. Reece and J. O'Keefe. The tetrode: a new technique for multi-unit extracellular recording. *Society of Neuroscience Abstracts* **15**, 1250 (1989).

[5] M.S. Fee, P. P. Mitra and D. Kleinfeld. Automatic sorting of multiple unit neuronal signals in the presence of anisotropic and non-Gaussian variability. *Journal of Neuroscience Methods* **69**, 175-188 (1996).

[6] M.S. Lewicki. A review of methods for spike sorting: the detection and classification of neural potentials. *Network: Compututational Neural Systems* **9**, R53-R78 (1998).

[7] A. Papoulis. *Probability, random variables and stochastic processes*, (McGraw-Hill, New-York, 1965).

[8] M. Abeles and G.L. Gerstein. Detecting spatio-temporal firing patterns among simultaneously recorded single neurons. *Journal of Neurophysiology* **60**(3), 909-924 (1988).

[9] J.M. Camhi and A. Levy. The code for stimulus direction in a cell assembly in the cockroach. *Journal of Comparative Physiology A* **165**, 83-97 (1989).

[10] L. Kolton and J.M. Camhi. Cartesian representation of stimulus direction: parallel processing by two sets of giant interneurons in the cockroach. *Journal of Comparative Physiology A* **176**, 691-702 (1995).

[11] J. Westin, J.J. Langberg and J.M. Camhi. Responses of Giant Interneurons of the cockroach *Periplaneta americana* to wind puffs of different directions and velocities. *Journal of Comparative Physiology A* **121**, 307-324 (1977).

Modeling Surround Suppression in V1 Neurons with a Statistically-Derived Normalization Model

Eero P. Simoncelli
Center for Neural Science, and
Courant Institute of Mathematical Sciences
New York University
eero.simoncelli@nyu.edu

Odelia Schwartz
Center for Neural Science
New York University
odelia@cns.nyu.edu

Abstract

We examine the statistics of natural monochromatic images decomposed using a multi-scale wavelet basis. Although the coefficients of this representation are nearly decorrelated, they exhibit important higher-order statistical dependencies that cannot be eliminated with purely linear processing. In particular, rectified coefficients corresponding to basis functions at neighboring spatial positions, orientations and scales are highly correlated. A method of removing these dependencies is to *divide* each coefficient by a weighted combination of its rectified neighbors. Several successful models of the steady-state behavior of neurons in primary visual cortex are based on such "divisive normalization" computations, and thus our analysis provides a theoretical justification for these models. Perhaps more importantly, the statistical measurements explicitly specify the weights that should be used in computing the normalization signal. We demonstrate that this weighting is qualitatively consistent with recent physiological experiments that characterize the suppressive effect of stimuli presented outside of the classical receptive field. Our observations thus provide evidence for the hypothesis that early visual neural processing is well matched to these statistical properties of images.

An appealing hypothesis for neural processing states that sensory systems develop in response to the statistical properties of the signals to which they are exposed [e.g., 1, 2]. This has led many researchers to look for a means of deriving a model of cortical processing purely from a statistical characterization of sensory signals. In particular, many such attempts are based on the notion that neural responses should be statistically independent.

The pixels of digitized natural images are highly redundant, but one can always find a linear decomposition (i.e., principal component analysis) that eliminates second-order cor-

---

Research supported by an Alfred P. Sloan Fellowship to EPS, and by the Sloan Center for Theoretical Neurobiology at NYU.

relation. A number of researchers have used such concepts to derive linear receptive fields similar to those determined from physiological measurements [e.g., 16, 20]. The principal components decomposition is, however, not unique. Because of this, these early attempts required additional constraints, such as spatial locality and/or symmetry, in order to achieve functions approximating cortical receptive fields.

More recently, a number of authors have shown that one may use higher-order statistical measurements to uniquely constrain the choice of linear decomposition [e.g., 7, 9]. This is commonly known as *independent components analysis*. Vision researchers have demonstrated that the resulting basis functions are similar to cortical receptive fields, in that they are localized in spatial position, orientation and scale [e.g., 17, 3]. The associated coefficients of such decompositions are (second-order) decorrelated, highly kurtotic, and generally more independent than principal components.

But the response properties of neurons in primary visual cortex are not adequately described by linear processes. Even if one chooses to describe only the mean firing rate of such neurons, one must at a minimum include a rectifying, saturating nonlinearity. A number of authors have shown that a gain control mechanism, known as *divisive normalization*, can explain a wide variety of the nonlinear behaviors of these neurons [18, 4, 11, 12, 6]. In most instantiations of normalization, the response of each linear basis function is rectified (and typically squared) and then divided by a uniformly weighted sum of the rectified responses of all other neurons. Physiologically, this is hypothesized to occur via feedback shunting inhibitory mechanisms [e.g., 13, 5]. Ruderman and Bialek [19] have discussed divisive normalization as a means of increasing entropy.

In this paper, we examine the joint statistics of coefficients of an orthonormal wavelet image decomposition that approximates the independent components of natural images. We show that the coefficients are second-order decorrelated, but *not* independent. In particular, pairs of rectified responses are highly correlated. These pairwise dependencies may be eliminated by dividing each coefficient by a *weighted* combination of the rectified responses of other neurons, with the weighting determined from image statistics. We show that the resulting model, with all parameters determined from the statistics of a set of images, can account for recent physiological observations regarding suppression of cortical responses by stimuli presented outside the classical receptive field. These concepts have been previously presented in [21, 25].

1 Joint Statistics of Orthonormal Wavelet Coefficients

Multi-scale linear transforms such as wavelets have become popular for image representation. Typically, the basis functions of these representations are localized in spatial position, orientation, and spatial frequency (scale). The coefficients resulting from projection of natural images onto these functions are essentially uncorrelated. In addition, a number of authors have noted that wavelet coefficients have significantly non-Gaussian marginal statistics [e.g., 10, 14]. Because of these properties, we believe that wavelet bases provide a close approximation to the independent components decomposition for natural images. For the purposes of this paper, we utilize a typical separable decomposition, based on symmetric quadrature mirror filters taken from [23]. The decomposition is constructed by splitting an image into four subbands (lowpass, vertical, horizontal, diagonal), and then recursively splitting the lowpass subband.

Despite the decorrelation properties of the wavelet decomposition, it is quite evident that wavelet coefficients are *not* statistically independent [26, 22]. Large-magnitude coefficients (either positive or negative) tend to lie along ridges with orientation matching that of the subband. Large-magnitude coefficients also tend to occur at the same relative spatial locations in subbands at adjacent scales, and orientations. To make these statistical relationships

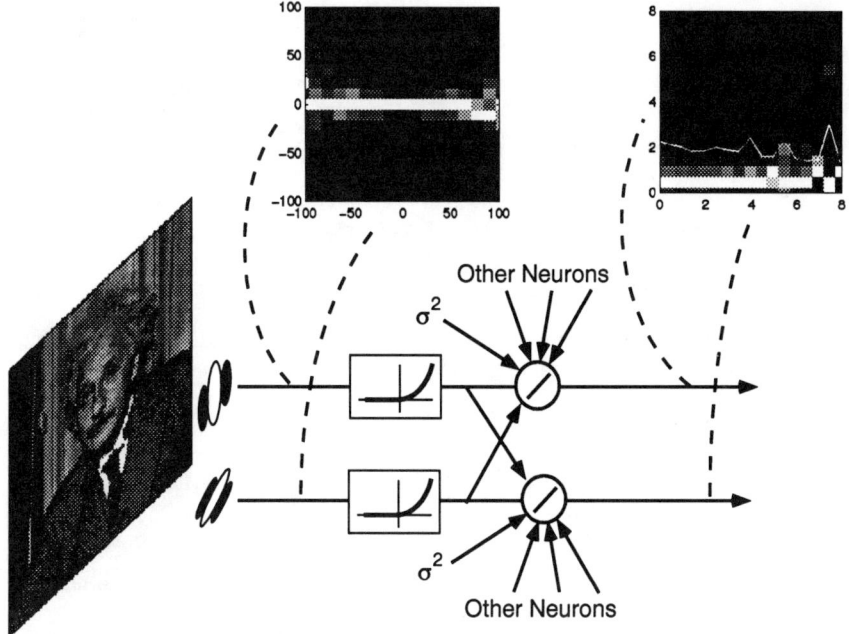

Figure 1: Illustration of image statistics as seen through two neighboring receptive fields. Left image: Joint conditional histogram of two linear coefficients. Pixel intensity corresponds to frequency of occurrence of a given pair of values, except that each column has been independently rescaled to fill the full intensity range. Right image: Joint histogram of divisively normalized coefficients (see text).

more explicit, the left panel of Fig. 1 shows a conditional histogram of coefficients associated with two neighboring receptive fields. Assuming stationarity, the statistics are gathered over all spatial positions of a single natural image. First, we see that the coefficients are well decorrelated: The expected value of the ordinate coefficient is approximately zero, independent of the value of the abscissa. But the *variance* of the ordinate clearly increases with the absolute value of the abscissa.

We have observed this type of dependency in pairs of coefficients at neighboring spatial positions, orientations and scales, and for a wide variety of imagery. We have previously used these relationships in applications of image compression, denoising, and synthesis [e.g., 22]. We have also shown that this dependency may be eliminated by *dividing*. Specifically, the squared coefficient, C^2 may be divided by a weighted sum of the neighboring squared coefficients plus a constant:

$$R = C^2 / \left[\sum_k w_k P_k^2 + \sigma^2 \right]. \tag{1}$$

The parameters $\{w_k\}$ and σ are chosen to minimize squared prediction error:

$$\{\hat{w}, \hat{\sigma}\} = \arg\min_{\{\vec{w}, \sigma\}} \mathbf{E}\left[C^2 - \sum_k w_k P_k^2 - \sigma^2 \right]^2,$$

where the P_k are the values of coefficients at adjacent spatial positions, orientations and scales, and $\mathbf{E}[\cdot]$ indicates expected value (computed by integrating over the full spatial

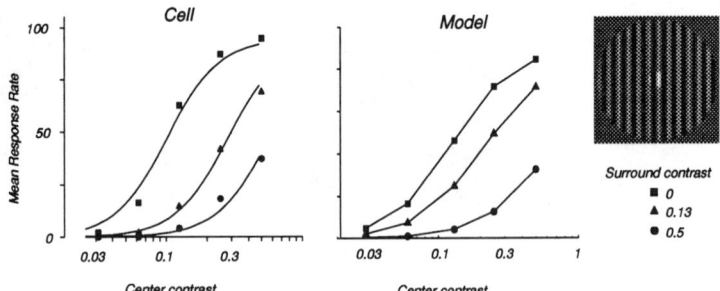

Figure 2: Response vs. center contrast, in the presence of a parallel surround stimulus of varying contrast. Physiological data from [8].

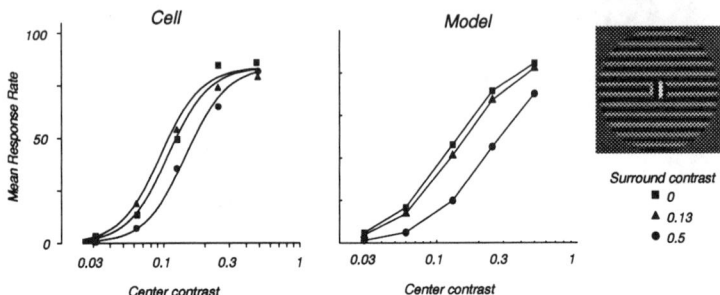

Figure 3: Response vs. center contrast in the presence of a perpendicular surround stimulus. Physiological data from [8].

extent of a set of images). A joint histogram of the square roots of two normalized coefficients is shown in the rightmost panel of Fig. 1, indicating that the resulting normalized components are nearly independent.

2 Physiological Comparisons

In this section, we examine predictions of the normalization model with weights determined from image statistics. The ability of normalization models to account for non-specific suppression within the classical receptive field has been documented [e.g., 12, 6]. Here we consider the influence of stimuli presented outside of the classical receptive field.

We examine electrophysiological data obtained from recordings of simple cells in area V1 of an anesthetized Macaque monkey in two different labs [8, 15]. In each example, an optimal drifting sinusoidal grating is presented in the classical receptive field of the neuron. Simultaneously, another drifting sine grating is presented in a large annular region surrounding the classical receptive field. Each experiment examines the effect of varying one parameter of the surround stimulus on the mean firing rate of the neuron.

For comparison, we show the normalized response, R, of a vertical basis function at the second recursion level of a wavelet pyramid, as specified by Eq. (1). Responses are averaged over all phases of the sinusoidal input, and scaled by a fixed constant α to produce response levels comparable to physiological responses. The normalization signal is a weighted combination of squared coefficients at two scales, all three orientations, and a spatial neighborhood of diameter 65 pixels (roughly 7 receptive fields). The normalization weights are optimized for the statistics of a set of three 512×512 images ("Goldhill",

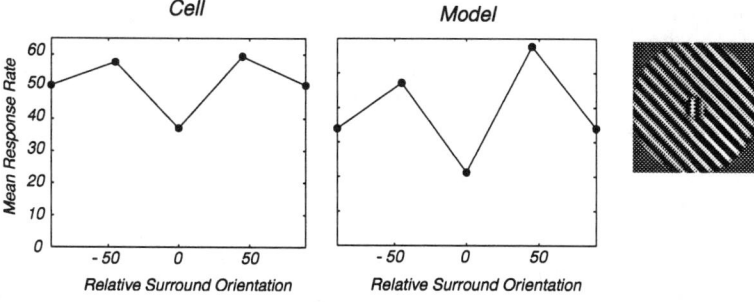

Figure 4: Response as a function of surround orientation. Physiological data from [8].

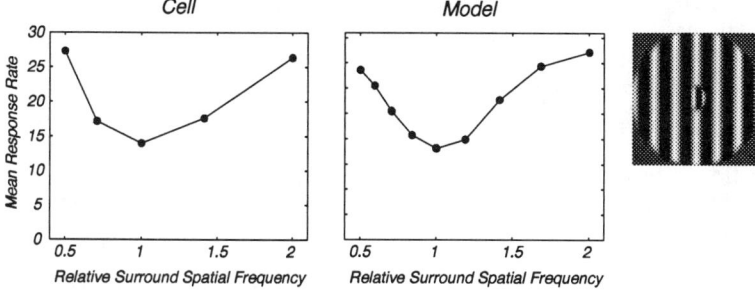

Figure 5: Response as a function of surround spatial frequency. Physiological data from [15].

"Boats", and "Lena").

The first two examples (Figs. 2 and 3) show response as a function of center stimulus contrast. Each curve corresponds to a different surround contrast. The physiological data are fit with a function of the form $R(c) = \alpha c^p/(c^p + \sigma^p)$. The model curves are less steep than those of the neurons, since the model uses a fixed exponent of two. As surround contrast increases, the entire curve shifts to the right (on a log scale), indicative of divisive suppression. The parallel surround stimulus produces a significantly larger shift than the perpendicular surround. In the model, this behavior is a direct consequence of the statistically-chosen normalization weights.

Figure 4 summarizes the suppressive effect of the surround (at the highest contrast) as a

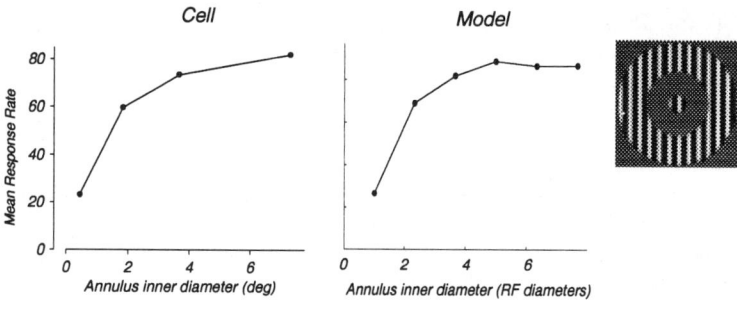

Figure 6: Response as a function of surround inner diameter. Physiological data from [8].

function of orientation. Figure 5 shows a similar behavior with respect to surround spatial frequency. The largest suppression is observed when the surround spatial frequency is the same as the center (i.e., the preferred spatial frequency of the cell). Figure 6 shows the effect of spatial proximity. As the surround stimulus is moved away from the receptive field, the suppressive effect is reduced.

3 Conclusions

We have presented a weighted normalization model for early visual processing. Both the form and the parameters of the model are specified by statistical measurements from natural images. Although the comparisons we have presented are somewhat anecdotal, we find the ability of this model to mimic physiological suppression behaviors quite remarkable.

Nevertheless, there are many tough issues to be resolved. Some of these are statistical. A fundamental question is whether statistical independence is a reasonable goal for neural processing. Additionally, one might ask if there is a statistical justification for cascaded sequences of normalization computations, as has been proposed in some models of cortical processing [e.g., 24]. More practically, the normalization procedure needs to be examined in the context of a proper independent components basis. The orthonormal wavelet approximation that we have used here has the disadvantage that the diagonal bands contain a mixture of orientations. Preliminary tests indicate substitution of a better basis produces qualitatively similar results.

An essential feature that is missing from our description is *time*. In particular, our normalization computation is simultaneous and instantaneous, and we have only modeled steady-state firing rates. A more realistic implementation would involve normalization of a population of neurons in parallel using feedback or lateral connections (necessarily delayed), and would thus introduce temporal dynamics as well as higher-order effects such as disinhibition. Furthermore, our modeling and implementation are based on still images and static receptive fields. This should be augmented to include spatio-temporal behaviors such as direction-selectivity: we suspect that these properties may be derived from statistics of image sequences.

Finally, an interesting issue is the plasticity of the normalization weights: Are these fixed (i.e., globally optimized over all images), or are they modified according to the statistics of the recent visual context? Our preliminary investigations indicate that such plasticity may account for adaptation effects that have been observed physiologically.

References

[1] F Attneave. Some informational aspects of visual perception. *Psych. Rev.*, 61:183–193, 1954.

[2] H B Barlow. Possible principles underlying the transformation of sensory messages. In W A Rosenblith, editor, *Sensory Communication*, page 217. MIT Press, Cambridge, MA, 1961.

[3] A J Bell and T J Sejnowski. The 'independent components' of natural scenes are edge filters. *Vision Research*, 37(23):3327–3338, 1997.

[4] A B Bonds. Role of inhibition in the specification of orientation selectivity of cells in the cat striate cortex. *Visual Neuroscience*, 2:41–55, 1989.

[5] M Carandini and D J Heeger. Summation and division by neurons in primate visual cortex. *Science*, 264:1333–1336, 1994.

[6] M Carandini, D J Heeger, and J A Movshon. Linearity and normalization in simple cells of the macaque primary visual cortex. *J. Neuroscience*, 17:8621–8644, 1997.

[7] J F Cardoso. Source separation using higer order moments. In *ICASSP*, pages 2109–2112, 1989.

[8] J R Cavanaugh, W Bair, and J A Movshon. Orientation-selective setting of contrast gain by the surrounds of macaque striate cortex neurons. In *Neurosci Abstracts*, volume 23, page 227.2, 1997.

[9] P Common. Independent component analysis, a new concept? *Signal Process.*, 36:387–314, 1994.

[10] D J Field. Relations between the statistics of natural images and the response properties of cortical cells. *J. Opt. Soc. Am. A*, 4(12):2379–2394, 1987.

[11] W S Geisler and D G Albrecht. Cortical neurons: Isolation of contrast gain control. *Vision Research*, 8:1409–1410, 1992.

[12] D J Heeger. Normalization of cell responses in cat striate cortex. *Visual Neuroscience*, 9:181–198, 1992.

[13] D J Heeger. Modeling simple cell direction selectivity with normalized, half-squared, linear operators. *J. Neurophysiology*, 70(5):1885–1898, 1993.

[14] S G Mallat. A theory for multiresolution signal decomposition: The wavelet representation. *IEEE Pat. Anal. Mach. Intell.*, 11:674–693, July 1989.

[15] J Müller, J Krauskopf, and P Lennie, 1998. Center for Visual Science, University of Rochester. Unpublished data.

[16] E Oja. A simplified neuron model as a principal component analyzer. *J. Mathematical Biology*, 15:267–273, 1982.

[17] B A Olshausen and D J Field. Natural image statistics and efficient coding. *Network: Computation in Neural Systems*, 7:333–339, 1996.

[18] W Reichhardt and T Poggio. Figure-ground discrimination by relative movement in the visual system of the fly. *Biol. Cybern.*, 35:81–100, 1979.

[19] D L Ruderman and W Bialek. Statistics of natural images: Scaling in the woods. *Phys Rev. Letters*, 73(6), 1994.

[20] T D Sanger. Optimal unsupervised learning in a single-layer linear feedforward neural network. *Neural Networks*, 2:459–473, 1989.

[21] E P Simoncelli. Normalized component analysis and the statistics of natural scenes. In *Natural Scene Statistics Meeting*, Hancock, MA, September 11-14 1997.

[22] E P Simoncelli. Statistical models for images: Compression, restoration and synthesis. In *31st Asilomar Conf Signals, Systems and Computers*, pages 673–678, Pacific Grove, CA, November 1997. Available from http://www.cns.nyu.edu/~eero/publications.html

[23] E P Simoncelli and E H Adelson. Subband transforms. In John W Woods, editor, *Subband Image Coding*, chapter 4, pages 143–192. Kluwer Academic Publishers, Norwell, MA, 1990.

[24] E P Simoncelli and D J Heeger. A model of neuronal responses in visual area MT. *Vision Research*, 38(5):743–761, 1998.

[25] E P Simoncelli and O Schwartz. Derivation of a cortical normalization model from the statistics of natural images. In *Investigative Opthalmology and Visual Science Supplement (ARVO)*, volume 39, pages S–424, May 1998.

[26] B Wegmann and C Zetzsche. Statistical dependence between orientation filter outputs used in an human vision based image code. In *Proc SPIE Visual Comm. and Image Processing*, volume 1360, pages 909–922, Lausanne, Switzerland, 1990.

Acknowledgement: Special thanks to James Cavanaugh and James Müller for providing physiological data shown in this paper.

Information Maximization in Single Neurons

Martin Stemmler and Christof Koch
Computation and Neural Systems Program
Caltech 139-74
Pasadena, CA 91125
Email: stemmler@klab.caltech.edu, koch@klab.caltech.edu

Abstract

Information from the senses must be compressed into the limited range of firing rates generated by spiking nerve cells. Optimal compression uses all firing rates equally often, implying that the nerve cell's response matches the statistics of naturally occurring stimuli. Since changing the voltage-dependent ionic conductances in the cell membrane alters the flow of information, an unsupervised, non-Hebbian, developmental learning rule is derived to adapt the conductances in Hodgkin-Huxley model neurons. By maximizing the rate of information transmission, each firing rate within the model neuron's limited dynamic range is used equally often.

An efficient neuronal representation of incoming sensory information should take advantage of the regularity and scale invariance of stimulus features in the natural world. In the case of vision, this regularity is reflected in the typical probabilities of encountering particular visual contrasts, spatial orientations, or colors [1]. Given these probabilities, an optimized neural code would eliminate any redundancy, while devoting increased representation to commonly encountered features.

At the level of a single spiking neuron, information about a potentially large range of stimuli is compressed into a finite range of firing rates, since the maximum firing rate of a neuron is limited. Optimizing the information transmission through a single neuron in the presence of uniform, additive noise has an intuitive interpretation: the most efficient representation of the input uses every firing rate with *equal* probability. An analogous principle for non-spiking neurons has been tested experimentally by Laughlin [2], who matched the statistics

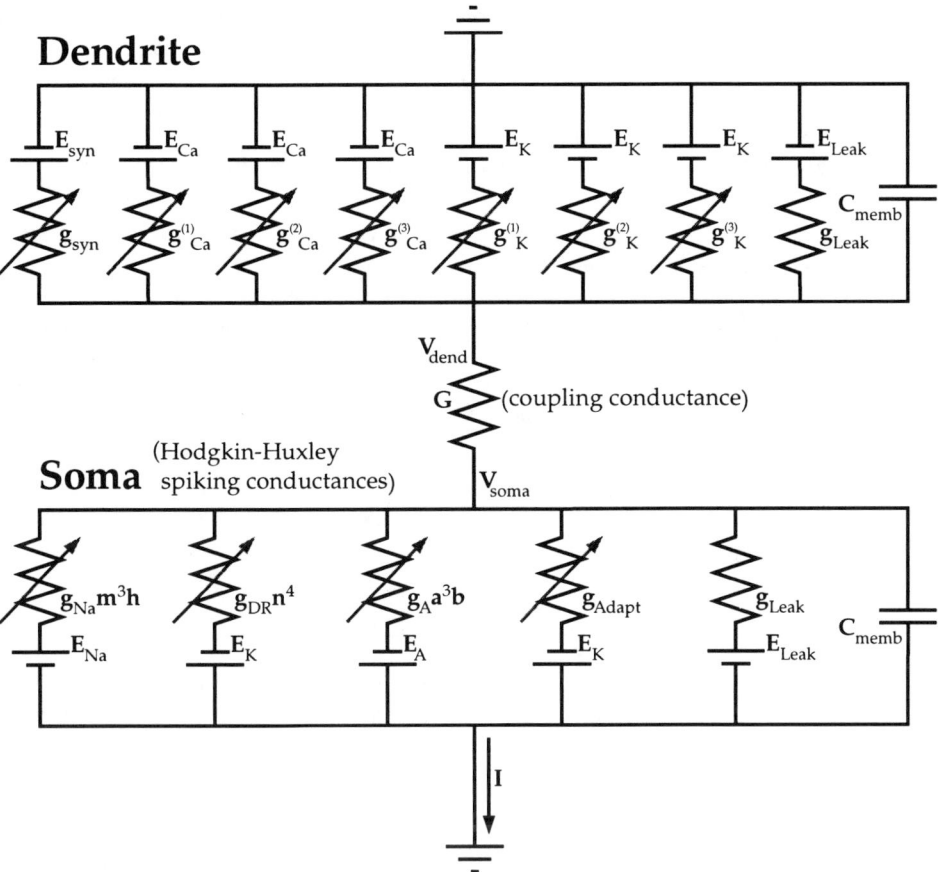

Figure 1: The model neuron contains two compartments to represent the cell's soma and dendrites. To maximize the information transfer, the parameters for six calcium and six potassium voltage-dependent conductances in the dendritic compartment are iteratively adjusted, while the somatic conductances responsible for the cell's spiking behavior are held fixed.

of naturally occurring visual contrasts to the response amplitudes of the blowfly's large monopolar cell.

From a theoretical perspective, the central question is whether a neuron can "learn" the best representation for natural stimuli through experience. During neuronal development, the nature and frequency of incoming stimuli are known to change both the anatomical structure of neurons and the distribution of ionic conductances throughout the cell [3]. We seek a guiding principle that governs the developmental timecourse of the Na^+, Ca^{2+} and K^+ conductances in the somatic and dendritic membrane by asking how a neuron would set its conductances to transmit as much information as possible. Spiking neurons must associate a range of different inputs to a set of distinct responses—a more difficult task than keeping the firing rate or excitatory postsynaptic potential (EPSP) amplitude constant under changing conditions, two tasks for which learning rules that change the voltage-dependent conductances have recently been proposed [4, 5]. Learning the proper representation of stimulus information goes beyond simply correlating input and output; an alternative to the classic postulate of Hebb [6], in which synaptic learning in networks is a consequence of correlated activity between pre- and postsynaptic neurons, is required for such learning in a single neuron.

To explore the feasibility of learning rules for information maximization, a simplified model of a neuron consisting of two electrotonic compartments, illustrated in fig. 1, was constructed. The soma (or cell body) contains the classic Hodgkin-Huxley sodium and delayed rectifier potassium conductances, with the addition of a transient potassium "A-"current and an effective calcium-dependent potassium current. The soma is coupled through an effective conductance G to the dendritic compartment, which contains the synaptic input conductance and three adjustable calcium and three adjustable potassium conductances.

The dynamics of this model are given by Hodgkin-Huxley-like equations that govern the membrane potential and a set of activation and inactivation variables, m_i and h_i, respectively. In each compartment of the neuron, the voltage V evolves as

$$C\frac{dV}{dt} = \sum_i g_i m_i^{p_i} h_i^{q_i} (E_i - V), \tag{1}$$

where C is the membrane capacitance, g_i is the (peak) value of the i-th conductance, p_i and q_i are integers, and E_i are the ion-specific reversal potentials. The variables h_i and m_i obey first order kinetics of the type $dm/dt = (m_\infty(V) - m)/\tau(V)$, where $m_\infty(V)$ denotes the steady state activation when the voltage is clamped to V and $\tau(V)$ is a voltage-dependent time constant.

All parameters for the somatic compartment, with the exception of the adaptation conductance, are given by the standard model of Connor *et al* (1977) [7]. This choice of somatic spiking conductances allows spiking to occur at arbitrarily low firing rates. Adaptation is modeled by a calcium-dependent potassium conductance that scales with the firing rate, such that the conductance has a mean value of 34 mS/cm² Hz. The calcium and potassium conductances in the dendritic compartment have simple activation and inactivation functions described by distinct Boltzmann functions. Together with the peak conductance values, the midpoint voltages $V_{\frac{1}{2}}$ and slopes s of these Boltzmann functions adapt to the statistics of stimuli. For simplicity, all time constants for the dendritic conductances are set to a constant 5 msec. For additional details and parameter values, see http://www.klab.caltech.edu/infomax.

Hodgkin-Huxley models can exhibit complex behaviors on several timescales, such as firing patterns consisting of "bursts"—sequences of multiple spikes interspersed with periods of silence. We will, however, focus on models of regularly spiking cells that adapt to a sustained stimulus by spiking periodically. To quantify how much information about a continuous stimulus variable x the time-averaged firing rate f of a regularly spiking neuron carries, we use a lower bound [8] on the mutual information $I(f;x)$ between the stimulus

x and the firing rate f:

$$I_{\text{LB}}(f; x) = -\int \ln\left(p(f)\,\sigma_f(x)\right) p(x)\,dx - \ln(\sqrt{2\pi e}), \tag{2}$$

where $p(f)$ is the probability, given the set of all stimuli, of a firing rate f, and $\sigma_f^2(x)$ is the variance of the firing rate in response to a given stimulus x.

To maximize the information transfer, does a neuron need to "know" the arrival rates of photons impinging on the retina or the frequencies of sound waves hitting the ear's tympanic membrane? Since the ion channels in the dendrites only sense a voltage and not the stimulus directly, the answer to this question, fortunately, is no: maximizing the information between the firing rate f and the dendritic voltage $V_{\text{dend}}(t)$ is equivalent to maximizing the information about the stimuli, as long as we can guarantee that the transformation from stimuli to firing rates is always one-to-one.

Since a neuron must be able to adapt to a changing environment and shifting intra- and extracellular conditions [4], learning and relearning of the proper conductance parameters, such as the channel densities, should occur on a continual basis. An alphabet zoo of different calcium (Ca^{2+}) conductances in neurons of the central nervous system, denoted 'L', 'N', 'P', 'R', and 'T'-conductances, reflects a wealth of different voltage and pharmacological properties [9], matching an equal diversity of potassium (K^+) channels. No fewer than ten different genes code for various Ca^{2+} subunits, allowing for a combinatorial number of functionally different channels [10]. A self-regulating neuron should be able to express different ionic channels and insert them into the membrane. In information maximization, the parameters for each of the conductances, such as the number of channels, are continually modified in the direction that most increases the mutual information $I[f; V_{\text{dend}}(t)]$ each time a stimulus occurs.

The standard approach to such a problem is known as stochastic approximation of the mutual information, which was recently applied to feedforward neural networks for blind source sound separation by Bell and Sejnowski [11]. We define a "free energy" $\mathcal{F} = E(f) - \beta^{-1} I_{\text{LB}}(f; x)$, where $E(f)$ incorporates constraints on the peak or mean firing rate f, and β is a Lagrangean parameter that balances the mutual information and constraint satisfaction. Stochastic approximation then consists of adjusting the parameter r of a voltage-dependent conductance by

$$\Delta r|_x = -\eta \frac{\partial}{\partial r} \frac{\delta \mathcal{F}(x)}{\delta p(x)} \tag{3}$$

whenever a stimulus x is presented; this will, by definition, occur with probability $p(x)$. In the model, the stimuli are taken to be maintained synaptic input conductances g_{syn} lasting 200 msec and drawn randomly from a fixed, continuous probability distribution. After an initial transient, we assume that the voltage waveform $V_{\text{dend}}(t)$ settles into a simple periodic limit cycle as dictated by the somatic spiking conductances. We thus posit the existence of the invertible composition of maps, such that the input conductance g_{syn} maps onto a periodic voltage waveform $V_{\text{dend}}(t)$ of period T, from thence onto an averaged current $\langle I \rangle = 1/T \int_0^T I(t)\,dt$ to the soma, and then finally onto an output firing rate f. The last element in this chain of transformations, the steady-state current-discharge

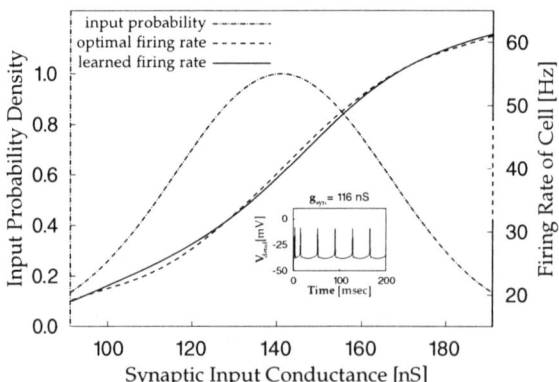

Figure 2: The inputs to the model are synaptic conductances, drawn randomly from a Gaussian distribution of mean 141 nS and standard deviation of 25 nS with the restriction that the conductance be non-negative (dot-dashed line). The learning rule in eq. 4—maximizing the information in the cell's firing rate—was used to adjust the peak conductances, midpoint voltages, and slopes of the "dendritic" Ca^{2+} and K^+ conductances over the course of 10.9 (simulated) minutes. . The learning rate decayed with time: $\eta(t) = \eta_0 \exp(-t/\tau_{\text{learning}})$, with $\eta_0 = 4.3 \times 10^{-3}$ and $\tau_{\text{learning}} = 4.4$ sec. The optimal firing rate response curve (dotted line) is asymptotically proportional to the cumulative probability distribution of inputs. The inset illustrates the typical timecourse of the dendritic voltage in the trained model.

relationship at the soma, can be predicted from the theory of dynamical systems (see http://www.klab.caltech.edu/~stemmler for details).

The voltage and the conductances are nonlinearly coupled: the conductances affect the voltage, which, in turn, sets the conductances. Since the mutual information is a *global* property of the stimulus set, the learning rule for any one conductance would depend on the values of all other conductances, were it not for the nonlinear feedback loop between voltages and conductances. This nonlinear coupling must satisfy the strict physical constraint of charge conservation: when the neuron is firing periodically, the average current injected by the synaptic and voltage-dependent conductances must equal the average current discharged by the neuron. Remarkably, charge conservation results in a learning mechanism that is strictly *local*, so that the mechanism for changing one conductance does not depend on the values of any other conductances.

For instance, information maximization predicts that the peak calcium or potassium conductance g_i changes by

$$\Delta g_i = \eta(t) \left\langle \frac{\delta}{\delta V_{\text{dend}}(t)} \langle m_i h_i (E_i - V_{\text{dend}}) \rangle + c(\langle V_{\text{dend}} \rangle) \, m_i h_i (E_i - V_{\text{dend}}) \right\rangle \quad (4)$$

each time a stimulus is presented. Here $\eta(t)$ is a time-dependent learning rate, the angular brackets indicate an average over the stimulus duration, and $c(\langle V_{\text{dend}} \rangle)$ is a simple function that is zero for most commonly encountered voltages, equal to a positive constant below some minimum, and equal to a negative constant above some maximum voltage. This

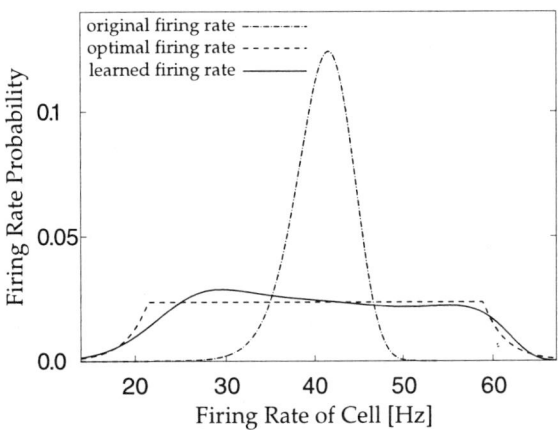

Figure 3: The probability distribution of firing rates before and after adaptation of voltage-dependent conductances. Learning shifts the distribution from a peaked distribution to a much flatter one, so that the neuron uses each firing rate within the range [22, 59] Hz equally often in response to randomly selected synaptic inputs.

function represents the constraint on the maximum and minimum firing rate, which sets the limit on the neuron's dynamic range. A constraint on the mean firing rate implies that $c(\langle V_{\text{dend}} \rangle)$ is simply a negative constant for all suprathreshold voltages. Under this constraint, the optimal distribution of firing rates becomes exponential (not shown). This latter case corresponds to transmitting as much information as possible in the rate while firing as little as possible.

Given a stimulus x, the dominant term $\delta/\delta V(t) \langle m_i h_i (E_i - V) \rangle$ of eq. 4 changes those conductances that increase the slope of the firing rate response to x. A higher slope means that more of the neuron's limited range of firing rates is devoted to representing the stimulus x and its immediate neighborhood. Since the learning rule is democratic yet competitive, only the most frequent inputs "win" and thereby gain the largest representation in the output firing rate.

In Fig. 2, the learning rule of eq. 4—generalized to also change the midpoint voltage and steepness of the activation and inactivation functions—has been used to train the model neuron as it responds to random, 200 msec long amplitude modulations of a synaptic input conductance to the dendritic compartment. The cell "learns" the statistical structure of the input, matching its adapted firing rate to the cumulative distribution function of the conductance inputs. The distribution of firing rates shifts from a peaked distribution to a much flatter one, so that all firing rates are used nearly equally often (Fig. 3). The information in the firing rate increases by a factor of three to 10.7 bits/sec, as estimated by adding a 5 msec, Gaussian-distributed noise jitter to the spike times.

Changing how tightly the stimulus amplitudes are clustered around the mean will increase or decrease the slope of the firing rate response to input, without necessarily changing the average firing rate. Neuronal systems are known to adapt not only to the mean of the stimulus intensity, but also to the variance of the stimulus [12]. We predict that such adaptation to stimulus variance will occur not just at the level of networks of neurons, but also at the single cell level.

While the detailed substrate for maximizing the information at both the single cell and network level awaits experimental elucidation, the terms in the learning rule of eq. 4 have simple biophysical correlates: the derivative term, for instance, is reflected in the stochastic flicker of ion channels switching between open and closed states. The transitions between simple open and closed states will occur at a rate proportional to $(\delta/\delta V \langle m(V) \rangle)^\gamma$ in equilibrium, where the exponent γ is $1/2$ or 1, depending on the kinetic model. To change the information transfer properties of the cell, a neuron could use state-dependent phosphorylation of ion channels or gene expression of particular ion channel subunits, possibly mediated by G-protein initiated second messenger cascades, to modify the properties of voltage-dependent conductances. The tools required to adaptively compress information from the senses are thus available at the subcellular level.

References

[1] D. L. Ruderman, *Network* **5**(4), 517 (1995), R. J. Baddeley and P. J. B. Hancock, *Proc. Roy. Soc. B* **246**, 219 (1991), J. J. Atick, *Network* **3**, 213 (1992).

[2] S. Laughlin, *Z. Naturforsch.* **36c**, 910 (1981).

[3] Purves, D. *Neural activity and the growth of the brain*, (Cambridge University Press, NY, 1994); X. Gu and N. C. Spitzer, *Nature* **375**, 784 (1995).

[4] G. LeMasson, E. Marder, and L. F. Abbott, *Science* **259**, 1915 (1993).

[5] A. J. Bell, *Neural Information Processing Systems* **4**, 59 (1992).

[6] D. O. Hebb, *The Organization of Behavior* (Wiley, New York, 1949).

[7] J. A. Connor, D. Walter, R. McKown, *Biophys. J.* **18**, 81 (1977).

[8] R. B. Stein, *Biophys. J.* **7**, 797 (1967).

[9] R. B. Avery and D. Johnston, *J. Neurosci.* **16**, 5567 (1996), F. Helmchen, K. Imoto, and B. Sakmann, *Biophys. J.* **70**, 1069 (1996).

[10] F. Hofmann, M. Biel, and V. Flockerzi, *Ann. Rev. Neurosci.* **17**, 399 (1994).

[11] Y. Z. Tsypkin, *Adaptation and Learning in Automatic Systems* (Academic Press, NY, 1971)], R. Linsker, *Neural Comp.* **4**, 691 (1992), and A. J. Bell and T. J. Sejnowski, *Neural Comp.* **7**, 1129 (1995).

[12] S. M. Smirnakis et al., *Nature* **386**, 69 (1997).

The Effect of Correlations on the Fisher Information of Population Codes

Hyoungsoo Yoon
hyoung@fiz.huji.ac.il

Haim Sompolinsky
haim@fiz.huji.ac.il

Racah Institute of Physics and Center for Neural Computation
Hebrew University, Jerusalem 91904, Israel

Abstract

We study the effect of correlated noise on the accuracy of population coding using a model of a population of neurons that are broadly tuned to an angle in two-dimension. The fluctuations in the neuronal activity is modeled as a Gaussian noise with pairwise correlations which decays exponentially with the difference between the preferred orientations of the pair. By calculating the Fisher information of the system, we show that in the biologically relevant regime of parameters positive correlations decrease the estimation capability of the network relative to the uncorrelated population. Moreover strong positive correlations result in information capacity which saturates to a finite value as the number of cells in the population grows. In contrast, negative correlations substantially increase the information capacity of the neuronal population.

1 Introduction

In many neural systems, information regarding sensory inputs or (intended) motor outputs is found to be distributed throughout a localized pool of neurons. It is generally believed that one of the main characteristics of the population coding scheme is its redundancy in representing information (Paradiso 1988; Snippe and Koenderink 1992a; Seung and Sompolinsky 1993). Hence the intrinsic neuronal noise, which has detrimental impact on the information processing capability, is expected to be compensated by increasing the number of neurons in a pool. Although this expectation is universally true for an ensemble of neurons whose stochastic variabilities are statistically independent, a general theory of the efficiency of population coding when the neuronal noise is correlated within the population, has been lacking. The conventional wisdom has been that the correlated variability limits the information processing capacity of neuronal ensembles (Zohary, Shadlen, and Newsome 1994).

However, detailed studies of simple models of a correlated population that code for a single real-valued parameter led to apparently contradicting claims. Snippe and Koenderink (Snippe and Koenderink 1992b) conclude that depending on the details of the correlations, such as their spatial range, they may either increase or decrease the information capacity relative to the uncorrelated one. Recently, Abbott and Dayan (Abbott and Dayan 1998) claimed that in many cases correlated noise improves the accuracy of population code. Furthermore, even when the information is decreased it still grows linearly with the size of the population. If true, this conclusion has an important implication on the utility of using a large population to improve the estimation accuracy. Since cross-correlations in neuronal activity are frequently observed in both primary sensory and motor areas (Fetz, Yoyama, and Smith 1991; Lee, Port, Kruse, and Georgopoulos 1998), understanding the effect of noise correlation in biologically relevant situations is of great importance.

In this paper we present an analytical study of the effect of noise correlations on the population coding of a pool of cells that code for a single one-dimensional variable, an angle on a plane, $e.g.$, an orientation of a visual stimulus, or the direction of an arm movement. By assuming that the noise follows the multivariate Gaussian distribution, we investigate analytically the effect of correlation on the Fisher information. This model is similar to that considered in (Snippe and Koenderink 1992b; Abbott and Dayan 1998). By analyzing its behavior in the biologically relevant regime of tuning width and correlation range, we derive general conclusions about the effect of the correlations on the information capacity of the population.

2 Population Coding with Correlated Noise

We consider a population of N neurons which respond to a stimulus characterized by an angle θ, where $-\pi < \theta \leq \pi$. The activity of each neuron (indexed by i) is assumed to be Gaussian with a mean $f_i(\theta)$ which represents its tuning curve, and a uniform variance a. The noise is assumed to be pairwise-correlated throughout the population. Hence the activity profile of the whole population, $R = \{r_1, r_2, \cdots, r_N\}$, given a stimulus θ, follows the following multivariate Gaussian distribution.

$$P(R|\theta) = \mathcal{N} \exp\left(-\frac{1}{2}\sum_{i,j}(r_i - f_i(\theta))C_{ij}^{-1}(r_j - f_j(\theta))\right) \quad (1)$$

where $\mathcal{N}$ is a normalization constant and C_{ij} is the correlation matrix.

$$C_{ij} = a\delta_{ij} + b_{ij}(1 - \delta_{ij}). \quad (2)$$

It is assumed that the tuning curves of all the neurons are identical in form but peaked at different angles, that is $f_i(\theta) = f(\theta - \phi_i)$ where the preferred angles ϕ_i are distributed *uniformly* from $-\pi$ to π with a lattice spacing, ω, which is equal to $2\pi/N$. We further assume that the noise correlation between a pair of neurons is only a function of their preferred angle difference, i.e., $b_{ij}(\theta) = b(\|\phi_i - \phi_j\|)$ where $\|\theta_1 - \theta_2\|$ is defined to be the relative angle between θ_1 and θ_2, and hence its maximum value is π. A decrease in the magnitude of neuronal correlations with the dissimilarity in the preferred stimulus is often observed in cortical areas. We model this by exponentially decaying correlations

$$b_{ij} = b \exp(-\frac{\|\phi_i - \phi_j\|}{\rho}) \quad (3)$$

where ρ specifies the angular correlation length.

The amount of information that can be extracted from the above population will depend on the decoding scheme. A convenient measure of the information capacity in the population is given by the Fisher information, which in our case is (for a given stimulus θ)

$$J(\theta) = \sum_{i,j} g_i C_{ij}^{-1} g_j \qquad (4)$$

where

$$g_i(\theta) \equiv \frac{\partial f_i(\theta)}{\partial \theta}. \qquad (5)$$

The utility of this measure follows from the well known Cramér-Rao bound for the variance of any unbiased estimators, i.e., $\langle(\theta - \hat{\theta})^2\rangle \geq 1/J(\theta)$. For the rest of this paper, we will concentrate on the Fisher information as a function of the noise correlation parameters, b and ρ, as well as the population size N.

3 Results

In the case of uncorrelated population ($b = 0$), the Fisher information is given by (Seung and Sompolinsky 1993)

$$J_o = \frac{N}{a} \sum_n |g_n|^2 \qquad (6)$$

where g_n is the Fourier transform of g_j, defined by

$$g_n \equiv \frac{1}{N} \sum_j e^{-in\phi_j} g_j. \qquad (7)$$

The mode number n is an integer running from $-\frac{N-1}{2}$ to $\frac{N-1}{2}$ (for odd N) and $\phi_i = -\pi(N+1)/N + i\omega$, $i = 1, \ldots, N$. Likewise, in the case of $b \neq 0$, J is given by

$$J = N \sum_n \frac{|g_n|^2}{C_n} \qquad (8)$$

where C_n are the eigenvalues of the covariance matrix,

$$C_n \equiv \frac{1}{N} \sum_{i,j} e^{-in(\phi_i - \phi_j)} C_{ij}$$

$$= (a - 2b) + 2b \frac{1 - \lambda \cos(n\omega) - (-1)^n \lambda^{\frac{N+1}{2}} \cos(n\omega)(1 - \lambda)}{1 - 2\lambda \cos(n\omega) + \lambda^2} \qquad (9)$$

where $\omega = \frac{2\pi}{N}$, $\lambda = e^{-\omega/\rho}$, and N is assumed to be an odd integer. Note that the covariance matrix C_{ij} remains positive definite as long as

$$-\frac{1}{2N} \frac{1 - \lambda}{\lambda(1 - \lambda^{\frac{N-1}{2}})} < \frac{b}{a} < 1 \qquad (10)$$

where the lower bound holds for general N while the upper bound is valid for large N.

To evaluate the effect of correlations in a large population it is important to specify the appropriate scales of the system parameters. We consider here the biologically relevant case of broadly tuned neurons that have a smoothly varying tuning curve with a single peak. When the tuning curve is smoothly varying, $|g_n|^2$ will be a rapidly decaying function as n increases beyond a characteristic value which is proportional to the inverse of the tuning width, σ. We further assume a broad tuning, namely that the tuning curve spans a substantial fraction of the angular extent. This is consistent with the observed typical values of half-width at half height in visual and motor areas, which range from 20 to 60 degrees. Likewise, it is reasonable to assume that the angular correlation length ρ spans a substantial fraction of the entire angular range. This broad tuning of correlations with respect to the difference in the preferred angles is commonly observed in cortex (Fetz, Yoyama, and Smith 1991; Lee, Port, Kruse, and Georgopoulos 1998). To capture these features we will consider the limit of large N while keeping the parameters ρ and σ constant. Note that keeping σ of order 1 implies that substantial contributions to Eq. (8) come only from n which remain of order 1 as N increases. On the other hand, given the enormous variability in the strength of the observed cross-correlations between pairs of neurons in cortex, we do not restrict the value of b at this point.

Incorporating the above scaling we find that when N is large J is given by

$$J = \frac{N}{a} \sum_n |g_n|^2 \frac{\rho^{-2} + n^2}{\rho^{-2} + n^2 + (\frac{2b}{a\omega\rho})(1 - (-1)^n e^{-\pi/\rho})}. \quad (11)$$

Inspection of the denominator in the above equation clearly shows that for all positive values of b, J is smaller than J_o. On the other hand, when b is negative J is larger than J_o. To estimate the magnitude of these effects we consider below three different regimes.

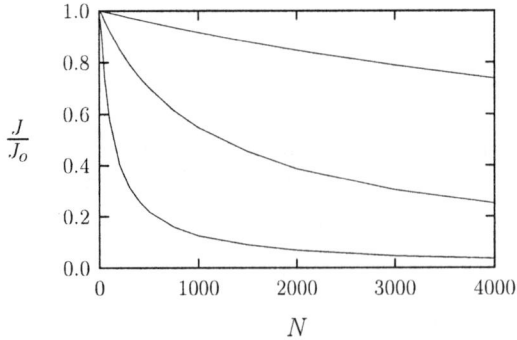

Figure 1: Normalized Fisher information when $\rho \sim \mathcal{O}(1)$ ($\rho = 0.25\pi$ was used). $a = 1$ and $b = 0.1, 0.01,$ and 0.001 from the bottom. We used a circular Gaussian tuning curve, Eq. (13), with $f_{\max} = 10$ and $\sigma = 0.2\pi$.

Strong positive correlations: We first discuss the regime of strong positive correlations, by which we mean that $0 < b/a \sim \mathcal{O}(1)$. In this case the second term in the denominator of Eq. (11) is of order N and Eq. (11) becomes

$$J = \frac{\pi\rho}{b} \sum_n |g_n|^2 \frac{\rho^{-2} + n^2}{1 - (-1)^n e^{-\pi/\rho}}. \quad (12)$$

This result implies that in this regime the Fisher information in the entire population does not scale linearly with the population size N but saturates to a size-independent finite limit. Thus, for these strong correlations, although the number of neurons in the population may be large, the number of independent degrees of freedom is small.

We demonstrate the above phenomenon by a numerical evaluation of J for the following choice of tuning curve

$$f(\theta) = f_{\max} \exp\left((\cos(\theta) - 1)/\sigma^2\right) \quad (13)$$

with $\sigma = 0.2\pi$. The results are shown in Fig. 1 and Fig. 2. The results of Fig. 1 clearly show the substantial decrease in J as b increases. The reduction in J/J_o when $b \sim \mathcal{O}(1)$ indicates that J does not scale with N in this limit. Fig. 2 shows the saturation of J when N increases. For $\rho = 0.1$ and 1 ((c) and (d)), J saturates at about $N = 100$, which means that for these parameter values the network contains at most 100 independent degrees of freedom. When the correlation range becomes either smaller or bigger, the saturation becomes less prominent ((a) and (b)), which is further explained later in the text.

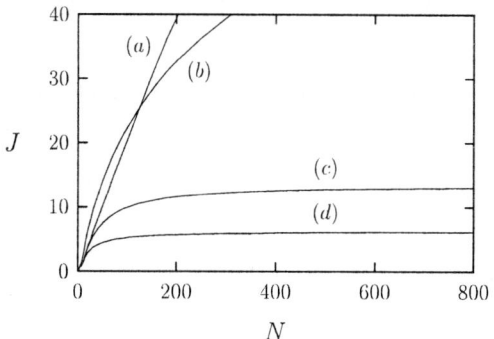

Figure 2: Saturation of Fisher information with the correlation coefficient kept fixed; $a = 1$ and $b = 0.5$. Both $\rho \sim \mathcal{O}(1)$ ((c) $\rho = 0.1$ and (d) $\rho = 1$) and other extreme limits ((a) $\rho = 0.01$ and (b) $\rho = 10$) are shown. Tuning curve with $f_{\max} = 1$ and $\sigma = 0.2\pi$ was used for all four curves.

Weak positive correlations: This regime is defined formally by positive values of b which scale as $b/a \sim \mathcal{O}(\frac{1}{N})$. In this case, while J is still smaller than J_o the suppressive effects of the correlations are not as strong as in the first case. This is shown in Fig. 3 (bottom traces) for $N = 1000$. While J is less than J_o, it is still a substantial fraction of J_o, indicating J is of order N.

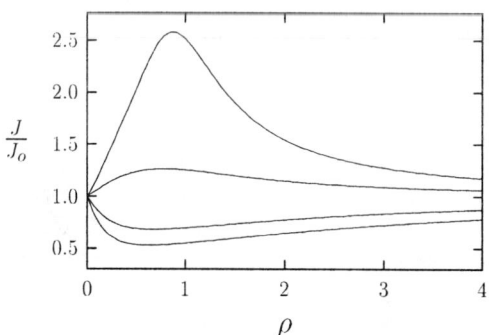

Figure 3: Normalized Fisher information when $\rho \sim \mathcal{O}(1)$ and $b/a \sim \mathcal{O}(\frac{1}{N})$. $N = 1000$, $a = 1$, $f_{\max} = 10$, and $\sigma = 0.2\pi$. The top curves represent negative b ($b = -0.005$ and -0.002 from the top) and the bottom ones positive b ($b = 0.01$ and 0.005 from the bottom).

Weak negative correlations: So far we have considered the case of positive b. As stated above, Eq. (11) implies that when $b < 0$, $J > J_o$. The lower bound of b (Eq. (10)) means that when the correlations are negative and ρ is of order 1 the amplitude of the correlations must be small. It scales as $b/a = \hat{b}/N$ with $\hat{b}$ which is of order 1 and is larger than $\hat{b}_{\min} = -(\pi/\rho)/(1 - \exp(-\pi/\rho))$. In this regime $(J - J_o)/N$ retains a finite positive value even for large N. This enhancement can be made large if $\hat{b}$ comes close to $\hat{b}_{\min}$. This behavior is shown in Fig. 3 (upper traces). Note that, for both positive and negative weak correlations, the curves have peaks around a characteristic length scale $\rho \sim \sigma$, which is 0.2π in this figure.

Extremely long and short range correlations: Calculation with strictly uniform correlations, i.e., $b_{ij} = b$, shows that in this case the positive correlations enhance the Fisher information of the system, leading to claims that this might be a generic result (Abbott and Dayan 1998). Here we show that this behavior is special to cases where the correlations essentially do not vary in strength. We consider the case $\rho \sim \mathcal{O}(N)$. This means that the strength of the correlations is the same for all the neurons up to a correction of order $1/N$. In this limit Eq. (11) is not valid, and the Fisher information is obtained from Eq. (8) and Eq. (9),

$$J = \frac{N}{a-b} \sum_{\text{even}} |g_n|^2 + N \sum_{\text{odd}} \frac{|g_n|^2}{a - b + b/(n^2 \varrho)} \qquad (14)$$

where $\varrho = \omega \rho / 4$. Note that even in this extreme regime, only for $\varrho > 1$ is J guaranteed to be always larger than J_o. Below this value the sign of $J - J_o$ depends on the particular shape of the tuning curve and the value of b. In fact, a more detailed analysis (Yoon and Sompolinsky 1998) shows that as soon as $\rho \ll \mathcal{O}(\sqrt{N})$, $J - J_o < 0$, as in the case of $\rho \sim \mathcal{O}(1)$ discussed above. The crossover between these two opposite behaviors is shown in Fig. 4. For comparison the case with $\rho \sim \mathcal{O}(1)$ is also shown.

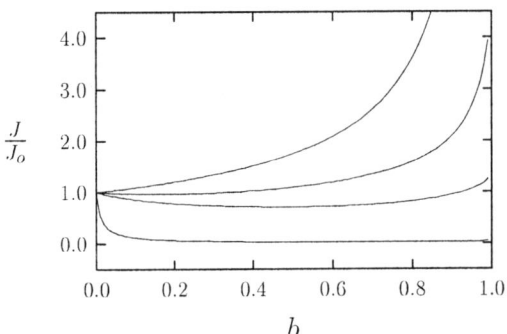

Figure 4: Normalized Fisher information when $b/a \sim \mathcal{O}(1)$. $N = 1000$ and $a = 1$. When $\rho \sim \mathcal{O}(1)$, increasing b always decreases the Fisher information (bottom curve $\rho = 0.25\pi$). However, this trend is reversed when $\rho \sim \mathcal{O}(\sqrt{N})$ and when $\rho > \frac{2}{\pi}N$ $J - J_o$ becomes always positive. From the top $\rho = 400$, 50, and 25.

Another extreme regime is where the correlation length ρ scales as $1/N$ but the tuning width remains of order 1. This means that a given neuron is correlated with a small number of its immediate neighbors, which remains finite as $N \to \infty$. In this limit, the Fisher information becomes, again from Eq. (8) and Eq. (9),

$$J = \frac{N(\lambda^{-1} - 1)}{a(\lambda^{-1} - 1) + 2b} \sum_n |g_n|^2. \qquad (15)$$

In this case, the behavior of J is similar to the cases of weak correlations discussed above. The information remains of order N but the sign of $J - J_o$ depends on the sign of b. Thus, when the amplitude of the positive correlation function is $\mathcal{O}(1)$, J increases linearly with N in the two opposite extremes of very large and very small ρ as shown in Fig. 2 ((a) and (b)).

4 Discussion

In this paper we have studied the effect of correlated variability of neuronal activity on the maximum accuracy of the population coding. We have shown that the effect of correlation on the information capacity of the population crucially depends on the scale of correlation length. We argue that for the sensory and motor areas which are presumed to utilize population coding, the tuning of both the correlations and the mean response profile is broad and of the same order. This implies that each neuron is correlated with a finite fraction of the total number of neurons, N, and a given stimulus activates a finite fraction of N. We show that in this regime positive correlations always decrease the information. When they are strong enough in amplitude they reduce the number of independent degrees of freedom to a finite number even for large population. Only in the extreme case of almost uniform correlations the information capacity is enhanced. This is reasonable since to overcome the positive correlations one needs to subtract the responses of different neurons. But in general this will reduce their signal by a larger amount. When the correlations are uniform, the reduction of the correlated noise by subtraction is perfect and can be made in a manner that will little affect the signal component.

Acknowledgments

H.S. acknowledges helpful discussions with Larry Abbott and Sebastian Seung. This research is partially supported by the Fund for Basic Research of the Israeli Academy of Science and by a grant from the United States-Israel Binational Science Foundation (BSF), Jerusalem, Israel.

References

L. F. Abbott and P. Dayan (1998). The effect of correlated variability on the accuracy of a population code. *Neural Comp.*, in press.

E. Fetz, K. Yoyama, and W. Smith (1991). Synaptic interactions between cortical neurons. In A. Peters and E. G. Jones (Eds.), *Cerebral Cortex*, Volume 9. New York: Plenum Press.

D. Lee, N. L. Port, W. Kruse, and A. P. Georgopoulos (1998). Variability and correlated noise in the discharge of neurons in motor and parietal areas of the primate cortex. *J. Neurosci. 18*, 1161–1170.

M. A. Paradiso (1988). A theory for the use of visual orientation information which exploits the columnar structure of striate cortex. *Biol. Cybern. 58*, 35–49.

H. S. Seung and H. Sompolinsky (1993). Simple models for reading neuronal population codes. *Proc. Natl. Acad. Sci. USA 90*, 10749–10753.

H. P. Snippe and J. J. Koenderink (1992a). Discrimination thresholds for channel-coded systems. *Biol. Cybern. 66*, 543–551.

H. P. Snippe and J. J. Koenderink (1992b). Information in channel-coded system: correlated receivers. *Biol. Cybern. 67*, 183–190.

H. Yoon and H. Sompolinsky (1998). Population coding in neuronal systems with correlated noise, preprint.

E. Zohary, M. N. Shadlen, and W. T. Newsome (1994). Correlated neuronal discharge rate and its implications for psychophysical performance. *Nature 370*, 140–143.

Distributional Population Codes and Multiple Motion Models

Richard S. Zemel
University of Arizona
zemel@u.arizona.edu

Peter Dayan
Gatsby Computational Neuroscience Unit
dayan@gatsby.ucl.ac.uk

Abstract

Most theoretical and empirical studies of population codes make the assumption that underlying neuronal activities is a unique and unambiguous value of an encoded quantity. However, population activities can contain additional information about such things as multiple values of or uncertainty about the quantity. We have previously suggested a method to recover extra information by treating the activities of the population of cells as coding for a complete distribution over the coded quantity rather than just a single value. We now show how this approach bears on psychophysical and neurophysiological studies of population codes for motion direction in tasks involving transparent motion stimuli. We show that, unlike standard approaches, it is able to recover multiple motions from population responses, and also that its output is consistent with both correct and erroneous human performance on psychophysical tasks.

A population code can be defined as a set of units whose activities collectively encode some underlying variable (or variables). The standard view is that population codes are useful for accurately encoding the underlying variable when the individual units are noisy. Current statistical approaches to interpreting population activity reflect this view, in that they determine the optimal single value that explains the observed activity pattern given a particular model of the noise (and possibly a loss function).

In our work, we have pursued an alternative hypothesis, that the population encodes additional information about the underlying variable, including *multiple values* and *uncertainty*. The **Distributional Population Coding** (DPC) framework finds the best probability distribution across values that fits the population activity (Zemel, Dayan, & Pouget, 1998).

The DPC framework is appealing since it makes clear how extra information can be conveyed in a population code. In this paper, we use it to address a particu-

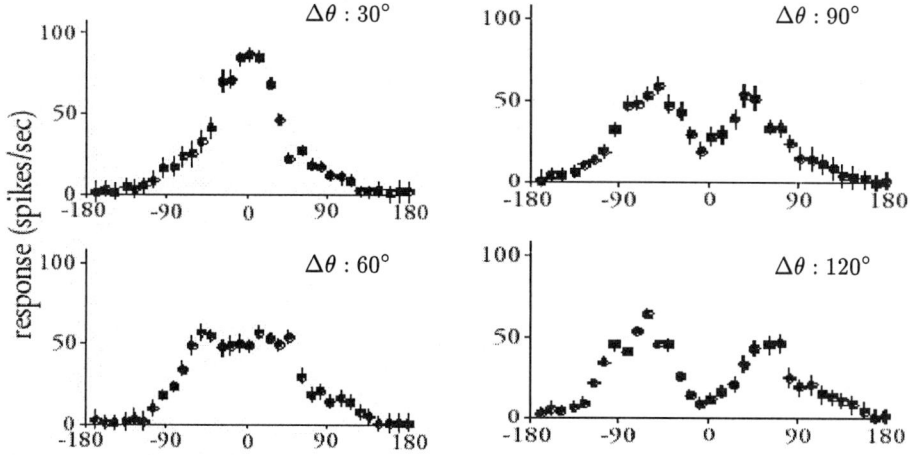

Figure 1: Each of the four plots depicts a single MT cell response (spikes per second) to a transparent motion stimulus of a fixed directional difference ($\Delta\theta$) between the two motion directions. The x-axis gives the average direction of stimulus motion relative to the cell's preferred direction (0°). From Treue, personal communication.

lar body of experimental data on transparent motion perception, due to Treue and colleagues (Hol & Treue, 1997; Rauber & Treue, 1997). These transparent motion experiments provide an ideal test of the DPC framework, in that the neurophysiological data reveal how the population responds to multiple values in the stimuli, and the psychophysical data describe how these values are actually decoded, putatively from the population response. We investigate how standard methods fare on these data, and compare their performance to that of DPC.

1 RESPONSES TO MULTIPLE MOTIONS

Many investigators have examined neural and behavioral responses to stimuli composed of two patterns sliding across each other. These often create the impression of two separate surfaces moving in different directions. The general neurophysiological finding is that an MT cell's response to these stimuli can be characterized as the average of its responses to the individual components (van Wezel et al., 1996; Recanzone et al., 1997). As an example, Figure 1 shows data obtained from single-cell recordings in MT to random dot patterns consisting of two distinct motion directions (Treue, personal communication). Each plot is for a different relative angle ($\Delta\theta$) between the two directions. A plot can equivalently be viewed as the response of an population of MT cells having different preferred directions to a single presentation of a stimulus containing two directions. If $\Delta\theta$ is large, the activity profile is bimodal, but as the directional difference shrinks, the profile becomes unimodal. The population response to a $\Delta\theta = 30°$ motion stimulus is merely a wider version of the response to a stimulus containing a single direction of motion. However, this transition from a bimodal to unimodal profiles in MT does not apparently correspond to subjects' percepts; subjects can reliably perceive both motions in superimposed transparent random patterns down to an angle of 10° (Mather & Moulden, 1983). If these MT activities play a determining role in motion perception, the challenge is to understand how the visual system can extract

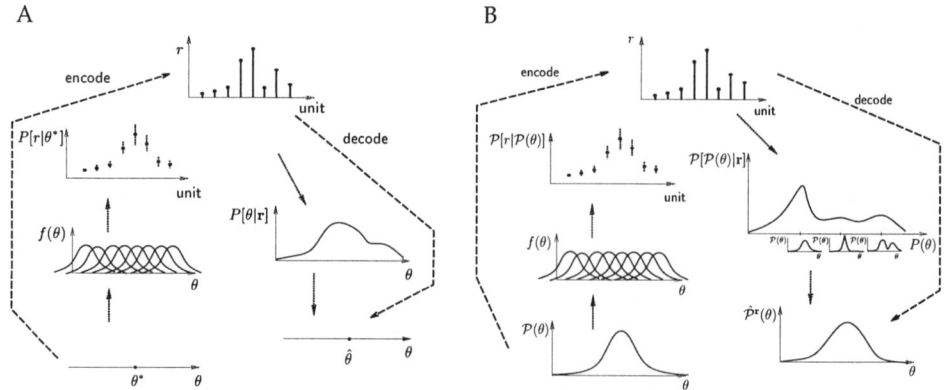

Figure 2: (A) The standard Bayesian population coding framework assumes that a single value is encoded in a set of noisy neural activities. (B) The distributional population coding framework shows how a distribution over θ can be encoded and then decoded from noisy population activities. From Zemel et al. (1998).

both motions from such unimodal (and bimodal) response profiles.

2 ENCODING & DECODING

Statistical population code decoding methods begin with the knowledge, collected over many experimental trials, of the tuning function $f_i(\theta)$ for each cell i, determined using simple stimuli (e.g., ones containing uni-directional motion). Figure 2A cartoons the framework used for standard decoding. Starting on the bottom left, encoding consists of taking a value θ to be coded and representing it by the noisy activities r_i of the elements of a population code. In the simulations described here, we have used a population of 200 model MT cells, with tuning functions defined by random sampling within physiologically-determined ranges for the parameters: baseline b, amplitude a and width σ. The encoding model comes from the MT data: for a single motion, $\langle r_i | \theta \rangle = f_i(\theta) = b_i + a_i \times \exp[-(\theta-\theta_i)^2/2\sigma_i^2]$, while for two motions, $\langle r_i|\theta_1, \theta_2\rangle = \frac{1}{2}[f_i(\theta_1) + f_i(\theta_2)]$. The noise is taken to be independent and Poisson.

Standard Bayesian decoding starts with the activities $\mathbf{r} = \{r_i\}$ and generates a distribution $\mathcal{P}[\theta|\mathbf{r}]$. Under the model with Poisson noise,

$$\mathcal{P}[\theta|\mathbf{r}] \sim \log\left\{\mathcal{P}[\theta]\prod_i \mathcal{P}[r_i|\theta]\right\} \sim \sum_i r_i \log f_i(\theta)$$

This method thus provides a multiplicative kernel density estimate, tending to produce a sharp distribution for a single motion direction θ. A single estimate $\hat{\theta}$ can be extracted from $\mathcal{P}[\theta|\mathbf{r}]$ using a loss function.

For this method to decode successfully when there are two motions in the input (θ_1 and θ_2), the extracted distribution must at least have two modes. Standard Bayesian decoding fails to satisfy this requirement. First, if the response profile $\mathbf{r}$ is unimodal (cf. the 30° plot in Figure 1), convolution with unimodal kernels $\{\log f_i(\theta)\}$ produces a unimodal $\log \mathcal{P}[\theta|\mathbf{r}]$, peaked about the average of the two directions. The additive kernel density estimate, an alternative distributional decoding method proposed by Anderson (1995), suffers from the same problem, and also fails to be adequately sharp for single value inputs.

Surprisingly, the standard Bayesian decoding method also fails on bimodal response profiles. If the baseline response $b_i = 0$, then $\mathcal{P}[\theta|\mathbf{r}]$ is Gaussian, with mean $\sum_i r_i \theta_i / \sum_{i'} r_{i'}$ and variance $1/\sum_i r_i/\sigma_i^2$ (Snippe, 1996; Zemel et al., 1998). If $b_i > 0$, then, for the extracted distribution to have two modes in the appropriate positions, $\log[\mathcal{P}[\theta_1|\mathbf{r}]/\mathcal{P}[\theta_2|\mathbf{r}]]$ must be small. However, the variance of this quantity is $\sum_i \langle r_i \rangle (\log[f_i(\theta_1)/f_i(\theta_2)])^2$, which is much greater than 0 unless the tuning curves are so flat as to be able to convey only little information about the stimuli. Intuitively, the noise in the rates causes $\sum r_i \log f_i(\theta)$ to be greater around one of the two values, and exponentiating to form $\mathcal{P}[\theta|\mathbf{r}]$ selects out this one value. Thus the standard method can only extract one of the two motion components from the population responses to transparent motion.

The distributional population coding method (Figure 2B) extends the standard encoding model to allow $\mathbf{r}$ to depend on general $\mathcal{P}[\theta]$:

$$\langle r_i \rangle = \int_\theta \mathcal{P}[\theta] f_i(\theta) d\theta \tag{1}$$

Bayesian decoding takes the observed activities $\mathbf{r}$ and produces probability distributions over probability distributions over θ, $\mathcal{P}[\mathcal{P}(\theta)|\mathbf{r}]$. For simplicity, we decode using an approximate form of maximum likelihood in distributions over θ, finding the $\hat{\mathcal{P}}^\mathbf{r}(\theta)$ that maximizes $L[\mathcal{P}(\theta)|\mathbf{r}] \sim \sum_i r_i \log[f_i(\theta) * \mathcal{P}(\theta)] - \alpha g[\mathcal{P}(\theta)]$ where the smoothness term $g[]$ acts as a regularizer.

The distributional *encoding* operation in Equation 1 is quite straightforward – by design, since this represents an assumption about what neural processing prior to (in this case) MT performs. However, the distributional *decoding* operation that we have used (Zemel et al., 1998) involves complicated and non-neural operations. The idea is to understand what information in principle may be conveyed by a population code under this interpretation, and then to judge actual neural operations in the light of this theoretical optimum. DPC is a statistical cousin of so-called line-element models, which attempt to account for subjects' performance in cases like transparency using the output of some fixed number of direction-selective mechanisms (Williams et al., 1991).

3 DECODING MULTIPLE MOTIONS

We have applied our model to simulated MT response patterns $\mathbf{r}$ generated via the DPC encoding model (Equation 1). For multiple motion stimuli, with $\mathcal{P}(\theta) = (\delta(\theta - \theta_1) + \delta(\theta - \theta_2))/2$, this encoding model produces the observed neurophysiological response: each unit's expected activity is the average of its responses to the component motions. For bimodal response patterns, DPC matches the generating distribution (Figure 3). For unimodal response patterns, such as those generated by double motion stimuli with $\Delta\theta = 30°$, DPC also consistently recovers the generating distribution. The bimodality of the reconstructed distribution begins to break down around $\Delta\theta = 10°$, which is also the point at which subjects are unable distinguish two motions from a single broader band of motion directions (Mather & Moulden, 1983).

It has been reported (Treue, personal communication) that for angles $\Delta\theta < 10°$, subjects can tell that all points are not moving in parallel, but are uncertain whether

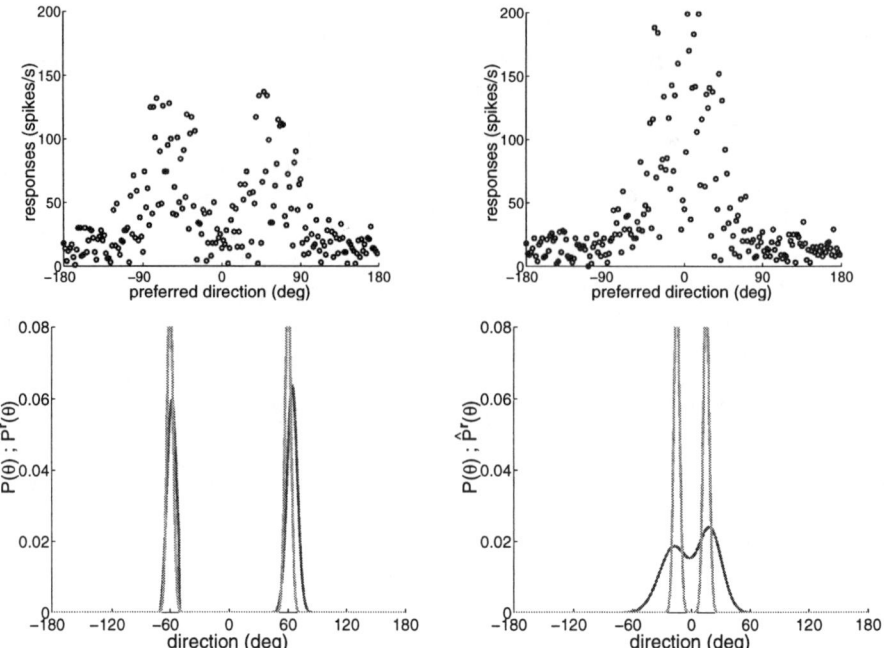

Figure 3: (A) On a single simulated trial, the population response forms a bimodal activity profile when $\Delta\theta = 120°$. (B) The reconstructed (darker) distribution closely matches the true input distribution for this trial. (C) As $\Delta\theta \to 10°$, the population response is no longer bimodal, instead has a noisy unimodal profile, and (D) the reconstructed distribution no longer has two clear modes.

they are moving in two discrete directions or within a directional band. Our model qualitatively captures this uncertainty, reconstructing a broad distribution with two small peaks for directional differences between 7° and 10°.

DPC also matches psychophysical performance on metameric stimuli. Rauber and Treue (1997) asked human subjects to report the directions in moving dot patterns consisting of 2, 3 or 5 directions of motion. The motion directions were -40° and +40°; -50°, 0° and +50°; and -50°, -30°, 0°, +30°, and +50°, respectively, but the proportions of dots moving in each direction were adjusted so that the population responses produced by an encoding model similar to Equation 1 would all be the same. Subjects reported the same two motion directions, at -40° and 40°, to all three types of stimuli.

DPC, like any reasonably deterministic decoding model, takes these (essentially identical) patterns of activity and, metamerically, reports the same answer for each case. Unlike most models, its answer—that there are two motions at roughly ±40°—matches human responses. The *fact* of metamerization is not due to any kind of prior in the model as to the number of directions to be recovered. However, that the actual report in each case includes just two motions (when clearly three or five motions would be equally consistent with the input) is a consequence of the smoothness prior. We can go further with DPC and predict how changing the proportion of dots moving in the central of three directions would lead to different percepts – from a single motion to two as this proportion decreases.

We can further evaluate the performance of DPC by comparing the quality of its

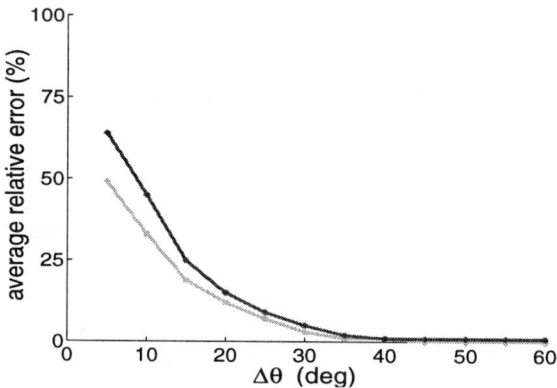

Figure 4: The average relative error E in direction judgments (Equation 2) for the DPC model (top curve) and for a model with the correct prior for this particular input set.

reconstruction to that obtained by fitting the correct model of the input distribution, a mixture of delta functions. We simulated MT responses to motion stimuli composed of two evenly-weighted directions, with 100 examples for each value of $\Delta\theta$ in a range from 5° to 60°. We fit a mixture of two delta functions to each population response, and measured the average relative error in direction judgments based on this fitted distribution versus the two true directions, θ_1 and θ_2 on that example t:

$$E = \frac{|\hat{\theta}_1^t - \theta_1| + |\hat{\theta}_2^t - \theta_2|}{2\Delta\theta} \qquad (2)$$

We then applied the DPC model to the same population codes. To measure the average error, we first fit the general distribution $\hat{\mathcal{P}}^r(\theta)$ produced by DPC with a pair of equal-weighted Gaussians, and determined $\hat{\theta}_1^t$ and $\hat{\theta}_2^t$ from the appropriate mean and variance. As can be seen in Figure 4, the DPC model, which only has a general smoothness prior over the form of the input distribution, preserves the information in the observed rates nearly as well as the model with the correct prior.

4 CONCLUSIONS

Transparent motion provides an ideal test of distributional population coding, since the encoding model is determined by neural activity and the decoding model by the behavioral data. Two existing kernel density estimate models, involving additive (Anderson, 1995) and multiplicative (standard Bayesian decoding) combination, perform poorly in this paradigm. DPC, a model in which neuronal responses and the animal's judgments are treated as being sensitive to the entire distribution of an encoded value, has been shown to be consistent with both single-cell responses and behavioral decisions, even matching subjects' threshold behavior.

We are currently applying this same model to several other motion experiments, including one in which subjects had to determine whether a motion stimulus consisted of a number of discrete directions or a uniform distribution (Williams et al., 1991). We are investigating whether our model can explain the nonmonotonic relationship between the number of directions and the judgments. We have also applied DPC to a notorious puzzle for population coding: that *single* MT cells are just as accurate as the whole monkey – one cell's output could directly support inference of the same quality as the monkeys. Our approach provides an alternative explanation for part of this apparent inefficiency to that of the noisy pooling model of Shadlen et al. (1996). Finally, experiments showing the effect of target uncertainty on population responses (Basso & Wurtz, 1998; Bastian et al,. 1998) are also handled naturally by the DPC approach.

The current model is intended to describe the information available at one stage in the processing stream. It does not address the precise mechanism of motion encoding, i.e., how responses in MT arise. We also have not considered the neural decoding and decision mechanisms. These could likely involve a layer of units that reaches decisions through a pattern of feedforward and lateral connections, as in the model proposed by Grunewald (1996) for the detection of transparent motion.

One critical issue that remains is normalization. It is not clear how to distinguish ambiguity about a *single* value for the encoded variable from the existence of *multiple* values of that variable (as in transparency for motion). Various factors are likely to be important, including the degree of separation of the modes and also prior expectations about the possibility of equivalents of transparency.

Acknowledgements: This work was funded by ONR Young Investigator Award N00014-98-1-0509 to RZ, and NIMH grant 1R29MH5541-01, and grants from the Surdna Foundation and the Gatsby Charitable Foundation to PD. We thank Stefan Treue for providing us with the data plot and for informative discussions of his experiments; Alexandre Pouget and Charlie Anderson for useful discussions of distributed coding and the standard model; and Zoubin Ghahramani and Geoff Hinton for helpful conversations about reconstruction in the log probability domain.

References

[1] Anderson, C. H. (1995). Unifying perspectives on neuronal codes and processing. In *XIX International workshop on condensed matter theories*. Caracas, Venezuela.

[2] Basso, M. A. & Wurtz, R. H. (1998). Modulation of neuronal activity in superior colliculus by changes in target probability. *Journal of Neuroscience*, 18(18), 7519-34.

[3] Bastian, A., Riehle, A., Erlhagen, W., & Schoner, G. (1998). Prior information preshapes the population representation of movement direction in motor cortex. *Neuroreport*, 9(2), 315-319.

[4] Britten, K. H., Shadlen, M. N., Newsome, W. T., & Movshon, J. A. (1992). The analysis of visual motion: A comparison of neuronal and psychophysical performance. *Journal of Neuroscience*, 12(12), 4745–4765.

[5] Grunewald, A. (1996). A model of transparent motion and non-transparent motion aftereffects. In D. S. Touretzky, M. C. Mozer, & M. E. Hasselmo (Eds.), *Advances in Neural Information Processing Systems 8* (pp. 837–843). Cambridge, MA: MIT Press.

[6] Hol, K. & Treue, S. (1997). Direction-selective responses in the superior temporal sulcus to transparent patterns moving at acute angles. *Society for Neuroscience Abstracts 23* (p. 179:11).

[7] Mather, G. & Moulden, B. (1983). Thresholds for movement direction: two directions are less detectable than one. *Quarterly Journal of Experimental Psychology*, 35, 513-518.

[8] Rauber, H. J. & Treue, S. (1997). Recovering the directions of visual motion in transparent patterns. *Society for Neuroscience Abstracts 23* (p. 179:10).

[9] Recanzone, G. H., Wurtz, R. H., & Schwarz, U. (1997). Responses of MT and MST neurons to one and two moving objects in the receptive field. *Journal of Neurophysiology*, 78(6), 2904–2915.

[10] Shadlen, M. N., Britten, K. H., Newsome, W. T., & Movshon, J. A. (1996). A computational analysis of the relationship between neuronal and behavioral responses to visual motion. *Journal of Neuroscience*, 16(4), 1486–510.

[11] Snippe, H. P. (1996). Theoretical considerations for the analysis of population coding in motor cortex. *Neural Computation*, 8(3):29–37.

[12] van Wezel, R. J., Lankheet, M. J., Verstraten, F. A., Maree, A. F., & van de Grind, W. A. (1996). Responses of complex cells in area 17 of the cat to bi-vectorial transparent motion. *Vision Research*, 36(18), 2805-13.

[13] Williams, D., Tweten, S., & Sekuler, R. (1991). Using metamers to explore motion perception. *Vision Research*, 31(2), 275–286.

[14] Zemel, R. S., Dayan, P., & Pouget, A. (1998). Probabilistic interpretation of population codes. *Neural Computation*, 10, 403–430.

Part III
Theory

Tractable Variational Structures for Approximating Graphical Models

David Barber   Wim Wiegerinck
{davidb,wimw}@mbfys.kun.nl
RWCP[*] Theoretical Foundation SNN[†] University of Nijmegen
6525 EZ Nijmegen, The Netherlands.

Abstract

Graphical models provide a broad probabilistic framework with applications in speech recognition (Hidden Markov Models), medical diagnosis (Belief networks) and artificial intelligence (Boltzmann Machines). However, the computing time is typically exponential in the number of nodes in the graph. Within the variational framework for approximating these models, we present two classes of distributions, decimatable Boltzmann Machines and Tractable Belief Networks that go beyond the standard factorized approach. We give generalised mean-field equations for both these directed and undirected approximations. Simulation results on a small benchmark problem suggest using these richer approximations compares favorably against others previously reported in the literature.

1 Introduction

Graphical models provide a powerful framework for probabilistic inference[1] but suffer intractability when applied to large scale problems. Recently, variational approximations have been popular [2, 3, 4, 5], and have the advantage of providing rigorous bounds on quantities of interest, such as the data likelihood, in contrast to other approximate procedures such as Monte Carlo methods[1]. One of the original models in the neural networks community, the Boltzmann machine (BM), belongs to the class of undirected graphical models. The lack of a suitable algorithm has hindered its application to larger problems. The deterministic BM algorithm[6], a variational procedure using a factorized approximating distribution, speeds up the learning of BMs, although the simplicity of this approximation can lead to undesirable effects[7]. Factorized approximations have also been successfully applied to sigmoid belief networks[4]. One approach to producing a more accurate approximation is to go beyond the class of factorized approximating models by using, for example, mixtures of factorized models. However, it may be that very many mixture components are needed to obtain a significant improvement beyond using the factorized approximation[5]. In this paper, after describing the variational learn-

---

[*]Real World Computing Partnership
[†]Foundation for Neural Networks

ing framework, we introduce two further classes of non-factorized approximations, one undirected (decimatable BMs in section (3)) and the other, directed (Tractable Belief Networks in section (4)). To demonstrate the potential benefits of these methods, we include results on a toy benchmark problem in section (5) and discuss their relation to other methods in section (6).

2 Variational Learning

We assume the existence of a graphical model P with known qualitative structure but for which the quantitative parameters of the structure remain to be learned from data. Given that the variables can be considered as either visible (V) or hidden (H), one approach to learning is to carry out maximum likelihood on the visible variables for each example in the dataset. Considering the KL divergence between the true distribution $P(H|V)$ and a distribution $Q(H)$,

$$KL(Q(H), P(H|V)) = \sum_H Q(H) \ln \frac{Q(H)}{P(H|V)} \geq 0$$

and using $P(H|V) = P(H,V)/P(V)$ gives the bound

$$\ln P(V) \geq -\sum_H Q(H) \ln Q(H) + \sum_H Q(H) \ln P(H,V) \tag{1}$$

Betraying the connection to statistical physics, the first term is termed the "entropy" and the second the "energy". One typically chooses a variational distribution Q so that the entropic term is "tractable". We assume that the energy $E(Q)$ is similarly computable, perhaps with recourse to some extra variational bound (as in section (5)). By tractable, we mean that all necessary marginals and desired quantities are computationally feasible, regardless of the issue of the scaling of the computational effort with the graph size. Learning consists of two iterating steps: first optimize the bound (1) with respect to the parameters of Q, and then with respect to the parameters of $P(H,V)$. We concentrate here on the first step. For clarity, we present our approach for the case of binary variables $s_i \in \{0,1\}, i = 1..N$. We now consider two classes of approximating distributions Q.

3 Undirected Q: Decimatable Boltzmann Machines

Boltzmann machines describe probability distributions parameterized by a symmetric weight matrix J

$$Q(s) = \frac{1}{Z} \exp \phi, \qquad \phi \equiv \sum_{ij} J_{ij} s_i s_j = s \cdot J s \tag{2}$$

where the normalization constant, or "partition function" is $Z = \sum_s \exp \phi$. For convenience we term the diagonals of J the "biases", $h_i = J_{ii}$. Since $\ln Z(J, h)$ is a generating function for the first and second order statistics of the variables s, the entropy is tractable provided that Z is tractable. For general connection structures, J, computing Z is intractable as it involves a sum over 2^N states; however, not all Boltzmann machines are intractable. A class of tractable structures is described by a set of so-called decimation rules in which nodes from the graph can be removed one by one, fig(1). Provided that appropriate local changes are made to the BM parameters, the partition function of the reduced graph remains unaltered (see eg [2]). For example, node c in fig(1) can be removed, provided that the weight matrix J and bias h are transformed, $J \to J'$, $h \to h'$, with $J'_{ac} = J'_{bc} = h'_c = 0$ and

$$J'_{ab} = J_{ab} + \frac{1}{2} \ln \frac{(1 + e^{h_c})(1 + e^{h_c + 2(J_{ac} + J_{bc})})}{(1 + e^{h_c + 2J_{ac}})(1 + e^{h_c + 2J_{bc}})}, \qquad h'_{a/b} = h_{a/b} + \ln \frac{1 + e^{h_c + 2J_{a/b,c}}}{1 + e^{h_c}} \tag{3}$$

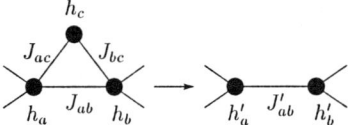

Figure 1: A decimation rule for BMs. We can remove the upper node on the left so that the partition function of the reduced graph is the same. This requires a simple change in the parameters J, h coupling the two nodes on the right (see text).

By repeatedly applying such rules, Z is calculable in time linear in N.

3.1 Fixed point (Mean Field) Equations

Using (2) in (1), the bound we wish to optimize with respect to the parameters $\theta = (J, h)$ of Q has the form ($\langle \ldots \rangle$ denotes averages with respect to Q)

$$B(\theta) = -\langle \phi \rangle + \ln Z + E(\theta) \qquad (4)$$

where $E(\theta)$ is the energy. Differentiating (4) with respect to J_{ij} ($i \neq j$) gives

$$\frac{\partial B}{\partial J_{ij}} = -\sum_{kl} F_{ij,kl} J_{kl} + \frac{\partial E}{\partial J_{ij}} \qquad (5)$$

where $F_{ij,kl} = \langle s_i s_j s_k s_l \rangle - \langle s_i s_j \rangle \langle s_k s_l \rangle$ is the Fisher information matrix. A similar expression holds for the bias parameters, h, so that we can form a linear fixed point equation in the total parameter set θ where the derivatives of the bound vanish. This suggests the iterative solution, $\theta^{new} = F^{-1} \nabla_\theta f$ where the right hand side is evaluated at the current parameter values, θ^{old}.

4 Directed Q: Tractable Belief Networks

Belief networks are products of conditional probability distributions,

$$Q(H) = \prod_{i \in H} Q(H_i | \pi_i) \qquad (6)$$

in which π_i denotes the parents of node i (see for example, [1]). The efficiency of computation depends on the underlying graphical structure of the model and is exponential in the maximal clique size (of the moralized triangulated graph [1]). We now assume that our model class consists of belief networks with a fixed, tractable graphical structure. The entropy can then be computed efficiently since it decouples into a sum of averaged entropies per site i ($Q(\pi_i) \equiv 1$ if $\pi_i = \phi$),

$$\sum_H Q(H) \ln Q(H) = \sum_{i \in H} \sum_{\pi_i} Q(\pi_i) \sum_{H_i} Q(H_i | \pi_i) \ln Q(H_i | \pi_i) \qquad (7)$$

Note that the conditional entropy at each site i is trivial to compute since the values required can be read off directly from the definition of Q (6). By assumption, the marginals $Q(\pi_i)$ are tractable, and can be found by standard methods, for example using the Junction Tree Algorithm[1].

To optimize the bound (1), we parameterize Q via its conditional probabilities, $q_i(\pi_i) \equiv Q(H_i = 1 | \pi_i)$. The remaining probability $Q(H_i = 0 | \pi_i)$ follows from normalization. We therefore have a set $\{q_i(\pi_i)|\pi_i = (0\ldots0),\ldots,(1\ldots1)\}$ of variational parameters for each node in the graph. Setting the gradient of the bound with respect to the $q_i(\pi_i)$'s equal to zero yields the equations

$$q_i(\pi_i) = \sigma\left(\frac{(\nabla_{i\pi_i} E(Q)) + L_{i\pi_i}}{Q(\pi_i)}\right) \qquad (8)$$

with

$$L_{i\pi_i} = -\sum_j \sum_{\pi_j} [\nabla_{i\pi_i} Q(\pi_j)] \sum_{H_j} Q(H_j|\pi_j) \ln Q(H_j|\pi_j) \qquad (9)$$

where $\sigma(z) = 1/(1+e^{-z})$. The gradient $\nabla_{i\pi_i}$ is with respect to $q_i(\pi_i)$. The explicit evaluation of the gradients can be performed efficiently, since all that need to be differentiated are at most scalar functions of quantities that depend again only linearly on the parameters $q_i(\pi_i)$. To optimize the bound, we iterate (8) till convergence, analogous to using factorized models[4]. However, the more powerful class of approximating distributions described by belief networks should enable a much tighter bound on the likelihood of the visible units.

5 Application to Sigmoid Belief Networks

We now describe an application of these non-factorized approximations to a particular class of directed graphical models, sigmoid belief networks[8] for which the conditional distributions have the form

$$P(s_i = 1|\pi_i) = \sigma\left(\sum_j W_{ij} s_j + k_i\right) \qquad (10)$$

$W_{ij} = 0$ if $j \notin \pi_i$. The joint distribution then has the form

$$P(H,V) = \prod_i \exp\left[z_i s_i - \ln(1+e^{z_i})\right] \qquad (11)$$

where $z_i = \sum_j W_{ij} s_j + k_i$. In (11) it is to be understood that the visible units are set to their observed values. In the lower bound (1), unfortunately, the average of $\ln P(H,V)$ is not tractable, since $\langle \ln[1+e^z]\rangle$ does not decouple into a polynomial number of single site averages. Following [4] we use therefore the bound

$$\langle \ln[1+e^z]\rangle \leq \xi\langle z\rangle + \ln\left\langle e^{-\xi z} + e^{(1-\xi)z}\right\rangle \qquad (12)$$

where ξ is a variational parameter in $[0,1]$. We can then define the energy function

$$E(Q,\xi) = \sum_{ij} W_{ij}\langle s_i s_j\rangle + \sum_i \tilde{k}_i \langle s_i\rangle - \sum_i k_i \xi_i - \sum_i \ln\left\langle e^{-\xi_i z_i} + e^{(1-\xi_i)z_i}\right\rangle \qquad (13)$$

where $\tilde{k}_i = k_i - \sum_j \xi_j W_{ji}$. Expect for the final term, the energy is a function of first or second order statistics of the variables. For using a BM as the variational distribution, the final terms of (13) $\langle e^{-\xi_i z_i}\rangle = \sum_H e^{\phi-\xi_i z_i}/Z$ are simply the ratio of two partition functions, with the one in the numerator having a shifted bias. This is therefore tractable, provided that we use a tractable BM Q.

Similarly, if we are using a Belief Network as the variational distribution, all but the last term in (13) is trivially tractable, provided that Q is tractable. We write the terms $\langle e^{-\xi_i z_i}\rangle = e^{-\xi_i h_i} \sum_H R(H)$, where $R(H) = \prod_j R(H_j|\pi_j)$ and $R(H_j|\pi_j) \equiv$

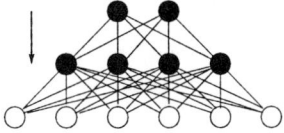

(a) Directed graph toy problem. Hidden units are black

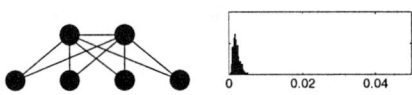

(b) Decimatable BM - 25 parameters, mean: 0.0020.

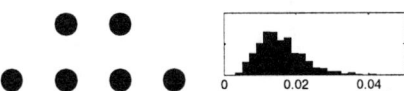

(c) disconnected ('standard mean field') - 16 parameters, mean: 0.01571. Max. clique size: 1

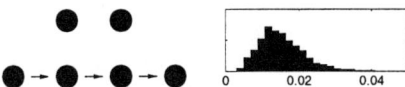

(d) chain - 19 parameters, mean: 0.01529. Max. clique size: 2

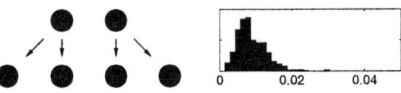

(e) trees - 20 parameters, mean: 0.0089. Max. clique size: 2

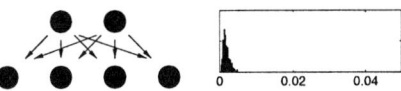

(f) network - 28 parameters, mean: 0.00183. Max. clique size: 3

Figure 2: (a) Sigmoid Belief Network for which we approximate $\ln P(V)$. (b): BM approximation. (c,d,e,f): Structures of the directed approximations on H. For each structure, histograms of the relative error between the true log likelihood and the lower bound is plotted. The horizontal scale has been fixed to [0,0.05] in all plots. The maximum clique size refers to the complexity of computation for each approximation, which is exponential in this quantity. The number of parameters includes the vector ξ.

$Q(H_j|\pi_j)\exp(-\xi_i J_{ij} H_j)$. R and Q have the same graphical structure and we can therefore use message propagation techniques again to compute $\langle e^{-\xi_i z_i}\rangle$.

To test our methods numerically, we generated 500 networks with parameters $\{W_{ij}, k_j\}$ drawn randomly from the uniform distribution over $[-1,1]$. The lower bounds $\mathcal{F}_V$ for several approximating structures are compared with the true log likelihood, using the relative error $\mathcal{E} = \mathcal{F}_V/\ln P(V) - 1$, fig. 2. These show that considerable improvements can be obtained when non-factorized variational distributions are used. Note that a 5 component mixture model ($\approx$ 80 variational parameters) yields $\mathcal{E} = 0.01139$ on this problem [5][1]. These results suggest therefore that exploiting knowledge of the graphical structure of the model is useful. For instance, the chain (fig. 2(b)) with no graphical overlap with the original graph shows hardly any improvement over the standard mean field approximation. On the other hand, the tree model (fig. 2(c)), which has about the same number of parameters, but a larger overlap with the original graph, does improve considerably over the mean field approximation (and even over the 5 component mixture model). By increasing the overlap, as in fig. 2(d), the improvement gained is even greater.

---

[1] In which $Q = \sum_j \lambda_j Q(H|\mu^j)$ where $Q(H|\mu) = \prod_i \mu_i^{H_i}(1-\mu_i)^{1-H_i}$ and $\sum_j \lambda_j = 1$.

6 Discussion

In this section, we briefly explain the relationship of the introduced methods to other, "non-factorized" methods in the literature, namely node-elimination[9] and substructure variation[10].

6.1 Graph Partitioning and Node Elimination

A further class of approximating distributions Q that could be considered are those in which the nodes can be partitioned into clusters, with independencies between the clusters. For expositional clarity, consider two partitions, $s = (s_1, s_2)$, and define Q to be factorized over these partitions[2], $Q = Q_1(s_1)Q_2(s_2)$. Using this Q in (1), we obtain (with obvious notational simplifications)

$$\ln P(V) \geq -\langle \ln Q_1 \rangle_1 - \langle \ln Q_2 \rangle_2 + \langle \ln P \rangle_{1,2} \qquad (14)$$

A functional derivative with respect to Q_1 and Q_2 gives the optimal forms:

$$Q_1 = \exp \langle \ln P \rangle_2 / Z_1 \qquad Q_2 = \exp \langle \ln P \rangle_1 / Z_2 \qquad (15)$$

If we substitute this form for Q_2 in (14) and use $Z_2 = \sum \exp \langle \ln P \rangle_1$, we obtain

$$\ln P(V) \geq -\langle \ln Q_1 \rangle_1 + \ln \sum_2 \exp \langle \ln P \rangle_1 \qquad (16)$$

In general, the final term may not have a simple form. In the case of approximating a BM P, $\ln P = s_1 \cdot J_{11} s_1 + 2 s_1 \cdot J_{12} s_2 + s_2 \cdot J_{22} s_2 - \ln Z_p$. Used in (16), we get:

$$\ln P(V) \geq -\langle \ln Q_1 \rangle_1 - \ln Z_p + \langle s_1 \cdot J_{11} s_1 \rangle_1 + \ln \sum_2 \exp \left(s_2 \cdot J_{22} s_2 + 2 s_2 \cdot J_{21} \langle s_1 \rangle_1 \right) \qquad (17)$$

so that the final term of (17) is the normalizing constant of a BM with connection matrix J_{22} and whose diagonals are shifted by $J_{21} \langle s_1 \rangle_1$. One can therefore identify a set of nodes s_1 which, when eliminated, reveal a tractable structure on the nodes s_2. The nodes that were removed are compensated for by using a variational distribution $Q_1(s_1)$. If P is a BM, then the optimal Q_1 has its weights fixed to those of P restricted to variables s_1, but with variable biases shifted by $J_{12} \langle s_2 \rangle_2$. Restricting Q_1 to factorized models, we recover the node elimination bound [9] which can readily be improved by considering *non-factorized* distributions Q_1 (for example those introduced in this paper), see fig(3). Note, however, that there is no a-priori guarantee that using such partitioned approximations will lead to a better approximation than that obtained from a tractable variational distribution defined on the whole graph, but which does not have such a product form. Using a product of *conditional* distributions over clusters of nodes is developed more fully in [11].

6.2 Substructure Variation

The process of using a Q defined on the whole graph but for which only a subset of the connections are adaptive is termed substructure variation [10]. In the context of BMs, Saul et al [2] identified weights in the original intractable distribution P that, if set to zero, would lead to a tractable graph $Q(s) = P(s|h, J, J_{intractable} = 0)$. To compensate for these removed weights they allowed the biases in Q to vary such that the KL divergence between Q and P is minimized. In general, this is a weaker method than one in which potentially all the parameters in the approximating network are adaptive, such as using a decimatable BM.

[2]In the case of fully connected BMs, for computing with a Q which is the product of K partitions (each of which is fully connected say), the computing time reduces from 2^N for the "intractable" P to $K 2^{N/K}$ for Q, which can be a considerable reduction.

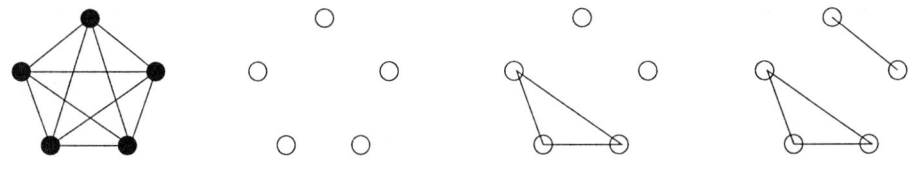

(a) Intractable Model (b) "Naive" mean field (c) Node elimination (d) Partioning

Figure 3: (a) A non-decimatable 5 node BM. (b) The standard factorized approximation. (c) Node Elimination (d) Partitioning, where a richer distribution is considered on the eliminated nodes. A solid line denotes a weight fixed to those in the original graph. A solid node is fixed, and an open node represents a variable bias.

7 Conclusion

Finding accurate, controllable approximations of graphical models is crucial if their application to large scale problems is to be realised. We have elucidated two general classes of tractable approximations, both based on the Kullback-Leibler divergence. Future interesting directions include extending the class of distributions to higher order Boltzmann Machines (for which the class of decimation rules is greater), and to mixtures of these approaches. Higher order perturbative approaches are considered in [12]. These techniques therefore facilitate the approximating power of tractable models which can lead to a considerable improvement in performance.

[1] E. Castillo, J. M. Gutierrez, and A. S. Hadi. *Expert Systems and Probabilistic Network Models*. Springer, 1997.

[2] L. K. Saul and M. I. Jordan. Boltzmann Chains and Hidden Markov Models. In G. Tesauro, D. S. Touretzky, and T. K. Leen, editors, Advances in Neural Information Processing Systems, pages 435–442. MIT Press, 1995. NIPS 7.

[3] T. Jaakkola. *Variational Methods for Inference and Estimation in Graphical Models*. PhD thesis, Massachusetts Institute of Technology, 1997

[4] L. K. Saul, T. Jaakkola, and M. I. Jordan. Mean Field Theory for Sigmoid Belief Networks. *Journal of Artificial Intelligence Research*, 4:61–76, 1996.

[5] C.M. Bishop, N. Lawrence, T. Jaakkola, and M. I. Jordan. Approximating Posterior Distributions in Belief Networks using Mixtures. MIT Press, 1998. NIPS 10.

[6] C. Peterson and J. R. Anderson. A Mean Field Theory Learning Algorithm for Neural Networks. *Complex Systems*, 1:995–1019, 1987.

[7] Conrad C. Galland. The limitations of deterministic Boltzmann machine learning. *Network: Computation in Neural Systems*, 4:355–379, 1993.

[8] R. Neal. Connectionist learning of Belief Networks. *Artificial Intelligence*, 56:71–113, 1992.

[9] T. S. Jaakkola and M. I. Jordan. Recursive Algorithms for Approximating Probabilities in Graphical Models. MIT Press, 1996. NIPS 9.

[10] L. K. Saul and M. I. Jordan. Exploiting Tractable Substructures in Intractable Networks. MIT Press, 1996. NIPS 8.

[11] W. Wiegerinck and D. Barber. Mean Field Theory based on Belief Networks for Approximate Inference. 1998. ICANN 98.

[12] D. Barber and P. van de Laar. Variational Cumulant Expansions for Intractable Distributions. *Journal of Artificial Intelligence Research*, 1998. Accepted.

Almost Linear VC Dimension Bounds for Piecewise Polynomial Networks

Peter L. Bartlett
Department of System Engineering
Australian National University
Canberra, ACT 0200
Australia
Peter.Bartlett@anu.edu.au

Vitaly Maiorov
Department of Mathematics
Technion, Haifa 32000
Israel

Ron Meir
Department of Electrical Engineering
Technion, Haifa 32000
Israel
rmeir@dumbo.technion.ac.il

Abstract

We compute upper and lower bounds on the VC dimension of feedforward networks of units with piecewise polynomial activation functions. We show that if the number of layers is fixed, then the VC dimension grows as $W \log W$, where W is the number of parameters in the network. This result stands in opposition to the case where the number of layers is unbounded, in which case the VC dimension grows as W^2.

1 MOTIVATION

The VC dimension is an important measure of the complexity of a class of binary-valued functions, since it characterizes the amount of data required for learning in the PAC setting (see [BEHW89, Vap82]). In this paper, we establish upper and lower bounds on the VC dimension of a specific class of multi-layered feedforward neural networks. Let $\mathcal{F}$ be the class of binary-valued functions computed by a feedforward neural network with W weights and k computational (non-input) units, each with a piecewise polynomial activation function. Goldberg and Jerrum [GJ95] have shown that $\text{VCdim}(\mathcal{F}) \leq c_1(W^2 + Wk) = O(W^2)$, where c_1 is a constant. Moreover, Koiran and Sontag [KS97] have demonstrated such a network that has $\text{VCdim}(\mathcal{F}) \geq c_2 W^2 = \Omega(W^2)$, which would lead one to conclude that the bounds are in fact tight up to a constant. However, the proof used in [KS97] to establish the lower bound made use of the fact that the number of layers can grow with W. In practical applications, this number is often a small constant. Thus, the question remains as to whether it is possible to obtain a better bound in the realistic scenario where the number of layers is fixed.

The contribution of this work is the proof of upper and lower bounds on the VC dimension of piecewise polynomial nets. The upper bound behaves as $O(WL^2 + WL \log WL)$, where L is the number of layers. If L is fixed, this is $O(W \log W)$, which is superior to the previous best result which behaves as $O(W^2)$. Moreover, using ideas from [KS97] and [GJ95] we are able to derive a lower bound on the VC dimension which is $\Omega(WL)$ for $L = O(W)$. Maass [Maa94] shows that three-layer networks with threshold activation functions and binary inputs have VC dimension $\Omega(W \log W)$, and Sakurai [Sak93] shows that this is also true for two-layer networks with threshold activation functions and real inputs. It is easy to show that these results imply similar lower bounds if the threshold activation function is replaced by any piecewise polynomial activation function f that has bounded and distinct limits $\lim_{x \to -\infty} f(x)$ and $\lim_{x \to \infty} f(x)$. We thus conclude that if the number of layers L is fixed, the VC dimension of piecewise polynomial networks with $L \geq 2$ layers and real inputs, and of piecewise polynomial networks with $L \geq 3$ layers and binary inputs, grows as $W \log W$. We note that for the piecewise polynomial networks considered in this work, it is easy to show that the VC dimension and pseudo-dimension are closely related (see e.g. [Vid96]), so that similar bounds (with different constants) hold for the pseudo-dimension. Independently, Sakurai has obtained similar upper bounds and improved lower bounds on the VC dimension of piecewise polynomial networks (see [Sak99]).

2 UPPER BOUNDS

We begin the technical discussion with precise definitions of the VC-dimension and the class of networks considered in this work.

Definition 1 *Let X be a set, and $\mathcal{A}$ a system of subsets of X. A set $S = \{x_1, \ldots, x_n\}$ is shattered by $\mathcal{A}$ if, for every subset $B \subseteq S$, there exists a set $A \in \mathcal{A}$ such that $S \cap A = B$. The VC-dimension of $\mathcal{A}$, denoted by $\mathrm{VCdim}(\mathcal{A})$, is the largest integer n such that there exists a set of cardinality n that is shattered by $\mathcal{A}$.*

Intuitively, the VC dimension measures the size, n, of the largest set of points for which all possible 2^n labelings may be achieved by sets $A \in \mathcal{A}$. It is often convenient to talk about the VC dimension of classes of indicator functions $\mathcal{F}$. In this case we simply identify the sets of points $x \in X$ for which $f(x) = 1$ with the subsets of $\mathcal{A}$, and use the notation $\mathrm{VCdim}(\mathcal{F})$.

A feedforward multi-layer network is a directed acyclic graph that represents a parametrized real-valued function of d real inputs. Each node is called either an input unit or a computation unit. The computation units are arranged in L layers. Edges are allowed from input units to computation units. There can also be an edge from a computation unit to another computation unit, but only if the first unit is in a lower layer than the second. There is a single unit in the final layer, called the output unit. Each input unit has an associated real value, which is one of the components of the input vector $x \in \mathbf{R}^d$. Each computation unit has an associated real value, called the unit's output value. Each edge has an associated real parameter, as does each computation unit. The output of a computation unit is given by $\sigma \left(\sum_e w_e z_e + w_0 \right)$, where the sum ranges over the set of edges leading to the unit, w_e is the parameter (weight) associated with edge e, z_e is the output value of the unit from which edge e emerges, w_0 is the parameter (bias) associated with the unit, and $\sigma : \mathbf{R} \to \mathbf{R}$ is called the activation function of the unit. The argument of σ is called the *net input* of the unit. We suppose that in each unit except the output unit, the activation function is a fixed piecewise polynomial function of the form

$$\sigma(u) = \phi_i(u) \qquad \text{for } u \in [t_{i-1}, t_i),$$

for $i = 1, \ldots, p+1$ (and set $t_0 = -\infty$ and $t_{p+1} = \infty$), where each ϕ_i is a polynomial of degree no more than l. We say that σ has p break-points, and degree l. The activation function in the output unit is the identity function. Let k_i denote the number of computational units in layer i and suppose there is a total of W parameters (weights and biases) and k computational units ($k = k_1 + k_2 + \cdots + k_{L-1} + 1$). For input x and parameter vector $a \in A = \mathbf{R}^W$, let $f(x, a)$ denote the output of this network, and let $\mathcal{F} = \{x \mapsto f(x, a) : a \in \mathbf{R}^W\}$ denote the class of functions computed by such an architecture, as we vary the W parameters. We first discuss the computation of the VC dimension, and thus consider the class of functions $\text{sgn}(\mathcal{F}) = \{x \mapsto \text{sgn}(f(x, a)) : a \in \mathbf{R}^W\}$.

Before giving the main theorem of this section, we present the following result, which is a slight improvement of a result due to Warren (see [ABar], Chapter 8).

Lemma 2.1 *Suppose $f_1(\cdot), f_2(\cdot), \ldots, f_m(\cdot)$ are fixed polynomials of degree at most l in $n \leq m$ variables. Then the number of distinct sign vectors $\{\text{sgn}(f_1(a)), \ldots, \text{sgn}(f_m(a))\}$ that can be generated by varying $a \in \mathbf{R}^n$ is at most $2(2eml/n)^n$.*

We then have our main result:

Theorem 2.1 *For any positive integers W, $k \leq W$, $L \leq W$, l, and p, consider a network with real inputs, up to W parameters, up to k computational units arranged in L layers, a single output unit with the identity activation function, and all other computation units with piecewise polynomial activation functions of degree l and with p break-points. Let $\mathcal{F}$ be the class of real-valued functions computed by this network. Then*

$$\text{VCdim}(\text{sgn}(\mathcal{F})) \leq 2WL \log(2eWLpk) + 2WL^2 \log(l+1) + 2L .$$

Since L and k are $O(W)$, for fixed l and p this implies that

$$\text{VCdim}(\text{sgn}(\mathcal{F})) = O(WL \log W + WL^2).$$

Before presenting the proof, we outline the main idea in the construction. For any fixed input x, the output of the network $f(x, a)$ corresponds to a piecewise polynomial function in the parameters a, of degree no larger than $(l+1)^{L-1}$ (recall that the last layer is linear). Thus, the parameter domain $A = \mathbf{R}^W$ can be split into regions, in each of which the function $f(x, \cdot)$ is polynomial. From Lemma 2.1, it is possible to obtain an upper bound on the number of sign assignments that can be attained by varying the parameters of a set of polynomials. The theorem will be established by combining this bound with a bound on the number of regions.

PROOF OF THEOREM 2.1 For an arbitrary choice of m points $x_1, x_2, \ldots, x_m$, we wish to bound

$$K = |\{(\text{sgn}(f(x_1, a)), \ldots, \text{sgn}(f(x_m, a))) : a \in A\}| .$$

Fix these m points, and consider a partition $\{S_1, S_2, \ldots, S_N\}$ of the parameter domain A. Clearly

$$K \leq \sum_{i=1}^{N} |\{(\mathrm{sgn}(f(x_1,a)), \ldots, \mathrm{sgn}(f(x_m,a))) : a \in S_i\}|.$$

We choose the partition so that within each region S_i, $f(x_1, \cdot), \ldots, f(x_m, \cdot)$ are all fixed polynomials of degree no more than $(l+1)^{L-1}$. Then, by Lemma 2.1, each term in the sum above is no more than

$$2\left(\frac{2em(l+1)^{L-1}}{W}\right)^W. \tag{1}$$

The only remaining point is to construct the partition and determine an upper bound on its size. The partition is constructed recursively, using the following procedure. Let $\mathcal{S}_1$ be a partition of A such that, for all $S \in \mathcal{S}_1$, there are constants $b_{h,i,j} \in \{0,1\}$ for which

$$\mathrm{sgn}(p_{h,x_j}(a) - t_i) = b_{h,i,j} \quad \text{for all } a \in S,$$

where $j \in \{1, \ldots, m\}$, $h \in \{1, \ldots, k_1\}$ and $i \in \{1, \ldots, p\}$. Here t_i are the breakpoints of the piecewise polynomial activation functions, and p_{h,x_j} is the affine function describing the net input to the h-th unit in the first layer, in response to x_j. That is,

$$p_{h,x_j} = a_h \cdot x_j + a_{h,0},$$

where $a_h \in \mathbf{R}^d$, $a_{h,0} \in \mathbf{R}$ are the weights of the h-th unit in the first layer. Note that the partition $\mathcal{S}_1$ is determined solely by the parameters corresponding to the first hidden layer, as the input to this layer is unaffected by the other parameters. Clearly, for $a \in S$, the output of any first layer unit in response to an x_j is a fixed polynomial in a.

Now, let $W_1, \ldots, W_L$ be the number of variables used in computing the unit outputs up to layer $1, \ldots, L$ respectively (so $W_L = W$), and let $k_1, \ldots, k_L$ be the number of computation units in layer $1, \ldots, L$ respectively (recall that $k_L = 1$). Then we can choose $\mathcal{S}_1$ so that $|\mathcal{S}_1|$ is no more than the number of sign assignments possible with mk_1p affine functions in W_1 variables. Lemma 2.1 shows that $|\mathcal{S}_1| \leq 2\left(\frac{2emk_1p}{W_1}\right)^{W_1}$.

Now, we define $\mathcal{S}_n$ (for $n > 1$) as follows. Assume that for all S in $\mathcal{S}_{n-1}$ and all x_j, the net input of every unit in layer n in response to x_j is a fixed polynomial function of $a \in S$, of degree no more than $(l+1)^{n-1}$. Let $\mathcal{S}_n$ be a partition of A that is a refinement of $\mathcal{S}_{n-1}$ (that is, for all $S \in \mathcal{S}_n$, there is an $S' \in \mathcal{S}_{n-1}$ with $S \subseteq S'$), such that for all $S \in \mathcal{S}_n$ there are constants $b_{h,i,j} \in \{0,1\}$ such that

$$\mathrm{sgn}(p_{h,x_j}(a) - t_i) = b_{h,i,j} \quad \text{for all } a \in S, \tag{2}$$

where p_{h,x_j} is the polynomial function describing the net input of the h-th unit in the n-th layer, in response to x_j, when $a \in S$. Since $S \subseteq S'$ for some $S' \in \mathcal{S}_{n-1}$, (2) implies that the output of each n-th layer unit in response to an x_j is a fixed polynomial in a of degree no more than $l(l+1)^{n-1}$, for all $a \in S$.

Finally, we can choose $\mathcal{S}_n$ such that, for all $S' \in \mathcal{S}_{n-1}$ we have $|\{S \in \mathcal{S}_n : S \subseteq S'\}|$ is no more than the number of sign assignments of mk_np polynomials in W_n variables of degree no more than $(l+1)^{n-1}$, and by Lemma 2.1 this is no more than $2\left(\frac{2emk_np(l+1)^{n-1}}{W_n}\right)^{W_n}$. Notice also that the net input of every unit in layer $n+1$ in response to x_j is a fixed polynomial function of $a \in S \in \mathcal{S}_n$ of degree no more than $(l+1)^n$.

Proceeding in this way we get a partition $\mathcal{S}_{L-1}$ of A such that for $S \in \mathcal{S}_{L-1}$ the network output in response to any x_j is a fixed polynomial of $a \in S$ of degree no more than $l(l+1)^{L-2}$. Furthermore,

$$|\mathcal{S}_{L-1}| \leq 2\left(\frac{2emk_1p}{W_1}\right)^{W_1} \prod_{i=2}^{L-1} 2\left(\frac{2emk_ip(l+1)^{i-1}}{W_i}\right)^{W_i}$$

$$\leq \prod_{i=1}^{L-1} 2\left(\frac{2emk_ip(l+1)^{i-1}}{W_i}\right)^{W_i}.$$

Multiplying by the bound (1) gives the result

$$K \leq \prod_{i=1}^{L} 2\left(\frac{2emk_ip(l+1)^{i-1}}{W_i}\right)^{W_i}.$$

Since the points $x_1, \ldots, x_m$ were chosen arbitrarily, this gives a bound on the maximal number of dichotomies induced by $a \in A$ on m points. An upper bound on the VC-dimension is then obtained by computing the largest value of m for which this number is at least 2^m, yielding

$$m < L + \sum_{i=1}^{L} W_i \log\left(\frac{2empk_i(l+1)^{i-1}}{W_i}\right)$$
$$< L\left[1 + (L-1)W\log(l+1) + W\log(2empk)\right],$$

where all logarithms are to the base 2. We conclude (see for example [Vid96] Lemma 4.4) that

$$\text{VCdim}(\mathcal{F}) \leq 2L\left[(L-1)W\log(l+1) + W\log(2eWLpk) + 1\right].$$

■

We briefly mention the application of this result to the problem of learning a regression function $\mathbf{E}[Y|X = x]$, from n input/output pairs $\{(X_i, Y_i)\}_{i=1}^n$, drawn independently at random from an unknown distribution $P(X, Y)$. In the case of quadratic loss, $L(f) = \mathbf{E}(Y - f(X))^2$, one can show that there exist constants $c_1 \geq 1$ and c_2 such that

$$\mathbf{E}L(\hat{f}_n) \leq s^2 + c_1 \inf_{f \in \mathcal{F}} \tilde{L}(f) + c_2 \frac{M\text{Pdim}(\mathcal{F})\log n}{n},$$

where $s^2 = \mathbf{E}\left[Y - \mathbf{E}[Y|X]\right]^2$ is the noise variance, $\tilde{L}(f) = \mathbf{E}\left[(\mathbf{E}[Y|X] - f(X))^2\right]$ is the approximation error of f, and $\hat{f}_n$ is a function from the class $\mathcal{F}$ that approximately minimizes the sample average of the quadratic loss. Making use of recently derived bounds [MM97] on the approximation error, $\inf_{f \in \mathcal{F}} \tilde{L}(f)$, which are equal, up to logarithmic factors, to those obtained for networks of units with the standard sigmoidal function $\sigma(u) = (1 + e^{-u})^{-1}$, and combining with the considerably lower pseudo-dimension bounds for piecewise polynomial networks, we obtain much better error rates than are currently available for sigmoid networks.

3 LOWER BOUND

We now compute a lower bound on the VC dimension of neural networks with continuous activation functions. This result generalizes the lower bound in [KS97], since it holds for any number of layers.

Theorem 3.1 *Suppose* $f : \mathbf{R} \to \mathbf{R}$ *has the following properties:*

1. $\lim_{\alpha \to \infty} f(\alpha) = 1$ *and* $\lim_{\alpha \to -\infty} f(\alpha) = 0$, *and*

2. f *is differentiable at some point x_0 with derivative $f'(x_0) \neq 0$.*

Then for any $L \geq 1$ and $W \geq 10L - 14$, there is a feedforward network with the following properties: The network has L layers and W parameters, the output unit is a linear unit, all other computation units have activation function f, and the set $\mathrm{sgn}(\mathcal{F})$ *of functions computed by the network has*

$$\mathrm{VCdim}(\mathrm{sgn}(\mathcal{F})) \geq \left\lfloor \frac{L}{2} \right\rfloor \left\lfloor \frac{W}{2} \right\rfloor,$$

where $\lfloor u \rfloor$ is the largest integer less than or equal to u.

PROOF As in [KS97], the proof follows that of Theorem 2.5 in [GJ95], but we show how the functions described in [GJ95] can be computed by a network, and keep track of the number of parameters and layers required. We first prove the lower bound for a network containing linear threshold units and linear units (with the identity activation function), and then show that all except the output unit can be replaced by units with activation function f, and the resulting network still shatters the same set. For further details of the proof, see the full paper [BMM98].

Fix positive integers $M, N \in \mathbf{N}$. We now construct a set of MN points, which may be shattered by a network with $O(N)$ weights and $O(M)$ layers. Let $\{a_i\}$, $i = 1, 2, \ldots, N$ denote a set of N parameters, where each $a_i \in [0,1)$ has an M-bit binary representation $a_i = \sum_{j=1}^{M} 2^{-j} a_{i,j}$, $a_{i,j} \in \{0,1\}$, i.e. the M-bit base two representation of a_i is $a_i = 0.a_{i,1} a_{i,2} \ldots a_{i,M}$. We will consider inputs in $B_N \times B_M$, where $B_N = \{e_i : 1 \leq i \leq N\}$, $e_i \in \{0,1\}^N$ has i-th bit 1 and all other bits 0, and B_M is defined similarly. We show how to extract the bits of the a_i, so that for input $x = (e_l, e_m)$ the network outputs $a_{l,m}$. Since there are NM inputs of the form (e_l, e_m), and $a_{l,m}$ can take on all possible 2^{MN} values, the result will follow. There are three stages to the computation of $a_{l,m}$: (1) computing a_l, (2) extracting $a_{l,k}$ from a_l, for every k, and (3) selecting $a_{l,m}$ among the $a_{l,k}$s.

Suppose the network input is $x = ((u_1, \ldots, u_N), (v_1, \ldots, v_M)) = (e_l, e_m)$. Using one linear unit we can compute $\sum_{i=1}^{N} u_i a_i = a_l$. This involves $N+1$ parameters and one computation unit in one layer. In fact, we only need N parameters, but we need the extra parameter when we show that this linear unit can be replaced by a unit with activation function f.

Consider the parameter $c_k = 0.a_{l,k} \ldots a_{l,M}$, that is, $c_k = \sum_{j=k}^{M} 2^{k-1-j} a_{l,j}$ for $k = 1, \ldots, M$. Since $c_k \geq 1/2$ iff $a_{l,k} = 1$, clearly $\mathrm{sgn}(c_k - 1/2) = a_{l,k}$ for all k. Also, $c_1 = a_l$ and $c_k = 2c_{k-1} - a_{l,k-1}$. Thus, consider the recursion

$$c_k = 2c_{k-1} - a_{l,k-1}$$
$$a_{l,k} = \mathrm{sgn}(c_k - 1/2),$$

with initial conditions $c_1 = a_l$ and $a_{l,1} = \mathrm{sgn}(a_l - 1/2)$. Clearly, we can compute $a_{l,1}, \ldots, a_{l,M-1}$ and $c_2, \ldots, c_{M-1}$ in another $2(M-2)+1$ layers, using $5(M-2)+2$ parameters in $2(M-2)+1$ computational units.

We could compute $a_{l,M}$ in the same way, but the following approach gives fewer layers. Set $b = \mathrm{sgn}\left(2c_{M-1} - a_{l,M-1} - \sum_{i=1}^{M-1} v_i\right)$. If $m \neq M$ then $b = 0$. If $m = M$ then the input vector $(v_1, \ldots, v_M) = e_M$, and thus $\sum_{i=1}^{M-1} v_i = 0$, implying that $b = \mathrm{sgn}(c_M) = \mathrm{sgn}(0.a_{l,M}) = a_{l,M}$.

In order to conclude the proof, we need to show how the variables $a_{l,m}$ may be recovered, depending on the inputs $(v_1, v_2, \ldots, v_M)$. We then have $a_{l,m} = b \vee \bigvee_{i=1}^{M-1}(a_{l,i} \wedge v_i)$. Since for boolean x and y, $x \wedge y = \text{sgn}(x + y - 3/2)$, and $\bigvee_{i=1}^{M} x_i = \text{sgn}(\sum_{i=1}^{M} x_i - 1/2)$, we see that the computation of $a_{l,m}$ involves an additional $5M$ parameters in $M+1$ computational units, and adds another 2 layers.

In total, there are $2M$ layers and $10M + N - 7$ parameters, and the network shatters a set of size NM. Clearly, we can add parameters and layers without affecting the function of the network. So for any $L, W \in \mathbf{N}$, we can set $M = \lfloor L/2 \rfloor$ and $N = W + 7 - 10M$, which is at least $\lfloor W/2 \rfloor$ provided $W \geq 10L - 14$. In that case, the VC-dimension is at least $\lfloor L/2 \rfloor \lfloor W/2 \rfloor$.

The network just constructed uses linear threshold units and linear units. However, it is easy to show (see [KS97], Theorem 5) that each unit except the output unit can be replaced by a unit with activation function f so that the network still shatters the set of size MN. For linear units, the input and output weights are scaled so that the linear function can be approximated to sufficient accuracy by f in the neighborhood of the point x_0. For linear threshold units, the input weights are scaled so that the behavior of f at infinity accurately approximates a linear threshold function. ∎

References

[ABar] M. Anthony and P. L. Bartlett. *Neural Network Learning: Theoretical Foundations*. Cambridge University Press, 1999 (to appear).

[BEHW89] A. Blumer, A. Ehrenfeucht, D. Haussler, and M. K. Warmuth. Learnability and the Vapnik-Chervonenkis dimension. *J. ACM*, 36(4):929–965, 1989.

[BMM98] P. L. Bartlett, V. Maiorov, and R. Meir. Almost linear VC-dimension bounds for piecewise polynomial networks. *Neural Computation*, 10:2159–2173, 1998.

[GJ95] P.W. Goldberg and M.R. Jerrum. Bounding the VC Dimension of Concept Classes Parameterized by Real Numbers. *Machine Learning*, 18:131–148, 1995.

[KS97] P. Koiran and E.D. Sontag. Neural Networks with Quadratic VC Dimension. *Journal of Computer and System Science*, 54:190–198, 1997.

[Maa94] W. Maass. Neural nets with superlinear VC-dimension. *Neural Computation*, 6(5):877–884, 1994.

[MM97] V. Maiorov and R. Meir. On the Near Optimality of the Stochastic Approximation of Smooth Functions by Neural Networks. Submitted for publication, 1997.

[Sak93] A. Sakurai. Tighter bounds on the VC-dimension of three-layer networks. In *World Congress on Neural Networks*, volume 3, pages 540–543, Hillsdale, NJ, 1993. Erlbaum.

[Sak99] A. Sakurai. Tight bounds for the VC-dimension of piecewise polynomial networks. In *Advances in Neural Information Processing Systems*, volume 11. MIT Press, 1999.

[Vap82] V. N. Vapnik. *Estimation of Dependences Based on Empirical Data*. Springer-Verlag, New York, 1982.

[Vid96] M Vidyasagar. *A Theory of Learning and Generalization*. Springer Verlag, New York, 1996.

Dynamics of Supervised Learning with Restricted Training Sets

A.C.C. Coolen
Dept of Mathematics
King's College London
Strand, London WC2R 2LS, UK
tcoolen@mth.kcl.ac.uk

D. Saad
Neural Computing Research Group
Aston University
Birmingham B4 7ET, UK
saadd@aston.ac.uk

Abstract

We study the dynamics of supervised learning in layered neural networks, in the regime where the size p of the training set is proportional to the number N of inputs. Here the local fields are no longer described by Gaussian distributions. We use dynamical replica theory to predict the evolution of macroscopic observables, including the relevant error measures, incorporating the old formalism in the limit $p/N \to \infty$.

1 INTRODUCTION

Much progress has been made in solving the dynamics of supervised learning in layered neural networks, using the strategy of statistical mechanics: by deriving closed laws for the evolution of suitably chosen macroscopic observables (order parameters) in the limit of an infinite system size [1, 2, 3, 4]. For a recent review and guide to references see e.g. [5]. The main successful procedure developed so far is built on the following cornerstones:
• *The task to be learned is defined by a 'teacher', which is itself a neural network.* This induces a natural set of order parameters (mutual weight vector overlaps between the teacher and the trained, 'student', network).
• *The number of network inputs is infinitely large.* This ensures that fluctuations in the order parameters will vanish, and enables usage of the central limit theorem.
• *The number of 'hidden' neurons is finite,* in both teacher and student, ensuring a finite number of order parameters and an insignificant cumulative impact of the fluctuations.
• *The size of the training set is much larger than the number of updates.* Each example presented is now different from the previous ones, so that the local fields will have Gaussian distributions, leading to closure of the dynamic equations.

In this paper we study the dynamics of learning in layered networks with *restricted* training sets, where the number p of examples scales linearly with the number N of inputs. Individual examples will now re-appear during the learning process as soon as the number of weight updates made is of the order of p. Correlations will develop between the weights

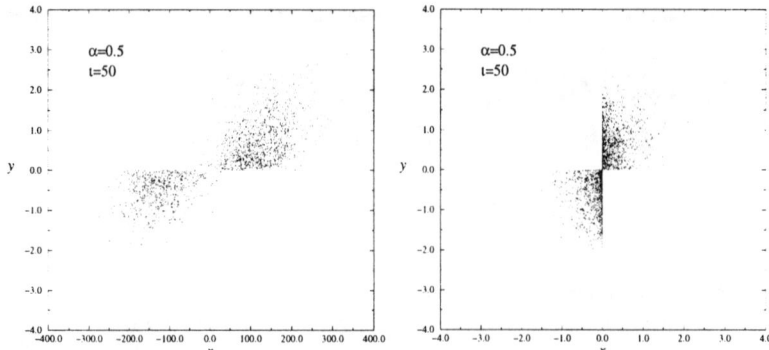

Figure 1: Student and teacher fields (x, y) (see text) observed during numerical simulations of on-line learning (learning rate $\eta = 1$) in a perceptron of size $N = 10,000$ at $t = 50$, using examples from a training set of size $p = \frac{1}{2}N$. Left: Hebbian learning. Right: AdaTron learning [5]. Both distributions are clearly non-Gaussian.

and the training set examples and the student's local fields (activations) will be described by non-Gaussian distributions (see e.g. Figure 1). This leads to a breakdown of the standard formalism: the field distributions are no longer characterized by a few moments, and the macroscopic laws must now be averaged over realizations of the training set. The first rigorous study of the dynamics of learning with restricted training sets in non-linear networks, via generating functionals [6], was carried out for networks with binary weights. Here we use dynamical replica theory (see e.g. [7]) to predict the evolution of macroscopic observables for finite α, incorporating the old formalism as a special case ($\alpha = p/N \to \infty$). For simplicity we restrict ourselves to single-layer systems and noise-free teachers.

2 FROM MICROSCOPIC TO MACROSCOPIC LAWS

A 'student' perceptron operates a rule which is parametrised by the weight vector $\boldsymbol{J} \in \Re^N$:

$$S : \{-1, 1\}^N \to \{-1, 1\} \qquad S(\boldsymbol{\xi}) = \text{sgn}\,[\boldsymbol{J} \cdot \boldsymbol{\xi}] \equiv \text{sgn}\,[x] \qquad (1)$$

It tries to emulate a teacher perceptron which operates a similar rule, characterized by a (fixed) weight vector $\boldsymbol{B} \in \Re^N$. The student modifies its weight vector $\boldsymbol{J}$ iteratively, using examples of input vectors $\boldsymbol{\xi}$ which are drawn at random from a fixed (randomly composed) training set $\tilde{D} = \{\boldsymbol{\xi}^1, \ldots, \boldsymbol{\xi}^p\} \subset D = \{-1, 1\}^N$, of size $p = \alpha N$ with $\alpha > 0$, and the corresponding values of the teacher outputs $T(\boldsymbol{\xi}) = \text{sgn}[\boldsymbol{B} \cdot \boldsymbol{\xi}] \equiv \text{sgn}\,[y]$. Averages over the training set $\tilde{D}$ and over the full set D will be denoted as $\langle \Phi(\boldsymbol{\xi}) \rangle_{\tilde{D}}$ and $\langle \Phi(\boldsymbol{\xi}) \rangle_D$, respectively. We will analyze the following two classes of learning rules:

$$\begin{aligned}\text{on-line:} &\quad \boldsymbol{J}(m+1) = \boldsymbol{J}(m) + \tfrac{\eta}{N}\, \boldsymbol{\xi}(m)\, \mathcal{G}\left[\boldsymbol{J}(m) \cdot \boldsymbol{\xi}(m), \boldsymbol{B} \cdot \boldsymbol{\xi}(m)\right] \\ \text{batch:} &\quad \boldsymbol{J}(m+1) = \boldsymbol{J}(m) + \tfrac{\eta}{N}\, \langle \boldsymbol{\xi}\, \mathcal{G}\left[\boldsymbol{J}(m) \cdot \boldsymbol{\xi}, \boldsymbol{B} \cdot \boldsymbol{\xi}\right] \rangle_{\tilde{D}} \end{aligned} \qquad (2)$$

In on-line learning one draws at each step m a question $\boldsymbol{\xi}(m)$ at random from the training set, the dynamics is a stochastic process; in batch learning one iterates a deterministic map. Our key dynamical observables are the training- and generalization errors, defined as

$$E_{\text{t}}(\boldsymbol{J}) = \langle \theta[-(\boldsymbol{J} \cdot \boldsymbol{\xi})(\boldsymbol{B} \cdot \boldsymbol{\xi})] \rangle_{\tilde{D}} \qquad E_{\text{g}}(\boldsymbol{J}) = \langle \theta[-(\boldsymbol{J} \cdot \boldsymbol{\xi})(\boldsymbol{B} \cdot \boldsymbol{\xi})] \rangle_D \qquad (3)$$

Only if the training set $\tilde{D}$ is sufficiently large, and if there are no correlations between $\boldsymbol{J}$ and the training set examples, will these two errors be identical. We now turn to *macroscopic* observables $\Omega[\boldsymbol{J}] = (\Omega_1[\boldsymbol{J}], \ldots, \Omega_k[\boldsymbol{J}])$. For $N \to \infty$ (with finite times $t = m/N$

and with finite k), and if our observables are of a so-called mean-field type, their associated macroscopic distribution $P_t(\Omega)$ is found to obey a Fokker-Planck type equation, with flow- and diffusion terms that depend on whether on-line or batch learning is used. We now choose a *specific* set of observables $\Omega[\boldsymbol{J}]$, taylored to the present problem:

$$Q[\boldsymbol{J}] = \boldsymbol{J}^2, \qquad R[\boldsymbol{J}] = \boldsymbol{J}\cdot\boldsymbol{B}, \qquad P[x,y;\boldsymbol{J}] = \langle\delta[x-\boldsymbol{J}\cdot\boldsymbol{\xi}]\,\delta[y-\boldsymbol{B}\cdot\boldsymbol{\xi}]\rangle_{\tilde{D}} \qquad (4)$$

This choice is motivated as follows: (i) in order to incorporate the old formalism we need $Q[\boldsymbol{J}]$ and $R[\boldsymbol{J}]$, (ii) the training error involves field statistics calculated over the training set, as given by $P[x,y;\boldsymbol{J}]$, and (iii) for $\alpha < \infty$ one cannot expect closed equations for a finite number of order parameters, the present choice effectively represents an infinite number. We will assume the number of arguments (x,y) for which $P[x,y;\boldsymbol{J}]$ is evaluated to go to infinity *after* the limit $N \to \infty$ has been taken. This eliminates technical subtleties and allows us to show that in the Fokker-Planck equation all diffusion terms vanish as $N \to \infty$. The latter thereby reduces to a Liouville equation, describing deterministic evolution of our macroscopic observables. For on-line learning one arrives at

$$\frac{d}{dt}Q = 2\eta \int dxdy\, P[x,y]\, x\, \mathcal{G}[x;y] + \eta^2 \int dxdy\, P[x,y]\, \mathcal{G}^2[x;y] \qquad (5)$$

$$\frac{d}{dt}R = \eta \int dxdy\, P[x,y]\, y\, \mathcal{G}[x;y] \qquad (6)$$

$$\frac{\partial}{\partial t}P[x,y] = \frac{1}{\alpha}\left[\int dx'\,P[x',y]\delta[x-x'-\eta\mathcal{G}[x',y]] - P[x,y]\right]$$

$$-\eta\frac{\partial}{\partial x}\int dx'dy'\,\mathcal{G}[x',y']\,\mathcal{A}[x,y;x',y']$$

$$+\frac{1}{2}\eta^2 \int dx'dy'\,P[x',y']\,\mathcal{G}^2[x',y']\,\frac{\partial^2}{\partial x^2}P[x,y] \qquad (7)$$

Expansion of these equations in powers of η, and retaining only the terms linear in η, gives the corresponding equations describing batch learning. The complexity of the problem is fully concentrated in a Green's function $\mathcal{A}[x,y;x',y']$, which is defined as

$$\mathcal{A}[x,y;x',y'] = \lim_{N\to\infty} \langle\langle\langle[1-\delta_{\boldsymbol{\xi}\boldsymbol{\xi}'}]\delta[x-\boldsymbol{J}\cdot\boldsymbol{\zeta}]\,\delta[y-\boldsymbol{B}\cdot\boldsymbol{\zeta}](\boldsymbol{\zeta}\cdot\boldsymbol{\zeta}')\,\delta[x'-\boldsymbol{J}\cdot\boldsymbol{\zeta}']\delta[y'-\boldsymbol{B}\cdot\boldsymbol{\zeta}']\rangle_D\rangle_D\rangle_{\text{QRP};t}$$

It involves a *sub-shell* average, in which $p_t(\boldsymbol{J})$ is the weight probability density at time t:

$$\langle K[\boldsymbol{J}]\rangle_{\text{QRP};t} = \frac{\int d\boldsymbol{J}\, K[\boldsymbol{J}]\, p_t(\boldsymbol{J})\delta[Q-Q[\boldsymbol{J}]]\delta[R-R[\boldsymbol{J}]]\prod_{xy}\delta[P[x,y]-P[x,y;\boldsymbol{J}]]}{\int d\boldsymbol{J}\, p_t(\boldsymbol{J})\delta[Q-Q[\boldsymbol{J}]]\delta[R-R[\boldsymbol{J}]]\prod_{xy}\delta[P[x,y]-P[x,y;\boldsymbol{J}]]}$$

where the sub-shells are defined with respect to the order parameters. The solution of (5,6,7) can be used to generate the errors of (3):

$$E_t = \int dxdy\, P[x,y]\theta[-xy] \qquad E_g = \frac{1}{\pi}\arccos[R/\sqrt{Q}] \qquad (8)$$

3 CLOSURE VIA DYNAMICAL REPLICA THEORY

So far our analysis is still exact. We now close the macroscopic laws (5,6,7) by making, for $N \to \infty$, the two key assumptions underlying dynamical replica theory [7]:

(i) Our macroscopic observables $\{Q, R, P\}$ obey *closed* dynamic equations.

(ii) These equations are self-averaging with respect to the realisation of $\tilde{D}$.

(i) implies that probability variations within the $\{Q, R, P\}$ subshells are either absent or irrelevant to the evolution of $\{Q, R, P\}$. We may thus make the simplest choice for $p_t(\boldsymbol{J})$:

$$p_t(\boldsymbol{J}) \to \bar{p}(\boldsymbol{J}) \sim \delta[Q-Q[\boldsymbol{J}]]\,\delta[R-R[\boldsymbol{J}]]\prod_{xy}\delta[P[x,y]-P[x,y;\boldsymbol{J}]] \qquad (9)$$

$\bar{p}(\boldsymbol{J})$ depends on time implicitly, via the order parameters $\{Q, R, P\}$. The procedure (9) leads to exact laws if our observables $\{Q, R, P\}$ indeed obey closed equations for $N \to \infty$. It gives an approximation if they don't. (ii) allows us to average the macroscopic laws over all training sets; it is observed in numerical simulations, and can probably be proven using the formalism of [6]. Our assumptions result in the closure of (5,6,7), since now $\mathcal{A}[\ldots]$ is expressed fully in terms of $\{Q, R, P\}$. The final ingredient of dynamical replica theory is the realization that averaging fractions is simplified with the replica identity [8]

$$\left\langle \frac{\int d\boldsymbol{J}\, W[\boldsymbol{J},z]G[\boldsymbol{J},z]}{\int d\boldsymbol{J}\, W[\boldsymbol{J},z]} \right\rangle_z = \lim_{n\to 0} \int d\boldsymbol{J}^1 \cdots d\boldsymbol{J}^n \left\langle G[\boldsymbol{J}^1,z] \prod_{\alpha=1}^n W[\boldsymbol{J}^\alpha,z]\right\rangle_z$$

What remains is to perform integrations. One finds that $P[x,y] = P[x|y]P[y]$ with $P[y] = (2\pi)^{-\frac{1}{2}} e^{-\frac{1}{2}y^2}$. Upon introducing the short-hands $Dy = (2\pi)^{-\frac{1}{2}} e^{-\frac{1}{2}y^2} dy$ and $\langle f(x,y)\rangle = \int Dy dx\, P[x|y]f(x,y)$ we can write the resulting macroscopic laws as follows:

$$\frac{d}{dt}Q = 2\eta V + \eta^2 Z \qquad \frac{d}{dt}R = \eta W \qquad (10)$$

$$\frac{\partial}{\partial t}P[x|y] = \frac{1}{\alpha}\int dx'\, P[x'|y]\{\delta[x-x'-\eta G[x',y]] - \delta[x-x']\} + \frac{1}{2}\eta^2 Z \frac{\partial^2}{\partial x^2} P[x|y]$$

$$-\eta \frac{\partial}{\partial x}\{P[x|y][U(x-Ry)+Wy+[V-RW-(Q-R^2)U]\Phi[x,y]]\} \qquad (11)$$

with

$$U = \langle \Phi[x,y]\mathcal{G}[x,y]\rangle, \quad V = \langle x\mathcal{G}[x,y]\rangle, \quad W = \langle y\mathcal{G}[x,y]\rangle, \quad Z = \langle \mathcal{G}^2[x,y]\rangle$$

As before the batch equations follow upon expanding in η and retaining only the linear terms. Finding the function $\Phi[x,y]$ (in replica symmetric ansatz) requires solving a saddle-point problem for a scalar observable q and a function $M[x|y]$. Upon introducing

$$B = \frac{\sqrt{qQ-R^2}}{Q(1-q)} \qquad \langle f[x,y,z]\rangle_\star = \frac{\int dx\, M[x|y]e^{Bxz}f[x,y,z]}{\int dx\, M[x|y]e^{Bxz}}$$

(with $\int dx\, M[x|y] = 1$ for all y) the saddle-point equations acquire the form

$$\text{for all } X, y: \quad P[X|y] = \int Dz\, \langle \delta[X-x]\rangle_\star$$

$$\langle (x-Ry)^2\rangle + (qQ-R^2)[1-\frac{1}{\alpha}] = [Q(1+q)-2R^2]\langle x\Phi[x,y]\rangle$$

The solution $M[x|y]$ of the functional saddle-point equation, given a value for q in the physical range $q\in[R^2/Q, 1]$, is unique [9]. The function $\Phi[x,y]$ is then given by

$$\Phi[X,y] = \left\{\sqrt{qQ-R^2}P[X|y]\right\}^{-1} \int Dz\, z\langle \delta[X-x]\rangle_\star \qquad (12)$$

4 THE LIMIT $\alpha \to \infty$

For consistency we show that our theory reduces to the simple (Q, R) formalism of infinite training sets in the limit $\alpha \to \infty$. Upon making the ansatz

$$P[x|y] = [2\pi(Q-R^2)]^{-\frac{1}{2}} e^{-\frac{1}{2}[x-Ry]^2/(Q-R^2)}$$

one finds that the saddle-point equations are simultaneously and uniquely solved by

$$M[x|y] = P[x|y], \qquad q = R^2/Q$$

and $\Phi[x,y]$ reduces to

$$\Phi[x,y] = (x-Ry)/(Q-R^2)$$

Insertion of our ansatz into equation (11), followed by rearranging of terms and usage of the above expression for $\Phi[x,y]$, shows that this equation is satisfied. Thus from our general theory we indeed recover for $\alpha \to \infty$ the standard theory for infinite training sets.

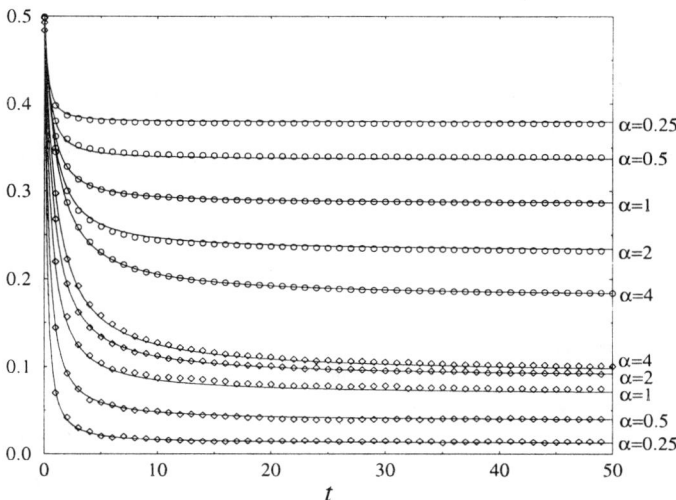

Figure 2: Simulation results for on-line Hebbian learning (system size $N = 10,000$) versus an approximate solution of the equations generated by dynamical replica theory (see main text), for $\alpha \in \{0.25, 0.5, 1.0, 2.0, 4.0\}$. Upper five curves: E_g as functions of time. Lower five curves: E_t as functions of time. Circles: simulation results for E_g; diamonds: simulation results for E_t. Solid lines: the corresponding theoretical predictions.

5 BENCHMARK TESTS: HEBBIAN LEARNING

Batch Hebbian Learning

For the Hebbian rule, where $\mathcal{G}[x, y] = \text{sgn}(y)$, one can calculate our order parameters exactly at any time, even for $\alpha < \infty$ [10], which provides an excellent benchmark for general theories such as ours. For batch execution all integrations in our present theory can be done and all equations solved explicitly, and our theory is found to predict the following:

$$R = R_0 + \eta t \sqrt{\frac{2}{\pi}} \qquad Q = Q_0 + 2\eta t R_0 \sqrt{\frac{2}{\pi}} + \eta^2 t^2 \left[\frac{2}{\pi} + \frac{1}{\alpha}\right] \qquad q = \frac{\alpha R^2 + \eta^2 t^2}{\alpha Q} \qquad (13)$$

$$P[x|y] = \frac{e^{-\frac{1}{2}[x - Ry - (\eta t/\alpha)\,\text{sgn}(y)]^2/(Q-R^2)}}{\sqrt{2\pi(Q - R^2)}} \qquad (14)$$

$$E_g = \frac{1}{\pi} \arccos\left[\frac{R}{\sqrt{Q}}\right] \qquad E_t = \frac{1}{2} - \frac{1}{2}\int Dy \,\text{erf}\left[\frac{|y|R + \eta t/\alpha}{\sqrt{2(Q - R^2)}}\right] \qquad (15)$$

Comparison with the exact solution, calculated along the lines of [10] (where this was done for on-line Hebbian learning) shows that the above expressions are all rigorously exact.

On-Line Hebbian Learning

For on-line execution we cannot (yet) solve the functional saddle-point equation analytically. However, some explicit analytical predictions can still be extracted [9]:

$$R = R_0 + \eta t \sqrt{\frac{2}{\pi}} \qquad Q = Q_0 + 2\eta t R_0 \sqrt{\frac{2}{\pi}} + \eta^2 t + \eta^2 t^2 \left[\frac{2}{\pi} + \frac{1}{\alpha}\right] \qquad (16)$$

$$\int dx\, x P[x|y] = Ry + (\eta t/\alpha)\,\text{sgn}(y) \qquad (17)$$

$$P[x|y] \sim \left[\frac{\alpha}{2\pi \eta^2 t^2}\right]^{\frac{1}{2}} \exp\left[-\frac{\alpha(x - Ry - (\eta t/\alpha)\,\text{sgn}(y))^2}{2\eta^2 t^2}\right] \qquad (t \to \infty) \qquad (18)$$

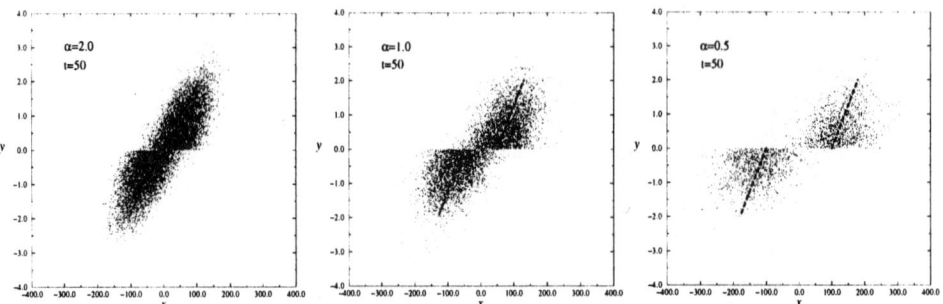

Figure 3: Simulation results for on-line Hebbian learning ($N = 10,000$) versus dynamical replica theory, for $\alpha \in \{2.0, 1.0, 0.5\}$. Dots: local fields $(x, y) = (\boldsymbol{J}\cdot\boldsymbol{\xi}, \boldsymbol{B}\cdot\boldsymbol{\xi})$ (calculated for examples in the training set), at time $t = 50$. Dashed lines: conditional average of student field x as a function of y, as predicted by the theory, $\overline{x}(y) = Ry + (\eta t/\alpha)\,\mathrm{sgn}(y)$.

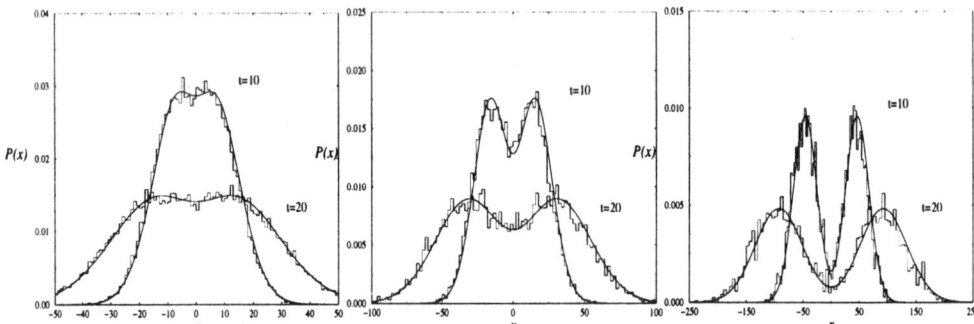

Figure 4: Simulations of Hebbian on-line learning with $N = 10,000$. Histograms: student field distributions measured at $t = 10$ and $t = 20$. Lines: theoretical predictions for student field distributions (using the approximate solution of the diffusion equation, see main text), for $\alpha = 4$ (left), $\alpha = 1$ (middle), $\alpha = 0.25$ (right).

Comparison with the exact result of [10] shows that the above expressions (16,17,18), and therefore also that of E_g at any time, are all rigorously exact.

At intermediate times it turns out that a good approximation of the solution of our dynamic equations for on-line Hebbian learning (exact for $t \ll \alpha$ and for $t \to \infty$) is given by

$$P[x|y] = \frac{e^{-\frac{1}{2}[x - Ry - (\eta t/\alpha)\,\mathrm{sgn}(y)]^2/(Q - R^2 + \eta^2 t/\alpha)}}{\sqrt{2\pi(Q - R^2 + \eta^2 t/\alpha)}} \tag{19}$$

$$E_g = \frac{1}{\pi}\arccos\left[\frac{R}{\sqrt{Q}}\right] \qquad E_t = \frac{1}{2} - \frac{1}{2}\int Dy\ \mathrm{erf}\left[\frac{|y|R + \eta t/\alpha}{\sqrt{2(Q - R^2 - \eta^2 t/\alpha)}}\right] \tag{20}$$

In Figure 2 we compare the approximate predictions (20) with the results obtained from numerical simulations ($N = 10,000$, $Q_0 = 1$, $R_0 = 0$, $\eta = 1$). All curves show excellent agreement between theory and experiment. We also compare the theoretical predictions for the distribution $P[x|y]$ with the results of numerical simulations. This is done in Figure 3 where we show the fields as observed at $t = 50$ in simulations (same parameters as in Figure 2) of on-line Hebbian learning, for three different values of α. In the same figure we draw (dashed lines) the theoretical prediction for the y-dependent average (17) of the conditional x-distribution $P[x|y]$. Finally we compare the student field distribution $P[x] =$

$\int Dy\, P[x|y]$ according to (19) with that observed in numerical simulations, see Figure 4. The agreement is again excellent (note: here the learning process has almost equilibrated).

6 DISCUSSION

In this paper we have shown how the formalism of dynamical replica theory [7] can be used successfully to build a general theory with which to predict the evolution of the relevant macroscopic performance measures, including the training- and generalisation errors, for supervised (on-line and batch) learning in layered neural networks with randomly composed but restricted training sets (i.e. for finite $\alpha = p/N$). Here the student fields are no longer described by Gaussian distributions, and the more familiar statistical mechanical formalism breaks down. For simplicity and transparency we have restricted ourselves to single-layer systems and realizable tasks. In our approach the joint distribution $P[x, y]$ for student and teacher fields is itself taken to be a dynamical order parameter, in addition to the conventional observables Q and R. From the order parameter set $\{Q, R, P\}$, in turn, we derive both the generalization error E_g and the training error E_t. Following the prescriptions of dynamical replica theory one finds a diffusion equation for $P[x, y]$, which we have evaluated by making the replica-symmetric ansatz in the saddle-point equations. This equation has Gaussian solutions only for $\alpha \to \infty$; in the latter case we indeed recover correctly from our theory the more familiar formalism of infinite training sets, with closed equations for Q and R only. For finite α our theory is by construction exact if for $N \to \infty$ the dynamical order parameters $\{Q, R, P\}$ obey closed, deterministic equations, which are self-averaging (i.e. independent of the microscopic realization of the training set). If this is not the case, our theory is an approximation.

We have worked out our general equations explicitly for the special case of Hebbian learning, where the existence of an exact solution [10], derived from the microscopic equations (for finite α), allows us to perform a critical test of our theory. Our theory is found to be fully exact for batch Hebbian learning. For on-line Hebbian learning full exactness is difficult to determine, but exactness can be establised at least for (i) $t \to \infty$, (ii) the predictions for Q, R, E_g and $\bar{x}(y) = \int dx\, xP[x|y]$ at any time. A simple approximate solution of our equations already shows excellent agreement between theory and experiment. The present study clearly represents only a first step, and many extensions, applications and generalizations are currently under way. More specifically, we study alternative learning rules as well as the extension of this work to the case of noisy data and of soft committee machines.

References

[1] Kinzel W. and Rujan P. (1990), *Europhys. Lett.* **13**, 473

[2] Kinouchi O. and Caticha N. (1992), *J. Phys. A: Math. Gen.* **25**, 6243

[3] Biehl M. and Schwarze H. (1992), *Europhys. Lett.* **20**, 733
   Biehl M. and Schwarze H. (1995), *J. Phys. A: Math. Gen.* **28**, 643

[4] Saad D. and Solla S. (1995), *Phys. Rev. Lett.* **74**, 4337

[5] Mace C.W.H. and Coolen A.C.C (1998), *Statistics and Computing* **8**, 55

[6] Horner H. (1992a), *Z. Phys. B* **86**, 291
   Horner H. (1992b), *Z. Phys. B* **87**, 371

[7] Coolen A.C.C., Laughton S.N. and Sherrington D. (1996), *Phys. Rev. B* **53**, 8184

[8] Mézard M., Parisi G. and Virasoro M.A. (1987), *Spin-Glass Theory and Beyond* (Singapore: World Scientific)

[9] Coolen A.C.C. and Saad D. (1998), in preparation.

[10] Rae H.C., Sollich P. and Coolen A.C.C. (1998), these proceedings

Dynamically Adapting Kernels in Support Vector Machines

Nello Cristianini
Dept. of Engineering Mathematics
University of Bristol, UK
nello.cristianini@bristol.ac.uk

Colin Campbell
Dept. of Engineering Mathematics
University of Bristol, UK
c.campbell@bristol.ac.uk

John Shawe-Taylor
Dept. of Computer Science
Royal Holloway College
john@dcs.rhbnc.ac.uk

Abstract

The kernel-parameter is one of the few tunable parameters in Support Vector machines, controlling the complexity of the resulting hypothesis. Its choice amounts to model selection and its value is usually found by means of a validation set. We present an algorithm which can automatically perform model selection with little additional computational cost and with no need of a validation set. In this procedure model selection and learning are not separate, but kernels are dynamically adjusted during the learning process to find the kernel parameter which provides the best possible upper bound on the generalisation error. Theoretical results motivating the approach and experimental results confirming its validity are presented.

1 Introduction

Support Vector Machines (SVMs) are learning systems designed to automatically trade-off accuracy and complexity by minimizing an upper bound on the generalisation error provided by VC theory. In practice, however, SVMs still have a few tunable parameters which need to be determined in order to achieve the right balance and the values of these are usually found by means of a validation set. One of the most important of these is the kernel-parameter which implicitly defines the structure of the high dimensional feature space where the maximal margin hyperplane is found. Too rich a feature space would cause the system to overfit the data, and conversely the system can be unable to separate the data if the kernels are too poor. Capacity control can therefore be performed by tuning the kernel parameter subject to the margin being maximized. For noisy datasets, yet another quantity needs to be set, namely the soft-margin parameter C.

SVMs therefore display a remarkable dimensionality reduction for model selection. Systems such as neural networks need many different architectures to be tested and decision trees are faced with a similar problem during the pruning phase. On the other hand SVMs can shift from one model complexity to another by simply tuning a continuous parameter.

Generally, model selection by SVMs is still performed in the standard way: by learning different SVMs and testing them on a validation set in order to determine the optimal value of the kernel-parameter. This is expensive in terms of computing time and training data. In this paper we propose a different scheme which dynamically adjusts the kernel-parameter to explore the space of possible models at little additional computational cost compared to fixed-kernel learning. Futhermore this approach only makes use of training-set information so it is more efficient in a sample complexity sense.

Before proposing the model selection procedure we first prove a theoretical result, namely that the margin and structural risk minimization (SRM) bound on the generalization error depend smoothly on the kernel parameter. This can be exploited by an algorithm which keeps the system close to maximal margin while the kernel parameter is changed smoothly. During this phase, the theoretical bound given by SRM theory can be computed. The best kernel-parameter is the one which gives the lowest possible bound. In section 4 we present experimental results showing that model selection can be efficiently performed using the proposed method (though we only consider Gaussian kernels in the simulations outlined).

2 Support Vector Learning

The decision function implemented by SV machines can be written as:

$$f(x) = \text{sign}\left(\sum_{i \in \text{SV}} y_i \alpha_i^o K(x, x_i) - \theta\right)$$

where the α_i^o are obtained by maximising the following Lagrangian (where m is the number of patterns):

$$L = \sum_{i=1}^{m} \alpha_i - 1/2 \sum_{i,j=1}^{m} \alpha_i \alpha_j y_i y_j K(x_i, x_j)$$

with respect to the α_i, subject to the constraints

$$\alpha_i \geq 0 \qquad \sum_{i=1}^{m} \alpha_i y_i = 0$$

and where the functions $K(x, x')$ are called *kernels*. The kernels provide an expression for dot-products in a high-dimensional *feature space* [1]:

$$K(x, x') = \langle \Phi(x), \Phi(x') \rangle$$

and also implicitly define the nonlinear mapping $\Phi(x)$ of the training data into feature space where they may be separated using the maximal margin hyperplane. A number of choices of kernel-function can be made e.g. Gaussians kernels:

$$K(x,x') = e^{-||x-x'||^2/2\sigma^2}$$

The following upper bound can be proven from VC theory for the generalisation error using hyperplanes in feature space [7, 9]:

$$\epsilon \leq O\left(\frac{R^2}{m\gamma^2}\right)$$

where R is the radius of the smallest ball containing the training set, m the number of training points and γ the margin (cf. [2] for a complete survey of the generalization properties of SV machines).

The Lagrange multipliers α_i are usually found by means of a Quadratic Programming optimization routine, while the kernel-parameters are found using a validation set. As illustrated in Figure 1 there is a minimum of the generalisation error for that value of the kernel-parameter which has the best trade-off between overfitting and ability to find an efficient solution.

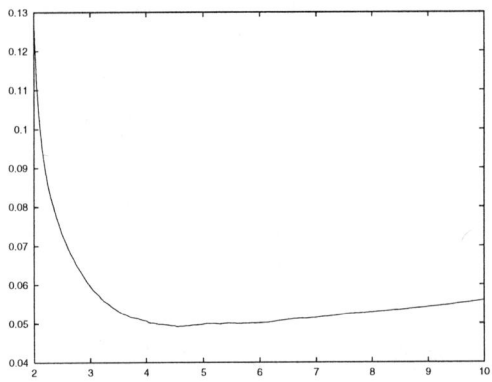

Figure 1: Generalization error (y-axis) as a function of σ (x-axis) for the mirror symmetry problem (for Gaussian kernels with zero training error and maximal margin, $m = 200$, $n = 30$ and averaged over 10^5 examples).

3 Automatic Model Order Selection

We now prove a theorem which shows that the margin of the optimal hyperplane is a smooth function of the kernel parameter, as is the upper bound on the generalisation error. First we state the Implicit Function Theorem.

Implicit Function Theorem [10]: Let $\overline{F}(x,\overline{y})$ be a continuously differentiable function,

$$\overline{F} : U \subseteq \Re \times V \subseteq \Re^p \to \Re$$

and let $(a,\overline{b}) \in U \times V$ be a solution to the equation $\overline{F}(x,\overline{y}) = 0$. Let the partial derivatives matrix $m_{i,j} = \left(\frac{\partial F_i}{\partial y_j}\right)$ w.r.t. y be full rank at $(a,\overline{b})$. Then, near $(a,\overline{b})$, there exists one and only one function $\overline{y} = \overline{g}(x)$ such that $\overline{F}(x, \overline{g}(x)) = 0$, and such function is continuous.

Theorem: The *margin* γ of SV machines depends smoothly on the kernel parameter σ.

Proof: Consider the function $\overline{g} : \Sigma \subseteq \Re \to A \subseteq \Re^p, \overline{g} : \sigma \mapsto (\overline{\alpha}^o, \lambda)$ which given the data maps the choice of σ to the optimal parameters α^o and lagrange parameter λ of the SV machine with Kernel matrix $G_{ij} = y_i y_j K(\sigma; x_i, x_j))$. Let

$$W_\sigma(\overline{\alpha}) = \sum_{i=1}^p \overline{\alpha}_i - 1/2 \sum_{i,j} \overline{\alpha}_i \overline{\alpha}_j y_i y_j K(\sigma; x_i, x_j) + \lambda (\sum_i y_i \overline{\alpha}_i)$$

be the functional that the SV machine maximizes. Fix a value of σ and let $\alpha^o(\sigma)$ be the corresponding solution of $W_\sigma(\overline{\alpha})$. Let I be the set of indices for which $\overline{\alpha}_j^o(\sigma) \neq 0$. We may assume that the submatrix of G indexed by I is non-singular since otherwise the maximal margin hyperplane could be expressed in terms of a subset of indices. Now choose a maximal set of indices J containing I such that the corresponding submatrix of G is non-singular and all of the points indexed by J have margin 1. Now consider the function $F(\sigma, \overline{\alpha}, \lambda)_i = \left(\frac{\partial W_\sigma}{\partial \overline{\alpha}}\right)_{j_i}, i \geq 1$, $F(\sigma, \overline{\alpha}, \lambda)_0 = \sum_j y_j \overline{\alpha}_j$ in the neighbourhood of σ, where j_i is an enumeration of the elements of J,

$$\frac{\partial W_\sigma}{\partial \alpha_j} = 1 - y_j \sum_i \overline{\alpha}_i y_i K(\sigma; x_i, x_j) + \lambda y_j$$

and satisfies the equation $F(\sigma, \overline{\alpha^o}(\sigma), \lambda(\sigma)) = \mathbf{0}$ at the extremal points of $W_\sigma(\overline{\alpha})$. Then the SV function is the implicit function, $(\overline{\alpha}^o, \lambda) = \overline{g}(\sigma)$, and is continuous (and unique) *iff* $\overline{F}$ is continuously differentiable and the partial derivatives matrix w.r.t. $\overline{\alpha}, \lambda$ is full rank. But the partial derivatives matrix H is given by

$$H_{ij} = \frac{\partial F_i}{\partial \alpha_{j_j}} = y_{j_i} y_{j_j} K(\sigma; x_{j_i}, x_{j_j}) = H_{ji}, i, j \geq 1,$$

for $j_i, j_j \in J$, which was non-degenerate by definition of J, while

$$H_{00} = \frac{\partial F_0}{\partial \lambda} = 0 \quad \text{and} \quad H_{0j} = \frac{\partial F_0}{\partial \alpha_{j_j}} = y_{j_j} = \frac{\partial F_j}{\partial \lambda} = H_{j0}, j \geq 1.$$

Consider any non-zero α satisfying $\sum_j \alpha_j y_j = 0$, and any λ. We have

$$(\alpha, \lambda)^T H(\alpha, \lambda) = \alpha^T G \alpha + 2\lambda \alpha^T y = \alpha^T G \alpha > 0.$$

Hence, the matrix H is non-singular for α satisfying the given linear constraint. Hence, by the implicit function theorem g is a continuous function of σ. The following is proven in [2]:

$$\gamma^2 = \left(\sum_{i=1}^p \overline{\alpha}_i^o\right)^{-1}$$

which shows that γ is a continuous function of σ. As the radius of the ball containing the points is also a continuous function of σ, and the generalization error bound has the form $\epsilon \leq CR(\sigma)^2 \|\alpha^o(\sigma)\|_1$ for some constant C, we have the following corollary.

Corollary: The bound on the generalization error is smooth in σ.

This means that, when the margin is optimal, small variations in the kernel parameter will produce small variations in the margin (and in the bound on the generalisation error). Thus $\gamma_\sigma \approx \gamma_{\sigma+\delta\sigma}$ and after updating the σ, the system will still be in a sub-optimal position. This suggests the following strategy for Gaussian kernels, for instance:

Kernel Selection Procedure

1. Initialize σ to a very small value
2. Maximize the margin, then
   - Compute the SRM bound (or observe the validation error)
   - Increase the kernel parameter: $\sigma \leftarrow \sigma + \delta\sigma$
3. Stop when a predetermined value of σ is reached else repeat step 2.

This procedure takes advantage of the fact that for very small σ convergence is generally very rapid (overfitting the data, of course), and that once the system is near the equilibrium, few iterations will always be sufficient to move it back to the maximal margin situation. In other words, this system is brought to a maximal margin state in the beginning, when this is computationally very cheap, and then it is actively kept in that situation by continuously adjusting the α while the kernel-parameter is gradually increased.

In the next section we will experimentally investigate this procedure for real-life datasets. In the numerical simulations we have used the Kernel-Adatron (KA) algorithm recently developed by two of the authors [4] which can be used to train SV machines. We have chosen this algorithm because it can be regarded as a gradient ascent procedure for maximising the Kuhn-Tucker Lagrangian L. Thus the α_i for a sub-optimal state are close to those for the optimum and so little computational effort will be needed to bring the system back to a maximal margin position:

The Kernel-Adatron Algorithm.

1. $\alpha_i = 1$.
2. FOR $i = 1$ TO m
   - $z_i = \sum_{j=1}^{m} \alpha_j y_j K(x_i, x_j)$
   - $\gamma_i = y_i z_i$
   - $\delta\alpha^i = \eta(1 - \gamma^i)$
   - IF $(\alpha^i + \delta\alpha^i) \leq 0$ THEN $\alpha^i = 0$ ELSE $\alpha^i \leftarrow \alpha^i + \delta\alpha^i$.
   - $margin = \frac{1}{2} \left(\min\left(z_i^+\right) - \max\left(z_i^-\right) \right)$
   (z_i^+ (z_i^-) = positively (negatively) labelled patterns)
3. IF$(margin = 1)$ THEN stop, ELSE go to step 2.

4 Experimental Results

In this section we implement the above algorithm for real-life datasets and plot the upper bound given by VC theory and the generalization error as functions of σ. In order to compute the bound, $\epsilon \leq R^2/m\gamma^2$ we need to estimate the radius of the ball in feature space. In general his can be done explicitly by maximising the following Lagrangian w.r.t. λ_i using convex quadratic programming routines:

$$L = \sum_i \lambda_i K(x_i, x_i) - \sum_{i,j} \lambda_i \lambda_j K(x_i, x_j)$$

subject to the constraints $\sum_i \lambda_i = 1$ and $\lambda_i \geq 0$. The radius is then found from [3]:

$$R = \sum_{i,j} \lambda_i \lambda_j K(x_i, x_j) - 2 \sum_{i,j} \lambda_j K(x_i, x_j) + \sum_i K(x_i, x_i)$$

However, we can also get an upper bound for this quantity by noting that Gaussian kernels always map training points to the surface of a sphere of radius 1 centered on the origin of the feature space. This can be easily seen by noting that the distance of a point from the origin is its norm:

$$||\Phi(x)|| = \sqrt{\langle \Phi(x), \Phi(x) \rangle} = \sqrt{K(x,x)} = \sqrt{e^{||x-x||/2\sigma^2}} = 1$$

In Figure 2 we give both these bounds (the upper bound is $\sum_i \alpha_i/m$) and generalisation error (on a test set) for two standard datasets: the aspect-angle dependent sonar classification dataset of Gorman and Sejnowski [5] and the Wisconsin breast cancer dataset [8]. As we see from these plots there is little need for the additional computational cost of determining R from the above quadratic progamming problem, at least for Gaussian kernels. In Fig. 3 we plot the bound $\sum_i \alpha_i/m$ and generalisation error for 2 figures from a United States Postal Service dataset of handwritten digits [6]. In these, and other instances we have investigated, the minimum of the bound approximately coincides with the minimum of the generalisation error. This gives a good criterion for the most suitable choice for σ. Furthermore, this estimate for the best σ is derived solely from training data without the need for an additional validation set.

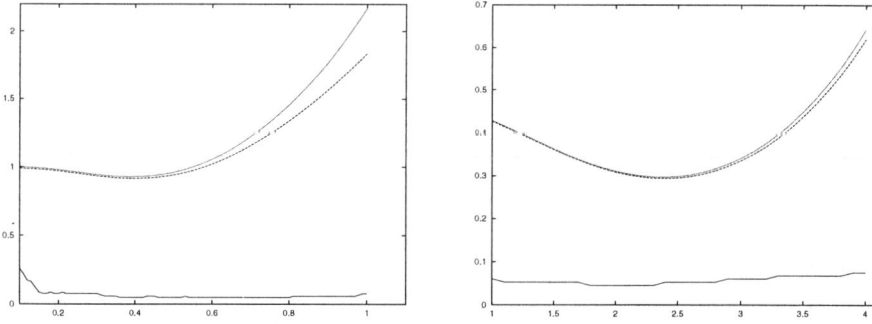

Figure 2: Generalisation error (solid curves) for the sonar classification (left Fig.) and Wisconsin breast cancer datasets (right Fig.). The upper curves (dotted) show the upper bounds from VC theory (for the top curves R=1).

Starting with a small σ-value we have observed that the margin can be maximised rapidly. Furthermore, the margin remains close to 1 if σ is incremented by a small amount. Consequently, we can study the performance of the system by traversing a range of σ-values, alternately incrementing σ then maximising the margin using the previous optimal set of α-values as a starting point. We have found that this procedure does not add a significant computational cost in general. For example, for the sonar classification dataset mentioned above and starting at $\sigma = 0.1$ with increments $\Delta\sigma = 0.1$ it took 186 iterations to reach $\sigma = 1.0$ and 4895 to reach $\sigma = 2.0$ as against 110 and 2624 iterations for learning at both these σ-values. For a rough doubling of the learning time it is possible to determine a reasonable value for σ for good generalisation without use of a validation set.

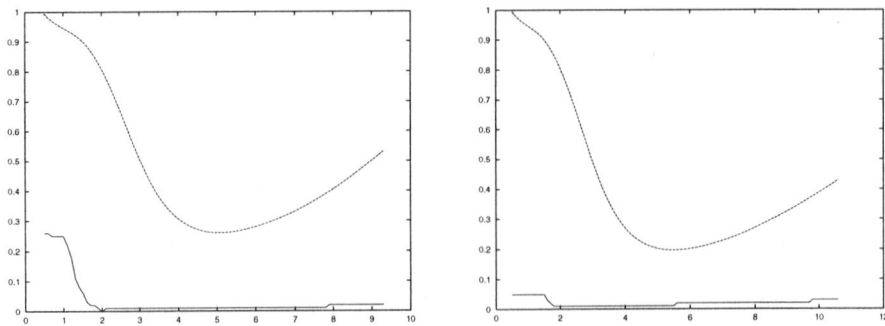

Figure 3: Generalisation error (solid curve) and upper bound from VC theory (dashed curve with R=1) for digits 0 and 3 from the USPS dataset of handwritten digits.

5 Conclusion

We have presented an algorithm which automatically learns the kernel parameter with little additional cost, both in a computational and sample-complexity sense. Model selection takes place during the learning process itself, and experimental results are provided showing that this strategy provides a good estimate of the correct model complexity.

References

[1] Aizerman, M., Braverman, E., and Rozonoer, L. (1964). Theoretical Foundations of the Potential Function Method in Pattern Recognition Learning, *Automations and Remote Control*, **25**:821-837.

[2] Bartlett P., Shawe-Taylor J., (1998). Generalization Performance of Support Vector Machines and Other Pattern Classifiers. 'Advances in Kernel Methods - Support Vector Learning', Bernhard Schölkopf, Christopher J. C. Burges, and Alexander J. Smola (eds.), MIT Press, Cambridge, USA.

[3] Burges C., (1998). A tutorial on support vector machines for pattern recognition. *Data Mining and Knowledge Discovery*, **2**:1.

[4] Friess T., Cristianini N., Campbell C., (1998) The Kernel-Adatron Algorithm: a Fast and Simple Learning Procedure for Support Vector Machines, in Shavlik, J., ed., *Machine Learning: Proceedings of the Fifteenth International Conference*, Morgan Kaufmann Publishers, San Francisco, CA.

[5] Gorman R.P. & Sejnowski, T.J. (1988) *Neural Networks* **1**:75-89.

[6] LeCun, Y., Jackel, L. D., Bottou, L., Brunot, A., Cortes, C., Denker, J. S., Drucker, H., Guyon, I., Muller, U. A., Sackinger, E., Simard, P. and Vapnik, V., (1995). Comparison of learning algorithms for handwritten digit recognition, *International Conference on Artificial Neural Networks*, Fogelman, F. and Gallinari, P. (Ed.), pp. 53-60.

[7] Shawe-Taylor, J., Bartlett, P., Williamson, R. & Anthony, M. (1996). Structural Risk Minimization over Data-Dependent Hierarchies NeuroCOLT Technical Report NC-TR-96-053 (ftp://ftp.dcs.rhbnc.ac.uk /pub/neurocolt/tech_reports).

[8] Ster, B., & Dobnikar, A. (1996) Neural networks in medical diagnosis: comparison with other methods. In A. Bulsari et al. (ed.) *Proceedings of the International Conference EANN'96*, p. 427-430.

[9] Vapnik, V. (1995) *The Nature of Statistical Learning Theory*, Springer Verlag.

[10] James, Robert C. (1966) *Advanced calculus* Belmont, Calif. : Wadsworth

Phase Diagram and Storage Capacity of Sequence Storing Neural Networks

A. Düring
Dept. of Physics
Oxford University
Oxford OX1 3NP
United Kingdom
a.during1@physics.oxford.ac.uk

A. C. C. Coolen
Dept. of Mathematics
King's College
London WC2R 2LS
United Kingdom
tcoolen@mth.kcl.ac.uk

D. Sherrington
Dept. of Physics
Oxford University
Oxford OX1 3NP
United Kingdom
d.sherrington1@physics.oxford.ac.uk

Abstract

We solve the dynamics of Hopfield–type neural networks which store sequences of patterns, close to saturation. The asymmetry of the interaction matrix in such models leads to violation of detailed balance, ruling out an equilibrium statistical mechanical analysis. Using generating functional methods we derive exact closed equations for dynamical order parameters, viz. the sequence overlap and correlation and response functions, in the limit of an infinite system size. We calculate the time translation invariant solutions of these equations, describing stationary limit–cycles, which leads to a phase diagram. The effective retarded self-interaction usually appearing in symmetric models is here found to vanish, which causes a significantly enlarged storage capacity of $\alpha_c \approx 0.269$, compared to $\alpha_c \approx 0.139$ for Hopfield networks storing static patterns. Our results are tested against extensive computer simulations and excellent agreement is found.

1 INTRODUCTION AND DEFINITIONS

We consider a system of N neurons $\boldsymbol{\sigma}(t) = \{\sigma_i(t) = \pm 1\}$, which can change their states collectively at discrete times (parallel dynamics). Each neuron changes its state with a probability $p_i(t) = \frac{1}{2}[1-\tanh \beta \sigma_i(t)[\sum_j J_{ij}\sigma_j(t)+\theta_i(t)]]$, so that the transition matrix is

$$W[\boldsymbol{\sigma}(s+1)|\boldsymbol{\sigma}(s)] = \prod_{i=1}^{N} e^{\beta \sigma_i(s+1)[\sum_{j=1}^{N} J_{ij}\sigma_j(s)+\theta_i(s)]-\ln 2\cosh(\beta[\sum_{j=1}^{N} J_{ij}\sigma_j(s)+\theta_i(s)])} \tag{1}$$

with the (non-symmetric) interaction strengths J_{ij} chosen as

$$J_{ij} = \frac{1}{N} \sum_{\mu=1}^{p} \xi_i^{\mu+1} \xi_j^{\mu}, \tag{2}$$

The ξ_i^μ represent components of an ordered sequence of patterns to be stored[1]. The gain parameter β can be interpreted as an inverse temperature governing the noise level in the dynamics (1) and the number of patterns is assumed to scale as N, i. e. $p = \alpha N$. If the interaction matrix would have been chosen symmetrically, the model would be accessible to methods originally developed for the equilibrium statistical mechanical analysis of physical spin systems and related models [1, 2], in particular the replica method. For the nonsymmetric interaction matrix proposed here this is ruled out, and no exact solution exists to our knowledge, although both models have been first mentioned at the same time and an approximate solution compatible with the numerical evidence at the time has been provided by Amari [3]. The difficulty for the analysis is that a system with the interactions (2) never reaches equilibrium in the thermodynamic sense, so that equilibrium methods are not applicable. One therefore has to apply dynamical methods and give a dynamical meaning to the notion of the recall state. Consequently, we will for this paper employ the dynamical method of path integrals, pioneered for spin glasses by de Dominicis [4] and applied to the Hopfield model by Rieger et al. [5].

We point out that our choice of parallel dynamics for the problem of sequence recall is deliberate in that simple sequential dynamics will not lead to stable recall of a sequence. This is due to the fact that the number of updates of a single neuron per time unit is not a constant for sequential dynamics. Schemes for using delayed asymmetric interactions combined with sequential updates have been proposed (see e. g. [6] for a review), but are outside the scope of this paper.

Our analysis starts with the introduction of a generating functional $Z[\boldsymbol{\psi}]$ of the form

$$Z[\boldsymbol{\psi}] = \sum_{\boldsymbol{\sigma}(0)...\boldsymbol{\sigma}(t)} p[\boldsymbol{\sigma}(0),\ldots,\boldsymbol{\sigma}(t)]\, e^{-i\sum_{s<t}\boldsymbol{\sigma}(s)\cdot\boldsymbol{\psi}(s)}, \tag{3}$$

which depends on real fields $\{\psi_i(t)\}$. These fields play a formal role only, allowing for the identification of interesting order parameters, such as

$$m_i(s) = \langle \sigma_i(s) \rangle = i \lim_{\psi \to 0} \frac{\partial Z[\boldsymbol{\psi}]}{\partial \psi_i(s)}$$

$$G_{ij}(s,s') = \frac{\partial}{\partial \theta_j(s')} \langle \sigma_i(s) \rangle = i \lim_{\psi \to 0} \frac{\partial^2 Z[\boldsymbol{\psi}]}{\partial \psi_i(s)\partial \theta_j(s')}$$

$$C_{ij}(s,s') = \langle \sigma_i(s)\sigma_j(s') \rangle = -\lim_{\psi \to 0} \frac{\partial^2 Z[\boldsymbol{\psi}]}{\partial \psi_i(s)\partial \psi_j(s')}.$$

---

[1]Upper (pattern) indices are understood to be taken modulo p unless otherwise stated.

for the average activation, response and correlation functions, respectively. Since this functional involves the probability $p[\sigma(0),\ldots,\sigma(t)]$ of finding a 'path' of neuron activations $\{\sigma(0),\ldots,\sigma(t)\}$, the task of the analysis is to express this probability in terms of the macroscopic order parameters itself to arrive at a set of closed macroscopic equations.

The first step in rewriting the path probability is to realise that (1) describes a one–step Markov process and the path probability is therefore just the product of the single–time transition probabilities, weighted by the probability of the initial state: $p[\sigma(0),\ldots,\sigma(t)] = p(\sigma(0)) \prod_{s=0}^{t-1} W[\sigma(s+1)|\sigma(s)]$. Furthermore, we will in the course of the analysis frequently isolate interesting variables by introducing appropriate δ-functions, such as

$$1 = \int d\mathbf{h}(s) \prod_{i=1}^{N} \delta\left[h_i(s) - \left(\sum_{j=1}^{N} J_{ij}\sigma_j(s) + \theta_i(s)\right)\right]$$

$$= \int \frac{d\mathbf{h}(s)\, d\hat{\mathbf{h}}(s)}{(2\pi)^N} \prod_{i=1}^{N} e^{i\hat{h}_i(s)(h_i(s) - \sum_{j=1}^{N} J_{ij}\sigma_j(s) - \theta_i(s))}$$

The variable $h_i(t)$ can be interpreted as the local field (or presynaptic potential) at site i and time t and their introduction transforms $Z[\psi]$ into

$$Z[\psi] = \sum_{\sigma(0)\ldots\sigma(t)} p(\sigma(0)) \int \frac{d\mathbf{h}\, d\hat{\mathbf{h}}}{(2\pi)^{Nt}} \prod_{s=0}^{t-1} \left[e^{\beta\sigma(s+1)\cdot\mathbf{h}(s) - \sum_i \ln 2\cosh(\beta h_i(s))} \right.$$

$$\left. e^{i(\hat{\mathbf{h}}(s)\cdot\mathbf{h}(s) - N^{-1}\sum_{i,j} \hat{h}_i(s)\sum_\mu \xi_i^{\mu+1}\xi_j^\mu \sigma_i(s) - \hat{\mathbf{h}}(s)\cdot\theta(s) - \psi(s)\cdot\sigma(s))} \right]. \quad (4)$$

This expression is the last general form of $Z[\psi]$ we consider. To proceed with the analysis, we have to make a specific ansatz for the system behaviour.

2 DYNAMIC MEAN FIELD THEORY

As sequence recall is the mode of operation we are most interested in, we make the ansatz that, for large systems, we have an overlap of order $\mathcal{O}(N^0)$ between the pattern ξ^s at time s, and that all other patterns are overlapping with order $\mathcal{O}(N^{-1/2})$ at most. Accordingly, we introduce the macroscopic order parameters for the condensed pattern $m(s) = N^{-1}\sum_i \xi_i^s \sigma_i(s)$ and for the quantity $k(s) = N^{-1}\sum_i \xi_i^s h_i(s)$, and their noncondensed equivalents $y^\mu(s) = N^{-1/2}\sum_i \xi_i^\mu \sigma_i(s)$ and $x(s) = N^{-1/2}\sum_i \xi_i^\mu \hat{h}_i(s)$ ($\mu \neq s$), where the scaling ansatz is reflected in the normalisation constants. Introducing these objects using δ functions, as with the local fields $h_i(s)$, removes the product of two patterns in the last line of eq. (4), so that the exponent will be linear in the pattern bits.

Because macroscopic observables will in general not depend on the microscopic realisation of the patterns, the values of these observables do not change if we average $Z[\psi]$ over the realisations of the patterns. Performing this average is complicated by the occurrence of some patterns in both the condensed and the noncondensed overlaps, depending on the current time index, which is an effect not occurring in the standard Hopfield model. Using some simple scaling arguments, this difficulty can be removed and we can perform the average over the noncondensed patterns. The disorder averaged $Z[\psi]$ acquires the form

$$Z[\psi] = \int d\mathbf{m}\, d\hat{\mathbf{m}}\, d\mathbf{k}\, d\hat{\mathbf{k}}\, d\mathbf{q}\, d\hat{\mathbf{q}}\, d\mathbf{Q}\, d\hat{\mathbf{Q}}\, d\mathbf{K}\, d\hat{\mathbf{K}}\, e^{N(\Psi[\ldots] + \Phi[\ldots] + \Omega[\ldots]) + \mathcal{O}(N^{1/2})} \quad (5)$$

where we have introduced the new observables $q(s,s') = 1/N \sum_i \sigma_i(s)\sigma_i(s')$, $Q(s,s') = 1/N \sum_i \hat{h}_i(s)\hat{h}_i(s')$, and $K(s,s') = 1/N \sum_i \sigma_i(s)\hat{h}_i(s')$, and their corresponding conjugate variables. The functions in the exponent turn out to be

$$\Psi[\mathbf{m},\hat{\mathbf{m}},\mathbf{k},\hat{\mathbf{k}},\mathbf{q},\hat{\mathbf{q}},\mathbf{Q},\hat{\mathbf{Q}},\mathbf{K},\hat{\mathbf{K}}] = i\sum_{s<t}\left[\hat{m}(s)m(s) + \hat{k}(s)k(s) - m(s)k(s)\right] +$$
$$i\sum_{s,s'<t}\left[\hat{q}(s,s')q(s,s') + \hat{Q}(s,s')Q(s,s') + \hat{K}(s,s')K(s,s')\right], \quad (6)$$

$$\Phi[\mathbf{m},\mathbf{k},\hat{\mathbf{q}},\hat{\mathbf{Q}},\hat{\mathbf{K}}] = \frac{1}{N}\sum_i \ln\left[\sum_{\sigma(0)...\sigma(t)} p_i(\sigma(0))\int\prod_{s<t}\left[\frac{dh(s)\,d\hat{h}(s)}{2\pi}\right]\right.$$
$$e^{\sum_{s<t}\left[\beta\sigma(s+1)h(s)-\ln 2\cosh(\beta h(s))\right]} \times$$
$$e^{-i\sum_{s,s'<t}\left[\hat{q}(s,s')\sigma(s)\sigma(s')+\hat{Q}(s,s')\hat{h}(s)\hat{h}(s')+\hat{K}(s,s')\sigma(s)\hat{h}(s')\right]} \times$$
$$\left. e^{i\sum_{s<t}\hat{h}(s)\left[h(s)-\theta_i(s)-\hat{k}(s)\xi_i^{s+1}\right]-i\sum_{s<t}\sigma(s)\left[\hat{m}(s)\xi_i^s+\psi_i(s)\right]}\right], \quad (7)$$

and

$$\Omega[\mathbf{q},\mathbf{Q},\hat{\mathbf{Q}}] = \frac{1}{N}\ln\int\prod_{s<t}\left[\frac{du(s)\,dv(s)}{(2\pi)^{(p-t)}}\right]e^{i\sum_{\mu>t}\sum_{s<t}u_{\mu+1}(s)v_\mu(s)} \times$$
$$e^{-\frac{1}{2}\sum_{\mu>t}\sum_{s,s'<t}\left[u_\mu(s)Q(s,s')u_\mu(s')+u_\mu(s)K(s',s)v_\mu(s')+v_\mu(s)K(s,s')u_\mu(s')+v_\mu(s)q(s,s')v_\mu(s')\right]}. \quad (8)$$

The first of these expressions is just a result of the introduction of δ functions, while the second will turn out to represent a probability measure given by the evolution of a *single* neuron under *prescribed* fields and the third reflects the disorder contribution to the local fields in that single neuron measure[2]. We have thus reduced the original problem involving N neurons in a one-step Markov process to one involving just a single neuron, but at the cost of introducing two–time observables.

3 DERIVATION OF SADDLE POINT EQUATIONS

The integral in (5) will be dominated by saddle points, in our case by a unique saddle point when causality is taken into account. Extremising the exponent with respect to all occurring variables gives a number of equations, the most important of which give the physical meanings of three observables: $q(s,s') = C(s,s')$, $K(s,s') = iG(s,s')$,

$$m(s) = \lim_{N\to\infty}\frac{1}{N}\sum_i \overline{\langle\sigma_i(s)\rangle}\xi_i^s \quad (9)$$

with

$$C(s,s') = \lim_{N\to\infty}\frac{1}{N}\sum_i \overline{\langle\sigma_i(s)\sigma_i(s')\rangle} \qquad G(s,s') = \lim_{N\to\infty}\frac{1}{N}\sum_i \frac{\partial\overline{\langle\sigma_i(s)\rangle}}{\partial\theta_i(s')}, \quad (10)$$

---
[2] We have assumed $p(\boldsymbol{\sigma}(0)) = \prod_i p_i(\sigma_i(0))$.

which are the single-site correlation and response functions, respectively. The overline $\overline{\ldots}$ is taken to represent disorder averaged values. Using also additional equations arising from the normalisation $Z[0] = 1$, we can rewrite the single neuron measure Φ as

$$\langle f[\{\sigma\}]\rangle_* = \sum_{\sigma_0\ldots\sigma(t)} \int \prod_{s<t} \left[\frac{dh(s)\,d\hat{h}(s)}{2\pi}\right] p(\sigma(0)) f[\{\sigma\}] e^{\sum_{s<t} \left[\beta\sigma(s+1)h(s) - \ln 2\cosh(\beta h(s))\right]}$$

$$\times e^{i\sum_{s<t} \hat{h}(s)\left[h(s) - \theta(s) - m(s)\right] - \frac{1}{2}\alpha \sum_{s,s'<t} R(s,s')\hat{h}(s)\hat{h}(s')} \quad (11)$$

with the short-hand $\mathbf{R} = \sum_{l=0}^{\infty} \mathbf{G}^{\dagger l} \mathbf{C} \mathbf{G}^{l}$. To simplify notation, we have here assumed that the initial probabilities $p_i(\sigma_i(0))$ are uniform and that the external fields $\theta_i(s)$ are so-called staggered ones, i.e. $\theta_i(s) = \theta \xi_i^{s+1}$, which makes the single neuron measure site–independent. This single neuron measure (11) represents the essential result of our calculations and is already properly normalised (i.e. $\langle 1 \rangle_* = 1$).

When one compares the present form of the single neuron measure with that obtained for the symmetric Hopfield network, one finds in the latter model an additional term which corresponds to a retarded self–interaction. The absence of such a term here suggests that the present model will have a higher storage capacity. It can be explained by the constant change of state of a large number of neurons as the network goes through the sequence, which prevents the build-up of microscopic memory of past activations.

However, as is the case for the standard Hopfield model, the measure (11) is still too complicated to find explicit equations for the observables we are interested in. Although it is possible to evaluate the necessary integrals numerically, we instead concentrate on the interesting behaviour when transients have died out and time–translation invariance is present.

4 STATIONARY STATE

We will now concentrate on the behaviour of the network at the stage when transients have subsided and the system is on a macroscopic limit cycle. Then the relations

$$m(s) = m \qquad C(s,s') = C(s-s') \qquad G(s,s') = C(s-s'). \quad (12)$$

hold and also $R(s,s') = R(s-s')$. We can then for simplicity shift the time origin $t_0 = -\infty$ and the upper temporal bound to $t = \infty$. Note, however, that this state is not to be confused with microscopic equilibrium in the thermodynamic sense. The stationary versions of the measure (11) for the interesting observables are then given by the following expressions (note that $C(0) = 1$):

$$m = \int \prod_s \frac{dv(s)\,dw(s)}{2\pi} e^{i\mathbf{v}\cdot\mathbf{w} - \frac{1}{2}\mathbf{w}\cdot\mathbf{R}\mathbf{w}} \tanh\beta\left[m + \theta + \alpha^{\frac{1}{2}} v(0)\right]$$

$$C(\tau \neq 0) = \int \prod_s \frac{dv(s)\,dw(s)}{2\pi} e^{i\mathbf{v}\cdot\mathbf{w} - \frac{1}{2}\mathbf{w}\cdot\mathbf{R}\mathbf{w}} \times$$

$$\tanh\beta\left[m + \theta + \alpha^{\frac{1}{2}} v(\tau)\right] \tanh\beta\left[m + \theta + \alpha^{\frac{1}{2}} v(0)\right]$$

$$G(\tau) = \beta\delta_{\tau,1}\left[1 - \int \prod_s \frac{dv(s)\,dw(s)}{2\pi} e^{i\mathbf{v}\cdot\mathbf{w} - \frac{1}{2}\mathbf{w}\cdot\mathbf{R}\mathbf{w}} \tanh^2\beta\left[m + \theta + \alpha^{\frac{1}{2}} v(0)\right]\right] \quad (13)$$

and we notice that the response function is now limited to a single time step, which again reflects the influence of the uncorrelated flips induced by the sequence recall. These equations can be solved by separating the persistent and fluctuating parts of $C(\tau)$ and $R(\tau)$,

$$C(\tau) = q + \tilde{C}(\tau), \qquad R(\tau) = r + \tilde{R}(\tau), \qquad \lim_{\tau = \pm\infty} \tilde{C}(\tau) = \lim_{\tau = \pm\infty} \tilde{R}(\tau) = 0.$$

Doing so eventually leads us to the coupled equations

$$\rho = \left[1 - \beta^2(1-\tilde{q})^2\right]^{-1} \tag{14}$$

$$m = \int Dz \, \tanh \beta \left[m + \theta + z\sqrt{\alpha\rho}\right] \tag{15}$$

$$\tilde{q} = \int Dz \, \tanh^2 \beta \left[m + \theta + z\sqrt{\alpha\rho}\right] \tag{16}$$

$$q = \int Dz \left[\int Dx \, \tanh \beta \left[m + \theta + z\sqrt{\alpha q \rho} + x\sqrt{\alpha(1-q)\rho}\right]\right]^2. \tag{17}$$

Note that the three equations (14—16) form a closed set, from which the persistent correlation q simply follows.

5 PHASE DIAGRAM AND STORAGE CAPACITY

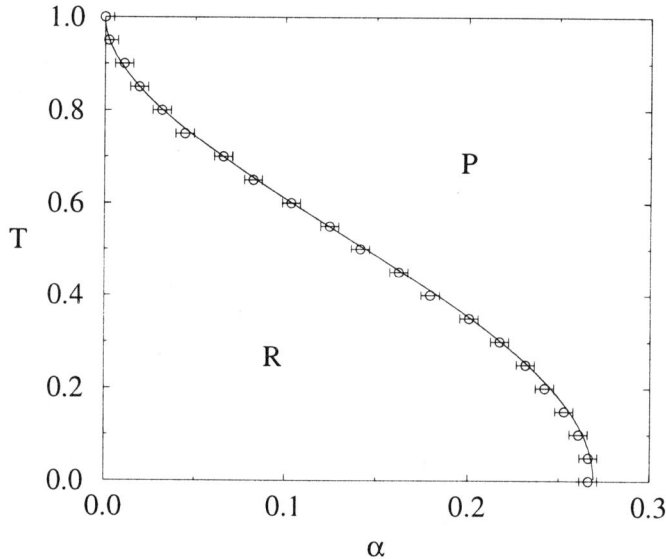

Figure 1: Phase diagram of the sequence storage network, in which one finds two phases: a recall phase (R), characterized by $\{m \neq 0, q > 0, \tilde{q} > 0\}$, and a paramagnetic phase (P), characterized by $\{m = 0, q = 0, \tilde{q} > 0\}$. The solid line separating the two phases is the theoretical prediction for the (discontinuous) phase transition. The markers represent simulation results, for systems of $N = 10,000$ neurons measured after $2,500$ iteration steps, and obtained by bisection in α. The precision in terms of α is at least $\Delta\alpha = 0.005$ (indicated by error bars); the values for T are exact.

The coupled equations (14—17) can be solved numerically for $\theta = 0$ to find the area in the α—T plane where solutions $m \neq 0$ — corresponding to sequence recall — exist. The boundary of this area describes the storage capacity of the system. This theoretical curve can then be compared with computer simulations directly performing the neural dynamics given by (1) and (2). We show the result of doing both in the same accompanying diagram. We find that there are only two types of solutions, namely a recall phase R where $m \neq 0$ and $q \neq 0$, and a paramagnetic phase where $m = q = 0$. Unlike the standard Hopfield model, the present model does not have a spin glass phase with $m = 0$ and $q \neq 0$. The agreement between simulations (done here for $N = 10,000$ neurons) and theoretical results is excellent and separate simulations of systems with up to $N = 50,000$ neurons to assess finite size effects confirm that the numerical data are reliable.

6 DISCUSSION

In this paper, we have used path integral methods to solve in the infinite system size limit the dynamics of a non-symmetric neural network model, designed to store and recall a sequence of patterns, close to saturation. This model has been known for over a decade from numerical simulations to possess a storage capacity roughly twice that of the symmetric Hopfield model, but no rigorous analytic results were available. We find here that in contrast to equilibrium statistical mechanical methods, which do not apply due to the absence of detailed balance, the powerful path integral formalism provides us with a solution and a transparent explanation of the increased storage capacity. It turns out that this higher capacity is due to the absence of a retarded self-interaction, viz. the absence of microscopic memory of activations.

The theoretically obtained phase diagram can be compared to the results of numerical simulations and we find excellent agreement. Our confidence in this agreement is supported by additional simulations to study the effect of finite size scaling. Full details of the calculations will be presented elsewhere [7].

References

[1] Sherrington D and Kirkpatrick S 1975 *Phys. Rev. Lett.* **35** 1972
[2] Amit D J, Gutfreund H, and Sompolinsky H 1985 *Phys. Rev. Lett.* **55** 1530
[3] Amari S and Maginu K 1988 *Neural Networks* **1** 63
[4] de Dominicis G 1978 *Phys. Rev. B* **18** 4913
[5] Rieger H, Schreckenberg M, and Zittartz J 1988 *J. Phys. A: Math. Gen.* **21** L263
[6] Kühn R and van Hemmen J L 1991 *Temporal Association* ed E Domany, J L van Hemmen, and K Schulten (Berlin, Heidelberg: Springer) p 213
[7] Düring A, Coolen A C C, and Sherrington D 1998 *J. Phys. A: Math. Gen.* **31** 8607

Finite-dimensional approximation of Gaussian processes

Giancarlo Ferrari Trecate
Dipartimento di Informatica e Sistemistica, Università di Pavia,
Via Ferrata 1, 27100 Pavia, Italy
ferrari@conpro.unipv.it

Christopher K. I. Williams
Department of Artificial Intelligence, University of Edinburgh,
5 Forrest Hill, Edinburgh EH1 2QL,
ckiw@dai.ed.ac.uk.

Manfred Opper
Neural Computing Research Group
Division of Electronic Engineering and Computer Science
Aston University, Birmingham, B4 7ET, UK
m.opper@aston.ac.uk

Abstract

Gaussian process (GP) prediction suffers from $O(n^3)$ scaling with the data set size n. By using a finite-dimensional basis to approximate the GP predictor, the computational complexity can be reduced. We derive optimal finite-dimensional predictors under a number of assumptions, and show the superiority of these predictors over the Projected Bayes Regression method (which is asymptotically optimal). We also show how to calculate the minimal model size for a given n. The calculations are backed up by numerical experiments.

1 Introduction

Over the last decade there has been a growing interest in the Bayesian approach to regression problems, using both neural networks and Gaussian process (GP) prediction, that is regression performed in function spaces when using a Gaussian random process as a prior.

The computational complexity of the GP predictor scales as $O(n^3)$, where n is the size of the dataset[1]. This suggests using a finite-dimensional approximating function space, which we will assume has dimension $m < n$. The use of the finite-dimensional model is motivated by the need for regression algorithms computationally cheaper than the GP one. Moreover, GP regression may be used for the identification of dynamical systems (De Nicolao and Ferrari Trecate, 1998), the next step being a model-based controller design. In many cases it is easier to accomplish this second task if the model is low dimensional.

Use of a finite-dimensional model leads naturally to the question as to which basis is optimal. Zhu et al. (1997) show that, in the asymptotic régime, one should use the first m eigenfunctions of the covariance function describing the Gaussian process. We call this method Projected Bayes Regression (PBR).

The main results of the paper are:

1. Although PBR is asymptotically optimal, for finite data we derive a predictor $h^o(x)$ with computational complexity $O(n^2 m)$ which outperforms PBR, and obtain an upper bound on the generalization error of $h^o(x)$.

2. In practice we need to know how large to make m. We show that this depends on n and provide a means of calculating the minimal m. We also provide empirical results to back up the theoretical calculation.

2 Problem statement

Consider the problem of estimating an unknown function $f(x) : \mathbb{R}^d \to \mathbb{R}$, from the noisy observations
$$t_i = f(x_i) + \epsilon_i, \quad i = 1, \ldots, n$$
where ϵ_i are i.i.d. zero-mean Gaussian random variables with variance σ^2 and the samples x_i are drawn independently at random from a distribution $p(x)$. The prior probability measure over the function $f(\cdot)$ is assumed to be Gaussian with zero mean and autocovariance function $C(\xi_1, \xi_2)$. Moreover we suppose that $f(\cdot)$, x_i, ϵ_i, are mutually independent. Given the data set $\mathcal{D}_n = \{\bar{x}, \bar{t}\}$, where $\bar{x} = [x_1, \ldots, x_n]$ and $\bar{t} = [t_1, \ldots, t_n]'$, it is well known that the posterior probability $P(f|\mathcal{D}_n)$ is Gaussian and the GP prediction can be computed via explicit formula (e.g. Whittle, 1963)
$$\hat{f}(x) = \mathrm{E}[f|\mathcal{D}_n](x) = [C(x, x_1) \quad \cdots \quad C(x, x_n)] \; H^{-1} \bar{t}, \quad \{H\}_{ij} \doteq C(x_i, x_j) + \sigma^2 \delta_{ij}$$
where H is a $n \times n$ matrix and δ_{ij} is the Kronecker delta.

In this work we are interested in approximating $\hat{f}$ in a suitable m-dimensional space that we are going to define. Consider the Mercer-Hilbert expansion of $C(\xi_1, \xi_2)$
$$\int_{\mathbb{R}^d} C(\xi_1, \xi_2) \varphi_i(\xi_2) p(\xi_2) d\xi_2 = \lambda_i \varphi_i(\xi_1), \quad \int_{\mathbb{R}^d} \varphi_i(\xi) \varphi_j(\xi) p(\xi) d\xi = \delta_{ij} \quad (1)$$
$$C(\xi_1, \xi_2) = \sum_{i=1}^{+\infty} \lambda_i \varphi_i(\xi_1) \varphi_i(\xi_2),$$
where the eigenvalues λ_i are ordered in a decreasing way.

Then, in (Zhu et al., 1997) is shown that, at least asymptotically, the optimal model belongs to $\mathcal{M} = \mathrm{Span}\{\varphi_i, i = 1, \ldots, m\}$. This motivates the choice of this space even when dealing with a finite amount of data.

Now we introduce the finite-dimensional approximator which we call Projected Bayes Regression.

---

[1] $O(n^3)$ arises from the inversion of a $n \times n$ matrix.

Definition 1 *The PBR approximator is* $b(x) = k'(x)w$, *where* $w \doteq \beta A^{-1}\Phi'\bar{t}$, $\beta \doteq 1/\sigma^2$, $A = \left(\Lambda^{-1} + \beta \Phi'\Phi\right)$, $(\Lambda)_{ij} \doteq \lambda_i \delta_{ij}$ *and*

$$k(x) \doteq \begin{bmatrix} \varphi_1(x) \\ \vdots \\ \varphi_m(x) \end{bmatrix}, \quad \Phi \doteq \begin{bmatrix} \varphi_1(x_1) & \cdots & \varphi_m(x_1) \\ \vdots & \ddots & \vdots \\ \varphi_1(x_n) & \cdots & \varphi_m(x_n) \end{bmatrix}.$$

The name PBR comes from the fact that $b(x)$ is the GP predictor when using the mis-specified prior

$$\tilde{f}(x) = \sum_{i=1}^{m} w_i \varphi_i(x), \quad w \sim N(0, \Lambda) \tag{2}$$

whose autocovariance function is the projection of $C(\xi_1, \xi_2)$ on $\mathcal{M}$. From the computational point of view, is interesting to note that the calculation of PBR scales with the data as $O(m^2 n)$, assuming that $n \gg m$ (this is the cost of computing the matrix product $A^{-1}\Phi'$).

Throughout the paper the following measures of performance will be extensively used.

Definition 2 *Let $s(x)$ be a predictor that uses only information from $\mathcal{D}_n$. Then its $\bar{x}$-error and generalization error are respectively defined as*

$$E_s(n, \bar{x}) \doteq \mathrm{E}_{t^*, x^*, \bar{t}}\left[(t^* - s(x^*))^2\right], \quad E_s^g(n) \doteq \mathrm{E}_{\bar{x}}\left[E_s(n, \bar{x})\right].$$

An estimator $s^o(x)$ belonging to a class $\mathcal{H}$ is said $\bar{x}$-optimal or simply optimal if, respectively, $E_{s^o}(n, \bar{x}) \leq E_s(n, \bar{x})$ or $E_{s^o}^g(n) \leq E_s^g(n)$, for all the $s(x) \in \mathcal{H}$ and the data sets $\bar{x}$.

Note that $\bar{x}$-optimality means optimality for each fixed vector $\bar{x}$ of data points. Obviously, if $s^o(x)$ is $\bar{x}$-optimal it is also simply optimal. These definitions are motivated by the fact that for Gaussian process priors over functions and a predictor s that depends linearly on $\bar{t}$, the computation of $E_s(n, \bar{x})$ can be carried out with finite-dimensional matrix calculations (see Lemma 4 below), although obtaining $E_s^g(n)$ is more difficult, as the average over $\bar{x}$ is usually analytically intractable.

3 Optimal finite-dimensional models

We start considering two classes of linear approximators, namely $\mathcal{H}_1 \doteq \left\{g(x) = k'(x)L\bar{t} | L \in \mathbb{R}^{m \times n}\right\}$ and $\mathcal{H}_2 \doteq \left\{h(x) = k'(x)F\Phi'\bar{t} | F \in \mathbb{R}^{m \times m}\right\}$, where the matrices L and F are possibly dependent on the x_i samples. We point out that $\mathcal{H}_2 \subset \mathcal{H}_1$ and that the PBR predictor $b(x) \in \mathcal{H}_2$. Our goal is the characterization of the optimal predictors in $\mathcal{H}_1$ and $\mathcal{H}_2$. Before stating the main result, two preliminary lemmas are given. The first one is proved in (Pilz, 1991) while the second follows from a straightforward calculation.

Lemma 3 *Let $A \in \mathbb{R}^{n \times n}$, $B \in \mathbb{R}^{n \times r}$, $A > 0$. Then it holds that*

$$\inf_{Z \in \mathbb{R}^{r \times n}} \mathrm{Tr}\left[(ZAZ' - ZB - B'Z')\right] = \mathrm{Tr}\left[-B'A^{-1}B\right]$$

and the minimum is achieved for the matrix $Z^* = B'A^{-1}$.

Lemma 4 *Let $g(x) \in \mathcal{H}_1$. Then it holds that*

$$E_g(n, \bar{x}) = \sum_{i=1}^{+\infty} \lambda_i + \sigma^2 + q(L), \quad q(L) \doteq \mathrm{Tr}\left[LHL' - 2L\Phi\Lambda\right].$$

Proof. In view of the $\bar{x}$-error definition, setting $r(x^*) = [C(x^*, x_1) \cdots C(x^*, x_n)]'$, it holds

$$\begin{aligned}
E_{t^*,\bar{t}}\left[(t^* - k'(x^*)L\bar{t})^2\right] &= \sigma^2 + C(x^*, x^*) + k'(x^*)LHL'k(x^*) \\
&\quad - 2k'(x^*)Lr(x^*) \quad (3) \\
&= \sigma^2 + C(x^*, x^*) \\
&\quad + \text{Tr}\left[LHL'k(x^*)k'(x^*) - 2Lr(x^*)k'(x^*)\right].
\end{aligned}$$

Note that $E_{x^*}\left[k(x^*)k'(x^*)\right] = I_m$, $E_{x^*}\left[r(x^*)k'(x^*)\right] = \Phi\Lambda$, and, from the Mercer-Hilbert expansion (1), $E_{x^*}[C(x^*, x^*)] = \sum_{i=1}^{+\infty} \lambda_i$. Then, taking the mean of (3) w.r.t. x^*, the result follows. $\square$

Theorem 5 *The predictors $g^o(x) \in \mathcal{H}_1$ given by $L = L^o = \Lambda\Phi'H^{-1}$ and $h^o(x) \in \mathcal{H}_2$ given by $F = F^o = \Lambda\Phi'\Phi(\Phi'H\Phi)^{-1}$, $\forall n \geq m$, are $\bar{x}$-optimal. Moreover*

$$E_{g^o}(n, \bar{x}) = \sum_{i=1}^{+\infty} \lambda_i + \sigma^2 - \text{Tr}\left[\Lambda\Phi'H^{-1}\Phi\Lambda\right] \quad (4)$$

$$E_{h^o}(n, \bar{x}) = \sum_{i=1}^{+\infty} \lambda_i + \sigma^2 - \text{Tr}\left[\Lambda\Phi'\Phi(\Phi'H\Phi)^{-1}\Phi'\Phi\Lambda\right]$$

Proof. We start considering the $g^o(x)$ case. In view of Lemma 4 we need only to minimize $q(L)$ w.r.t. to the matrix L. By applying Lemma 3 with $B = \Phi\Lambda$, $A = H > 0$, $Z = L$, one obtains

$$\arg\min_L q(L) \doteq L^o = \Lambda\Phi'H^{-1} \quad \min_L q(L) = -\text{Tr}\left[\Lambda\Phi'H^{-1}\Phi\Lambda\right] \quad (5)$$

so proving the first result. For the second case, we apply Lemma 4 with $L = F\Phi'$ and then perform the minimization of $q(F\Phi')$, w.r.t. the matrix F. This can be done as before noting that $\Phi'H^{-1}\Phi > 0$ only when $n \geq m$. $\square$

Note that the only difference between $g^o(x)$ and the GP predictor derives from the approximation of the functions $C(x, x_k)$ with $\sum_{i=1}^{m} \lambda_i \varphi_i(x)\varphi_i(x_k)$. Moreover the complexity of $g^o(x)$ is $O(n^3)$ the same of $\hat{f}(x)$. On the other hand $h^o(x)$ scales as $O(n^2m)$, so having a computational cost intermediate between the GP predictor and PBR. Intuitively, the PBR method is inferior to h^o as it does not take into account the $\bar{x}$ locations in setting up its prior. We can also show that the PBR predictor $b(x)$ and $h^o(x)$ are asymptotically equivalent.

¿From (4) is clear that the explicit evaluations of $E^g_{g^o}(n)$ and $E^g_{h^o}(n)$ are in general very hard problems, because the mean w.r.t. the x_i samples that enters in the Φ and H matrices. In the remainder of this section we will derive an upper bound on $E^g_{h^o}(n)$. Consider the class of approximators $\mathcal{H}_3 \doteq \left\{u(x) = k'(x)D\Phi'\bar{t}|D \in \mathbb{R}^{m \times m}, (D)_{ij} = d_i\delta_{ij}\right\}$. Because of the inclusions $\mathcal{H}_3 \subset \mathcal{H}_2 \subset \mathcal{H}_1$, if $u^o(x)$ is the $\bar{x}$-optimal predictor in $\mathcal{H}_3$, then $E^g_{g^o}(n) \leq E^g_{h^o}(n) \leq E^g_{u^o}(n)$. Due the diagonal structure of the matrix D, an upper bound to $E^g_{u^o}(n)$ may be explicitly computed, as stated in the next Theorem.

Theorem 6 *The approximator $u^o(x) \in \mathcal{H}_3$ given by*

$$(D)_{ij} = (D^o)_{ij} = \frac{\left(\Phi'\Phi\Lambda\right)_{ij}}{\left(\Phi'H\Phi\right)_{ij}}\delta_{ij}, \quad (6)$$

is $\bar{x}$-optimal. Moreover an upper-bound on its generalization error is given by

$$E_{u^o}^g \leq \sum_{i=1}^{+\infty} \lambda_i + \sigma^2 - n \sum_{k=1}^{m} q_k \lambda_k, \quad q_k = \frac{\lambda_k}{c_k} \quad (7)$$

$$c_k = (n-1)\lambda_k + \int C(x,x)\varphi_k^2(x)p(x)dx + \sigma^2.$$

Proof. In order to find the $\bar{x}$-optimal approximator in $\mathcal{H}_3$, we start applying the Lemma 4 with $L = D\Phi'$. Then we need to minimize

$$q(D\Phi') = \sum_{i=1}^{m} d_i^2 \left(\Phi' H \Phi\right)_{ii} - 2\sum_{i=1}^{m} d_i \left(\Phi' \Phi \Lambda\right)_{ii}. \quad (8)$$

w.r.t. d_i so obtaining (6). To bound $E_{u^o}^g(n)$, we first compute the generalization error of a generic approximation $u(x)$ that is $E_u^g = \mathrm{E}_{\bar{x}}\left[q(D\Phi')\right] + \sum_{i=1}^{+\infty} \lambda_i + \sigma^2$. After verifying that

$$\mathrm{E}_{\bar{x}}\left[\left(\Phi'\Phi\Lambda\right)_{ii}\right] = \lambda_i n, \quad \mathrm{E}_{\bar{x}}\left[\left(\Phi' H \Phi\right)_{ii}\right] = nc_i,$$

we obtain from (8), assuming the d_i constant,

$$E_u^g = \sum_{i=1}^{+\infty} \lambda_i + \sigma^2 + n \sum_{i=1}^{m} d_i^2 c_i - 2n \sum_{i=1}^{m} d_i \lambda_i.$$

Minimizing E_u^g w.r.t. d_i, and recalling that $u^o(x)$ is also simply optimal the formula (7) follows.□ When $C(\xi_1, \xi_2)$ is stationary, the expression of the c_i coefficient becomes simply $c_i = (n-1)\lambda_i + \sum_{i=1}^{+\infty} \lambda_i + \sigma^2$.

Remark : A naive approach to estimating the coefficients in the estimator $\sum_{i=1}^{\infty} w_i \phi_i(x)$ would be to set $\hat{w}_i = n^{-1}(\Phi' \underline{t})_i$ as an approximation to the integral $w_i = \int \phi_i(x) f(x) p(x) dx$. The effect of the matrix D is to "shrink" the $\hat{w}_i$'s of the higher-frequency eigenfunctions. If there was no shrinkage it would be necessary to limit m to stop the poorly-determined w_i's from dominating, but equation 7 shows that in fact the upper bound is improved as m increases. (In fact equation 7 can be used as an upper bound on the GP prediction error; it is tightest when $m \to \infty$.) This is consistent with the idea that increasing m under a Bayesian scheme should lead to improved predictions. In practice one would keep $m < n$, otherwise the approximate algorithm would be computationally more expensive than the $O(n^3)$ GP predictor.

4 Choosing m

For large n, we can show that

$$b(x) \simeq \beta \sum_{i=1}^{m} \varphi_i(x) \left(\frac{1}{\lambda_i} + \beta n\right)^{-1} \sum_{j=1}^{n} \varphi_i(x_j) t_j, \quad (9)$$

where $b(x)$ is the PBR approximator of Definition 1. (This arises because the matrix $\Phi'\Phi$ becomes diagonal in the limit $n \to \infty$ due to the orthogonality of the eigenfunctions.)

In equation 9, the factor $(\lambda_i^{-1} + \beta n)^{-1}$ indicates by how much the prior variance of the ith eigenfunction ϕ_i has been reduced by the observation of the n datapoints. (Note that this expression is exactly the same as the posterior variance of the mean

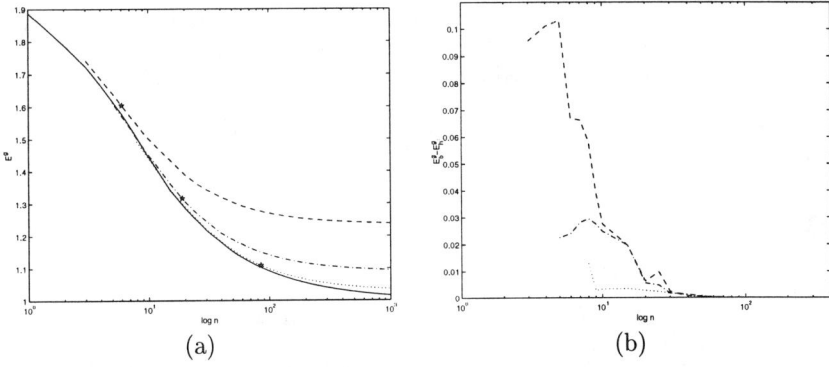

Figure 1: (a) $E^g_{h^o}(n)$ and detaching points for various model orders. Dashed: $m = 3$, dash-dot: $m = 5$, dotted: $m = 8$, solid: $E^g_{\hat{f}}(n)$. (b) $E^g_b(n) - E^g_{h^o}(n)$ plotted against n.

of a Gaussian with prior $N(0, \lambda_i)$ given n observations corrupted by Gaussian noise of variance β^{-1}.) For an eigenfunction with $\lambda_i \gg \sigma^2/n$, the posterior is considerably tighter than the prior, but when $\lambda_i \ll \sigma^2/n$, the prior and posterior have almost the same width, which suggests that there is little point in including these eigenfunctions in the finite-dimensional model. By omitting all but the first m eigenfunctions we add a term $\sum_{i=m+1}^{\infty} \lambda_i$ to the expected generalization error.

This means that for a finite-dimensional model using the first m eigenfunctions, we expect that $E^g_b(n) \simeq E^g_{\hat{f}}(n)$ up to a training set size $\bar{n}$ determined by $\bar{n} = 1/(\beta\lambda_m)$. We call $\bar{n}$ the *detatching point* for the m-dimensional approximator. Conversely, in practical regression problems the data set size n is known. Then, from the knowledge of the autocovariance eigenvalues, is possible to determine, via the detatching points formula, the order m of the approximation that should be used in order to guarantee $E^g_{h^o}(n) \sim E^g_{\hat{f}}(n)$.

5 Experimental results

We have conducted experiments using the prior covariance function $C(\xi_1, \xi_2) = (1 + h)e^{-h}$ where $h = |\xi_1 - \xi_2|/\mu$. with $\mu = 0.1$. This covariance function corresponds to a Gaussian process which is once mean-squared differentiable. It lies in the family of stationary covariance functions $C(h) = h^{\nu} K_{\nu}(h)$ (where $K_{\nu}(\cdot)$ is a modified Bessel function), with $\nu = 3/2$. The eigenvalues and eigenfunctions of this covariance kernel for the density $p(x) \sim U(0, 1)$ have been calculated in Vivarelli (1998).

In our first experiment (using $\sigma^2 = 1$) the learning curves of $b(x)$, $h^o(x)$ and $\hat{f}(x)$ were obtained; the average over the choice of training data sets was estimated by using 100 different $\bar{x}$ samples. It was noticed that $E^g_b(n)$ and $E^g_{h^o}(n)$ practically coincide, so only the latter curve is drawn in the pictures.

In Figure 1(a) we have plotted the learning curves for GP regression and the approximation $h^o(x)$ for various model orders. The corresponding detaching points are also plotted, showing their effectiveness in determining the size of data sets for which $E^g_{h^o}(n) \simeq E^g_{\hat{f}}(n)$. The minimum possible error attainable is $\sigma^2 = 1.0$ For finite-dimensional models this is increased by $\sum_{i=m+1}^{\infty} \lambda_i$; these "plateaux" can be clearly seen on the right hand side of Figure 1(a).

Our second experiment demonstrates the differences in performance for the $h^o(x)$ and $b(x)$ estimators, using $\sigma^2 = 0.1$. In Figure 1(b) we have plotted the average difference $E_b^g(n) - E_{h^o}^g(n)$. This was obtained by averaging $E_b(n, \bar{x}) - E_{h^o}(n, \bar{x})$ (computed with the *same* $\bar{x}$, i.e. a paired comparison) over 100 choices of $\bar{x}$, for each n. Notice that h^o is superior to the PBR estimator for small n (as expected), but that they are asymptotically equivalent.

6 Discussion

In this paper we have shown that a finite-dimensional predictor h^o can be constructed which has lower generalization error than the PBR predictor. Its computational complexity is $O(n^2 m)$, lying between the $O(n^3)$ complexity of the GP predictor and $O(m^2 n)$ complexity of PBR. We have also shown how to calculate m, the number of basis functions required, according to the data set size.

We have used finite-dimensional models to approximate GP regression. An interesting alternative is found in the work of Gibbs and MacKay (1997), where approximate matrix inversion methods that have $O(n^2)$ scaling have been investigated. It would be interesting to compare the relative merits of these two methods.

Acknowledgements

We thank Francesco Vivarelli for his help in providing the learning curves for $E_f^g(n)$ and the eigenfunctions/values in section 5.

References

[1] De Nicolao, G., and Ferrari Trecate, G. (1998). *Identification of NARX models using regularization networks: a consistency result.*.IEEE Int. Joint Conf. on Neural Networks, Anchorage, US, pp. 2407-2412.

[2] Gibbs, M. and MacKay, D. J. C.´(1997). *Efficient Implementation of Gaussian Processes.* Cavendish Laboratory, Cambridge, UK. Draft manuscript, available from http://wol.ra.phy.cam.ac.uk/mackay/homepage.html.

[3] Opper, M. (1997). *Regression with Gaussian processes: Average case performance.* In I. K. Kwok-Yee, M. Wong and D.-Y. Yeung (eds), *Theoretical Aspects of Neural Computation: A Multidisciplinary Perspective.* Springer-Verlag.

[4] Pilz, J. (1991). Bayesian estimation and experimental design in linear regression models. Wiley & Sons.

[5] Ripley, B. D. (1996). *Pattern recognition and neural networks.* CUP.

[6] Wahba, G. (1990). *Spline models for observational data.* Society for Industrial and Applied Mathematics. CBMS-NSF Regional Conf. series in applied mathematics.

[7] Whittle, P. (1963). *Prediction and regulation by linear least-square methods.* English Universities Press.

[8] Williams C. K. I. (1998). Prediction with Gaussian processes: from linear regression to linear prediction and beyond. In Jordan, M.I. editor, *Learning and inference in graphical models.* Kluwer Academic Press.

[9] Vivarelli, F. (1998).*Studies on generalization in Gaussian processes and Bayesian Neural Networks.* Forthcoming PhD thesis, Aston University, Birmingham, UK.

[10] Zhu, H., and Rohwer, R. (1996). *Bayesian regression filters and the issue of priors.* Neural Computing and Applications, 4:130-142.

[11] Zhu, H., Williams, C. K. I. Rohwer, R. and Morciniec, M. (1997). *Gaussian regression and optimal finite dimensional linear models.* Tech. Rep. NCRG/97/011. Aston University, Birmingham, UK.

Linear Hinge Loss and Average Margin

Claudio Gentile
DSI, Universita' di Milano,
Via Comelico 39,
20135 Milano, Italy
gentile@dsi.unimi.it

Manfred K. Warmuth[*]
Computer Science Department,
University of California,
95064 Santa Cruz, USA
manfred@cse.ucsc.edu

Abstract

We describe a unifying method for proving relative loss bounds for on-line linear threshold classification algorithms, such as the Perceptron and the Winnow algorithms. For classification problems the discrete loss is used, i.e., the total number of prediction mistakes. We introduce a continuous loss function, called the "linear hinge loss", that can be employed to derive the updates of the algorithms. We first prove bounds w.r.t. the linear hinge loss and then convert them to the discrete loss. We introduce a notion of "average margin" of a set of examples. We show how relative loss bounds based on the linear hinge loss can be converted to relative loss bounds i.t.o. the discrete loss using the average margin.

1 Introduction

Consider the classical Perceptron algorithm. The hypothesis of this algorithm at trial t is a linear threshold function determined by a weight vector $w_t \subset \mathcal{R}^n$. For an instance $x_t \in \mathcal{R}^n$ the linear activation $\hat{a}_t = w_t \cdot x_t$ is passed through a threshold function σ_r which is -1 on arguments less than the threshold r and $+1$ otherwise. Thus the prediction of the algorithm is binary and $-1, +1$ denote the two classes. The Perceptron algorithm is aimed at learning a classification problem where the examples have the form $(x_t, y_t) \in \mathcal{R}^n \times \{-1, +1\}$.

After seeing T examples $(x_t, y_t)_{1 \leq t \leq T}$, the algorithm predicts with $\hat{y}_{T+1} = \sigma_r(w_{T+1} \cdot x_{T+1})$ on the next instance x_{T+1}. If the algorithm's prediction $\hat{y}_{T+1}$ agrees with the label y_{T+1} on the instance x_{T+1}, then its loss is zero. If the prediction and the label disagree, then the loss is one. We call this loss the discrete loss.

The convergence of the Perceptron algorithm is established in the Perceptron convergence theorem. There is a second by now classical algorithm for learning with linear threshold functions: the Winnow algorithm of Nick Littlestone [Lit88]. This algorithm also maintains a weight vector and predicts with the same linear threshold function defined by the current weight vector w_t. However, the update of the weight vector $w_t = (w_{t,1}, ..., w_{t,n})$

---

[*] Supported by NSF grant CCR-9700201.

performed by the two algorithms is radically different:

$$\text{Perceptron: } \boldsymbol{w}_{t+1} := \boldsymbol{w}_t - \eta\,\delta_t\,\boldsymbol{x}_t$$
$$\text{Winnow: } \ln w_{t+1,i} := \ln w_{t,i} - \eta\,\delta_t\,x_{t,i}$$

The Perceptron algorithm performs a simple additive update. The parameter η is a positive learning rate and δ_t equals $(\hat{y}_t - y_t)/2$, which lies in $\{-1, 0, +1\}$. When $\delta_t = 0$ the prediction of the algorithm is correct and no update occurs. Both the Perceptron algorithm and Winnow update *conservatively*, i.e., they update only when the prediction of the algorithm is wrong. If $\hat{y}_t = +1$ and $y_t = -1$ then the algorithm overshot and $\delta_t = +1$. This causes the Perceptron to subtract $\eta\,\boldsymbol{x}_t$ from the current weight $\boldsymbol{w}_t$. Similarly if $\hat{y}_t = -1$ and $y_t = +1$ then the algorithm undershot and $\delta_t = -1$. Now the Perceptron adds $\eta\,\boldsymbol{x}_t$ to the current weight $\boldsymbol{w}_t$. We will later interpret $\delta_t\,\boldsymbol{x}_t$ as a gradient of a loss function. Winnow uses the same gradient but the update is done through the componentwise logarithm of the weight vector. One can also rewrite Winnow's update as

$$w_{t+1,i} := w_{t,i}\exp\left(-\eta\,\delta_t x_{t,i}\right),\ i = 1,...,n,$$

so that the gradient appears in the exponents of factors that multiply the old weights. The factors are now used to correct the weights in the right direction when the algorithm under or overshot.

The algorithms are good for different purposes and, generally speaking, incomparable (see [KWA97] for a discussion). In [KW97] a framework was introduced for deriving simple on-line learning updates. This framework has been applied to a variety of different learning algorithms and *differentiable* loss functions [HKW95, KW98]. The updates are always derived by approximately solving the following minimization problem

$$\boldsymbol{w}_{t+1} := \mathrm{argmin}_{\boldsymbol{w}} U(\boldsymbol{w}),\text{ where } U(\boldsymbol{w}) = d(\boldsymbol{w}, \boldsymbol{w}_t) + \eta\,\mathbf{loss}(y_t, \sigma_r(\boldsymbol{w}\cdot\boldsymbol{x}_t)). \quad (1)$$

Here **loss** denotes the chosen loss function. In our setting this would be the discrete loss. What is different now is that the prediction of the algorithm $\hat{y}_t = \sigma_r(\boldsymbol{w}_t\cdot\boldsymbol{x}_t)$ and the discrete loss are *discontinuous* in the weight vector $\boldsymbol{w}_t$. We will return to this point later after discussing the other parts of the above minimization problem. The parameter η is the learning rate mentioned above and, most importantly, $d(\boldsymbol{w}, \boldsymbol{w}_t)$ is a divergence measuring how far $\boldsymbol{w}$ is from $\boldsymbol{w}_t$. The divergence function has two purposes. It motivates the update and it becomes the potential function in the amortized analysis used to prove loss bounds for the corresponding algorithm.

The use of an amortized analysis in the context of learning essentially goes back to [Lit89] and the method for deriving updates based on the divergence was introduced in [KW97]. The divergence may be seen as a regularization term and may also serve as a barrier function in the optimization problem (1) for the purpose of keeping the weights in a particular region. The additive algorithms, such as gradient descent and the Perceptron algorithm, use $d(\boldsymbol{w}, \boldsymbol{w}_t) = ||\boldsymbol{w} - \boldsymbol{w}_t||^2/2$ as the divergence. This can be used as a potential function for the proof of the Perceptron convergence theorem. Multiplicative update algorithms such as Winnow and various exponentiated gradient algorithms use entropy-based divergences as potential functions [HKW95, KW98]. The function U in (1) is minimized by differentiating w.r.t. $\boldsymbol{w}$. This works very well when the loss function is convex and differentiable. For example for linear regression, when the loss function is the square loss $(\boldsymbol{w}_t\cdot\boldsymbol{x}_t - y_t)^2/2$, then minimizing $U(\boldsymbol{w})$ with the divergence $||\boldsymbol{w} - \boldsymbol{w}_t||^2/2$ gives the Widrow-Hoff update:

$$\boldsymbol{w}_{t+1} := \boldsymbol{w}_t - \eta(\boldsymbol{w}_{t+1}\cdot\boldsymbol{x}_t - y_t)\boldsymbol{x}_t \approx \boldsymbol{w}_t - \eta(\boldsymbol{w}_t\cdot\boldsymbol{x}_t - y_t)\boldsymbol{x}_t.$$

Various exponentiated gradient algorithms [KW97] can be derived in the same way when entropic divergences are used instead. However, in our case we cannot differentiate the discrete loss since it is discontinuous.

We asked ourselves which loss function motivates the Perceptron and Winnow algorithms in this framework. We will see that the loss function that achieves this is continuous and its gradient w.r.t. w_t is $\delta_t x_t$, where $\delta_t \in \{-1, 0, +1\}$. We call this loss the (linear) *hinge loss* (HL) and we believe this is the key tool for understanding linear threshold algorithms such as the Perceptron and Winnow. However, in the process of changing the discrete loss to the HL we also changed our learning problem from a classification to a regression problem. There are now two versions of each algorithm, a classification version and a regression version. The classification version predicts with a binary label using its linearly thresholded prediction. The loss function is the discrete loss. The regression version, on the other hand, predicts on the next instance x_t with its linear activation $\hat{a}_t = w_t \cdot x_t$. In the classification problem the labels y_t of the examples are -1 and $+1$, while in the regression problem the labels a_t are $-\infty$ and $+\infty$. We will see that both versions of each algorithm use the same rule to update the weight vector w_t.

Another strong hint that the HL is related to Perceptron and Winnow comes from the fact that this loss may be seen as a limiting case of the entropic loss used in logistic regression. In logistic regression the threshold function σ_r is replaced by the smooth tanh function. There is a technical way of associating a "matching loss function" with a given increasing transfer function [HKW95]. The matching loss for the tanh transfer function is the entropic loss. We will show that by making this transfer function steeper and by taking the right viewpoint of the matching loss, the entropic loss converges to the HL. In the limiting case the slope of the transfer function is infinite, i.e., it becomes the threshold function σ_r.

The question is whether this introduction of the HL buys us anything. We believe so. We can prove a unifying meta-theorem for the whole class of *general additive algorithms* [GLS97, KW98], when defined w.r.t. the HL. The bounds for the regression versions of the Perceptron and Winnow are simple special cases. These loss bounds can then be converted to loss bounds for the corresponding classification problems w.r.t. the discrete loss. This conversion is carried out through working with the "average margin" of a set of examples relative to a linear threshold classifier. The conversion of the HL described in this paper can then be considered a principled way of deriving average margin-based mistake bounds. The average margin reveals the inner structure of mistake bound results that have been proven thus far for conservative on-line algorithms. Previously used definitions, such as the deviation [FS98] and the attribute error [Lit91], can easily be related to the average margin or reinterpreted in terms of the HL and the average margin.

2 Preliminaries and the linear hinge loss

We define two subsets of $\mathcal{R}^n$: the *weight domain* $\mathcal{W}$ and the *instance domain* $\mathcal{X}$. The weights w maintained by the algorithms always lie in the weight domain and the instances x of the examples always lie in the instance domain. We require $\mathcal{W}$ be convex.

A general additive algorithm and a divergence are defined in terms of a *link function* **f**. Such a function is a vector valued function from the interior int $\mathcal{W}$ of the weight domain $\mathcal{W}$ onto $\mathcal{R}^n$, with the property that its Jacobian is strictly positive definite everywhere in int $\mathcal{W}$. A link function **f** has a unique inverse $\mathbf{f}^{-1} : \mathcal{R}^n \to$ int $\mathcal{W}$. We assume that **f** is the gradient of a (potential) function $P_\mathbf{f}$ from int $\mathcal{W}$ to $\mathcal{R}$, i.e., $\mathbf{f}(w) = \nabla P_\mathbf{f}(w)$ for $w \in$ int $\mathcal{W}$. It is easy to extend the domain of $P_\mathbf{f}$ such that it includes the boundary of $\mathcal{W}$.

For any link function **f**, a *(Bregman) divergence* function $d_\mathbf{f} : \mathcal{W} \times$ int $\mathcal{W} \to [0, \infty)$ is defined as [Bre67]:
$$d_\mathbf{f}(u, w) = P_\mathbf{f}(u) - P_\mathbf{f}(w) - (u - w) \cdot \mathbf{f}(w). \tag{2}$$
Thus $d_\mathbf{f}(u, w)$ is the difference between $P_\mathbf{f}(u)$ and its first order Taylor expansion around w. Since **f** has a strictly positive definite Jacobian everywhere in int $\mathcal{W}$, the potential $P_\mathbf{f}$ is strictly convex over $\mathcal{W}$. Thus $d_\mathbf{f}(u, w) \geq 0$ with equality holding iff $u = w$.

The Perceptron algorithm is motivated by the identity link $\mathbf{f}(w) = w$, with weight domain $\mathcal{W} = \mathcal{R}^n$. The corresponding divergence is $d_\mathbf{f}(u, w) = ||u - w||^2/2$. For Winnow the

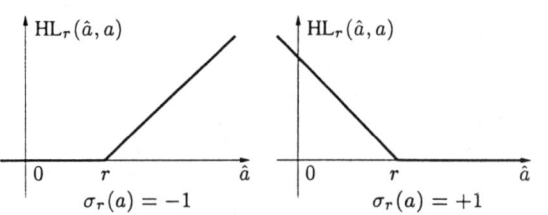
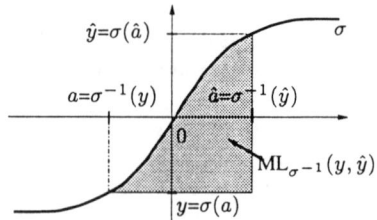

Figure 1: $\mathrm{HL}(\hat{a}, a)$ as a function of $\hat{a}$ for the two cases $\sigma_r(a) = -1, +1$.

Figure 2: The matching loss $\mathrm{ML}_{\sigma^{-1}}(y, \hat{y})$.

weight domain is $\mathcal{W} = [0, \infty)^n$. The link function is the componentwise logarithm. The divergence related to this link function is the un-normalized relative entropy $d_{\mathbf{f}}(\boldsymbol{u}, \boldsymbol{w}) = \sum_{i=1}^{n} u_i \ln \frac{u_i}{w_i} + w_i - u_i$. Note that now $\boldsymbol{u} \in \mathcal{W}$, but $\boldsymbol{w}$ must lie in int $\mathcal{W}$.

The following key property immediately follows from the definition of the divergence $d_{\mathbf{f}}$.

Lemma 1 *[KW98] For any $\boldsymbol{u} \in \mathcal{W}$ and $\boldsymbol{w}_1, \boldsymbol{w}_2 \in$ int $\mathcal{W}$:*

$$d_{\mathbf{f}}(\boldsymbol{u}, \boldsymbol{w}_2) - d_{\mathbf{f}}(\boldsymbol{u}, \boldsymbol{w}_1) - d_{\mathbf{f}}(\boldsymbol{w}_1, \boldsymbol{w}_2) = (\boldsymbol{u} - \boldsymbol{w}_1) \cdot (\mathbf{f}(\boldsymbol{w}_1) - \mathbf{f}(\boldsymbol{w}_2)).$$

In this paper we focus on a single neuron using a hard threshold as the transfer function (see beginning of the introduction). We will view such a neuron in two ways. In the standard view the neuron is used for binary classification. It outputs $\hat{y} = \sigma_r(\hat{a})$ trying to predict the desired label y using a threshold r. In the new view the neuron is a regressor. It outputs the linear activation $\hat{a} \in \mathcal{R}$ and is trying to predict $a \in \mathcal{R}$.

For classification we use the discrete loss $\mathrm{DL}(y, \hat{y}) = \frac{1}{2}|\hat{y} - y| \in \{0, 1\}$. For regression we use the linear hinge loss (HL) parameterized by a threshold r:

$$\text{For any } a, \hat{a} \in \mathcal{R}: \quad \mathrm{HL}_r(\hat{a}, a) := \frac{1}{2}(\sigma_r(\hat{a}) - \sigma_r(a))(\hat{a} - r) = \mathrm{DL}(y, \hat{y})|\hat{a} - r|.$$

Note that the arguments in the two losses DL and HL_r are switched. This is intentional and will be discussed later on.

It can be easily shown that $\mathrm{HL}_r(\boldsymbol{w} \cdot \boldsymbol{x}, a)$ is convex in $\boldsymbol{w}$ and that the gradient of this loss w.r.t. $\boldsymbol{w}$ is $\nabla_{\boldsymbol{w}} \mathrm{HL}_r(\boldsymbol{w} \cdot \boldsymbol{x}, a) = \frac{1}{2}(\sigma_r(\hat{a}) - \sigma_r(a)) \boldsymbol{x}$. Note that $\delta = (\sigma_r(\hat{a}) - \sigma_r(a))/2$ can only take the three values $0, -1,$ and $+1$ mentioned in the introduction. Strictly speaking, this gradient is not defined when $\boldsymbol{w} \cdot \boldsymbol{x}$ equals the threshold r. But we will show in the subsequent sections that even in that case $\delta \boldsymbol{x}$ has the properties we need. Figure 1 provides a graphical representation of HL_r. The threshold function σ_r "transfers" the linear activation $\hat{a} = \boldsymbol{w} \cdot \boldsymbol{x}$ to a prediction $\hat{y}$ which is a hard classification in $\{-1, +1\}$. (For the remaining discussion of this section we can assume with no loss of generality that the threshold r is 0.) Smooth transfer functions such as the tanh are commonly used in neural networks, e.g., $\hat{y} = \tanh(\hat{a})$, and relative loss bounds have been proven when the comparison class consists of single neurons with any increasing differentiable transfer function σ [HKW95, KW98]. However, for this to work a loss function that "matches" the transfer function has to be used. This loss is defined[1] as follows [HKW95] (see Figure 2):

$$\mathrm{ML}_{\sigma^{-1}}(y, \hat{y}) := \int_{\sigma^{-1}(y)}^{\sigma^{-1}(\hat{y})} \sigma(z) - y \; dz = d_{\sigma^{-1}}(y, \hat{y}).$$

The matching loss for $\sigma(z) = z$ is the square loss (linear regression) and the matching loss for $\sigma(z) = \tanh(z)$ is the entropic loss (logistic regression), which is defined as:

---

[1]In [HKW95] the notation $L_\sigma(y, \hat{y})$ is used for the matching loss $\mathrm{ML}_{\sigma^{-1}}(y, \hat{y})$. We use here the subscript σ^{-1} instead of σ to stress a connection between the matching loss and the divergence that is discussed at the end of this section.

$\mathrm{ML}_{\sigma^{-1}}(y,\hat{y}) = \frac{1}{2}(1-y)\ln\frac{1-y}{1-\hat{y}} + \frac{1}{2}(1+y)\ln\frac{1+y}{1+\hat{y}}$. The entropic loss is finite when $y \in [-1,+1]$ and $\hat{y} = \tanh(\hat{a}) \in (-1,+1)$. These are the ranges for y and $\hat{y}$ needed for logistic regression. We now want to use this type of loss for classification with linear threshold functions, i.e., when $y, \hat{y} \in \{-1,+1\}$ and the slope s of the tanh function is increased until in the limit it becomes the hard threshold σ_0. Obviously, $\sigma^{-1}(-1) = -\infty$ and $\sigma^{-1}(+1) = +\infty$ for any slope s. Thus the matching loss is infinite for all slopes. Also, the known relative loss bounds based on the above notion of matching loss grow with the slope of the transfer function. Thus it seems to be impossible to use the matching loss when the transfer function is the hard threshold σ_0. However, we can still make sense of the matching loss by viewing the neuron as a regressor. The matching loss is now rewritten as another Bregman divergence:

$$\widetilde{\mathrm{ML}}_\sigma(\hat{a},a) = \int_a^{\hat{a}} \sigma(z) - \sigma(a) \ dz = P_\sigma(\hat{a}) - P_\sigma(a) - (\hat{a}-a)\sigma(a) = d_\sigma(\hat{a},a), \quad (3)$$

where P_σ is any function such that $P'_\sigma(a) = \sigma(a)$. We now increase the slope of the transfer function tanh while keeping $\hat{a}$ and a fixed. In the limiting case (hard threshold σ_0) the above loss becomes twice the linear hinge loss with threshold zero, i.e., $\widetilde{\mathrm{ML}}_{\sigma_0}(\hat{a},a) = 2\,\mathrm{HL}_0(\hat{a},a) = (\sigma_0(\hat{a}) - \sigma_0(a))(\hat{a} - 0)$. Finally, observe that the two views of the neuron are related to a duality property [AW98] of Bregman divergences:

$$d_{\sigma^{-1}}(y,\hat{y}) = \mathrm{ML}_{\sigma^{-1}}(y,\hat{y}) = \widetilde{\mathrm{ML}}_\sigma(\hat{a},a) = d_\sigma(\hat{a},a). \quad (4)$$

3 The algorithms

In this paper we always associate two general additive algorithms with a given link function: a classification algorithm and a regression algorithm. Such algorithms, given in the next table, correspond to the two views of a linear threshold neuron discussed in the last section. For brevity, we will call the two algorithms "the classification algorithm" and "the regression algorithm", respectively.

Gen. add. classification algorithm:	Gen. add. regression algorithm:
For $t = 1, 2, \ldots$	For $t = 1, 2, \ldots$
Instance: $\boldsymbol{x}_t \in \mathcal{R}^n$	Instance: $\boldsymbol{x}_t \in \mathcal{R}^n$
Prediction: $\hat{y}_t = \sigma_r(\boldsymbol{w}_t \cdot \boldsymbol{x}_t)$	Prediction: $\hat{a}_t = \boldsymbol{w}_t \cdot \boldsymbol{x}_t$
Label: $y_t \in \{-1,+1\}$	Label:[2] $a_t = y_t \infty$
Update:	Update:
$\boldsymbol{w}_{t+1} = \mathbf{f}^{-1}\big(\mathbf{f}(\boldsymbol{w}_t) - \frac{\eta}{2}(\hat{y}_t - y_t)\boldsymbol{x}_t\big)$	$\boldsymbol{w}_{t+1} = \mathbf{f}^{-1}\big(\mathbf{f}(\boldsymbol{w}_t) - \frac{\eta}{2}(\sigma_r(\hat{a}_t) - \sigma_r(a_t))\boldsymbol{x}_t\big)$
Discrete loss:	Linear hinge loss:
$\mathrm{DL}(y_t,\hat{y}_t) = \frac{1}{2}|\hat{y}_t - y_t|$	$\mathrm{HL}_r(\hat{a}_t,a_t) = \frac{1}{2}(\sigma_r(\hat{a}_t) - \sigma_r(a_t))(\hat{a}_t - r)$

The classification algorithm receives a label $y_t \in \{-1,+1\}$, while the regression algorithm receives the infinite label a_t with the sign of y_t. This assures that $y_t = \sigma_r(a_t)$. The classification algorithm predicts with $\hat{y}_t = \sigma_r(\hat{a}_t)$, and the regression algorithm with its linear activation $\hat{a}_t$. The loss for the classification algorithm is the discrete loss $\mathrm{DL}(y_t,\hat{y}_t)$, while for the regression algorithm we use $\mathrm{HL}_r(\hat{a}_t,a_t)$. The updates of the two algorithms are equivalent. The update of the regression algorithm is motivated by the minimization problem:

$$\boldsymbol{w}_{t+1} := \mathrm{argmin}_{\boldsymbol{w}} U(\boldsymbol{w}) \text{ where } U(\boldsymbol{w}) = d_{\mathbf{f}}(\boldsymbol{w},\boldsymbol{w}_t) + \eta\,\mathrm{HL}_r(\boldsymbol{w}\cdot\boldsymbol{x}_t,a_t).$$

By setting the gradient of $U(\boldsymbol{w})$ w.r.t. $\boldsymbol{w}$ to zero we get the following equilibrium equation that holds at the minimum of $U(\boldsymbol{w})$: $\boldsymbol{w}_{t+1} = \mathbf{f}^{-1}\big(\mathbf{f}(\boldsymbol{w}_t) - \frac{\eta}{2}(\sigma_r(\boldsymbol{w}_{t+1}\cdot\boldsymbol{x}_t) - \sigma_r(a_t))\boldsymbol{x}_t\big)$. We approximately solve this equation by replacing $\boldsymbol{w}_{t+1}\cdot\boldsymbol{x}_t$ by $\hat{a}_t = \boldsymbol{w}_t\cdot\boldsymbol{x}_t$, i.e., $\boldsymbol{w}_{t+1} = \mathbf{f}^{-1}\big(\mathbf{f}(\boldsymbol{w}_t) - \frac{\eta}{2}(\sigma_r(\hat{a}_t) - \sigma_r(a_t))\boldsymbol{x}_t\big)$.

---

[2] This is a short-hand meaning $a_t = +\infty$ if $y_t = +1$ and $a_t = -\infty$ if $y_t = -1$.

Both versions of the Perceptron and Winnow are obtained by using the link functions $\mathbf{f}(\mathbf{w}) = \mathbf{w}$ and $\mathbf{f}(\mathbf{w}) = (\ln(w_1), ..., \ln(w_n))$, respectively.

4 Relative loss bounds

The following lemma relates the hinge loss of the regression algorithm to the hinge loss of an arbitrary linear predictor $\mathbf{u}$.

Lemma 2 *For all* $\mathbf{u} \in \mathcal{W}$, $\mathbf{w}_t \in \text{int } \mathcal{W}$, $\mathbf{x}_t \in \mathcal{X}$, $a_t, r \in \mathcal{R}$ *and* $\eta > 0$:

$$\text{HL}_r(\hat{a}_t, a_t) - \text{HL}_r(\mathbf{u} \cdot \mathbf{x}_t, a_t) + \text{HL}_r(\mathbf{u} \cdot \mathbf{x}_t, \hat{a}_t)$$
$$= \tfrac{1}{\eta}\left(d_{\mathbf{f}}(\mathbf{u}, \mathbf{w}_t) - d_{\mathbf{f}}(\mathbf{u}, \mathbf{w}_{t+1}) + d_{\mathbf{f}}(\mathbf{w}_t, \mathbf{w}_{t+1})\right) = \tfrac{1}{2}(\hat{y}_t - y_t)(\hat{a}_t - \mathbf{u} \cdot \mathbf{x}_t) \quad (5)$$

Proof. We have $d_{\mathbf{f}}(\mathbf{u}, \mathbf{w}_t) - d_{\mathbf{f}}(\mathbf{u}, \mathbf{w}_{t+1}) + d_{\mathbf{f}}(\mathbf{w}_t, \mathbf{w}_{t+1}) = (\mathbf{u} - \mathbf{w}_t) \cdot (\mathbf{f}(\mathbf{w}_{t+1}) - \mathbf{f}(\mathbf{w}_t)) = (\mathbf{w}_t - \mathbf{u}) \cdot \tfrac{\eta}{2}(\sigma_r(\hat{a}_t) - \sigma_r(a_t))\mathbf{x}_t = \tfrac{\eta}{2}(\sigma_r(\hat{a}_t) - \sigma_r(a_t))(\hat{a}_t - \mathbf{u} \cdot \mathbf{x}_t) = \eta\left(\text{HL}_r(\hat{a}_t, a_t) - \text{HL}_r(\mathbf{u} \cdot \mathbf{x}_t, a_t) + \text{HL}_r(\mathbf{u} \cdot \mathbf{x}_t, \hat{a}_t)\right)$. The first equality follows Lemma 1 and the second follows from the update rule of the regression algorithm. The last equality uses $\text{HL}_r(\hat{a}_t, a_t)$ as a divergence $d_{\sigma_r}(\hat{a}_t, a_t)$ (see (4)) and again Lemma 1. □

By summing the first equality of (5) over all trials t we could relate the total HL_r of the regression algorithm to the total HL_r of the regressor $\mathbf{u}$. However, our goal is to obtain bounds on the number of mistakes on the classification algorithm. It is therefore natural to *interpret* $\mathbf{u}$ too as a linear threshold classifier, with the same threshold r used by the classification algorithm. We use the second equality of (5) and sum up over all T trials:

$$\sum_{t=1}^{T} \tfrac{1}{2}(\hat{y}_t - y_t)(\hat{a} - \mathbf{u} \cdot \mathbf{x}_t) = \tfrac{1}{\eta}\left(d_{\mathbf{f}}(\mathbf{u}, \mathbf{w}_1) - d_{\mathbf{f}}(\mathbf{u}, \mathbf{w}_{T+1}) + \sum_{t=1}^{T} d_{\mathbf{f}}(\mathbf{w}_t, \mathbf{w}_{t+1})\right).$$

Note that the sums in the above equality are unaffected by trials in which no mistake occurs. In such trials, $\hat{y}_t = y_t$ and $\mathbf{w}_{t+1} = \mathbf{w}_t$. Thus the above is equivalent to the following, where $\mathcal{M}$ is the set of trials in which a mistake occurs:

$$\sum_{t \in \mathcal{M}} \tfrac{1}{2}(\hat{y}_t - y_t)(\hat{a}_t - \mathbf{u} \cdot \mathbf{x}_t) = \tfrac{1}{\eta}\left(d_{\mathbf{f}}(\mathbf{u}, \mathbf{w}_1) - d_{\mathbf{f}}(\mathbf{u}, \mathbf{w}_{T+1}) + \sum_{t \in \mathcal{M}} d_{\mathbf{f}}(\mathbf{w}_t, \mathbf{w}_{t+1})\right).$$

Since $\tfrac{1}{2}(\hat{y}_t - y_t) = -y_t$ when $t \in \mathcal{M}$ and $d_{\mathbf{f}}(\mathbf{u}, \mathbf{w}_{T+1}) \geq 0$ we get the following theorem:

Theorem 3 *Let* $\mathcal{M} \subseteq \{1, \ldots, T\}$ *be the set of trials in which the classification algorithm makes a mistake. Then for every* $\mathbf{u} \in \mathcal{W}$ *we have*

$$\sum_{t \in \mathcal{M}} y_t(\mathbf{u} \cdot \mathbf{x}_t - \hat{a}_t) \leq \tfrac{1}{\eta}\left(d_{\mathbf{f}}(\mathbf{u}, \mathbf{w}_1) + \sum_{t \in \mathcal{M}} d_{\mathbf{f}}(\mathbf{w}_t, \mathbf{w}_{t+1})\right). \quad □$$

Throughout the rest of this section the classification algorithm is compared to the performance of a linear threshold classifier $\mathbf{u}$ with threshold $r = 0$. We now apply Theorem 3 to the Perceptron algorithm with $\mathbf{w}_1 = \mathbf{0}$, giving a bound i.t.o. the *average margin* of a linear threshold classifier $\mathbf{u}$ with threshold 0 on a trial sequence $\mathcal{M}$:

$$\hat{\gamma}_{\mathbf{u}, \mathcal{M}} := \tfrac{1}{|\mathcal{M}|} \sum_{t \in \mathcal{M}} y_t \mathbf{u} \cdot \mathbf{x}_t.$$

Since $y_t \hat{a}_t \leq 0$ for $t \in \mathcal{M}$, the l.h.s. of the inequality of Theorem 3 is at least $|\mathcal{M}|\hat{\gamma}_{\mathbf{u}, \mathcal{M}}$. By the update rule, $\sum_{t \in \mathcal{M}} d_{\mathbf{f}}(\mathbf{w}_t, \mathbf{w}_{t+1}) = \sum_{t \in \mathcal{M}} \tfrac{\eta^2}{2}\|\mathbf{x}_t\|_2^2 \leq \tfrac{\eta^2}{2}|\mathcal{M}|X_2^2$, where $\|\mathbf{x}\|_2 \leq X_2$ for $t \in \mathcal{M}$. Since in Theorem 3 $\mathbf{u}$ is an arbitrary vector, we replace $\mathbf{u}$ by $\lambda \mathbf{u}$ therein, and set $\lambda = \tfrac{X_2^2 \eta}{\hat{\gamma}_{\mathbf{u}, \mathcal{M}}}$. When we solve the resulting inequality for $|\mathcal{M}|$ the dependence on η cancels out. This gives us the following bound on the number of mistakes:

$$|\mathcal{M}| \leq \left(\frac{\|\mathbf{u}\|_2 X}{\hat{\gamma}_{\mathbf{u}, \mathcal{M}}}\right)^2.$$

Note that in the usual mistake bound for the Perceptron algorithm the average $\hat{\gamma}_{u,\mathcal{M}}$ is replaced by $\min_{t \in \mathcal{M}} y_t u \cdot x_t$.[3] Also, observe that the predictions of the Perceptron algorithm with $r = 0$ and $w_1 = 0$ are not affected by η. Hence the previous bound holds for any $\eta > 0$.

Next, we apply Theorem 3 to a normalized version of Winnow. This version of Winnow keeps weights in the probability simplex and is obtained by a slight modification of Winnow's link function. We assume $r = 0$ and choose $\mathcal{X} = \{x \in \mathcal{R}^n : ||x||_\infty \leq X_\infty\}$. Unlike the Perceptron algorithm, a Winnow-like algorithm heavily depends on the learning rate, so a careful tuning is needed. One can show (details omitted due to space limitations) that if η is such that $\eta \hat{\gamma}_{u,\mathcal{M}} + \eta X_\infty - \ln\left(\frac{e^{2\eta X_\infty}+1}{2}\right) > 0$ then this normalized version of Winnow achieves the bound

$$|\mathcal{M}| \leq \frac{d_\mathbf{f}(u, w_1)}{\eta \hat{\gamma}_{u,\mathcal{M}} + \eta X_\infty - \ln\left(\frac{e^{2\eta X_\infty}+1}{2}\right)},$$

where $d_\mathbf{f}(u, w_1)$ is the relative entropy between the two probability vectors u and w_1.

Conclusions: In the full paper we study the case when there is no consistent threshold u more carefully and give more involved bounds for the Winnow and normalized Winnow algorithms as well as for the p-norm Perceptron algorithm [GLS97].

References

[AW98]   K. Azoury and M. K. Warmuth", "Relative loss bounds and the exponential family of distributions", "1998", Unpublished manuscript.

[Bre67]   L.M. Bregman. The relaxation method of finding the common point of convex sets and its application to the solution of problems in convex programming. *USSR Computational Mathematics and Physics*, 7:200–217, 1967.

[FS98]   Y. Freund and R. Schapire. Large margin classification using the perceptron algorithm. In *11th COLT*, pp. 209–217, ACM, 1998.

[GLS97]   A. J. Grove, N. Littlestone, and D. Schuurmans. General convergence results for linear discriminant updates. In *10th COLT*, pp. 171–183. ACM, 1997.

[HKW95]   D. P. Helmbold, J. Kivinen, and M. K. Warmuth. Worst-case loss bounds for sigmoided linear neurons. In *NIPS 1995*, pp. 309–315. MIT Press, 1995.

[KW97]   J. Kivinen and M. K. Warmuth. Additive versus exponentiated gradient updates for linear prediction. *Inform. and Comput.*, 132(1):1–64, 1997.

[KW98]   J. Kivinen and M. K. Warmuth. Relative loss bounds for multidimensional regression problems. In *NIPS 10*, pp. 287–293. MIT Press, 1998.

[KWA97]   J. Kivinen, M. K. Warmuth, and P. Auer. The perceptron algorithm vs. winnow: linear vs. logarithmic mistake bounds when few input variables are relevant. *Artificial Intelligence*, 97:325–343, 1997.

[Lit88]   N. Littlestone. Learning when irrelevant attributes abound: A new linear-threshold algorithm. *Machine Learning*, 2:285–318, 1988.

[Lit89]   N. Littlestone. *Mistake Bounds and Logarithmic Linear-threshold Learning Algorithms*. PhD thesis, University of California Santa Cruz, 1989.

[Lit91]   N. Littlestone. Redundant noisy attributes, attribute errors, and linear threshold learning using Winnow. In *4th COLT*, pp. 147–156, Morgan Kaufmann, 1991.

---

[3] The average margin $\hat{\gamma}_{u,\mathcal{M}}$ may be positive even though u is not consistent.

Unsupervised and supervised clustering: the mutual information between parameters and observations

Didier Herschkowitz   Jean-Pierre Nadal

Laboratoire de Physique Statistique de l'E.N.S.*
Ecole Normale Supérieure
24, rue Lhomond - 75231 Paris cedex 05, France
herschko@lps.ens.fr   nadal@lps.ens.fr
http://www.lps.ens.fr/~risc/rescomp

Abstract

Recent works in parameter estimation and neural coding have demonstrated that optimal performance are related to the mutual information between parameters and data. We consider the mutual information in the case where the dependency in the parameter (a vector θ) of the conditional p.d.f. of each observation (a vector ξ), is through the scalar product $\theta.\xi$ only. We derive bounds and asymptotic behaviour for the mutual information and compare with results obtained on the same model with the "replica technique".

1 INTRODUCTION

In this contribution we consider an unsupervised clustering task. Recent results on neural coding and parameter estimation (supervised and unsupervised learning tasks) show that the mutual information between data and parameters (equivalently between neural activities and stimulus) is a relevant tool for deriving optimal performances (Clarke and Barron, 1990; Nadal and Parga, 1994; Opper and Kinzel, 1995; Haussler and Opper, 1995; Opper and Haussler, 1995; Rissanen, 1996; Brunel and Nadal 1998).

---

*Laboratory associated with C.N.R.S. (U.R.A. 1306), ENS, and Universities Paris VI and Paris VII.

With this tool we analyze a particular case which has been studied extensively with the "replica technique" in the framework of statistical mechanics (Watkin and Nadal, 1994; Reimann and Van den Broeck, 1996; Buhot and Gordon, 1998). After introducing the model in the next section, we consider the mutual information between the patterns and the parameter. We derive a bound on it which is of interest for not too large p. We show how the "free energy" associated to *Gibbs learning* is related to the mutual information. We then compare the exact results with replica calculations. We show that the asymptotic behaviour ($p \gg N$) of the mutual information is in agreement with the exact result which is known to be related to the *Fisher information* (Clarke and Barron, 1990; Rissanen, 1996; Brunel and Nadal 1998). However for moderate values of $\alpha = p/N$, we can eliminate false solutions of the replica calculation. Finally, we give bounds related to the mutual information between the parameter and its estimators, and discuss common features of parameter estimation and neural coding.

2   THE MODEL

We consider the problem where a direction θ (a unit vector) of dimension N has to be found based on the observation of p patterns. The probability distribution of the patterns is uniform except in the unknown symmetry-breaking direction θ. Various instances of this problem have been studied recently within the satistical mechanics framework, making use of the *replica technique* (Watkin and Nadal, 1994; Reimann and Van den Broeck, 1996; Buhot and Gordon, 1998). More specifically it is assumed that a set of patterns $D = \{\xi^\mu\}_{\mu=1}^p$ is generated by p independant samplings from a non-uniform probability distribution $P(\xi|\theta)$ where $\theta = \{\theta_1, ..., \theta_N\}$ represents the symmetry-breaking orientation. The probability is written in the form:

$$P(\xi|\theta) = \frac{1}{\sqrt[N]{2\pi}} exp(-\frac{\xi^2}{2} - V(\lambda)) \qquad (1)$$

where N is the dimension of the space, $\lambda = \theta.\xi$ is the overlap and $V(\lambda)$ characterizes the structure of the data in the breaking direction. As justified within the Bayesian and Statistical Physics frameworks, one has to consider a *prior* distribution on the parameter space, $\rho(\theta)$, e.g. the uniform distribution on the sphere.

The mutual information $I(D|\theta)$ between the data and θ is defined by

$$I(D|\theta) = \int d\theta dD P(\theta) P(D|\theta) ln(\frac{P(D|\theta)}{P(D)}) \qquad (2)$$

It can be rewritten:

$$\frac{I(D|\theta)}{N} = -\alpha < V(\lambda) > - \frac{<< ln(Z) >>}{N}. \qquad (3)$$

where

$$Z = \int_{-\infty}^{\infty} d\theta \rho(\theta) exp(-\sum_{\mu=1}^p V(\lambda^\mu)) \qquad (4)$$

In the statistical physics literature $- \ln Z$ is a "free energy". The brackets $<< .. >>$ stand for the average over the pattern distribution, and $< .. >$ is the average over the resulting overlap distribution. We will consider properties valid for any N and any p, others for $p \gg N$, and the replica calculations are valid for N and p large at any given value of $\alpha = \frac{p}{N}$.

3 LINEAR BOUND

The mutual information, a positive quantity, cannot grow faster than linearly in the amount of data, p. We derive the simple linear bound:

$$I(D|\theta) \leq -p <V(\lambda)> \tag{5}$$

We proove the inequality for the case $<\lambda> = 0$. The extension to the case $<\lambda> \neq 0$ is straightforward. The mutual information can be written as $I = H(D) - H(D|\theta)$. The calculation of $H(D|\theta)$ is straightforward:

$$H(D|\theta) = \frac{pN}{2}ln(e2\pi) + \frac{p}{2}(<\lambda^2> -1) + p<V> \tag{6}$$

Now, the entropy of the data $H(D) = -\int dD P(D) ln P(D)$ is lower or equal to the entropy of a Gaussian distribution with the same variance. We thus calculate the covariance matrix of the data

$$<<\xi_i^\mu \xi_j^\nu>> = \delta_{\mu\nu}(\delta_{ij} + (<\lambda^2> -1)\overline{\theta_i \theta_j}) \tag{7}$$

where $\overline{(.)}$ denotes the average over the parameter distribution. We then have

$$H(D) \leq \frac{pN}{2}ln(2\pi e) + \frac{p}{2}\sum_{i=1}^{N} ln(1 + (<\lambda^2> -1)\gamma_i) \tag{8}$$

where γ_i are the eigen value of the matrix $\overline{\theta_i \theta_j}$. Using $\sum_{i=1}^{N}\overline{\theta_i^2} = 1$ and the property $ln(1+x) \leq x$ we obtain

$$H(D) \leq \frac{pN}{2}ln(2\pi e) + \frac{p}{2}(<\lambda^2> -1) \tag{9}$$

Putting (9) and (6) together, we find the inequality (5). ¿From this and (3) it follows also

$$p<V> \leq -<<ln(Z)>> \leq 0 \tag{10}$$

4 REPLICA CALCULATIONS

In the limit $N \to \infty$ with α finite, the free energy becomes self-averaging, that is equal to its average, and its calculation can be performed by standard replica technique. This calculation is the same as calculations related to Gibbs learning, done in (Reimann and van den Broeck, 1996, Buhot and Gordon, 1998), but the interpretation of the order parameters is different. Assuming replica symmetry, we reproduce in fig.2 results from (Buhot and Gordon, 1998) for the behaviour with α of Q which is the typical overlap between two directions compatible with the data. The overlap distribution $P(\lambda)$ was chosen to get patterns distributed according to two clusters along the symmetry-breaking direction

$$P(\lambda) = \frac{1}{2\sigma\sqrt{2\pi}}\sum_{\epsilon=\pm 1} exp(-\frac{(\lambda-\epsilon\rho)^2}{2\sigma^2}) \tag{11}$$

In fig.2 and fig.1 we show the corresponding behaviour of the average free energy and of the mutual information.

4.1 Discussion

Up to α_1, $Q = 0$ and the mutual information is in a purely linear phase $\frac{I(\theta|D)}{N} = -\alpha < V(\lambda) >$. This correspond to a regime where the data have no correlations. For $\alpha \geq \alpha_1$, the replica calculation admits up to three differents solutions. In view of the fact that the mutual information can never decrease with α and that the average free energy can not be positive, it follows that only two behaviours are acceptable. In the first, Q leaves the solution $Q = 0$ at α_1, and follows the lower branch until α_3 where it jumps to the upper branch. This is the stable way. The second possibility is that $Q = 0$ until α_2 where it directly jumps to the upper branch. In (Buhot and Gordon, 1998), it has been suggested that one can reach the upper branch, well before α_3. Here we have thus shown that it is only possible from α_2. It remains also the possibility of a replica symetry breacking phase in this range of α.

In the limit $\alpha \to \infty$ the replica calculus gives for the behaviour of the mutual information

$$I(D|\theta) \cong \frac{N}{2} ln(\alpha < (\frac{dV(\lambda)}{d\lambda})^2 >) \quad (12)$$

The r.h.s can be shown to be equal to half the logarithm of the determinant of the *Fisher information* matrix, which is the exact asymptotic behaviour (Clarke and Barron, 1990; Brunel and Nadal, 1998). It can be shown that this behaviour for $p >> N$ implies that the best possible estimator based on the data will saturate the *Cramer-Rao* bound (see e.g. Blahut, 1988). It has already been noted that the asymptotics performance in estimating the direction, as computed by the replica technique, saturate this bound (Van den Broeck, 1997). What we have check here is that this manifests itself in the behaviour of the mutual information for large α.

4.2 Bounds for specific estimators

Given the data D, one wants to find an estimate J of the parameter. The amount of information $I(D|\theta)$ limits the performance of the estimator. Indeed, one has $I(J|\theta) \leq I(D|\theta)$. This basic relationship allows to derive interesting bounds based on the choice of particular estimators. We consider first *Gibbs learning*, which consists in sampling a direction J from the 'a posteriori' probability $P(J|D) = P(D|J)\rho(J) / P(D)$. In this particular case, the differential entropy of the estimator J and of the parameter θ are equal $H(J) = H(\theta)$. If $1 - Q_g^2$ is the variance of the *Gibbs* estimator one gets, for a Gaussian prior on θ, the relations

$$-\frac{N}{2} ln(1 - Q_g^2) \leq I_{Gibbs}(J|\theta) \leq I(D|\theta) \quad (13)$$

These relations together with the linear bound (5) allows to bound the order parameter Q_g for small α where this bound is of interest.

The *Bayes estimator* consists in taking for J the center of mass of the 'a posteriori' probability. In the limit $\alpha \to \infty$, this distribution becomes Gaussian centered at its most probable value. We can thus assume $P_{Bayes}(J|\theta)$ to be Gaussian with mean $Q_b\theta$ and variance $1 - Q_b^2$, then the first inequality in (13) (with Q_g replaced by Q_b and *Gibbs* by *Bayes*) is an equality. Then using the Cramer-Rao bound on the variance of the estimator, that is $(1 - Q_b^2)/Q_b^2 \geq (\alpha < (dV/d\lambda)^2 >)^{-1}$, one can bound the mutual information for the Bayes estimator

$$I_{Bayes}(J|\theta) \leq \frac{N}{2} ln(1 + \alpha < (\frac{dV(\lambda)}{d\lambda})^2 >) \quad (14)$$

These different quantities are shown on fig.1.

5 CONCLUSION

We have studied the mutual information between data and parameter in a problem of unsupervised clustering: we derived bounds, asymptotic behaviour, and compared these results with replica calculations. Most of the results concerning the behaviour of the mutual information, observed for this particular clustering task, are "universal", in that they will be qualitatively the same for any problem which can be formulated as either a parameter estimation task or a neural coding/signal processing task. In particular, there is a linear regime for small enough amount of data (number of coding cells), up to a maximal value related to the VC dimension of the system. For large data size, the behaviour is logarithmic - that is $I \sim \ln p$ (Nadal and Parga, 1994; Opper and Haussler, 1995) or $\frac{1}{2} \ln p$ (Clarke and Barron, 1990; Opper and Haussler, 1995; Brunel and Nadal, 1998) depending on the smoothness of the model. A more detailed review with more such universal features, exact bounds and relations between unsupervised and supervised learning will be presented elsewhere. (Nadal, Herschkowitz, to appear in Phys. rev. E).

Acknowledgements

We thank Arnaud Buhot and Mirta Gordon for stimulating discussions. This work has been partly supported by the French contract DGA 96 2557A/DSP.

References

[B88]   R. E. Blahut, Addison-Wesley, Cambridge MA, 1998.

[BG98]   A. Buhot and M. Gordon. *Phys. Rev. E*, 57(3):3326–3333, 1998.

[BN98]   N. Brunel and J.-P. Nadal. *Neural Computation*, to appear, 1998.

[CB90]   B. S. Clarke and A. R. Barron. *IEEE Trans. on Information Theory*, 36 (3):453–471, 1990.

[HO95]   D. Haussler and M. Opper. conditionally independent observations. In *VIIIth Ann. Workshop on Computational Learning Theory (COLT95)*, pages 402–411, Santa Cruz, 1995 (ACM, New-York).

[OH95]   M. Opper and D. Haussler supervised learning, *Phys. Rev. Lett.*, 75:3772-3775, 1995.

[NP94a] J.-P. Nadal and N. Parga. unsupervised learning. *Neural Computation*, 6:489–506, 1994.

[OK95]   M. Opper and W. Kinzel. In E. Domany J.L. van Hemmen and K. Schulten, editors, *Physics of Neural Networks*, pages 151–. Springer, 1995.

[Ris]   J. Rissanen. *IEEE Trans. on Information Theory*, 42 (1):40-47, 1996.

[RVdB96]   P. Reimann and C. Van den Broeck. *Phys. Rev. E*, 53 (4):3989–3998, 1996.

[VdB98]   C. Van den Broeck. In *proceedings of the TANC workshop* (Hong-Kong May 26-28, 1997).

[WN94]   T. Watkin and J.-P. Nadal. *J. Phys. A: Math. and Gen.*, 27:1899–1915, 1994.

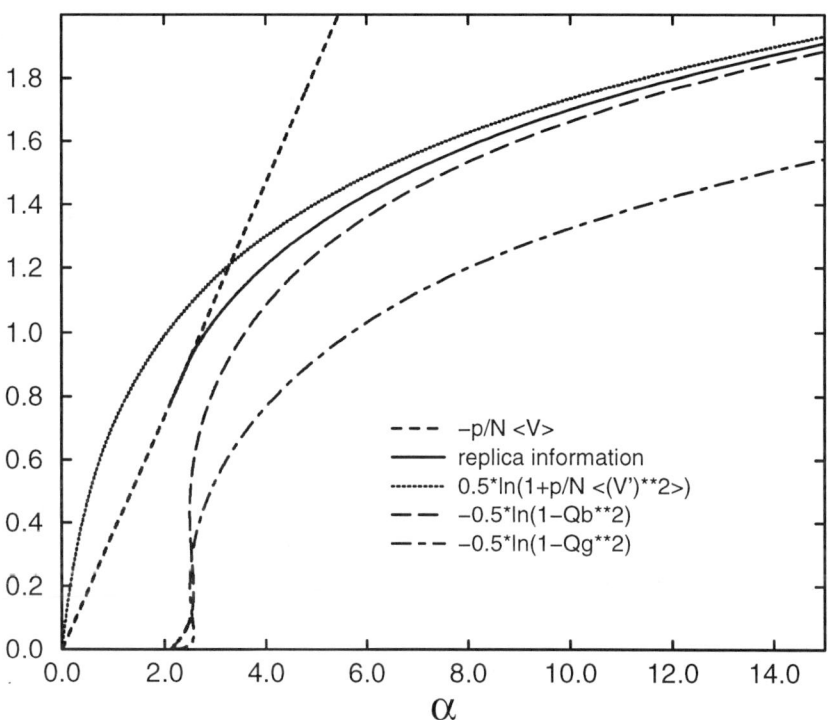

Figure 1: Dashed line is the linear bound on the mutual information $I(D|\theta)/N$. The latter, calculated with the replica technique, saturates the bound for $\alpha \leq \alpha_1$, and is the (lower) solid line for $\alpha > \alpha_1$. The special structure on fig.2 is not visible here due to the graph scale. The curve $-\frac{1}{2}ln(1 - Q_g^2)$ is a lower bound on the mutual information between the *Gibbs* estimator and θ (which would be equal to this bound if the conditional probability distribution of the estimator were Gaussian with mean $Q_g\theta$ and variance $1 - Q_g^2$). Shown also is the analogous curve $-\frac{1}{2}ln(1 - Q_b^2)$ for the *Bayes* estimator. In the limit $\alpha \to \infty$ these two latter Gaussian curves and the replica information $I(D|\theta)$, all converge toward the exact asymptotic behaviour, which can be expressed as $\frac{1}{2}ln(1 + \alpha < (\frac{dV(\lambda)}{d\lambda})^2 >)$ (upper solid line). This latter expression is, for any p, an upper bound for the two Gaussian curves.

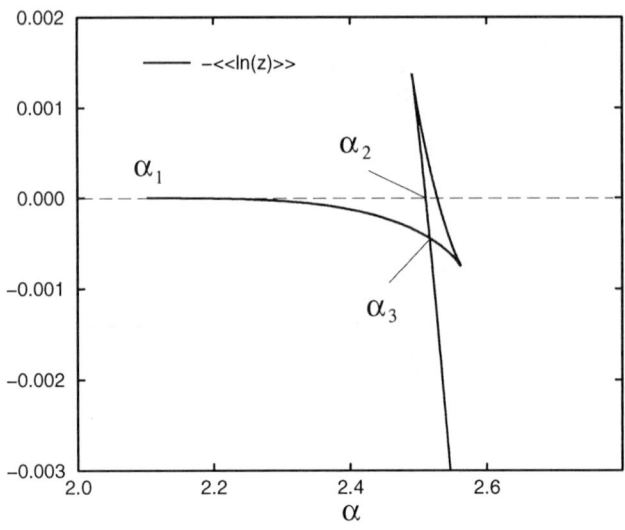

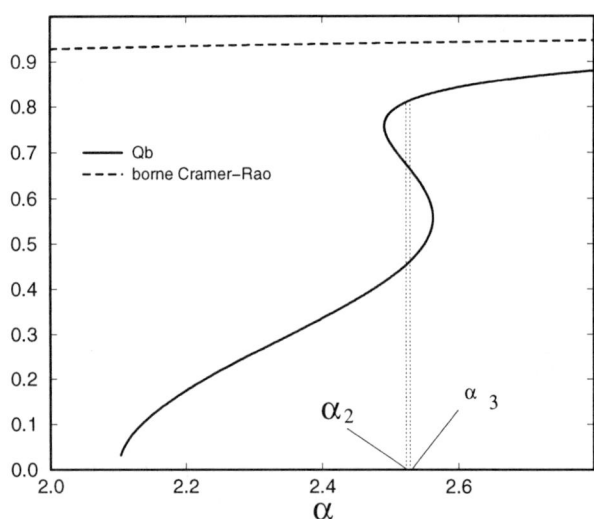

Figure 2: In the lower figure, the optimal learning curve $Q_b(\alpha)$ for $\rho = 1.2$ and $\sigma = 0.5$, as computed in (Buhot and Gordon, 1998) under the replica symetric ansatz. We have put the Cramer-Rao bound for this quantity. In the upper figure, the average free energy $- \ll lnZ \gg /N$. All the part above zero has to be rejected.
$\alpha_1 = 2.10$, $\alpha_2 = 2.515$ and $\alpha_3 = 2.527$

Convergence of The Wake-Sleep Algorithm

Shiro Ikeda
PRESTO, JST
Wako, Saitama, 351-0198, Japan
shiro@brain.riken.go.jp

Shun-ichi Amari
RIKEN Brain Science Institute
Wako, Saitama, 351-0198, Japan
amari@brain.riken.go.jp

Hiroyuki Nakahara
RIKEN Brain Science Institute
hiro@brain.riken.go.jp

Abstract

The W-S (Wake-Sleep) algorithm is a simple learning rule for the models with hidden variables. It is shown that this algorithm can be applied to a factor analysis model which is a linear version of the Helmholtz machine. But even for a factor analysis model, the general convergence is not proved theoretically. In this article, we describe the geometrical understanding of the W-S algorithm in contrast with the EM (Expectation-Maximization) algorithm and the em algorithm. As the result, we prove the convergence of the W-S algorithm for the factor analysis model. We also show the condition for the convergence in general models.

1 INTRODUCTION

The W-S algorithm[5] is a simple Hebbian learning algorithm. Neal and Dayan applied the W-S algorithm to a factor analysis model[7]. This model can be seen as a linear version of the Helmholtz machine[3]. As it is mentioned in[7], the convergence of the W-S algorithm has not been proved theoretically even for this simple model.

From the similarity of the W-S and the EM algorithms and also from empirical results, the W-S algorithm seems to work for a factor analysis model. But there is an essential difference between the W-S and the EM algorithms. In this article, we show the em algorithm[2], which is the information geometrical version of the EM algorithm, and describe the essential difference. From the result, we show that we cannot rely on the similarity for the reason of the W-S algorithm to work. However, even with this difference, the W-S algorithm works on the factor analysis model and we can prove it theoretically. We show the proof and also show the condition of the W-S algorithm to work in general models.

2 FACTOR ANALYSIS MODEL AND THE W-S ALGORITHM

A factor analysis model with a single factor is defined as the following generative model,

Generative model $\quad x = \mu + yg + \epsilon,$
where $x = (x_1, \cdots, x_n)^T$ is a n dimensional real-valued visible inputs, $y \sim \mathcal{N}(0, 1)$ is the single invisible factor, g is a vector of "factor loadings", μ is the overall means vector which is set to be zero in this article, and $\epsilon \sim \mathcal{N}(0, \Sigma)$ is the noise with a diagonal covariance matrix, $\Sigma = \text{diag}(\sigma_i^2)$. In a Helmholtz machine, this generative model is accompanied by a recognition model which is defined as,

Recognition model $\quad y = r^T x + \delta,$
where r is the vector of recognition weights and $\delta \sim \mathcal{N}(0, s^2)$ is the noise.

When data $x_1, \cdots, x_N$ is given, we want to estimate the MLE(Maximum Likelihood Estimator) of g and Σ. The W-S algorithm can be applied[7] for learning of this model.

Wake-phase: From the training set $\{x_s\}$ choose a number of x randomly and for each data, generate y according to the recognition model $y = r_t^T x + \delta, \delta \sim \mathcal{N}(0, s_t^2)$. Update g and Σ as follows using these x's and y's, where α is a small positive number and β is slightly less than 1.

$$g_{t+1} = g_t + \alpha \overline{(x - g_t y) y} \tag{1}$$
$$\sigma_{i,t+1}^2 = \beta \sigma_{i,t}^2 + (1 - \beta) \overline{(x_i - g_{i,t} y)^2}, \tag{2}$$

where $\overline{}$ denotes the averaging over the chosen data.

Sleep-phase: According to the updated generative model $x = y g_{t+1} + \epsilon, y \sim \mathcal{N}(0, 1), \epsilon \sim \mathcal{N}(0, \text{diag}(\sigma_{t+1}^2))$, generate a number of x and y. And update r and s^2 as,

$$r_{t+1} = r_t + \alpha \overline{(y - r_t^T x) x} \tag{3}$$
$$s_{t+1}^2 = \beta s_t^2 + (1 - \beta) \overline{(y - r_t^T x)^2}. \tag{4}$$

By iterating these phases, they try to find the MLE as the converged point.

For the following discussion, let us define two probability densities p and q, where p is the density of the generative model, and q is that of the recognition model.

Let $\theta = (g, \Sigma)$, and the generative model gives the density function of x and y as,

$$p(y, x; \theta) = \exp\left(-\frac{1}{2}(y \; x^T) A \begin{pmatrix} y \\ x \end{pmatrix} - \psi(\theta)\right) \tag{5}$$

$$A = \begin{pmatrix} 1 + g^T \Sigma^{-1} g & -g^T \Sigma^{-1} \\ -\Sigma^{-1} g & \Sigma^{-1} \end{pmatrix}, \psi(\theta) = \frac{1}{2}\left(\sum \log \sigma_i^2 + (n+1) \log 2\pi\right),$$

while the recognition model gives the distribution of y conditional to x as the following,

$$q(y|x; \eta) \sim \mathcal{N}(r^T x, s^2),$$

where, $\eta = (r, s^2)$. From the data $x_1, \cdots, x_N$, we define,

$$C = \frac{1}{N} \sum_{s=1}^{N} x_s x_s^T, \quad q(x) \sim \mathcal{N}(0, C).$$

With this $q(x)$, we define $q(y, x; \eta)$ as,

$$q(y, x; \eta) = q(x) q(y|x; \eta) = \exp\left(-\frac{1}{2}(y \; x^T) B \begin{pmatrix} y \\ x \end{pmatrix} - \psi(\eta)\right) \tag{6}$$

$$B = \frac{1}{s^2}\begin{pmatrix} 1 & -r^T \\ -r & s^2 C^{-1} + r r^T \end{pmatrix}, \psi(\eta) = \frac{1}{2}\left(\log s^2 + \log |C| + (n+1) \log 2\pi\right).$$

3 THE EM AND THE *em* ALGORITHMS FOR A FACTOR ANALYSIS MODEL

It is mentioned that the W-S algorithm is similar to the EM algorithm[4]([5][7]). But there is an essential difference between them. In this section, first, we show the EM algorithm. We also describe the *em* algorithm[2] which gives us the information geometrical understanding of the EM algorithm. With these results, we will show the difference between W-S and the EM algorithms in the next section.

The EM algorithm consists of the following two steps.

E-step: Define $Q(\theta, \theta_t)$ as,

$$Q(\theta, \theta_t) = \frac{1}{N} \sum_{s=1}^{N} E_{p(y|x_s;\theta_t)} [\log p(y, x_s; \theta)]$$

M-step: Update θ as,

$$\theta_{t+1} = \underset{\theta}{\operatorname{argmax}} \, Q(\theta, \theta_t),$$

$$g_{t+1} = \frac{(1 + g_t^T \Sigma_t^{-1} g_t) C \Sigma_t^{-1} g_t}{g_t^T \Sigma_t^{-1} C \Sigma_t^{-1} g_t + 1 + g_t^T \Sigma_t^{-1} g_t}, \quad \Sigma_{t+1} = \operatorname{diag}\left(C - g_{t+1} \frac{g_t^T \Sigma_t^{-1} C}{1 + g_t^T \Sigma_t^{-1} g_t}\right). \tag{7}$$

$E_p[\cdot]$ denotes taking the average with the probability distribution p. The iteration of these two steps converges to give the MLE.

The EM algorithm only uses the generative model, but the *em* algorithm[2] also uses the recognition model. The *em* algorithm consists of the *e* and *m* steps which are defined as the *e* and *m* projections[1] between the two manifolds M and D. The manifolds are defined as follows.

Model manifold M: $M \stackrel{\text{def}}{=} \{p(y, x; \theta) | \theta = (g, \operatorname{diag}(\sigma_i^2)), g \in \mathbb{R}^n, 0 < \sigma_i < \infty\}$.

Data manifold D: $D \stackrel{\text{def}}{=} \{q(y, x; \eta) | \eta = (r, s^2), r \in \mathbb{R}^n, 0 < s < \infty\}$, $q(x)$ include the matrix C which is defined by the data, and this is called the "data manifold".

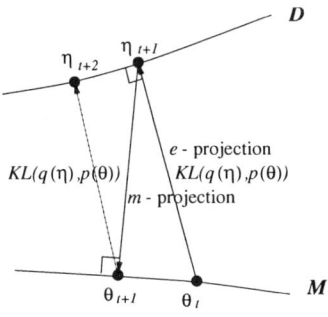

Figure 1: Information geometrical understanding of the *em* algorithm

Figure 1 schematically shows the *em* algorithm. It consists of two steps, *e* and *m* steps. On each step, parameters of recognition and generative models are updated respectively.

e-step: Update η as the e projection of $p(y, x; \theta_t)$ on D.

$$\eta_{t+1} = \operatorname*{argmin}_{\eta} KL(q(\eta), p(\theta_t)) \tag{8}$$

$$r_{t+1} = \frac{\Sigma_t^{-1} g_t}{1 + g_t^T \Sigma_t^{-1} g_t}, \quad s_{t+1}^2 = \frac{1}{1 + g_t^T \Sigma_t^{-1} g_t}. \tag{9}$$

where $KL(q(\eta), p(\theta))$ is the Kullback-Leibler divergence defined as,

$$KL(q(\eta), p(\theta)) = E_{q(y,x;\eta)}\left[\log \frac{q(y,x;\eta)}{p(y,x;\theta)}\right]$$

m-step: Update θ as the m projection of $q(y, x; \eta_t)$ on M.

$$\theta_{t+1} = \operatorname*{argmin}_{\theta} KL(q(\eta_{t+1}), p(\theta)) \tag{10}$$

$$g_{t+1} = \frac{Cr_{t+1}}{s_{t+1}^2 + r_{t+1}^T C r_{t+1}}, \quad \Sigma_{t+1} = \operatorname{diag}\left(C - g_{t+1} r_{t+1}^T C\right). \tag{11}$$

By substituting (9) for r_{t+1} and s_{t+1}^2 in (11), it is easily proved that (11) is equivalent to (7), and the em and EM algorithms are equivalent.

4 THE DIFFERENCE BETWEEN THE W-S AND THE EM ALGORITHMS

The wake-phase corresponds to a gradient flow of the M-step[7] in the stochastic sense. But the sleep-phase is not a gradient flow of the E-step. In order to see these clear, we show the detail of the W-S phases in this section.

First, we show the averages of (1), (2), (3) and (4),

$$g_{t+1} = g_t - \alpha(s_t^2 + r_t^T C r_t)\left(g_t - \frac{Cr_t}{s_t^2 + r_t^T C r_t}\right) \tag{12}$$

$$\Sigma_{t+1} = \Sigma_t - (1-\beta)\left(\Sigma_t - \operatorname{diag}\left(C - 2(Cr_t)g_t^T + (s_t^2 + r_t^T C r_t)g_t g_t^T\right)\right) \tag{13}$$

$$r_{t+1} = r_t - \alpha(\Sigma_{t+1} + g_{t+1} g_{t+1}^T)\left(r_t - \frac{\Sigma_{t+1}^{-1} g_{t+1}}{1 + g_{t+1}^T \Sigma_{t+1}^{-1} g_{t+1}}\right) \tag{14}$$

$$s_{t+1}^2 = s_t^2 - (1-\beta)\left(s_t^2 - ((1 - g_{t+1}^T r_t)^2 + r_t^T \Sigma_{t+1} r_t)\right). \tag{15}$$

As the K-L divergence is rewritten as $KL(q(\eta), p(\theta))$,

$$KL(q(\eta), p(\theta)) = \frac{1}{2}\operatorname{tr}(B^{-1}A) - \frac{n+1}{2} + \psi(\theta) - \psi(\eta),$$

the derivatives of this K-L divergence with respect to $\theta = (g, \Sigma)$ are,

$$\frac{\partial}{\partial g} KL(q(\eta), p(\theta)) = 2\left((s^2 + r^T C r)\Sigma^{-1}\right)\left(g - \frac{Cr}{s^2 + r^T C r}\right) \tag{16}$$

$$\frac{\partial}{\partial \Sigma} KL(q(\eta), p(\theta)) = \Sigma^{-2}\left(\Sigma - \operatorname{diag}\left(C - 2Crg^T + (s^2 + r^T C r)gg^T\right)\right). \tag{17}$$

With these results, we can rewrite the wake-phase as,

$$g_{t+1} = g_t - \frac{\alpha}{2}\Sigma_t \frac{\partial}{\partial g_t} KL(q(\eta_t), p(\theta_t)) \tag{18}$$

$$\Sigma_{t+1} = \Sigma_t - (1-\beta)\Sigma_t^2 \frac{\partial}{\partial \Sigma_t} KL(q(\eta_t), p(\theta_t)) \tag{19}$$

Since Σ is a positive definite matrix, the wake-phase is a gradient flow of m-step which is defined as (10).

On the other hand, $KL(p(\boldsymbol{\theta}), q(\boldsymbol{\eta}))$ is,

$$KL(p(\boldsymbol{\theta}), q(\boldsymbol{\eta})) = \frac{1}{2} tr(A^{-1}B) - \frac{n}{2} + \psi(\boldsymbol{\eta}) - \psi(\boldsymbol{\theta}).$$

The derivatives of this K-L divergence respect to r and s^2 are,

$$\frac{\partial}{\partial r} KL(p(\boldsymbol{\theta}), q(\boldsymbol{\eta})) = \frac{2}{s^2}(\Sigma + gg^T)\left(r - \frac{\Sigma^{-1}g}{1 + g^T \Sigma^{-1}g}\right) \quad (20)$$

$$\frac{\partial}{\partial(s^2)} KL(p(\boldsymbol{\theta}), q(\boldsymbol{\eta})) = \frac{1}{(s^2)^2}\left(s^2 - ((1 - g^T r)^2 + r^T \Sigma r)\right). \quad (21)$$

Therefore, the sleep-phase can be rewritten as,

$$r_{t+1} = r_t - \frac{\alpha}{2} s_t^2 \frac{\partial}{\partial r_t} KL(p(\boldsymbol{\theta}_{t+1}), q(\boldsymbol{\eta}_t)) \quad (22)$$

$$s_{t+1}^2 = s_t^2 - (1 - \beta)(s_t^2)^2 \frac{\partial}{\partial(s_t^2)} KL(p(\boldsymbol{\theta}_{t+1}), q(\boldsymbol{\eta}_t)). \quad (23)$$

These are also a gradient flow, but because of the asymmetricity of K-L divergence, (22), (23) are different from the on-line version of the m-step. This is the essential difference between the EM and W-S algorithms. Therefore, we cannot prove the convergence of the W-S algorithm based on the similarity of these two algorithms[7].

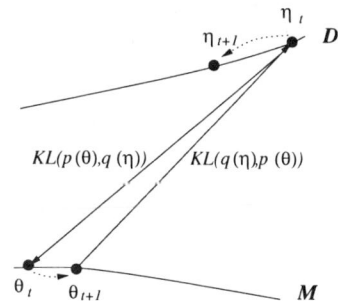

Figure 2: The Wake-Sleep algorithm

5 CONVERGENCE PROPERTY

We want to prove the convergence property of the W-S algorithm. If we can find a Lyapnov function for the W-S algorithm, the convergence is guaranteed[7]. But we couldn't find it. Instead of finding a Lyapnov function, we take the continuous time, and see the behavior of the parameters and K-L divergence, $KL(q(\boldsymbol{\eta}_t), p(\boldsymbol{\theta}_t))$.

$KL(q(\boldsymbol{\eta}), p(\boldsymbol{\theta}))$ is a function of g, r, Σ and s^2. The derivatives with respect to g and Σ are given in (16) and (17). The derivatives with respect to r and s^2 are,

$$\frac{\partial}{\partial r} KL(q(\boldsymbol{\eta}), p(\boldsymbol{\theta})) = 2(1 + g^T \Sigma^{-1} g) C \left(r - \frac{\Sigma^{-1} g}{1 + g^T \Sigma^{-1} g}\right) \quad (24)$$

$$\frac{\partial}{\partial(s^2)} KL(q(\boldsymbol{\eta}), p(\boldsymbol{\theta})) = 1 + g^T \Sigma^{-1} g - \frac{1}{s^2}. \quad (25)$$

On the other hand, we set the flows of g, r, Σ and s^2 to follow the updating due to the W-S algorithm, that is,

$$\frac{d}{dt}g = -\alpha'(s_t^2 + r_t^T C r_t)\left(g_t - \frac{C r_t}{s_t^2 + r_t^T C r_t}\right) \quad (26)$$

$$\frac{d}{dt}r = -\alpha'(\Sigma_t + g_t g_t^T)\left(r_t - \frac{\Sigma_t^{-1} g_t}{1 + g_t^T \Sigma_t^{-1} g_t}\right) \quad (27)$$

$$\frac{d}{dt}\Sigma = -\beta'\left(\Sigma_t - \text{diag}\left(C - 2 C r_t g^T{}_t + (s_t^2 + r_t^T C r_t) g_t g_t^T\right)\right) \quad (28)$$

$$\frac{d}{dt}(s^2) = -\beta'\left(s_t^2 - ((1 - g_t^T r_t)^2 + r_t^T \Sigma_t r_t)\right) \quad (29)$$

With theses results, $dKL(q(\eta_t), p(\theta_t))/dt$ is,

$$\frac{dKL(q(\eta_t), p(\theta_t))}{dt} = \frac{\partial KL}{\partial g}\frac{dg}{dt} + \frac{\partial KL}{\partial r}\frac{dr}{dt} + \frac{\partial KL}{\partial \Sigma}\frac{d\Sigma}{dt} + \frac{\partial KL}{\partial (s^2)}\frac{d(s^2)}{dt}. \quad (30)$$

First 3 terms in the right side of (30) are apparently non-positive. Only the 4th one is not clear.

$$\frac{\partial KL}{\partial (s^2)}\frac{d(s^2)}{dt} = -\beta'\left(s_t^2 - ((1 - g_t^T r_t)^2 + r_t^T \Sigma_t r_t)\right)\left(1 + g_t^T \Sigma_t^{-1} g_t - \frac{1}{s_t^2}\right)$$

$$= -\frac{1 + g_t^T \Sigma_t^{-1} g_t}{s_t^2}\left(s_t^2 - ((1 - g_t^T r_t)^2 + r_t^T \Sigma_t r_t)\right)\left(s_t^2 - \frac{1}{1 + g_t^T \Sigma_t^{-1} g_t}\right).$$

The $KL(q(\eta_t), p(\theta_t))$ does not decrease when s_t^2 stays between $((1 - g_t^T r_t)^2 + r_t^T \Sigma_t r_t)$ and $1/(1 + g_t^T \Sigma_t^{-1} g_t)$, but if the following equation holds, these two are equivalent,

$$r_t = \frac{\Sigma_t^{-1} g_t}{1 + g_t^T \Sigma_t^{-1} g_t}. \quad (31)$$

From the above results, the flows of g, r and Σ decrease $KL(q(\eta_t), p(\theta_t))$ at any time. s_t^2 converges to $((1 - g_t^T r_t)^2 + r_t^T \Sigma_t r_t)$ but it does not always decrease $KL(q(\eta_t), p(\theta_t))$. But since r does converge to satisfy (31) independently of s_t^2, finally s_t^2 converges to $1/(1 + g_t^T \Sigma_t^{-1} g_t)$.

6 DISCUSSION

This factor analysis model has a special property that $p(y|x; \theta)$ and $q(y|x; \eta)$ are equivalent when following conditions are satisfied[7],

$$r = \frac{\Sigma^{-1} g}{1 + g^T \Sigma^{-1} g}, \qquad s^2 = \frac{1}{1 + g^T \Sigma^{-1} g}. \quad (32)$$

From this property, minimizing $KL(p(\theta), q(\eta))$ and $KL(q(\eta), p(\theta))$ with respect to η leads to the same point.

$$KL(p(\theta), q(\eta)) = E_{p(x;\theta)}\left[\log \frac{p(x;\theta)}{q(x)}\right] + E_{p(y,x;\theta)}\left[\log \frac{p(y|x;\theta)}{q(y|x;\eta)}\right] \quad (33)$$

$$KL(q(\eta), p(\theta)) = E_{q(x)}\left[\log \frac{q(x)}{p(x;\theta)}\right] + E_{q(y,x;\eta)}\left[\log \frac{q(y|x;\eta)}{p(y|x;\theta)}\right], \quad (34)$$

both of (33) and (34) include η only in the second term of the right side. If (32) holds, those two terms are 0. Therefore $KL(p(\theta), q(\eta))$ and $KL(q(\eta), p(\theta))$ are minimized at the same point.

We can use this result to modify the W-S algorithm. If the factor analysis model does not try wake- and sleep- phase alternately but "sleeps well" untill convergence, it will find the η which is equivalent to the e-step in the em algorithm. Since the wake-phase is a gradient flow of the m-step, this procedure will converge to the MLE. This algorithm is equivalent to what is called the GEM(Generalized EM) algorithm[6].

The reason of the GEM and the W-S algorithms work is that $p(y|x;\theta)$ is realizable with the recognition model $q(y|x;\eta)$. If the recognition model is not realizable, the W-S algorithm won't converge to the MLE. We are going to show an example and conclude this article.

Suppose the case that the average of y in the recognition model is not a linear function of r and x but comes through a nonlinear function $f(\cdot)$ as,

Recognition model $\qquad\qquad\qquad y = f(r^T x) + \delta,$

where $f(\cdot)$ is a function of single input and output and $\delta \sim \mathcal{N}(0, s^2)$ is the noise. In this case, the generative model is not realizable by the recognition model in general. And minimizing (33) with respect to η leads to a different point from minimizing (34). $KL(p(\theta), q(\eta))$ is minimized when r and s^2 satisfies,

$$E_{p(x;\theta)}\left[f(r^T x)f'(r^T x)x\right] = E_{p(y,x;\theta)}\left[yf'(r^T x)x\right] \qquad (35)$$

$$s^2 = 1 - E_{p(y,x;\theta)}\left[-2yf(r^T x) + f^2(r^T x)\right], \qquad (36)$$

while $KL(q(\eta), p(\theta))$ is minimized when r and s^2 satisfies,

$$(1 + g^T \Sigma^{-1} g) E_{q(x;\eta)}\left[f(r^T x)f'(r^T x)x\right] = E_{q(x;\eta)}\left[f'(r^T x)xx^T\right]\Sigma^{-1}g \qquad (37)$$

$$s^2 = \frac{1}{1 + g^T \Sigma^{-1} g}. \qquad (38)$$

Here, $f'(\cdot)$ is the derivative of $f(\cdot)$. If $f(\cdot)$ is a linear function, $f'(\cdot)$ is a constant value and (35), (36) and (37), (38) give the same η as (32), but these are different in general.

We studied a factor analysis model, and showed that the W-S algorithm works on this model. From further analysis, we could show that the reason why the algorithm works on the model is that the generative model is realizable by the recognition model. We also showed that the W-S algorithm doesn't converge to the MLE if the generative model is not realizable with a simple example.

Acknowledgment

We thank Dr. Noboru Murata for very useful discussions on this work.

References

[1] Shun-ichi Amari. *Differential-Geometrical Methods in Statistics*, volume 28 of *Lecture Notes in Statistics*. Springer-Verlag, Berlin, 1985.

[2] Shun-ichi Amari. Information geometry of the EM and em algorithms for neural networks. *Neural Networks*, 8(9):1379–1408, 1995.

[3] Peter Dayan, Geoffrey E. Hinton, and Radford M. Neal. The Helmholtz machine. *Neural Computation*, 7(5):889–904, 1995.

[4] A. P. Dempster, N. M. Laird, and D. B. Rubin. Maximum likelihood from incomplete data via the EM algorithm. *J. R. Statistical Society, Series B*, 39:1–38, 1977.

[5] G. E. Hinton, P. Dayan, B. J. Frey, and R. M. Neal. The "wake-sleep" algorithm for unsupervised neural networks. *Science*, 268:1158–1160, 1995.

[6] Geoffrey J. McLachlan and Thriyambakam Krishnan. *The EM Algorithm and Extensions*. Wiley series in probability and statistics. John Wiley & Sons, Inc., 1997.

[7] Radford M. Neal and Peter Dayan. Factor analysis using delta-rule wake-sleep learning. *Neural Computation*, 9(8):1781–1803, 1997.

The Belief in TAP

Yoshiyuki Kabashima
Dept. of Compt. Intl. & Syst. Sci.
Tokyo Institute of Technology
Yokohama 226, Japan

David Saad
Neural Computing Research Group
Aston University
Birmingham B4 7ET, UK

Abstract

We show the similarity between belief propagation and TAP, for decoding corrupted messages encoded by Sourlas's method. The latter is a special case of the Gallager error-correcting code, where the code word comprises products of K bits selected randomly from the original message. We examine the efficacy of solutions obtained by the two methods for various values of K and show that solutions for $K \geq 3$ may be sensitive to the choice of initial conditions in the case of unbiased patterns. Good approximations are obtained generally for $K = 2$ and for biased patterns in the case of $K \geq 3$, especially when Nishimori's temperature is being used.

1 Introduction

Belief networks [1] are diagrammatic representations of joint probability distributions over a set of variables. This set is usually represented by the vertices of a graph, while arcs between vertices represent probabilistic dependencies between variables. Belief propagation provides a convenient mathematical tool for calculating iteratively joint probability distributions between variables and have been used in a variety of cases, most recently in the field of error correcting codes, for decoding corrupted messages [2] (for a review of graphical models and their use in the context of error-correcting codes see [3]).

Error-correcting codes provide a mechanism for retrieving the original message after corruption due to noise during transmission. Of a particular interest to the current paper is an error-correcting code presented by Sourlas [4] which is a special case of the Gallager codes [5]. The latter have been recently re-discovered by MacKay and Neal [2] and seem to have a significant practical potential.

In this paper we will examine the similarities between the belief propagation (BP) and TAP approaches, used to decode corrupted messaged encoded by Sourlas's method, and compare the solutions obtained by both approaches to the exact results obtained using the replica method [8]. The statistical mechanics approach will then allow us to draw some conclusion on the efficacy of the TAP/BP approach in the context of error correcting codes.

The paper is arranged in the following manner: In section 2 we will introduce the encoding method and describe the decoding task. The Belief Propagation approach to the decoding process will be introduced in section 3 and will be compared to the TAP approach for diluted spin systems in section 4. Numerical solutions for various cases will be presented in section 5 and we will summarize our results and discuss their implications in section 6.

2 The decoding problem

In a general scenario, a message represented by an N dimensional binary vector $\boldsymbol{\xi}$ is encoded by a vector $\boldsymbol{J}^0$ which is then transmitted through a noisy channel with some flipping probability p per bit. The received message $\boldsymbol{J}$ is then decoded to retrieve the original message. Sourlas's code [4], is based on encoded message bits of the form $J^0_{i_1,i_2...i_K} = \xi_{i_1}\xi_{i_2}\ldots\xi_{i_K}$, taking the product of different K message sites for each code word bit.

In the statistical mechanics approach we will attempt to retrieve the original message by exploring the ground state of the following Hamiltonian which corresponds to the preferred state of the system in terms of 'energy'

$$\mathcal{H} = -\sum_{\langle i_1,...i_K \rangle} \mathcal{A}_{\langle i_1,...i_K \rangle} J_{\langle i_1,...i_K \rangle} S_{i_1}...S_{i_K} - F/\beta \sum_k S_k , \qquad (1)$$

where $\boldsymbol{S}$ is an N dimensional binary vector of dynamical variables and $\mathcal{A}$ is a sparse tensor with C unit elements per index (other elements are zero), which determines the components of $\boldsymbol{J}^0$. The last term on the right is required in the case of sparse (biased) messages and will require assigning a certain value to the additive field F/β, related to the prior belief in the Bayesian framework.

The statistical mechanical analysis can be easily linked to the Bayesian framework [4] in which one focuses on the posterior probability using Bayes theorem $\mathcal{P}(\boldsymbol{S}|\boldsymbol{J}) \sim \prod_\mu \mathcal{P}(J_\mu|\boldsymbol{S}) \mathcal{P}_0(\boldsymbol{S})$ where μ runs over the message components and $\mathcal{P}_0(\boldsymbol{S})$ represents the prior. Knowing the posterior one can calculate the typical retrieved message elements and their alignment, which correspond to the Bayes-optimal decoding. The logarithms of the likelihood and prior terms are directly related to the first and second components of the Hamiltonian (Eq.1).

One should also note that $\mathcal{A}_{\langle i_1,...i_K \rangle} J_{\langle i_1,...i_K \rangle}$ represents a similar encoding scheme to that of Ref. [2] where a sparse matrix with K non-zero elements per row multiplies the original message $\boldsymbol{\xi}$ and the resulting vector, modulo 2, is transmitted.

Sourlas analyzed this code in the cases of $K = 2$ and $K \to \infty$, where the ratio $C/K \to \infty$, by mapping them onto the SK [9] and Random Energy [10] models respectively. However, the ratio $R = K/C$ constitutes the code rate and the scenarios examined by Sourlas therefore correspond to the limited case of a vanishing code rate. The case of finite code rate, which we will consider here, has only recently been analyzed [8].

3 Decoding by belief propagation

As our goal, of calculating the posterior of the system $\mathcal{P}(\boldsymbol{S}|\boldsymbol{J})$ is rather difficult, we resort to the methods of BP, focusing on the calculation of conditional probabilities when some elements of the system are set to specific values or removed.

The approach adopted in this case, which is quite similar to the practical approach employed in the case of Gallager codes [2], assumes a two layer system corresponding to the elements of the corrupted message $\boldsymbol{J}$ and the dynamical variables $\boldsymbol{S}$ respectively, defining conditional probabilities which relate elements in the two layers:

$$q_{\mu l}^x = \mathcal{P}(S_l = x | \{J_{\nu \neq \mu}\}) \tag{2}$$
$$r_{\mu l}^x = \mathcal{P}(J_\mu | S_l = x, \{J_{\nu \neq \mu}\}) = \sum_{\{S_{k \neq l}\}} \mathcal{P}(J_\mu | S_l = x, \{S_{k \neq l}\}) \, \mathcal{P}(\{S_{k \neq l}\} | \{J_{\nu \neq \mu}\}) \, ,$$

where the index μ represents *an element* of the received vector message $\boldsymbol{J}$, constituted by a particular choice of indices $i_1, \ldots i_K$, which is connected to the corresponding index of $\boldsymbol{S}$ (l in the first equation), i.e., for which the corresponding element $\mathcal{A}_{(i_1, \ldots i_K)}$ is non-zero; the notation $\{S_{k \neq l}\}$ refers to all elements of $\boldsymbol{S}$, excluding the l-th element, which are connected to the corresponding index of $\boldsymbol{J}$ (μ in this case for the second equation); the index x can take values of ± 1. The conditional probabilities $q_{\mu l}^x$ and $r_{\mu l}^x$ will enable us, through recursive calculations to obtain an approximated expression to the posterior.

Employing Bayes rule and the assumption that the dependency of S_l on an element J_ν is factorizable and vice versa: $\mathcal{P}(S_{l_1}, S_{l_2} \ldots S_{l_K} | \{J_{\nu \neq \mu}\}) = \prod_{k=1}^K \mathcal{P}(S_{l_k} | \{J_{\nu \neq \mu}\})$ and $\mathcal{P}(\{J_{\nu \neq \mu}\} | S_l = x) = \prod_{\nu \neq \mu} \mathcal{P}(J_\nu | S_l = x, \{J_{\sigma \neq \nu}\})$, one can rewrite a set of coupled equations for $q_{\mu l}^1$, $q_{\mu l}^{-1}$, $r_{\mu l}^1$ and $r_{\mu l}^{-1}$ of the form

$$q_{\mu l}^x = a_{\mu l} \, p_l^x \prod_{\nu \neq \mu} r_{\nu l}^x \quad \text{and} \quad r_{\mu l}^x = \sum_{\{S_{k \neq l}\}} \mathcal{P}(J_\mu | S_l = x, \{S_{k \neq l}\}) \prod_{k \neq l} q_{\mu k}^{S_k} \, , \tag{3}$$

where $a_{\mu l}$ is a normalizing factor such that $q_{\mu l}^1 + q_{\mu l}^{-1} = 1$ and $p_l^x = \mathcal{P}(S_l = x)$ are our prior beliefs in the value of the source bits S_l.

This set of equations can be solved iteratively [2] by updating a coupled set of difference equations for $\delta q_{\mu l} = q_{\mu l}^1 - q_{\mu l}^{-1}$ and $\delta r_{\mu l} = r_{\mu l}^1 - r_{\mu l}^{-1}$, derived for this specific model, making use of the fact that the variables $r_{\mu l}^x$, and sub-sequentially the variables $q_{\mu l}^x$, can be calculated by exploiting the relation $r_{\mu l}^{\pm 1} = (1 \pm \delta r_{\mu l})/2$ and Eq.(3). At each iteration we can also calculate the pseudo-posterior probabilities $q_l^x = a_l p_l^x \prod_\nu r_{\nu l}^x$, where a_l are normalizing factors, to determine the current estimated value of S_l.

Two points that are worthwhile noting: Firstly, the iterative solution makes use of the normalization $r_{\mu l}^1 + r_{\mu l}^{-1} = 1$, which is *not* derived from the basic probability rules and makes implicit assumptions about the probabilities of obtaining $S_l = \pm 1$ for all elements l. Secondly, the iterative solution would have provided the true posterior probabilities q_l^x if the graph connecting the message $\boldsymbol{J}$ and the encoded bits $\boldsymbol{S}$ would have been free of cycles, i.e., if the graph would have been a tree with no recurrent dependencies among the variables. The fact that the framework provides adequate practical solutions has only recently been explained [13].

4 Decoding by TAP

We will now show that for this particular problem it is possible to obtain a similar set of equations from the corresponding statistical mechanics framework based on Bethe approximation [11] or the TAP (Thouless-Anderson-Palmer) approach [12] to diluted systems [1]. In the statistical mechanics approach we assign a Boltzmann

---

[1] The terminology in the case of diluted systems is slightly vague. Unlike in the case of fully connected systems, self consistent equations of diluted systems cannot be derived

weight to each set comprising an encoded message bit J_μ and a dynamical vector S

$$w_B(J_\mu|S) = e^{-\beta\, g(J_\mu|S)}, \qquad (4)$$

such that the first term of the system's Hamiltonian (Eq.1) can be rewritten as $\sum_\mu g(J_\mu|S)$, where the index μ runs over all non-zero sites in the multidimensional tensor $\mathcal{A}$. We will now employ two straightforward assumptions to write a set of coupled equations for the mean field $q_{\mu l}^{S_l} = \mathcal{P}(S_l|\{J_{\nu\neq\mu}\})$, which may be identified as the same variable as in the belief network framework (Eq.2), and the effective Boltzmann weight $w_{\text{eff}}(J_\mu|S_l,\{J_{\nu\neq\mu}\})$:

1) we assume a mean field behavior for the dependence of the dynamical variables S on a certain realization of the message sites J, i.e., the dependence is factorizable and may be replaced by a product of mean fields.

2) Boltzmann weights (effective) for site S_l are factorizable with respect to J_μ.

The resulting set of equations are of the form

$$w_{\text{eff}}(J_\mu \mid S_l, \{J_{\nu\neq\mu}\}) = \text{Tr}_{\{S_{k\neq l}\}}\, w_B(J_\mu \mid S) \prod_{k\neq l} q_{\mu l}^{S_k}$$

$$q_{\mu l}^{S_l} = \tilde{a}_{\mu l}\, p_l^{S_l} \prod_{\nu\neq\mu} w_{\text{eff}}(J_\nu \mid S_l, \{J_{\sigma\neq\nu}\}), \qquad (5)$$

where $\tilde{a}_{\mu l}$ is a normalization factor and $p_l^{S_l}$ is our prior knowledge of the source's bias. Replacing the effective Boltzmann weight by a normalized field, which may be identified as the variable $r_{\mu l}^{S_l}$ of Eq.(2), we obtain

$$r_{\mu l}^{S_l} = \mathcal{P}(S_l \mid J_\mu, \{J_{\nu\neq\mu}\}) = a_{\mu l}\, w_{\text{eff}}(J_\mu \mid S_l, \{J_{\nu\neq\mu}\}), \qquad (6)$$

i.e., a set of equations equivalent to Eq.(3). The explicit expressions of the normalization coefficients, $a_{\mu l}$ and $\tilde{a}_{\mu l}$, are

$$a_{\mu l}^{-1} = \text{Tr}_{\{S\}}\, w_B(J_\mu|S) \prod_{k\neq l} q_{\mu l}^{S_k} \quad \text{and} \quad \tilde{a}_{\mu l}^{-1} = \text{Tr}_{\{S_l\}}\, p_l^{S_l} \prod_{\nu\neq\mu} r_{\nu l}^{S_l}, \qquad (7)$$

The somewhat arbitrary use of the differences $\delta q_{\mu l} = \langle S_l^\mu \rangle_q$ and $\delta r_{\mu l} = \langle S_l^\mu \rangle_r$ in the BP approach becomes clear form the statistical mechanics description, where they represent the expectation values of the dynamical variables with respect to the fields. The statistical mechanics formulation also provides a partial answer to the successful use of the BP methods to loopy systems, as we consider a finite number of steps on an infinite lattice [14]. However, it does not provide an explanation in the case of small systems which should be examined using other methods.

The formulation so far has been general; however, in the case of Sourlas's code we can make use of the explicit expression for g to derive the relation between $q_{\mu l}^{S_l}$, $r_{\mu l}^{S_l}$, $\delta q_{\mu l}$ and $\delta r_{\mu l}$ as well as an explicit expression for $w_B(J_\mu|S,\beta)$

$$q_{\mu l}^{S_l} = \frac{1}{2}(1+\delta q_{\mu l}S_l), \quad r_{\mu l}^{S_l} = \frac{1}{2}(1+\delta r_{\mu l}S_l) \quad \text{and} \qquad (8)$$

$$w_B(J_\mu|S,\beta) = \frac{1}{2}\cosh\beta J_\mu \left(1+\tanh\beta J_\mu \prod_{l\in\mathcal{L}(\mu)} S_l\right), \qquad (9)$$

by the perturbation expansion of the mean field equations with respect to Onsager reaction fields since these fields are too large in diluted systems. Consequently, the resulting equations are different than those obtained for fully connected systems [12]. We termed our approach TAP, following the convention for the Bethe approximation when applied to disordered systems subject to mean field type random interactions.

where $\mathcal{L}(\mu)$ is the set of all sites of $\boldsymbol{S}$ connected to J_μ, i.e., for which the corresponding element of the tensor $\mathcal{A}$ is non-zero. The explicit form of the equations for $\delta q_{\mu l}$ and $\delta r_{\mu l}$ becomes

$$\delta r_{\mu l} = \tanh \beta J_\mu \prod_{l \in \mathcal{L}(\mu)/l} \delta q_{\mu l} \quad \text{and} \quad \delta q_{\mu l} = \tanh \left(\sum_{\nu \in \mathcal{M}(l)/\mu} \tanh^{-1} \delta r_{\nu l} + F \right), \quad (10)$$

where $\mathcal{M}(l)/\mu$ is the set of all indices of the tensor $\boldsymbol{J}$, excluding μ, which are connected to the vector site l; the external field F which previously appeared in the last term of Eq.(1) is directly related to our prior belief of the message bias

$$p_l^{S_l} = \frac{1}{2}(1 + \tanh F S_l). \quad (11)$$

We therefore showed that there is a direct relation between the equations derived from the BP approach and from TAP in this particular case. One should note that the TAP approach allows for the use of finite inverse-temperatures β which is not naturally included in the BP approach.

5 Numerical solutions

To examine the efficacy of TAP/BP decoding we used the method for decoding corrupted messages encoded by the Sourlas scheme [4], for which we have previously obtained analytical solutions using the replica method [8]. We solved iteratively Eq.(10) for specific cases by making use of differences $\delta q_{\mu l}$ and $\delta r_{\mu l}$ to obtain the values of $q_{\mu l}^{\pm 1}$ and $r_{\mu l}^{\pm 1}$ and of the magnetization M.

Numerical solutions of 10 individual runs for each value of the flip rate p starting from different initial conditions, obtained for the case $K = 2$ and $C = 4$, different biases ($f = p_l^1 = 0.1, 0.5$ - the probability of $+1$ bit in the original message $\boldsymbol{\xi}$) and temperatures ($T = 0.26, T_n$) are shown in Fig. 1a. For each run, 20000 bit code words $\boldsymbol{J}^0$ were generated from 10000 bit message $\boldsymbol{\xi}$ using a fixed random sparse tensor $\mathcal{A}$. The noise corrupted code word $\boldsymbol{J}$ was decoded to retrieve the original message $\boldsymbol{\xi}$. Initial conditions are set to $\delta r_{\mu l} = 0$ and $\delta q_{\mu l} = \tanh F$ reflecting the prior belief; whenever the TAP/BP approach was successful in predicting the theoretical values we observed convergence in most runs corresponding to the ferromagnetic phase while almost all runs at low temperatures did not converged to a stable solution above the critical flip-rate (although the magnetization M did converge as one may expect). We obtain good agreement between the TAP/BP solutions and the theoretical values calculated using the methods of [8] (diamond symbols and dashed line respectively). The results for biased patterns at $T = 0.26$ presented in the form of mean values and standard deviation, show a sub-optimal improvement in performance as expected. Obtaining solutions under similar conditions but at Nishimori's temperature - $1/T_n = 1/2 \ln[(1-p)/p]$ [7], we see that pattern sparsity is exploited optimally resulting in a magnetization $M \approx 0.8$ for high corruption rates, as T_n simulates accurately the loss of information due to channel noise [6, 7]; results for unbiased patterns (not shown) are not affected significantly by the use of Nishimori's temperature.

The replica-based theoretical solutions [8] indicate a profoundly different behaviour for $K = 2$ in comparison to other K values. We therefore obtained solutions for $K = 5$ under similar conditions (which are representative of results obtained in other cases of $K \neq 2$). The results presented in Fig. 1b, in terms of means and standard deviation of 10 individual runs per flip rate value p, are less encouraging as the iterative solutions are sensitive to the choice of initial conditions and tend to

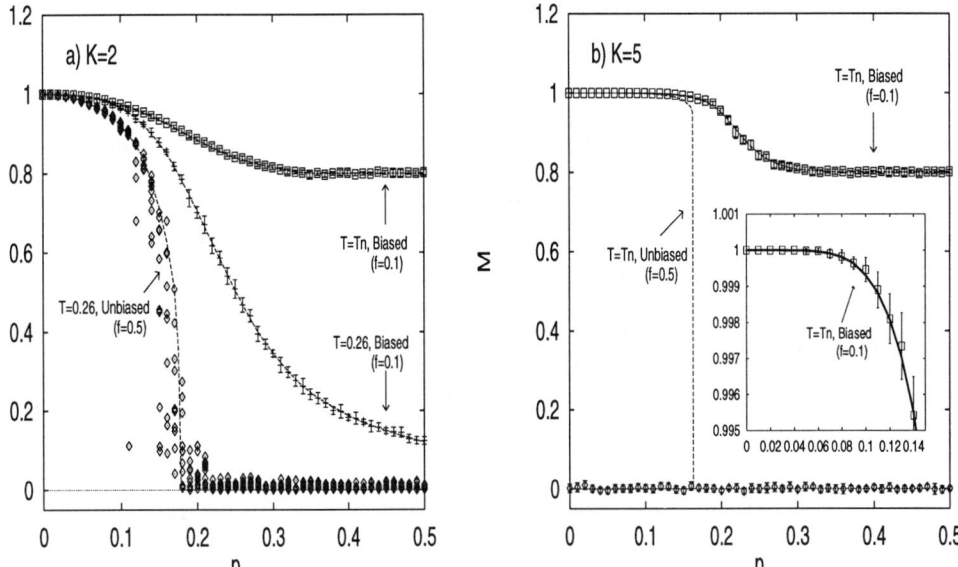

Figure 1: Numerical solutions for M and different flip rate p. (a) For $K = 2$, different biases ($f = p_l^1 = 0.1, 0.5$) and temperatures ($T = 0.26, T_n$). Results for the unbiased patterns are shown as raw data (10 runs per flip rate value p - diamond), while the theoretical solution is marked by the dashed line. Results for biased patterns are presented by their mean and standard deviation, showing a suboptimal performance as expected for $T = 0.26$ and an optimal one at Nishimori's temperature -T_n. The standard deviation is significantly smaller than the symbol size. Figure (b) shows results for the case $K = 5$ and $T = T_n$ in similar conditions to (a). Also here iterative solutions may generally drift away from the theoretical values where temperatures other than T_n are employed (not shown); using Nishimori's temperature alleviates the problem only in the case of biased messages and the results are in close agreement with the theoretical solutions (inset - focusing on low p values).

converge to sub-optimal values unless high sparsity and the appropriate choice of temperature (T_n) forces them to the correct values, showing then good agreement with the theoretical results (solid line, see inset). This phenomena is indicative of the fact that the ground state of the non-biased system is macroscopically degenerate with multiple equally good ground states.

We conclude that the TAP/BP approach may be highly useful in the case of biased patterns but may lead to errors for unbiased patterns and $K \geq 3$, and that the use of the appropriate temperature, i.e., Nishimori's temperature, enables one to obtain improved results, in agreement with results presented elsewhere [4, 6, 7].

6 Summary and discussion

We compared the use of BP to that of TAP for decoding corrupted messages encoded by Sourlas's method to discover that in this particular case the two methods provide a similar set of equations. We then solved the equations iteratively for specific cases and compared the results to those obtained by the replica method. The solutions indicate that the method is particularly useful in the case of biased messages and that using Nishimori's temperature is highly beneficial; solutions obtained using other temperature values may be sub-optimal. For non-sparse messages and $K \geq 3$ we may obtain erroneous solutions using these methods.

It would be desirable to explore whether the similarity in the equations derived using TAP and BP is restricted to this particular case or whether there is a more general link between the two methods. Another important question that remains open is the generality of our conclusions on the efficacy of these methods for decoding corrupted messages, as they are currently being applied in a variety of state-of-the-art coding schemes (e.g., [2, 3]). Understanding the limitations of these methods and the proper way to use them in general, especially in the context of error-correcting codes, may be highly beneficial to practitioners.

Acknowledgment This work was partially supported by the RFTF program of the JSPS (YK) and by EPSRC grant GR/L19232 (DS).

References

[1] J. Pearl, *Probabilistic Reasoning in Intelligent Systems: Networks of Plausible Inference* (Morgan Kaufmann) 1988.

[2] D.J.C. MacKay and R.M. Neal, *Elect. Lett.*, **33**, 457 and preprint (1997).

[3] B.J. Frey, *Graphical Models for Machine Learning and Digital Communication* (MIT Press), 1998.

[4] N. Sourlas, *Nature*, **339**, 693 (1989) and *Europhys. Lett.*, **25**, 159 (1994).

[5] R.G. Gallager, *IRE Trans. Info. Theory*, **IT-8**, 21 (1962).

[6] P. Ruján, *Phys. Rev. Lett.*, **70**, 2968 (1993).

[7] H. Nishimori, *J. Phys. C*, **13**, 4071 (1980) and *J. Phys. Soc. of Japan*, **62**, 1169 (1993).

[8] Y. Kabashima and D. Saad, *Europhys. Lett.*, **45**, in press (1999).

[9] D. Sherrington and S. Kirkpatrick, *Phys. Rev. Lett.*, **35**, 1792 (1975).

[10] B. Derrida, *Phys. Rev. B*, **24**, 2613 (1981).

[11] H. Bethe, *Proc. R. Soc. A*, **151**, 540 (1935).

[12] D. Thouless, P.W. Anderson and R.G. Palmer, *Phil. Mag.*, **35**, 593 (1977).

[13] Y. Weiss, MIT preprint CBCL155 (1997).

[14] D. Sherrington and K.Y.M. Wong *J. Phys. A*, **20**, L785 (1987).

Optimizing Classifiers for Imbalanced Training Sets

Grigoris Karakoulas
Global Analytics Group
Canadian Imperial Bank of Commerce
161 Bay St., BCE-11,
Toronto ON, Canada M5J 2S8
Email: karakoul@cibc.ca

John Shawe-Taylor
Department of Computer Science
Royal Holloway, University of London
Egham, TW20 0EX
England
Email: jst@dcs.rhbnc.ac.uk

Abstract

Following recent results [9, 8] showing the importance of the fat-shattering dimension in explaining the beneficial effect of a large margin on generalization performance, the current paper investigates the implications of these results for the case of imbalanced datasets and develops two approaches to setting the threshold. The approaches are incorporated into ThetaBoost, a boosting algorithm for dealing with unequal loss functions. The performance of ThetaBoost and the two approaches are tested experimentally.

Keywords: Computational Learning Theory, Generalization, fat-shattering, large margin, pac estimates, unequal loss, imbalanced datasets

1 Introduction

Shawe-Taylor [8] demonstrated that the output margin can also be used as an estimate of the confidence with which a particular classification is made. In other words if a new example has an output value well clear of the threshold we can be more confident of the associated classification than when the output value is closer to the threshold. The current paper applies this result to the case where there are different losses associated with a false positive, than with a false negative. If a significant number of data points are misclassified we can use the criterion of minimising the empirical loss. If, however, the data is correctly classified the empirical loss is zero for all correctly separating hyperplanes. It is in this case that the approach can provide insight into how to choose the hyperplane and threshold. In summary, the paper suggests ways in which a hyperplane should be optimised for imbalanced datasets where the loss associated with misclassifying the less prevalent class is higher.

2 Background to the Analysis

Definition 2.1 *[3] Let $\mathcal{F}$ be a set of real-valued functions. We say that a set of points X is γ-shattered by $\mathcal{F}$ if there are real numbers r_x indexed by $x \in X$ such that for all binary vectors b indexed by X, there is a function $f_b \in \mathcal{F}$ realising dichotomy b with margin γ. The fat-shattering dimension $\mathrm{Fat}_{\mathcal{F}}$ of the set $\mathcal{F}$ is a function from the positive real numbers to the integers which maps a value γ to the size of the largest γ-shattered set, if this is finite, or infinity otherwise.*

In general we are concerned with classifications obtained by thresholding real-valued functions. The classification values will be $\{-1, 1\}$ instead of the usual $\{0, 1\}$ in order to simplify some expressions. Hence, typically we will consider a set $\mathcal{F}$ of functions mapping from an input space X to the reals. For the sake of simplifying the presentation of our results we will assume that the threshold used for classification is 0. The results can be extended to other thresholds without difficulty. Hence we implicitly use the classification functions $H = T(\mathcal{F}) = \{T(f) : f \in \mathcal{F}\}$, where $T(f)$ is the function f thresholded at 0. We will say that f has γ margin on the training set $\{(x_i, y_i) : i = 1, \ldots, m\}$, if $\min_{1 \leq i \leq m}\{y_i f(x_i)\} = \gamma$. Note that a positive margin implies that $T(f)$ is consistent.

Definition 2.2 *Given a real-valued function $f : X \to [-1, 1]$ used for classification by thresholding at 0, and probability distribution P on $X \times \{-1, 1\}$, we use $\mathrm{er}_P(f)$ to denote the following probability $\mathrm{er}_P(f) = P\{(x, y) : yf(x) \leq 0\}$. Further suppose $0 \leq \eta \leq 1$, then we use $\mathrm{er}_P(f|\eta)$ to denote the probability*

$$\mathrm{er}_P(f|\eta) = P\{(x, y) : yf(x) \leq 0 \| |f(x)| \geq \eta\}.$$

The probability $\mathrm{er}_P(f|\eta)$ is the probability of misclassification of a randomly chosen example given that it has a margin of η or more.

We consider the following restriction on the set of real-valued functions.

Definition 2.3 *The real-valued function class $\mathcal{F}$ is closed under addition of constants if*

$$\eta \in \mathbb{R}, f \in \mathcal{F} \Rightarrow f + \eta \in \mathcal{F}.$$

Note that the linear functions (with threshold weights) used in perceptrons [9] satisfy this property as do neural networks with linear output units. Hence, this property applies to the Support Vector Machine, and the neural network examples. We now quote a result from [8].

Theorem 2.4 *[8] Let $\mathcal{F}$ be a class of real-valued functions closed under addition of constants with fat-shattering dimension bounded by $\mathrm{Fat}_{\mathcal{F}}(\gamma)$ which is continuous from the right. With probability at least $1-\delta$ over the choice of a random m sample (x_i, y_i) drawn according to P the following holds. Suppose that for some $f \in \mathcal{F}$, $\eta > 0$,*

1. *$y_i f(x_i) \geq -\eta + 2\gamma$ for all (x_i, y_i) in the sample,*

2. *$n = |\{i : y_i f(x_i) \geq \eta + 2\gamma\}|$,*

3. *$n \geq 3\sqrt{2m(2d\ln(288m)\log_2(12em) + \ln(32m^2/\delta))}$,*

Let $d = \mathrm{Fat}_{\mathcal{F}}(\gamma/6)$. Then the probability that a new example with margin η is misclassified is bounded by

$$\frac{3}{n}\left(2d\log_2(288m)\log_2(12em) + \log_2\frac{32m^2}{\delta}\right).$$

3 Unequal Loss Functions

We consider the situation where the loss associated with an example is different for misclassification of positive and negative examples. Let $L_h(x,y)$ be the loss associated with the classification function h on example (x,y). For the analysis considered above the loss function is taken to be $L_h(x,y) = |h(x) - y|$, that is 1 if the point x is misclassified and 0 otherwise. This is also known as the discrete loss. In this paper we consider a different loss function for classification functions.

Definition 3.1 *The loss function L^β is defined as $L^\beta(x,y) = \beta y + (1-y)$, if $h(x) \neq y$, and 0, otherwise.*

We first consider the classical approach of minimizing the empirical loss, that is the loss on the training set. Since, the loss function is no longer binary the standard theoretical results that can be applied are much weaker than for the binary case. The algorithmic implications will, however, be investigated under the assumption we are using a hyperplane parallel to the maximal margin hyperplane. The empirical risk is given by $ER(h) = \sum_{i=1}^{m} L^\beta(x_i, y_i)$, for the training set $\{(x_i, y_i) : i = 1, \ldots, m\}$.

Assuming that the training set can be correctly classified by the hypothesis class this criterion will not be able to distinguish between consistent hypotheses, hence giving no reason not to choose the standard maximal margin choice. However, there is a natural way to introduce the different losses into the maximal margin quadratic programming procedure [1]. Here, the constraints given are specified as $y_i(\langle w \cdot x_i \rangle + \theta) \geq 1, i = 1, 2, \ldots, m$. In order to force the hyperplane away from the positive points which will incur greater loss, a natural heuristic is to set $y_i = -1$ for negative examples and $y_i = 1/\beta$ for positive points, hence making them further from the decision boundary. In the case where consistent classification is possible, the effect of this will be to move the hyperplane parallel to itself so that the margin on the positive side is β times that on the negative side. Hence, to solve the problem we simply use the standard maximal margin algorithm [1] and then replace the threshold θ with

$$b = \frac{1}{1+\beta}[(w \cdot x^+) + \beta(w \cdot x^-)], \tag{1}$$

where x^+ (x^-) is one of the closest positive (negative) points.

The alternative approach we wish to employ is to consider other movements of the hyperplane parallel to itself while retaining consistency. Let γ_0 be the margin of the maximal margin hyperplane. We consider a consistent hyperplane h_η with margin $\gamma_0 + \eta$ to the positive examples, and $\gamma_0 - \eta$ to the negative example. The basic analytic tool is Theorem 2.4 which will be applied once for the positive examples and once for the negative examples (note that classifications are in the set $\{-1, 1\}$).

Theorem 3.2 *Let h_0 be the maximal margin hyperplane with margin γ_0, while h_η is as above with $\eta < \gamma_0$. Set $\gamma^+ = (\gamma_0 + \eta)/2$ and $\gamma^- = (\gamma_0 - \eta)/2$. With probability at least $1 - \delta$ over the choice of a random m sample (x_i, y_i) drawn according to P the following holds. Suppose that for h_0*

1. $n_0 = |\{i : y_i h_0(x_i) \geq 2\eta + \gamma_0\}|$,
2. $n_0 \geq 3\sqrt{2m(d\ln(288m)\log_2(12em) + \ln(8/\delta))}$,

Let $d^+ = \text{Fat}_{\mathcal{F}}(\gamma^+/6)$ and $d^- = \text{Fat}_{\mathcal{F}}(\gamma^-/6)$. Then we can bound the expected loss by

$$\frac{3}{n_0}(2\max(\beta d^+, d^-)\log_2(288m)\log_2(12em) + \beta\log_2(32m^2/\delta))$$

Proof: Using Theorem 2.4 we can bound the probability of error given that the correct classification is positive in terms of the expression with the fat shattering dimension d^+ and $n = n_0$, while for a negative example we can bound the probability of error in terms of the expression with fat shattering dimension d^- and $n = m$. Hence, the expected loss can be bounded by taking the maximum of the second bound with n^+ in place of m together with a factor β in front of the second log term and the first bound multiplied by β. ∎

The bound obtained suggests a way of optimising the choice of η, namely to minimise the expression for the fat shattering dimension of linear functions [9]. Solving for η in terms of γ_0 and β gives

$$\eta = \gamma_0 \left((\sqrt[3]{\beta} - 1)/(\sqrt[3]{\beta} + 1)\right). \tag{2}$$

This choice of η does not in general agree with that suggested by the choice of the threshold b in the previous section. In a later section we report on initial experiments for investigating the performance of these different choices.

4 The ThetaBoost Algorithm

The above idea for adjusting the margin in the case of unequal loss function can also be applied to the AdaBoost algorithm [2] which has been shown to maximise the margin on the training examples and hence the generalization can be bounded in terms of the margin and the fat-shattering dimension of the functions that can be produced by the algorithm [6]. We will first develop a boosting algorithm for unequal loss functions and then extend it for adjustable margin. More specifically, assume: (i) a set of training examples $(x_1, y_1), ..., (x_m, y_m)$ where $x_i \in X$ and $y \in Y = \{-1, +1\}$; (ii) a weak learner that outputs hypotheses $h : X \to \{-1, +1\}$ and (iii) the unequal loss function $L^\beta(y)$ of Definition 3.1.

We assign initial weight $D_1(i) = w^+$ to the n^+ positive examples and $D_1(i) = w^-$ to the n^- negative examples, where $w^+ n^+ + w^- n^- = 1$. The values can be set so that $w^+/w^- = \beta$ or they can be adjusted using a validation set. The generalization of AdaBoost to the case of an unequal loss function is given as the AdaUBoost algorithm in Figure 1. We adapt theorem 1 in [7] for this algorithm.

Theorem 4.1 *Assuming the notation and algorithm of Figure 1, the following bound holds on the training error of H*

$$w^+|i : H(x_i) \neq y_i = 1| + w^-|i : H(x_i) \neq y_i = -1| \leq \prod_{t=1}^{T} Z_t. \tag{3}$$

The choice of w^+ and w^- will force uneven probabilities of misclassification on the training set, but to ensure that the weak learners concentrate on misclassified positive examples we define Z (suppressing the subscript) as

$$Z = \sum_i D(i) \exp(-\alpha \beta_i y_i h(x_i)). \tag{4}$$

Thus, to minimize training error we should seek to minimize Z with respect to α (the voting coefficient) on each iteration of boosting. Following [7], we introduce the notation W_{++}, W_{-+}, W_{+-} and W_{--}, where for s_1 and $s_2 \in \{-1, +1\}$

$$W_{s_1 s_2} = \sum_{i: y_i = s_1, h(x_i) = s_2} D(i) \tag{5}$$

By equating to zero the first derivative of (4) with respect to α, $Z'(\alpha)$, and using (5) we have $-\exp(-\alpha/\beta)W_{++}/\beta+\exp(\alpha/\beta)W_{-+}/\beta+\exp(\alpha)W_{+-}-\exp(-\alpha)W_{--}=0$. Letting $Y = \exp(\alpha)$ we get a polynomial in Y:

$$C_1 Y^{1-1/\beta} + C_2 Y^{1+1/\beta} + C_3 Y^2 + C_4 = 0 \qquad (6)$$

where $C_1 = -W_{++}/\beta$, $C_2 = W_{-+}/\beta$, $C_3 = W_{+-}$, and $C_4 = -W_{--}$.

The root of this polynomial can be found numerically. Since $Z''(\alpha) > 0$, $Z'(\alpha)$ can have at most one zero and this gives the unique minimum of $Z(\alpha)$. The solution for α from (6) is used (as α_t) when taking the distance of a training example from the standard threshold on each iteration of the AdaUBoost algorithm in Figure 1 as well as when combining the weak learners in $H(x)$.

The ThetaBoost algorithm searches for a positive and a negative support vector (SV) point such that the hyperplane separating them has the largest margin. Once these SV points are found we can then apply the formulas (1) and (2) of Sections 3.1 and 3.2 respectively to compute values for adjusting the threshold. See Figure 2 for the complete algorithm.

Algorithm AdaUBoost(X, Y, β)

1. Initialize $D_1(i)$ as described above.
2. For $t = 1, ..., T$
   - train weak learner using distribution D_t;
   - get weak hypothesis h_t;
   - choose $\alpha_t \in \mathbb{R}$;
   - update: $D_{t+1}(i) = D_t(i) \exp[-\alpha_t \beta_i y_i h(x_i)]/Z_t$
   - where $\beta_i = 1/\beta$ if $y_i = 1$ and 1 if otherwise, and Z_t is a normalization factor such that $\sum_i D_{t+1}(i) = 1$;
3. Output the final hypothesis: $H(x) = \text{sgn}\left(\sum_{t=1}^{T} \alpha_t h_t(x)\right)$.

Algorithm ThetaBoost(X, Y, β, δ_M)

1. $H(x) = \text{AdaUBoost}(X, Y, \beta)$;
2. Remove from the training dataset the false positive and borderline points;
3. Find the smallest $H(x_+)$ and mark this as the SV_+; and remove any negative points with value greater than $H(SV_+)$;
4. Find the first negative point that is next in ranking to the SV_+ and mark this as SV_-; and compute the margin as the sum of distances, d_+ and d_-, of SV_+ and SV_- from the standard threshold;
5. Check for candidate SV_-'s that are near to the current one and change the margin by at least δ_M;
6. Use SV_+ and SV_- to compute the theta threshold from Eqn (1) and (2);
7. Output the final hypothesis: $H(x) = \text{sgn}\left(\sum_{t=1}^{T} \alpha_t h_t(x) - \theta\right)$

Figure 1: The AdaUBoost and Theta-Boost algorithms.

5 Experiments

The purpose of the experiments reported in this section is two-fold:

(i) to compare the generalization performance of AdaUBoost against that of standard Adaboost on imbalanced datasets;

(ii) to examine the two formulas for choosing the threshold in ThetaBoost and evaluate their effect on generalization performance.

For the evaluations in (i) and (ii) we use two performance measures: the average L^β and the geometric mean of accuracy (g-mean) [4]. The latter is defined as $g = \sqrt{\text{precision} \cdot \text{recall}}$, where

$$\text{precision} = \frac{\text{\# positives correct}}{\text{\# positives predicted}}; \quad \text{recall} = \frac{\text{\# positives correct}}{\text{\# true positives}}.$$

The g-mean has recently been proposed as a performance measure that, in contrast to accuracy, can capture the "specificity" trade-off between false positives and true positives in imbalanced datasets [4]. It is also independent of the distribution of examples between classes.

For our initial experiments we used the satimage dataset from the UCI repository [5] and used a uniform D_1. The dataset is about classifying neigborhoods of pixels in a satelite image. It has 36 continuous attributes and 6 classes. We picked class 4 as the goal class since it is the less prevalent one (9.73% of the dataset). The dataset comes in a training (4435 examples) and a test (2000 examples) set.

Table 1 shows the performance on the test set of AdaUBoost, AdaBoost and C4.5 for different values of the beta parameter. It should be pointed out that the latter two algorithms minimize the total error assuming an equal loss function ($\beta = 1$). In the case of equal loss AdaUBoost simply reduces to AdaBoost. As observed from the table the higher the loss parameter the bigger the improvement of AdaUBoost over the other two algorithms. This is particularly apparent in the values of g-mean.

	AdaUBoost		AdaBoost		C4.5	
β values	avgLoss	g-mean	avgLoss	g-mean	avgLoss	g-mean
1	0.0545	0.773	0.0545	0.773	0.0885	0.724
2	0.0895	0.865	0.0831	0.773	0.136	0.724
4	0.13	0.889	0.1662	0.773	0.231	0.724
8	0.1785	0.898	0.3324	0.773	0.421	0.724
16	0.267	0.89	0.664	0.773	0.801	0.724

Table 1: Generalization performance in the SatImage dataset.

Figure 2 shows the generalization performance of ThetaBoost in terms of average loss ($\beta = 2$) for different values of the threshold θ. The latter ranges from the largest margin of negative examples that corresponds to SV_- to the smallest margin of positive examples that corresponds to SV_+. This range includes the values of b and η given by formulas (1) and (2). In this experiment δ_M was set to 0.2. As depicted in the figure, the margin defined by b achieves better generalization performance than the margin defined by η. In particular, b is closer to the value of θ that gives the minimum loss on this test set. In addition, ThetaBoost with b performs better than AdaUBoost on this test set. We should emphasise, however, that the differences are not significant and that more extensive experiments are required before the two approaches can be ranked reliably.

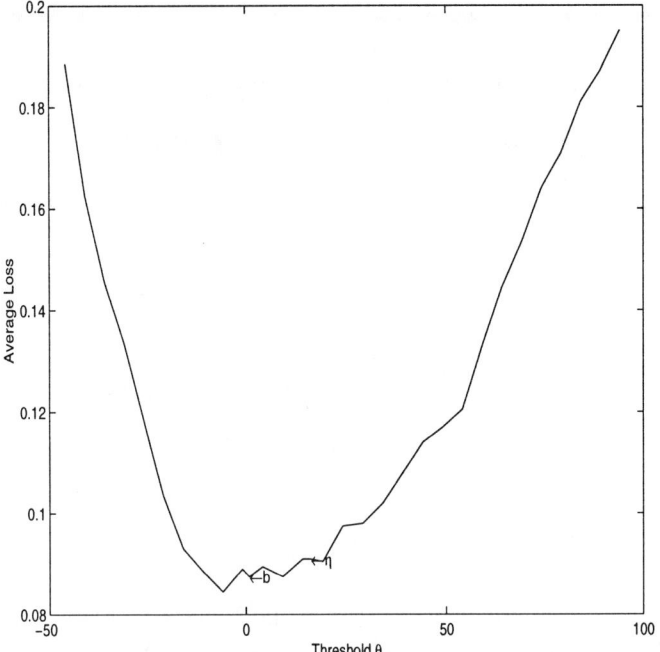

Figure 2: Average Loss L^β ($\beta = 2$) on test set as a function of θ

6 Discussion

In the above we built a theoretical framework for optimally setting the margin given an unequal loss function. By applying this framework to boosting we developed AdaUBoost and ThetaBoost that generalize Adaboost, a well known boosting algorithm, for taking into account unequal loss functions and adjusting the margin in imbalanced datasets. Initial experiments have shown that both these factors improve the generalization performance of the boosted classifier.

References

[1] Corinna Cortes and Vladimir Vapnik, *Machine Learning*, **20**, 273–297, 1995.

[2] Yoav Freund and Robert Schapire, pages 148–156 in *Proceedings of the International Conference on Machine Learning, ICML'96*, 1996.

[3] Michael J. Kearns and Robert E. Schapire, pages 382–391 in *Proceedings of the 31st Symposium on the Foundations of Computer Science, FOCS'90*, 1990.

[4] Kubat, M., Holte, R. and Matwin, S., Machine Learning, **30**, 195-215, 1998.

[5] Merz, C.J. and Murphy, P.M. (1997). UCI repository of machine learning databases. http://www.ics.uci.edu/ mlearn/MLRepository.html.

[6] R. Schapire, Y. Freund, P. Bartlett, W. Sun Lee, pages 322–330 in *Proceedings of International Conference on Machine Learning, ICML'97*, 1997.

[7] Robert Schapire and Yoram Singer, in *Proceedings of the Eleventh Annual Conference on Computational Learning Theory, COLT'98*, 1998.

[8] John Shawe-Taylor, Algorithmica, **22**, 157–172, 1998.

[9] John Shawe-Taylor, Peter Bartlett, Robert Williamson and Martin Anthony, IEEE Trans. Inf. Theory, **44** (5) 1926–1940, 1998.

Inference in Multilayer Networks via Large Deviation Bounds

Michael Kearns and Lawrence Saul
AT&T Labs — Research
Shannon Laboratory
180 Park Avenue A-235
Florham Park, NJ 07932
{mkearns,lsaul}@research.att.com

Abstract

We study probabilistic inference in large, layered Bayesian networks represented as directed acyclic graphs. We show that the intractability of exact inference in such networks does not preclude their effective use. We give algorithms for approximate probabilistic inference that exploit averaging phenomena occurring at nodes with large numbers of parents. We show that these algorithms compute rigorous lower and upper bounds on marginal probabilities of interest, prove that these bounds become exact in the limit of large networks, and provide rates of convergence.

1 Introduction

The promise of neural computation lies in exploiting the information processing abilities of simple computing elements organized into large networks. Arguably one of the most important types of information processing is the capacity for probabilistic reasoning.

The properties of *undirected* probabilistic models represented as symmetric networks have been studied extensively using methods from statistical mechanics (Hertz et al, 1991). Detailed analyses of these models are possible by exploiting averaging phenomena that occur in the thermodynamic limit of large networks.

In this paper, we analyze the limit of large, multilayer networks for probabilistic models represented as *directed* acyclic graphs. These models are known as *Bayesian networks* (Pearl, 1988; Neal, 1992), and they have different probabilistic semantics than symmetric neural networks (such as Hopfield models or Boltzmann machines). We show that the intractability of exact inference in multilayer Bayesian networks does not preclude their effective use. Our work builds on earlier studies of variational methods (Jordan et al, 1997). We give algorithms for approximate probabilistic inference that exploit averaging phenomena occurring at nodes with $N \gg 1$ parents. We show that these algorithms compute rigorous lower and upper bounds on marginal probabilities of interest, prove that these bounds become exact in the limit $N \to \infty$, and provide rates of convergence.

2 Definitions and Preliminaries

A Bayesian network is a *directed* graphical probabilistic model, in which the nodes represent random variables, and the links represent causal dependencies. The joint distribution of this model is obtained by *composing* the local conditional probability distributions (or *tables*), **Pr**[child|parents], specified at each node in the network. For networks of binary random variables, so-called *transfer functions* provide a convenient way to parameterize conditional probability tables (CPTs). A transfer function is a mapping $f : [-\infty, \infty] \to [0, 1]$ that is everywhere differentiable and satisfies $f'(x) \geq 0$ for all x (thus, f is nondecreasing). If $f'(x) \leq \alpha$ for all x, we say that f has *slope* α. Common examples of transfer functions of bounded slope include the sigmoid $f(x) = 1/(1+e^{-x})$, the cumulative gaussian $f(x) = \int_{-\infty}^{x} dt\, e^{-t^2}/\sqrt{\pi}$, and the noisy-OR $f(x) = 1 - e^{-x}$. Because the value of a transfer function f is bounded between 0 and 1, it can be interpreted as the conditional probability that a binary random variable takes on a particular value. One use of transfer functions is to endow multilayer networks of soft-thresholding computing elements with probabilistic semantics. This motivates the following definition:

Definition 1 *For a transfer function f, a* **layered probabilistic f-network** *has:*

- *Nodes representing binary variables $\{X_i^\ell\}$, $\ell = 1, \ldots, L$ and $i = 1, \ldots, N$. Thus, L is the number of layers, and each layer contains N nodes.*

- *For every pair of nodes $X_j^{\ell-1}$ and X_i^ℓ in adjacent layers, a real-valued weight $\theta_{ij}^{\ell-1}$ from $X_j^{\ell-1}$ to X_i^ℓ.*

- *For every node X_i^1 in the first layer, a* **bias** *p_i.*

We will sometimes refer to nodes in layer 1 as **inputs**, and to nodes in layer L as **outputs**. A layered probabilistic f-network defines a joint probability distribution over all of the variables $\{X_i^\ell\}$ as follows: each input node X_i^1 is independently set to 1 with probability p_i, and to 0 with probability $1 - p_i$. Inductively, given binary values $X_j^{\ell-1} = x_j^{\ell-1} \in \{0, 1\}$ for all of the nodes in layer $\ell - 1$, the node X_i^ℓ is set to 1 with probability $f(\sum_{j=1}^{N} \theta_{ij}^{\ell-1} x_j^{\ell-1})$.

Among other uses, multilayer networks of this form have been studied as hierarchical generative models of sensory data (Hinton et al, 1995). In such applications, the fundamental computational problem (known as *inference*) is that of estimating the marginal probability of evidence at some number of *output* nodes, say the first $K \leq N$. (The computation of conditional probabilities, such as diagnostic queries, can be reduced to marginals via Bayes rule.) More precisely, one wishes to estimate $\mathbf{Pr}[X_1^L = x_1, \ldots, X_K^L = x_K]$ (where $x_i \in \{0,1\}$), a quantity whose exact computation involves an exponential sum over all the possible settings of the uninstantiated nodes in layers 1 through $L - 1$, and is known to be computationally intractable (Cooper, 1990).

3 Large Deviation and Union Bounds

One of our main weapons will be the theory of *large deviations*. As a first illustration of this theory, consider the input nodes $\{X_j^1\}$ (which are independently set to 0 or 1 according to their biases p_j) and the weighted sum $\sum_{j=1}^{N} \theta_{ij}^1 X_j^1$ that feeds into the ith node X_i^2 in the second layer. A typical large deviation bound (Kearns & Saul, 1997) states that for all $\epsilon > 0$, $\mathbf{Pr}[|\sum_{j=1}^{N} \theta_{ij}^1 (X_j^1 - p_j)| > \epsilon] \leq 2e^{-2\epsilon^2/(N\Theta^2)}$ where Θ is the largest weight in the network. If we make the scaling assumption that each weight θ_{ij}^1 is bounded by τ/N for some constant τ (thus, $\Theta \leq \tau/N$), then we see that the probability of large (order 1) deviations of this weighted sum from its mean decays exponentially with N. (Our methods can also provide results under the weaker assumption that all weights are bounded by $O(N^{-a})$ for $a > 1/2$.)

How can we apply this observation to the problem of inference? Suppose we are interested in the marginal probability $\mathbf{Pr}[X_i^2 = 1]$. Then the large deviation bound tells us that with probability at least $1 - \delta$ (where we define $\delta = 2e^{-2N\epsilon^2/\tau^2}$), the weighted sum at node X_i^2 will be within ϵ of its mean value $\mu_i = \sum_{j=1}^{N} \theta_{ij}^1 p_j$. Thus, with probability at least $1 - \delta$, we are assured that $\mathbf{Pr}[X_i^2 = 1]$ is at least $f(\mu_i - \epsilon)$ and at most $f(\mu_i + \epsilon)$. Of course, the flip side of the large deviation bound is that with probability at most δ, the weighted sum may fall more than ϵ away from μ_i. In this case we can make no guarantees on $\mathbf{Pr}[X_i^2 = 1]$ aside from the trivial lower and upper bounds of 0 and 1. Combining both eventualities, however, we obtain the overall bounds:

$$(1-\delta)f(\mu_i - \epsilon) \leq \mathbf{Pr}[X_i^2 = 1] \leq (1-\delta)f(\mu_i + \epsilon) + \delta. \qquad (1)$$

Equation (1) is based on a simple *two-point* approximation to the distribution over the weighted sum of inputs, $\sum_{j=1}^{N} \theta_{ij}^1 X_j^1$. This approximation places one point, with weight $1 - \delta$, at either ϵ above or below the mean μ_i (depending on whether we are deriving the upper or lower bound); and the other point, with weight δ, at either $-\infty$ or $+\infty$. The value of δ depends on the choice of ϵ: in particular, as ϵ becomes smaller, we give more weight to the $\pm\infty$ point, with the trade-off governed by the large deviation bound. We regard the weight given to the $\pm\infty$ point as a *throw-away* probability, since with this weight we resort to the trivial bounds of 0 or 1 on the marginal probability $\mathbf{Pr}[X_i^2 = 1]$.

Note that the very simple bounds in Equation (1) already exhibit an interesting trade-off, governed by the choice of the parameter ϵ—namely, as ϵ becomes smaller, the throw-away probability δ becomes larger, while the terms $f(\mu_i \pm \epsilon)$ converge to the same value. Since the overall bounds involve products of $f(\mu_i \pm \epsilon)$ and $1 - \delta$, the optimal value of ϵ is the one that balances this competition between probable explanations of the evidence and improbable deviations from the mean. This trade-off is reminiscent of that encountered between energy and entropy in mean-field approximations for symmetric networks (Hertz et al, 1991).

So far we have considered the marginal probability involving a single node in the second layer. We can also compute bounds on the marginal probabilities involving $K > 1$ nodes in this layer (which without loss of generality we take to be the nodes X_1^2 through X_K^2). This is done by considering the probability that *one or more* of the weighted sums entering these K nodes in the second layer deviate by more than ϵ from their means. We can upper bound this probability by $K\delta$ by appealing to the so-called *union bound*, which simply states that the probability of a union of events is bounded by the sum of their individual probabilities. The union bound allows us to bound marginal probabilities involving multiple variables. For example, consider the marginal probability $\mathbf{Pr}[X_1^2 = 1, \ldots, X_K^2 = 1]$. Combining the large deviation and union bounds, we find:

$$(1-K\delta)\prod_{i=1}^{K} f(\mu_i-\epsilon) \leq \mathbf{Pr}[X_1^2 = 1, \ldots, X_K^2 = 1] \leq (1-K\delta)\prod_{i=1}^{K} f(\mu_i+\epsilon)+K\delta. \quad (2)$$

A number of observations are in order here. First, Equation (2) directly leads to *efficient algorithms* for computing the upper and lower bounds. Second, although for simplicity we have considered ϵ-deviations of the same size at each node in the second layer, the same methods apply to different choices of ϵ_i (and therefore δ_i) at each node. Indeed, variations in ϵ_i can lead to significantly tighter bounds, and thus we exploit the freedom to choose different ϵ_i in the rest of the paper. This results, for example, in bounds of the form:

$$\left(1-\sum_{i=1}^{K}\delta_i\right)\prod_{i=1}^{K} f(\mu_i - \epsilon_i) \leq \mathbf{Pr}[X_1^2 = 1, \ldots, X_K^2 = 1], \text{ where } \delta_i = 2e^{-2N\epsilon_i^2/\tau^2}. \quad (3)$$

The reader is invited to study the small but important differences between this lower bound and the one in Equation (2). Third, the arguments leading to bounds on the marginal probability $\mathbf{Pr}[X_1^2 = 1, \ldots, X_K^2 = 1]$ generalize in a straightforward manner to other patterns of evidence besides all 1's. For instance, again just considering the lower bound, we have:

$$\left(1-\sum_{i=1}^{K}\delta_i\right)\prod_{x_i=0}[1-f(\mu_i+\epsilon_i)]\prod_{x_i=1} f(\mu_i-\epsilon_i) \leq \mathbf{Pr}[X_1^2 = x_1, \ldots, X_K^2 = x_K] \quad (4)$$

where $x_i \in \{0,1\}$ are arbitrary binary values. Thus together the large deviation and union bounds provide the means to compute upper and lower bounds on the marginal probabilities over nodes in the second layer. Further details and consequences of these bounds for the special case of *two-layer* networks are given in a companion paper (Kearns & Saul, 1997); our interest here, however, is in the more challenging generalization to multilayer networks.

4 Multilayer Networks: Inference via Induction

In extending the ideas of the previous section to multilayer networks, we face the problem that the nodes in the second layer, unlike those in the first, are *not* independent. But we can still adopt an inductive strategy to derive bounds on marginal probabilities. The crucial observation is that *conditioned* on the values of the incoming weighted sums at the nodes in the second layer, the variables $\{X_i^2\}$ do become independent. More generally, conditioned on these weighted sums all falling "near" their means — an event whose probability we quantified in the last section — the nodes $\{X_i^2\}$ become "almost" independent. It is exactly this near-independence that we now formalize and exploit inductively to compute bounds for multilayer networks. The first tool we require is an appropriate generalization of the large deviation bound, which does not rely on precise knowledge of the means of the random variables being summed.

Theorem 1 *For all $1 \leq j \leq N$, let $X_j \in \{0,1\}$ denote independent binary random variables, and let $|\tau_j| \leq \tau$. Suppose that the means are bounded by $|\mathbf{E}[X_j]-p_j| \leq \Delta_j$, where $0 < \Delta_j \leq p_j \leq 1 - \Delta_j$. Then for all $\epsilon > \frac{1}{N}\sum_{j=1}^{N}|\tau_j|\Delta_j$:*

$$\mathbf{Pr}\left[\left|\frac{1}{N}\sum_{j=1}^{N}\tau_j(X_j-p_j)\right| > \epsilon\right] \leq 2e^{-\frac{2N}{\tau^2}\left(\epsilon-\frac{1}{N}\sum_{j=1}^{N}|\tau_j|\Delta_j\right)^2}. \quad (5)$$

The proof of this result is omitted due to space considerations. Now for induction, consider the nodes in the ℓth layer of the network. Suppose we are told that for every i, the weighted sum $\sum_{j=1}^{N} \theta_{ij}^{\ell-1} X_j^{\ell-1}$ entering into the node X_i^{ℓ} lies in the interval $[\mu_i^{\ell} - \epsilon_i^{\ell}, \mu_i^{\ell} + \epsilon_i^{\ell}]$, for some choice of the μ_i^{ℓ} and the ϵ_i^{ℓ}. Then the mean of node X_i^{ℓ} is constrained to lie in the interval $[p_i^{\ell} - \Delta_i^{\ell}, p_i^{\ell} + \Delta_i^{\ell}]$, where

$$p_i^{\ell} = \frac{1}{2}\left[f(\mu_i^{\ell} - \epsilon_i^{\ell}) + f(\mu_i^{\ell} + \epsilon_i^{\ell})\right] \tag{6}$$

$$\Delta_i^{\ell} = \frac{1}{2}\left[f(\mu_i^{\ell} + \epsilon_i^{\ell}) - f(\mu_i^{\ell} - \epsilon_i^{\ell})\right]. \tag{7}$$

Here we have simply run the leftmost and rightmost allowed values for the incoming weighted sums through the transfer function, and defined the interval around the mean of unit X_i^{ℓ} to be centered around p_i^{ℓ}. Thus we have translated uncertainties on the incoming weighted sums to layer ℓ into conditional uncertainties on the means of the nodes X_i^{ℓ} in layer ℓ. To complete the cycle, we now translate these into conditional uncertainties on the incoming weighted sums to layer $\ell + 1$. In particular, conditioned on the original intervals $[\mu_i^{\ell} - \epsilon_i^{\ell}, \mu_i^{\ell} + \epsilon_i^{\ell}]$, what is probability that for each i, $\sum_{j=1}^{N} \theta_{ij}^{\ell} X_j^{\ell}$ lies inside some new interval $[\mu_i^{\ell+1} - \epsilon_i^{\ell+1}, \mu_i^{\ell+1} + \epsilon_i^{\ell+1}]$? In order to make some guarantee on this probability, we set $\mu_i^{\ell+1} = \sum_{j=1}^{N} \theta_{ij}^{\ell} p_j^{\ell}$ and assume that $\epsilon_i^{\ell+1} > \sum_{j=1}^{N} |\theta_{ij}^{\ell}| \Delta_j^{\ell}$. These conditions suffice to ensure that the new intervals contain the (conditional) *expected values* of the weighted sums $\sum_{j=1}^{N} \theta_{ij}^{\ell} X_j^{\ell}$, and that the new intervals are large enough to encompass the incoming uncertainties. Because these conditions are a minimal requirement for establishing any probabilistic guarantees, we shall say that the $[\mu_i^{\ell} - \epsilon_i^{\ell}, \mu_i^{\ell} + \epsilon_i^{\ell}]$ define a *valid set of ϵ-intervals* if they meet these conditions for all $1 \leq i \leq N$. Given a valid set of ϵ-intervals at the $(\ell+1)$th layer, it follows from Theorem 1 and the union bound that the weighted sums entering nodes in layer $\ell + 1$ obey

$$\mathbf{Pr}\left[\left|\sum_{j=1}^{N} \theta_{ij}^{\ell} X_j^{\ell} - \mu_i^{\ell+1}\right| > \epsilon_i^{\ell+1} \text{ for some } 1 \leq i \leq N\right] \leq \sum_{i=1}^{N} \delta_i^{\ell+1} \tag{8}$$

where

$$\delta_i^{\ell+1} = 2e^{-\frac{2N}{r^2}\left(\epsilon_i^{\ell+1} - \sum_{j=1}^{N} |\theta_{ij}^{\ell}| \Delta_j^{\ell}\right)^2}. \tag{9}$$

In what follows, we shall frequently make use of the fact that the weighted sums $\sum_{j=1}^{N} \theta_{ij}^{\ell} X_i^{\ell}$ are bounded by intervals $[\mu_i^{\ell+1} - \epsilon_i^{\ell+1}, \mu_i^{\ell+1} + \epsilon_i^{\ell+1}]$. This motivates the following definitions.

Definition 2 *Given a valid set of ϵ-intervals and binary values $\{X_i^{\ell} = x_i^{\ell}\}$ for the nodes in the ℓth layer, we say that the $(\ell+1)$st layer of the network* **satisfies** *its ϵ-intervals if $\left|\sum_{j=1}^{N} \theta_{ij}^{\ell} x_j^{\ell} - \mu_i^{\ell+1}\right| < \epsilon_i^{\ell+1}$ for all $1 \leq i \leq N$. Otherwise, we say that the $(\ell+1)$st layer* **violates** *its ϵ-intervals.*

Suppose that we are given a valid set of ϵ-intervals and that we sample from the joint distribution defined by the probabilistic f-network. The right hand side of Equation (8) provides an upper bound on the conditional probability that the $(\ell+1)$st layer violates its ϵ-intervals, given that the ℓth layer did not. This upper bound may be vacuous (that is, larger than 1), so let us denote by $\delta^{\ell+1}$ whichever is smaller — the right hand side of Equation (8), or 1; in other words, $\delta^{\ell+1} = \min\left\{\sum_{i=1}^{N} \delta_i^{\ell+1}, 1\right\}$. Since at the ℓth layer, the probability of violating the ϵ-intervals is at most δ^{ℓ} we

Inference in Multilayer Networks via Large Deviation Bounds

are guaranteed that with probability at least $\prod_{\ell>1}[1-\delta^\ell]$, all the layers satisfy their ϵ-intervals. Conversely, we are guaranteed that the probability that any layer violates its ϵ-intervals is at most $1 - \prod_{\ell>1}[1-\delta^\ell]$. Treating this as a throw-away probability, we can now compute upper and lower bounds on marginal probabilities involving nodes at the Lth layer exactly as in the case of nodes at the second layer. This yields the following theorem.

Theorem 2 *For any subset $\{X_1^L, \ldots, X_K^L\}$ of the outputs of a probabilistic f-network, for any setting $x_1, \ldots, x_K$, and for any valid set of ϵ-intervals, the marginal probability of partial evidence in the output layer obeys:*

$$\prod_{\ell>1}[1-\delta^\ell] \prod_{x_i=1} f(\mu_i^L - \epsilon_i^L) \prod_{x_i=0}[1 - f(\mu_i^L + \epsilon_i^L)] \tag{10}$$

$$\leq \Pr[X_1^L = x_1, \ldots, X_K^L = x_K]$$

$$\leq \prod_{\ell>1}[1-\delta^\ell] \prod_{x_i=1} f(\mu_i^L + \epsilon_i^L) \prod_{x_i=0}[1 - f(\mu_i^L - \epsilon_i^L)] + \left(1 - \prod_{\ell>1}[1-\delta^\ell]\right) \tag{11}$$

Theorem 2 generalizes our earlier results for marginal probabilities over nodes in the second layer; for example, compare Equation (10) to Equation (4). Again, the upper and lower bounds can be efficiently computed for all common transfer functions.

5 Rates of Convergence

To demonstrate the power of Theorem 2, we consider how the gap (or additive difference) between these upper and lower bounds on $\Pr[X_1^L = x_1, \ldots, X_K^L = x_K]$ behaves for some crude (but informed) choices of the $\{\epsilon_i^\ell\}$. Our goal is to derive the *rate* at which these upper and lower bounds converge to the same value as we examine larger and larger networks. Suppose we choose the ϵ-intervals inductively by defining $\Delta_i^1 = 0$ and setting

$$\epsilon_i^{\ell+1} = \sum_{j=1}^N |\theta_{ij}^\ell| \Delta_j^\ell + \sqrt{\frac{\gamma \tau^2 \ln N}{N}} \tag{12}$$

for some $\gamma > 1$. From Equations (8) and (9), this choice gives $\delta^{\ell+1} \leq 2N^{1-2\gamma}$ as an upper bound on the probability that the $(\ell+1)$th layer violates its ϵ-intervals. Moreover, denoting the gap between the upper and lower bounds in Theorem 2 by G, it can be shown that:

$$G \leq 2\alpha \sqrt{\frac{\gamma \tau^2 \ln N}{N}} \left[\frac{1 - (\alpha\tau)^L}{1 - \alpha\tau}\right] \sum_{i=1}^K \prod_{\substack{v_j = 1 \\ j \neq i}} f(\mu_j^L + \epsilon_j^L) \prod_{\substack{v_j = 0 \\ j \neq i}} [1 - f(\mu_j^L - \epsilon_j^L)] + \frac{2L}{N^{2\gamma-1}}. \tag{13}$$

Let us briefly recall the definitions of the parameters on the right hand side of this equation: α is the maximal slope of the transfer function f, N is the number of nodes in each layer, K is the number of nodes with evidence, $\tau = N\Theta$ is N times the largest weight in the network, L is the number of layers, and $\gamma > 1$ is a parameter at our disposal. The first term of this bound essentially has a $1/\sqrt{N}$ dependence on N, but is multiplied by a damping factor that we might typically expect to decay exponentially with the number K of outputs examined. To see this, simply notice that each of the factors $f(\mu_j + \epsilon_j)$ and $[1 - f(\mu_j - \epsilon_j)]$ is bounded by 1; furthermore, since all the means μ_j are bounded, if N is large compared to γ then the ϵ_i are small, and each of these factors is in fact bounded by some value $\beta < 1$. Thus the first term in Equation (13) is bounded by a constant times $\beta^{K-1} K \sqrt{\ln(N)/N}$. Since it is natural to expect the marginal probability of interest itself to decrease exponentially with K, this is desirable and natural behavior.

Of course, in the case of large K, the behavior of the resulting overall bound can be dominated by the second term $2L/N^{2\gamma-1}$ of Equation (13). In such situations, however, we can consider larger values of γ, possibly even of order K; indeed, for sufficiently large γ, the first term (which scales like $\sqrt{\gamma}$) must necessarily overtake the second one. Thus there is a clear trade-off between the two terms, as well as optimal value of γ that sets them to be (roughly) the same magnitude. Generally speaking, for fixed K and large N, we observe that the difference between our upper and lower bounds on $\mathbf{Pr}[X_1^L = x_1, \ldots, X_K^L = x_K]$ vanishes as $O\left(\sqrt{\ln(N)/N}\right)$.

6 An Algorithm for Fixed Multilayer Networks

We conclude by noting that the specific choices made for the parameters ϵ_i in Section 5 to derive rates of convergence may be far from the optimal choices for a fixed network of interest. However, Theorem 2 directly suggests a natural algorithm for approximate probabilistic inference. In particular, regarding the upper and lower bounds on $\mathbf{Pr}[X_1^L = x_1, \ldots, X_K^L = x_K]$ as functions of $\{\epsilon_i^\ell\}$, we can optimize these bounds by standard numerical methods. For the upper bound, we may perform gradient descent in the $\{\epsilon_i^\ell\}$ to find a local minimum, while for the lower bound, we may perform gradient ascent to find a local maximum. The components of these gradients in both cases are easily computable for all the commonly studied transfer functions. Moreover, the constraint of maintaining valid ϵ-intervals can be enforced by maintaining a floor on the ϵ-intervals in one layer in terms of those at the previous one. The practical application of this algorithm to interesting Bayesian networks will be studied in future work.

References

Cooper, G. (1990). Computational complexity of probabilistic inference using Bayesian belief networks. *Artificial Intelligence* **42**:393-405.

Hertz, J,. Krogh, A., & Palmer, R. (1991). *Introduction to the theory of neural computation*. Addison-Wesley, Redwood City, CA.

Hinton, G., Dayan, P., Frey, B., and Neal, R. (1995). The wake-sleep algorithm for unsupervised neural networks. *Science* **268**:1158-1161.

Jordan, M., Ghahramani, Z., Jaakkola, T., & Saul, L. (1997). An introduction to variational methods for graphical models. In M. Jordan, ed. *Learning in Graphical Models*. Kluwer Academic.

Kearns, M., & Saul, L. (1998). Large deviation methods for approximate probabilistic inference. In *Proceedings of the 14th Annual Conference on Uncertainty in Artificial Intelligence*.

Neal, R. (1992). Connectionist learning of belief networks. *Artificial Intelligence* **56**:71-113.

Pearl, J. (1988). *Probabilistic Reasoning in Intelligent Systems: Networks of Plausible Inference*. Morgan Kaufmann, San Mateo, CA.

Stationarity and Stability of Autoregressive Neural Network Processes

Friedrich Leisch[1], Adrian Trapletti[2] & Kurt Hornik[1]

[1] Institut für Statistik
Technische Universität Wien
Wiedner Hauptstraße 8–10 / 1071
A-1040 Wien, Austria
firstname.lastname@ci.tuwien.ac.at

[2] Institut für Unternehmensführung
Wirtschaftsuniversität Wien
Augasse 2–6
A-1090 Wien, Austria
adrian.trapletti@wu-wien.ac.at

Abstract

We analyze the asymptotic behavior of autoregressive neural network (AR-NN) processes using techniques from Markov chains and non-linear time series analysis. It is shown that standard AR-NNs without shortcut connections are asymptotically stationary. If linear shortcut connections are allowed, only the shortcut weights determine whether the overall system is stationary, hence standard conditions for linear AR processes can be used.

1 Introduction

In this paper we consider the popular class of nonlinear autoregressive processes driven by additive noise, which are defined by stochastic difference equations of form

$$\xi_t = g(\xi_{t-1}, \ldots, \xi_{t-p}, \theta) + \epsilon_t \tag{1}$$

where ϵ_t is an iid. noise process. If $g(\cdots, \theta)$ is a feedforward neural network with parameter ("weight") vector θ, we call Equation 1 an autoregressive neural network process of order p, short AR-NN(p) in the following.

AR-NNs are a natural generalization of the classic linear autoregressive AR(p) process

$$\xi_t = \alpha_1 \xi_{t-1} + \cdots + \alpha_p \xi_{t-p} + \epsilon_t. \tag{2}$$

See, e.g., Brockwell & Davis (1987) for a comprehensive introduction into AR and ARMA (autoregressive moving average) models.

One of the most central questions in linear time series theory is the stationarity of the model, i.e., whether the probabilistic structure of the series is constant over time or at least asymptotically constant (when not started in equilibrium). Surprisingly, this question has not gained much interest in the NN literature, especially there are—up to our knowledge—no results giving conditions for the stationarity of AR-NN models. There are results on the stationarity of Hopfield nets (Wang & Sheng, 1996), but these nets cannot be used to estimate conditional expectations for time series prediction.

The rest of this paper is organized as follows: In Section 2 we recall some results from time series analysis and Markov chain theory defining the relationship between a time series and its associated Markov chain. In Section 3 we use these results to establish that standard AR-NN models without shortcut connections are stationary. We also give conditions for AR-NN models with shortcut connections to be stationary. Section 4 examines the NN modeling of an important class of non-stationary time series, namely integrated series. All proofs are deferred to the appendix.

2 Some Time Series and Markov Chain Theory

2.1 Stationarity

Let ξ_t denote a time series generated by a (possibly nonlinear) autoregressive process as defined in (1). If $\mathbb{E}\epsilon_t = 0$, then g equals the conditional expectation $\mathbb{E}(\xi_t|\xi_{t-1}, \ldots, \xi_{t-p})$ and $g(\xi_{t-1}, \ldots, \xi_{t-p})$ is the best prediction for ξ_t in the mean square sense.

If we are interested in the long term properties of the series, we may ask whether certain features such as mean or variance change over time or remain constant. The time series is called *weakly stationary* if $\mathbb{E}\xi_t = \mu$ and $cov(\xi_t, \xi_{t+h}) = \gamma_h$, $\forall t$, i.e., mean and covariances do not depend on the time t. A stronger criterion is that the whole distribution (and not only mean and covariance) of the process does not depend on the time, in this case the series is called *strictly stationary*. Strong stationarity implies weak stationarity if the second moments of the series exist. For details see standard time series textbooks such as Brockwell & Davis (1987).

If ξ_t is strictly stationary, then $\mathbb{P}(\xi_t \in A) = \pi(A)$, $\forall t$ and $\pi(\cdot)$ is called the *stationary distribution* of the series. Obviously the series can only be stationary from the beginning if it is started with the stationary distribution such that $\xi_0 \sim \pi$. If it is not started with π, e.g., because ξ_0 is a constant, then we call the series *asymptotically stationary* if it converges to its stationary distribution:

$$\lim_{t \to \infty} \mathbb{P}(\xi_t \in A) = \pi(A)$$

2.2 Time Series as Markov Chains

Using the notation

$$x_{t-1} = (\xi_{t-1}, \ldots, \xi_{t-p})' \qquad (3)$$
$$G(x_{t-1}) = (g(x_{t-1}), \xi_{t-1}, \ldots, \xi_{t-p+1})' \qquad (4)$$
$$e_t = (\epsilon_t, 0, \ldots, 0)' \qquad (5)$$

we can write scalar autoregressive models of order p such as (1) or (2) as a first order vector model

$$x_t = G(x_{t-1}) + e_t \qquad (6)$$

with $x_t, e_t \in \mathbb{R}^p$ (e.g., Chan & Tong, 1985). If we write

$$p^n(x, A) = \mathbb{P}\{x_{t+n} \in A | x_t = x\}$$
$$p(x, A) = p^1(x, A)$$

for the probability of going from point x to set $A \in \mathcal{B}$ in n steps, then $\{x_t\}$ with $p(x, A)$ forms a Markov chain with state space $(\mathbb{R}^p, \mathcal{B}, \lambda)$, where $\mathcal{B}$ are the Borel sets on $\mathbb{R}^p$ and λ is the usual Lebesgue measure.

The Markov chain $\{x_t\}$ is called φ-*irreducible*, if for some σ-finite measure φ on $(\mathbb{R}^p, \mathcal{B}, \lambda)$

$$\forall x \in \mathbb{R}^p : \quad \sum_{n=1}^{\infty} p^n(x, A) > 0$$

whenever $\varphi(A) > 0$. This means essentially, that all parts of the state space can be reached by the Markov chain irrespective of the starting point. Another important property of Markov chains is *aperiodicity*, which loosely speaking means that there are no (infinitely often repeated) cycles. See, e.g., Tong (1990) for details.

The Markov chain $\{x_t\}$ is called *geometrically ergodic*, if there exists a probability measure $\pi(A)$ on $(\mathbb{R}^p, \mathcal{B}, \lambda)$ and a $\rho > 1$ such that

$$\forall x \in \mathbb{R}^p : \quad \lim_{n \to \infty} \rho^n ||p^n(x, \cdot) - \pi(\cdot)|| = 0$$

where $|| \cdot ||$ denotes the total variation. Then π satisfies the invariance equation

$$\pi(A) = \int p(x, A) \, \pi(dx), \quad \forall A \in \mathcal{B}$$

There is a close relationship between a time series and its associated Markov chain. If the Markov chain is geometrically ergodic, then its distribution will converge to π and the time series is asymptotically stationary. If the time series is started with distribution π, i.e., $x_0 \sim \pi$, then the series $\{\xi_t\}$ is strictly stationary.

3 Stationarity of AR-NN Models

We now apply the concepts defined in Section 2 to the case where g is defined by a neural network. Let x denote a p-dimensional input vector, then we consider the following standard network architectures:

Single hidden layer perceptrons:

$$g(x) = \gamma_0 + \sum_i \beta_i \sigma(\alpha_i + a'_i x) \qquad (7)$$

where α_i, β_i and γ_0 are scalar weights, a_i are p-dimensional weight vectors, and $\sigma(\cdot)$ is a bounded sigmoid function such as $\tanh(\cdot)$.

Single hidden layer perceptrons with shortcut connections:

$$g(x) = \gamma_0 + c'x + \sum_i \beta_i \sigma(\alpha_i + a'_i x) \qquad (8)$$

where c is an additional weight vector for shortcut connections between inputs and output. In this case we define the characteristic polynomial $c(z)$ associated with the linear shortcuts as

$$c(z) = 1 - c_1 z - c_2 z^2 - \ldots - c^p z^p, \quad z \in \mathbb{C}.$$

Radial basis function networks:

$$g(x) = \gamma_0 + \sum_i \beta_i \phi(\alpha_i |x - m_i|) \tag{9}$$

where m_i are center vectors and $\phi(\cdots)$ is one of the usual bounded radial basis functions such as $\phi(x) = \exp(-x^2)$.

Lemma 1 *Let $\{x_t\}$ be defined by (6), let $\mathbb{E}|\epsilon_t| < \infty$ and let the PDF of ϵ_t be positive everywhere in $\mathbb{R}$. Then if g is defined by any of (7), (8) or (9), the Markov chain $\{x_t\}$ is ϕ-irreducible and aperiodic.*

Lemma 1 basically says that the state space of the Markov chain, i.e., the points that can be reached, cannot be reduced depending on the starting point. An example for a reducible Markov chain would be a series that is always positive if only $x_0 > 0$ (and negative otherwise). This cannot happen in the AR-NN(p) case due to the unbounded additive noise term.

Theorem 1 *Let $\{\xi_t\}$ be defined by (1), $\{x_t\}$ by (6), further let $\mathbb{E}|\epsilon_t| < \infty$ and the PDF of ϵ_t be positive everywhere in $\mathbb{R}$. Then*

1. *If g is a network without linear shortcuts as defined in (7) and (9), then $\{x_t\}$ is geometrically ergodic and $\{\xi_t\}$ is asymptotically stationary.*

2. *If g is a network with linear shortcuts as defined in (8) and additionally $c(z) \neq 0, \forall z \in \mathbb{C} : |z| \leq 1$, then $\{x_t\}$ is geometrically ergodic and $\{\xi_t\}$ is asymptotically stationary.*

The time series $\{\xi_t\}$ remains stationary if we allow for more than one hidden layer ($\rightarrow$ multi layer perceptron, MLP) or non-linear output units, as long as the overall mapping has bounded range. An MLP with shortcut connections combines a (possibly non-stationary) linear AR(p) process with a non-linear stationary NN part. Thus, the NN part can be used to model non-linear fluctuations around a linear process like a random walk.

The only part of the network that controls whether the overall process is stationary are the linear shortcut connections (if present). If there are no shortcuts, then the process is always stationary. With shortcuts, the usual test for stability of a linear system applies.

4 Integrated Models

An important method in classic time series analysis is to first transform a non-stationary series into a stationary one and then model the remainder by a stationary process. The probably most popular models of this kind are autoregressive integrated moving average (ARIMA) models, which can be transformed into stationary ARMA processes by simple differencing.

Let Δ^k denote the k-th order difference operator

$$\Delta \xi_t = \xi_t - \xi_{t-1} \tag{10}$$

$$\Delta^2 \xi_t = \Delta(\xi_t - \xi_{t-1}) = \xi_t - 2\xi_{t-1} + \xi_{t-2} \tag{11}$$

$$\cdots$$

$$\Delta^k \xi_t = \Delta(\Delta \cdots (\Delta \xi_t)) = \sum_{n=0}^{k} (-1)^n \binom{k}{n} \xi_{t-n} \tag{12}$$

with $\Delta^1 = \Delta$. E.g., a standard random walk $\xi_t = \xi_{t-1} + \epsilon_t$ is non-stationary because of the growing variance, but can be transformed into the iid (and hence stationary) noise process ϵ_t by taking first differences.

If a time series is non-stationary, but can be transformed into a stationary series by taking k-th differences, we call the series *integrated of order k*. Standard MLPs or RBFs without shortcuts are asymptotically stationary. It is therefore important to take care that these networks are only used to model stationary processes. Of course the network can be trained to mimic a non-stationary process on a finite time interval, but the out-of-sample or prediction performance will be poor, because the network inherently cannot capture some important features of the process. One way to overcome this problem is to first transform the process into a stationary series (e.g., by differencing an integrated series) and train the network on the transformed series (Chng et al., 1996).

As differencing is a linear operation, this transformation can also be easily incorporated into the network by choosing the shortcut connections and weights from input to hidden units accordingly. Assume we want to model an integrated series of integration order k, such that

$$\Delta^k \xi_t = g(\Delta^k \xi_{t-1}, \ldots, \Delta^k \xi_{t-p}) + \epsilon_t$$

where $\Delta^k \xi_t$ is stationary. By (12) this is equivalent to

$$\begin{aligned} \xi_t &= \sum_{n=1}^{k} (-1)^{n-1} \binom{k}{n} \xi_{t-n} + g(\Delta^k \xi_{t-1}, \ldots, \Delta^k \xi_{t-p}) + \epsilon_t \\ &= \sum_{n=1}^{k} (-1)^{n-1} \binom{k}{n} \xi_{t-n} + \tilde{g}(\xi_{t-1}, \ldots, \xi_{t-p-k}) + \epsilon_t \end{aligned}$$

which (for $p > k$) can be modeled by an MLP with shortcut connections as defined by (8) where the shortcut weight vector c is *fixed* to

$$c = \left(\binom{k}{1}, \ldots, (-1)^{p-1} \binom{k}{p} \right)', \qquad \binom{k}{n} := 0 \text{ for } n > k$$

and $\tilde{g}$ is such that $\tilde{g}(\xi_{t-1}, \ldots, \xi_{t-p-k}) = g(\Delta^k x_{t-1})$. This is always possible and can basically be obtained by adding c to all weights between input and first hidden layer of g.

An AR-NN(p) can model integrated series up to integration order p. If the order of integration is known, the shortcut weights can either be fixed, or the differenced series is used as input. If the order is unknown, we can also train the complete network including the shortcut connections and implicitly estimate the order of integration. After training the final model can be checked for stationarity by looking at the characteristic roots of the polynomial defined by the shortcut connections.

4.1 Fractional Integration

Up to now we have only considered integrated series with positive integer order of integration, i.e., $k \in \mathbb{N}$. In the last years models with *fractional* integration order became very popular (again). Series with integration order of $0.5 < k < 1$ can be shown to exhibit self-similar or fractal behavior, and have long memory. These type of processes were introduced by Mandelbrot in a series of paper modeling river flows, e.g., see Mandelbrot & Ness (1968). More recently, self-similar processes were used to model Ethernet traffic by Leland et al. (1994). Also some financial time series such as foreign exchange data series exhibit long memory and self-similarity.

The fractional differencing operator $\Delta^k, k \in [-1, 1]$ is defined by the series expansion

$$\Delta^k \xi_t = \sum_{n=0}^{\infty} \frac{\Gamma(-k+n)}{\Gamma(-k)\Gamma(n+1)} \xi_{t-n} \tag{13}$$

which is obtained from the Taylor series of $(1-z)^k$. For $k > 1$ we first use Equation (12) and then the above series for the fractional remainder. For practical computation, the series (13) is of course truncated at some term $n = N$. An AR-NN(p) model with shortcut connections can approximate the series up to the first p terms.

5 Summary

We have shown that AR-NN models using standard NN architectures without shortcuts are asymptotically stationary. If linear shortcuts between inputs and outputs are included—which many popular software packages have already implemented—then only the weights of the shortcut connections determine if the overall system is stationary. It is also possible to model many integrated time series by this kind of networks. The asymptotic behavior of AR-NNs is especially important for parameter estimation, predictions over larger intervals of time, or when using the network to generate artificial time series. Limiting (normal) distributions of parameter estimates are only guaranteed for stationary series. We therefore always recommend to transform a non-stationary series to a stationary series if possible (e.g., by differencing) before training a network on it.

Another important aspect of stationarity is that a single trajectory displays the complete probability law of the process. If we have observed one long enough trajectory of the process we can (in theory) estimate all interesting quantities of the process by averaging over time. This need not be true for non-stationary processes in general, where some quantities may only be estimated by averaging over several independent trajectories. E.g., one might train the network on an available sample and then use the trained network afterwards—driven by artificial noise from a random number generator—to generate new data with similar properties than the training sample. The asymptotic stationarity guarantees that the AR-NN model cannot show "explosive" behavior or growing variance with time.

We currently are working on extensions of this paper in several directions. AR-NN processes can be shown to be strong mixing (the memory of the process vanishes exponentially fast) and have autocorrelations going to zero at an exponential rate. Another question is a thorough analysis of the properties of parameter estimates (weights) and tests for the order of integration. Finally we want to extend the univariate results to the multivariate case with a special interest towards cointegrated processes.

Acknowledgement

This piece of research was supported by the Austrian Science Foundation (FWF) under grant SFB#010 ('Adaptive Information Systems and Modeling in Economics and Management Science').

Appendix: Mathematical Proofs

Proof of Lemma 1

It can easily be shown that $\{x_t\}$ is φ-irreducible if the support of the probability density function (PDF) of ϵ_t is the whole real line, i.e., the PDF is positive everywhere in $\mathbb{R}$ (Chan & Tong, 1985). In this case every non-null p-dimensional hypercube is reached in p steps with positive probability (and hence every non-null Borel set A).

A necessary and sufficient condition for $\{x_t\}$ to be aperiodic is that there exists a set A and positive integer n such that $p^n(x, A) > 0$ and $p^{n+1}(x, A) > 0$ for all $x \in A$ (Tong, 1990, p. 455). In our case this is true for all n due to the unbounded additive noise.

Proof of Theorem 1

We use the following result from nonlinear time series theory:

Theorem 2 (Chan & Tong 1985) *Let $\{x_t\}$ be defined by (1), (6) and let G be compact, i.e. preserve compact sets. If G can be decomposed as $G = G_h + G_d$ and $G_d(\cdot)$ is of bounded range, $G_h(\cdot)$ is continuous and homogeneous, i.e., $G_h(\alpha x) = \alpha G_h(x)$, the origin is a fixed point of G_h and G_h is uniform asymptotically stable, $\mathbb{E}|\epsilon_t| < \infty$ and the PDF of ϵ_t is positive everywhere in $\mathbb{R}$, then $\{x_t\}$ is geometrically ergodic.*

The noise process ϵ_t fulfills the conditions by assumption. Clearly all networks are continuous compact functions. Standard MLPs without shortcut connections and RBFs have a bounded range, hence $G_h \equiv 0$ and $G \equiv G_d$, and the series $\{\xi_t\}$ is asymptotically stationary. If we allow for linear shortcut connections between the input and the outputs, we get $G_h = c'x$ and $G_d = \gamma_0 + \sum_i \beta_i \sigma(\alpha_i + a'_i x)$ i.e., G_h is the linear shortcut part of the network, and G_d is a standard MLP without shortcut connections. Clearly, G_h is continuous, homogeneous, and has the origin as a fixed point. Hence, the series $\{\xi_t\}$ is asymptotically stationary if G_h is asymptotically stable, i.e., when all characteristic roots of G_h have a magnitude less than unity. Obviously the same is true for RBFs with shortcut connections. Note that the model reduces to a standard linear AR(p) model if $G_d \equiv 0$.

References

Brockwell, P. J. & Davis, R. A. (1987). *Time Series: Theory and Methods.* Springer Series in Statistics. New York, USA: Springer Verlag.

Chan, K. S. & Tong, H. (1985). On the use of the deterministic Lyapunov function for the ergodicity of stochastic difference equations. *Advances in Applied Probability*, **17**, 666–678.

Chng, E. S., Chen, S., & Mulgrew, B. (1996). Gradient radial basis function networks for nonlinear and nonstationary time series prediction. *IEEE Transactions on Neural Networks*, **7**(1), 190–194.

Husmeier, D. & Taylor, J. G. (1997). Predicting conditional probability densities of stationary stochastic time series. *Neural Networks*, **10**(3), 479–497.

Jones, D. A. (1978). Nonlinear autoregressive processes. *Proceedings of the Royal Society London A*, **360**, 71–95.

Leland, W. E., Taqqu, M. S., Willinger, W., & Wilson, D. V. (1994). On the self-similar nature of ethernet traffic (extended version). *IEEE/ACM Transactions on Networking*, **2**(1), 1–15.

Mandelbrot, B. B. & Ness, J. W. V. (1968). Fractional brownian motions, fractional noises and applications. *SIAM Review*, **10**(4), 422–437.

Tong, H. (1990). *Non-linear time series: A dynamical system approach.* New York, USA: Oxford University Press.

Wang, T. & Sheng, Z. (1996). Asymptotic stationarity of discrete-time stochastic neural networks. *Neural Networks*, **9**(6), 957–963.

Computational Differences between Asymmetrical and Symmetrical Networks

Zhaoping Li   Peter Dayan
Gatsby Computational Neuroscience Unit
17 Queen Square, London, England, WC1N 3AR.
zhaoping@gatsby.ucl.ac.uk   dayan@gatsby.ucl.ac.uk

Abstract

Symmetrically connected recurrent networks have recently been used as models of a host of neural computations. However, because of the separation between excitation and inhibition, biological neural networks are asymmetrical. We study characteristic differences between asymmetrical networks and their symmetrical counterparts, showing that they have dramatically different dynamical behavior and also how the differences can be exploited for computational ends. We illustrate our results in the case of a network that is a selective amplifier.

1 Introduction

A large class of non-linear recurrent networks, including those studied by Grossberg,[9] the Hopfield net,[10,11] and many more recent proposals for the head direction system,[27] orientation tuning in primary visual cortex,[25,1,3,18] eye position,[20] and spatial location in the hippocampus[19] make a key simplifying assumption that the connections between the neurons are symmetric. Analysis is relatively straightforward in this case, since there is a Lyapunov (or energy) function[4,11] that often guarantees the convergence of the motion trajectory to an equilibrium point. However, the assumption of symmetry is broadly false. Networks in the brain are almost never symmetrical, if for no other reason than the separation between excitation and inhibition. In fact, the question of whether ignoring the polarity of the cells is simplification or over-simplification has yet to be fully answered.

Networks with excitatory and inhibitory cells (EI systems, for short) have long been studied,[6] for instance from the perspective of pattern generation in invertebrates,[23] and oscillations in the thalamus[7,24] and the olfactory system.[17,13] Further, since the discovery of 40 Hz oscillations or synchronization amongst cells in primary visual cortex of anesthetised cat,[8,5] oscillatory models of V1 involving separate excitatory and inhibitory cells have also been popular, mainly from the perspective of how the oscillations can be created and sustained and how they can be used for feature linking or binding.[26,22,12] However the scope for computing with dynamically stable behaviors such as limit cycles is not yet clear.

In this paper, we study the computational differences between a family of EI systems and their symmetric counterparts (which we call S systems). One inspiration for this work is Li's nonlinear EI system modeling how the primary visual cortex performs contour enhancement and pre-attentive region segmentation.[14,15] Studies by Braun[2] had suggested that an S system model of the cortex can not perform contour enhancement unless additional (and biologically questionable) mechanisms are used. This posed a question about the true differences between EI and S systems that we answer. We show that EI systems can take advantage of dynamically stable modes that are not available to S systems. The computational significance of this result is discussed and demonstrated in the context of models of orientation selectivity. More details of this work, especially its significance for models of the primary visual cortical system, can be found in Li & Dayan (1999).[16]

2 Theory and Experiment

Consider a simple, but biologically significant, EI system in which excitatory and inhibitory cells come in pairs and there are no 'long-range' connections from the inhibitory cells[14,15] (to which the Lyapunov theory[13,21] does not yet apply):

$$\dot{x}_i = -x_i + \sum_j J_{ij} g(x_j) - h(y_i) + I_i \qquad \tau_y \dot{y}_i = -y_i + \sum_j W_{ij} g(x_j), \qquad (1)$$

where x_i are the principal excitatory cells, which receive external or sensory input I_i, and generate the network outputs $g(x_i)$; y_i are the inhibitory interneurons (which are taken here as having no external input); function $g(x) = [x - T]_+$ is the threshold non-linear activation function for the excitatory cells; $h(y)$ is the activation function for the inhibitory cells (for analytical convenience, we use the linear form $h(y) = (y - T_y)$ although the results are similar with the non-linear $h(y) = [y - T_y]_+$); τ_y is a time-constant for the inhibitory cells; and J_{ij} and W_{ij} are the output connections of the excitatory cells. Excitatory and inhibitory cells can also be perturbed by Gaussian noise.

In the limit that the inhibitory cells are made infinitely fast ($\tau_y = 0$), we have $y_i = \sum_j W_{ij} g(x_j)$, leaving the excitatory cells to interact directly with each other:

$$\dot{x}_i = -x_i + \sum_j J_{ij} g(x_j) - h(\sum_j W_{ij} g(x_j)) + I_i \qquad (2)$$
$$= -x_i + \sum_j (J_{ij} - W_{ij}) g(x_j) + I_i + \kappa_i \qquad (3)$$

where κ_i are constants. In this network, the neural connections $J_{ij} - W_{ij}$ between any two cells x can be either excitatory or inhibitory, as in many abstract neural network models. When $J_{ij} = J_{ji}$ and $W_{ij} = W_{ji}$, the network has symmetric connections. This paper compares EI systems with such connections and the corresponding S systems. Since there are many ways of setting J_{ij} and W_{ij} in the EI system whilst keeping constant $J_{ij} - W_{ij}$, which is the effective weight in the S system, one may intuitively expect the EI system to have a broader computational range.

The response of either system to given inputs is governed by the location and linear stability of their fixed points. The S network is so defined as to have fixed points $\bar{x}$ (where $\dot{x} = 0$ in equation 3) that are the same as those $(\bar{x}, \bar{y})$ of the EI network. In particular, $\bar{x}$ depends on inputs $\mathbf{I}$ (the input-output sensitivity) via $d\bar{x} = (\mathbb{I} - \mathbf{J}\mathbf{D}_g + \mathbf{W}\mathbf{D}_g)^{-1} d\mathbf{I}$, where $\mathbb{I}$ is the identity matrix, $\mathbf{J}$ and $\mathbf{W}$ are the connection matrices, and $\mathbf{D}_g$ is a diagonal matrix with elements $[\mathbf{D}_g]_{ii} = g'(\bar{x}_i)$. However, although the locations of the fixed points are the same for the EI and S systems, the dynamical behavior of the systems about those fixed points are quite different, and this is what leads to their differing computational power.

To analyse the stability of the fixed points, consider, for simplicity the case that $\tau_y = 1$ in the EI system, and that the matrices $\mathbf{JD}_g$ and $\mathbf{WD}_g$ commute with eigenvalues λ_k^J and λ_k^W respectively for $k = 1, \ldots, N$ where N is the dimension of $\mathbf{x}$. The local deviations near the fixed points along each of the N modes will grow in time if the real parts of the following values are positive

$$\gamma_k^{EI} = -1 + (1/2\lambda_k^J \pm (\tfrac{1}{4}\left(\lambda_k^J\right)^2 - \lambda_k^W)^{1/2} \quad \text{for the EI system}$$
$$\gamma_k^S = -1 - \lambda_k^W + \lambda_k^J \quad \text{for the S system}$$

In the case that λ^J and λ^W are real, then *if* the S system is unstable, *then* the EI system is also unstable. For if $-1 + \lambda_i^J - \lambda_i^W > 0$ then $(\lambda_i^J)^2 - 4\lambda_i^W > (\lambda_i^J - 2)^2$, and so $2\gamma_i^{EI} = -2 + \lambda_i^J + ((\lambda_i^J)^2 - 4\lambda^W)^{1/2} > 0$. However, if the EI system is oscillatory, $4\lambda^W > (\lambda^J)^2$, then the S system is stable since $-1 + \lambda^J - \lambda^W < -1 + \lambda^J - (\lambda^J)^2/4 = -(1 - \lambda^J/2)^2 \leq 0$. Hence the EI system can be unstable and oscillatory while the S system is stable.

We are interested in the capacity of both systems to be selective *amplifiers*. This means that there is a class of inputs $\mathbf{I}$ that should be comparatively boosted by the system; whereas others should be comparatively suppressed. For instance, if the cells represent the orientation of a bar at a point, then the mode containing a unimodal, well-tuned, 'bump' in orientation space should be enhanced compared with poorly tuned inputs.[25,1,18] However, if the cells represent oriented small bars at multiple points in visual space, then isolated smooth and straight contours should be enhanced compared with extended homogeneous textures.[14,15]

The quality of the systems will be judged according to how much selective amplification they can stably deliver. The critical trade-off is that the more the selected mode is amplified, the more likely it is that, when the input is non-specific, the system will be *unstable* to fluctuations in the direction of the selected mode, and therefore will hallucinate spurious answers.

3 The Two Point System

A particularly simple case to consider has just two neurons (for the S system; two pairs of neurons for the EI system) and weights

$$\mathbf{J} = \begin{pmatrix} j_o & j \\ j & j_o \end{pmatrix} \quad \mathbf{W} = \begin{pmatrix} w_o & w \\ w & w_o \end{pmatrix}$$

The idea is that each node coarsely models a group of neurons, and the interactions between neurons within a group (j_o and w_o) are qualitatively different from interactions between neurons between groups (j and w). The form of selective amplification here is that symmetric or ambiguous inputs $\mathbf{I}^a = I(1,1)$ should be suppressed compared with asymmetric inputs $\mathbf{I}^b = I(1,0)$ (and, equivalently, $I(0,1)$). In particular, given, $\mathbf{I}^a$, the system should not spontaneously generate a response with x_1 significantly different from x_2. Define the fixed points to be $\bar{x}_1^a = \bar{x}_2^a > T$ under $\mathbf{I}^a$ and $\bar{x}_1^b > T > \bar{x}_2^b$ under $\mathbf{I}^b$, where T is the threshold of the excitatory neurons. These relationships will be true across a wide range of input levels I. The ratio

$$R = \frac{d\bar{x}_1^b/dI}{d\bar{x}_1^a/dI} = \frac{1 + ((w_o + w) - (j_o + j))}{1 + (w_o - j_o)} = 1 + \frac{(w - j)}{1 + (w_o - j_o)} \quad (4)$$

of the average relative responses as the input level I changes is a measure of how the system selectively amplifies the preferred or consistent inputs against ambiguous ones. This measure is appropriate only when the fluctuations of the system

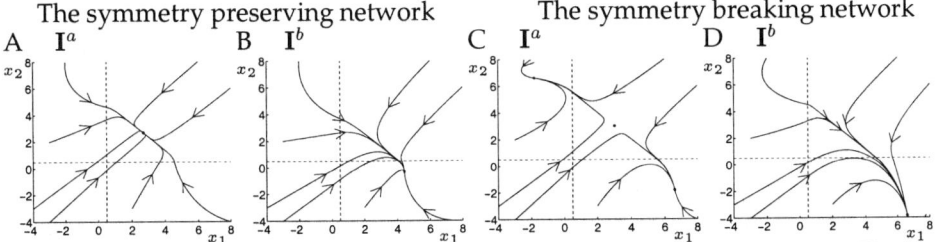

Figure 1: Phase portraits for the S system in the 2 point case. A;B) Evolution in response to $\mathbf{I}^a \propto (1,1)$ and $\mathbf{I}^b \propto (1,0)$ for parameters for which the response to $\mathbf{I}^a$ is stably symmetric. C;D) Evolution in response to $\mathbf{I}^a$ and $\mathbf{I}^b$ for parameters for which the symmetric response to $\mathbf{I}^a$ is unstable, inducing two extra equilibrium points. The dotted lines show the thresholds T for $g(x)$.

from the fixed points $\bar{x}^a$ and $\bar{x}^b$ are well behaved. We will show that this requirement permits larger values of R in the EI system than the S system, suggesting that the EI system can be a more powerful selective amplifier.

In the S system, the stabilities are governed by $\gamma^S = -(1 + w_o - j_o)$ for the single mode of deviation $x_1 - \bar{x}_1^b$ around fixed point b and $\gamma^S_\pm = -(1 + (w_o \pm w) - (j_o \pm j))$ for the two modes of deviation $x_\pm \equiv (x_1 - \bar{x}_1^a) \pm (x_2 - \bar{x}_2^a)$ around fixed point a. Since we only consider cases when the input-output relationship $d\bar{x}/d\mathbf{I}$ of the fixed points is well defined, this means $\gamma^S < 0$ and $\gamma^S_+ < 0$. However, for some interaction parameters, there are two extra (uneven) fixed points $\bar{x}_1^a \neq \bar{x}_2^a$ for (the even) input I^a. Dynamic systems theory dictates these two uneven fixed points will be stable and that they will appear when the '−' mode of the perturbation around the even fixed point $\bar{x}_1^a = \bar{x}_2^a$ is unstable. The system breaks symmetry in inputs, ie the motion trajectory diverges from the (unstable) even fixed point to one of the (stable) uneven ones. To avoid such cases, it is necessary that $\gamma^S_- < 0$. Combining this condition with equation 4 and $\gamma^S < 0$ leads to a upper bound on the amplification ratio $R^S < 2$. Figure 1 shows phase portraits and the equilibrium points of the S system under input I^a and I^b for the two different system parameter regions.

As we have described, the EI system has exactly the same fixed points as the S system, but they are more unstable. The stability around the symmetric fixed point under $\mathbf{I}^a$ is governed by $\gamma^{EI}_\pm = -1 + (j_o \pm j)/2 \pm \sqrt{(j_o \pm j)^2/4 - (w_o \pm w)}$, while that of the asymmetric fixed point under $\mathbf{I}^b$ or $\mathbf{I}^a$ by $\gamma^{EI} = -1 + j_o/2 \pm \sqrt{j_o^2/4 - w_o}$. Consequently, when there are three fixed points under $\mathbf{I}^a$, all of them can be unstable in the EI system, and the motion trajectory cannot converge to any of them. In this case, when both the '+' and '−' modes around the symmetric fixed point $\bar{x}_1^a = \bar{x}_2^a$ are unstable, the global dynamics constrains the motion trajectory to a limit cycle around the fixed points. If $x_1^a \approx x_2^a$ on this limit cycle, then the EI system will not break symmetry, even though the selective amplification ratio $R > 2$. Figure 2 demonstrates the performance of the EI system in this regime. Figure 2A;B show various aspects of the response to input $\mathbf{I}^a$ which should be comparatively suppressed. The system oscillates in such a way that x_1 and x_2 tend to be extremely similar (including being synchronised). Figure 2C;D show the same aspects of the response to $\mathbf{I}^b$, which should be amplified. Again the network oscillates, and, although $g(x_2)$ is not driven completely to 0 (it peaks at 15), it is very strongly dominated by $g(x_1)$, and further, the overall response is much stronger than in figure 2A;B.

The pertinent difference between the EI and S systems is that while the S system (when $h(y)$ is linear) can only roll down the energy landscape to a stable fixed

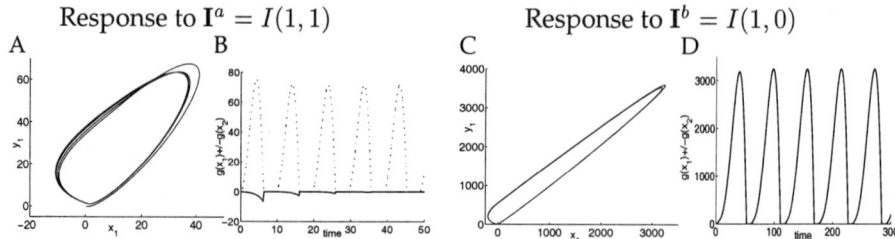

Figure 2: Projections of the response of the EI system. A;B) Evolution of response to $\mathbf{I}^a$. A) x_1 vs y_1 and B) $g(x_1)-g(x_2)$ (solid); $g(x_1)+g(x_2)$ (dotted) across time show that the $x_1=x_2$ mode dominates and the growth of x_1-x_2 is strongly suppressed. C;D) Evolution of the response to $\mathbf{I}^b$. Here, the response of x_1 always dominates that of x_2 over oscillations. The difference between $g(x_1)+g(x_2)$ and $g(x_1)-g(x_2)$ is too small to be evident on the figure. Note the difference in scales between A;B and C;D. Here $j_0=2.1; j=0.4; w_0=1.11; w=0.9$.

point and break the input symmetry, the EI system can resort to global limit cycles $x_1(t) \approx x_2(t)$ between unstable fixed points and maintain input symmetry. This is often (robustly over a large range of parameters) the case even when the '−' mode is locally *more* unstable (at the symmetric fixed point) than the '+' mode, because the '−' mode is much strongly suppressed when the motion trajectory enters the subthreshold region $x_1 < T$ and $x_2 < T$. As we can see in figure 2A;B, this acts to suppress any overall growth in the '−' mode. Since the asymmetric fixed point under $\mathbf{I}^b$ is just as unstable as that under $\mathbf{I}^a$, the EI system responds to asymmetric input $\mathbf{I}^b$ also by a stable limit cycle around the asymmetric fixed point.

Since the response of the system in response to either pattern is oscillatory, there are various reasonable ways of evaluating the relative response ratio. Using the mean responses of the system during a cycle to define $\tilde{\mathbf{x}}$, the selective amplification ratio in figure 2 is $R^{EI}=97$, which is significantly higher than the $R^S=2$ available from the S system. This is a simple existence proof of the superiority of the EI system for amplification, albeit at the expense of oscillations. In fact, in this two point case, it can be shown that any meaningful behavior of the S system (including symmetry breaking) can be qualitatively replicated in the EI system, but not vice-versa.

4 The Orientation System

Symmetric recurrent networks have recently been investigated in great depth for representing and calculating a wide variety of quantities, including orientation tuning. The idea behind the recurrent networks is that they should take noisy (and perhaps weakly tuned) input and selectively amplify the component that represents an orientation θ in the input, leaving a tuned pattern of excitation across the population that faithfully represents the underlying input. Based on the analysis above, we can expect that if an S network amplifies a tuned input enough, then it will break input symmetry given an untuned input and thus hallucinate a tuned response. However, an EI system, in the same oscillatory regime as for the two point system, can maintain untuned and suppressed response to untuned inputs.

We designed a particular EI system with a high selective amplification factor for tuned inputs $\mathbf{I}(\theta)$. In this case, units x_i, y_i have preferred orientations $\theta_i = (i-N/2)\pi/N$ for $i=1\ldots n$. the connection matrices $\mathbf{J}$ is Töplitz with Gaussian tuning, and, for simplicity, $[\mathbf{W}]_{ij}$ does not depend on i,j. Figure 3B (and inset) shows the output of two units in the network in response to a tuned input, showing the nature of the oscillations and the way that selectivity builds up over the course of each period. Figure 3C shows the activities of all the units at three particular phases of the oscillation. Figure 3A shows how the mean activity of the most

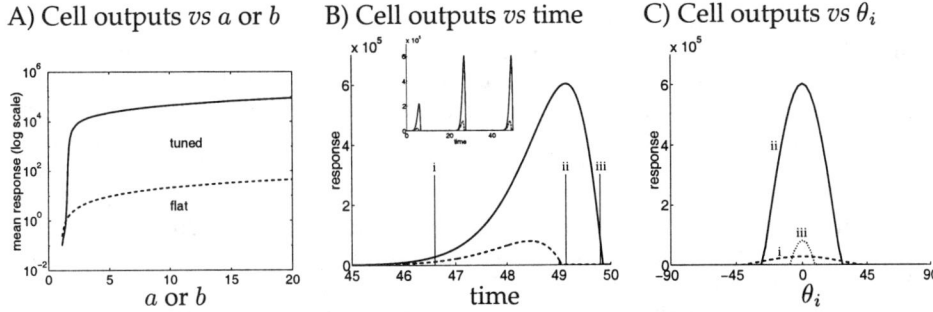

Figure 3: The Gaussian orientation network. A) Mean response of the $\theta_i = 0°$ unit in the network as a function of a (untuned) or b (tuned) with a log scale. B) Activity of the $\theta_i = 0°$ (solid) and $\theta_i = 30°$ (dashed) units in the network over the course of the positive part of an oscillation. Inset – activity of these units over all time. C) Activity of all the units at the three times shown as (i), (ii) and (iii) in (B) (i) (dashed) is in the rising phase of the oscillation; (ii) (solid) is at the peak; and (iii) (dotted) is during the falling phase. Here, the input is $I_i = a + be^{-\theta_i^2/2\sigma^2}$, with $\sigma = 13°$, and the Töplitz weights are $J_{ij} = (3 + 21e^{-(\theta_i-\theta_j)^2/2\sigma'^2})/N$, with $\sigma' = 20°$ and $\mathbf{W}_{ij} = 23.5/N$.

activated unit scales with the levels of tuned and untuned input. The network amplifies the tuned inputs dramatically more – note the logarithmic scale. The S system breaks symmetry to the untuned input ($b = 0$) for these weights. If the weights are scaled uniformly by a factor of 0.22, then the S system is appropriately stable. However, the magnification ratio is 4.2 rather than something greater than 1000 in the EI system.

The orientation system can be understood to a large qualitative degree by looking at its two-point cousins. Many of the essential constraints on the system are determined by the behavior of the system when the mode with $x_i = x_j$ dominates, in which case the complex non-linearities induced by orientation tuning or cut off and its equivalents are irrelevant. Let $\tilde{J}(f)$ and $\tilde{W}(f)$ for (angular) frequency f be the Fourier transforms of $J(i-j) \equiv [\mathbf{J}]_{ij}$ and $W(i-j) \equiv [\mathbf{W}]_{ij}$ and define $\lambda(f) = Re\{-1 + \tilde{J}(f)/2 + i\sqrt{(\tilde{W}(f) - \tilde{J}^2(f)/4)}\}$. Then, let $f^* > 0$ be the frequency such that $\lambda(f^*) \geq \lambda(f)$ for all $f > 0$. This is the non-translation-invariant mode that is most likely to cause instabilities for translation invariant behavior. A two point system that closely corresponds to the full system can be found by solving the simultaneous equations:

$$j_o + j = \tilde{J}(0) \quad w_o + w = \tilde{W}(0) \quad j_o - j = \tilde{J}(f^*) \quad w_o - w = \tilde{W}(f^*)$$

This design equates the $x_1 = x_2$ mode in the two point system with the $f = 0$ mode in the orientation system and the $x_1 = -x_2$ mode with the $f = f^*$ mode. For smooth J and W, f^* is often the smallest or one of the smallest non-zero spatial frequencies. It is easy to see that the two systems are exactly equivalent in the translation invariant mode $x_i = x_j$ under translation invariant input $I_i = I_j$ in both the linear and nonlinear regimes. The close correspondence between the two systems in other dynamic regimes is supported by simulation results.[16] Quantitatively, however, the amplification ratio differs between the two systems.

5 Conclusions

We have studied the dynamical behavior of networks with symmetrical and asymmetrical connections and have shown that the extra degrees of dynamical freedom of the latter can be put to good computational use, *eg* global dynamic stability via local instability. Many applications of recurrent networks involve selective amplification – and the selective amplification factors for asymmetrical networks can greatly exceed those of symmetrical networks. We showed this in the case of orientation selectivity. However, it was originally inspired by a similar result in contour enhancement and texture segregation for which the activity of isolated oriented line elements should be enhanced if they form part of a smooth contour in the input and suppressed if they form part of an extended homogeneous texture. Further, the output should be homogeneous if the input is homogeneous (in the same way that the orientation network should not hallucinate orientations from untuned input). In this case, similar analysis[16] shows that stable contour enhancement is limited to just a factor of 3.0 for the S system (but not for the EI system), suggesting an explanation for the poor performance of a slew of S systems in the literature designed for this purpose. We used a very simple system with just two pairs of neurons to develop analytical intuitions which are powerful enough to guide our design of the more complex systems. We expect that the details of our model, with the exact pairing of excitatory and inhibitory cells and the threshold non-linearity, are not crucial for the results.

Inhibition in the cortex is, of course, substantially more complicated than we have suggested. In particular, inhibitory cells do have somewhat faster (though finite) time constants than excitatory cells, and are also not so subject to short term plasticity effects such as spike rate adaptation. Nevertheless, oscillations of various sorts can certainly occur, suggesting the relevance of the computational regime that we have studied.

References

[1] Ben-Yishai, R, Bar-Or, RL & Sompolinsky, H (1995) *PNAS* **92**:3844-3848.
[2] Braun, J, Neibur, E, Schuster, HG & Koch, C (1994) *Society for Neuroscience Abstracts* **20**:1665.
[3] Carandini, M & Ringach, DL (1997) *Vision Research* **37**:3061-3071.
[4] Cohen, MA & Grossberg, S (1983) *IEEE Transactions on Systems, Man and Cybernetics* **13**:815-826.
[5] Eckhorn, R, et al (1988) *Biological Cybernetics* **60**:121-130.
[6] Ermentrout, GB & Cowan, JD (1979). *Journal of Mathematical Biology* **7**:265-280.
[7] Golomb, D, Wang, XJ & Rinzel, J (1996). *Journal of Neurophysiology* **75**:750-769.
[8] Gray, CM, Konig, P, Engel, AK & Singer, W (1989) *Nature* **338**:334-337.
[9] Grossberg, S (1988) *Neural Networks* **1**:17-61.
[10] Hopfield, JJ (1982) *PNAS* **79**:2554-2558.
[11] Hopfield, JJ (1984) *PNAS* **81**:3088-3092.
[12] Konig, P, Janosch, B & Schillen, TB (1992) *Neural Computation* **4**:666-681.
[13] Li, Z (1995) In JL van Hemmen *et al*, eds, *Models of Neural Networks*. Vol. 2. NY: Springer.
[14] Li, Z (1997) In KYM Wong, I King & DY Yeung, editors, *Theoretical Aspects of Neural Computation*. Hong Kong: Springer-Verlag.
[15] Li, Z (1998) *Neural Computation* **10**:903-940.
[16] Li, Z. and Dayan, P. (1999) to be published in *Network: Computations in Neural Systems*.
[17] Li, Z & Hopfield, JJ (1989). *Biological Cybernetics* **61**:379-392.
[18] Pouget, A, Zhang, KC, Deneve, S & Latham, PE (1998) *Neural Computation*, **10**373-401.
[19] Samsonovich A & McNaughton, BL (1997) *Journal of Neuroscience* **17**:5900-5920.
[20] Seung, HS (1996) *PNAS* **93**:13339-13344.
[21] Seung, HS *et al* (1998). *NIPS 10*.
[22] Sompolinsky, H, Golomb, D & Kleinfeld, D (1990) *PNAS* **87**:7200-7204.
[23] Stein, PSG, *et al* (1997) *Neurons, Networks, and Motor Behavior*. Cambridge, MA: MIT Press.
[24] Steriade, M, McCormick, DA & Sejnowski, TJ (1993). *Science* **262**:679-685.
[25] Suarez, H, Koch, C & Douglas, R (1995) *Journal of Neuroscience* **15**:6700-6719.
[26] von der Malsburg, C (1988) *Neural Networks* **1**:141-148.
[27] Zhang, K (1996) *Journal of Neuroscience* **16**:2112-2126.

A Precise Characterization of the Class of Languages Recognized by Neural Nets under Gaussian and other Common Noise Distributions

Wolfgang Maass*
Inst. for Theoretical Computer Science,
Technische Universität Graz
Klosterwiesgasse 32/2,
A-8010 Graz, Austria
email: maass@igi.tu-graz.ac.at

Eduardo D. Sontag
Dep. of Mathematics
Rutgers University
New Brunswick, NJ 08903, USA
email: sontag@hilbert.rutgers.edu

Abstract

We consider recurrent analog neural nets where each gate is subject to Gaussian noise, or any other common noise distribution whose probability density function is nonzero on a large set. We show that many regular languages cannot be recognized by networks of this type, for example the language $\{w \in \{0,1\}^* |\ w$ begins with $0\}$, and we give a precise characterization of those languages which can be recognized. This result implies severe constraints on possibilities for constructing recurrent analog neural nets that are robust against realistic types of analog noise. On the other hand we present a method for constructing *feedforward* analog neural nets that are robust with regard to analog noise of this type.

1 Introduction

A fairly large literature (see [Omlin, Giles, 1996] and the references therein) is devoted to the construction of analog neural nets that recognize regular languages. Any physical realization of the analog computational units of an analog neural net in technological or biological systems is bound to encounter some form of "imprecision" or analog noise at its analog computational units. We show in this article that this effect has serious consequences for the computational power of recurrent analog neural nets. We show that any analog neural net whose computational units are subject to Gaussian or other common noise distributions cannot recognize arbitrary regular languages. For example, such analog neural net cannot recognize the regular language $\{w \in \{0,1\}^* |\ w$ begins with $0\}$.

---
*Partially supported by the Fonds zur Förderung der wissenschaftlichen Forschung (FWF), Austria, project P12153.

A precise characterization of those regular languages which can be recognized by such analog neural nets is given in Theorem 1.1. In section 3 we introduce a simple technique for making feedforward neural nets robust with regard to the same types of analog noise. This method is employed to prove the positive part of Theorem 1.1. The main difficulty in proving Theorem 1.1 is its negative part, for which adequate theoretical tools are introduced in section 2.

Before we can give the exact statement of Theorem 1.1 and discuss related preceding work we have to give a precise definition of computations in *noisy* neural networks. From the conceptual point of view this definition is basically the same as for computations in noisy boolean circuits (see [Pippenger, 1985] and [Pippenger, 1990]). However it is technically more involved since we have to deal here with an infinite state space.

We will first illustrate this definition for a concrete case, a recurrent sigmoidal neural net with Gaussian noise, and then indicate the full generality of our result, which makes it applicable to a very large class of other types of analog computational systems with analog noise. Consider a recurrent sigmoidal neural net $\mathcal{N}$ consisting of n units, that receives at each time step t an input u_t from some finite alphabet U (for example $U = \{0, 1\}$). The internal state of $\mathcal{N}$ at the end of step t is described by a vector $x_t \in [-1, 1]^n$, which consists of the outputs of the n sigmoidal units at the end of step t. A computation step of the network $\mathcal{N}$ is described by

$$x_{t+1} = \sigma(W x_t + h + u_t c + V_t)$$

where $W \in \mathbb{R}^{n \times n}$ and $c, h \in \mathbb{R}^n$ represent weight matrix and vectors, σ is a sigmoidal activation function (e.g., $\sigma(y) = 1/(1 + e^{-y})$) applied to each vector component, and $V_1, V_2, \ldots$ is a sequence of n-vectors drawn independently from some Gaussian distribution. In analogy to the case of noisy boolean circuits [Pippenger, 1990] one says that this network $\mathcal{N}$ *recognizes a language* $L \subseteq U^*$ *with reliability* ε (where $\varepsilon \in (0, \frac{1}{2}]$ is some given constant) if immediately after reading an arbitrary word $w \in U^*$ the network $\mathcal{N}$ is with probability $\geq \frac{1}{2} + \varepsilon$ in an accepting state in case that $w \in L$, and with probability $\leq \frac{1}{2} - \varepsilon$ in an accepting state in case that $w \notin L$[1].

We will show in this article that even if the parameters of the Gaussian noise distribution for each sigmoidal unit can be determined by the designer of the neural net, it is impossible to find a size n, weight matrix W, vectors h, c and a reliability $\varepsilon \in (0, \frac{1}{2}]$ so that the resulting recurrent sigmoidal neural net with Gaussian noise accepts the simple regular language $\{w \in \{0, 1\}^* | \ w$ begins with $0\}$ with reliability ε. This result exhibits a fundamental limitation for making a recurrent analog neural net noise robust, even in a case where the noise distribution is known and of a rather benign type. This quite startling negative result should be contrasted with the large number of known techniques for making a feedforward boolean circuit robust against noise, see [Pippenger, 1990].

Our negative result turns out to be of a very general nature, that holds for virtually all related definitions of noisy analog neural nets and also for completely different models for analog computation in the presence of Gaussian or similar noise. Instead of the state set $[-1, 1]^n$ one can take any compact set $\Omega \subseteq \mathbb{R}^n$, and instead of the map $(x, u) \mapsto Wx + h + uc$ one can consider an arbitrary map $f : \Omega \times U \to \widehat{\Omega}$ for a compact set $\widehat{\Omega} \subseteq \mathbb{R}^n$ where $f(\cdot, u)$ is Borel measurable for each fixed $u \in U$. Instead of a sigmoidal activation function σ and a Gaussian distributed noise vector V it suffices to assume that $\sigma : \mathbb{R}^n \to \Omega$ is some arbitrary Borel measurable function and V is some $\mathbb{R}^n$-valued random variable with a density $\phi(\cdot)$ that has a wide support[2]. In order to define a computation in such system we consider for

---

[1]According to this definition a network $\mathcal{N}$ that is after reading some $w \in U^*$ in an accepting state with probability strictly between $\frac{1}{2} - \varepsilon$ and $\frac{1}{2} + \varepsilon$ does not recognize any language $L \subseteq U^*$.

[2]More precisely: We assume that there exists a subset Ω_0 of Ω and some constant $c_0 > 0$ such

each $u \in U$ the stochastic kernel K_u defined by $K_u(x, A) := \text{Prob}\,[\sigma(f(x, u) + V) \in A]$ for $x \in \Omega$ and $A \subseteq \Omega$. For each (signed, Borel) measure μ on Ω, and each $u \in U$, we let $\mathbb{K}_u \mu$ be the (signed, Borel) measure defined on Ω by $(\mathbb{K}_u \mu)(A) := \int K_u(x, A) d\mu(x)$. Note that $\mathbb{K}_u \mu$ is a probability measure whenever μ is. For any sequence of inputs $w = u_1, \ldots, u_r$, we consider the composition of the evolution operators $\mathbb{K}_{u_i}$:

$$\mathbb{K}_w = \mathbb{K}_{u_r} \circ \mathbb{K}_{u_{r-1}} \circ \ldots \circ \mathbb{K}_{u_1}. \tag{1}$$

If the probability distribution of states at any given instant is given by the measure μ, then the distribution of states after a single computation step on input $u \in U$ is given by $\mathbb{K}_u \mu$, and after r computation steps on inputs $w = u_1, \ldots, u_r$, the new distribution is $\mathbb{K}_w \mu$, where we are using the notation (1). In particular, if the system starts at a particular initial state ξ, then the distribution of states after r computation steps on w is $\mathbb{K}_w \delta_\xi$, where δ_ξ is the probability measure concentrated on $\{\xi\}$. That is to say, for each measurable subset $F \subseteq \Omega$

$$\text{Prob}\,[x_{r+1} \in F \mid x_1 = \xi, \text{ input } = w] = (\mathbb{K}_w \delta_\xi)(F).$$

We fix an initial state $\xi \in \Omega$, a set of "accepting" or "final" states F, and a "reliability" level $\varepsilon > 0$, and say that the resulting noisy analog computational system M *recognizes the language* $L \subseteq U^*$ if for all $w \in U^*$:

$$w \in L \iff (\mathbb{K}_w \delta_\xi)(F) \geq \frac{1}{2} + \varepsilon$$

$$w \notin L \iff (\mathbb{K}_w \delta_\xi)(F) \leq \frac{1}{2} - \varepsilon.$$

In general a neural network that simulates a DFA will carry out not just one, but a fixed number k of computation steps (=state transitions) of the form $x' = \sigma(Wx + h + uc + V)$ for each input symbol $u \in U$ that it reads (see the constructions described in [Omlin, Giles, 1996], and in section 3 of this article). This can easily be reflected in our model by formally replacing any input sequence $w = u_1, u_2, \ldots, u_r$ from U^* by a padded sequence $\tilde{w} = u_1, b^{k-1}, u_2, b^{k-1}, \ldots, u_r, b^{k-1}$ from $(U \cup \{b\})^*$, where b is a blank symbol not in U, and b^{k-1} denotes a sequence of $k - 1$ copies of b (for some arbitrarily fixed $k \geq 1$). This completes our definition of language recognition by a noisy analog computational system M with discrete time. This definition essentially agrees with that given in [Maass, Orponen, 1997].

We employ the following common notations from formal language theory: We write $w_1 w_2$ for the concatenation of two strings w_1 and w_2, U^r for the set of all concatenations of r strings from U, U^* for the set of all concatenations of any finite number of strings from U, and UV for the set of all strings $w_1 w_2$ with $w_1 \in U$ and $w_2 \in V$. The main result of this article is the following:

Theorem 1.1 *Assume that U is some arbitrary finite alphabet. A language $L \subseteq U^*$ can be recognized by a noisy analog computational system of the previously specified type if and only if $L = E_1 \bigcup U^* E_2$ for two finite subsets E_1 and E_2 of U^*.*

A corresponding version of Theorem 1.1 for *discrete* computational systems was previously shown in [Rabin, 1963]. More precisely, Rabin had shown that probabilistic automata with strictly positive matrices can recognize exactly the same class of languages L that occur in our Theorem 1.1. Rabin referred to these languages as *definite languages*. Language recognition by *analog* computational systems with *analog* noise has previously been investigated in [Casey, 1996] for the special case of bounded noise and perfect reliability

---

that the following two properties hold: $\phi(v) \geq c_0$ for all $v \in Q := \sigma^{-1}(\Omega_0) - \widehat{\Omega}$ (that is, Q is the set consisting of all possible differences $z - y$, with $\sigma(z) \in \Omega_0$ and $y \in \widehat{\Omega}$) *and* $\sigma^{-1}(\Omega_0)$ has finite and nonzero Lebesgue measure $m_0 = \lambda\left(\sigma^{-1}(\Omega_0)\right)$.

(i.e. $\int_{\|v\|\leq \eta} \phi(v)dv = 1$ for some small $\eta > 0$ and $\varepsilon = 1/2$ in our terminology), and in [Maass, Orponen, 1997] for the general case. It was shown in [Maass, Orponen, 1997] that any such system can only recognize regular languages. Furthermore it was shown there that if $\int_{\|v\|\leq \eta} \phi(v)dv = 1$ for some small $\eta > 0$ then all regular languages *can* be recognized by such systems. In the present paper we focus on the complementary case where the condition "$\int_{\|v\|\leq \eta} \phi(v)dv = 1$ for some small $\eta > 0$" is not satisfied, i.e. analog noise may move states over larger distances in the state space. We show that even if the probability of such event is arbitrarily small, the neural net will no longer be able to recognize arbitrary regular languages.

2 A Constraint on Language Recognition

We prove in this section the following result for arbitrary noisy computational systems M as specified at the end of section 1:

Theorem 2.1 *Assume that U is some arbitrary alphabet. If a language $L \subseteq U^*$ is recognized by M, then there are subsets E_1 and E_2 of $U^{\leq r}$, for some integer r, such that $L = E_1 \bigcup U^* E_2$. In other words: whether a string $w \in U^*$ belongs to the language L can be decided by just inspecting the first r and the last r symbols of w.*

2.1 A General Fact about Stochastic Kernels

Let $(S, \mathcal{S})$ be a measure space, and let K be a stochastic kernel[3]. As in the special case of the K_u's above, for each (signed) measure μ on $(S, \mathcal{S})$, we let $\mathbb{K}\mu$ be the (signed) measure defined on $\mathcal{S}$ by $(\mathbb{K}\mu)(A) := \int K(x, A)d\mu(x)$. Observe that $\mathbb{K}\mu$ is a probability measure whenever μ is. Let $c > 0$ be arbitrary. We say that K satisfies *Doeblin's condition (with constant c)* if there is some probability measure ρ on $(S, \mathcal{S})$ so that

$$K(x, A) \geq c\rho(A) \quad \text{for all } x \in S, A \in \mathcal{S}. \tag{2}$$

(Necessarily $c \leq 1$, as is seen by considering the special case $A = S$.) This condition is due to [Doeblin, 1937].

We denote by $\|\mu\|$ the *total variation* of the (signed) measure μ. Recall that $\|\mu\|$ is defined as follows. One may decompose S into a disjoint union of two sets A and B, in such a manner that μ is nonnegative on A and nonpositive on B. Letting the restrictions of μ to A and B be "μ_+" and "$-\mu_-$" respectively (and zero on B and A respectively), we may decompose μ as a difference of nonnegative measures with disjoint supports, $\mu = \mu_+ - \mu_-$. Then, $\|\mu\| = \mu_+(A) + \mu_-(B)$. The following Lemma is a "folk" fact ([Papinicolaou, 1978]).

Lemma 2.2 *Assume that K satisfies Doeblin's condition with constant c. Let μ be any (signed) measure such that $\mu(S) = 0$. Then $\|\mathbb{K}\mu\| \leq (1-c)\|\mu\|$.* ∎

2.2 Proof of Theorem 2.1

Lemma 2.3 *There is a constant $c > 0$ such that K_u satisfies Doeblin's condition with constant c, for every $u \in U$.*

Proof. Let Ω_0, c_0, and $0 < m_0 < 1$ be as in the second footnote, and introduce the following (Borel) probability measure on Ω_0:

$$\lambda_0(A) := \frac{1}{m_0}\lambda\left(\sigma^{-1}(A)\right).$$

---
[3]That is to say, $K(x, \cdot)$ is a probability distribution for each x, and $K(\cdot, A)$ is a measurable function for each Borel measurable set A.

Pick any measurable $A \subseteq \Omega_0$ and any $y \in \widehat{\Omega}$. Then,

$$Z(y, A) = \text{Prob}[\sigma(y + V) \in A] = \text{Prob}[y + V \in \sigma^{-1}(A)]$$
$$= \int_{A_y} \phi(v)\, dv \geq c_0 \lambda(A_y) = c_0 \lambda(\sigma^{-1}(A)) = c_0 m_0 \lambda_0(A),$$

where $A_y := \sigma^{-1}(A) - \{y\} \subseteq Q$. We conclude that $Z(y, A) \geq c\lambda_0(A)$ for all y, A, where $c = c_0 m_0$. Finally, we extend the measure λ_0 to all of Ω by assigning zero measure to the complement of Ω_0, that is, $\rho(A) := \lambda_0(A \cap \Omega_0)$ for all measurable subsets A of Ω. Pick $u \in U$; we will show that K_u satisfies Doeblin's condition with the above constant c (and using ρ as the "comparison" measure in the definition). Consider any $x \in \Omega$ and measurable $A \subseteq \Omega$. Then,

$$K_u(x, A) = Z(f(x, u), A) \geq Z(f(x, u), A \cap \Omega_0) \geq c\lambda_0(A \cap \Omega_0) = c\rho(A),$$

as required. ∎

For every two probability measures μ_1, μ_2 on Ω, applying Lemma 2.2 to $\mu := \mu_1 - \mu_2$, we know that $\|\mathbb{K}_u \mu_1 - \mathbb{K}_u \mu_2\| \leq (1 - c)\|\mu_1 - \mu_2\|$ for each $u \in U$. Recursively, then, we conclude:

$$\|\mathbb{K}_w \mu_1 - \mathbb{K}_w \mu_2\| \leq (1 - c)^r \|\mu_1 - \mu_2\| \leq 2(1 - c)^r \quad (3)$$

for all words w of length $\geq r$.

Now pick any integer r such that $(1 - c)^r < 2\varepsilon$. From Equation (3), we have that

$$\|\mathbb{K}_w \mu_1 - \mathbb{K}_w \mu_2\| < 4\varepsilon$$

for all w of length $\geq r$ and any two probability measures μ_1, μ_2. In particular, this means that, for each measurable set A,

$$|(\mathbb{K}_w \mu_1)(A) - (\mathbb{K}_w \mu_2)(A)| < 2\varepsilon \quad (4)$$

for all such w. (Because, for any two probability measures ν_1 and ν_2, and any measurable set A, $2|\nu_1(A) - \nu_2(A)| \leq \|\nu_1 - \nu_2\|$.)

Lemma 2.4 *Pick any $v \in U^*$ and $w \in U^r$. Then*

$$w \in L \iff vw \in L.$$

Proof. Assume that $w \in L$, that is, $(\mathbb{K}_w \delta_\xi)(F) \geq \frac{1}{2} + \varepsilon$. Applying inequality (4) to the measures $\mu_1 := \delta_\xi$ and $\mu_2 := \mathbb{K}_v \delta_\xi$ and $A = F$, we have that $|(\mathbb{K}_w \delta_\xi)(F) - (\mathbb{K}_{vw} \delta_\xi)(F)| < 2\varepsilon$, and this implies that $(\mathbb{K}_{vw} \delta_\xi)(F) > \frac{1}{2} - \varepsilon$, i.e., $vw \in L$. (Since $\frac{1}{2} - \varepsilon < (\mathbb{K}_{vw} \delta_\xi)(F) < \frac{1}{2} + \varepsilon$ is ruled out.) If $w \notin L$, the argument is similar. ∎

We have proved that

$$L \cap (U^* U^r) = U^* (L \cap U^r).$$

So,

$$L = \left(L \cap U^{\leq r}\right) \cup \left(L \cap U^* U^r\right) = E_1 \cup U^* E_2$$

where $E_1 := L \cap U^{\leq r}$ and $E_2 := L \cap U^r$ are both included in $U^{\leq r}$. This completes the proof of Theorem 2.1. ∎

3 Construction of Noise Robust Analog Neural Nets

In this section we exhibit a method for making feedforward analog neural nets robust with regard to arbitrary analog noise of the type considered in the preceding sections. This method will be used to prove in Corollary 3.2 the missing positive part of the claim of the main result (Theorem 1.1) of this article.

Theorem 3.1 *Let $\mathcal{C}$ be any (noiseless) feedforward threshold circuit, and let $\sigma : \mathbb{R} \to [-1,1]$ be some arbitrary function with $\sigma(u) \to 1$ for $u \to \infty$ and $\sigma(u) \to -1$ for $u \to -\infty$. Furthermore assume that $\delta, \rho \in (0,1)$ are some arbitrary given parameters. Then one can transform for any given analog noise of the type considered in section 1 the noiseless threshold circuit $\mathcal{C}$ into an analog neural net $\mathcal{N}_\mathcal{C}$ with the same number of gates, whose gates employ the given function σ as activation function, so that for any circuit input $\underline{x} \in \{-1,1\}^m$ the output of the noisy analog neural net $\mathcal{N}_\mathcal{C}$ differs with probability $\geq 1 - \delta$ by at most ρ from the output of $\mathcal{C}$.*

Idea of the *proof:* Let k be the maximal fan-in of a gate in $\mathcal{C}$, and let w be the maximal absolute value of a weight in $\mathcal{C}$. We choose $R > 0$ so large that the density function $\phi(\cdot)$ of the noise vector V satisfies for each gate with n inputs in $\mathcal{C}$

$$\int_{|v_i| \geq R} \phi(v)\, dv \leq \frac{\delta}{2n} \quad \text{for } i = 1, \ldots, n.$$

Furthermore we choose $u_0 > 0$ so large that $\sigma(u) \geq 1 - \rho/(wk)$ for $u \geq u_0$ and $\sigma(u) \leq -1 + \rho/(wk)$ for $u \leq -u_0$. Finally we choose a factor $\gamma > 0$ so large that $\gamma(1-\rho) - R \geq u_0$. Let $\mathcal{N}_\mathcal{C}$ be the analog neural net that results from $\mathcal{C}$ through multiplication of all weights and thresholds with γ and through replacement of the Heaviside activation functions of the gates in $\mathcal{C}$ by the given activation function σ. ∎

The following Corollary provides the proof of the positive part of our main result Theorem 1.1. It holds for any σ considered in Theorem 3.1.

Corollary 3.2 *Assume that U is some arbitrary finite alphabet, and language $L \subseteq U^*$ is of the form $L = E_1 \bigcup U^* E_2$ for two arbitrary finite subsets E_1 and E_2 of U^*. Then the language L can be recognized by a noisy analog neural net $\mathcal{N}$ with any desired reliability $\varepsilon \in (0, \frac{1}{2})$, in spite of arbitrary analog noise of the type considered in section 1.*

Proof. We first construct a feedforward threshold circuit $\mathcal{C}$ for recognizing L, that receives each input symbol from U in the form of a bitstring $u \in \{0,1\}^l$ (for some fixed $l \geq \log_2 |U|$), that is encoded as the binary states of l input units of the boolean circuit $\mathcal{C}$. Via a tapped delay line of fixed length d (which can easily be implemented in a feedforward threshold circuit by d layers, each consisting of l gates that compute the identity function on a single binary input from the preceding layer) one can achieve that the feedforward circuit $\mathcal{C}$ computes *any* given boolean function of the last d sequences from $\{0,1\}^l$ that were presented to the circuit. On the other hand for any language of the form $L = E_1 \cup U^* E_2$ with E_1, E_2 finite there exists some $d \in \mathbb{N}$ such that for each $w \in U^*$ one can decide whether $w \in L$ by just inspecting the last d characters of w. Therefore a feedforward threshold circuit $\mathcal{C}$ with a tapped delay line of the type described above can decide whether $w \in L$.

We apply Theorem 3.1 to this circuit $\mathcal{C}$ for $\delta = \rho = \min(\frac{1}{2} - \varepsilon, \frac{1}{4})$. We define the set F of accepting states for the resulting analog neural net $\mathcal{N}_\mathcal{C}$ as the set of those states where the computation is completed and the output gate of $\mathcal{N}_\mathcal{C}$ assumes a value $\geq 3/4$. Then according to Theorem 3.1 the analog neural net $\mathcal{N}_\mathcal{C}$ recognizes L with reliability ε. To be formally precise, one has to apply Theorem 3.1 to a threshold circuit $\mathcal{C}$ that receives its input not in a single batch, but through a sequence of d batches. The proof of Theorem 3.1 readily extends to this case. ∎

4 Conclusions

We have exhibited a fundamental limitation of analog neural nets with Gaussian or other common noise distributions whose probability density function is nonzero on a large set: They cannot accept the very simple regular language $\{w \in \{0,1\}^* |\ w \text{ begins with } 0\}$. This holds even if the designer of the neural net is allowed to choose the parameters of the Gaussian noise distribution and the architecture and parameters of the neural net. The proof of this result introduces new mathematical arguments into the investigation of neural computation, which can also be applied to other stochastic analog computational systems.

We also have presented a method for making *feedforward* analog neural nets robust against the same type of noise. This implies that certain regular languages, such as for example $\{w \in \{0,1\}^* |\ w \text{ ends with } 0\}$ *can* be recognized by a recurrent analog neural net with Gaussian noise. In combination with our negative result this yields a *precise characterization* of all regular languages that can be recognized by recurrent analog neural nets with Gaussian noise, or with any other noise distribution that has a large support.

References

[Casey, 1996] Casey, M., "The dynamics of discrete-time computation, with application to recurrent neural networks and finite state machine extraction", *Neural Computation* 8, 1135–1178, 1996.

[Doeblin, 1937] Doeblin, W., "Sur le propriétés asymtotiques de mouvement régis par certain types de chaînes simples", *Bull. Math. Soc. Roumaine Sci. 39(1)*: 57–115; (2) 3–61, 1937.

[Maass, Orponen, 1997] Maass, W., and Orponen, P. "On the effect of analog noise on discrete-time analog computations", *Advances in Neural Information Processing Systems 9*, 1997, 218–224; journal version: *Neural Computation* 10(5), 1071–1095, 1998.

[Omlin, Giles, 1996] Omlin, C. W., Giles, C. L. "Constructing deterministic finite-state automata in recurrent neural networks", *J. Assoc. Comput. Mach. 43* (1996), 937–972.

[Papinicolaou, 1978] Papinicolaou, G., "Asymptotic Analysis of Stochastic Equations", in *Studies in Probability Theory, MAA Studies in Mathematics*, vol. 18, 111–179, edited by M. Rosenblatt, Math. Assoc. of America, 1978.

[Pippenger, 1985] Pippenger, N., "On networks of noisy gates", *IEEE Sympos. on Foundations of Computer Science*, vol. 26, IEEE Press, New York, 30–38, 1985.

[Pippenger, 1989] Pippenger, N., "Invariance of complexity measures for networks with unreliable gates", *J. of the ACM*, vol. 36, 531–539, 1989.

[Pippenger, 1990] Pippenger, N., "Developments in 'The Synthesis of Reliable Organisms from Unreliable Components' ", *Proc. of Symposia in Pure Mathematics*, vol. 50, 311–324, 1990.

[Rabin, 1963] Rabin, M., "Probabilistic automata", *Information and Control*, vol. 6, 230–245, 1963.

Direct Optimization of Margins Improves Generalization in Combined Classifiers

Llew Mason, Peter Bartlett, Jonathan Baxter
Department of Systems Engineering
Australian National University, Canberra, ACT 0200, Australia
{lmason, bartlett, jon}@syseng.anu.edu.au

Abstract

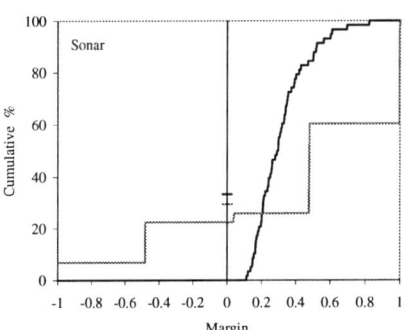

Cumulative training margin distributions for AdaBoost versus our "Direct Optimization Of Margins" (DOOM) algorithm. The dark curve is AdaBoost, the light curve is DOOM. DOOM sacrifices significant training error for improved test error (horizontal marks on margin= 0 line).

1 Introduction

Many learning algorithms for pattern classification minimize some cost function of the training data, with the aim of minimizing error (the probability of misclassifying an example). One example of such a cost function is simply the classifier's error on the training data. Recent results have examined alternative cost functions that provide better error estimates in some cases. For example, results in [Bar98] show that the error of a sigmoid network classifier $f(\cdot)$ is no more than the sample average of the cost function $\text{sgn}(\theta - yf(x))$ (which takes value 1 when $yf(x)$ is no more than θ and 0 otherwise) plus a complexity penalty term that scales as $\|w\|_1/\theta$, where $(x,y) \in X \times \{\pm 1\}$ is a labelled training example, and $\|w\|_1$ is the sum of the magnitudes of the output node weights. The quantity $yf(x)$ is the *margin* of the real-valued function f, and reflects the extent to which $f(x)$ agrees with the label $y \in \{\pm 1\}$. By minimizing squared error, neural network learning algorithms implicitly maximize margins, which may explain their good generalization performance.

More recently, Schapire *et al* [SFBL98] have shown a similar result for convex combinations of classifiers, such as those produced by boosting algorithms. They show that, with high probability over m random examples, every convex combination of classifiers from some finite class H has error satisfying

$$\Pr[yf(x) \leq 0] \leq \mathbf{E}_S\left[\mathrm{sgn}(\theta - yf(x))\right] + O\left(\frac{1}{\sqrt{m}}\left(\frac{\log m \log |H|}{\theta^2} + \log(1/\delta)\right)^{\frac{1}{2}}\right) \quad (1)$$

for all $\theta > 0$, where $\mathbf{E}_S$ denotes the average over the sample S.

One way to think of these results is as a technique for adjusting the effective complexity of the function class by adjusting θ. Large values of θ correspond to low complexity and small values to high complexity. If the learning algorithm were to optimize the parametrized cost function $\mathbf{E}_S\mathrm{sgn}(\theta - yf(x))$ for large values of θ, it would not be able to make fine distinctions between different functions in the class, and so the effective complexity of the class would be reduced. The second term in the error bounds (the regularization term involving the complexity parameter θ and the size of the base hypothesis class H) would be correspondingly reduced. In both the neural network and boosting settings, the learning algorithms do not directly minimize these cost functions; we use different values of the complexity parameter in the cost functions only in explaining their generalization performance.

In this paper, we address the question: what are suitable cost functions for convex combinations of classifiers? In the next section, we give general conditions on parametrized families of cost functions that ensure that they can be used to give error bounds for convex combinations of classifiers. In the remainder of the paper, we investigate learning algorithms that choose the convex coefficients of a combined classifier by minimizing a suitable family of piecewise linear cost functions using gradient descent. Even when the base hypotheses are chosen by the AdaBoost algorithm, and we only use the new cost functions to adjust the convex coefficients, we obtained an improvement on the test error of AdaBoost in all but one of the UC Irvine data sets we used. Margin distribution plots show that in many cases the algorithm achieves these lower errors by sacrificing training error, in the interests of reducing the new cost function.

2 Theory

In this section, we derive an error bound that generalizes the result for convex combinations of classifiers described in the previous section. The result involves a family of *margin cost functions* (functions mapping from the interval $[-1, 1]$ to $\mathbb{R}^+$), indexed by an integer-valued complexity parameter N, which measures the resolution at which we examine the margins. The following definition gives conditions on the margin cost functions that relate the complexity N to the amount by which the margin cost function is larger than the function $\mathrm{sgn}(-yf(x))$. The particular form of this definition is not important. In particular, the functions Ψ_N are only used in the analysis in this section, and will not concern us later in the paper.

Definition 1 *A family* $\{C_N : N \in \mathbb{N}\}$ *of margin cost functions is B-admissible for $B \geq 0$ if for all $N \in \mathbb{N}$ there is an interval $Y \subset \mathbb{R}$ of length no more than B and a function $\Psi_N : [-1, 1] \to Y$ that satisfies*

$$\mathrm{sgn}(-\alpha) \leq \mathbf{E}_{Z \sim Q_{N,\alpha}}\left(\Psi_N(Z)\right) \leq C_N(\alpha)$$

for all $\alpha \in [-1, 1]$, where $\mathbf{E}_{Z \sim Q_{N,\alpha}}(\cdot)$ denotes the expectation when Z is chosen randomly as $Z = (1/N)\sum_{i=1}^{N} Z_i$ with $Z_i \in \{-1, 1\}$ and $\Pr(Z_i = 1) = (1 + \alpha)/2$.

As an example, let $C_N(\alpha) = \mathrm{sgn}(\theta - \alpha) + c$, for $\theta = 1/\sqrt{N}$ and some constant c. This is a B-admissible family of margin cost functions, for suitably large B. (This is exhibited by the functions $\Psi_N(\alpha) = \text{sgn}(\theta/2 - \alpha) + c/2$; the proof involves Chernoff bounds.) Clearly, for larger values of N, the cost functions C_N are closer to the threshold function $\text{sgn}(-\alpha)$. Inequality (1) is implied by the following theorem. In this theorem, $\text{co}(H)$ is the set of convex combinations of functions from H. A similar proof gives the same result with $\text{VCdim}(H) \ln m$ replacing $\ln |H|$.

Theorem 2 *For any B-admissible family $\{C_N : N \in \mathbb{N}\}$ of margin cost functions, any finite hypothesis class H and any distribution P on $X \times \{-1, 1\}$, with probability at least $1 - \delta$ over a random sample S of m labelled examples chosen according to P, every N and every f in $\text{co}(H)$ satisfies*

$$\Pr[yf(x) \leq 0] < \mathbf{E}_S[C_N(yf(x))] + \sqrt{\frac{B^2}{2m}(N \ln |H| + \ln(N(N+1)/\delta))}.$$

Proof Fix N and $f \in \text{co}(H)$, and suppose that $f = \sum_i \alpha_i h_i$ for $h_i \in H$. Define $\text{co}_N(H) = \left\{(1/N) \sum_{j=1}^{N} h_j : h_j \in H\right\}$, and notice that $|\text{co}_N(H)| \leq |H|^N$. As in the proof of (1) in [SFBL98], we show using the probabilistic method that there is a function g in $\text{co}_N(H)$ that closely approximates f. Let Q be the distribution on $\text{co}_N(H)$ corresponding to the average of N independent draws from $\{h_i\}$ according to the distribution $\{\alpha_i\}$, and let $Q_{N,\alpha}$ be the distribution given in Definition 1. Then for any fixed pair x, y, when g is chosen according to Q the distribution of $yg(x)$ is $Q_{N,yf(x)}$. Now, fix the function Ψ_N implied by the B-admissibility condition. By the definition of B-admissibility,

$$\mathbf{E}_{g \sim Q} \mathbf{E}_P [\Psi_N(yg(x))] = \mathbf{E}_P \mathbf{E}_{Z \sim Q_{N,yf(x)}}[\Psi_N(Z)] \geq \mathbf{E}_P \text{sgn}(-yf(x)) = P[yf(x) \leq 0].$$

Similarly, $\mathbf{E}_S[C_N(yf(x))] \geq \mathbf{E}_{g \sim Q} \mathbf{E}_S[\Psi_N(yg(x))]$. Hence, if $\Pr[yf(x) \leq 0] - \mathbf{E}_S[C_N(yf(x))] \geq \epsilon_N$, then $\mathbf{E}_{g \sim Q}[\mathbf{E}_P[\Psi_N(yg(x))] - \mathbf{E}_S[\Psi_N(yg(x))]] \geq \epsilon_N$. Thus,

$$\Pr[\exists f \in \text{co}(H) \colon \Pr[yf(x) \leq 0] \geq \mathbf{E}_S[C_N(yf(x))] + \epsilon_N]$$
$$\leq \Pr[\exists g \in \text{co}_N(H) \colon \mathbf{E}_P[\Psi_N(yg(x))] \geq \mathbf{E}_S[\Psi_N(yg(x))] + \epsilon_N]$$
$$\leq |H|^N \exp(-2m\epsilon_N^2/B^2),$$

where the last inequality follows from the union bound and Hoeffding's inequality. Setting this probability to $\delta_N = \delta/(N(N+1))$, solving for ϵ_N, and summing over values of N completes the proof, since $\sum_{N \in \mathbb{N}} \delta_N = \delta$. □

For the best bounds, we want Ψ_N to satisfy $\mathbf{E}_{Z \sim Q_{N,\alpha}}[\Psi_N(Z)] \geq \text{sgn}(-\alpha)$, but with the difference $\mathbf{E}_{Z \sim Q_{N,\alpha}}[\Psi_N(Z) - \text{sgn}(-\alpha)]$ as small as possible for $\alpha \in [-1, 1]$. One approach would be to minimize the expectation of this difference, for α chosen uniformly in $[-1, 1]$. However, this yields a non-monotone solution for $C_N(\alpha)$. Figure 1a illustrates an example of a monotone B-admissible family; it shows the cost functions $C_N(\alpha) = \mathbf{E}_{Z \sim Q_{N,\alpha}} \Psi_N(Z)$, for $N = 20, 50$ and 200, where $\Psi_N(\alpha) = \text{sgn}(\sqrt{2 \log N/N} - \alpha) + 1/N$.

3 Algorithm

We now consider how to select convex coefficients $w_1, \ldots, w_T$ for a sequence of $\{-1, 1\}$ classifiers $h_1, \ldots, h_T$ so that the combined classifier $f(x) = \sum_{t=1}^{T} w_t h_t(x)$ has small error. In the experiments we used the hypotheses provided by AdaBoost. (The aim was to investigate how useful are the error estimates provided by the cost functions of the previous section.)

If we take Theorem 2 at face value and ignore log terms, the best error bound is obtained if the weights $w_1, \ldots, w_T$ and the complexity N are chosen to minimize

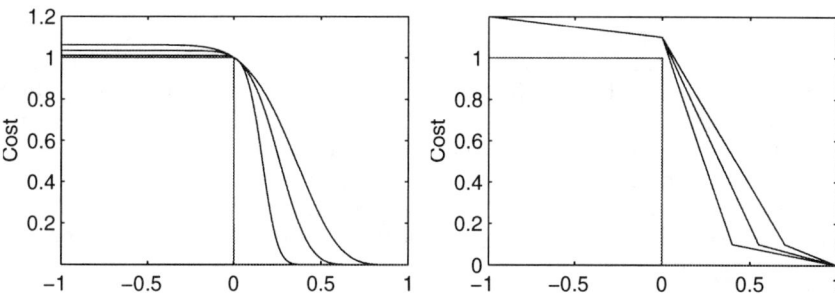

Figure 1: (a) The margin cost functions $C_N(\alpha)$, for $N = 20, 50$ and 200, compared to the function $\text{sgn}(-\alpha)$. Larger values of N correspond to closer approximations to $\text{sgn}(-\alpha)$. (b) Piecewise linear upper bounds on the functions $C_N(\alpha)$, and the function $\text{sgn}(-\alpha)$.

$(1/m) \sum_{i=1}^{m} C_N(y_i f(x_i)) + \kappa \sqrt{N/m}$, where κ is a constant and $\{C_N\}$ is a family of B-admissible cost functions. Although Theorem 2 provides an expression for the constant κ, in practical problems this will almost certainly be an overestimate and so our penalty for even moderately complex models will be too great. To solve this problem, instead of optimizing the average cost of the margins plus a penalty term over all values of the parameter θ, we estimated the optimal value of θ using a cross-validation set. That is, for fixed values of θ in a discrete but fairly dense set we selected weights optimizing the average cost $\frac{1}{m} \sum_{i=1}^{m} C_\theta(y_i f(x_i))$ and then chose the solution with smallest error on an independent cross-validation set.

We considered the use of the cost functions plotted in Figure 1a, but the existence of flat regions caused difficulties for gradient descent approaches. Instead we adopted a piecewise linear family of cost functions C_θ that are linear in the intervals $[-1, 0]$, $[0, \theta]$, and $[\theta, 1]$, and pass through the points $(-1, 1.2)$, $(0, 0.1)$, $(\theta, 0.1)$, and $(1, 0)$, for $\theta \in (0, 1)$. The numbers were chosen to ensure the C_θ are upper bounds on the cost functions of Figure 1a (see Figure 1b). Note that θ plays the role of a complexity parameter, except that in this case smaller values of θ correspond to higher complexity classes.

Even with the restriction to piecewise linear cost functions, the problem of optimizing $\frac{1}{m} \sum_{i=1}^{m} C_\theta(y_i f(x_i))$ is still hard. Fortunately, the nature of this cost function makes it possible to find successful heuristics (which is why we chose it). The algorithm we have devised to optimize the C_θ family of cost functions is called Direct Optimization Of Margins (DOOM). (The pseudo-code of the algorithm is given in the full version [MBB98].) DOOM is basically a form of gradient descent, with two complications: it takes account of the fact that the cost function is not differentiable at 0 and θ, and it ensures that the weight vector lies on the unit ball in l_1. In order to avoid problems with local minima we actually allow the weight vector to lie within the l_1-ball throughout optimization rather than on the l_1-ball. If the weight vector reaches the surface of the l_1-ball and the update direction points out of the l_1-ball, it is projected back to the surface of the l_1-ball.

Observe that the gradient of $\frac{1}{m} \sum_{i=1}^{m} C_\theta(y_i f(x_i))$ is a constant function of the weights $w = (w_1, \ldots, w_T)$ provided no example (x_i, y_i) "crosses" one of the discontinuities at 0 or θ (i.e. provided the margin $y_i f(x_i)$ does not cross 0 or θ). Hence, the central operation of DOOM is to step in the negative gradient direction until an example's margin hits one of the discontinuities (projecting where necessary to ensure the weight vector lies within the l_1 ball). At this point the gradient vector becomes multi-valued (generally two-valued but it can be more). Each of the possible gradient directions is then tested by taking a small step in that direction (a random subset of the gradient directions is chosen if there are too many of them). If none of the directions lead to a decrease in the cost, the examples whose margins lie on discontinuities of the cost function are added to a constraint set E. In subsequent iterations the same stepping procedure above is followed except that the direction step is modified to ensure that the examples in E do not move (i.e. they remain on the discontinuity points of C_θ). That is, the weight vector moves within the subspace defined by the examples in E. If no progress is made in any iteration, the constraint set E is reset to zero. If still no progress is made the procedure terminates.

4 Experiments

We used the following two-class problems from the UC Irvine database [CBM98] : Cleveland Heart Disease, Credit Application, German, Glass, Ionosphere, King Rook vs King Pawn, Pima Indians Diabetes, Sonar, Tic-Tac-Toe, and Wisconsin Breast Cancer. For the sake of simplicity we did not consider multi-class problems. Each data set was randomly separated into train, test and validation sets, with the test and validation sets being equal in size. This was repeated 10 times independently and the results were averaged.

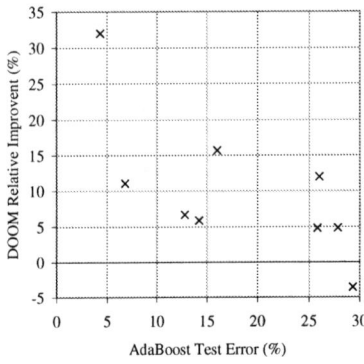

Figure 2: Relative improvement of DOOM over AdaBoost for all examined datasets.

Each experiment consisted of the following steps. First, AdaBoost was run on the training data to produce a sequence of base classifiers and their corresponding weights. In all of the experiments the base classifiers were axis-orthogonal hyperplanes (also known as decision stumps); this choice ensured that the complexity of the class of base classifiers was constant. Boosting was halted when adding a new classifier failed to decrease the error on the validation set. DOOM was then run on the classifiers produced by AdaBoost for a large range of θ values and 1000 random initial weight vectors for each value of θ. The weight vector (and θ value) with minimum misclassification on the validation set was chosen as the final solution.

In some cases the training sets were reduced in size to make overfitting more likely, so that complexity regularization with DOOM could have an effect. (The details are given in the full version [MBB98].) In three of the datasets (Credit Application, Wisconsin Breast Cancer and Pima Indians Diabetes), AdaBoost gained no advantage from using more than a single classifier. In these datasets, the number of classifiers was chosen so that the validation error was reasonably stable.

A comparison between the test errors generated by AdaBoost and DOOM is shown in Figure 2. In only one data set did DOOM produce a classifier which performed worse than AdaBoost in terms of test error; for most data sets DOOM's test error was a significant improvement over AdaBoost's.

Figure 3 shows cumulative training margin distribution graphs for four of the datasets for both AdaBoost and DOOM (with optimal θ chosen by cross-validation). For a given margin the value on the curve corresponds to the proportion of training examples with margin no more than this value. The test errors for both algorithms are also shown for comparison, as short horizontal lines on the vertical axis.

The margin distributions show that the value of the minimum training margin has no real impact on generalization performance. (See also [Bre97] and [GS98].) As

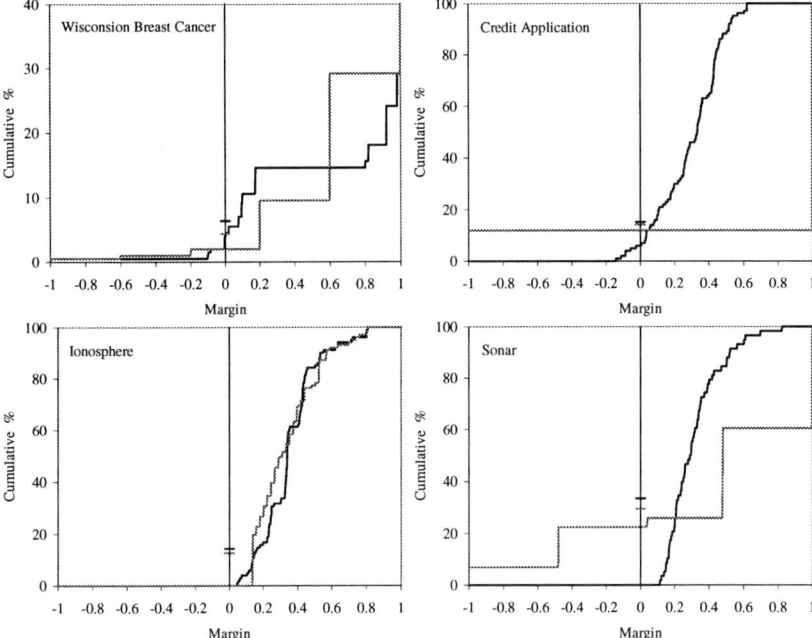

Figure 3: Cumulative training margin distributions for four datasets. The dark curve is AdaBoost, the light curve is DOOM with θ selected by cross-validation. The test errors for both algorithms are marked on the vertical axis at margin 0.

can be seen in Figure 3 (Credit Application and Sonar data sets), the generalization performance of the combined classifier produced by DOOM can be as good as or better than that of the classifier produced by AdaBoost, despite having dramatically worse minimum training margin. Conversely, Figure 3 (Ionosphere data set) shows that improved generalization performance can be associated with an improved minimum margin.

The margin distributions also show that there is a balance to be found between training error and complexity (as measured by θ). DOOM is willing to sacrifice training error in order to reduce complexity and thereby obtain a better margin distribution. For instance, in Figure 3 (Sonar data set), DOOM's training error is over 20% while AdaBoost's is 0%, but DOOM's test error is 5% less than that of AdaBoost's. The reason for this success can be seen in Figure 4, which illustrates the changes in the cost function, training error, and test error as a function of θ. The optimal complexity for this data set is low (corresponding to a large optimal θ). In this case, a reduction in complexity is more important to generalization error than a reduction in training error.

5 Conclusion

In this paper we have addressed the question: what are suitable cost functions for convex combinations of base hypotheses? For general families of cost functions that are functions of the *margin* of a sample, we proved (Theorem 2) that the error of a convex combination is no more than the sample average of the cost function plus a regularization term involving the complexity of the cost function and the size of the base hypothesis class.

We constructed a piecewise linear family of cost functions satisfying the conditions of Theorem 2 and presented a heuristic algorithm (DOOM) for optimizing the sample

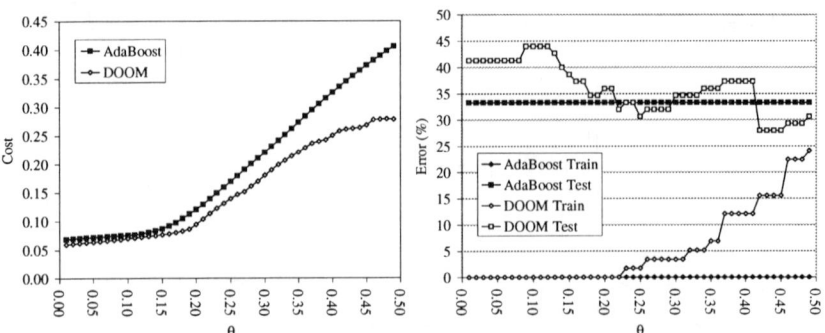

Figure 4: Sonar data set. **Left:** Plot of cost ($\frac{1}{m}\sum_{i=1}^{m} C_\theta(y_i f(x_i))$) against θ for AdaBoost and DOOM. **Right:** Plot of training and test error against θ.

average of the cost.

We ran experiments on several of the datasets in the UC Irvine database, in which AdaBoost was used to generate a set of base classifiers and then DOOM was used to find the optimal convex combination of those classifiers. In all but one case the convex combination generated by DOOM had lower test error than AdaBoost's combination. Margin distribution plots show that in many cases DOOM achieves these lower test errors by sacrificing training error, in the interests of reducing the new cost function. The margin plots also show that the size of the minimum margin is not relevant to generalization performance.

Acknowledgments

Thanks to Yoav Freund, Wee Sun Lee and Rob Schapire for helpful comments and suggestions. This research was supported in part by a grant from the Australian Research Council. Jonathan Baxter was supported by an Australian Research Council Fellowship and Llew Mason was supported by an Australian Postgraduate Award.

References

[Bar98] P. L. Bartlett. The sample complexity of pattern classification with neural networks: the size of the weights is more important than the size of the network. *IEEE Transactions on Information Theory*, 44(2):525–536, 1998.

[Bre97] L. Breiman. Prediction games and arcing algorithms. Technical Report 504, Department of Statistics, University of California, Berkeley, 1997.

[CBM98] E. Keogh C. Blake and C.J. Merz. UCI repository of machine learning databases, 1998. http://www.ics.uci.edu/~mlearn/MLRepository.html.

[GS98] A. Grove and D. Schuurmans. Boosting in the limit: Maximizing the margin of learned ensembles. In *Proceedings of the Fifteenth National Conference on Artificial Intelligence*, pages 692–699, 1998.

[MBB98] L. Mason, P. L. Bartlett, and J. Baxter. Improved generalization through explicit optimization of margins. Technical report, Department of Systems Engineering, Australian National University, 1998. (Available from http://syseng.anu.edu.au/lsg).

[SFBL98] R. E. Schapire, Y. Freund, P. L. Bartlett, and W. S. Lee. Boosting the margin: a new explanation for the effectiveness of voting methods. *Annals of Statistics*, (to appear), 1998.

On the optimality of incremental neural network algorithms

Ron Meir*
Department of Electrical Engineering
Technion, Haifa 32000, Israel
rmeir@dumbo.technion.ac.il

Vitaly Maiorov[†]
Department of Mathematics
Technion, Haifa 32000, Israel
maiorov@tx.technion.ac.il

Abstract

We study the approximation of functions by two-layer feedforward neural networks, focusing on incremental algorithms which greedily add units, estimating single unit parameters at each stage. As opposed to standard algorithms for fixed architectures, the optimization at each stage is performed over a small number of parameters, mitigating many of the difficult numerical problems inherent in high-dimensional non-linear optimization. We establish upper bounds on the error incurred by the algorithm, when approximating functions from the Sobolev class, thereby extending previous results which only provided rates of convergence for functions in certain convex hulls of functional spaces. By comparing our results to recently derived lower bounds, we show that the greedy algorithms are nearly optimal. Combined with estimation error results for greedy algorithms, a strong case can be made for this type of approach.

1 Introduction and background

A major problem in the application of neural networks to real world problems is the excessively long time required for training large networks of a fixed architecture. Moreover, theoretical results establish the intractability of such training in the worst case [9][4]. Additionally, the problem of determining the architecture and size of the network required to solve a certain task is left open. Due to these problems, several authors have considered incremental algorithms for constructing the network by the addition of hidden units, and estimation of each unit's parameters incrementally. These approaches possess two desirable attributes: first, the optimization is done step-wise, so that only a small number of parameters need to be optimized at each stage; and second, the structure of the network

---

*This work was supported in part by the a grant from the Israel Science Foundation

[†]The author was partially supported by the center for Absorption in Science, Ministry of Immigrant Absorption, State of Israel.

is established concomitantly with the learning, rather than specifying it in advance. However, until recently these algorithms have been rather heuristic in nature, as no guaranteed performance bounds had been established. Note that while there has been a recent surge of interest in these types of algorithms, they in fact date back to work done in the early seventies (see [3] for a historical survey).

The first theoretical result establishing performance bounds for incremental approximations in Hilbert space, was given by Jones [8]. This work was later extended by Barron [2], and applied to neural network approximation of functions characterized by certain conditions on their Fourier coefficients. The work of Barron has been extended in two main directions. First, Lee et al. [10] have considered approximating general functions using Hilbert space techniques, while Donahue et al. [7] have provided powerful extensions of Jones' and Barron's results to general Banach spaces. One of the most impressive results of the latter work is the demonstration that iterative algorithms can, in many cases, achieve nearly optimal rates of convergence, when approximating convex hulls.

While this paper is concerned mainly with issues of approximation, we comment that it is highly relevant to the statistical problem of learning from data in neural networks. First, Lee et al. [10] give estimation error bounds for algorithms performing incremental optimization with respect to the training error. Under certain regularity conditions, they are able to achieve rates of convergence comparable to those obtained by the much more computationally demanding algorithm of empirical error minimization. Moreover, it is well known that upper bounds on the approximation error are needed in order to obtain performance bounds, both for parametric and nonparametric estimation, where the latter is achieved using the method of complexity regularization. Finally, as pointed out by Donahue et al. [7], lower bounds on the approximation error are crucial in establishing worst case speed limitations for learning.

The main contribution of this paper is as follows. For functions belonging to the Sobolev class (see definition below), we establish, under appropriate conditions, near-optimal rates of convergence for the incremental approach, and obtain explicit bounds on the parameter values of the network. The latter bounds are often crucial for establishing estimation error rates. In contrast to the work in [10] and [7], we characterize approximation rates for functions belonging to standard smoothness classes, such as the Sobolev class. The former work establishes rates of convergence with respect to the convex hulls of certain subsets of functions, which do not relate in a any simple way to standard functional classes (such as Lipschitz, Sobolev, Hölder, etc.). As far as we are aware, the results reported here are the first to report on such bounds for incremental neural network procedures. A detailed version of this work, complete with the detailed proofs, is available in [13].

2 Problem statement

We make use of the nomenclature and definitions from [7]. Let $\mathcal{H}$ be a Banach space of functions with norm $\|\cdot\|$. For concreteness we assume henceforth that the norm is given by the L_q norm, $1 < q < \infty$, denoted by $\|\cdot\|_q$. Let $\lin_n \mathcal{H}$ consist of all sums of the form $\sum_{i=1}^n a_i g_i$, $g_i \in \mathcal{H}$ and arbitrary a_i, and $\co_n \mathcal{H}$ is the set of such sums with $a_i \in [0, 1]$ and $\sum_{i=1}^n a_i = 1$. The distances, measured in the L_q norm, from a function f are given by

$$\dist(\lin_n \mathcal{H}, f) = \inf \{\|h - f\|_q : h \in \lin_n \mathcal{H}\},$$
$$\dist(\co_n \mathcal{H}, f) = \inf \{\|h - f\|_q : h \in \co_n \mathcal{H}\}.$$

The *linear span* of $\mathcal{H}$ is given by $\lin \mathcal{H} = \cup_n \lin_n \mathcal{H}$, while the *convex-hull* of $\mathcal{H}$ is $\co \mathcal{H} = \cup_n \co_n \mathcal{H}$. We follow standard notation and denote closures of sets by a bar, e.g. $\overline{\co \mathcal{H}}$ is the closure of the convex hull of $\mathcal{H}$. In this work we focus on the special case where

$$\mathcal{H} = \mathcal{H}_\eta \triangleq \left\{ g : g(x) = c\sigma(a^T x + b), |c| \leq \eta, \|\sigma(\cdot)\|_q \leq 1 \right\}, \tag{1}$$

corresponding to the basic building blocks of multilayer neural networks. The restriction $\|\sigma(\cdot)\| \leq 1$ is not very demanding as many sigmoidal functions can be expressed as a sum of functions of bounded norm. It should be obvious that $\lin_n \mathcal{H}_\eta$ corresponds to a two-layer neural network with a linear output unit and σ-activation functions in the single hidden layer, while $\co_n \mathcal{H}_\eta$ is equivalent to a restricted form of such a network, where restrictions are placed on the hidden-to-output weights. In terms of the definitions introduced above, the by now well known property of universal function approximation over compacta can be stated as $\overline{\lin \mathcal{H}} = C(M)$, where $C(M)$ is the class of continuous real valued functions defined over M, a compact subset of $\mathbf{R}^d$. A necessary and sufficient condition for this has been established by Leshno et al. [11], and essentially requires that $\sigma(\cdot)$ be locally integrable and non-polynomial. We comment that if $\eta = \infty$ in (1), and c is unrestricted in sign, then $\co \mathcal{H}_\infty = \lin \mathcal{H}_\infty$. The distinction becomes important only if $\eta < \infty$, in which case $\co \mathcal{H}_\eta \subset \lin \mathcal{H}_\eta$.

For the purpose of incremental approximation, it turns out to be useful to consider the convex hull $\co \mathcal{H}$, rather than the usual linear span, as powerful algorithms and performance bounds can be developed in this case. In this context several authors have considered bounds for the approximation of a function f belonging to $\overline{\co \mathcal{H}}$ by sequences of functions belonging to $\co_n \mathcal{H}$. However, it is not clear in general how well convex hulls of *bounded* functions approximate general functions. One contribution of this work is to show how one may control the rate of growth of the bound η in (1), so that general functions, belonging to certain smoothness classes (e.g. Sobolev), may be well approximated. In fact, we show that the incremental approximation scheme described below achieves nearly optimal approximation error for functions in the Sobolev space.

Following Donahue et al. [7], we consider ε-greedy algorithms. Let $\varepsilon = (\varepsilon_1, \varepsilon_2, \ldots)$ be a positive sequence, and similarly for $(\alpha_1, \alpha_2, \ldots)$, $0 < \alpha_n < 1$. A sequence of functions $h_1, h_2, \ldots$ is ε-greedy with respect to f if for $n = 0, 1, 2, \ldots$,

$$\|h_{n+1} - f\|_q < \inf \{\|\alpha_n h_n + (1 - \alpha_n) g - f\|_q : g \in \mathcal{H}_\eta\} + \varepsilon_n, \qquad (2)$$

where we set $h_0 = 0$. For simplicity we set $\alpha_n = (n-1)/n$, although other schemes are also possible. It should be clear that at each stage n, the function h_n belongs to $\co_n \mathcal{H}_\eta$. Observe also that at each step, the infimum is taken with respect to $g \in \mathcal{H}_\eta$, the function h_n being fixed. In terms of neural networks, this implies that the optimization over each hidden unit parameters (a, b, c) is performed independently of the others. We note in passing, that while this greatly facilitates the optimization process in practice, no theoretical guarantee can be made as to the convexity of the single-node error function (see [1] for counter-examples). The variables ε_n are slack variables, allowing the extra freedom of only approximate minimization. In this paper we do not optimize over α_n, but rather fix a sequence in advance, forfeiting some generality at the price of a simpler presentation. In any event, the rates we obtain are unchanged by such a restriction.

In the sequel we consider ε-greedy approximations of smooth functions belonging to the Sobolev class of functions,

$$W_2^r = \left\{ f : \max_{0 \leq \vec{k} \leq r} \|\mathcal{D}^{\vec{k}} f\|_2 \leq 1 \right\},$$

where $\vec{k} = (k_1, \ldots, k_d)$, $k_i \geq 0$ and $|\vec{k}| = k_1 + \cdots k_d$. Here $\mathcal{D}^{\vec{k}}$ is the partial derivative operator of order $\vec{k}$. All functions are defined over a compact domain $K \subset \mathbf{R}^d$.

3 Upper bound for the L_2 norm

First, we consider the approximation of functions from W_2^r using the L_2 norm. In distinction with other L_q norms, there exists an inner product in this case, defined through

$(\cdot, \cdot) = \|\cdot\|_2^2$. This simplification is essential to the proof in this case.

We begin by recalling a result from [12], demonstrating that any function in L_2 may be exactly expressed as a *convex* integral representation of the form

$$f(x) = Q \int h(x,\theta) w(\theta) d\theta, \tag{3}$$

where $0 < Q < \infty$ depends on f, and $w(\theta)$ is a probability density function (pdf) with respect to the multi-dimensional variable θ. Thus, we may write $f(x) = Q E_w\{h(x,\Theta)\}$, where E_w denotes the expectation operator with respect to the pdf w. Moreover, it was shown in [12], using the Radon and wavelet transforms, that the function $h(x,\theta)$ can be taken to be a ridge function with $\theta = (a,b,c)$ and $h(x,\theta) = c\sigma(a^T x + b)$.

In the case of neural networks, this type of convex representation was first exploited by Barron in [2], assuming f belongs to a class of functions characterized by certain moment conditions on their Fourier transforms. Later, Delyon et al. [6] and Maiorov and Meir [12] extended Barron's results to the case of wavelets and neural networks, respectively, obtaining rates of convergence for functions in the Sobolev class.

The basic idea at this point is to generate an approximation, $h_n(x)$, based on n draws of random variables $\Theta^n = \{\Theta_1, \Theta_2, \ldots, \Theta_n\}$, $\Theta_i \sim w(\cdot)$, resulting in the random function

$$h_n(x; \Theta^n) = \frac{Q}{n} \sum_{i=1}^n h(x, \Theta_i). \tag{4}$$

Throughout the paper we conform to standard notation, and denote random variables by uppercase letters, as in Θ, and their realization by lower case letters, as in θ. Let $w^n = \prod_{i=1}^n w_i$ represent the product pdf for $\{\Theta_1, \ldots, \Theta_n\}$. Our first result demonstrates that, on the average, the above procedure leads to good approximation of functions belonging to W_2^r.

Theorem 3.1 *Let $K \subset \mathbf{R}^d$ be a compact set. Then for any $f \in W_2^r$, $n > 0$ and $\varepsilon > 0$ there exists a constant $c > 0$, such that*

$$E_{w^n} \|f - h_n(x; \Theta^n)\|_2 \leq c n^{-r/d + \varepsilon}, \tag{5}$$

where $Q < c n^{(1/2 - r/d)_+}$, and $(x)_+ = \max(0, x)$.

The implication of the upper bound on the expected value, is that there exists a set of values $\theta^{*,n} = \{\theta_1^*, \ldots, \theta_n^*\}$, for which the rate (5) can be achieved. Moreover, as long as the functions $h(x, \theta_i)$ in (4) are bounded in the L_2 norm, a bound on Q implies a bound on the size of the function h_n itself.

Proof sketch The proof proceeds by expressing f as the sum of two functions, f_1 and f_2. The function f_1 is the best approximation to f from the class of multi-variate splines of degree r. From [12] we know that there exist parameters θ^n such that $\|f_1(\cdot) - h_n(\cdot, \theta^n)\|_2 \leq c n^{-r/d}$. Moreover, using the results of [5] it can be shown that $\|f_2\|_2 \leq c n^{-r/d}$. Using these two observations, together with the triangle inequality $\|f - h_n\|_2 \leq \|f_1 - h_n\|_2 + \|f_2\|_2$, yields the desired result. ∎

Next, we show that given the approximation rates attained in Theorem 3.1, the same rates may be obtained using an ε-greedy algorithm. Moreover, since in [12] we have established the optimality of the upper bound (up to a logarithmic factor in n), we conclude that greedy approximations can indeed yield near-optimal performance, while at the same time being much more attractive computationally. In fact, in this section we use a weaker algorithm, which does not perform a full minimization at each stage.

Incremental algorithm: ($q = 2$) Let $\alpha_n = 1 - 1/n$, $\bar{\alpha}_n = 1 - \alpha_n = 1/n$.

1. Let θ_1^* be chosen to satisfy
$$\|f(x) - Qh(x, \theta_1^*)\|_2^2 = \mathrm{E}_{w_1}\left\{\|f(x) - Qh(x, \Theta_1)\|_2^2\right\}.$$

2. Assume that $\theta_1^*, \theta_2^*, \ldots, \theta_{n-1}^*$ have been generated. Select θ_n^* to obey
$$\left\| f(x) - \frac{Q\alpha_n}{n-1}\sum_{i=1}^{n-1} h(x, \theta_i^*) - \bar{\alpha}_n Q h(x, \theta_n^*) \right\|_2^2$$
$$= \mathrm{E}_{w_n}\left\{ \left\| f(x) - \frac{Q\alpha_n}{n-1}\sum_{i=1}^{n-1} h(x, \theta_i^*) - \bar{\alpha}_n Q h(x, \Theta_n) \right\|_2^2 \right\}.$$

Define
$$\mathrm{E}_n^{(i)} \triangleq \mathrm{E}_{w_n}\left\{ \left\| f(x) - \frac{Q\alpha_n}{n-1}\sum_{i=1}^{n-1} h(x, \theta_i^*) - \bar{\alpha}_n Q h(x, \Theta_n) \right\|_2^2 \right\},$$
which measures the error incurred at the n-th stage by this incremental procedure. The main result of this section then follows.

Theorem 3.2 *For any $f \in W_2^r$ and $\varepsilon > 0$, the error of the incremental algorithm above is bounded as*
$$\mathrm{E}_n^{(i)} \leq cn^{-\frac{r}{d}+\varepsilon},$$
for some finite constant c.

Proof sketch The claim will be established upon showing that
$$\mathrm{E}_n^{(i)} \triangleq \mathrm{E}_{w^n}\left\{ \left\| f(x) - \frac{Q}{n}\sum_{i=1}^{n} h(x, \Theta_i) \right\|_2^2 \right\}, \tag{6}$$
namely, the error incurred by the incremental procedure is identical to that of the non-incremental one described preceding Theorem 3.1. The result will then follow upon using Hölder's inequality and the upper bound (5) for the r.h.s. of (6). The remaining details are straightforward, but tedious, and can be found in the full paper [13]. ∎

4 Upper bound for general L_q norms

Having established rates of convergence for incremental approximation of W_2^r in the L_2 norm, we move now to general L_q norms. First, note that the proof of Theorem 3.2 relies heavily on the existence on an inner product. This useful tool is no longer available in the case of general Banach spaces such as L_q. In order to extend the results to the latter norm, we need to use more advanced ideas from the theory of the geometry of Banach spaces. In particular, we will make use of recent results from the work of Donahue et al. [7]. Second, we must keep in mind that the approximation of the Sobolev space W_2^r using the L_q norm only makes sense if the *embedding condition $r/d > (1/2 - 1/q)_+$* holds, since otherwise the L_q norm may be infinite (the embedding condition guarantees its finiteness; see [14] for details).

We first present the main result of this section, followed by a sketch of the proof. The full details of the rather technical proof can be found in [13]. Note that in this case we need to use the greedy algorithm (2) rather than the algorithm of Section 3.

Theorem 4.1 *Let the embedding condition $r/d > (1/2 - 1/q)_+$ hold for $1 < q < \infty$, $0 < r < r^*$, $r^* = \frac{d}{2} + \left(\frac{1}{2} - \frac{1}{q}\right)_+$ and assume that $\|h(\cdot, \theta)\|_q \leq 1$ for all θ. Then for any $f \in W_2^r$ and $\epsilon > 0$*

$$\|f(\cdot) - h_n(\cdot, \theta^n)\|_q \leq cn^{-\gamma+\varepsilon},$$

where

$$\gamma = \begin{cases} \frac{\frac{r}{d} - \left(\frac{1}{2} - \frac{1}{q}\right)}{\frac{1}{d} + \frac{2}{q} - \frac{2}{qd}} & q > 2, \\ \frac{r}{d} & q \leq 2, \end{cases} \tag{7}$$

$c = c(r, d, K)$ and $h_n(\cdot, \theta^n)$ is obtained via the incremental greedy algorithm (2) with $\varepsilon_n = 0$.

Proof sketch The main idea in the proof of Theorem 4.1 is a two-part approximation scheme. First, based on [13], we show that any $f \in W_2^r$ may be well approximated by functions in the convex class $\text{co}_n(\mathcal{H}_\eta)$ for an appropriate value of η (see Lemma 5.2 in [13]), where H_η is defined in (1). Then, it is argued, making use of results from [7] (in particular, using Corollary 3.6), that an incremental greedy algorithm can be used to approximate the closure of the class $\text{co}(H_\eta)$ by the class $\text{co}_n(\mathcal{H}_\eta)$. The proof is completed by using the triangle inequality. The proof along the above lines is done for the case $q > 2$. In the case $q \leq 2$, a simple use of the Hölder inequality in the form $\|f\|_q \leq |K|^{1/q-1/2}\|f\|_2$, where $|K|$ is the volume of the region K, yields the desired result, which, given the lower bounds in [12], is nearly optimal. ∎

5 Discussion

We have presented a theoretical analysis of an increasingly popular approach to incremental learning in neural networks. Extending previous results, we have shown that near-optimal rates of convergence may be obtained for approximating functions in the Sobolev class W_2^r. These results extend and clarify previous work dealing solely with the approximation of functions belonging to the closure of convex hulls of certain sets of functions. Moreover, we have given explicit bounds on the parameters used in the algorithm, and shown that the restriction to $\text{co}_n \mathcal{H}_\eta$ is not too stringent. In the case $q \leq 2$ the rates obtained are as good (up to logarithmic factors) to the rates obtained for general spline functions, which are known to be optimal for approximating Sobolev spaces. The rates obtained in the case $q > 2$ are sub-optimal as compared to spline functions, but can be shown to be provably better than any *linear* approach. In any event, we have shown that the rates obtained are equal, up to logarithmic factors, to approximation from $\text{lin}_n \mathcal{H}_\eta$, when the size of η is chosen appropriately, implying that positive input-to-output weights suffice for approximation. An open problem remaining at this point is to demonstrate whether incremental algorithms for neural network construction can be shown to be optimal for every value of q. In fact, this is not even known at this stage for neural network approximation in general.

References

[1] P. Auer, M. Herbster, and M. Warmuth. Exponentially many local minima for single neurons. In D.S. Touretzky, M.C. Mozer, and M.E. Hasselmo, editors, *Advances in Neural Information Processing Systems 8*, pages 316–322. MIT Press, 1996.

[2] A.R. Barron. Universal approximation bound for superpositions of a sigmoidal function. *IEEE Trans. Inf. Th.*, 39:930–945, 1993.

[3] A.R. Barron and R.L. Barron. Statistical learning networks: a unifying view. In E. Wegman, editor, *Computing Science and Statistics: Proceedings 20th Symposium Interface*, pages 192–203, Washington D.C., 1988. Amer. Statis. Assoc.

[4] A. Blum and R. Rivest. Training a 3-node neural net is np-complete. In D.S. Touretzky, editor, *Advances in Neural Information Processing Systems I*, pages 494–501. Morgan Kaufmann, 1989.

[5] C. de Boor and G. Fix. Spline approximation by quasi-interpolation. *J. Approx. Theory*, 7:19–45, 1973.

[6] B. Delyon, A. Juditsky, and A. Benveniste. Accuracy nalysis for wavelet approximations. *IEEE Transaction on Neural Networks*, 6:332–348, 1995.

[7] M.J. Donahue, L. Gurvits, C. Darken, and E. Sontag. Rates of convex approximation in non-hilbert spaces. *Constructive Approx.*, 13:187–220, 1997.

[8] L. Jones. A simple lemma on greedy approximation in Hilbert space and convergence rate for projection pursuit regression and neural network training. *Ann. Statis.*, 20:608–613, 1992.

[9] S. Judd. *Neural Network Design and the Complexity of Learning*. MIT Press, Boston, USA, 1990.

[10] W.S. Lee, P.S. Bartlett, and R.C. Williamson. Efficient Agnostic learning of neural networks with bounded fan-in. *IEEE Trans. Inf. Theory*, 42(6):2118–2132, 1996.

[11] M. Leshno, V. Lin, A. Pinkus, and S. Schocken. Multilayer Feedforward Networks with a Nonpolynomial Activation Function Can Approximate any Function. *Neural Networks*, 6:861–867, 1993.

[12] V.E. Maiorov and R. Meir. On the near optimality of the stochastic approximation of smooth functions by neural networks. Technical Report CC-223, Technion, Department of Electrical Engineering, November 1997. Submitted to *Advances in Computational Mathematics*.

[13] R. Meir and V. Maiorov. On the optimality of neural network approximation using incremental algorithms. *Submitted for publication*, October 1998. ftp://dumbo.technion.ac.il/pub/PAPERS/incremental.pdf.

[14] H. Triebel. *Theory of Function Spaces*. Birkhauser, Basel, 1983.

General Bounds on Bayes Errors for Regression with Gaussian Processes

Manfred Opper
Neural Computing Research Group
Dept. of Electronic Engineering
and Computer Science,
Aston University,
Birmingham, B4 7ET
United Kingdom
opperm@aston.ac.uk

Francesco Vivarelli
Centro Ricerche Ambientali
Montecatini,

via Ciro Menotti, 48
48023 Marina di Ravenna,
Italy
fvivarelli@cramont.it

Abstract

Based on a simple convexity lemma, we develop bounds for different types of Bayesian prediction errors for regression with Gaussian processes. The basic bounds are formulated for a fixed training set. Simpler expressions are obtained for sampling from an input distribution which equals the weight function of the covariance kernel, yielding asymptotically tight results. The results are compared with numerical experiments.

1 Introduction

Nonparametric Bayesian models which are based on Gaussian priors on function spaces are becoming increasingly popular in the Neural Computation Community (see e.g.[2, 3, 4, 7, 1]). Since the model classes considered in this approach are infinite dimensional, the application of Vapnik - Chervonenkis type of methods to determine bounds for the learning curves is nontrivial and has not been performed so far (to our knowledge). In these methods, the target function to be learnt is fixed and input data are drawn independently at random from a fixed (unknown) distribution. The approach of this paper is different. Here, we assume that the *target* is actually drawn at random from a known prior distribution, and we are interested in developing simple bounds on the average prediction performance (with respect to the prior) which hold for a fixed set of inputs. Only at a later stage, an average over the input distribution is made.

2 Regression with Gaussian processes

To explain the Gaussian process scenario for regression problems [4], we assume that observations $y \in R$ at input points $x \in R^D$ are corrupted values of a function $\theta(x)$ by an independent Gaussian noise with variance σ^2. The appropriate stochastic model is given by the likelihood

$$p_\theta(y|x) = \frac{e^{-\frac{(y-\theta(x))^2}{2\sigma^2}}}{\sqrt{2\pi\sigma^2}}. \tag{1}$$

The goal of a learner is to give an estimate of the function $\theta(x)$, based on a set of observed example data $D_t = ((x_1, y_1), \ldots, (x_t, y_t))$. As the prior information about the unknown function $\theta(x)$ we asume that θ is a realization of a Gaussian random field with zero mean and covariance

$$C(x, x') = \mathbb{E}[\theta(x)\theta(x')]. \tag{2}$$

It is useful to expand the random functions as

$$\theta(x) = \sum_{k=0}^{\infty} w_k \phi_k(x) \tag{3}$$

in a complete set of deterministic functions $\phi_k(x)$ with random Gaussian coefficients w_k. As is well known, if the ϕ_k are chosen as orthonormal eigenfunctions of the integral equation

$$\int C(x, x')\phi_k(x')p(x')dx' = \lambda_k \phi_k(x), \tag{4}$$

with eigenvalues λ_k and a nonnegative weight function $p(x)$, the a priori statistics of w_l is simple. They are *independent* Gaussian variables which satisfy $\mathbb{E}[w_k w_l] = \lambda_k \delta_{kl}$.

3 Prediction and Bayes error

Usually, the posterior mean of $\theta(x)$ is chosen as the prediction $\hat\theta(x)$ on a new point x based on a dataset $D_n = (x_1, y_1), \ldots, (x_n, y_n)$. Its explicit form can be easily derived by using the expansion $\hat\theta(x) = \sum_k \hat w_k \phi_k(x)$, and the fact that for Gaussian random variables, their mean coincides with their most probable value. Maximizing the log posterior, with respect to the w_k, one finds for the infinite dimensional vector $\hat w \doteq (w_k)_{k=0,\ldots,\infty}$ the result $\hat w = (\sigma^2 I + \Lambda V)^{-1} b$ where $V_{kl} = \sum_{i=1}^n \phi_k(x_i)\phi_l(x_i)$ $\Lambda_{kl} = \lambda_k \delta_{kl}$ and $b_k = \sum_{i=1}^n \lambda_k y_i \phi_k(x_i)$ Fixing the set of inputs x^n, the Bayesian prediction error at a point x is given by

$$\varepsilon(x|x^n) \doteq \mathbb{E}\left(\theta(x) - \hat\theta(x)\right)^2 \tag{5}$$

Evaluating (5) yields, after some work, the expression

$$\varepsilon(x|x^n) = \sigma^2 \operatorname{Tr}\left\{(\sigma^2 I + \Lambda V)^{-1} \Lambda U(x)\right\} \tag{6}$$

with the matrix $U_{kl}(x) = \phi_k(x)\phi_l(x)$. U has the properties that $\frac{1}{n}\sum_{i=1}^n U(x_i) = V$ and $\int dx\, p(x)U(x) = I$. We define the Bayesian *training error* as the empirical average of the error (5) at the n datapoints of the training set and the Bayesian *generalization error* as the average error over all x weighted by the function $p(x)$. We get

$$\varepsilon_t(x^n) = \frac{1}{n}\operatorname{Tr}\left\{\Lambda V \left(I + \Lambda V/\sigma^2\right)^{-1}\right\} \tag{7}$$

$$\varepsilon_g(x^n) = \operatorname{Tr}\left\{\Lambda \left(I + \Lambda V/\sigma^2\right)^{-1}\right\}. \tag{8}$$

4 Entropic error

In order to understand the next type of error [9], we assume that the data arrive sequentially, one after the other. The *predictive distribution* after $t-1$ training data at the new input x_t is the posterior expectation of the likelihood (1), i.e.

$$\hat{P}(y|x_t, D_{t-1}) = \mathbb{E}[P_\theta(y|x_t)|D_{t-1}].$$

Let L_t as the Bayesian average of the relative entropy (or Kullback Leibler divergence) between the predictive distribution and the true distribution P_θ from which the data were generated, i.e. $L_t = \mathbb{E}\left[D_{KL}\left(P_\theta || \hat{P}\right)\right]$. It can also be shown that $L_t = \frac{1}{2}\ln\left(1 + \frac{\varepsilon_g(x_t|x^{t-1})}{\sigma^2}\right)$. Hence, when the prediction error is small, we will have

$$L_t \approx \frac{1}{2} \frac{\varepsilon_g(x_t|x^{t-1})}{\sigma^2}. \tag{9}$$

The *cumulative* entropic error $E_e(x^n)$ is defined by summing up all the losses (which gives an integrated learning curve) from $t=1$ up to time n and one can show that

$$E(x_n) = \sum_{t=1}^{n} L_t(x_t, D_{t-1}) = \mathbb{E}D_{KL}\left(P_\theta^n || \hat{P}^n\right) = \frac{1}{2}\operatorname{Tr}\ln\left(I + \Lambda V/\sigma^2\right) \tag{10}$$

where $P_\theta^n = \prod_{i=1}^{n} P_\theta(y_i|x_i)$ and $\hat{P}^n = \mathbb{E}[\prod_{i=1}^{n} P_\theta(y_i|x_i)]$. The first equality may be found e.g. in [9], and the second follows from direct calculation.

5 Bounds for fixed set of inputs

In order to get bounds on (7),(8) and (10), we use a lemma, which has been used in Quantum Statistical Mechanics to get bounds on the free energy. The lemma (for the special function $f(x) = e^{-\beta x}$) was proved by Sir Rudolf Peierls in 1938 [10]. In order to keep the paper self contained, we have included the proof in the appendix.

Lemma 1 *Let H be a real symmetric matrix and f a convex real function. Then $\operatorname{Tr} f(H) \geq \sum_k f(H_{kk})$.*

By noting, that for concave functions the bound goes in the other direction, we immediately get

$$\varepsilon_t \leq \frac{\sigma^2}{n}\sum_k \frac{\lambda_k V_{kk}}{\sigma^2 + \lambda_k V_{kk}} \leq \sigma^2 \sum_k \frac{\lambda_k v_k}{\sigma^2 + n\lambda_k v_k} \tag{11}$$

$$\varepsilon_g \geq \sum_k \frac{\sigma^2 \lambda_k}{\sigma^2 + \lambda_k V_{kk}} \geq \sum_k \frac{\sigma^2 \lambda_k}{\sigma^2 + n\lambda_k v_k} \tag{12}$$

$$E(x^n) \leq \frac{1}{2}\sum_k \ln\left(1 + V_{kk}\lambda_k/\sigma^2\right) \leq \frac{1}{2}\sum_k \ln\left(1 + nv_k\lambda_k/\sigma^2\right) \tag{13}$$

where in the rightmost inequalities, we assume that all n inputs are in a compact region $\mathcal{D}$, and we define $v_k = \sup_{x \in \mathcal{D}} \phi_k^2(x)$. [1]

---

[1] The entropic case may also be proved by Hadamard's inequality.

6 Average case bounds

Next, we assume that the input data are drawn at random and denote by $\langle \ldots \rangle$ the expectations with respect to the distribution. *We do not have to assume independence here, but only the fact that all marginal distributions for the n inputs are identical!* Using Jensen's inequality

$$\varepsilon_t = \langle \varepsilon_t(x^n) \rangle \leq \sigma^2 \sum_k \frac{\lambda_k u_k}{\sigma^2 + n\lambda_k u_k} \tag{14}$$

$$\varepsilon_g = \langle \varepsilon_g(x^n) \rangle \geq \sum_k \frac{\sigma^2 \lambda_k}{\sigma^2 + n\lambda_k u_k} \tag{15}$$

$$E = \langle E(x^n) \rangle \leq \frac{1}{2} \sum_k \ln\left(1 + n u_k \lambda_k / \sigma^2\right) \tag{16}$$

where now $u_k = \langle \phi_k^2(x) \rangle$. This result is especially simple, when the weighting function $p(x)$ is a probability density and the inputs have the marginal distribution $p(x)$. In this case, we simply have $u_k = 1$. In this case, training and generalization error sandwich the bound

$$\varepsilon_b = \sigma^2 \sum_k \frac{\lambda_k}{\sigma^2 + n\lambda_k}. \tag{17}$$

We expect that the bound ε_b becomes asymptotically exact, when $n \to \infty$. This should be intuitively clear, because training and generalization error approach each other asymptotically. This fact may also be understood from (9), which shows that the cumulative entropic error is within a factor of $\frac{1}{2}$ asymptotically equal to the cumulative generalization error. By integrating the lower bound (17) over n, we obtain precisely the upper bound on E with a factor 2, showing that upper and lower bounds show the same behaviour.

7 Simulations

We have compared our bounds with simulations for the average training error and generalization error for the case that the data are drawn from $p(x)$. Results for the entropic error will be given elsewhere.

We have specialized on the case, where the covariance kernel is of the RBF form $C(x, x') = \exp[(x - x')^2/\lambda^2]$, and $p(x) = (2\pi)^{-\frac{1}{2}} e^{-\frac{1}{2}x^2}$, for which, following Zhu et al. (1997), the k-th eigenvalue of the spectrum ($k = 0 \ldots \infty$) can be written as $\lambda_k = ab^k$, where $a = \sqrt{c}, b = c/\lambda^2, c = 2\left(1 + 2/\lambda^2 + \sqrt{1 + 4/\lambda^2}\right)^{-1}$, and λ is the lengthscale of the process. We estimated the average generalisation error for each training set based on the exact analytical expressions (8) and (7) over the distribution of the datasets by using a Monte Carlo approximation. To begin with, let us consider $x \in R$. We sampled the 1-dimensional input space generating 100 training sets whose data points were normally distributed around zero with unit variance. For each generation, the expected training and generalisation errors for a GP have been evaluated using up to 1000 data points. We set the value of the lengthscale[2] λ to 0.1 and we let the noise level σ^2 assume several values ($\sigma^2 = 10^{-4}, 10^{-3}, 10^{-2}, 10^{-1}, 1$). Figure 1 shows the results we obtained when

---

[2] The value of the lengthscale λ has the effect of stretching the training and learning curves; thus the results of the experiments performed with different λ are qualitatively similar to those presented.

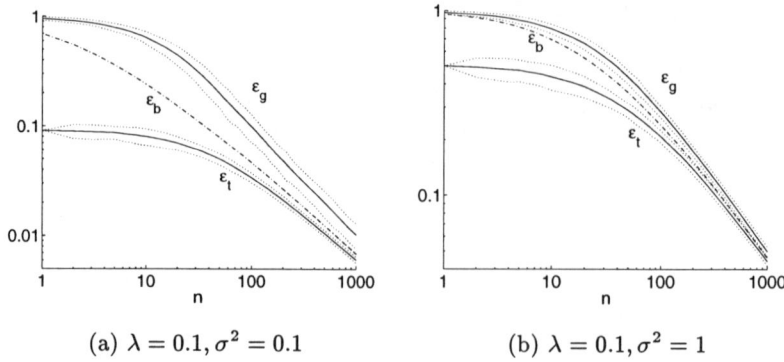

(a) $\lambda = 0.1, \sigma^2 = 0.1$ (b) $\lambda = 0.1, \sigma^2 = 1$

Figure 1: The Figures show the graphs of the training and learning curves with their bound $\epsilon_b(n)$ obtained with $\lambda = 0.1$; the noise level is set to 0.1 in Figure 1(a) and to 1 in Figure 1(b). In all the graphs, ϵ_t and $\epsilon_g(n)$ are drawn by the solid line and their 95% confidence interval is signed by the dotted curves. The bound $\epsilon_b(n)$ is drawn by the dash-dotted lines.

$\sigma^2 = 0.1$ (Figure 1(a)) and $\sigma^2 = 1$ (Figure 1(b)). The bound $\epsilon_b(n)$ lies within the training and learning curves, being an upper bound for $\epsilon_t(n)$ and a lower bound for $\epsilon_g(n)$. This bound is tighter for the processes with higher noise level; in particular, for large datasets the error bars on the curves $\epsilon_t(n)$ and $\epsilon_g(n)$ overlap the bound $\epsilon_b(n)$. The curves $\epsilon_t(n)$, $\epsilon_g(n)$ and $\epsilon_b(n)$ approach zero as $O(\log(n)/n)$.

Our bounds can also be applied to higher dimensions $D > 1$ using the covariance

$$C(x, x') = \exp\left(-||x - x'||^2/\lambda^2\right) \qquad (18)$$

for $x, x' \in R^D$. Obviously the integral kernel C is just a direct product of RBF kernels, one for each coordinate of x and x'. The eigenvalue problem (4) can be immediately reduced to the one for a single variable. Eigenfunctions and eigenvalues are simply products of those for the single coordinate problems. Hence, using a bit of combinatorics, the bound ε_b can be written as

$$\varepsilon_b = \sum_{k=0}^{\infty} \binom{k+D-1}{k} \frac{\sigma^2 a^D b^k}{\sigma^2 + n a^D b^k}, \qquad (19)$$

where a and b have been defined above. We performed experiments when $x \in R^2$ and $x \in R^5$. The correlation lengths along each direction of the input space has been set to 1 and the noise level was $\sigma^2 = 1.0$. The graphs of the curves, with their error bars are reported in Figure 2(a) (for $x \in R^2$) and in Figure 2(b) (for $x \in R^5$).

8 Discussion

Based on the minimal requirements on training inputs and covariances, we conjecture that our bounds cannot be improved much without making more detailed assumptions on models and distributions. We can observe from the simulations that the tightness of the bound $\epsilon_b(n)$ depends on the dimension of the input space. In particular, for large datasets $\epsilon_b(n)$ is tighter for small dimension of the input space; Figure 2(a) shows this quite clearly since $\epsilon_b(n)$ overlaps the error bars of the

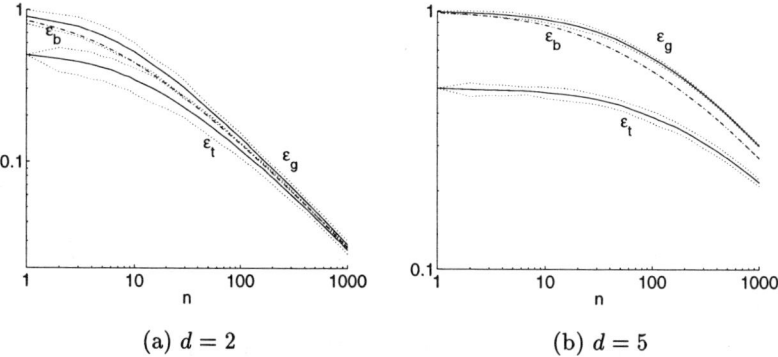

(a) $d = 2$ (b) $d = 5$

Figure 2: The Figures show the graphs of the training and learning curves with their bound $\epsilon_b(n)$ obtained with the squared exponential covariance function with $\lambda = 1$ and $\sigma^2 = 1$; the input space is R^2 (Figure 2(a)) and R^5 (Figure 2(b)). In all the Figures, ϵ_t and $\epsilon_g(n)$ are drawn by the solid line and their 95% confidence interval is signed by the dotted curves. The bound $\epsilon_b(n)$ is drawn by the dash-dotted lines.

training and learning curves for large n. Numerical simulations performed using modified Bessel covariance functions of order r (describing random processes $r - 1$ time mean square differentiable) have shown that the bound $\epsilon_b(n)$ becomes tighter for smoother processes.

Acknowledgement: We are grateful for many inspiring discussions with C.K.I. Williams. M.O. would like to thank Peter Sollich for his conjecture that (17) is an exact lower bound on the generalization error, which motivated part of this work. F. V. was supported by a studentship of British Aerospace.

9 Appendix: Proof of the lemma 1

Let $\{\Phi^{(j)}\}$ be a complete set of orthonormal eigenvectors and $\{E_i\}$ the corresponding set of eigenvalues of H, i.e. we have the properties $\sum_l H_{kl}\Phi_l^{(i)} = E_i\Phi_k^{(i)}$, $\sum_i \Phi_k^{(i)}\Phi_l^{(i)} = \delta_{kl}$, and $\sum_k \Phi_k^{(i)}\Phi_k^{(j)} = \delta_{ij}$. Then we get

$$\begin{aligned} \operatorname{Tr} f(H) &= \sum_i f(E_i) = \sum_k \sum_i (\Phi_k^{(i)})^2 f(E_i) \\ &\geq \sum_k f\left(\sum_i (\Phi_k^{(i)})^2 E_i\right) = \sum_k f\left(\sum_i \Phi_k^{(i)} \sum_l H_{kl}\Phi_l^{(i)}\right) \\ &= \sum_k f(H_{kk}) \end{aligned}$$

The second equality follows from orthonormality, because $\sum_k (\Phi_k^{(i)})^2 = 1$. The inequality uses the fact that by completeness, for any k, we have $\sum_i (\Phi_k^{(i)})^2 = 1$ and we may regard the $(\Phi_k^{(i)})^2$ as probabilities, such that by convexity, Jensen's inequality can be used. After using the eigenvalue equation, the sum over i was carried out with the help of the completeness relation, in order to obtain the last line.

References

[1] D. J. C. Mackay, Gaussian Processes, A Replacement for Neural Networks, NIPS tutorial 1997. May be obtained from http://wol.ra.phy.cam.ac.uk/pub/mackay/.

[2] R. Neal, *Bayesian Learning for Neural Networks*, Lecture Notes in Statistics, Springer (1996).

[3] C. K. I. Williams, Computing with Infinite Networks, in *Neural Information Processing Systems 9*, M. C. Mozer, M. I. Jordan and T. Petsche, eds., 295-301. MIT Press (1997).

[4] C. K. I. Williams and C. E. Rasmussen, Gaussian Processes for Regression, in *Neural Information Processing Systems 8*, D. S. Touretzky, M. C. Mozer and M. E. Hasselmo eds., 514-520, MIT Press (1996).

[5] R. M. Neal, Monte Carlo Implementation of Gaussian Process Models for Bayesian Regression and Classification, Technical Report CRG-TR-97-2, Dept. of Computer Science, University of Toronto (1997).

[6] M. N. Gibbs and D. J. C. Mackay, Variational Gaussian Process Classifiers, Preprint Cambridge University (1997).

[7] D. Barber and C. K. I. Williams, Gaussian Processes for Bayesian Classification via Hybrid Monte Carlo, in *Neural Information Processing Systems 9*, M. C. Mozer, M. I. Jordan and T. Petsche, eds., 340-346. MIT Press (1997).

[8] C. K. I. Williams and D. Barber, Bayesian Classification with Gaussian Processes, Preprint Aston University (1997).

[9] D. Haussler and M. Opper, Mutual Information, Metric Entropy and Cumulative Relative Entropy Risk, The Annals of Statistics, Vol 25, No 6, 2451 (1997).

[10] R. Peierls, Phys. Rev. 54, 918 (1938).

[11] H. Zhu, C. K. I. Williams, R. Rohwer and M. Morciniec, Gaussian Regression and Optimal Finite Dimensional Linear Models, Technical report NCRG/97/011, Aston University (1997).

Mean field methods for classification with Gaussian processes

Manfred Opper
Neural Computing Research Group
Division of Electronic Engineering and Computer Science
Aston University Birmingham B4 7ET, UK.
opperm@aston.ac.uk

Ole Winther
Theoretical Physics II, Lund University, Sölvegatan 14 A
S-223 62 Lund, Sweden
CONNECT, The Niels Bohr Institute, University of Copenhagen
Blegdamsvej 17, 2100 Copenhagen Ø, Denmark
winther@thep.lu.se

Abstract

We discuss the application of TAP mean field methods known from the Statistical Mechanics of disordered systems to Bayesian classification models with Gaussian processes. In contrast to previous approaches, no knowledge about the distribution of inputs is needed. Simulation results for the Sonar data set are given.

1 Modeling with Gaussian Processes

Bayesian models which are based on Gaussian prior distributions on function spaces are promising non-parametric statistical tools. They have been recently introduced into the Neural Computation community (Neal 1996, Williams & Rasmussen 1996, Mackay 1997). To give their basic definition, we assume that the likelihood of the output or target variable τ for a given input $\mathbf{s} \in R^N$ can be written in the form $p(\tau|h(\mathbf{s}))$ where $h : R^N \to R$ is a priori assumed to be a Gaussian random field. If we assume fields with zero prior mean, the statistics of h is entirely defined by the second order correlations $C(\mathbf{s}, \mathbf{s}') \doteq E[h(\mathbf{s})h(\mathbf{s}')]$, where E denotes expectations with respect to the prior. Interesting examples are

$$C(\mathbf{s},\mathbf{s}') = \frac{2}{\pi}\arcsin\left(\frac{\sum_i w_i s_i s'_i}{\sqrt{(1+\sum_i w_i s_i s_i)(1+\sum_i w_i s'_i s'_i)}}\right) \quad (1)$$

$$C(\mathbf{s},\mathbf{s}') = \exp\left(-\frac{1}{2}\sum_i w_i(s_i - s'_i)^2\right) \quad (2)$$

The choice (1) can be motivated as a limit of a two-layered neural network with infinitely many hidden units with factorizable input-hidden weight priors (Williams 1997). w_i are hyperparameters determining the relevant prior lengthscales of $h(\mathbf{s})$. The simplest choice $C(\mathbf{s},\mathbf{s}') = \sum_i w_i s_i s'_i$ corresponds to a single layer perceptron with independent Gaussian weight priors.

In this Bayesian framework, one can make predictions on a novel input $\mathbf{s}$ after having received a set D_m of m training examples $(\tau^\mu, \mathbf{s}^\mu)$, $\mu = 1,\ldots,m$ by using the posterior distribution of the field at the test point $\mathbf{s}$ which is given by

$$p(h(\mathbf{s})|D_m) = \int p(h(\mathbf{s})|\{h^\nu\})\, p(\{h^\nu\}|D_m) \prod_\mu dh^\mu. \quad (3)$$

$p(h(\mathbf{s})|\{h^\nu\})$ is a conditional Gaussian distribution and

$$p(\{h^\nu\}|D_m) = \frac{1}{Z}p(\{h^\nu\})\prod_\mu p(\tau^\mu|h^\mu). \quad (4)$$

is the posterior distribution of the field variables at the training points. Z is a normalizing partition function and

$$p(\{h^\mu\}) = \frac{1}{\sqrt{(2\pi)^m \det C}} e^{-\frac{1}{2}\sum_{\mu\nu} h^\mu (C^{-1})_{\mu\nu} h^\nu}. \quad (5)$$

is the prior distribution of the fields at the training points. Here, we have introduced the abbreviations $h^\mu = h(\mathbf{s}^\mu)$ and $C_{\mu\nu} \doteq C(\mathbf{s}^\mu, \mathbf{s}^\nu)$.

The major technical problem of this approach comes from the difficulty in performing the high dimensional integrations. Non-Gaussian likelihoods can be only treated by approximations, where e.g. Monte Carlo sampling (Neal 1997), Laplace integration (Barber & Williams 1997) or bounds on the likelihood (Gibbs & Mackay 1997) have been used so far. In this paper, we introduce a further approach, which is based on a mean field method known in the Statistical Physics of disordered systems (Mézard, Parisi & Virasoro 1987).

We specialize on the case of a binary classification problem, where a binary class label $\tau = \pm 1$ must be predicted using a training set corrupted by i.i.d label noise. The likelihood for this problem is taken as

$$p(\tau|h) = \kappa + (1-2\kappa)\Theta(\tau h),$$

where κ is the probability that the true classification label is corrupted, i.e. flipped and the step function, $\Theta(x)$ is defined as $\Theta(x) = 1$ for $x > 0$ and 0 otherwise. For such a case, we expect that (by the non-smoothness of the model), e.g. Laplace's method and the bounds introduced in (Gibbs & Mackay 1997) are not directly applicable.

2 Exact posterior averages

In order to make a prediction on an input $\mathbf{s}$, ideally the label with maximum posterior probability should be chosen, i.e. $\tau^{\text{Bayes}} = \mathrm{argmax}_\tau\, p(\tau|D_m)$, where the predictive probability is given by $p(\tau|D_m) = \int dh\, p(\tau|h)\, p(h|D_m)$. For the binary case the Bayes classifier becomes $\tau^{\text{Bayes}} = \mathrm{sign}\langle \mathrm{sign} h(\mathbf{s})\rangle$, where we throughout the paper let brackets $\langle \ldots \rangle$ denote posterior averages. Here, we use a somewhat simpler approach by using the prediction

$$\tau = \mathrm{sign}(\langle h(\mathbf{s})\rangle)\ .$$

This would reduce to the ideal prediction, when the posterior distribution of $h(\mathbf{s})$ is symmetric around its mean $\langle h(\mathbf{s})\rangle$. The goal of our mean field approach will be to provide a set of equations for approximately determining $\langle h(\mathbf{s})\rangle$. The starting point of our analysis is the partition function

$$Z = \int \prod_\mu \frac{dx^\mu dh^\mu}{2\pi i} \prod_\mu p(\tau^\mu|h^\mu) e^{\frac{1}{2}\sum_{\mu,\nu} C_{\mu\nu} x^\mu x^\nu - \sum_\mu h^\mu x^\mu}\ , \qquad (6)$$

where the new auxiliary variables x^μ (integrated along the imaginary axis) have been introduced in order to get rid of C^{-1} in (5).

It is not hard to show from (6) that the posterior averages of the fields at the m training inputs and at a new test point $\mathbf{s}$ are given by

$$\langle h^\mu \rangle = \sum_\nu C_{\mu\nu} \langle x^\nu \rangle \qquad \langle h(\mathbf{s})\rangle = \sum_\nu C(\mathbf{s}, \mathbf{s}^\nu) \langle x^\nu \rangle. \qquad (7)$$

We have thus reduced our problem to the calculation of the "microscopic orderparameters" $\langle x^\mu \rangle$.[1] Averages in Statistical Physics can be calculated from derivatives of $-\ln Z$ with respect to small external fields, which are then set to zero. An equivalent formulation uses the *Legendre transform* of $-\ln Z$ as a function of the expectations, which in our case is given by

$$G(\{\langle x^\mu \rangle, \langle (x^\mu)^2\rangle\}) = -\ln Z(\gamma^\mu, \lambda) + \sum_\mu \langle x^\mu \rangle \gamma^\mu + \frac{1}{2}\sum_\mu \lambda_\mu \langle (x^\mu)^2 \rangle\ . \qquad (8)$$

with

$$Z(\{\gamma^\mu, \lambda_\mu\}) = \int \prod_\mu \frac{dx^\mu dh^\mu}{2\pi i} \prod_\mu p(\tau^\mu|h^\mu) e^{\frac{1}{2}\sum_{\mu,\nu}(\lambda_\mu \delta_{\mu\nu} + C_{\mu\nu}) x^\mu x^\nu + \sum_\mu x^\mu(\gamma^\mu - h^\mu)}\ . \qquad (9)$$

The additional averages $\langle (x^\mu)^2 \rangle$ have been introduced, because the dynamical variables x^μ (unlike Ising spins) do not have fixed length. The external fields γ^μ, λ_μ must be eliminated from $\frac{\partial G}{\partial \lambda_\mu} = \frac{\partial G}{\partial \gamma^\mu} = 0$ and the true expectation values of x^μ and $(x^\mu)^2$ are those which satisfy $\frac{\partial G}{\partial \langle (x^\mu)^2 \rangle} = \frac{\partial G}{\partial \langle x^\mu \rangle} = 0$.

3 Naive mean field theory

So far, this description does not give anything new. Usually G cannot be calculated exactly for the non-Gaussian likelihood models of interest. Nevertheless, based on mean field theory (MFT) it is possible to guess an approximate form for G.

---

[1] Although the integrations are over the imaginary axis, these expectations come out positive. This is due to the fact that the integration "measure" is complex as well.

Mean field methods have found interesting applications in Neural Computing within the framework of *ensemble learning*, where the the exact posterior distribution is approximated by a simpler one using product distributions in a variational treatment. Such a "standard" mean field method for the posterior of the h^μ (for the case of Gaussian process classification) is in preparation and will be discussed somewhere else. In this paper, we suggest a different route, which introduces nontrivial corrections to a simple or "naive" MFT for the variables x^μ. Besides the variational method (which would be purely formal because the distribution of the x^μ is complex and does not define a probability), there are other ways to define the simple MFT. E.g., by truncating a perturbation expansion with respect to the "interactions" $C_{\mu\nu}$ in G after the first order (Plefka 1982). These approaches yield the result

$$G \approx G_{naive} = G_0 - \frac{1}{2}\sum_\mu C_{\mu\mu}\langle(x^\mu)^2\rangle - \frac{1}{2}\sum_{\mu,\nu,\mu\neq\mu} C_{\mu\nu}\langle x^\mu\rangle\langle x^\nu\rangle \; . \tag{10}$$

G_0 is the contribution to G for a model without any interactions i.e. when $C_{\mu\nu} = 0$ in (9), i.e. it is the Legendre transform of

$$-\ln Z_0 = \sum_\mu \ln\left[\kappa + (1-2\kappa)\Phi\left(\tau^\mu \frac{\gamma^\mu}{\sqrt{\lambda^\mu}}\right)\right] \; ,$$

where $\Phi(z) = \int_{-\infty}^z \frac{dt}{\sqrt{2\pi}} e^{-t^2/2}$ is an error function. For simple models in Statistical Physics, where *all* interactions $C_{\mu\nu}$ are positive and equal, it is easy to show that G_{naive} will become exact in the limit of an infinite number of variables x^μ. Hence, for systems with a large number of nonzero interactions having the same orders of magnitude, one may expect that the approximation is not too bad.

4 The TAP approach

Nevertheless, when the interactions $C_{\mu\nu}$ can be both positive and negative (as one would expect e.g. when inputs have zero mean), even in the thermodynamic limit and for nice distributions of inputs, an additional contribution ΔG must be added to the "naive" mean field theory (10). Such a correction (often called an *Onsager reaction term*) has been introduced for a spin glass model by (Thouless, Anderson & Palmer 1977) (TAP). It was later applied to the statistical mechanics of single layer perceptrons by (Mézard 1989) and then generalized to the Bayesian framework by (Opper & Winther 1996, 1997). For an application to multilayer networks, see (Wong 1995). In the thermodynamic limit of infinitely large dimension of the input space, and for nice input distributions, the results can be shown coincide with the results of the replica framework. The drawback of the previous derivations of the TAP MFT for neural networks was the fact that special assumptions on the input distribution had been made and certain fluctuating terms have been replaced by their averages over the distribution of random data, which in practice would not be available. In this paper, we will use the approach of (Parisi & Potters 1995), which allows to circumvent this problem. They concluded (applied to the case of a spin model with random interactions of a specific type), that the functional form of ΔG should not depend on the type of the "single particle" contribution G_0. Hence, one may use any model in G_0, for which G can be calculated exactly (e.g. the Gaussian regression model) and subtract the naive mean field contribution to obtain the desired ΔG. For the sake of simplicity, we have chosen the even simpler model $p(\tau^\mu|h^\mu) \sim \delta(h^\mu)$ without changing the final result. A lengthy but straightforward calculation for this problem leads to the result

$$\Delta G = \frac{1}{2}\ln\det(\Lambda + C) + \frac{1}{2}\sum_\mu (\Lambda_\mu - C_{\mu\mu})R_\mu + \frac{m}{2} + \frac{1}{2}\sum_\mu \ln(-R_\mu) . \quad (11)$$

with $R_\mu \doteq \langle (x^\mu)^2 \rangle - \langle x^\mu \rangle^2$. The Λ_μ must be eliminated using $\frac{\partial G}{\partial \Lambda_\mu} = 0$, which leads to the equation

$$R_\mu = -\left[(\Lambda + C)^{-1}\right]_{\mu\mu} . \quad (12)$$

Note, that with this choice, the TAP mean field theory becomes exact for Gaussian likelihoods, i.e. for standard regression problems.

Finally, setting the derivatives of $G_{TAP} = G_{naive} + \Delta G$ with respect to the 4 variables $\langle x^\mu \rangle, \langle (x^\mu)^2 \rangle, \gamma_\mu, \lambda_\mu$ equal to zero, we obtain the equations

$$\gamma^\mu = \sum_\nu C_{\mu\nu}\langle x^\nu \rangle - \lambda_\mu \langle x^\mu \rangle \qquad \lambda_\mu = -(\Lambda_\mu + \frac{1}{R_\mu}) \quad (13)$$

$$\langle x^\mu \rangle = \frac{\tau^\mu}{\sqrt{\lambda_\mu}} \frac{(1-2\kappa)D\left(\frac{\gamma^\mu}{\sqrt{\lambda_\mu}}\right)}{\kappa + (1-2\kappa)\Phi\left(\tau^\mu \frac{\gamma^\mu}{\sqrt{\lambda_\mu}}\right)} \qquad R_\mu = -\langle x^\mu \rangle \left(\frac{\gamma^\mu}{\lambda_\mu} + \langle x^\mu \rangle\right) ,$$

where $D(z) = e^{-z^2/2}/\sqrt{2\pi}$ is the Gaussian measure. These eqs. have to be solved numerically together with (12). In contrast, for the naive MFT, the simpler result $\lambda_\mu = C_{\mu\mu}$ is found.

5 Simulations

Solving the nonlinear system of equations (12,13) by iteration turns out to be quite straightforward. For some data sets to get convergence, one has to add a diagonal term v to the covariance matrix C: $C_{ij} \to C_{ij} + \delta_{ij}v$. It may be shown that this term corresponds to learning with Gaussian noise (with variance v) added the Gaussian random field.

Here, we present simulation results for a single data set, the *Sonar – Mines versus Rocks* using the same training/test set split as in the original study by (Gorman & Sejnowski 1988). The input data were pre-processed by linear rescaling such that over the training set each input variable has zero mean and unit variance. In some cases the mean field equations failed to converge using the raw data.

A further important feature of TAP MFT is the fact that the method also gives an approximate leave-one-out estimator for the generalization error, ϵ_{loo} expressed in terms of the solution to the mean field equations (see (Opper & Winther 1996, 1997) for more details). It is also possible to derive a leave-one-out estimator for the naive MFT (Opper & Winther to be published).

Since we so far haven't dealt with the problem of automatically estimating the hyperparameters, their number was drastically reduced by setting $w_i = \frac{1}{\sigma^2 N}$ in the covariances (1) and (2). The remaining hyperparameters, σ^2, κ and v were chosen

Table 1: The result for the Sonar data.

Algorithm	Covariance Function	ϵ_{test}	$\epsilon_{\text{loo}}^{\text{exact}}$	ϵ_{loo}
TAP Mean Field	(1)	0.183	0.260	0.260
	(2)	0.077	0.212	0.212
Naive Mean Field	(1)	0.154	0.269	0.269
	(2)	0.077	0.221	0.221
Back-Prop	Simple Perceptron	0.269($\pm$0.048)		
	Best 2layer – 12 Hidden	0.096($\pm$0.018)		

as to minimize ϵ_{loo}. It turned out that the lowest ϵ_{loo} was found from modeling without noise: $\kappa = v = 0$.

The simulation results are shown in table 1. The comparisons for back-propagation is taken from (Gorman & Sejnowski 1988). The solution found by the algorithm turned out to be unique, i.e. different order presentation of the examples and different initial values for the $\langle x^\mu \rangle$ converged to the same solution.

In table 1, we have also compared the estimate given by the algorithm with the exact leave-one-out estimate $\epsilon_{\text{loo}}^{\text{exact}}$ obtained by going through the training set and keeping an example out for testing and running the mean field algorithm on the rest. The estimate and exact value are in complete agreement. Comparing with the test error we see that the training set is 'hard' and the test set is 'easy'. The small difference for test error between the naive and full mean field algorithms also indicate that the mean field scheme is quite robust with respect to choice of λ_μ.

6 Discussion

More work has to be done to make the TAP approach a practical tool for Bayesian modeling. One has to find better methods for solving the equations. A conversion into a direct minimization problem for a free energy maybe helpful. To achieve this, one may probably work with the real field variables h^μ instead of the imaginary x^μ. A further problem is the determination of the hyperparameters of the covariance functions. Two ways seem to be interesting here. One may use the approximate free energy G, which is essentially the negative logarithm of the Bayesian *evidence* to estimate the most probable values of the hyperparameters. However, an estimate on the errors made in the TAP approach would be necessary. Second, one may use the built-in leave-one-out estimate to estimate the generalization error. Again an estimate on the validity of the approximation is necessary. It will further be interesting to apply our way of deriving the TAP equations to other models (Boltzmann machines, belief nets, combinatorial optimization problems), for which standard mean field theories have been applied successfully.

Acknowledgments

This research is supported by the Swedish Foundation for Strategic Research and by the Danish Research Councils for the Natural and Technical Sciences through the Danish Computational Neural Network Center (CONNECT).

References

D. Barber and C. K. I. Williams, Gaussian Processes for Bayesian Classification via Hybrid Monte Carlo, in *Neural Information Processing Systems 9*, M . C. Mozer, M. I. Jordan and T. Petsche, eds., 340-346. MIT Press (1997).

M. N. Gibbs and D. J. C. Mackay, Variational Gaussian Process Classifiers, Preprint Cambridge University (1997).

R. P. Gorman and T. J. Sejnowski, Analysis of Hidden Units in a Layered Network Trained to Classify Sonar Targets, Neural Networks **1**, 75 (1988).

D. J. C. Mackay, Gaussian Processes, A Replacement for Neural Networks, NIPS tutorial 1997, May be obtained from http://wol.ra.phy.cam.ac.uk/pub/mackay/.

M. Mézard, The Space of interactions in Neural Networks: Gardner's Computation with the Cavity Method, J. Phys. A **22**, 2181 (1989).

M. Mézard and G. Parisi and M. A. Virasoro, *Spin Glass Theory and Beyond*, Lecture Notes in Physics, 9, World Scientific (1987).

R. Neal, *Bayesian Learning for Neural Networks*, Lecture Notes in Statistics, Springer (1996).

R. M. Neal, Monte Carlo Implementation of Gaussian Process Models for Bayesian Regression and Classification, Technical Report CRG-TR-97-2, Dept. of Computer Science, University of Toronto (1997).

M. Opper and O. Winther, A Mean Field Approach to Bayes Learning in Feed-Forward Neural Networks, Phys. Rev. Lett. **76**, 1964 (1996).

M. Opper and O. Winther, A Mean Field Algorithm for Bayes Learning in Large Feed-Forward Neural Networks, in *Neural Information Processing Systems 9*, M. C. Mozer, M. I. Jordan and T. Petsche, eds., 225-231. MIT Press (1997).

G. Parisi and M. Potters, Mean-Field Equations for Spin Models with Orthogonal Interaction Matrices, J. Phys. A: Math. Gen. **28** 5267 (1995).

T. Plefka, Convergence Condition of the TAP Equation for the Infinite-Range Ising Spin Glass, J. Phys. A **15**, 1971 (1982).

D. J. Thouless, P. W. Anderson and R. G. Palmer, Solution of a 'Solvable Model of a Spin Glass', Phil. Mag. **35**, 593 (1977).

C. K. I. Williams, Computing with Infinite Networks, in *Neural Information Processing Systems 9*, M. C. Mozer, M. I. Jordan and T. Petsche, eds., 295-301. MIT Press (1997).

C. K. I. Williams and C. E. Rasmussen, Gaussian Processes for Regression, in *Neural Information Processing Systems 8*, D. S. Touretzky, M. C. Mozer and M. E. Hasselmo eds., 514-520, MIT Press (1996).

K. Y. M. Wong, Microscopic Equations and Stability Conditions in Optimal Neural Networks, Europhys. Lett. **30**, 245 (1995).

On-Line Learning with Restricted Training Sets: Exact Solution as Benchmark for General Theories

H.C. Rae	P. Sollich	A.C.C. Coolen
hamish.rae@kcl.ac.uk	psollich@mth.kcl.ac.uk	tcoolen@mth.kcl.ac.uk

Department of Mathematics
King's College London
The Strand
London WC2R 2LS, UK

Abstract

We solve the dynamics of on-line Hebbian learning in perceptrons exactly, for the regime where the size of the training set scales linearly with the number of inputs. We consider both noiseless and noisy teachers. Our calculation cannot be extended to non-Hebbian rules, but the solution provides a nice benchmark to test more general and advanced theories for solving the dynamics of learning with restricted training sets.

1 Introduction

Considerable progress has been made in understanding the dynamics of supervised learning in layered neural networks through the application of the methods of statistical mechanics. A recent review of work in this field is contained in [1]. For the most part, such theories have concentrated on systems where the training set is much larger than the number of updates. In such circumstances the probability that a question will be repeated during the training process is negligible and it is possible to assume for large networks, via the central limit theorem, that the local field distribution is Gaussian. In this paper we consider *restricted training sets*; we suppose that the size of the training set scales linearly with N, the number of inputs. The probability that a question will reappear during the training process is no longer negligible, the assumption that the local fields have Gaussian distributions is not tenable, and it is clear that correlations will develop between the weights and the questions in the training set as training progresses. In fact, the non-Gaussian character of the local fields should be a *prediction* of any satisfactory theory of learning with restricted training sets, as this is clearly demanded by numerical simulations. Several authors [2, 3, 4, 5, 6, 7] have discussed learning with restricted training sets but a general theory is difficult. A simple model of learning with restricted training sets which can be solved *exactly* is therefore particularly attractive and provides a yardstick against which more difficult and sophisticated general theories can, in due course, be tested and compared. We show how this can be accomplished for on-line Hebbian learning in perceptrons with restricted training sets and we obtain exact solutions for the generalisation error and the training error for a class of noisy teachers and students with arbitrary weight decay. Our theory is in excellent agreement with numerical simulations and our prediction of the probability density of the student field is a striking confirmation of them, making it clear that we are indeed dealing with local fields which are non-Gaussian.

2 Definitions

We study on-line learning in a student perceptron S, which tries to perform a task defined by a teacher perceptron characterised by a fixed weight vector $\boldsymbol{B}^* \in \Re^N$. We assume, however, that the teacher is noisy and that the *actual* teacher output T and the corresponding student response S are given by

$$T : \{-1,1\}^N \to \{-1,1\} \qquad T(\boldsymbol{\xi}) = \mathrm{sgn}[\boldsymbol{B} \cdot \boldsymbol{\xi}],$$
$$S : \{-1,1\}^N \to \{-1,1\} \qquad S(\boldsymbol{\xi}) = \mathrm{sgn}[\boldsymbol{J} \cdot \boldsymbol{\xi}],$$

where the vector $\boldsymbol{B}$ is drawn *independently* of $\boldsymbol{\xi}$ with probability $p(\boldsymbol{B})$ which may depend explicitly on the correct teacher vector $\boldsymbol{B}^*$. Of particular interest are the following two choices, described in literature as output noise and Gaussian input noise, respectively:

$$p(\boldsymbol{B}) = \lambda\, \delta(\boldsymbol{B}+\boldsymbol{B}^*) + (1-\lambda)\, \delta(\boldsymbol{B}-\boldsymbol{B}^*) \tag{1}$$

where $\lambda \geq 0$ represents the probability that the teacher output is incorrect, and

$$p(\boldsymbol{B}) = \left[\frac{N}{2\pi\Sigma^2}\right]^{\frac{N}{2}} e^{-\frac{N}{2}(\boldsymbol{B}-\boldsymbol{B}^*)^2/\Sigma^2}. \tag{2}$$

The variance Σ^2/N has been chosen so as to achieve appropriate scaling for $N \to \infty$.

Our learning rule will be the on-line Hebbian rule, i.e.

$$\boldsymbol{J}(\ell+1) = \left(1 - \frac{\gamma}{N}\right)\boldsymbol{J}(\ell) + \frac{\eta}{N}\, \boldsymbol{\xi}(\ell)\, \mathrm{sgn}[\boldsymbol{B}(\ell) \cdot \boldsymbol{\xi}(\ell)] \tag{3}$$

where the non-negative parameters γ and η are the decay rate and the learning rate, respectively. At each iteration step ℓ an input vector $\boldsymbol{\xi}(\ell)$ is picked at random from a training set consisting of $p = \alpha N$ randomly drawn vectors $\boldsymbol{\xi}^\mu \in \{-1,1\}^N$, $\mu = 1,\ldots p$. This set remains unchanged during the learning dynamics. At the same time the teacher selects at random, and independently of $\boldsymbol{\xi}(\ell)$, the vector $\boldsymbol{B}(\ell)$, according to the probability distribution $p(\boldsymbol{B})$. Iterating equation (3) gives

$$\boldsymbol{J}(m) = \left(1 - \frac{\gamma}{N}\right)^m \boldsymbol{J}_0 + \frac{\eta}{N} \sum_{\ell=0}^{m-1} \left(1 - \frac{\gamma}{N}\right)^{m-\ell-1} \boldsymbol{\xi}(\ell)\, \mathrm{sgn}[\boldsymbol{B}(\ell) \cdot \boldsymbol{\xi}(\ell)] \tag{4}$$

We assume that the (noisy) teacher output is *consistent* in the sense that if a question $\boldsymbol{\xi}$ reappears at some stage during the training process the teacher makes the same choice of $\boldsymbol{B}$ in both cases, i.e. if $\boldsymbol{\xi}(\ell) = \boldsymbol{\xi}(\ell')$ then also $\boldsymbol{B}(\ell) = \boldsymbol{B}(\ell')$. This consistency allows us to define a generalised training set $\tilde{D}$ by including with the p

questions the corresponding teacher vectors:
$$\tilde{D} = \{(\boldsymbol{\xi}^1, \boldsymbol{B}^1), \ldots, (\boldsymbol{\xi}^p, \boldsymbol{B}^p)\}$$
There are two sources of randomness in this problem. First of all there is the random realisation of the 'path' $\Omega = \{(\boldsymbol{\xi}(0), \boldsymbol{B}(0)), (\boldsymbol{\xi}(1), \boldsymbol{B}(1)), \ldots, (\boldsymbol{\xi}(\ell), \boldsymbol{B}(\ell)), \ldots\}$. This is simply the randomness of the stochastic process that gives the evolution of the vector $\boldsymbol{J}$. Averages over this process will be denoted as $\langle \ldots \rangle$. Secondly there is the randomness in the composition of the training set. We will write averages over all training sets as $\langle \ldots \rangle_{\text{sets}}$. We note that

$$\langle f[\boldsymbol{\xi}(\ell), \boldsymbol{B}(\ell)] \rangle = \frac{1}{p} \sum_{\mu=1}^{p} f(\boldsymbol{\xi}^\mu, \boldsymbol{B}^\mu) \qquad \text{(for all } \ell\text{)}$$

and that averages over all possible realisations of the training set are given by

$$\langle f[(\boldsymbol{\xi}^1, \boldsymbol{B}^1), (\boldsymbol{\xi}^2, \boldsymbol{B}^2), \ldots, (\boldsymbol{\xi}^p, \boldsymbol{B}^p)] \rangle_{\text{sets}}$$
$$= \sum_{\boldsymbol{\xi}^1} \sum_{\boldsymbol{\xi}^2} \cdots \sum_{\boldsymbol{\xi}^p} \frac{1}{2^{Np}} \int \left[\prod_{\mu=1}^{p} p(\boldsymbol{B}^\mu) \, d\boldsymbol{B}^\mu \right] f[(\boldsymbol{\xi}^1, \boldsymbol{B}^1), (\boldsymbol{\xi}^2, \boldsymbol{B}^2), \ldots, (\boldsymbol{\xi}^p, \boldsymbol{B}^p)]$$

where $\boldsymbol{\xi}^\mu \in \{-1, 1\}^N$. We normalise $\boldsymbol{B}^*$ so that $[\boldsymbol{B}^*]^2 = 1$ and choose the time unit $t = m/N$. We finally assume that $\boldsymbol{J}_0$ and $\boldsymbol{B}^*$ are statistically independent of the training vectors $\boldsymbol{\xi}^\mu$, and that they obey $J_i(0), B_i^* = \mathcal{O}(N^{-\frac{1}{2}})$ for all i.

3 Explicit Microscopic Expressions

At the m-th stage of the learning process the two simple scalar observables $Q[\boldsymbol{J}] = \boldsymbol{J}^2$ and $R[\boldsymbol{J}] = \boldsymbol{B}^* \cdot \boldsymbol{J}$, and the joint distribution of fields $x = \boldsymbol{J} \cdot \boldsymbol{\xi}$, $y = \boldsymbol{B}^* \cdot \boldsymbol{\xi}$, $z = \boldsymbol{B} \cdot \boldsymbol{\xi}$ (calculated over the questions in the training set $\tilde{D}$), are given by

$$Q[\boldsymbol{J}(m)] = \boldsymbol{J}^2(m) \qquad R[\boldsymbol{J}(m)] = \boldsymbol{B}^* \cdot \boldsymbol{J}(m) \qquad (5)$$

$$P[x, y, z; \boldsymbol{J}(m)] = \frac{1}{p} \sum_{\mu=1}^{p} \delta[x - \boldsymbol{J}(m) \cdot \boldsymbol{\xi}^\mu] \, \delta[y - \boldsymbol{B}^* \cdot \boldsymbol{\xi}^\mu] \, \delta[z - \boldsymbol{B}^\mu \cdot \boldsymbol{\xi}^\mu] \qquad (6)$$

For infinitely large systems one can prove that the fluctuations in mean-field observables such as $\{Q, R, P\}$, due to the randomness in the dynamics, will vanish [6]. Furthermore one assumes, with convincing support from numerical simulations, that for $N \to \infty$ the evolution of such observables, observed for different random realisations of the training set, will be reproducible (i.e. the sample-to-sample fluctuations will also vanish, which is called 'self-averaging'). Both properties are central ingredients of all current theories. We are thus led to the introduction of the averages of the observables in (5,6), with respect to the dynamical randomness and with respect to the randomness in the training set (to be carried out in precisely this order):

$$Q(t) = \lim_{N \to \infty} \langle \, \langle Q[\boldsymbol{J}(tN)] \rangle \, \rangle_{\text{sets}} \qquad R(t) = \lim_{N \to \infty} \langle \, \langle R[\boldsymbol{J}(tN)] \rangle \, \rangle_{\text{sets}} \qquad (7)$$

$$P_t(x, y, z) = \lim_{N \to \infty} \langle \, \langle P[x, y, z; \boldsymbol{J}(tN)] \rangle \, \rangle_{\text{sets}} \qquad (8)$$

A fundamental ingredient of our calculations will be the average $\langle \xi_i \, \text{sgn}(\boldsymbol{B} \cdot \boldsymbol{\xi}) \rangle_{(\boldsymbol{\xi}, \boldsymbol{B})}$, calculated over all realisations of $(\boldsymbol{\xi}, \boldsymbol{B})$. We find, for a wide class of $p(\boldsymbol{B})$, that

$$\langle \xi_i \, \text{sgn}(\boldsymbol{B} \cdot \boldsymbol{\xi}) \rangle_{(\boldsymbol{\xi}, \boldsymbol{B})} = \rho B_i^* + \mathcal{O}(N^{-3/2}) \qquad (9)$$

where, for example,

$$\rho = \sqrt{\frac{2}{\pi}}\,(1-2\lambda) \qquad \text{(output noise)} \tag{10}$$

$$\rho = \sqrt{\frac{2}{\pi}}\,\frac{1}{\sqrt{1+\Sigma^2}} \qquad \text{(Gaussian input noise)} \tag{11}$$

4 Averages of Simple Scalar Observables

Calculation of $Q(t)$ and $R(t)$ using (4, 5, 7, 9) to execute the path average and the average over sets is relatively straightforward, albeit tedious. We find that

$$Q(t) = e^{-2\gamma t}Q_0 + 2\eta\rho R_0 \frac{e^{-\gamma t}(1-e^{-\gamma t})}{\gamma} + \frac{\eta^2}{2\gamma}(1-e^{-2\gamma t})$$
$$+ \eta^2 \frac{(1-e^{-\gamma t})^2}{\gamma^2}\left(\frac{1}{\alpha}+\rho^2\right) \tag{12}$$

and that
$$R(t) = e^{-\gamma t}R_0 + \eta\rho\gamma^{-1}(1-e^{-\gamma t}) \tag{13}$$

where ρ is given by equations (10, 11) in the examples of output noise and Gaussian input noise, respectively. We note that the generalisation error is given by

$$E_g = \frac{1}{\pi}\arccos\left[R(t)/\sqrt{Q(t)}\right] \tag{14}$$

All models of the teacher noise which have the same ρ will thus have the same generalisation error at any time. This is true, in particular, of output noise and Gaussian input noise when their respective parameters λ and Σ are related by

$$1 - 2\lambda = \frac{1}{\sqrt{1+\Sigma^2}}. \tag{15}$$

With each type of teacher noise for which (9) holds, one can thus associate an effective output noise parameter λ. Note, however, that this effective teacher error probability λ will in general not be identical to the *true* teacher error probability associated with a given $p(B)$, as can immediately be seen by calculating the latter for the Gaussian input noise (2).

5 Average of the Joint Field Distribution

The calculation of the average of the joint field distribution starting from equation (8) is more difficult. Writing $\sigma = (1-\gamma/N)$, and expressing the δ functions in terms of complex exponentials, we find that

$$P_t(x,y,z) = \int \frac{d\hat{x}d\hat{y}d\hat{z}}{8\pi^3}\,e^{i(x\hat{x}+y\hat{y}+z\hat{z})} \lim_{N\to\infty} \left\langle e^{-i[\hat{x}e^{-\gamma t}\boldsymbol{J}_0\cdot\boldsymbol{\xi}^1 + \hat{y}\boldsymbol{B}^*\cdot\boldsymbol{\xi}^1 + \hat{z}\boldsymbol{B}^1\cdot\boldsymbol{\xi}^1]} \right.$$
$$\left. \times \prod_{\ell=0}^{tN}\left[\frac{1}{p}\sum_{\nu=1}^{p} e^{-[i\eta\hat{x}N^{-1}\sigma^{tN-\ell}(\boldsymbol{\xi}^1\cdot\boldsymbol{\xi}^\nu)\,\mathrm{sgn}(\boldsymbol{B}^\nu\cdot\boldsymbol{\xi}^\nu)]}\right]\right\rangle_{\text{sets}} \tag{16}$$

In this expression we replace $\boldsymbol{\xi}^1$ by $\boldsymbol{\xi}$ and $\boldsymbol{B}^1$ by $\boldsymbol{B}$, and abbreviate $S = \prod_{\ell=0}^{tN}[\cdots]$. Upon writing the latter product in terms of the auxiliary variables $v_\nu = (\boldsymbol{\xi}^1\cdot\boldsymbol{\xi}^\nu)/\sqrt{N}$ and $\omega_\nu = \boldsymbol{B}^\nu\cdot\boldsymbol{\xi}^\nu$, we find that for large N

$$\log S \sim \chi(\hat{x}\,\mathrm{sgn}[\boldsymbol{B}\cdot\boldsymbol{\xi}],t) - \frac{i\eta\hat{x}u_1}{\gamma}(1-e^{-\gamma t}) - \frac{\eta^2\hat{x}^2 u_2}{4\gamma}(1-e^{-2\gamma t}) \tag{17}$$

where u_1, u_2 are the random variables given by

$$u_1 = \frac{1}{\alpha\sqrt{N}} \sum_{\nu>1} v_\nu \, \text{sgn}(\omega_\nu), \qquad u_2 = \frac{1}{p} \sum_{\nu>1} v_\nu^{\,2}.$$

and with
$$\chi(w,t) = \frac{1}{\alpha} \int_0^t ds \, [e^{-[i\eta w e^{\gamma(s-t)}]} - 1] \qquad (18)$$

A study of the statistics of u_1 and u_2 shows that $\lim_{N\to\infty} u_2 = 1$, and that

$$u_1 = \rho \boldsymbol{B}^* \cdot \boldsymbol{\xi} + \alpha^{-1/2} u \qquad (N \to \infty),$$

where u is a Gaussian random variable with mean equal to zero and variance unity. On the basis of these results and equations (16, 17) we find that

$$P_t(x,y,z) = \int \frac{d\hat{x}\,d\hat{y}\,d\hat{z}}{8\pi^3} \, e^{i(x\hat{x}+y\hat{y}+z\hat{z}) - \frac{1}{2}\hat{x}^2[Q-R^2 - e^{-2\gamma t}(Q_0 - R_0^2)] + \chi(\hat{x}\,\text{sgn}[z], t) - i\hat{x}y(R - R_0 e^{-\gamma t}}$$

$$\times \lim_{N\to\infty} \langle e^{-i[\hat{x}e^{-\gamma t} \boldsymbol{J}_0 \cdot \boldsymbol{\xi} + \hat{y}\boldsymbol{B}^* \cdot \boldsymbol{\xi} + \hat{z}\boldsymbol{B}\cdot\boldsymbol{\xi}]} \rangle_{(\boldsymbol{\xi},\boldsymbol{B})} \qquad (19)$$

where Q and R are given by the expressions (12,13) (note: $Q - R^2$ is independent of ρ, i.e. of the distribution $p(\boldsymbol{B})$). Let $x_0 = \boldsymbol{J}_0 \cdot \boldsymbol{\xi}$, $y = \boldsymbol{B}^* \cdot \boldsymbol{\xi}$, $z = \boldsymbol{B} \cdot \boldsymbol{\xi}$. We assume that, given y, z is independent of x_0. This condition, which reflects in some sense the property that the teacher noise preserves the perceptron structure, is certainly satisfied for the models which we are considering and is probably true of all reasonable noise models. The joint probability density then has the form $p(x_0, y, z) = p(x_0|y)p(y,z)$. Equation (19) then leads to the following expression for the conditional probability of x, given y and z:

$$P_t(x|y,z) = \int \frac{d\hat{x}}{2\pi} \, e^{i\hat{x}[x - Ry] - \frac{1}{2}\hat{x}^2[Q-R^2] + \chi(\hat{x}\,\text{sgn}[z], t)} \qquad (20)$$

We observe that this probability distribution is the same for all models with the same ρ and that the dependence on z is through $\tau = \text{sgn}[z]$, a directly observable quantity. The training error and the student field probability density are given by

$$E_{\text{tr}} = \int dx\,dy \sum_{\tau=\pm 1} \theta(-x\tau) P_t(x|y,\tau) P(\tau|y) P(y) \qquad (21)$$

$$P_t(x) = \int dy \sum_{\tau=\pm 1} P_t(x|y,\tau) P(\tau|y) P(y) \qquad (22)$$

in which $P(y) = (2\pi)^{-\frac{1}{2}} e^{-\frac{1}{2}y^2}$. We note that the dependence of E_{tr} and $P_t(x)$ on the specific noise model arises solely through $P(\tau|y)$ which we find is given by

$$P(\tau|y) = \lambda \theta(-\tau y) + (1-\lambda)\theta(\tau y) \qquad P(\tau|y) = \frac{1}{2}(1 + \tau\,\text{erf}[y/\sqrt{2}\Sigma])$$

in the output noise and Gaussian input noise models, respectively. In order to simplify the numerical computation of the remaining integrals one can further reduce the number of integrations analytically. Details will be reported elsewhere.

6 Comparison with Numerical Simulations

It will be clear that there is a large number of parameters that one could vary in order to generate different simulation experiments with which to test our theory. Here we have to restrict ourselves to presenting a number of representative results. Figure 1 shows, for the output noise model, how the probability density $P_t(x)$ of

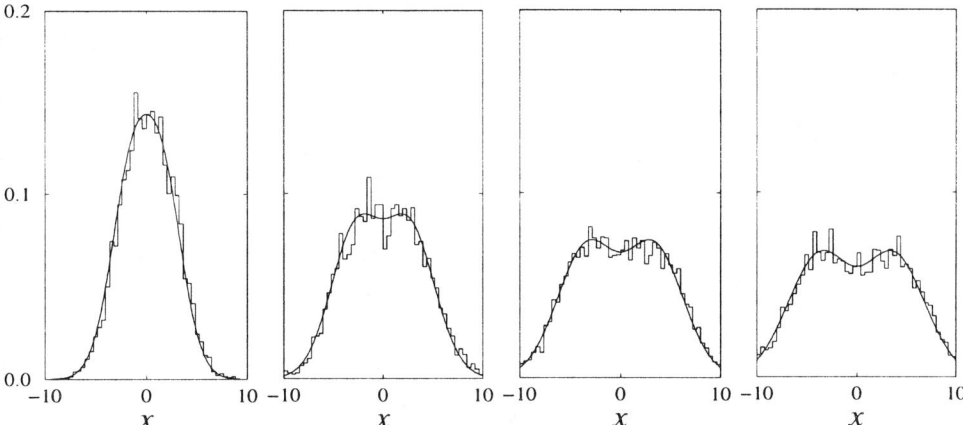

Figure 1: Student field distribution $P(x)$ for the case of output noise, at different times (left to right: $t = 1, 2, 3, 4$), for $\alpha = \gamma = \frac{1}{2}$, $J_0 = \eta = 1$, $\lambda = 0.2$. Histograms: distributions measured in simulations, ($N = 10{,}000$). Lines: theoretical predictions.

the student field $x = \boldsymbol{J} \cdot \boldsymbol{\xi}$ develops in time, starting as a Gaussian at $t = 0$ and evolving to a highly non-Gaussian distribution with a double peak by time $t = 4$. The theoretical results give an extremely satisfactory account of the numerical simulations. Figure 2 compares our predictions for the generalisation and training errors E_g and $E_{\rm tr}$ with the results of numerical simulations, for different initial conditions, $E_g(0) = 0$ and $E_g(0) = 0.5$, and for different choices of the two most important parameters λ (which controls the amount of teacher noise) and α (which measures the relative size of the training set). The theoretical results are again in excellent agreement with the simulations. The system is found to have no memory of its past (which will be different for some other learning rules), the asymptotic values of E_g and $E_{\rm tr}$ being independent of the initial student vector. In our examples E_g is consistently larger than $E_{\rm tr}$, the difference becoming less pronounced as α increases. Note, however, that in some circumstances $E_{\rm tr}$ can also be larger then E_g. Careful inspection shows that for Hebbian learning there are no true overfitting effects, not even in the case of large λ and small γ (for large amounts of teacher noise, without regularisation via weight decay). Minor finite time minima of the generalisation error are only found for very short times ($t < 1$), in combination with special choices for parameters and initial conditions.

7 Discussion

Starting from a microscopic description of Hebbian on-line learning in perceptrons with restricted training sets, of size $p = \alpha N$ where N is the number of inputs, we have developed an exact theory in terms of macroscopic observables which has enabled us to predict the generalisation error and the training error, as well as the probability density of the student local fields in the limit $N \to \infty$. Our results are in execellent agreement with numerical simulations (as carried out for systems of size $N = 5{,}000$) in the case of output noise; our predictions for the Gaussian input noise model are currently being compared with the results of simulations. Generalisations of our calculations to scenarios involving, for instance, time-dependent learning rates or time-dependent decay rates are straightforward. Although it will be clear that our present calculations cannot be extended to non-Hebbian rules, since they

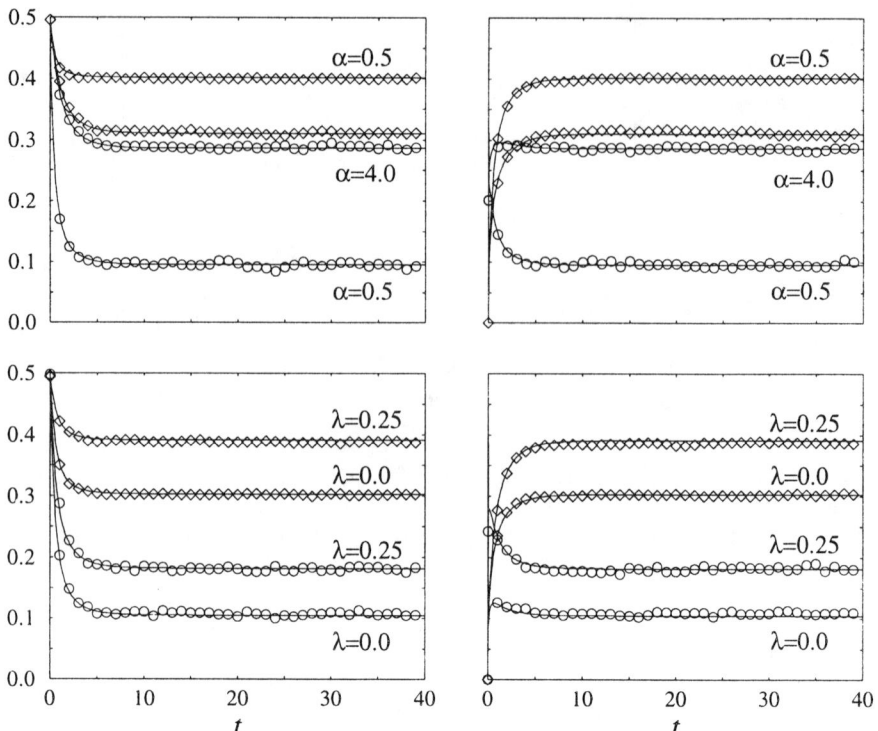

Figure 2: Generalisation errors (diamonds/lines) and training errors (circles/lines) as observed during on-line Hebbian learning, as functions of time. Upper two graphs: $\lambda = 0.2$ and $\alpha \in \{0.5, 4.0\}$ (upper left: $E_g(0) = 0.5$, upper right: $E_g(0) = 0$). Lower two graphs: $\alpha = 1$ and $\lambda \in \{0.0, 0.25\}$ (lower left: $E_g(0) = 0.5$, lower right: $E_g(0) = 0.0$). Markers: simulation results for an $N = 5,000$ system. Solid lines: predictions of the theory. In all cases $J_0 = \eta = 1$ and $\gamma = 0.5$.

ultimately rely on our ability to write down the microscopic weight vector $\boldsymbol{J}$ at any time in explicit form (4), they do indeed provide a significant yardstick against which more sophisticated and more general theories can be tested. In particular, they have already played a valuable role in assessing the conditions under which a recent general theory of learning with restricted training sets, based on a dynamical version of the replica formalism, is exact [6, 7].

References

[1] Mace C.W.H. and Coolen A.C.C. (1998) *Statistics and Computing* **8**, 55

[2] Horner H. (1992a), Z.Phys. B **86**, 291; (1992b), Z.Phys. B **87**, 371

[3] Krogh A. and Hertz J.A. (1992) *J.Phys. A: Math. Gen.* **25**, 1135

[4] Sollich P. and Barber D. (1997) *Europhys. Lett.* **38**, 477

[5] Sollich P. and Barber D. (1998) *Advances in Neural Information Processing Systems 10*, Eds. Jordan M., Kearns M. and Solla S. (Cambridge: MIT)

[6] Coolen A.C.C. and Saad D., King's College London preprint KCL-MTH-98-08

[7] Coolen A.C.C. and Saad D. (1998) (in preparation)

Tight Bounds for the VC-Dimension of Piecewise Polynomial Networks

Akito Sakurai
School of Knowledge Science
Japan Advanced Institute of Science and Technology
Nomi-gun, Ishikawa 923-1211, Japan.
CREST, Japan Science and Technology Corporation.
ASakurai@jaist.ac.jp

Abstract

$O(ws(s \log d + \log(dqh/s)))$ and $O(ws((h/s) \log q) + \log(dqh/s))$ are upper bounds for the VC-dimension of a set of neural networks of units with piecewise polynomial activation functions, where s is the depth of the network, h is the number of hidden units, w is the number of adjustable parameters, q is the maximum of the number of polynomial segments of the activation function, and d is the maximum degree of the polynomials; also $\Omega(ws \log(dqh/s))$ is a lower bound for the VC-dimension of such a network set, which are tight for the cases $s = \Theta(h)$ and s is constant. For the special case $q = 1$, the VC-dimension is $\Theta(ws \log d)$.

1 Introduction

In spite of its importance, we had been unable to obtain VC-dimension values for practical types of networks, until fairly tight upper and lower bounds were obtained ([6], [8], [9], and [10]) for linear threshold element networks in which all elements perform a threshold function on weighted sum of inputs. Roughly, the lower bound for the networks is $(1/2)w \log h$ and the upper bound is $w \log h$ where h is the number of hidden elements and w is the number of connecting weights (for one-hidden-layer case $w \approx nh$ where n is the input dimension of the network).

In many applications, though, sigmoidal functions, specifically a typical sigmoid function $1/(1 + \exp(-x))$, or piecewise linear functions for economy of calculation, are used instead of the threshold function. This is mainly because the differentiability of the functions is needed to perform backpropagation or other learning algorithms. Unfortunately explicit bounds obtained so far for the VC-dimension of sigmoidal networks exhibit large gaps ($O(w^2h^2)$ ([3]), $\Omega(w \log h)$ for bounded depth and $\Omega(wh)$ for unbounded depth) and are hard to improve. For the piecewise linear case, Maass obtained a result that the VC-dimension is $O(w^2 \log q)$, where q is the number of linear pieces of the function ([5]).

Recently Koiran and Sontag ([4]) proved a lower bound $\Omega(w^2)$ for the piecewise polynomial case and they claimed that an open problem that Maass posed if there is a matching w^2 lower bound for the type of networks is solved. But we still have something to do, since they showed it only for the case $w = \Theta(h)$ and the number of hidden layers being unbounded; also $O(w^2)$ bound has room to improve.

We in this paper improve the bounds obtained by Maass, Koiran and Sontag and consequently show the role of polynomials, which can not be played by linear functions, and the role of the constant functions that could appear for piecewise polynomial case, which cannot be played by polynomial functions.

After submission of the draft, we found that Bartlett, Maiorov, and Meir had obtained similar results prior to ours (also in this proceedings). Our advantage is that we clarified the role played by the degree and number of segments concerning the both bounds.

2 Terminology and Notation

log stands for the logarithm base 2 throughout the paper.

The *depth* of a network is the length of the longest path from its external inputs to its external output, where the length is the number of units on the path. Likewise we can assign a *depth* to each unit in a network as the length of the longest path from the external input to the output of the unit. A *hidden layer* is a set of units at the same depth other than the depth of the network. Therefore a depth L network has $L - 1$ hidden layers.

In many cases $\mathbf{w}$ will stand for a vector composed of all the connection weights in the network (including threshold values for the threshold units) and w is the length of $\mathbf{w}$. The number of units in the network, excluding "input units," will be denoted by h; in other words, the number of hidden units plus one, or sometimes just the number of hidden units. A function whose range is $\{0, 1\}$ (a set of 0 and 1) is called a *Boolean-valued function*.

3 Upper Bounds

To obtain upper bounds for the VC-dimension we use a *region counting argument*, developed by Goldberg and Jerrum [2]. The VC-dimension of the network, that is, the VC-dimension of the function set $\{f_G(\mathbf{w}; \cdot) \mid \mathbf{w} \in \mathcal{R}^w\}$ is upper bounded by

$$\max\left\{N \mid 2^N \leq \max_{\mathbf{x}_1,\ldots,\mathbf{x}_N} N_{cc}\left(\mathcal{R}^w - \bigcup_{i=1}^N \mathcal{N}(f_G(\mathbf{w}; \mathbf{x}_i))\right)\right\} \tag{3.1}$$

where $N_{cc}(\cdot)$ is the number of connected components and $\mathcal{N}(f)$ is the set $\{\mathbf{w} \mid f(\mathbf{w}) = 0\}$.

The following two theorems are convenient. Refer [11] and [7] for the first theorem. The lemma followed is easily proven.

Theorem 3.1. *Let $f_G(\mathbf{w}; \mathbf{x}_i)$ ($1 \leq i \leq N$) be real polynomials in $\mathbf{w}$, each of degree d or less. The number of connected components of the set $\bigcap_{i=1}^m \{\mathbf{w} \mid f_G(\mathbf{w}; \mathbf{x}_i) = 0\}$ is bounded from above by $2(2d)^w$ where w is the length of $\mathbf{w}$.*

Lemma 3.2. *If $m \geq w(\log C + \log\log C + 1)$, then $2^m > (mC/w)^w$ for $C \geq 4$.*

First let us consider the polynomial activation function case.

Theorem 3.3. *Suppose that the activation function are polynomials of degree at most d. $O(ws\log d)$ is an upper bound of the VC-dimension for the networks with depth s. When $s = \Theta(h)$ the bound is $O(wh\log d)$. More precisely $ws(\log d + \log\log d + 2)$ is an upper bound. Note that if we allow a polynomial as the input function, $d_1 d_2$ will replace d above where d_1 is the maximum degree of the input functions and d_2 is that of the activation functions.*

The theorem is clear from the facts that the network function (f_G in (3.1)) is a polynomial of degree at most $d^s + d^{s-1} + \cdots + d$, Theorem 3.1 and Lemma 3.2.

For the piecewise linear case, we have two types of bounds. The first one is suitable for bounded depth cases (*i.e.* the depth $s = o(h)$) and the second one for the unbounded depth case (*i.e.* $s = \Theta(h)$).

Theorem 3.4. *Suppose that the activation functions are piecewise polynomials with at most q segments of polynomials degree at most d. $O(ws(s\log d + \log(dqh/s)))$ and $O(ws((h/s)\log q) + \log(dqh/s))$ are upper bounds for the VC-dimension, where s is the depth of the network. More precisely, $ws((s/2)\log d + \log(qh))$ and $ws((h/s)\log q + \log d)$ are asymptotic upper bounds. Note that if we allow a polynomial as the input function then $d_1 d_2$ will replace d above where d_1 is the maximum degree of the input functions and d_2 is that of the activation functions.*

Proof. We have two different ways to calculate the bounds. First

$$N_{cc}\left(\mathcal{R}^w - \bigcup_{i=1}^{N}\mathcal{N}(f_G(\mathbf{w};\mathbf{x}_i))\right)$$
$$\leq \prod_{j=1}^{s} \max N_{cc}\left(\mathcal{R}^{w_1+\cdots+w_j} - \bigcup\mathcal{N}(f_{G_1}(\mathbf{w}_1\circ\cdots\circ\mathbf{w}_j;\mathbf{x}_i))\right)$$
$$\leq \prod_{j=1}^{s}\left(\frac{8eNqh_s(d^{j-1}+\cdots+d+1)d}{w_1+\cdots+w_j}\right)^{w_1+\cdots+w_j}$$
$$\leq \left(\frac{8eNqd^{(s+3)/2}(h/s)}{w}\right)^{ws}.$$

where h_i is the number of hidden units in the i-th layer and $\circ$ is an operator to form a new vector by concatenating the two. From this we get an asymptotic upper bound $ws((s/2)\log d + \log(qh))$ for the VC-dimension.

Secondly

$$N_{cc}\left(\mathcal{R}^w - \bigcup_{i=1}^{N}\mathcal{N}(f_G(\mathbf{w};\mathbf{x}_i))\right) \leq N_{cc}\left(\mathcal{R}^w - \bigcup_{i=1}^{N}\bigcup_{j=1}^{q^h}\mathcal{N}(f_{G,j}(\mathbf{w};\mathbf{x}_i))\right) \leq \left(\frac{8eNq^h d^s}{w}\right)^w$$

From this we get an asymptotic upper bound $ws((h/s)\log q + \log d)$ for the VC-dimension. Combining these two bounds we get the result. Note that s in $\log(dqh/s)$ in it is introduced to eliminate unduly large term emerging when $s = \Theta(h)$. □

4 Lower Bounds for Polynomial Networks

Theorem 4.1 *Let us consider the case that the activation function are polynomials of degree at most d. $\Omega(ws\log d)$ is a lower bound of the VC-dimension for the networks with depth s. When $s = \Theta(h)$ the bound is $\Omega(wh\log d)$, More precisely,*

$(1/16)w(s-6)\log d$ is an asymptotic lower bound where d is the degree of activation functions and is a power of two and h is restricted to $O(n^2)$ for input dimension n.

The proof consists of several lemmas. The network we are constructing will have two parts: an encoder and a decoder. We deliberately fix the N input points. The decoder part has fixed underlying architecture but also fixed connecting weights whereas the encoder part has variable weights so that for any given binary outputs for the input points the decoder could output the specified value from the codes in which the output value is encoded by the encoder.

First we consider the decoder, which has two real inputs and one real output. One of the two inputs y holds a code of a binary sequence $b_1, b_2, \ldots, b_m$ and the other x holds a code of a binary sequence $c_1, c_2, \ldots, c_m$. The elements of the latter sequence are all 0's except for $c_j = 1$, where $c_j = 1$ orders the decoder to output b_j from it and consequently from the network.

We show two types of networks; one of which has activation functions of degree at most two and has the VC-dimension $w(s-1)$ and the other has activation functions of degree d a power of two and has the VC-dimension $w(s-5)\log d$.

We use for convenience two functions $\mathcal{H}_\theta(x) = 1$ if $x \geq \theta$ and 0 otherwise and $\mathcal{H}_{\theta,\phi}(x) = 1$ if $x \geq \phi$, 0 if $x \leq \theta$, and undefined otherwise. Throughout this section we will use a simple logistic function $\rho(x) = (16/3)x(1-x)$ which has the following property.

Lemma 4.2. *For any binary sequence $b_1, b_2, \ldots, b_m$, there exists an interval $[x_1, x_2]$ such that $b_i = \mathcal{H}_{1/4,3/4}(\rho^i(x))$ and $0 \leq \rho^i(x) \leq 1$ for any $x \in [x_1, x_2]$.*

The next lemmas are easily proven.

Lemma 4.3. *For any binary sequence $c_1, c_2, \ldots, c_m$ which are all 0's except for $c_j = 1$, there exists x_0 such that $c_i = \mathcal{H}_{1/4,3/4}(\rho^i(x_0))$. Specifically we will take $x_0 = \rho_L^{-(j-1)}(1/4)$, where $\rho_L^{-1}(x)$ is the inverse of $\rho(x)$ on $[0, 1/2]$. Then $\rho^{j-1}(x_0) = 1/4$, $\rho^j(x_0) = 1$, $\rho^i(x_0) = 0$ for all $i > j$, and $\rho^{j-i}(x_0) \leq (1/4)^i$ for all positive $i \leq j$.*

Proof. Clear from the fact that $\rho(x) \geq 4x$ on $[0, 1/4]$. □

Lemma 4.4. *For any binary sequence $b_1, b_2, \ldots, b_m$, take y such that $b_i = \mathcal{H}_{1/4,3/4}(\rho^i(y))$ and $0 \leq \rho^i(y) \leq 1$ for all i and $x_0 = \rho_L^{-(j-1)}(1/4)$, then $\mathcal{H}_{7/12,3/4}\left(\sum_{i=1}^m \rho^i(x_0)\rho^i(y)\right) = b_j$, i.e. $\mathcal{H}_0\left(\sum_{i=1}^m \rho^i(x_0)\rho^i(y) - 2/3\right) = b_j$.*

Proof. If $b_j = 0$, $\sum_{i=1}^m \rho^i(x_0)\rho^i(y) = \sum_{i=1}^j \rho^i(x_0)\rho^i(y) \leq \rho^j(y) + \sum_{i=1}^{j-1}(1/4)^i < \rho^j(y) + (1/3) \leq 7/12$. If $b_j = 1$, $\sum_{i=1}^m \rho^i(x_0)\rho^i(y) > \rho^j(x_0)\rho^j(y) \geq 3/4$. □

By the above lemmas, the network in Figure 1 (left) has the following function:

- Suppose that a binary sequence $b_1, \ldots, b_m$ and an integer j is given. Then we can present y that depends only on $b_1, \ldots, b_m$ and x_0 that depends only on j such that b_j is output from the decoder.

Note that we use $(x+y)^2 - (x-y)^2 = 4xy$ to realize a multiplication unit.

For the case of degree of higher than two we have to construct a bit more complicated one by using another simple logistic function $\mu(x) = (36/5)x(1-x)$. We need the next lemma.

Lemma 4.5. *Take $x_0 = \mu_L^{-(j-1)}(1/6)$, where $\mu_L^{-1}(x)$ is the inverse of $\mu(x)$ on $[0, 1/2]$. Then $\mu^{j-1}(x_0) = 1/6$, $\mu^j(x_0) = 1$, $\mu^i(x_0) = 0$ for all $i > j$, and $\mu^{j-i}(x_0) =$*

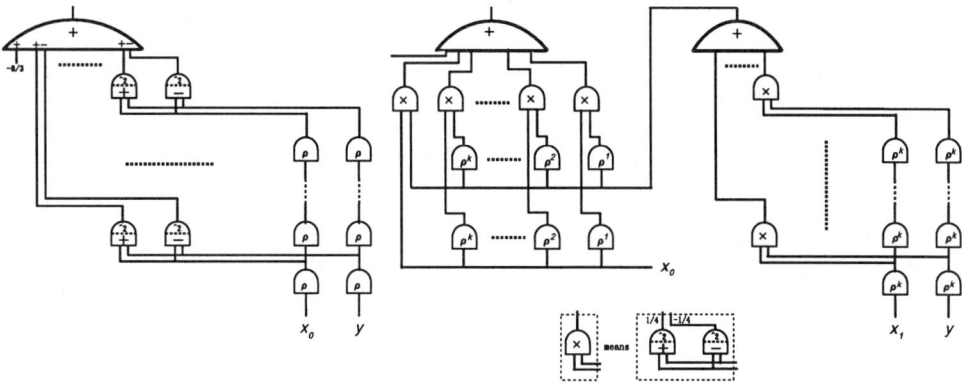

Figure 1: Network architecture consisting of polynomials of order two (left) and those of order of power of two (right).

$(1/6)^i$ for all $i > 0$ and $\leq j$.

Proof. Clear from the fact that $\mu(x) \geq 6x$ on $[0, 1/6]$. □

Lemma 4.6. *For any binary sequence $b_1, b_2, \ldots, b_k$, $b_{k+1}, b_{k+2}, \ldots, b_{2k}$, $\ldots, b_{(m-1)k+1}, \ldots, b_{mk}$ take y such that $b_i = \mathcal{H}_{1/4,3/4}(\rho^i(y))$ and $0 \leq \rho^i(y) \leq 1$ for all i. Moreover for any $1 \leq j \leq m$ and any $1 \leq l \leq k$ take $x_1 = \mu_L^{-(j-1)}(1/6)$, and $x_0 = \mu_L^{-(l-1)}(1/6^k)$. Then for $z = \sum_{i=1}^{m} \rho^{ik}(y)\mu^{ik}(x_1)$, $\mathcal{H}_0\left(\sum_{i=0}^{k-1} \rho^i(z)\mu^i(x_0) - (1/2)\right) = b_{kj+l}$ holds.*

Lemma 4.7. *If $0 < \rho^i(x) < 1$ for any $0 < i \leq l$, take an ϵ such that $(16/3)^l\epsilon < 1/4$. Then $\rho^l(x) - (16/3)^l\epsilon < \rho^l(x+\epsilon) < \rho^l(x) + (16/3)^l\epsilon$.*

Proof. There are four cases depending on whether $\rho^{l-1}(x+\epsilon)$ is on the uphill or downhill of ρ and whether x is on the uphill or downhill of ρ^{l-1}. The proofs are done by induction.

First suppose that the two are on the uphill. Then $\rho^l(x+\epsilon) = \rho(\rho^{l-1}(x+\epsilon)) < \rho(\rho^{l-1}(x) + (16/3)^{l-1}\epsilon)) < \rho^l(x) + (16/3)^l\epsilon$. Secondly suppose that $\rho^{l-1}(x+\epsilon)$ is on the uphill but x is on the downhill. Then $\rho^l(x+\epsilon) = \rho(\rho^{l-1}(x+\epsilon)) > \rho(\rho^{l-1}(x) - (16/3)^{l-1}\epsilon)) > \rho^l(x) - (16/3)^l\epsilon$. The other two cases are similar. □

Proof of Lemma 4.6. We will show that the difference between $\rho^{jk+l}(y)$ and $\sum_{i=0}^{k-1} \rho^i(z)\mu^i(x_0)$ is sufficiently small. Clearly $z = \sum_{i=1}^{m} \mu^{ik}(x_1)\rho^{ik}(y) = \sum_{i=1}^{j} \mu^{ik}(x_1)\rho^{ik}(y) \leq \rho^{jk}(y) + \sum_{i=1}^{j-1}(1/6^k)^i < \rho^{jk}(y) + 1/(6^k - 1)$ and $\rho^{jk}(y) < z$. If z is on the uphill of ρ^l then by using the above lemma, we get $\sum_{i=0}^{k-1} \rho^i(z)\mu^i(x_0) = \sum_{i=0}^{l} \rho^i(z)\mu^i(x_0) < \rho^l(z) + 1/(6^k - 1) < \rho^{jk+l}(y) + (1 + (16/3)^l)(1/(6^k - 1)) < \rho^{jk+l}(y) + 1/4$ (note that $l \leq k - 1$ and $k \geq 2$). If z is on the downhill of ρ^l then by using the above lemma, we get $\sum_{i=0}^{k-1} \rho^i(z)\mu^i(x_0) = \sum_{i=0}^{l} \rho^i(z)\mu^i(x_0) > \rho^l(z) > \rho^l(\rho^{jk}(y)) - (16/3)^l(1/(6^k - 1)) > \rho^{jk+l}(y) - 1/4$. □

Next we show the encoding scheme we adopted. We show only the case $w = \Theta(h^2)$ since the case $w = \Theta(h)$ or more generally $w = O(h^2)$ is easily obtained from this.

Theorem 4.8 *There is a network of $2n$ inputs, $2h$ hidden units with h^2 weights $\mathbf{w}$,* and h^2 sets of input values $\mathbf{x}_1, \ldots, \mathbf{x}_{h^2}$ such that for any set of values $y_1, \ldots, y_{h^2}$ we can chose $\mathbf{w}$ to satisfy $y_i = f_G(\mathbf{w}; \mathbf{x}_i)$.

Proof. We extensively utilize the fact that monomials obtained by choosing at most k variables from n variables with repetition allowed (say $x_1^2 x_2 x_6$) are all linearly independent ([1]). Note that the number of monomials thus formed is $\binom{n+m}{m}$.

Suppose for simplicity that we have $2n$ inputs and $2h$ main hidden units (we have other hidden units too), and $h = \binom{n+m}{m}$. By using multiplication units (in fact each is a composite of two squaring units and the outputs are supposed to be summed up as in Figure 1), we can form $h = \binom{n+m}{m}$ linearly independent monomials composed of variables $x_1, \ldots, x_n$ by using at most $(m-1)h$ multiplication units (or h nominal units when $m = 1$). In the same way, we can form h linearly independent monomials composed of variables $x_{n+1}, \ldots, x_{2n}$. Let us denote the monomials by $u_1, \ldots, u_h$ and $v_1, \ldots, v_h$.

We form a subnetwork to calculate $\sum_{j=1}^{h}(\sum_{i=1}^{h} w_{i,j} u_i) v_j$ by using h multiplication units. Clearly the calculated result y is the weighted sum of monomials described above where the weights are $w_{i,j}$ for $1 \leq i,j \leq h$.

Since $y = f_G(\mathbf{w}; \mathbf{x})$ is a linear combination of linearly independent terms, if we choose appropriately h^2 sets of values $\mathbf{x}_1, \ldots, \mathbf{x}_{h^2}$ for $\mathbf{x} = (x_1, \ldots, x_{2n})$, then for any assignment of h^2 values $y_1, \ldots, y_{h^2}$ to y we have a set of weights $\mathbf{w}$ such that $y_i = f(\mathbf{x}_i, \mathbf{w})$. □

Proof of Theorem 4.1. The whole network consists of the decoder and the encoder. The input points are the Cartesian product of the above $\mathbf{x}_1, \ldots, \mathbf{x}_{h^2}$ and $\{x_0$ defined in Lemma 4.4 for $b_j = 1 \mid 1 \leq j \leq s'\}$ for some h where s' is the number of bits to be encoded. This means that we have $h^2 s$ points that can be shattered.

Let the number of hidden layers of the decoder be s. The number of units used for the decoder is $4(s-1)+1$ (for the degree 2 case which can decode at most s bits) or $4(s-3)+4(k-1)+1$ (for the degree 2^k case which can decode at most $(s-2)k$ bits). The number of units used for the encoder is less than $4h$; we though have constraints on s (which dominates the depth of the network) and h (which dominates the number of units in the network) that $h \leq \binom{n+m}{m}$ and $m = O(s)$ or roughly $\log h = O(s)$ be satisfied.

Let us chose $m = 2$ ($m = \log s$ is a better choise). As a result, by using $4h+4(s-1)+1$ (or $4h+4(s-3)+4(k-1)+1$) units in $s+2$ layers, we can shatter $h^2 s$ (or $h^2(s-2)\log d$) points; or asymptotically by using h units s layers we can shatter $(1/16)w(s-3)$ (or $(1/16)w(s-5)\log d$) points. □

5 Piecewise Polynomial Case

Theorem 5.1. *Let us consider a set of networks of units with linear input functions and piecewise polynomial (with q polynomial segments) activation functions. $\Omega(ws\log(dqh/s))$ is a lower bound of the VC-dimension, where s is the depth of the network and d is the maximum degree of the activation functions. More precisely, $(1/16)w(s-6)(\log d + \log(h/s) + \log q)$ is an asymptotic lower bound.*

For the scarcity of space, we give just an outline of the proof. Our proof is based on that of the polynomial networks. We will use h units with activation function of $q \geq 2$ polynomial segments of degree at most d in place of each of ρ^k unit in the decoder, which give the ability of decoding $\log dqh$ bits in one layer and $s \log dqh$ bits in total by $\Theta(sh)$ units in total. If h designates the total number of units, the number of the decodable bits is represented as $\log(dqh/s)$.

In the following for simplicity we suppose that dqh is a power of 2. Let $\rho^k(x)$ be the k composition of $\rho(x)$ as usual i.e. $\rho^k(x) = \rho(\rho^{k-1}(x))$ and $\rho^1(x) = \rho(x)$. Let $\rho^{\log d,l}(x) = \rho^{\log d}(\lambda^l(x))$, where $\lambda(x) = 4x$ if $x \leq 1/2$ and $4 - 4x$ otherwise, which by the way has 2^l polynomial segments.

Now the ρ^k unit in the polynomial case is replaced by the array $\rho^{\log d, \log q, \log h}(x)$ of h units that is defined as follows:

(i) $\rho^{\log d, \log q, 1}(x)$ is an array of two units; one is $\rho^{\log d, \log q}(\lambda^+(x))$ where $\lambda^+(x) = 4x$ if $x \leq 1/2$ and 0 otherwise and the other is $\rho^{\log d, \log q}(\lambda^-(x))$ where $\lambda^-(x) = 0$ if $x \leq 1/2$ and $4 - 4x$ otherwise.

(ii) $\rho^{\log d, \log q, m}(x)$ is the array of 2^m units, each with one of the functions $\rho^{\log d, \log q}(\lambda^{\pm}(\cdots(\lambda^{\pm}(x))\cdots))$ where $\lambda^{\pm}(\cdots(\lambda^{\pm}(x))\cdots)$ is the m composition of $\lambda^+(x)$ or $\lambda^-(x)$. Note that $\lambda^{\pm}(\cdots(\lambda^{\pm}(x))\cdots)$ has at most three linear segments (one is linear and the others are constant 0) and the sum of 2^m possible combinations $f(\lambda^{\pm}(\cdots(\lambda^{\pm}(x))\cdots))$ is equal to $f(\lambda^m(x))$ for any function f such that $f(0) = 0$.

Then lemmas similar to the ones in the polynomial case follow.

References

[1] Anthony, M: Classification by polynomial surfaces, *NeuroCOLT Technical Report Series*, NC-TR-95-011 (1995).

[2] Goldberg, P. and M. Jerrum: Bounding the Vapnik-Chervonenkis dimension of concept classes parameterized by real numbers, *Proc. Sixth Annual ACM Conference on Computational Learning Theory*, 361–369 (1993).

[3] Karpinski, M. and A. Macintyre, Polynomial bounds for VC dimension of sigmoidal neural networks, *Proc. 27th ACM Symposium on Theory of Computing*, 200–208 (1995).

[4] Koiran, P. and E. D. Sontag: Neural networks with quadratic VC dimension, *Journ. Comp. Syst. Sci.*, 54, 190–198(1997).

[5] Maass, W. G.: Bounds for the computational power and learning complexity of analog neural nets, *Proc. 25th Annual Symposium of the Theory of Computing*, 335-344 (1993).

[6] Maass, W. G.: Neural nets with superlinear VC-dimension, *Neural Computation*, 6, 877–884 (1994)

[7] Milnor, J.: On the Betti numbers of real varieties, *Proc. of the AMS*, 15, 275–280 (1964).

[8] Sakurai, A.: Tighter Bounds of the VC-Dimension of Three-layer Networks, *Proc. WCNN'93*, III, 540–543 (1993).

[9] Sakurai, A.: On the VC-dimension of depth four threshold circuits and the complexity of Boolean-valued functions, *Proc. ALT93 (LNAI 744)*, 251–264 (1993); refined version is in *Theoretical Computer Science*, 137, 109-127 (1995).

[10] Sakurai, A.: On the VC-dimension of neural networks with a large number of hidden layers, *Proc. NOLTA'93*, IEICE, 239–242 (1993).

[11] Warren, H. E.: Lower bounds for approximation by nonlinear manifolds, *Trans. AMS*, 133, 167–178, (1968).

Shrinking the Tube:
A New Support Vector Regression Algorithm

Bernhard Schölkopf[§,*], **Peter Bartlett**[*], **Alex Smola**[§,*], **Robert Williamson**[*]
[§] GMD FIRST, Rudower Chaussee 5, 12489 Berlin, Germany
[*] FEIT/RSISE, Australian National University, Canberra 0200, Australia
bs, smola@first.gmd.de, Peter.Bartlett, Bob.Williamson@anu.edu.au

Abstract

A new algorithm for Support Vector regression is described. For a priori chosen ν, it automatically adjusts a flexible tube of minimal radius to the data such that at most a fraction ν of the data points lie outside. Moreover, it is shown how to use parametric tube shapes with non-constant radius. The algorithm is analysed theoretically and experimentally.

1 INTRODUCTION

Support Vector (SV) machines comprise a new class of learning algorithms, motivated by results of statistical learning theory (Vapnik, 1995). Originally developed for pattern recognition, they represent the decision boundary in terms of a typically small subset (Schölkopf et al., 1995) of all training examples, called the Support Vectors. In order for this property to carry over to the case of SV Regression, Vapnik devised the so-called ε-insensitive loss function $|y - f(\mathbf{x})|_\varepsilon = \max\{0, |y - f(\mathbf{x})| - \varepsilon\}$, which does not penalize errors below some $\varepsilon > 0$, chosen a priori. His algorithm, which we will henceforth call ε-**SVR**, seeks to estimate functions
$$f(\mathbf{x}) = (\mathbf{w} \cdot \mathbf{x}) + b, \quad \mathbf{w}, \mathbf{x} \in \mathbb{R}^N, b \in \mathbb{R}, \quad (1)$$
based on data
$$(\mathbf{x}_1, y_1), \ldots, (\mathbf{x}_\ell, y_\ell) \in \mathbb{R}^N \times \mathbb{R}, \quad (2)$$
by minimizing the regularized risk functional
$$\|\mathbf{w}\|^2/2 + C \cdot R_{emp}^\varepsilon, \quad (3)$$
where C is a constant determining the trade-off between minimizing training errors and minimizing the model complexity term $\|\mathbf{w}\|^2$, and $R_{emp}^\varepsilon := \frac{1}{\ell} \sum_{i=1}^{\ell} |y_i - f(\mathbf{x}_i)|_\varepsilon$.

The parameter ε can be useful if the desired accuracy of the approximation can be specified beforehand. In some cases, however, we just want the estimate to be as accurate as possible, without having to commit ourselves to a certain level of accuracy.

We present a modification of the ε-SVR algorithm which automatically minimizes ε, thus adjusting the accuracy level to the data at hand.

2 ν-SV REGRESSION AND ε-SV REGRESSION

To estimate functions (1) from empirical data (2) we proceed as follows (Schölkopf et al., 1998a). At each point $\mathbf{x}_i$, we allow an error of ε. Everything above ε is captured in slack variables $\xi_i^{(*)}$ ($(*)$ being a shorthand implying both the variables with and without asterisks), which are penalized in the objective function via a regularization constant C, chosen a priori (Vapnik, 1995). The tube size ε is traded off against model complexity and slack variables via a constant $\nu \geq 0$:

$$\text{minimize} \quad \tau(\mathbf{w}, \boldsymbol{\xi}^{(*)}, \varepsilon) = \|\mathbf{w}\|^2/2 + C \cdot \left(\nu\varepsilon + \frac{1}{\ell}\sum_{i=1}^{\ell}(\xi_i + \xi_i^*)\right) \quad (4)$$

$$\text{subject to} \quad ((\mathbf{w} \cdot \mathbf{x}_i) + b) - y_i \leq \varepsilon + \xi_i \quad (5)$$

$$y_i - ((\mathbf{w} \cdot \mathbf{x}_i) + b) \leq \varepsilon + \xi_i^* \quad (6)$$

$$\xi_i^{(*)} \geq 0, \quad \varepsilon \geq 0. \quad (7)$$

Here and below, it is understood that $i = 1, \ldots, \ell$, and that bold face greek letters denote ℓ-dimensional vectors of the corresponding variables. Introducing a Lagrangian with multipliers $\alpha_i^{(*)}, \eta_i^{(*)}, \beta \geq 0$, we obtain the the Wolfe dual problem. Moreover, as Boser et al. (1992), we substitute a kernel k for the dot product, corresponding to a dot product in some feature space related to input space via a nonlinear map Φ,

$$k(\mathbf{x}, \mathbf{y}) = (\Phi(\mathbf{x}) \cdot \Phi(\mathbf{y})). \quad (8)$$

This leads to the ν-**SVR Optimization Problem:** for $\nu \geq 0, C > 0$,

$$\text{maximize} \quad W(\boldsymbol{\alpha}^{(*)}) = \sum_{i=1}^{\ell}(\alpha_i^* - \alpha_i)y_i - \frac{1}{2}\sum_{i,j=1}^{\ell}(\alpha_i^* - \alpha_i)(\alpha_j^* - \alpha_j)k(\mathbf{x}_i, \mathbf{x}_j) \quad (9)$$

subject to

$$\sum_{i=1}^{\ell}(\alpha_i - \alpha_i^*) = 0, \quad (10) \qquad 0 \leq \alpha_i^{(*)} \leq \frac{C}{\ell}, \quad (11) \qquad \sum_{i=1}^{\ell}(\alpha_i + \alpha_i^*) \leq C \cdot \nu. \quad (12)$$

The regression estimate can be shown to take the form

$$f(\mathbf{x}) = \sum_{i=1}^{\ell}(\alpha_i^* - \alpha_i)k(\mathbf{x}_i, \mathbf{x}) + b, \quad (13)$$

where b (and ε) can be computed by taking into account that (5) and (6) (substitution of $\sum_j(\alpha_j^* - \alpha_j)k(\mathbf{x}_j, \mathbf{x})$ for $(\mathbf{w} \cdot \mathbf{x})$ is understood) become equalities with $\xi_i^{(*)} = 0$ for points with $0 < \alpha_i^{(*)} < C/\ell$, respectively, due to the Karush-Kuhn-Tucker conditions (cf. Vapnik, 1995). The latter moreover imply that in the kernel expansion (13), only those $\alpha_i^{(*)}$ will be nonzero that correspond to a constraint (5)/(6) which is precisely met. The respective patterns $\mathbf{x}_i$ are referred to as *Support Vectors*.

Before we give theoretical results explaining the significance of the parameter ν, the following observation concerning ε is helpful. If $\nu > 1$, then $\varepsilon = 0$, since it does not pay to increase ε (cf. (4)). If $\nu \leq 1$, it can still happen that $\varepsilon = 0$, e.g. if the data are noise-free and can perfectly be interpolated with a low capacity model. The case $\varepsilon = 0$, however, is not what we are interested in; it corresponds to plain L_1 loss regression. Below, we will use the term **errors** to refer to training points lying outside of the tube, and the term **fraction** of errors/SVs to denote the relative numbers of errors/SVs, i.e. divided by ℓ.

Proposition 1 *Assume $\varepsilon > 0$. The following statements hold:*

(i) ν is an upper bound on the fraction of errors.

(ii) ν is a lower bound on the fraction of SVs.

(iii) Suppose the data (2) were generated iid from a distribution $P(\mathbf{x}, y) = P(\mathbf{x})P(y|\mathbf{x})$ with $P(y|\mathbf{x})$ continuous. With probability 1, asymptotically, ν equals both the fraction of SVs and the fraction of errors.

The first two statements of this proposition can be proven from the structure of the dual optimization problem, with (12) playing a crucial role. Presently, we instead give a graphical proof based on the primal problem (Fig. 1).

To understand the third statement, note that all errors are also SVs, but there can be SVs which are not errors: namely, if they lie exactly at the edge of the tube. Asymptotically, however, these SVs form a negligible fraction of the whole SV set, and the set of errors and the one of SVs essentially coincide. This is due to the fact that for a class of functions with well-behaved capacity (such as SV regression functions), and for a distribution satisfying the above continuity condition, the number of points that the tube edges $f \pm \varepsilon$ can pass through cannot asymptotically increase linearly with the sample size. Interestingly, the proof (Schölkopf et al., 1998a) uses a uniform convergence argument similar in spirit to those used in statistical learning theory.

Due to this proposition, $0 \leq \nu \leq 1$ can be used to control the number of errors (note that for $\nu \geq 1$, (11) implies (12), since $\alpha_i \cdot \alpha_i^* = 0$ for all i (Vapnik, 1995)). Moreover, since the constraint (10) implies that (12) is equivalent to $\sum_i \alpha_i^{(*)} \leq C\nu/2$, we conclude that Proposition 1 actually holds for the upper and the lower edge of the tube separately, with $\nu/2$ each. As an aside, note that by the same argument, the number of SVs at the two edges of the standard ε-SVR tube asymptotically agree.

Moreover, note that this bears on the *robustness* of ν-SVR. At first glance, SVR seems all but robust: using the ε-insensitive loss function, only the patterns *outside* of the ε-tube contribute to the empirical risk term, whereas the patterns *closest* to the estimated regression have zero loss. This, however, does not mean that it is only the outliers that determine the regression. In fact, the contrary is the case: one can show that local movements of target values y_i of points $\mathbf{x}_i$ outside the tube do not influence the regression (Schölkopf et al., 1998c). Hence, ν-SVR is a generalization of an estimator for the mean of a random variable which throws away the largest and smallest examples (a fraction of at most $\nu/2$ of either category), and estimates the mean by taking the average of the two extremal ones of the remaining examples. This is close in spirit to robust estimators like the *trimmed mean*.

Let us briefly discuss how the new algorithm relates to ε-SVR (Vapnik, 1995). By rewriting (3) as a constrained optimization problem, and deriving a dual much like we did for ν-SVR,

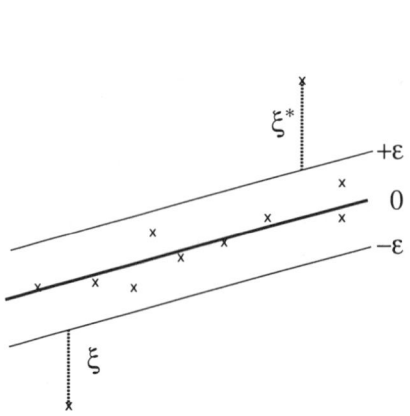

Figure 1: Graphical depiction of the ν-trick. Imagine increasing ε, starting from 0. The first term in $\nu\varepsilon + \frac{1}{\ell}\sum_{i=1}^{\ell}(\xi_i + \xi_i^*)$ (cf. (4)) will increase proportionally to ν, while the second term will decrease proportionally to the fraction of points outside of the tube. Hence, ε will grow as long as the latter fraction is larger than ν. At the optimum, it therefore must be $\leq \nu$ (Proposition 1, (i)). Next, imagine decreasing ε, starting from some large value. Again, the change in the first term is proportional to ν, but this time, the change in the second term is proportional to the fraction of SVs (even points *on* the edge of the tube will contribute). Hence, ε will shrink as long as the fraction of SVs is smaller than ν, eventually leading to Proposition 1, (ii).

one arrives at the following quadratic program: maximize

$$W(\boldsymbol{\alpha}, \boldsymbol{\alpha}^*) = -\varepsilon \sum_{i=1}^{\ell}(\alpha_i^*+\alpha_i)+\sum_{i=1}^{\ell}(\alpha_i^*-\alpha_i)y_i - \frac{1}{2}\sum_{i,j=1}^{\ell}(\alpha_i^*-\alpha_i)(\alpha_j^*-\alpha_j)k(\mathbf{x}_i, \mathbf{x}_j) \quad (14)$$

subject to (10) and (11). Compared to (9), we have an additional term $-\varepsilon \sum_{i=1}^{\ell}(\alpha_i^* + \alpha_i)$, which makes it plausible that the constraint (12) is not needed.

In the following sense, ν-SVR includes ε-SVR. Note that in the general case, using kernels, $\bar{\mathbf{w}}$ is a vector in feature space.

Proposition 2 *If ν-SVR leads to the solution $\bar{\varepsilon}, \bar{\mathbf{w}}, \bar{b}$, then ε-SVR with ε set a priori to $\bar{\varepsilon}$, and the same value of C, has the solution $\bar{\mathbf{w}}, \bar{b}$.*

Proof If we minimize (4), then fix ε and minimize only over the remaining variables, the solution does not change. ∎

3 PARAMETRIC INSENSITIVITY MODELS

We generalized ε-SVR by considering the tube as not given but instead estimated it as a model parameter. What we have so far retained is the assumption that the ε-insensitive zone has a tube (or slab) shape. We now go one step further and use parametric models of arbitrary shape. Let $\{\zeta_q^{(*)}\}$ (here and below, $q = 1, \ldots, p$ is understood) be a set of $2p$ positive functions on $\mathbb{R}^N$. Consider the following quadratic program: for given $\nu_1^{(*)}, \ldots, \nu_p^{(*)} \geq 0$, minimize

$$\tau(\mathbf{w}, \boldsymbol{\xi}^{(*)}, \boldsymbol{\varepsilon}^{(*)}) = \|\mathbf{w}\|^2/2 + C \cdot \left(\sum_{q=1}^{p}(\nu_q \varepsilon_q + \nu_q^* \varepsilon_q^*) + \frac{1}{\ell}\sum_{i=1}^{\ell}(\xi_i + \xi_i^*) \right) \quad (15)$$

$$\text{subject to} \quad ((\mathbf{w} \cdot \mathbf{x}_i) + b) - y_i \leq \sum_q \varepsilon_q \zeta_q(\mathbf{x}_i) + \xi_i \quad (16)$$

$$y_i - ((\mathbf{w} \cdot \mathbf{x}_i) + b) \leq \sum_q \varepsilon_q^* \zeta_q^*(\mathbf{x}_i) + \xi_i^* \quad (17)$$

$$\xi_i^{(*)} \geq 0, \quad \varepsilon_q^{(*)} \geq 0. \quad (18)$$

A calculation analogous to Sec. 2 shows that the Wolfe dual consists of maximizing (9) subject to (10), (11), and, instead of (12), the modified constraints $\sum_{i=1}^{\ell} \alpha_i^{(*)} \zeta_q^{(*)}(\mathbf{x}_i) \leq C \cdot \nu_q^{(*)}$. In the experiments in Sec. 4, we use a simplified version of this optimization problem, where we drop the term $\nu_q^* \varepsilon_q^*$ from the objective function (15), and use ε_q and ζ_q in (17). By this, we render the problem symmetric with respect to the two edges of the tube. In addition, we use $p = 1$. This leads to the same Wolfe dual, except for the last constraint, which becomes (cf. (12))

$$\sum_{i=1}^{\ell}(\alpha_i + \alpha_i^*)\zeta(\mathbf{x}_i) \leq C \cdot \nu. \quad (19)$$

The advantage of this setting is that since the same ν is used for both sides of the tube, the computation of ε, b is straightforward: for instance, by solving a linear system, using two conditions as those described following (13). Otherwise, general statements are harder to make: the linear system can have a zero determinant, depending on whether the functions $\zeta_p^{(*)}$, evaluated on the $\mathbf{x}_i$ with $0 < \alpha_i^{(*)} < C/\ell$, are linearly dependent. The latter occurs, for instance, if we use constant functions $\zeta^{(*)} \equiv 1$. In this case, it is pointless to use two different values ν, ν^*; for, the constraint (10) then implies that *both* sums $\sum_{i=1}^{\ell} \alpha_i^{(*)}$ will be bounded by $C \cdot \min\{\nu, \nu^*\}$. We conclude this section by giving, without proof, a generalization of Proposition 1, (iii), to the optimization problem with constraint (19):

Proposition 3 *Assume $\varepsilon > 0$. Suppose the data (2) were generated iid from a distribution $P(\mathbf{x}, y) = P(\mathbf{x})P(y|\mathbf{x})$ with $P(y|\mathbf{x})$ continuous. With probability 1, asymptotically, the fractions of SVs and errors equal $\nu \cdot (\int \zeta(\mathbf{x}) \, d\tilde{P}(\mathbf{x}))^{-1}$, where $\tilde{P}$ is the asymptotic distribution of SVs over $\mathbf{x}$.*

4 EXPERIMENTS AND DISCUSSION

In the experiments, we used the optimizer LOQO (http://www.princeton.edu/˜rvdb/). This has the serendipitous advantage that the primal variables b and ε can be recovered as the dual variables of the Wolfe dual (9) (i.e. the double dual variables) fed into the optimizer.

In Fig. 2, the task was to estimate a regression of a noisy sinc function, given ℓ examples (x_i, y_i), with x_i drawn uniformly from $[-3, 3]$, and $y_i = \sin(\pi x_i)/(\pi x_i) + v_i$, with v_i drawn from a Gaussian with zero mean and variance σ^2. We used the default parameters $\ell = 50$, $C = 100$, $\sigma = 0.2$, and the RBF kernel $k(x, x') = \exp(-|x - x'|^2)$.

Figure 3 gives an illustration of how one can make use of parametric insensitivity models as proposed in Sec. 3. Using the proper model, the estimate gets much better. In the parametric case, we used $\nu = 0.1$ and $\zeta(x) = \sin^2((2\pi/3)x)$, which, due to $\int \zeta(x) \, dP(x) = 1/2$, corresponds to our standard choice $\nu = 0.2$ in ν-SVR (cf. Proposition 3). The experimental findings are consistent with the asymptotics predicted theoretically even if we assume a uniform distribution of SVs: for $\ell = 200$, we got 0.24 and 0.19 for the fraction of SVs and errors, respectively.

This method allows the incorporation of prior knowledge into the loss function. Although this approach at first glance seems fundamentally different from incorporating prior knowledge directly into the kernel (Schölkopf et al., 1998b), from the point of view of statistical

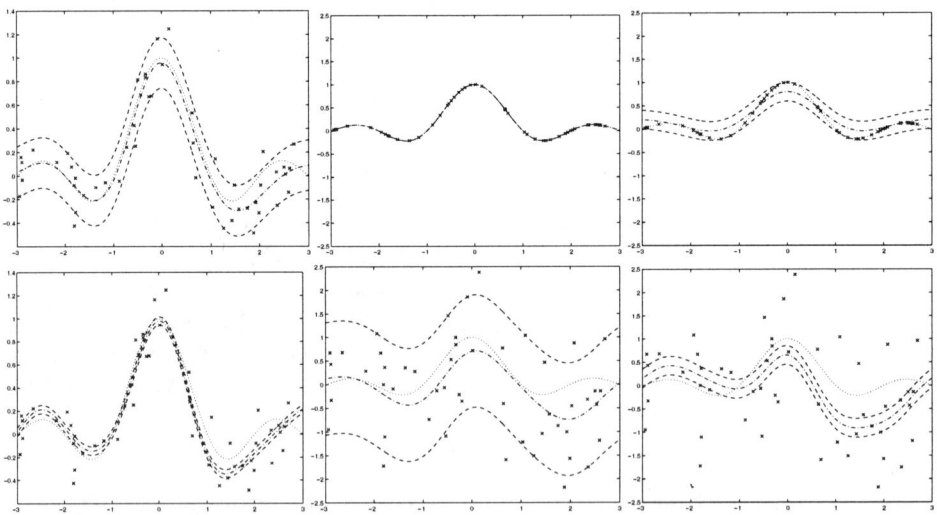

Figure 2: *Left:* ν-SV regression with $\nu = 0.2$ (top) and $\nu = 0.8$ (bottom). The larger ν allows more points to lie outside the tube (see Sec. 2). The algorithm automatically adjusts ε to 0.22 (top) and 0.04 (bottom). Shown are the sinc function (dotted), the regression f and the tube $f \pm \varepsilon$. *Middle:* ν-SV regression on data with noise $\sigma = 0$ (top) and $\sigma = 1$ (bottom). In both cases, $\nu = 0.2$. The tube width automatically adjusts to the noise (top: $\varepsilon = 0$, bottom: $\varepsilon = 1.19$). *Right:* ε-SV regression (Vapnik, 1995) on data with noise $\sigma = 0$ (top) and $\sigma = 1$ (bottom). In both cases, $\varepsilon = 0.2$ — this choice, which has to be specified a priori, is ideal for neither case: in the top figure, the regression estimate is biased; in the bottom figure, ε does not match the external noise (cf. Smola et al., 1998).

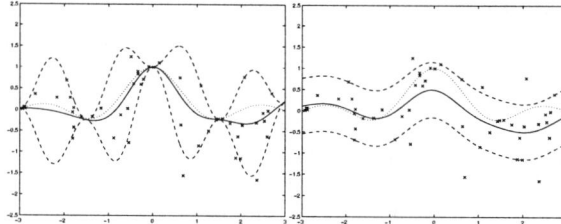

Figure 3: Toy example, using prior knowledge about an x-dependence of the noise. Additive noise ($\sigma = 1$) was multiplied by $\sin^2((2\pi/3)x)$. *Left:* the *same* function was used as ζ as a parametric insensitivity tube (Sec. 3). *Right:* ν-SVR with standard tube.

Table 1: Results for the Boston housing benchmark; *top:* ν-SVR, *bottom:* ε-SVR. <u>MSE:</u> Mean squared errors, <u>STD:</u> standard deviations thereof (100 trials), <u>Errors:</u> fraction of training points outside the tube, <u>SVs:</u> fraction of training points which are SVs.

ν	0.1	0.2	0.3	0.4	0.5	0.6	0.7	0.8	0.9	1.0
automatic ε	2.6	1.7	1.2	0.8	0.6	0.3	0.0	0.0	0.0	0.0
MSE	9.4	8.7	9.3	9.5	10.0	10.6	11.3	11.3	11.3	11.3
STD	6.4	6.8	7.6	7.9	8.4	9.0	9.6	9.5	9.5	9.5
Errors	0.0	0.1	0.2	0.2	0.3	0.4	0.5	0.5	0.5	0.5
SVs	0.3	0.4	0.6	0.7	0.8	0.9	1.0	1.0	1.0	1.0

ε	0	1	2	3	4	5	6	7	8	9	10
MSE	11.3	9.5	8.8	9.7	11.2	13.1	15.6	18.2	22.1	27.0	34.3
STD	9.5	7.7	6.8	6.2	6.3	6.0	6.1	6.2	6.6	7.3	8.4
Errors	0.5	0.2	0.1	0.0	0.0	0.0	0.0	0.0	0.0	0.0	0.0
SVs	1.0	0.6	0.4	0.3	0.2	0.1	0.1	0.1	0.1	0.1	0.1

learning theory the two approaches are closely related: in both cases, the structure of the loss-function-induced class of functions (which is the object of interest for generalization error bounds) is customized, in the first case, by changing the loss function, in the second case, by changing the class of functions that the estimate is taken from.

Empirical studies using ε-SVR have reported excellent performance on the widely used **Boston housing regression benchmark** set (Stitson et al., 1999). Due to Proposition 2, the only difference between ν-SVR and standard ε-SVR lies in the fact that different parameters, ε vs. ν, have to be specified a priori. Consequently, we are in this experiment only interested in these parameters and simply adjusted C and the width $2\sigma^2$ in $k(\mathbf{x}, \mathbf{y}) = \exp(-\|\mathbf{x} - \mathbf{y}\|^2/(2\sigma^2))$ as Schölkopf et al. (1997): we used $2\sigma^2 = 0.3 \cdot N$, where $N = 13$ is the input dimensionality, and $C/\ell = 10 \cdot 50$ (i.e. the original value of 10 was corrected since in the present case, the maximal y-value is 50). We performed 100 runs, where each time the overall set of 506 examples was randomly split into a training set of $\ell = 481$ examples and a test set of 25 examples. Table 1 shows that in a wide range of ν (note that only $0 \le \nu \le 1$ makes sense), we obtained performances which are close to the best performances that can be achieved by selecting ε a priori by looking at the test set. Finally, note that although we did not use validation techniques to select the optimal values for C and $2\sigma^2$, we obtained performance which are state of the art (Stitson et al. (1999) report an MSE of 7.6 for ε-SVR using ANOVA kernels, and 11.7 for Bagging trees). Table 1 moreover shows that ν can be used to control the fraction of SVs/errors.

Discussion. The theoretical and experimental analysis suggest that ν provides a way to control an upper bound on the number of training errors which is tighter than the one used in the soft margin hyperplane (Vapnik, 1995). In many cases, this makes it a parameter which is more convenient than the one in ε-SVR. Asymptotically, it directly controls the number of Support Vectors, and the latter can be used to give a leave-one-out generalization bound (Vapnik, 1995). In addition, ν characterizes the compression ratio: it suffices to train the algorithm only on the SVs, leading to the same solution (Schölkopf et al., 1995). In ε-SVR, the tube width ε must be specified a priori; in ν-SVR, which generalizes the idea of the *trimmed mean*, it is computed automatically. Desirable properties of ε-SVR, including the formulation as a definite quadratic program, and the sparse SV representation of the solution, are retained. We are optimistic that in many applications, ν-SVR will be more robust than ε-SVR. Among these should be the reduced set algorithm of Osuna and Girosi (1999), which approximates the SV pattern recognition decision surface by ε-SVR. Here, ν should give a direct handle on the desired speed-up.

One of the immediate questions that a ν-approach to SV regression raises is whether a similar algorithm is possible for the case of pattern recognition. This question has recently been answered to the affirmative (Schölkopf et al., 1998c). Since the pattern recognition algorithm (Vapnik, 1995) does not use ε, the only parameter that we can dispose of by using ν is the regularization constant C. This leads to a dual optimization problem with a homogeneous quadratic form, and ν lower bounding the sum of the Lagrange multipliers. Whether we could have abolished C in the regression case, too, is an open problem.

Acknowledgement This work was supported by the ARC and the DFG (# Ja 379/71).

References

B. E. Boser, I. M. Guyon, and V. N. Vapnik. A training algorithm for optimal margin classifiers. In D. Haussler, editor, *Proceedings of the 5th Annual ACM Workshop on Computational Learning Theory*, pages 144–152, Pittsburgh, PA, 1992. ACM Press.

E. Osuna and F. Girosi. Reducing run-time complexity in support vector machines. In B. Schölkopf, C. Burges, and A. Smola, editors, *Advances in Kernel Methods — Support Vector Learning*, pages 271–283. MIT Press, Cambridge, MA, 1999.

B. Schölkopf, C. Burges, and V. Vapnik. Extracting support data for a given task. In U. M. Fayyad and R. Uthurusamy, editors, *Proceedings, First International Conference on Knowledge Discovery & Data Mining*. AAAI Press, Menlo Park, CA, 1995.

B. Schölkopf, P. Bartlett, A. Smola, and R. Williamson. Support vector regression with automatic accuracy control. In L. Niklasson, M. Bodén, and T. Ziemke, editors, *Proceedings of the 8th International Conference on Artificial Neural Networks*, Perspectives in Neural Computing, pages 111–116, Berlin, 1998a. Springer Verlag.

B. Schölkopf, P. Simard, A. Smola, and V. Vapnik. Prior knowledge in support vector kernels. In M. Jordan, M. Kearns, and S. Solla, editors, *Advances in Neural Information Processing Systems 10*, pages 640–646, Cambridge, MA, 1998b. MIT Press.

B. Schölkopf, A. Smola, R. Williamson, and P. Bartlett. New support vector algorithms. 1998c. NeuroColt2-TR 1998-031; cf. http://www.neurocolt.com

B. Schölkopf, K. Sung, C. Burges, F. Girosi, P. Niyogi, T. Poggio, and V. Vapnik. Comparing support vector machines with gaussian kernels to radial basis function classifiers. *IEEE Trans. Sign. Processing*, 45:2758–2765, 1997.

A. Smola, N. Murata, B. Schölkopf, and K.-R. Müller. Asymptotically optimal choice of ε-loss for support vector machines. In L. Niklasson, M. Bodén, and T. Ziemke, editors, *Proceedings of the 8th International Conference on Artificial Neural Networks*, Perspectives in Neural Computing, pages 105–110, Berlin, 1998. Springer Verlag.

M. Stitson, A. Gammerman, V. Vapnik, V. Vovk, C. Watkins, and J. Weston. Support vector regression with ANOVA decomposition kernels. In B. Schölkopf, C. Burges, and A. Smola, editors, *Advances in Kernel Methods — Support Vector Learning*, pages 285–291. MIT Press, Cambridge, MA, 1999.

V. Vapnik. *The Nature of Statistical Learning Theory*. Springer Verlag, New York, 1995.

Discontinuous Recall Transitions Induced By Competition Between Short- and Long-Range Interactions in Recurrent Networks

N.S. Skantzos, C.F. Beckmann and A.C.C. Coolen
Dept of Mathematics, King's College London, Strand, London WC2R 2LS, UK
E-mail: skantzos@mth.kcl.ac.uk tcoolen@mth.kcl.ac.uk

Abstract

We present exact analytical equilibrium solutions for a class of recurrent neural network models, with both sequential and parallel neuronal dynamics, in which there is a tunable competition between nearest-neighbour and long-range synaptic interactions. This competition is found to induce novel coexistence phenomena as well as discontinuous transitions between pattern recall states, 2-cycles and non-recall states.

1 INTRODUCTION

Analytically solvable models of large recurrent neural networks are bound to be simplified representations of biological reality. In early analytical studies such as [1, 2] neurons were, for instance, only allowed to interact with a strength which was independent of their spatial distance (these are the so-called mean field models). At present both the statics of infinitely large mean-field models of recurrent networks, as well as their dynamics away from saturation are well understood, and have obtained the status of textbook or review paper material [3, 4]. The focus in theoretical research of recurrent networks has consequently turned to new areas such as solving the dynamics of large networks close to saturation [5], the analysis of finite size phenomenology [6], solving biologically more realistic (e.g. spike-based) models [7] or analysing systems with spatial structure. In this paper we analyse models of recurrent networks with spatial structure, in which there are two types of synapses: long-range ones (operating between any pair of neurons), and short-range ones (operating between nearest neighbours only). In contrast to early papers on spatially structured networks [8], one here finds that, due to the nearest neighbour interactions, exact solutions based on simple mean-field approaches are ruled out. Instead, the present models can be solved exactly by a combination of mean-field techniques and the so-called transfer matrix method (see [9]). In parameter regimes where the two synapse types compete (where one has long-range excitation with short-range inhibition, or long-range Hebbian synapses with short-range anti-Hebbian synapses) we find interesting and potentially useful novel phenomena, such as coexistence of states and discontinuous transitions between them.

2 MODEL DEFINITIONS

We study models with N binary neuron variables $\sigma_i = \pm 1$, which evolve in time stochastically on the basis of post-synaptic potentials $h_i(\vec{\sigma})$, following

$$\text{Prob}[\sigma_i(t+1) = \pm 1] = \frac{1}{2}[1 \pm \tanh[\beta h_i(\vec{\sigma}(t))]] \qquad h_i(\vec{\sigma}) = \sum_{j \neq i} J_{ij}\sigma_j + \theta_i \qquad (1)$$

The variables J_{ij} and θ_i represent synaptic interactions and firing thresholds, respectively. The (non-negative) parameter β controls the amount of noise, with $\beta = 0$ and $\beta = \infty$ corresponding to purely random and purely deterministic response, respectively. If the synaptic matrix is symmetric, both a random sequential execution and a fully parallel execution of the stochastic dynamics (1) will evolve to a unique equilibrium state. The corresponding microscopic state probabilities can then both formally be written in the Boltzmann form $p_\infty(\vec{\sigma}) \sim \exp[-\beta H(\vec{\sigma})]$, with [10]

$$H_{\text{seq}}(\vec{\sigma}) = -\sum_{i<j} \sigma_i J_{ij} \sigma_j - \sum_i \theta_i \sigma_i \qquad H_{\text{par}}(\vec{\sigma}) = -\frac{1}{\beta} \sum_i \log\cosh[\beta h_i(\vec{\sigma})] - \sum_i \theta_i \sigma_i \qquad (2)$$

For large systems the macroscopic observables of interest can be obtained by differentiation of the free energy per neuron $f = -\lim_{N \to \infty} (\beta N)^{-1} \log \sum_{\vec{\sigma}} \exp[-\beta H(\vec{\sigma})]$, which acts as a generating function. For the synaptic interactions J_{ij} and the thresholds θ_i we now make the following choice:

$$\text{model I}: \qquad J_{ij} = \frac{J_\ell}{N} \xi_i \xi_j + J_s(\delta_{i,j+1} + \delta_{i,j-1})\xi_i \xi_j \qquad \theta_i = \theta \xi_i \qquad (3)$$

(which corresponds to the result of having stored a binary pattern $\vec{\xi} \in \{-1, 1\}^N$ through Hebbian-type learning), with $J_\ell, J_s, \theta \in \Re$ and $i + N \equiv i$. The neurons can be thought of as being arranged on a periodic one-dimensional array, with uniform interactions of strength $J_\ell \xi_i \xi_j / N$, in combination with nearest neighbour interactions of strength $J_s \xi_i \xi_j$. Note that model I behaves in exactly the same way as the following

$$\text{model II}: \qquad J_{ij} = \frac{J_\ell}{N} + J_s(\delta_{i,j+1} + \delta_{i,j-1}) \qquad \theta_i = \theta \qquad (4)$$

since a simple transformation $\sigma_i \to \sigma_i \xi_i$ maps one model into the other. Taking derivatives of f with respect to the parameters θ and J_s for model II produces our order parameters, expressed as equilibrium expectation values. For sequential dynamics we have

$$m = -\frac{\partial f}{\partial \theta} = \lim_{N \to \infty} \frac{1}{N} \sum_i \langle \sigma_i \rangle \qquad a = -\frac{\partial f}{\partial J_s} = \lim_{N \to \infty} \frac{1}{N} \sum_i \langle \sigma_{i+1} \sigma_i \rangle \qquad (5)$$

For parallel dynamics the corresponding expressions turn out to be

$$m = -\frac{1}{2}\frac{\partial f}{\partial \theta} = \lim_{N \to \infty} \frac{1}{N} \sum_i \langle \sigma_i \rangle \qquad a = -\frac{1}{2}\frac{\partial f}{\partial J_s} = \lim_{N \to \infty} \frac{1}{N} \sum_i \langle \sigma_{i+1} \tanh[\beta h_i(\vec{\sigma})] \rangle \qquad (6)$$

We have simplified (6) with the identities $\langle \sigma_{i+1} \tanh[\beta h_i(\vec{\sigma})] \rangle = \langle \sigma_{i-1} \tanh[\beta h_i(\vec{\sigma})] \rangle$ and $\langle \tanh[\beta h_i(\vec{\sigma})] \rangle = \langle \sigma_i \rangle$, which follow from (1) and from invariance under the transformation $i \to N + 1 - i$ (for all i). For sequential dynamics a describes the average equilibrium state covariances of neighbouring neurons. For parallel dynamics a gives the average equilibrium state covariances of neurons *at a given time* t, and their neighbours *at time* $t + 1$ (the difference between the two meanings of a will be important in the presence of 2-cycles). In model II m is the average activity in equilibrium, whereas for model I one finds

$$m = \lim_{N \to \infty} \frac{1}{N} \sum_i \xi_i \langle \sigma_i \rangle$$

This is the familiar overlap order parameter of associative memory models [1, 2], which measures the quality of pattern recall in equilibrium. The observable a transforms similarly.

3 SOLUTION VIA TRANSFER MATRICES

From this stage onwards our analysis will refer to model II, i.e eqn (4); the results can immediately be translated into the language of model I (3) via the transformation $\sigma_i \to \sigma_i \xi_i$. In calculating f it is advantageous to separate terms induced by the long-range synapses from those induced by the short-range ones, via insertion of $1 = \int dm\, \delta[m - \frac{1}{N}\sum_i \sigma_i]$. Upon using the integral representation of the δ-function, we then arrive at

$$f = -\lim_{N\to\infty} \frac{1}{\beta N} \log \int dm\, d\hat{m}\, e^{-\beta N \phi(m,\hat{m})}$$

with

$$\phi_{\text{seq}}(m,\hat{m}) = -im\hat{m} - m\theta - \frac{1}{2}J_\ell m^2 - \frac{1}{\beta N} \log R_{\text{seq}}(\hat{m}) \tag{7}$$

$$\phi_{\text{par}}(m,\hat{m}) = -im\hat{m} - m\theta - \frac{1}{\beta N} \log R_{\text{par}}(m,\hat{m}) \tag{8}$$

The quantities R contain all complexities due to the short-range interactions in the model (they describe a periodic one-dimensional system with neighbour interactions only):

$$R_{\text{seq}}(\hat{m}) = \sum_{\vec{\sigma}\in\{-1,1\}^N} e^{-i\beta\hat{m}\sum_i \sigma_i}\, e^{\beta J_s \sum_i \sigma_i \sigma_{i+1}}$$

$$R_{\text{par}}(m,\hat{m}) = \sum_{\vec{\sigma}\in\{-1,1\}^N} e^{-i\beta\hat{m}\sum_i \sigma_i}\, e^{\sum_i \log\cosh\beta[J_\ell m + \theta + J_s(\sigma_{i+1}+\sigma_{i-1})]}$$

They can be calculated using the transfer-matrix technique [9], which exploits an interpretation of the summations over the N neuron states σ_i as matrix multiplications, giving

$$R_{\text{seq}}(\hat{m}) = \text{Tr}\,[T_{\text{seq}}^N] \qquad T_{\text{seq}} = \begin{pmatrix} e^{\beta J_s - i\beta\hat{m}} & e^{-\beta J_s} \\ e^{-\beta J_s} & e^{\beta J_s + i\beta\hat{m}} \end{pmatrix}$$

$$R_{\text{par}}(m,\hat{m}) = \text{Tr}\,[T_{\text{par}}^N] \qquad T_{\text{par}} = \begin{pmatrix} \cosh[\beta w_+]e^{-i\beta\hat{m}} & \cosh[\beta w_0] \\ \cosh[\beta w_0] & \cosh[\beta w_-]e^{i\beta\hat{m}} \end{pmatrix}$$

where $w_0 = J_\ell m + \theta$ and $w_\pm = w_0 \pm 2J_s$. The identity $\text{Tr}\,[T^N] = \lambda_+^N + \lambda_-^N$, in which $\lambda_\pm$ are the eigenvalues of the 2×2 matrix T, enables us to take the limit $N\to\infty$ in our equations. The integral over $(m,\hat{m})$ is for $N\to\infty$ evaluated by gradient descent, and is dominated by the saddle points of the exponent ϕ. We thus arrive at the transparent result

$$f = \text{extr}\,\phi(m,\hat{m}) \quad \begin{cases} \phi_{\text{seq}}(m,\hat{m}) = -im\hat{m} - m\theta - \frac{1}{2}J_\ell m^2 - \frac{1}{\beta}\log\lambda_+^{\text{seq}} \\ \phi_{\text{par}}(m,\hat{m}) = -im\hat{m} - m\theta - \frac{1}{\beta}\log\lambda_+^{\text{par}} \end{cases} \tag{9}$$

where λ_+^{seq} and λ_+^{par} are the largest eigenvalues of T_{seq} and T_{par}. For simplicity, we will restrict ourselves to the case where $\theta = 0$; generalisation of what follows to the case of arbitrary θ, by using the full form of (9), is not significantly more difficult. The expressions defining the value(s) of the order parameter m can now be obtained from the saddle point equations $\partial_m \phi(m,\hat{m}) = \partial_{\hat{m}} \phi(m,\hat{m}) = 0$. Straightforward differentiation shows that

$$\text{sequential:} \quad \hat{m} = imJ_\ell, \qquad m = G(m; J_\ell, J_s)$$

$$\text{parallel:} \quad \hat{m} = imJ_\ell, \qquad m = G(m; J_\ell, J_s) \qquad \text{for } J_\ell \geq 0 \tag{10}$$
$$\hat{m} = -imJ_\ell, \qquad m = G(m; -J_\ell, -J_s) \qquad \text{for } J_\ell < 0$$

with

$$G(m; J_\ell, J_s) = \frac{\sinh[\beta J_\ell m]}{\sqrt{\sinh^2[\beta J_\ell m] + e^{-4\beta J_s}}} \tag{11}$$

Note that equations (10,11) allow us to derive the physical properties of the parallel dynamics model from those of the sequential dynamics model via simple transformations.

4 PHASE TRANSITIONS

Our main order parameter m is to be determined by solving an equation of the form $m = G(m)$, in which $G(m) = G(m; J_\ell, J_s)$ for both sequential and parallel dynamics with $J_\ell \geq 0$, whereas $G(m) = G(m; -J_\ell, -J_s)$ for parallel dynamics with $J_\ell < 0$. Note that, due to $G(0; J_\ell, J_s) = 0$, the trivial solution $m = 0$ always exists. In order to obtain a phase diagram we have to perform a bifurcation analysis of the equations (10,11), and determine the combinations of parameter values for which specific non-zero solutions are created or annihilated (the transition lines). Bifurcations of non-zero solutions occur when

$$m = G(m) \quad \text{and} \quad 1 = G'(m) \quad (12)$$

The first equation in (12) states that m must be a solution of the saddle-point problem, the second one states that this solution is in the process of being created/annihilated. Nonzero solutions of $m = G(m)$ can come into existence in two qualitatively different ways: as continuous bifurcations away from the trivial solution $m = 0$, and as discontinuous bifurcations away from the trivial solution. These two types will have to be treated differently.

4.1 Continuous Transitions

An analytical expression for the lines in the $(\beta J_s, \beta J_\ell)$ plane where continuous transitions occur between recall states (where $m \neq 0$) and non-recall states (where $m = 0$) is obtained by solving the coupled equations (12) for $m = 0$. This gives:

$$\text{cont. trans.}: \quad \begin{array}{ll} \text{sequential}: & \beta J_\ell = e^{-2\beta J_s} \\ \text{parallel}: & \beta J_\ell = e^{-2\beta J_s} \quad \text{and} \quad \beta J_\ell = -e^{2\beta J_s} \end{array} \quad (13)$$

If along the transition lines (13) we inspect the behaviour of $G(m)$ close to $m = 0$ we can anticipate the possible existence of discontinuous ones, using the properties of $G(m)$ for $m \to \pm\infty$, in combination with $G(-m) = -G(m)$. Precisely *at* the lines (13) we have $G(m) = m + \frac{1}{6}G'''(0).m^3 + \mathcal{O}(m^5)$. Since $\lim_{m \to \infty} G(m) = 1$ one knows that for $G'''(0) > 0$ the function $G(m)$ will have to cross the diagonal $G(m) = m$ again at some value $m > 0$ in order to reach the limit $G(\infty) = 1$. This implies, in combination with $G(-m) = -G(m)$, that a discontinuous transition must have already taken place earlier, and that away from the lines (13) there will consequently be regions where one finds five solutions of $m = G(m)$ (two positive ones, two negative ones). Along the lines (13) the condition $G'''(0) > 0$, pointing at discontinuous transitions elsewhere, translates into

$$\begin{array}{ll} \text{sequential}: & \beta J_\ell > \sqrt{3} \quad \text{and} \quad \beta J_s < -\frac{1}{4}\log 3 \\ \text{parallel}: & |\beta J_\ell| > \sqrt{3} \quad \text{and} \quad |\beta J_s| < -\frac{1}{4}\log 3 \end{array} \quad (14)$$

4.2 Discontinuous Transitions

In the present models it turns out that one can also find an analytical expression for the discontinuous transition lines in the $(\beta J_s, \beta J_\ell)$ plane, in the form of a parametrisation. For sequential dynamics one finds a single line, parametrised by $x = \beta J_\ell m \in [0, \infty)$:

$$\text{discont. trans.}: \quad \beta J_\ell(x) = \sqrt{\frac{x^3}{x - \tanh(x)}}, \quad \beta J_s(x) = -\frac{1}{4}\log\left[\frac{\tanh(x)\sinh^2(x)}{x - \tanh(x)}\right] \quad (15)$$

Since this parametrisation (15) obeys $\beta J_s(0) = -\frac{1}{4}\log 3$ and $\beta J_\ell(0) = \sqrt{3}$, the discontinuous transition indeed starts precisely at the point predicted by the convexity of $G(m)$ at $m = 0$, see (14). For sequential dynamics the line (15) gives all non-zero solutions of the coupled equations (12). For parallel dynamics one finds, in addition to (15), a second 'mirror image' transition line, generated by the transformation $\{\beta J_\ell, \beta J_s\} \mapsto \{-\beta J_\ell, -\beta J_s\}$.

5 PHASE DIAGRAMS

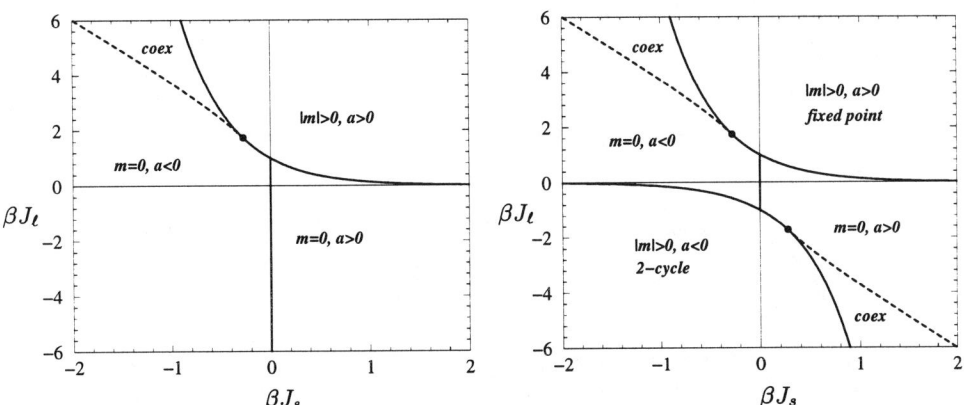

Figure 1: Left: phase diagram for sequential dynamics, involving three regions: (i) a region with $m = 0$ only (here $a = \tanh[\beta J_s]$), (ii) a region with two $m \neq 0$ fixed-point states (with opposite sign, and with identical $a > 0$), and (iii) a region where the $m = 0$ state and the two $m \neq 0$ states coexist. The (i) → (ii) and (ii) → (iii) transitions are continuous (solid lines), whereas the (i) → (iii) transition is discontinuous (dashed line). Right: phase diagram for parallel dynamics, involving the above regions and transitions, as well as a second set of transition lines (in the region $J_\ell < 0$) which are exact reflections in the origin of the first set. Here, however, the $m = 0$ region has $a = \tanh[2\beta J_s]$, the two $m \neq 0$ physical solutions describe 2-cycles rather than fixed-points, and the $J_\ell < 0$ coexistence region describes the coexistence of an $m = 0$ fixed-point and 2-cycles.

Having determined the transition lines in parameter space, we can turn to the phase diagrams. A detailed expose of the various procedures followed to determine the nature of the various phases, which are also dependent on the type of dynamics used, goes beyond the scope of this presentation; here we can only present the resulting picture.[1] Figure 1 shows the phase diagram for the two types of dynamics, in the $(\beta J_s, \beta J_\ell)$ plane (note: of the three parameters $\{\beta, J_s, J_\ell\}$ one is redundant). In contrast to models with nearest neighbour interactions only ($J_\ell = 0$, where no pattern recall ever will occur), and to models with mean-field interactions only ($J_s = 0$, where pattern recall can occur), the combination of the two interaction types leads to qualitatively new modes of operation. This especially in the competition region, where $J_\ell > 0$ and $J_s < 0$ (Hebbian long-range synapses, combined with anti-Hebbian short range ones). The novel features of the diagram can play a useful role: phase coexistence ensures that only sufficiently strong recall cues will evoke pattern recognition; the discontinuity of the transition subsequently ensures that in the latter case the recall will be of a substantial quality. In the case of parallel dynamics, similar statements can be made in the opposite region of synaptic competition, but now involving 2-cycles. Since figure 1 cannot show the zero noise region ($\beta = T^{-1} = \infty$), we have also drawn the interesting competition region of the sequential dynamics phase diagram in the (J_ℓ, T) plane, for $J_s = -1$ (see figure 3, left picture). At $T = 0$ one finds coexistence of recall states ($m \neq 0$) and non-recall states ($m = 0$) for any $J_\ell > 0$, as soon as $J_s < 0$. In the same figure (right picture) we show the magnitude of the discontinuity in the order parameter m at the discontinuous transition, as a function of βJ_ℓ.

---

[1]Due to the occurrence of imaginary saddle-points in (10) and our strategy to eliminate the variable $\hat{m}$ by using the equation $\partial_m \phi(m, \hat{m}) = 0$, it need not be true that the saddle-point with the lowest value of $\phi(m, \hat{m})$ is the minimum of ϕ (complex conjugation can induce curvature sign changes, and in addition the minimum could occur at boundaries or as special limits). Inspection of the status of saddle-points and identification of the physical ones in those cases where there are multiple solutions is thus a somewhat technical issue, details of which will be published elsewhere [11].

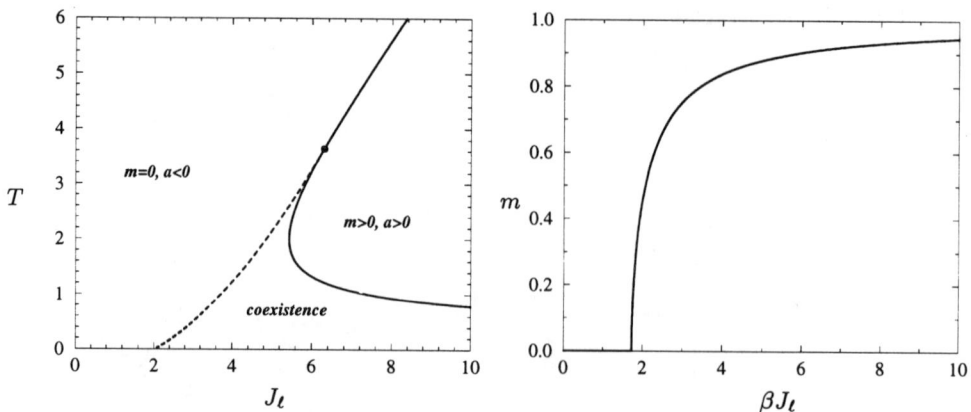

Figure 2: Left picture: alternative presentation of the competition region of the sequential dynamics phase diagram in figure 1. Here the system states and transitions are drawn in the (J_ℓ, T) plane $(T = \beta^{-1})$, for $J_s = -1$. Right picture: the magnitude of the 'jump' of the overlap m along the discontinuous transition line, as a function of βJ_ℓ.

The fact that for parallel dynamics one finds 2-cycles in the lower left corner of the phase diagram (figure 1) can be inferred from the exact dynamical solution available along the line $J_s = 0$ (see e.g. [4]), provided by the deterministic map $m(t+1) = \tanh[\beta J_\ell m(t)]$.

Finally we show, by way of further illustration of the coexistence mechanism, the value of reduced exponent $\phi_{\text{seq}}(m)$ given in (9), evaluated upon elimination of the auxiliary order parameter $\hat{m}$: $\phi(m) \equiv \phi_{\text{seq}}(m, imJ_\ell)$. The result, for the parameter choice $(\beta, J_\ell) = (2, 3)$ and for three different short-range coupling stengths (corresponding to the three phase regimes: non-zero recall, coexistence and zero recall) is given in figure 3. In the same figure we also give the sequential dynamics bifurcation diagram displaying the value(s) of the overlap m as a function of βJ_ℓ and for $\beta J_s = -0.6$ (a line crossing all three phase regimes in figure (1)).

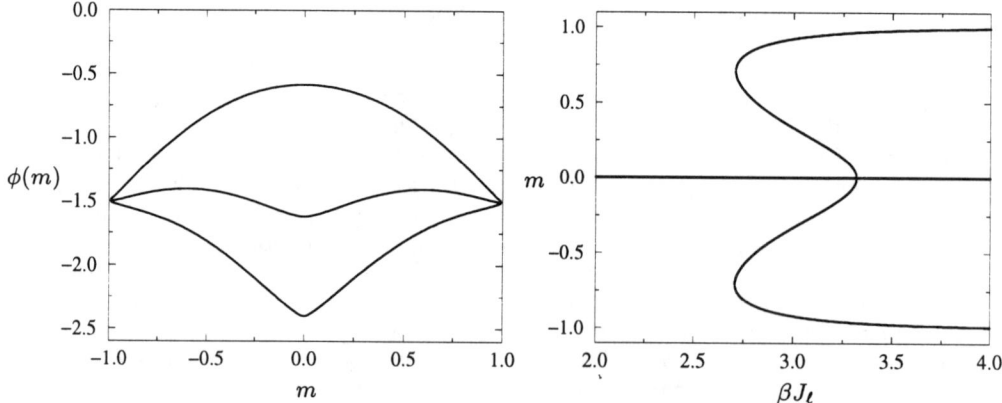

Figure 3: Left: Graph of the reduced exponent $\phi(m) = \phi_{\text{seq}}(m, imJ_\ell)$ for the parameter choice $(\beta, J_\ell) = (2,3)$. The three lines (from upper to lower: $J_s = -1.2, -0.8, -0.2$) correspond to regimes where (i) $m' \neq 0$ only (ii) coexistence of trivial and non-trivial recall states occurs and (iii) $m = 0$ only. Right: Sequential dynamics bifurcation diagram displaying for $\beta J_s = -0.6$ the possible recall solutions. For a critical βJ_ℓ given by (15) m jumps discontinuously to non-zero values. For increasing values of βJ_ℓ the unstable $m \neq 0$ solutions converge towards the trivial one until $\beta J_\ell = \exp(1.2)$ where a continuous phase transition takes place and $m = 0$ becomes unstable.

6 DISCUSSION

In this paper we have presented exact analytical equilibrium solutions, for sequential and parallel neuronal dynamics, for a class of recurrent neural network models which allow for a tunable competition between short-range synapses (operating between nearest neighbours only) and long-range ones (operating between any pair of neurons). The present models have been solved exactly by a combination of mean-field techniques and transfer matrix techniques. We found that there exist regions in parameter space where discontinuous transitions take place between states without pattern recall and either states of partial/full pattern recall or 2-cycles. These regions correspond to the ranges of the network parameters where the competition is most evident, for instance, where one has strongly *excitatory* long-range interactions and strongly *inhibitory* short-range ones. In addition this competition is found to generate a coexistence of pattern recall states or 2-cycles with the non-recall state, which (in turn) induces a dependence on initial conditions of whether or not recall will at all take place.

This study is, however, only a first step. In a similar fashion one can now study more complicated systems, where (in addition to the long-range synapses) the short-range synapses reach beyond nearest neighbours, or where the system is effectively on a two-dimensional (rather than one-dimensional) array. Such models can still be solved using the techniques employed here. A different type of generalisation would be to allow for a competition between synapses which would not all be of a Hebbian form, e.g. by having long-range Hebbian synapses (modeling processing via pyramidal neurons) in combination with short-range inhibitory synapses without any effect of learning (modeling processing via simple inhibitory inter-neurons). In addition, one could increase the complexity of the model by storing more than just a single pattern. In the latter types of models the various pattern components can no longer be transformed away, and one has to turn to the methods of random field Ising models (see e.g. [12]).

References

[1] D.J. Amit, H. Gutfreund and H. Sompolinsky (1985), *Phys. Rev.* **A32**, 1007-1018

[2] D.J. Amit, H. Gutfreund and H. Sompolinsky (1985), *Phys. Rev. Lett.* **55**, 1530-1533

[3] A.C.C. Coolen and D. Sherrington (1993), in J.G.Taylor (editor) *Mathematical Approaches to Neural Networks*, Elsevier Science Publishers, 293-306

[4] A.C.C. Coolen (1997), *Statistical Mechanics of Neural Networks*, King's College London Lecture Notes

[5] A.C.C. Coolen, S.N. Laughton and D. Sherrington (1996), in D.S. Touretzky, M.C. Mozer and M.E. Hasselmo (eds) *Advances in Neural Information Processing Systems 8*, MIT Press

[6] A. Castellanos, A.C.C. Coolen and L. Viana (1998), *J. Phys. A* **31**, 6615-6634

[7] E. Domany, J.L. van Hemmen and K. Schulten (eds) (1994), *Models of Neural Networks II*, Springer

[8] A.C.C. Coolen and L.G.V.M. Lenders (1992), *J. Phys A* **25**, 2593-2606

[9] J.M. Yeomans (1992), *Statistical Mechanics of Phase Transitions*, Oxford U.P.

[10] P. Peretto (1984), *Biol. Cybern.* **50**, 51-62

[11] N.S. Skantzos and A.C.C. Coolen (1998), *in preparation*

[12] U. Brandt and W. Gross (1978), *Z. Physik B* **31**, 237-245

Learning curves for Gaussian processes

Peter Sollich[*]
Department of Physics, University of Edinburgh
Edinburgh EH9 3JZ, U.K. Email: P.Sollich@ed.ac.uk

Abstract

I consider the problem of calculating learning curves (i.e., average generalization performance) of Gaussian processes used for regression. A simple expression for the generalization error in terms of the eigenvalue decomposition of the covariance function is derived, and used as the starting point for several approximation schemes. I identify where these become exact, and compare with existing bounds on learning curves; the new approximations, which can be used for any input space dimension, generally get substantially closer to the truth.

1 INTRODUCTION: GAUSSIAN PROCESSES

Within the neural networks community, there has in the last few years been a good deal of excitement about the use of Gaussian processes as an alternative to feedforward networks [1]. The advantages of Gaussian processes are that prior assumptions about the problem to be learned are encoded in a very transparent way, and that inference—at least in the case of regression that I will consider—is relatively straightforward. One crucial question for applications is then how 'fast' Gaussian processes learn, i.e., how many training examples are needed to achieve a certain level of generalization performance. The typical (as opposed to worst case) behaviour is captured in the *learning curve*, which gives the average generalization error ϵ as a function of the number of training examples n. Several workers have derived bounds on $\epsilon(n)$ [2, 3, 4] or studied its large n asymptotics. As I will illustrate below, however, the existing bounds are often far from tight; and asymptotic results will not necessarily apply for realistic sample sizes n. My main aim in this paper is therefore to derive approximations to $\epsilon(n)$ which get closer to the true learning curves than existing bounds, and apply both for small and large n.

In its simplest form, the regression problem that I am considering is this: We are trying to learn a function θ^* which maps inputs x (real-valued vectors) to (real-valued scalar) outputs $\theta^*(x)$. We are given a set of training data D, consisting of n

---

[*]Present address: Department of Mathematics, King's College London, Strand, London WC2R 2LS, U.K. Email peter.sollich@kcl.ac.uk

input-output pairs (x_l, y_l); the training outputs y_l may differ from the 'clean' target outputs $\theta^*(x_l)$ due to corruption by noise. Given a test input x, we are then asked to come up with a prediction $\theta(x)$ for the corresponding output, expressed either in the simple form of a mean prediction $\hat{\theta}(x)$ plus error bars, or more comprehensively in terms of a 'predictive distribution' $P(\theta(x)|x, D)$. In a Bayesian setting, we do this by specifying a prior $P(\theta)$ over our hypothesis functions, and a likelihood $P(D|\theta)$ with which each θ could have generated the training data; from this we deduce the posterior distribution $P(\theta|D) \propto P(D|\theta)P(\theta)$. In the case of feedforward networks, where the hypothesis functions θ are parameterized by a set of network weights, the predictive distribution then needs to be extracted by integration over this posterior, either by computationally intensive Monte Carlo techniques or by approximations which lead to analytically tractable integrals. For a Gaussian process, on the other hand, obtaining the predictive distribution is trivial (see below); one reason for this is that the prior $P(\theta)$ is defined directly over input-output functions θ. How is this done? Any θ is uniquely determined by its output values $\theta(x)$ for all x from the input domain, and for a Gaussian process, these are simply assumed to have a joint Gaussian distribution (hence the name). This distribution can be specified by the mean values $\langle \theta(x) \rangle_\theta$ (which I assume to be zero in the following, as is commonly done), and the covariances $\langle \theta(x)\theta(x') \rangle_\theta = C(x, x')$; $C(x, x')$ is called the *covariance function* of the Gaussian process. It encodes in an easily interpretable way prior assumptions about the function to be learned. Smoothness, for example, is controlled by the behaviour of $C(x, x')$ for $x' \to x$: The Ornstein-Uhlenbeck (OU) covariance function $C(x, x') \propto \exp(-|x-x'|/l)$ produces very rough (non-differentiable) functions, while functions sampled from the squared exponential (SE) prior with $C(x, x') \propto \exp(-|x-x'|^2/(2l^2))$ are infinitely differentiable. The 'length scale' parameter l, on the other hand, corresponds directly to the distance in input space over which we expect our function to vary significantly. More complex properties can also be encoded; by replacing l with different length scales for each input component, for example, relevant (small l) and irrelevant (large l) inputs can be distinguished.

How does inference with Gaussian processes work? I only give a brief summary here and refer to existing reviews on the subject (see *e.g.* [5, 1]) for details. It is simplest to assume that outputs y are generated from the 'clean' values of a hypothesis function $\theta(x)$ by adding Gaussian noise of x-independent variance σ^2. The joint distribution of a set of training outputs $\{y_l\}$ and the function values $\theta(x)$ is then also Gaussian, with covariances given by

$$\langle y_l y_m \rangle = C(x_l, x_m) + \sigma^2 \delta_{lm} = (\mathbf{K})_{lm}, \qquad \langle y_l \theta(x) \rangle = C(x_l, x) = (\mathbf{k}(x))_l;$$

here I have defined an $n \times n$ matrix $\mathbf{K}$ and x-dependent n-component vectors $\mathbf{k}(x)$. The posterior distribution $P(\theta|D)$ is then obtained by simply conditioning on the $\{y_l\}$. It is again Gaussian and has mean and variance

$$\langle \theta(x) \rangle_{\theta|D} = \hat{\theta}(x) = \mathbf{k}(x)^\mathrm{T} \mathbf{K}^{-1} \mathbf{y} \tag{1}$$

$$\left\langle (\theta(x) - \hat{\theta}(x))^2 \right\rangle_{\theta|D} = C(x, x) - \mathbf{k}(x)^\mathrm{T} \mathbf{K}^{-1} \mathbf{k}(x) \tag{2}$$

Eqs. (1,2) solve the inference problem for Gaussian process: They provide us directly with the predictive distribution $P(\theta(x)|x, D)$. The posterior variance, eq. (2), in fact also gives us the expected generalization error at x. Why? If the teacher is θ^*, the squared deviation between our mean prediction and the teacher output is[1] $(\hat{\theta}(x) - \theta^*(x))^2$; averaging this over the posterior distribution of teachers $P(\theta^*|D)$ just gives (2). The underlying assumption is that our assumed Gaussian process

---
[1] One can also one measure the generalization by the squared deviation between the prediction $\hat{\theta}(x)$ and the *noisy* teacher output; this simply adds a term σ^2 to eq. (3).

prior is the true one from which teachers are actually generated (and that we are using the correct noise model). Otherwise, a more complicated expression for the expected generalization error results; in line with most other work on the subject, I only consider the 'correct prior' case in the following. Averaging the generalization error at x over the distribution of inputs gives then

$$\epsilon(D) = \langle C(x,x) - \mathbf{k}(x)^{\mathbf{T}}\mathbf{K}^{-1}\mathbf{k}(x)\rangle_x \qquad (3)$$

This form of the generalization error (which is well known [2, 3, 4, 5]) still depends on the training inputs (the fact that the training outputs have dropped out already is a signature of the fact that Gaussian processes are *linear* predictors, compare (1)). Averaging over data sets yields the quantity we are after,

$$\epsilon = \langle \epsilon(D) \rangle_D. \qquad (4)$$

This average expected generalization error (I will drop the 'average expected' in the following) only depends on the number of training examples n; the function $\epsilon(n)$ is called the *learning curve*. Its exact calculation is difficult because of the joint average in eqs. (3,4) over the training inputs x_l and the test input x.

2 LEARNING CURVES

As a starting point for an approximate calculation of $\epsilon(n)$, I first derive a representation of the generalization error in terms of the eigenvalue decomposition of the covariance function. Mercer's theorem (see e.g. [6]) tells us that the covariance function can be decomposed into its eigenvalues λ_i and eigenfunctions $\phi_i(x)$:

$$C(x,x') = \sum_{i=1}^{\infty} \lambda_i \phi_i(x)\phi_i(x') \qquad (5)$$

This is simply the analogue of the eigenvalue decomposition of a finite symmetric matrix; the eigenfunctions can be taken to be normalized such that $\langle \phi_i(x)\phi_j(x) \rangle_x = \delta_{ij}$. Now write the data-dependent generalization error (3) as $\epsilon(D) = \langle C(x,x) \rangle_x -$ tr $\langle \mathbf{k}(x)\mathbf{k}(x)^{\mathbf{T}} \rangle_x \mathbf{K}^{-1}$ and perform the x-average in the second term:

$$\langle (\mathbf{k}(x)\mathbf{k}(x)^{\mathbf{T}})_{lm} \rangle_x = \sum_{ij} \lambda_i \lambda_j \phi_i(x_l) \langle \phi_i(x)\phi_j(x) \rangle \phi_j(x_m) = \sum_i \lambda_i^2 \phi_i(x_l)\phi_i(x_m)$$

This suggests introducing the diagonal matrix $(\mathbf{\Lambda})_{ij} = \lambda_i \delta_{ij}$ and the 'design matrix' $(\mathbf{\Phi})_{li} = \phi_i(x_l)$, so that $\langle \mathbf{k}(x)\mathbf{k}(x)^{\mathbf{T}} \rangle_x = \mathbf{\Phi}\mathbf{\Lambda}^2 \mathbf{\Phi}^{\mathbf{T}}$. One then also has $\langle C(x,x) \rangle_x = $ tr $\mathbf{\Lambda}$, and the matrix $\mathbf{K}$ is expressed as $\mathbf{K} = \sigma^2 \mathbf{I} + \mathbf{\Phi}\mathbf{\Lambda}\mathbf{\Phi}^{\mathbf{T}}$, $\mathbf{I}$ being the identity matrix. Collecting these results, we have

$$\epsilon(D) = \text{tr } \mathbf{\Lambda} - \text{tr}\,(\sigma^2 \mathbf{I} + \mathbf{\Phi}\mathbf{\Lambda}\mathbf{\Phi}^{\mathbf{T}})^{-1}\mathbf{\Phi}\mathbf{\Lambda}^2\mathbf{\Phi}^{\mathbf{T}}$$

This can be simplified using the Woodbury formula for matrix inverses (see *e.g.* [7]), which applied to our case gives $(\sigma^2\mathbf{I}+\mathbf{\Phi}\mathbf{\Lambda}\mathbf{\Phi}^{\mathbf{T}})^{-1} = \sigma^{-2}[\mathbf{I}-\mathbf{\Phi}(\sigma^2\mathbf{I}+\mathbf{\Lambda}\mathbf{\Phi}^{\mathbf{T}}\mathbf{\Phi})^{-1}\mathbf{\Lambda}\mathbf{\Phi}^{\mathbf{T}}]$; after a few lines of algebra, one then obtains the final result

$$\epsilon = \langle \epsilon(D) \rangle_D, \qquad \epsilon(D) = \text{tr}\,\sigma^2 \mathbf{\Lambda}(\sigma^2 \mathbf{I} + \mathbf{\Lambda}\mathbf{\Phi}^{\mathbf{T}}\mathbf{\Phi})^{-1} = \text{tr}\,(\mathbf{\Lambda}^{-1} + \sigma^{-2}\mathbf{\Phi}^{\mathbf{T}}\mathbf{\Phi})^{-1} \qquad (6)$$

This exact representation of the generalization error is one of the main results of this paper. Its advantages are that the average over the test input x has already been carried out, and that the remaining dependence on the training data is contained entirely in the matrix $\mathbf{\Phi}^{\mathbf{T}}\mathbf{\Phi}$. It also includes as a special case the well-known result for linear regression (see *e.g.* [8]); $\mathbf{\Lambda}^{-1}$ and $\mathbf{\Phi}^{\mathbf{T}}\mathbf{\Phi}$ can be interpreted as suitably generalized versions of the weight decay (matrix) and input correlation matrix. Starting from (6), one can now derive approximate expressions for the learning curve $\epsilon(n)$. The most naive approach is to entirely neglect the fluctuations in $\mathbf{\Phi^T\Phi}$ over different data sets and replace it by its average, which is simply $\langle(\mathbf{\Phi^T\Phi})_{ij}\rangle_D = \sum_l \langle\phi_i(x_l)\phi_j(x_l)\rangle_D = n\delta_{ij}$. This leads to the Naive approximation

$$\epsilon_N(n) = \text{tr}\,(\mathbf{\Lambda}^{-1} + \sigma^{-2}n\mathbf{I})^{-1} \tag{7}$$

which is not, in general, very good. It does however become exact in the large noise limit $\sigma^2 \to \infty$ at constant n/σ^2: The fluctuations of the elements of the matrix $\sigma^{-2}\mathbf{\Phi^T\Phi}$ then become vanishingly small (of order $\sqrt{n}\sigma^{-2} = (n/\sigma^2)/\sqrt{n} \to 0$) and so replacing $\mathbf{\Phi^T\Phi}$ by its average is justified.

To derive better approximations, it is useful to see how the matrix $\mathcal{G} = (\mathbf{\Lambda}^{-1} + \sigma^{-2}\mathbf{\Phi^T\Phi})^{-1}$ changes when a new example is added to the training set. One has

$$\mathcal{G}(n+1) - \mathcal{G}(n) = [\mathcal{G}^{-1}(n) + \sigma^{-2}\psi\psi^\mathbf{T}]^{-1} - \mathcal{G}(n) = -\frac{\mathcal{G}(n)\psi\psi^\mathbf{T}\mathcal{G}(n)}{\sigma^2 + \psi^\mathbf{T}\mathcal{G}(n)\psi} \tag{8}$$

in terms of the vector ψ with elements $(\psi)_i = \phi_i(x_{n+1})$; the second identity uses again the Woodbury formula. To get exact learning curves, one would have to average this update formula over both the new training input x_{n+1} and all previous ones. This is difficult, but progress can be made by again neglecting some fluctuations: The average over x_{n+1} is approximated by replacing $\psi\psi^\mathbf{T}$ by its average, which is simply the identity matrix; the average over the previous training inputs by replacing $\mathcal{G}(n)$ by its average $\mathbf{G}(n) = \langle\mathcal{G}(n)\rangle_D$. This yields the approximation

$$\mathbf{G}(n+1) - \mathbf{G}(n) = -\frac{\mathbf{G}^2(n)}{\sigma^2 + \text{tr}\,\mathbf{G}(n)} \tag{9}$$

Iterating from $\mathbf{G}(n=0) = \mathbf{\Lambda}$, one sees that $\mathbf{G}(n)$ remains diagonal for all n, and so (9) is trivial to implement numerically. I call the resulting $\epsilon_D(n) = \text{tr}\,\mathbf{G}(n)$ the Discrete approximation to the learning curve, because it still correctly treats n as a variable with discrete, integer values. One can further approximate (9) by taking n as continuously varying, replacing the difference on the left-hand side by the derivative $d\mathbf{G}(n)/dn$. The resulting differential equation for $\mathbf{G}(n)$ is readily solved; taking the trace, one obtains the generalization error

$$\epsilon_{UC}(n) = \text{tr}\,(\mathbf{\Lambda}^{-1} + \sigma^{-2}n'\mathbf{I})^{-1} \tag{10}$$

with n' determined by the self-consistency equation $n' + \text{tr}\,\ln(\mathbf{I} + \sigma^{-2}n'\mathbf{\Lambda}) = n$. By comparison with (7), n' can be thought of as an 'effective number of training examples'. The subscript UC in (10) stands for Upper Continuous approximation. As the name suggests, there is another, lower approximation also derived by treating n as continuous. It has the same form as (10), but a different self-consistent equation for n', and is derived as follows. Introduce an auxiliary offset parameter v (whose usefulness will become clear shortly) by $\mathcal{G}^{-1} = v\mathbf{I} + \mathbf{\Lambda}^{-1} + \sigma^{-2}\mathbf{\Phi^T\Phi}$; at the end of the calculation, v will be set to zero again. As before, start from (8)—which also holds for nonzero v—and approximate $\psi\psi^\mathbf{T}$ and $\text{tr}\,\mathcal{G}$ by their averages, but retain possible fluctuations of $\mathcal{G}$ in the numerator. This gives $\mathbf{G}(n+1) - \mathbf{G}(n) = -\langle\mathcal{G}^2(n)\rangle/[\sigma^2 + \text{tr}\,\mathbf{G}(n)]$. Taking the trace yields an update formula for the generalization error ϵ, where the extra parameter v lets us rewrite the average on the right-hand side as $-\text{tr}\,\langle\mathcal{G}^2\rangle = (\partial/\partial v)\text{tr}\,\langle\mathcal{G}\rangle = \partial\epsilon/\partial v$. Treating n again as continuous, we thus arrive at the partial differential equation $\partial\epsilon/\partial n = (\partial\epsilon/\partial v)/(\sigma^2 + \epsilon)$. This can be solved using the method of characteristics [8] and (for $v = 0$) gives the Lower Continuous approximation to the learning curve,

$$\epsilon_{LC}(n) = \text{tr}\,(\mathbf{\Lambda}^{-1} + \sigma^{-2}n'\mathbf{I})^{-1}, \qquad n' = \frac{n\sigma^2}{\sigma^2 + \epsilon_{LC}} \tag{11}$$

By comparing derivatives w.r.t. n, it is easy to show that this is always lower than the UC approximation (10). One can also check that all three approximations that I have derived (D, LC and UC) converge to the exact result (7) in the large noise limit as defined above.

3 COMPARISON WITH BOUNDS AND SIMULATIONS

I now compare the D, LC and UC approximations with existing bounds, and with the 'true' learning curves as obtained by simulations. A lower bound on the generalization error was given by Michelli and Wahba [2] as

$$\epsilon(n) \geq \epsilon_{\text{MW}}(n) = \sum_{i=n+1}^{\infty} \lambda_i \qquad (12)$$

This is derived for the noiseless case by allowing 'generalized observations' (projections of $\theta^*(x)$ along the first n eigenfunctions of $C(x,x')$), and so is unlikely to be tight for the case of 'real' observations at discrete input points. Based on information theoretic methods, a different Lower bound was obtained by Opper [3]:

$$\epsilon(n) \geq \epsilon_{\text{LO}}(n) = \frac{1}{4}\text{tr}\,(\boldsymbol{\Lambda}^{-1} + 2\sigma^{-2}n\mathbf{I})^{-1} \times [\mathbf{I} + (\mathbf{I} + 2\sigma^{-2}n\boldsymbol{\Lambda})^{-1}]$$

This is always lower than the naive approximation (7); both incorrectly suggest that ϵ decreases to zero for $\sigma^2 \to 0$ at fixed n, which is clearly not the case (compare (12)). There is also an Upper bound due to Opper [3],

$$\tilde{\epsilon}(n) \leq \epsilon_{\text{UO}}(n) = (\sigma^{-2}n)^{-1}\,\text{tr}\,\ln(\mathbf{I} + \sigma^{-2}n\boldsymbol{\Lambda}) + \text{tr}\,(\boldsymbol{\Lambda}^{-1} + \sigma^{-2}n\mathbf{I})^{-1} \qquad (13)$$

Here $\tilde{\epsilon}$ is a modified version of ϵ which (in the rescaled version that I am using) becomes identical to ϵ in the limit of small generalization errors ($\epsilon \ll \sigma^2$), but never gets larger that $2\sigma^2$; for small n in particular, $\epsilon(n)$ can therefore actually be much larger than $\tilde{\epsilon}(n)$ and its bound (13). An upper bound on $\epsilon(n)$ itself was derived by Williams and Vivarelli [4] for one-dimensional inputs and stationary covariance functions (for which $C(x,x')$ is a function of $x - x'$ alone). They considered the generalization error at x that would be obtained from each individual training example, and then took the minimum over all n examples; the training set average of this 'lower envelope' can be evaluated explicitly in terms of integrals over the covariance function [4]. The resulting upper bound, $\epsilon_{\text{WV}}(n)$, never decays below σ^2 and therefore complements the range of applicability of the UO bound (13).

In the examples in Fig. 1, I consider a very simple input domain, $x \in [0,1]^d$, with a uniform input distribution. I also restrict myself to stationary covariance functions, and in fact I use what physicists call periodic boundary conditions. This is simply a trick that makes it easy to calculate the required eigenvalue spectra of the covariance function, but otherwise has little effect on the results as long as the length scale of the covariance function is smaller than the size of the input domain[2], $l \ll 1$. To cover the two extremes of 'rough' and 'smooth' Gaussian priors, I consider the OU [$C(x,x') = \exp(-|x-x'|/l)$] and SE [$C(x,x') = \exp(-|x-x'|^2/2l^2)$] covariance functions. The prior variance of the values of the function to be learned is simply $C(x,x) = 1$; one generically expects this 'prior ignorance' to be significantly larger than the noise on the training data, so I only consider values of $\sigma^2 < 1$. I also fix the covariance function length scale to $l = 0.1$; results for $l = 0.01$ are qualitatively similar. Several observations can be made from Figure 1. (1) The MW lower bound is not tight, as expected. (2) The bracket between Opper's lower and upper bounds (LO/UO) is rather wide (1-2 orders of magnitude); both give good representations of the overall shape of the learning curve only in the asymptotic regime (most clearly visible for the SE covariance function), i.e., once ϵ has dropped below σ^2. (3) The WV upper bound (available only in $d = 1$) works

---

[2]In $d = 1$ dimension, for example, a 'periodically continued' stationary covariance function on $[0,1]$ can be written as $C(x,x') = \sum_{r=-\infty}^{\infty} c(x - x' + r)$. For $l \ll 1$, only the $r = 0$ term makes a significant contribution, except when x and x' are within $\approx l$ of opposite ends of the input space. With this definition, the eigenvalues of $C(x,x')$ are given by the Fourier transform $\int_{-\infty}^{\infty} dx\, c(x)\exp(-2\pi i q x)$, for integer q.

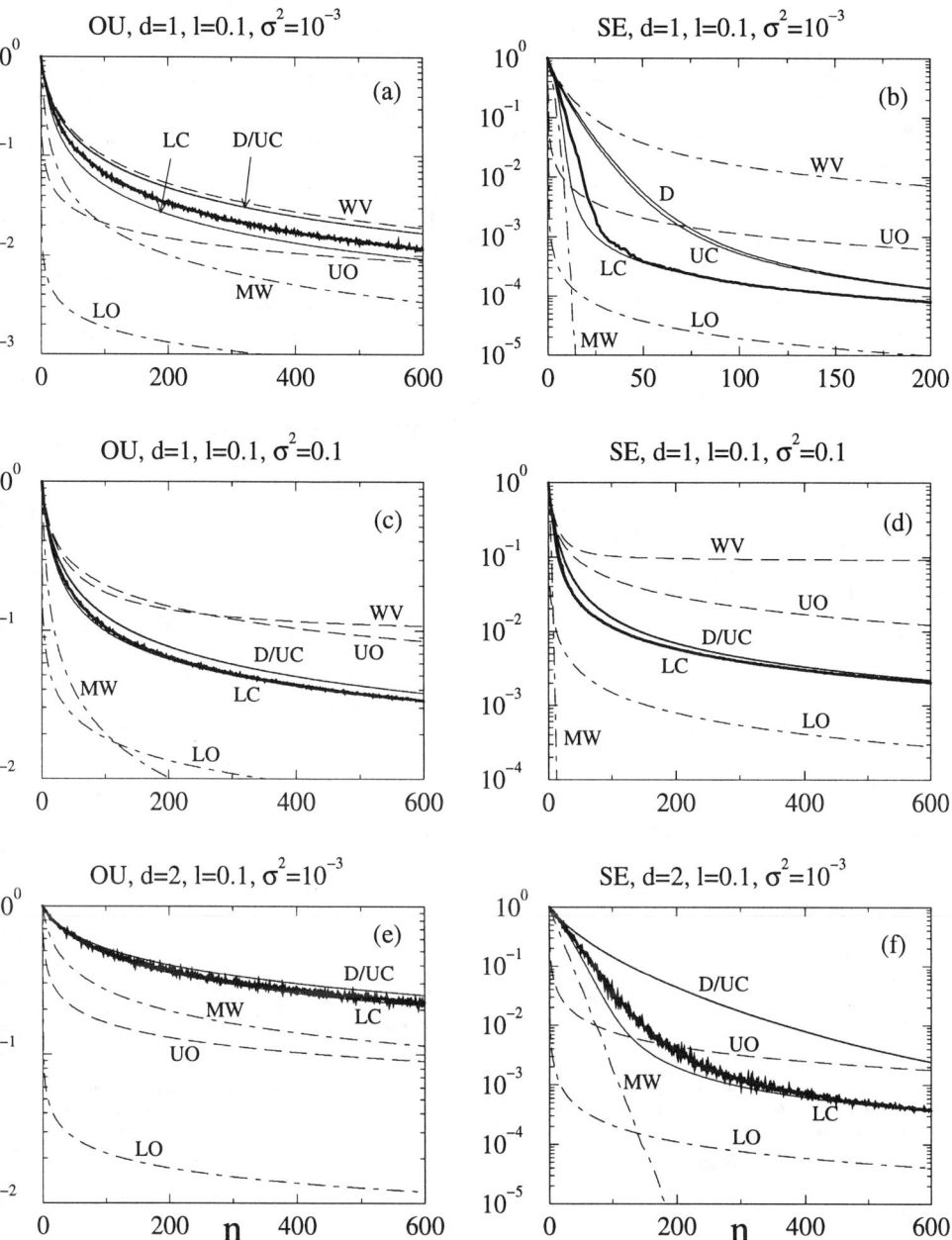

Figure 1: Learning curves $\epsilon(n)$: Comparison of simulation results (thick solid lines; the small fluctuations indicate the order of magnitude of error bars), approximations derived in this paper (thin solid lines; D = discrete, UC/LC = upper/lower continuous), and existing upper (dashed; UO = upper Opper, WV = Williams-Vivarelli) and lower (dot-dashed; LO = lower Opper, MW = Michelli-Wahba) bounds. The type of covariance function (Ornstein-Uhlenbeck/Squared Exponential), its length scale l, the dimension d of the input space, and the noise level σ^2 are as shown. Note the logarithmic y-axes. On the scale of the plots, D and UC coincide (except in (b)); the simulation results are essentially on top of the LC curve in (c-e).

well for the OU covariance function, but less so for the SE case. As expected, it is not useful in the asymptotic regime because it always remains above σ^2. (4) The discrete (D) and upper continuous (UC) approximations are very similar, and in fact indistinguishable on the scale of most plots. This makes the UC version preferable in practice, because it can be evaluated for any chosen n without having to step through all smaller values of n. (5) In all the examples, the true learning curve lies between the UC and LC curves. In fact I would conjecture that these two approximations provide upper and lower bounds on the learning curves, at least for stationary covariance functions. (6) Finally, the LC approximation comes out as the clear winner: For $\sigma^2 = 0.1$ (Fig. 1c,d), it is indistinguishable from the true learning curves. But even in the other cases it represents the overall shape of the learning curves very well, both for small n and in the asymptotic regime; the largest deviations occur in the crossover region between these two regimes.

In summary, I have derived an exact representation of the average generalization ϵ error of Gaussian processes used for regression, in terms of the eigenvalue decomposition of the covariance function. Starting from this, I have obtained three different approximations to the learning curve $\epsilon(n)$. All of them become exact in the large noise limit; in practice, one generically expects the opposite case ($\sigma^2/C(x,x) \ll 1$), but comparison with simulation results shows that even in this regime the new approximations perform well. The LC approximation in particular represents the overall shape of the learning curves very well, both for 'rough' (OU) and 'smooth' (SE) Gaussian priors, and for small as well as for large numbers of training examples n. It is not perfect, but does get substantially closer to the true learning curves than existing bounds. Future work will have to show how well the new approximations work for non-stationary covariance functions and/or non-uniform input distributions, and whether the treatment of fluctuations in the generalization error (due to the random selection of training sets) can be improved, by analogy with fluctuation corrections in linear perceptron learning [8].

Acknowledgements: I would like to thank Chris Williams and Manfred Opper for stimulating discussions, and for providing me with copies of their papers [3, 4] prior to publication. I am grateful to the Royal Society for financial support through a Dorothy Hodgkin Research Fellowship.

[1] See *e.g.* D J C MacKay, Gaussian Processes, Tutorial at *NIPS 10*, and recent papers by Goldberg/Williams/Bishop (in *NIPS 10*), Williams and Barber/Williams (*NIPS 9*), Williams/Rasmussen (*NIPS 8*).

[2] C A Michelli and G Wahba. Design problems for optimal surface interpolation. In Z Ziegler, editor, *Approximation theory and applications*, pages 329–348. Academic Press, 1981.

[3] M Opper. Regression with Gaussian processes: Average case performance. In I K Kwok-Yee, M Wong, and D-Y Yeung, editors, *Theoretical Aspects of Neural Computation: A Multidisciplinary Perspective*. Springer, 1997.

[4] C K I Williams and F Vivarelli. An upper bound on the learning curve for Gaussian processes. Submitted for publication.

[5] C K I Williams. Prediction with Gaussian processes: From linear regression to linear prediction and beyond. In M I Jordan, editor, *Learning and Inference in Graphical Models*. Kluwer Academic. In press.

[6] E Wong. *Stochastic Processes in Information and Dynamical Systems*. McGraw-Hill, New York, 1971.

[7] W H Press, S A Teukolsky, W T Vetterling, and B P Flannery. *Numerical Recipes in C (2nd ed.)*. Cambridge University Press, Cambridge, 1992.

[8] P Sollich. Finite-size effects in learning and generalization in linear perceptrons. *Journal of Physics A*, 27:7771–7784, 1994.

A Theory of Mean Field Approximation

T. Tanaka
Department of Electronics and Information Engineering
Tokyo Metropolitan University
1-1, Minami-Osawa, Hachioji, Tokyo 192-0397 Japan

Abstract

I present a theory of mean field approximation based on information geometry. This theory includes in a consistent way the naive mean field approximation, as well as the TAP approach and the linear response theorem in statistical physics, giving clear information-theoretic interpretations to them.

1 INTRODUCTION

Many problems of neural networks, such as learning and pattern recognition, can be cast into a framework of statistical estimation problem. How difficult it is to solve a particular problem depends on a statistical model one employs in solving the problem. For Boltzmann machines[1] for example, it is computationally very hard to evaluate expectations of state variables from the model parameters.

Mean field approximation[2], which is originated in statistical physics, has been frequently used in practical situations in order to circumvent this difficulty. In the context of statistical physics several advanced theories have been known, such as the TAP approach[3], linear response theorem[4], and so on. For neural networks, application of mean field approximation has been mostly confined to that of the so-called naive mean field approximation, but there are also attempts to utilize those advanced theories[5, 6, 7, 8].

In this paper I present an information-theoretic formulation of mean field approximation. It is based on information geometry[9], which has been successfully applied to several problems in neural networks[10]. This formulation includes the naive mean field approximation as well as the advanced theories in a consistent way. I give the formulation for Boltzmann machines, but its extension to wider classes of statistical models is possible, as described elsewhere[11].

2 BOLTZMANN MACHINES

A Boltzmann machine is a statistical model with N binary random variables $s_i \in \{-1, 1\}$, $i = 1, \ldots, N$. The vector $s = (s_1, \ldots, s_N)$ is called the state of the Boltzmann machine.

The state s is also a random variable, and its probability law is given by the Boltzmann-Gibbs distribution

$$p(s) = e^{-E(s)-\psi(p)}, \quad (1)$$

where $E(s)$ is the "energy" defined by

$$E(s) = -\sum_i h^i s_i - \sum_{\langle ij \rangle} w^{ij} s_i s_j \quad (2)$$

with h^i and w^{ij} the parameters, and $-\psi(p)$ is determined by the normalization condition and is called the Helmholtz free energy of p. The notation $\langle ij \rangle$ means that the summation should be taken over all distinct pairs.

Let $\eta_i(p) \equiv \langle s_i \rangle_p$ and $\eta_{ij}(p) \equiv \langle s_i s_j \rangle_p$, where $\langle \cdot \rangle_p$ means the expectation with respect to p. The following problem is essential for Boltzmann machines:

Problem 1 Evaluate the expectations $\eta_i(p)$ and $\eta_{ij}(p)$ from the parameters h^i and w^{ij} of the Boltzmann machine p.

3 INFORMATION GEOMETRY

3.1 ORTHOGONAL DUAL FOLIATIONS

A whole set $\mathcal{M}$ of the Boltzmann-Gibbs distribution (1) realizable by a Boltzmann machine is regarded as an exponential family. Let us use shorthand notations $I, J, \ldots$, to represent distinct pairs of indices, such as ij. The parameters h^i and w^I constitute a coordinate system of $\mathcal{M}$, called the canonical parameters of $\mathcal{M}$. The expectations η_i and η_I constitute another coordinate system of $\mathcal{M}$, called the expectation parameters of $\mathcal{M}$.

Let $\mathcal{F}_0$ be a subset of $\mathcal{M}$ on which w^I are all equal to zero. I call $\mathcal{F}_0$ the factorizable submodel of $\mathcal{M}$ since $p(s) \in \mathcal{F}_0$ can be factorized with respect to s_i. On $\mathcal{F}_0$ the problem is easy: Since w^I are all zero, s_i are statistically independent of others, and therefore $\eta_i = \tanh^{-1} h^i$ and $\eta_{ij} = \eta_i \eta_j$ hold.

Mean field approximation systematically reduces the problem onto the factorizable submodel $\mathcal{F}_0$. For this reduction, I introduce dual foliations $\mathcal{F}$ and $\mathcal{A}$ onto $\mathcal{M}$. The foliation $\mathcal{F} = \{\mathcal{F}(w)\}$, $\mathcal{M} = \bigcup_w \mathcal{F}(w)$, is parametrized by $w \equiv (w^I)$ and each leaf $\mathcal{F}(w)$ is defined as

$$\mathcal{F}(w) = \{p(s) \mid w^I(p) = w^I\}. \quad (3)$$

The leaf $\mathcal{F}(0)$ is the same as $\mathcal{F}_0$, the factorizable submodel. Each leaf $\mathcal{F}(w)$ is again an exponential family with h^i and η_i the canonical and the expectation parameters, respectively. A pair of dual potentials is defined on each leaf, one is the Helmholtz free energy $\tilde{\psi}(p) \equiv \psi(p)$ and another is its Legendre transform, or the Gibbs free energy,

$$\tilde{\phi}(p) \equiv \sum_i h^i(p)\eta_i(p) - \tilde{\psi}(p), \quad (4)$$

and the parameters of $p \in \mathcal{F}(w)$ are given by

$$\eta_i(p) = \partial_i \tilde{\psi}(p), \quad h^i(p) = \partial^i \tilde{\phi}(p), \quad (5)$$

where $\partial_i \equiv (\partial/\partial h^i)$ and $\partial^i \equiv (\partial/\partial \eta_i)$. Another foliation $\mathcal{A} = \{\mathcal{A}(m)\}$, $\mathcal{M} = \bigcup_m \mathcal{A}(m)$, is parametrized by $m \equiv (m_i)$ and each leaf $\mathcal{A}(m)$ is defined as

$$\mathcal{A}(m) = \{p(s) \mid \eta_i(p) = m_i\}. \quad (6)$$

A Theory of Mean Field Approximation

Each leaf $\mathcal{A}(\boldsymbol{m})$ is not an exponential family, but again a pair of dual potentials $\bar{\psi}$ and $\bar{\phi}$ is defined on each leaf, the former is given by

$$\bar{\psi}(p) = \psi(p) - \sum_i h^i(p)\eta_i(p) \quad (= -\bar{\phi}(p)) \tag{7}$$

and the latter by its Legendre transform as

$$\bar{\phi}(p) = \sum_I w^I(p)\eta_I(p) - \bar{\psi}(p), \tag{8}$$

and the parameters of $p \in \mathcal{A}(\boldsymbol{m})$ are given by

$$\eta_I(p) = \partial_I \bar{\psi}(p), \quad w^I(p) = \partial^I \bar{\phi}(p), \tag{9}$$

where $\partial_I \equiv (\partial/\partial w^I)$ and $\partial^I \equiv (\partial/\partial \eta_I)$. These two foliations form the orthogonal dual foliations, since the leaves $\mathcal{F}(\boldsymbol{w})$ and $\mathcal{A}(\boldsymbol{m})$ are orthogonal at their intersecting point. I introduce still another coordinate system on $\mathcal{M}$, called the mixed coordinate system, on the basis of the orthogonal dual foliations. It uses a pair $(\boldsymbol{m}, \boldsymbol{w})$ of the expectation and the canonical parameters to specify a single element $p \in \mathcal{M}$. The $\boldsymbol{m}$ part specifies the leaf $\mathcal{A}(\boldsymbol{m})$ on which p resides, and the $\boldsymbol{w}$ part specifies the leaf $\mathcal{F}(\boldsymbol{w})$.

3.2 REFORMULATION OF PROBLEM

Assume that a target Boltzmann machine q is given by specifying its parameters $h^i(q)$ and $w^I(q)$. Problem 1 is restated as follows: evaluate its expectations $\eta_i(q)$ and $\eta_I(q)$ from those parameters. To evaluate η_i mean field approximation translates the problem into the following one:

Problem 2 Let $\mathcal{F}(\boldsymbol{w})$ be a leaf on which q resides. Find $p \in \mathcal{F}(\boldsymbol{w})$ which is the closest to q.

At first sight this problem is trivial, since one immediately finds the solution $p = q$. However, solving this problem with respect to $\eta_i(p)$ is nontrivial, and it is the key to understanding of mean field approximation including advanced theories.

Let us measure the proximity of p to q by the Kullback divergence

$$D(p\|q) = \sum_s p(s) \log \frac{p(s)}{q(s)}, \tag{10}$$

then solving Problem 2 reduces to finding a minimizer $p \in \mathcal{F}(\boldsymbol{w})$ of $D(p\|q)$ for a given q. For $p, q \in \mathcal{F}(\boldsymbol{w})$, $D(p\|q)$ is expressed in terms of the dual potentials $\bar{\psi}$ and $\bar{\phi}$ of $\mathcal{F}(\boldsymbol{w})$ as

$$D(p\|q) = \bar{\psi}(q) + \bar{\phi}(p) - \sum_i h^i(q)\eta_i(p). \tag{11}$$

The minimization problem is thus equivalent to minimizing

$$G(p) \equiv \bar{\phi}(p) - \sum_i h^i(q)\eta_i(p), \tag{12}$$

since $\bar{\psi}(q)$ in eq. (11) does not depend on p. Solving the stationary condition $\partial G(p) = 0$ with respect to $\eta_i(p)$ will give the correct expectations $\eta_i(q)$, since the true minimizer is $p = q$. However, the scenario is in general intractable since $\bar{\phi}(p)$ cannot be given explicitly as a function of $\eta_i(p)$.

3.3 PLEFKA EXPANSION

The problem is easy if $w^I = 0$. In this case $\tilde{\phi}(p)$ is given explicitly as a function of $m_i \equiv \eta_i(p)$ as

$$\tilde{\phi}(p) = \frac{1}{2} \sum_i \left[(1 + m_i) \log \frac{1 + m_i}{2} + (1 - m_i) \log \frac{1 - m_i}{2}\right]. \tag{13}$$

Minimization of $G(p)$ with respect to m_i gives the solution $m_i = \tanh h^i$ as expected. When $w^I \neq 0$ the expression (13) is no longer exact, but to compensate the error one may use, leaving convergence problem aside, the Taylor expansion of $\tilde{\phi}(w) \equiv \tilde{\phi}(p)$ with respect to $w = 0$,

$$\begin{aligned}\tilde{\phi}(w) &= \tilde{\phi}(0) + \sum_I (\partial_I \tilde{\phi}(0)) w^I + \frac{1}{2} \sum_{IJ} (\partial_I \partial_J \tilde{\phi}(0)) w^I w^J \\ &\quad + \frac{1}{6} \sum_{IJK} (\partial_I \partial_J \partial_K \tilde{\phi}(0)) w^I w^J w^K + \cdots.\end{aligned} \tag{14}$$

This expansion has been called the Plefka expansion[12] in the literature of spin glasses. Note that in considering the expansion one should temporarily assume that m is fixed: One can rely on the solution m evaluated from the stationary condition $\partial G(p) = 0$ only if the expansion does not change the value of m.

The coefficients in the expansion can be efficiently computed by fully utilizing the orthogonal dual structure of the foliations. First, we have the following theorem:

Theorem 1 *The coefficients of the expansion (14) are given by the cumulant tensors of the corresponding orders, defined on $\mathcal{A}(m)$.*

Because $\tilde{\phi} = -\tilde{\psi}$ holds, one can consider derivatives of $\tilde{\psi}$ instead of those of $\tilde{\phi}$. The first-order derivatives $\partial_I \tilde{\psi}$ are immediately given by the property of the potential of the leaf $\mathcal{A}(m)$ (eq. (9)), yielding

$$\partial_I \tilde{\psi}(0) = \eta_I(p_0), \tag{15}$$

where p_0 denotes the distribution on $\mathcal{A}(m)$ corresponding to $w = 0$. The coefficients of the lowest-orders, including the first-order one, are given by the following theorem.

Theorem 2 *The first-, second-, and third-order coefficients of the expansion (14) are given by:*

$$\begin{aligned}\partial_I \tilde{\psi}(0) &= \eta_I(p_0) \\ \partial_I \partial_J \tilde{\psi}(0) &= \langle (\partial_I \ell)(\partial_J \ell) \rangle_{p_0} \\ \partial_I \partial_J \partial_K \tilde{\psi}(0) &= \langle (\partial_I \ell)(\partial_J \ell)(\partial_K \ell) \rangle_{p_0}\end{aligned} \tag{16}$$

where $\ell \equiv \log p_0$.

The proofs will be found in [11]. It should be noted that, although these results happen to be the same as the ones which would be obtained by regarding $\mathcal{A}(m)$ as an exponential family, they are not the same in general since actually $\mathcal{A}(m)$ is not an exponential family; for example, they are different for the fourth-order coefficients.

The explicit formulas for these coefficients for Boltzmann machines are given as follows:

- For the first-order,
$$\partial_I \tilde{\psi}(0) = m_i m_{i'} \quad (I = ii'). \tag{17}$$

A Theory of Mean Field Approximation

- For the second-order,
$$(\partial_I)^2 \bar{\psi}(0) = (1 - m_i^2)(1 - m_{i'}^2) \quad (I = ii'), \tag{18}$$
and
$$\partial_I \partial_J \bar{\psi}(0) = 0 \quad (I \neq J). \tag{19}$$

- For the third-order,
$$(\partial_I)^3 \bar{\psi}(0) = 4 m_i m_{i'} (1 - m_i^2)(1 - m_{i'}^2) \quad (I = ii'), \tag{20}$$
and for $I = ij$, $J = jk$, $K = ik$ for three distinct indices i, j, and k,
$$\partial_I \partial_J \partial_K \bar{\psi}(0) = (1 - m_i^2)(1 - m_j^2)(1 - m_k^2) \tag{21}$$
For other combinations of I, J, and K,
$$\partial_I \partial_J \partial_K \bar{\psi}(0) = 0. \tag{22}$$

4 MEAN FIELD APPROXIMATION

4.1 MEAN FIELD EQUATION

Truncating the Plefka expansion (14) up to n-th order term gives n-th order approximations, $\tilde{\phi}_n(p)$ and $G_n(p) \equiv \tilde{\phi}_n(p) - \sum_i h^i(q) m_i$. The Weiss free energy, which is used in the naive mean field approximation, is given by $\tilde{\phi}_1(p)$. The TAP approach picks up all relevant terms of the Plefka expansion[12], and for the SK model it gives the second-order approximation $\tilde{\phi}_2(p)$.

The stationary condition $\partial^i G_n(p) = 0$ gives the so-called mean field equation, from which a solution of the approximate minimization problem is to be determined. For $n = 1$ it takes the following familiar form,
$$\tanh^{-1} m_i - h^i - \sum_{j \neq i} w^{ij} m_j = 0 \tag{23}$$
and for $n = 2$ it includes the so-called Onsager reaction term.
$$\tanh^{-1} m_i - h^i - \sum_{j \neq i} w^{ij} m_j + \sum_{j \neq i} (w^{ij})^2 (1 - m_j^2) m_i = 0 \tag{24}$$
Note that all of these are expressed as functions of m_i.

Geometrically, the mean field equation approximately represents the "surface" $\overset{*}{h}{}^i(p) = h^i(q)$ in terms of the mixed coordinate system of $\mathcal{M}$, since for the exact Gibbs free energy G, the stationary condition $\partial^i G(p) = 0$ gives $h^i(p) - h^i(q) = 0$. Accordingly, the approximate relation $h^i(p) = \partial^i \tilde{\phi}_n(p)$, for fixed m, represents the n-th order approximate expression of the leaf $\mathcal{A}(m)$ in the canonical coordinate system. The fit of this expression to the true leaf $\mathcal{A}(m)$ around the point $w = 0$ becomes better as the order of approximation gets higher, as seen in Fig. 1. Such a behavior is well expected, since the Plefka expansion is essentially a Taylor expansion.

4.2 LINEAR RESPONSE

For estimating $\eta_I(p)$ one can utilize the linear response theorem. In information geometrical framework it is represented as a trivial identity relation for the Fisher information on the leaf $\mathcal{F}(w)$. The Fisher information matrix (g_{ij}), or the Riemannian metric tensor, on the leaf $\mathcal{F}(w)$, and its inverse (g^{ij}) are given by
$$g_{ij} = \partial_i \partial_j \bar{\psi}(p) = \eta_{ij}(p) - \eta_i(p) \eta_j(p) \tag{25}$$

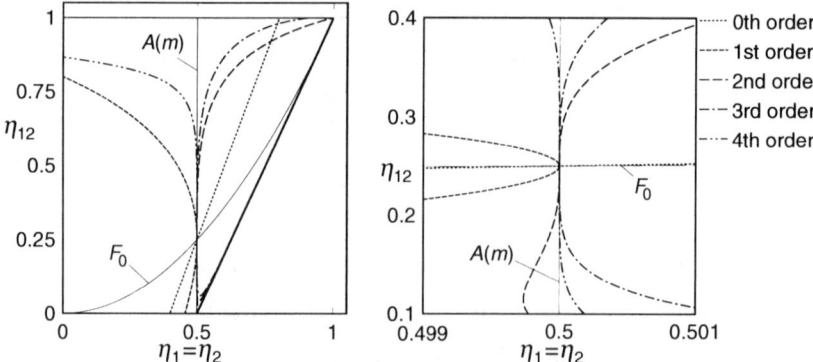

Figure 1: Approximate expressions of $\mathcal{A}(m)$ by mean field approximations of several orders for 2-unit Boltzmann machine, with $(m_1, m_2) = (0.5, 0.5)$ (left), and their magnified view (right).

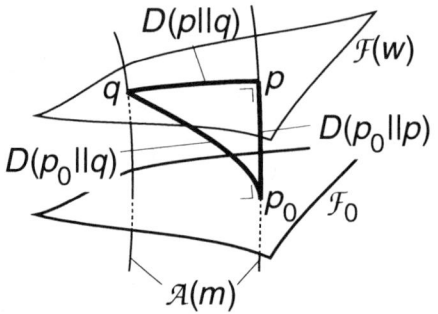

Figure 2: Relation between "naive" approximation and present theory.

and
$$g^{ij} = \partial^i \partial^j \tilde{\phi}(p), \qquad (26)$$
respectively. In the framework here, the linear response theorem states the trivial fact that those are the inverse of the other. In mean field approximation, one substitutes an approximation $\tilde{\phi}_n(p)$ in place of $\tilde{\phi}(p)$ in eq. (26) to get an approximate inverse of the metric (g_n^{ij}). The derivatives in eq. (26) can be analytically calculated, and therefore (g_n^{ij}) can be numerically evaluated by substituting to it a solution m_i of the mean field equation. Equating its inverse to (g_{ij}) gives an estimate of $\eta_{ij}(p)$ by using eq. (25). So far, Problem 1 has been solved within the framework of mean field approximation, with m_i and η_{ij} obtained by the mean field equation and the linear response theorem, respectively.

5 DISCUSSION

Following the framework presented so far, one can in principle construct algorithms of mean field approximation of desired orders. The first-order algorithm with linear response has been first proposed and examined by Kappen and Rodríguez[7, 8]. Tanaka[13] has formulated second- and third-order algorithms and explored them by computer simulations. It is also possible to extend the present formulation so that it can be applicable to higher-order Boltzmann machines. Tanaka[14] discusses an extension of the present formulation to third-order Boltzmann machines: It is possible to extend linear response theorem to higher-orders, and it allows us to treat higher-order correlations within the framework of mean field approximation.

The common understanding about the "naive" mean field approximation is that it minimizes Kullback divergence $D(p_0\|q)$ with respect to $p_0 \in \mathcal{F}_0$ for a given q. It can be shown that this view is consistent with the theory presented in this paper. Assume that $q \in \mathcal{F}(w)$ and $p_0 \in \mathcal{A}(m)$, and let p be a distribution corresponding the intersecting point of the leaves $\mathcal{F}(w)$ and $\mathcal{A}(m)$. Because of the orthogonality of the two foliations $\mathcal{F}$ and $\mathcal{A}$ the following "Pythagorean law[9]" holds (Fig. 2).

$$D(p_0\|q) = D(p_0\|p) + D(p\|q) \tag{27}$$

Intuitively, $D(p_0\|p)$ measures the squared distance between $\mathcal{F}(w)$ and $\mathcal{F}_0$, and is a second-order quantity in w. It should be ignored in the first-order approximation, and thus $D(p_0\|q) \approx D(p\|q)$ holds. Under this approximation minimization of the former with respect to p_0 is equivalent to that of the latter with respect to p, which establishes the relation between the "naive" approximation and the present theory. It can also be checked directly that the first-order approximation of $D(p\|q)$ exactly gives $D(p_0\|q)$, the Weiss free energy.

The present theory provides an alternative view about the validity of mean field approximation: As opposed to a common "belief" that mean field approximation is a good one when N is sufficiently large, one can state from the present formulation that it is so whenever higher-order contribution of the Plefka expansion vanishes, *regardless of whether N is large or not*. This provides a theoretical basis for the observation that mean field approximation often works well for small networks.

The author would like to thank the Telecommunications Advancement Foundation for financial support.

References

[1] Ackley, D. H., Hinton, G. E., and Sejnowski, T. J. (1985) A learning algorithm for Boltzmann machines. *Cognitive Science* **9**: 147–169.

[2] Peterson, C., and Anderson, J. R. (1987) A mean field theory learning algorithm for neural networks. *Complex Systems* **1**: 995–1019.

[3] Thouless, D. J., Anderson, P. W., and Palmer, R. G. (1977) Solution of 'Solvable model of a spin glass'. *Phil. Mag.* **35** (3): 593–601.

[4] Parisi, G. (1988) *Statistical Field Theory*. Addison-Wesley.

[5] Galland, C. C. (1993) The limitations of deterministic Boltzmann machine learning. *Network* **4** (3): 355–379.

[6] Hofmann, T. and Buhmann, J. M. (1997) Pairwise data clustering by deterministic annealing. *IEEE Trans. Patt. Anal. & Machine Intell.* **19** (1): 1–14; Errata, *ibid.* **19** (2): 197 (1997).

[7] Kappen, H. J. and Rodríguez, F. B. (1998) Efficient learning in Boltzmann machines using linear response theory. *Neural Computation.* **10** (5): 1137–1156.

[8] Kappen, H. J. and Rodríguez, F. B. (1998) Boltzmann machine learning using mean field theory and linear response correction. In M. I. Jordan, M. J. Kearns, and S. A. Solla (Eds.), *Advances in Neural Information Processing Systems* 10, pp. 280–286. The MIT Press.

[9] Amari, S.-I. (1985) *Differential-Geometrical Method in Statistics*. Lecture Notes in Statistics **28**, Springer-Verlag.

[10] Amari, S.-I., Kurata, K., and Nagaoka, H. (1992) Information geometry of Boltzmann machines. *IEEE Trans. Neural Networks* **3** (2): 260–271.

[11] Tanaka, T. Information geometry of mean field approximation. preprint.

[12] Plefka, P. (1982) Convergence condition of the TAP equation for the infinite-ranged Ising spin glass model. *J. Phys. A: Math. Gen.* **15** (6): 1971–1978.

[13] Tanaka, T. (1998) Mean field theory of Boltzmann machine learning. *Phys. Rev. E.* **58** (2): 2302–2310.

[14] Tanaka, T. (1998) Estimation of third-order correlations within mean field approximation. In S. Usui and T. Omori (Eds.), *Proc. Fifth International Conference on Neural Information Processing*, vol. 1, pp. 554–557.

PART IV
ALGORITHMS AND ARCHITECTURE

Learning a Hierarchical Belief Network of Independent Factor Analyzers

H. Attias[*]
hagai@gatsby.ucl.ac.uk
Sloan Center for Theoretical Neurobiology, Box 0444
University of California at San Francisco
San Francisco, CA 94143-0444

Abstract

Many belief networks have been proposed that are composed of binary units. However, for tasks such as object and speech recognition which produce real-valued data, binary network models are usually inadequate. Independent component analysis (ICA) learns a model from real data, but the descriptive power of this model is severly limited. We begin by describing the independent factor analysis (IFA) technique, which overcomes some of the limitations of ICA. We then create a multilayer network by cascading single-layer IFA models. At each level, the IFA network extracts real-valued latent variables that are non-linear functions of the input data with a highly adaptive functional form, resulting in a hierarchical distributed representation of these data. Whereas exact maximum-likelihood learning of the network is intractable, we derive an algorithm that maximizes a lower bound on the likelihood, based on a variational approach.

1 Introduction

An intriguing hypothesis for how the brain represents incoming sensory information holds that it constructs a hierarchical probabilistic model of the observed data. The model parameters are learned in an unsupervised manner by maximizing the likelihood that these data are generated by the model. A multilayer belief network is a realization of such a model. Many belief networks have been proposed that are composed of binary units. The hidden units in such networks represent latent variables that explain different features of the data, and whose relation to the

---
[*]Current address: Gatsby Computational Neuroscience Unit, University College London, 17 Queen Square, London WC1N 3AR, U.K.

data is highly non-linear. However, for tasks such as object and speech recognition which produce real-valued data, the models provided by binary networks are often inadequate. Independent component analysis (ICA) learns a generative model from real data, and extracts real-valued latent variables that are mutually statistically independent. Unfortunately, this model is restricted to a single layer and the latent variables are simple linear functions of the data; hence, underlying degrees of freedom that are non-linear cannot be extracted by ICA. In addition, the requirement of equal numbers of hidden and observed variables and the assumption of noiseless data render the ICA model inappropriate.

This paper begins by introducing the independent factor analysis (IFA) technique. IFA is an extension of ICA, that allows different numbers of latent and observed variables and can handle noisy data. The paper proceeds to create a multilayer network by cascading single-layer IFA models. The resulting generative model produces a hierarchical distributed representation of the input data, where the latent variables extracted at each level are *non-linear* functions of the data with a highly adaptive functional form. Whereas exact maximum-likelihood (ML) learning in this network is intractable due to the difficulty in computing the posterior density over the hidden layers, we present an algorithm that maximizes a lower bound on the likelihood. This algorithm is based on a general variational approach that we develop for the IFA network.

2 Independent Component and Independent Factor Analysis

Although the concept of ICA originated in the field of signal processing, it is actually a density estimation problem. Given an $L' \times 1$ observed data vector $\mathbf{y}$, the task is to explain it in terms of an $L \times 1$ vector $\mathbf{x}$ of unobserved 'sources' that are mutually statistically independent. The relation between the two is assumed linear,

$$\mathbf{y} = \mathbf{Hx} + \mathbf{u}, \qquad (1)$$

where $\mathbf{H}$ is the 'mixing' matrix; the noise vector $\mathbf{u}$ is usually assumed zero-mean Gaussian with a covariance matrix $\mathbf{\Lambda}$. In the context of blind source separation [1]-[4], the source signals $\mathbf{x}$ should be recovered from the mixed noisy signals $\mathbf{y}$ with no knowledge of $\mathbf{H}$, $\mathbf{\Lambda}$, or the source densities $p(x_i)$, hence the term 'blind'. In the density estimation approach, one regards (1) as a probabilistic generative model for the observed $p(\mathbf{y})$, with the mixing matrix, noise covariance, and source densities serving as model parameters. In principle, these parameters should be learned by ML, followed by inferring the sources via a MAP estimator.

For Gaussian sources, (1) is the factor analysis model, for which an EM algorithm exists and the MAP estimator is linear. The problem becomes interesting and more difficult for non-Gaussian sources. Most ICA algorithms focus on square ($L' = L$), noiseless ($\mathbf{y} = \mathbf{Hx}$) mixing, and fix $p(x_i)$ using prior knowledge (but see [5] for the case of noisy mixing with a fixed Laplacian source prior). Learning $\mathbf{H}$ occurs via gradient-ascent maximization of the likelihood [1]-[4]. Source density parameters can also be adapted in this way [3],[4], but the resulting gradient-ascent learning is rather slow. This state of affairs presented a problem to ICA algorithms, since the ability to learn arbitrary source densities that are not known in advance is crucial: using an inaccurate $p(x_i)$ often leads to a bad $\mathbf{H}$ estimate and failed separation.

This problem was recently solved by introducing the IFA technique [6]. IFA employs a semi-parametric model of the source densities, which allows learning them (as well as the mixing matrix) using expectation-maximization (EM). Specifically, $p(x_i)$ is described as a mixture of Gaussians (MOG), where the mixture components are labeled by $s = 1, ..., n_i$ and have means $\mu_{i,s}$ and variances $\gamma_{i,s}$: $p(x_i) = \sum_s p(s_i = s) \mathcal{G}(x_i - \mu_{i,s}, \gamma_{i,s})$. [1] The mixing proportions are parametrized using the softmax form: $p(s_i = s) = \exp(a_{i,s}) / \sum_{s'} \exp(a_{i,s'})$. Beyond noiseless ICA, an EM algorithm for the noisy case (1) with any L, L' was also derived in [6] using the MOG description. [2] This algorithm learns a probabilistic model $p(\mathbf{y} \mid W)$ for the observed data, parametrized by $W = (\mathbf{H}, \mathbf{\Lambda}, \{a_{i,s}, \mu_{i,s}, \gamma_{i,s}\})$. A graphical representation of this model is provided by Fig. 1, if we set $n = 1$ and $y_j^0 = b_{j,s}^1 = \nu_{j,s}^1 = 0$.

3 Hierarchical Independent Factor Analysis

In the following we develop a multilayer generalization of IFA, by cascading duplicates of the generative model introduced in [6]. Each layer $n = 1, ..., N$ is composed of two sublayers: a source sublayer which consists of the units x_i^n, $i = 1, ..., L_n$, and an output sublayer which consists of y_j^n, $j = 1, ..., L'_n$. The two are linearly related via $\mathbf{y}^n = \mathbf{H}^n \mathbf{x}^n + \mathbf{u}^n$ as in (1); $\mathbf{u}^n$ is a Gaussian noise vector with covariance $\mathbf{\Lambda}^n$. The nth-layer source x_i^n is described by a MOG density model with parameters $a_{i,s}^n$, $\mu_{i,s}^n$, and $\gamma_{i,s}^n$, in analogy to the IFA sources above.

The important step is to determine how layer n depends on the previous layers. We choose to introduce a dependence of the ith source of layer n only on the ith output of layer $n - 1$. Notice that matching $L_n = L'_{n-1}$ is now required. This dependence is implemented by making the means and mixture proportions of the Gaussians which compose $p(x_i^n)$ dependent on y_i^{n-1}. Specifically, we make the replacements $\mu_{i,s}^n \to \mu_{i,s}^n + \nu_{i,s}^n y_i^{n-1}$ and $a_{i,s}^n \to a_{i,s}^n + b_{i,s}^n y_i^{n-1}$. The resulting joint density for layer n, conditioned on layer $n - 1$, is

$$p(\mathbf{s}^n, \mathbf{x}^n, \mathbf{y}^n \mid \mathbf{y}^{n-1}, W^n) = \prod_{i=1}^{L_n} p(s_i^n \mid y_i^{n-1}) \, p(x_i^n \mid s_i^n, y_i^{n-1}) \, p(\mathbf{y}^n \mid \mathbf{x}^n) \,, \qquad (2)$$

where W^n are the parameters of layer n and

$$p(s_i^n = s \mid y_i^{n-1}) = \frac{\exp(a_{i,s}^n + b_{i,s}^n y_i^{n-1})}{\sum_{s'} \exp(a_{i,s'}^n + b_{i,s'}^n y_i^{n-1})} \,, \qquad p(\mathbf{y}^n \mid \mathbf{x}^n) = \mathcal{G}(\mathbf{y}^n - \mathbf{H}^n \mathbf{x}^n, \mathbf{\Lambda}^n) \,,$$

$$p(x_i^n \mid s_i^n = s, y_i^{n-1}) = \mathcal{G}(x_i^n - \mu_{i,s}^n - \nu_{i,s}^n y_i^{n-1}, \gamma_{i,s}^n) \,.$$

The full model joint density is given by the product of (2) over $n = 1, ..., N$ (setting $\mathbf{y}^0 = 0$). A graphical representation of layer n of the hierarchical IFA network is given in Fig. 1. All units are hidden except $\mathbf{y}^N$.

To gain some insight into our network, we examine the relation between the nth-layer source x_i^n and the $n - 1$th-layer output y_i^{n-1}. This relation is probabilistic and is determined by the conditional density $p(x_i^n \mid y_i^{n-1}) = \sum_{s_i^n} p(s_i^n \mid y_i^{n-1}) p(x_i^n \mid s_i^n, y_i^{n-1})$. Notice from (2) that this is a MOG density. Its y_i^{n-1}-dependent mean is given by

$$\overline{x_i^n} = f_i^n(y_i^{n-1}) = \sum_s p(s_i^n = s \mid y_i^{n-1}) \, (\mu_{i,s}^n + \nu_{i,s}^n y_i^{n-1}) \,, \qquad (3)$$

---

[1] Throughout this paper, $\mathcal{G}(\mathbf{x}, \mathbf{\Sigma}) = \mid 2\pi \mathbf{\Sigma} \mid^{-1/2} \exp(-\mathbf{x}^T \mathbf{\Sigma}^{-1} \mathbf{x}/2)$.
[2] However, for many sources the E-step becomes intractable, since the number $\prod_i n_i$ of source state configurations $\mathbf{s} = (s_1, ..., s_L)$ depends exponentially on L. Such cases are treated in [6] using a variational approximation.

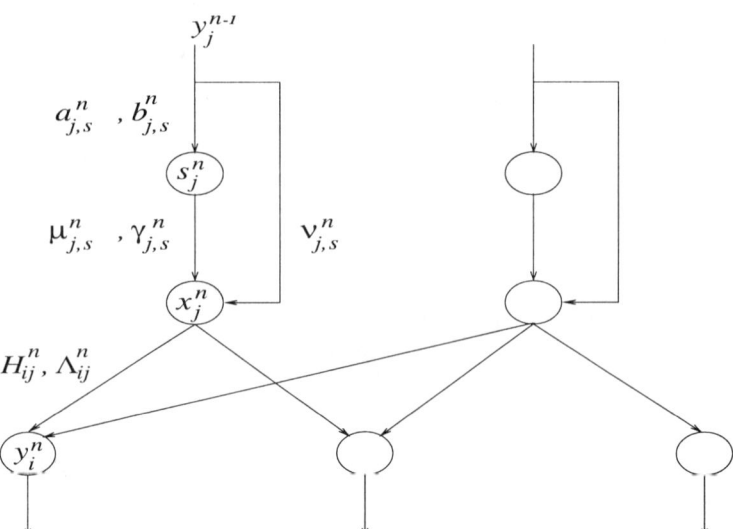

Figure 1: Layer n of the hierarchical ICA generative model.

and is a non-linear function of y_i^{n-1} due to the softmax form of $p(s_i^n \mid y_i^{n-1})$. By adjusting the parameters, the function f_i^n can assume a very wide range of forms: suppose that for state s_i^n, $a_{i,s}^n$ and $b_{i,s}^n$ are set so that $p(s_i^n = s \mid y_i^{n-1})$ is significant only in a small, continuous range of y_i^{n-1} values, with different ranges associated with different s's. In this range, f_i^n will be dominated by the linear term $\mu_{i,s}^n + \nu_{i,s}^n y_i^{n-1}$. Hence, a desired f_i^n can be produced by placing oriented line segments at appropriate points above the y_i^{n-1}-axis, then smoothly join them together by the $p(s_i^n \mid y_i^{n-1})$. Using the algorithm below, the optimal form of f_i^n will be learned from the data. Therefore, our model describes the data y_i^N as a potentially highly complex function of the top layer sources, produced by repeated application of linear mixing followed by a non-linearity, with noise allowed at each stage.

4 Learning and Inference by Variational EM

The need for summing over an exponentially large number of source state configurations $(s_1^n, ..., s_L^n)$, and integrating over the softmax functions $p(s_i^n \mid y_i^n)$, makes exact learning intractable in our network. Thus, approximations must be made. In the following we develop a variational approach, in the spirit of [8], to hierarchical IFA. We begin, following the approach of [7] to EM, by bounding the log-likelihood from below: $\mathcal{L} = \log p(\mathbf{y}^N) \geq \sum_n \{E \log p(\mathbf{y}^n \mid \mathbf{x}^n) + \sum_{i,s_i^n} [E \log p(x_i^n \mid s_i^n, y_i^{n-1}) + E \log p(s_i^n \mid y_i^{n-1})]\} - E \log q$, where E denotes averaging over the hidden layers using an arbitrary posterior $q = q(\mathbf{s}^{1...N}, \mathbf{x}^{1...N}, \mathbf{y}^{1...N-1} \mid \mathbf{y}^N)$. In exact EM, q at each iteration is the true posterior, parametrized by $W^{1...N}$ from the previous iteration. In variational EM, q is chosen to have a form which makes learning tractable, and is parametrized by a separate set of parameters $V^{1...N}$. These are optimized to bring q as close to the true posterior as possible.

E-step. We use a variational posterior that is factorized across layers. Within layer n it has the form

$$q(\mathbf{s}^n, \mathbf{x}^n, \mathbf{y}^n \mid V^n) = \prod_{i=1}^{L_n} v_{i,s_i}^n \, \mathcal{G}(\mathbf{z}^n - \boldsymbol{\rho}^n, \boldsymbol{\Sigma}^n), \quad \mathbf{z}^n = (\mathbf{x}^n, \mathbf{y}^n)^T \tag{4}$$

for $n < N$, and $q(\mathbf{s}^N, \mathbf{x}^N \mid V^N) = \prod_i v_{i,s_i}^N \mathcal{G}(\mathbf{x}^N - \boldsymbol{\rho}^N, \boldsymbol{\Sigma}^N)$. The variational parameters $V^n = (\boldsymbol{\rho}^n, \boldsymbol{\Sigma}^n, \{v_{i,s}^n\})$ depend on the data $\mathbf{y}^N$. The full N-layer posterior is simply a product of (4) over n. Hence, given the data, the nth-layer sources and outputs are jointly Gaussian whereas the states s_i^n are independent. [3]

Even with the variational posterior (4), the term $E \log p(s_i^n \mid y_i^{n-1})$ in the lower bound cannot be calculated analytically, since it involves integration over the softmax function. Instead, we calculate yet a lower bound on this term. Let $c_{i,s}^n = a_{i,s}^n + b_{i,s}^n y_i^{n-1}$ and drop the unit and layer indices i, n, then $\log p(s \mid y) = -\log(1 + e^{-c_s} \sum_{s' \neq s} e^{c_{s'}})$. Borrowing an idea from [8], we multiply and divide by e^{η_s} under the logarithm sign and use Jensen's inequality to get $E \log p(s \mid y) \geq -\eta_s E c_s - \log E\left[e^{-\eta_s c_s} + e^{-(1+\eta_s)c_s} \sum_{s' \neq s} e^{c_{s'}}\right]$. This results in a bound that can be calculated in closed form:

$$E \log p(s_i^n = s \mid y_i^{n-1}) \geq -v_s^n \eta_s^n \bar{c}_s^n - v_s^n \log \left(e^{f_s^n} + \sum_{s' \neq s} e^{f_{ss'}^n} \right) \equiv \mathcal{F}_{i,s}^n, \tag{5}$$

where $\bar{c}_s^n = a_s^n + b_s^n \rho_y^{n-1}$, $f_s^n = -\eta_s^n \bar{c}_s^n + (\eta_s^n b_s^n)^2 \Sigma_{yy}^{n-1}/2$, $f_{ss'}^n = -(1+\eta_s^n)\bar{c}_s^n + \bar{c}_{s'}^n + [(1+\eta_s^n)b_s^n - b_{s'}^n]^2 \Sigma_{yy}^{n-1}/2$, and the subscript i is omitted. We also defined $\boldsymbol{\rho}^n = (\rho_x^n, \rho_y^n)^T$ and similarly $\boldsymbol{\Sigma}_{xx}, \boldsymbol{\Sigma}_{yy}, \boldsymbol{\Sigma}_{xy} = \boldsymbol{\Sigma}_{yx}^T$ are the subblocks of $\boldsymbol{\Sigma}$. Since (5) holds for arbitrary $\eta_{i,s}^n$, the latter are treated as additional variational parameters which are optimized to tighten this bound. [4]

To optimize the variational parameters $V^{1 \cdots N}$, we equate the gradient of the lower bound on $\mathcal{L}$ to zero and obtain

$$\begin{pmatrix} (\mathbf{H}^T \boldsymbol{\Lambda}^{-1} \mathbf{H})^n + \mathbf{A}^n & -(\mathbf{H}^T \boldsymbol{\Lambda}^{-1})^n \\ -(\boldsymbol{\Lambda}^{-1} \mathbf{H})^n & (\boldsymbol{\Lambda}^{-1})^n + \mathbf{B}^{n+1} \end{pmatrix} \boldsymbol{\rho}^n - \begin{pmatrix} 0 & \mathbf{B}^n \\ \mathbf{A}^{n+1} & 0 \end{pmatrix} \begin{pmatrix} \rho_x^{n+1} \\ \rho_y^{n-1} \end{pmatrix}$$
$$= \begin{pmatrix} \alpha^n \\ \beta^{n+1} + \mathcal{F}_\rho^{n+1} \end{pmatrix}, \tag{6}$$

$$\boldsymbol{\Sigma}^n = \begin{pmatrix} (\mathbf{H}^T \boldsymbol{\Lambda}^{-1} \mathbf{H})^n + \mathbf{A}^n & -(\mathbf{H}^T \boldsymbol{\Lambda}^{-1})^n \\ -(\boldsymbol{\Lambda}^{-1} \mathbf{H})^n & (\boldsymbol{\Lambda}^{-1})^n + \mathbf{B}^{n+1} - \mathcal{F}_\Sigma^{n+1} \end{pmatrix}^{-1}, \tag{7}$$

where $A_{ij}^n = \sum_s (v_{i,s}/\gamma_{i,s})^n \delta_{ij}$, $B_{ij}^n = \sum_s (v_{i,s}\nu_{i,s}/\gamma_{i,s})^n \delta_{ij}$, $\alpha_i^n = \sum_s (v_{i,s}\mu_{i,s}/\gamma_{i,s})^n$, and $\beta_i^n = \sum_s (v_{i,s}\mu_{i,s}\nu_{i,s}/\gamma_{i,s})^n$. (All parameters within $(\cdots)^n$ belong to layer n). $\mathcal{F}_{\rho,\Sigma}^{n+1}$ contain the corresponding derivatives of $\mathcal{F}_s^{n+1}$ (5), summed over s. For the state posteriors we have

$$v_s^n = \frac{1}{Z^n} \exp\left(\frac{\gamma_s^n}{2} + \frac{1}{2\gamma_s^n}[(\rho_x^n - \mu_s^n - \nu_s^n \rho_y^{n-1})^2 + \Sigma_{xx}^n + (\nu_s^n)^2 \Sigma_{yy}^{n-1}] + \frac{\partial \mathcal{F}_s^n}{\partial v_s^n} \right), \tag{8}$$

---

[3] It is easy to introduce more structure into (4) by allowing the means ρ_i^n to depend on s_i^n, and the covariances Σ_{ij}^n to depend on s_i^n, s_j^n, thus making the approximation more accurate (but more complex) while maintaining tractability.

[4] An alternative approach to handle $E \log p(s_i^n \mid y_i^{n-1})$ is to approximate the required integral by, e.g., the maximum value of the integrand, possibly including Gaussian corrections. The resulting approximation is simpler than (5); however, it is no longer guaranteed to bound the log-likelihood from below.

where the unit subscript i is omitted (i.e., $\Sigma_{xx}^n = \Sigma_{xx,ii}^n$); $Z^n = Z_i^n$ is set such that $\sum_s v_{i,s}^n = 1$. A simple modification of these equations is required for layer $n = N$.

The optimal $V^{1\cdots N}$ are obtained by solving the fixed-point equations (6–8) iteratively for each data vector $\mathbf{y}^N$, keeping the generative parameters $W^{1\cdots N}$ fixed. Notice that these equations couple layer n to layers $n \pm 1$. The additional parameters $\eta_{i,s}^n$ are adjusted using gradient ascent on $\mathcal{F}_{i,s}^n$. Once learning is complete, the inference problem is solved since the MAP estimate of the hidden unit values given the data is readily available from ρ_i^n and $v_{i,s}^n$.

M-Step. In terms of the variational parameters obtained in the E-step, the new generative parameters are given by

$$\mathbf{H}^n = (\rho_y^n \rho_x^{n\,T} + \Sigma_{yx}^n)(\rho_x^n \rho_x^{n\,T} + \Sigma_{xx}^n)^{-1},$$

$$\Lambda^n = \rho_y^n \rho_y^{n\,T} + \Sigma_{yy}^n - \mathbf{H}^n(\rho_x^n \rho_y^{n\,T} + \Sigma_{xy}^n), \tag{9}$$

$$\begin{pmatrix} \mu_s^n \\ \nu_s^n \end{pmatrix} = \begin{pmatrix} v_s^n & \rho_y^{n-1} v_s^n \\ \rho_y^{n-1} v_s^n & [(\rho_y^{n-1})^2 + \Sigma_{yy}^{n-1}] v_s^n \end{pmatrix}^{-1} \begin{pmatrix} \rho_x^n v_s^n \\ \rho_x^n \rho_y^{n-1} v_s^n \end{pmatrix},$$

$$\gamma_s^n = \frac{1}{v_s^n}\left[(\rho_x^n - \mu_s^n - \nu_s^n \rho_y^{n-1})^2 + \Sigma_{xx}^n + (\nu_s^n)^2 \Sigma_{yy}^{n-1}\right] v_s^n, \tag{10}$$

omitting the subscript i as in (8), and are slightly modified for layer N. In batch mode, averaging over the data is implied and the v_s^n do not cancel out. Finally, the softmax parameters $a_{i,s}^n, b_{i,s}^n$ are adapted by gradient ascent on the bound (5).

5 Discussion

The hierarchical IFA network presented here constitutes a quite general framework for learning and inference using real-valued probabilistic models that are strongly non-linear but highly adaptive. Notice that this network includes both continuous x_i^n, y_i^n and binary s_i^n units, and can thus extract both types of latent variables. In particular, the uppermost units s_i^1 may represent class labels in classification tasks. The models proposed in [9]-[11] can be viewed as special cases where x_i^n is a prescribed deterministic function (e.g., rectifier) of the previous outputs y_j^{n-1}: in the IFA network, a deterministic (but still adaptive) dependence can be obtained by setting the variances $\gamma_{i,s}^n = 0$. Note that the source x_i^n in such a case assumes only the values $\mu_{i,s}^n$, and thus corresponds to a discrete latent variable.

The learning and inference algorithm presented here is based on the variational approach. Unlike variational approximations in other belief networks [8],[10] which use a completely factorized approximation, the structure of the hierarchical IFA network facilitates using a variational posterior that allows correlations among hidden units occupying the same layer, thus providing a more accurate description of the true posterior. It would be interesting to compare the performance of our variational algorithm with the belief propagation algorithm [12] which, when adapted to the densely connected IFA network, would also be an approximation. Markov chain Monte Carlo methods, including the more recent slice sampling procedure used in [11], would become very slow as the network size increases.

It is possible to consider a more general non-linear network along the lines of hierarchical IFA. Notice from (2) that given the previous layer output $\mathbf{y}^{n-1}$, the mean output of the next layer is $\overline{y_i^n} = \sum_j H_{ij}^n f_j^n(y_j^{n-1})$ (see (3)), i.e. a linear mixing preceded by a non-linear function operating on each output component separately. However, if we eliminate the sources x_j^n, replace the individual source states s^n_j by collective states s^n, and allow the linear transformation to depend on s^n, we arrive at the following model: $p(s^n = s \mid \mathbf{y}^{n-1}) \propto \exp(a^n_s + \mathbf{b}^n_s{}^T \mathbf{y}^{n-1})$, $p(\mathbf{y}^n \mid s^n = s, \mathbf{y}^{n-1}) = \mathcal{G}(\mathbf{y}^n - \mathbf{h}^n_s - \mathbf{H}^n_s \mathbf{y}^{n-1}, \mathbf{\Lambda}^n)$. Now we have $\overline{\mathbf{y}^n} = \sum_s p(s^n = s \mid \mathbf{y}^{n-1})(\mathbf{h}^n_s + \mathbf{H}^n_s \mathbf{y}^{n-1}) \equiv F(\mathbf{y}^{n-1})$, which is a more general non-linearity.

Finally, the blocks $\{\mathbf{y}^n, \mathbf{x}^n, s^n \mid \mathbf{y}^{n-1}\}$ (Fig. 1), or alternatively the blocks $\{\mathbf{y}^n, s^n \mid \mathbf{y}^{n-1}\}$ described above, can be connected not only vertically (as in this paper) and horizontally (creating layers with multiple blocks), but in any directed acyclic graph architecture, with the variational EM algorithm extended accordingly.

Acknowledgements

I thank V. de Sa for helpful discussions. Supported by The Office of Naval Research (N00014-94-1-0547), NIDCD (R01-02260), and the Sloan Foundation.

References

[1] Bell, A.J. and Sejnowski, T.J. (1995). An information-maximization approach to blind separation and blind deconvolution. *Neural Computation* **7**, 1129-1159.

[2] Cardoso, J.-F. (1997). Infomax and maximum likelihood for source separation. *IEEE Signal Processing Letters* **4**, 112-114.

[3] Pearlmutter, B.A. and Parra, L.C. (1997). Maximum likelihood blind source separation: A context-sensitive generalization of ICA. *Advances in Neural Information Processing Systems* **9** (Ed. Mozer, M.C. et al), 613-619. MIT Press.

[4] Attias, H. and Schreiner, C.E. (1998). Blind source separation and deconvolution: the dynamic component analysis algorithm. *Neural Computation* **10**, 1373-1424.

[5] Lewicki, M.S. and Sejnowski, T.J. (1998). Learning nonlinear overcomplete representations for efficient coding. *Advances in Neural Information Processing Systems* **10** (Ed. Jordan, M.I. et al), MIT Press.

[6] Attias, H. (1999). Independent factor analysis. *Neural Computation*, in press.

[7] Neal, R.M. and Hinton, G.E. (1998). A view of the EM algorithm that justifies incremental, sparse, and other variants. *Learning in Graphical Models* (Ed. Jordan, M.I.), Kluwer Academic Press.

[8] Saul, L.K., Jaakkola, T., and Jordan, M.I. (1996). Mean field theory of sigmoid belief networks. *Journal of Artificial Intelligence Research* **4**, 61-76.

[9] Frey, B.J. (1997) Continuous sigmoidal belief networks trained using slice sampling. *Advances in Neural Information Processing Systems* **9** (Ed. Mozer, M.C. et al). MIT Press.

[10] Frey, B.J. and Hinton, G.E. (1999). Variational learning in non-linear Gaussian belief networks. *Neural Computation*, in press.

[11] Ghahramani, Z. and Hinton, G.E. (1998). Hierarchical non-linear factor analysis and topographic maps. *Advances in Neural Information Processing Systems* **10** (Ed. Jordan, M.I. et al), MIT Press.

[12] Pearl, J. (1988). *Probabilistic Reasoning in Intelligent Systems*. Morgan Kaufmann, San Mateo, CA.

Semi-Supervised Support Vector Machines

Kristin P. Bennett
Department of Mathematical Sciences
Rensselaer Polytechnic Institute
Troy, NY 12180   bennek@rpi.edu

Ayhan Demiriz
Department of Decision Sciences and Engineering Systems
Rensselaer Polytechnic Institute
Troy, NY 12180   demira@rpi.edu

Abstract

We introduce a semi-supervised support vector machine (S^3VM) method. Given a training set of labeled data and a working set of unlabeled data, S^3VM constructs a support vector machine using both the training and working sets. We use S^3VM to solve the transduction problem using overall risk minimization (ORM) posed by Vapnik. The transduction problem is to estimate the value of a classification function at the given points in the working set. This contrasts with the standard inductive learning problem of estimating the classification function at all possible values and then using the fixed function to deduce the classes of the working set data. We propose a general S^3VM model that minimizes both the misclassification error and the function capacity based on all the available data. We show how the S^3VM model for 1-norm linear support vector machines can be converted to a mixed-integer program and then solved exactly using integer programming. Results of S^3VM and the standard 1-norm support vector machine approach are compared on ten data sets. Our computational results support the statistical learning theory results showing that incorporating working data improves generalization when insufficient training information is available. In every case, S^3VM either improved or showed no significant difference in generalization compared to the traditional approach.

1 INTRODUCTION

In this work we propose a method for semi-supervised support vector machines (S^3VM). S^3VM are constructed using a mixture of labeled data (the training set) and unlabeled data (the working set). The objective is to assign class labels to the working set such that the "best" support vector machine (SVM) is constructed. If the working set is empty the method becomes the standard SVM approach to classification [20, 9, 8]. If the training set is empty, then the method becomes a form of unsupervised learning. *Semi-supervised* learning occurs when both training and working sets are nonempty. Semi-supervised learning for problems with small training sets and large working sets is a form of semi-supervised clustering. There are successful semi-supervised algorithms for k-means and fuzzy c-means clustering [4, 18]. Clustering is a potential application for S^3VM as well. When the training set is large relative to the working set, S^3VM can be viewed as a method for solving the *transduction* problem according to the principle of *overall risk minimization* (ORM) posed by Vapnik at the NIPS 1998 SVM Workshop and in [19, Chapter 10]. S^3VM for ORM is the focus of this paper.

In classification, the transduction problem is to estimate the class of each given point in the unlabeled working set. The usual support vector machine (SVM) approach estimates the entire classification function using the principle of *statistical risk minimization* (SRM). In transduction, one estimates the classification function at points within the working set using information from both the training and working set data. Theoretically, if there is adequate training data to estimate the function satisfactorily, then SRM will be sufficient. We would expect transduction to yield no significant improvement over SRM alone. If, however, there is inadequate training data, then ORM may improve generalization on the working set. Intuitively, we would expect ORM to yield improvements when the training sets are small or when there is a significant deviation between the training and working set subsamples of the total population. Indeed, the theoretical results in [19] support these hypotheses.

In Section 2, we briefly review the standard SVM model for structural risk minimization. According to the principles of structural risk minimization, SVM minimize both the empirical misclassification rate and the capacity of the classification function [19, 20] using the training data. The capacity of the function is determined by margin of separation between the two classes based on the training set. ORM also minimizes the both the empirical misclassification rate and the function capacity. But the capacity of the function is determined using both the training and working sets. In Section 3, we show how SVM can be extended to the semi-supervised case and how mixed integer programming can be used practically to solve the resulting problem. We compare support vector machines constructed by structural risk minimization and overall risk minimization computationally on ten problems in Section 4. Our computational results support past theoretical results that improved generalization can be obtained by incorporating working set information during training when there is a deviation between the working set and training set sample distributions. In three of ten real-world problems the semi-supervised approach, S^3VM , achieved a significant increase in generalization. In no case did S^3VM ever obtain a significant decrease in generalization. We conclude with a discussion of more general S^3VM algorithms.

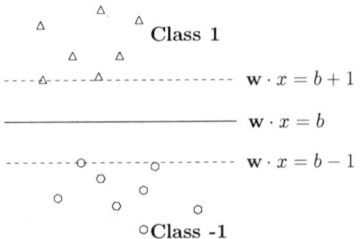

Figure 1: Optimal plane maximizes margin.

2 SVM using Structural Risk Minimization

The basic SRM task is to estimate a classification function $f : R^N \to \{\pm 1\}$ using input-output training data from two classes

$$(\mathbf{x}_1, y_1), \ldots, (\mathbf{x}_\ell, y_\ell) \in R^n \times \{\pm 1\}. \tag{1}$$

The function f should correctly classify unseen examples $(\mathbf{x}, y)$, i.e. $f(\mathbf{x}) = y$ if $(\mathbf{x}, y)$ is generated from the same underlying probability distribution as the training data. In this work we limit discussion to linear classification functions. We will discuss extensions to the nonlinear case in Section 5. If the points are linearly separable, then there exist an n-vector $\mathbf{w}$ and scalar b such that

$$\begin{array}{ll} \mathbf{w} \cdot x_i - b \geq 1 & if\ y_i = 1,\ and \\ \mathbf{w} \cdot x_i - b \leq -1 & if\ y_i = -1,\ i = 1,\ldots,\ell \end{array} \tag{2}$$

or equivalently

$$y_i[\mathbf{w} \cdot x_i - b] \geq 1,\ i = 1, \ldots, \ell. \tag{3}$$

The "optimal" separating plane, $\mathbf{w} \cdot x = b$, is the one which is furthest from the closest points in the two classes. Geometrically this is equivalent to maximizing the separation margin or distance between the two parallel planes $\mathbf{w} \cdot x = b + 1$ and $\mathbf{w} \cdot x = b - 1$ (see Figure 1.)

The "margin of separation" in Euclidean distance is $2/\|\mathbf{w}\|_2$ where $\|\mathbf{w}\|_2 = \sum_{i=1}^n \mathbf{w}_i^2$ is the 2-norm. To maximize the margin, we minimize $\|\mathbf{w}\|_2 / 2$ subject to the constraints (3). According to structural risk minimization, for a fixed empirical misclassification rate, larger margins should lead to better generalization and prevent overfitting in high-dimensional attribute spaces. The classifier is called a support vector machine because the solution depends only on the points (called support vectors) located on the two supporting planes $\mathbf{w} \cdot x = b - 1$ and $\mathbf{w} \cdot x = b + 1$.

In general the classes will not be separable, so the generalized optimal plane (GOP) problem (4) [9, 20] is used. A slack term η_i is added for each point such that if the point is misclassified, $\eta_i \geq 1$. The final GOP formulation is:

$$\begin{array}{ll} \min_{\mathbf{w},b,\eta} & C\sum_{i=1}^\ell \eta_i + \frac{1}{2}\|\mathbf{w}\|^2 \\ s.t. & y_i[\mathbf{w} \cdot x_i - b] + \eta_i \geq 1 \\ & \eta_i \geq 0,\ i = 1, \ldots, \ell \end{array} \tag{4}$$

where $C > 0$ is a fixed penalty parameter. The capacity control provided by the margin maximization is imperative to achieve good generalization [21, 19].

The Robust Linear Programming (RLP) approach to SVM is identical to GOP except the margin term is changed from the 2-norm $\|\mathbf{w}\|_2$ to the 1-norm, $\|\mathbf{w}\|_1 =$

$\sum_{j=1}^{n} |w_j|$. The problem becomes the following robust linear program (RLP) [2, 7, 1]:

$$\min_{\mathbf{w},b,s,\eta} \quad C\sum_{i=1}^{\ell} \eta_i + \sum_{j=1}^{n} s_j \qquad (5)$$
$$\text{s.t.} \quad y_i[\mathbf{w} \cdot x_i - b] + \eta_i \geq 1$$
$$\eta_i \geq 0, \quad i = 1, \ldots, \ell$$
$$-s_j <= w_j <= s_j, \quad j = 1, \ldots, n.$$

The RLP formulation is a useful variation of SVM with some nice characteristics. The 1-norm weight reduction still provides capacity control. The results in [13] can be used to show that minimizing $\|\mathbf{w}\|_1$ corresponds to maximizing the separation margin using the infinity norm. Statistical learning theory could potentially be extended to incorporate alternative norms. One major benefit of RLP over GOP is dimensionality reduction. Both RLP and GOP minimize the magnitude of the weights $\mathbf{w}$. But RLP forces more of the weights to be 0 due to the properties of the 1-norm. Another benefit of RLP over GOP is that it can be solved using linear programming instead of quadratic programming. Both approaches can be extended to handle nonlinear discrimination using kernel functions [8, 12]. Empirical comparisons of the approaches have not found any significant difference in generalization between the formulations [5, 7, 3, 12].

3 Semi-supervised support vector machines

To formulate the S^3VM, we start with either SVM formulation, (4) or (5), and then add two constraints for each point in the working set. One constraint calculates the misclassification error as if the point were in class 1 and the other constraint calculates the misclassification error as if the point were in class -1. The objective function calculates the minimum of the two possible misclassification errors. The final class of the points corresponds to the one that results in the smallest error. Specifically we define the semi-supervised support vector machine problem (S^3VM) as:

$$\min_{\mathbf{w},b,\eta,\xi,z} \quad C\left[\sum_{i=1}^{\ell} \eta_i + \sum_{j=\ell+1}^{\ell+k} \min(\xi_j, z_j)\right] + \|\mathbf{w}\| \qquad (6)$$
$$\text{subject to} \quad y_i(\mathbf{w} \cdot x_i + b) + \eta_i \geq 1 \quad \eta_i \geq 0 \quad i = 1, \ldots, \ell$$
$$\mathbf{w} \cdot x_j - b + \xi_j \geq 1 \quad \xi_j \geq 0 \quad j = \ell+1, \ldots, \ell+k$$
$$-(\mathbf{w} \cdot x_j - b) + z_j \geq 1 \quad z_j \geq 0$$

where $C > 0$ is a fixed misclassification penalty.

Integer programming can be used to solve this problem. The basic idea is to add a 0 or 1 decision variable, d_j, for each point $\mathbf{x}_j$ in the working set. This variable indicates the class of the point. If $d_j = 1$ then the point is in class 1 and if $d_j = 0$ then the point is in class -1. This results in the following mixed integer program:

$$\min_{\mathbf{w},b,\eta,\xi,z,d} \quad C\left[\sum_{i=1}^{\ell} \eta_i + \sum_{j=\ell+1}^{\ell+k} (\xi_j + z_j)\right] + \|\mathbf{w}\| \qquad (7)$$
$$\text{subject to} \quad y_i(\mathbf{w} \cdot x_i - b) + \eta_i \geq 1 \quad \eta_i \geq 0 \quad i = 1, \ldots, \ell$$
$$\mathbf{w} \cdot x_j - b + \xi_j + M(1 - d_j) \geq 1 \quad \xi_j \geq 0 \quad j = \ell+1, \ldots, \ell+k$$
$$-(\mathbf{w} \cdot x_j - b) + z_j + Md_j \geq 1 \quad z_j \geq 0 \quad d_j = \{0, 1\}$$

The constant $M > 0$ is chosen sufficiently large such that if $d_j = 0$ then $\xi_j = 0$ is feasible for any optimal $\mathbf{w}$ and b. Likewise if $d_j = 1$ then $z_j = 0$. A globally optimal

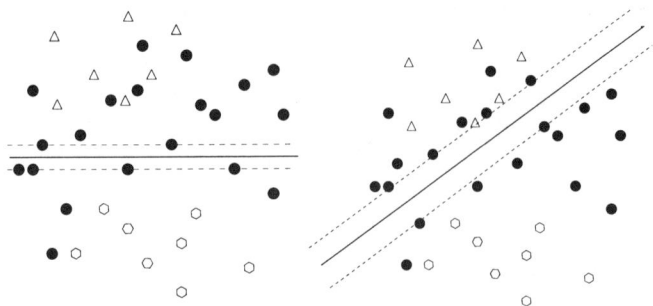

Figure 2: Left = solution found by RLP; Right = solution found by S^{3}VM

solution to this problem can be found using CPLEX or other commercial mixed integer programming codes [10] provided computer resources are sufficient for the problem size. Using the mathematical programming modeling language AMPL [11], we were able to express the problem in thirty lines of code plus a data file and solve it using CPLEX.

4 S^{3}VM and Overall Risk Minimization

An integer S^{3}VM can be used to solve the Overall Risk Minimization problem. Consider the simple problem given in Figure 20 of [19]. Using RLP alone on the training data results in the separation shown in Figure 1. Figure 2 illustrates what happens when working set data is added. The training set points are shown as transparent triangles and hexagons. The working set points are shown as filled circles. The left picture in Figure 2 shows the solution found by RLP. Note that when the working set points are added, the resulting separation has very a small margin. The right picture shows the S^{3}VM solution constructed using the unlabeled working set. Note that a much larger and clearer separation margin is found. These computational solutions are identical to those presented in [19].

We also tested S^{3}VM on ten real-world data sets (eight from [14] and the bright and dim galaxy sets from [15]). There have been many algorithms applied successfully to these problems without incorporate working set information. Thus it was not clear *a priori* that S^{3}VM would improve generalization on these data sets. For the data sets where no improvement is possible, we would like transduction using ORM to not degrade the performance of the induction via SRM approach. For each data set, we performed 10-fold cross-validation. For the three starred data sets, our integer programming solver failed due to excessive branching required within the CPLEX algorithm. On those data sets we randomly extracted 50 point working sets for each trial. The same C parameter was used for each data set in both the RLP and S^{3}VM problems[1]. In all ten problems, S^{3}VM never performed significantly worse than RLP. In three of the problems, S^{3}VM performed significantly better. So ORM did not hurt generalization and in some cases it helped significantly. We would expect this based on ORM theory. The generalization bounds for ORM depend on the difference between the training and working sets. If there is little difference, we would not expect any improvement using ORM.

---

[1]The formula for C was $C = \frac{(1-\lambda)}{\lambda(\ell+k)}$ with $\lambda = .001$, ℓ is the size of training set, and k is the size of the working set. This formula was chosen because it worked well empirically for both methods.

Data Set	Dim	Points	CV-size	RLP	S^{3}VM	p-value
Bright	14	2462	50*	0.02	0.018	0.343
Cancer	9	699	70	0.036	0.034	0.591
Cancer(Prognostic)	30	569	57	0.035	0.033	0.678
Dim	14	4192	50*	0.064	0.054	0.096
Heart	13	297	30	0.173	0.160	0.104
Housing	13	506	51	0.155	0.151	0.590
Ionosphere	34	351	35	0.109	0.106	0.59
Musk	166	476	48	0.173	0.173	0.999
Pima	8	769	50*	0.220	0.222	0.678
Sonar	60	208	21	0.281	0.219	0.045

5 Conclusion

We introduced a semi-supervised SVM model. S^{3}VM constructs a support vector machine using all the available data from both the training and working sets. We show how the S^{3}VM model for 1-norm linear support vector machines can be converted to a mixed-integer program. One great advantage of solving S^{3}VM using integer programming is that the globally optimal solution can be found using packages such as CPLEX. Using the integer S^{3}VM we performed an empirical investigation of transduction using overall risk minimization, a problem posed by Vapnik. Our results support the statistical learning theory results that incorporating working data improves generalization when insufficient training information is available. In every case, S^{3}VM either improved or showed no significant difference in generalization compared to the usual structural risk minimization approach. Our empirical results combined with the theoretical results in [19], indicate that transduction via ORM constitutes a very promising research direction.

Many research questions remain. Since transduction via overall risk minimization is not always be better than the basic induction via structural risk minimization, can we identify *a priori* problems likely to benefit from transduction? The best methods of constructing S^{3}VM for the 2-norm case and for nonlinear functions are still open questions. Kernel based methods can be incorporated into S^{3}VM. The practical scalability of the approach needs to be explored. We were able to solve moderately-sized problems with on the order of 50 working set points using a general purpose integer programming code. The recent success of special purpose algorithms for support vector machines [16, 17, 6] indicate that such approaches may produce improvement for S^{3}VM as well.

References

[1] K. P. Bennett and E. J. Bredensteiner. Geometry in learning. In C. Gorini, E. Hart, W. Meyer, and T. Phillips, editors, *Geometry at Work*, Washington, D.C., 1997. Mathematical Association of America. To appear.

[2] K. P. Bennett and O. L. Mangasarian. Robust linear programming discrimination of two linearly inseparable sets. *Optimization Methods and Software*, 1:23–34, 1992.

[3] K. P. Bennett, D. H. Wu, and L. Auslender. On support vector decision trees for database marketing. R.P.I. Math Report No. 98-100, Rensselaer Polytechnic

Institute, Troy, NY, 1998.

[4] A.M. Bensaid, L.O. Hall, J.C. Bezdek, and L.P. Clarke. Partially supervised clustering for image segmentation. *Pattern Recognition*, 29(5):859–871, 199.

[5] P. S. Bradley and O. L. Mangasarian. Feature selection via concave minimization and support vector machines. Technical Report Mathematical Programming Technical Report 98-03, University of Wisconsin-Madison, 1998. To appear in ICML-98.

[6] P. S. Bradley and O. L. Mangasarian. Massive data discrimination via linear support vector machines. Technical Report Mathematical Programming Technical Report 98-05, University of Wisconsin-Madison, 1998. Submitted for publication.

[7] E. J. Bredensteiner and K. P. Bennett. Feature minimization within decision trees. *Computational Optimization and Applications*, 10:110–126, 1997.

[8] C. J. C Burges. A tutorial on support vector machines for pattern recognition. *Data Mining and Knowledge Discovery*, 1998. to appear.

[9] C. Cortes and V. N. Vapnik. Support vector networks. *Machine Learning*, 20:273–297, 1995.

[10] CPLEX Optimization Incorporated, Incline Village, Nevada. *Using the CPLEX Callable Library*, 1994.

[11] R. Fourer, D. Gay, and B. Kernighan. *AMPL A Modeling Language for Mathematical Programming*. Boyd and Frazer, Danvers, Massachusetts, 1993.

[12] T. T. Fries and R. Harrison Fries. Linear programming support vector machines for pattern classification and regression estimation: and the sr algorithm. Research report 706, University of Sheffield, 1998.

[13] O. L. Mangasarian. Parsimonious least norm approximation. Technical Report Mathematical Programming Technical Report 97-03, University of Wisconsin-Madison, 1997. To appear in *Computational Optimization and Applications*.

[14] P.M. Murphy and D.W. Aha. UCI repository of machine learning databases. Department of Information and Computer Science, University of California, Irvine, California, 1992.

[15] S. Odewahn, E. Stockwell, R. Pennington, R Humphreys, and W Zumach. Automated star/galaxy discrimination with neural networks. *Astronomical Journal*, 103(1):318–331, 1992.

[16] E. Osuna, R. Freund, and F. Girosi. Support vector machines: Training and applications. AI Memo 1602, Maassachusets Institute of Technology, 1997.

[17] J. Platt. Sequentional minimal optimization: A fast algorithm for training support vector machines. Technical Report Technical Report 98-14, Microsoft Research, 1998.

[18] M. Vaidyanathan, R.P. Velthuizen, P. Venugopal, L.P. Clarke, and L.O. Hall. Tumor volume measurements using supervised and semi-supervised mri segmentation. In *Artificial Neural Networks in Engineering Conference, ANNIE(1994)*, 1994.

[19] V. N. Vapnik. *Estimation of dependencies based on empirical Data*. Springer, New York, 1982. English translation, Russian version 1979.

[20] V. N. Vapnik. *The Nature of Statistical Learning Theory*. Springer Verlag, New York, 1995.

[21] V. N. Vapnik and A. Ja. Chervonenkis. *Theory of Pattern Recognition*. Nauka, Moscow, 1974. In Russian.

Lazy Learning Meets
the Recursive Least Squares Algorithm

Mauro Birattari, Gianluca Bontempi, and Hugues Bersini
Iridia - Université Libre de Bruxelles
Bruxelles, Belgium
{mbiro, gbonte, bersini}@ulb.ac.be

Abstract

Lazy learning is a memory-based technique that, once a query is received, extracts a prediction interpolating locally the neighboring examples of the query which are considered relevant according to a distance measure. In this paper we propose a data-driven method to select on a query-by-query basis the optimal number of neighbors to be considered for each prediction. As an efficient way to identify and validate local models, the recursive least squares algorithm is introduced in the context of local approximation and lazy learning. Furthermore, beside the *winner-takes-all* strategy for model selection, a local combination of the most promising models is explored. The method proposed is tested on six different datasets and compared with a state-of-the-art approach.

1 Introduction

Lazy learning (Aha, 1997) postpones all the computation until an explicit request for a prediction is received. The request is fulfilled interpolating locally the examples considered relevant according to a distance measure. Each prediction requires therefore a local modeling procedure that can be seen as composed of a *structural* and of a *parametric* identification. The parametric identification consists in the optimization of the parameters of the local approximator. On the other hand, structural identification involves, among other things, the selection of a family of local approximators, the selection of a metric to evaluate which examples are more relevant, and the selection of the *bandwidth* which indicates the size of the region in which the data are correctly modeled by members of the chosen family of approximators. For a comprehensive tutorial on local learning and for further references see Atkeson *et al.* (1997).

As far as the problem of bandwidth selection is concerned, different approaches exist. The choice of the bandwidth may be performed either based on some *a priori* assumption or on the data themselves. A further sub-classification of data-driven approaches is of interest here. On the one hand, a constant bandwidth may be used; in this case it is set by a global optimization that minimizes an error criterion over the available dataset. On the other hand, the bandwidth may be selected locally and tailored for each query point.

In the present work, we propose a method that belongs to the latter class of local data-driven approaches. Assuming a given fixed metric and local linear approximators, the method we introduce selects the bandwidth on a query-by-query basis by means of a local leave-one-out cross-validation. The problem of bandwidth selection is reduced to the selection of the number k of neighboring examples which are given a non-zero weight in the local modeling procedure. Each time a prediction is required for a specific query point, a set of local models is identified, each including a different number of neighbors. The generalization ability of each model is then assessed through a local cross-validation procedure. Finally, a prediction is obtained either combining or selecting the different models on the basis of some statistic of their cross-validation errors.

The main reason to favor a query-by-query bandwidth selection is that it allows better adaptation to the local characteristics of the problem at hand. Moreover, this approach is able to handle directly the case in which the database is updated on-line (Bontempi et al., 1997). On the other hand, a globally optimized bandwidth approach would, in principle, require the global optimization to be repeated each time the distribution of the examples changes.

The major contribution of the paper consists in the adoption of the *recursive least squares* algorithm in the context of lazy learning. This is an appealing and efficient solution to the intrinsically incremental problem of identifying and validating a sequence of local linear models centered in the query point, each including a growing number of neighbors. It is worth noticing here that a leave-one-out cross-validation of each model considered does not involve any significant computational overload, since it is obtained though the PRESS statistic (Myers, 1990) which simply uses partial results returned by the recursive least squares algorithm. Schaal and Atkeson (1998) used already the recursive least squares algorithm for the incremental update of a set of local models. In the present paper, we use for the first time this algorithm in a query-by-query perspective as an effective way to explore the neighborhood of each query point.

As a second contribution, we propose a comparison, on a local scale, between a *competitive* and a *cooperative* approach to model selection. On the problem of extracting a final prediction from a set of alternatives, we compared a *winner-takes-all* strategy with a strategy based on the *combination of estimators* (Wolpert, 1992).

In Section 5 an experimental analysis of the recursive algorithm for local identification and validation is presented. The algorithm proposed, used in conjunction with different strategies for model selection or combination, is compared experimentally with Cubist, the rule-based tool developed by Ross Quinlan for generating piecewise-linear models.

2 Local Weighted Regression

Given two variables $\mathbf{x} \in \Re^m$ and $y \in \Re$, let us consider the mapping $f: \Re^m \to \Re$, known only through a set of n examples $\{(\mathbf{x}_i, y_i)\}_{i=1}^{n}$ obtained as follows:

$$y_i = f(\mathbf{x}_i) + \varepsilon_i, \tag{1}$$

where $\forall i$, ε_i is a random variable such that $E[\varepsilon_i] = 0$ and $E[\varepsilon_i \varepsilon_j] = 0$, $\forall j \neq i$, and such that $E[\varepsilon_i^m] = \mu_m(\mathbf{x}_i)$, $\forall m \geq 2$, where $\mu_m(\cdot)$ is the unknown m^{th} moment of the distribution of ε_i and is defined as a function of $\mathbf{x}_i$. In particular for $m = 2$, the last of the above mentioned properties implies that no assumption of global homoscedasticity is made.

The problem of local regression can be stated as the problem of estimating the value that the regression function $f(\mathbf{x}) = E[y|\mathbf{x}]$ assumes for a specific query point $\mathbf{x}$, using information pertaining only to a neighborhood of $\mathbf{x}$.

Given a query point $\mathbf{x}_q$, and under the hypothesis of a local homoscedasticity of ε_i, the parameter β of a local linear approximation of $f(\cdot)$ in a neighborhood of $\mathbf{x}_q$ can be obtained solving the local polynomial regression:

$$\sum_{i=1}^{n} \left\{ (y_i - \mathbf{x}'_i \beta)^2 K\left(\frac{d(\mathbf{x}_i, \mathbf{x}_q)}{h}\right) \right\}, \qquad (2)$$

where, given a metric on the space $\Re^m$, $d(\mathbf{x}_i, \mathbf{x}_q)$ is the distance from the query point to the ith example, $K(\cdot)$ is a weight function, h is the bandwidth, and where a constant value 1 has been appended to each vector $\mathbf{x}_i$ in order to consider a constant term in the regression.

In matrix notation, the solution of the above stated weighted least squares problem is given by:

$$\hat{\beta} = (\mathbf{X}'\mathbf{W}'\mathbf{W}\mathbf{X})^{-1}\mathbf{X}'\mathbf{W}'\mathbf{W}\mathbf{y} = (\mathbf{Z}'\mathbf{Z})^{-1}\mathbf{Z}'\mathbf{v} = \mathbf{PZ}'\mathbf{v}, \qquad (3)$$

where $\mathbf{X}$ is a matrix whose i^{th} row is $\mathbf{x}'_i$, $\mathbf{y}$ is a vector whose i^{th} element is y_i, $\mathbf{W}$ is a diagonal matrix whose i^{th} diagonal element is $w_{ii} = \sqrt{K\left(d(\mathbf{x}_i, \mathbf{x}_q)/h\right)}$, $\mathbf{Z} = \mathbf{WX}$, $\mathbf{v} = \mathbf{Wy}$, and the matrix $\mathbf{X}'\mathbf{W}'\mathbf{WX} = \mathbf{Z}'\mathbf{Z}$ is assumed to be non-singular so that its inverse $\mathbf{P} = (\mathbf{Z}'\mathbf{Z})^{-1}$ is defined.

Once obtained the local linear polynomial approximation, a prediction of $y_q = f(\mathbf{x}_q)$, is finally given by:

$$\hat{y}_q = \mathbf{x}'_q \hat{\beta}. \qquad (4)$$

Moreover, exploiting the linearity of the local approximator, a leave-one-out cross-validation estimation of the error variance $E[(y_q - \hat{y}_q)^2]$ can be obtained without any significant overload. In fact, using the PRESS statistic (Myers, 1990), it is possible to calculate the error $e_j^{\text{cv}} = y_j - \mathbf{x}'_j \hat{\beta}_{-j}$, without explicitly identifying the parameters $\hat{\beta}_{-j}$ from the examples available with the jth removed. The formulation of the PRESS statistic for the case at hand is the following:

$$e_j^{\text{cv}} = y_j - \mathbf{x}'_j \hat{\beta}_{-j} = \frac{y_j - \mathbf{x}'_j \mathbf{PZ}'\mathbf{v}}{1 - \mathbf{z}'_j \mathbf{P}\mathbf{z}_j} = \frac{y_j - \mathbf{x}'_j \hat{\beta}}{1 - h_{jj}}, \qquad (5)$$

where $\mathbf{z}'_j$ is the jth row of $\mathbf{Z}$ and therefore $\mathbf{z}_j = w_{jj}\mathbf{x}_j$, and where h_{jj} is the jth diagonal element of the *Hat matrix* $\mathbf{H} = \mathbf{ZPZ}' = \mathbf{Z}(\mathbf{Z}'\mathbf{Z})^{-1}\mathbf{Z}'$.

3 Recursive Local Regression

In what follows, for the sake of simplicity, we will focus on linear approximator. An extension to generic polynomial approximators of any degree is straightforward. We will assume also that a metric on the space $\Re^m$ is given. All the attention will be thus centered on the problem of bandwidth selection.

If as a weight function $K(\cdot)$ the indicator function

$$K\left(\frac{d(\mathbf{x}_i, \mathbf{x}_q)}{h}\right) = \begin{cases} 1 & \text{if } d(\mathbf{x}_i, \mathbf{x}_q) \leq h, \\ 0 & \text{otherwise;} \end{cases} \qquad (6)$$

is adopted, the optimization of the parameter h can be conveniently reduced to the optimization of the number k of neighbors to which a unitary weight is assigned in the local regression evaluation. In other words, we reduce the problem of bandwidth selection to a search in the space of $h(k) = d(\mathbf{x}(k), \mathbf{x}_q)$, where $\mathbf{x}(k)$ is the kth nearest neighbor of the query point.

The main advantage deriving from the adoption of the weight function defined in Eq. 6, is that, simply by updating the parameter $\hat{\beta}(k)$ of the model identified using the k nearest neighbors, it is straightforward and inexpensive to obtain $\hat{\beta}(k+1)$. In fact, performing a step of the standard recursive least squares algorithm (Bierman, 1977), we have:

$$\begin{cases} \mathbf{P}(k+1) = \mathbf{P}(k) - \dfrac{\mathbf{P}(k)\mathbf{x}(k+1)\mathbf{x}'(k+1)\mathbf{P}(k)}{1 + \mathbf{x}'(k+1)\mathbf{P}(k)\mathbf{x}(k+1)} \\ \gamma(k+1) = \mathbf{P}(k+1)\mathbf{x}(k+1) \\ e(k+1) = y(k+1) - \mathbf{x}'(k+1)\hat{\beta}(k) \\ \hat{\beta}(k+1) = \hat{\beta}(k) + \gamma(k+1)e(k+1) \end{cases} \quad (7)$$

where $\mathbf{P}(k) = (\mathbf{Z}'\mathbf{Z})^{-1}$ when $h = h(k)$, and where $\mathbf{x}(k+1)$ is the $(k+1)^{\text{th}}$ nearest neighbor of the query point.

Moreover, once the matrix $\mathbf{P}(k+1)$ is available, the leave-one-out cross-validation errors can be directly calculated without the need of any further model identification:

$$e_j^{\text{cv}}(k+1) = \frac{y_j - \mathbf{x}_j'\hat{\beta}(k+1)}{1 - \mathbf{x}_j'\mathbf{P}(k+1)\mathbf{x}_j}, \quad \forall j : d(\mathbf{x}_j, \mathbf{x}_q) \leq h(k+1). \quad (8)$$

It will be useful in the following to define for each value of k the $[k \times 1]$ vector $\mathbf{e}^{\text{cv}}(k)$ that contains all the leave-one-out errors associated to the model $\hat{\beta}(k)$.

Once an initialization $\hat{\beta}(0) = \tilde{\beta}$ and $\mathbf{P}(0) = \tilde{\mathbf{P}}$ is given, Eq. 7 and Eq. 8 recursively evaluate for different values of k a local approximation of the regression function $f(\cdot)$, a prediction of the value of the regression function in the query point, and the vector of leave-one-out errors from which it is possible to extract an estimate of the variance of the prediction error. Notice that $\tilde{\beta}$ is an *a priori* estimate of the parameter and $\tilde{\mathbf{P}}$ is the covariance matrix that reflects the reliability of $\tilde{\beta}$ (Bierman, 1977). For non-reliable initialization, the following is usually adopted: $\tilde{\mathbf{P}} = \lambda \mathbf{I}$, with λ large and where $\mathbf{I}$ is the identity matrix.

4 Local Model Selection and Combination

The recursive algorithm described by Eq. 7 and Eq. 8 returns for a given query point $\mathbf{x}_q$, a set of predictions $\hat{y}_q(k) = \mathbf{x}_q'\hat{\beta}(k)$, together with a set of associated leave-one-out error vectors $\mathbf{e}^{\text{cv}}(k)$.

From the information available, a final prediction $\hat{y}_q$ of the value of the regression function can be obtained in different ways. Two main paradigms deserve to be considered: the first is based on the selection of the *best* approximator according to a given criterion, while the second returns a prediction as a combination of more local models.

If the selection paradigm, frequently called *winner-takes-all*, is adopted, the most natural way to extract a final prediction $\hat{y}_q$, consists in comparing the prediction obtained for each value of k on the basis of the classical *mean square error* criterion:

$$\hat{y}_q = \mathbf{x}_q'\hat{\beta}(\hat{k}), \quad \text{with } \hat{k} = \arg\min_k \text{MSE}(k) = \arg\min_k \frac{\sum_{i=1}^k \omega_i \left(e_i^{\text{cv}}(k)\right)^2}{\sum_{i=1}^k \omega_i}; \quad (9)$$

Table 1: A summary of the characteristics of the datasets considered.

Dataset	Housing	Cpu	Prices	Mpg	Servo	Ozone
Number of examples	506	209	159	392	167	330
Number of regressors	13	6	16	7	8	8

where ω_i are weights than can be conveniently used to discount each error according to the distance from the query point to the point to which the error corresponds (Atkeson *et al.*, 1997).

As an alternative to the *winner-takes-all* paradigm, we explored also the effectiveness of local combinations of estimates (Wolpert, 1992). Adopting also in this case the *mean square error* criterion, the final prediction of the value y_q is obtained as a weighted average of the best b models, where b is a parameter of the algorithm. Suppose the predictions $\hat{y}_q(k)$ and the error vectors $\mathbf{e}^{\text{cv}}(k)$ have been ordered creating a sequence of integers $\{k_i\}$ so that $\text{MSE}(k_i) \leq \text{MSE}(k_j), \forall i < j$. The prediction of $\hat{y}_q$ is given by

$$\hat{y}_q = \frac{\sum_{i=1}^{b} \zeta_i \hat{y}_q(k_i)}{\sum_{i=1}^{b} \zeta_i}, \tag{10}$$

where the weights are the inverse of the mean square errors: $\zeta_i = 1/\text{MSE}(k_i)$. This is an example of the *generalized ensemble method* (Perrone & Cooper, 1993).

5 Experiments and Results

The experimental evaluation of the incremental local identification and validation algorithm was performed on six datasets. The first five, described by Quinlan (1993), were obtained from the UCI Repository of machine learning databases (Merz & Murphy, 1998), while the last one was provided by Leo Breiman. A summary of the characteristics of each dataset is presented in Table 1.

The methods compared adopt the recursive identification and validation algorithm, combined with different strategies for model selection or combination. We considered also two approaches in which k is selected globally:

lb1: Local bandwidth selection for linear local models. The number of neighbors is selected on a query-by-query basis and the prediction returned is the one of the best model according to the mean square error criterion.

lb0: Local bandwidth selection for constant local models. The algorithm for constant models is derived directly from the recursive method described in Eq. 7 and Eq. 8. The best model is selected according to the mean square error criterion.

lbC: Local combination of estimators. This is an example of the method described in Eq. 10. On the datasets proposed, for each query the best 2 linear local models and the best 2 constant models are combined.

gb1: Global bandwidth selection for linear local models. The value of k is obtained minimizing the prediction error in 20-fold cross-validation on the dataset available. This value is then used for all the query points.

gb0: Global bandwidth selection for constant local models. As in **gb1**, the value of k is optimized globally and kept constant for all the queries.

Table 2: Mean absolute error on unseen cases.

Method	Housing	Cpu	Prices	Mpg	Servo	Ozone
lb1	2.21	28.38	1509	1.94	0.48	3.52
lb0	2.60	31.54	1627	1.97	0.32	3.33
lbC	2.12	26.79	1488	1.83	0.29	3.31
gb1	2.30	28.69	1492	1.92	0.52	3.46
gb0	2.59	32.19	1639	1.99	0.34	3.19
Cubist	2.17	28.37	1331	1.90	0.36	3.15

Table 3: Relative error (%) on unseen cases.

Method	Housing	Cpu	Prices	Mpg	Servo	Ozone
lb1	12.63	9.20	15.87	12.65	28.66	35.25
lb0	18.06	20.37	22.19	12.64	22.04	31.11
lbC	12.35	9.29	17.62	11.82	19.72	30.28
gb1	13.47	9.93	15.95	12.83	30.46	32.58
gb0	17.99	21.43	22.29	13.48	24.30	28.21
Cubist	16.02	12.71	11.67	12.57	18.53	26.59

As far as the metric is concerned, we adopted a global Euclidean metric based on the relative influence (*relevance*) of the regressors (Friedman, 1994). We are confident that the adoption of a local metric could improve the performance of our lazy learning method.

The results of the methods introduced are compared with those we obtained, in the same experimental settings, with Cubist, the rule-based tool developed by Quinlan for generating piecewise-linear models. Each approach was tested on each dataset using the same 10-fold cross-validation strategy. Each dataset was divided randomly into 10 groups of nearly equal size. In turn, each of these groups was used as a testing set while the remaining ones together were providing the examples. Thus all the methods performed a prediction on the same unseen cases, using for each of them the same set of examples. In Table 2 we present the results obtained by all the methods, and averaged on the 10 cross-validation groups. Since the methods were compared on the same examples in exactly the same conditions, the sensitive one-tailed paired test of significance can be used. In what follows, by "significantly better" we mean better at least at a 5% significance level.

The first consideration about the results concerns the local combination of estimators. According to Table 2, the method **lbC** performs in average always better than the *winner-takes-all* linear and constant. On two dataset **lbC** is significantly better than both **lb1** and **lb0**; and on three dataset it is significantly better than one of the two, and better in average than the other.

The second consideration is about the comparison between our query-by-query bandwidth selection and a global optimization of the number of neighbors: in average **lb1** and **lb0** performs better than their counterparts **gb1** and **gb0**. On two datasets **lb1** is significantly better than **gb1**, while is about the same on the other four. On one dataset **lb0** is significantly better than **gb0**.

As far as the comparison with Cubist is concerned, the recursive lazy identification and validation proposed obtains results comparable with those obtained by the state-of-the-art method implemented in Cubist. On the six datasets, **lbC** performs one time significantly better than Cubist, and one time significantly worse.

The second index of performance we investigated is the *relative error*, defined as the mean square error on unseen cases, normalized by the variance of the test set. The relative errors are presented in Table 3 and show a similar picture to Table 2, although the mean square errors considered here penalize larger absolute errors.

6 Conclusion and Future Work

The experimental results confirm that the recursive least squares algorithm can be effectively used in a local context. Despite the trivial metric adopted, the local combination of estimators, identified and validated recursively, showed to be able to compete with a state-of-the-art approach.

Future work will focus on the problem of local metric selection. Moreover, we will explore more sophisticated ways to combine local estimators and we will extend this work to polynomial approximators of higher degree.

Acknowledgments

The work of Mauro Birattari was supported by the FIRST program of the Région Wallonne, Belgium. The work of Gianluca Bontempi was supported by the European Union TMR Grant FMBICT960692. The authors thank Ross Quinlan and gratefully acknowledge using his software Cubist. For more details on Cubist see http://www.rulequest.com. We also thank Leo Breiman for the dataset *ozone* and the UCI Repository for the other datasets used in this paper.

References

Aha D. W. 1997. Editorial. *Artificial Intelligence Review*, **11**(1–5), 1–6. Special Issue on Lazy Learning.

Atkeson C. G., Moore A. W. & Schaal S. 1997. Locally weighted learning. *Artificial Intelligence Review*, **11**(1–5), 11–73.

Bierman G. J. 1977. *Factorization Methods for Discrete Sequential Estimation*. New York, NY: Academic Press.

Bontempi G., Birattari M. & Bersini H. 1997. Lazy learning for local modeling and control design. *International Journal of Control*. Accepted for publication.

Friedman J. H. 1994. *Flexible metric nearest neighbor classification*. Tech. rept. Department of Statistics, Stanford University.

Merz C. J. & Murphy P. M. 1998. *UCI Repository of machine learning databases*.

Myers R. H. 1990. *Classical and Modern Regression with Applications*. Boston, MA: PWS-KENT.

Perrone M. P. & Cooper L. N. 1993. When networks disagree: Ensemble methods for hybrid neural networks. *Pages 126–142 of:* Mammone R. J. (ed), *Artificial Neural Networks for Speech and Vision*. Chapman and Hall.

Quinlan J. R. 1993. Combining instance-based and model-based learning. *Pages 236–243 of: Machine Learning. Proceedings of the Tenth International Conference*. Morgan Kaufmann.

Schaal S. & Atkeson C. G. 1998. Constructive incremental learning from only local information. *Neural Computation*, **10**(8), 2047–2084.

Wolpert D. 1992. Stacked Generalization. *Neural Networks*, **5**, 241–259.

Bayesian PCA

Christopher M. Bishop

Microsoft Research
St. George House, 1 Guildhall Street
Cambridge CB2 3NH, U.K.
cmbishop@microsoft.com

Abstract

The technique of principal component analysis (PCA) has recently been expressed as the maximum likelihood solution for a generative latent variable model. In this paper we use this probabilistic reformulation as the basis for a Bayesian treatment of PCA. Our key result is that *effective* dimensionality of the latent space (equivalent to the number of retained principal components) can be determined automatically as part of the Bayesian inference procedure. An important application of this framework is to mixtures of probabilistic PCA models, in which each component can determine its own effective complexity.

1 Introduction

Principal component analysis (PCA) is a widely used technique for data analysis. Recently Tipping and Bishop (1997b) showed that a specific form of generative latent variable model has the property that its maximum likelihood solution extracts the principal sub-space of the observed data set. This probabilistic reformulation of PCA permits many extensions including a principled formulation of mixtures of principal component analyzers, as discussed by Tipping and Bishop (1997a).

A central issue in maximum likelihood (as well as conventional) PCA is the choice of the number of principal components to be retained. This is particularly problematic in a mixture modelling context since ideally we would like the components to have potentially different dimensionalities. However, an exhaustive search over the choice of dimensionality for each of the components in a mixture distribution can quickly become computationally intractable. In this paper we develop a Bayesian treatment of PCA, and we show how this leads to an *automatic* selection of the appropriate model dimensionality. Our approach avoids a discrete model search, involving instead the use of continuous hyper-parameters to determine an *effective* number of principal components.

2 Maximum Likelihood PCA

Consider a data set D of observed d-dimensional vectors $D = \{\mathbf{t}_n\}$ where $n \in \{1, \ldots, N\}$. Conventional principal component analysis is obtained by first computing the sample covariance matrix given by

$$\mathbf{S} = \frac{1}{N} \sum_{n=1}^{N} (\mathbf{t}_n - \bar{\mathbf{t}})(\mathbf{t}_n - \bar{\mathbf{t}})^{\mathrm{T}} \quad (1)$$

where $\bar{\mathbf{t}} = N^{-1} \sum_n \mathbf{t}_n$ is the sample mean. Next the eigenvectors $\mathbf{u}_i$ and eigenvalues λ_i of $\mathbf{S}$ are found, where $\mathbf{S}\mathbf{u}_i = \lambda_i \mathbf{u}_i$ and $i = 1, \ldots, d$. The eigenvectors corresponding to the q largest eigenvalues (where $q < d$) are retained, and a reduced-dimensionality representation of the data set is defined by $\mathbf{x}_n = \mathbf{U}^{\mathrm{T}}(\mathbf{t}_n - \bar{\mathbf{t}})$ where $\mathbf{U}_q = (\mathbf{u}_1, \ldots, \mathbf{u}_q)$. It is easily shown that PCA corresponds to the linear projection of a data set under which the retained variance is a maximum, or equivalently the linear projection for which the sum-of-squares reconstruction cost is minimized.

A significant limitation of conventional PCA is that it does not define a probability distribution. Recently, however, Tipping and Bishop (1997b) showed how PCA can be reformulated as the maximum likelihood solution of a specific latent variable model, as follows. We first introduce a q-dimensional latent variable $\mathbf{x}$ whose prior distribution is a zero mean Gaussian $p(\mathbf{x}) = \mathcal{N}(\mathbf{0}, \mathbf{I}_q)$ and $\mathbf{I}_q$ is the q-dimensional unit matrix. The observed variable $\mathbf{t}$ is then defined as a linear transformation of $\mathbf{x}$ with additive Gaussian noise $\mathbf{t} = \mathbf{W}\mathbf{x} + \boldsymbol{\mu} + \boldsymbol{\epsilon}$ where $\mathbf{W}$ is a $d \times q$ matrix, $\boldsymbol{\mu}$ is a d-dimensional vector and $\boldsymbol{\epsilon}$ is a zero-mean Gaussian-distributed vector with covariance $\sigma^2 \mathbf{I}_d$. Thus $p(\mathbf{t}|\mathbf{x}) = \mathcal{N}(\mathbf{W}\mathbf{x} + \boldsymbol{\mu}, \sigma^2 \mathbf{I}_d)$. The marginal distribution of the observed variable is then given by the convolution of two Gaussians and is itself Gaussian

$$p(\mathbf{t}) = \int p(\mathbf{t}|\mathbf{x}) p(\mathbf{x}) \, d\mathbf{x} = \mathcal{N}(\boldsymbol{\mu}, \mathbf{C}) \quad (2)$$

where the covariance matrix $\mathbf{C} = \mathbf{W}\mathbf{W}^{\mathrm{T}} + \sigma^2 \mathbf{I}_d$. The model (2) represents a constrained Gaussian distribution governed by the parameters $\boldsymbol{\mu}$, $\mathbf{W}$ and σ^2.

The log probability of the parameters under the observed data set D is then given by

$$L(\boldsymbol{\mu}, \mathbf{W}, \sigma^2) = -\frac{N}{2} \left\{ d \ln(2\pi) + \ln |\mathbf{C}| + \mathrm{Tr}\left[\mathbf{C}^{-1} \mathbf{S}\right] \right\} \quad (3)$$

where $\mathbf{S}$ is the sample covariance matrix given by (1). The maximum likelihood solution for $\boldsymbol{\mu}$ is easily seen to be $\boldsymbol{\mu}_{\mathrm{ML}} = \bar{\mathbf{t}}$. It was shown by Tipping and Bishop (1997b) that the stationary points of the log likelihood with respect to $\mathbf{W}$ satisfy

$$\mathbf{W}_{\mathrm{ML}} = \mathbf{U}_q (\boldsymbol{\Lambda}_q - \sigma^2 \mathbf{I}_q)^{1/2} \quad (4)$$

where the columns of $\mathbf{U}_q$ are eigenvectors of $\mathbf{S}$, with corresponding eigenvalues in the diagonal matrix $\boldsymbol{\Lambda}_q$. It was also shown that the *maximum* of the likelihood is achieved when the q largest eigenvalues are chosen, so that the columns of $\mathbf{U}_q$ correspond to the *principal* eigenvectors, with all other choices of eigenvalues corresponding to saddle points. The maximum likelihood solution for σ^2 is then given by

$$\sigma^2_{\mathrm{ML}} = \frac{1}{d-q} \sum_{i=q+1}^{d} \lambda_i \quad (5)$$

which has a natural interpretation as the average variance lost per discarded dimension. The density model (2) thus represents a probabilistic formulation of PCA. It is easily verified that conventional PCA is recovered in the limit $\sigma^2 \to 0$.

Probabilistic PCA has been successfully applied to problems in data compression, density estimation and data visualization, and has been extended to mixture and hierarchical mixture models. As with conventional PCA, however, the model itself provides no mechanism for determining the value of the latent-space dimensionality q. For $q = d - 1$ the model is equivalent to a full-covariance Gaussian distribution, while for $q < d - 1$ it represents a constrained Gaussian in which the variance in the remaining $d - q$ directions is modelled by the single parameter σ^2. Thus the choice of q corresponds to a problem in model complexity optimization. If data is plentiful, then cross-validation to compare all possible values of q offers a possible approach. However, this can quickly become intractable for mixtures of probabilistic PCA models if we wish to allow each component to have its own q value.

3 Bayesian PCA

The issue of model complexity can be handled naturally within a Bayesian paradigm. Armed with the probabilistic reformulation of PCA defined in Section 2, a Bayesian treatment of PCA is obtained by first introducing a prior distribution $p(\boldsymbol{\mu}, \mathbf{W}, \sigma^2)$ over the parameters of the model. The corresponding posterior distribution $p(\boldsymbol{\mu}, \mathbf{W}, \sigma^2|D)$ is then obtained by multiplying the prior by the likelihood function, whose logarithm is given by (3), and normalizing. Finally, the predictive density is obtained by marginalizing over the parameters, so that

$$p(\mathbf{t}|D) = \iiint p(\mathbf{t}|\boldsymbol{\mu}, \mathbf{W}, \sigma^2) p(\boldsymbol{\mu}, \mathbf{W}, \sigma^2|D) \, d\boldsymbol{\mu} \, d\mathbf{W} \, d\sigma^2. \tag{6}$$

In order to implement this framework we must address two issues: (i) the choice of prior distribution, and (ii) the formulation of a tractable algorithm. Our focus in this paper is on the specific issue of controlling the effective dimensionality of the latent space (corresponding to the number of retained principal components). Furthermore, we seek to avoid discrete model selection and instead use continuous hyper-parameters to determine automatically an appropriate *effective* dimensionality for the latent space as part of the process of Bayesian inference. This is achieved by introducing a *hierarchical* prior $p(\mathbf{W}|\boldsymbol{\alpha})$ over the matrix $\mathbf{W}$, governed by a q-dimensional vector of hyper-parameters $\boldsymbol{\alpha} = \{\alpha_1, \ldots, \alpha_q\}$. The dimensionality of the latent space is set to its maximum possible value $q = d - 1$, and each hyper-parameter controls one of the columns of the matrix $\mathbf{W}$ through a conditional Gaussian distribution of the form

$$p(\mathbf{W}|\boldsymbol{\alpha}) = \prod_{i=1}^{d-1} \left(\frac{\alpha_i}{2\pi}\right)^{d/2} \exp\left\{-\frac{1}{2}\alpha_i \|\mathbf{w}_i\|^2\right\} \tag{7}$$

where $\{\mathbf{w}_i\}$ are the columns of $\mathbf{W}$. This form of prior is motivated by the framework of *automatic relevance determination* (ARD) introduced in the context of neural networks by Neal and MacKay (see MacKay, 1995). Each α_i controls the inverse variance of the corresponding $\mathbf{w}_i$, so that if a particular α_i has a posterior distribution concentrated at large values, the corresponding $\mathbf{w}_i$ will tend to be small, and that direction in latent space will be effectively 'switched off'. The probabilistic structure of the model is displayed graphically in Figure 1.

In order to make use of this model in practice we must be able to marginalize over the posterior distribution of $\mathbf{W}$. Since this is analytically intractable we have developed three alternative approaches based on (i) type-II maximum likelihood using a local Gaussian approximation to a mode of the posterior distribution (MacKay, 1995), (ii) Markov chain Monte Carlo using Gibbs sampling, and (iii) variational inference using a factorized approximation to the posterior distribution. Here we describe the first of these in more detail.

Bayesian PCA

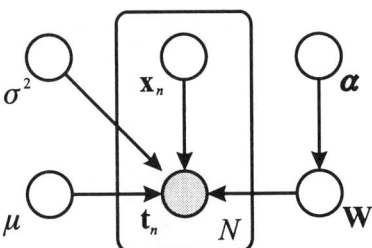

Figure 1: Representation of Bayesian PCA as a probabilistic graphical model showing the hierarchical prior over $\mathbf{W}$ governed by the vector of hyper-parameters $\boldsymbol{\alpha}$. The box denotes a 'plate' comprising a data set of N independent observations of the visible vector $\mathbf{t}_n$ (shown shaded) together with the corresponding hidden variables $\mathbf{x}_n$.

The location $\mathbf{W}_{\text{MP}}$ of the mode can be found by maximizing the log posterior distribution given, from Bayes' theorem, by

$$\ln p(\mathbf{W}|D) = L - \frac{1}{2}\sum_{i=1}^{d-1} \alpha_i \|\mathbf{w}_i\|^2 + \text{const.} \qquad (8)$$

where L is given by (3). For the purpose of controlling the effective dimensionality of the latent space, it is sufficient to treat $\boldsymbol{\mu}$, σ^2 and $\boldsymbol{\alpha}$ as parameters whose values are to be estimated, rather than as random variables. In this case there is no need to introduce priors over these variables, and we can determine $\boldsymbol{\mu}$ and σ^2 by maximum likelihood. To estimate $\boldsymbol{\alpha}$ we use type-II maximum likelihood, corresponding to maximizing the marginal likelihood $p(D|\boldsymbol{\alpha})$ in which we have integrated over $\mathbf{W}$ using the quadratic approximation. It is easily shown (Bishop, 1995) that this leads to a re-estimation formula for the hyper-parameters α_i of the form

$$\alpha_i := \frac{\gamma_i}{\|\mathbf{w}_i\|^2} \qquad (9)$$

where $\gamma_i = d - \alpha_i \text{Tr}_i(\mathbf{H}^{-1})$ is the effective number of parameters in $\mathbf{w}_i$, $\mathbf{H}$ is the Hessian matrix given by the second derivatives of $\ln p(\mathbf{W}|D)$ with respect to the elements of $\mathbf{W}$ (evaluated at $\mathbf{W}_{\text{MP}}$), and $\text{Tr}_i(\cdot)$ denotes the trace of the sub-matrix corresponding to the vector $\mathbf{w}_i$.

For the results presented in this paper, we make the further simplification of replacing γ_i in (9) by d, corresponding to the assumption that all model parameters are 'well-determined'. This significantly reduces the computational cost since it avoids evaluation and manipulation of the Hessian matrix. An additional consequence is that vectors $\mathbf{w}_i$ for which there is insufficient support from the data will be driven to zero, with the corresponding $\alpha_i \to \infty$, so that un-used dimensions are switched off completely. We define the *effective* dimensionality of the model to be the number of vectors $\mathbf{w}_i$ whose values remain non-zero.

The solution for $\mathbf{W}_{\text{MP}}$ can be found efficiently using the EM algorithm, in which the E-step involves evaluation of the expected sufficient statistics of the latent-space posterior distribution, given by

$$\begin{aligned}
\langle \mathbf{x}_n \rangle &= \mathbf{M}^{-1}\mathbf{W}^{\text{T}}(\mathbf{t}_n - \boldsymbol{\mu}) & (10)\\
\langle \mathbf{x}_n \mathbf{x}_n^{\text{T}} \rangle &= \sigma^2 \mathbf{M} + \langle \mathbf{x}_n \rangle \langle \mathbf{x}_n \rangle^{\text{T}} & (11)
\end{aligned}$$

where $\mathbf{M} = (\mathbf{W}^T\mathbf{W} + \sigma^2\mathbf{I}_q)$. The M-step involves updating the model parameters using

$$\widetilde{\mathbf{W}} = \left[\sum_n (\mathbf{t}_n - \boldsymbol{\mu})\langle\mathbf{x}_n^T\rangle\right]\left[\sum_n \langle\mathbf{x}_n\mathbf{x}_n^T\rangle + \sigma^2\mathbf{A}\right]^{-1} \quad (12)$$

$$\widetilde{\sigma}^2 = \frac{1}{Nd}\sum_{n=1}^{N}\left\{\|\mathbf{t}_n - \boldsymbol{\mu}\|^2 - 2\langle\mathbf{x}_n^T\rangle\widetilde{\mathbf{W}}^T(\mathbf{t}_n - \boldsymbol{\mu}) + \text{Tr}\left[\langle\mathbf{x}_n\mathbf{x}_n^T\rangle\widetilde{\mathbf{W}}^T\widetilde{\mathbf{W}}\right]\right\} \quad (13)$$

where $\mathbf{A} = \text{diag}(\alpha_i)$. Optimization of $\mathbf{W}$ and σ^2 is alternated with re-estimation of $\boldsymbol{\alpha}$, using (9) with $\gamma_i = d$, until all of the parameters satisfy a suitable convergence criterion.

As an illustration of the operation of this algorithm, we consider a data set consisting of 300 points in 10 dimensions, in which the data is drawn from a Gaussian distribution having standard deviation 1.0 in 3 directions and standard deviation 0.5 in the remaining 7 directions. The result of fitting both maximum likelihood and Bayesian PCA models is shown in Figure 2. In this case the Bayesian model has an effective dimensionality of $q_{\text{eff}} = 3$.

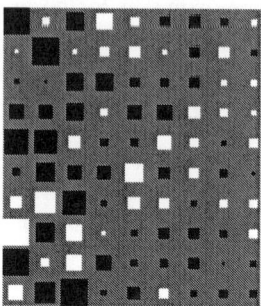

Figure 2: Hinton diagrams of the matrix $\mathbf{W}$ for a data set in 10 dimensions having $m = 3$ directions with larger variance than the remaining 7 directions. The left plot shows $\mathbf{W}$ from maximum likelihood PCA while the right plot shows $\mathbf{W}_{\text{MP}}$ from the Bayesian approach, showing how the model is able to discover the appropriate dimensionality by suppressing the 6 surplus degrees of freedom.

The effective dimensionality found by Bayesian PCA will be dependent on the number N of points in the data set. For $N \to \infty$ we expect $q_{\text{eff}} \to d-1$, and in this limit the maximum likelihood framework and the Bayesian approach will give identical results. For finite data sets the effective dimensionality may be reduced, with degrees of freedom for which there is insufficient evidence in the data set being suppressed. The variance of the data in the remaining $d - q_{\text{eff}}$ directions is then accounted for by the single degree of freedom defined by σ^2. This is illustrated by considering data in 10 dimensions generated from a Gaussian distribution with standard deviations given by $\{1.0, 0.9, 0.8, 0.7, 0.6, 0.5, 0.4, 0.3, 0.2, 0.1\}$. In Figure 3 we plot q_{eff} (averaged over 50 independent experiments) versus the number N of points in the data set.

These results indicate that Bayesian PCA is able to determine automatically a suitable effective dimensionality q_{eff} for the principal component subspace, and therefore offers a practical alternative to exhaustive comparison of dimensionalities using techniques such as cross-validation. As an illustration of the generalization capability of the resulting model we consider a data set of 20 points in 10 dimensions generated from a Gaussian distribution having standard deviations in 5 directions given by $(1.0, 0.8, 0.6, 0.4, 0.2)$ and standard deviation 0.04 in the remaining 5 directions. We fit maximum likelihood PCA models to this data having q values in the range 1–9 and compare their log likelihoods on both the training data and on an independent test set, with the results (averaged over 10 independent experiments) shown in Figure 4. Also shown are the corresponding results obtained from Bayesian PCA.

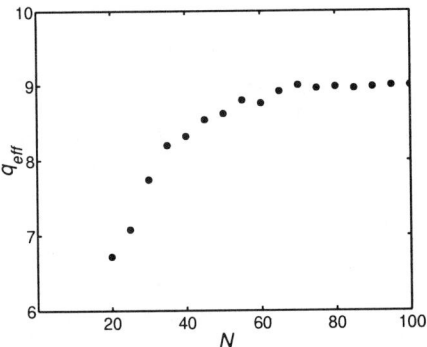

Figure 3: Plot of the average effective dimensionality of the Bayesian PCA model versus the number N of data points for data in a 10-dimensional space.

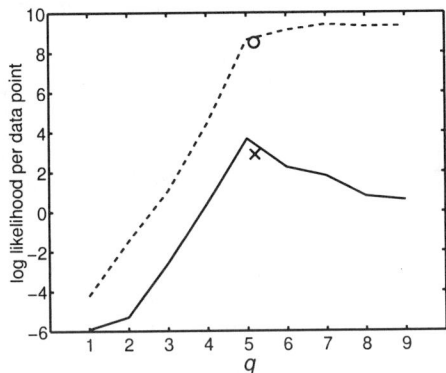

Figure 4: Plot of the log likelihood for the training set (dashed curve) and the test set (solid curve) for maximum likelihood PCA models having q values in the range 1–9, showing that the best generalization is achieved for $q = 5$ which corresponds to the number of directions of significant variance in the data set. Also shown are the training (circle) and test (cross) results from a Bayesian PCA model, plotted at the average effective q value given by $q_{\text{eff}} = 5.2$. We see that the Bayesian PCA model automatically discovers the appropriate dimensionality for the principal component subspace, and furthermore that it has a generalization performance which is close to that of the optimal fixed q model.

4 Mixtures of Bayesian PCA Models

Given a probabilistic formulation of PCA it is straightforward to construct a mixture distribution comprising a linear superposition of principal component analyzers. In the case of maximum likelihood PCA we have to choose both the number M of components and the latent space dimensionality q for each component. For moderate numbers of components and data spaces of several dimensions it quickly becomes intractable to explore the exponentially large number of combinations of q values for a given value of M. Here Bayesian PCA offers a significant advantage in allowing the effective dimensionalities of the models to be determined automatically.

As an illustration we consider a density estimation problem involving hand-written digits from the CEDAR database. The data set comprises 8×8 scaled and smoothed gray-scale images of the digits '2', '3' and '4', partitioned randomly into 1500 training, 900 validation and 900 test points. For mixtures of maximum likelihood PCA the model parameters can be determined using the EM algorithm in which the M-step uses (4) and (5), with eigenvector and eigenvalues obtained from the weighted covariance matrices in which the weighting coefficients are the posterior probabilities for the components determined in the E-step. Since, for maximum likelihood PCA, it is computationally impractical to explore independent q values for each component we consider mixtures in which every component has the same dimensionality. We therefore train mixtures having $M \in \{2, 4, 6, 8, 10, 12, 14, 16, 18\}$ for all values $q \in \{2, 4, 8, 12, 16, 20, 25, 30, 40, 50\}$. In order to avoid singularities associated with the more complex models we omit any component from the mixture for which the value of σ^2 goes to zero during the optimization. The highest log likelihood on the validation set (-295) is obtained for $M = 6$ and $q = 50$.

For mixtures of Bayesian PCA models we need only explore alternative values for M, which are taken from the same set as for the mixtures of maximum likelihood PCA. Again, the best performance on the validation set (-293) is obtained for $M = 6$. The values of the log likelihood for the test set were -295 (maximum likelihood PCA) and -293 (Bayesian PCA). The mean vectors μ_i for each of the 6 components of the Bayesian PCA mixture model are shown in Figure 5.

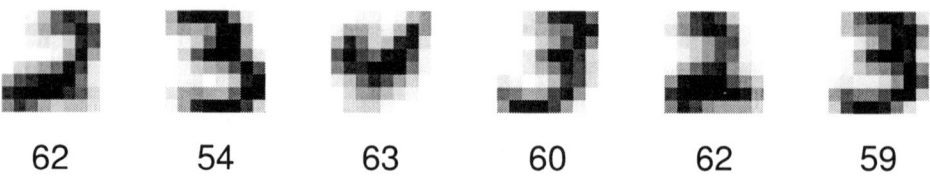

Figure 5: The mean vectors for each of the 6 components in the Bayesian PCA mixture model, displayed as an 8×8 image, together with the corresponding values of the effective dimensionality.

The Bayesian treatment of PCA discussed in this paper can be particularly advantageous for small data sets in high dimensions as it can avoid the singularities associated with maximum likelihood (or conventional) PCA by suppressing unwanted degrees of freedom in the model. This is especially helpful in a mixture modelling context, since the effective number of data points associated with specific 'clusters' can be small even when the total number of data points appears to be large.

References

Bishop, C. M. (1995). *Neural Networks for Pattern Recognition*. Oxford University Press.

MacKay, D. J. C. (1995). Probable networks and plausible predictions – a review of practical Bayesian methods for supervised neural networks. *Network: Computation in Neural Systems* **6** (3), 469–505.

Tipping, M. E. and C. M. Bishop (1997a). Mixtures of principal component analysers. In *Proceedings IEE Fifth International Conference on Artificial Neural Networks, Cambridge, U.K., July.*, pp. 13–18.

Tipping, M. E. and C. M. Bishop (1997b). Probabilistic principal component analysis. Accepted for publication in the Journal of the Royal Statistical Society, B.

Learning multi-class dynamics

A. Blake, B. North and M. Isard
Department of Engineering Science, University of Oxford, Oxford OX1 3PJ, UK.
Web: http://www.robots.ox.ac.uk/~vdg/

Abstract

Standard techniques (eg. Yule-Walker) are available for learning Auto-Regressive process models of simple, directly observable, dynamical processes. When sensor noise means that dynamics are observed only approximately, learning can still been achieved via Expectation-Maximisation (EM) together with Kalman Filtering. However, this does not handle more complex dynamics, involving multiple classes of motion. For that problem, we show here how EM can be combined with the CONDENSATION algorithm, which is based on propagation of random sample-sets. Experiments have been performed with visually observed juggling, and plausible dynamical models are found to emerge from the learning process.

1 Introduction

The paper presents a probabilistic framework for estimation (perception) and classification of complex time-varying signals, represented as temporal streams of states. Automated learning of dynamics is of crucial importance as practical models may be too complex for parameters to be set by hand. The framework is particularly general, in several respects, as follows.

1. Mixed states: each state comprises a continuous and a discrete component. The continuous component can be thought of as representing the instantaneous position of some object in a continuum. The discrete state represents the current class of the motion, and acts as a label, selecting the current member from a set of dynamical models.

2. Multi-dimensionality: the continuous component of a state is, in general, allowed to be multi-dimensional. This could represent motion in a higher dimensional continuum, for example, two-dimensional translation as in figure 1. Other examples include multi-spectral acoustic or image signals, or multi-channel sensors such as an electro-encephalograph.

Figure 1: **Learning the dynamics of juggling.** *Three motion classes, emerging from dynamical learning, turn out to correspond accurately to ballistic motion (mid grey), catch/throw (light grey) and carry (dark grey).*

3. Arbitrary order: each dynamical system is modelled as an Auto-Regressive Process (ARP) and allowed to have arbitrary order (the number of time-steps of "memory" that it carries.)

4. Stochastic observations: the sequence of mixed states is "hidden" — not observable directly, but only via observations, which may be multi-dimensional, and are stochastically related to the continuous component of states. This aspect is essential to represent the inherent variability of response of any real signal sensing system.

Estimation for processes with properties 2,3,4 has been widely discussed both in the control-theory literature as "estimation" and "Kalman filtering" (Gelb, 1974) and in statistics as "forecasting" (Brockwell and Davis, 1996). Learning of models with properties 2,3 is well understood (Gelb, 1974) and once learned can be used to drive pattern classification procedures, as in Linear Predictive Coding (LPC) in speech analysis (Rabiner and Bing-Hwang, 1993), or in classification of EEG signals (Pardey et al., 1995). When property 4 is added, the learning problem becomes harder (Ljung, 1987) because the training sets are no longer observed directly.

Mixed states (property 1) allow for combining perception with classification. Allowing properties 2,4, but restricted to a 0th order ARP (in breach of property 3), gives

Hidden Markov Models (HMM) (Rabiner and Bing-Hwang, 1993), which have been used effectively for visual classification (Bregler, 1997). Learning HMMs is accomplished by the "Baum-Welch" algorithm, a form of Expectation-Maximisation (EM) (Dempster et al., 1977). Baum-Welch learning has been extended to "graphical-models" of quite general topology (Lauritzen, 1996). In this paper, graph topology is a simple chain-pair as in standard HMMs, and the complexity of the problem lies elsewhere — in the generality of the dynamical model.

Generally then, restoring non-zero order to the ARPs (property 3), there is no exact algorithm for estimation. However the estimation problem can be solved by random sampling algorithms, known variously as bootstrap filters (Gordon et al., 1993), particle filters (Kitagawa, 1996), and CONDENSATION (Blake and Isard, 1997). Here we show how such algorithms can be used, with EM, in dynamical learning theory and experiments (figure 1).

2 Multi-class dynamics

Continuous dynamical systems can be specified in terms of a continuous state vector $\mathbf{x}_t \in \mathcal{R}^{N_x}$. In machine vision, for example, $\mathbf{x}_t$ represents the parameters of a time-varying shape at time t. Multi-class dynamics are represented by appending to the continuous state vector $\mathbf{x}_t$, a discrete state component y_t to make a "mixed" state

$$\mathbf{X}_t = \begin{pmatrix} \mathbf{x}_t \\ y_t \end{pmatrix},$$

where $y_t \in \mathcal{Y} = \{1, \ldots, N_y\}$ is the discrete component of the state, drawn from a finite set of integer labels. Each discrete state represents a class of motion, for example "stroke", "rest" and "shade" for a hand engaged in drawing.

Corresponding to each state $y_t = y$ there is a dynamical model, taken to be a Markov model of order K^y that specifies $p_i(\mathbf{x}_t | \mathbf{x}_{t-1}, \ldots \mathbf{x}_{t-K^y})$. A linear-Gaussian Markov model of order K is an Auto-Regressive Process (ARP) defined by

$$\mathbf{x}_t = \sum_{k=1}^{K} A_k \mathbf{x}_{t-k} + \mathbf{d} + B\mathbf{w}_t$$

in which each $\mathbf{w}_t$ is a vector of N_x independent random $\mathcal{N}(0,1)$ variables and $\mathbf{w}_t, \mathbf{w}_{t'}$ are independent for $t \neq t'$. The dynamical parameters of the model are

- deterministic parameters $A_1, A_2, \ldots, A_K$
- stochastic parameters B, which are multipliers for the stochastic process $\mathbf{w}_t$, and determine the "coupling" of noise $\mathbf{w}_t$ into the vector valued process $\mathbf{x}_t$.

For convenience of notation, let

$$A = \begin{pmatrix} A_1 & A_2 & \cdots & A_K \end{pmatrix}.$$

Each state $y \in \mathcal{Y}$ has a set $\{A^y, B^y, d^y\}$ of dynamical parameters, and the goal is to learn these from example trajectories. Note that the stochastic parameter B^y is a first-class part of a dynamical model, representing the degree and the shape of uncertainty in motion, allowing the representation of an entire distribution of possible motions for each state y. In addition, and independently, state transitions are governed by the transition matrix for a 1st order Markov chain:

$$P(y_t = y' | y_{t-1} = y) = M_{y,y'}.$$

Observations $\mathbf{z}_t$ are assumed to be conditioned purely on the continuous part $\mathbf{x}$ of the mixed state, independent of y_t, and this maintains a healthy separation between the modelling of dynamics and of observations. Observations are also assumed to be independent, both mutually and with respect to the dynamical process. The observation process is defined by specifying, at each time t, the conditional density $p(\mathbf{z}_t|\mathbf{x}_t)$ which is taken to be Gaussian in experiments here.

3 Maximum Likelihood learning

When observations are exact, maximum likelihood estimates (MLE) for dynamical parameters can be obtained from a training sequence $\mathbf{X}_1^* \ldots \mathbf{X}_T^*$ of mixed states. The well known Yule-Walker formula approximates MLE (Gelb, 1974; Ljung, 1987), but generalisations are needed to allow for short training sets (small T), to include stochastic parameters B, to allow a non-zero offset $\mathbf{d}$ (this proves essential in experiments later) and to encompass multiple dynamical classes.

The resulting MLE learning rule is as follows

$$A^y \bar{R}^y = \bar{\mathbf{R}}_0^y, \quad \mathbf{d}^y = \frac{1}{T^y - K^y}(R_0^y - A^y \mathbf{R}^y), \quad C^y = \frac{1}{T^y - K^y}\left(\bar{R}_{0,0}^y - A^y (\bar{\mathbf{R}}_0^y)^\top\right),$$

where (omitting the ^{y} superscripts for clarity) $C = BB^\top$ and

$$\bar{R} = \begin{pmatrix} \bar{R}_{1,1} & \cdots & \bar{R}_{1,K} \\ \vdots & \ddots & \vdots \\ \bar{R}_{K,1} & \cdots & \bar{R}_{K,K} \end{pmatrix}, \quad \bar{\mathbf{R}}_0 = \begin{pmatrix} \bar{R}_{0,1} & \cdots & \bar{R}_{0,K} \end{pmatrix}, \quad \mathbf{R} = \begin{pmatrix} R_1 \\ \vdots \\ R_K \end{pmatrix},$$

and the first-order moments R_i and (offset-invariant) autocorrelations $\bar{R}_{i,j}$, for each class y, are given by

$$R_i^y = \sum_{y_t^* = y} \mathbf{x}_{t-i}^* \quad \text{and} \quad \bar{R}_{i,j}^y = R_{i,j}^y - \frac{1}{T_y - K} R_i^y R_j^{y\top},$$

where

$$R_{i,j}^y = \sum_{y_t = y} \mathbf{x}_{t-i}^* \mathbf{x}_{t-j}^{*\top}; \qquad T_y = \#\{t : y_t^* = y\} \equiv \sum_{t: y_t = y} 1.$$

The MLE for the transition matrix M is constructed from relative frequencies as:

$$M_{y,y'} = \frac{T_{y,y'}}{\sum_{y' \in \mathcal{Y}} T_{y,y'}} \quad \text{where} \quad T_{y,y'} = \#\{t : y_{t-1}^* = y, y_t^* = y'\}.$$

4 Learning with stochastic observations

To allow for stochastic observations, direct MLE is no longer possible, but an EM learning algorithm can be formulated. Its M-step is simply the MLE estimate of the previous section. It might be thought that the E-step should consist simply of computing expectations, for instance $\mathcal{E}[\mathbf{x}_t|\mathcal{Z}_1^T]$, (where $\mathcal{Z}_1^t = (\mathbf{z}_1, \ldots, \mathbf{z}_t)$ denotes a sequence of observations) and treating them as training values $\mathbf{x}_t^*$. This would be incorrect however because the log-likelihood function $\mathcal{L}$ for the problem is not linear in the $\mathbf{x}_t^*$ but quadratic. Instead, we need expectations

$$\mathcal{E}[R_i|\mathcal{Z}_1^T], \quad \mathcal{E}[R_{i,j}|\mathcal{Z}_1^T], \quad \mathcal{E}[T_i|\mathcal{Z}_1^T], \quad \mathcal{E}[T_{i,j}|\mathcal{Z}_1^T],$$

conditioned on the entire training set $\mathcal{Z}_1^T$ of observations, given that $\mathcal{L}$ is linear in the R_i, $R_{i,j}$ etc. (Shumway and Stoffer, 1982). These expected values of autocorrelations and frequencies are to be used in place of actual autocorrelations and frequencies in the learning formulae of section 3. The question is, how to compute them. In the special case $\mathcal{Y} = \{1\}$ of single-class dynamics, and assuming a Gaussian observation density, exact methods are available for computing expected moments, using Kalman and smoothing filters (Gelb, 1974), in an "augmented state" filter (North and Blake, 1998). For multi-class dynamics, exact computation is infeasible, but good approximations can be achieved based on propagation of sample sets, using CONDENSATION.

Forward sampling with backward chaining

For the purposes of learning, an extended and generalised form of the CONDENSATION algorithm is required. The generalisations allow for mixed states, arbitrary order for the ARP, and backward-chaining of samples. In backward chaining, sample-sets for successive times are built up and stored together with a complete state history back to time $t = 0$. The extended CONDENSATION algorithm is given in figure 2. Note that the algorithm needs to be initialised. This requires that the y_0 and $(\mathbf{X}_{-k|0}^{(n)}, k = 0, \ldots, K^{y_0} - 1)$ be drawn from a suitable (joint) prior for the multi-class process. One way to do this is to ensure that the training set starts in a known state and to fix the initial sample-values accordingly. Normally, the choice of prior is not too important as it is dominated by data.

At time $t = T$, when the entire training sequence has been processed, the final sample set is

$$\{(\mathbf{X}_{T|T}^{(n)}, \ldots, \mathbf{X}_{0|T}^{(n)}), \pi_T^{(n)}\}, n = 1, \ldots, N\}$$

represents fairly (in the limit, weakly, as $N \to \infty$) the posterior distribution for the entire state sequence $\mathbf{X}_0, \ldots, \mathbf{X}_T$, conditioned on the entire training set $\mathcal{Z}_1^T$ of observations. The expectations of the autocorrelation and frequency measures required for learning can be estimated from the sample set, for example:

$$\mathcal{E}[R_{i,j}^y] \approx \sum_{n=1}^{N} \pi_T^{(n)} \sum_{\{t:\, y_{t|T}^{(n)} = y\}} \mathbf{x}_{t-i|T}^{(n)} \left(\mathbf{x}_{t-j|T}^{(n)}\right)^\top.$$

An alternative algorithm is a sample-set version of forward-backward propagation (Kitagawa, 1996). Experiments have suggested that probability densities generated by this form of smoothing converge far more quickly with respect to sample set size N, but at the expense of computational complexity — $O(N^2)$ as opposed to $O(N \log N)$ for the algorithm above.

5 Practical applications

Experiments are reported briefly here on learning the dynamics of juggling using the EM-Condensation algorithm, as in figure 1. An offset $\mathbf{d}^y$ is learned for each class in $\mathcal{Y} = \{1, 2, 3\}$; other dynamical parameters are fixed such that that learning $\mathbf{d}^y$ amounts to learning mean accelerations $\mathbf{a}^y$ for each class. The transition matrix is also learned. From a more or less neutral starting point, learned structure emerges as in figure 3. Around 60 iterations of EM suffice, with $N = 2048$, to learn dynamics in this case. It is clear from the figure that the learned structure is an altogether plausible model for the juggling process.

Iterate for $t = 1, \ldots, T$.

Construct the sample-set $\{(\mathbf{X}_{1|t}^{(n)}, \ldots, \mathbf{X}_{t|t}^{(n)}), \pi_t^{(n)}\}, n = 1, \ldots, N$ for time t.

For each n:

1. **Choose** (with replacement) $m \in \{1, \ldots, N\}$ with prob. $\pi_{t-1}^{(m)}$.

2. **Predict** by sampling from

$$p\left(\mathbf{X}_t \mid \mathcal{X}_1^{t-1} = (\mathbf{X}_{1|t-1}^{(m)}, \ldots, \mathbf{X}_{t-1|t-1}^{(m)})\right)$$

to choose $\mathbf{X}_{t|t}^{(n)}$. For multi-class ARPs this is done in two steps.

Discrete: Choose $y_t^{(n)} = y' \in \mathcal{Y}$ with probability $M_{y,y'}$, where $y = y_{t-1}^{(m)}$.

Continuous: Compute

$$\mathbf{x}_{t|t}^{(n)} = \sum_{k=1}^{K} A_k^y \mathbf{x}_{t-k|t-1}^{(m)} + \mathbf{d} + B\mathbf{w}_t^{(n)},$$

where $y = y_t^{(n)}$ and $\mathbf{w}_t^{(n)}$ is a vector of standard normal r.v.

3. **Observation weights** $\pi_t^{(n)}$ are computed from the observation density, evaluated for the current observations $\mathbf{z}_t$:

$$\pi_t^{(n)} = p(\mathbf{z}_t | \mathbf{x}_t = \mathbf{x}_{t|t}^{(n)}),$$

then normalised multiplicatively so that $\sum_n \pi_t^{(n)} = 1$.

4. **Update sample history:**

$$\mathbf{X}_{t'|t}^{(n)} = \mathbf{X}_{t'|t-1}^{(m)}, \ t' = 1, \ldots, t - 1.$$

Figure 2: **The CONDENSATION algorithm for forward propagation with backward chaining.**

Acknowledgements

We are grateful for the support of the EPSRC (AB,BN) and Magdalen College Oxford (MI).

References

Blake, A. and Isard, M. (1997). The Condensation algorithm — conditional density propagation and applications to visual tracking. In *Advances in Neural Information Processing Systems 9*, pages 361–368. MIT Press.

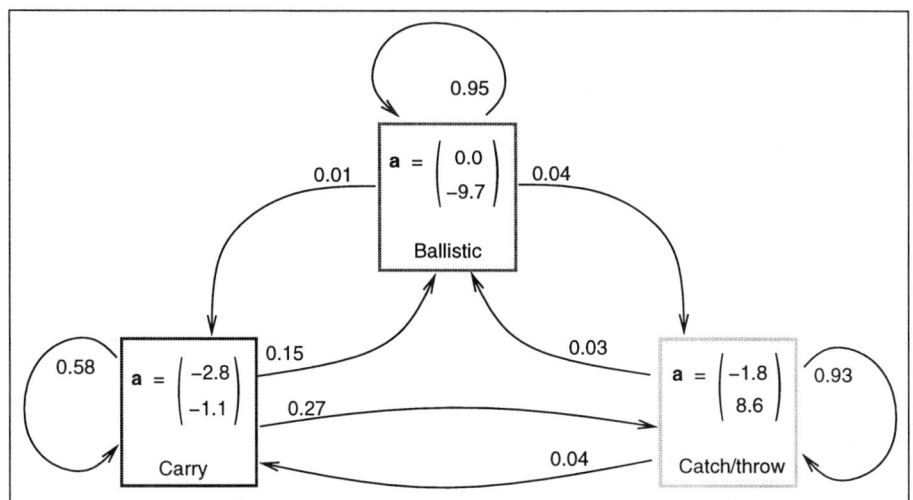

Figure 3: **Learned dynamical model for juggling.** *The three motion classes allowed in this experiment organise themselves into: ballistic motion (acceleration* **a** $\approx -g$); *catch/throw; carry. As expected, life-time in the ballistic state is longest, the transition probability of* 0.95 *corresponding to 20 time-steps or about 0.7 seconds. Transitions tend to be directed, as expected; for example ballistic motion is more likely to be followed by a catch/throw* ($p = 0.04$) *than by a carry* ($p = 0.01$). *(Acceleration* **a** *shown here in units of* m/s^2.)

Bregler, C. (1997). Learning and recognising human dynamics in video sequences. In *Proc. Conf. Computer Vision and Pattern Recognition*.

Brockwell, P. and Davis, R. (1996). *Introduction to time-series and forecasting.* Springer-Verlag.

Dempster, A., Laird, M., and Rubin, D. (1977). Maximum likelihood from incomplete data via the EM algorithm. *J. Roy. Stat. Soc. B.*, 39:1–38.

Gelb, A., editor (1974). *Applied Optimal Estimation.* MIT Press, Cambridge, MA.

Gordon, N., Salmond, D., and Smith, A. (1993). Novel approach to nonlinear/non-Gaussian Bayesian state estimation. *IEE Proc. F*, 140(2):107–113.

Kitagawa, G. (1996). Monte Carlo filter and smoother for non-Gaussian nonlinear state space models. *Journal of Computational and Graphical Statistics*, 5(1):1–25.

Lauritzen, S. (1996). *Graphical models.* Oxford.

Ljung, L. (1987). *System identification: theory for the user.* Prentice-Hall.

North, B. and Blake, A. (1998). Learning dynamical models using expectation-maximisation. In *Proc. 6th Int. Conf. on Computer Vision*, pages 384–389.

Pardey, J., Roberts, S., and Tarassenko, L. (1995). A review of parametric modelling techniques for EEG analysis. *Medical Engineering Physics*, 18(1):2–11.

Rabiner, L. and Bing-Hwang, J. (1993). *Fundamentals of speech recognition.* Prentice-Hall.

Shumway, R. and Stoffer, D. (1982). An approach to time series smoothing and forecasting using the EM algorithm. *J. Time Series Analysis*, 3:253–226.

Approximate Learning of Dynamic Models

Xavier Boyen
Computer Science Dept. 1A
Stanford, CA 94305-9010
xb@cs.stanford.edu

Daphne Koller
Computer Science Dept. 1A
Stanford, CA 94305-9010
koller@cs.stanford.edu

Abstract

Inference is a key component in learning probabilistic models from partially observable data. When learning temporal models, each of the many inference phases requires a traversal over an entire long data sequence; furthermore, the data structures manipulated are exponentially large, making this process computationally expensive. In [2], we describe an approximate inference algorithm for monitoring stochastic processes, and prove bounds on its approximation error. In this paper, we apply this algorithm as an approximate forward propagation step in an EM algorithm for learning temporal Bayesian networks. We provide a related approximation for the backward step, and prove error bounds for the combined algorithm. We show empirically that, for a real-life domain, EM using our inference algorithm is much faster than EM using exact inference, with almost no degradation in quality of the learned model. We extend our analysis to the online learning task, showing a bound on the error resulting from restricting attention to a small window of observations. We present an online EM learning algorithm for dynamic systems, and show that it learns much faster than standard offline EM.

1 Introduction

In many real-life situations, we are faced with the task of inducing the dynamics of a complex stochastic process from limited observations about its state over time. Until now, *hidden Markov models (HMMs)* [12] have played the largest role as a representation for learning models of stochastic processes. Recently, however, there has been increasing use of more structured models of stochastic processes, such as *factorial HMMs* [8] or *dynamic Bayesian networks (DBNs)* [4]. Such structured decomposed representations allow complex processes over a large number of states to be encoded using a much smaller number of parameters, thereby allowing better generalization from limited data [8, 7, 13]. Furthermore, the natural structure of such processes makes it easier for a human expert to incorporate prior knowledge about the domain structure into the model, thereby improving its inductive bias.

Both parameter and structure learning algorithms for dynamic models [12, 7] use probabilistic inference as a crucial component. An inference routine is called multiple times in order to "fill in" missing data with its expected value according to the current hypothesis; the resulting *expected sufficient statistics* are then used to construct a new hypothesis. The inference step is used many times, each of which iterates over the entire sequence. This behavior is problematic in two important respects. First, in many settings, we may not have access to the entire sequence in advance. Second, the various structured representations of stochastic processes do not admit an effective inference procedure. The messages propagated by exact inference algorithms include an entry for each possible state of the system; the number of states is exponential in the size of our model, rendering this type of computation infeasible in all but the smallest of problems. In this paper, we describe and analyze an approach that helps us address both of these problems.

In [2], we proposed a new approach to approximate inference in stochastic processes, where *approximate* distributions that admit compact representation are maintained and propagated. Our approach can achieve exponential savings over exact inference for DBNs. We showed empirically that, for a practical DBN [6], our approach results in a factor 15–20 reduction in running time at only a small cost in accuracy. We also proved that the accumulated error arising from the repeated approximations remains bounded indefinitely over time. This result relied on an analysis showing that transition through a stochastic process is a contraction for relative entropy (KL-divergence) [3].

Here, we apply this approach to the parameter learning task. This application is not completely straightforward, since our algorithm of [2] and the associated analysis only applied to the forward propagation of messages, whereas the inference used in learning algorithms require propagation of information from the entire sequence. In this paper, we provide an analysis of the error accumulated by an approximate inference process in the backward propagation phase of inference. This analysis is quite different from the contraction analysis for the forward phase. We combine these two results to prove bounds on the error of the expected sufficient statistics relayed to the learning algorithm at each stage. We then present empirical results for a practical DBN, illustrating the performance of this approximate learning algorithm. We show that speedups of 15–20 can be obtained easily, with no discernable loss in the quality of the learned hypothesis.

Our theoretical analysis also suggests a way of dealing with the problematic need to reason about the entire sequence of temporal observations at once. Our contraction results show that it is legitimate to ignore observations that are very far in the future. Thus, we can compute a very accurate approximation to the backward message by considering only a small window of observations in the future. This idea leads to an efficient online learning algorithm. We show that it converges to a good hypothesis much faster than the standard offline EM algorithm, even in settings favorable to the latter.

2 Preliminaries

A model for a dynamic system is specified as a tuple $\langle \mathcal{B}, \Theta \rangle$ where $\mathcal{B}$ represents the qualitative structure of the model, and Θ the appropriate parameterization. In a DBN, the instantaneous state of a process is specified in terms of a set of variables $X_1, ..., X_n$. Here, $\mathcal{B}$ encodes a network fragment which specifies, for each time t variable $X_k^{(t)}$, the set of parents $\mathit{Parents}(X_k^{(t)})$; an example fragment is shown in Figure 1(a). The parameters Θ define for each $X_k^{(t)}$ a conditional probability table $\boldsymbol{P}[X_k^{(t)} \mid \mathit{Parents}(X_k^{(t)})]$. For simplicity, we assume that the variables are partitioned into *state* variables, which are never observed, and *observation* variables, which are always observed. We also assume that the observation variables at time t depend only on state variables at time t. We use $\mathcal{T}$ to denote the transition matrix over the state variables in the stochastic process; i.e., $\mathcal{T}_{i,j}$ is the transition probability from state s_i to state s_j. Note that this concept is well-defined even for a DBN, although in that case, the matrix is represented implicitly via the other parameters. We use $\mathcal{O}$ to denote the observation matrix; i.e., $\mathcal{O}_{i,j}$ is the probability of observing response r_j in state s_i.

Our goal is to learn the model for stochastic process from partially observable data. To simplify our discussion, we focus on the problem of learning parameters for a known structure using the *EM (Expectation Maximization)* algorithm [5]; most of our discussion applies equally to other contexts (e.g., [7]). EM is an iterative procedure that searches over the space of parameter vectors for one which is a local maximum of the likelihood function— the probability of the observed data D given Θ. We describe the EM algorithm for the task of learning HMMs; the extension to DBNs is straightforward. The EM algorithm starts with some initial (often random) parameter vector $\tilde{\Theta}$, which specifies a current estimate of the transition and observation matrices of the process $\tilde{\mathcal{T}}$ and $\tilde{\mathcal{O}}$. The EM algorithm computes the *expected sufficient statistics (ESS)* for D, using $\tilde{\mathcal{T}}$ and $\tilde{\mathcal{O}}$ to compute the expectation. In the case of HMMs, the ESS are an average, over t, of the joint distributions $\boldsymbol{\psi}^{(t)}$ over the variables at time $t - 1$ and the variables at time t. A new parameter vector $\tilde{\Theta}'$ can then be computed from the ESS by a simple maximum likelihood step. These two steps are iterated until an appropriate stopping condition is met.

The $\boldsymbol{\psi}^{(t)}$ for the entire sequence can be computed by a simple forward-backward algorithm. Let $r^{(t)}$ be the response observed at time t, and let $\mathcal{O}_{r^{(t)}}$ be its likelihood vector ($\mathcal{O}_{r_j}(i) \triangleq \mathcal{O}_{i,j}$). The forward messages $\boldsymbol{\alpha}^{(t)}$ are propagated as follows: $\boldsymbol{\alpha}^{(t)} \propto (\boldsymbol{\alpha}^{(t-1)} \cdot \mathcal{T}) \times \mathcal{O}_{r^{(t)}}$, where $\times$ is the outer product. The backward messages $\boldsymbol{\beta}^{(t)}$ are propagated as $\boldsymbol{\beta}^{(t)} \propto (\mathcal{T} \cdot (\boldsymbol{\beta}^{(t+1)} \times \mathcal{O}_{r^{(t+1)}})')'$. The estimated belief at time t is now simply $\boldsymbol{\alpha}^{(t)} \times \boldsymbol{\beta}^{(t)}$ (suitably renormalized); similarly, the joint belief $\boldsymbol{\psi}^{(t)}$ is proportional to $(\boldsymbol{\alpha}^{(t-1)} \times \boldsymbol{\beta}^{(t)} \times \mathcal{T} \times \mathcal{O}_{r^{(t)}})$.

This message passing algorithm has an obvious extension to DBNs. Unfortunately, it is feasible only for very small DBNs. Essentially, the messages passed in this algorithm have an entry for every possible state at time t; in a DBN, the number of states is exponential in the number of state variables, rendering such an explicit representation infeasible in most cases. Furthermore even highly structured processes do not admit a more compact representation of these messages [8, 2].

3 Belief state approximation

In [2], we described a new approach to approximate inference in dynamic systems, which avoids the problem of explicitly maintaining distributions over large spaces. We maintain our *belief state* (distribution over the current state) using some computationally tractable representation of a distribution. We propagate the time t approximate belief state through the transition model and condition it on our evidence at time $t+1$. We then approximate the resulting time $t+1$ distribution using one that admits a compact representation, allowing the algorithm to continue. We also showed that the errors arising from the repeated approximation do not accumulate unboundedly, as the stochasticity of the process attenuates their effect.

In particular, for DBNs we considered belief state approximations where certain subsets of less correlated variables are grouped into distinct clusters which are approximated as being independent. In this case, the approximation at each step consists of a simple projection onto the relevant marginals, which are used as a factored representation of the time $t + 1$ approximate belief state. This algorithm can be implemented efficiently using the clique tree algorithm [10]. To compute $\tilde{\boldsymbol{\alpha}}^{(t+1)}$ from $\tilde{\boldsymbol{\alpha}}^{(t)}$, we generate a clique tree over these two time slices of the DBN, ensuring that both the time t and time $t + 1$ clusters appear as a subset of some clique. We then incorporate $\tilde{\boldsymbol{\alpha}}^{(t)}$ into the time t cliques; $\tilde{\boldsymbol{\alpha}}^{(t+1)}$ is obtained by calibrating the tree (doing inference) and reading off the relevant marginals from the tree ($\tilde{\alpha}^{(t+1)}$ is implicitly defined as their product).

These results are directly applicable to the learning task, as the belief state is the forward message in the forward-backward algorithm. Thus, we can apply this approach to the forward step, with the guarantee that the approximation will not lead to a big difference in the ESS. However, this technique does not resolve our computational problems, as the backward propagation phase is as expensive as the forward phase. We can apply the same idea to the backward propagation, i.e., we maintain and propagate a compactly represented approximate backward message $\tilde{\beta}^{(t)}$. The implementation of this idea is a simple extension of our algorithm for forward messages. To compute $\tilde{\beta}^{(t)}$ from $\tilde{\beta}^{(t+1)}$, we simply incorporate $\tilde{\beta}^{(t+1)}$ into our clique tree over these two time slices, then read off the relevant marginals for computing $\tilde{\beta}^{(t)}$.

However, extending the analysis is not as straightforward. It is not completely straightforward to apply the techniques of [2] to get relative error bounds for the backward message. Furthermore, even if we have bounds on relative entropy error of both the forward and backward messages, bounds for the error of the $\psi^{(t)}$ do not follow. The solution turns out to use an alternative notion of distance, which combines additively under Bayesian updating, albeit at the cost of weaker contraction rates.

Definition 1 Let ρ and $\tilde{\rho}$ be two positive vectors of same dimension. Their *projective distance* is defined as $\boldsymbol{D}_{\text{Proj}}[\rho, \tilde{\rho}] \triangleq \max_{i,i'} \ln[(\rho_i \cdot \tilde{\rho}_{i'})/(\rho_{i'} \cdot \tilde{\rho}_i)]$.

We note that the projective distance is a (weak) upper bound on the relative entropy.

Lemma 1 $\boldsymbol{D}_{\text{Proj}}[\psi^{(t)}, \tilde{\psi}^{(t)}] \leq \boldsymbol{D}_{\text{Proj}}[\alpha^{(t-1)}, \tilde{\alpha}^{(t-1)}] + \boldsymbol{D}_{\text{Proj}}[\beta^{(t)}, \tilde{\beta}^{(t)}]$.

Based on the results of [1], we show that projective distance contracts when messages are propagated through the stochastic transition matrix, in either direction. Of course, the rate of contraction depends on ergodicity properties of the matrix:

Lemma 2 Let $k = \min_{\{i,j,i',j' : \mathcal{T}_{i,j} \cdot \mathcal{T}_{i',j'} \neq 0\}} \sqrt{(\mathcal{T}_{i,j'} \cdot \mathcal{T}_{i',j})/(\mathcal{T}_{i,j} \cdot \mathcal{T}_{i',j'})}$, and define $\kappa_{\mathcal{T}} \triangleq 2 \cdot k/(1+k)$. Then $\boldsymbol{D}_{\text{Proj}}[\alpha^{(t)}, \tilde{\alpha}^{(t)}] \leq (1 - \kappa_{\mathcal{T}}) \cdot \boldsymbol{D}_{\text{Proj}}[\alpha^{(t-1)}, \tilde{\alpha}^{(t-1)}]$, and $\boldsymbol{D}_{\text{Proj}}[\beta^{(t)}, \tilde{\beta}^{(t)}] \leq (1 - \kappa_{\mathcal{T}}) \cdot \boldsymbol{D}_{\text{Proj}}[\beta^{(t+1)}, \tilde{\beta}^{(t+1)}]$.

We can now show that, if our approximations do not introduce too large an error, then the expected sufficient statistics will remain close to their correct value.

Theorem 3 *Let S be the ESS computed via exact inference, and let $\tilde{S}$ be its approximation. If the forward (backward) approximation step is guaranteed to introduce at most ε (δ) projective error, then $\boldsymbol{D}_{\text{Proj}}[S, \tilde{S}] \leq (\varepsilon + \delta)/\kappa_{\mathcal{T}}$. Therefore $\boldsymbol{D}_{\text{KL}}[S \| \tilde{S}] \leq (\varepsilon + \delta)/\kappa_{\mathcal{T}}$.*

Note that even small fluctuations in the sufficient statistics can cause the EM algorithm to reach a different local maximum. Thus, we cannot analytically compare the quality of the resulting algorithms. However, as our experimental results show, there is no divergence between exact EM and aproximate EM in practice.

We tested our algorithms on the task of learning the parameters for the BAT network shown in Figure 1(a), used for traffic monitoring [6]. The training set was a fixed sequence of 1000 slices, generated from the correct network distribution. Our test metric was the average log-likelihood (per slice) of a fixed test sequence of 50 slices. All experiments were conducted using three different random starting points for the parameters (the same

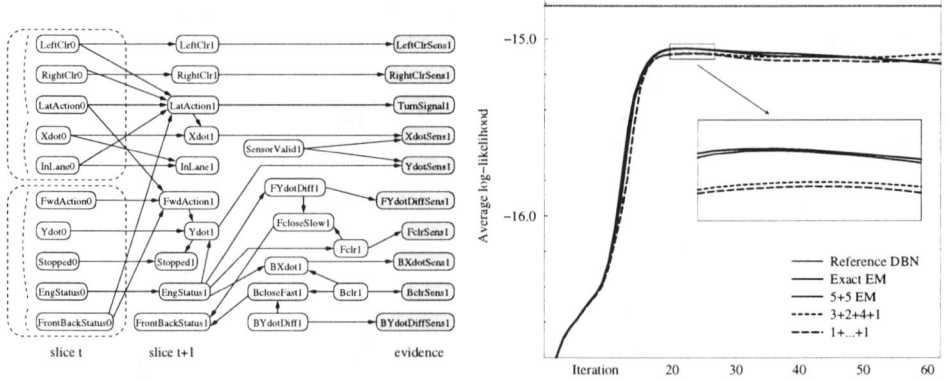

Figure 1: (a) The BAT DBN. (b) Structural approximations for batch EM.

in all the experiments). We ran EM with different types of structural approximations, and evaluated the quality of the model after each iteration of the algorithm. We used four different structural approximations: (i) exact propagation; (ii) a 5+5 clustering of the ten state variables; (iii) a 3+2+4+1 clustering; (iv) each variable in a separate cluster. The results for one random starting point are shown on Figure 1(b). As we can see, the impact of (even severe) structural approximation on learning accuracy is negligible. In all of the runs, the approximate algorithm tracked the exact one very closely, and the largest difference in the peak log-likelihood was at most 0.04. This phenomenon is rather remarkable, especially in view of the substantial savings caused by the approximations: on a Sun Ultra II, the computational cost of learning was 138 min/iteration in the exact case, vs. 6 min/iteration for the 5+5 clustering, and less than 5 min/iteration for the other two.

4 Online learning

Our analysis also gives us the tools to address another important problem with learning dynamic models: the need to reason about the entire temporal sequence at once. One consequence of our contraction result is that the effect of approximations done far away in the sequence decays exponentially with the time difference. In particular, the effect of an approximation which ignores observations that are far in the future is also limited. Therefore, if we do inference for a time slice based on a small window of observations into the future, the result should still be fairly accurate. More precisely, assume that we are at time t and are considering a window of size w. We can view the uniform message as a very bad approximation to $\beta^{(t+w)}$. But as we propagate this approximate backward message from $t+w$ to t, the error will decay exponentially with w.

Based on these insights, we experimented with various online algorithms that use a small window approximation. Our online algorithms are based on the approach of [11], in which ESS are updated with an exponential decay every few data cases; the parameters are then updated correspondingly. The main problem with frequent parameter updates in the online setting is that they require a recomputation of the messages computed using the old parameters. For long sequences, the computational cost of such a scheme would be prohibitive. In our algorithms, we simply leave the forward messages unchanged, under the assumption that the most recent time slices used parameters that are very close to the new ones. Our contraction result tells us that the use of old parameters far back in the sequence has a negligible effect on the message. We tried several schemes for the update of the backward messages. In the *dynamic-1000* approach, we use a backward message computed over 1000 slices, with the closer messages recomputed very frequently as the parameters are changed, based on cached messages that used older parameters. The 8

Approximate Learning of Dynamic Models

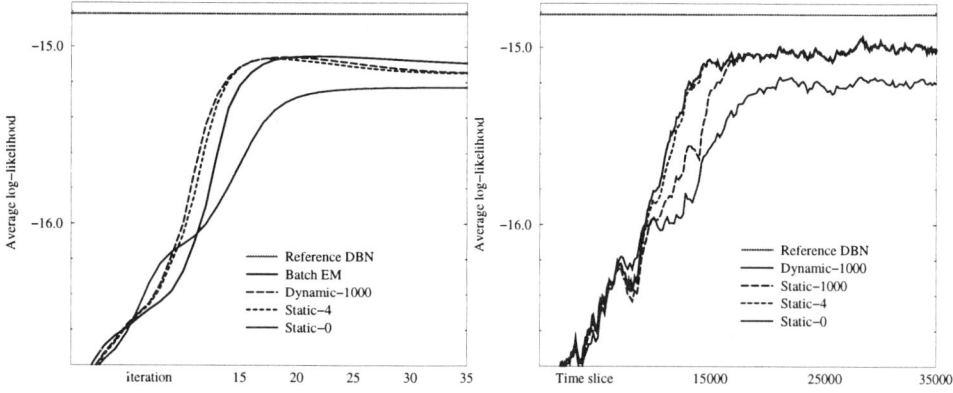

Figure 2: Temporal approximations for (a) batch setting; (b) online setting.

closest messages are updated every parameter update, the next 16 every other update, etc. This approach is the closest realistic alternative to a full update of backward messages. In the *static-1000* approach, we use a very long window (1000 slices), but do not recompute messages; when the window ends, we use the current parameters to compute the messages for the entire next window. In the *static-4* approach, we do the same, but use a very short window of 4 slices. Finally, in the *static-0* approach, there is no lookahead at all; only the past and present evidence is used to compute the joint beliefs. The latter case is often used (e.g., in the context of Kalman filters [9]) for online learning of the process parameters. To minimize the computational burden, all tests were conducted using the 5+5 structural approximation. The running time for the various algorithms are: 0.4 sec/slice for batch EM; 1.4 for dynamic-1000; 0.5 for static-1000 and for static-4; and 0.3 for static-0.

We evaluated these temporal approximations both in an online and in a batch setting. In the batch experiments, we used the same 1000-step sequence used above. The results are shown in Figure 2(a). We see that the dynamic-1000 algorithm reaches the same quality model as standard batch EM, but converges sooner. As in [11], the difference is due to the frequent update of the sufficient statistics based on more accurate parameters. More interestingly, we see that the static-4 algorithm, which uses a lookahead of only 4, also reaches the same accuracy. Thus, our approximation—ignoring evidence far in the future—is a good one, even for a very weak notion of "far". By contrast, we see that the quality reached by the static-0 approach is significantly lower: the sufficient statistics used by the EM algorithm in this case are consistently worse, as they ignore all future evidence. Thus, in this network, a window of size 4 is as good as full forward-backward, whereas one of size 0 is clearly worse. Our online learning experiments, shown in Figure 2(b), used a single long sequence of 40,000 slices. Again, we see that the static-4 approach is almost indistinguishable in terms of accuracy from the dynamic-1000 approach, and that both converge more rapidly than the static-1000 algorithm. Thus, frequent updates over short windows are better than infrequent updates over longer ones. Finally, we see again that the static-0 algorithm converges to a hypothesis of much lower quality. Thus, even a very short window allows rapid convergence to the "best possible" answer, but a window of size 0 does not.

5 Conclusion and extensions

In this paper, we suggested the use of simple structural approximations in the inference algorithm used in an E-step. Our results suggest that even severe structural approximations have almost negligible effects on the accuracy of learning. The advantages of approximate inference in the learning setting are even more pronounced than in the inference task [2], as the small errors caused by approximation are negligible compared to the larger ones induced by the learning process. Our techniques provide a new and simple approach for learning structured models of complex dynamic systems, with the resulting advantages of generalization and the ability to incorporate prior knowledge. We also presented a new algorithm for the online learning task, showing that we can learn high-quality models using a very small time window of future observations.

The work most comparable to ours is the variational approach to approximate inference applied to learning factorial HMMs [8]. While we have not done a direct empirical comparison, it seems likely that the variational approach would work better for densely connected models, whereas our approach would dominate for structured models such as the one in our experiments. Indeed, for this model, our algorithms track exact EM so closely that any significant improvement in accuracy is unlikely. Our algorithm is also simpler and easier to implement. Most importantly, it is applicable to the task of online learning.

The most obvious extension to our results is an integration of our ideas with structure learning algorithm for DBNs [7]. We believe that the resulting algorithm will be able to learn structured models for real-life complex systems.

Acknowledgements. We thank Tim Huang for providing us with the BAT network, and Nir Friedman and Leonid Gurvits for useful discussions. This research was supported by ARO under the MURI program "Integrated Approach to Intelligent Systems", and by DARPA contract DACA76-93-C-0025 under subcontract to IET, Inc.

References

[1] M. Artzrouni and X. Li. A note on the coefficient of ergodicity of a column-allowable nonnegative matrix. *Linear algebra and applications*, 214:93–101, 1995.

[2] X. Boyen and D. Koller. Tractable inference for complex stochastic processes. In *Proc. UAI*, pages 33–42, 1998.

[3] T. Cover and J. Thomas. *Elements of Information Theory*. Wiley, 1991.

[4] T. Dean and K. Kanazawa. A model for reasoning about persistence and causation. *Comp. Int.*, 5(3), 1989.

[5] A.P. Dempster, N.M. Laird, and D.B. Rubin. Maximum-likelihood from incomplete data via the EM algorithm. *Journal of the Royal Statistical Society*, B39:1–38, 1977.

[6] J. Forbes, T. Huang, K. Kanazawa, and S.J. Russell. The BATmobile: Towards a Bayesian automated taxi. In *Proc. IJCAI*, 1995.

[7] N. Friedman, K. Murphy, and S.J. Russell. Learning the structure of dynamic probabilistic networks. In *Proc. UAI*, pages 139–147, 1998.

[8] Z. Ghahramani and M.I. Jordan. Factorial hidden Markov models. In *NIPS 8*, 1996.

[9] R.E. Kalman. A new approach to linear filtering and prediction problems. *J. of Basic Engineering*, 82:34–45, 1960.

[10] S.L. Lauritzen and D.J. Spiegelhalter. Local computations with probabilities on graphical structures and their application to expert systems. *J. Roy. Stat. Soc.*, B 50, 1988.

[11] R.M. Neal and G.E. Hinton. A view of the EM algorithm that justifies incremental, sparse, and other variants. In M.I. Jordan, editor, *Learning in Graphical Models*. Kluwer, 1998.

[12] L. Rabiner and B. Juang. An introduction to hidden Markov models. *IEEE Acoustics, Speech & Signal Processing*, 1986.

[13] G. Zweig and S.J. Russell. Speech recognition with dynamic bayesian networks. In *Proc. AAAI*, pages 173–180, 1998.

Fisher Scoring and a Mixture of Modes Approach for Approximate Inference and Learning in Nonlinear State Space Models

Thomas Briegel and Volker Tresp
Siemens AG, Corporate Technology
Dept. Information and Communications
Otto-Hahn-Ring 6, 81730 Munich, Germany
{Thomas.Briegel, Volker.Tresp}@mchp.siemens.de

Abstract

We present Monte-Carlo generalized EM equations for learning in nonlinear state space models. The difficulties lie in the Monte-Carlo E-step which consists of sampling from the posterior distribution of the hidden variables given the observations. The new idea presented in this paper is to generate samples from a Gaussian approximation to the true posterior from which it is easy to obtain independent samples. The parameters of the Gaussian approximation are either derived from the extended Kalman filter or the Fisher scoring algorithm. In case the posterior density is multimodal we propose to approximate the posterior by a sum of Gaussians (mixture of modes approach). We show that sampling from the approximate posterior densities obtained by the above algorithms leads to better models than using point estimates for the hidden states. In our experiment, the Fisher scoring algorithm obtained a better approximation of the posterior mode than the EKF. For a multimodal distribution, the mixture of modes approach gave superior results.

1 INTRODUCTION

Nonlinear state space models (NSSM) are a general framework for representing nonlinear time series. In particular, any NARMAX model (nonlinear auto-regressive moving average model with external inputs) can be translated into an equivalent NSSM. Mathematically, a NSSM is described by the system equation

$$x_t = f_w(x_{t-1}, u_t) + \epsilon_t \tag{1}$$

where x_t denotes a hidden state variable, ϵ_t denotes zero-mean uncorrelated Gaussian noise with covariance Q_t and u_t is an exogenous (deterministic) input vector. The time-series measurements y_t are related to the unobserved hidden states x_t through the observation equation

$$y_t = g_v(x_t, u_t) + v_t \tag{2}$$

where v_t is uncorrelated Gaussian noise with covariance V_t. In the following we assume that the nonlinear mappings $f_w(.)$ and $g_v(.)$ are neural networks with weight vectors w and v, respectively. The initial state x_0 is assumed to be Gaussian distributed with mean a_0 and covariance Q_0. All variables are in general multidimensional. The two challenges in NSSMs are the interrelated tasks of inference and learning. In inference we try to estimate the states of unknown variables x_s given some measurements $y_1, \ldots, y_t$ (typically the states of past $(s < t)$, present $(s = t)$ or future $(s > t)$ values of x_t) and in learning we want to adapt some unknown parameters in the model (i.e. neural network weight vectors w and v) given a set of measurements.[1] In the special case of linear state space models with Gaussian noise, efficient algorithms for inference and maximum likelihood learning exist. The latter can be implemented using EM update equations in which the E-step is implemented using forward-backward Kalman filtering (Shumway & Stoffer, 1982). If the system is nonlinear, however, the problem of inference and learning leads to complex integrals which are usually considered intractable (Anderson & Moore, 1979). A useful approximation is presented in section 3 where we show how the learning equations for NSSMs can be implemented using two steps which are repeated until convergence. First in the (Monte-Carlo) E-step, random samples are generated from the unknown variables (e.g. the hidden variables x_t) given the measurements. In the second step (a generalized M-step) those samples are treated as real data and are used to adapt $f_w(.)$ and $g_v(.)$ using some version of the backpropagation algorithm. The problem lies in the first step, since it is difficult to generate independent samples from a general multidimensional distribution. Since it is difficult to generate samples from the *proper* distribution the next best thing might be to generate samples using an *approximation* to the proper distribution which is the idea pursued in this paper. The first thing which might come to mind is to approximate the posterior distribution of the hidden variables by a multidimensional Gaussian distribution since generating samples from such a distribution is simple. In the first approach we use the extended Kalman filter and smoother to obtain mode and covariance of this Gaussian.[2] Alternatively, we estimate the mode and the covariance of the posterior distribution using an efficient implementation of Fisher scoring derived by Fahrmeir and Kaufmann (1991) and use those as parameters of the Gaussian. In some cases the approximation of the posterior mode by a single Gaussian might be considered too crude. Therefore, as a third solution, we approximate the posterior distribution by a sum of Gaussians (mixture of modes approach). Modes and covariances of those Gaussians are obtained using the Fisher scoring algorithm. The weights of the Gaussians are derived from the likelihood of the observed data given the individual Gaussian. In the following section we derive the gradient of the log-likelihood with respect to the weights in $f_w(.)$ and $g_v(.)$. In section 3, we show that the network weights can be updated using a Monte-Carlo E-step and a generalized M-step. Furthermore, we derive the different Gaussian approximations to the posterior distribution and introduce the mixture of modes approach. In section 4 we validate our algorithms using a standard nonlinear stochastic time-series model. In section 5 we present conclusions.

2 THE GRADIENTS FOR NONLINEAR STATE SPACE MODELS

Given our assumptions we can write the joint probability of the complete data for $t = 1, \ldots, T$ as[3]

$$p(X_T, Y_T, U_T) = p(U_T)\, p(x_0) \prod_{t=1}^{T} p(x_t|x_{t-1}, u_t) \prod_{t=1}^{T} p(y_t|x_t, u_t) \qquad (3)$$

---

[1] In this paper we focus on the case $s \leq t$ (smoothing and offline learning, respectively).

[2] Independently from our work, a single Gaussian approximation to the E-step using the EKFS has been proposed by Ghahramani & Roweis (1998) for the special case of a RBF network. They show that one obtains a closed form M-step when just adapting the *linear* parameters by holding the nonlinear parameters fixed. Although avoiding sampling, the computational load of their M-step seems to be significant.

[3] In the following, each probability density is conditioned on the current model. For notational convenience, we do not indicate this fact explicitly.

where $U_T = \{u_1, \ldots, u_T\}$ is a set of *known* inputs which means that $p(U_T)$ is irrelevant in the following. Since only $Y_T = \{y_1, \ldots, y_T\}$ and U_T are observed, the log-likelihood of the model is

$$\log L = \log \int p(X_T, Y_T|U_T) p(U_T) \, dX_T \propto \log \int p(X_T, Y_T|U_T) \, dX_T \quad (4)$$

with $X_T = \{x_0, \ldots, x_T\}$. By inserting the Gaussian noise assumptions we obtain the gradients of the log-likelihood with respect to the neural network weight vectors w and v, respectively (Tresp & Hofmann, 1995)

$$\frac{\partial \log L}{\partial w} \propto \sum_{t=1}^{T} \iint \frac{\partial f_w(x_{t-1}, u_t)}{\partial w} (x_t - f_w(x_{t-1}, u_t)) \, p(x_t, x_{t-1}|Y_T, U_T) \, dx_{t-1} \, dx_t$$

$$\frac{\partial \log L}{\partial v} \propto \sum_{t=1}^{T} \int \frac{\partial g_v(x_t, u_t)}{\partial v} (y_t - g_v(x_t, u_t)) \, p(x_t|Y_T, U_T) \, dx_t. \quad (5)$$

3 APPROXIMATIONS TO THE E-STEP

3.1 Monte-Carlo Generalized EM Learning

The integrals in the previous equations can be solved using Monte-Carlo integration which leads to the following learning algorithm.

1. Generate S samples $\{\hat{x}_0^s, \ldots, \hat{x}_T^s\}_{s=1}^{S}$ from $p(X_T|Y_T, U_T)$ assuming the current model is correct (Monte-Carlo E-Step).

2. Treat those samples as real data and update $w^{\text{new}} = w^{\text{old}} + \eta \frac{\partial \log L}{\partial w}$ and $v^{\text{new}} = v^{\text{old}} + \eta \frac{\partial \log L}{\partial v}$ with stepsize η and

$$\frac{\partial \log L}{\partial w} \propto \frac{1}{S} \sum_{t=1}^{T} \sum_{s=1}^{S} \frac{\partial f_w(x_{t-1}, u_t)}{\partial w} \bigg|_{x_{t-1} = \hat{x}_{t-1}^s} (\hat{x}_t^s - f_w(\hat{x}_{t-1}^s, u_t)) \quad (6)$$

$$\frac{\partial \log L}{\partial v} \propto \frac{1}{S} \sum_{t=1}^{T} \sum_{s=1}^{S} \frac{\partial g_v(x_t, u_t)}{\partial v} \bigg|_{x_t = \hat{x}_t^s} (y_t - g_v(\hat{x}_t^s, u_t)) \quad (7)$$

(generalized M-step). Go back to step one.

The second step is simply a stochastic gradient step. The computational difficulties lie in the first step. Methods which produce samples from multivariate distributions such as Gibbs sampling and other Markov chain Monte-Carlo methods have (at least) two problems. First, the sampling process has to "forget" its initial condition which means that the first samples have to be discarded and there are no simple analytical tools available to determine how many samples must be discarded. Secondly, subsequent samples are highly correlated which means that many samples have to be generated before a sufficient amount of independent samples is available. Since it is so difficult to sample from the correct posterior distribution $p(X_T|Y_T, U_T)$ the idea in this paper is to generate samples from an approximate distribution from which it is easy to draw samples. In the next sections we present approximations using a multivariate Gaussian and a mixture of Gaussians.

3.2 Approximate Mode Estimation Using the Extended Kalman Filter

Whereas the Kalman filter is an optimal state estimator for linear state space models the extended Kalman filter is a suboptimal state estimator for NSSMs based on local linearizations of the nonlinearities.[4] The *extended Kalman filter and smoother* (EKFS) algorithm is

---
[4] Note that we do not include the parameters in the NSSM as additional states to be estimated as done by other authors, e.g. Puskorius & Feldkamp (1994).

a forward-backward algorithm and can be derived as an approximation to posterior mode estimation for Gaussian error sequences (Sage & Melsa, 1971). Its application to our framework amounts to approximating $x_t^{\text{mode}} \approx \hat{x}_t^{\text{EKFS}}$ where $\hat{x}_t^{\text{EKFS}}$ is the smoothed estimate of x_t obtained from forward-backward extended Kalman filtering over the set of measurements Y_T and x_t^{mode} is the mode of the posterior distribution $p(x_t|Y_T, U_T)$. We use $\hat{x}_t^{\text{EKFS}}$ as the center of the approximating Gaussian. The EKFS also provides an estimate of the error covariance of the state vector at each time step t which can be used to form the covariance matrix of the approximating Gaussian. The EKFS equations can be found in Anderson & Moore (1979). To generate samples we recursively apply the following algorithm. Given $\hat{x}_{t-1}^s$ is a sample from the Gaussian approximation of $p(x_{t-1}|Y_T, U_T)$ at time $t-1$ draw a sample $\hat{x}_t^s$ from $p(x_t|x_{t-1} = \hat{x}_{t-1}^s, Y_T, U_T)$. The last conditional density is Gaussian with mean and covariance calculated from the EKFS approximation and the lag-one error covariances derived in Shumway & Stoffer (1982), respectively.

3.3 Exact Mode Estimation Using the Fisher Scoring Algorithm

If the system is highly nonlinear, however, the EKFS can perform badly in finding the posterior mode due to the fact that it uses a first order Taylor series expansion of the nonlinearities $f_w(.)$ and $g_v(.)$ (for an illustration, see Figure 1). A useful – and computationally tractable – alternative to the EKFS is to compute the "exact" posterior mode by maximizing $\log p(X_T|Y_T, U_T)$ with respect to X_T. A suitable way to determine a stationary point of the log posterior, or equivalently, of $p(X_T, Y_T|U_T)$ (derived from (3) by dropping $p(U_T)$) is to apply *Fisher scoring*. With the current estimate $X_T^{\text{FS,old}}$ we get a better estimate $X_T^{\text{FS,new}} = X_T^{\text{FS,old}} + \eta\,\delta$ for the unknown state sequence X_T where δ is the solution of

$$\mathcal{S}(X_T^{\text{FS,old}})\,\delta = s(X_T^{\text{FS,old}}) \tag{8}$$

with the score function $s(X_T) = \frac{\partial \log p(X_T, Y_T|U_T)}{\partial X_T}$ and the expected information matrix $\mathcal{S}(X_T) = \mathrm{E}\big[-\frac{\partial^2 \log p(X_T, Y_T|U_T)}{\partial X_T \partial X_T^T}\big]$.[5] By extending the arguments given in Fahrmeir & Kaufmann (1991) to nonlinear state space models it turns out that solving equation (8) – e.g. to compute the inverse of the expected information matrix – can be performed by Cholesky decomposition in one forward and backward pass.[6] The forward-backward steps can be implemented as a fast EKFS-like algorithm which has to be iterated to obtain the maximum posterior estimates $x_t^{\text{mode}} = \hat{x}_t^{\text{FS}}$ (see Appendix). Figure 1 shows the estimate obtained by the Fisher scoring procedure for a bimodal posterior density. Fisher scoring is successful in finding the "exact" mode, the EKFS algorithm is not. Samples of the approximating Gaussian are generated in the same way as in the last section.

3.4 The Mixture of Modes Approach

The previous two approaches to posterior mode smoothing can be viewed as single Gaussian approximations of the mode of $p(X_T|Y_T, U_T)$. In some cases the approximation of the posterior density by a single Gaussian might be considered too crude, in particular if the posterior distribution is multimodal. In this section we approximate the posterior by a *weighted sum* of m Gaussians $p(X_T|Y_T, U_T) \approx \sum_{k=1}^{m} \alpha^k p(X_T|k)$ where $p(X_T|k)$ is the k-th Gaussian. If the individual Gaussians model the different modes we are able to model multimodal posterior distributions accurately. The approximations of the individual modes are local maxima of the Fisher scoring algorithm which are found by starting the algorithm using different initial conditions. Given the different Gaussians, the optimal weighting factors are $\alpha^k = p(Y_T|k)p(k)/p(Y_T)$ where $p(Y_T|k) = \int p(Y_T|X_T)p(X_T|k)\,dX_T$ is the

---

[5]Note that the difference between the Fisher scoring and the Gauss-Newton update is that in the former we take the expectation of the information matrix.

[6]The expected information matrix is a positive definite block-tridiagonal matrix.

likelihood of the data given mode k. If we approximate that integral by inserting the Fisher scoring solutions $\hat{x}_t^{FS,k}$ for each time step t and linearize the nonlinearity $g_v(.)$ about the Fisher scoring solutions, we obtain a closed form solution for computing the α^k (see Appendix). The resulting estimator is a weighted sum of the m single Fisher scoring estimates $\hat{x}_t^{MM} = \sum_{k=1}^{m} \alpha^k \hat{x}_t^{FS,k}$. The mixture of modes algorithm can be found in the Appendix. For the learning task samples of the mixture of Gaussians are based on samples of each of the m single Gaussians which are obtained the same way as in subsection 3.2.

4 EXPERIMENTAL RESULTS

In the first experiment we want to test how well the different approaches can approximate the posterior distribution of a nonlinear time series (inference). As a time-series model we chose

$$f(x_{t-1}, u_t) = 0.5 x_{t-1} + 25 \frac{x_{t-1}}{1 + x_{t-1}^2} + 8\cos(1.2(t-1)), \quad g(x_t) = \frac{1}{20} x_t^2, \quad (9)$$

the covariances $Q_t = 10$, $V_t = 1$ and initial conditions $a_0 = 0$ and $Q_0 = 5$ which is considered a hard inference problem (Kitagawa, 1987). At each time step we calculate the expected value of the hidden variables $x_t, t = 1, ..., 400$ based on a set of measurements $Y_{400} = \{y_1, ..., y_{400}\}$ (which is the optimal estimator in the mean squared sense) and based on the different approximations presented in the last section. Note that for the single mode approximation, x_t^{mode} is the best estimate of x_t based on the approximating Gaussian. For the mixture of modes approach, the best estimate is $\sum_{k=1}^{m} \alpha^k \hat{x}_t^{FS,k}$ where $\hat{x}_t^{FS,k}$ is the mode of the k-th Gaussian in the dimension of x_t. Figure 2 (left) shows the mean squared error (MSE) of the smoothed estimates using the different approaches. The Fisher scoring (FS) algorithm is significantly better than the EKFS approach. In this experiment, the mixture of modes (MM) approach is significantly better than both the EKFS and Fisher scoring. The reason is that the posterior probability is multimodal as shown in Figure 1.

In the second experiment we used the same time-series model and trained a neural network to approximate $f_w(.)$ where all covariances were assumed to be fixed and known. For adaptation we used the learning rules of section 3 using the various approximations to the posterior distribution of X_T. Figure 2 (right) shows the results. The experiments show that truly sampling from the approximating Gaussians gives significantly better results than using the expected value as a point estimate. Furthermore, using the mixture of modes approach in conjunction with sampling gave significantly better results than the approximations using a single Gaussian. When used for inference, the network trained using the mixture of modes approach was not significantly worse than the true model (5% significance level, based on 20 experiments).

5 CONCLUSIONS

In our paper we presented novel approaches for inference and learning in NSSMs. The application of Fisher scoring and the mixture of modes approach to nonlinear models as presented in our paper is new. Also the idea of sampling from an approximation to the posterior distribution of the hidden variables is presented here for the first time. Our results indicate that the Fisher scoring algorithm gives better estimates of the expected value of the hidden variable than the EKFS based approximations. Note that the Fisher scoring algorithm is more complex in requiring typically 5 forward-backward passes instead of only one forward-backward pass for the EKFS approach. Our experiments also showed that if the posterior distribution is multimodal, the mixture of modes approach gives significantly better estimates if compared to the approaches based on a single Gaussian approximation. Our learning experiments show that it is important to sample from the approximate distributions and that it is not sufficient to simply substitute point estimates. Based on the

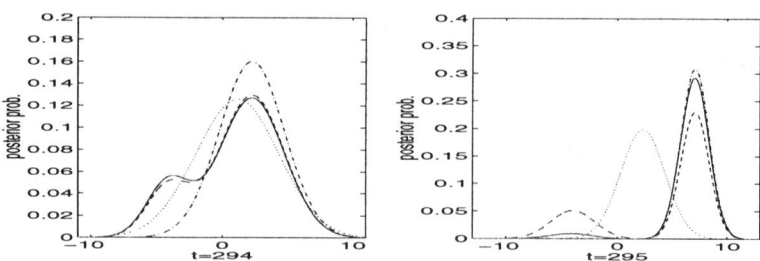

Figure 1: Approximations to the posterior distribution $p(x_t|Y_{400}, U_{400})$ for $t = 294$ and $t = 295$. The continuous line shows the posterior distribution based on Gibbs sampling using 1000 samples and can be considered a close approximation to the true posterior. The EKFS approximation (dotted) does not converge to a mode. The Fisher scoring solution (dash-dotted) finds the largest mode. The mixture of modes approach with 50 modes (dashed) correctly finds the two modes.

sampling approach it is also possible to estimate hyperparameters (e.g. the covariance matrices) which was not done in this paper. The approaches can also be extended towards online learning and estimation in various ways (e.g. missing data problems).

Appendix: Mixture of Modes Algorithm

The *mixture of modes* estimate $\hat{x}_t^{\mathrm{MM}}$ is derived as a weighted sum of $k = 1, \ldots, m$ individual Fisher scoring (mode) estimates $\hat{x}_t^{\mathrm{FS},k}$. For $m = 1$ we obtain the *Fisher scoring* algorithm of subsection 3.3.

First, one performs the set of forward recursions $(t = 1, \ldots, T)$ for each single mode estimator k.

$$\Sigma_{t|t-1}^k = F_t(\hat{x}_{t-1}^{\mathrm{FS},k})\Sigma_{t-1|t-1}^k F_t^\top(\hat{x}_{t-1}^{\mathrm{FS},k}) + Q_t \tag{10}$$

$$B_t^k = \Sigma_{t-1|t-1}^k F_t^\top(\hat{x}_{t-1}^{\mathrm{FS},k})(\Sigma_{t|t-1}^k)^{-1} \tag{11}$$

$$\Sigma_{t|t}^k = \left((\Sigma_{t|t-1}^k)^{-1} + G_t(\hat{x}_t^{\mathrm{FS},k})V_t^{-1}G_t^\top(\hat{x}_t^{\mathrm{FS},k})\right)^{-1} \tag{12}$$

$$\gamma_t^k = s_t(\hat{x}_t^{\mathrm{FS},k}) + {B_t^k}^\top \gamma_{t-1}^k \tag{13}$$

with the initialization $\Sigma_{0|0}^k = Q_0, \gamma_0 = s_0(\hat{x}_0^{\mathrm{FS},k})$. Then, one performs the set of backward smoothing recursions $(t = T, \ldots, 1)$

$$(D_{t-1}^k)^{-1} = \Sigma_{t-1|t-1}^k - B_t^k \Sigma_{t|t-1}^k {B_t^k}^\top \tag{14}$$

$$\Sigma_{t-1}^k = (D_{t-1}^k)^{-1} + B_t^k \Sigma_t^k {B_t^k}^\top \tag{15}$$

$$\delta_{t-1}^k = (D_{t-1}^k)^{-1}\gamma_{t-1}^k + B_t^k \delta_t^k \tag{16}$$

with $F_t(z) = \frac{\partial f_w(x_{t-1}, u_t)}{\partial x_{t-1}}|_{x_{t-1}=z}$, $G_t(z) = \frac{\partial g_v(x_t, u_t)}{\partial x_t}|_{x_t=z}$, $s_t(z) = \frac{\partial \log p(X_T, Y_T|U_T)}{\partial x_t}|_{x_t=z}$ and initialization $\delta_T^k = \Sigma_T^k \gamma_T^k$. The k individual mode estimates $\hat{x}_t^{\mathrm{FS},k}$ are obtained by iterative application of the update rule $X_T^{\mathrm{FS},k} := \eta \delta^k + X_T^{\mathrm{FS},k}$ with stepsize η where $X_T^{\mathrm{FS},k} = \{\hat{x}_0^{\mathrm{FS},k}, \ldots, \hat{x}_T^{\mathrm{FS},k}\}$ and $\delta^k = \{\delta_0^k, \ldots, \delta_T^k\}$. After convergence we obtain the mixture of modes estimate as the weighted sum $\hat{x}_t^{\mathrm{MM}} = \sum_{k=1}^m \alpha^k \hat{x}_t^{\mathrm{FS},k}$ with weighting coefficients $\alpha^k := \alpha_0^k$ where $\alpha_t^k(t = T-1, \ldots, 0)$ are computed recursively starting with a uniform prior $\alpha_T^k = \frac{1}{m}$ ($\mathcal{N}(x|\mu, \Sigma)$ stands for a Gaussian with center μ and covariance Σ evaluated at x):

$$\alpha_t^k = \frac{\alpha_{t+1}^k \mathcal{N}(y_t|g_v(\hat{x}_t^{\mathrm{FS},k}, u_t), \Omega_t^k)}{\sum_{j=1}^m \alpha_{t+1}^j \mathcal{N}(y_t|g_v(\hat{x}_t^{\mathrm{FS},j}, u_t), \Omega_t^j)} \tag{17}$$

$$\Omega_t^k = G_t(\hat{x}_t^{\mathrm{FS},k})\Sigma_t^k G_t(\hat{x}_t^{\mathrm{FS},k})^\top + V_t \tag{18}$$

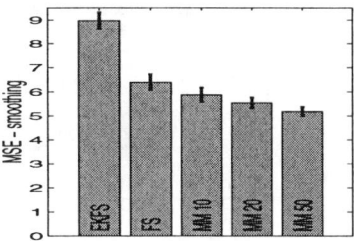 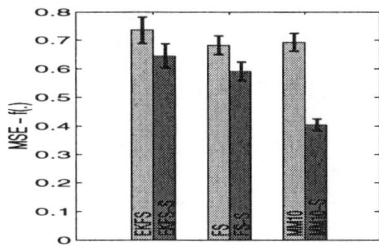

Figure 2: Left (inference): The heights of the bars indicate the mean squared error between the true x_t (which we know since we simulated the system) and the estimates using the various approximations. The error bars show the standard deviation derived from 20 repetitions of the experiment. Based on the paired t-test, Fisher scoring is significantly better than the EKFS and all mixture of modes approaches are significantly better than both EKFS and Fisher scoring based on a 1% rejection region. The mixture of modes approximation with 50 modes (MM 50) is significantly better than the approximation using 20 modes. The improvement of the approximation using 20 modes (MM 20) is not significantly better than the approximation with 10 (MM 10) modes using a 5% rejection region.

Right (learning): The heights of the bars indicate the mean squared error between the true $f_w(.)$ (which is known) and the approximations using a multi-layer perceptron with 3 hidden units and $T = 200$. Shown are results using the EKFS approximation, (left) the Fisher scoring approximation (center) and the mixture of modes approximation (right). There are two bars for each experiment: The left bars show results where the expected value of x_t calculated using the approximating Gaussians are used as (single) samples for the generalized M-step – in other words – we use a point estimate for x_t. Using the point estimates, the results of all three approximations are not significantly different based on a 5% significance level. The right bars shows the result where $S = 50$ samples are generated for approximating the gradient using the Gaussian approximations. The results using sampling are all significantly better than the results using point estimates (1% significance level). The sampling approach using the mixture of modes approximation is significantly better than the other two sampling based approaches (1% significance level). If compared to the inference results of the experiments shown on the left, we achieved a mean squared error of 6.02 for the mixture of modes approach with 10 modes which is not significantly worse than the results the with the true model of 5.87 (5% significance level).

References

Anderson, B. and Moore, J. (1979) *Optimal Filtering*, Prentice-Hall, New Jersey.

Fahrmeir, L. and Kaufmann, H. (1991) *On Kalman Filtering, Posterior Mode Estimation and Fisher Scoring in Dynamic Exponential Family Regression*, Metrika, 38, pp. 37-60.

Ghahramani, Z. and Roweis, S. (1999) *Learning Nonlinear Stochastic Dynamics using the Generalized EM Algorithm*, Advances in Neural Information Processing Systems 11, eds. M. Kearns, S. Solla, D. Cohn, MIT Press, Cambridge, MA.

Kitagawa, G. (1987) *Non-Gaussian State Space Modeling of Nonstationary Time Series (with Comments)*, JASA 82, pp. 1032-1063.

Puskorius, G. and Feldkamp, L. (1994) *Neurocontrol of Nonlinear Dynamical Systems with Kalman Filter Trained Recurrent Networks*, IEEE Transactions on Neural Networks, 5:2, pp. 279-297.

Sage, A. and Melsa, J. (1971) *Estimation Theory with Applications to Communications and Control*, McGraw-Hill, New York.

Shumway, R. and Stoffer, D. (1982) *Time Series Smoothing and Forecasting Using the EM Algorithm*, Technical Report No. 27, Division of Statistics, UC Davis.

Tresp, V. and Hofmann, R. (1995) *Missing and Noisy Data in Nonlinear Time-Series Prediction*, Neural Networks for Signal Processing 5, IEEE Sig. Proc. Soc., pp. 1-10.

Global Optimisation of Neural Network Models Via Sequential Sampling

João FG de Freitas
Cambridge University
Engineering Department
Cambridge CB2 1PZ England
jfgf@eng.cam.ac.uk
[Corresponding author]

Arnaud Doucet
Cambridge University
Engineering Department
Cambridge CB2 1PZ England
ad2@eng.cam.ac.uk

Mahesan Niranjan
Cambridge University
Engineering Department
Cambridge CB2 1PZ England
niranjan@eng.cam.ac.uk

Andrew H Gee
Cambridge University
Engineering Department
Cambridge CB2 1PZ England
ahg@eng.cam.ac.uk

Abstract

We propose a novel strategy for training neural networks using sequential sampling-importance resampling algorithms. This global optimisation strategy allows us to learn the probability distribution of the network weights in a sequential framework. It is well suited to applications involving on-line, nonlinear, non-Gaussian or non-stationary signal processing.

1 INTRODUCTION

This paper addresses sequential training of neural networks using powerful sampling techniques. Sequential techniques are important in many applications of neural networks involving real-time signal processing, where data arrival is inherently sequential. Furthermore, one might wish to adopt a sequential training strategy to deal with non-stationarity in signals, so that information from the recent past is lent more credence than information from the distant past. One way to sequentially estimate neural network models is to use a state space formulation and the extended Kalman filter (Singhal and Wu 1988, de Freitas, Niranjan and Gee 1998). This involves local linearisation of the output equation, which can be easily performed, since we only need the derivatives of the output with respect to the unknown parameters. This approach has been employed by several authors, including ourselves.

However, local linearisation leading to the EKF algorithm is a gross simplification of the probability densities involved. Nonlinearity of the output model induces multi-modality of the resulting distributions. Gaussian approximation of these densities will loose important details. The approach we adopt in this paper is one of sampling. In particular, we discuss the use of 'sampling-importance resampling' and 'sequential importance sampling' algorithms, also known as particle filters (Gordon, Salmond and Smith 1993, Pitt and Shephard 1997), to train multi-layer neural networks.

2 STATE SPACE NEURAL NETWORK MODELLING

We start from a state space representation to model the neural network's evolution in time. A transition equation describes the evolution of the network weights, while a measurements equation describes the nonlinear relation between the inputs and outputs of a particular physical process, as follows:

$$\mathbf{w}_{k+1} = \mathbf{w}_k + \mathbf{d}_k \tag{1}$$
$$\mathbf{y}_k = \mathbf{g}(\mathbf{w}_k, \mathbf{x}_k) + \mathbf{v}_k \tag{2}$$

where ($\mathbf{y}_k \in \Re^o$) denotes the output measurements, ($\mathbf{x}_k \in \Re^d$) the input measurements and ($\mathbf{w}_k \in \Re^m$) the neural network weights. The measurements nonlinear mapping $\mathbf{g}(.)$ is approximated by a multi-layer perceptron (MLP). The measurements are assumed to be corrupted by noise $\mathbf{v}_k$. In the sequential Monte Carlo framework, the probability distribution of the noise is specified by the user. In our examples we shall choose a zero mean Gaussian distribution with covariance R. The measurement noise is assumed to be uncorrelated with the network weights and initial conditions.

We model the evolution of the network weights by assuming that they depend on the previous value $\mathbf{w}_k$ and a stochastic component $\mathbf{d}_k$. The process noise $\mathbf{d}_k$ may represent our uncertainty in how the parameters evolve, modelling errors or unknown inputs. We assume the process noise to be a zero mean Gaussian process with covariance Q, however other distributions can also be adopted. This choice of distributions for the network weights requires further research. The process noise is also assumed to be uncorrelated with the network weights.

The posterior density $p(W_k|Y_k)$, where $Y_k = \{\mathbf{y}_1, \mathbf{y}_2, \cdots, \mathbf{y}_k\}$ and $W_k = \{\mathbf{w}_1, \mathbf{w}_2, \cdots, \mathbf{w}_k\}$, constitutes the complete solution to the sequential estimation problem. In many applications, such as tracking, it is of interest to estimate one of its marginals, namely the filtering density $p(\mathbf{w}_k|Y_k)$. By computing the filtering density recursively, we do not need to keep track of the complete history of the weights. Thus, from a storage point of view, the filtering density turns out to be more parsimonious than the full posterior density function. If we know the filtering density of the network weights, we can easily derive various estimates of the network weights, including centroids, modes, medians and confidence intervals.

3 SEQUENTIAL IMPORTANCE SAMPLING

In the sequential importance sampling optimisation framework, a set of representative samples is used to describe the posterior density function of the network parameters. Each sample consists of a complete set of network parameters. More specifically, we make use of the following Monte Carlo approximation:

$$\hat{p}(W_k|Y_k) = \frac{1}{N} \sum_{i=1}^{N} \delta(W_k - W_k^{(i)})$$

where $W_k^{(i)}$ represents the samples used to describe the posterior density and $\delta(.)$ denotes the Dirac delta function. Consequently, any expectations of the form:

$$\mathbf{E}[f_k(W_k)] = \int f_k(W_k)\mathrm{p}(W_k|Y_k)\mathrm{d}W_k$$

may be approximated by the following estimate:

$$\mathbf{E}[f_k(W_k)] \approx \frac{1}{N}\sum_{i=1}^{N} f_k(W_k^{(i)})$$

where the samples $W_k^{(i)}$ are drawn from the posterior density function. Typically, one cannot draw samples directly from the posterior density. Yet, if we can draw samples from a proposal density function $\pi(W_k|Y_k)$, we can transform the expectation under $\mathrm{p}(W_k|Y_k)$ to an expectation under $\pi(W_k|Y_k)$ as follows:

$$\begin{aligned}\mathbf{E}[f_k(W_k)] &= \int f_k(W_k)\frac{\mathrm{p}(W_k|Y_k)}{\pi(W_k|Y_k)}\pi(W_k|Y_k)\mathrm{d}W_k \\ &= \frac{\int f_k(W_k)q_k(W_k)\pi(W_k|Y_k)\mathrm{d}W_k}{\int q_k(W_k)\pi(W_k|Y_k)\mathrm{d}W_k} \\ &= \frac{\mathbf{E}_\pi[q_k(W_k)f_k(W_k)]}{\mathbf{E}_\pi[q_k(W_k)]}\end{aligned}$$

where the variables $q_k(W_k)$ are known as the unnormalised importance ratios:

$$q_k = \frac{\mathrm{p}(Y_k|W_k)\mathrm{p}(W_k)}{\pi(W_k|Y_k)} \qquad (3)$$

Hence, by drawing samples from the proposal function $\pi(.)$, we can approximate the expectations of interest by the following estimate:

$$\begin{aligned}\mathbf{E}[f_k(W_k)] &\approx \frac{1/N \sum_{i=1}^{N} f_k(W_k^{(i)})q_k(W_k^{(i)})}{1/N \sum_{i=1}^{N} q_k(W_k^{(i)})} \\ &= \sum_{i=1}^{N} f_k(W_k^{(i)})\tilde{q}_k(W_k^{(i)}) \qquad (4)\end{aligned}$$

where the normalised importance ratios $\tilde{q}_k^{(i)}$ are given by:

$$\tilde{q}_k^{(i)} = \frac{q_k^{(i)}}{\sum_{j=1}^{N} q_k^{(j)}}$$

It is not difficult to show (de Freitas, Niranjan, Gee and Doucet 1998) that, if we assume **w** to be a hidden Markov process with initial density $\mathrm{p}(\mathbf{w}_0)$ and transition density $\mathrm{p}(\mathbf{w}_k|\mathbf{w}_{k-1})$, various recursive algorithms can be derived. One of these algorithms (HySIR), which we derive in (de Freitas, Niranjan, Gee and Doucet 1998), has been shown to perform well in neural network training. Here we extended the algorithm to deal with multiple noise levels. The pseudo-code for the HySIR algorithm with EKF updating is as follows[1]:

---

[1] We have made available the software for the implementation of the HySIR algorithm at the following web-site: http://svr-www.eng.cam.ac.uk/~jfgf/software.html.

1. INITIALISE NETWORK WEIGHTS ($k=0$):
2. For $k=1,\cdots,L$
   (a) SAMPLING STAGE:
   For $i=1,\cdots,N$
   - Predict via the dynamics equation:
   $$\hat{\mathbf{w}}_{k+1}^{(i)} = \mathbf{w}_k^{(i)} + \mathbf{d}_k^{(i)}$$
   where $\mathbf{d}_k^{(i)}$ is a sample from $p(\mathbf{d}_k)$ ($\mathcal{N}(0,Q_k)$ in our case).
   - Update samples with the EKF equations.

   $$\begin{aligned}
   \mathbf{w}_{k+1|k}^{(i)} &= \hat{\mathbf{w}}_{k+1}^{(i)} \\
   P_{k+1|k}^{(i)} &= P_k^{T(i)} + Q^{*(i)} I_{mm} \\
   K_{k+1}^{(i)} &= P_{k+1|k}^{(i)} G_{k+1}^{(i)} [R^* I_{oo} + G_{k+1}^{T(i)} P_{k+1|k}^{(i)} G_{k+1}^{(i)}]^{-1} \\
   \hat{\mathbf{w}}_{k+1}^{(i)} &= \mathbf{w}_{k+1|K}^{(i)} + K_{k+1}^{(i)}(\mathbf{y}_{k+1} - \mathbf{g}(\mathbf{x}_{k+1}, \mathbf{w}_{k+1|k}^{(i)})) \\
   \hat{P}_{k+1}^{(i)} &= P_{k+1|k}^{(i)} - K_{k+1}^{(i)} G_{k+1}^{T(i)} P_{k+1|k}^{(i)}
   \end{aligned}$$

   - Evaluate the importance ratios:
   $$q_{k+1}^{(i)} = q_k^{(i)} p(\mathbf{y}_{k+1}|\hat{\mathbf{w}}_{k+1}^{(i)}) = q_k^{(i)} \mathcal{N}(\mathbf{g}(\mathbf{x}_{k+1}, \hat{\mathbf{w}}_{k+1}^{(i)}), R_k)$$

   - Normalise the importance ratios:
   $$\tilde{q}_{k+1}^{(i)} = \frac{q_{k+1}^{(i)}}{\sum_{j=1}^{N} q_{k+1}^{(j)}}$$

   (b) RESAMPLING STAGE:
   For $i=1,\cdots,N$
   If $N_{eff} \geq$ Threshold:
   - $\mathbf{w}_{k+1}^{(i)} = \hat{\mathbf{w}}_{k+1}^{(i)}$
   - $P_{k+1}^{(i)} = \hat{P}_{k+1}^{(i)}$
   - $Q_{k+1}^{*(i)} = Q_{k+1}^{*(i)}$
   Else
   - Resample new index j from the discrete set $\{\hat{\mathbf{w}}_{k+1}^{(i)}, \tilde{q}_{k+1}^{(i)}\}$
   - $\mathbf{w}_{k+1}^{(i)} = \hat{\mathbf{w}}_{k+1}^{(j)}$, $P_{k+1}^{(i)} = \hat{P}_{k+1}^{(j)}$ and $Q_{k+1}^{*(i)} = Q_{k+1}^{*(j)}$
   - $q_{k+1}^{(i)} = \frac{1}{N}$

where K_{k+1} is known as the Kalman gain matrix, I_{mm} denotes the identity matrix of size $m \times m$, and R^* and Q^* are two tuning parameters, whose roles are explained in detail in (de Freitas, Niranjan and Gee 1997). G represents the Jacobian matrix and, strictly speaking, P_k is an approximation to the covariance matrix of the network weights. The resampling stage is used to eliminate samples with low probability and multiply samples with high probability. Various authors have described efficient algorithms for accomplishing this task in $\mathcal{O}(N)$ operations (Pitt and Shephard 1997, Carpenter, Clifford and Fearnhead 1997, Doucet 1998).

4 EXPERIMENT

To assess the ability of the hybrid algorithm to estimate time-varying hidden parameters, we generated input-output data from a logistic function followed by a linear scaling and a displacement as shown in Figure 1. This simple model is equivalent to an MLP with one hidden neuron and an output linear neuron. We applied two Gaussian ($\mathcal{N}(0, 10)$) input sequences to the model and corrupted the weights and output values with Gaussian noise ($\mathcal{N}(0, 1 \times 10^{-3})$ and $\mathcal{N}(0, 1 \times 10^{-4})$ respectively). We then trained a second model with the same structure using the input-output

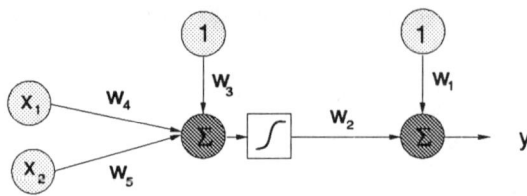

Figure 1: Logistic function with linear scaling and displacement used in the experiment. The weights were chosen as follows: $\mathbf{w}_1(k) = 1 + k/100$, $\mathbf{w}_2(k) = \sin(0.06k) - 2$, $\mathbf{w}_3(k) = 0.1$, $\mathbf{w}_4(k) = 1$, $\mathbf{w}_5(k) = -0.5$.

data generated by the first model. In so doing, we chose 100 sampling trajectories and set R to 10, Q to $1 \times 10^{-3} I_{55}$, the initial weights variance to 5, P_0 to $100 I_{55}$, R^* to 1×10^{-5}. The process noise parameter Q^* was set to three levels: 5×10^{-3}, 1×10^{-3} and 1×10^{-10}, as shown in the plot of Figure 2 at time zero. In the training

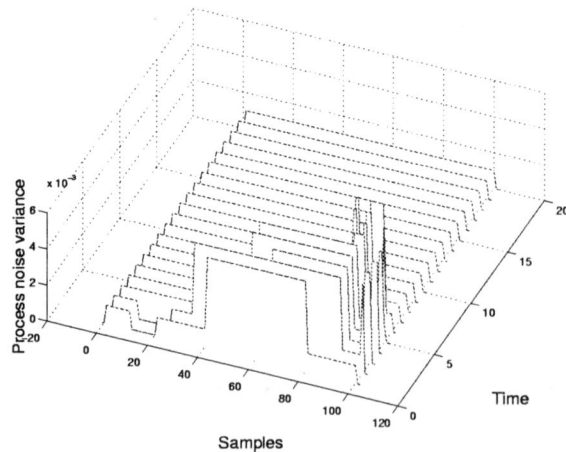

Figure 2: Noise level estimation with the HySIR algorithm.

phase, of 200 time steps, we allowed the model weights to vary with time. During this phase, the HySIR algorithm was used to track the input-output training data and estimate the latent model weights. In addition, we assumed three possible noise variance levels at the begining of the training session. After the 200-th time step, we fixed the values of the weights and generated another 200 input-output data test sets from the original model. The input test data was then fed to the trained model, using the weights values estimated at the 200-th time step. Subsequently, the output prediction of the trained model was compared to the output data from the original model to assess the generalisation performance of the training process. As shown in Figure 2, the noise level of the trajectories converged to the true value (1×10^{-3}). In addition, it was possible to track the network weights and obtain accurate output predictions as shown in Figures 3 and 4.

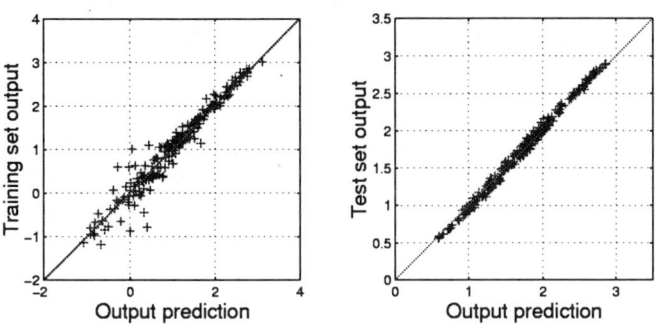

Figure 3: One step ahead predictions during the training phase (left) and stationary predictions in the test phase (right).

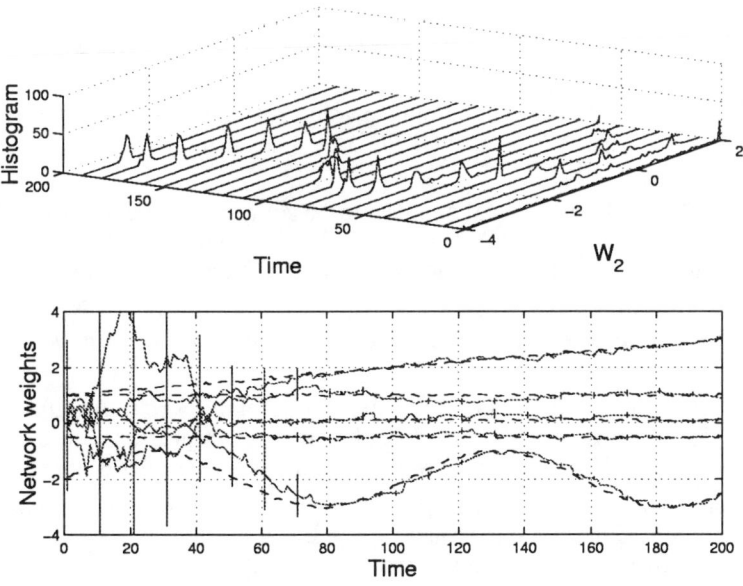

Figure 4: Weights tracking performance with the HySIR algorithm. As indicated by the histograms of $\mathbf{w}_2$, the algorithm performs a global search in parameter space.

5 CONCLUSIONS

In this paper, we have presented a sequential Monte Carlo approach for training neural networks in a Bayesian setting. In particular, we proposed an algorithm (HySIR) that makes use of both gradient and sampling information. HySIR can be interpreted as a Gaussian mixture filter, in that only a few sampling trajectories need to be employed. Yet, as the number of trajectories increases, the computational requirements increase only linearly. Therefore, the method is also suitable as a sampling strategy for approximating multi-modal distributions. Further avenues of research include the design of algorithms for adapting the noise covariances R and Q, studying the effect of different noise models for the network weights and improving the computational efficiency of the algorithms.

ACKNOWLEDGEMENTS

João FG de Freitas is financially supported by two University of the Witwatersrand Merit Scholarships, a Foundation for Research Development Scholarship (South Africa), an ORS award and a Trinity College External Studentship (Cambridge).

References

Carpenter, J., Clifford, P. and Fearnhead, P. (1997). An improved particle filter for non-linear problems, *Technical report*, Department of Statistics, Oxford University, England. Available at http://www.stats.ox.ac.uk/~clifford/index.htm.

de Freitas, J. F. G., Niranjan, M. and Gee, A. H. (1997). Hierarchichal Bayesian-Kalman models for regularisation and ARD in sequential learning, *Technical Report CUED/F-INFENG/TR 307*, Cambridge University, http://svr-www.eng.cam.ac.uk/~jfgf.

de Freitas, J. F. G., Niranjan, M. and Gee, A. H. (1998). Regularisation in sequential learning algorithms, *in* M. I. Jordan, M. J. Kearns and S. A. Solla (eds), *Advances in Neural Information Processing Systems*, Vol. 10, MIT Press.

de Freitas, J. F. G., Niranjan, M., Gee, A. H. and Doucet, A. (1998). Sequential Monte Carlo methods for optimisation of neural network models, *Technical Report CUED/F-INFENG/TR 328*, Cambridge University, http://svr-www.eng.cam.ac.uk/~jfgf.

Doucet, A. (1998). On sequential simulation-based methods for Bayesian filtering, *Technical Report CUED/F-INFENG/TR 310*, Cambridge University. Available at http://www.stats.bris.ac.uk:81/MCMC/pages/list.html.

Gordon, N. J., Salmond, D. J. and Smith, A. F. M. (1993). Novel approach to nonlinear/non-Gaussian Bayesian state estimation, *IEE Proceedings-F* **140**(2): 107–113.

Pitt, M. K. and Shephard, N. (1997). Filtering via simulation: Auxiliary particle filters, *Technical report*, Department of Statistics, Imperial College of London, England. Available at http://www.nuff.ox.ac.uk/economics/papers.

Singhal, S. and Wu, L. (1988). Training multilayer perceptrons with the extended Kalman algorithm, *in* D. S. Touretzky (ed.), *Advances in Neural Information Processing Systems*, Vol. 1, San Mateo, CA, pp. 133–140.

Efficient Bayesian Parameter Estimation in Large Discrete Domains

Nir Friedman
Hebrew University
nir@cs.huji.ac.il

Yoram Singer
AT&T Labs
singer@research.att.com

Abstract

We examine the problem of estimating the parameters of a multinomial distribution over a large number of discrete outcomes, most of which do not appear in the training data. We analyze this problem from a Bayesian perspective and develop a hierarchical prior that incorporates the assumption that the observed outcomes constitute only a small subset of the possible outcomes. We show how to *efficiently* perform *exact* inference with this form of hierarchical prior and compare it to standard approaches.

1 Introduction

One of the most important problems in statistical inference is *multinomial* estimation: Given a past history of observations independent trials with a discrete set of outcomes, predict the probability of the next trial. Such estimators are the basic building blocks in more complex statistical models, such as prediction trees [1, 12, 11], hidden Markov models [9] and Bayesian networks [3, 6]. The roots of multinomial estimation go back to Laplace's work in the 18th century [7].

In Bayesian theory, the classic approach to multinomial estimation is via the use of the *Dirichlet* distribution (see for instance [4]). Laplace's "law of succession" and other common methods can be derived using Bayesian inference with the Dirichlet distribution as a prior distribution. The Dirichlet distribution has several properties that are useful in statistical inference. In particular, estimates with Dirichlet priors are *consistent* (the estimate converges with probability one to the true distribution), *conjugate* (the posterior distribution is also a Dirichlet distribution), and can be computed efficiently (queries of interest have a closed-form solution). Furthermore, theoretical studies of online prediction of individual sequences show that prediction using Dirichlet priors is competitive with *any* other prior distribution (see for instance [2] and the references therein).

Unfortunately, in some key applications, Dirichlet priors are unwieldy. These applications are characterized by several features: (a) The set of possible outcomes is extremely large, and often not known in advance. (b) The number of training examples is small compared to the number of possible outcomes. (c) The outcomes that have positive probability constitute a relatively small subset of the possible outcomes; this subset, however, is not known in advance. In these situations, predictions based on a Dirichlet priors tend to assign most of the probability mass to outcomes that were not seen in the training set.

For example, consider a natural language application, where outcomes are words drawn from an English dictionary, and the problem is predicting the probability of words that follow a particular word, say "Bosnia". If we do not have any prior knowledge, we can consider any word in the dictionary as a possible candidate. Yet, our knowledge of language would lead us to believe that in fact, only few words, such as "Herzegovina", should naturally follow the word "Bosnia". Furthermore, even in a large corpus, we do not expect to see many training examples that involve this phrase. As another example consider the problem of estimating the parameters of a discrete dynamical system. Here the task is to find a distribution over the states that can be reached from a particular state s (possibly after the system receives an external control signal). Again, in many domains it is natural to assume that the system is sparse: only a small subset of states is reachable from any state.

In this paper, we present a Bayesian treatment of this problem using an *hierarchical* prior that averages over an exponential number of hypotheses each of which represents a subset of the feasible outcomes. Such a prior was previously used in a specific context of online prediction using suffix tree transducers [11]. As we show, although this prior involves exponentially many hypotheses, we can *efficiently* perform predictions. Moreover, our approach allows us to deal with countably infinite number of outcomes.

2 Dirichlet priors

Let X be a random variable that can take L possible values from a set Σ. Without loss of generality, let $\Sigma = \{1, \ldots L\}$. We are given a training set D that contains the outcomes of N independent draws $x^1, \ldots, x^N$ of X from an unknown multinomial distribution P^*. We denote by N_i be the number of occurrences of the symbol i in the training data. The *multinomial estimation* problem is to find a good approximation for P^*.

This problem can be stated as the problem of predicting the outcome x^{N+1} given $x^1, \ldots, x^N$. Given a prior distribution over the possible multinomial distributions, the Bayesian estimate is:

$$P(x^{N+1} \mid x^1, \ldots, x^N, \xi) = \int P(x^{N+1} \mid \theta, \xi) P(\theta \mid x^1, \ldots, x^N, \xi) d\theta \quad (1)$$

where $\theta = \langle \theta_1, \ldots, \theta_L \rangle$ is a vector that describes possible values of the (unknown) probabilities $P^*(1), \ldots, P^*(L)$, and ξ is the "context" variable that denotes all other assumptions about the domain. (We consider particular contexts in the next section.)

The posterior probability of θ can rewritten using Bayes law as:

$$P(\theta \mid x^1, \ldots, x^N, \xi) \propto P(x^1, \ldots, x^N \mid \theta, \xi) P(\theta \mid \xi) = P(\theta \mid \xi) \prod_i \theta_i^{N_i} \quad (2)$$

The family of *Dirichlet* distributions is *conjugate* to the multinomial distribution. That is, if the prior distribution is from this family, so is the posterior. A Dirichlet prior for X is specified by *hyperparameters* $\alpha_1, \ldots, \alpha_L$, and has the form:

$$P(\theta \mid \xi) = \frac{\Gamma(\sum_i \alpha_i)}{\prod_i \Gamma(\alpha_i)} \prod_i \theta_i^{\alpha_i - 1} \quad (\sum_i \theta_i = 1 \text{ and } \theta_i \geq 0 \text{ for all } i)$$

where $\Gamma(x) = \int_0^\infty t^{x-1} e^{-t} dt$ is the *gamma* function. Given a Dirichlet prior, the initial prediction for each value of X is $P(X^1 = i \mid \xi) = \int \theta_i P(\theta \mid \xi) d\theta = \alpha_i / \sum_j \alpha_j$. It is easy to see that, if the prior is a Dirichlet prior with hyperparameters $\alpha_1, \ldots, \alpha_L$, then the posterior is a Dirichlet with hyperparameters $\alpha_1 + N_1, \ldots, \alpha_L + N_L$. Thus, we get that the prediction for X^{N+1} is $P(X^{N+1} = i \mid x^1, \ldots, x^N, \xi) = (\alpha_i + N_i)/\sum_j (\alpha_j + N_j)$. We can think of the hyperparameters α_i as the number of "imaginary" examples in which we saw outcome i. Thus, the ratio between hyperparameters corresponds to our initial assessment of the relative probability of the corresponding outcomes. The total weight of the hyperparameters represent our confidence (or entrenchment) in the prior knowledge. As we can see, if this weight is large, our estimates for the parameters tend to be further off from the empirical frequencies observed in the training data.

3 Hierarchical priors

We now describe structured priors that capture our uncertainty about the set of "feasible" values of X. We define a random variable V that takes values from the set 2^Σ of possible subsets of Σ. The intended semantics for this variable is that $\theta_i > 0$ iff $i \in V$.

Clearly, the hypothesis $V = \Sigma'$ (for $\Sigma' \subseteq \Sigma$) is consistent with training data only if Σ' contains all the indices i for which $N_i > 0$. We denote by Σ^o the set of observed symbols. That is, $\Sigma^o = \{i : N_i > 0\}$, and we let $k^o = |\Sigma^o|$.

Suppose we know the value of V. Given this assumption, we can define a Dirichlet prior over possible multinomial distributions θ if we use the same hyper-parameter α for each symbol in V. Formally, we define the prior:

$$P(\theta|V) = \frac{\Gamma(|V|\alpha)}{\Gamma(\alpha)^{|V|}} \prod_{i \in V} \theta_i^{\alpha-1} \quad (\sum_i \theta_i = 1, \forall i, \theta_i \geq 0, \text{ and } \theta_i = 0 \text{ for all } i \notin V) \quad (3)$$

Using Eq. (2), we have that:

$$P(X^{N+1} = i \mid x^1, \ldots, x^n, V) = \begin{cases} \frac{\alpha + N_i}{|V|\alpha + N} & \text{if } i \in V \\ 0 & \text{otherwise} \end{cases} \quad (4)$$

Now consider the case where we are uncertain about the actual set of feasible outcomes. We construct a two tiered prior over the values of V. We start with a prior over the size of V, and then assume that all sets of the same cardinality have the same prior probability. We let the random variable S denote the cardinality of V. We assume that we are given a distribution $P(S = k)$ for $k = 1, \ldots, L$. We define the prior over sets to be:

$$P(V \mid S = k) = \binom{L}{k}^{-1} \quad (5)$$

We now examine how to compute the posterior predictions given this hierarchical prior. Let D denote the training data $x^1, \ldots, x^N$. Then it is easy to verify that

$$P(X^{N+1} = i \mid D) = \sum_k \frac{\alpha + N_i}{k\alpha + N} \sum_{V, |V|=k, i \in V} P(V \mid D) \quad (6)$$

Let us now examine which sets V actually contribute to this sum.

First, we note that sets that do not contain Σ^o have zero posterior probability, since they are inconsistent with the observed data. Thus, we can examine only sets V that contain Σ^o. Second, as we noted above, $P(D \mid V)$ is the same for all sets of cardinality k that contain Σ^o. Moreover, by definition the prior for all these sets is the same. Using Bayes rule, we conclude that $P(V \mid D)$ is the same for all sets of size k that contain Σ^o. Thus, we can simplify the inner summation in Eq. (6), by multiplying the number of sets in the score of the summation by the posterior probability of such sets.

There are two cases. If $i \in \Sigma^o$, then any set V that has non-zero posterior probability for i appears in the sum. Thus, in this case we can write:

$$P(X^{N+1} = i \mid D) = \sum_k \frac{\alpha + N_i}{k\alpha + N} P(S = k \mid D) \qquad \text{if } i \in \Sigma^o$$

If $i \notin \Sigma^o$, then we need to estimate the fraction of subsets of V with non-zero posterior that contain i. This leads to an equation similar to the one above, but with a correction for this fraction. By symmetry all unobserved outcomes have the same posterior probability. Thus, we can simply divide the mass that was not assigned to the observed outcomes among the unseen symbols.

Notice that the single term in Eq. (3) that depends on N_i can be moved outside the summation. Thus, to make predictions, we only need to estimate the quantity:

$$C(D, L) = \sum_{k=k^o}^{L} \frac{k^o \alpha + N}{k \alpha + N} P(k \mid D)$$

and then

$$P(X^{N+1} = i \mid D) = \begin{cases} \frac{\alpha + N_i}{k^o \alpha + N} C(D, L) & \text{if } i \in \Sigma^o \\ \frac{1}{n - k^o}(1 - C(D, L)) & \text{if } i \notin \Sigma^o \end{cases}$$

We can therefore think of $C(D, L)$ as scaling factor that we apply to the Dirichlet prediction that assumes that we have seen all of the feasible symbols. The quantity $1 - C(D, L)$ is the probability mass assigned to *novel* (i.e., unseen) outcomes. Using properties of Dirichlet priors we get the following characterization of $C(D, L)$.

Proposition 3.1: $P(S = k \mid D) = \frac{m_k}{\sum_{k' \geq k^o} m_{k'}}$ where $m_k = P(S = k) \frac{k!}{(k-k^o)!} \cdot \frac{\Gamma(k\alpha)}{\Gamma(k\alpha+N)}$.

Proof: To compute $C(D, L)$, we need to compute $P(S = k \mid D)$. Using Bayes rule, we have that

$$P(k \mid D) = \frac{P(D \mid S = k) P(S = k)}{\sum_{k'} P(D \mid S = k') P(S = k')} \qquad (7)$$

By introduction of variables, we have that:

$$P(D \mid S = k) = \sum_{V \supseteq \Sigma^o, |V| = k} P(D \mid V) P(V \mid S = k).$$

Using standard properties of Dirichlet priors, we have that if $\Sigma^o \subseteq V$, then

$$P(D|V) = \frac{\Gamma(|V|\alpha)}{\Gamma(|V|\alpha + N)} \prod_{i \in V^o} \frac{\Gamma(\alpha + N_i)}{\Gamma(\alpha)} \qquad (8)$$

Now, using Eq. (8) and (5), we get that if $\Sigma^o \subseteq V$, and $k = |V|$, then

$$P(D \mid V) P(V \mid S = k) = \binom{L}{k}^{-1} \frac{\Gamma(k\alpha)}{\Gamma(k\alpha + N)} \Gamma(\alpha)^{-k^o} \prod_{i \in \Sigma^o} \Gamma(\alpha + N_i). \qquad (9)$$

Thus,

$$\begin{aligned}
P(D \mid S = k) &= \binom{L - k^o}{k - k^o} \binom{L}{k}^{-1} \frac{\Gamma(k\alpha)}{\Gamma(k\alpha + N)} \Gamma(\alpha)^{-k^o} \prod_{i \in \Sigma^o} \Gamma(\alpha + N_i) \\
&= \left[\frac{(L - k^o)!}{L!} \Gamma(\alpha)^{-k^o} \prod_{i \in \Sigma^o} \Gamma(\alpha + N_i) \right] \frac{k!}{(k - k^o)!} \cdot \frac{\Gamma(k\alpha)}{\Gamma(k\alpha + N)} \quad (10)
\end{aligned}$$

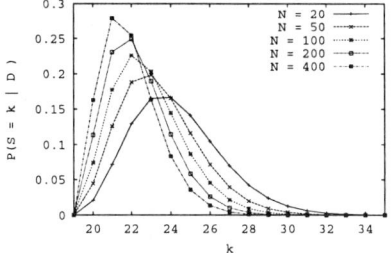
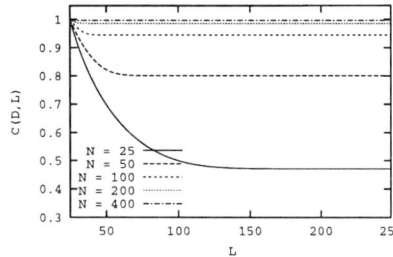

Figure 1: Left: Illustration of the posterior distribution $P(S \mid D)$ for different values of N, with $k^o = 20$, $L = 100$, $\alpha = .25$, and $P(S = k) \propto 0.25^k$. Right: Illustration showing the change in $C(D, L)$ for different values of N, with $k^o = 25$, $\alpha = 1$, and $P(S = k) \propto 0.9^k$.

The term in the square brackets does not depend on the choice of k. Thus, it cancels out when plug Eq. (10) in Eq.(7). The desired equality follows directly. ∎

From the above proposition we immediately get that

$$C(D, L) = \left(\sum_{k=k^o}^{L} \frac{k^o \alpha + N}{k\alpha + N} m_k \right) \left(\sum_{k' \geq k^o} m_k \right)^{-1}. \quad (11)$$

Note that $P(S = k \mid D)$ and $C(D, L)$ depend only on k^o and N and does not depend on the distribution of counts among the k^o observed symbols. Also note that when N is sufficiently larger than k^o (and this depends on the choice of α), then the term $\frac{k!}{(k-k^o)!} \cdot \frac{\Gamma(k\alpha)}{\Gamma(k\alpha+N)}$ is much smaller than 1. This implies that the posterior for larger sets decays rapidly. We can see this behavior on the left hand side of Figure 1 that shows the posterior distribution of $P(S \mid D)$ for different dataset sizes.

4 Unbounded alphabets

By examining the analytic form of $C(D, L)$, we see that the dependency on L is expressed only in the number of terms in the summation. If the terms m_k vanish for large k, then $C(D, L)$ becomes insensitive to the exact size of the alphabet. We can see this behavior on the right hand side of Figure 1, which shows $C(D, L)$ as a function of L. As we can see, when L is close to k^o, then $C(D, L)$ is close to 1. As L grows, $C(D, L)$ asymptotes to a value that depends on N and k^o (as well as α and the prior $P(S = k)$).

This discussion suggests that we can apply our prior in cases where we do not know L in advance. In fact, we can assume that L is unbounded. That is, Σ is isomorphic to $\{1, 2, \ldots\}$. Assume that we assign the prior $P(S = k)$ for each choice of L, and that $\lim_{L \to \infty} P(S = k)$ exists for all k. We define $C(D, \infty) = \lim_{L \to \infty} C(D, L)$. We then use for prediction the term $P(X^{N+1} = i \mid D) = \frac{\alpha + N_i}{k^o \alpha + N} C(D, \infty)$.

For this method to work, we have to ensure that $C(D, \infty)$ is well defined; that is, that the limit exists. Two such cases are identified by the following proposition (proof omitted).

Proposition 4.1: *If $P(S = k)$ is exponentially decreasing in k or if $\alpha \geq 1$ and $P(S = k)$ is polynomially decreasing in k, then $C(D, \infty)$ is well-defined.*

In practice we evaluate $C(D, \infty)$ by computing successive values of (the logarithm of) m_k, until we reach values that are significantly smaller than the largest value beforehand.

	Perplexity		
Method	Observed	Novel	Overall
A ($\frac{N_i}{N+r}$)	28.19	141.7	28.20
B (Approximated Good-Turing)	28.15	802.7	28.19
Sparse-Multinomial (Poly)	27.97	3812.9	28.02
Sparse-Multinomial (Exp)	27.97	3913.1	28.03

Table 1: Perplexity results on heterogeneous character data.

Since m_k is exponentially decaying, we can ignore the mass in the tail of the sequence. As we can see from the right hand side of Figure 1, there is not much difference between the prediction using a large L, and unbounded one.

5 Empirical evaluation

We used the proposed estimation method to construct statistical models for predicting the probability of characters in the context of the previously observed character. Such models, often referred to as bigram models, are of great interest in applications such as optical character recognition and text compression. We tested two of prior distributions for the alphabet size $P_0(S = k)$: an exponential prior, $P_0(S = k) \propto \beta^k$, and a polynomial prior, $P_0(S = k) \propto k^{-\beta}$. The training and test material were derived from various archives and included different types of files such C programs, core dumps, and ascii text files. The alphabet for the algorithm consists of all the (ascii and non-ascii) 256 possible characters. The training data consisted of around 170 mega bytes and for testing we used 35 mega bytes.

Each model we compared had to assign a probability to any character. If a character was not observed in the context of the previous character, the new character is assigned the probability of the total mass of novel events. We compared our approach with two estimation techniques that have been shown to perform well on natural data sets [13]. The first estimates the probability of a symbol i in the context of a given word as $\frac{N_i}{N+r}$ where r is the number of different characters observed at given context (the previous character). The second method, based on an approximation of the Good-Turing estimation scheme [5], estimates the probability of a symbol i as $\frac{(1-f_1/N)N_i}{N}$, where f_1 is the number of different characters that have been observed only once at for the given context (for more details see [13]). For evaluation we used the perplexity which is simply the exponentiation of the average log-loss on the test data. Table 1 summarizes the average test-set perplexity for observed characters, novel events, and the overall perplexity. In the experiments we fixed $\alpha = 1/2$ for the parameters of the Dirichlet priors and $\beta = 2$ for the exponentially and polynomially decaying priors of the alphabet size.

One can see from the table that predictions using sparse-multinomials achieve the lowest overall perplexity. (The differences are statistically significant due to the size of the data.) The performance based on the two different priors for the alphabet size is comparable. The results indicate the all the leverage in using sparse-multinomials for prediction is due to more accurate predictions for observed events. Indeed, the perplexity of novel events using sparse-multinomials is much higher than when using either method A or B. Put another way, our approach prefers to "sacrifice" events with low probability (novel events) and suffer high loss in favor of more accurate predictions for frequently occurring events. The net effect is a lower overall perplexity.

6 Discussion

In this paper we presented a Bayesian approach for the problem of estimating the parameters of a multinomial source over a large alphabet. Our method is based on hierarchical priors. We clearly identify the assumptions made by these priors. Given these assumptions, prediction reduces to probabilistic inference. Our main result is showing how to perform this inference *exactly* in an efficient manner. Among the numerous techniques that have been used for multinomial estimation the one proposed by Ristad [10] is the closest to ours. Though the methodology used by Ristad is substantially different than ours, his method can been seen as a special case of sparse-multinomials with α set to 1 and with a specific prior on alphabet sizes. The main advantage of these choices is a simpler inference procedure. This simplicity comes at the price of losing flexibility. In addition, our method explicitly represents the posterior distribution. Hence, it is more suitable for tasks, such as stochastic sampling, where an explicit representation of the approximated distribution is required. Finally, our method can be combined with other Bayesian approaches for language modeling such as the one proposed by MacKay and Peto [8], and with Bayesian approaches for learning complex models such as Bayesian networks [6].

Acknowledgments We are grateful to Fernando Pereira and Stuart Russell for discussions related to this work. This work was done while Nir Friedman was at U.C. Berkeley and supported by ARO under grant number DAAH04-96-1-0341 and by ONR under grant number N00014-97-1-0941.

References

[1] W. Buntine. Learning classification trees. In *Artificial Intelligence Frontiers in Statistics*. Chapman & Hall, 1993.

[2] B.S. Clarke and A.R. Barron. Jeffrey's prior is asymptotically least favorable under entropic risk. *J. Stat. Planning and Inference*, 41:37–60, 1994.

[3] G. F. Cooper and E. Herskovits. A Bayesian method for the induction of probabilistic networks from data. *Machine Learning*, 9:309–347, 1992.

[4] M. H. DeGroot. *Optimal Statistical Decisions*. McGraw-Hill, 1970.

[5] I.J. Good. The population frequencies of species and the estimation of population parameters. *Biometrika*, 40(3):237–264, 1953.

[6] D. Heckerman, D. Geiger, and D. M. Chickering. Learning Bayesian networks: The combination of knowledge and statistical data. *Machine Learning*, 20:197–243, 1995.

[7] P.S. Laplace. *Philosophical Essay on Probabilities*. Springer-Verlag, 1995.

[8] D.J.C. MacKay and L. Peto. A hierarchical Dirichlet language model. *Natural Language Eng.*, 1(3):1–19, 1995.

[9] L. R. Rabiner and B. H. Juang. An introduction to hidden Markov models. *IEEE ASSP Mag.*, 3(1):4–16, 1986.

[10] E. Ristad. A natural law of succession. Tech. Report CS-TR-495-95, Princeton Univ., 1995.

[11] Y. Singer. Adaptive mixtures of probabilistic transducers. *Neur. Comp.*, 9(8):1711–1734, 1997.

[12] F.M.J. Willems, Y.M. Shtarkov, and T.J. Tjalkens. The context tree weighting method: basic properties. *IEEE Trans. on Info. Theory*, 41(3):653–664, 1995.

[13] I.H. Witten and T.C. Bell. The zero-frequency problem: estimating the probabilities of novel events in adaptive text compression. *IEEE Trans. on Info. Theory*, 37(4):1085–1094, 1991.

A Randomized Algorithm for Pairwise Clustering

Yoram Gdalyahu, Daphna Weinshall, Michael Werman
Institute of Computer Science, The Hebrew University, 91904 Jerusalem, Israel
{yoram,daphna,werman}@cs.huji.ac.il

Abstract

We present a stochastic clustering algorithm based on pairwise similarity of datapoints. Our method extends existing deterministic methods, including agglomerative algorithms, min-cut graph algorithms, and connected components. Thus it provides a common framework for all these methods. Our graph-based method differs from existing stochastic methods which are based on analogy to physical systems. The stochastic nature of our method makes it more robust against noise, including accidental edges and small spurious clusters. We demonstrate the superiority of our algorithm using an example with 3 spiraling bands and a lot of noise.

1 Introduction

Clustering algorithms can be divided into two categories: those that require a vectorial representation of the data, and those which use only pairwise representation. In the former case, every data item must be represented as a vector in a real normed space, while in the second case only pairwise relations of similarity or dissimilarity are used. The pairwise information can be represented by a weighted graph $G(V, E)$: the nodes V represent data items, and the positive weight w_{ij} of an edge (i, j) representing the amount of similarity or dissimilarity between items i and j. The graph G might not be a complete graph. In the rest of this paper w_{ij} represents a similarity value.

A vectorial representation is very convenient when one has either an explicit or an implicit parametric model for the data. An implicit model means that the data distribution function is not known, but it is assumed, e.g., that every cluster is symmetrically distributed around some center. An explicit model specifically describes the *shape* of the distribution (e.g., Gaussian). In these cases, if a vectorial representation is available, the clustering procedure may rely on iterative estimation of means (e.g., [2, 8]).

In the absence of a vectorial representation, one can either try to embed the graph of distances in a vector space, or use a direct pairwise clustering method. The embedding problem is difficult, since it is desirable to use a representation that is both low dimensional and has a low distortion of distances [6, 7, 3]. Moreover, even if such embedding is achieved, it can help to cluster the data only if at least an implicit parametric model is valid. Hence, direct methods for pairwise clustering are of great value.

One strategy of pairwise clustering is to use a similarity threshold θ, remove edges with weight less than θ, and identify the connected components that remain as clusters. A transformation of weights may precede the thresholding[1]. The physically motivated transformation in [1] uses a granular magnet model and replaces weights by "spin correlations". Our algorithm is similar to this model, see Section 2.4.

A second pairwise clustering strategy is used by agglomerative algorithms [2], which start with the trivial partition of N points into N clusters of size one, and continue by subsequently merging pairs of clusters. At every step the two clusters which are most similar are merged together, until the similarity of the closest clusters is lower than some threshold. Different similarity measures between clusters distinguish between different agglomerative algorithms. In particular, the single linkage algorithm defines the similarity between clusters as the maximal similarity between two of their members, and the complete linkage algorithm uses the minimal value.

A third strategy of pairwise clustering uses the notion of cuts in a graph. A cut (A, B) in a graph $G(V, E)$ is a partition of V into two disjoint sets A and B. The capacity of the cut is the sum of weights of all edges that cross the cut, namely: $c(A, B) = \sum_{i \in A, j \in B} w_{ij}$. Among all the cuts that separate two marked vertices, the *minimal cut* is the one which has minimal capacity. The minimal cut clustering algorithm [11] divides the graph into components using a cascade of minimal cuts[2].

The normalized cut algorithm [9] uses the association of A (sum of weights incident on A) and the association of B to normalize the capacity $c(A, B)$. In contrast with the easy min-cut problem, the problem of finding a minimal normalized cut (Ncut) is NP-hard, but with certain approximations it reduces to a generalized eigenvalue problem [9].

Other pairwise clustering methods include techniques of non parametric density estimation [4] and pairwise deterministic annealing [3]. However, the three categories of methods above are of special importance to us, since our current work provides a common framework for all of them. Specifically, our new algorithm may be viewed as a randomized version of an agglomerative clustering procedure, and in the same time it generalizes the minimal cut algorithm. It is also strongly related to the physically motivated granular magnet model algorithm. By showing the connection between these methods, which may seem very different at a first glance, we provide a better understanding of pairwise clustering.

Our method is unique in its stochastic nature while provenly maintaining low complexity. Thus our method performs as well as the aforementioned methods in "easy" cases, while keeping the good performance in "difficult" cases. In particular, it is more robust against noise and pathological configurations: (i) A *minimal cut* algorithm is intuitively reasonable since it optimizes so that as much of the similarity

---

[1]For example, the mutual neighborhood clustering algorithm [10] substitutes the edge weight w_{ij} with a new weight $w'_{ij} = m + n$ where i is the mth nearest neighbor of j and j is the nth nearest neighbor of i.

[2]The reader who is familiar with flow theory may notice that this algorithm also belongs to the first category of methods, as it is equivalent to a weight transformation followed by thresholding. The weight transformation replaces w_{ij} by the maximal flow between i and j.

weight remains within the parts of the clusters, and as little as possible is "wasted" between the clusters. However, it tends to fail when there is no clean separation into 2 parts, or when there are many small spurious parts due, e.g., to noise. Our stochastic approach avoids these problems and behaves more robustly. (ii) The *single linkage* algorithm deals well with chained data, where items in a cluster are connected by transitive relations. Unfortunately the deterministic construction of chains can be harmful in the presence of noise, where a few points can make a "bridge" between two large clusters and merge them together. Our algorithm inherits the ability to cluster chained data; at the same time it is robust against such noisy bridges as long as the probability to select all the edges in the bridge remains small.

2 Stochastic pairwise clustering

Our randomized clustering algorithm is constructed of two main steps:

1. Stochastic partition of the similarity graph into r parts (by randomized agglomeration). For each partition index r ($r = N \ldots 1$):
   (a) for every pair of points, the probability that they remain in the same part is computed;
   (b) the weight of the edge between the two points is replaced by this probability;
   (c) clusters are formed using connected components and threshold of 0.5.

   This is described in Sections 2.1 and 2.2.

2. Selection of proper r values, which reflect "interesting" structure in our problem. This is described in Section 2.3.

2.1 The similarity transformation

At each level r, our algorithm performs a similarity transformation followed by thresholding. In introducing this process, our starting point is a generalization of the minimal cut algorithm; then we show how this generalization is obtained by the randomization of a single linkage algorithm.

First, instead of considering only the minimal cuts, let us induce a probability distribution on the set of *all* cuts. We assign to each cut a probability which decreases with increasing capacity. Hence the minimal cut is the most probable cut in the graph, but it does not determine the graph partition on its own.

As a second generalization to the min-cut algorithm we consider multi-way cuts. An *r-way cut* is a partition of G into r connected components. The capacity of an r-way cut is the sum of weights of all edges that connect different components. In the rest of this paper we may refer to r-way cuts simply as "cuts".

Using the distribution induced on r-way cuts, we apply the following family of *weight transformations*. The weight w_{ij} is replaced by the probability that nodes i and j are in the same side of a random r-way cut: $w_{ij} \to p_{ij}^r$. This transformation is defined for every integer r between 1 and N.

Since the number of cuts in a graph is exponentially large, one must ask whether p_{ij}^r is computable. Here the decaying rate of the cut probability plays an essential role. The induced probability is found to decay fast enough with the capacity, hence p_{ij}^r is dominated by the low capacity cuts. Thus, since there exists a polynomial bound on the number of low capacity cuts in any graph [5], the problem becomes computable.

This strong property suggests a sampling scheme to estimate the pairing probabilities. Assume that a sampling tool is available, which generates cuts according to their probability. Under this condition, a sample of polynomial size is sufficient to estimate the p_{ij}^r's.

The sampling tool that we use is called the "contraction algorithm" [5]. Its discovery led to an efficient probabilistic algorithm for the minimal cut problem. It was shown that for a given r, the probability that the contraction algorithm returns the minimal r-way cut of any graph is at least $N^{-2(r-1)}$, and it decays with increasing capacity[3]. For a graph which is really made of clusters this is a rough underestimation.

The contraction algorithm can be implemented in several ways. We describe here its simplest form, which is constructed from N-1 *edge contraction* steps. Each edge contraction follows the procedure below:

- Select edge (i, j) with probability proportional to w_{ij}.
- Replace nodes i and j by a single node $\{ij\}$.
- Let the set of edges incident on $\{ij\}$ be the union of the sets of edges incident on i and j, but remove self loops formed by edges originally connecting i to j.

It is shown in [5] that each step of edge contraction can be implemented in $O(N)$ time, hence this simple form of the contraction algorithm has complexity of $O(N^2)$. For sparse graphs an $O(N \log N)$ implementation can be shown.

The contraction algorithm as described above is a randomized version of the agglomerative single linkage procedure. If the probabilistic selection rule is replaced by a greedy selection of the maximal weight edge, the single linkage algorithm is obtained.

In terms of similarity transformations, a single linkage algorithm which halts with r clusters may be associated with the transformation $w_{ij} \to 0,1$ (1 if i and j are returned at the same cluster, 0 otherwise). Our similarity transformation (p_{ij}^r) uses the expected value (or the average) of of this binary assignment under the probabilistic relaxation of the selection rule.

We could estimate p_{ij}^r by repeating the contraction algorithm M times and averaging these binary indicators (a better way is described below). Using Chernoff inequality it can be shown[4] that if $M \geq (2 \ln 2 + 4 \ln N - 2 \ln \delta)/\epsilon^2$ then each p_{ij}^r is estimated, with probability $\geq 1 - \delta$, within ϵ from its true value.

2.2 Construction of partitions

To compute a partition at every r level, it is sufficient to know for every i-j pair which r satisfies $p_{ij}^r = 0.5$.

This is found by repeating the contraction algorithm M times. In each iteration there exists a single r at which the edge between points $i - j$ is marked and the points are merged. Denote by r_m the level r which joins i and j at the m-th iteration ($m = 1 \ldots M$). The median r' of the sequence $\{r_1, r_2 \ldots r_M\}$ is the sample estimate

---

[3]The exact decay rate is not known, but found experimentally to be adequate. Otherwise we would ignore cuts generated with high capacity.
[4]Thanks to Ido Bergman for pointing this out.

for the level r that satisfies $p_{ij}^r = 0.5$. We use an on-line technique (not described here) to estimate the median r' using constant and small memory.

Having computed the matrix r', where the entry r'_{ij} is the estimator for r that satisfies $p_{ij}^r = 0.5$, we find the connected components at a given r value after disconnecting every edge (i,j) for which $r'_{ij} > r$. This gives the r level partition.

2.3 Hierarchical clustering

We now address the problem of choosing "good" r values.

The transformed weight p_{ij}^r has the advantage of reflecting transitive relations between data items i and j. For a selected value of r (which defines a specification level) the partition of data items into clusters is obtained by eliminating edges whose weight (p_{ij}^r) is less than a fixed threshold (0.5). That is: nodes are assigned to the same cluster if at level r their probability to be on the same side of a random r-way cut is larger than half.

Partitions which correspond to subsequent r values might be very similar to each other, or even identical, in the sense that only a few nodes (if at all) change the component to which they belong. Events which are of interest, therefore, are when the variation between subsequent partitions is of the order of the size of a cluster. This typically happens when two clusters combine to form one cluster which corresponds to a higher scale (less resolution).

In accordance, using the hierarchical partition obtained in Section 2.2, we measure the variation between subsequent partitions by $\sum_{k=1}^{K} \Delta N_k$, where K is a small constant (of the order of the number of clusters) and N_k is the size of the kth largest component of the partition.

2.4 The granular magnet model

Our algorithm is closely related to the successful granular magnet model recently proposed in [1]. However, the two methods draw the random cuts effectively from different distributions. In our case the distribution is data driven, imposed by the contraction algorithm. The physical model imposes the Boltzmann distribution, where a cut of capacity E is assigned a probability proportional to $\exp(-E/T)$, and T is a temperature parameter.

The probability p_{ij}^T measures whether nodes i and j are on the same side of a cut at temperature T (originally called "spin-spin correlation function"). The magnetic model uses the similarity transformation $w_{ij} \to p_{ij}^T$ and a threshold (0.5) to break the graph into components. However, even if identical distributions were used, p_{ij}^T is inherently different from p_{ij}^r since at a fixed temperature the random cuts may have different numbers of components.

Superficially, the parameter T plays in the magnetic model a similar role to our parameter r. But the two parameterizations are quite different. First, r is a discrete parameter while T is a continuous one. Moreover, in order to find the pairing probabilities p_{ij}^T for different temperatures, the stochastic process should be employed for every T value separately. On the other hand, our algorithm estimates p_{ij}^r for every $1 \leq r \leq N$ at once. For hard clustering (v.s. soft clustering) it was shown above that even this is not necessary, since we can get a direct estimation of r which satisfies $p_{ij}^r = 0.5$.

3 Example

Pairwise clustering has the advantage that a vectorial representation of the data is not needed. However, graphs of distances are hard to visualize and we therefore demonstrate our algorithm using vectorial data. In spite of having vectorial representation, the information which is made available to the clustering algorithm includes only the matrix of pairwise Euclidean distances[5] d_{ij}. Since our algorithm works with similarity values and not with distances, it is necessary to invert the distances using $w_{ij} = f(d_{ij})$. We choose f to be similar to the function used in [1]: $w_{ij} = \exp(-d_{ij}^2/a^2)$ where a is the average distance to the n-th nearest neighbor (we used $n=10$, but the results remain the same as long as a reasonable value is selected).

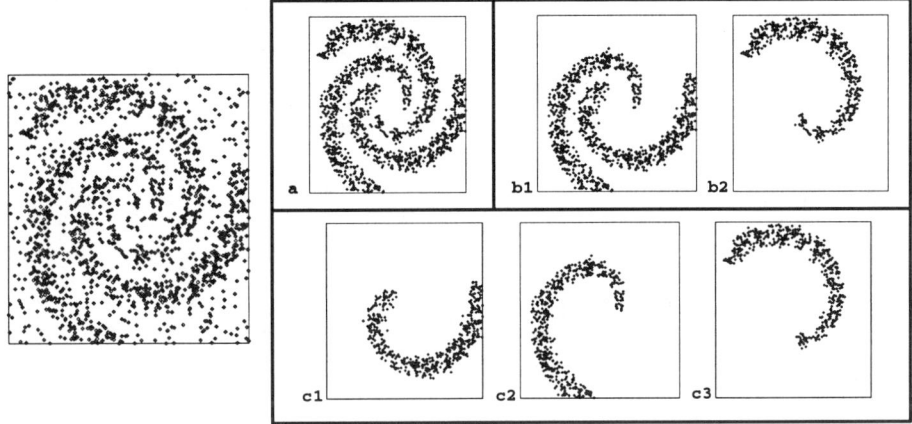

Figure 1: The 2000 data points (left), and the three most pronounced hierarchical levels of clustering (right). At $r=353$ the three spirals form one cluster (figure a). This cluster splits at $r=354$ into two (figures b1,b2), and into three parts at $r=368$ (figures c1,c2,c3). The background points form isolated clusters, usualy of size 1 (not shown).

Figure 1 shows 2000 data points in the Euclidean plane. In the stochastic stage of the algorithm we used only 200 iterations of graph contraction, during which we estimated for every pair i-j the value of r which satisfies $p_{ij}^r = 0.5$ (see Section 2.2).

As expected, subsequent partitions are typically identical or differ only slightly from each other (Figure 2). The variation between subsequent partitions was measured using the 10 largest parts ($K = 10$, see Section 2.3). The results did not depend on the exact value of K since the sum was dominated by its first terms.

At low r values (partition into a small number of components) a typical partition is composed of one giant component and a few tiny components that capture isolated noise points. The incorporation of these tiny components into the giant one produce negligible variations between subsequent partitions. At high r values all the components are small, and therefore the variation between subsequent partitions must decay. At intermediate r values a small number of sharp peaks appear.

The two highest peaks in Figure 2 are at $r=354$ and $r=368$; they mark meaningful hierarchies for the data clustering, as shown in Figure 1. We compare our results with two other methods in Figures 3 and 4.

---

[5]The vectorial representation of data points is not useful even if it was available, since the parametric model is not known (see Section 1)

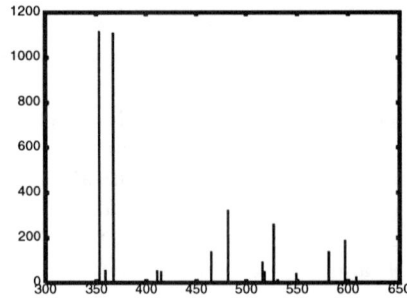

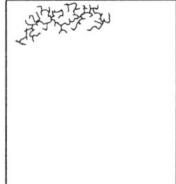

Figure 2: The variation between subsequent partitions (see text) as a function of the number of components (r). The variation is computed for every integer r (the spacing between peaks is *not* due to sparse sampling). Outside the displayed range the variation vanishes.

Figure 3: The best bi-partition according to the normalized cut algorithm [9]. Since the first partition breaks one of the spirals, a satisfactory solution cannot be achieved in any of the later stages.

Figure 4: A three (macroscopic) clusters partition by a deterministic single linkage algorithm. The probabilistic scheme avoids the "bridging effect" thanks to the small probability of selecting the particular chain of edges.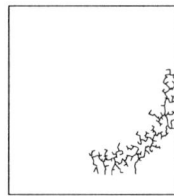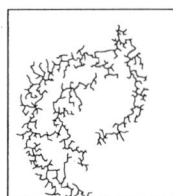

References

[1] Blatt M., Wiseman S. and Domany E., "Data clustering using a model granular magnet", Neural Computation 9, 1805-1842, 1997.

[2] Duda O. and Hart E., *"Pattern classification and scene analysis"*, Wiley-Interscience, New York, 1973.

[3] Hofmann T. and Buhmann J., "Pairwise data clustering by deterministic annealing", PAMI 19, 1-14, 1997.

[4] Jain A. and Dubes R., *"Algorithms for clustering data"*, Prentice Hall, NJ, 1988.

[5] Karger D., "A new approach to the minimum cut problem", Journal of the ACM, 43(4) 1996.

[6] Klock H. and Buhmann J., "Data visualization by multidimensional scaling: a deterministic annealing approach", Technical Report IAI-TR-96-8, Institut fur Informatik III, University of Bonn. October 1996.

[7] Linial N., London E. and Rabinovich Y., "The geometry of graphs and some of its algorithmic applications", Combinatorica 15, 215-245, 1995.

[8] Rose K., Gurewitz E. and Fox G., "Constrained clustering as an optimization method", PAMI 15, 785-794, 1993.

[9] Shi J. and Malik J., "Normalized cuts and image segmentation", Proc. CVPR, 731-737, 1997.

[10] Smith S., "Threshold validity for mutual neighborhood clustering", PAMI 15, 89-92, 1993.

[11] Wu Z. and Leahy R., "An optimal graph theoretic approach to data clustering: theory and its application to image segmentation", PAMI 15, 1101-1113, 1993.

Learning Nonlinear Dynamical Systems using an EM Algorithm

Zoubin Ghahramani and Sam T. Roweis

Gatsby Computational Neuroscience Unit
University College London
London WC1N 3AR, U.K.
http://www.gatsby.ucl.ac.uk/

Abstract

The Expectation–Maximization (EM) algorithm is an iterative procedure for maximum likelihood parameter estimation from data sets with missing or hidden variables [2]. It has been applied to system identification in linear stochastic state-space models, where the state variables are hidden from the observer and both the state and the parameters of the model have to be estimated simultaneously [9]. We present a generalization of the EM algorithm for parameter estimation in *nonlinear* dynamical systems. The "expectation" step makes use of Extended Kalman Smoothing to estimate the state, while the "maximization" step re-estimates the parameters using these uncertain state estimates. In general, the nonlinear maximization step is difficult because it requires integrating out the uncertainty in the states. However, if Gaussian radial basis function (RBF) approximators are used to model the nonlinearities, the integrals become tractable and the maximization step can be solved via systems of linear equations.

1 Stochastic Nonlinear Dynamical Systems

We examine inference and learning in discrete-time dynamical systems with hidden state x_t, inputs u_t, and outputs y_t.[1] The state evolves according to stationary nonlinear dynamics driven by the inputs and by additive noise

$$x_{t+1} = f(x_t, u_t) + w \qquad (1)$$

---

[1] All lowercase characters (except indices) denote vectors. Matrices are represented by uppercase characters.

where w is zero-mean Gaussian noise with covariance Q.[2] The outputs are non-linearly related to the states and inputs by

$$y_t = g(x_t, u_t) + v \tag{2}$$

where v is zero-mean Gaussian noise with covariance R. The vector-valued nonlinearities f and g are assumed to be differentiable, but otherwise arbitrary.

Models of this kind have been examined for decades in various communities. Most notably, nonlinear state-space models form one of the cornerstones of modern systems and control engineering. In this paper, we examine these models within the framework of probabilistic graphical models and derive a novel learning algorithm for them based on EM. With one exception,[3] this is to the best of our knowledge the first paper addressing learning of stochastic nonlinear dynamical systems of the kind we have described within the framework of the EM algorithm.

The classical approach to system identification treats the parameters as hidden variables, and applies the Extended Kalman Filtering algorithm (described in section 2) to the nonlinear system with the state vector augmented by the parameters [5].[4] This approach is inherently on-line, which may be important in certain applications. Furthermore, it provides an estimate of the covariance of the parameters at each time step. In contrast, the EM algorithm we present is a batch algorithm and does not attempt to estimate the covariance of the parameters.

There are three important advantages the EM algorithm has over the classical approach. First, the EM algorithm provides a straightforward and principled method for handing missing inputs or outputs. Second, EM generalizes readily to more complex models with combinations of discrete and real-valued hidden variables. For example, one can formulate EM for a *mixture* of nonlinear dynamical systems. Third, whereas it is often very difficult to prove or analyze stability within the classical on-line approach, the EM algorithm is always attempting to maximize the likelihood, which acts as a Lyapunov function for stable learning.

In the next sections we will describe the basic components of the learning algorithm. For the expectation step of the algorithm, we infer the conditional distribution of the hidden states using Extended Kalman Smoothing (section 2). For the maximization step we first discuss the general case (section 3) and then describe the particular case where the nonlinearities are represented using Gaussian radial basis function (RBF; [6]) networks (section 4).

2 Extended Kalman Smoothing

Given a system described by equations (1) and (2), we need to infer the hidden states from a history of observed inputs and outputs. The quantity at the heart of this inference problem is the conditional density $P(x_t|u_1, \ldots, u_T, y_1, \ldots, y_T)$, for $1 \leq t \leq T$, which captures the fact that the system is stochastic and therefore our inferences about x will be uncertain.

---

[2] The Gaussian noise assumption is less restrictive for nonlinear systems than for linear systems since the nonlinearity can be used to generate non-Gaussian state noise.

[3] The authors have just become aware that Briegel and Tresp (this volume) have applied EM to essentially the same model. Briegel and Tresp's method uses multilayer perceptrons (MLP) to approximate the nonlinearities, and requires sampling from the hidden states to fit the MLP. We use Gaussian radial basis functions (RBFs) to model the nonlinearities, which can be fit analytically without sampling (see section 4).

[4] It is important not to confuse this use of the Extended Kalman algorithm, to simultaneously estimate parameters and hidden states, with our use of EKS, to estimate just the hidden state as part of the E step of EM.

For linear dynamical systems with Gaussian state evolution and observation noises, this conditional density is Gaussian and the recursive algorithm for computing its mean and covariance is known as *Kalman smoothing* [4, 8]. Kalman smoothing is directly analogous to the forward–backward algorithm for computing the conditional hidden state distribution in a hidden Markov model, and is also a special case of the belief propagation algorithm.[5]

For nonlinear systems this conditional density is in general non-Gaussian and can in fact be quite complex. Multiple approaches exist for inferring the hidden state distribution of such nonlinear systems, including sampling methods [7] and variational approximations [3]. We focus instead in this paper on a classic approach from engineering, *Extended Kalman Smoothing* (EKS).

Extended Kalman Smoothing simply applies Kalman smoothing to a local *linearization* of the nonlinear system. At every point $\tilde{x}$ in x-space, the derivatives of the vector-valued functions f and g define the matrices, $A_{\tilde{x}} \equiv \frac{\partial f}{\partial x}\big|_{x=\tilde{x}}$ and $C_{\tilde{x}} \equiv \frac{\partial g}{\partial x}\big|_{x=\tilde{x}}$, respectively. The dynamics are linearized about $\hat{x}_t$, the mean of the Kalman filter state estimate at time t:

$$x_{t+1} = f(\hat{x}_t, u_t) + A_{\hat{x}_t}(x_t - \hat{x}_t) + w. \tag{3}$$

The output equation (2) can be similarly linearized. If the prior distribution of the hidden state at $t = 1$ was Gaussian, then, in this linearized system, the conditional distribution of the hidden state at any time t given the history of inputs and outputs will also be Gaussian. Thus, Kalman smoothing can be used on the linearized system to infer this conditional distribution (see figure 1, left panel).

3 Learning

The M step of the EM algorithm re-estimates the parameters given the observed inputs, outputs, and the conditional distributions over the hidden states. For the model we have described, the parameters define the nonlinearities f and g, and the noise covariances Q and R.

Two complications arise in the M step. First, it may not be computationally feasible to fully re-estimate f and g. For example, if they are represented by neural network regressors, a single full M step would be a lengthy training procedure using backpropagation, conjugate gradients, or some other optimization method. Alternatively, one could use partial M steps, for example, each consisting of one or a few gradient steps.

The second complication is that f and g have to be trained using the uncertain state estimates output by the EKS algorithm. Consider fitting f, which takes as inputs x_t and u_t and outputs x_{t+1}. For each t, the conditional density estimated by EKS is a full-covariance Gaussian in (x_t, x_{t+1})-space. So f has to be fit not to a set of data points but instead to a mixture of full-covariance Gaussians in input-output space (Gaussian "clouds" of data). Integrating over this type of noise is non-trivial for almost any form of f. One simple but inefficient approach to bypass this problem is to draw a large sample from these Gaussian clouds of uncertain data and then fit f to these samples in the usual way. A similar situation occurs with g.

In the next section we show how, by choosing Gaussian radial basis functions to model f and g, both of these complications vanish.

---

[5]The forward part of the Kalman smoother is the Kalman filter.

4 Fitting Radial Basis Functions to Gaussian Clouds

We will present a general formulation of an RBF network from which it should be clear how to fit special forms for f and g. Consider the following nonlinear mapping from input vectors x and u to an output vector z:

$$z = \sum_{i=1}^{I} h_i \, \rho_i(x) + Ax + Bu + b + w, \quad (4)$$

where w is a zero-mean Gaussian noise variable with covariance Q. For example, one form of f can be represented using (4) with the substitutions $x \leftarrow x_t$, $u \leftarrow u_t$, and $z \leftarrow x_{t+1}$; another with $x \leftarrow (x_t, u_t)$, $u \leftarrow \emptyset$, and $z \leftarrow x_{t+1}$. The parameters are: the coefficients of the I RBFs, h_i; the matrices A and B multiplying inputs x and u, respectively; and an output bias vector b. Each RBF is assumed to be a Gaussian in x-space, with center c_i and width given by the covariance matrix S_i:

$$\rho_i(x) = |2\pi S_i|^{-1/2} \exp\left\{-\frac{1}{2}(x - c_i)^\top S_i^{-1}(x - c_i)\right\}. \quad (5)$$

The goal is to fit this model to data (u, x, z). The complication is that the data set comes in the form of a mixture of Gaussian distributions. Here we show how to analytically integrate over this mixture distribution to fit the RBF model.

Assume the data set is:

$$P(x, z, u) = \frac{1}{J} \sum_j \mathcal{N}_j(x, z) \, \delta(u - u_j). \quad (6)$$

That is, we observe samples from the u variables, each paired with a Gaussian "cloud" of data, $\mathcal{N}_j$, over (x, z). The Gaussian $\mathcal{N}_j$ has mean μ_j and covariance matrix C_j.

Let $\hat{z}_\theta(x, u) = \sum_{i=1}^{I} h_i \, \rho_i(x) + Ax + Bu + b$, where θ is the set of parameters $\theta = \{h_1 \ldots h_I, A, B, b\}$. The log likelihood of a single data point under the model is:

$$-\frac{1}{2}[z - \hat{z}_\theta(x, u)]^\top Q^{-1} [z - \hat{z}_\theta(x, u)] - \frac{1}{2} \ln |Q| + \text{const.}$$

The maximum likelihood RBF fit to the mixture of Gaussian data is obtained by minimizing the following integrated quadratic form:

$$\min_{\theta, Q} \left\{ \sum_j \int_x \int_z \mathcal{N}_j(x, z) \, [z - \hat{z}_\theta(x, u_j)]^\top Q^{-1} [z - \hat{z}_\theta(x, u_j)] \, dx \, dz + J \ln |Q| \right\}. \quad (7)$$

We rewrite this in a slightly different notation, using angled brackets $\langle \cdot \rangle_j$ to denote expectation over $\mathcal{N}_j$, and defining

$$\theta \equiv [h_1^\top \, h_2^\top \, \ldots \, h_I^\top \, A^\top \, B^\top \, b^\top]^\top$$
$$\Phi \equiv [\rho_1(x) \, \rho_2(x) \ldots \rho_I(x) \, x \, u \, 1].$$

Then, the objective can be written

$$\min_{\theta, Q} \left\{ \sum_j \langle (z - \theta \, \Phi)^\top Q^{-1} (z - \theta \, \Phi) \rangle_j + J \ln |Q| \right\}. \quad (8)$$

Taking derivatives with respect to θ, premultiplying by $-Q^{-1}$, and setting to zero gives the linear equations $\sum_j \langle (z - \theta\Phi)\Phi^\top \rangle_j = 0$, which we can solve for θ and Q:

$$\hat{\theta} = \left(\sum_j \langle z\Phi^\top \rangle_j\right)\left(\sum_j \langle \Phi\Phi^\top \rangle_j\right)^{-1}, \quad \hat{Q} = \frac{1}{J}\left(\sum_j \langle zz^\top \rangle_j - \hat{\theta}\sum_j \langle \Phi z^\top \rangle_j\right). \quad (9)$$

In other words, given the expectations in the angled brackets, the optimal parameters can be solved for via a set of linear equations. In appendix A we show that these expectations can be computed analytically. The derivation is somewhat laborious, but the intuition is very simple: the Gaussian RBFs multiply with the Gaussian densities $\mathcal{N}_j$ to form new unnormalized Gaussians in (x, y)-space. Expectations under these new Gaussians are easy to compute. This fitting algorithm is illustrated in the right panel of figure 1.

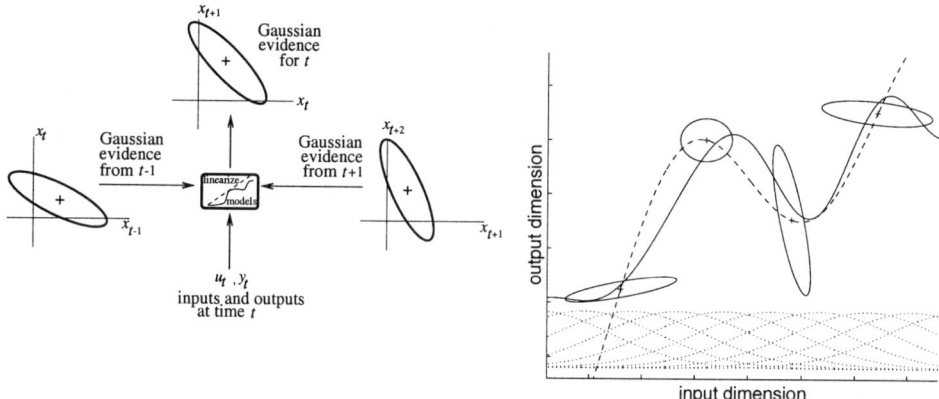

Figure 1: Illustrations of the E and M steps of the algorithm. The left panel shows the information used in Extended Kalman Smoothing (EKS), which infers the hidden state distribution during the E-step. The right panel illustrates the regression technique employed during the M-step. A fit to a mixture of Gaussian densities is required; if Gaussian RBF networks are used then this fit can be solved analytically. The dashed line shows a regular RBF fit to the centres of the four Gaussian densities while the solid line shows the analytic RBF fit using the covariance information. The dotted lines below show the support of the RBF kernels.

5 Results

We tested how well our algorithm could learn the dynamics of a nonlinear system by observing only its inputs and outputs. The system consisted of a single input, state and output variable at each time, where the relation of the state from one time step to the next was given by a tanh nonlinearity. Sample outputs of this system in response to white noise are shown in figure 2 (left panel).

We initialized the nonlinear model with a linear dynamical model trained with EM, which in turn we initialized with a variant of factor analysis. The model was given 11 RBFs in x_t-space, which were uniformly spaced within a range which was automatically determined from the density of points in x_t-space. After the initialization was over, the algorithm discovered the sigmoid nonlinearity in the dynamics within less than 10 iterations of EM (figure 2, middle and right panels).

Further experiments need to be done to determine how practical this method will be in real domains.

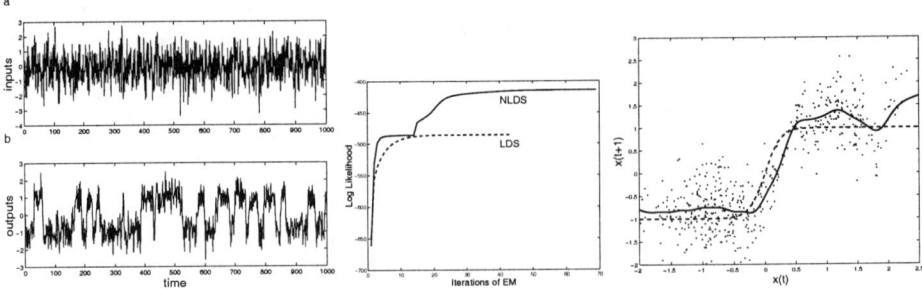

Figure 2: **(left):** Data set used for training (first half) and testing (rest), which consists of a time series of inputs, u_t **(a)**, and outputs y_t **(b)**. **(middle):** Representative plots of log likelihood vs iterations of EM for linear dynamical systems (dashed line) and nonlinear dynamical systems trained as described in this paper (solid line). Note that the actual likelihood for nonlinear dynamical systems cannot generally be computed analytically; what is shown here is the approximate likelihood computed by EKS. The kink in the solid curve comes when initialization with linear dynamics ends and the nonlinearity starts to be learned. **(right):** Means of (x_t, x_{t+1}) Gaussian posteriors computed by EKS (dots), along with the sigmoid nonlinearity (dashed line) and the RBF nonlinearity learned by the algorithm. At no point does the algorithm actually observe (x_t, x_{t+1}) pairs; these are inferred from inputs, outputs, and the current model parameters.

6 Discussion

This paper brings together two classic algorithms, one from statistics and another from systems engineering, to address the learning of stochastic nonlinear dynamical systems. We have shown that by pairing the Extended Kalman Smoothing algorithm for state estimation in the E-step, with a radial basis function learning model that permits analytic solution of the M-step, the EM algorithm is capable of learning a nonlinear dynamical model from data. As a side effect we have derived an algorithm for training a radial basis function network to fit data in the form of a mixture of Gaussians.

Our initial approach has three potential limitations. First, the M-step presented does not modify the centres or widths of the RBF kernels. It is possible to compute the expectations required to change the centres and widths, but it requires resorting to a partial M-step. For low dimensional state spaces, filling the space with pre-fixed kernels is feasible, but this strategy needs exponentially many RBFs in high dimensions. Second, EM training can be slow, especially if initialized poorly. Understanding how different hidden variable models are related can help devise sensible initialization heuristics. For example, for this model we used a nested initialization which first learned a simple linear dynamical system, which in turn was initialized with a variant of factor analysis. Third, the method presented here learns from batches of data and assumes stationary dynamics. We have recently extended it to handle online learning of nonstationary dynamics.

The belief network literature has recently been dominated by two methods for approximate inference, Markov chain Monte Carlo [7] and variational approximations [3]. To our knowledge this paper is the first instance where extended Kalman smoothing has been used to perform approximate inference in the E step of EM. While EKS does not have the theoretical guarantees of variational methods, its simplicity has gained it wide acceptance in the estimation and control literatures as a method for doing inference in nonlinear dynamical systems. We are now exploring generalizations of this method to learning nonlinear multilayer belief networks.

Acknowledgements

ZG would like to acknowledge the support of the CITO (Ontario) and the Gatsby Charitable Fund. STR was supported in part by the NSF Center for Neuromorphic Systems Engineering and by an NSERC of Canada 1967 Award.

A Expectations Required to Fit the RBFs

The expectations we need to compute for equation 9 are $\langle x \rangle_j$, $\langle z \rangle_j$, $\langle xx^\top \rangle_j$, $\langle xz^\top \rangle_j$, $\langle zz^\top \rangle_j$, $\langle \rho_i(x) \rangle_j$, $\langle x\, \rho_i(x) \rangle_j$, $\langle z\, \rho_i(x) \rangle_j$, $\langle \rho_i(x)\, \rho_\ell(x) \rangle_j$.

Starting with some of the easier ones that do not depend on the RBF kernel ρ:

$$\langle x \rangle_j = \mu_j^x \qquad \langle z \rangle_j = \mu_j^z$$
$$\langle xx^\top \rangle_j = \mu_j^x \mu_j^{x,\top} + C_j^{xx} \qquad \langle xz^\top \rangle_j = \mu_j^x \mu_j^{z,\top} + C_j^{xz}$$
$$\langle zz^\top \rangle_j = \mu_j^z \mu_j^{z,\top} + C_j^{zz}$$

Observe that when we multiply the Gaussian RBF kernel $\rho_i(x)$ (equation 5) and $\mathcal{N}_j$ we get a Gaussian density over (x, z) with mean and covariance

$$\mu_{ij} = C_{ij}\left(C_j^{-1} \mu_j + \begin{bmatrix} S_i^{-1} c_i \\ 0 \end{bmatrix} \right) \quad \text{and} \quad C_{ij} = \left(C_j^{-1} + \begin{bmatrix} S_i^{-1} & 0 \\ 0 & 0 \end{bmatrix} \right)^{-1},$$

and an extra constant (due to lack of normalization),

$$\beta_{ij} = (2\pi)^{-d_x/2} |S_i|^{-1/2} |C_j|^{-1/2} |C_{ij}|^{1/2} \exp\{-\delta_{ij}/2\}$$

where $\delta_{ij} = c_i^\top S_i^{-1} c_i + \mu_j^\top C_j^{-1} \mu_j - \mu_{ij}^\top C_{ij}^{-1} \mu_{ij}$. Using β_{ij} and μ_{ij}, we can evaluate the other expectations:

$$\langle \rho_i(x) \rangle_j = \beta_{ij}, \qquad \langle x\, \rho_i(x) \rangle_j = \beta_{ij} \mu_{ij}^x, \quad \text{and} \quad \langle z\, \rho_i(x) \rangle_j = \beta_{ij} \mu_{ij}^z.$$

Finally, $\langle \rho_i(x)\, \rho_\ell(x) \rangle_j = (2\pi)^{-d_x} |C_j|^{-1/2} |S_i|^{-1/2} |S_\ell|^{-1/2} |C_{i\ell j}|^{1/2} \exp\{-\gamma_{i\ell j}/2\}$, where

$$C_{i\ell j} = \left(C_j^{-1} + \begin{bmatrix} S_i^{-1} + S_\ell^{-1} & 0 \\ 0 & 0 \end{bmatrix} \right)^{-1} \quad \text{and} \quad \mu_{i\ell j} = C_{i\ell j}\left(C_j^{-1} \mu_j + \begin{bmatrix} S_i^{-1} c_i + S_\ell^{-1} c_\ell \\ 0 \end{bmatrix} \right),$$

and $\gamma_{i\ell j} = c_i^\top S_i^{-1} c_i + c_\ell^\top S_\ell^{-1} c_\ell + \mu_j^\top C_j^{-1} \mu_j - \mu_{i\ell j}^\top C_{i\ell j}^{-1} \mu_{i\ell j}$.

References

[1] T. Briegel and V. Tresp. Fisher Scoring and a Mixture of Modes Approach for Approximate Inference and Learning in Nonlinear State Space Models. In *This Volume*. MIT Press, 1999.

[2] A.P. Dempster, N.M. Laird, and D.B. Rubin. Maximum likelihood from incomplete data via the EM algorithm. *J. Royal Statistical Society Series B*, 39:1–38, 1977.

[3] M. I. Jordan, Z. Ghahramani, T. S. Jaakkola, and L. K. Saul. An Introduction to variational methods in graphical models. *Machine Learning*, 1999.

[4] R. E. Kalman and R. S. Bucy. New results in linear filtering and prediction. *Journal of Basic Engineering (ASME)*, 83D:95–108, 1961.

[5] L. Ljung and T. Söderström. *Theory and Practice of Recursive Identification*. MIT Press, Cambridge, MA, 1983.

[6] J. Moody and C. Darken. Fast learning in networks of locally-tuned processing units. *Neural Computation*, 1(2):281–294, 1989.

[7] R. M. Neal. Probabilistic inference using Markov chain monte carlo methods. Technical Report CRG-TR-93-1, 1993.

[8] H. E. Rauch. Solutions to the linear smoothing problem. *IEEE Transactions on Automatic Control*, 8:371–372, 1963.

[9] R. H. Shumway and D. S. Stoffer. An approach to time series smoothing and forecasting using the EM algorithm. *J. Time Series Analysis*, 3(4):253–264, 1982.

Classification on Pairwise Proximity Data

Thore Graepel[†], Ralf Herbrich[‡],
Peter Bollmann-Sdorra[‡], Klaus Obermayer[†]
Technical University of Berlin,
[‡] Statistics Research Group, Sekr. FR 6-9,
[†] Neural Information Processing Group, Sekr. FR 2-1,
Franklinstr. 28/29, 10587 Berlin, Germany

Abstract

We investigate the problem of learning a classification task on data represented in terms of their pairwise proximities. This representation does not refer to an explicit feature representation of the data items and is thus more general than the standard approach of using Euclidean feature vectors, from which pairwise proximities can always be calculated. Our first approach is based on a combined linear embedding and classification procedure resulting in an extension of the Optimal Hyperplane algorithm to pseudo-Euclidean data. As an alternative we present another approach based on a linear threshold model in the proximity values themselves, which is optimized using Structural Risk Minimization. We show that prior knowledge about the problem can be incorporated by the choice of distance measures and examine different metrics w.r.t. their generalization. Finally, the algorithms are successfully applied to protein structure data and to data from the cat's cerebral cortex. They show better performance than K-nearest-neighbor classification.

1 Introduction

In most areas of pattern recognition, machine learning, and neural computation it has become common practice to represent data as feature vectors in a Euclidean vector space. This kind of representation is very convenient because the Euclidean vector space offers powerful analytical tools for data analysis not available in other representations. However, such a representation incorporates assumptions about the data that may not hold and of which the practitioner may not even be aware. And – an even more severe restriction – no domain-independent procedures for the construction of features are known [3].

A more general approach to the characterization of a set of data items is to define a proximity or distance measure between data items – not necessarily given as feature vectors – and to provide a learning algorithm with a proximity matrix of a set of training data. Since pairwise proximity measures can be defined on structured objects like graphs this procedure provides a bridge between the classical and the "structural" approaches to pattern recognition [3]. Additionally, pairwise data occur frequently in empirical sciences like psychology, psychophysics, economics, biochemistry etc., and most of the algorithms developed for this kind of data – predominantly clustering [5, 4] and multidimensional scaling [8, 6]– fall into the realm of unsupervised learning.

In contrast to nearest-neighbor classification schemes [10] we suggest algorithms which operate on the given proximity data via linear models. After a brief discussion of different kinds of proximity data in terms of possible embeddings, we suggest how the Optimal Hyperplane (OHC) algorithm for classification [2, 9] can be applied to distance data from both Euclidean and pseudo-Euclidean spaces. Subsequently, a more general model is introduced which is formulated as a linear threshold model on the proximities, and is optimized using the principle of Structural Risk Minimization [9]. We demonstrate how the choice of proximity measure influences the generalization behavior of the algorithm and apply both algorithms to real-world data from biochemistry and neuroanatomy.

2 The Nature of Proximity Data

When faced with proximity data in the form of a matrix $\mathbf{P} = \{p_{ij}\}$ of pairwise proximity values between data items, one idea is to embed the data in a suitable space for visualization and analysis. This is referred to as multidimensional scaling, and Torgerson [8] suggested a procedure for the linear embedding of proximity data. Interpreting the proximities as Euclidean distances in some unknown Euclidean space one can calculate an inner product matrix $\mathbf{H} = \mathbf{X}^T \mathbf{X}$ w.r.t. to the center of mass of the data from the proximities according to [8]

$$(\mathbf{H})_{ij} = -\frac{1}{2}\left(|p_{ij}|^2 - \frac{1}{\ell}\sum_{m=1}^{\ell}|p_{mj}|^2 - \frac{1}{\ell}\sum_{n=1}^{\ell}|p_{in}|^2 + \frac{1}{\ell^2}\sum_{m,n=1}^{\ell}|p_{mn}|^2\right). \quad (1)$$

Let us perform a spectral decomposition $\mathbf{H} = \mathbf{U}\mathbf{D}\mathbf{U}^T = \mathbf{X}^T\mathbf{X}$ and choose $\mathbf{D}$ and $\mathbf{U}$ such that their columns are sorted in decreasing order of magnitude of the eigenvalues λ_i of $\mathbf{H}$. The embedding in an n-dimensional space is achieved by calculating the first n rows of $\mathbf{X} = \mathbf{D}^{\frac{1}{2}}\mathbf{U}^T$. In order to embed a new data item characterized by a vector $\mathbf{p}$ consisting of its pairwise proximities p_i w.r.t. to the previously known data items, one calculates the corresponding inner product vector $\mathbf{h}$ using (1) with $(\mathbf{H})_{ij}$, p_{ij}, and p_{mj} replaced by h_i, p_i, and p_m respectively, and then obtains the embedding $\mathbf{x} = \mathbf{D}^{-\frac{1}{2}}\mathbf{U}^T\mathbf{h}$.

The matrix $\mathbf{H}$ has negative eigenvalues if the distance data $\mathbf{P}$ were not Euclidean. Then the data can be isometrically embedded only in a pseudo-Euclidean or Minkowski space $\Re^{(n^+,n^-)}$, equipped with a bilinear form Φ, which is not positive definite. In this case the distance measure takes the form $p(\mathbf{x}_i, \mathbf{x}_j) = \sqrt{\Phi(\mathbf{x}_i - \mathbf{x}_j)} = \sqrt{(\mathbf{x}_i - \mathbf{x}_j)^T \mathbf{M}(\mathbf{x}_i - \mathbf{x}_j)}$, where $\mathbf{M}$ is any $n \times n$ symmetric matrix assumed to have full rank, but not necessarily positive definite. However, we can always find a basis such that the matrix $\mathbf{M}$ assumes the form $\mathbf{M} = \text{diag}(\mathbf{I}_{n^+}, -\mathbf{I}_{n^-})$ with $n = n^+ + n^-$, where the pair (n^+, n^-) is called the signature of the pseudo-Euclidean space [3]. Also in this case (1) serves to reconstruct the symmetric bilinear form, and the embedding proceeds as above with $\mathbf{D}$ replaced by $\tilde{\mathbf{D}}$, whose diagonal contains the modules of the eigenvalues of $\mathbf{H}$.

From the eigenvalue spectrum of $\mathbf{H}$ the effective dimensionality of the proximity preserving embedding can be obtained. (i) If there is only a small number of large positive eigenvalues, the data items can be reasonably embedded in a Euclidean space. (ii) If there is a small number of positive and negative eigenvalues of large absolute value, then an embedding in a pseudo-Euclidean space is possible. (iii) If the spectrum is continuous and relatively flat, then no linear embedding is possible in less than $\ell - 1$ dimensions.

3 Classification in Euclidean and Pseudo-Euclidean Space

Let the training set S be given by an $\ell \times \ell$ matrix $\mathbf{P}$ of pairwise distances of unknown data vectors $\mathbf{x}$ in a Euclidean space, and a target class $y_i \in \{-1, +1\}$ for each data item. Assuming that the data are linearly separable, we follow the OHC algorithm [2] and set up a linear model for the classification in data space,

$$y(\mathbf{x}) = \text{sign}(\mathbf{x}^T \mathbf{w} + b). \tag{2}$$

Then we can always find a weight vector $\mathbf{w}$ and threshold b such that

$$y_i(\mathbf{x}_i^T \mathbf{w} + b) \geq 1 \quad i = 1, \ldots, \ell. \tag{3}$$

Now the optimal hyperplane with maximal margin is found by minimizing $\|\mathbf{w}\|^2$ under the constraints (3). This is equivalent to maximizing the Wolfe dual $W(\boldsymbol{\alpha})$ w.r.t. $\boldsymbol{\alpha}$,

$$W(\boldsymbol{\alpha}) = \boldsymbol{\alpha}^T \mathbf{1} - \frac{1}{2} \boldsymbol{\alpha}^T \mathbf{Y} \mathbf{X}^T \mathbf{X} \mathbf{Y} \boldsymbol{\alpha}, \tag{4}$$

with $\mathbf{Y} = \text{diag}(\mathbf{y})$, and the ℓ-vector $\mathbf{1}$. The constraints are $\alpha_i \geq 0, \forall i$, and $\mathbf{1}^T \mathbf{Y} \boldsymbol{\alpha}^* = 0$. Since the optimal weight vector $\mathbf{w}^*$ can be expressed as a linear combination of training examples

$$\mathbf{w}^* = \mathbf{X} \mathbf{Y} \boldsymbol{\alpha}^*, \tag{5}$$

and the optimal threshold b^* is obtained by evaluating $b^* = y_i - \mathbf{x}_i^T \mathbf{w}^*$ for any training example $\mathbf{x}_i$ with $\alpha_i \neq 0$, the decision function (2) can be fully evaluated using inner products between data vectors only. This formulation allows us to learn on the distance data directly.

In the Euclidean case we can apply (1) to the distance matrix $\mathbf{P}$ of the training data, obtain the inner product matrix $\mathbf{H} = \mathbf{X}^T \mathbf{X}$, and introduce it directly – without explicit embedding of the data – into the Wolfe dual (4). The same is true for the test phase, where only the inner products of the test vector with the training examples are needed.

In the case of pseudo-Euclidean distance data the inner product matrix $\mathbf{H}$ obtained from the distance matrix $\mathbf{P}$ via (1) has negative eigenvalues. This means that the corresponding data vectors can only be embedded in a pseudo-Euclidean space $\Re^{(n^+,n^-)}$ as explained in the previous section. Also $\mathbf{H}$ cannot serve as the Hessian in the quadratic programming (QP) problem (4). It turns out, however, that the indefiniteness of the bilinear form in pseudo-Euclidean spaces does not forestall linear classification [3]. A decision plane is characterized by the equation $\mathbf{x}^T \mathbf{M} \mathbf{w} = 0$, as illustrated in Fig. 1. However, Fig. 1 also shows that the same plane can just as well be described by $\mathbf{x}^T \bar{\mathbf{w}} = 0$ – as if the space were Euclidean – where $\bar{\mathbf{w}} = \mathbf{M}\mathbf{w}$ is simply the mirror image of $\mathbf{w}$ w.r.t. the axes of negative signature. For the OHC algorithm this means, that if we can reconstruct the Euclidean inner product matrix $\bar{\mathbf{X}}^T \bar{\mathbf{X}}$ from the distance data, we can proceed with the OHC algorithm as usual. $\bar{\mathbf{H}} = \bar{\mathbf{X}}^T \bar{\mathbf{X}}$ is calculated by "flipping" the axes of negative signature, i.e., with $\bar{\mathbf{D}} = \text{diag}(|\lambda_1|, \ldots, |\lambda_\ell|)$, we can calculate $\bar{\mathbf{H}}$ according to

$$\bar{\mathbf{H}} = \mathbf{U} \bar{\mathbf{D}} \mathbf{U}^T, \tag{6}$$

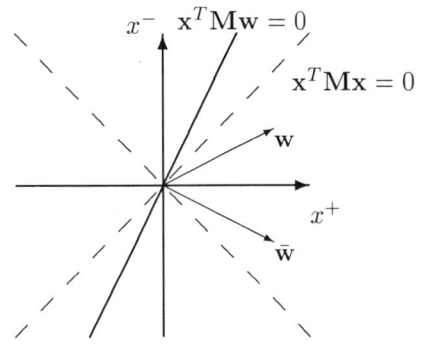

Figure 1: Plot of a decision line (thick) in a 2D pseudo-Euclidean space with signature $(1,1)$, i.e., $\mathbf{M} = \mathrm{diag}(1,-1)$. The decision line is described by $\mathbf{x}^T \mathbf{M} \mathbf{w} = 0$. When interpreted as Euclidean it is at right angles with $\bar{\mathbf{w}}$, which is the mirror image of $\mathbf{w}$ w.r.t. the axis x^- of negative signature. In physics this plot is referred to as a Minkowski space-time diagram, where x^+ corresponds to the space axis and x^- to the time axis. The dashed diagonal lines indicate the points $\mathbf{x}^T \mathbf{M} \mathbf{x} = 0$ of zero length, the light cone.

which serves now as the Hessian matrix for normal OHC classification. Note, that $\bar{\mathbf{H}}$ is positive semi-definite, which ensures a unique solution for the QP problem (4).

4 Learning a Linear Decision Function in Proximity Space

In order to cope with general proximity data (case (iii) of Section 2) let the training set S be given by an $\ell \times \ell$ proximity matrix $\mathbf{P}$ whose elements $p_{ij} = p(x_i, x_j)$ are the pairwise proximity values between data items $x_i, i = 1, \ldots, \ell$, and a target class $y_i \in \{-1, +1\}$ for each data item. Let us assume that the proximity values satisfy reflexivity, $p_{ii} = 0, \forall i$, and symmetry, $p_{ij} = p_{ji}, \forall i, j$. We can make a linear model for the classification of a new data item x represented by a vector of proximities $\mathbf{p} = (p_1, \ldots, p_\ell)^T$ where $p_i = p(x, x_i)$ are the proximities of x w.r.t. to the items x_i in the training set,

$$y(x) = \mathrm{sign}(\mathbf{p}^T \mathbf{w} + b). \qquad (7)$$

Comparing (7) to (2) we note, that this is equivalent to using the vector of proximities $\mathbf{p}$ as the feature vector $\mathbf{x}$ characterizing data item x. Consequently, the OHC algorithm from the previous section can be used to learn a proximity model when $\mathbf{x}$ is replaced by $\mathbf{p}$ in (2), $\mathbf{X}^T \mathbf{X}$ is replaced by $\mathbf{P}^2$ in the Wolfe dual (4), and the columns $\mathbf{p}_i$ of $\mathbf{P}$ serve as the training data.

Note that the formal correspondence does not imply that the columns of the proximity matrix are Euclidean feature vectors as used in the SV setting. We merely consider a linear threshold model on the proximities of a data item to all the training data items. Since the Hessian of the QP problem (4) is the square of the proximity matrix, it is always at least positive semi-definite, which guarantees a unique solution of the QP problem. Once the optimal coefficients α_i^* have been found, a test data item can be classified by determining its proximities p_i from the elements x_i of the training set and by using conditions (2) together with (5) for its classification.

5 Metric Proximities

Let us consider two examples in order to see, what learning on pairwise metric data amounts to. The first example is the minimalistic 0-1-metric, which for two objects x_i and x_j is defined as follows:

$$p_0(x_i, x_j) = \begin{cases} 0 & \text{if } x_i = x_j \\ 1 & \text{otherwise} \end{cases}. \qquad (8)$$

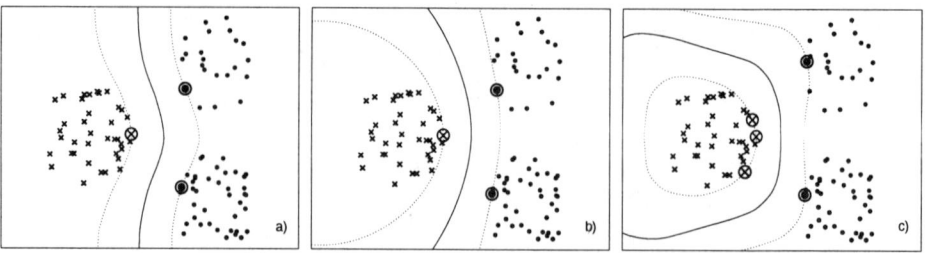

Figure 2: Decision functions in a simple two-class classification problem for different Minkowski metrics. The algorithm described in Sect. 4 was applied with (a) the city-block metric ($r = 1$), (b) the Euclidean metric ($r = 2$), and (c) the maximum metric ($r \to \infty$). The three metrics result in considerably different generalization behavior, and use different Support Vectors (circled).

The corresponding $\ell \times \ell$ proximity matrix $\mathbf{P}_0$ has full rank as can be seen from its non-vanishing determinant $\det(\mathbf{P}_0) = (-1)^{\ell-1}(\ell - 1)$. From the definition of the 0-1 metric it is clear that every data item x not contained in the training set is represented by the same proximity vector $\mathbf{p} = \mathbf{1}$, and will be assigned to the same class. For the 0-1 metric the QP problem (4) can be solved analytically by matrix inversion, and using $\mathbf{P}_0^{-1} = (\ell - 1)^{-1}\mathbf{1}\mathbf{1}^T - \mathbf{I}$ we obtain for the classification

$$y = \text{sign}\left(\mathbf{1}^T((\ell-1)^{-1}\mathbf{1}\mathbf{1}^T - \mathbf{I})\mathbf{Y}\mathbf{1}\right) = \text{sign}\left(\frac{1}{\ell-1}\sum_{i=1}^{\ell} y_i\right). \quad (9)$$

This result means, that each new data item is assigned to the majority class of the training sample, which is – given the available information – the Bayes optimal decision. This example demonstrates, how the prior information – in the case of the 0-1 metric the minimal information of identity – is encoded in the chosen distance measure.

As an easy-to-visualize example of metric distance measures on vectors $\mathbf{x} \in \Re^n$ let us consider the Minkowski r-metrics defined for $r \geq 1$ as

$$p(\mathbf{x}_i, \mathbf{x}_j) = \left(\sum_{\mu} |x_i^{\mu} - x_j^{\mu}|^r\right)^{1/r}. \quad (10)$$

For $r = 2$ the Minkowski metric is equivalent to the Euclidean distance. The case $r = 1$ corresponds to the so-called city-block metric, in which the distance is given by the sum of absolute differences for each feature. On the other extreme, the maximum norm, $r \to \infty$, takes only the largest absolute difference in feature values as the distance between objects. Note that with increasing r more weight is given to the larger differences in feature values, and that in the literature on multidimensional scaling [1] Minkowski metrics have been used to examine the dominance of features in human perception. Using the Minkowski metrics for classification in a toy example, we observed that different values of r lead to very different generalization behavior on the same set of data points, as can be seen in Fig. 2. Since there is no apriori reason to prefer one metric over the other, using a particular metric is equivalent to incorporating prior knowledge into the solution of the problem.

	Cat Cortex (leave-one-out)				Proteins (10-fold)			
	A	V	SS	FL	H-α	H-β	M	GH
Size of Class	10	19	17	19	72	72	37	30
OHC-cut-off	**3.08**	4.62	6.15	3.08	0.91	4.01	0.45	**0.00**
OHC-flip-axis	**3.08**	**1.54**	4.62	3.08	0.91	4.01	0.45	**0.00**
OHC-proximity	**3.08**	4.62	3.08	**1.54**	**0.45**	3.60	0.45	**0.00**
1-NN	5.82	6.00	6.09	6.74	1.65	3.66	**0.00**	2.01
2-NN	6.09	4.46	7.91	5.09	2.01	5.27	**0.00**	3.44
3-NN	5.29	2.29	4.18	4.71	2.14	6.34	**0.00**	2.68
4-NN	6.45	5.14	3.68	5.17	2.46	5.13	**0.00**	4.87
5-NN	5.55	2.75	**2.72**	5.29	1.65	5.09	**0.00**	4.11

Table 1: Classification results for Cat Cortex and Protein data. Bold numbers indicate best results.

6 Real-World Proximity Data

In the numerical experiments we focused on two real-world data sets, which are both given in terms of a proximity matrix **P** and class labels y for each data item. The data set called "cat cortex" consists of a matrix of connection strengths between 65 cortical areas of the cat. The data was collected by Scannell [7] from text and figures of the available anatomical literature and the connections are assigned proximity values p as follows: self-connection ($p = 0$), strong and dense connection ($p = 1$), intermediate connection ($p = 2$), weak connection ($p = 3$), and absent or unreported connection ($p = 4$). From functional considerations the areas can be assigned to four different regions: auditory (A), visual (V), somatosensory (SS), and frontolimbic (FL). The classification task is to discriminate between these four regions, each time one against the three others.

The second data set consists of a proximity matrix from the structural comparison of 224 protein sequences based upon the concept of evolutionary distance. The majority of these proteins can be assigned to one of four classes of globins: hemoglobin-α (H-α), hemoglobin-β (H-β), myoglobin (M), and heterogenous globins (GH). The classification task is to assign proteins to one of these classes, one against the rest.

We compared three different procedures for the described two-class classification problems, performing leave-one-out cross-validation for the "cat cortex" dataset and 10-fold cross-validation for the "protein" data set to estimate the generalization error. Table 1 shows the results. OHC-cut-off refers to the simple method of making the inner product matrix **H** positive semi-definite by neglecting projections to those eigenvectors with negative eigenvalues. OHC-flip-axis flips the axes of negative signature as described in (6) and thus preserves the information contained in those directions for classification. OHC-proximity, finally, refers to the model linear in the proximities as introduced in Section 4. It can be seen that OHC-proximity shows a better generalization than OHC-flip-axis, which in turn performs slightly better than OHC-cut-off. This is especially the case on the cat cortex data set, whose inner product matrix **H** has negative eigenvalues. For comparison, the lower part of Table 1 shows the corresponding cross-validation results for K-nearest-neighbor, which is a natural choice to use, because it only needs the pairwise proximities to determine the training data to participate in the voting. The presented algorithms OHC-flip-axis and OHC-proximity perform consistently better than K-nearest-neighbor, even when the value of K is optimally chosen.

7 Conclusion and Future work

In this contribution we investigated the nature of proximity data and suggested ways for performing classification on them. Due to the generality of the proximity approach we expect that many other problems can be fruitfully cast into this framework. Although we focused on classification problems, regression can be considered on proximity data in an analogous way. Noting that Support Vector kernels and covariance functions for Gaussian processes are similarity measures for vector spaces, we see that this approach has recently gained a lot of popularity. However, one problem with pairwise proximities is that their number scales quadratically with the number of objects under consideration. Hence, for large scale practical applications the problems of missing data and active data selection for proximity data will be of increasing importance.

Acknowledgments

We thank Prof. U. Kockelkorn for fruitful discussions. We also thank S. Gunn for providing his Support Vector implementation. Finally, we are indebted to M. Vingron and T. Hofmann for providing the protein data set. This project was funded by the Technical University of Berlin via the Forschungsinitiativprojekt FIP 13/41.

References

[1] I. Borg and J. Lingoes. *Multidimensional Similarity Structure Analysis*, volume 13 of *Springer Series in Statistics*. Springer-Verlag, Berlin, Heidelberg, 1987.

[2] B. Boser, I. Guyon, and V. N. Vapnik. A training algorithm for optimal margin classifiers. In *Proceedings of the Fifth Annual Workshop on Computational Learning Theory*, pages 144–152, 1992.

[3] L. Goldfarb. *Progress in Pattern Recognition*, volume 2, chapter 9: A New Approach To Pattern Recognition, pages 241–402. Elsevier Science Publishers, 1985.

[4] T. Graepel and K. Obermayer. A stochastic self-organizing map for proximity data. Neural Computation (accepted for publication), 1998.

[5] T. Hofmann and J. Buhmann. Pairwise data clustering by deterministic annealing. *IEEE Transactions on Pattern Analysis and Machine Intelligence*, 19(1):1–14, 1997.

[6] H. Klock and J. M. Buhmann. Multidimensional scaling by deterministic annealing. In M. Pelillo and E. R. Hancock, editors, *Energy Minimization Methods in Computer Vision and Pattern Recognition*, volume 1223, pages 246–260, Berlin, Heidelberg, 1997. Springer-Verlag.

[7] J. W. Scannell, C. Blakemore, and M. P. Young. Analysis of connectivity in the cat cerebral cortex. *The Journal of Neuroscience*, 15(2):1463–1483, 1995.

[8] W. S. Torgerson. *Theory and Methods of Scaling*. Wiley, New York, 1958.

[9] V. Vapnik. *The Nature of Statistical Learning*. Springer-Verlag, Berlin, Heidelberg, Germany, 1995.

[10] D. Weinshall, D. W. Jacobs, and Y. Gdalyahu. Classification in non–metric space. In *Advances in Neural Information Processing Systems*, volume 11, 1999. in press.

Outcomes of the Equivalence of Adaptive Ridge with Least Absolute Shrinkage

Yves Grandvalet   **Stéphane Canu**
Heudiasyc, UMR CNRS 6599, Université de Technologie de Compiègne,
BP 20.529, 60205 Compiègne cedex, France
Yves.Grandvalet@hds.utc.fr

Abstract

Adaptive Ridge is a special form of Ridge regression, balancing the quadratic penalization on each parameter of the model. It was shown to be equivalent to Lasso (least absolute shrinkage and selection operator), in the sense that both procedures produce the same estimate. Lasso can thus be viewed as a particular quadratic penalizer.

From this observation, we derive a fixed point algorithm to compute the Lasso solution. The analogy provides also a new hyper-parameter for tuning effectively the model complexity. We finally present a series of possible extensions of lasso performing sparse regression in kernel smoothing, additive modeling and neural net training.

1 INTRODUCTION

In supervised learning, we have a set of explicative variables x from which we wish to predict a response variable y. To solve this problem, a learning algorithm is used to produce a predictor $\widehat{f}(x)$ from a learning set $s_\ell = \{(x_i, y_i)\}_{i=1}^{\ell}$ of examples. The goal of prediction may be: 1) to provide an accurate prediction of future responses, accuracy being measured by a user-defined loss function; 2) to quantify the effect of each explicative variable in the response; 3) to better understand the underlying phenomenon.

Penalization is extensively used in learning algorithms. It decreases the predictor variability to improve the prediction accuracy. It is also expected to produce models with few non-zero coefficients if interpretation is planned.

Ridge regression and Subset Selection are the two main penalization procedures. The former is stable, but does not shrink parameters to zero, the latter gives simple models, but is unstable [1]. These observations motivated the search for new penalization techniques such as Garrotte, Non-Negative Garrotte [1], and Lasso (least absolute shrinkage and selection operator) [10].

Adaptive Ridge was proposed as a means to automatically balance penalization on different coefficients. It was shown to be equivalent to Lasso [4]. Section 2 presents Adaptive Ridge and recalls the equivalence statement. The following sections give some of the main outcomes of this connection. They concern algorithmic issues in section 3, complexity control in section 4, and some possible generalizations of lasso to non-linear regression in section 5.

2 ADAPTIVE RIDGE REGRESSION

For clarity of exposure, the formulae are given here for linear regression with quadratic loss. The predictor is defined as $\widehat{f}(x) = \beta^T x$, with $\beta^T = (\beta_1, \ldots, \beta_d)$. Adaptive Ridge is a modification of the Ridge estimate, which is defined by the quadratic constraint $\sum_{j=1}^d \beta_j^2 \leq C$ applied to the parameters. It is usually computed by minimizing the Lagrangian

$$\widehat{\beta} = \underset{\beta}{\text{Argmin}} \sum_{i=1}^{\ell} \Big(\sum_{j=1}^{d} \beta_j x_{ij} - y_i \Big)^2 + \lambda \sum_{j=1}^{d} \beta_j^2 , \qquad (1)$$

where λ is the Lagrange multiplier varying with the bound C on the norm of the parameters.

When the ordinary least squares (OLS) estimate maximizes likelihood[1], the Ridge estimate may be seen as a maximum a posteriori estimate. The Bayes prior distribution is a centered normal distribution, with variance proportional to $1/\lambda$. This prior distribution treats all covariates similarly. It is not appropriate when we know that all covariates are not equally relevant.

The garrotte estimate [1] is based on the OLS estimate $\widehat{\beta}^{\circ}$. The standard quadratic constraint is replaced by $\sum_{j=1}^d \beta_j^2 / \widehat{\beta}_j^{\circ\,2} \leq C$. The coefficients with smaller OLS estimate are thus more heavily penalized. Other modifications are better explained with the prior distribution viewpoint. Mixtures of Gaussians may be used to cluster different set of covariates. Several models have been proposed, with data dependent clusters [9], or classes defined a priori [7]. The Automatic Relevance Determination model [8] ranks in the latter type. In [4], we propose to use such a mixture, in the form

$$\widehat{\beta} = \underset{\beta}{\text{Argmin}} \sum_{i=1}^{\ell} \Big(\sum_{j=1}^{d} \beta_j x_{ij} - y_i \Big)^2 + \sum_{j=1}^{d} \lambda_j \beta_j^2 . \qquad (2)$$

Here, each coefficient has its own prior distribution. The priors are centered normal distributions with variances proportional to $1/\lambda_j$. To avoid the simultaneous estimation of these d hyper-parameters by trial, the constraint

$$\frac{1}{d} \sum_{j=1}^{d} \frac{1}{\lambda_j} = \frac{1}{\lambda} \quad , \lambda_j > 0 \qquad (3)$$

is applied on $\boldsymbol{\lambda} = (\lambda_1, \ldots, \lambda_d)^T$, where λ is a predefined value. This constraint is a link between the d prior distributions. Their mean variance is proportional to $1/\lambda$. The values of λ_j are automatically[2] induced from the sample, hence the qualifier adaptative. Adaptativity refers here to the penalization balance on $\{\widehat{\beta}_j\}$, not to the tuning of the hyper-parameter λ.

---

[1] If $\{x_i\}$ are independently and identically drawn from some distribution, and that some β^* exists, such that $Y_i = \beta^{*T} x_i + \varepsilon$, where ε is a centered normal random variable, then the empirical cost based on the quadratic loss is proportional to the log-likelihood of the sample. The OLS estimate $\widehat{\beta}^{\circ}$ is thus the maximum likelihood estimate of β^*.

[2] Adaptive Ridge, as Ridge or Lasso, is not scale invariant, so that the covariates should be normalized to produce sensible estimates.

It was shown [4] that Adaptive Ridge and least absolute value shrinkage are equivalent, in the sense that they yield the same estimate. We remind that the Lasso estimate is defined by

$$\widehat{\beta} = \underset{\beta}{\text{Argmin}} \sum_{i=1}^{\ell} \left(\sum_{j=1}^{d} \beta_j x_{ij} - y_i \right)^2 \quad \text{subject to} \quad \sum_{j=1}^{d} |\beta_j| \leq K \ . \tag{4}$$

The only difference in the definition of the Adaptive Ridge and the Lasso estimate is that the Lagrangian form of Adaptive Ridge uses the constraint $(\sum_{j=1}^{d} |\beta_j|)^2/d \leq K^2$.

3 OPTIMIZATION ALGORITHM

Tibshirani [10] proposed to use quadratic programming to find the lasso solution, with $2d$ variables (positive and negative parts of β_j) and $2d+1$ constraints (signs of positive and negative parts of β_j plus constraint (4)). Equations (2) and (3) suggest to use a fixed point (FP) algorithm. At each step s, the FP algorithm estimates the optimal parameters $\lambda_j^{(s)}$ of the Bayes prior based on the estimate $\beta_j^{(s-1)}$, and then maximizes the posterior to compute the current estimate $\beta_j^{(s)}$.

As the parameterization (β, λ) may lead to divergent solutions, we define new variables

$$\gamma_j = \sqrt{\frac{\lambda_j}{\lambda}} \beta_j \ , \quad \text{and} \quad c_j = \sqrt{\frac{\lambda}{\lambda_j}} \quad \text{for } j = 1, \ldots, d \ . \tag{5}$$

The FP algorithm updates alternatively c and γ as follows:

$$\begin{cases} c_j^{(s)2} = \dfrac{d\gamma_j^{(s-1)2}}{\sum_{k=1}^{d} \gamma_k^{(s-1)2}} \\ \gamma^{(s)} = \left(\text{diag}(c^{(s)}) X^T X \text{diag}(c^{(s)}) + \lambda I\right)^{-1} \text{diag}(c^{(s)}) X^T y \ , \end{cases} \tag{6}$$

where $X_{ij} = x_{ij}$, I is the identity matrix, and $\text{diag}(c)$ is the square matrix with the vector c on its diagonal.

The algorithm can be initialized by the Ridge or the OLS estimate. In the latter case, $\beta^{(1)}$ is the garrotte estimate.

Practically, if $\gamma_j^{(s-1)}$ is small compared to numerical accuracy, then $c_j^{(s)}$ is set to zero. In turn, $\gamma_j^{(s)}$ is zero, and the system to be solved in the second step to determine γ can be reduced to the other variables. If c_j is set to zero at any time during the optimization process, the final estimate $\widehat{\beta}_j$ will be zero. The computations are simplified, but it is not clear whether global convergence can be obtained with this algorithm. It is easy to show the convergence towards a local minimum, but we did not find general conditions ensuring global convergence. If these conditions exist, they rely on initial conditions.

Finally, we stress that the optimality conditions for c (or in a less rigorous sense for λ) do not depend on the first part of the cost minimized in (2). In consequence, *the equivalence between Adaptive Ridge and lasso holds for any model or loss function.* The FP algorithm can be applied to these other problems, without modifying the first step.

4 COMPLEXITY TUNING

The Adaptive Ridge estimate depends on the learning set s_ℓ and on the hyper-parameter λ. When the estimate is defined by (2) and (3), the analogy with Ridge suggests λ as the "natural" hyper-parameter for tuning the complexity of the regressor. As λ goes to zero, $\widehat{\beta}$ approaches the OLS estimate $\widehat{\beta}^o$, and the number of effective parameters is d. As λ goes to infinity, $\widehat{\beta}$ goes to zero and the number of effective parameters is zero.

When the estimate is defined by (4), there is no obvious choice for the hyper-parameter controlling complexity. Tibshirani [10] proposed to use $\nu = \sum_{j=1}^{d} |\widehat{\beta}_j| / \sum_{j=1}^{d} |\widehat{\beta}_j^o|$. As ν goes to one, $\widehat{\beta}$ approaches $\widehat{\beta}^o$; as ν goes to infinity, $\widehat{\beta}$ goes to zero.

The weakness of ν is that it is explicitly defined from the OLS estimate. As a result, it is variable when the design matrix is badly conditioned. The estimation of ν is thus harder, and the overall procedure looses in stability. This is illustrated on an experiment following Breiman's benchmark [1] with 30 highly correlated predictors $\mathbb{E}(X_j X_k) = \rho^{|j-k|}$, with $\rho = 1 - 10^{-3}$.

We generate 1000 i.i.d. samples of size $\ell = 60$. For each sample s_ℓ^k, the modeling error (ME) is computed for several values of ν and λ. We select ν^k and λ^k achieving the lowest ME. For one sample, there is a one to one mapping from ν to λ. Thus ME is the same for ν^k and λ^k. Then, we compute ν^* and λ^* achieving the best average ME on the 1000 samples. As ν^k and λ^k achieve the lowest ME for s_ℓ^k, the ME for s_ℓ^k is higher or equal for ν^* and λ^*. Due to the wide spread of $\{\nu_k\}$, the average loss encountered is twice for ν^* than for λ^*: $1/1000 \sum_{k=1}^{1000} \left(\text{ME}(s_\ell^k, \nu^*) - \text{ME}(s_\ell^k, \nu^k) \right) = 4.6 \ 10^{-2}$, and $1/1000 \sum_{k=1}^{1000} \left(\text{ME}(s_\ell^k, \lambda^*) - \text{ME}(s_\ell^k, \lambda^k) \right) = 2.3 \ 10^{-2}$. The average modeling error are $\overline{\text{ME}}(\nu^*) = 1.9 \ 10^{-1}$ and $\overline{\text{ME}}(\lambda^*) = 1.7 \ 10^{-1}$.

The estimates of prediction error, such as leave-one-out cross-validation tend to be variable. Hence, complexity tuning is often based on the minimization of some estimate of the mean prediction error (*e.g* bootstrap, K-fold cross-validation). Our experiment supports that, regarding mean prediction error, the optimal λ performs better than the optimal ν. Thus, λ is the best candidate for complexity tuning.

Although λ and ν are respectively the control parameter of the FP and QP algorithms, the preceding statement does not imply that we should use the FP algorithm. Once the solution $\widehat{\beta}$ is known, ν or λ are easily computed. The choice of one hyper-parameter is not linked to the choice of the optimization algorithm.

5 APPLICATIONS

Adaptive Ridge may be applied to a variety of regression techniques. They include kernel smoothing, additive and neural net modeling.

5.1 KERNEL SMOOTHING

Soft-thresholding was proved to be efficient in wavelet functional estimation [2]. Kernel smoothers [5] can also benefit from the sparse representation given by soft-thresholding methods. For these regressors, $\widehat{f}(\boldsymbol{x}) = \sum_{i=1}^{\ell} \beta_i K(\boldsymbol{x}, \boldsymbol{x}_i) + \beta_0$, there are as many covariates as pairs in the sample. The quadratic procedure of Lasso with $2\ell + 1$ constraints becomes computationally expensive, but the FP algorithm of Adaptive Ridge is reasonably fast to converge.

An example of least squares fitting is shown in fig. 1 for the motorcycle dataset [5]. On this example, the hyperparameter λ has been estimated by .632 bootstrap (with 50 bootstrap replicates) for Ridge and Adaptive Ridge regressions. For tuning λ, it is not necessary to determine the coefficients β with high accuracy. Hence, compared to Ridge regression, the overall amount of computation required to get the Adaptive Ridge estimate was about six times more important. For evaluation, Adaptive Ridge is ten times faster as Ridge regression as the final fitting uses only a few kernels (11 out of 133).

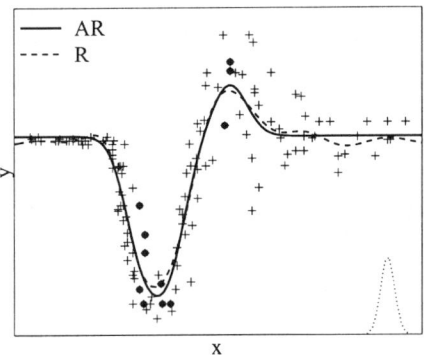

Figure 1: Adaptive Ridge (AR) and Ridge (R) in kernel smoothing on the motorcycle data. The + are data points, and • are the prototypes corresponding to the kernels with non-zero coefficients in AR. The Gaussian kernel used is represented dotted in the lower right-hand corner.

Girosi [3] showed an equivalence between a version of least absolute shrinkage applied to kernel smoothing, and Support Vector Machine (SVM). However, Adaptive Ridge, as applied here, is not equivalent to SVM, as the cost minimized is different. The fit and prototypes are thus different from the fit and support vectors that would be obtained from SVM.

5.2 ADDITIVE MODELS

Additive models [6] are sums of univariate functions, $\widehat{f}(x) = \sum_{j=1}^{d} \widehat{f}_j(x_j)$. In the nonparametric setting, $\{\widehat{f}_j\}$ are smooth but unspecified functions. Additive models are easily represented and thus interpretable, but they require the choice of the relevant covariates to be included in the model, and of the smoothness of each $\widehat{f}_j$.

In the form presented in the two previous sections, Adaptive Ridge regression penalizes differently each individual coefficient, but it is easily extended to the pooled penalization of coefficients. Adaptive Ridge may thus be used as an alternative to BRUTO [6] to balance the penalization parameters on each $\widehat{f}_j$.

A classical choice for $\widehat{f}_j$ is cubic spline smoothing. Let B_j denote the $\ell \times (\ell+2)$ matrix of the unconstrained B-spline basis, evaluated at x_{ij}. Let Ω_j be the $(\ell+2) \times (\ell+2)$ matrix corresponding to the penalization of the second derivative of $\widehat{f}_j$. The coefficients of $\widehat{f}_j$ in the unconstrained B-spline basis are noted β_j. The "natural" extension of Adaptive Ridge is to minimize

$$\|\sum_{j=1}^{d} B_j \beta_j - y\|^2 + \sum_{j=1}^{d} \lambda_j \beta_j^T \Omega_j \beta_j \; , \tag{7}$$

subject to constraint (3). This problem is easily shown to have the same solution as the minimization of

$$\|\sum_{j=1}^{d} B_j \beta_j - y\|^2 + \lambda \left(\sum_{j=1}^{d} \sqrt{\beta_j^T \Omega_j \beta_j} \right)^2 . \tag{8}$$

Note that if the cost (8) is optimized with respect to a single covariate, the solution is a usual smoothing spline regression (with quadratic penalization). In the multidimensional case,

$\alpha_j^2 = \beta_j^T \Omega_j \beta_j = \int \{f_j''(t)\}^2 dt$ may be used to summarize the non-linearity of f_j, thus $|\widehat{\alpha}_j|$ can be interpreted as a relevance index operating besides linear dependence of feature j. The penalizer in (8) is a least absolute shrinkage operator applied to α_j. Hence, formula (8) may be interpreted as "quadratic penalization within, and soft-thresholding between covariates". The FP algorithm of section 3 is easily modified to minimize (8), and backfitting may be used to solve the second step of this procedure.

A simulated example in dimension five is shown in fig. 2. The fitted univariate functions are plotted for five values of λ. There is no dependency between the the explained variable and the last covariate. The other covariates affect the response, but the dependency on the first features is smoother, hence easier to capture and more relevant for the spline smoother. For a small value of λ, the univariate functions are unsmooth, and the additive model is interpolating the data. For $\lambda = 10^{-4}$, the dependencies are well estimated on all covariates. As λ increases, the covariates with higher coordinate number are more heavily penalized, and the corresponding $\widehat{f}_j$ tend to be linear.

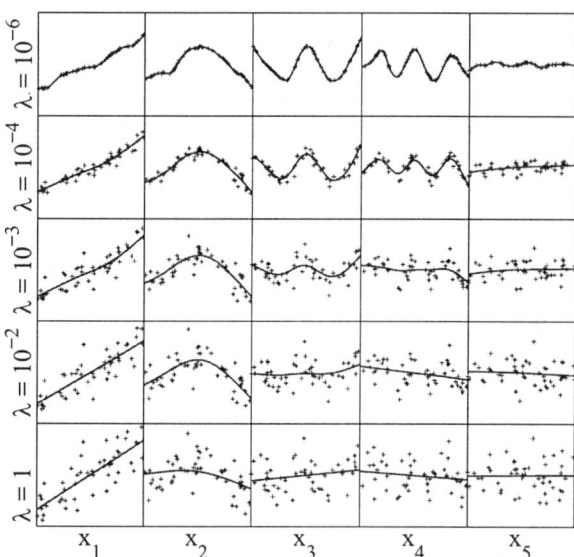

Figure 2: Adaptive Ridge in additive modeling on simulated data. The true model is $y = x_1 + \cos(\pi x_2) + \cos(2\pi x_3) + \cos(3\pi x_4) + \varepsilon$. The covariates are independently drawn from a uniform distribution on $[-1, 1]$ and ε is a Gaussian noise of standard deviation $\sigma = 0.3$. The solid curves are the estimated univariate functions for different values of λ, and + are partial residuals.

Linear trends are not penalized in cubic spline smoothing. Thus, when after convergence $\widehat{\beta}_j^T \Omega_j \widehat{\beta}_j = 0$, the jth covariate is not eliminated. This can be corrected by applying Adaptive Ridge a second time. To test if a significant linear trend can be detected, a linear (penalized) model may be used for $\widehat{f}_j$, the remaining $\widehat{f}_k$, $k \neq j$ being cubic splines.

5.3 MLP FITTING

The generalization to the pooled penalization of coefficients can also be applied to Multi-Layered Perceptrons to control the complexity of the fit. If weights are penalized individually, Adaptive Ridge is equivalent to the Lasso. If weights are pooled by layer, Adaptive Ridge automatically tunes the amount of penalization on each layer, thus avoiding the multiple hyper-parameter tuning necessary in weight-decay [7].

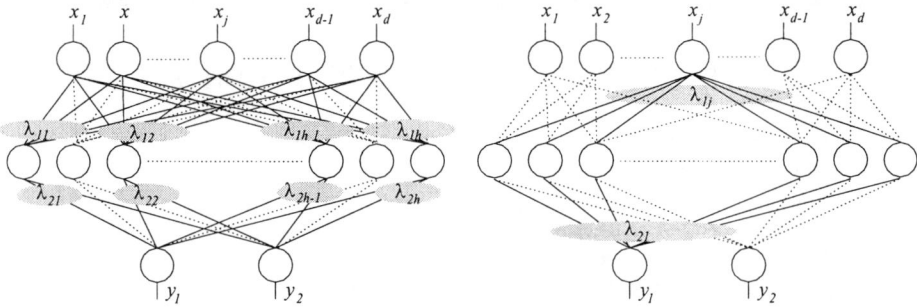

Figure 3: groups of weights for two examples of Adaptive Ridge in MLP fitting. Left: hidden node soft-thresholding. Right: input penalization and selection, and individual smoothing coefficient for each output unit.

Two other interesting configurations are shown in fig. 3. If weights are pooled by incoming and outcoming weights of a unit, node penalization/pruning is performed. The weight groups may also gather the outcoming weights from each input unit, or the incoming weights from each output unit (one set per input plus one per output). The goal here is to penalize/select the input variables according to their relevance, and each output variable according to the smoothness of the corresponding mapping. This configuration proves itself especially useful in time series prediction, where the number of inputs to be fed into the network is not known in advance. There are also more complex choices of pooling, such as the one proposed to encourage additive modeling in Automatic Relevance Determination [8].

References

[1] L. Breiman. Heuristics of instability and stabilization in model selection. *The Annals of Statistics*, 24(6):2350–2383, 1996.

[2] D.L Donoho and I.M. Johnstone. Minimax estimation via wavelet shrinkage. *Ann. Statist.*, 26(3):879–921, 1998.

[3] F. Girosi. An equivalence between sparse approximation and support vector machines. Technical Report 1606, M.I.T. AI Laboratory, Cambridge, MA., 1997.

[4] Y. Grandvalet. Least absolute shrinkage is equivalent to quadratic penalization. In L. Niklasson, M. Bodén, and T. Ziemske, editors, *ICANN'98*, volume 1 of *Perspectives in Neural Computing*, pages 201–206. Springer, 1998.

[5] W. Härdle. *Applied Nonparametric Regression*, volume 19 of *Economic Society Monographs*. Cambridge University Press, New York, 1990.

[6] T.J. Hastie and R.J. Tibshirani. *Generalized Additive Models*, volume 43 of *Monographs on Statistics and Applied Probability*. Chapman & Hall, New York, 1990.

[7] D.J.C. MacKay. A practical Bayesian framework for backprop networks. *Neural Computation*, 4(3):448–472, 1992.

[8] R. M. Neal. *Bayesian Learning for Neural Networks*. Lecture Notes in Statistics. Springer, New York, 1996.

[9] S.J. Nowlan and G.E. Hinton. Simplifying neural networks by soft weight-sharing. *Neural Computation*, 4(4):473–493, 1992.

[10] R.J. Tibshirani. Regression shrinkage and selection via the lasso. *Journal of the Royal Statistical Society, B*, 58(1):267–288, 1995.

Visualizing Group Structure*

Marcus Held, Jan Puzicha, and Joachim M. Buhmann
Institut für Informatik III,
Römerstraße 164, D-53117 Bonn, Germany
email: {held,jan,jb}.cs.uni-bonn.de,
WWW: http://www-dbv.cs.uni-bonn.de

Abstract

Cluster analysis is a fundamental principle in exploratory data analysis, providing the user with a description of the group structure of given data. A key problem in this context is the interpretation and visualization of clustering solutions in high–dimensional or abstract data spaces. In particular, probabilistic descriptions of the group structure, essential to capture inter–cluster relationships, are hardly assessable by simple inspection of the probabilistic assignment variables. We present a novel approach to the visualization of group structure. It is based on a statistical model of the object assignments which have been observed or estimated by a probabilistic clustering procedure. The objects or data points are embedded in a low dimensional Euclidean space by approximating the observed data statistics with a Gaussian mixture model. The algorithm provides a new approach to the visualization of the inherent structure for a broad variety of data types, e.g. histogram data, proximity data and co–occurrence data. To demonstrate the power of the approach, histograms of textured images are visualized as an example of a large–scale data mining application.

1 Introduction

Clustering and visualization are key issues in exploratory data analysis and are fundamental principles of many unsupervised learning schemes. For a given data set, the aim of any clustering approach is to extract a description of the inherent group structure. The object space is partitioned into groups where each partition

---

*This work has been supported by the German Research Foundation (DFG) under grant #BU 914/3–1, by the German Israel Foundation for Science and Research Development (GIF) under grant #1-0403-001.06/95 and by the Federal Ministry for Education, Science and Technology (BMBF #01 M 3021 A/4).

is as homogeneous as possible and two partitions are maximally heterogeneous. For several reasons it is useful to deal with probabilistic partitioning approaches:

1. The data generation process itself might be stochastic, resulting in overlapping partitions. Thus, a probabilistic group description is adequate and provides additional information about the inter–cluster relations.
2. The number of clusters might be chosen too large. Forcing the algorithm to a hard clustering solution creates artificial structure not supported by the data. On the other hand, superfluous clusters can be identified by a probabilistic group description.
3. There exists theoretical and empirical evidence that probabilistic assignments avoid over-fitting phenomena [7].

Several well-known clustering schemes result in fuzzy cluster assignments: For the most common type of vector–valued data, heuristic fuzzy clustering methods were suggested [4, 5]. In a more principled way, *deterministic annealing* algorithms provide fuzzy clustering solutions for a given cost function with a rigorous statistical foundation and have been developed for vectorial [9], proximity [6] and histogram data [8]. In mixture model approaches the assignments of objects to groups are interpreted as missing data. Its conditional expectations given the data and the estimated cluster parameters are computed during the E–step in the corresponding EM–algorithm and can be understood as assignment probabilities.

The aim of this contribution is to develop a generic framework to visualize such probabilities as distances in a low dimensional Euclidean space. Especially in high dimensional or abstract object spaces, the interpretation of fuzzy group structure is rather difficult, as humans do not perform very well in interpreting probabilities. It is, therefore, a key issue to make an interpretation of the cluster structure more feasible. In contrast to multidimensional scaling (MDS), where objects are embedded in low dimensional Euclidean spaces by preserving the original inter object distances [3], our approach yields a mixture model in low dimensions, where the probabilities for assigning objects to clusters are maximally preserved. The proposed approach is similar in spirit to data visualization methods like projection pursuit clustering, GTM [1], simultaneous clustering and embedding [6], and hierarchical latent variable models [2]. It also aims on visualizing high dimensional data. But while the other methods try to model the data itself by a low dimensional generator model, we seek to model the inferred probabilistic grouping structure. As a consequence, the framework is generic in the sense that it is applicable to any probabilistic or fuzzy group description.

The key idea is to interpret a given probabilistic group description as an observation of an underlying random process. We estimate a low–dimensional statistical model by maximum likelihood inference which provides the visualization. To our knowledge the proposed algorithm provides the first solution to the visualization of distributional data, where the observations of an object consists of a histogram of measured features. Such data is common in data mining applications like image retrieval where image similarity is often based on histograms of color or texture features. Moreover, our method is applicable to proximity and co–occurrence data.

2 Visualizing Probabilistic Group Structure

Let a set of N (abstract) objects $\mathcal{O} = \{o_1, \ldots, o_N\}$ be given which have been partitioned into K groups or clusters. Let the fuzzy assignment of object o_i to cluster $\mathcal{C}_\nu$ be given by $q_{i\nu} \in [0, 1]$, where we assume $\sum_{\nu=1}^{K} q_{i\nu} = 1$ to enable a probabilistic interpretation. We assume that there exists an underlying "true" assignment of objects to clusters which we encode by Boolean variables $M_{i\nu}$ denoting whether object o_i belongs to (has been generated by) cluster C_ν. We thus interpret $q_{i\nu}$ as an *empirical estimate* of the probability $\mathbf{P}(M_{i\nu} = 1)$. For notational simplicity, we summarize the assignment variables in matrices $\mathbf{Q} = (q_{i\nu})$ and $\mathbf{M} = (M_{i\nu})$.

The key idea for visualizing group structure is to exploit a low–dimensional statistical model which "explains" the observed $q_{i\nu}$. The parameters are estimated by maximum likelihood inference and provide a natural data visualization. Gaussian mixture models in low dimensions (typically $d = 2$ or $d = 3$) are often appropriate but the scheme could be easily extended to other classes, e.g. hierarchical models. To define the Gaussian mixture model, we first introduce a set of prototypes $\mathcal{Y} = \{\mathbf{y}_1, \ldots, \mathbf{y}_K\} \subset \mathbb{R}^d$ representing the K clusters, and a set vector–valued object parameters $\mathcal{X} = \{\mathbf{x}_1, \ldots, \mathbf{x}_N\} \subset \mathbb{R}^d$. To model the assignment probabilities, the prototypes $\mathcal{Y}$ and the data points $\mathcal{X}$ are chosen such that the resulting assignment probabilities are maximally similar to the given frequencies $\mathbf{Q}$. For the Gaussian mixture model we have

$$\mathbf{P}(\mathbf{M}|\mathcal{X},\mathcal{Y}) = \prod_{i=1}^{N}\prod_{\nu=1}^{K}(m_{i\nu})^{M_{i\nu}}, \text{ with } m_{i\nu} = \frac{\exp\left(-\beta\|\mathbf{x}_i - \mathbf{y}_\nu\|^2\right)}{\sum_{\mu=1}^{K}\exp\left(-\beta\|\mathbf{x}_i - \mathbf{y}_\mu\|^2\right)} . \quad (1)$$

Note that the probability distribution is invariant under translation and rotation of the complete parameter sets $\mathcal{X}, \mathcal{Y}$. In addition, the scale parameter β could be dropped since a change of β only results in a rescaling of the prototypes $\mathcal{Y}$ and the data points $\mathcal{X}$. For the observation $\mathbf{Q}$ the log–likelihood is given by[1]

$$\mathcal{L}_\mathbf{Q}(\mathcal{X},\mathcal{Y}) = \sum_{i=1}^{N}\sum_{\nu=1}^{K} q_{i\nu} \log m_{i\nu} . \quad (2)$$

It is worth to note that when the $q_{i\nu} = \langle M_{i\nu}\rangle_{\mathbf{P}^{\text{true}}}$ are estimates obtained by a factorial distribution, i.e. $\mathbf{P}^{\text{true}}(\mathbf{M}) = \prod_i \sum_\nu M_{i\nu} q_{i\nu}$, then maximizing (2) is identical to minimizing the Kullback–Leibler (KL–)divergence $D_{\text{KL}}(\mathbf{P}^{\text{true}}\|\mathbf{P}) = \sum_\mathbf{M}\mathbf{P}^{\text{true}}\log(\mathbf{P}^{\text{true}}/\mathbf{P})$. In that case the similarity to the recent approach of Hofmann et al. [6] proposed as the minimization of $D_{\text{KL}}(\mathbf{P}\|\mathbf{P}^{\text{true}})$ becomes apparent. Compared to [6] the role of $\mathbf{P}$ and $\mathbf{P}^{\text{true}}$ is interchanged. From an information–theoretic viewpoint $D_{\text{KL}}(\mathbf{P}^{\text{true}}\|\mathbf{P})$ is a better choice as it quantifies the coding inefficiency of assuming the distribution $\mathbf{P}$ when the true distribution is $\mathbf{P}^{\text{true}}$. Note that the choice of the KL–divergence as a distortion measure for distributions follows intrinsically from the likelihood principle. Maximum likelihood estimates are derived by differentiation:

$$\frac{\partial \mathcal{L}_\mathbf{Q}}{\partial \mathbf{x}_i} = \sum_{\nu=1}^{K}\frac{q_{i\nu}}{m_{i\nu}}\frac{\partial m_{i\nu}}{\partial \mathbf{x}_i} = -2\beta\sum_{\nu=1}^{K} q_{i\nu}\left(\sum_{\mu=1}^{K}m_{i\mu}\mathbf{y}_\mu - \mathbf{y}_\nu\right) , \quad (3)$$

$$\frac{\partial \mathcal{L}_\mathbf{Q}}{\partial \mathbf{y}_\alpha} = \sum_{i=1}^{N}\sum_{\nu=1}^{K}\frac{q_{i\nu}}{m_{i\nu}}\frac{\partial m_{i\nu}}{\partial \mathbf{y}_\alpha} = -2\beta\sum_{i=1}^{N}\sum_{\nu=1}^{K} q_{i\nu}(m_{i\alpha} - \delta_{\alpha\nu})(\mathbf{x}_i - \mathbf{y}_\alpha)$$

$$= -2\beta\sum_{i=1}^{N}(m_{i\alpha} - q_{i\alpha})(\mathbf{x}_i - \mathbf{y}_\alpha) . \quad (4)$$

The gradients can be used for any gradient descent scheme. In the experiments, we used (3)–(4) in conjunction with a simple gradient descent technique, which has

---

[1] Here, it is implicitly assumed that all $q_{i\nu}$ have been estimated based on the same amount of information.

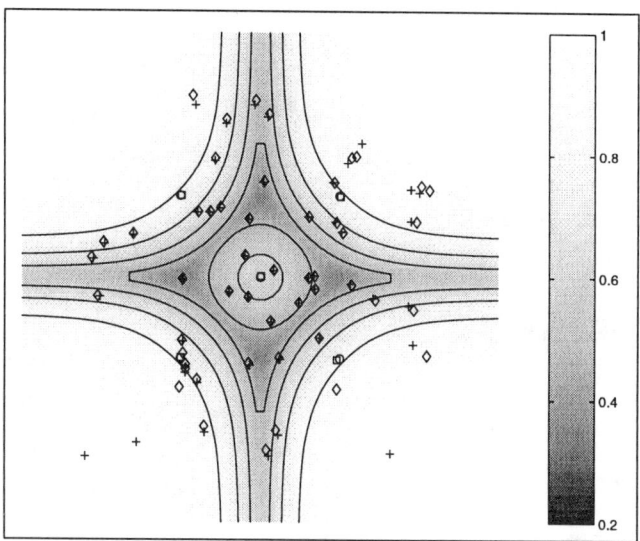

Figure 1: Visualization of two–dimensional artificial data. Original data generated by the mixture model with $\beta = 1.0$ and 5 prototypes. Crosses denote the data points x_i, circles the prototypes y_α. The embedding prototypes are plotted as squares, while the embedding data points are diamonds. The contours are given by $f(x) = \max_\alpha \left(\exp\left(-\beta ||\mathbf{x} - \mathbf{y}_\alpha||^2\right) / \sum_{\mu=1}^{K} \exp\left(-\beta ||\mathbf{x} - \mathbf{y}_\mu||^2\right) \right)$. For visualization purposes the embedding is translated and rotated in the correct position.

been observed to be efficient and reliable up to a few hundred objects. From (4) an explicit formula for the prototypes may be recovered

$$\mathbf{y}_\alpha = \sum_{i=1}^{N} (m_{i\alpha} - q_{i\alpha}) \mathbf{x}_i / \sum_{i=1}^{N} (m_{i\alpha} - q_{i\alpha}) \qquad (5)$$

which can be interpreted as an alternative centroid rule. The position of the prototypes is dominated by objects with a large deviation between modeled and measured assignment probabilities. Note that (5) should not be used as an iterative equation as the corresponding fixed point is not contractive.

3 Results

As a first experiment we discuss the approximately recoverable case, where we sample from (1) to generate artificial two–dimensional data and infer the positions of the sample points and of the prototypes by the visualizing group structure approach (see Fig. 1). Due to iso–contour lines in the generator density and in the visualization density not all data positions are recovered exactly. We like to emphasize that the complete information available on the grouping structure of the data is preserved, since the mean KL–divergence is quite small ($\approx 2.10 \cdot 10^{-5}$). It is worth mentioning that the rank–order of the assignments of objects i to clusters α is completely preserved.

For many image retrieval systems image similarity has been defined as similarity of occurring feature coefficients, e.g. colors or texture features. In [7], a novel statistical mixture model for distributional data, the probabilistic histogram clustering (ACM), has been proposed which we applied to extract the group structure inherent in image databases based on histograms of textured image features. The ACM explains the observed data by the generative model:

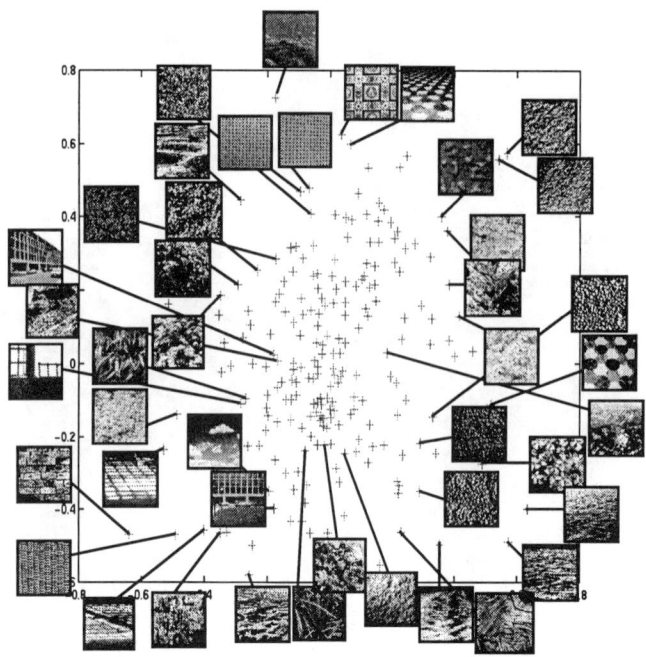

Figure 2: Embedding of the VisTex database with MDS.

1. select an object $o_i \in \mathcal{O}$ with probability p_i,
2. choose a cluster $\mathcal{C}_\alpha$ according to the cluster membership $M_{i\alpha}$ of o_i,
3. sample a feature $v_j \in \mathcal{V}$ from the cluster conditional distribution $q_{j|\alpha}$.

This generative model is formalized by

$$P(o_i, v_j | \mathbf{M}, p, q) = p_i \sum_{\alpha=1}^{K} M_{i\alpha} q_{j|\alpha} . \quad (6)$$

The parameters are estimated by maximum likelihood inference. The assignments $M_{i\alpha}$ are treated as unobserved data in an (annealed) EM procedure, which provides a probabilistic group description. For the details we refer to [7].

In the experiments, texture features are extracted by a bank of 12 Gabor filters with 3 scales and 4 orientations. Different Gabor channels are assumed to be independently distributed, which results in a concatenated histogram of the empirically measured channel distributions. Each channel was discretized into 40 bins resulting in a 480 dimensional histogram representing one image. For the experiments two different databases were used.

In Fig. 3 a probabilistic $K = 10$ cluster solution with 160 images containing different textures taken from the Brodatz album is visualized. The clustering algorithm produces 8 well separated clusters, while the two clusters in the mid region exhibit substantial overlap. A close inspection of these two clusters indicates that the fuzziness of the assignments in this area is plausible as the textures in this area have similar frequency components in common.

The result for a more complex database of 220 textured images taken from the MIT VisTex image database with a large range of uniformly and non-uniformly textured images is depicted in Fig. 4. This plot indicates that the proposed approach provides a structured view on image databases. Especially the upper left cluster yields some insight in the clustering solution, as this cluster consists of a large range of non–uniformly textured images, enabling the user to decide that a higher number of clusters might yield a better solution. The visualization approach fits naturally in an interactive scenario, where the user can choose interactively data points to focus his examination to certain areas of interest in the clustering solution.

For comparison, we present in Fig. 2 a multidimensional scaling (Sammon's mapping [3]) solution for the VisTex database. A detailed inspection of this plot indicates, that the embedding is locally quiet satisfactory, while no global structure of the database is visible. This is explained by the fact, that Sammon's mapping only tries to preserve the object distances, while our novel approach first extracts group structure in a high dimensional feature space and than embeds this group structure in a low dimensional Euclidean space. While MDS completely neglects the grouping structure we do not care for the exact inter object distances.

4 Conclusion

In this contribution, a generic framework for the low–dimensional visualization of probabilistic group structure was presented. The effectiveness of this approach was demonstrated by experiments on artificial data as well as on databases of textured images. While we have focussed on histogram data the generality of the approach makes it feasible to visualize a broad range of different data types, e.g. vectorial, proximity or co–occurrence data. Thus, it is useful in a broad variety of applications, ranging from image or document retrieval tasks, the analysis of marketing data to the inspection of protein data. We believe that this technique provides the user substantial insight in the validity of clustering solutions making the inspection and interpretation of large databases more practicable.

A natural extension of the proposed approach leads to the visualization of hierarchical cluster structures by a hierarchy of visualization plots.

References

[1] C.M. Bishop, M. Svensén, and C.K.I. Williams. GTM: the generative topographic mapping. *Neural Computation*, 10(1):215–234, 1998.

[2] C.M. Bishop and M. E. Tipping. A hierarchical latent variable model for data visualization. Technical Report NCRG/96/028, Neural Computing Research Group Dept. Of Computer Science & Applied Mathematics, Aston University, 1998.

[3] T.F. Cox and M.A.A. Cox. *Multidimensional Scaling*, volume 59 of *Mongraphs on statistics and applied probability*. Chapman & Hall, London, New York, 1994.

[4] J.C. Dunn. A fuzzy relative of the ISODATA process and its use in detecting well–separated clusters. *Journal of Cybernetics*, 3:32–57, 1975.

[5] I. Gath and A. Geva. Unsupervised optimal fuzzy clustering. *IEEE Transactions on Pattern Analysis and Machine Intelligence*, 11:773–781, 1989.

[6] T. Hofmann and J. M. Buhmann. Pairwise data clustering by deterministic annealing. *PAMI*, 19(1):1–25, 1997.

[7] T. Hofmann, J. Puzicha, and M. I. Jordan. Learning from dyadic data. In *Advances in Neural Information Processing Systens 11*. MIT Press, 1999.

[8] F.C.N. Pereira, N.Z. Tishby, and L. Lee. Distributional clustering of English words. In *30th Annual Meeting of the Association for Computational Linguistics, Columbus, Ohio*, pages 183–190, 1993.

[9] K. Rose, E. Gurewitz, and G.C. Fox. A deterministic annealing approach to clustering. *Pattern Recognition Letters*, 11(9):589–594, September 1990.

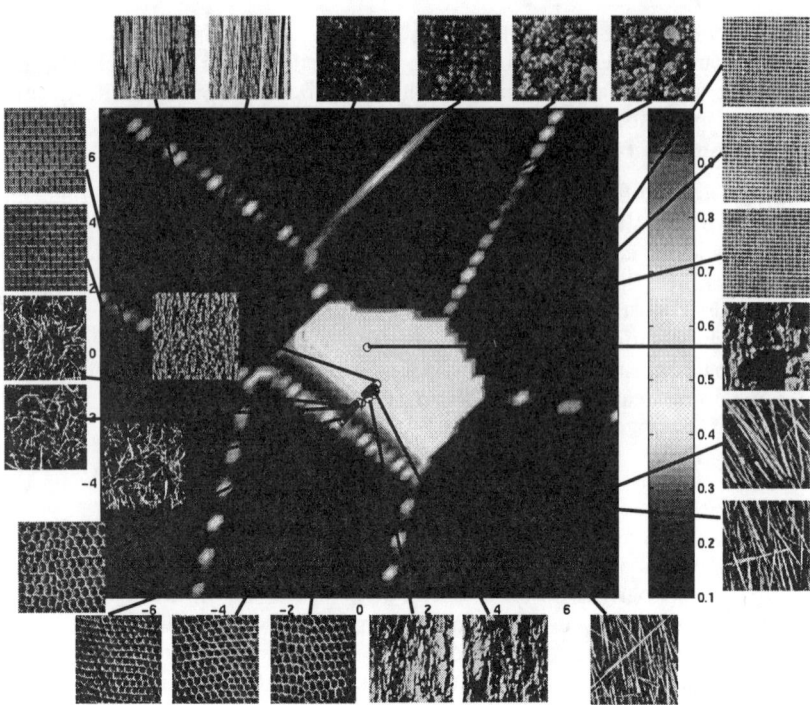

Figure 3: Visualization of a probabilistic grouping structure inferred for a database of 160 Brodatz textures. A mean KL–divergence of 0.031 is obtained.

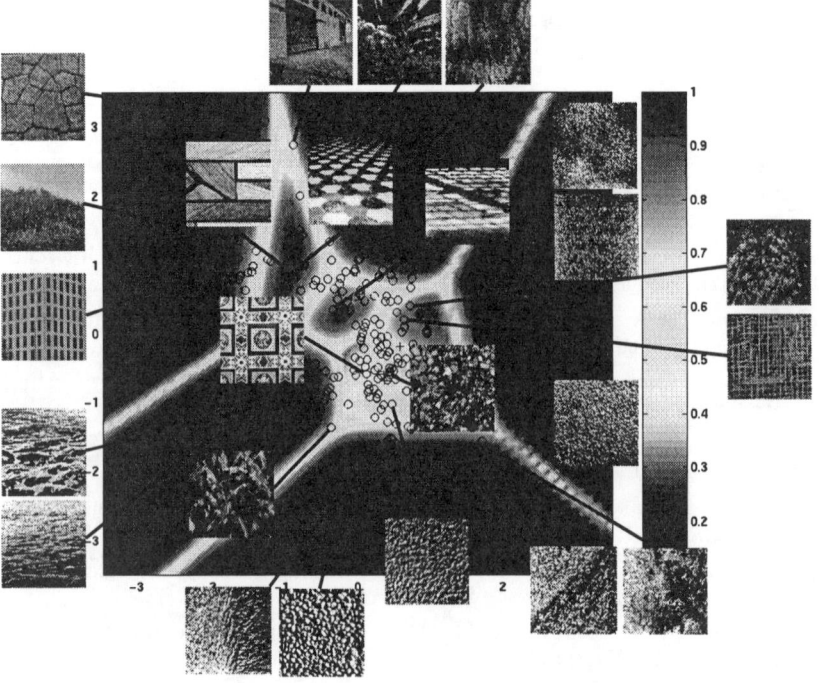

Figure 4: Visualization of a probabilistic grouping structure inferred for 220 images of the VisTex database. A mean KL–divergence of 0.0018 is obtained.

Source Separation as a By-Product of Regularization

Sepp Hochreiter
Fakultät für Informatik
Technische Universität München
80290 München, Germany
hochreit@informatik.tu-muenchen.de

Jürgen Schmidhuber
IDSIA
Corso Elvezia 36
6900 Lugano, Switzerland
juergen@idsia.ch

Abstract

This paper reveals a previously ignored connection between two important fields: regularization and independent component analysis (ICA). We show that at least one representative of a broad class of algorithms (regularizers that reduce network complexity) extracts independent features as a by-product. This algorithm is *Flat Minimum Search* (FMS), a recent general method for finding low-complexity networks with high generalization capability. FMS works by minimizing both training error and required weight precision. According to our theoretical analysis the hidden layer of an FMS-trained autoassociator attempts at coding each input by a sparse code with as few simple features as possible. In experiments the method extracts optimal codes for difficult versions of the "noisy bars" benchmark problem by separating the underlying sources, whereas ICA and PCA fail. Real world images are coded with fewer bits per pixel than by ICA or PCA.

1 INTRODUCTION

In the field of unsupervised learning several information-theoretic objective functions (OFs) have been proposed to evaluate the quality of sensory codes. Most OFs focus on properties of the code components — we refer to them as code component-oriented OFs, or COCOFs. Some COCOFs explicitly favor near-factorial, minimally redundant codes of the input data [2, 17, 23, 7, 24] while others favor local codes [22, 3, 15]. Recently there has also been much work on COCOFs encouraging biologically plausible sparse distributed codes [19, 9, 25, 8, 6, 21, 11, 16].

While COCOFs express desirable properties of the code itself they neglect the costs of constructing the code from the data. E.g., coding input data without redundancy may be very expensive in terms of information required to describe the code-generating network, which may need many finely tuned free parameters. We believe that one of sensory coding's objectives should be to reduce the cost of code *generation* through data transformations, and postulate that an important scarce resource is the bits required to describe the mappings that generate and process the codes.

Hence we shift the point of view and focus on the information-theoretic costs of code generation. We use a novel approach to unsupervised learning called *"low-complexity coding and decoding"* (LOCOCODE [14]). Without assuming particular goals such as data compression, subsequent classification, etc., but in the spirit of research on minimum description length (MDL), LOCOCODE generates so-called *lococodes* that (1) convey information about the input data, (2) can be computed from the data by a low-complexity mapping (LCM), and (3) can be decoded by an LCM. We will see that by minimizing coding/decoding costs LOCOCODE can yield efficient, robust, noise-tolerant mappings for processing inputs and codes.

Lococodes through regularizers. To implement LOCOCODE we apply regularization to an autoassociator (AA) whose hidden layer activations represent the code. The hidden layer is forced to code information about the input data by minimizing training error; the regularizer reduces coding/decoding costs. Our regularizer of choice will be *Flat Minimum Search* (FMS) [13].

2 FLAT MINIMUM SEARCH: REVIEW AND ANALYSIS

FMS is a general gradient-based method for finding low-complexity networks with high generalization capability. FMS finds a large region in weight space such that each weight vector from that region has *similar* small error. Such regions are called "flat minima". In MDL terminology, few bits of information are required to pick a weight vector in a "flat" minimum (corresponding to a low-complexity network) — the weights may be given with low precision. FMS automatically prunes weights and units, and reduces output sensitivity with respect to remaining weights and units. Previous FMS applications focused on supervised learning [12, 13].

Notation. Let O, H, I denote index sets for output, hidden, and input units, respectively. For $l \in O \cup H$, the activation y^l of unit l is $y^l = f(s_l)$, where $s_l = \sum_m w_{lm} y^m$ is the net input of unit l ($m \in H$ for $l \in O$ and $m \in I$ for $l \in H$), w_{lm} denotes the weight on the connection from unit m to unit l, f denotes the activation function, and for $m \in I$, y^m denotes the m-th component of an input vector. $W = |(O \times H) \cup (H \times I)|$ is the number of weights.

Algorithm. FMS' objective function E features an unconventional error term:

$$B = \sum_{i,j:\ i \in O \cup H} \log \sum_{k \in O} \left(\frac{\partial y^k}{\partial w_{ij}}\right)^2 + W \log \sum_{k \in O} \left(\sum_{i,j: i \in O \cup H} \frac{\left|\frac{\partial y^k}{\partial w_{ij}}\right|}{\sqrt{\sum_{k \in O} \left(\frac{\partial y^k}{\partial w_{ij}}\right)^2}} \right)^2.$$

$E = E_q + \lambda B$ is minimized by gradient descent, where E_q is the training set mean squared error (MSE), and λ a positive "regularization constant" scaling B's influence. Choosing λ corresponds to choosing a tolerable error level (there is no *a priori* "optimal" way of doing so). B measures the weight precision (number of bits needed to describe all weights in the net). Given a constant number of output units, FMS can be implemented efficiently, namely, with standard backprop's order of computational complexity [13].

2.1 FMS: A Novel Analysis

Simple basis functions (BFs). A BF is the function determining the activation of a code component in response to a given input. Minimizing B's term

$$T1 := \sum_{i,j:\ i \in O \cup H} \log \sum_{k \in O} \left(\frac{\partial y^k}{\partial w_{ij}}\right)^2$$

obviously reduces output sensitivity with respect to weights (and therefore units). $T1$ is responsible for pruning weights (and, therefore, units). $T1$ is one reason why low-complexity (or simple) BFs are preferred: weight precision (or complexity) is mainly determined by $\frac{\partial y^k}{\partial w_{ij}}$.

Sparseness. Because $T1$ tends to make unit activations decrease to zero it favors sparse codes. But $T1$ also favors a sparse hidden layer in the sense that *few hidden units contribute to producing the output*. B's second term

$$T2 := W \log \sum_{k \in O} \left(\sum_{i,j:\ i \in O \cup H} \frac{\left|\frac{\partial y^k}{\partial w_{ij}}\right|}{\sqrt{\sum_{k \in O} \left(\frac{\partial y^k}{\partial w_{ij}}\right)^2}} \right)^2$$

punishes units with similar influence on the output. We reformulate it:

$$T2 = W \log \left(\sum_{i,j:\ i \in O \cup H} \sum_{u,v:\ u \in O \cup H} \frac{\sum_{k \in O} \left|\frac{\partial y^k}{\partial y^i}\right| \left|\frac{\partial y^k}{\partial y^u}\right|}{\sqrt{\sum_{k \in O} \left(\frac{\partial y^k}{\partial y^i}\right)^2} \sqrt{\sum_{k \in O} \left(\frac{\partial y^k}{\partial y^u}\right)^2}} \right) =$$

$$W \log \left(|O|\ |O \times H|^2 + |I|^2 \sum_{k \in O} \sum_{i \in H} \sum_{u \in H} \frac{\left|\frac{\partial y^k}{\partial y^i}\right| \left|\frac{\partial y^k}{\partial y^u}\right|}{\sqrt{\sum_{k \in O} \left(\frac{\partial y^k}{\partial y^i}\right)^2} \sqrt{\sum_{k \in O} \left(\frac{\partial y^k}{\partial y^u}\right)^2}} \right).$$

See intermediate steps in [14]. We observe: (1) an output unit that is very sensitive with respect to two given hidden units will heavily contribute to $T2$ (compare the numerator in the last term of $T2$). (2) This large contribution can be reduced by making both hidden units have large impact on other output units (see denominator in the last term of $T2$).

Few separated basis functions. Hence FMS tries to figure out a way of using (1) as few BFs as possible for determining the activation of each output unit, while simultaneously (2) using the same BFs for determining the activations of as many output units as possible (common BFs). (1) and $T1$ separate the BFs: the force towards simplicity (see $T1$) prevents input information from being channelled through a single BF; the force towards few BFs per output makes them non-redundant. (1) and (2) cause few BFs to determine all outputs.

Summary. Collectively $T1$ and $T2$ (which make up B) encourage *sparse codes* based on *few separated simple basis functions* producing all outputs. Due to space limitations a more detailed analysis (e.g. linear output activation) had to be left to a TR [14] (on the WWW).

3 EXPERIMENTS

We compare LOCOCODE to "independent component analysis" (ICA, e.g., [5, 1, 4, 18]) and "principal component analysis" (PCA, e.g., [20]). ICA is realized by Cardoso's JADE algorithm, which is based on whitening and subsequent joint diagonalization of 4th-order cumulant matrices. To measure the information conveyed by resulting codes we train a standard backprop net on the training set used for code generation. Its inputs are the code components; its task is to reconstruct the original input. The test set consists of 500 off-training set exemplars (in the case of real world images we use a separate test image). *Coding efficiency* is the average number of bits needed to code a test set input pixel. The code components are scaled to the interval [0, 1] and partitioned into discrete intervals. Assuming independence of the code components we estimate the probability of each discrete code value by Monte Carlo sampling on the training set. To obtain the test set codes' bits per pixel (Shannon's optimal value) the average sum of all negative logarithms of code component probabilities is divided by the number of input components. All details necessary for reimplementation are given in [14].

Noisy bars adapted from [10, 11]. The input is a 5×5 pixel grid with horizontal and vertical bars at random positions. The task is to extract the independent features (the bars). Each of the 10 possible bars appears with probability $\frac{1}{5}$. In contrast to [10, 11] we allow for bar type mixing — *this makes the task harder*. Bar intensities vary in $[0.1, 0.5]$; input units that see a pixel of a bar are activated correspondingly others adopt activation -0.5. We add Gaussian noise with variance 0.05 and mean 0 to each pixel. For ICA and PCA we have to provide information about the number (ten) of independent sources (tests with n assumed sources will be denoted by ICA-n and PCA-n). LOCOCODE does not require this — using 25 hidden units (HUs) we expect LOCOCODE to *prune* the 15 superfluous HUs.

Results. See Table 1. While the reconstruction errors of all methods are similar, LOCOCODE has the best coding efficiency. 15 of the 25 HUs are indeed automatically pruned: LOCOCODE finds an optimal factorial code which exactly mirrors the pattern generation process. PCA codes and ICA-15 codes, however, are unstructured and dense. While ICA-10 codes are almost sparse and do recognize some sources, the sources are not clearly separated like with LOCOCODE — compare the weight patterns shown in [14].

Real world images. Now we use more realistic input data, namely subsections of: 1) the aerial shot of a village, 2) an image of wood cells, and 3) an image of striped piece of wood. Each image has 150×150 pixels, each taking on one of 256 gray levels. 7×7 (5×5 for village) pixels subsections are randomly chosen as training inputs. Test sets stem from images similar to 1), 2), and 3).

Results. For the village image LOCOCODE discovers on-center-off-surround hidden units forming a sparse code. For the other two images LOCOCODE also finds appropriate feature detectors — see weight patterns shown in [14]. Using its compact, low-complexity features it always codes more efficiently than ICA and PCA.

exp.	input field	meth.	num. comp.	rec. error	code type	bits per pixel: # intervals			
						10	20	50	100
bars	5 × 5	LOC	10	1.05	sparse	0.584	0.836	1.163	1.367
bars	5 × 5	ICA	10	1.02	sparse	0.811	1.086	1.446	1.678
bars	5 × 5	PCA	10	1.03	dense	0.796	1.062	1.418	1.655
bars	5 × 5	ICA	15	0.71	dense	1.189	1.604	2.142	2.502
bars	5 × 5	PCA	15	0.72	dense	1.174	1.584	2.108	2.469
village	5 × 5	LOC	8	1.05	sparse	0.436	0.622	0.895	1.068
village	5 × 5	ICA	8	1.04	sparse	0.520	0.710	0.978	1.165
village	5 × 5	PCA	8	1.04	dense	0.474	0.663	0.916	1.098
village	5 × 5	ICA	10	1.11	sparse	0.679	0.934	1.273	1.495
village	5 × 5	PCA	10	0.97	dense	0.578	0.807	1.123	1.355
village	7 × 7	LOC	10	8.29	sparse	0.250	0.368	0.547	0.688
village	7 × 7	ICA	10	7.90	dense	0.318	0.463	0.652	0.796
village	7 × 7	PCA	10	9.21	dense	0.315	0.461	0.648	0.795
village	7 × 7	ICA	15	6.57	dense	0.477	0.694	0.981	1.198
village	7 × 7	PCA	15	8.03	dense	0.474	0.690	0.972	1.189
cell	7 × 7	LOC	11	0.840	sparse	0.457	0.611	0.814	0.961
cell	7 × 7	ICA	11	0.871	sparse	0.468	0.622	0.829	0.983
cell	7 × 7	PCA	11	0.722	sparse	0.452	0.610	0.811	0.960
cell	7 × 7	ICA	15	0.360	sparse	0.609	0.818	1.099	1.315
cell	7 × 7	PCA	15	0.329	dense	0.581	0.798	1.073	1.283
piece	7 × 7	LOC	4	0.831	sparse	0.207	0.269	0.347	0.392
piece	7 × 7	ICA	4	0.856	sparse	0.207	0.276	0.352	0.400
piece	7 × 7	PCA	4	0.830	sparse	0.207	0.269	0.348	0.397
piece	7 × 7	ICA	10	0.716	sparse	0.535	0.697	0.878	1.004
piece	7 × 7	PCA	10	0.534	sparse	0.448	0.590	0.775	0.908

Table 1: *Overview of experiments: name of experiment, input field size, coding method, number of relevant code components (code size), reconstruction error, nature of code observed on the test set. PCA's and ICA's code sizes need to be prewired.* LOCOCODE's, *however, are found automatically (we always start with 25 HUs). The final 4 columns show the coding efficiency measured in bits per pixel, assuming the real-valued HU activations are partitioned into 10, 20, 50, and 100 discrete intervals.* LOCOCODE *codes most efficiently.*

4 CONCLUSION

According to our analysis LOCOCODE attempts to describe single inputs with as few and as simple features as possible. Given the statistical properties of many visual inputs (with few defining features), this typically results in sparse codes. Unlike objective functions of previous methods, however, LOCOCODE's does *not* contain an explicit term enforcing, say, sparse codes — sparseness or independence are not viewed as a good things *a priori*. Instead we focus on the information-theoretic complexity of the mappings used for coding and decoding. The resulting codes typically compromise between conflicting goals. They tend to be sparse and exhibit *low but not minimal* redundancy — if the cost of minimal redundancy is too high.

Our results suggest that LOCOCODE's objective may embody a general principle of unsupervised learning going beyond previous, more specialized ones. We see that there is at least one representative (FMS) of a broad class of algorithms (regularizers that reduce network complexity) which (1) can do optimal feature extraction as a by-product, (2) outperforms traditional ICA and PCA on visual source separation tasks, and (3) unlike ICA does not even need to know the number of independent sources in advance. This reveals an interesting, previously ignored connection between regularization and ICA, and may represent a first step towards unification of regularization and unsupervised learning.

More. Due to space limitations, much additional theoretical and experimental analysis had to be left to a tech report (29 pages, 20 figures) on the WWW: see [14].

Acknowledgments. This work was supported by *DFG grant SCHM 942/3-1* and *DFG grant BR 609/10-2* from "Deutsche Forschungsgemeinschaft".

References

[1] S. Amari, A. Cichocki, and H.H. Yang. A new learning algorithm for blind signal separation. In David S. Touretzky, Michael C. Mozer, and Michael E. Hasselmo, editors, *Advances in Neural Information Processing Systems 8*, pages 757–763. The MIT Press, Cambridge, MA, 1996.

[2] H. B. Barlow, T. P. Kaushal, and G. J. Mitchison. Finding minimum entropy codes. *Neural Computation*, 1(3):412–423, 1989.

[3] H. G. Barrow. Learning receptive fields. In *Proceedings of the IEEE 1st Annual Conference on Neural Networks*, volume IV, pages 115–121. IEEE, 1987.

[4] A. J. Bell and T. J. Sejnowski. An information-maximization approach to blind separation and blind deconvolution. *Neural Computation*, 7(6):1129–1159, 1995.

[5] J.-F. Cardoso and A. Souloumiac. Blind beamforming for non Gaussian signals. *IEE Proceedings-F*, 140(6):362–370, 1993.

[6] P. Dayan and R. Zemel. Competition and multiple cause models. *Neural Computation*, 7:565–579, 1995.

[7] G. Deco and L. Parra. Nonlinear features extraction by unsupervised redundancy reduction with a stochastic neural network. Technical report, Siemens AG, ZFE ST SN 41, 1994.

[8] D. J. Field. What is the goal of sensory coding? *Neural Computation*, 6:559–601, 1994.

[9] P. Földiák and M. P. Young. Sparse coding in the primate cortex. In M. A. Arbib, editor, *The Handbook of Brain Theory and Neural Networks*, pages 895–898. The MIT Press, Cambridge, Massachusetts, 1995.

[10] G. E. Hinton, P. Dayan, B. J. Frey, and R. M. Neal. The wake-sleep algorithm for unsupervised neural networks. *Science*, 268:1158–1161, 1995.

[11] G. E. Hinton and Z. Ghahramani. Generative models for discovering sparse distributed representations. *Philosophical Transactions of the Royal Society* **B**, 352:1177–1190, 1997.

[12] S. Hochreiter and J. Schmidhuber. Simplifying nets by discovering flat minima. In G. Tesauro, D. S. Touretzky, and T. K. Leen, editors, *Advances in Neural Information Processing Systems 7*, pages 529–536. MIT Press, Cambridge MA, 1995.

[13] S. Hochreiter and J. Schmidhuber. Flat minima. *Neural Computation*, 9(1):1–42, 1997.

[14] S. Hochreiter and J. Schmidhuber. LOCOCODE. Technical Report FKI-222-97, Revised Version, Fakultät für Informatik, Technische Universität München, 1998.

[15] T. Kohonen. *Self-Organization and Associative Memory.* Springer, second ed., 1988.

[16] M. S. Lewicki and B. A. Olshausen. Inferring sparse, overcomplete image codes using an efficient coding framework. In M. I. Jordan, M. J. Kearns, and S. A. Solla, editors, *Advances in Neural Information Processing Systems 10*, 1998. To appear.

[17] R. Linsker. Self-organization in a perceptual network. *IEEE Computer*, 21:105–117, 1988.

[18] L. Molgedey and H. G. Schuster. Separation of independent signals using time-delayed correlations. *Phys. Reviews Letters*, 72(23):3634–3637, 1994.

[19] M. C. Mozer. Discovering discrete distributed representations with iterative competitive learning. In R. P. Lippmann, J. E. Moody, and D. S. Touretzky, editors, *Advances in Neural Information Processing Systems 3*, pages 627–634. San Mateo, CA: Morgan Kaufmann, 1991.

[20] E. Oja. Neural networks, principal components, and subspaces. *International Journal of Neural Systems*, 1(1):61–68, 1989.

[21] B. A. Olshausen and D. J. Field. Emergence of simple-cell receptive field properties by learning a sparse code for natural images. *Nature*, 381(6583):607–609, 1996.

[22] D. E. Rumelhart and D. Zipser. Feature discovery by competitive learning. In *Parallel Distributed Processing*, pages 151–193. MIT Press, 1986.

[23] J. Schmidhuber. Learning factorial codes by predictability minimization. *Neural Computation*, 4(6):863–879, 1992.

[24] S. Watanabe. *Pattern Recognition: Human and Mechanical.* Willey, New York, 1985.

[25] R. S. Zemel and G. E. Hinton. Developing population codes by minimizing description length. In J. D. Cowan, G. Tesauro, and J. Alspector, editors, *Advances in Neural Information Processing Systems 6*, pages 11–18. San Mateo, CA: Morgan Kaufmann, 1994.

Learning from Dyadic Data

Thomas Hofmann*, Jan Puzicha[+], Michael I. Jordan*
* Center for Biological and Computational Learning, M.I.T
Cambridge, MA, {hofmann, jordan}@ai.mit.edu
[+] Institut für Informatik III, Universität Bonn, Germany, jan@cs.uni-bonn.de

Abstract

Dyadic data refers to a domain with two finite sets of objects in which observations are made for *dyads*, i.e., pairs with one element from either set. This type of data arises naturally in many application ranging from computational linguistics and information retrieval to preference analysis and computer vision. In this paper, we present a systematic, domain-independent framework of learning from dyadic data by statistical *mixture models*. Our approach covers different models with flat and hierarchical latent class structures. We propose an *annealed* version of the standard EM algorithm for model fitting which is empirically evaluated on a variety of data sets from different domains.

1 Introduction

Over the past decade *learning from data* has become a highly active field of research distributed over many disciplines like pattern recognition, neural computation, statistics, machine learning, and data mining. Most domain-independent learning architectures as well as the underlying theories of learning have been focusing on a feature-based data representation by vectors in an Euclidean space. For this restricted case substantial progress has been achieved. However, a variety of important problems does not fit into this setting and far less advances have been made for data types based on different representations.

In this paper, we will present a general framework for unsupervised learning from *dyadic data*. The notion *dyadic* refers to a domain with two (abstract) sets of objects, $\mathcal{X} = \{x_1, \ldots, x_N\}$ and $\mathcal{Y} = \{y_1, \ldots, y_M\}$ in which observations $\mathcal{S}$ are made for *dyads* (x_i, y_k). In the simplest case – on which we focus – an elementary observation consists just of (x_i, y_k) itself, i.e., a *co-occurrence* of x_i and y_k, while other cases may also provide a scalar value w_{ik} (strength of preference or association). Some exemplary application areas are: (i) *Computational linguistics* with the corpus-based statistical analysis of word co-occurrences with applications in language modeling, word clustering, word sense disambiguation, and thesaurus construction. (ii) *Text-based information retrieval*, where $\mathcal{X}$ may correspond to a document collection, $\mathcal{Y}$

to keywords, and (x_i, y_k) would represent the occurrence of a term y_k in a document x_i. (iii) *Modeling of preference and consumption behavior* by identifying $\mathcal{X}$ with individuals and $\mathcal{Y}$ with objects or stimuli as in *collaborative filtering*. (iv) *Computer vision*, in particular in the context of image segmentation, where $\mathcal{X}$ corresponds to image locations, $\mathcal{Y}$ to discretized or categorical feature values, and a dyad (x_i, y_k) represents a feature y_k observed at a particular location x_i.

2 Mixture Models for Dyadic Data

Across different domains there are at least two tasks which play a fundamental role in unsupervised learning from dyadic data: (i) probabilistic modeling, i.e., learning a joint or conditional probability model over $\mathcal{X} \times \mathcal{Y}$, and (ii) structure discovery, e.g., identifying clusters and data hierarchies. The key problem in probabilistic modeling is the *data sparseness*: How can probabilities for rarely observed or even unobserved co-occurrences be reliably estimated? As an answer we propose a model-based approach and formulate *latent class* or *mixture models*. The latter have the further advantage to offer a unifying method for probabilistic modeling and structure discovery. There are at least three (four, if both variants in (ii) are counted) different ways of defining latent class models:

i. The most direct way is to introduce an (unobserved) mapping $c : \mathcal{X} \times \mathcal{Y} \to \{c_1, \ldots, c_K\}$ that partitions $\mathcal{X} \times \mathcal{Y}$ into K classes. This type of model is called *aspect-based* and the pre-image $c^{-1}(c_\alpha)$ is referred to as an *aspect*.

ii. Alternatively, a class can be defined as a subset of *one* of the spaces $\mathcal{X}$ (or $\mathcal{Y}$ by symmetry, yielding a different model), i.e., $c : \mathcal{X} \to \{c_1, \ldots, c_K\}$ which induces a unique partitioning on $\mathcal{X} \times \mathcal{Y}$ by $c(x_i, y_k) \equiv c(x_i)$. This model is referred to as *one-sided clustering* and $c^{-1}(c_\alpha) \subseteq \mathcal{X}$ is called a *cluster*.

iii. If latent classes are defined for both sets, $c : \mathcal{X} \to \{c_1^x, \ldots, c_K^x\}$ and $c : \mathcal{Y} \to \{c_1^y, \ldots, c_L^y\}$, respectively, this induces a mapping c which is a $K \cdot L-$partitioning of $\mathcal{X} \times \mathcal{Y}$. This model is called *two-sided clustering*.

2.1 Aspect Model for Dyadic Data

In order to specify an aspect model we make the assumption that all co-occurrences in the sample set $\mathcal{S}$ are i.i.d. and that x_i and y_k are conditionally independent given the class. With parameters $P(x_i|c_\alpha)$, $P(y_k|c_\alpha)$ for the class-conditional distributions and prior probabilities $P(c_\alpha)$ the complete data probability can be written as

$$P(\mathcal{S}, c) = \prod_{i,k} [P(c_{ik})P(x_i|c_{ik})P(y_k|c_{ik})]^{n(x_i, y_k)}, \qquad (1)$$

where $n(x_i, y_k)$ are the empirical counts for dyads in $\mathcal{S}$ and $c_{ik} \equiv c(x_i, y_k)$. By summing over the latent variables c the usual mixture formulation is obtained

$$P(\mathcal{S}) = \prod_{i,k} P(x_i, y_k)^{n(x_i, y_k)}, \quad \text{where} \quad P(x_i, y_k) = \sum_\alpha P(c_\alpha)P(x_i|c_\alpha)P(y_k|c_\alpha) . \qquad (2)$$

Following the standard *Expectation Maximization* approach for maximum likelihood estimation [Dempster *et al.*, 1977], the E-step equations for the class posterior probabilities are given by[1]

$$P\{c_{ik} = c_\alpha\} \propto P(c_\alpha)P(x_i|c_\alpha)P(y_j|c_\alpha) . \qquad (3)$$

---

[1] In the case of multiple observations of dyads it has been assumed that each observation may have a different latent class. If only one latent class variable is introduced for each dyad, slightly different equations are obtained.

$P(c_\alpha)$	#1, 0.004	#2, 0.005	#3, 0.008	#4, 0.002	#5, 0.040	#6, 0.011	#7, 0.029	#8, 0.007
maximal $P(x_i\|c_\alpha)$	two 0.18 seven 0.10 three 0.10 four 0.06 five 0.06	went 0.10 go 0.08 come 0.04 came 0.04 brought 0.03	have 0.38 hath 0.22 had 0.11 hast 0.09 be 0.02	shalt 0.18 hast 0.08 wilt 0.08 art 0.07 if 0.05	the 0.95 his 0.006 my 0.005 our 0.003 thy 0.003	he 0.51 god 0.08 lord 0.05 and 0.04 who 0.03	<,> 0.52 <:> 0.16 <,> 0.14 <;> 0.07 <?> 0.04	thee 0.04 me 0.03 him 0.03 it 0.02 you 0.02
maximal $P(y_k\|c_\alpha)$	years 0.11 thousand 0.1 hundred 0.1 days 0.07 cubits 0.05	up 0.40 down 0.17 forth 0.15 out 0.09 in 0.01	not 0.04 done 0.04 given 0.03 made 0.03 been 0.03	thou 0.85 not 0.01 also 0.004 indeed 0.003 anoint 0.003	lord 0.09 children 0.02 son 0.02 land 0.02 people 0.02	hath 0.14 shall 0.07 said 0.05 is 0.04 was 0.04	and 0.33 for 0.08 but 0.07 then 0.05 so 0.02	<?> 0.27 <,> 0.23 <,> 0.12 <:> 0.06 <;> 0.04

Figure 1: Some aspects of the *Bible* (bigrams).

It is straightforward to derive the M-step re-estimation formulae

$$P(c_\alpha) \propto \sum_{i,k} n(x_i, y_k) P\{c_{ik} = c_\alpha\}, \ P(x_i|c_\alpha) \propto \sum_k n(x_i, y_k) P\{c_{ik} = c_\alpha\}, \quad (4)$$

and an analogous equation for $P(y_k|c_\alpha)$. By re-parameterization the aspect model can also be characterized by a cross-entropy criterion. Moreover, formal equivalence to the *aggregate Markov model*, independently proposed for language modeling in [Saul, Pereira, 1997], has been established (cf. [Hofmann, Puzicha, 1998] for details).

2.2 One-Sided Clustering Model

The complete data model proposed for the one-sided clustering model is

$$P(\mathcal{S}, c) = P(c)P(\mathcal{S}|c) = \left(\prod_i P(c(x_i))\right) \left(\prod_{i,k} [P(x_i)P(y_k|c(x_i))]^{n(x_i, y_k)}\right), \quad (5)$$

where we have made the assumption that observations (x_i, y_k) for a particular x_i are conditionally independent given $c(x_i)$. This effectively defines the mixture

$$P(\mathcal{S}) = \prod_i P(\mathcal{S}_i), \quad P(\mathcal{S}_i) = \sum_\alpha P(c_\alpha) \prod_k [P(x_i)P(y_k|c_\alpha)]^{n(x_i, y_k)}, \quad (6)$$

where $\mathcal{S}_i$ are all observations involving x_i. Notice that co-occurrences in $\mathcal{S}_i$ are not independent (as they are in the aspect model), but get coupled by the (shared) latent variable $c(x_i)$. As before, it is straightforward to derive an EM algorithm with update equations

$$P\{c(x_i) = c_\alpha\} \propto P(c_\alpha) \prod_k P(y_k|c_\alpha)^{n(x_i, y_k)}, \ P(y_k|c_\alpha) \propto \sum_i n(x_i, y_k) P\{c(x_i) = c_\alpha\} \quad (7)$$

and $P(c_\alpha) \propto \sum_i P\{c(x_i) = c_\alpha\}$, $P(x_i) \propto \sum_j n(x_i, y_j)$. The one-sided clustering model is similar to the distributional clustering model [Pereira *et al.*, 1993], however, there are two important differences: (i) the number of likelihood contributions in (7) scales with the number of observations – a fact which follows from Bayes' rule – and (ii) mixing proportions are missing in the original distributional clustering model. The one-sided clustering model corresponds to an unsupervised version of the naive Bayes' classifier, if we interpret $\mathcal{Y}$ as a feature space for objects $x_i \in \mathcal{X}$. There are also ways to weaken the conditional independence assumption, e.g., by utilizing a mixture of tree dependency models [Meila, Jordan, 1998].

2.3 Two-Sided Clustering Model

The latent variable structure of the two-sided clustering model significantly reduces the degrees of freedom in the specification of the class conditional distribution. We

Learning from Dyadic Data

Figure 2: Exemplary segmentation results on *Aerial* by one-sided clustering.

propose the following complete data model

$$P(\mathcal{S}, c) = \prod_{i,k} P(c(x_i)) P(c(y_k)) \left[P(x_i) P(y_k) \pi_{c(x_i), c(y_k)} \right]^{n(x_i, y_k)} \quad (8)$$

where $\pi_{c_\alpha^x, c_\gamma^y}$ are cluster association parameters. In this model the latent variables in the $\mathcal{X}$ and $\mathcal{Y}$ space are coupled by the π-parameters. Therefore, there exists no simple mixture model representation for $P(\mathcal{S})$. Skipping some of the technical details (cf. [Hofmann, Puzicha, 1998]) we obtain $P(x_i) \propto \sum_k n(x_i, y_k)$, $P(y_k) \propto \sum_i n(x_i, y_k)$ and the M-step equations

$$\pi_{c_\alpha^x, c_\gamma^y} = \frac{\sum_{i,k} n(x_i, y_k) P\{c(x_i) = c_\alpha^x \wedge c(y_k) = c_\gamma^y\}}{[\sum_i P\{c(x_i) = c_\alpha^x\} \sum_k n(x_i, y_k)][\sum_k P\{c(y_k) = c_\gamma^y\} \sum_i n(x_i, y_k)]} \quad (9)$$

as well as $P(c_\alpha^x) = \sum_i P\{c(x_i) = c_\alpha^x\}$ and $P(c_\gamma^y) = \sum_k P\{c(x_k) = c_\gamma^y\}$. To preserve tractability for the remaining problem of computing the posterior probabilities in the E-step, we apply a factorial approximation (*mean field* approximation), i.e., $P\{c(x_i) = c_\alpha^x \wedge c(y_k) = c_\gamma^y\} \approx P\{c(x_i) = c_\alpha^x\} P\{c(y_k) = c_\gamma^y\}$. This results in the following coupled approximation equations for the marginal posterior probabilities

$$P\{c(x_i) = c_\alpha^x\} \propto P(c_\alpha^x) \exp\left[\sum_k n(x_i, y_k) \sum_\gamma P\{c(y_k) = c_\gamma^y\} \log \pi_{c_\alpha^x, c_\gamma^y}\right] \quad (10)$$

and a similar equation for $P\{c(y_k) = c_\gamma^y\}$. The resulting approximate EM algorithm performs updates according to the sequence (c^x-post., π, c^y-post., π). Intuitively the (probabilistic) clustering in one set is optimized in alternation for a given clustering in the other space and vice versa. The two-sided clustering model can also be shown to maximize a mutual information criterion [Hofmann, Puzicha, 1998].

2.4 Discussion: Aspects and Clusters

To better understand the differences of the presented models it is elucidating to systematically compare the conditional probabilities $P(c_\alpha | x_i)$ and $P(c_\alpha | y_k)$:

	Aspect Model	One-sided $\mathcal{X}$ Clustering	One-sided $\mathcal{Y}$ Clustering	Two-sided Clustering
$P(c_\alpha\|x_i)$	$\frac{P(x_i\|c_\alpha) P(c_\alpha)}{P(x_i)}$	$P\{c(x_i) = c_\alpha\}$	$\frac{P(x_i\|c_\alpha) P(c_\alpha)}{P(x_i)}$	$P\{c(x_i) = c_\alpha^x\}$
$P(c_\alpha\|y_k)$	$\frac{P(y_k\|c_\alpha) P(c_\alpha)}{P(y_k)}$	$\frac{P(y_k\|c_\alpha) P(c_\alpha)}{P(y_k)}$	$P\{c(y_k) = c_\alpha\}$	$P\{c(y_k) = c_\alpha^y\}$

As can be seen from the above table, probabilities $P(c_\alpha | x_i)$ and $P(c_\alpha | y_k)$ correspond to posterior probabilities of latent variables if clusters are defined in the $\mathcal{X}$- and $\mathcal{Y}$-space, respectively. Otherwise, they are computed from model *parameters*. This is a crucial difference as, for example, the posterior probabilities are approaching

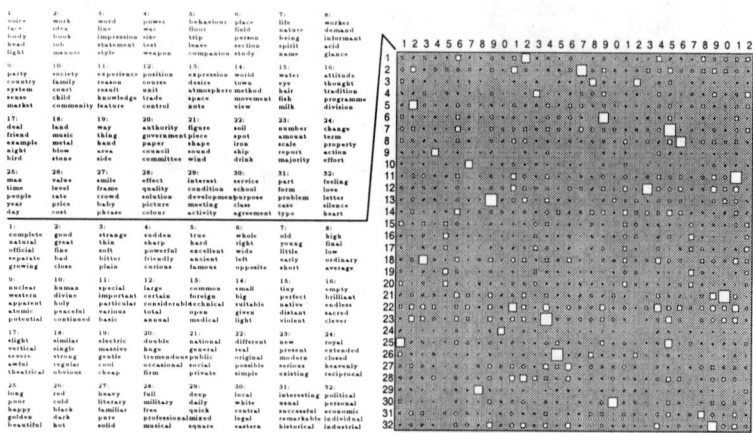

Figure 3: Two-sided clustering of LOB: π matrix and most probable words.

Boolean values in the infinite data limit and $P(y_k|x_i) = \sum_\alpha P\{c(x_i) = c_\alpha\} P(y_k|c_\alpha)$ are converging to one of the class-conditional distributions. Yet, in the aspect model $P(y_k|x_i) = \sum_\alpha P(c_\alpha|x_i) P(y_k|c_\alpha)$ and $P(c_\alpha|x_i) \propto P(c_\alpha) P(x_i|c_\alpha)$ are typically not peaking more sharply with an increasing number of observations. In the aspect model, conditionals $P(y_k|x_i)$ are inherently a weighted sum of the 'prototypical' distributions $P(y_k|c_\alpha)$. Cluster models in turn ultimately look for the 'best' class-conditional and weights are only indirectly induced by the posterior uncertainty.

3 The Cluster-Abstraction Model

The models discussed in Section 2 all define a non-hierarchical, 'flat' latent class structure. However, for structure discovery it is important to find hierarchical data organizations. There are well-known architectures like the *Hierarchical Mixtures of Experts* [Jordan, Jacobs, 1994] which fit hierarchical models. Yet, in the case of dyadic data there is an alternative possibility to define a hierarchical model. The *Cluster-Abstraction Model* (CAM) is a clustering model (e.g., in $\mathcal{X}$) where the conditionals $P(y_k|c_\alpha)$ are itself x_i-specific aspect mixtures, $P(y_k|c_\alpha, x_i) = \sum_\nu P(y_k|a_\nu) P(a_\nu|c_\alpha, x_i)$ with a latent aspect mapping a. To obtain a hierarchical organization, clusters c_α are identified with the terminal nodes of a hierarchy (e.g., a complete binary tree) and aspects a_ν with inner *and* terminal nodes. As a compatibility constraint it is imposed that $P(a_\nu|c_\alpha, x_i) = 0$ whenever the node corresponding to a_ν is not on the path to the terminal node c_α. Intuitively, conditioned on a 'horizontal' clustering c all observations $(x_i, y_k) \in S_i$ for a particular x_i have to be generated from one of the 'vertical' abstraction levels on the path to $c(x_i)$. Since different clusters share aspects according to their topological relation, this favors a meaningful hierarchical organization of clusters. Moreover, aspects at inner nodes do not simply represent averages over clusters in their subtree as they are forced to explicitly represent what is *common* to all subsequent clusters.

Skipping the technical details, the E-step is given by

$$P\{a(x_i, y_k) = a_\nu | c(x_i) = c_\alpha\} \propto P(a_\nu|c_\alpha, x_i) P(y_k|a_\nu) \qquad (11)$$

$$P\{c(x_i) = c_\alpha\} \propto P(c_\alpha) \prod_k \sum_\nu [P(a_\nu|c_\alpha, x_i) P(y_k|a_\nu)]^{n(x_i, y_k)} \qquad (12)$$

and the M-step formulae are $P(y_k|a_\nu) \propto \sum_i P\{a(x_i, y_k) = a_\nu\} n(x_i, y_k)$, $P(c_\alpha) \propto \sum_i P\{c(x_i) = c_\alpha\}$, and $P(a_\nu|c_\alpha, x_i) \propto \sum_k P\{a(x_i, y_k) = a_\nu | c(x_i) = c_\alpha\} n(x_i, y_k)$.

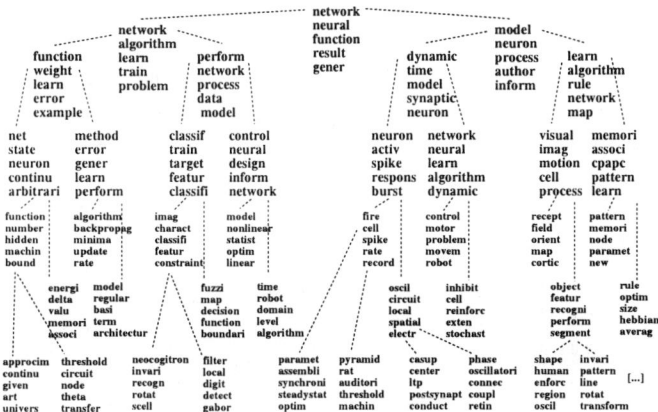

Figure 4: Parts of the top levels of a hierarchical clustering solution for the *Neural* document collection, aspects are represented by their 5 most probable word stems.

4 Annealed Expectation Maximization

Annealed EM is a generalization of EM based on the idea of *deterministic annealing* [Rose et al., 1990] that has been successfully applied as a heuristic optimization technique to many clustering and mixture problems. Annealing reduces the sensitivity to local maxima, but, even more importantly in this context, it may also improve the generalization performance compared to maximum likelihood estimation.[2] The key idea in annealed EM is to introduce an (inverse temperature) parameter β, and to replace the negative (averaged) complete data log-likelihood by a substitute known as the *free energy* (both are in fact equivalent at $\beta = 1$). This effectively results in a simple modification of the E-step by taking the likelihood contribution in Bayes' rule to the power of β. In order to determine the optimal value for β we used an additional validation set in a cross validation procedure.

5 Results and Conclusions

In our experiments we have utilized the following real-world data sets: (i) *Cranfield*: a standard test collection from information retrieval ($N = 1400$, $M = 4898$), (ii) *Penn*: adjective-noun co-occurrences from the Penn Treebank corpus ($N = 6931$, $M = 4995$) and the LOB corpus ($N = 5448$, $M = 6052$), (iii) *Neural*: a document collection with abstracts of journal papers on neural networks ($N = 1278$, $M = 6065$), (iv) *Bible*: word bigrams from the bible edition of the Gutenberg project ($N = M = 12858$), (v) *Aerial*: Textured aerial images for segmentation ($N = 128 \times 128$, $M = 192$).

In Fig. 1 we have visualized an aspect model fitted to the *Bible* bigram data. Notice that although $\mathcal{X} = \mathcal{Y}$ the role of the preceding and the subsequent words in bigrams is quite different. Segmentation results obtained on *Aerial* applying the one-sided clustering model are depicted in Fig. 2. A multi-scale Gabor filter bank (3 octaves, 4 orientations) was utilized as an image representation (cf. [Hofmann et al., 1998]). In Fig. 3 a two-sided clustering solution of LOB is shown. Fig. 4 shows the top levels of the hierarchy found by the Cluster-Abstraction Model in *Neural*. The inner node distributions provide resolution-specific descriptors for the documents in the corresponding subtree which can be utilized, e.g., in interactive browsing for information retrieval. Fig. 5 shows typical test set perplexity curves of the

---

[2] Moreover, the tree topology for the CAM is heuristically grown via phase transitions.

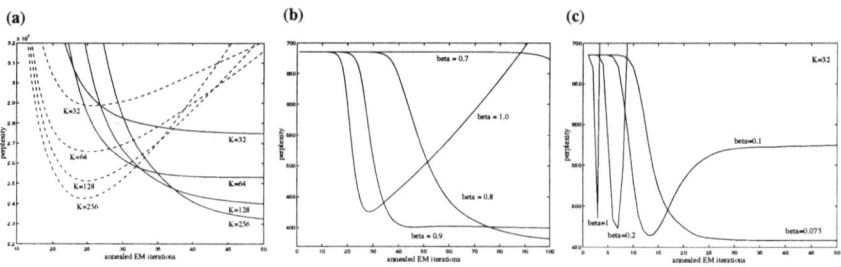

Figure 5: Perplexity curves for annealed EM (aspect (a), (b) and one-sided clustering model (c)) on the *Bible* and *Cran* data.

	Aspect		$\mathcal{X}$-cluster		CAM		$\mathcal{X}/\mathcal{Y}$-cluster		Aspect		$\mathcal{X}$-cluster		CAM		$\mathcal{X}/\mathcal{Y}$-cluster	
K	β	$\mathcal{P}$	β	$\mathcal{P}$	β	$\mathcal{P}$	β	$\mathcal{P}$	β	$\mathcal{P}$	β	$\mathcal{P}$	β	$\mathcal{P}$	β	$\mathcal{P}$
	Cran								Penn							
1	-	685	-	-	-	-	-	-	-	639	-	-	-	-	-	-
8	0.88	482	0.09	527	0.18	511	0.67	615	0.73	312	0.08	352	0.13	322	0.55	394
16	0.72	255	0.07	302	0.10	268	0.51	335	0.72	255	0.07	302	0.10	268	0.51	335
32	0.83	386	0.07	**452**	0.12	438	0.53	506	0.71	205	0.07	254	0.08	226	0.46	286
64	0.79	360	0.06	527	0.11	422	0.48	477	0.69	182	0.07	**223**	0.07	204	0.44	272
128	0.78	**353**	0.04	663	0.10	**410**	0.45	**462**	0.68	**166**	0.06	231	0.06	**179**	0.40	**241**

Table 1: Perplexity results for different models on the *Cran* (predicting words conditioned on documents) and *Penn* data (predicting nouns conditioned on adjectives).

annealed EM algorithm for the aspect and clustering model ($\mathcal{P} = e^{-l}$ where l is the per-observation log-likelihood). At $\beta = 1$ (standard EM) overfitting is clearly visible, an effect that vanishes with decreasing β. Annealed learning performs also better than standard EM with early stopping. Tab. 1 systematically summarizes perplexity results for different models and data sets.

In *conclusion* mixture models for dyadic data have shown a broad application potential. Annealing yields a substantial improvement in generalization performance compared to standard EM, in particular for clustering models, and also outperforms a complexity control via K. In terms of perplexity, the aspect model has the best performance. Detailed performance studies and comparisons with other state-of-the-art techniques will appear in forthcoming papers.

References

[Dempster et al., 1977] Dempster, A.P., Laird, N.M., Rubin, D.B. (1977). Maximum likelihood from incomplete data via the EM algorithm. *J. Royal Statist. Soc. B*, **39**, 1–38.

[Hofmann, Puzicha, 1998] Hofmann, T., Puzicha, J. 1998. *Statistical models for co-occurrence data*. Tech. rept. Artifical Intelligence Laboratory Memo 1625, M.I.T.

[Hofmann et al., 1998] Hofmann, T., Puzicha, J., Buhmann, J.M. (1998). Unsupervised texture segmentation in a deterministic annealing framework. *IEEE Transactions on Pattern Analysis and Machine Intelligence*, **20**(8), 803–818.

[Jordan, Jacobs, 1994] Jordan, M.I., Jacobs, R.A. (1994). Hierarchical mixtures of experts and the EM algorithm. *Neural Computation*, **6**(2), 181–214.

[Meila, Jordan, 1998] Meila, M., Jordan, M. I. 1998. Estimating Dependency Structure as a Hidden Variable. *In: Advances in Neural Information Processing Systems 10*.

[Pereira et al., 1993] Pereira, F.C.N., Tishby, N.Z., Lee, L. 1993. Distributional clustering of English words. *Pages 183–190 of: Proceedings of the ACL*.

[Rose et al., 1990] Rose, K., Gurewitz, E., Fox, G. (1990). Statistical mechanics and phase transitions in clustering. *Physical Review Letters*, **65**(8), 945–948.

[Saul, Pereira, 1997] Saul, L., Pereira, F. 1997. Aggregate and mixed–order Markov models for statistical language processing. *In: Proceedings of the 2nd International Conference on Empirical Methods in Natural Language Processing*.

Sparse Code Shrinkage: Denoising by Nonlinear Maximum Likelihood Estimation

Aapo Hyvärinen, Patrik Hoyer and Erkki Oja
Helsinki University of Technology
Laboratory of Computer and Information Science
P.O. Box 5400, FIN-02015 HUT, Finland
aapo.hyvarinen@hut.fi,patrik.hoyer@hut.fi,erkki.oja@hut.fi
http://www.cis.hut.fi/projects/ica/

Abstract

Sparse coding is a method for finding a representation of data in which each of the components of the representation is only rarely significantly active. Such a representation is closely related to redundancy reduction and independent component analysis, and has some neurophysiological plausibility. In this paper, we show how sparse coding can be used for denoising. Using maximum likelihood estimation of nongaussian variables corrupted by gaussian noise, we show how to apply a shrinkage nonlinearity on the components of sparse coding so as to reduce noise. Furthermore, we show how to choose the optimal sparse coding basis for denoising. Our method is closely related to the method of wavelet shrinkage, but has the important benefit over wavelet methods that both the features and the shrinkage parameters are estimated directly from the data.

1 Introduction

A fundamental problem in neural network research is to find a suitable representation for the data. One of the simplest methods is to use linear transformations of the observed data. Denote by $\mathbf{x} = (x_1, x_2, ..., x_n)^T$ the observed n-dimensional random vector that is the input data (e.g., an image window), and by $\mathbf{s} = (s_1, s_2, ..., s_n)^T$ the vector of the linearly transformed component variables. Denoting further the $n \times n$ transformation matrix by $\mathbf{W}$, the linear representation is given by

$$\mathbf{s} = \mathbf{W}\mathbf{x}. \qquad (1)$$

We assume here that the number of transformed components equals the number of observed variables, but this need not be the case in general.

An important representation method is given by (linear) sparse coding [1, 10], in which the representation of the form (1) has the property that only a small number of the components s_i of the representation are significantly non-zero at the same time. Equivalently, this means that a given component has a 'sparse' distribution. A random variable s_i is called sparse when s_i has a distribution with a peak at zero, and heavy tails, as is the case, for example, with the double exponential (or Laplace) distribution [6]; for all practical purposes, sparsity is equivalent to supergaussianity or leptokurtosis [8]. Sparse coding is an adaptive method, meaning that the matrix $\mathbf{W}$ is estimated for a given class of data so that the components s_i are as sparse as possible; such an estimation procedure is closely related to independent component analysis [2].

Sparse coding of sensory data has been shown to have advantages from both physiological and information processing viewpoints [1]. However, thorough analyses of the utility of such a coding scheme have been few. In this paper, we introduce and analyze a statistical method based on sparse coding. Given a signal corrupted by additive gaussian noise, we attempt to *reduce gaussian noise* by soft thresholding ('shrinkage') of the sparse components. Intuitively, because only a few of the components are significantly active in the sparse code of a given data point, one may assume that the activities of components with small absolute values are purely noise and set them to zero, retaining just a few components with large activities. This method is closely connected to the wavelet shrinkage method [3]. In fact, sparse coding may be viewed as a principled way for determining a wavelet-like basis and the corresponding shrinkage nonlinearities, based on data alone.

2 Maximum likelihood estimation of sparse components

The starting point of a rigorous derivation of our denoising method is the fact that the distributions of the sparse components are nongaussian. Therefore, we shall begin by developing a general theory that shows how to remove gaussian noise from nongaussian variables, making minimal assumptions on the data.

Denote by s the original nongaussian random variable (corresponding here to a noise-free version of one of the sparse components s_i), and by ν gaussian noise of zero mean and variance σ^2. Assume that we only observe the random variable y:

$$y = s + \nu \qquad (2)$$

and we want to estimate the original s. Denoting by p the probability density of s, and by $f = -\log p$ its negative log-density, the maximum likelihood (ML) method gives the following estimator for s:

$$\hat{s} = \arg\min_u \frac{1}{2\sigma^2}(y-u)^2 + f(u). \qquad (3)$$

Assuming f to be strictly convex and differentiable, this can be solved [6] to yield $\hat{s} = g(y)$, where the function g can be obtained from the relation

$$g^{-1}(u) = u + \sigma^2 f'(u). \qquad (4)$$

This nonlinear estimator forms the basis of our method.

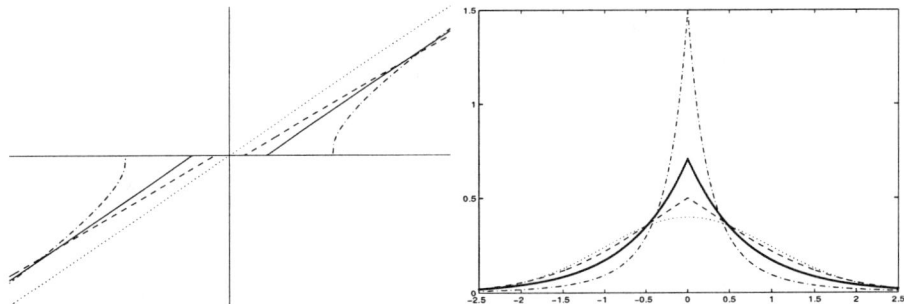

Figure 1: Shrinkage nonlinearities and associated probability densities. Left: Plots of the different shrinkage functions. Solid line: shrinkage corresponding to Laplace density. Dashed line: typical shrinkage function obtained from (6). Dash-dotted line: typical shrinkage function obtained from (8). For comparison, the line $x = y$ is given by dotted line. All the densities were normalized to unit variance, and noise variance was fixed to .3. Right: Plots of corresponding model densities of the sparse components. Solid line: Laplace density. Dashed line: a typical moderately supergaussian density given by (5). Dash-dotted line: a typical strongly supergaussian density given by (7). For comparison, gaussian density is given by dotted line.

3 Parameterizations of sparse densities

To use the estimator defined by (3) in practice, the densities of the s_i need to be modelled with a parameterization that is rich enough. We have developed two parameterizations that seem to describe very well most of the densities encountered in image denoising. Moreover, the parameters are easy to estimate, and the inversion in (4) can be performed analytically. Both models use two parameters and are thus able to model different degrees of supergaussianity, in addition to different scales, i.e. variances. The densities are here assumed to be symmetric and of zero mean.

The *first model* is suitable for supergaussian densities that are not sparser than the Laplace distribution [6], and is given by the family of densities

$$p(s) = C \exp(-as^2/2 - b|s|), \qquad (5)$$

where $a, b > 0$ are parameters to be estimated, and C is an irrelevant scaling constant. The classical Laplace density is obtained when $a = 0$, and gaussian densities correspond to $b = 0$. A simple method for estimating a and b was given in [6]. For this density, the nonlinearity g takes the form:

$$g(u) = \frac{1}{1 + \sigma^2 a} \mathrm{sign}(u) \max(0, |u| - b\sigma^2) \qquad (6)$$

where σ^2 is the noise variance. The effect of the *shrinkage* function in (6) is to reduce the absolute value of its argument by a certain amount, which depends on the parameters, and then rescale. Small arguments are thus set to zero. Examples of the obtained shrinkage functions are given in Fig. 1.

The *second model* describes densities that are sparser than the Laplace density:

$$p(s) = \frac{1}{2d} \frac{(\alpha + 2)[\alpha(\alpha+1)/2]^{(\alpha/2+1)}}{[\sqrt{\alpha(\alpha+1)/2} + |s/d|]^{(\alpha+3)}}. \qquad (7)$$

When $\alpha \to \infty$, the Laplace density is obtained as the limit. A simple consistent method for estimating the parameters $d, \alpha > 0$ in (7) can be obtained from the relations $d = \sqrt{E\{s^2\}}$ and $\alpha = (2 - k + \sqrt{k(k+4)})/(2k-1)$ with $k = d^2 p_s(0)^2$, see [6]. The resulting shrinkage function can be obtained as [6]

$$g(u) = \text{sign}(u) \max(0, \frac{|u| - ad}{2} + \frac{1}{2}\sqrt{(|u| + ad)^2 - 4\sigma^2(\alpha + 3)}) \qquad (8)$$

where $a = \sqrt{\alpha(\alpha + 1)/2}$, and $g(u)$ is set to zero in case the square root in (8) is imaginary. This is a shrinkage function that has a certain hard-thresholding flavor, as depicted in Fig. 1.

Examples of the shapes of the densities given by (5) and (7) are given in Fig. 1, together with a Laplace density and a gaussian density. For illustration purposes, the densities in the plot are normalized to unit variance, but these parameterizations allow the variance to be choosen freely.

Choosing whether model (5) or (7) should be used can be based on moments of the distributions; see [6]. Methods for estimating the noise variance σ^2 are given in [3, 6].

4 Sparse code shrinkage

The above results imply the following *sparse code shrinkage* method for denoising. Assume that we observe a noisy version $\tilde{\mathbf{x}} = \mathbf{x} + \boldsymbol{\nu}$ of the data $\mathbf{x}$, where $\boldsymbol{\nu}$ is gaussian white noise vector. To denoise $\tilde{\mathbf{x}}$, we transform the data to a sparse code, apply the above ML estimation procedure component-wise, and then transform back to the original variables. Here, we constrain the transformation to be orthogonal; this is motivated in Section 5. To summarize:

1. First, using a noise-free training set of $\mathbf{x}$, use some sparse coding method for determining the orthogonal matrix $\mathbf{W}$ so that the components s_i in $\mathbf{s} = \mathbf{W}\mathbf{x}$ have as sparse distributions as possible. Estimate a density model $p_i(s_i)$ for each sparse component, using the models in (5) and (7).

2. Compute for each noisy observation $\tilde{\mathbf{x}}(t)$ of $\mathbf{x}$ the corresponding noisy sparse components $\mathbf{y}(t) = \mathbf{W}\tilde{\mathbf{x}}(t)$. Apply the shrinkage non-linearity $g_i(.)$ as defined in (6), or in (8), on each component $y_i(t)$, for every observation index t. Denote the obtained components by $\hat{s}_i(t) = g_i(y_i(t))$.

3. Invert the relation (1) to obtain estimates of the noise-free $\mathbf{x}$, given by $\hat{\mathbf{x}}(t) = \mathbf{W}^T \hat{\mathbf{s}}(t)$.

To estimate the sparsifying transform $\mathbf{W}$, we assume that we have access to a noise-free realization of the underlying random vector. This assumption is not unrealistic on many applications: for example, in image denoising it simply means that we can observe noise-free images that are somewhat similar to the noisy image to be treated, i.e., they belong to the same environment or context. This assumption can be, however, relaxed in many cases, see [7]. The problem of finding an optimal sparse code in step 1 is treated in the next section.

In fact, it turns out that the shrinkage operation given above is quite similar to the one used in the wavelet shrinkage method derived earlier by Donoho et al [3] from a very different approach. Their estimator consisted of applying the shrinkage operator in (6), with different values for the parameters, on the coefficients of the wavelet transform. There are two main differences between the two methods. The first is the choice of the transformation. We choose the transformation using the statistical properties of the data at hand, whereas Donoho et al use a predetermined wavelet transform. The second important difference is that we estimate the shrinkage nonlinearities by the ML principle, again adapting to the data at hand, whereas Donoho et al use fixed thresholding operators derived by the minimax principle.

5 Choosing the optimal sparse code

Different measures of sparseness (or nongaussianity) have been proposed in the literature [1, 4, 8, 10]. In this section, we show which measures are optimal for our method. We shall here restrict ourselves to the class of linear, orthogonal transformations. This restriction is justified by the fact that orthogonal transformations leave the gaussian noise structure intact, which makes the problem more simply tractable. This restriction can be relaxed, however, see [7].

A simple, yet very attractive principle for choosing the basis for sparse coding is to consider the data to be generated by a noisy independent component analysis (ICA) model [10, 6, 9]:

$$\mathbf{x} = \mathbf{A}\mathbf{s} + \boldsymbol{\nu}, \tag{9}$$

where the s_i are now the independent components, and $\boldsymbol{\nu}$ is multivariate gaussian noise. We could then estimate $\mathbf{A}$ using ordinary maximum likelihood estimation of the ICA model. Under the restriction that $\mathbf{A}$ is constrained to be orthogonal, estimation of the noise-free components s_i then amounts to the above method of shrinking the values of $\mathbf{A}^T\mathbf{x}$, see [6]. In this ML sense, the optimal transformation matrix is thus given by $\mathbf{W} = \mathbf{A}^T$. In particular, using this principle means that ordinary ICA algorithms can be used to estimate the sparse coding basis. This is very fortunate since the computationally efficient methods for ICA estimation enable the basis estimation even in spaces of rather high dimensions [8, 5].

An alternative principle for determining the optimal sparsifying transformation is to minimize the mean-square error (MSE). In [6], a theorem is given that shows that the optimal basis in minimum MSE sense is obtained by maximizing $\sum_{i=1}^{n} I_F(\mathbf{w}_i^T\mathbf{x})$ where $I_F(s) = E\{[p'(s)/p(s)]^2\}$ is the Fisher information of the density of s, and the $\mathbf{w}_i^T$ are the rows of $\mathbf{W}$. Fisher information of a density [4] can be considered as a measure of its nongaussianity. It is well-known [4] that in the set of probability densities of unit variance, Fisher information is minimized by the gaussian density, and the minimum equals 1. Thus the theorem shows that the more nongaussian (sparse) s is, the better we can reduce noise. Note, however, that Fisher information is not scale-invariant.

The former (ML) method of determining the basis matrix gives usually sparser components than the latter method based on minimizing MSE. In the case of image denoising, however, these two methods give essentially equivalent bases if a perceptually weighted MSE is used [6]. Thus we luckily avoid the classical dilemma of choosing between these two optimality criteria.

6 Experiments

Image data seems to fulfill the assumptions inherent in sparse code shrinkage: It is possible to find linear representations whose components have sparse distributions, using wavelet-like filters [10]. Thus we performed a set of experiments to explore the utility of sparse code shrinkage in image denoising. The experiments are reported in more detail in [7].

Data. The data consisted of real-life images, mainly natural scenes. The images were randomly divided into two sets. The first set was used in estimating the matrix $\mathbf{W}$ that gives the sparse coding transformation, as well as in estimating the shrinkage nonlinearities. The second set was used as a test set. It was artificially corrupted by Gaussian noise, and sparse code shrinkage was used to reduce the noise. The images were used in the method in the form of subwindows of 8×8 pixels.

Methods. The sparse coding matrix $\mathbf{W}$ was determined by first estimating the ICA model for the image windows (with DC component removed) using the FastICA algorithm [8, 5], and projecting the obtained estimate on the space of orthogonal matrices. The training images were also used to estimate the parametric density models of the sparse components. In the first series of experiments, the local variance was equalized as a preprocessing step [7]. This implied that the density in (5) was a more suitable model for the densities of the sparse components; thus the shrinkage function in (6) was used. In the second series, no such equalization was made, and the density model (7) and the shrinkage function (8) were used [7].

Results. Fig. 2 shows, on the left, a test image which was artificially corrupted with Gaussian noise with standard deviation 0.5 (the standard deviations of the original images were normalized to 1). The result of applying our denoising method (without local variance equalization) on that image is shown on the right. Visual comparison of the images in Fig. 2 shows that our sparse code shrinkage method cancels noise quite effectively. One sees that contours and other sharp details are conserved quite well, while the overall reduction of noise is quite strong, which in is contrast to methods based on low-pass filtering. This result is in line with those obtained by wavelet shrinkage [3]. More experimental results are given in [7].

7 Conclusion

Sparse coding and ICA can be applied for image feature extraction, resulting in a wavelet-like basis for image windows [10]. As a practical application of such a basis, we introduced the method of sparse code shrinkage. It is based on the fact that in sparse coding the energy of the signal is concentrated on only a few components, which are different for each observed vector. By shrinking the absolute values of the sparse components towards zero, noise can be reduced. The method is also closely connected to modeling image data with noisy independent component analysis [9]. We showed how to find the optimal sparse coding basis for denoising, and we developed families of probability densities that allow the shrinkage nonlinearities to adapt accurately to the data at hand. Experiments on image data showed that the performance of the method is very appealing. The method reduces noise without blurring edges or other sharp features as much as linear low-pass or median filtering. This is made possible by the strongly non-linear nature of the shrinkage operator that takes advantage of the inherent statistical structure of natural images.

Figure 2: An experiment in image denoising. A noisy image, depicted on the left, was denoised by sparse code shrinkage to obtain the image on the right.

References

[1] H.B. Barlow. What is the computational goal of the neocortex ? In C. Koch and J.L. Davis, editors, *Large-scale neuronal theories of the brain*. MIT Press, Cambridge, MA, 1994.

[2] P. Comon. Independent component analysis – a new concept? *Signal Processing*, 36:287–314, 1994.

[3] D. L. Donoho, I. M. Johnstone, G. Kerkyacharian, and D. Picard. Wavelet shrinkage: asymptopia? *Journal of the Royal Statistical Society ser. B*, 57:301–337, 1995.

[4] P.J. Huber. Projection pursuit. *The Annals of Statistics*, 13(2):435–475, 1985.

[5] A. Hyvärinen. A family of fixed-point algorithms for independent component analysis. In *Proc. IEEE Int. Conf. on Acoustics, Speech and Signal Processing (ICASSP'97)*, pages 3917–3920, Munich, Germany, 1997.

[6] A. Hyvärinen. Sparse code shrinkage: Denoising of nongaussian data by maximum likelihood estimation. Technical Report A51, Helsinki University of Technology, Laboratory of Computer and Information Science, 1998.

[7] A. Hyvärinen, P. Hoyer, and E. Oja. Applications of sparse code shrinkage to image denoising. Technical report, Helsinki University of Technology, Laboratory of Computer and Information Science, 1998. To appear.

[8] A. Hyvärinen and E. Oja. A fast fixed-point algorithm for independent component analysis. *Neural Computation*, 9(7):1483–1492, 1997.

[9] M. Lewicki and B. Olshausen. Inferring sparse, overcomplete image codes using an efficient coding framework. In *Advances in Neural Information Processing 10 (Proc. NIPS*97)*, pages 815–821. MIT Press, 1998.

[10] B. A. Olshausen and D. J. Field. Emergence of simple-cell receptive field properties by learning a sparse code for natural images. *Nature*, 381:607–609, 1996.

Restructuring Sparse High Dimensional Data for Effective Retrieval

Charles Lee Isbell, Jr.
AT&T Labs
180 Park Avenue Room A255
Florham Park, NJ 07932-0971

Paul Viola
Artificial Intelligence Laboratory
Massachusetts Institute of Technology
Cambridge, MA 02139

Abstract

The task in text retrieval is to find the subset of a collection of documents relevant to a user's information request, usually expressed as a set of words. Classically, documents and queries are represented as vectors of word counts. In its simplest form, relevance is defined to be the dot product between a document and a query vector–a measure of the number of common terms. A central difficulty in text retrieval is that the presence or absence of a word is not sufficient to determine relevance to a query. Linear dimensionality reduction has been proposed as a technique for extracting underlying structure from the document collection. In some domains (such as vision) dimensionality reduction reduces computational complexity. In text retrieval it is more often used to improve retrieval performance. We propose an alternative and novel technique that produces *sparse* representations constructed from sets of highly-related words. Documents and queries are represented by their distance to these sets, and relevance is measured by the number of common clusters. This technique significantly improves retrieval performance, is efficient to compute and shares properties with the optimal linear projection operator and the *independent components* of documents.

1 Introduction

The task in text retrieval is to find the subset of a collection of documents relevant to a user's information request, usually expressed as a set of words. Naturally, we would like to apply techniques from natural language understanding to this problem. Unfortunately, the sheer size of the data to be represented makes this difficult. We wish to process tens or hundreds of thousands of documents, each of which may contain hundreds of thousands of different words. It is clear that any useful approach must be time and space efficient.

Following (Salton, 1971), we adopt a modified Vector Space Model (VSM) for document representation. A document is a vector where each dimension is a count of occurrences for a different word[1].

---
[1] In practice, suffixes are removed and counts are re-weighted by some function of their natural frequency

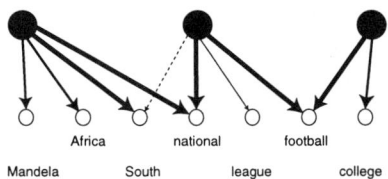

Figure 1: A Model of Word Generation. Independent topics give rise to specific words words according an unknown probability distribution (Line thickness indicates the likelihood of generating a word).

A collection of documents is a matrix, D, where each column is a document vector d_i. Queries are similarly represented.

We propose a topic based model for the generation of words in documents. Each document is generated by the interaction of a set of independent hidden random variables called *topics*. When a topic is active it causes words to appear in documents. Some words are very likely to be generated by a topic and others less so. Different topics may give rise to some of the same words. The final set of observed words results from a linear combination of topics. See Figure 1 for an example.

In this view of word generation, individual words are only weak indicators of underlying topics. Our task is to discover from data those collections of words that best predict the (unknown) underlying topics. The assumption that words are neither independent of one another or conditionally independent of topics motivates our belief that this is possible.

Our approach is to construct a set of linear operators which extract the independent topic structure of documents. We have explored different algorithms for discovering these operators include independent components analysis (Bell and Sejnowski, 1995). The inferred topics are then used to represent and compare documents.

Below we describe our approach and contrast it with Latent Semantic Indexing (LSI), a technique that also attempts to linearly transform the documents from "word space" into one more appropriate for comparison (Hull, 1994; Deerwester et al., 1990). We show that the LSI transformation has very different properties than the optimal linear transformation. We characterize some of these properties and derive an unsupervised method that searches for them. Finally, we present experiments demonstrating the robustness of this method and describe several computational and space advantages.

2 The Vector Space Model and Latent Semantic Indexing

The similarity between two documents using the VSM model is their inner product, $d_i^T d_j$. Queries are just short documents, so the relevance of documents to a query, q, is $D^T q$. There are several advantages to this approach beyond its mathematical simplicity. Above all, it is efficient to compute and store the word counts. While the word-document matrix has a very large number of potential entries, most documents do not contain very many of the possible words, so it is sparsely populated. Thus, algorithms for manipulating the matrix only require space and time proportional to the average number of different words that appear in a document, a number likely to be much smaller than the full dimensionality of the document matrix (in practice, non-zero elements represent about 2% of the total number of elements). Nevertheless, VSM makes an important tradeoff by sacrificing a great deal of document structure, losing context that may disambiguate meaning.

Any text retrieval system must overcome the fundamental difficulty that the presence or absence of a word is insufficient to determine relevance. This is due to two intrinsic problems of natural

---

(Frakes and Baeza-Yates, 1992). We incorporate these methods; however, such details are unimportant for this discussion.

language: *synonymy* and *polysemy*. Synonymy refers to the fact that a single underlying concept can be represented by many different words (e.g. "car" and "automobile" refer to the same class of objects). Polysemy refers to the fact that a single word can refer to more than one underlying concept (e.g. "apple" is both a fruit and a computer company). Synonymy results in false negatives and polysemy results in false positives.

Latent semantic indexing is one proposal for addressing this problem. LSI constructs a smaller document matrix that retains only the most important information from the original, by using the Singular Value Decomposition (SVD). Briefly, the SVD of a matrix D is: USV^T where U and V contain orthogonal vectors and S is diagonal (see (Golub and Loan, 1993) for further properties and algorithms). Note that the co-occurrence matrix, DD^T, can be written as US^2U^T; U contains the eigenvectors of the co-occurrence matrix while the diagonal elements of S (referred to as *singular values*) contain the square roots of their corresponding eigenvalues. The eigenvectors with the largest eigenvalues capture the axes of largest variation in the data.

In LSI, each document is projected into a lower dimensional space $\hat{D} = \hat{S}_k^{-1}\hat{U}_k^T D$ where $\hat{S}_k$ and $\hat{U}_k$ which contain only the largest k singular values and the corresponding eigenvectors, respectively. The resulting document matrix is of smaller size but still provably represents the most variation in the original matrix. Thus, LSI represents documents as linear combinations of orthogonal features. It is hoped that these features represent meaningful underlying "topics" present in the collection. Queries are also projected into this space, so the relevance of documents to a query is $D^T\hat{U}_k\hat{S}_k^{-2}\hat{U}_k^T q$.

This type of dimensionality reduction is very similar to principal components analysis (PCA), which has been used in other domains, including visual object recognition (Turk and Pentland, 1991). In practice, there is some evidence to suggest that LSI can improve retrieval performance; however, it is often the case that LSI improves text retrieval performance by only a small amount or not at all (see (Hull, 1994) and (Deerwester et al., 1990) for a discussion).

3 Do Optimal Projections for Retrieval Exist?

Hypotheses abound for the success of LSI, including: i) LSI removes noise from the document set; ii) LSI finds words that are synonyms; iii) LSI finds clusters of documents. Whatever it does, LSI operates without knowledge of the queries that will be presented to the system. We could instead attempt a supervised approach, searching for a matrix P such that $D^T PP^T q$ results in large values for documents in D that are known to be relevant for a particular query, q. The choice for the structure of P embodies assumptions about the structure of D and q and what it means for documents and queries to be related.

For example, imagine that we are given a collection of documents, D, and queries, Q. For each query we are told which documents are relevant. We can use this information to construct an optimal P such that: $D^T PP^T Q \approx R$, where R_{ij} equals 1 if document i is relevant to query j, and 0 otherwise.

We find P in two steps. First we find an X minimizing $\|D^T XQ - R\|_F$, where $\|\cdot\|_F$ denotes the Frobenius norm of a matrix[2]. Second, we find P by decomposing X into PP^T. Unfortunately, this may not be simple. The matrix PP^T has properties that are not necessarily shared by X. In particular, while PP^T is symmetric, there is no guarantee that X will be (in our experiments X is far from symmetric). We can however take SVD of $X = U_x S_x V_x^T$, using matrix U_x to project the documents and V_x to project the queries.

We can now compare LSI's projection axes, U with the optimal U_x computed as above. One measure of comparison is the distribution of documents as projected onto these axes. Figure 2a shows the distribution of Medline documents[3] projected onto the first axis of U_x. Notice that there is a large

---
[2]First find M that minimizes $\|D^T M - R\|_F$. X is the matrix that minimizes $\|XQ - M\|_F$

[3]Medline is a small test collection, consisting of 1033 documents and about 8500 distinct words. We have found similar results for other, larger collections.

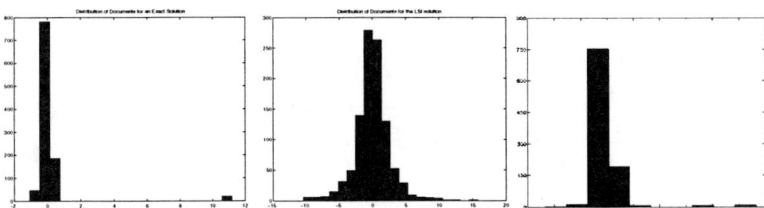

Figure 2: **(A)**. The distribution of medline documents projected onto one of the "optimal" axes. The kurtosis of this distribution is 44. **(B)**. The distribution of medline documents projected onto one of the LSI axes. The kurtosis of this distribution is 6.9. **(C)**. The distribution of medline documents projected onto one of the ICA axes. The kurtosis of this distribution is 60.

spike near zero, and a well-separated outlier spike. The kurtosis of this distribution is 44. Subsequent axes of U_x result in similar distributions. We might hope that these axes each represent a topic shared by a few documents. Figure 2b shows the distribution of documents projected onto the first LSI axis. This axis yields a distribution with a much lower kurtosis of 6.9 (a normal distribution has kurtosis 3). This induces a distribution that looks nothing like a cluster: there is a smooth continuum of values. Similar distributions result for many of the first 100 axes.

These results suggest that LSI-like approaches may well be searching for projections that are suboptimal. In the next section, we describe an algorithm designed to find projections that look more like those in Figure 2a than in Figure 2b.

4 Topic Centered Representations

There are several problems with the "optimal" approach described in the previous section. Aside from its completely supervised nature, there may be a problem of over-fitting: the number of parameters in X (the number of words squared) can be large compared to the number of documents and queries. It is not clear how to move towards a solution that will likely have low generalization error, our ultimate goal. Further, computing X is expensive, involving several full-rank singular value decompositions.

On the other hand, while we may not be able to take advantage of supervision, it seems reasonable to search for projections like those in Figure 2a. There are several unsupervised techniques we might use. We begin with independent component analysis (Bell and Sejnowski, 1995), a technique that has recently gained popularity. Extensions such as (Amari, Cichocki and Yang, 1996) have made the algorithm more efficient and robust.

4.1 What are the Independent Components of Documents?

Figure 2C shows the distribution of Medline documents along one of the ICA axes (kurtosis 60). It is representative of other axes found for that collection, and for other, larger collections.

Like the optimal axes found earlier, this axis also separates documents. This is desirable because it means that the axes are distinguishing groups of (presumably related) documents. Still, we can ask a more interesting question; namely, how do these axes group words? Rather than project our documents onto the ICA space, we can project individual words (this amounts to projecting the identity matrix onto that space) and observe how ICA redistributes them.

Figure 3 shows a typical distribution of all the words along one of the axes found by ICA on the

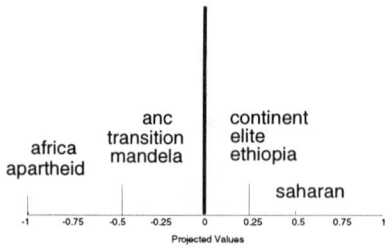

Figure 3: The distribution of words with large magnitude along an ICA axis from the White House collection.

White House collection.[4] ICA induces a highly kurtotic distribution over the words. It is also quite sparse: most words have a value very close to zero. The histogram shows only the words large values, both positive and negative. One group of words is made up of highly-related words; namely, "africa," "apartheid," and "mandela." The other is made up of words that have no obvious relationship to one another. In fact, these words are not directly related, but each co-occurs with different individual words in the first group. For example, "saharan" and "africa" occur together many times, but not in the context of apartheid and South Africa; rather, in documents concerning US policy toward Africa in general. As it so happens, "saharan" acts as a discriminating word for these subtopics.

4.2 Topic Centered Representations

It appears that ICA is finding a set of words, S, that selects for related documents, H, along with another set of words, T, whose elements do not select for H, but co-occur with elements of S. Intuitively, S selects for documents in a general subject area, and T removes a specific subset of those documents, leaving a small set of highly related documents. This suggests a straightforward algorithm to achieve the same goal directly:

```
foreach topic, C^k, you wish to define:
    -Choose a source document d_c from D
    -Let D̂ be the documents of D sorted by similarity to d_c
    -Divide D̂ into into three groups:  those assumed to be relevant,
     those assumed to be completely irrelevant,
     and those assumed to be weakly relevant.
    -Let G^k, B^k, and M^k be the centroid of each respective group
    -Let C^k = f(G^k - B^k) - f(M^k - G^k)
     where f(x) = max(x,0).
```

The three groups of documents are used to drive the discovery of two sets of words. One set selects for documents in a general topic area by finding the set of words that distinguish the relevant documents from documents in general, a form of global clustering. The other set of words distinguish the weakly-related documents from the relevant documents. Assigning them negative weight results in their removal. This leaves only a set of closely related documents. This local clustering approach is similar to an unsupervised version of Rocchio with Query Zoning (Singhal, 1997).

---

[4]The White House collection contains transcripts of press releases and press conferences from 1993. There are 1585 documents and 18675 distinct words.

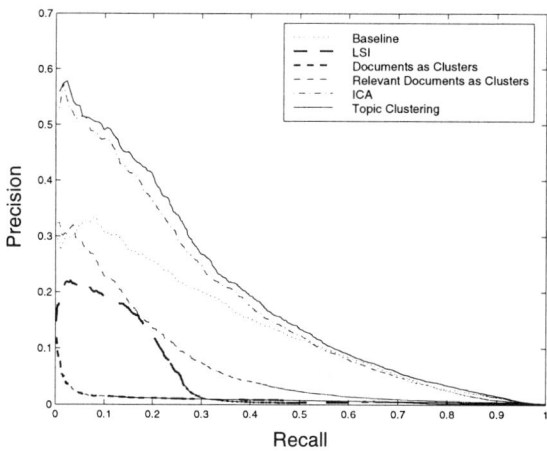

Figure 4: A comparison of different algorithms on the Wall Street Journal

5 Experiments

In this section, we show results of experiments with the Wall Street Journal collection. It contains 42,652 documents and 89757 words. Following convention, we measure the success of a text retrieval system using precision-recall curves[5]. Figure 4 illustrates the performance of several algorithms:

1. Baseline: the standard inner product measure, $D^T q$.
2. LSI: Latent Semantic Indexing.
3. Documents as Clusters: each document is a projection axis. This is equivalent to a modified inner product measure, $D^T D D^T q$.
4. Relevant Documents as Clusters: In order to simulate psuedo-relevance feedback, we use the centroid of the top few documents returned by the $D^T q$ similarity measure.
5. ICA: Independent Component Analysis.
6. Topic Clustering: The algorithm described in Section 4.2.

In this graph, we restrict queries to those that have at least fifty relevant documents. The topic clustering approach and ICA perform best, maintaining higher average precision over all ranges. Unlike smaller collections such as Medline, documents from this collection do not tend to cluster around the queries naturally. As a result, the baseline inner product measure performs poorly. Other clustering techniques that tend to work well on collections such as Medline perform even worse. Finally, LSI does not perform well.

Figure 5 illustrates different approaches on subsets of Wall Street Journal queries. In general, as each query has more and more relevant documents, overall performance improves. In particular, the simple clustering scheme using only relevant documents performs very well. Nonetheless, our approach improves upon this standard technique with minimal additional computation.

---

[5] When asked to return n documents *precision* is the percentage of those which are relevant. *Recall* is the percentage of the total relevant documents which are returned.

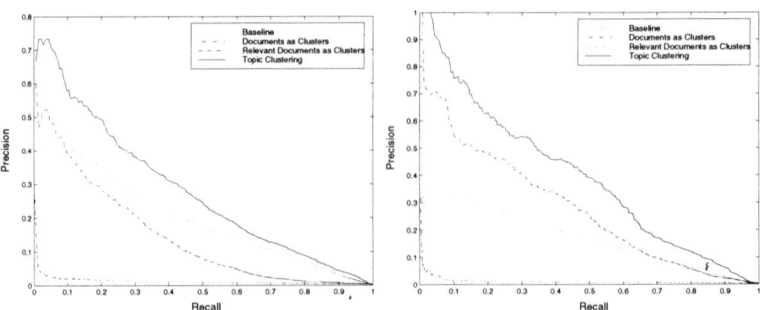

Figure 5: **(A)**. Performance of various clustering techniques for those queries with more than 75 relevant documents. **(B)**. Performance for those queries with more than 100 relevant documents.

6 Discussion

We have described typical dimension reduction techniques used in text retrieval and shown that these techniques make strong assumptions about the form of projection axes. We have characterized another set of assumptions and derived an algorithm that enjoys significant computational and space advantages. Further, we have described experiments that suggest that this approach is robust. Finally, much of what we have described here is not specific to text retrieval. Hopefully, similar characterizations will apply to other sparse high-dimensional domains.

References

Amari, S., Cichocki, A., and Yang, H. (1996). A new learning algorithm for blind source separation. In *Advances in Neural Information Processing Systems*.

Bell, A. and Sejnowski, T. (1995). An information-maximizaton approach to blind source separation and blind deconvolution. *Neural Computation*, 7:1129–1159.

Deerwester, S., Dumais, S. T., Landauer, T. K., Furnas, G. W., and Harshman, R. A. (1990). Indexing by latent semantic analysis. *Journal of the Society for Information Science*, 41(6):391–407.

Frakes, W. B. and Baeza-Yates, R., editors (1992). *Information Retrieval: Data Structures and Algorithms*. Prentice-Hall.

Golub, G. H. and Loan, C. F. V. (1993). *Matrix Computations*. The Johns Hopkins University Press.

Hull, D. (1994). Improving text retrieval for the routing problem using latent semantic indexing. In *Proceedings of the 17th ACM/SIGIR Conference*, pages 282–290.

Kwok, K. L. (1996). A new method of weighting query terms for ad-hoc retrieval. In *Proceedings of the 19th ACM/SIGIR Conference*, pages 187–195.

O'Brien, G. W. (1994). Information management tools for updating an svd-encoded indexing scheme. Technical Report UT-CS-94-259, University of Tennessee.

Sahami, M., Hearst, M., and Saund, E. (1996). Applying the multiple cause mixture model to text categorization. In *Proceedings of the 13th International Machine Learning Conference*.

Salton, G., editor (1971). *The SMART Retrieval System: Experiments in Automatic Document Processing*. Prentice-Hall.

Singhal, A. (1997). Learning routing queries in a query zone. In *Proceedings of the 20th International Conference on Research and Development in Information Retrieval*.

Turk, M. A. and Pentland, A. P. (1991). Face recognition using eigenfaces. In *IEEE Conference on Computer Vision and Pattern Recognition*, pages 586–591.

Exploiting generative models in discriminative classifiers

Tommi S. Jaakkola[*]
MIT Artificial Intelligence Laboratorio
545 Technology Square
Cambridge, MA 02139

David Haussler
Department of Computer Science
University of California
Santa Cruz, CA 95064

Abstract

Generative probability models such as hidden Markov models provide a principled way of treating missing information and dealing with variable length sequences. On the other hand, discriminative methods such as support vector machines enable us to construct flexible decision boundaries and often result in classification performance superior to that of the model based approaches. An ideal classifier should combine these two complementary approaches. In this paper, we develop a natural way of achieving this combination by deriving kernel functions for use in discriminative methods such as support vector machines from generative probability models. We provide a theoretical justification for this combination as well as demonstrate a substantial improvement in the classification performance in the context of DNA and protein sequence analysis.

1 Introduction

Speech, vision, text and biosequence data can be difficult to deal with in the context of simple statistical classification problems. Because the examples to be classified are often sequences or arrays of variable size that may have been distorted in particular ways, it is common to estimate a generative model for such data, and then use Bayes rule to obtain a classifier from this model. However, many discriminative methods, which directly estimate a posterior probability for a class label (as in Gaussian process classifiers [5]) or a discriminant function for the class label (as in support vector machines [6]) have in other areas proven to be superior to

---

[*]Corresponding author.

generative models for classification problems. The problem is that there has been no systematic way to extract features or metric relations between examples for use with discriminative methods in the context of difficult data types such as those listed above. Here we propose a general method for extracting these discriminatory features using a generative model. While the features we propose are generally applicable, they are most naturally suited to kernel methods.

2 Kernel methods

Here we provide a brief introduction to kernel methods; see, e.g., [6] [5] for more details. Suppose now that we have a training set of examples X_i and corresponding binary labels S_i (± 1). In kernel methods, as we define them, the label for a new example X is obtained from a weighted sum of the training labels. The weighting of each training label S_i consists of two parts: 1) the overall importance of the example X_i as summarized with a coefficient λ_i and 2) a measure of pairwise "similarity" between between X_i and X, expressed in terms of a kernel function $K(X_i, X)$. The predicted label $\hat{S}$ for the new example X is derived from the following rule:

$$\hat{S} = \text{sign}\left(\sum_i S_i \lambda_i K(X_i, X)\right) \qquad (1)$$

We note that this class of kernel methods also includes probabilistic classifiers, in which case the above rule refers to the label with the maximum probability. The free parameters in the classification rule are the coefficients λ_i and to some degree also the kernel function K. To pin down a particular kernel method, two things need to be clarified. First, we must define a classification loss, or equivalently, the optimization problem to solve to determine appropriate values for the coefficients λ_i. Slight variations in the optimization problem can take us from support vector machines to generalized linear models. The second and the more important issue is the choice of the kernel function – the main topic of this paper. We begin with a brief illustration of generalized linear models as kernel methods.

2.1 Generalized linear models

For concreteness we consider here only logistic regression models, while emphasizing that the ideas are applicable to a larger class of models[1]. In logistic regression models, the probability of the label S given the example X and a parameter vector θ is given by[2]

$$P(S|X, \theta) = \sigma\left(S\theta^T X\right) \qquad (2)$$

where $\sigma(z) = (1 + e^{-z})^{-1}$ is the logistic function. To control the complexity of the model when the number of training examples is small we can assign a prior distribution $P(\theta)$ over the parameters. We assume here that the prior is a zero mean Gaussian with a possibly full covariance matrix Σ. The maximum a posteriori (MAP) estimate for the parameters θ given a training set of examples is found by

---

[1] Specifically, it applies to all generalized linear models whose transfer functions are log-concave.

[2] Here we assume that the constant $+1$ is appended to every feature vector X so that an adjustable bias term is included in the inner product $\theta^T X$.

maximizing the following penalized log-likelihood:

$$\sum_i \log P(S_i|X_i, \theta) + \log P(\theta) = \sum_i \log \sigma\left(S_i \theta^T X_i\right) - \frac{1}{2}\theta^T \Sigma^{-1}\theta + c \quad (3)$$

where the constant c does not depend on θ. It is straightforward to show, simply by taking the gradient with respect to the parameters, that the solution to this (concave) maximization problem can be written as[3]

$$\hat{\theta} = \sum_i S_i \lambda_i \Sigma X_i, \text{ where } \lambda_i = \left.\frac{\partial}{\partial z}\log \sigma(z)\right|_{z=S_i\hat{\theta}^T X_i} \quad (4)$$

Note that the coefficients λ_i appear as weights on the training examples as in the definition of the kernel methods. Indeed, inserting the above solution back into the conditional probability model gives

$$P(S|X, \hat{\theta}) = \sigma\left(S \sum_i S_i \lambda_i \left(X_i^T \Sigma X\right)\right) \quad (5)$$

By identifying $K(X_i, X) = X_i^T \Sigma X$ and noting that the label with the maximum probability is the one that has the same sign as the sum in the argument, this gives the decision rule (1).

Through the above derivation, we have written the primal parameters θ in terms of the dual coefficients λ_i.[4] Consequently, the penalized log-likelihood function can be also written entirely in terms of λ_i; the resulting likelihood function specifies how the coefficients are to be optimized. This optimization problem has a unique solution and can be put into a generic form. Also, the form of the kernel function that establishes the connection between the logistic regression model and a kernel classifier is rather specific, i.e., has the inner product form $K(X_i, X) = X_i^T \Sigma X$. However, as long as the examples here can be replaced with feature vectors derived from the examples, this form of the kernel function is the most general. We discuss this further in the next section.

3 The kernel function

For a general kernel function to be valid, roughly speaking it only needs to be positive semi-definite (see e.g. [7]). According to the Mercer's theorem, any such valid kernel function admits a representation as a simple inner product between suitably defined feature vectors, i.e., $K(X_i, X_j) = \phi_{X_i}^T \phi_{X_j}$. where the feature vectors come from some fixed mapping $X \to \phi_X$. For example, in the previous section the kernel function had the form $X_i^T \Sigma X_j$, which is a simple inner product for the transformed feature vector $\phi_X = \Sigma^{\frac{1}{2}} X$.

Specifying a simple inner product in the feature space defines a Euclidean metric space. Consequently, the Euclidean distances between the feature vectors are obtained directly from the kernel function: with the shorthand notation $K_{ij} =$

---

[3] This corresponds to a Legendre transformation of the loss functions $\log \sigma(z)$.
[4] This is possible for all those θ that could arise as solutions to the maximum penalized likelihood problem; in other words, for all relevant θ.

$K(X_i, X_j)$ we get $||\phi_{X_i} - \phi_{X_j}||^2 = K_{ii} - 2K_{ij} + K_{jj}$. In addition to defining the metric structure in the feature space, the kernel defines a pseudo metric in the original example space through $D(X_i, X_j) = ||\phi_{X_i} - \phi_{X_j}||$. Thus the kernel embodies prior assumptions about the metric relations between the original examples. No systematic procedure has been proposed for finding kernel functions, let alone finding ones that naturally handle variable length examples etc. This is the topic of the next section.

4 Kernels from generative probability models: the Fisher kernel

The key idea here is to derive the kernel function from a generative probability model. We arrive at the same kernel function from two different perspectives, that of enhancing the discriminative power of the model and from an attempt to find a natural comparison between examples induced by the generative model. Both of these ideas are developed in more detail in the longer version of this paper[4].

We have seen in the previous section that defining the kernel function automatically implies assumptions about metric relations between the examples. We argue that these metric relations should be defined directly from a generative probability model $P(X|\theta)$. To capture the generative process in a metric between examples we use the gradient space of the generative model. The gradient of the log-likelihood with respect to a parameter describes how that parameter contributes to the process of generating a particular example[5]. This gradient space also naturally preserves all the structural assumptions that the model encodes about the generation process.

To develop this idea more generally, consider a parametric class of models $P(X|\theta)$, $\theta \in \Theta$. This class of probability models defines a Riemannian manifold M_Θ with a local metric given by the Fisher information matrix[6] I, where $I = E_X\{U_X U_X^T\}$, $U_X = \nabla_\theta \log P(X|\theta)$, and the expectation is over $P(X|\theta)$ (see e.g. [1]). The gradient of the log-likelihood, U_X, is called the *Fisher score*, and plays a fundamental role in our development. The local metric on M_Θ defines a distance between the current model $P(X|\theta)$ and a nearby model $P(X|\theta+\delta)$. This distance is given by $D(\theta, \theta+\delta) = \frac{1}{2}\delta^T I \delta$, which also approximates the KL-divergence between the two models for a sufficiently small δ.

The Fisher score $U_X = \nabla_\theta \log P(X|\theta)$ maps an example X into a feature vector that is a point in the gradient space of the manifold M_Θ. We call this the *Fisher score mapping*. This gradient U_X can be used to define the direction of steepest ascent in $\log P(X|\theta)$ for the example X *along the manifold*, i.e., the gradient in the direction δ that maximizes $\log P(X|\theta)$ while traversing the minimum distance in the manifold as defined by $D(\theta, \theta+\delta)$. This latter gradient is known as the natural gradient (see e.g. [1]) and is obtained from the ordinary gradient via $\phi_X = I^{-1} U_X$. We will call the mapping $X \to \phi_X$ the *natural mapping* of examples into feature vectors[7]. The natural kernel of this mapping is the inner product between these

---

[5]For the exponential family of distributions, under the natural parameterization θ, these gradients, less a normalization constant that depends on θ, form sufficient statistics for the example.

[6]For simplicity we have suppressed the dependence of I and U_X on the parameter setting θ, or equivalently, on the position in the manifold.

[7]Again, we have suppressed dependence on the parameter setting θ here.

feature vectors relative to the local Riemannian metric:

$$K(X_i, X_j) \propto \phi_{X_i}^T I \phi_{X_j} = U_{X_i}^T I^{-1} U_{X_j} \tag{6}$$

We call this the Fisher kernel owing to the fundamental role played by the Fisher scores in its definition. The role of the information matrix is less significant; indeed, in the context of logistic regression models, the matrix appearing in the middle of the feature vectors relates to the covariance matrix of a Gaussian prior, as show above. Thus, asymptotically, the information matrix is immaterial, and the simpler kernel $K_U(X_i, X_j) \propto U_{X_i}^T U_{X_j}$ provides a suitable substitute for the Fisher kernel.

We emphasize that the Fisher kernel defined above provides only the basic comparison between the examples, defining what is meant by an "inner product" between the examples when the examples are objects of various types (e.g. variable length sequences). The way such a kernel function is used in a discriminative classifier is not specified here. Using the Fisher kernel directly in a kernel classifier, for example, amounts to finding a linear separating hyper-plane in the natural gradient (or Fisher score) feature space. The examples may not be linearly separable in this feature space even though the natural metric structure is given by the Fisher kernel. It may be advantageous to search in the space of quadratic (or higher order) decision boundaries, which is equivalent to transforming the Fisher kernel according to $\tilde{K}(X_i, X_j) = (1 + K(X_i, X_j))^m$ and using the resulting kernel $\tilde{K}$ in the classifier.

We are now ready to state a few properties of the Fisher kernel function. So long as the probability model $P(X|\theta)$ is suitably regular then the Fisher kernel derived from it is a) a valid kernel function and b) invariant to any invertible (and differentiable) transformation of the model parameters. The rather informally stated theorem below motivates the use of this kernel function in a classification setting.

Theorem 1 *Given any suitably regular probability model $P(X|\theta)$ with parameters θ and assuming that the classification label is included as a latent variable, the Fisher kernel $K(X_i, X_j) = U_{X_i}^T I^{-1} U_{X_j}$ derived from this model and employed in a kernel classifier is, asymptotically, never inferior to the MAP decision rule from this model.*

The proofs and other related theorems are presented in the longer version of this paper [4].

To summarize, we have defined a generic procedure for obtaining kernel functions from generative probability models. Consequently the benefits of generative models are immediately available to the discriminative classifier employing this kernel function. We now turn the experimental demonstration of the effectiveness of such a combined classifier.

5 Experimental results

Here we consider two relevant examples from biosequence analysis and compare the performance of the combined classifier to the best generative models used in these problems. We start with a DNA splice site classification problem, where the objective is to recognize true splice sites, i.e., the boundaries between expressed regions (exons) in a gene and the intermediate regions (introns). The data set used in our experiments consisted of 9350 DNA fragments from *C. elegans*. Each of the

2029 true examples is a sequence X over the DNA alphabet $\{A, G, T, C\}$ of length 25; the 7321 false examples are similar sequences that occur near but not at 5' splice sites. All recognition rates we report on this data set are averages from 7-fold cross-validation.

To use the combined classifier in this setting requires us to choose a generative model for the purpose of deriving the kernel function. In order to test how much the performance of the combined classifier depends on the quality of the underlying generative model, we chose the poorest model possible. This is the model where the DNA residue in each position in the fragment is chosen independently of others, i.e., $P(X|\theta) = \prod_{i=1}^{25} P(X_i|\theta_i)$ and, furthermore, the parameters θ_i are set such that $P(X_i|\theta_i) = 1/4$ for all i and all $X_i \in \{A, G, T, C\}$. This model assigns the same probability to all examples X. We can still derive the Fisher kernel from such a model and use it in a discriminative classifier. In this case we used a logistic regression model as in (5) with a quadratic Fisher kernel $\tilde{K}(X_i, X_j) = (1 + K(X_i, X_j))^2$. Figure 1 shows the recognition performance of this kernel method, using the poor generative model, in comparison to the recognition performance of a naive Bayes model or a hierarchical mixture model. The comparison is summarized in ROC style curves plotting false positive errors (the errors of accepting false examples) as a function of false negative errors (the errors of missing true examples) when we vary the classification bias for the labels. The curves show that even with such a poor underlying generative model, the combined classifier is consistently better than either of the better generative models alone.

In the second and more serious application of the combined classifier, we consider the well-known problem of recognizing remote homologies (evolutionary/structural similarities) between protein sequences[8] that have low residue identity. Considerable recent work has been done in refining hidden Markov models for this purpose as reviewed in [2], and such models current achieve the best performance. We use these state-of-the-art HMMs as comparison cases and also as sources for deriving the kernel function. Here we used logistic regression with the simple kernel $K_U(X_i, X_j)$, as the number of parameters in the HMMs was several thousand.

The experiment was set up as follows. We picked a particular superfamily (glycosyltransferases) from the TIM-barrel fold in the SCOP protein structure classification [3], and left out one of the four major families in this superfamily for testing while training the HMM as well as the combined classifier on sequences corresponding to the remaining three families. The false training examples for the discriminative method came from those sequences in the same fold but not in the same superfamily. The test sequences consisted of the left-out family (true examples) and proteins outside the TIM barrel fold (false examples). The number of training examples varied around 100 depending on the left-out family. As the sequences among the four glycosyltransferase families are extremely different, this is a challenging discrimination problem. Figure 1c shows the recognition performance curves for the HMM and the corresponding kernel method, averaged over the four-way cross validation. The combined classifier yields a substantial improvement in performance over the HMM alone.

---

[8]These are variable length sequences thus rendering many discriminative methods inapplicable.

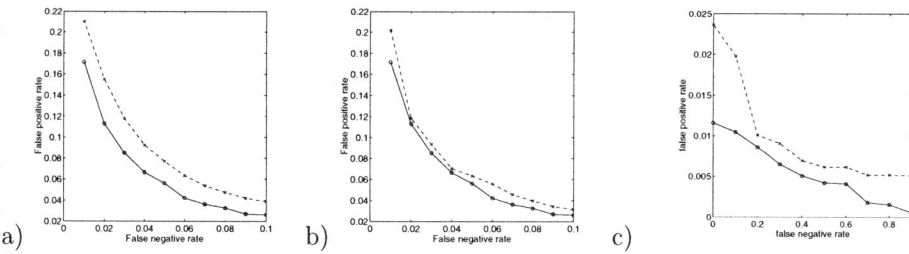

Figure 1: a) & b) Comparison of classification performance between a kernel classifiers from the uniform model (solid line) and a mixture model (dashed line). In a) the mixture model is a naive Bayes model and in b) it has three components in each class. c) Comparison of homology recognition performance between a hidden Markov model (dashed line) and the corresponding kernel classifier (solid line).

6 Discussion

The model based kernel function derived in this paper provides a generic mechanism for incorporating generative models into discriminative classifiers. For discrimination, the resulting combined classifier is guaranteed to be superior to the generative model alone with little additional computational cost. We note that the power of the new classifier arises to a large extent from the use of Fisher scores as features in place of original examples. It is possible to use these features with any classifier, e.g. a feed-forward neural net, but kernel methods are most naturally suited for incorporating them.

Finally we note that while we have used classification to guide the development of the kernel function, the results are directly applicable to regression, clustering, or even interpolation problems, all of which can easily exploit metric relations among the examples defined by the Fisher kernel.

References

[1] S.-I. Amari. Natural gradient works efficiently in learning. *Neural Computation*, 10:251–276, 1998.

[2] R. Durbin, S. Eddy, A. Krogh, and G. Mitchison. *Biological Sequence Analysis: Probabilistic Models of Proteins and Nucleic Acids*. Cambridge University Press, 1998.

[3] T. Hubbard, A. Murzin, S. Brenner, and C. Chothia. SCOP: a structural classification of proteins database. *NAR*, 25(1):236–9, Jan. 1997.

[4] T. S. Jaakkola and D. Haussler. Exploiting generative models in discriminative classifiers. 1998. Revised and extended version. Will be available from http://www.ai.mit.edu/~tommi.

[5] D. J. C. MacKay. Introduction to gaussian processes. 1997. Available from http://wol.ra.phy.cam.ac.uk/mackay/.

[6] V. Vapnik. *The nature of statistical learning theory*. Springer-Verlag, 1995.

[7] G. Wahba. *Spline models for observational data*. CBMS-NSF Regional Conference Series in Applied Mathematics, 1990.

Maximum Conditional Likelihood via Bound Maximization and the CEM Algorithm

Tony Jebara and Alex Pentland
Vision and Modeling, MIT Media Laboratory, Cambridge MA
http://www.media.mit.edu/ ~ jebara
{ jebara,sandy }@media.mit.edu

Abstract

We present the CEM (*Conditional Expectation Maximization*) algorithm as an extension of the EM (*Expectation Maximization*) algorithm to conditional density estimation under missing data. A bounding and maximization process is given to specifically optimize conditional likelihood instead of the usual joint likelihood. We apply the method to conditioned mixture models and use bounding techniques to derive the model's update rules. Monotonic convergence, computational efficiency and regression results superior to EM are demonstrated.

1 Introduction

Conditional densities have played an important role in statistics and their merits over joint density models have been debated. Advantages in feature selection, robustness and limited resource allocation have been studied. Ultimately, tasks such as regression and classification reduce to the evaluation of a conditional density.

However, popularity of maximum joint likelihood and EM techniques remains strong in part due to their elegance and convergence properties. Thus, many conditional problems are solved by first estimating joint models then conditioning them. This results in concise solutions such as the Nadarya-Watson estimator [2], Xu's mixture of experts [7], and Amari's em-neural networks [1]. However, direct conditional density approaches [2, 4] can offer solutions with higher conditional likelihood on test data than their joint counter-parts.

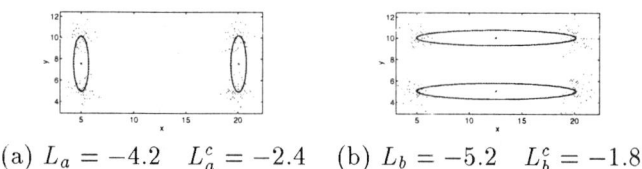

(a) $L_a = -4.2$ $L_a^c = -2.4$ (b) $L_b = -5.2$ $L_b^c = -1.8$

Figure 1: Average Joint (x,y) vs. Conditional $(y|x)$ Likelihood Visualization

Popat [6] describes a simple visualization example where 4 clusters must be fit with 2 Gaussian models as in Figure 1. Here, the model in (a) has a superior joint likelihood ($L_a > L_b$) and hence a better $p(x,y)$ solution. However, when the models are conditioned to estimate $p(y|x)$, model (b) is superior ($L_b^c > L_a^c$). Model (a) yields a poor unimodal conditional density in y and (b) yields a bi-modal conditional density. It is therefore of interest to directly optimize conditional models using conditional likelihood. We introduce the CEM (*Conditional Expectation Maximization*) algorithm for this purpose and apply it to the case of Gaussian mixture models.

2 EM and Conditional Likelihood

For joint densities, the tried and true EM algorithm [3] maximizes joint likelihood over data. However, EM is not as useful when applied to conditional density estimation and maximum conditional likelihood problems. Here, one typically resorts to other local optimization techniques such as gradient descent or second order Hessian methods [2]. We therefore introduce CEM, a variant of EM, which targets conditional likelihood while maintaining desirable convergence properties. The CEM algorithm operates by directly bounding and decoupling conditional likelihood and simplifies M-step calculations.

In EM, a complex density optimization is broken down into a two-step iteration using the notion of missing data. The unknown data components are estimated via the E-step and a simplified maximization over complete data is done in the M-step. In more practical terms, EM is a bound maximization: the E-step finds a lower bound for the likelihood and the M-step maximizes the bound.

$$p(\mathbf{x}_i, \mathbf{y}_i | \Theta) = \sum_{m=1}^{M} p(m, \mathbf{x}_i, \mathbf{y}_i | \Theta) \qquad (1)$$

Consider a complex joint density $p(\mathbf{x}_i, \mathbf{y}_i|\Theta)$ which is best described by a discrete (or continuous) summation of simpler models (Equation 1). Summation is over the 'missing components' m.

$$\begin{aligned}\Delta l &= \sum_{i=1}^{N} \log(p(\mathbf{x}_i, \mathbf{y}_i|\Theta^t)) - \log(p(\mathbf{x}_i, \mathbf{y}_i|\Theta^{t-1})) \\ &\geq \sum_{i=1}^{N} \sum_{m=1}^{M} h_{im} \log \frac{p(m,\mathbf{x}_i,\mathbf{y}_i|\Theta^t)}{p(m,\mathbf{x}_i,\mathbf{y}_i|\Theta^{t-1})} \quad \text{where} \quad h_{im} = \frac{p(m,\mathbf{x}_i,\mathbf{y}_i|\Theta^{t-1})}{\sum_{n=1}^{M} p(n,\mathbf{x}_i,\mathbf{y}_i|\Theta^{t-1})}\end{aligned} \qquad (2)$$

By appealing to Jensen's inequality, EM obtains a lower bound for the incremental log-likelihood over a data set (Equation 2). Jensen's inequality bounds the logarithm of the sum and the result is that the logarithm is applied to each simple model $p(m, \mathbf{x}_i, \mathbf{y}_i|\Theta)$ individually. It then becomes straightforward to compute the derivatives with respect to Θ and set to zero for maximization (M-step).

$$p(\mathbf{y}_i|\mathbf{x}_i, \Theta) = \sum_{m=1}^{M} p(m, \mathbf{y}_i|\mathbf{x}_i, \Theta) = \frac{\sum_{m=1}^{M} p(m, \mathbf{x}_i, \mathbf{y}_i|\Theta)}{\sum_{m=1}^{M} p(m, \mathbf{x}_i|\Theta)} \tag{3}$$

However, the elegance of EM is compromised when we consider a conditioned density as in Equation 3. The corresponding incremental conditional log-likelihood, Δl^c, is shown in Equation 4.

$$\begin{aligned}\Delta l^c &= \sum_{i=1}^{N} \log(p(\mathbf{y}_i|\mathbf{x}_i, \Theta^t)) - \log(p(\mathbf{y}_i|\mathbf{x}_i, \Theta^{t-1})) \\ &= \sum_{i=1}^{N} \log \frac{\sum_{m=1}^{M} p(m, \mathbf{x}_i, \mathbf{y}_i|\Theta^t)}{\sum_{m=1}^{M} p(m, \mathbf{x}_i, \mathbf{y}_i|\Theta^{t-1})} - \log \frac{\sum_{n=1}^{M} p(n, \mathbf{x}_i|\Theta^t)}{\sum_{n=1}^{M} p(n, \mathbf{x}_i|\Theta^{t-1})}\end{aligned} \tag{4}$$

The above is a difference between a ratio of joints *and* a ratio of marginals. If Jensen's inequality is applied to the second term in Equation 4 it yields an *upper* bound since the term is subtracted (this would compromise convergence). Thus, only the first ratio can be lower bounded with Jensen (Equation 5).

$$\Delta l^c \geq \sum_{i=1}^{N} \sum_{m=1}^{M} h_{im} \log \frac{p(m, \mathbf{x}_i, \mathbf{y}_i|\Theta^t)}{p(m, \mathbf{x}_i, \mathbf{y}_i|\Theta^{t-1})} - \log \frac{\sum_{n=1}^{M} p(n, \mathbf{x}_i|\Theta^t)}{\sum_{n=1}^{M} p(n, \mathbf{x}_i|\Theta^{t-1})} \tag{5}$$

Note the lingering logarithm of a sum which prevents a simple M-Step. At this point, one would resort to a Generalized EM (GEM) approach which requires gradient or second-order ascent techniques for the M-step. For example, Jordan *et al.* overcome the difficult M-step caused by EM with an Iteratively Re-Weighted Least Squares algorithm in the mixtures of experts architecture [4].

3 Conditional Expectation Maximization

The EM algorithm can be extended by substituting Jensen's inequality for a different bound. Consider the upper variational bound of a logarithm $x - 1 \geq \log(x)$ (which becomes a lower bound on the negative log). The proposed logarithm's bound satisfies a number of desiderata: (1) it makes contact at the current operating point[1], (2) it is tangential to the logarithm, (3) it is a tight bound, (4) it is simple and (5) it is the variational dual of the logarithm. Substituting this linear bound into the incremental conditional log-likelihood maintains a true lower bounding function Q (Equation 6).

$$\Delta l^c \geq Q(\Theta^t, \Theta^{t-1}) = \sum_{i=1}^{N} \sum_{m=1}^{M} h_{im} \log \frac{p(m, \mathbf{x}_i, \mathbf{y}_i|\Theta^t)}{p(m, \mathbf{x}_i, \mathbf{y}_i|\Theta^{t-1})} - \frac{\sum_{n=1}^{M} p(n, \mathbf{x}_i|\Theta^t)}{\sum_{n=1}^{M} p(n, \mathbf{x}_i|\Theta^{t-1})} + 1 \tag{6}$$

The Mixture of Experts formalism [4] offers a graceful representation of a conditional density using experts (conditional sub-models) and gates (marginal sub-models). The Q function adopts this form in Equation 7.

---

[1] The current operating point is 1 since the Θ^t model in the ratio is held fixed at the previous iteration's value Θ^{t-1}.

$$\sum_{i=1}^{N}\sum_{m=1}^{M}\{h_{im}(\log p(\mathbf{y}_i|m,\mathbf{x}_i,\Theta^t)+\log p(m,\mathbf{x}_i|\Theta^t)-z_{im})-r_ip(m,\mathbf{x}_i|\Theta)+\tfrac{1}{M}\} \quad (7)$$
where $z_{im}=\log(p(m,\mathbf{x}_i,\mathbf{y}_i|\Theta^{t-1}))$ and $r_i=(\sum_{n=1}^{M}p(n,\mathbf{x}_i|\Theta^{t-1}))^{-1}$

Computing this Q function forms the CE-step in the Conditional Expectation Maximization algorithm and it results in a simplified M-step. Note the absence of the logarithm of a sum and the *decoupled* models. The form here allows a more straightforward computation of derivatives with respect to Θ^t and a more tractable M-Step. For continuous missing data, a similar derivation holds.

At this point, without loss of generality, we specifically attend to the case of a conditioned Gaussian mixture model and derive the corresponding M-Step calculations. This serves as an implementation example for comparison purposes.

4 CEM and Bound Maximization for Gaussian Mixtures

In deriving an efficient M-step for the mixture of Gaussians, we call upon more bounding techniques that follow the CE-step and provide a monotonically convergent learning algorithm. The form of the conditional model we will train is obtained by conditioning a joint mixture of Gaussians. We write the conditional density in a experts-gates form as in Equation 8. We use unnormalized Gaussian gates $\bar{\mathcal{N}}(\mathbf{x};\mu,\Sigma)=\exp(-\tfrac{1}{2}(\mathbf{x}-\mu)^T\Sigma^{-1}(\mathbf{x}-\mu))$ since conditional models do not require true marginal densities over $\mathbf{x}$ (i.e. that necessarily integrate to 1). Also, note that the parameters of the gates $(\alpha,\mu_x,\Sigma_{xx})$ are independent of the parameters of the experts $(\nu^m,\Gamma^m,\Omega^m)$.

Both gates and experts are optimized independently and have no variables in common. An update is performed over the experts and then over the gates. If each of those causes an increase, we converge to a local maximum of conditional log-likelihood (as in Expectation Conditional Maximization [5]).

$$\begin{aligned}p(\mathbf{y}|\mathbf{x},\Theta) &= \frac{\sum_{m=1}^{M}\alpha_n\bar{\mathcal{N}}(\mathbf{x};\mu_x^n,\Sigma_{xx}^n)\times\mathcal{N}(\mathbf{y};\mu_y^m+\Sigma_{yx}^m(\Sigma_{xx}^m)^{-1}(\mathbf{X}-\mu_x^m),\Sigma_{yy}^m-\Sigma_{yx}^m(\Sigma_{xx}^m)^{-1}\Sigma_{xy}^m)}{\sum_{n=1}^{M}\alpha_n\bar{\mathcal{N}}(\mathbf{x};\mu_x^n,\Sigma_{xx}^n)}\\ &= \frac{\sum_{m=1}^{M}\alpha_n\bar{\mathcal{N}}(\mathbf{x};\mu_x^n,\Sigma_{xx}^n)\times\mathcal{N}(\mathbf{y};\nu^m+\Gamma^m\mathbf{x},\Omega^m)}{\sum_{n=1}^{M}\alpha_n\bar{\mathcal{N}}(\mathbf{x};\mu_x^n,\Sigma_{xx}^n)}\end{aligned} \quad (8)$$

To update the experts, we hold the gates fixed and merely take derivatives of the Q function with respect to the expert parameters ($\Phi^m=\{\nu^m,\Gamma^m,\Omega^m\}$) and set them to 0. Each expert is effectively decoupled from other terms (gates, other experts, etc.). The solution reduces to maximizing the log of a single conditioned Gaussian and is analytically straightforward.

$$\frac{\partial Q(\Theta^t,\Theta^{(t-1)})}{\partial\Phi^m} = \sum_{i=1}^{N}h_{im}\frac{\partial\log\mathcal{N}(\mathbf{y}_i;\nu^m+\Gamma^m\mathbf{x}_i,\Omega^m)}{\partial\Phi^m} := 0 \quad (9)$$

Similarly, to update the gate mixing proportions, derivatives of the Q function are taken with respect to α_m and set to 0. By holding the other parameters fixed, the update equation for the mixing proportions is numerically evaluated (Equation 10).

$$\alpha_m := \sum_{i=1}^{N}r_i\hat{\mathcal{N}}(\mathbf{x}_i;\mu_x^m,\Sigma_{xx}^m)|_{\Theta^{(t-1)}}\{\sum_{i=1}^{N}\hat{h}_{im}\}^{-1} \quad (10)$$

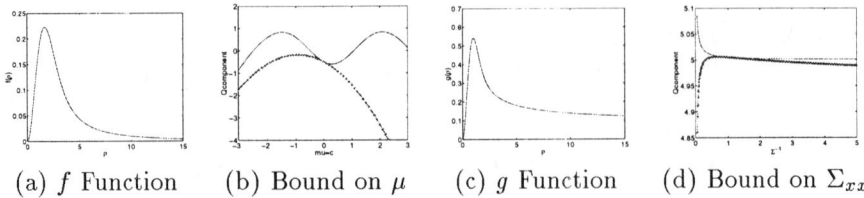

(a) f Function (b) Bound on μ (c) g Function (d) Bound on Σ_{xx}

Figure 2: Bound Width Computation and Example Bounds

4.1 Bounding Gate Means

Taking derivatives of Q and setting to 0 is not as straightforward for the case of the gate means (even though they are decoupled). What is desired is a simple update rule (i.e. computing an empirical mean). Therefore, we further bound the Q function for the M-step. The Q function is actually a summation of sub-elements Q_{im} and we bound it instead by a summation of quadratic functions on the means (Equation 11).

$$Q(\Theta^t, \Theta^{(t-1)}) = \sum_{i=1}^{N} \sum_{m=1}^{M} Q(\Theta^t, \Theta^{(t-1)})_{im} \geq \sum_{i=1}^{N} \sum_{m=1}^{M} k_{im} - w_{im}\|\mu_x^m - c_{im}\|^2 \quad (11)$$

Each quadratic bound has a location parameter c_{im} (a centroid), a scale parameter w_{im} (narrowness), and a peak value at k_{im}. The sum of quadratic bounds makes contact with the Q function at the old values of the model Θ^{t-1} where the gate mean was originally μ_x^{m*} and the covariance is Σ_{xx}^{m*}. To facilitate the derivation, one may assume that the previous mean was zero and the covariance was identity if the data is appropriately whitened with respect to a given gate.

The parameters of each quadratic bound are solved by ensuring that it contacts the corresponding Q_{im} function at Θ^{t-1} and they have equal derivatives at contact (i.e. tangential contact). Solving these constraints yields quadratic parameters for each gate m and data point i in Equation 12 (k_{im} is omitted for brevity).

$$\begin{aligned} c_{im} &= \frac{1}{2w_{im}}(\hat{h}_{im} - r_i \alpha_m e^{-\frac{1}{2}\mathbf{X}_i^T \mathbf{X}_i})\mathbf{x} \\ w_{im} &\geq r_i \alpha_m \frac{e^{-\frac{1}{2}(\mathbf{X}_i - \mu_x^m)^T(\mathbf{X}_i - \mu_x^m)} - e^{-\frac{1}{2}\mathbf{X}_i^T \mathbf{X}_i} - e^{-\frac{1}{2}\mathbf{X}_i^T \mathbf{X}_i}\mathbf{X}_i^T \mu_x^m}{\mu_x^{m T} \mu_x^m} + \frac{\hat{h}_{im}}{2} \end{aligned} \quad (12)$$

The tightest quadratic bound occurs when w_{im} is minimal (without violating the inequality). The expression for w_{im} reduces to finding the minimal value, w_{im}^*, as in Equation 13 (here $\rho^2 = \mathbf{x}_i^T \mathbf{x}_i$). The f function is computed numerically only *once* and stored as a lookup table (see Figure 2(a)). We thus immediately compute the optimal w_{im}^* and the rest of the quadratic bound's parameters obtaining bounds as in Figure 2(b) where a Q_{im} is lower bounded.

$$w_{im}^* = r_i \alpha_m \max_c \{e^{-\frac{1}{2}\rho^2} \frac{e^{-\frac{1}{2}c^2}e^{c\rho} - c\rho - 1}{c^2}\} + \frac{\hat{h}_{im}}{2} = r_i \alpha_m e^{-\frac{1}{2}\rho^2} f(\rho) + \frac{\hat{h}_{im}}{2} \quad (13)$$

The gate means μ_x^m are solved by maximizing the sum of the $M \times N$ parabolas which bound Q. The update is $\mu_x^m = (\sum w_{im}^* c_{im})(\sum w_{im}^*)^{-1}$. This mean is subsequently unwhitened to undo earlier data transformations.

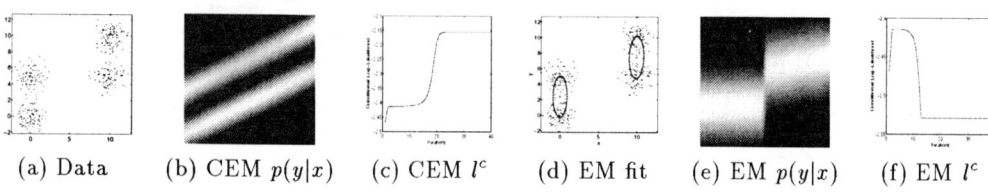

(a) Data (b) CEM $p(y|x)$ (c) CEM l^c (d) EM fit (e) EM $p(y|x)$ (f) EM l^c

Figure 3: Conditional Density Estimation for CEM and EM

4.2 Bounding Gate Covariances

Having derived the update equation for gate means, we now turn our attention to the gate covariances. We bound the Q function with logarithms of Gaussians. Maximizing this bound (a sum of log-Gaussians) reduces to the maximum-likelihood estimation of a covariance matrix. The bound for a Q_{im} sub-component is shown in Equation 14. Once again, we assume the data has been appropriately whitened with respect to the gate's previous parameters (the gate's previous mean is 0 and previous covariance is identity). Equation 15 solves for the log-Gaussian parameters (again $\rho^2 = \mathbf{x}_i^T \mathbf{x}_i$).

$$Q(\Theta^t, \Theta^{(t-1)})_{im} \geq \log(\mathcal{N}) = k_{im} - w_{im} \mathbf{c}_{im}^T {\Sigma_{xx}^m}^{-1} \mathbf{c}_{im} - w_{im} \log|\Sigma_{xx}^m| \quad (14)$$

$$\mathbf{c}_{im} \mathbf{c}_{im}^T = \frac{1}{2w_{im}} \left(\hat{h}_{im} - r_i \alpha_m e^{-\frac{1}{2}\rho^2} \right) \mathbf{x}_i \mathbf{x}_i^T + I$$

$$w_{im} \geq r_i \alpha_m \frac{\frac{1}{2}\exp(-\frac{1}{2}\rho^2)\rho^2 - \frac{1}{2}\exp(-\frac{1}{2}\rho^2)\mathbf{x}_i^T \Sigma^{-1} \mathbf{x}_i + \exp(-\frac{1}{2}\rho^2) - \exp(-\frac{1}{2}\mathbf{x}_i^T \Sigma^{-1} \mathbf{x}_i)}{tr(I) - tr(\Sigma^{-1}) + \log|\Sigma^{-1}|} \quad (15)$$

The computation for the minimal w_{im} simplifies to $w_{im}^* = r_i \alpha_m g(\rho)$. The g function is derived and plotted in Figure 2(c). An example of a log-Gaussian bound is shown in Figure 2(d) a sub-component of the Q function. Each sub-component corresponds to a single data point as we vary one gate's covariance. All $M \times N$ log-Gaussian bounds are computed (one for each data point and gate combination) and are summed to bound the Q function in its entirety.

To obtain a final answer for the update of the gate covariances Σ_{xx}^m we simply maximize the sum of log Gaussians (parametrized by $w_{im}^*, k_{im}, \mathbf{c}_{im}$). The update is $\Sigma_{xx}^m = (\sum w_{im}^* \mathbf{c}_{im} \mathbf{c}_{im}^T)(\sum w_{im}^*)^{-1}$. This covariance is subsequently unwhitened, inverting the whitening transform applied to the data.

5 Results

The CEM algorithm updates the conditioned mixture of Gaussians by computing h_{im} and r_{im} in the CE steps and interlaces these with updates on the experts, mixing proportions, gate means and gate covariances. For the mixture of Gaussians, each CEM update has a computation time that is comparable with that of an EM update (even for high dimensions). However, conditional likelihood (not joint) is monotonically increased.

Consider the 4-cluster (x, y) data in Figure 3(a). The data is modeled with a conditional density $p(y|x)$ using *only 2* Gaussian models. Estimating the density with CEM yields the $p(y|x)$ shown in Figure 3(b). CEM exhibits monotonic conditional likelihood growth (Figure 3(c)) and obtains a more conditionally likely model. In

Algorithm	CCN0	CCN5	C4.5	LD	EM2	CEM2
Abalone	24.86%	26.25%	21.5%	0.0%	22.32%	26.63%

Table 1: Test Results. Class label regression accuracy data. (CNN0=cascade-correlation, 0 hidden units, CCN5=5 hidden LD=linear discriminant).

the EM case, a joint $p(x,y)$ clusters the data as in Figure 3(d). Conditioning it yields the $p(y|x)$ in Figure 3(e). Figure 3(f) depicts EM's non-monotonic evolution of conditional log-likelihood. EM produces a superior joint likelihood but an inferior conditional likelihood. Note how the CEM algorithm utilized limited resources to capture the multimodal nature of the distribution in y and ignored spurious bimodal clustering in the x feature space. These properties are critical for a good conditional density $p(y|x)$.

For comparison, standard databases were used from UCI [2]. Mixture models were trained with EM and CEM, maximizing joint and conditional likelihood respectively. Regression results are shown in Table 1. CEM exhibited, monotonic conditional log-likelihood growth and out-performed other methods including EM with the same 2-Gaussian model (EM2 and CEM2).

6 Discussion

We have demonstrated a variant of EM called CEM which optimizes conditional likelihood efficiently and monotonically. The application of CEM and bound maximization to a mixture of Gaussians exhibited promising results and better regression than EM. In other work, a MAP framework with various priors and a deterministic annealing approach have been formulated. Applications of the CEM algorithm to non-linear regressor experts and hidden Markov models are currently being investigated. Nevertheless, many applications CEM remain to be explored and hopefully others will be motivated to extend the initial results.

Acknowledgements

Many thanks to Michael Jordan and Kris Popat for insightful discussions.

References

[1] S. Amari. Information geometry of em and em algorithms for neural networks. *Neural Networks*, 8(9), 1995.
[2] C. Bishop. *Neural Networks for Pattern Recognition*. Oxford Press, 1996.
[3] A. Dempster, N. Laird, and D. Rubin. Maximum likelihood from incomplete data via the em algorithm. *Journal of the Royal Statistical Society*, B39, 1977.
[4] M. Jordan and R. Jacobs. Hierarchical mixtures of experts and the em algorithm. *Neural Computation*, 6:181–214, 1994.
[5] X. Meng and D. Rubin. Maximum likelihood estimation via the ecm algorithm: A general framework. *Biometrika*, 80(2), 1993.
[6] A. Popat. Conjoint probabilistic subband modeling (phd. thesis). Technical Report 461, M.I.T. Media Laboratory, 1997.
[7] L. Xu, M. Jordan, and G. Hinton. An alternative model for mixtures of experts. In *Neural Information Processing Systems 7*, 1995.

---

[2] http://www.ics.uci.edu/~mlearn/MLRepository.html

A Polygonal Line Algorithm for Constructing Principal Curves

Balázs Kégl, Adam Krzyżak
Dept. of Computer Science
Concordia University
1450 de Maisonneuve Blvd. W.
Montreal, Canada H3G 1M8
kegl@cs.concordia.ca
krzyzak@cs.concordia.ca

Tamás Linder
Dept. of Mathematics
and Statistics
Queen's University
Kingston, Ontario
Canada K7L 3N6
linder@mast.queensu.ca

Kenneth Zeger
Dept. of Electrical and
Computer Engineering
University of California
San Diego, La Jolla
CA 92093-0407
zeger@ucsd.edu

Abstract

Principal curves have been defined as "self consistent" smooth curves which pass through the "middle" of a d-dimensional probability distribution or data cloud. Recently, we [1] have offered a new approach by defining principal curves as continuous curves of a given length which minimize the expected squared distance between the curve and points of the space randomly chosen according to a given distribution. The new definition made it possible to carry out a theoretical analysis of learning principal curves from training data. In this paper we propose a practical construction based on the new definition. Simulation results demonstrate that the new algorithm compares favorably with previous methods both in terms of performance and computational complexity.

1 Introduction

Hastie [2] and Hastie and Stuetzle [3] (hereafter HS) generalized the self consistency property of principal components and introduced the notion of *principal curves*. Consider a d-dimensional random vector $\mathbf{X} = (X^{(1)}, \ldots, X^{(d)})$ with finite second moments, and let $\mathbf{f}(t) = (f_1(t), \ldots, f_d(t))$ be a smooth curve in $\mathcal{R}^d$ parameterized by $t \in \mathcal{R}$. For any $\mathbf{x} \in \mathcal{R}^d$ let $t_\mathbf{f}(\mathbf{x})$ denote the parameter value t for which the distance between $\mathbf{x}$ and $\mathbf{f}(t)$ is minimized. By the HS definition, $\mathbf{f}(t)$ is a principal curve if it does not intersect itself and is self consistent, that is, $\mathbf{f}(t) = E(\mathbf{X}|t_\mathbf{f}(\mathbf{X}) = t)$. Intuitively speaking, self-consistency means that each point of $\mathbf{f}$ is the average (under the distribution of $\mathbf{X}$) of points that project there. Based on their defining property HS developed an algorithm for constructing principal curves for distributions or data sets, and described an application in the Stanford Linear Collider Project [3].

Principal curves have been applied by Banfield and Raftery [4] to identify the outlines of ice floes in satellite images. Their method of clustering about principal curves led to a fully automatic method for identifying ice floes and their outlines. On the theoretical side, Tibshirani [5] introduced a semiparametric model for principal curves and proposed a method for estimating principal curves using the EM algorithm. Recently, Delicado [6] proposed yet another definition based on a property of the first principal components of multivariate normal distributions. Close connections between principal curves and Kohonen's self-organizing maps were pointed out by Mulier and Cherkassky [7]. Self-organizing maps were also used by Der et al. [8] for constructing principal curves.

There is an unsatisfactory aspect of the definition of principal curves in the original HS paper as well as in subsequent works. Although principal curves have been defined to be *nonparametric*, their existence for a given distribution or probability density is an open question, except for very special cases such as elliptical distributions. This also makes it difficult to theoretically analyze any learning schemes for principal curves.

Recently, we [1] have proposed a new definition of principal curves which resolves this problem. In the new definition, a curve $\mathbf{f}^*$ is called a principal curve of length L for $\mathbf{X}$ if $\mathbf{f}^*$ minimizes $\Delta(\mathbf{f}) = E\left[\inf_t \|\mathbf{X} - \mathbf{f}(t)\|^2\right] = E\|\mathbf{X} - \mathbf{f}(t_\mathbf{f}(\mathbf{X}))\|^2$, the expected squared distance between $\mathbf{X}$ and the curve, over all curves of length less than or equal to L. It was proved in [1] that for any $\mathbf{X}$ with finite second moments there always exists a principal curve in the new sense.

A theoretical algorithm has also been developed to estimate principal curves based on a common model in statistical learning theory (e.g. see [9]). Suppose that the distribution of $\mathbf{X}$ is concentrated on a closed and bounded convex set $K \subset \mathcal{R}^d$, and we are given n training points $\mathbf{X}_1, \ldots, \mathbf{X}_n$ drawn independently from the distribution of $\mathbf{X}$. Let S denote the family of curves taking values in K and having length not greater than L. For $k \geq 1$ let S_k be the set of polygonal (piecewise linear) curves in K which have k segments and whose lengths do not exceed L. Let

$$\Delta(\mathbf{x}, \mathbf{f}) = \min_t \|\mathbf{x} - \mathbf{f}(t)\|^2 \tag{1}$$

denote the squared distance between $\mathbf{x}$ and $\mathbf{f}$. For any $\mathbf{f} \in S$ the empirical squared error of $\mathbf{f}$ on the training data is the sample average $\Delta_n(\mathbf{f}) = \frac{1}{n}\sum_{i=1}^n \Delta(\mathbf{X}_i, \mathbf{f})$. Let the theoretical algorithm choose an $\mathbf{f}_{k,n} \in S_k$ which minimizes the empirical error, i.e, let $\mathbf{f}_{k,n} = \arg\min_{\mathbf{f} \in S_k} \Delta_n(\mathbf{f})$. It was shown in [1] that if k is chosen to be proportional to $n^{1/3}$, then the expected squared loss of the empirically optimal polygonal curve with k segments and length at most L converges, as $n \to \infty$, to the squared loss of the principal curve of length L at a rate $\Delta(\mathbf{f}_{k,n}) - \Delta(\mathbf{f}^*) = O(n^{-1/3})$.

Although amenable to theoretical analysis, the algorithm in [1] is computationally burdensome for implementation. In this paper we develop a suboptimal algorithm for learning principal curves. This practical algorithm produces polygonal curve approximations to the principal curve just as the theoretical method does, but global optimization is replaced by a less complex iterative descent method. We give simulation results and compare our algorithm with previous work. In general, on examples considered by HS the performance of the new algorithm is comparable with the HS algorithm, while it proves to be more robust to changes in the data generating model.

2 A Polygonal Line Algorithm

Given a set of data points $\mathcal{X}_n = \{\mathbf{x}_1, \ldots, \mathbf{x}_n\} \subset \mathcal{R}^d$, the task of finding the polygonal curve with k segments and length L which minimizes $\frac{1}{n}\sum_{i=1}^n \Delta(\mathbf{x}_i, \mathbf{f})$ is computationally difficult. We propose a suboptimal method with reasonable complexity. The basic idea is to start with a straight line segment $\mathbf{f}_{1,n}$ ($k = 1$) and in each iteration of the algorithm to increase the number of segments by one by adding a new vertex to the polygonal curve $\mathbf{f}_{k,n}$ produced by the previous iteration. After adding a new vertex, the positions of all vertices are updated in an inner loop.

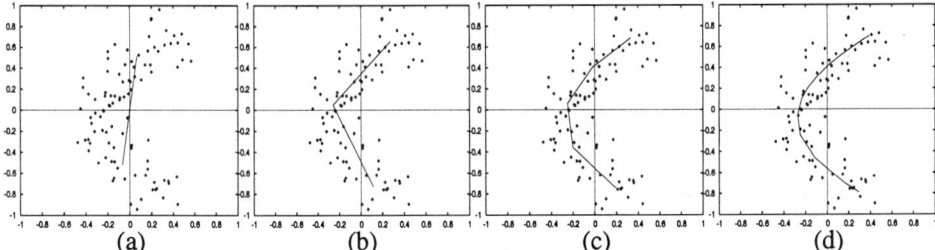

Figure 1: The curves $\mathbf{f}_{k,n}$ produced by the polygonal line algorithm for $n = 100$ data points. The data was generated by adding independent Gaussian errors to both coordinates of a point chosen randomly on a half circle. (a) $\mathbf{f}_{1,n}$, (b) $\mathbf{f}_{2,n}$, (c) $\mathbf{f}_{4,n}$, (d) $\mathbf{f}_{11,n}$ (the output of the algorithm).

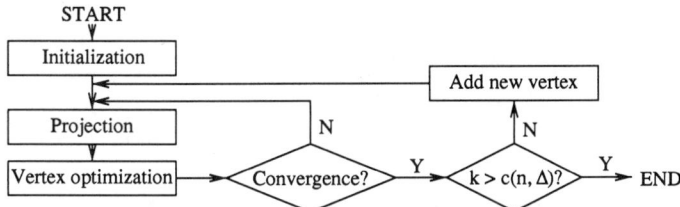

Figure 2: The flow chart of the polygonal line algorithm.

The inner loop consists of a projection step and an optimization step. In the projection step the data points are partitioned into "Voronoi regions" according to which segment or vertex they project. In the optimization step the new position of each vertex is determined by minimizing an average squared distance criterion penalized by a measure of the local curvature. These two steps are iterated until convergence is achieved and $f_{k,n}$ is produced. Then a new vertex is added.

The algorithm stops when k exceeds a threshold $c(n, \Delta)$. This stopping criterion is based on a heuristic complexity measure, determined by the number segments k, the number of data points n, and the average squared distance $\Delta_n(\mathbf{f}_{k,n})$.

THE INITIALIZATION STEP. To obtain $\mathbf{f}_{1,n}$, take the shortest segment of the first principal component line which contains all of the projected data points.

THE PROJECTION STEP. Let $\mathbf{f}$ denote a polygonal curve with vertices $\mathbf{v}_1, \ldots, \mathbf{v}_{k+1}$ and closed line segments $\mathbf{s}_1, \ldots, \mathbf{s}_k$, such that $\mathbf{s}_i$ connects vertices $\mathbf{v}_i$ and $\mathbf{v}_{i+1}$. In this step the data set $\mathcal{X}_n$ is partitioned into (at most) $2k+1$ disjoint sets $V_1, \ldots, V_{k+1}$ and $S_1, \ldots, S_k$, the Voronoi regions of the vertices and segments of $\mathbf{f}$, in the following manner. For any $\mathbf{x} \in \mathcal{R}^d$ let $\Delta(\mathbf{x}, \mathbf{s}_i)$ be the squared distance from $\mathbf{x}$ to $\mathbf{s}_i$ (see definition (1)), and let $\Delta(\mathbf{x}, \mathbf{v}_i) = \|\mathbf{x} - \mathbf{v}_i\|^2$. Then let

$$V_i = \{\mathbf{x} \in \mathcal{X}_n : \Delta(\mathbf{x}, \mathbf{v}_i) = \Delta(\mathbf{x}, \mathbf{f}), \quad \Delta(\mathbf{x}, \mathbf{v}_i) < \Delta(\mathbf{x}, \mathbf{v}_m), m = 1, \ldots, i-1\}.$$

Upon setting $V = \bigcup_{i=1}^{k+1} V_i$, the S_i sets are defined by

$$S_i = \{\mathbf{x} \in \mathcal{X}_n : \mathbf{x} \notin V, \Delta(\mathbf{x}, \mathbf{s}_i) = \Delta(\mathbf{x}, \mathbf{f}), \quad \Delta(\mathbf{x}, \mathbf{s}_i) < \Delta(\mathbf{x}, \mathbf{s}_m), m = 1, \ldots, i-1\}.$$

The resulting partition is illustrated in Figure 3.

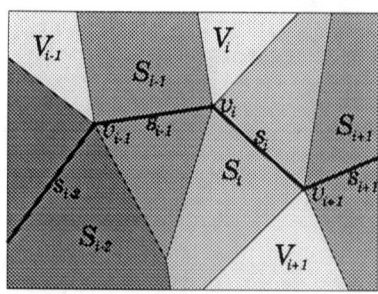

Figure 3: The Voronoi partition induced by the vertices and segments of $\mathbf{f}$

THE VERTEX OPTIMIZATION STEP. In this step we iterate over the vertices, and relocate each vertex while all the others are kept fixed. For each vertex, we minimize $\Delta_n(\mathbf{v}_i) + \lambda_p P(\mathbf{v}_i)$, a local average squared distance criterion penalized by a measure of the local curvature by using a gradient (steepest descent) method.

The local measure of the average squared distance is calculated from the data points which project to $\mathbf{v}_i$ or to the line segment(s) starting at $\mathbf{v}_i$ (see Projection Step). Accordingly, let $\sigma_+(\mathbf{v}_i) = \sum_{\mathbf{x} \in S_i} \Delta(\mathbf{x}, \mathbf{s}_i)$, $\sigma_-(\mathbf{v}_i) = \sum_{\mathbf{x} \in S_{i-1}} \Delta(\mathbf{x}, \mathbf{s}_{i-1})$, and $\nu(\mathbf{v}_i) = \sum_{\mathbf{x} \in V_i} \Delta(\mathbf{x}, \mathbf{v}_i)$. Now define the local average squared distance as a function of $\mathbf{v}_i$ by

$$\Delta_n(\mathbf{v}_i) = \begin{cases} \dfrac{\nu(\mathbf{v}_i) + \sigma_+(\mathbf{v}_i)}{|V_i| + |S_i|} & \text{if } i = 1 \\[2mm] \dfrac{\sigma_-(\mathbf{v}_i) + \nu(\mathbf{v}_i) + \sigma_+(\mathbf{v}_i)}{|S_{i-1}| + |V_i| + |S_i|} & \text{if } 1 < i < k+1 \\[2mm] \dfrac{\sigma_-(\mathbf{v}_i) + \nu(\mathbf{v}_i)}{|S_{i-1}| + |V_i|} & \text{if } i = k+1. \end{cases} \qquad (2)$$

In the theoretical algorithm the average squared distance $\Delta_n(\mathbf{x}, \mathbf{f})$ is minimized subject to the constraint that $\mathbf{f}$ is a polygonal curve with k segments and length not exceeding L. One could use a Lagrangian formulation and attempt to find a new position for $\mathbf{v}_i$ (while all other vertices are fixed) such that the penalized squared error $\Delta_n(\mathbf{f}) + \lambda l(\mathbf{f})^2$ is minimum. However, we have observed that this approach is very sensitive to the choice of λ, and reproduces the estimation bias of the HS algorithm which flattens the curve at areas of high curvature. So, instead of directly penalizing the lengths of the line segments, we chose to penalize sharp angles to obtain a smooth curve solution. Nonetheless, note that if only one vertex is moved at a time, penalizing sharp angles will indirectly penalize long line segments. At inner vertices $\mathbf{v}_i$, $3 \leq i \leq k-1$ we penalize the sum of the cosines of the three angles at vertices $\mathbf{v}_{i-1}$, $\mathbf{v}_i$, and $\mathbf{v}_{i+1}$. The cosine function was picked because of its regular behavior around π, which makes it especially suitable for the steepest descent algorithm. To make the algorithm invariant under scaling, we multiply the cosines by the squared radius of the data, that is, $r = 1/2 \max_{\mathbf{x} \in X_n, \mathbf{y} \in X_n} \|\mathbf{x} - \mathbf{y}\|$. At the endpoints and at their immediate neighbors ($\mathbf{v}_i$, $i = 1, 2, k, k+1$), where penalizing sharp angles does not translate to penalizing long line segments, the penalty on a nonexistent angle is replaced by a direct penalty on the squared length of the first (or last) segment. Formally, let γ_i denote the angle at vertex $\mathbf{v}_i$, let $\pi(\mathbf{v}_i) = r^2(1 + \cos \gamma_i)$, let $\mu_+(\mathbf{v}_i) = \|\mathbf{v}_i - \mathbf{v}_{i+1}\|^2$, and let $\mu_-(\mathbf{v}_i) = \|\mathbf{v}_i - \mathbf{v}_{i-1}\|^2$. Then the penalty at vertex $\mathbf{v}_i$ is

$$P(\mathbf{v}_i) = \begin{cases} 2\mu_+(\mathbf{v}_i) + \pi(\mathbf{v}_{i+1}) & \text{if } i = 1 \\ \mu_-(\mathbf{v}_i) + \pi(\mathbf{v}_i) + \pi(\mathbf{v}_{i+1}) & \text{if } i = 2 \\ \pi(\mathbf{v}_{i-1}) + \pi(\mathbf{v}_i) + \pi(\mathbf{v}_{i+1}) & \text{if } 2 \leq i \leq k-1 \\ \pi(\mathbf{v}_{i-1}) + \pi(\mathbf{v}_i) + \mu_+(\mathbf{v}_i) & \text{if } i = k \\ \pi(\mathbf{v}_{i-1}) + 2\mu_-(\mathbf{v}_i) & \text{if } i = k+1. \end{cases}$$

One important issue is the amount of smoothing required for a given data set. In the HS algorithm one needs to set the penalty coefficient of the spline smoother, or the span of the scatterplot smoother. In our algorithm, the corresponding parameter is the curvature penalty factor λ_p. If some a priori knowledge about the distribution is available, one can use it to determine the smoothing parameter. However in the absence of such knowledge, the coefficient should be data-dependent. Intuitively, λ_p should increase with the number of segments and the size of the average squared error, and it should decrease with the data size. Based on heuristic considerations and after carrying out practical experiments, we set $\lambda_p = \lambda'_p n^{-1/3} \Delta_n(\mathbf{f}_{k,n})^{1/2} r^{-1}$, where λ'_p is a parameter of the algorithm, and can be kept fixed for substantially different data sets.

ADDING A NEW VERTEX. We start with the optimized $\mathbf{f}_{k,n}$ and choose the segment that has the largest number of data points projecting to it. If more then one such segment exists, we choose the longest one. The midpoint of this segment is selected as the new vertex. Formally, let $I = \{i : |S_i| \geq |S_j|, \, j = 1, \ldots, k\}$, and $\ell = \arg\max_{i \in I} \|\mathbf{v}_i - \mathbf{v}_{i+1}\|$. Then the new vertex is $\mathbf{v}_{new} = (\mathbf{v}_\ell + \mathbf{v}_{\ell+1})/2$.

STOPPING CONDITION. According to the theoretical results of [1], the number of segments k should be proportional to $n^{1/3}$ to achieve the $O(n^{1/3})$ convergence rate for the expected squared distance. Although the theoretical bounds are not tight enough to determine the optimal number of segments for a given data size, we found that $k \sim n^{1/3}$ also works in practice. To achieve robustness we need to make k sensitive to the average squared distance. The stopping condition blends these two considerations. The algorithm stops when k exceeds $c(n, \Delta_n(\mathbf{f}_{k,n})) = \lambda_k n^{1/3} \Delta_n(\mathbf{f}_{k,n})^{-1/2} r$.

COMPUTATIONAL COMPLEXITY. The complexity of the inner loop is dominated by the complexity of the projection step, which is $O(nk)$. Increasing the number of segments by one at a time (as described in Section 2), and using the stopping condition of Section 2, the computational complexity of the algorithm becomes $O(n^{5/3})$. This is slightly better than the $O(n^2)$ complexity of the HS algorithm. The complexity can be dramatically decreased if, instead of adding only one vertex, a new vertex is placed at the midpoint of every segment, giving $O(n^{4/3} \log n)$, or if k is set to be a constant, giving $O(n)$. These simplifications work well in certain situations, but the original algorithm is more robust.

3 Experimental Results

We have extensively tested our algorithm on two-dimensional data sets. In most experiments the data was generated by a commonly used (see, e.g., [3] [5] [7]) additive model $\mathbf{X} = \mathbf{Y} + \mathbf{e}$, where $\mathbf{Y}$ is uniformly distributed on a smooth planar curve (hereafter called the *generating curve*) and $\mathbf{e}$ is bivariate additive noise which is independent of $\mathbf{Y}$.

Since the "true" principal curve is not known (note that the generating curve in the model $\mathbf{X} = \mathbf{Y} + \mathbf{e}$ is in general not a principal curve either in the HS sense or in our definition), it is hard to give an objective measure of performance. For this reason, in what follows, the performance is judged subjectively, mainly on the basis of how closely the resulting curve follows the shape of the generating curve.

In general, in simulation examples considered by HS the performance of the new algorithm is comparable with the HS algorithm. Due to the data-dependence of the curvature penalty factor and the stopping condition, our algorithm turns out to be more robust to alterations in the data generating model, as well as to changes in the parameters of the particular model.

We use varying generating shapes, noise parameters, and data sizes to demonstrate the robustness of the polygonal line algorithm. All of the plots in Figure 4 show the generating curve (Generator Curve), the curve produced by our polygonal line algorithm (Principal

Curve), and the curve produced by the HS algorithm with spline smoothing (HS Principal Curve), which we have found to perform better than the HS algorithm using scatterplot smoothing. For closed generating curves we also include the curve produced by the Banfield and Raftery (BR) algorithm [4], which extends the HS algorithm to closed curves (BR Principal Curve). The two coefficients of the polygonal line algorithm are set in all experiments to the constant values $\lambda_k = 0.3$ and $\lambda'_p = 0.1$. All plots have been normalized to fit in a 2×2 square. The parameters given below refer to values before this normalization.

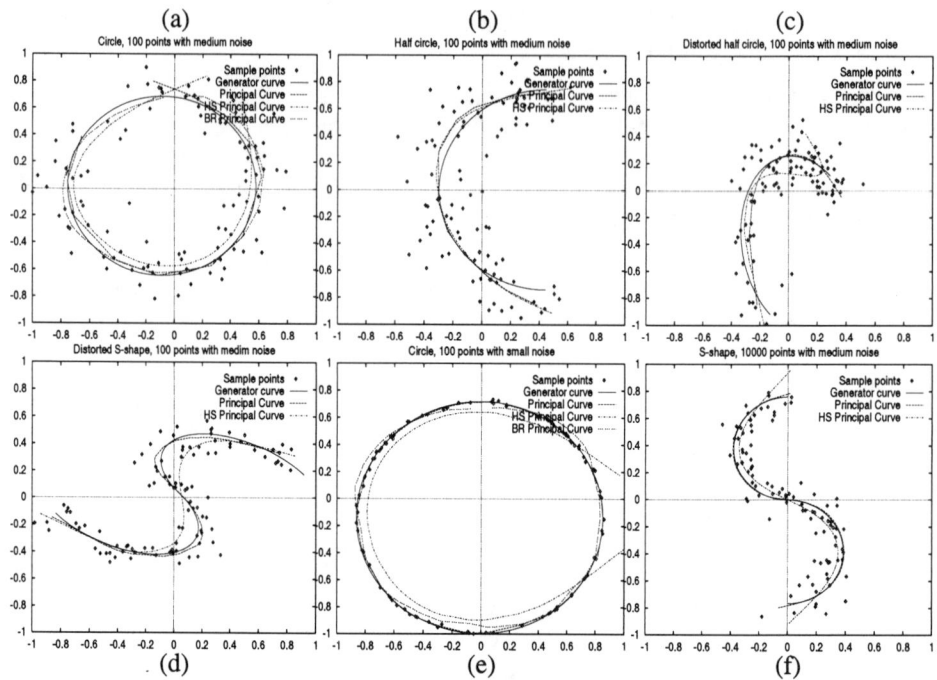

Figure 4: (a) **The Circle Example**: the BR and the polygonal line algorithm show less bias than the HS algorithm. (b) **The Half Circle Example**: the HS and the polygonal line algorithms produce similar curves. (c) and (d) **Transformed Data Sets**: the polygonal line algorithm still follows fairly closely the "distorted" shapes. (e) **Small Noise Variance** and (f) **Large Sample Size**: the curves produced by the polygonal line algorithm are nearly indistinguishable from the generating curves.

In Figure 4(a) the generating curve is a circle of radius $r = 1$, and $\mathbf{e} = (e_1, e_2)$ is a zero mean bivariate uncorrelated Gaussian with variance $E(e_i^2) = 0.04$, $i = 1, 2$. The performance of the three algorithms (HS, BR, and the polygonal line algorithm) is comparable, although the HS algorithm exhibits more bias than the other two. Note that the BR algorithm [4] has been tailored to fit closed curves and to reduce the estimation bias. In Figure 4(b), only half of the circle is used as a generating curve and the other parameters remain the same. Here, too, both the HS and our algorithm behave similarly.

When we depart from these usual settings the polygonal line algorithm exhibits better behavior than the HS algorithm. In Figure 4(c) the data set of Figure 4(b) was linearly transformed using the matrix $\begin{pmatrix} 0.6 & 0.6 \\ -1.0 & 1.2 \end{pmatrix}$. In Figure 4(d) the transformation $\begin{pmatrix} -1.0 & -1.2 \\ 1.0 & -0.2 \end{pmatrix}$ was used. The original data set was generated by an S-shaped generating curve, consisting of two half circles of unit radii, to which the same Gaussian noise was added as in Figure 4(b). In both cases the polygonal line algorithm produces curves that fit the generator curve more closely. This is especially noticeable in Figure 4(c) where the HS principal curve fails to follow the shape of the distorted half circle.

There are two situations when we expect our algorithm to perform particularly well. If the distribution is concentrated on a curve, then according to both the HS and our definitions the principal curve is the generating curve itself. Thus, if the noise variance is small, we expect both algorithms to very closely approximate the generating curve. The data in Figure 4(e) was generated using the same additive Gaussian model as in Figure 4(a), but the noise variance was reduced to $E(e_i^2) = 0.001$ for $i = 1, 2$. In this case we found that the polygonal line algorithm outperformed both the HS and the BR algorithms.

The second case is when the sample size is large. Although the generating curve is not necessarily the principal curve of the distribution, it is natural to expect the algorithm to well approximate the generating curve as the sample size grows. Such a case is shown in Figure 4(f), where $n = 10000$ data points were generated (but only a small subset of these was actually plotted). Here the polygonal line algorithm approximates the generating curve with much better accuracy than the HS algorithm.

The Java implementation of the algorithm is available at the WWW site
http://www.cs.concordia.ca/~grad/kegl/pcurvedemo.html

4 Conclusion

We offered a new definition of principal curves and presented a practical algorithm for constructing principal curves for data sets. One significant difference between our method and previous principal curve algorithms ([3],[4], and [8]) is that, motivated by the new definition, our algorithm minimizes a distance criterion (2) between the data points and the *polygonal curve* rather than minimizing a distance criterion between the data points and the vertices of the polygonal curve. This and the introduction of the data-dependent smoothing factor λ_p made our algorithm more robust to variations in the data distribution, while we could keep computational complexity low.

Acknowledgments

This work was supported in part by NSERC grant OGP000270, Canadian National Networks of Centers of Excellence grant 293, and the National Science Foundation.

References

[1] B. Kégl, A. Krzyżak, T. Linder, and K. Zeger, "Principal curves: Learning and convergence," in *Proceedings of IEEE Int. Symp. on Information Theory*, p. 387, 1998.

[2] T. Hastie, *Principal curves and surfaces*. PhD thesis, Stanford University, 1984.

[3] T. Hastie and W. Stuetzle, "Principal curves," *Journal of the American Statistical Association*, vol. 84, no. 406, pp. 502–516, 1989.

[4] J. D. Banfield and A. E. Raftery, "Ice floe identification in satellite images using mathematical morphology and clustering about principal curves," *Journal of the American Statistical Association*, vol. 87, no. 417, pp. 7–16, 1992.

[5] R. Tibshirani, "Principal curves revisited," *Statistics and Computation*, vol. 2, pp. 183–190, 1992.

[6] P. Delicado, "Principal curves and principal oriented points," Tech. Rep. 309, Department d'Economia i Empresa, Universitat Pompeu Fabra, 1998.
http://www.econ.upf.es/deehome/what/wpapers/postscripts/309.pdf.

[7] F. Mulier and V. Cherkassky, "Self-organization as an iterative kernel smoothing process," *Neural Computation*, vol. 7, pp. 1165–1177, 1995.

[8] R. Der, U. Steinmetz, and G. Balzuweit, "Nonlinear principal component analysis," tech. rep., Institut für Informatik, Universität Leipzig, 1998.
http://www.informatik.uni-leipzig.de/~der/Veroeff/npcafin.ps.

[9] V. N. Vapnik, *The Nature of Statistical Learning Theory*. New York: Springer-Verlag, 1995.

Unsupervised Classification with Non-Gaussian Mixture Models using ICA

Te-Won Lee, Michael S. Lewicki and Terrence Sejnowski

Howard Hughes Medical Institute
Computational Neurobiology Laboratory
The Salk Institute
10010 N. Torrey Pines Road
La Jolla, California 92037, USA
{tewon,lewicki,terry}@salk.edu

Abstract

We present an unsupervised classification algorithm based on an ICA mixture model. The ICA mixture model assumes that the observed data can be categorized into several mutually exclusive data classes in which the components in each class are generated by a linear mixture of independent sources. The algorithm finds the independent sources, the mixing matrix for each class and also computes the class membership probability for each data point. This approach extends the Gaussian mixture model so that the classes can have non-Gaussian structure. We demonstrate that this method can learn efficient codes to represent images of natural scenes and text. The learned classes of basis functions yield a better approximation of the underlying distributions of the data, and thus can provide greater coding efficiency. We believe that this method is well suited to modeling structure in high-dimensional data and has many potential applications.

1 Introduction

Recently, Blind Source Separation (BSS) by Independent Component Analysis (ICA) has shown promise in signal processing applications including speech enhancement systems, telecommunications and medical signal processing. ICA is a technique for finding a linear non-orthogonal coordinate system in multivariate data. The directions of the axes of this coordinate system are determined by the data's second- and higher-order statistics. The goal of the ICA is to linearly transform the data such that the transformed variables are as statistically independent from each other as possible (Bell and Sejnowski, 1995; Cardoso and Laheld, 1996; Lee et al., 1999a). ICA generalizes the technique of Principal Component Analysis (PCA) and, like PCA, has proven a useful tool for finding structure in data.

One limitation of ICA is the assumption that the sources are independent. Here, we present an approach for relaxing this assumption using mixture models. In a mixture model (Duda and Hart, 1973), the observed data can be categorized into several mutually exclusive classes. When the class variables are modeled as multivariate Gaussian densities, it is called a Gaussian mixture model. We generalize the Gaussian mixture model by modeling each class with independent variables (ICA mixture model). This allows modeling of classes with non-Gaussian (e.g., platykurtic or leptokurtic) structure. An algorithm for learning the parameters is derived using the expectation maximization (EM) algorithm. In Lee et al. (1999c), we demonstrated that this approach showed improved performance in data classification problems. Here, we apply the algorithm to learning efficient codes for representing different types of images.

2 The ICA Mixture Model

We assume that the data were generated by a mixture density (Duda and Hart, 1973):

$$p(\mathbf{x}|\Theta) = \sum_{k=1}^{K} p(\mathbf{x}|C_k, \theta_k) p(C_k), \quad (1)$$

where $\Theta = (\theta_1, \cdots, \theta_K)$ are the unknown parameters for each $p(\mathbf{x}|C_k, \theta_k)$, called the component densities. We further assume that the number of classes, K, and the a priori probability, $p(C_k)$, for each class are known. In the case of a Gaussian mixture model, $p(\mathbf{x}|C_k, \theta_k) \propto N(\mu_k, \Sigma_k)$. Here we assume that the form of the component densities is non-Gaussian and the data within each class are described by an ICA model.

$$\mathbf{x}_k = \mathbf{A}_k \mathbf{s}_k + \mathbf{b}_k, \quad (2)$$

where $\mathbf{A}_k$ is a $N \times M$ scalar matrix (called the basis or mixing matrix) and $\mathbf{b}_k$ is the bias vector for class k. The vector $\mathbf{s}_k$ is called the source vector (these are also the coefficients for each basis vector). It is assumed that the individual sources s_i within each class are mutually independent across a data ensemble. For simplicity, we consider the case where $\mathbf{A}_k$ is full rank, i.e. the number of sources (M) is equal to the number of mixtures (N). Figure 1 shows a simple example of a dataset that can be described by ICA mixture model. Each class was generated from eq.2 using a different $\mathbf{A}$ and $\mathbf{b}$. Class (o) was generated by two uniform distributed sources, whereas class (+) was generated by two Laplacian distributed sources ($p(s) \propto \exp(-|s|)$). The task is to model the unlabeled data points and to determine the parameters for each class, $\mathbf{A}_k, \mathbf{b}_k$ and the probability of each class $p(C_k|\mathbf{x}, \theta_{1:K})$ for each data point. A learning algorithm can be derived by an expectation maximization approach (Ghahramani, 1994) and implemented in the following steps:

- Compute the log-likelihood of the data for each class:
$$\log p(\mathbf{x}|C_k, \theta_k) = \log p(\mathbf{s}_k) - \log(\det|\mathbf{A}_k|), \quad (3)$$
where $\theta_k = \{\mathbf{A}_k, \mathbf{b}_k, \mathbf{s}_k\}$.

- Compute the probability for each class given the data vector $\mathbf{x}$
$$p(C_k|\mathbf{x}, \theta_{1:K}) = \frac{p(\mathbf{x}|\theta_k, C_k) p(C_k)}{\sum_k p(\mathbf{x}|\theta_k, C_k) p(C_k)}. \quad (4)$$

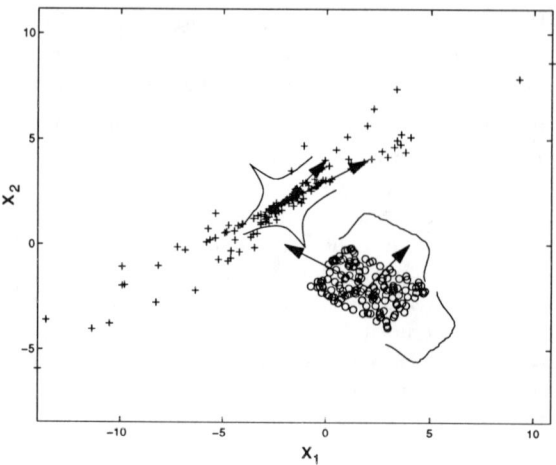

Figure 1: A simple example for classifying an ICA mixture model. There are two classes (+) and (o); each class was generated by two independent variables, two bias terms and two basis vectors. Class (o) was generated by two uniform distributed sources as indicated next to the data class. Class (+) was generated by two Laplacian distributed sources with a sharp peak at the bias and heavy tails. The inset graphs show the distributions of the source variables, $s_{i,k}$, for each basis vector.

- Adapt the basis functions $\mathbf{A}$ and the bias terms $\mathbf{b}$ for each class. The basis functions are adapted using gradient ascent

$$\Delta \mathbf{A}_k \propto \frac{\partial}{\partial \mathbf{A}_k} \log p(\mathbf{x}|\theta_{1:K})$$
$$= p(C_k|\mathbf{x}, \theta_{1:K}) \frac{\partial}{\partial \mathbf{A}_k} \log p(\mathbf{x}|C_k, \theta_k). \quad (5)$$

Note that this simply weights any standard ICA algorithm gradient by $p(C_k|\mathbf{x}, \theta_{1:K})$. The gradient can also be summed over multiple data points. The bias term is updated according to

$$\mathbf{b}_k = \frac{\sum_t \mathbf{x}_t p(C_k|\mathbf{x}_t, \theta_{1:K})}{\sum_t p(C_k|\mathbf{x}_t, \theta_{1:K})}, \quad (6)$$

where t is the data index ($t = 1, \ldots, T$).

The three steps in the learning algorithm perform gradient ascent on the total likelihood of the data in eq.1.

The extended infomax ICA learning rule is able to blindly separate mixed sources with sub- and super-Gaussian distributions. This is achieved by using a simple type of learning rule first derived by Girolami (1998). The learning rule in Lee et al. (1999b) uses the stability analysis of Cardoso and Laheld (1996) to switch between sub- and super-Gaussian regimes. The learning rule expressed in terms of $\mathbf{W} = \mathbf{A}^{-1}$, called the filter matrix is:

$$\Delta \mathbf{W} \propto \left[\mathbf{I} - \mathbf{K} \tanh(\mathbf{u})\mathbf{u}^T - \mathbf{u}\mathbf{u}^T \right] \mathbf{W}, \quad (7)$$

where k_i are elements of the N-dimensional diagonal matrix $\mathbf{K}$ and $\mathbf{u} = \mathbf{W}\mathbf{x}$. The unmixed sources $\mathbf{u}$ are the source estimate $\mathbf{s}$ (Bell and Sejnowski, 1995). The k_i's are (Lee et al., 1999b)

$$k_i = \text{sign}\left(E[\text{sech}^2 u_i]E[u_i^2] - E[u_i \tanh u_i]\right). \quad (8)$$

The source distribution is super-Gaussian when $k_i = 1$ and sub-Gaussian when $k_i = -1$. For the log-likelihood estimation in eq.3 the term $\log p(\mathbf{s})$ can be approximated as follows

$$\log p(\mathbf{s}) \propto -\sum_n \log \cosh s_n - \frac{s_n^2}{2} \quad \text{super-Gaussian}$$

$$\log p(\mathbf{s}) \propto +\sum_n \log \cosh s_n - \frac{s_n^2}{2} \quad \text{sub-Gaussian} \quad (9)$$

Super-Gaussian densities, are approximated by a density model with heavier tail than the Gaussian density; Sub-Gaussian densities are approximated by a bimodal density (Girolami, 1998). Although the source density approximation is crude it has been demonstrated that they are sufficient for standard ICA problems (Lee et al., 1999b). When learning sparse representations only, a Laplacian prior ($p(s) \propto \exp(-|s|)$) can be used for the weight update which simplifies the infomax learning rule to

$$\Delta \mathbf{W} \propto [\mathbf{I} - \text{sign}(\mathbf{u})\mathbf{u}^T]\mathbf{W}, \quad (10)$$

$$\log p(\mathbf{s}) \propto -\sum_n |s_n| \quad \text{Laplacian prior}$$

3 Learning efficient codes for images

Recently, several approaches have been proposed to learn image codes that utilize a set of linear basis functions. Olshausen and Field (1996) used a sparseness criterion and found codes that were similar to localized and oriented receptive fields. Similar results were presented by Bell and Sejnowski (1997) using the infomax algorithm and by Lewicki and Olshausen (1998) using a Bayesian approach. By applying the ICA mixture model we present results which show a higher degree of flexibility in encoding the images. We used images of natural scenes obtained from Olshausen and Field (1996) and text images of scanned newspaper articles. The training set consisted of 12 by 12 pixel patches selected randomly from both image types. Figure 2 illustrates examples of those image patches. Two complete basis vectors $\mathbf{A}_1$ and $\mathbf{A}_2$ were randomly initialized. Then, for each gradient in eq.5 a stepsize was computed as a function of the amplitude of the basis vectors and the number of iterations. The algorithm converged after 100,000 iterations and learned two classes of basis functions as shown in figure 3. Figure 3 (top) shows basis functions corresponding to natural images. The basis functions show Gabor[1]-like structure as previously reported in (Olshausen and Field, 1996; Bell and Sejnowski, 1997; Lewicki and Olshausen, 1998). However, figure 3 (bottom) shows basis functions corresponding to text images. These basis functions resemble bars with different lengths and widths that capture the high-frequency structure present in the text images.

3.1 Comparing coding efficiency

We have compared the coding efficiency between the ICA mixture model and similar models using Shannon's theorem to obtain a lower bound on the number of bits

---
[1] Gaussian modulated siusoidal

 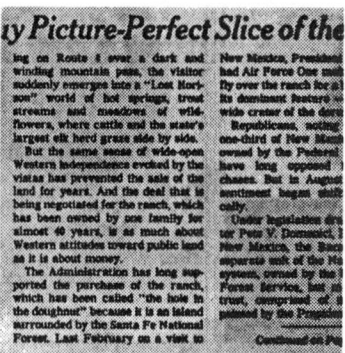

Figure 2: Example of natural scene and text image. The 12 by 12 pixel image patches were randomly sampled from the images and used as inputs to the ICA mixture model.

required to encode the pattern.

$$\#\text{bits} \geq -\log_2 P(\mathbf{x}|\mathbf{A}) - N\log_2(\sigma_x), \qquad (11)$$

where N is the dimensionality of the input pattern $\mathbf{x}$ and σ_x is the coding precision (standard deviation of the noise introduced by errors in encoding). Table 1 compares the coding efficiency of five different methods. It shows the number of bits required to encode three different test data sets (5000 image patches from natural scenes, 5000 image patches from text images and 5000 image patches from both image types) using five different encoding methods (ICA mixture model, nature trained ICA, text trained ICA, nature and text trained ICA, and PCA trained on all three test sets). It is clear that ICA basis functions trained on natural scene images exhibit the best encoding when only natural scenes are presented (column: nature). The same applies to text images (column: text). Note that text training yields a reasonable basis for both data sets but nature training gives a good basis only for nature. The ICA mixture model shows the same encoding power for the individual test data sets, and it gives the best encoding when both image types are present. In this case, the encoding difference between the ICA mixture model and PCA is significant (more than 20%). ICA mixtures yielded a small improvement over ICA trained on both image types. We expect the size of the improvement to be greater in situations where there are greater differences among the classes. An advantage of the mixture model is that each image patch is automatically classified.

4 Discussion

The new algorithm for unsupervised classification presented here is based on a maximum likelihood mixture model using ICA to model the structure of the classes. We have demonstrated here that the algorithm can learn efficient codes to represent different image types such as natural scenes and text images. In this case, the learned classes of basis functions show a 20% improvement over PCA encoding. ICA mixture model should show better image compression rates than traditional compression algorithm such as JPEG.

The ICA mixture model is a nonlinear model in which each class is modeled as a linear process and the choice of class is modeled using probabilities. This model

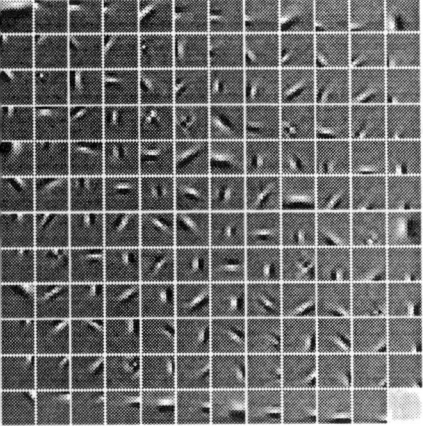 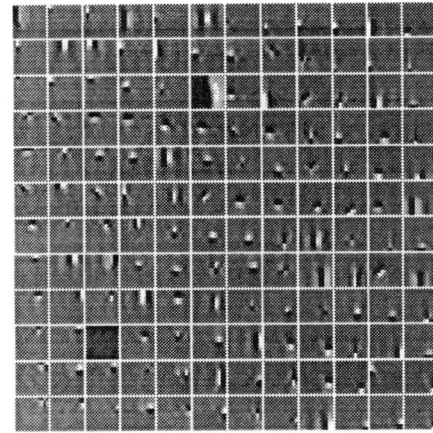

Figure 3: (Left) Basis function class corresponding to natural images. (Right) Basis function class corresponding to text images.

Table 1: Comparing coding efficiency

Training set and model	Test data		
	Nature	Text	Nature and Text
ICA mixtures	4.72	5.20	4.96
Nature trained ICA	4.72	9.57	7.15
Text trained ICA	5.00	5.19	5.10
Nature and text trained ICA	4.83	5.29	5.07
PCA	6.22	5.97	6.09

Coding efficiency (bits per pixel) of five methods is compared for three test sets. Coding precision was set to 7 bits (Nature: $\sigma_x = 0.016$ and Text: $\sigma_x = 0.029$).

can therefore be seen as a nonlinear ICA model. Furthermore, it is one way of relaxing the independence assumption over the whole data set. The ICA mixture model is a conditional independence model, i.e., the independence assumption holds within only each class and there may be dependencies among classes. A different view of the ICA mixture model is to think of the classes of being an overcomplete representation. Compared to the approach of Lewicki and Sejnowski (1998), the main difference is that the basis functions learned here are mutually exclusive, i.e. each class uses its own set of basis functions.

This method is similar to other approaches including the mixture density networks by Bishop (1994) in which a neural network was used to find arbitrary density functions. This algorithm reduces to the Gaussian mixture model when the source priors are Gaussian. Purely Gaussian structure, however, is rare in real data sets. Here we have used priors of the form of super-Gaussian and sub-Gaussian densities. But these could be extended as proposed by Attias (1999). The proposed model was used for learning a complete set of basis functions without additive noise. However, the method can be extended to take into account additive Gaussian noise and an overcomplete set of basis vectors (Lewicki and Sejnowski, 1998).

In (Lee et al., 1999c), we have performed several experiments on benchmark data sets for classification problems. The results were comparable or improved over those obtained by AutoClass (Stutz and Cheeseman, 1994) which uses a Gaussian mixture model. Furthermore, we showed that the algorithm can be applied to blind source separation in nonstationary environments. The method can switch automatically between learned mixing matrices in different environments (Lee et al., 1999c). This may prove to be useful in the automatic detection of sleep stages by observing EEG signals. The method can identify these stages due to the changing source priors and their mixing.

Potential applications of the proposed method include the problem of noise removal and the problem of filling in missing pixels. We believe that this method provides greater flexibility in modeling structure in high-dimensional data and has many potential applications.

References

Attias, H. (1999). Blind separation of noisy mixtures: An EM algorithm for independent factor analysis. *Neural Computation*, in press.

Bell, A. J. and Sejnowski, T. J. (1995). An Information-Maximization Approach to Blind Separation and Blind Deconvolution. *Neural Computation*, 7:1129–1159.

Bell, A. J. and Sejnowski, T. J. (1997). The 'independent components' of natural scenes are edge filters. *Vision Research*, 37(23):3327–3338.

Bishop, C. (1994). Mixture density networks. *Technical Report*, NCRG/4288.

Cardoso, J.-F. and Laheld, B. (1996). Equivariant adaptive source separation. *IEEE Trans. on S.P.*, 45(2):434–444.

Duda, R. and Hart, P. (1973). *Pattern classification and scene analysis*. Wiley, New York.

Ghahramani, Z. (1994). Solving inverse problems using an em approach to density estimation. *Proceedings of the 1993 Connectionist Models Summer School*, pages 316–323.

Girolami, M. (1998). An alternative perspective on adaptive independent component analysis algorithms. *Neural Computation*, 10(8):2103–2114.

Lee, T.-W., Girolami, M., Bell, A. J., and Sejnowski, T. J. (1999a). A unifying framework for independent component analysis. *International Journal on Mathematical and Computer Models*, in press.

Lee, T.-W., Girolami, M., and Sejnowski, T. J. (1999b). Independent component analysis using an extended infomax algorithm for mixed sub-gaussian and super-gaussian sources. *Neural Computation*, 11(2):409–433.

Lee, T.-W., Lewicki, M. S., and Sejnowski, T. J. (1999c). ICA mixture models for unsupervised classification and automatic context switching. In *International Workshop on ICA*, Aussois, in press.

Lewicki, M. and Olshausen, B. (1998). Inferring sparse, overcomplete image codes using an efficient coding framework. In *Advances in Neural Information Processing Systems 10*, pages 556–562.

Lewicki, M. and Sejnowski, T. J. (1998). Learning nonlinear overcomplete representations for efficient coding. In *Advances in Neural Information Processing Systems 10*, pages 815–821.

Olshausen, B. and Field, D. (1996). Emergence of simple-cell receptive field properties by learning a sparse code for natural images. *Nature*, 381:607–609.

Stutz, J. and Cheeseman, P. (1994). Autoclass - a Bayesian approach to classification. *Maximum Entropy and Bayesian Methods*, Kluwer Academic Publishers.

Learning a Continuous Hidden Variable Model for Binary Data

Daniel D. Lee
Bell Laboratories
Lucent Technologies
Murray Hill, NJ 07974
ddlee@bell-labs.com

Haim Sompolinsky
Racah Institute of Physics and
Center for Neural Computation
Hebrew University
Jerusalem, 91904, Israel
haim@fiz.huji.ac.il

Abstract

A directed generative model for binary data using a small number of hidden continuous units is investigated. A clipping nonlinearity distinguishes the model from conventional principal components analysis. The relationships between the correlations of the underlying continuous Gaussian variables and the binary output variables are utilized to learn the appropriate weights of the network. The advantages of this approach are illustrated on a translationally invariant binary distribution and on handwritten digit images.

Introduction

Principal Components Analysis (PCA) is a widely used statistical technique for representing data with a large number of variables [1]. It is based upon the assumption that although the data is embedded in a high dimensional vector space, most of the variability in the data is captured by a much lower dimensional manifold. In particular for PCA, this manifold is described by a linear hyperplane whose characteristic directions are given by the eigenvectors of the correlation matrix with the largest eigenvalues. The success of PCA and closely related techniques such as Factor Analysis (FA) and PCA mixtures clearly indicate that much real world data exhibit the low dimensional manifold structure assumed by these models [2, 3].

However, the linear manifold structure of PCA is not appropriate for data with binary valued variables. Binary values commonly occur in data such as computer bit streams, black-and-white images, on-off outputs of feature detectors, and electrophysiological spike train data [4]. The Boltzmann machine is a neural network model that incorporates hidden binary spin variables, and in principle, it should be able to model binary data with arbitrary spin correlations [5]. Unfortunately, the

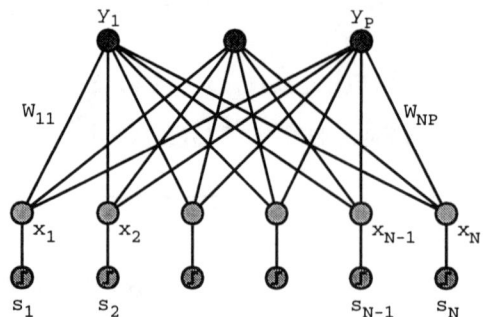

Figure 1: Generative model for N-dimensional binary data using a small number P of continuous hidden variables.

computational time needed for training a Boltzmann machine renders it impractical for most applications.

In these proceedings, we present a model that uses a small number of continuous hidden variables rather than hidden binary variables to capture the variability of binary valued visible data. The generative model differs from conventional PCA because it incorporates a clipping nonlinearity. The resulting spin configurations have an entropy related to the number of hidden variables used, and the resulting states are connected by small numbers of spin flips. The learning algorithm is particularly simple, and is related to PCA by a scalar transformation of the correlation matrix.

Generative Model

Figure 1 shows a schematic diagram of the generative process. As in PCA, the model assumes that the data is generated by a small number P of continuous hidden variables y_i. Each of the hidden variables are assumed to be drawn independently from a normal distribution with unit variance:

$$P(y_i) = \exp(-y_i^2/2)/\sqrt{2\pi}. \qquad (1)$$

The continuous hidden variables are combined using the feedforward weights W_{ij}, and the N binary output units are then calculated using the sign of the feedforward activations:

$$x_i = \sum_{j=1}^{P} W_{ij} y_j \qquad (2)$$

$$s_i = \mathrm{sgn}(x_i). \qquad (3)$$

Since binary data is commonly obtained by thresholding, it seems reasonable that a proper generative model should incorporate such a clipping nonlinearity. The generative process is similar to that of a sigmoidal belief network with continuous hidden units at zero temperature. The nonlinearity will alter the relationship between the correlations of the binary variables and the weight matrix W as described below.

The real-valued Gaussian variables x_i are exactly analogous to the visible variables of conventional PCA. They lie on a linear hyperplane determined by the span of the matrix W, and their correlation matrix is given by:

$$C^{xx} = \langle xx^T \rangle = WW^T. \qquad (4)$$

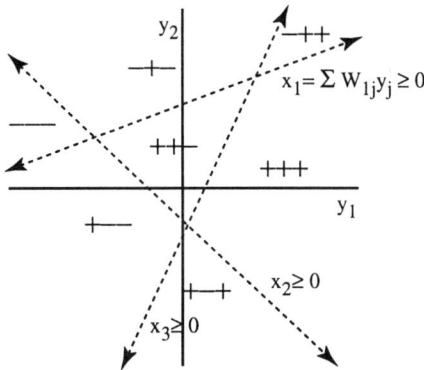

Figure 2: Binary spin configurations s_i in the vector space of continuous hidden variables y_j with $P = 2$ and $N = 3$.

By construction, the correlation matrix C^{xx} has rank P which is much smaller than the number of components N. Now consider the binary output variables $s_i = \text{sgn}(x_i)$. Their correlations can be calculated from the probability distribution of the Gaussian variables x_i:

$$(C^{ss})_{ij} = \langle s_i s_j \rangle = \int \prod_k dy_k \, P(x_k) \, \text{sgn}(x_i) \, \text{sgn}(x_j) \tag{5}$$

where

$$P(\mathbf{x}) = \frac{1}{(2\pi)^{N/2}\sqrt{|C^{xx}|}} \exp\left(-\frac{1}{2}\mathbf{x}^T (C^{xx})^{-1} \mathbf{x}\right). \tag{6}$$

The integrals in Equation 5 can be done analytically, and yield the surprisingly simple result:

$$(C^{ss})_{ij} = \left(\frac{2}{\pi}\right) \sin^{-1}\left[\frac{C^{xx}_{ij}}{\sqrt{C^{xx}_{ii} C^{xx}_{jj}}}\right]. \tag{7}$$

Thus, the correlations of the clipped binary variables C^{ss} are related to the correlations of the corresponding Gaussian variables C^{xx} through the nonlinear arcsine function. The normalization in the denominator of the arcsine argument reflects the fact that the sign function is unchanged by a scale change in the Gaussian variables.

Although the correlation matrix C^{ss} and the generating correlation matrix C^{xx} are easily related through Equation 7, they have qualitatively very different properties. In general, the correlation matrix C^{ss} will no longer have the low rank structure of C^{xx}. As illustrated by the translationally invariant example in the next section, the spectrum of C^{ss} may contain a whole continuum of eigenvalues even though C^{xx} has only a few nonzero eigenvalues.

PCA is typically used for dimensionality reduction of real variables; can this model be used for compressing the binary outputs s_i? Although the output correlations C^{ss} no longer display the low rank structure of the generating C^{xx}, a more appropriate measure of data compression is the entropy of the binary output states. Consider how many of the 2^N possible binary states will be generated by the clipping process. The equation $x_i = \sum_j W_{ij} y_j = 0$ defines a $P-1$ dimensional hyperplane in the P-dimensional state space of hidden variables y_j, which are shown as dashed lines in Figure 2. These hyperplanes partition the half-space where $s_i = +1$ from the

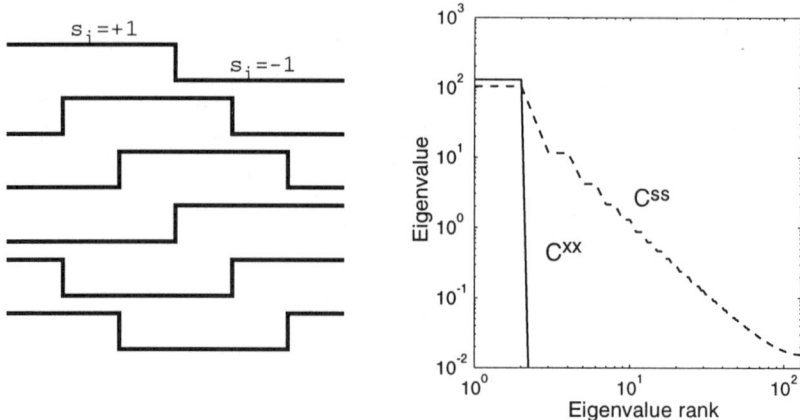

Figure 3: Translationally invariant binary spin distribution with $N = 256$ units. Representative samples from the distribution are illustrated on the left, while the eigenvalue spectrum of C^{ss} and C^{xx} are plotted on the right.

region where $s_i = -1$. Each of the N spin variables will have such a dividing hyperplane in this P-dimensional state space, and all of these hyperplanes will generically be unique. Thus, the total number of spin configurations s_i is determined by the number of cells bounded by N dividing hyperplanes in P dimensions. The number of such cells is approximately N^P for $N \gg P$, a well-known result from perceptrons [6]. To leading order for large N, the entropy of the binary states generated by this process is then given by $S = P \log N$. Thus, the entropy of the spin configurations generated by this model is directly proportional to the number of hidden variables P.

How is the topology of the binary spin configurations s_i related to the PCA manifold structure of the continuous variables x_i? Each of the generated spin states is represented by a polytope cell in the P dimensional vector space of hidden variables. Each polytope has at least $P+1$ neighboring polytopes which are related to it by a single or small number of spin flips. Therefore, although the state space of binary spin configurations is discrete, the continuous manifold structure of the underlying Gaussian variables in this model is manifested as binary output configurations with low entropy that are connected with small Hamming distances.

Translationally Invariant Example

In principle, the weights W could be learned by applying maximum likelihood to this generative model; however, the resulting learning algorithm involves analytically intractable multi-dimensional integrals. Alternatively, approximations based upon mean field theory or importance sampling could be used to learn the appropriate parameters [7]. However, Equation 7 suggests a simple learning rule that is also approximate, but is much more computationally efficient [8]. First, the binary correlation matrix C^{ss} is computed from the data. Then the empirical C^{ss} is mapped into the appropriate Gaussian correlation matrix using the nonlinear transformation: $C^{xx} = \sin(\pi C^{ss}/2)$. This results in a Gaussian correlation matrix where the variances of the individual x_i are fixed at unity. The weights W are then calculated using the conventional PCA algorithm. The correlation matrix C^{xx} is diagonalized, and the eigenvectors with the largest eigenvalues are used to form the columns of

W to yield the best low rank approximation $C^{xx} \approx WW^T$. Scaling the variables x_i will result in a correlation matrix C^{xx} with slightly different eigenvalues but with the same rank.

The utility of this transformation is illustrated by the following simple example. Consider the distribution of $N = 256$ binary spins shown in Figure 3. Half of the spins are chosen to be positive, and the location of the positive bump is arbitrary under the periodic boundary conditions. Since the distribution is translationally invariant, the correlations C_{ij}^{ss} depend only on the relative distance between spins $|i - j|$. The eigenvectors are the Fourier modes, and their eigenvalues correspond to their overlap with a triangle wave. The eigenvalue spectrum of C^{ss} is plotted in Figure 3 as sorted by their rank. In this particular case, the correlation matrix C^{ss} has $N/2$ positive eigenvalues with a corresponding range of values.

Now consider the matrix $C^{xx} = \sin(\pi C^{ss}/2)$. The eigenvalues of C^{xx} are also shown in Figure 3. In contrast to the many different eigenvalues C^{ss}, the spectrum of the Gaussian correlation matrix C^{xx} has only two positive eigenvalues, with all the rest exactly equal to zero. The corresponding eigenvectors are a cosine and sine function. The generative process can thus be understood as a linear combination of the two eigenmodes to yield a sine function with arbitary phase. This function is then clipped to yield the positive bump seen in the original binary distribution.

In comparison with the eigenvalues of C^{ss}, the eigenvalue spectrum of C^{xx} makes obvious the low rank structure of the generative process. In this case, the original binary distribution can be constructed using only $P = 2$ hidden variables, whereas it is not clear from the eigenvalues of C^{ss} what the appropriate number of modes is. This illustrates the utility of determining the principal components from the calculated Gaussian correlation matrix C^{xx} rather than working directly with the observable binary correlation matrix C^{ss}.

Handwritten Digits Example

This model was also applied to a more complex data set. A large set of 16×16 black and white images of handwritten twos were taken from the US Post Office digit database [9]. The pixel means and pixel correlations were directly computed from the images. The generative model needs to be slightly modified to account for the non-zero means in the binary outputs. This is accomplished by adding fixed biases ξ_i to the Gaussian variables x_i before clipping:

$$s_i = \mathrm{sgn}(\xi_i + x_i). \tag{8}$$

The biases ξ_i can be related to the means of the binary outputs through the expression:

$$\xi_i = \sqrt{2C_{ii}^{xx}}\,\mathrm{erf}^{-1}\langle s_i \rangle. \tag{9}$$

This allows the biases to be directly computed from the observed means of the binary variables. Unfortunately, with non-zero biases, the relationship between the Gaussian correlations C^{xx} and binary correlations C^{ss} is no longer the simple expression found in Equation 7. Instead, the correlations are related by the following integral equation:

$$C_{ij}^{ss} = \langle s_i \rangle \langle s_j \rangle + \frac{2}{\pi}\int_0^{\frac{C_{ij}^{xx}}{\sqrt{C_{ii}^{xx}C_{jj}^{xx}}}} d\rho\, \frac{1}{\sqrt{1-\rho^2}}\exp\left[-\frac{1}{2(1-\rho^2)}(\xi_i^2 + \xi_j^2 - 2\rho\xi_i\xi_j)\right]. \tag{10}$$

Given the empirical pixel correlations C^{ss} for the handwritten digits, the integral in Equation 10 is numerically solved for each pair of indices to yield the appropriate

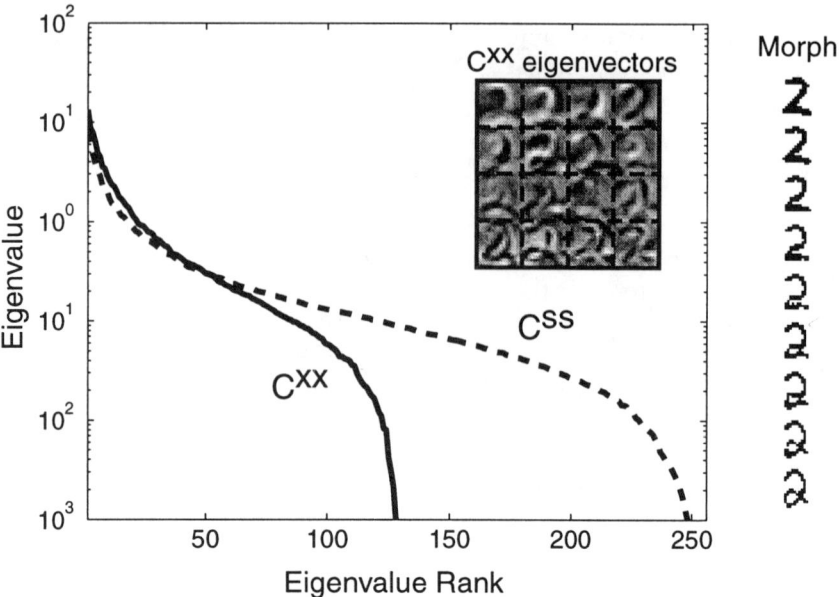

Figure 4: Eigenvalue spectrum of C^{ss} and C^{xx} for handwritten images of twos. The inset shows the $P = 16$ most significant eigenvectors for C^{xx} arranged by rows. The right side of the figure shows a nonlinear morph between two different instances of a handwritten two using these eigenvectors.

Gaussian correlation matrix C^{xx}. The correlation matrices are diagonalized and the resulting eigenvalue spectra are shown in Figure 4. The eigenvalues for C^{xx} again exhibit a characteristic drop that is steeper than the falloff in the spectrum of the binary correlations C^{ss}. The corresponding eigenvectors of C^{xx} with the 16 largest positive eigenvalues are depicted in the inset of Figure 4. These eigenmodes represent common image distortions such as rotations and stretching and appear qualitatively similar to those found by the standard PCA algorithm.

A generative model with weights W corresponding to the $P = 16$ eigenvectors shown in Figure 4 is used to fit the handwritten twos, and the utility of this nonlinear generative model is illustrated in the right side of Figure 4. The top and bottom images in the figure are two different examples of a handwritten two from the data set, and the generative model is used to morph between the two examples. The hidden values y_i for the original images are first determined for the different examples, and the intermediate images in the morph are constructed by linearly interpolating in the vector space of the hidden units. Because of the clipping nonlinearity, this induces a nonlinear mapping in the outputs with binary units being flipped in a particular order as determined by the generative model. In contrast, morphing using conventional PCA would result in a simple linear interpolation between the two images, and the intermediate images would not look anything like the original binary distribution [10].

The correlation matrix C^{xx} also happens to contain some small negative eigenvalues. Even though the binary correlation matrix C^{ss} is positive definite, the transformation in Equation 10 does not guarantee that the resulting matrix C^{xx} will also be positive definite. The presence of these negative eigenvalues indicates a shortcoming of the generative processs for modelling this data. In particular, the clipped Gaussian model is unable to capture correlations induced by global constraints in the data. As a simple illustration of this shortcoming in the generative model, consider the binary distribution defined by the probability density: $P(\{s\}) \propto \lim_{\beta \to \infty} \exp(-\beta \sum_{ij} s_i s_j)$. The states in this distribution are defined by the constraint that the sum of the binary variables is exactly zero: $\sum_i s_i = 0$. Now, for $N \geq 4$, it can be shown that it is impossible to find a Gaussian distribution whose visible binary variables match the negative correlations induced by this sum constraint.

These examples illustrate the value of using the clipped generative model to learn the correlation matrix of the underlying Gaussian variables rather than using the correlations of the outputs directly. The clipping nonlinearity is convenient because the relationship between the hidden variables and the output variables is particularly easy to understand. The learning algorithm differs from other nonlinear PCA models and autoencoders because the inverse mapping function need not be explicitly learned [11, 12]. Instead, the correlation matrix is directly transformed from the observable variables to the underlying Gaussian variables. The correlation matrix is then diagonalized to determine the appropriate feedforward weights. This results in a extremely efficient training procedure that is directly analogous to PCA for continuous variables.

We acknowledge the support of Bell Laboratories, Lucent Technologies, and the US-Israel Binational Science Foundation. We also thank H. S. Seung for helpful discussions.

References

[1] Jolliffe, IT (1986). *Principal Component Analysis*. New York: Springer-Verlag.

[2] Bartholomew, DJ (1987). *Latent variable models and factor analysis*. London: Charles Griffin & Co. Ltd.

[3] Hinton, GE, Dayan, P & Revow, M (1996). Modeling the manifolds of images of handwritten digits. *IEEE Transactions on Neural networks* **8**, 65–74.

[4] Van Vreeswijk, C, Sompolinsky, H, & Abeles, M. (1999). Nonlinear statistics of spike trains. In preparation.

[5] Ackley, DH, Hinton, GE, & Sejnowski, TJ (1985). A learning algorithm for Boltzmann machines. *Cognitive Science* **9**, 147–169.

[6] Cover, TM (1965). Geometrical and statistical properties of systems of linear inequalities with applications in pattern recognition. *IEEE Trans. Electronic Comput.* **14**, 326–334.

[7] Tipping, ME (1999). Probabilistic visualisation of high-dimensional binary data. *Advances in Neural Information Processing Systems* **11**.

[8] Christoffersson, A (1975). Factor analysis of dichotomized variables. *Psychometrika* **40**, 5–32.

[9] LeCun, Y et al. (1989). Backpropagation applied to handwritten zip code recognition. *Neural Computation* **1**, 541–551.

[10] Bregler, C, & Omohundro, SM (1995). Nonlinear image interpolation using manifold learning. *Advances in Neural Information Processing Systems* **7**, 973–980.

[11] Hastie, T and Stuetzle, W (1989). Principal curves. *Journal of the American Statistical Association* **84**, 502–516.

[12] Demers, D, & Cottrell, G (1993). Nonlinear dimensionality reduction. *Advances in Neural Information Processing Systems* **5**, 580–587.

Neural Networks for Density Estimation

Malik Magdon-Ismail[*]
magdon@cco.caltech.edu
Caltech Learning Systems Group
Department of Electrical Engineering
California Institute of Technology
136-93 Pasadena, CA, 91125

Amir Atiya
amir@deep.caltech.edu
Caltech Learning Systems Group
Department of Electrical Engineering
California Institute of Technology
136-93 Pasadena, CA, 91125

Abstract

We introduce two new techniques for density estimation. Our approach poses the problem as a supervised learning task which can be performed using Neural Networks. We introduce a stochastic method for learning the cumulative distribution and an analogous deterministic technique. We demonstrate convergence of our methods both theoretically and experimentally, and provide comparisons with the Parzen estimate. Our theoretical results demonstrate better convergence properties than the Parzen estimate.

1 Introduction and Background

A majority of problems in science and engineering have to be modeled in a probabilistic manner. Even if the underlying phenomena are inherently deterministic, the complexity of these phenomena often makes a probabilistic formulation the only feasible approach from the computational point of view. Although quantities such as the mean, the variance, and possibly higher order moments of a random variable have often been sufficient to characterize a particular problem, the quest for higher modeling accuracy, and for more realistic assumptions drives us towards modeling the available random variables using their probability density. This of course leads us to the problem of density estimation (see [6]).

The most common approach for density estimation is the nonparametric approach, where the density is determined according to a formula involving the data points available. The most common non parametric methods are the kernel density estimator, also known as the Parzen window estimator [4] and the k-nearest neighbor technique [1]. Non parametric density estimation belongs to the class of ill-posed problems in the sense that small changes in the data can lead to large changes in

---
[*]To whom correspondence should be addressed.

the estimated density. Therefore it is important to have methods that are robust to slight changes in the data. For this reason some amount of regularization is needed [7]. This regularization is embedded in the choice of the smoothing parameter (kernel width or k). The problem with these non-parametric techniques is their extreme sensitivity to the choice of the smoothing parameter. A wrong choice can lead to either undersmoothing or oversmoothing.

In spite of the importance of the density estimation problem, proposed methods using neural networks have been very sporadic. We propose two new methods for density estimation which can be implemented using multilayer networks. In addition to being able to approximate any function to any given precision, multilayer networks give us the flexibility to choose an error function to suit our application. The methods developed here are based on approximating the distribution function, in contrast to most previous works which focus on approximating the density itself. Straightforward differentiation gives us the estimate of the density function. The distribution function is often useful in its own right - one can directly evaluate quantiles or the probability that the random variable occurs in a particular interval.

One of the techniques is a stochastic algorithm (SLC), and the second is a deterministic technique based on learning the cumulative (SIC). The stochastic technique will generally be smoother on smaller numbers of data points, however, the deterministic technique is faster and applies to more that one dimension. We will present a result on the consistency and the convergence rate of the estimation error for our methods in the univariate case. When the unknown density is bounded and has bounded derivatives up to order K, we find that the estimation error is $O((\log \log(N)/N)^{-(1-\frac{1}{K})})$, where N is the number of data points. As a comparison, for the kernel density estimator (with non-negative kernels), the estimation error is $O(N^{-4/5})$, under the assumptions that the unknown density has a square integrable second derivative (see [6]), and that the *optimal* kernel width is used, which is not possible in practice because computing the optimal kernel width requires knowledge of the true density. One can see that for smooth density functions with bounded derivatives, our methods achieve an error rate that approaches $O(N^{-1})$.

2 New Density Estimation Techniques

To illustrate our methods, we will use neural networks, but stress that any sufficiently general learning model will do just as well. The network's output will represent an estimate of the distribution function, and its derivative will be an estimate of the density. We will now proceed to a description of the two methods.

2.1 SLC (Stochastic Learning of the Cumulative)

Let $x_n \in \mathbf{R}$, $n = 1, ..., N$ be the data points. Let the underlying density be $g(x)$ and its distribution function $G(x) = \int_{-\infty}^{x} g(t)dt$. Let the neural network output be $H(x, w)$, where w represents the set of weights of the network. Ideally, after training the neural network, we would like to have $H(x, w) = G(x)$. It can easily be shown that the density of the random variable $G(x)$ (x being generated according to $g(x)$) is uniform in $[0, 1]$. Thus, if $H(x, w)$ is to be as close as possible to $G(x)$, then the network output should have a density that is close to uniform in $[0, 1]$. This is what our goal will be. We will attempt to train the network such that its output density is uniform, then the network mapping should represent the distribution function $G(x)$. The basic idea behind the proposed algorithm is to use the N data points as inputs to the network. For every training cycle, we generate a different set of N network targets randomly from a uniform distribution in $[0, 1]$, and adjust the weights to map the data points (sorted in ascending order) to these generated targets (also sorted in ascending order). Thus we are training the network to map the data to a uniform distribution.

Before describing the steps of the algorithm, we note that the resulting network has to represent a monotonically nondecreasing mapping, otherwise it will not represent a legitimate distribution function. In our simulations, we used a hint penalty to enforce monotonicity [5]. The algorithm is as follows.

1. Let $x_1 \leq x_2 \leq \cdots \leq x_N$ be the data points. Set $t = 1$, where t is the training cycle number. Initialize the weights (usually randomly) to $w(1)$.
2. Generate randomly from a uniform distribution in $[0, 1]$ N points (and sort them): $u_1 \leq u_2 \leq ... \leq u_N$. The point u_n is the target output for x_n.
3. Adjust the network weights according to the backpropagation scheme:

$$w(t+1) = w(t) - \eta(t)\frac{\partial \mathcal{E}}{\partial w} \quad (1)$$

where $\mathcal{E}$ is the objective function that includes the error term and the monotonicity hint penalty term [5]:

$$\mathcal{E} = \sum_{n=1}^{N}\Big[H(x_n) - u_n\Big]^2 + \lambda\sum_{k=1}^{N_h}\Theta\Big(H(y_k) - H(y_k + \Delta)\Big)\Big[H(y_k) - H(y_k + \Delta)\Big]^2 \quad (2)$$

where we have suppressed the w dependence. The second term is the monotonicity penalty term, λ is a positive weighting constant, Δ is a small positive number, $\Theta(x)$ is the familiar unit step function, and the y_k's are any set of points where we wish to enforce the monotonicity.

4. Set $t = t + 1$, and go to step 2. Repeat until the error is small enough. Upon convergence, the density estimate is the derivative of H.

Note that as presented, the randomly generated targets are different for every cycle, which will have a smoothing effect that will allow convergence to a truly uniform distribution. One other version, that we have implemented in our simulation studies, is to generate new targets after every fixed number L of cycles, rather than every cycle. This will generally improve the speed of convergence as there is more "continuity" in the learning process. Also note that it is preferable to choose the activation function for the output node to be in the range of 0 to 1, to ensure that the estimate of the distribution function is in this range.

SLC is only applicable to estimating univariate densities, because, for the multivariate case, the nonlinear mapping $y = G(x)$ will not necessarily result in a uniformly distributed output y. Fortunately, many, if not the majority of problems encountered in practice are univariate. This is because multivariate problems, with even a modest number of dimensions, need a huge amount of data to obtain statistically accurate results. The next method, is applicable to the multivariate case as well.

2.2 SIC (Smooth Interpolation of the Cumulative)

Again, we have a multilayer network, to which we input the point $\mathbf{x}$, and the network outputs the estimate of the distribution function. Let $g(\mathbf{x})$ be the true density function, and let $G(\mathbf{x})$ be the corresponding distribution function. Let $\mathbf{x} = (x^1, ..., x^d)^T$. The distribution function is given by

$$G(\mathbf{x}) = \int_{-\infty}^{x^1} \cdots \int_{-\infty}^{x^d} g(\mathbf{x}) dx^1 \cdots x^d, \quad (3)$$

a straightforward estimate of $G(\mathbf{x})$ could be the fraction of data points falling in the area of integration:

$$\hat{G}(\mathbf{x}) = \frac{1}{N}\sum_{n=1}^{N}\Theta(\mathbf{x} - \mathbf{x}_n), \qquad (4)$$

where Θ is defined as

$$\Theta(\mathbf{x}) = \begin{cases} 1 & \text{if } x^i \geq 0 \text{ for all } i = 1,\ldots,d, \\ 0 & \text{otherwise.} \end{cases}$$

The method we propose uses such an estimate for the target outputs of the neural network. The estimate given by (4) is discontinuous. The neural network method developed here provides a smooth, and hence more realistic estimate of the distribution function. The density can be obtained by differentiating the output of the network with respect to its inputs.

For the low-dimensional case, we can uniformly sample (4) using a grid, to obtain the examples for the network. Beyond two or three dimensions, this becomes computationally intensive. Alternatively, one could sample the input space randomly (using say a uniform distribution over the approximate range of $\mathbf{x}_n$'s), and for every point determine the network target according to (4). Another option is to use the data points themselves as examples. The target for a point $\mathbf{x}_m$ would then be

$$\hat{G}(x_m) = \frac{1}{N-1}\sum_{n=1,\,n\neq m}^{N}\Theta(x_m - x_n). \qquad (5)$$

We also use monotonicity as a hint to guide the training. Once training is performed, and $H(\mathbf{x}, w)$ approximates $G(\mathbf{x})$, the density estimate can be obtained as

$$\hat{g}(\mathbf{x}) = \frac{\partial^d H(\mathbf{x}, w)}{\partial x^1 \cdots \partial x^d}. \qquad (6)$$

3 Simulation Results

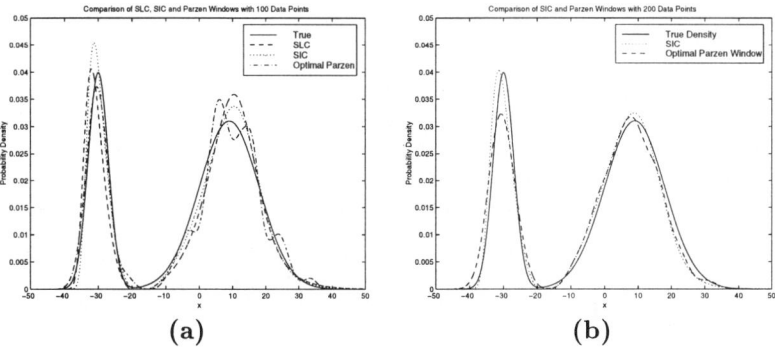

Figure 1: Comparison of optimal Parzen windows, with neural network estimators. Plotted are the true density and the estimates (SLC, SIC, Parzen window with optimal kernel width [6, pg 40]). Notice that even the optimal Parzen window is bumpy as compared to the neural network.

We tested our techniques for density estimation on data drawn from a mixture of two Gaussians:

$$g(x) = \frac{3}{10}\frac{1}{\sqrt{18\pi}}e^{-\frac{(x+30)^2}{18}} + \frac{7}{10}\frac{1}{\sqrt{162\pi}}e^{-\frac{(x-9)^2}{162}} \qquad (7)$$

Data points were randomly generated and the density estimates using SLC or SIC (for 100 and 200 data points) were compared to the Parzen technique. Learning was performed with a standard 1 hidden layer neural network with 3 hidden units. The hidden unit activation function used was *tanh* and the output unit was an *erf* function[1]. A set of typical density estimates are shown in figure 1.

4 Convergence of the Density Estimation Techniques

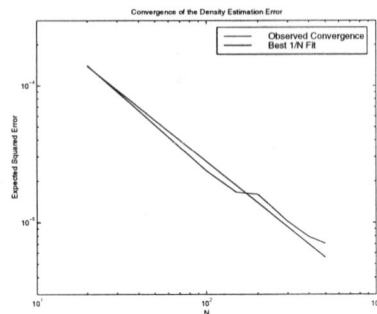

Figure 2: Convergence of the density estimation error for SIC. A five hidden unit two layer neural network was used to perform the mapping $x_i \to i/(N+1)$, trained according to SIC. For various N, the resulting density estimation error was computed for over 100 runs. Plotted are the results on a Log-Log scale. For comparison, also shown is the best $1/N$ fit.

Using techniques from stochastic approximation theory, it can be shown that SLC converges to a similar solution to SIC [3], so, we focus our attention on the convergence of SIC. Figure 2 shows an empirical study of the convergence behavior. The optimal linear fit between $\log(E)$ and $\log(N)$ has a slope of -0.97. This indicates that the convergence rate is about $1/N$. The theoretically derived convergence rate is $\log\log(N)/N$ as we will shortly discuss.

To analyze SIC, we introduce so called approximate generalized distribution functions. We will assume that the true distribution function has bounded derivatives. Therefore the cumulative will be "approximately" implementable by generalized distributions with bounded derivatives (in the asymptotic limit, with probability 1). We will then obtain the convergence to the true density.

Let $\mathcal{G}$ be the space of distribution functions on the real line that possess continuous densities, i.e., $X \in \mathcal{G}$ if $X : \mathbf{R} \to [0,1]$; $X'(t)$ exists everywhere, is continuous and $X'(t) \geq 0$; $X(-\infty) = 0$ and $X(\infty) = 1$. This is the class of functions that we will be interested in. We define a metric with respect to $\mathcal{G}$ as follows

$$\|f\|_X^2 = \int_{-\infty}^{\infty} f(t)^2 X'(t) dt \qquad (8)$$

$\|f\|_X^2$ is the expectation of the squared value of f with respect to the distribution $X \in \mathcal{G}$. Let us name this the L_2 X-norm of f. Let the data set (D) be $\{x_1 \leq x_2 \leq \ldots \leq x_N\}$, and corresponding to each x_i, let the target be $y_i = i/N + 1$. We will assume that the true distribution function has bounded derivatives up to order K. We define the set of approximate sample distribution functions $\mathcal{H}_D^\nu$ as follows

---

[1] $erf(x) = \frac{1}{\sqrt{2\pi}} \int_{-\infty}^{x} e^{-\frac{x^2}{2}}$.

Definition 4.1 *Fix $\nu > 0$. A ν-approximate sample distribution function, H, satisfies the following two conditions*

- $H \in \mathcal{G}$
- $|H(x_i) - y_i| \leq \nu \sqrt{\frac{\log \log(N)}{2N}}$, $\forall i$

We will denote the set of all ν-approximate sample distribution functions for a data set, D, and a given ν by $\mathcal{H}_D^\nu$.

Let $A_i = \sup_x |G^{(i)}|$, $i = 1 \ldots K$ where we use the notation $f^{(i)}$ to denote the ith derivative. Define $B_i^\nu(D)$ by

$$B_i^\nu(D) = \inf_{Q \in \mathcal{H}_D^\nu} \sup_x \left| Q^{(i)} \right| \tag{9}$$

for fixed $\nu > 0$. Note that by definition, for all $\epsilon > 0$, $\exists H \in \mathcal{H}_D^\nu$ such that $\sup_x |H^{(i)}(x)| \leq B_i^\nu + \epsilon$. $B_i^\nu(D)$ is the lowest possible bound on the ith derivative for the ν-approximate sample distribution functions given a particular data set. In a sense, the "smoothest" approximating sample distribution function with respect to the ith derivative has an ith derivative bounded by $B_i^\nu(D)$. One expects that $B_i \leq A_i$, at least in the limit $N \to \infty$.

In the next theorem, we present the main theoretical result of the paper, namely a bound on the estimation error for the density estimator obtained by using the approximate sample distribution functions. It is embedded in a large amount of technical machinery, but its essential content is that if the true distribution function has bounded derivatives to order K, then, picking the approximate distribution function obeying certain bounds, we obtain a convergence rate for the estimation error of $O((\log \log(N)/N)^{1-1/K})$.

Theorem 4.2 (L_2 convergence to the true density) *Let N data points, x_i be drawn i.i.d. from the distribution $G \in \mathcal{G}$. Let $\sup_x |G^{(i)}| = A_i$ for $i = 0 \ldots K$, where $K \geq 2$. Fix $\nu > 2$ and $\epsilon > 0$. Let $B_K^\nu(D) = \inf_{Q \in \mathcal{H}_D^\nu} \sup_x |Q^{(K)}|$. Let $H \in \mathcal{H}_D^\nu$ be a ν-approximate distribution function with $B_K = \sup_x |H^K| \leq B_K^\nu + \epsilon$ (by the definition of B_K^ν, such a ν-approximate sample distribution function must exist). Then, for any $F \in \mathcal{G}$, as $N \to \infty$, the inequality*

$$\| H' - G' \|_F^2 \leq 2^{2(K-1)} (2A_K + \epsilon)^{\frac{2}{K}} \mathcal{F}(N) \tag{10}$$

where

$$\mathcal{F}(N) = \left[(1+\nu) \left(\frac{2 \log \log(N)}{N} \right)^{\frac{1}{2}} + \frac{2}{N+1} \right]^{2 - \frac{2}{K}} \tag{11}$$

holds with probability 1, as $N \to \infty$.

We present the proof elsewhere [3]. ∎

Note 1: The theorem applies uniformly to *any* interpolator $H \in \mathcal{H}_D^\nu$. In particular, a large enough neural network will be one such monotonic interpolator, provided that the network can be trained to small enough error. This is possible by the universal approximation results for multilayer networks [2].

Note 2: This theorem holds for any $\epsilon > 0$ and $\nu > 1$. For smooth density functions, with bounded higher derivatives, the convergence rate approaches $O(\log \log(N)/N)$ which is faster convergence than the kernel density estimator (for which the optimal rate is $O(N^{-4/5})$).

Note 3: No smoothing parameter needs to be determined.

Note 4: One should try to find an approximate distribution function with the smallest possible derivatives. Specifically, of all the sample distribution functions, pick the one that "minimizes" B_K, the bound on the Kth derivative. This could be done by introducing penalty terms, penalizing the magnitudes of the derivatives (for example Tikhonov type regularizers [7]).

5 Comments

We developed two techniques for density estimation based on the idea of learning the cumulative by mapping the data points to a uniform density. Two techniques were presented, a stochastic technique (SLC), which is expected to inherit the characteristics of most stochastic iterative algorithms, and a deterministic technique (SIC). SLC tends to be slow in practice, however, because each set of targets is drawn from the uniform distribution, this is anticipated to have a smoothing/regularizing effect – this can be seen by comparing SLC and SIC in figure 1 (a). We presented experimental comparison of our techniques with the Parzen technique.

We presented a theoretical result that demonstrated the consistency of our techniques as well as giving a convergence rate of $O(\log \log(N)/N)$, which is better than the optimal Parzen technique. No smoothing parameter needs to be chosen – smoothing occurs naturally by picking the interpolator with the lowest bound for a certain derivative. For our methods, the majority of time is spent in the learning phase, but once learning is done, evaluating the density is fast.

6 Acknowledgments

We would like to acknowledge Yaser Abu-Mostafa and the Caltech Learning Systems Group for their useful input.

References

[1] K. Fukunaga and L. D. Hostetler. Optimization of k-nearest neighbor density estimates. *IEEE Transactions on Information Theory*, 19(3):320–326, 1973.

[2] K. Hornik, M. Stinchcombe, and H. White. Universal approximation of an unknown mapping and its derivatives using multilayer feedforward networks. *Neural Networks*, 3:551–560, 1990.

[3] M. Magdon-Ismail and A. Atiya. Consistent density estimation from the sample distribution function. *manuscript in preparation for submission*, 1998.

[4] E. Parzen. On the estimation of a probability density function and mode. *Annals of Mathematical Statistics*, 33:1065–1076, 1962.

[5] J. Sill and Y. S. Abu-Mostafa. Monotonicity hints. In M. C. Mozer, M. I. Jordan, and T. Petsche, editors, *Advances in Neural Information Processing Systems (NIPS)*, volume 9, pages 634–640. Morgan Kaufmann, 1997.

[6] B. Silverman. *Density Estimation for Statistics and Data Analysis*. Chapman and Hall, London, UK, 1993.

[7] A. N. Tikhonov and V. I. Arsenin. *Solutions of Ill-Posed Problems*. Scripta Series in Mathematics. Distributed solely by Halsted Press, Winston; New York, 1977. Translation Editor: Fritz, John.

Exploratory Data Analysis Using Radial Basis Function Latent Variable Models

Alan D. Marrs and Andrew R. Webb
DERA
St Andrews Road, Malvern
Worcestershire U.K. WR14 3PS
{marrs,webb}@signal.dera.gov.uk
©British Crown Copyright 1998

Abstract

Two developments of nonlinear latent variable models based on radial basis functions are discussed: in the first, the use of priors or constraints on allowable models is considered as a means of preserving data structure in low-dimensional representations for visualisation purposes. Also, a resampling approach is introduced which makes more effective use of the latent samples in evaluating the likelihood.

1 INTRODUCTION

Radial basis functions (RBF) have been extensively used for problems in discrimination and regression. Here we consider their application for obtaining low–dimensional representations of high–dimensional data as part of the exploratory data analysis process. There has been a great deal of research over the years into linear and nonlinear techniques for dimensionality reduction. The technique most commonly used is principal components analysis (PCA) and there have been several nonlinear generalisations, each taking a particular definition of PCA and generalising it to the nonlinear situation.

One approach is to find surfaces of closest fit (as a generalisation of the PCA definition due to the work of Pearson (1901) for finding lines and planes of closest fit). This has been explored by Hastie and Stuetzle (1989), Tibshirani (1992) (and further by LeBlanc and Tibshirani, 1994) and various authors using a neural network approach (for example, Kramer, 1991). Another approach is one of variance maximisation subject to constraints on the transformation (Hotelling, 1933). This has been investigated by Webb (1996), using a transformation modelled as an RBF network, and in a supervised context in Webb (1998).

An alternative strategy also using RBFs, based on metric multidimensional scaling, is described by Webb (1995) and Lowe and Tipping (1996). Here, an optimisation criterion, termed *stress*, is defined in the transformed space and the weights in an RBF model determined by minimising the stress.

The above methods use a radial basis function to model a transformation from the high–dimensional *data space* to a low–dimensional *representation space*. A complementary approach is provided by Bishop et al (1998) in which the structure of the data is modelled as a function of hidden or latent variables. Termed *generative topographic mapping* (GTM), the model may be regarded as a nonlinear generalisation of factor analysis in which the mapping from latent space to data space is characterised by an RBF.

Such generative models are relevant to a wide range of applications including radar target modelling, speech recognition and handwritten character recognition.

However, one of the problems with GTM that limits its practical use for visualising data on manifolds in high dimensional space arises from distortions in the structure that it imposes. This is acknowledged in Bishop et al (1997) where 'magnification factors' are introduced to correct for the GTM's deficiency as a means of data visualisation.

This paper considers two developments: constraints on the permissible models and resampling of the latent space. Section 2 presents the background to latent variable models; Model constraints are discussed in Section 3. Section 4 describes a re–sampling approach to estimation of the posterior pdf on the latent samples. An illustration is provided in Section 5.

2 BACKGROUND

Briefly, we shall re–state the basic GTM model, retaining the notation of Bishop et al (1998). Let $\{t_i, i = 1, \ldots, N\}$, $t_i \in \mathbb{R}^D$ represent measurements on the data space variables; $x \in \mathbb{R}^L$ represent the latent variables.

Let t be normally–distributed with mean $y(x; W)$ and covariance matrix $\beta^{-1}I$; $y(x; W)$ is a nonlinear transformation that depends on a set of parameters W. Specifically, we shall assume a basis function model

$$y(x; W) = \sum_{i=1}^{M} w_i \phi_i(x)$$

where the vectors $w_i \in \mathbb{R}^D$ are to be determined through optimisation and $\{\phi_i, i = 1, \ldots, M\}$ is a set of basis functions defined on the latent space.

The data distribution may be written

$$p(t|W, \beta) = \int p(t|x; W, \beta) p(x) dx \qquad (1)$$

where, under the assumptions of normality,

$$p(t|x; W, \beta) = \left(\frac{\beta}{2\pi}\right)^{D/2} \exp\left\{-\frac{\beta}{2} \|y(x; W) - t\|^2\right\}$$

Approximating the integral by a finite sum (assuming the functions $p(x)$ and $y(x)$ do not vary too greatly compared with the sample spacing), we have

$$p(t|W, \beta) = \sum_{i=1}^{K} p_i p(t|x_i; W, \beta) \qquad (2)$$

which may be regarded as a function of the parameters W and β that characterise y.

Given the data set $\{t_i, i = 1, \ldots, N\}$, the log likelihood is given by

$$L(\boldsymbol{W}, \beta) = \sum_{j=1}^{N} \ln[p(t_j|\boldsymbol{W}, \beta)]$$

which may be maximised using a standard EM approach (Bishop et al, 1998). In this case, we have

$$\hat{p}_j = \frac{1}{N} \sum_{n=1}^{N} R_{in} \qquad (3)$$

as the re–estimate of the mixture component weights, p_j, at the $(m+1)$ step, where

$$R_{in} = \frac{p_i^{(m)} p(t_n|\boldsymbol{x}_i; \boldsymbol{W}^{(m)}, \beta^{(m)})}{\sum_i p_i^{(m)} p(t_n|\boldsymbol{x}_i; \boldsymbol{W}^{(m)}, \beta^{(m)})} \qquad (4)$$

and $(.)^{(m)}$ denotes values at the mth step. Note that Bishop et al (1998) do not re–estimate p_j; all values are taken to be equal.

The number of p_j terms to be re–estimated is K, the number of terms used to approximate the integral (1). We might expect that the density is smoothly varying and governed by a much fewer number of parameters (not dependent on K).

The re–estimation equation for the $D \times M$ matrix $\boldsymbol{W} = [\boldsymbol{w}_1|\ldots|\boldsymbol{w}_M]$ is

$$\boldsymbol{W}^{(m+1)} = \boldsymbol{T}^T \boldsymbol{R}^T \boldsymbol{\Phi} [\boldsymbol{\Phi}^T \boldsymbol{G} \boldsymbol{\Phi}]^{-1} \qquad (5)$$

where $\boldsymbol{G}$ is the $K \times K$ diagonal matrix with

$$G_{jj} = \sum_{n=1}^{N} R_{jn}$$

and $\boldsymbol{T}^T = [\boldsymbol{t}_1|\ldots|\boldsymbol{t}_N]$, $\boldsymbol{\Phi}^T = [\phi(\boldsymbol{x}_1)|\ldots|\phi(\boldsymbol{x}_K)]$. The term β is re–estimated as $1/\beta^{(m)} = 1/(ND) \sum_{i=1}^{N} \sum_{j=1}^{K} R_{ji} |t_i - \boldsymbol{W}^{(m+1)} \phi(\boldsymbol{x}_j)|^2$.

Once we have determined parameters of the transformation, we may invert the model by asking for the distribution of x given a measurement t_i. That is, we require

$$p(\boldsymbol{x}|t_i) = \frac{p(t_i|\boldsymbol{x}) p(\boldsymbol{x})}{\int p(t_i|\boldsymbol{x}) p(\boldsymbol{x}) d\boldsymbol{x}} \qquad (6)$$

For example, we may plot the position of the peak of the distribution $p(\boldsymbol{x}|t_i)$ for each data sample t_i.

3 APPLYING A CONSTRAINT

One way to retain structure is to impose a condition that ensures that a unit step in the latent space corresponds to a unit step in the data space (more or less). For a single latent variable, x_1, we may impose the constraints that

$$\left|\frac{\partial \boldsymbol{y}}{\partial x_1}\right|^2 = 1$$

which may be written, in terms of $\boldsymbol{W}$ as

$$\boldsymbol{j}_1^T \boldsymbol{W}^T \boldsymbol{W} \boldsymbol{j}_1 = 1$$

where $j_1 = \frac{\partial \phi}{\partial x_1}$.

The derivative of the data space variable with respect to the latent variable has unit magnitude. The derivative is of course a function of x_1 and imposing such a condition at each sample point in latent space would not be possible owing to the smoothness of the RBF model. However, we may average over the latent space,

$$\overline{\left|\frac{\partial y}{\partial x_1}\right|^2} = 1$$

where $\overline{(.)}$ denotes average over the latent space.

In general, for L latent variables we may impose a constraint $\overline{J^T W^T W J} = I_L$ leading to the penalty term

$$\text{Tr}\left\{\Lambda(\overline{J^T W^T W J} - I_L)\right\}$$

where J is an $M \times L$ matrix with jth column $\partial \phi / \partial x_j$ and Λ is a symmetric matrix of Lagrange multipliers. This is very similar to regularisation terms. It is a condition on the norm of W; it incorporates the Jacobian matrix J and a symmetric $L \times L$ matrix of Lagrange multipliers, Λ. The re-estimation solution for W may be written

$$W = T^T R^T \Phi (\Phi^T G \Phi + \overline{J \Lambda J^T})^{-1} \tag{7}$$

with Λ chosen so that the constraint $\overline{J^T W^T W J} = I_L$ is satisfied.

We may also use the derivatives of the transformation to define a distortion measure or *magnification factor*,

$$M(x; W) = \|J^T W^T W J - I\|^2$$

which is a function of the latent variables and the model parameters. A value of zero shows that there is no distortion[1].

An alternative to the constraint approach above is to introduce a prior on the allowable transformations using the magnification factor; for example,

$$P(W) \approx \exp(-\lambda \overline{M(x; W)}) \tag{8}$$

where λ is a regularisation parameter. This leads to a modification to the M-step re-estimation equation for W, providing a maximum a posteriori estimate. Equation (8) provides a natural generalisation of PCA since for the special case of a linear transformation ($\phi_i = x_i$, $M = L$), the solution for W is the PCA space as $\lambda \to \infty$.

4 RESAMPLING THE LATENT SPACE

Having obtained a mapping from latent space to data space using the above constraint, we seek a better estimate to the posterior pdf of the latent samples. Current versions of GTM require the latent samples to be uniformly distributed in the latent space which leads to distortions when the data of interest are projected into the latent space for visualisation. Since the responsibility matrix R can be used to determine a weight for each of the latent samples it is possible to update these samples using a resampling scheme.

We propose to use a resampling scheme based upon adaptive kernel density estimation. The basic procedure places a Gaussian kernel on each latent sample. This results in a Gaussian

---

[1] Note that this differs from the measure in the paper by Bishop *et al*, where a ratio-of-areas criterion is used, a factor which is unity for zero distortion, but may also be unity for some distortions.

mixture representation of the pdf of the latent samples $p(\boldsymbol{x}|\boldsymbol{t})$,

$$p(\boldsymbol{x}|\boldsymbol{t}) = \sum_{i=1}^{K} p_i N(\boldsymbol{\mu}_i, \boldsymbol{\Sigma}_i), \quad (9)$$

where each mixture component is weighted according to the latent sample weight p_i. Initially, the $\boldsymbol{\Sigma}_i$'s are all equal, taking their value from the standard formula of Silverman (1986),

$$\boldsymbol{\Sigma}_i = h^L \boldsymbol{V}, \quad (10)$$

where matrix $\boldsymbol{V}$ is an estimate of the covariance of $p(\boldsymbol{x})$ and,

$$h = [\{4/(L+2)\}^{1/(L+4)} K^{-1/(L+4)}]^L. \quad (11)$$

If the kernels are centered exactly on the latent samples, this model artificially inflates the variance of the latent samples. Following West (1993) we perform kernel shrinkage by making the $\boldsymbol{\mu}_i$ take the values

$$\boldsymbol{\mu}_i = \sqrt{1-h^L}\boldsymbol{x}_i + (1-\sqrt{1-h^L})\hat{\boldsymbol{\mu}} \quad (12)$$

where $\hat{\boldsymbol{\mu}}$ is the mean of the latent samples. This ensures that there is no artificial inflation of the variance.

To reduce the redundancy in our initially large number of mixture components, we propose a kernel reduction scheme in a similar manner to West. However, the scheme used here differs from that of West and follows a scheme proposed by Salmond (1990). Essentially, we chose the component with the smallest weight and its nearest neighbour, denoting these with subscripts 1 and 2 respectively. These components are then combined into a single component denoted with subscript c as follows,

$$p_c = p_1 + p_2 \quad (13)$$

$$\boldsymbol{\mu}_c = \frac{p_1 \boldsymbol{\mu}_1 + p_2 \boldsymbol{\mu}_2}{p_c} \quad (14)$$

$$\boldsymbol{\Sigma}_c = \frac{p_1[\boldsymbol{\Sigma}_1 + (\boldsymbol{\mu}_c - \boldsymbol{\mu}_1)(\boldsymbol{\mu}_c - \boldsymbol{\mu}_1)^T] + p_2[\boldsymbol{\Sigma}_2 + (\boldsymbol{\mu}_c - \boldsymbol{\mu}_2)(\boldsymbol{\mu}_c - \boldsymbol{\mu}_2)^T]}{p_c}. \quad (15)$$

This procedure is repeated until some stopping criterion is met. The stopping criterion could be a simple limit upon the number of mixture components ie; smaller than K but sufficiently large to model the data structure. Alternatively, the average kernel covariance and between kernel covariance can be monitored and the reduction stopped before some multiple (eg. 10) of the average kernel covariance exceeds the between kernel covariance.

Once a final mixture density estimate is obtained, a new set of equally weighted latent samples can be drawn from it. The new latent samples represent a better estimate of the posterior pdf of the latent samples and can be used, along with the existing RBF mapping, to calculate a new responsibility matrix R. This procedure can be repeated to obtain a further improved estimate of the posterior pdf which, after only a couple of iterations can lead to good estimates of the posterior pdf which further iterations fail to improve upon.

5 RESULTS

A latent variable model based on a spherically–symmetric Gaussian RBF has been implemented. The weights and the centres of the RBF were initialised so that the solution best approximated the zero–distortion principal components solution for two–dimensional projection.

For our example we chose to construct a simulated data set with easily identifiable structure. Four hundred points lying on the letters "NIPS" were sampled and projected onto a sphere of radius 50 such that the points lay between $25°$ and $175°$ longitude and $75°$ and $125°$ latitude with Gaussian noise of variance 4.0 on the radius of each point. The resulting data are shown in figure 1.

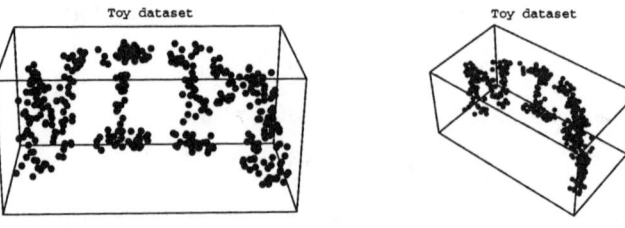

Figure 1: Simulated data.

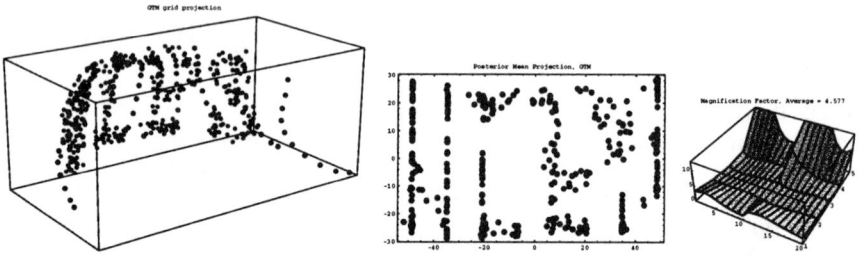

Figure 2: Results for standard GTM model.

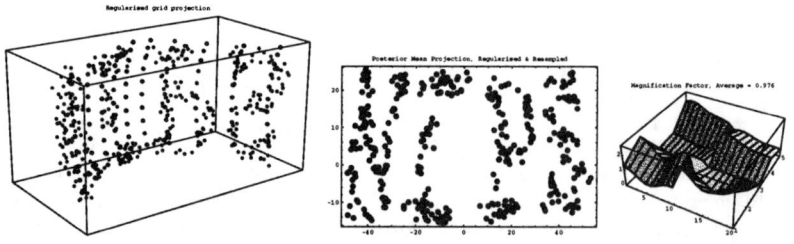

Figure 3: Results for regularised/resampled model.

Figure 2 shows results for the standard GTM (uniform grid of latent samples) projection of the data to two dimensions. The central figure shows the projection onto the latent space, exhibiting significant distortion. The left figure shows the projection of the regular grid of latent samples (red points) into the data space. Distortion of this grid can be easily seen. The right figure is a plot of the magnification factor as defined in section 3, with mean value of 4.577. For this data set most stretching occurs at the edges of the latent variable space.

Figure 3 shows results for the regularised/resampled version of the latent variable model for $\lambda = 1.0$. Again the central figure shows the projection onto the latent space after 2 iterations of the resampling procedure. The left-hand figure shows the projection of the initial regular grid of latent samples into the data space. The effect of regularisation is evident by the lack of severe distortions. Finally the magnification factors can be seen in the right-hand figure to be lower, with a mean value of 0.976.

6 DISCUSSION

We have considered two developments of the GTM latent variable model: the incorporation of priors on the allowable model and a resampling approach to the maximum likelihood parameter estimation. Results have been presented for this regularised/resampling approach and magnification factors lower than the standard model achieved, using the same RBF model. However, further reduction in magnification factor is possible with different RBF models, but the example illustrates that resampling offers a more robust approach. Current work is aimed at assessing the approach on realistic data sets.

References

Bishop, C.M. and Svensén, M. and Williams, C.K.I. (1997). Magnification factors for the GTM algorithm. *IEE International Conference on Artificial Neural Networks*, 465–471.

Bishop, C.M. and Svensén, M. and Williams, C.K.I. (1998). GTM: the generative topographic mapping. *Neural Computation*, 10, 215–234.

Hastie, T. and Stuetzle, W. (1989). Principal curves, *Journal of the American Statistical Association*, 84, 502–516.

Hotelling, H. (1933). Analysis of a complex of statistical variables into principal components. *Journal of Educational Psychology*, 24, 417–441, 498–520.

Kramer, M.A. (1991). Nonlinear principal component analysis using autoassociative neural networks. *American Institute of Chemical Engineers Journal*, 37(2), 233–243.

LeBlanc, M. and Tibshirani, R. (1994). Adaptive principal surfaces. *Journal of the American Statistical Association*, 89(425), 53–664.

Lowe, D. and Tipping, M. (1996). Feed–forward neural networks and topographic mappings for exploratory data analysis. *Neural Computing and Applications*, 4, 83–95.

Pearson, K. (1901). On lines and planes of closest fit. *Philosophical Magazine*, 6, 559–572.

Salmond, D.J. (1990). Mixture reduction algorithms for target tracking in clutter. *Signal & Data processing of small targets, edited by O. Drummond, SPIE*, 1305.

Silverman, B.W. (1986). Density Estimation for Statistics and Data Analysis. *Chapman & Hall*, 1986.

Tibshirani, R. (1992). Principal curves revisited. *Statistics and Computing*, 2(4), 183–190.

Webb, A.R. (1995). Multidimensional scaling by iterative majorisation using radial basis functions. Pattern Recognition, 28(5), 753-759.

Webb, A.R. (1996). An approach to nonlinear principal components analysis using radially-symmetric kernel functions. *Statistics and Computing*, 6, 159-168.

Webb, A.R. (1997). Radial basis functions for exploratory data analysis: an iterative majorisation approach for Minkowski distances based on multidimensional scaling. *Journal of Classification*, 14(2), 249-267.

Webb, A.R. (1998). Supervised nonlinear principal components analysis. (submitted for publication).

West, M. (1993). Approximating posterior distributions by mixtures. *J. R. Statist. Soc B*, 55(2), 409-422.

Kernel PCA and De-Noising in Feature Spaces

Sebastian Mika, Bernhard Schölkopf, Alex Smola
Klaus-Robert Müller, Matthias Scholz, Gunnar Rätsch
GMD FIRST, Rudower Chaussee 5, 12489 Berlin, Germany
{mika, bs, smola, klaus, scholz, raetsch}@first.gmd.de

Abstract

Kernel PCA as a nonlinear feature extractor has proven powerful as a preprocessing step for classification algorithms. But it can also be considered as a natural generalization of linear principal component analysis. This gives rise to the question how to use nonlinear features for data compression, reconstruction, and de-noising, applications common in linear PCA. This is a nontrivial task, as the results provided by kernel PCA live in some high dimensional feature space and need not have pre-images in input space. This work presents ideas for finding approximate pre-images, focusing on Gaussian kernels, and shows experimental results using these pre-images in data reconstruction and de-noising on toy examples as well as on real world data.

1 PCA and Feature Spaces

Principal Component Analysis (PCA) (e.g. [3]) is an orthogonal basis transformation. The new basis is found by diagonalizing the centered covariance matrix of a data set $\{x_k \in \mathbf{R}^N | k = 1, \ldots, \ell\}$, defined by $C = \langle(x_i - \langle x_k \rangle)(x_i - \langle x_k \rangle)^T\rangle$. The coordinates in the Eigenvector basis are called *principal components*. The size of an Eigenvalue λ corresponding to an Eigenvector v of C equals the amount of variance in the direction of v. Furthermore, the directions of the first n Eigenvectors corresponding to the biggest n Eigenvalues cover as much variance as possible by n orthogonal directions. In many applications they contain the most interesting information: for instance, in data compression, where we project onto the directions with biggest variance to retain as much information as possible, or in de-noising, where we deliberately drop directions with small variance.

Clearly, one cannot assert that linear PCA will always detect all structure in a given data set. By the use of suitable *nonlinear* features, one can extract more information. Kernel PCA is very well suited to extract interesting nonlinear structures in the data [9]. The purpose of this work is therefore (i) to consider nonlinear de-noising based on Kernel PCA and (ii) to clarify the connection between feature space expansions and meaningful patterns in input space. Kernel PCA first maps the data into some feature space $\mathbf{F}$ via a (usually nonlinear) function Φ and then performs linear PCA on the mapped data. As the feature space $\mathbf{F}$ might be very high dimensional (e.g. when mapping into the space of all possible d-th order monomials of input space), kernel PCA employs Mercer kernels instead of carrying out the mapping Φ explicitly. A Mercer kernel is a function k(x, y) which for all data sets $\{x_i\}$ gives rise to a positive matrix $K_{ij} =$ k(x_i, x_j) [6]. One can show that using k instead of a dot product in input space corresponds to mapping the data with some Φ to a feature space $\mathbf{F}$ [1], i.e. k$(x, y) = (\Phi(x) \cdot \Phi(y))$. Kernels that have proven useful include Gaussian kernels k$(x, y) = \exp(-\|x - y\|^2/c)$ and polynomial kernels k$(x, y) = (x \cdot y)^d$. Clearly, all algorithms that can be formulated in terms of dot products, e.g. *Support Vector Machines* [1], can be carried out in some feature space $\mathbf{F}$ without mapping the data explicitly. All these algorithms construct their solutions as expansions in the potentially infinite-dimensional feature space.

The paper is organized as follows: in the next section, we briefly describe the kernel PCA algorithm. In section 3, we present an algorithm for finding approximate pre-images of expansions in feature space. Experimental results on toy and real world data are given in section 4, followed by a discussion of our findings (section 5).

2 Kernel PCA and Reconstruction

To perform PCA in feature space, we need to find Eigenvalues $\lambda > 0$ and Eigenvectors $V \in \mathbf{F}\backslash\{0\}$ satisfying $\lambda V = \bar{C}V$ with $\bar{C} = \langle \Phi(x_k)\Phi(x_k)^T \rangle$.[1] Substituting $\bar{C}$ into the Eigenvector equation, we note that all solutions V must lie in the span of Φ-images of the training data. This implies that we can consider the equivalent system

$$\lambda(\Phi(x_k) \cdot V) = (\Phi(x_k) \cdot \bar{C}V) \text{ for all } k = 1, \ldots, \ell \tag{1}$$

and that there exist coefficients $\alpha_1, \ldots, \alpha_\ell$ such that

$$V = \sum_{i=1}^{\ell} \alpha_i \Phi(x_i) \tag{2}$$

Substituting $\bar{C}$ and (2) into (1), and defining an $\ell \times \ell$ matrix K by $K_{ij} := (\Phi(x_i) \cdot \Phi(x_j)) =$ k(x_i, x_j), we arrive at a problem which is cast in terms of dot products: solve

$$\ell \lambda \alpha = K \alpha \tag{3}$$

where $\alpha = (\alpha_1, \ldots, \alpha_\ell)^T$ (for details see [7]). Normalizing the solutions V^k, i.e. $(V^k \cdot V^k) = 1$, translates into $\lambda_k(\alpha^k \cdot \alpha^k) = 1$. To extract nonlinear principal components for the Φ-image of a test point x we compute the projection onto the k-th component by $\beta_k := (V^k \cdot \Phi(x)) = \sum_{i=1}^{\ell} \alpha_i^k$ k(x, x_i). For feature extraction, we thus have to evaluate ℓ kernel functions instead of a dot product in $\mathbf{F}$, which is expensive if $\mathbf{F}$ is high-dimensional (or, as for Gaussian kernels, infinite-dimensional). To reconstruct the Φ-image of a vector x from its projections β_k onto the first n principal components in $\mathbf{F}$ (assuming that the Eigenvectors are ordered by decreasing Eigenvalue size), we define a projection operator P_n by

$$P_n \Phi(x) = \sum_{k=1}^{n} \beta_k V^k \tag{4}$$

If n is large enough to take into account all directions belonging to Eigenvectors with non-zero Eigenvalue, we have $P_n \Phi(x_i) = \Phi(x_i)$. Otherwise (kernel) PCA still satisfies (i) that the overall squared reconstruction error $\sum_i \|P_n \Phi(x_i) - \Phi(x_i)\|^2$ is minimal and (ii) the retained variance is maximal among all projections onto orthogonal directions in $\mathbf{F}$. In common applications, however, we are interested in a reconstruction in input space rather than in $\mathbf{F}$. The present work attempts to achieve this by computing a vector z satisfying $\Phi(z) = P_n \Phi(x)$. The hope is that for the kernel used, such a z will be a good approximation of x in input space. However, (i) such a z will not always exist and (ii) if it exists,

---

[1]For simplicity, we assume that the mapped data are centered in $\mathbf{F}$. Otherwise, we have to go through the same algebra using $\tilde{\Phi}(x) := \Phi(x) - \langle \Phi(x_i) \rangle$.

it need be not unique.[2] As an example for (i), we consider a possible representation of **F**. One can show [7] that Φ can be thought of as a map $\Phi(x) = \mathrm{k}(x, .)$ into a Hilbert space $\mathcal{H}_k$ of functions $\sum_i \alpha_i \mathrm{k}(x_i, .)$ with a dot product satisfying $(\mathrm{k}(x, .) \cdot \mathrm{k}(y, .)) = \mathrm{k}(x, y)$. Then $\mathcal{H}_k$ is called *reproducing kernel Hilbert space* (e.g. [6]). Now, for a Gaussian kernel, $\mathcal{H}_k$ contains all linear superpositions of Gaussian bumps on $\mathbf{R}^N$ (plus limit points), whereas by definition of Φ only single bumps $\mathrm{k}(x, .)$ have pre-images under Φ. When the vector $\mathrm{P}_n \Phi(x)$ has no pre-image z we try to approximate it by minimizing

$$\rho(z) = \|\Phi(z) - \mathrm{P}_n\Phi(x)\|^2 \tag{5}$$

This is a special case of the reduced set method [2]. Replacing terms independent of z by Ω, we obtain

$$\rho(z) = \|\Phi(z)\|^2 - 2(\Phi(z) \cdot \mathrm{P}_n\Phi(x)) + \Omega \tag{6}$$

Substituting (4) and (2) into (6), we arrive at an expression which is written in terms of dot products. Consequently, we can introduce a kernel to obtain a formula for ρ (and thus $\nabla_z \rho$) which does not rely on carrying out Φ explicitly

$$\rho(z) = \mathrm{k}(z, z) - 2 \sum_{k=1}^n \beta_k \sum_{i=1}^\ell \alpha_i^k \mathrm{k}(z, x_i) + \Omega \tag{7}$$

3 Pre-Images for Gaussian Kernels

To optimize (7) we employed standard gradient descent methods. If we restrict our attention to kernels of the form $\mathrm{k}(x, y) = \mathrm{k}(\|x - y\|^2)$ (and thus satisfying $\mathrm{k}(x, x) \equiv$ const. for all x), an optimal z can be determined as follows (cf. [8]): we deduce from (6) that we have to maximize

$$\rho(z) = (\Phi(z) \cdot \mathrm{P}_n\Phi(x)) + \Omega' = \sum_{i=1}^\ell \gamma_i \mathrm{k}(z, x_i) + \Omega' \tag{8}$$

where we set $\gamma_i = \sum_{k=1}^n \beta_k \alpha_i^k$ (for some Ω' independent of z). For an extremum, the gradient with respect to z has to vanish: $\nabla_z \rho(z) = \sum_{i=1}^\ell \gamma_i \mathrm{k}'(\|z - x_i\|^2)(z - x_i) = 0$. This leads to a necessary condition for the extremum: $z = \sum_i \delta_i x_i / \sum_j \delta_j$, with $\delta_i = \gamma_i \mathrm{k}'(\|z - x_i\|^2)$. For a Gaussian kernel $\mathrm{k}(x, y) = \exp(-\|x - y\|^2/c)$ we get

$$z = \frac{\sum_{i=1}^\ell \gamma_i \exp(-\|z - x_i\|^2/c) x_i}{\sum_{i=1}^\ell \gamma_i \exp(-\|z - x_i\|^2/c)}. \tag{9}$$

We note that the denominator equals $(\Phi(z) \cdot \mathrm{P}_n\Phi(x))$ (cf. (8)). Making the assumption that $\mathrm{P}_n\Phi(x) \neq \mathbf{0}$, we have $(\Phi(x) \cdot \mathrm{P}_n\Phi(x)) = (\mathrm{P}_n\Phi(x) \cdot \mathrm{P}_n\Phi(x)) > 0$. As k is smooth, we conclude that there exists a neighborhood of the extremum of (8) in which the denominator of (9) is $\neq 0$. Thus we can devise an iteration scheme for z by

$$z_{t+1} = \frac{\sum_{i=1}^\ell \gamma_i \exp(-\|z_t - x_i\|^2/c) x_i}{\sum_{i=1}^\ell \gamma_i \exp(-\|z_t - x_i\|^2/c)} \tag{10}$$

Numerical instabilities related to $(\Phi(z) \cdot \mathrm{P}_n\Phi(x))$ being small can be dealt with by restarting the iteration with a different starting value. Furthermore we note that any fixed-point of (10) will be a linear combination of the kernel PCA training data x_i. If we regard (10) in the context of clustering we see that it resembles an iteration step for the estimation of

---

[2] If the kernel allows reconstruction of the dot–product in input space, and under the assumption that a pre–image exists, it is possible to construct it explicitly (cf. [7]). But clearly, these conditions do not hold true in general.

the center of a single Gaussian cluster. The weights or 'probabilities' γ_i reflect the (anti-) correlation between the amount of $\Phi(x)$ in Eigenvector direction V^k and the contribution of $\Phi(x_i)$ to this Eigenvector. So the 'cluster center' z is drawn towards training patterns with positive γ_i and pushed away from those with negative γ_i, i.e. for a fixed-point z_∞ the influence of training patterns with smaller distance to x will tend to be bigger.

4 Experiments

To test the feasibility of the proposed algorithm, we run several toy and real world experiments. They were performed using (10) and Gaussian kernels of the form $k(x,y) = \exp(-(\|x-y\|^2)/(nc))$ where n equals the dimension of input space. We mainly focused on the application of *de-noising*, which differs from *reconstruction* by the fact that we are allowed to make use of the original test data as starting points in the iteration.

Toy examples: In the first experiment (table 1), we generated a data set from eleven Gaussians in $\mathbf{R}^{10}$ with zero mean and variance σ^2 in each component, by selecting from each source 100 points as a training set and 33 points for a test set (centers of the Gaussians randomly chosen in $[-1,1]^{10}$). Then we applied kernel PCA to the training set and computed the projections β_k of the points in the test set. With these, we carried out de-noising, yielding an approximate pre-image in $\mathbf{R}^{10}$ for each test point. This procedure was repeated for different numbers of components in reconstruction, and for different values of σ. For the kernel, we used $c = 2\sigma^2$. We compared the results provided by our algorithm to those of linear PCA via the mean squared distance of all de-noised test points to their corresponding center. Table 1 shows the *ratio* of these values; here and below, ratios larger than one indicate that kernel PCA performed better than linear PCA. For almost every choice of n and σ, kernel PCA did better. Note that using all 10 components, linear PCA is just a basis transformation and hence cannot de-noise. The extreme superiority of kernel PCA for small σ is due to the fact that all test points are in this case located close to the eleven spots in input space, and linear PCA has to cover them with less than ten directions. Kernel PCA moves each point to the correct source even when using only a small number of components.

σ	$n=1$	2	3	4	5	6	7	8	9
0.05	2058.42	1238.36	846.14	565.41	309.64	170.36	125.97	104.40	92.23
0.1	10.22	31.32	21.51	29.24	27.66	23.53	29.64	40.07	63.41
0.2	0.99	1.12	1.18	1.50	2.11	2.73	3.72	5.09	6.32
0.4	1.07	1.26	1.44	1.64	1.91	2.08	2.22	2.34	2.47
0.8	1.23	1.39	1.54	1.70	1.80	1.96	2.10	2.25	2.39

Table 1: De-noising Gaussians in $\mathbf{R}^{10}$ (see text). Performance ratios larger than one indicate how much better kernel PCA did, compared to linear PCA, for different choices of the Gaussians' std. dev. σ, and different numbers of components used in reconstruction.

To get some intuitive understanding in a low-dimensional case, figure 1 depicts the results of de-noising a half circle and a square in the plane, using kernel PCA, a *nonlinear autoencoder*, *principal curves*, and linear PCA. The principal curves algorithm [4] iteratively estimates a curve capturing the structure of the data. The data are projected to the closest point on a curve which the algorithm tries to construct such that each point is the average of all data points projecting onto it. It can be shown that the only straight lines satisfying the latter are principal components, so principal curves are a generalization of the latter. The algorithm uses a smoothing parameter which is annealed during the iteration. In the nonlinear autoencoder algorithm, a 'bottleneck' 5-layer network is trained to reproduce the input values as outputs (i.e. it is used in autoassociative mode). The hidden unit activations in the third layer form a lower-dimensional representation of the data, closely related to

PCA (see for instance [3]). Training is done by conjugate gradient descent. In all algorithms, parameter values were selected such that the best possible de-noising result was obtained. The figure shows that on the closed square problem, kernel PCA does (subjectively) best, followed by principal curves and the nonlinear autoencoder; linear PCA fails completely. However, note that all algorithms except for kernel PCA actually provide an explicit one-dimensional parameterization of the data, whereas kernel PCA only provides us with a means of mapping points to their de-noised versions (in this case, we used four kernel PCA features, and hence obtain a four-dimensional parameterization).

kernel PCA	nonlinear autoencoder	Principal Curves	linear PCA

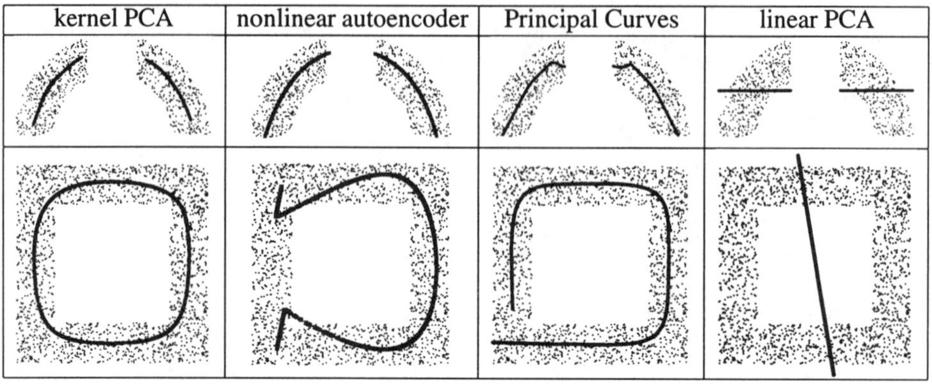

Figure 1: De-noising in 2-d (see text). Depicted are the data set (small points) and its de-noised version (big points, joining up to solid lines). For linear PCA, we used one component for reconstruction, as using two components, reconstruction is perfect and thus does not de-noise. Note that all algorithms except for our approach have problems in capturing the circular structure in the bottom example.

USPS example: To test our approach on real-world data, we also applied the algorithm to the USPS database of 256-dimensional handwritten digits. For each of the ten digits, we randomly chose 300 examples from the training set and 50 examples from the test set. We used (10) and Gaussian kernels with $c = 0.50$, equaling twice the average of the data's variance in each dimensions. In figure 4, we give two possible depictions of

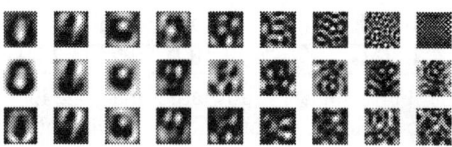

Figure 2: Visualization of Eigenvectors (see text). Depicted are the $2^0, \ldots, 2^8$-th Eigenvector (from left to right). First row: linear PCA, second and third row: different visualizations for kernel PCA.

the Eigenvectors found by kernel PCA, compared to those found by linear PCA for the USPS set. The second row shows the approximate pre-images of the Eigenvectors V^k, $k = 2^0, \ldots, 2^8$, found by our algorithm. In the third row each image is computed as follows: Pixel i is the projection of the Φ-image of the i-th canonical basis vector in input space onto the corresponding Eigenvector in features space (upper left $\Phi(e_1) \cdot V^k$, lower right $\Phi(e_{256}) \cdot V^k$). In the linear case, both methods would simply yield the Eigenvectors of linear PCA depicted in the first row; in this sense, they may be considered as generalized Eigenvectors in input space. We see that the first Eigenvectors are almost identical (except for signs). But we also see, that Eigenvectors in linear PCA start to concentrate on high-frequency structures already at smaller Eigenvalue size. To understand this, note that in linear PCA we only have a maximum number of 256 Eigenvectors, contrary to kernel PCA which gives us the number of training examples (here 3000) possible Eigenvectors. This

Figure 3: Reconstruction of USPS data. Depicted are the reconstructions of the first digit in the test set (original in last column) from the first $n = 1, \ldots, 20$ components for linear PCA (first row) and kernel PCA (second row) case. The numbers in between denote the fraction of squared distance measured towards the original example. For a small number of components both algorithms do nearly the same. For more components, we see that linear PCA yields a result resembling the original digit, whereas kernel PCA gives a result resembling a more prototypical 'three'

also explains some of the results we found when working with the USPS set. In these experiments, linear and kernel PCA were trained with the original data. Then we added (i) additive Gaussian noise with zero mean and standard deviation $\sigma = 0.5$ or (ii) 'speckle' noise with probability $p = 0.4$ (i.e. each pixel flips to black or white with probability $p/2$) to the test set. For the noisy test sets we computed the projections onto the first n linear and nonlinear components, and carried out reconstruction for each case. The results were compared by taking the mean squared distance of each reconstructed digit from the noisy test set to its original counterpart. As a third experiment we did the same for the original test set (hence doing reconstruction, not de-noising). In the latter case, where the task is to reconstruct a given example as exactly as possible, linear PCA did better, at least when using more than about 10 components (figure 3). This is due to the fact that linear PCA starts earlier to account for fine structures, but at the same time it starts to reconstruct noise, as we will see in figure 4. Kernel PCA, on the other hand, yields recognizable results even for a small number of components, representing a prototype of the desired example. This is one reason why our approach did better than linear PCA for the de-noising example (figure 4). Taking the mean squared distance measured over the whole test set for the optimal number of components in linear and kernel PCA, our approach did better by a factor of 1.6 for the Gaussian noise, and 1.2 times better for the 'speckle' noise (the optimal number of components were 32 in linear PCA, and 512 and 256 in kernel PCA, respectively). Taking identical numbers of components in both algorithms, kernel PCA becomes up to 8 (!) times better than linear PCA. However, note that kernel PCA comes with a higher computational complexity.

5 Discussion

We have studied the problem of finding approximate pre-images of vectors in feature space, and proposed an algorithm to solve it. The algorithm can be applied to both reconstruction and de-noising. In the former case, results were comparable to linear PCA, while in the latter case, we obtained significantly better results. Our interpretation of this finding is as follows. Linear PCA can extract at most N components, where N is the dimensionality of the data. Being a basis transform, all N components together fully describe the data. If the data are noisy, this implies that a certain fraction of the components will be devoted to the extraction of noise. Kernel PCA, on the other hand, allows the extraction of up to ℓ features, where ℓ is the number of training examples. Accordingly, kernel PCA can provide a larger number of features carrying information about the structure in the data (in our experiments, we had $\ell > N$). In addition, if the structure to be extracted is nonlinear, then linear PCA must necessarily fail, as we have illustrated with toy examples.

These methods, along with depictions of pre-images of vectors in feature space, provide some understanding of kernel methods which have recently attracted increasing attention. Open questions include (i) what kind of results kernels other than Gaussians will provide,

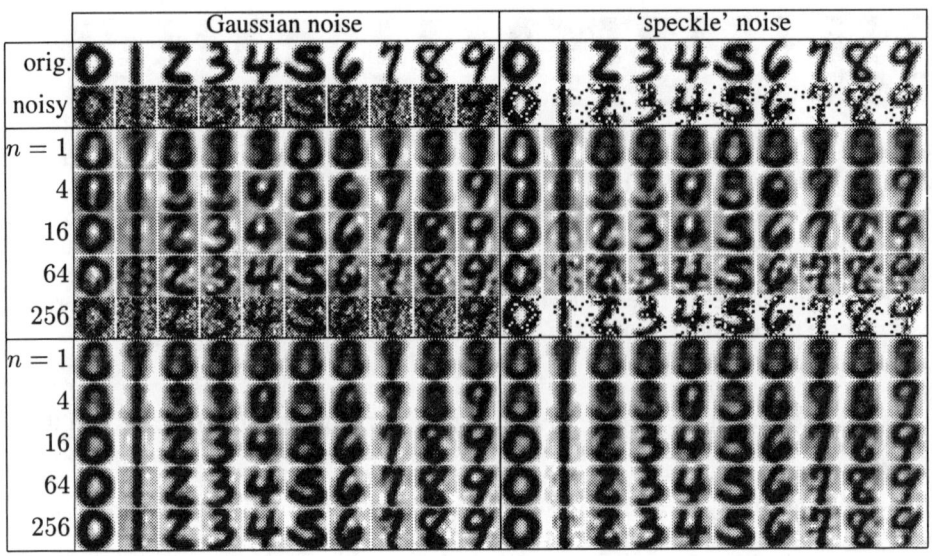

Figure 4: De-Noising of USPS data (see text). The left half shows: *top:* the first occurrence of each digit in the test set, *second row:* the upper digit with additive Gaussian noise ($\sigma = 0.5$), *following five rows:* the reconstruction for linear PCA using $n = 1, 4, 16, 64, 256$ components, and, *last five rows:* the results of our approach using the same number of components. In the right half we show the same but for 'speckle' noise with probability $p = 0.4$.

(ii) whether there is a more efficient way to solve either (6) or (8), and (iii) the comparison (and connection) to alternative nonlinear de-noising methods (cf. [5]).

References

[1] B. Boser, I. Guyon, and V.N. Vapnik. A training algorithm for optimal margin classifiers. In D. Haussler, editor, *Proc. COLT*, pages 144–152, Pittsburgh, 1992. ACM Press.

[2] C.J.C. Burges. Simplified support vector decision rules. In L. Saitta, editor, *Prooceedings, 13th ICML*, pages 71–77, San Mateo, CA, 1996.

[3] K.I. Diamantaras and S.Y. Kung. *Principal Component Neural Networks*. Wiley, New York, 1996.

[4] T. Hastie and W. Stuetzle. Principal curves. *JASA*, 84:502–516, 1989.

[5] S. Mallat and Z. Zhang. Matching Pursuits with time-frequency dictionaries. *IEEE Transactions on Signal Processing*, 41(12):3397–3415, December 1993.

[6] S. Saitoh. *Theory of Reproducing Kernels and its Applications*. Longman Scientific & Technical, Harlow, England, 1988.

[7] B. Schölkopf. *Support vector learning*. Oldenbourg Verlag, Munich, 1997.

[8] B. Schölkopf, P. Knirsch, A. Smola, and C. Burges. Fast approximation of support vector kernel expansions, and an interpretation of clustering as approximation in feature spaces. In P. Levi et. al., editor, *DAGM'98*, pages 124 – 132, Berlin, 1998. Springer.

[9] B. Schölkopf, A.J. Smola, and K.-R. Müller. Nonlinear component analysis as a kernel eigenvalue problem. *Neural Computation*, 10:1299–1319, 1998.

Very Fast EM-based Mixture Model Clustering using Multiresolution kd-trees

Andrew W. Moore
Robotics Institute, Carnegie Mellon University
Pittsburgh, PA 15213, awm@cs.cmu.edu

Abstract

Clustering is important in many fields including manufacturing, biology, finance, and astronomy. Mixture models are a popular approach due to their statistical foundations, and EM is a very popular method for finding mixture models. EM, however, requires many accesses of the data, and thus has been dismissed as impractical (e.g. [9]) for data mining of enormous datasets. We present a new algorithm, based on the multiresolution kd-trees of [5], which dramatically reduces the cost of EM-based clustering, with savings rising linearly with the number of datapoints. Although presented here for maximum likelihood estimation of Gaussian mixture models, it is also applicable to non-Gaussian models (provided class densities are monotonic in Mahalanobis distance), mixed categorical/numeric clusters, and Bayesian methods such as Autoclass [1].

1 Learning Mixture Models

In a Gaussian mixture model (e.g. [3]), we assume that datapoints $\{\mathbf{x}_1 \ldots \mathbf{x}_R\}$ have been generated independently by the following process. For each $\mathbf{x}_i$ in turn, nature begins by randomly picking a class, c_j, from a discrete set of classes $\{c_1 \ldots c_N\}$. Then nature draws $\mathbf{x}_i$ from an M-dimensional Gaussian whose mean μ_j and covariance Σ_j depend on the class. Thus we have

$$P(\mathbf{x}_i \mid c_j, \boldsymbol{\theta}) \sim ((2\pi)^M ||\Sigma_j||)^{-1/2} \exp(-\frac{1}{2}(\mathbf{x}_i - \mu_j)^T \Sigma_j^{-1} (\mathbf{x}_i - \mu_j)) \qquad (1)$$

where $\boldsymbol{\theta}$ denotes all the parameters of the mixture: the class probabilities p_j (where $p_j = P(c_j \mid \boldsymbol{\theta})$), the class centers μ_j and the class covariances Σ_j.

The job of a mixture model learner is to find a good estimate of the model, and Expectation Maximization (EM), also known as "Fuzzy k-means", is a popular algorithm for doing so. The tth iteration of EM begins with an estimate $\boldsymbol{\theta}^t$ of the model, and ends with an improved estimate $\boldsymbol{\theta}^{t+1}$. Write

$$\boldsymbol{\theta}^t = (p_1, \ldots p_N, \mu_1, \ldots \mu_N, \Sigma_1, \ldots, \Sigma_N) \qquad (2)$$

EM iterates over each point-class combination, computing for each class c_j and each datapoint $\mathbf{x}_i$, the extent to which $\mathbf{x}_i$ is "owned" by c_j. The ownership is simply $w_{ij} = P(c_j \mid \mathbf{x}_i, \boldsymbol{\theta}^t)$. Throughout this paper we will use the following notation:

$$\begin{aligned}
a_{ij} &= P(\mathbf{x}_i \mid c_j, \boldsymbol{\theta}^t) \\
w_{ij} &= P(c_j \mid \mathbf{x}_i, \boldsymbol{\theta}^t) = a_{ij} p_j / \sum_{k=1}^N a_{ik} p_k \text{(by Bayes' Rule)}
\end{aligned}$$

Then the new value of the centroid, μ_j, of the jth class in the new model $\boldsymbol{\theta}^{t+1}$ is simply the weighted mean of all the datapoints, using the values $\{w_{1j}, w_{2j}, \ldots w_{Rj}\}$ as the weights. A similar weighted procedure gives the new estimates of the class probabilities and the class covariances:

$$p_j \leftarrow \frac{\mathrm{sw}_j}{R} \quad , \quad \mu_j \leftarrow \frac{1}{\mathrm{sw}_j} \sum_{i=1}^R w_{ij} \mathbf{x}_i \quad , \quad \Sigma_j \leftarrow \frac{1}{\mathrm{sw}_j} \sum_{i=1}^R w_{ij} (\mathbf{x}_i - \mu_j)(\mathbf{x}_i - \mu_j)^T \qquad (3)$$

where $\mathrm{sw}_j = \sum_{i=1}^R w_{ij}$. Thus each iteration of EM visits every datapoint-class pair, meaning NR evaluations of a M-dimensional Gaussian, and so needing $O(M^2 NR)$ arithmetic operations per iteration. This paper aims to reduce that cost.

An mrkd-tree (Multiresolution KD-tree), introduced in [2] and developed further in [5], is a binary tree in which each node is associated with a subset of the datapoints. The root node owns all the datapoints. Each non-leaf-node has two children, defined by a splitting dimension ND.SPLITDIM and a splitting value ND.SPLITVAL. The two children divide their parent's datapoints between them, with the left child owing those datapoints that are strictly less than the splitting value in the splitting dimension, and the right child owning the remainder of the parent's datapoints:

$$\begin{aligned}
\mathbf{x}_i \in \text{ND.LEFT} &\Leftrightarrow \mathbf{x}_i[\text{ND.SPLITDIM}] < \text{ND.SPLITVAL and } \mathbf{x}_i \in \text{ND} \qquad (4) \\
\mathbf{x}_i \in \text{ND.RIGHT} &\Leftrightarrow \mathbf{x}_i[\text{ND.SPLITDIM}] \geq \text{ND.SPLITVAL and } \mathbf{x}_i \in \text{ND} \qquad (5)
\end{aligned}$$

The distinguishing feature of mrkd-trees is that their nodes contain the following:

- ND.NUMPOINTS: The number of points owned by ND (equivalently, the average density in ND).
- ND.CENTROID: The centroid of the points owned by ND (equivalently, the first moment of the density below ND).
- ND.COV: The covariance of the points owned by ND (equivalently, the second moment of the density below ND).
- ND.HYPERRECT: The bounding hyper-rectangle of the points below ND

We construct mrkd-trees top-down, identifying the bounding box of the current node, and splitting in the center of the widest dimension. A node is declared to be a leaf, and is left unsplit, if the widest dimension of its bounding box is $\leq$ some threshold, MBW. If MBW is zero, then all leaf nodes denote singleton or coincident points, the tree has $O(R)$ nodes and so requires $O(M^2 R)$ memory, and (with some care) the construction cost is $O(M^2 R + MR \log R)$. In practice, we set MBW to 1% of the range of the datapoint components. The tree size and construction thus cost considerably less than these bounds because in dense regions, tiny leaf nodes were able to summarize dozens of datapoints. Note too that the cost of tree-building is amortized—the tree must be built once, yet EM performs many iterations.

To perform an iteration of EM with the mrkd-tree, we call the function MAKESTATS (described below) on the root of the tree. MAKESTATS(ND, $\boldsymbol{\theta}^t$) outputs $3N$ values: (SW$_1$, SW$_2$, ...SW$_N$, SWX$_1$, ...SWX$_N$, SWXX$_1$, ...SWXX$_N$) where

$$\text{SW}_j = \sum_{\mathbf{x}_i \in \text{ND}} w_{ij} \quad , \quad \text{SWX}_j = \sum_{\mathbf{x}_i \in \text{ND}} w_{ij}\mathbf{x}_i \quad , \quad \text{SWXX}_j = \sum_{\mathbf{x}_i \in \text{ND}} w_{ij}\mathbf{x}_i\mathbf{x}_i^T \quad (6)$$

The results of MAKESTATS(ROOT) provide sufficient statistics to construct $\boldsymbol{\theta}^{t+1}$:

$$p_j \leftarrow \text{SW}_j/R \quad , \quad \mu_j \leftarrow \text{SWX}_j/\text{SW}_j \quad , \quad \Sigma_j \leftarrow (\text{SWXX}_j/\text{SW}_j) - \mu_j\mu_j^T \quad (7)$$

If MAKESTATS is called on a leaf node, we simply compute, for each j,

$$\bar{w}_j = P(c_j \mid \bar{\mathbf{x}}, \boldsymbol{\theta}^t) = P(\bar{\mathbf{x}} \mid c_j, \boldsymbol{\theta}^t)P(c_j \mid \boldsymbol{\theta}^t)/\sum_{k=1}^{N} P(\bar{\mathbf{x}} \mid c_k, \boldsymbol{\theta}^t)P(c_k \mid \boldsymbol{\theta}^t) \quad (8)$$

where $\bar{\mathbf{x}} =$ ND.CENTROID, and where all the items in the right hand equation are easily computed. We then return SW$_j = \bar{w}_j \times$ ND.NUMPOINTS, SWX$_j = \bar{w}_j \times$ ND.NUMPOINTS $\times \bar{\mathbf{x}}$ and SWXX$_j = \bar{w}_j \times$ ND.NUMPOINTS $\times$ ND.COV. The reason we can do this is that, if the leaf node is very small, there will be little variation in w_{ij} for the points owned by the node and so, for example $\sum w_{ij}\mathbf{x}_i \approx \bar{w}_j \sum \mathbf{x}_i$. In the experiments below we use very tiny leaf nodes, ensuring accuracy.

If MAKESTATS is called on a non-leaf-node, it can easily compute its answer by recursively calling MAKESTATS on its two children and then returning the sum of the two sets of answers. In general, that is exactly how we will proceed. If that was the end of the story, we would have little computational improvement over conventional EM, because one pass would fully traverse the tree, which contains $O(R)$ nodes, doing $O(NM^2)$ work per node.

We will win if we ever spot that, at some intermediate node, we can *prune*, i.e. evaluate the node as if it were a leaf, without searching its descendents, but without introducing significant error into the computation.

To do this, we will compute, for each j, the minimum and maximum w_{ij} that any point inside the node could have. This procedure is more complex than in the case of locally weighted regression [5].

We wish to compute $w_j^{\min}$ and $w_j^{\max}$ for each j, where $w_j^{\min}$ is a lower bound on $\min_{\mathbf{x}_i \in \text{ND}} w_{ij}$ and $w_j^{\max}$ is an upper bound on $\max_{\mathbf{x}_i \in \text{ND}} w_{ij}$. This is hard because $w_j^{\min}$ is determined not only by the mean and covariance of the jth class but also the other classes. For example, in Figure 1, w_{32} is approximately 0.5, but it would be much larger if c_1 were further to the left, or had a thinner covariance.

But remember that the w_{ij}'s are defined in terms of a_{ij}'s, thus: $w_{ij} = a_{ij}p_j/\sum_{k=1}^{N} a_{ik}p_k$. We *can* put bounds on the a_{ij}'s relatively easily. It simply requires that for each j we compute[1] the closest and furthest point from μ_j within

---

[1] Computing these points requires non-trivial computational geometry because the covariance matrices are not necessarily axis-aligned. There is no space here for details.

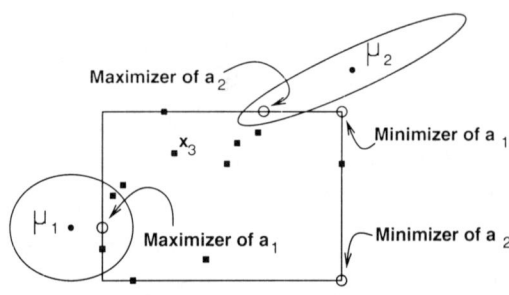

Figure 1: The rectangle denotes a hyper-rectangle in the mrkd-tree. The small squares denote datapoints "owned" by the node. Suppose there are just two classes, with the given means, and covariances depicted by the ellipses. Small circles indicate the locations within the node for which a_j (i.e. $P(x \mid c_j)$) would be extremized.

ND.HYPERRECT, using the Mahalanobis distance $MHD(\mathbf{x}, \mathbf{x}') = (\mathbf{x}-\mathbf{x}')^T \Sigma_j^{-1} (\mathbf{x}-\mathbf{x}')$. Call these shortest and furthest squared distances $MHD^{\min}$ and $MHD^{\max}$. Then

$$a_j^{\min} = ((2\pi)^M \|\Sigma_j\|)^{-1/2} \exp(-\frac{1}{2} MHD^{\max}) \tag{9}$$

is a lower bound for $\min_{\mathbf{x}_i \in \text{ND}} a_{ij}$, with a similar definition of $a_j^{\max}$. Then write

$$\min_{\mathbf{x}_i \in \text{ND}} w_{ij} = \min_{\mathbf{x}_i \in \text{ND}} (a_{ij} p_j / \sum_k a_{ik} p_k) = \min_{\mathbf{x}_i \in \text{ND}} (a_{ij} p_j / (a_{ij} p_j + \sum_{k \neq j} a_{ik} p_k))$$
$$\geq a_j^{\min} p_j / (a_j^{\min} p_j + \sum_{k \neq j} a_k^{\max} p_k) = w_j^{\min}$$

where $w_j^{\min}$ is our lower bound. There is a similar definition for $w_j^{\max}$. The inequality is proved by elementary algebra, and requires that all quantities are positive (which they are). We can often tighten the bounds further using a procedure that exploits the fact that $\sum_j w_{ij} = 1$, but space does not permit further discussion.

We will prune if $w_j^{\min}$ and $w_j^{\max}$ are close for all j. What should be the criterion for closeness? The first idea that springs to mind is: Prune if $\forall j$. $(w_j^{\max} - w_j^{\min} < \epsilon)$. But such a simple criterion is not suitable: some classes may be accumulating very large sums of weights, whilst others may be accumulating very small sums. The large-sum-weight classes can tolerate far looser bounds than the small-sum-weight classes. Here, then, is a more satisfactory pruning criterion: Prune if $\forall j$. $(w_j^{\max} - w_j^{\min} < \tau w_j^{\text{total}})$ where w_j^{total} is the total weight awarded to class j over the entire dataset, and τ is some small constant. Sadly, w_j^{total} is not known in advance, but happily we can find a lower bound on w_j^{total} of $w_j^{\text{sofar}} + \text{ND.NUMPOINTS} \times w_j^{\min}$, where w_j^{sofar} is the total weight awarded to class j so far during the search over the kd-tree.

The algorithm as described so far performs divide-and-conquer-with-cutoffs on the set of datapoints. In addition, it is possible to achieve an extra acceleration by means of divide and conquer on the class centers. Suppose there were $N = 100$ classes. Instead of considering all 100 classes at all nodes, it is frequently possible to determine at some node that the maximum possible weight $w_j^{\max}$ for some class j is less than a miniscule fraction of the minimum possible weight $w_k^{\min}$ for some other class k. Thus if we ever find that in some node $w_j^{\max} < \lambda w_k^{\min}$ where $\lambda = 10^{-4}$, then class c_j is removed from consideration from all descendents of the current node. Frequently this means that near the tree's leaves, only a tiny fraction of the classes compete for ownership of the datapoints, and this leads to large time savings.

2 Results

We have subjected this approach to numerous Monte-Carlo empirical tests. Here we report on one set of such tests, created with the following methodology.

- We randomly generate a mixture of Gaussians in M-dimensional space (by default $M = 2$). The number of Gaussians, N is, by default, 20. Each Gaussian has a mean lying within the unit hypercube, and a covariance matrix randomly generated with diagonal elements between 0 up to $4\sigma^2$ (by default, $\sigma = 0.05$) and random non-diagonal elements that ensure symmetric positive definiteness. Thus the distance from a Gaussian center to its 1-standard-deviation contour is of the order of magnitude of σ.
- We randomly generate a dataset from the mixture model. The number of points, R, is (by default) 160,000. Figure 2 shows a typical generated set of Gaussians and datapoints.
- We then build an mrkd-tree for the dataset, and record the memory requirements and real time to build (on a Pentium 200Mhz, in seconds).
- We then run EM on the data. EM begins with an entirely different set of Gaussians, randomly generated using the same procedure.
- We run 5 iterations of the conventional EM algorithm and the new mrkd-tree-based algorithm. The new algorithm uses a default value of 0.1 for τ. We record the real time (in seconds) for each iteration of each algorithm, and we also record the mean log-likelihood score $(1/R) \sum_{i=1}^{R} \log P(\mathbf{x}_i \mid \boldsymbol{\theta}^t)$ for the tth model for both algorithms.

Figure 3 shows the nodes that are visited during Iteration 2 of the Fast EM with $N = 6$ classes. Table 1 shows the detailed results as the experimental parameters are varied. Speedups vary from 8-fold to 1000-fold. There are 100-fold speedups even with very wide (non-local) Gaussians. In other experiments, similar results were also obtained on real datasets that disobey the Gaussian assumption. There too, we find one- and two-order-of-magnitude computational advantages with indistinguishable statistical behavior (no better and no worse) compared with conventional EM.

Real Data: Preliminary experiments in applying this to large datasets have been encouraging. For three-dimensional galaxy clustering with 800,000 galaxies and 1000 clusters, traditional EM needed 35 minutes per iteration, while the mrkd-trees required only 13 seconds. With 1.6 million galaxies, traditional EM needed 70 minutes and mrkd-trees required 14 seconds.

3 Conclusion

The use of variable resolution structures for clustering has been suggested in many places (e.g. [7, 8, 4, 9]). The BIRCH system, in particular, is popular in the database community. BIRCH is, however, unable to identify second-moment features of clusters (such as non-axis-aligned spread). Our contributions have been the use of a multi-resolution approach, with associated computational benefits, and the introduction of an efficient algorithm that leaves the statistical aspects of mixture model estimation unchanged. The growth of recent data mining algorihms that are *not* based on statistical foundations has freqently been justified by the following statement: Using state-of-the-art statistical techniques is too expensive because such techniques were not designed to handle large datasets and become intractable with millions of datapoints. In earlier work we provided evidence that this statement may

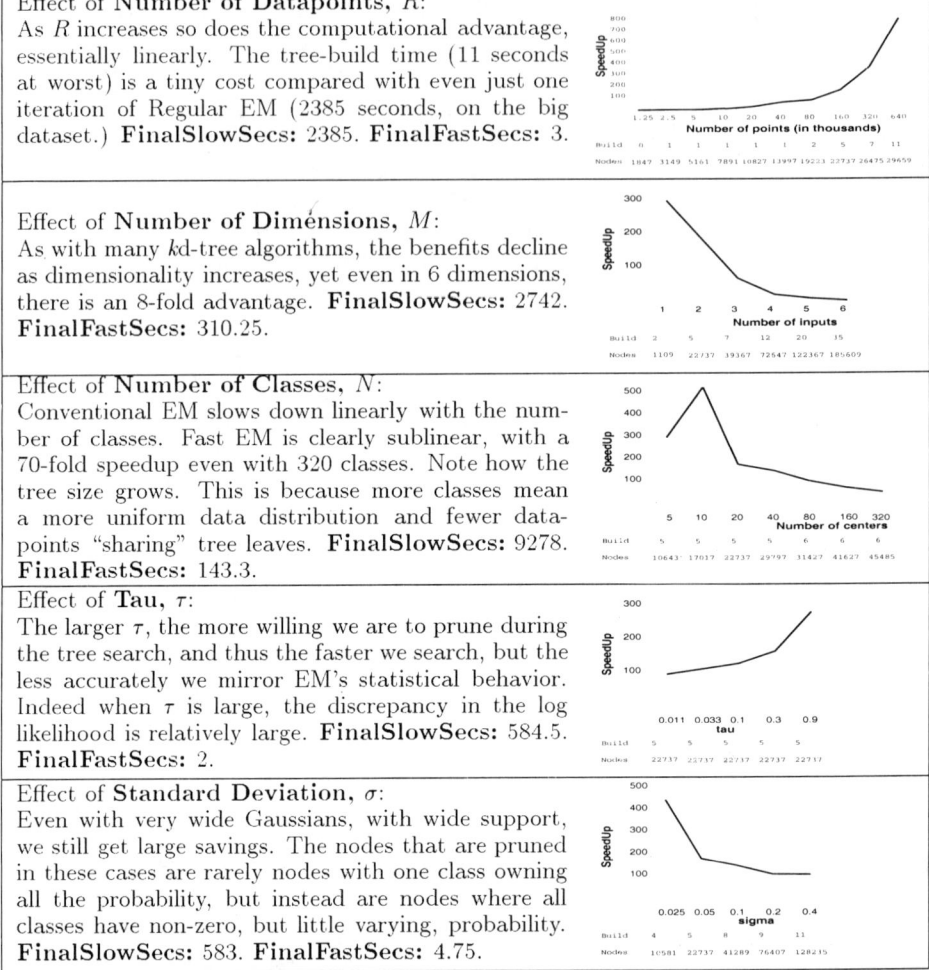

Effect of **Number of Datapoints, R**:
As R increases so does the computational advantage, essentially linearly. The tree-build time (11 seconds at worst) is a tiny cost compared with even just one iteration of Regular EM (2385 seconds, on the big dataset.) **FinalSlowSecs**: 2385. **FinalFastSecs**: 3.

Effect of **Number of Dimensions, M**:
As with many kd-tree algorithms, the benefits decline as dimensionality increases, yet even in 6 dimensions, there is an 8-fold advantage. **FinalSlowSecs**: 2742. **FinalFastSecs**: 310.25.

Effect of **Number of Classes, N**:
Conventional EM slows down linearly with the number of classes. Fast EM is clearly sublinear, with a 70-fold speedup even with 320 classes. Note how the tree size grows. This is because more classes mean a more uniform data distribution and fewer datapoints "sharing" tree leaves. **FinalSlowSecs**: 9278. **FinalFastSecs**: 143.3.

Effect of **Tau, τ**:
The larger τ, the more willing we are to prune during the tree search, and thus the faster we search, but the less accurately we mirror EM's statistical behavior. Indeed when τ is large, the discrepancy in the log likelihood is relatively large. **FinalSlowSecs**: 584.5. **FinalFastSecs**: 2.

Effect of **Standard Deviation, σ**:
Even with very wide Gaussians, with wide support, we still get large savings. The nodes that are pruned in these cases are rarely nodes with one class owning all the probability, but instead are nodes where all classes have non-zero, but little varying, probability. **FinalSlowSecs**: 583. **FinalFastSecs**: 4.75.

Table 1: In all the above results all parameters were held at their default values except for one, which varied as shown in the graphs. Each graph shows the factor by which the new EM is faster than the conventional EM. Below each graph is the time to build the mrkd-tree in seconds and the number of nodes in the tree. Note that although the tree building cost is not included in the speedup calculation, it is negligible in all cases, especially considering that only one tree build is needed for all EM iterations. Does the approximate nature of this process result in inferior clusters? The answer is no: the quality of clusters is indistinguishable between the slow and fast methods when measured by log-likelihood and when viewed visually.

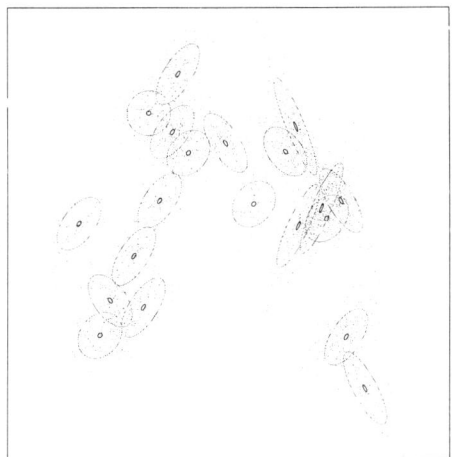
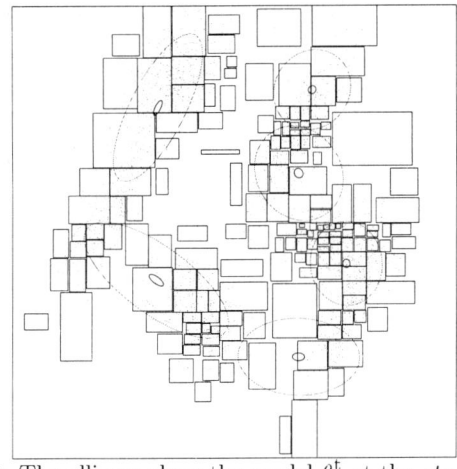

Figure 2: A typical set of Gaussians generated by our random procedure. They in turn generate the datasets upon which we compare the performance of the old and new implementations of EM.

Figure 3: The ellipses show the model θ^t at the *start* of an EM iteration. The rectangles depict the *mrkd*-tree nodes that were pruned. Observe larger rectangles (and larger savings) in areas with less variation in class probabilities. Note this is not merely able to only prune where the data density is low.

not apply for locally weighted regression [5] or Bayesian network learning [6], and we hope this paper provides some evidence that it also needn't apply to clustering.

References

[1] P. Cheeseman and R. Oldford. *Selecting Models from Data: Artificial Intelligence and Statistics IV. Lecture Notes in Statistics, vol. 89*. Springer Verlag, 1994.

[2] K. Deng and A. W. Moore. Multiresolution Instance-based Learning. In *Proceedings of IJCAI-95*. Morgan Kaufmann, 1995.

[3] R. O. Duda and P. E. Hart. *Pattern Classification and Scene Analysis*. John Wiley & Sons, 1973.

[4] M. Ester, H. P. Kriegel, and X. Xu. A Database Interface for Clustering in Large Spatial Databases. In *Proceedings of the First International Conference on Knowledge Discovery and Data Mining*. AAAI Press, 1995.

[5] A. W. Moore, J. Schneider, and K. Deng. Efficient Locally Weighted Polynomial Regression Predictions. In D. Fisher, editor, *Proceedings of the 1997 International Machine Learning Conference*. Morgan Kaufmann, 1997.

[6] Andrew W. Moore and M. S. Lee. Cached Sufficient Statistics for Efficient Machine Learning with Large Datasets. *Journal of Artificial Intelligence Research*, 8, March 1998.

[7] S. M. Omohundro. Efficient Algorithms with Neural Network Behaviour. *Journal of Complex Systems*, 1(2):273–347, 1987.

[8] S. M. Omohundro. Bumptrees for Efficient Function, Constraint, and Classification Learning. In R. P. Lippmann, J. E. Moody, and D. S. Touretzky, editors, *Advances in Neural Information Processing Systems 3*. Morgan Kaufmann, 1991.

[9] T. Zhang, R. Ramakrishnan, and M. Livny. BIRCH: An Efficient Data Clustering Method for Very Large Databases. In *Proceedings of the Fifteenth ACM SIGACT-SIGMOD-SIGART Symposium on Principles of Database Systems : PODS 1996*. Assn for Computing Machinery, 1996.

Replicator Equations, Maximal Cliques, and Graph Isomorphism

Marcello Pelillo
Dipartimento di Informatica
Università Ca' Foscari di Venezia
Via Torino 155, 30172 Venezia Mestre, Italy
E-mail: `pelillo@dsi.unive.it`

Abstract

We present a new energy-minimization framework for the graph isomorphism problem which is based on an equivalent maximum clique formulation. The approach is centered around a fundamental result proved by Motzkin and Straus in the mid-1960s, and recently expanded in various ways, which allows us to formulate the maximum clique problem in terms of a standard quadratic program. To solve the program we use "replicator" equations, a class of simple continuous- and discrete-time dynamical systems developed in various branches of theoretical biology. We show how, despite their inability to escape from local solutions, they nevertheless provide experimental results which are competitive with those obtained using more elaborate mean-field annealing heuristics.

1 INTRODUCTION

The graph isomorphism problem is one of those few combinatorial optimization problems which still resist any computational complexity characterization [6]. Despite decades of active research, no polynomial-time algorithm for it has yet been found. At the same time, while clearly belonging to NP, no proof has been provided that it is NP-complete. Indeed, there is strong evidence that this cannot be the case for, otherwise, the polynomial hierarchy would collapse [5]. The current belief is that the problem lies strictly between the P and NP-complete classes.

Because of its theoretical as well as practical importance, the problem has attracted much attention in the neural network community, and various powerful heuristics have been developed [11, 18, 19, 20]. Following Hopfield and Tank's seminal work [10], the typical approach has been to write down a (continuous) energy function whose minimizers correspond to the (discrete) solutions being sought, and then construct a dynamical system which converges toward them. Almost invariably, all the algorithms developed so far are based on techniques borrowed from statistical mechanics, in particular mean field theory, which allow one to escape from poor local solutions.

In this paper, we develop a new energy-minimization framework for the graph isomorphism problem which is based on the idea of reducing it to the maximum clique problem, another well-known combinatorial optimization problem. Central to our approach is a powerful result originally proved by Motzkin and Straus [13], and recently extended in various ways [3, 7, 16], which allows us to formulate the maximum clique problem in terms of an indefinite quadratic program. We then present a class of straightforward continuous- and discrete-time dynamical systems known in mathematical biology as *replicator equations*, and show how, thanks to their dynamical properties, they naturally suggest themselves as a useful heuristic for solving the proposed graph isomorphism program. The extensive experimental results presented show that, despite their simplicity and their inherent inability to escape from local optima, replicator dynamics are nevertheless competitive with more sophisticated deterministic annealing algorithms. The proposed formulation seems therefore a promising framework within which powerful continuous-based graph matching heuristics can be developed, and is in fact being employed for solving practical computer vision problems [17]. More details on the work presented here can be found in [15].

2 A QUADRATIC PROGRAM FOR GRAPH ISOMORPHISM

2.1 GRAPH ISOMORPHISM AS CLIQUE SEARCH

Let $G = (V, E)$ be an undirected graph, where V is the set of vertices and $E \subseteq V \times V$ is the set of edges. The *order* of G is the number of its vertices, and its *size* is the number of edges. Two vertices $i, j \in V$ are said to be *adjacent* if $(i, j) \in E$. The *adjacency matrix* of G is the $n \times n$ symmetric matrix $A = (a_{ij})$ defined as follows: $a_{ij} = 1$ if $(i, j) \in E$, $a_{ij} = 0$ otherwise.

Given two graphs $G' = (V', E')$ and $G'' = (V'', E'')$ having the same order and size, an *isomorphism* between them is any bijection $\phi : V' \to V''$ such that $(i, j) \in E' \Leftrightarrow (\phi(i), \phi(j)) \in E''$, for all $i, j \in V'$. Two graphs are said to be *isomorphic* if there exists an isomorphism between them. The graph isomorphism problem is therefore to decide whether two graphs are isomorphic and, in the affirmative, to find an isomorphism. Barrow and Burstall [1] introduced the notion of an *association graph* as a useful auxiliary graph structure for solving general graph/subgraph isomorphism problems. The association graph derived from G' and G'' is the undirected graph $G = (V, E)$, where $V = V' \times V''$ and

$$E = \{((i, h), (j, k)) \in V \times V : i \neq j, h \neq k, \text{ and } (i, j) \in E' \Leftrightarrow (h, k) \in E''\} .$$

Given an arbitrary undirected graph $G = (V, E)$, a subset of vertices C is called a *clique* if all its vertices are mutually adjacent, i.e., for all $i, j \in C$ we have $(i, j) \in E$. A clique is said to be *maximal* if it is not contained in any larger clique, and *maximum* if it is the largest clique in the graph. The *clique number*, denoted by $\omega(G)$, is defined as the cardinality of the maximum clique.

The following result establishes an equivalence between the graph isomorphism problem and the maximum clique problem (see [15] for proof).

Theorem 2.1 *Let G' and G'' be two graphs of order n, and let G be the corresponding association graph. Then, G' and G'' are isomorphic if and only if $\omega(G) = n$. In this case, any maximum clique of G induces an isomorphism between G' and G'', and vice versa.*

2.2 CONTINUOUS FORMULATION OF MAX-CLIQUE

Let $G = (V, E)$ be an arbitrary undirected graph of order n, and let S_n denote the standard simplex of $\mathbb{R}^n$:

$$S_n = \left\{ \mathbf{x} \in \mathbb{R}^n \; : \; x_i \geq 0 \text{ for all } i = 1 \ldots n, \text{ and } \sum_{i=1}^{n} x_i = 1 \right\}.$$

Given a subset of vertices C of G, we will denote by $\mathbf{x}^c$ its *characteristic vector* which is the point in S_n defined as $x_i^c = 1/|C|$ if $i \in C$, $x_i^c = 0$ otherwise, where $|C|$ denotes the cardinality of C.

Now, consider the following quadratic function:

$$f(\mathbf{x}) = \mathbf{x}^T A \mathbf{x} \tag{1}$$

where "T" denotes transposition. The Motzkin-Straus theorem [13] establishes a remarkable connection between global (local) maximizers of f in S_n and maximum (maximal) cliques of G. Specifically, it states that a subset of vertices C of a graph G is a maximum clique if and only if its characteristic vector $\mathbf{x}^c$ is a global maximizer of the function f in S_n. A similiar relationship holds between (strict) local maximizers and maximal cliques [7, 16].

One drawback associated with the original Motzkin-Straus formulation relates to the existence of spurious solutions, i.e., maximizers of f which are not in the form of characteristic vectors [16]. In principle, spurious solutions represent a problem since, while providing information about the *order* of the maximum clique, do not allow us to extract the vertices comprising the clique. Fortunately, there is straightforward solution to this problem which has recently been introduced and studied by Bomze [3]. Consider the following regularized version of function f:

$$\hat{f}(\mathbf{x}) = \mathbf{x}^T A \mathbf{x} + \frac{1}{2} \mathbf{x}^T \mathbf{x} . \tag{2}$$

The following is the spurious-free counterpart of the original Motzkin-Straus theorem (see [3] for proof).

Theorem 2.2 *Let C be a subset of vertices of a graph G, and let $\mathbf{x}^c$ be its characteristic vector. Then the following statements hold:*

(a) C is a maximum clique of G if and only if $\mathbf{x}^c$ is a global maximizer of $\hat{f}$ over the simplex S_n. Its order is then given by $|C| = 1/2(1 - f(\mathbf{x}^c))$.

(b) C is a maximal clique of G if and only if $\mathbf{x}^c$ is a local maximizer of $\hat{f}$ in S_n.

(c) All local (and hence global) maximizers of $\hat{f}$ over S_n are strict.

Unlike the Motzkin-Straus formulation, the previous result guarantees that *all* maximizers of $\hat{f}$ on S_n are strict, and are characteristic vectors of maximal/maximum cliques in the graph. In an exact sense, therefore, a one-to-one correspondence exists between maximal cliques and local maximizers of $\hat{f}$ in S_n on the one hand, and maximum cliques and global maximizers on the other hand.

2.3 A QUADRATIC PROGRAM FOR GRAPH ISOMORPHISM

Let G' and G'' be two arbitrary graphs of order n, and let A denote the adjacency matrix of the corresponding association graph, whose order is assumed to be N. The graph isomorphism problem is equivalent to the following program:

$$\begin{array}{ll} \text{maximize} & \hat{f}(\mathbf{x}) = \mathbf{x}^T (A + \frac{1}{2} I_N) \mathbf{x} \\ \text{subject to} & \mathbf{x} \in S_N \end{array} \tag{3}$$

More precisely, the following result holds, which is a straightforward consequence of Theorems 2.1 and 2.2.

Theorem 2.3 *Let G' and G'' be two graphs of order n, and let $\mathbf{x}^*$ be a global solution of program (3), where A is the adjacency matrix of the association graph of G' and G''. Then, G' and G'' are isomorphic if and only if $\hat{f}(\mathbf{x}^*) = 1 - 1/2n$. In this case, any global solution to (3) induces an isomorphism between G' and G'', and vice versa.*

In [15] we discuss the analogies between our objective function and those proposed in the literature (e.g., [18, 19]).

3 REPLICATOR EQUATIONS AND GRAPH ISOMORPHISM

Let W be a non-negative $n \times n$ matrix, and consider the following dynamical system:

$$\frac{d}{dt}x_i(t) = x_i(t)\left(\pi_i(t) - \sum_{j=1}^{n} x_j(t)\pi_j(t)\right), \quad i = 1\ldots n \quad (4)$$

where $\pi_i(t) = \sum_{j=1}^{n} w_{ij}x_j(t)$, $i = 1\ldots n$, and its discrete-time counterpart:

$$x_i(t+1) = \frac{x_i(t)\pi_i(t)}{\sum_{j=1}^{n} x_j(t)\pi_j(t)}, \quad i = 1\ldots n. \quad (5)$$

It is readily seen that the simplex S_n is invariant under these dynamics, which means that every trajectory starting in S_n will remain in S_n for all future times.

Both (4) and (5) are called *replicator equations* in theoretical biology, since they are used to model evolution over time of relative frequencies of interacting, self-replicating entities [9]. The discrete-time dynamical equations turn also out to be a special case of a general class of dynamical systems introduced by Baum and Eagon [2] in the context of Markov chain theory.

Theorem 3.1 *If W is symmetric, then the quadratic polynomial $F(\mathbf{x}) = \mathbf{x}^T W \mathbf{x}$ is strictly increasing along any non-constant trajectory of both continuous-time (4) and discrete-time (5) replicator equations. Furthermore, any such trajectory converges to a (unique) stationary point. Finally, a vector $\mathbf{x} \in S_n$ is asymptotically stable under (4) and (5) if and only if $\mathbf{x}$ is a strict local maximizer of F on S_n.*

The previous result is known in mathematical biology as the Fundamental Theorem of Natural Selection [9, 21]. As far as the discrete-time model is concerned, it can be regarded as a straightforward implication of the more general Baum-Eagon theorem [2]. The fact that all trajectories of the replicator dynamics converge to a stationary point is proven in [12].

Recently, there has been much interest in evolutionary game theory around the following exponential version of replicator equations, which arises as a model of evolution guided by imitation [8, 21]:

$$\frac{d}{dt}x_i(t) = x_i(t)\left(\frac{e^{\kappa \pi_i(t)}}{\sum_{j=1}^{n} x_j(t)e^{\kappa \pi_j(t)}} - 1\right), \quad i = 1\ldots n \quad (6)$$

where κ is a positive constant. As κ tends to 0, the orbits of this dynamics approach those of the standard, first-order replicator model (4), slowed down by the factor

κ. Hofbauer [8] has recently proven that when the matrix W is symmetric, the quadratic polynomial F defined in Theorem 3.1 is also strictly increasing, as in the first-order case. After discussing various properties of this, and more general dynamics, he concluded that the model behaves essentially in the same way as the standard replicator equations, the only difference being the size of the basins of attraction around stable equilibria. A customary way of discretizing equation (6) is given by the following difference equations:

$$x_i(t+1) = \frac{x_i(t)e^{\kappa \pi_i(t)}}{\sum_{j=1}^{n} x_j(t)e^{\kappa \pi_j(t)}} , \quad i = 1 \ldots n \qquad (7)$$

which enjoys many of the properties of the first-order system (5), e.g., they have the same set of equilibria.

The properties discussed above naturally suggest using replicator equations as a useful heuristic for the graph isomorphism problem. Let G' and G'' be two graphs of order n, and let A denote the adjacency matrix of the corresponding N-vertex association graph G. By letting

$$W = A + \frac{1}{2}I_N$$

we know that the replicator dynamical systems, starting from an arbitrary initial state, will iteratively maximize the function $\hat{f}(\mathbf{x}) = \mathbf{x}^T(A + \frac{1}{2}I_N)\mathbf{x}$ in S_N, and will eventually converge to a strict local maximizer which, by virtue of Theorem 2.2 will then correspond to the characteristic vector of a maximal clique in the association graph. This will in turn induce an isomorphism between two subgraphs of G' and G'' which is "maximal," in the sense that there is no other isomorphism between subgraphs of G' and G'' which includes the one found. Clearly, in theory there is no guarantee that the converged solution will be a *global* maximizer of $\hat{f}$, and therefore that it will induce an isomorphism between the two original graphs. Previous work done on the maximum clique problem [4, 14], and also the results presented in this paper, however, suggest that the basins of attraction of global maximizers are quite large, and very frequently the algorithm converges to one of them.

4 EXPERIMENTAL RESULTS

In the experiments reported here, the discrete-time replicator equation (5) and its exponential counterpart (7) with $\kappa = 10$ were used. The algorithms were started from the barycenter of the simplex and they were stopped when either a maximal clique was found or the distance between two successive points was smaller than a fixed threshold, which was set to 10^{-17}. In the latter case the converged vector was randomly perturbed, and the algorithm restarted from the perturbed point. Because of the one-to-one correspondence between local maximizers and maximal cliques, this situation corresponds to convergence to a saddle point. All the experiments were run on a Sparc20.

Undirected 100-vertex random graphs were generated with expected connectivities ranging from 1% to 99%. For each connectivity value, 100 graphs were produced and each of them had its vertices randomly permuted so as to obtain a pair of isomorphic graphs. Overall, therefore, 1500 pairs of isomorphic graphs were used. Each pair was given as input to the replicator models and, after convergence, a success was recorded when the cardinality of the returned clique was equal to the order of the graphs given as input (i.e., 100).[1] Because of the stopping criterion employed, this

---

[1] Due to the high computational time required, in the 1% and 99% cases the first-order replicator algorithm (5) was tested only on 10 pairs, instead of 100.

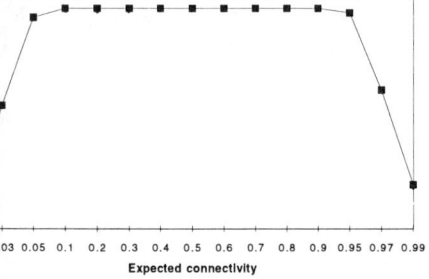
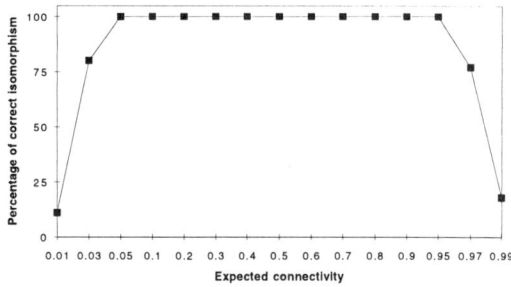

Figure 1: Percentage of correct isomorphisms obtained using the first-order (left) and the exponential (right) replicator equations, as a function of the expected connectivity.

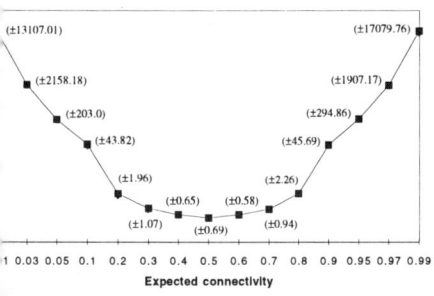
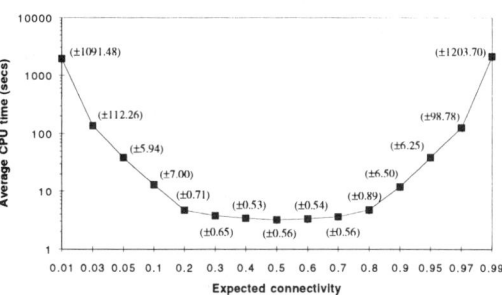

Figure 2: Average computational time taken by the first-order (left) and the exponential (right) replicator equations, as a function of the expected connectivity. The vertical axes are in logarithmic scale, and the numbers in parentheses represent the standard deviation.

guarantees that a maximum clique, and therefore a correct isomorphism, was found. The proportion of successes as a function of the expected connectivities for both replicator models is plotted in Fig. 1, whereas Fig. 2 shows the average CPU time taken by the two algorithms to converge (in logarithmic scale). Notice how the exponential replicator system (7) is dramatically faster and also performs better than the first-order model (5).

These results are significantly superior to those reported by Simić [20] who obtained poor results at connectivities less than 40% even on smaller graphs (i.e., up to 75 vertices). They also compare favorably with the results obtained more recently by Rangarajan et al. [18] on 100-vertex random graphs for connectivities up to 50%. Specifically, at 1% and 3% connectivities they report a percentage of correct isomorphisms of about 30% and 0%, respectively. Using our approach we obtained, on the same kind of graphs, a percentage of success of 80% and 11%, respectively. Rangarajan and Mjolsness [19] also ran experiments on 100-vertex random graphs with various connectivities, using a powerful Lagrangian relaxation network. Except for a few instances, they always obtained a correct solution. The computational time required by their model, however, turns out to largely exceed ours. As an example, the average time taken by their algorithm to match two 100-vertex 50%-connectivity graphs was about 30 minutes on an SGI workstation. As shown in Fig. 2, we obtained identical results in about 3 seconds.

It should be emphasized that all the algorithms mentioned above do incorporate sophisticated annealing mechanisms to escape from poor local minima. By contrast, in the presented work no attempt was made to prevent the algorithms from converging to such solutions.

Acknowledgments. This work has been done while the author was visiting the Department of Computer Science at the Yale University. Funding for this research has been provided by the Consiglio Nazionale delle Ricerche, Italy. The author would like to thank I. M. Bomze, A. Rangarajan, K. Siddiqi, and S. W. Zucker for many stimulating discussions.

References

[1] H. G. Barrow and R. M. Burstall, "Subgraph isomorphism, matching relational structures and maximal cliques," *Inform. Process. Lett.*, vol. 4, no. 4, pp. 83–84, 1976.

[2] L. E. Baum and J. A. Eagon, "An inequality with applications to statistical estimation for probabilistic functions of Markov processes and to a model for ecology," *Bull. Amer. Math. Soc.*, vol. 73, pp. 360–363, 1967.

[3] I. M. Bomze, "Evolution towards the maximum clique," *J. Global Optim.*, vol. 10, pp. 143–164, 1997.

[4] I. M. Bomze, M. Pelillo, and R. Giacomini, "Evolutionary approach to the maximum clique problem: Empirical evidence on a larger scale," in *Developments in Global Optimization*, I. M. Bomze et al., eds., Kluwer, The Netherlands, 1997, pp. 95–108.

[5] R. B. Boppana, J. Hastad, and S. Zachos, "Does co-NP have short interactive proofs?" *Inform. Process. Lett.*, vol. 25, pp. 127–132, 1987.

[6] M. R. Garey and D. S. Johnson, *Computers and Intractability: A Guide to the Theory of NP-Completeness*. Freeman, San Francisco, CA, 1979.

[7] L. E. Gibbons, D. W. Hearn, P. M. Pardalos, and M. V. Ramana, "Continuous characterizations of the maximum clique problem," *Math. Oper. Res.*, vol. 22, no. 3, pp. 754–768, 1997.

[8] J. Hofbauer, "Imitation dynamics for games," Collegium Budapest, preprint, 1995.

[9] J. Hofbauer and K. Sigmund, *The Theory of Evolution and Dynamical Systems*. Cambridge University Press, Cambridge, UK, 1988.

[10] J. J. Hopfield and D. W. Tank, "Neural computation of decisions in optimization problems," *Biol. Cybern.*, vol. 52, pp. 141–152, 1985.

[11] R. Kree and A. Zippelius, "Recognition of topological features of graphs and images in neural networks," *J. Phys. A: Math. Gen.*, vol. 21, pp. L813–L818, 1988.

[12] V. Losert and E. Akin, "Dynamics of games and genes: Discrete versus continuous time," *J. Math. Biol.*, vol. 17, pp. 241–251, 1983.

[13] T. S. Motzkin and E. G. Straus, "Maxima for graphs and a new proof of a theorem of Turán," *Canad. J. Math.*, vol. 17, pp. 533–540, 1965.

[14] M. Pelillo, "Relaxation labeling networks for the maximum clique problem," *J. Artif. Neural Networks*, vol. 2, no. 4, pp. 313–328, 1995.

[15] M. Pelillo, "Replicator equations, maximal cliques, and graph isomorphism," *Neural Computation*, to appear.

[16] M. Pelillo and A. Jagota, "Feasible and infeasible maxima in a quadratic program for maximum clique," *J. Artif. Neural Networks*, vol. 2, no. 4, pp. 411–420, 1995.

[17] M. Pelillo, K. Siddiqi, and S. W Zucker, "Matching hierarchical structures using association graphs," in *Computer Vision—ECCV'98, Vol. II*, H. Burkhardt and B. Neumann, eds., Springer-Verlag, Berlin, 1998, pp. 3–16.

[18] A. Rangarajan, S. Gold, and E. Mjolsness, "A novel optimizing network architecture with applications," *Neural Computation*, vol. 8, pp. 1041–1060, 1996.

[19] A. Rangarajan and E. Mjolsness, "A Lagrangian relaxation network for graph matching," *IEEE Trans. Neural Networks*, vol. 7, no. 6, pp. 1365–1381, 1996.

[20] P. D. Simić, "Constrained nets for graph matching and other quadratic assignment problems," *Neural Computation*, vol. 3, pp. 268–281, 1991.

[21] J. W. Weibull, *Evolutionary Game Theory*. MIT Press, Cambridge, MA, 1995.

Using Analytic QP and Sparseness to Speed Training of Support Vector Machines

John C. Platt
Microsoft Research
1 Microsoft Way
Redmond, WA 98052
jplatt@microsoft.com

Abstract

Training a Support Vector Machine (SVM) requires the solution of a very large quadratic programming (QP) problem. This paper proposes an algorithm for training SVMs: *Sequential Minimal Optimization*, or *SMO*. SMO breaks the large QP problem into a series of smallest possible QP problems which are analytically solvable. Thus, SMO does not require a numerical QP library. SMO's computation time is dominated by evaluation of the kernel, hence kernel optimizations substantially quicken SMO. For the MNIST database, SMO is 1.7 times as fast as PCG chunking; while for the UCI Adult database and linear SVMs, SMO can be 1500 times faster than the PCG chunking algorithm.

1 INTRODUCTION

In the last few years, there has been a surge of interest in Support Vector Machines (SVMs) [1]. SVMs have empirically been shown to give good generalization performance on a wide variety of problems. However, the use of SVMs is still limited to a small group of researchers. One possible reason is that training algorithms for SVMs are slow, especially for large problems. Another explanation is that SVM training algorithms are complex, subtle, and sometimes difficult to implement. This paper describes a new SVM learning algorithm that is easy to implement, often faster, and has better scaling properties than the standard SVM training algorithm. The new SVM learning algorithm is called Sequential Minimal Optimization (or SMO).

1.1 OVERVIEW OF SUPPORT VECTOR MACHINES

A general non-linear SVM can be expressed as

$$u = \sum_i \alpha_i y_i K(\vec{x}_i, \vec{x}) - b \qquad (1)$$

where u is the output of the SVM, K is a kernel function which measures the similarity of a stored training example $\vec{x}_i$ to the input $\vec{x}$, $y_i \in \{-1, +1\}$ is the desired output of the classifier, b is a threshold, and α_i are weights which blend the different kernels [1]. For linear SVMs, the kernel function K is linear, hence equation (1) can be expressed as

$$u = \vec{w} \cdot \vec{x} - b \qquad (2)$$

where $\vec{w} = \sum_i \alpha_i y_i \vec{x}_i$.

Training of an SVM consists of finding the α_i. The training is expressed as a minimization of a dual quadratic form:

$$\min_{\vec{\alpha}} \Psi(\alpha) = \min_{\vec{\alpha}} \frac{1}{2} \sum_{i=1}^{N} \sum_{j=1}^{N} y_i y_j K(\vec{x}_i, \vec{x}_j) \alpha_i \alpha_j - \sum_{i=1}^{N} \alpha_i, \qquad (3)$$

subject to box constraints,

$$0 \leq \alpha_i \leq C, \quad \forall i, \qquad (4)$$

and one linear equality constraint

$$\sum_{i=1}^{N} y_i \alpha_i = 0. \qquad (5)$$

The α_i are Lagrange multipliers of a primal quadratic programming (QP) problem: there is a one-to-one correspondence between each α_i and each training example $\vec{x}_i$.

Equations (3–5) form a QP problem that the SMO algorithm will solve. The SMO algorithm will terminate when all of the Karush-Kuhn-Tucker (KKT) optimality conditions of the QP problem are fulfilled. These KKT conditions are particularly simple:

$$\alpha_i = 0 \Rightarrow y_i u_i \geq 1, \quad 0 < \alpha_i < C \Rightarrow y_i u_i = 1, \quad \alpha_i = C \Rightarrow y_i u_i \leq 1, \qquad (6)$$

where u_i is the output of the SVM for the ith training example.

1.2 PREVIOUS METHODS FOR TRAINING SUPPORT VECTOR MACHINES

Due to its immense size, the QP problem that arises from SVMs cannot be easily solved via standard QP techniques. The quadratic form in (3) involves a Hessian matrix of dimension equal to the number of training examples. This matrix cannot be fit into 128 Megabytes if there are more than 4000 training examples.

Vapnik [9] describes a method to solve the SVM QP, which has since been known as "chunking." Chunking relies on the fact that removing training examples with $\alpha_i = 0$ does not change the solution. Chunking thus breaks down the large QP problem into a series of smaller QP sub-problems, whose object is to identify the training examples with non-zero α_i. Every QP sub-problem updates the subset of the α_i that are associated with the sub-problem, while leaving the rest of the α_i unchanged. The QP sub-problem consists of every non-zero α_i from the previous sub-problem combined with the M worst examples that violate the KKT conditions (6), for some M [1]. At the last step, the entire set of non-zero α_i has been identified, hence the last step solves the entire QP problem.

Chunking reduces the dimension of the matrix from the number of training examples to approximately the number of non-zero α_i. If standard QP techniques are used, chunking cannot handle large-scale training problems, because even this reduced matrix cannot fit into memory. Kaufman [3] has described a QP algorithm that does not require the storage of the entire Hessian.

The decomposition technique [6] is similar to chunking: decomposition breaks the large QP problem into smaller QP sub-problems. However, Osuna et al. [6] suggest keeping a

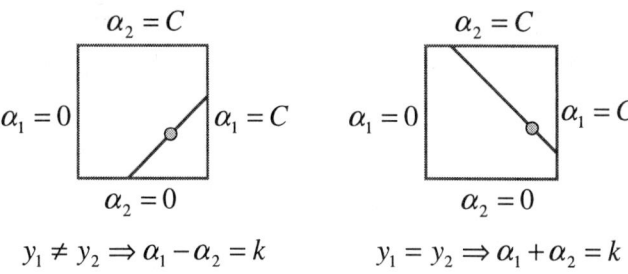

Figure 1: The Lagrange multipliers α_1 and α_2 must fulfill all of the constraints of the full problem. The inequality constraints cause the Lagrange multipliers to lie in the box. The linear equality constraint causes them to lie on a diagonal line.

fixed size matrix for every sub-problem, deleting some examples and adding others which violate the KKT conditions. Using a fixed-size matrix allows SVMs to be trained on very large training sets. Joachims [2] suggests adding and subtracting examples according to heuristics for rapid convergence. However, until SMO, decomposition required the use of a numerical QP library, which can be costly or slow.

2 SEQUENTIAL MINIMAL OPTIMIZATION

Sequential Minimal Optimization quickly solves the SVM QP problem without using numerical QP optimization steps at all. SMO decomposes the overall QP problem into fixed-size QP sub-problems, similar to the decomposition method [7].

Unlike previous methods, however, SMO chooses to solve the smallest possible optimization problem at each step. For the standard SVM, the smallest possible optimization problem involves two elements of $\vec{\alpha}$ because the $\vec{\alpha}$ must obey one linear equality constraint. At each step, SMO chooses two α_i to jointly optimize, finds the optimal values for these α_i, and updates the SVM to reflect these new values.

The advantage of SMO lies in the fact that solving for two α_i can be done analytically. Thus, numerical QP optimization is avoided entirely. The inner loop of the algorithm can be expressed in a short amount of C code, rather than invoking an entire QP library routine.

By avoiding numerical QP, the computation time is shifted from QP to kernel evaluation. Kernel evaluation time can be dramatically reduced in certain common situations, e.g., when a linear SVM is used, or when the input data is sparse (mostly zero). The result of kernel evaluations can also be cached in memory [1].

There are two components to SMO: an analytic method for solving for the two α_i, and a heuristic for choosing which multipliers to optimize. Pseudo-code for the SMO algorithm can be found in [8, 7], along with the relationship to other optimization and machine learning algorithms.

2.1 SOLVING FOR TWO LAGRANGE MULTIPLIERS

To solve for the two Lagrange multipliers α_1 and α_2, SMO first computes the constraints on these multipliers and then solves for the constrained minimum. For convenience, all quantities that refer to the first multiplier will have a subscript 1, while all quantities that refer to the second multiplier will have a subscript 2. Because there are only two multipliers, the constraints can easily be displayed in two dimensions (see figure 1). The constrained minimum of the objective function must lie on a diagonal line segment.

The ends of the diagonal line segment can be expressed quite simply in terms of α_2. Let $s = y_1 y_2$. The following bounds apply to α_2:

$$L = \max(0, \alpha_2 + s\alpha_1 - \frac{1}{2}(s+1)C), \qquad H = \min(C, \alpha_2 + s\alpha_1 - \frac{1}{2}(s-1)C). \quad (7)$$

Under normal circumstances, the objective function is positive definite, and there is a minimum along the direction of the linear equality constraint. In this case, SMO computes the minimum along the direction of the linear equality constraint:

$$\alpha_2^{\text{new}} = \alpha_2 + \frac{y_2(E_1 - E_2)}{K(\vec{x}_1, \vec{x}_1) + K(\vec{x}_2, \vec{x}_2) - 2K(\vec{x}_1, \vec{x}_2)}, \quad (8)$$

where $E_i = u_i - y_i$ is the error on the ith training example. As a next step, the constrained minimum is found by clipping α_2^{new} into the interval $[L, H]$. The value of α_1 is then computed from the new, clipped, α_2:

$$\alpha_1^{\text{new}} = \alpha_1 + s(\alpha_2 - \alpha_2^{\text{new,clipped}}). \quad (9)$$

For both linear and non-linear SVMs, the threshold b is re-computed after each step, so that the KKT conditions are fulfilled for both optimized examples.

2.2 HEURISTICS FOR CHOOSING WHICH MULTIPLIERS TO OPTIMIZE

In order to speed convergence, SMO uses heuristics to choose which two Lagrange multipliers to jointly optimize.

There are two separate choice heuristics: one for α_1 and one for α_2. The choice of α_1 provides the outer loop of the SMO algorithm. If an example is found to violate the KKT conditions by the outer loop, it is eligible for optimization. The outer loop alternates single passes through the entire training set with multiple passes through the non-bound α_i ($\alpha_i \neq \{0, C\}$). The multiple passes terminate when all of the non-bound examples obey the KKT conditions within ϵ. The entire SMO algorithm terminates when the entire training set obeys the KKT conditions within ϵ. Typically, $\epsilon = 10^{-3}$.

The first choice heuristic concentrates the CPU time on the examples that are most likely to violate the KKT conditions, i.e., the non-bound subset. As the SMO algorithm progresses, α_i that are at the bounds are likely to stay at the bounds, while α_i that are not at the bounds will move as other examples are optimized.

As a further optimization, SMO uses the shrinking heuristic proposed in [2]. After the pass through the entire training set, shrinking finds examples which fulfill the KKT conditions more than the worst example failed the KKT conditions. Further passes through the training set ignore these fulfilled conditions until a final pass at the end of training, which ensures that every example fulfills its KKT condition.

Once an α_1 is chosen, SMO chooses an α_2 to maximize the size of the step taken during joint optimization. SMO approximates the step size by the absolute value of the numerator in equation (8): $|E_1 - E_2|$. SMO keeps a cached error value E for every non-bound example in the training set and then chooses an error to approximately maximize the step size. If E_1 is positive, SMO chooses an example with minimum error E_2. If E_1 is negative, SMO chooses an example with maximum error E_2.

2.3 KERNEL OPTIMIZATIONS

Because the computation time for SMO is dominated by kernel evaluations, SMO can be accelerated by optimizing these kernel evaluations. Utilizing sparse inputs is a generally

Experiment	Kernel	Sparse Inputs Used	Kernel Caching Used	Training Set Size	Number of Support Vectors	C	% Sparse Inputs
AdultLin	Linear	Y	mix	11221	4158	0.05	89
AdultLinD	Linear	N	mix	11221	4158	0.05	0
WebLin	Linear	Y	mix	49749	1723	1	96
WebLinD	Linear	N	mix	49749	1723	1	0
AdultGaussK	Gaussian	Y	Y	11221	4206	1	89
AdultGauss	Gaussian	Y	N	11221	4206	1	89
AdultGaussKD	Gaussian	N	Y	11221	4206	1	0
AdultGaussD	Gaussian	N	N	11221	4206	1	0
WebGaussK	Gaussian	Y	Y	49749	4484	5	96
WebGauss	Gaussian	Y	N	49749	4484	5	96
WebGaussKD	Gaussian	N	Y	49749	4484	5	0
WebGaussD	Gaussian	N	N	49749	4484	5	0
MNIST	Polynom.	Y	N	60000	3450	100	81

Table 1: Parameters for various experiments

applicable kernel optimization. For commonly-used kernels, equations (1) and (2) can be dramatically sped up by exploiting the sparseness of the input. For example, a Gaussian kernel can be expressed as an exponential of a linear combination of sparse dot products. Sparsely storing the training set also achieves substantial reduction in memory consumption.

To compute a linear SVM, only a single weight vector needs to be stored, rather than all of the training examples that correspond to non-zero α_i. If the QP sub-problem succeeds, the stored weight vector is updated to reflect the new α_i values.

3 BENCHMARKING SMO

The SMO algorithm is tested against the standard chunking algorithm and against the decomposition method on a series of benchmarks. Both SMO and chunking are written in C++, using Microsoft's Visual C++ 6.0 compiler. Joachims' package SVM^{light} (version 2.01) with a default working set size of 10 is used to test the decomposition method. The CPU time of all algorithms are measured on an unloaded 266 MHz Pentium II processor running Windows NT 4.

The chunking algorithm uses the projected conjugate gradient algorithm as its QP solver, as suggested by Burges [1]. All algorithms use sparse dot product code and kernel caching, as appropriate [1, 2]. Both SMO and chunking share folded linear SVM code.

The SMO algorithm is tested on three real-world data sets. The results of the experiments are shown in Tables 1 and 2. Further tests on artificial data sets can be found in [8, 7].

The first test set is the UCI Adult data set [5]. The SVM is given 14 attributes of a census form of a household and asked to predict whether that household has an income greater than $50,000. Out of the 14 attributes, eight are categorical and six are continuous. The six continuous attributes are discretized into quintiles, yielding a total of 123 binary attributes.

The second test set is text categorization: classifying whether a web page belongs to a category or not. Each web page is represented as 300 sparse binary keywords attributes.

The third test set is the MNIST database of handwritten digits, from AT&T Research Labs [4]. One classifier of MNIST, class 8, is trained. The inputs are 784-dimensional

Experiment	SMO Time (sec)	SVM^{light} Time (sec)	Chunking Time (sec)	SMO Scaling Exponent	SVM^{light} Scaling Exponent	Chunking Scaling Exponent
AdultLin	**13.7**	217.9	20711.3	**1.8**	2.1	3.1
AdultLinD	**21.9**	n/a	21141.1	**1.0**	n/a	3.0
WebLin	**339.9**	3980.8	17164.7	**1.6**	2.2	2.5
WebLinD	**4589.1**	n/a	17332.8	**1.5**	n/a	2.5
AdultGaussK	442.4	**284.7**	11910.6	2.0	2.0	2.9
AdultGauss	**523.3**	737.5	n/a	2.0	2.0	n/a
AdultGaussKD	**1433.0**	n/a	14740.4	**2.5**	n/a	2.8
AdultGaussD	1810.2	n/a	n/a	2.0	n/a	n/a
WebGaussK	**2477.9**	2949.5	23877.6	**1.6**	2.0	2.0
WebGauss	**2538.0**	6923.5	n/a	**1.6**	1.8	n/a
WebGaussKD	**23365.3**	n/a	50371.9	2.6	n/a	**2.0**
WebGaussD	24758.0	n/a	n/a	1.6	n/a	n/a
MNIST	**19387.9**	38452.3	33109.0	n/a	n/a	n/a

Table 2: Timings of algorithms on various data sets.

non-binary vectors and are stored as sparse vectors. A fifth-order polynomial kernel is used to match the AT&T accuracy results.

The Adult set and the Web set are trained both with linear SVMs and Gaussian SVMs with variance of 10. For the Adult and Web data sets, the C parameter is chosen to optimize accuracy on a validation set. Experiments on the Adult and Web sets are performed with and without sparse inputs and with and without kernel caching, in order to determine the effect these kernel optimizations have on computation time. When a kernel cache is used, the cache size for SMO and SVM^{light} is 40 megabytes. The chunking algorithm always uses kernel caching: matrix values from the previous QP step are re-used. For the linear experiments, SMO does not use kernel caching, while SVM^{light} does.

In Table 2, the scaling of each algorithm is measured as a function of the training set size, which is varied by taking random nested subsets of the full training set. A line is fitted to the log of the training time versus the log of the set size. The slope of the line is an empirical scaling exponent.

4 CONCLUSIONS

As can be seen in Table 2, standard PCG chunking is slower than SMO for the data sets shown, even for dense inputs. Decomposition and SMO have the advantage, over standard PCG chunking, of ignoring the examples whose Lagrange multipliers are at C. This advantage is reflected in the scaling exponents for PCG chunking versus SMO and SVM^{light}. PCG chunking can be altered to have a similar property [3]. Notice that PCG chunking uses the same sparse dot product code and linear SVM folding code as SMO. However, these optimizations do not speed up PCG chunking due to the overhead of numerically solving large QP sub-problems.

SMO and SVM^{light} are similar: they decompose the large QP problem into very small QP sub-problems. SMO decomposes into even smaller sub-problems: it uses analytical solutions of two-dimensional sub-problems, while SVM^{light} uses numerical QP to solve 10-dimensional sub-problems. The difference in timings between the two methods is partly due to the numerical QP overhead, but mostly due to the difference in heuristics and kernel optimizations. For example, SMO is faster than SVM^{light} by an order of magnitude on linear problems, due to linear SVM folding. However, SVM^{light} can also potentially use linear SVM folding. In these experiments, SMO uses a very simple least-recently-used kernel cache of Hessian rows, while SVM^{light} uses a more complex kernel cache and modifies its heuristics to utilize the kernel effectively [2]. Therefore, SMO does not benefit from the kernel cache at the largest problem sizes, while SVM^{light} speeds up by a factor of 2.5.

Utilizing sparseness to compute kernels yields a large advantage for SMO due to the lack of heavy numerical QP overhead. For the sparse data sets shown, SMO can speed up by a factor of between 3 and 13, while PCG chunking only obtained a maximum speed up of 2.1 times.

The MNIST experiments were performed without a kernel cache, because the MNIST data set takes up most of the memory of the benchmark machine. Due to sparse inputs, SMO is a factor of 1.7 faster than PCG chunking, even though none of the Lagrange multipliers are at C. On a machine with more memory, SVM^{light} would be as fast or faster than SMO for MNIST, due to kernel caching.

In summary, SMO is a simple method for training support vector machines which does not require a numerical QP library. Because its CPU time is dominated by kernel evaluation, SMO can be dramatically quickened by the use of kernel optimizations, such as linear SVM folding and sparse dot products. SMO can be anywhere from 1.7 to 1500 times faster than the standard PCG chunking algorithm, depending on the data set.

Acknowledgements

Thanks to Chris Burges for running data sets through his projected conjugate gradient code and for various helpful suggestions.

References

[1] C. J. C. Burges. A tutorial on support vector machines for pattern recognition. *Data Mining and Knowledge Discovery*, 2(2), 1998.

[2] T. Joachims. Making large-scale SVM learning practical. In B. Schölkopf, C. J. C. Burges, and A. J. Smola, editors, *Advances in Kernel Methods — Support Vector Learning*, pages 169–184. MIT Press, 1998.

[3] L. Kaufman. Solving the quadratic programming problem arising in support vector classification. In B. Schölkopf, C. J. C. Burges, and A. J. Smola, editors, *Advances in Kernel Methods — Support Vector Learning*, pages 147–168. MIT Press, 1998.

[4] Y. LeCun. MNIST handwritten digit database. Available on the web at http://www.research.att.com/~yann/ocr/mnist/.

[5] C. J. Merz and P. M. Murphy. UCI repository of machine learning databases, 1998. [http://www.ics.uci.edu/~mlearn/MLRepository.html]. Irvine, CA: University of California, Department of Information and Computer Science.

[6] E. Osuna, R. Freund, and F. Girosi. Improved training algorithm for support vector machines. In *Proc. IEEE Neural Networks in Signal Processing '97*, 1997.

[7] J. C. Platt. Fast training of SVMs using sequential minimal optimization. In B. Schölkopf, C. J. C. Burges, and A. J. Smola, editors, *Advances in Kernel Methods — Support Vector Learning*, pages 185–208. MIT Press, 1998.

[8] J. C. Platt. Sequential minimal optimization: A fast algorithm for training support vector machines. Technical Report MSR–TR–98–14, Microsoft Research, 1998. Available at http://www.research.microsoft.com/~jplatt/smo.html.

[9] V. Vapnik. *Estimation of Dependences Based on Empirical Data*. Springer-Verlag, 1982.

Regularizing AdaBoost

Gunnar Rätsch, Takashi Onoda*, Klaus R. Müller
GMD FIRST, Rudower Chaussee 5, 12489 Berlin, Germany
{raetsch, onoda, klaus}@first.gmd.de

Abstract

Boosting methods maximize a hard classification margin and are known as powerful techniques that do not exhibit overfitting for low noise cases. Also for noisy data boosting will try to enforce a hard margin and thereby give too much weight to outliers, which then leads to the dilemma of non-smooth fits and overfitting. Therefore we propose three algorithms to allow for soft margin classification by introducing regularization with slack variables into the boosting concept: (1) AdaBoost$_{reg}$ and regularized versions of (2) linear and (3) quadratic programming AdaBoost. Experiments show the usefulness of the proposed algorithms in comparison to another soft margin classifier: the support vector machine.

1 Introduction

Boosting and other ensemble methods have been used with success in several applications, e.g. OCR [13, 8]. For **low noise** cases several lines of explanation have been proposed as candidates for explaining the well functioning of boosting methods. (a) Breiman proposed that during boosting also a "bagging effect" takes place [3] which reduces the variance and effectively limits the capacity of the system and (b) Freund et al. [12] show that boosting classifies with large margins, since the error function of boosting can be written as a function of the margin and every boosting step tries to minimize this function by maximizing the margin [9, 11].

Recently, studies with **noisy** patterns have shown that boosting does indeed overfit on noisy data, this holds for boosted decision trees [10], RBF nets [11] and also other kinds of classifiers (e.g. [7]). So it is clearly a myth that boosting methods will not overfit. The fact that boosting is trying to maximize the margin, is exactly also the argument that can be used to understand why boosting must necessarily overfit for noisy patterns or overlapping distributions and we give asymptotic arguments for this statement in section 3. Because the hard margin (smallest margin in the trainings set) plays a central role in causing overfitting, we propose to relax the hard margin classification and allow for misclassifications by using the soft margin classifier concept that has been applied to support vector machines successfully [5].

---

*permanent address: Communication & Information Research Lab. CRIEPI, 2-11-1 Iwado kita, Komae-shi, Tokyo 201-8511, Japan.

Our view is that the margin concept is central for the understanding of both support vector machines and boosting methods. So far it is not clear what the optimal margin distribution should be that a learner has to achieve for optimal classification in the noisy case. For data without noise a hard margin might be the best choice. However, for noisy data there is always the trade-off in believing in the data or mistrusting it, as the very data point could be an outlier. In general (e.g. neural network) learning strategies this leads to the introduction of regularization which reflects the prior that we have about a problem. We will also introduce a regularization strategy (analogous to weight decay) into boosting. This strategy uses slack variables to achieve a soft margin (section 4). Numerical experiments show the validity of our regularization approach in section 5 and finally a brief conclusion is given.

2 AdaBoost Algorithm

Let $\{h_t(\mathbf{x}) : t = 1, \ldots, T\}$ be an ensemble of T hypotheses defined on input vector $\mathbf{x}$ and $\mathbf{c} = [c_1 \ldots c_T]$ their weights satisfying $c_t > 0$ and $|\mathbf{c}| = \sum_t c_t = 1$. In the binary classification case, the output is one of two class labels, i.e. $h_t(\mathbf{x}) = \pm 1$. The ensemble generates the label which is the weighted majority of the votes: $\text{sgn}\left(\sum_t c_t h_t(\mathbf{x})\right)$. In order to train this ensemble of T hypotheses $\{h_t(\mathbf{x})\}$ and $\mathbf{c}$, several algorithms have been proposed: bagging, where the weighting is simply $c_t = 1/T$ [2] and AdaBoost/Arcing, where the weighting scheme is more complicated [12]. In the following we give a brief description of AdaBoost/Arcing. We use a special form of Arcing, which is equivalent to AdaBoost [4]. In the binary classification case we define the margin for an input-output pair $\mathbf{z}_i = (\mathbf{x}_i, y_i), i = 1, \ldots, l$ by

$$mg(\mathbf{z}_i, \mathbf{c}) = y_i \sum_{t=1}^{T} c_t h_t(\mathbf{x}_i), \qquad (1)$$

which is between -1 and 1, if $|\mathbf{c}| = 1$. The correct class is predicted, if the margin at $\mathbf{z}$ is positive. When the positivity of the margin value increases, the decision correctness becomes larger. AdaBoost maximizes the margin by (asymptotically) minimizing a function of the margin $mg(\mathbf{z}_i, \mathbf{c})$ [9, 11]

$$g(\mathbf{b}) = \sum_{i=1}^{l} \exp\left\{-\frac{|\mathbf{b}|}{2} mg(\mathbf{z}_i, \mathbf{c})\right\}, \qquad (2)$$

where $\mathbf{b} = [b_1 \ldots b_T]$ and $|\mathbf{b}| = \sum_t b_t$ (starting from $\mathbf{b} = 0$). Note that b_t is the unnormalized weighting of the hypothesis h_t, whereas $\mathbf{c}$ is simply a normalized version of $\mathbf{b}$, i.e. $\mathbf{c} = \mathbf{b}/|\mathbf{b}|$. In order to find the hypothesis h_t the learning examples $\mathbf{z}_i$ are weighted in each iteration t with $w_t(\mathbf{z}_i)$. Using a bootstrap on this weighted sample we train h_t; alternatively a weighted error function can be used (e.g. weighted MSE). The weights $w_t(\mathbf{z}_i)$ are computed according to[1]

$$w_t(\mathbf{z}_i) = \frac{\exp\{-|\mathbf{b}_{t-1}|mg(\mathbf{z}_i, \mathbf{c}_{t-1})/2\}}{\sum_{j=1}^{l} \exp\{-|\mathbf{b}_{t-1}|mg(\mathbf{z}_j, \mathbf{c}_{t-1})/2\}} \qquad (3)$$

and the training error ϵ_t of h_t is computed as $\epsilon_t = \sum_{i=1}^{l} w_t(\mathbf{z}_i) I(y_i \neq h_t(\mathbf{x}_i))$, where $I(true) = 1$ and $I(false) = 0$. For each given hypothesis h_t we have to find a weight b_t, such that $g(\mathbf{b})$ is minimized. One can optimize this parameter by a line search

---
[1] This direct way for computing the weights is equivalent to the update rule of AdaBoost.

or directly by analytic minimization [4], which gives $b_t = \log(1 - \epsilon_t) - \log \epsilon_t$. Interestingly, we can write

$$w_t(\mathbf{z}_i) = \frac{\partial g(\mathbf{b}_{t-1})/\partial mg(\mathbf{z}_i, \mathbf{b}_{t-1})}{\sum_{j=1}^{l} \partial g(\mathbf{b}_{t-1})/\partial mg(\mathbf{z}_j, \mathbf{b}_{t-1})}, \quad (4)$$

as a gradient of $g(\mathbf{b}_{t-1})$ with respect to the margins. The weighted minimization with $w_t(\mathbf{z}_i)$ will give a hypothesis h_t which is an approximation to the best possible hypothesis h_t^* that would be obtained by minimizing g directly. Note that, the weighted minimization (bootstrap, weighted LS) will not necessarily give h_t^*, even if ϵ_t is minimized [11]. AdaBoost is therefore an *approximate* gradient descent method which minimizes g asymptotically.

3 Hard margins

A decrease of $g(\mathbf{c}, |\mathbf{b}|) := g(\mathbf{b})$ is predominantly achieved by improvements of the margin $mg(\mathbf{z}_i, \mathbf{c})$. If the margin $mg(\mathbf{z}_i, \mathbf{c})$ is negative, then the error $g(\mathbf{c}, |\mathbf{b}|)$ takes clearly a big value, which is additionally amplified by $|\mathbf{b}|$. So, AdaBoost tries to decrease the negative margin efficiently to improve the error $g(\mathbf{c}, |\mathbf{b}|)$.

Now, let us consider the asymptotic case, where the number of iterations and therefore also $|\mathbf{b}|$ take large values [9]. In this case, when the values of all $mg(\mathbf{z}_i, \mathbf{c}), i = 1, \cdots, l$, are almost the same but have small differences, these differences are amplified strongly in $g(\mathbf{c}, |\mathbf{b}|)$. Obviously the function $g(\mathbf{c}, |\mathbf{b}|)$ is asymptotically very sensitive to small differences between margins. Therefore, the margins $mg(\mathbf{z}_i, \mathbf{c})$ of the training patterns from the margin area (boundary area between classes) should asymptotically converge to the same value. From Eq. (3), when $|\mathbf{b}|$ takes a very big value, AdaBoost learning becomes a "hard competition" case: only the pattern with smallest margin will get high weights, the other patterns are effectively neglected in the learning process. In order to confirm that the above reasoning is correct, Fig. 1 shows margin distributions after 10^4 AdaBoost iterations for a toy example [9] at different noise levels generated by uniform distribution $U(0.0, \sigma^2)$ (left). From this figure, it becomes apparent that the margin distribution asymptotically makes a step at a fixed size of the margin for training patterns which are in the margin area. In previous studies [9, 11] we observed that those patterns exhibit a large overlap to support vectors in support vector machines. The numerical results support our theoretical asymptotic analysis. The property of AdaBoost to produce a big margin area (no pattern in the area, i.e. a hard margin), will not always lead to the best generalization ability (cf. [5, 11]). This is especially true,

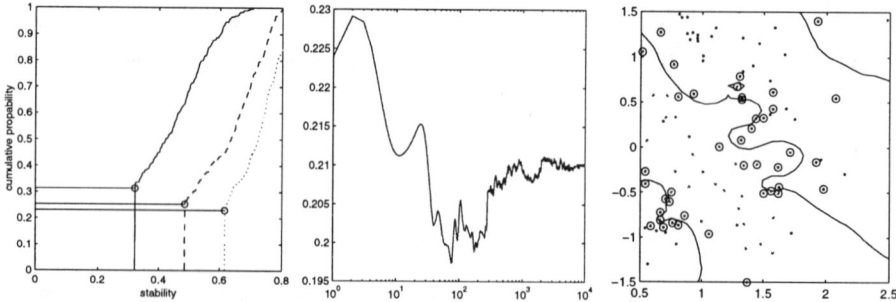

Figure 1: Margin distributions for AdaBoost (left) for different noise levels (σ^2 = 0%(dotted), 9%(dashed), 16%(solid)) with fixed number of RBF-centers for the base hypothesis and typical overfitting behaviour in the generalization error as a function of the number of iterations (middle) and a typical decision line (right) generated by AdaBoost using RBF networks in the case with noise (here: 30 centers and $\sigma^2 = 16\%$; smoothed)

if the training patterns have classification or input noise. In our experiments with noisy data, we often observed that AdaBoost made overfitting (for a high number of boosting iterations). Fig. 1 (middle) shows a typical overfitting behaviour in the generalization error for AdaBoost: after only 80 boosting iterations the best generalization performance is already achieved. Quinlan [10] and Grove et al. [7] also observed overfitting and that the generalization performance of AdaBoost is often worse than that of the single classifier, if the data has classification noise.

The first reason for overfitting is the increasing value of $|\mathbf{b}|$: noisy patterns (e.g. bad labelled) can asymptotically have an "unlimited" influence to the decision line leading to overfitting (cf. Eq. (3)). Another reason is the classification with a hard margin, which also means that all training patterns will asymptotically be correctly classified (without any capacity limitation!). In the presence of noise this will certainly be not the right concept, because the best decision line (e.g. Bayes) usually will not give a training error of zero. So, the achievement of large hard margins for noisy data will produce hypotheses which are too complex for the problem.

4 How to get Soft Margins

Changing AdaBoost's error function   In order to avoid overfitting, we introduce slack variables, which are similar to those of the support vector algorithm [5, 14], into AdaBoost.

We know that all training patterns will get non-negative stabilities after many iterations(see Fig. 1(left)), i.e. $mg(\mathbf{z}_i, \mathbf{c}) \geq \rho$ for all $i = 1, \ldots, l$, where ρ is the minimum margin of the patterns. Due to this fact, AdaBoost often produces high weights for the difficult training patterns by enforcing a non-negative margin $\rho \geq 0$ (for every pattern including outliers) and this property will eventually lead to overfitting, as observed in Fig. 1. Therefore, we introduce some variables ξ_i - the slack variables - and get

$$mg(\mathbf{z}_i, \mathbf{c}) \geq \rho - C\xi_i^t, \quad \xi_i^t > 0. \quad (5)$$

In these inequalities, ξ_i^t are positive and if a training pattern has high weights in the previous iterations, the ξ_i^t should be increasing. In this way, for example, we do not force outliers to be classified according to their possibly wrong labels, but we allow for some errors. In this sense we get a trade-off between the margin and the importance of a pattern in the training process (depending on the constant $C \geq 0$). If we choose $C = 0$ in Eq. (5), the original AdaBoost algorithm is retrieved. If C is chosen too high, the data is not taken seriously. We adopt a prior on the weights $w_r(\mathbf{z}_i)$ that punishes large weights in analogy to weight decay and choose

$$\xi_i^t = \left(\sum_{r=1}^{t} c_r w_r(\mathbf{z}_i) \right)^2, \quad (6)$$

where the inner sum is the cumulative weight of the pattern in the previous iterations (we call it *influence* of a pattern – similar to Lagrange multipliers in SVMs). By this ξ_i^t, AdaBoost is not changed for easy classifiable patterns, but is changed for difficult patterns. From Eq. (5), we can derive a new error function:

$$\tilde{g}_{reg}(\mathbf{c}_t, |\mathbf{b}_t|) = \sum_{i=1}^{l} \exp\left\{ -\frac{|\mathbf{b}_t|}{2} mg(\mathbf{z}_i, \mathbf{c_t}) - C\xi_i^t \right\} \quad (7)$$

By this error function, we can control the trade-off between the weights, which the pattern had in the last iterations, and the achieved margin. The weight $w_t(\mathbf{z}_i)$ of a pattern is computed as the derivative of Eq. (7) subject to $mg(\mathbf{z}_i, \mathbf{b}^{t-1})$ (cf. Eq. (4)) and is given by

$$w_t(\mathbf{z}_i) = \frac{\exp\left\{ |\mathbf{b}_{t-1}|(mg(\mathbf{z}_i, c_{t-1}) - \xi_i^{t-1})/2 \right\}}{\sum_{j=1}^{l} \exp\left\{ |\mathbf{b}_{t-1}|(mg(\mathbf{z}_j, c_{t-1}) - \xi_j^{t-1})/2 \right\}}. \quad (8)$$

Table 1: Pseudocode description of the algorithms

LP-AdaBoost(Z,T)	**LP$_{reg}$-AdaBoost(Z,T,C)**	**QP$_{reg}$-AdaBoost(Z,T,C)**
Run AdaBoost on dataset **Z** to get T hypotheses **h** and their weights **c**		
Construct loss matrix $L_{i,t} = \begin{cases} -1 & \text{if } h_t(\mathbf{x}_i) \neq y_i \\ 1 & \text{otherwise} \end{cases}$		
minimize $-\rho$	minimize $-\rho + C \sum_i \xi_i$	minimize $\|\mathbf{b}\|^2 + C \sum_i \xi_i$
s.t. $\sum_{t=1}^{T} c_t L_{i,t} \geq \rho$ $c_t \geq 0, \sum c_t = 1$	s.t. $\sum_{t=1}^{T} c_t L_{i,t} \geq \rho + \xi_i$ $c_t \geq 0, \sum c_t = 1$ $\xi_i \geq 0$	s.t. $\sum_{t=1}^{T} b_t L_{i,t} \geq 1 - \xi_i$ $b_t \geq 0$ $\xi_i \geq 0$

Thus we can get an update rule for the weight of a training pattern [11]

$$w_t(\mathbf{z}_i) = w_{t-1}(\mathbf{z}_i) \exp\{b_{t-1} I(y_i \neq h_{t-1}(\mathbf{x}_i)) + C\xi_i^{t-2}|\mathbf{b}_{t-2}| - C\xi_i^{t-1}|\mathbf{b}_{t-1}|\}. \quad (9)$$

It is more difficult to compute the weight b_t of the t-th hypothesis analytically. However, we can get b_t by a line search procedure over Eq. (7), which has an unique solution because $\frac{\partial}{\partial b_t} g_{reg} > 0$ is satisfied. This line search can be implemented very efficiently. With this line-search, we can now also use real-valued outputs of the base hypotheses, while the original AdaBoost algorithm could not (cf. also [6]).

Optimizing a given ensemble In Grove et al. [7], it was shown how to use linear programming to maximize the minimum margin for a given ensemble and LP-AdaBoost was proposed (table 1 left). This algorithm maximizes the minimum margin on the training patterns. It achieves a hard margin (as AdaBoost asymptotically does) for small number of iterations. For the reasoning for a hard margin (section 3) this can not generalize well. If we introduce slack variables to LP-AdaBoost, one gets the algorithm LP$_{reg}$-AdaBoost (table 1 middle) [11]. This modification allows that some patterns have lower margins than ρ (especially lower than 0). There is a trade-off: (a) make all margins bigger than ρ and (b) maximize ρ. This trade-off is controlled by the constant C.

Another formulation of a optimization problem can be derived from the support vector algorithm. The optimization objective of a SVM is to find a function $h^{\mathbf{w}}$ which minimizes a functional of the form $E = \|\mathbf{w}\|^2 + C \sum_i \xi_i$, where $y_i h(\mathbf{x}_i) \geq 1 - \xi_i$ and the norm of the parameter vector $\mathbf{w}$ is the measure for the complexity of the hypothesis $h^{\mathbf{w}}$ [14]. For ensemble learning we do not have such a measure of complexity and so we use the norm of the hypotheses weight vector $\mathbf{b}$. For $|\mathbf{b}| = 1$ this is a small value, if the elements are approximately equal (analogy to bagging) and has high values, when there are some strongly emphasized hypotheses (far away from bagging). Experimentally, we found that $\|\mathbf{b}\|^2$ is often larger for more complex hypothesis. Thus, we can apply the optimization principles of SVMs to AdaBoost and get the algorithm QP$_{reg}$-AdaBoost (table 1 right). We effectively use a linear SVM on top of the results of the base hypotheses.

5 Experiments

In order to evaluate the performance of our new algorithms, we make a comparison among the single RBF classifier, the original AdaBoost algorithm, AdaBoost$_{reg}$ (with RBF nets), L/QP$_{reg}$-AdaBoost and a Support Vector Machine (with RBF kernel). We use ten artificial and real world datasets from the UCI and DELVE benchmark repositories: banana (toy dataset as in [9, 11]), breast cancer, image segment, ringnorm, flare sonar, splice, new-thyroid, titanic, twonorm, waveform. Some of the problems are originally not binary classification problems, hence a (random) partition into two classes was used. At first we generate 20 partitions into training and test set (mostly $\approx$ 60% : 40%). On each partition we train the classifier and get its test set error. The performance is averaged and we get table 2.

Regularizing AdaBoost

Table 2: Comparison among the six methods: Single RBF classifier, AdaBoost(AB), AdaBoost$_{reg}$(AB$_{reg}$), L/QP$_{reg}$-AdaBoost (L/QPR) and a Support Vector Machine(SVM): Estimation of generalization error in % on 10 datasets (best method in bold face). Clearly, AdaBoost$_{reg}$ gives the best overall performance. For further explanation see text.

	RBF	AB	AB$_{reg}$	LPR	QPR	SVM
Banana	10.9±0.5	12.3±0.7	**10.7±0.5**	10.8±0.4	10.9±0.5	11.5±4.7
Cancer	28.7±5.3	30.5±4.5	26.3±4.3	31.0±4.2	26.2±4.7	**26.1±4.8**
Image	2.8±0.7	2.5±0.7	2.5±0.7	2.6±0.6	**2.4±0.5**	2.9±0.7
Ringnorm	1.7±0.3	2.0±0.2	1.7±0.2	2.2±0.4	1.9±0.2	**1.7±0.1**
FSonar	34.6±2.1	35.6±1.9	33.6±1.7	35.7±4.5	36.2±1.7	**32.5±1.7**
Splice	10.0±0.3	10.1±0.3	**9.5±0.2**	10.2±1.6	10.1±0.5	10.9±0.7
Thyroid	4.8±2.4	**4.4±1.9**	4.4±2.1	4.4±2.0	4.4±2.2	4.8±2.2
Titanic	23.4±1.7	22.7±1.2	22.5±1.0	22.9±1.9	22.7±1.0	**22.4±1.0**
Twonorm	2.8±0.2	3.1±0.3	**2.7±2.1**	3.4±0.6	3.0±0.3	3.0±0.2
Waveform	10.7±1.0	10.8±0.4	9.9±0.9	10.6±1.0	10.1±0.5	**9.8±0.3**
Mean %	6.7	9.6	1.0	11.1	4.7	6.3
Winner %	16.4	8.2	28.5	15.0	15.3	16.6

We used RBF nets with adaptive centers (some conjugate gradient iterations to optimize positions and widths of the centers) as base hypotheses as described in [1, 11]. In all experiments, we combined 200 hypotheses. Clearly, this number of hypotheses may be not optimal, however Adaboost with optimal early stopping is not better than AdaBoost$_{reg}$. The parameter C of the regularized versions of AdaBoost and the parameters (C, σ) of the SVM are optimized by the first five training datasets. On each training set 5-fold-cross validation is used to find the best model for this dataset[2]. Finally, the model parameters are computed as the median of the five estimations. This way of estimating the parameters is surely not possible in practice, but will make this comparison more robust and the results more reliable. The last but one line in Tab. 2 shows the line 'Mean %', which is computed as follows: For each dataset the average error rate of all classifier types are divided by the minimum error rate and 1 is subtracted. These resulting numbers are averaged over the 10 datasets. The last line shows the probabilities that a method wins, i.e. gives the smallest generalization error, on the basis of our experiments (averaged over all ten datasets). Our experiments on noisy data show that (a) the results of AdaBoost are in almost all cases worse than the single classifier (clear overfitting effect) and (b) the results of AdaBoost$_{reg}$ are in all cases (much) better than those of AdaBoost and better than that of the single classifier. Furthermore, we see clearly, that (c) the single classifier wins as often as the SVM, (d) L/QP$_{reg}$-AdaBoost improves the results of AdaBoost, (e) AdaBoost$_{reg}$ wins most often. L/QP$_{reg}$-AdaBoost improves the results of AdaBoost in almost cases due to established the soft margin. But the results are not as good as the results of AdaBoost$_{reg}$ and the SVM, because the hypotheses generated by AdaBoost (aimed to construct a hard margin) may be not the appropriate ones generate a good soft margin. We also observe that quadratic programming gives slightly better results than linear programming. This may be due to the fact that the hypotheses coefficients generated by LP$_{reg}$-AdaBoost are more sparse (smaller ensemble). Bigger ensembles may have a better generalization ability (due to the reduction of variance [3]). The worse performance of SVM compared to AdaBoost$_{reg}$ and the unexpected tie between SVM and RBF net may be explained with (a) the fixed σ of the RBF-kernel (loosing multi-scale information), (b) coarse model selection, (c) worse error function of the SV algorithm (noise model). Sumarizing, AdaBoost is useful for low noise cases, where the classes are separable (as shown for OCR[13, 8]). AdaBoost$_{reg}$ extends the applicability of boosting to "difficult separable" cases and should be applied, if the data is noisy.

---

[2]The parameters are only near-optimal. Only 10 values for each parameter are tested.

6 Conclusion

We introduced three algorithms to alleviate the overfitting problems of boosting algorithms for high noise data: (1) direct incorporation of the regularization term into the error function (Eq.(7)), use of (2) linear and (3) quadratic programming with constraints given by the slack variables. The essence of our proposal is to introduce slack variables for regularization in order to allow for soft margin classification in contrast to the hard margin classification used before. The slack variables basically allow to control how much we trust the data, so we are permitted to ignore outliers which would otherwise have spoiled our classification. This generalization is very much in the spirit of support vector machines that also trade-off the maximization of the margin and the minimization of the classification errors in the slack variables. In our experiments, $AdaBoost_{reg}$ showed a better overall generalization performance than all other algorithms including the Support Vector Machines. We conjecture that this unexpected result is mostly due to the fact that SVM can only use one σ and therefore loose scaling information. AdaBoost does not have this limitation.

So far we balance our trust in the data and the margin maximization by cross validation. Better would be, if we knew the "optimal" margin distribution that we could achieve for classifying noisy patterns, then we could of course balance the errors and the margin sizes optimally.

In future works, we plan to establish more connections between AdaBoost and SVM.

Acknowledgements: We thank for valuable discussions with A. Smola, B. Schölkopf, T. Frieß and D. Schuurmans. Partial funding from EC STORM project grant number 25387 is greatfully acknowledged. The breast cancer domain was obtained from the University Medical Centre, Inst. of Oncology, Ljubljana, Yugoslavia. Thanks go to M. Zwitter and M. Soklic for providing the data.

References

[1] C. M. Bishop. *Neural Networks for Pattern Recognition*. Clarendon, 1995.
[2] L. Breiman. Bagging predictors. *Machine Learning*, 26(2):123–140, 1996.
[3] L. Breiman. Arcing classifiers. Tech.Rep. 460, Berkeley Stat.Dept., 1997.
[4] L. Breiman. Prediction games and arcing algorithms. Tech.Rep. 504, Berkeley Stat.Dept., 1997.
[5] C. Cortes, V. Vapnik. Support vector network. *Mach.Learn.*, 20:273–297, 1995.
[6] R. Schapire, Y. Singer. Improved Boosting Algorithms Using Confidence-rated Predictions. In *Proc. of COLT'98*.
[7] A.J. Grove, D. Schuurmans. Boosting in the limit: Maximizing the margin of learned ensembles. In *Proc. 15th Nat. Conf. on AI*, 1998. To appear.
[8] Y. LeCun et al. Learning algorithms for classification: A comparism on handwritten digit recognistion. *Neural Networks*, pages 261–276, 1995.
[9] T. Onoda, G. Rätsch, and K.-R. Müller. An asymptotic analysis of adaboost in the binary classification case. In *Proc. of ICANN'98*, April 1998.
[10] J. Quinlan. Boosting first-order learning. In *Proc. of the 7th Internat. Workshop on Algorithmic Learning Theory, LNAI*, 1160, 143–155. Springer.
[11] G. Rätsch. Soft Margins for AdaBoost. August 1998. Royal Holloway College, Technical Report NC-TR-1998-021. Submitted to Machine Learning.
[12] R. Schapire, Y. Freund, P. Bartlett, W. Lee. Boosting the margin: A new explanation for the effectiveness of voting methods. *Mach.Learn.*, 148–156, 1998.
[13] H. Schwenk and Y. Bengio. Adaboosting neural networks: Application to online character recognition. In *ICANN'97*, LNCS, 1327, 967–972, 1997. Springer.
[14] V. Vapnik. *The Nature of Statistical Learning Theory*. Springer, 1995.

Boxlets: a Fast Convolution Algorithm for Signal Processing and Neural Networks

Patrice Y. Simard[*], Léon Bottou, Patrick Haffner and Yann LeCun
AT&T Labs-Research
100 Schultz Drive, Red Bank, NJ 07701-7033
patrice@microsoft.com
{leonb,haffner,yann}@research.att.com

Abstract

Signal processing and pattern recognition algorithms make extensive use of convolution. In many cases, computational accuracy is not as important as computational speed. In feature extraction, for instance, the features of interest in a signal are usually quite distorted. This form of noise justifies some level of quantization in order to achieve faster feature extraction. Our approach consists of approximating regions of the signal with low degree polynomials, and then differentiating the resulting signals in order to obtain impulse functions (or derivatives of impulse functions). With this representation, convolution becomes extremely simple and can be implemented quite effectively. The true convolution can be recovered by integrating the result of the convolution. This method yields substantial speed up in feature extraction and is applicable to convolutional neural networks.

1 Introduction

In pattern recognition, convolution is an important tool because of its translation invariance properties. Feature extraction is a typical example: The distance between a small pattern (i.e. feature) is computed at all positions (i.e. translations) inside a larger one. The resulting "distance image" is typically obtained by convolving the feature template with the larger pattern. In the remainder of this paper we will use the terms image and pattern interchangeably (because of the topology implied by translation invariance).

There are many ways to convolve images efficiently. For instance, a multiplication of images of the same size in the Fourier domain corresponds to a convolution of the two images in the original space. Of course this requires $KN \log N$ operations (where N is the number of pixels of the image and K is a constant) just to go in and out of the Fourier domain. These methods are usually not appropriate for feature extraction because the feature to be extracted is small with respect to the image. For instance, if the image and the feature have respectively 32×32 and 5×5 pixels,

---

[*] Now with Microsoft, One Microsoft Way, Redmond, WA 98052

the full convolution can be done in 25 × 1024 multiply-adds. In contrast, it would require $2 \times K \times 1024 \times 10$ to go in and out of the Fourier domain.

Fortunately, in most pattern recognition applications, the interesting features are already quite distorted when they appear in real images. Because of this inherent noise, the feature extraction process can usually be approximated (to a certain degree) without affecting the performance. For example, the result of the convolution is often quantized or thresholded to yield the presence and location of distinctive features [1]. Because precision is typically not critical at this stage (features are rarely optimal, thresholding is a crude operation), it is often possible to quantize the signals before the convolution with negligible degradation of performance.

The subtlety lies in choosing a quantization scheme which can speed up the convolution while maintaining the same level of performance. We now introduce the convolution algorithm, from which we will deduce the constraints it imposes on quantization.

The main algorithm introduced in this paper is based on a fundamental property of convolutions. Assuming that f and g have finite support and that f^n denotes the n-th integral of f (or the n-th derivative if n is negative), we can write the following convolution identity:

$$(f * g)^n = f^n * g = f * g^n \tag{1}$$

where $*$ denotes the convolution operator. Note that f or g are not necessarily differentiable. For instance, the impulse function (also called Dirac delta function), denoted δ, verifies the identity:

$$\delta_a^n * \delta_b^m = \delta_{a+b}^{m+n} \tag{2}$$

where δ_a^n denotes the n-th integral of the delta function, translated by a ($\delta_a(x) = \delta(x-a)$). Equations 1 and 2 are not new to signal processing. Heckbert has developed an effective filtering algorithm [2] where the filter g is a simple combination of polynomial of degree $n-1$. Convolution between a signal f and the filter g can be written as

$$f * g = f^n * g^{-n} \tag{3}$$

where f^n is the n-th integral of the signal, and the n-th derivative of the filter g can be written exclusively with delta functions (resulting from differentiating $n-1$ degree polynomials n times). Since convolving with an impulse function is a trivial operation, the computation of Equation 3 can be carried out effectively. Unfortunately, Heckbert's algorithm is limited to simple polynomial filters and is only interesting when the filter is wide and when the Fourier transform is unavailable (such as in variable length filters).

In contrast, in feature extraction, we are interested in small and arbitrary filters (the features). Under these conditions, the key to fast convolution is to quantize the images to combinations of low degree polynomials, which are differentiated, convolved and then integrated. The algorithm is summarized by equation:

$$f * g \approx F * G = (F^{-n} * G^{-m})^{m+n} \tag{4}$$

where F and G are polynomial approximation of f and g, such that F^{-n} and G^{-m} can be written as sums of impulse functions and their derivatives. Since the convolution $F^{-n} * G^{-m}$ only involves applying Equation 2, it can be computed quite effectively. The computation of the convolution is illustrated in Figure 1. Let f and g be two arbitrary 1-dimensional signals (top of the figure). Let's assume that f and g can both be approximated by partitions of polynomials, F and G. On the figure, the polynomials are of degree 0 (they are constant), and are depicted in the second line. The details on how to compute F and G will be explained in the next section. In the next step, F and G are differentiated once, yielding successions of impulse functions (third line in the figure). The impulse representation has the advantage of having a finite support, and of being easy to convolve. Indeed two impulse functions can be convolved using Equation 2 ($4 \times 3 = 12$ multiply-adds on the figure). Finally the result of the convolution must be integrated twice to yield

$$F * G = (F^{-1} * G^{-1})^2 \tag{5}$$

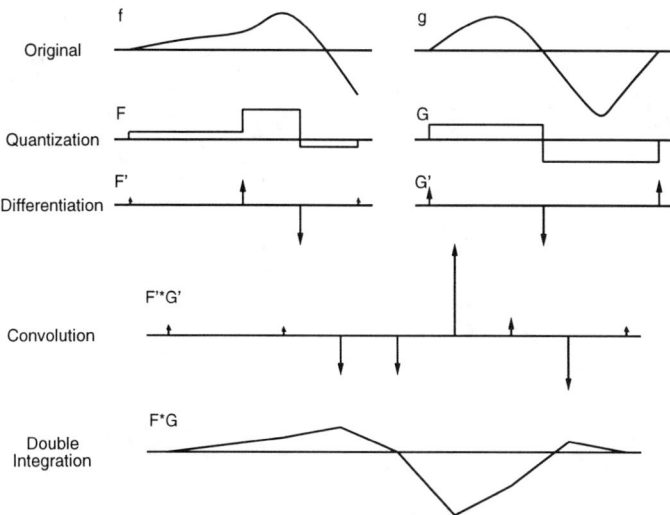

Figure 1: Example of convolution between 1-dimensional function f and g, where the approximations of f and g are piecewise constant.

2 Quantization: from Images to Boxlets

The goal of this section is to suggest efficient ways to approximate an image f by cover of polynomials of degree d suited for convolution. Let S be the space on which f is defined, and let $C = \{c_i\}$ be a partition of S ($c_i \cap c_j = \emptyset$ for $i \neq j$, and $\bigcup_i c_i = S$). For each c_i, let p_i be a polynomial of degree d which minimizes equation:

$$e_i = \int_{x \in c_i} (f(x) - p_i(x))^2 dx \qquad (6)$$

The uniqueness of p_i is guaranteed if c_i is convex. The problem is to find a cover C which minimizes both the number of c_i and $\sum_i e_i$. Many different compromises are possible, but since the computational cost of the convolution is proportional to the number of regions, it seemed reasonable to chose the largest regions with a *maximum error* bounded by a threshold K. Since each region will be differentiated and integrated along the directions of the axes, the boundaries of the c_is are restricted to be parallel to the axes, hence the appellation *boxlet*. There are still many ways to compute valid partitions of boxlets and polynomials. We have investigated two very different approaches which both yield a polynomial cover of the image in reasonable time. The first algorithm is greedy. It uses a procedure which, starting from a top left corner, finds the biggest boxlet c_i which satisfies $e_i < K$ without overlapping another boxlet. The algorithm starts with the top left corner of the image, and keeps a list of all possible starting points (uncovered top left corners) sorted by X and Y positions. When the list is exhausted, the algorithm terminates. Surprisingly, this algorithm can run in $O(d(N + P \log N))$, where N is the number of pixels, P is the number of boxlets and d is the order of the polynomials p_is. Another much simpler algorithm consists of recursively splitting boxlets, starting from a boxlet which encompass the whole image, until $e_i < K$ for all the leaves of the tree. This algorithm runs in $O(dN)$, is much easier to implement, and is faster (better time constant). Furthermore, even though the first algorithm yields a polynomial coverage with less boxlets, the second algorithm yields less impulse functions after differentiation because more impulse functions can be combined (see next section). Both algorithms rely on the fact that Equation 6 can be computed

Figure 2: *Effects of boxletization: original (top left), greedy (bottom left) with a threshold of 10,000, and recursive (top and bottom right) with a threshold of 10,000.*

in constant time. This computation requires the following quantities

$$\underbrace{\sum f(x,y), \sum f(x,y)^2}_{\text{degree 0}}, \underbrace{\sum f(x,y)x, \sum f(x,y)y, \sum f(x,y)xy}_{\text{degree 1}}, \ldots \quad (7)$$

to be pre-computed over the whole image, for the greedy algorithm, or over recursively embedded regions, for the recursive algorithm. In the case of the recursive algorithm these quantities are computed bottom up and very efficiently. To prevent the sums to become too large a limit can be imposed on the maximum size of c_i. The coefficients of the polynomials are quickly evaluated by solving a small linear system using the first two sums for polynomials of degree 0 (constants), the first 5 sums for polynomials of degree 1, and so on.

Figure 2 illustrates the results of the quantization algorithms. The top left corner is a fraction of the original image. The bottom left image illustrates the boxletization of the greedy algorithm, with polynomials of degree 1, and $e_i <= 10,000$ (13000 boxlets, 62000 impulse (and its derivative) functions). The top right image illustrates the boxletization of the recursive algorithm, with polynomials of degree 0 and $e_i <= 10,000$ (47000 boxlets, 58000 impulse functions). The bottom right is the same as top right without displaying the boxlet boundaries. In this case the pixel to impulse function ratio 5.8.

3 Differentiation: from Boxlets to Impulse Functions

If p_i is a polynomial of degree d, its $(d+1)$-th derivative can be written as a sum of impulse function's derivatives, which are zero everywhere but at the corners of c_i. These impulse functions summarize the boundary conditions and completely characterize p_i. They can be represented by four $(d+1)$-dimensional vectors associated with the 4 corners of c_i. Figure 3 (top) illustrates the impulse functions at the 4

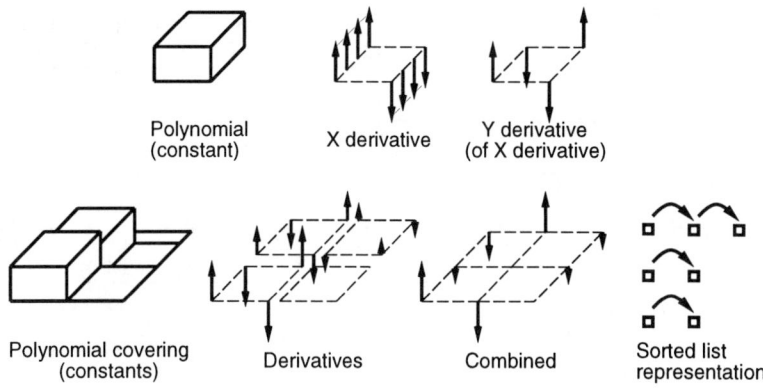

Figure 3: *Differentiation of a constant polynomial in 2D (top). Combining the derivative of adjacent polynomials (bottom)*

corners when the polynomial is a constant (degree zero). Note that the polynomial must be differentiated $d+1$ times (in this example the polynomial is a constant, so $d=0$), with respect to each dimension of the input space. This is illustrated at the top of Figure 3. The cover C being a partition, boundary conditions between adjacent squares do simplify, that is, the same derivatives of a impulse functions at the same location can be combined by adding their coefficients. It is very advantageous to do so because it will reduce the computation of the convolution in the next step. This is illustrated in Figure 3 (bottom). This combining of impulse functions is one of the reason why the recursive algorithm for the quantization is preferred to the greedy algorithm. In the recursive algorithm, the boundaries of boxlets are often aligned, so that the impulse functions of adjacent boxlets can be combined. Typically, after simplification, there are only 20% more impulse functions than there are boxlets. In contrast, the greedy algorithm generates up to 60% more impulse functions than boxlets, due to the fact that there are no alignment constraints. For the same threshold the recursive algorithm generates 20% to 30% less impulse functions than the greedy algorithm.

Finding which impulse functions can be combined is a difficult task because the recursive representation returned by the recursive algorithm does not provide any means for matching the bottom of squares on one line, with the top of squares from below that line. Sorting takes $O(P \log P)$ computational steps (where P is the number of impulse functions) and is therefore too expensive. A better algorithm is to visit the recursive tree and accumulate all the top corners into sorted (horizontal) lists. A similar procedure sorts all the bottom corners (also into horizontal lists). The horizontal lists corresponding to the same vertical positions can then be merged in $O(P)$ operations. The complete algorithm which quantizes an image of N pixels and returns sorted lists of impulse functions runs in $O(dN)$ (where d is the degree of the polynomials).

4 Results

The convolution speed of the algorithm was tested with feature extraction on the image shown on the top left of Figure 2. The image is quantized, but the feature is not. The feature is tabulated in kernels of sizes 5×5, 10×10, 15×15 and 20×20. If the kernel is decomposable, the algorithm can be modified to do two 1D convolutions instead of the present 2D convolution.

The quantization of the image is done with constant polynomials, and with thresholds varying from 1,000 to 40,000. This corresponds to varying the pixel to impulse function ratio from 2.3 to 13.7. Since the feature is not quantized, these ratios correspond exactly to the ratios of number of multiply-adds for the standard convolution versus the boxlet convolution (excluding quantization and integration). The

Threshold	Image			Convolution kernel size			
	Boxlets	Impls f.	Ratio	5x5	10x10	15x15	20x20
1,000	125,685	144,520	2.3	1.5	2.2	2.4	2.4
				2.3	2.6	2.6	2.5
5,000	68,994	84.382	4.0	2.3	3.2	3.8	4.0
				3.8	3.8	4.0	4.0
10,000	47,253	58,120	5.8	2.8	4.8	5.4	5.5
				4.7	6.0	6.1	5.9
40,000	20,244	24,661	13.7	5.2	9.2	11.3	12.4
				8.4	12.5	13.4	13.8

Table 1: *Convolution speed-up factors*

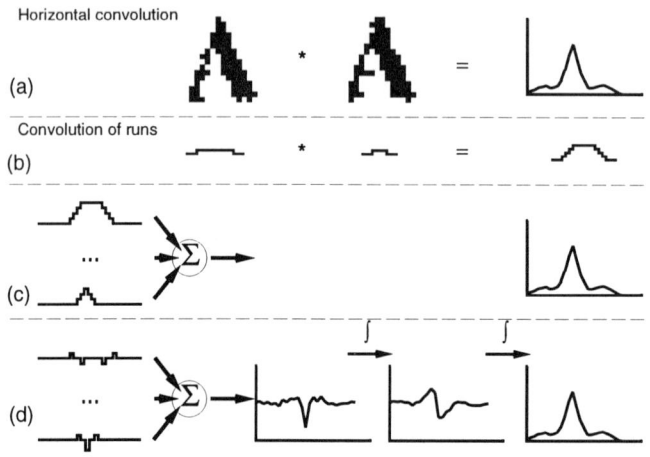

Figure 4: *Run length X convolution*

actual speed up factors are summarized in Table 1. The four last columns indicate the measured time ratios between the standard convolution and the boxlet convolution. For each threshold value, the top line indicates the time ratio of standard convolution versus quantization, convolution and integration time for the boxlet convolution. The bottom line does not take into account the quantization time. The feature size was varied from 5×5 to 20×20. Thus with a threshold of 10,000 and a 5×5 kernel, the quantization ratio is 5.8, and the speed up factor is 2.8. The loss in image quality can be seen by comparing the top left and the bottom right images. If several features are extracted, the quantization time of the image is shared amongst the features and the speed up factor is closer to 4.7.

It should be noted that these speed up factors depend on the quantization level which depends on the data and affects the accuracy of the result. The good news is that for each application the optimal threshold (the maximum level of quantization which has negligible effect on the result) can be evaluated quickly. Once the optimal threshold has been determined, one can enjoy the speed up factor. It is remarkable that with a quantization factor as low as 2.3, the speed up ratio can range from 1.5 to 2.3, depending on the number of features. We believe that this method is directly applicable to forward propagation in convolutional neural nets (although no results are available at this time).

The next application shows a case where quantization has no adverse effect on the accuracy of the convolution, and yet large speed ups are obtained.

5 Binary images and run-length encoding

The quantization steps described in Sections 2 and 3 become particularly simple when the image is binary. If the threshold is set to zero, and if only the X derivative is considered, the impulse representation is equivalent to run-length encoding. Indeed the position of each positive impulse function codes the beginning of a run, while the position of each negative impulses code the end of a run. The horizontal convolution can be computed effectively using the boxlet convolution algorithm. This is illustrated in Figure 4. In (a), the distance between two binary images must be evaluated for every horizontal position (horizontal translation invariant distance). The result is obtained by convolving each horizontal line and by computing the sum of each of the convolution functions. The convolution of two runs, is depicted in (b), while the summation of all the convolutions of two runs is depicted in (c). If an impulse representation is used for the runs (a first derivative), each summation of a convolution between two runs requires only 4 additions of impulse functions, as depicted in (d). The result must be integrated twice, according to Equation 5. The speed up factors can be considerable depending on the width of the images (an order of magnitude if the width is 40 pixels), and there is no accuracy penalty.

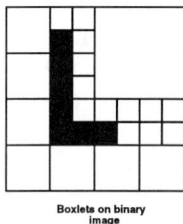
Boxlets on binary image

Compact Dirac representation

Figure 5: Binary image (left) and compact impulse function encoding (right).

This speed up also generalizes to 2-dimensional encoding of binary images. The gain comes from the frequent cancellations of impulse functions of adjacent boxlets. The number of impulse functions is proportional to the contour length of the binary shapes. In this case, the boxlet computation is mostly an efficient algorithm for 2-dimensional run-length encoding. This is illustrated in Figure 5. As with run-length encoding, a considerable speed up is obtained for convolution, at no accuracy penalty cost.

6 Conclusion

When convolutions are used for feature extraction, precision can often be sacrificed for speed with negligible degradation of performance. The boxlet convolution method combines quantization and convolution to offer a continuous adjustable trade-off between accuracy and speed. In some cases (such as in relatively simple binary images) large speed ups can come with no adverse effects. The algorithm is directly applicable to the forward propagation in convolutional neural networks and in pattern matching when translation invariance results from the use of convolution.

References

[1] Yann LeCun and Yoshua Bengio, "Convolutional networks for images, speech, and time-series," in *The Handbook of Brain Theory and Neural Networks*, M. A. Arbib, Ed. 1995, MIT Press.

[2] Paul S. Heckbert, "Filtering by repeated integration," in *ACM SIGGRAPH conference on Computer graphics*, Dallas, TX, August 1986, vol. 20, pp. 315–321.

Batch and On-line Parameter Estimation of Gaussian Mixtures Based on the Joint Entropy

Yoram Singer
AT&T Labs
singer@research.att.com

Manfred K. Warmuth
University of California, Santa Cruz
manfred@cse.ucsc.edu

Abstract

We describe a new iterative method for parameter estimation of Gaussian mixtures. The new method is based on a framework developed by Kivinen and Warmuth for supervised on-line learning. In contrast to gradient descent and EM, which estimate the mixture's covariance matrices, the proposed method estimates the *inverses* of the covariance matrices. Furthermore, the new parameter estimation procedure can be applied in both on-line and batch settings. We show experimentally that it is typically faster than EM, and usually requires about half as many iterations as EM.

1 Introduction

Mixture models, in particular mixtures of Gaussians, have been a popular tool for density estimation, clustering, and un-supervised learning with a wide range of applications (see for instance [5, 2] and the references therein). Mixture models are one of the most useful tools for handling incomplete data, in particular hidden variables. For Gaussian mixtures the hidden variables indicate for each data point the index of the Gaussian that generated it. Thus, the model is specified by a joint density between the observed and hidden variables. The common technique used for estimating the parameters of a stochastic source with hidden variables is the EM algorithm. In this paper we describe a new technique for estimating the parameters of Gaussian mixtures. The new parameter estimation method is based on a framework developed by Kivinen and Warmuth [8] for supervised on-line learning. This framework was successfully used in a large number of supervised and un-supervised problems (see for instance [7, 6, 9, 1]).

Our goal is to find a local minimum of a loss function which, in our case, is the negative log likelihood induced by a mixture of Gaussians. However, rather than minimizing the loss directly we add a term measuring the distance of the new parameters to the old ones. This distance is useful for iterative parameter estimation procedures. Its purpose is to keep the new parameters close to the old ones. The method for deriving iterative parameter estimation can be used in batch settings as well as on-line settings where the parameters are updated after each observation. The distance used for deriving the parameter estimation method in this paper is the relative entropy between the old and new joint density of the observed and hidden variables. For brevity we term the new iterative parameter estimation method the *joint-entropy* (JE) update.

The JE update shares a common characteristic with the Expectation Maximization [4, 10] algorithm as it first calculates the same expectations. However, it replaces the maximization step with a different update of the parameters. For instance, it updates the inverse of the covariance matrix of each Gaussian in the mixture, rather than the covariance matrices themselves. We found in our experiments that the JE update often requires half as many iterations as EM. It is also straightforward to modify the proposed parameter estimation method for on-line setting where the parameters are updated after each new observation. As we demonstrate in our experiments with digit recognition, the on-line version of the JE update is especially useful in situations where the observations are generated by a non-stationary stochastic source.

2 Notation and preliminaries

Let S be a sequence of training examples $\langle x_1, x_2, \ldots, x_N \rangle$ where each x_i is a d-dimensional vector in $\mathbb{R}^d$. To model the distribution of the examples we use m d-dimensional Gaussians. The parameters of the i-th Gaussian are denoted by Θ_i and they include the mean-vector and the covariance matrix

$$\mu_i = E(\mathbf{x}|\Theta_i) \quad C_i = E((\mathbf{x}-\mu_i)(\mathbf{x}-\mu_i)^T|\Theta_i) .$$

The density function of the ith Gaussian, denoted $P(\mathbf{x}|\Theta_i)$, is

$$P(\mathbf{x}|\Theta_i) = (2\pi)^{-d/2}|\mathbf{C}_i|^{-1/2}e^{-\frac{1}{2}(\mathbf{x}-\mu_i)^T \mathbf{C}_i^{-1}(\mathbf{x}-\mu_i)} .$$

We denote the entire set of parameters of a Gaussian mixture by $\Theta = \{\Theta_i\}_{i=1}^m = \{w_i, \mu_i, \mathbf{C}_i\}_{i=1}^m$ where $\mathbf{w} = (w_1, \ldots, w_m)$ is a non-negative vector of mixture coefficients such that $\sum_{i=1}^m w_i = 1$. We denote by $P(\mathbf{x}|\Theta) = \sum_{i=1}^m w_i P(\mathbf{x}|\Theta_i)$ the likelihood of an observation $\mathbf{x}$ according to a Gaussian mixture with parameters Θ. Let Θ_i and $\widetilde{\Theta}_i$ be two Gaussian distributions. For brevity, we denote by $E_i(Z)$ and $\widetilde{E}_i(Z)$ the expectation of a random variable Z with respect to Θ_i and $\widetilde{\Theta}_i$. Let f be a parametric function whose parameters constitute a matrix $A = (a_{ij})$. We denote by $\partial f/\partial A$ the matrix of partial derivatives of f with respect to the elements in A. That is, the ij element of $\partial f/\partial A$ is $\partial f/\partial a_{ij}$. Similarly, let $B = (b_{ij}(x))$ a matrix whose elements are functions of a scalar x. Then, we denote by dB/dx the matrix of derivatives of the elements in B with respect to x, namely, the ij element of dB/dx is $db_{ij}(x)/dx$.

3 The framework for deriving updates

Kivinen and Warmuth [8] introduced a general framework for deriving on-line parameter updates. In this section we describe how to apply their framework for the problem of parameter estimation of Gaussian mixtures in a batch setting. We later discuss how a simple modification gives the on-line updates.

Given a set of data points S in $\mathbb{R}^d$ and a number m, the goal is to find a set of m Gaussians that minimize the loss on the data, denoted as $\text{loss}(S|\Theta)$. For density estimation the natural loss function is the negative log-likelihood of the data $\text{loss}(S|\Theta) = -(1/|S|) \ln P(S|\Theta) \stackrel{\text{def}}{=} -(1/|S|) \sum_{x \in S} \ln P(x|\Theta)$. The best parameters which minimize the above loss cannot be found analytically. The common approach is to use iterative methods such as EM [4, 10] to find a local minimizer of the loss.

In an iterative parameter estimation framework we are given the old set of parameters Θ^t and we need to find a set of new parameters Θ^{t+1} that induce smaller loss. The framework introduced by Kivinen and Warmuth [8] deviates from the common approaches as it also requires to the new parameter vector to stay "close" to the old set of parameters which incorporates all that was learned in the previous iterations. The distance of the new parameter setting Θ^{t+1} from the old setting Θ^t is measured by a non-negative distance function $\Delta(\Theta^{t+1}, \Theta^t)$. We now search for a new set of parameters Θ^{t+1} that minimizes the distance summed with the loss multiplied by η. Here η is a non-negative number measuring the relative importance of the distance versus the loss. This parameter η will become the learning rate of the update. More formally, the update is found by setting $\Theta^{t+1} = \arg\min_{\widetilde{\Theta}} U^t(\widetilde{\Theta})$ where $U^t(\widetilde{\Theta}) = \Delta(\widetilde{\Theta}, \Theta^t) + \eta \, \text{loss}(S|\widetilde{\Theta}) + \lambda(\sum_{i=1}^m \widetilde{w}_i - 1)$. (We use a Lagrange multiplier λ to enforce the constraint that the mixture coefficients sum to one.) By choosing the apropriate distance function and $\eta = 1$ one can show that EM becomes the above update.

For most distance functions and learning rates the minimizer of the function $U^t(\widetilde{\Theta})$ cannot be found analytically as both the distance function and the log-likelihood are usually non-linear in $\widetilde{\Theta}$. Instead, we expand the log-likelihood using a first order Taylor expansion around the old parameter setting. This approximation degrades the further the new parameter values are from the old ones, which further motivates the use of the distance function $\Delta(\widetilde{\Theta}, \Theta^t)$ (see also the discussion in [7]). We now seek a new set of parameters $\Theta^{t+1} = \arg\min_{\widetilde{\Theta}} V^t(\widetilde{\Theta})$ where

$$V^t(\widetilde{\Theta}) = \Delta(\widetilde{\Theta}, \Theta^t) + \eta \left(\text{loss}(S|\Theta^t) + (\widetilde{\Theta} - \Theta^t) \cdot \nabla_\Theta \text{loss}(S|\Theta^t) \right) + \lambda(\sum_{i=1}^m \widetilde{w}_i - 1). \quad (1)$$

Here $\nabla_\Theta \text{loss}(S|\Theta^t)$ denotes the gradient of the loss at Θ^t. We use the above method Eq. (1) to derive the updates of this paper. For density estimation, it is natural to use the relative entropy between the new and old density as a distance. In this paper we use the joint density between the observed (data points) and hidden variables (the indices of the Gaussians). This motivates the name joint-entropy update.

4 Entropy based distance functions

We first consider the relative entropy between the new and old parameter parameters of a *single* Gaussian. Using the notation introduced in Sec. 2, the relative entropy between two Gaussian distributions denoted by $\widetilde{\Theta}_i, \Theta_i$ is

$$\Delta(\widetilde{\Theta}_i, \Theta_i) \stackrel{\text{def}}{=} \int_{x \in \mathbb{R}^d} P(x|\widetilde{\Theta}_i) \ln \frac{P(x|\widetilde{\Theta}_i)}{P(x|\Theta_i)} dx$$

$$= \tfrac{1}{2} \ln \frac{|\mathbf{C}_i|}{|\widetilde{\mathbf{C}}_i|} - \tfrac{1}{2} \widetilde{E}_i \left((x - \widetilde{\mu}_i)^T \widetilde{\mathbf{C}}_i^{-1} (x - \widetilde{\mu}_i) \right) + \tfrac{1}{2} \widetilde{E}_i \left((x - \mu_i)^T \mathbf{C}_i^{-1} (x - \mu_i) \right)$$

Parameter Estimation of Gaussian Mixtures

Using standard (though tedious) algebra we can rewrite the expectations as follows:

$$\Delta(\widetilde{\Theta}_i, \Theta_i) = \tfrac{1}{2}\ln\frac{|C_i|}{|\widetilde{C}_i|} - \frac{d}{2} + \tfrac{1}{2}\mathrm{tr}(C_i^{-1}\widetilde{C}_i) + \tfrac{1}{2}(\widetilde{\mu}_i - \mu)^T C_i^{-1}(\widetilde{\mu}_i - \mu_i) . \quad (2)$$

The relative entropy between the new and the old *mixture* models is the following

$$\Delta(\widetilde{\Theta}, \Theta) \stackrel{\text{def}}{=} \int_X P(\mathbf{x}|\widetilde{\Theta}) \ln\frac{P(\mathbf{x}|\widetilde{\Theta})}{P(\mathbf{x}|\Theta)} d\mathbf{x} = \int_X \sum_{i=1}^m \widetilde{w}_i P(\mathbf{x}|\widetilde{\Theta}_i) \ln \frac{\sum_{i=1}^m \widetilde{w}_i P(\mathbf{x}|\widetilde{\Theta}_i)}{\sum_{i=1}^m w_i P(\mathbf{x}|\Theta_i)} d\mathbf{x} . \quad (3)$$

Ideally, we would like to use the above distance function in V^t to give us an update of $\widetilde{\Theta}$ in terms of Θ. However, there isn't a closed form expression for Eq. (3). Although the relative entropy between two Gaussians is a convex function in their parameters, the relative entropy between two Gaussian mixtures is non-convex. Thus, the loss function $V^t(\widetilde{\Theta})$ may have multiple minima, making the problem of finding $\arg\min_{\widetilde{\Theta}} V^t(\widetilde{\Theta})$ difficult.

In order to sidestep this problem we use the log-sum inequality [3] to obtain an upper bound for the distance function $\Delta(\widetilde{\Theta}, \Theta)$. We denote this upper bound as $\widehat{\Delta}(\widetilde{\Theta}, \Theta)$.

$$\Delta(\widetilde{\Theta}, \Theta) \leq \widehat{\Delta}(\widetilde{\Theta}, \Theta) \stackrel{\text{def}}{=} \int_\mathbf{x} \sum_{i=1}^m (\mathbf{x}, i|\widetilde{\Theta}) \ln \frac{P(\mathbf{x}, i|\widetilde{\Theta})}{P(\mathbf{x}, i|\Theta)} d\mathbf{x} = \int_\mathbf{x} \sum_{i=1}^m \widetilde{w}_i P(\mathbf{x}|\widetilde{\Theta}_i) \ln \frac{\widetilde{w}_i P(\mathbf{x}|\widetilde{\Theta}_i)}{w_i P(\mathbf{x}|\Theta_i)} d\mathbf{x}$$

$$= \sum_{i=1}^m \widetilde{w}_i \ln \frac{\widetilde{w}_i}{w_i} + \sum_{i=1}^m \widetilde{w}_i \int_\mathbf{x} P(\mathbf{x}|\widetilde{\Theta}_i) \ln \frac{P(\mathbf{x}|\widetilde{\Theta}_i)}{P(\mathbf{x}|\Theta_i)} d\mathbf{x} = \sum_{i=1}^m \widetilde{w}_i \ln \frac{\widetilde{w}_i}{w_i} + \sum_{i=1}^m \widetilde{w}_i \Delta(\widetilde{\Theta}_i, \Theta_i) . \quad (4)$$

We call the new distance function $\widehat{\Delta}(\widetilde{\Theta}, \Theta)$ the *joint-entropy distance*. Note that in this distance the parameters of $\widetilde{w}_i$ and w_i are "coupled" in the sense that it is a convex combination of the distances $\Delta(\widetilde{\Theta}_i, \Theta_i)$. In particular, $\widehat{\Delta}(\widetilde{\Theta}, \Theta)$ as a function of the parameters $\widetilde{w}_i, \widetilde{\mu}_i, \widetilde{C}_i$ does not remain constant any more when the parameters of the individual Gaussians are permuted. Furthermore, $\widehat{\Delta}(\widetilde{\Theta}, \Theta)$ is also is sufficiently convex so that finding the minimizer of V^t is possible (see below).

5 The updates

We are now ready to derive the new parameter estimation scheme. This is done by setting the partial derivatives of V^t, with respect to $\widetilde{\Theta}$, to 0. That is, our problem consists of solving the following equations

$$\frac{\partial \widehat{\Delta}(\widetilde{\Theta}, \Theta)}{\partial \widetilde{w}_i} - \frac{\eta}{|S|}\frac{\partial \ln P(S|\Theta)}{\partial w_i} + \lambda = 0, \quad \frac{\partial \widehat{\Delta}(\widetilde{\Theta}, \Theta)}{\partial \widetilde{\mu}_i} - \frac{\eta}{|S|}\frac{\partial \ln P(S|\Theta)}{\partial \mu_i} = 0, \quad \frac{\partial \widehat{\Delta}(\widetilde{\Theta}, \Theta)}{\partial \widetilde{C}_i} - \frac{\eta}{|S|}\frac{\partial \ln P(S|\Theta)}{\partial C_i} = 0.$$

We now use the fact that C_i and thus C_i^{-1} is symmetric. The derivatives of $\widehat{\Delta}(\widetilde{\Theta}, \Theta)$, as defined by Eq. (4) and Eq. (2), with respect to $\widetilde{w}_i, \widetilde{\mu}_i$ and $\widetilde{C}_i$, are

$$\frac{\partial \widehat{\Delta}(\widetilde{\Theta}, \Theta)}{\partial \widetilde{w}_i} = \ln\frac{\widetilde{w}_i}{w_i} + 1 + \tfrac{1}{2}\ln\frac{|C_i|}{|\widetilde{C}_i|} - \frac{d}{2} + \tfrac{1}{2}\mathrm{tr}(C_i^{-1}\widetilde{C}_i) + \tfrac{1}{2}(\widetilde{\mu}_i - \mu)^T C_i^{-1}(\widetilde{\mu}_i - \mu_i) \quad (5)$$

$$\frac{\partial \widehat{\Delta}(\widetilde{\Theta}, \Theta)}{\partial \widetilde{\mu}_i} = \widetilde{w}_i C_i^{-1}(\widetilde{\mu}_i - \mu_i) \quad (6)$$

$$\frac{\partial \widehat{\Delta}(\widetilde{\Theta}, \Theta)}{\partial \widetilde{C}_i} = \tfrac{1}{2}\widetilde{w}_i(-\widetilde{C}_i^{-1} + C_i^{-1}) . \quad (7)$$

To simplify the notation throughout the rest of the paper we define the following variables

$$\beta_i(\mathbf{x}) \stackrel{\text{def}}{=} \frac{P(\mathbf{x}|\Theta_i)}{P(\mathbf{x}|\Theta)} \quad \text{and} \quad \alpha_i(\mathbf{x}) \stackrel{\text{def}}{=} \frac{w_i P(\mathbf{x}|\Theta_i)}{P(\mathbf{x}|\Theta)} = P(i|\mathbf{x}, \Theta_i) = w_i \beta_i(\mathbf{x}).$$

The partial derivatives of the log-likelihood are computed similarly:

$$\frac{\partial \ln P(S|\Theta)}{\partial w_i} = \sum_{\mathbf{x} \in S} \frac{P(\mathbf{x}|\Theta_i)}{P(\mathbf{x}|\Theta)} = \sum_{\mathbf{x} \in S} \beta_i(\mathbf{x}) \tag{8}$$

$$\frac{\partial \ln P(S|\Theta)}{\partial \mu_i} = \sum_{\mathbf{x} \in S} \frac{w_i P(\mathbf{x}|\Theta_i)}{P(\mathbf{x}|\Theta)} \mathbf{C}_i^{-1}(\mathbf{x} - \mu_i) = \sum_{\mathbf{x} \in S} \alpha_i(\mathbf{x}) \mathbf{C}_i^{-1}(\mathbf{x} - \mu_i) \tag{9}$$

$$\frac{\partial \ln P(S|\Theta)}{\partial \mathbf{C}_i} = -\tfrac{1}{2} \sum_{\mathbf{x} \in S} \frac{w_i P(\mathbf{x}|\Theta_i)}{P(\mathbf{x}|\Theta)} (\mathbf{C}_i^{-1} - \mathbf{C}_i^{-1}(\mathbf{x} - \mu_i)(\mathbf{x} - \mu_i)^T \mathbf{C}_i^{-1})$$

$$= -\tfrac{1}{2} \sum_{\mathbf{x} \in S} \alpha_i(\mathbf{x}) (\mathbf{C}_i^{-1} - \mathbf{C}_i^{-1}(\mathbf{x} - \mu_i)(\mathbf{x} - \mu_i)^T \mathbf{C}_i^{-1}). \tag{10}$$

We now need to decide on an order for updating the parameter classes w_i, μ_i, and $\mathbf{C}_i$. We use the same order that EM uses, namely, w_i, then μ_i, and finally, $\mathbf{C}_i$. (After doing one pass over all three groups we start again using the same order.) Using this order results in a simplified set of equations as several terms in Eq. (5) cancel out. Denote the size of the sample by $N = |S|$. We now need to sum the derivatives from Eq. (5) and Eq. (8) while using the fact that the Lagrange multiplier λ simply assures that the new weight $\widetilde{w}_i$ sum to one. By setting the result to zero, we get that

$$w_i \leftarrow \frac{w_i \exp\left(-\frac{\eta}{N} \sum_{\mathbf{x} \in S} \beta_i(\mathbf{x})\right)}{\sum_{j=1}^m w_j \exp\left(-\frac{\eta}{N} \sum_{\mathbf{x} \in S} \beta_i(\mathbf{x})\right)}. \tag{11}$$

Similarly, we sum Eq. (6) and Eq. (9), set the result to zero, and get that

$$\mu_i \leftarrow \mu_i + \frac{\eta}{N} \sum_{\mathbf{x} \in S} \beta_i(\mathbf{x})(\mathbf{x} - \mu_i). \tag{12}$$

Finally, we do the same for $\mathbf{C}_i$. We sum Eq. (7) and Eq. (10) using the newly obtained μ_i,

$$\mathbf{C}_i^{-1} \leftarrow \mathbf{C}_i^{-1} + \frac{\eta}{N} \sum_{\mathbf{x} \in S} \beta_i(\mathbf{x})(\mathbf{C}_i^{-1} - \mathbf{C}_i^{-1}(\mathbf{x} - \mu_i)(\mathbf{x} - \mu_i)^T \mathbf{C}_i^{-1}). \tag{13}$$

We call the new iterative parameter estimation procedure the joint-entropy (JE) update. To summarize, the JE update is composed of the following alternating steps: We first calculate for each observation $\mathbf{x}$ the value $\beta_i(\mathbf{x}) = P(\mathbf{x}|\Theta_i)/P(\mathbf{x}|\Theta)$ and then update the parameters as given by Eq. (11), Eq. (12), and Eq. (13). The JE update and EM differ in several aspects. First, EM uses a simple update for the mixture weights $\mathbf{w}$. Second, EM uses the expectations (with respect to the current parameters) of the sufficient statistics [4] for μ_i and C_i to find new sets of mean vectors and covariance matrices. The JE uses a (slightly different) weighted average of the observation and, in addition, it adds the old parameters. The learning rate η determines the proportion to be used in summing the old parameters and the newly estimated parameters. Last, EM estimates the covariance matrices $\mathbf{C}_i$ whereas the new update estimates the *inverses*, $\mathbf{C}_i^{-1}$, of these matrices. Thus, it is potentially be more stable numerically in cases where the covariance matrices have small condition number.

To obtain an on-line procedure we need to update the parameters after each new observation at a time. That is, rather than summing over all $\mathbf{x} \in S$, for a new observation $\mathbf{x}_t$, we update

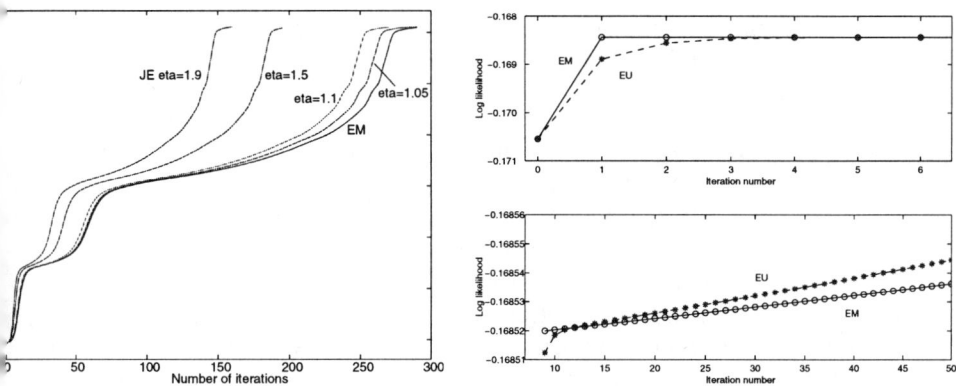

Figure 1: Left: comparison of the convergence rate of EM and the JE update with different learning rates. Right: example of a case where EM *initially* increases the likelihood faster than the JE update.

the parameters and get a new set of parameters Θ^{t+1} using the current parameters Θ^t. The new parameters are then used for inducing the likelihood of the next observation $\mathbf{x}_{t+1}$. The on-line parameter estimation procedure is composed of the following steps:

1. Set: $\beta_i(\mathbf{x}_t) = \frac{P(\mathbf{x}_t|\Theta_i)}{P(\mathbf{x}_t|\Theta)}$.
2. Parameter updates:
   (a) $w_i \leftarrow w_i \exp(-\eta_t \beta_i(\mathbf{x}_t)) / \sum_{j=1}^{m} w_j \exp(-\eta_t \beta_i(\mathbf{x}_t))$
   (b) $\mu_i \leftarrow \mu_i + \eta_t \beta_i(\mathbf{x}_t)(\mathbf{x}_t - \mu_i)$
   (c) $\mathbf{C}_i^{-1} \leftarrow \mathbf{C}_i^{-1} + \eta_t \beta_i(\mathbf{x}_t)(\mathbf{C}_i^{-1} - \mathbf{C}_i^{-1}(\mathbf{x}_t - \mu_i)(\mathbf{x}_t - \mu_i)^T \mathbf{C}_i^{-1})$.

To guarantee convergence of the on-line update one should use a diminishing learning rate, that is $\eta_t \to 0$ as $t \to \infty$ (for further motivation see [11]).

6 Experiments

We conducted numerous experiments with the new update. Due to the lack of space we describe here only two. In the first experiment we compared the JE update and EM in batch settings. We generated data from Gaussian mixture distributions with varying number of components ($m = 2$ to 100) and dimensions ($d = 2$ to 20). Due to the lack of space we describe here results obtained from only one setting. In this setting the examples were generated by a mixture of 5 components with $\mathbf{w} = (0.4, 0.3, 0.2, 0.05, 0.05)$. The mean vectors were the 5 standard unit vectors in the Euclidean space $\mathbb{R}^5$ and we set all of covariances matrices to the identity matrix. We generated 1000 examples. We then run EM and the JE update with different learning rates ($\eta = 1.9, 1.5, 1.1, 1.05$). To make sure that all the runs will end in the same local maximum we fist performed three EM iterations. The results are shown on the left hand side of Figure 1. In this setting, the JE update with high learning rates achieves much faster convergence than EM. We would like to note that this behavior is by no means esoteric – most of our experiments data yielded similar results.

We found a different behavior in low dimensional settings. On the right hand side of Figure 1 we show convergence rate results for a mixture containing two components each of which is a single dimension Gaussians. The mean of the two components were located at 1 and -1 with the same variance of 2. Thus, there is a significant "overlap" between the two Gaussian constituting the mixture. The mixture weight vector was $(0.5, 0.5)$. We generated 50 examples according to this distribution and initialized the parameters as follows: $\mu_1 = 0.01, \mu_2 = -0.01$, $\sigma_1 = \sigma_2 = 2$, $w_1 = w_2 = 0.5$ We see that initially EM increases the likelihood much faster than the JE update. Eventually, the JE update convergences faster than EM when using a small learning rate (in the example appearing in Figure 1 we set $\eta = 1.05$). However, in this setting, the JE update diverges when learning rates larger than $\eta = 1.1$ are used. This behavior underscores the advantages of both methods. EM uses a fixed learning rate and is guaranteed to converge to a local maximum of the likelihood, under conditions that typically hold for mixture of Gaussians [4, 12]. the JE update, on the other hand, encompasses a learning rate and in many settings it converges much faster than EM. However, the superior performance in high dimensional cases demands its price in low dimensional "dense" cases. Namely, a very conservative learning rate, which is hard to tune, need to be used. In these cases, EM is a better alternative, offering almost the same convergence rate without the need to tune any parameters.

Acknowledgments Thanks to Duncan Herring for careful proof reading and providing us with interesting data sets.

References

[1] E. Bauer, D. Koller, and Y. Singer. Update rules for parameter estimation in Bayesian networks. In *Proc. of the 13th Annual Conf. on Uncertainty in AI*, pages 3–13, 1997.

[2] C.M. Bishop. *Neural Networks and Pattern Recognition*. Oxford Univ. Press, 1995.

[3] Thomas M. Cover and Joy A. Thomas. *Elements of Information Theory*. Wiley, 1991.

[4] A.P. Dempster, N.M. Laird, and D.B. Rubin. Maximum-likelihood from incomplete data via the EM algorithm. *Journal of the Royal Statistical Society*, B39:1–38, 1977.

[5] R.O. Duda and P.E. Hart. *Pattern Classification and Scene Analysis*. Wiley, 1973.

[6] D. P. Helmbold, J. Kivinen, and M.K. Warmuth. Worst-case loss bounds for sigmoided neurons. In *Advances in Neural Information Processing Systems 7*, pages 309–315, 1995.

[7] D.P. Helmbold, R.E. Schapire, Y.Singer, and M.K. Warmuth. A comparison of new and old algorithms for a mixture estimation problem. *Machine Learning*, Vol. 7, 1997.

[8] J. Kivinen and M.K. Warmuth. Additive versus exponentiated gradient updates for linear prediction. *Information and Computation*, 132(1):1–64, January 1997.

[9] J. Kivinen and M.K. Warmuth. Relative loss bounds for multidimensional regression problems. In *Advances in Neural Information Processing Systems 10*, 1997.

[10] R.A. Redner and H.F. Walker. Mixture densities, maximum likelihood and the EM algorithm. *SIAM Review*, 26(2), 1984.

[11] D.M. Titterington, A.F.M. Smith, and U.E. Makov. *Statistical Analysis of Finite Mixture Distributions*. Wiley, 1985.

[12] C.F. Wu. On the convergence properties of the EM algorithm. *Annals of Stat.*, 11:95–103, 1983.

Semiparametric Support Vector and Linear Programming Machines

Alex J. Smola, Thilo T. Frieß, and Bernhard Schölkopf
GMD FIRST, Rudower Chaussee 5, 12489 Berlin
{smola, friess, bs}@first.gmd.de

Abstract

Semiparametric models are useful tools in the case where domain knowledge exists about the function to be estimated or emphasis is put onto understandability of the model. We extend two learning algorithms - Support Vector machines and Linear Programming machines to this case and give experimental results for SV machines.

1 Introduction

One of the strengths of Support Vector (SV) machines is that they are *nonparametric* techniques, where one does not have to e.g. specify the number of basis functions beforehand. In fact, for many of the kernels used (not the polynomial kernels) like Gaussian rbf–kernels it can be shown [6] that SV machines are universal approximators.

While this is advantageous in general, parametric models are useful techniques in their own right. Especially if one happens to have additional knowledge about the problem, it would be unwise not to take advantage of it. For instance it might be the case that the major properties of the data are described by a combination of a small set of linear independent basis functions $\{\phi_1(\cdot), \ldots, \phi_n(\cdot)\}$. Or one may want to correct the data for some (e.g. linear) trends. Secondly it also may be the case that the user wants to have an *understandable* model, without sacrificing accuracy. For instance many people in life sciences tend to have a preference for linear models. This may be some motivation to construct *semiparametric* models, which are both easy to understand (for the parametric part) and perform well (often due to the nonparametric term). For more advocacy on semiparametric models see [1].

A common approach is to fit the data with the parametric model and train the nonparametric add–on on the errors of the parametric part, i.e. fit the nonparametric part to the errors. We show in Sec. 4 that this is useful only in a very restricted situation. In general it is impossible to find the best model amongst a given class for different cost functions by doing so. The better way is to solve a convex optimization problem like in standard SV machines, however with a different set of admissible functions

$$f(x) = \langle w, \psi(x) \rangle + \sum_{i=1}^{n} \beta_i \phi_i(x). \qquad (1)$$

Note that this is not so much different from the classical SV [10] setting where one uses functions of the type

$$f(x) = \langle w, \psi(x) \rangle + b. \qquad (2)$$

2 Semiparametric Support Vector Machines

Let us now treat this setting more formally. For the sake of simplicity in the exposition we will restrict ourselves to the case of SV regression and only deal with the ε-insensitive loss function $|\xi|_\varepsilon = \max\{0, |\xi| - \varepsilon\}$. Extensions of this setting are straightforward and follow the lines of [7].

Given a training set of size ℓ, $X := \{(x_1, y_1), \ldots, (x_\ell, y_\ell)\}$ one tries to find a function f that minimizes the functional of the expected risk[1]

$$R[f] = \int c(f(x) - y) p(x, y) dx dy. \qquad (3)$$

Here $c(\xi)$ denotes a cost function, i.e. how much deviations between prediction and actual training data should be penalized. Unless stated otherwise we will use $c(\xi) = |\xi|_\varepsilon$.

As we do not know $p(x, y)$ we can only compute the empirical risk $R_{\text{emp}}[f]$ (i.e. the training error). Yet, minimizing the latter is not a good idea if the model class is sufficiently rich and will lead to overfitting. Hence one adds a regularization term $T[f]$ and minimzes the regularized risk functional

$$R_{\text{reg}}[f] = \sum_{i=1}^{\ell} c(f(x_i) - y_i) + \lambda T[f] \quad \text{with} \quad \lambda > 0. \qquad (4)$$

The standard choice in SV regression is to set $T[f] = \frac{1}{2}\|w\|^2$.

This is the point of departure from the standard SV approach. While in the latter f is described by (2), we will expand f in terms of (1). Effectively this means that there exist functions $\phi_1(\cdot), \ldots, \phi_n(\cdot)$ whose contribution is not regularized at all. If n is sufficiently smaller than ℓ this need not be a major concern, as the VC–dimension of this additional class of linear models is n, hence the overall capacity control will still work, provided the nonparametric part is restricted sufficiently. Figure 1 explains the effect of choosing a different structure in detail.

Solving the optimization equations for this particular choice of a regularization term, with expansion (1), the ε–insensitive loss function and introducing kernels

---

[1] More general definitions, mainly in terms of the cost function, do exist but for the sake of clarity in the exposition we ignored these cases. See [10] or [7] for further details on alternative definitions of risk functionals.

Semiparametric Support Vector and Linear Programming Machines

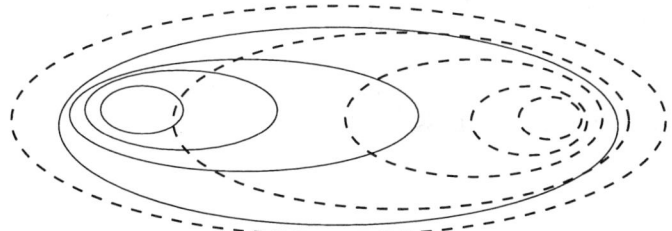

Figure 1: Two different nested subsets (solid and dotted lines) of hypotheses and the optimal model (+) in the realizable case. Observe that the optimal model is already contained in much a smaller (in this diagram size corresponds to the capacity of a subset) subset of the structure with solid lines than in the structure denoted by the dotted lines. Hence prior knowledge in choosing the structure can have a large effect on generalization bounds and performance.

following [2] we arrive at the following primal optimization problem:

$$\text{minimize} \quad \tfrac{\lambda}{2}\|w\|^2 + \sum_{i=1}^{\ell} \xi_i + \xi_i^*$$

$$\text{subject to} \quad \begin{cases} \langle w, \psi(x_i) \rangle + \sum_{j=1}^{n} \beta_j \phi_j(x_i) - y_i \leq \epsilon + \xi_i^* \\ y_i - \langle w, \psi(x_i) \rangle - \sum_{j=1}^{n} \beta_j \phi_j(x_i) \leq \epsilon + \xi_i \\ \xi_i, \xi_i^* \geq 0 \end{cases} \quad (5)$$

Here $k(x, x')$ has been written as $\langle \psi(x), \psi(x') \rangle$. Solving (5) for its Wolfe dual yields

$$\text{maximize} \quad \begin{cases} -\tfrac{1}{2} \sum_{i,j=1}^{\ell} (\alpha_i - \alpha_i^*)(\alpha_j - \alpha_j^*) k(x_i, x_j) \\ -\varepsilon \sum_{i=1}^{\ell} (\alpha_i + \alpha_i^*) + \sum_{i=1}^{\ell} y_i (\alpha_i - \alpha_i^*) \end{cases} \quad (6)$$

$$\text{subject to} \quad \begin{cases} \sum_{i=1}^{\ell} (\alpha_i - \alpha_i^*) \phi_j(x_i) = 0 \text{ for all } 1 \leq j \leq n \\ \alpha_i, \alpha_i^* \in [0, 1/\lambda] \end{cases}$$

Note the similarity to the standard SV regression model. The objective function and the box constraints on the Lagrange multipliers α_i, α_i^* remain unchanged. The only modification comes from the additional unregularized basis functions. Whereas in the standard SV case we only had a single (constant) function $b \cdot 1$ we now have an expansion in the basis $\beta_i \phi_i(\cdot)$. This gives rise to n constraints instead of one. Finally f can be found as

$$f(x) = \sum_{i=1}^{\ell} (\alpha_i - \alpha_i^*) k(x_i, x) + \sum_{i=1}^{n} \beta_i \phi_i(x) \quad \text{since} \quad w = \sum_{i=1}^{\ell} (\alpha_i - \alpha_i^*) \psi(x_i). \quad (7)$$

The only difficulty remaining is how to determine β_i. This can be done by exploiting the Karush–Kuhn–Tucker optimality conditions, or much more easily, by using an interior point optimization code [9]. In the latter case the variables β_i can be obtained as the dual variables of the dual (dual dual = primal) optimization problem (6) as a by product of the optimization process. This is also how these variables have been obtained in the experiments in the current paper.

3 Semiparametric Linear Programming Machines

Equation (4) gives rise to the question whether not completely different choices of regularization functionals would also lead to good algorithms. Again we will allow functions as described in (7). Possible choices are

$$T[f] = \frac{1}{2}\|w\|^2 + \sum_{i=1}^{n} |\beta_i| \tag{8}$$

or

$$T[f] = \sum_{i=1}^{\ell} |\alpha_i - \alpha_i^*| \tag{9}$$

or

$$T[f] = \sum_{i=1}^{\ell} |\alpha_i - \alpha_i^*| + \frac{1}{2} \sum_{i,j=1}^{n} \beta_i \beta_j M_{ij} \tag{10}$$

for some positive semidefinite matrix M. This is a simple extension of existing methods like Basis Pursuit [3] or Linear Programming Machines for classification (see e.g. [4]). The basic idea in all these approaches is to have two different sets of basis functions that are regularized differently, or where a subset may not be regularized at all. This is an efficient way of encoding prior knowledge or the preference of the user as the emphasis obviously will be put mainly on the functions with little or no regularization at all. Eq. (8) is essentially the SV estimation model where an additional linear regularization term has been added for the parametric part. In this case the constraints of the optimization problem (6) change into

$$-1 \leq \sum_{i=1}^{\ell} (\alpha_i - \alpha_i^*) \phi_j(x_i) \leq 1 \quad \text{for all } 1 \leq j \leq n$$
$$\alpha_i, \alpha_i^* \in [0, 1/\lambda] \tag{11}$$

It makes little sense (from a technical viewpoint) to compute Wolfe's dual objective function in (10) as the problem does not get significantly easier by doing so. The best approach is to solve the corresponding optimization problem directly by some linear or quadratic programming code, e.g. [9]. Finally (10) can be reduced to the case of (8) by renaming variables accordingly and a proper choice of M.

4 Why Backfitting is not sufficient

One might think that the approach presented above is quite unnecessary and overly complicated for semiparametric modelling. In fact, one could try to fit the data to the parametric model first, and then fit the nonparametric part to the residuals. In most cases, however, this does not lead to finding the minimum of (4). We will show this at a simple example.

Take a SV machine with linear kernel (i.e. $k(x, x') = \langle x, x' \rangle$) in one dimension and a constant term as parametric part (i.e. $f(x) = wx + \beta$). This is one of the simplest semiparametric SV machines possible. Now suppose the data was generated by

$$y_i = x_i \quad \text{where } x_i \geq 1 \tag{12}$$

without noise. Clearly then also $y_i \geq 1$ for all i. By construction the best overall fit of the pair (β, w) will be arbitrarily close to $(0, 1)$ if the regularization parameter λ is chosen sufficiently small.

For backfitting one first carries out the parametric fit to find a constant β minimizing the term $\sum_{i=1}^{\ell} c(y_i - \beta)$. Depending on the chosen cost function $c(\cdot)$, β will be the mean (L_2-error), the median (L_1-error), etc., of the set $\{y_1, \ldots, y_\ell\}$. As all $y_i \geq 1$

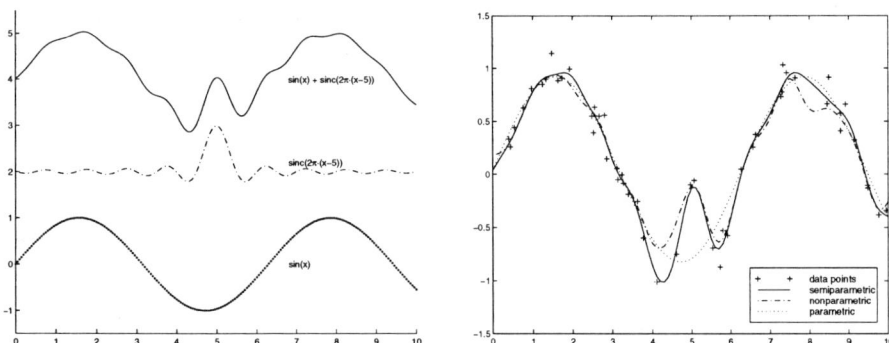

Figure 2: Left: Basis functions used in the toy example. Note the different length scales of $\sin x$ and $\operatorname{sinc} 2\pi x$. For convenience the functions were shifted by an offset of 2 and 4 respectively. Right: Training data denoted by '+', nonparametric (dash–dotted line), semiparametric (solid line), and parametric regression (dots). The regularization constant was set to $\lambda = 2$. Observe that the semiparametric model picks up the characteristic *wiggles* of the original function.

also $\beta \geq 1$ which is surely not the optimal solution of the overall problem as there β would be close to 0 as seen above. Hence not even in the simplest of all settings backfitting minimizes the regularized risk functional, thus one cannot expect the latter to happen in the more complex case either. There exists only one case in which backfitting would suffice, namely if the function spaces spanned by the kernel expansion $\{k(x_i, \cdot)\}$ and $\{\phi_i(\cdot)\}$ were orthogonal. Consequently in general one has to jointly solve for both the parametric and the semiparametric part.

5 Experiments

The main goal of the experiments shown is a proof of concept and to display the properties of the new algorithm. We study a modification of the *Mexican hat* function, namely

$$f(x) = \sin x + \operatorname{sinc}(2\pi(x-5)). \tag{13}$$

Data is generated by an additive noise process, i.e. $y_i = f(x_i) + \xi_i$, where ξ_i is additive noise. For the experiments we choose Gaussian rbf–kernels with width $\sigma = 1/4$, normalized to maximum output 1. The noise is uniform with 0.2 standard deviation, the ε–insensitive cost function $|\cdot|_\varepsilon$ with $\varepsilon = 0.05$. Unless stated otherwise averaging is done over 100 datasets with 50 samples each. The x_i are drawn uniformly from the interval $[0, 10]$. L_1 and L_2 errors are computed on the interval $[0, 10]$ with uniform measure. Figure 2 shows the function and typical predictions in the nonparametric, semiparametric, and parametric setting. One can observe that the semiparametric model including $\sin x$, $\cos x$ and the constant function as basis functions generalizes better than the standard SV machine. Fig. 3 shows that the generalization performance is better in the semiparametric case. The length of the weight vector of the kernel expansion $\|w\|$ is displayed in Fig. 4. It is smaller in the semiparametric case for practical values of the regularization strength. To make a more realistic comparison, model selection (how to determine $1/\lambda$) was carried out by 10–fold cross validation for both algorithms independently for all 100 datasets. Table 1 shows generalization performance for both a nonparametric model, a correctly chosen and an incorrectly chosen semiparametric model. The experiments indicate that cases in which prior knowledge exists on the type of functions to be used will benefit from semiparametric modelling. Future experiments will show how much can be gained in real world examples.

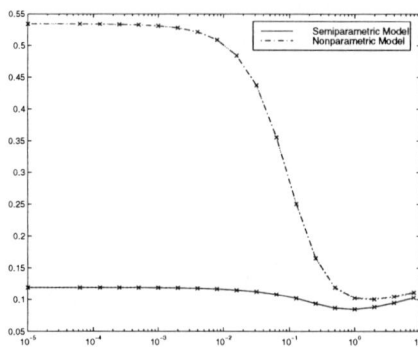
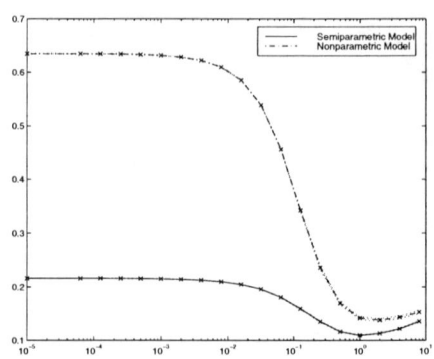

Figure 3: L_1 error (left) and L_2 error (right) of the nonparametric / semiparametric regression computed on the interval $[0, 10]$ vs. the regularization strength $1/\lambda$. The dotted lines (although hardly visible) denote the variance of the estimate. Note that in both error measures the semiparametric model consistently outperforms the nonparametric one.

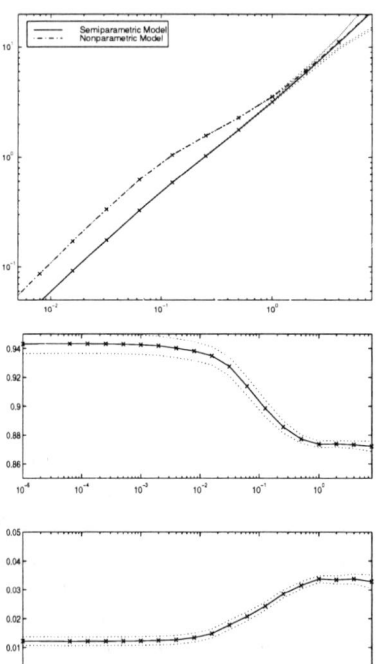

Figure 4: Length of the weight vector w in feature space $(\sum_{i,j}(\alpha_i - \alpha_i^*)(\alpha_j - \alpha_j^*)k(x_i, x_j))^{1/2}$ vs. regularization strength. Note that $\|w\|$, controlling the capacity of that part of the function, belonging to the kernel expansion, is smaller (for practical choices of the regularization term) in the semiparametric than in the nonparametric model. If this difference is sufficiently large the overall capacity of the resulting model is smaller in the semiparametric approach. As before dotted lines indicates the variance.

Figure 5: Estimate of the parameters for $\sin x$ (top picture) and $\cos x$ (bottom picture) in the semiparametric model vs. regularization strength $1/\lambda$. The dotted lines above and below show the variation of the estimate given by its variance. Training set size was $\ell = 50$. Note the small variation of the estimate. Also note that even in the parametric case $1/\lambda \approx 0$ neither the coefficient for $\sin x$ converges to 1, nor does the corresponding term for $\cos x$ converge to 0. This is due to the additional frequency contributions of $\mathrm{sinc}\, 2\pi x$.

	Nonparam.	Semiparam. $\sin x, \cos x, 1$	Semiparam. $\sin 2x, \cos 2x, 1$
L_1 error	0.1263 ± 0.0064 (12)	0.0887 ± 0.0018 (82)	0.1267 ± 0.0064 (6)
L_2 error	0.1760 ± 0.0097 (12)	0.1197 ± 0.0046 (82)	0.1864 ± 0.0124 (6)

Table 1: L_1 and L_2 error for model selection by 10–fold crossvalidation. The *correct* semiparametric model $(\sin x, \cos x, 1)$ outperforms the nonparametric model by at least 30%, and has significantly smaller variance. The wrongly chosen nonparametric model $(\sin 2x, \cos 2x, 1)$, on the other hand, gives performance comparable to the nonparametric one, in fact, no significant performance degradation was noticeable. The number in parentheses denotes the number of trials in which the corresponding model was the best among the three models.

6 Discussion and Outlook

Similar models have been proposed and explored in the context of smoothing splines. In fact, expansion (7) is a direct result of the representer theorem, however only in the case of regularization in feature space (aka Reproducing Kernel Hilbert Space, RKHS). One can show [5] that the expansion (7) is optimal in the space spanned by the RKHS and the additional set of basis functions.

Moreover the semiparametric setting arises naturally in the context of conditionally positive definite kernels of order m (see [8]). There, in order to use a set of kernels which do not satisfy Mercer's condition, one has to exclude polynomials up to order $m - 1$. Hence, to with that one has to add polynomials back in 'manually' and our approach presents a way of doing that.

Another application of semiparametric models besides the conventional approach of treating the nonparametric part as *nuisance parameters* [1] is the domain of hypothesis testing, e.g. to test whether a parametric model fits the data sufficiently well. This can be achieved in the framework of structural risk minimization [10] — given the different models (nonparametric vs. semiparametric vs. parametric) one can evaluate the bounds on the expected risk and then choose the model with the lowest error bound. Future work will tackle the problem of computing good error bounds of compound hypothesis classes. Moreover it should be easily possible to apply the methods proposed in this paper to Gaussian processes.

Acknowledgements This work was supported in part by grants of the DFG Ja 379/51 and ESPRIT Project Nr. 25387–STORM. The authors thank Peter Bartlett, Klaus–Robert Müller, Noboru Murata, Takashi Onoda, and Bob Williamson for helpful discussions and comments.

References

[1] P.J. Bickel, C.A.J. Klaassen, Y. Ritov, and J.A. Wellner. *Efficient and adaptive estimation for semiparametric models*. J. Hopkins Press, Baltimore, ML, 1994.

[2] B. E. Boser, I. M. Guyon, and V. N. Vapnik. A training algorithm for optimal margin classifiers. In *COLT'92*, pages 144–152, Pittsburgh, PA, 1992.

[3] S. Chen, D. Donoho, and M. Saunders. Atomic decomposition by basis pursuit. Technical Report 479, Department of Statistics, Stanford University, 1995.

[4] T.T. Frieß and R.F. Harrison. Perceptrons in kernei feature spaces. TR RR-720, University of Sheffield, Sheffield, UK, 1998.

[5] G.S. Kimeldorf and G. Wahba. A correspondence between Bayesan estimation on stochastic processes and smoothing by splines. *Ann. Math. Statist.*, 2:495–502, 1971.

[6] C.A. Micchelli. Interpolation of scattered data: distance matrices and conditionally positive definite functions. *Constructive Approximation*, 2:11–22, 1986.

[7] A. J. Smola and B. Schölkopf. On a kernel–based method for pattern recognition, regression, approximation and operator inversion. *Algorithmica*, 22:211–231, 1998.

[8] A.J. Smola, B. Schölkopf, and K. Müller. The connection between regularization operators and support vector kernels. *Neural Netw.*, 11:637–649, 1998.

[9] R.J. Vanderbei. LOQO: An interior point code for quadratic programming. TR SOR-94-15, Statistics and Operations Research, Princeton Univ., NJ, 1994.

[10] V. Vapnik. *The Nature of Statistical Learning Theory*. Springer, N.Y., 1995.

Probabilistic Visualisation of High-dimensional Binary Data

Michael E. Tipping

Microsoft Research,
St George House, 1 Guildhall Street,
Cambridge CB2 3NH, U.K.

mtipping@microsoft.com

Abstract

We present a probabilistic latent-variable framework for data visualisation, a key feature of which is its applicability to binary and categorical data types for which few established methods exist. A variational approximation to the likelihood is exploited to derive a fast algorithm for determining the model parameters. Illustrations of application to real and synthetic binary data sets are given.

1 Introduction

Visualisation is a powerful tool in the exploratory analysis of multivariate data. The rendering of high-dimensional data in two dimensions, while generally implying loss of information, often reveals interesting structure to the human eye. Standard dimensionality-reduction methods from multivariate analysis, notably the principal component projection, are often utilised for this purpose, while techniques such as 'projection pursuit' have been tailored specifically to this end. With the current trend for larger databases and the need for effective 'data mining' methods, visualisation is becoming increasingly topical, and recent novel developments include nonlinear topographic methods (Lowe and Tipping 1997; Bishop, Svensén, and Williams 1998) and hierarchical combinations of linear models (Bishop and Tipping 1998). However, a disadvantageous aspect of many proposed techniques is their applicability only to continuous variables; there are very few such methods proposed specifically for the visualisation of discrete *binary* data types, which are commonplace in real-world datasets.

We approach this difficulty by proposing a probabilistic framework for the visualisation of arbitrary data types, based on an underlying latent variable density model. This leads to an algorithm which permits the visualisation of structure within data, while also defining a generative observation probability model. A further, and intuitively pleasing, result is that the specialisation of the model to continuous variables recovers principal component analysis. Continuous, binary and categorical data types may thus be combined and visualised together within this framework, but for reasons of space, we concentrate on binary types alone in this paper.

In the next section we outline the proposed latent variable approach, and in Section 3 consider the difficulties involved in estimating the parameters in this model, giving an efficient variational scheme to this end in Section 4. In Section 5 we illustrate the application of the model and consider the accuracy of the variational approximation.

2 Latent Variable Models for Visualisation

In an ideal visualisation model, we would wish all of the dependencies between variables to be evident in the visualisation space, while the information that we lose in the dimensionality-reduction process should represent "noise", independent to each variable. This principle is captured by the following probability density model for a dataset comprising d-dimensional observation vectors $\mathbf{t} = (t_1, t_2, \ldots, t_d)$:

$$p(\mathbf{t}) = \int \left\{ \prod_{i=1}^{d} p(t_i|\mathbf{x}, \boldsymbol{\theta}) \right\} p(\mathbf{x}) d\mathbf{x}, \qquad (1)$$

where $\mathbf{x}$ is a two-dimensional *latent* variable vector, the distribution of which must be *a priori* specified, and $\boldsymbol{\theta}$ are the model parameters. Now, for a given value of $\mathbf{x}$ (or location in the visualisation space), the observations are independent under the model. (In general, of course, the model and conditional independence assumption will only hold approximately.) However, the unconditional observation model $p(\mathbf{t})$ does not, in general, factorise and so can still capture dependencies between the d variables, given the constraint implied by the use of just two underlying latent variables. So, having estimated the parameters $\boldsymbol{\theta}$, data could be visualised by 'inverting' the generative model using Bayes' rule: $p(\mathbf{x}|\mathbf{t}) = p(\mathbf{t}|\mathbf{x})p(\mathbf{x})/p(\mathbf{t})$. Each data point then induces a distribution in the latent space, which for the purposes of visualisation, we might summarise with the conditional mean value $\langle \mathbf{x}|\mathbf{t} \rangle$.

That this form of model can be appropriate for visualisation was demonstrated by Bishop and Tipping (1998), who showed that if the latent variables are defined to be independent and Gaussian, $\mathbf{x} \sim \mathcal{N}(\mathbf{0}, \mathbf{I})$, and the conditional observation model is also Gaussian, $t_i|\mathbf{x} \sim \mathcal{N}(\mathbf{w}_i^T\mathbf{x} + \mu_i, \sigma_i^2\mathbf{I})$, then maximum-likelihood estimation of the model parameters $\{\mathbf{w}_i, \mu_i, \sigma_i^2\}$ leads to a model where the the posterior mean $\langle \mathbf{x}|\mathbf{t} \rangle$ is equivalent to a probabilistic principal component projection.

A visualisation method for binary variables now follows naturally. Retaining the Gaussian latent distribution $\mathbf{x} \sim \mathcal{N}(\mathbf{0}, \mathbf{I})$, we specify an appropriate conditional distribution for $P(t_i|\mathbf{x}, \boldsymbol{\theta})$. Given that principal components corresponds to a linear model for continuous data types, we adopt the appropriate generalised linear model in the binary case:

$$P(t_i|\mathbf{x}) = \sigma(A_i)^{t_i} \left\{ 1 - \sigma(A_i) \right\}^{1-t_i}, \qquad (2)$$

where $\sigma(A) = \{1 + \exp(-A)\}^{-1}$ and $A_i = \mathbf{w}_i^T\mathbf{x} + b_i$ with parameters $\mathbf{w}_i$ and b_i.

3 Maximum-likelihood Parameter Estimation

The proposed model for binary data already exists in the literature under various guises, most historically as a *latent trait* model (Bartholomew 1987), although it is not utilised for data visualisation. While in the case of probabilistic principal component analysis, ML parameter estimates can be obtained in closed-form, a disadvantageous feature of the binary model is that, with $P(t_i|\mathbf{x})$ defined by (2), the integral of (1) is analytically intractable and $P(\mathbf{t})$ cannot be computed directly. Fitting a latent trait model thus necessitates a numerical integration, and recent papers have considered both Gauss-Hermite (Moustaki 1996) and Monte-Carlo sampling approximations (Mackay 1995; Sammel, Ryan, and Legler 1997).

In this latter case, the log-likelihood for a dataset of N observation vectors $\{\mathbf{t}_1, \ldots, \mathbf{t}_N\}$ would be approximated by

$$\mathcal{L} \approx \sum_{n=1}^{N} \ln \left\{ \frac{1}{L} \sum_{l=1}^{L} \prod_{i=1}^{d} P(t_{in}|\mathbf{x}_l, \mathbf{w}_i, b_i) \right\} \qquad (3)$$

where $\mathbf{x}_l$, $l = 1 \ldots L$, are samples from the two-dimensional latent distribution.

To obtain parameter estimates we may utilise an expectation-maximisation (EM) approach by noting that (3) is equivalent in form to an L-component *latent class* model (Bartholomew 1987) where the component probabilities are mutually constrained from (2). Applying standard methodology leads to an E-step which requires computation of $N \times L$ posterior 'responsibilities' $P(\mathbf{x}_l|\mathbf{t}_n)$, and a logistic regression M-step which is unfortunately iterative, although it can be performed relatively efficiently by an iteratively re-weighted least-squares algorithm. Because of these difficulties in implementation, in the next section we describe a variational approximation to the likelihood which can be maximised more efficiently.

4 A Variational Approximation to the Likelihood

Jaakkola and Jordan (1997) introduced a variational approximation for the predictive likelihood in a Bayesian logistic regression model and also briefly considered the "dual" problem, which is closely related to the proposed visualisation model. In this approach, the integral in (1) is approximated by:

$$\widetilde{P}(\mathbf{t}) = \int \left\{ \prod_{i=1}^{d} \widetilde{P}(t_i|\mathbf{x}, \xi_i) \right\} p(\mathbf{x}) \, d\mathbf{x}, \qquad (4)$$

where

$$\widetilde{P}(t_i|\mathbf{x}, \xi_i) = \sigma(\xi_i) \exp \left\{ (A_i - \xi_i)/2 + \lambda(\xi_i)(A_i^2 - \xi_i^2) \right\}, \qquad (5)$$

with $A_i = (2t_i - 1)(\mathbf{w}_i^T \mathbf{x} + b_i)$ and $\lambda(\xi_i) = \{0.5 - \sigma(\xi_i)\}/2\xi_i$. The parameters ξ_i are the 'variational' parameters, and this approximation has the property that $\widetilde{P}(t_i|\mathbf{x}, \xi_i) \leq P(t_i|\mathbf{x})$, with equality at $\xi_i = A_i$, and thus it follows that $\widetilde{P}(\mathbf{t}) \leq P(\mathbf{t})$.

Now because the exponential in (5) is quadratic in $\mathbf{x}$, then the integral in (4), and also the likelihood, can be computed in closed form. This suggests an alternative algorithm for finding parameter estimates where we iteratively maximise the variational approximation to the likelihood. Each iteration of this algorithm is guaranteed to increase a lower bound on, but will not necessarily maximise, the true likelihood. Nevertheless, we would hope that it will be a close approximation, the accuracy of which is investigated later. At each step in the algorithm, then, we:

1. Obtain the sufficient statistics for the approximated posterior distribution of latent variables given each observation, $\widetilde{p}(\mathbf{x}_n|\mathbf{t}_n, \boldsymbol{\xi}_n)$.

2. Optimise the variational parameters ξ_{in} in order to make the approximation $\widetilde{P}(\mathbf{t}_n)$ as close as possible to $P(\mathbf{t}_n)$ for all $\mathbf{t}_n$.

3. Update the model parameters $\mathbf{w}_i$ and b_i to increase $\widetilde{P}(\mathbf{t})$.

Jaakkola and Jordan (1997) give formulae for the above computations, but these do not include provision for the 'biases' b_i, and so the necessary expressions are re-derived below. Note that although we have introduced $N \times d$ additional variational parameters, it is no longer necessary to sample from $p(\mathbf{x})$ and compute responsibilities, and no iterative logistic regression step is needed.

Computing the Latent Posterior Statistics. From Bayes' rule, the posterior approximation $\widetilde{p}(\mathbf{x}_n|\mathbf{t}_n, \boldsymbol{\xi}_n)$ is Gaussian with covariance and mean given by

$$\mathbf{C}_n = \left[\mathbf{I} - 2\sum_{i=1}^{d} \lambda(\xi_{in})\mathbf{w}_i\mathbf{w}_i^\mathrm{T}\right]^{-1}, \tag{6}$$

$$\boldsymbol{\mu}_n = \mathbf{C}_n \left\{\sum_{i=1}^{d}\left[t_{in} - \frac{1}{2} + 2\lambda(\xi_{in})b_i\right]\mathbf{w}_i\right\}. \tag{7}$$

Optimising the Variational Parameters. Because $P(\mathbf{t}) \geq \widetilde{P}(\mathbf{t})$, the variational approximation can be optimised by maximising $\widetilde{P}(\mathbf{t}_n)$ with respect to each ξ_{in}. We use the EM methodology to obtain updates

$$\xi_{in}^2 = \mathbf{w}_i^\mathrm{T}\langle\mathbf{x}_n\mathbf{x}_n^\mathrm{T}\rangle\mathbf{w}_i + 2b_i\mathbf{w}_i^\mathrm{T}\langle\mathbf{x}_n\rangle + b_i^2, \tag{8}$$

where the angle brackets $\langle\cdot\rangle$ denote expectations with respect to $\widetilde{p}(\mathbf{x}_n|\mathbf{t}_n, \boldsymbol{\xi}_n^{\mathrm{old}})$ and where, from (6) and (7) earlier, the necessary posterior statistics are given by:

$$\langle\mathbf{x}_n\rangle = \boldsymbol{\mu}_n, \tag{9}$$
$$\langle\mathbf{x}_n\mathbf{x}_n^\mathrm{T}\rangle = \mathbf{C}_n + \boldsymbol{\mu}_n\boldsymbol{\mu}_n^\mathrm{T}. \tag{10}$$

Since (6) and (7) depend on the variational parameters, $\mathbf{C}_n$ and $\boldsymbol{\mu}_n$ are computed followed by the update for each ξ_{in} from (8). Iteration of this two-stage process is guaranteed to improve monotonically the approximation of $P(\mathbf{t}_n)$ and typically only two iterations are necessary for convergence.

Optimising the Model Parameters. We again use EM to increase the variational likelihood approximation with respect to $\mathbf{w}_i$ and b_i. Defining

$$\widehat{\mathbf{w}}_i = (\mathbf{w}_i^\mathrm{T}, b_i)^\mathrm{T},$$
$$\widehat{\mathbf{x}} = (\mathbf{x}^\mathrm{T}, 1)^\mathrm{T},$$

leads to updates for both $\mathbf{w}_i$ and b_i given by:

$$\widehat{\mathbf{w}}_i = -\left[\sum_{n=1}^{N} 2\lambda(\xi_{in})\langle\widehat{\mathbf{x}}_n\widehat{\mathbf{x}}_n^\mathrm{T}\rangle\right]^{-1}\left[\sum_{n=1}^{N}(t_{in}-1/2)\langle\widehat{\mathbf{x}}_n\rangle\right], \tag{11}$$

where

$$\langle\widehat{\mathbf{x}}_n\widehat{\mathbf{x}}_n^\mathrm{T}\rangle = \begin{pmatrix}\mathbf{C}_n + \boldsymbol{\mu}_n\boldsymbol{\mu}_n^\mathrm{T} & \boldsymbol{\mu}_n \\ \boldsymbol{\mu}_n^\mathrm{T} & 1\end{pmatrix}. \tag{12}$$

5 Visualisation

Synthetic clustered data. We firstly give an example of visualisation of artificially-generated data to illustrate the operation and features of the method. Binary data was synthesised by first generating three random 16-bit prototype vectors, where each bit was set with probability 0.5. Next a 600-point dataset was generated by taking 200 examples of each prototype and inverting each bit with probability 0.05. We generated a second dataset in the same manner, but where the probability of bit inversion was 0.15, simulating more "noise" about each prototype. The final values of $\boldsymbol{\mu}_n$ from (7) for each data point are plotted in Figure 1. In the left plot for the low-noise dataset, the three clusters are clear, as are the prototype vectors. On the right, the bit-noise is sufficiently high such that clusters now overlap to a degree and the prototypes are no longer evident. However, we can elucidate further information from the model by drawing lines representing $P(t_i|\mathbf{x}) = 0.5$, or $\mathbf{w}_i^T\mathbf{x} + b_i = 0$, which may be considered to be 'decision boundaries' for each bit. These offer more convincing evidence of the presence of three clusters.

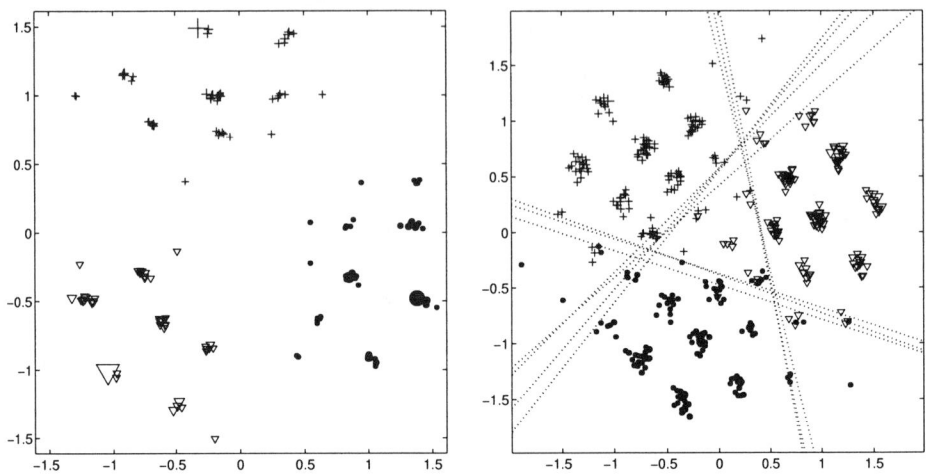

Figure 1: Visualisation of two synthetic clustered datasets. The three clusters have been denoted by separate glyphs, the size of which reflects the number of examples whose posterior means are located at that point in the latent space. In the right plot, lines corresponding to $P(t_i|\mathbf{x}) = 0.5$ have been drawn.

Handwritten digit data. On the left of Figure 2, a visualisation is given of 1000 examples derived from 16 × 16 images of handwritten digit '2's. There is visual evidence of the natural variability of writing styles in the plot as the posterior latent means in Figure 2 describe an approximate 'horseshoe' structure. On the right of the figure we examine the nature of this by plotting gray-scale images of the vectors $P(\mathbf{t}|\mathbf{x}_j)$, where $\mathbf{x}_j$ are four numbered samples in the visualisation space. These images illustrate the expected value of each bit given the latent-space location and demonstrate that the location is indeed indicative of the style of the digit, notably the presence of a loop.

Accuracy of the variational approximation. To investigate the accuracy of the approximation, the sampling algorithm of Section 3 for likelihood maximisation was implemented and applied to the above two datasets. The evolution of error (negative log-likelihood per data-point) was plotted against time for both algorithms, using identical initialisations. The 'true' error for the variational approach was estimated using the same 500-point Monte-Carlo sample. Typical results are shown in Figure 3, and the final running time and error (using a sensible stopping criterion) are given for both datasets in Table 1.

For these two example datasets, the variational algorithm converges considerably more quickly than in the sampling case, and the difference in final error is relatively small, particularly so for the larger-dimensionality dataset. The approximation of the posterior distributions $p(\mathbf{x}_n|\mathbf{t}_n)$ is the key factor in the accuracy of the algorithm. In Figure 4, contours of the posterior distribution in the latent space induced

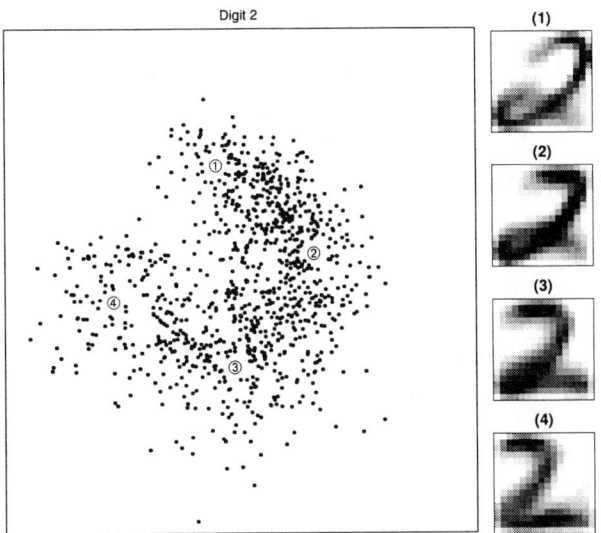

Figure 2: Left: visualisation of 256-dimensional digit '2' data. Right: gray-scale images of the conditional probability of each bit at the latent space locations marked.

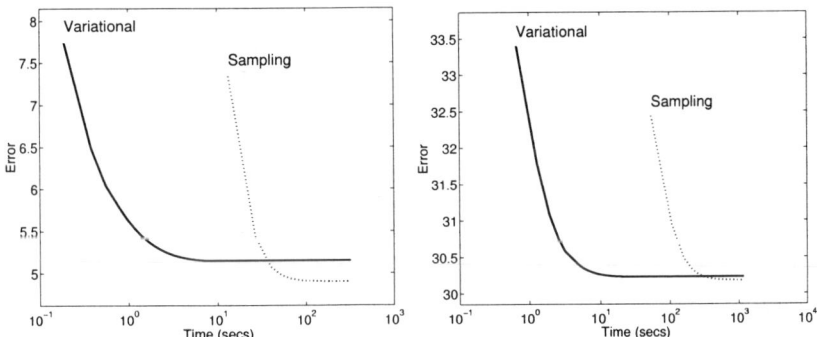

Figure 3: Error vs. time for the synthetic data (left) and the digit '2' data (right).

by a typical data point are shown for both algorithms and datasets. This approximation is more accurate as dimensionality increases (a phenomenon observed with other datasets too), as the true posterior becomes more Gaussian in form.

6 Conclusions

We have outlined a variational approximation for parameter estimation in a probabilistic visualisation model and although we have only considered its application to binary variables here, the extension to mixtures of arbitrary data types is readily implemented. For the two comparisons shown (and others not illustrated here), the approximation appears acceptably accurate, and particularly so for data of higher dimensionality. The algorithm is considerably faster than a sampling approach, which would permit incorporation of multiple models in a more complex hierarchical architecture, of a sort that has been effectively implemented for visualisation of continuous variables (Bishop and Tipping 1998).

	Synthetic-16		Digit-256	
	Time	Error	Time	Error
Variational	7.8	5.14	25.6	30.23
Sampling	331.1	4.93	1204.5	30.19

Table 1: Comparison of final error and running time for the two algorithms.

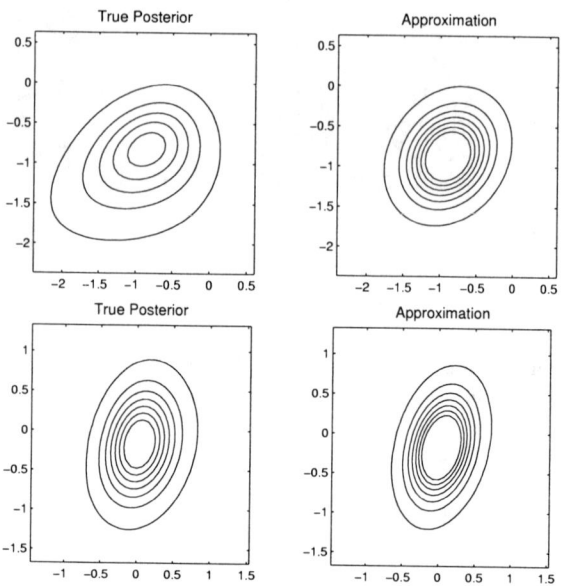

Figure 4: True and approximated posteriors for a single example from the synthetic data set (top) and the digit '2' data (bottom).

7 References

Bartholomew, D. J. (1987). *Latent Variable Models and Factor Analysis*. London: Charles Griffin & Co. Ltd.

Bishop, C. M., M. Svensén, and C. K. I. Williams (1998). GTM: the Generative Topographic Mapping. *Neural Computation* 10(1), 215–234.

Bishop, C. M. and M. E. Tipping (1998). A hierarchical latent variable model for data visualization. *IEEE Transactions on Pattern Analysis and Machine Intelligence* 20(3), 281–293.

Jaakkola, T. S. and M. I. Jordan (1997). Bayesian logistic regression: a variational approach. In D. Madigan and P. Smyth (Eds.), *Proceedings of the 1997 Conference on Artificial Intelligence and Statistics*, Ft Lauderdale, FL.

Lowe, D. and M. E. Tipping (1997). Neuroscale: Novel topographic feature extraction with radial basis function networks. In M. Mozer, M. Jordan, and T. Petsche (Eds.), *Advances in Neural Information Processing Systems 9*, pp. 543–549. Cambridge, Mass: MIT Press.

Mackay, D. J. C. (1995). Bayesian neural networks and density networks. *Nuclear Instruments and Methods in Physics Research, Section A* 354(1), 73–80.

Moustaki, I. (1996). A latent trait and a latent class model for mixed observed variables. *British Journal of Mathematical and Statistical Psychology* 49, 313–334.

Sammel, M. D., L. M. Ryan, and J. M. Legler (1997). Latent variable models for mixed discrete and continuous outcomes. *Journal of the Royal Statistical Society, Series B* 59, 667–678.

SMEM Algorithm for Mixture Models

Naonori Ueda   Ryohei Nakano
{ueda, nakano}@cslab.kecl.ntt.co.jp
NTT Communication Science Laboratories
Hikaridai, Seika-cho, Soraku-gun, Kyoto 619-0237 Japan

Zoubin Ghahramani   Geoffrey E. Hinton
zoubin@gatsby.ucl.ac.uk g.hinton@ucl.ac.uk
Gatsby Computational Neuroscience Unit, University College London
17 Queen Square, London WC1N 3AR, UK

Abstract

We present a split and merge EM (SMEM) algorithm to overcome the local maximum problem in parameter estimation of finite mixture models. In the case of mixture models, non-global maxima often involve having too many components of a mixture model in one part of the space and too few in another, widely separated part of the space. To escape from such configurations we repeatedly perform simultaneous split and merge operations using a new criterion for efficiently selecting the split and merge candidates. We apply the proposed algorithm to the training of Gaussian mixtures and mixtures of factor analyzers using synthetic and real data and show the effectiveness of using the split and merge operations to improve the likelihood of both the training data and of held-out test data.

1 INTRODUCTION

Mixture density models, in particular normal mixtures, have been extensively used in the field of statistical pattern recognition [1]. Recently, more sophisticated mixture density models such as mixtures of latent variable models (*e.g.,* probabilistic PCA or factor analysis) have been proposed to approximate the underlying data manifold [2]-[4]. The parameter of these mixture models can be estimated using the EM algorithm [5] based on the maximum likelihood framework [3][4]. A common and serious problem associated with these EM algorithm is the local maxima problem. Although this problem has been pointed out by many researchers, the best way to solve it in practice is still an open question.

Two of the authors have proposed the deterministic annealing EM (DAEM) algorithm [6], where a modified posterior probability parameterized by *temperature* is derived to avoid local maxima. However, in the case of mixture density models, local maxima arise when there are too many components of a mixture models in one part of the space and too few in another. It is not possible to move a component from the overpopulated region to the underpopulated region without passing through positions that give lower likelihood. We therefore introduce a discrete move that simultaneously merges two components in an overpopulated region and splits a component in an underpopulated region.

The idea of split and merge operations has been successfully applied to clustering or vector quantization (*e.g.*, [7]). To our knowledge, this is the first time that simultaneous split and merge operations have been applied to improve mixture density estimation. New criteria presented in this paper can efficiently select the split and merge candidates. Although the proposed method, unlike the DAEM algorithm, is limited to mixture models, we have experimentally comfirmed that our split and merge EM algorithm obtains better solutions than the DAEM algorithm.

2 Split and Merge EM (SMEM) Algorithm

The probability density function (pdf) of a mixture of M density models is given by

$$p(\boldsymbol{x};\Theta) = \sum_{m=1}^{M} \alpha_m p(\boldsymbol{x}|\omega_m;\theta_m), \quad \text{where} \quad \alpha_m \geq 0 \quad \text{and} \quad \sum_{m=1}^{M} \alpha_m = 1. \quad (1)$$

The $p(\boldsymbol{x}|\omega_m;\theta_m)$ is a d-dimensional density model corresponding to the component ω_m. The EM algorithm, as is well known, iteratively estimates the parameters $\Theta = \{(\alpha_m, \theta_m), m = 1, \ldots, M\}$ using two steps. The E-step computes the expectation of the complete data log-likelihood.

$$Q(\Theta|\Theta^{(t)}) = \sum_{\boldsymbol{x}} \sum_{m} P(\omega_m|\boldsymbol{x};\Theta^{(t)}) \log \alpha_m p(\boldsymbol{x}|\omega_m;\theta_m), \quad (2)$$

where $P(\omega_m|\boldsymbol{x};\Theta^{(t)})$ is the posterior probability which can be computed by

$$P(\omega_m|\boldsymbol{x};\Theta^{(t)}) = \frac{\alpha_m^{(t)} p(\boldsymbol{x}|\omega_m;\theta_m^{(t)})}{\sum_{m'=1}^{M} \alpha_{m'}^{(t)} p(\boldsymbol{x}|\omega_{m'};\theta_{m'}^{(t)})}. \quad (3)$$

Next, the M-step maximizes this Q function with respect to Θ to estimate the new parameter values $\Theta^{(t+1)}$.

Looking at (2) carefully, one can see that the Q function can be represented in the form of a direct sum; *i.e.*, $Q(\Theta|\Theta^{(t)}) = \sum_{m=1}^{M} q_m(\Theta|\Theta^{(t)})$, where $q_m(\Theta|\Theta^{(t)}) = \sum_{\boldsymbol{x} \in \mathcal{X}} P(\omega_m|\boldsymbol{x};\Theta^{(t)}) \log \alpha_m p(\boldsymbol{x}|\omega_m;\theta_m)$ and depends only on α_m and θ_m. Let Θ^* denote the parameter values estimated by the usual EM algorithm. Then after the EM algorithm has converged, the Q function can be rewritten as

$$Q^* = q_i^* + q_j^* + q_k^* + \sum_{m, m \neq i,j,k} q_m^*. \quad (4)$$

We then try to increase the first three terms of the right-hand side of (4) by merging two components ω_i and ω_j to produce a component $\omega_{i'}$, and splitting the component ω_k into two components $\omega_{j'}$ and $\omega_{k'}$. To reestimate the parameters of these new components, we have to initialize the parameters corresponding to them using Θ^*.

The initial parameter values for the merged component $\omega_{i'}$ can be set as a linear combination of the original ones before merge:

$$\alpha_{i'} = \alpha_i^* + \alpha_j^* \quad \text{and} \quad \theta_{i'} = \frac{\theta_i^* \sum_{\boldsymbol{x}} P(\omega_i|\boldsymbol{x};\Theta^*) + \theta_j^* \sum_{\boldsymbol{x}} P(\omega_j|\boldsymbol{x};\Theta^*)}{\sum_{\boldsymbol{x}} P(\omega_i|\boldsymbol{x};\Theta^*) + \sum_{\boldsymbol{x}} P(\omega_j|\boldsymbol{x};\Theta^*)}. \quad (5)$$

On the other hand, as for two components $\omega_{j'}$ and $\omega_{k'}$, we set

$$\alpha_{j'} = \alpha_{k'} = \alpha_k^*/2 \qquad \theta_{j'} = \theta_k^* + \epsilon \quad \text{and} \quad \theta_{k'} = \theta_k^* + \epsilon', \tag{6}$$

where ϵ is some small random perturbation vector or matrix (i.e., $\|\epsilon\| \ll \|\theta_k^*\|$)[1]. The parameter reestimation for $m = i', j'$ and k' can be done by using EM steps, but note that the posterior probability (3) should be replaced with (7) so that this reestimation does not affect the other components.

$$P(\omega_m|\boldsymbol{x};\Theta^{(t)}) = \frac{\alpha_m^{(t)} p(\boldsymbol{x}|\omega_m;\theta_m^{(t)})}{\sum_{m'=i',j',k'} \alpha_{m'}^{(t)} p(\boldsymbol{x}|\omega_m;\theta_{m'}^{(t)})} \times \sum_{m'=i,j,k} P(\omega_{m'}|\boldsymbol{x};\Theta^*), \quad m = i', j', k'. \tag{7}$$

Clearly $\sum_{m'=i',j',k'} P(\omega_{m'}|\boldsymbol{x};\Theta^{(t)}) = \sum_{m=i,j,k} P(\omega_m|\boldsymbol{x};\Theta^*)$ always holds during the reestimation process. For convenience, we call this EM procedure the *partial EM procedure*. After this partial EM procedure, the usual EM steps, called the *full EM procedure*, are performed as a post processing. After these procedures, if Q is improved, then we accept the new estimate and repeat the above after setting the new paramters to Θ^*. Otherwise reject and go back to Θ^* and try another candidate. We summarize these procedures as follows:

[SMEM Algorithm]
1. Perform the usual EM updates. Let Θ^* and Q^* denote the estimated parameters and corresponding Q function value, respectively.
2. Sort the split and merge candidates by computing split and merge criteria (described in the next section) based on Θ^*. Let $\{i,j,k\}_c$ denote the cth candidate.
3. For $c = 1, \ldots, C_{max}$, perform the following: After initial parameter settings based on Θ^*, perform the *partial EM procedure* for $\{i,j,k\}_c$ and then perform the *full EM procedure*. Let Θ^{**} be the obtained parameters and Q^{**} be the corresponding Q function value. If $Q^{**} > Q^*$, then set $Q^* \leftarrow Q^{**}$, $\Theta^* \leftarrow \Theta^{**}$ and go to Step 2.
4. Halt with Θ^* as the final parameters.

Note that when a certain split and merge candidate which improves the Q function value is found at Step 3, the other successive candidates are ignored. There is therefore no guarantee that the split and the merge candidates that are chosen will give the largest possible improvement in Q. This is not a major problem, however, because the split and merge operations are performed repeatedly. Strictly speaking, $C_{max} = M(M-1)(M-2)/2$, but experimentally we have confirmed that $C_{max} \sim 5$ may be enough.

3 Split and Merge Criteria

Each of the split and merge candidates can be evaluated by its Q function value after Step 3 of the SMEM algorithm mentioned in Sec.2. However, since there are so many candidates, some reasonable criteria for ordering the split and merge candidates should be utilized to accelerate the SMEM algorithm.

In general, when there are many data points each of which has almost equal posterior probabilities for any two components, it can be thought that these two components

---
[1] In the case of mixture Gaussians, covariance matrices $\Sigma_{j'}$ and $\Sigma_{k'}$ should be positive definite. In this case, we can initialize them as $\Sigma_{j'} = \Sigma_{k'} = \det(\Sigma_k^*)^{1/d} I_d$ indtead of (6).

might be merged. To numerically evaluate this, we define the following merge criterion:

$$J_{merge}(i,j;\Theta^*) = \mathbf{P}_i(\Theta^*)^T \mathbf{P}_j(\Theta^*), \tag{8}$$

where $\mathbf{P}_i(\Theta^*) = (P(\omega_i|\boldsymbol{x}_1;\Theta^*),\ldots,P(\omega_i|\boldsymbol{x}_N;\Theta^*))^T \in \mathcal{R}^N$ is the N-dimensional vector consisting of posterior probabilities for the component ω_i. Clearly, two components ω_i and ω_j with larger $J_{merge}(i,j;\Theta^*)$ should be merged.

As a split criterion (J_{split}), we define the *local Kullback divergence* as:

$$J_{split}(k;\Theta^*) = \int p_k(\boldsymbol{x};\Theta^*) \log \frac{p_k(\boldsymbol{x};\Theta^*)}{p(\boldsymbol{x}|\omega_k;\theta_k^*)} d\boldsymbol{x}, \tag{9}$$

which is the distance between two distributions: the local data density $p_k(\boldsymbol{x})$ around the component ω_k and the density of the component ω_k specified by the current parameter estimate $\boldsymbol{\mu}_k^*$ and Σ_k^*. The local data density is defined as:

$$p_k(\boldsymbol{x};\Theta^*) = \frac{\sum_{n=1}^N \delta(\boldsymbol{x}-\boldsymbol{x}_n)P(\omega_k|\boldsymbol{x}_n;\Theta^*)}{\sum_{n=1}^N P(\omega_k|\boldsymbol{x}_n;\Theta^*)}. \tag{10}$$

This is a modified empirical distribution weighted by the posterior probability so that the data around the component ω_k are focused. Note that when the weights are equal, i.e., $P(\omega_k|\boldsymbol{x};\Theta^*) = 1/M$, (10) is the usual empirical distribution, i.e., $p_k(\boldsymbol{x};\Theta^*) = (1/N)\sum_{n=1}^N \delta(\boldsymbol{x}-\boldsymbol{x}_n)$. Since it can be thought that the component with the largest $J_{split}(k;\Theta^*)$ has the worst estimate of the local density, we should try to split it. Using J_{merge} and J_{split}, we sort the split and merge candidates as follows. First, merge candidates are sorted based on J_{merge}. Then, for each sorted merge candidate $\{i,j\}_c$, split candidates excluding $\{i,j\}_c$ are sorted as $\{k\}_c$. By combining these results and renumbering them, we obtain $\{i,j,k\}_c$.

4 Experiments

4.1 Gaussian mixtures

First, we show the results of two-dimensional synthetic data in Fig. 1 to visually demonstrate the usefulness of the split and merge operations. Initial mean vectors and covariance matrices were set to near mean of all data and unit matrix, respectively. The usual EM algorithm converged to the local maximum solution shown in Fig. 1(b), whereas the SMEM algorithm converged to the superior solution shown in Fig. 1(d) very close to the true one. The split of the 1st Gaussian shown in Fig. 1(c) seems to be redundant, but as shown in Fig. 1(d) they are successfully merged and the original two Gaussians were improved. This indicates that the split and merge operations not only appropriately assign the number of Gaussians in a local data space, but can also improve the Gaussian parameters themselves.

Next, we tested the proposed algorithm using 20-dimensional real data (facial images) where the local maxima make the optimization difficult. The data size was 103 for training and 103 for test. We ran three algorithms (EM, DAEM, and SMEM) for ten different initializations using the K-means algorithm. We set $M = 5$ and used a diagonal covariance for each Gaussian. As shown in Table 1, the worst solution found by the SMEM algorithm was better than the best solutions found by the other algorithms on both training and test data.

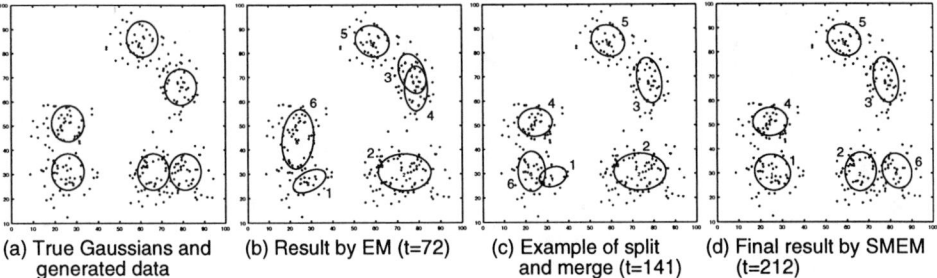

(a) True Gaussians and generated data (b) Result by EM (t=72) (c) Example of split and merge (t=141) (d) Final result by SMEM (t=212)

Figure 1: Gaussian mixture estimation results.

Table 1: Log-likelihood / data point

		initiall value	EM	DAEM	SMEM
Training data	mean	−159.1	−148.2	−147.9	−145.1
	std	1.77	0.24	0.04	0.08
	max	−157.3	−147.7	−147.8	−145.0
	min	−163.2	−148.6	−147.9	−145.2
Test data	mean	−168.2	−159.8	−159.7	−155.9
	std	2.80	1.00	0.37	0.09
	max	−165.5	−158.0	−159.6	−155.9
	min	−174.2	−160.8	−159.8	−156.0

Table 2: No. of iterations

	EM	DAEM	SMEM
mean	47	147	155
std	16	39	44
max	65	189	219
min	37	103	109

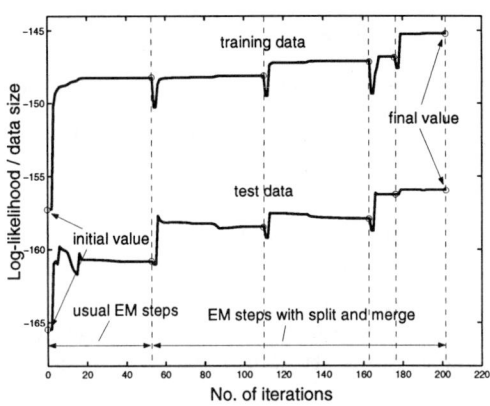

Figure 2: Trajectories of loglikelihood. Upper (lower) corresponds to training (test) data.

Figure 2 shows log-likelihood value trajectories accepted at Step 3 of the SMEM algorithm during the estimation process [2]. Comparing the convergence points at Step 3 marked by the 'o' symbol in Fig. 2, one can see that the successive split and merge operations improved the log-likelihood for both the training and test data, as we expected. Table 2 compares the number of iterations executed by the three algorithms. Note that in the SMEM algorithm, the EM-steps corresponding to rejected split and merge operations are not counted. The average rank of the accepted split and merge candidates was 1.8 (STD=0.9), which indicates that the proposed split and merge criteria work very well. Therefore, the SMEM algorithm was about $155 \times 1.8/47 \simeq 6$ times slower than the original EM algorithm.

4.2 Mixtures of factor analyzers

A mixture of factor analyzers (MFA) can be thought of as a reduced dimension mixture of Gaussians [4]. That is, it can extract locally linear low-dimensional manifold underlying given high-dimensional data. A single FA model assumes that an observed D-dimensional variable x are generated as a linear transformation of some lower K-dimensional *latent* variable $z \sim \mathcal{N}(0, I)$ plus additive Gaussian noise $v \sim \mathcal{N}(0, \Psi)$. Ψ is diagonal. That is, the generative model can be written as

---

[2] Dotted lines in Fig. 2 denote the starting points of Step 2. Note that it is due to the initialization at Step 3 that the log-likelihood decreases just after the split and merge.

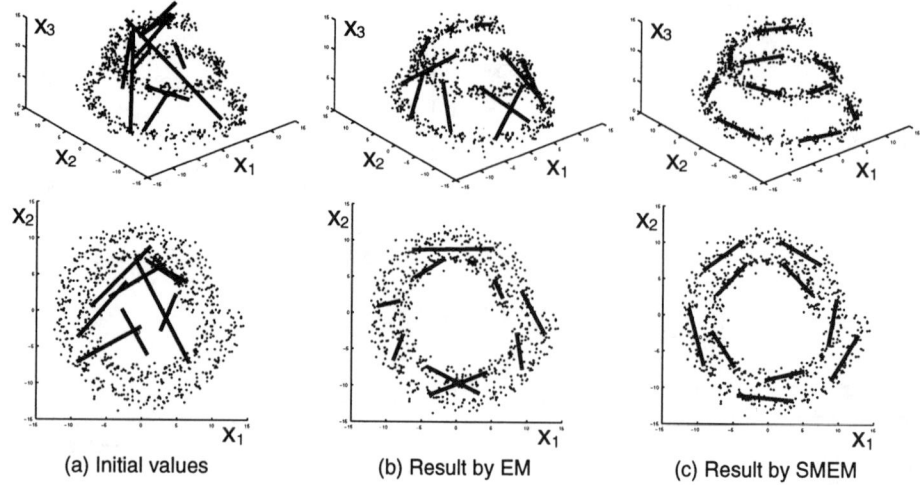

Figure 3: Extraction of 1D manifold by using a mixture of factor analyzers.

$x = \Lambda z + v + \mu$. Here μ is a mean vector. Then from simple calculation, we can see that $x \sim \mathcal{N}(\mu, \Lambda\Lambda^T + \Psi)$. Therefore, in the case of a M mixture of FAs, $x \sim \sum_{m=1}^{M} \alpha_m \mathcal{N}(\mu_m, \Lambda_m\Lambda_m^T + \Psi_m)$. See [4] for the details. Then, in this case, the Q function is also decomposable into M components and therefore the SMEM algorithm is straightforwardly applicable to the parameter estimation of the MFA models.

Figure 3 shows the results of extracting a one-dimensional manifold from three-dimensional data (noisy shrinking spiral) using the EM and the SMEM algorithms[3]. Although the EM algorithm converged to a poor local maxima, the SMEM algorithm successfully extracted data manifold. Table 3 compares average log-likelihood per data point over ten different initializations. The log-likelihood values were drastically improved on both training and test data by the SMEM algorithm.

The MFA model is applicable to pattern recognition tasks [2][3] since once an MFA model is fitted to each class, we can compute the posterior probabilities for each data point. We tried a digit recognition task (10 digits (classes))[4] using the MFA model. The computed log-likelihood averaged over ten classes and recognition accuracy for test data are given in Table 4. Clearly, the SMEM algorithm consistently improved the EM algorithm on both log-likelihood and recognition accuracy. Note that the recognition accuracy by the 3-nearest neighbor (3NN) classifier was 88.3%. It is interesting that the MFA approach by both the EM and SMEM algorithms could outperform the nearest neighbor approach when $K = 3$ and $M = 5$. This suggests that the intrinsic dimensionality of the data would be three or so.

---

[3]In this case, each factor loading matrix Λ_m becomes a three dimensional column vector corresponding to each thick line in Fig. 3. More correctly, the center position and the direction of each thick line are μ_m and Λ_m, respectively. And the length of each thick line is $2 \|\Lambda_m\|$.

[4]The data were created using the degenerate Glucksman's feature (16 dimensional data) by NTT labs.[8]. The data size was 200/class for training and 200/class for test.

Table 3: Log-likelihood / data point

	EM	SMEM
Training	−7.68 (0.151)	−7.26 (0.017)
Test	−7.75 (0.171)	−7.33 (0.032)

( ) : STD

Table 4: Digit recognition results

		Log-likelihood / data point		Recognition rate (%)	
		EM	SMEM	EM	SMEM
K=3	M=5	−3.18	−3.15	89.0	91.3
	M=10	−3.09	−3.05	87.5	88.7
K=8	M=5	−3.14	−3.11	85.3	87.3
	M=10	−3.04	−3.01	82.5	85.1

5 Conclusion

We have shown how simultaneous split and merge operations can be used to move components of a mixture model from regions of the space in which there are too many components to regions in which there are too few. Such moves cannot be accomplished by methods that continuously move components through intermediate locations because the likelihood is lower at these locations. A simultaneous split and merge can be viewed as a way of tunneling through low-likelihood barriers, thereby eliminating many non-global optima. In this respect, it has some similarities with simulated annealing but the moves that are considered are long-range and are very specific to the particular problems that arise when fitting a mixture model. Note that the SMEM algorithm is applicable to a wide variety of mixture models, as long as the decomposition (4) holds. To make the split and merge method efficient we have introduced criteria for deciding which splits and merges to consider and have shown that these criteria work well for low-dimensional synthetic datasets and for higher-dimensional real datasets. Our SMEM algorithm consistently outperforms standard EM and therefore it would be very useful in practice.

References

[1] MacLachlan, G. and Basford K., "Mixture models: Inference and application to clustering," Marcel Dekker, 1988.

[2] Hinton G. E., Dayan P., and Revow M., "Modeling the minifolds of images of handwritten digits," *IEEE Trans. PAMI*, vol.8, no.1, pp. 65–74, 1997.

[3] Tipping M. E. and Bishop C. M., "Mixtures of probabilistic principal component analysers," Tech. Rep. NCRG-97-3, Aston Univ. Birmingham, UK, 1997.

[4] Ghahramani Z. and Hinton G. E., "The EM algorithm for mixtures of factor analyzers," Tech. Report CRG-TR-96-1, Univ. of Toronto, 1997.

[5] Dempster A. P., Laird N. M. and Rubin D. B., "Maximum likelihood from incomplete data via the EM algorithm," *Journal of Royal Statistical Society B*, vol. 39, pp. 1–38, 1977.

[6] Ueda N. and Nakano R., "Deterministic annealing EM algorithm," *Neural Networks*, vol.11, no.2, pp.271–282, 1998.

[7] Ueda N. and Nakano R., "A new competitive learning approach based on an equidistortion principle for designing optimal vector quantizers," *Neural Networks*, vol.7, no.8, pp.1211–1227, 1994.

[8] Ishii K., "Design of a recognition dictionary using artificially distorted characters," *Systems and computers in Japan*, vol.21, no.9, pp. 669–677, 1989.

Learning Mixture Hierarchies

Nuno Vasconcelos   **Andrew Lippman**
MIT Media Laboratory, 20 Ames St, E15-320M, Cambridge, MA 02139,
{nuno,lip}@media.mit.edu,   http://www.media.mit.edu/~nuno

Abstract

The hierarchical representation of data has various applications in domains such as data mining, machine vision, or information retrieval. In this paper we introduce an extension of the *Expectation-Maximization* (EM) algorithm that learns mixture hierarchies in a computationally efficient manner. Efficiency is achieved by progressing in a bottom-up fashion, i.e. by clustering the mixture components of a given level in the hierarchy to obtain those of the level above. This clustering requires only knowledge of the mixture parameters, there being no need to resort to intermediate samples. In addition to practical applications, the algorithm allows a new interpretation of EM that makes clear the relationship with non-parametric *kernel-based* estimation methods, provides explicit control over the trade-off between the bias and variance of EM estimates, and offers new insights about the behavior of deterministic annealing methods commonly used with EM to escape local minima of the likelihood.

1 Introduction

There are many practical applications of statistical learning where it is useful to characterize data hierarchically. Such characterization can be done according to either top-down or bottom-up strategies. While the former start by generating a coarse model that roughly describes the entire space, and then successively refine the description by partitioning the space and generating sub-models for each of the regions in the partition; the later start from a fine description, and successively agglomerate sub-models to generate the coarser descriptions at the higher levels in the hierarchy.

Bottom-up strategies are particularly useful when not all the data is available at once, or when the dataset is so big that processing it as whole is computationally infeasible. This is the case of machine vision tasks such as object recognition, or the indexing of video databases. In object recognition, it is many times convenient to determine not only which object is present in the scene but also its pose [2], a goal that can be attained by a hierarchical, description where at the lowest level a model is learned for each object pose and all pose models are then combined into a generic model at the top level of the hierarchy. Similarly, for video indexing, one may be interested in learning a description for each frame and then combine these into shot descriptions or descriptions for some other sort of high level temporal unit [6].

In this paper we present an extension of the EM algorithm [1] for the estimation of hierarchical mixture models in a bottom-up fashion. It turns out that the attainment of this goal has far more reaching consequences than the practical applications above. In particular, because a kernel density estimate can be seen as a limiting case of a mixture model (where a mixture component is superimposed on each sample), this extension establishes a direct connection between so-called parametric and non-parametric density estimation methods making it possible to exploit results from the vast non-parametric smoothing literature [4] to improve the accuracy of parametric estimates. Furthermore, the original EM algorithm becomes a particular case of the one now presented, and a new intuitive interpretation becomes available for an important variation of EM (known as *deterministic annealing*) that had previously been derived from statistical physics. With regards to practical applications, the algorithm leads to computationally efficient methods for estimating density hierarchies capable of describing data at different resolutions.

2   Hierarchical mixture density estimation

Our model consists of a hierarchy of mixture densities, where the data at a given level is described by

$$P(\mathbf{X}) = \sum_{k=1}^{C^l} \pi_k^l p(\mathbf{X}|z_k^l = 1, \mathcal{M}_l), \qquad (1)$$

where l is the level in the hierarchy ($l = 0$ providing the coarsest characterization of the data), $\mathcal{M}_l$ the mixture model at this level, C^l the number of mixture components that compose it, π_k^l the prior probability of the kth component, and z_k^l a binary variable that takes the value 1 if and only if the sample $\mathbf{X}$ was drawn from this component. The only restriction on the model is that if node j of level $l+1$ is a child of node i of level l, then

$$\pi_j^{l+1} = \pi_{j|k}^{l+1} \pi_k^l, \qquad (2)$$

where k is the parent of j in the hierarchy of hidden variables.

The basic problem is to compute the mixture parameters of the description at level l given the knowledge of the parameters at level $l+1$. This can also be seen as a problem of clustering mixture components. A straightforward solution would be to draw a sample from the mixture density at level $l+1$ and simply run EM with the number of classes of the level l to estimate the corresponding parameters. Such a solution would have at least two major limitations. First, there would be no guarantee that the constraint of equation (2) would be enforced, i.e. there would be no guarantee of structure in the resulting mixture hierarchy, and second it would be computationally expensive, as all the models in the hierarchy would have to be learned from a large sample. In the next section, we show that this is really not necessary.

3   Estimating mixture hierarchies

The basic idea behind our approach is, instead of generating a real sample from the mixture model at level $l+1$, to consider a *virtual sample* generated from the same model, use EM to find the expressions for the parameters of the mixture model of level l that best explain this virtual sample, and establish a closed-form relationship between these parameters and those of the model at level $l+1$. For this, we start by considering a virtual sample $\mathbf{X} = \{\mathbf{X}_1, \ldots, \mathbf{X}_{C^{l+1}}\}$ from $\mathcal{M}_{l+1}$, where each of the $\mathbf{X}_i$ is a virtual sample from one of the C^{l+1} components of this model, with size $M_i = \pi_i^l N$, where N is the total number of virtual points.

We next establish the likelihood for the virtual sample under the model $\mathcal{M}_l$. For this, as is usual in the EM literature, we assume that samples from different blocks are independent, i.e.
$$P(\mathbf{X}|\mathcal{M}_l) = \prod_{i=1}^{C^{l+1}} P(\mathbf{X}_i|\mathcal{M}_l), \tag{3}$$
but, to ensure that the constraint of equation (2) is enforced, samples within the same block are assigned to the same component of $\mathcal{M}_l$. Assuming further that, given the knowledge of the assignment the samples are drawn independently from the corresponding mixture component, the likelihood of each block is given by
$$P(\mathbf{X}_i|\mathcal{M}_l) = \sum_{j=1}^{C^l} \pi_j^l P(\mathbf{X}_i|z_{ij}=1,\mathcal{M}_l) = \sum_{j=1}^{C^l} \pi_j^l \prod_{m=1}^{M_i} P(\mathbf{x}_i^m|z_{ij}=1,\mathcal{M}_l), \tag{4}$$
where $z_{ij} = z_i^{l+1} z_j^l$ is a binary variable with value one if and only if the block $\mathbf{X}_i$ is assigned to the jth component of $\mathcal{M}_l$, and $\mathbf{x}_i^m$ is the mth data point in $\mathbf{X}_i$. Combining equations (3) and (4) we obtain the *incomplete data* likelihood, under $\mathcal{M}_l$, for the whole sample
$$P(\mathbf{X}|\mathcal{M}_l) = \prod_{i=1}^{C^{l+1}} \sum_{j=1}^{C^l} \pi_j^l \prod_{m=1}^{M_i} P(\mathbf{x}_i^m|z_{ij}=1,\mathcal{M}_l). \tag{5}$$
This equation is similar to the incomplete data likelihood of standard EM, the main difference being that instead of having an hidden variable for each sample point, we now have one for each sample block. The likelihood of the *complete data* is given by
$$P(\mathbf{X},\mathbf{Z}|\mathcal{M}_l) = \prod_{i=1}^{C^{l+1}} \prod_{j=1}^{C^l} \left[\pi_j^l P(\mathbf{X}_i|z_{ij}=1,\mathcal{M}_l)\right]^{z_{ij}}, \tag{6}$$
where $\mathbf{Z}$ is a vector containing all the z_{ij}, and the log-likelihood becomes
$$\log P(\mathbf{X},\mathbf{Z}|\mathcal{M}_l) = \sum_{i=1}^{C^{l+1}} \sum_{j=1}^{C^l} z_{ij} \log(\pi_j^l P(\mathbf{X}_i|z_{ij}=1,\mathcal{M}_l)). \tag{7}$$
Relying on EM to estimate the parameters of $\mathcal{M}_l$ leads to the the following E-step
$$h_{ij} = E[z_{ij}|\mathbf{X}_i,\mathcal{M}_l] = P(z_{ij}=1|\mathbf{X}_i,\mathcal{M}_l) = \frac{P(\mathbf{X}_i|z_{ij}=1,\mathcal{M}_l)\pi_j^l}{\sum_k P(\mathbf{X}_i|z_{ik}=1,\mathcal{M}_l)\pi_k^l}. \tag{8}$$
The key quantity to compute is therefore $P(\mathbf{X}_i|z_{ij}=1,\mathcal{M}_l)$. Taking its logarithm
$$\log P(\mathbf{X}_i|z_{ij}=1,\mathcal{M}_l) = M_i[\frac{1}{M_i}\sum_{i=1}^{M_i} \log P(\mathbf{x}_i^m|z_{ij}=1,\mathcal{M}_l)]$$
$$= M_i E_{\mathcal{M}_{l+1,i}}[\log P(\mathbf{x}|z_{ij}=1,\mathcal{M}_l)], \tag{9}$$
where we have used the law of large numbers, and $E_{\mathcal{M}_{l+1,i}}[\mathbf{x}]$ is the expected value of $\mathbf{x}$ according the ith mixture component of $\mathcal{M}_{l+1}$ (the one from which $\mathbf{X}_i$ was drawn). This is an easy computation for most densities commonly used in mixture modeling. It can be shown [5] that for the Gaussian case it leads to
$$h_{ij} = \frac{\left[\mathcal{G}(\mu_i^{l+1},\mu_j^l,\mathbf{\Sigma}_j^l)e^{-\frac{1}{2}trace\{(\mathbf{\Sigma}_j^l)^{-1}\mathbf{\Sigma}_i^{l+1}\}}\right]^{M_i} \pi_j^l}{\sum_k \left[\mathcal{G}(\mu_i^{l+1},\mu_k^l,\mathbf{\Sigma}_k^l)e^{-\frac{1}{2}trace\{(\mathbf{\Sigma}_k^l)^{-1}\mathbf{\Sigma}_i^{l+1}\}}\right]^{M_i} \pi_k^l}, \tag{10}$$

where $\mathcal{G}(\mathbf{x}, \mu, \Sigma)$ is the expression for a Gaussian with mean μ and covariance Σ.

The M-step consists of maximizing

$$Q = \sum_{i=1}^{C^{l+1}} \sum_{j=1}^{C^l} h_{ij} \log(\pi_j^l P(\mathbf{X}_i | z_{ij} = 1, \mathcal{M}_l)) \quad (11)$$

subject to the constraint $\sum_j \pi_j^l = 1$. Once again, this is a relatively simple task for common mixture models and in [5] we show that for the Gaussian case it leads to the following parameter update equations

$$\pi_j^l = \frac{\sum_i h_{ij}}{C^{l+1}} \quad (12)$$

$$\mu_j^l = \frac{\sum_i h_{ij} M_i \mu_i^{l+1}}{\sum_i h_{ij} M_i} \quad (13)$$

$$\Sigma_j^l = \frac{1}{\sum_i h_{ij} M_i} \left[\sum_i h_{ij} M_i \Sigma_i^{l+1} + \sum_i h_{ij} M_i (\mu_i^{l+1} - \mu_j^l)(\mu_i^{l+1} - \mu_j^l)^T \right]. \quad (14)$$

Notice that neither equation (10) nor equations (12) to (14) depend explicitly on the underlying sample $\mathbf{X}_i$ and can be computed directly from the parameters of $\mathcal{M}_{l+1}$. The algorithm is thus very efficient from a computational standpoint as the number of mixture components in $\mathcal{M}_{l+1}$ is typically much smaller than the size of the sample at the bottom of the hierarchy.

4 Relationships with standard EM

There are interesting relationships between the algorithm derived above and the standard EM procedure. The first thing to notice is that by making $M_i = 1$ and $\Sigma_i^{l+1} = 0$, the E and M-steps become those obtained by applying standard EM to the sample composed of the points μ_i^{l+1}.

Thus, standard EM can be seen as a particular case of the new algorithm, that learns a two level mixture hierarchy. An initial estimate is first obtained at the bottom of this hierarchy by placing a Gaussian with zero covariance on top of each data point, the model at the second level being then computed from this estimate. The fact that the estimate at the bottom level is nothing more than a kernel estimate with zero bandwidth suggests that other choices of the kernel bandwidth may lead to better overall EM estimates.

Under this interpretation, the Σ_i^{l+1} become free parameters that can be used to control the smoothness of the density estimates and the whole procedure is equivalent to the composition of three steps: 1) find the kernel density estimate that best fits the sample under analysis, 2) draw a larger virtual sample from that density, and 3) compute EM estimates from this larger sample. In section 5, we show that this can leave to significant improvements in estimation accuracy, particularly when the initial sample is small, the free parameters allowing explicit control over the trade-off between the bias and variance of the estimator.

Another interesting relationship between the hierarchical method and standard EM can be derived by investigating the role of the size of the underlying virtual sample (which determines M_i) on the estimates. Assuming M_i constant, $M_i = M, \forall i$, it factors out of all summations in equations (12) to (14), the contributions of numerator and denominator canceling each other. In this case, the only significance of the choice of M is its impact on the E-step. Assuming, as before, that $\Sigma_i^{l+1} = 0$ we once again have the EM algorithm, but where the class-conditional likelihoods of the E-step are now raised to the Mth power. If

M is seen as the inverse of temperature, both the E and M steps become those of standard EM under deterministic annealing (DA) [1] [3].

The DA process is therefore naturally derived from our hierarchical formulation, which gives it a new interpretation that is significantly simpler and more intuitive than those derived from statistical physics. At the start of the process M is set to zero, i.e. no virtual samples are drawn from the Gaussian superimposed on the real dataset, and there is no virtual data. Thus, the assignments h_{ij} of the E-step simply become the prior mixing proportions π_j^l and the M-step simply sets the parameters of all Gaussians in the model to the sample mean and sample covariance of the real sample. As M increases, the number of virtual points drawn from each Gaussian also increases and for $M = 1$ we have a single point that coincides with the point on the real training sample. We therefore obtain the standard EM equations. Increasing M further will make the E-step assignments harder (in the limit of $M = \infty$ each point is assigned to a single mixture component) because a larger virtual probability mass is attached to each real point leading to much higher certainty with regards to the reliability of the assignment.

Overall, while in the beginning of the process the reduced size of the virtual sample allows the points in the real sample to switch from mixture to mixture easily, as M is increased the switching becomes much less likely. The "exploratory" nature of the initial iterations drives the process towards solutions that are globally good, therefore allowing it to escape local minima.

5 Experimental results

In this section, we present experimental results that illustrate the properties of the hierarchical EM algorithm now proposed. We start by a simple example that illustrates how the algorithm can be used to estimate hierarchical mixtures.

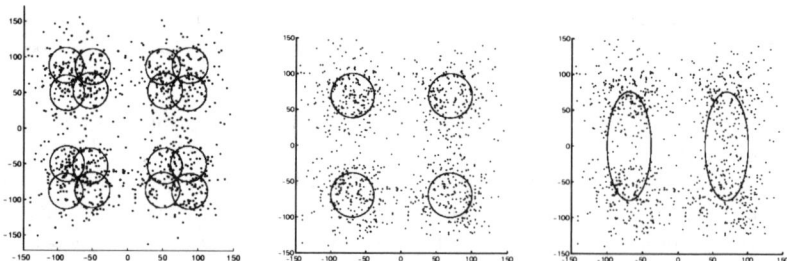

Figure 1: Mixture hierarchy derived from the model shown in the left. The plot relative to each level of the hierarchy is superimposed on a sample drawn from this model. Only the one-standard deviation contours are shown for each Gaussian.

The plot on the left of Figure 1 presents a Gaussian mixture with 16 uniformly weighted components. A sample with 1000 points was drawn from this model, and the algorithm used to find the best descriptions for it at three resolutions (mixtures with 16, 4, and 2 Gaussian). These descriptions are shown in the figure. Notice how the mixture hierarchy naturally captures the various levels of structure exhibited by the data.

This example suggests how the algorithm could be useful for applications such as object recognition or image retrieval. Suppose that each of the Gaussians in the leftmost plot of

---

[1]DA is a technique drawn from analogies with statistical physics that avoids local maxima of the likelihood function (in which standard EM can get trapped) by performing a succession of optimizations at various temperatures [3].

Learning Mixture Hierarchies

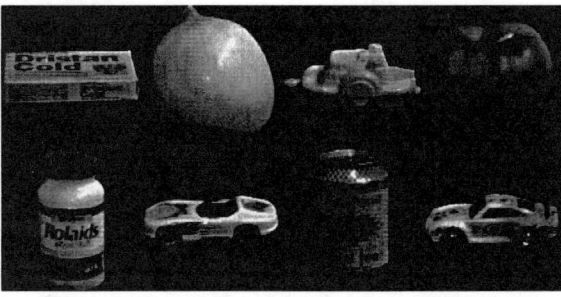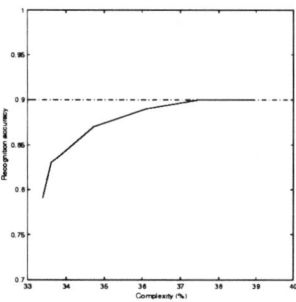

Figure 2: Object recognition task. Left: 8 of the 100 objects in the database. Right: computational savings achieved with hierarchical recognition vs full search.

the figure describes how a given pose of a given object populates a 2-D feature space on which object recognition is to be performed. In this case, higher levels in the hierarchical representation provide a more generic description of the object. E.g. each of the Gaussians in the model shown in the middle of the figure might provide a description for all the poses in which the camera is on the same quadrant of the viewing sphere, while those in the model shown in the right might represent views from the same hemisphere. The advantage, for recognition or retrieval, of relying on a hierarchal structure is that the search can be performed first at the highest resolution, where it is much less expensive, only the best matches being considered at the subsequent levels.

Figure 2 illustrates the application of hierarchical mixture modeling to a real object recognition task. Shown on the left side of the figure are 8 objects from the 100 contained in the Columbia object database [2]. The database consists of 72 views (obtained by positioning the camera in 5° intervals along a circle on the viewing sphere), which were evenly separated into a training and a test set. A set of features was computed for each image, and a hierarchical model was then learned for each object in the resulting feature space. While the process could be extended to any number of levels, here we only report on the case of a two-level hierarchy: at the bottom each image is described by a mixture of 8 Gaussians, and at the top each mixture (also with 8 Gaussians) describes 3 consecutive views. Thus, the entire training set is described by 3600 mixtures at the bottom resolution and 1200 at the top.

Given an image of an object to recognize, recognition takes place by computing its projection into the feature space, measuring the likelihood of the resulting sample according to each of the models in the database, and choosing the most likely. The complexity of the process is proportional to the database size. The plot on the left of Figure 2 presents the recognition accuracy achieved with the hierarchical representation vs the corresponding complexity, shown as a percent of the complexity required by full search. The full-search accuracy is in this case 90%, and is also shown as a straight line in the graph. As can be seen from the figure, the hierarchical search achieves the full search accuracy with less than 40% of its complexity. We are now repeating this experiments with deeper trees, where we expect the gains to be even more impressive.

We finalize by reporting on the impact of smoothing on the quality of EM estimates. For this, we conducted the following Monte Carlo experiment: 1) draw 200 datasets $S_i, i = 1, \ldots, 200$ from the model shown on the left of Figure 1, 2) fit each dataset with EM, 3) measure the correlation coefficient $\rho_i, i = 1, \ldots, 200$ between each of the EM fits and the original model, and 4) compute the sample mean $\hat{\rho}$ and variance $\hat{\sigma}_\rho$. The correlation coefficient is defined by $\rho_i = \int f(\mathbf{x})\hat{f}_i(\mathbf{x})d\mathbf{x}/(\int f(\mathbf{x})d\mathbf{x} \int \hat{f}_i(\mathbf{x})d\mathbf{x})$, where $f(\mathbf{x})$ is the

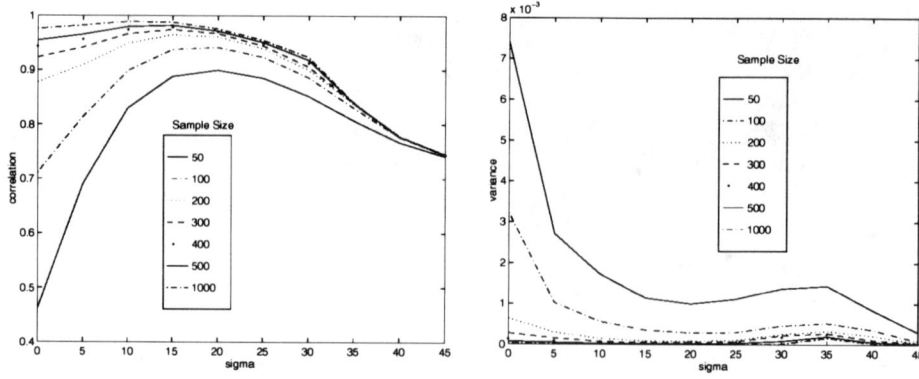

Figure 3: Results of the Monte Carlo experiment described on the text. Left: $\hat{\rho}$ as a function σ_k. Right: $\hat{\sigma}_\rho$ as a function of σ_k. The various curves in each graph correspond to to different sample sizes.

true model and $f_i(\mathbf{x})$ the ith estimate, and can be computed in closed form for Gaussian mixtures. The experiment was repeated with various dataset sizes and various degrees of smoothing (by setting the bandwidth of the underlying Gaussian kernel to $\sigma_k^2 \mathbf{I}$ for various values of σ_k).

Figure 3 presents the results of this experiment. It is clear, from the graph on the left, that smoothing can have a significant impact on the quality of the EM estimates. This impact is largest for small samples, where smoothing can provide up to a two fold improvement estimation accuracy, but can be found even for large samples.

The kernel bandwidth allows control over the trade-off between the bias and variance of the estimates. When σ_k is zero (standard EM), bias is small but variance can be large, as illustrated by the graph on the right of the figure. As σ_k is increased, variance decreases at the cost of an increase in bias (the reason why for large σ_k all lines in the graph of the left meet at the same point regardless of the sample size). The point where $\hat{\rho}$ is the highest is the point at which the bias-variance trade off is optimal. Operating at this point leads to a much smaller dependence of the accuracy of the estimates on the sample size or, conversely, the need for much smaller samples to achieve a given degree of accuracy.

References

[1] A. Dempster, N. Laird, and D. Rubin. Maximum-likelihood from Incomplete Data via the EM Algorithm. *J. of the Royal Statistical Society*, B-39, 1977.

[2] H. Murase and S. Nayar. Visual Learning and Recognition of 3-D Objects from Appeerence. *International Journal of Computer Vision*, 14:5-24, 1995.

[3] K. Rose, E. Gurewitz, and G. Fox. Vector Quantization by Determinisc Annealing. *IEEE Trans. on Information Theory*, Vol. 38, July 1992.

[4] J. Simonoff. *Smoothing Methods in Statistics*. Springer-Verlag, 1996.

[5] N. Vasconcelos and A. Lippman. Learning Mixture Hierarchies. Technical report, MIT Media Laboratory, 1998. Available from ftp://ftp.media.mit.edu/pub/nuno/HierMix.ps.gz.

[6] N. Vasconcelos and A. Lippman. Content-based Pre-Indexed Video. In *Proc. Int. Conf. Image Processing*, Santa Barbara, California, 1997.

Discovering hidden features with Gaussian processes regression

Francesco Vivarelli
Centro Ricerche Ambientali
Montecatini,
via Ciro Menotti, 48
48023 Marina di Ravenna
Italy
fvivarelli@cramont.it

Christopher K. I. Williams
Division of Informatics
The University of Edinburgh,
5 Forrest Hill,
Edinburgh, EH1 2QL
United Kingdom
ckiw@dai.ed.ac.uk

Abstract

In Gaussian process regression the covariance between the outputs at input locations $\mathbf{x}$ and $\mathbf{x}'$ is usually assumed to depend on the distance $(\mathbf{x} - \mathbf{x}')^T W (\mathbf{x} - \mathbf{x}')$, where W is a positive definite matrix. W is often taken to be diagonal, but if we allow W to be a general positive definite matrix which can be tuned on the basis of training data, then an eigen-analysis of W shows that we are effectively creating hidden features, where the dimensionality of the hidden-feature space is determined by the data. We demonstrate the superiority of predictions using the general matrix over those based on a diagonal matrix on two test problems.

1 Introduction

Over the last few years Bayesian approaches to prediction with neural networks have come to the fore. Following an argument in Neal (1996) concerning the equivalence between infinite neural networks and certain Gaussian processes, Gaussian process (GP) prediction has also become popular, and Rasmussen (1996) has demonstrated good performance of GP predictors on a number of tasks.

In Gaussian process prediction as applied by Rasmussen (1996), Williams and Rasmussen (1996) and others, the covariance between the outputs at locations $\mathbf{x}$ and $\mathbf{x}'$ is usually assumed to depend on the distance $(\mathbf{x} - \mathbf{x}')^T W(\mathbf{x} - \mathbf{x}')$, where W is a positive definite, *diagonal* matrix. This means that different dimensions in the input space can have different relevances to the prediction problem (c.f.MacKay and Neal's idea of Automatic Relevance Determination (Neal, 1996)). However, some of the reasoning about the success of neural networks and methods such as projection pursuit regression suggests that discovering relevant *directions* in feature space is important; clearly the ARD model is a special case, where these directions are parallel to the axes in the input feature space. In this paper we allow W to be a general positive semidefinite matrix (defining a Mahalanobis distance in the input space), thereby allowing general directions in the input space to be selected. We then compare the performance of GP predictors using the diagonal and full distance matrices on some regression problems.

The structure of the paper is as follows. GPs for regression are introduced in Section 2, where we also explain the rôle played by the distance matrix W and the criterion used to compare the generalisation performances of the diagonal and the general distance matrices. The two methods have been compared on two regression tasks and the results of our experiments are shown in Section 3. A summary of the work done and some open questions are presented in Section 4.

2 Gaussian processes and prediction

In this paper we use Gaussian process models as predictors. Consider a stochastic process $Y(\mathbf{x})$, with the input observable $\mathbf{x}$ belonging to some input space $\mathcal{X} \subseteq \mathbb{R}^d$. Gaussian processes are a subset of stochastic processes that can be defined by specifying the mean and covariance functions, $\mu(\mathbf{x}) = \mathcal{E}[Y(\mathbf{x})]$ and $C_p(\mathbf{x}, \mathbf{x}') = \mathcal{E}[Y(\mathbf{x})Y(\mathbf{x}')]$ respectively. For the work below we shall set $\mu(\mathbf{x}) \equiv 0$. Although the GP formulation provides a prior over functions, for our purposes it suffices to note that the y-values $Y(\mathbf{x}^1), Y(\mathbf{x}^2), \ldots, Y(\mathbf{x}^n)$ corresponding to $\mathbf{x}$-values $\mathbf{x}^1, \mathbf{x}^2, \ldots, \mathbf{x}^n$ have a multivariate Gaussian distribution $\mathcal{N}(\mathbf{0}, K_p)$, where $(K_p)_{ij} = C_p(\mathbf{x}^i, \mathbf{x}^j)$. The specific form of the covariance function that we shall use is

$$C_p(\mathbf{x}, \mathbf{x}') = \sigma_p^2 \exp\left[-\frac{1}{2}(\mathbf{x} - \mathbf{x}')^T W (\mathbf{x} - \mathbf{x}')\right]. \tag{1}$$

When W is a diagonal matrix the entry w_{ii} is the inverse of the squared *correlation length-scale* of the process along the direction i. In particular, we note that this model is closely related to the Automatic Relevance Determination method of MacKay and Neal (Neal, 1996), as a small lengthscale along a certain direction of the space highlights the relevance of the corresponding input feature (assuming that the inputs are normalised).

For the prediction problem, let us suppose to have n data points $\mathcal{D}_n = \{(\mathbf{x}^1, t^1), (\mathbf{x}^2, t^2), \ldots, (\mathbf{x}^n, t^n)\}$, where t^i is the output-value corresponding to the input $\mathbf{x}^i$. The t's are assumed to be generated from the true y-values by adding Gaussian noise of variance σ_ν^2. Given the assumption of a Gaussian process prior over functions, it is a standard result (e.g. Whittle, 1963) that the predictive distribution $p(t|\mathbf{x}, \mathcal{D}_n)$ corresponding to a new input is $\mathcal{N}(\hat{y}(\mathbf{x}), \sigma^2(\mathbf{x}))$, with mean and variance

$$\hat{y}(\mathbf{x}) = \mathbf{k}^T(\mathbf{x}) K^{-1} \mathbf{t} \tag{2}$$

$$\sigma^2(\mathbf{x}) = C_p(\mathbf{x}, \mathbf{x}) + \sigma_\nu^2 - \mathbf{k}^T(\mathbf{x}) K^{-1} \mathbf{k}(\mathbf{x}), \tag{3}$$

where $K = K_p + \sigma_\nu^2 I$, $\mathbf{k}^T(\mathbf{x}) = (C_p(\mathbf{x}, \mathbf{x}^1), C_p(\mathbf{x}, \mathbf{x}^2), \ldots, C_p(\mathbf{x}, \mathbf{x}^n))$ and $\mathbf{t}^T = (t^1, t^2, \ldots t^n)$.

This method of prediction assumes that the process $y(\mathbf{x})$ we are modelling is really a function of the observable $\mathbf{x}$. However it is often the case that for real world problems the y is actually a function of a set of hidden features $\mathbf{z} \in \mathcal{Z} \subseteq \mathbb{R}^q$ which arise from a combination of the manifest variables $\mathbf{x}$. In particular we wish to study the problem in which the hidden features are a linear combination of the observable coordinates through a $q \times d$ matrix M, where $q < d$ (i.e. $\mathbf{z} = M\mathbf{x}$). In this case, the covariance of the function y is specified by Equation 1 but turns out to depend upon the estimation of the distance between hidden features $(\mathbf{z} - \mathbf{z}')^T \Psi (\mathbf{z} - \mathbf{z}')$. Since $\mathbf{z} = M\mathbf{x}$, $(\mathbf{z} - \mathbf{z}') = M(\mathbf{x} - \mathbf{x}')$ and $W = M^T \Psi M$.

A GP model depends on the parameters which describe the covariance function (i.e. σ_p^2, σ_ν^2 and the elements of W). The training of a GP can be carried out by either estimating the parameters of the covariance function (for example, using the maximum likelihood method) or using a Bayesian approach and sampling from the posterior distribution over the parameters (Williams and Rasmussen, 1996). We follow the first approach, maximising the logarithm of the likelihood

$$\mathcal{L} = \log p(\mathcal{D}_n | \theta) = -\frac{1}{2} \log \det K - \frac{1}{2} \mathbf{t}^T K^{-1} \mathbf{t} - \frac{n}{2} \log 2\pi \quad (4)$$

where K^{-1} depends upon θ, the vector of parameters of the covariance function.

The number of free parameters depends on the number of non-zero elements of the matrix W. Usually, W is chosen to be diagonal and the number of free parameters is $d + 2$ (the d diagonal elements, σ_p^2 and σ_ν^2). We notice that this parametrisation of W allows the discovery of relevant directions in the observed space; it does not lead to an estimation of a general mapping of $\mathcal{X}$ onto the feature space $\mathcal{Z}$ as the relevant directions are parallel to the axes in the input manifest space.

If q is not known in advance, it is preferable to use a general symmetric positive semidefinite matrix W. A parametrisation of such a matrix follows from the Choleski decomposition as $W = U^T U$, where U is an upper triangular matrix with positive entries on the diagonal (Williams, 1996). Hence the factorisation of U turns out to be

$$U = \begin{pmatrix} \exp[u_{1,1}] & u_{1,2} & \cdots & u_{1,d} \\ 0 & \exp[u_{2,2}] & \cdots & u_{2,d} \\ 0 & 0 & \cdots & u_{3,d} \\ \cdots & \cdots & \cdots & \exp[u_{d,d}] \end{pmatrix}. \quad (5)$$

The elements on the diagonal are positive because of the exponential. Being symmetric, W has at most $d(d+1)/2$ independent entries and thus the total number of free parameters of the GP model is $2 + d(d+1)/2$.

We note that such a full distance matrix W allows an estimation of the matrix M from an eigenvalue decomposition of $W = V\Lambda V^T$, where Λ is a diagonal matrix of the eigenvalues of W and V is the matrix of the eigenvectors. The dimension of the hidden feature space $\mathcal{Z}$ can be inferred by the number of relevant eigenvalues of the matrix Λ (which are the inverse of the squared correlation lengths of the process along the directions of the hidden space). The directions of the hidden feature space are defined by the eigenvectors corresponding to the relevant eigenvalues; in particular the matrix composed by these eigenvectors gives an estimate of the mapping from $\mathcal{X}$ to $\mathcal{Z}$. In the following the diagonal and the general full correlation matrices are designated by W_d and W_f.

It is important to observe that the predictor obtained using W_f is not equivalent to an additive model (Hastie and Tibshirani, 1990), as the predictor is a multivariate function of $\mathbf{z}$ rather than being an additive function of the components of $\mathbf{z}$. However, it would be possible to produce an additive function in the GP context, using a covariance function which is the sum of one-dimensional covariance functions based on projections of $\mathbf{x}$.

2.1 Generalisation error

Consider predicting the value of a function $y(\mathbf{x})$ with a predictor $\hat{y}(\mathbf{x})$. A commonly-used measure of the generalisation error given a dataset $\mathcal{D}_n$ is the average squared error

$$E^g(\mathcal{D}_n) = \int (y(\mathbf{x}) - \hat{y}_{\mathcal{D}_n}(\mathbf{x}))^2 p(\mathbf{x}) d\mathbf{x}. \tag{6}$$

The average generalisation error $E^g(n)$ for a dataset of size n is obtained by averaging over the choice of training dataset, i.e. $E^g(n) = \mathcal{E}_\mathcal{D}[E^g(\mathcal{D}_n)]$. $E^g(\mathcal{D}_n)$ can sometimes be evaluated analytically or by numerical integration, but it is usually necessary to use samples to perform the average over training datasets $\mathcal{D}_n$.

In order to investigate the generalisation capabilities of GPs using a diagonal and full distance matrices W_d and W_f, we trained the GP predictors on some regression tasks. The generalisation errors are compared by looking at the relative error

$$\rho(\mathcal{D}_n) = \frac{E^g_d(\mathcal{D}_n) - E^g_f(\mathcal{D}_n)}{E^g_d(\mathcal{D}_n)} \tag{7}$$

where $E^g_d(\mathcal{D}_n)$ and $E^g_f(\mathcal{D}_n)$ are the generalisation errors reported using a diagonal and a full distance matrix respectively. This ratio allow us to perform a fair comparison between the pairwise differences of the generalisation errors for each dataset and the actual value $E^g_d(\mathcal{D}_n)$. The expected value $\rho(n)$ is the average over the sampling of the training data $\mathcal{D}_n$: $\rho(n) = \mathcal{E}_\mathcal{D}[\rho(\mathcal{D}_n)]$.

3 Results

We have conducted experiments to compare the generalisation capabilities of a GP predictor with full and diagonal distance matrices. In this section we illustrate the results we obtained by training a GP on two regression tasks, the regression of a trigonometric function (Section 3.1), and the regression of a high-interaction surface (Section 3.2).

3.1 Regression of a trigonometric function

In the first experiments, a GP has been trained on observations drawn from the function $y(z) = \sin(2\pi z)$ corrupted by Gaussian noise of mean zero and variance $\sigma^2_\nu = 10^{-4}, 10^{-3}, 10^{-2}, 10^{-1}, 1$. The hidden feature $z \in \mathbb{R}$ has been generated from the observable variables $\mathbf{x} \in \mathbb{R}^2$ through the transformation $z = \mathbf{m}^T\mathbf{x}$, where $\mathbf{m}^T = (1/\sqrt{2}, 1/\sqrt{2})$ and $\mathbf{x} \sim \mathcal{N}(\mathbf{0}, \mathbb{I})$. We wish to infer the process $y(z)$ (which is actually a function of the one-dimensional feature z) by using a GP on the manifest space $\mathbb{R}^2$. We evaluated the expected generalisation errors of Equation 6 by Gaussian quadrature (Press et al., 1992) and estimated the expected relative error $\rho(n)$ by averaging over 10 different samples of the training set.

The parameters of the covariance function are optimised on each of the 10 training datasets by maximising the likelihood (see Equation 4) with the conjugate gradient algorithm (Press et al., 1992) with 50 (for W_d) and 70 (for W_f) iterations for the largest training sets with 256 data.

Figure 1 reports the value of $\rho(n)$ on the vertical axis as a function of the amount of training data (x axis). The variance of the noise has been set to 0.01 in Figure 1(a) and 0.1 in Figure 1(b).

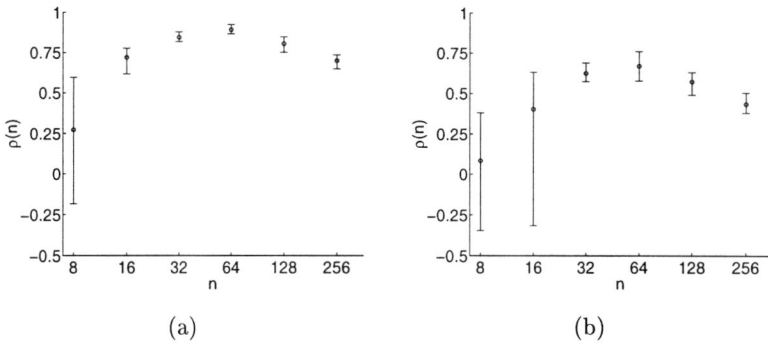

Figure 1: The Figures report on the y axis the graphs of $\rho(n)$ (see Equation 7) as a function of the amount of training data (x axis); the noise level is set to 0.01 (Figure 1(a)) and to 0.1 (Figure 1(b)). The error bars are generated by the minimum and the maximum value of $\rho(\mathcal{D}_n)$ which occurred over the 10 training datasets.

The plots show that the use of W_f significantly improves the generalisation performance with respect to a diagonal matrix as the relative error $\rho(n)$ lies well above zero, within its confidence interval. This is particularly highlighted in Figure 1(a) where for datasets larger than 32 data, $\rho(n)$ is larger than 75%. We notice that for small datasets, $\rho(n)$ is close to zero, as the distribution of its values are spread out around zero with wide confidence intervals. This is due to the fact that with small amounts of data it is not possible to train the GP properly; in particular, as the number of free parameters of W_f is larger than that of W_d, the former needs larger datasets for the training than the latter in order to avoid overfitting. A fully Bayesian treatment of the training of a GP (see Section 2) would not be so seriously affected by this problem since the prediction of the GP would be marginalised over the posterior distribution of the parameters. For large datasets, the relative error declines after having reached its maximum value; this agrees with the intuition that with large amounts of data, both methods will be become good predictors. Similar remarks apply also to Figure 1(b) (where $\sigma_\nu^2 = 0.1$) although we notice that the relative error $\rho(n)$ assumes lower values due to the higher noise variance.

The better perfomance of W_f with respect to W_d can be explained by an eigenanalysis of the two distance matrices. Since one eigenvalue of W_f is much larger than the other ($O(10)$ vs. $O(10^{-4})$), the full rank distance matrix is able to discover the relevant true dimension of the process. The eigenvector corresponding to the larger eigenvalue represents the operator which maps the space of the observables onto the hidden feature space. W_d fails to find out the effective dimension of the problem as it is characterised by two eigenvalues of similar magnitude ($O(10)$).

3.2 A high-interaction surface

We also tested our method on an example taken from Breiman (1993) which is concerned with a regression problem of a surface in a high dimensional space. The target function is $y(\mathbf{x}) = \sigma(z_1) + \sigma(z_2) + \sigma(z_3)$, where $\sigma(z)$ is the sigmoid function $\sigma(z) = \exp[z]/(1+\exp[z])$. The hidden features z_1, z_2 and z_3 are derived from the transformation $z_i = 2(l_i - 2)$, $i = 1\ldots3$, where the l_i are the normalised inner products $\mathbf{m}_i^T \mathbf{x}$. The observed variables $\mathbf{x} \in \mathbb{R}^{10}$ are uniformly distributed over

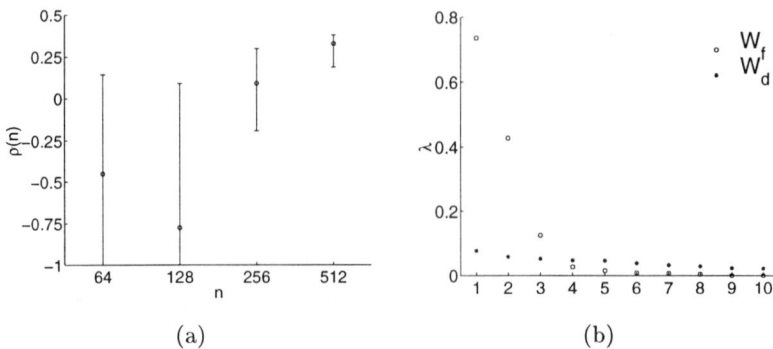

Figure 2: Figure 2(a) reports on the y axis the graph of $\rho(n)$ (see Equation 7) as a function of the amount of training data (x axis); the error bars are generated by the minimum and the maximum value of $\rho(\mathcal{D}_n)$ that occurred over the 10 training datasets. Figure 2(a) shows the graph of the ten eigenvalues of the W_d ($*$) and the W_f (o) distance matrices obtained using one training set of 512 data. The lower values reached by training sets with 64 and 128 data are -1.06 and -1.97 respectively.

$[0,1]^{10}$; the three vectors $\mathbf{m}_i$ are $\mathbf{m}_1^T = (10, 9, 3, 7, -6, -5, -9, -3, -2, -1)$, $\mathbf{m}_2^T = (-1, -2, -3, -4, -5, -6, 7, 8, 9, 10)$ and $\mathbf{m}_3^T = (-1, -2, -3, 4, 5, 4, -3, -2, -1, 0)$. The values of the true function are also corrupted by Gaussian noise of mean zero; the variance of the noise was such that the ratio between the standard deviations of the signal $y(\mathbf{x})$ and the the noise was 4.0, as in Breiman (1993).

We have run experiments, training GPs with diagonal and full distance matrices on 10 data sets of size 64, 128, 256 and 512; in his work, Breiman used training sets with 400 datapoints. The GP's parameters are optimised on each of the 10 training datasets by maximising the likelihood (see Equation 4) with the conjugate gradient algorithm (Press et al., 1992). The generalisation errors of W_d and W_f have been estimated using 1024 test data points; the relative generalisation error $\rho(n)$ (c.f.Equation 7) is shown in Figure 2(a). We observe that for datasets of size 512 the use of W_f significantly reduces the relative error with respect the diagonal matrix. Models trained with smaller training sets do not have such good generalisation performance because the larger number of parameters in W_f (57) overfits the data.

An eigenvalue decomposition of the distance matrices shows that W_f is able to discover the underlying structure of the process. Figure 2(b) displays the eigenvalues of W_f and W_d optimised for one of the training sets of 512 data. W_f is characterised by three large eigenvalues, whose eigenvectors indicate the three main directions in the feature space; thus the full matrix is able to find out three out of ten directions which are responsible of the variation of the function. Conversely, W_d fails to discover the hidden features in the data; since all the eigenvalues have almost the same magnitude, all the input dimensions of the observed variable are equally relevant in training the GP.

The eigenvectors $\mathbf{e}_i^f, i = 1, 2, 3$ of W_f define a basis in the space generating a subspace of features. In order to verify the subspace spanned by the $\mathbf{e}_i^f$ actually overlaps the hidden feature space, we tried to express the former set of vectors as a linear combination the latter. Thus we computed the singular values (Press et al., 1992) of the matrix composed by the normalised vectors $\mathbf{m}_i$ and the basis $\mathbf{e}_i^f$'s. As three out of six singular values are negligible with respect to the others ($O\left(10^{-2}\right)$ vs. $O\left(1\right)$), the original hidden transformation can be well approximated as a linear combination of the new basis of eigenvectors showing that the eigenspace of W_f is a good approximation of the hidden feature space.

4 Discussion

In this paper we have shown how to discover hidden features with GP regression. We also note that this technique could be applied to problems where Gaussian process predictors are used in classification problems. An attractive feature of the method is that it allows the appropriate dimensionality of the **z** space to be discovered. If we wish to restrict the maximum dimensionality of $\mathcal{Z}$ to be q then one could use a distance matrix of rank-q, i.e. $(\Psi^{\frac{1}{2}} M)^T (\Psi^{\frac{1}{2}} M)$.

The idea of allowing a general transformation of the input space has been mentioned before in the literature, for example in (Girosi et al., 1995). However, Girosi *et al* suggest setting the parameters in W_f by cross-validation; we believe that this is not very practical in high-dimensional spaces. The results obtained show that the use of a full distance matrix can reduce significantly the relative error with respect to the use of a diagonal distance matrix. As the training of the GP has been carried out maximising the logarithm of the likelihood, this effect was particularly evident when larger amounts of data were used; this problem can be reduced when a full Bayesian approach to the GP regression is used.

Currently we are investigating how the input-dimensionality of the affects GP regression with a general distance matrix W (for a fixed dimensionality of $\mathcal{Z}$).

Acknowledgements

This research forms part of the "Validation and Verification of Neural Network Systems" project funded jointly by EPSRC (GR/K 51792) and British Aerospace. We thank Dr. Andy Wright of BAe for helpful discussions.

References

Breiman, L. (1993). Hinging hyperplanes for regression, classification and function approximation. *IEEE Trans. on Information Theory*, 39(3):999–1013.

Girosi, F., Jones, M., and Poggio, T. (1995). Regularization Theory and Neural Networks Architectures. *Neural Computation*, 7(2):219–269.

Hastie, T. J. and Tibshirani, R. J. (1990). *Generalized Additive Models*. Chapman and Hall, London.

Neal, R. M. (1996). *Bayesian Learning for Neural Networks*. Springer. Lecture Notes in Statistics 118.

Press, W., Teukolsky, S., Vetterling, W., and Flannery, B. (1992). *Numerical Recipes in C. The Art of Scientific Computing*. Cambridge University Press. second edition.

Rasmussen, C. E. (1996). *Evaluation of Gaussian Processes and Other Methods for Nonlinear Regression*. PhD thesis, Dept. of Computer Science, University of Toronto.

Whittle, P. (1963). *Prediction and regulation by linear least square methods*. English Universities Press.

Williams, C. K. I. and Rasmussen, C. E. (1996). Gaussian processes for regression. In Touretzky, M. C. and Mozer, M. C. and Hasselmo, M. E., editors, *Advances in Neural Information Processing Systems 8*, pages 514–520. MIT Press.

Williams, P. M. (1996). Conditional multivariate densities. *Neural Computation*, 8(4).

The Bias-Variance Tradeoff and the Randomized GACV

Grace Wahba, Xiwu Lin and Fangyu Gao
Dept of Statistics
Univ of Wisconsin
1210 W Dayton Street
Madison, WI 53706
wahba,xiwu,fgao@stat.wisc.edu

Dong Xiang
SAS Institute, Inc.
SAS Campus Drive
Cary, NC 27513
sasdxx@unx.sas.com

Ronald Klein, MD and Barbara Klein, MD
Dept of Ophthalmology
610 North Walnut Street
Madison, WI 53706
kleinr,kleinb@epi.ophth.wisc.edu

Abstract

We propose a new in-sample cross validation based method (randomized GACV) for choosing smoothing or bandwidth parameters that govern the bias-variance or fit-complexity tradeoff in 'soft' classification. Soft classification refers to a learning procedure which estimates the probability that an example with a given attribute vector is in class 1 *vs* class 0. The target for optimizing the the tradeoff is the Kullback-Liebler distance between the estimated probability distribution and the 'true' probability distribution, representing knowledge of an infinite population. The method uses a randomized estimate of the trace of a Hessian and mimics cross validation at the cost of a single relearning with perturbed outcome data.

1 INTRODUCTION

We propose and test a new in-sample cross-validation based method for optimizing the bias-variance tradeoff in 'soft classification' (Wahba *et al* 1994), called $ranGACV$ (randomized Generalized Approximate Cross Validation). Summarizing from Wahba *et al*(1994) we are given a training set consisting of n examples, where for each example we have a vector $t \in \mathcal{T}$ of attribute values, and an outcome y, which is either 0 or 1. Based on the training data it is desired to estimate the probability p of the outcome 1 for any new examples in the future. In 'soft' classification the estimate $\hat{p}(t)$ of $p(t)$ is of particular interest, and might be used by a physician to tell patients how they might modify their risk p by changing (some component of) t, for example, cholesterol as a risk factor for heart attack. Penalized likelihood estimates are obtained for p by assuming that the logit $f(t), t \in \mathcal{T}$, which satisfies $p(t) = e^{f(t)}/(1 + e^{f(t)})$ is in some space $\mathcal{H}$ of functions. Technically $\mathcal{H}$ is a reproducing kernel Hilbert space, but you don't need to know what that is to read on. Let the training set be $\{y_i, t_i, i = 1, \cdots, n\}$. Letting $f_i = f(t_i)$, the negative log likelihood $\mathcal{L}\{y_i, t_i, f_i\}$ of the observations, given f is

$$\mathcal{L}\{y_i, t_i, f_i\} = \sum_{i=1}^{n}[-y_i f_i + b(f_i)], \qquad (1)$$

where $b(f) = log(1 + e^f)$. The penalized likelihood estimate of the function f is the solution to: Find $f \in \mathcal{H}$ to minimize $I_\lambda(f)$:

$$I_\lambda(f) = \sum_{i=1}^{n}[-y_i f_i + b(f_i)] + J_\lambda(f), \qquad (2)$$

where $J_\lambda(f)$ is a quadratic penalty functional depending on parameter(s) $\lambda = (\lambda_1, ..., \lambda_q)$ which govern the so called bias-variance tradeoff. Equivalently the components of λ control the tradeoff between the complexity of f and the fit to the training data. In this paper we sketch the derivation of the $ranGACV$ method for choosing λ, and present some preliminary but favorable simulation results, demonstrating its efficacy. This method is designed for use with penalized likelihood estimates, but it is clear that it can be used with a variety of other methods which contain bias-variance parameters to be chosen, and for which minimizing the Kullback-Liebler (KL) distance is the target. In the work of which this is a part, we are concerned with λ having multiple components. Thus, it will be highly convenient to have an in-sample method for selecting λ, if one that is accurate and computationally convenient can be found.

Let p_λ be the the estimate and p be the 'true' but unknown probability function and let $p_i = p(t_i), p_{\lambda i} = p_\lambda(t_i)$. For in-sample tuning, our criteria for a good choice of λ is the KL distance $KL(p, p_\lambda) = \frac{1}{n}\sum_{i=1}^{n}[p_i log \frac{p_i}{p_{\lambda i}} + (1 - p_i)log \frac{(1-p_i)}{(1-p_{\lambda i})}]$. We may replace $KL(p, p_\lambda)$ by the comparative KL distance (CKL), which differs from KL by a quantity which does not depend on λ. Letting $f_{\lambda i} = f_\lambda(t_i)$, the CKL is given by

$$CKL(p, p_\lambda) \equiv CKL(\lambda) = \frac{1}{n}\sum_{i=1}^{n}[-p_i f_{\lambda i} + b(f_{\lambda i})]. \qquad (3)$$

$CKL(\lambda)$ depends on the unknown p, and it is desired is to have a good estimate or proxy for it, which can then be minimized with respect to λ.

It is known (Wong 1992) that no exact unbiased estimate of $CKL(\lambda)$ exists in this case, so that only approximate methods are possible. A number of authors have tackled this problem, including Utans and Moody(1993), Liu(1993), Gu(1992). The iterative UBR method of Gu(1992) is included in GRKPACK (Wang 1997), which implements general smoothing spline ANOVA penalized likelihood estimates with multiple smoothing parameters. It has been successfully used in a number of practical problems, see, for example, Wahba et al (1994,1995). The present work represents an approach in the spirit of GRKPACK but which employs several approximations, and may be used with any data set, no matter how large, provided that an algorithm for solving the penalized likelihood equations, either exactly or approximately, can be implemented.

2 THE GACV ESTIMATE

In the general penalized likelihood problem the minimizer $f_\lambda(\cdot)$ of (2) has a representation

$$f_\lambda(t) = \sum_{\nu=1}^{M} d_\nu \phi_\nu(t) + \sum_{i=1}^{n} c_i Q_\lambda(t_i, t) \tag{4}$$

where the ϕ_ν span the null space of J_λ, $Q_\lambda(s,t)$ is a reproducing kernel (positive definite function) for the penalized part of $\mathcal{H}$, and $c = (c_1, \cdots, c_n)'$ satisfies M linear conditions, so that there are (at most) n free parameters in f_λ. Typically the unpenalized functions ϕ_ν are low degree polynomials. Examples of $Q(t_i, \cdot)$ include radial basis functions and various kinds of splines; minor modifications include sigmoidal basis functions, tree basis functions and so on. See, for example Wahba(1990,1995), Girosi, Jones and Poggio(1995). If $f_\lambda(\cdot)$ is of the form (4) then $J_\lambda(f_\lambda)$ is a quadratic form in c. Substituting (4) into (2) results in I_λ a convex functional in c and d, and c and d are obtained numerically via a Newton Raphson iteration, subject to the conditions on c. For large n, the second sum on the right of (4) may be replaced by $\sum_{k=1}^{K} c_{i_k} Q_\lambda(t_{i_k}, t)$, where the t_{i_k} are chosen via one of several principled methods.

To obtain the $GACV$ we begin with the ordinary leaving-out-one cross validation function $CV(\lambda)$ for the CKL:

$$CV(\lambda) = \frac{1}{n} \sum_{i=1}^{n} [-y_i f_{\lambda i}^{[-i]} + b(f_{\lambda i})], \tag{5}$$

where $f_\lambda^{[-i]}$ the solution to the variational problem of (2) with the ith data point left out and $f_{\lambda i}^{[-i]}$ is the value of $f_\lambda^{[-i]}$ at t_i. Although $f_\lambda(\cdot)$ is computed by solving for c and d the $GACV$ is derived in terms of the values $(f_1, \cdots, f_n)'$ of f at the t_i. Where there is no confusion between functions $f(\cdot)$ and vectors $(f_1, \cdots, f_n)'$ of values of f at $t_1, \cdots, t_n$, we let $f = (f_1, \cdots, f_n)'$. For any $f(\cdot)$ of the form (4), $J_\lambda(f)$ also has a representation as a non-negative definite quadratic form in $(f_1, \cdots, f_n)'$. Letting Σ_λ be twice the matrix of this quadratic form we can rewrite (2) as

$$I_\lambda(f, y) = \sum_{i=1}^{n} [-y_i f_i + b(f_i)] + \frac{1}{2} f' \Sigma_\lambda f. \tag{6}$$

Let $W = W(f)$ be the $n \times n$ diagonal matrix with $\sigma_{ii} \equiv p_i(1 - p_i)$ in the iith position. Using the fact that σ_{ii} is the second derivative of $b(f_i)$, we have that $H = [W + \Sigma_\lambda]^{-1}$ is the inverse Hessian of the variational problem (6). In Xiang and Wahba (1996), several Taylor series approximations, along with a generalization of the leaving-out-one lemma (see Wahba 1990) are applied to (5) to obtain an approximate cross validation function $ACV(\lambda)$, which is a second order approximation to $CV(\lambda)$. Letting h_{ii} be the iith entry of H, the result is

$$CV(\lambda) \approx ACV(\lambda) = \frac{1}{n} \sum_{i=1}^{n} [-y_i f_{\lambda i} + b(f_{\lambda i})] + \frac{1}{n} \sum_{i=1}^{n} \frac{h_{ii} y_i (y_i - p_{\lambda i})}{[1 - h_{ii} \sigma_{ii}]}. \tag{7}$$

Then the $GACV$ is obtained from the ACV by replacing h_{ii} by $\frac{1}{n} \sum_{i=1}^{n} h_{ii} \equiv \frac{1}{n} tr(H)$ and replacing $1 - h_{ii}\sigma_{ii}$ by $\frac{1}{n} tr[I - (W^{1/2} H W^{1/2})]$, giving

$$GACV(\lambda) = \frac{1}{n} \sum_{i=1}^{n} [-y_i f_{\lambda i} + b(f_{\lambda i})] + \frac{tr(H)}{n} \frac{\sum_{i=1}^{n} y_i(y_i - p_{\lambda i})}{tr[I - (W^{1/2} H W^{1/2})]}, \tag{8}$$

where W is evaluated at f_λ. Numerical results based on an exact calculation of (8) appear in Xiang and Wahba (1996). The exact calculation is limited to small n however.

3 THE RANDOMIZED GACV ESTIMATE

Given any 'black box' which, given λ, and a training set $\{y_i, t_i\}$ produces $f_\lambda(\cdot)$ as the minimizer of (2), and thence $f_\lambda = (f_{\lambda 1}, \cdots, f_{\lambda n})'$, we can produce randomized estimates of trH and $tr[I - W^{1/2}HW^{1/2}]$ without having any explicit calculations of these matrices. This is done by running the 'black box' on perturbed data $\{y_i + \delta_i, t_i\}$. For the y_i Gaussian, randomized trace estimates of the Hessian of the variational problem (the 'influence matrix') have been studied extensively and shown to be essentially as good as exact calculations for large n, see for example Girard(1998). Randomized trace estimates are based on the fact that if A is any square matrix and δ is a zero mean random n-vector with independent components with variance σ_δ^2, then $E\delta' A\delta = \frac{1}{\sigma_\delta^2} trA$. See Gong et al(1998) and references cited there for experimental results with multiple regularization parameters. Returning to the 0-1 data case, it is easy to see that the minimizer $f_\lambda(\cdot)$ of I_λ is continuous in y, not withstanding the fact that in our training set the y_i take on only values 0 or 1. Letting $f_\lambda^y = (f_{\lambda 1}, \cdots, f_{\lambda n})'$ be the minimizer of (6) given $y = (y_1, \cdots, y_n)'$, and $f_\lambda^{y+\delta}$ be the minimizer given data $y+\delta = (y_1+\delta_1, \cdots, y_n+\delta_n)'$ (the t_i remain fixed), Xiang and Wahba (1997) show, again using Taylor series expansions, that $f_\lambda^{y+\delta} - f_\lambda^y \sim [W(f_\lambda^y) + \Sigma_\lambda]^{-1}\delta$. This suggests that $\frac{1}{\sigma_\delta^2}\delta'(f_\lambda^{y+\delta} - f_\lambda^y)$ provides an estimate of $tr[W(f_\lambda^y) + \Sigma_\lambda]^{-1}$. However, if we take the solution f_λ^y to the nonlinear system for the original data y as the initial value for a Newton-Raphson calculation of $f_\lambda^{y+\delta}$ things become even simpler. Applying a one step Newton-Raphson iteration gives

$$f_\lambda^{y+\delta,1} = f_\lambda^y - [\frac{\partial^2 I_\lambda}{\partial f' \partial f}(f_\lambda^y, y+\delta)]^{-1}\frac{\partial I_\lambda}{\partial f}(f_\lambda^y, y+\delta). \quad (9)$$

Since $\frac{\partial I_\lambda}{\partial f}(f_\lambda^y, y+\delta) = -\delta + \frac{\partial I_\lambda}{\partial f}(f_\lambda^y, y) = -\delta$, and $[\frac{\partial^2 I_\lambda}{\partial f'\partial f}(f_\lambda^y, y+\delta)]^{-1} = [\frac{\partial^2 I_\lambda}{\partial f'\partial f}(f_\lambda^y, y)]^{-1}$, we have $f_\lambda^{y+\delta,1} = f_\lambda^y + [\frac{\partial^2 I_\lambda}{\partial f'\partial f}(f_\lambda^y, y)]^{-1}\delta$ so that $f_\lambda^{y+\delta,1} - f_\lambda^y = [W(f_\lambda^y) + \Sigma_\lambda]^{-1}\delta$. The result is the following $ranGACV$ function:

$$ranGACV(\lambda) = \frac{1}{n}\sum_{i=1}^n [-y_i f_{\lambda i} + b(f_{\lambda i})] + \frac{\delta'(f_\lambda^{y+\delta,1} - f_\lambda^y)}{n} \frac{\sum_{i=1}^n y_i(y_i - p_{\lambda i})}{[\delta'\delta - \delta' W(f_\lambda^y)(f_\lambda^{y+\delta,1} - f_\lambda^y)]}. \quad (10)$$

To reduce the variance in the term after the '+' in (10), we may draw R independent replicate vectors $\delta_1, \cdots, \delta_R$, and replace the term after the '+' in (10) by $\frac{1}{R}\sum_{r=1}^R \frac{\delta_r'(f_\lambda^{y+\delta_r,1} - f_\lambda^y)}{n} \frac{\sum_{i=1}^n y_i(y_i - p_{\lambda i})}{[\delta_r'\delta_r - \delta_r' W(f_\lambda^y)(f_\lambda^{y+\delta_r,1} - f_\lambda^y)]}$ to obtain an R-replicated $ranGACV(\lambda)$ function.

4 NUMERICAL RESULTS

In this section we present simulation results which are representative of more extensive simulations to appear elsewhere. In each case, $K \ll n$ was chosen by a sequential clustering algorithm. In that case, the t_i were grouped into K clusters and one member of each cluster selected at random. The model is fit. Then the number of clusters is doubled and the model is fit again. This procedure continues until the fit does not change. In the randomized trace estimates the random variates were Gaussian. Penalty functionals were (multivariate generalizations of) the cubic spline penalty functional $\lambda \int_0^1 (f''(x))^2$, and smoothing spline ANOVA models were fit.

4.1 EXPERIMENT 1. SINGLE SMOOTHING PARAMETER

In this experiment $t \in [0,1]$, $f(t) = 2sin(10t)$, $t_i = (i - .5)/500, i = 1, \cdots, 500$. A random number generator produced 'observations' $y_i = 1$ with probability $p_i = e^{f_i}/(1 + e^{f_i})$, to get the training set. Q_λ is given in Wahba(1990) for this cubic spline case, $K = 50$. Since the true p is known, the true CKL can be computed. Fig. 1(a) gives a plot of $CKL(\lambda)$ and 10 replicates of $ranGACV(\lambda)$. In each replicate R was taken as 1, and δ was generated anew as a Gaussian random vector with $\sigma_\delta = .001$. Extensive simulations with different σ_δ showed that the results were insensitive to σ_δ from 1.0 to 10^{-6}. The minimizer of CKL is at the filled-in circle and the 10 minimizers of the 10 replicates of $ranGACV$ are the open circles. Any one of these 10 provides a rather good estimate of the λ that goes with the filled-in circle. Fig. 1(b) gives the same experiment, except that this time $R = 5$. It can be seen that the minimizers $ranGACV$ become even more reliable estimates of the minimizer of CKL, and the CKL at all of the $ranGACV$ estimates are actually quite close to its minimum value.

4.2 EXPERIMENT 2. ADDITIVE MODEL WITH $\lambda = (\lambda_1, \lambda_2)$

Here $t \in [0,1] \otimes [0,1]$. $n = 500$ values of t_i were generated randomly according to a uniform distribution on the unit square and the y_i were generated according to $p_i = e^{f_i}/(1 + e^{f_i})$ with $t = (x_1, x_2)$ and $f(t) = 5\sin 2\pi x_1 - 3sin 2\pi x_2$. An additive model as a special case of the smoothing spline ANOVA model (see Wahba et al, 1995), of the form $f(t) = \mu + f_1(x_1) + f_2(x_2)$ with cubic spline penalties on f_1 and f_2 were used. $K = 50, \sigma_\delta = .001, R = 5$. Figure 1(c) gives a plot of $CKL(\lambda_1, \lambda_2)$ and Figure 1(d) gives a plot of $ranGACV(\lambda_1, \lambda_2)$. The open circles mark the minimizer of $ranGACV$ in both plots and the filled in circle marks the minimizer of CKL. The inefficiency, as measured by $CKL(\hat{\lambda})/min_\lambda CKL(\lambda)$ is 1.01. Inefficiencies near 1 are typical of our other similar simulations.

4.3 EXPERIMENT 3. COMPARISON OF ranGACV AND UBR

This experiment used a model similar to the model fit by GRKPACK for the risk of progression of diabetic retinopathy given $t = (x_1, x_2, x_3) =$ (duration, glycosylated hemoglobin, body mass index) in Wahba et al(1995) as 'truth'. A training set of 669 examples was generated according to that model, which had the structure $f(x_1, x_2, x_3) = \mu + f_1(x_1) + f_2(x_2) + f_3(x_3) + f_{1,3}(x_1, x_3)$. This (synthetic) training set was fit by GRKPACK and also using $K = 50$ basis functions with $ranGACV$. Here there are $p = 6$ smoothing parameters (there are 3 smoothing parameters in f_{13}) and the $ranGACV$ function was searched by a downhill simplex method to find its minimizer. Since the 'truth' is known, the CKL for $\hat{\lambda}$ and for the GRKPACK fit using the iterative UBR method were computed. This was repeated 100 times, and the 100 pairs of CKL values appears in Figure 1(e). It can be seen that the UBR and $ranGACV$ give similar CKL values about 90% of the time, while the $ranGACV$ has lower CKL for most of the remaining cases.

4.4 DATA ANALYSIS: AN APPLICATION

Figure 1(f) represents part of the results of a study of association at baseline of pigmentary abnormalities with various risk factors in 2585 women between the ages of 43 and 86 in the Beaver Dam Eye Study, R. Klein et al(1995). The attributes are: $x_1 =$ age, $x_2 =$ body mass index, $x_3 =$ systolic blood pressure, $x_4 =$ cholesterol. x_5 and x_6 are indicator variables for taking hormones, and history of drinking. The smoothing spline ANOVA model fitted was $f(t) = \mu + d_1 x_1 + d_2 x_2 + f_3(x_3) + f_4(x_4) + f_{34}(x_3, x_4) + d_5 I(x_5) + d_6 I(x_6)$, where I is the indicator function. Figure 1(e) represents a cross section of the fit for $x_5 = no, x_6 = no$,

x_2, x_3 fixed at their medians and x_1 fixed at the 75th percentile. The dotted lines are the Bayesian confidence intervals, see Wahba et al(1995). There is a suggestion of a borderline inverse association of cholesterol. The reason for this association is uncertain. More details will appear elsewhere.

Principled soft classification procedures can now be implemented in much larger data sets than previously possible, and the $ranGACV$ should be applicable in general learning.

References

Girard, D. (1998), 'Asymptotic comparison of (partial) cross-validation, GCV and randomized GCV in nonparametric regression', *Ann. Statist.* **126**, 315–334.

Girosi, F., Jones, M. & Poggio, T. (1995), 'Regularization theory and neural networks architectures', *Neural Computation* **7**, 219–269.

Gong, J., Wahba, G., Johnson, D. & Tribbia, J. (1998), 'Adaptive tuning of numerical weather prediction models: simultaneous estimation of weighting, smoothing and physical parameters', *Monthly Weather Review* **125**, 210–231.

Gu, C. (1992), 'Penalized likelihood regression: a Bayesian analysis', *Statistica Sinica* **2**, 255–264.

Klein, R., Klein, B. & Moss, S. (1995), 'Age-related eye disease and survival. the Beaver Dam Eye Study', *Arch Ophthalmol* **113**, 1995.

Liu, Y. (1993), Unbiased estimate of generalization error and model selection in neural network, manuscript, Department of Physics, Institute of Brain and Neural Systems, Brown University.

Utans, J. & Moody, J. (1993), Selecting neural network architectures via the prediction risk: application to corporate bond rating prediction, *in* 'Proc. First Int'l Conf. on Artificial Intelligence Applications on Wall Street', IEEE Computer Society Press.

Wahba, G. (1990), *Spline Models for Observational Data*, SIAM. CBMS-NSF Regional Conference Series in Applied Mathematics, v. 59.

Wahba, G. (1995), Generalization and regularization in nonlinear learning systems, *in* M. Arbib, ed., 'Handbook of Brain Theory and Neural Networks', MIT Press, pp. 426–430.

Wahba, G., Wang, Y., Gu, C., Klein, R. & Klein, B. (1994), Structured machine learning for 'soft' classification with smoothing spline ANOVA and stacked tuning, testing and evaluation, *in* J. Cowan, G. Tesauro & J. Alspector, eds, 'Advances in Neural Information Processing Systems 6', Morgan Kauffman, pp. 415–422.

Wahba, G., Wang, Y., Gu, C., Klein, R. & Klein, B. (1995), 'Smoothing spline ANOVA for exponential families, with application to the Wisconsin Epidemiological Study of Diabetic Retinopathy', *Ann. Statist.* **23**, 1865–1895.

Wang, Y. (1997), 'GRKPACK: Fitting smoothing spline analysis of variance models to data from exponential families', *Commun. Statist. Sim. Comp.* **26**, 765–782.

Wong, W. (1992), Estimation of the loss of an estimate, Technical Report 356, Dept. of Statistics, University of Chicago, Chicago, Il.

Xiang, D. & Wahba, G. (1996), 'A generalized approximate cross validation for smoothing splines with non-Gaussian data', *Statistica Sinica* **6**, 675–692, preprint TR 930 available via www.stat.wisc.edu/~wahba − > TRLIST.

Xiang, D. & Wahba, G. (1997), Approximate smoothing spline methods for large data sets in the binary case, Technical Report 982, Department of Statistics, University of Wisconsin, Madison WI. To appear in the Proceedings of the 1997 ASA Joint Statistical Meetings, Biometrics Section, pp 94-98 (1998). Also in TRLIST as above.

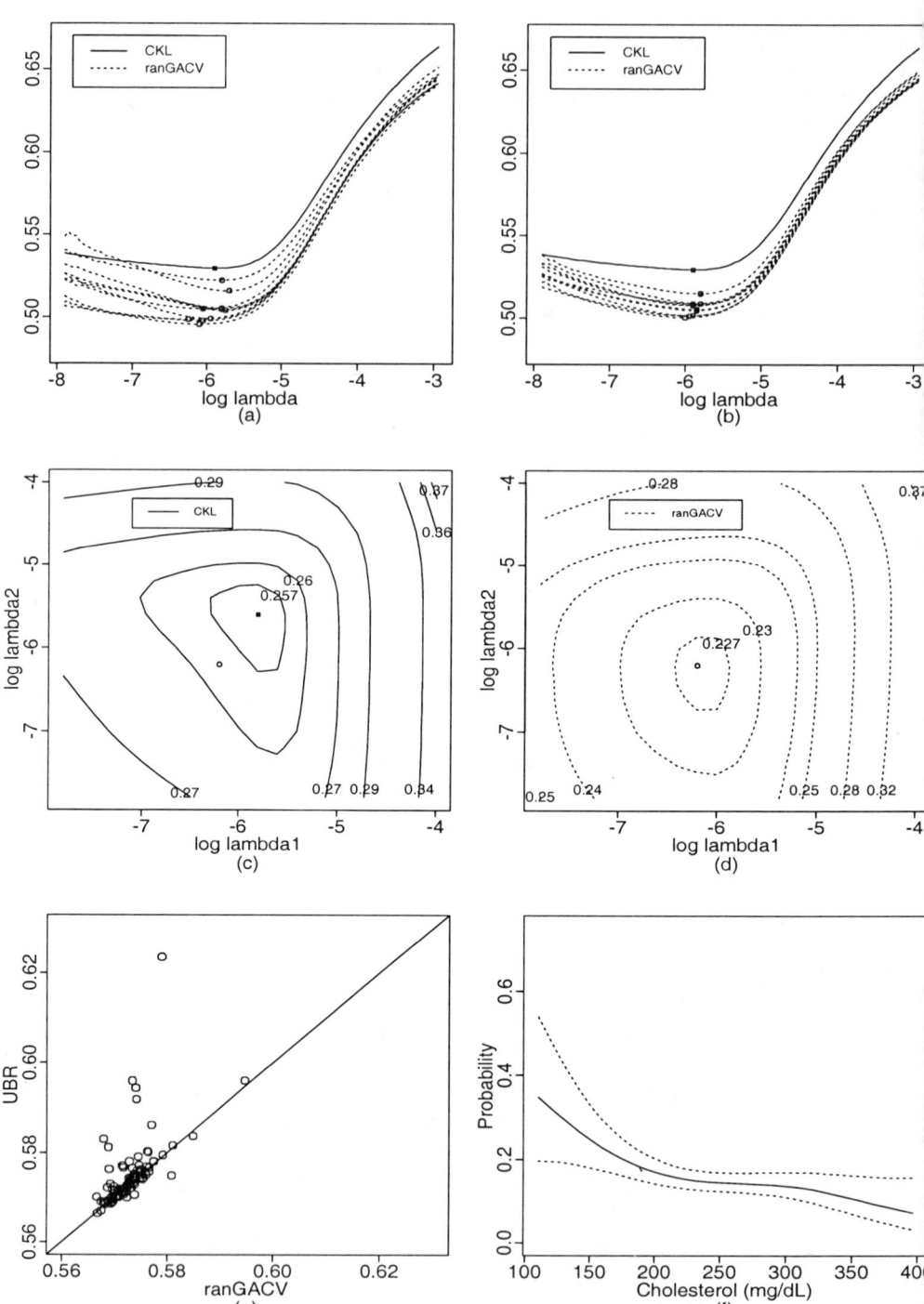

Figure 1: (a) and (b): Single smoothing parameter comparison of $ranGACV$ and CKL. (c) and (d): Two smoothing parameter comparison of $ranGACV$ and CKL. (e): Comparison of $ranGACV$ and UBR. (f): Probability estimate from Beaver Dam Study

Basis Selection For Wavelet Regression

Kevin R. Wheeler
Caelum Research Corporation
NASA Ames Research Center
Mail Stop 269-1
Moffett Field, CA 94035
kwheeler@mail.arc.nasa.gov

Atam P. Dhawan
College of Engineering
University of Toledo
2801 W. Bancroft Street
Toledo, OH 43606
adhawan@eng.utoledo.edu

Abstract

A wavelet basis selection procedure is presented for wavelet regression. Both the basis and threshold are selected using cross-validation. The method includes the capability of incorporating prior knowledge on the smoothness (or shape of the basis functions) into the basis selection procedure. The results of the method are demonstrated using widely published sampled functions. The results of the method are contrasted with other basis function based methods.

1 INTRODUCTION

Wavelet regression is a technique which attempts to reduce noise in a sampled function corrupted with noise. This is done by thresholding the small wavelet decomposition coefficients which represent mostly noise. Most of the papers published on wavelet regression have concentrated on the threshold selection process. This paper focuses on the effect that different wavelet bases have on cross-validation based threshold selection, and the error in the final result. This paper also suggests how prior information may be incorporated into the basis selection process, and the effects of choosing a wrong prior. Both orthogonal and biorthogonal wavelet bases were explored.

Wavelet regression is performed in three steps. The first step is to apply a discrete wavelet transform to the sampled data to produce decomposition coefficients. Next a threshold is applied to the coefficients. Then an inverse discrete wavelet transform is applied to these modified coefficients.

The basis selection procedure is demonstrated to perform better than other wavelet regression methods even when the wrong prior on the space of the basis selections is specified.

This paper is broken into the following sections. The background section gives a brief summary of the mathematical requirements of the discrete wavelet transform. This section is followed by a methodology section which outlines the basis selection algorithms, and the process for obtaining the presented results. This is followed by a results section and then a conclusion.

2 BACKGROUND

2.1 DISCRETE WAVELET TRANSFORM

The Discrete Wavelet Transform (DWT) [Daubechies, 92] is implemented as a series of projections onto scaling functions in $L_2(\Re)$. The initial assumption is that the original data samples lie in the finest space V_0, which is spanned by the scaling function $\phi \in V_0$ such that the collection $\{\phi(x-l) \mid l \in \mathcal{Z}\}$ is a Riesz basis of V_0. The first level of the dyadic decomposition then consists of projecting the data samples onto scaling functions which have been dilated to be twice as wide as the original ϕ. These span the coarser space $V_{-1} : \{\phi(2x - 2l) \mid l \in \mathcal{Z}\}$. The information that is lost going from the finer to coarser scale is retained in what is known as wavelet coefficients. Instead of taking the difference, the wavelet coefficients can be obtained via a projection operation onto the wavelet basis functions ψ which span a space known as W_0. The projections are typically implemented using Quadrature Mirror Filters (QMF) which are implemented as Finite Impulse Response filters (FIR). The next level of decomposition is obtained by again doubling the scaling functions and projecting the first scaling decomposition coefficients onto these functions. The difference in information between this level and the last one is contained in the wavelet coefficients for this level. In general, the scaling functions for level j and translation m may be represented by: $\phi_j^m(t) = 2^{\frac{-j}{2}}\phi(2^{-j}t-m)$ where $t \in [0, 2^k-1]$, $k \geq 1, 1 \leq j \leq k, 0 \leq m \leq 2^{k-j} - 1$.

2.1.1 Orthogonal

An orthogonal wavelet decomposition is defined such that the difference space W_j is the orthogonal complement of V_j in $V_{j+1} : W_0 \perp V_0$ which means that the projection of the wavelet functions onto the scaling functions on a level is zero: $\langle \psi, \phi(\cdot - l) \rangle = 0, l \in Z$

This results in the wavelet spaces W_j with $j \in Z$ being all mutually orthogonal. The refinement relations for an orthogonal decomposition may be written as: $\phi(x) = 2\sum_k h_k \phi(2x - k)$ and $\psi(x) = 2\sum_k g_k \phi(2x - k)$.

2.1.2 Biorthogonal

Symmetry is as an important property when the scaling functions are used as interpolatory functions. Most commonly used interpolatory functions are symmetric. It is well known in the subband filtering community that symmetry and exact reconstruction are incompatible if the same FIR filters are used for reconstruction and decomposition (except for the Haar filter) [Daubechies, 92]. If we are willing to use different filters for the analysis and synthesis banks, then symmetry and exact reconstruction are possible using biorthogonal wavelets. Biorthogonal wavelets have dual scaling $\tilde{\phi}$ and dual wavelet $\tilde{\psi}$ functions. These generate a dual multiresolution analysis with subspaces $\tilde{V}_j$ and $\tilde{W}_j$ so that: $\tilde{V}_j \perp W_j$ and $V_j \perp \tilde{W}_j$ and the orthogonality conditions can now be written as:

$$\langle \tilde{\phi}, \psi(\cdot - l) \rangle = \langle \tilde{\psi}, \phi(\cdot - l) \rangle = 0$$

$$\langle \tilde{\phi}_{j,l}, \phi_{k,m} \rangle = \delta_{j-k}, \delta_{l-m} \text{ for } l, m, j, k \in Z$$

$$\langle \tilde{\psi}_{j,l}, \psi_{k,m} \rangle = \delta_{j-k}, \delta_{l-m} \text{ for } l, m, j, k \in Z$$

where $\delta_{j-k} = 1$ when $j = k$, and zero otherwise.

The refinement relations for biorthogonal wavelets can be written:

$$\phi(x) = 2 \sum_k h_k \phi(2x - k) \text{ and } \psi(x) = 2 \sum_k g_k \phi(2x - k)$$

$$\tilde{\phi}(x) = 2 \sum_k \tilde{h}_k \tilde{\phi}(2x - k) \text{ and } \tilde{\psi}(x) = 2 \sum_k \tilde{g}_k \tilde{\phi}(2x - k)$$

Basically, this means that the scaling functions at one level are composed of linear combinations of scaling functions at the next finer level. The wavelet functions at one level are also composed of linear combinations of the scaling functions at the next finer level.

2.2 LIFTING AND SECOND GENERATION WAVELETS

Swelden's lifting scheme [Sweldens, 95a] is a way to transform a biorthogonal wavelet decomposition obtained from low order filters to one that could be obtained from higher order filters (more FIR filter coefficients), without applying the longer filters and thus saving computations. This method can be used to increase the number of vanishing moments of the wavelet, or change the shape of the wavelet. This means that several different filters (i.e. sets of basis functions) may be applied with properties relevant to the problem domain in a manner more efficient than directly applying the filters individually. This is beneficial to performing a search over the space of admissible basis functions meeting the problem domain requirements.

Swelden's Second Generation Wavelets [Sweldens, 95b] are a result of applying lifting to simple interpolating biorthogonal wavelets, and redefining the refinement relation of the dual wavelet to be:

$$\tilde{\psi}(x) = \tilde{\phi}(2x - 1) - \sum_k a_k \tilde{\phi}(x - k)$$

where the a_k are the lifting parameters. The lifting parameters may be selected to achieve desired properties in the basis functions relevant to the problem domain.

Prior information for a particular application domain may now be incorporated into the basis selection for wavelet regression. For example, if a particular application requires that there be a certain degree of smoothness (or a certain number of vanishing moments in the basis), then only those lifting parameters which result in a number of vanishing moments within this range are used. Another way to think about this is to form a probability distribution over the space of lifting parameters. The most likely lifting parameters will be those which most closely match one's intuition for the given problem domain.

2.3 THRESHOLD SELECTION

Since the wavelet transform is a linear operator the decomposition coefficients will have the same form of noise as the sampled data. The idea behind wavelet regression is that the decomposition coefficients that have a small magnitude are substantially representative of the noise component of the sampled data. A threshold is selected and then all coefficients which are below the threshold in magntiude are either set to zero (a hard threshold) or a moved towards zero (a soft threshold). The soft threshold $\eta_t(y) = \text{sgn}(y)(|y|-t)$ is used in this study.

There are two basic methods of threshold selection: 1. Donoho's [Donoho, 95] analytic method which relies on knowledge of the noise distribution (such as a Gaussian noise source with a certain variance); 2. a cross-validation approach (many of which are reviewed in [Nason, 96]). It is beyond the scope of this paper to review these methods. Leave-one-out cross-validation with padding was used in this study.

3 METHODOLOGY

The test functions used in this study are the four functions published by Donoho and Johnstone [Donoho and Johnstone, 94]. These functions have been adopted by the wavelet regression community to aid in comparison of algorithms across publications.

Each function was uniformly sampled to contain 2048 points. Gaussian white noise was added so that the signal to noise ratio (SNR) was 7.0. Fifty replicates of each noisy function were created, of which four instantiations are depicted in Figure 1.

The noise removal process involved three steps. The first step was to perform a discrete wavelet transform using a paticular basis. A threshold was selected for the resulting decomposition coefficients using leave-one-out cross validation with padding.

The soft threshold was then applied to the decomposition. Next, the inverse wavelet transform was applied to obtain a cleaner version of the original signal. These steps were repeated for each basis set or for each set of lifting parameters.

3.1 WAVELET BASIS SELECTION

To demonstrate the effect of basis selection on the threshold found and the error in the resulting recovered signal, the following experiments were conducted. In the first trial two well studied orthogonal wavelet families were used: Daubechies most compactly supported (DMCS), and Symlets (S) [Daubechies, 92]. For the DMCS family, filters of order 1 (which corresponds to the Haar wavelet) through 7 were used. For the Symlets, filters of order 2 through 8 were used. For each filter, leave-one-out cross-validation was used to find a threshold which minimized the mean square error for each of the 50 replicates for the four test functions. The median threshold found was then applied to the decomposition of each of the replicates for each test function. The resulting reconstructed signals are compared to the ideal function (the original before noise was added) and the Normalized Root Mean Square Error (NRMSE) is presented.

3.2 INCORPORATING PRIOR INFORMATION: LIFTING PARAMETERS

If the function that we are sampling is known to have certain smoothness properties, then a distribution of the admissible lifting coefficients representing a similar smoothness characteristic can be formed. However, it is not necessary to cautiously pick a prior. The performance of this method with a piecewise linear prior (the (2,2) biorthogonal wavelet of Cohen-Daubechies-Feauveau [Cohen, 92]) has been applied to the non-linear smooth test functions Bumps, Doppler, and Heavysin. This method has been compared with several standard techniques [Wheeler, 96]. The Smoothing Spline method (SS) [Wahba, 90], Donoho's Sure Shrink method (SureShrink)[Donoho, 95], and an optimized Radial Basis Function Neural Network (RBFNN).

4 RESULTS

In the first experiment, the procedure was only allowed to select between two well known bases (Daubechies most compactly supported and symmlet wavelets) with the desired filter order. Table 1 shows the filter order resulting in lowest cross-validation error for each filter and function. The NRMSE is presented with respect to the original noise-free functions for comparison. As expected the best basis for the noisy blocks function was the piecewise linear basis (Daubechies, order 1). The doppler, which had very high frequency components required the highest filter order. Figure 2 represents typical denoised versions for the functions recovered by the filters listed in **bold** in the table.

The method selected the basis having similar properties to the underlying function without knowing the original function. When higher order filters were applied to the noisy Blocks data, the resulting NRMSE was higher.

The basis selection procedure (labelled CV-Wavelets in Table 2) was compared with Donoho's SureShrink, Wahba's Smoothing Splines (SS), and an optimized RBFNN [Wheeler, 96]. The prior information specified incorrectly to the procedure to prefer bases near piecewise linear. The remarkable observation is that the method did better than the others as measured by Mean Square Error.

5 CONCLUSION

A basis selection procedure for wavelet regression was presented. The method was shown to select bases appropriate to the characteristics of the underlying functions. The shape of the basis was determined with cross-validation selecting from either a pre-set library of filters or from previously calculated lifting coefficients. The lifting coefficients were calculated to be appropriate for the particular problem domain. The method was compared for various bases and against other popular methods. Even with the wrong lifting parameters, the method was able to reduce error better than other standard algorithms.

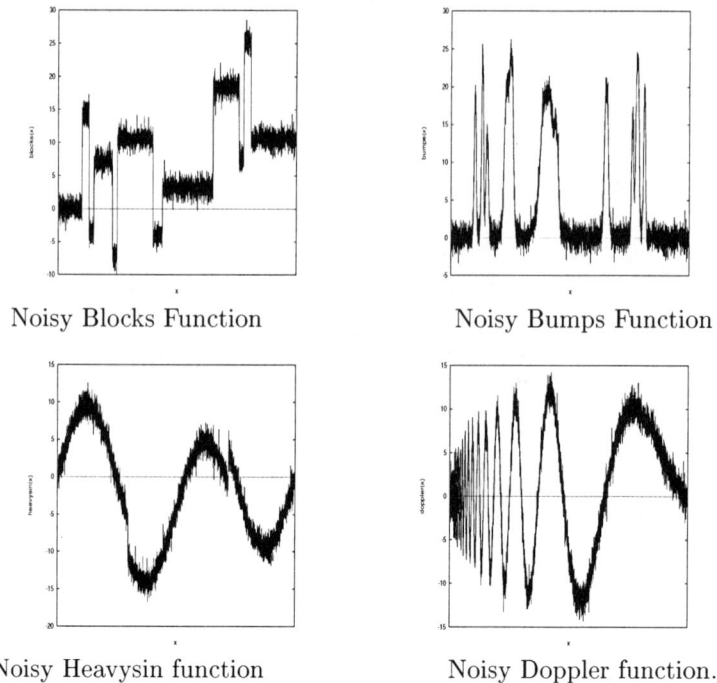

Figure 1: Noisy Test Functions

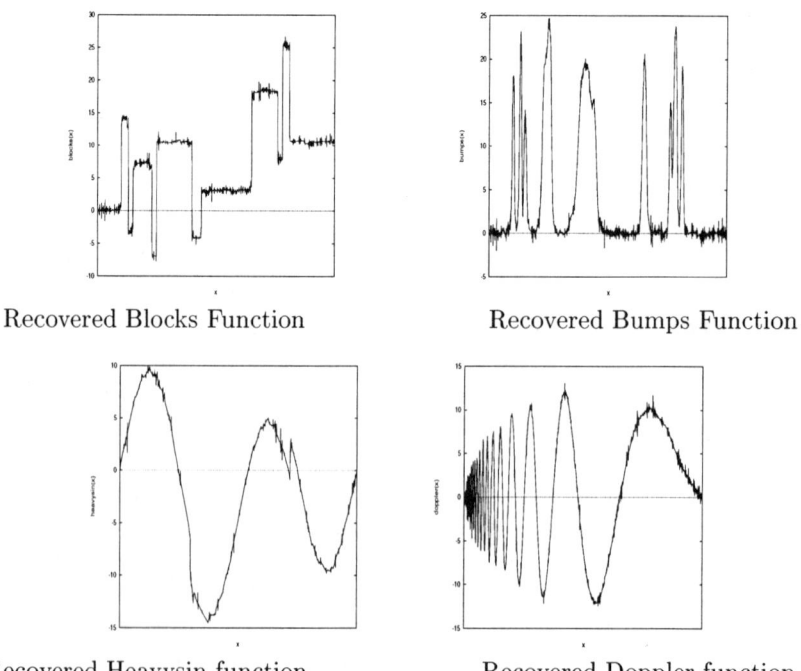

Figure 2: Recovered Functions

Table 1: Effects of Basis Selection

Function	Filter Order	Family	Median Thr. (MT)	NRMSE Using MT	Median True Thr.	NRMSE using MTT
Blocks	1	**Daubechies**	**1.33**	**0.038**	**1.61**	**0.036**
Blocks	2	Symmlets	1.245	0.045	1.40	0.045
Bumps	4	Daubechies	1.11	0.059	1.47	0.056
Bumps	5	**Symmlets**	**1.13**	**0.058**	**1.48**	**0.055**
Doppler	8	Daubechies	1.27	0.058	1.65	0.054
Doppler	8	**Symmlets**	**1.36**	**0.054**	**1.74**	**0.050**
Heavysin	2	**Daubechies**	**1.97**	**0.039**	**2.17**	**0.038**
Heavysin	5	Symmlets	1.985	0.039	2.16	0.038

Table 2: Methods Comparison Table of MSE

Function	SS	SureShrink	RBFNN	CV-Wavelets
Blocks	0.546	0.398	1.281	0.362
Heavysin	0.075	0.062	0.113	0.051
Doppler	0.205	0.145	0.287	0.116

References

A. Cohen, I. Daubechies, and J. C. Feauveau (1992), "Biorthogonal bases of compactly supported wavelets," *Communications on Pure and Applied Mathematics*, vol. 45, no. 5, pp. 485 - 560, June.

I. Daubechies (1992), *Ten Lectures on Wavelets*, CBMS-NSF Regional Conference Series in Applied Mathematics, vol. 61, SIAM, Philadelphia, PA.

D. L. Donoho (1995), "De-noising by soft-thresholding," *IEEE Transactions on Information Theory*, vol. 41, no. 3, pp.613-627, May.

D. L. Donoho, I. M. Johnstone (1994), "Ideal spatial adaptation by wavelet shrinkage," *Biometrika*, vol. 81, no. 3, pp. 425-455, September.

G. P. Nason (1996), "Wavelet shrinkage using cross-validation," *Journal of the Royal Statistical Society, Series B*, vol. 58, pp. 463 - 479.

W. Sweldens (1995), "The lifting scheme: a custom-design construction of biorthogonal wavelets," Technical Report, no. IMI 1994:7, Dept. of Mathematics, University of South Carolina.

W. Sweldens (1995), "The lifting scheme: a construction of second generation wavelets," Technical Report, no. IMI 1995:6, Dept. of Mathematics, University of South Carolina.

G. Wahba (1990), *Spline Models for Observational Data*, SIAM, Philadelphia, PA.

K. Wheeler (1996), *Smoothing Non-uniform Data Samples With Wavelets*, Ph.D. Thesis, University of Cincinnati, Dept. of Electrical and Computer Engineering, Cincinnati, OH.

DTs: Dynamic Trees

Christopher K. I. Williams   **Nicholas J. Adams**
Institute for Adaptive and Neural Computation
Division of Informatics, 5 Forrest Hill
Edinburgh, EH1 2QL, UK.   http://www.anc.ed.ac.uk/
ckiw@dai.ed.ac.uk   nicka@dai.ed.ac.uk

Abstract

In this paper we introduce a new class of image models, which we call dynamic trees or DTs. A dynamic tree model specifies a prior over a large number of trees, each one of which is a tree-structured belief net (TSBN). Experiments show that DTs are capable of generating images that are less blocky, and the models have better translation invariance properties than a fixed, "balanced" TSBN. We also show that Simulated Annealing is effective at finding trees which have high posterior probability.

1 Introduction

In this paper we introduce a new class of image models, which we call dynamic trees or DTs. A dynamic tree model specifies a prior over a large number of trees, each one of which is a tree-structured belief net (TSBN). Our aim is to retain the advantages of tree-structured belief networks, namely the hierarchical structure of the model and (in part) the efficient inference algorithms, while avoiding the "blocky" artifacts that derive from a single, fixed TSBN structure. One use for DTs is as prior models over labellings for image segmentation problems.

Section 2 of the paper gives the theory of DTs, and experiments are described in section 3.

2 Theory

There are two essential components that make up a dynamic tree network (i) the tree architecture and (ii) the nodes and conditional probability tables (CPTs) in the given tree. We consider the architecture question first.

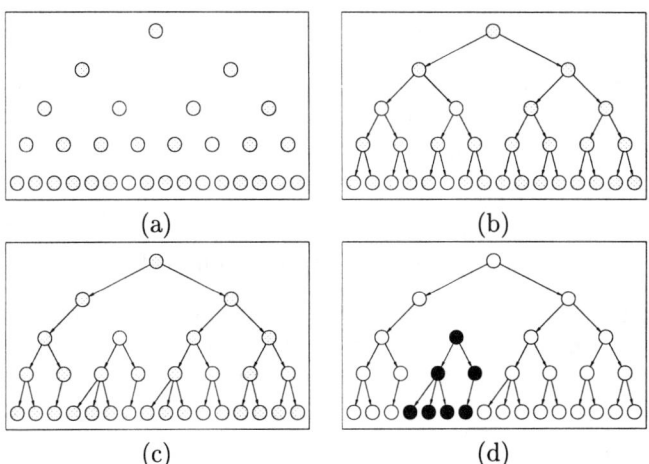

Figure 1: (a) "Naked" nodes, (b) the "balanced" tree architecture, (c) a sample from the prior over Z, (d) data generated from the tree in (c).

Consider a number of nodes arranged into layers, as in Figure 1(a). We wish to construct a tree structure so that any child node in a particular layer will be connected to a parent in the layer above. We also allow there to be a null parent for each layer, so that any child connected to it will become a new root. (Technically we are constructing a forest rather than a tree.) An example of a structure generated using this method is shown in Figure 1(c).

There are a number of ways of specifying a prior over trees. If we denote by z_i the indicator vector which shows to which parent node i belongs, then the tree structure is specified by a matrix Z whose columns are the individual z_i vectors (one for each node). The scheme that we have investigated so far is to set $P(Z) = \prod_i P(z_i)$.

In our work we have specified $P(z_i)$ as follows. Each child node is considered to have a "natural" parent—its parent in the balanced structure shown in Figure 1(b). Each node in the parent layer is assigned an "affinity" for each child node, and the "natural" parent has the highest affinity. Denote the affinity of node k in the parent layer by a_k. Then we choose $P(z_i = e_k) = e^{\beta a_k} / \sum_{j \in Pa_i} e^{\beta a_j}$, where β is some positive constant and e_k is the unit vector with a 1 in position k. Note that the "null" parent is included in the sum, and has affinity a_{null} associated with it, which affects the relative probability of "orphans". We have named this prior the "full-time-node-employment" prior as all the nodes participate in the creation of the tree structure to some degree.

Having specified the prior over architectures, we now need to translate this into a TSBN. The units in the tree are taken to be C-class multinomial random variables. Each *layer* of the structure has associated with it a prior probability vector π_l and CPT M_l. Given a particular Z matrix which specifies a forest structure, the probability of a particular instantiation of all of the random variables is simply the product of the probabilities of all of the trees, where the appropriate root probabilities and CPTs are picked up from the π_ls and M_ls. A sample generated from the tree structure in Figure 1(c) is shown in Figure 1(d).

Our intuition as to why DTs may be useful image models is based on the idea that most pixels in an image are derived from a single object. We think of an object as being described by a root of a tree, with the scale of the object being determined by the level in the tree at which the root occurs. In this interpretation the CPTs will have most of their probability mass on the diagonal.

Given some data at the bottom layer of units, we can form a posterior over the tree structures and node instantiations of the layers above. This is rather like obtaining a set of parses for a number of sentences using a context-free grammar[1].

In the DT model as described above different examples are explained by different trees. This is an important difference with the usual priors over belief networks as used, e.g. in Bayesian averaging over model structures. Also, in the usual case of model averaging, there is normally no restriction to TSBN structures, or to tying the parameters (π_ls and M_ls) between different structures.

2.1 Inference in DTs

We now consider the problem of inference in DTs, i.e. obtaining the posterior $P(Z, X_h|X_v)$ where Z denotes the tree-structure, X_v the visible units (the image clamped on the lowest level) and X_h the hidden units. In fact, we shall concentrate on obtaining the posterior marginal $P(Z|X_v)$, as we can obtain samples from $P(X_h|X_v, Z)$ using standard techniques for TSBNs.

There are a very large number of possible structures; in fact for a set of nodes created from a balanced tree with branching factor b and depth D (with the top level indexed by 1) there are $\prod_{d=2}^{D}(b^{(d-2)} + 1)^{b^{(d-1)}}$ possible forest structures. Our objective will be to obtain the maximum a posteriori (MAP) state from the posterior $P(Z|X_v) \propto P(Z)P(X_v|Z)$ using Simulated Annealing.[2] This is possible because two components $P(Z)$ and $P(X_v|Z)$ are readily evaluated. $P(X_v|Z)$ can be computed from $\prod_r (\sum_{x_r} \lambda(x_r)\pi(x_r))$, where $\lambda(x_r)$ and $\pi(x_r)$ are the Pearl-style vectors of each root r of the forest.

An alternative to sampling from the posterior $P(Z, X_h|X_v)$ is to use approximate inference. One possibility is to use a mean-field-type approximation to the posterior of the form $Q_Z(Z)Q_h(X_h)$ (Zoubin Ghahramani, personal communication, 1998).

2.2 Comparing DTs to other image models

Fixed-structure TSBNs have been used by a number of authors as models of images (Bouman and Shapiro, 1994), (Luettgen and Willsky, 1995). They have an attractive multi-scale structure, but suffer from problems due to the fixed tree structure, which can lead to very "blocky" segmentations. Markov Random Field (MRF) models are also popular image models; however, one of their main limitations is that inference in a MRF is NP-hard. Also, they lack an hierarchical structure. On the other hand, stationarity of the process they define can be easily ensured, which

---

[1]CFGs have a $O(n^3)$ algorithm to infer the MAP parse; however, this algorithm depends crucially on the one-dimensional ordering of the inputs. We believe that the possibility of crossed links in the DT architecture means that this kind of algorithm is not applicable to the DT case. Also, the DT model can be applied to 2-d images, where the $O(n^3)$ algorithm is not applicable.

[2]It is also possible to sample from the posterior using, e.g. Gibbs Sampling.

is not the case for fixed-structure TSBNs. One strategy to overcome the fixed structure of TSBNs is to break away from the tree structure, and use belief networks with cross connections e.g. (Dayan et al., 1995). However, this means losing the linear-time belief-propagation algorithms that can be used in trees (Pearl, 1988) and using approximate algorithms. While it is true that inference over DTs is also NP-hard, we do retain a "clean" semantics based on the fact that we expect that each pixel should belong to one object, which may lead to useful approximation schemes.

3 Experiments

In this section we describe two experiments conducted on the DT models. The first has been designed to compare the translation performance of DTs with that of the balanced TSBN structure and is described in section 3.1. In section 3.2 we generate 2-d images from the DT model, find the MAP Dynamic Tree for these images, and contrast their performance in relative to the balanced TSBN.

3.1 Comparing DTs with the balanced TSBN

We consider a 5-layer binary tree with 16 leaf nodes, as shown in Figure 1. Each node in the tree is a binary variable, taking on values of white/black. The π_l's, M_l's and affinities were set to be equal in each layer. The values used were $\pi = (0.75, 0.25)$ with 0.75 referring to white, and M had values 0.99 on the diagonal and 0.01 off-diagonal. The affinities[3] were set as 1 for the natural parent, 0 for the nearest neighbour(s) of the natural parent, $-\infty$ for non-nearest neighbours and $a_{null} = 0$, with $\beta = 1.25$.

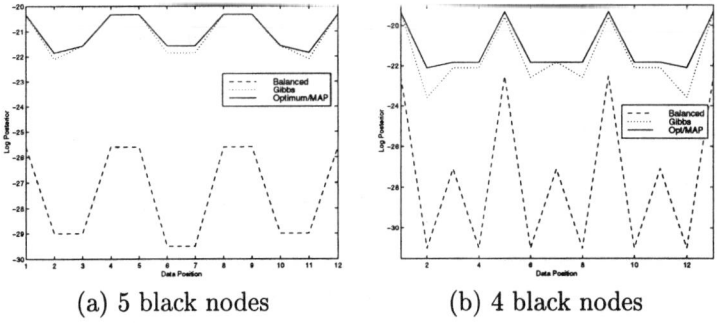

(a) 5 black nodes   (b) 4 black nodes

Figure 2: Plots of the unnormalised log posterior vs position of the input pattern for (a) the 5-black-nodes pattern and (b) 4-black-nodes pattern.

To illustrate the effects of translation, we have taken a stimulus made up of a bar of five black pixels, and moved it across the image. The unnormalised log posterior for a particular Z configuration is $\log P(Z) + \log P(X_v|Z)$. This is computed for the balanced TSBN architecture, and compared to the highest value that can be found by conducting a search over Z. These results are plotted in Figure 2(a). The x-axis denotes the position of the left hand end of the bar (running from 1 to

---

[3]The affinities are defined up to the addition of an arbitrary constant.

12), and the y-axis shows the posterior probability. Note that due to symmetries there are in reality fewer than 12 distinct configurations. Figure 2(a) shows clearly that the balanced TSBN is a poor model for this stimulus, and that much better interpretations can be found using DTs, even though the "natural parent" idea ensures that the $\log P(Z)$ is always larger for the balanced tree.

Notice also how the balanced TSBN displays greater sensitivity of the log posterior with respect to position than the DT model. Figure 2 shows both the "optimal" log posterior (found "by hand", using intuitions as to the best trees), and the those of the MAP models discovered by Simulated Annealing. Annealing was conducted from a starting temperature of 1.0 and exponentially decreased by a factor of 0.9. At each temperature up to 2000 proposals could be made, although transition to the next temperature would occur after 200 accepted steps. The run was deemed to have converged after five successive temperature steps were made without accepting a single step. We also show the log posterior of trees found by Gibbs sampling from which we report the best configuration found from four separate runs (with different random starting positions), each of which was run for 25,000 sweeps through all of the nodes.

In Figure 2(b) we have shown the log posterior for a stimulus made up of *four* black nodes[4]. In this case the balanced TSBN is even more sensitive to the stimulus location, as the four black nodes fit exactly under one sub-tree when they are in positions 1, 5, 9 or 13. By contrast, the dynamic tree is less sensitive to the alignment, although it does retain a preference for the configuration most favoured by the balanced TSBN. This is due to the concept of a "natural" parent built into the (current) architecture (but see Section 4 for further discussion).

Clearly these results are somewhat sensitive to settings of the parameters. One of the most important parameters is the diagonal entry in the CPT. This controls the relative desirability of having a disconnection against a transition in the tree that involves a colour change. For example, if the diagonal entry in the CPT is reduced to 0.95, the gap between the optimal and balanced trees in Figure 2(b) is decreased. We have experimented with CPT entries of 0.90, 0.95 and 0.99, but otherwise have not needed to explore the parameter space to obtain the results shown.

3.2 Generating from the prior and finding the MAP Tree in 2-d

We now turn our attention to 2-d images. Considering a 5 layer quad-tree node arrangement gives a total of 256 leaf nodes or a 16x16 pixel image. A structural plot of such a tree generated from the prior is shown in figure 3.

Each sub-plot is a slice through the tree showing the nodes on successive levels. The boxes represent a single node on the current level and their shading indicates the tree to which they belong. Nodes in the parent layer above are superimposed as circles and the lines emanating from them shows their connectivity. Black circles with a smaller white circle inside are used to indicate root nodes. Thus in the example above we see that the forest consists of five trees, four of whose roots lie at level 3 (which between them account for most of the black in the image, Figure 3(f)), while the root node at level 1 is responsible for the background.

---

[4]The parameters are the same as above, except that a_{null} in level 3 was set to 10.0 to encourage disconnections at this level.

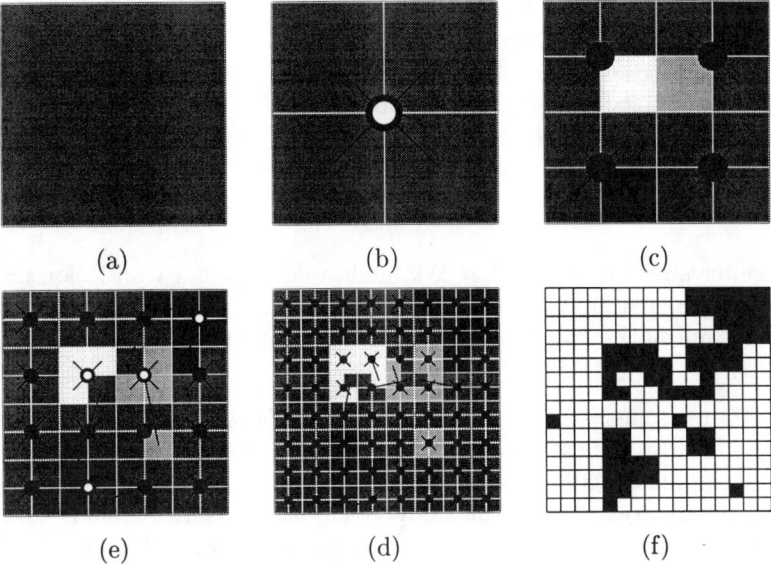

Figure 3: Plot of the MAP Dynamic Tree of the accompanying image (f).

Broadly speaking the parameters for the 2-d DTs were set to be similar to the 1-d trees of the previous section, except that the disconnection affinities were set to favour disconnections higher up the tree, and to values for the leaf level such that leaf disconnection probabilities tend to zero. In practice this resulted in all leaves being connected to parent nodes (which is desirable as we believe that single-pixel objects are unlikely). The β values increase with tree depth so that lower levels nodes choose parents from a tighter neighbourhood. The m_l and M_l values were unchanged, and again we consider binary valued nodes.

A suite of 600 images were created by sampling DTs from the above prior and then generating 5 images from each. Figure 3(f) shows an example of an image generated by the DT and it can be seen that the "blockiness" exhibited by balanced TSBNs is not present.

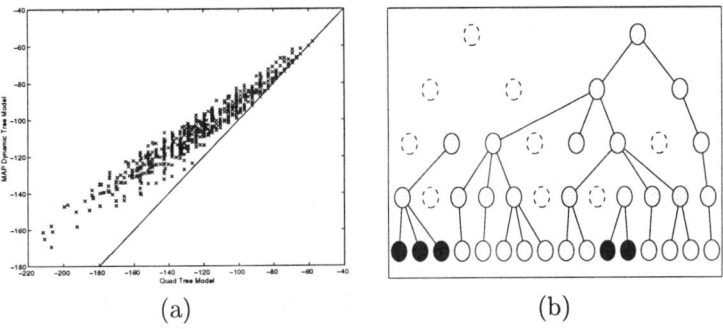

Figure 4: (a) Comparison of the MAP DT log posterior against that of the quad-tree for 600 images, (b) tree generated from the "part-time-node-employment" prior.

The MAP Dynamic Tree for each of these images was found by Simulated Annealing using the same exponential strategy described earlier, and their log posteriors are compared with those of the balanced TSBN in the plot 4(a). The line denotes the boundary of equal log posterior and the location of all the points above this clearly shows that in every case the MAP tree found has a higher posterior.

4 Discussion

Above we have demonstrated that DT models have greater translation invariance and do not exhibit the blockiness of the balanced TSBN model. We also see that Simulated Annealing methods are successful at finding trees that have high posterior probability.

We now discuss some extensions to the model. In the work above we have kept the balanced tree arrangement of nodes. However, this could be relaxed, giving rise to roughly equal numbers of nodes at the various levels (*cf stationary* wavelets). This would be useful (a) for providing better translation invariance and (b) to avoid slight shortages of hidden units that can occur when patterns that are "misaligned" wrt the balanced tree are presented. In this case the prior over Z would need to be adjusted to ensure a high proportion of tree-like structures, by generating the z's and x's in layers, so that the z's can be contingent on the states of the units in the layer above. We have devised a prior of this nature and called it the "part-time-employment" prior as the nodes can decide whether or not they wish to be employed in the tree structure or remain redundant and inactive. An example tree generated from this prior is shown in figure 4(b); we plan to explore this direction further in on-going research. Other research directions include the learning of parameters in the networks (e.g. using EM), and the introduction of additional information at the nodes; for example one might use real-valued variables in addition to the multinomial variables considered above. These additional variables might be used to encode information such as that concerning the instantiation parameters of objects.

Acknowledgements

This work stems from a conversation between CW and Zoubin Gharahmani at the Isaac Newton Institute in October 1997. We thank Zoubin Ghahramani, Geoff Hinton and Peter Dayan for helpful conversations, and the Isaac Newton Institute for Mathematical Sciences (Cambridge, UK) for hospitality during the "Neural Networks and Machine Learning" programme. NJA is supported by an EPSRC research studentship, and the work of CW is partially supported by EPSRC grant GR/L03088, *Combining Spatially Distributed Predictions From Neural Networks*.

References

Bouman, C. A. and M. Shapiro (1994). A Multiscale Random Field Model for Bayesian Image Segmentation. *IEEE Transactions on Image Processing* **3(2)**, 162–177.

Dayan, P., G. E. Hinton, R. M. Neal, and R. S. Zemel (1995). The Helmholtz Machine. *Neural Computation* **7(5)**, 889–904.

Luettgen, M. R. and A. S. Willsky (1995). Likelihood Calculation for a Class of Multiscale Stocahstic Models, with Application to Texture Discrimination. *IEEE Trans. Image Processing* **4(2))**, 194–207.

Pearl, J. (1988). *Probabilistic Reasoning in Intelligent Systems: Networks of Plausible Inference*. San Mateo, CA: Morgan Kaufmann.

Convergence Rates of Algorithms for Visual Search: Detecting Visual Contours

A.L. Yuille
Smith-Kettlewell Inst.
San Francisco, CA 94115

James M. Coughlan
Smith-Kettlewell Inst.
San Francisco, CA 94115

Abstract

This paper formulates the problem of visual search as Bayesian inference and defines a Bayesian ensemble of problem instances. In particular, we address the problem of the detection of visual contours in noise/clutter by optimizing a global criterion which combines local intensity and geometry information. We analyze the convergence rates of A* search algorithms using results from information theory to bound the probability of rare events within the Bayesian ensemble. This analysis determines characteristics of the domain, which we call order parameters, that determine the convergence rates. In particular, we present a specific admissible A* algorithm with pruning which converges, with high probability, with expected time $O(N)$ in the size of the problem. In addition, we briefly summarize extensions of this work which address fundamental limits of target contour detectability (i.e. algorithm independent results) and the use of non-admissible heuristics.

1 Introduction

Many problems in vision, such as the detection of edges and object boundaries in noise/clutter, see figure (1), require the use of search algorithms. Though many algorithms have been proposed , see Yuille and Coughlan (1997) for a review, none of them are clearly optimal and it is difficult to judge their relative effectiveness. One approach has been to compare the results of algorithms on a representative dataset of images. This is clearly highly desirable though determining a representative dataset is often rather subjective.

In this paper we are specifically interested in the convergence rates of A* algorithms (Pearl 1984). It can be shown (Yuille and Coughlan 1997) that many algorithms proposed to detect visual contours are special cases of A* . We would like to understand what characteristics of the problem domain determine the convergence

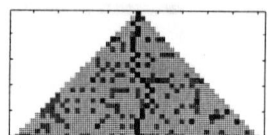 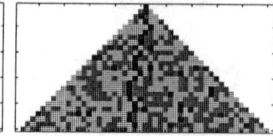 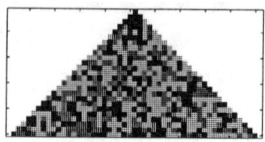

Figure 1: The difficulty of detecting the target path in clutter depends, by our theory (Yuille and Coughlan 1998), on the order parameter K. The larger K the less computation required. Left, an easy detection task with $K = 3.1$. Middle, a hard detection task $K = 1.6$. Right, an impossible task with $K = -0.7$.

rates.

We formulate the problem of detecting object curves in images to be one of statistical estimation. This assumes statistical knowledge of the images and the curves, see section (2). Such statistical knowledge has often been used in computer vision for determining optimization criteria to be minimized. We want to go one step further and use this statistical knowledge to determine good search strategies by defining a *Bayesian ensemble* of problem instances. For this ensemble, we can prove certain curve and boundary detection algorithms, with high probability, achieve expected time convergence in time linear with the size of the problem. Our analysis helps determine important characteristics of the problem, which we call *order parameters*, which quantify the difficulty of the problem.

The next section (2) of this paper describes the basic statistical assumptions we make about the domain and describes the mathematical tools used in the remaining sections. In section (3) we specify our search algorithm and establish convergence rates. We conclude by placing this work in a larger context and summarizing recent extensions.

2 Statistical Background

Our approach assumes that both the intensity properties and the geometrical shapes of the target path (i.e. the edge contour) can be determined statistically. This path can be considered to be a set of elementary path segments joined together. We first consider the intensity properties along the edge and then the geometric properties. The set of all possible paths can be represented by a tree structure, see figure (2).

The image properties at segments lying on the path are assumed to differ, in a statistical sense, from those off the path. More precisely, we can design a filter $\phi(.)$ with output $\{y_x = \phi(I(x))\}$ for a segment at point x so that:

$$P(y_x) = P_{on}(y_x), \quad if \text{ "}x\text{" } lies \ on \ the \ true \ path$$
$$P(y_x) = P_{off}(y_x), \quad if \text{ "}x\text{" } lies \ off \ the \ true \ path. \qquad (1)$$

For example, we can think of the $\{y_x\}$ as being values of the edge strength at point x and P_{on}, P_{off} being the probability distributions of the response of $\phi(.)$ on and off an edge. The set of possible values of the random variable y_x is the *alphabet* with *alphabet size* M (i.e. y_x can take any of M possible values). See (Geman and Jedynak 1996) for examples of distributions for P_{on}, P_{off} used in computer vision applications.

We now consider the geometry of the target contour. We require the path to be made up of connected segments $x_1, x_2, \ldots, x_N$. There will be a Markov probability distribution $P_g(x_{i+1}|x_i)$ which specifies prior probabilistic knowledge of the target.

It is convenient, in terms of the graph search algorithms we will use, to consider that each point x has a set of Q neighbours. Following terminology from graph theory, we refer to Q as the *branching factor*. We will assume that the distribution P_g depends only on the relative positions of x_{i+1} and x_i. In other words, $P_g(x_{i+1}|x_i) = P_{\Delta g}(x_{i+1} - x_i)$. An important special case is when the probability distribution is uniform for all branches (i.e. $P_{\Delta g}(\Delta x) = U(\Delta x) = 1/Q, \forall \Delta x$). The joint distribution $P(X,Y)$ of the road geometry X and filter responses Y determines the *Bayesian Ensemble*.

By standard Bayesian analysis, the optimal path $X^* = \{x_1^*, \ldots, x_N^*\}$ maximizes the sum of the log posterior:

$$E(X) = \sum_i \log \frac{P_{on}(y_{(x_i)})}{P_{off}(y_{(x_i)})} + \sum_i \log \frac{P_{\Delta g}(x_{i+1} - x_i)}{U(x_{i+1} - x_i)}, \quad (2)$$

where the sum i is taken over all points on the target. $U(x_{i+1} - x_i)$ is the uniform distribution and its presence merely changes the log posterior $E(X)$ by a constant value. It is included to make the form of the intensity and geometric terms similar, which simplifies our later analysis.

We will refer to $E(X)$ as the *reward* of the path X which is the sum of the *intensity rewards* $\log \frac{P_{on}(y_{(x_i)})}{P_{off}(y_{(x_i)})}$ and the *geometric rewards* $\log \frac{P_{\Delta g}(x_{i+1} - x_i)}{U(x_{i+1} - x_i)}$.

It is important to emphasize that our results can be extended to higher-order Markov chain models (provided they are shift-invariant). We can, for example, define the x variable to represent spatial orientation *and* position of a small edge segment. This will allow our theory to apply to models, such as snakes, used in recent successful vision applications (Geman and Jedynak 1996). (It is straightforward to transform the standard energy function formulation of snakes into a Markov chain by discretizing and replacing the derivatives by differences. The smoothness constraints, such as membranes and thin plate terms, will transform into first and second order Markov chain connections respectively). Recent work by Zhu (1998) shows that Markov chain models of this type can be learnt using Minimax Entropy Learning theory from a representative set of examples. Indeed Zhu goes further by demonstrating that other Gestalt grouping laws can be expressed in this framework and learnt from representative data.

Most Bayesian vision theories have stopped at this point. The statistics of the problem domain are used only to determine the optimization criterion to be minimized and are not exploited to analyze the complexity of algorithms for performing the optimization. In this paper, we go a stage further. We use the statistics of the problem domain to define a Bayesian ensemble and hence to *determine the effectiveness of algorithms for optimizing* criteria such as (2). To do this requires the use of Sanov's theorem for calculating the probability of rare events (Cover and Thomas 1991). For the road tracking problem this can be re-expressed as the following theorem, derived in (Yuille and Coughlan 1998):

Theorem 1. *The probabilities that the spatially averaged log-likelihoods on, and off, the true curve are above, or below, threshold T are bounded above as follows:*

$$Pr\{\frac{1}{n}\sum_{i=1}^n \{\log \frac{P_{on}(y_{(x_i)})}{P_{off}(y_{(x_i)})}\}_{on} < T\} \leq (n+1)^M 2^{-nD(P_T||P_{on})} \quad (3)$$

$$Pr\{\frac{1}{n}\sum_{i=1}^n \{\log \frac{P_{on}(y_{(x_i)})}{P_{off}(y_{(x_i)})}\}_{off} > T\} \leq (n+1)^M 2^{-nD(P_T||P_{off})}, \quad (4)$$

where the subscripts $_{on}$ and $_{off}$ mean that the data is generated by P_{on}, P_{off}, $P_T(y) = P_{on}^{1-\lambda(T)}(y) P_{off}^{\lambda(T)}/Z(T)$ where $0 \leq \lambda(T) \leq 1$ is a scalar which depends on the threshold T and $Z(T)$ is a normalization factor. The value of $\lambda(T)$ is determined by the constraint $\sum_y P_T(y) \log \frac{P_{on}(y)}{P_{off}(y)} = T$.

In the next section, we will use Theorem 1 to determine a criterion for pruning the search based on comparing the intensity reward to a threshold T (pruning will also be done using the geometric reward). The choice of T involves a trade-off. If T is large (i.e. close to $D(P_{on}||P_{off})$) then we will rapidly reject false paths but we might also prune out the target (true) path. Conversely, if T is small (close to $-D(P_{off}||P_{on})$) then it is unlikely we will prune out the target path but we may waste a lot of time exploring false paths. In this paper we choose T large and write the fall-off factors (i.e. the exponents in the bounds of equations (3,4)) as $D(P_T||P_{on}) = \epsilon_1(T)$, $D(P_T||P_{off}) = D(P_{on}||P_{off}) - \epsilon_2(T)$ where $\epsilon_1(T), \epsilon_2(T)$ are positive and $(\epsilon_1(T), \epsilon_2(T)) \mapsto (0,0)$ as $T \mapsto D(P_{on}||P_{off})$. We perform a similar analysis for the geometric rewards by substituting $P_{\Delta g}, U$ for P_{on}, P_{off}. We choose a threshold $\hat{T}$ satisfying $-D(U||P_{\Delta g}) < \hat{T} < D(P_{\Delta g}||U)$. The results of Theorem 1 apply with the obvious substitutions. In particular, the alphabet factor becomes Q (the branching factor). Once again, in this paper, we choose $\hat{T}$ to be large and obtain fall-off factors $D(P_{\hat{T}}||P_{\Delta g}) = \hat{\epsilon}_1(\hat{T})$, $D(P_{\hat{T}}||U) = D(P_{\Delta g}||U) - \hat{\epsilon}_2(\hat{T})$.

3 Tree Search: A*, heuristics, and block pruning

We now consider a specific example, motivated by Geman and Jedynak (1996), of searching for a path through a search tree. In Geman and Jedynak the path corresponds to a road in an aerial image and they assume that they are given an initial point and direction on the target path. They have a branching factor $Q = 3$ and, in their first version, the prior probability of branching is considered to be the uniform distribution (later they consider more sophisticated priors). They assume that no path segments overlap which means that the search space is a tree of size Q^N where N is the size of the problem (i.e. the longest length). The size of the problem requires an algorithm that converges in $O(N)$ time and they demonstrate an algorithm which empirically performs at this speed. But no proof of convergence rates are given in their paper. It can be shown, see (Yuille and Coughlan 1997), that the Geman and Jedynak algorithm is a close approximation to A* which uses pruning. (Observe that Geman and Jedynak's tree representation is a simplifying assumption of the Bayesian model which assumes that once a path diverges from the true path it can never recover, although we stress that the *algorithm* is able to recover from false starts – for more details see Coughlan and Yuille 1998).

We consider an algorithm which uses an admissible A* heuristic and a pruning mechanism. The idea is to examine the paths chosen by the A* heuristic. As the length of the candidate path reaches an integer multiple of N_0 we prune it based on its intensity reward and its geometric reward evaluated on the previous N_0 segments, which we call a *segment block*. The reasoning is that few false paths will survive this pruning for long but the target path will survive with high probability.

We prune on the intensity by eliminating all paths whose intensity reward, averaged over the last N_0 segments, is below a threshold T (recall that $-D(P_{off}||P_{on}) < T < D(P_{on}||P_{off})$ and we will usually select T to take values close to $D(P_{on}||P_{off})$). In addition, we prune on the geometry by eliminating all paths whose geometric rewards, averaged over the last N_0 segments, are below $\hat{T}$ (where $-D(U||P_{\Delta g}) < \hat{T} < D(P_{\Delta g}||U)$ with $\hat{T}$ typically being close to $D(P_{\Delta g}||U)$). More precisely, we discard a path provided (for any integer $z \geq 0$):

$$\frac{1}{N_0} \sum_{i=zN_0+1}^{(z+1)N_0} \log \frac{P_{on}(y_i)}{P_{off}(y_i)} < T, \text{ or } \frac{1}{N_0} \sum_{i=zN_0+1}^{(z+1)N_0} \log \frac{P_{\Delta g}(\Delta x_i)}{U(\Delta x_i)} < \hat{T}. \quad (5)$$

There are two important issues to address: (i) With what probability will the algorithm converge?, (ii) How long will we expect it take to converge? The next two subsections put bounds on these issues.

3.1 Probability of Convergence

Because of the pruning, there is a chance that there will be no paths which survive pruning. To put a bound on this we calculate the probability that the target (true) path survives the pruning. This gives a lower bound on the probability of convergence (because there could be false paths which survive even if the target path is mistakenly pruned out).

The pruning rules removes path segments for which the intensity reward r_I or the geometric reward r_g fails the pruning test. The probability of failure by removing a block segment of the true path, with rewards r_I^t, r_g^t, is $Pr(r_I^t < T \text{ or } r_g^t < \hat{T}) \leq Pr(r_I^t < T) + Pr(r_g^t < \hat{T}) \leq (N_0 + 1)^M 2^{-N_0 \epsilon_1(T)} + (N_0 + 1)^Q 2^{-N_0 \hat{\epsilon}_1(\hat{T})}$, where we have used Theorem 1 to put bounds on the probabilities. The probability of pruning out any N_0 segments of the true path can therefore be made arbitrarily small by choosing $N_0, T, \hat{T}$ so as to make $N_0 \epsilon_1$ and $N_0 \hat{\epsilon}_1$ large.

It should be emphasized that the algorithm will not necessarily converge to the exact target path. The admissible nature of the heuristic means that the algorithm will converge to the path with highest reward which has survived the pruning. It is highly probable that this path is close to the target path. Our recent results (Coughlan and Yuille 1998, Yuille and Coughlan 1998) enable us to quantify this claim.

3.2 Bounding the Number of False Paths

Suppose we face a Q-nary tree. We can order the false paths by the stage at which they diverge from the target (true) path, see figure (2). For example, at the first branch point the target path lies on only one of the Q branches and there are $Q-1$ false branches which generate the first set of false paths F_1. Now consider all the $Q-1$ false branches at the second target branch, these generate set F_2. As we follow along the true path we keep generating these false sets F_i. The set of all paths is therefore the target path plus the union of the F_i ($i = 1, \ldots, N$). To determine convergence rates we must bound the amount of time we spend searching the F_i. If the expected time to search each F_i is constant then searching for the target path will at most take $constant \cdot N$ steps.

Consider the set F_i of false paths which leave the true path at stage i. We will apply our analysis to block segments of F_i which are completely off the true path. If $(i-1)$ is an integer multiple of N_0 then all block segments of F_i will satisfy this condition. Otherwise, we will start our analysis at the next block and make the worse case assumption that all path segments up till this next block will be searched. Since the distance to the next block is at most $N_0 - 1$, this gives a maximum number of Q^{N_0-1} starting blocks for any branch of F_i. Each F_i also has $Q-1$ branches and so this gives a generous upper bound of $(Q-1)Q^{N_0-1}$ starting blocks for each F_i.

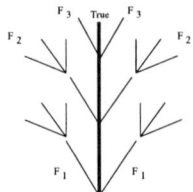

Figure 2: The target path is shown as the heavy line. The false path sets are labelled as F_1, F_2, etc. with the numbering depending on how soon they leave the target path. The branching factor $Q = 3$.

For each starting block, we wish to compute (or bound) the expected number of blocks that are explored thereafter. This requires computing the *fertility* of a block, the average number of paths in the block that survive pruning. Provided the fertility is smaller than one, we can then apply results from the theory of branching processes to determine the expected number of blocks searched in F_i.

The fertility q is the number of paths that survive the geometric pruning times the probability that each survives the intensity pruning. This can be bounded (using Theorem 1) by $q \leq \hat{q}$ where:

$$\hat{q} = Q^{N_0}(N_0 + 1)^Q 2^{-N_0\{D(P_{\Delta g}||U) - \hat{\epsilon}_2(\hat{T})\}}(N_0 + 1)^M 2^{-N_0\{D(P_{on}||P_{off}) - \epsilon_2(T)\}}$$
$$= (N_0 + 1)^{Q+M} 2^{-N_0\{D(P_{on}||P_{off}) - H(P_{\Delta g}) - \epsilon_2(T) - \hat{\epsilon}_2(\hat{T})\}}, \quad (6)$$

where we used the fact that $D(P_{\Delta g}||U) = \log Q - H(P_{\Delta g})$.

Observe that the condition $\hat{q} < 1$ can be satisfied provided $D(P_{on}||P_{off}) - H(P_{\Delta g}) > 0$. This condition is intuitive, it requires that the edge detector information, quantified by $D(P_{on}||P_{off})$, must be greater than the uncertainty in the geometry measured by $H(P_{\Delta g})$. In other words, the better the edge detector and the more predictable the path geometry then the smaller $\hat{q}$ will be.

We now apply the theory of branching processes to determine the expected number of blocks explored from a starting block in F_i, $\sum_{z=0}^{\infty} \hat{q}^z = 1/(1 - \hat{q})$. The number of branches of F_i is $(Q - 1)$, the total number of segments explored per block is at most Q^{N_0}, and we explore at most $Q^{N_0 - 1}$ segments before reaching the first block. The total number of F_i is N. Therefore the total number of segments wastefully explored is at most $N(Q - 1)\frac{1}{1-\hat{q}}Q^{2N_0 - 1}$. We summarize this result in a theorem:

Theorem 2. *Provided $\hat{q} = (N_0 + 1)^{Q+M} 2^{-N_0 K} < 1$, where the order parameter $K = D(P_{on}||P_{off}) - H(P_{\Delta g}) - \epsilon_2(T) - \hat{\epsilon}_2(\hat{T})$, then the expected number of false segments explored is at most $N(Q - 1)\frac{1}{1-\hat{q}}Q^{2N_0 - 1}$.*

Comment The requirement that $\hat{q} < 1$ is chiefly determined by the *order parameter* $K = D(P_{on}||P_{off}) - H(P_{\Delta g}) - \epsilon_2(T) - \hat{\epsilon}_2(\hat{T})$. Our convergence proof requires that $K > 0$ and will break down if $K < 0$. Is this a limitation of our proof? Or does it correspond to a fundamental difficulty in solving this tracking problem?

In more recent work (Yuille and Coughlan 1998) we extend the concept of order parameters and show that they characterize the difficulty of visual search problem *independently of the algorithm*. In other words, as $K \mapsto 0$ the problem becomes impossible to solve by any algorithm. There will be too many false paths which have better rewards than the target path. As $K \mapsto 0$ there is a phase transition in the ease of solving the problem.

4 Conclusion

Our analysis shows it is possible to detect certain types of image contours in linear expected time (with given starting points). We have shown how the convergence rates depend on order parameters which characterize the problem domain. In particular, the entropy of the geometric prior and the Kullback-Leibler distance between P_{on} and P_{off} allow us to quantify intuitions about the power of geometrical assumptions and edge detectors to solve these tasks.

Our more recent work (Yuille and Coughlan 1998) has extended this work by showing that the order parameters can be used to specify the intrinsic (algorithm independent) difficulty of the search problem and that phase transitions occur when these order parameters take critical values. In addition, we have proved convergence rates for A* algorithms which use inadmissible heuristics or combinations of heuristics and pruning (Coughlan and Yuille 1998).

As shown in (Yuille and Coughlan 1997) many of the search algorithms proposed to solve vision search problems, such as (Geman and Jedynak 1996), are special cases of A* (or close approximations). We therefore hope that the results of this paper will throw light on the success of the algorithms and may suggest practical improvements and speed ups.

Acknowledgements

We want to acknowledge funding from NSF with award number IRI-9700446, from the Center for Imaging Sciences funded by ARO DAAH049510494, and from an ASOSRF contract 49620-98-1-0197 to ALY. We would like to thank L. Xu, D. Snow, S. Konishi, D. Geiger, J. Malik, and D. Forsyth for helpful discussions.

References

[1] J.M. Coughlan and A.L. Yuille. "Bayesian A* Tree Search with Expected O(N) Convergence Rates for Road Tracking." Submitted to *Artificial Intelligence*. 1998.

[2] T.M. Cover and J.A. Thomas. **Elements of Information Theory**. Wiley Interscience Press. New York. 1991.

[3] D. Geman. and B. Jedynak. "An active testing model for tracking roads in satellite images". *IEEE Trans. Patt. Anal. and Machine Intel.* Vol. 18. No. 1, pp 1-14. January. 1996.

[4] J. Pearl. **Heuristics**. Addison-Wesley. 1984.

[5] A.L. Yuille and J. Coughlan. "Twenty Questions, Focus of Attention, and A*". In **Energy Minimization Methods in Computer Vision and Pattern Recognition**. Ed. M. Pellilo and E. Hancock. Springer-Verlag. (Lecture Notes in Computer Science 1223). 1997.

[6] A.L. Yuille and J.M. Coughlan. "Visual Search: Fundamental Bounds, Order Parameters, Phase Transitions, and Convergence Rates." Submitted to *Pattern Analysis and Machine Intelligence*. 1998.

[7] S.C. Zhu. "Embedding Gestalt Laws in Markov Random Fields". Submitted to *IEEE Computer Society Workshop on Perceptual Organization in Computer Vision*.

Blind Separation of Filtered Sources Using State-Space Approach

Liqing Zhang* and Andrzej Cichocki[†]
Laboratory for Open Information Systems,
Brain Science Institute, RIKEN
Saitama 351-0198, Wako shi, JAPAN
Email: {zha, cia}@open.brain.riken.go.jp

Abstract

In this paper we present a novel approach to multichannel blind separation/generalized deconvolution, assuming that both mixing and demixing models are described by stable linear state-space systems. We decompose the blind separation problem into two process: separation and state estimation. Based on the minimization of Kullback-Leibler Divergence, we develop a novel learning algorithm to train the matrices in the output equation. To estimate the state of the demixing model, we introduce a new concept, called hidden innovation, to numerically implement the Kalman filter. Computer simulations are given to show the validity and high effectiveness of the state-space approach.

1 Introduction

The field of blind separation and deconvolution has grown dramatically during recent years due to its similarity to the separation feature in human brain, as well as its rapidly growing applications in various fields, such as telecommunication systems, image enhancement and biomedical signal processing. The blind source separation problem is to recover independent sources from sensor outputs without assuming any priori knowledge of the original signals besides certain statistic features. Refer to review papers [1] and [5] for the current state of theory and methods in the field.

Although there exist a number of models and methods, such as the infomax, natural gradient approach and equivariant adaptive algorithms, for separating blindly independent sources, there still are several challenges in generalizing mixture to dy-

---
*On leave from South China University of Technology, China
[†]On leave from Warsaw University of Technology, Poland

namic and nonlinear systems, as well as in developing more rigorous and effective algorithms with general convergence.[1-9], [11-13]

The state-space description of systems is a new model for blind separation and deconvolution[9,12]. There are several reasons why we use linear state-space systems as blind deconvolution models. Although transfer function models are equivalent to the state-space ones, it is difficult to exploit any common features that may be present in the real dynamic systems. The main advantage of the state space description for blind deconvolution is that it not only gives the internal description of a system, but there are various equivalent types of state-space realizations for a system, such as balanced realization and observable canonical forms. In particular it is known how to parameterize some specific classes of models which are of interest in applications. Also it is much easy to tackle the stability problem of state-space systems using the Kalman Filter. Moreover, the state-space model enables much more general description than standard finite impulse response (FIR) convolutive filtering. All known filtering (dynamic) models, like AR, MA, ARMA, ARMAX and Gamma filterings, could also be considered as special cases of flexible state-space models.

2 Formulation of Problem

Assume that the source signals are a stationary zero-mean i.i.d processes and mutually statistically independent. Let $s(t) = (s_1(t), \cdots, s_n(t))$ be an unknown vector of independent i.i.d. sources. Suppose that the mixing model is described by a stable linear state discrete-time system

$$\overline{x}(k+1) = \overline{A}\overline{x}(k) + \overline{B}s(k) + \overline{L}\xi_P(k), \quad (1)$$
$$u(k) = \overline{C}\overline{x}(k) + \overline{D}s(k) + \theta(k), \quad (2)$$

where $\overline{x} \in \mathbf{R}^r$ is the state vector of system, $s(k) \in \mathbf{R}^n$ is the vector of source signals and $u(k) \in \mathbf{R}^m$ is the vector of sensor signals. $\overline{A}$, $\overline{B}$, $\overline{C}$ and $\overline{D}$ are the mixing matrices of the state space model with consistent dimensions. $\xi_P(k)$ is the process noise and $\theta(k)$ is sensor noise of the mixing system. If we ignore the noise terms in the mixing model, its transfer function matrix is described by a $m \times n$ matrix of the form

$$H(z) = \overline{C}(z\mathbf{I} - \overline{A})^{-1}\overline{B} + \overline{D}, \quad (3)$$

where z^{-1} is a delay operator.

We formulate the blind separation problem as a task to recover original signals from observations $u(t)$ without prior knowledge on the source signals and the state space matrices $[\overline{A}, \overline{B}, \overline{C}, \overline{D}]$ besides certain statistic features of source signals. We propose that the demixing model here is another linear state-space system, which is described as follows, (see Fig. 1)

$$x(k+1) = Ax(k) + Bu(k) + L\xi_R(k), \quad (4)$$
$$y(k) = Cx(k) + Du(k), \quad (5)$$

where the input $u(k)$ of the demixing model is just the output (sensor signals) of the mixing model and the $\xi_R(k)$ is the reference model noise. A, B, C and D are the demixing matrices of consistent dimensions. In general, the matrices $W = [A, B, C, D, L]$ are parameters to be determined in learning process.

For simplicity, we do not consider, at this moment, the noise terms both in the mixing and demixing models. The transfer function of the demixing model is $W(z) = C(z\mathbf{I} - A)^{-1}B + D$. The output $y(k)$ is designed to recover the source signals in the following sense

$$y(k) = W(z)H(z)s(k) = P\Lambda(z)s(k), \quad (6)$$

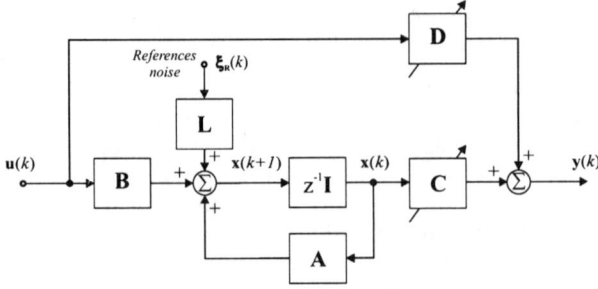

Figure 1: General state-space model for blind deconvolution

where P is any permutation matrix and $\Lambda(z)$ is a diagonal matrix with $\lambda_i z^{-\tau_i}$ in diagonal entry (i,i), here λ_i is a nonzero constant and τ_i is any nonnegative integer. It is easy to see that the linear state space model mixture is an extension of instantaneous mixture. When both the matrices $\overline{A}, \overline{B}, \overline{C}$ in the mixing model and A, B, C in the demixing model are null matrices, the problem is simplified to standard ICA problem [1-8].

The question here is whether exist matrices $[A, B, C, D]$ in the demixing model (4) and (5), such that its transfer function $W(z)$ satisfies (6). It is proven [12] that if the matrix $\overline{D}$ in the mixing model is of full rank, $rank(\overline{D}) = n$, then there exist matrices $[A, B, C, D]$, such that the output signal y of state-space system (4) and (5) recovers the independent source signal s in the sense of (6).

3 Learning Algorithm

Assume that $p(y, W), p_i(y_i, W)$ are the joint probability density function of y and marginal pdf of y_i, $(i = 1, \cdots, n)$ respectively. We employ the mutual information of the output signals, which measures the mutual independence of the output signals $y_i(k)$, as a risk function [1,2]

$$l(W) = -H(y, W) + \sum_{i=1}^{n} H(y_i, W), \qquad (7)$$

where

$$H(y, W) = -\int p(y, W) \log p(y, W) dy, \quad H(y_i, W) = -\int p_i(y_i, W) \log p_i(y_i, W) dy_i.$$

In this paper we do not directly develop learning algorithms to update all parameters $W = [A, B, C, D]$ in demixing model. We separate the blind deconvolution problem into two procedures: separation and state-estimation. In the separation procedure we develop a novel learning algorithm, using a new search direction, to update the matrices C and D in output equation (5). Then we define a hidden innovation of the output and use Kalman filter to estimate the state vector $x(k)$.

For simplicity we suppose that the matrix D in the demixing model (5) is nonsingular $n \times n$ matrix. From the risk function (7), we can obtain a cost function for on line learning

$$l(y, W) = -\frac{1}{2} \log det(D^T D)) - \sum_{i=1}^{n} \log p_i(y_i, W), \qquad (8)$$

where $det(\boldsymbol{D}^T\boldsymbol{D})$ is the determinant of symmetric positive definite matrix $\boldsymbol{D}^T\boldsymbol{D}$. For the gradient of l with respect to $\boldsymbol{W}$, we calculate the total differential dl of $l(\boldsymbol{y},\boldsymbol{W})$ when we takes a differential $d\boldsymbol{W}$ on $\boldsymbol{W}$

$$dl(\boldsymbol{y},\boldsymbol{W}) = l(\boldsymbol{y},\boldsymbol{W}+d\boldsymbol{W}) - l(\boldsymbol{y},\boldsymbol{W}). \tag{9}$$

Following Amari's derivation for natural gradient methods [1-3], we have

$$dl(\boldsymbol{y},\boldsymbol{W}) = -tr(d\boldsymbol{D}\boldsymbol{D}^{-1}) + \boldsymbol{\varphi}^T(\boldsymbol{y})d\boldsymbol{y}, \tag{10}$$

where tr is the trace of a matrix and $\boldsymbol{\varphi}(\boldsymbol{y})$ is a vector of nonlinear activation functions

$$\varphi_i(y_i) = -\frac{d\log p_i(y_i)}{dy_i} = -\frac{p'_i(y_i)}{p_i(y_i)}. \tag{11}$$

Taking the derivative on equation (5), we have following approximation

$$d\boldsymbol{y} = d\boldsymbol{C}\boldsymbol{x}(k) + d\boldsymbol{D}\boldsymbol{u}(k). \tag{12}$$

On the other hand, from (5), we have

$$\boldsymbol{u}(k) = \boldsymbol{D}^{-1}(\boldsymbol{y}(k) - \boldsymbol{C}\boldsymbol{x}(k)) \tag{13}$$

Substituting (13) into (12), we obtain

$$d\boldsymbol{y} = (d\boldsymbol{C} - d\boldsymbol{D}\boldsymbol{D}^{-1}\boldsymbol{C})\boldsymbol{x} + d\boldsymbol{D}\boldsymbol{D}^{-1}\boldsymbol{y}. \tag{14}$$

In order to improve the computing efficiency of learning algorithms, we introduce a new search direction

$$d\boldsymbol{X}_1 = d\boldsymbol{C} - d\boldsymbol{D}\boldsymbol{D}^{-1}\boldsymbol{C}, \tag{15}$$
$$d\boldsymbol{X}_2 = d\boldsymbol{D}\boldsymbol{D}^{-1}. \tag{16}$$

Then the total differential dl can be expressed by

$$dl = -tr(d\boldsymbol{X}_2) + \boldsymbol{\varphi}^T(\boldsymbol{y})(d\boldsymbol{X}_1\boldsymbol{x} + d\boldsymbol{X}_2\boldsymbol{y}). \tag{17}$$

It is easy to obtain the derivatives of the cost function l with respect to matrices $\boldsymbol{X}_1$ and $\boldsymbol{X}_2$ as

$$\frac{\partial l}{\partial \boldsymbol{X}_1} = \boldsymbol{\varphi}(\boldsymbol{y}(k))\boldsymbol{x}^T(k), \tag{18}$$

$$\frac{\partial l}{\partial \boldsymbol{X}_2} = \boldsymbol{\varphi}(\boldsymbol{y}(k))\boldsymbol{y}^T(k) - \boldsymbol{I}. \tag{19}$$

From (15) and (16), we derive a novel learning algorithm to update matrices $\boldsymbol{C}$ and $\boldsymbol{D}$.

$$\Delta\boldsymbol{C}(k) = \eta\left(-\boldsymbol{\varphi}(\boldsymbol{y}(k))\boldsymbol{x}^T(k) + (\boldsymbol{I} - \boldsymbol{\varphi}(\boldsymbol{y}(k))\boldsymbol{y}^T(k))\boldsymbol{C}(k)\right), \tag{20}$$
$$\Delta\boldsymbol{D}(k) = \eta\left(\boldsymbol{I} - \boldsymbol{\varphi}(\boldsymbol{y}(k))\boldsymbol{y}^T(k)\right)\boldsymbol{D}(k). \tag{21}$$

The equilibrium points of the learning algorithm satisfy the following equations

$$E[\boldsymbol{\varphi}(\boldsymbol{y}(k))\boldsymbol{x}^T(k)] = 0, \tag{22}$$
$$E\left[\boldsymbol{I} - \boldsymbol{\varphi}(\boldsymbol{y}(k))\boldsymbol{y}^T(k)\right] = 0. \tag{23}$$

This means that separated signals $\boldsymbol{y}$ could achieve as mutually independent as possible if the nonlinear activation function $\boldsymbol{\varphi}(\boldsymbol{y})$ are suitably chosen and the state vector $\boldsymbol{x}(k)$ is well estimated. From (20) and (21), we see that the natural gradient learning algorithm [2] is covered as a special case of the learning algorithm when the mixture is simplified to instantaneous case.

The above derived learning algorithm enable to solve the blind separation problem under assumption that state matrices $\boldsymbol{A}$ and $\boldsymbol{B}$ are known or designed appropriately. In the next section instead of adjusting state matrices $\boldsymbol{A}$ and $\boldsymbol{B}$ directly, we propose new approaches how to estimate state vector $\boldsymbol{x}$.

4 State Estimator

From output equation (5), it is observed that if we can accurately estimate the state vector $x(k)$ of the system, then we can separate mixed signals using the learning algorithm (20) and (21).

4.1 Kalman Filter

The Kalman filter is a useful technique to estimate the state vector in state-space models. The function of the Kalman Filter is to generate on line the state estimate of the state $x(k)$. The Kalman filter dynamics are given as follows

$$x(k+1) = Ax(k) + Bu(k) + Kr(k) + \xi_R(k), \tag{24}$$

where K is the Kalman filter gain matrix, and $r(k)$ is the innovation or residual vector which measures the error between the measured(or expected) output $y(k)$ and the predicted output $Cx(k) + Du(k)$. There are varieties of algorithms to update the Kalman filter gain matrix K as well as the state $x(k)$, refer to [10] for more details.

However in the blind deconvolution problem there exists no explicit residual $r(k)$ to estimate the state vector $x(k)$ because the expected output $y(t)$ means the unavailable source signals. In order to solve this problem, we present a new concept called hidden innovation to implement the Kalman filter in blind deconvolution case. Since updating matrices C and D will produces an innovation in each learning step, we introduce a hidden innovation as follows

$$r(k) = \Delta y(k) = \Delta C x(k) + \Delta D u(k), \tag{25}$$

where $\Delta C = C(k+1) - C(k)$ and $\Delta D = D(k+1) - D(k)$. The hidden innovation presents the adjusting direction of the output of the demixing system and is used to generate an a posteriori state estimate. Once we define the hidden innovation, we can employ the commonly used Kalman filter to estimate the state vector $x(k)$, as well as to update Kalman gain matrix K. The updating rule in this paper is described as follows:

(1) Compute the Kalman gain matrix

$$K(k) = P(k)C(k)^T (C(k)P(k)C^T(k) + R(k))^{-1}$$

(2) Update state vector with hidden innovation

$$\hat{x}(k) = x(k) + K(k)r(k)$$

(3) Update the error covariance matrix

$$\hat{P}(k) = (I - K(k)C(k))P(k)$$

(4) evaluate the state vector ahead

$$x_{k+1} = A(k)\hat{x}(k) + B(k)u(k)$$

(5) evaluate the error covariance matrix ahead

$$P(k) = A(k)\hat{P}(k)A(k)^T + Q(k)$$

with the initial condition $P(0) = I$, where $Q(k)$, $R(k)$ are the covariance matrices of the noise vector ξ_R and output measurement noise n_k.

The theoretic problems, such as convergence and stability, remain to be elaborated. Simulation experiments show that the proposed algorithm, based on the Kalman filter, can separate the convolved signals well.

4.2 Information Back-propagation

Another solution to estimating the state of a system is to propagate backward the mutual information. If we consider the cost function is also a function of the vector x, than we have the partial derivative of $l(y, W)$ with respect to x

$$\frac{\partial l(y, W)}{\partial x} = C^T \varphi(y). \qquad (26)$$

Then we adjust the state vector $x(k)$ according to the following rule

$$\hat{x}(k) = x(k) - \eta C(k)^T \varphi(y(k)). \qquad (27)$$

Then the estimated state vector is used as a new state of the system.

5 Numerical Implementation

Several numerical simulations have been done to demonstrate the validity and effectiveness of the proposed algorithm. Here we give a typical example

Example 1. Consider the following MIMO mixing model

$$u(k) + \sum_{i=1}^{10} A_i u(k-i) = s(k) + \sum_{i=1}^{10} B_i s(k-i) + v(k),$$

where $u, s, v \in \mathbf{R}^3$, and

$$A_2 = \begin{pmatrix} -0.48 & -0.16 & -0.64 \\ -0.16 & -0.48 & -0.24 \\ -0.16 & -0.16 & -0.08 \end{pmatrix}, \quad A_8 = \begin{pmatrix} -0.50 & -0.10 & -0.40 \\ -0.10 & -0.50 & -0.20 \\ -0.10 & -0.10 & -0.10 \end{pmatrix},$$

$$A_{10} = \begin{pmatrix} 0.32 & 0.19 & 0.38 \\ 0.16 & 0.29 & 0.20 \\ 0.08 & 0.08 & 0.10 \end{pmatrix}, \quad B_2 = \begin{pmatrix} 0.42 & 0.21 & 0.14 \\ 0.10 & 0.56 & 0.14 \\ 0.21 & 0.21 & 0.35 \end{pmatrix},$$

$$B_8 = \begin{pmatrix} -0.40 & -0.08 & -0.08 \\ -0.08 & -0.40 & -0.16 \\ -0.08 & -0.08 & -0.56 \end{pmatrix}, \quad B_{10} = \begin{pmatrix} -0.19 & -0.15 & -0.10 \\ -0.11 & -0.27 & -0.12 \\ -0.16 & -0.18 & -0.22 \end{pmatrix},$$

and other matrices are set to the null matrix. The sources s are chosen to be i.i.d signals uniformly distributed in the range (-1,1), and v are the Gaussian noises with zero mean and a covariance matrix $0.1I$. We employ the state space approach to separate mixing signals. The nonlinear activation function is chosen $\varphi(y) = y^3$. The initial value for matrices A and B in the state equation are chosen as in canonical controller form. The initial values for matrix C is set to null matrix or given randomly in the range (-1,1), and $D = I_3$. A large number of simulations show that the state space method can easily recover source signals in the sense of $W(z)H(z) = P\Lambda$. Figure 2 illustrates the coefficients of global transfer function $G(z) = W(z)H(z)$ after 3000 iterations, where the (i,j)th sub-figure plots the coefficients of the transfer function $G_{ij}(z) = \sum_{k=0}^{\infty} g_{ijk} z^{-k}$ up to order of 50.

References

[1] S. Amari and A. Cichocki, "Adaptive blind signal processing– neural network approaches", *Proceedings of the IEEE*, 86(10):2026-2048, 1998.

[2] S. Amari, A. Cichocki, and H.H. Yang, "A new learning algorithm for blind signal separation", *Advances in Neural Information Processing Systems 1995* (Boston, MA: MIT Press, 1996), pp. 752–763.

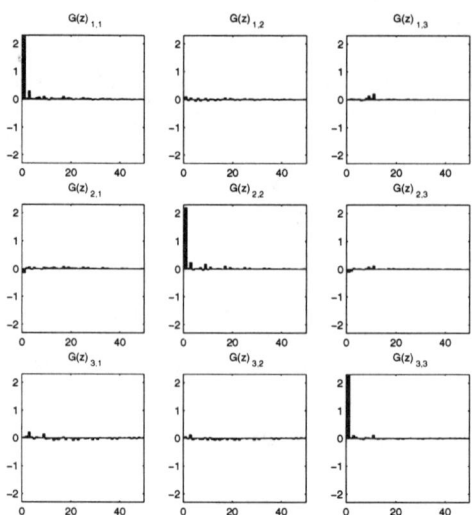

Figure 2: The coefficients of global transfer function after 3000 iterations

[3] S. Amari "Natural gradient works efficiently in learning", *Neural Computation*, Vol.10, pp251-276, 1998.

[4] A. J. Bell and T. J. Sejnowski, " An information-maximization approach to blind separation and blind deconvolution", *Neural Computation*, Vol.7, pp 1129-1159, 1995.

[5] J.-F Cardoso, "Blind signal separation: statistical principles", *Proceedings of the IEEE*, 86(10):2009-2025, 1998.

[6] J.-F. Cardoso and B. Laheld, "Equivariant adaptive source separation," *IEEE Trans. Signal Processing*, vol. SP-43, pp. 3017–3029, Dec. 1996.

[7] A.Cichocki and R. Unbehauen, "Robust neural networks with on-line learning for blind identification and blind separation of sources" IEEE Trans Circuits and Systems I : Fundamentals Theory and Applications, vol 43, No.11, pp. 894-906, Nov. 1996.

[8] P. Comon, "Independent component analysis: a new concept?", *Signal Processing*, vol.36, pp.287–314, 1994.

[9] A. Gharbi and F. Salam, " Algorithm for blind signal separation and recovery in static and dynamics environments", *IEEE Symposium on Circuits and Systems*, Hong Kong, June, 713-716, 1997.

[10] O. L. R. Jacobs, "Introduction to Control Theory", Second Edition, Oxford University Press, 1993.

[11] T. W. Lee, A.J. Bell, and R. Lambert, "Blind separation of delayed and convolved sources", *NIPS 9*, 1997, MIT Press, Cambridge MA, pp758-764.

[12] L. -Q. Zhang and A. Cichocki, "Blind deconvolution/equalization using state-space models", Proc. '98 IEEE Signal Processing Society Workshop on NNSP, pp123-131, Cambridge, 1998.

[13] S. Choi, A. Cichocki and S. Amari, "Blind equalization of simo channels via spatio-temporal anti-Hebbian learning rule", Proc. '98 IEEE Signal Processing Society Workshop on NNSP, pp93-102, Cambridge, 1998.

PART V
IMPLEMENTATION

Analog VLSI Cellular Implementation of the Boundary Contour System

Gert Cauwenberghs and James Waskiewicz
Department of Electrical and Computer Engineering
Johns Hopkins University
3400 North Charles Street
Baltimore, MD 21218-2686
E-mail: {gert,davros}@bach.ece.jhu.edu

Abstract

We present an analog VLSI cellular architecture implementing a simplified version of the Boundary Contour System (BCS) for real-time image processing. Inspired by neuromorphic models across several layers of visual cortex, the design integrates in each pixel the functions of simple cells, complex cells, hyper-complex cells, and bipole cells, in three orientations interconnected on a hexagonal grid. Analog current-mode CMOS circuits are used throughout to perform edge detection, local inhibition, directionally selective long-range diffusive kernels, and renormalizing global gain control. Experimental results from a fabricated 12×10 pixel prototype in 1.2 μm CMOS technology demonstrate the robustness of the architecture in selecting image contours in a cluttered and noisy background.

1 Introduction

The Boundary Contour System (BCS) and Feature Contour System (FCS) combine models for processes of image segmentation, feature filling, and surface reconstruction in biological vision systems [1],[2]. They provide a powerful technique to recognize patterns and restore image quality under excessive fixed pattern noise, such as in SAR images [3]. A related model with similar functional and structural properties is presented in [4].

The motivation for implementing a relatively complex model such as BCS and FCS on the focal-plane is dual. First, as argued in [5], complex neuromorphic active pixel designs become viable engineering solutions as the feature size of the VLSI technology shrinks significantly below the optical diffraction limit, and more transistors can be stuffed in each pixel. The pixel design that we present contains 88 transistors, likely the most complex

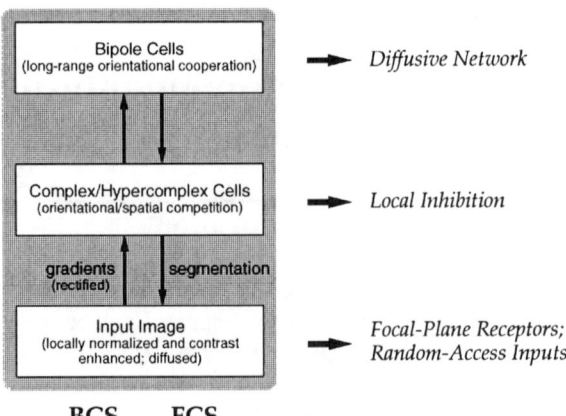

Figure 1: *Diagram of BCS/FCS model for image segmentation, feature filling, and surface reconstruction. Three layers represent simple, complex and bipole cells.*

active pixel imager ever put on silicon. Second, our motivation is to extend the functionality of previous work on analog VLSI neuromorphic image processors for image boundary segmentation, *e.g.* [6, 7, 5, 8, 9] which are based on simplified physical models that do not include directional selectivity and/or long-range signal aggregation for boundary formation in the presence of significant noise and clutter. The analog VLSI implementation of BCS reported here is a first step towards this goal, with the additional objectives of real-time, low-power operation as required for demanding target recognition applications. As an alternative to focal-plane optical input, the image can be loaded electronically through random-access pixel addressing.

The BCS model encompasses visual processing at different levels, including several layers of cells interacting through shunting inhibition, long-range cooperative excitation, and renormalization. The implementation architecture, shown schematically in Figure 1, partitions the BCS model into three levels: simple cells, complex and hypercomplex cells, and bipole cells.

Simple cells compute unidirectional gradients of normalized intensity obtained from the photoreceptors. Complex (hyper-complex) cells perform spatial and directional competition (inhibition) for edge formation. Bipole cells perform long-range cooperation for boundary contour enhancement, and exert positive feedback (excitation) onto the hypercomplex cells. Our present implementation does not include the FCS model, which completes and fills features through diffusive spatial filtering of the image blocked by the edges formed in BCS.

2 Modified BCS Algorithm and Implementation

We adopted the BCS algorithm for analog continuous-time implementation on a hexagonal grid, extending in three directions u, v and w on the focal plane as indicated schematically in Figure 2. For notational convenience, let *subscript* 0 denote the center pixel and $\pm u$, $\pm v$ and $\pm w$ its six neighbors. Components of each complex cell "vector" $\mathbf{C}_i$ at grid location i, along three directions of edge selectivity, are indicated with *superscript* indices u, v and w.

In the implemented circuit model, a pixel unit consists of a photosensor (or random-access analog memory) sourcing a current indicating light intensity, gradient computation and rectification circuits implementing simple cells in three directions, and one complex (hyper-

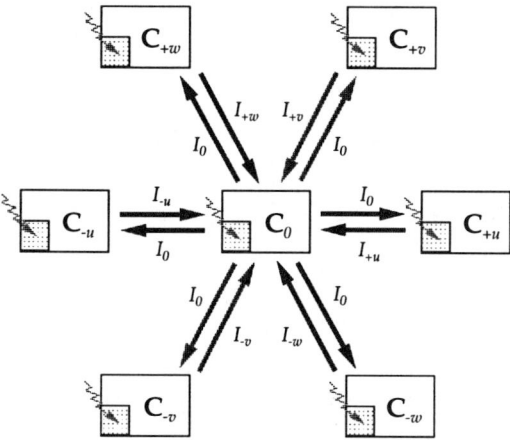

Figure 2: *Hexagonal arrangement of BCS pixels, at the level of simple and complex cells, extending in three directions u, v and w in the focal plane.*

complex) cell and one bipole cell for each of the three directions.

The photosensors generate a current I_i that is proportional to intensity. Through current mirrors, the currents I_i propagate in the three directions u, v, and w as noted in Figure 2. Rectified finite-difference gradient estimates of I_i are obtained for each of the three hexagonal directions. These gradients excite the complex cells C_i^j.

Lateral inhibition among spatially (i) and directionally (j) adjacent complex cells implement the function of hypercomplex cells for edge enhancement and noise reduction. The complex output (C_i^j) is inhibited by local complex cell outputs in the two competing directions of j. C_0 is additionally inhibited by the complex cells of the four nearest neighbors in competing locations i with parallel orientation.

A directionally selective interconnected diffusive network of bipole cells B_i^j, interacting with the complex cells C_i^j, provides long range cooperative feedback, and enhances smooth edge contours while reducing spurious edges due to image clutter. C_i^j is excited by bipole interaction received from the bipole cell B_i^j on the line crossing i in the same direction j.

The operation of the (hyper-)complex cells in the hexagonal arrangement is summarized in the following equation, for one of the three directions u:

$$C_0^u = \left| \frac{1}{2}(I_v + I_w) - I_0 \right| - \alpha(C_0^v + C_0^w) - \alpha'(C_v^u + C_w^u + C_{-v}^u + C_{-w}^u) + \beta B_0^u \quad (1)$$

where:

1. $\left| \frac{1}{2}(I_v + I_w) - I_0 \right|$ represents the rectified gradient input as approximated on the hexagonal grid;

2. $\alpha(C_0^v + C_0^w)$ is the inhibition from locally opposing directions;

3. $\alpha'(C_v^u + C_w^u + C_{-v}^u + C_{-w}^u)$ is inhibition from non-aligned neighbors in the same direction; and

4. βB_0^u is the excitation through long-range cooperation from the bipole cell.

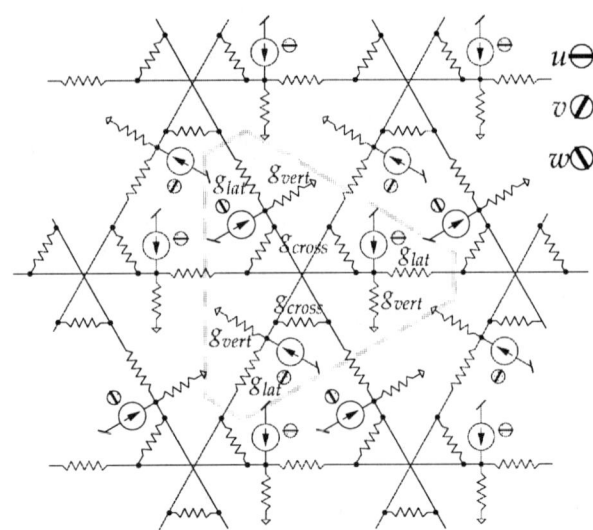

Figure 3: *Network of bipole cells, implemented on a hexagonal resistive grid using orientationally tuned diffusors extending in three directions. g_{lat}/g_{vert} determines the spatial extent of the dipole, whereas g_{lat}/g_{cross} sets the directional selectivity.*

The bipole cell resistive grid (Figure 3) implements a three-fold cross-coupled, directionally polarized, long-range diffusive kernel, formulated as follows:

$$B_0^u = K_u^u C_0^u + K_v^u C_0^v + K_w^u C_0^w \qquad (2)$$

where K_u^u, K_v^u, and K_w^u represent spatial convolutional kernels implementing bipole fields symmetrically polarized in the u, v and w directions. Diffusive kernels can be efficiently implemented with a distributed representation using resistive diffusive elements [7, 10]. Three linear networks of diffusor elements are used, complemented with cross-links of adjustable strength, to control the degree of direction selectivity and the spatial spread of the kernel. Finally, the result (2) is locally normalized, before it is fed back onto the complex cells.

3 Analog VLSI Implementation

The simplified circuit diagram of the BCS cell, including simple, complex and bipole cell functions on a hexagonal grid, is shown in Figure 4.

The image is acquired either optically from phototransistors on the focal-plane, or in direct electronic format through random-access pixel addressing, Figure 4 (a). The simple cell portion in Figure 4 (b) combines the local intensity I_0 with intensities I_v and I_w received from neighboring cells to compute the rectified gradient in (1), using distributed current mirrors and an absolute value circuit. A pMOS load converts the complex cell output into a voltage representation C_0^u for distribution to neighboring nodes and complementary orientations: local inhibition for spatial and directional competition in Figure 4 (c), and long-range cooperation through the bipole layer in Figure 4 (d). The linear diffusive kernel is implemented in current-mode using ladder structures of subthreshold MOS transistors [7], three families extending in each direction with cross-links for directional dispersion as indicated in Figure 3.

Voltage biases control the spatial extent and directional selectivity of the interactions, as

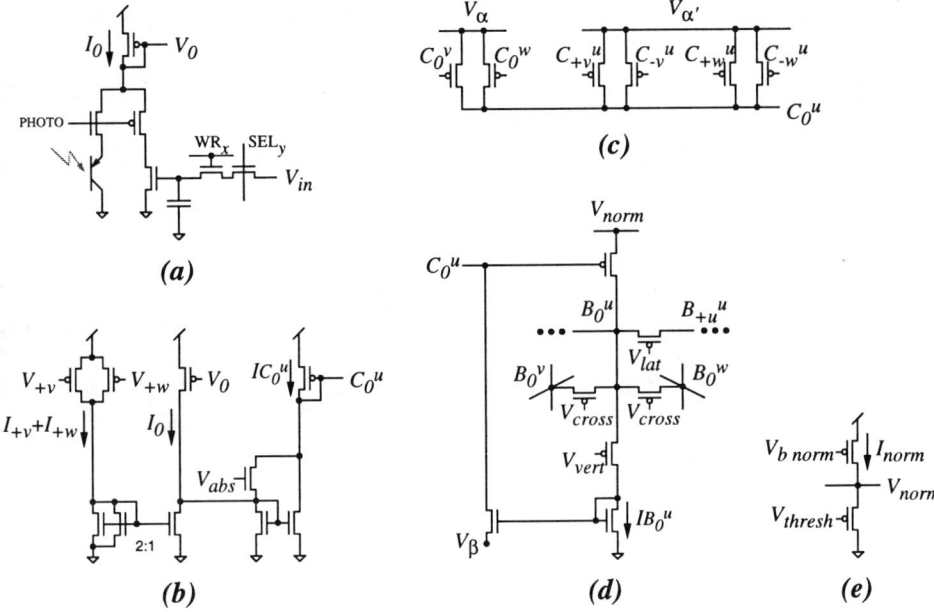

Figure 4: Simplified circuit schematic of one BCS cell in the hexagonal array, showing only one of three directions, the other directions being symmetrical in implementation. (a) Photosensor and random-access input selection circuit. (b) Simple cell rectified gradient calculation. (c) Complex cell spatial and orientational inhibition. (d) Bipole cell directional long range cooperation. (e) Bipole global gain and threshold control.

well as the relative strength of inhibition and excitation, and the level of renormalization, for the complex and bipole cells. The values for g_{vert}, g_{lat} and g_{cross} controlling the bipole kernel are set externally by applying gate bias voltages V_{vert}, V_{lat} and V_{cross}, respectively. Likewise, the constants α, α' and β in (1) are set independently by the applied source voltages V_α, $V_{\alpha'}$ and V_β. Global normalization and thresholding of the bipole response for improved stability of edge formation is achieved through an additional diffusive network that acts as a localized Gilbert-type current normalizer (only partially shown in Figure 4 (e)).

4 Experimental Results

A prototype 12×10 pixel array has been fabricated and tested. The pixel unit, illustrated in Figure 5 (a), has been designed for testability, and has not been optimized for density. The pixel contains 88 transistors including a phototransistor, a large sample-and-hold capacitor, and three networks of interconnections in each of the three directions, requiring a fan-in/fan-out of 18 node voltages across the interface of each pixel unit. A micrograph of the Tiny 2.2×2.2 sq. mm chip, fabricated through MOSIS in 1.2 μm CMOS technology, is shown in Figure 5 (b).

We have tested the BCS chip both under focal-plane optical inputs, and random-access direct electronic inputs. Input currents from optical input under ambient room lighting conditions are around 30 nA. The experimental results reported here are obtained by feeding test inputs electronically. The response of the BCS chip to two test images of interest are shown in Figures 6 and 7.

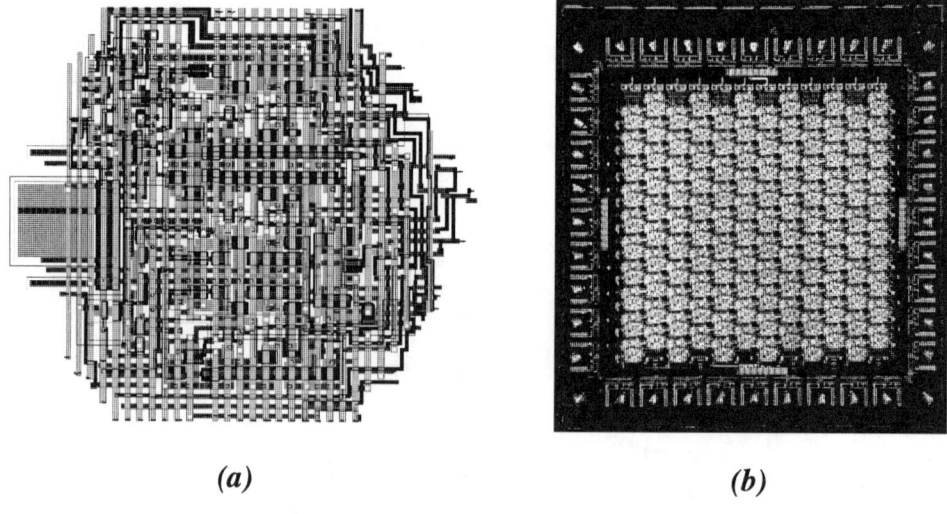

Figure 5: *BCS processor.* *(a) Pixel layout.* *(b) Chip micrograph.*

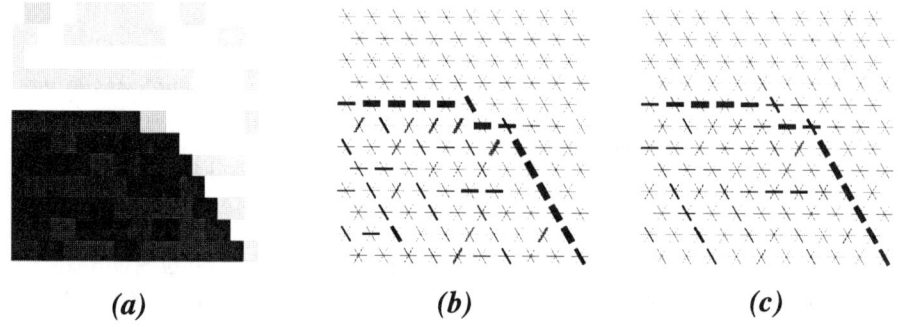

Figure 6: *Experimental response of the BCS chip to a curved edge.* *(a) Reconstructed input image.* *(b) Complex field.* *(c) Bipole field.* *The thickness of the bars on the grid represent the measured components in the three directions.*

Figure 6 illustrates the interpolating directional response to a curved edge in the input, varying in direction between two of the principal axes (u and w in the example). Interpolation between quantized directions is important since implementing more axes on the grid incurs a quadratic cost in complexity. The second example image contains a bar with two gaps of different diameter, for the purpose of testing BCS's capacity to extend contour boundaries across clutter. The response in Figure 7 illustrates a characteristic of bipole operation, in which short-range discontinuities are bridged but large ones are preserved.

5 Conclusions

An analog VLSI cellular architecture implementing the Boundary Contour System (BCS) on the focal plane has been presented. A diffusive kernel with distributed resistive networks has been used to implement long-range interactions of bipole cells without the need of excessive global interconnects across the array of pixels. The cellular model is fairly easy to implement, and succeeds in selecting boundary contours in images with significant clutter.

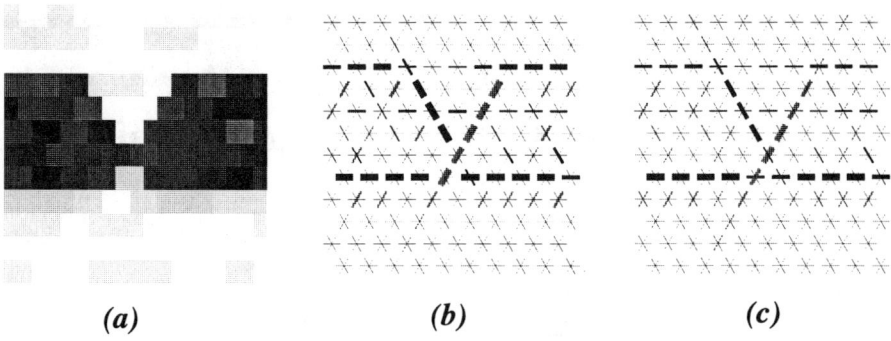

Figure 7: *Experimental response of the BCS chip to a bar with two gaps of different size. (a) Reconstructed input image. (b) Complex field. (c) Bipole field.*

Experimental results from a 12 × 10 pixel prototype demonstrate expected BCS operation on simple examples. While this size is small for practical applications, the analog cellular architecture is fully scalable towards higher resolutions. Based on the current design, a 10,000-pixel array in 0.5 μm CMOS technology would fit a 1 cm^2 die.

Acknowledgments

This research was supported by DARPA and ONR under MURI grant N00014-95-1-0409. Chip fabrication was provided through the MOSIS service.

References

[1] S. Grossberg, "Neural Networks for Visual Perception in Variable Illumination," *Optics News*, pp. 5–10, August 1988.

[2] S. Grossberg, "A Solution of the Figure-Ground Problem for Biological Vision," *Neural Networks*, vol. 6, pp. 463–482, 1993.

[3] S. Grossberg, E. Mingolla, and J. Williamson, "Synthetic Aperture Radar Processing by a Multiple Scale Neural System for Boundary and Surface Representation," *Neural Networks*, vol. 9 (1), January 1996.

[4] Z.P. Li, "A Neural Model of Contour Integration in the Primary Visual Cortex," *Neural Computation*, vol. 10 (4), pp. 903-940, 1998.

[5] K.A. Boahen, "A Retinomorphic Vision System," *IEEE Micro*, vol. 16 (5), pp. 30-39, Oct. 1996.

[6] J.G. Harris, C. Koch, and J. Luo, "A Two-Dimensional Analog VLSI Circuit for Detecting Discontinuities in Early Vision," *Science*, vol. 248, pp. 1209-1211, June 1990.

[7] A.G. Andreou, K.A. Boahen, P.O. Pouliquen, A. Pavasovic, R.E. Jenkins, and K. Strohbehn, "Current-Mode Subthreshold MOS Circuits for Analog VLSI Neural Systems," *IEEE Transactions on Neural Networks*, vol. 2 (2), pp 205-213, 1991.

[8] L. Dron McIlrath, "A CCD/CMOS Focal-Plane Array Edge Detection Processor Implementing the Multiscale Veto Algorithm," *IEEE J. Solid State Circuits*, vol. 31 (9), pp 1239-1248, 1996.

[9] P. Venier, A. Mortara, X. Arreguit and E.A. Vittoz, "An Integrated Cortical Layer for Orientation Enhancement," *IEEE J. Solid State Circuits*, vol. 32 (2), pp 177-186, Febr. 1997.

[10] E. Fragniere, A. van Schaik and E. Vittoz, "Reactive Components for Pseudo-Resistive Networks," Electronic Letters, vol. 33 (23), pp 1913-1914, Nov. 1997.

Active Noise Canceling using Analog Neuro-Chip with On-Chip Learning Capability

Jung-Wook Cho and Soo-Young Lee
Computation and Neural Systems Laboratory
Department of Electrical Engineering
Korea Advanced Institute of Science and Technology
373-1 Kusong-dong, Yusong-gu, Taejon 305-701, Korea
sylee@ee.kaist.ac.kr

Abstract

A modular analogue neuro-chip set with on-chip learning capability is developed for active noise canceling. The analogue neuro-chip set incorporates the error backpropagation learning rule for practical applications, and allows pin-to-pin interconnections for multi-chip boards. The developed neuro-board demonstrated active noise canceling without any digital signal processor. Multi-path fading of acoustic channels, random noise, and nonlinear distortion of the loud speaker are compensated by the adaptive learning circuits of the neuro-chips. Experimental results are reported for cancellation of car noise in real time.

1 INTRODUCTION

Both analog and digital implementations of neural networks have been reported. Digital neuro-chips can be designed and fabricated with the help of well-established CAD tools and digital VLSI fabrication technology [1]. Although analogue neuro-chips have potential advantages on integration density and speed over digital chips[2], they suffer from non-ideal characteristics of the fabricated chips such as offset and nonlinearity, and the fabricated chips are not flexible enough to be used for many different applications. Also, much careful design is required, and the fabricated chip characteristics are fairly dependent upon fabrication processes.

For the implementation of analog neuro-chips, there exist two different approaches, i.e., with and without on-chip learning capability [3,4]. Currently the majority of analog neuro-chips does not have learning capability, while many practical applications require on-line adaptation to continuously changing environments, and must have on-line adaptation learning capability. Therefore neuro-chips with on-chip learning capability are essential for such practical applications. Modular architecture is also advantageous to provide flexibility of implementing many large complex systems from same chips.

Although many applications have been studied for analog neuro-chips, it is very important to find proper problems where analog neuro-chips may have potential advantages over popular DSPs. We believe applications with analog input/output signals and high computational requirements are those good problems. For example, active noise controls [5] and adaptive equalizers [6,7] are good applications for analog neuro-chips.

In this paper we report a demonstration of the active noise canceling, which may have many applications in real world. A modular analog neuro-chip set is developed with on-chip learning capability, and a neuro-board is fabricated from multiple chips with PC interfaces for input and output measurements. Unlike our previous implementations for adaptive equalizers with binary outputs [7], both input and output values are analogue in this noise canceling.

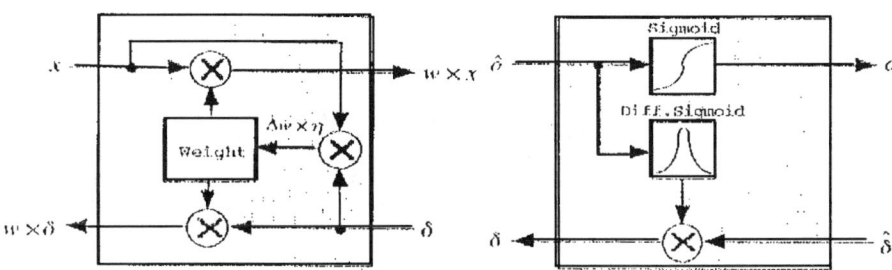

Figure 1. Block diagram of a synapse cell   Figure 2. Block diagram of a neuron cell

2 ANALOG NEURO-CHIP WITH ON-CHIP LEARNING

We had developed analog neuro-chips with error backpropagation learning capability. With the modular architecture the developed analog neuro-chip set consists of a synapse chip and a neuron chip.[8] The basic cell of the synapse chip is shown in Figure 1. Each synapse cell receives two inputs, i.e., pre-synaptic neural activation x and error correction term δ, and generates two outputs, i.e., feed-forward signal wx and back-propagated error $w\delta$. Also it updates a stored weight w by the amount of $x\delta$. Therefore, a synapse cell consists of three multiplier circuits and one analogue storage for the synaptic weight. Figure 2 shows the basic cell in the neuron chip, which collects signals from synapses in the previous layer and distributes to synapses in the following layer. Each neuron body receives two inputs, i.e., post-synaptic neural activation $\hat{o}$ and back-propagated error δ from the following layer, and generates two outputs, i.e., Sigmoid-squashed neural activation o and a new backpropagated error δ multiplied by a bell-shaped Sigmoid-derivative. The backpropagated error may be input to the synapse cells in the previous layer.

To provide easy connectivity with other chips, the two inputs of the synapse cell are represented as voltage, while the two outputs are as currents for simple current summation. On the other hand the inputs and outputs of the neuron cell are represented as currents and voltages, respectively. For simple pin-to-pin connections between chips, one package pin is maintained to each input and output of the chip. No time-multiplexing is introduced, and no other control is required for multi-chip and multi-layer systems. However, it makes the number of package pins the main limiting factor for the number of synapse and neuron cells in the developed chip sets.

Although many simplified multipliers had been reported for high-density integration, their performance is limited in linearity, resolution, and speed. For on-chip learning, it is desirable to have high precision, and a faithful implementation of the 4-quadranr Gilbert multipliers is used. Especially, the multiplier for weight updates in the synapse cell requires high precision.[9] The synaptic weight is stored on a capacitor, and an MOS switch is used to allow current flow from the multiplier to the capacitor during a short time interval for weight adaptation. For applications like active noise controls [5] and telecommunications [6,7], tapped analog delay lines are also designed and integrated in the synapse chip. To reduce offset accumulation, a parallel analog delay line is adopted. Same offset voltage is introduced for operational amplifiers at all nodes [10]. Diffusion capacitors with 2.2 pF are used for the storage of the tapped analog delay line.

In a synapse chip 250 synapse cells are integrated in a 25x10 array with a 25-tap analog delay line. Inputs may be applied either from the analog delay line or from external pins in parallel. To select a capacitor in the cell for refresh, decoders are placed in columns and rows. The actual size of the synapse cell is 141μm x 179μm, and the size of the synapse chip is 5.05mm x 5.05mm. The chip is fabricated in a 0.8μm single-poly CMOS process. On the other hand, the neuron chip has a very simple structure, which consists of 20 neuron cells without additional circuits. The Sigmoid circuit [3] in the neuron cell uses a differential pair, and the slope and amplitude are controlled by a voltage-controlled resistor [11]. Sigmoid-derivative circuit is also using differential pair with min-select circuit. The size of the neuron cell is 177.2μm x 62.4μm.

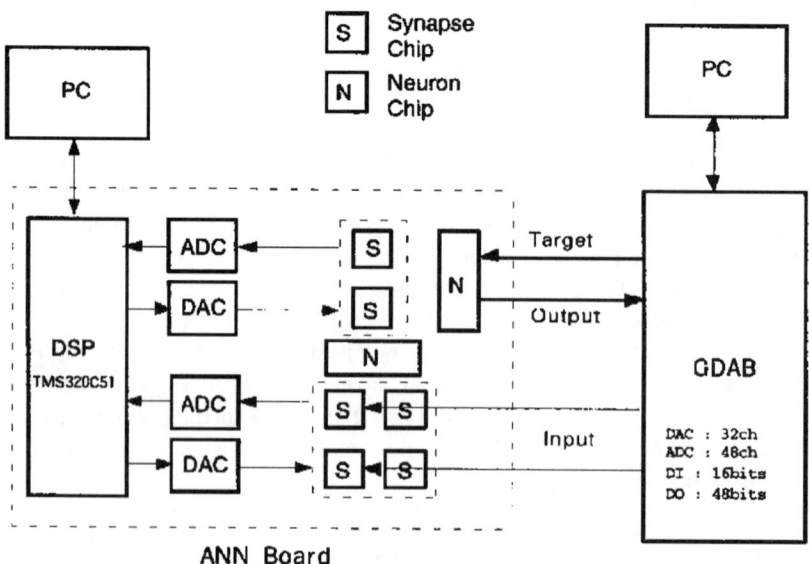

Figure 3: Block diagram of the analog neuro-board

Using these chip sets, an analog neuro-system is constructed. Figure 3 shows a brief block diagram of the analog neuro-system, where an analogue neuro-board is interfaced to a host computer through a GDAB (General Data Acquisition Board). The GDAB board is specially designed for the data interface with the analogue neuro-chips. The neuro-board has 6 synapse chips and 2 neuron chips with the 2-layer Perceptron architecture. For test and development purposes, a DSP, ADC and DAC are installed on the neuro-board to refresh and adjust weights.

Forward propagation time of the 2 layers Perceptron is measured as about 30 μsec. Therefore the computation speed of the neuro-board is about 266 MCPS (Mega Connections Per Second) for recall and about 200 MCUPS (Mega Connections Updates Per Second) for error backpropagation learning. To achieve this speed with a DSP, about 400 MIPS is required for recall and at least 600 MIPS for error-back propagation learning.

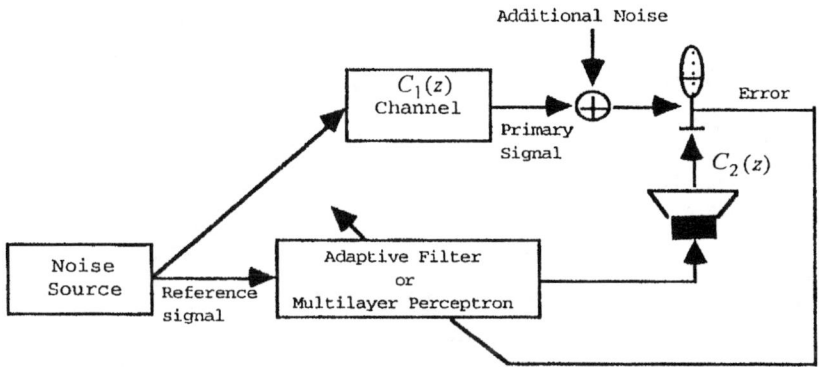

Figure 4: Structure of a feedforward active noise canceling

3 ACTIVE NOISE CANCELING USING NEURO-CHIP

Basic architecture of the feedforward active noise canceling is shown in Figure 4. An area near the microphone is called "quiet zone," which actually means noise should be small in this area. Noise propagates from a source to the quiet zone through a dispersive medium, of which characteristics are modeled as a finite impulse response (FIR) filter with additional random noise. An active noise canceller should generate electric signals for a loud speaker, which creates acoustic signals to cancel the noise at the quiet zone. In general the electric-to-acoustic signal transfer characteristics of the loud speaker is nonlinear, and the overall active noise canceling (ANC) system also becomes nonlinear. Therefore, multilayer Perceptron has a potential advantage over popular transversal adaptive filters based on linear-mean.-square (LMS) error minimization.

Experiments had been conducted for car noise canceling. The reference signal for the noise source was extracted from an engine room, while a compact car was running at 60 km/hour. The difference of the two acoustic channels, i.e., $H(z) = C_1(z)/C_2(z)$, addition noise n, and nonlinear characteristics of the loud speaker need be compensated. Two different acoustic channels are used for the experiments. The first channel $H_1(z) = 0.894 + 0.447z^{-1}$ is a minimum phase channel, while the second non-minimum phase channel $H_2(z) = 0.174 + 0.6z^{-1} + 0.6z^{-2} + 0.174z^{-3}$ characterizes frequency-selective multipath fading with a deep spectral amplitude null. A simple cubic distortion model was used for the characteristics of the loud speaker.[12] To compare performance of the neuro-chip with digital processors, computer simulation was first conducted with error backpropagation algorithm for a single hidden-layer Perceptron as well as the LMS algorithm for a transversal adaptive filter. Then, the same experimental data were provided to the developed neuro-board by a personal computer through the GDAB.

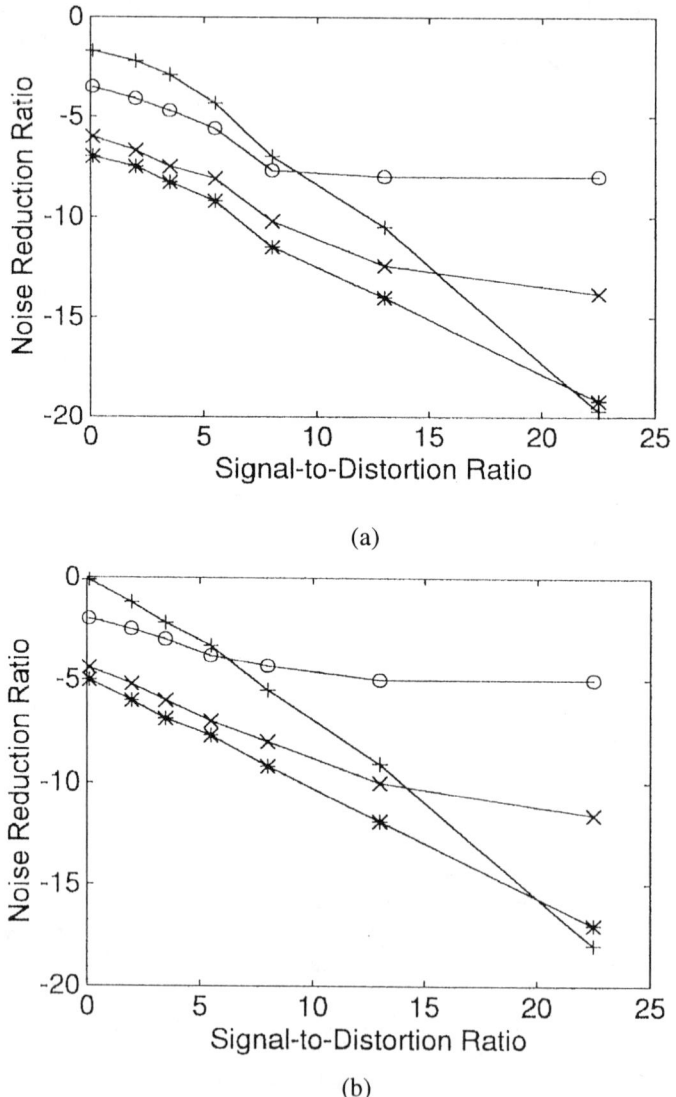

Figure 5: Noise Reduction Ratio (dB) versus Signal-to-Distortion Ratio (dB) for (a) a simple acoustic channel $H_1(z)$ and (b) a multi-path fading acoustic channel $H_2(z)$.
Here, '+', '*', 'x', and 'o' denote results of LMS algorithm, neural networks simulation, neural network simulation with 8-bit input quantization, and neuro-chips, respectively.

Results for the channels $H_1(z)$ and $H_2(z)$ are shown in Figures 5(a) and 5(b), respectively. Each point in these figures denotes the result of one experiment with different parameters. The horizontal axes represent Signal-to-Distortion Ratio (SDR) of the speaker nonlinear characteristics. The vertical axes represent Noise Reduction Ratio (NRR) of the active noise canceling systems. As expected, severe nonlinear distortion of the loud speaker resulted in poor noise canceling for the LMS canceller. However, the performance degradation was greatly reduced by neural network canceller. With the neuro-chips the performance was worse than that of computer simulation. Although the neuro-chip demonstrated active noise canceling and worked better than LMS cancellers for very small SDRs, i.e., very high nonlinear distortions, its performance became saturated to -8 dB and -5 dB NRRs, respectively. The performance saturation was more severe for the harder problem with the complicated $H_2(z)$ channel.

The performance degradation with neuro-chips may come from inherent limitations of analogue chips such as limited dynamic ranges of synaptic weights and signals, unwanted offsets and nonlinearity, and limited resolution of the learning rate and sigmoid slope.[9] However, other side effects of the GDAB board, i.e., fixed resolution of A/D converters and D/A converters for data I/O, also contributed to the performance degradation. The input and output resolutions of the GDAB were 16 bit and 8 bit, respectively. Unlike actual real-world systems the input values of the experimental analogue neuro-chips are these 8-bit quantized values. As shown in Figures 5, results of the computer simulation with 8-bit quantized target values showed much degraded performance compared to the floating-point simulations. Therefore, a significant portion of the poor performance in the experimental analogue system may be contributed from the A/D converters, and the analogue system may work better in real world systems.

Actual acoustic signals are plotted in Figure 6. The top, middle, and bottom signals denote noise, negated speaker signal, and residual noise at the quiet zone, respectively.

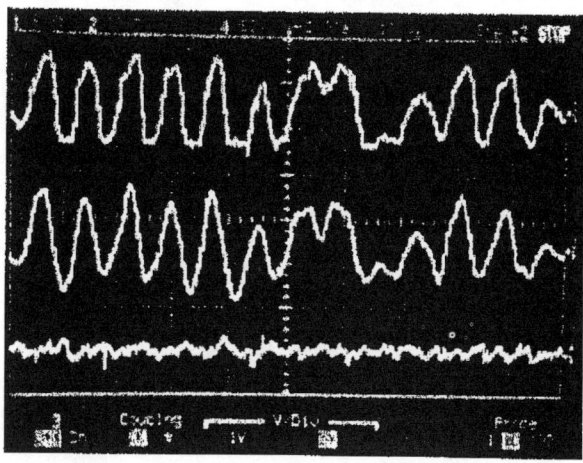

Figure 6: Examples of noise, negated loud-speaker canceling signal, and residual error

4 CONCLUSION

In this paper we report an experimental results of active noise canceling using analogue neuro-chips with on-chip learning capability. Although the its performance is limited due to nonideal characteristics of analogue chip itself and also peripheral devices, it clearly demonstrates feasibility of analogue chips for real world applications.

Acknowledgements

This research was supported by Korean Ministry of Information and Telecommunications.

References

[1] T. Watanabe, K. Kimura, M. Aoki, T. Sakata & K. Ito (1993) A Single 1.5-V Digital Chip for a 106 Synapse Neural Network, *IEEE Trans. Neural Network,* Vol.4, No.3, pp.387-393.

[2] T. Morie and Y. Amemiya (1994) An All-Analog Expandable Neural Network LSI with On-Chip Backpropagation Learning, *IEEE Journal of Solid State Circuits,* vol.29, No.9, pp.1086-1093.

[3] J.-W. Cho, Y. K. Choi, S.-Y. Lee (1996) Modular Neuro-Chip with On-Chip Learning and Adjustable Learning Parameters, *Neural Processing Letters,* Vol.4, No.1.

[4] J. Alspector, A. Jayakumar, S. Luna (1992) Experimental evaluation of learning in neural microsystem, *Advances in Neural Information Processing Systems* **4**, pp. 871-878.

[5] B. Widrow, et al. (1975) Adative Noise Cancelling: Principles and Applications, *Proceeding of IEEE,* Vol.63, No.12, pp.1692-1716.

[6] J. Choi, S.H. Bang, B.J. Sheu (1993) A Programmable Analog VLSI Neural Network Processor for Communication Receivers, *IEEE Transaction on Neural Network,* Vol.4, No.3, pp.484-495.

[7] J.-W. Cho and S.-Y. Lee (1998) Analog neuro-chips with on-chip learning capability for adaptive nonlinear equalizer, *Proc. IJCNN,* pp. 581-586, May 4-9, Anchorage, USA.

[8] J. Van der Spiegel, C. Donham, R. Etienne-Cummings, S. Fernando (1994) Large scale analog neural computer with programmable architecture and programmable time constants for temporal pattern analysis, *Proc. ICNN, pp. 1830-1835.*

[9] Y.K. Choi, K.H. Ahn, and S.Y. Lee (1996) Effects of multiplier offsets on on-chip learning for analog neuro-chip, *Neural Processing Letters,* vol. 4, No.1, 1-8.

[10] T. Enomoto, T. Ishihara and M. Yasumoto (1982) Integrated tapped MOS analogue delay line using switched-capacitor technique, *Electronics Lertters,* Vol.18, pp.193-194.

[11] P.B. Allen, D.R. Holberg (1987) *CMOS Analog Circuit Design,* Holt, Douglas Rinehart and Winston.

[12] F. Gao and W.M. Snelgrove (1991) Adaptive linearization of a loudspeaker, *Proc. International Conference on Acoustics, Speech and Signal processing,* pp. 3589-3592.

A Micropower CMOS Adaptive Amplitude and Shift Invariant Vector Quantiser

Richard J. Coggins, Raymond J.W. Wang and Marwan A. Jabri
Computer Engineering Laboratory
School of Electrical and Information Engineering, J03
University of Sydney, 2006, Australia.
{richardc, jwwang, marwan}@sedal.usyd.edu.au

Abstract

In this paper we describe the architecture, implementation and experimental results for an Intracardiac Electrogram (ICEG) classification and compression chip. The chip processes and vector-quantises 30 dimensional analogue vectors while consuming a maximum of 2.5 μW power for a heart rate of 60 beats per minute (1 vector per second) from a 3.3 V supply. This represents a significant advance on previous work which achieved ultra low power supervised morphology classification since the template matching scheme used in this chip enables unsupervised blind classification of abnormal rhythms and the computational support for low bit rate data compression. The adaptive template matching scheme used is tolerant to amplitude variations, and inter- and intra-sample time shifts.

1 INTRODUCTION

Implantable cardioverter defibrillators (ICDs) are devices used to monitor the electrical activity of the heart muscle and to apply appropriate levels of electrical stimulation if abnormal conditions are detected. Despite the considerable success of ICDs they suffer from a number of limitations including an inability to detect and treat some abnormal heart rhythms and limited data recording capabilities.

We have previously shown that micropower analogue Multi-Layer Perceptron (MLP) neural networks can be trained to separate such arrhythmia [4]. However, MLPs are best suited to learning the boundary between classes whereas a vector quantization scheme allows a measure of the probability density of the morphological types to be estimated.

Many analogue vector quantiser (VQ) chips have been reported in the literature. For example, a 16×256 500 kHz 50 mW 2 μm CMOS vector A/D converter [10] and a 16 × 16 300 kHz 0.7 mW 2 μm CMOS analogue VQ [1]. These correspond to an energy per match per dimension of 24 pJ and 9 pJ respectively. The integrated circuit (IC) described in this paper is distinguished from these approaches in that it is specifically targeted for the low power, low bandwidth application of ICEG classification and compression. Our chip achieves vector matching (without the winner take all function) to 7 bit 30 dimensional vectors with three coefficient linear prediction, at an energy consumption of 15 pJ per template per dimension using a 1.2 μm CMOS process. Although this figure is greater than that for [1] it should be noted that in [1] the mean absolute error metric is used rather than the squared Euclidean distance and no provision is provided for linear transformation of the incoming analogue vector.

2 ADAPTIVE DATA COMPRESSION

Recording of ICEGs in ICDs is currently very limited due to the amount of memory available and the power/area cost of implementing all but the simplest compression techniques. Micropower template matching however, enables large amounts of the signal to be encoded as template indices plus amplitude parameters. Effective compression of the ICEG requires adaptation to the short term non-stationary behaviour of the ICEG [2]. In particular, short term amplitude variations, lag variation, phase variation and ectopic beats (which originate from the ventricles of the heart and have differing morphology) reduce the achievable compression. The impact of ectopic beats can be reduced by increasing the number of templates. This can often be achieved without increasing the code book search complexity by using associated timing features. The amplitude and shift variations require short term adaptation of the template matching in order to minimise the residual error and hence raise the compression ratio at fixed distortion.

2.1 Amplitude and Shift Invariant Matching

In order to facilitate analogue implementation, a backward prediction procedure is used rather than the usual forward prediction [8]. This approach allows the incoming analogue template to be manipulated in the analogue domain for amplitude and shift invariance purposes. Consider the long term backward prediction problem described by,

$$r_b(n) = \tilde{x}(n) - b_0 x(n+\alpha) - b_1 \frac{\{x(n+\alpha+1) - x(n+\alpha-1)\}}{2} \quad (1)$$

where $r_b(n)$ denotes the backward residuals, $\tilde{x}$ is a template which is a function of previous beats, $x(\alpha)$ is the sampled ICEG signal, α the time index, n is the template index and b_0 and b_1 are the amplitude and phase coefficients respectively. b_0 scales the current beat to match the template and hence is an amplitude term. b_1 scales the central difference of the current beat and is a function of the amplitude and phase corrections required to minimise the residuals. To see why this is a phase term consider the Taylor expansion of $Ax(t+\phi)$ to the first derivative term around t,

$$Ax(t+\phi) = Ax(t) + A\phi x'(t) \quad (2)$$

where ϕ is a small phase shift of $x(t)$ and A is the amplitude factor. When ϕ is due to sampling jitter then, $-\frac{T}{2} \leq \phi \leq \frac{T}{2}$, where T is the sampling period. Provided that $x(t)$ is sampled according to the Nyquist criterion, ϕ is sufficiently small for the first derivative term to adequately account for the sampling jitter. Hence, $b1$ accounts for the residual error remaining after optimisation of the integer α. α is approximately determined by the beat detector of the ICD which attempts to detect the fiducial point of heart beats using filters and comparators. b_0 and b_1 can be determined by minimising the squared error between the current signal window and the previously recorded template which in this case has a closed form solution in terms of correlation coefficients. However, in Section 3 we present an alternative iterative procedure suited to low-power analogue implementations.

3 SYSTEM ARCHITECTURE & IMPLEMENTATION

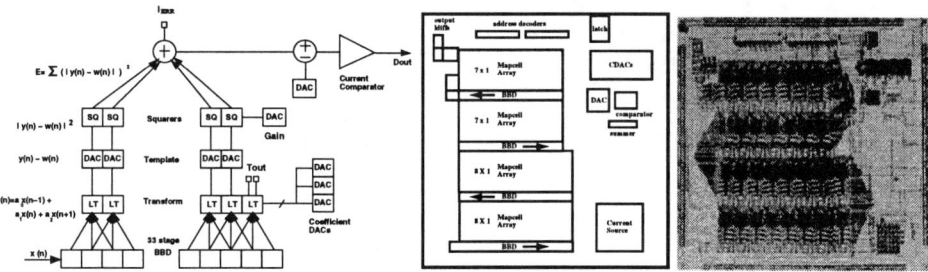

Figure 1: Left: Block diagram of the adaptive linear transform VQ chip. Middle: Floorplan of the chip. Right: Photomicrograph of the chip.

The ICEG is first high pass filtered to remove the DC and then is bandpass filtered to prevent aliasing and enhance the high frequency component for beat detection. (This is the filtering approach already existing in an ICD and therefore not implemented by us). This then feeds the discrete time analogue delay line, which is continuously sampling the signal at 250 Hz. The analogue samples are then transformed by a two layer network. The first layer implements the linear prediction by adjusting the amplitude b_0 and the phase of the analogue vector. Note that the phase consists of two components, the coarse part α corresponding to sample lags and the fine part b_1 corresponding to intra-sample lags. The second layer calculates the distance between the linearly predicted vector and the template $w(n)$ to be matched. A comparator is provided so that a match to within a given threshold may be detected.

3.1 Chip Architecture

Input to the IC is via a single analogue channel which is sampled by a bucket brigade device of length 30. The resultant 30 dimensional analogue vector is adaptively linear transformed to facilitate a shift and scale invariant match to a digital (7 bit per dimension) template. The IC generates digital representations of the square of the Euclidean distance between the transformed analogue vector and the digital template. A block diagram of the IC appears in Figure 1. The IC has been fabricated. Performance figures in this paper are based on measurements of the chip fabricated in a $1.2\mu m$ CMOS MOSIS process.

The block diagram shows the input signal being sampled by the bucket brigade device (BBD)[4]. The signal is sampled at a rate of 250 Hz. Existing circuitry in the defibrillator detects the peak of the heart beat and hence indicates a coarse alignment (due to detection jitter) to the template stored in the template DACs (TDACs). The BBD continues to sample until the coarse alignment is attained at which point the IC is biased up. The BBD now contains a segment of the ICEG corresponding to one heart beat. The digital error output is then monitored with the linear transform blocks configured to 1:1 mappings until an error minimum is detected indicating optimal sampling alignment. The three linear transform coefficient DACs (CDACs) which are common to the 30 linear transform blocks may then be adapted to further reduce the matching error. The transformation can be represented by $y(n) = a_0 x(n-1) + a_1 x(n) + a_2 x(n+1)$ where a_0 corresponds to CDAC0 etc. This constitutes a general linear long term prediction [8]. Constraining CDAC0 and CDAC2 to be equal magnitudes and opposite signs results in a minimisation of errors due to phase and amplitude variation and a simpler adaptation procedure. The matching error is computed via the squarer blocks and the summing node. The matching error consists of both a magnitude and exponent thereby increasing the dynamic range of the error representation.

The magnitude is the output of the squarer block. The exponent is determined by control of a current reference in the squaring circuit. A reference DAC and precision current comparator provide the means of successive approximation A/D conversion of the matching error current I_{ERR}. Using this scheme heart beat morphology can be classified by loading different templates (TDAC values). A stream of beats may be compressed by identifying matches with continuously updated representations of previous beats. Close matches are encoded by an index and an amplitude coefficent while poor matches are encoded by quantised residuals which have been minimised by the linear prediction.

3.2 Adaptation and Learning

The first step in the learning process is to determine α, the coarse phase lag. This can be achieved by shifting the delay line and evaluating the error until a minimum is reached. Once the coarse phase lag α has been determined the error function to be minimised to compensate for amplitude and phase variations is given by $E = \sum_{i=1}^{N}(b_0 x_i + b_1 \Delta x_i - w_i)^2$, where the subscript i implicitly incorporates the coarse phase α. This is a quadratic in b_0 and b_1. b_0 and b_1 can be optimised separately provided cross terms in E are negligible. Here the cross terms are given by $\sum_{i=1}^{N} 2 b_0 b_1 x_i \Delta x_i = b_0 b_1 (x_{N+1} x_N - x_1 x_0)$. Thus, if the end points of the N point window have approximately the same value (as is usually the case for ICEG beats) then the cross terms in E are negligible and b_0 and b_1 can be optimised separately.

So the only remaining issue is how to optimise a single parameter. A simple linear search takes at most 2^b evaluations of E where b is the number of bits. A search based on bisection takes $b + 2$ evaluations. Techniques involving gradient descent and conjugate gradient lead to more complex learning logic with minor reductions in the number of evaluations. Therefore, bisection is the best compromise between the number of evaluations and the complexity of the learning state machine.

Once the best template match has been achieved, learning may also then be applied to the template itself depending on the application and context. For example, in the case of adaptive classification a weight perturbation algorithm [6] could be used to adapt the template for morphological drift based on heart rate information. Similarly, for a data compression application, if the template match exceeds a fidelity criterion the template may be adapted and the template changes logged in the compression record.

3.3 Building Blocks

In order to implement the template matcher, sub-threshold analogue VLSI building blocks were designed. All transistors in the building blocks operate in weak inversion exclusively. We do not have the space to describe all of the building blocks, so we will focus here on the linear transform and squarer cells.

3.3.1 Linear Transform Cell

The linear transform (LT) cell consists of three linearised differential pairs [7] with their biases controlled by the coefficient DACs (CDACs) (see Figure 2(a)). The nature of the linearisation is controlled by the ratio of the aspect ratios of M3 to M5 and M4 to M6. Methods for choosing this ratio are discussed in [5]. Denoting the aspect ratio of a transistor by S we chose $S_3/S_5 = S_4/S_6 = 4$. This introduces some ripple in the transconductance while increasing the asymptotic saturation voltage to $4nU_T$ compared to nU_T for the ordinary differential pair. Signed coefficients are achieved by switches at the outputs of the differential pairs. The template DACs (TDACs) have differential outputs to form the difference $y(n) - w(n)$ where $w(n)$ is the nth template value.

3.3.2 Squaring Cell

The squaring function must meet the following design constraints. It should have current inputs and outputs in order to avoid linear current to voltage conversion at low currents. The squared current must be normalised to the original linear range to avoid excessive power consumption. The squaring function should avoid the MOS square law approach in order to conserve space and power, and the the available voltage range should be 3.3 V rail to rail.

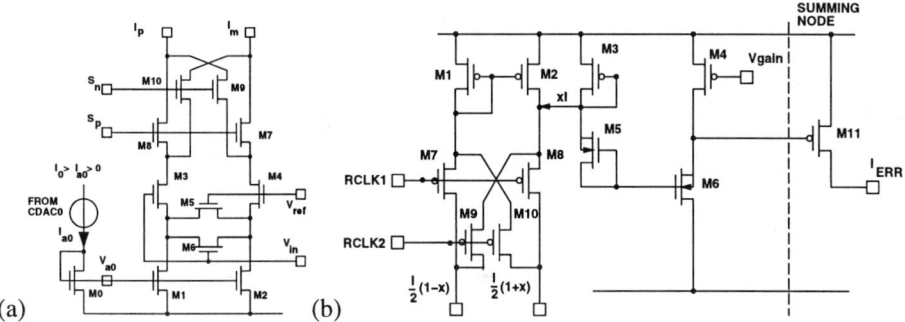

Figure 2: (a) Circuit diagram of one of three the linear transform linearised differential pairs in the LT cell. (b) Circuit diagram of the squarer (SQ cell) and the summing node.

The choices available then are restricted to weak inversion circuits. The circuit (see Figure 2(b)) used relies on the translinear principle [9]. Here, loops of MOS g-s diode structures operating in weak inversion are used to form a normalised squared current which is summed to form the final normalised output. The translinear loops are implemented with P-type transistors in separate N-wells to avoid the body effect. Positive and negative inputs are squared separately using the RCLK signals and then added at the output.

3.4 Circuit Performance

Table 1: Summary of electrical specifications of the chip.

Item	Conditions	Value
Template dimension		30
Adaptation coefficients	Excludes squarer error gain control	3
DAC Precision	Weighted lateral PNP	7 bits
Max. Error per dimension[a]	CDACx=64, DCBBD, w/r to TDACs	2 bits
LSB bias		2 nA
Power comsumption	TDACs=CDAC1=64, duty cycle[b] = 3.2%	2.5 μW

[a] Excludes error at 1st CDAC0 stage. [b] For 1 bpm, chip biased up 8/250 of the time.

We provide three measures of the performance of the chip along with a summary of its basic electrical characteristics which is shown in Table 1. The first measure characterises the accuracy of the template matching function relative to the available precision of the template. This is summarised by the Maximum Error per dimension in Table 1 which was produced by inputing a zero offset DC signal into the BBD and setting each CDAC in turn to one half of its maximum value. The TDACs were then adjusted so as to minimise the output of the squarer. Therefore, the resulting TDAC values indicate the accumulated effects of transistor mismatches through each path to the squarer output. The curves generated are averages over 80 trials to remove noise influences (where as the classification performance shown in Table /refvterr-tab includes such influences). The curves showed that except for the input stage corresponding to CDAC0 (stage 30) the accumulated mismatches influence the two least significant bits of the TDACs. A larger error of 4 bits for the first stage feeding CDAC0 was due to a design oversight of not providing a dummy capacitive load to the input end of the BBD (stage 30 of CDAC0 derives its input from the input BBD cell, which does not have the full capacitive loading of three linearised differential pairs as on the rest of the cells).

Table 2: Relative impact on the error output of the chip for the adaptation steps of alignment, amplitude and phase correction for patient No. 2s ST rhythm. The errors are normalised to the non-aligned error. A numerical simulation is provided for comparison to the chip performance.

Adaptation step	Chip Error	Std. Dev.	Simulation Error	Std. Dev.
No align	1.0	0.04	1.0	0.28
Align	0.31	0.07	0.41	0.35
Amplitude	0.16	0.05	0.37	0.22
Phase	0.07	0.01	0.32	0.16

The second performance measure uses real heart patients ICEG (Sinus Tachycardia) ST data. Table 2 shows the normalised output error of the chip averaged over 107 heart beats while being compared to the 10th beat in the series. The normalised error was measured from a mirrored version of the current at the output of the chip. The adaptation steps shown in the table are as follows. "No align" implies that the error for the template match is determined only by the approximate alignment provided by a numerical simulation of the beat detector of the ICD. "Align" corresponds to coarse alignment where the matching error is calculated up to two samples either side to determine the best positioning of the input in the BBD. "Amplitude" corresponds to adaptation of the amplitude coefficient by adjustment of CDAC1. "Phase" corresponds to adaptation of the difference between CDAC2 and CDAC0. Each of the adaptations reduces the error of the match with the coarse alignment being most significant. An idealised limited precision numerical simulation of the error calculation is also provided in the table for comparison. It can be seen that the amplitude and phase adaptation steps lower the relative error more for the chip than in the simulation. This is most likely due to the adaptation on the chip also compensating for the analogue noise and imprecision as well as the variability of the original data.

The third performance measure illustrates the ability of the chip to solve a blind classification problem and is summarised in Table 3. The safe rhythm of the patient is Sinus Tachycardia (ST). For each patient one beat is chosen at random as the template and is loaded into the TDACs of the chip. The 20 beats subsequent to the chosen template are then used to determine the average error between templates after adaptation. Twice this error is then used as the classifier threshold for "safe" versus "unknown". The ST and VT data sets for the patient are then passed through the chip and classified giving the column "% Correct chip". For comparison the expected best performance for the data set are also reproduced in the table from previous work by the authors [3]. The results indicate that a very simple blind classification algorithm when combined with the adaptive template matching capabilities of the chip shows good performance for 4 out of 5 patients.

4 CONCLUSION

We have presented a micropower learning vector quantization system that can provide hardware support for both signal classification and compression of ICEG signals. The analogue block can be used to implement several different classification and compression algorithms

Table 3: Performance of the chip on a blind classification task for 5 patients with Ventricular Tachycardia (VT) 1:1 retrograde conduction compared to classification bounds.

Patient	No. of Complexes		% Correct chip		% Correct Bounds	
	ST	VT	ST	VT	ST	VT
1[a]	440	61	99	100	99	100
2	107	71	99	100	99	100
3	177	75	89	100	98	100
4	110	71	92	100	99	100
5	38	90	97	87	99	100

[a] The R point search interval was increased to 4 for this patient.

depending on how the template matching capability is utilised. By providing significant compression capability in an ICD, a larger data base of natural onset cardiac arrhythmia should become available, leading to improved designs of ICD based adaptive classification and compression systems.

5 ACKNOWLEDGEMENTS

The work in this paper was funded by the Australian Research Council and Telectronics Pacing Systems Ltd, Sydney, Australia.

References

[1] G. Cauwenberghs and V. Pedroni. A Charge-Based CMOS Parallel Analog Vector Quantiser. In *NIPS*, volume 7, pages 779–786. MIT Press, 1995.

[2] R.J. Coggins. *Low Power Signal Compression and Classification for Implantable Defibrillators*. PhD thesis, University of Sydney, Sydney, Australia, 1996.

[3] R.J. Coggins and M.A. Jabri. Classification and Compression of ICEGs using Gaussian Mixture Models. In J. Principe, L. Giles, N. Morgan, and E. Wilson, editors, *Neural Networks for Signal Processing*, volume 7, pages 226–235. IEEE, 1997.

[4] R.J. Coggins, M.A. Jabri, B.G. Flower, and S.J. Pickard. A Hybrid Analog and Digital VLSI Neural Network for Intracardiac Morphology Classification. *IEEE Journal of Solid-State Circuits*, 30(5):542–550, May 1995.

[5] M. Furth and A. Andreou. Linearised Differential Transconductors in Subthreshold CMOS. *Electronics Letters*, 31(7):545–547, 1995.

[6] M.A. Jabri and B.G. Flower. Weight Perturbation: An Optimal Architecture and Learning Technique for Analog VLSI Feedforward and Recurrent Multilayer Networks. *IEEE Transactions on Neural Networks*, 3(1):154–157, January 1992.

[7] F. Krummenacher and N Joehl. A 4Mhz CMOS Continuous Time Filter with On Chip Automatic Tuning. *IEEE Journal of Solid-State Circuits*, 23(3):750–758, June 1986.

[8] G. Nave and A. Cohen. ECG Compression Using Long Term Prediction. *IEEE Trans. Biomed. Eng.*, 40(9):877–885, 1993.

[9] E. Seevinck. *Analysis and Synthesis of Translinear Integrated Circuits*. Elsevier, 1988.

[10] G.T. Tyson, S. Fallahi, and A.A. Abidi. An 8b CMOS Vector A/D converter. In *Proceedings of the International Solid State Circuits Conference*, pages 38–39, 1993.

Optimizing Correlation Algorithms for Hardware-based Transient Classification

R. Timothy Edwards[1], Gert Cauwenberghs[1], and Fernando J. Pineda[2]

[1]Electrical and Computer Engineering, Johns Hopkins University, Baltimore, MD 21218
[2]Applied Physics Laboratory, Johns Hopkins University, Laurel, MD 20723
e-mail: {tim,gert,fernando}@bach.ece.jhu.edu

Abstract

The performance of dedicated VLSI neural processing hardware depends critically on the design of the implemented algorithms. We have previously proposed an algorithm for acoustic transient classification [1]. Having implemented and demonstrated this algorithm in a mixed-mode architecture, we now investigate variants on the algorithm, using time and frequency channel differencing, input and output normalization, and schemes to binarize and train the template values, with the goal of achieving optimal classification performance for the chosen hardware.

1 Introduction

At the NIPS conference in 1996 [1], we introduced an algorithm for classifying acoustic transient signals using template correlation. While many pattern classification systems use template correlation [2], our system differs in directly addressing the issue of efficient implementation in analog hardware, to overcome the area and power consumption drawbacks of equivalent digital systems. In the intervening two years, we have developed analog circuits and built VLSI hardware implementing both the template correlation and the frontend acoustic processing necessary to map the transient signal into a time-frequency representation corresponding to the template [3, 4]. In the course of hardware development, we have been led to reevaluate the algorithm in the light of the possibilities and the limitations of the chosen hardware.

The general architecture is depicted in Figure 1 (a), and excellent agreement between simulations and experimental output from a prototype is illustrated in Figure 1 (b). Issues of implementation efficiency and circuit technology aside, the this paper specifically addresses further improvements in classification performance achievable by algorithmic modifications, tailored to the constraints and strengths of the implementation medium.

Optimizing Correlation Algorithms for Transient Classification

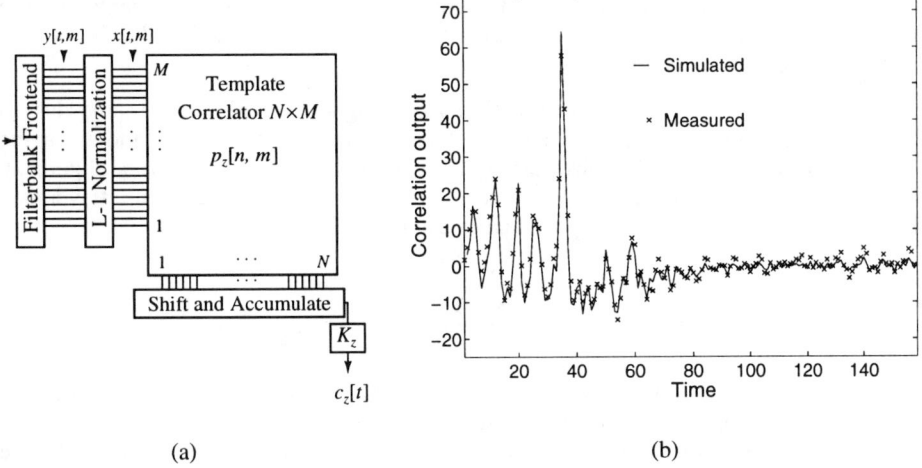

Figure 1: (a) System architecture of the acoustic transient classifier (b) Demonstration of accurate computation in the analog correlator on a transient classification task.

2 The transient classification algorithm

The core of our architecture performs the running correlation between an acoustic input and a set of templates for distiguishing between Z distinct classes. A simple template correlation equation for the acoustic transient classification can be written:

$$c_z[t] = K_z \sum_{m=1}^{M} \sum_{n=1}^{N} x[t-n,m] \, p_z[n,m] \qquad (1)$$

where M is the number of frequency channels of the input, N is the maximum number of time bins in the window, and x is the array of input signals representing the energy content in each of the M bandpass frequency channels. The inputs x are normalized across channels using an L-1 normalization so that the correlation is less affected by volume changes in the input. The matrix p_z contains the template pattern values for pattern z out of a total of Z classes; K_z is a constant gain coefficient for class z, and t is the current time. This formula produces a running correlation $c_z[t]$ of the input array with the template for class z. A signal is classified as belonging to class z when the output c_z exceeds the output for all other classes at a point in time t determined by simple segmentation of the input.

To train and evaluate the system, we used a database of 22 recorded samples of 10 different classes of "everyday" transients such as the sounds made by aluminum cans, plastic tubs, handclaps, and the like.

Each example transient recording was processed through a thirty-two channel constant-Q analog cochlear filter with output taps spaced on a logarithmic frequency scale [6]. For the simulations, the frontend system outputs were sampled and saved to disk, then digitally rectified and smoothed with a lowpass filter function with a 2 ms time constant. These thirty-two channel outputs representing short-term average energy in each frequency band were decimated to 500 Hz and normalized with the function

$$x[t,m] = y[t,m] / \sum_{k=1}^{M+1} y[t,k], \qquad (2)$$

where $y[t, M+1]$ is a constant-valued input added to the system in order to supress noise in the normalized outputs during periods of silence. The additional output $x[t, M+1]$

becomes maximum during the periods of silence and minimum during presentation of a transient event. This extra output can be used to detect onsets of transients, but is not used in the correlation computation of equation (1).

Template values p_z are learned by automatically aligning all examples of the same class in the training set using a threshold on the normalization output $x[t, M + 1]$, and averaging the values together over N samples, starting a few samples before the point of alignment. Class outputs are normalized relative to one another by multiplying each output by a gain factor K_z, computed from the template values using the L-2 norm function

$$K_z = \sqrt{\sum_{m=1}^{M} \sum_{n=1}^{N} p_z[n,m]^2}. \qquad (3)$$

We evaluated the accuracy of the system with a cross-validation loop in which we train the system on all of the database except one example of one class, then test on that remaining example, repeating the test for each of the 220 examples in the database. The baseline algorithm gives a classification accuracy of 96.4%.

3 Single-bit template values

A major consideration for hardware implementations (both digital and analog) is the memory storage required by the templates, one of which is required for each class. Minimal storage space in terms of bits per template is practical only if the algorithm can be proved to perform acceptably well under decreased levels of quantization of the template values.

At one bit per template location (i.e., $M \times N$ bits per template), the complexity of the hardware is greatly simplified, but it is no longer obvious what method is best to use for learning the template values, or for calculating the per-class gains. The choice of the method is guided by knowledge about the acoustic transients themselves, and simulation to evaluate its effect on the accuracy of a typical classification task.

4 Simulations of different zero-mean representations

One bit per template value is a desirable goal, but realizing this goal requires reevaluating the original correlation equation. The input values to be correlated represent band-limited energy spectra, and range from zero to some maximum determined by the L-1 normalization. To determine the value of a template bit, the averaged value over all examples of the class in the training set must be compared to a threshold (which itself must be determined), or else the input itself must be transformed into a form with zero average mean value. In the latter method, the template value is determined by the sign of the transformed input, averaged over all examples of the class in the training set.

The obvious transformations of the input which provide a vector of zero-mean signals to the correlator are the time derivative of each input channel, and the difference between neighboring channels. Certain variations of these are possible, such as a center-surround computation of channel differences, and zero-mean combinations of time and channel differences. While there is evidence that center-surround mechanisms are common to neurobiological signal processing of various sensory modalities in the brain, including processing in the mammalian auditory cortex [5], time derivatives of the input are also plausible in light of the short time base of acoustic transient events. Indeed, there is no reason to assume *a priori* that channel differences are even meaningful on the time scale of transients.

Table 1 shows simulation results, where classification accuracy on the cross-validation test is given for different combinations of continuous-valued and binary inputs and templates,

Table 1: Simulation results with different architectures.

Method	Both Cont.	Binary Input	Both Binary	Binary $(1,-1)$ Template	Binary $(1,0)$ Template
One-to-One	96.40%	—	—	—	—
Time Difference	85.59%	65.32%	59.46%	82.43%	81.98%
Channel Difference	90.54%	53.60%	95.05%	94.59%	94.14%
Center-Surround	92.79%	53.60%	95.05%	92.34%	92.34%

and different zero-mean transformations of the input. There are several significant points to the results of these classification tasks. The first is to note that in spite of the fact that acoustic transient events are short-term and the time steps between the bins in the template as low as 2 ms, using time differences between samples does not yield reliable classification when either the input or the template or both is reduced to binary form. However, reliability remains high when the correlation is performed using channel differences. The implication is that even the shortest transient events have stable and reliable structure in the frequency domain, a somewhat surprising conclusion given the impulsive nature of most transients.

Another interesting point is that we observe no significant difference between the use of pairwise channel differences and the more complicated center-surround mechanism (twice the channel value minus the value of the two neighboring channels). The slight decrease in accuracy for the center-surround in some instances is most likely due only to the fact that one less channel contributes information to the correlator than in the pairwise channel difference computation. When accuracy is constant, a hardware implementation will always prefer the simpler mechanism.

Very little difference in accuracy is seen between the use of a binary $(1, -1)$ representation and a binary $(1, 0)$ representation, in spite of the fact that all zero-valued template positions do not contribute to the correlation output. This lack of difference is a result of the choice of the L-1 normalization across the input vector, which ensures that the part of the correlation due to positive template values is roughly the same magnitude as that due to negative template values, leading to a redundant representation which can be removed without affecting classification results. In analog hardware, particularly current-mode circuits, the $(1, 0)$ template representation is much simpler to implement.

Time differencing of the input can be efficiently realized in analog hardware by commuting the time-difference calculation to the end of the correlation computation and implementing it with a simple switch-capacitor circuit. Taking differences between input channel values, on the other hand, is no so easily reduced to a simple hardware form. To find a reasonable solution, we simulated a number of different combinations of channel differencing and binarization. Table 2 shows a few examples. The first row is our standard implementation of channel differences using binary $(1, 0)$ templates and continuous-valued input. The drawback of this method in analog hardware is the matching between negative and positive parts of the correlation sum. We found two ways to get around this problem without greatly compromising the system performance: The first, shown in the second row of Table 2 is to add to the correlation sum only if the channel difference is positive and the template value is 1 (one-quadrant multiplication). Another (shown in the last row) is to add the maximum of each pair of channels if the template value is 1, which is preferable in that it uses the input values directly and does not require computing a difference at all. Unfortunately, it also adds a large component to the output which is related only to the total energy of the input and therefore is common to all class outputs, reducing the dynamic range of the system.

Table 2: Simulation results for different methods of computing channel differences

method	accuracy
channel difference	94.14%
one-quadrant multiply	92.34%
maximum channel	93.69%

5 Optimization of the classifier using per-class gains

The per-class gain values K_z in equation (1) are optimal for the baseline algorithm when using the L-2 normalization. The same normalization applied to the binary templates (when the template value is assumed to be either $+1$ or -1) yields the same K_z value for all classes. This unity gain on all class outputs is assumed in all the simulations of the previous section. A careful evaluation of errors from several runs indicated the possibility that different gains on each channel could improve recognition rates, and simple experiments with values tweaked by hand proved this suspicion to be true.

To automate the process of gain optimization, we consider the templates, as determined by averaging together examples of each class in the training set, to be fixed. Then we compute the correlation between each template and the aligned, averaged inputs for each class which were used to generate the templates. The result is a $Z \times Z$ matrix, which we denote C, of expected values for the correlation between a typical example of a transient input and the template for its own class (diagonal elements C_{ii}) and the templates for all other classes (off-diagonal elements C_{ij}, $i \neq j$). Each column of C is like the correlator outputs on which we make a classification decision by choosing the maximum. Therefore we wish to maximize C_{ii} with respect to all other elements in the same column. The only degree of freedom for adjusting these values is to multiply the correlation output of each template z by a constant coefficient K_z. This corresponds to multiplying each row of C by K_z. This per-class gain mechanism is easily transferred to the analog hardware domain.

In the case of continuous-valued templates, an optimal solution can be directly evaluated and yields the L-2 normalization. However, for all binary forms of the template and/or the input, direct evaluation is impossible and the solution must be found by choosing an error function $\mathcal{E}$ to minimize or maximize. The error function must assign a large error to any off-diagonal element in a column that approaches or exceeds the diagonal element in that column, but must not force the cross-correlations to arbitrarily low negative values. A minimizing function that fits this description is

$$\mathcal{E} = \sum_i \sum_{j \neq i} \exp\left(K_j C_{ji} - K_i C_{ii}\right). \tag{4}$$

This function unfortunately has no closed-form solution for the coefficients K_i, which must be determined numerically using Newton-Raphson or some other iterative method.

Improvements in the recognition rates of the classification task using this optimization of per-class gains is shown in Table 3, where we have considered only the case of inputs and templates encoding channel differences. Although the database is small, the gains of 2 to 4% for the quantized cases are significant. For this particular simulation we used a different type of frontend section to verify that the performance of the correlation algorithm was not linked to a specific frontend architecture. To generate these performance values, we used sixteen channels with the inputs digitally processed through a constant-Q bandpass filter having a Q of 5.0 and with center frequencies spaced on a mel scale from 100 Hz to 4500 Hz. The bandpass filtering was followed by rectification and smoothing with a lowpass filter function with a cutoff frequency scaled logarithmically across channels, from 60 Hz to 600 Hz. The channel output data were decimated to a 500 Hz rate. Half of the database was used to train the system, and half used to test. Performance is similar to that reported in the previous section in spite of the fact that the number of channels was cut in half, and the number of training examples was also cut in half. Slight gains in performance are most likely due to the cleaner digital filtering of the recorded data.

Table 3: System accuracy with and without per-class normalization.

binarization	accuracy, optimized	accuracy, non-optimized
none	100%	100%
template only	93%	91%
template & input	95%	91%

6 System Robustness

We performed several additional experiment in addition to those covered in the previous sections. One of these was an evaluation of recognition accuracy as a function of the template length N (number of time bins), to determine what is a proper size for the templates. The result is shown in Figure 2 (a). This curve reaches a reliable maximum at about 50 time bins, from which our chosen size for the hardware implementation of 64 bins provides a safe margin of error. However, it is interesting to note that recognition accuracy does not drop to that of random chance until only two time bins are used (64 bits per template), and accuracy is nearly 50% with only 3 time bins (96 bits per template).

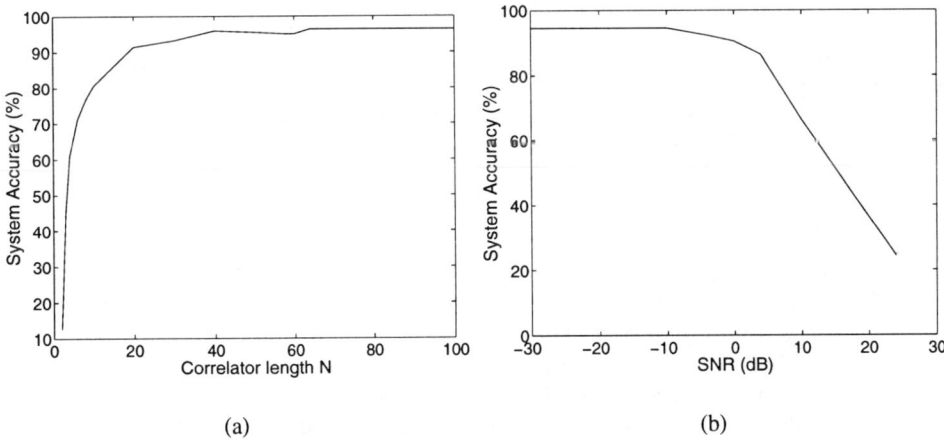

Figure 2: (a) Effect of decreasing the number of time-bins. (b) Effect of white noise added to the correlator inputs.

We made one evaluation of the robustness of the algorithm in the presence of noise by introducing additional white noise at the correlator inputs. The graph of Figure 2 (right) shows that accuracy remains high until the signal-to-noise ratio is roughly 0 dB.

An interesting question to ask about the L-1 normalization at the frontend is how the added constant normalization channel ($y[t, M+1]$) affects the classification performance. If this channel is omitted, then the total instantaneous value of all outputs must equal the same value, even during periods of silence, in which low-level noise gets amplified. The nominal value of this channel was chosen to match the levels of noise in the transient recordings. For one of the cases of Table 1 (real input, binary $(1,0)$ template, channel differencing at the input), we tried two other tests, one with the normalization constant doubled, and one with it omitted (zero). Doubling the normalization constant had no effect on the error rate, while omitting it caused the accuracy to drop only from 94.1% to 92.3%. The conclusion is that for large templates, random noise has a low probability of producing a spurious positive correlation that would be classified as a transient. The classification algorithm is not largely dependent on input signal normalization.

7 Conclusions

Starting from a template correlation architecture for acoustic transient classification targeted for high-density, low-power analog VLSI implementation, we have investigated several variants on the correlation algorithms, accounting for the strengths and constraints of the VLSI implementation medium while maintaining acceptable classification performance.

Reduction of input and templates to binary form does not significantly affect performance, as long as they are transformed to encode the difference in neighboring channels of the original filterbank frontend outputs. This suggests that acoustic transient classification is not only amenable to implementation in simple analog hardware, but also in reasonably simple digital hardware.

In looking for zero-mean representations of the input compatible with a binary template, we found that computing pairwise differences between channels gives a more robust representation than a time-differential form, as was reported previously in [1]. We have found that computing a center-surround function of the inputs yields virtually the same results as taking pairwise channel differences. Where hardware implementation is the goal, the pairwise difference function is preferred due to its greater simplicity.

We have additionally shown that cross-correlations between aligned, averaged inputs and templates can be used with an iterative method to solve for optimal gain coefficients per class output, which yield better classification performance. This is a method which can be applied in general to all template correlation systems.

References

[1] F. J. Pineda, G. Cauwenberghs, R. T. Edwards, "Bangs, Clicks, Snaps, Thuds, and Whacks: An Architecture for Acoustic Transient Processing," *Neural Information Processing Systems (NIPS)*, Denver, 1996.

[2] K. P. Unnikrishnan, J. J. Hopfield, and D. W. Tank, "Connected-Digit Speaker-Dependent Speech Recognition Using a Neural Network with Time-Delayed Connections," *IEEE Transactions on Signal Processing*, **39**, pp. 698–713, 1991.

[3] R. T. Edwards, G. Cauwenberghs, and F. J. Pineda, "A Mixed-Signal Correlator for Acoustic Transient Classification," *International Symposium on Circuits and Systems (ISCAS)*, Hong Kong, June 1997.

[4] R. T. Edwards and G. Cauwenberghs, "A Second-Order Log-Domain Bandpass Filter for Audio Frequency Applications," *International Symposium on Circuits and Systems (ISCAS)*, Monterey, CA, June 1998.

[5] K. Wang and S. Shamma, "Representation of Acoustic Signals in the Primary Auditory Cortex," *IEEE Trans. Audio and Speech Processing*, **3**(5), pp. 382–395, 1995.

[6] F. J. Pineda, K. Ryals, D. Steigerwald, and P. Furth, "Acoustic Transient Processing using the Hopkins Electronic Ear," World Conference on Neural Networks, Washington, D.C., 1995.

VLSI Implementation of Motion Centroid Localization for Autonomous Navigation

Ralph Etienne-Cummings
Dept. of ECE,
Johns Hopkins University,
Baltimore, MD

Viktor Gruev
Dept. of ECE,
Johns Hopkins University,
Baltimore, MD

Mohammed Abdel Ghani
Dept. of EE,
S. Illinois University,
Carbondale, IL

Abstract

A circuit for fast, compact and low-power focal-plane motion centroid localization is presented. This chip, which uses mixed signal CMOS components to implement photodetection, edge detection, ON-set detection and centroid localization, models the retina and superior colliculus. The centroid localization circuit uses time-windowed asynchronously triggered row and column address events and two linear resistive grids to provide the analog coordinates of the motion centroid. This VLSI chip is used to realize fast lightweight autonavigating vehicles. The obstacle avoiding line-following algorithm is discussed.

1 INTRODUCTION

Many neuromorphic chips which mimic the analog and parallel characteristics of visual, auditory and cortical neural circuits have been designed [Mead, 1989; Koch, 1995]. Recently researchers have started to combine digital circuits with neuromorphic aVLSI systems [Boahen, 1996]. The persistent doctrine, however, has been that computation should be performed in analog, and only communication should use digital circuits. We have argued that hybrid computational systems are better equipped to handle the high speed processing required for real-world problem solving, while maintaining compatibility with the ubiquitous digital computer [Etienne, 1998]. As a further illustration of this point of view, this paper presents a departure form traditional approaches for focal plane centroid localization by offering a mixed signal solution that is simultaneously high-speed, low power and compact. In addition, the chip is interfaced with an 8-bit microcomputer to implement fast autonomous navigation.

Implementation of centroid localization has been either completely analog or completely digital. The analog implementations, realized in the early 1990s, used focal plane current mode circuits to find a global continuos time centroid of the pixels' intensities [DeWeerth, 1992]. Due to their sub-threshold operation, these circuits are low power, but slow. On the other hand, the digital solutions do not compute the centroid at the focal plane. They use standard CCD cameras, A/D converters and DSP/CPU to compute the intensity centroid [Mansfield, 1996]. These software approaches offer multiple centroid localization with complex mathematical processing. However, they suffer from the usual high power consumption and non-scalability of traditional digital visual processing systems. Our approach is novel in many aspects. We benefit from the low power, compactness and parallel organization of focal plane analog circuits and the speed, robustness and standard architecture of asynchronous digital circuits. Furthermore, it uses event triggered analog address read-out, which is ideal for the visual centroid localization problem. Moreover, our chip responds to moving targets only by using the ON-set of each pixel in the centroid computation. Lastly, our chip models the retina and two dimensional saccade motor error maps of superior colliculus on a single chip [Sparks, 1990]. Subsequently, this chip is interfaced with a µC for autonomous obstacle avoidance during line-following navigation. The line-following task is similar to target tracking using the saccadic system, except that the "eye" is fixed and the "head" (the vehicle) moves to maintain fixation on the target. Control signals provided to the vehicle based on decisions made by the µC are used for steering and accelerating/braking. Here the computational flexibility and programmability of the µC allows rapid prototyping of complex and robust algorithms.

2 CENTROID LOCALIZATION

The mathematical computation of the centroid of an object on the focal plane uses intensity weighted average of the position of the pixels forming the object [DeWeerth, 1992]. Equation (1) shows this formulation. The implementation of this representation

$$\hat{x} = \frac{\sum_{i=1}^{N} I_i x_i}{\sum_{i=1}^{N} I_i} \quad \text{and} \quad \hat{y} = \frac{\sum_{i=1}^{N} I_i y_i}{\sum_{i=1}^{N} I_i} \quad (1)$$

can be quite involved since a product between the intensity and position is implied. To eliminate this requirement, the intensity of the pixels can be normalized to a single value within the object. This gives equation (2) since the intensity can be factored out of the summations. Normalization of the intensity using a simple threshold is not advised since

$$\hat{x} = \frac{\sum_{i=1}^{N} x_i}{N} \quad \text{and} \quad \hat{y} = \frac{\sum_{i=1}^{N} y_i}{N} \quad (2)$$

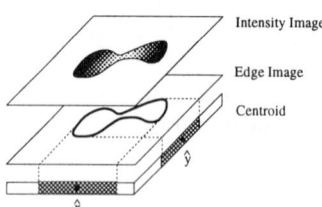

Figure 1: Centroid computation architecture.

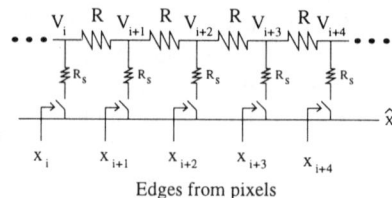

Figure 2: Centroid computation method.

the value of the threshold is dependent on the brightness of the image and number of pixels forming the object may be altered by the thresholding process. To circumvent these problems, we take the view that the centroid of the object is defined in relation to its boundaries. This implies that edge detection (second order spatial derivative of intensity) can be used to highlight the boundaries, and edge labeling (the zero-crossing of the edges) can be used to normalize the magnitude of the edges. Subsequently, the centroid of the zero-crossings is computed. Equation (2) is then realized by projecting the zero-crossing image onto the x- and y-axis and performing two linear centroid determinations. Figure (1) shows this process.

The determination of the centroid is computed using a resistance grid to associate the position of a column (row) with a voltage. In figure 2, the positions are given by the voltages V_i. By activating the column (row) switch when a pixel of the edge image appears in that column (row), the position voltage is connected to the output line through the switch impedance, R_s. As more switches are activated, the voltage on the output line approximates equation (2). Clearly, since no buffers are used to isolate the position voltages, as more switches are activated, the position voltages will also change. This does not pose a problem since the switch resistors are design to be larger than the position resistors (the switch currents are small compared to the grid current). Equation (3) gives the error between the ideal centroid and the switch loaded centroid in the worst case when $R_s = 0\Omega$. In the equation, N is the number of nodes, M is the number of switches set and x_1 and x_M are the locations of the first and last set switches, respectively. This error is improved as R_s gets larger, and vanishes as N (M≤N) approaches infinity. The terms x_i represent an ascending ordered list of the activated switches; x_1 may correspond to column five, for example. This circuit is compact since it uses only a simple linear resistive grid and MOS switches. It is low power because the total grid resistance, N x R, can be large. It can be fast when the parasitic capacitors are kept small. It provides an analog position value, but it is triggered by fast digital signals that activate the switches.

$$error = \frac{V_{max} - V_{min}}{M(N+1)} \sum_{i=1}^{M} \left[x_i - \frac{x_1(N+1)}{N+1+x_1-x_m} \right] \quad (3)$$

3 MODELING THE RETINA AND SUPERIOR COLLICULUS

3.1 System Overview

The centroid computation approach presented in section 2 is used to isolate the location of moving targets on a 2D focal plane array. Consequently, a chip which realizes a neuromorphic visual target acquisition system based on the saccadic generation mechanism of primates can be implemented. The biological saccade generation process is mediated by the superior colliculus, which contains a map of the visual field [Sparks, 1990]. In laboratory experiments, cellular recordings suggest that the superior colliculus provides the spatial location of targets to be foveated. Clearly, a great deal of neural circuitry exists between the superior colliculus and the eye muscle. Horiuchi has built an analog system which replicates most of the neural circuits (including the motor system) which are believed to form the saccadic system [Horiuchi, 1996]. Staying true to the anatomy forced his implementation to be a complex multi-chip system with many control parameters. On the other hand, our approach focuses on realizing a compact single chip solution by only mimicking the behavior of the saccadic system, but not its structure.

3.2 Hardware Implementation

Our approach uses a combination of analog and digital circuits to implement the functions of the retina and superior colliculus at the focal plane. We use simple digital control ideas, such as pulse-width modulation and stepper motors, to position the "eye". The retina portion of this chip uses photodiodes, logarithmic compression, edge detection and zero-crossing circuits. These circuits mimic the first three layers of cells in the retina with mixed sub-threshold and strong inversion circuits. The edge detection circuit is realized with an approximation of the Laplacian operator implemented using the difference between a smooth (with a resistive grid) and unsmoothed version of the image [Mead, 1989]. The high gain of the difference circuit creates a binary image of approximate zero-crossings. After this point, the computation is performed using mixed analog/digital circuits. The zero-crossings are fed to ON-set detectors (positive temporal derivatives) which signal the location of moving or flashing targets. These circuits model the behavior of some of the amacrine and ganglion cells of the primate retina [Barlow, 1982]. These first layers of processing constitute all the "direct" mimicry of the biological models. Figure 3 shows the schematic of these early processing layers.

The ON-set detectors provide inputs to the model of the superior colliculus circuits. The ON-set detectors allow us to segment moving targets against textured backgrounds. This is an improvement on earlier centroid and saccade chips that used pixel intensity. The essence of the superior colliculus map is to locate the target that is to be foveated. In our case, the target chosen to be foveated will be moving. Here motion is define simply as the change in contrast over time. Motion, in this sense, can be seen as being the earliest measurable attribute of the target which can trigger a saccade without requiring any high level decision making. Subsequently, the coordinates of the motion must be extracted and provided to the motor drivers.

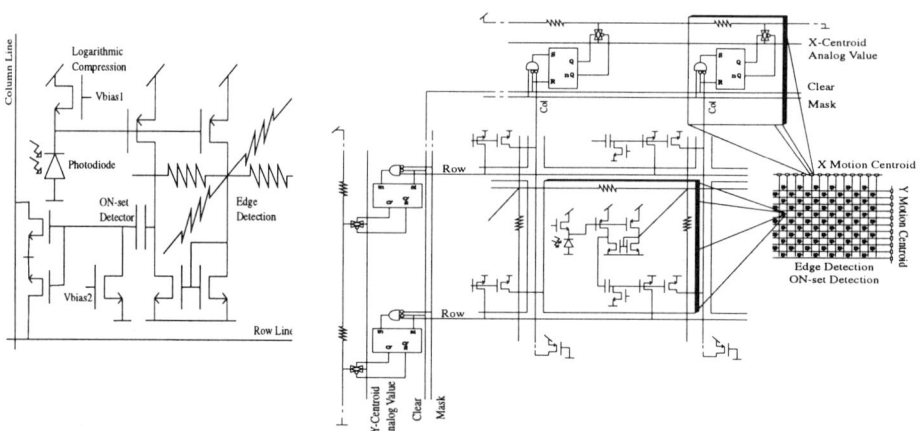

Figure 3: Schematic of the model of the retina.

Figure 4: Schematic of the model of the superior colliculus.

The circuits for locating the target are implemented entirely with mixed signal, non-neuromorphic circuits. The theoretical foundation for our approach is presented in section 2. The ON-set detector is triggered when an edge of the target appears at a pixel. At this time, the pixel broadcasts its location to the edge of the array by activating row and column lines. This row (column) signal sets a latch at the right (top) of the array. The latches asynchronously activate switches and the centroid of the activated positions is provided. The latches remain set until they are cleared by an external control signal. This control signal provides a time-window over which the centroid output is integrated. This has the effect of reducing noise by combining the outputs of pixels which are activated at different instances even if they are triggered by the same motion (an artifact of small fill factor focal plane image processing). Furthermore, the latches can be masked from the pixels' output with a second control signal. This signal is used to de-activate the centroid circuit during a saccade (saccadic suppression). A centroid valid signal is also generated by the chip. Figure 4 shows a portion of the schematic of the superior colliculus model.

3.3 Results

In contrast to previous work, this chip provides the 2-D coordinates of the centroid of a moving target. Figure 5 shows the oscilloscope trace of the coordinates as a target moves back and forth, in and out of the chip's field of view. The y-coordinate does change while the x-coordinate increases and decreases as the target moves to the left and right, respectively. The chip has been used to track targets in 2-D by making micro-saccades. In this case, the chip chases the target as it attempts to escape from the center. The eye movement is performed by converting the analog coordinates into PWM signals, which are used to drive stepper motors. The system performance is limited by the contrast sensitivity of the edge detection circuit, and the frequency response of the edge (high frequency cut-off) and ON-set (low frequency cut-off) detectors. With the appropriate optics, it can track walking or running persons under indoor or outdoor lighting conditions at close or far distances. Table I gives a summary of the chip characteristics.

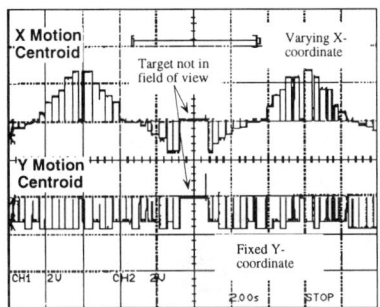

Figure 5: Oscilloscope trace of 2D centroid for a moving target.

Technology	1.2um ORBIT
Chip Size	4 mm^2
Array Size	12 x 10
Pixel Size	110 x 110 um
Fill Factor	11%
Intensity	0.1u - 100m W/cm^2
Min. Contrast	10%
Response Time	$2 - 10^6$ Hz (@1 m W/cm^2)
Power (chip)	5 mW (@1 m W/cm^2, Vdd = 6V)

Table I: Chip characteristics.

4 APPLICATION: OBSTACLE AVOIDANCE DURING LINE-FOLLOWING AUTONAVIGATION

4.1 System Overview

The frenzy of activity towards developing neuromorphic systems over the pass 10 years has been mainly driven by the promise that one day engineers will develop machines that can interact with the environment in a similar way as biological organisms. The prospect of having a robot that can help humans in their daily tasks has been a dream of science fiction for many decades. As can be expected, the key to success is premised on the development of compact systems, with large computational capabilities, at low cost (in terms of hardware and power). Neuromorphic VLSI systems have closed the gap between dreams and reality, but we are still very far from the android robot. For all these robots, autonomous behavior, in the form of auto-navigation in natural environments, must be one of their primary skills. For miniaturization, neuromorphic vision systems performing most of the pre-processing, can be coupled with small fast computers to realize these compact yet powerful sensor/processor modules.

4.2 Navigation Algorithm

The simplest form of data driven auto-navigation is the line-following task. In this task, the robot must maintain a certain relationship with some visual cues that guide its motion. In the case of the line-follower, the visual system provides data regarding the state of the line relative to the vehicle, which results in controlling steering and/or speed. If obstacle avoidance is also required, auto-navigation is considerably more difficult. Our system handles line-following and obstacle avoidance by using two neuromorphic visual sensors that provide information to a micro-controller (μC) to steer, accelerate or decelerate the vehicle. The sensors, which uses the centroid location system outlined above, provides information on the position of the line and obstacles to the μC, which provides PWM signals to the servos for controlling the vehicle. The algorithm implemented in the μC places the two sensors in competition with each other to force the line into a blind zone between the sensors. Simultaneously, if an object enters the visual field from outside, it is treated as an obstacle and the μC turns the car away from the object. Obstacle avoidance is given higher priority than line-following to avoid collisions. The μC also keeps track of the direction of avoidance such that the vehicle can be re-oriented towards the line after the obstacle is pushed out of the field of view. Lastly, for line following, the position, orientation and velocity of drift, determined from the temporal derivative of the centroid, are used to track the line. The control strategy is to keep the line in the blind zone, while slowing down at corners, speeding up on straight aways and avoiding obstacles. The angle which the line or obstacle form with the x-axis also affects the speed. The value of the x-centroid relative to the y-centroid provides rudimentary estimate of the orientation of the line or obstacle to the vehicle. For example, angles less

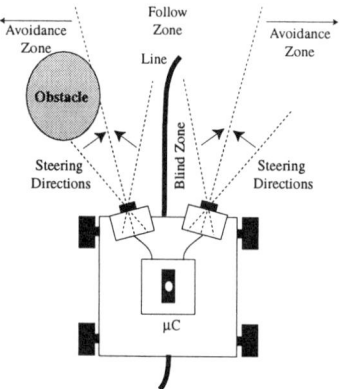 

Figure 6: Block diagram of the autonomous line-follower system.

Figure 7: A picture of the vehicle.

(greater) than +/- 45 degrees tend to have small (large) x-coordinates and large (small) y-coordinates and require deceleration (acceleration). Figure 6 shows the organization of the sensors on the vehicle and control spatial zones. Figure 7 shows the vehicle and samples of the line and obstacles.

4.3 Hardware Implementation

The coordinates from the centroid localization circuits are presented to the μC for analysis. The μC used is the Microchip PIC16C74. This chip is chosen because of its five A/D inputs and three PWM outputs. The analog coordinates are presented directly to the A/D inputs. Two of the PWM outputs are connected to the steering and speed control servos. The PIC16C74 runs at 20 MHz and has 35 instructions, 4K by 8-b ROM and 80 by 20-b RAM. The program which runs on the PIC determines the control action to take, based on the signal provided by the neuromorphic visual sensors. The vehicle used is a four-wheel drive radio controlled model car (the radio receiver is disconnected) with Digital Proportional Steering (DPS).

4.4 Results

The vehicle was tested on a track composed of black tape on a gray linoleum floor with black and white obstacles. The track formed a closed loop with two sharp turns and some smooth S-curves. The neuromorphic vision chip was equipped with a 12.5 mm variable iris lens, which limited its field of view to about 10°. Despite the narrow field of view, the car was able to navigate the track at an average speed of 1 m/s without making any errors. On less curvy parts of the track, it accelerated to about 2 m/s and slowed down at the corners. When the speed of the vehicle is scaled up, the errors made are mainly due to over steering.

5 CONCLUSION

A 2D model of the saccade generating components of the superior colliculus is presented. This model only mimics the functionality the saccadic system using mixed signal focal plane circuits that realize motion centroid localization. The single chip combines a silicon retina with the superior colliculus model using compact, low power and fast circuits. Finally, the centroid chip is interfaced with an 8-bit μC and vehicle for fast line-following autonavigation with obstacle avoidance. Here all of the required computation is performed at the visual sensor, and a standard μC is the high-level decision maker.

References

Barlow H., *The Senses: Physiology of the Retina*, Cambridge University Press, Cambridge, England, 1982.

Boahen K., "Retinomorphic Vision Systems II: Communication Channel Design," *ISCAS 96*, Atlanta, GA, 1996.

DeWeerth, S. P., "Analog VLSI Circuits for Stimulus Localization and Centroid Computation," *Int'l J. Computer Vision*, Vol. 8, No. 2, pp. 191-202, 1992.

Etienne-Cummings R., J Van der Spiegel and P. Mueller, "Neuromorphic and Digital Hybrid Systems," *Neuromorphic Systems: Engineering Silicon from Neurobiology*, L. Smith and A. Hamilton (Eds.), World Scientific, 1998.

Horiuchi T., T. Morris, C. Koch and S. P. DeWeerth, "Analog VLSI Circuits for Attention-Based Visual Tracking," *Advances in Neural Information Processing Systems*, Vol. 9, Denver, CO, 1996.

Koch C. and H. Li (Eds.), *Vision Chips: Implementing Vision Algorithms with Analog VLSI Circuits*, IEEE Computer Press, 1995.

Mansfield, P., "Machine Vision Tackles Star Tracking," *Laser Focus World*, Vol. 30, No. 26, pp. S21-S24, 1996.

Mead C. and M. Ismail (Eds.), *Analog VLSI Implementation of Neural Networks*, Kluwer Academic Press, Newell, MA, 1989.

Sparks D., C. Lee and W. Rohrer, "Population Coding of the Direction, Amplitude and Velocity of Saccadic Eye Movements by Neurons in the Superior Colliculus," *Proc. Cold Spring Harbor Symp. Quantitative Biology*, Vol. LV, 1990.

A Neuromorphic Monaural Sound Localizer

John G. Harris, Chiang-Jung Pu, and Jose C. Principe
Department of Electrical & Computer Engineering
University of Florida
Gainesville, FL 32611

Abstract

We describe the first single microphone sound localization system and its inspiration from theories of human monaural sound localization. Reflections and diffractions caused by the external ear (pinna) allow humans to estimate sound source elevations using only one ear. Our single microphone localization model relies on a specially shaped reflecting structure that serves the role of the pinna. Specially designed analog VLSI circuitry uses echo-time processing to localize the sound. A CMOS integrated circuit has been designed, fabricated, and successfully demonstrated on actual sounds.

1 Introduction

The principal cues for human sound localization arise from time and intensity differences between the signals received at the two ears. For *low-frequency* components of sounds (below 1500Hz for humans), the phase-derived interaural time difference (ITD) can be used to localize the sound source. For these frequencies, the sound wavelength is at least several times larger than the head and the amount of shadowing (which depends on the wavelength of the sound compared with the dimensions of the head) is negligible. ITD localization is a well-studied system in biology (see e.g., [5]) and has even been mapped to neuromorphic analog VLSI circuits with limited success on actual sound signals [6] [2]. Above 3000Hz, interaural phase differences become ambiguous by multiples of 360° and are no longer viable localization cues. For these high frequencies, the wavelength of the sound is small enough that the sound amplitude is attenuated by the head. The intensity difference of the log magnitudes at the ears provides a unique interaural intensity difference (IID) that can be used to localize.

Many studies have shown that when one ear is completely blocked, humans can still localize sounds in space, albeit at a worse resolution in the horizontal direc-

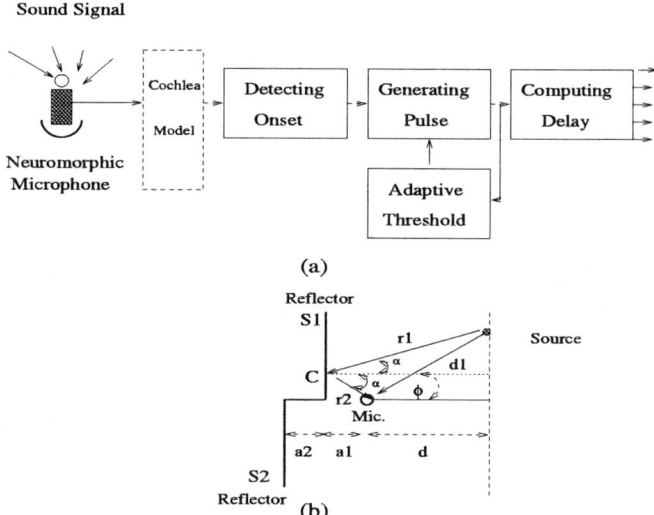

Figure 1: *(a) Proposed localization model is inspired from the biological model (b) Special reflection surface to serve the role of the pinna*

tion. Monaural localization requires that information is somehow extracted from the direction-dependent effects of the reflections and diffractions of sound off of the external ear (pinna), head, shoulder, and torso. The so-called "Head Related Transfer Function" (HRTF) is the effective direction-dependent transfer function that is applied to the incoming sound to produce the sound in the middle ear. Section 2 of this paper introduces our monaural sound localization model and Section 3 discusses the simulation and measurement results.

2 Monaural Sound Localization Model

Batteau [1] was one of the first to emphasize that the external ear, specifically the pinna, could be a source of spatial cues that account for vertical localization. He concluded that the physical structure of the external ear introduced two significant echoes in addition to the original sound. One echo varies with the azimuthal position of the sound source, having a latency in the 0 to 80μs range, while the other varies with elevation in the 100μs to 300μs range. The output $y(t)$ at the inner ear is related to the original sound source $x(t)$ as

$$y(t) = x(t) + a_1 x(t - \tau_a) + a_2 x(t - \tau_v) \qquad (1)$$

where τ_a, τ_v refer to azimuth and elevation echoes respectively; a_1 and a_2 are two reflection constants. Other researchers subsequently verified these results [11] [4].

Our localizer system (shown in Figure 1(a)) is composed of a special reflection surface that encodes the sound source's direction, a silicon cochlea that functions as a band-pass filter bank, onset detecting circuitry that detects and amplifies the energy change at each frequency tap, pulse generating circuitry that transfers analog sound signals into pulse signals based on adaptively thresholding the onset signal, and delay time computation circuitry that computes the echo's time delay then decodes the sound source's direction.

Since our recorded signal is composed of a direct sound and an echo, the sound is a simplified version of actual HRTF recordings that are composed of the direct sound

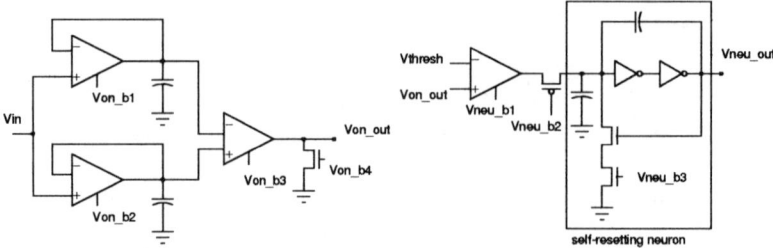

Figure 2: (a) Sound signal's onset is detected by taking the difference of two low-pass filters with different time constants. (b) Pulse generating circuit.

and its reflections from the external ear, head, shoulder, and torso. To achieve localization in a 1D plane, we may use any shape of reflection surface as long as the reflection echo caused by the surface provides a one-to-one mapping between the echo's delay time and the source's direction. Thus, we propose two flat surfaces to compose the reflection structure in our proposed model depicted in Figure 1(b). A microphone is placed at distances a_1 and a_2 from two flat surfaces (S_1 and S_2), d is the distance between the microphone and the sound source moving line (the dotted line in Figure 1(b). As shown in Figure 1(b), a sound source is at $\angle \phi$ position. If the source is far enough from the reflection surface, the ray diagram is valid to analyze the sound's behavior. We skip the complete derivation but the echo's delay time can be expressed as

$$\tau = \frac{r_1 + r_2 - d_1}{c} \quad (2)$$

where d_1 is the length of the direct path, $r_1 + r_2$ is reflected path length, and c is the speed of sound. The path distance are easily solved in terms of the source direction and the geometry of the setup (see [9] for complete details).

The echo's delay time τ decreases as the source position ϕ moves from 0 to 90 degrees. A similar analysis can be made if the source moves in the opposite direction, and the reflection is caused by the other reflection surface S_2. Since the reflection path is longer for reflection surface S_2 than for reflection surface S_1, the echo's delay time can be segmented into two ranges. Therefore, the echo's delay time encodes the source's directions in a one-to-one mapping relation.

In the setup, an Earthworks M30 microphone and Lab1 amplifier were used to record and amplify the sound signals [3]. For this preliminary study of monaural localization, we have chosen to localize simple impulse sounds generated through speakers and therefore can drop the silicon cochlea from our model. In the future, more complicated signals, such as speech, will require a silicon cochlea implementation.

Inspired by ideas from visual processing, onset detection is used to segment sounds [10]. The detection of an onset is produced by first taking the difference of two first-order, low-pass filters given by [10]

$$O(t,k,r) = \int_0^t f_z(t-x,k)s(x)dx - \int_0^t f_z(t-x,k/r)s(x)dx \quad (3)$$

where r>1, k is a time constant, $s(x)$ is the input sound signal, and $f_z(x,k) = k\exp(-kx)$.

A hardware implementation of the above equation is depicted in Figure 2a. In our model, sound signals from the special reflection surface microphone are fed into two low-pass filters which have different time constants determined by two bias

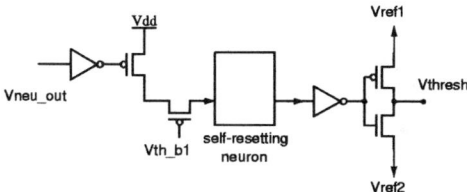

Figure 3: *Adaptive threshold circuit used to remove unwanted reflections.*

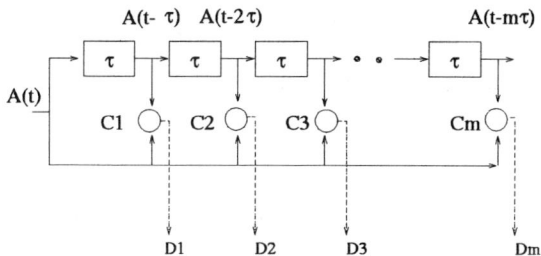

Figure 4: *Neural signal processing model*

voltages $V_{on_{b1}}$ and $V_{on_{b2}}$. The bias voltage $V_{on_{b3}}$ determines the amplification of the difference. The output of the onset detecting circuit is $V_{on_{out}}$. The onset detection circuit determines significant increases in the signal energy and therefore segments sound events. By computing the delay time between two sound events (direct sound and its echo caused by the reflection surface), the system is able to decode the source's direction. Each sound event is then transformed into a fixed-width pulse so that the delay time can be computed with binary autocorrelators.

The fixed-width pulse generating circuit is depicted in Figure 2b. The pulse generating circuit includes a self-resetting neuron circuit [8] that controls the pulse duration based on the bias voltage $V_{neu_{b3}}$. As discussed above, an appropriate threshold is required to discriminate sound events from noise. One input of the pulse generating circuit is the output of the onset detecting signal, $V_{on_{out}}$. V_{thresh} is set properly in the pulse generating circuit in order to generate a fixed width pulse when $V_{on_{out}}$ exceeds V_{thresh}. Unfortunately the system may be confused by unwanted sound events due to extraneous reflections from the desks and walls. However, since we know the expect range of echo delays, we can inhibit many of the environmental echoes that fall outside this range using an adaptive threshold circuit.

In order to cancel unwanted signals, we need to design an inhibition mechanism which suppresses signals arriving to our system outside of the expected time range. This inhibition is implemented in Figure 3. As the pulse generating circuit detects the first sound event (which is the direct sound signal), the threshold becomes high in a certain period of time to suppress the detection of the unwanted reflections (not from our reflection surfaces). The input of the adaptive threshold circuit is $V_{neu_{out}}$ which is the output of the pulse generating circuit. The output of the threshold circuit is V_{thresh} which is the input of the pulse generating circuit. When the pulse generating circuit detects a sound event, $V_{neu_{out}}$ becomes high, which increases V_{thresh} from V_{ref2} to V_{ref1} as shown in Figure 3. The higher V_{thresh} suppresses the detection. The suppression time is determined by the other self-resetting neuron circuit.

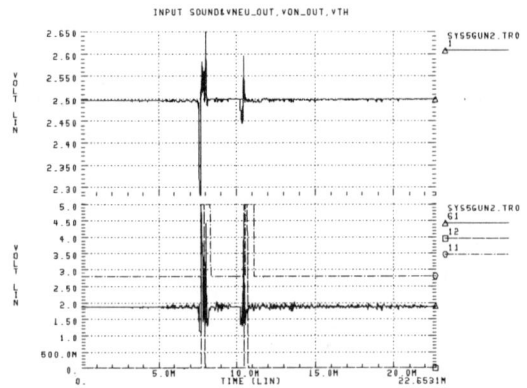

Figure 5: (a) The input sound signal: impulse signal recorded in typical office environment (b) HSPICE simulation of the output of the detecting onset circuit (label 61), the output of the pulse generating circuit (label 12), and the adaptive threshold circuit response (label 11)

The nervous system likely uses a running autocorrelation analysis to measure the time delay between signals. The basic neural connections are shown in Figure 4 [7]. $A(t)$ is the input neuron, $A(t - \tau)$, $A(t - 2\tau)$,...$A(t - m\tau)$ is a delay chain. The original signal and the delayed signal are multiplied when $A(t)$ and $A(t - k\tau)$ feed C_k. Assuming the state of neuron A is $N_A(t)$. If each synaptic delay in the chain is τ, the chain gives us $N_A(t)$ under various delays. C_k fires simultaneously when both $A(t)$ and $A(t - k\tau)$ fire. Neuron C_k connects neuron D_k. Excitation is built up at D_k by the charge and discharge of C_k. The excitation at D_k is therefore

$$D_k(t) = N_{C_k}(t) = N_A(t)N_A(t - k\tau) \qquad (4)$$

Viewing the arrangement of Figure 4 as a neuron autocorrelator, the time-varying excitation at $D_1, D_2,..D_k$ provides a spatial representation of the autocorrelation function. The localization resolution of this system depends on the delay time τ, and the number of the correlators. As τ decreases, the localization resolution is improved provided there are enough correlators. In this paper, 30 unit delay taps, and 10 correlators have been implemented on chip. The outputs of the 10 correlators display the time difference between two sound events. The delay time decodes the source's direction. Therefore, the 10 correlators provide a unit encoding of the source location in the 1D plane.

3 Simulation and Measurement Results

The complete system has been successfully simulated in HSPICE using database we have recorded. Figure 5(a) shows the input sound signal which is an impulse signal recording in our lab (a typical student office environment). Figure 5(b) shows the output of the onset detector (labeled 61), the pulse generating output (labeled 12), and the adaptive threshold (labeled 11). When the onset output exceeds the threshold, the output of the pulse generating circuit becomes high. Simultaneously, the high value of the generated pulse turns on the adaptive threshold circuit to increase the threshold voltage. The adaptive threshold voltage suppresses the unwanted re-

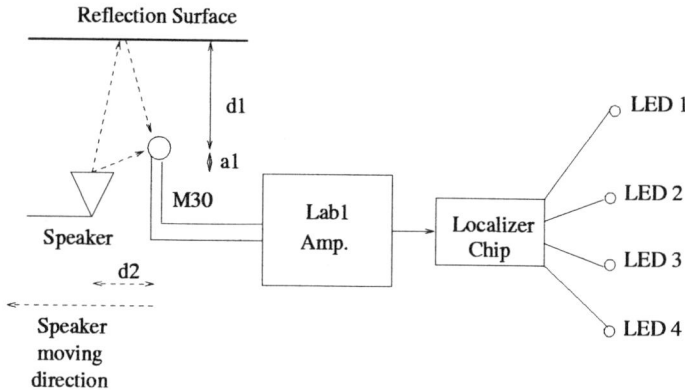

Figure 6: *Block diagram of the test setup*

flection which can be seen right after the direct signal (we believe the unwanted reflection is caused by the table). Further simulation results are discussed in [9].

The single microphone sound localizer circuit has been fabricated through the MOSIS $2\mu m$ N-well CMOS process. Impulse signals are played through speakers to test the fabricated localizer chip. Figure 6 depicts the block diagram of the test setup. The M30 microphone picks up the direct impulse signal and echoes from the reflection surface. Since the reflection surface in our test is just a single flat surface, localization is only tested in one-half of the 1D plane. The composite signals are fed into the input of the sound localizer after amplification. Our sound localizer chip receives the composite signal, computes the echo time delay, and sends out the localization result to a display circuit. The display circuit is composed of 4 LEDs with each LED representing a specific sound source location. The sound localizer sends the computational result to turn on a specific LED signifying the echo time delay. In the test, the M30 microphone and the reflection surface are placed at fixed locations. The speaker is moved along the dotted line shown in Figure 6. The M30 microphone is d_1 (33cm) from the reflection surface and a_1 (24cm) from the speaker moving line. The speaker's location is defined as d_2 as depicted in Figure 6.

Figure 7(a) shows the theoretical echo's delay at various speaker locations. Figure 7(b) is the measurement of the setup depicted in Figure 6. The y-axis indicates LED 1 through LED 4. The x-axis represents the distance between the speaker's location (d_2 in Figure 6). The solid horizontal line in Figure 7(b) represents the theoretical results for which LED should respond for each displacement. The results show that localization is accurate within each region with possibilities of two LEDs responding in the overlap regions.

4 Conclusion

We have developed the first monaural sound localization system. This system provides a real-time model for human sound localization and has potential use in such applications as low-cost teleconferencing. More work is needed to further develop the system. We need to characterize the accuracy of our system and to test more interesting sound signals, such as speech. Our flat reflection surface is straightforward and simple, but it lacks sufficient flexibility to encode the source's direction in more than a 1-D plane. We plan to replace the flat surfaces with a more complicated surface to provide more reflections to encode a richer set of source directions.

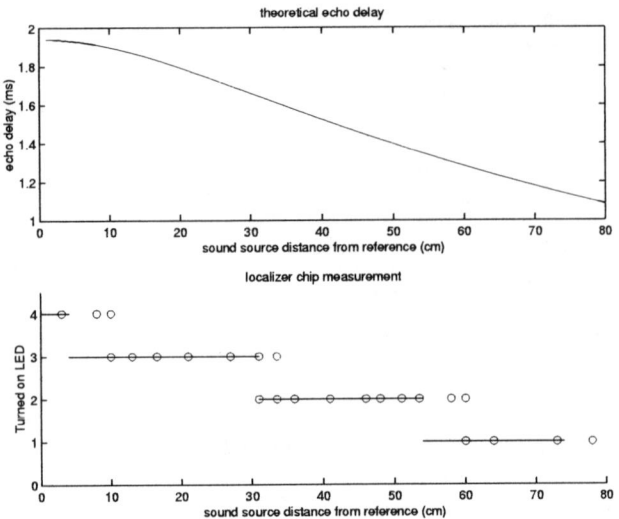

Figure 7: *Sound localizer chip test result*

Acknowledgments

This work was supported by an ONR contract #N00014-94-1-0858 and an NSF CAREER award #MIP-9502307. We gratefully acknowledge MOSIS chip fabrication and Earthworks Inc. for loaning the M30 microphone and amplifier.

References

[1] D. W. Batteau. The role of the pinna in human localization. *Proc. R. Soc. London, Ser. B*, 168:158–180, 1967.

[2] Neal A. Bhadkamkar. Binaural source localizer chip using subthreshold analog cmos. In *Proceeding of ICNN*, pages 1866–1870, 1994.

[3] Earthworks, Inc., P.O. Box 517, Wilton, NH 03086. *M30 Microphone*.

[4] Y. Hiranaka and H. Yamasaki. Envelop representations of pinna impulse responses relating to three-dimensional localization of sound sources. *J. Acoust. Soc. Am.*, 73:29, 1983.

[5] E. Knudsen, G. Blasdel, and M. Konishi. Mechanisms of sound localization in the barn owl (tyto alba). *J. Comp. Physiol*, 133:13–21, 1979.

[6] J. Lazzaro and C. A. Mead. A silicon model of auditory localization. *Neural Computation*, 1:47–57, 1989.

[7] J.C. Licklider. A duplex theory of pitch perception. *Experientia*, 7:128–133, 1951.

[8] C. Mead. *Analog VLSI and Neural Systems*. Addison-Wesley, 1989.

[9] Chiang-Jung Pu. *A neuromorphic microphone for sound localization*. PhD thesis, University of Florida, Gainesville, FL, May 1998.

[10] L.S. Smith. Sound segmentation using onsets and offsets. *J. of New Music Research*, 23, 1994.

[11] A.J. Watkins. Psychoacoustical aspects of synthesized vertical locale cues. *J. Acoust. Soc. Am.*, 63:1152–1165, 1978.

An Integrated Vision Sensor for the Computation of Optical Flow Singular Points

Charles M. Higgins and Christof Koch

Division of Biology, 139-74
California Institute of Technology
Pasadena, CA 91125
[chuck,koch]@klab.caltech.edu

Abstract

A robust, integrative algorithm is presented for computing the position of the focus of expansion or axis of rotation (the singular point) in optical flow fields such as those generated by self-motion. Measurements are shown of a fully parallel CMOS analog VLSI motion sensor array which computes the direction of local motion (sign of optical flow) at each pixel and can directly implement this algorithm. The flow field singular point is computed in real time with a power consumption of less than 2 mW. Computation of the singular point for more general flow fields requires measures of field expansion and rotation, which it is shown can also be computed in real-time hardware, again using only the sign of the optical flow field. These measures, along with the location of the singular point, provide robust real-time self-motion information for the visual guidance of a moving platform such as a robot.

1 INTRODUCTION

Visually guided navigation of autonomous vehicles requires robust measures of self-motion in the environment. The heading direction, which corresponds to the focus of expansion in the visual scene for a fixed viewing angle, is one of the primary sources of guidance information. Psychophysical experiments [WH88] show that humans can determine their heading direction very precisely. In general, the location of the singular point in the visual field provides important self-motion information.

Optical flow, representing the motion seen in each local area of the visual field, is particularly compute-intensive to process in real time. We have previously shown [DHK97] a fully parallel, low power, CMOS analog VLSI vision processor for computing the local direction of motion. With onboard photoreceptors, each pixel computes in continuous time a vector corresponding to the sign of the local normal flow. In this article, we show how these motion vectors can be integrated in hardware to compute the singular point of the optical flow field. While each individual pixel suffers from transistor mismatch and spatial variability with respect to its neighbors, the integration of many pixels serves to average out these irregularities and results in a highly robust computation. This compact, low power self-motion processor is well suited for autonomous vehicle applications.

Extraction of self-motion information has been a topic of research in the machine vision community for decades, and has generated volumes of research; see [FA97] for a good review. While many algorithms exist for determining flow field singular points in complex self-motion situations, few are suitable for real-time implementation. Integrated hardware attempts at self-motion processing have only begun recently, with the work of Indiveri et al [IKK96]. The zero crossing in a 1D array of CMOS velocity sensors was used to detect one component of the focus of expansion. In a separate chip, the sum of a radial array of velocity sensors was used to compute the rate of flow field expansion, from which the time-to-contact can be calculated. McQuirk [McQ96] built a CCD-based image processor which used an iterative algorithm to locate consistent stable points in the image, and thus the focus of expansion. More recently, Deutschmann et al. [DW98] have extended Indiveri et al.'s work to 2D by summing rows and columns in a 2D CMOS motion sensor array and using software to detect zero crossings and find the flow field singular point.

2 SINGULAR POINT ALGORITHM

In order to compute the flow field singular point, we compute the sum of the *sign* of optical flow over the entire field of view. Let the field of view be centered at $(0,0)$ and bounded by $\pm L$ in both spatial dimensions; then (vector quantities are indicated in boldface)

$$\mathbf{S} = \int_{-L}^{L} \int_{-L}^{L} \mathbf{U}(x,y) \, dx \, dy \quad (1)$$

where $\mathbf{U}(x,y) = (U_x(x,y), U_y(x,y)) = \text{sgn}(\mathbf{V}(x,y))$ and $\mathbf{V}(x,y)$ is the optical flow field. Consider a purely expanding flow field with the focus of expansion (FOE) at the center of the visual field. Intuitively, the vector sum of the sign of optical flow will be zero, because each component is balanced by a spatially symmetric component with opposite sign. As the FOE moves away from the center of the visual field, the sum will increase or decrease depending on the FOE position.

An expanding flow field may be expressed as

$$\mathbf{V_e}(x,y) = A(x,y) \cdot ((x - X_e), (y - Y_e)) \quad (2)$$

where $A(x,y)$ denotes the local rate of expansion and (X_e, Y_e) is the focus of expansion. The integral (1) applied to this flow field yields

$$\mathbf{S} = -4L \cdot (X_e, Y_e)$$

as long as A is positive. Note that, due to the use of optical flow *sign* only, this quantity is independent of the speed of the flow field components. We will discuss in Section 5 how the positivity requirement of A can be relaxed somewhat.

Similarly, a clockwise rotating flow field may be expressed as

$$\mathbf{V_r}(x, y) = B(x, y) \cdot ((y - Y_r), -(x - X_r)) \tag{3}$$

where $B(x, y)$ denotes the local rate of rotation and (X_r, Y_r) is the axis of rotation (AOR). The integral (1) applied to this flow field yields

$$\mathbf{S} = -4L \cdot (Y_r, -X_r)$$

as long as B is positive.

Let us now consider the case of a combination of these expanding and rotating fields (2) and (3):

$$\mathbf{V}(x, y) = \theta \mathbf{V_e} + (1 - \theta) \mathbf{V_r} \tag{4}$$

This flow field is spiral in shape; the parameter θ defines the mix of the two field types. The sum in this case is more complex to evaluate, but for θ small (rotation dominating),

$$\mathbf{S} = -4L \cdot (CX_e + Y_r, CY_e - X_r) \tag{5}$$

and for θ large (expansion dominating),

$$\mathbf{S} = -4L \cdot (X_e + (1/C)Y_r, Y_e - (1/C)X_r) \tag{6}$$

where $C = \frac{\theta A}{1-\theta B}$. Since it is mathematically impossible to recover *both* the FOE and AOR with only two equations,[1] let us equate the FOE and AOR and concentrate on recovering the unique singular point of this spiral flow field. In order to do this, we need a measurement of the quantity C, which reflects the relative mix and strength of the expanding and rotating flow fields.

2.1 COEFFICIENTS OF EXPANSION AND ROTATION

Consider a contour integral around the periphery of the visual field of the sign of optical flow components *normal* to the contour of integration. If we let this contour be a square of size $2L$ centered at $(0, 0)$, we can express this integral as

$$8LC_{exp} = \int_{-L}^{L} (U_y(x, L) - U_y(x, -L)) \, dx + \int_{-L}^{L} (U_x(L, y) - U_x(-L, y)) \, dy \tag{7}$$

This integral can be considered as a 'template' for expanding flow fields. The quantity C_{exp} reaches unity for a purely expanding flow field with FOE within the visual field, and reaches zero for a purely rotating flow field. A similar quantity for rotation may be defined by an integral of the sign of optical flow components *parallel* to the contour of integration:

$$8LC_{rot} = \int_{-L}^{L} (U_x(x, L) - U_x(x, -L)) \, dx + \int_{-L}^{L} (U_y(-L, y) - U_y(L, y)) \, dy \tag{8}$$

It can be shown that for θ small (rotation dominating), $C_{exp} \approx C$. As θ increases, C_{exp} saturates at unity. Similarly, for θ large (expansion dominating), $C_{rot} \approx (1/C)$. As θ decreases, C_{rot} saturates at unity. This suggests the following approximation to equations (5) and (6), letting $X_s = X_e = X_r$ and $Y_s = Y_e = Y_r$

$$\mathbf{S} = -4L \cdot (C_{exp}X_s + C_{rot}Y_s, C_{exp}Y_s - C_{rot}X_s) \tag{9}$$

from which equation the singular point (X_s, Y_s) may be uniquely calculated. Note that this generalized expression also covers contracting and counterclockwise rotating fields (for which the quantities C_{exp} and C_{rot} would be negative).

---

[1] In fact, if A and B are constant, there exists no unique solution for the FOE and AOR.

3 HARDWARE IMPLEMENTATION

The real-time hardware implementation of the above algorithm utilizes a fully parallel 14×13 CMOS analog VLSI motion sensor array. The elementary motion detectors are briefly described below. Each pixel in the array creates a local motion vector when crossed by a spatial edge; this vector is represented by two currents encoding the x and y components. These currents persist for an adjustable period of time after stimulation. By using the serial pixel scanners at the periphery of the chip (normally used to address each pixel individually), it is possible to connect all of these currents to the same output wire, thus implementing the sum required by the algorithm. In this mode, the current outputs of the chip directly represent the sum S in equation (1), and power consumption is less than $2\ mW$.

A similar sum combining sensor row and column outputs around the periphery of the chip could be used to implement the quantities C_{exp} and C_{rot} in equations (7) and (8). Due to the sign changes necessary, this sum cannot be directly implemented with the present implementation. However, it is possible to emulate this sum by scanning off the vector field and performing the sum in real-time software.

3.1 ELEMENTARY MOTION DETECTOR

The 1D elementary motion detector used in this processor is the ITI (Inhibit, Trigger, and Inhibit) sensor. Its basic operation is described in Figure 1; see [DHK97] for details. The sensor is edge sensitive, approximately invariant to stimulus contrast above 20% and functions over a stimulus velocity range from 10-800 pixels/sec.

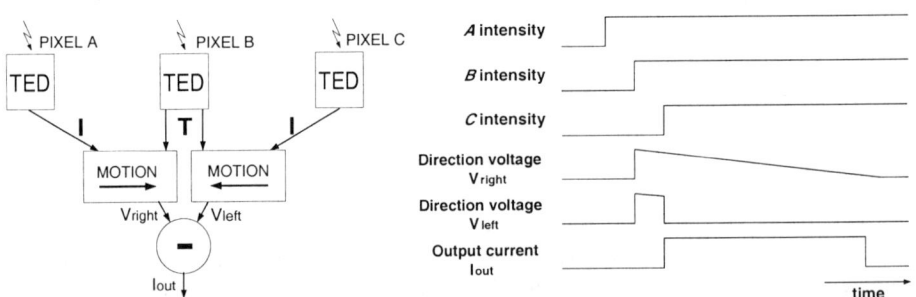

Figure 1: ITI sensor: a spatial edge crossing the sensor from left to right triggers direction voltages for both directions V_{right} and V_{left} in pixel B. The same edge subsequently crossing pixel C inhibits the null direction voltage V_{left}. The output current is continuously computed as the difference between V_{right} and V_{left}; the resulting positive output current I_{out} indicates rightward motion. Pixels B and A interact similarly to detect leftward motion, resulting in a negative output current.

The output of each 1D ITI sensor represents the order in which the three involved photoreceptors were crossed by a spatial edge. Like all local motion sensors, it suffers from the aperture problem, and thus can only respond to the optical flow normal to the local gradients of intensity. The final result of this computation is the sign of the projection of the normal flow onto the sensor orientation. Two such sensors placed orthogonally effectively compute the sign of the normal flow vector.

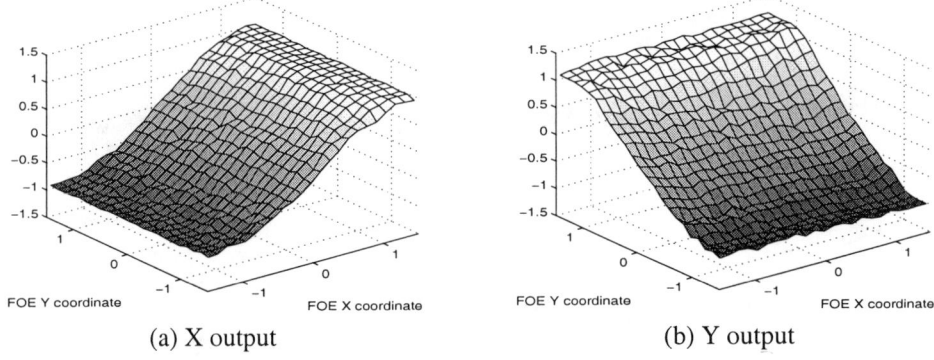

(a) X output   (b) Y output

Figure 2: Hardware FOE computation: the chip was presented with a computer-generated image of high-contrast expanding circles; the FOE location was varied under computer control on a 2D grid. The measured chip current output has been scaled by a factor of 6×10^5 chip radii per Ampere. All FOE locations are shown in chip radii, where a radius of 1.0 corresponds to the periphery of the sensor array. Data shown is the mean output over one stimulus period; RMS variation is 0.27 chip radii.

4 SENSOR MEASUREMENTS

In Figure 2, we demonstrate the hardware computation of the FOE. To generate this data, the chip was presented with a computer-generated image of high-contrast expanding circles. The focus of expansion was varied on a 2D grid under computer control, and the mean of the chip's output current over one period of the stimulus was calculated for each FOE position. This output varies periodically with the stimulus because each motion sensor stops generating output while being crossed by a stimulus edge. The RMS value of this variation for the expanding circles stimulus is 0.27 chip radii; this variation can be decreased by increasing the resolution of the sensor array. The data shows that the FOE is precisely located when it is within the chip's visual field. Each component of the chip output is virtually independent of the other. When the FOE is outside the chip's visual field, the chip output saturates, but continues to indicate the correct direction towards the FOE.

The chip's AOR response to a rotating 'wagon wheel' stimulus is qualitatively and quantitatively very similar, and is not shown for lack of space.

In Figure 3, the coefficients of expansion and rotation are shown for the same expanding circles stimulus used in Figure 2. Since these coefficients cannot be calculated directly by the present hardware, the flow field was scanned out of the chip and these quantities were calculated in real-time software. While the FOE is on the chip, C_{exp} remains near unity, dropping off as the FOE leaves the chip. As expected, C_{rot} remains near zero regardless of the FOE position. Note that, because these coefficients are calculated by integrating a ring of only 48 sensors near the chip periphery, they have more spatial noise than the FOE calculation which integrates all 182 motion sensors.

In Figure 4, a spiral stimulus is presented, creating an equal combination of expansion and rotation ($\theta = 0.5$ in equation (4)). The singular point is calculated from equation (9) using the optical flow field scanned from the chip. Due to the combination of the coefficients with the sum computation, more spatial noise has been introduced than was seen in the FOE case. However, the singular point is still clearly located when within the chip. When the

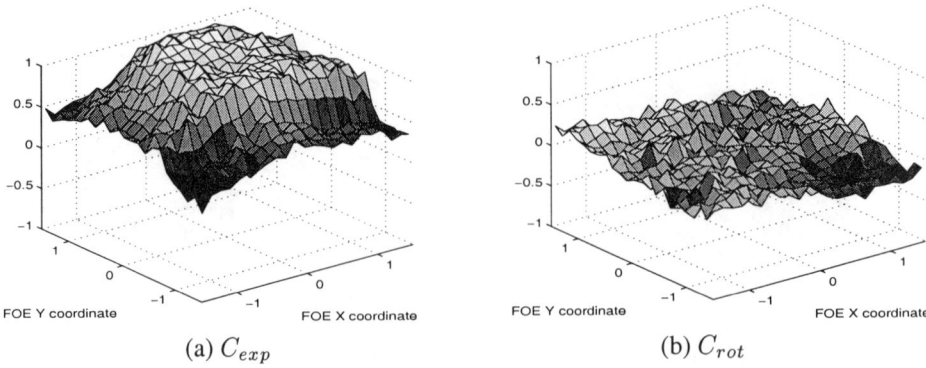

(a) C_{exp} (b) C_{rot}

Figure 3: Coefficients of expansion and rotation: again using the computer-generated expanding circles stimulus, the FOE was varied on a 2D grid. All FOE locations are shown in chip radii, where a radius of 1.0 corresponds to the periphery of the sensor array. Data shown is the mean output over one stimulus period.

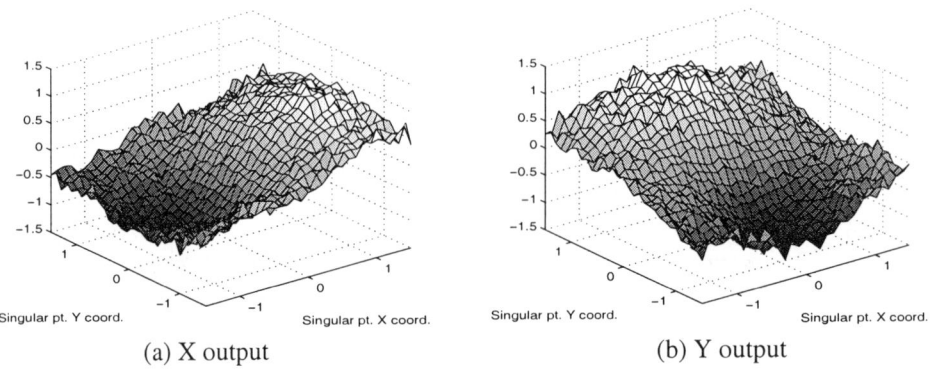

(a) X output   (b) Y output

Figure 4: Singular point calculation: the chip was shown a computer-generated image of a rotating spiral; the singular point location was varied under computer control on a 2D grid. All singular point locations are shown in chip radii, where a radius of 1.0 corresponds to the periphery of the sensor array. Data shown is the mean output over one stimulus period.

singular point leaves the chip, the calculated position drops towards zero as the algorithm can no longer compute the mix of expansion and rotation.

5 DISCUSSION

We have presented a simple, robust algorithm for computing the singular point of an optical flow field and demonstrated a real-time hardware implementation. Due to the use of the *sign* of optical flow only, the solution is independent of the relative velocities of components of the flow field. Because a large number of individual sensors are integrated to produce this output, it is quite robust to the spatial variability of the individual motion sensors. We have also shown how coefficients indicating the mix of expansion and rotation may be computed in hardware. A motion sensor array which directly computes these coefficients, as well as the flow field singular point, is currently in fabrication.

In order to derive the equations relating the flow field sums to the FOE, it was necessary in Section 2 to make the unrealistic assumption that the optical flow field contains no areas of zero optical flow. Due to the persistence time of the motion sensor used, it is possible to relax this assumption significantly. As long as all parts of the visual field receive stimulation *within the persistence time of the motion output*, the optical flow field seen by the motion sensor array will contain no zeros and the singular point output will remain correct. This is a simple example of temporal motion integration. In fact, it is possible in practice to relax this assumption even further: as long as the location of zeros in the optical flow field is spatially random, the magnitude of the output will be reduced but it will continue to provide a clear error signal pointing towards the flow field singular point.

Because of the fully parallel design of the motion sensor array, larger arrays may be obtained by simply replicating pixels. The FOE summing algorithm is not affected by this increase in the number of pixels. As the number of pixels is increased, the average power consumption will increase sublinearly, because the sum output current (the dominant source of prolonged power consumption) can be maintained at approximately the same absolute value regardless of the number of pixels integrated. However, the periodic variation of the output with the stimulus will be decreased, the precision of the FOE output will be improved, and the need for temporal averaging will be reduced.

Acknowledgments

This research was supported by the Caltech Center for Neuromorphic Systems Engineering as a part of the National Science Foundation's Engineering Research Center program, as well as by the Office of Naval Research. The authors wish to thank Rainer Deutschmann for stimulating discussions.

References

[DHK97] R. Deutschmann, C. Higgins, and C. Koch. Real-time analog VLSI sensors for 2-D direction of motion. In *Proceedings of the Int. Conf. on Artificial Neural Networks*, pages 1163–1168. Springer Verlag, 1997.

[DW98] R. A. Deutschmann and O. G. Wenisch. Compressive computation in analog VLSI motion sensors. In *Proceedings of Deutsche Arbeitsgemeinschaft für Mustererkennung*, 1998.

[FA97] C. Fermüller and Y. Aloimonos. On the geometry of visual correspondence. *International Journal of Computer Vision*, 21(3):233–247, 1997.

[IKK96] G. Indiveri, J. Kramer, and C. Koch. Parallel analog VLSI architectures for computation of heading direction and time-to-contact. In D.S. Touretzky, M.C. Mozer, and M.E. Hasselmo, editors, *Advances in Neural Information Processing Systems*, volume 8, pages 720–726, Cambridge, MA, 1996. MIT.

[McQ96] I. McQuirk. An analog VLSI chip for estimating the focus of expansion. Technical Report 1577, Massachusetts Institute of Technology, Artificial Intelligence Laboratory, 1996.

[WH88] W. Warren and D. Hannon. Direction of self-motion is perceived from optical-flow. *Nature*, 336(6195):162–163, 1988.

Computation of Smooth Optical Flow in a Feedback Connected Analog Network

Alan Stocker *
Institute of Neuroinformatics
University and ETH Zürich
Winterthurerstrasse 190
8057 Zürich, Switzerland

Rodney Douglas
Institute of Neuroinformatics
University and ETH Zürich
Winterthurerstrasse 190
8057 Zürich, Switzerland

Abstract

In 1986, Tanner and Mead [1] implemented an interesting constraint satisfaction circuit for global motion sensing in aVLSI. We report here a new and improved aVLSI implementation that provides smooth optical flow as well as global motion in a two dimensional visual field. The computation of optical flow is an ill-posed problem, which expresses itself as the aperture problem. However, the optical flow can be estimated by the use of regularization methods, in which additional constraints are introduced in terms of a global energy functional that must be minimized. We show how the algorithmic constraints of Horn and Schunck [2] on computing smooth optical flow can be mapped onto the physical constraints of an equivalent electronic network.

1 Motivation

The perception of apparent motion is crucial for navigation. Knowledge of local motion of the environment relative to the observer simplifies the calculation of important tasks such as time-to-contact or focus-of-expansion. There are several methods to compute optical flow. They have the common problem that their computational load is large. This is a severe disadvantage for autonomous agents, whose computational power is restricted by energy, size and weight. Here we show how the global regularization approach which is necessary to solve for the ill-posed nature of computing optical flow, can be formulated as a local feedback constraint, and implemented as a physical analog device that is computationally efficient.

---

* correspondence to: alan@ini.phys.ethz.ch

2 Smooth Optical Flow

Horn and Schunck [2] defined optical flow in relation to the spatial and temporal changes in image brightness. Their model assumes that the total image brightness $E(x, y, t)$ does not change over time;

$$\frac{d}{dt} E(x, y, t) = 0. \tag{1}$$

Expanding equation (1) according to the chain rule of differentiation leads to

$$F \equiv \frac{\delta}{\delta x} E(x, y, t) u + \frac{\delta}{\delta y} E(x, y, t) v + \frac{\delta}{\delta t} E(x, y, t) = 0, \tag{2}$$

where $u = dx/dt$ and $v = dy/dt$ represent the two components of the local optical flow vector.

Since there is one equation for two unknowns at each spatial location, the problem is ill-posed, and there are an infinite number of possible solutions lying on the *constraint line* for every location (x, y). However, by introducing an additional constraint the problem can be regularized and a unique solution can be found.

For example, Horn and Schunck require the optical flow field to be smooth. As a measure of smoothness they choose the squares of of the spatial derivatives of the flow vectors,

$$S^2 = \left(\frac{\delta u}{\delta x}\right)^2 + \left(\frac{\delta u}{\delta y}\right)^2 + \left(\frac{\delta v}{\delta x}\right)^2 + \left(\frac{\delta v}{\delta y}\right)^2. \tag{3}$$

One can also view this constraint as introducing *a priori* knowledge: the closer two points are in the image space the more likely they belong to the projection of the same object. Under the assumption of rigid objects undergoing translational motion, this constraint implies that the points have the same, or at least very similar motion vectors. This assumption is obviously not valid at boundaries of moving objects, and so this algorithm fails to detect motion discontinuities [3].

The computation of smooth optical flow can now be formulated as the minimization problem of a global energy functional,

$$\iint \underbrace{F^2 + \lambda S^2}_{L} \, dx \, dy \longrightarrow min \tag{4}$$

with F and S^2 as in equation (2) and (3) respectively. Thus, we exactly apply the approach of *standard regularization theory* [4]:

$$\mathbf{A}\mathbf{x} = \mathbf{y} \qquad \qquad \text{y: data}$$
$$\mathbf{x} = \mathbf{A}^{-1}\mathbf{y} \qquad \qquad \text{inverse problem, ill-posed}$$
$$\| \mathbf{A}\mathbf{x} - \mathbf{y} \| + \lambda \| \mathbf{P} \| = min \qquad \qquad \text{regularization}$$

The regularization parameter, λ, controls the degree of smoothing of the solution and its closeness to the data. The norm, $\| \cdot \|$, is quadratic. A difference in our case is that $\mathbf{A}$ is not constant but depends on the data. However, if we consider motion on a discrete time-axis and look at snapshots rather than continuously changing images, $\mathbf{A}$ is *quasi-stationary*.[1] The energy functional (4) is convex and so, a simple numerical technique like gradient descent would be able to find the global minimum. To compute optical flow while preserving motion discontinuities one can modify the energy functional to include a binary line process that prevents smoothing over discontinuities [4]. However, such an functional will not be convex. Gradient descent methods would probably fail to find the global amongst all local minima and other methods have to be applied.

---

[1] In the aVLSI implementation this requires a much shorter settling time constant for the network than the brightness changes in the image.

3 A Physical Analog Model

3.1 Continuous space

Standard regularization problems can be mapped onto electronic networks consisting of conductances and capacitors [5]. Hutchinson et al. [6] showed how resistive networks can be used to compute optical flow and Poggio et al. [7] introduced electronic network solutions for second-order-derivative optic flow computation. However, these proposed network architectures all require complicated and sometimes negative conductances although Harris et al. [8] outlined a similar approach as proposed in this paper independently. Furthermore, such networks were not implemented practically, whereas our implementation with constant nearest neighbor conductances is intuitive and straightforward.
Consider equation (4):
$$L = L(u, v, \nabla u, \nabla v, x, y).$$
The *Lagrange function* L is sufficiently regular ($L \in C^2$), and thus it follows from calculus of variation that the solution of equation (4) also suffices the linear Euler-Lagrange equations
$$\lambda \nabla^2 u - E_x(E_x u + E_y v + E_t) = 0 \qquad (5)$$
$$\lambda \nabla^2 v - E_y(E_x u + E_y v + E_t) = 0.$$
The Euler-Lagrange equations are only necessary conditions for equation (4). The sufficient condition for solutions of equations (5) to be a weak minimum is the strong Legendre-condition, that is
$$L_{\nabla u \nabla u} > 0 \quad \text{and} \quad L_{\nabla v \nabla v} > 0,$$
which is easily shown to be true.

3.2 Discrete Space – Mapping to Resistive Network

By using a discrete five-point approximation of the Laplacian ∇^2 on a regular grid, equations (5) can be rewritten as
$$\lambda(u_{i+1,j} + u_{i-1,j} + u_{i,j+1} + u_{i,j-1} - 4u_{i,j}) - E_{x_{i,j}}(E_{x_{i,j}} u_{i,j} + E_{y_{i,j}} v_{i,j} + E_{t_{i,j}}) = 0$$
$$\lambda(v_{i+1,j} + v_{i-1,j} + v_{i,j+1} + v_{i,j-1} - 4v_{i,j}) - E_{y_{i,j}}(E_{x_{i,j}} u_{i,j} + E_{y_{i,j}} v_{i,j} + E_{t_{i,j}}) = 0$$
where i and j are the indices for the sampling nodes. Consider a single node of the resistive network shown in Figure 1:

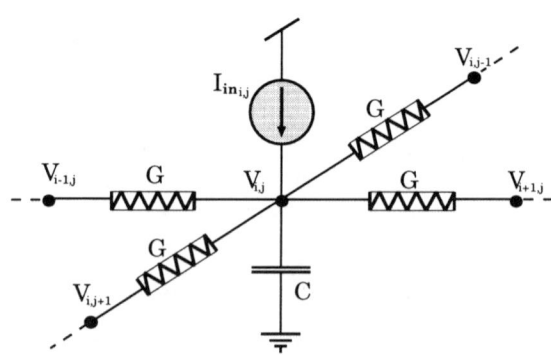

Figure 1: Single node of a resistive network.

From Kirchhoff's law it follows that
$$C \frac{dV_{i,j}}{dt} = G(V_{i+1,j} + V_{i-1,j} + V_{i,j+1} + V_{i,j-1} - 4V_{i,j}) + I_{in_{i,j}} \qquad (7)$$

where $V_{i,j}$ represents the voltage and $I_{in_{i,j}}$ the input current. G is the conductance between two neighboring nodes and C the node capacitance.

In steady state, equation (7) becomes

$$G(V_{i+1,j} + V_{i-1,j} + V_{i,j+1} + V_{i,j-1} - 4V_{i,j}) + I_{in_{i,j}} = 0. \tag{8}$$

The analogy with equations (6) is obvious:

$$\begin{aligned}
G &\longleftrightarrow \lambda \\
Iu_{in_{i,j}} &\longleftrightarrow -E_{x_{i,j}}(E_{x_{i,j}} u_{i,j} + E_{y_{i,j}} v_{i,j} + E_{t_{i,j}}) \\
Iv_{in_{i,j}} &\longleftrightarrow -E_{y_{i,j}}(E_{x_{i,j}} u_{i,j} + E_{y_{i,j}} v_{i,j} + E_{t_{i,j}})
\end{aligned} \tag{9}$$

To create the full system we use two parallel resistive networks in which the node voltages $U_{i,j}$ and $V_{i,j}$ represent the two components of the optical flow vector u and v. The input currents $Iu_{in_{i,j}}$ and $Iv_{in_{i,j}}$ are computed by a negative *recurrent feedback loop* modulated by the input data, which are the spatial and temporal intensity gradients.
Notice that the input currents are proportional to the deviation of the *local brightness constraint*: the less the local optical flow solution fits the data the higher the current $I_{in_{i,j}}$ will be to correct the solution and vice versa.
Stability and convergence of the network are guaranteed by Maxwell's minimum power principle [4, 9].

4 The Smooth Optical Flow Chip

4.1 Implementation

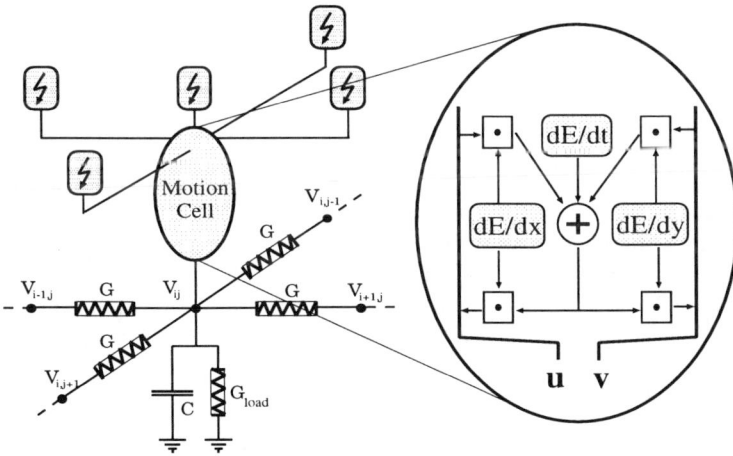

Figure 2: A single motion cell within the three layer network. For simplicity only one resistive network is shown.

The circuitry consists of three functional layers (Figure 2). The input layer includes an array of adaptive photoreceptors [10] and provides the derivatives of the image brightness to the second layer. The spatial gradients are the first-order linear approximation obtained by subtracting the two neighboring photoreceptor outputs. The second layer computes the input current to the third layer according to equations (9). Finally these currents are fed into the two resistive networks that report the optical flow components.
The schematics of the core of a single motion cell are drawn in Figure 3. The photoreceptor and the temporal differentiator are not shown as well as the other half of the circuitry that computes the y-component of the flow vector.

A few remarks are appropriate here: First, the two components of the optical flow vector have to be able to take on positive and negative values with respect to some reference potential. Therefore, a symmetrical circuit scheme is applied where the positive and negative (reference voltage) values are carried on separate signal lines. Thus, the actual value is encoded as the difference of the two potentials.

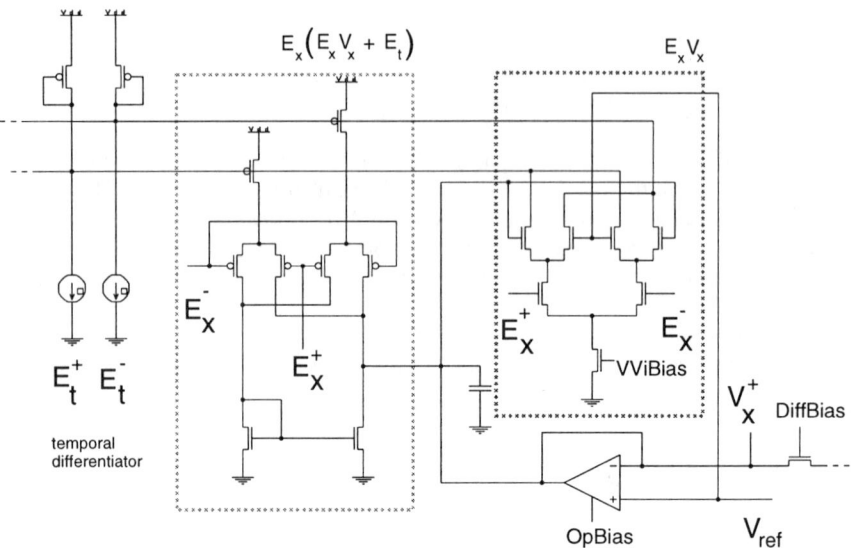

Figure 3: Cell core schematics; only the circuitry related to the computation of the x-component of the flow vector is shown.

Second, the limited linear range of the Gilbert multipliers leads to a narrow span of flow velocities that can be computed reliably. However, the tuning can be such that the operational range is either at high or very low velocities. Newer implementations are using modified multipliers with a larger linear range.

Third, consider a single motion cell (Figure 2). In principle, this cell would be able to satisfy the local constraint perfectly. In practice (see Figure 3), the finite output impedance of the p-type Gilbert multiplier slightly degrades this ideal solution by imposing an effective conductance G_{load}. Thus, a constant voltage on the capacitor representing a non-zero motion signal requires a net output current of the multiplier to maintain it. This requirement has two interesting consequences:

i) The reported optical flow is dependent on the spatial gradients (contrast). A single uncoupled cell according to Figure 2 has a steady state solution with

$$U_{i,j} \sim \frac{-E_{t_{i,j}} E_{x_{i,j}}}{(G_{load} + E_{x_{i,j}}^2 + E_{y_{i,j}}^2)} \quad \text{and} \quad V_{i,j} \sim \frac{-E_{t_{i,j}} E_{y_{i,j}}}{(G_{load} + E_{x_{i,j}}^2 + E_{y_{i,j}}^2)}$$

respectively. For the same object speed, the chip reports higher velocity signals for higher spatial gradients. Preferably, G_{load} should be as low as possible to minimize its influence on the solution.

ii) On the other hand, the locally ill-posed problem is now well-posed because G_{load} imposes a second constraint. Thus, the chip behaves sensibly in the case of low contrast input (small gradients), reporting zero motion where otherwise, unreliable high values would occur. This is convenient because the signal-to-noise ratio at low contrast is very poor. Furthermore, a single cell is forced to report the velocity on the constraint line with smallest absolute value, which is normal to the spatial gradient. That means that the chip reports *normal flow* when there is no neighbor connection. Since there is an trade-off between the robustness of the optical flow computation and a low conductance G_{load}, the follower-connected transconductance amplifier in our implementation allows us to control G_{load} above its small intrinsic value.

4.2 Results

The results reported below were obtained from a MOSIS tinychip containing a 7x7 array of motion cells each 325x325 λ^2 in size. The chip was fabricated in 1.2 μm technology at AMI.

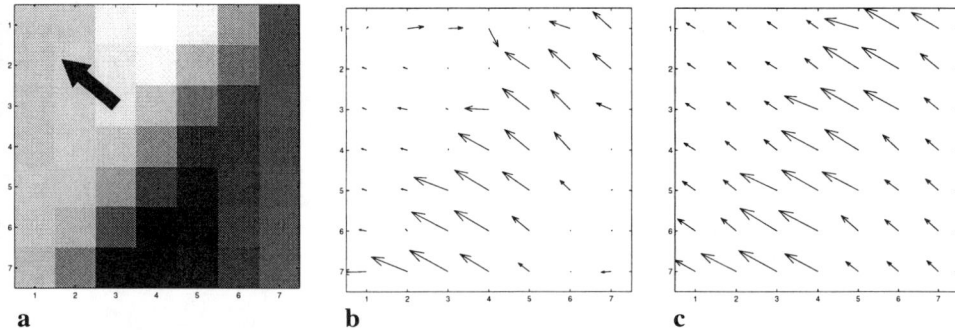

Figure 4: Smooth optical flow response of the chip to an left-upwards moving edge.
a: photoreceptor output, the arrow indicates the actual motion direction. **b**: weak coupling (small conductance G). **c**: strong coupling.

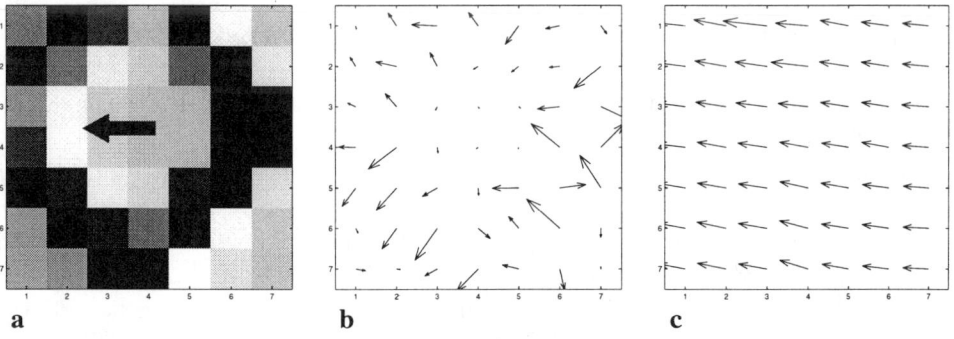

Figure 5: Response of the optical flow chip to a plaid stimulus moving towards the left: **a**: photoreceptor output; **b** shows the normal flow computation with disabled coupling between the motion cells in the network while in **c** the coupling strength is at maximum.

The chip is able to compute smooth optical flow in a qualitative manner. The smoothness can be set by adjusting the coupling conductances (Figure 4). Figure 5b presents the normal flow computation that occurs when the coupling between the motion cells is disabled. The limited resolution of this prototype chip together with the small size of the stimulus leads to a noisy response. However it is clear that the chip perceives the two gratings as separate moving objects with motion normal to their edge orientation. When the network conductance is set very high the chip performs a collective computation solving the aperture problem under the assumption of single object motion. Figure 5c shows how the chip can compute the correct motion of a plaid pattern.

5 Conclusion

We have presented here an aVLSI implementation of a network that computes 2D smooth optical flow. The strength of the resistive coupling can be varied continuously to obtain different degrees of smoothing, from a purely local up to a single global motion signal. The chip ideally computes smooth optical flow in the classical definition of Horn and Schunck. Instead of using negative and complex conductances we implemented a network solution where each motion cell is performing a local constraint satisfaction task in a recurrent negative feedback loop.
It is significant that the solution of a global energy minimization task can be achieved within a network of local constraint solving cells that do not have explicit access to the global computational goal.

Acknowledgments

This article is dedicated to Misha Mahowald. We would like to thank Eric Vittoz, Jörg Kramer, Giacomo Indiveri and Tobi Delbrück for fruitful discussions. We thank the Swiss National Foundation for supporting this work and MOSIS for chip fabrication.

References

[1] J. Tanner and C.A. Mead. An integrated analog optical motion sensor. In S.-Y. Kung, R. Owen, and G. Nash, editors, *VLSI Signal Processing, 2*, page 59 ff. IEEE Press, 1986.

[2] B.K. Horn and B.G. Schunck. Determining optical flow. *Artificial Intelligence*, 17:185–203, 1981.

[3] A. Yuille. Energy functions for early vision and analog networks. *Biological Cybernetics*, 61:115–123, 1989.

[4] T. Poggio, V. Torre, and C. Koch. Computational vision and regularization theory. *Nature*, 317(26):314–319, September 1985.

[5] B. K. Horn. Parallel networks for machine vision. Technical Report 1071, MIT AI Lab, December 1988.

[6] J. Hutchinson, C. Koch, J. Luo, and C. Mead. Computing motion using analog and binary resistive networks. *Computer*, 21:52–64, March 1988.

[7] T. Poggio, W. Yang, and V. Torre. Optical flow: Computational properties and networks, biological and analog. *The Computing Neuron*, pages 355–370, 1989.

[8] J.G. Harris, C. Koch, E. Staats, and J. Luo. Analog hardware for detecting discontinuities in early vision. *Int. Journal of Computer Vision*, 4:211–223, 1990.

[9] J. Wyatt. Little-known properties of resistive grids that are useful in analog vision chip designs. In C. Koch and H. Li, editors, *Vision Chips: Implementing Vision Algorithms with Analog VLSI Circuits*, pages 72–89. IEEE Computer Society Press, 1995.

[10] S.C. Liu. Silicon retina with adaptive filtering properties. In *Advances in Neural Information Processing Systems 10*, November 1997.

A High Performance k-NN Classifier Using a Binary Correlation Matrix Memory

Ping Zhou
zhoup@cs.york.ac.uk

Jim Austin
austin@cs.york.ac.uk

John Kennedy
johnk@cs.york.ac.uk

Advanced Computer Architecture Group
Department of Computer Science
University of York, York YO10 5DD, UK

Abstract

This paper presents a novel and fast k-NN classifier that is based on a binary CMM (Correlation Matrix Memory) neural network. A robust encoding method is developed to meet CMM input requirements. A hardware implementation of the CMM is described, which gives over 200 times the speed of a current mid-range workstation, and is scaleable to very large problems. When tested on several benchmarks and compared with a simple k-NN method, the CMM classifier gave less than 1% lower accuracy and over 4 and 12 times speed-up in software and hardware respectively.

1 INTRODUCTION

Pattern classification is one of most fundamental and important tasks, and a k-NN rule is applicable to a wide range of classification problems. As this method is too slow for many applications with large amounts of data, a great deal of effort has been put into speeding it up via complex pre-processing of training data, such as reducing training data (Dasarathy 1994) and improving computational efficiency (Grother & Candela 1997). This work investigates a novel k-NN classification method that uses a binary correlation matrix memory (CMM) neural network as a pattern store and match engine. Whereas most neural networks need a long iterative training time, a CMM is simple and quick to train. It requires only one-shot storage mechanism and simple binary operations (Willshaw & Buneman 1969), and it has highly flexible and fast pattern search ability. Therefore, the combination of CMM and k-NN techniques is likely to result in a generic and fast classifier. For most classification problems, patterns are in the form of multi-dimensional real numbers, and appropriate quantisation and encoding are needed to convert them into binary inputs to a CMM. A robust quantisation and encoding method is developed to meet requirements for CMM input codes, and to overcome the common problem of identical data points in many applications, e.g. background of images or normal features in a diagnostic problem.

Many research projects have applied the CMM successfully to commercial problems, e.g. symbolic reasoning in the AURA (Advanced Uncertain Reasoning Architecture) approach

(Austin 1996), chemical structure matching and post code matching. The execution of the CMM has been identified as the bottleneck. Motivated by the needs of these applications for a further high speed processing, the CMM has been implemented in dedicated hardware, i.e. the PRESENCE architecture. The primary aim is to improve the execution speed over conventional workstations in a cost-effective way.

The following sections discuss the CMM for pattern classification, describe the PRESENCE architecture (the hardware implementation of CMM), and present experimental results on several benchmarks.

2 BINARY CMM k-NN CLASSIFIER

The key idea (Figure 1) is to use a CMM to pre-select a small sub-set of training patterns from a large number of training data, and then to apply the k-NN rule to the sub-set. The CMM is fast but produces spurious errors as a side effect (Turner & Austin 1997); these are removed through the application of the k-NN rule. The architecture of the CMM classifier (Figure 1) includes an encoder (detailed in 2.2) for quantising numerical inputs and generating binary codes, a CMM pattern store and match engine and a conventional k-NN module as detailed below.

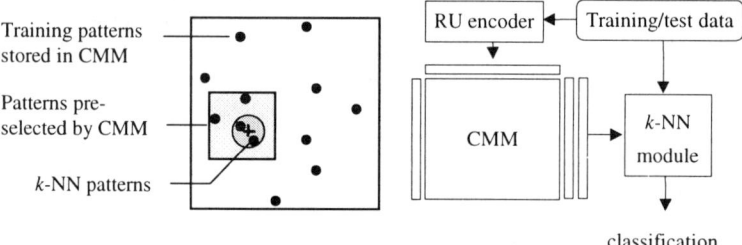

Figure 1: Architecture of the binary CMM k-NN classifier

2.1 PATTERN MATCH AND CLASSIFICATION WITH CMM

A correlation matrix memory is basically a single layer network with binary weights M. In the training process a unique binary vector or separator s_i is generated to label an unseen input binary vector p_i; the CMM learns their association by performing the following logical ORing operation:

$$M = \bigvee_i s_i^T p_i \quad (1)$$

In a recall process, for a given test input vector p_k, the CMM performs:

$$v_k = M p_k^T = \left(\bigvee_i s_i^T p_i \right) p_k^T \quad (2)$$

followed by thresholding v_k and recovering individual separators. For speed, it is appropriate to use a fixed thresholding method and the threshold is set to a level proportional to the number of '1' bits in the input pattern to allow an exact or partial match. To understand the recall properties of the CMM, consider the case where a known pattern p_k is represented, then Equation 2 can be written as the following when two different patterns are orthogonal to each other:

$$v_k = s_k^T p_k p_k^T + \bigvee_{i \neq k} s_i^T p_i p_k^T = n_p s_k^T \quad (3)$$

where n_p is a scalar, i.e. the number of '1' bits in p_k, and $p_i p_k^T = 0$ for $i \neq k$. Hence a perfect recall of s_k can be obtained by thresholding v_k at the level n_p. In practice 'partially orthogonal' codes may be used to increase the storage capacity of the CMM and the recall noise can be removed via appropriately thresholding v_k (as $p_i p_k^T \leq n_p$ for $i \neq k$)

and post-processing (e.g. applying k-NN rule). Sparse codes are usually used, i.e. only a few bits in s_k and p_i being set to '1', as this maximises the number of codes and minimises the computation time (Turner & Austin 1997). These requirements for input codes are often met by an encoder as detailed below.

The CMM exhibits an interesting 'partial match' property when the data dimensionality d is larger than one and input vector p_i consists of d concatenated components. If two different patterns have some common components, v_k also contains separators for partially matched patterns, which can be obtained at lower threshold levels. This partial or near match property is useful for pattern classification as it allows the retrieval of stored patterns that are close to the test pattern in Hamming distance.

From those training patterns matched by the CMM engine, a test pattern is classified using the k-NN rule. Distances are computed in the original input space to minimise the information loss due to quantisation and noise in the above match process. As the number of matches returned by the CMM is much smaller than the number of training data, the distance computation and comparison are dramatically reduced compared with the simple k-NN method. Therefore, the speed of the classifier benefits from fast training and matching of the CMM, and the accuracy gains from the application of the k-NN rule for reducing information loss and noise in the encoding and match processes.

2.2 ROBUST UNIFORM ENCODING

Figure 2 shows three stages of the encoding process. d-dimensional real numbers, x_i, are quantised as y_i; sparse and orthogonal binary vectors, c_i, are generated and concatenated to form a CMM input vector.

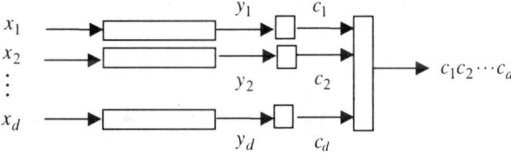

Figure 2: Quantisation, code generation and concatenation

CMM input codes should be distributed as uniformly as possible in order to avoid some parts of the CMM being used heavily while others are rarely used. The code uniformity is met at the quantisation stage. For a given set of N training samples in some dimension (or axis), it is required to divide the axis into N_b small intervals, called bins, such that they contain uniform numbers of data points. As the data often have a non-uniform distribution, the sizes of these bins should be different. It is also quite common for real world problems that many data points are identical. For instance, there are 11%-99.9% identical data in benchmarks used in this work. Our robust quantisation method described below is designed to cope with the above problems and to achieve a maximal uniformity.

In our method data points are first sorted in ascending order, N_i identical points are then identified, and the number of non-identical data points in each bin is estimated as $N_p = (N - N_i)/N_b$. Bin boundaries or partitions are determined as follows. The right boundary of a bin is initially set to the next N_p-th data point in the ordered data sequence; the number of identical points on both sides of the boundary is identified; these are either included in the current or next bin. If the number of non-identical data points in the last bin is N_l and $N_l \geq (N_p + N_b)$, N_p may be increased by $(N_l - N_p)/N_b$ and the above partition process may be repeated to increase the uniformity. Boundaries of bins obtained become parameters of the encoder in Figure 2. In general it is appropriate to choose N_b such that each bin contains a number of samples, which is larger than k nearest neighbours for the optimal classification.

3 THE PRESENCE ARCHITECTURE

The pattern match and store engine of the CMM k-NN classifier has been implemented using a novel hardware based CMM architecture, i.e. the PRESENCE.

3.1 ARCHITECTURE DESIGN

Important design decisions include the use of cheap memory, and not embedding both the weight storage and the training and testing in hardware (VLSI). This arises because the applications commonly use CMMs with over 100Mb of weight memory, which would be difficult and expensive to implement in custom silicon. VME and PCI are chosen to host on industry standard buses and to allow widespread application.

The PRESENCE architecture implements the control logic and accumulators, i.e. the core of the CMM. As shown in Figure 3a binary input selects rows from the CMM that are added, thresholded using L-max (Austin & Stonham 1987) or fixed global thresholding, and then returned to the host for further processing. The PRESENCE architecture shown in Figure 3b consists of a bus interface, a buffer memory which allows interleaving of memory transfer and operation of the PRESENCE system, a SATCON and SATSUM combination that accumulates and thresholds the weights. The data bus connects to a pair of memory spaces, each of which contains a control block, an input block and an output block. Thus the PRESENCE card is a memory mapping device, that uses interrupts to confirm the completion of each operation. For efficiency, two memory input/output areas are provided to be acted on from the external bus and used by the card. The control memory input block feeds to the control unit, which is a FPGA device. The input data are fed to the weights and the memory area read is then passed to a block of accumulators. In our current implementation the data width of each FPGA device is 32 bits, which allows us to add a 32 bit row from the weights memory in one cycle per device.

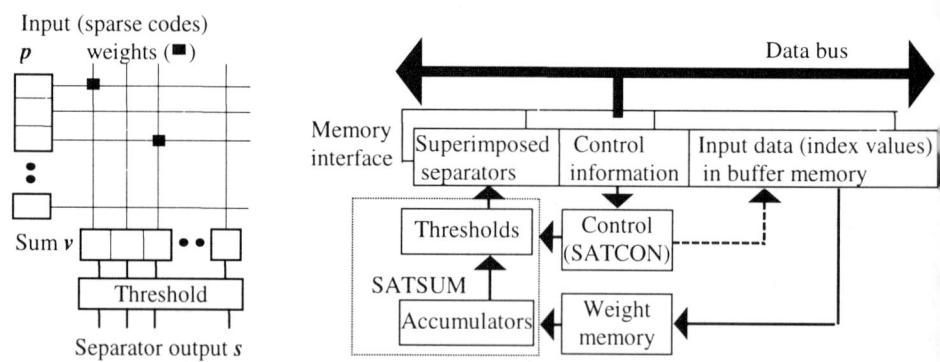

Figure 3: (a) correlation matrix memory, and (b) overall architecture of PRESENCE

Currently we have 16Mb of 25ns static memory implemented on the VME card, and 128 Mb of dynamic (60ns) memory on the PCI card. The accumulators are implemented along with the thresholding logic on another FPGA device (SATSUM). To enable the SATSUM processors to operate faster, a 5 stage pipeline architecture was used, and the data accumulation time is reduced from 175ns to 50ns. All PRESENCE operations are supported by a C++ library that is used in all AURA applications. The design of the SATCON allows many SATSUM devices to be used in parallel in a SIMD configuration. The VME implementation uses 4 devices per board giving a 128 bit wide data path. In addition the PCI version allows daisy chaining of cards allowing a 4 card set for a 512 bit wide data path. The complete VME card assembly is shown in Figure 4. The SATCON and SATSUM devices are mounted on a daughter board for simple upgrading and alteration. The weights memory, buffer memory and VME interface are held on the mother board.

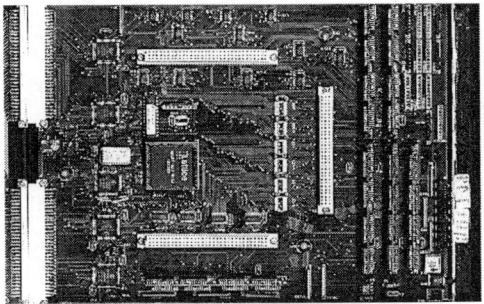 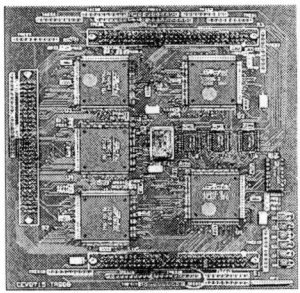

Figure 4: The VME based PRESENCE card (a) motherboard, and (b) daughterboard

3.2 PERFORMANCE

By an analysis of the state machines used in the SATCON device the time complexity of the approach can be calculated. Equation 4 is used to calculate the processing time, T, in seconds to recall the data with N index values, a separator size of S, R 32 bit SATSUM devices, and the clock period of C.

$$T = C[23 + ((s-1)/32R + 1)(N + 38 + 2R)] \qquad (4)$$

A comparison with a Silicon Graphics 133MHz R4600SC Indy in Table 1 shows the speed up of the matrix operation (Equation 2) for our VME implementation (128 bits wide) using a fixed threshold. The values for processing rate are given in millions of binary weight additions per-second (MW/s). The system cycle time needed to sum a row of weights into the counters (i.e. time to accumulate one line) is 50ns for the VME version and 100ns for the PCI version. In the PCI form, we will use 4 closely coupled cards, which result in a speed-up of 432. The build cost of the VME card was half the cost of the baseline SGI Indy machine, when using 4Mb of 20ns static RAM. In the PCI version the cost is greatly reduced through the use of dynamic RAM devices allowing a 128Mb memory to be used for the same cost, allowing only a 2x slower system with 32x as much memory per card (note that 4 cards used in Table 1 hold 512Mb of memory).

Table 1: Relative speed-up of the PRESENCE architecture

Platform	Processing Rate	Relative Speed
Workstation	11.8 MW/s	1
1 Card VME implementation	2557MW/s	216
Four card PCI system (estimate)	17,114MW/s	432

The training and recognition speed of the system are approximately equal. This is particularly useful in on-line applications, where the system must learn to solve the problem incrementally as it is presented. In particular, the use of the system for high speed reasoning allows the rules in the system to be altered without the long training times of other systems. Furthermore our use of the system for a k-NN classifier also allows high speed operation compared with a conventional implementation of the classifier, while still allowing very fast training times.

4 RESULTS ON BENCHMARKS

Performance of the robust quantisation method and the CMM classifier have been evaluated on four benchmarks consisting of large sets of real world problems from the Statlog project (Michie & Spiegelhalter 1994), including a satellite image database, letter image recognition database, shuttle data set and image segmentation data set. To visualise the result of quantisation, Figure 5a shows the distribution of numbers of data points of the 8th feature of the image segment data for equal-size bins. The distribution represents the inherent characteristics of the data. Figure 5b shows our robust quantisation (RQ) has resulted in the uniform distribution desired.

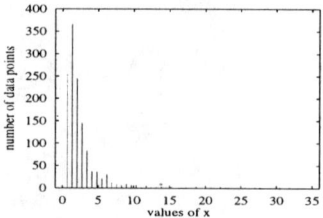 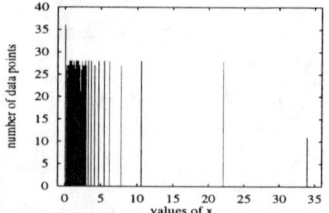

Figure 5: Distributions of the image segment data for (a) equal bins, (b) RQ bins

We compared the CMM classifier with the simple k-NN method, multi-layer perceptron (MLP) and radial basis function (RBF) networks (Zhou and Austin 1997). In the evaluation we used the CMM software libraries developed in the project AURA at the University of York. Between 1 and 3 '1' bits are set in input vectors and separators. Experiments were conducted to study influences of a CMM's size on classification rate (c-rate) on test data sets and speed-up measured against the k-NN method (as shown in Figure 6). The speed-up of the CMM classifier includes the encoding, training and test time. The effects of the number of bins N_b on the performance were also studied.

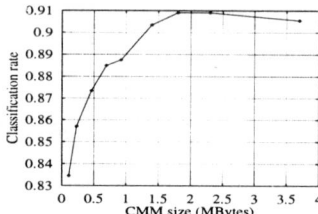 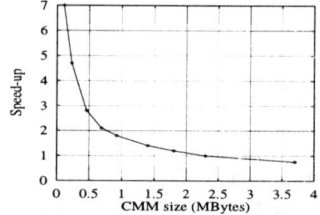

Figure 6: Effects of the CMM size on (a) c-rate and (b) speed-up on the satellite image data

Choices of the CMM size and the number of bins may be application dependent, for instance, in favour of the speed or accuracy. In the experiment it was required that the speed-up is not 4 times less and c-rate is not 1% lower than that of the k-NN method. Table 2 contains the speed-up of MLP and RBF networks and the CMM on the four benchmarks. It is interesting to note that the k-NN method needed no training. The recall of MLP and RBF networks was very faster but their training was much slower than that of the CMM classifier. The recall speed-up of the CMM was 6-23 times, and the overall speed-up (including training and recall time) was 4-15x. When using the PRESENCE, i.e. the dedicated CMM hardware, the speed of the CMM was further increased over 3 times. This is much less than the speed-up of 216 given in Table 1 because of recovering separators and k-NN classification are performed in software.

Table 2: Speed-up of MLP, RBF and CMM relative to the simple k-NN method

	Image segment		Satellite image		Letter		Shuttle	
method	training	test	training	Test	training	test	training	test
MLPN	0.04	18	0.2	28.4	0.2	96.5	4.2	587.2
RBFN	0.09	9	0.07	20.3	0.3	66.4	1.8	469.7
simple k-NN	-	1	-	1	-	1	-	1
CMM	18	9	15.8	5.7	24.6	6.8	43	23

The classification rates by the four methods are given in Table 3, which shows the CMM classifier performed only 0-1% less accurate than the k-NN method.

Table 3: Classification rates of four methods on four benchmarks

	Image segment	Satellite image	Letter	Shuttle
MLPN	0.950	0.914	0.923	0.998
RBFN	0.939	0.914	0.941	0.997
simple k-NN	0.956	0.906	0.954	0.999
CMM	0.948	0.901	0.945	0.999

5 CONCLUSIONS

A novel classifier is presented, which uses a binary CMM for storing and matching a large amount of patterns efficiently, and the k-NN rule for classification. The RU encoder converts numerical inputs into binary ones with the maximally achievable uniformity to meet requirements of the CMM. Experimental results on the four benchmarks show that the CMM classifier, compared with the simple k-NN method, gave slightly lower classification accuracy (less than 1% lower) and over 4 times speed in software and 12 times speed in hardware. Therefore our method has resulted in a generic and fast classifier.

This paper has also described a hardware implementation of a FPGA based chip set and a processor card that will support the execution of binary CMM. It has shown the viability of using a simple binary neural network to achieve high processing rates. The approach allows both recognition and training to be achieved at speeds well above two orders of magnitude faster than conventional workstations at a much lower cost than the workstation. The system is scaleable to very large problems with very large weight arrays. Current research is aimed at showing that the system is scaleable, evaluating methods for the acceleration of the pre- and post processing tasks and considering greater integration of the elements of the processor through VLSI. For more details of the AURA project and the hardware described in this paper see http://www.cs.york.ac.uk/arch/nn/aura.html.

Acknowledgements

We acknowledge British Aerospace and the Engineering and Physical Sciences Research Council (grant no. GR/K 41090 and GR/L 74651) for sponsoring the research. Our thanks are given to R Pack, A Moulds, Z Ulanowski, R Jennison and K Lees for their support.

References

Willshaw, D.J., Buneman, O.P. & Longuet-Higgins, H.C. (1969) Non-holographic associative memory. Nature, Vol. 222, p960-962.

Austin, J. (1996) AURA, A distributed associative memory for high speed symbolic reasoning. In: Ron Sun (ed), Connectionist Symbolic Integration. Kluwer.

Turner, M. & Austin, J. (1997) Matching performance of binary correlation matrix memories. Neural Networks; 10:1637-1648.

Dasarathy, B.V. (1994) Minimal consistent set (MCS) identification for optimal nearest neighbor decision system design. IEEE Trans. Systems Man Cybernet; 24:511-517.

Grother, P.J., Candela, G.T. & Blue, J.L. (1997) Fast implementations of nearest neighbor classifiers. Pattern Recognition; 30:459-465.

Austin, J., Stonham, T.J. (1987) An associative memory for use in image recognition and occlusion analysis. Image and Vision Computing; 5:251-261.

Michie, D., Spiegelhalter, D.J. & Taylor, C.C. (1994) Machine learning, neural and statistical classification (Chapter 9). New York, Ellis Horwood.

Zhou, P. & Austin J. (1998) Learning criteria for training neural network classifiers. Neural Computing and Applications Forum; 7:334-342.

PART VI
SPEECH, HANDWRITING AND SIGNAL PROCESSING

An entropic estimator for structure discovery

Matthew Brand
Mitsubishi Electric Research Laboratories, 201 Broadway, Cambridge MA 02139
brand@merl.com

Abstract

We introduce a novel framework for simultaneous structure and parameter learning in hidden-variable conditional probability models, based on an entropic prior and a solution for its maximum *a posteriori* (MAP) estimator. The MAP estimate minimizes uncertainty in all respects: cross-entropy between model and data; entropy of the model; entropy of the data's descriptive statistics. Iterative estimation extinguishes weakly supported parameters, compressing and sparsifying the model. Trimming operators accelerate this process by removing excess parameters and, unlike most pruning schemes, guarantee an increase in posterior probability. *Entropic estimation* takes a overcomplete random model and simplifies it, inducing the structure of relations between hidden and observed variables. Applied to hidden Markov models (HMMs), it finds a concise finite-state machine representing the hidden structure of a signal. We entropically model music, handwriting, and video time-series, and show that the resulting models are highly concise, structured, predictive, and *interpretable*: Surviving states tend to be highly correlated with meaningful partitions of the data, while surviving transitions provide a low-perplexity model of the signal dynamics.

1 An entropic prior

In entropic estimation we seek to maximize the information content of parameters. For conditional probabilities, parameters values near chance add virtually no information to the model, and are therefore wasted degrees of freedom. In contrast, parameters near the extrema $\{0,1\}$ are informative because they impose strong constraints on the class of signals accepted by the model. In Bayesian terms, our prior should assert that parameters that do not reduce uncertainty are improbable. We can capture this intuition in a surprisingly simple form: For a model of N conditional probabilities $\boldsymbol{\theta} = \{\theta_1, \ldots, \theta_N\}$ we write

$$P_e(\boldsymbol{\theta}) = \boldsymbol{\theta}^{\boldsymbol{\theta}} = \prod_i^N \theta_i^{\theta_i} = \exp\left[\sum_i^N \theta_i \log \theta_i\right] = e^{-H(\boldsymbol{\theta})} \tag{1}$$

whence we can see that the prior measures a model's freedom from ambiguity ($H(\boldsymbol{\theta})$ is an entropy measure). Applying $P_e(\cdot)$ to a multinomial yields the posterior

$$P_e(\boldsymbol{\theta}|\boldsymbol{\omega}) \propto \frac{P(\boldsymbol{\omega}|\boldsymbol{\theta})P_e(\boldsymbol{\theta})}{P(\boldsymbol{\omega})} \propto \left[\prod_i \theta_i^{\omega_i}\right] \frac{P_e(\boldsymbol{\theta})}{P(\boldsymbol{\omega})} \propto \prod_i \theta_i^{\theta_i + \omega_i} \tag{2}$$

where ω_i is evidence for event type i. With extensive evidence this distribution converges to "fair"(ML) odds for $\boldsymbol{\omega}$, but with scant evidence it skews to stronger odds.

1.1 MAP estimator

To obtain MAP estimates we set the derivative of log-posterior to zero, using Lagrange multipliers to ensure $\sum_i \theta_i = 1$,

$$0 = \frac{\partial}{\partial \theta_i}\left(\log \prod_i \theta_i^{\omega_i+\theta_i} + \lambda\left(\sum_i \theta_i - 1\right)\right) = \sum_i \frac{\partial}{\partial \theta_i}(\omega_i + \theta_i)\log \theta_i + \lambda \sum_i \frac{\partial}{\partial \theta_i}\theta_i$$

$$= 1 + \frac{\omega_i}{\theta_i} + \log \theta_i + \lambda \quad (3)$$

We obtain θ_i by working backward from the Lambert W function, a multi-valued inverse function satisfying $W(x)e^{W(x)} = x$. Taking logarithms and setting $y = \log x$,

$$0 = -W(x) - \log W(x) + \log x = -W(e^y) - \log W(e^y) + y$$

$$= \frac{-1}{1/W(e^y)} + \log 1/W(e^y) + \log z + y - \log z$$

$$= \frac{-z}{z/W(e^y)} + \log z/W(e^y) + y - \log z \quad (4)$$

Setting $\theta_i = z/W(e^y)$, $y = 1 + \lambda + \log z$, and $z = -\omega_i$, eqn. 4 simplifies to eqn. 3, implying

$$\hat{\theta}_i = \frac{-\omega_i}{W(-\omega_i e^{1+\lambda})} \quad (5)$$

Equations 3 and 5 together yield a quickly converging fix-point equation for λ and therefore for the entropic MAP estimate. Solutions lie in the W_{-1} branch of Lambert's function. See [Brand, 1997] for methods we developed to calculate the little-known W function.

1.2 Interpretation

The negated log-posterior is equivalent to a sum of entropies:

$$-\log \prod_i \theta_i^{\theta_i + \omega_i} = -\sum_i (\theta_i + \omega_i) \log \theta_i$$

$$= -\sum_i (\theta_i \log \theta_i + \omega_i \log \theta_i - \omega_i \log \omega_i + \omega_i \log \omega_i)$$

$$= -\sum_i \theta_i \log \theta_i + \sum_i \omega_i \log \frac{\omega_i}{\theta_i} - \sum_i \omega_i \log \omega_i$$

$$= H(\boldsymbol{\theta}) + D(\boldsymbol{\omega}\|\boldsymbol{\theta}) + H(\boldsymbol{\omega}) \quad (6)$$

Maximizing $P_e(\boldsymbol{\theta}|\boldsymbol{\omega})$ minimizes entropy in all respects: the parameter entropy $H(\boldsymbol{\theta})$; the cross-entropy $D(\boldsymbol{\omega}\|\boldsymbol{\theta})$ between the parameters $\boldsymbol{\theta}$ and the data's descriptive statistics $\boldsymbol{\omega}$; and the entropy of those statistics $H(\boldsymbol{\omega})$, which are calculated relative to the structure of the model. Equivalently, the MAP estimator minimizes the expected coding length, making it a maximally efficient compressor of messages consisting of the model and the data coded relative to the model. Since compression involves separating essential from accidental structure, this can be understood as a form of noise removal. Noise inflates the apparent entropy of a sampled process; this systematically biases maximum likelihood (ML) estimates toward weaker odds, more so in smaller samples. Consequently, the entropic prior is a countervailing bias toward stronger odds.

1.3 Model trimming

Because the prior rewards sparse models, it is possible to remove weakly supported parameters from the model while improving its posterior probability, such that $P_e(\boldsymbol{\theta}\backslash\theta_i|\boldsymbol{X}) > P_e(\boldsymbol{\theta}|\boldsymbol{X})$. This stands in contrast to most pruning schemes, which typically try to minimize damage to the posterior. Expanding via Bayes rule and taking logarithms we obtain

$$h_i(\theta_i) = H(\boldsymbol{\theta}) - H(\boldsymbol{\theta}\backslash\theta_i) > \log P(\boldsymbol{X}|\boldsymbol{\theta}) - \log P(\boldsymbol{X}|\boldsymbol{\theta}\backslash\theta_i) \tag{7}$$

where $h_i(\theta_i)$ is the entropy due to θ_i. For small θ_i, we can approximate via differentials:

$$\theta_i \frac{\partial H(\boldsymbol{\theta})}{\partial \theta_i} > \theta_i \frac{\partial \log P(\boldsymbol{X}|\boldsymbol{\theta})}{\partial \theta_i} \tag{8}$$

By mixing the left- and right-hand sides of equations 7 and 8, we can easily identify trimmable parameters—those that contribute more to the entropy than the log-likelihood. E.g., for multinomials we set $h_i(\theta_i) = -\theta_i \log \theta_i$ against r.h.s. eqn. 8 and simplify to obtain

$$\theta_i < \exp\left[-\frac{\partial \log P(\boldsymbol{X}|\boldsymbol{\theta})}{\partial \theta_i}\right] \tag{9}$$

Parameters can be trimmed at any time during training; at convergence trimming can bump the model out of a local probability maximum, allowing further training in a lower-dimensional and possibly smoother parameter subspace.

2 Entropic HMM training and trimming

In entropic estimation of HMM transition probabilities, we follow the conventional E-step, calculating the probability mass for each transition to be used as evidence $\boldsymbol{\omega}$:

$$\gamma_{j,i} = \sum_{t}^{T-1} \alpha_j(t) P_{i|j} p_i(x_{t+1}) \beta_i(t+1) \tag{10}$$

where $P_{i|j}$ is the current estimate of the transition probability from state j to state i; $p_i(x_{t+1})$ is the output probability of observation x_{t+1} given state i, and $\boldsymbol{\alpha}, \boldsymbol{\beta}$ are obtained from forward-backward analysis and follow the notation of Rabiner [1989]. For the M-step, we calculate new estimates $\{\hat{P}_{i|j}\}_i = \boldsymbol{\theta}$ by applying the MAP estimator in §1.1 to each $\boldsymbol{\omega} = \{\gamma_{j,i}\}_i$. That is, $\boldsymbol{\omega}$ is a vector of the evidence for each kind of transition out of a single state; from this evidence the MAP estimator calculates probabilities $\boldsymbol{\theta}$. (In Baum-Welch re-estimation, the maximum-likelihood estimator simply sets $\hat{P}_{i|j} = \gamma_{j,i}/\sum_i \gamma_{j,i}$.)

In iterative estimation, e.g., expectation-maximization (EM), the entropic estimator drives weakly supported parameters toward zero, skeletonizing the model and concentrating evidence on surviving parameters until their estimates converge to near the ML estimate. Trimming appears to accelerate this process by allowing slowly dying parameters to leapfrog to extinction. It also averts numerical underflow errors.

For HMM transition parameters, the trimming criterion of eqn. 9 becomes

$$P_{i|j} < \exp\left[-\frac{\sum_{t=1}^{T-1} \alpha_j(t) p(x_{t+1}|s_i) \beta_i(t+1)}{\sum_k^N \alpha_k(T)}\right] = \exp\left[-\sum_{t=1}^{T-1} \gamma_j(t)\right] \tag{11}$$

where $\gamma_j(t)$ is the probability of state j at time t. The multinomial output distributions of a discrete-output HMM can be entropically re-estimated and trimmed in the same manner.

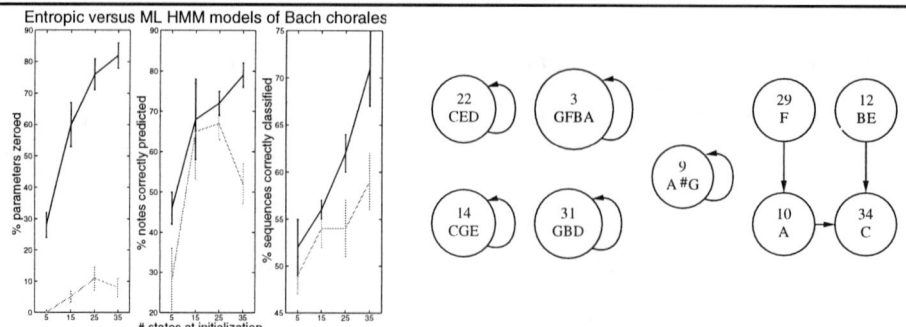

Figure 1: **Left:** Sparsification, classification, and prediction superiority of entropically estimated HMMs modeling Bach chorales. Lines indicate mean performance over 10 trials; error bars are 2 standard deviations. **Right:** High-probability states and subgraphs of interest from an entropically estimated 35-state chorale HMM. Tones output by each state are listed in order of probability. Extraneous arcs have been removed for clarity.

3 Structure learning experiments

To explore the practical utility of this framework, we will use entropically estimated HMMs as a window into the hidden structure of some human-generated time-series.

Bach Chorales: We obtained a dataset of melodic lines from 100 of J.S. Bach's 371 surviving chorales from the UCI repository [Merz and Murphy, 1998], and transposed all into the key of C. We compared entropically and conventionally estimated HMMs in prediction and classification tasks, training both from identical random initial conditions and trying a variety of different initial state-counts. We trained with 90 chorales and testing with the remaining 10. In ten trials, all chorales were rotated into the test set. Figure 1 illustrates that despite substantial loss of parameters to sparsification, the entropically estimated HMMs were, on average, better predictors of notes. (Each test sequence was truncated to a random length and the HMMs were used to predict the first missing note.) They also were better at discriminating between test chorales and temporally reversed test chorales—challenging because Bach famously employed melodic reversal as a compositional device. With larger models, parameter-trimming became state-trimming: An average of 1.6 states were "pinched off" the 35-state models when all incoming transitions were deleted.

While the conventionally estimated HMMs were wholly uninterpretable, in the entropically estimated HMMs one can discern several basic musical structures (figure 1, right), including self-transitioning states that output only tonic (C-E-G) or dominant (G-B-D) triads, lower- or upper-register diatonic tones (C-D-E or F-G-A-B), and mordents (A-♯G-A). We also found chordal state sequences (F-A-C) and states that lead to the tonic (C) via the mediant (E) or the leading tone (B).

Handwriting: We used 2D Gaussian-output HMMs to analyze handwriting data. Training data, obtained from the UNIPEN web site [Reynolds, 1992], consisted of sequences of normalized pen-position coordinates taken at 5msec intervals from 10 different individuals writing the digits 0-9. The HMMs were estimated from identical data and initial conditions (random upper-diagonal transition matrices; random output parameters). The diagrams in Figure 2 depict transition graphs of two HMMs modeling the pen-strokes for the digit "5," mapped onto the data. Ellipses indicate each state's output probability iso-contours (receptive field); ×s and arcs indicate state dwell and transition probabilities, respectively, by their thicknesses. Entropic estimation induces an interpretable automaton that captures essential structure and timing of the pen-strokes. 50 of the 80 original transition parameters

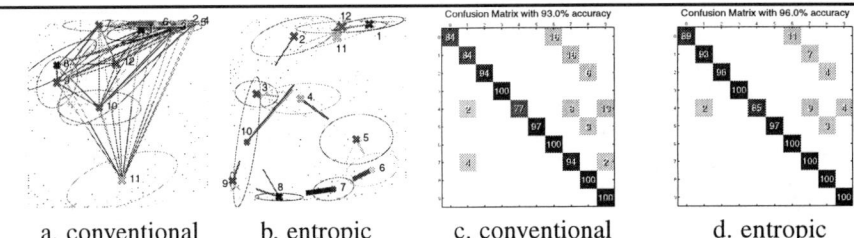

| a. conventional | b. entropic | c. conventional | d. entropic |

Figure 2: (a & b): State machines of conventionally and entropically estimated hidden Markov models of writing "5." (c & d): Confusion matrices for all digits.

were trimmed. Estimation without the entropic prior results in a wholly opaque model, in which none of the original dynamical parameters were trimmed. Model concision leads to better classification—the confusion matrices show cumulative classification error over ten trials with random initializations. Inspection of the parameters for the model in 2b showed that all writers began in states 1 or 2. From there it is possible to follow the state diagram to reconstruct the possible sequences of pen-strokes: Some writers start with the cap (state 1) while others start with the vertical (state 2); all loop through states 3-8 and some return to the top (via state 10) to add a horizontal (state 12) or diagonal (state 11) cap.

Office activity: Here we demonstrate a model of human activity learned from medium- to long-term ambient video. By activity, we mean spatio-temporal patterns in the pose, position, and movement of one's body. To make the vision tractable, we consider the activity of a single person in a relatively stable visual environment, namely, an office.

We track the gross shape and position of the office occupant by segmenting each image into foreground and background pixels. Foreground pixels are identified with reference to an acquired statistical model of the background texture and camera noise. Their ensemble properties such as motion or color are modeled via adaptive multivariate Gaussian distributions, re-estimated in each frame. A single bivariate Gaussian is fitted to the foreground pixels and we record the associated ellipse parameters [$mean_x$, $mean_y$, $\Delta mean_x$, $\Delta mean_y$, $mass$, $\Delta mass$, $elongation$, $eccentricity$]. Sequences of these observation vectors are used to train and test the HMMs.

Approximately 30 minutes of data were taken at 5Hz from an SGI IndyCam. Data was collected automatically and at random over several days by a program that started recording whenever someone entered the room after it had been empty 5+ minutes. Backgrounds were re-learned during absences to accommodate changes in lighting and room configuration. Prior to training, HMM states were initialized to tile the image with their receptive fields, and transition probabilities were initialized to prefer motion to adjoining tiles. Three sequences ranging from 1000 to 1900 frames in length were used for entropic training of 12, 16, 20, 25, and 30-state HMMs.

Entropic training yielded a substantially sparsified model with an easily interpreted state machine (see figure 3). Grouping of states into activities (done only to improve readability) was done by adaptive clustering on a proximity matrix which combined Mahalonobis distance and transition probability between states. The labels are the author's description of the set of frames claimed by each state cluster during forward-backward analysis of test data. Figure 4 illustrates this analysis, showing frames from a test sequence to which specific states are strongly tuned. State 5 (figure 3 right) is particularly interesting—it has a very non-specific receptive field, no self-transition, and an extremely low rate of occupancy. Instead of modeling data, it serves to *compress* the model by summarizing transition patterns that are common to several other states. The entropic model has proven to be quite superior for segmented new video into activities and detecting anomalous behavior.

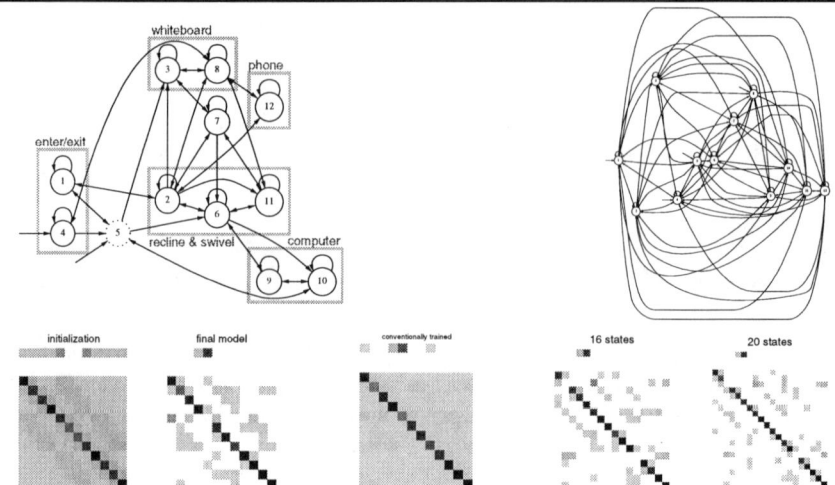

Figure 3: **Top:** The state machine found by entropic training (left) is easily labeled and interpreted. The state machine found by conventional training (right) is not, begin fully connected. **Bottom:** Transition matrices after (1) initialization, (2) entropic training, (3) conventional training, and (4 & 5) entropic training from larger initializations. The top row indicates initial probabilities of each state; each subsequent row indicates the transition probabilities out of a state. Color key: $\square = 0$; $\blacksquare = 1$. The state machines above are extracted from 2 & 3. Note that 4 & 5 show the same qualitative structure as 2, but sparser, while 3 shows no almost no structure at all.

Figure 4: Some sample frames assigned high state-specific probabilities by the model. Note that some states are tuned to velocities, hence the difference between states 6 and 11.

4 Related work

HMMs: The literature of structure-learning in HMMs is based almost entirely on generate-and-test algorithms. These algorithms work by merging [Stolcke and Omohundro, 1994] or splitting [Takami and Sagayama, 1991] states, then retraining the model to see if any advantage has been gained. Space constraints force us to summarize a recent literature review: There are now more than 20 variations and improvements on these approaches, plus some heuristic constructive algorithms (e.g., [Wolfertstetter and Ruske, 1995]). Though these efforts use a variety of heuristic techniques and priors (including MDL) to avoid detrimental model changes, much of the computation is squandered and reported run-times often range from hours to days. Entropic estimation is exact, monotonic, and orders of magnitude faster—only slightly longer than standard EM parameter estimation.

MDL: Description length minimization is typically done via gradient ascent or search via model comparison; few estimators are known. Rissanen [1989] introduced an estimator for binary fractions, from which Vovk [1995] derived an approximate estimator for Bernoulli models over discrete sample spaces. It approximates a special case of our exact estimator, which handles multinomial models in continuous sample spaces. Our framework provides a unified Bayesian framework for two issues that are often treated separately in MDL: estimating the number of parameters and estimating their values.

MaxEnt: Our prior has different premises and an effect opposite that of the "standard" MaxEnt prior $e^{-\alpha D(\theta\|\theta_0)}$. Nonetheless, our prior can be derived via MaxEnt reasoning from the premise that the expectation of the perplexity over all possible models is finite [Brand, 1998]. More colloquially, we almost always expect there to be learnable structure.

Extensions: For simplicity of exposition (and for results that are independent of model class), we have assumed prior independence of the parameters and taken $H(\theta)$ to be the combined parameter entropies of the model's component distributions. Depending on the model class, we can also provide variants of eqns. 1-8 for $H(\theta)$ =conditional entropy or $H(\theta)$ =entropy rate of the model. In Brand [1998] we present entropic MAP estimators for spread and covariance parameters with applications to mixtures-of-Gaussians, radial basis functions, and other popular models. In the same paper we generalize eqns. 1-8 with a temperature term, obtaining a MAP estimator that minimizes the free energy of the model. This folds deterministic annealing into EM, turning it into a quasi-global optimizer. It also provides a workaround for one known limitation of entropy minimization: It is inappropriate for learning from data that is atypical of the source process.

Open questions: Our framework is currently agnostic w.r.t. two important questions: Is there an optimal trimming policy? Is there a best entropy measure? Other questions naturally arise: Can we use the entropy to estimate the peakedness of the posterior distribution, and thereby judge the appropriateness of MAP models? Can we also directly minimize the entropy of the hidden variables, thereby obtaining discriminant training?

5 Conclusion

Entropic estimation is highly efficient hillclimbing procedure for simultaneously estimating model structure and parameters. It provides a clean Bayesian framework for minimizing all entropies associated with modeling, and an E-MAP algorithm that brings the structure of a randomly initialized model into alignment with hidden structures in the data via parameter extinction. The applications detailed here are three of many in which entropically estimated models have consistently outperformed maximum likelihood models in classification and prediction tasks. Most notably, it tends to produce interpretable models that shed light on the structure of relations between hidden variables and observed effects.

References

Brand, M. (1997). Structure discovery in conditional probability models via an entropic prior and parameter extinction. *Neural Computation* To appear; accepted 8/98.

Brand, M. (1998). Pattern discovery via entropy minimization. To appear in *Proc., Artificial Intelligence and Statistics #7*.

Merz, C. and Murphy, P. (1998). UCI repository of machine learning databases.

Rabiner, L. R. (1989). A tutorial on hidden Markov models and selected applications in speech recognition. *Proceedings of the IEEE*, 77(2):257–286.

Reynolds, D. (1992). Handwritten digit data. UNIPEN web site, http://hwr.nici.kun.nl/unipen/. Donated by HP Labs, Bristol, England.

Rissanen, J. (1989). *Stochastic Complexity and Statistical Inquiry*. World Scientific.

Stolcke, A. and Omohundro, S. (1994). Best-first model merging for hidden Markov model induction. TR-94-003, International Computer Science Institute, U.C. Berkeley.

Takami, J.-I. and Sagayama, S. (1991). Automatic generation of the hidden Markov model by successive state splitting on the contextual domain and the temporal domain. TR SP91-88, IEICE.

Vovk, V. G. (1995). Minimum description length estimators under the optimal coding scheme. In Vitányi, P., editor, *Proc. Computational Learning Theory / Europe*, pages 237–251. Springer-Verlag.

Wolfertstetter, F. and Ruske, G. (1995). Structured Markov models for speech recognition. In *International Conference on Acoustics, Speech, and Signal Processing*, volume 1, pages 544–7.

Coding time-varying signals using sparse, shift-invariant representations

Michael S. Lewicki*
lewicki@salk.edu

Terrence J. Sejnowski
terry@salk.edu

Howard Hughes Medical Institute
Computational Neurobiology Laboratory
The Salk Institute
10010 N. Torrey Pines Rd.
La Jolla, CA 92037

Abstract

A common way to represent a time series is to divide it into short-duration blocks, each of which is then represented by a set of basis functions. A limitation of this approach, however, is that the temporal alignment of the basis functions with the underlying structure in the time series is arbitrary. We present an algorithm for encoding a time series that does not require blocking the data. The algorithm finds an efficient representation by inferring the best temporal positions for functions in a kernel basis. These can have arbitrary temporal extent and are not constrained to be orthogonal. This allows the model to capture structure in the signal that may occur at arbitrary temporal positions and preserves the relative temporal structure of underlying events. The model is shown to be equivalent to a very sparse and highly overcomplete basis. Under this model, the mapping from the data to the representation is nonlinear, but can be computed efficiently. This form also allows the use of existing methods for adapting the basis itself to data. This approach is applied to speech data and results in a shift invariant, spike-like representation that resembles coding in the cochlear nerve.

1 Introduction

Time series are often encoded by first dividing the signal into a sequence of blocks. The data within each block is then fit with a standard basis such as a Fourier or wavelet. This has a limitation that the components of the bases are arbitrarily aligned with respect to structure in the time series. Figure 1 shows a short segment of speech data and the boundaries of the blocks. Although the structure in the signal is largely periodic, each large oscillation appears in a different position within the blocks and is sometimes split across blocks. This problem is particularly present for acoustic events with sharp onset, such as plosives in speech. It also presents

---

*To whom correspondence should be addressed.

difficulties for encoding the signal efficiently, because any basis that is adapted to the underlying structure must represent all possible phases. This can be somewhat circumvented by techniques such as windowing or averaging sliding blocks, but it would be more desirable if the representation were *shift invariant*.

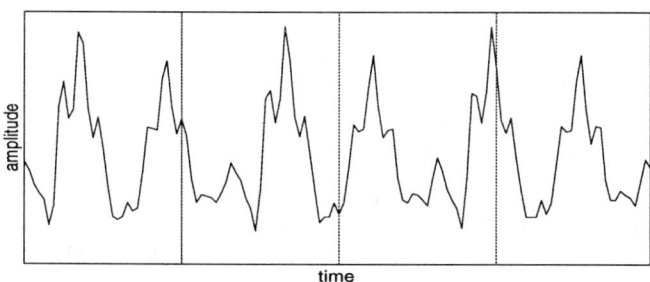

Figure 1: Blocking results in arbitrary phase alignment the underlying structure.

2 The Model

Our goal is to model a signal by using a small set of *kernel* functions that can be placed at arbitrary time points. Ultimately, we want to find the minimal set of functions and time points that fit the signal within a given noise level. We expect this type of model to work well for signals composed of events whose onset can occur at arbitrary temporal positions. Examples of these include, musical instruments sounds with sharp attack or plosive sounds in speech.

We assume time series $x(t)$ is modeled by

$$x(t) = \sum_i s_i \phi_{m[i]}(t - \tau_i) + \epsilon(t), \qquad (1)$$

where τ_i indicates the temporal position of the ith kernel function, $\phi_{m[i]}$, which is scaled by s_i. The notation $m[i]$ represents an index function that specifies which of the M kernel functions is present at time τ_i. A single kernel function can occur at multiple times during the time series. Additive noise at time t is given by $\epsilon(t)$.

A more general way to express (1) is to assume that the kernel functions exist at all time points during the signal, and let the non-zero coefficients determine the positions of the kernel functions. In this case, the model can be expressed in convolutional form

$$\begin{align}x(t) &= \sum_m \int s_m(\tau)\phi_m(t-\tau)d\tau + \epsilon(t) & (2)\\ &= \sum_m s_m(t) * \phi_m(t) + \epsilon(t), & (3)\end{align}$$

where $s_m(\tau)$ is the coefficient at time τ for kernel function ϕ_m.

It is also helpful to express the model in matrix form using a discrete sampling of the continuous time series:

$$x = As + \epsilon. \qquad (4)$$

The basis matrix, A, is defined by

$$A = [C(\phi_1)\, C(\phi_2) \cdots C(\phi_M)], \tag{5}$$

where $C(a)$ is an N-by-N circulant matrix parameterized by the vector a. This matrix is constructed by replicating the kernel functions at each sample position

$$C(a) = \begin{bmatrix} a_0 & a_{N-1} & \cdots & a_2 & a_1 \\ a_1 & a_0 & \cdots & a_3 & a_2 \\ \cdots & & \cdots & & \cdots \\ a_{N-2} & a_{N-3} & \cdots & a_0 & a_{N-1} \\ a_{N-1} & a_{N-2} & \cdots & a_1 & a_0 \end{bmatrix} \tag{6}$$

The kernels are zero padded to be of length N. The length of each kernel is typically much less than the length of the signal, making A very sparse. This can be viewed as a special case of a Toeplitz matrix. Note that the size of A is MN-by-N, and is thus an example of an overcomplete basis, i.e. a basis with more basis functions than dimensions in the data space (Simoncelli et al., 1992; Coifman and Wickerhauser, 1992; Mallat and Zhang, 1993; Lewicki and Sejnowski, 1998).

3 A probabilistic formulation

The optimal coefficient values for a signal are found by maximizing the posterior distribution

$$\hat{s} = \arg\max_{s} P(s|x, A) = \arg\max_{s} P(x|A, s) P(s) \tag{7}$$

where $\hat{s}$ is the most probable representation of the signal. Note that omission of the normalizing constant $P(x|A)$ does not change the location of the maximum. This formulation of the problem offers the advantage that the model can fit more general types of distributions and naturally "denoises" the signal. Note that the mapping from x to $\hat{s}$ is *nonlinear* with non-zero additive noise and an overcomplete basis (Chen et al., 1996; Lewicki and Sejnowski, 1998). Optimizing (7) essentially selects out the subset of basis functions that best account for the data.

To define a probabilistic model, we follow previous conventions for linear generative models with additive noise (Cardoso, 1997; Lewicki and Sejnowski, 1998). We assume the noise, ϵ, to have a Gaussian distribution which yields a data likelihood for a given representation of

$$\log P(x|A, s) \propto -\frac{1}{2\sigma^2}(x - As)^2. \tag{8}$$

The function $P(s)$ describes the a priori distribution of the coefficients. Under the assumption that $P(s)$ is sparse (highly peaked around zero), maximizing (7) results in very few nonzero coefficients. A compact representation of $\hat{s}$ is to describe the values of the non-zero coefficients and their temporal positions

$$P(s) = \prod_m P(u_m, \tau_m) = \prod_{m=1}^{M} \prod_{i=1}^{n_m} P(u_{m,i}) P(\tau_{m,i}), \tag{9}$$

where the prior for the non-zero coefficient values, $u_{m,i}$, is assumed to be Laplacian, and the prior for the temporal positions (or intervals), $\tau_{m,i}$, is assumed to be a gamma distribution.

4 Finding the best encoding

A difficult challenge presented by the proposed model is finding a computationally tractable method for fitting it to the data. The brute-force approach of generating the basis matrix A generates an intractable number basis functions for signals of any reasonable length, so we need to look for ways of making the optimization of (7) more efficient. The gradient of the log posterior is given by

$$\frac{\partial}{\partial s} \log P(s|A,x) \propto A^T(x - As) + z(s), \tag{10}$$

where $z(s) = (\log P(s))'$. A basic operation required is $v = A^T u$. We saw that $x = As$ can be computed efficiently using convolution (2). Because A^T is also block circulant

$$A^T = \begin{bmatrix} C(\phi_1') \\ \ldots \\ C(\phi_M') \end{bmatrix} \tag{11}$$

where $\phi'(1:N) = \phi(N:-1:1)$. Thus, terms involving A^T can also be computed efficiently using convolution

$$v = A^T u = \begin{bmatrix} \phi_1(-t) * u(t) \\ \ldots \\ \phi_M(-t) * u(t) \end{bmatrix} \tag{12}$$

Obtaining an initial representation

An alternative approach to optimizing (7) is to make use of the fact that if the kernel functions are short enough in length, direct multiplication is faster than convolution, and that, for this highly overcomplete basis, most of the coefficients will be zero after being fit to the data. The central problem in encoding the signal then is to determine which coefficients are non-zero, ideally finding a description of the time series with the minimal number of non-zero coefficients. This is equivalent to determining the best set of temporal positions for each of the kernel functions (1).

A crucial step in this approach is to obtain a good initial estimate of the coefficients. One way to do this is to consider the projection of the signal onto each of the basis functions, i.e. $A^T x$. This estimate will be exact (i.e. zero residual error) in the case of zero noise and A orthogonal. For the non-orthogonal, overcomplete case the solution will be approximate, but for certain choices of the basis matrix, an exact representation can still be obtained efficiently (Daubechies, 1990; Simoncelli et al., 1992).

Figure 2 shows examples of convolving two different kernel functions with data. One disadvantage with this initial solution is that the coefficient functions $s_m^0(t)$ are not sparse. For example, even though the signal in figure 2a is composed of only three instances of the kernel function, the convolution is mostly non-zero.

A simple procedure for obtaining a better initial estimate of the most probable coefficients is to select the time locations of the maxima (or extrema) in the convolutions. These are positions where the kernel functions capture the greatest amount of signal structure and where the optimal coefficients are likely to be non-zero. This generates a large number of positions, but their number can be reduced further by selecting only those that contribute significantly, i.e. where the average power is greater than some fraction of the noise level. From these, a basis for the entire signal is constructed by replicating the kernel functions at the appropriate time positions.

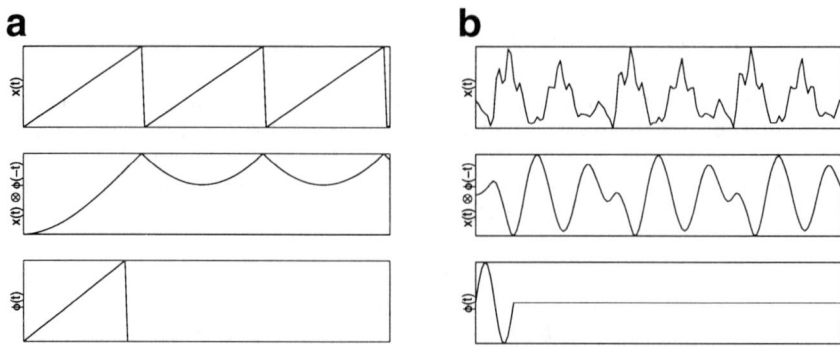

Figure 2: Convolution using the fast Fourier transform is an efficient way to select an initial solution for the temporal positions of the kernel functions. (a) The convolution of a sawtooth-shaped kernel function, $\phi(t)$, with a sawtooth waveform, $x(t)$. (b) A single period sine-wave kernel function convolved with a speech segment.

Once an initial estimate and basis are formed, the most probable coefficient values are estimated using a modified conjugate gradient procedure. The size of the generated basis does not pose a problem for optimization, because it is has very few non-zero elements (the number of which is roughly constant per unit time). This arises because each column is non-zero only around the position of the kernel function, which is typically much shorter in duration than the data waveform. This structure affords the use of sparse matrix routines for all the key computations in the conjugate gradient routine. After the initial fit, there typically are a large number of basis functions that give a very small contribution. These can be pruned to yield, after refitting, a more probable representation that has significantly fewer coefficients.

5 Properties of the representation

Figure 3 shows the results of fitting a segment of speech with a sine wave kernel. The 64 kernel functions were constructed using a single period of a sine function whose log frequencies were evenly distributed between 0 and Nyquist (4 kHz), which yielded kernel functions that were minimally correlated (they are not orthogonal because each has only one cycle and is zero elsewhere). The kernel function lengths varied between 2 and 64 samples. The plots show the positions of the non-zero coefficients superimposed on the waveform. The residual errors curves from the fitted waveforms are shown offset, below each waveform. The right axes indicate the kernel function number which increase with frequency. The dots show the starting position of the kernels with non-zero coefficients, with the dot size scaled according to the mean power contribution. This plot is essentially a time/frequency analysis, similar to a wavelet decomposition, but on a finer temporal scale.

Figure 3a shows that the structure in the coefficients repeats for each oscillation in the waveform. Adding a delay leaves the relative temporal structure of the non-zero coefficients mostly unchanged (figure 3b). The small variations between the two sets of coefficients are due to variations in the fitting of the small-magnitude coefficients. Representing the signal in figure 3b with a standard complete basis would result in a very different representation.

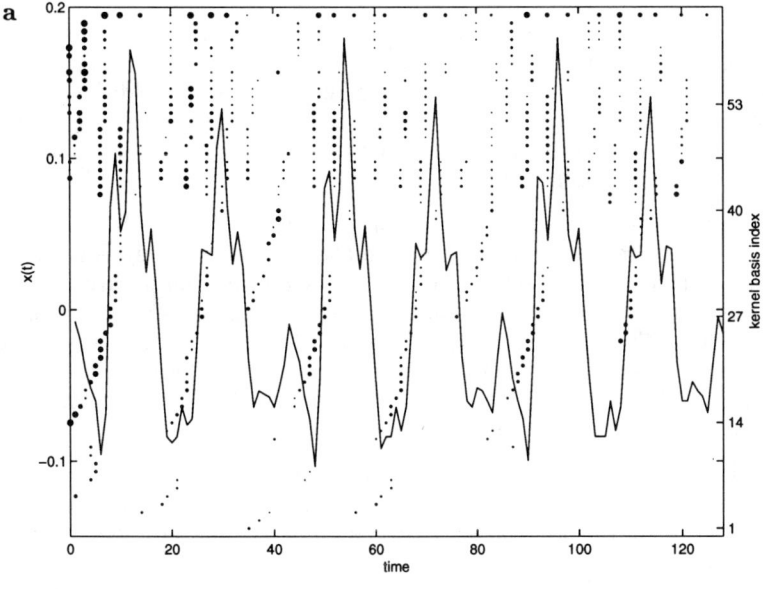

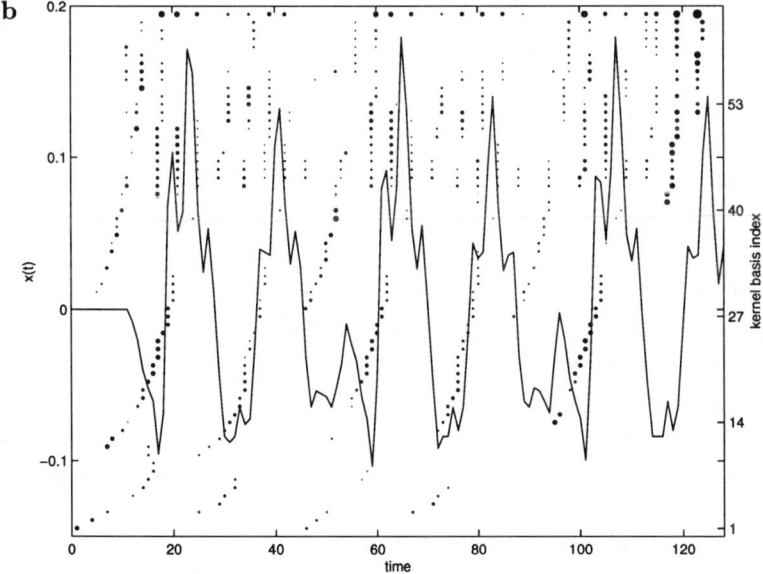

Figure 3: Fitting a shift-invariant model to a segment of speech, x(t). Dots indicate positions of kernels (right axis) with size scaled by the mean power contribution. Fitting error is plotted below speech signal.

6 Discussion

The model presented here can be viewed as an extension of the shiftable transforms of Simoncelli et al. (1992). One difference is that here no constraints are placed on the kernel functions. Furthermore, this model accounts for additive noise, which yields automatic signal denoising and provides sensible criteria for selecting significant coefficients. An important unresolved issue is how well the algorithm works for increasingly non-orthogonal kernels.

One interesting property of this representation is that it results in a spike-like representation. In the resulting set of non-zero coefficients, not only is their value important for representing the signal, but also their relative temporal position, which indicate when an underlying event has occurred. This shares many properties with cochlear models. The model described here also has capacity to have an overcomplete representation at any given timepoint, e.g. a kernel basis with an arbitrarily large number of frequencies. These properties make this model potentially useful for binaural signal processing applications.

The effectiveness of this method for efficient coding remains to be proved. A trivial example of a shift-invariant basis is a delta-function model. For a model to encode information efficiently, the representation should be non-redundant. Each basis function should "grab" as much structure in the data as possible and achieve the same level of coding efficiency for arbitrary shifts of the data. The matrix form of the model (4) suggests that it is possible to achieve this optimum by adapting the kernel functions themselves using the methods of Lewicki and Sejnowski (1998). Initial results suggest that this approach is promising. Beyond this, it is evident that modeling the higher-order structure in the coefficients themselves will be necessary both to achieve an efficient representation and to capture structure that is relevant to such tasks as speech recognition or auditory stream segmentation. These results are a step toward these goals.

Acknowledgments. We thank Tony Bell, Bruno Olshausen, and David Donoho for helpful discussions.

References

Cardoso, J.-F. (1997). Infomax and maximum likelihood for blind source separation. *IEEE Signal Processing Letters*, 4:109–111.

Chen, S., Donoho, D. L., and Saunders, M. A. (1996). Atomic decomposition by basis pursuit. Technical report, Dept. Stat., Stanford Univ., Stanford, CA.

Coifman, R. R. and Wickerhauser, M. V. (1992). Entropy-based algorithms for best basis selection. *IEEE Transactions on Information Theory*, 38(2):713–718.

Daubechies, I. (1990). The wavelet transform, time-frequency localization, and signal analysis. *IEEE Transactions on Information Theory*, 36(5):961–1004.

Lewicki, M. S. and Sejnowski, T. J. (1998). Learning overcomplete representations. *Neural Computation.* submitted.

Mallat, S. G. and Zhang, Z. F. (1993). Matching pursuits with time-frequency dictionaries. *IEEE Transactions on Signal Processing*, 41(12):3397–3415.

Simoncelli, E. P., Freeman, W. T., Adelson, E. H., and J., H. D. (1992). Shiftable multiscale transforms. *IEEE Trans. Info. Theory*, 38:587–607.

Controlling the Complexity of HMM Systems by Regularization

Christoph Neukirchen, Gerhard Rigoll
Department of Computer Science
Gerhard-Mercator-University Duisburg
47057 Duisburg, Germany
email: {chn,rigoll}@fb9-ti.uni-duisburg.de

Abstract

This paper introduces a method for regularization of HMM systems that avoids parameter overfitting caused by insufficient training data. Regularization is done by augmenting the EM training method by a penalty term that favors simple and smooth HMM systems. The penalty term is constructed as a mixture model of negative exponential distributions that is assumed to generate the state dependent emission probabilities of the HMMs. This new method is the successful transfer of a well known regularization approach in neural networks to the HMM domain and can be interpreted as a generalization of traditional state-tying for HMM systems. The effect of regularization is demonstrated for continuous speech recognition tasks by improving overfitted triphone models and by speaker adaptation with limited training data.

1 Introduction

One general problem when constructing statistical pattern recognition systems is to ensure the capability to generalize well, i.e. the system must be able to classify data that is not contained in the training data set. Hence the classifier should learn the true underlying data distribution instead of overfitting to the few data examples seen during system training. One way to cope with the problem of overfitting is to balance the system's complexity and flexibility against the limited amount of data that is available for training.

In the neural network community it is well known that the amount of information used in system training that is required for a good generalization performance should be larger than the number of adjustable weights (Baum, 1989). A common method to train a large size neural network sufficiently well is to reduce the number of adjustable parameters either by removing those weights that seem to be less important (in (le Cun, 1990) the sensitivity of individual network weights is estimated by the second order gradient) or by sharing the weights among many network connections (in (Lang, 1990) the connections that share identical weight values are determined in advance by using prior knowledge about invariances in the problem to be solved). A second approach to avoid overfitting in neural networks is to make use of regularization methods. Regularization adds an extra term to the training objective function that penalizes network complexity. The simplest regularization method is weight decay (Plaut, 1986) that assigns high penalties to large weights. A more complex regularization term is used in soft weight-sharing (Nowlan, 1992) by favoring neural network weights that fall into a finite set of small weight-clusters. The traditional neural weight sharing technique can be interpreted as a special case of soft weight-sharing regularization when the cluster variances tend towards zero.

In continuous speech recognition the Hidden Markov Model (HMM) method is common. When using detailed context-dependent triphone HMMs, the number of HMM-states and parameters to estimate in the state-dependent probability density functions (pdfs) is increasingly large and overfitting becomes a serious problem. The most common approach to balance the complexity of triphone HMM systems against the training data set is to reduce the number of parameters by tying, i.e. parameter sharing (Young, 1992). A popular sharing method is state-tying with selecting the HMM-states to be tied in advance, either by data-driven state-clustering based on a pdf-dependent distance metric (Young, 1993), or by constructing binary decision trees that incorporate higher phonetic knowledge (Bahl, 1991). In these methods, the number of state-clusters and the decision tree sizes, respectively, must be chosen adequately to match the training data size. However, a possible drawback of both methods is that two different states may be selected to be tied (and their pdfs are forced to be identical) although there is enough training data to estimate the different pdfs of both states sufficiently well. In the following, a method to reduce the complexity of general HMM systems based on a regularization term is presented. Due to its close relationship to the soft weight-sharing method for neural networks this novel approach can be interpreted as soft state-tying.

2 Maximum likelihood training in HMM systems

Traditionally, the method most commonly used to determine the set of adjustable parameters Θ in a HMM system is maximum likelihood (ML) estimation via the expectation maximization (EM) algorithm. If the training observation vector sequence is denoted as $X = (\mathbf{x}(1), \ldots, \mathbf{x}(T))$ and the corresponding HMM is denoted as W the ML estimator is given by:

$$\hat{\theta}^{ML} = \arg\max_\theta \{\log p_\Theta(X|W)\} \tag{1}$$

In the following, the total number of different HMM states is given by K. The emission pdf of the k-th state is denoted as $b_k(\mathbf{x})$; for continuous HMMs $b_k(\mathbf{x})$ is a mixture of Gaussian pdfs most commonly; in the case of discrete HMMs the observation vector $\mathbf{x}$ is mapped by a vector quantizer (VQ) on the discrete VQ-label $\hat{m}(\mathbf{x})$ and the emission pdf is replaced by the discrete output probability $b_k(\hat{m})$. By the forward-backward algorithm the probabilistic state counts $\gamma_k(t)$ can be determined for each training observation and the log-likelihood over the training data can be decomposed into the auxiliary function $Q(\Theta)$ optimized in the EM steps (state transition probabilities are neglected here):

$$Q(\Theta) = \sum_{t=1}^{T} \sum_{k=1}^{K} \gamma_k(t) \cdot \log b_k(\mathbf{x}(t)) \tag{2}$$

Sometimes, the observation vector $\mathbf{x}$ is split up into several independent streams. If the total number of streams is given by Z, the features in the z-th stream comprise the subvector $\mathbf{x}^{(z)}$ and in the case of application of a VQ the corresponding VQ label is denoted as $\hat{m}^{(z)}(\mathbf{x}^{(z)})$.

The observation subvectors in different streams are assumed to be statistically independent thus the states' pdfs can be written as:

$$b_k(\mathbf{x}) = \prod_{z=1}^{Z} b_k^{(z)}(\mathbf{x}^{(z)}) \qquad (3)$$

3 A complexity measure for HMM systems

When using regularization methods to train the HMM system, the traditional objective training function $Q(\Theta)$ is augmented by a complexity penalization term Ω and the new optimization problem becomes:

$$\hat{\theta}^{reg} = \mathop{\mathrm{argmax}}_{\theta} \{Q(\Theta) + \nu \cdot \Omega(\Theta)\} \qquad (4)$$

Here, the regulizer term Ω should be small if the HMM system has high complexity and parameter overfitting becomes a problem; Ω should be large if the HMM-states' pdfs are shaped smoothly and system generalization works well. The constant $\nu \geq 0$ is a control parameter that adjusts the tradeoff between the pure ML solution and the smoothness of penalization. In Eqn. (4) the term $Q(\Theta)$ becomes larger the more data is used for training (which makes the ML estimation become more reliable) and the influence of the term $\nu \cdot \Omega$ gets less important, relatively.

The basic idea when constructing an expression for the regulizer Ω that favors smooth HMM systems is, that in the case of simple and smooth systems the state-dependent emission pdfs $b_k(\cdot)$ should fall into several groups of similar pdfs. This is in contrast to the traditional state-tying that forces identical pdfs in each group. In the following, these clusters of similar emission pdfs are described by a probabilistic mixture model. Each pdf is assumed to be generated by a mixture of I different mixture components $p_i(\cdot)$. In this case the probability (-density) of generating the emission pdf $b_k(\cdot)$ is given by:

$$p(b_k(\cdot)) = \sum_{i=1}^{I} c_i \cdot p_i(b_k(\cdot)) \qquad (5)$$

with the mixture weights c_i that are constrained to $0 \leq c_i \leq 1$ and $1 = \sum_{i=1}^{I} c_i$. The i-th mixture component $p_i(\cdot)$ is used to model the i-th cluster of HMM-emission pdfs. Each cluster is represented by a prototype pdf that is denoted as $\beta_i(\cdot)$ for the i-th cluster; the distance (using a suitable metric) between a HMM emission pdf $b_k(\cdot)$ and the i-th prototype pdf is denoted as $D_i(b_k(\cdot))$. If these distances are small for all HMM emission probabilities there are several small clusters of emission probabilities and the regulizer term Ω should be large. Now, it is assumed that the distances follow a negative exponential distribution (with a deviation parameter λ_i), yielding an expression for the mixture components:

$$p_i(b_k(\cdot)) \sim \left(\prod_{z=1}^{Z} \lambda_{i,z}\right) \cdot \exp\left(-\sum_{z=1}^{Z} \lambda_{i,z} \cdot D_{i,z}(b_k^{(z)}(\cdot))\right) \qquad (6)$$

In Eqn. (6) the more general case of Z independent streams is given. Hence, the HMM emission pdfs and the cluster prototype pdfs are split up into Z different pdfs $b_k^{(z)}(\cdot)$ and $\beta_i^{(z)}(\cdot)$, respectively and the stream dependent distances $D_{i,z}$ and parameters $\lambda_{i,z}$ are used.

Now, for the regulizer term Ω the log-likelihood of the mixture model in Eqn. (5) over all emission pdfs in the HMM system can be used:

$$\Omega(\Theta) = \sum_{k=1}^{K} \log p(b_k(\cdot)) \qquad (7)$$

4 Regularization example: discrete HMMs

As an example for parameter estimation in the regularization framework, a discrete HMM system with different VQs for each of the Z streams is considered here: Each VQ subdivides the feature space into J_z different partitions (i.e. the z-th codebook size is J_z) and the VQ-partition labels are denoted $m_j^{(z)}$. If the observation subvector $\mathbf{x}^{(z)}$ is in the j-th VQ-partition the VQ output is $\hat{m}^{(z)}(\mathbf{x}^{(z)}) = m_j^{(z)}$.

Since the discrete kind HMM output probabilities $b_k^{(z)}(\hat{m}^{(z)})$ are used here, the regularizer's prototypes are the discrete probabilities $\beta_i^{(z)}(m_j^{(z)})$. As a distance metric between the HMM emission probabilities and the prototype probabilities used in Eqn. (6) the asymmetric Kullback-Leibler divergence is applied:

$$D_{i,z}(b_k^{(z)}(\hat{m}^{(z)})) = -\sum_{j=1}^{J_z} \beta_i^{(z)}(m_j^{(z)}) \cdot \log \frac{b_k^{(z)}(m_j^{(z)})}{\beta_i^{(z)}(m_j^{(z)})} \qquad (8)$$

4.1 Estimation of HMM parameters using regularization

The parameter set Θ of the HMM system to be estimated mainly consists of the discrete HMM emission probabilities (transition probabilities are not subject of regularization here). To get an iterative parameter estimation in the EM style, Eqn. (4) must be maximized; e.g. by setting the derivative of Eqn. (4) with respect to the HMM-parameter $b_k^{(z)}(m_j^{(z)})$ to zero and application of Lagrange multipliers with regard to the constraint $1 = \sum_{j=1}^{J_z} b_k^{(z)}(m_j^{(z)})$. This leads to a quite complex solution that can be only solved numerically.

The optimization problem can be simplified if the mixture in Eqn. (5) is replaced by the maximum approximation; i.e. only the maximum component in the sum is considered. The corresponding index of the maximum component is denoted i^*:

$$p(b_k(\cdot)) \approx c_{i^*} \cdot p_{i^*}(b_k(\cdot)) = \max_{1 \leq i \leq I} \{c_i \cdot p_i(b_k(\cdot))\} \qquad (9)$$

In this simplified case the HMM parameter estimation is given by:

$$\hat{b}_k^{(z)}(m_j^{(z)}) = \frac{\frac{\nu}{\lambda_{i^*,z}} \cdot \beta_{i^*}^{(z)}(m_j^{(z)}) + \sum_{t=1}^{T} \gamma_k(t) \cdot \delta_{\hat{m}^{(z)}(t), m_j^{(z)}}}{\frac{\nu}{\lambda_{i^*,z}} + \sum_{t=1}^{T} \gamma_k(t)} \qquad (10)$$

This is a weighted sum of the well known ML solution and the regularizer's prototype probability $\beta_{i^*}^{(z)}(\cdot)$ that is selected by the maximum search in Eqn. (9). The larger the value of the constant ν, the stronger is the force that pushes the estimate of the HMM emission probability $\hat{b}_k^{(z)}(m_j^{(z)})$ towards the prototype probability $\beta_{i^*}^{(z)}(\cdot)$. The situation when ν tends towards infinity corresponds to the case of traditional state-tying, because all different states that fall into the same cluster i^* make use of $\beta_{i^*}^{(z)}(\cdot)$ as emission probability in the z-th stream.

4.2 Estimation of regulizer parameters

The parameter set ξ of the regulizer consists of the mixture weights c_i, the deviation parameters $\lambda_{i,z}$, and of the discrete prototype probabilities $\beta_i^{(z)}(m_j^{(z)})$ in the case of regulizing discrete HMMs. These parameters can be set in advance by making use of prior knowledge; e.g. the prototype probabilities can be obtained from a simple HMM system that uses a small number of states. Alternatively, the regulizer's parameters can be estimated in a similar way as in (Nowlan, 1992) by maximizing Eqn. (7). Since there is no direct solution to this optimization problem, maximization must be performed in an EM-like iterative procedure that uses the HMM emission pdfs $b_k(\cdot)$ as training data for the mixture model and by increasing the following auxiliary function in each step:

$$R(\xi) = \sum_{k=1}^{K}\sum_{i=1}^{I} P(i|b_k(\cdot)) \cdot \log p(i, b_k(\cdot))$$

$$= \sum_{k=1}^{K}\sum_{i=1}^{I} P(i|b_k(\cdot)) \cdot \log\left(c_i \cdot p_i(b_k(\cdot))\right) \qquad (11)$$

with the posterior probability used as weighting factor given by:

$$P(i|b_k(\cdot)) = \frac{c_i \cdot p_i(b_k(\cdot))}{\sum_{l=1}^{I} c_l \cdot p_l(b_k(\cdot))} \qquad (12)$$

Again, maximization of Eqn. (11) can be performed by setting the derivative of $R(\xi)$ with respect to the regulizer's parameters to zero under consideration of the constraints $1 = \sum_{i=1}^{I} c_i$ and $1 = \sum_{j=1}^{J_z} \beta_i^{(z)}(m_j^{(z)})$ by application of Lagrange multipliers. For the estimation of the regulizer parameters this yields:

$$\hat{c}_i = \frac{1}{K} \cdot \sum_{k=1}^{K} P(i|b_k(\cdot)) \qquad (13)$$

$$\hat{\lambda}_{i,z} = \frac{\sum_{k=1}^{K} P(i|b_k(\cdot))}{\sum_{k=1}^{K} D_{i,z}(b_k^{(z)}(\cdot)) \cdot P(i|b_k(\cdot))} \qquad (14)$$

$$\hat{\beta}_i^{(z)}(m_j^{(z)}) = \frac{\exp\left(\frac{\sum_{k=1}^{K} P(i|b_k(\cdot)) \cdot \log b_k^{(z)}(m_j^{(z)})}{\sum_{k=1}^{K} P(i|b_k(\cdot))}\right)}{\sum_{l=1}^{I} \exp\left(\frac{\sum_{k=1}^{K} P(l|b_k(\cdot)) \cdot \log b_k^{(z)}(m_j^{(z)})}{\sum_{k=1}^{K} P(l|b_k(\cdot))}\right)} \qquad (15)$$

The estimate $\hat{c}_i$ can be interpreted as the average probability that a HMM emission probability falls into the i-th mixture cluster; $\hat{\lambda}_{i,z}$ is the inverse of the weighted average distance between the emission probabilities and the prototype probability $\beta_i^{(z)}(\cdot)$. The estimate $\hat{\beta}_i^{(z)}(m_j^{(z)})$ is the average probability over all emission probabilities for the VQ-label $m_j^{(z)}$ weighted in the log-domain.

If the Euclidean distance between the discrete probabilities is used instead of Eqn. (8) to measure the differences between the HMM emission probabilities and the prototypes

$$D_{i,z}(b_k^{(z)}(\hat{m}^{(z)})) = \sum_{j=1}^{J_z} \left(\beta_i^{(z)}(m_j^{(z)}) - b_k^{(z)}(m_j^{(z)})\right)^2 \qquad (16)$$

the estimate of the prototype probabilities is given by the average of the HMM probabilities weighted in the original space:

$$\hat{\beta}_i^{(z)}(m_j^{(z)}) = \frac{\sum_{k=1}^{K} P(i|b_k(\cdot)) \cdot b_k^{(z)}(m_j^{(z)})}{\sum_{k=1}^{K} P(i|b_k(\cdot))} \qquad (17)$$

5 Experimental results

To investigate the performance of the regularization methods described above a HMM speech recognition system for the speaker-independent resource management (RM) continuous speech task is built up. For training 3990 sentences from 109 different speakers are used. Recognition results are given as word error rates averaged over the official DARPA RM test sets feb'89, oct'89, feb'91 and sep'92, consisting of 1200 sentences from 40 different speakers, totally. Recognition is done via a beam search guided Viterbi decoder using the DARPA RM word pair grammar (perplexity: 60).

As acoustic features every 10 ms 12 MFCC coefficients and the relative signal power are extracted from the speech signal along with the dynamic Δ- and $\Delta\Delta$-features, comprising 39 features per frame. The HMM system makes use of standard 3-state discrete probability phonetic models. Four different neural networks, trained by the MMI method, that is described in in (Rigoll, 1997) and extended in (Neukirchen, 1998), are used as VQ to quantize the features into $Z = 4$ different streams of discrete labels. The codebook size in each stream is set to 200.

A simple system with models for 47 monophones and for the most prominent 33 function words (totally 394 states) yields a word error rate of 8.6%. A system that makes use of the more detailed (but untied) word internal triphone models (totally 6921 states) yields 12.2% word error. Hence HMM overfitting because of insufficient training data is a severe problem in this case. Traditional methods to overcome the effects of overfitting like interpolating between triphones and monophones (Bahl, 1983), data driven state-clustering and decision tree clustering yield error rates of 6.5%, 8.3% and 6.4%, respectively. It must be noted that in contrast to the usual training procedure in (Rigoll, 1996) no further smoothing methods are applied to the HMM emission probabilities here.

In a first series of experiments the untied triphone system is regulized by a quite simple mixture of $I = 394$ density components, i.e. the number of clusters in the penalty term is identical to the number of states in the monophone system. In this case the prototype probabilities are initialized by the emission probabilities of the monophone system; the mixture weights and the deviation parameters in the regulizer are set to be uniform, initially. In order to test the inluence of the tradeoff parameter ν it is set to 50, 10 and 2, respectively. The corresponding word error rates are 8.4%, 6.9% and 6.3%, respectively. In the case of large νs regularization degrades to a tying of triphone states to monophone states and the error rate tends towards the monophone system performance. For smaller νs there is a good tradeoff between data fitting and HMM smoothness yielding improved system performance. The initial prototype probability settings provided by the monophone system do not seem to be changed much by regulizer parameter estimation, since the system performance only changes slightly when the regulizer's parameter reestimation is not incorporated.

In preliminary experiments the regularization method is also used for speaker adaptation. A speaker-independent system trained on the Wall Street Journal (WSJ) database yields an error rate of 32.4% on the Nov. 93 S3_P0 test set with 10 different non-native speakers. The speaker-independent HMM emission probabilities are used to initialize the prototype probabilities of the regulizer. Then, speaker-dependent systems are built up for each speaker using only 40 fast enrollment sentences for training along with regularization (ν is set to 10). Now, the error rate drops to 25.7% what is better than the speaker adaptation method described in (Rottland, 1998) that yields 27.3% by a linear feature space transformation. In combination both methods achieve 23.0% word error.

6 Summary and Discussion

A method to avoid parameter overfitting in HMM systems by application of a regularization term that favor smooth and simple models has been presented here. The complexity measure applied to the HMMs is based on a finite mixture of negative exponential distributions, that generates the state-dependent emission probabilities. This kind of regularization term can be interpreted as a soft state-tying, since it forces the HMM emission probabilities to form a finite set of clusters. The effect of regularization has been demonstrated on the RM task by improving overfitted triphone models. On a WSJ non-native speaker adaption task with limited training data, regularization outperforms feature space transformations.

Eqn. (4) may be also interpreted from a perspective of Bayesian inference: the term $\nu \cdot \Omega$ plays the role of setting a prior distribution on the HMM parameters to be estimated. Hence, the use of a mixture model for Ω is equivalent to using a special kind of prior in the framework of MAP estimation for HMMs (Gauvain, 1994).

References

L.R. Bahl, F. Jelinek, L.R. Mercer, 'A Maximum Likelihood Approach to Continuous Speech Recognition', *IEEE Trans. Pattern Analysis and Machine Intelligence,* Vol. 5, No. 2 Mar. 1983, pp. 179–190.

L.R. Bahl, P.V. de Souza, P.S. Gopalakrishnan, D. Nahamoo, M.A. Picheny, (1991) Context dependent modeling of phones in continuous speech using decision trees. *Proc. DARPA speech and natural language processing workshop,* 264–270.

E.B. Baum, D. Haussler, (1989) What size net gives valid generalization? *Neural Computation,* 1:151–160.

Y. le Cun, J. Denker, S. Solla, R.E. Howard, L.D. Jackel, (1990) Optimal brain damage. *Advances in Neural Information Processing Systems 2,* San Mateo, CA, Morgan Kauffman.

J.L. Gauvain, C.H. Lee, (1994) Maximum a posteriori estimation for multivariate Gaussian mixture observations of markov chains. *IEEE Transaction Speech and Audio Proc.,* Vol. 2, 2:291–298.

K.J. Lang, A.H. Waibel, G.E. Hinton, (1990) A time-delay neural network architecture for isolated word recognition. *Neural Networks,* 3:23–43.

Ch. Neukirchen, D. Willett, S. Eickeler, S. Müller, (1998) Exploiting acoustic feature correlations by joint neural vector quantizer design in a discrete HMM system. *Proc. ICASSP'98,* 5-8.

S.J. Nowlan, G.E. Hinton, (1992) Simplifying neural networks by soft weight-sharing. *Neural Computation,* 4:473–493.

D.C. Plaut, S.J. Nowlan, G.E. Hinton, (1986) Experiments on learning by backpropagation. *technical report CMU-CS-86-126,* Carnegie-Mellon University, Pittsburgh, PA.

G. Rigoll, Ch. Neukirchen, J. Rottland, (1996) A new hybrid system based on MMI-neural networks for the RM speech recognition task. *Proc. ICASSP'96,* 865–868.

G. Rigoll, Ch. Neukirchen, (1997) A new approach to hybrid HMM/ANN speech recognition using mutual information neural networks. *Advances in Neural Information Processing Systems 9,* Cambridge, MA, MIT Press, 772-778.

J. Rottland, Ch. Neukirchen, G. Rigoll, (1998) Speaker adaptation for hybrid MMI-connectionist speech recognition systems. *Proc. ICASSP'98,* 465–468.

S.J. Young, (1992) The general use of tying in phoneme-based HMM speech recognizers. *Proc. ICASSP'92,* 569–572.

S.J. Young, P.C. Woodland (1993) The use of state tying in continuous speech recognition. *Proc. Eurospeech'93,* 2203–2206.

Maximum-Likelihood Continuity Mapping (MALCOM): An Alternative to HMMs

David A. Nix
dnix@lanl.gov
Computer Research & Applications
CIC-3, MS B265
Los Alamos National Laboratory
Los Alamos, NM 87545

John E. Hogden
hogden@lanl.gov
Computer Research & Applications
CIC-3, MS B265
Los Alamos National Laboratory
Los Alamos, NM 87545

Abstract

We describe Maximum-Likelihood Continuity Mapping (MALCOM), an alternative to hidden Markov models (HMMs) for processing sequence data such as speech. While HMMs have a discrete "hidden" space constrained by a fixed finite-automaton architecture, MALCOM has a continuous hidden space—a *continuity map*—that is constrained only by a smoothness requirement on paths through the space. MALCOM fits into the same probabilistic framework for speech recognition as HMMs, but it represents a more realistic model of the speech production process. To evaluate the extent to which MALCOM captures speech production information, we generated continuous speech continuity maps for three speakers and used the paths through them to predict measured speech articulator data. The median correlation between the MALCOM paths *obtained from only the speech acoustics* and articulator measurements was 0.77 on an independent test set not used to train MALCOM or the predictor. This unsupervised model achieved correlations over speakers and articulators only 0.02 to 0.15 lower than those obtained using an analogous supervised method which *used articulatory measurements as well as acoustics.*.

1 INTRODUCTION

Hidden Markov models (HMMs) are generally considered to be the state of the art in speech recognition (e.g., Young, 1996). The strengths of the HMM framework include a rich mathematical foundation, powerful training and recognition algorithms for large speech corpora, and a probabilistic framework that can incorporate statistical phonology and syntax (Morgan & Bourlard, 1995). However, HMMs are known to be a poor model of the speech production process. While speech production is a continuous, temporally evolving process, HMMs treat speech production as a discrete, finite-state system where the current state depends only on the immediately preceding state. Furthermore, while HMMs are designed to capture temporal information as state transition probabilities, Bourlard *et al.*,

(1995) suggest that when the transition probabilities are replaced by constant values, recognition results do not significantly deteriorate. That is, while transitions are often considered the most perceptually relevent component of speech, the conventional HMM framework is poor at capturing transition information.

Given these deficiencies, we are considering alternatives to the HMM approach that maintain its strengths while improving upon its weaknesses. This paper describes one such model called Maximum-Likelihood Continuity Mapping (MALCOM). We first review a general statistical framework for speech recognition so that we can compare the HMM and MALCOM formulations. Then we consider what the abstract hidden state represents in MALCOM, demonstrating empirically that the paths through MALCOM's hidden space are closely related to the movements of the speech production articulators.

2 A GENERAL FRAMEWORK FOR SPEECH RECOGNITION

Consider an unknown speech waveform that is converted by a front-end signal-processing module into a sequence of acoustic vectors $\mathbf{X}$. Given a space of possible utterances, W, the task of speech recognition is to return the most likely utterance W^* given the observed acoustic sequence $\mathbf{X}$. Using Bayes' rule this corresponds to

$$W^* = \operatorname*{argmax}_W P(W|\mathbf{X}) = \operatorname*{argmax}_W \frac{P(\mathbf{X}|W)P(W)}{P(\mathbf{X})}. \tag{1}$$

In recognition, $P(\mathbf{X})$ is typically ignored because it is constant over all W, and the posterior $P(W|\mathbf{X})$ is estimated as the product of the prior probability of the word sequence, $P(W)$, and the probability that the observed acoustics were generated by the word sequence, $P(\mathbf{X}|W)$. The prior $P(W)$ is estimated by a *language model*, while the production probability $P(\mathbf{X}|W)$ is estimated by an *acoustic model*. In continuous speech recognition, the product of these terms must be maximized over W; however, in this paper, we will restrict our attention to the form of the acoustical model only. Every candidate utterance W corresponds to a sequence of word/phone models $\mathcal{M}_w$ such that $P(\mathbf{X}|W) = P(\mathbf{X}|\mathcal{M}_w)$, and each $\mathcal{M}_w$ considers all possible paths through some "hidden" space. Thus, for each candidate utterance, we must calculate

$$P(\mathbf{X}|\mathcal{M}_w) = \int_{\mathbf{Y}} P(\mathbf{X}|\mathbf{Y}, \mathcal{M}_w) P(\mathbf{Y}|\mathcal{M}_w) d\mathbf{Y}, \tag{2}$$

where $\mathbf{Y}$ is some path through the hidden space.

2.1 HIDDEN MARKOV MODELS

Because HMMs are finite-state machines with a given fixed architecture, the path $\mathbf{Y}$ through the hidden space corresponds to series of discrete states, simplifying the integral of Eq. (2) to a sum. However, to avoid computing the contribution of all possible paths, the *Viterbi approximation*—considering only the single path that maximizes Eq. (2)—is frequently used without much loss in recognition performance (Morgan & Bourlard, 1995). Thus,

$$P(\mathbf{X}|\mathcal{M}_w) \approx \operatorname*{argmax}_Y P(\mathbf{X}|\mathbf{Y}, \mathcal{M}_w) P(\mathbf{Y}|\mathcal{M}_w). \tag{3}$$

The first term corresponds to the product of the emission probabilities of the acoustics given the state sequence and is typically estimated by mixtures of high-dimensional Gaussian densities. The second term corresponds to the product of the state transition probabilities. However, because Bourlard *et al.* (1995) found that this second term contributes little to recognition performance, the modeling power of the conventional HMM must reside in the first term. Training the HMM system involves estimating both the emission and the transition probabilities from real speech data. The Baum-Welch/forward-backward algorithm (e.g., Morgan & Scofield, 1994) is the standard computationally efficient algorithm for iteratively estimating these distributions.

2.2 MAXIMUM-LIKELIHOOD CONTINUITY MAPPING (MALCOM)

In contrast to HMMs, the multi-dimensional MALCOM hidden space is continuous—there are an infinite number states and paths through them. While the HMM is constrained by a fixed architecture, MALCOM is constrained by the notion of continuity of the hidden path. That is, the path must be smooth and continuous: it may not carry any energy above a given cutoff frequency. Unlike the discrete path in an HMM, the smooth hidden path in MALCOM attempts to emulate the motion of the speech articulators in what we call a *continuity map* (CM).

Unless we know how to evaluate the integral of Eq. (2) (which we currently do not), we must also make the Viterbi approximation and approximate $P(\mathbf{X}|\mathcal{M}_w)$ by considering only the single path that maximizes the likelihood of the acoustics $\mathbf{X}$ given the utterance model $\mathcal{M}_w$, resulting in Eq. (3) once again. Analogously, the first term, $P(\mathbf{X}|\mathbf{Y}, \mathcal{M}_w)$, corresponds to the acoustic generation probability given the hidden path, and the second term corresponds to the probability of the hidden path given the utterance model. This paper focuses on the first term because this is the term that produces conventional HMM performance.[1]

Common to all $\mathcal{M}_w$ is a set of N probability density functions (pdfs) Φ that define the CM hidden space, modeling the likelihood of $\mathbf{Y}$ given $\mathbf{X}$ for an N-code vector quantization (VQ) of the acoustic space. Because these pdfs are defined over the low-dimensional CM space instead of the high-dimensional acoustic space (e.g., 6 vs. 40+), MALCOM requires many fewer parameters to be estimated than the corresponding HMM.

3 THE MALCOM ALGORITHM

We now turn to developing an algorithm to estimate both the CM pdfs Φ and the corresponding paths $\mathbf{Y}$ that together maximize the likelihood of a given time series of acoustics, $\mathcal{L} = P(\mathbf{X}|\mathbf{Y}, \Phi)$. This is an extension of the method first proposed by Hogden (1995), in which he instead maximized $P(\mathbf{Y}|\mathbf{X}, \Phi)$ using vowel data from a single speaker. Starting with random but smooth $\mathbf{Y}$, the MALCOM training algorithm generates a CM by iterating between the following two steps: (1) Given $\mathbf{Y}$, reestimate Φ to maximize $\mathcal{L}$; and (2) Given Φ, reestimate smooth paths $\mathbf{Y}$ to maximize $\mathcal{L}$.

3.1 LOG LIKELIHOOD FUNCTION

To specify the log likelihood function $\mathcal{L}$, we make two dependence claims and one independence assumption. First we claim that $\mathbf{y}_t$ depends (to at least some small extent) on all other $\mathbf{y}$ in the utterance, an expression of the continuity constraint described above. We make another natural claim that $\mathbf{x}_t$ depends on $\mathbf{y}_t$, that the path configuration at time t influences the corresponding acoustics. However, we do make the conditional independence assumption that

$$\mathcal{L} = P(\mathbf{X}|\mathbf{Y}, \Phi) = \prod_{t=1}^{n} P(\mathbf{x}_t|\mathbf{y}_t, \Phi). \qquad (4)$$

Note that Eq. (4) does not assume that each $\mathbf{x}_t$ is independent of $\mathbf{x}_{t-1}$ (as is often assumed in data modeling); it only assumes that the *conditioning* of $\mathbf{x}_t$ on $\mathbf{y}_t$ is independent from

---

[1] However, we are currently developing a model of $P(\mathbf{Y}|\mathcal{M}_w)$ to replace the corresponding (and useless) term in the conventional HMM formulation as well (Hogden et al., 1998).

$t-1$ to t. For example, because $\mathbf{x}_t$ depends on $\mathbf{y}_t$, $\mathbf{y}_t$ depends on all other $\mathbf{y}$ (the smoothness constraint), and $\mathbf{x}_{t-1}$ depends on $\mathbf{y}_{t-1}$, $\mathbf{x}_t$ is *not* assumed to be independent of all other $\mathbf{x}$s in the utterance.

With a log transformation and an invocation of Bayes' rule, we obtain the MALCOM log likelihood function:

$$\ln \mathcal{L} = \sum_{t=1}^{n} \left[\ln P(\mathbf{y}_t|\mathbf{x}_t, \Phi) + \ln P(\mathbf{x}_t) - \ln P(\mathbf{y}_t|\Phi) \right]. \tag{5}$$

We model each $P(\mathbf{y}_t|\mathbf{x}_t, \Phi)$ by a probability density function (pdf) $p[\mathbf{y}_t|\mathbf{x}_t, \Phi_j(\mathbf{x}_t)]$, where the particular model Φ_j depends on which of the N VQ codes $\mathbf{x}_t$ is assigned to. Here we use a simple multi-dimensional Gaussian for each pdf, but we are currently exploring the use of multi-modal mixtures of Gaussians to represent the pdfs for sounds such as stop consonants for which the inverse map from acoustics to articulation may not be unique (Nix, 1998). Next, we need an estimate of $P(\mathbf{y}_t|\Phi)$, which can be obtained by summing over all VQ partitions: $P(\mathbf{y}_t|\Phi) \approx \sum_{j=1}^{N} p(\mathbf{y}_t|\mathbf{x}_j, \Phi_j) P(\mathbf{x}_j)$. We estimate $P(\mathbf{x}_j)$ by calculating the relative frequency of each acoustic code in the VQ codebook.

3.2 PDF ESTIMATION

For step (1) of training, we use gradient-based optimization to reestimate the means of the Gaussian pdfs for each acoustic partition, where the gradient of Eq.(5) with respect to the mean of pdf i is

$$\nabla_{\boldsymbol{\mu}_i} \ln \mathcal{L} = \sum_{t \in \mathbf{x}(t) = \mathbf{x}_i} \Sigma_i^{-1}(\mathbf{y}_t - \boldsymbol{\mu}_i) - \sum_{i=1}^{t} \left\{ \frac{\sum_{j=1}^{N} p[\mathbf{y}_t|\mathbf{x}_j, \Phi(\mathbf{x}_j)] P(\mathbf{x}_j) \Sigma_j^{-1}(\mathbf{y}_t - \boldsymbol{\mu}_j)}{\sum_{j=1}^{N} p[\mathbf{y}_t|\mathbf{x}_j, \Phi(\mathbf{x}_j)] P(\mathbf{x}_j)} \right\} \tag{6}$$

where Σ is the covariance matrix for each pdf. For the results in this paper, we use a common radially symmetric covariance matrix for all pdfs and reestimate the covariance matrix after each path optimization step.[2] In doing the optimization, we employ the following algorithm:

1. Make an initial guess of each $\boldsymbol{\mu}_i$ as the means of the path configurations corresponding to the observed acoustics $\mathbf{X} \in \mathbf{x}_i$.
2. Construct $\nabla_{\boldsymbol{\mu}} \ln \mathcal{L}$ by considering Eq. (6) over all N acoustic partitions.
3. Determine a search direction for the optimization using, for example, conjugate gradients and perform a line search along this direction (Press *et al.*, 1988).
4. Repeat steps [2]–[3] until convergence.

To avoid potential degenerate solutions, after each pdf optimization step, the dimensions of the CM are orthogonalized. Furthermore, because the scale of the continuity map is meaningless (only its topological arrangement matters), the N pdf means are scaled to zero mean, unit variance before each path optimization step.

3.3 PATH ESTIMATION

For step (2) of training, we use gradient-based optimization to reestimate $\mathbf{Y}$, where the gradient of the log likelihood function with respect to a specific $\mathbf{y}_t$ is given by

$$\nabla_{\mathbf{y}_t} \ln \mathcal{L} = \frac{\nabla_{\mathbf{y}_t} p[\mathbf{y}_t|\mathbf{x}_t, \Phi(\mathbf{x}_t)]}{p[\mathbf{y}_t|\mathbf{x}_t, \Phi(\mathbf{x}_t)]} - \frac{\nabla_{\mathbf{y}_t} \sum_{j=1}^{N} p[\mathbf{y}_t|\mathbf{x}_j, \Phi(\mathbf{x}_j)] P(\mathbf{x}_j)}{\sum_{j=1}^{N} p[\mathbf{y}_t|\mathbf{x}_j, \Phi(\mathbf{x}_j)] P(\mathbf{x}_j)}. \tag{7}$$

---

[2] However, we are currently exploring the effects of individual and diagonal covariance matrices.

In doing the optimization, we employ the following gradient-based algorithm:

1. Make an initial guess of the path $\mathbf{Y}^0$ as the means of the pdfs corresponding to the observed acoustic sequence $\mathbf{X}$.
2. Low pass filter $\mathbf{Y}^0$.
3. Construct $\nabla_\mathbf{Y} \ln \mathcal{L}$ by considering Eq. (7) over all t.
4. Determine a search direction for the optimization using, for example, conjugate gradients (Press et al., 1988).
5. Low-pass filter this search direction using the same filter as in step [2].
6. Perform a line search along the filtered direction (Press et al., 1988).
7. Repeat steps [3]–[6] until convergence.

Because neither the line search direction nor the initial estimate $\mathbf{Y}^0$ contains energy above the cutoff frequency of the low-pass filter, their linear addition—the next estimate of $\mathbf{Y}$—will not contain energy above the cutoff frequency either. Thus, steps [2] and [5] implement the desired smoothness constraint.

4 COMPARNG MALCOM PATHS TO SPEECH ARTICULATION

To evaluate our claim that MALCOM paths are topologically related to articulator motions, we construct a regression predictor from $\mathbf{Y}$ to measured articulator data using the training data and test the quality of this predictor on an independent test set.

Our speech corpus consists of data from two male and one female native speakers of German. This data was obtained from Dr. Igor Zlokarnik and recorded at the Technical University of Munich, Germany using electro-magnetic articulography (EMA) (Perkell et al., 1992). Each speaker's articulatory measurements and acoustics were recorded for the same 108 sentences, where each sentence was about 4 seconds long.

The acoustics were recorded using a room-placed microphone and sampled using 16-bit resolution at 16 kHz. Prior to receiving the data from Munich, the data were resampled at 11025 Hz. To represent the acoustic signal in compact vector time-series, we used 256-sample (23.2 msec) Hamming-windowed frames, with a new frame starting every 5.8 msec (75% overlap). We transform each frame into a 13th-order LPC-cepstral coefficient vector $\mathbf{a}_t$ (12 cepstral features plus log gain—see Morgan& Scofield, 1994). A full acoustical feature vector $\mathbf{x}_t$ consists of a window of seven frames such that $\mathbf{x}_t$ is made up of the frames $\{\mathbf{a}_{t-6}, \mathbf{a}_{t-4}, \mathbf{a}_{t-2}, \mathbf{a}_t, \mathbf{a}_{t+2}, \mathbf{a}_{t+4}, \mathbf{a}_{t+6}\}$. To VQ the acoustic space we used the classical k-means algorithm (e.g., Bishop, 1995), but we used 512 codes to model the vowel data, and 256 codes each to model the stop consonants, the fricatives, the nasals, and the liquids (1536 codes combined).[3]

The articulatory data consist of the (x, y) coordinates of 4 coils along the tongue and the y-coordinates of coils on the jaw and lower lip. Figure 1 illustrates the approximate location of each coil. The data were originally sampled at 250 Hz but were resampled to 172.26 Hz to match one articulatory sample for each 75%-overlapping acoustic frame of 256 samples. The articulatory data were subsequently low-pass filtered at 15 Hz to remove measurement noise.

Sentences 1–90 were used as a training set, and sentences 91–108 were withheld for evaluation. A separate CM was generated for each speaker using the training data. We used an 8 Hz cutoff frequency because the measured articulatory data had very little energy above 8 Hz, and a 6-dimensional continuity map was used because the first six principal components capture 99% of the variance of the corresponding articulator data (Nix, 1998).

---

[3]This acoustic representation and VQ scheme were determined to work well for modeling real articulator data (Nix, 1998), so they were used here as well.

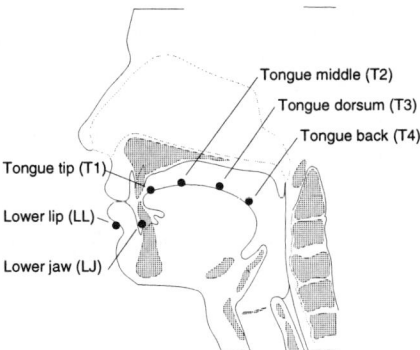

Figure 1: Approximate positions of EMA coils for speech articulation measurements.

Because the third term in Eq. (5) is computationally complex, we approximated Eq. (5) by only its first term (the second term is constant during training) until $\ln \mathcal{L}$, calculated at the end of each iteration using all terms, started to decrease. At this point we started using both the first and third terms of Eq. (5). In each pdf and path optimization step, our convergence criterion was when the maximum movement of a mean or a path was $< 10^{-4}$. Our convergence criterion for the entire algorithm was when the correlation of the paths from one full iteration of pdf and path optimization to another was > 0.99 in all dimensions. This usually took about 30 iterations.

To evaluate the extent to which MALCOM hidden paths capture information related to articulation, we used the same training set to estimate a non-linear regression function from the output generated by MALCOM to the corresponding measured articulator data. We used an ensemble of 10 single-hidden-layer, 32-hidden unit, multi-layer perceptrons trained on different 2/3-training, 1/3-early stopping partitions of the training set, where the results of the ensemble on the test set were averaged (e.g., Bishop, 1995). A linear regression produced results approximately 10% worse than those we report here.

To contrast with the unsupervised MALCOM method, we also tested a supervised method in which the articulatory data was available for training as well as evaluation. This involved only the pdf optimization step of MALCOM because the paths were fixed as the articulator measurements. The resulting pdfs were then used in the path optimization step to determine paths for the test data acoustics. We could then measure what fraction of this supervised performance the unsupervised MALCOM attained.

5 RESULTS AND CONCLUSIONS

The results of this regression on the test set are plotted in Figure 2. The MALCOM paths had a median correlation of 0.77 with the actual articulator data, compared to 0.84 for the comparable supervised method. Thus, *using only the speech acoustics*, MALCOM generated continuity maps with correlations to real articulator measurements only 0.02 to 0.15 lower than the corresponding supervised model which *used articulatory measurements as well as acoustics*.

Given that (1) MALCOM fits into the same probabilistic framework for speech recognition as HMMs and (2) MALCOM's hidden paths capture considerable information about the speech production process, we believe that MALCOM will prove to be a viable alternative to the HMM for speech processing tasks. Our current work emphasizes developing a word model to complete the MALCOM formulation and test a full speech recognition system. Furthermore, MALCOM is applicable to any other task to which HMMs can be applied,

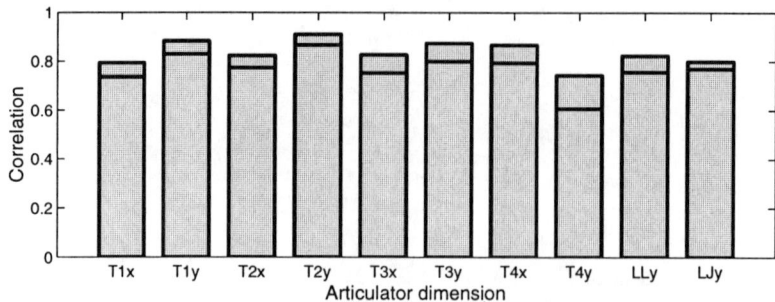

Figure 2: Correlation between estimated and actual articulator trajectories on the independent test set averaged across speakers. Each full bar is the performance of the supervised analogy to MALCOM, and the horizontal line on each bar is the performance of MALCOM itself.

including fraud detection (Hogden, 1997) and text processing.

Acknowledgments

We would like to thank James Howse and Mike Mozer for their helpful comments on this manuscript and Igor Zlokarnik for sharing his data with us. This work was performed under the auspices of the U.S. Department of Energy.

References

Bishop, C.M. (1995). *Neural Networks for Pattern Recognition*, NY: Oxford University Press, Inc.

Bourlard, H. Konig, Y., & Morgan, N. (1995). "REMAP: Recursive estimation and maximization of a posteriori probabilities, application to transition-based connectionist speech recognition," International Computer Science Institute Technical Report TR-94-064.

Hogden, J. (1995). "Improving on hidden Markov models: an articulatorily constrained, maximum-likelihood approach to speech recognition and speech coding," Los Alamos National Laboratory Technical Report, LA-UR-96-3945.

Hogden, J. (1997). "Maximum likelihood continuity mapping for fraud detection," Los Alamos National Laboratory Technical Report, LA-UR-97-992.

Hogden, J., Nix, D.A., Gracco, V., & Rubin, P. (1998). "Stochastic word nodels for articulatorily constrained speech recognition and synthesis," submitted to Acoustical Society of America Conference, 1998.

Morgan, N. & Bourlard, H.A. (1995). "Neural Networks for Statistical Recognition of Continuous Speech," *Proceedings of the IEEE*, **83**(5), 742–770.

Morgan, D.P., & Scofield, C.L. (1992). *Neural Networks and Speech Processing*, Boston, MA: Kluwer Academic Publishers.

Nix, D.A. (1998). *Probabilistic methods for inferring vocal-tract articulation from speech acoustics*, Ph.D. Dissertation, U. of CO at Boulder, Dept. of Computer Science, in preparation.

Perkell, J.S., Cohen, M.H., Svirsky, M.A., Matthies, M.L., Garabieta, I., & Jackson, M.T.T. (1992). "Electromagnetic midsagittal articulometer systems for transducing speech articulatory movements," *Journal of the Acoustical Society of America*, **92**(6), 3078–3096.

Press, W.H., Teukolsky, S.A., Vetterling, W.T., & Flannery, B.P. (1988). *Numerical Recipes in C* Cambridge University Press.

Young, S.J. (1996). "A review of large-vocabulary continuous speech recognition," *IEEE Signal Processing Magazine*, September, 45–57.

Markov processes on curves for automatic speech recognition

Lawrence Saul and Mazin Rahim
AT&T Labs — Research
Shannon Laboratory
180 Park Ave E-171
Florham Park, NJ 07932
{lsaul,mazin}@research.att.com

Abstract

We investigate a probabilistic framework for automatic speech recognition based on the intrinsic geometric properties of curves. In particular, we analyze the setting in which two variables—one continuous (x), one discrete (s)—evolve jointly in time. We suppose that the vector x traces out a smooth multidimensional curve and that the variable s evolves stochastically as a function of the *arc length* traversed along this curve. Since arc length does not depend on the rate at which a curve is traversed, this gives rise to a family of Markov processes whose predictions, $\Pr[s|x]$, are invariant to nonlinear warpings of time. We describe the use of such models, known as *Markov processes on curves* (MPCs), for automatic speech recognition, where x are acoustic feature trajectories and s are phonetic transcriptions. On two tasks—recognizing New Jersey town names and connected alpha-digits—we find that MPCs yield lower word error rates than comparably trained hidden Markov models.

1 Introduction

Variations in speaking rate currently present a serious challenge for automatic speech recognition (ASR) (Siegler & Stern, 1995). It is widely observed, for example, that fast speech is more prone to recognition errors than slow speech. A related effect, occurring at the phoneme level, is that consonants are more frequently botched than vowels. Generally speaking, consonants have short-lived, non-stationary acoustic signatures; vowels, just the opposite. Thus, at the phoneme level, we can view the increased confusability of consonants as a consequence of *locally* fast speech.

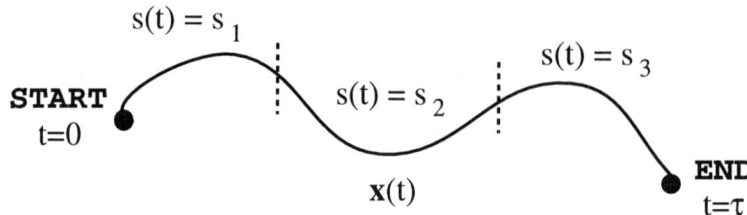

Figure 1: Two variables—one continuous (x), one discrete (s)—evolve jointly in time. The trace of s partitions the curve of x into different segments whose boundaries occur where s changes value.

In this paper, we investigate a probabilistic framework for ASR that models variations in speaking rate as arising from *nonlinear warpings of time* (Tishby, 1990). Our framework is based on the observation that acoustic feature vectors trace out continuous trajectories (Ostendorf et al, 1996). We view these trajectories as multidimensional curves whose intrinsic geometric properties (such as arc length or radius) do not depend on the rate at which they are traversed (do Carmo, 1976). We describe a probabilistic model whose predictions are based on these intrinsic geometric properties and—as such—are invariant to nonlinear warpings of time. The handling of this invariance distinguishes our methods from traditional hidden Markov models (HMMs) (Rabiner & Juang, 1993).

The probabilistic models studied in this paper are known as *Markov processes on curves* (MPCs). The theoretical framework for MPCs was introduced in an earlier paper (Saul, 1997), which also discussed the problems of decoding and parameter estimation. In the present work, we report the first *experimental* results for MPCs on two difficult benchmark problems in ASR. On these problems—recognizing New Jersey town names and connected alpha-digits—our results show that MPCs generally match or exceed the performance of comparably trained HMMs.

The organization of this paper is as follows. In section 2, we review the basic elements of MPCs and discuss important differences between MPCs and HMMs. In section 3, we present our experimental results and evaluate their significance.

2 Markov processes on curves

Speech recognizers take a continuous acoustic signal as input and return a sequence of discrete labels representing phonemes, syllables, or words as output. Typically the short-time properties of the speech signal are summarized by acoustic feature vectors. Thus the abstract mathematical problem is to describe a multidimensional trajectory $\{x(t)|t \in [0,\tau]\}$ by a sequence of discrete labels $s_1 s_2 \ldots s_n$. As shown in figure 1, this is done by specifying consecutive time intervals such that $s(t) = s_k$ for $t \in [t_{k-1}, t_k]$ and attaching the labels s_k to contiguous arcs along the trajectory. To formulate a probabilistic model of this process, we consider two variables—one continuous (x), one discrete (s)—that evolve jointly in time. Thus the vector x traces out a smooth multidimensional curve, to each point of which the variable s attaches a discrete label.

Markov processes on curves are based on the concept of *arc length*. After reviewing how to compute arc lengths along curves, we introduce a family of Markov processes whose predictions are invariant to nonlinear warpings of time. We then consider the ways in which these processes (and various generalizations) differ from HMMs.

2.1 Arc length

Let $g(x)$ define a $D \times D$ matrix-valued function over $x \in \mathcal{R}^D$. If $g(x)$ is everywhere non-negative definite, then we can use it as a *metric* to compute distances along curves. In particular, consider two nearby points separated by the infinitesimal vector dx. We define the squared distance between these two points as:

$$d\ell^2 = dx^T g(x) \, dx. \tag{1}$$

Arc length along a curve is the non-decreasing function computed by integrating these local distances. Thus, for the trajectory $x(t)$, the arc length between the points $x(t_1)$ and $x(t_2)$ is given by:

$$\ell = \int_{t_1}^{t_2} dt \, \left[\dot{x}^T g(x) \, \dot{x}\right]^{\frac{1}{2}}, \tag{2}$$

where $\dot{x} = \frac{d}{dt}[x(t)]$ denotes the time derivative of x. Note that the arc length defined by eq. (2) is invariant under reparameterizations of the trajectory, $x(t) \to x(f(t))$, where $f(t)$ is any smooth monotonic function of time that maps the interval $[t_1, t_2]$ into itself.

In the special case where $g(x)$ is the identity matrix, eq. (2) reduces to the standard definition of arc length in Euclidean space. More generally, however, eq. (1) defines a non-Euclidean metric for computing arc lengths. Thus, for example, if the metric $g(x)$ varies as a function of x, then eq. (2) can assign different arc lengths to the trajectories $x(t)$ and $x(t) + x_0$, where x_0 is a constant displacement.

2.2 States and lifelengths

We now return to the problem of segmentation, as illustrated in figure 1. We refer to the possible values of s as *states*. MPCs are conditional random processes that evolve the state variable s stochastically as a function of the arc length traversed along the curve of x. In MPCs, *the probability of remaining in a particular state decays exponentially with the cumulative arc length traversed in that state*. The signature of a state is the particular way in which it computes arc length.

To formalize this idea, we associate with each state i the following quantities: (i) a feature-dependent matrix $g_i(x)$ that can be used to compute arc lengths, as in eq. (2); (ii) a decay parameter λ_i that measures the probability per unit arc length that s makes a transition from state i to some other state; and (iii) a set of transition probabilities a_{ij}, where a_{ij} represents the probability that—having decayed out of state i—the variable s makes a transition to state j. Thus, a_{ij} defines a stochastic transition matrix with zero elements along the diagonal and rows that sum to one: $a_{ii} = 0$ and $\sum_j a_{ij} = 1$. A Markov process is defined by the set of differential equations:

$$\frac{dp_i}{dt} = -\lambda_i p_i \left[\dot{x}^T g_i(x) \, \dot{x}\right]^{\frac{1}{2}} + \sum_{j \neq i} \lambda_j p_j a_{ji} \left[\dot{x}^T g_j(x) \, \dot{x}\right]^{\frac{1}{2}}, \tag{3}$$

where $p_i(t)$ denotes the (forward) probability that s is in state i at time t, based on its history up to that point in time. The right hand side of eq. (3) consists of two competing terms. The first term computes the probability that s decays out of state i; the second computes the probability that s decays into state i. Both terms are proportional to measures of arc length, making the evolution of p_i along the curve of x invariant to nonlinear warpings of time. The decay parameter, λ_i, controls the typical amount of arc length traversed in state i; it may be viewed as an inverse lifetime or—to be more precise—an inverse *lifelength*. The entire process is Markovian because the evolution of p_i depends only on quantities available at time t.

2.3 Decoding

Given a trajectory $x(t)$, the Markov process in eq. (3) gives rise to a conditional probability distribution over possible segmentations, $s(t)$. Consider the segmentation in which $s(t)$ takes the value s_k between times t_{k-1} and t_k, and let

$$\ell_{s_k} = \int_{t_{k-1}}^{t_k} dt \left[\dot{x}^T g_{s_k}(x) \dot{x}\right]^{\frac{1}{2}} \quad (4)$$

denote the arc length traversed in state s_k. By integrating eq. (3), one can show that the probability of remaining in state s_k decays exponentially with the arc length ℓ_{s_k}. Thus, the conditional probability of the overall segmentation is given by:

$$\Pr[s, \ell | x] = \prod_{k=1}^{n} \lambda_{s_k} e^{-\lambda_{s_k} \ell_{s_k}} \prod_{k=0}^{n} a_{s_k s_{k+1}}, \quad (5)$$

where we have used s_0 and s_{n+1} to denote the START and END states of the Markov process. The first product in eq. (5) multiplies the probabilities that each segment traverses exactly its observed arc length. The second product multiplies the probabilities for transitions between states s_k and s_{k+1}. The leading factors of λ_{s_k} are included to normalize each state's distribution over observed arc lengths.

There are many important quantities that can be computed from the distribution, $\Pr[s|x]$. Of particular interest for ASR is the most probable segmentation: $s^*(x) = \text{argmax}_{s,\ell} \{\ln \Pr[s, \ell | x]\}$. As described elsewhere (Saul, 1997), this maximization can be performed by discretizing the time axis and applying a dynamic programming procedure. The resulting algorithm is similar to the Viterbi procedure for maximum likelihood decoding (Rabiner & Juang, 1993).

2.4 Parameter estimation

The parameters $\{\lambda_i, a_{ij}, g_i(x)\}$ in MPCs are estimated from training data to maximize the log-likelihood of target segmentations. In our preliminary experiments with MPCs, we estimated only the metric parameters, $g_i(x)$; the others were assigned the default values $\lambda_i = 1$ and $a_{ij} = 1/f_i$, where f_i is the fanout of state i. The metrics $g_i(x)$ were assumed to have the parameterized form:

$$g_i(x) = \sigma_i^{-1} \Phi_i^2(x), \quad (6)$$

where σ_i is a positive definite matrix with unit determinant, and $\Phi_i(x)$ is a non-negative scalar-valued function of x. For the experiments in this paper, the form of $\Phi_i(x)$ was fixed so that the MPCs reduced to HMMs as a special case, as described in the next section. Thus the only learning problem was to estimate the matrix parameters σ_i. This was done using the reestimation formula:

$$\sigma_i \leftarrow C \int dt \frac{\dot{x}\dot{x}^T}{[\dot{x}^T \sigma_i^{-1} \dot{x}]^{\frac{1}{2}}} \Phi_i(x(t)), \quad (7)$$

where the integral is over all speech segments belonging to state i, and the constant C is chosen to enforce the determinant constraint $|\sigma_i| = 1$. For fixed $\Phi_i(x)$, we have shown previously (Saul, 1997) that this iterative update leads to monotonic increases in the log-likelihood.

2.5 Relation to HMMs and previous work

There are several important differences between HMMs and MPCs. HMMs parameterize joint distributions of the form: $\Pr[s, x] = \prod_t \Pr[s_{t+1}|s_t]\Pr[x_t|s_t]$. Thus, in HMMs, parameter estimation is directed at learning a *synthesis* model, $\Pr[x|s]$, while in MPCs, it is directed at learning a *segmentation* model, $\Pr[s, \ell|x]$. The direction of conditioning on x is a crucial difference. MPCs do not attempt to learn anything as ambitious as a joint distribution over acoustic feature trajectories.

HMMs and MPCs also differ in how they weight the speech signal. In HMMs, each state contributes an amount to the overall log-likelihood that grows in proportion to its duration in time. In MPCs, on the other hand, each state contributes an amount that grows in proportion to its arc length. Naturally, the weighting by arc length attaches a more important role to short-lived but *non-stationary* phonemes, such as consonants. It also guarantees the invariance to nonlinear warpings of time (to which the predictions of HMMs are quite sensitive).

In terms of previous work, our motivation for MPCs resembles that of Tishby (1990), who several years ago proposed a dynamical systems approach to speech processing. Because MPCs exploit the continuity of acoustic feature trajectories, they also bear some resemblance to so-called *segmental* HMMs (Ostendorf et al, 1996). MPCs nevertheless differ from segmental HMMs in two important respects: the invariance to nonlinear warpings of time, and the emphasis on learning a segmentation model $\Pr[s, \ell|x]$, as opposed to a synthesis model, $\Pr[x|s]$.

Finally, we note that admitting a slight generalization in the concept of arc length, we can essentially realize HMMs as a *special case* of MPCs. This is done by computing arc lengths along the *spacetime* trajectories $z(t) = \{x(t), t\}$—that is to say, replacing eq. (1) by $dL^2 = [\dot{z}^T g(z) \dot{z}]dt^2$, where $\dot{z} = \{\dot{x}, 1\}$ and $g(z)$ is a spacetime metric. This relaxes the invariance to nonlinear warpings of time and incorporates both movement in acoustic feature space *and* duration in time as measures of phonemic evolution. Moreover, in this setting, one can mimic the predictions of HMMs by setting the σ_i matrices to have only one non-zero element (namely, the diagonal element for delta-time contributions to the arc length) and by defining the functions $\Phi_i(x)$ in terms of HMM emission probabilities $P(x|i)$ as:

$$\Phi_i(x) = -\ln\left[\frac{P(x|i)}{\sum_k P(x|k)}\right]. \qquad (8)$$

This relation is important because it allows us to *initialize* the parameters of an MPC by those of a continuous-density HMM. This initialization was used in all the experiments reported below.

3 Automatic speech recognition

Both HMMs and MPCs were used to build connected speech recognizers. Training and test data came from speaker-independent databases of telephone speech. All data was digitized at the caller's local switch and transmitted in this form to the receiver. For feature extraction, input telephone signals (sampled at 8 kHz and band-limited between 100-3800 Hz) were pre-emphasized and blocked into 30ms frames with a frame shift of 10ms. Each frame was Hamming windowed, autocorrelated, and processed by LPC cepstral analysis to produce a vector of 12 liftered cepstral coefficients (Rabiner & Juang, 1993). The feature vector was then augmented by its normalized log energy value, as well as temporal derivatives of first and second order. Overall, each frame of speech was described by 39 features. These features were used differently by HMMs and MPCs, as described below.

Mixtures	HMM (%)	MPC (%)
2	22.3	20.9
4	18.9	17.5
8	16.5	15.1
16	14.6	13.3
32	13.5	12.3
64	11.7	11.4

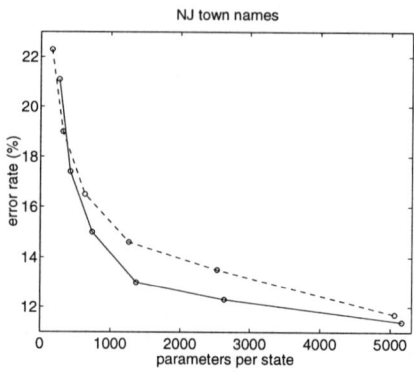

Table 1: Word error rates for HMMs (dashed) and MPCs (solid) on the task of recognizing NJ town names. The table shows the error rates versus the number of mixture components; the graph, versus the number of parameters per hidden state.

Recognizers were evaluated on two tasks. The first task was recognizing New Jersey town names (e.g., Newark). The training data for this task (Sachs et al, 1994) consisted of 12100 short phrases, spoken in the seven major dialects of American English. These phrases, ranging from two to four words in length, were selected to provide maximum phonetic coverage. The test data consisted of 2426 isolated utterances of 1219 New Jersey town names and was collected from nearly 100 speakers. Note that the training and test data for this task have non-overlapping vocabularies.

Baseline recognizers were built using 43 left-to-right continuous-density HMMs, each corresponding to a context-independent English phone. Phones were modeled by three-state HMMs, with the exception of background noise, which was modeled by a single state. State emission probabilities were computed by mixtures of Gaussians with diagonal covariance matrices. Different sized models were trained using $M = 2$, 4, 8, 16, 32, and 64 mixture components per hidden state; for a particular model, the number of mixture components was the same across all states. Parameter estimation was handled by a Viterbi implementation of the Baum-Welch algorithm.

MPC recognizers were built using the same overall grammar. Each hidden state in the MPCs was assigned a metric $g_i(\boldsymbol{x}) = \sigma_i^{-1} \Phi_i^2(\boldsymbol{x})$. The functions $\Phi_i(\boldsymbol{x})$ were initialized (and fixed) by the state emission probabilities of the HMMs, as given by eq. (8). The matrices σ_i were estimated by iterating eq. (7). We computed arc lengths along the 14 dimensional spacetime trajectories through cepstra, log-energy, and time. Thus each σ_i was a 14 × 14 symmetric matrix applied to tangent vectors consisting of delta-cepstra, delta-log-energy, and delta-time.

The table in figure 1 shows the results of these experiments comparing MPCs to HMMs. For various model sizes (as measured by the number of mixture components), we found the MPCs to yield consistently lower error rates than the HMMs. The graph in figure 1 plots these word error rates versus the number of modeling parameters per hidden state. This graph shows that the MPCs are not outperforming the HMMs merely because they have extra modeling parameters (i.e., the σ_i matrices). The beam widths for the decoding procedures in these experiments were chosen so that corresponding recognizers activated roughly equal numbers of arcs.

The second task in our experiments involved the recognition of connected alpha-digits (e.g., N Z 3 V J 4 E 3 U 2). The training and test data consisted of

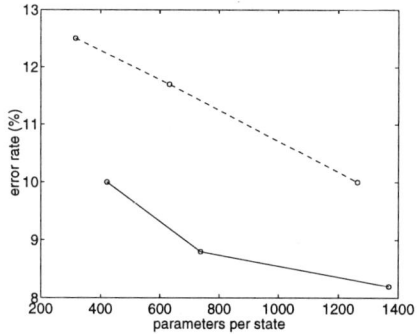

Mixtures	HMM (%)	MPC (%)
2	12.5	10.0
4	10.7	8.8
8	10.0	8.2

Figure 2: Word error rates for HMMs and MPCs on the task of recognizing connected alpha-digits. The table shows the error rates versus the number of mixture components; the graph, versus the number of parameters per hidden state.

14622 and 7255 utterances, respectively. Recognizers were built from 285 sub-word HMMs/MPCs, each corresponding to a context-dependent English phone. The recognizers were trained and evaluated in the same way as the previous task. Results are shown in figure 2.

While these results demonstrate the viability of MPCs for automatic speech recognition, several issues require further attention. The most important issues are feature selection—how to define meaningful acoustic trajectories from the raw speech signal—and learning—how to parameterize and estimate the hidden state metrics $g_i(x)$ from sampled trajectories $\{x(t)\}$. These issues and others will be studied in future work.

References

M. P. do Carmo (1976). *Differential Geometry of Curves and Surfaces*. Prentice Hall.

M. Ostendorf, V. Digalakis, and O. Kimball (1996). From HMMs to segment models: a unified view of stochastic modeling for speech recognition. *IEEE Transactions on Acoustics, Speech and Signal Processing*, 4:360-378.

L. Rabiner and B. Juang (1993). *Fundamentals of Speech Recognition*. Prentice Hall, Englewood Cliffs, NJ.

R. Sachs, M. Tikijian, and E. Roskos (1994). United States English subword speech data. *AT&T unpublished report*.

L. Saul (1998). Automatic segmentation of continuous trajectories with invariance to nonlinear warpings of time. In *Proceedings of the Fifteenth International Conference on Machine Learning*, 506-514.

M. A. Siegler and R. M. Stern (1995). On the effects of speech rate in large vocabulary speech recognition systems. In *Proceedings of the 1995 IEEE International Conference on Acoustics, Speech, and Signal Processing*, 612-615.

N. Tishby (1990). A dynamical system approach to speech processing. In *Proceedings of the 1990 IEEE International Conference on Acoustics, Speech, and Signal Processing*, 365-368.

Part VII
Visual Processing

A Phase Space Approach to Minimax Entropy Learning and the Minutemax Approximations

James M. Coughlan
Smith-Kettlewell Inst.
San Francisco, CA 94115

A. L. Yuille
Smith-Kettlewell Inst.
San Francisco, CA 94115

Abstract

There has been much recent work on measuring image statistics and on learning probability distributions on images. We observe that the mapping from images to statistics is many-to-one and show it can be quantified by a phase space factor. This phase space approach throws light on the Minimax Entropy technique for learning Gibbs distributions on images with potentials derived from image statistics and elucidates the ambiguities that are inherent to determining the potentials. In addition, it shows that if the phase factor can be approximated by an analytic distribution then this approximation yields a swift "Minutemax" algorithm that vastly reduces the computation time for Minimax entropy learning. An illustration of this concept, using a Gaussian to approximate the phase factor, gives a good approximation to the results of Zhu and Mumford (1997) in just seconds of CPU time. The phase space approach also gives insight into the multi-scale potentials found by Zhu and Mumford (1997) and suggests that the forms of the potentials are influenced greatly by phase space considerations. Finally, we prove that probability distributions learned in feature space alone are equivalent to Minimax Entropy learning with a multinomial approximation of the phase factor.

1 Introduction

Bayesian probability theory gives a powerful framework for visual perception (Knill and Richards 1996). This approach, however, requires specifying prior probabilities and likelihood functions. Learning these probabilities is difficult because it requires estimating distributions on random variables of very high dimensions (for example, images with 200 × 200 pixels, or shape curves of length 400 pixels). An important recent advance is the Minimax Entropy Learning theory. This theory was developed by Zhu, Wu and Mumford (1997 and 1998) and enables them to learn probability distributions for the intensity properties and shapes of natural stimuli and clutter. In addition, when applied to real world images it has an interesting link to the work on natural image statistics (Field 1987), (Ruderman and Bialek 1994), (Olshaussen and Field 1996). We wish to simplify Minimax and make the learning easier, faster and more transparent.

In this paper we present a phase space approach to Minimax Entropy learning. This approach is based on the observation that the mapping from images to statistics is many-to-one and can be quantified by a phase space factor. If this phase space factor can be approximated by an analytic function then we obtain approximate "Minutemax" algorithms which greatly speed up the learning process. In one version of this approximation, the unknown parameters of the distribution to be learned are related linearly to the empirical statistics of the image data set, and may be solved for in seconds or less. Independent of this approximation, the Minutemax framework also illuminates an important combinatoric aspect of Minimax, namely the fact that many different images can give rise to the same image statistics. This "phase space" factor explains the ambiguities inherent in learning the parameters of the unknown distribution, and motivates the approximation that reduces the problem to linear algebra. Finally, we prove that probability distributions learned in feature space alone are equivalent to Minimax Entropy learning with a multinomial approximation of the phase factor.

2   A Phase Space Perspective on Minimax

We wish to learn a distribution $P(\mathbf{I})$ on images, where $\mathbf{I}$ denotes the set of pixel values $I(x,y)$ on a finite image lattice, and each value $I(x,y)$ is quantized to a finite set of intensity values. (In fact, this approach is general and applies to any patterns, not just images.) We define a set of image statistics $\phi_1(\mathbf{I}), \phi_2(\mathbf{I}), \ldots, \phi_S(\mathbf{I})$, which we concatenate as a single vector function $\vec{\phi}(\mathbf{I})$. If these statistics have empirical mean $\vec{d} \equiv <\vec{\phi}(\mathbf{I})>$ on a dataset of images (we assume a large enough dataset for the law of large numbers to apply; see Zhu and Mumford (1997) for an analysis of the errors inherent in this assumption) then the maximum entropy distribution $P_M(\mathbf{I})$ with these empirical statistics is an exponential (Gibbs) distribution of the form

$$P_M(\mathbf{I}) = \frac{e^{\vec{\lambda}\cdot\vec{\phi}(\mathbf{I})}}{Z(\vec{\lambda})}, \qquad (1)$$

where the potential $\vec{\lambda}$ is set so that $<\vec{\phi}(\mathbf{I})>_M = \vec{d}$.

In summary, the goal of Minimax Learning is to to find an appropriate set of image filters for the domain of interest (i.e. maximally informative filters) and to estimate $\vec{\lambda}$ given $\vec{d}$. Extensive computation is required to determine $\vec{\lambda}$; the phase space approach to Minimax Learning motivates approximations that make $\vec{\lambda}$ easy to estimate.

2.1   Image Histogram Statistics

The statistics we consider (following Zhu, Wu and Mumford (1997, 1998)) are defined as histograms of the responses of one or more filters applied across an entire image. Consider a single filter f (linear or non-linear) with response $f_\mathbf{x}(\mathbf{I})$ centered at position $\mathbf{x}$ in the image. Without loss of generality, we will assume the filter has quantized integer responses from 1 through f_{max}.

For notational convenience we transform the filter response $f_{\mathbf{x}}(\mathbf{I})$ to a binary representation $\vec{b}_{\mathbf{x}}(\mathbf{I})$, defined as a column vector with f_{max} components: $\vec{b}_{\mathbf{x},z}(\mathbf{I}) = \delta_{z,f_{\mathbf{x}}(\mathbf{I})}$, where index z ranges from 1 through f_{max}. This vector is composed of all zeros except for the entry corresponding to the filter response, which is set to one. The image statistics vector is then a histogram vector defined as the average of the $\vec{b}_{\mathbf{x}}(\mathbf{I})$'s over all N pixels: $\vec{\phi}(\mathbf{I}) = \frac{1}{N}\sum_{\mathbf{x}}\vec{b}_{\mathbf{x}}(\mathbf{I})$. The entries in $\vec{\phi}(\mathbf{I})$ then sum to 1. (We can generalize to the case of multiple filters $f^{(1)}, f^{(2)}, \ldots, f^{(m)}$, as detailed in Coughlan and Yuille (1999).)

2.2 The Phase Factor

The original Minimax distribution $P_M(\mathbf{I})$ induces a distribution $P_M(\vec{\phi})$ on the statistics themselves, without reference to a particular image:

$$P_M(\vec{\phi}_0) = \sum_{\mathbf{I}} \delta_{\vec{\phi}_0,\vec{\phi}(\mathbf{I})} P_M(\mathbf{I}) = g(\vec{\phi}_0)\frac{e^{\vec{\lambda}\cdot\vec{\phi}_0}}{Z(\vec{\lambda})} \qquad (2)$$

where $g(\vec{\phi})$ is a combinatoric *phase space factor*, with a corresponding *normalized* combinatoric distribution $\hat{g}(\vec{\phi})$, defined by:

$$g(\vec{\phi}_0) = \sum_{\mathbf{I}} \delta_{\vec{\phi}_0,\vec{\phi}(\mathbf{I})}, \text{ and } \hat{g}(\vec{\phi}) = g(\vec{\phi})/Q^N, \qquad (3)$$

where the phase space factor $g(\vec{\phi})$ counts the number of images $\mathbf{I}$ having statistics $\vec{\phi}$. N is the number of pixels and Q is the number of pixel intensity levels, i.e. Q^N is the total number of possible images $\mathbf{I}$. It should be emphasized that *the phase factor depends only on the set of filters chosen and is independent of the true distribution $P(\mathbf{I})$*. Thus the phase factor can be computed offline, independent of the image data set.

In this paper we will discuss two useful approximations to $g(\vec{\phi})$: a Gaussian approximation, which yields the swift approximation for learning, and a multinomial approximation, which establishes a connection between Minimax and standard feature learning.

2.3 The Non-Uniqueness of the Potential $\vec{\lambda}$

Given a set of filters and their empirical mean statistics $\vec{d}$, is the potential $\vec{\lambda}$ uniquely specified? Clearly, any solution for $\vec{\lambda}$ may be shifted by an additive constant ($\lambda_i \to \lambda_i' = \lambda_i + k$ for all i), yielding a different normalization constant $Z(\vec{\lambda}')$ but preserving $P_M(\mathbf{I})$. In this section we show that other, non-trivial ambiguities in $\vec{\lambda}$ which preserve $P_M(\mathbf{I})$ can exist, stemming from the fact that some values of $\vec{\phi}$ are inconsistent with every possible image $\mathbf{I}$ and hence never arise (in *any* possible image dataset). These "intrinsic" ambiguities are inherent to Minimax and are independent of the true distribution $P(\mathbf{I})$. We will also discuss a second type of possible ambiguity which depends on the characteristics of the image dataset used for learning.

We can uncover the intrinsic ambiguities in $\vec{\lambda}$ by examining the covariance C of $\hat{g}(\vec{\phi})$. (See Coughlan and Yuille (1999) for details on calculating the mean $\vec{c}$ and covariance C for any set of linear filters or non-linear filters that are scalar functions of linear filters.) Defining the set of all possible statistics values $\Phi = \{\vec{\phi} : g(\vec{\phi}) \neq 0\}$, the null space of C reflects degeneracy (i.e. flatness) in Φ. The following theorem, proved in Coughlan and Yuille (1999), shows that $\vec{\lambda}$ is determined only up to a hyperplane whose dimension is the nullity of C.

Theorem 1 (Intrinsic Ambiguity in $\vec{\lambda}$). $C\vec{\mu} = 0$ if and only if $e^{(\vec{\lambda}+\vec{\mu}) \cdot \vec{\phi}(\mathbf{I})}/Z(\vec{\lambda}+\vec{\mu})$ and $e^{\vec{\lambda} \cdot \vec{\phi}(\mathbf{I})}/Z(\vec{\lambda})$ are identical distributions on $\mathbf{I}$.

In addition to this intrinsic ambiguity in $\vec{\lambda}$, it is also possible that different values of $\vec{\lambda}$ may yield distinct distributions which nevertheless have the same mean statistics $<\vec{\phi}>$ on the image dataset. (As shown in Coughlan and Yuille (1999), there is a *convex set of distributions*, of which the true distribution $P(\mathbf{I})$ is a member, which share the same mean statistics $<\vec{\phi}>$.) This second kind of ambiguity stems from the fact that the mean statistics convey only a fraction of the information that is contained in the true distribution $P(\mathbf{I})$. To resolve this second ambiguity it is necessary to extract more information from the image data set. The simplest way to achieve this is to use a larger (or more informative) set of filters to lower the entropy of $P_M(\mathbf{I})$ (this topic is discussed in more detail in Zhu, Wu and Mumford (1997, 1998), Coughlan and Yuille (1999)). Alternatively, one can extend Minimax to include second-order statistics, i.e. the covariance of $\vec{\phi}$ in addition to its mean $\vec{d}$. This is an important topic for future research.

3 The Minutemax Approximations

We now illustrate the phase space approach by showing that suitable approximations of the phase space factor $g(\vec{\phi})$ make it easy to estimate the potential $\vec{\lambda}$ given the empirical mean $\vec{d}$. The resulting fast approximations to Minimax Learning are called "Minutemax" algorithms.

3.1 The Gaussian Approximation of $g(\vec{\phi})$

If the phase space factor $g(\vec{\phi})$ may be approximated as a multi-variate Gaussian (see Coughlan and Yuille (1999) for a justification of this approximation) then the probability distribution $P_M(\vec{\phi}) = g(\vec{\phi})e^{\vec{\lambda} \cdot \vec{\phi}}/Z(\vec{\lambda})$ reduces to another multi-variate Gaussian. (Note that we are making the Gaussian approximation in $\vec{\phi}$ space–the space of all possible image statistics histograms–and not filter response (feature) space.) As we will see, this result greatly simplifies the problem of estimating the potential $\vec{\lambda}$.

Recall that the mean and covariance of $\hat{g}(\vec{\phi})$ are denoted by $\vec{c}$ and C, respectively. The null space of C has dimension n and is spanned by vectors $\vec{u}^{(1)}, \vec{u}^{(2)} \ldots \vec{u}^{(n)}$. As discussed in Theorem 1, for all *feasible* values of $\vec{\phi}$ (i.e. all $\vec{\phi} \in \Phi$) and all $\vec{\mu}$ in the null space, $\vec{\mu} \cdot \vec{\phi}$ is a constant k. Thus we have that

$$g_{gauss}(\vec{\phi}) \propto \{\prod_{i=1}^{n} \delta_{\vec{\phi} \cdot \vec{u}_i, k}\} e^{-\frac{1}{2}(\vec{\phi}_r - \vec{c}_r)^T C_r^{-1}(\vec{\phi}_r - \vec{c}_r)}, \quad (4)$$

where the subscript r denotes projection onto the rank of C. Thus $P_{gauss}(\vec{\phi}) \propto g_{gauss}(\vec{\phi})e^{\vec{\lambda} \cdot \vec{\phi}} \propto \{\prod_{i=1}^{n} \delta_{\vec{\phi} \cdot \vec{u}_i, k}\} e^{-\frac{1}{2}(\vec{\phi}_r - \vec{c}_r)^T C_r^{-1}(\vec{\phi}_r - \vec{c}_r) + \vec{\lambda} \cdot \vec{\phi}}$. Completing the square in the exponent yields $P_{gauss}(\vec{\phi}) \propto \{\prod_{i=1}^{n} \delta_{\vec{\phi} \cdot \vec{u}_i, k}\} e^{-\frac{1}{2}(\vec{\phi}_r - \vec{\psi}_r)^T C_r^{-1}(\vec{\phi}_r - \vec{\psi}_r)}$ where $\vec{\psi}_r$

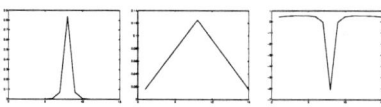

Figure 1: From left to right: $\vec{d}$, $\vec{c}$ and $-\vec{\lambda}$ (as computed by the Gaussian Minutemax approximation) for first filter alone.

is the projection of any $\vec{\psi}$ that satisfies $\vec{\psi} = \vec{c} + C\vec{\lambda}$. Since $P_{gauss}(\vec{\phi})$ is a Gaussian we have $<\vec{\phi}>_{gauss} = \vec{\psi} = \vec{d}$, and so we can write a linear equation relating $\vec{\lambda}$ and $\vec{d}$: $\vec{d} = \vec{c} + C\vec{\lambda}$.

It can be shown (Zhu – private communication) that solving this equation is equivalent to one step of Newton-Raphson for minimization of an appropriate cost function. This will fail to be a good approximation if the cost function is highly non-quadratic. As explained in Coughlan and Yuille (1999), the Gaussian approximation is also equivalent to a second-order perturbation expansion of the partition function $Z(\vec{\lambda})$; higher-order corrections can be made by computing higher-order moments of $g(\vec{\phi})$.

3.2 Experimental Results

We tested the Gaussian Minutemax procedure on two sets of filters: a single (fine scale) image gradient filter $\partial I/\partial x$, and a set of multi-scale image gradient filters defined at three scales, similar to those used by Zhu and Mumford (1997). In both sets, the fine scale gradient filter is linear with kernel $(1, -1)$, representing a discretization of $\partial/\partial x$. In the second set, the medium scale filter kernel is $(U_2, -U_2)/4$ and the coarse scale kernel is $(U_4, -U_4)/16$, where U_n denotes the $n \times n$ matrix of all ones. The responses of the medium and coarse filters were rounded (i.e. quantized) to the nearest integer, thus adding a non-linearity to these filters. Finally, $\vec{d}$ was measured on a data set of over 100 natural images; the fine scale components of $\vec{d}$ are shown in the first panel of Figure (1) and were empirically very similar to the medium and coarse scale components.

A $\vec{\lambda}$ that solves $\vec{d} = \vec{c} + C\vec{\lambda}$ is shown in the third panel of Figure (1) for the first filter (along with $\vec{c}$ in the second panel) and in the three panels of Figure (2) for the multi-scale filter set. The form of $\vec{\lambda}$ is qualitatively similar to that obtained by Zhu and Mumford (1997) (bearing in mind that Zhu disregarded any filter responses with magnitude above $Q/2$, i.e. his filter response range is half of ours). In addition, the eigenvectors of C with small eigenvalues are large away from the origin, so one should not trust the values of the potentials there (obtained by *any* algorithm).

Zhu and Mumford (1997) report interactions between filters applied at different scales. This is because the resulting potentials appear different than the potential at the fine scale even though the histograms appear similar at all scales. We argue, however, that some of this "interaction" is due to *the different phase factors at different scales*. In other words the potentials would look different at different scales *even if the empirical histograms were identical* because of differing phase factors.

3.3 The Multinomial Approximation of $g(\vec{\phi})$

Many learning theories simply make probability distributions on feature space. How do they differ from Minimax Entropy Learning which works on image space? By

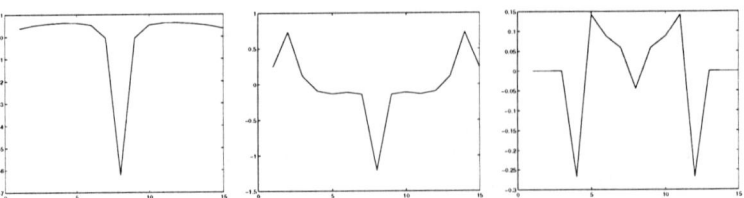

Figure 2: From left to right: the fine, medium and coarse components of $-\vec{\lambda}$ as computed by the Gaussian Minutemax approximation.

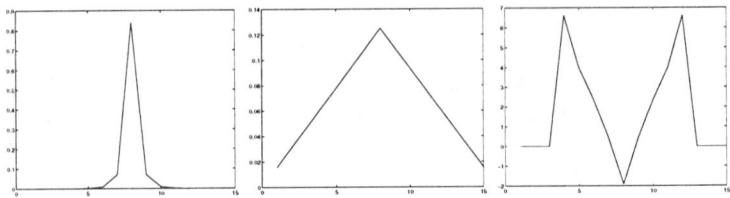

Figure 3: Left to right: $\vec{d}, \vec{c}$, and $-\vec{\lambda}$ as given by multinomial approximation for the $\partial/\partial x$ filter at fine scale.

examining the phase factor we will show that the two approaches are not identical in general. The feature space learning ignores the coupling between the filters which arise due to how the statistics are obtained. More precisely, the probability distribution obtained on feature space, P_F, is equivalent to the Minimax distribution P_M if, and only if, the phase factor is multinomial.

We begin the analysis by considering a single filter. As before we define the combinatoric mean $\vec{c} = \sum_{\vec{\phi}} \hat{g}(\vec{\phi})\vec{\phi}$. The multinomial approximation of $\hat{g}(\vec{\phi})$ is equivalent to assuming that the combinatoric frequencies of filter responses are *independent* from pixel to pixel. Since the combinatoric frequency of filter response $j \in \{1, 2, \ldots, f_{max}\}$ is c_j and there are $N\phi_j$ pixels with response j, we have:

$$\hat{g}_{mult}(\vec{\phi}) = \prod_{j=1}^{f_{max}} c_j^{N\phi_j} \frac{N!}{\prod_{j=1}^{f_{max}} (N\phi_j)!}, \text{ and } P_{mult}(\vec{\phi}) \propto \prod_{j=1}^{f_{max}} (c_j e^{\lambda_j/N})^{N\phi_j} \frac{N!}{\prod_{j=1}^{f_{max}} (N\phi_j)!} \quad (5)$$

using $P_{mult}(\vec{\phi}) \propto g_{mult}(\vec{\phi})e^{\vec{\lambda}\cdot\vec{\phi}}$. Therefore $P_{mult}(\vec{\phi})$ is also a multinomial. Shifting the λ_j's by an appropriate additive constant, we can make the constant of proportionality in the above equation equal to 1. In this case we have $<\phi_j>_{mult} = c_j e^{\lambda_j/N}$ and $\lambda_j = N \log(d_j/c_j)$ by setting $<\phi_j>_{mult}$ to the empirical mean d_j.

Note that if any component d_j of the empirical mean is close to 0 then by the previous equation any small perturbations in d_j (e.g. from sampling error) will yield large changes in λ_j, making the estimate of that component unstable.

We can generalize the multinomial approximation of $g(\vec{\phi})$ to the multiple filter case merely by factoring $\hat{g}_{mult}(\vec{\phi})$ into separate multinomials, one for each filter. Of course, this approximation neglects all interactions among filters (and among pixels).

3.4 The Multinomial Approximation and Feature Learning

The connection between the multinomial approximation and feature learning is straightforward once we consider a distribution on the feature vector $\vec{f}$. This distribution (denoted P_F for "feature") is constructed assuming independent filter responses from pixel to pixel and with statistics matching the empirical mean $\vec{d}$: $P_F(\vec{f}) = \prod_{i=1}^{N} d_{(f_i)}$, where f_i denotes the filter response at pixel i. Then it follows that $P_F(\vec{\phi})$ is a multinomial: $P_F(\vec{\phi}) = \prod_{j=1}^{f_{max}} d_j^{N\phi_j} \frac{N!}{\prod_{j=1}^{f_{max}}(N\phi_j)!}$. Since $d_j = c_j e^{\lambda_j/N}$, we have our main result that $P_F(\vec{\phi}) = P_{mult}(\vec{\phi})$.

4 Conclusion

The main point of this paper is to introduce the phase space factor to quantify the mapping between images and their feature statistics. This phase space approach can: (i) provide fast approximate "Minutemax" algorithms, (ii) clarify the relationship between probability distributions learned in feature and image space, and (iii) to determine intrinsic ambiguities in the $\vec{\lambda}$ potentials.

Acknowledgements

We acknowledge stimulating discussions with Song Chun Zhu. Funding was provided by the Smith-Kettlewell Institute Core Grant and the Center for Imaging Sciences ARO grant DAANO4-95-1-0494.

References

Coughlan, J.M. and Yuille, A.L. "The Phase Space of Minimax Entropy Learning". In preparation. 1999.

Field, D. J. "Relations between the statistics of natural images and the response properties of cortical cells". *Journal of the Optical Society* 4,(12), 2379-2394. 1987.

D.C. Knill and W. Richards. (Eds). **Perception as Bayesian Inference**. Cambridge University Press. 1996.

Olshausen, B. A. and Field, D. J. "Emergence of simple-cell receptive field properties by learning a sparse code for natural images". *Nature*. 381, 607-609. 1996.

B.D. Ripley. **Pattern Recognition and Neural Networks**. Cambridge University Press. 1996.

Ruderman, D. and Bialek, W. "Statistics of Natural Images: Scaling in the Woods". *Physical Review Letters*. 73, Number 6,(8 August 1994), 814-817. 1994.

S.C. Zhu, Y. Wu, and D. Mumford. "Minimax Entropy Principle and Its Application to Texture Modeling". Neural Computation. Vol. 9. no. 8. Nov. 1997.

S.C. Zhu and D. Mumford. "Prior Learning and Gibbs Reaction-Diffusion". IEEE Trans. on PAMI vol. 19, no. 11. Nov. 1997.

S-C Zhu, Y-N Wu and D. Mumford. FRAME: Filters, Random field And Maximum Entropy: — Towards a Unified Theory for Texture Modeling. Int'l Journal of Computer Vision 27(2) 1-20, March/April. 1998.

Example Based Image Synthesis of Articulated Figures

Trevor Darrell
Interval Research, 1801C Page Mill Road, Palo Alto CA 94304
trevor@interval.com, http://www.interval.com/~trevor/

Abstract

We present a method for learning complex appearance mappings, such as occur with images of articulated objects. Traditional interpolation networks fail on this case since appearance is not necessarily a smooth function nor a linear manifold for articulated objects. We define an appearance mapping from examples by constructing a set of independently smooth interpolation networks; these networks can cover overlapping regions of parameter space. A set growing procedure is used to find example clusters which are well-approximated within their convex hull; interpolation then proceeds only within these sets of examples. With this method physically valid images are produced even in regions of parameter space where nearby examples have different appearances. We show results generating both simulated and real arm images.

1 Introduction

Image-based view synthesis is an important application of learning networks, offering the ability to render realistic images without requiring detailed models of object shape and illumination effects. To date, much attention has been given to the problem of view synthesis under varying camera pose or rigid object transformation. Several successful solutions have been proposed in the computer graphics and vision literature, including view morphing [12], plenoptic modeling/depth recovery [8], "lightfields" [7], and recent approaches using the trifocal tensor for view extrapolation [13].

For non-rigid view synthesis, networks for model-based interpolation and manifold learning have been used successfully in some cases [14, 2, 4, 11]. Techniques based on Radial Basis Function (RBF) interpolation or on Principle Components Analysis (PCA), have been able to interpolate face images under varying pose, expression and identity [1, 5, 6]. How-

extends the notion of example clustering to the case of coupled shape and texture appearance models.

Our basic method is to find sets of examples which can be well-approximated from their convex hull in parameter space. We define a set growing criterion which enforces compactness and the good-interpolation property. To add a new point to an example set, we require both that the new point must be well approximated by the previous set alone and that all interior points in the resulting set be well interpolated from the exterior examples. We define exterior examples to be those on the convex hull of the set in parameter space. Given a training subset $s \subset \Omega$ and new point $p \in \Omega$,

$$E(s,p) = \max(E_I(s \cup \{p\}), E_E(s,p)) ,$$

with the interior and extrapolation error defined as

$$E_I(s) = \max_{p' \in (s - \mathcal{H}_x(s))} ||y_{p'} - \hat{y}(\mathcal{H}_x(s), x_{p'})|| , \qquad E_E(s,p) = ||y_p - \hat{y}(\mathcal{H}_x(s), x_p)|| .$$

$\mathcal{H}_x(s)$ is the subset of s whose x vectors lie on the convex hull of all such vectors in s. To add a new point, we require $E < \epsilon$, where ϵ is a free parameter of the clustering method.

Given a seed example set, we look to nearest neighbors in appearance space to find the next candidate to add. Unless we are willing to test the extrapolation error of the current model to all points, we have to rely on precomputed non-vectorized appearance distance (e.g., MSE between example images). If the examples are sparse in the appearance domain, this may not lead to effective groupings.

If examples are provided in sequence and are based on observations from an object with realistic dynamics, then we can find effective groupings even if observations are sparse in appearance space. We make the assumption that along the trajectory of example observations over time, the underlying object is likely to remain smooth and locally span regions of appearance which are possible to interpolate. We thus perform set growing along examples on their input trajectory. Specifically, in the results reported below, we select K seed points on the trajectory to form initial clusters. At each point p we find the set s which is the smallest interval on the example trajectory which contains p, has a non-zero interior region $(s - \mathcal{H}_x(s))$, and for which $E_I(s) < \epsilon$. If such set exists, we continue to expand it, growing the set along the example trajectory until the above set growing criterion is violated. Once we can no longer grow any set, we test whether any set is a proper subset of another, and delete it if so. We keep the remaining sets, and use them for interpolation as described below.

4 Synthesis using example sets

We generate new views using sets of examples: interpolation is restricted to only occur inside the convex hull of an example set found as above for which $E_I(s) \leq \epsilon$. Given a new parameter vector x, we test whether it is in the convex hull of parameters in any example set. If the point does not lie in the convex hull of any example set, we find the nearest point on the convex hull of one of the example sets, and use that instead. This prevents erroneous extrapolation.

If a new parameter is in the convex hull of more than one example set, we first select the set whose median example parameter is closest to the desired example parameter. Once a set has been selected, we interpolate a new function value from examples using the RBF method summarized above. To enforce temporal consistency of rendered images over time,

Figure 2: (a) Images of a real arm (from a sequence of 33 images) with changing appearance and elbow configuration. (b,c) Interpolated shape of arms tracked in previous figure. (b) shows results using all examples in a single interpolation network; (c) shows results using example sets algorithm. Open contours show arms example locations; filled contour shows interpolation result. Near regions of appearance singularity in parameter space the full network method generates physically-invalid arm shapes; the example sets method produces realistic images.

The method presented below for grouping examples into locally valid spaces is generally applicable to both the PCA and RBF-based view synthesis techniques. However our initial implementation, and the results reported in this paper, have been with RBF-based models.

3 Finding consistent example sets

Given examples from a complicated (non-linear, non-smooth) appearance mapping, we find local regions of appearance which are well-behaved as smooth, possibly linear, functions. We wish to cluster our examples into sets which can be used for successful interpolation using our local appearance model.

Conceptually, this problem is similar to that faced by Bregler and Omohundro [2], who built image manifolds using a mixture of local PCA models. Their work was limited to modeling shape (lip outlines); they used K-means clustering of image appearance to form the initial groupings for PCA analysis. However this approach had no model of texture and performed clustering using a mean-squared-error distance metric in simple appearance. Simple appearance clustering drastically over-partitions the appearance space compared to a model that jointly represent shape and texture. Examples which are distant in simple appearance can often be close when considered in 'vectorized' representation. Our work

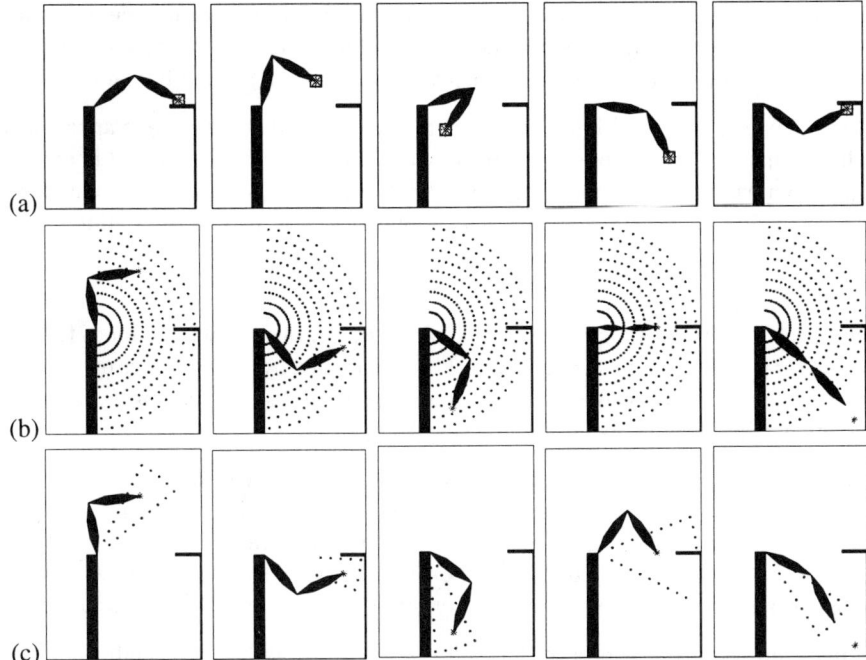

Figure 1: Arm appearance interpolated from examples using approximation network. (a) A 2DOF planar arm. Discontinuities in appearance due to workspace constraints make this a difficult function to learn from examples; the first and last example are very close in parameter space, but far in appearance space. (b) shows results using all examples in a single network; (c) using the example sets algorithm described in text. Note poor approximation on last two examples in (a); appearance discontinuities and extrapolation cause problems for full network, but are handled well in examples sets method.

In PCA-based approaches, G projects a portion of u onto a optimal linear subspace found from D, and F projects a portion of u onto a subspace found from T [6, 5]. For example $G_D(u) = P_D^m S_g u$, where S_g is a diagonal boolean matrix which selects the texture parameters from u and P_D^m is a matrix containing the m-th largest principle components of D. F warps the reconstructed texture according to the given shape: $F_T(u, s) = [P_T^m S_t u] \circ s$. While interpolation is simple using a PCA approach, the parameters used in PCA models often do not have any direct physical interpretation. For the task of view synthesis, an additional mapping $u = H(x)$ is needed to map from task parameters to PCA input values; a backpropagation neural net was used to perform this function for the task of eye gaze analysis [10].

Using the RBF-based approach [1], the application to view synthesis is straightforward. Both G and F are networks which compute locally-weighted regression, and parameters are used directly ($u = x$). G computes an interpolated shape, and F warps and blends the example texture images according to that shape: $G_D(x) = \sum_i c_i f(x - x_i)$, $F_T(x, s) = [\sum_i c'_i f(x - x_i)] \circ s$, where f is a radial basis function. The coefficients c and c' are derived from D and T, respectively: $C = DR^+$, where $r_{ij} = f(x_i - x_j)$ and C is the matrix of row vectors c_i; similarly $C' = TR^+$ [9]. We have found both vector norm and Gaussian basis functions give good results when appearance data is from a smooth function; the results below use $f(r) = ||r||$.

ever, these methods are limited in the types of object appearance they can accurately model. PCA-based face analysis typically assumes images of face shape and texture fall in a linear subspace; RBF approaches fare poorly when appearance is not a smooth function.

We want to extend non-rigid interpolation networks to handle cases where appearance is not a linear manifold and is not a smooth function, such as with articulated bodies. The mapping from parameter to appearance for articulated bodies is often one-to-many due to the multiple solutions possible for a given endpoint. It will also be discontinuous when constraints call for different solutions across a boundary in parameter space, such as the example shown in Figure 1.

Our approach represents an appearance mapping as a set of piecewise smooth functions. We search for sets of examples which are well approximated by the examples on the convex hull of the set's parameter values. Once we have these 'safe' sets of examples we perform interpolation using only the examples in a single set.

The clear advantage of this approach is that it will prevent inconsistent examples from being combined during interpolation. It also can reduce the number of examples needed to fully interpolate the function, as only those examples which are on the convex hull of one or more example sets are needed. If a new example is provided and it falls within and is well-approximated by the convex hull of an existing set, it can be safely ignored.

The remainder of this paper proceeds as follows. First, we will review methods for modeling appearance when it can be well approximated with a smooth and/or linear function. Next, we will present a technique for clustering examples to find maximal subsets which are well approximated in their interior. We will then detail how we select among the subsets during interpolation, and finally show results with both synthetic and real imagery.

2 Modeling smooth and/or linear appearance functions

Traditional interpolation networks work well when object appearance can be modeled either as a linear manifold or as a smooth function over the parameters of interest (describing pose, expression, identity, configuration, etc.). As mentioned above, both PCA and RBF approaches have been successfully applied to model facial expression.

In both approaches, a key step in modeling non-rigid shape appearance from examples is to couple shape and texture into a single representation. Interpolation of shape has been well studied in the computer graphics literature (e.g., splines for key-frame animation) but does not alone render realistic images. PCA or RBF models of images without a shape model can only represent and interpolate within a very limited range of pose or object configuration.

In a coupled representation, texture is modeled in shape-normalized coordinates, and shape is modeled as disparity between examples or displacement from a canonical example to all examples. Image warping is used to generate images for a particular texture and shape. Given a training set $\Omega = \{(y_i, x_i, d_i), 0 \leq i \leq n\}$, where y_i is the image of example i, x_i is the associated pose or configuration parameter, and d_i is a dense correspondence map relative to a canonical pose, a set of shape-aligned texture images can be computed such that texture t_i warped with displacement d_i renders example image y_i: $y_i = t_i \circ d_i$ [5, 1, 6]. A new image is constructed using a coupled shape model G and texture model F, based on input u:

$$\hat{y}(\Omega, u) = F_T(G_D(u), u) ,$$

where D, T are the matrices $[d_0 d_1 ... d_n]$, $[t_0 t_1 ... t_n]$, respectively.

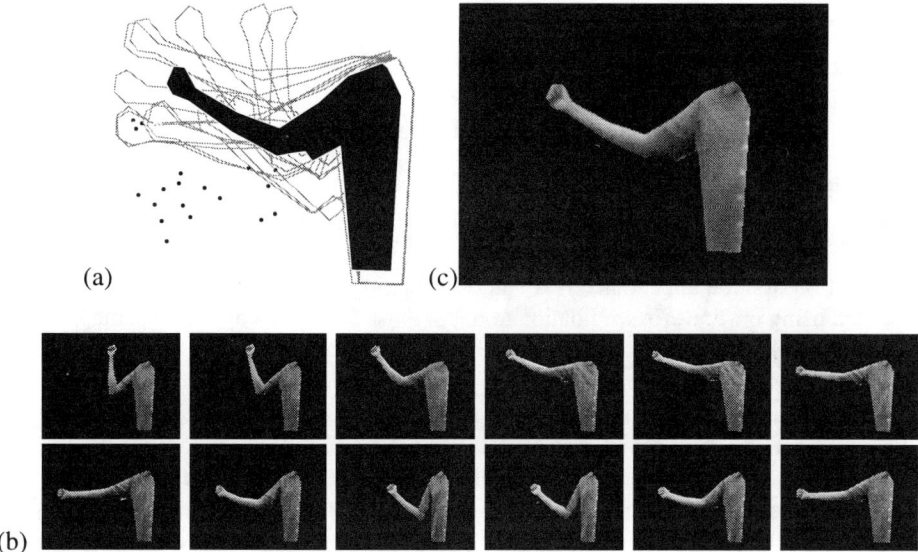

Figure 3: Interpolated shape and texture result. (a) shows exemplar contours (open) and interpolated shape (filled). (b) shows example texture images. (c) shows final interpolated image.

we can use a simple additional constraint on subsequent frames. Once we have selected an example set, we keep using it until the desired parameter value leaves the valid region (convex hull) of that set. When this occurs, we allow transitions only to "adjacent" example sets; adjacency is defined as those pairs of sets for which at least one example on each convex hull are sufficiently close ($||y_i - y_j|| < \epsilon$) in appearance space.

5 Results

First we show examples using a synthetic arm with several workspace constraints. Figure 1(a) shows examples of a simple planar 2DOF arm and the inverse kinematic solution for a variety of endpoints. Due to an artificial obstacle in the world, the arm is forced to switch between arm-up and arm-down configurations to avoid collision.

We trained an interpolation network using a single RBF to model the appearance of the arm as a function of endpoint location. Appearance was modeled as the vector of contour point locations, obtained from the synthetic arm rendering function. We first trained a single RBF network on a dense set of examples of this appearance function. Figure 1(b) shows results interpolating new arm images from these examples; results are accurate except where there are regions of appearance discontinuity due to workspace constraints, or when the network extrapolates erroneously.

We applied our clustering method described above to this data, yielding the results shown in Figure 1(c). None of the problems with discontinuities or erroneous extrapolation can be seen in these results, since our method enforces the constraint that an interpolated result must be returned from on or within the convex hull of a valid example set.

Next we applied our method to the images of real arms shown in Figure 2(a). Arm contours were obtained in a sequence of 33 such images using a semi-automated deformable contour tracker augmented with a local image distance metric [3]. Dense correspondences were interpolated from the values on the contour. Figure 2(b) shows interpolated arm shapes using a single RBF on all examples; dramatic errors can be seen near where multiple different appearances exist within a small region of parameter space.

Figure 2(c) shows the results on the same points using sets of examples found using our clustering method; physically realistic arms are generated in each case. Figure 3 shows the final interpolated result rendered with both shape and texture.

6 Conclusion

View-based image interpolation is a powerful paradigm for generating realistic imagery without full models of the underlying scene geometry. Current techniques for non-rigid interpolation assume appearance is a smooth function. We apply an example clustering approach using on-line cross validation to decompose a complex appearance mapping into sets of examples which can be smoothly interpolated. We show results on real imagery of human arms, with correspondences recovered from deformable contour tracking. Given images of an arm moving on a plane with various configuration conditions (elbow up and elbow down), and with associated parameter vectors marking the hand location, our method is able to discover a small set of manifolds with a small number of exemplars each can render new examples which are always physically correct. A single interpolating manifold for this same data has errors near the boundary between different arm configurations, and where multiple images have the same parameter value.

References

[1] D. Beymer, A. Shashua and T. Poggio, Example Based Image Analysis and Synthesis, MIT AI Lab Memo No. 1431, MIT, 1993. also see D. Beymer and T. Poggio, *Science* 272:1905-1909, 1996.

[2] C. Bregler and S. Omohundro, Nonlinear Image Interpolation using Manifold Learning, NIPS-7, MIT Press, 1995.

[3] T. Darrell, A Radial Cumulative Similarity Transform for Robust Image Correspondence, Proc. CVPR-98, Santa Barbara, CA, IEEE CS Press, 1998.

[4] M. Jagersand, Image Based View Synthesis of Articulated Agents, Proc. CVPR-97, San Jaun, Pureto Rico, pp. 1047-1053, IEEE CS Press, 1997.

[5] M. Jones and T. Poggio, Multidimensional Morphable Models, Proc. ICCV-98, Bombay, India, pp. 683-688, 1998.

[6] A. Lanitis, C.J. Taylor, T.F. Cootes, A Unified Approach to Coding and Interpreting Face Images, Proc. ICCV-95, pp. 368-373, Cambridge, MA, 1995.

[7] M. Levoy and P. Hanrahan, Light Field Rendering, In SIGGRAPH-96, pp. 31-42, 1996.

[8] L. McMillan and G. Bishop, Plenoptic Modeling: An image-based rendering system. In Proc. SIGGRAPH-95, pp. 39-46, 1995.

[9] T. Poggio and F. Girosi, A Theory of Networks for Approximation and Learning, MIT AI Lab Memo No. 1140. 1989.

[10] T. Rikert and M. Jones, Gaze Estimation using Morphable Models, Proc. IEEE Conf. Face and Gesture Recognition '98, pp. 436-441, Nara, Japan, IEEE CS Press, 1998.

[11] L. Saul and M. Jordan, A Variational Principle for Model-based Morphing, NIPS-9, MIT Press, 1997.

[12] S. Seitz and C. Dyer, View Morphing, in Proc. SIGGRAPH-96, pp. 21-30, 1996.

[13] A. Shashua and M. Werman, Trilinearity of Three Perspective Views and its Associated Tensor, in Proc. ICCV-95, pp. 920-935, Cambridge, MA, IEEE CS Press, 1995.

[14] J. Tenenbaum, Mapping a manifold of perceptual observations, NIPS-10, MIT Press, 1998.

Learning to estimate scenes from images

William T. Freeman and Egon C. Pasztor
MERL, Mitsubishi Electric Research Laboratory
201 Broadway; Cambridge, MA 02139
freeman@merl.com, pasztor@merl.com

Abstract

We seek the scene interpretation that best explains image data. For example, we may want to infer the projected velocities (scene) which best explain two consecutive image frames (image). From synthetic data, we model the relationship between image and scene patches, and between a scene patch and neighboring scene patches. Given a new image, we propagate likelihoods in a Markov network (ignoring the effect of loops) to infer the underlying scene. This yields an efficient method to form low-level scene interpretations. We demonstrate the technique for motion analysis and estimating high resolution images from low-resolution ones.

1 Introduction

There has been recent interest in studying the statistical properties of the visual world. Olshausen and Field [23] and Bell and Sejnowski [2] have derived V1-like receptive fields from ensembles of images; Simoncelli and Schwartz [30] account for contrast normalization effects by redundancy reduction. Li and Atick [1] explain retinal color coding by information processing arguments. Various research groups have developed realistic texture synthesis methods by studying the response statistics of V1-like multi-scale, oriented receptive fields [12, 7, 33, 29]. These methods help us understand the early stages of image representation and processing in the brain.

Unfortunately, they don't address how a visual system might *interpret* images, i.e., estimate the underlying scene. In this work, we study the statistical properties of a *labelled* visual world, images together with scenes, in order to infer scenes from images. The image data might be single or multiple frames; the scene quantities to be estimated could be projected object velocities, surface shapes, reflectance patterns, or colors.

We ask: can a visual system correctly interpret a visual scene if it models (1) the probability that any local scene patch generated the local image, and (2) the probability that any local scene is the neighbor to any other? The first probabilities allow making scene estimates from local image data, and the second allow these local estimates to propagate. This leads to a Bayesian method for low level vision problems, constrained by Markov assumptions. We describe this method, and show it working for two low-level vision problems.

2 Markov networks for scene estimation

First, we synthetically generate images and their underlying scene representations, using computer graphics. The synthetic world should typify the visual world in which the algorithm will operate.

For example, for the motion estimation problem of Sect. 3, our training images were irregularly shaped blobs, which could occlude each other, moving in randomized directions at speeds up to 2 pixels per frame. The contrast values of the blobs and the background were randomized. The image data were the concatenated image intensities from two successive frames of an image sequence. The scene data were the velocities of the visible objects at each pixel in the two frames.

Second, we place the image and scene data in a Markov network [24]. We break the images and scenes into localized patches where image patches connect with underlying scene patches; scene patches also connect with neighboring scene patches. The neighbor relationship can be with regard to position, scale, orientation, etc.

For the motion problem, we represented both the images and the velocities in 4-level Gaussian pyramids [6], to efficiently communicate across space. Each scene patch then additionally connects with the patches at neighboring resolution levels. Figure 2 shows the multiresolution representation (at one time frame) for images and scenes.[1]

Third, we propagate probabilities. Weiss showed the advantage of belief propagation over regularization methods for several 1-d problems [31]; we apply related methods to our 2-d problems. Let the ith and jth image and scene patches be y_i and x_j, respectively. For the MAP estimate [3] of the scene data,[2] we want to find $\mathrm{argmax}_{x_1,x_2,\ldots,x_N} P(x_1, x_2, \ldots, x_N | y_1, y_2, \ldots, y_M)$, where N and M are the number of scene and image patches. Because the joint probability is simpler to compute, we find, equivalently, $\mathrm{argmax}_{x_1,x_2,\ldots,x_N} P(x_1, x_2, \ldots, x_N, y_1, y_2, \ldots, y_M)$.

The conditional independence assumptions of the Markov network let us factorize the desired joint probability into quantities involving only local measurements and calculations [24, 32]. Consider the two-patch system of Fig. 1. We can factorize $P(x_1, x_2, y_1, y_2)$ in three steps: (1) $P(x_1, x_2, y_1, y_2) = P(x_2, y_1, y_2 | x_1) P(x_1)$ (by elementary probability); (2) $P(x_2, y_1, y_2 | x_1) = P(y_1 | x_1) P(x_2, y_2 | x_1)$ (by conditional

---

[1] To maintain the desired conditional independence relationships, we appended the image data to the scenes. This provided the scene elements with image contrast information, which they would otherwise lack.

[2] Related arguments follow for the MMSE or other estimators.

independence); (3) $P(x_2, y_2|x_1) = P(x_2|x_1)P(y_2|x_2)$ (by elementary probability and the Markov assumption). To estimate just x_1 at node 1, the argmax$_{x_2}$ becomes max$_{x_2}$, and then slides over constants, giving terms involving only local computations at each node:

$$\text{argmax}_{x_1} \max_{x_2} P(x_1, x_2, y_1, y_2) = \text{argmax}_{x_1}[P(x_1)P(y_1|x_1)\max_{x_2}[P(x_2|x_1)P(y_2|x_2)]]. \tag{1}$$

This factorization generalizes to any network structure without loops. We use a *different* factorization at each scene node: we turn the initial joint probability into a conditional by factoring out *that* node's prior, $P(x_j)$, then proceeding analogously to the example above. The resulting factorized computations give local propagation rules, similar to those of [24, 32]: Each node, j, receives a message from each neighbor, k, which is an accumulated likelihood function, $L_{kj} = P(y_k \ldots y_z | x_j)$, where $y_k \ldots y_z$ are all image nodes that lie at or beyond scene node k, relative to scene node j. At each iteration, more image nodes y enter that likelihood function. After each iteration, the MAP estimate at node j is argmax$_{x_j} P(x_j)P(y_j|x_j) \prod_k L_{kj}$, where k runs over all scene node neighbors of node j. We calculate L_{kj} from:

$$L_{kj} = \max_{x_k} P(x_k|x_j)P(y_k|x_k) \prod_{l \neq j} \tilde{L}_{lk}, \tag{2}$$

where $\tilde{L}_{lk}$ is L_{lk} from the previous iteration. The initial $\tilde{L}_{lk}$'s are 1. Using the

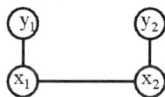

Figure 1: Markov network nodes used in example.

factorization rules described above, one can verify that the local computations will compute argmax$_{x_1, x_2, \ldots, x_N} P(x_1, x_2, \ldots, x_N | y_1, y_2, \ldots, y_M)$, as desired. To learn the network parameters, we measure $P(x_j)$, $P(y_j|x_j)$, and $P(x_k|x_j)$, directly from the synthetic training data.

If the network contains loops, the above factorization does not hold. Both learning and inference then require more computationally intensive methods [15]. Alternatively, one can use multi-resolution quad-tree networks [20], for which the factorization rules apply, to propagate information spatially. However, this gives results with artifacts along quad-tree boundaries, statistical boundaries in the model not present in the real problem. We found good results by including the loop-causing connections between adjacent nodes at the same tree level but applying the factorized propagation rules, anyway. Others have obtained good results using the same approach for inference [8, 21, 32]; Weiss provides theoretical arguments why this works for certain cases [32].

3 Discrete Probability Representation (motion example)

We applied the training method and propagation rules to motion estimation, using a vector code representation [11] for both images and scenes. We wrote a tree-structured vector quantizer, to code 4 by 4 pixel by 2 frame blocks of image data for each pyramid level into one of 300 codes for each level. We also coded scene patches into one of 300 codes.

During training, we presented approximately 200,000 examples of irregularly shaped moving blobs, some overlapping, of a contrast with the background randomized to one of 4 values. Using co-occurance histograms, we measured the statistical relationships that embody our algorithm: $P(x)$, $P(y|x)$, and $P(x_n|x)$, for scene x_n neighboring scene x.

Figure 2 shows an input test image, (a) before and (b) after vector quantization. The true underlying scene, the desired output, is shown (c) before and (d) after vector quantization. Figure 3 shows six iterations of the algorithm (Eq. 2) as it converges to a good estimate for the underlying scene velocities. The local probabilities we learned ($P(x)$, $P(y|x)$, and $P(x_n|x)$) lead to figure/ground segmentation, aperture problem constraint propagation, and filling-in (see caption).

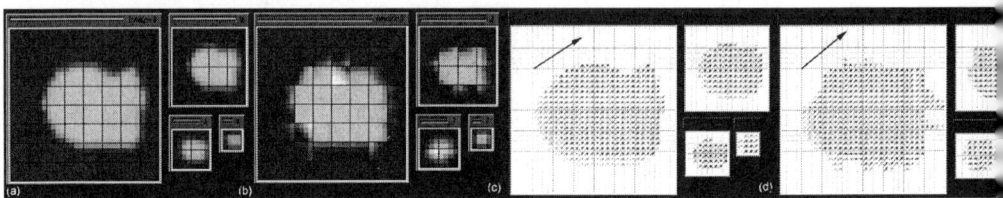

Figure 2: (a) First of two frames of image data (in gaussian pyramid), and (b) vector quantized. (c) The optical flow scene information, and (d) vector quantized. Large arrow added to show small vectors' orientation.

4 Density Representation (super-resolution example)

For super-resolution, the input "image" is the high-frequency components (sharpest details) of a sub-sampled image. The "scene" to be estimated is the high-frequency components of the full-resolution image, Fig. 4.

We improved our method for this second problem. A faithful image representation requires so many vector codes that it becomes infeasible to measure the prior and co-occurance statistics (note unfaithful fit of Fig. 2). On the other hand, a discrete representation allows fast propagation. We developed a hybrid method that allows both good fitting and fast propagation.

We describe the image and scene patches as vectors in a continuous space, and first modelled the probability densities, $P(x)$, $P(y,x)$, and $P(x_n,x)$, as gaussian mixtures [4]. (We reduced the dimensionality some by principal components analysis [4]). We then evaluated the prior and conditional distributions of Eq. 2 only at a discrete set of scene values, different for each node. (This sample-based approach relates to [14, 7]). The scenes were a sampling of those scenes which render to the image at that node. This focusses the computation to the locally feasible scene interpretations. $P(x_k|x_j)$ in Eq. 2 becomes the ratios of the gaussian mixtures $P(x_k, x_j)$ and $P(x_j)$, evaluated at the scene samples at nodes k and j, respectively. $P(y_k|x_k)$ is $P(y_k, x_k)/P(x_k)$ evaluated at the scene samples of node k.

To select the scene samples, we could condition the mixture $P(y,x)$ on the y observed at each node, and sample x's from the resulting mixture of gaussians. We obtained somewhat better results by using the scenes from the training set whose

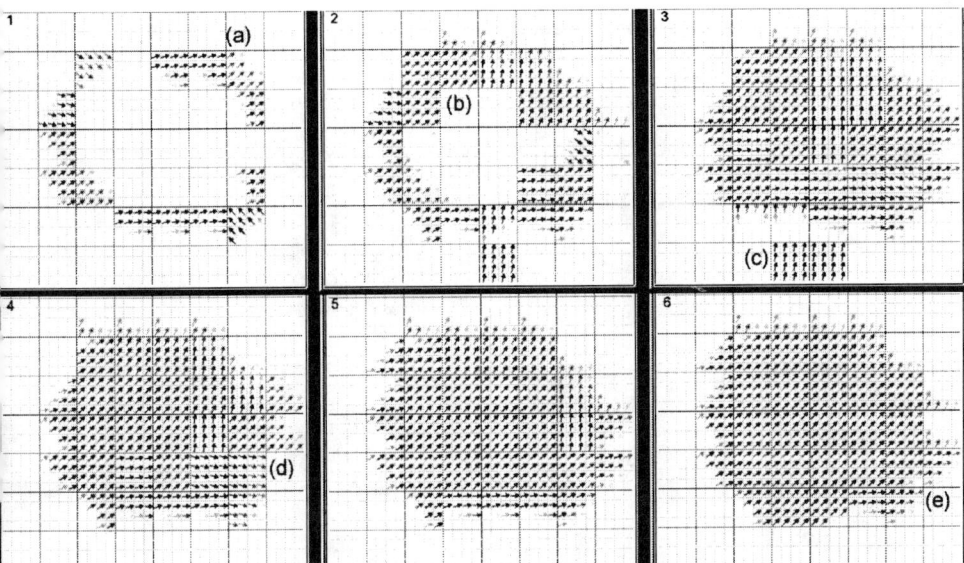

Figure 3: The most probable scene code for Fig. 2b at first 6 iterations of Bayesian belief propagation. (a) Note initial motion estimates occur only at edges. Due to the "aperture problem", initial estimates do not agree. (b) Filling-in of motion estimate occurs. Cues for figure/ground determination may include edge curvature, and information from lower resolution levels. Both are included implicitly in the learned probabilities. (c) Figure/ground still undetermined in this region of low edge curvature. (d) Velocities have filled-in, but do not yet all agree. (e) Velocities have filled-in, and agree with each other and with the correct velocity direction, shown in Fig. 2.

images most closely matched the image observed at that node (thus avoiding one gaussian mixture modeling step).

Using 40 scene samples per node, setting up the $P(x_k|x_j)$ matrix for each link took several minutes for 96x96 pixel images. The scene (high resolution) patch size was 3x3; the image (low resolution) patch size was 7x7. We didn't feel long-range scene propagation was critical here, so we used a flat, not a pyramid, node structure. Once the matrices were computed, the iterations of Eq. 2 were completed within seconds.

Figure 4 shows the results. The training images were random shaded and painted blobs such as the test image shown. After 5 iterations, the synthesized maximum likelihood estimate of the high resolution image is visually close to the actual high frequency image (top row). (Including $P(x)$ gave too flat results, we suspect due to errors modeling that highly peaked distribution). The dominant structures are all in approximately the correct position. This may enable high quality zooming of low-resolution images, attempted with limited success by others [28, 25].

5 Discussion

In related applications of Markov random fields to vision, researchers typically use relatively simple, heuristically derived expressions (rather than learned) for the likelihood function $P(y|x)$ or for the spatial relationships in the prior term on scenes

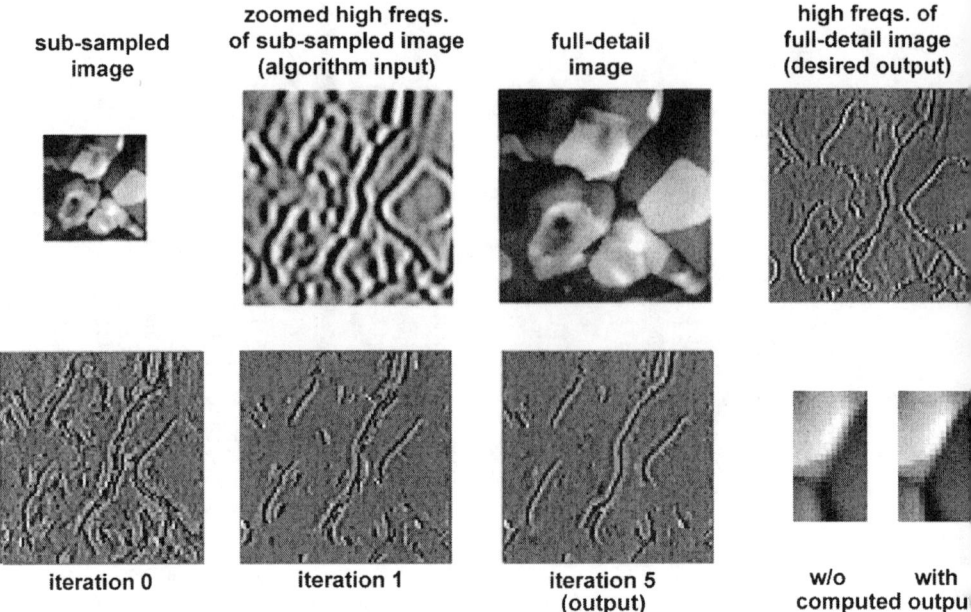

Figure 4: Superresolution example. Top row: Input and desired output (contrast normalized, only those orientations around vertical). Bottom row: algorithm output and comparison of image with and without estimated high vertical frequencies.

[10, 26, 9, 17, 5, 20, 19, 27]. Some researchers have applied related learning approaches to low-level vision problems, but restricted themselves to linear models [18, 13]. For other learning or constraint propagation approaches in motion analysis, see [20, 22, 16].

In summary, we have developed a principled and practical learning based method for low-level vision problems. Markov assumptions lead to factorizing the posterior probability. The parameters of our Markov random field are probabilities specified by the training data. For our two examples (programmed in C and Matlab, respectively), the training can take several hours but the running takes only several minutes. Scene estimation by Markov networks may be useful for other low-level vision problems, such as extracting intrinsic images from line drawings or photographs.

Acknowledgements We thank E. Adelson, J. Tenenbaum, P. Viola, and Y. Weiss for helpful discussions.

References

[1] J. J. Atick, Z. Li, and A. N. Redlich. Understanding retinal color coding from first principles. *Neural Computation*, 4:559–572, 1992.
[2] A. J. Bell and T. J. Senjowski. The independent components of natural scenes are edge filters. *Vision Research*, 37(23):3327–3338, 1997.
[3] J. O. Berger. *Statistical decision theory and Bayesian analysis*. Springer, 1985.
[4] C. M. Bishop. *Neural networks for pattern recognition*. Oxford, 1995.
[5] M. J. Black and P. Anandan. A framework for the robust estimation of optical flow. In *Proc. 4th Intl. Conf. Computer Vision*, pages 231–236. IEEE, 1993.
[6] P. J. Burt and E. H. Adelson. The Laplacian pyramid as a compact image code. *IEEE Trans. Comm.*, 31(4):532–540, 1983.
[7] J. S. DeBonet and P. Viola. Texture recognition using a non-parametric multi-scale

statistical model. In *Proc. IEEE Computer Vision and Pattern Recognition*, 1998.
[8] B. J. Frey. *Bayesian networks for pattern classification*. MIT Press, 1997.
[9] D. Geiger and F. Girosi. Parallel and deterministic algorithms from MRF's: surface reconstruction. *IEEE Pattern Analysis and Machine Intelligence*, 13(5):401–412, May 1991.
[10] S. Geman and D. Geman. Stochastic relaxation, Gibbs distribution, and the Bayesian restoration of images. *IEEE Pattern Analysis and Machine Intelligence*, 6:721–741, 1984.
[11] R. M. Gray, P. C. Cosman, and K. L. Oehler. Incorporating visual factors into vector quantizers for image compression. In A. B. Watson, editor, *Digital images and human vision*. MIT Press, 1993.
[12] D. J. Heeger and J. R. Bergen. Pyramid-based texture analysis/synthesis. In *ACM SIGGRAPH*, pages 229–236, 1995. In *Computer Graphics* Proceedings, Annual Conference Series.
[13] A. C. Hurlbert and T. A. Poggio. Synthesizing a color algorithm from examples. *Science*, 239:482–485, 1988.
[14] M. Isard and A. Blake. Contour tracking by stochastic propagation of conditional density. In *Proc. European Conf. on Computer Vision*, pages 343–356, 1996.
[15] M. I. Jordan, editor. *Learning in graphical models*. MIT Press, 1998.
[16] S. Ju, M. J. Black, and A. D. Jepson. Skin and bones: Multi-layer, locally affine, optical flow and regularization with transparency. In *Proc. IEEE Computer Vision and Pattern Recognition*, pages 307–314, 1996.
[17] D. Kersten. Transparancy and the cooperative computation of scene attributes. In M. S. Landy and J. A. Movshon, editors, *Computational Models of Visual Processing*, chapter 15. MIT Press, Cambridge, MA, 1991.
[18] D. Kersten, A. J. O'Toole, M. E. Sereno, D. C. Knill, and J. A. Anderson. Associative learning of scene parameters from images. *Applied Optics*, 26(23):4999–5006, 1987.
[19] D. Knill and W. Richards, editors. *Perception as Bayesian inference*. Cambridge Univ. Press, 1996.
[20] M. R. Luettgen, W. C. Karl, and A. S. Willsky. Efficient multiscale regularization with applications to the computation of optical flow. *IEEE Trans. Image Processing*, 3(1):41–64, 1994.
[21] D. J. C. Mackay and R. M. Neal. Good error–correcting codes based on very sparse matrices. In *Cryptoqraphy and coding – LNCS 1025*, 1995.
[22] S. Nowlan and T. J. Senjowski. A selection model for motion processing in area MT of primates. *J. Neuroscience*, 15:1195–1214, 1995.
[23] B. A. Olshausen and D. J. Field. Emergence of simple-cell receptive field properties by learning a sparse code for natural images. *Nature*, 381:607–609, 1996.
[24] J. Pearl. *Probabilistic reasoning in intelligent systems: networks of plausible inference*. Morgan Kaufmann, 1988.
[25] A. Pentland and B. Horowitz. A practical approach to fractal-based image compression. In A. B. Watson, editor, *Digital images and human vision*. MIT Press, 1993.
[26] T. Poggio, V. Torre, and C. Koch. Computational vision and regularization theory. *Nature*, 317(26):314–139, 1985.
[27] E. Saund. Perceptual organization of occluding contours of opaque surfaces. In *CVPR '98 Workshop on Perceptual Organization*, Santa Barbara, CA, 1998.
[28] R. R. Schultz and R. L. Stevenson. A Bayesian approach to image expansion for improved definition. *IEEE Trans. Image Processing*, 3(3):233–242, 1994.
[29] E. P. Simoncelli. Statistical models for images: Compression, restoration and synthesis. In *31st Asilomar Conf. on Sig., Sys. and Computers*, Pacific Grove, CA, 1997.
[30] E. P. Simoncelli and O. Schwartz. Modeling surround suppression in v1 neurons with a statistically-derived normalization model. In *Adv. in Neural Information Processing Systems*, volume 11, 1999.
[31] Y. Weiss. Interpreting images by propagating Bayesian beliefs. In *Adv. in Neural Information Processing Systems*, volume 9, pages 908–915, 1997.
[32] Y. Weiss. Belief propagation and revision in networks with loops. Technical Report 1616, AI Lab Memo, MIT, Cambridge, MA 02139, 1998.
[33] S. C. Zhu and D. Mumford. Prior learning and Gibbs reaction-diffusion. *IEEE Pattern Analysis and Machine Intelligence*, 19(11), 1997.

Learning to Find Pictures of People

Sergey Ioffe
Computer Science Division
U.C. Berkeley
Berkeley CA 94720
ioffe@cs.berkeley.edu

David Forsyth
Computer Science Division
U.C. Berkeley
Berkeley CA 94720
daf@cs.berkeley.edu

Abstract

Finding articulated objects, like people, in pictures presents a particularly difficult object recognition problem. We show how to find people by finding putative body segments, and then constructing assemblies of those segments that are consistent with the constraints on the appearance of a person that result from kinematic properties. Since a reasonable model of a person requires at least nine segments, it is not possible to present every group to a classifier. Instead, the search can be pruned by using projected versions of a classifier that accepts groups corresponding to people. We describe an efficient projection algorithm for one popular classifier, and demonstrate that our approach can be used to determine whether images of real scenes contain people.

1 Introduction

Several typical collections containing over ten million images are listed in [2]. There is an extensive literature on obtaining images from large collections using features computed from the whole image, including colour histograms, texture measures and shape measures; a partial review appears in [5].

However, in the most comprehensive field study of usage practices (a paper by Enser [2] surveying the use of the Hulton Deutsch collection), there is a clear user preference for searching these collections on image semantics. An ideal search tool would be a quite general object recognition system that could be adapted quickly and easily to the types of objects sought by a user. An important special case is finding people and determining what they are doing. This is hard, because people have many internal degrees of freedom. We follow the approach of [3], and represent people as collections of cylinders, each representing a body segment. Regions that could be the projections of cylinders are easily found using techniques similar to those of [1]. Once these regions are found, they must be assembled into collections that are consistent with the appearance of images of real people, which are constrained by the kinematics of human joints; consistency is tested with a classifier. Since there are many candidate segments, a brute force search is impossible. We show how this search can be pruned using projections of the classifier.

2 Learning to Build Segment Configurations

Suppose that N segments have been found in an image, and there are m body parts. We will define a *labeling* as a set $L = \{(l_1, s_1), (l_2, s_2), \ldots, (l_k, s_k)\}$ of pairs where each segment $s_i \in \{1 \ldots N\}$ is labeled with the *label* $l_i \in \{1 \ldots m\}$. A labeling is *complete* if it represents a full m-segment configuration (Fig. 2(a,b)).

Assume we have a classifier C that for any complete labeling L outputs $C(L) > 0$ if L corresponds to a person-like configuration, and $C(L) < 0$ otherwise. Finding all the possible body configurations in an image is equivalent to finding all the complete labelings L for which $C(L) > 0$. This cannot be done with brute-force search through the entire set. The search can be pruned if, for an (incomplete) labeling L' there is no complete $L \supseteq L'$ such that $C(L) > 0$. For instance, if two segments cannot represent the upper and lower left arm, as in Figure 1a, then we do not consider any complete labelings where they are labeled as such.

Projected classifiers make the search for body configurations efficient by pruning labelings using the properties of smaller sub-labelings (as in [7], who use manually determined bounds and do not learn the tests). Given a classifier C which is a function of a set of features whose values depend on segments with labels $l_1 \ldots l_m$, the *projected classifier* $C_{l_1 \ldots l_k}$ is a function of of all those features that depend only on the segments with labels $l_1 \ldots l_k$. In particular, $C_{l_1 \ldots l_k}(L') > 0$ if there is some extension L of L' such that $C(L) > 0$ (see figure 1). The converse need not be true: the feature values required to bring a projected point inside the positive volume of C may not be realized with any labeling of the current set of segments $1, \ldots, N$. For a projected classifier to be useful, it must be easy to compute the projection, and it must be effective in rejecting labelings at an early stage. These are strong requirements which are not satisfied by most good classifiers; for example, in our experience a support vector machine with a positive definite quadratic kernel projects easily but typically yields unrestrictive projected classifiers.

2.1 Building Labelings Incrementally

Assume we have a classifier C that accepts assemblies corresponding to people and that we can construct projected classifiers as we need them. We will now show how to use them to construct labelings, using a *pyramid of classifiers*.

A pyramid of classifiers (Fig. 1(c)), determined by the classifier C and a permutation of labels $(l_1 \ldots l_k)$ consists of nodes $N_{l_i \ldots l_j}$ corresponding to each of the projected classifiers $C_{l_i \ldots l_j}$, $i \leq j$. Each of the bottom-level nodes N_{l_i} receives the set of all segments in the image as the input. The top node $N_{l_1 \ldots l_m}$ outputs the set of all complete labelings $L = \{(l_1, s_1) \ldots (l_m, s_m)\}$ such that $C(L) > 0$, i.e. the set of all assemblies in the image classified as people. Further, each node $N_{l_i \ldots l_j}$ outputs the set of all sub-labelings $L = \{(l_i, s_i) \ldots (l_j, s_j)\}$ such that $C_{l_i \ldots l_j}(L) > 0$.

The nodes N_{l_i} at the bottom level work by selecting all segments s_i in the image for which $C_{l_i}\{(l_i, s_i)\} > 0$. Each of the remaining nodes has two parts: merging and filtering. The *merging* stage of node $N_{l_i \ldots l_j}$ merges the outputs of its children by computing the set of all labelings $\{(l_i, s_i) \ldots (l_j, s_j)\}$ where $\{(l_i, s_i) \ldots (l_{j-1}, s_{j-1})\}$

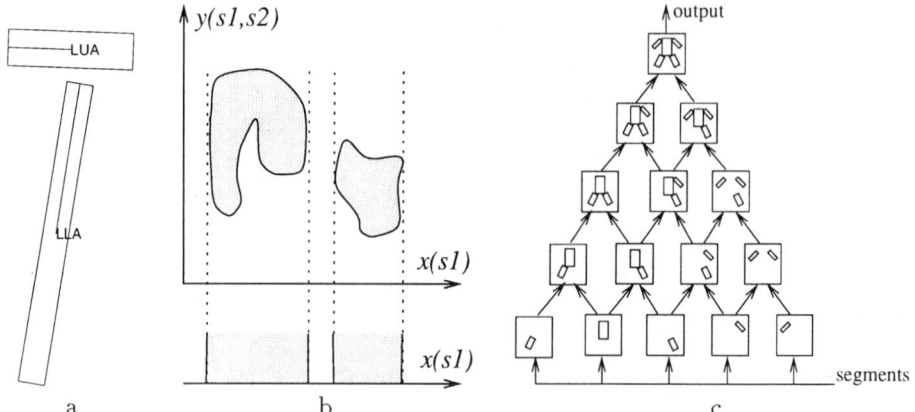

Figure 1: (a) *Two segments that cannot correspond to the left upper and lower arm. Any configuration where they do can be rejected using a projected classifier regardless of the other segments that might appear in the configuration.* (b) *Projecting a classifier $C\{(l_1, s_1), (l_2, s_2)\}$. The shaded area is the volume classified as positive, for the feature set $\{x(s_1), y(s_1, s_2)\}$. Finding the projection C_{l_1} amounts to projecting off the features that cannot be computed from s_1 only, i.e., $y(s_1, s_2)$.* (c) *A pyramid of classifiers. Each node outputs sub-assemblies accepted by the corresponding projected classifier. Each node except those in the bottom row works by forming labelings from the outputs of its two children, and filtering the result using the corresponding projected classifier. The top node outputs the set of all complete labelings that correspond to body configurations.*

and $\{(l_{i+1}, s_{i+1}) \ldots (l_j, s_j)\}$ are in the outputs of $N_{l_i \ldots l_{j-1}}$ and $N_{l_{i+1} \ldots l_j}$, respectively. The *filtering* stage then selects, from the resulting set of labelings, those for which $C_{l_i \ldots l_j}(\cdot) > 0$, and the resulting set is the output of $N_{l_i \ldots l_j}$. It is clear, from the definition of projected classifiers, that the output of the pyramid is, in fact, the set of all complete L for which $C(L) > 0$ (note that $C_{l_1 \ldots l_m} = C$).

The only constraint on the order in which the outputs of nodes are computed is that children nodes have to be applied before parents. In our implementation, we use nodes $N_{l_i \ldots l_j}$ where j changes from 1 to m, and, for each j, i changes from j down to 1. This is equivalent to computing sets of labelings of the form $\{(l_1, s_1) \ldots (l_j, s_j)\}$ in order, where getting $(j+1)$-segment labelings from j-segment ones is itself an incremental process, whereby we check labels against l_{j+1} in the order $l_j, l_{j-1}, \ldots, l_1$. In practice, we choose the latter order on the fly for each increment step using a greedy algorithm, to minimize the size of labeling sets that are constructed (note that in this case the classifiers no longer form a pyramid). The order $(l_1 \ldots l_m)$ in which labels are added to an assembly needs to be fixed. We determine this order with a greedy algorithm by running a large segment set through the labeling builder and choosing the next label to add so as to minimize the number of labelings that result.

2.2 Classifiers that Project

In our problem, each *segment* from the set $\{1 \ldots N\}$ is a rectangle in some position and orientation. Given a complete labeling $L = \{(1, s_1), \ldots, (m, s_m)\}$, we want to have $C(L) > 0$ iff the segment arrangement produced by L looks like a person.

Learning to Find Pictures of People 785

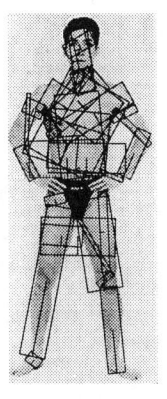
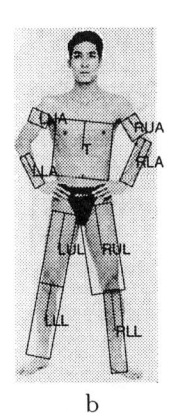
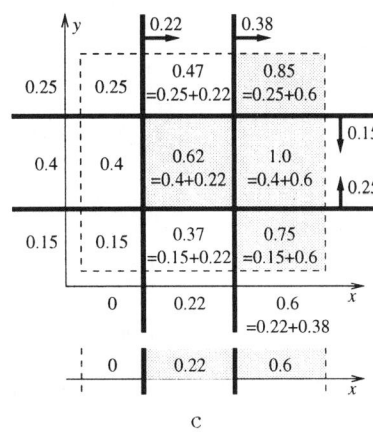

a b c

Figure 2: (a) *All segments extracted for an image.* (b) *A labeled segment configuration corresponding to a person, where* T=*torso,* LUA=*left upper arm, etc. The head is not marked because we are not looking for it with our method. The single left leg segment in (a) has been broken in (b) to generate the upper and lower leg segments.* (c) *(top) A combination of a bounding box (the dashed line) and a boosted classifier, for two features x and y. Each plane in the boosted classifier is a thick line with the positive half-space indicated by an arrow; the associated weight β is shown next to the arrow. The shaded area is the positive volume of the classifier, which are the points P where* $\sum_f w_f(P(f)) > 1/2$. *The weights* $w_x(\cdot)$ *and* $w_y(\cdot)$ *are shown along the x- and y-axes, respectively, and the total weight* $w_x(P(x)) + w_y(P(y))$ *is shown for each region of the bounding box. (bottom) The projected classifier, given by* $w_x(P(x)) > 1/2 - \delta = 0.1$ *where* $\delta = \max_{P(y)} w_y(P(y)) = \max\{0.25, 0.4, 0.15\} = 0.4.$

Each feature will depend on a few segments (1 to 3 in our experiments). Our kinematic features are invariant to translation, uniform scaling or rotation of the segment set, and include angles between segments and ratios of lengths, widths and distances. We expect the features that correspond to human configurations to lie within small fractions of their possible value ranges. This suggests using an axis-aligned bounding box, with bounds learned from a collection of positive labelings, for a good first separation, and then using a boosted version of a weak classifier that splits the feature space on a single feature value (as in [6]). This classifier projects particularly well, using a simple algorithm described in section 2.3.

Each weak classifier (Fig. 2(c)) is defined by the feature f_j on which the split is made, the position p_j of the splitting hyperplane, and the direction $d_j \in \{1, -1\}$ that determines which half-space is positive. A point P is classified as positive iff $d_j(P(f_j) - p_j) > 0$, where $P(f_j)$ is the value of feature f_j. The boosting algorithm will associate a weight β_j with each plane (so that $\sum_j \beta_j = 1$), and the resulting classifier will classify a point as positive iff $\sum_{d_j(P(f_j)-p_j)>0} \beta_j > 1/2$, that is, iff the total weight of the weak classifiers that classify the point as positive is at least a half of the total weight of the classifiers. The set $\{f_j\}$ may have repeating features (which may have different p_j, d_j and w_j values), and does not need to span the entire feature set.

By grouping together the weights corresponding to planes splitting on the same feature, we finally rewrite the classifier as $\sum_f w_f(P(f)) > 1/2$, where $w_f(P(f)) =$

$\sum_{f_j=f,\ d_j(P(f)-p_j)>0} \beta_j$ is the weight associated with the particular value of feature f, is a piece-wise constant function and depends on in which of the intervals given by $\{p_j|f_j = f\}$ this value falls.

2.3 Projecting a Boosted Classifier

Given a classifier constructed as above, we need to construct classifiers that depend on on some identified subset of the features. The geometry of our classifiers — whose positive regions consist of unions of axis-aligned bounding boxes — makes this easy to do.

Let g be the feature to be projected away — perhaps because the value depends on a label that is not available. The projection of the classifier should classify a point P' in the (lower-dimensional) feature space as positive iff $\max_P \sum_f w_f(P(f)) > 1/2$ where P is a point which projects into P' but can have any value for $P(g)$. We can rewrite this expression as $\sum_{f \neq g} w_f(P'(f)) + \max_{P(g)} w_g(P(g)) > 1/2$. The value of $\delta = \max w_g(P(g))$ is readily available and independent of P'. We can see that, with the feature projected away, we obtain $\sum_f w_f(P'(f)) > 1/2 - \delta$. Any number of features can be projected away in a sequence in this fashion. An example of the projected classifier is shown in Figure 2(c).

The classifier C we are using allows for an efficient building of labelings, in that the features do not need to be recomputed when we move from $C_{l_1...l_k}$ to $C_{l_1...l_{k+1}}$. We achieve this efficiency by carrying along with a labeling $L = \{(l_1, s_1)...(l_k, s_k)\}$ the sum $\sigma(L) = \sum_{f \in F(l_1...l_k)} w_f(P(f))$ where $F(l_1...l_k)$ is the set of all features computable from the segments labeled as $l_1, ..., l_k$, and $\{P(f)\}$ — the values of these features. When we add another segment to get $L' = \{(l_1, s_1)...(l_{k+1}, s_{k+1})\}$, we can compute $\sigma(L') = \sigma(L) + \sum_{f \in F(l_1...l_{k+1}) \setminus F(l_1...l_k)} w_f(P'(f))$. In other words, when we add a label l_{k+1}, we need to compute only those features that require s_{k+1} for their computation.

3 Experimental Results

We report results for a system that automatically identifies potential body segments (using the techniques described in [4]), and then applies the assembly process described above. Images for which assemblies that are kinematically consistent with a person are reported as having people in them. The segment finder may find either 1 or 2 segments for each limb, depending on whether it is bent or straight; because the pruning is so effective, we can allow segments to be broken into two equal halves lengthwise (like the left leg in Fig. 2(b)), both of which are tested.

3.1 Training

The training set included 79 images without people, selected randomly from the COREL database, and 274 images each with a single person on uniform background. The images with people have been scanned from books of human models [10]. All segments in the test images were reported; in the control images, only segments whose interior corresponded to human skin in colour and texture were reported. Control images, both for the training and for the test set, were chosen so that all had at least 30% of their pixels similar to human skin in colour and texture. This gives a more realistic test of the system performance by excluding regions that are obviously not human, and reduces the number of segments in the control images to the same order of magnitude as those in the test images.

Learning to Find Pictures of People

Features	Test	Control
367	120	28
567	120	86

a

Features	False Neg.	False Pos.
367	37 %	4 %
567	49 %	10 %

b

Table 1: *(a) Number of images of people (test) and without people (control) processed by the classifiers with 367 and 567 features. (b) False negative (images with a person where no body configuration was found) and false positive (images with no people where a person was detected) rates.*

The models are all wearing either swim suits or no clothes, otherwise segment finding fails; it is an open problem to segment people wearing loose clothing. There is a wide variation in the poses of the training examples, although all body segments are visible. The sets of segments corresponding to people were then hand-labeled. Of the 274 images with people, segments for each body part were found in 193 images. The remaining 81 resulted in incomplete configurations, which could still be used for computing the bounding box used to obtain a first separation. Since we assume that if a configuration looks like a person then its mirror image would too, we double the number of body configurations by flipping each one about a vertical axis. The bounding box is then computed from the resulting 548 points in the feature space, without looking at the images without people.

The boosted classifier was trained to separate two classes: the $193 \times 2 = 386$ points corresponding to body configurations, and 60727 points that did not correspond to people but lay in the bounding box, obtained by using the bounding box classifier to incrementally build labelings for the images with no people. We added 1178 synthetic positive configurations obtained by randomly selecting each limb and the torso from one of the 386 real images of body configurations (which were rotated and scaled so the torso positions were the same in all of them) to give an effect of joining limbs and torsos from different images rather like children's flip-books. Remarkably, the boosted classifier classified each of the real data points correctly but misclassified 976 out of the 1178 synthetic configurations as negative; the synthetic examples were unexpectedly more similar to the negative examples than the real positive examples were.

3.2 Results

The test dataset was separate from the training set and included 120 images with a person on a uniform background, and varying numbers of control images, reported in Table 1. We report results for two classifiers, one using 567 features and the other using a subset of 367 of those features. Table 1b shows the false positive and false negative rates achieved for each of the two classifiers. By marking 51% of test images and only 10% of control images, the classifier using 567 features compares extremely favorably with that of [3], which marked 54% of test images and 38% of control images using hand-tuned tests to form groups of four segments. In 55 of the 59 images where there was a false negative, a segment corresponding to a body part was missed by the segment finder, meaning that the overall system performance significantly understates the classifier performance. There are few signs of overfitting, probably because the features are highly redundant. Using the larger set of features makes labeling faster (by a factor of about five), because more configurations are rejected earlier.

4 Conclusions and Future Work

Groups of segments that satisfy kinematic constraints, learned from images of real people, quite reliably correspond to people and can be used to identify them. Our trick of projecting classifiers is effective at pruning an otherwise completely unmanageable correspondence search. Future issues include: fusing responses from face finders (such as those of [11, 9]; exploiting patterns of shading on human limbs to get better selectivity (as in [8]); determining the configuration of the person, which might tell what they are doing; and exploiting the kinematic similarities between humans and many animals to build systems that can find many different types of animal without searching the classes one by one.

References

[1] J.M. Brady and H. Asada. Smoothed local symmetries and their implementation. *International Journal of Robotics Research*, 3(3), 1984.

[2] P.G.B. Enser. Query analysis in a visual information retrieval context. *J. Document and Text Management*, 1(1):25–52, 1993.

[3] M. M. Fleck, D. A. Forsyth, and C. Bregler. Finding naked people. In *European Conference on Computer Vision 1996, Vol. II*, pages 592–602, 1996.

[4] D.A. Forsyth and M.M. Fleck. Body plans. In *IEEE Conf. on Computer Vision and Pattern Recognition*, 1997.

[5] D.A. Forsyth, J. Malik, M.M. Fleck, H. Greenspan, T. Leung, S. Belongie, C. Carson, and C. Bregler. Finding pictures of objects in large collections of images. In *Proc. 2'nd International Workshop on Object Representation in Computer Vision*, 1996.

[6] Y. Freund and R.E. Schapire. Experiments with a new boosting algorithm. In *Machine Learning - 13*, 1996.

[7] W.E.L. Grimson and T. Lozano-Pérez. Localizing overlapping parts by searching the interpretation tree. *IEEE Trans. Patt. Anal. Mach. Intell.*, 9(4):469–482, 1987.

[8] J. Haddon and D.A. Forsyth. Shading primitives. In *Int. Conf. on Computer Vision*, 1997. to appear.

[9] H.A. Rowley, S. Baluja, and T. Kanade. Human face detection in visual scenes. In D.S. Touretzky, M.C. Mozer, and M.E. Hasselmo, editors, *Advances in Neural Information Processing 8*, pages 875–881, 1996.

[10] Elte Shuppan. *Pose file*, volume 1-7. Books Nippan, 1993-1996. A collection of photographs of human models, annotated in Japanese.

[11] K-K Sung and T. Poggio. Example based learning for view based face detection. Ai memo 1521, MIT, 1994.

Attentional Modulation of Human Pattern Discrimination Psychophysics Reproduced by a Quantitative Model

Laurent Itti, Jochen Braun, Dale K. Lee and Christof Koch
{itti, achim, jjwen, koch}@klab.caltech.edu
Computation & Neural Systems, MSC 139-74
California Institute of Technology, Pasadena, CA 91125, U.S.A.

Abstract

We previously proposed a quantitative model of early visual processing in primates, based on non-linearly interacting visual filters and statistically efficient decision. We now use this model to interpret the observed modulation of a range of human psychophysical thresholds with and without focal visual attention. Our model – calibrated by an automatic fitting procedure – simultaneously reproduces thresholds for four classical pattern discrimination tasks, performed while attention was engaged by another concurrent task. Our model then predicts that the seemingly complex improvements of certain thresholds, which we observed when attention was fully available for the discrimination tasks, can best be explained by a strengthening of competition among early visual filters.

1 INTRODUCTION

What happens when we voluntarily focus our attention to a restricted part of our visual field? Focal attention is often thought as a gating mechanism, which selectively allows a certain spatial location and and certain types of visual features to reach higher visual processes. We here investigate the possibility that attention might have a specific computational modulatory effect on early visual processing.

We and others have observed that focal visual attention can modulate human psychophysical thresholds for simple pattern discrimination tasks [7, 8, 5] When attention is drawn away from a task, for example by "cueing" [12] to another location of the display, or by a second, concurrent task [1, 7, 8], an apparently complex pattern of performance degradation is observed: For some tasks, attention has little or no effect on performance (e.g., detection of luminance increments), while for other tasks, attention dramatically improves performance (e.g., discrimination of orientation). Our specific findings with dual-task psychophysics are detailed below.

These observations have been paralleled by electrophysiological studies of attention. In the awake macaque, neuronal responses to attended stimuli can be 20% to 100% higher than to otherwise identical unattended stimuli. This has been demonstrated in visual cortical areas V1, V2, and V4 [16, 11, 10, 9] when the animal discriminates stimulus orientation, and in areas MT and MST when the animal discriminates the speed of stimulus motion [17]. Even spontaneous firing rates are 40% larger when attention is directed at a neuron's receptive field [9]. Whether neuronal responses to attended stimuli are merely enhanced [17] or whether they are also more sharply tuned for certain stimulus dimensions [16] remains controversial. Very recently, fMRI studies have shown similar enhancement (as measured with BOLD contrast) in area V1 of humans, specifically at the retinotopic location where subjects had been instructed to focus their attention to [2, 14].

All of these observations directly address the issue of the "top-down" computational effect of attentional focusing onto early visual processing stages. This issue should be distinguished from that of the "bottom-up" control of visual attention [6], which studies which visual features are likely to attract the attention focusing mechanism (e.g., pop-out phenomena and studies of visual search). Top-down attentional modulation happens after attention has been focused to a location of the visual field, and most probably involves the massive feedback circuits which anatomically project from higher cortical areas back to early visual processing areas.

In the present study, we quantify the modulatory effect of attention observed in human psychophysics using a model of early visual processing. The model is based on non-linearly interacting visual filters and statistically efficient decision [4, 5]. Although attention could modulate virtually any visual processing stage (e.g., the decision stage, which compares internal responses from different stimuli), our basic hypothesis here – supported by electrophysiology and fMRI [16, 11, 10, 17, 9, 2, 14] – is that this modulation might happen very early in the visual processing hierarchy. Given this basic hypothesis, we investigate how attention should affect early visual processing in order to quantitatively reproduce the psychophysical results.

2 PSYCHOPHYSICAL EXPERIMENTS

We measured attentional modulation of spatial vision thresholds using a dual-task paradigm [15, 7]: At the center of the visual field, a letter discrimination task is presented, while a pattern discrimination task is simultaneously presented at a random peripheral location (4° eccentricity). The central task consists of discriminating between five letters "T" or four "T" and one "L". It has been shown to efficiently engage attention [7]. The peripheral task is chosen from a battery of a classical pattern discrimination tasks, and is the task of interest for this study. Psychophysical thresholds are measured for two distinct conditions: In the **"fully attended"** condition, observers are asked to devote their entire attention to the peripheral

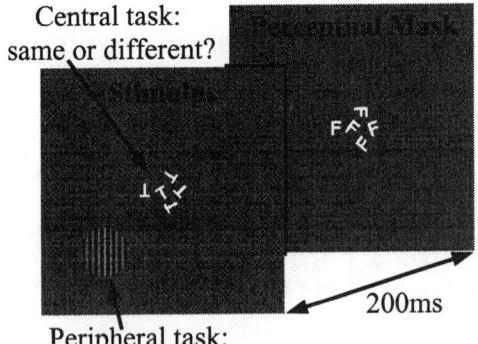

task, and to ignore the central task (while still fixating the center of the screen). In the **"poorly attended"** condition, observers are asked to pay full attention to the central task (and the blocks of trials for which performance for the central task falls below a certain cut-off are discarded).

Four classical pattern discrimination tasks were investigated, each with two volunteer subjects (average shown in **Figure 1**), similarly to our previous experiments [7, 8]. Screen luminance resolution was 0.2%. Screen luminance varied from 1 to $90cd/m^2$ (mean $45cd/m^2$), room illumination was $5cd/m^2$ and viewing distance 80cm. The Yes/No (present/absent) paradigm was used (one stimulus presentation per trial). Threshold (75% correct peformance) was reached using a staircase procedure, and computed through a maximum-likelihood fit of a Weibull function with two degrees of freedom to the psychometric curves.

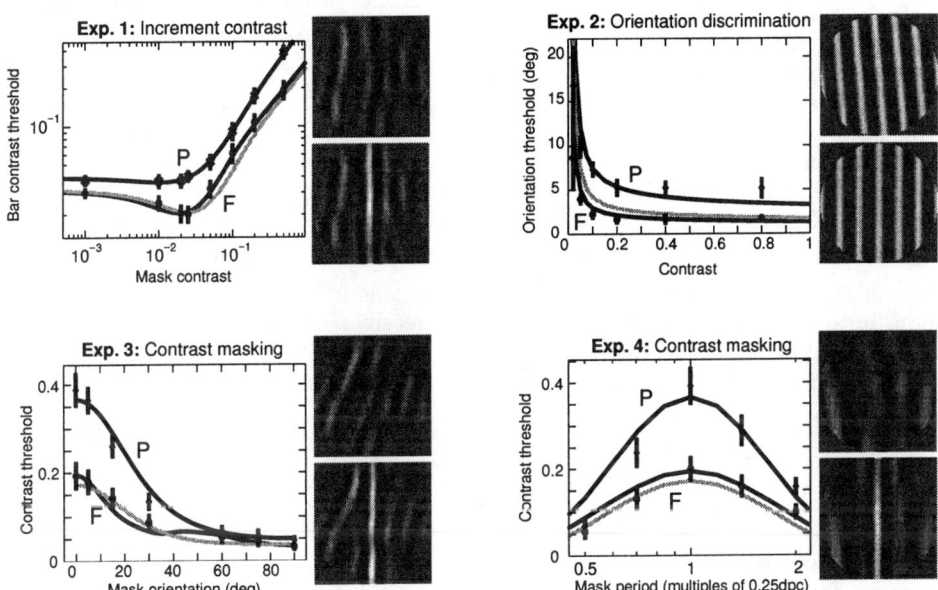

Figure 1: Psychophysical data and model fits using the parameters from Table 1 (P=poorly and F=fully attended). Gray curves: Model predictions for fully attended data, using the poorly attended parameters, except for $\gamma = 2.9$ and $\delta = 2.1$ (see Results).

Exp. 1 measured increment contrast discrimination threshold: The observer discriminates between a 4cpd (cycles per degree) stochastic oriented mask [7] at fixed contrast, and the same mask plus a low-contrast sixth-derivative-of-Gaussian (D6G) bar; threshold is measured for bar contrast [8]. **Exp. 2** measured orientation discrimination thresholds: The observer discriminates between a vertical and tilted grating at 4cpd; threshold for the angle difference is measured. In addition, two contrast masking tasks were investigated for their sensitivity to non-linearities in visual processing. A 4cpd stochastic mask (50% contrast) was always present, and threshold was measured for the contrast of a vertical superimposed D6G bar. In **Exp. 3**, the orientation of the masker was varied and its spatial frequency fixed (4cpd), while in **Exp. 4** the spatial period of the masker was varied and its orientation vertical. Our aim was to investigate very dissimilar tasks, in particular with respect to the decision strategy used by the observer.

Using the dual-task paradigm, we found mixed attentional effects on psychophysical thresholds, including the appearance of a more pronounced contrast discrimination "dipper" in **Exp. 1**, substantial improvement of orientation thresholds in **Exp. 2**, and reduced contrast elevations due to masking in **Exps. 3**–**4** (also see [7, 8]).

3 MODEL

The model consists of three successive stages [4, 5]. In the first stage, a bank of Gabor-like linear filters analyzes a fixed location of the visual scene. Here, a single-scale model composed of 12 pairs of filters in quadrature phase, tuned for orientations $\theta \in \Theta$ evenly spanning 180°, was sufficient to account for the data (although a multi-scale model may account for

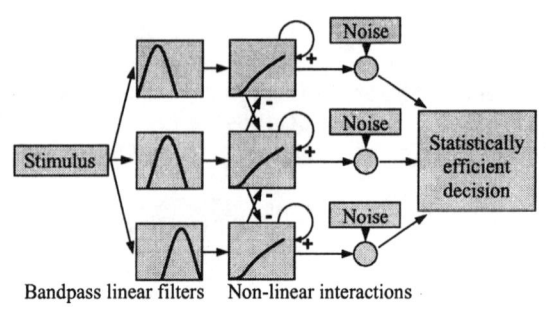

Bandpass linear filters   Non-linear interactions

a wider range of psychophysical thresholds). The linear filters take values between 0.0 and 100.0, then multiplied by a gain factor A (one of the ten free parameters of the model), and to which a small background activity ϵ is added.

In the second stage, filters non-linearly interact as follows: (1) Each unit receives non-linear self-excitation, and (2) each unit receives non-linear divisive inhibition from a pool of similarly-tuned units: With E_θ being the linear response from a unit tuned for orientation θ, the pooled response R_θ is given by:

$$R_\theta = \frac{(E_\theta)^\gamma}{(S)^\delta + \sum_{\theta' \in \Theta} W_\theta(\theta')(E_{\theta'})^\delta} + \eta, \qquad \text{where} \qquad W_\theta(\theta') = e^{-\frac{(\theta'-\theta)^2}{2\Sigma_\theta^2}}$$

is a Gaussian weighting function centered around θ, and η a positive constant to account for background activity in the pooling stage. This stage is inspired from Heeger's model of gain control in cat V1 [3, 4]. Our formulation, in which none of the parameters is given a particular value, however allows for multiple outcomes, to be determined by fitting the model to our psychophysical data: A sigmoidal ($S > 0, \gamma > \delta$) as well as simple power-law ($S = 0$) or even linear ($\gamma = 1, \delta = 0$) contrast response characteristic could emerge, the responses could be saturating ($\gamma = \delta$) or not ($\gamma \neq \delta$), and the inhibitory pool size (Σ_θ) could be broad or narrow. Because striate neurons are noisy, physiological noise is assumed in the model at the outputs of the second stage. The noise level is chosen close to what is typically observed in cortical pyramidal cells, and modeled by Gaussian noise with variance equal to mean taken to some power α determined by fitting.

Because the decision stage – which quantitatively relates activity in the population of pooled noisy units to behavioral discrimination performance – is not fully characterized in humans, we are not in a position to model it in any detail. Instead, we trained our subjects (for 2-3 hours on each task), and assume that they perform close to an "optimal detector". Such optimal detector may be characterized in a formal manner, using Statistical Estimation Theory [4, 5]. We assume that a brain mechanism exists, which, for a given stimulus presentation, builds an internal estimate of some stimulus attribute ζ (e.g., contrast, orientation, period). The central assumption of our decision stage is that this brain mechanism will perform close to an *unbiased efficient statistic* T, which is the best possible estimator of ζ

given the noisy population response from the second stage. The accuracy (variance) with which T estimates ζ can be computed formally, and is the inverse of the Fisher Information with respect to ζ [13, 4]. Simply put, this means that, from the first two stages of the model alone, we have a means of computing the best possible estimation performance for ζ, and consequently, the best possible discrimination performance between two stimuli with parameters ζ_1 and ζ_2 [4, 5]. Such statistically efficient decision stage is implementable as a neural network [13].

This decision stage provides a unified framework for optimal discrimination in any behavioral situation, and eliminates the need for task-dependent assumptions about the strategy used by the observers to perform the task in a near optimal manner. Our model allows for a quantitative prediction of human psychophysical thresholds, based on a crude simulation of the physiology of primary visual cortex (area V1).

4 RESULTS

All parameters in the model were automatically adjusted in order to best fit the psychophysical data from all experiments. A multidimensional downhill simplex with simulated annealing overhead was used to minimize the root-mean-square distance between the quantitative predictions of the model and the human data [4]. The best-fit parameters obtained independently for the "fully attended" and "poorly attended" conditions are reported in **Table 1**. The model's simultaneous fits to our entire dataset are plotted in **Figure 1** for both conditions. After convergence of the fitting procedure, a measure of how well constrained each parameter was by the data was computed as follows: Each parameter was systematically varied around its best-fit value, in 0.5% steps, and the fitting error was recomputed; the amplitude by which each parameter could be varied before the fitting error increased by more than 10% of its optimum is noted as a standard deviation in **Table 1**. A lower deviation indicates that the parameter is more strongly constrained by the dataset.

Table 1. Model parameters for both attentional conditions.

Name	Symbol	fully attended	poorly attended
Linear gain[†]	A	1.7 ± 0.2	8.2 ± 0.9
Activity-independent inhibition[†]	S	14.1 ± 2.3	101.5 ± 16.6
Excitatory exponent	γ	3.36 ± 0.02	2.09 ± 0.01
Inhibitory exponent	δ	2.48 ± 0.02	1.51 ± 0.02
Noise exponent	α	1.34 ± 0.07	1.39 ± 0.08
Background activity, linear stage	ϵ	1.13 ± 0.35	1.25 ± 0.60
Background activity, pooling stage	η	0.18 ± 0.05	0.77 ± 0.11
Spatial period tuning width[×]	σ_λ	0.85 ± 0.06 oct.	0.85 ± 0.09 oct.
Orientation tuning width[×]	σ_θ	$26° \pm 2.4°$	$38° \pm 5.5°$
Orientation pooling width[×]	Σ_θ	$48° \pm 25°$	$50° \pm 26°$

[†] Dynamic range of linear filters is $[\epsilon \ldots 100.0 \times A + \epsilon]$.
[×] For clarity, FWHM values are given rather than σ values (FWHM = $2\sigma\sqrt{2\ln(2)}$).

Although no human bias was introduced during the fitting procedure, interestingly, all of the model's internal parameters reached physiologically plausible best-fit values, such as, for example, slightly supra-Poisson noise level ($\alpha \approx 1.35$), $\approx 30°$ orientation tuning FWHM (full-width at half-maximum), and ≈ 0.85 octave spatial period tuning FWHM. Some of the internal characteristics of the model which more closely relate to the putative underlying physiological mechanisms are shown in **Figure 2**.

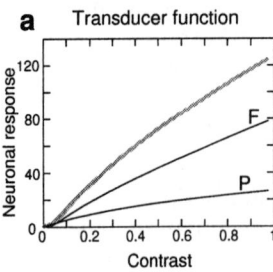 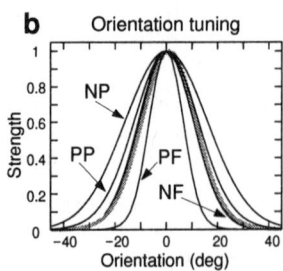 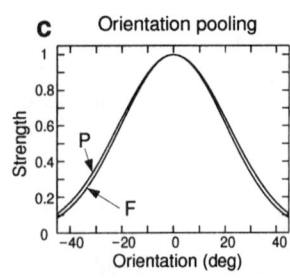

Figure 2: Internals of the model. (a) The response function of individual units to contrast was sigmoidal under full (F) and almost linear under poor (P) attention. (b) Native linear orientation tuning was broader under poor (NP) than full (NF) attention, but it was sharpened in both cases by pooling (PP=pooled poor, and PF=pooled full attention). (c) There was no difference in orientation pooling width under poor (P) or full (F) attention. Using poorly attended parameters, except for $\gamma = 2.9$ and $\delta = 2.1$ (grey curves), yielded steep non-linear contrast response, and intermediary tuning (same width as NF).

In **Table 1**, attention had the following significant effects on the model's parameters: 1) Both pooling exponents (γ, δ) were higher; 2) the tuning width (σ_θ) was narrower; 3) the linear gain (A) and associated activity-independent inhibition (S) were lower; and 4) the background activity of the pooling stage was lower. This yielded increased competition between filters: The network behaved more like a winner-take-all under full attention, and more like a linear network of independent units under poor attention. While the attentional modulation of γ, δ and σ_θ are easy to interpret, its effect on the A, S and η is more difficult to understand.

Consequently, we conducted a further automatic fit, which, starting from the "poorly attended" parameters, was only allowed to alter γ and δ to fit the "fully attended" data. The motivation for not varying σ_θ was that we observed significant sharpening of the tuning induced by higher exponents γ, δ **(Figure 2)**. Also, slight changes in the difference $\gamma - \delta$ can easily produce large changes in the overall gain of the system, hence compensating for changes in A, S and η. (We however do not imply here that σ_θ, A, S and η are redundant parameters; there is only a small range around the best-fit point over which γ and δ can compensate for variations in the other parameters, without dramatically impairing the quality of fit).

Although the new fit was not as accurate as that obtained with all parameters allowed to vary, it appeared that a simple modification of the pooling exponents well captured the effect of attention **(Figure 1)**. Hence, the "poorly attended" parameters of **Table 1** well described the "poorly attended" data, and the same parameters except for $\gamma = 2.9$ and $\delta = 2.1$ well described the "fully attended" data.

A variety of other simple parameter modifications were also tested, but none except for the pooling exponents (γ, δ) could fully account for the attentional modulation. These modifications include: Changes in gain (obtained by modifying A only, γ only, or δ only), in tuning (σ_θ), in the extent of the inhibitory pool (Σ_θ), and in the noise level (α). A more systematic study, in which all possible parameter subsets are successively examined, is currently in progress in our laboratory.

5 DISCUSSION and CONCLUSION

At the basis of our results is the hypothesis that attention might modulate the earlier rather than the later stages of visual processing. We found that a very simple, prototypical, task-independent enhancement of the amount of competition between early visual filters accounts well for the human data. This enhancement resulted from increases in parameters γ and δ in the model, and was paralleled by an increase in contrast gain and a sharpening in orientation tuning. Although it is not possible from our data to rule out any attentional modulation at later stages, our hypothesis has recently received experimental support that attention indeed modulates early visual processing in humans [2, 14].

More psychophysical experiments are needed to investigate attentional modulation at later processing stages. For example, it might be possible to study the effect of attention on the decision stage by manipulating attention during experiments involving decision uncertainty. In the absence of such results, we have attempted in our experiments to minimize the possible impact of attention on later stages, by using only simple stimulus patterns devoid of conceptual or emotional meaning, such as to involve as little as possible the more cognitive stages of visual processing.

Our finding that attention may increase the amount of competition between early visual filters is accompanied by an enhancement of the gain and sensitivity of the filters, and by a sharpening of their tuning properties. The existence of two such processing states – one, more sensitive and selective inside the focus of attention, and the other, more broadly-tuned and non-specific outside – can be justified by at least two observations: First, the higher level of activity in attended neurons consumes more energy, which may not be desirable over the entire extent of visual cortices. Second, although less efficient for fine discriminations, the broadly-tuned and non-specific state may have greater ability at catching unexpected, non-specific visual events. In this perspective, this state would be desirable as an input to bottom-up, visual alerting mechanisms, which monitor the rest of our visual world while we are focusing on a specific task requiring high focal accuracy.

Acknowledgements

This research was supported by ONR and NSF (Caltech ERC).

References

[1] Bonnel AM, Stein JF, Bertucci P. *Q J Exp Psychol [A]* 1992;44(4):601-26
[2] Gandhi SP, Heeger DJ, Boynton GM. *Inv Opht Vis Sci (ARVO'98)* 1998;39(4):5194
[3] Heeger DJ. *Vis Neurosci* 1992;9:181-97
[4] Itti L, Braun J, Lee DK, Koch C. *Proc NIPS*97* (in press)
[5] Itti L, Koch C, Braun J. *Inv Opht Vis Sci (Proc ARVO'98)* 1998;39(4):2934
[6] Koch C, Ullman S. *Hum Neurobiol* 1985;4:219-27
[7] Lee DK, Koch C, Braun J. *Vis Res* 1997:37(17):2409-18
[8] Lee DK, Koch C, Itti L, Braun J. *Inv Opht Vis Sci (Proc ARVO'98)* 1998;39(4):2938
[9] Luck SJ, Chelazzi L, Hillyard SA, Desimone R. *J Neurophysiol* 1997;77(1):24-42
[10] Maunsell JH. *Science* 1995;270(5237)764-9
[11] Motter BC. *J Neurophysiol* 1993;70(3):909-19
[12] Nakayama K, Mackeben M. *Vis Res* 1989;29(11):1631-47
[13] Pouget A, Zhang K, Deneve S, Latham PE. *Neur Comp* 1998;10:373-401
[14] Somers DC, et al. *Inv Opht Vis Sci (Proc ARVO'98)* 1998;39(4):5192
[15] Sperling G, Melchner MJ. *Science* 1978;202:315-8
[16] Spitzer H, Desimone R, Moran J. *Science* 1988;240(4850):338-40
[17] Treue S, Maunsell JH. *Nature* 1996;382(6591):539-41

A V1 model of pop out and asymmetry in visual search

Zhaoping Li
University College London, z.li@ucl.ac.uk

Abstract

Visual search is the task of finding a target in an image against a background of distractors. Unique features of targets enable them to pop out against the background, while targets defined by lacks of features or conjunctions of features are more difficult to spot. It is known that the ease of target detection can change when the roles of figure and ground are switched. The mechanisms underlying the ease of pop out and asymmetry in visual search have been elusive. This paper shows that a model of segmentation in V1 based on intracortical interactions can explain many of the qualitative aspects of visual search.

1 Introduction

Visual search is closely related to visual segmentation, and therefore can be used to diagnose the mechanisms of visual segmentation. For instance, a red dot can pop-out against a background of green distractor dots instantaneously, suggesting that only pre-attentive mechanisms are necessary (Treisman et al, 1990). On the other hand, it is much more difficult to search for a red 'X' among green 'X's and red 'O's – the time it takes to detect the target's presence increases with the number of background distractors, suggesting some form of attentive serial search. Sometimes, the search times change when the role of the figure (target) and ground (distractors) are switched -- *asymmetry* in visual search. For instance, it is easier to find a longer bar in a background of shorter bars than vice-versa.

It has been unclear which visual areas or neural mechanisms are responsible for the pop out and asymmetry in visual search. There are, however, psychophysical theories (Treisman et al 1990, Treisman and Gormican 1988) which argue that visual inputs are coded in a number of primitive or basic feature dimensions: orientation, color, brightness, motion direction, disparity, line ends, line intersections, and closure. A target can pop-out preattentively if it has a feature in one of these dimensions, such as a particular color or orientation, which is absent in the distractors. Hence, a red dot pops out among green ones. However, red 'X' is difficult to spot among green 'X's and red 'O's because neither being red nor being 'X' is unique for the target, and therefore serial search is required. While a vertical line pops out of horizontal ones and vice versa without any search asymmetry, search asymmetry will arise when a single feature in which target and distractors differ is present in one of the two and absent or reduced in the other. Hence, a long line is more easily spotted among short lines than the reserve. This theory has been very helpful in understanding search phenomena. However, it has to make assumptions about what are the primitive feature dimensions, as well as what constitutes larger or smaller values along a given dimension. For instance, to explain that a curved line is more easily spotted among straight lines than the reverse, the theory has to define straightness as the default or standard, and curvaciousness as the deviation from this standard and thus an added feature. Empirically, other pairs of standard and deviant properties include vertical versus tilted, parallel versus convergent, short vs long lines, circle vs ellipse, and complete versus incomplete circles. The basis behind these assumptions are not completely clear. Other related theories have similar problems. For instance, Julesz's texton theory (Julesz 1981) for visual segmentation or pop out starts off by assuming a complete set of special features that constitute textons.

This paper proposes and demonstrates in a model that pre-attentive mechanisms in V1 can qualitatively explain many of the phenomena of visual search. It is assumed that the ease of search is determined by the relative saliencies of the target and distractors. Intracortical interactions in V1 alter the saliencies of targets and distractors according to their own image features as well as those of the distractor or targets images that form the context. Hence, the relative saliency depends on the particular target-distractor pair involved. In particular, asymmetry is a natural consequence of contextual influences.

2 The V1 model

We use a V1 model of pre-attentive visual segmentation which has been shown to be able to detect and highlight smooth contours in noisy backgrounds and find boundaries between texture regions in images (Li 1998a, 1998b). Its behavior agrees with physiological observations (Knierim and van Essen 1992, Kapadia et al 1995). Without loss of generality, the model ignores color, motion, and stereo dimensions, includes mainly layer 2-3 orientation selective cells, and ignores the intra-hypercolumnar mechanism by which their receptive fields are formed. Inputs to the model are images filtered by the edge- or bar-like local receptive fields (RFs) of V1 cells.[1] The cells influence each other contextually via horizontal intra-cortical connections (Rockland and Lund 1983, Gilbert, 1992), transforming patterns of inputs to patterns of cell responses. Fig. 1 shows the elements of the model and their interactions. At each location i there is a model V1 hypercolumn composed of K neuron pairs. Each pair (i, θ) has RF center i and preferred orientation $\theta = k\pi/K$ for $k = 1, 2, ...K$, and is called (the neural representation of) an edge segment. Based on experimental data (White, 1989, Douglas and Martin 1990), each edge segment consists of an excitatory and an inhibitory neuron that are interconnected, and each model cell represents a collection of local cells of similar types. The excitatory cell receives the visual input; its output is used as a measure of the response or salience of the edge segment and projects to higher visual areas. The inhibitory cells are treated as interneurons. Based on observations by Gilbert, Lund and their colleagues (Rockland and Lund, 1983, Gilbert 1992) horizontal connections $J_{i\theta,j\theta'}$

---

[1]The terms 'edge' and 'bar' will be used interchangeably.

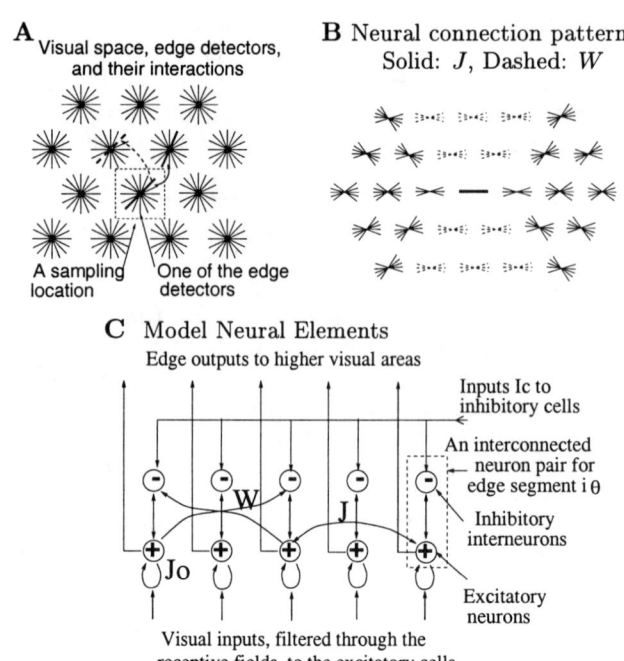

Figure 1: **A**: Visual inputs are sampled in a discrete grid of edge/bar detectors. Each grid point i has K neuron pairs (see **C**), one per bar segment, tuned to different orientations θ spanning $180°$. Two segments at different grid points can interact with each other via monosynaptic excitation J (the solid arrow from one thick bar to anothe r) or disynaptic inhibition W (the dashed arrow to a thick dashed bar). See also **C**. **B**: A schematic of the neural connection pattern from the center (thick solid) bar to neighboring bars within a few sampling unit distances. J's contacts are shown by thin solid bars. W's are shown by thin dashed bars. The connection pattern is translation and rotation invariant. **C**: An input bar segment is directly processed by an interconnected pair of excitatory and inhibitory cells, each cell models abstractly a local group of cells of the same type. The excitatory cell receives visual input and sends output $g_x(x_{i\theta})$ to higher centers. The inhibitory cell is an interneuron. Visual space is taken as having periodic boundary conditions.

(respectively $W_{i\theta,j\theta'}$) mediate contextual influences via monosynaptic excitation (respectively disynaptic inhibition) from $j\theta'$ to $i\theta$ which have nearby but different RF centers, $i \neq j$, and similar orientation preferences, $\theta \sim \theta'$. The membrane potentials follow the equations:

$$\dot{x}_{i\theta} = -\alpha_x x_{i\theta} - \sum_{\Delta\theta} \psi(\Delta\theta) g_y(y_{i,\theta+\Delta\theta}) + J_o g_x(x_{i\theta}) + \sum_{j\neq i,\theta'} J_{i\theta,j\theta'} g_x(x_{j\theta'}) + I_{i\theta} + I_o$$

$$\dot{y}_{i\theta} = -\alpha_y y_{i\theta} + g_x(x_{i\theta}) + \sum_{j\neq i,\theta'} W_{i\theta,j\theta'} g_x(x_{j\theta'}) + I_c$$

where $\alpha_x x_{i\theta}$ and $\alpha_y y_{i\theta}$ model the decay to resting potential, $g_x(x)$ and $g_y(y)$ are sigmoid-like functions modeling cells' firing rates in response to membrane potentials x and y, respectively, $\psi(\Delta\theta)$ is the spread of inhibition within a hypercolumn, $J_o g_x(x_{i\theta})$ is self excitation, I_c and I_o are background inputs, including noise and inputs modeling the general and local normalization of activities (see Li (1998b) for more details). Visual input $I_{i\theta}$ persists after onset, and initializes the activity levels $g_x(x_{i\theta})$. The activities are then modified by the contextual influences. Depending on the visual input, the system often settles into an oscillatory state (Gray

A V1 Model of Pop Out and Asymmetry in Visual Search

and Singer, 1989, see the details in Li 1998b). Temporal averages of $g_x(x_{i\theta})$ over several oscillation cycles are used as the model's output. The nature of the computation performed by the model is determined largely by the horizontal connections J and W, which are local (spanning only a few hypercolumns), and translation and rotation invariant (Fig. 1B).

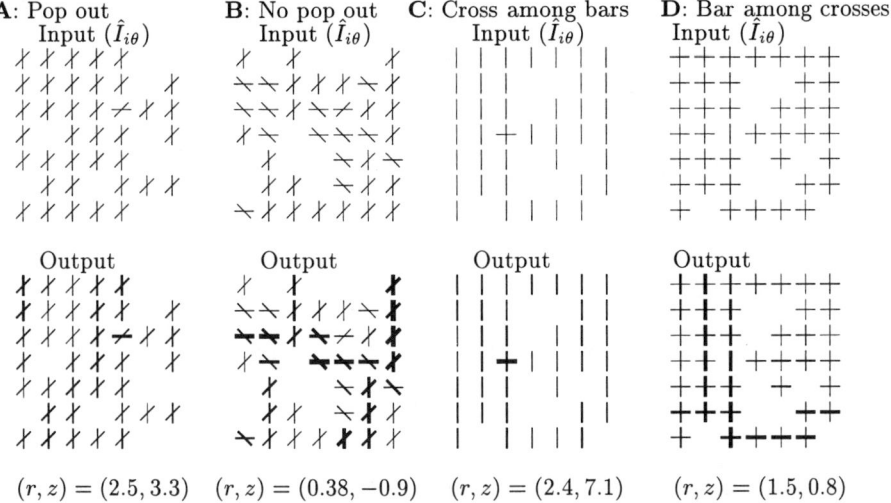

Figure 2: Visual search examples plotted by the model inputs and outputs. A: A single distinctive feature, the horizontal bar in the target, enables pop out. This target is the most salient (measured as the saliency of the horizontal bar in target) spot in the image. B: The target does not pop out since neither of its features, a horizontal and a 45° bars, is unique in the image. The target is less salient than average in the image. C and D demonstrate the asymmetry in a target-distractor pair. C: The cross is the most salient (measured by the saliency of the horizontal bar) spot in the image. The popout strength is stronger than in A. D: The target bar does not pop out,

The model was applied to a variety of input patterns, as shown in examples in the figures. The input values $\hat{I}_{i\theta}$ are the same for all visible bars in each example. The differences in the outputs are caused by intracortical interactions. They become significant about one membrane time constant after the initial neural response (Li, 1998b). The widths of the bars in the figures are proportional to input and output strengths. The plotted region in each picture is often a small region of an extended image. The same model parameters (*e.g.* the dependence of the synaptic weights on distances and orientations, the thresholds and gains in the functions $g_x()$ and $g_y()$, and the level of input noise in I_o) are used for all the simulation examples.

We define the net saliency S_i at each grid point i as that of the most activated bar. Define $\bar{S}$ and σ_s be the mean and standard deviation of the saliencies of all grid points with visible stimuli. Let $r_i \equiv S_i/\bar{S}$ and $z_i \equiv (S_i - \bar{S})/\sigma_s$. A highly salient point i should have large values of (r_i, z_i) – in particular, both r_i and z_i should be larger than 1. For larger targets that occupy more than one grid point, the relative saliency measure of the target is that of the most salient grid point on the target.

Fig. (2)A,B compare the state of the target '⊬' in two different contexts. Against a texture of '⊬' it is highly salient because of its unique horizontal bar. Against '⊬' and '⊻' it is much less salient because only the conjunction of '—' and '╱' distinguishes it. Fig. (2)C,D exhibit search asymmetry. The horizontal bar in the target is unique in the image of Fig. (2)A,C, which leads to pop out, and each target sits at the most salient location in the respective images. On the other hand, no feature in the targets of Fig. (2)B,D is unique. These examples are consistent with the psychophysical

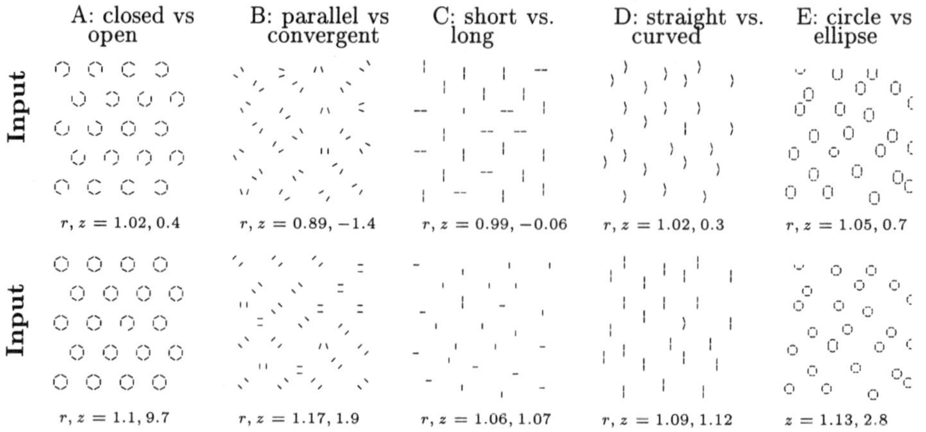

Figure 3: Five typical examples, one column each, of visual search asymmetry as simulated in the model. The input stimuli are plotted, the target saliency r, z scores are indicated below each of them. All input bars are of the same intermediate input contrast. The role of figure and ground is switched from the top to the bottom rows.

theories mentioned in introduction. Further, we note that because intracortical interactions link mostly neurons preferring similar orientations, two very different orientations can be viewed as independent features. The pop out is stronger in Fig. (2)C than Fig. (2)A since horizontal differs more from vertical ($90°$) than from $45°$. The V1 orientation selective RFs and orientation specific horizontal connnections provide the neural basis for orientation as one of the primitive feature dimensions. In fact, the contextual influences between image features imply that saliency values depend on detailed geometrical relationships between features within and between a target or distrator and its nearby target or distractors (see Fig. (2)B). The relative ease in searches varies continuously from extreme pop out to slow serial searches depending on the specific stimuli, as suggested by Duncan and Humphreys (1989).

Further interesting examples of search asymmetry include cases for which neither target nor distractors have a primitive feature (such as color or orientation) that is absent in the other. Asymmetry is much weaker but still present. Figure 3 shows some typical examples. Although the saliencies of the more salient targets are only fractionally higher than the average feature saliency in rest of the image, this fraction is significant when the standard deviation σ_s of the saliencies is small or when z is large enough, thus making the search task easier.

3 Summary and Discussion

Early psychophysical studies (Treisman et al 1990) suggested that most aspects of visual search involve mechanisms of early vision. However, it has never been clear which visual areas or neural mechanisms might be responsible. To the best of my knowledge, this model is the first non-phenomenological model to understand the

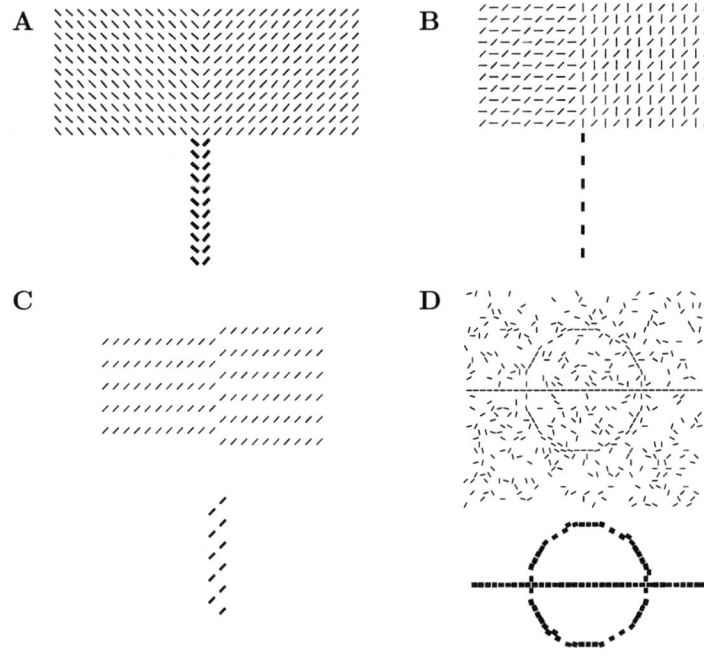

Figure 4: Four examples of model performance under various inputs. Each plots the visual input image at the top and the most activated bars in V1 cell outputs (using a threshold) at the bottom. Every visible bar in a given input image has the same input strength. A, B, and C demonstrate that the texture region boundaries have the highest output saliencies. D shows that the smooth contours are detected as the most salient against a background of noise.

neural bases of visual search phenomena (see Rubenstein and Sagi (1990) for a model of asymmetry using variances of the local image filter responses). This paper has shown that intra-cortical interactions in V1 can account for the qualitative phenomena of pop-out and asymmetry in visual search, assuming that the ease of detection is directly determined by the saliencies of targets. Of course, the task of search requires decision making and often visual attention, especially when the target does not spontaneously pop-out. The quantitative search times can only be modeled on the basis of an assumption of specific mechanisms for attention and decision making. Our model suggests, nevertheless, that pre-attentive V1 mechanisms play a significant and controlling role in such tasks. Furthermore, it suggests that some otherwise intractable phenomena can be understood without resorting to additional concepts such as textons (Julesz 1981) or defining certain image properties (such as closure and straightness) as having standard or reference values.

Our current implementation of V1 is still very simplistic. We have not yet included color, motion, or stereo inputs, nor multiscale sampling. Further, our input sampling density is very low. Consequently, the model cannot simulate many of the more complex input stimuli used in psychophysical experiments (Treisman and Gormican, 1988). An extended implementation is needed to test whether V1 mechanisms alone can qualitatively account for all or most types of search pop-out and asymmetries. Physiological evidence (Gilbert 1992) suggests that intracortical connections tend to link neurons with similar selectivities in other dimensions, such as color and stereo, in addition to orientation. This supports the idea that color, motion, and disparity are also primitive visual coding dimensions like orientation. We believe that the example in Fig. 2A,B demonstrating pop-out versus serial search would be more convincing if color were included to simulate, for instance, a red 'X' among green 'X's with and without red 'O's in the background. Our current model does not explain why a slightly tilted line pops out more readily from vertical line distractors than the reverse. This is because our V1 model idealistically assumes rotational symmetry, and so vertical is not distinguished from other orientations. Neither our visual environment nor our visual system is in fact rotationally invariant.

The V1 model was originally proposed to account for pre-attentive contour enhancement and visual segmentation (Li 1998a, 1998b). The contextual influences mediated by the intracortical interactions enable each V1 neuron to process inputs from a local image area larger than its classical receptive field. This enables cortical neurons to detect image locations where translation invariance in the input image breaks down, and highlight these image locations with higher neural activities, making them conspicuous. These highlights mark candidate locations for image region (or object surface) boundaries, smooth contours and small figures against backgrounds, serving the purpose of pre-attentive segmentation. Fig. 4 demonstrates the performance of the model for pre-attentive segmentation. In each example, the visual inputs and the most salient outputs are shown. All examples are simulated using exactly the same model parameters as those used in examples of visual search. It is not too surprising that a model of pre-attentive segmentation in V1 can explain visual search phenomena. Indeed, pop out has been commonly understood as a sign of pre-attentive segmentation. Our model further suggests that asymmetry in visual search is partly a side-effect of pre-attentive segmentation. Our V1 model can in turn be improved using visual search as a diagnostic tool.

References

[1] R. J. Douglas and K. A. Martin (1990) "Neocortex" in *Synaptic Organization of the Brain* ed. G. M. Shepherd. (Oxford University Press), 3rd Edition, pp389-438

[2] Duncan J. Humphreys G. *Psychological Review* 96: p1-26, (1989).

[3] C. D. Gilbert (1992) *Neuron.* **9**(1), 1-13.

[4] C. M. Gray and W. Singer (1989) *Proc. Natl. Acad. Sci. USA* **86**, 1698-1702.

[5] B. Julesz. (1981) *Nature* **290**, 91-97.

[6] M. K. Kapadia, M. Ito, C. D. Gilbert, and G. Westheimer (1995) *Neuron.* **15**(4), 843-56.

[7] J. J. Knierim and D. C. van Essen (1992) *J. Neurophysiol.* **67**, 961-980.

[8] Z. Li (1998a) in *Theoretical aspects of neural computation* Eds. Wong, K.Y.M, King, I, and D-Y Yeung, Springer-Verlag, 1998.

[9] Z. Li (1998b) *Neural Computation* 10(4) p 903-940.

[10] K.S. Rockland and J. S. Lund (1983) *J. Comp. Neurol.* **216**, 303-318

[11] Rubenstein B. and Sagi D. asymmetries" *J. Opt. Soc. Am. A* 9: 1632-1643 (1990).

[12] Treisman A, Cavanagh, P, Fischer B, Ramachandran V.S., and R. von der Heydt in *Visual perception, the Neurophysiological Foundations* Eds. L. Spillmann and J S. Werner, 1990 Academic Press.

[13] Treisman A. and Gormican S. (1988) *Psychological Rev.* **95**, 15-48.

[14] E. L. White (1989) *Cortical circuits* (Birkhauser).

Support Vector Machines Applied to Face Recognition

P. Jonathon Phillips

National Institute of Standards and Technology
Bldg 225 / Rm A216
Gaithersburg, MD 20899
Tel 301.975.5348; Fax 301.975.5287
jonathon@nist.gov

Abstract

Face recognition is a K class problem, where K is the number of known individuals; and support vector machines (SVMs) are a binary classification method. By reformulating the face recognition problem and re-interpreting the output of the SVM classifier, we developed a SVM-based face recognition algorithm. The face recognition problem is formulated as a problem in *difference space*, which models dissimilarities between two facial images. In difference space we formulate face recognition as a two class problem. The classes are: dissimilarities between faces of the same person, and dissimilarities between faces of different people. By modifying the interpretation of the decision surface generated by SVM, we generated a similarity metric between faces that is learned from examples of differences between faces. The SVM-based algorithm is compared with a principal component analysis (PCA) based algorithm on a difficult set of images from the FERET database. Performance was measured for both verification and identification scenarios. The identification performance for SVM is 77-78% versus 54% for PCA. For verification, the equal error rate is 7% for SVM and 13% for PCA.

1 Introduction

Face recognition has developed into a major research area in pattern recognition and computer vision. Face recognition is different from classical pattern-recognition problems such as character recognition. In classical pattern recognition, there are relatively few classes, and many samples per class. With many samples per class, algorithms can classify samples not previously seen by *interpolating* among the training samples. On the other hand, in face recognition, there are many individuals (classes), and only a few images (samples) per person, and algorithms must recognize faces by *extrapolating* from the training samples. In numerous applications there can be only one training sample (image) of each person.

Support vector machines (SVMs) are formulated to solve a classical two class pattern recognition problem. We adapt SVM to face recognition by modifying the interpretation of the output of a SVM classifier and devising a representation of facial images that is concordant with a two class problem. Traditional SVM returns a binary value, the class of the object. To train our SVM algorithm, we formulate the problem in a *difference space*, which explicitly captures the dissimilarities between two facial images. This is a departure from traditional *face space* or *view-based* approaches, which encodes each facial image as a separate view of a face.

In difference space, we are interested in the following two classes: the dissimilarities between images of the same individual, and dissimilarities between images of different people. These two classes are the input to a SVM algorithm. A SVM algorithm generates a decision surface separating the two classes. For face recognition, we re-interpret the decision surface to produce a similarity metric between two facial images. This allows us to construct face-recognition algorithms. The work of Moghaddam et al. [3] uses a Bayesian method in a difference space, but they do not derive a similarity distance from both positive and negative samples.

We demonstrate our SVM-based algorithm on both verification and identification applications. In identification, the algorithm is presented with an image of an unknown person. The algorithm reports its best estimate of the identity of an unknown person from a database of known individuals. In a more general response, the algorithm will report a list of the most similar individuals in the database. In verification (also referred to as authentication), the algorithm is presented with an image and a claimed identity of the person. The algorithm either accepts or rejects the claim. Or, the algorithm can return a confidence measure of the validity of the claim.

To provide a benchmark for comparison, we compared our algorithm with a principal component analysis (PCA) based algorithm. We report results on images from the FERET database of images, which is the de facto standard in the face recognition community. From our experience with the FERET database, we selected harder sets of images on which to test the algorithms. Thus, we avoided saturating performance of either algorithm and providing a robust comparison between the algorithms. To test the ability of our algorithm to generalize to new faces, we trained and tested the algorithms on separate sets of faces.

2 Background

In this section we will give a brief overview of SVM to present the notation used in this paper. For details of SVM see Vapnik [7], or for a tutorial see Burges [1]. SVM is a binary classification method that finds the optimal linear decision surface based on the concept of structural risk minimization. The decision surface is a weighted combination of elements of the training set. These elements are called support vectors and characterize the boundary between the two classes. The input to a SVM algorithm is a set $\{(\mathbf{x_i}, y_i)\}$ of labeled training data, where $\mathbf{x_i}$ is the data and $y_i = -1$ or 1 is the label. The output of a SVM algorithm is a set of N_S support vectors $\mathbf{s_i}$, coefficient weights α_i, class labels y_i of the support vectors, and a constant term b. The linear decision surface is

$$\mathbf{w} \cdot \mathbf{z} + b = 0,$$

where

$$\mathbf{w} = \sum_{i=1}^{N_S} \alpha_i y_i \mathbf{s_i}.$$

SVM can be extended to nonlinear decision surfaces by using a kernel $K(\cdot, \cdot)$ that satisfies Mercer's condition [1, 7]. The nonlinear decision surface is

$$\sum_{i=1}^{N_S} \alpha_i y_i K(\mathbf{s_i}, \mathbf{z}) + b = 0.$$

A facial image is represented as a vector $\mathbf{p} \in \Re^N$, where $\Re^N$ is referred to as *face space*. Face space can be the original pixel values vectorized or another feature space; for example, projecting the facial image on the eigenvectors generated by performing PCA on a training set of faces [6] (also referred to as *eigenfaces*).

We write $\mathbf{p_1} \sim \mathbf{p_2}$ if $\mathbf{p_1}$ and $\mathbf{p_2}$ are images of the same face, and $\mathbf{p_1} \not\sim \mathbf{p_2}$ if they are images of different faces. To avoid confusion we adopted the following terminology for identification and verification. The *gallery* is the set of images of known people and a *probe* is an unknown face that is presented to the system. In identification, the face in a probe is identified. In verification, a probe is the facial image presented to the system whose identity is to be verified. The set of unknown faces is call the *probe set*.

3 Verification as a two class problem

Verification is fundamentally a two class problem. A verification algorithm is presented with an image p and a claimed identity. Either the algorithm accepts or rejects the claim. A straightforward method for constructing a classifier for person X, is to feed a SVM algorithm a training set with one class consisting of facial images of person X and the other class consisting of facial images of other people. A SVM algorithm will generated a linear decision surface, and the identity of the face in image p is accepted if

$$\mathbf{w} \cdot \mathbf{p} + b \leq 0,$$

otherwise the claim is rejected.

This classifier is designed to minimizes the structural risk. Structural risk is an overall measure of classifier performance. However, verification performance is usually measured by two statistics, the probability of correct verification, P_V, and the probability of false acceptance, P_F. There is a tradeoff between P_V and P_F. At one extreme all claims are rejected and $P_V = P_F = 0$; and at the other extreme, all claims are accepted and $P_V = P_F = 1$. The operating values for P_V and P_F are dictated by the application.

Unfortunately, the decision surface generated by a SVM algorithm produces a single performance point for P_V and P_F. To allow for adjusting P_V and P_F, we parameterize a SVM decision surface by Δ. The parametrized decision surface is

$$\mathbf{w} \cdot \mathbf{z} + b = \Delta,$$

and the identity of the face image p is accepted if

$$\mathbf{w} \cdot \mathbf{p} + b \leq \Delta.$$

If $\Delta = -\infty$, then all claims are rejected and $P_V = P_F = 0$; if $\Delta = +\infty$, all claims are accepted and $P_V = P_F = 0$. By varying Δ between negative and positive infinity, all possible combinations of P_V and P_F are found.

Nonlinear parametrized decision surfaces are described by

$$\sum_{i=1}^{N_S} \alpha_i y_i K(\mathbf{s_i}, \mathbf{z}) + b = \Delta.$$

4 Representation

In a canonical face recognition algorithm, each individual is a class and the distribution of each face is estimated or approximated. In this method, for a gallery of K individuals, the identification problem is a K class problem, and the verification problem is K instances of a two class problems. To reduce face recognition to a single instance of a two class problem, we introduce a new representation. We model the dissimilarities between faces. Let $T = \{t_1, \ldots, t_M\}$ be a training set of faces of K individuals, with multiple images of each of the K individuals. From T, we generate two classes. The first is the *within-class differences set*, which are the dissimilarities in facial images of the same person. Formally the within-class difference set is

$$C_1 = \{\mathbf{t_i} - \mathbf{t_j} | \mathbf{t_i} \sim \mathbf{t_j}\}.$$

The set C_1 contains within-class differences for all K individuals in T, not dissimilarities for one of the K individuals in the training set. The second is the *between-class differences set*, which are the dissimilarities among images of different individuals in the training set. Formally,

$$C_2 = \{\mathbf{t_i} - \mathbf{t_j} | \mathbf{t_i} \not\sim \mathbf{t_j}\}.$$

Classes C_1 and C_2 are the inputs to our SVM algorithm, which generates a decision surface. In the pure SVM paradigm, given the difference between facial images $\mathbf{p_1}$ and $\mathbf{p_2}$, the classifier estimates if the faces in the two images are from the same person. In the modification described in section 3, the classification returns a measure of similarity $\delta = \mathbf{w} \cdot (\mathbf{p_1} - \mathbf{p_2}) + b$. This similarity measure is the basis for the SVM-based verification and identification algorithms presented in this paper.

5 Verification

In verification, there is a gallery $\{g_j\}$ of m known individuals. The algorithm is presented with a probe p and a claim to be person j in the gallery. The first step of the verification algorithm computes the similarity score

$$\delta = \sum_{i=1}^{N_S} \alpha_i y_i K(\mathbf{s_i}, \mathbf{g_j} - \mathbf{p}) + b.$$

The second step accepts the claim if $\delta \leq \Delta$. Otherwise, the claim is rejected. The value of Δ is set to meet the desired tradeoff between P_V and P_F.

6 Identification

In identification, there is a gallery $\{g_j\}$ of m known individuals. The algorithm is presented with a probe p to be identified. The first step of the identification algorithm computes a similarity score between the probe and each of the gallery images. The similar score between p and g_j is

$$\delta_j = \sum_{i=1}^{N_S} \alpha_i y_i K(\mathbf{s_i}, \mathbf{g_j} - \mathbf{p}) + b.$$

In the second step, the probe is identified as person j that has minimum similarity score δ_j. An alternative method of reporting identification results is to order the gallery by the similarity measure δ_j.

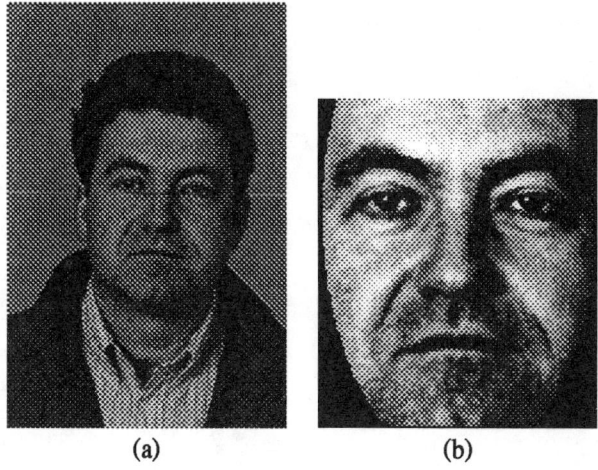

Figure 1: (a) Original image from the FERET database. (b) Image after preprocessing.

7 Experiments

We demonstrate our SVM-based verification and identification algorithms on 400 frontal images from the FERET database of facial images [5]. To provide a benchmark for algorithm performance, we provide performance for a PCA-based algorithm on the same set of images. The PCA algorithm identifies faces with a L_2 nearest neighbor classifier. For the SVM-based algorithms, a radial basis kernel was used.

The 400 images consisted of two images of 200 individuals, and were divided into disjoint training and testing sets. Each set consisted of two images of 100 people. All 400 images were preprocessed to normalize geometry and illumination, and to remove background and hair (figure 1). The preprocessing procedure consisted of manually locating the centers of the eyes; translating, rotating, and scaling the faces to place the center of the eyes on specific pixels; masking the faces to remove background and hair; histogram equalizing the non-masked facial pixels; and scaling the non-masked facial pixels to have zero mean and unit variance.

PCA was performed on 100 preprocessed images (one image of each person in the training set). This produced 99 eigenvectors $\{e_\ell\}$ and eigenvalues $\{\lambda_\ell\}$. The eigenvectors were ordered so that $\lambda_i < \lambda_j$ when $i < j$. Thus, the low order eigenvectors encode the majority of the variance in the training set. The faces were represented by projecting them on a subset of the eigenvectors and this is the face space. We varied the dimension of face space by changing the number of eigenvectors in the representation.

In all experiments, the SVM training set consisted of the same images. The SVM-training set T consisted of two images of 50 individuals from the general training set of 100 individuals. The set C_1 consisted of all 50 within-class differences from faces of the same individuals. The set C_2 consisted of 50 randomly selected between-class differences.

The verification and identification algorithms were tested on a gallery consisted of 100 images from the test set, with one image person. The probe set consisted of the remaining images in the test set (100 individuals, with one image per person).

We report results for verification on a face space that consisted of the first 30 eigenfeatures (an eigenfeature is the projection of the image onto an eigenvector). The results are reported as a receiver operator curve (ROC) in figure 2. The ROC in figure 2 was computed

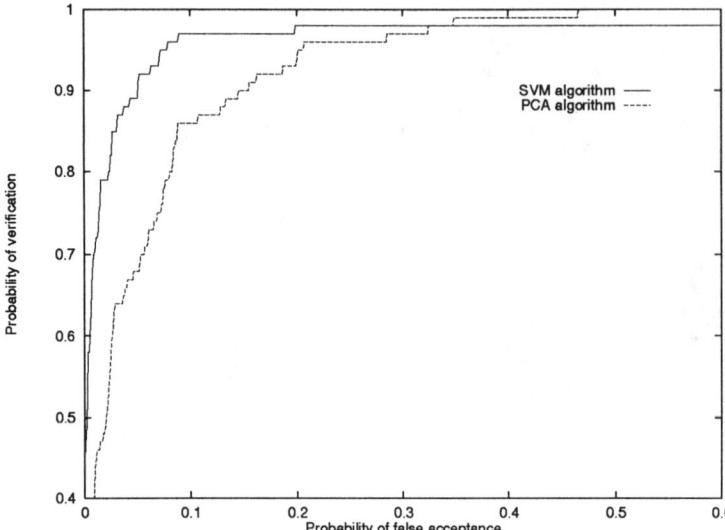

Figure 2: ROC for verification (using first 30 eigenfeatures).

by averaging the ROC for each of the 100 individuals in the gallery. For person g_j, the probe set consisted of one image of person g_j and 99 faces of different people. A summary statistic for verification is the equal error rate. The equal error rate is the point where the probability of false acceptance is equal to the probability of false verification, or mathematically, $P_F = 1 - P_V$. For the SVM-based algorithm the equal error rate is 0.07, and for the PCA-based algorithm is 0.13.

For identification, the algorithm estimated the identity of each of the probes in the probe set. We compute the probability of correctly identifying the probes for a set of face spaces parametrized by the number of eigenfeatures. We always use the first n eigenfeatures, thus we are slowly increasing the amount of information, as measured by variance, available to the classifier. Figure 3 shows probability of identification as a function of representing faces by the first n eigenfeatures. PCA achieves a correct identification rate of 54% and SVM achieves an identification rate of 77-78%. (The PCA results we report are significantly lower than those reported in the literature [2, 3]. This is because we selected a set of images that are more difficult to recognize. The results are consistent with experimentations in our group with PCA-based algorithms on the FERET database [4]. We selected this set of images so that performance of neither the PCA or SVM algorithms are saturated.)

8 Conclusion

We introduced a new technique for applying SVM to face recognition. We demonstrated the algorithm on both verification and identification applications. We compared the performance of our algorithm to a PCA-based algorithm. For verification, the equal error rate of our algorithm was almost half that of the PCA algorithm, 7% versus 13%. For identification, the error of SVM was half that of PCA, 22-23% versus 46%. This indicates that SVM is making more efficient use of the information in face space than the baseline PCA algorithm.

One of the major concerns in practical face recognition applications is the ability of the

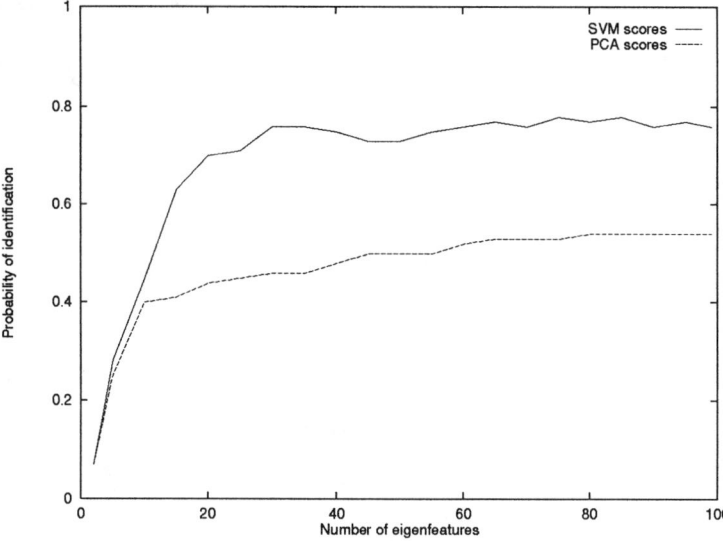

Figure 3: Probability of identification as a function of the number eigenfeatures.

algorithm to generalize from a training set of faces to faces outside of the training set. We demonstrated the ability of the SVM-based algorithm to generalize by training and testing on separate sets.

Future research directions include varying the kernel K, changing the representation space, and expanding the size of the gallery and probe set. There is nothing in our method that is specific to faces, and it should generalize to other biometrics such as fingerprints.

References

[1] C. J. C. Burges. A tuturial on support vector machines for pattern recognition. *Data mining and knowledge discovery*, (submitted), 1998.

[2] B. Moghaddam and A. Pentland. Face recognition using view-based and modular eigenspaces. In *Proc. SPIE Conference on Automatic Systems for the Identification and Inspection of Humans*, volume SPIE Vol. 2277, pages 12–21, 1994.

[3] B. Moghaddam, W. Wahid, and A. Pentland. Beyond eigenfaces: probablistic matching for face recognition. In *3rd International Conference on Automatic Face and Gesture Recognition*, pages 30–35, 1998.

[4] H. Moon and P. J. Phillips. Analysis of PCA-based face recognition algorithms. In K. W. Bowyer and P. J. Phillips, editors, *Empirical Evaluation Techniques in Computer Vision*. IEEE Computer Society Press, Los Alamitos, CA, 1998.

[5] P. J. Phillips, H. Wechsler, J. Huang, and P. Rauss. The FERET database and evaluation procedure for face-recognition algorithms. *Image and Vision Computing Journal*, 16(5):295–306, 1998.

[6] M. Turk and A. Pentland. Eigenfaces for recognition. *J. Cognitive Neuroscience*, 3(1):71–86, 1991.

[7] V. Vapnik. *The nature of statistical learning theory*. Springer, New York, 1995.

Learning Lie Groups for Invariant Visual Perception[*]

Rajesh P. N. Rao and Daniel L. Ruderman
Sloan Center for Theoretical Neurobiology
The Salk Institute
La Jolla, CA 92037
{rao,ruderman}@salk.edu

Abstract

One of the most important problems in visual perception is that of visual invariance: how are objects perceived to be the same despite undergoing transformations such as translations, rotations or scaling? In this paper, we describe a Bayesian method for learning invariances based on Lie group theory. We show that previous approaches based on first-order Taylor series expansions of inputs can be regarded as special cases of the Lie group approach, the latter being capable of handling in principle arbitrarily large transformations. Using a matrix-exponential based generative model of images, we derive an unsupervised algorithm for learning Lie group operators from input data containing infinitesimal transformations. The on-line unsupervised learning algorithm maximizes the posterior probability of generating the training data. We provide experimental results suggesting that the proposed method can learn Lie group operators for handling reasonably large 1-D translations and 2-D rotations.

1 INTRODUCTION

A fundamental problem faced by both biological and machine vision systems is the recognition of familiar objects and patterns in the presence of transformations such as translations, rotations and scaling. The importance of this problem was recognized early by visual scientists such as J. J. Gibson who hypothesized that "constant perception depends on the ability of the individual to detect the invariants" [6]. Among computational neuroscientists, Pitts and McCulloch were perhaps the first to propose a method for perceptual invariance ("knowing universals") [12]. A number of other approaches have since been proposed [5, 7, 10], some relying on temporal sequences of input patterns undergoing transformations (e.g. [4]) and others relying on modifications to the distance metric for comparing input images to stored templates (e.g. [15]).

In this paper, we describe a Bayesian method for learning invariances based on the notion of continuous transformations and Lie group theory. We show that previous approaches based on first-order Taylor series expansions of images [1, 14] can be regarded as special cases of the Lie group approach. Approaches based on first-order models can account only for small transformations due to their assumption of a linear generative model for the transformed images. The Lie approach on the other hand utilizes a matrix-exponential based generative model which can in principle handle arbitrarily large transformations once the correct transformation operators have been learned. Using Bayesian principles, we derive an on-line unsupervised algorithm for learning Lie group operators from input data containing infinitesimal transformations. Although Lie groups have previously

---

[*]This research was supported by the Alfred P. Sloan Foundation.

been used in visual perception [2], computer vision [16] and image processing [9], the question of whether it is possible to learn these groups directly from input data has remained open. Our preliminary experimental results suggest that in the two examined cases of 1-D translations and 2-D rotations, the proposed method can learn the corresponding Lie group operators with a reasonably high degree of accuracy, allowing the use of these learned operators in transformation-invariant vision.

2 CONTINUOUS TRANSFORMATIONS AND LIE GROUPS

Suppose we have a point (in general, a vector) I_0 which is an element in a space F. Let TI_0 denote a transformation of the point I_0 to another point, say I_1. The transformation operator T is completely specified by its actions on all points in the space F. Suppose T belongs to a family of operators $\mathcal{T}$. We will be interested in the cases where $\mathcal{T}$ is a group i.e. there exists a mapping $f : \mathcal{T} \times \mathcal{T} \rightarrow \mathcal{T}$ from pairs of transformations to another transformation such that (a) f is associative, (b) there exists a unique identity transformation, and (c) for every $T \in \mathcal{T}$, there exists a unique inverse transformation of T. These properties seem reasonable to expect in general for transformations on images.

Continuous transformations are those which can be made infinitesimally small. Due to their favorable properties as described below, we will be especially concerned with *continuous transformation groups* or *Lie groups*. Continuity is associated with both the transformation operators T and the group $\mathcal{T}$. Each $T \in \mathcal{T}$ is assumed to implement a continuous mapping from $F \rightarrow F$. To be concrete, suppose T is parameterized by a single real number x. Then, the group $\mathcal{T}$ is continuous if the function $T(x) : \Re \rightarrow \mathcal{T}$ is continuous i.e. any $T \in \mathcal{T}$ is the image of some $x \in \Re$ and any continuous variation of x results in a continuous variation of T. Let $T(0)$ be equivalent to the identity transformation. Then, as $x \rightarrow 0$, the transformation $T(x)$ gets arbitrarily close to identity. Its effect on I_0 can be written as (to first order in x): $T(x)I_0 \approx (1 + xG)I_0$ for some matrix G which is known as the *generator* of the transformation group. A macroscopic transformation $I_1 = I(x) = T(x)I_0$ can be produced by chaining together a number of these infinitesimal transformations. For example, by dividing the parameter x into N equal parts and performing each transformation in turn, we obtain:

$$I(x) = (1 + (x/N)G)^N I_0 \qquad (1)$$

In the limit $N \rightarrow \infty$, this expression reduces to the matrix exponential equation:

$$I(x) = e^{xG} I_0 \qquad (2)$$

where I_0 is the initial or "reference" input. Thus, each of the elements of our one-parameter Lie group can be written as: $T(x) = e^{xG}$. The generator G of the Lie group is related to the derivative of $T(x)$ with respect to x: $\frac{d}{dx}T = GT$. This suggests an alternate way of deriving Equation 2. Consider the Taylor series expansion of a transformed input $I(x)$ in terms of a previous input $I(0)$:

$$I(x) = I(0) + \frac{dI(0)}{dx}x + \frac{d^2I(0)}{dx^2}\frac{x^2}{2} + \ldots \qquad (3)$$

where x denotes the relative transformation between $I(x)$ and $I(0)$. Defining $\frac{d}{dx}I = GI$ for some operator matrix G, we can rewrite Equation 3 as: $I(x) = e^{xG}I_0$ which is the same as equation 2 with $I_0 = I(0)$. Thus, some previous approaches based on first-order Taylor series expansions [1, 14] can be viewed as special cases of the Lie group model.

3 LEARNING LIE TRANSFORMATION GROUPS

Our goal is to learn the generators G of particular Lie transformation groups directly from input data containing examples of infinitesimal transformations. Note that learning the generator of a transformation effectively allows us to remain invariant to that transformation (see below). We assume that during natural temporal sequences of images containing transformations, there are "small" image changes corresponding to deterministic sets of pixel changes that are *independent* of what the

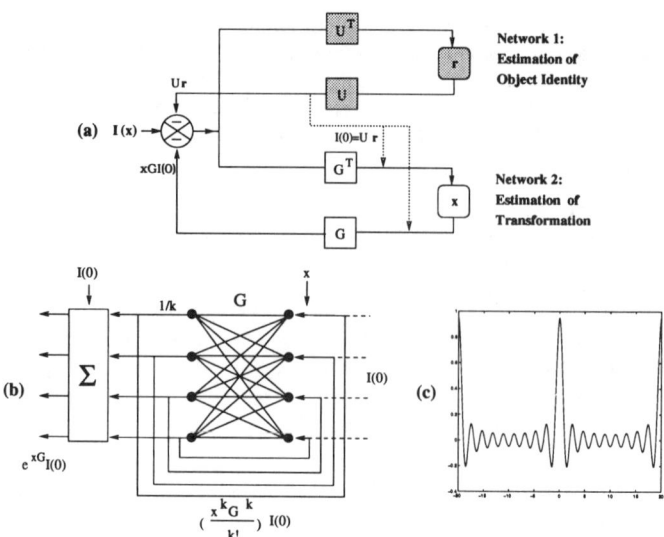

Figure 1: **Network Architecture and Interpolation Function.** (a) An implementation of the proposed approach to invariant vision involving two cooperating recurrent networks, one estimating transformations and the other estimating object features. The latter supplies the reference image $\mathbf{I}(0)$ to the transformation network. (b) A locally recurrent elaboration of the transformation network for implementing Equation 9. The network computes $e^{xG}\mathbf{I}(0) = \mathbf{I}(0) + \sum_k (x^k G^k/k!)\mathbf{I}(0)$. (c) The interpolation function Q used to generate training data (assuming periodic, band-limited signals).

actual pixels are. The rearrangements themselves are universal as in for example image translations. The question we address is: can we learn the Lie group operator G given simply a series of "before" and "after" images?

Let the $n \times 1$ vector $\mathbf{I}(0)$ be the "before" image and $\mathbf{I}(x)$ the "after" image containing the infinitesimal transformation. Then, using results from the previous section, we can write the following stochastic generative model for images:

$$\mathbf{I}(x) = e^{xG}\mathbf{I}(0) + \mathbf{n} \qquad (4)$$

where $\mathbf{n}$ is assumed to be a zero-mean Gaussian white noise process with variance σ^2. Since learning using this full exponential generative model is difficult due to multiple local minima, we restrict ourselves to transformations that are infinitesimal. The higher order terms then become negligible and we can rewrite the above equation in a more tractable form:

$$\Delta \mathbf{I} = xG\mathbf{I}(0) + \mathbf{n} \qquad (5)$$

where $\Delta \mathbf{I} = \mathbf{I}(x) - \mathbf{I}(0)$ is the difference image. Note that although this model is linear, the generator G learned using infinitesimal transformations is the same matrix that is used in the exponential model. Thus, once learned, this matrix can be used to handle larger transformations as well (see experimental results).

Suppose we are given M image pairs as data. We wish to find the $n \times n$ matrix G and the transformations x which generated the data set. To do so, we take a Bayesian maximum a posteriori approach using Gaussian priors on x and G. The negative log of the posterior probability of generating the data is given by:

$$E = -\log P[G, x|\mathbf{I}(x), \mathbf{I}(0)] = \frac{1}{2\sigma^2}(\Delta\mathbf{I} - xG\mathbf{I}(0))^T(\Delta\mathbf{I} - xG\mathbf{I}(0)) + \frac{1}{2\sigma_x^2}x^2 + \frac{1}{2}\mathbf{g}^T C^{-1}\mathbf{g} \qquad (6)$$

where σ_x^2 is the variance of the zero-mean Gaussian prior on x, $\mathbf{g}$ is the $n^2 \times 1$ vector form of G and C is the covariance matrix associated with the Gaussian prior on G. Extending this equation to multiple image data is accomplished straightforwardly by summing the data-driven term over the image pairs (we assume G is fixed for all images although the transformation x may vary). For the experiments, σ, σ_x and C were chosen to be fixed scalar values but it may be possible to speed up learning and improve accuracy by choosing C based on some knowledge of what we expect for infinitesimal image transformations (for example, we may define each entry in C to be a function only of the distance between pixels associated with the entry and exploit the fact that C needs to be symmetric; the efficacy of this choice is currently under investigation).

The $n \times n$ generator matrix G can be learned in an unsupervised manner by performing gradient descent on E, thereby maximizing the posterior probability of generating the data:

$$\dot{G} = -\alpha \frac{\partial E}{\partial G} = \alpha(\Delta \mathbf{I} - xG\mathbf{I}(0))(x\mathbf{I}(0))^T - \alpha c(G) \tag{7}$$

where α is a positive constant that governs the learning rate and $c(G)$ is the $n \times n$ matrix form of the $n^2 \times 1$ vector $C^{-1}\mathbf{g}$. The learning rule for G above requires the value of x for the current image pair to be known. We can estimate x by performing gradient descent on E with respect to x (using a fixed previously learned value for G):

$$\dot{x} = -\beta \frac{\partial E}{\partial x} = \beta(G\mathbf{I}(0))^T(\Delta \mathbf{I} - xG\mathbf{I}(0)) - \frac{\beta}{\sigma_x^2}x \tag{8}$$

The learning process thus involves alternating between the fast estimation of x for the given image pair and the slower adaptation of the generator matrix G using this x. Figure 1 (a) depicts a possible network implementation of the proposed approach to invariant vision. The implementation, which is reminiscent of the division of labor between the dorsal and ventral streams in primate visual cortex [3], uses two parallel but cooperating networks, one estimating object identity and the other estimating object transformations. The object network is based on a standard linear generative model of the form: $\mathbf{I}(0) = U\mathbf{r} + \mathbf{n}_0$ where U is a matrix of learned object "features" and $\mathbf{r}$ is the feature vector for the object in $\mathbf{I}(0)$ (see, for example, [11, 13]). Perceptual constancy is achieved due to the fact that the estimate of object identity remains stable in the first network as the second network attempts to account for any transformations being induced in the image, appropriately conveying the type of transformation being induced in its estimate for x (see [14] for more details).

The estimation rule for x given above is based on a first-order model (Equation 5) and is therefore useful only for estimating small (infinitesimal) transformations. A more general rule for estimating larger transformations is obtaining by performing gradient descent on the optimization function given by the matrix-exponential generative model (Equation 4):

$$\dot{x} = \gamma(e^{xG}G\mathbf{I}(0))^T(\mathbf{I}(x) - e^{xG}\mathbf{I}(0)) - \frac{\gamma}{\sigma_x^2}x \tag{9}$$

Figure 1 (b) shows a locally recurrent network implementation of the matrix exponential computation required by the above equation.

4 EXPERIMENTAL RESULTS

Training Data and Interpolation Function. For the purpose of evaluating the algorithm, we generated synthetic training data by subjecting a randomly generated image (containing uniformly random pixel intensities) to a known transformation. Consider a given 1-D image $\mathbf{I}(0)$ with image pixels given by $I(j)$, $j = 1, \ldots, N$. To be able to continuously transform $\mathbf{I}(0)$ sampled at discrete pixel locations by infinitesimal (sub-pixel) amounts, we need to employ an interpolation function. We make use of the Shannon-Whittaker theorem [8] stating that any band-limited signal $I(j)$, with j being any real number, is uniquely specified by its sufficiently close equally spaced discrete samples. Assuming that our signal is periodic i.e. $I(j + N) = I(j)$ for all j, the Shannon-Whittaker theorem in one dimension can be written as: $I(j) = \sum_{m=0}^{N-1} I(m) \sum_{r=-\infty}^{\infty} \text{sinc}[\pi(j - m - Nr)]$ where $\text{sinc}[x] = \sin(x)/x$. After some algebraic manipulation and simplification, this can be reduced to: $I(j) = \sum_{m=0}^{N-1} I(m) Q(j - m)$ where the interpolation function Q is given by:

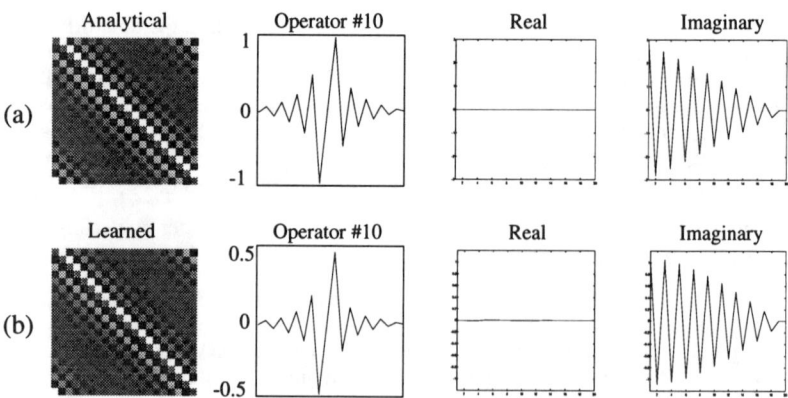

Figure 2: **Learned Lie Operators for 1-D Translations.** (a) Analytically-derived 20 × 20 Lie operator matrix G, operator for the 10th pixel (10th row of G), and plot of real and imaginary parts of the eigenvalues of G. (b) Learned G matrix, 10th operator, and plot of eigenvalues of the learned matrix.

$Q(x) = (1/N)[1 + 2\sum_{p=1}^{N/2-1} \cos(2\pi px/N)]$. Figure 1 (c) shows this interpolation function. To translate $\mathbf{I}(0)$ by an infinitesimal amount $x \in \Re$, we use: $I(j+x) = \sum_{m=0}^{N-1} I(m)Q(j+x-m)$. Similarly, to rotate or translate 2-D images, we use the 2-D analog of the above. In addition to being able to generate images with known transformations, the interpolation function also allows one to derive an analytical expression for the Lie operator matrix directly from the derivative of Q. This allows us to evaluate the results of learning. Figure 2 (a) shows the analytically-derived G matrix for 1-D infinitesimal translations of 20-pixel images (bright pixels = positive values, dark = negative). Also shown alongside is one of the rows of G (row 10) representing the Lie operator centered on pixel 10.

Learning 1-D Translations. Figure 2 (b) shows the results of using Equation 7 and 50,000 training image pairs for learning the generator matrix for 1-D translations in 20-pixel images. The randomly generated first image of a training pair was translated left or right by 0.5 pixels ($C^{-1} = 0.0001$ and learning rate $\alpha = 0.4$ was decreased by 1.0001 after each training pair). Note that as expected for translations, the rows of the learned G matrix are identical except for a shift: the same differential operator (shown in Figure 2 (b)) is applied at each image location. A comparison of the eigenvalues of the learned matrix with those of the analytical matrix (Figure 2) suggests that the learning algorithm was able to learn a reasonably good approximation of the true generator matrix (to within an arbitrary multiplicative scaling factor). To further evaluate the learned matrix G, we ascertained whether G could be used to generate arbitrary translations of a given reference image using Equation 2. The results are encouraging as shown in Figure 3 (a), although we have noticed a tendency for the appearance of some artifacts in translated images if there is significant high-frequency content in the reference image.

Estimating Large Transformations. The learned generator matrix can be used to estimate large translations in images using Equation 9. Unfortunately, the optimization function can contain local minima (Figure 3 (b)). The local minima however tend to be shallow and of approximately the same value, with a unique well-defined global minimum. We therefore searched for the global minimum by performing gradient descent with several equally spaced starting values and picked the minimum of the estimated values after convergence. Figure 3 (c) shows results of this estimation process.

Learning 2-D Rotations. We have also tested the learning algorithm in 2-D images using image plane rotations. Training image pairs were generated by infinitesimally rotating images with random pixel intensities 0.2 radians clockwise or counterclockwise. The learned operator matrix (for three different spatial scales) is shown in Figure 4 (a). The accuracy of these matrices was tested

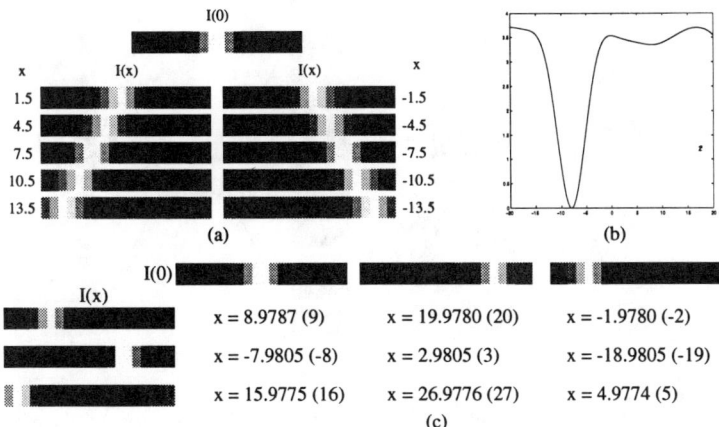

Figure 3: **Generating and Estimating Large Transformations.** (a) An original reference image $\mathbf{I}(0)$ was translated to varying degrees by using the learned generator matrix G and varying x in Equation 2. (b) The negative log likelihood optimization function for the matrix-exponential generative model (Equation 4) which was used for estimating large translations. The globally minimum value for x was found by using gradient descent with multiple starting points. (c) Comparison of estimated translation values with actual values (in parenthesis) for different pairs of reference ($\mathbf{I}(0)$) and translated images ($\mathbf{I}(x)$) shown in the form of a table.

by using them in Equation 2 for various rotations x. As shown in Figure 4 (b) for the 5×5 case, the learned matrix appears to be able to rotate a given reference image between $-180°$ and $+180°$ about an initial position (for the larger rotations, some minor artifacts appear near the edges).

5 CONCLUSIONS

Our results suggest that it is possible for an unsupervised network to learn visual invariances by learning operators (or generators) for the corresponding Lie transformation groups. An important issue is how local minima can be avoided during the estimation of large transformations. Apart from performing multiple searches, one possibility is to use coarse-to-fine techniques, where transformation estimates obtained at a coarse scale are used as starting points for estimating transformations at finer scales (see, for example, [1]). A second possibility is to use stochastic techniques that exploit the specialized stucture of the optimization function (Figure 1 (c)). Besides these directions of research, we are also investigating the use of structured priors on the generator matrix G to improve learning accuracy and speed. A concurrent effort involves testing the approach on more realistic natural image sequences containing a richer variety of transformations.[1]

References

[1] M. J. Black and A. D. Jepson. Eigentracking: Robust matching and tracking of articulated objects using a view-based representation. In *Proc. of the Fourth European Conference on Computer Vision (ECCV)*, pages 329–342, 1996.

[2] P. C. Dodwell. The Lie transformation group model of visual perception. *Perception and Psychophysics*, 34(1):1–16, 1983.

[3] D. J. Felleman and D. C. Van Essen. Distributed hierarchical processing in the primate cerebral cortex. *Cerebral Cortex*, 1:1–47, 1991.

---

[1]The generative model in the case of multiple transformations is given by: $\mathbf{I}(\mathbf{x}) = e^{\sum_{i=1}^{m} x_i G_i} \mathbf{I}(0) + \mathbf{n}$ where G_i is the generator for the ith type of transformation and x_i is the value of that transformation in the input image.

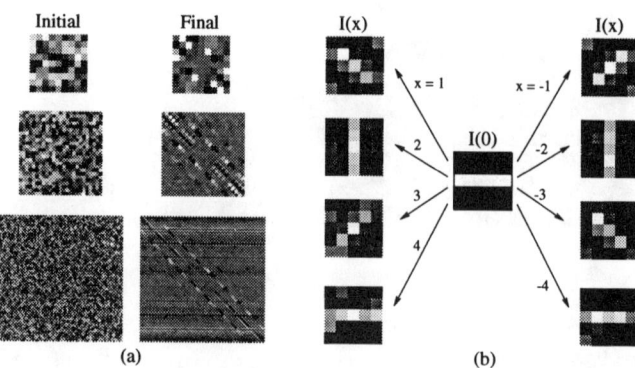

Figure 4: **Learned Lie Operators for 2-D Rotations.** (a) The initial and converged values of the Lie operator matrix for 2D rotations at three different scales (3 × 3, 5 × 5 and 9 × 9). (b) Examples of arbitrary rotations of a 5 × 5 reference image $\mathbf{I}(0)$ generated by using the learned Lie operator matrix (although only results for integer-valued x between -4 and 4 are shown, rotations can be generated for any real-valued x).

[4] P. Földiák. Learning invariance from transformation sequences. *Neural Computation*, 3(2):194–200, 1991.

[5] K. Fukushima. Neocognitron: A self-organizing neural network model for a mechanism of pattern recognition unaffected by shift in position. *Biological Cybernetics*, 36:193–202, 1980.

[6] J.J. Gibson. *The Senses Considered as Perceptual Systems*. Houghton-Mifflin, Boston, 1966.

[7] Y. LeCun, B. Boser, J. S. Denker, B. Henderson, R. E. Howard, W. Hubbard, and L. D. Jackel. Backpropagation applied to handwritten zip code recognition. *Neural Computation*, 1(4):541–551, 1989.

[8] R. J. Marks II. *Introduction to Shannon Sampling and Interpolation Theory*. New York: Springer-Verlag, 1991.

[9] K. Nordberg. Signal representation and processing using operator groups. Technical Report Linköping Studies in Science and Technology, Dissertations No. 366, Department of Electrical Engineering, Linköping University, 1994.

[10] B. A. Olshausen, C. H. Anderson, and D. C. Van Essen. A multiscale dynamic routing circuit for forming size- and position-invariant object representations. *Journal of Computational Neuroscience*, 2:45–62, 1995.

[11] B. A. Olshausen and D. J. Field. Emergence of simple-cell receptive field properties by learning a sparse code for natural images. *Nature*, 381:607–609, 1996.

[12] W. Pitts and W.S. McCulloch. How we know universals: the perception of auditory and visual forms. *Bulletin of Mathematical Biophysics*, 9:127–147, 1947.

[13] R. P. N. Rao and D. H. Ballard. Dynamic model of visual recognition predicts neural response properties in the visual cortex. *Neural Computation*, 9(4):721–763, 1997.

[14] R. P. N. Rao and D. H. Ballard. Development of localized oriented receptive fields by learning a translation-invariant code for natural images. *Network: Computation in Neural Systems*, 9(2):219–234, 1998.

[15] P. Simard, Y. LeCun, and J. Denker. Efficient pattern recognition using a new transformation distance. In *Advances in Neural Information Processing Systems V*, pages 50–58, San Mateo, CA, 1993. Morgan Kaufmann Publishers.

[16] L. Van Gool, T. Moons, E. Pauwels, and A. Oosterlinck. Vision and Lie's approach to invariance. *Image and Vision Computing*, 13(4):259–277, 1995.

General-purpose localization of textured image regions

Ruth Rosenholtz*
Xerox PARC
3333 Coyote Hill Rd.
Palo Alto, CA 94304

Abstract

We suggest a working definition of texture: Texture is stuff that is more compactly represented by its statistics than by specifying the configuration of its parts. This definition suggests that to find texture we look for outliers to the local statistics, and label as texture the regions with no outliers. We present a method, based upon this idea, for labeling points in natural scenes as belonging to texture regions, while simultaneously allowing us to label low-level, bottom-up cues for visual attention. This method is based upon recent psychophysics results on processing of texture and popout.

1 WHAT IS TEXTURE, AND WHY DO WE WANT TO FIND IT?

In a number of problems in computer vision and image processing, one must distinguish between image regions that correspond to objects and those which correspond to texture, and perform different processing depending upon the type of region. Current computer vision algorithms assume one magically knows this region labeling. But what is texture? We have the notion that texture involves a pattern that is somehow homogeneous, or in which signal changes are "too complex" to describe, so that aggregate properties must be used instead (Saund, 1998). There is by no means a firm division between texture and objects; rather, the characterization often depends upon the scale of interest (Saund, 1998).

---

* Email: rruth@parc.xerox.com

Ideally the definition of texture should probably depend upon the application. We investigate a definition that we believe will be of fairly general utility: Texture is stuff that seems to belong to the local statistics. We propose extracting several texture features, at several different scales, and labeling as texture those regions whose feature values are likely to have come from the local distribution.

Outliers to the local statistics tend to draw our attention (Rosenholtz, 1997, 1998). The phenomenon is often referred to as "popout." Thus while labeling (locally) statistically homogeneous regions as texture, we can simultaneously highlight salient outliers to the local statistics. Our revised definition is that texture is the absence of popout.

In Section 2, we discuss previous work in both human perception and in finding texture and regions of interest in an image. In Section 3, we describe our method. We present and discuss results on a number of real images in Section 4.

2 PREVIOUS WORK

See (Wolfe, 1998) for a review of the visual search literature. Popout is typically studied using simple displays, in which an experimental subject searches for the unusual, target item, among the other, distractor items. One typically attempts to judge the "saliency," or degree to which the target pops out, by studying the efficiency of search for that item. Typically popout is modeled by a relatively low-level operator, which operates independently on a number of basic features of the image, including orientation, contrast/color, depth, and motion. In this paper, we look only at the features of contrast and orientation.

Within the image-processing field, much of the work in finding texture has defined as texture any region with a high luminance variance, e.g. Vaisey & Gersho (1992). Unfortunately, the luminance variance in a region containing an edge can be as high as that in a textured region. Won & Park (1997) use model fitting to detect image blocks containing an edge, and then label blocks with high variance as containing texture.

Recently, several computer vision researchers have also tackled this problem. Leung & Malik (1996) found regions of completely deterministic texture. Other researchers have used the definition that if the luminance goes up and then down again (or vice versa) it's texture (Forsyth et al, 1996). However, this method will treat lines as if they were texture. Also, with no notion of similarity within a texture (also lacking in the image-processing work), one would mark a "fault" in a texture as belonging to that texture. This would be unacceptable for a texture synthesis application, in which a routine that tried to synthesize such a texture would most likely fail to reproduce the (highly visible) fault. More recently, Shi and Malik (1998) presented a method for segmenting images based upon texture features. Their method performs extremely well at the segmentation task, dividing an image into regions with internal similarity that is high compared to the similarity across regions. However, it is difficult to compare with their results, since they do not explicitly label a subset of the resulting regions as texture. Furthermore, this method may also tend to mark a "fault" in a texture as belonging to that texture. This is both because the method is biased against separating out small regions, and because the grouping of a patch with one region depends as much upon the difference between that patch and other regions as it does upon the similarity between the patch and the given region.

Very little computer vision work has been done on attentional cues. Milanese et al (1993) found salient image regions using both top-down information and a bottom-up "conspicuity" operator, which marks a local region as more salient the greater the difference between a local feature value and the mean feature value in the surrounding region. However, for the same difference in means, a local region is less salient when there is a greater variance in the feature values in the surrounding region (Duncan & Humphreys, 1989; Rosenholtz, 1997). We use as our saliency measure a test for outliers to the local distribution. This captures, in many cases, the dependence of saliency on difference between a given feature value and the local mean, relative to the local standard deviation. We will discuss our saliency measure in greater detail in the following section.

3 FINDING TEXTURE AND REGIONS OF INTEREST

We compute multiresolution feature maps for orientation and contrast, and then look for outliers in the local orientation and contrast statistics. We do this by first creating a 3-level Gaussian pyramid representation of the image. To extract contrast, we filter the pyramid with a difference of circularly symmetric Gaussians. The response of these filters will oscillate, even in a region with constant-contrast texture (e.g. a sinewave pattern). We approximate a computation of the maximum response of these filters over a small region by first squaring the filter responses, and then filtering the contrast energy with an appropriate Gaussian. Finally, we threshold the contrast to eliminate low-contrast regions ("flat" texture). These thresholds (one for each scale) were set by examining the visibility of sinewave patterns of various spatial frequencies.

We compute orientation in a simple and biologically plausible way, using Bergen & Landy's (1991) "back pocket model" for low-level computations:

1. Filter the pyramid with horizontal, vertical, and ±45° oriented Gaussian second derivatives.

2. Compute opponent energy by squaring the filter outputs, pooling them over a region 4 times the scale of the second derivative filters, and subtracting the vertical from the horizontal response and the +45° from the -45° response.

3. Normalize the opponent energy at each scale by dividing by the total energy in the 4 orientation energy bands at that scale.

The result is two images at each scale of the pyramid. To a good approximation, in regions which are strongly oriented, these images represent $k\cos(2\theta)$ and $k\sin(2\theta)$, where θ is the local orientation at that scale, and k is a value between 0 and 1 which is related to the local orientation specificity. Orientation estimates from points with low specificity tend to be very noisy. In images of white noise, 80% of the estimates of k fall below 0.5, therefore with 80% confidence, an orientation specificity of $k>0.5$ did not occur due to chance. We use this value to threshold out orientation estimates with low "orientedness."

We then estimate D, the local feature distribution, for each feature and scale, using the method of Parzen windows. The blurring of the distribution estimate by the Parzen window mimics uncertainty in estimates of feature values by the visual system. We collect statistics over a local *integration* region. For texture processing, the size of this region is independent of viewing distance, and is roughly $10S$ in diameter, where S is the support of the Gaussian 2nd derivative filters used to extract the texture features (Kingdom & Keeble, 1997; Kingdom et al, 1995).

We next compute a non-parametric measure of saliency:

$$\text{saliency} = -\log\left(\frac{P(v|D)}{\max_x P(x|D)}\right) \quad (1)$$

Note that if D were Gaussian $N(\mu,\sigma^2)$, this simplifies to

$$\frac{(x-\mu)^2}{2\sigma^2} \qquad (2)$$

which should be compared to the standard parametric test for outliers, which uses the measure $(x-\mu)/\sigma$. Our saliency measure is essentially a more general, non-parametric form of this measure (i.e. it does not assume a Gaussian distribution).

Points with saliency less than 0.5 are labeled as candidate texture points. If D were Gaussian, this would correspond to feature estimates within one standard deviation of the mean. Points with saliency greater than 3.1 are labeled as candidates for bottom-up attentional cues. If D were Gaussian, this would correspond to feature estimates more than 2.5σ from the mean, a standard parametric test for outliers. One could, of course, keep the raw saliency values, as a measure of the likelihood that a region contained texture, rather than setting a hard threshold. We use a hard threshold in our examples to better display the results. Both the texture images and the region of interest images are median-filtered to remove extraneous points.

4 EXPERIMENTAL RESULTS

Figure 3 shows several example images. Figures 2, 3, and 4 show texture found at each scale of processing. The striped and checkered patterns represent oriented and homogeneous contrast texture, respectively. The absence of an image in any of these figures means that no texture of the given type was found in that image at the given scale. Note that we perform no segmentation of one texture from another.

For the building image, the algorithm labeled bricks and window panes as fine-scale texture, and windows and shutters as coarser-scale texture. The leopard skin and low-frequency stripes in the lower right corner of the leopard image were correctly labeled as texture. In the desk image, the "wood" texture was correctly identified. The regular pattern of windows were marked as texture in the hotel image. In the house image, the wood siding, trees, and part of the grass were labeled as texture (much of the grass was low contrast and labeled as "flat" texture). One of the bushes is correctly identified as having coarser texture than the other has. In the lighthouse image, the house sans window, fence, and tower were marked, as well as a low-frequency oriented pattern in the clouds.

Figure 5 shows the regions of interest that were found (the striped and plaid patterns here have no meaning but were chosen for maximum visibility). Most complex natural scenes had few interesting low-level attentional areas. In the lighthouse image, the life preserver is marked. In the hotel, curved or unusual angular windows are identified as attentional cues, as well as the top of the building. Both of these results are in agreement with psychophysical results showing that observers quickly identify curved or bent lines among straight lines (reviewed in Wolfe, 1998). The simpler desk scene yields more intuitive results, with each of the 3 objects labeled, as well as the phone cord.

Bottom-up attentional cues are outliers to the local distribution of features, and we have suggested that texture is the absence of such outliers. This definition captures some of the intuition that texture is homogeneous and statistical in nature. We presented a method for finding contrast and orientation outliers, and results both on localizing texture and on finding popout in natural images. For the simple desk image, the algorithm highlights salient regions that correspond to our notions of the important objects in the scene. On complicated natural scenes, its results are less intuitive; suggesting that search in natural scenes makes use of higher-level processing such as grouping into objects. This result should not be terribly surprising, but serves as a useful check on simple low-level models of visual attention. The algorithm does a good job of identifying textured regions at a number of different scales, with the results perhaps more intuitive at finer scales.

Acknowledgments

This work was partially supported by an NRC postdoctoral award at NASA Ames. Many thanks to David Marimont and Eric Saund for useful discussions.

References

J. R. Bergen and M. S. Landy (1991), "Computational modeling of visual texture segmentation," *Computational Models of Visual Processing*, Landy and Movshon (eds.), pp. 252-271, MIT Press, Cambridge, MA.

J. Duncan and G. Humphreys (1989), "Visual search and stimulus similarity," *Psych. Review* **96**, pp. 433-458.

D. Forsyth, J. Malik, M. Fleck, H. Greenspan, T. Leung, S. Belongie, C. Carson, and C. Bregler (1996), "Finding pictures of objects in collections of images," *ECCV Workshop on Object Representation*, Cambridge.

F. A. A. Kingdom, D. Keeble, D., and B. Moulden (1995), "Sensitivity to orientation modulation in micropattern-based textures," *Vis. Res.* **35**, 1, pp. 79-91.

F. A. A. Kingdom and D. Keeble (1997), "The mechanism for scale invariance in orientation-defined textures." *Invest. Ophthal. and Vis. Sci. (Suppl.)* **38**, 4, p. 636.

T. K. Leung and J. Malik (1996), "Detecting, localizing, and grouping repeated scene elements from an image," *Proc. 4th European Conf. On Computer Vision*, **1064**, 1, pp. 546-555, Springer-Verlag, Cambridge.

R. Milanese, H. Wechsler, S. Gil, J. -M. Bost, and T. Pun (1993), "Integration of bottom-up and top-down cues for visual attention using non-linear relaxation," *Proc. IEEE CVPR*, pp. 781-785, IEEE Computer Society Press, Seattle.

R. Rosenholtz (1997), "Basic signal detection theory model does not explain search among heterogeneous distractors." *Invest. Ophthal. and Vis. Sci. (Suppl.)* **38**, 4, p. 687.

R. Rosenholtz (1998), "A simple saliency model explains a number of motion popout phenomena." *Invest. Ophthal. and Vis. Sci. (Suppl.)* **39**, 4, p. 629.

E. Saund (1998), "Scale and the Shape/Texture Continuum," Xerox Internal Technical Memorandum.

J. Shi and J. Malik (1998), "Self Inducing Relational Distance and its Application to Image Segmentation," *Proc. 5th European Conf. on Computer Vision*, Burkhardt and Neumann (eds.), **1406**, 1, pp. 528-543, Springer, Freiburg.

J. Vaisey and A. Gersho (1992), "Image compression with variable block size segmentation." *IEEE Trans. Signal Processing* **40**, 8, pp. 2040-2060.

J. M. Wolfe (1998), "Visual search: a review," *Attention*, H. Pashler (ed.), pp. 13-74, Psychology Press Ltd., Hove, East Sussex, UK.

C. S. Won and D. K. Park (1997), "Image block classification and variable block size segmentation using a model-fitting criterion," *Opt. Eng.* **36**, 8, pp. 2204-2209.

Figure 1: Original images.

Figure 2: Fine-scale texture. (a) oriented texture, (b) homogeneous contrast texture.

Figure 3: Medium-scale texture. (a) oriented texture, (b) homogeneous contrast texture.

General-Purpose Localization of Textured Image Regions   823

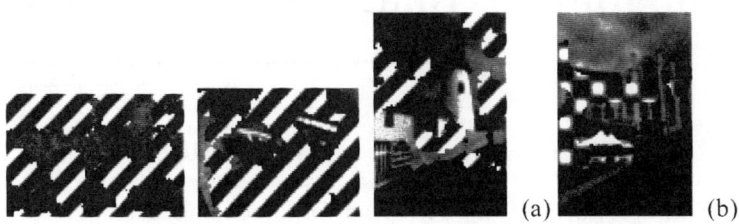

Figure 4: Coarse-scale texture. (a) oriented texture, (b) homogeneous contrast texture.

Figure 5: Regions of interest.

Probabilistic Image Sensor Fusion

Ravi K. Sharma[1], Todd K. Leen[2] and Misha Pavel[1]

[1]Department of Electrical and Computer Engineering
[2]Department of Computer Science and Engineering
Oregon Graduate Institute of Science and Technology
P.O. Box 91000, Portland, OR 97291-1000
Email: {ravi,pavel}@ece.ogi.edu, tleen@cse.ogi.edu

Abstract

We present a probabilistic method for fusion of images produced by multiple sensors. The approach is based on an image formation model in which the sensor images are noisy, locally linear functions of an *underlying, true scene*. A Bayesian framework then provides for maximum likelihood or maximum a posteriori estimates of the true scene from the sensor images. Maximum likelihood estimates of the parameters of the image formation model involve (local) second order image statistics, and thus are related to local principal component analysis. We demonstrate the efficacy of the method on images from visible-band and infrared sensors.

1 Introduction

Advances in sensing devices have fueled the deployment of multiple sensors in several computational vision systems [1, for example]. Using multiple sensors can increase reliability with respect to single sensor systems. This work was motivated by a need for an aircraft autonomous landing guidance (ALG) system [2, 3] that uses visible-band, infrared (IR) and radar-based imaging sensors to provide guidance to pilots for landing aircraft in low visibility. IR is suitable for night operation, whereas radar can penetrate fog. The application requires fusion algorithms [4] to combine the different sensor images.

Images from different sensors have different characteristics arising from the varied physical imaging processes. Local contrast may be polarity reversed between visible-band and IR images [5, 6]. A particular sensor image may contain local features not found in another sensor image, i.e., sensors may report complementary features. Finally, individual sensors are subject to noise. Fig. 1(a) and 1(b) are visible-band and IR images respectively, of a runway scene showing polarity reversed (rectangle) and complementary (circle) features. These effects pose difficulties for fusion.

An obvious approach to fusion is to average the pixel intensities from different sensors. Averaging, Fig. 1(c), increases the signal to noise ratio, but reduces the contrast where there are polarity reversed or complementary features [7].

Transform-based fusion methods [8, 5, 9] *select* from one sensor or another for fusion. They consist of three steps: (i) decompose the sensor images using a specified transform e.g. a multiresolution Laplacian pyramid, (ii) fuse at each level of the pyramid by selecting the highest energy transform coefficient, and (iii) invert the transform to synthesize the fused image. Since features are selected rather than averaged, they are rendered at full contrast, but the methods are sensitive to sensor noise, see Fig. 1(d).

To overcome the limitations of averaging or selection methods, and put sensor fusion on firm theoretical grounds, we explicitly model the production of sensor images from the true scene, including the effects of sensor noise. From the model, and sensor images, one can ask *What is the most probable true scene?* This forms the basis for fusing the sensor images. Our technique uses the Laplacian pyramid representation [5], with the step (ii) above replaced by our probabilistic fusion. A similar probabilistic framework for sensor fusion is discussed in ([10]).

2 The Image Formation Model

The true scene, denoted s, gives rise to a sensor image through a noisy, non-linear transformation. For ALG, s would be an image of the landing scene under conditions of uniform lighting, unlimited visibility, and perfect sensors. We model the map from the true scene to a sensor image by a noisy, *locally affine transformation* whose parameters are allowed to vary across the image (actually across the Laplacian pyramid)

$$a_i(\vec{l},t) = \beta_i(\vec{l},t)\, s(\vec{l},t) + \alpha_i(\vec{l},t) + \epsilon_i(\vec{l},t) \qquad (1)$$

where, s is the true scene, a_i is i^{th} sensor image, $\vec{l} \equiv (x,y,k)$ is the hyperpixel location, with x,y the pixel coordinates and k the level of the pyramid, t is the time, α is the sensor offset, β is the sensor gain (which includes the effects of local polarity reversals and complementarity), and ϵ is the (zero-mean) sensor noise. To simplify notation, we adopt the matrix form

$$\boldsymbol{a} = \boldsymbol{\beta} s + \boldsymbol{\alpha} + \boldsymbol{\epsilon} \qquad (2)$$

where $\boldsymbol{a} = [a_1, a_2, \ldots, a_q]^T$, $\boldsymbol{\beta} = [\beta_1, \beta_2, \ldots, \beta_q]^T$, $\boldsymbol{\alpha} = [\alpha_1, \alpha_2, \ldots, \alpha_q]^T$, s is a scalar and $\boldsymbol{\epsilon} = [\epsilon_1, \epsilon_2, \ldots, \epsilon_q]^T$, and we have dropped the reference to location and time.

Since the image formation parameters $\boldsymbol{\beta}$, $\boldsymbol{\alpha}$, and the sensor noise covariance Σ_ϵ can vary from hyperpixel to hyperpixel, the model can express local polarity reversals, complementary features, spatial variation of sensor gain, and noise.

We do assume, however, that the image formation parameters and sensor noise distribution vary *slowly* with location[1]. Hence, a particular set of parameters is considered to hold true over a spatial region of several square hyperpixels. We will use this assumption implicitly when we estimate these parameters from data.

The model (2) fits the framework of the factor analysis model in statistics [11, 12]. Here the hyperpixel values of the true scene s are the latent variables or

---
[1]Specifically the parameters vary slowly on the spatio-temporal scales over which the true scene s may exhibit large variations.

common factors, $\boldsymbol{\beta}$ contains the factor loadings, and the sensor noise $\boldsymbol{\epsilon}$ values are the independent factors. Estimation of the true scene is equivalent to estimating the common factors from the observations $\boldsymbol{a}$.

3 Bayesian Fusion

Given the sensor intensities $\boldsymbol{a}$, we will estimate the true scene s by appeal to a Bayesian framework. We assume that the probability density function of the latent variables s is a Gaussian with local mean $s_0(\vec{l}, t)$ and local variance $\sigma_s^2(\vec{l}, t)$. An attractive benefit of this setup is that the *prior mean* s_0 might be obtained from knowledge in the form of maps, or clear-weather images of the scene. Thus, such database information can be folded into the sensor fusion in a natural way.

The density on the sensor images conditioned on the true scene, $\mathcal{P}(\boldsymbol{a}|s)$, is normal with mean $\boldsymbol{\beta} s + \boldsymbol{\alpha}$ and covariance $\boldsymbol{\Sigma}_{\boldsymbol{\epsilon}} = \mathrm{diag}[\sigma_{\epsilon_1}^2, \sigma_{\epsilon_2}^2, \ldots, \sigma_{\epsilon_q}^2]$. The marginal density $\mathcal{P}(\boldsymbol{a})$ is normal with mean $\boldsymbol{\mu}_m = \boldsymbol{\beta} s_0 + \boldsymbol{\alpha}$ and covariance

$$\mathbf{C} = \boldsymbol{\Sigma}_{\boldsymbol{\epsilon}} + \sigma_s^2 \boldsymbol{\beta}\boldsymbol{\beta}^\mathrm{T} \tag{3}$$

Finally, the posterior density on s, given the sensor data $\boldsymbol{a}$, $\mathcal{P}(s|\boldsymbol{a})$ is also normal with mean $\mathbf{M}^{-1}(\boldsymbol{\beta}^\mathrm{T} \boldsymbol{\Sigma}_{\boldsymbol{\epsilon}}^{-1}(\boldsymbol{a}-\boldsymbol{\alpha}) + s_0/\sigma_s^2)$, and covariance $\mathbf{M}^{-1} = (\boldsymbol{\beta}^\mathrm{T} \boldsymbol{\Sigma}_{\boldsymbol{\epsilon}}^{-1} \boldsymbol{\beta} + 1/\sigma_s^2)^{-1}$.

Given these densities, there are two obvious candidates for probabilistic fusion: *maximum likelihood* (ML) $\hat{s} = \max_s \mathcal{P}(\boldsymbol{a}|s)$, and *maximum a posteriori* (MAP) $\hat{s} = \max_s \mathcal{P}(s|\boldsymbol{a})$.

The MAP fusion estimate is simply the posterior mean

$$\hat{s} = [\boldsymbol{\beta}^\mathrm{T} \boldsymbol{\Sigma}_{\boldsymbol{\epsilon}}^{-1} \boldsymbol{\beta} + 1/\sigma_s^2]^{-1} \left(\boldsymbol{\beta}^\mathrm{T} \boldsymbol{\Sigma}_{\boldsymbol{\epsilon}}^{-1} (\boldsymbol{a} - \boldsymbol{\alpha}) + s_0/\sigma_s^2 \right) \tag{4}$$

which for two sensors reads

$$\hat{s} = \left(\frac{\beta_1(a_1 - \alpha_1)}{\sigma_{\epsilon_1}^2} + \frac{\beta_2(a_2 - \alpha_2)}{\sigma_{\epsilon_2}^2} + \frac{s_0}{\sigma_s^2} \right) \Big/ \left(\frac{\beta_1^2}{\sigma_{\epsilon_1}^2} + \frac{\beta_2^2}{\sigma_{\epsilon_2}^2} + \frac{1}{\sigma_s^2} \right). \tag{5}$$

To obtain the ML fusion estimate we take the limit $\sigma_s^2 \to \infty$ in either (4) or (5).

For both ML and MAP, the fused image $\hat{s}$ is a locally linear combination of the sensor images that can, through the spatio-temporal variations in $\boldsymbol{\beta}$, $\boldsymbol{\alpha}$, and $\boldsymbol{\Sigma}_{\boldsymbol{\epsilon}}$, properly respond to changes in the sensor characteristics that tax averaging or selection schemes. For example, if the second sensor has a polarity reversal relative to the first, then β_2 is negative and the two sensor contributions are properly *subtracted*. If the first sensor has high noise (large $\sigma_{\epsilon_1}^2$), its contribution to the fused image is attenuated. Finally, a feature missing from sensor 1 corresponds to $\beta_1 = 0$. The model compensates by accentuating the contribution from sensor 2.

4 Model Parameter Estimates

We need to estimate the local image formation model parameters $\boldsymbol{\alpha}(\vec{l}, t), \boldsymbol{\beta}(\vec{l}, t)$ and the local sensor noise covariance $\boldsymbol{\Sigma}_{\boldsymbol{\epsilon}}(\vec{l}, t)$. We estimate the latter from successive, motion compensated video frames from each sensor. First we estimate the average value at each hyperpixel $(\overline{a_i}(t))$, and the average square $(\overline{a_i^2}(t))$ by exponential moving averages. We next estimate the noise variance by the difference $\sigma_{\epsilon_i}^2(t) = \overline{a_i^2}(t) - \overline{a_i}^2(t)$.

To estimate $\boldsymbol{\beta}$ and $\boldsymbol{\alpha}$, we assume that $\boldsymbol{\beta}$, $\boldsymbol{\alpha}$, $\boldsymbol{\Sigma}_{\boldsymbol{\epsilon}}$, s_0 and σ_s^2 are nearly constant over small spatial regions (5 × 5 blocks) surrounding the hyperpixel for which the parameters are desired. Essentially we are invoking a spatial analog of ergodicity, where ensemble averages are replaced by spatial averages, carried out locally over regions in which the statistics are approximately constant.

To form a maximum likelihood (ML) estimate of $\boldsymbol{\alpha}$, we extremize the data log-likelihood $\mathcal{L} = \sum_{n=1}^{N} \log[\mathcal{P}(\boldsymbol{a}_n)]$ with respect to $\boldsymbol{\alpha}$ to obtain

$$\boldsymbol{\alpha}_{\mathrm{ML}} = \boldsymbol{\mu}_a - \boldsymbol{\beta} s_0 , \quad (6)$$

where $\boldsymbol{\mu}_a$ is the data mean, computed over a 5×5 hyperpixel local region ($N = 25$ points).

To obtain a ML estimate of $\boldsymbol{\beta}$, we set the derivatives of $\mathcal{L}$ with respect to $\boldsymbol{\beta}$ equal to zero and recover

$$(\mathbf{C} - \boldsymbol{\Sigma}_a) \mathbf{C}^{-1} \boldsymbol{\beta} = 0 \quad (7)$$

where $\boldsymbol{\Sigma}_a$ is the data covariance matrix, also computed over a 5×5 hyperpixel local region. The only non-trivial solution to (7) is

$$\boldsymbol{\beta}_{\mathrm{ML}} = \boldsymbol{\Sigma}_\epsilon^{\frac{1}{2}} \widetilde{\mathbf{U}} \frac{(\widetilde{\lambda} - 1)^{\frac{1}{2}}}{\sigma_s} r \quad (8)$$

where $\widetilde{\mathbf{U}}, \widetilde{\lambda}$ are the principal eigenvector and eigenvalue of the weighted data covariance matrix, $\widetilde{\boldsymbol{\Sigma}}_a \equiv \boldsymbol{\Sigma}_\epsilon^{-\frac{1}{2}} \boldsymbol{\Sigma}_a \boldsymbol{\Sigma}_\epsilon^{-\frac{1}{2}}$, and $r = \pm 1$.

An alternative to maximum likelihood estimation is the least squares (LS) approach [11]. We obtain the LS estimate $\boldsymbol{\alpha}_{\mathrm{LS}}$ by minimizing

$$E_\alpha = \| \boldsymbol{\mu}_a - \boldsymbol{\mu}_m \|^2 \quad (9)$$

with respect to $\boldsymbol{\alpha}$. This gives

$$\boldsymbol{\alpha}_{\mathrm{LS}} = \boldsymbol{\mu}_a - \boldsymbol{\beta} s_0 . \quad (10)$$

The least squares estimate $\boldsymbol{\beta}_{\mathrm{LS}}$ is obtained by minimizing

$$E_\beta = \| \boldsymbol{\Sigma}_a - \mathbf{C} \|^2 \quad (11)$$

with respect to $\boldsymbol{\beta}$. The solution to this minimization is

$$\boldsymbol{\beta}_{\mathrm{LS}} = \frac{\lambda^{\frac{1}{2}}}{\sigma_s} \mathbf{U} r \quad (12)$$

where $\mathbf{U}, \lambda$ are the principal eigenvector and eigenvalue of the noise-corrected covariance matrix $(\boldsymbol{\Sigma}_a - \boldsymbol{\Sigma}_\epsilon)$, and $r = \pm 1$.[2]

The estimation procedures cannot provide values of the priors σ_s^2 and s_0. Were we dealing with a single global model, this would pose no problem. But we must impose a constraint in order to smoothly piece together our local models. We impose that $\|\beta\| = 1$ everywhere, or by (12) $\sigma_s^2 = \lambda$. Recall that λ is the leading eigenvalue of $\boldsymbol{\Sigma}_a - \boldsymbol{\Sigma}_\epsilon$ and thus captures the scale of variations in $\boldsymbol{a}$ that arise from variations in s. Thus we would expect $\lambda \propto \sigma_s^2$. Our constraint insures that the proportionality constant be the same for each local model. Next, note that changing s_0 causes a shift

---

[2] The least squares and maximum likelihood solutions are *identical* when the model is exact $\boldsymbol{\Sigma}_a \equiv \mathbf{C}$, i.e. the observed data covariance is *exactly* of the form dictated by the model. Under this condition, $\widetilde{\mathbf{U}} = (\mathbf{U}^T \boldsymbol{\Sigma}_\epsilon^{-1} \mathbf{U})^{-1/2} \boldsymbol{\Sigma}_\epsilon^{-1/2} \mathbf{U}$ and $(\widetilde{\lambda} - 1) = \lambda(\mathbf{U}^T \boldsymbol{\Sigma}_\epsilon^{-1} \mathbf{U})$. The LS and ML solutions are also identical when the noise covariance is homoscedastic $\boldsymbol{\Sigma}_\epsilon = \sigma_\epsilon^2 \mathbf{I}$, even if the model is *not* exact.

in $\hat{s}$. To maintain consistency between local regions, we take $s_0 = 0$ everywhere. These choices for σ_s^2 and s_0 constrain the parameter estimates to

$$\beta_{\text{LS}} = r\,\mathbf{U} \text{ and}$$
$$\alpha_{\text{LS}} = \boldsymbol{\mu}_a \; . \qquad (13)$$

In (5) σ_s^2 and s_0 are defined at each hyperpixel. However, to estimate β and α, we used spatial averages to compute the sample mean and covariance. This is somewhat inconsistent, since the spatial variation of s_0 (e.g. when there are edges in the scene) is not explicitly captured in the model mean and covariance. These variations are, instead, attributed to σ_s^2, resulting in overestimation of the latter. A more complete model would explicitly model the spatial variations of s_0, though we expect this will produce only minor changes in the results.

Finally, the sign parameter r is not specified. In order to properly piece together our local models, we must choose r at each hyperpixel in such a way that β changes direction *slowly* as we move from hyperpixel to hyperpixel and encounter changes in the local image statistics. That is, large direction changes due to arbitrary sign reversals are not allowed. We use a simple heuristic to accomplish this.

5 Relation to PCA

The MAP and ML fusion rules are closely related to PCA. To see this, assume that the noise is homoscedastic $\boldsymbol{\Sigma}_\epsilon = \sigma_\epsilon^2 \mathbf{I}$ and use the parameter estimates (13) in the MAP fusion rule (5), reducing the latter to

$$\hat{s} = \frac{1}{1 + \sigma_\epsilon^2/\sigma_s^2}\, \mathbf{U}_a^{\mathrm{T}}(\boldsymbol{a} - \boldsymbol{\mu}_a) + \frac{1}{1 + \sigma_s^2/\sigma_\epsilon^2}\, s_0 \qquad (14)$$

where $\mathbf{U}_a$ is the principal eigenvector of the data covariance matrix $\boldsymbol{\Sigma}_a$. The MAP estimate $\hat{s}$ is simply a scaled and shifted local PCA projection of the sensor data.

Both the scaling and shift arise because the prior distribution on s tends to bias $\hat{s}$ towards s_0. When the prior is flat $\sigma_s^2 \to \infty$, (or equivalently when using the ML fusion estimate), or when the noise variance vanishes, the fused image is given by a simple local PCA projection

$$\hat{s} = \mathbf{U}_a^{\mathrm{T}}(\boldsymbol{a} - \boldsymbol{\mu}_a) \; . \qquad (15)$$

6 Experiments and Results

We applied our fusion method to visible-band and IR runway images, Fig. 1, containing additive Gaussian noise. Fig. 1(e) shows the result of ML fusion with β and α estimated using (13). ML fusion performs better than either averaging or selection in regions that contain local polarity reversals or complementary features. ML fusion gives higher weight to IR in regions where the features in the two images are common, thus reducing the effects of noise in the visible-band image. ML fusion gives higher weight to the appropriate sensor in regions with complementary features.

Fig. 1(f) shows the result of MAP fusion (5) with the priors σ_s^2 and s_0 those dictated by the consistency requirements discussed in section 4. Clearly, the MAP image is less noisy than the ML image. In regions of low sensor image contrast, σ_s^2 is low (since λ is low), thus the contribution from the sensor images is attenuated compared to the ML fusion rule. Hence the noise is attenuated. In regions containing features such as edges, σ_s^2 is high (since λ is high); hence the contribution from the sensor images is similar to that in ML fusion.

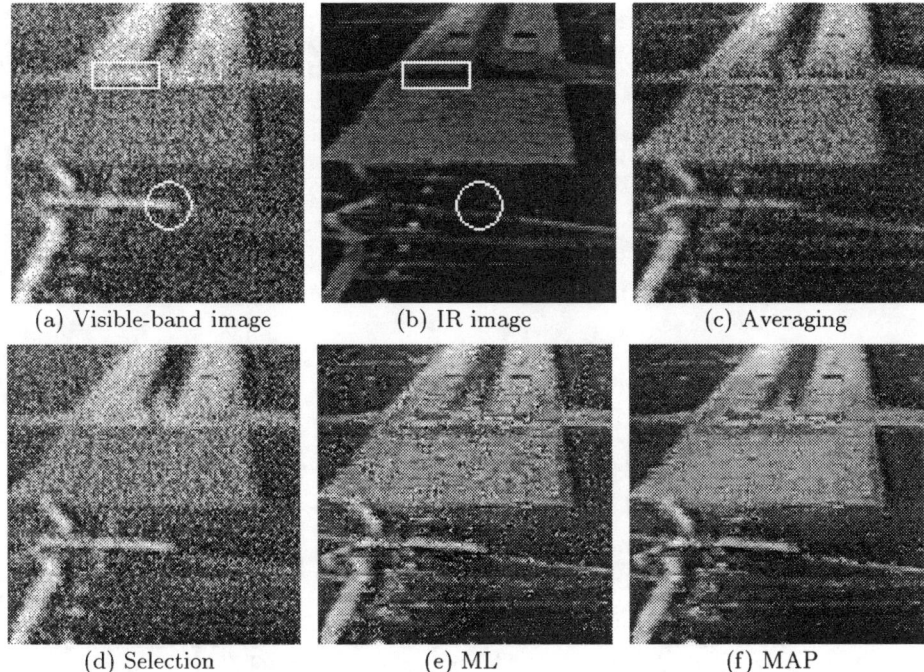

Figure 1: Fusion of visible-band and IR images containing additive Gaussian noise

In Fig. 2 we demonstrate the use of a database image for fusion. Fig. 2(a) and 2(b) are simulated noisy sensor images from visible-band and IR, that depict a runway with an aircraft on it. Fig. 2(c) is an image of the same scene as might be obtained from a terrain database. Although this image is clean, it does not show the actual situation on the runway. One can use the database image pixel intensities as the prior mean s_0 in the MAP fusion rule (5). The prior variance σ_s^2 in (5) can be regarded as a measure of confidence in the database image – it's value controls the relative contribution of the sensors vs. the database image in the fused image. (The parameters β and α, and the sensor noise covariance Σ_ϵ were estimated exactly as before.) Fig. 2(d), 2(e) and 2(f) show the MAP-fused image as a function of increasing σ_s^2. Higher values of σ_s^2 accentuate the contribution of the sensor images, whereas lower values of σ_s^2 accentuate the contribution of the database.

7 Discussion

We presented a model-based probabilistic framework for fusion of images from multiple sensors and exercised the approach on visible-band and IR images. The approach provides both a rigorous framework for PCA-like fusion rules, and a principled way to combine information from a terrain database with sensor images.

We envision several refinements of the approach given here. Writing new image formation models at each hyperpixel produces an overabundance of models. Early experiments show that this can be relaxed by using the same model parameters over regions of several square hyperpixels, rather than recalculating for each hyperpixel. A further refinement could be provided by adopting a mixture of linear models to build up the non-linear image formation model. Finally, we have used multiple frames from a video sequence to obtain ML and MAP fused sequences, and one should be able to produce superior parameter estimates by suitable use of the video sequence.

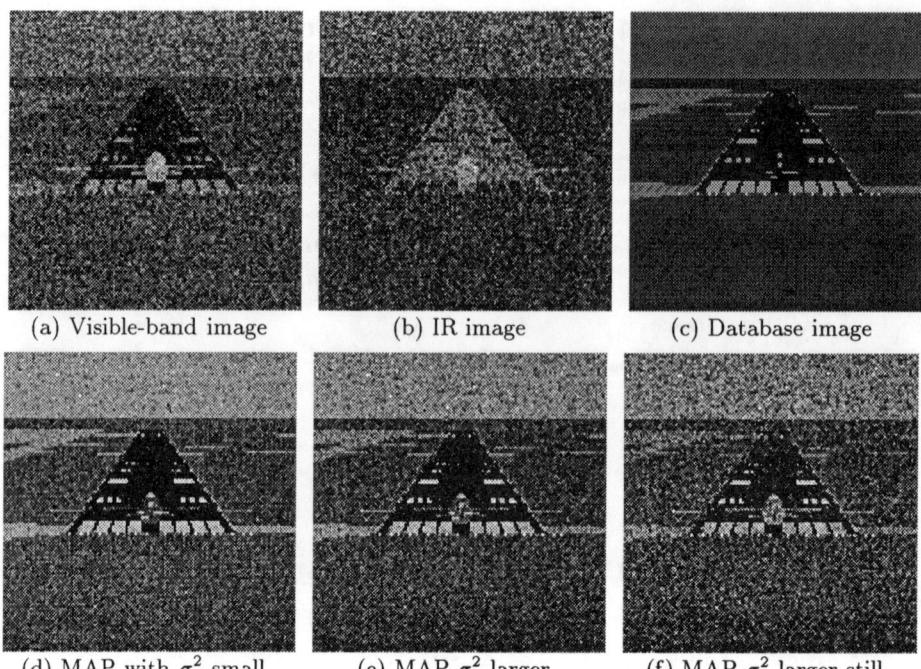

Figure 2: Fusion of simulated visible-band and IR images using database image

Acknowledgments – This work was supported by NASA Ames Research Center grant NCC2-811. TKL was partially supported by NSF grant ECS-9704094.

References

[1] L. A. Klein. *Sensor and Data Fusion Concepts and Applications*. SPIE, 1993.

[2] J. R. Kerr, D. P. Pond, and S. Inman. Infrared-optical multisensor for autonomous landing guidance. *Proceedings of SPIE*, 2463:38–45, 1995.

[3] B. Roberts and P. Symosek. Image processing for flight crew situation awareness. *Proceedings of SPIE*, 2220:246–255, 1994.

[4] M. Pavel and R. K. Sharma. Model-based sensor fusion for aviation. In J. G. Verly, editor, *Enhanced and Synthetic Vision 1997*, volume 3088, pages 169–176. SPIE, 1997.

[5] P. J. Burt and R. J. Kolczynski. Enhanced image capture through fusion. In *Fourth Int. Conf. on Computer Vision*, pages 173–182. IEEE Comp. Soc., 1993.

[6] H. Li and Y. Zhou. Automatic visual/IR image registration. *Optical Engineering*, 35(2):391–400, 1996.

[7] M. Pavel, J. Larimer, and A. Ahumada. Sensor fusion for synthetic vision. In *Proceedings of the Society for Information Display*, pages 475–478. SPIE, 1992.

[8] P. Burt. A gradient pyramid basis for pattern-selective image fusion. In *Proceedings of the Society for Information Display*, pages 467–470. SPIE, 1992.

[9] A. Toet. Hierarchical image fusion. *Machine Vision and Applications*, 3:1–11, 1990.

[10] J. J. Clark and A. L. Yuille. *Data Fusion for Sensory Information Processing Systems*. Kluwer, Boston, 1990.

[11] A. Basilevsky. *Statistical Factor Analysis and Related Methods*. Wiley, 1994.

[12] M. E. Tipping and C. M. Bishop. Probabilistic principal component analysis. Technical report, NCRG/97/010, Neural Computing Research Group, Aston University, UK, 1997.

Orientation, Scale, and Discontinuity as Emergent Properties of Illusory Contour Shape

Karvel K. Thornber
NEC Research Institute
4 Independence Way
Princeton, NJ 08540

Lance R. Williams
Dept. of Computer Science
University of New Mexico
Albuquerque, NM 87131

Abstract

A recent neural model of illusory contour formation is based on a distribution of natural shapes traced by particles moving with constant speed in directions given by Brownian motions. The input to that model consists of pairs of position and direction constraints and the output consists of the distribution of contours joining all such pairs. In general, these contours will not be closed and their distribution will not be scale-invariant. In this paper, we show how to compute a scale-invariant distribution of closed contours given position constraints alone and use this result to explain a well known illusory contour effect.

1 INTRODUCTION

It has been proposed by Mumford[3] that the distribution of illusory contour shapes can be modeled by particles travelling with constant speed in directions given by Brownian motions. More recently, Williams and Jacobs[7, 8] introduced the notion of a *stochastic completion field*, the distribution of particle trajectories joining pairs of position and direction constraints, and showed how it could be computed in a local parallel network. They argued that the mode, magnitude and variance of the completion field are related to the observed shape, salience, and sharpness of illusory contours.

Unfortunately, the Williams and Jacobs model, as described, has some shortcomings. Recent psychophysics suggests that contour salience is greatly enhanced by closure[2]. Yet, in general, the distribution computed by the Williams and Jacobs model does not consist of closed contours. Nor is it scale-invariant—doubling the distances between the constraints does not produce a comparable completion field of double the size without a corresponding doubling of the particle's speeds. However, the Williams and Jacobs model contains no intrinsic mechanism for speed selection. The speeds (like the directions) must be specified *a priori*. In this paper, we show how to compute a scale-invariant distribution of closed contours given position constraints alone.

2 TECHNICAL DETAILS

2.1 SHAPE DISTRIBUTION

Consistent with our earlier work[5, 6], in this paper we do not use the same distribution described by Mumford[3] but instead assume a distribution of completion shapes consisting of straight-line base-trajectories modified by random impulses drawn from a mixture of two limiting distributions. The first distribution consists of weak but frequently acting impulses (we call this the Gaussian-limit). The distribution of these weak impulses has zero mean and variance equal to σ_g^2. The weak impulses act at Poisson times with rate R_g. The second distribution consists of strong but infrequently acting impulses (we call this the Poisson-limit). Here, the magnitude of the random impulses is Gaussian distributed with zero mean. However, the variance is equal to σ_p^2 (where $\sigma_p^2 >> \sigma_g^2$). The strong impulses act at Poisson times with rate $R_p << R_g$. Particles decay with half-life equal to a parameter τ. The effect is that particles tend to travel in smooth, short paths punctuated by occasional orientation discontinuities. See [5, 6].

2.2 EIGENSOURCES

Let i and j be position and velocity constraints, $(\mathbf{x}_i, \dot{\mathbf{x}}_i)$ and $(\mathbf{x}_j, \dot{\mathbf{x}}_j)$. Then $P(j|i)$ is the conditional probability that a particle beginning at i will reach j. Note that these transition probabilities are not symmetric, i.e., $P(j|i) \neq P(i|j)$. However, by time-reversal symmetry, $P(j|i) = P(\bar{i}|\bar{j})$ where $\bar{i} = (\mathbf{x}_i, -\dot{\mathbf{x}}_i)$ and $\bar{j} = (\mathbf{x}_j, -\dot{\mathbf{x}}_j)$.

Given only the matrix of transition probabilities, $\mathbf{P}$, we would like to compute the relative number of closed contours satisfying a given position and velocity constraint. We begin by noting that, due to their randomness, only increasingly smaller and smaller fractions of contours are likely to satisfy increasing numbers of constraints. Suppose we let $s_i^{(1)}$ contours start at $\mathbf{x}_i$ with $\dot{\mathbf{x}}_i$. Then

$$s_j^{(2)} = \sum_i P(j|i) s_i^{(1)}$$

is the relative number of contours through $\mathbf{x}_j$ with $\dot{\mathbf{x}}_j$, i.e., which satisfy two constraints. In general,

$$s_j^{(n+1)} = \sum_i P(j|i) s_i^{(n)}$$

Now suppose we compute the eigenvector,

$$\lambda s_j = \sum_i P(j|i) s_i$$

with largest, real positive eigenvalue, and take $s_i^{(1)} = s_i$. Then clearly $s_i^{(n+1)} = \lambda^n s_i$. This implies that as the number of constraints satisfied increases by one, the number of contours remaining in the sample of interest decreases by λ. However, the ratios of the s_i remain invariant. Letting n pass to infinity, we see that the s_i are just the relative number of contours through i. To summarize, having started with all possible contours, we are now left with only those bridging pairs of constraints at all past-times. By solving $\lambda \mathbf{s} = \mathbf{P}\mathbf{s}$ for $\mathbf{s}$ we know their relative numbers. We refer to the components of $\mathbf{s}$ as the *eigensources* of the stochastic completion field.

Emergent Properties of Illusory Contour Shape

2.3 STOCHASTIC COMPLETION FIELDS

Note that the eigensources alone do not represent a distribution of closed contours. In fact, the majority of contours contributing to s will not satisfy a single additional constraint. However, the following recurrence equation gives the number of contours which begin at constraint i and end at constraint j and satisfy $n-1$ intermediate constraints

$$P^{(n+1)}(j\,|\,i) = \sum_k P(j\,|\,k)P^{(n)}(k\,|\,i)$$

where $P^{(1)}(j\,|\,i) = P(j\,|\,i)$. Given the above recurrence equation, we can define an expression for the relative number of contours of any length which begin and end at constraint i:

$$c_i = \lim_{n\to\infty} P^{(n)}(i\,|\,i) / \sum_j P^{(n)}(j\,|\,j)$$

Using a result from the theory of positive matrices[1], it is possible to show that the above expression is simply

$$c_i = s_i \bar{s}_i / \sum_j s_j \bar{s}_j$$

where s and $\bar{\mathbf{s}}$ are the right and left eigenvectors of $\mathbf{P}$ with largest positive real eigenvalue, i.e., $\lambda \mathbf{s} = \mathbf{Ps}$ and $\lambda \bar{\mathbf{s}} = \mathbf{P}^T \bar{\mathbf{s}}$. Because of the time-reversal symmetry of $\mathbf{P}$, the right and left eigenvectors are related by a permutation which exchanges opposite directions, i.e., $\bar{s}_i = s_{\bar{i}}$.

Finally, given s and $\bar{\mathbf{s}}$, it is possible to compute the relative number of closed contours through an *arbitrary* position and velocity in the plane, i.e., to compute the stochastic completion field. If $\eta = (\mathbf{x}, \dot{\mathbf{x}})$ is an arbitrary position and velocity in the plane, then

$$C(\eta) = \tfrac{1}{\lambda \mathbf{s}^T \bar{\mathbf{s}}} \sum_i P(\eta\,|\,i) s_i \cdot \sum_j P(j\,|\,\eta) \bar{s}_j$$

gives the relative probability that a closed contour will pass through η. Note, that this is a natural generalization of the Williams and Jacobs[7] factorization of the completion field into the product of source and sink fields.

2.4 SCALE-INVARIANCE

Under the restriction that particles have constant speed, the transition probability matrix, $\mathbf{P}$, becomes block-diagonal. Each block corresponds to a different possible speed, γ. Since the components of any given eigenvector will be confined to a single block, we can consider $\mathbf{P}$ to be a function of γ and solve:

$$\lambda(\gamma)\mathbf{s}(\gamma) = \mathbf{P}(\gamma)\mathbf{s}(\gamma)$$

Let $\lambda_{max}(\gamma)$ be the largest positive real eigenvalue of $\mathbf{P}(\gamma)$ and let γ_{max} be the speed where $\lambda_{max}(\gamma)$ is maximized. Then $\mathbf{s}_{max}(\gamma_{max})$, i.e., the eigenvector of $\mathbf{P}(\gamma_{max})$ associated with $\lambda_{max}(\gamma_{max})$, is the limiting distribution over all spatial scales.

3 EXPERIMENTS

3.1 EIGHT POINT CIRCLE

Given eight points spaced uniformly around the perimeter of a circle of diameter, $d = 16$, we would like to find the distribution of directions through each point and the corresponding completion field (Figure 1 (left)). Neither the order of traversal, directions, i.e., $\dot{\mathbf{x}}_i / |\dot{\mathbf{x}}_i|$, or speed, i.e., $\gamma = |\dot{\mathbf{x}}_i|$, are specified *a priori*. In all of our experiments, we sample direction at $5°$ intervals. Consequently, there are 72 discrete directions and 576 position-direction pairs, i.e., $\mathbf{P}(\gamma)$ is of size 576×576.[1]

---

[1]The parameters defining the distribution of completion shapes are $T = R_g \sigma_g^2 = 0.0005$ and $\tau = 9.5$. For simplicity, we assume the pure Gaussian-limit case described in [6].

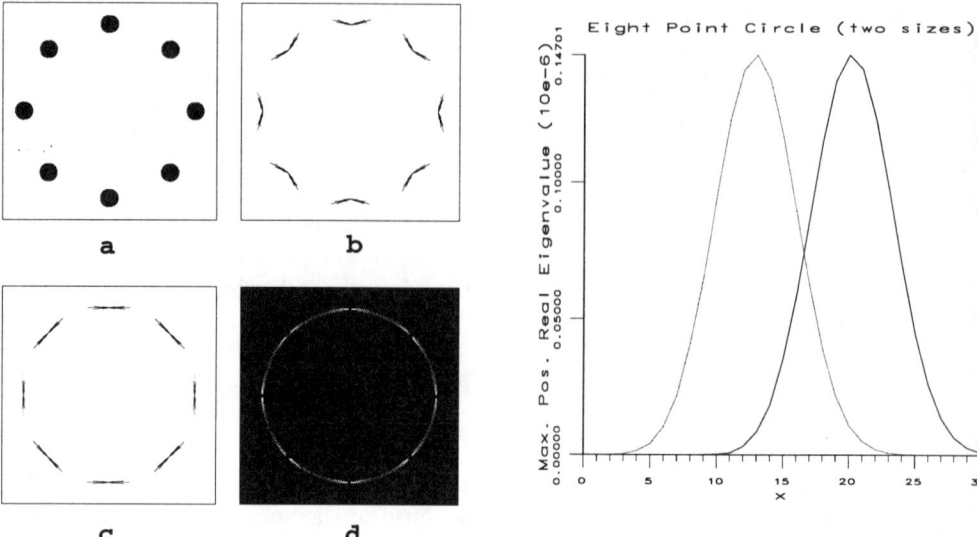

Figure 1: Left: (a) The eight position constraints. Neither the order of traversal, directions, or speed are specified *a priori*. (b) The eigenvector, $\mathbf{s}_{max}(\gamma_{max})$ represents the limiting distribution over all spatial scales. (c) The product of $\mathbf{s}_{max}(\gamma_{max})$ and $\bar{\mathbf{s}}_{max}(\gamma_{max})$. Orientations tangent to the circle dominate the distribution of closed contours. (d) The stochastic completion field, C, due to $\mathbf{s}_{max}(\gamma_{max})$. Right: Plot of magnitude of maximum positive real eigenvalue, λ_{max}, vs. $\log_{1.1}(1/\gamma)$ for eight point circle with $d = 16.0$ (solid) and $d = 32.0$ (dashed).

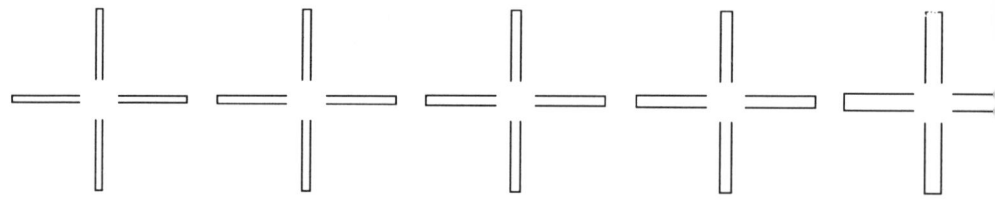

Figure 2: Observers report that as the width of the arms increases, the shape of the illusory contour changes from a circle to a square[4].

First, we evaluated $\lambda_{max}(\gamma)$ over the velocity interval $[1.1^{-1}, 1.1^{-30}]$ using standard numerical routines and plotted the magnitude of the largest, real positive eigenvalue, λ_{max} vs. $\log_{1.1}(1/\gamma)$. The function reaches its maximum value at $\gamma_{max} \approx 1.1^{-20}$. Consequently, the eigenvector, $\mathbf{s}_{max}(1.1^{-20})$ represents the limiting distribution over all spatial scales (Figure 1 (right)).

Next, we scaled the test Figure by a factor of two, i.e., $d' = 32.0$ and plotted $\lambda'_{max}(\gamma)$ over the same interval (Figure 1 (right)). We observe that $\lambda'_{max}(1.1^{-x+7}) \approx \lambda_{max}(1.1^{-x})$, i.e., when plotted using a logarithmic x-axis, the functions are identical except for a translation. It follows that $\gamma'_{max} \approx \log_{1.1} 7 \times \gamma_{max} \approx 2.0 \times \gamma_{max}$. This confirms the scale-invariance of the system—doubling the size of the Figure results in a doubling of the selected speed.

3.2 KOFFKA CROSS

The Koffka Cross stimulus (Figure 2) has two basic degrees of freedom which we call diameter (i.e., d) and arm width (i.e., w) (Figure 3 (a)). We are interested in how

Emergent Properties of Illusory Contour Shape

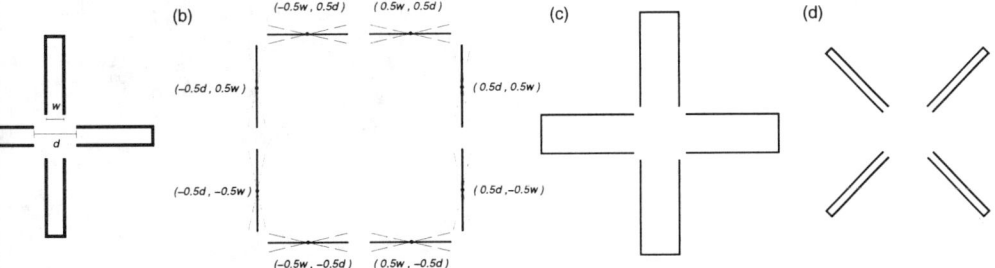

Figure 3: (a) Koffka Cross showing diameter, d, and width, w. (b) Orientation and position constraints in terms of d and w. The normal orientation at each endpoint is indicated by the solid lines while the dashed lines represent plus or minus one standard deviation (i.e., $12.8°$) of the Gaussian weighting function. (c) Typically perceived as square. (d) Typically perceived as circle. The positions of the line endpoints is the same.

the stochastic completion field changes as these parameters are varied. Observers report that as the width of the arms increases, the shape of the illusory contour changes from a circle to a square[4]. The endpoints of the lines comprising the Koffka Cross can be used to define a set of position and orientation constraints (Figure 3 (b)). The position constraints are specified in terms of the parameters, d and w. The orientation constraints take the form of a Gaussian weighting function which assigns higher probabilities to contours passing through the endpoints with orientations normal to the lines.[2] The prior probabilities assigned to each position-direction pair by the Gaussian weighting function form a diagonal matrix, $\mathbf{D}$:

$$\lambda(\gamma)\,\mathbf{s}(\gamma) = \mathbf{D}^{\frac{1}{2}}\mathbf{P}(\gamma)\mathbf{D}^{\frac{1}{2}}\mathbf{s}(\gamma) = \mathbf{Q}(\gamma)\mathbf{s}(\gamma)$$

where $\mathbf{P}(\gamma)$ is the transition probability matrix for the random process at scale γ, $\lambda(\gamma)$ is an eigenvalue of $\mathbf{Q}(\gamma)$, and $\mathbf{s}(\gamma)$ is the corresponding eigenvector. Let $\lambda_{max}(\gamma)$ be the largest positive real eigenvalue of $\mathbf{Q}(\gamma)$ and let γ_{max} be the scale where $\lambda_{max}(\gamma)$ is maximized. Then $\mathbf{s}_{max}(\gamma_{max})$, i.e., the eigenvector of $\mathbf{Q}(\gamma_{max})$ associated with $\lambda_{max}(\gamma_{max})$, is the limiting distribution over all spatial scales.

First, we used a Koffka Cross where $d = 2.0$ and $w = 0.5$ and evaluated $\lambda_{max}(\gamma)$ over the velocity interval $[8.0 \times 1.1^{-1}, 8.0 \times 1.1^{-80}]$ using standard numerical routines.[3] The function reaches its maximum value at $\gamma_{max} \approx 8.0 \times 1.1^{-62}$ (Figure 4 (left)). Observe that the completion field due to the eigenvector, $\mathbf{s}_{max}(8.0 \times 1.1^{-62})$, is dominated by contours of a predominantly circular shape (Figure 4 (right)). We then uniformly scaled the Koffka Cross Figure by a factor of two, i.e., $d' = 4.0$ and

---

[2]Observe that Figure 3 (c) is perceived as a square while Figure 3 (d) is perceived as a circle. Yet the positions of the line endpoints is the same. It follows that the orientations of the lines affect the percept. We have chosen to model this dependence through the use of a Gaussian weighting function which favors contours passing through the endpoints of the lines in the normal direction. It is possible to motivate this based on the statistics of natural scenes. The distribution of relative orientations at contour crossings is maximum at $90°$ and drops to nearly zero at $0°$ and $180°$.

[3]The parameters defining the distribution of completion shapes were: $T = R_g \sigma_g^2 = 0.0005$, $\tau = 9.5$, $\xi_p = \sigma_p^2/T = 100.0$ and $R_p = 1.0 \times 10^{-8}$. As an anti-aliasing measure, the transition probabilities, $P(j\,|\,i)$, were averaged over initial conditions modeled as Gaussians of variance $\sigma_x^2 = \sigma_y^2 = 0.00024$ and $\sigma_\theta^2 = 0.0019$. See [6].

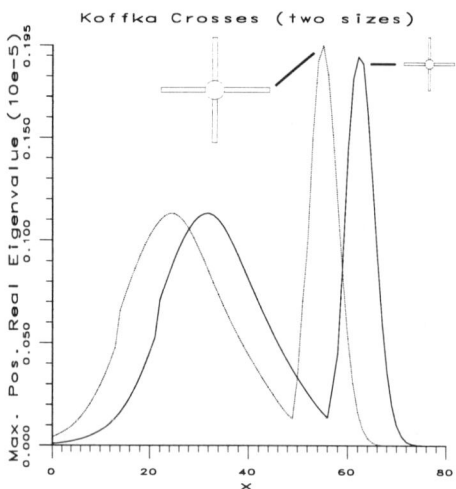 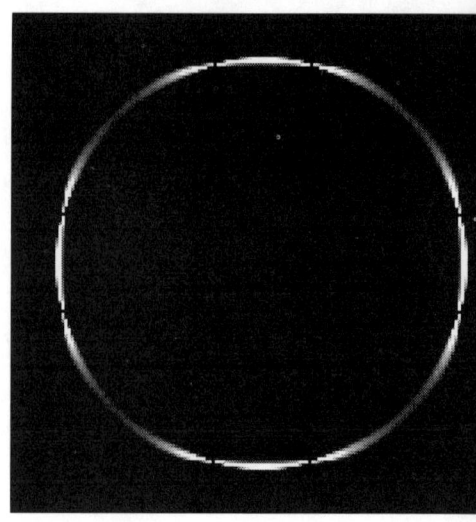

Figure 4: Left: Plot of magnitude of maximum positive real eigenvalue, λ_{max}, vs. $\log_{1.1}(1/\gamma)$ for Koffka Crosses with $d = 2.0$ and $w = 0.5$ (solid) and $d = 4.0$ and $w = 1.0$ (dashed). Right: The completion field due to the eigenvector, $\mathbf{s}_{max}(8.0 \times 1.1^{-62})$.

$w' = 1.0$ and plotted $\lambda'_{max}(\gamma)$ over the same interval (Figure 4 (left)). Observe that $\lambda'_{max}(8.0 \times 1.1^{-x+7}) \approx \lambda_{max}(8.0 \times 1.1^{-x})$. As before, this confirms the scale-invariance of the system.

Next, we studied how the relative magnitudes of the local maxima of $\lambda_{max}(\gamma)$ change as the parameter w is varied. We begin with a Koffka Cross where $d = 2.0$ and $w = 0.5$ and observe that $\lambda_{max}(\gamma)$ has two local maxima (Figure 5 (left)). We refer to the larger of these maxima as γ_{circle}. As previously noted, this maximum is located at approximately 8.0×1.1^{-62}. The second maximum is located at approximately 8.0×1.1^{-32}. When the completion field due to the eigenvector, $\mathbf{s}_{max}(8.0 \times 1.1^{-32})$, is rendered, we observe that the distribution is dominated by contours of predominantly square shape (Figure 5(a)). For this reason, we refer to this local maximum as γ_{square}. Now consider a Koffka Cross where the widths of the arms are doubled but the diameter remains the same, i.e., $d' = 2.0$ and $w' = 1.0$. We observe that $\lambda'_{max}(\gamma)$ still has two local maxima, one at approximately 8.0×1.1^{-63} and a second at approximately 8.0×1.1^{-29} (Figure 5 (left)). When we render the completion fields due to the eigenvectors, $\mathbf{s}'_{max}(8.0 \times 1.1^{-63})$ and $\mathbf{s}'_{max}(8.0 \times 1.1^{-29})$, we find that the completion fields have the same general character as before—the contours associated with the smaller spatial scale (i.e., lower speed) are approximately circular and those associated with the larger spatial scale (i.e., higher speed) are approximately square (Figure 5 (d) and (c)). Accordingly, we refer to the locations of the respective local maxima as γ'_{circle} and γ'_{square}. However, what is most interesting is that the relative magnitudes of the local maxima have reversed. Whereas we previously observed that $\lambda_{max}(\gamma_{circle}) > \lambda_{max}(\gamma_{square})$, we now observe that $\lambda'_{max}(\gamma'_{square}) > \lambda'_{max}(\gamma'_{circle})$. Therefore, the completion field due to the eigenvector, $\mathbf{s}'_{max}(\gamma'_{square})$ [not $\mathbf{s}'_{max}(\gamma'_{circle})$!] represents the limiting distribution over all spatial scales. This is consistent with the transition from circle to square reported by human observers when the widths of the arms of the Koffka Cross are increased.

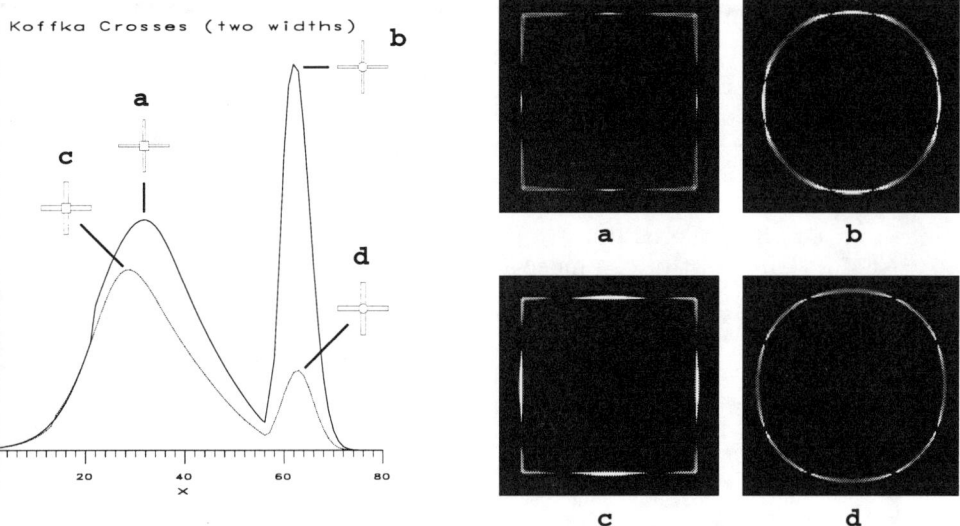

Figure 5: Plot of magnitude of maximum positive real eigenvalue, λ_{max}, vs. $\log_{1.1}(1/\gamma)$ for Koffka Crosses with $d = 2.0$ and $w = 0.5$ (solid) and $d = 2.0$ and $w = 1.0$ (dashed). Stochastic completion fields for Koffka Cross due to (a) $\mathbf{s}_{max}(\gamma_{square})$ is a local optimum for $w = 0.5$ (b) $\mathbf{s}_{max}(\gamma_{circle})$ is the global optimum for $w = 0.5$ (c) $\mathbf{s}'_{max}(\gamma'_{square})$ is the global optimum for $w = 1.0$ (d) $\mathbf{s}'_{max}(\gamma'_{square})$ is a local optimum for $w = 1.0$. These results are consistent with the circle-to-square transition perceived by human subjects when the width of the arms of the Koffka Cross are increased.

4 CONCLUSION

We have improved upon a previous model of illusory contour formation by showing how to compute a scale-invariant distribution of closed contours given position constraints alone. We also used our model to explain a previously unexplained perceptual effect.

References

[1] Horn, R.A., and C.R. Johnson, *Matrix Analysis*, Cambridge Univ. Press, p. 500, 1985.

[2] Kovacs, I. and B. Julesz, A Closed Curve is Much More than an Incomplete One: Effect of Closure in Figure-Ground Segmentation, *Proc. Natl. Acad. Sci. USA*, **90**, pp. 7495-7497, 1993.

[3] Mumford, D., Elastica and Computer Vision, *Algebraic Geometry and Its Applications*, Chandrajit Bajaj (ed.), Springer-Verlag, New York, 1994.

[4] Sambin, M., Angular Margins without Gradients, *Italian Journal of Psychology* **1**, pp. 355-361, 1974.

[5] Thornber, K.K. and L.R. Williams, Analytic Solution of Stochastic Completion Fields, *Biological Cybernetics* **75**, pp. 141-151, 1996.

[6] Thornber, K.K. and L.R. Williams, Characterizing the Distribution of Completion Shapes with Corners Using a Mixture of Random Processes, *Intl. Workshop on Energy Minimization Methods in Computer Vision*, Venice, Italy, 1997.

[7] Williams, L.R. and D.W. Jacobs, Stochastic Completion Fields: A Neural Model of Illusory Contour Shape and Salience, *Neural Computation* **9**(4), pp. 837-858, 1997.

[8] Williams, L.R. and D.W. Jacobs, Local Parallel Computation of Stochastic Completion Fields, *Neural Computation* **9**(4), pp. 859-881, 1997.

Classification in Non-Metric Spaces

Daphna Weinshall[1,2] **David W. Jacobs**[1] **Yoram Gdalyahu**[2]
[1]NEC Research Institute, 4 Independence Way, Princeton, NJ 08540, USA
[2]Inst. of Computer Science, Hebrew University of Jerusalem, Jerusalem 91904, Is

Abstract

A key question in vision is how to represent our knowledge of previously encountered objects to classify new ones. The answer depends on how we determine the similarity of two objects. Similarity tells us how relevant each previously seen object is in determining the category to which a new object belongs. Here a dichotomy emerges. Complex notions of similarity appear necessary for cognitive models and applications, while simple notions of similarity form a tractable basis for current computational approaches to classification. We explore the nature of this dichotomy and why it calls for new approaches to well-studied problems in learning. We begin this process by demonstrating new computational methods for supervised learning that can handle complex notions of similarity. (1) We discuss how to implement parametric methods that represent a class by its *mean* when using non-metric similarity functions; and (2) We review non-parametric methods that we have developed using nearest neighbor classification in non-metric spaces. Point (2), and some of the background of our work have been described in more detail in [8].

1 Supervised Learning and Non-Metric Distances

How can one represent one's knowledge of previously encountered objects in order to classify new objects? We study this question within the framework of supervised learning: it is assumed that one is given a number of *training* objects, each labeled as belonging to a category; one wishes to use this experience to label new *test* instances of objects. This problem emerges both in the modeling of cognitive processes and in many practical applications. For example, one might want to identify risky applicants for credit based on past experience with clients who have proven to be good or bad credit risks. Our work is motivated by computer vision applications.

Most current computational approaches to supervised learning suppose that objects can be thought of as vectors of numbers, or equivalently as points lying in an n-dimensional space. They further suppose that the similarity between objects can be determined from the Euclidean distance between these vectors, or from some other simple metric. This classic notion of similarity as Euclidean or metric distance leads to considerable mathematical and computational simplification.

However, work in cognitive psychology has challenged such simple notions of similarity as models of human judgment, while applications frequently employ non-Euclidean distances to measure object similarity. We consider the need for similarity measures that are not only non-Euclidean, but that are non-*metric*. We focus on proposed similarities that violate one requirement of a metric distance, the triangle inequality. This states that if we denote the distance between objects A and B by $d(A, B)$, then: $\forall A, B, C : d(A, B) + d(B, C) \geq d(A, C)$. Distances violating the triangle inequality must also be non-Euclidean.

Data from cognitive psychology has demonstrated that similarity judgments may not be well modeled by Euclidean distances. Tversky [12] has demonstrated instances in which similarity judgments may violate the triangle inequality. For example, close similarity between Jamaica and Cuba and between Cuba and Russia does not imply close similarity between Jamaica and Russia (see also [10]). Non-metric similarity measures are frequently employed for practical reasons, too (cf. [5]). In part, work in robust statistics [7] has shown that methods that will survive the presence of outliers, which are extraneous pieces of information or information containing extreme errors, must employ non-Euclidean distances that in fact violate the triangle inequality; related insights have spurred the widespread use of robust methods in computer vision (reviewed in [5] and [9]).

We are interested in handling a wide range of non-metric distance functions, including those that are so complex that they must be treated as a black box. However, to be concrete, we will focus here on two simple examples of such distances:

median distance: This distance assumes that objects are representable as a set of features whose individual differences can be measured, so that the difference between two objects is representable as a vector: $\vec{d} = (d_1, d_2, ...d_n)$. The median distance between the two objects is just the median value in this vector. Similarly, one can define a k-*median* distance by choosing the k'th lowest element in this list. k-median distances are often used in applications (cf. [9]), because they are unaffected by the exact values of the most extreme differences between the objects. Only these features that are most similar determine its value. The k-median distance can violate the triangle inequality to an arbitrary degree (i.e., there are no constraints on the pairwise distances between three points).

robust non-metric L^p distances: Given a difference vector $\vec{d}$, an L^p distance has the form:

$$\left(\sum_{i=1}^{n} d_i^p\right)^{\frac{1}{p}} \tag{1}$$

and is non-metric for $p < 1$.

Figure 1 illustrates why these distances present significant new challenges in supervised learning. Suppose that given some datapoints (two in Fig. 1), we wish to classify each new point as coming from the same category as its nearest neighbor. Then we need to determine the Voronoi diagram generated by our data: a division of the plane into regions in which the points all have the same nearest neighbor. Fig. 1 shows how the Voronoi diagram changes with the function used to compute the distance between datapoints; the non-metric diagrams (rightmost three pictures in Fig. 1) are more complex and more likely to make non-intuitive predictions. In fact, very little is known about the computation of non-metric Voronoi diagrams.

We now describe new parametric methods for supervised learning with non-metric

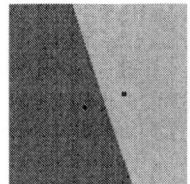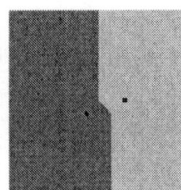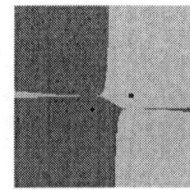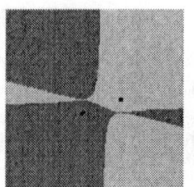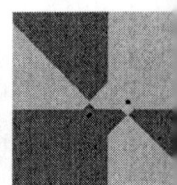

Figure 1: The Voronoi diagram for two points using, from left to right, p-distances with $p = 2$ (Euclidean), $p = 1$ (Manhattan, which is still metric), the non-metric distances arising from $p = 0.5$, $p = 0.2$, and the min (1-median) distance. The min distance in 2-D illustrates the behavior of the other median distances in higher dimensions. The region of the plane closer to one point is shown in black, and closer to the other in white.

distances, and review non-parametric methods that we described in [8].

2 Parametric methods: what should replace the mean

Parametric methods typically represent objects as vectors in a high-dimensional space, and represent classes and the boundaries between them in this space using geometric constructions or probability distributions with a limited number of parameters. One can attempt to extend these techniques to specific non-metric distances, such as the median distance, or non-metric L^p distances. We discuss the example of the mean of a class below. One can also redefine geometric objects such as linear separators, for specific non-metric distances. However, existing algorithms for finding such objects in Euclidean spaces will no longer be directly suitable, nor will theoretical results about such representations hold. Many problems are therefore open in determining how to best apply parametric supervised learning techniques to specific non-metric distances.

We analyze k-means clustering where each class is represented by its average member; new elements are then classified according to which of these prototypical examples is nearest. In Euclidean space, the mean is the point $\bar{q}$ whose sum of squared distances to all the class members $\{q_i\}_{i=1}^n$ - $\left(\sum_{i=1}^n d(\bar{q}, q_i)^2\right)^{\frac{1}{2}}$ - is minimized.

Suppose now that our data come from a vector space where the correct distance is the L^p distance from (1). Using the natural extension of the above definition, we should represent each class by the point $\bar{q}$ whose sum of distances to all the class members - $\left(\sum_{i=1}^n d(\bar{q}, q_i)^p\right)^{\frac{1}{p}}$ - is minimal. It is now possible to show (proof is omitted) that for $p < 1$ (the non-metric cases), the exact value of every feature of the representative point $\bar{q}$ must have already appeared in at least one element in the class. Moreover, the value of these features can be determined separately with complexity $O(n^2)$, and total complexity of $O(dn^2)$ given d features. $\bar{q}$ is therefore determined by a mixture of up to d exemplars, where d is the dimension of the vector space. Thus there are efficient algorithms for finding the "mean" element of a class, even using certain non-metric distances.

We will illustrate these results with a concrete example using the corel database, a commercial database of images pre-labeled by categories (such as "lions"), where non-metric distance functions have proven effective in determining the similarity of images [1]. The corel database is very large, making the use of prototypes desirable.

We represent each image using a vector of 11 numbers describing general image properties, such as color histograms, as described in [1]. We consider the Euclidean and $L^{0.5}$ distances, and their corresponding prototypes: the mean and the $L^{0.5}$-prototype computed according to the result above. Given the first 45 classes, each containing 100 images, we found their corresponding prototypes; we then computed the percentage of images in each class that are closest to their own prototype, using either the Euclidean or the $L^{0.5}$ distance and one of the two prototypes. The results are the following:

prototype:	mean	d existing features
$L^{0.5}$ distance	18%	25%
Euclidean distance	20%	20%

In the first column, the prototype is computed using the Euclidean mean. In the second column the prototype is computed using an $L^{0.5}$ distance. In each row, a different function is used to compute the distance from each item to the cluster prototype. Best results are indeed obtained with the non-metric $L^{0.5}$ distance and the correct prototype for this particular distance. While performance in absolute terms depends on how well this data clusters using distances derived from a simple feature vector, relative performance of different methods reveals the advantage of using a prototype computed with a non-metric distance.

Another important distance function is the generalized Hamming distance: given two vectors of features, their distance is the number of features which are different in the two vectors. This distance was assumed in psychophysical experiments which used artificial objects (Fribbles) to investigate human categorization and object recognition [13]. In agreement with experimental results, the prototype $\bar{q}$ for this distance computed according to the definition above is the vector of "modal" features - the most common feature value computed independently at each feature.

3 Non-Parametric Methods: Nearest Neighbors

Non-parametric classification methods typically represent a class directly by its exemplars. Specifically, nearest-neighbor techniques classify new objects using only their distance to labeled exemplars. Such methods can be applied using any non-metric distance function, treating the function as a black-box. However, nearest-neighbor techniques must also be modified to apply well to non-metric distances. The insights we gain below from doing this can form the basis of more efficient and effective computer algorithms, and of cognitive models for which examples of a class are worth remembering. This section summarizes work described in [8].

Current efficient algorithms for finding the nearest neighbor of a class work only for metric distances [3]. The alternative of a brute-force approach, in which a new object is explicitly compared to every previously seen object, is desirable neither computationally nor as a cognitive model. A natural approach to handling this problem is to represent each class by a subset of its labeled examples. Such methods are called *condensing* algorithms. Below we develop condensing methods for selecting a subset of the training set which minimizes errors in the classification of new datapoints, taking into account the non-metric nature of the distance.

In designing a condensing method, one needs to answer the question *when is one object a good substitute for another?* Earlier methods (e.g., [6, 2]) make use of the fact that the triangle inequality guarantees that when two points are similar to each other, their pattern of similarities to other points are not very different. Thus, in a metric space, there is no reason to store two similar datapoints, one can easily substitute for the other. Things are different in non-metric spaces.

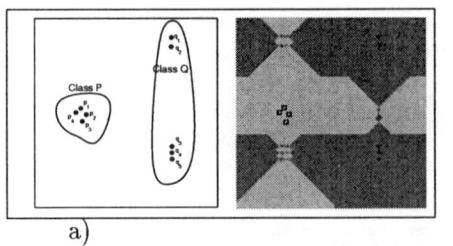
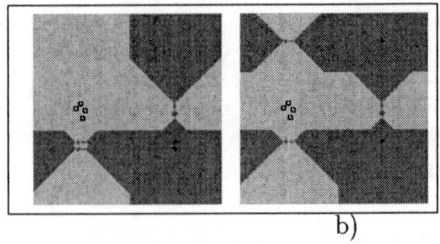

a) b)

Figure 2: a) Two clusters of labeled points (left) and their Voronoi diagram (right) computed using the 1-median (min) distance. Cluster P consists of four points (black squares) all close together both according to the median distance and the Euclidean distance. Cluster Q consists of five points (black crosses) all having the same x coordinate, and so all are separated by zero distance using the median (but not Euclidean) distance. We wish to select a subset of points to represent each class, while changing this Voronoi diagram as little as possible. b) All points in class Q have zero distance to each other, using the min distance. So distance provides no clue as to which are interchangeable. However, the top points (q_1, q_2) have distances to the points in class P that are highly correlated with each other, and poorly correlated with the bottom points (q_3, q_4, q_5). Without using correlation as a clue, we might represent Q with two points from the bottom (which are nearer the boundary with P, a factor preferred in existing approaches). This changes the Voronoi diagram drastically, as shown on the left. Using correlation as a clue, we select points from the top and bottom, changing the Voronoi diagram much less, as shown on the right.

Specifically, what we really need to know is when two objects will have similar distances to other objects, yet unseen. We estimate this quantity using the correlation between two vectors: the vector of distances from one datapoint to all the other training data, and the vector of distances from the second datapoint to all the remaining training data[1]. It can be shown (proof is omitted) that in a Euclidean space the similarity between two points is the best measure of how well one can substitute the other, whereas in a non-metric space the aforementioned vector correlation is a substantially better measure. Fig. 2 illustrates this result.

We now draw on these insights to produce concrete methods for representing classes in non-metric spaces, for nearest neighbor classification. We compare three algorithms. The first two algorithms, **random selection** (cf. [6]) and **boundary detection** (e.g., [11]), represent old condensing ideas: in the first we pick a random selection of class representatives, in the second we use points close to class boundaries as representatives. The last algorithm uses new ideas: **correlation selection** includes in the representative set points which are least correlated with the other class members and representatives. To be fair in our comparison, all algorithms were constrained to select the same number of representative points for each class.

During the simulation, each of 1000 test datapoints was classified based on: (1) all the data, (2) the representatives computed by each of the three algorithms. For each algorithm, the test is successful if the two methods (classification based on all the data and based on the chosen representatives) give the same results. Fig. 3a-c summarizes representative results of our simulations. See [8] for details.

---

[1] Given two datapoints X, Y and $\mathbf{x}, \mathbf{y} \in \mathcal{R}^n$, where $\mathbf{x}$ is the vector of distances from X to all the other training points and $\mathbf{y}$ is the corresponding vector for Y, we measure the correlation between the datapoints using the statistical correlation coefficient between $\mathbf{x}, \mathbf{y}$: $corr(X,Y) = corr(\mathbf{x}, \mathbf{y}) = \frac{\mathbf{x}-\mu_x}{\sigma_x} \cdot \frac{\mathbf{y}-\mu_y}{\sigma_y}$, where μ_x, μ_y denote the mean of $\mathbf{x}, \mathbf{y}$ respectively, and σ_x, σ_y denote the standard deviation of $\mathbf{x}, \mathbf{y}$ respectively.

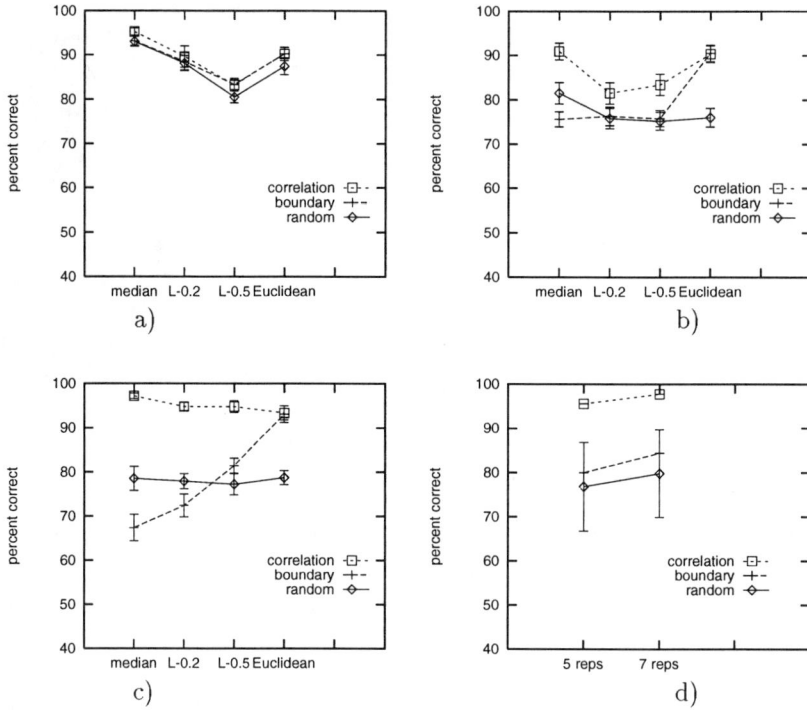

Figure 3: Results: values of percent correct scores, as well as error bars giving the standard deviation calculated over 20 repetitions of each test block when appropriate. Each graph contains 3 plots, giving the percent correct score for each of the three algorithms described above: random (selection), boundary (detection), and (selection based on) correlation. (a-c) Simulation results: data is chosen from $\mathcal{R}^{25}$. 30 clusters were randomly chosen, each with 30 datapoints. The distribution of points in each class was: (a) normal; (b) normal, where in half the datapoints one random coordinate was modified (thus the points cluster around a prototype, but many class members vary widely in one random dimension); (c) union of 2 concentric normal distributions, one spherical and one elongated elliptical (thus the points cluster around a prototype, but may vary significantly in a few non-defining dimensions). Each plot gives 4 values, for each of the different distance functions used here: median, $L^{0.2}$, $L^{0.5}$ and L^2. (d) Real data: the number of representatives chosen by the algorithm was limited to 5 (first column) and 7 (second column).

To test our method with real images, we used the local curve matching algorithm described in [4]. This non-metric curve matching algorithm was specifically designed to compare curves which may be quite different, and return the distance between them. The training and test data are shown in Fig. 4. Results are given in Fig. 3d.

The simulations and the real data demonstrate a significant advantage to our new method. Almost as important, in metric spaces (4th column in Fig. 3a-c) or when the classes lack any "interesting" structure (Fig. 3a), our method is not worse than existing methods. Thus it should be used to guarantee good performance when the nature of the data and the distance function is not known a priori.

References

[1] Cox, I., Miller, M., Omohundro, S., and Yianilos, P., 1996, "PicHunter: Bayesian Relevance Feedback for Image Retrieval," *Proc. of ICPR*, C:361-369.

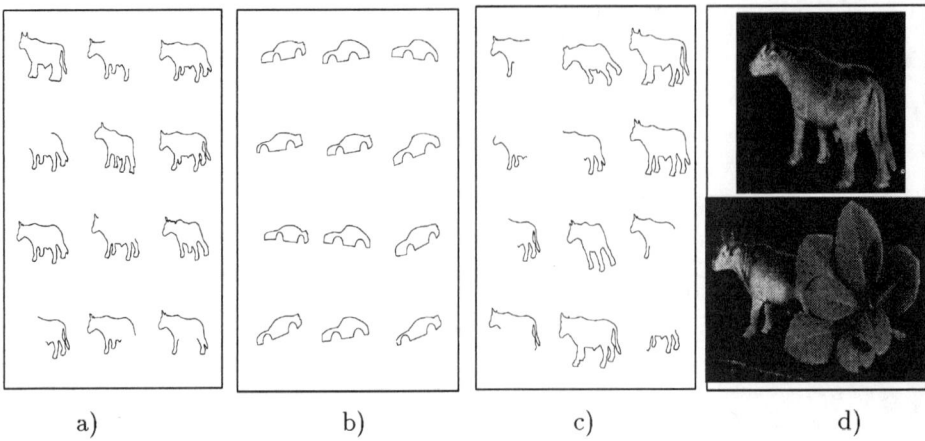

Figure 4: Real data used to test the three algorithms, including 2 classes with 30 images each: a) 12 examples from the first class of 30 cow contours, obtained from different viewpoints of the same cow. b) 12 examples from the second class of 30 car contours, obtained from different viewpoints of 2 similar cars. c) 12 examples from the set of 30 test cow contours, obtained from different viewpoints of the same cow with possibly additional occlusion. d) 2 examples of the real images from which the contours in a) are obtained.

[2] Dasarathy, B., 1994, "Minimal Consistent Set (MCS) Identification for Optimal Nearest Neighbor Decision Systems Design," *IEEE Trans. on Systems, Man and Cybernetics*, **24**(3):511–517.

[3] Friedman, J., Bently, J., Finkel, R., 1977, "An Algorithm for Finding Best Matches in Logarithmic Expected Time," *ACM Trans. on Math. Software*, **3:3** 209–226.

[4] Gdalyahu, Y. and D. Weinshall, 1997, "Local Curve Matching for Object Recognition without Prior Knowledge", *Proc.: DARPA Image Understanding Workshop*, 1997.

[5] Haralick, R. and L. Shapiro, 1993, *Computer and Robot Vision, Vol. 2*, Addison-Wesley Publishing.

[6] Hart, P., 1968, "The Condensed Nearest Neighbor Rule," *IEEE Trans. on Information Theory*, **14**(3):515–516.

[7] Huber, P., 1981, *Robust Statistics*, John Wiley and Sons.

[8] Jacobs, D., Weinshall, D., and Gdalyahu, Y., 1998, "Condensing Image Databases when Retrieval is based on Non-Metric Distances," *Int. Conf. on Computer vis.*:596–601.

[9] Meer, P., D. Mintz, D. Kim and A. Rosenfeld, 1991, "Robust Regression Methods for Computer Vision: A Review," *Int. J. of Comp. Vis.* **6**(1):59-70.

[10] Rosch, E., 1975, "Cognitive Reference Points," *Cognitive Psychology*, **7**:532–547.

[11] Tomek, I., 1976, "Two modifications of CNN," *IEEE Trans. Syst., Man, Cyber.*,, **SMC-6(11)**:769–772.

[12] Tversky, A., 1977, "Features of Similarity," *Psychological Review*, **84**(4):327–352.

[13] Williams, P., "Prototypes, Exemplars, and Object Recognition", submitted.

Part VIII
Applications

Making Templates Rotationally Invariant: An Application to Rotated Digit Recognition

Shumeet Baluja
baluja@cs.cmu.edu
Justsystem Pittsburgh Research Center &
School of Computer Science, Carnegie Mellon University

Abstract

This paper describes a simple and efficient method to make template-based object classification invariant to in-plane rotations. The task is divided into two parts: orientation discrimination and classification. The key idea is to perform the orientation discrimination *before* the classification. This can be accomplished by hypothesizing, in turn, that the input image belongs to each class of interest. The image can then be rotated to maximize its similarity to the training images in each class (these contain the prototype object in an upright orientation). This process yields a set of images, at least one of which will have the object in an upright position. The resulting images can then be classified by models which have been trained with only upright examples. This approach has been successfully applied to two real-world vision-based tasks: rotated handwritten digit recognition and rotated face detection in cluttered scenes.

1 Introduction

Rotated text is commonly used in a variety of situations, ranging from advertisements, logos, official post-office stamps, and headlines in magazines, to name a few. For examples, see Figure 1. We would like to be able to recognize these digits or characters, regardless of their rotation.

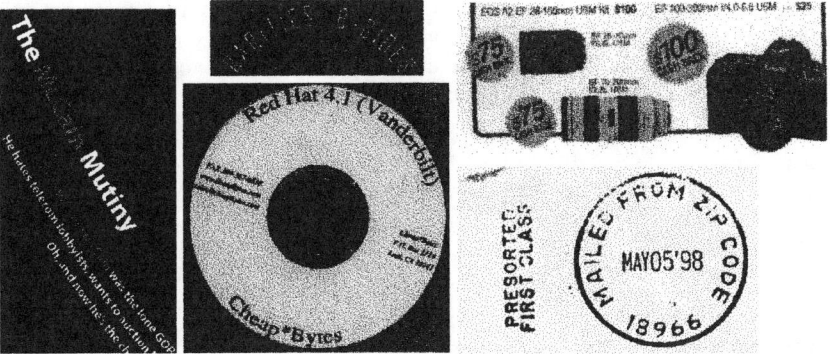

Figure 1: Common examples of images which contain text that is not axis aligned include logos, post-office stamps, magazine headlines and consumer advertisements.

The focus of this paper is on the recognition of rotated digits. The simplest method for creating a system which can recognize digits rotated within the image-plane is to employ existing systems which are designed only for upright digit recognition [Le Cun et al., 1990][Le Cun et al., 1995a][Le Cun et al., 1995b][Lee, 1991][Guyon et al., 1989]. By repeatedly rotating the input image by small increments and applying the recognition system at each rotation, the digit will eventually be recognized. As will be discussed in this paper, besides being extremely computationally expensive, this approach is also error-prone. Because the classification of each digit must occur in many orientations, the likelihood of an incorrect match is high.

The procedure presented in this paper to make templates rotationally invariant is significantly faster and more accurate than the one described above. Detailed descriptions of the procedure are given in Section 2. Section 3 demonstrates the applicability of this approach to a real-world vision-based task, rotated handwritten digit recognition. Section 4 closes the paper with conclusions and suggestions for future research. It also briefly describes the second application to which this method has been successfully applied, face detection in cluttered scenes.

2 Making Templates Rotationally Invariant

The process to make templates rotationally invariant is easiest to describe in the context of a binary classification problem; the extension to multiple classes is discussed later in this section. Imagine a simplified version of the digit recognition task: we want a detector for a single digit. Suppose we wish to tell whether the input contains the digit '3' or not. The challenge is that the '3' can be rotated within the image plane by an arbitrary amount.

Recognizing rotated objects is a two step process. In the first step, a "De-Rotation" network is applied to the input image. This network analyzes the input before it is given to a "Detection" network. If the input contains a '3', the De-Rotation network returns the digit's angle of rotation. The window can then be rotated by the negative of that angle to make the '3' upright. Note that the De-Rotation network *does not* require a '3' as input. If a non-'3' image is encountered, the De-Rotation network will return an unspecified rotation. However, a rotation of a non-'3' will yield another (perhaps different) image of a non-'3'. When the resulting image is given to the Detection network it will not detect a '3'. On the other hand, a rotated '3', which may not have been detected by the Detection network alone, will be rotated to an upright position by the De-Rotation network, and will subsequently be detected as a '3' by the Detection network.

The Detection network is trained to output a positive value only if the input contains an *upright* '3', and a negative value otherwise (even if it contains a rotated '3'). It should be noted that the methods described here do not require neural networks. As shown in [Le Cun et al., 1995a, Le Cun et al., 1995b] a number of other classifiers can be used.

The De-Rotation and Detection networks are used sequentially. First, the input image is processed by the De-Rotation network which returns an angle of rotation, assuming the image contains a '3'. A simple geometric transformation of the image is performed to undo this rotation. If the original image contained a '3', it would now be upright. The resulting image is then passed to the Detection network. If the original image contained a '3', it can now be successfully detected.

This idea can easily be extended to multiple-class classification problems: a De-Rotation network is trained for each object class to be recognized. For the digit recognition problem, 10 De-Rotation networks are trained, one for each of the digits $0..9$. To classify the digits once they are upright, a single classification network is used with 10 outputs (instead of the detection networks trained on individual digits – alternative approaches will be described later in this paper). The classification network is used in the standard manner; the output with the maximum value is taken as the classification. To classify a new image, the following procedure is used:

For each digit D $(0 \leq D \leq 9)$:

1. Pass image through De-Rotation-network-D. This returns the rotation angle.
2. Rotate the image by (-1.0 * returned rotation angle).
3. Pass the de-rotated image to the classification network.
4. If the classification network's maximum output is output D, the activation of output D is recorded. Otherwise digit D is eliminated as a candidate.

In most cases, this will eliminate all but one of the candidates. However, in some cases more than one candidate will remain. In these cases, the digit with the maximum recorded activation (from Step 4) is returned. In the unlikely event that no candidates remain, either the system can reject the sample as one it cannot classify, or it can return the maximum value which would have been recorded in Step 4 if none of the examples were rejected.

2.1 Network Specifics

To train the De-Rotation networks, images of rotated digits were input, with the rotation angle as the target output. Examples of rotated digits are shown in Figure 2. Each image is 28x28 pixels. The upright data sets are from the MNIST database [Le Cun et al., 1995a].

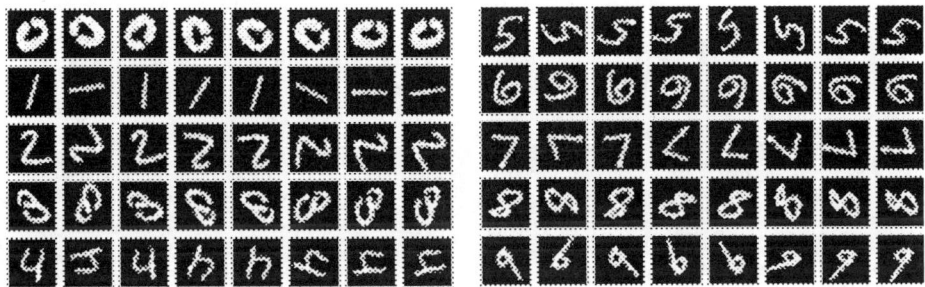

Figure 2: 8 examples of each of the 10 digits to be recognized. The first example in each group of eight is shown with no rotation; it is as it appears in the MNIST data set. The second through eighth examples show the same digit rotated in-plane by random amounts.

In the classification network, each output represents a distinct class; therefore, the standard 1-of-N output representation was used with 10 outputs. To represent a continuous variable (the angle of rotation) in the outputs of the De-Rotation network, we used a Gaussian output encoding [Pomerleau, 1992] with 90 output units. With the Gaussian encoding, instead of only training the network to activate a single output (as is done in 1-of-N encoding), outputs close to the desired output are also activated in proportion to their distance from the desired output. This representation avoids the imposed discontinuities of the strict 1-of-N encoding for images which are similar, but have only slight differences in rotations. Further, this representation allows finer granularity with the same number of output units than would be possible if a 1-of-N encoding was used [Pomerleau, 1992].

The network architecture for both the classification and the De-Rotation networks consists of a single hidden layer. However, unlike a standard fully-connected network, each hidden unit was only connected to a small patch of the 28x28 input. The De-Rotation networks used groups of hidden units in which each hidden unit was connected to only 2x2, 3x3, 4x4 & 5x5 patches of the inputs (in each of these groups, the patches were spaced 2x2 pixels apart; therefore, the last three groups had overlapping patches). This is similar to the networks used in [Baluja, 1997][Rowley et. al, 1998a, 1998b] for face detection. Unlike the convolution networks used by [Le Cun et al., 1990], the weights into the hidden units were not shared.[1] Note that many different local receptive field configurations were tried; almost all had equivalent performance.

3 Rotated Handwritten Digit Recognition

To create a complete rotationally invariant digit recognition system, the first step is to segment each digit from the background. The second is to recognize the digit which has been segmented. Many systems have been proposed for segmenting written digits from background clutter [Jain & Yu, 1997][Sato et al., 1998][Satoh & Kanade, 1997]. In this paper, we concentrate on the recognition portion of the task. Given a segmented image of a potentially rotated digit, how do we recognize the digit?

The first experiment conducted was to establish the base-line performance. We used only the standard, upright training set to train a classification network (this training set consists of 60,000 digits). This network was then tested on the testing set (the testing set contains 10,000 digits). In addition to measuring the performance on the upright testing set, the entire testing set was also rotated. As expected, performance rapidly degrades with rotation. A graph of the performance with respect to the rotation angle is shown in Figure 3.

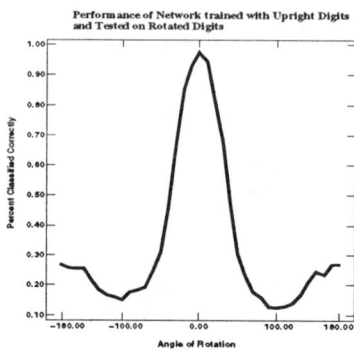

Figure 3: Performance of the classification network trained only with upright images when tested on rotated images. As the angle of rotation increases, performance degrades. Note the spike around 180 degrees, this is because some digits look the same even when they are upside-down. The peak performance is approximately 97.5% (when the digits are upright).

It is interesting to note that around 180° rotation, performance slightly rises. This is because some of the digits are symmetric across the center horizontal axis – for example the digits '8', '1', '2' & '5' can be recognized upside-down. Therefore, at these orientations, the upright detector works well for these digits.

As mentioned earlier, the simplest method to make an upright digit classifier handle rotations is to repeatedly rotate the input image and classify it at each rotation. The first drawback to this approach is the severe computational expense. The second drawback is that because the digit is examined at many rotations, it may appear similar to numerous digits in different orientations. One approach to avoid the latter problem is to classify the digit as the one that is voted for most often when examined over all rotations. To ensure that this process is not biased by the size of the increments by which the image is rotated, various angle increments are tried. As shown in the first row of Table I, this method yields low

Table I: Exhaustive Search over all possible rotations

Exhaustive Search Method	Number of Angle Increments Tried		
	360 (1 degree/increment)	100 (3.6 degree/increment)	50 (7.2 degrees/increment)
Most frequent vote (over all rotations)	59.5%	66.0%	65.0%
Most frequent vote – counted only when votes are positive (over all rotations)	75.2%	74.5%	74.0%

---

1. Note that in the empirical comparisons presented in [Le Cun et al., 1995a], convolution networks performed extremely well in the upright digit recognition task. However, due to limited computation resources, we were unable to train these networks, as each takes 14-20 days to train. The network used here was trained in 3 hours, and had approximately a 2.6% misclassification rate on the upright test set. The best networks reported in [Le Cun et al, 1995a] have less than 1% error. It should be noted that the De-Rotation networks trained in this study can easily be used in conjunction with any classification procedure, including convolutional networks.

classification accuracies. One reason for this is that a vote is counted even when the classification network predicts all outputs to be less than 0 (the network is trained to predict +1 when a digit is recognized, and -1 when it is not). The above experiment was repeated with the following modification: a vote was only counted when the maximum output of the classification network was above 0. The result is shown in the second row of Table I. The classification rate improved by more than 10%.

Given these base-line performance measures[2], we now have quantitative measurements with which to compare the effectiveness of the approach described in this paper. The performance of the procedure used here, with 10 "De-Rotation" networks and a single classification network, is shown in Figure 4. Note that unlike the graph shown in Figure 3, there is very little effect on the classification performance with the rotation angle.

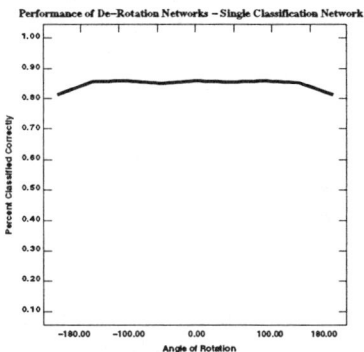

Figure 4: Performance of the combined De-Rotation network and classification network system proposed in this paper. Note that the performance is largely unaffected by the rotation. The average performance, over all rotations, is 85.0%.

To provide some intuition of how the De-Rotation networks perform, Figure 5 shows examples of how each De-Rotation networks transform each digit. Each De-Rotation network suggests a rotation which makes the digit look as much like the one with which the network was trained. For example, De-Rotation-Network-5 will suggest a rotation that will make the input digit look as much like the digit '5' as possible; for example, see De-Rotation-Network-5's effect on the digit '4'.

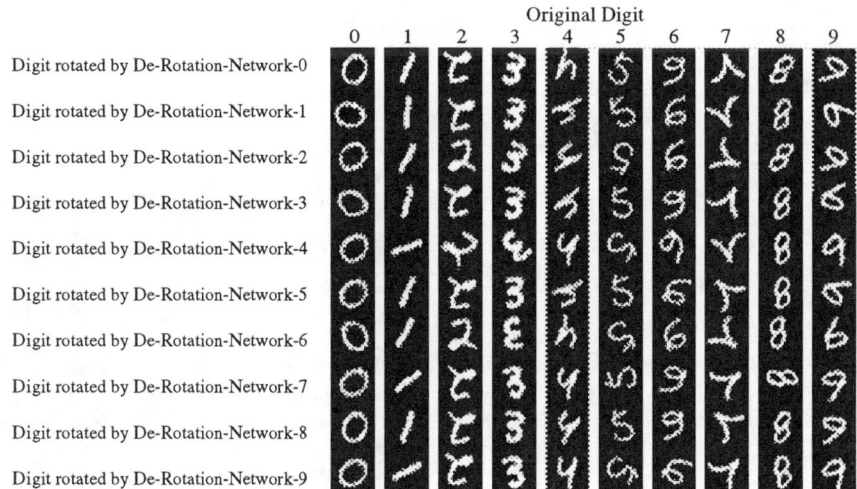

Figure 5: Digits which have been rotated by the angles specified by each of the De-rotation networks. As expected (if the method is working), the digits on the diagonal (upper left to bottom right) appear upright.

---

2. Another approach is to train a single network to handle both rotation and classification by using rotated digits as inputs, and the digit's classification as the target output. Experiments with the approach yielded results far below the techniques presented here.

As shown in Figure 4, the average classification accuracy is approximately 85.0%. The performance is not as good as with the upright case alone, which had a peak performance of approximately 97.5% (Figure 3). The high level of performance achieved in the upright case is unlikely for rotated digits: if all rotations are admissible, some characters are ambiguous. The problem is that when working correctly, De-Rotation-Network-*D* will suggest an angle of rotation that will make any input image look as much like the digit *D* as possible through rotation. In most cases when the input image is not the digit *D*, the rotation will not cause the image to look like *D*. However, in some cases, such as those shown in Figure 6(right), the digit will be transformed enough to cause a classification error. Some of these errors will most likely never be correctable (for example, '6' and '9' in some instances); however, there is hope for correcting some of the others.

Figure 6 presents the complete confusion matrix. As can be seen in the examples in Figure 6(right), the digit '4' can be rotated to appear similar to a '5'. Nonetheless, there often remain distinctive features that allow real '5's to be differentiated from the rotated '4's. However, the classification network is unable to make these distinctions because it was not trained with the appropriate examples. Remember, that since the classification network was only trained with the upright digit training set, rotated '4's are never encountered during training. This reflects a fundamental discrepancy in the training/testing procedure. The distributions of images which were used to train the classification network is different than the distributions on which the network is tested.

To address this problem, the classification mechanism is modified. Rather than using the single *1-of-10* neural network classifier used previously, 10 individual Detection networks are used. Each detection network has a single binary output that signifies whether the input contains the digit (upright) with which the network was trained. Each De-Rotation network is paired with the respective Detection network. *The crucial point is that rather than training the Detection-Network-D with the original upright images in the training set, each image (whether it is a positive or negative example) is first passed through De-Rotation-Network-D.* Although this makes training Detection-Network-*D* difficult since all the digits are rotated to appear as much like upright-*D*'s as possible by De-Rotation-Network-*D*, the distribution of training images matches the testing distribution more closely. In use, when a new image is presented, it is passed through the 10 network pairs. Candidate digits are eliminated if the binary output from the detection network does not signal a detection. Preliminary results with this new approach are extremely promising; the classification accuracy increases dramatically – to 93% when averaged over all rotations. This is a more than a 50% reduction in error over the previously described approach.

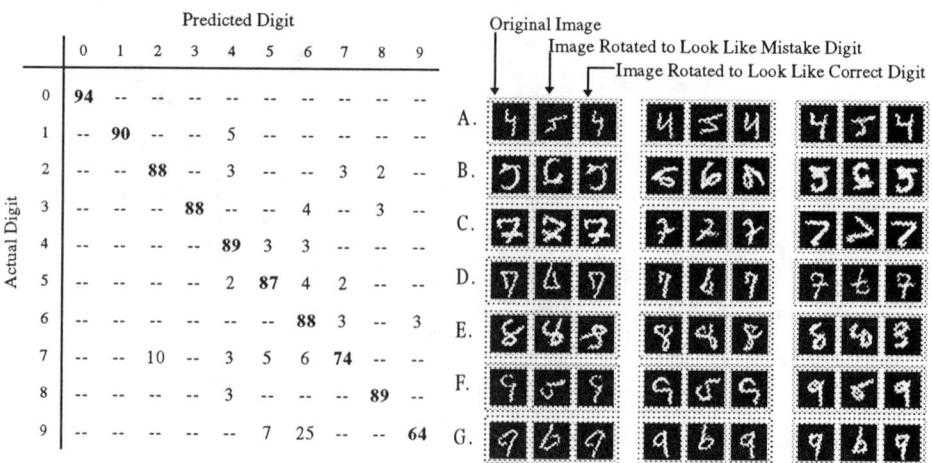

	Predicted Digit									
		0	1	2	3	4	5	6	7	8	9
Actual Digit	0	94	--	--	--	--	--	--	--	--	--
	1	--	90	--	--	5	--	--	--	--	--
	2	--	--	88	--	3	--	--	3	2	--
	3	--	--	--	88	--	--	4	--	3	--
	4	--	--	--	--	89	3	3	--	--	--
	5	--	--	--	--	2	87	4	2	--	--
	6	--	--	--	--	--	--	88	3	--	3
	7	--	--	10	--	3	5	6	74	--	--
	8	--	--	--	--	3	--	--	--	89	--
	9	--	--	--	--	--	7	25	--	--	64

Figure 6: Example errors. (LEFT) Confusion Matrix (only entries account for 2% or more entries are filled in for ease of reading). (RIGHT) some of the errors made in classification. 3 examples of each of the errors are shown. Row A: '4' mistaken as '5'. Row B: '5' mistaken as '6'. Row C: '7' mistaken as '2'. Row D: '7' mistaken as '6'. Row E: '8' mistaken as '4'. Row F: '9' mistaken as '5'. Row G: '9' mistaken as '6'.

4 Conclusions and Future Work

This paper has presented results on the difficult problem of rotated digit recognition. First, we presented base-line results with naive approaches such as exhaustively checking all rotations. These approaches are both slow and have large error rates. Second, we presented results with a novel two-stage approach which is both faster and more effective than the naive approaches. Finally, we presented preliminary results with a new approach that more closely models the training and testing distributions.

We have recently applied the techniques presented in this paper to the detection of faces in cluttered scenes. In previous studies, we presented methods for finding all upright frontal faces [Rowley et al., 1998a]. By using the techniques presented here, we were able to detect all frontal faces, including those which were rotated within the image plane [Baluja, 1997][Rowley et al., 1998b]. The methods presented in this paper should also be directly applicable to full alphabet rotated character recognition.

In this paper, we examined each digit individually. A straight-forward method to eliminate some of the ambiguities between rotationally similar digits is to use contextual information. For example, if surrounding digits are all rotated to the same amount, this provides strong hints about the rotation of nearby digits. Further, in most real-world cases, we might expect digits to be close to upright; therefore, one method of incorporating this information is to penalize matches which rely on large rotation angles.

This paper presented a general way to make template-based recognition rotation invariant. In this study, both the rotation estimation procedures and the recognition templates were implemented with neural-networks. Nonetheless, for classification, any technique which implements a form of templates, such as correlation templates, support vector machines, probabilistic networks, K-Nearest Neighbor, or principal component-based methods, could have easily been employed.

Acknowledgements

The author would like to thank Kaari Flagstad for her reviews of many successive drafts of this paper.

References

Baluja, S. (1997) "Face Detection with In-Plane Rotation: Early Concepts and Preliminary Results," Justsystem Pittsburgh Research Center Technical Report. JPRC-TR-97-001.

Guyon, I, Poujaud, I., Personnaz, L, Dreyfus, G., Denker, J. LeCun, Y. (1989) "Comparing Different Neural Net Architectures for Classifying Handwritten Digits", in *IJCNN II* 127-132.

Jain, A. & Yu, B. (1997) "Automatic Text Location in Images and Video Frames", TR: MSUCPS: TR 97-33.

Le Cun, Y., Jackel, D., Bottou, L, Cortes, C., Denker, J. Drucker, J. Guyon, I, Miller, U. Sackinger, E. Simard, P. Vapnik, V. (1995a) "Learning Algorithms for Classification: A Comparison on Handwritten Digit Recognition". *Neural Networks: The Statistical Mechanics Perspective*, Oh, J., Kwon, C. & Cho, S. (Ed.), pp. 261-276.

LeCun, Y., Jackel, L. D., Bottou, L., Brunot, A., Cortes, C., Denker, J. S., Drucker, H., Guyon, I., Muller, U. A., Sackinger, E., Simard, P. and Vapnik, V. (1995b), Comparison of learning algorithms for handwritten digit recognition," *ICANN*, Fogelman, F. and Gallinari, P., 1995, pp. 53-60.

LeCun, Y., Boser, B., Denker, J. S., Henderson, D., Howard, R. E., Hubbard, W. and Jackel, L. D. (1990), "Handwritten digit recognition with a back-propagation network," *Advances in Neural Information Processing Systems 2 (NIPS '89)*, Touretzky, David (Ed.), Morgan Kaufman.

Lee, Y. (1991) "Handwritten Digit Recognition using K-NN, RBF and Backpropagation Neural Networks", *Neural Computation*, 3, 3.

Pomerleau, D.A. (1993) *Neural Network Perception for Mobile Robot Guidance*, Kluwer Academic

Rowley, H., Baluja, S. & Kanade, T. (1998a) "Neural Network-Based Face Detection," *IEEE-Transactions on Pattern Analysis and Machine Intelligence (PAMI)*, Vol. 20, No. 1, January, 1998.

Rowley, H., Baluja, S. & Kanade, T. (1998b) "Rotation Invariant Neural Network-Based Face Detection," to appear in *Proceedings of Computer Vision and Pattern Recognition, 1998*.

Sato, T, Kanade, T., Hughes, E. & Smith, M. (1998) "Video OCR for Digital News Archives" to appear in *IEEE International Workshop on Content-Based Access of Image and Video Databases*.

Satoh, S. & Kanade, T. (1997) "Name-It: Association of face and name in Video", in *Proceedings of IEEE Conference on Computer Vision and Pattern Recognition, 1997*.

Probabilistic Modeling for Face Orientation Discrimination:
Learning from Labeled and Unlabeled Data

Shumeet Baluja
baluja@cs.cmu.edu
Justsystem Pittsburgh Research Center &
School of Computer Science, Carnegie Mellon University

Abstract

This paper presents probabilistic modeling methods to solve the problem of discriminating between five facial orientations with very little labeled data. Three models are explored. The first model maintains no inter-pixel dependencies, the second model is capable of modeling a set of arbitrary pair-wise dependencies, and the last model allows dependencies only between neighboring pixels. We show that for all three of these models, the accuracy of the learned models can be greatly improved by augmenting a small number of labeled training images with a large set of unlabeled images using Expectation-Maximization. This is important because it is often difficult to obtain image labels, while many unlabeled images are readily available. Through a large set of empirical tests, we examine the benefits of unlabeled data for each of the models. By using only two randomly selected labeled examples per class, we can discriminate between the five facial orientations with an accuracy of 94%; with six labeled examples, we achieve an accuracy of 98%.

1 Introduction

This paper examines probabilistic modeling techniques for discriminating between five face orientations: left profile, left semi-profile, frontal, right semi-profile, and right profile. Three models are explored: the first model represents no inter-pixel dependencies, the second model is capable of modeling a set of arbitrary pair-wise dependencies, and the last model allows dependencies only between neighboring pixels.

Models which capture inter-pixel dependencies can provide better classification performance than those that do not capture dependencies. The difficulty in using the more complex models, however, is that as more dependencies are modeled, more parameters must be estimated – which requires more training data. We show that by using Expectation-Maximization, the accuracy of what is learned can be greatly improved by augmenting a small number of labeled training images with unlabeled images, which are much easier to obtain.

The remainder of this section describes the problem of face orientation discrimination in detail. Section 2 provides a brief description of the probabilistic models explored. Section 3 presents results with these models with varying amounts of training data. Also shown is how Expectation-Maximization can be used to augment the limited labeled training data with unlabeled training data. Section 4 briefly discusses related work. Finally, Section 5 closes the paper with conclusions and suggestions for future work.

1.1 Detailed Problem Description

The interest in face orientation discrimination arises from two areas. First, the rapid increase in the availability of inexpensive cameras makes it practical to create systems which automatically monitor a person while using a computer. By using motion, color, and size cues, it is possible to quickly find and segment a person's face when he/she is sitting in front of a computer monitor. By determining whether the person is looking directly at the computer, or is staring away from the computer, we can provide feedback to any user interface that could benefit from knowing whether a user is paying attention or is distracted (such as computer-based tutoring systems for children, computer games, or even car-mounted cameras that monitor drivers).

Second, to perform accurate *face detection* for use in video-indexing or content-based image retrieval systems, one approach is to design detectors specific to each face orientation, such as [Rowley et al., 1998, Sung 1996]. Rather than applying all detectors to every location, a face-orientation system can be applied to each candidate face location to "route" the candidate to the appropriate detector, thereby reducing the potential for false-positives, and also reducing the computational cost of applying each detector. This approach was taken in [Rowley et al., 1998].

For the experiments in this paper, each image to be classified is 20x20 pixels. The face is centered in the image, and comprises most of the image. Sample faces are shown in Figure 1. Empirically, our experiments show that accurate pose discrimination is possible from binary versions of the images. First, the images were histogram-equalized to values between 0 and 255. This is a standard non-linear transformation that maps an approximately equal number of pixels to each value within the 0-255 range. It is used to improve the contrast in images. Second, to "binarize" the images, pixels with intensity above 128 were mapped to a value of 255, otherwise the pixels were mapped to a value of 0.

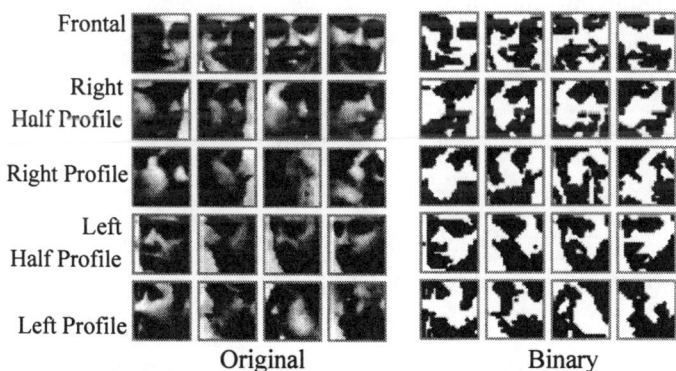

Figure 1: 4 images of each of the 5 classes to be discriminated. Note the variability in the images. **Left:** Original Images. **Right:** Images after histogram equalization and binary quantization.

2 Methods Explored

This section provides a description of the probabilistic models explored: Naive-Bayes, Dependency Trees (as proposed by [Chow and Liu, 1968]), and a dependence network which models dependencies only between neighboring pixels. For more details on using Bayesian "multinets" (independent networks trained to model each class) for classification in a manner very similar to that used in this paper, see [Friedman, et al., 1997].

2.1 The Naive-Bayes Model

The first, and simplest, model assumes that each pixel is independent of every other pixel. Although this assumption is clearly violated in real images, the model often yields good results with limited training data since it requires the estimation of the fewest parameters.

Assuming that each image belongs exclusively to one of the five face classes to be discriminated, the probability of the image belonging to a particular class is given as follows:

$$P(Class_c|Image) = \frac{P(Image|Class_c) \times P(Class_c)}{P(Image)} \qquad P(Image|Class_c) = \prod_{i=1}^{400} P(Pixel_i|Class_c)$$

$P(Pixel_i|Class_c)$ is estimated directly from the training data by:

$$P(Pixel_i|Class_c) = \frac{k + \sum_{TrainingImages} Pixel_i \times P(Class_c|Image)}{2k + \sum_{TrainingImages} P(Class_c|Image)}$$

Since we are only counting examples from the training images, $P(Class_c|Image)$ is known. The notation $P(Class_c|Image)$ is used to represent image labels because it is convenient for describing the counting process with both labeled and unlabeled data (this will be described in detail in Section 3). With the labeled data, $P(Class_c|Image) \in \{0,1\}$. Later, $P(Class_c|Image)$ may not be binary; instead, the probability mass may be divided between classes. $Pixel_i \in \{0,1\}$ since the images are binary. k is a smoothing constant, set to 0.001.

When used for classification, we compute the posterior probabilities and take the maximum, $C_{predicted}$, where: $C_{predicted} = \text{argmax}_c \ P(Class_c|Image) \cong P(Image|Class_c)$. For simplicity, $P(Class_c)$ is assumed equal for all c; $P(Image)$ is a normalization constant which can be ignored since we are only interested in finding the maximum posterior probability.

2.2 Optimal Pair-Wise Dependency Trees

We wish to model a probability distribution $P(X_1, ..., X_{400}|Class_c)$, where each X corresponds to a pixel in the image. Instead of assuming pixel independence, we restrict our model to the following form:

$$P(X_1...X_n|Class_c) = \prod_{i=1}^{n} P\left(X_i | \Pi_{X_i}, Class_c\right)$$

where Π_{X_i} is X_i's single "parent" variable. We require that there be no cycles in these "parent-of" relationships: formally, there must exist some permutation $m = (m_1, ..., m_n)$ of $(1, ..., n)$ such that $\left(\Pi_{X_i} = X_j\right) \Rightarrow m(i) < m(j)$ for all i. In other words, we restrict P' to factorizations representable by Bayesian networks in which each node (except the root) has one parent, *i.e.*, tree-shaped graphs.

A method for finding the optimal model within these restrictions is presented in [Chow and Liu, 1968]. A complete weighted graph G is created in which each variable X_i is represented by a corresponding vertex V_i, and in which the weight W_{ij} for the edge between vertices V_i and V_j is set to the mutual information $I(X_i, X_j)$ between X_i and X_j. The edges in the maximum spanning tree of G determine an optimal set of (n-1) conditional probabilities with which to construct a tree-based model of the original probability distribution.

We calculate the probabilities $P(X_i)$ and $P(X_i, X_j)$ directly from the dataset. From these, we calculate the mutual information, $I(X_i, X_j)$, between all pairs of variables X_i and X_j:

$$I(X_i, X_j) = \sum_{a,b} P(X_i = a, X_j = b) \cdot \log \frac{P(X_i = a, X_j = b)}{P(X_i = a) \cdot P(X_j = b)}$$

The maximum spanning tree minimizes the Kullback-Leibler divergence $D(P\|P')$ between

Probabilistic Modeling for Face Orientation Discrimination

the true and estimated distributions:

$$D(P \| P') = \sum_X P(X) \log \frac{P(X)}{P'(X)}$$

as shown in [Chow & Liu, 1968]. Among all distributions of the same form, this distribution maximizes the likelihood of the data when the data is a set of empirical observations drawn from any unknown distribution.

2.3 Local Dependency Models

Unlike the Dependency Trees presented in the previous section, the local dependency networks only model dependencies between adjacent pixels. The most obvious dependencies to model are each pixel's eight neighbors. The dependencies are shown graphically in Figure 2(left). The difficulty with the above representation is that two pixels may be dependent upon each other (if this above model was represented as a Bayesian network, it would contain cycles). Therefore, to avoid problems with circular dependencies, we use the following model instead. Each pixel is still connected to each of its eight neighbors; however, the arcs are directed such that the dependencies are acyclic. In this local dependence network, each pixel is only dependent on four of its neighbors: the three neighbors to the right and the one immediately below. The dependencies which are modeled are shown graphically in Figure 2 (right). The dependencies are:

$$P(Image | Class_c) = \prod_{i=1}^{400} P(Pixel_i | \Pi_{Pixel_i}, Class_c)$$

$$P(Pixel_{i,j} | \Pi_{Pixel_{i,j}}, Class_c) = P(Pixel_{i,j} | Pixel_{i+1,j}, Pixel_{i+1,j+1}, Pixel_{i+1,j-1}, Pixel_{i,j+1}, Class_c)$$

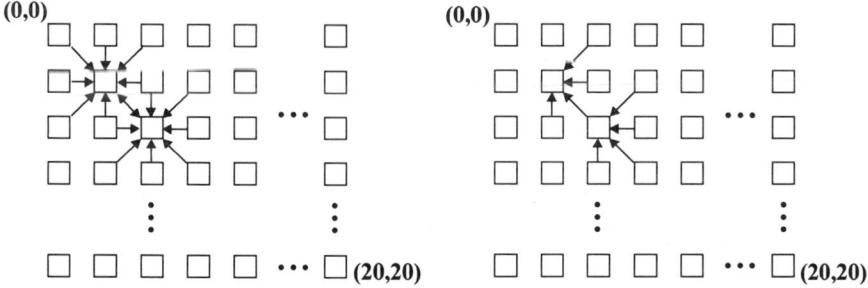

Figure 2: Diagram of the dependencies maintained. Each square represents a pixel in the image. Dependencies are shown only for two pixels. (Left) Model with 8 dependencies – note that because this model has circular dependencies, we do not use it. Instead, we use the model shown on the Right. (Right) Model used has 4 dependencies per pixel. By imposing an ordering on the pixels, circular dependencies are avoided.

3 Performance with Labeled and Unlabeled Data

In this section, we compare the results of the three probabilistic models with varying amounts of labeled training data. The training set consists of between 1 and 500 labeled training examples, and the testing set contains 5500 examples. Each experiment is repeated at least 20 times with random train/test splits of the data.

3.1 Using only Labeled Data

In this section, experiments are conducted with only labeled data. Figure 3(left) shows each model's accuracy in classifying the images in the test set into the five classes. As expected, as more training data is used, the performance improves for all models.

Note that the model with no-dependencies performs the best when there is little data. However, as the amount of data increases, the relative performance of this model, compared to the other models which account for dependencies, decreases. It is interesting to note that when there is little data, the Dependency Trees perform poorly. Since these trees can select dependencies between any two pixels, they are the most susceptible to finding spurious dependencies. However, as the amount of data increases, the performance of this model rapidly improves. By using all of the labeled data (500 examples total), the Dependency Tree and the Local-Dependence network perform approximately the same, achieving a correct classification rate of approximately 99%.

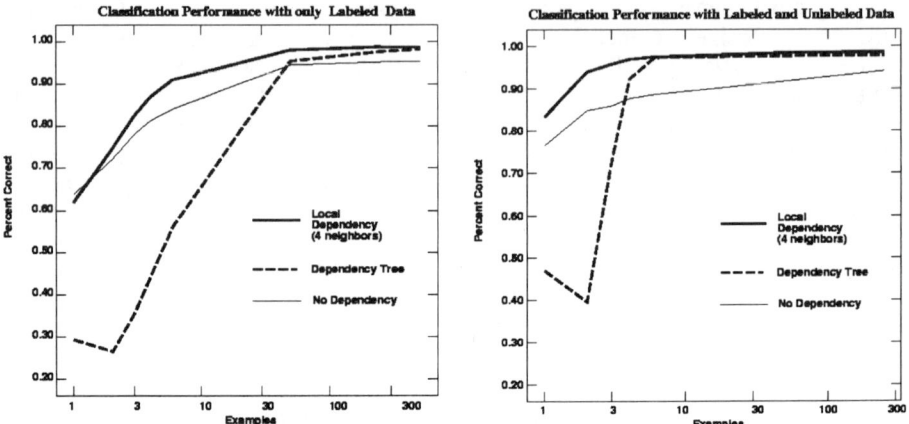

Figure 3: Performance of the three models. **X Axis:** Amount of labeled training data used. **Y Axis:** Percent correct on an independent test set. In the left graph, only labeled data was used. In the right graph, unlabeled and labeled data was used (the total number of examples were 500, with varying amounts of labeled data).

3.2 Augmenting the Models with Unlabeled Data

We can augment what is learned from only using the labeled examples by incorporating unlabeled examples through the use of the Expectation-Maximization (EM) algorithm. Although the details of EM are beyond the scope of this paper, the resulting algorithm is easily described (for a description of EM and applications to filling in missing values, see [Dempster et al., 1977] and [Ghahramani & Jordan, 1994]):

1. Build the models using only the labeled data (as in Section 2).

2. Use the models to probabilistically label the unlabeled images.

3. Using the images with the probabilistically assigned labels, and the images with the given labels, recalculate the models' parameters. As mentioned in section 2, for the images labeled by this process, $P(Class_c|Image)$ is **not** restricted to $\{0,1\}$; the probability mass for an image may be spread to multiple classes.

4. If a pre-specified termination condition is not met, go to step 2.

This process is used for each classifier. The termination condition was five iterations; after five iterations, there was little change in the models' parameters.

The performance of the three classifiers with unlabeled data is shown in Figure 3(right). Note that with small amounts of data, the performance of all of the classifiers improved dramatically when the unlabeled data is used. Figure 4 shows the percent improvement by using the unlabeled data to augment the labeled data. Note that the error is reduced by almost 90% with the use of unlabeled data (see the case with Dependency Trees with only 4 labeled examples, in which the accuracy rates increase from 44% to 92.5%). With only 50 labeled examples, a classification accuracy of 99% was obtained. This accuracy was obtained with almost an order of magnitude fewer labeled examples than required with classifiers which used only labeled examples.

In almost every case examined, the addition of unlabeled data helped performance. However, unlabeled data actually hurt the no-dependency model when a large amount of labeled data already existed. With large amounts of labeled data, the parameters of the model were estimated well. Incorporating unlabeled data may have hurt performance because the underlying generative process modeled did not match the real generative process. Therefore, the additional data provided may not have been labeled with the accuracy required to improve the model's classification performance. It is interesting to note that with the more complex models, such as the dependency trees or local dependence networks, even with the same amount of labeled data, unlabeled data improved performance. [Nigam, et al., 1998] have reported similar performance degradation when using a large number of labeled examples and EM with a naive-Bayesian model to classify text documents. They describe two methods for overcoming this problem. First, they adjust the relative weight of the labeled and unlabeled data in the M-step by using cross-validation. Second, they providing multiple centroids per class, which improves the data/model fit. Although not presented here due to space limitations, the first method was attempted – it improved the performance on the face orientation discrimination task.

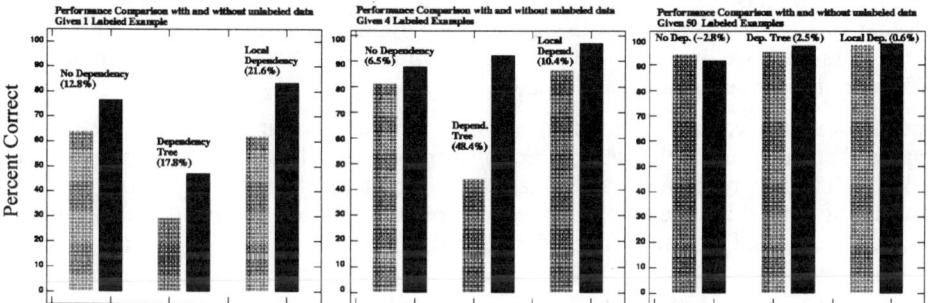

Figure 4: Improvement for each model by using unlabeled data to augment the labeled data. **Left:** with only 1 labeled example, **Middle:** 4 labeled, **Right:** 50 labeled. The bars in light gray represent the performance with only labeled data, the dark bars indicate the performance with the unlabeled data. The number in parentheses indicates the *absolute (in contrast to relative)* percentage change in classification performance with the use of unlabeled data.

4 Related Work

There is a large amount of work which attempts to discover attributes of faces, including (but not limited to) face detection, face expression discrimination, face recognition, and face orientation discrimination (for example [Rowley et al., 1998][Sung, 1996][Bartlett & Sejnowski, 1997][Cottrell & Metcalfe, 1991][Turk & Pentland, 1991]). The work presented in this paper demonstrates the effective incorporation of unlabeled data into image classification procedures; it should be possible to use unlabeled data in any of these tasks.

The closest related work is presented in [Nigam et al, 1998]. They used naive-Bayes methods to classify text documents into a pre-specified number of groups. By using unlabeled data, they achieve significant classification performance improvement over using labeled documents alone. Other work which has employed EM for learning from labeled and unlabeled data include [Miller and Uyar, 1997] who used a mixture of experts classifier, and [Shahshahani & Landgrebe, 1994] who used a mixture of Gaussians. However, the dimensionality of their input was at least an order of magnitude smaller than used here. There is a wealth of other related work, such as [Ghahramani & Jordan, 1994] who have used EM to fill in missing values in the training examples. In their work, class labels can be regarded as another feature value to fill-in.

Other approaches to reducing the need for large amounts of labeled data take the form of *active learning* in which the learner can ask for the labels of particular examples. [Cohn, et. al 1996] [McCallum & Nigam, 1998] provide good overviews of active learning.

5 Conclusions & Future Work

This paper has made two contributions. The first contribution is to solve the problem of discriminating between five face orientations with very little data. With only two labeled example images per class, we were able to obtain classification accuracies of 94% on separate test sets (with the local dependence networks with 4 parents). With only a few more examples, this was increased to greater than 98% accuracy. This task has a range of applications in the design of user-interfaces and user monitoring.

We also explored the use of multiple probabilistic models with unlabeled data. The models varied in their complexity, ranging from modeling no dependencies between pixels, to modeling four dependencies per pixel. While the no-dependency model performs well with very little labeled data, when given a large amount of labeled data, it is unable to match the performance of the other models presented. The Dependency-Tree models perform the worst when given small amounts of data because they are most susceptible to finding spurious dependencies in the data. The local dependency models performed the best overall, both by working well with little data, and by being able to exploit more data, whether labeled or unlabeled. By using EM to incorporate unlabeled data into the training of the classifiers, we improved the performance of the classifiers by up to approximately 90% when little labeled data was available.

The use of unlabeled data is vital in this domain. It is time-consuming to hand label many images, but many unlabeled images are often readily available. Because many similar tasks, such as face recognition and facial expression discrimination, suffer from the same problem of limited labeled data, we hope to apply the methods described in this paper to these applications. Preliminary results on related recognition tasks have been promising.

Acknowledgments

Scott Davies helped tremendously with discussions about modeling dependencies. I would also like to acknowledge the help of Andrew McCallum for discussions of EM, unlabeled data and the related work. Many thanks are given to Henry Rowley who graciously provided the data set. Finally, thanks are given to Kaari Flagstad for comments on drafts of this paper.

References

Bartlett, M. & Sejnowski, T. (1997) "Viewpoint Invariant Face Recognition using ICA and Attractor Networks", in *Adv. in Neural Information Processing Systems (NIPS) 9*.
Chow, C. & Liu, C. (1968) "Approximating Discrete Probability Distributions with Dependence Trees". *IEEE-Transactions on Information Theory*, 14: 462-467.
Cohn, D.A., Ghahramani, Z. & Jordan, M. (1996) "Active Learning with Statistical Models", *Journal of Artificial Intelligence Research* 4: 129-145.
Cottrell, G. & Metcalfe, (1991) "Face, Gender and Emotion Recognition using Holons", *NIPS 3*.
Dempster, A. P., Laird, N.M., Rubin, D.B. (1977) "Maximum Likelihood from Incomplete Data via the EM Algorithm", *J. Royal Statistical Society Series B*, 39 1-38.
Friedman, N., Geiger, D. Goldszmidt, M. (1997) "Bayesian Network Classifiers", *Machine Learning* 1:29.
Ghahramani & Jordan (1994) "Supervised Learning from Incomplete Data Via an EM Approach" *NIPS 6*.
McCallum, A. & Nigam, K. (1998) "Employing EM in Pool-Based Active Learning", in *ICML98*.
Miller, D. & Uyar, H. (1997) "A Mixture of Experts Classifier with Learning based on both Labeled and Unlabeled data", in *Adv. in Neural Information Processing Systems 9*.
Nigam, K. McCallum, A., Thrun, S., Mitchell, T. (1998), "Learning to Classify Text from Labeled and Unlabeled Examples", to appear in *AAAI-98*.
Rowley, H., Baluja, S. & Kanade, T. (1998) "Neural Network-Based Face Detection", *IEEE-Transactions on Pattern Analysis and Machine Intelligence (PAMI)*, Vol. 20, No. 1, January, 1998.
Shahshahani, B. & Landgrebe, D. (1994) "The Effect of Unlabeled samples in reducing the small sample size problem and mitigating the Hughes Phenomenon", *IEEE Trans. on Geosc. and Remote Sensing* 32.
Sung, K.K. (1996), *Learning and Example Selection for Object and Pattern Detection*, Ph.D. Thesis, MIT AI Lab - AI Memo 1572.
Turk, M. & Pentland, A. (1991) "Eigenfaces for Recognition". *J. Cog Neurosci.* 3 (1).

Adding Constrained Discontinuities to Gaussian Process Models of Wind Fields

Dan Cornford*   Ian T. Nabney   Christopher K. I. Williams[†]
Neural Computing Research Group
Aston University, BIRMINGHAM, B4 7ET, UK
d.cornford@aston.ac.uk

Abstract

Gaussian Processes provide good prior models for spatial data, but can be too smooth. In many physical situations there are discontinuities along bounding surfaces, for example fronts in near-surface wind fields. We describe a modelling method for such a constrained discontinuity and demonstrate how to infer the model parameters in wind fields with MCMC sampling.

1 INTRODUCTION

We introduce a model for wind fields based on Gaussian Processes (GPs) with 'constrained discontinuities'. GPs provide a flexible framework for modelling various systems. They have been adopted in the neural network community and are interpreted as placing priors over functions.

Stationary vector-valued GP models (Daley, 1991) can produce realistic wind fields when run as a generative model; however, the resulting wind fields do not contain some features typical of the atmosphere. The most difficult features to include are surface fronts. Fronts are generated by complex atmospheric dynamics and are marked by large changes in the surface wind direction (see for example Figures 2a and 3b) and temperature. In order to account for such features, which appear discontinuous at our observation scale, we have developed a model for vector-valued GPs with constrained discontinuities which could also be applied to surface reconstruction in computer vision, and geostatistics.

In section 2 we illustrate the generative model for wind fields with fronts. Section 3 explains what we mean by GPs with constrained discontinuities and derives the likelihood of data under the model. Results of Bayesian estimation of the model parameters are given,

---

*To whom correspondence should be addressed.

[†]Now at: Division of Informatics, University of Edinburgh, 5 Forrest Hill, Edinburgh EH1 2QL, Scotland, UK

using a Markov Chain Monte Carlo (MCMC) procedure. In the final section, the strengths and weaknesses of the model are discussed and improvements suggested.

2 A GENERATIVE WIND FIELD MODEL

We are primarily interested in retrieving wind fields from satellite scatterometer observations of the ocean surface[1]. A probabilistic prior model for wind fields will be used in a Bayesian procedure to resolve ambiguities in local predictions of wind direction. The generative model for a wind field including a front is taken to be a combination of two vector-valued GPs with a constrained discontinuity.

A common method for representing wind fields is to put GP priors over the velocity potential Φ and stream function Ψ, assuming the processes are uncorrelated (Daley, 1991). The horizontal wind vector $\bm{u} = (u, v)$ can then be derived from:

$$u = -\frac{\partial \Psi}{\partial y} + \frac{\partial \Phi}{\partial x}, \qquad v = \frac{\partial \Psi}{\partial x} + \frac{\partial \Phi}{\partial y}. \tag{1}$$

This produces good prior models for wind fields when a suitable choice of covariance function for Φ and Ψ is made. We have investigated using a modified Bessel function based covariance[2] (Handcock and Wallis, 1994) but found, using three years of wind data for the North Atlantic, that the maximum *a posteriori* value for the smoothness parameter[3] in this covariance function was ~ 2.5. Thus we used the correlation function:

$$\rho(r) = \left(1 + \frac{r}{L} + \frac{r^2}{3L^2}\right) \exp\left(-\frac{r}{L}\right) \tag{2}$$

where L is the correlation length scale, which is equivalent to the modified Bessel function and less computationally demanding (Cornford, 1998).

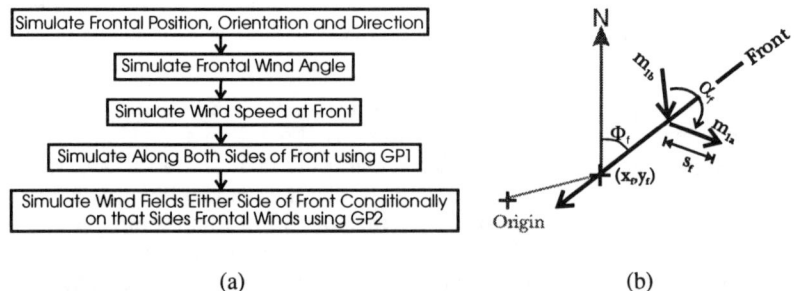

Figure 1: (a) Flowchart describing the generative frontal model. See text for full description. (b) A description of the frontal model.

The generative model has the form outlined in Figure 1a. Initially the frontal position and orientation are simulated. They are defined by the angle clockwise from north (ϕ_f) that the front makes and a point on the line (x_f, y_f). Having defined the position of the front,

---

[1] See http://www.ncrg.aston.ac.uk/Projects/NEUROSAT/NEUROSAT.html for details of the scatterometer work. Technical reports describing, in more detail, methods for generating prior wind field models can also be accessed from the same page.

[2] The modified Bessel function allows us to control the differentiability of the sample realisations through the 'smoothness parameter', as well as the length scales and variances.

[3] This varies with season, but is the most temporally stable parameter in the covariance function.

the angle of the wind across the front (α_f) is simulated from a distribution covering the range $[0, \pi)$. This angle is related to the vertical component of vorticity (ζ) across the front through $\zeta = k \cdot \nabla \times u \propto \cos\left(\frac{\alpha_f}{2}\right)$ and the constraint $\alpha_f \in [0, \pi)$ ensures cyclonic vorticity at the front. It is assumed that the front bisects α_f. The wind speed (s_f) is then simulated at the front. Since there is generally little change in wind speed across the front, one value is simulated for both sides of the front. These components $\theta_f = (\phi_f, x_f, y_f, \alpha_f, s_f)$ define the line of the front and the mean wind vectors just ahead of and just behind the front (Figure 1b):

$$m_{1a} = (u_{1a}^m, v_{1a}^m) = \left(s_f \sin\left(\phi_f + \frac{\alpha_f}{2}\right), s_f \cos\left(\phi_f + \frac{\alpha_f}{2}\right)\right) \quad (3)$$

$$m_{1b} = (u_{1b}^m, v_{1b}^m) = \left(-s_f \sin\left(\phi_f - \frac{\alpha_f}{2}\right), -s_f \cos\left(\phi_f - \frac{\alpha_f}{2}\right)\right) \quad (4)$$

A realistic model requires some variability in wind vectors along the front. Thus we use a GP with a non-zero mean (m_{1a} or m_{1b}) along the line of the front. In the real atmosphere we observe a smaller variability in the wind vectors along the line of the front compared with regions away from fronts. Thus we use different GP parameters along the front (GP_1), from those used in the wind field away from the front (GP_2), although the same GP_1 parameters are used both sides of the front, just with different means. The winds just ahead of and behind the front are assumed conditionally independent given m_{1a} and m_{1b}, and are simulated at a regular $50\ km$ spacing. The final step in the generative model is to simulate wind vectors using GP_2 in both regions either side of the front, conditionally on the values along that side of the front. This model is flexible enough to represent fronts, yet has the required constraints derived from meteorological principles, for example that fronts should always be associated with cyclonic vorticity and that discontinuities at the model scale should be in wind direction but not in wind speed[4]. To make this generative model useful for inference, we need to be able to compute the data likelihood, which is the subject of the next section.

3 GPs WITH CONSTRAINED DISCONTINUITIES

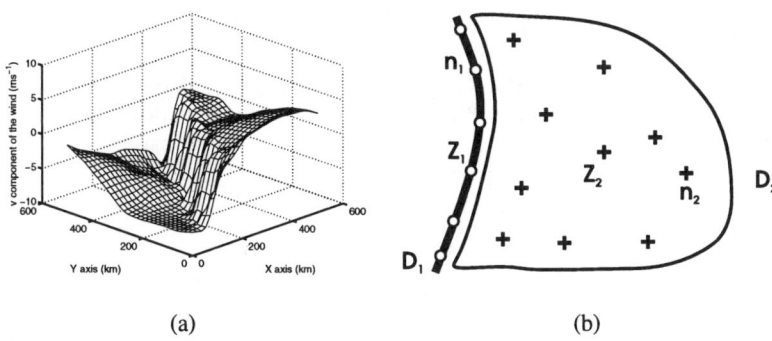

(a)   (b)

Figure 2: (a) The discontinuity in one of the vector components in a simulation. (b) Framework for GPs with boundary conditions. The curve D_1 has n_1 sample points with values Z_1. The domain D_2 has n_2 points with values Z_2.

---

[4]The model allows small discontinuities in wind speed, which are consistent with frontal dynamics.

We consider data from two domains D_1 and D_2 (Figure 2b), where in this case D_1 is a curve in the plane which is intended to be the front and D_2 is a region of the plane. We obtain n_1 variables Z_1 at points x_1 along the curve, and we assume these are generated under GP_1 (a GP which depends on parameters θ_1 and has mean $m_1 = m_1 \mathbf{1}$ which will be determined by (3) or (4)). We are interested in determining the likelihood of the variables Z_2 observed at n_2 points x_2 under GP_2 which depends on parameters θ_2, conditioned on the 'constrained discontinuities' at the front.

We evaluate this by calculating the likelihood of Z_2 conditioned on the n_1 values of Z_1 from GP_1 along the front and marginalising out Z_1:

$$p(Z_2|\theta_2,\theta_1) = \int_{-\infty}^{\infty} p(Z_2|Z_1,\theta_2,\theta_1,m_1) p(Z_1|\theta_1,m_1) \, dZ_1. \tag{5}$$

From the definition of the likelihood of a GP (Cressie, 1993) we find:

$$p(Z_2|Z_1,\theta_2,\theta_1,m_1) = \frac{1}{(2\pi)^{\frac{n_2}{2}} |S_{22}|^{\frac{1}{2}}} \exp\left(-\frac{1}{2} Z_2^{*\prime} S_{22}^{-1} Z_2^*\right) \tag{6}$$

where:

$$S_{22} = K_{22|2} - K'_{12|2} K_{11|2}^{-1} K_{12|2}, \qquad Z_2^* = Z_2 - K'_{12|2} K_{11|2}^{-1} Z_1.$$

To understand the notation consider the joint distribution of Z_1, Z_2 and in particular its covariance matrix:

$$K = \begin{bmatrix} K_{11|2} & K_{12|2} \\ K_{21|2} & K_{22|2} \end{bmatrix} \tag{7}$$

where $K_{11|2}$ is the $n_1 \times n_1$ covariance matrix between the points in D_1 evaluated using θ_2, $K_{12|2} = K'_{21|2}$ the $n_1 \times n_2$ (cross) covariance matrix between the points in D_1 and D_2 evaluated using θ_2 and $K_{22|2}$ is the usual $n_2 \times n_2$ covariance for points in D_2. Thus we can see that S_{22} is the $n_2 \times n_2$ modified covariance for the points in D_2 given the points along D_1, while the Z_2^* is the corrected mean that accounts for the values at the points in D_1, which have non-zero mean.

We remove the dependency on the values Z_1 by evaluating the integral in (5). $p(Z_1|\theta_1,m_1)$ is given by:

$$p(Z_1|\theta_1,m_1) = \frac{1}{(2\pi)^{\frac{n_1}{2}} |K_{11|1}|^{\frac{1}{2}}} \exp\left(-\frac{1}{2} (Z_1 - m_1)' K_{11|1}^{-1} (Z_1 - m_1)\right) \tag{8}$$

where $K_{11|1}$ is the $n_1 \times n_1$ covariance matrix between the points in D_1 evaluated under the covariance given by θ_1. Completing the square in Z_1 in the exponent, the integral (5) can be evaluated to give:

$$p(Z_2|\theta_2,\theta_1,m_1) = \frac{1}{(2\pi)^{\frac{n_2}{2}}} \frac{1}{|S_{22}|^{\frac{1}{2}}} \frac{1}{|K_{11|1}|^{\frac{1}{2}}} \frac{1}{|B|^{\frac{1}{2}}} \times \tag{9}$$

$$\exp\left(\frac{1}{2}\left(C' B^{-1} C - Z_2' S_{22}^{-1} Z_2 - m_1' K_{11|1}^{-1} m_1\right)\right)$$

where:

$$B = (K'_{12|2} K_{11|2}^{-1})' S_{22}^{-1} K'_{12|2} K_{11|2}^{-1} + K_{11|1}^{-1}$$
$$C' = Z_2' S_{22}^{-1} K'_{12|2} K_{11|2}^{-1} + m_1' K_{11|1}^{-1}$$

The algorithm has been coded in MATLAB and can deal with reasonably large numbers of points quickly. For a two dimensional vector-valued GP with $n_1 = 12$ and $n_2 = 200$ [5] and

---

[5]This is equivalent to $n_1 = 24$ and $n_2 = 400$ for a scalar GP.

a covariance function given by (2), computation of the log likelihood takes 4.13 seconds on an SGI Indy R5000.

The mean value just ahead and behind the front define the mean values for the constrained discontinuity (i.e. m_1 in (9)). Conditional on the frontal parameters the wind fields either side (Figure 3a) are assumed independent:

$$p(Z_{2a}, Z_{2b}|\theta_2, \theta_1, \theta_f) = p(Z_{2a}|\theta_2, \theta_1, m_{1a})p(m_{1a}|\theta_f) \times$$
$$p(Z_{2b}|\theta_2, \theta_1, m_{1b})p(m_{1b}|\theta_f)$$

where we have performed the integration (5) to remove the dependency on Z_{1a} and Z_{1b}. Thus the likelihood of the data $Z_2 = (Z_{2a}, Z_{2b})$ given the model parameters $\theta_2, \theta_1, \theta_f$ is simply the product of the likelihoods of two GPs with a constrained discontinuity which can be computed using (9).

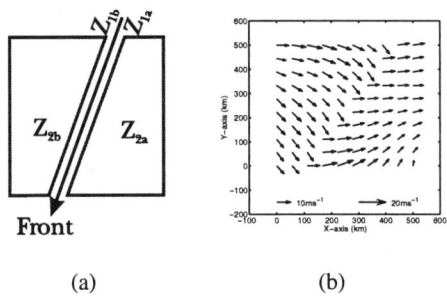

(a) (b)

Figure 3: (a) The division of the wind field using the generative frontal model. Z_{1a}, Z_{1b} are the wind fields just ahead and behind the front, along its length, respectively. Z_{2a}, Z_{2b} are the wind fields in the regions ahead of and behind the front respectively. (b) An example from the generative frontal model: the wind field looks like a typical 'cold front'.

The model outlined above was tested on simulated data generated from the model to assess parameter sensitivity. We generated a wind field $Z^o = (Z^o_{2a}, Z^o_{2b})$ using known model parameters (e.g. Figure 3b). We then sampled the model parameters from the posterior distribution:

$$p(\theta_2, \theta_1, \theta_f|Z^o) \propto p(Z^o|\theta_2, \theta_1, \theta_f)p(\theta_2)p(\theta_1)p(\theta_f) \qquad (10)$$

where $p(\theta_2), p(\theta_1), p(\theta_f)$ are prior distributions over the parameters in the GPs and front models. This brings out one advantage of the proposed model. All the model parameters have a physical interpretation and thus expert knowledge was used to set priors which produce realistic wind fields. We will also use (10) to help set (hyper)priors using real data in Z^o.

MCMC using the Metropolis algorithm (Neal, 1993) is used to sample from (10) using the NETLAB[6] library. Convergence of the Markov chain is currently assessed using visual inspection of the univariate sample paths since the generating parameters are known, although other diagnostics could be used (Cowles and Carlin, 1996). We find that the procedure is insensitive to the initial value of the GP parameters, but that the parameters describing the location of the front (ϕ_f, d_f) need to be initialised 'close' to the correct values if the chain is to converge on a reasonable time-scale. In the application some preliminary analysis of the wind field would be necessary to identify possible fronts and thus set the initial parameters to 'sensible' values. We intend to fit a vector-valued GP without any discontinuities

---

[6] Available from http://www.ncrg.aston.ac.uk/netlab/index.html.

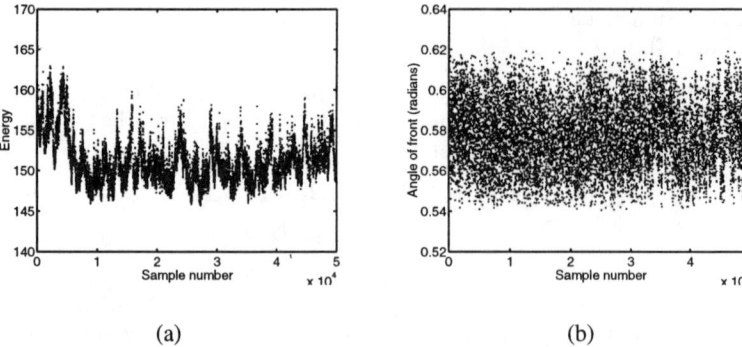

Figure 4: Examples from the Markov chain of the posterior distribution (10). (a) The energy = negative log posterior probability. Note that the energy when the chain was initialised was 2789 and the first 27 values are outside the range of the y-axis. (b) The angle of the front relative to north (ϕ_f).

and then measure the 'strain' or misfit of the locally predicted winds with the winds fitted by the GP. Lines of large 'strain' will be used to initialise the front parameters.

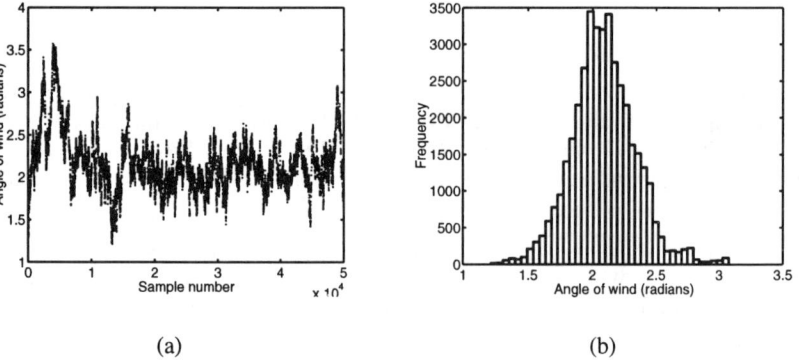

Figure 5: Examples from the Markov chain of the posterior distribution (10). (a) The angle of the wind across the front (α_f). (b) Histogram of the posterior distribution of α_f allowing a 10000 iteration burn-in period.

Examples of samples from the Markov chain from the simulated wind field shown in Figure 3a can be seen in Figures 4 and 5. Figure 4a shows that the energy level (= negative log posterior probability) falls very rapidly to near its minimum value from its large starting value of 2789. In these plots the true parameters for the front were $\phi_f = 0.555, \alpha_f = 2.125$ while the initial values were set at $\phi_f = 0.89, \alpha_f = 1.49$. Other parameters were also incorrectly set. The Metropolis algorithm seems to be able to find the minimum and then stays in it.

Figure 4b and 5a show the Markov chains for ϕ_f and α_f. Both converge quickly to an apparently stationary distributions, which have mean values very close to the 'true' generating parameters. The histogram of the distribution of α_f is shown in Figure 5b.

4 DISCUSSION AND CONCLUSIONS

Simulations from our model are meteorologically plausible wind fields which contain fronts. It is possible similar models could usefully be applied to other modelling problems where there are discontinuities with known properties. A method for the computation of the likelihood of data given two GP models, one with non-zero mean on the boundary and another in the domain in which the data is observed, has been given. This allows us to perform inference on the parameters in the frontal model using a Bayesian approach of sampling from the posterior distribution using a MCMC algorithm.

There are several weaknesses in the model specifically for fronts, which could be improved with further work. Real atmospheric fronts are not straight, thus the model would be improved by allowing 'curved' fronts. We could represent the position of the front, oriented along the angle defined by ϕ_f using either another smooth GP, B-splines or possibly polynomials.

Currently the points along the line of the front are simulated at the mean observation spacing in the rest of the wind field ($\sim 50\ km$). Interesting questions remain about the (in-fill) asymptotics (Cressie, 1993) as the distance between the points along the front tends to zero. Empirical evidence suggests that as long as the spacing along the front is 'much less' than the length scale of the GP along the front (which is typically $\sim 1000\ km$) then the spacing does not significantly affect the results.

Although we currently use a Metropolis algorithm for sampling from the Markov chain, the derivative of (9) with respect to the GP parameters $\boldsymbol{\theta_1}$ and $\boldsymbol{\theta_2}$ could be computed analytically and used in a hybrid Monte Carlo procedure (Neal, 1993).

These improvements should lead to a relatively robust procedure for putting priors over wind fields which will be used with real data when retrieving wind vectors from scatterometer observations over the ocean.

Acknowledgements

This work was partially supported by the European Union funded NEUROSAT programme (grant number ENV4 CT96-0314) and also EPSRC grant GR/L03088 *Combining Spatially Distributed Predictions from Neural Networks*.

References

Cornford, D. 1998. Flexible Gaussian Process Wind Field Models. Technical Report NCRG/98/017, Neural Computing Research Group, Aston University, Aston Triangle, Birmingham, UK.

Cowles, M. K. and B. P. Carlin 1996. Markov-Chain Monte-Carlo Convergence Diagnostics—A Comparative Review. *Journal of the American Statistical Association* **91**, 883–904.

Cressie, N. A. C. 1993. *Statistics for Spatial Data*. New York: John Wiley and Sons.

Daley, R. 1991. *Atmospheric Data Analysis*. Cambridge: Cambridge University Press.

Handcock, M. S. and J. R. Wallis 1994. An Approach to Statistical Spatio-Temporal Modelling of Meteorological Fields. *Journal of the American Statistical Association* **89**, 368–378.

Neal, R. M. 1993. Probabilistic Inference Using Markov Chain Monte Carlo Methods. Technical Report CRG-TR-93-1, Department of Computer Science, University of Toronto. URL: http://www.cs.utoronto.ca/~radford.

Vertex Identification in High Energy Physics Experiments

Gideon Dror[*]
Department of Computer Science
The Academic College of Tel-Aviv-Yaffo, Tel Aviv 64044, Israel

Halina Abramowicz[†] **David Horn**[‡]
School of Physics and Astronomy
Raymond and Beverly Sackler Faculty of Exact Sciences
Tel-Aviv University, Tel Aviv 69978, Israel

Abstract

In High Energy Physics experiments one has to sort through a high flux of events, at a rate of tens of MHz, and select the few that are of interest. One of the key factors in making this decision is the location of the vertex where the interaction, that led to the event, took place. Here we present a novel solution to the problem of finding the location of the vertex, based on two feedforward neural networks with fixed architectures, whose parameters are chosen so as to obtain a high accuracy. The system is tested on simulated data sets, and is shown to perform better than conventional algorithms.

1 Introduction

An event in High Energy Physics (HEP) is the experimental result of an interaction during the collision of particles in an accelerator. The result of this interaction is the production of tens of particles, each of which is ejected in a different direction and energy. Due to the quantum mechanical effects involved, the events differ from one another in the number of particles produced, the types of particles, and their energies. The trajectories of produced particles are detected by a very large and sophisticated detector.

---

[*]gideon@server.mta.ac.il
[†]halina@post.tau.ac.il
[‡]horn@neuron.tau.ac.il

Vertex Identification in High Energy Physics Experiments

Events are typically produced at a rate of 10 MHz, in conjunction with a data volume of up to 500 kBytes per event. The signal is very small, and is selected from the background by multilevel triggers that perform filtering either through hardware or software. In the present paper we confront one problem that is of interest in these experiments and is part of the triggering consideration. This is the location of the vertex of the interaction. To be specific we will use a simulation of data collected by the central tracking detector [1] of the ZEUS experiment [2] at the HEP laboratory DESY in Hamburg, Germany. This detector, placed in a magnetic field, surrounds the interaction point and is sensitive to the path of charged particles. It has a cylindrical shape around the axis, z, where the interaction between the incoming particles takes place. The challenge is to find an efficient and fast method to extract the exact location of the vertex along this axis.

2 The Input Data

An example of an event, projected onto the $z = 0$ plane, is shown in Figure 1. Only the information relevant to triggering is used and displayed. The relevant points, which denote hits by the outgoing particles on wires in the detector, form five rings due to the concentric structure of the detector. Several slightly curved particle tracks emanating from the origin, which is marked with a + sign, and crossing all five rings, can easily be seen. Each track is made of 30-40 data points. All tracks appear in this projection as arcs, and indeed, when viewed in 3 dimensions, every particle follows a helical trajectory due to the solenoidal magnetic field in the detector.

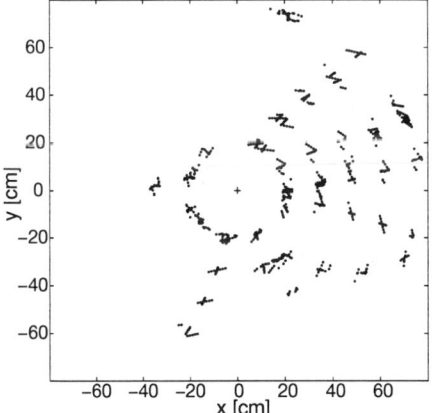

Figure 1: A typical event projected onto the $z = 0$ plane. The dots, or hits, have a two-fold ambiguity in the determination of the xy coordinates through which the particle has moved. The correct solutions lie on curved tracks that emanate from the origin.

Each physical hit is represented twice in Fig. 1 due to an inherent two-fold ambiguity in the determination of its xy coordinates. The correct solutions form curved tracks emanating from the origin. Some of those can be readily seen in the data. Due to the limited time available for decision making at the trigger level, the z coordinate is obtained from the difference in arrival times of a pulse at both ends of the CTD and is available for only a fraction of these points. The hit resolution in xy is $\sim 230\,\mu\text{m}$, while that of z-by-timing is $\simeq 4\,\text{cm}$. The quality of the z coordinate information is exemplified in figure 2. Figure 2(a) shows points forming a track of a single particle on the $z = 0$ projection. Since the corresponding track forms a helix with small curvature, one expects a linear dependence of the z coordinate of the hits on their radial position, $r = \sqrt{x^2 + y^2}$. Figure 2(b) compares the values of r with the measured z values for these points. The scatter of the data around the linear regression fit is considerable.

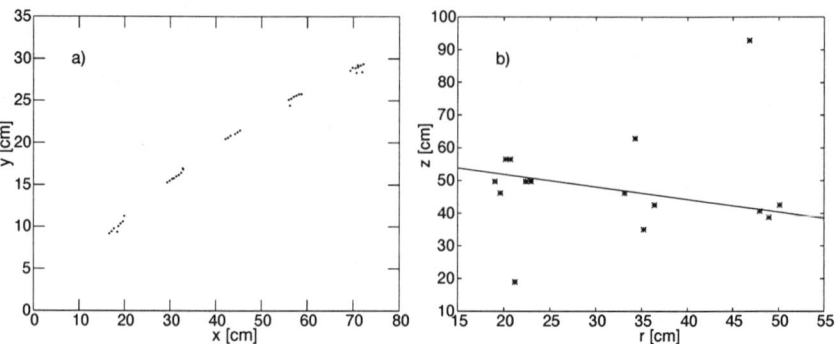

Figure 2: A typical example of uncertainties in the measured z values: (a) a single track taken from the event shown in figure 1, (b) the z coordinate vs $r = \sqrt{x^2 + y^2}$ the distance from the z axis for the data points shown in (a). The full line is a linear regression fit.

3 The Network

Our network is based on step-wise changes in the representation of the data, moving from the input points, to local line segments and to global arcs. The nature of the data and the problem suggest it is best to separate the treatment of the xy coordinates from that of the z coordinate. Two parallel networks which perform entirely different computations, form our final system. The first network, which handles the xy information is responsible for constructing arcs that correctly identify some of the particle tracks in the event. The second network uses this information to evaluate the z location of the point where all tracks meet.

3.1 Arc Identification Network

The arc identification network processes information in a fashion akin to the method visual information is processed by the primary visual system [3].

The input layer for this network is made of a large number of neurons (several tens of thousands) and corresponds to the function of the retina. Each input neuron has its distinct receptive field. The sum of all fields covers completely the relevant domain in the xy plane. This domain has 5 concentric rings, which show up in figure 1. The total area of the rings is about 5000 cm^2, and covering it with 100000 input neurons leads to satisfactory resolution. A neuron in the input level fires when a hit is present in its receptive field. We shall label each input neuron by the (xy) coordinates of the center of its receptive field.

Neurons of the second layer are line segment detectors. Each second layer neuron is labeled by $(XY\alpha)$, where (X,Y) are the coordinates of the center of the segment and α denotes its orientation. The activation of second layer neurons is given by

$$V_{XY\alpha} = g(\sum_{xy} J_{XY\alpha,xy} V_{xy} - \theta_2),\tag{1}$$

where

$$J_{XY\alpha,xy} = \begin{cases} 1 & \text{if } r_\perp < 0.5\,\text{cm} \wedge r_\parallel < 2\,\text{cm} \\ -1 & \text{if } 0.5\,\text{cm} < r_\perp < 1\,\text{cm} \wedge r_\parallel < 2\,\text{cm} \\ 0 & \text{otherwise} \end{cases}\tag{2}$$

and $g(x)$ is the standard Heaviside step function. $r_\parallel$ and $r_\perp$ are the parallel and perpendicular distances between (X,Y) and (x,y) with respect to the axis of the line segment, defined by α. It is important to note that at this level, values of the threshold θ_2 which are slightly lower than optimum are preferable, taking the risk of obtaining superfluous line segments in order to reduce the probability of missing one. Superfluous line segments are filtered out very efficiently in higher layers.

Figure 3 represents the output of the second layer neurons for the input illustrated by the event of figure 1. An active second layer neuron $(XY\alpha)$ is represented in this figure by a line segment centered at the point (X,Y) making an angle α with the x axis. The length of the line segments is immaterial and was chosen only for the purpose of visual clarity.

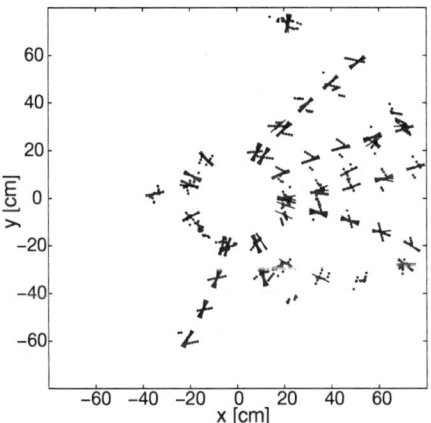

Figure 3: Representation of the activity of second layer neurons $XY\alpha$ for the input of figure 1 taken by plotting the appropriate line segments in the xy plane. At some XY locations several line segments with different directions occur due to the rather low threshold parameter used, $\theta_2 = 4$.

Neurons of the third layer transform the representation of local line segments into local arc segments. An arc which passes through the origin is uniquely defined by its radius of curvature R and its slope at the origin. Thus, each third layer neuron is labeled by $\kappa\,\theta\,i$, where $|\kappa| = 1/R$ is the curvature and the sign of κ determines the orientation of the arc. $1 \leq i \leq 5$ is an index which relates each arc segment to the ring it belongs to.

The mapping between second and third layers is based on a winner-take-all mechanism. Namely, for a given local arc segment, we take the arc segment which is closest to being tangent to the local arc segment.

Denoting the average radius of the ring i (i=1,2,...5) by r_i and using $\beta_i = \sin^{-1}(\frac{\kappa r_i}{2})$

the final expression for the activation of the third layer neurons is

$$V_{\kappa\theta i} = \max_{\delta<3} e^{-\delta^2} \cos^2(\theta - 2\beta_i - \alpha), \qquad (3)$$

where $\delta = \delta(X, Y, \kappa, \theta, i) = \sqrt{(X - r_i \cos(\theta - \beta_i))^2 + (Y - r_i \sin(\theta - \beta_i))^2}$ is simply the distance of the center of the receptive field of the $(XY\alpha)$ neuron to the $(\kappa\theta)$ arc.

The fourth layer is the last one in the arc identification network. Neurons belonging to this layer are global arc detectors. In other words, they detect projected tracks on the $z = 0$ plane. A fourth level neuron is denoted by $\kappa\theta$, where κ and θ have the previous meaning, now describing global arcs. Fourth layer neurons are connected to third layer neurons in a simple fashion,

$$V_{\kappa\theta} = g(\sum_{\kappa'\theta'i} \delta_{\kappa,\kappa'} \delta_{\theta,\theta'} V_{\kappa'\theta'i} - \theta_4). \qquad (4)$$

Figure 4 represents the activity of fourth layer neurons. Each active neuron $\kappa\theta$ is equivalent in the xy plane to one arc appearing in the figure.

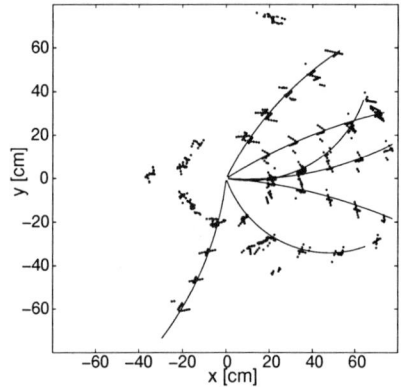

Figure 4: Representation of the activity of fourth layer neurons $\kappa\theta$ for the input of figure 1 taken by plotting the appropriate arcs in the xy plane. The arcs are not precisely congruent to the activity of the input layer which is also shown, due to the finite widths which were used, $\Delta\kappa = 0.004$ and $\Delta\theta = \pi/20$. This figure was produced with $\theta_4 = 3$.

3.2 z Location Network

The architecture of the second network has a structure which is identical to the first one, although its computational task is different. We will use an identical labeling system for its neurons, but denote their activities by v_{xy}. The latter will assume continuous values in this network.

A first layer neuron of the z-location network receives its input from the same receptive field as its corresponding neuron in the first network. Its value, v_{xy}, is the mean value of the z values of the points within its receptive field. If no z values are available for these points, a null value is assigned to it.

The second layer neurons compute the mean value $v_{XY\alpha} = \langle v_{xy} \rangle$ of the z coordinate of the first layer neurons in their receptive field, averaging over all neurons within

the section
$$\{xy \,|\, |(x-X)\sin\alpha - (y-Y)\cos\alpha| < 0.5\,\text{cm} \wedge (x-X)^2 + (y-Y)^2 < 4\,\text{cm}^2\}\,,$$
which corresponds to the excitatory part of the synaptic connections of equation (2). If null values appear within that section they are disregarded by the averaging procedure. If all values are null, $v_{XY\alpha}$ is assigned a null value too. This z averaging procedure is similarly propagated to the third layer neurons.

The fourth layer neurons evaluate the z value of the origin of each arc identified by the first network. This is performed by a simple linear extrapolation. The final z estimate of the vertex, z_{net}, which should be the common origin of all arcs, is calculated by averaging the outputs of all active fourth layer neurons.

4 Results

In order to test the network, we ran it over a set of 1000 events generated by a Monte-Carlo simulator as well as over a sample of physical events taken from the ZEUS experiment at the HEP laboratory DESY in Hamburg. For the former set we compared the estimate of the net z_{net} with the nominal location of the vertex z, whereas for the real events in the latter set, we compared it with an estimate z_{rec} obtained by full reconstruction algorithm, which runs off-line and uses all available data. Results of the two tests can be compared since it is well established that the result of the full reconstruction algorithm is within 1 mm from the exact location of the vertex.

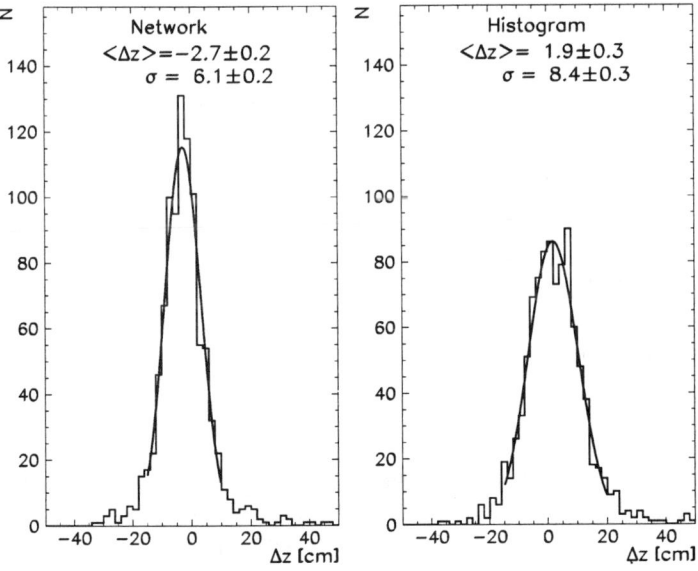

Figure 5: Distribution of $\Delta z = z_{estimate} - z_{exact}$ values for two types of estimates, (a) the one proposed in this paper and (b) the one based on a commonly used histogram method.

We also compared our results with those of an algorithmic method used for triggering at ZEUS [4]. We shall refer to this method as the 'histogram method'. The performance of the two methods was compared on a sample of 1000 Monte-Carlo events. The network was unable to get an estimate for 16 events from the set, as compared with 15 for the histogram method (15 of those events were common failures). In Figure 5 we compare the distributions of $\Delta z = z_{net} - z_{exact}$ and $\Delta z = z_{hist} - z_{exact}$ for the sample of Monte-Carlo events, where z_{exact} is the generated location of the vertex. Both methods lead to small biases, -2.7 cm for z_{net} and 1.9 cm for z_{hist}. The resolution, as obtained from a Gaussian fit, was found to be better for the network approach ($\sigma = 6.1$ cm) as compared to the histogram method ($\sigma = 8.4$ cm). In addition, it should be noted that the histogram method yields discrete results, with a step of 10 cm, whereas the current method gives continuous values. This can be of great advantage for further processing. Note that off-line, after using the whole CTD information, the resolution is better than 1 mm.

5 Discussion

We have described a feedforward double neural network that performs a task of pattern identification by thresholding and selecting subsets of data on which a simple computation can lead to the final answer. The network uses a fixed architecture, which allows for its implementation in hardware, crucial for fast triggering purposes.

The basic idea of using a fixed architecture that is inspired by the way our brain processes visual information, is similar to the the raison d'être of the orientation selective neural network employed by [5]. The latter was based on orientation selective cells only, which were sufficient to select linear tracks that are of interest in HEP experiments. Here we develop an arc identification method, following similar steps. Both methods can also be viewed as generalizations of the Hough transform [6] that was originally proposed for straight line identification and may be regarded as a basic element of pattern recognition problems [7]. Neither [5] nor our present proposal were considered by previous neural network analyses of HEP data [8]. The results that we have obtained are very promising. We hope that they open the possibility for a new type of neural network implementation in triggering devices of HEP experiments.

Acknowledgments

We are indebted to the ZEUS Collaboration whose data were used for this study. This research was partially supported by the Israel National Science Foundation.

References

[1] B. Foster et al., Nuclear Instrum. and Methods in Phys. Res. A338 (1994) 254.
[2] ZEUS Collab., The ZEUS Detector, Status Report 1993, DESY 1993; M. Derrick et al., Phys. Lett. B 293 (1992) 465.
[3] D. H. Hubel and T. N. Wiesel, J. Physiol. 195 (1968) 215.
[4] A. Quadt, MSc thesis, University of Oxford (1997).
[5] H. Abramowicz, D. Horn, U. Naftaly and C. Sahar-Pikielny, Nuclear Instrum. and Methods in Phys. Res. A378 (1996) 305; *Advances in Neural Information Processing Systems 9*, eds. M. C. Mozer, M. J. Jordan and T. Petsche, MIT Press 1997, pp. 925–931.
[6] P. V. Hough, "Methods and means to recognize complex patterns", U.S. patent 3.069.654.
[7] R. O. Duda and P. E. Hart, "Pattern classification and scene analysis", Wiley, New York, 1973.
[8] B. Denby, Neural Computation, 5 (1993) 505.

Familiarity Discrimination of Radar Pulses

Eric Granger[1], Stephen Grossberg[2]
Mark A. Rubin[2], William W. Streilein[2]

[1]Department of Electrical and Computer Engineering
École Polytechnique de Montréal
Montreal, Qc. H3C 3A7 CANADA

[2]Department of Cognitive and Neural Systems, Boston University
Boston, MA 02215 USA

Abstract

The ARTMAP-FD neural network performs both identification (placing test patterns in classes encountered during training) and familiarity discrimination (judging whether a test pattern belongs to any of the classes encountered during training). The performance of ARTMAP-FD is tested on radar pulse data obtained in the field, and compared to that of the nearest-neighbor-based NEN algorithm and to a $k > 1$ extension of NEN.

1 Introduction

The recognition process involves both identification and familiarity discrimination. Consider, for example, a neural network designed to identify aircraft based on their radar reflections and trained on sample reflections from ten types of aircraft $A \ldots J$. After training, the network should correctly classify radar reflections belonging to the familiar classes $A \ldots J$, but it should also abstain from making a meaningless guess when presented with a radar reflection from an object belonging to a different, unfamiliar class. Familiarity discrimination is also referred to as "novelty detection," a "reject option," and "recognition in partially exposed environments."

ARTMAP-FD, an extension of fuzzy ARTMAP that performs familiarity discrimination, has shown its effectiveness on datasets consisting of simulated radar range profiles from aircraft targets [1, 2]. In the present paper we examine the performance of ARTMAP-FD on radar pulse data obtained in the field, and compare it to that of NEN, a nearest-neighbor-based familiarity discrimination algorithm, and to a $k > 1$ extension of NEN.

2 Fuzzy ARTMAP

Fuzzy ARTMAP [3] is a self-organizing neural network for learning, recognition, and prediction. Each input **a** learns to predict an output class K. During training, the network creates internal recognition categories, with the number of categories determined on-line by predictive success. Components of the vector **a** are scaled so that each $a_i \in [0,1]$ ($i = 1\ldots M$). Complement coding [4] doubles the number of components in the input vector, which becomes $\mathbf{A} \equiv (\mathbf{a}, \mathbf{a}^c)$, where the ith component of $\mathbf{a}^c$ is $a_i^c \equiv (1-a_i)$. With fast learning, the weight vector $\mathbf{w}_j$ records the largest and smallest component values of input vectors placed in the jth category. The $2M$-dimensional vector $\mathbf{w}_j$ may be visualized as the hyperbox R_j that just encloses all the vectors **a** that selected category j during training.

Activation of the coding field F_2 is determined by the Weber law choice function $T_j(\mathbf{A}) = |\mathbf{A} \wedge \mathbf{w}_j| / (\alpha + |\mathbf{w}_j|)$, where $(\mathbf{P} \wedge \mathbf{Q})_i \equiv \min(P_i, Q_i)$ and $|\mathbf{P}| \equiv \sum_{i=1}^{2M} |P_i|$. With winner-take-all coding, the F_2 node J that receives the largest $F_1 \to F_2$ input T_j becomes active. Node J remains active if it satisfies the matching criterion: $|\mathbf{A} \wedge \mathbf{w}_j| / |\mathbf{A}| = |\mathbf{A} \wedge \mathbf{w}_j| / M > \rho$, where $\rho \in [0,1]$ is the dimensionless *vigilance parameter*. Otherwise, the network resets the active F_2 node and searches until J satisfies the matching criterion. If node J then makes an incorrect class prediction, a *match tracking* signal raises vigilance just enough to induce a search, which continues until either some F_2 node becomes active for the first time, in which case J learns the correct output class label $k(J) = K$; or a node J that has previously learned to predict K becomes active. During testing, a pattern **a** that activates node J is predicted to belong to the class $K = k(J)$.

3 ARTMAP-FD

Familiarity measure. During testing, an input pattern **a** is defined as *familiar* when a familiarity function $\phi(\mathbf{A})$ is greater than a decision threshold γ. Once a category choice has been made by the winner-take-all rule, fuzzy ARTMAP ignores the size of the input T_J. In contrast, ARTMAP-FD uses T_J to define familiarity, taking

$$\phi(\mathbf{A}) = \frac{T_J(\mathbf{A})}{T_J^{MAX}} = \frac{|\mathbf{A} \wedge \mathbf{w}_J|}{|\mathbf{w}_J|}, \tag{1}$$

where $T_J^{MAX} = |\mathbf{w}_J| / (\alpha + |\mathbf{w}_J|)$. This maximal value of T_J is attained by each input **a** that lies in the hyperbox R_J, since $|\mathbf{A} \wedge \mathbf{w}_J| = |\mathbf{w}_J|$ for these points. An input that chooses category J during testing is then assigned the maximum familiarity value 1 if and only if **a** lies within R_J.

Familiarity discrimination algorithm. ARTMAP-FD is identical to fuzzy ARTMAP during training. During testing, $\phi(\mathbf{A})$ is computed after fuzzy ARTMAP has yielded a winning node J and a predicted class $K = k(J)$. If $\phi(\mathbf{A}) > \gamma$, ARTMAP-FD predicts class K for the input **a**. If $\phi(\mathbf{A}) \leq \gamma$, **a** is regarded as belonging to an unfamiliar class and the network makes no prediction.

Note that fuzzy ARTMAP can also abstain from classification, when the baseline vigilance parameter $\bar{\rho}$ is greater than zero during testing. Typically $\bar{\rho} = 0$ during training, to maximize code compression. In radar range profile simulations such as those described below, fuzzy ARTMAP can perform familiarity discrimination when $\bar{\rho} > 0$ during both training and testing. However, accurate discrimination requires that $\bar{\rho}$ be close to 1, which causes category proliferation during training.

Range profile simulations have also set $\bar{\rho} = 0$ during both training and testing, but with the familiarity measure set equal to the fuzzy ARTMAP match function:

$$\phi(\mathbf{A}) = \frac{|\mathbf{A} \wedge \mathbf{w}_J|}{M}. \quad (2)$$

This approach is essentially equivalent to taking $\bar{\rho} = 0$ during training and $\bar{\rho} > 0$ during testing, with $\bar{\rho} = \gamma$. However, for a test set input $\mathbf{a} \in R_J$, the function defined by (2) sets $\phi(\mathbf{A}) = |\mathbf{w}_J|/M$, which may be large or small although $\mathbf{a}$ is familiar. Thus this function does not provide as good familiarity discrimination as the one defined by (1), which always sets $\phi(\mathbf{A}) = 1$ when $\mathbf{a} \in R_J$. Except as noted, all the simulations below employ the function (1), with $\bar{\rho} = 0$.

Sequential evidence accumulation. ART-EMAP (Stage 3) [5] identifies a test set object's class after exposure to a sequence of input patterns, such as differing views, all identified with that one object. Training is identical to that of fuzzy ARTMAP, with winner-take-all coding at F_2. ART-EMAP generally employs distributed F_2 coding during testing. With winner-take-all coding during testing as well as training, ART-EMAP predicts the object's class to be the one selected by the largest number of inputs in the sequence. Extending this approach, ARTMAP-FD accumulates familiarity measures for each predicted class K as the test set sequence is presented. Once the winning class is determined, the object's familiarity is defined as the average accumulated familiarity measure of the predicted class during the test sequence.

4 Familiarity discrimination simulations

Since familiarity discrimination involves placing an input into one of two sets, familiar and unfamiliar, the receiver operating characteristic (ROC) formalism can be used to evaluate the effectiveness of ARTMAP-FD on this task. The *hit rate* H is the fraction of familiar targets the network correctly identifies as familiar and the *false alarm rate* F is the fraction of unfamiliar targets the network incorrectly identifies as familiar. An ROC curve is a plot of H vs. F, parameterized by the threshold γ (*i.e.*, it is equivalent to the two curves $F(\gamma)$ and $H(\gamma)$). The area under the ROC curve is the *c-index*, a measure of predictive accuracy that is independent of both the fraction of positive (familiar) cases in the test set and the positive-case decision threshold γ.

An ARTMAP-FD network was trained on simulated radar range profiles from 18 targets out of a 36-target set (Fig. 1a). Simulations tested sequential evidence accumulation performance for 1, 3, and 100 observations, corresponding to 0.05, 0.15, and 5.0 sec. of observation (smooth curves, Fig. 1b). As in the case of identification [6], a combination of multiwavelength range profiles and sequential evidence accumulation produces good familiarity discrimination, with the c-index approaching 1 as the number of sequential observations grows.

Fig. 1b also demonstrates the importance of the proper choice of familiarity measure. The jagged ROC curve was produced by a familiarity discrimination simulation identical to that which resulted in the 100-sequential-view smooth curve, but using the match function (2) instead of ϕ as given by (1).

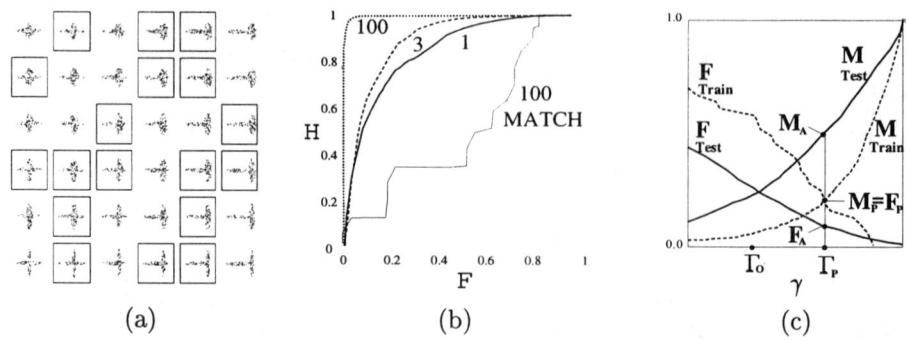

Figure 1:(a) 36 simulation targets with 6 wing positions and 6 wing lengths, and 100 scattering centers per target. Boxes indicate randomly selected familiar targets. (b) ROC curves from ARTMAP-FD simulations, with multiwavelength range profiles having 40 center frequencies. Sequential evidence accumulation for 1, 3 and 100 views uses familiarity measure (1) (smooth curves); and for 100 views uses the match function (2) (jagged curve). (c) Training and test curves of miss rate $M = (1 - H)$ and false alarm rate F vs threshold γ, for 36 targets and one view. Training curves intersect at the point where $\gamma = \Gamma_P$ (predicted); and test curves intersect near the point where $\gamma = \Gamma_O$ (optimal). The training curves are based on data from the first training epoch, the test curves on data from 3 training epochs.

5 Familiarity threshold selection

When a system is placed in operation, one particular decision threshold $\gamma = \Gamma$ must be chosen. In a given application, selection of Γ depends upon the relative cost of errors due to missed targets and false alarms. The optimal Γ corresponds to a point on the parameterized ROC curve that is typically close to the upper left-hand corner of the unit square, to maximize correct selection of familiar targets (H) while minimizing incorrect selection of unfamiliar targets (F).

Validation set method. To determine a predicted threshold Γ_P, the training data is partitioned into a training subset and a validation subset. The network is trained on the training subset, and an ROC curve $(F(\gamma), H(\gamma))$ is calculated for the validation subset. Γ_P is then taken to be the point on the curve that maximizes $[H(\gamma) - F(\gamma)]$. (For ease of computation the symmetry point on the curve, where $1 - H(\gamma) = F(\gamma)$, can yield a good approximation.) For a familiarity discrimination task the validation set must include examples of classes not present in the training set. Once Γ_P is determined, the training subset and validation subset should be recombined and the network retrained on the complete training set. The retrained network and the predicted threshold Γ_P are then employed for familiarity discrimination on the test set.

On-line threshold determination. During ARTMAP-FD training, category nodes compete for new patterns as they are presented. When a node J wins the competition, learning expands the category hyperbox R_J enough to enclose the training pattern **a**. The familiarity measure ϕ for each training set input then becomes equal to 1. However, *before* this learning takes place, ϕ can be less than 1, and the degree to which this initial value of ϕ is less than 1 reflects the distance from the training pattern to R_J. An event of this type—a training pattern successfully coded by a category node—is taken to be representative of familiar test-set patterns. The corresponding initial values of ϕ are thus used to generate a training hit rate curve, where $H(\gamma)$ equals the fraction of training inputs with $\phi > \gamma$.

What about false alarms? By definition, all patterns presented during training are familiar. However, a reset event during training (Sec. 2) resembles the arrival of an unfamiliar pattern during testing. Recall that a reset occurs when a category node that predicts class K wins the competition for a pattern that actually belongs to a different class k. The corresponding values of ϕ for these events can thus be used to generate a training false-alarm rate curve, where $F(\gamma)$ equals the fraction of match-tracking inputs with initial $\phi > \gamma$.

Predictive accuracy is improved by use of a reduced set of ϕ values in the training-set ROC curve construction process. Namely, training patterns that fall inside R_J, where $\phi = 1$, are not used because these exemplars tend to distort the miss rate curve. In addition, the *first* incorrect response to a training input is the best predictor of the network's response to an unfamiliar testing input, since sequential search will not be available during testing. Finally, giving more weight to events occurring later in the training process improves accuracy. This can be accomplished by first computing training curves $H(\gamma)$ and $F(\gamma)$ and a preliminary predicted threshold Γ_P using the reduced training set; then recomputing the curves and Γ_P from data presented only after the system has activated the final category node of the training process (Fig. 1c). The final predicted threshold Γ_P averages these values. This calculation can still be made on-line, by taking the "final" node to be the last one activated.

Table 1 shows that applying on-line threshold determination to simulated radar range profile data gives good predictions for the actual hit and false alarm rates, H_A and F_A. Furthermore, the H_A and F_A so obtained are close to optimal, particularly when the ROC curve has a c-index close to one. The method is effective even when testing involves sequential evidence accumulation, despite the fact that the training curves use only single views of each target.

6 NEN

Near-enough-neighbor (NEN) [7, 8] is a familiarity discrimination algorithm based on the single nearest neighbor classifier. For each familiar class K, the familiarity threshold Δ_K is the largest distance between any training pattern of class K and its nearest neighbor also of class K. During testing, a test pattern is declared unfamiliar if the distance to its nearest neighbor is greater than the threshold Δ_K corresponding to the class K of that nearest neighbor.

We have extended NEN to $k > 1$ by retaining the above definition of the Δ_K's, while taking the comparison during testing to be between Δ_K and the distance between the test pattern and the closest of its k nearest neighbors which is of the class K to which the test pattern is deemed to belong.

7 Radar pulse data

Identifying the type of emitter from which a radar signal was transmitted is an important task for radar electronic support measures (ESM) systems. Familiarity discrimination is a key component of this task, particularly as the continual proliferation of new emitters outstrips the ability of emitter libraries to document every sort of emitter which may be encountered.

The data analyzed here, gathered by Defense Research Establishment Ottawa, con-

	3x3		6x6		6x6*	
	actual	optimal	actual	optimal	actual	optimal
hit rate	0.81	0.86	0.77	0.77	0.99	0.98
false alarm rate	0.11	0.14	0.24	0.23	0.06	0.02
accuracy	0.95	1.00	0.93	1.00	1.00	1.00

Table 1: Familiarity discrimination, using ARTMAP-FD with on-line threshold prediction, of simulated radar range profile data. Training on half the target classes (boxed "aircraft" in Fig. 1a), testing on all target classes. (In 3x3 case, 4 classes out of 9 total used for training.) Accuracy equals the fraction of correctly-classified targets out of familiar targets selected by the network as familiar. The results for the 6x6* dataset involve sequential evidence accumulation, with 100 observations (5 sec.) per test target. Radar range profile simulations use 40 center frequencies evenly spaced between 18GHz and 22GHz, and $wp \times wl$ simulated targets, where wp =number of wing positions and wl =number of wing lengths. The number of range bins (2/3 m. per bin) is 60, so each pattern vector has (60 range bins) × (40 center frequencies) = 2400 components. Training patterns are at 21 evenly spaced aspects in a 10° angular range and, for each viewing angle, at 15 downrange shifts evenly spaced within a single bin width. Testing patterns are at random aspects and downrange shifts within the angular range and half the total range profile extent of (60 bins) × (2/3 m.) =40 m.

method	ARTMAP-FD	NEN					
		city-block metric			Euclidean metric		
		$k=1$	$k=5$	$k=25$	$k=1$	$k=5$	$k=25$
hit rate	0.95	0.94	0.94	0.93	0.94	0.93	0.92
f. a. rate	0.02	0.13	0.04	0.02	0.14	0.05	0.02
accuracy	1.00	1.00	1.00	1.00	0.99	1.00	1.00
memory	21	446					

Table 2: Familiarity discrimination of radar pulse data set, using ARTMAP-FD and NEN with different metrics and values of k. Figure given for memory is twice number of F_2 nodes (due to complement coding) for ARTMAP-FD, number of training patterns for NEN. Training (single epoch) on first three quarters of data in classes 1-9, testing on other quarter of data in classes 1-9 and all data in classes 10-12. (Values given are averages over four cyclic permutations of the the 12 classes.) ARTMAP-FD familiarity threshold determined by validation-set method with retraining.

sist of radar pulses from 12 shipborne navigation radars [9]. Fifty pulses were collected from each radar, with the exception of radars #7 (100 pulses) and #8 (200 pulses). The pulses were preprocessed to yield 800 15-component vectors, with the components taking values between 0 and 1.

8 Results

From Table 2, ARTMAP-FD is seen to perform effective familiarity discrimination on the radar pulse data. NEN ($k = 1$) performs comparatively poorly. Extensions of NEN to $k > 1$ perform well. During fielded operation these would incur the cost of the additional computation required to find the k nearest neighbors of the current test pattern, as well as the cost of higher memory requirements[1] relative to ARTMAP-FD. The combination of low hit rate with low false alarm rate obtained by NEN on the simulated radar range profile datasets (Table 3) suggests that the algorithm performs poorly here because it selects a familiarity threshold which is

---

[1]The memory requirements of kNN pattern classifiers can be reduced by editing techniques[8], but how the use of these methods affects performance of kNN-based familiarity discrimination methods is an open question.

method	ARTMAP-FD		NEN				
			$k=1$	$k=5$	$k=99$	$k=1$	$k=5$
dataset	3x3	6x6	3x3			6x6	
hit rate	0.81	0.77	0.11	0.11	0.11	0.14	0.14
false alarm rate	0.11	0.24	0.00	0.00	0.00	0.00	0.00
accuracy	0.95	0.93	1.00	1.00	1.00	1.00	1.00
memory	12	88	1260			5670	

Table 3: Familiarity discrimination of simulated radar range profiles using ARTMAP-FD and NEN with different values of k. Training and testing as in Table 1. ARTMAP-FD familiarity threshold determined by on-line method. City-block metric used with NEN; results with Euclidean metric were slighlty poorer.

too high. ARTMAP-FD on-line threshold selection, on the other hand, yields a value for the familiarity threshold which balances the desiderata of high hit rate and low false alarm rate.

This research was supported in part by grants from the Office of Naval Research, ONR N00014-95-1-0657 (S. G.) and ONR N00014-96-1-0659 (M. A. R., W. W. S.), and by a grant from the Defense Advanced Research Projects Agency and the Office of Naval Research, ONR N00014-95-1-0409 (S. G., M. A. R., W. W. S.). E. G. was supported in part by the Defense Research Establishment Ottawa and the Natural Sciences and Engineering Research Council of Canada.

References

[1] Carpenter, G. A., Rubin, M. A., & Streilein, W. W., ARTMAP-FD: Familiarity discrimination applied to radar target recognition, in *ICNN'97: Proceedings of the IEEE International Conference on Neural Networks*, Houston, June 1997;

[2] Carpenter, G. A., Rubin, M. A., & Streilein, W. W., Threshold Determination for ARTMAP-FD Familiarity Discrimination, in C. H. Dagli et al., eds., *Intelligent Engineering Systems Through Artificial Neural Networks*, **7**, 23-28, ASME, New York, 1997.

[3] Carpenter, G. A., Grossberg, S., Markuzon, N., Reynolds, J. H., & Rosen, D. B., Fuzzy ARTMAP: A neural network architecture for incremental supervised learning of analog multidimensional maps, *IEEE Transactions on Neural Networks*, **3**, 698-713, 1992.

[4] Carpenter, G. A., Grossberg, S., & Rosen, D. B., Fuzzy ART: Fast stable learning and categorization of analog patterns by an adaptive resonance system, *Neural Networks*, **4**, 759-771, 1991.

[5] Carpenter, G. A., & Ross, W. D., ART-EMAP: A neural network architecture for object recognition by evidence accumulation, *IEEE Transactions on Neural Networks*, **6**, 805-818, 1995.

[6] Rubin, M. A., Application of fuzzy ARTMAP and ART-EMAP to automatic target recognition using radar range profiles, *Neural Networks*, **8**, 1109-1116, 1995.

[7] Dasarathy, B. V., Is your nearest neighbor near enough a neighbor?, in Lainious, D. G. and Tzannes, N. S., eds. *Applications and Research in Informations Systems and Sciences*, **1**, 114-117, Hemisphere Publishing Corp., Washington, 1977.

[8] Dasarathy, B. V., ed., *Nearest Neighbor(NN) Norm: NN Pattern Classification Techniques*, IEEE Computer Society Press, Los Alamitos, CA, 1991.

[9] Granger, E., Savaria, Y., Lavoie, P., & Cantin, M.-A., A comparison of self-organizing neural networks for fast clustering of radar pulses, *Signal Processing*, **64**, 249-269, 1998.

Fast Neural Network Emulation of Dynamical Systems for Computer Animation

Radek Grzeszczuk [1]   Demetri Terzopoulos [2]   Geoffrey Hinton [2]

[1] Intel Corporation
Microcomputer Research Lab
2200 Mission College Blvd.
Santa Clara, CA 95052, USA

[2] University of Toronto
Department of Computer Science
10 King's College Road
Toronto, ON M5S 3H5, Canada

Abstract

Computer animation through the numerical simulation of physics-based graphics models offers unsurpassed realism, but it can be computationally demanding. This paper demonstrates the possibility of replacing the numerical simulation of nontrivial dynamic models with a dramatically more efficient "NeuroAnimator" that exploits neural networks. NeuroAnimators are automatically trained off-line to emulate physical dynamics through the observation of physics-based models in action. Depending on the model, its neural network emulator can yield physically realistic animation one or two orders of magnitude faster than conventional numerical simulation. We demonstrate NeuroAnimators for a variety of physics-based models.

1 Introduction

Animation based on physical principles has been an influential trend in computer graphics for over a decade (see, e.g., [1, 2, 3]). This is not only due to the unsurpassed realism that physics-based techniques offer. In conjunction with suitable control and constraint mechanisms, physical models also facilitate the production of copious quantities of realistic animation in a highly automated fashion. Physics-based animation techniques are beginning to find their way into high-end commercial systems. However, a well-known drawback has retarded their broader penetration—compared to geometric models, physical models typically entail formidable numerical simulation costs.

This paper proposes a new approach to creating physically realistic animation that differs radically from the conventional approach of numerically simulating the equations of motion of physics-based models. We replace physics-based models by fast *emulators* which automatically learn to produce similar motions by observing the models in action. Our emulators have a neural network structure, hence we dub them *NeuroAnimators*.

Our work is inspired in part by that of Nguyen and Widrow [4]. Their "truck backer-upper" demonstrated the neural network based approximation and control of a nonlinear kinematic system. We introduce several generalizations that enable us to tackle a variety of complex, fully dynamic models in the context of computer animation. Connectionist approximations of dynamical systems have been also been applied to robot control (see, e.g., [5, 6]).

2 The NeuroAnimator Approach

Our approach is motivated by the following considerations: Whether we are dealing with rigid [2], articulated [3], or nonrigid [1] dynamic animation models, the numerical simulation of the associated equations of motion leads to the computation of a discrete-time dynamical system of the form $s_{t+\delta t} = \Phi[s_t, u_t, f_t]$. These (generally nonlinear) equations express the vector $s_{t+\delta t}$ of state variables of the system (values of the system's degrees of freedom and their velocities) at time $t + \delta t$ in the future as a function Φ of the state vector s_t, the vector u_t of control inputs, and the vector f_t of external forces acting on the system at time t.

Physics-based animation through the numerical simulation of a dynamical system requires the evaluation of the map Φ at every timestep, which usually involves a non-trivial computation. Evaluating Φ using explicit time integration methods incurs a computational cost of $O(N)$ operations, where N is proportional to the dimensionality of the state space. Unfortunately, for many dynamic models of interest, explicit methods are plagued by instability, necessitating numerous tiny timesteps δt per unit simulation time. Alternatively, implicit time-integration methods usually permit larger timesteps, but they compute Φ by solving a system of N algebraic equations, generally incurring a cost of $O(N^3)$ per timestep.

Is it possible to replace the conventional numerical simulator by a significantly cheaper alternative? A crucial realization is that the substitute, or emulator, need not compute the map Φ exactly, but merely approximate it to a degree of precision that preserves the perceived faithfulness of the resulting animation to the simulated dynamics of the physical model. Neural networks offer a general mechanism for approximating complex maps in higher dimensional spaces [7].[1] Our premise is that, to a sufficient degree of accuracy and at significant computational savings, trained neural networks can approximate maps Φ not just for simple dynamical systems, but also for those associated with dynamic models that are among the most complex reported in the graphics literature to date.

The NeuroAnimator, which uses neural networks to emulate physics-based animation, learns an approximation to the dynamic model by observing instances of state transitions, as well as control inputs and/or external forces that cause these transitions. By generalizing from the sparse examples presented to it, a trained NeuroAnimator can emulate an infinite variety of continuous animations that it has never actually seen. Each emulation step costs only $O(N^2)$ operations, but it is possible to gain additional efficiency relative to a numerical simulator by training neural networks to approximate a lengthy chain of evaluations of the discrete-time dynamical system. Thus, the emulator network can perform "super

---

[1] Note that Φ is in general a high-dimensional map from $\Re^{s+u+f} \mapsto \Re^s$, where s, u, and f denote the dimensionalities of the state, control, and external force vectors.

timesteps" $\Delta t = n\delta t$, typically one or two orders of magnitude larger than δt for the competing implicit time-integration scheme, thereby achieving outstanding efficiency without serious loss of accuracy.

3 From Physics-Based Models to NeuroAnimators

Our task is to construct neural networks that approximate Φ in the dynamical system. We propose to employ backpropagation to train feedforward networks N_Φ, with a single layer of sigmoidal hidden units, to predict future states using super timesteps $\Delta t = n\delta t$ while containing the approximation error so as not to appreciably degrade the physical realism of the resulting animation. The basic emulation step is $s_{t+\Delta t} = N_\Phi[s_t, u_t, f_t]$. The trained emulator network N_Φ takes as input the state of the model, its control inputs, and the external forces acting on it at time t, and produces as output the state of the model at time $t + \Delta t$ by evaluating the network. The emulation process is a sequence of these evaluations. After each evaluation, the network control and force inputs receive new values, and the network state inputs receive the emulator outputs from the previous evaluation. Since the emulation step is large compared with the numerical simulation step, we resample the motion trajectory at the animation frame rate, computing intermediate states through linear interpolation of states obtained from the emulation.

3.1 Network Input/Output Structure

Fig. 1(a) illustrates different emulator input/output structures. The emulator network has a single set of output variables specifying $s_{t+\Delta t}$. In general, for a so-called active model, which includes control inputs, under the influence of unpredictable applied forces, we employ a full network with three sets of input variables: s_t, u_t, and f_t, as shown in the figure. For passive models, the control $u_t = 0$ and the network simplifies to one with two sets of inputs, s_t and f_t. In the special case when the forces f_t are completely determined by the state of the system s_t, we can suppress the f_t inputs, allowing the network to learn the effects of these forces from the state transition training data, thus yielding a simpler emulator with two input sets s_t and u_t. The simplest type of emulator has only a single set of inputs s_t. This emulator suffices to approximate passive models acted upon by deterministic external forces.

3.2 Input and Output Transformations

The accurate approximation of complex functional mappings using neural networks can be challenging. We have observed that a simple feedforward neural network with a single layer of sigmoid units has difficulty producing an accurate approximation to the dynamics of physical models. In practice, we often must transform the emulator to ensure a good approximation of the map Φ.

A fundamental problem is that the state variables of a dynamical system can have a large dynamic range (in principle, from $-\infty$ to $+\infty$). To approximate a nonlinear map Φ accurately over a large domain, we would need to use a neural network with many sigmoid units, each shifted and scaled so that their nonlinear segments cover different parts of the domain. The direct approximation of Φ is therefore impractical. A successful strategy is to train networks to emulate *changes* in state variables rather than their actual values, since state changes over small timesteps will have a significantly smaller dynamic range. Hence, in Fig. 1(b) (top) we restructure our simple network N_Φ as a network N_Φ^Δ which is trained

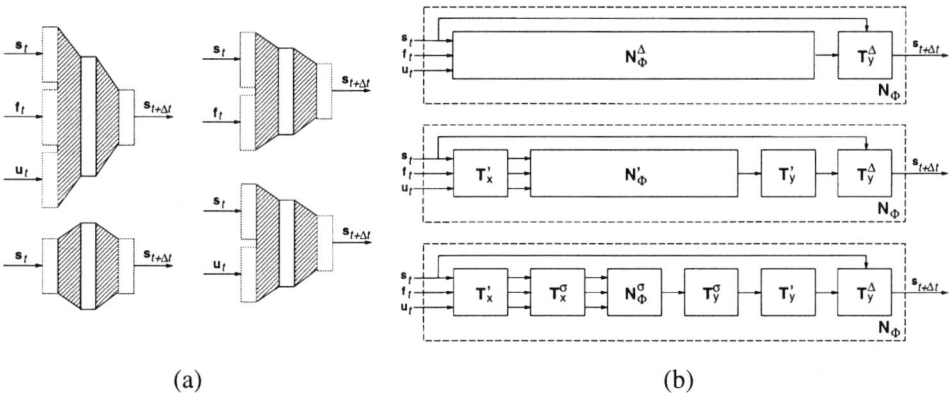

Figure 1: (a) Different types of emulators. (b) Transforming a simple feedforward neural network $\mathbf{N}_\Phi$ into a practical emulator network $\mathbf{N}_\Phi^\sigma$ that is easily trained to emulate physics-based models. The following operators perform the appropriate pre- and post-processing: $\mathbf{T}'_x$ transforms inputs to local coordinates, $\mathbf{T}_x^\sigma$ normalizes inputs, $\mathbf{T}_y^\sigma$ unnormalizes outputs, $\mathbf{T}'_y$ transforms outputs to global coordinates, $\mathbf{T}_y^\Delta$ converts from a state change to the next state (see text and [8] for the details).

to emulate the change in the state vector $\Delta \mathbf{s}_t$ for given state, external force, and control inputs, followed by an operator $\mathbf{T}_y^\Delta$ that computes $\mathbf{s}_{t+\Delta t} = \mathbf{s}_t + \Delta \mathbf{s}_t$ to recover the next state.

We can further improve the approximation power of the emulator network by exploiting natural invariances. In particular, since the map Φ is invariant under rotation and translation, we replace $\mathbf{N}_\Phi^\Delta$ with an operator $\mathbf{T}'_x$ that converts the inputs from the world coordinate system to the local coordinate system of the model, a network $\mathbf{N}'_\Phi$ that is trained to emulate state changes represented in the local coordinate system, and an operator $\mathbf{T}'_y$ that converts the output of $\mathbf{N}'_\Phi$ back to world coordinates (Fig. 1(b) (center)).

Since the values of state, force, and control variables can deviate significantly, their effect on the network outputs is uneven, causing problems when large inputs must have a small influence on outputs. To make inputs contribute more evenly to the network outputs, we normalize groups of variables so that they have zero means and unit variances. With normalization, we can furthermore expect the weights of the trained network to be of order unity and they can be given a simple random initialization prior to training. Hence, in Fig. 1(b)) (bottom) we replace $\mathbf{N}'_\Phi$ with an operator $\mathbf{T}_x^\sigma$ that normalizes its inputs, a network $\mathbf{N}_\Phi^\sigma$ that assumes zero mean, unit variance inputs and outputs, and an operator $\mathbf{T}_y^\sigma$ that unnormalizes the outputs to recover their original distributions.

Although the final emulator in Fig. 1(b) is structurally more complex than the standard feedforward neural network $\mathbf{N}_\Phi$ that it replaces, the operators denoted by $\mathbf{T}$ are completely determined by the state of the model and the distribution of the training data, and the emulator network $\mathbf{N}_\Phi^\sigma$ is much easier to train.

3.3 Hierarchical Networks

As a universal function approximator, a neural network should in principle be able to approximate the map Φ for any dynamical system, given enough sigmoid hidden units and training data. In practice, however, the number of hidden layer neurons needed and the training data requirements grow quickly with the size of the network, often making the training of large networks impractical. To overcome the "curse of dimensionality," we have found it prudent to structure NeuroAnimators for all but the simplest physics-based models as hierarchies of smaller networks rather than as large, monolithic networks. The strategy behind a hierarchical representation is to group state variables according to their dependencies and approximate each tightly coupled group with a subnet that takes part of its input from a parent network.

3.4 Training NeuroAnimators

To arrive at a NeuroAnimator for a given physics-based model, we train the constituent neural network(s) through backpropagation on training examples generated by simulating the model. Training requires the generation and processing of many examples, hence it is typically slow, often requiring several CPU hours. However, once a NeuroAnimator is trained offline, it can be reused online to produce an infinite variety of fast animations. The important point is that by generalizing from the sparse training examples, a trained NeuroAnimator will produce an infinite variety of extended, continuous animations that it has never "seen".

More specifically, each training example consists of an input vector $\mathbf{x}$ and an output vector $\mathbf{y}$. In the general case, the input vector $\mathbf{x} = [\mathbf{s}_0^T, \mathbf{f}_0^T, \mathbf{u}_0^T]^T$ comprises the state of the model, the external forces, and the control inputs at time $t = 0$. The output vector $\mathbf{y} = \mathbf{s}_{\Delta t}$ is the state of the model at time $t = \Delta t$, where Δt is the duration of the super timestep. To generate each training example, we could start the numerical simulator of the physics-based model with the initial conditions $\mathbf{s}_0$, $\mathbf{f}_0$, and $\mathbf{u}_0$, and run the dynamic simulation for n numerical time steps δt such that $\Delta t = n\delta t$. In principle, we could generate an arbitrarily large set of training examples $\{\mathbf{x}^\tau; \mathbf{y}^\tau\}$, $\tau = 1, 2, \ldots$, by repeating this process with different initial conditions. To learn a good neural network approximation N_Φ of the map Φ, we would like ideally to sample Φ as uniformly as possible over its domain, with randomly chosen initial conditions among all valid state, external force, and control combinations. However, we can make better use of computational resources by sampling those state, force, and control inputs that typically occur as a physics-based model is used in practice.

We employ a neural network simulator called *Xerion* which was developed at the University of Toronto. We begin the off-line training process by initializing the weights of N_Φ^σ to random values from a uniform distribution in the range $[0, 1]$ (due to the normalization of inputs and outputs). Xerion automatically terminates the backpropagation learning algorithm when it can no longer reduce the network approximation error significantly. We use the conjugate gradient method to train networks of small and moderate size. For large networks, we use gradient descent with momentum. We divide the training examples into mini-batches, each consisting of approximately 30 uncorrelated examples, and update the network weights after processing each mini-batch.

4 Results

We have successfully constructed and trained several NeuroAnimators to emulate a variety of physics-based models (Fig. 2). We used SD/FAST (a rigid body dynamics simulator marketed by Symbolic Dynamics, Inc.) to simulate the dynamics of the rigid body

Emulation for Animation

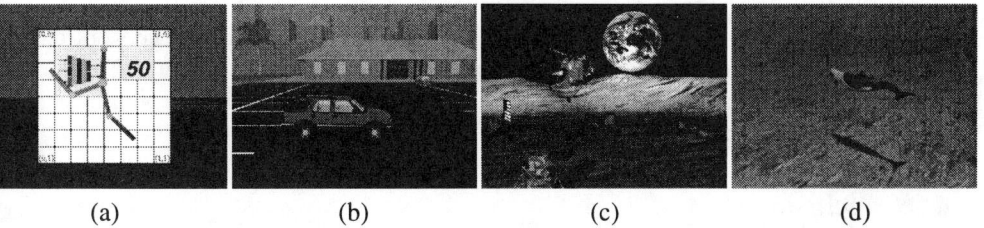

(a) (b) (c) (d)

Figure 2: NeuroAnimators used in our experiments. (a) Emulator of a physics-based model of a planar multi-link pendulum suspended in gravity, subject to joint friction forces, external forces applied on the links, and controlled by independent motor torques at each of the three joints. (b) Emulator of a physics-based model of a truck implemented as a rigid body, subject to friction forces where the tires contact the ground, controlled by rear-wheel drive (forward and reverse) and steerable front wheels. (c) Emulator of a physics-based model of a lunar lander, implemented as a rigid body subject to gravitational forces and controlled by a main rocket thruster and three independent attitude jets. (d) Emulator of a biomechanical (mass-spring-damper) model of a dolphin capable of swimming in simulated water via the coordinated contraction of 6 independently controlled muscle actuators which deform its body, producing hydrodynamic propulsion forces.

and articulated models, and we employ the simulator developed in [10] to simulate the deformable-body dynamics of the dolphin.

In our experiments we have not attempted to minimize the number of network weights required for successful training. We have also not tried to minimize the number of sigmoidal hidden units, but rather used enough units to obtain networks that generalize well while not overfitting the training data. We can always expect to be able to satisfy these guidelines in view of our ability to generate sufficient training data.

An important advantage of using neural networks to emulate dynamical systems is the speed at which they can be iterated to produce animation. Since the emulator for a dynamical system with the state vector of size N never uses more than $O(N)$ hidden units, it can be evaluated using only $O(N^2)$ operations. By comparison, a single simulation timestep using an implicit time integration scheme requires $O(N^3)$ operations. Moreover, a forward pass through the neural network is often equivalent to as many as 50 physical simulation steps, so the efficiency is even more dramatic, yielding performance improvements up to two orders of magnitude faster than the physical simulator. A NeuroAnimator that predicts 100 physical simulation steps offers a speedup of anywhere between 50 and 100 times depending on the type of physical model.

5 Control Learning

An additional benefit of the NeuroAnimator is that it enables a novel, highly efficient approach to the difficult problem of controlling physics-based models to synthesize motions that satisfy prescribed animation goals. The neural network approximation to the physical model is differentiable; hence, it can be used to discover the causal effects that control force inputs have on the actions of the models. Outstanding efficiency stems from exploiting the trained NeuroAnimator to compute partial derivatives of output states with respect to control inputs. The efficient computation of the approximate gradient enables the utilization of fast gradient-based optimization for controller synthesis.

Nguyen and Widrow's [4] "truck backer-upper" demonstrated the neural network based approximation and control of a nonlinear kinematic system. Our technique offers a new controller synthesis algorithm that works well in dynamic environments with changing control objectives. See [8, 9] for the details.

6 Conclusion

We have introduced an efficient alternative to the conventional approach of producing physically realistic animation through numerical simulation. Our approach involves the learning of neural network emulators of physics-based models by observing the dynamic state transitions produced by such models in action. The emulators approximate physical dynamics with dramatic efficiency, yet without serious loss of apparent fidelity. Our performance benchmarks indicate that the neural network emulators can yield physically realistic animation one or two orders of magnitude faster than conventional numerical simulation of the associated physics-based models. Our new control learning algorithm, which exploits fast emulation and the differentiability of the network approximation, is orders of magnitude faster than competing controller synthesis algorithms for computer animation.

Acknowledgements

We thank Zoubin Ghahramani for valuable discussions leading to the idea of the rotation and translation invariant emulator, which was crucial to the success of this work. We are indebted to Steve Hunt, John Funge, Alexander Reshetov, Sonja Jeter and Mike Gendimenico at Intel, and Mike Revow, Drew van Camp and Michiel van de Panne at the University of Toronto for their assistance.

References

[1] D. Terzopoulos, J. Platt, A. Barr, K. Fleischer. Elastically deformable models. In M.C. Stone, ed., *Computer Graphics (SIGGRAPH '87 Proceedings)*, **21**, 205–214, July 1987.

[2] J.K. Hahn. Realistic animation of rigid bodies. In J. Dill, ed., *Computer Graphics (SIGGRAPH '88 Proceedings)*, **22**, 299–308, August 1988.

[3] J.K. Hodgins, W.L. Wooten, D.C. Brogan, J.F. O'Brien. Animating human athletics. In R. Cook, ed., *Proc. of ACM SIGGRAPH 95 Conf.*, 71–78, August, 1995.

[4] D. Nguyen, B. Widrow. The truck backer-upper: An example of self-learning in neural networks. In *Proc. Inter. Joint Conf. Neural Networks*, 357–363. IEEE Press, 1989.

[5] M. I. Jordan. Supervised learning and systems with excess degrees of freedom. Technical Report 88-27, Univ. of Massachusetts, Comp.& Info. Sci., Amherst, MA, 1988.

[6] K. S. Narendra, K. Parthasarathy. Gradient methods for the optimization of dynamical systems containing neural networks. *IEEE Trans. on Neural Networks*, **2**(2):252–262, 1991.

[7] G. Cybenko. Approximation by superposition of sigmoidal function. *Math. of Control Signals & Systems*, **2**(4):303–314, 1989.

[8] R. Grzeszczuk. *NeuroAnimator: Fast Neural Network Emulation and Control of Physics-Based Models*. PhD thesis, Dept. of Comp. Sci., Univ. of Toronto, May 1998.

[9] R. Grzeszczuk, D. Terzopoulos, G. Hinton. NeuroAnimator: Fast neural network emulation and control of physics-based models. In M. Cohen, ed., *Proc. of ACM SIGGRAPH 98 Conf.*, 9–20, July 1998.

[10] X. Tu, D. Terzopoulos. Artificial fishes: Physics, locomotion, perception, behavior. In A. Glassner, ed., *Proc. of ACM SIGGRAPH 94 Conf.*, 43–50. July 1994.

Call-based Fraud Detection in Mobile Communication Networks using a Hierarchical Regime-Switching Model

Jaakko Hollmén
Helsinki University of Technology
Lab. of Computer and Information Science
P.O. Box 5400, 02015 HUT, Finland
Jaakko.Hollmen@hut.fi

Volker Tresp
Siemens AG, Corporate Technology
Dept. Information and Communications
81730 Munich, Germany
Volker.Tresp@mchp.siemens.de

Abstract

Fraud causes substantial losses to telecommunication carriers. Detection systems which automatically detect illegal use of the network can be used to alleviate the problem. Previous approaches worked on features derived from the call patterns of individual users. In this paper we present a call-based detection system based on a hierarchical regime-switching model. The detection problem is formulated as an inference problem on the regime probabilities. Inference is implemented by applying the junction tree algorithm to the underlying graphical model. The dynamics are learned from data using the EM algorithm and subsequent discriminative training. The methods are assessed using fraud data from a real mobile communication network.

1 INTRODUCTION

Fraud is costly to a network carrier both in terms of lost income and wasted capacity. It has been estimated that the telecommunication industry looses approximately 2-5% of its total revenue to fraud. The true losses are expected to be even higher since telecommunication companies are reluctant to admit fraud in their systems. A fraudulent attack causes lots of inconveniences to the victimized subscriber which might motivate the subscriber to switch to a competing carrier. Furthermore, potential new customers would be very reluctant to switch to a carrier which is troubled with fraud.

Mobile communication networks —which are the focus of this work— are particularly appealing to fraudsters as the calling from the mobile terminal is not bound to a physical place and a subscription is easy to get. This provides means for an illegal high-profit business requiring minimal investment and relatively low risk of getting caught. Fraud is usually initiated by a mobile phone theft, by cloning the mobile phone card or by acquiring a subscription with false identification. After intrusion the subscription can be used for gaining free services either for the intruder himself or for his illegal customers in form of call-selling. In the latter case, the fraudster sells calls to customers for reduced rates.

The earliest means of detecting fraud were to register overlapping calls originating from one subscription, evidencing card cloning. While this procedure efficiently detects cloning, it misses a large share of other fraud cases. A more advanced system is a velocity trap which detects card cloning by using an upper speed limit at which a mobile phone user can travel. Subsequent calls from distant places provide evidence for card cloning. Although a velocity trap is a powerful method of detecting card cloning, it is ineffective against other types of fraud. Therefore there is great interest in detection systems which detect fraud based on an analysis of behavioral patterns (Barson et al., 1996, Burge et al., 1997, Fawcett and Provost, 1997, Taniguchi et al., 1998).

In an absolute analysis, a user is classified as a fraudster based on features derived from daily statistics summarizing the call pattern such as the average number of calls. In a differential analysis, the detection is based on measures describing the changes in those features capturing the transition from a normal use to fraud. Both approaches have the problem of finding efficient feature representations describing normal and fraudulent behavior. As they usually derive features as summary statistics over one day, they are plagued with a latency time of up to a day to detect fraudulent behavior. The resulting delay in detection can already lead to unacceptable losses and can be exploited by the fraudster. For these reasons real-time fraud detection is seen to be the most important development in fraud detection (Pequeno, 1997).

In this paper we present a real-time fraud detection system which is based on a stochastic generative model. In the generative model we assume a variable *victimized* which indicates if the account has been victimized by a fraudster and a second variable *fraud* which indicates if the fraudster is currently performing fraud. Both variables are hidden. Furthermore, we have an observed variable *call* which indicates if a call being is performed or not. The transition probabilities from no-call to call and from call to no-call are dependent on the state of the variable *fraud*. Overall, we obtain a regime-switching time-series model as described by Hamilton (1994), with the modifications that first, the variables in the time series are not continuous but binary and second, the switching variable has a hierarchical structure. The benefit of the hierarchical structure is that it allows us to model the time-series at different time scales. At the lowest hierarchical level, we model the dynamical behavior of the individual calls, at the next level the transition from normal behavior to fraudulent behavior and at the highest level the transition to being victimized. To be able to model a time-series at different temporal resolutions was also the reason for introducing a hierarchy into a hidden Markov model for Jordan, Ghahramani and Saul (1997). Fortunately, our hidden variables have only a small number of states such that we do not have to work with the approximation techniques those authors have introduced.

Section 2 introduces our hierarchical regime-switching fraud model. The detection problem is formulated as an inference problem on the regime probabilities based on subscriber data. We derive iterative algorithms for estimating the hidden variables *fraud* and *victimized* based on past and present data (filtering) or based on the complete set of observed data (smoothing). We present EM learning rules for learning the parameters in the model using observed data. We develop a gradient based approach for fine tuning the emission probabilities in the non-fraud state to enhance the discrimination capability of the model. In Section 3 we present experimental results. We show that a system which is fine-tuned on real data can be used for detecting fraudulent behavior on-line based on the call patterns. In Section 4 we present conclusions and discuss further applications and extensions of our fraud model.

2 THE HIERARCHICAL REGIME-SWITCHING FRAUD MODEL

2.1 THE GENERATIVE MODEL

The hierarchical regime-switching model consists of three variables which evolve in time stochastically according to first-order Markov chains. The first binary variable v_t (victimized) is equal to one if the account is currently being victimized by a fraudster and zero otherwise. The states of this variable evolve according to the state transition probabilities $p_{ij}^v = P(v_t = i | v_{t-1} = j); i,j = 0,1$. The second binary variable s_t (fraud) is equal to one if the fraudster currently performs fraud and is equal to zero if the fraudster is inactive. The change between actively performing fraud and intermittent silence is typical for a victimized account as is apparent from Figure 3. Note that this transient bursty behavior of a victimized account would be difficult to capture with a pure feature based approach. The states of this variable evolve following the state transition probabilities $p_{ijk}^s = P(s_t = i | v_t = j, s_{t-1} = k,); i,j,k = 0,1$. Finally, the binary variable y_t (call) is equal to one if the mobile phone is being used and zero otherwise with state transition matrix $p_{ijk}^y = P(y_t = i | s_t = j, y_{t-1} = k); i,j,k = 0,1$. Note that this corresponds to the assumption of exponentially distributed call duration. Although not quite realistic, this is the general assumption in telecommunications. Typically, both the frequency of calls and the lengths of the calls are increased when fraud is executed. The joint probability of the time series up to time T is then

$$P(V_T, S_T, Y_T) = P(v_0, s_0, y_0) \prod_{t=1}^{T} P(v_t | v_{t-1}) \prod_{t=1}^{T} P(s_t | v_t, s_{t-1}) \prod_{t=1}^{T} P(y_t | s_t, y_{t-1}) \quad (1)$$

where in the experiments we used a sampling time of one minute. Furthermore, $V_T = \{v_0, \ldots, v_T\}$, $S_T = \{s_0, \ldots, s_T\}$, $Y_T = \{y_0, \ldots, y_T\}$ and $P(v_0, s_0, y_0)$ is the prior distribution of the initial states.

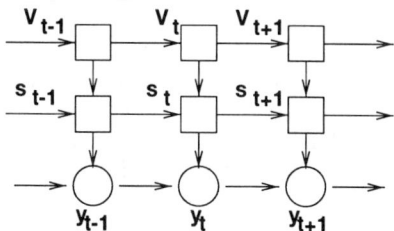

Figure 1: Dependency graph of the hierarchical regime-switching fraud model. The square boxes denote hidden variables and the circles observed variables. The hidden variable v_t on the top describes whether the subscriber account is victimized by fraud. The hidden variable s_t indicates if fraud is currently being executed. The state of s_t determines the statistics of the variable call y_t.

2.2 INFERENCE: FILTERING AND SMOOTHING

When using the fraud detection system, we are interested to estimate the probability that an account is victimized or that fraud is currently occurring based on the call patterns up to the current point in time (filtering). We can calculate the probabilities of the states of the hidden variables by applying the following equations recursively with $t = 1, \ldots, T$.

$$P(v_t = i, s_{t-1} = k|Y_{t-1}) = \sum_l p_{il}^v P(v_{t-1} = l, s_{t-1} = k|Y_{t-1})$$

$$P(v_t = i, s_t = j|Y_{t-1}) = \sum_k p_{jik}^s P(v_t = i, s_{t-1} = k|Y_{t-1})$$

$$P(v_t = i, s_t = j|Y_t) = c \cdot p_{y_t j y_{t-1}}^y P(v_t = i, s_t = j|Y_{t-1})$$

where c is a scaling factor. These equations can be derived from the junction tree algorithm for the Bayesian networks (Jensen, 1996). We obtain the probability of victimization and fraud by simple marginalization

$$P(v_t = i|Y_t) = \sum_j P(v_t = i, s_t = j|Y_t) \; ; \; P(s_t = j|Y_t) = \sum_i P(v_t = i, s_t = j|Y_t).$$

In some cases —in particular for the EM learning rules in the next section— we might be interested in estimating the probabilities of the hidden states at some time in the past (smoothing). In this case we can use a variation of the smoothing equations described in Hamilton (1994) and Kim (1994). After performing the forward recursion, we can calculate the probability of the hidden states at time t' given data up to time $T > t'$ iterating the following equations with $t = T, T-1, \ldots, 1$.

$$P(v_{t+1} = k, s_t = j|Y_T) = \sum_l \frac{P(v_{t+1} = k, s_{t+1} = l|Y_T)}{P(v_{t+1} = k, s_{t+1} = l|Y_t)} P(v_{t+1} = k, s_t = j|Y_t) p_{lkj}^s$$

$$P(v_t = i, s_t = j|Y_T) = \sum_k \frac{P(v_{t+1} = k, s_t = j|Y_T)}{P(v_{t+1} = k, s_t = j|Y_t)} P(v_t = i, s_t = j|Y_t) p_{ki}^v$$

2.3 EM LEARNING RULES

Parameter estimation in the regime-switching model is conveniently formulated as an incomplete data problem, which can be solved using the EM algorithm (Hamilton, 1994). Each iteration of the EM algorithm is guaranteed to increase the value of the marginal log-likelihood function until a fixed point is reached. This fixed point is a local optimum of the marginal log-likelihood function.

In the M-step the model parameters are optimized using the estimates of the hidden states using the current parameter estimates. Let $\theta = \{p_{ij}^v, p_{ijk}^s, p_{ikj}^y\}$ denote the current parameter estimates. The new estimates are obtained using

$$p_{ij}^v = \frac{\sum_{t=1}^T P(v_t = i, v_{t-1} = j|Y_T; \theta)}{\sum_{t=1}^T P(v_{t-1} = j|Y_T; \theta)}$$

$$p_{ijk}^s = \frac{\sum_{t=1}^T P(s_t = i, v_t = j, s_{t-1} = k|Y_T; \theta)}{\sum_{t=1}^T P(v_t = j, s_{t-1} = k|Y_T; \theta)}$$

$$p_{ikj}^y = \frac{\sum_{t=1, if\ y_t=i\ and\ y_{t-1}=j}^T P(s_{t-1} = k|Y_T; \theta)}{\sum_{t=1,\ if\ y_{t-1}=j}^T P(s_{t-1} = k|Y_T; \theta)}$$

The E-step determines the probabilities on the right sides of the equations using the current parameter estimates. These can be determined using the smoothing equations from the previous section directly by marginalizing

$$P(v_t = k, s_t = l, v_{t+1} = i, s_{t+1} = j | Y_T)$$

$$= P(v_{t+1} = i, s_{t+1} = j | Y_T) \frac{p^v_{ik} p^s_{jkl} P(v_t = k, s_t = l | Y_t)}{P(v_{t+1} = i, s_{t+1} = j | Y_t)}$$

where the terms on the right side are obtained from the equations in the last Section.

2.4 DISCRIMINATIVE TRAINING

In our data setting, it is not known when the fraudulent accounts were victimized by fraud. This is why we use the EM algorithm to learn the two regimes from data in an incomplete data setting. We know, however, which accounts were victimized by fraud. After EM learning the discrimination ability of the model was not satisfactory. We therefore used the labeled sequences to improve the model. The reason for the poor performance was credited to unsuitable call emission probabilities in the normal state. We therefore minimize the error function $E = \sum_i \left(\max_t P(v_t^{(i)} | Y_t^{(i)}) - t^{(i)} \right)^2$ with regard to the parameter $p^y_{i=0, j=0, k=0}$, where the $t^{(i)} = \{0, 1\}$ is the label for the sequence i. The error function was minimized with Quasi-Newton procedure with numerical differentiation.

3 EXPERIMENTS

To test our approach we used a data set consisting of 600 accounts which were not affected by fraud and 304 accounts which were affected by fraud. The time period for non-fraud and fraud accounts were 49 and 92 days, respectively. We divided the data equally into training data and test data. From the non-fraud data we estimated the parameters describing the normal calling behavior, i.e. $p^y_{i,j=0,k}$. Next, we fixed the probability that an account is victimized from one time step to the next to $p^v_{i=1,j=0} = 10^{-5}$ and the probability that a victimized account becomes de-victimized as $p^v_{i=0,j=1} = 5 \times 10^{-4}$. Leaving those parameters fixed the remaining parameters were trained using the fraudulent accounts and the EM algorithm described in Section 2. We had to do unsupervised training since it was known by velocity check that the accounts were affected but it was not clear when the intrusion occurred. After unsupervised training, we further enhanced the discrimination capability of the system which helped us reduce the amount of false alarms. The final model parameters can be found in the Appendix.

After training, the system was tested using the test data. Unfortunately, it is not known when the accounts were attacked by fraud, but only on per-account basis if an account was at some point a victim of fraud. Therefore, we declare an account to be victimized if the victimized variable at some point exceeds the threshold. Also, it is interesting to study the results shown in Figure 3. We show data and posterior time-evolving probabilities for an account which is known to be victimized. From the call pattern it is obvious that there are periods of suspiciously high traffic at which the probability of victimization is recognized to be very high. We also see that the variable fraud s_t follows the bursty behavior of the fraudulent behavior correctly. Note, that for smoothing which is important both for a retrospective analysis of call data and for learning, we achieve smoother curves for the victimized variable.

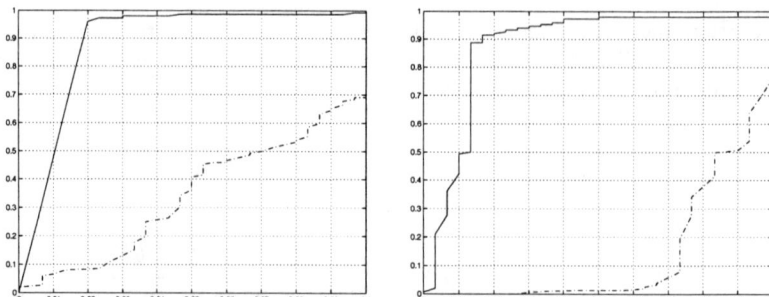

Figure 2: The Receiver Operating Characteristic (ROC) curves are shown for on-line detection (left figure) and for retrospective classification (right figure). In the figures, detection probability is plotted against the false alarm probability. The dash-dotted lines are results before, the solid lines after discriminative training. We can see that the discriminative training improves the model considerably.

After EM training and discriminative training, we tested the model both in on-line detection mode (filtering) and in retrospective classification (smoothing) with smoothed probabilities. The detection results are shown in Figure 2. With a fixed false alarm probability of 0.003, the detection probabilities for the training set were found to be 0.974 and 0.934 using on-line detection mode and with smoothed probabilities, respectively. With a testing set and a fixed false alarm probability of 0.020, we obtain the detection probabilities of 0.928 and 0.921, for the on-line detection and for retrospective classification, respectively.

4 CONCLUSIONS

We presented a call-based on-line fraud detection system which is based on a hierarchical regime-switching generative model. The inference rules are obtained from the junction tree algorithm for the underlying graphical model. The model is trained using the EM algorithm in an incomplete data setting and is further refined with gradient-based discriminative training, which considerably improves the results.

A few extensions are in the process of being implemented. First of all, it makes sense to use more than one fraud model for the different fraud scenarios and several user models to account for different user profiles. For these more complex models we might have to rely on approximations techniques such as the ones introduced by Jordan, Ghahramani and Saul (1997).

Appendix

The model parameters after EM training and discriminative training. Note that entering the fraud state without first entering the victimized state is impossible.

$$p^y_{i,j=0,k} = \begin{pmatrix} 0.9559 & 0.0441 \\ 0.3533 & 0.6467 \end{pmatrix} \quad p^y_{i,j=1,k} = \begin{pmatrix} 0.9292 & 0.0708 \\ 0.0570 & 0.9430 \end{pmatrix}$$

$$p^s_{i,j=0,k} = \begin{pmatrix} 1.0000 & 0.0000 \\ 0.0000 & 1.0000 \end{pmatrix} \quad p^s_{i,j=1,k} = \begin{pmatrix} 0.9979 & 0.0021 \\ 0.0086 & 0.9914 \end{pmatrix}$$

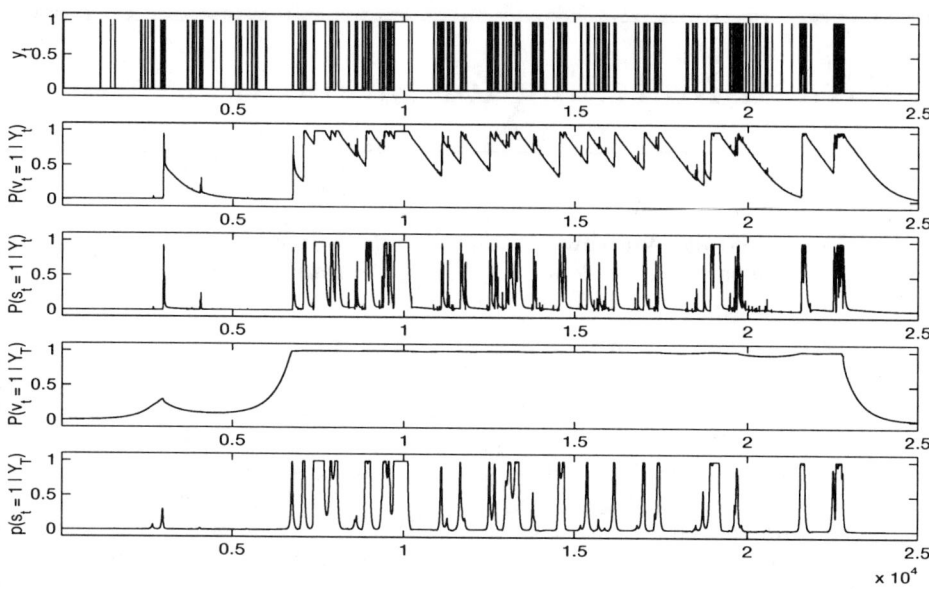

Figure 3: The first line shows the calling data y_t from a victimized account. The second and third lines show the states of the victimized and fraud variables, respectively. Both are calculated with the filtering equations. The fourth and fifth lines show the same variables using the smoothing equations. The displayed time window period is seventeen days.

References

Barson P., Field, S., Davey, N., McAskie, G., and Frank, R. (1996). The Detection of Fraud in Mobile Phone Networks. *Neural Network World,* Vol. 6, No. 4.

Bengio, Y. (1996). Markovian Models for Sequential Data. *Technical Report # 1049, Université de Montreal.*

Burge, P., Shawe-Taylor J., Moreau Y., Verrelst, H., Störmann C. and Gosset, P. (1997). BRUTUS - A Hybrid Detection Tool. *Proc. of ACTS Mobile Telecommunications Summit, Aalborg, Denmark.*

Fawcett, T. and Provost, F. (1997). Adaptive Fraud Detection. *Journal of Data Mining and Knowledge Discovery,* , Vol. 1, No. 3, pp. 1-28.

Hamilton, J. D. (1994). *Time Series Analysis.* Princeton University Press.

Jensen, Finn V. (1996). *Introduction to Bayesian Networks.* UCL Press.

Jordan, M. I, Ghahramani, Z. and Saul, L. K. (1997). Hidden Markov Decision Trees, in *Advances in Neural Information Processing Systems: Proceedings of the 1996 Conference (NIPS'9),* MIT-Press, pp. 501-507.

Kim, C.-J. (1994). Dynamical linear models with Markov-switching. *Journal of Econometrics,* Vol. 60, pp. 1-22.

Pequeno, K. A.(1997). Real-Time fraud detection: Telecom's next big step. *Telecommunications (America Edition),* Vol. 31, No. 5, pp. 59-60.

Taniguchi, M., Haft, M., Hollmén, J. and Tresp, V. (1998). Fraud detection in communications networks using neural and probabilistic methods. *Proceedings of the 1998 IEEE Int. Conf. in Acoustics, Speech and Signal Processing (ICASSP'98),* Vol. 2, pp. 1241-1244.

Graph Matching for Shape Retrieval

Benoit Huet, Andrew D.J. Cross and Edwin R. Hancock*
Department of Computer Science, University of York
York, Y01 5DD, UK

Abstract

This paper describes a Bayesian graph matching algorithm for data-mining from large structural data-bases. The matching algorithm uses edge-consistency and node attribute similarity to determine the *a posteriori* probability of a query graph for each of the candidate matches in the data-base. The node feature-vectors are constructed by computing normalised histograms of pairwise geometric attributes. Attribute similarity is assessed by computing the Bhattacharyya distance between the histograms. Recognition is realised by selecting the candidate from the data-base which has the largest *a posteriori* probability. We illustrate the recognition technique on a data-base containing 2500 line patterns extracted from real-world imagery. Here the recognition technique is shown to significantly outperform a number of algorithm alternatives.

1 Introduction

Since Barrow and Popplestone [1] first suggested that relational structures could be used to represent and interpret 2D scenes, there has been considerable interest in the machine vision literature in developing practical graph-matching algorithms [8, 3, 10]. The main computational issues are how to compare relational descriptions when there is significant structural corruption [8, 10] and how to search for the best match [3]. Despite resulting in significant improvements in the available methodology for graph-matching, there has been little progress in applying the resulting algorithms to large-scale object recognition problems. Most of the algorithms developed in the literature are evaluated for the relatively simple problem of matching a model-graph against a scene known to contain the relevant structure. A more realistic problem is that of taking a large number (maybe thousands) of scenes and retrieving the ones that best match the model. Although this problem is key to data-mining from large libraries of visual information, it has invariably been approached using low-level feature comparison techniques. Very little effort [7, 4] has been devoted to matching

---

*corresponding author erh@cs.york.ac.uk

higher-level structural primitives such as lines, curves or regions. Moreover, because of the perceived fragility of the graph matching process, there has been even less effort directed at attempting to retrieve shapes using relational information.

Here we aim to fill this gap in the literature by using graph-matching as a means of retrieving the shape from a large data-based that most closely resembles a query shape. Although the indexation images in large data-bases is a problem of current topicality in the computer vision literature [5, 6, 9], the work presented in this paper is more ambitious. Firstly, we adopt a structural abstraction of the shape recognition problem and match using attributed relational graphs. Each shape in our data-base is a pattern of line-segments. The structural abstraction is a nearest neighbour graph for the centre-points of the line-segments. In addition, we exploit attribute information for the line patterns. Here the geometric arrangement of the line-segments is encapsulated using a histogram of Euclidean invariant pairwise (binary) attributes. For each line-segment in turn we construct a normalised histogram of relative angle and length with the remaining line-segments in the pattern. These histograms capture the global geometric context of each line-segment. Moreover, we interpret the pairwise geometric histograms as measurement densities for the line-segments which we compare using the Bhattacharyya distance.

Once we have established the pattern representation, we realise object recognition using a Bayesian graph-matching algorithm. This is a two-step process. Firstly, we establish correspondence matches between the individual tokens in the query pattern and each of the patterns in the data-base. The correspondences matches are sought so as to maximise the *a posteriori* measurement probability. Once the MAP correspondence matches have been established, then the second step in our recognition architecture involves selecting the line-pattern from the data-base which has maximum matching probability.

2 MAP Framework

Formally our recognition problem is posed as follows. Each ARG in the database is a triple, $G = (V_G, E_G, A_G)$, where V_G is the set of vertices (nodes), E_G is the edge set ($E_G \subset V_G \times V_G$), and A_G is the set of node attributes. In our experimental example, the nodes represent line-structures segmented from 2D images. The edges are established by computing the N-nearest neighbour graph for the line-centres. Each node $j \in V_G$ is characterised by a vector of attributes, $\underline{x}_j$ and hence $A_G = \{\underline{x}_j | j \in V_G\}$. In the work reported here the attribute-vector is represents the contents of a normalised pairwise attribute histogram.

The data-base of line-patterns is represented by the set of ARG's $\mathcal{D} = \{G\}$. The goal is to retrieve from the data-base $\mathcal{D}$, the individual ARG that most closely resembles a query pattern $Q = (V_Q, E_Q, A_Q)$. We pose the retrieval process as one of associating with the query the graph from the data-base that has the largest *a posteriori* probability. In other words, the class identity of the graph which most closely corresponds to the query is

$$\omega_Q = \arg\max_{G' \in \mathcal{D}} P(G'|Q)$$

However, since we wish to make a detailed structural comparison of the graphs, rather than comparing their overall statistical properties, we must first establish a set of best-match correspondences between each ARG in the data-base and the query Q. The set of correspondences between the query Q and the ARG G is a relation $f_G : V_G \mapsto V_Q$ over the vertex sets of the two graphs. The mapping function consists of a set of Cartesian pairings between the nodes of the two graphs, i.e. $f_G = \{(a, \alpha); a \in V_G, \alpha \in V_Q\} \subseteq V_G \times V_Q$. Although this may appear to be a brute force method, it must be stressed that we view this process of correspondence matching as the final step in the filtering of the line-patterns. We provide more details of practical implementation in the experimental section of this paper.

With the correspondences to hand we can re-state our maximum *a posteriori* probability recognition objective as a two step process. For each graph G in turn, we locate the maximum *a posteriori* probability mapping function f_G onto the query Q. The second step is to perform recognition by selecting the graph whose mapping function results in the largest matching probability. These two steps are succinctly captured by the following statement of the recognition condition

$$\omega_Q = \arg \max_{G' \in \mathcal{D}} \max_{f_{G'}} P(f_{G'}|G', Q)$$

This global MAP condition is developed into a useful local update formula by applying the Bayes formula to the *a posteriori* matching probability. The simplification is as follows

$$P(f_G|G, Q) = \frac{p(A_G, A_Q|f_G)P(f_G|V_G, E_G, V_Q, E_Q)P(V_G, E_G)P(V_Q, E_Q)}{P(G)P(Q)}$$

The terms on the right-hand side of the Bayes formula convey the following meaning. The conditional measurement density $p(A_G, A_Q|f_G)$ models the measurement similarity of the node-sets of the two graphs. The conditional probability $P(f_G|E_G, E_Q)$ models the structural similarity of the two graphs under the current set of correspondence matches. The assumptions used in developing our simplification of the *a posteriori* matching probability are as follows. Firstly, we assume that the joint measurements are conditionally independent of the structure of the two graphs provided that the set of correspondences is known, i.e. $P(A_G, A_Q|f_G, E_G, V_G, E_Q, V_Q) = P(A_G, A_Q|f_G)$. Secondly, we assume that there is conditional independence of the two graphs in the absence of correspondences. In other words, $P(V_G, E_G, V_Q, E_Q) = P(V_Q, E_Q)P(V_G, E_G)$ and $P(G, Q) = P(G)P(Q)$. Finally, the graph priors $P(V_G, E_G)$, $P(V_Q, E_Q)$ $P(G)$ and $P(Q)$ are taken as uniform and are eliminated from the decision making process.

To continue our development, we first focus on the conditional measurement density, $p(A_G, A_Q|f_G)$ which models the process of comparing attribute similarity on the nodes of the two graphs. Assuming statistical independence of node attributes, the conditional measurement density $p(A_G, A_Q|f_G)$, can be factorised over the Cartesian pairs $(a, \alpha) \in V_G \times V_Q$ which constitute the the correspondence match f_G in the following manner

$$p(A_G, A_Q|f_G) = \prod_{(a,\alpha) \in f_G} p(\underline{x}_a, \underline{x}_\alpha | f_G(a) = \alpha)$$

As a result the correspondence matches may be optimised using a simple node-by-node discrete relaxation procedure. The rule for updating the match assigned to the node a of the graph G is

$$f_G(a) = \arg \max_{\alpha \in V_Q \cup \{\Phi\}} p(\underline{x}_a, \underline{x}_\alpha)|f(a) = \alpha)P(f_G|E_G, E_Q)$$

In order to model the structural consistency of the set of assigned matches, we turn to the framework recently reported by Finch, Wilson and Hancock [2]. This work provides a framework for computing graph-matching energies using the weighted Hamming distance between matched cliques. Since we are dealing with a large-scale object recognition system, we would like to minimise the computational overheads associated with establishing correspondence matches. For this reason, rather than working with graph neighbourhoods or cliques, we chose to work with the relational units of the smallest practical size. In other words we satisfy ourself with measuring consistency at the edge level. For edge-units, the structural matching probability $P(f_G|V_G, E_G, V_Q, E_Q)$ is computed from the formula

$$\ln P(f_G|V_G, E_G, V_G, E_Q) = \sum_{(a,b)\in E_G} \sum_{(\alpha,\beta)\in E_Q} \{\ln(1-P_e)s_{a,\alpha}s_{b,\beta} + \ln P_e(1-s_{a,\alpha}s_{b,\beta})\}$$

where P_e is the probability of an error appearing on one of the edges of the matched structure. The $s_{a,\alpha}$ are assignment variables which are used to represent the current state of match and convey the following meaning

$$s_{a,\alpha} = \begin{cases} 1 & \text{if } f_G(a) = \alpha \\ 0 & \text{otherwise} \end{cases}$$

3 Histogram-based consistency

We now furnish some details of the shape retrieval task used in our experimental evaluation of the recognition method. In particular, we focus on the problem of recognising 2D line patterns in a manner which is invariant to rotation, translation and scale. The raw information available for each line segment are its orientation (angle with respect to the horizontal axis) and its length (see figure 1). To illustrate how the Euclidean invariant pairwise feature attributes are computed, suppose that we denote the line segments associated with the nodes indexed a and b by the vectors $\underline{v}_a$ and $\underline{v}_b$ respectively. The vectors are directed away from their point of intersection. The pairwise relative angle attribute is given by

$$\theta_{a,b} = \arccos\left[\frac{\underline{v}_a \cdot \underline{v}_b}{|\underline{v}_a||\underline{v}_b|}\right]$$

From the relative angle we compute the directed relative angle. This involves giving

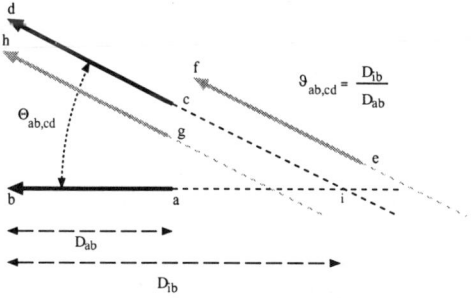

Figure 1: Geometry for shape representation

the relative angle a positive sign if the direction of the angle from the baseline $\underline{v}_a$ to its partner $\underline{v}_b$ is clockwise and a negative sign if it is counter-clockwise. This allows us to extend the range of angles describing pairs of segments from $[0,\pi]$ to $[-\pi,\pi]$.

The directed relative position $\vartheta_{a,b}$ is represented by the normalised length ratio between the oriented baseline vector $\underline{v}_a$ and the vector $\underline{v}'$ joining the end (b) of the baseline segment (ab) to the intersection of the segment pair (cd).

$$\vartheta_{a,b} = \frac{1}{\frac{1}{2} + \frac{D_{ib}}{D_{ab}}}$$

The physical range of this attribute is $(0, 1]$. A relative position of 0 indicates that the two segments are parallel, while a relative position of 1 indicates that the two segments intersect at the middle point of the baseline.

The Euclidean invariant angle and position attributes $\theta_{a,b}$ and $\vartheta_{a,b}$ are binned in a histogram. Suppose that $S_a(\mu, \nu) = \{(a,b)|\theta_{a,b} \in A_\mu \wedge \vartheta_{a,b} \in R_\nu \wedge b \in V_D\}$ is the set of nodes whose pairwise geometric attributes with the node a are spanned by the range of directed relative angles A_μ and the relative position attribute range R_ν. The contents of the histogram bin spanning the two attribute ranges is given by $H_a(\mu, \nu) = |S_a(\mu, \nu)|$. Each histogram contains n_A relative angle bins and n_R length ratio bins. The normalised geometric histogram bin-entries are computed as follows

$$h_a(\mu, \nu) = \frac{H_a(\mu, \nu)}{\sum_{\mu'=1}^{n_A} \sum_{\nu'=1}^{n_R} H_a(\mu, \nu)}$$

The probability of match between the pattern-vectors is computed using the Bhattacharyya distance between the normalised histograms.

$$P(f(a) = \alpha | \underline{x}_a, \underline{x}_\alpha) = \frac{\sum_{\mu=1}^{n_A} \sum_{\nu=1}^{n_R} h_a(\mu, \nu) h_\alpha(\mu, \nu)}{\sum_{j' \in Q} \sum_{\mu'=1}^{n_A} \sum_{\nu'=1}^{n_R} h_a(\mu, \nu) h_\alpha(\mu, \nu)} = \exp[-B_{a,\alpha}]$$

With this modelling ingredient, the condition for recognition is

$$\omega_Q = \arg\min_{G' \in \mathcal{D}} \sum_{(a,b) \in E'_G} \sum_{(\alpha,\beta) \in E_Q} \left\{ -B_{a,\alpha} - B_{b,\beta} + \ln(1-P_e) s_{a,\alpha} s_{b,\beta} + \ln P_e (1 - s_{a,\alpha} s_{b,\beta}) \right\}$$

4 Experiments

The aim in this section is to evaluate the graph-based recognition scheme on a data-base of real-world line-patterns. We have conducted our recognition experiments with a data-base of 2500 line-patterns each containing over a hundred lines. The line-patterns have been obtained by applying line/edge detection algorithms to the raw grey-scale images followed by polygonisation. For each line-pattern in the data-base, we construct the six-nearest neighbour graph. The feature extraction process together with other details of the data used in our study are described in recent papers where we have focussed on the issues of histogram representation [4] and the optimal choice of the relational structure for the purposes of recognition. In order to prune the set of line-patterns for detailed graph-matching we select about 10% of the data-base using a two-step process. This consists of first refining the data-base using a global histogram of pairwise attributes [4]. The top quartile of matches selected in this way are then further refined using a variant of the Haussdorff distance to select the set of pairwise attributes that best match against the query.

The recognition task is posed as one of recovering the line-pattern which most closely resembles a digital map. The original images from which our line-patterns have been obtained are from a number of diverse sources. However, a subset of the images are aerial infra-red line-scan views of southern England. Two of these infra-red images correspond to different views of the area covered by the digital map. These views are obtained when the line-scan device is flying at different altitudes. The line-scan device used to obtain the aerial images introduces severe barrel distortions and hence the map and aerial images are not simply related via a Euclidean or affine transformation. The remaining line-patterns in the data-base have been extracted from trademarks and logos. It is important to stress that although the raw images are obtained from different sources, there is nothing salient about their associated line-pattern representations that allows us to distinguish them from one-another.

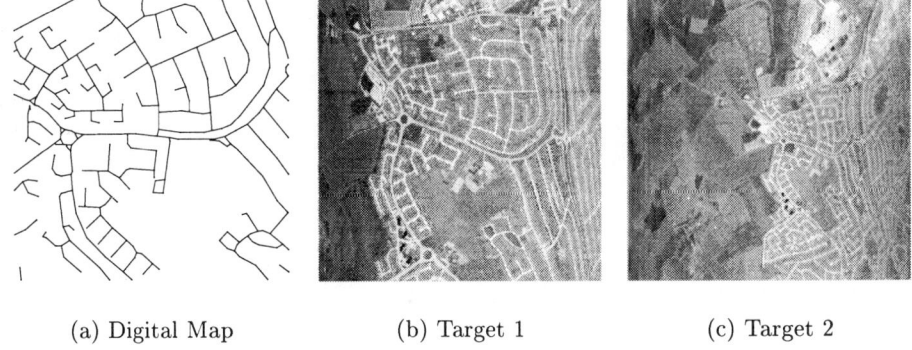

(a) Digital Map (b) Target 1 (c) Target 2

Figure 2: Images from the data-base

Moreover, since it is derived from a digital map rather than one of the images in the data-base, the query is not identical to any of the line-patterns in the model library.

We aim to assess the importance of different attributes representation on the retrieval process. To this end, we compare node-based and the histogram-based attribute representation. We also consider the effect of taking the relative angle and relative position attributes both singly and in tandem. The final aspect of the comparison is to consider the effects of using the attributes purely for initialisation purposes and also in a persistent way during the iteration of the matching process. To this end we consider the following variants of our algorithm.

- **Non-Persistent Attributes:** Here we ignore the attribute information provided by the node-histograms after the first iteration and attempt to maximise the structural congruence of the graphs.

- **Local attributes:** Here we use only the single node attributes rather than an attribute histogram to model the *a posteriori* matching probabilities.

Graph Matching Strategy	Retrieval Accuracy	Iterations per recall
Rel. Position Attribute (Initialisation only)	39%	5.2
Rel. Angle Attribute (Initialisation only)	45%	4.75
Rel. Angle + Position Attributes (Initialisation only)	58%	4.27
1D Rel. Position Histogram (Initialisation only)	42%	4.7
1D Rel. Angle Histogram (Initialisation only)	59%	4.2
2D Histogram (Initialisation only)	68%	3.9
Rel. Position Attribute (Persistent)	63%	3.96
Rel. Angle Attribute (Persistent)	89%	3.59
Rel. Angle + Position Attributes (Persistent)	98%	3.31
1D Rel. Position Histogram (Persistent)	66%	3.46
1D Rel. Angle Histogram (Persistent)	92%	3.23
2D Histogram (Persistent)	100%	3.12

Table 1: Recognition performance of various recognition strategies averaged over 26 queries in a database of 260 line-patterns

In Table 1 we present the recognition performance for each of the recognition strategies in turn. The table lists the recall performance together with the average number of iterations per recall for each of the recognition strategies in turn. The main features to note from this table are as follows. Firstly, the iterative recall using the full histogram representation outperforms each of the remaining recognition methods in terms of both accuracy and computational overheads. Secondly, it is interesting to compare the effect of using the histogram in the initialisation-only and iteration persistent modes. In the latter case the recall performance is some 32% better than in the former case. In the non-persistent mode the best recognition accuracy that can be obtained is 68%. Moreover, the recall is typically achieved in only 3.12 iterations as opposed to 3.9 (average over 26 queries on a database of 260 images). Finally, the histogram representation provides better performance, and more significantly, much faster recall than the single-attribute similarity measure. When the attributes are used singly, rather than in tandem, then it is the relative angle that appears to be the most powerful.

5 Conclusions

We have presented a practical graph-matching algorithm for data-mining in large structural libraries. The main conclusion to be drawn from this study is that the combined use of structural and histogram information improves both recognition performance and recall speed. There are a number of ways in which the ideas presented in this paper can be extended. Firstly, we intend to explore more a perceptually meaningful representation of the line patterns, using grouping principals derived from Gestalt psychology. Secondly, we are exploring the possibility of formulating the filtering of line-patterns prior to graph matching using Bayes decision trees.

References

[1] H. Barrow and R. Popplestone. Relational descriptions in picture processing. *Machine Intelligence*, 5:377–396, 1971.

[2] A. Finch, R. Wilson, and E. Hancock. Softening discrete relaxation. *Advances in NIPS 9, Edited by M. Mozer, M. Jordan and T. Petsche, MIT Press*, pages 438–444, 1997.

[3] S. Gold and A. Rangarajan. A graduated assignment algorithm for graph matching. *IEEE PAMI*, 18:377–388, 1996.

[4] B. Huet and E. Hancock. Relational histograms for shape indexing. *IEEE ICCV*, pages 563–569, 1998.

[5] W. Niblack et al.. The QBIC project: Querying images by content using color, texture and shape. *Image and Vision Storage and Retrieval*, 173–187, 1993.

[6] A. P. Pentland, R. W. Picard, and S. Scarloff. Photobook: tools for content-based manipulation of image databases. *Storage and Retrieval for Image and Video Database II*, pages 34–47, February 1994.

[7] K. Sengupta and K. Boyer. Organising large structural databases. *IEEE PAMI*, 17(4):321–332, 1995.

[8] L. Shapiro and R. Haralick. A metric for comparing relational descriptions. *IEEE PAMI*, 7(1):90–94, 1985.

[9] M. Swain and D. Ballard. Color indexing. *International Journal of Computer Vision*, 7(1):11–32, 1991.

[10] R. Wilson and E. R. Hancock. Structural matching by discrete relaxation. *IEEE PAMI*, 19(6):634–648, June 1997.

Scheduling Straight-Line Code Using Reinforcement Learning and Rollouts

Amy McGovern and Eliot Moss
{amy|moss@cs.umass.edu}
Department of Computer Science
University of Massachusetts, Amherst
Amherst, MA 01003

Abstract

The execution order of a block of computer instructions can make a difference in its running time by a factor of two or more. In order to achieve the best possible speed, compilers use heuristic schedulers appropriate to each specific architecture implementation. However, these heuristic schedulers are time-consuming and expensive to build. In this paper, we present results using both rollouts and reinforcement learning to construct heuristics for scheduling basic blocks. The rollout scheduler outperformed a commercial scheduler, and the reinforcement learning scheduler performed almost as well as the commercial scheduler.

1 Introduction

Although high-level code is generally written as if it were going to be executed sequentially, many modern computers are pipelined and allow for the simultaneous issue of multiple instructions. In order to take advantage of this feature, a scheduler needs to reorder the instructions in a way that preserves the semantics of the original high-level code while executing it as quickly as possible. An efficient schedule can produce a speedup in execution of a factor of two or more. However, building a scheduler can be an arduous process. Architects developing a new computer must manually develop a specialized instruction scheduler each time a change is made in the proposed system. Building a scheduler automatically can save time and money. It can allow the architects to explore the design space more thoroughly and to use more accurate metrics in evaluating designs.

Moss et al. (1997) showed that supervised learning techniques can induce excellent basic block instruction schedulers for the Digital Alpha 21064 processor. Although all of the supervised learning methods performed quite well, they shared several limitations. Supervised learning requires exact input/output pairs. Generating these training pairs requires an optimal scheduler that searches every valid permutation of the instructions within a basic block and saves the optimal permutation (the schedule with the smallest running time). However, this search was too time-consuming to perform on blocks with more than 10 instructions, because optimal instruction scheduling is NP-hard. Using a semi-supervised method such as reinforcement learning or rollouts does not require generating training pairs, so the method can be applied to larger basic blocks and can be trained without knowing optimal schedules.

2 Domain Overview

Moss et al. (1997) gave a full description of the domain. This study presents an overview, necessary details, our experimental method and detailed results for both rollouts and reinforcement learning.

We focused on scheduling *basic blocks* of instructions on the 21064 version (DEC, 1992) of the Digital Alpha processor (Sites, 1992). A basic block is a set of instructions with a single entry point and a single exit point. Our schedulers could reorder instructions within a basic block but could not rewrite, add, or remove any instructions. The goal of each scheduler is to find a least-cost valid ordering of the instructions. The cost is defined as the simulated execution time of the block. A valid ordering is one that preserves the semantically necessary ordering constraints of the original code. We insure validity by creating a dependency graph that directly represents those necessary ordering relationships. This graph is a directed acyclic graph (DAG).

The Alpha 21064 is a dual-issue machine with two different execution pipelines. Dual issue occurs only if a number of detailed conditions hold, e.g., the two instructions match the two pipelines. An instruction can take anywhere from one to many tens of cycles to execute. Researchers at Digital have a publicly available 21064 simulator that also includes a heuristic scheduler for basic blocks. We call that scheduler *DEC*. The simulator gives the running time for a given scheduled block assuming all memory references hit the cache and all resources are available at the beginning of the block. All of our schedulers used a greedy algorithm to schedule the instructions, i.e., they built schedules sequentially from beginning to end with no backtracking.

In order to test each scheduling algorithm, we used the 18 SPEC95 benchmark programs. Ten of these programs are written in FORTRAN and contain mostly floating point calculations. Eight of the programs are written in C and focus more on integer, string, and pointer calculations. Each program was compiled using the commercial Digital compiler at the highest level of optimization. We call the schedules output by the compiler *ORIG*. This collection has 447,127 basic blocks, containing 2,205,466 instructions.

3 Rollouts

Rollouts are a form of Monte Carlo search, first introduced by Tesauro and Galperin (1996) for use in backgammon. Bertsekas et al. (1997a,b) have explored rollouts in other domains and proven important theoretical results. In the instruction scheduling domain, rollouts work as follows: suppose the scheduler comes to a point where it has a partial schedule and a set of (more than one) candidate instructions to add to the schedule. For each candidate, the scheduler appends it to the partial schedule and then follows a fixed policy π to schedule the remaining instructions. When the schedule is complete, the scheduler evaluates the running time and returns. When π is stochastic, this rollout can be repeated many times for each instruction to achieve a measure of the average expected outcome. After rolling out each candidate, the scheduler picks the one with the best average running time.

Our first set of rollout experiments compared three different rollout policies π. The theory developed by Bertsekas et al. (1997a,b) proved that if we used the DEC scheduler as π, we would perform no worse than DEC. An architect proposing a new machine might not have a good heuristic available to use as π, so we also considered policies more likely to be available. The first was the random policy, *RANDOM-π*, which is a choice that is clearly always available. Under this policy, the rollout makes all choices randomly. We also used the ordering produced by the optimizing compiler ORIG, denoted *ORIG-π*. The last rollout policy tested was the DEC scheduler itself, denoted *DEC-π*.

The scheduler performed only one rollout per candidate instruction when using ORIG-π and DEC-π because they are deterministic. We used 25 rollouts for RANDOM-π. After performing a number of rollouts for each candidate instruction, we chose the instruction with the best average running time. As a baseline scheduler, we also scheduled each block randomly. Because the running time increases quadratically with the number of rollouts, we focused our rollout experiments on one program in the SPEC95 suite: *applu*.

Table 1 gives the performance of each rollout scheduler as compared to the DEC scheduler on all 33,007 basic blocks of size 200 or less from applu. To assess the performance of each rollout policy π, we used the ratio of the weighted execution time of the rollout scheduler to the weighted execution time of the DEC scheduler. More concisely, the performance measure was:

$$\text{ratio} = \frac{\sum_{\text{all blocks}} \text{rollout scheduler execution time} * \text{number of times block is executed}}{\sum_{\text{all blocks}} \text{DEC scheduler execution time} * \text{number of times block is executed}}$$

This means that a faster running time on the part of our scheduler would give a smaller ratio.

Scheduler	Ratio	Scheduler	Ratio
Random	1.3150	RANDOM-π	1.0560
ORIG-π	0.9895	DEC-π	0.9875

Table 1: Ratios of the weighted execution time of the rollout scheduler to the DEC scheduler. A ratio of less than one means that the rollouts outperformed the DEC scheduler.

All of the rollout schedulers far outperformed the random scheduler which was 31% slower than DEC. By only adding rollouts, RANDOM-π was able to achieve a running time only 5% slower than DEC. Only the schedulers using ORIG-π and DEC-π as a model outperformed the DEC scheduler. Using ORIG-π and DEC-π for rollouts produced a schedule that was 1.1% faster than the DEC scheduler on average. Although this improvement may seem small, the DEC scheduler is known to make optimal choices 99.13% of the time for blocks of size 10 or less (Stefanović, 1997).

Rollouts were tested only on applu rather than on the entire SPEC95 benchmark suite due to the lengthy computation time. Rollouts are costly because performing m rollouts on n instructions is $O(n^2 m)$, whereas a greedy scheduling algorithm is $O(n)$. Again, because of the time required, we only performed five runs of RANDOM-π. Since DEC-π and ORIG-π are deterministic, only one run was necessary. We also ran the random scheduler 5 times. Each number reported above is the geometric mean of the ratios across the five runs.

Part of the motivation behind using rollouts in a scheduler is to obtain fast schedules without spending the time to build a precise heuristic. With this in mind, we explored RANDOM-π more closely in a follow-up experiment.

Evaluation of the number of rollouts

This experiment considered how performance varies with the number of rollouts. We tested 1, 5, 10, 25, and 50 rollouts per candidate instruction. We also varied the metric for choosing among candidates. Instead of always choosing the instruction with the best average performance, we also experimented with selecting the instruction with the absolute best running time among its rollouts. We hypothesized that selection of the absolute best path might lead to better performance overall. These experiments were performed on all 33,007 basic blocks of size 200 or less from applu.

Figure 1 shows the performance of the rollout scheduler as a function of the number of rollouts. Performance is assessed in the same way as before: ratio of weighted execution

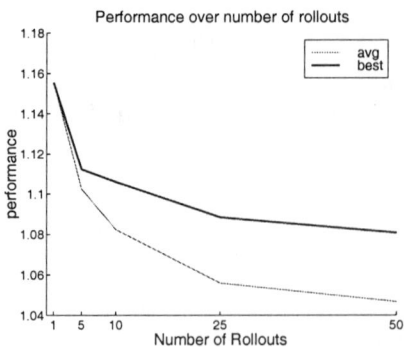

Figure 1: Performance of rollout scheduler with the random model as a function of the number of rollouts and the choice of evaluation function.

times. Thus, a lower number is better. Each data point represents the geometric mean over five different runs. The difference in performance between one rollout and five rollouts using the average choice for each rollout is 1.16 versus 1.10. However, the difference between 25 rollouts and 50 rollouts is only 1.06 versus 1.05. This indicates the tradeoff between schedule quality and the number of rollouts. Also, choosing the instructions with the best rollout schedule did not yield better performance over any numbers of rollouts. We hypothesize that this is due to the stochastic nature of the rollouts. Once the scheduler chooses an instruction, it repeats the rollout process again. By choosing the instruction with the absolute best rollout, there is no guarantee that the scheduler will find that permutation of instructions again on the next rollout. When it chooses the instruction with the best average rollout, the scheduler has a better chance of finding a good schedule on the next rollout.

Although the rollout schedulers performed quite well, the extremely long scheduling time is a major drawback. Using 25 rollouts per block took over 6 hours to schedule one program. Unless this aspect can be improved, rollouts cannot be used for all blocks in a commercial scheduler or in evaluating more than a few proposed machine architectures. However, because rollout scheduling performance is high, rollouts could be used to optimize the schedules on important (long running times or frequently executed) blocks within a program.

4 Reinforcement Learning Results

4.1 Overview

Reinforcement learning (RL) is a collection of methods for discovering near-optimal solutions to stochastic sequential decision problems (Sutton & Barto, 1998). A reinforcement learning system does not require a teacher to specify correct actions. Instead, the learning agent tries different actions and observes their consequences to determine which actions are best. More specifically, in the reinforcement learning framework, a learning *agent* interacts with an *environment* over a series of discrete time steps $t = 0, 1, 2, 3, \ldots$. At each time t, the agent is in some *state*, denoted s_t, and chooses an action, denoted a_t, which causes the environment to transition to state s_{t+1} and to emit a reward, denoted r_{t+1}. The next state and reward depend only on the preceding state and action, but they may depend on it in a stochastic fashion. The objective is to learn a (possibly stochastic) mapping from states to actions called a *policy*, which maximizes the cumulative discounted reward received by the agent. More precisely, the objective is to choose action a_t so as to maximize the expected *return*, $E\left\{\sum_{i=0}^{\infty} \gamma^i r_{t+i+1}\right\}$, where $\gamma \in [0, 1)$ is a discount-rate parameter.

A common solution strategy is to approximate the *optimal value function* V^*, which maps states to the maximal expected return that can be obtained starting in each state and taking the best action. In this paper we use *temporal difference (TD) learning* (Sutton, 1988). In this method, the approximation to V^* is represented by a table with an entry $V(s)$ for every state. After each transition from state s_t to state s_{t+1}, under an action with reward r_{t+1}, the estimated value function $V(s_t)$ is updated by:

$$V(s_t) \leftarrow V(s_t) + \alpha \left[r_{t+1} + \gamma V(s_{t+1}) - V(s_t) \right]$$

where α is a positive step-size parameter.

4.2 Experimental Results

Scheeff et al. (1997) have previously experimented with reinforcement learning in this domain. However, the results were not as good as hoped. Finding the right reward structure was the difficult part of using RL in this domain. Rewarding based on number of cycles to execute the block does not work well as it punishes the learner on long blocks. To normalize for this effect, Scheeff et al. (1997) rewarded based on the cycles per instruction (CPI). However, learning with this reward also did not work well as some blocks have more unavoidable idle time than others. A reward based solely on CPI does not account for this aspect. To account for this variation across blocks, we gave the RL scheduler a final reward of:

$$r = \text{time to execute block} - \max \left(\text{minimum weighted critical path}, \left(\frac{\text{\# of instructions}}{2} \right) \right)$$

The scheduler received a reward of zero unless the schedule was complete. As the 21064 processor can only issue two instructions at a time, the number of instructions divided by 2 gives an absolute lower bound on the running time. The weighted critical path (wcp) helps to solve the problem of the same size blocks being easier or harder to schedule than others. When a block is harder to execute than another block of the same size, the wcp tends to be higher, thus causing the learner to get a different reward. The wcp is correlated with the predicted number of execution cycles for the DEC scheduler ($r = 0.9$) and the number of instructions divided by 2 is also correlated ($r = 0.78$) with the DEC scheduler. Future experiments will use a weighted combination of these two features to compute the reward.

As with the supervised learning results presented in Moss et al. (1997), the RL system learned a preferential value function between candidate instructions. That is, instead of learning the value of instruction A or instruction B, RL learned the value of choosing instruction A over instruction B. The state space consisted of a tuple of features from a current partial schedule and the two candidate instructions. These features were derived from knowledge of the DEC simulator. The features and our intuition for their importance are summarized in Table 2.

Previous experiments (Moss et al. 1997) showed that the actual value of wcp and e did not matter as much as their relative values. Thus, for those features we used the signum (σ) of the difference of their values for the two candidate instruction. Signum returns $-1, 0$, or 1 depending on whether the value is less than, equal to, or greater than zero. Using this representation, the RL state space consisted of the following tuple, given candidate instruction x and y and partial schedule p:

$$\text{state\_vec}(p, x, y) = \langle \text{odd}(p), \text{ic}(x), \text{ic}(y), \text{d}(x), \text{d}(y), \sigma(\text{wcp}(x) - \text{wcp}(y)), \sigma(\text{e}(x) - \text{e}(y)) \rangle$$

This yields 28,800 unique states. Figure 2 shows an example partial schedule, a set of candidate instructions, and the resulting states for the RL system.

The RL scheduler does not learn over states where there are no choices to be made. The last choice point in a trajectory is given the final reward even if further instructions are scheduled from that point. The values of multiple states are updated at each time step because the instruction that is chosen affects the preference function of multiple states. For

Heuristic Name	Heuristic Description	Intuition for Use
Odd Partial (odd)	Is the current number of instructions scheduled odd or even?	If TRUE, we're interested in scheduling instructions that can dual-issue with the previous instruction.
Instruction Class (ic)	The Alpha's instructions can be divided into equivalence classes with respect to timing properties.	The instructions in each class can be executed only in certain execution pipelines, etc.
Weighted Critical Path (wcp)	The height of the instruction in the DAG (the length of the longest chain of instructions dependent on this one), with edges weighted by expected latency of the result produced by the instruction	Instructions on longer critical paths should be scheduled first, since they affect the lower bound of the schedule cost.
Actual Dual (d)	Can the instruction dual-issue with the previous scheduled instruction?	If Odd Partial is TRUE, it is important that we find an instruction, if there is one, that can issue in the same cycle with the previous scheduled instruction.
Max Delay (e)	The earliest cycle when the instruction can begin to execute, relative to the current cycle; this takes into account any wait for inputs for functional units to become available	We want to schedule instructions that will have their data and functional unit available earliest.

Table 2: Features for Instructions and Partial Schedule

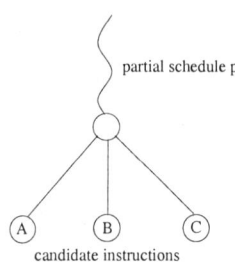

States for RL system	
State label	State
AB	state_vec(p,A,B)
AC	state_vec(p,A,C)
BC	state_vec(p,B,C)
BA	state_vec(p,B,A)
CA	state_vec(p,C,A)
CB	state_vec(p,C,B)

Figure 2: On the left is a graphical depiction of a partial schedule and three candidate instructions. The table on the right shows how the RL system makes its states from this.

example, using the partial schedule and candidate instructions shown in Figure 2, scheduling instruction A, the RL system would backup values for AB, AC, and the opposite values for BA and CA.

Using this system, we performed leave-one-out cross validation across all blocks of the SPEC95 benchmark suite. Blocks with more than 800 instructions were broken into blocks of 800 or less because of memory limitations on the DEC simulator. This was true for only two applications: applu and fpppp. The RL system was trained online for 19 of the 20 applications using $\alpha = 0.05$ and an ϵ-greedy exploration method with $\epsilon = 0.05$. This was repeated 20 different times, holding one program from SPEC95 out of the training each time. We then evaluated the greedy policy ($\epsilon = 0$) learned by the RL system on each program that had been held out. All ties were broken randomly. Performance was assessed the same way as before. The results for each benchmark are shown in Table 3. Overall, the RL scheduler performed only 2% slower than DEC. This is a geometric mean over all applications in the suite and on all blocks. Although the RL system did not outperform the DEC scheduler overall, it significantly outperformed DEC on the large blocks (applu-big and fpppp-big).

5 Conclusions

The advantages of the RL scheduler are its performance on the task, its speed, and the fact that it does not rely on any heuristics for training. Each run was much faster than with rollouts and the performance came close to the performance of the DEC scheduler. In a

App	Ratio	App	Ratio	App	Ratio	App	Ratio
applu	1.001	*applu-big*	*0.959*	apsi	1.018	cc1	1.022
compress95	*0.977*	fpppp	1.055	*fpppp-big*	*0.977*	go	1.028
hydro2d	1.022	*ijpeg*	*0.975*	li	1.012	m88ksim	1.042
mgrid	1.009	perl	1.014	su2cor	1.018	swim	1.040
tomcatv	1.019	turb3d	1.218	vortex	1.032	wave5	1.032

Table 3: Performance of the greedy RL-scheduler on each application in SPEC95 over all leave-one-out cross-validation runs as compared to DEC. Applications whose running time was better than DEC are shown in italics.

system where multiple architectures are being tested, RL could provide a good scheduler with minimal setup and training.

We have demonstrated two methods of instruction scheduling that do not rely on having heuristics and that perform quite well. Future work could address tying the two methods together while retaining the speed of the RL learner, issues of global instruction scheduling, scheduling loops, and validating the techniques on other architectures.

Acknowledgments

We thank John Cavazos and Darko Stefanović for setting up the simulator and for prior work in this domain, along with Paul Utgoff, Doina Precup, Carla Brodley, and David Scheeff. We also wish to thank Andrew Barto, Andrew Fagg, and Doina Precup for comments on earlier versions of the paper. This work is supported in part by the National Physical Science Consortium, Lockheed Martin, Advanced Technology Labs, and NSF grant IRI-9503687 to Roderic A. Grupen and Andrew G. Barto. We thank various people of Digital Equipment Corporation, for the DEC scheduler and the ATOM program instrumentation tool (Srivastava & Eustace, 1994), essential to this work. We also thank Sun Microsystems and Hewlett-Packard for their support.

References

Bertsekas, D. P. (1997). Differential training of rollout policies. In *Proc. of the 35th Allerton Conference on Communication, Control, and Computing*. Allerton Park, Ill.

Bertsekas, D. P., Tsitsiklis, J. N. & Wu, C. (1997). Rollout algorithms for combinatorial optimization. *Journal of Heuristics*.

DEC (1992). *DEC chip 21064-AA Microprocessor Hardware Reference Manual* (first edition Ed.). Maynard, MA: Digital Equipment Corporation.

Moss, J. E. B., Utgoff, P. E., Cavazos, J., Precup, D., Stefanović, D., Brodley, C. E. & Scheeff, D. T. (1997). Learning to schedule straight-line code. In *Proceedings of Advances in Neural Information Processing Systems 10 (Proceedings of NIPS'97)*. MIT Press.

Scheeff, D., Brodley, C., Moss, E., Cavazos, J. & Stefanović, D. (1997). Applying reinforcement learning to instruction scheduling within basic blocks. Technical report, University of Massachusetts, Amherst.

Sites, R. (1992). *Alpha Architecture Reference Manual*. Maynard, MA: Digital Equipment Corporation.

Srivastava, A. & Eustace, A. (1994). ATOM: A system for building customized program analysis tools. In *Proc. ACM SIGPLAN '94 Conf. on Prog. Lang. Design and Impl.* (pp. 196–205).

Stefanović, D. (1997). The character of the instruction scheduling problem. University of Massachusetts, Amherst.

Sutton, R. S. (1988). Learning to predict by the method of temporal differences. *Machine Learning*, *3*, 9–44.

Sutton, R. S. & Barto, A. G. (1998). *Reinforcement Learning. An Introduction*. Cambridge, MA: MIT Press.

Tesauro, G. & Galperin, G. R. (1996). On-line policy improvement using monte-carlo search. In *Advances in Neural Information Processing: Proceedings of the Ninth Conference*. MIT Press.

Bayesian Modeling of Facial Similarity

Baback Moghaddam
Mitsubishi Electric Research Laboratory
201 Broadway
Cambridge, MA 02139, USA
baback@merl.com

Tony Jebara and Alex Pentland
Massachusettes Institute of Technology
20 Ames St.
Cambridge, MA 02139, USA
{jebara,sandy}@media.mit.edu

Abstract

In previous work [6, 9, 10], we advanced a new technique for direct visual matching of images for the purposes of face recognition and image retrieval, using a *probabilistic* measure of similarity based primarily on a Bayesian (MAP) analysis of image differences, leading to a "dual" basis similar to eigenfaces [13]. The performance advantage of this probabilistic matching technique over standard Euclidean nearest-neighbor eigenface matching was recently demonstrated using results from DARPA's 1996 "FERET" face recognition competition, in which this probabilistic matching algorithm was found to be the top performer. We have further developed a simple method of replacing the costly compution of *nonlinear* (online) Bayesian similarity measures by the relatively inexpensive computation of *linear* (offline) subspace projections and simple (online) Euclidean norms, thus resulting in a significant computational speed-up for implementation with very large image databases as typically encountered in real-world applications.

1 Introduction

Current approaches to image matching for visual object recognition and image database retrieval often make use of simple image similarity metrics such as Euclidean distance or normalized correlation, which correspond to a template-matching approach to recognition [2, 5]. For example, in its simplest form, the similarity measure $S(I_1, I_2)$ between two images I_1 and I_2 can be set to be inversely proportional to the norm $||I_1 - I_2||$. Such a simple formulation suffers from a major drawback: it does not exploit knowledge of which types of variation are critical (as opposed to incidental) in expressing similarity. In this paper, we formulate a *probabilistic* similarity measure which is based on the probability that the image intensity differences, denoted by $\Delta = I_1 - I_2$, are characteristic of typical variations in appearance of the *same* object. For example, for purposes of face recognition, we can define two classes of facial image variations: *intrapersonal* variations Ω_I (corresponding, for example, to different facial expressions of the *same* individual) and *extrapersonal* variations Ω_E (corresponding to variations between *different* individuals). Our similarity measure is then expressed in terms of the probability

$$S(I_1, I_2) = P(\Delta \in \Omega_I) = P(\Omega_I | \Delta) \tag{1}$$

where $P(\Omega_I | \Delta)$ is the *a posteriori* probability given by Bayes rule, using estimates of the likelihoods $P(\Delta | \Omega_I)$ and $P(\Delta | \Omega_E)$. The likelihoods are derived from training data using an efficient subspace method for density estimation of high-dimensional data [7, 8]. This Bayesian (MAP) approach can also be viewed as a generalized nonlinear extension of Linear Discriminant Analysis (LDA) [12, 3] or "FisherFace" techniques [1] for face recognition. Moreover, our nonlinear generalization has distinct computational/storage advantages over some of these linear methods for large databases.

2 Difference Density Modeling

Consider the problem of characterizing the type of intensity differences which occur when matching two images in a face recognition task. We have two classes (intrapersonal Ω_I and extrapersonal Ω_E) which we will assume form Gaussian distributions whose likelihoods can be estimated as $P(\Delta | \Omega_I)$ and $P(\Delta | \Omega_E)$ for a given intensity difference $\Delta = I_1 - I_2$.

Given these likelihoods we can evaluate a similarity score $S(I_1, I_2)$ between a pair of images directly in terms of the intrapersonal *a posteriori* probability as given by Bayes rule:

$$S = \frac{P(\Delta|\Omega_I)P(\Omega_I)}{P(\Delta|\Omega_I)P(\Omega_I) + P(\Delta|\Omega_E)P(\Omega_E)} \tag{2}$$

where the priors $P(\Omega)$ can be set to reflect specific operating conditions (*e.g.*, number of test images *vs.* the size of the database) or other sources of *a priori* knowledge regarding the two images being matched. Additionally, this particular Bayesian formulation casts the standard face recognition task (essentially an M-ary classification problem for M individuals) into a *binary* pattern classification problem with Ω_I and Ω_E. This much simpler problem is then solved using the maximum *a posteriori* (MAP) rule — *i.e.*, two images are determined to belong to the same individual if $P(\Omega_I|\Delta) > P(\Omega_E|\Delta)$, or equivalently, if $S(I_1, I_2) > \frac{1}{2}$.

To deal with the high-dimensionality of Δ, we make use of the efficient density estimation method proposed by Moghaddam & Pentland [7, 8] which divides the vector space $\mathcal{R}^N$ into two complementary subspaces using an eigenspace decomposition. This method relies on a Principal Components Analysis (PCA) [4] to form a low-dimensional estimate of the complete likelihood which can be evaluated using only the first M principal components, where $M << N$.

3 Efficient Similarity Computation

Consider now a feature space of Δ vectors, the differences between two images (I_j and I_k). The two classes of interest in this space correspond to intrapersonal and extrapersonal variations and each is modeled as a high-dimensional Gaussian density as in Equation 3. The densities are zero-mean since for each $\Delta = I_j - I_k$ there exists a $\Delta = I_k - I_j$.

$$P(\Delta|\Omega_E) = \frac{e^{-\frac{1}{2}\Delta^T \Sigma_E^{-1} \Delta}}{(2\pi)^{D/2}|\Sigma_E|^{1/2}}$$
$$P(\Delta|\Omega_I) = \frac{e^{-\frac{1}{2}\Delta^T \Sigma_I^{-1} \Delta}}{(2\pi)^{D/2}|\Sigma_I|^{1/2}} \tag{3}$$

By PCA, the Gaussians are known to only occupy a subspace of image space (face-space) and thus, only the top few eigenvectors of the Gaussian densities are relevant for modeling. These densities are used to evaluate the *similarity score* in Equation 2.

Computing the similarity score involves first subtracting a candidate image I_j from a database entry I_k. The resulting Δ image is then projected onto the eigenvectors of the extrapersonal Gaussian and also the eigenvectors of the intrapersonal Gaussian. The exponentials are computed, normalized and then combined as in Equation 2. This operation is iterated over all members of the database (many I_k images) until the maximum score is found (i.e. the match). Thus, for large databases, this evaluation is expensive but can be simplified by offline transformations.

To compute the likelihoods $P(\Delta|\Omega_I)$ and $P(\Delta|\Omega_E)$ we pre-process the I_k images with whitening transformations. Each image is converted and stored as whitened subspace coefficients; $\mathbf{i}$ for intrapersonal space and $\mathbf{e}$ for extrapersonal space (see Equation 4). Here, Λ and V are matrices of the largest eigenvalues and eigenvectors of Σ_E or Σ_I. Typically, we have used $M_I = 100$ and $M_E = 100$ for Ω_I and Ω_E respectively.

$$\mathbf{i}_j = \Lambda_I^{-\frac{1}{2}} V_I I_j \qquad \mathbf{e}_j = \Lambda_E^{-\frac{1}{2}} V_E I_j \tag{4}$$

After this pre-processing, evaluating the Gaussians can be reduced to simple Euclidean distances as in Equation 5. Denominators are of course pre-computed. These likelihoods are evaluated and used to compute the MAP similarity S in Equation 2. Euclidean distances are computed between the 100-dimensional $\mathbf{i}$ vectors as well as the 100-dimensional $\mathbf{e}$ vectors. Thus, roughly $2 \times (M_E + M_I) = 400$ arithmetic operations are required for each similarity computation, avoiding repeated image differencing and projections.

$$P(\Delta|\Omega_E) = P(I_j - I_k|\Omega_E) = \frac{e^{-\frac{1}{2}\|\mathbf{e}_j - \mathbf{e}_k\|^2}}{(2\pi)^{D/2}|\Sigma_E|^{1/2}}$$
$$P(\Delta|\Omega_I) = P(I_j - I_k|\Omega_I) = \frac{e^{-\frac{1}{2}\|\mathbf{i}_j - \mathbf{i}_k\|^2}}{(2\pi)^{D/2}|\Sigma_I|^{1/2}} \tag{5}$$

The ML similarity matching is even simpler since only the intra-personal class is evaluated, leading to the following modified form for the similarity measure

$$S' = P(\Delta|\Omega_I) = \frac{e^{-\frac{1}{2}\|\mathbf{i}_j - \mathbf{i}_k\|^2}}{(2\pi)^{D/2}|\Sigma_I|^{1/2}} \tag{6}$$

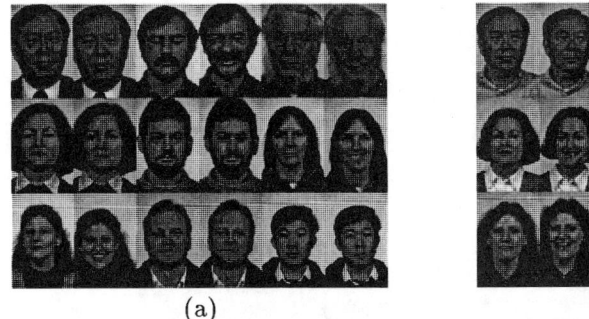 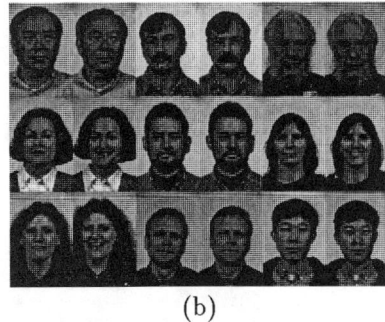

Figure 1: Examples of FERET frontal-view image pairs used for (a) the Gallery set (training) and (b) the Probe set (testing).

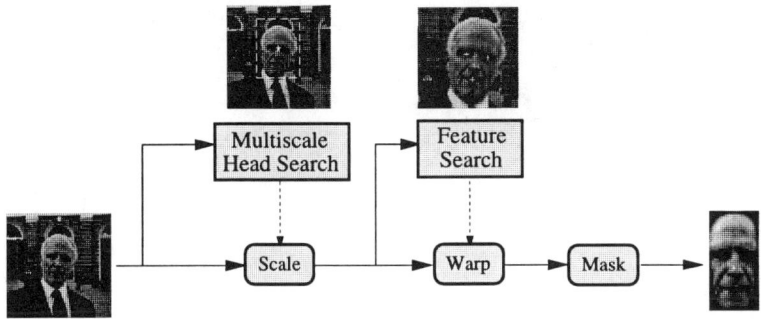

Figure 2: Face alignment system [7].

4 Experimental Results

To test our recognition strategy we used a collection of images from the ARPA FERET face database. The set of images consists of pairs of frontal-views (FA/FB) and are divided into two subsets: the "gallery" (training set) and the "probes" (testing set). The gallery images consisted of 74 pairs of images (2 per individual) and the probe set consisted of 38 pairs of images, corresponding to a subset of the gallery members. The probe and gallery datasets were captured a week apart and exhibit differences in clothing, hair and lighting (see Figure 1).

Each of these images were affine normalized with a canonical model using an automatic face-processing system which normalizes for translation, scale as well as slight rotations (both in-plane and out-of-plane). This system is described in detail in [7, 8] and uses maximum-likelihood estimation of object location (in this case the position and scale of a face and the location of individual facial features) to geometrically align faces into standard normalized form as shown in Figure 2. All the faces in our experiments were geometrically aligned and normalized in this manner prior to further analysis.

4.1 Eigenface Matching

As a baseline comparison, we first used an eigenface matching technique for recognition [13]. The normalized images from the gallery and the probe sets were projected onto a 100-dimensional eigenspace similar to that shown in Figure 3 and a nearest-neighbor rule based on a Euclidean distance measure was used to match

Figure 3: Standard Eigenfaces.

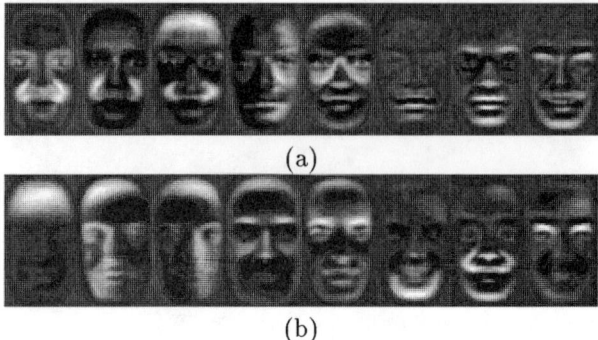

Figure 4: "Dual" Eigenfaces: (a) Intrapersonal, (b) Extrapersonal

each probe image to a gallery image. We note that this method corresponds to a generalized template-matching method which uses a Euclidean norm measure of similarity which is, however, restricted to the principal subspace of the data. The rank-1 recognition rate obtained with this method was found to be 84%.

4.2 Bayesian Matching

For our probabilistic algorithm, we first gathered training data by computing the intensity differences for a training subset of 74 intrapersonal differences (by matching the two views of every individual in the gallery) and a random subset of 296 extrapersonal differences (by matching images of *different* individuals in the gallery), corresponding to the classes Ω_I and Ω_E, respectively, and performing a separate PCA analysis on each.

We note that the two mutually exclusive classes Ω_I and Ω_E correspond to a "dual" set of eigenfaces as shown in Figure 4. Note that the intrapersonal variations shown in Figure 4-(a) represent subtle variations due mostly to expression changes (and lighting) whereas the extrapersonal variations in Figure 4-(b) are more representative of general eigenfaces which code variations such as hair color, facial hair and glasses. These extrapersonal eigenfaces are qualitatively similar to the standard normalized intensity eigenfaces shown in Figure 3.

We next computed the likelihood estimates $P(\Delta|\Omega_I)$ and $P(\Delta|\Omega_E)$ using the PCA-based method [7, 8], using subspace dimensions of $M_I = 10$ and $M_E = 30$ for Ω_I and Ω_E, respectively. These density estimates were then used with a default setting of equal priors, $P(\Omega_I) = P(\Omega_E)$, to evaluate the *a posteriori* intrapersonal probability $P(\Omega_I|\Delta)$ for matching probe images to those in the gallery. Therefore, for each probe image we computed probe-to-gallery differences and sorted the matching order, this time using the *a posteriori* probability $P(\Omega_I|\Delta)$ as the similarity measure. This probabilistic ranking yielded an improved rank-1 recognition rate of 90%.

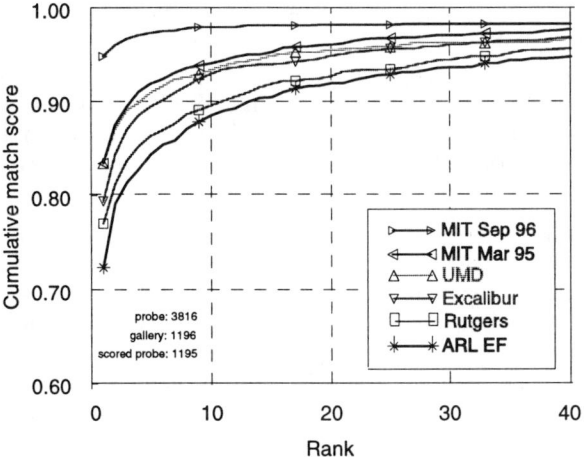

Figure 5: Cumulative recognition rates for frontal FA/FB views for the competing algorithms in the FERET 1996 test. The top curve (labeled "MIT Sep 96") corresponds to our Bayesian matching technique. Note that second placed is standard eigenface matching (labeled "MIT Mar 95").

4.3 The 1996 FERET Competition

Our Bayesian approach to recognition has yielded even more significant improvement over simple eigenface techniques with very large face databases. The probabilistic similarity measure was tested in the September 1996 ARPA FERET face recognition competition and yielded a surprising 95% recognition accuracy (on nearly 1200 individuals) making it the top-performing system by a typical margin of 10-20% over the other competing algorithms [11] (see Figure 5). A comparison between standard eigenfaces and the Bayesian method from this test shows a 10% gain in performance afforded by the new similarity measure. Thus we note that, in this particular case, the probabilistic similarity measure has effectively *halved* the error rate of eigenface matching.

Note that we can also use the simplified similarity measure based on the *intrapersonal* eigenfaces for a *maximum likelihood* (ML) matching technique using

$$S' = P(\Delta|\Omega_I) \qquad (7)$$

instead of the *maximum a posteriori* (MAP) approach defined by Equation 2. Although this simplified measure has not been officially FERET tested, our own internal experiments with a database of size 2000 have shown that using S' instead of S results in only a minor (2-3%) deficit in the recognition rate while at the same time cutting the computational cost by a further factor of 2.

5 Conclusions

The performance advantage of our probabilistic matching technique has been demonstrated using both a small database (internally tested) as well as a large (800+) database with an independent double-blind test as part of ARPA's September 1996 "FERET" competition, in which Bayesian similarity out-performed all competing algorithms (at least one of which was using an LDA/Fisher type method). We believe that these results clearly demonstrate the superior performance of probabilistic matching over eigenface, LDA/Fisher and other existing techniques.

The results obtained with the simplified ML similarity measure (S' in Eq. 7) suggest a computationally equivalent yet superior alternative to standard eigenface matching. In other words, a likelihood similarity based on the intrapersonal density $P(\Delta|\Omega_I)$ alone is far superior to nearest-neighbor matching in eigenspace while essentially requiring the same number of projections. For completeness (and a slightly better performance) however, one should use the *a posteriori* similarity S in Eq. 2, at twice the computational cost of standard eigenfaces.

This probabilistic framework is particularly advantageous in that the intra/extra density estimates explicitly characterize the type of appearance variations which are critical in formulating a meaningful measure of similarity. For example, the deformations corresponding to facial expression changes (which may have high image-difference norms) are, in fact, *irrelevant* when the measure of similarity is to be based on *identity*. The subspace density estimation method used for representing these classes thus corresponds to a *learning* method for discovering the principal modes of variation important to the classification task.

References

[1] V.I. Belhumeur, J.P. Hespanha, and D.J. Kriegman. Eigenfaces vs. fisherfaces: Recognition using class specific linear projection. *IEEE Transactions on Pattern Analysis and Machine Intelligence*, PAMI-19(7):711–720, July 1997.

[2] R. Brunelli and T. Poggio. Face recognition : Features vs. templates. *IEEE Transactions on Pattern Analysis and Machine Intelligence*, 15(10), October 1993.

[3] K. Etemad and R. Chellappa. Discriminant analysis for recognition of human faces. In *Proc. of Int'l Conf. on Acoustics, Speech and Signal Processing*, pages 2148–2151, 1996.

[4] I.T. Jolliffe. *Principal Component Analysis*. Springer-Verlag, New York, 1986.

[5] M. J. Jones and T. Poggio. Model-based matching by linear combination of prototypes. AI Memo No. 1583, Artificial Intelligence Laboratory, Massachusetts Institute of Technology, November 1996.

[6] B. Moghaddam, C. Nastar, and A. Pentland. Bayesian face recognition using deformable intensity differences. In *Proc. of IEEE Conf. on Computer Vision and Pattern Recognition*, June 1996.

[7] B. Moghaddam and A. Pentland. Probabilistic visual learning for object detection. In *IEEE Proceedings of the Fifth International Conference on Computer Vision (ICCV'95)*, Cambridge, USA, June 1995.

[8] B. Moghaddam and A. Pentland. Probabilistic visual learning for object representation. *IEEE Transactions on Pattern Analysis and Machine Intelligence*, PAMI-19(7):696–710, July 1997.

[9] B. Moghaddam, W. Wahid, and Alex Pentland. Beyond eigenfaces: Probabilistic matching for face recognition. In *Proc. of Int'l Conf. on Automatic Face and Gesture Recognition*, pages 30–35, Nara, Japan, April 1998.

[10] C. Nastar, B. Moghaddam, and A. Pentland. Generalized image matching: Statistical learning of physically-based deformations. In *Proceedings of the Fourth European Conference on Computer Vision (ECCV'96)*, Cambridge, UK, April 1996.

[11] P. J. Phillips, H. Moon, P. Rauss, and S. Rizvi. The FERET evaluation methodology for face-recognition algorithms. In *IEEE Proceedings of Computer Vision and Pattern Recognition*, pages 137–143, June 1997.

[12] D. Swets and J. Weng. Using discriminant eigenfeatures for image retrieval. *IEEE Transactions on Pattern Analysis and Machine Intelligence*, PAMI-18(8):831–836, August 1996.

[13] M. Turk and A. Pentland. Eigenfaces for recognition. *Journal of Cognitive Neuroscience*, 3(1), 1991.

Reinforcement Learning for Trading

John Moody and Matthew Saffell[*]
Oregon Graduate Institute, CSE Dept.
P.O. Box 91000, Portland, OR 97291-1000
{moody, saffell}@cse.ogi.edu

Abstract

We propose to train trading systems by optimizing financial objective functions via reinforcement learning. The performance functions that we consider are profit or wealth, the Sharpe ratio and our recently proposed *differential Sharpe ratio* for online learning. In Moody & Wu (1997), we presented empirical results that demonstrate the advantages of reinforcement learning relative to supervised learning. Here we extend our previous work to compare Q-Learning to our Recurrent Reinforcement Learning (RRL) algorithm. We provide new simulation results that demonstrate the presence of predictability in the monthly S&P 500 Stock Index for the 25 year period 1970 through 1994, as well as a sensitivity analysis that provides economic insight into the trader's structure.

1 Introduction: Reinforcement Learning for Trading

The investor's or trader's ultimate goal is to optimize some relevant measure of trading system performance, such as profit, economic utility or risk-adjusted return. In this paper, we propose to use recurrent reinforcement learning to directly optimize such trading system performance functions, and we compare two different reinforcement learning methods. The first, Recurrent Reinforcement Learning, uses immediate rewards to train the trading systems, while the second (Q-Learning (Watkins 1989)) approximates discounted future rewards. These methodologies can be applied to optimizing systems designed to trade a single security or to trade portfolios. In addition, we propose a novel value function for risk-adjusted return that enables learning to be done online: the *differential Sharpe ratio*.

Trading system profits depend upon sequences of interdependent decisions, and are thus path-dependent. Optimal trading decisions when the effects of transactions costs, market impact and taxes are included require knowledge of the current system state. In Moody, Wu, Liao & Saffell (1998), we demonstrate that reinforcement learning provides a more elegant and effective means for training trading systems when transaction costs are included, than do more standard supervised approaches.

[*] The authors are also with Nonlinear Prediction Systems.

Though much theoretical progress has been made in recent years in the area of reinforcement learning, there have been relatively few successful, practical applications of the techniques. Notable examples include Neuro-gammon (Tesauro 1989), the asset trader of Neuneier (1996), an elevator scheduler (Crites & Barto 1996) and a space-shuttle payload scheduler (Zhang & Dietterich 1996).

In this paper we present results for reinforcement learning trading systems that outperform the S&P 500 Stock Index over a 25-year test period, thus demonstrating the presence of predictable structure in US stock prices. The reinforcement learning algorithms compared here include our new recurrent reinforcement learning (RRL) method (Moody & Wu 1997, Moody et al. 1998) and Q-Learning (Watkins 1989).

2 Trading Systems and Financial Performance Functions

2.1 Structure, Profit and Wealth for Trading Systems

We consider performance functions for systems that trade a single [1] security with price series z_t. The trader is assumed to take only long, neutral or short positions $F_t \in \{-1, 0, 1\}$ of constant magnitude. The constant magnitude assumption can be easily relaxed to enable better risk control. The position F_t is established or maintained at the end of each time interval t, and is re-assessed at the end of period $t + 1$. A trade is thus possible at the end of each time period, although nonzero trading costs will discourage excessive trading. A trading system return R_t is realized at the end of the time interval $(t - 1, t]$ and includes the profit or loss resulting from the position F_{t-1} held during that interval and any transaction cost incurred at time t due to a difference in the positions F_{t-1} and F_t.

In order to properly incorporate the effects of transactions costs, market impact and taxes in a trader's decision making, the trader must have internal state information and must therefore be recurrent. An example of a single asset trading system that takes into account transactions costs and market impact has following decision function: $F_t = F(\theta_t; F_{t-1}, I_t)$ with $I_t = \{z_t, z_{t-1}, z_{t-2}, \ldots; y_t, y_{t-1}, y_{t-2}, \ldots\}$ where θ_t denotes the (learned) system parameters at time t and I_t denotes the information set at time t, which includes present and past values of the price series z_t and an arbitrary number of other external variables denoted y_t.

Trading systems can be optimized by maximizing performance functions $U()$ such as profit, wealth, utility functions of wealth or performance ratios like the Sharpe ratio. The simplest and most natural performance function for a risk-insensitive trader is profit. The transactions cost rate is denoted δ.

Additive profits are appropriate to consider if each trade is for a fixed number of shares or contracts of security z_t. This is often the case, for example, when trading small futures accounts or when trading standard US$ FX contracts in dollar-denominated foreign currencies. With the definitions $r_t = z_t - z_{t-1}$ and $r_t^f = z_t^f - z_{t-1}^f$ for the price returns of a risky (traded) asset and a risk-free asset (like T-Bills) respectively, the additive profit accumulated over T time periods with trading position size $\mu > 0$ is then defined as:

$$P_T = \sum_{t=1}^{T} R_t = \mu \sum_{t=1}^{T} \left\{ r_t^f + F_{t-1}(r_t - r_t^f) - \delta |F_t - F_{t-1}| \right\} \quad (1)$$

---

[1] See Moody et al. (1998) for a detailed discussion of multiple asset portfolios.

with $P_0 = 0$ and typically $F_T = F_0 = 0$. Equation (1) holds for continuous quantities also. The wealth is defined as $W_T = W_0 + P_T$.

Multiplicative profits are appropriate when a fixed fraction of accumulated wealth $\nu > 0$ is invested in each long or short trade. Here, $r_t = (z_t/z_{t-1} - 1)$ and $r_t^f = (z_t^f/z_{t-1}^f - 1)$. If no short sales are allowed and the leverage factor is set fixed at $\nu = 1$, the wealth at time T is:

$$W_T = W_0 \prod_{t=1}^{T} \{1 + R_t\} = W_0 \prod_{t=1}^{T} \left\{1 + (1 - F_{t-1})r_t^f + F_{t-1}r_t\right\} \{1 - \delta|F_t - F_{t-1}|\}. \quad (2)$$

2.2 The *Differential* Sharpe Ratio for On-line Learning

Rather than maximizing profits, most modern fund managers attempt to maximize risk-adjusted return as advocated by Modern Portfolio Theory. The Sharpe ratio is the most widely-used measure of risk-adjusted return (Sharpe 1966). Denoting as before the trading system returns for period t (including transactions costs) as R_t, the Sharpe ratio is defined to be

$$S_T = \frac{\text{Average}(R_t)}{\text{Standard Deviation}(R_t)} \quad (3)$$

where the average and standard deviation are estimated for periods $t = \{1, \ldots, T\}$.

Proper on-line learning requires that we compute the influence on the Sharpe ratio of the return at time t. To accomplish this, we have derived a new objective function called the *differential Sharpe ratio* for on-line optimization of trading system performance (Moody et al. 1998). It is obtained by considering exponential moving averages of the returns and standard deviation of returns in (3), and expanding to first order in the decay rate η: $S_t \approx S_{t-1} + \eta \frac{dS_t}{d\eta}|_{\eta=0} + O(\eta^2)$. Noting that only the first order term in this expansion depends upon the return R_t at time t, we define the *differential Sharpe ratio* as:

$$D_t \equiv \frac{dS_t}{d\eta} = \frac{B_{t-1}\Delta A_t - \frac{1}{2}A_{t-1}\Delta B_t}{(B_{t-1} - A_{t-1}^2)^{3/2}}. \quad (4)$$

where the quantities A_t and B_t are exponential moving estimates of the first and second moments of R_t:

$$\begin{aligned} A_t &= A_{t-1} + \eta \Delta A_t = A_{t-1} + \eta(R_t - A_{t-1}) \\ B_t &= B_{t-1} + \eta \Delta B_t = B_{t-1} + \eta(R_t^2 - B_{t-1}) \;. \end{aligned} \quad (5)$$

Treating A_{t-1} and B_{t-1} as numerical constants, note that η in the update equations controls the magnitude of the influence of the return R_t on the Sharpe ratio S_t. Hence, the *differential Sharpe ratio* represents the influence of the trading return R_t realized at time t on S_t.

3 Reinforcement Learning for Trading Systems

The goal in using reinforcement learning to adjust the parameters of a system is to maximize the expected payoff or reward that is generated due to the actions of the system. This is accomplished through trial and error exploration of the environment. The system receives a reinforcement signal from its environment (a *reward*) that provides information on whether its actions are good or bad. The performance function at time T can be expressed as a function of the sequence of trading returns $U_T = U(R_1, R_2, \ldots, R_T)$.

Given a trading system model $F_t(\theta)$, the goal is to adjust the parameters θ in order to maximize U_T. This maximization for a complete sequence of T trades can be done off-line using dynamic programming or batch versions of recurrent reinforcement learning algorithms. Here we do the optimization on-line using a reinforcement learning technique. This reinforcement learning algorithm is based on stochastic gradient ascent. The gradient of U_T with respect to the parameters θ of the system after a sequence of T trades is

$$\frac{dU_T(\theta)}{d\theta} = \sum_{t=1}^{T} \frac{dU_T}{dR_t} \left\{ \frac{dR_t}{dF_t} \frac{dF_t}{d\theta} + \frac{dR_t}{dF_{t-1}} \frac{dF_{t-1}}{d\theta} \right\} . \tag{6}$$

A simple on-line stochastic optimization can be obtained by considering only the term in (6) that depends on the most recently realized return R_t during a forward pass through the data:

$$\frac{dU_t(\theta)}{d\theta} = \frac{dU_t}{dR_t} \left\{ \frac{dR_t}{dF_t} \frac{dF_t}{d\theta} + \frac{dR_t}{dF_{t-1}} \frac{dF_{t-1}}{d\theta} \right\} . \tag{7}$$

The parameters are then updated on-line using $\Delta\theta_t = \rho dU_t(\theta_t)/d\theta_t$. Because of the recurrent structure of the problem (necessary when transaction costs are included), we use a reinforcement learning algorithm based on real-time recurrent learning (Williams & Zipser 1989). This approach, which we call recurrent reinforcement learning (RRL), is described in (Moody & Wu 1997, Moody et al. 1998) along with extensive simulation results.

4 Empirical Results: S&P 500 / TBill Asset Allocation

A long/short trading system is trained on monthly S&P 500 stock index and 3-month TBill data to maximize the differential Sharpe ratio. The S&P 500 target series is the total return index computed by reinvesting dividends. The 84 input series used in the trading systems include both financial and macroeconomic data. All data are obtained from Citibase, and the macroeconomic series are lagged by one month to reflect reporting delays.

A total of 45 years of monthly data are used, from January 1950 through December 1994. The first 20 years of data are used only for the initial training of the system. The test period is the 25 year period from January 1970 through December 1994. The experimental results for the 25 year test period are true *ex ante* simulated trading results.

For each year during 1970 through 1994, the system is trained on a moving window of the previous 20 years of data. For 1970, the system is initialized with random parameters. For the 24 subsequent years, the previously learned parameters are used to initialize the training. In this way, the system is able to adapt to changing market and economic conditions. Within the moving training window, the "RRL" systems use the first 10 years for stochastic optimization of system parameters, and the subsequent 10 years for validating early stopping of training. The networks are linear, and are regularized using quadratic weight decay during training with a regularization parameter of 0.01. The "Qtrader" systems use a bootstrap sample of the 20 year training window for training, and the final 10 years of the training window are used for validating early stopping of training. The networks are two-layer feedforward networks with 30 tanh units in the hidden layer.

4.1 Experimental Results

The left panel in Figure 1 shows box plots summarizing the test performance for the full 25 year test period of the trading systems with various realizations of the initial system parameters over 30 trials for the "RRL" system, and 10 trials for the "Qtrader" system[2]. The transaction cost is set at 0.5%. Profits are reinvested during trading, and multiplicative profits are used when calculating the wealth. The notches in the box plots indicate robust estimates of the 95% confidence intervals on the hypothesis that the median is equal to the performance of the buy and hold strategy. The horizontal lines show the performance of the "RRL" voting, "Qtrader" voting and buy and hold strategies for the same test period. The annualized monthly Sharpe ratios of the buy and hold strategy, the "Qtrader" voting strategy and the "RRL" voting strategy are 0.34, 0.63 and 0.83 respectively. The Sharpe ratios calculated here are for the returns in excess of the 3-month treasury bill rate.

The right panel of Figure 1 shows results for following the strategy of taking positions based on a majority vote of the ensembles of trading systems compared with the buy and hold strategy. We can see that the trading systems go short the S&P 500 during critical periods, such as the oil price shock of 1974, the tight money periods of the early 1980's, the market correction of 1984 and the 1987 crash. This ability to take advantage of high treasury bill rates or to avoid periods of substantial stock market loss is the major factor in the long term success of these trading models. One exception is that the "RRL" trading system remains long during the 1991 stock market correction associated with the Persian Gulf war, though the "Qtrader" system does identify the correction. On the whole though, the "Qtrader" system trades much more frequently than the "RRL" system, and in the end does not perform as well on this data set.

From these results we find that both trading systems outperform the buy and hold strategy, as measured by both accumulated wealth and Sharpe ratio. These differences are statistically significant and support the proposition that there is predictability in the U.S. stock and treasury bill markets during the 25 year period 1970 through 1994. A more detailed presentation of the "RRL" results appears in (Moody et al. 1998).

4.2 Gaining Economic Insight Through Sensitivity Analysis

A sensitivity analysis of the "RRL" systems was performed in an attempt to determine on which economic factors the traders are basing their decisions. Figure 2 shows the absolute normalized sensitivities for 3 of the more salient input series as a function of time, averaged over the 30 members of the "RRL" committee. The sensitivity of input i is defined as:

$$S_i = \left|\frac{dF}{dx_i}\right| \bigg/ \max_j \left|\frac{dF}{dx_j}\right| \qquad (8)$$

where F is the unthresholded trading output and x_i denotes input i.

---

[2] Ten trials were done for the "Qtrader" system due to the amount of computation required in training the systems

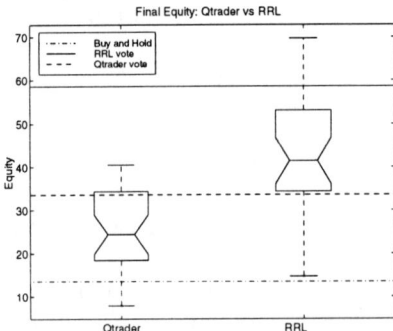 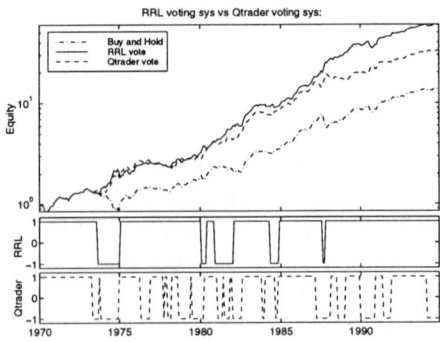

Figure 1: Test results for ensembles of simulations using the S&P 500 stock index and 3-month Treasury Bill data over the 1970-1994 time period. The solid curves correspond to the "RRL" voting system performance, dashed curves to the "Qtrader" voting system and the dashed and dotted curves indicate the buy and hold performance. The boxplots in (a) show the performance for the ensembles of "RRL" and "Qtrader" trading systems The horizontal lines indicate the performance of the voting systems and the buy and hold strategy. Both systems significantly outperform the buy and hold strategy. (b) shows the equity curves associated with the voting systems and the buy and hold strategy, as well as the voting trading signals produced by the systems. In both cases, the traders avoid the dramatic losses that the buy and hold strategy incurred during 1974 and 1987.

The time-varying sensitivities in Figure 2 emphasize the nonstationarity of economic relationships. For example, the yield curve slope (which measures inflation expectations) is found to be a very important factor in the 1970's, while trends in long term interest rates (measured by the 6 month difference in the AAA bond yield) becomes more important in the 1980's, and trends in short term interest rates (measured by the 6 month difference in the treasury bill yield) dominate in the early 1990's.

5 Conclusions and Extensions

In this paper, we have trained trading systems via reinforcement learning to optimize financial objective functions including our *differential Sharpe ratio* for online learning. We have also provided results that demonstrate the presence of predictability in the monthly S&P 500 Stock Index for the 25 year period 1970 through 1994.

We have previously shown with extensive simulation results (Moody & Wu 1997, Moody et al. 1998) that the "RRL" trading system significantly outperforms systems trained using supervised methods for traders of both single securities and portfolios. The superiority of reinforcement learning over supervised learning is most striking when state-dependent transaction costs are taken into account. Here, we present results for asset allocation systems trained using two different reinforcement learning algorithms on a real, economic dataset. We find that the "Qtrader" system does not perform as well as the "RRL" system on the S&P 500 / TBill asset allocation problem, possibly due to its more frequent trading. This effect deserves further exploration. In general, we find that Q-learning can suffer from the curse of dimensionality and is more difficult to use than our RRL approach.

Finally, we apply sensitivity analysis to the trading systems, and find that certain interest rate variables have an influential role in making asset allocation decisions.

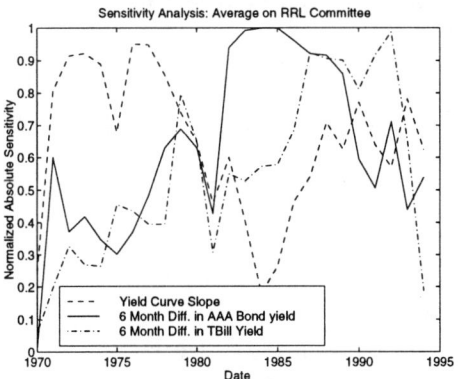

Figure 2: Sensitivity traces for three of the inputs to the "RRL" trading system averaged over the ensemble of traders. The nonstationary relationships typical among economic variables is evident from the time-varying sensitivities.

We also find that these influences exhibit nonstationarity over time.

Acknowledgements

We gratefully acknowledge support for this work from Nonlinear Prediction Systems and from DARPA under contract DAAH01-96-C-R026 and AASERT grant DAAH04-95-1-0485.

References

Crites, R. H. & Barto, A. G. (1996), Improving elevator performance using reinforcement learning, in D. S. Touretzky, M. C. Mozer & M. E. Hasselmo, eds, 'Advances in NIPS', Vol. 8, pp. 1017–1023.

Moody, J. & Wu, L. (1997), Optimization of trading systems and portfolios, in Y. Abu-Mostafa, A. N. Refenes & A. S. Weigend, eds, 'Decision Technologies for Financial Engineering', World Scientific, London, pp. 23–35. This is a slightly revised version of the original paper that appeared in the NNCM*96 Conference Record, published by Caltech, Pasadena, 1996.

Moody, J., Wu, L., Liao, Y. & Saffell, M. (1998), 'Performance functions and reinforcement learning for trading systems and portfolios', *Journal of Forecasting* 17, 441–470.

Neuneier, R. (1996), Optimal asset allocation using adaptive dynamic programming, in D. S. Touretzky, M. C. Mozer & M. E. Hasselmo, eds, 'Advances in NIPS', Vol. 8, pp. 952–958.

Sharpe, W. F. (1966), 'Mutual fund performance', *Journal of Business* pp. 119–138.

Tesauro, G. (1989), 'Neurogammon wins the computer olympiad', *Neural Computation* 1, 321–323.

Watkins, C. J. C. H. (1989), Learning with Delayed Rewards, PhD thesis, Cambridge University, Psychology Department.

Williams, R. J. & Zipser, D. (1989), 'A learning algorithm for continually running fully recurrent neural networks', *Neural Computation* 1, 270–280.

Zhang, W. & Dietterich, T. G. (1996), High-performance job-shop scheduling with a time-delay td(λ) network, in D. S. Touretzky, M. C. Mozer & M. E. Hasselmo, eds, 'Advances in NIPS', Vol. 8, pp. 1024–1030.

Graphical Models for Recognizing Human Interactions

Nuria M. Oliver, Barbara Rosario and Alex Pentland
20 Ames Street, E15-384C,
Media Arts and Sciences Laboratory, MIT
Cambridge, MA 02139
{nuria, rosario, sandy}@media.mit.edu

Abstract

We describe a real-time computer vision and machine learning system for modeling and recognizing human actions and interactions. Two different domains are explored: recognition of two-handed motions in the martial art 'Tai Chi', and multiple-person interactions in a visual surveillance task. Our system combines top-down with bottom-up information using a feedback loop, and is formulated with a Bayesian framework. Two different graphical models (HMMs and Coupled HMMs) are used for modeling both individual actions and multiple-agent interactions, and CHMMs are shown to work more efficiently and accurately for a given amount of training. Finally, to overcome the limited amounts of training data, we demonstrate that 'synthetic agents' (Alife-style agents) can be used to develop flexible prior models of the person-to-person interactions.

1 INTRODUCTION

We describe a real-time computer vision and machine learning system for modeling and recognizing human behaviors in two different scenarios: (1) complex, two-handed action recognition in the martial art of *Tai Chi* and (2) detection and recognition of individual human behaviors and multiple-person interactions in a visual surveillance task. In the latter case, the system is particularly concerned with detecting when interactions between people occur, and classifying them.

Graphical models, such as Hidden Markov Models (HMMs) [6] and Coupled Hidden Markov Models (CHMMs) [3, 2], seem appropriate for modeling and classifying human behaviors because they offer dynamic time warping, a well-understood training algorithm, and a clear Bayesian semantics for both individual (HMMs) and interacting or coupled (CHMMs) generative processes. A major problem with this data-driven statistical approach, especially when modeling rare or anomalous behaviors, is the limited number of training examples. A major emphasis of our work, therefore, is on efficient Bayesian integration of both prior knowledge with evidence from data. We will show that for situations involving multiple independent (or partially independent) agents the Coupled HMM approach generates much better results than traditional HMM methods.

In addition, we have developed a *synthetic agent or Alife* modeling environment for building and training flexible a *priori* models of various behaviors using software agents. Simulation with these software agents yields synthetic data that can be used to train prior models. These prior models can then be used recursively in a Bayesian framework to fit real behavioral data.

This synthetic agent approach is a straightforward and flexible method for developing prior models, one that does not require strong analytical assumptions to be made about the form of the priors[1]. In addition, it has allowed us to develop robust models even when there are only a few examples of some target behaviors. In our experiments we have found that by combining such synthetic priors with limited real data we can easily achieve very high accuracies at recognition of different human-to-human interactions.

The paper is structured as follows: section 2 presents an overview of the system, the statistical models used for behavior modeling and recognition are described in section 3. Section 4 contains experimental results in two different real situations. Finally section 5 summarizes the main conclusions and our future lines of research.

2 VISUAL INPUT

We have experimented using two different types of visual input. The first is a real-time, self-calibrating 3-D stereo blob tracker (used for the *Tai Chi* scenario) [1], and the second is a real-time blob-tracking system [5] (used in the visual surveillance task). In both cases an Extended Kalman filter (EKF) tracks the blobs' location, coarse shape, color pattern, and velocity. This information is represented as a low-dimensional, parametric probability distribution function (PDF) composed of a mixture of Gaussians, whose parameters (sufficient statistics and mixing weights for each of the components) are estimated using Expectation Maximization (EM).

This visual input module detects and tracks moving objects — body parts in *Tai Chi* and pedestrians in the visual surveillance task — and outputs a feature vector describing their motion, heading, and spatial relationship to all nearby moving objects. These output feature vectors constitute the temporally ordered stream of data input to our stochastic state-based behavior models. Both HMMs and CHMMs, with varying structures depending on the complexity of the behavior, are used for classifying the observed behaviors.

Both *top-down* and *bottom-up* flows of information are continuously managed and combined for each moving object within the scene. The Bayesian graphical models offer a mathematical framework for combining the observations (bottom-up) with complex behavioral priors (top-down) to provide expectations that will be fed back to the input visual system.

3 VISUAL UNDERSTANDING VIA GRAPHICAL MODELS: HMMs and CHMMs

Statistical directed acyclic graphs (DAGs) or probabilistic inference networks (PINs hereafter) can provide a computationally efficient solution to the problem of time series analysis and modeling. HMMs and some of their extensions, in particular CHMMs, can be viewed as a particular and simple case of temporal PIN or DAG. Graphically Markov Models are often depicted 'rolled-out in time' as Probabilistic Inference Networks, such as in figure 1. PINs present important advantages that are relevant to our problem: they can handle incomplete data as well as uncertainty; they are trainable and easier to avoid overfitting; they encode causality in a natural way; there are algorithms for both doing prediction and probabilistic inference; they offer a framework for combining prior knowledge and data; and finally they are modular and parallelizable.

Traditional HMMs offer a probabilistic framework for modeling processes that have structure in time. They offer clear Bayesian semantics, efficient algorithms for state and parameter estimation, and they automatically perform dynamic time warping. An HMM is essentially a quantization of a system's configuration space into a small number of discrete states, together with probabilities for transitions between

---

[1] Note that our priors have the same form as our posteriors, namely, they are graphical models.

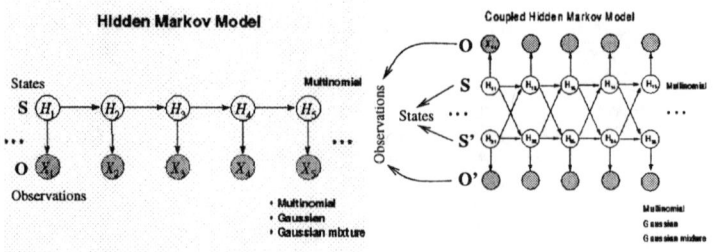

Figure 1: Graphical representation of a HMM and a CHMM rolled-out in time

states. A single finite discrete variable indexes the current state of the system. Any information about the history of the process needed for future inferences must be reflected in the current value of this state variable.

However many interesting real-life problems are composed of multiple interacting processes, and thus merit a compositional representation of two or more variables. This is typically the case for systems that have structure both in time and space. With a single state variable, Markov models are ill-suited to these problems. In order to model these interactions a more complex architecture is needed.

Extensions to the basic Markov model generally increase the memory of the system (durational modeling), providing it with compositional state in time. We are interested in systems that have compositional state in *space*, e.g., more than one simultaneous state variable. It is well known that the exact solution of extensions of the basic HMM to 3 or more chains is intractable. In those cases approximation techniques are needed ([7, 4, 8, 9]). However, it is also known that there exists an exact solution for the case of 2 interacting chains, as it is our case [7, 2].

We therefore use two Coupled Hidden Markov Models (CHMMs) for modeling two interacting processes, whether they are separate body parts or individual humans. In this architecture state chains are coupled via matrices of conditional probabilities modeling causal (temporal) influences between their hidden state variables. The graphical representation of CHMMs is shown in figure 1. From the graph it can be seen that for each chain, the state at time t depends on the state at time $t-1$ in both chains. The influence of one chain on the other is through a causal link.

In this paper we compare performance of HMMs and CHMMs for maximum *a posteriori* (MAP) state estimation. We compute the most likely sequence of states $\hat{S}$ within a model given the observation sequence $O = \{o_1, \ldots, o_n\}$. This most likely sequence is obtained by $\hat{S} = argmax_S P(S|O)$.

In the case of HMMs the posterior state sequence probability $P(S|O)$ is given by

$$P(S|O) = P_{s_1} p_{s_1}(o_1) \prod_{t=2}^{T} p_{s_t}(o_t) P_{s_t|s_{t-1}} \qquad (1)$$

where $S = \{a_1, \ldots, a_N\}$ is the set of discrete states, $s_t \in S$ corresponds to the state at time t. $P_{i|j} \doteq P_{s_t=a_i|s_{t-1}=a_j}$ is the state-to-state transition probability (i.e. probability of being in state a_i at time t given that the system was in state a_j at time $t-1$). In the following we will write them as $P_{s_t|s_{t-1}}$. $P_i \doteq P_{s_1=a_i} = P_{s_1}$ are the prior probabilities for the initial state. Finally $p_i(o_t) \doteq p_{s_t=a_i}(o_t) = p_{s_t}(o_t)$ are the output probabilities for each state[2].

For CHMMs we need to introduce another set of probabilities, $P_{s_t|s'_{t-1}}$, which cor-

---

[2]The output probability is the probability of observing o_t given state a_i at time t

respond to the probability of state s_t at time t in one chain given that the other chain –denoted hereafter by superscript $'$ – was in state s'_{t-1} at time $t-1$. These new probabilities express the causal influence (coupling) of one chain to the other. The posterior state probability for CHMMs is expressed as

$$P(S|O) = \frac{P_{s_1} p_{s_1}(o_1) P_{s'_1} p_{s'_1}(o'_1)}{P(O)} \times \prod_{t=2}^{T} P_{s_t|s_{t-1}} P_{s'_t|s'_{t-1}} P_{s'_t|s_{t-1}} P_{s_t|s'_{t-1}} p_{s_t}(o_t) p_{s'_t}(o'_t) \quad (2)$$

where $s_t, s'_t; o_t, o'_t$ denote states and observations for each of the Markov chains that compose the CHMMs.

In [2] a deterministic approximation for maximum *a posterior* (MAP) state estimation is introduced. It enables fast classification and parameter estimation via EM, and also obtains an upper bound on the cross entropy with the full (combinatoric) posterior which can be minimized using a subspace that is linear in the number of state variables. An "N-heads" dynamic programming algorithm samples from the $O(N)$ highest probability paths through a compacted state trellis, with complexity $O(T(CN)^2)$ for C chains of N states apiece observing T data points. The cartesian product equivalent HMM would involve a combinatoric number of states, typically requiring $O(TN^{2C})$ computations. We are particularly interested in efficient, compact algorithms that can perform in real-time.

4 EXPERIMENTAL RESULTS

Our first experiment is with a version of Tai Chi Ch'uan (a Chinese martial and meditative art) that is practiced while sitting. Using our self-calibrating, 3-D stereo blob tracker [1], we obtained 3D hand tracking data for three Tai Chi gestures involving two, semi-independent arm motions: the left single whip, the left cobra, and the left brush knee. Figure 4 illustrates one of the gestures and the blob-tracking. A detailed description of this set of *Tai Chi* experimental results can be found in [3] and viewed at http://nuria.www.media.mit.edu/~nuria/chmm/taichi.html.

Figure 2: Selected frames from 'left brush knee.'

We collected 52 sequences, roughly 17 of each gesture and created a feature vector consisting of the 3-D (x, y, z) centroid (mean position) of each of the blobs that characterize the hands. The resulting six-dimensional time series was used for training both HMMs and CHMMs.

We used the best trained HMMs and CHMMs — using 10-crossvalidation — to classify the full data set of 52 gestures. The Viterbi algorithm was used to find the maximum likelihood model for HMMs and CHMMs. Two-thirds of the testing data had not been seen in training, including gestures performed at varying speeds and from slightly different views. It can be seen from the classification accuracies, shown in table 1, that the CHMMs outperform the HMMs. This difference is not due to intrinsic modeling power, however; from earlier experiments we know that when a large number of training samples is available then HMMs can reach similar accuracies. We conclude thus that for data where there are two partially-independent processes (e.g., coordinated but not exactly linked), the CHMM method requires much less training to achieve a high classification accuracy.

Table 1 illustrates the source of this training advantage. The numbers between

Table 1: Recognition accuracies for HMMs and CHMMs on Tai Chi gestures. The expressions between parenthesis correspond to the number of parameters of the largest best-scoring model.

Recognition Results on Tai Chi Gestures	
Single HMMs	Coupled HMMs (CHMMs)
Accuracy 69.2% (25+30+180)	100% (27+18+54)

parenthesis correspond to the number of degrees of freedom in the largest best-scoring model: state-to-state probabilities + output means + output covariances. The conventional HMM has a large number of covariance parameters because it has a 6-D output variable; whereas the CHMM architecture has two 3-D output variables. In consequence, due to their larger dimensionality HMMs need much more training data than equivalent CHMMs before yielding good generalization results.

Our second experiment was with a pedestrian video surveillance task [3]; the goal was first to recognize typical pedestrian behaviors in an open plaza (e.g., walk from A to B, run from C to D), and second to recognize interactions between the pedestrians (e.g., person X greets person Y). The task is to reliably and robustly detect and track the pedestrians in the scene. We use in this case 2-D *blob features* for modeling each pedestrian. In our system one of the main cues for clustering the pixels into blobs is motion, because we have a static background with moving objects. To detect these moving objects we build an eigenspace that models the background. Depending on the dynamics of the background scene the system can *adaptively* relearn the eigenbackground to compensate for changes such as big shadows.

The trajectories of each blob are computed and saved into a *dynamic track memory*. Each trajectory has associated a first order EKF that predicts the blob's position and velocity in the next frame As before, the appearance of each blob is modeled by a Gaussian PDF in RGB color space, allowing us to handle occlusions.

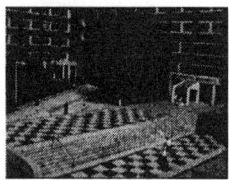  

Figure 3: Typical Image from pedestrian plaza. Background mean image, input image with blob bounding boxes and blob segmentation image

The behaviors we examine are generated by pedestrians walking in an open outdoor environment. Our goal is to develop a generic, compositional analysis of the observed behaviors in terms of states and transitions between states over time in such a manner that (1) the states correspond to our common sense notions of human behaviors, and (2) they are immediately applicable to a wide range of sites and viewing situations. Figure 3 shows a typical image for our pedestrian scenario, the pedestrians found, and the final segmentation. Two people (each modeled as its own generative process) may interact without wholly determining each others' behavior. Instead, each of them has its own internal dynamics and is influenced (either weakly or strongly) by others. The probabilities $P_{s_t|s'_{t-1}}$ and $P_{s'_t|s_{t-1}}$ from equation 2 describe this kind of interactions and CHMMs are intended to model them in as efficient a manner as is possible.

We would like to have a system that will accurately interpret behaviors and interactions within almost any pedestrian scene with at most minimal training. As we have

---

[3] Further information about this system can be found at http://www.vismod.www.media.mit.edu/ nuria/humanBehavior/humanBehavior.html

already mentioned, one critical problem is the generation of models that capture our prior knowledge about human behavior. To achieve this goal we have developed a modeling environment that uses synthetic agents to mimic pedestrian behavior in a virtual environment. The agents can be assigned different behaviors and they can interact with each other as well. Currently they can generate 5 different interacting behaviors and various kinds of individual behaviors (with no interaction). These behaviors are: following, meet and walk together (inter1); approach, meet and go on separately (inter2) or go on together (inter3); change direction in order to meet, approach, meet and continue together (inter4) or go on separately (inter5). The parameters of this virtual environment are modeled using data drawn from a 'generic' set of real scenes.

By training the models of the synthetic agents to have good generalization and invariance properties, we can obtain flexible prior models for use when learning the human behavior models from real scenes. Thus the synthetic prior models allow us to learn robust behavior models from a small number of real behavior examples. This capability is of special importance in a visual surveillance task, where typically the behaviors of greatest interest are also the rarest.

To test our behavior modeling in the pedestrian scenario, we first used the detection and tracking system previously described to obtain 2-D blob features for each person in several hours of video. More than 20 examples of *following* and the two first types of *meeting* behaviors were detected and processed.

CHMMs were then used for modeling three different behaviors: following, meet and continue together, and meet and go on separately. Furthermore, an *interaction* versus *no interaction* detection test was also performed (HMMs performed so poorly at this task that their results are not reported). In addition to velocity, heading, and position, the feature vectors consisted of the derivative of the relative distance between two agents, their degree of alignment (dot product of their velocity vectors) and the magnitude of the difference in their velocity vectors.

We tested on this video data using models trained with two types of data: (1) 'Prior-only models', that is, models learned entirely from our synthetic-agents environment and then applied directly to the real data with no additional training or tuning of the parameters; and (2) 'Posterior models', or prior-plus-real data behavior models trained by starting with the prior-only model and then 'tuning' the models with data from this specific site, using eight examples of each type of interaction. Recognition accuracies for both these 'prior' and 'posterior' CHMMs are summarized in table 2. It is noteworthy that with only 8 training examples, the recognition accuracy on the remaining data could be raised to 100%. This demonstrates the ability to accomplish extremely rapid refinement of our behavior models from the initial a priori models.

Table 2: Accuracies on real pedestrian data, (a) only a priori models, (b) posterior models (with site-specific training)

	Accuracy on Real Pedestrian Data			
	No-inter	Inter1	Inter2	Inter3
(a)**Prior CHMMs**	90.9	93.7	100	100
(b)**Posterior CHMMs**	100	100	100	100

In a visual surveillance system the *false alarm* rate is often as important as the classification accuracy[4] To analyze this aspect of our system's performance, we calculated the system's ROC curve. For accuracies of 95% the false alarm rate was less than 0.01.

---

[4]In an ideal automatic surveillance system, all the targeted behaviors should be detected with a close-to-zero false alarm rate, so that we can reasonably alert a human operator to examine them further.

5 SUMMARY, CONCLUSIONS AND FUTURE WORK

In this paper we have described a computer vision system and a mathematical modeling framework for recognizing different human behaviors and interactions in two different real domains: human actions in the martial art of *Tai Chi* and human interactions in a visual surveillance task. Our system combines top-down with bottom-up information in a closed feedback loop, with both components employing a statistical Bayesian approach.

Two different state-based statistical learning architectures, namely HMMs and CHMMs, have been proposed and compared for modeling behaviors and interactions. The superiority of the CHMM formulation has been demonstrated in terms of both training efficiency and classification accuracy. A synthetic agent training system has been created in order to develop flexible prior behavior models, and we have demonstrated the ability to use these prior models to accurately classify real behaviors with no additional training on real data. This fact is specially important, given the limited amount of training data available.

Future directions under current investigation include: extending our agent interactions to more than two interacting processes; developing a hierarchical system where complex behaviors are expressed in terms of simpler behaviors; automatic discovery and modeling of new behaviors (both structure and parameters); automatic determination of priors, their evaluation and interpretation; developing an attentional mechanism with a foveated camera along with a more detailed representation of the behaviors; evaluating the adaptability of off-line learned behavior structures to different real situations; and exploring a sampling approach for recognizing behaviors by sampling the interactions generated by our synthetic agents.

Acknowledgments

Sincere thanks to Michael Jordan, Tony Jebara and Matthew Brand for their inestimable help.

References

1. A. Azarbayejani and A. Pentland. Real-time self-calibrating stereo person-tracker using 3-D shape estimation from blob features. In *Proceedings, International Conference on Pattern Recognition*, Vienna, August 1996. IEEE.

2. M. Brand. Coupled hidden markov models for modeling interacting processes. November 1996. Submitted to Neural Computation.

3. M. Brand and N. Oliver. Coupled hidden markov models for complex action recognition. In *In Proceedings of IEEE CVPR97*, 1996.

4. Z. Ghahramani and M. I. Jordan. Factorial hidden Markov models. In D. S. Touretzky, M. C. Mozer, and M. Hasselmo, editors, *NIPS*, volume 8, Cambridge, MA, 1996. MITP.

5. N. Oliver, B. Rosario, and A. Pentland. Statistical modeling of human behaviors. In *To appear in Proceedings of CVPR98, Perception of Action Workshop*, 1998.

6. L. R. Rabiner. A tutorial on hidden markov models and selected applications in speech recognition. *PIEEE*, 77(2):257–285, 1989.

7. L. K. Saul and M. I. Jordan. Boltzmann chains and hidden Markov models. In G. Tesauro, D. S. Touretzky, and T. Leen, editors, *NIPS*, volume 7, Cambridge, MA, 1995. MITP.

8. P. Smyth, D. Heckerman, and M. Jordan. Probabilistic independence networks for hidden Markov probability models. AI memo 1565, MIT, Cambridge, MA, Feb 1996.

9. C. Williams and G. E. Hinton. Mean field networks that learn to discriminate temporally distorted strings. In *Proceedings, connectionist models summer school*, pages 18–22, San Mateo, CA, 1990. Morgan Kaufmann.

Independent Component Analysis of Intracellular Calcium Spike Data

Klaus Prank, Julia Börger, Alexander von zur Mühlen,
Georg Brabant, Christof Schöfl
Department of Clinical Endocrinology
Medical School Hannover
D-30625 Hannover
Germany

Abstract

Calcium (Ca^{2+}) is an ubiquitous intracellular messenger which regulates cellular processes, such as secretion, contraction, and cell proliferation. A number of different cell types respond to hormonal stimuli with periodic oscillations of the intracellular free calcium concentration ($[Ca^{2+}]_i$). These Ca^{2+} signals are often organized in complex temporal and spatial patterns even under conditions of sustained stimulation. Here we study the spatio-temporal aspects of intracellular calcium ($[Ca^{2+}]_i$) oscillations in clonal β-cells (hamster insulin secreting cells, HIT) under pharmacological stimulation (Schöfl et al., 1996). We use a novel fast fixed-point algorithm (Hyvärinen and Oja, 1997) for *Independent Component Analysis* (ICA) to blind source separation of the spatio-temporal dynamics of $[Ca^{2+}]_i$ in a HIT-cell. Using this approach we find two significant independent components out of five differently mixed input signals: one $[Ca^{2+}]_i$ signal with a mean oscillatory period of $68s$ and a high frequency signal with a broadband power spectrum with considerable spectral density. This results is in good agreement with a study on high-frequency $[Ca^{2+}]_i$ oscillations (Paluš et al., 1998) Further theoretical and experimental studies have to be performed to resolve the question on the functional impact of intracellular signaling of these independent $[Ca^{2+}]_i$ signals.

1 INTRODUCTION

Independent component analysis (ICA) (Comon, 1994; Jutten and Herault, 1991) has recently received much attention as a signal processing method which has been successfully applied to blind source separation and feature extraction. The goal of ICA is to find independent sources in an unknown linear mixture of measured sensory data. This goal is obtained by reducing 2nd-order and higher order statistical dependencies to make the signals as independent as possible. Mainly three different approaches for ICA exist. The first approach is based on batch computations minimizing or maximizing some relevant criterion functions (Cardoso, 1992; Comon, 1994). The second category contains adaptive algorithms based on stochastic gradient methods, which may have implementations in neural networks (Amari et al., 1996; Bell and Sejnowski, 1995; Delfosse and Loubaton, 1995; Hyvärinen and Oja, 1996; Jutten and Herault, 1991; Moreau and Macchi, 1993; Oja and Karhunen, 1995). The third class of algorithms is based on a *fixed-point iteration scheme* for finding the local extrema of the kurtosis of a linear combination of the observed variables which is equivalent to estimating the non-Gaussian independent components (Hyvärinen and Oja 1997). Here we use the *fast fixed-point algorithm* for independent component analysis proposed by Hyvärinen and Oja (1997) to analyze the spatio-temporal dynamics of intracellular free calcium ($[Ca^{2+}]_i$) in a hamster insulin secreting cell (HIT).

Oscillations of $[Ca^{2+}]_i$ have been reported in a number of electrically excitable and non-excitable cells and the hypotheses of frequency coding were proposed a decade ago (Berridge and Galione, 1988). Recent experimental results clearly demonstrate that $[Ca^{2+}]_i$ oscillations and their frequency can be specific for gene activation concerning the efficiency as well as the selectivity (Dolmetsch et al., 1998). Cells are highly compartmentalized structures which can not be regarded as homogenous entities. Thus, $[Ca^{2+}]_i$ oscillations do not occur uniformly throughout the cell but are initiated at specific sites which are distributed in a functional and nonuniformtm manner. These $[Ca^{2+}]_i$ oscillations spread across individual cells in the form of Ca^{2+} waves. $[Ca^{2+}]_i$ gradients within cells have been proposed to initiate cell migration, exocytosis, lymphocyte, killer cell activity, acid secretion, transcellular ion transport, neurotransmitter release, gap junction regulation, and numerous other functions (Tsien and Tsien, 1990). Due to this fact it is of major importance to study the spatio-temporal aspects of $[Ca^{2+}]_i$ signaling in small subcompartments using calcium-specific fluorescent reporter dyes and digital videomicroscopy rather than studying the cell as a uniform entity. The aim of this study was to define the independent components of the spatio-temporal $[Ca^{2+}]_i$ signal.

2 METHODS

2.1 FAST FIXED-POINT ALGORITHM USING KURTOSIS FOR INDEPENDENT COMPONENT ANALYSIS

In *Independent Component Analysis (ICA)* the original independent sources are unknown. In this study we have recorded the $[Ca^{2+}]_i$ signal in single HIT-cells under pharmacological stimulation at different subcellular regions ($m = 5$) in parallel. The $[Ca^{2+}]_i$ signals (mixtures of sources) are denoted as $x_1, x_2, \ldots, x_m$. Each x_i is expressed as the weighted sum of n unknown statistically independent components (ICs), denoted as $s_1, s_2, \ldots, s_n$. The components are assumed to be mutually statistically independent and zero-mean. The measured signals x_i as well as the independent component variables can be arranged into vectors $\mathbf{x} = (\mathbf{x_1}, \mathbf{x_2}, \ldots, \mathbf{x_m})$ and $\mathbf{s} = (\mathbf{s_1}, \mathbf{s_2}, \ldots, \mathbf{s_n})$ respectively. The linear relationship is given by:

$$\mathbf{x} = \mathbf{A}\mathbf{s} \tag{1}$$

Here $\mathbf{A}$ is a constant mixing matrix whose elements a_{ij} are the unknown coefficients of the mixtures. The basic problem of ICA is to estimate both the mixing matrix $\mathbf{A}$ and the realizations of the s_i using only observations of the mixtures x_j. In order to perform ICA, it is necessary to have at least as many mixtures as there are independent sources ($m \geq n$). The assumption of zero mean of the ICs is no restriction, as this can always be accomplished by subtracting the mean from the random vector $\mathbf{x}$. The ICs and the columns of $\mathbf{A}$ can only be estimated up to a multiplicative constant, because any constant multiplying an IC in eq. 1 could be cancelled by dividing the corresponding column of the mixing matrix $\mathbf{A}$ by the same constant. For mathematical convenience, the ICs are defined to have unit variance making the (non-Gaussian) ICs unique, up to their signs (Comon, 1994). Here we use a novel *fixed-point algorithm* for ICA estimation which is based on 'contrast' functions whose extrema are closely connected to the estimation of ICs (Hyvärinen and Oja, 1997). This method denoted as *fast fixed-point algorithm* has a number of desirable properties. First, it is easy to use, since there are no user-defined parameters. Furthermore, the convergence is fast, conventionally in less than 15 steps and for an appropriate contrast function, the fixed-point algorithm is much more robust against outliers than most ICA algorithms.

Most solutions to the ICA problem use the fourth-order cumulant or *kurtosis* of the signals, defined for a zero-mean random variable x as:

$$kurt(x) = E\{x^4\} - 3(E\{x^2\})^2, \tag{2}$$

where $E\{x\}$ denotes the mathematical expectation of x. The kurtosis is negative for source signals whose amplitude has sub-Gaussian probability densitites (distribution flatter than Gaussian, positive for super Gaussian) sharper than Gaussian, and zero for Gausssian densities. Kurtosis is a contrast function for ICA in the following sense. Consider a linear combination of the measured mixtures $\mathbf{x}$, say $\mathbf{w}^T\mathbf{x}$, where the vector $\mathbf{w}$ is constrained so that $E\{(w^Tx)^2\} = 1$. When $w^Tx = \pm s_i$, for some i, i.e. when the linear combination equals, up to the sign, one of the ICs, the kurtosis of w^Tx is locally minimized or maximized. This property is widely used in ICA algorithms and forms the basis of the *fixed-point algorithm* used in this study which finds the relevant extrema of kurtosis also for non-whitened data. Based on this fact, Hyvärinen and Oja (1997) introduced a very simple and highly efficient *fixed-point algorithm* for computing ICA, calculated over sphered zero-mean vectors $\mathbf{x}$, that is able to find the rows of the separation matrix (denoted as $\mathbf{w}$) and so identify one independent source at a time. The algorithm which computes a gradient descent over the kurtosis is defined as follows:

1. Take a random initial vector w_0 of unit norm. Let $l = 1$.

2. Let $w_l = E\{v(w_{l-1}^T v)^3\} - 3w_{l-1}$. The expectation can be estimated using a large sample of v_k vectors.

3. Divide w_l by its norm (e.g. the Euclidean norm $\| w \| = \sqrt{\sum_i w_i^2}$).

4. If $| w_l^T w_{l-1} |$ is not close enough to 1, let $l = l + 1$ and go back to step 2. Otherwise, output the vector w_l.

To calculate more than one solution, the algorithm may be run as many times as required. It is nevertheless, necessary to remove the information contained in the solutions already found, to estimate each time a different independent component. This can be achieved, after the fourth step of the algorithm, by simply subtracting the estimated solution $\hat{s} = w^T v$ from the unsphered data $\mathbf{x}$.

In the first step of analysis we determined the eigenvalues of the covariance matrix of the measured $[Ca^{2+}]_i$ signals s_i to reduce the dimensionality of the system. Then the *fast fixed-point algorithm* was run using the experimental $[Ca^{2+}]_i$ data to determine the ICs. The resulting ICs were analyzed in respect to their frequency content by computing the Fourier power spectrum.

2.2 MEASUREMENT OF INTRACELLULAR CALCIUM IN HIT-CELLS

To measure $[Ca^{2+}]_i$, HIT (hamster insulin secreting tumor)-cells were loaded with the fluorescent indicator Fura-2/AM and Fura-2 fluorescence was recorded at five different subcellular regions in parallel using a dual excitation spectrofluorometer videoimaging system. The emission wavelength was 510 nm and the excitation wavelengths were 340 nm and 380 nm respectively. The ration between the excitation wavelength (F_{340nm}/F_{380nm}) which correlates to $[Ca^{2+}]_i$ was sampled at a rate of 1 Hz over 360 s. $[Ca^{2+}]_i$ spikes in this cell were induced by the administration of 1 nM arginine vasopressin (AVP).

3 RESULTS

From the five experimental $[Ca^{2+}]_i$ signals (Fig. 1) we determined two significant eigenvalues of the covariance matrix. The *fixed-point algorithm* converged in less than 15 steps and yielded two different ICs, one slowly oscillating component with a mean period of 68 s and one component with fast irregular oscillations with a flat broadband power spectrum (Fig. 2). The spectral density of the second component was considerably larger than that for the high-frequency content of the first slowly oscillating component.

4 CONCLUSIONS

Changes in $[Ca^{2+}]_i$ associated with Ca^{2+} oscillations generally do not occur uniformly throughout the cell but are initiated at specific sites and are able to spread across individual cells in the form of intracellular Ca^{2+} waves. Furthermore, Ca^{2+} signaling is not limited to single cells but occurs between adjacent cells in the form of intercellular Ca^{2+} waves. The reasons for these spatio-temporal patterns of $[Ca^{2+}]_i$ are not yet fully understood. It has been suggested that information is encoded in the frequency, rather than the amplitude, of Ca^{2+} oscillations, which has the advantage of avoiding prolonged exposures to high $[Ca^{2+}]_i$. Another advantage of

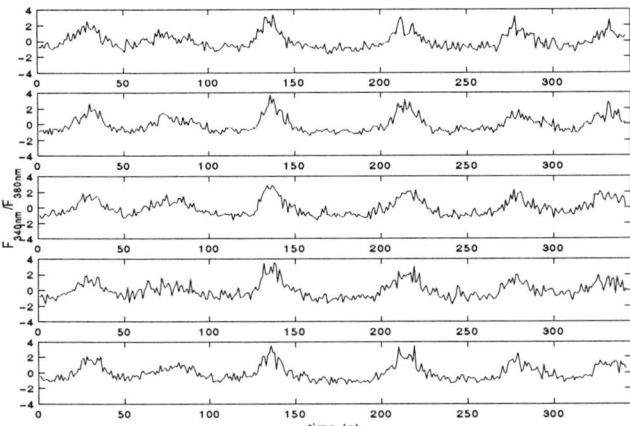

Figure 1: Experimental time series of $[Ca^{2+}]_i$ in a β-cell (insulin secreting cell from a hamster, HIT-cell) determined in five subcellular regions. The data are given as the ratio between both excitation wavelengths of 340 nm and 380 nm respectively which correspond to $[Ca^{2+}]_i$. $[Ca^{2+}]_i$ can be calculated from this ratio. The plotted time series are whitened.

frequency modulated signaling is its high signal-to-noise ratio. In the spatial domain, the spreading of a Ca^{2+} oscillation as a Ca^{2+} wave provides a mechanism by which the regulatory signal can be distributed throughout the cell. The extension of Ca^{2+} waves to adjacent cells by intercellular communication provides one mechanism by which multicellular systems can effect coordinated and cooperative cell responses to localized stimuli. In this study we demonstrated that the $[Ca^{2+}]_i$ signal in clonal β-cells (HIT cells) is composed of two independent components using spatio-temporal $[Ca^{2+}]_i$ data for analysis. One component can be described as large amplitude slow frequency oscillations whereas the other one is a high frequency component which exhibits a broadband power spectrum. These results are in good agreement with a previous study where only the temporal dynamics of $[Ca^{2+}]_i$ in HIT cells has been studied. Using coarse-grained entropy rates computed from information-theoretic functionals we could demonstrate in that study that a fast oscillatory component of the $[Ca^{2+}]_i$ signal can be modulated pharmacologically suggesting deterministic structure in the temporal dynamics (Paluš et al., 1998). Since Ca^{2+} is central to the stimulation of insulin secretion from pancreatic β-cells future experimental and theoretical studies should evaluate the impact of the different oscillatory components of $[Ca^{2+}]_i$ onto the secretory process as well as gene transcription. One possibility to resolve that question is to use a recently proposed mathematical model which allows for the on-line decoding of the $[Ca^{2+}]_i$ into the cellular response represented by the activation (phospho-

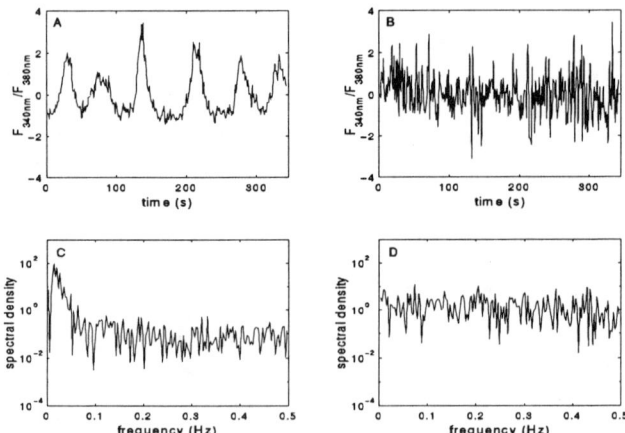

Figure 2: Results from the *independent component analysis* by the *fast fixed-point algorithm*. Two independent components of $[Ca^{2+}]_i$ were found. A: slowly oscillating $[Ca^{2+}]_i$ signal, B: fast oscillating $[Ca^{2+}]_i$ signal. Fourier power spectra of the independent components. C: the major $[Ca^{2+}]_i$ oscillatory period is 68 s, D: flat broadband power spectrum.

rylation) of target proteins (Prank et al., 1998). Very recent experimental data clearly demonstrate that specificty is encoded in the frequency of $[Ca^{2+}]_i$ oscillations. Rapid oscillations of $[Ca^{2+}]_i$ are able to stimulate a set of transcription factors in T-lymphocytes whereas slow oscillations activate only one transcription factor (Dolmetsch et al., 1998). Frequency-dependent gene expression is likely to be a widespread phenomenon and oscillations of $[Ca^{2+}]_i$ can occur with periods of seconds to hours. The technique of independent component analyis should be able to extract the spatio-temporal features of the $[Ca^{2+}]_i$ signal in a variety of cells and should help to understand the differential regulation of $[Ca^{2+}]_i$-dependent intracellular processes such as gene transcription or secretion.

Acknowledgements

This study was supported by Deutsche Forschungsgemeinschaft under grants Scho 466/1-3 and Br 915/4-4.

References

Amari, S., Cichocki, A. & Yang, H. (1996) A new learning algorithm for blind source separation. In Touretzky, D.S., Mozer, M. C. & Hasselmo, M. E., (eds.), *Advances in Neural Information Processing 8*, pp. 757-763. Cambridge, MA: MIT Press.

Bell, A. & Sejnowski, T. (1995) An information-maximization approach to blind separation and blind deconvolution. *Neural Computation* **7**:1129-1159.

Berridge, M. & Galione, A. (1988) Cytosolic calcium oscillators. *FASEB* **2**:3074-3082.

Cardoso, J. F. (1992) Iterative techniques for blind source separation using only fourth-order cumulants. In *Proc. EUSIPCO* (pp. 739-742). Brussels.

Comon, P. (1994) Independent component analysis - a new concept? *Signal Procesing* **36**:287-314.

Delfosse, N. & Loubaton, P. (1995) Adaptive blind separation of independent sources: a deflation approach. *Signal Processing* **45**:59-83.

Dolmetsch, R. E., Xu, K. & Lewis, R. S. (1998) Calcium oscillations increase the efficiency and specificity of gene expression. *Nature* **392**:933-936.

Hyvärinen, A. & Oja, E. (1996) A neuron that learns to separate one independent component from linear mixtures. In *Proc. IEEE Int. Conf. on Neural Networks*, pp. 62-67, Washington, D.C.

Hyvärinen, A. & Oja, E. (1997) A fast fixed-point algorithm for independent component analysis. *Neural Computation* **9**:1483-1492.

Jutten, C. & Herault, J. (1991) Blind separation of sources, part I: An adaptive algorithm based on neuromimetic architecture. *Signal Processing* **24**:1-10.

Moureau, E., & Macchi, O. (1993) New self-adaptive algorithms for source separation based on contrast functions. In *Proc. IEEE Signal Processing Workshop on Higher Order Statistics*, pp. 215-219, Lake Tahoe, USA.

Oja, E. & Karhunen, J. (1995) Signal separation by nonlinear hebbian learning. In Palaniswami, M., Attikiouzel, Y., Marks, R., Fogel, D. & Fukuda, T. (eds.) *Computational Intelligence - a Dynamic System Perspective* pp. 83-97. IEEE Press, New York.

Paluš, M., Schöfl, C., von zur Mühlen, A., Brabant, G. & Prank, K. (1998) Coarse-grained entropy rates quantify fast Ca^{2+} dynamics modulated by pharmacological stimulation. *Pacific Symposium on Biocomputing 1998*:645-656.

Prank, K., Läer, L., Wagner, M., von zur Mühlen, A., Brabant, G. & Schöfl, C. (1998) Decoding of intracellular calcium spike trains. *Europhys. Lett.* **42**:143-147.

Schöfl, C., Rössig, L., Leitolf, H., Mader, T., von zur Mühlen, A. & Brabant, G. (1996) Generation of repetitive Ca^{2+} transients by bombesin requires intracellular release and influx of Ca^{2+} through voltage-dependent and voltage independent channels in single HIT cells. *Cell Calcium* **19**(6):485-493.

Tsien, R. W. & Tsien, R. Y. (1990) Calcium channels, stores, and oscillations. *Annu. Rev. Cell Biol.* **6**:715-760.

Applications of multi-resolution neural networks to mammography

Clay D. Spence and Paul Sajda
Sarnoff Corporation
CN5300
Princeton, NJ 08543-5300
{cspence, psajda}@sarnoff.com

Abstract

We have previously presented a coarse-to-fine hierarchical pyramid/neural network (HPNN) architecture which combines multi-scale image processing techniques with neural networks. In this paper we present applications of this general architecture to two problems in mammographic Computer-Aided Diagnosis (CAD). The first application is the detection of microcalcifications. The coarse-to-fine HPNN was designed to learn large-scale context information for detecting small objects like microcalcifications. Receiver operating characteristic (ROC) analysis suggests that the hierarchical architecture improves detection performance of a well established CAD system by roughly 50 %. The second application is to detect mammographic masses directly. Since masses are large, extended objects, the coarse-to-fine HPNN architecture is not suitable for this problem. Instead we construct a fine-to-coarse HPNN architecture which is designed to learn small-scale detail structure associated with the extended objects. Our initial results applying the fine-to-coarse HPNN to mass detection are encouraging, with detection performance improvements of about 36 %. We conclude that the ability of the HPNN architecture to integrate information across scales, both coarse-to-fine and fine-to-coarse, makes it well suited for detecting objects which may have contextual clues or detail structure occurring at scales other than the natural scale of the object.

1 Introduction

In a previous paper [8] we presented a coarse-to-fine hierarchical pyramid/neural network (*HPNN*) architecture that combines multi-scale image processing techniques with neural networks to search for small targets in images (see figure 1A). To *search* an image we apply the network at a position and use its output as an estimate of the probability that a target (an object of the class we wish to find) is present there. We then repeat this at each position in the image. In the coarse-to-fine HPNN, the hidden units of networks operating at low resolution or coarse scale learn associated *context* information, since the targets themselves are difficult to detect at low resolution. The context is then passed to networks searching at higher resolution. The use of context can significantly improve detection performance since small objects have few distinguishing features. In the HPNN each of the networks receives information directly from only a small part of several feature images, and so the networks can be relatively simple. The network at the highest resolution integrates the contextual information learned at coarser resolutions to detect the object of interest.

The HPNN architecture can be extended by considering the implications of inverting the information flow in the coarse-to-fine architecture. This fine-to-coarse HPNN would have networks extracting detail structure at fine resolutions of the image and then passing this detail information to networks operating at coarser scales (see figure 1B). For many types of objects, information about the fine structure is important for discriminating between different classes. The fine-to-coarse HPNN is therefore a natural architecture for exploiting fine detail information for detecting extended objects.

In this paper, we present our experiences in applying the HPNN framework to two problems in mammographic Computer-Aided Diagnosis (CAD); that of detecting microcalcifications in mammograms and that of detecting malignant masses in mammograms. The coarse-to-fine HPNN architecture is well-suited for the microcalcification problem, while the fine-to-coarse HPNN is suited for mass detection. We evaluate the performance and utility of the HPNN framework by considering its effects on reducing false positive rates in a well characterized CAD system.

The University of Chicago (UofC) has been actively developing mammographic CAD systems for microcalcification and mass detection [6] and has been evaluating their performance clinically. A general block diagram showing the basic processing elements of these CAD systems is shown in figure 2. First, a pre-processing step is used to segment the breast area and increase the overall signal-to-noise levels in the image. Regions of interest ($ROIs$) are defined at this stage, representing local areas of the breast which potentially contain a cluster of microcalcifications or a mass. The next stage typically involves feature extraction and rule-based/heuristic analysis, in order to prune false positives. The remaining ROIs are classified as positive or negative by a statistical classifier or neural network. The CAD system is used as a "second reader", aiding the radiologist by pointing out spots to double check. One of the key requirements of CAD is that false positive rates be low enough that radiologists will not ignore the CAD system output. Therefore it is critical to reduce false positive rates of CAD systems without significant reductions in sensitivity. In this paper we evaluate the HPNN framework within the context of reducing the false positive rates of the UofC CAD systems for microcalcification and mass detection. In both cases the HPNN acts as a post-processor of the UofC CAD system.

2 Microcalcification detection

Microcalcifications are calcium deposits in breast tissue that appear as very small bright dots in mammograms. Clusters of microcalcifications frequently occur around tumors. Unfortunately microcalcification clusters are sometimes missed, since they

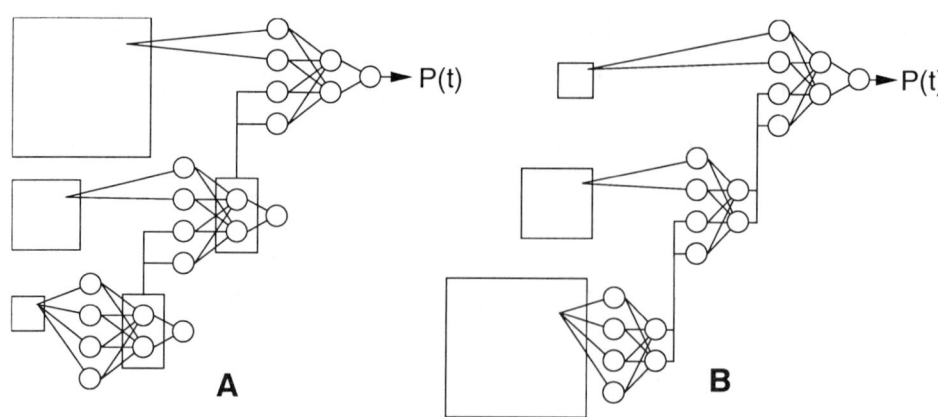

Figure 1: Hierarchical pyramid/neural network architectures for (A) detecting microcalcifications and (B) detecting masses. In (A) context is propagated from low to high resolution via the hidden units of low resolution networks. In (B) small scale detail information is propagated from high to low resolution. In both cases the output of the last integration network is an estimate of the probability that a target is present.

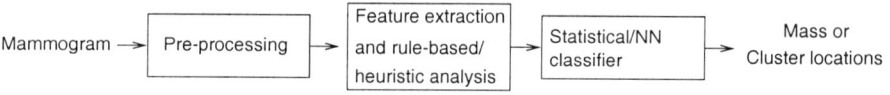

Figure 2: Block diagram for a typical CAD detection system.

can be quite subtle and the radiologists can only spend about a minute evaluating a patient's mammograms.

Data used for the microcalcification experiments was provided by The University of Chicago. The first set of data consists of 50 true positive and 86 false positive ROIs. These ROIs are 99x99 pixels and digitized at 100 micron resolution. A second set of data from the UofC clinical testing database included 47 true positives and 103 false positives, also 99x99 and sampled at 100 micron resolution.

We trained the coarse-to-fine HPNN architecture in figure 1A as a detector for individual calcifications. For each level in the pyramid a network is trained, beginning with the network at low resolution. The network at a particular pyramid level is applied to one pixel at a time in the image at that resolution, and so produces an output at each pixel. All of the networks are trained to detect microcalcifications, however, at low resolutions the microcalcifications are not directly detectable. To achieve better than chance performance, the networks at those levels must learn something about the context in which microcalcifications appear. To integrate context information with the other features the outputs of hidden units from low resolution networks are propagated hierarchically as inputs to networks operating at higher resolutions.

Input to the neural networks come from an integrated feature pyramid (IFP) [1]. To construct the IFP, we used steerable filters [3] to compute local orientation energy. The steering properties of these filters enable the direct computation of the orientation having maximum energy. We constructed features which represent, at each pixel location, the maximum energy (energy at θ_{max}), the energy at the

cc	HPNN				Chicago NN			
	A_z	σ_{A_z}	FPF TPF=1.0	σ_{FPF}	A_z	σ_{A_z}	FPF TPF=1.0	σ_{FPF}
1	.93	.03	.24	.11	.88	.04	.50	.11
2	.94	.02	.21	.11	.91	.02	.43	.10
3	.94	.03	.39	.19	.91	.03	.48	.19
4	.93	.03	.48	.15	.90	.05	.56	.21
5	.93	.03	.51	.06	.88	.05	.68	.21

Table 1: Comparison of HPNN and Chicago networks.

orientation perpendicular to θ_{max} ($\theta_{max} - 90^o$), and the energy at the diagonal (energy at $\theta_{max} - 45^o$).[1] The resulting features are input into the coarse-to-fine network hierarchy.

In examining the truth data for the ROI data set, we found that the experts who specified the microcalcification positions often made errors in these positions of up to ±2 pixels of the correct position. To take this uncertainty in position into account, we used the following error function

$$E_{UOP} = - \sum_{p \in Pos} \log\left(1 - \prod_{x \in p}(1 - y(x))\right) - \sum_{x \in Neg} \log(1 - y(x)) \quad (1)$$

which we have called the Uncertain Object Position (*UOP*) error function [7].[2] ($y(x)$ is the network's output when applied to position x.) It is essentially the cross-entropy error, but for positive examples the probability of generating a positive output ($y(x)$, in this case) has been replaced by the probability of generating at least one positive output in a region or set of pixels p in the image. In our case each p is a five-by-five pixel square centered on the location specified by the expert. To this we added the standard weight decay regularization term. The regularization constant was adjusted to minimize the ten-fold cross-validation error.

The coarse-to-fine HPNN was applied to each input ROI, and an image was constructed from the output of the Level 0 network at each pixel. Each of these pixel values is the network's estimate of the probability that a microcalcification is present there. Training and testing were done using as jackknife protocol [5], whereby one half of the data (25 TPs and 43 FPs) was used for training and the other half for testing. We used five different random splits of the data into training and test sets. For a given ROI, the probability map produced by the network was thresholded at a given value to produce a binary detection map. Region growing was used to count the number of distinct detected regions. The ROI was classified as a positive if the number of regions was greater than or equal to a certain cluster criterion.

Table 1 compares ROC results for the HPNN and another network that had been used in the University of Chicago CAD system [9] using five different cluster criterion (cc). Reported are the area under the ROC curve (A_z), the standard deviation of A_z across the subsets of the jackknife (σ_{A_z}), the false positive fraction at a true positive fraction of 1.0 ($FPF@TPF = 1.0$) and the standard deviation of the FPF across the subsets of the jackknife (σ_{FPF}). A_z and $FPF@TPF = 1.0$ represent

---

[1] We found that the energies in the two diagonal directions were nearly identical.
[2] Keeler et al. [4] developed a network for object recognition that had some similarities to the UOP error. In fact the way in which the outputs of units are combined for their error function can be shown to be an approximation to the UOP error.

the averages of the subsets of the jackknife. Note that both networks operate best when the cluster criterion is set to two. For this case the HPNN has a higher A_z than the Chicago network while also halving the false positive rate. This difference, between the two networks' A_z and FPF values, is statistically significant (z-test; $p_{A_z} = .0018$, $p_{FPF} = .00001$).

A second set of data was also tested. 150 ROIs taken from a clinical prospective study and classified as positive by the full Chicago CAD system (including the Chicago neural network) were used to test the HPNN. Though the Chicago CAD system classified all 150 ROIs as positive, only 47 were in fact positive while 103 were negatives. We applied the HPNN trained on the entire previous data set to this new set of ROIs. The HPNN was able to reclassify 47/103 negatives as negative, without loss in sensitivity (no false negatives were introduced).

On examining the negative examples rejected by the coarse-to-fine HPNN, we found that many of these ROIs contained linear, high-contrast structure which would otherwise be false positives for the Chicago network. The Chicago neural network presumably interprets the "peaks" on the linear structure as calcifications. However because the coarse-to-fine HPNN also integrates information from low resolution it can associate these "peaks" with the low-resolution linear structure and reject them.

3 Mass detection

Although microcalcifications are an important cue for malignant masses in mammograms, they are not visible or even present in all cases. Thus mammographic CAD systems include algorithms to directly detect the presence of masses. We have started to apply a fine-to-coarse HPNN architecture to detect malignant masses in digitized mammograms. Radiologists often distinguish malignant from benign masses based on the detailed shape of the mass border and the presence of spicules alone the border. Thus to integrate this high resolution information to detect malignant masses, which are extended objects, we apply the fine-to-coarse HPNN of figure 1B.

As for microcalcifications, we apply the HPNN as a post-processor, but here it processes the output of the mass-detection component of UofC CAD system. The data in our study consists of 72 positive and 100 negative ROIs. These are 256-by-256 pixels and are sampled at 200 micron resolution.

At each level of the fine-to-coarse HPNN several hidden units process the feature images. The outputs of each unit at all of the positions in an image make up a new feature image. This is reduced in resolution by the usual pyramid blur-and-subsample operation to make an input feature image for the network units at the next lower resolution. We trained the entire fine-to-coarse HPNN as one network instead of training a network for each level, one level at a time. This training is quite straightforward. Back-propagating error through the network units is the same as in conventional networks. We must also back-propagate through the pyramid reduction operation, but this is linear and therefore quite simple. In addition we use the same UOP error function (Equation 1) used to train the coarse-to-fine architecture. The rationale for this application of the UOP error function is that the truth data specifies the location of the center of the mass at the highest resolution. However, because of the sub-sampling the center cannot be unambiguously assigned to a particular pixel at low resolution.

The features input to the fine-to-coarse HPNN are filtered versions of the image, with filter kernels given by $\psi_{q,p}(r,\theta) = \left(\frac{q!}{\pi(q+|p|)!}\right)^{1/2} r^{|p|} e^{-r^2/2} L_q^{|p|}(r^2) e^{ip\phi}$ in polar

Sensitivity	Coarse-to-Fine HPNN Microcalcification	Fine-to-Coarse HPNN Mass
100 %	45 %	32 %
95 %	47 %	36 %
90 %	63 %	40 %
80 %	69 %	78 %

Table 2: Detector Specificity (% reduction in false positive rate of UofC CAD system).

coordinates, with $(q,p) \in \{(0,1),(1,0),(0,2)\}$. These are combinations of derivatives of Gaussians, and can be written as combinations of separable filter kernels (products of purely horizontal and vertical filters), so they can be computed at relatively low cost. They are also easy to steer, since this is just multiplication by a complex phase factor. We steered these in the radial and tangential directions relative to the tentative mass centers, and used the real and imaginary parts and their squares and products as features. The center coordinates of the are generated by the earlier stages of the CAD system. These features were extracted at each level of the Gaussian pyramid representation of the mass ROI, and used as inputs only to the network units at the same level.

The fine-to-coarse HPNN is quite similar to the convolution network proposed by Le Cun, et al [2], however with a few notable differences. The fine-to-coarse HPNN receives as inputs preset features extracted from the image (in this case radial and tangential gradients) at each resolution, compared to the convolution network, whose inputs are the original pixel values at the highest resolution. Secondly, in the fine-to-coarse HPNN, the inputs to a hidden unit at a particular position are the pixel values at that position in each of the feature images, one pixel value per feature image. Thus the HPNN's hidden units do not learn linear filters, except as linear combinations of the filters used to form the features. Finally the fine-to-coarse HPNN is trained using the UOP error function, which is not used in the Le Cun network.

Currently our best performing fine-to-coarse HPNN system for mass detection has two hidden units per pyramid level. This gives an ROC area of $A_z = 0.85$ and eliminates 36 % of the false-positives at a cost of missing 5 % of the actual positives. To improve performance further, we are investigating different regularizers, richer feature sets, and more complex architectures, i.e., more hidden units.

4 Conclusion

We have presented the application of multi-resolution neural network architectures to two problems in computer-aided diagnosis, the detection of microcalcifications in mammograms and the direct detection of malignant masses in mammograms. A summary of the performance of these architectures is given in Table 2. In the case of microcalcifications, the coarse-to-fine HPNN architecture successfully discovered large-scale context information that improves the system's performance in detecting small objects. A coarse-to-fine HPNN has been directly integrated with the UofC CAD system for microcalcification detection and the complete system is undergoing clinical evaluation.

In the case of malignant masses, a fine-to-coarse HPNN architecture was used to exploit information from fine resolution detail which could be used to differentiate malignant from benign masses. The results of this network are encouraging, but additional improvement is needed. In general, we have found that the multi-resolution HPNNs are a useful class of network architecture for exploiting and integrating information at multiple scales.

5 Acknowledgments

This work was funded by the National Information Display Laboratory, DARPA through ONR contract No. N00014-93-C-0202, and the Murray Foundation. We would like to thank Drs. Robert Nishikawa and Maryellen Giger of The University of Chicago for useful discussions and providing the data.

References

[1] Peter Burt. Smart sensing within a pyramid vision machine. *Proceedings IEEE*, 76(8):1006–1015, 1988. Also in *Neuro-Vision Systems*, Gupta and Knopf, eds., 1994.

[2] Y. Le Cun, B. Boser, J. S. Denker, and D. Henderson. Handwritten digit recognition with a back-propagation network. In David S. Touretzky, editor, *Advances in Neural Information Processing Systems 2*, pages 396–404, 2929 Campus Drive, San Mateo, CA 94403, 1991. Morgan-Kaufmann Publishers.

[3] William T. Freeman and Edward H. Adelson. The design and use of steerable filters. *IEEE Transactions on Pattern Analysis and Machine Intelligence*, PAMI-13(9):891–906, 1991.

[4] James D. Keeler, David E. Rumelhart, and Wee-Keng Leow. Integrated segmentation and recognition of hand-printed numerals. In Richard P. Lippmann, John E. Moody, and David S. Touretzky, editors, *Advances in Neural Information Processing Systems 3*, pages 557–563, 2929 Campus Drive, San Mateo, CA 94403, 1991. Morgan-Kaufmann Publishers.

[5] Charles Metz. Current problems in ROC analysis. In *Proceedings of the Chest Imaging Conference*, pages 315–33, Madison, WI, November 1988.

[6] R. M. Nishikawa, R. C. Haldemann, J. Papaioannou, M. L. Giger, P. Lu, R. A. Schmidt, D. E. Wolverton, U. Bick, and K. Doi. Initial experience with a prototype clinical intelligent mammography workstation for computer-aided diagnosis. In Murray H. Loew and Kenneth M. Hanson, editors, *Medical Imaging 1995*, volume 2434, pages 65–71, P.O. Box 10, Bellingham WA 98227-0010, 1995. SPIE.

[7] Clay D. Spence. Supervised learning of detection and classification tasks with uncertain training data. In *Image Understanding Workshop*. ARPA, 1996. This Volume.

[8] Clay D. Spence, John C. Pearson, and Jim Bergen. Coarse-to-fine image search using neural networks. In Gerald Tesauro, David S. Touretzky, and Todd K. Leen, editors, *Advances in Neural Information Processing Systems 7*, pages 981–988, Massachusetts Institute of Technology, Cambridge, MA 02142, 1994. MIT Press.

[9] W. Zhang, K. Doi, M. L. Giger, Y. Wu, R. M. Nishikawa, and R. Schmidt. Computerized detection of clustered microcalcifications in digital mammograms using a shift-invariant artificial neural network. *Medical Physics*, 21(4):517–524, April 1994.

Robot Docking using Mixtures of Gaussians

Matthew Williamson[*]   Roderick Murray-Smith[†]   Volker Hansen[‡]

Abstract

This paper applies the *Mixture of Gaussians* probabilistic model, combined with Expectation Maximization optimization to the task of summarizing three dimensional range data for a mobile robot. This provides a flexible way of dealing with uncertainties in sensor information, and allows the introduction of prior knowledge into low-level perception modules. Problems with the basic approach were solved in several ways: the mixture of Gaussians was reparameterized to reflect the types of objects expected in the scene, and priors on model parameters were included in the optimization process. Both approaches force the optimization to find 'interesting' objects, given the sensor and object characteristics. A higher level classifier was used to interpret the results provided by the model, and to reject spurious solutions.

1 Introduction

This paper concerns an application of the *Mixture of Gaussians* (MoG) probabilistic model (Titterington et al., 1985) for a robot docking application. We use the Expectation-Maximization (EM) approach (Dempster et al., 1977) to fit Gaussian sub-models to a sparse 3d representation of the robot's environment, finding walls, boxes, etc.. We have modified the MoG formulation in three ways to incorporate prior knowledge about the task, and the sensor characteristics: the parameters of the Gaussians are recast to constrain how they fit the data, priors on these parameters are calculated and incorporated into the EM algorithm, and a higher level processing stage is included which interprets the fit of the Gaussians on the data, detects misclassifications, and providing prior information to guide the model-fitting.

The robot is equipped with a LIDAR 3d laser range-finder (PIAP, 1995) which it uses to identify possible docking objects. The range-finder calculates the time of flight for a light pulse reflected off objects in the scene. The particular LIDAR used is not very powerful, making objects with poor reflectance (e.g., dark, shiny, or surfaces not perpendicular to the

---

[*]Corresponding author: MIT AI Lab, Cambridge, MA, USA. matt@ai.mit.edu
[†]Dept. of Mathematical Modelling, Technical University of Denmark. rod@imm.dtu.dk
[‡]DaimlerChrysler, Alt-Moabit 96a, Berlin, Germany. hansen@dbag.bln.daimlerbenz.com

laser beam) invisible. The scan pattern is also very sparse, especially in the vertical direction, as shown in the scan of a wall in Figure 1. However, if an object is detected, the range returned is accurate (±1-2cm). When the range data is plotted in Cartesian space it forms a number of sparse clusters, leading naturally to the use of MoG clustering algorithms to make sense of the scene. While the Gaussian assumption is not an ideal model of the data, the generality of MoG, and its ease of implementation and analysis motivated its use over a more specialized approach. The sparse nature of the data inspired the modifications to the MoG formulation described in this paper.

Model-based object recognition from dense range images has been widely reported (see (Arman and Aggarwal, 1993) for a review), but is not relevant in this case given the sparseness of the data. Denser range images could be collected by combining multiple scans, but the poor visibility of the sensor hampers the application of these techniques. The advantage of the MoG technique is that the segmentation is "soft", and perception proceeds iteratively during learning. This is especially useful for mobile robots where evidence accumulates over time, and the allocation of attention is time and state-dependent. The EM algorithm is useful since it is guaranteed to converge to a local maximum.

The following sections of the paper describe the re-parameterization of the Gaussians to model plane-like clusters, the formulation of the priors, and the higher level processing which interprets the clustered data in order to both move the robot and provide prior information to the model-fitting algorithm.

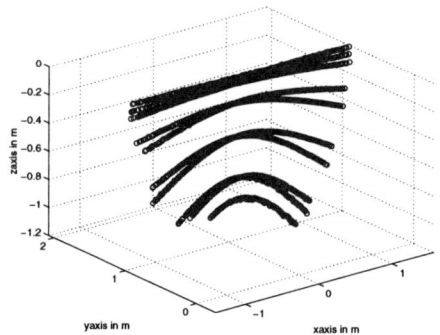

Figure 1: Plot showing data from a LIDAR scan of a wall, plotted in Cartesian space. The robot is located at the origin, with the y axis pointing forward, x to the right, and z up. The sparse scan pattern is visible, as well as the visibility constraint: the wall extends beyond where the scan ends, but is invisible to the LIDAR due to the orientation of the wall

2 Mixture of Gaussians model

The range-finder returns a set of data, each of which is a position in Cartesian space $\mathbf{x}_i = (x_i, y_i, z_i)$. The complete set of data $D = \{\mathbf{x}_1 \ldots \mathbf{x}_N\}$ is modeled as being generated by a mixture density

$$P(\mathbf{x}_n) = \sum_{i=1}^{M} P(\mathbf{x}_n | i, \mu_i, \Sigma_i, \pi_i) P(i),$$

where we use a Gaussian as the sub-model, with mean μ_i, variance Σ_i and weight π_i, which makes the probability of a particular data point:

$$P(\mathbf{x}_n | \mu, \Sigma, \pi) = \sum_{i=1}^{M} \frac{\pi_i}{(2\pi)^{3/2} |\Sigma_i|^{1/2}} \exp\left(-\frac{1}{2}(\mathbf{x}_n - \mu_i)^T \Sigma_i^{-1} (\mathbf{x}_n - \mu_i)\right)$$

Given a set of data D, the most likely set of parameters is found using the EM algorithm. This algorithm has a number of advantages, such as guaranteed convergence to a local minimum, and efficient computational performance.

In 3D Cartesian space, the Gaussian sub-models form ellipsoids, where the size and orientation are determined by the covariance matrix Σ_i. In the general case, the EM algorithm can be used to learn all the parameters of Σ_i. The sparseness of the LIDAR data makes this parameterization inappropriate, as various odd collections of points could be clustered together. By changing the parameterization of Σ_i to better model plane-like structures, the system can be improved. The reparameterization is most readily expressed in terms of the eigenvalues Λ_i and eigenvectors V_i of the covariance matrix $\Sigma_i = V_i \Lambda_i V_i^{-1}$.

The covariance matrix of a normal approximation to a plane-like vertical structure will have a large eigenvalue in the z direction, and in the x–y plane one large and one small eigenvalue. Since Σ_i is symmetrical, the eigenvectors are orthogonal, $V_i^{-1} = V_i^T = V_i$, and Σ_i can be written:

$$\Sigma_i = \begin{pmatrix} \sin\theta_i & \cos\theta_i & 0 \\ \cos\theta_i & -\sin\theta_i & 0 \\ 0 & 0 & 1 \end{pmatrix} \begin{pmatrix} a_i & 0 & 0 \\ 0 & \gamma a_i & 0 \\ 0 & 0 & b_i \end{pmatrix} \begin{pmatrix} \sin\theta_i & \cos\theta_i & 0 \\ \cos\theta_i & -\sin\theta_i & 0 \\ 0 & 0 & 1 \end{pmatrix},$$

where θ_i is the angle of orientation of the ith sub-model in the x–y plane, a_i scales the cluster in the x and y directions, and b_i scales in the z direction. The constant γ controls the aspect ratio of the ellipsoid in the x–y plane.[1]

The optimal values of these parameters (a, b) are found using EM, first calculating the probability that data point $\mathbf{x}_n$ is modeled by Gaussian i, (h_{in}) for every data point $\mathbf{x}_n$ and every Gaussian i,

$$h_{in} = \frac{\pi_i |\Sigma_i|^{-1/2} \exp\left(-\frac{1}{2}(\mathbf{x}_n - \mu_i)^T \Sigma_i^{-1} (\mathbf{x}_n - \mu_i)\right)}{\sum_{i=1}^M \pi_i |\Sigma_i|^{-1/2} \exp\left(-\frac{1}{2}(\mathbf{x}_n - \mu_i)^T \Sigma_i^{-1} (\mathbf{x}_n - \mu_i)\right)}.$$

This "responsibility" is then used as a weighting for the updates to the other parameters,

$$\hat{\mu}_i = \frac{\sum_n h_{in} \mathbf{x}_n}{\sum_n h_{in}}, \quad \hat{\theta}_i = \frac{1}{2} \tan^{-1}\left(\frac{2 \sum_n h_{in}(\mathbf{x}_{n1} - \mu_{i1})(\mathbf{x}_{n2} - \mu_{i2})}{\sum_n h_{in}[(\mathbf{x}_{n1} - \mu_{i1})^2 - (\mathbf{x}_{n2} - \mu_{i2})^2]}\right)$$

$$\zeta = (\gamma - 1)((\mathbf{x}_{n1} - \mu_{i1})\sin\theta + (\mathbf{x}_{n2} - \mu_{i2})\cos\theta)^2 + (\mathbf{x}_{n1} - \mu_{i1})^2 + (\mathbf{x}_{n2} - \mu_{i2})^2$$

$$\hat{a}_i = \frac{\sum_n h_{in} \zeta}{2\gamma \sum_n h_{in}}, \quad \hat{b}_i = \frac{\sum_n h_{in}(\mathbf{x}_{n3} - \mu_{n3})^2}{\sum_n h_{in}},$$

where $\mathbf{x}_{n1}$ is the first element of $\mathbf{x}_n$ etc. and ζ corresponds to the projection of the data into the plane of the cluster. It is important to update the means μ_i first, and use the new values to update the other parameters.[2] Figure 2 shows a typical model response on real LIDAR data.

2.1 Practicalities of application, and results

Starting values for the model parameters are important, as EM is only guaranteed to find a local optimum. The Gaussian mixture components are initialized with a large covariance, allowing them to pick up data and move to the correct positions. We found that initializing the means μ_i to random data points, rather than randomly in the input space, tended to

---

[1] By experimentation, a value of γ of 0.01 was found to be reasonable for this application.

[2] Intuition for the $\hat{\theta}_i$ update can be obtained by considering that $(\mathbf{x}_{n1} - \mu_{i1})$ is the x component of the distance between $\mathbf{x}_n$ and μ_i, which is $|\mathbf{x}_n - \mu_i|\cos\theta$, and similarly $(\mathbf{x}_{n2} - \mu_{i2})$ is $|\mathbf{x}_n - \mu_i|\sin\theta$, so $\tan 2\theta = \frac{\sin 2\theta}{\cos 2\theta} = \frac{2\sin\theta\cos\theta}{\cos^2\theta - \sin^2\theta} = \frac{2(\mathbf{x}_{n1} - \mu_{i1})(\mathbf{x}_{n2} - \mu_{i2})}{(\mathbf{x}_{n1} - \mu_{i1})^2 - (\mathbf{x}_{n2} - \mu_{i2})^2}$.

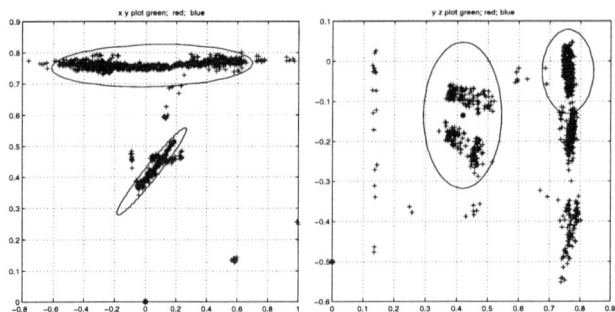

Figure 2: Example of clustering of the 3d data points. The left hand graph shows the view from above (the x–y plane), and the right graph shows the view from the side (the y–z plane), with the robot positioned at the origin. The scene shows a box at an oblique angle, with a wall behind. The extent of the plane-like Gaussian sub-models is illustrated using the ellipses, which are drawn at a probability of 0.5.

work better, especially given the sensor characteristics—if the LIDAR returned a range measurement, it was likely to be part of an interesting object.

Despite the accuracy of measurement, there are still outlying data points, and it is impossible to fully segment the data into separate objects. One simple solution we found was to define a "junk" Gaussian. This is a sub-model placed in the center of the data, with a large covariance Σ. This Gaussian then becomes responsible for the outliers in the data (i.e. sparsely distributed data over the whole scene, none of which are associated with a specific object), allowing the object-modeling Gaussians to work undistracted.

The use of EM with the a, b, θ parameterization found and represented plane-like data clusters better than models where all the elements of the covariance matrix were free to adapt. It also tended to converge faster, probably due to the reduced numbers of parameters in the covariance matrix (3 as opposed to 6). Although the algorithm is constrained to find planes, the parameterization was flexible enough to model other objects such as thin vertical lines (say from a table leg). The only problem with the algorithm was that it occasionally found poor local minimum solutions, such as illustrated in Figure 3. This is a common problem with least squares based clustering methods (Duda and Hart, 1973).

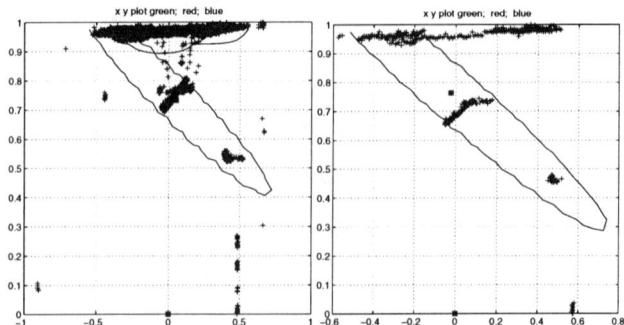

Figure 3: Two examples of 'undesirable' local minimum solutions found by EM. Both graphs show the top view of a scene of a box in front of a wall. The algorithm has incorrectly clustered the box with the left hand side of the wall.

3 Incorporating prior information

As well as reformulating the Gaussian models to suit our application, we also incorporated prior knowledge on the parameters of the sub-models. Sensor characteristics are often well-defined, and it makes sense to use these as early as possible in perception, rather than dealing with their side-effects at higher levels of reasoning. Here, e.g., the visibility constraint, by which only planes which are almost perpendicular to the lidar rays are visible, could be included by writing $P(\mathbf{x}_n) = \sum_{i=1}^{M} P(\mathbf{x}_n|i, \beta_i)P(i)P(visible|\beta_i)$, the updates could be recalculated, and the feature immediately brought into the modeling process. In addition, prior knowledge about the locations and sizes of objects, maybe from other sensors, can be used to influence the modeling procedure. This allows the sensor to make better use of the sparse data.

For a model with parameters β and data D, Bayes rule gives:

$$P(\beta|D) = \frac{P(\beta)}{P(D)} \prod P(\mathbf{x}_n|\beta).$$

Normally the logarithm of this is taken, to give the log-likelihood, which in the case of mixtures of Gaussians is

$$L(D|\beta) = \log(p(\{\mu_i, \pi_i, a_i, b_i, \theta_i\})) - \log(p(D)) + \sum_n \log \sum_i p(\mathbf{x}_n|i, \mu_i, \pi_i, a_i, b_i, \theta_i)$$

To include the parameter priors in the EM algorithm, distributions for the different parameters are chosen, then the log-likelihood is differentiated as usual to find the updates to the parameters (McMichael, 1995). The calculations are simplified if the priors on all the parameters are assumed to be independent, $p(\{\mu_i, \pi_i, a_i, b_i, \theta_i\}) = \prod_i p(\mu_i)p(\pi_i)p(a_i)p(b_i)p(\theta_i)$.

The exact form of the prior distributions varies for different parameters, both to capture different behavior and for ease of implementation. For the element means (μ_i), a flat distribution over the data is used, specifying that the means should be among the data points. For the element weights, a multinomial Dirichlet prior can be used, $p(\pi_i|\alpha) = \frac{\Gamma(\alpha|M)}{\Gamma(\alpha+1)^M} \prod_{i=1}^{M} \pi_i^\alpha$. When the hyperparameter $\alpha > 0$, the algorithm favours weights around $1/M$, and when $-1 < \alpha < 0$, weights close to 0 or 1.[3] The expected value of a_i (written as $\overline{a_i}$) can be encoded using a truncated inverse exponential prior (McMichael, 1995), setting $p(a_i|\overline{a_i}) = K \exp(-\overline{a_i}/(2a_i))$, where K is a normalizing factor.[4] The prior for b_i has the same form. Priors for θ_i were not used, but could be useful to capture the visibility constraint. Given these distributions, the updates to the parameters become

$$\hat{\mu}_i = \frac{\sum_n h_{in}\mathbf{x}_n}{\sum_n h_{in}}, \quad \hat{\pi}_i = \frac{\sum_n h_{in} + \alpha}{\sum_n \sum_j h_{jn} + \alpha}$$

$$\hat{a}_i = \frac{\sum_n h_{in}\zeta/\gamma + \overline{a_i}}{2\sum_n h_{in}}, \quad \hat{b}_i = \frac{\sum_n h_{in}(\mathbf{x}_{n3} - \mu_{n3})^2 + \overline{b_i}}{\sum_n h_{in}}.$$

The update for μ_i is the same as before, the prior having no effect. The update for a_i and b_i forces them to be near $\overline{a_i}$ and $\overline{b_i}$, and the update for π_i is affected by the hyperparameter α.

The priors on a_i and b_i had noticeable effects on the models obtained. Figure 4 shows the results from two fits, starting from identical initial conditions. By adjusting the size of the prior, the algorithm can be guided into finding different sized clusters. Large values of the prior are shown here to demonstrate its effect.

---

[3] In this paper we make little use of the α priors, but introducing separate α_i's for each object could be a useful next step for scenes with varying object sizes.

[4] To deal with the case when $a_i = 0$, the prior is truncated, setting $p(a_i|\overline{a_i}) = 0$ when $a_i < \rho_{crit}$.

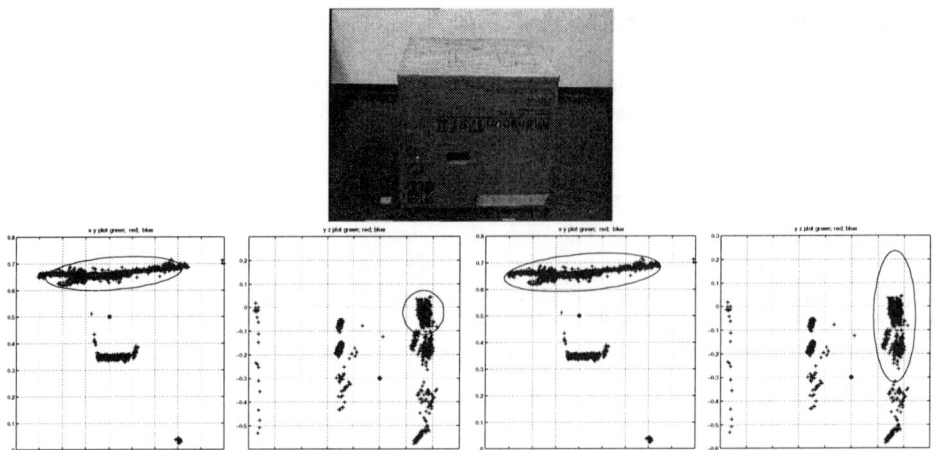

Figure 4: Example of the action of the priors on a_i and b_i. The photograph shows a visual image of the scene: a box in front of a wall, and the priors were chosen to prefer a distribution matching the wall. The two left hand graphs show the top and side view of the scene clustered without priors, while the two right hand graphs use priors on a_i and b_i. The priors give a preference for large values of a_i and b_i, so biasing the optimization to find a mixture component matching the whole wall as opposed to just the top of it.

4 Classification and diagnosis

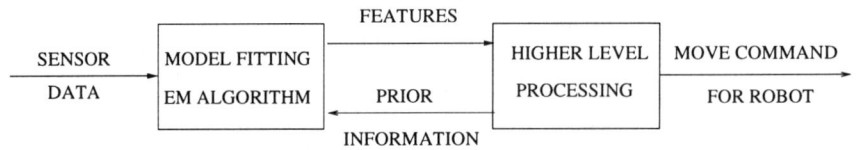

Figure 5: Schematic of system

This section describes how higher-level processing can be used to not only interpret the clusters fitted by the EM algorithm, but also affect the model-fitting using prior information. The processes of model-fitting and analysis are thus coupled, and not sequential.

The results of the model fitting are primarily processed to steer the robot. Once the cluster has been recognized as a box/wall/etc., the location and orientation are used to calculate a move command. To perform the object-recognition, we used a simple classifier on a feature vector extracted from the clustered data. The labels used were specific to docking, and commonly clustered objects – boxes, walls, thin vertical lines, but also included labels for clustering errors (like those shown in Figure 3). The features used were the values of the parameters a_i, b_i, giving the size of the clusters, but also measures of the visibility of the clusters, and the skewness of the within-cluster data. The classification used simple models of the probability distributions of the features f_i, given the objects O_j (i.e. $P(f_i|O_j)$), using a set of training data. In addition to moving the robot, the classifier can modify the behavior of the model fitting algorithm. If a poor clustering solution is found, EM can be re-run with slightly different initial conditions. If the probable locations or sizes of objects are known from previous scans, or indeed from other sensors, then these can constrain the clustering through priors, or provide initial means.

5 Summary

This paper shows that the Mixture of Gaussians architecture combined with EM optimization and the use of parameter priors can be used to segment and analyze real data from the 3D range-finder of a mobile robot. The approach was successfully used to guide a mobile robot towards a docking object, using only its range-finder for perception.

For the learning community this provides more than an example of the application of a probabilistic model to a real task. We have shown how the usual Mixture of Gaussians model can be parameterized to include expectations about the environment in a way which can be readily extended. We have included prior knowledge at three different levels: 1. The use of problem-specific parameterization of the covariance matrix to find expected patterns (e.g. planes at particular angles). 2. The use of problem-specific parameter priors to automatically rule-out unlikely objects at the lowest level of perception. 3. The results of the clustering process were post-processed by higher-level classification algorithms which interpreted the parameters of the mixture components, diagnosed typical misclassification, provided new priors for future perception, and gave the robot control system new targets.

It is expected that the basic approach can be fruitfully applied to other sensors, to problems which track dynamically changing scenes, or to problems which require relationships between objects in the scene to be accounted for and interpreted. A problem common to all modeling approaches is that it is not trivial to determine the number and types of clusters needed to represent a given scene. Recent work with Markov-Chain Monte-Carlo approaches has been successfully applied to mixtures of Gaussians (Richardson and Green, 1997), allowing a Bayesian solution to this problem, which could provide control systems with even richer probabilistic information (a series of models conditioned on number of clusters).

Acknowledgements

All authors were employed by Daimler-Benz AG during stages of the work. R. Murray-Smith gratefully acknowledges the support of Marie Curie TMR grant FMBICT961369.

References

Arman, F. and Aggarwal, J. K. (1993). Model-based object recognition in dense-range images—a review. *ACM Computing Surveys*, **25** (**1**), 5–43.

Dempster, A. P., Laird, N. M., and Rubin, D. B. (1977). Maximum likelihood from incomplete data via the EM algorithm. *J. Royal Statistical Society Series B*, **39**, 1–38.

Duda, R. O. and Hart, P. E. (1973). *Pattern Classification and Scene Analysis*. New York, Wiley.

McMichael, D. W. (1995). Bayesian growing and pruning strategies for MAP-optimal estimation of gaussian mixture models. In *4th IEE International Conf. on Artificial Neural Networks*, pp. 364–368.

PIAP (1995). PIAP impact report on TRC lidar performance. Technical Report 1, Industrial Research Institute for Automation and Measure ments, 02-486 Warszawa, Al. Jerozolimskie 202, Poland.

Richardson, S. and Green, P. J. (1997). On Bayesian anaysis of mixtures with an unknown number of components. *Journal of the Royal Statistical Society B*, **50** (**4**), 700–792.

Titterington, D., Smith, A., and Makov, U. (1985). *Statistical Analysis of Finite Mixture Distributions*. Chichester, John Wiley & Sons.

USING COLLECTIVE INTELLIGENCE TO ROUTE INTERNET TRAFFIC

David H. Wolpert
NASA Ames Research Center
Moffett Field, CA 94035
dhw@ptolemy.arc.nasa.gov

Kagan Tumer
NASA Ames Research Center
Moffett Field, CA 94035
kagan@ptolemy.arc.nasa.gov

Jeremy Frank
NASA Ames Research Center
Moffett Field, CA 94035
frank@ptolemy.arc.nasa.gov

Abstract

A COllective INtelligence (COIN) is a set of interacting reinforcement learning (RL) algorithms designed in an automated fashion so that their collective behavior optimizes a global utility function. We summarize the theory of COINs, then present experiments using that theory to design COINs to control internet traffic routing. These experiments indicate that COINs outperform all previously investigated RL-based, shortest path routing algorithms.

1 INTRODUCTION

COllective INtelligences (COINs) are large, sparsely connected recurrent neural networks, whose "neurons" are reinforcement learning (RL) algorithms. The distinguishing feature of COINs is that their dynamics involves no centralized control, but only the collective effects of the individual neurons each modifying their behavior via their individual RL algorithms. This restriction holds even though the goal of the COIN concerns the system's global behavior. One naturally-occurring COIN is a human economy, where the "neurons" consist of individual humans trying to maximize their reward, and the "goal", for example, can be viewed as having the overall system achieve high gross domestic product. This paper presents a preliminary investigation of designing and using artificial COINs as controllers of distributed systems. The domain we consider is routing of internet traffic.

The design of a COIN starts with a global utility function specifying the desired global behavior. Our task is to initialize and then update the neurons' "local" utility functions, without centralized control, so that as the neurons improve their utilities, global utility also improves. (We may also wish to update the local topology of the COIN.) In particular, we need to ensure that the neurons do not "frustrate" each other as they attempt to increase their utilities. The RL algorithms at each neuron that aim to optimize that neuron's local utility are *microlearners*. The learning algorithms that update the neuron's utility functions are *macrolearners*.

For robustness and breadth of applicability, we assume essentially no knowledge concerning the dynamics of the full system, i.e., the macrolearning and/or microlearning must "learn" that dynamics, implicitly or otherwise. This rules out any approach that models the full system. It also means that rather than use domain knowledge to hand-craft the local utilities as is done in multi-agent systems, in COINs the local utility functions must be automatically initialized and updated using only the provided global utility and (locally) observed dynamics.

The problem of designing a COIN has never previously been addressed in full — hence the need for the new formalism described below. Nonetheless, this problem is related to previous work in many fields: distributed artificial intelligence, multi-agent systems, computational ecologies, adaptive control, game theory [6], computational markets [2], Markov decision theory, and ant-based optimization.

For the particular problem of routing, examples of relevant work include [4, 5, 8, 9, 10]. Most of that previous work uses microlearning to set the internal parameters of routers running conventional shortest path algorithms (SPAs). However the microlearning occurs, they do not address the problem of ensuring that the associated local utilities do not cause the microlearners to work at cross purposes.

This paper concentrates on COIN-based setting of local utilities rather than macrolearning. We used simulations to compare three algorithms. The first two are an SPA and a COIN. Both had "full knowledge" (FK) of the true reward-maximizing path, with reward being the routing time of the associated router's packets for the SPAs, but set by COIN theory for the COINs. The third algorithm was a COIN using a memory-based (MB) microlearner [1] whose knowledge was limited to local observations.

The performance of the FK COIN was the theoretical optimum. The performance of the FK SPA was 12.5 ± 3 % worse than optimum. Despite limited knowledge, the MB COIN outperformed the FK SPA, achieving performance 36 ± 8 % closer to optimum. Note that the performance of the FK SPA is an upper bound on the performance of any RL-based SPA. Accordingly, the performance of the MB COIN is at least 36% superior to that of any RL-based SPA.

Section 2 below presents a cursory overview of the mathematics behind COINs. Section 3 discusses how the network routing problem is mapped into the COIN formalism, and introduces our experiments. Section 4 presents results of those experiments, which establish the power of COINs in the context of routing problems. Finally, Section 5 presents conclusions and summarizes future research directions.

2 MATHEMATICS OF COINS

The mathematical framework for COINs is quite extensive [11, 12]. This paper concentrates on four of the concepts from that framework: subworlds, factored systems, constraint-alignment, and the wonderful-life utility function.

We consider the state of the system across a set of discrete, time steps, $t \in \{0, 1, ...\}$. All characteristics of a neuron at time t — including its internal parameters at that time as well as its externally visible actions — are encapsulated in a real-valued vector $\underline{\zeta}_{\eta,t}$. We call this the "state" of neuron η at time t, and let $\underline{\zeta}$ be the state of all neurons across all time. World utility, $G(\underline{\zeta})$, is a function of the state of all neurons across all time, potentially not expressible as a discounted sum.

A subworld is a set of neurons. All neurons in the same subworld ω share the same *subworld utility function* $g_\omega(\underline{\zeta})$. So when each subworld is a set of neurons that have the most effect on each other, neurons are unlikely to work at cross-purposes — all neurons that affect each other substantially share the same local utility.

Associated with subworlds is the concept of a (perfectly) *constraint-aligned* system. In such systems any change to the neurons in subworld ω at time 0 will have no effects on the neurons outside of ω at times later than 0. Intuitively, a system is constraint-aligned if the neurons in separate subworlds do not affect each other directly, so that the rationale behind the use of subworlds holds.

A *subworld-factored* system is one where for each subworld ω considered by itself, a change at time 0 to the states of the neurons in that subworld results in an increased value for $g_\omega(\underline{\zeta})$ if and only if it results in an increased value for $G(\underline{\zeta})$. For a subworld-factored system, the side effects on the rest of the system of ω's increasing its own utility (which perhaps decrease other subworlds' utilities) do not end up decreasing world utility. For these systems, the separate subworlds successfully pursuing their separate goals do not frustrate each other as far as world utility is concerned.

The desideratum of subworld-factored is carefully crafted. In particular, it does *not* concern changes in the value of the utility of subworlds other than the one changing its actions. Nor does it concern changes to the states of neurons in more than one subworld at once. Indeed, consider the following alternative desideratum: any change to the $t = 0$ state of the entire system that improves all subworld utilities simultaneously also improves world utility. Reasonable as it may appear, one can construct examples of systems that obey this desideratum and yet quickly evolve to a *minimum* of world utility [12].

It can be proven that for a subworld-factored system, when each of the neurons' reinforcement learning algorithms are performing as well as they can, given each others' behavior, world utility is at a critical point. Correct global behavior corresponds to learners reaching a (Nash) equilibrium [8, 13]. There can be no tragedy of the commons for a subworld-factored system [7, 11, 12].

Let $\mathrm{CL}_\omega(\underline{\zeta})$ be defined as the vector $\underline{\zeta}$ modified by clamping the states of all neurons in subworld ω, across all time, to an arbitrary fixed value, here taken to be 0. The *wonderful life subworld utility* (WLU) is:

$$g_\omega(\underline{\zeta}) \equiv G(\underline{\zeta}) - G(\mathrm{CL}_\omega(\underline{\zeta})) \qquad (1)$$

When the system is constraint-aligned, so that, loosely speaking, subworld ω's "absence" would not affect the rest of the system, we can view the WLU as analogous to the change in world utility that would have arisen if subworld ω "had never existed". (Hence the name of this utility - cf. the Frank Capra movie.) Note however, that CL is a purely mathematical operation. Indeed, no assumption is even being made that $\mathrm{CL}_\omega(\underline{\zeta})$ is consistent with the dynamics of the system. The sequence of states the neurons in ω are clamped to in the definition of the WLU need not be consistent with the dynamical laws of the system.

This dynamics-independence is a crucial strength of the WLU. It means that to evaluate the WLU we do *not* try to infer how the system would have evolved if all neurons in ω were set to 0 at time 0 and the system evolved from there. So long as we know ζ extending over all time, and so long as we know G, we know the value of WLU. This is true even if we know nothing of the dynamics of the system.

In addition to assuring the correct equilibrium behavior, there exist many other theoretical advantages to having a system be subworld-factored. In particular, the experiments in this paper revolve around the following fact: a constraint-aligned system with wonderful life subworld utilities is subworld-factored. Combining this with our previous result that subworld-factored systems are at Nash equilibrium at critical points of world utility, this result leads us to expect that a constraint-aligned system using WL utilities in the microlearning will approach near-optimal values of the world utility. No such assurances accrue to WL utilities if the system is not constraint-aligned however. Accordingly our experiments constitute an investigation of how well a particular system performs when WL utilities are used but little attention is paid to ensuring that the system is constraint-aligned.

3 COINS FOR NETWORK ROUTING

In our experiments we concentrated on the two networks in Figure 1, both slightly larger than those in [9]. To facilitate the analysis, traffic originated only at routers indicated with white boxes and had only the routers indicated by dark boxes as ultimate destinations. Note that in both networks there is a bottleneck at router 2.

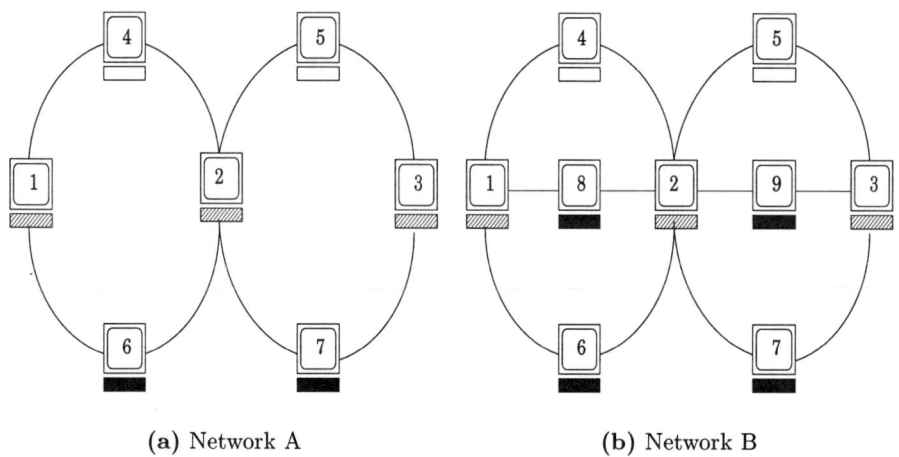

(a) Network A (b) Network B

Figure 1: Network Architectures.

As is standard in much of traffic network analysis [3], at any time all *traffic* at a router is a real-valued number together with an ultimate destination tag. At each timestep, each router sums all traffic received from upstream routers in this timestep, to get a *load*. The router then decides which downstream router to send its load to, and the cycle repeats.

A running average is kept of the total value of each router's load over a window of the previous L timesteps. This average is run through a *load-to-delay* function, $W(x)$, to get the summed *delay* accrued at this timestep by all those packets traversing this router at this timestep. Different routers had different $W(x)$, to reflect the fact that real networks have differences in router software and hardware (response time, queue length, processing speed etc). In our experiments $W(x) = x^3$ for routers 1 and 3, and $W(x) = log(x+1)$ for router 2, for both networks. The global goal is to minimize total delay encountered by all traffic.

In terms of the COIN formalism, we identified the neurons η as individual pairs of routers and ultimate destinations. So $\underline{\zeta}_{\eta,t}$ was the vector of traffic sent along all links exiting η's router, tagged for η's ultimate destination, at time t. Each subworld consisted of the set all neurons that shared a particular ultimate destination.

In the SPA each node η tries to set $\underline{\zeta}_{\eta,t}$ to minimize the sum of the delays to be accrued by that traffic on the way to its ultimate destination. In contrast, in a COIN η tries to set $\underline{\zeta}_{\eta,t}$ to optimize g_ω for the subworld ω containing η. For both algorithms, "full knowledge" means that at time t all of the routers know the window-averaged loads for all routers for time $t-1$, and assume that those values will be the same at t. For large enough L, this assumption will be arbitrarily good, and therefore will allow the routers to make arbitrarily accurate estimates of how best to route their traffic, according to their respective routing criteria.

In contrast, having limited knowledge, the MB COIN could only *predict* the WLU value resulting from each routing decision. More precisely, for each router-ultimate-destination pair, the associated microlearner estimates the map from traffic on all outgoing links (the inputs) to WLU-based reward (the outputs – see below). This was done with a single-nearest-neighbor algorithm. Next, each router could send the packets along the path that results in outbound traffic with the best (estimated) reward. However to be conservative, in these experiments we instead had the router randomly select between that path and the path selected by the FK SPA.

The load at router r at time t is determined by $\underline{\zeta}$. Accordingly, we can encapsulate the load-to-delay functions at the nodes by writing the delay at node r at time t as $W_{r,t}(\underline{\zeta})$. In our experiments world utility was the total delay, i.e., $G(\underline{\zeta}) = \sum_{r,t} W_{r,t}(\underline{\zeta})$. So using the WLU, $g_\omega(\underline{\zeta}) = \sum_{r,t} \Delta_{\omega,r,t}(\underline{\zeta})$, where $\Delta_{\omega,r,t}(\underline{\zeta}) = [W_{r,t}(\underline{\zeta}) - W_{r,t}(CL_\omega(\underline{\zeta}))]$. At each time t, the MB COIN used $\sum_r \Delta_{\omega,r,t}(\underline{\zeta})$ as the "WLU-based" reward signal for trying optimize this full WLU.

In the MB COIN, evaluating this reward in a decentralized fashion was straightforward. All packets have a header containing a running sum of the Δ's encountered in all the routers it has traversed so far. Each ultimate destination sums all such headers it received and echoes that sum back to all routers that had routed to it. In this way each neuron is apprised of the WLU-based reward of its subworld.

4 EXPERIMENTAL RESULTS

The networks discussed above were tested under light, medium and heavy traffic loads. Table 1 shows the associated destinations (cf. fig. 1).

Table 1: Source–Destination Pairings for the Three Traffic Loads

Network	Source	Dest. (Light)	Dest. (Medium)	Dest. (Heavy)
A	4	6	6,7	6,7
	5	7	7	6,7
B	4	7,8	7,8,9	6,7,8,9
	5	6,9	6,7,9	6,7,8,9

In our experiments one new packet was fed to each source router at each time step. Table 2 reports the average total delay (i.e., average per packet time to traverse the total network) in each of the traffic regimes, for the shortest path algorithm with full knowledge, the COIN with full knowledge, and the MB COIN. Each table entry is based on 50 runs with a window size of 50, and the errors reported are errors in the mean[1]. All the entries in Table 2 are statistically different at the .05 level, including FK SPA vs. MB COIN for Network A under light traffic conditions.

Table 2: Average Total Delay

Network	Load	FK SPA	FK COIN	MB COIN
A	light	0.53 ± .007	0.45 ± .001	0.50 ± .008
	medium	1.26 ± .010	1.10 ± .001	1.21 ± .009
	heavy	2.17 ± .012	1.93 ± .001	2.06 ± .010
B	light	2.13 ± .012	1.92 ± .001	2.05 ± .010
	medium	4.37 ± .014	3.96 ± .001	4.19 ± .012
	heavy	6.94 ± .015	6.35 ± .001	6.82 ± .024

Table 2 provides two important observations: First, the WLU-based COIN outperformed the SPA when both have full knowledge, thereby demonstrating the superiority of the new routing strategy. By not having its routers greedily strive for the shortest paths for their packets, the COIN settles into a more desirable state that reduces the average total delay for *all* packets. Second, even when the WLU is estimated through a memory-based learner (using only information available to the local routers), the performance of the COIN still surpasses that of the FK SPA. This result not only establishes the feasibility of COIN-based routers, but also demonstrates that for this task COINs will outperform *any* algorithm that can only estimate the shortest path, since the performance of the FK SPA is a ceiling on the performance of any such RL-based SPA.

Figure 2 shows how total delay varies with time for the medium traffic regime (each plot is based on 50 runs). The "ringing" is an artifact caused by the starting conditions and the window size (50). Note that for both networks the FK COIN not only provides the shortest delays, but also settles into that solution very rapidly.

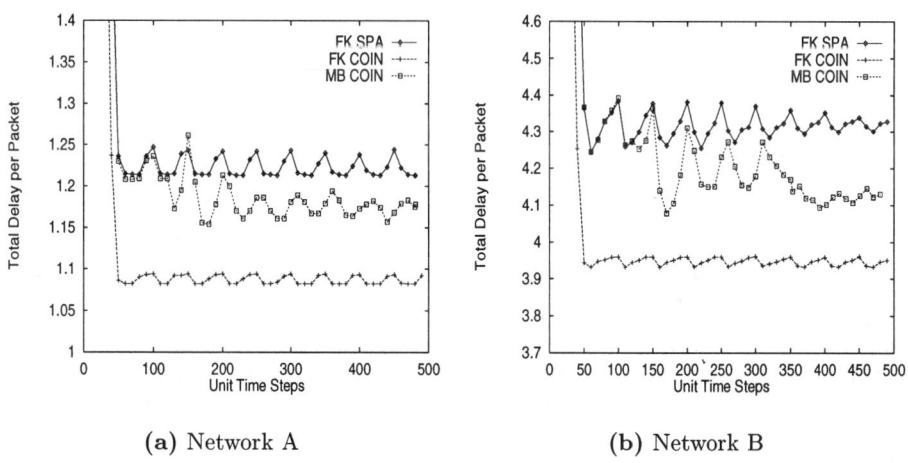

(a) Network A   (b) Network B

Figure 2: Total Delay.

5 DISCUSSION

Many distributed computational tasks are naturally addressed as recurrent neural networks of reinforcement learning algorithms (i.e., COINs). The difficulty in doing so is ensuring that, despite the absence of centralized communication and control,

---

[1] The results are qualitatively identical for window sizes 20 and 100 along with total timesteps of 100 and 500.

the reward functions of the separate neurons work in synchrony to foster good global performance, rather than cause their associated neurons to work at cross-purposes.

The mathematical framework synopsized in this paper is a theoretical solution to this difficulty. To assess its real-world applicability, we employed it to design a full-knowledge (FK) COIN as well as a memory-based (RL-based) COIN, for the task of packet routing on a network. We compared the performance of those algorithms to that of a FK shortest-path algorithm (SPA). Not only did the FK COIN beat the FK SPA, but also the memory-based COIN, despite having only limited knowledge, beat the full-knowledge SPA. This latter result is all the more remarkable in that the performance of the FK SPA is an upper bound on the performance of previously investigated RL-based routing schemes, which use the RL to try to provide accurate knowledge to an SPA.

There are many directions for future work on COINs, even restricting attention to domain of packet routing. Within that particular domain, currently we are extending our experiments to larger networks, using industrial event-driven network simulators. Concurrently, we are investigating the use of macrolearning for COIN-based packet-routing, i.e., the run-time modification of the neurons' utility functions to improve the subworld-factoredness of the COIN.

References

[1] C. G. Atkenson, A. W. Moore, and S. Schaal. Locally weighted learning. *Artificial Intelligence Review*, Submitted, 1996.

[2] E. Baum. Manifesto for an evolutionary economics of intelligence. In C. M. Bishop, editor, *Neural Networks and Machine Learning*. Springer-Verlag, 1998.

[3] D. Bertsekas and R. Gallager. *Data Networks*. Prentice Hall, NJ, 1992.

[4] J. Boyan and M. Littman. Packet routing in dynamically changing networks: A reinforcement learning approach. In *Advances in Neural Information Processing Systems - 6*, pages 671–678. Morgan Kaufmann, 1994.

[5] S. P. M. Choi and D. Y. Yeung. Predictive Q-routing: A memory based reinforcement learning approach to adaptive traffic control. In *Advances in Neural Information Processing Systems - 8*, pages 945–951. MIT Press, 1996.

[6] D. Fudenberg and J. Tirole. *Game Theory*. MIT Press, Cambridge, MA, 1991.

[7] G. Hardin. The tragedy of the commons. *Science*, 162:1243–1248, 1968.

[8] Y. A. Korilis, A. A. Lazar, and A. Orda. Achieving network optima using Stackelberg routing strategies. *IEEE Tran. on Networking*, 5(1):161–173, 1997.

[9] P. Marbach, O. Mihatsch, M. Schulte, and J. Tsisiklis. Reinforcement learning for call admission control and routing in integrated service networks. In *Adv. in Neural Info. Proc. Systems - 10*, pages 922–928. MIT Press, 1998.

[10] D. Subramanian, P. Druschel, and J. Chen. Ants and reinforcement learning: A case study in routing in dynamic networks. In *Proceedings of the Fifteenth International Conference on Artificial Intelligence*, pages 832–838, 1997.

[11] D. Wolpert and K. Tumer. Collective Intelligence. In J. M. Bradshaw, editor, *Handbook of Agent technology*. AAAI Press/MIT Press, 1999. to appear.

[12] D. Wolpert, K. Wheeler, and K. Tumer. Automated design of multi-agent systems. In *Proc. of the 3rd Int. Conf. of Autonomous Agents*, 1999. to appear.

[13] D. Wolpert, K. Wheeler, and K. Tumer. Collective intelligence for distributed control. 1999. (pre-print).

Part IX
Control, Navigation and Planning

Robust, Efficient, Globally-Optimized Reinforcement Learning with the Parti-Game Algorithm

Mohammad A. Al-Ansari and **Ronald J. Williams**
College of Computer Science, 161 CN
Northeastern University
Boston, MA 02115
alansar@ccs.neu.edu, rjw@ccs.neu.edu

Abstract

Parti-game (Moore 1994a; Moore 1994b; Moore and Atkeson 1995) is a reinforcement learning (RL) algorithm that has a lot of promise in overcoming the curse of dimensionality that can plague RL algorithms when applied to high-dimensional problems. In this paper we introduce modifications to the algorithm that further improve its performance and robustness. In addition, while parti-game solutions can be improved locally by standard local path-improvement techniques, we introduce an add-on algorithm in the same spirit as parti-game that instead tries to improve solutions in a non-local manner.

1 INTRODUCTION

Parti-game operates on goal problems by dynamically partitioning the space into hyper-rectangular cells of varying sizes, represented using a k-d tree data structure. It assumes the existence of a pre-specified local controller that can be commanded to proceed from the current state to a given state. The algorithm uses a game-theoretic approach to assign costs to cells based on past experiences using a minimax algorithm. A cell's cost can be either a finite positive integer or infinity. The former represents the number of cells that have to be traveled through to get to the goal cell and the latter represents the belief that there is no reliable way of getting from that cell to the goal. Cells with a cost of infinity are called *losing* cells while others are called *winning* ones.

The algorithm starts out with one cell representing the entire space and another, contained within it, representing the goal region. In a typical step, the local controller is commanded to proceed to the center of the most promising neighboring cell. Upon entering a neighboring cell (whether the one aimed at or not), or upon failing to leave the current cell within

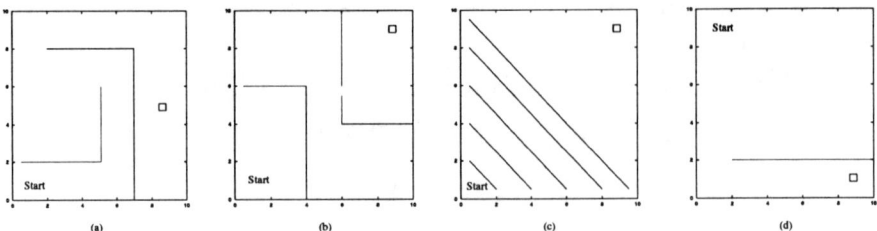

Figure 1: In these mazes, the agent is required to start from the point marked Start and reach the square goal cell.

a timeout period, the result of this attempt is added to the database of experiences the algorithm has collected, cell costs are recomputed based on the updated database, and the process repeats. The costs are computed using a Dijkstra-like, one-pass minimax version of dynamic programming. The algorithm terminates upon entering the goal cell.

If at any point the algorithm determines that it can not proceed because the agent is in a losing cell, each cell lying on the boundary between losing and winning cells is split across the dimension in which it is largest and all experiences involving cells that are split are discarded. Since parti-game assumes, in the absence of evidence to the contrary, that from any given cell every neighboring cell is reachable, discarding experiences in this way encourages exploration of the newly created cells.

2 PARTITIONING ONLY LOSING CELLS

The win-lose boundary mentioned above represents a barrier the algorithm perceives that is preventing the agent from reaching the goal. The reason behind partitioning cells along this boundary is to increase the resolution along these areas that are crucial to reaching the goal and thus creating more regions along this boundary for the agent to try to get through. By partitioning on both sides of the boundary, parti-game guarantees that neighboring cells along the boundary remain close in size. Along with the strategy of aiming towards centers of neighboring cells, this produces pairings of winner-loser cells that form proposed "corridors" for the agent to try to go through to penetrate the barrier it perceives.

In this section we investigate doing away with partitioning on the winning side, and only partition losing cells. Because partitioning can only be triggered with the agent on the losing side of the win-lose boundary, partitioning only losing cells would still give the agent the same kind of access to the boundary through the newly formed cells. However, this would result in a size disparity between winner- and loser-side cells and, thus, would not produce the winner side of the pairings mentioned above. To produce a similar effect to the pairings of parti-game, we change the aiming strategy of the algorithm. Under the new strategy, when the agent decides to go from the cell it currently occupies to a neighboring one, it aims towards the center point of the common surface between the two cells. While this does not reproduce the same line of motion of the original aiming strategy exactly, it achieves a very similar objective.

Parti-game's success in high-dimensional problems stems from its variable resolution strategy, which partitions finely only in regions where it is needed. By limiting partitioning to losing cells only, we hope to increase the resolution in even fewer parts of the state space and thereby make the algorithm even more efficient.

To compare the performance of parti-game to the modified algorithm, we applied both algorithms to the set of continuous mazes shown in Figure 1. For all maze problems we used a simple local controller that can move directly toward the specified target state. We also

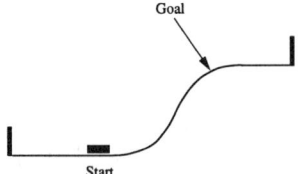

Figure 2: An ice puck on a hill. The puck can thrust horizontally to the left and to the right with a maximum force of 1 Newton. The state space is two-dimensional consisting of the horizontal position and velocity. The agent starts at the position marked Start at velocity zero and its goal is to reach the position marked Goal at velocity zero. Maximum thrust is not adequate to get the puck up the ramp so it has to learn to move to the left first to build up momentum.

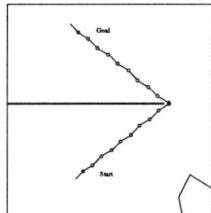

Figure 3: A nine degree of freedom, snake-like arm that moves in a plane and is fixed at one tip, as depicted in Figure 3. The objective is to move the arm from the start configuration to the goal one, which requires curling and uncurling to avoid the barrier and the wall.

applied both algorithms to the non-linear dynamics problem of the ice puck on a hill, depicted in Figure 2, which has been studied extensively in reinforcement learning literature. We used a local controller very similar to the one described in Moore and Atkeson (1995). Finally, we applied the algorithm to the nine-degree of freedom planar robot introduced in Moore and Atkeson (1995) and shown in Figure 3 and we used the same local controller described there. Additional results on the Acrobot problem (Sutton and Barto 1998) were not included here for space limitations but can be found in Al-Ansari and Williams (1998).

We applied both algorithms to each of these problems, in each case performing as many trials as was needed for the solution to stabilize. The agent was placed back in the start state at the end of each trial. In the puck problem, the agent was also reset to the start state whenever it hit either of the barriers at the bottom and top of the slope. The results are shown in Table 1. The table compares the number of trials needed, the number of partitions, total number of steps taken in the world, and the length of the final trajectory.

The table shows that the new algorithm indeed resulted in fewer total partitions in all prob-

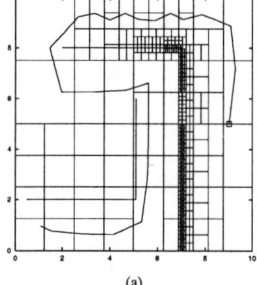 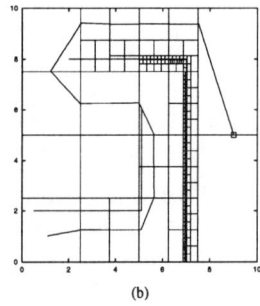 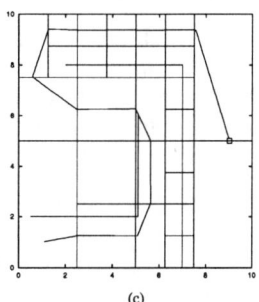

Figure 4: The final trial of applying the various algorithms to the maze in Figure 1(a). (a) parti-game, (b) parti-game with partitioning only losing cells and (c) parti-game with partitioning only the largest losing cells.

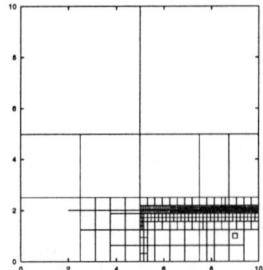

Figure 5: Parti-game needed 1194 partitions to reach the goal in the maze of Figure 1(d).

lems. It also improved in all problems in the number of trials required to stabilization. It improved in all but one problem (maze d) in the length of the final trajectory, however the difference in length is very small. Finally, it resulted in fewer total steps taken in three of the six problems, but the total steps taken increased in the remaining three.

To see the effect of the modification in detail, we show the result of applying parti-game and the modified algorithm on the maze of Figure 1(a) in Figures 4(a) and 4(b), respectively. We can see how areas with higher resolution are more localized in Figure 4(b).

3 BALANCED PARTITIONING

Upon close observation of Figure 4(a), we see that parti-game partitions very finely along the right wall of the maze. This behavior is even more clearly seen in parti-game's solution to the maze in Figure 1(d), which is a simple maze with a single barrier between the start state and the goal. As we see in Table 1, parti-game has a very hard time reaching the goal in this maze. Figure 5 shows the 1194 partitions that parti-game generated in trying to reach the goal. We can see that partitioning along the barrier is very uneven, being extremely fine near the goal and growing coarser as the distance from the goal increases. Putting higher focus on places where the highest gain could be attained if a hole is found can be a desirable feature, but what happens in cases like this one is obviously excessive.

One of the factors contributing to this problem of continuing to search at ever-higher resolutions in the part of the barrier nearest the goal is that any version of parti-game searches for solutions using an implicit trade-off between the shortness of a potential solution path and the resolution required to find this path. Only when the resolution becomes so fine that the number of cells through which the agent would have to pass in this potential shortcut exceeds the number of cells to be traversed when traveling around the barrier is the algorithm forced to look elsewhere for the actual opening.

A conceptually appealing way to bias this search is to maintain a more explicit coarse-to-fine search strategy. One way to do this is to try to keep the smallest cell size the algorithm generates as large as possible. In addition to achieving the balance we are seeking, this would tend to lower the total number of partitions and result in shallower tree structures needed to represent the state space, which, in turn, results in higher efficiency.

To achieve these goals, we modified the algorithm from the previous section such that whenever partitioning is required, instead of partitioning all losing cells, we only partition those among them that are of maximum size. This has the effect of postponing splits that would lower the minimum cell size as long as possible. The results of applying the modified algorithm on the test problems are also shown in Table 1.

Comparing the results of this version of the algorithm to those of partitioning all losing cells

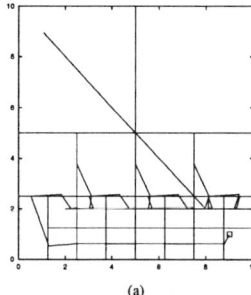
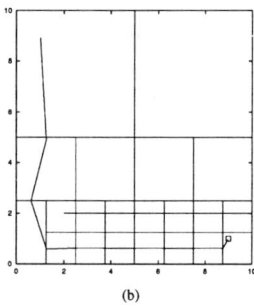

(a) (b)

Figure 6: The result of partitioning largest cells on the losing side in the maze of Figure 1(d). Only two trials are required to stabilize. The first requires 1304 steps and 21 partitions. The second trial adds no new partitions and produces a path of only 165 steps.

Problem	Algorithm	Trials	Partitions	Total Steps	Final Trajectory Length
maze a	original parti-game	3	444	35131	279
	partition losing side	3	239	16652	**256**
	partition largest losing	3	**27**	**1977**	270
maze b	original parti-game	6	98	**5180**	183
	partition losing side	5	**76**	7187	175
	partition largest losing	6	**76**	5635	**174**
maze c	original parti-game	3	176	7768	416
	partition losing side	2	120	10429	**165**
	partition largest losing	2	**96**	**6803**	**165**
maze d	original parti-game	2	1194	553340	**149**
	partition losing side	2	350	18639	155
	partition largest losing	2	**21**	**1469**	165
puck	original parti-game	6	80	6764	240
	partition losing side	2	**18**	**3237**	**151**
	partition largest losing	2	**18**	**3237**	**151**
nine-joint arm	original parti-game	25	104	2970	58
	partition losing side	17	61	3041	**56**
	partition largest losing	**7**	**37**	**2694**	112

Table 1: Results of applying parti-game, parti-game with partitioning only losing cells and parti-game with partitioning the largest losing cells on three of the problem domains. Smaller numbers are better. Best numbers are shown in **bold**.

on the win-lose boundary shows that this algorithm improves on parti-game's performance even further. It outperforms the above algorithm in four problems in the total number of partitions required, while it ties it in the remaining two. It outperforms the above algorithm in total steps taken in five problems and ties it in one. It improves in the number of trials needed to stabilize in one problem, ties the above algorithm in four cases and ties parti-game in the remaining one. In the length of the final trajectory, partitioning the largest losing cells does better in one case, ties partitioning only losing cells in two cases and does worse in three. This latter result is due to the generally larger partition sizes that result from the lower resolution that this algorithm produces. However, the increase in the number of steps is very minimal in all but the nine-joint arm problem.

Figure 4(c) shows the result of applying the new algorithm to the maze of Figure 1(a). In contrast to the other two algorithms depicted in the same figure, we can see that the new algorithm partitions very uniformly around the barrier. In addition, it requires the fewest number of partitions and total steps out of the three algorithms. Figure 6 shows that the new algorithm vastly outperforms parti-game on the maze in Figure 1(d). Here, too, it partitions very evenly around the barrier and finds the goal very quickly, requiring far fewer steps and partitions.

4 GLOBAL PATH IMPROVEMENT

Parti-game does not claim to find optimal solutions. As we see in Figure 4, parti-game and the two modified algorithms settle on the longer of the two possible routes to the goal in this maze. In this section we investigate ways we could improve parti-game so that it could find paths of optimal form. It is important to note that we are not seeking paths that are optimal, since that is not possible to achieve using the cell shapes and aiming strategies we are using here. By a path of optimal form we mean a path that could be continuously deformed into an optimal path.

4.1 OTHER GRADIENTS

As mentioned above, parti-game partitions only when the agent has no winning cells to aim for and the only cells partitioned are those that lie on the win-lose boundary. The win-lose boundary falls on the gradient between finite- and infinite-cost cells and it appears when the algorithm knows of no reliable way to get to the goal. Consistently partitioning along this gradient guarantees that the algorithm will eventually find a path to the goal, if one exists.

However, gradients across which the difference in cost is finite also exist in a state space partitioned by parti-game (or any of the variants introduced in this paper). Like the win-lose boundary, these gradients are boundaries through which the agent does not believe it can move directly. Although finding an opening in such a boundary is not essential to reaching the goal, these boundaries do represent potential shortcuts that might improve the agent's policy. Any gradient with a difference in cost of two or more is a location of such a potentially useful shortcut.

Because such gradients appear throughout the space, we need to be selective about which ones to partition along. There are many possible strategies one might consider using to incorporate these ideas into parti-game. For example, since parti-game focuses on the highest gradients only, the first thing that comes to mind is to follow in parti-game's footsteps and assign partitioning priorities to cells along gradients based on the differences in values across those gradients. However, since the true cost function typically has discontinuities, it is clear that the effect of such a strategy would be to continue refining the partitioning indefinitely along such a discontinuity in a vain search for a nonexistent shortcut.

4.2 THE ALGORITHM

A much better idea is to try to pick cells to partition in a way that would achieve balanced partitioning, following the rationale we introduced in section 3. Again, such a strategy would result in a uniform coarse-to-fine search for better paths along those other gradients.

The following discussion could, in principle, apply to any of the three forms of parti-game studied up to this point. Because of the superior behavior of the version where we partition the largest cells on the losing side, this is the specific version we report on here, and we use the term *modified parti-game* to refer to it.

The way we incorporated partitioning along other gradients is as follows. At the end of any trial in which the agent is able to go from the start state to the goal without any unexpected results of any of its aiming attempts, we partition the largest "losing cells" (i.e., higher-cost cells) that fall on any gradient across which costs differ by more than one. Because data about experiences involving cells that are partitioned is discarded, the next time modified parti-game is run, the agent will try to go through the newly formed cells in search of a shortcut.

This algorithm amounts to simply running modified parti-game until a stable solution is

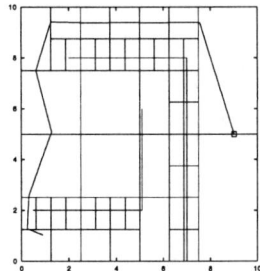

Figure 7: The solution found by applying the global improvement algorithm on the maze of Figure 1(a). The solution proceeded exactly like that of the algorithm of section 3 until the solution in Figure 4(d) was reached. After that, eight additional iterations were needed to find the better trajectory, resulting in 22 additional partitions, for a total of 49.

reached. At that point, it introduces new cells along some of the other gradients, and when it is subsequently run, modified parti-game is applied again until stabilization is achieved, and so on. The results of applying this algorithm to the maze of Figure 1(a) is shown in Figure 7. As we can see, the algorithm finds the better solution by increasing the resolution around the relevant part of the barrier above the start state.

In the absence of information about the form of the optimal trajectory, there is no natural termination criterion for this algorithm. It is designed to be run continually in search of better solutions. If, however, the form of the optimal solution is known in advance, the extra partitioning could be turned off after such a solution is found.

5 CONCLUSIONS

In this paper we have presented three successive modifications to parti-game. The combination of the first two appears to improve its robustness and efficiency, sometimes dramatically, and generally yields better solutions. The third provides a novel way of performing non-local search for higher quality solutions that are closer to optimal.

Acknowledgments

Mohammad Al-Ansari acknowledges the continued support of King Saud University, Riyadh, Saudi Arabia and the Saudi Arabian Cultural Mission to the U.S.A.

References

Al-Ansari, M. A. and R. J. Williams (1998). Modifying the parti-game algorithm for increased robustness, higher efficiency and better policies. Technical Report NU-CCS-98-13, College of Computer Science, Northeastern University, Boston, MA.

Moore, A. (1994a). Variable resolution reinforcement learning. In *Proceedings of the Eighth Yale Workshop on Adaptive and Learning Systems*. Center for Systems Science, Yale University.

Moore, A. W. (1994b). The parti-game algorithm for variable resolution reinforcement learning in multidimensional state spaces. In *Proceedings of Neural Information Processing Systems Conference 6*. Morgan Kaufman.

Moore, A. W. and C. G. Atkeson (1995). The parti-game algorithm for variable resolution reinforcement learning in multidimensional state-spaces. *Machine Learning 21*.

Sutton, R. S. and A. G. Barto (1998). *Reinforcement Learning: An Introduction*. MIT Press.

Gradient Descent for General Reinforcement Learning

Leemon Baird
leemon@cs.cmu.edu
www.cs.cmu.edu/~leemon
Computer Science Department
5000 Forbes Avenue
Carnegie Mellon University
Pittsburgh, PA 15213-3891

Andrew Moore
awm@cs.cmu.edu
www.cs.cmu.edu/~awm
Computer Science Department
5000 Forbes Avenue
Carnegie Mellon University
Pittsburgh, PA 15213-3891

Abstract

A simple learning rule is derived, the *VAPS* algorithm, which can be instantiated to generate a wide range of new reinforcement-learning algorithms. These algorithms solve a number of open problems, define several new approaches to reinforcement learning, and unify different approaches to reinforcement learning under a single theory. These algorithms all have guaranteed convergence, and include modifications of several existing algorithms that were known to fail to converge on simple MDPs. These include Q-learning, SARSA, and advantage learning. In addition to these *value-based* algorithms it also generates pure *policy-search* reinforcement-learning algorithms, which learn optimal policies without learning a value function. In addition, it allows policy-search and value-based algorithms to be combined, thus unifying two very different approaches to reinforcement learning into a single Value and Policy Search (VAPS) algorithm. And these algorithms converge for POMDPs without requiring a proper belief state. Simulations results are given, and several areas for future research are discussed.

1 CONVERGENCE OF GREEDY EXPLORATION

Many reinforcement-learning algorithms are known that use a parameterized function approximator to represent a value function, and adjust the weights incrementally during learning. Examples include Q-learning, SARSA, and advantage learning. There are simple MDPs where the original form of these algorithms fails to converge, as summarized in Table 1. For the cases with √, the algorithms are guaranteed to converge under reasonable assumptions such as

Table 1. Current convergence results for incremental, value-based RL algorithms. Residual algorithms changed every **X** in the first two columns to √. The new algorithms proposed in this paper change every **X** to a √.

		Fixed distribution (on-policy)	Fixed distribution	Usually-greedy distribution
Markov chain	Lookup table	√	√	
	Averager	√	√	
	Linear	√	X	
	Nonlinear	X	X	
MDP	Lookup table	√	√	√
	Averager	√	√	X
	Linear	X	X	X
	Nonlinear	X	X	X
POMDP	Lookup table	√	√	X
	Averager	√	√	X
	Linear	X	X	X
	Nonlinear	X	X	X

√=convergence guaranteed
X=counterexample is known that either diverges or oscillates between the best and worst possible policies.

decaying learning rates. For the cases with **X**, there are known counterexamples where it will either diverge or oscillate between the best and worst possible policies, which have very-different values. This can happen even with infinite training time and slowly-decreasing learning rates (Baird, 95, Gordon, 96). Each **X** in the first two columns can be changed to a √ and made to converge by using a modified form of the algorithm, the *residual* form (Baird 95). But this is only possible when learning with a fixed training distribution, and that is rarely practical. For most large problems, it is useful to explore with a policy that is usually-greedy with respect to the current value function, and that changes as the value function changes. In that case (the rightmost column of the chart), the current convergence guarantees are not very good. One way to guarantee convergence in all three columns is to modify the algorithm so that it is performing stochastic gradient descent on some average error function, where the average is weighted by state-visitation frequencies for the current usually-greedy policy. Then the weighting changes as the policy changes. It might appear that this gradient is difficult to compute. Consider Q-learning exploring with a Boltzman distribution that is usually greedy with respect to the learned Q function. It seems difficult to calculate gradients, since changing a single weight will change many Q values, changing a single Q value will change many action-choice probabilities in that state, and changing a single action-choice probability may affect the frequency with which every state in the MDP is visited. Although this might seem difficult, it is not. Surprisingly, unbiased estimates of the gradients of visitation distributions with respect to the weights can be calculated quickly, and the resulting algorithms can put a √ in every case in Table 1.

2 DERIVATION OF THE VAPS EQUATION

Consider a sequence of transitions observed while following a particular stochastic policy on an MDP. Let $s_t = \{x_0, u_0, R_0, x_1, u_1, R_1, \ldots x_{t-1}, u_{t-1}, R_{t-1}, x_t, u_t, R_t\}$ be the sequence of states, actions, and reinforcements up to time t, where performing action u_i in state x_i yields reinforcement R_i and a transition to state x_{i+1}. The stochastic policy may be a function of a vector of weights **w**. Assume the MDP has a single start state named x_0. If the MDP has terminal states, and x_i is a terminal state, then $x_{i+1}=x_0$. Let S_t be the set of all possible sequences from time 0 to t. Let $e(s_t)$ be a given error function that calculates an error on each time step, such as the squared Bellman residual at time t, or some other error occurring at time t. If e is a function of the weights, then it must be a smooth function of the weights. Consider a period of time starting at time 0 and ending with probability $P(\text{end}|s_t)$ after the sequence s_t occurs. The probabilities must be such that the expected squared period length is finite. Let B be the expected total error during that period, where the expectation is weighted according to the state-visitation frequencies generated by the given policy:

$$B = \sum_{T=0}^{\infty} \sum_{s_T \in S_T} P(\text{period ends at time } T \text{ after trajectory } s_T) \sum_{i=0}^{T} e(s_i) \qquad (1)$$

$$= \sum_{t=0}^{\infty} \sum_{s_t \in S_t} e(s_t) P(s_t) \qquad (2)$$

where:

$$P(s_t) = P(u_t \mid s_t) P(R_t \mid s_t) \prod_{i=0}^{t-1} P(u_i \mid s_i) P(R_i \mid s_i) P(s_{i+1} \mid s_i) [1 - P(\text{end} \mid s_i)] \qquad (3)$$

Note that on the first line, for a particular s_t, the error $e(s_t)$ will be added in to B once for every sequence that starts with s_t. Each of these terms will be weighted by the probability of a complete trajectory that starts with s_t. The sum of the probabilities of all trajectories that start with s_t is simply the probability of s_t being observed, since the period is assumed to end eventually with probability one. So the second line equals the first. The third line is the probability of the sequence, of which only the $P(u_i|x_i)$ factor might be a function of **w**. If so, this probability must be a smooth function of the weights and nonzero everywhere. The partial derivative of B with respect to w, a particular element of the weight vector **w**, is:

$$\frac{\partial}{\partial w} B = \sum_{t=0}^{\infty} \sum_{s_t \in S_t} \left(\left(\frac{\partial}{\partial w} e(s_t) \right) P(s_t) + e(s_t) P(s_t) \sum_{j=1}^{t} \frac{\frac{\partial}{\partial w}[P(u_{j-1} \mid s_{j-1})]}{P(u_{j-1} \mid s_{j-1})} \right) \qquad (4)$$

$$= \sum_{t=0}^{\infty} \sum_{s_t \in S_t} P(s_t) \left[\frac{\partial}{\partial w} e(s_t) + e(s_t) \sum_{j=1}^{t} \frac{\partial}{\partial w} \ln(P(u_{j-1} \mid s_{j-1})) \right] \qquad (5)$$

Space here is limited, and it may not be clear from the short sketch of this derivation, but summing (5) over an entire period does give an unbiased estimate of B, the expected total error during a period. An incremental algorithm to perform stochastic gradient descent on B is the weight update given on the left side of Table 2, where the summation over previous time steps is replaced with a trace T_t for each weight. This algorithm is more general than previously-published algorithms of this form, in that e can be a function of all previous states, actions, and reinforcements, rather than just the current reinforcement. This is what allows VAPS to do both value and policy search.

Every algorithm proposed in this paper is a special case of the VAPS equation on the left side of Table 2. Note that no model is needed for this algorithm. The only probability needed in the algorithm is the policy, not the transition probability from the MDP. This is stochastic gradient descent on B, and the update rule is only correct if the observed transitions are sampled from trajectories found by following

Gradient Descent for General Reinforcement Learning   971

Table 2. The general VAPS algorithm (left), and several instantiations of it (right).
This single algorithm includes both value-based and policy-search approaches and
their combination, and gives guaranteed convergence in every case.

$\Delta w_t = -\alpha \left[\frac{\partial}{\partial w} e(s_t) + e(s_t) T_t \right]$ $\Delta T_t = \frac{\partial}{\partial w} \ln(P(u_{t-1} \mid s_{t-1}))$	$e_{SARSA}(s_t) = \frac{1}{2} E^2 \left[R_{t-1} + \gamma Q(x_t, u_t) - Q(x_{t-1}, u_{t-1}) \right]$ $e_{Q-learning}(s_t) = \frac{1}{2} E^2 \left[R_{t-1} + \gamma \max_u Q(x_t, u) - Q(x_{t-1}, u_{t-1}) \right]$ $e_{advantage}(s_t) = \frac{1}{2} E^2 \left[\begin{array}{l} R_{t-1} + \gamma \max_u A(x_t, u) - \frac{M}{K} A(x_{t-1}, u_{t-1}) \\ + \left(\frac{M}{K} - 1 \right) \max_u A(x_{t-1}, u) \end{array} \right]$ $e_{value-iteration}(s_t) = \frac{1}{2} \left[\max_{u_{t-1}} E \left[R_{t-1} + \gamma V(x_t) \right] - V(x_{t-1}) \right]^2$ $e_{SARSA-policy}(s_t) = (1 - \beta) e_{SARSA}(s_t) + \beta (b - \gamma' R_t)$

the current, stochastic policy. Both e and P should be smooth functions of **w**, and
for any given **w** vector, e should be bounded. The algorithm is simple, but actually
generates a large class of different algorithms depending on the choice of e and
when the trace is reset to zero. For a single sequence, sampled by following the
current policy, the sum of Δw along the sequence will give an unbiased estimate of
the true gradient, with finite variance. Therefore, during learning, if weight updates
are made at the end of each trial, and if the weights stay within a bounded region,
and the learning rate approaches zero, then B will converge with probability one.
Adding a weight-decay term (a constant times the 2-norm of the weight vector) onto
B will prevent weight divergence for small initial learning rates. There is no
guarantee that a global minimum will be found when using general function
approximators, but at least it will converge. This is true for backprop as well.

3 INSTANTIATING THE VAPS ALGORITHM

Many reinforcement-learning algorithms are *value-based*; they try to learn a value
function that satisfies the Bellman equation. Examples are Q-learning, which learns
a value function, actor-critic algorithms, which learn a value function and the policy
which is greedy with respect to it, and TD(1), which learns a value function based
on future rewards. Other algorithms are pure *policy-search* algorithms; they
directly learn a policy that returns high rewards. These include REINFORCE
(Williams, 1988), backprop through time, learning automata, and genetic
algorithms. The algorithms proposed here combine the two approaches: they
perform *Value And Policy Search* (VAPS). The general VAPS equation is
instantiated by choosing an expression for e. This can be a Bellman residual
(yielding value-based), the reinforcement (yielding policy-search), or a linear
combination of the two (yielding Value And Policy Search). The single VAPS
update rule on the left side of Table 2 generates a variety of different types of
algorithms, some of which are described in the following sections.

3.1 REDUCING MEAN SQUARED RESIDUAL PER TRIAL

If the MDP has terminal states, and a *trial* is the time from the start until a terminal
state is reached, then it is possible to minimize the expected total error per trial by
resetting the trace to zero at the start of each trial. Then, a convergent form of
SARSA, Q-learning, incremental value iteration, or advantage learning can be
generated by choosing e to be the squared Bellman residual, as shown on the right
side of Table 2. In each case, the expected value is taken over all possible (x_t, u_t, R_t)

triplets, given s_{t-1}. The policy must be a smooth, nonzero function of the weights. So it could not be an ε-greedy policy that chooses the greedy action with probability (1-ε) and chooses uniformly otherwise. That would cause a discontinuity in the gradient when two Q values in a state were equal. But the policy could be something that approaches ε-greedy as a positive temperature c approaches zero:

$$P(u \mid x) = \frac{\varepsilon}{n} + (1-\varepsilon)\frac{1 + e^{Q(x,u)/c}}{\sum_{u'}\left(1 + e^{Q(x,u')/c}\right)} \qquad (6)$$

where n is the number of possible actions in each state. For each instance in Table 2 other than value iteration, the gradient of e can be estimated using two, independent, unbiased estimates of the expected value. For example:

$$\frac{\partial}{\partial w}e_{SARSA}(s_t) \doteq e_{SARSA}(s_t)\left(\gamma\phi\frac{\partial}{\partial w}Q(x'_t, u'_t) - \frac{\partial}{\partial w}Q(x_{t-1}, u_{t-1})\right) \qquad (7)$$

When $\phi=1$, this is an estimate of the true gradient. When $\phi<1$, this is a *residual* algorithm, as described in (Baird, 96), and it retains guaranteed convergence, but may learn more quickly than pure gradient descent for some values of ϕ. Note that the gradient of $Q(x,u)$ at time t uses primed variables. That means a new state and action at time t were generated independently from the state and action at time t-1. Of course, if the MDP is deterministic, then the primed variables are the same as the unprimed. If the MDP is nondeterministic but the model is known, then the model must be evaluated one additional time to get the other state. If the model is not known, then there are three choices. First, a model could be learned from past data, and then evaluated to give this independent sample. Second, the issue could be ignored, simply reusing the unprimed variables in place of the primed variables. This may affect the quality of the learned function (depending on how random the MDP is), but doesn't stop convergence, and be an acceptable approximation in practice. Third, all past transitions could be recorded, and the primed variables could be found by searching for all the times (x_{t-1}, u_{t-1}) has been seen before, and randomly choosing one of those transitions and using its successor state and action as the primed variables. This is equivalent to learning the certainty equivalence model, and sampling from it, and so is a special case of the first choice. For extremely large state-action spaces with many starting states, this is likely to give the same result in practice as simply reusing the unprimed variables as the primed variables. Note, that when weights do not effect the policy at all, these algorithms reduce to standard residual algorithms (Baird, 95).

It is also possible to reduce the mean squared residual per step, rather than per trial. This is done by making period lengths independent of the policy, so minimizing error per period will also minimize the error per step. For example, a period might be defined to be the first 100 steps, after which the traces are reset, and the state is returned to the start state. Note that if every state-action pair has a positive chance of being seen in the first 100 steps, then this will *not* just be solving a finite-horizon problem. It will be actually be solving the discounted, infinite-horizon problem, by reducing the Bellman residual in every state. But the weighting of the residuals will be determined only by what happens during the first 100 steps. Many different problems can be solved by the VAPS algorithm by instantiating the definition of "period" in different ways.

3.2 POLICY-SEARCH AND VALUE-BASED LEARNING

It is also possible to add a term that tries to maximize reinforcement directly. For example, e could be defined to be $e_{SARSA\text{-}policy}$ rather than e_{SARSA} from Table 2, and

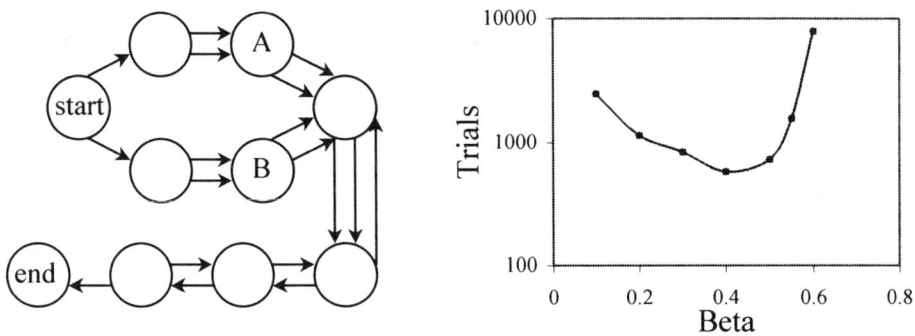

Figure 1. A POMDP and the number of trials needed to learn it vs. β.
A combination of policy-search and value-based RL outperforms either alone.

the trace reset to zero after each terminal state is reached. The constant b does not affect the expected gradient, but does affect the noise distribution, as discussed in (Williams, 88). When β=0, the algorithm will try to learn a Q function that satisfies the Bellman equation, just as before. When β=1, it directly learns a policy that will minimize the expected total discounted reinforcement. The resulting "Q function" may not even be close to containing true Q values or to satisfying the Bellman equation, it will just give a good policy. When β is in between, this algorithm tries to both satisfy the Bellman equation and give good greedy policies. A similar modification can be made to any of the algorithms in Table 2. In the special case where β=1, this algorithm reduces to the REINFORCE algorithm (Williams, 1988). REINFORCE has been rederived for the special case of gaussian action distributions (Tresp & Hofman, 1995), and extensions of it appear in (Marbach, 1998). This case of pure policy search is particularly interesting, because for β=1, there is no need for any kind of model or of generating two independent successors. Other algorithms have been proposed for finding policies directly, such as those given in (Gullapalli, 92) and the various algorithms from learning automata theory summarized in (Narendra & Thathachar, 89). The VAPS algorithms proposed here appears to be the first one unifying these two approaches to reinforcement learning, finding a value function that both approximates a Bellman-equation solution and directly optimizes the greedy policy.

Figure 1 shows simulation results for the combined algorithm. A run is said to have learned when the greedy policy is optimal for 1000 consecutive trials. The graph shows the average plot of 100 runs, with different initial random weights between $\pm 10^{-6}$. The learning rate was optimized separately for each β value. $R=1$ when leaving state A, $R=2$ when leaving state B or entering end, and $R=0$ otherwise. $\gamma=0.9$. The algorithm used was the modified Q-learning from Table 2, with exploration as in equation 13, and $\varphi=c=1$, $b=0$, $\varepsilon=0.1$. States A and B share the same parameters, so ordinary SARSA or greedy Q-learning could never converge, as shown in (Gordon, 96). When β=0 (pure value-based), the new algorithm converges, but of course it cannot learn the optimal policy in the start state, since those two Q values learn to be equal. When β=1 (pure policy-search), learning converges to optimality, but slowly, since there is no value function caching the results in the long sequence of states near the end. By combining the two approaches, the new algorithm learns much more quickly than either alone.

It is interesting that the VAPS algorithms described in the last three sections can be applied directly to a Partially Observable Markov Decision Process (POMDP), where the true state is hidden, and all that is available on each time step is an ambiguous "observation", which is a function of the true state. Normally, an algorithm such as SARSA only has guaranteed convergance when applied to an MDP. The VAPS algorithms will converge in such cases.

4 CONCLUSION

A new algorithm has been presented. Special cases of it give new algorithms similar to Q-learning, SARSA, and advantage learning, but with guaranteed convergence for a wider range of problems than was previously possible, including POMDPs. For the first time, these can be guaranteed to converge, even when the exploration policy changes during learning. Other special cases allow new approaches to reinforcement learning, where there is a tradeoff between satisfying the Bellman equation and improving the greedy policy. For one MDP, simulation showed that this combined algorithm learned more quickly than either approach alone. This unified theory, unifying for the first time both value-based and policy-search reinforcement learning, is of theoretical interest, and also was of practical value for the simulations performed. Future research with this unified framework may be able to empirically or analytically address the old question of when it is better to learn value functions and when it is better to learn the policy directly. It may also shed light on the new question, of when it is best to do both at once.

Acknowledgments

This research was sponsored in part by the U.S. Air Force.

References

Baird, L. C. (1995). Residual Algorithms: Reinforcement Learning with Function Approximation. In Armand Prieditis & Stuart Russell, eds. Machine Learning: Proceedings of the Twelfth International Conference, 9-12 July, Morgan Kaufman Publishers, San Francisco, CA.

Gordon, G. (1996). "Stable fitted reinforcement learning". In G. Tesauro, M. Mozer, and M. Hasselmo (eds.), Advances in Neural Information Processing Systems 8, pp. 1052-1058. MIT Press, Cambridge, MA.

Gullapalli, V. (1992). *Reinforcement Learning and Its Application to Control.* Dissertation and COINS Technical Report 92-10, University of Massachusetts, Amherst, MA.

Kaelbling, L. P., Littman, M. L. & Cassandra, A., "Planning and Acting in Partially Observable Stochastic Domains". Artificial Intelligence, to appear. Available now at http://www.cs.brown.edu/people/lpk.

Marbach, P. (1998). Simulation-Based Optimization of Markov Decision Processes. Thesis LIDS-TH 2429, Massachusetts Institute of Technology.

McCallum (1995), A. *Reinforcement learning with selective perception and hidden state.* Dissertation, Department of Computer Science, University of Rochester, Rochester, NY.

Narendra, K., & Thathachar, M.A.L. (1989). *Learning automata: An introduction.* Prentice Hall, Englewood Cliffs, NJ.

Tresp, V., & R. Hofman (1995). "Missing and noisy data in nonlinear time-series prediction". In *Proceedings of Neural Networks for Signal Processing 5*, F. Girosi, J. Makhoul, E. Manolakos and E. Wilson, eds., IEEE Signal Processing Society, New York, New York, 1995, pp. 1-10.

Williams, R. J. (1988). *Toward a theory of reinforcement-learning connectionist systems.* Technical report NU-CCS-88-3, Northeastern University, Boston, MA.

Non-linear PI Control Inspired by Biological Control Systems

Lyndon J. Brown   Gregory E. Gonye   James S. Schwaber [*]
Experimental Station, E.I. DuPont deNemours & Co. Wilmington, DE 19880

Abstract

A non-linear modification to PI control is motivated by a model of a signal transduction pathway active in mammalian blood pressure regulation. This control algorithm, labeled PII (proportional with intermittent integral), is appropriate for plants requiring exact set-point matching and disturbance attenuation in the presence of infrequent step changes in load disturbances or set-point. The proportional aspect of the controller is independently designed to be a disturbance attenuator and set-point matching is achieved by intermittently invoking an integral controller. The mechanisms observed in the Angiotensin II/AT1 signaling pathway are used to control the switching of the integral control. Improved performance over PI control is shown on a model of cyclopentenol production. A sign change in plant gain at the desirable operating point causes traditional PI control to result in an unstable system. Application of this new approach to this problem results in stable exact set-point matching for achievable set-points.

Biological processes have evolved sophisticated mechanisms for solving difficult control problems. By analyzing and understanding these natural systems it is possible that principles can be derived which are applicable to general control systems. This approach has already been the basis for the field of artificial neural networks, which are loosely based on a model of the electrical signaling of neurons. A suitable candidate system for analysis is blood pressure control. Tight control of blood pressure is critical for survival of an animal. Chronically high levels can lead to premature death. Low blood pressure can lead to oxygen and nutrient deprivation and sudden load changes must be quickly responded to or loss of consciousness can result. The baroreflex, reflexive change of heart rate in response to blood pressure challenge, has been previously studied in order to develop some insights into biological control systems [1, 2, 3].

---

[*]lyndon.j.brown@usa.dupont.com   Address correspondence to this author
Gregory.E.Gonye-PHD@usa.dupont.com James.S.Scwhaber@usa.dupont.com

Neurons exhibit complex dynamic behavior that is not directly revealed by their electrical behavior, but is incorporated in biochemical signal transduction pathways. This is an important basis for plasticity of neural networks. The area of the brain to which the baroreceptor afferents project is the nucleus of tractus solitarus (NTS). The neurons in the NTS are rich with diverse receptors for signaling pathways. It is logical that this richness and diversity play a crucial role in the signal processing that occurs here. Hormonal and neurotransmitter signals can activate signal transduction pathways in the cell, which result in physical modification of some components of a cell, or altered gene regulation. Fuxe et al [4] have shown the presence of the angiotensin II/AT1 receptor pathway in NTS neurons, and Herbert [5] has demonstrated its ability to affect the baroreflex.

To develop understanding of the effects of biochemical pathways, a detailed kinetic model of the angiotensin/AT1 pathway was developed. Certain features of this model and the baroreflex have interesting characteristics from a control engineering perspective. These features have been used to develop a novel control strategy. The resulting control algorithm utilizes a proportional controller that intermittently invokes integral action to achieve set-point matching. Thus the controller will be labeled PII.

The use of integral control is popular as it guarantees cancellation of offsets and ensures exact set-point matching. However, the use of integral control does have drawbacks. It introduces significant lag in the feedback system, which limits the bandwidth of the system. Increasing the integral gain, in order to improve response time, can lead to systems with excessive overshoot, excessive settling times, and less robustness to plant changes or uncertainty. Many processes in the chemical industry have a steady-state response curve with a maximum and frequently, the optimal operating condition is at this peak. Unfortunately, any controller with true integral action will be unstable at this operating point.

In a crude sense, the integrator learns the constant control action required to achieve set-point matching. If the integral control is viewed as a simple learning device, than a logical step is to remove it from the feedback loop once the necessary offset has been learned. If the offset is being successfully compensated for, only noise remains as a source for learning. It has been well established that learning based on nothing but noise leads to undesirable results. The maxim, 'garbage in, garbage out' will apply. Without integral control, the proportional controller can be made more aggressive while maintaining stability margins and/or control actions at similar levels. This control strategy will be appropriate for plants with infrequent step changes in set-points or loads. The challenge becomes deciding when, and how to perform this switching so that the resulting controller provides significant improvements.

1 Angiotensin II/AT1 receptor Signal Transduction Model

Regulation of blood pressure is a vital control problem in mammals. Blood pressure is sensed by stretch sensitive cells in the aortic arch and carotid sinus. These cells transmit signals to neurons in the NTS which are combined with other signals from the central nervous system (CNS) resulting in changes to the cardiac output and vascular tone [6]. This control is implemented by two parallel systems in the CNS, the sympathetic and parasympathetic nervous systems. The sympathetic system primarily affects the vascular tone and the parasympathetic system affects cardiac output [7]. Cardiac control can have a larger and faster effect, but long term application of this control is injurious to the overall health of the animal. Pottman et al [2] have suggested that these two systems separately control for long term set-point control and fast disturbance rejection.

One receptor in NTS neuronal cells is the AT1 receptor which binds Angiotensin II. The NTS is located in the brain stem where much of the processing of the autonomic regulatory systems reside. Angiotensin infusion in this region of the brain has been shown to significantly affect blood pressure control. In order to understand this aspect of neuronal behavior, a detailed kinetic model of this signaling pathway was developed. The pathway is presented in Figure 2. The outputs can be considered to be the concentrations of $G_q \cdot$GTP, $G_{\beta\gamma}$, activated protein kinase C, and/or calmodulin dependent protein kinase.

Several reactions in the cascade are of interest. The binding of phospholipase C is significantly slower than the other steps in the reaction. This can be modeled as a first order transfer function with a long time constant or as a pure integrator. The IP_3 receptor is a ligand gated channel on the membrane of the endoplasmic reticulum (ER). As Figure 2 shows, when IP_3 binds to this receptor, calcium is released from the ER into the cells cytoplasm. However the IP_3 receptor also has 2 binding sites on its cytoplasmic domain for binding calcium. The first has relatively fast dynamics and causes a substantial increase in the channel opening. The second calcium binding site has slower dynamics and inactivates the channel. The effect of this first binding site is to introduce positive feedback into the model. In traditional control literature, positive feedback is generally undesirable. Thus it is very interesting to see positive feedback in neuronal control systems.

A typical surface response for the model, comparing the time response of activated calmodulin versus the peak concentration of a pulse of angiotensin, is shown in Figure 1. The results are consistent with behavior of cells measured by Li and Guyenet [8]. The output level is seen to abruptly rise after a delay, which is a decreasing function of the magnitude of the input. Unlike a linear system, both the magnitude and speed of the response of the system are functions of the magnitude of the input. Further, the relaxing of the system to its equilibrium is a very slow response as compared to its activation. This behavior can be attributed to the positive feedback response inherent to the IP3 receptor. The effect of the slow dynamics of the phospholipase C binding, and the IP3 receptor dynamics results in an activation behavior similar to a threshold detector on the integrated input signal. However, removal of the input results in a slow recovery back to zero. The activation of the calcium calmodulin dependent protein kinase can lead to phosphorilation of channels that result in synaptic conductance changes that are functionally related to the amount of activated kinase. The activation of calcium calmodulin can also lead to changes in gene regulation that could potentially result in long term changes in the neurons synaptic conductances.

2 Proportional with Intermittent Integral Control

Key features from the model that are incorporated in the control law are:

1. separate controllers for set-point control and disturbance attenuation;
2. activation of set-point controller when integrated error exceeds threshold;
3. strength of integral action when activated will be a function of the speed with which activation was achieved;
4. smooth removal of integral action, without disruption of control action.

The PII controller begins initially as a proportional controller with a nominal offset added to its output. The integrated error is monitored. The integral controller is turned on when the integrated error exceeds a threshold. Once the integral control action is activated, it remains active as long as the error is excessive. Once the error is not significant, then the integral control action can be removed in a

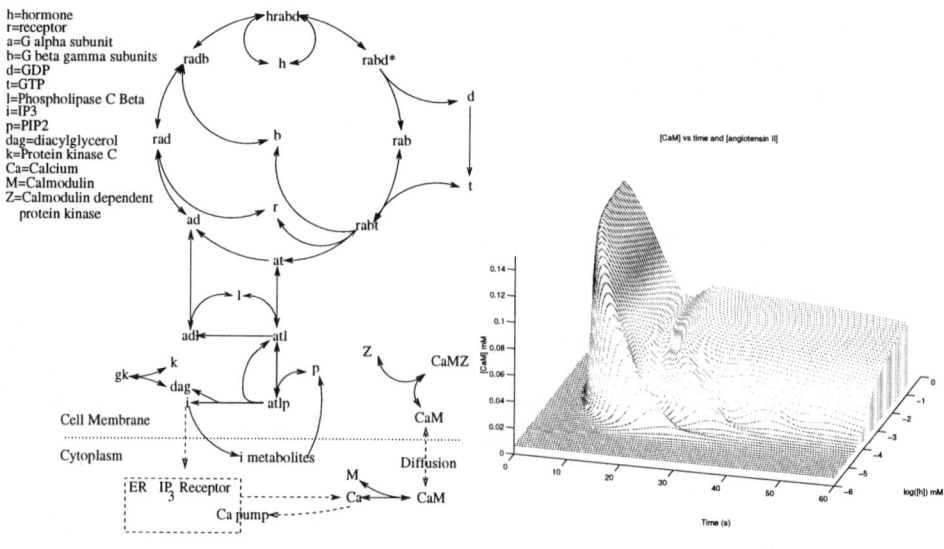

Figure 1: Schematic and Surface Responses of Angiotensin II / AT1 Model

smooth manner. This has been achieved by allowing the value of the integral gain, K_i, to decay exponentially. It is important that this is done in such a manner as not to affect the actual control signal. This can be achieved by adjusting the offset appropriately. Since $u = K_p e + K_i e/s$ and $\dot{K}_i \propto -K_i$, then u can be made constant for constant e by adding offset K_o where $\dot{K}_o \propto K_i e/s$. The integral action is completely removed once K_i has decayed to the point where it is no longer significant. In order to make the effect of activation of the integrator correspond to the behavior of the angiotensin model, the integrated error is scaled by the time spent reaching the threshold when the integrator is turned on. This corresponds to point 3 above.

If the error undergoes significant change when the integrator is already fully active the system will behave similarly to a system with a PI controller whose gains have been set too high. This may result in significant overshoot and possibly instability. There is a small chance that even with infrequent step changes, the residual error, or random disturbance could trigger the integrator immediately before a step change. In a biological control system, control does not rest in one neuron or necessarily in one signal transduction pathway but in multiple pathways. Furthermore, study of individual cells shows a great deal of variability in the details of their behavior. By implementing the intermittent integral control as a sum of many equivalent controllers, as in left side of Figure 2, with variability in their threshold parameters, a controller can be developed that is not subject to the chance of being fully activated by random disturbance or residual error. During steady-state operation these integrators will quickly deactivate when noise or small disturbances trigger them, as the error will be less than the threshold. However, an actual step change in the error signal will result in all or most of the integrators activating, and remaining active until the error is compensated for.

The block diagram on right side of Figure 2 and the time dependent definitions in Table 1 precisely define the control algorithm for the single integrator case.

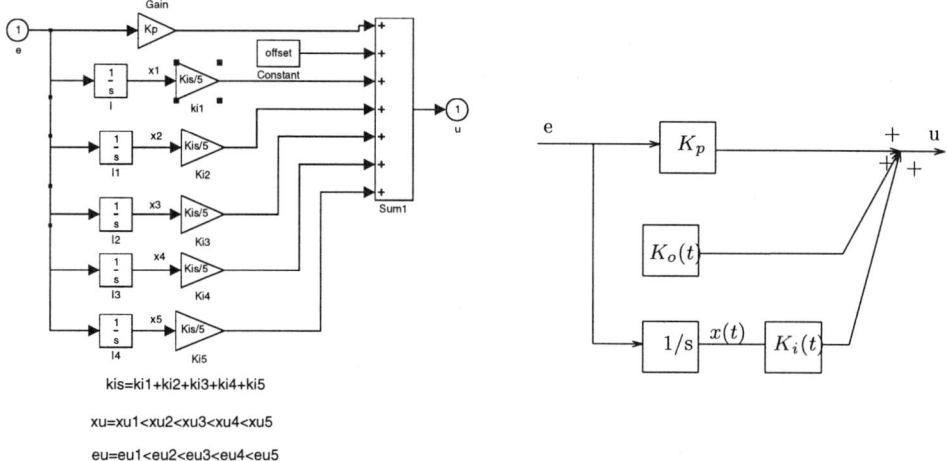

Figure 2: Block Diagrams for Control Algorithm Implementations

If	then
$t = t_0$	$x(t_0) = 0$, $K_i(t_0) = 0$, $K_o(t_0) = K_o^*$, $t_l(t_0) = t_0$.
$K_i(t) = 0$ and $|x(t)| > x_u$	$K_i(t) = K_i^*$, $x(t^+) = \dfrac{x(t)}{\max(1, K_s(t-t_l))}$.
$|K_i(t)| > K_i^l$ and $|e(t)| < e_u$	$\dot{K}_i(t) = -K_{decay}K_i(t)$, $\dot{K}_o(t) = K_{decay}K_i(t)x(t)$.
$0 < |K_i(t)| < K_i^l$	$K_o(t^+) = K_o(t) + K_i(t)x(t)$,
	$K_i(t^+) = 0$, $x(t^+) = 0$, $t_l(t^+) = t$.
Otherwise	$\dot{K}_i(t) = 0$, $\dot{K}_o(t) = 0$, $\dot{x} = e$, $\dot{t}_l(t) = 0$.

Table 1: Definition of Gains for PII Control

3 Control of CSTR Reactor for Cyclopentenol Production

The model of the CSTR reactor is taken from [9]. The basic process converts cyclopentadiene to cyclopentenol. Cyclopentenol can undergo a further undesirable reaction to form cyclopentadiol, and cyclopentadiene can undergo an alternative reaction to form dicyclopentadiene. The rates of the reactions are temperature dependent. Inputs to the model are flow rate, and the jacket temperature. The first input is the control input, and the jacket temperature is an unmeasured disturbance, with a root mean square deviation of 0.1 C about a nominal value of 130 C. The regulated output will be the cyclopentenol concentration in the outflow.

The steady-state response of this process is shown in Figure 3. Operation in the region labeled II up to the peak of the curve labeled VIII has been considered. At the point labeled VIII, the steady-state gain of the plant goes to 0. Plants with steady-state gains which change sign can not be stably controlled with PI control. An additional complicating factor is that the plant has significant inverse response in this region.

Criteria for this control design problem, in order of importance are

- operate between 45 and 60 l/hour with reasonable high frequency gain
- minimize the overshoot
- minimize rise time

- minimize the inverse response

Satisfying the first and last criteria should ensure a robust controller. Precise numerical performance criteria for the rise time have not been specified as no fixed values are reasonable for the entire region.

A PI controller, as well as a PII controller have been designed and the results are displayed in Figures 3. The controller parameters were $K_p = 75$, $K_i = 7500$ for the standard PI controller. The PII controller used 5 equally weighted parallel integrators with $K_p = 125$, total $K_i^* = 10000$ and $K_{decay} = 100$. The threshold parameters were chosen as $e_u = [4\ 3\ 2\ 1\ 1] * 0.00025$, $x_n = [16\ 8\ 4\ 2\ 1] * 0.00004$, and $K_i^l = K_i^*/5$.

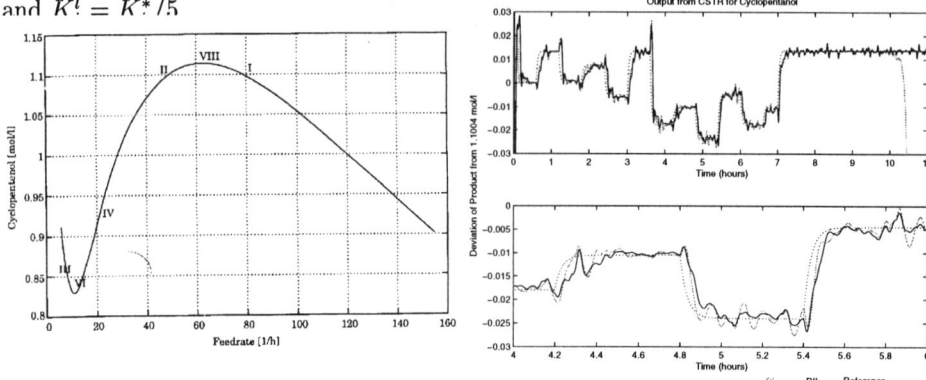

Figure 3: Steady-State Response of Cyclopentenol CSTR Reactor and Output Concentration from CSTR Reactor

The set-point was chosen to be a series of smoothed steps. Smoothing was performed with a first-order, low-pass filter with unity DC gain and a time constant of 30 hours^{-1}. While operating in the region of design from 0 to 4.8 hours and 5.4 to 7 hours, the PII controlled system, as compared to the PI controlled system, had reduced inverse response, less worst-case overshoot, similar response times and greater disturbance attenuation. A closer examination of the PI controlled system, during the interval 4.8-5.4 hours, showed that at this extreme operating point, oscillations of a fixed period begin to appear. This indicates the existence of poorly damped poles. The PII controlled system did not show this degradation of performance.

The set-point was raised to nearly the maximum achievable concentration. This allows examination of the behavior of the controller when operating near regions of uncertainty in the sign of the plant gain. This operating point achieves the maximum possible conversion to cyclopentenol and thus has significant economic advantages. In the region from 7.2s to 10s, there is a 10% reduction in the disturbance response with the PII controller. At this operating point, the PI controlled system can be shown to be locally stable. However, the effects of integrated noise easily allow the system trajectory to escape the region of attraction. As expected, the PI controlled system went unstable. The PII controlled system remains well behaved. The simulation was run for a total simulated time of 43 hours at this operating point, and repeated many times without seeing any loss of stability with PII controller. With PI control, the system went unstable within 10 hours for each trial. Thus, PII control allows operation at set-points closer to maximums or minimums.

4 Conclusion

The mechanisms that biological control systems employ to successfully control nonlinear, time varying, multivariable physiological systems under very demanding performance requirements are likely to have application in process control problems. In addition to neural networks already incorporated in advanced controllers, cells process information through biochemical signal transduction networks that may also contain useful non-linear mechanisms. A model of one such pathway has been developed, and features have been identified which can be used to develop an improved control system.

The fundamental idea is to design two separate control laws, one intermittently used for cancelling infrequently changing but mostly predictable disturbances, and another for attenuating white disturbances. The first controller learns the simple characteristics of the predictable disturbance. When the predictable disturbance is learned, it can be canceled with an open loop controller, and no further learning takes place. However if it appears that the open loop controller is not cancelling the disturbance, further learning takes place until the disturbance is again successfully cancelled. The second controller is designed strictly for fast disturbance attenuation. Without the lag inherent in integration, the controller can be made more aggressive resulting in better performance. The two controllers can be integrated by applying the threshold and switching mechanisms identified in the signal transduction model.

References

[1] M. A. Henson, B. A. Ogunnaike, J. S. Schwaber, and F. J. Doyle III, "The baroreceptor reflex: A biological control system with applications in chemical process control," *I&EC Research*, vol. 33, pp. 2453–2465, 1994.

[2] M. Pottman, M. A. Henson, B. A. Ogunnaike, and J. S. Schwaber, "A parrallel control strategy abstracted from the baroreceptor reflex," *Chemical Engineering Science*, vol. 51, pp. 931–945, 1996.

[3] H. S. Kwatra, F. J. Doyle III, and J. S. Schwaber, "Dynamic gain scheduled process control," *Chemical Engineering Science*, 1997.

[4] K. Fuxe and B. B. et al, "Pre- and post-synaptic features of the central angiotensin systems: Indications for a role of angiotensin peptides in volume transmission and for interactions with central monamine neurons," *Clin Exp Hypertens [Theory Pract]*, vol. A10, pp. 143–168, 1988.

[5] J. Herbert, "Studying the central actions of angiotensin using the expression of immediate-early genes: Expectations and limitations," *Regulatory Peptides*, vol. 66, pp. 13–18, 1996.

[6] K. M. Spyer, "The central nervous organization of reflex circulatory control," in *Clin Exp Hypertens [Theory Pract]Central Regulation of Automanomic Fuctions* (A. D. Loewy and K. M. Spyer, eds.), p. 168, New York: Oxford University Press, 1990.

[7] M. N. Kumada, N. Terui, and T. Kuwaki, "Arterial baroreceptor reflex: Its central and peripheral neural mechanisms," *Progr. Neurophysiol.*, vol. 35, p. 331, 1988.

[8] Y. Li and P. G. Guyenet, "Angiotensin II decreases a resting K^+ conductance in rat bulbospinal neurons of the c1 area," *Circulatiob Research*, vol. 78, pp. 274–282, 1996.

[9] B. Ogunnaike and W. H. Ray, *Process dynamics, Modeling and Control*. New York: Oxford University Press, 1995.

Optimizing admission control while ensuring quality of service in multimedia networks via reinforcement learning[*]

Timothy X Brown[†], Hui Tong[†], Satinder Singh[‡]
[†] Electrical and Computer Engineering
[‡] Computer Science
University of Colorado
Boulder, CO 80309-0425
{timxb, tongh, baveja}@colorado.edu

Abstract

This paper examines the application of reinforcement learning to a telecommunications networking problem. The problem requires that revenue be maximized while simultaneously meeting a quality of service constraint that forbids entry into certain states. We present a general solution to this multi-criteria problem that is able to earn significantly higher revenues than alternatives.

1 Introduction

A number of researchers have recently explored the application of reinforcement learning (RL) to resource allocation and admission control problems in telecommunications. e.g., channel allocation in wireless systems, network routing, and admission control in telecommunication networks [1, 6, 7, 8]. Telecom problems are attractive applications for RL research because good, simple to implement, simulation models exist for them in the engineering literature that are both widely used and results on which are trusted, because there are existing solutions to compare with, because small improvements over existing methods can lead to significant savings in the long run, because they have discrete states, and because there are many potential commercial applications. However, existing RL applications have ignored an issue of great practical importance to telecom engineers, that of ensuring *quality of service* (QoS) while simultaneously optimizing whatever resource allocation performance criterion is of interest.

This paper will focus on admission control for broadband multimedia communication networks. These networks are unlike the current internet in that voice, video, and data calls arrive and depart over time and, in exchange for giving QoS guarantees to customers, the network collects revenue for calls that it accepts into the network. In this environment, admission control decides what calls to accept into the network so as to maximize the earned revenue while meeting the QoS guarantees of all carried customers.

---
[*]Timothy Brown and Hui Tong were funded by NSF CAREER Award NCR-9624791. Satinder Singh was funded by NSF grant IIS-9711753.

Meeting QoS requires a decision function that decides when adding a new call will violate QoS guarantees. Given the diverse nature of voice, video, and data traffic, and their often complex underlying statistics, finding good QoS decision functions has been the subject of intense research [2, 5]. Recent results have emphasized that robust and efficient QoS decision functions require on-line adaptive methods [3].

Given we have a QoS decision function, deciding which of the heterogeneous arriving calls to accept and which to reject in order to maximize revenue can be framed as a dynamic program problem. The rapid growth in the number of states with problem complexity has led to reinforcement learning approaches to the problem [6].

In this paper we consider the problem of finding a control policy that simultaneously meets QoS guarantees and maximizes the network's earned revenue. We show that the straightforward approach of mixing positive rewards for revenue with negative rewards for violating QoS leads to sub-optimal policies. Ideally we would like to find the optimal policy from the subset of policies that never violate the QoS constraint. But there is no a priori useful way to characterize the space of policies that don't violate the QoS constraint. We present a general approach to meeting such multicriteria that solves this problem and potentially many other applications. Experiments show that incorporating QoS and RL yield significant gains over some alternative heuristics.

2 Problem Description

This section describes the admission control problem model that will be used. To emphasize the main features of the problem, networking issues such as queueing that are not essential have been simplified or eliminated. It should be emphasized that these aspects can readily be incorporated back into the problem.

We focus on a single network link. Users attempt to access the link over time and the network immediately chooses to accept or reject the call. If accepted, the call generates traffic in terms of bandwidth as a function of time. At a later time, the call terminates and departs from the network. For each call accepted, the network receives revenue at a fixed rate over the duration of the call. The network measures QoS metrics such as transmission delays or packet loss rates and compares them against the guarantees given to the calls. Thus, the problem is described by the call arrival, traffic, and departure processes; the revenue rates; QoS metrics; QoS constraints; and link model. The choices used in this paper are given in the next paragraph.

Calls are divided into discrete classes indexed by i. The calls are generated via a Poisson arrival process (arrival rate λ_i) and exponential holding times (mean holding time $1/\mu_i$). Within a call the bandwidth is an ON/OFF process where the traffic is either ON at rate r_i or OFF at rate zero with mean holding times ν_i^{ON}, and ν_i^{OFF}. The effective immediate revenue are c_i. The link has a fixed bandwidth B. The total bandwidth used by accepted calls varies over time. The QoS metric is the fraction of time that the total bandwidth exceeds the link bandwidth (i.e. the overload probability, p). The QoS guarantee is an upper limit, p^*.

In previous work each call had a constant bandwidth over time so that the effect on QoS was predictable. Variable rate traffic is safely approximated by assuming that it always transmits at its maximum or peak rate. Such so-called *peak rate* allocation under-utilizes the network; in some cases by orders of magnitude less than what is possible. Stochastic traffic rates in real traffic, the desire for high network utilization/revenue, and the resulting potential for QoS violations distinguish the problem in this paper.

3 Semi-Markov Decision Processes

At any given point of time, the system is in a particular configuration, x, defined by the number of each type of ongoing calls. At random times a call arrival or a call termination event, e, can occur. The configuration and event together determine the state of the system, $s = (x, e)$. When an event occurs, the learner has to choose an action feasible for that event. The choice of action, the event, and the configuration deterministically define the next configuration and the payoff received by the learner. Then after an interval the next event occurs, and this cycle repeats. The task of the learner is to determine a policy that maximizes the discounted sum of payoffs over an infinite horizon. Such a system constitutes a finite state, finite action, semi-Markov decision process (SMDP).

3.1 Multi-criteria Objective

The admission control objective is to learn a policy that assigns an accept or reject decision to each possible state of the system so as to *maximize*

$$J = E\left\{\int_0^\infty \gamma^t c(t) dt\right\},$$

where $E\{\cdot\}$ is the expectation operator, $c(t)$ is the total revenue rate of ongoing calls at time t, and $\gamma \in (0, 1)$ is a discount factor that makes immediate profit more valuable than future profit.[1]

In this paper we restrict the maximization to policies that never enter states that violate QoS guarantees. In general SMDP, due to stochastic state transitions, meeting such constraints may not be possible (e.g. from any state no matter what actions are taken there is a possibility of entering restricted states). In this problem service quality decreases with more calls in the system and adding calls is strictly controlled by the admission controller so that meeting this QoS constraint is possible.

3.2 Q-learning

RL methods solve SMDP problems by learning good approximations to the optimal value function, J^*, given by the solution to the Bellman optimality equation which takes the following form for the dynamic call admission problem:

$$J^*(s) = \max_{a \in A(s)} [E_{\Delta t, s'}\{c(s, a, \Delta t) + \gamma(\Delta t) J^*(s')\}] \quad (1)$$

where $A(s)$ is the set of actions available in the current state s, Δt is the random time until the next event, $c(s, a, \Delta t)$ is the effective *immediate* payoff with the discounting, and $\gamma(\Delta t)$ is the effective discount for the next state s'.

We learn an approximation to J^* using Watkin's Q-learning algorithm. To focus on the dynamics of this paper's problem and not on the confounding dynamics of function approximation, the problem state space is kept small enough so that table lookup can be used. Bellman's equation can be rewritten in Q-values as

$$J^*(s) = \max_{a \in A(s)} Q^*(s, a) \quad (2)$$

Call Arrival: When a call arrives, the Q-value of accepting the call and the Q-value of rejecting the call is determined. If rejection has the higher value, we drop the call. Else, if acceptance has the higher value, we accept the call.

Call Termination: No action needs to be taken.

Whatever our decision, we update our value function as follows: on a transition from state s to s' on action a in time Δt,

$$Q(s, a) = (1 - \alpha) Q(s, a) + \alpha \left(c(s, a, \Delta t) + \gamma(\Delta t) \max_{b \in A(s')} Q(s', b) \right) \quad (3)$$

---

[1] Since we will compare policies based on total reward rather than discounted sum of reward, we can use the Tauberian approximation [4], i.e., γ is chosen to be sufficiently close to 1.

where $\alpha \in [0, 1]$ is the learning rate.

In order for Q-learning to perform well, all potentially important state-action pairs (s, a) must be explored. At each state, with probability ϵ we apply an action that will lead to a less visited configuration, instead of the action recommended by the Q-value. However, to update Q-values we still use the action b recommended by the Q-learning.

4 Combining Revenue and Quality of Service

The primary question addressed in this paper is how to combine the QoS constraint with the objective of maximizing revenue within this constraint. Let $\rho(s, a, \Delta t)$ and $q(s, a, \Delta t)$ be the revenue and measured QoS components of the reward, $c(s, a, \Delta t)$. Ideally $c(s, a, \Delta t) = \rho(s, a, \Delta t)$ when the QoS constraint is met and $c(s, a, \Delta t) = -\text{Large}$ (where $-\text{Large}$ is any large negative value) when QoS is not met. If the QoS parameters could be accurately measured between each state transition then this approach would be a valid solution to the problem. In network systems, the QoS metrics contain a high-degree of variability. For example, overload probabilities can be much smaller than 10^{-3} while the interarrival periods can be only a few ON/OFF cycles so that except for states with the most egregious QoS violations, most interarrival periods will have no overloads.

If the reward is a general function of revenue and QoS:

$$c(s, a, \Delta t) = f(\rho(s, a, \Delta t), q(s, a, \Delta t)), \tag{4}$$

sufficient and necessary condition for inducing optimal policy with the QoS constraint is given by:

$$E\{f(\rho(s, a, \Delta t), q(s, a, \Delta t))\} = \begin{cases} E\{\rho(s, a, \Delta t)\} & \text{if } E\{q(s, a, \Delta t)\} < p^* \\ -\text{Large} & \text{otherwise} \end{cases} \tag{5}$$

For $f(\cdot)$ satisfying this condition, states that violate QoS will be highly penalized and never visited. The actions for states that are visited will be based solely on revenue.

The Appendix gives a simple example showing that finding a $f(\cdot)$ that yields the optimal policy is unlikely without significant prior knowledge about each state. Several attempts at using (4) to combine QoS and revenue into the reward either violated QoS or had significantly lower reward.

A straight-forward alternative exists to meeting the multicriteria formulated as follows. For each criteria, j, we estimate a separate set of Q-factors, $Q^j(s, a)$. Each is updated via on-line Q-learning. These are then combined post facto at the time of decision via some function $\mathcal{Q}(\cdot)$ so that:

$$Q(s, a) = \mathcal{Q}(\{Q^j(s, a)\}). \tag{6}$$

For example in this paper the two criteria are estimated separately as Q^ρ and Q^q and

$$Q(s, a) = \mathcal{Q}(Q^\rho(s, a), Q^q(s, a)) = \begin{cases} Q^\rho(s, a) & \text{if } Q^q(s, a) < p^* \\ -\text{Large} & \text{otherwise} \end{cases} \tag{7}$$

The structure of this problem allows us to estimate Q^q without using (3). As stated, the QoS is an intrinsic property of a state and not of future states so it is independent of the policy. This allows us to collect QoS statistics about each state and treat them in a principled way (e.g. computing confidence intervals on the estimates). Using these QoS estimates, the set of allowable states contracts monotonically over time eventually converging to a fixed set of allowable states. Since the QoS constraint is guaranteed to reach a fixed point asymptotically, the Q-learned policy also approaches a fixed point at the optimal policy via standard Q-learning proofs. A related scheme is analyzed in [4] suggesting that similar cases will also converge to optimal policies.

Many other QoS criteria do depend on the policy and require using (3). A constraint on the expected overload probability with a given policy is an example.

5 Simulation Results

The experiment uses the following model. The total bandwidth is normalized to 1.0 unit of traffic per unit time. The target overflow probability is $p^* = 10^{-3}$. Two source types are considered with the properties shown in Table 1. As noted before, call holding times are exponential and the arrivals are Poisson. For the first experiment, the ON/OFF holding times are exponentially distributed, while for the second experiment, they are Pareto distributed. The Pareto distribution is considered to be a more accurate representation of data traffic.

Table 1: Experimental parameters

Parameter	Source Type I	Source Type II
ON rate, r	0.08	0.2
Mean ON period, $1/\nu^{ON}$	5	5
Mean OFF period, $1/\nu^{OFF}$	15	45
Hyperbolic exponent, $u+1$	2.08	2.12
Call arrival rate, λ	0.067	0.2
Call holding time, $1/\mu$	60	60
Immediate payoff, c	5	1

In the experiments, for each state-action pair, (s, a), $Q^\rho(s, a)$ is updated using (3). As stated, in this case the update of $Q^q(s, a)$ does not need to use (3). Since random exploration is employed to ensure that all potentially important state-action pairs be tried, it naturally enables us to collect statistics that can be used to estimate QoS at these state-action pairs, $Q^q(s, a)$. As the number of visits to each state-action pair increases, the estimated $Q^q(s, a)$ becomes more and more accurate and, with confidence, we can gradually eliminate those state-action pairs that will violate QoS requirement. As a consequence, $Q^\rho(s, a)$ is updated in a gradually correct subset of state-action space in the sense that QoS is met for any action within this subspace. Initial Q-values for RL are artificially set such that Q-learning started with the *greedy* policy (the greedy policy always accepts).

After training is completed, we apply a test data set to compare the policy obtained through RL with alternative heuristic policies. The final QoS measurements obtained at the end of the RL training while learning QoS are used for testing different policies. To test the RL policies, when there is a new call arrival, the algorithm first determines if accepting this call will violate QoS. If it will, the call is rejected, else the action is chosen according to $a = \arg\max_{a \in A(s)} Q(s, a)$, where $A(s) = \{1=\text{accept}, 0=\text{reject}\}$. For the QoS constraint we use three cases: Peak rate allocation; Statistical multiplexing function learned on-line, denoted QoS learned; Given statistical multiplexing function a priori, denoted QoS given. We examine six different cases: (1) RL: QoS given; (2) RL: QoS learned; (3) RL: peak rate; (4) A heuristic that only accepts calls from the most valuable class, i.e., type I, with given QoS; (5) Greedy: QoS given; (6) Greedy: peak rate.

From the results shown in Fig. 1, it is clear that simultaneously doing Q-learning and QoS learning converges correctly to the RL policy obtained by giving the QoS a priori and doing standard Q-learning only. We see significant gains (about 15%) due to statistical multiplexing: (6) vs (5), and (3) vs (1). The gains due to RL are about 25%: (6) vs (3), and (5) vs (2). Together they yield about 45% increase in revenue over conservative peak rate allocation in this example. It is also clear from the figure that the RL policies perform better than the heuristic policies. Fig. (2) shows the rejection ratios for different policies.

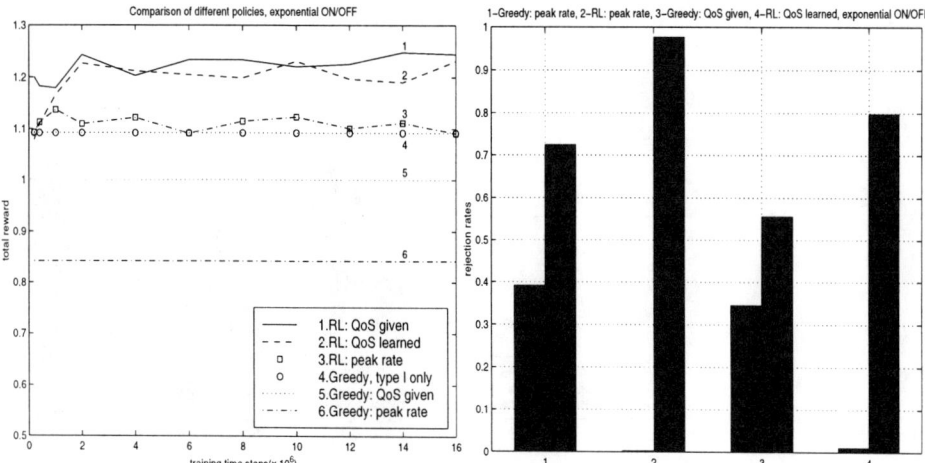

Figure 1: Comparison of total rewards of RL while learning QoS, RL with given QoS measurements, RL with peak rate, greedy policies and peak rate allocation, normalized by the greedy total reward – exponential ON/OFF.

Figure 2: Comparison of rejection ratios for the policies learned in Fig. 1.

We repeat the above experiments with Pareto distributed ON and OFF periods, using the same parameters listed in Table 1. The results are shown in Figs. 3–4. Clearly, the different ON/OFF distributions yield similar gains for RL.

6 Conclusion

This paper shows that a QoS constraint could be incorporated into a RL solution to maximizing a network's revenue, using a vector value Q-learning function. The formulation is quite general and can be applied to many possible constraints. The approach, when applied to a simple networking problem, increases revenue by up to 45%. Future research includes: using neural networks or other function approximators to deal with more complex problems for which lookup tables are infeasible; and extending admission control to multi-link routing.

7 Appendix: Simple One-State Example

A simple example will show that a function with property (5) is unlikely. Consider a link that can accept only one type of call and it can accept no more than one call. With no actions possible when carrying a call there is only one state. Only two rewards are possible, $c(R)$ for reject and $c(A)$ for accept. To fix the value function let $c(R) = 0$ and let ρ and q be the random revenues and QoS experienced. Analysis of (1) and (2) shows that the accept action will be chosen if and only if $E\{f(\rho, q)\} > 0$.

In this example, the revenues are random and possibly negative (e.g. if they are net after cost of billing and transport). The call should be accepted if $E\{\rho\} > 0$ and $E\{q\} < p^*$. Therefore the correct reward function has the property:

$$E\{f(\rho, q)\} > 0 \qquad \text{if } E\{\rho\} > 0 \text{ and } E\{q\} < p^* \qquad (8)$$

The point of the example is that an $f(\cdot)$ satisfying (8) requires prior knowledge about the distributions of the revenue and the QoS as a function of the state. Even if it were possible

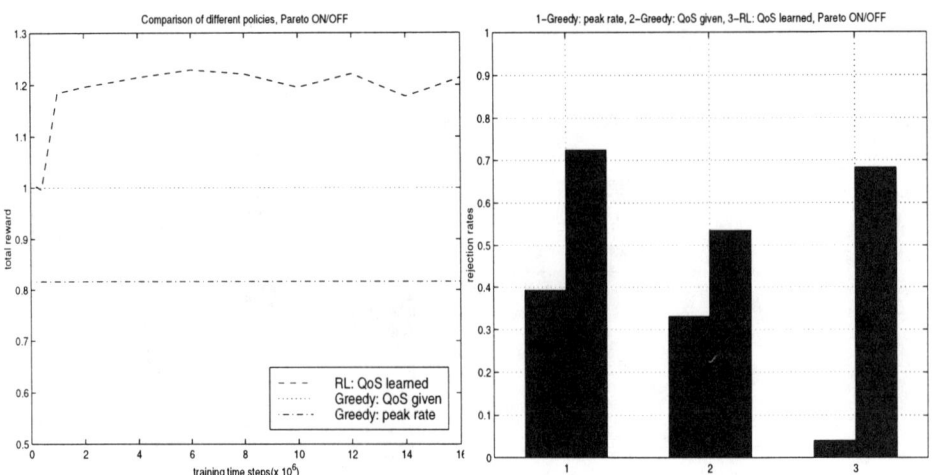

Figure 3: Comparison of total rewards of RL while learning QoS, greedy policy and peak rate allocation, normalized by the greedy total reward – Pareto ON/OFF.

Figure 4: Comparison of rejection ratios for the policies learned in Fig. 3.

for this example, setting up constraints such as (8) for a real problem with a huge state space would be non-trivial because p and q are functions of the many state and action pairs.

References

[1] Boyan, J.A., Littman, M.L., "Packet routing in dynamically changing networks: a reinforcement learning approach," in Cowan, J.D., et al., ed. *Advances in NIPS 6*, Morgan Kauffman, SF, 1994. pp. 671–678.

[2] Brown, T.X, "Adaptive Access Control Applied to Ethernet Data," *Advances in NIPS 9*, ed. M. Mozer et al., MIT Press, 1997. pp. 932–938.

[3] Brown, T.X, "Adaptive Statistical Multiplexing for Broadband Communications," Invited Tutorial *Fifth IFIP Workshop on Performance Modeling & Evaluation of ATM Networks*, Ilkley, U.K., July, 1997.

[4] Gabor, Z., Kalmar, Z., Szepesvari, C., "Multi-criteria Reinforcement Learning," to appear in *International Conference on Machine Learning*, Madison, WI, July, 1998.

[5] Hiramatsu, A., "ATM Communications Network Control by Neural Networks," *IEEE T. on Neural Networks*, v. 1, n. 1, pp. 122–130, 1990.

[6] Marbach, P., Mihatsch, O., Schulte, M., Tsitsiklis, J.N., "Reinforcement learning for call admission control and routing in integrated service networks," in Jordan, M., et al., ed. *Advances in NIPS 10*, MIT Press, 1998.

[7] Nie, J., Haykin, S., "A Q-learning based dynamic channel assignment technique for mobile communication systems," to appear in *IEEE T. on Vehicular Technology*.

[8] Singh, S.P., Bertsekas, D.P., "Reinforcement learning for dynamic channel allocation in cellular telephone systems," in *Advances in NIPS 9*, ed. Mozer, M., et al., MIT Press, 1997. pp. 974–980.

Viewing Classifier Systems as Model Free Learning in POMDPs

Akira Hayashi and Nobuo Suematsu
Faculty of Information Sciences
Hiroshima City University
3-4-1 Ozuka-higashi, Asaminami-ku, Hiroshima, 731-3194 Japan
{akira,suematsu}@im.hiroshima-cu.ac.jp

Abstract

Classifier systems are now viewed disappointing because of their problems such as the rule strength vs rule set performance problem and the credit assignment problem. In order to solve the problems, we have developed a hybrid classifier system: GLS (Generalization Learning System). In designing GLS, we view CSs as model free learning in POMDPs and take a hybrid approach to finding the best generalization, given the total number of rules. GLS uses the policy improvement procedure by Jaakkola et al. for an locally optimal stochastic policy when a set of rule conditions is given. GLS uses GA to search for the best set of rule conditions.

1 INTRODUCTION

Classifier systems (CSs) (Holland 1986) have been among the most used in reinforcement learning. Some of the advantages of CSs are (1) they have a built-in feature (the use of don't care symbols "#") for input generalization, and (2) the complexity of policies can be controlled by restricting the number of rules. In spite of these attractive features, CSs are now viewed somewhat disappointing because of their problems (Wilson and Goldberg 1989; Westerdale 1997). Among them are the rule strength vs rule set performance problem, the definition of the rule strength parameter, and the credit assignment (BBA vs PSP) problem.

In order to solve the problems, we have developed a hybrid classifier system: GLS (Generalization Learning System). GLS is based on the recent progress of RL research in partially observable Markov decision processes (POMDPs). In POMDPs, the environments are really Markovian, but the agent cannot identify the state from the current observation. It may be due to noisy sensing or *perceptual aliasing*. Perceptual aliasing occurs when the sensor returns the same observation in multiple states. Note that even for a completely observable

MDP, the use of don't care symbols for input generalization will make the process as if it were partially observable.

In designing GLS, we view CSs as RL in POMDPs and take a hybrid approach to finding the best generalization, given the total number of rules. GLS uses the policy improvement procedure in Jaakkola et al. (1994) for an locally optimal stochastic policy when a set of rule conditions is given. GLS uses GA to search for the best set of rule conditions.

The paper is organized as follows. Since CS problems are easier to understand from GLS perspective, we introduce Jaakkola et al. (1994), propose GLS, and then discuss CS problems.

2 LEARNING IN POMDPS

Jaakkola et al. (1994) consider POMDPs with perceptual aliasing and memoryless stochastic policies. Following the authors, let us call the observations *messages*. Therefore, a policy is a mapping from messages to probability distributions (PDs) over the actions.

Given a policy π, the value of a state s, $V^\pi(s)$, is defined for POMDPs just as for MDPs. Then, the value of a message m under policy π, $V^\pi(m)$, can be defined as follows:

$$V^\pi(m) = \sum_{s \in S} P^\pi(s|m) V^\pi(s) \tag{1}$$

where $P^\pi(s|m)$ is the probability that the state is s when the message is m under the policy π.

Then, the following holds.

$$V^\pi(s) = \lim_{N \to \infty} \sum_{t=1}^{N} E\{R(s_t, a_t) - \overline{R} \mid s_1 = s\} \tag{2}$$

$$V^\pi(m) = E\{V(s) \mid s \to m\} \tag{3}$$

where s_t and a_t refer to the state and the action taken at the tth step respectively, $R(s_t, a_t)$ is the immediate reward at the tth step, $\overline{R}$ is the (unknown) gain (i.e. the average reward per step). $s \to m$ refers to all the instances where m is observed in s and $E\{\cdot \mid s \to m\}$ is a Monte-Carlo expectation.

In order to compute $E\{V(s) \mid s \to m\}$, Jaakkola et al. showed a Monte-Carlo procedure:

$$\begin{aligned} V_t^\pi(m) = \frac{1}{k} \{ \quad & R_{t_1} & +\Gamma_{1,1} R_{t_1+1} + \Gamma_{1,2} R_{t_1+2} + \cdots + \Gamma_{1,t-t_1} R_t \\ + \; & R_{t_2} & +\Gamma_{2,1} R_{t_2+1} + \Gamma_{2,2} R_{t_2+2} + \cdots + \Gamma_{2,t-t_2} R_t \\ & \vdots & \\ + \; & R_{t_k} & +\Gamma_{k,1} R_{t_k+1} + \cdots + \Gamma_{k,t-t_k} R_t \} \end{aligned} \tag{4}$$

where t_k denotes the time step corresponding to the kth occurrence of the message m, $R_t = R(s_t, a_t) - \overline{R}$ for every t, $\Gamma_{k,T}$ indicates the discounting at the Tth step in the kth sequence. By estimating $\overline{R}$ and by suitably setting $\Gamma_{k,T}$, $V_t^\pi(m)$ converges to $V^\pi(m)$. $Q^\pi(m, a)$, Q-value of the message m for the action a under the policy π, is also defined and computed in the same way.

Jaakkola et al. have developed a policy improvement method:

Step 1 Evaluate the current policy π by computing $V^\pi(m)$ and $Q^\pi(m, a)$ for each m and a.

Step 2 Test for any m whether $\max_a Q^\pi(m,a) > V^\pi(m)$ holds. If *not*, then return π.
Step 3 For each m and a, define $\pi^1(a|m)$ as follows:
$\pi^1(a|m) = 1.0$ when $a = argmax_a Q^\pi(m,a)$, $\pi^1(a|m) = 0.0$ otherwise.
Then, define π^ϵ as $\pi^\epsilon(a|m) = (1-\epsilon)\pi(a|m) + \epsilon\pi^1(a|m)$
Step 4 Set the new policy as $\pi = \pi^\epsilon$, and goto Step1.

3 GLS

Each rule in GLS consists of a condition part, an action part, and an evaluation part: $Rule = (Condition, Action, Evaluation)$. The condition part is a string c over the alphabet $\{0, 1, \#\}$, and is compared with a binary sensor message. $\#$ is a don't care symbol, and matches 0 and 1. When the condition c matches the message, the action is randomly selected using the PD in the action part: $Action = (p(a_1|c), p(a_2|c), \ldots, p(a_{|A|}|c))$, $\sum_{j=1}^{|A|} p(a_j|c) = 1.0$ where $|A|$ is the total number of actions. The evaluation part records the value of the condition $V(c)$ and the Q-values of the condition action pairs $Q(c,a)$: $Evaluation = (V(c), Q(c, a_1), Q(c, a_2), \ldots, Q(c, a_{|A|}))$. Each *rule set* consists of N rules, $\{Rule_1, Rule_2, \ldots, Rule_N\}$. N, the total number of rules in a rule set, is a design parameter to control the complexity of policies. All the rules except the last one are called *standard* rules. The last rule $Rule_N$ is a special rule which is called the *default* rule. The condition part of the default rule is a string of $\#$'s and matches any message.

Learning in GLS proceeds as follows: (1)Initialization: randomly generate an initial population of M rule sets, (2)Policy Evaluation and Improvement: for each rule set, repeat a policy evaluation and improvement cycle for a suboptimal policy, then, record the gain of the policy for each rule set, (3)Genetic Algorithm: use the gain of each rule set as its fitness measure and produce a new generation of rule sets, (4) Repeat: repeat from the policy evaluation and improvement step with the new generation of rule sets.

In (2)Policy Evaluation and Improvement, GLS repeats the following cycle for each rule set.

Step 1 Set ϵ sufficiently small. Set t^{max} sufficiently large.
Step 2 Repeat for $1 \leq t \leq t^{max}$.

1. Make an observation of the environment and receive a message m_t from the sensor.
2. From all the rules whose condition matches the message m_t, find the rule whose condition is the most *specific*[1]. Let us call the rule the *active* rule.
3. Select the next action a_t randomly according to the PD in the action part of the active rule, execute the action, and receive the reward $R(s_t, a_t)$ from the environment. (The state s_t is not observable.)
4. Update the current estimate of the gain $\overline{R}$ from its previous estimate and $R(s_t, a_t)$. Let $R_t = R(s_t, a_t) - \overline{R}$. For each rule, consider its condition c_i as (a generalization of) a message, and update its evaluation part $V(c_i)$ and $Q(c_i, a)(a \in A)$ using Eq.(4).

Step 3 Check whether the following holds. If *not*, exit.
$\exists i(1 \leq i \leq N), \quad \max_a Q(c_i, a) > V(c_i)$
Step 4 Improve the current policy according to the method in the previous section, and update the action part of the corresponding rules and goto Step 2.

---
[1] The most specific rule has the least number of $\#$'s. This is intended only for saving the number of rules.

GLS extracts the condition parts of all the rules in a rule set and concatenates them to form a string. The string will be an individual to be manipulated by the genetic algorithm (GA). The genetic algorithm used in GLS is a fairly standard one. GLS combines the SGA (the simple genetic algorithm) (Goldberg 1989) with the elitist keeping strategy. The SGA is composed of three genetic operators: selection, crossover, and mutation. The fitness proportional selection and the single-point crossover are used. The three operators are applied to an entire population at each generation. Since the original SGA does not consider #'s in the rule conditions, we modified SGA as follows. When GLS randomly generates an initial population of rule sets, it generates # at each allele position in rule conditions according to the probability $P_\#$.

4 CS PROBLEMS AND GLS

In the history of classifier systems, there were two quite different approaches: the Michigan approach (Holland and Reitman 1978), and the Pittsburgh (Pitt) approach (DeJong 1988). In the Michigan approach, each rule is considered as an individual and the rule set as the population in GA. Each rule has its strength parameter, which is based on its future payoff and is used as the fitness measure in GA. These aspects of the approach cause many problems. One is the rule strength vs rule set performance problem. Can we collect only strong rules and get the best rule set performance? Not necessarily. A strong rule may cooperate with weak rules to increase its payoff. Then, how can we define and compute the strength parameter for the best rule set performance? In spite of its problems, this approach is now so much more popular than the other, that when people simply say classifier systems, they refer to Michigan type classifier systems. In the Pitt approach, the problems of the Michigan approach are avoided by requiring GA to evaluate a whole rule set. In the approach, a rule set is considered as an individual and multiple rule sets are kept as the population. The problem of the Pitt approach is its computational difficulties.

GLS can be considered as a combination of the Michigan and Pitt approaches. GA in GLS works as that in the Pitt approach. It evaluates a total rule set, and completely avoids the rule strength vs rule set performance problem in the Michigan approach. As the Michigan type CSs, GLS evaluates each rule to improve the policy. This alleviates the computational burden in the Pitt approach. Moreover, GLS evaluates each rule in a more formal and sound way than the Michigan approach. The values, $V(c)$, and $Q(c, a)$, are defined on the basis of POMDPs, and the policy improvement procedure using the values is guaranteed to find a local maximum.

Westerdale (1997) has recently made an excellent analysis of problematic behaviors of Michigan type CSs. Two popular methods for credit assignment in CSs are the bucket brigade algorithm (BBA) (Holland 1986) and the profit sharing plan (PSP) (Grefenstette 1988). Westerdale shows that BBA does not work in POMDPs. He insists that PSP with infinite time span is necessary for the right credit assignment, although he does not show how to carry out the computation. GLS does not use BBA or PSP. GLS uses the Monte Carlo procedure, Eq.(4), to compute the value of each condition action pair. The series in Eq.(4) is slow to converge. But, this is the cost we have to pay for the right credit assignment in POMDPs. Westerdale points out another CS problem. He claims that a distinction must be made between the *availability* and the payoff of rules. We agree with him. As he says, if the expected payoff of Rule 1 is twice as much as Rule 2, then we want to *always* choose Rule 1. GLS makes the distinction. The probability of a stochastic policy $\pi(a|c)$ in GLS corresponds to the availability, and the value of a condition action pair $Q(c, a)$ corresponds to the payoff.

Samuel System (Grefenstette et al. 1990) can also be considered as a combination of the Michigan and Pitt approaches. Samuel is a highly sophisticated system which has lots of features. We conjecture, however, that Samuel is not free from the CS problems which

Westerdale has analyzed. This is because Samuel uses PSP for credit assignment, and Samuel uses the payoff of each rule for action selection, and does not make a distinction between the availability and the payoff of rules.

XCS (Wilson 1995) seems to be an exceptionally reliable Michigan-type CS. In XCS, each rule's fitness is based *not* on its future payoff *but* on the prediction accuracy of its future payoff (XCS uses BBA for credit assignment). Wilson reports that XCS's population tends to form a complete and accurate mapping from sensor messages and actions to payoff predictions. We conjecture that XCS tries to build the most general Markovian model of the environment. Therefore, it will be difficult to apply XCS when the environment is not Markovian, or when we cannot afford the number of rules enough to build a Markovian model of the environment, even if the environment itself is Markovian. As we will see in the next section, GLS is intended exactly for these situations.

Kaelbling et al. (1996) surveys methods for input generalization when reward is delayed. The methods use a function approximator to represent the value function by mapping a state description to a value. Since they use value iteration or Q-learning anyway, it is difficult to apply the methods when the generalization violates the Markov assumption and induces a POMDP.

5 EXPERIMENTS

We have tested GLS with some of the representative problems in CS literature. Fig. 1 shows Gref1 world (Grefenstette 1987). In Gref1 world, we used GLS to find the smallest rule set which is necessary for the optimal performance. Since this is not a POMDP but an MDP, the optimal policy can easily be learned when we have a corresponding rule for each of the 16 states. However, when the total number of rules is less than that of states, the environment looks like a POMDP to the learning agent, even if the environment itself is an MDP. The graph shows how the gain of the best rule set in the population changes with the generation. We can see from the figure that four rules are enough for the optimal performance. Also note that the saving of the rules is achieved by selecting the most specific matching rule as an active rule. The rule set with this rule selection is called the *default hierarchy* in CS literature.

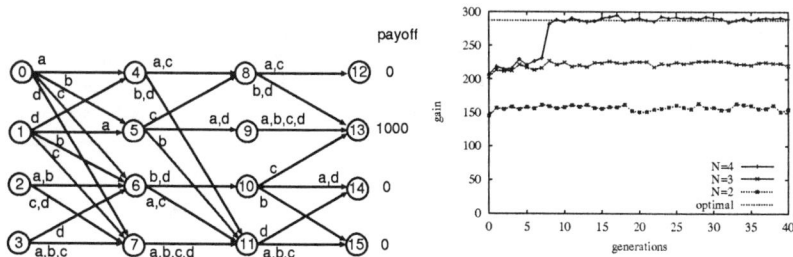

Figure 1: LEFT: GREF1 World. States $\{0, 1, 2, 3\}$ are the start states and states $\{12, 13, 14, 15\}$ are the end states. In each state, the agent gets the state number (4 bits) as a message, and chooses an action a,b,c, or d. When the agent reaches the end states, he receives reward 1000 in state 13, but reward 0 in other states. Then the agent is put in one of the start states with equal probability. We added 10% action errors to make the process ergodic. When an action error occurs, the agent moves to one of the 16 states with equal probability.
RIGHT: Gain of the best rule set. Parameters: $t^{max} = 10000, \epsilon = 0.10, M = 10, N = 2, 3, 4, P_\# = 0.33$. For $N = 4$, the best rule set at the 40th generation was { if 0101 (State 5) then a 1.0, if 1010 (State 10) then c 1.0, if ##11 (States 3,7,11,15) then d 1.0, if #### (Default Rule) then b 1.0}.

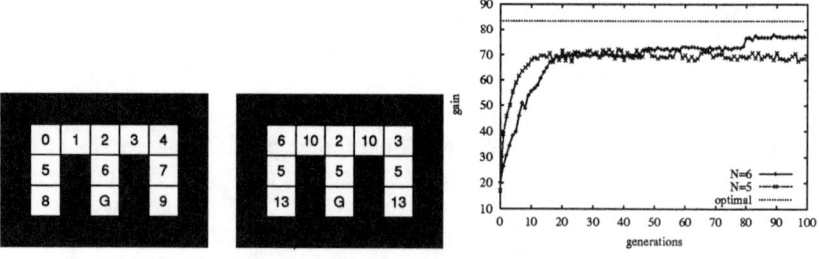

Figure 2: LEFT: McCallum's Maze. We show the state numbers in the left, and the messages in the right. States 8 and 9 are the start states, and state G is the goal state. In each state, the agent receives a sensor message which is 4 bit long, Each bit in the message tells whether a wall exists in each of the four directions. From each state, the agent moves to one of the adjacent states. When the agent reaches the goal state, he receives reward 1000. The agent is then put in one of the start states with equal probability.
RIGHT: Gain of the best rule set. Parameters: $t^{max} = 50000, \epsilon = 0.10, M = 10, N = 5, 6, P_\# = 0.33$.

Fig. 2 is a POMDP known as as McCallum's Maze (McCallum 1993). Thanks to the use of stochastic policies, GLS achieves near optimal gain for memoryless policies. Note that no memoryless deterministic policy can take the agent to the goal for this problem.

We have seen GLS's generalization capability for an MDP in Gref1 World, the advantage of stochastic policies for a POMDP in McCallum's maze. In Woods7 (Wilson 1994), we attempt to test GLS's generalization capability for a POMDP. See Fig. 3. Since each sensor message is 16 bit long, and the conditions of GLS rules can have either 0,1,or # for each of the 16 bits, there are 3^{16} possible conditions in total. When we notice that there are only 92 different actual sensor messages in the environment, it seems quite difficult to discover them only by using GA. In fact, when we ran GLS for the first time, the standard rules very rarely matched the messages and the default rule took over most of the time. In order to avoid the no matching rule problem, we made the number of rules in a rule set large ($N = 100$), increased $P_\#$ from 0.33 in the previous problems to 0.70.

The problem was independently attacked by other methods. Wilson applied his ZCS, zeroth level classifier system, to Woods7 (Wilson 1994). The gain was 0.20. ZCS has a special covering procedure to turn around the no matching rule problem. The covering procedure generates a rule which matches a message when none of the current rules matches the message. We expect further improvement on the gain, if we equip GLS with some covering procedure.

6 SUMMARY

In order to solve the CS problems such as the rule strength vs rule set performance problem and the credit assignment problem, we have developed a hybrid classifier system: GLS. We notice that generalization often leads to state aliasing. Therefore, in designing GLS, we view CSs as model free learning in POMDPs and take a hybrid approach to finding the best generalization, given the total number of rules. GLS uses the policy improvement procedure by Jaakkola et al. for an locally optimal stochastic policy when a set of rule conditions is given. GLS uses GA to search for the best set of rule conditions.

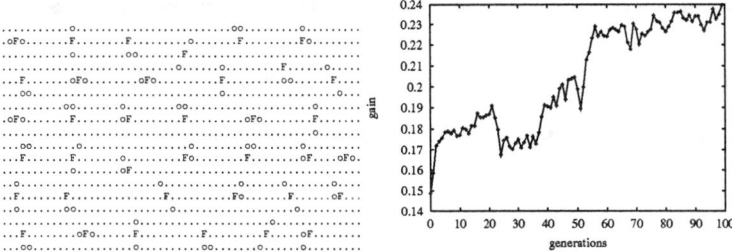

Figure 3: LEFT: Woods7.Each cell is either empty ".", contains a stone "o", or contains food "F". The cells which contain a stone are not passable, and the cells which contain food are goals. In each cell, the agent receives a $2 * 8 = 16$ bit long sensor message, which tells the contents of the eight adjacent cells. From each cell, the agent can move to one of the eight adjacent cells. When the agent reaches a cell which contains food, he receives reward 1. The agent is then put in one of the empty cells with equal probability.
RIGHT:Gain of the best rule set. Parameters: $t^{max} = 10000, \epsilon = 0.10, M = 10, N = 100, P_\# = 0.70$.

References

DeJong, K. A. (1988). Learning with genetic algorithms: An overview. *Machine Learning*, 3:121–138.

Goldberg, D. E. (1989). *Genetic Algorithms in Search, Optimization, and Machine Learning*. Addison-Wesley.

Grefenstette, J. J. (1987). Multilevel credit assignment in a genetic learning system. In *Proc. Second Int. Conf. on Genetic Algorithms*, pp. 202–209.

Grefenstette, J. J. (1988). Credit assignment in rule discovery systems based on genetic algorithms. *Machine Learning*, 3:225–245.

Grefenstette, J. J., C. L. Ramsey, and A. C. Schultz (1990). Learning sequential decision rules using simulation and competition. *Machine Learning*, 5:355–381.

Holland, J. H. (1986). Escaping brittleness: the possibilities of general purpose learning algorithms applied to parallel rule-based systems. In *Machine Learning II*, pp. 593–623. Morgan Kaufmann.

Holland, J. H. and J. S. Reitman (1978). Cognitive systems based on adaptive algorithms. In D. A. Waterman and F. Hayes-Roth (Eds.), *Pattern-directed inference systems*. Academic Press.

Jaakkola, T., S. P. Singh, and M. I. Jordan (1994). Reinforcement learning algorithm for partially observable markov decision problems. In *Advances of Neural Information Processing Systems 7*, pp. 345–352.

Kaelbling, L. P., M. L. Littman, and A. W. Moore (1996). Reinforcement learning: A survey. *Journal of Artificial Intelligence Research*, 4:237–285.

McCallum, R. A. (1993). Overcoming incomplete perception with utile distinction memory. In *Proc. the Tenth Int. Conf. on Machine Learning*, pp. 190–196.

Westerdale, T. H. (1997). Classifier systems - no wonder they don't work. In *Proc. Second Annual Genetic Programming Conference*, pp. 529–537.

Wilson, S. W. (1994). Zcs: A zeroth order classifier system. *Evolutionary Computation*, 2(1):1–18.

Wilson, S. W. (1995). Classifier fitness based on accuracy. *Evolutionary Computation*, 3(2):149–175.

Wilson, S. W. and D. E. Goldberg (1989). A critical review of classifier systems. In *Proc. Third Int. Conf. on Genetic Algorithms*, pp. 244–255.

Finite-Sample Convergence Rates for Q-Learning and Indirect Algorithms

Michael Kearns and Satinder Singh
AT&T Labs
180 Park Avenue
Florham Park, NJ 07932
{mkearns,baveja}@research.att.com

Abstract

In this paper, we address two issues of long-standing interest in the reinforcement learning literature. First, what kinds of performance guarantees can be made for Q-learning after only a finite number of actions? Second, what quantitative comparisons can be made between Q-learning and model-based (indirect) approaches, which use experience to estimate next-state distributions for off-line value iteration?

We first show that both Q-learning and the indirect approach enjoy rather rapid convergence to the optimal policy as a function of the number of state transitions observed. In particular, on the order of only $(N \log(1/\epsilon)/\epsilon^2)(\log(N) + \log\log(1/\epsilon))$ transitions are sufficient for both algorithms to come within ϵ of the optimal policy, in an idealized model that assumes the observed transitions are "well-mixed" throughout an N-state MDP. Thus, the two approaches have roughly the same sample complexity. Perhaps surprisingly, this sample complexity is far less than what is required for the model-based approach to actually construct a good approximation to the next-state distribution. The result also shows that the amount of memory required by the model-based approach is closer to N than to N^2.

For either approach, to remove the assumption that the observed transitions are well-mixed, we consider a model in which the transitions are determined by a fixed, arbitrary exploration policy. Bounds on the number of transitions required in order to achieve a desired level of performance are then related to the stationary distribution and mixing time of this policy.

1 Introduction

There are at least two different approaches to learning in Markov decision processes: *indirect* approaches, which use control experience (observed transitions and payoffs) to estimate a model, and then apply dynamic programming to compute policies from the estimated model; and *direct* approaches such as Q-learning [2], which use control experience to directly learn policies (through value functions) without ever explicitly estimating a model. Both are known to converge *asymptotically* to the optimal policy [1, 3]. However, little is known about the performance of these two approaches after only a finite amount of experience.

A common argument offered by proponents of direct methods is that it may require much more experience to learn an accurate model than to simply learn a good policy. This argument is predicated on the seemingly reasonable assumption that an indirect method must first learn an accurate model in order to compute a good policy. On the other hand, proponents of indirect methods argue that such methods can do unlimited off-line computation on the estimated model, which may give an advantage over direct methods, at least if the model is accurate. Learning a good model may also be useful across tasks, permitting the computation of good policies for multiple reward functions [4]. To date, these arguments have lacked a formal framework for analysis and verification.

In this paper, we provide such a framework, and use it to derive the first finite-time convergence rates (sample size bounds) for both Q-learning and the standard indirect algorithm. An important aspect of our analysis is that we *separate* the quality of the policy generating experience from the quality of the two learning algorithms. In addition to demonstrating that both methods enjoy rather rapid convergence to the optimal policy as a function of the amount of control experience, the convergence rates have a number of specific and perhaps surprising implications for the hypothetical differences between the two approaches outlined above. Some of these implications, as well as the rates of convergence we derive, were briefly mentioned in the abstract; in the interests of brevity, we will not repeat them here, but instead proceed directly into the technical material.

2 MDP Basics

Let M be an unknown N-state MDP with A actions. We use $P_M^a(ij)$ to denote the probability of going to state j, given that we are in state i and execute action a; and $R_M^a(i)$ to denote the reward received for executing a from i (which we assume is fixed and bounded between 0 and 1 without loss of generality). A policy π assigns an action to each state. The value of state i under policy π, $V_M^\pi(i)$, is the expected discounted sum of rewards received upon starting in state i and executing π forever: $V_M^\pi(i) = \mathbf{E}_\pi[r_1 + \gamma r_2 + \gamma^2 r_3 + \cdots]$, where r_t is the reward received at time step t under a random walk governed by π from start state i, and $0 \leq \gamma < 1$ is the discount factor. It is also convenient to define values for state-action pairs (i,a): $Q_M^\pi(i,a) = R_M^a(i) + \gamma \sum_j P_M^a(ij) V_M^\pi(j)$. The goal of learning is to approximate the optimal policy π^* that maximizes the value at every state; the optimal value function is denoted Q_M^*. Given Q_M^*, we can compute the optimal policy as $\pi^*(i) = \mathrm{argmax}_a\{Q_M^*(i,a)\}$.

If M is given, *value iteration* can be used to compute a good approximation to the optimal value function. Setting our initial guess as $Q_0(i,a) = 0$ for all (i,a), we iterate as follows:

$$Q_{\ell+1}(i,a) = R_M^a(i) + \gamma \sum_j [P_M^a(ij) V_\ell(j)] \qquad (1)$$

where we define $V_\ell(j) = \max_b\{Q_\ell(j,b)\}$. It can be shown that after ℓ iterations, $\max_{(i,a)}\{|Q_\ell(i,a) - Q_M^*(i,a)|\} \leq \gamma^\ell$. Given any approximation Q to Q_M^* we can compute the greedy approximation π to the optimal policy π^* as $\pi(i) = \mathrm{argmax}_a\{Q(i,a)\}$.

3 The Parallel Sampling Model

In reinforcement learning, the transition probabilities $P_M^a(ij)$ are not given, and a good policy must be *learned* on the basis of observed experience (transitions) in M. Classical convergence results for algorithms such as Q-learning [1] implicitly assume that the observed experience is generated by an *arbitrary* "exploration policy" π, and then proceed to prove convergence to the optimal policy *if* π meets certain minimal conditions — namely, π must try every state-action pair infinitely often, with probability 1. This approach conflates two distinct issues: the quality of the exploration policy π, and the quality of reinforcement learning algorithms using experience generated by π. In contrast, we choose to separate these issues. If the exploration policy never or only very rarely visits some state-action pair, we would like to have this reflected as a factor in our bounds that depends *only on* π; a separate factor depending *only on the learning algorithm* will in turn reflect how efficiently a particular learning algorithm uses the experience generated by π. Thus, for a fixed π, all learning algorithms are placed on equal footing, and can be directly compared.

There are probably various ways in which this separation can be accomplished; we now introduce one that is particularly clean and simple. We would like a model of the *ideal* exploration policy — one that produces experiences that are "well-mixed", in the sense that every state-action pair is tried with equal frequency. Thus, let us define a *parallel sampling* subroutine PS(M) that behaves as follows: a *single* call to PS(M) returns, for *every* state-action pair (i,a), a random next state j distributed according to $P_M^a(ij)$. Thus, every state-action pair is executed simultaneously, and the resulting $N \times A$ next states are reported. A single call to PS(M) is therefore really simulating $N \times A$ transitions in M, and we must be careful to multiply the number of calls to PS(M) by this factor if we wish to count the *total* number of transitions witnessed.

What is PS(M) modeling? It is modeling the idealized exploration policy that manages to visit every state-action pair in succession, without duplication, and without fail. It should be intuitively obvious that such an exploration policy would be optimal, from the viewpoint of gathering experience everywhere as rapidly as possible.

We shall first provide an analysis, in Section 5, of both direct and indirect reinforcement learning algorithms, in a setting in which the observed experience is generated by calls to PS(M). Of course, in any given MDP M, there may not be *any* exploration policy that meets the ideal captured by PS(M) — for instance, there may simply be some states that are very difficult for any policy to reach, and thus the experience generated by any policy will certainly not be equally mixed around the entire MDP. (Indeed, a call to PS(M) will typically return a set of transitions that does not even correspond to a trajectory in M.) Furthermore, even if PS(M) could be simulated by *some* exploration policy, we would like to provide more general results that express the amount of experience required for reinforcement learning algorithms under *any* exploration policy (where the amount of experience will, of course, depend on properties of the exploration policy).

Thus, in Section 6, we sketch how one can bound the amount of experience required under any π in order to simulate calls to PS(M). (More detail will be provided in a longer version of this paper.) The bound depends on natural properties of π, such as its stationary distribution and mixing time. Combined with the results of Section 5, we get the desired two-factor bounds discussed above: for both the direct and indirect approaches, a bound on the total number of transitions required, consisting of one factor that depends only on the algorithm, and another factor that depends only on the exploration policy.

4 The Learning Algorithms

We now explicitly state the two reinforcement learning algorithms we shall analyze and compare. In keeping with the separation between algorithms and exploration policies already discussed, we will phrase these algorithms in the parallel sampling framework, and Section 6 indicates how they generalize to the case of arbitrary exploration policies. We begin with the direct approach.

Rather than directly studying standard Q-learning, we will here instead examine a variant that is slightly easier to analyze, and is called *phased* Q-learning. However, we emphasize that *all of our results can be generalized to apply to standard Q-learning* (with learning rate $\alpha(i,a) = \frac{1}{t(i,a)}$, where $t(i,a)$ is the number of trials of (i,a) so far). Basically, rather than updating the value function with *every* observed transition from (i,a), phased Q-learning estimates the expected value of the next state from (i,a) on the basis of *many* transitions, and only then makes an update. The memory requirements for phased Q-learning are essentially the same as those for standard Q-learning.

Direct Algorithm — Phased Q-Learning: As suggested by the name, the algorithm operates in phases. In each phase, the algorithm will make m_D calls to PS(M) (where m_D will be determined by the analysis), thus gathering m_D trials of every state-action pair (i,a). At the ℓth phase, the algorithm updates the estimated value function as follows: for every (i,a),

$$\widehat{Q}_{\ell+1}(i,a) = R^a_M(i) + \gamma \frac{1}{m_D} \sum_{k=1}^{m_D} \widehat{V}_\ell(j^\ell_k) \qquad (2)$$

where $j^\ell_1, \ldots, j^\ell_{m_D}$ are the m_D next states observed from (i,a) on the m_D calls to PS(M) during the ℓth phase. The policy computed by the algorithm is then the greedy policy determined by the final value function. Note that phased Q-learning is quite like standard Q-learning, except that we gather statistics (the summation in Equation (2)) before making an update.

We now proceed to describe the standard indirect approach.

Indirect Algorithm: The algorithm first makes m_I calls to PS(M) to obtain m_I next state samples for each (i,a). It then builds an empirical model of the transition probabilities as follows: $\widehat{P}^a_M(ij) = \frac{\#(i \to_a j)}{m_I}$, where $\#(i \to_a j)$ is the number of times state j was reached on the m_I trials of (i,a). The algorithm then does value iteration (as described in Section 2) on the fixed model $\widehat{P}^a_M(ij)$ for ℓ_I phases. Again, the policy computed by the algorithm is the greedy policy dictated by the final value function.

Thus, in phased Q-learning, the algorithm runs for some number ℓ_D phases, and *each phase* requires m_D calls to PS(M), for a total number of transitions $\ell_D \times m_D \times N \times A$. The direct algorithm first makes m_I calls to PS(M), and then runs ℓ_I phases of value iteration (which requires no additional data), for a total number of transitions $m_I \times N \times A$. The question we now address is: how large must m_D, m_I, ℓ_D, ℓ_I be so that, with probability at least $1-\delta$, the resulting policies have expected return within ϵ of the optimal policy in M? The answers we give yield perhaps surprisingly similar bounds on the total number of transitions required for the two approaches in the parallel sampling model.

5 Bounds on the Number of Transitions

We now state our main result.

Theorem 1 *For any MDP M:*

- *For an appropriate choice of the parameters m_I and and ℓ_I, the total number of calls to $\text{PS}(M)$ required by the indirect algorithm in order to ensure that, with probability at least $1 - \delta$, the expected return of the resulting policy will be within ϵ of the optimal policy, is*

$$O((1/\epsilon^2)(\log(N/\delta) + \log\log(1/\epsilon)). \tag{3}$$

- *For an appropriate choice of the parameters m_D and ℓ_D, the total number of calls to $\text{PS}(M)$ required by phased Q-learning in order to ensure that, with probability at least $1 - \delta$, the expected return of the resulting policy will be within ϵ of the optimal policy, is*

$$O((\log(1/\epsilon)/\epsilon^2)(\log(N/\delta) + \log\log(1/\epsilon)). \tag{4}$$

The bound for phased Q-learning is thus only $O(\log(1/\epsilon))$ larger than that for the indirect algorithm. Bounds on the total number of transitions witnessed in either case are obtained by multiplying the given bounds by $N \times A$.

Before sketching some of the ideas behind the proof of this result, we first discuss some of its implications for the debate on direct versus indirect approaches. First of all, for *both* approaches, convergence is rather fast: with a total number of transitions only on the order of $N \log(N)$ (fixing ϵ and δ for simplicity), near-optimal policies are obtained. This represents a considerable advance over the classical asymptotic results: instead of saying that an infinite number of visits to every state-action pair are required to converge to the optimal policy, we are claiming that a rather small number of visits are required to get close to the optimal policy. Second, by our analysis, the two approaches have similar complexities, with the number of transitions required differing by only a $\log(1/\epsilon)$ factor in favor of the indirect algorithm. Third — and perhaps surprisingly — note that since only $O(\log(N))$ calls are being made to $\text{PS}(M)$ (again fixing ϵ and δ), and since the number of trials *per state-action pair* is exactly the number of calls to $\text{PS}(M)$, the total number of non-zero entries in the model $\hat{P}_M^a(ij)$ built by the indirect approach is in fact only $O(\log(N))$. In other words, $\hat{P}_M^a(ij)$ will be extremely sparse — and thus, a terrible approximation to the true transition probabilities — yet still good enough to derive a near-optimal policy! Clever representation of $\hat{P}_M^a(ij)$ will thus result in total memory requirements that are only $O(N \log(N))$ rather than $O(N^2)$. Fourth, although we do not have space to provide any details, if instead of a single reward function, we are provided with L reward functions (where the L reward functions are given in advance of observing any experience), then for both algorithms, the number of transitions required to compute near-optimal policies for all L reward functions simultaneously is only a factor of $O(\log(L))$ greater than the bounds given above.

Our own view of the result and its implications is:

- Both algorithms enjoy rapid convergence to the optimal policy as a function of the amount of experience.
- In general, neither approach enjoys a significant advantage in convergence rate, memory requirements, or handling multiple reward functions. Both are quite efficient on all counts.

We do not have space to provide a detailed proof of Theorem 1, but instead provide some highlights of the main ideas. The proofs for both the indirect algorithm and phased Q-learning are actually quite similar, and have at their heart two slightly different *uniform convergence* lemmas. For phased Q-learning, it is possible to show that, for any bound ℓ_D on the number of phases to be executed, and for any $\tau > 0$, we can choose m_D so that

$$\left| (1/m_D) \sum_{k=1}^{m_D} \widehat{V}_\ell(j_k^\ell) - \sum_j P_{ij}^a \widehat{V}_\ell(j) \right| \leq \tau \tag{5}$$

will hold *simultaneously* for *every* (i,a) and for *every* phase $\ell = 1, \ldots, \ell_D$. In other words, at the end of every phase, the empirical estimate of the expected next-state value for every (i,a) will be close to the true expectation, where here the expectation is with respect to the current estimated value function $\widehat{V}_\ell$.

For the indirect algorithm, a slightly more subtle uniform convergence argument is required. Here we show that it is possible to choose, for any bound ℓ_I on the number of iterations of value iteration to be executed on the $\widehat{P}_M^a(ij)$, and for any $\tau > 0$, a value m_I such that

$$\left| \sum_j \widehat{P}_{ij}^a V_\ell(j) - \sum_j P_{ij}^a V_\ell(j) \right| \leq \tau \tag{6}$$

for every (i,a) and every phase $\ell = 1, \ldots, \ell_I$, where the $V_\ell(j)$ are the value functions resulting from performing *true* value iteration (that is, on the $P_M^a(ij)$). Equation (6) essentially says that expectations of the true value functions are quite similar under either the true or estimated model, even though the indirect algorithm never has access to the true value functions.

In either case, the uniform convergence results allow us to argue that the corresponding algorithms still achieve successive *contractions*, as in the classical proof of value iteration. For instance, in the case of phased Q-learning, if we define $\Delta_\ell = \max_{(i,a)}\{|\widehat{Q}_\ell(i,a) - Q_\ell(i,a)|\}$, we can derive a recurrence relation for $\Delta_{\ell+1}$ as follows:

$$|\widehat{Q}_{\ell+1}(i,a) - Q_{\ell+1}(i,a)| = \left| \gamma(1/m) \sum_{k=1}^m \widehat{V}_\ell(j_k^\ell) - \gamma \sum_j P_{ij}^a V_\ell(j) \right| \tag{7}$$

$$\leq \gamma \max_{\alpha \in \{\tau, -\tau\}} \left\{ \left| \left(\sum_j P_{ij}^a \widehat{V}_\ell(j) + \alpha \right) - \sum_j P_{ij}^a V_\ell(j) \right| \right\} \tag{8}$$

$$\leq \gamma\tau + \gamma\Delta_\ell. \tag{9}$$

Here we have made use of Equation (5). Since $\Delta_0 = 0$ ($\widehat{Q}_0 = Q_0$), this recurrence gives $\Delta_\ell \leq \tau(\gamma/(1-\gamma))$ for any ℓ. From this it is not hard to show that for any (i,a)

$$|\widehat{Q}_\ell(i,a) - Q^*(i,a)| \leq \tau(\gamma/(1-\gamma)) + \gamma^\ell. \tag{10}$$

From this it can be shown that the regret in expected return suffered by the policy computed by phased Q-Learning after ℓ phases is at most $(\tau\gamma/(1-\gamma) + \gamma^\ell)(2/(1-\gamma))$. The proof proceeds by setting this regret smaller than the desired ϵ, solving for ℓ and τ, and obtaining the resulting bound on m_D. The derivation of bounds for the indirect algorithm is similar.

6 Handling General Exploration Policies

As promised, we conclude our technical results by briefly sketching how we can translate the bounds obtained in Section 5 under the idealized parallel sampling model into bounds applicable when *any* fixed policy π is guiding the exploration. Such bounds must, of course, depend on properties of π. Due to space limitations, we can only outline the main ideas; the formal statements and proofs are deferred to a longer version of the paper.

Let us assume for simplicity that π (which may be a stochastic policy) defines an *ergodic* Markov process in the MDP M. Thus, π induces a unique *stationary distribution* $P_{M,\pi}(i,a)$ over state-action pairs — intuitively, $P_{M,\pi}(i,a)$ is the frequency of executing action a from state i during an infinite random walk in M according to π. Furthermore, we can introduce the standard notion of the *mixing time* of π to its stationary distribution — informally, this is the number T_π of steps required such that the distribution induced on state-action pairs by T_π-step walks according to π will be "very close" to $P_{M,\pi}$ [1]. Finally, let us define $\rho_\pi = \min_{(i,a)}\{P_{M,\pi}(i,a)\}$.

Armed with these notions, it is not difficult to show that the number of steps we must take under π in order to simulate, with high probability, a call to the oracle PS(M), is polynomial in the quantity T_π/ρ_π. The intuition is straightforward: at most every T_π steps, we obtain an "almost independent" draw from $P_{M,\pi}(i,a)$; and with each independent draw, we have at least probability ρ of drawing any particular (i,a) pair. Once we have sampled every (i,a) pair, we have simulated a call to PS(M). The formalization of these intuitions leads to a version of Theorem 1 applicable to any π, in which the bound is multiplied by a factor polynomial in T_π/ρ_π, as desired.

However, a better result is possible. In cases where ρ_π may be small or even 0 (which would occur when π simply does not ever execute some action from some state), the factor T_π/ρ_π is large or infinite and our bounds become weak or vacuous. In such cases, it is better to define the sub-MDP $M_\pi(\alpha)$, which is obtained from M by simply deleting any (i,a) for which $P_{M,\pi}(i,a) < \alpha$, where $\alpha > 0$ is a parameter of our choosing. In $M_\pi(\alpha)$, $\rho_\pi > \alpha$ by construction, and we may now obtain convergence rates to the optimal policy in $M_\pi(\alpha)$ for both Q-learning and the indirect approach like those given in Theorem 1, multiplied by a factor polynomial in T_π/α. (Technically, we must slightly alter the algorithms to have an initial phase that detects and eliminates small-probability state-action pairs, but this is a minor detail.) By allowing α to become smaller as the amount of experience we receive from π grows, we can obtain an "anytime" result, since the sub-MDP $M_\pi(\alpha)$ approaches the full MDP M as $\alpha \to 0$.

References

[1] Jaakkola, T., Jordan, M. I., Singh, S. On the convergence of stochastic iterative dynamic programming algorithms. *Neural Computation*, 6(6), 1185–1201, 1994.

[2] C. J. C. H. Watkins. Learning from Delayed Rewards. Ph.D. thesis, Cambridge University, 1989.

[3] R. S. Sutton and A. G. Barto. *Reinforcement Learning: An Introduction.* MIT Press, 1998.

[4] S. Mahadevan. Enhancing Transfer in Reinforcement Learning by Building Stochastic Models of Robot Actions. In *Machine Learning: Proceedings of the Ninth International Conference*, 1992.

---

[1] Formally, the degree of closeness is measured by the distance between the transient and stationary distributions. For brevity here we will simply assume this parameter is set to a very small, constant value.

Exploring Unknown Environments with Real-Time Search or Reinforcement Learning

Sven Koenig
College of Computing, Georgia Institute of Technology
skoenig@cc.gatech.edu

Abstract

Learning Real-Time A* (LRTA*) is a popular control method that interleaves planning and plan execution and has been shown to solve search problems in known environments efficiently. In this paper, we apply LRTA* to the problem of getting to a given goal location in an initially unknown environment. Uninformed LRTA* with maximal lookahead always moves on a shortest path to the closest unvisited state, that is, to the closest potential goal state. This was believed to be a good exploration heuristic, but we show that it does not minimize the worst-case plan-execution time compared to other uninformed exploration methods. This result is also of interest to reinforcement-learning researchers since many reinforcement learning methods use asynchronous dynamic programming, interleave planning and plan execution, and exhibit optimism in the face of uncertainty, just like LRTA*.

1 Introduction

Real-time (heuristic) search methods are domain-independent control methods that interleave planning and plan execution. They are based on agent-centered search [Dasgupta *et al.*, 1994; Koenig, 1996], which restricts the search to a small part of the environment that can be reached from the current state of the agent with a small number of action executions. This is the part of the environment that is immediately relevant for the agent in its current situation. The most popular real-time search method is probably the Learning Real-Time A* (LRTA*) method [Korf, 1990]. It has a solid theoretical foundation and the following advantageous properties: First, it allows for fine-grained control over how much planning to do between plan executions and thus is an any-time contract algorithm [Russell and Zilberstein, 1991]. Second, it can use heuristic knowledge to guide planning, which reduces planning time without sacrificing solution quality. Third, it can be interrupted at any state and resume execution at a different state. Fourth, it amortizes learning over several search episodes, which allows it to find plans with suboptimal plan-execution time fast and then improve the plan-execution time as it solves similar planning tasks, until its plan-execution time is optimal. Thus, LRTA* always has a small sum of planning and plan-execution

Initially, $u(s) = 0$ for all $s \in S$.

1. $s_{current} := s_{start}$.
2. If $s_{current} \in G$, then stop successfully.
3. Generate a local search space $S_{lss} \subseteq S$ with $s_{current} \in S_{lss}$ and $S_{lss} \cap G = \emptyset$.
4. Update $u(s)$ for all $s \in S_{lss}$ (Figure 2).
5. $a := $ one-of arg $\min_{a \in A(s_{current})} u(succ(s_{current}, a))$.
6. Execute action a.
7. $s_{current} := succ(s_{current}, a)$.
8. If $s_{current} \in S_{lss}$, then go to 5.
9. Go to 2.

Figure 1: Uninformed LRTA*

1. For all $s \in S_{lss}$: $u(s) := \infty$.
2. If $u(s) < \infty$ for all $s \in S_{lss}$, then return.
3. $s' := $ one-of arg $\min_{s \in S_{lss}: u(s) = \infty} \min_{a \in A(s)} u(succ(s, a))$.
4. If $\min_{a \in A(s')} u(succ(s', a)) = \infty$, then return.
5. $u(s') := 1 + \min_{a \in A(s')} u(succ(s', a))$.
6. Go to 2.

Figure 2: Value-Update Step

time, and it minimizes the plan-execution time in the long run in case similar planning tasks unexpectedly repeat. This is important since no search method that executes actions before it has solved a planning task completely can guarantee to minimize the plan-execution time right away.

Real-time search methods have been shown to be efficient alternatives to traditional search methods in known environments. In this paper, we investigate real-time search methods in unknown environments. In such environments, real-time search methods allow agents to gather information early. This information can then be used to resolve some of the uncertainty and thus reduce the amount of planning done for unencountered situations.

We study robot-exploration tasks without actuator and sensor uncertainty, where the sensors on-board the robot can uniquely identify its location and the neighboring locations. The robot does not know the map in advance, and thus has to explore its environment sufficiently to find the goal and a path to it. A variety of methods can solve these tasks, including LRTA*. The proceedings of the AAAI-97 Workshop on On-Line Search [Koenig et al., 1997] give a good overview of some of these techniques. In this paper, we study whether uninformed LRTA* is able to minimize the worst-case plan-execution time over all state spaces with the same number of states provided that its lookahead is sufficiently large. Uninformed LRTA* with maximal lookahead always moves on a shortest path to the closest unvisited state, that is, to the closest potential goal state – it exhibits optimism in the face of uncertainty [Moore and Atkeson, 1993]. We show that this exploration heuristic is not as good as it was believed to be. This solves the central problem left open in [Pemberton and Korf, 1992] and improves our understanding of LRTA*. Our results also apply to learning control for tasks other than robot exploration, for example the control tasks studied in [Davies et al., 1998]. They are also of interest to reinforcement-learning researchers since many reinforcement learning methods use asynchronous dynamic programming, interleave planning and plan execution, and exhibit optimism in the face of uncertainty, just like LRTA* [Barto et al., 1995; Kearns and Singh, 1998].

2 LRTA*

We use the following notation to describe LRTA*: S denotes the finite set of states of the environment, $s_{start} \in S$ the start state, and $\emptyset \neq G \subseteq S$ the set of goal states. The number of states is $n := |S|$. $A(s) \neq \emptyset$ is the finite, nonempty set of actions that can be executed in state $s \in S$. $succ(s, a)$ denotes the successor state that results from the execution of action $a \in A(s)$ in state $s \in S$. We also use two operators with the following semantics: Given a set X, the expression "one-of X" returns an element of X according to an arbitrary rule. A subsequent invocation of "one-of X" can return the same or a different element. The expression "arg $\min_{x \in X} f(x)$" returns the elements $x \in X$ that minimize $f(x)$, that is, the set $\{x \in X | f(x) = \min_{x' \in X} f(x')\}$.

We model environments (topological maps) as state spaces that correspond to undirected graphs, and assume that it is indeed possible to reach a goal state from the start state. We measure the distances and thus plan-execution time in action executions, which is reasonable if every action can be executed in about the same amount of time. The graph is initially unknown. The robot can always observe whether its current state is a goal state, how many actions can be executed in it, and which successor states they lead to but not whether the successor states are goal states. Furthermore, the robot can identify the successor states when it observes them again at a later point in time. This assumption is realistic, for example, if the states look sufficiently different or the robot has a global positioning system (GPS) available.

LRTA* learns a map of the environment and thus needs memory proportional to the number of states and actions observed. It associates a small amount of information with the states in its map. In particular, it associates a *u-value* $u(s)$ with each state $s \in S$. The u-values approximate the goal distances of the states. They are updated as the search progresses and used to determine which actions to execute. Figure 1 describes LRTA*: LRTA* first checks whether it has already reached a goal state and thus can terminate successfully (Line 2). If not, it generates the local search space $S_{lss} \subseteq S$ (Line 3). While we require only that the current state is part of the local search space and the goal states are not [Barto *et al.*, 1995], in practice LRTA* constructs S_{lss} by searching forward from the current state. LRTA* then updates the u-values of all states in the local search space (Line 4), as shown in Figure 2. The value-update step assigns each state its goal distance under the assumption that the u-values of all states outside of the local search space correspond to their correct goal distances. Formally, if $u(s) \in [0, \infty]$ denotes the u-values before the value-update step and $\bar{u}(s) \in [0, \infty]$ denotes the u-values afterwards, then $\bar{u}(s) = 1 + \min_{a \in A(s)} \bar{u}(succ(s, a))$ for all $s \in S_{lss}$ and $\bar{u}(s) = u(s)$ otherwise. Based on these u-values, LRTA* decides which action to execute next (Line 5). It greedily chooses the action that minimizes the u-value of the successor state (ties are broken arbitrarily) because the u-values approximate the goal distances and LRTA* attempts to decrease its goal distance as much as possible. Finally, LRTA* executes the selected action (Line 6) and updates its current state (Line 7). Then, if the new state is still part of the local search space used previously, LRTA* selects another action for execution based on the current u-values (Line 8). Otherwise, it iterates (Line 9). (The behavior of LRTA* with either minimal or maximal lookahead does not change if Line 8 is deleted.)

3 Plan-Execution Time of LRTA* for Exploration

In this section, we study the behavior of LRTA* with minimal and maximal lookaheads in unknown environments. We assume that no a-priori heuristic knowledge is available and, thus, that LRTA* is uninformed. In this case, the u-values of all unvisited states are zero and do not need to be maintained explicitly.

Minimal Lookahead: The lookahead of LRTA* is minimal if the local search space contains only the current state. LRTA* with minimal lookahead performs almost no planning between plan executions. Its behavior in initially known and unknown environments is identical. Figure 3 shows an example.

Let $gd(s)$ denote the goal distance of state s. Then, according to one of our previous results, uninformed LRTA* with any lookahead reaches a goal state after at most $\sum_{s \in S} gd(s)$ action executions [Koenig and Simmons, 1995]. Since $\sum_{s \in S} gd(s) \leq \sum_{i=0}^{n-1} i = 1/2n^2 - 1/2n$,

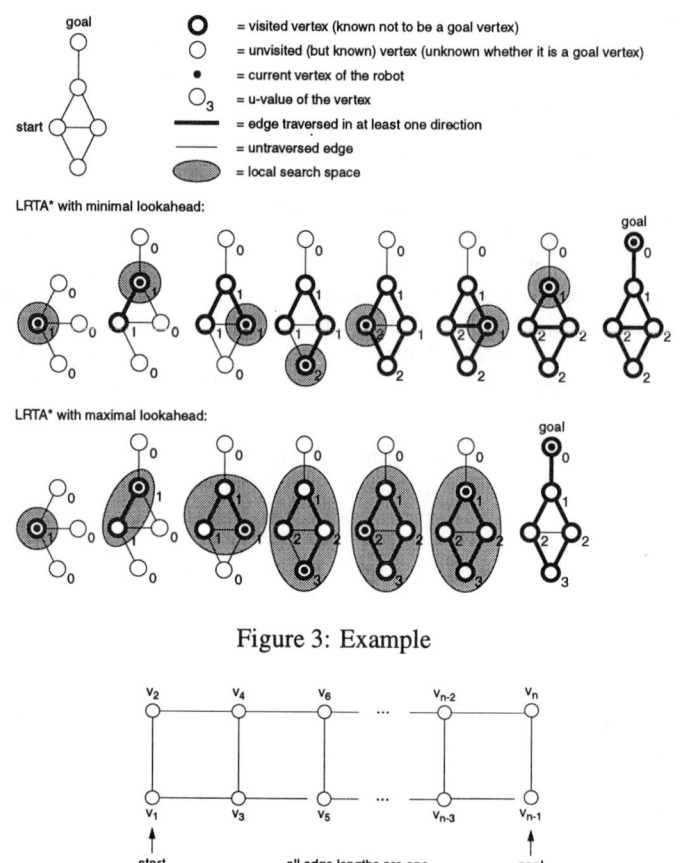

Figure 3: Example

Figure 4: A Planar Undirected Graph

uninformed LRTA* with any lookahead reaches a goal state after $O(n^2)$ action executions.

This upper bound on the plan-execution time is tight in the worst case for uninformed LRTA* with minimal lookahead, even if the number of actions that can be executed in any state is bounded from above by a small constant (here: three). Figure 4, for example, shows a rectangular grid-world for which uninformed LRTA* with minimal lookahead reaches a goal state in the worst case only after $\Theta(n^2)$ action executions. In particular, LRTA* can traverse the state sequence that is printed by the following program in pseudo code. The scope of the for-statements is shown by indentation.

```
for i := n-3 downto n/2 step 2
  for j := 1 to i step 2
    print j
  for j := i+1 downto 2 step 2
    print j
for i := 1 to n-1 step 2
  print i
```

In this case, LRTA* executes $3n^2/16 - 3/4$ actions before it reaches the goal state (for $n \geq 2$ with $n \bmod 4 = 2$). For example, for $n = 10$, it traverses the state sequence s_1, s_3, s_5, s_7, s_8, s_6, s_4, s_2, s_1, s_3, s_5, s_6, s_4, s_2, s_1, s_3, s_5, s_7, and s_9.

Maximal Lookahead: As we increase the lookahead of LRTA*, we expect that its plan-execution time tends to decrease because LRTA* uses more information to decide which

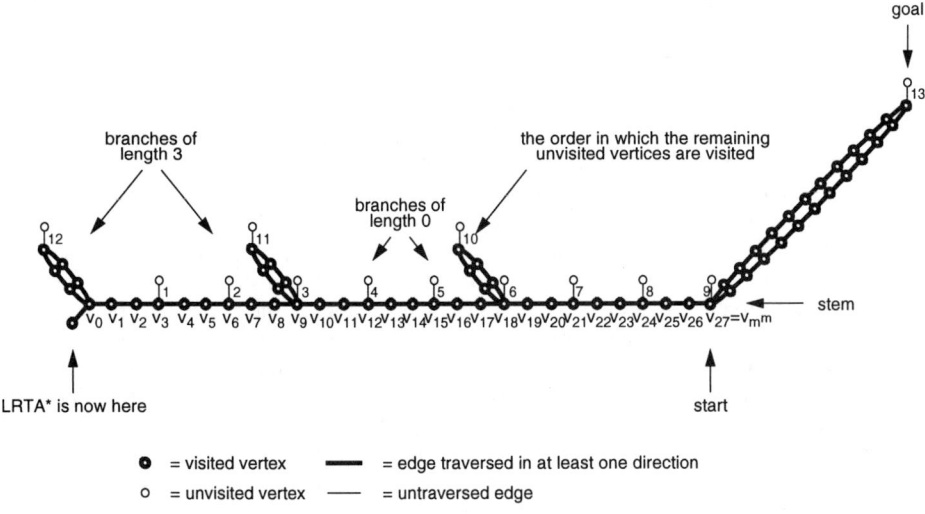

Figure 5: Another Planar Undirected Graph ($m = 3$)

action to execute next. This makes it interesting to study LRTA* with maximal lookahead.

The lookahead of LRTA* is maximal in known environments if the local search space contains all non-goal states. In this case, LRTA* performs a complete search without interleaving planning and plan execution and follows a shortest path from the start state to a closest goal state. Thus, it needs $gd(s_{start})$ action executions. No other method can do better than that.

The maximal lookahead of LRTA* is necessarily smaller in initially unknown environments than in known environments because its value-update step can only search the known part of the environment. Therefore, the lookahead of LRTA* is maximal in unknown environments if the local search space contains all *visited* non-goal states. Figure 3 shows an example.

Uninformed LRTA* with maximal lookahead always moves on a shortest path to the closest unvisited state, that is, to the closest potential goal state. This appears to be a good exploration heuristic. [Pemberton and Korf, 1992] call this behavior "incremental best-first search," but were not able to prove or disprove whether this locally optimal search strategy is also globally optimal. Since this exploration heuristic has been used on real mobile robots [Thrun et al., 1998], we study how well its plan-execution time compares to the plan-execution time of other uninformed exploration methods. We show that the worst-case plan-execution time of uninformed LRTA* with maximal lookahead in unknown environments is $\Omega(\frac{\log n}{\log \log n} n)$ action executions and thus grows faster than linearly in the number of states n. It follows that the plan-execution time of LRTA* is not optimal in the worst case, since depth-first search needs a number of action executions in the worst case that grows only linearly in the number of states.

Consider the graph shown in Figure 5, that is a variation of a graph in [Koenig and Smirnov, 1996]. It consists of a stem with several branches. Each branch consists of two parallel paths of the same length that connect the stem to a single edge. The length of the branch is the length of each of the two paths. The stem has length m^m for some integer $m \geq 3$ and consists of the vertices $v_0, v_1, \ldots, v_{m^m}$. For each integer i with $1 \leq i \leq m$ there are m^{m-i} branches of length $\sum_{j=1}^{i-1} m^j$ each (including branches of length zero). These branches attach to the stem at the vertices $v_{j\,m^i}$ for integers j; if i is even, then $0 \leq j \leq m^{m-i} - 1$, otherwise $1 \leq j \leq m^{m-i}$. There is one additional single edge that attaches to vertex v_0.

v_{m^m} is the starting vertex. The vertex at the end of the single edge of the longest branch is the goal vertex. Notice that the graph is planar. This is a desirable property since non-planar graphs are, in general, rather unrealistic models of maps.

Uninformed LRTA* with maximal lookahead can traverse the stem repeatedly forward and backward, and the resulting plan-execution time is large compared to the number of vertices that are necessary to mislead LRTA* into this behavior. In particular, LRTA* can behave as follows: It starts at vertex v_{m^m} and traverses the whole stem and all branches, excluding the single edges at their end, and finally traverses the additional edge attached to vertex v_0, as shown in Figure 5. At this point, LRTA* knows all vertices. It then traverses the whole stem, visiting the vertices at the ends of the single edges of the branches of length 0. It then switches directions and travels along the whole stem in the opposite direction, this time visiting the vertices at the end of the single edges of the branches of length m, and so forth, switching directions repeatedly. It succeeds when it finally uses the longest branch and discovers the goal vertex. To summarize, the vertices at the ends of the branches are tried out in the order indicated in Figure 5. The total number of edge traversals is $\Omega(m^{m+1})$ since the stem of length m^m is traversed $m+1$ times. To be precise, the total number of edge traversals is $(m^{m+3} + 3m^{m+2} - 8m^{m+1} + 2m^2 - m + 3)/(m^2 - 2m + 1)$. It holds that $n = \Theta(m^m)$ since $n = (3m^{m+2} - 5m^{m+1} - m^m + m^{m-1} + 2m^2 - 2m + 2)/(m^2 - 2m + 1)$. This implies that $m = \Omega(\frac{\log n}{\log \log n})$ since it holds that, for $k > 1$ and all sufficiently large m (to be precise: m with $m \geq k$)

$$\frac{\log_k(m^m)}{\log_k \log_k(m^m)} = \frac{1}{\frac{\log_k \log_k(m^m)}{\log_k(m^m)}} = \frac{1}{\frac{\log_k m + \log_k \log_k m}{m \log_k m}} = \frac{1}{\frac{1}{m} + \frac{\log_k \log_k m}{m \log_k m}} \leq \frac{1}{\frac{1}{m} + 0} = m.$$

Put together, it follows that the total number of edge traversals is $\Omega(m^{m+1}) = \Omega(m\,n) = \Omega(\frac{\log n}{\log \log n} n)$. (We also performed a simulation that confirmed our theoretical results.)

The graph from Figure 5 can be modified to cause LRTA* to behave similarly even if the assumptions of the capabilities of the robot or the environment vary from our assumptions here, including the case where the robot can observe only the actions that lead to unvisited states but not the states themselves.

4 Future Work

Our example provided a lower bound on the plan-execution time of uninformed LRTA* with maximal lookahead in unknown environments. The lower bound is barely super-linear in the number of states. A tight bound is currently unknown, although upper bounds are known. A trivial upper bound, for example, is $O(n^2)$ since LRTA* executes at most $n-1$ actions before it visits another state that it has not visited before and there are only n states to visit. A tighter upper bound follows directly from [Koenig and Smirnov, 1996]. It was surprisingly difficult to construct our example. It is currently unknown, and therefore a topic of future research, for which classes of graphs the worst-case plan-execution time of LRTA* is optimal up to a constant factor and whether these classes of graphs correspond to interesting and realistic environments. It is also currently unknown how the bounds change as LRTA* becomes more informed about where the goal states are.

5 Conclusions

Our work provides a first analysis of uninformed LRTA* in unknown environments. We studied versions of LRTA* with minimal and maximal lookaheads and showed that their worst-case plan-execution time is not optimal, not even up to a constant factor. The worst-case plan-execution time of depth-first search, for example, is smaller than that of LRTA* with either minimal or maximal lookahead. This is not to say that one should always prefer depth-first search over LRTA* since, for example, LRTA* can use heuristic knowledge to direct its search towards the goal states. LRTA* can also be interrupted at any location and get restarted at a different location. If the batteries of the robot need to get recharged during exploration, for instance, LRTA* can be interrupted and later get restarted at the charging station. While depth-first search could be modified to have these properties as well, it would lose some of its simplicity.

Acknowledgments

Thanks to Yury Smirnov for our collaboration on previous work which this paper extends. Thanks also to the reviewers for their suggestions for improvements and future research directions. Unfortunately, space limitations prevented us from implementing all of their suggestions in this paper.

References

(Barto et al., 1995) Barto, A.; Bradtke, S.; and Singh, S. 1995. Learning to act using real-time dynamic programming. *Artificial Intelligence* 73(1):81–138.

(Dasgupta et al., 1994) Dasgupta, P.; Chakrabarti, P.; and DeSarkar, S. 1994. Agent searching in a tree and the optimality of iterative deepening. *Artificial Intelligence* 71:195–208.

(Davies et al., 1998) Davies, S.; Ng, A.; and Moore, A. 1998. Applying online search techniques to reinforcement learning. In *Proceedings of the National Conference on Artificial Intelligence.* 753–760.

(Kearns and Singh, 1998) Kearns, M. and Singh, S. 1998. Near-optimal reinforcement learning in polynomial time. In *Proceedings of the International Conference on Machine Learning.* 260–268.

(Koenig and Simmons, 1995) Koenig, S. and Simmons, R.G. 1995. Real-time search in non-deterministic domains. In *Proceedings of the International Joint Conference on Artificial Intelligence.* 1660–1667.

(Koenig and Smirnov, 1996) Koenig, S. and Smirnov, Y. 1996. Graph learning with a nearest neighbor approach. In *Proceedings of the Conference on Computational Learning Theory.* 19–28.

(Koenig et al., 1997) Koenig, S.; Blum, A.; Ishida, T.; and Korf, R., editors 1997. *Proceedings of the AAAI-97 Workshop on On-Line Search.* AAAI Press.

(Koenig, 1996) Koenig, S. 1996. Agent-centered search: Situated search with small look-ahead. In *Proceedings of the National Conference on Artificial Intelligence.* 1365.

(Korf, 1990) Korf, R. 1990. Real-time heuristic search. *Artificial Intelligence* 42(2-3):189–211.

(Moore and Atkeson, 1993) Moore, A. and Atkeson, C. 1993. Prioritized sweeping: Reinforcement learning with less data and less time. *Machine Learning* 13:103–130.

(Pemberton and Korf, 1992) Pemberton, J. and Korf, R. 1992. Incremental path planning on graphs with cycles. In *Proceedings of the International Conference on Artificial Intelligence Planning Systems.* 179–188.

(Russell and Zilberstein, 1991) Russell, S. and Zilberstein, S. 1991. Composing real-time systems. In *Proceedings of the International Joint Conference on Artificial Intelligence.* 212–217.

(Thrun et al., 1998) Thrun, S.; Bücken, A.; Burgard, W.; Fox, D.; Fröhlinghaus, T.; Hennig, D.; Hofmann, T.; Krell, M.; and Schmidt, T. 1998. Map learning and high-speed navigation in rhino. In Kortenkamp, D.; Bonasso, R.; and Murphy, R., editors 1998, *Artificial Intelligence Based Mobile Robotics: Case Studies of Successful Robot Systems.* MIT Press. 21–52.

The effect of eligibility traces on finding optimal memoryless policies in partially observable Markov decision processes

John Loch
Department of Computer Science
University of Colorado
Boulder, CO 80309-0430
loch@cs.colorado.edu

Abstract

Agents acting in the real world are confronted with the problem of making good decisions with limited knowledge of the environment. Partially observable Markov decision processes (POMDPs) model decision problems in which an agent tries to maximize its reward in the face of limited sensor feedback. Recent work has shown empirically that a reinforcement learning (RL) algorithm called Sarsa(λ) can efficiently find optimal memoryless policies, which map current observations to actions, for POMDP problems (Loch and Singh 1998). The Sarsa(λ) algorithm uses a form of short-term memory called an eligibility trace, which distributes temporally delayed rewards to observation-action pairs which lead up to the reward. This paper explores the effect of eligibility traces on the ability of the Sarsa(λ) algorithm to find optimal memoryless policies. A variant of Sarsa(λ) called k-step truncated Sarsa(λ) is applied to four test problems taken from the recent work of Littman, Littman, Cassandra and Kaelbling, Parr and Russell, and Chrisman. The empirical results show that eligibility traces can be significantly truncated without affecting the ability of Sarsa(λ) to find optimal memoryless policies for POMDPs.

1 Introduction

Agents which operate in the real world, such as mobile robots, must use sensors which at best give only partial information about the state of the environment. Information about the robot's surroundings is necessarily incomplete due to noisy and/or imperfect sensors, occluded objects, and the inability of the robot to know precisely where it is. Such agent-environment systems can be modeled as partially observable Markov decision processes or POMDPs (Sondik, 1978).

A variety of algorithms have been developed for solving POMDPs (Lovejoy, 1991). However most of these techniques do not scale well to problems involving more than a few dozen states due to the computational complexity of the solution methods (Cassandra, 1994; Littman 1994). Therefore, finding efficient reinforcement learning methods for solving POMDPs is of great practical interest to the Artificial Intelligence and engineering fields.

Recent work has shown empirically that the Sarsa(λ) algorithm can efficiently find the best deterministic memoryless policy for several POMDPs problems from the recent literature (Loch and Singh 1998). The empirical results from Loch and Singh (1998) suggest that eligibility traces are necessary for finding the best or optimal memoryless policy. For this reason, a variant of Sarsa(λ) called k-step truncated Sarsa(λ) is formulated to explore the effect of eligibility traces on the ability of Sarsa(λ) to find the best memoryless policy.

The main contribution of this paper is to show empirically that a variant of Sarsa(λ) using truncated eligibility traces can find the optimal memoryless policy for several POMDP problems from the literature. Specifically we show that the k-step truncated Sarsa(λ) method can find the optimal memoryless policy for the four POMDP problems tested when $k \leq 2$.

2 Sarsa(λ) and POMDPs

An environment is defined by a finite set of states S, the agent can choose from a finite set of actions A, and the agent's sensors provide it observations from a finite set X. On executing action a ε A in state s ε S the agent receives expected reward r_s^a and the environment transitions to a state s' ε S with probability $P^a_{ss'}$. The probability of the agent observing x ε X given that the state is s is $O(x|s)$.

A straightforward way to extend RL algorithms to POMDPs is to learn Q-value functions of observation-action pairs, i.e. to simply treat the agents observations as states. Below we describe the standard Sarsa(λ) algorithm applied to POMDPs. At time step t the Q-value function is denoted Q_t; the eligibility trace function is denoted η_t; and the reward received is denoted r_t. On experiencing transition $<x_t, a_t, r_t, x_{t+1}>$ the following updates are performed in order:

$$\eta_t(x_t, a_t) = 1$$

$$\eta_t(x, a) = \gamma\lambda\ \eta_{t-1}(x, a)\ ; \text{for all } x \neq x_t \text{ and } a \neq a_t$$

$$Q_{t+1}(x, a) = Q_t(x, a) + \alpha * \delta_t * \eta_t(x, a)$$

where $\delta_t = r_t + \gamma\ Q_t(x_{t+1}, a_{t+1}) - Q_t(x_t, a_t)$ and α is the step-size (learning rate). The eligibility traces are initialized to zero, and in episodic tasks they are reinitialized to zero after every episode. The greedy policy at time step t assigns to each observation x the action $a = \text{argmax}_b\ Q_t(x, b)$.

2.1 Sarsa(λ) Using Truncated Eligibility Traces

Sarsa(λ) with truncated eligibility traces uses a parameter k which sets the eligibility trace for an observation-action pair to zero if that observation-action pair was not visited within the last k-1 time steps. Thus 1-step truncated Sarsa(λ) is equivalent to Sarsa(0) and 2-step truncated Sarsa(λ) updates the Q-values of the current observation-action pair and the immediately preceding observation-action pair.

3 Empirical Results

The truncated Sarsa(λ) algorithm was applied in an identical manner to four POMDP problems taken from the recent literature. Complete descriptions of the states, actions, observations, and rewards for each problem are provided in Loch and Singh (1998). Here we describe the aspects of the empirical results common to all four problems. At each step, the agent selected a random action with a probability equal to the exploration rate parameter and selected a greedy action otherwise. An initial exploration rate of 35% was used, decreasing linearly with each action (step) until the 350000th action from there onward the exploration rate remain fixed at 0%. Q-values were initialized to 0. Both the step-size α and the λ values are held constant in each experiment. A discount factor γ of 0.95 and a λ value of 1.0 were used for all four problems.

3.1 Sutton's Grid World

Sutton's grid world (Littman 1994) is an agent-environment system with 46 states, 30 observations, and 4 actions. State transitions and observations are deterministic.

The 1-step truncated eligibility trace, equivalent to Sarsa(0), was able to find a policy which could only reach the goal from start states within 7 steps of the goal state as shown in Figure 1. The optimal memoryless policy yielding 416 total steps to the goal state was found by the 2-step, 4-step and 8-step truncated eligibility trace methods shown in Figure 1.

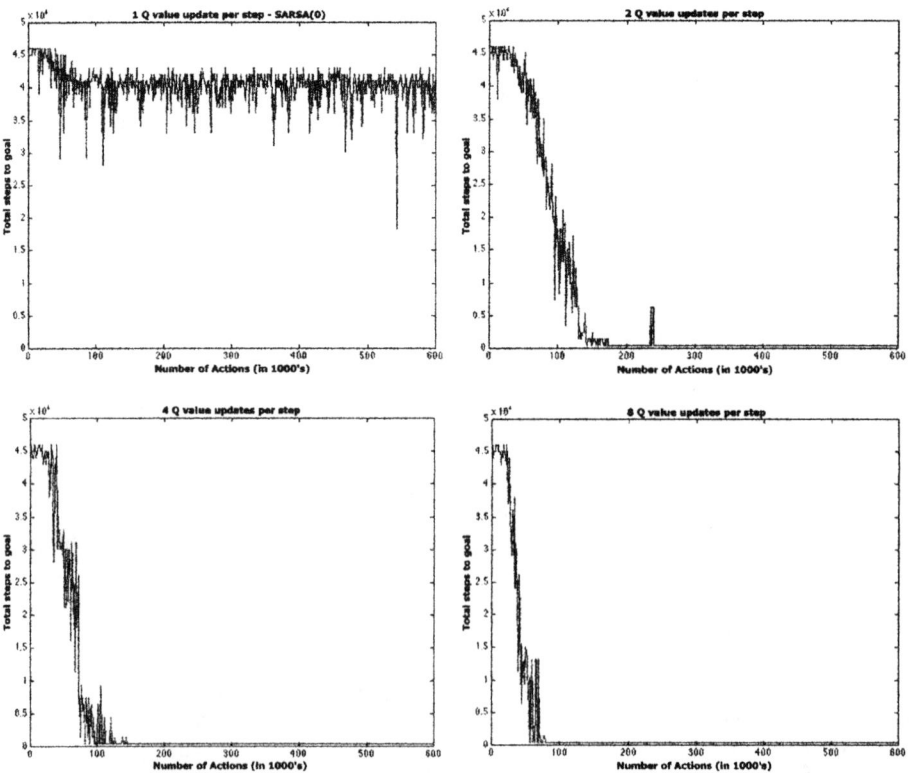

Figure 1: Sutton's Grid World (from Littman, 1994). Total steps to goal performance as a function of the number of learning steps for 1, 2, 4, and 8-step eligibility traces.

Effect of Eligibility Traces on Finding Optimal Memoryless Policies

3.2 Chrisman's Shuttle Problem

Chrisman's shuttle problem is an agent-environment system with 8 states, 5 observations, and 3 actions. State transitions and observations are stochastic.

The 1-step truncated eligibility trace, equivalent to Sarsa(0), was unable to find a policy which could could reach the goal state (Figure 2). The optimal memoryless policy yielding an average reward per step of 1.02 was found by the 2-step, 4-step, and 8-step truncated eligibility trace methods shown in Figure 2.

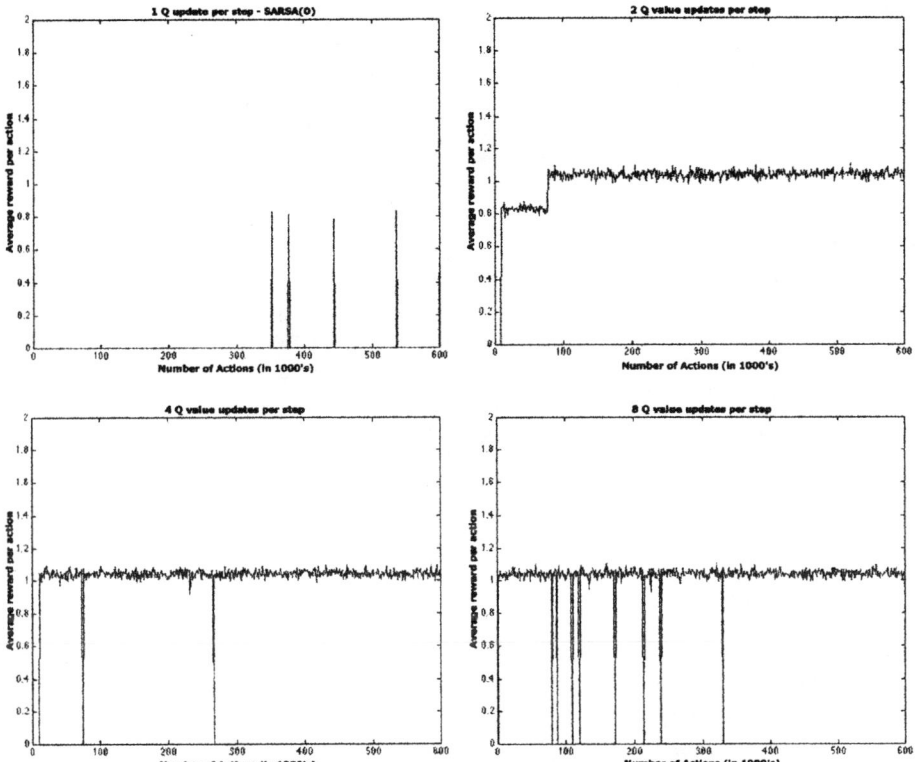

Figure 2: Chrisman's shuttle problem. Average reward per step performance as a function of the number of learning steps for 1, 2, 4, and 8-step eligibility traces.

3.3 Littman, Cassandra, and Kaelbling's 89 State Office World

Littman et al.'s 89 state office world (Littman 1995) is an agent-environment system with 89 states, 17 observations, and 5 actions. State transitions and observations are stochastic.

The 1-step truncated eligibility trace, equivalent to Sarsa(0), was able to find a policy which could reach the goal state in only 51% of the 251 trials (Figure 3). The 2-step, 4-step and 8-step truncated eligibility trace methods converged to the best memoryless policy found by Loch & Singh (1998) yielding a 77% success rate in reaching the goal state (Figure 3).

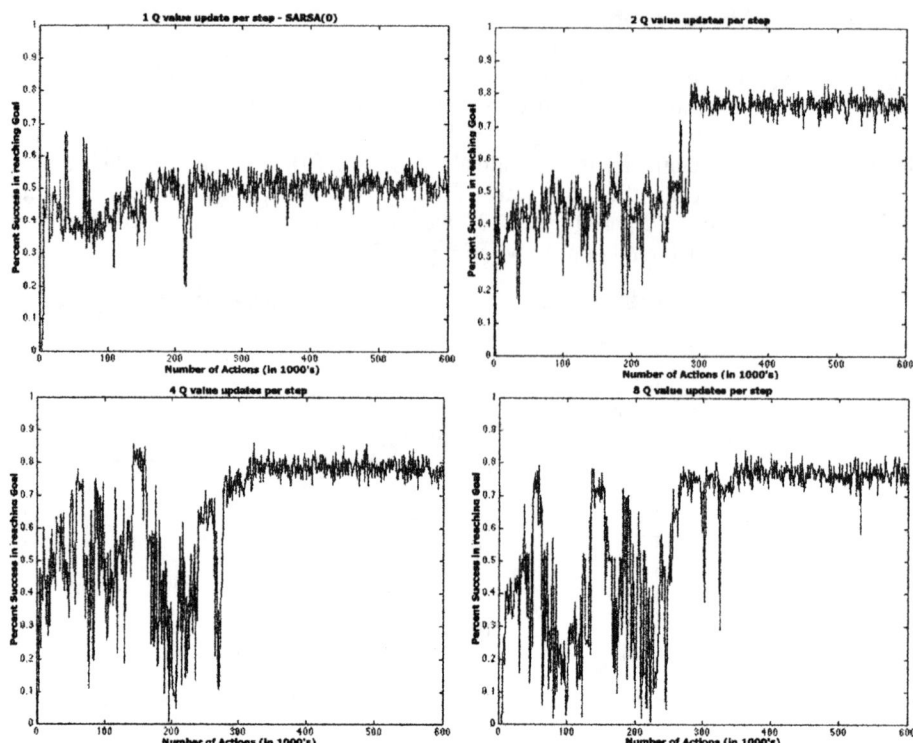

Figure 3: Littman et al.'s 89 state office world. Percent successful trials in reaching goal performance as a function of the number of learning steps for 1, 2, 4, and 8-step eligibility traces.

3.4 Parr & Russell's Grid World

Parr and Russell's grid world (Parr and Russell 1995) is an agent-environment system with 11 states, 6 observations, and 4 actions. State transitions are stochastic while observations are deterministic.

The optimal memoryless policy yielding an average reward per step of 0.024 was found by both the 1-step and 2-step truncated eligibility trace methods (Figure 4). Policies found by the 4-step and 8-step methods were not optimal. This result can be attributed to the sharp eligibility trace cutoff as this effect was not observed with smoothly decaying eligibility traces.

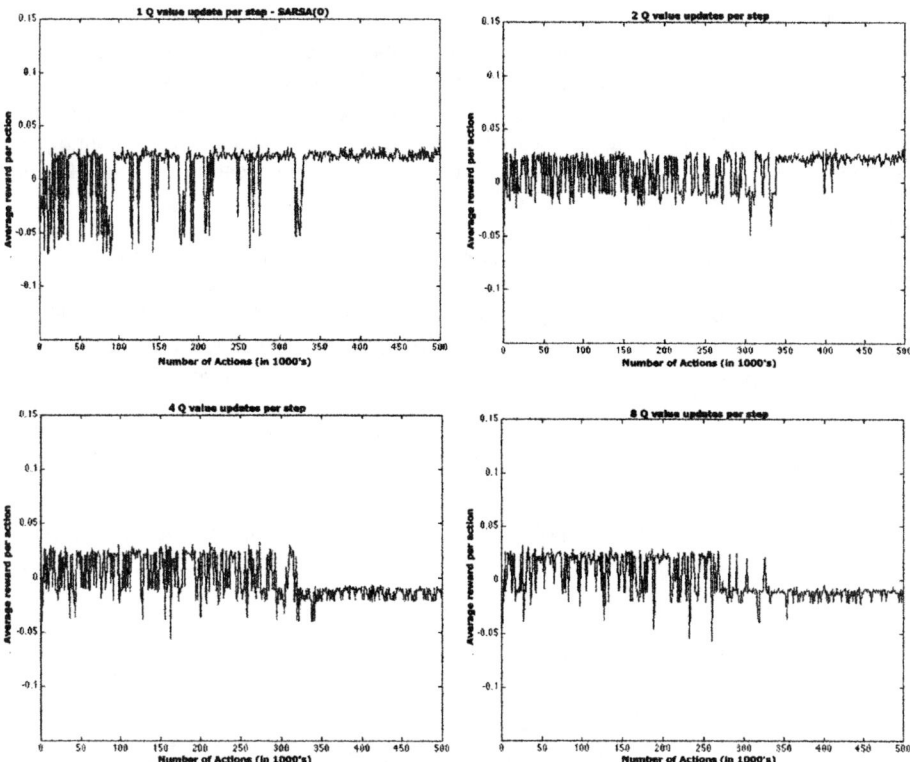

Figure 4: Parr & Russell's Grid World. Average reward per step performance as a function of the number of learning steps for 1, 2, 4, and 8-step eligibility traces.

3.5 Discussion

In all the empirical results presented above, we have shown that the k-step truncated Sarsa(λ) algorithm was able to find the best or the optimal deterministic memoryless policy when k=2.

This result is surprising since it was expected that the length of the eligibility trace required to find a good or optimal policy would vary widely depending on problem specific factors such as landmark (unique observation) spacing and the delay between critical decisions and rewards. Several additional POMDP problems were formulated in an attempt to create a POMDP which would require a k value greater than 2 to find the optimal policy. However, for all trial POMDPs tested the optimal memoryless policy could be found with $k \leq 2$.

4 Conclusions and Future Work

The ability of the Sarsa(λ) algorithm and the k-step truncated Sarsa(λ) algorithm to find optimal deterministic memoryless policies for a class of POMDP problems is important for several reasons. For POMDPs with good memoryless policies the Sarsa(λ) algorithm provides an efficient method for finding the best policy in that space.

If the performance of the memoryless policy is unsatisfactory, the observation and action spaces of the agent can be modified so as to produce an agent with a good memoryless policy. The designer of the autonomous system or agent can modify the observation space of the agent by either adding sensors or making finer distinctions in the current sensor values. In addition, the designer can add attributes from past observations into the current observation space. The action space can be modified by adding lower-level actions and by adding new actions to the space. Thus one method for designing a capable agent is to iterate between selecting an observation and action space for the agent, using Sarsa(λ) to find the best memoryless policy in that space, and repeating until satisfactory performance is achieved.

This suggests a future line of research into how to automate the process of observation and action space selection so as to acheive an acceptable performance level. Other avenues of research include an exploration into theoretical reasons why Sarsa(λ) and k-step truncated Sarsa(λ) are able to solve POMDPs. In addition, further research needs to be conducted as to why short ($k \leq 2$) eligibility traces work well over a wide class of POMDPs.

References

Cassandra, A. (1994). Optimal policies for partially observable Markov decision processes. Technical Report CS-94-14, Brown University, Department of Computer Science, Providence RI.

Littman, M. (1994). The Witness Algorithm: Solving partially observable Markov decision processes. Technical Report CS-94-40, Brown University, Department of Computer Science, Providence RI.

Littman, M., Cassandra, A., & Kaelbling, L. (1995). Learning policies for partially observable environments: Scaling up. In *Proceedings of the Twelfth International Conference on Machine Learning*, pages 362-370, San Francisco, CA, 1995. Morgan Kaufmann.

Loch, J., & Singh, S. (1998). Using eligibility traces to find the best memoryless policy in partially observable Markov decision processes. To appear In *Proceedings of the Fifteenth International Conference on Machine Learning,*, Madison, WI, 1998. Morgan Kaufmann. (Available from http://www.cs.colorado.edu/~baveja/papers.html)

Lovejoy, W. S. (1991). A survey of algorithmic methods for partially observable Markov decision processes. In *Annals of Operations Research*, 28:47-66.

Parr, R. & Russell, S. (1995). Approximating optimal policies for partially observable stochastic domains. In *Proceedings of the International Joint Conference on Artificial Intelligence*.

Sondik, E. J. (1978). The optimal control of partially observable Markov decision processes over the infinite horizon: Discounted costs. In*Operations Research*, 26(2).

Sutton, R.S. (1990). Integrated architectures for learning, planning, and reacting based on approximating dynamic programming. In *Proceedings of the Seventh International Conference of Machine Learning*, pages 216-224, San Mateo, CA. Morgan Kaufman.

Littman, M. (1994). Memoryless policies: theoretical limitations and practical results. In *From Animals to Animats 3: Proceedings of the Third International Conference on Simulation of Adaptive Behavior*, Cambridge, MA. MIT Press.

Learning Instance-Independent Value Functions to Enhance Local Search

Robert Moll Andrew G. Barto Theodore J. Perkins
Department of Computer Science
University of Massachusetts, Amherst, MA 01003

Richard S. Sutton
AT&T Shannon Laboratory, 180 Park Avenue, Florham Park, NJ 07932

Abstract

Reinforcement learning methods can be used to improve the performance of local search algorithms for combinatorial optimization by learning an evaluation function that predicts the outcome of search. The evaluation function is therefore able to guide search to low-cost solutions better than can the original cost function. We describe a reinforcement learning method for enhancing local search that combines aspects of previous work by Zhang and Dietterich (1995) and Boyan and Moore (1997, Boyan 1998). In an off-line learning phase, a value function is learned that is useful for guiding search for multiple problem sizes and instances. We illustrate our technique by developing several such functions for the Dial-A-Ride Problem. Our learning-enhanced local search algorithm exhibits an improvement of more then 30% over a standard local search algorithm.

1 INTRODUCTION

Combinatorial optimization is of great importance in computer science, engineering, and operations research. We investigated the use of reinforcement learning (RL) to enhance traditional local search optimization (hillclimbing). Since local search is a sequential decision process, RL can be used to improve search performance by learning an evaluation function that predicts the outcome of search and is therefore able to guide search to low-cost solutions better than can the original cost function.

Three approaches to using RL to improve combinatorial optimization have been described in the literature. One is to learn a value function over multiple search trajectories of a single problem instance. As the value function improves in its predictive accuracy, its guidance enhances additional search trajectories on the same instance. Boyan and Moore's STAGE algorithm (Boyan and Moore 1997, Boyan 1998) falls into this category, showing excellent performance on a range of optimization problems. Another approach is to learn a value function off-line and then use it over multiple new instances of the same problem. Zhang and Dietterich's (1995) application of RL to a NASA space shuttle mission scheduling problem takes this approach (although it does not strictly involve local search as we define it below). A key issue here is the need to normalize state representations and rewards so that trajectories from instances of different sizes and difficulties yield consistent training data. In each of the above approaches, a state of the RL problem is an entire solution (e.g., a complete tour in a Traveling Salesman Problem (TSP)) and the actions select next solutions from the current solutions' neighborhoods. A third approach, described by Bertsekas and Tsitsiklis (1996), uses a learned value function for guiding the direct construction of solutions rather than for moving between them.

We focused on combining aspects of first two of these approaches with the goal of carefully examining how well the TD(λ) algorithm can learn an instance-independent value function for a given problem to produce an enhanced local search algorithm applicable to all instances of that problem. Our approach combines an off-line learning phase with STAGE's alternation between using the learned value function and the original cost function to guide search. We present an extended case study of this algorithm's application to a somewhat complicated variant of TSP known as the Dial-A-Ride Problem, which exhibits some of the non-uniform structure present in real-world transportation and logistics problems.

2 ENHANCING LOCAL SEARCH

The components of local search for combinatorial optimization are 1) a finite set of *feasible solutions*, S; 2) an *objective, or cost, function*, $c : S \to \Re$; and 3) a *neighborhood function*, $A : S \to \mathcal{P}(S)$ (the power set of S). Local search starts with an initial feasible solution, s_0, of a problem instance and then at each step $k = 1, 2, \ldots$, it selects a solution $s_k \in A(s_{k-1})$ such that $c(s_k) < c(s_{k-1})$. This process continues until further local improvement is impossible, and the current *local optimum* is returned. If the algorithm always moves to the *first* less expensive neighboring solution encountered in an enumeration of a neighborhood, it is called *first improvement* local search.

Following Zhang and Dietterich (1995) and Boyan and Moore (1997), we note that local search can be viewed as a policy of a Markov decision process (MDP) with state set S and action sets $A(s)$, $s \in S$, where an action is identified with the neighboring solution selected. Local search selects actions which decrease the value of c, eventually absorbing at a state with a locally minimum cost. But c is not the optimal value function for the local search problem, whose objective is to reach the lowest-cost absorbing state (possibly including some tradeoff involving the number of search steps required to do so). RL used with a function approximator can learn an approximate optimal value function, V, thereby producing an enhanced search algorithm that is locally guided by V instead of by c. One way to do this is to give a small penalty, ϵ, for each transition and a terminal reward upon absorption that is inversely related to the cost of the terminal state. Maximizing the expected undiscounted return accomplishes the desired tradeoff (determined by the value of ϵ) between quality of final solution and search time (cf. Zhang and Dietterich, 1995).

Since each instance of an optimization problem corresponds to a different MDP, a value function V learned in this way is instance-specific. Whereas Boyan's STAGE algorithm in effect uses such a V to enhance additional searches that start from different states of the same instance, we are interested in learning a V off-line, and then using it for arbitrary instances of the given problem. In this case, the relevant sequential decision problem is more complicated than a single-instance MDP since it is a summary of aspects of all problem instances. It would be extremely difficult to make the structure of this process explicit, but fortunately RL requires only the generation of sample trajectories, which is relatively easy in this case.

In addition to their cost, secondary characteristics of feasible solutions can provide valuable information for search algorithms. By adjusting the parameters of a function approximation system whose inputs are feature vectors describing feasible solutions, an RL algorithm can produce a compact representation of V. Our approach operates in two distinct phases. In the *learning phase*, it learns a value function by applying the TD(λ) algorithm to a number of randomly chosen instances of the problem. In the *performance phase*, it uses the resulting value function, now held fixed, to guide local search for additional problem instances. This approach is in principle applicable to any combinatorial optimization problem, but we describe its details in the context of the Dial-A-Ride problem.

3 THE DIAL-A-RIDE PROBLEM

The Dial-a-Ride Problem (DARP) has the following formulation. A van is parked at a terminal. The driver receives calls from N customers who need rides. Each call identifies the location of a customer, as well as that customer's destination. After the calls have been received, the van must be routed so that it starts from the terminal, visits each pick-up and drop-off site in some order, and then returns to the terminal. The tour must pick up a passenger before eventually dropping that passenger off. The tour should be of minimal length. Failing this goal—and DARP is NP-complete, so it is unlikely that optimal DARP tours will be found easily—at least a good quality tour should be constructed. We assume that the van has unlimited capacity and that the distances between pick-up and drop-off locations are represented by a symmetric Euclidean distance matrix.

We use the notation
$$0\ 1\ 2\ -1\ 3\ -3\ -2$$
to denote the following tour: "start at the terminal (0), then pick up 1, then 2, then drop off 1 (thus: -1), pick up 3, drop off 3, drop off 2 and then return to the terminal (site 0)." Given a tour s, the *2-opt neighborhood* of s, $A_2(s)$, is the set of legal tours obtainable from s by subsequence reversal. For example, for the tour above, the new tour created by the following subsequence reversal
$$0\ 1\ /\ 2\ -1\ 3\ /\ -3\ -2\ \longrightarrow\ 0\ 1\ 3\ -1\ 2\ -3\ -2$$
is an element of $A_2(T)$. However, this reversal
$$0\ 1\ 2\ /\ -1\ 3\ -3\ /\ -2\ \longrightarrow\ 0\ 1\ 2\ -3\ 3\ -1\ -2$$
leads to an infeasible tour, since it asserts that passenger 3 is dropped off first, then picked up. The neighborhood structure of DARP is highly non-uniform, varying between A_2 neighborhood sizes of $O(N)$ and $O(N^2)$.

Let s be a feasible DARP tour. By 2-opt(s) we mean the tour obtained by first-improvement local search using the A_2 neighborhood structure (presented in a fixed, standard enumeration), with tour length as the cost function. As with TSP, there is a 3-opt algorithm for

DARP, where a 3-opt neighborhood $A_3(s)$ is defined and searched in a fixed, systematic way, again in first-improvement style. This neighborhood is created by inserting three rather than two "breaks" in a tour. 3-opt is much slower than 2-opt, more than 100 times as slow for $N = 50$, but it is much more effective, even when 2-opt is given equal time to generate multiple random starting tours and then complete its improvement scheme.

Psaraftis (1983) was the first to study 2-opt and 3-opt algorithms for DARP. He studied tours up to size $N = 30$, reporting that at that size, 3-opt tours are about 30% shorter on average than 2-opt tours. In theoretical studies of DARP, Stein (1978) showed that for sites placed in the unit square, the globally optimal tour for problem size N has a length that asymptotically approaches $1.02\sqrt{2N}$ with probability 1 as N increases. This bound applies to our study—although we multiply position coordinates by 100 and then truncate to get integer distance matrices—and thus, for example, a value of 1020 gives us a baseline estimate of the globally optimal tour cost for $N = 50$. Healy and Moll (1995) considered using a secondary cost function to extend local search on DARP. In addition to primary cost (tour length) they considered as a secondary cost the ratio of tour cost to neighborhood size, which they called *cost-hood*. Their algorithm employed a STAGE-like alternation between these two cost functions: starting from a random tour s, it first found 2opt(s); then it performed a limited local search using the cost-hood function, which had the effect of driving the search to a new tour with a decent cost and a large neighborhood. These alternating processes were repeated until a time bound was exhausted, at which point the least cost tour seen so far was reported as the result of the search. This technique worked well, with effectiveness falling midway between that of 2-opt and 3-opt.

4 ENHANCED 2-OPT FOR DARP

We restrict our description to a learning method for enhancing 2-opt for DARP, but the same method can be used for other problems. In the learning phase, after initializing the function approximator, we conduct a number training episodes until we are satisfied that the weights have stabilized. For each episode k, we select a problem size N at random (from a predetermined range) and generate a random DARP instance of that size, i.e., we generate a symmetric Euclidean distance matrix by generating random points in the plane inside the square bounded by the points (0,0), (0,100), (100,100) and (100,0). We set the "terminal site" to point (50,50) and the initial tour to a randomly generated feasible tour. We then conduct a modified first-improvement 2-opt local search using the negated current value function, $-V_k$, as the cost function. The modification is that termination is controlled by a parameter $\epsilon > 0$ as follows: the search terminates at a tour s if there is no $s' \in A(s)$ such that $V_k(s') > V_k(s) + \epsilon$. In other words, a step is taken only if it produces an improvement of at least ϵ according to the current value function. The episode returns a final tour s_f. We run one unmodified 2-opt local search, this time using the DARP cost function c (tour length), from s_f to compute 2-opt(s_f). We then apply a batch version of undiscounted TD(λ) to the saved search trajectory using the following immediate rewards: $-\epsilon$ for each transition, and $-c(2\text{-opt}(s_f))/Stein_N$ as a terminal reward, where $Stein_N$ is the Stein estimate for instance size N. Normalization by $Stein_N$ helps make the terminal reward consistent across instance sizes. At the end of this learning phase, we have a final value function, V. V is used in the performance phase, which consists of applying the modified first-improvement 2-opt local search with cost function $-V$ on new instances, followed by a 2-opt application to the resulting tour.

The results described here were obtained using a simple linear approximator with a bias

Table 1: Weight Vectors for Learned Value Functions.

Value Function	Weight Vector
V	$<.951, .033, .0153>$
V_{20}	$<.981, .019, .00017>$
V_{30}	$<.984, .014, .0006>$
V_{40}	$<.977, .022, .0009>$
V_{50}	$<.980, .019, .0015>$
V_{60}	$<.971, .022, .0069>$

weight and features developed from the following base features: 1) $normcost_N(s) = c(s)/Stein_N$; 2) $normhood_N = |A(s)|/a_N$, where a_N is a normalization coefficient defined below; and 3) $normprox_N$, which considers a list of the $N/4$ least expensive edges of the distance matrix, as follows. Let e be one of the edges, with endpoints u and v. The $normprox_N$ feature examines the current tour, and counts the number of sites on the tour that appear between u and v. $normprox_N$ is the sum of these counts over the edges on the proximity list divided by a normalizing coefficient b_N described below. Our function approximator is then give by $w_0 + normcost_N/(normhood_N)^2 w_1 + normprox_N/(normhood_N)^2 w_2$. The coefficients a_N and b_N are the result of running linear regression on randomly sampled instances of random sizes to determine coefficients that will yield the closest fit to a constant target value for normalized neighborhood size and proximity. The results were $a_N = .383N^2 + .28.5N - 244.5$ and $b_N = .43N^2 + .736N - 68.9\sqrt{N} + 181.75$. The motivation for the quotient features comes from Healy and Moll (1995) who found that using a similar term improved 2-opt on DARP by allowing it to sacrifice cost improvements to gain large neighborhoods.

5 EXPERIMENTAL RESULTS

Comparisons among algorithms were done at five representative sizes $N = 20, 30, 40, 50$, and 60. For the learning phase, we conducted approximately 3,000 learning episodes, each one using a randomly generated instance of size selected randomly between 20 and 60 inclusive. The result of the learning phase was a value function V. To assess the influence of this multi-instance learning, we also repeated the above learning phase 5 times, except that in each we held the instance size fixed to a different one of the 5 representative sizes, yielding in each case a distinct value function V_N, where N is the training instance size. Table 1 shows the resulting weight vector $<$ bias weight, $costhood_N$ weight, $proximity_N$ weight $>$. With the exception of the $proximity_N$ weight, these are quite consistent across training instance size. We do not yet understand why training on multiple-sized instances led to this pattern of variation.

Table 2 compares the tour quality found by six different local search algorithms. For the algorithms using learned value functions, the results are for the performance phase after learning using the algorithm listed. Table entries are the percent by which tour length exceeded $Stein_N$ for instance size N averaged over 100 instances of each representative size. Thus, 2-opt exceeded $Stein_{20} = 645$ on the 100 instance sample set by an average of 42%. The last row in the table gives the results of using the five different value functions V_N, for the corresponding N. Results for TD(.8) are shown because they were better than

Table 2: Comparison of Six Algorithms at Sizes $N = 20, 30, 40, 50, 60$. Entries are percentage above $Stein_N$ averaged over 100 random instances of size N.

Algorithm	N=20	N=30	N=40	N=50	N=60
2-opt	42	47	53	56	60
3-opt	8	8	11	10	10
TD(1)	28	31	34	39	40
TD(.8) $\epsilon = 0$	27	30	35	37	39
TD(.8) $\epsilon = .01/N$	29	35	37	41	44
TD(.8) $\epsilon = 0, V_N$	29	30	32	36	40

Table 3: Average Relative Running Times. Times for 2-opt are in seconds; other entries give time divided by 2-opt time.

Algorithm	N=20	N=30	N=40	N=50	N=60
2-opt	.237	.770	1.09	1.95	3.55
3-opt	32	45	100	162	238
TD(.8) $\epsilon = 0$	3.2	3.4	6.3	6.9	7.1
TD(.8) $\epsilon = .01/N$	2.2	1.8	2.6	2.9	3.0

those for other values of λ. The learning-enhanced algorithms do well against 2-opt when running time is ignored, and indeed TD(.8), $\epsilon = 0$, is about 35% percent better (according to this measure) by size 60. Note that 3-opt clearly produces the best tours, and a non-zero ϵ for TD(.8) decreases tour quality, as expected since it causes shorter search trajectories.

Table 3 gives the relative running times of the various algorithms. The raw running times for 2-opt are given in seconds (Common Lisp on 266 Mhz Mac G-3) at each of five sizes in the first row. Subsequent rows give approximate running times divided by the corresponding 2-opt running time. Times are averages over 30 instances. The algorithms using learned value functions are slower mainly due to the necessity to evaluate the features. Note that TD(.8) becomes significantly faster with ϵ non-zero.

Finally, Table 4 gives the relative performance of seven algorithms, normalized for time, including the STAGE algorithm using linear regression with our features. We generated 20 random instances at each of the representative sizes, and we allowed each algorithm to run for the indicated amount of time on each instance. If time remained when a local optimum was reached, we restarted the algorithm at that point, except in the case of 2-opt, where we selected a new random starting tour. The restarting regime for the learning-enhanced algorithms is the regime employed by STAGE. Each algorithm reports the best result found in the allotted time, and the chart reports the averages of these values across the 20 instances. Notice that the algorithms that take advantage of extensive off-line learning significantly outperform the other algorithms, including STAGE, which relies on single-instance learning.

6 DISCUSSION

We have presented an extension to local search that uses RL to enhance the local search cost function for a particular optimization problem. Our method combines aspects of work

Table 4: Performance Comparisons, Equalized for Running Time.

Algorithm	Size and Running Time				
	N=20 10 sec	N=30 20 sec	N=40 40 sec	N=50 100 sec	N=60 150 sec
2-opt	16	29	28	30	38
STAGE	18	20	32	24	27
TD(.8) $\epsilon = 0$	12	13	16	22	20
TD(.8) $\epsilon = .01/N$	13	11	14	24	28

by Zhang and Dietterich (1995) and Boyan and Moore (1997; Boyan 1998). We have applied our method to a relatively pure optimization problem—DARP—which possesses a relatively consistent structure across problem instances. This has allowed the method to learn a value function that can be applied across all problem instances at all sizes. Our method yields significant improvement over a traditional local search approach to DARP on the basis of a very simple linear approximator, built using a relatively impoverished set of features. It also improves upon Boyan and Moore's (1997) STAGE algorithm in our example problem, benefiting from extensive off-line learning whose cost was not included in our assessment. We think this is appropriate for some types of problems; since it is a one-time learning cost, it can be amortized over many future problem instances of practical importance.

Acknowledgement

We thank Justin Boyan for very helpful discussions of this subject. This research was supported by a grant from the Air Force Office of Scientific Research, Bolling AFB (AFOSR F49620-96-1-0254).

References

Boyan, J. A. (1998). Learning Evaluation Functions for Global Optimization. Ph.D. Thesis, Carnegie-Mellon University.

Boyan, J. A., and Moore, A. W. (1997). Using Prediction to Improve Combinatorial Optimization Search. Proceedings of AI-STATS-97.

D. P. Bertsekas, D. P., and Tsitsiklis, J. N. (1996). *Neuro-Dynamic Programming*. Athena Scientific, Belmont, MA.

Healy, P., and Moll, R. (1995). A New Extension to Local Search Applied to the Dial-A-Ride Problem. *European Journal of Operations Research*, 8: 83–104.

Psaraftis, H. N. (1983). K-interchange Procedures for Local Search in a Precedence-Constrained Routing Problem. *European Journal of Operations Research*, 13:391–402.

Zhang, W. and Dietterich, T. G. (1995). A Reinforcement Learning Approach to Job-Shop Scheduling. In *Proceedings of the Fourteenth International Joint Conference on Artificial Intelligence*, pp. 1114–1120. Morgan Kaufmann, San Francisco.

Stein, D. M. (1978). An Asymptotic Probabilistic Analysis of a Routing Problem. *Math. Operations Res. J.*, 3: 89–101.

Barycentric Interpolators for Continuous Space & Time Reinforcement Learning

Rémi Munos & Andrew Moore
Robotics Institute, Carnegie Mellon University
Pittsburgh, PA 15213, USA.
E-mail:{munos, awm}@cs.cmu.edu

Abstract

In order to find the optimal control of continuous state-space and time reinforcement learning (RL) problems, we approximate the value function (VF) with a particular class of functions called the *barycentric interpolators*. We establish sufficient conditions under which a RL algorithm converges to the optimal VF, even when we use approximate models of the state dynamics and the reinforcement functions.

1 INTRODUCTION

In order to approximate the value function (VF) of a continuous state-space and time reinforcement learning (RL) problem, we define a particular class of functions called the *barycentric interpolator*, that use some interpolation process based on finite sets of points. This class of functions, including continuous or discontinuous piecewise linear and multi-linear functions, provides us with a general method for designing RL algorithms that converge to the optimal value function. Indeed these functions permit us to discretize the HJB equation of the continuous control problem by a *consistent* (and thus convergent) approximation scheme, which is solved by using some model of the state dynamics and the reinforcement functions.

Section 2 defines the barycentric interpolators. *Section 3* describes the optimal control problem in the deterministic continuous case. *Section 4* states the convergence result for RL algorithms by giving sufficient conditions on the applied model. *Section 5* gives some computational issues for this method, and *Section 6* describes the approximation scheme used here and proves the convergence result.

2 DEFINITION OF BARYCENTRIC INTERPOLATORS

Let $\Sigma^\delta = \{\xi_i\}_i$ be a set of points distributed at some resolution δ (see (4) below) on the state space of dimension d.

For any state x inside some simplex $(\xi_1, ..., \xi_n)$, we say that x is the *barycenter* of the $\{\xi_i\}_{i=1..n}$ inside this simplex with positive coefficients $p(x|\xi_i)$ of sum 1, called the *barycentric coordinates*, if $x = \sum_{i=1..n} p(x|\xi_i).\xi_i$.

Let $V^\delta(\xi_i)$ be the value of the function at the points ξ_i. V^δ is a **barycentric interpolator** if for any state x which is the barycenter of the points $\{\xi_i\}_{i=1..n}$ for some simplex $(\xi_1, ..., \xi_n)$, with the barycentric coordinates $p(x|\xi_i)$, we have :

$$V^\delta(x) = \sum_{i=1..n} p(x|\xi_i).V^\delta(\xi_i) \tag{1}$$

Moreover we assume that the simplex $(\xi_1, ..., \xi_n)$ is of diameter $O(\delta)$. Let us describe some simple barycentric interpolators :

- **Piecewise linear functions** defined by some triangulation on the state space (thus defining continuous functions), see figure 1.a, or defined at any x by a linear combination of $(d+1)$ values at any points $(\xi_1, ..., \xi_{d+1}) \ni x$ (such functions may be discontinuous at some boundaries), see figure 1.b.

- **Piecewise multi-linear functions** defined by a multi-linear combination of the 2^d values at the vertices of d-dimensional rectangles, see figure 1.c. In this case as well, we can build continuous interpolations or allow discontinuities at the boundaries of the rectangles.

An important point is that the convergence result stated in Section 4 does not require the continuity of the function. This permits us to build variable resolution triangulations (see figure 1.b) or grid (figure 1.c) easily.

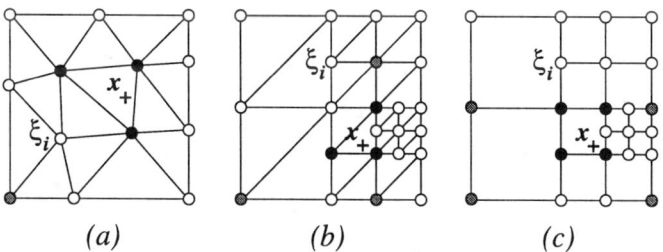

Figure 1: Some examples of barycentric approximators. These are piecewise continuous (a) or discontinuous (b) linear or multi-linear (c) interpolators.

Remark 1 *In the general case, for a given x, the choice of a simplex $(\xi_1, ..., \xi_n) \ni x$ is not unique (see the two sets of grey and black points in figure 1.b and 1.c), and once the simplex $(\xi_1, ..., \xi_n) \ni x$ is defined, if $n > d+1$ (for example in figure 1.c), then the choice of the barycentric coordinates $p(x|\xi_i)$ is also not unique.*

Remark 2 *Depending on the interpolation method we use, the time needed for computing the values will vary. Following [Dav96], the continuous multi-linear interpolation must process 2^d values, whereas the linear continuous interpolation inside a simplex processes $(d+1)$ values in $O(d \log d)$ time.*

In comparison to [Gor95], the functions used here are *averagers* that satisfy the barycentric interpolation property (1). This additional geometric constraint permits us to prove the consistency (see (15) below) of the approximation scheme and thus the convergence to the optimal value in the continuous time case.

3 THE OPTIMAL CONTROL PROBLEM

Let us describe the optimal control problem in the *deterministic* and *discounted* case for *continuous state-space* and *time* variables and define the value function that we intend to approximate. We consider a dynamical system whose *state dynamics* depends on the *current state* $x(t) \in \bar{O}$ (the *state-space*, with O an open subset of $\mathbb{R}^d$) and *control* $u(t) \in U$ (compact subset) by a differential equation:

$$\frac{dx}{dt} = f(x(t), u(t)) \tag{2}$$

From equation (2), the choice of an initial state x and a control function $u(t)$ leads to a unique trajectories $x(t)$ (see figure 2). Let τ be the *exit time* from $\bar{O}$ (with the convention that if $x(t)$ always stays in $\bar{O}$, then $\tau = \infty$). Then, we define the *functional* J as the discounted cumulative reinforcement:

$$J(x; u(.)) = \int_0^\tau \gamma^t r(x(t), u(t)) dt + \gamma^\tau R(x(\tau))$$

where $r(x, u)$ is the *running reinforcement* and $R(x)$ the *boundary reinforcement*. γ is the *discount factor* ($0 \leq \gamma < 1$). We assume that f, r and R are bounded and Lipschitzian, and that the boundary ∂O is $\mathcal{C}^2$.

RL uses the method of Dynamic Programming (DP) that introduces the *value function* (VF) : the maximal value of J as a function of initial state x :

$$V(x) = \sup_{u(.)} J(x; u(.)).$$

From the DP principle, we deduce that V satisfies a first-order differential equation, called the Hamilton-Jacobi-Bellman (HJB) equation (see [FS93] for a survey) :

Theorem 1 *If V is differentiable at $x \in O$, let $DV(x)$ be the gradient of V at x, then the following HJB equation holds at x.*

$$H(V, DV, x) \stackrel{\text{def}}{=} V(x) \ln \gamma + \sup_{u \in U}[DV(x).f(x, u) + r(x, u)] = 0 \tag{3}$$

The challenge of RL is to get a good approximation of the VF, because from V we can deduce the optimal control : for state x, the control $u^*(x)$ that realizes the supremum in the HJB equation provides an optimal (feed-back) control law.

The following hypothesis is a sufficient condition for V to be continuous within O (see [Bar94]) and is required for proving the convergence result of the next section.

Hyp 1: For $x \in \partial O$, let $\vec{n}(x)$ be the outward normal of O at x, we assume that :
-If $\exists u \in U$, s.t. $f(x, u).\vec{n}(x) \leq 0$ then $\exists v \in U$, s.t. $f(x, v) \vec{n}(x) < 0$.
-If $\exists u \in U$, s.t. $f(x, u).\vec{n}(x) \geq 0$ then $\exists v \in U$, s.t. $f(x, v) \vec{n}(x) > 0$.

which means that at the states (if there exist any) where some trajectory is tangent to the boundary, there exists, for some control, a trajectory strictly coming inside and one strictly leaving the state space.

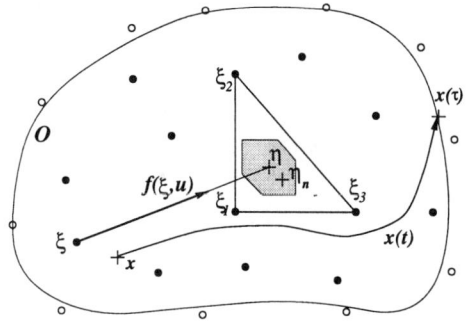

Figure 2: The state space and the set of points Σ^δ (the black dots belong to the interior and the white ones to the boundary). The value at some point ξ is updated, at step n, by the discounted value at point $\eta_n \in (\xi_1, \xi_2, \xi_3)$. The main requirement for convergence is that the points η_n approximate η in the sense: $p(\eta_n|\xi_i) = p(\eta|\xi_i) + O(\delta)$ (i.e. the η_n belong to the grey area).

4 THE CONVERGENCE RESULT

Let us introduce the set of points $\Sigma^\delta = \{\xi_i\}_i$, composed of the *interior* ($\Sigma^\delta \cap O$) and the *boundary* ($\partial\Sigma^\delta = \Sigma^\delta \setminus O$), such that its convex hull covers the state space $\overline{O}$, and performing a discretization at some resolution δ:

$$\forall x \in O, \inf_{\xi_i \in \Sigma^\delta \cap O} ||x - \xi_i|| \leq \delta \text{ and } \forall x \in \partial O \inf_{\xi_j \in \partial\Sigma^\delta} ||x - \xi_j|| \leq \delta \quad (4)$$

Moreover, we approximate the control space U by some finite control spaces $U^\delta \subset U$ such that for $\delta \leq \delta'$, $U^{\delta'} \subset U^\delta$ and $\lim_{\delta \to 0} U^\delta = U$.

We would like to update the value of any:

- *interior point* $\xi \in \Sigma^\delta \cap O$ with the discounted values at state $\eta_n(\xi, u)$ (figure 2):

$$V^\delta_{n+1}(\xi) \leftarrow \sup_{u \in U^\delta} \left[\gamma^{\tau_n(\xi,u)} V^\delta_n(\eta_n(\xi, u)) + \tau_n(\xi, u).r_n(\xi, u) \right] \quad (5)$$

for some state $\eta_n(\xi, u)$, some time delay $\tau_n(\xi, u)$ and some reinforcement $r_n(\xi, u)$.

- *boundary point* $\xi \in \partial\Sigma^\delta$ with some terminal reinforcement $R_n(\xi)$:

$$V^\delta_{n+1}(\xi) \leftarrow R_n(\xi) \quad (6)$$

The following theorem states that the values V^δ_n computed by a RL algorithm using the model (because of some a priori partial uncertainty of the state dynamics and the reinforcement functions) $\eta_n(\xi, u)$, $\tau_n(\xi, u)$, $r_n(\xi, u)$ and $R_n(\xi)$ converge to the optimal value function as the number of iterations $n \to \infty$ and the resolution $\delta \to 0$.

Let us define the state $\eta(\xi, u)$ (see figure 2):

$$\eta(\xi, u) = \xi + \tau(\xi, u).f(\xi, u) \quad (7)$$

for some time delay $\tau(\xi, u)$ (with $k_1 \delta \leq \tau(\xi, u) \leq k_2 \delta$ for some constants $k_1 > 0$ and $k_2 > 0$), and let $p(\eta|\xi_i)$ (resp. $p(\eta_n|\xi_i)$) be the barycentric coordinate of η inside a simplex containing it (resp. η_n inside the same simplex). We will write η, η_n, τ, r, ..., instead of $\eta(\xi, u)$, $\eta_n(\xi, u)$, $\tau(\xi, u)$, $r(\xi, u)$, ... when no confusion is possible.

Theorem 2 *Assume that the hypotheses of the previous sections hold, and that for any resolution δ, we use barycentric interpolators V^δ defined on state spaces Σ^δ (satisfying (4)) such that all points of $\Sigma^\delta \cap O$ are regularly updated with rule (5) and all points of $\partial\Sigma^\delta$ are updated with rule (6) at least once. Suppose that η_n, τ_n, r_n and R_n approximate η, τ, r and R in the sense:*

$$\forall \xi_i, \; p(\eta_n|\xi_i) = p(\eta|\xi_i) + O(\delta) \quad (8)$$
$$\tau_n = \tau + O(\delta^2) \quad (9)$$
$$r_n = r + O(\delta) \quad (10)$$
$$R_n = R + O(\delta) \quad (11)$$

then we have $\lim_{\substack{n\to\infty \\ \delta\to 0}} V_n^\delta = V$ uniformly on any compact $\Omega \subset O$ (i.e. $\forall \varepsilon > 0, \forall \Omega$ compact $\subset O, \exists \Delta, \exists N$, such that $\forall \delta \leq \Delta, \forall n \geq N, \sup_{\Sigma^\delta \cap \Omega} |V_n^\delta - V| \leq \varepsilon$).

Remark 3 *For a given value of δ, the rule (5) is not a DP updating rule for some Markov Decision Problem (MDP) since the values η_n, τ_n, r_n depend on n. This point is important in the RL framework since this allows on-line improvement of the model of the state dynamics and the reinforcement functions.*

Remark 4 *This result extends the previous results of convergence obtained by Finite-Element or Finite-Difference methods (see [Mun97]).*

This theoretical result can be applied by starting from a rough Σ^δ (high δ) and by combining to the iteration process ($n \to \infty$) some learning process of the model ($\eta_n \to \eta$) and a increasing process of the number of points ($\delta \to 0$).

5 COMPUTATIONAL ISSUES

From (8) we deduce that the method will also converge if we use an *approximate barycentric interpolator*, defined at any state $x \in (\xi_1, ..., \xi_n)$ by the value of the barycentric interpolator at some state $x' \in (\xi_1, ..., \xi_n)$ such that $p(x'|\xi_i) = p(x|\xi_i) + O(\delta)$ (see figure 3). The fact that we need not be completely accurate can be

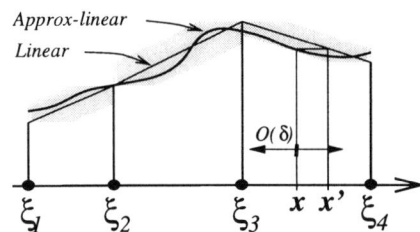

Figure 3: The linear function and the approximation error around it (the grey area). The value of the approximate linear function plotted here at some state x is equal to the value of the linear one at x'. Any such approximate barycenter interpolator can be used in (5).

used to our advantage. First, the computation of barycentric coordinates can use very fast approximate matrix methods. Second, the model we use to integrate the dynamics need not be perfect. We can make an $O(\delta^2)$ error, which is useful if we are learning a model from data: we need simply arrange to not gather more data than is necessary for the current δ. For example, if we use nearest neighbor for our dynamics learning, we need to ensure enough data so that every observation is $O(\delta^2)$ from its nearest neighbor. If we use local regression, then a mere $O(\delta)$ density is all that is required [Omo87, AMS97].

6 PROOF OF THE CONVERGENCE RESULT

6.1 Description of the approximation scheme

We use a convergent scheme derived from Kushner (see [Kus90]) in order to approximate the continuous control problem by a finite MDP. The HJB equation is discretized, at some resolution δ, into the following DP equation : for $\xi \in \Sigma^\delta \cap O$,

$$V^\delta(\xi) = F^\delta[V^\delta(.)](\xi) \stackrel{\text{def}}{=} \sup_{u \in U^\delta} \left\{ \gamma^\tau \sum_{\xi_i} p(\eta|\xi_i).V^\delta(\xi_i) + \tau.r \right\} \quad (12)$$

and for $\xi \in \partial \Sigma^\delta$, $V^\delta(\xi) = R(\xi)$. This is a fixed-point equation and we can prove that, thanks to the discount factor γ, it satisfies the **"strong" contraction** property :

$$\sup_{\Sigma^\delta} |V_{n+1}^\delta - V^\delta| \leq \lambda . \sup_{\Sigma^\delta} |V_n^\delta - V^\delta| \text{ for some } \lambda < 1 \quad (13)$$

from which we deduce that there exists exactly one solution V^δ to the DP equation, which can be computed by some value iteration process : for any initial V_0^δ, we iterate $V_{n+1}^\delta \leftarrow F^\delta \left[V_n^\delta\right]$. Thus for any resolution δ, the values $V_n^\delta \to V^\delta$ as $n \to \infty$.

Moreover, as V^δ is a barycentric interpolator and from the definition (7) of η,

$$F^\delta \left[V^\delta(.)\right](\xi) = \sup_{u \in U^\delta} \left\{\gamma^\tau V^\delta(\xi + \tau.f(\xi, u)) + \tau.r\right\} \tag{14}$$

from which we deduce that the scheme F^δ is *consistent* : in a formal sense,

$$\limsup_{\delta \to 0} \tfrac{1}{\delta}|F^\delta[W](x) - W(x)| \sim H(W, DW, x) \tag{15}$$

and obtain, from the general convergence theorem of [BS91] (and a result of strong unicity obtained from hyp.1), the convergence of the scheme : $V^\delta \to V$ as $\delta \to 0$.

6.2 Use of the "weak contraction" result of convergence

Since in the RL approach used here, we only have an approximation η_n, τ_n, ... of the true values η, τ, ..., the strong contraction property (13) does not hold any more. However, in previous work ([Mun98]), we have proven the convergence for some weakened conditions, recalled here :

If the values V_n^δ updated by some algorithm satisfy the **"weak" contraction** property with respect to a solution V^δ of a convergent approximation scheme (such as the previous one (12)) :

$$\sup_{\Sigma^\delta \cap O} \left|V_{n+1}^\delta - V^\delta\right| \leq (1 - k.\delta).\sup_{\Sigma^\delta} \left|V_n^\delta - V^\delta\right| + o(\delta) \tag{16}$$

$$\sup_{\partial \Sigma^\delta} \left|V_{n+1}^\delta - V^\delta\right| = O(\delta) \tag{17}$$

for some positive constant k, (with the notation $f(\delta) \leq o(\delta)$ iff $\exists g(\delta) = o(\delta)$ with $f(\delta) \leq g(\delta)$) then we have $\lim_{\substack{n \to \infty \\ \delta \to 0}} V_n^\delta = V$ uniformly on any compact $\Omega \subset O$ (i.e. $\forall \varepsilon > 0$, $\forall \Omega$ compact $\subset O$, $\exists \Delta$ and N such that $\forall \delta \leq \Delta, \forall n \geq N$, $\sup_{\Sigma^\delta \cap \Omega} |V_n^\delta - V| \leq \varepsilon$).

6.3 Proof of theorem 2

We are going to use the approximations (8), (9), (10) and (11) to deduce that the weak contraction property holds, and then use the result of the previous section to prove theorem 2.

The proof of (17) is immediate since, from (6) and (11) we have : $\forall \xi \in \partial \Sigma^\delta$,

$$\left|V_{n+1}^\delta(\xi) - V^\delta(\xi)\right| = |R_n(\xi) - R(\xi)| = O(\delta)$$

Now we need to prove (16). Let us estimate the error $E_n(\xi) = V^\delta(\xi) - V_n^\delta(\xi)$ between the value V^δ of the DP equation (12) and the values V_n^δ computed by rule (5) after one iteration :

$$E_{n+1}(\xi) = \sup_{u \in U^\delta} \left\{\sum_{\xi_i} \left[\gamma^\tau p(\eta|\xi_i).V^\delta(\xi_i) - \gamma^{\tau_n} p(\eta_n|\xi_i).V_n^\delta(\xi_i)\right] + \tau.r - \tau_n.r_n\right\}$$

$$E_{n+1}(\xi) = \sup_{u \in U^\delta} \left\{\gamma^\tau \sum_{\xi_i} [p(\eta|\xi_i) - p(\eta_n|\xi_i)] V^\delta(\xi_i) + [\gamma^\tau - \gamma^{\tau_n}] \sum_{\xi_i} p(\eta_n|\xi_i).V^\delta(\xi_i) \right.$$
$$\left. + \gamma^{\tau_n} \sum_{\xi_i} p(\eta_n|\xi_i).\left[V^\delta(\xi_i) - V_n^\delta(\xi_i)\right] + \tau_n [r - r_n] + [\tau - \tau_n] r\right\}$$

By using (9) (from which we deduce : $\gamma^\tau = \gamma^{\tau_n} + O(\delta^2)$) and (10), we deduce :

$$|E_{n+1}(\xi)| \leq \sup_{u \in U^\delta} \left\{\gamma^\tau . \left|\sum_{\xi_i} [p(\eta|\xi_i) - p(\eta_n|\xi_i)] V^\delta(\xi_i)\right| \right. \tag{18}$$
$$\left. + \gamma^{\tau_n} \sum_{\xi_i} p(\eta_n|\xi_i). \left|V^\delta(\xi_i) - V_n^\delta(\xi_i)\right|\right\} + O(\delta^2).$$

From the basic properties of the coefficients $p(\eta|\xi_i)$ and $p(\eta_n|\xi_i)$ we have:

$$\sum_{\xi_i} [p(\eta|\xi_i) - p(\eta_n|\xi_i)] V^\delta(\xi_i) = \sum_{\xi_i} [p(\eta|\xi_i) - p(\eta_n|\xi_i)] [V^\delta(\xi_i) - V^\delta(\xi)] \quad (19)$$

Moreover, $|V^\delta(\xi_i) - V^\delta(\xi)| \leq |V^\delta(\xi_i) - V(\xi_i)| + |V(\xi_i) - V(\xi)| + |V(\xi) - V^\delta(\xi)|$. From the convergence of the scheme V^δ, we have $\sup_{\Sigma^\delta \cap \Omega} |V^\delta - V| \overset{\delta \downarrow 0}{\to} 0$ for any compact $\Omega \subset O$ and from the continuity of V and the fact that the support of the simplex $\{\xi\} \ni \eta$ is $O(\delta)$, we have $\sup_{\Sigma^\delta \cap \Omega} |V(\xi_i) - V(\xi)| \overset{\delta \downarrow 0}{\to} 0$ and deduce that:
$\sup_{\Sigma^\delta \cap \Omega} |V^\delta(\xi_i) - V^\delta(\xi)| \overset{\delta \downarrow 0}{\to} 0$. Thus, from (19) and (8), we obtain:

$$\left| \sum_{\xi_i} [p(\eta|\xi) - p(\eta_n|\xi)] V^\delta(\xi_i) \right| = o(\delta) \quad (20)$$

The "weak" contraction property (16) holds: from the property of the exponential function $\gamma^{\tau_n} \leq 1 - \frac{\tau_n}{2} \ln \frac{1}{\gamma}$ for small values of τ_n, from (9) and that $\tau \geq k_1 \delta$, we deduce that $\gamma^{\tau_n} \leq 1 - \frac{k_1 \delta}{2} \ln \frac{1}{\gamma} + O(\delta^2)$, and from (18) and (20) we deduce that:

$$\left| V_{n+1}^\delta(\xi) - V^\delta(\xi) \right| \leq (1 - k.\delta) \sup_{\Sigma^\delta} \left| V_{n+1}^\delta(\xi) - V^\delta(\xi) \right| + o(\delta)$$

with $k = \frac{k_1 \delta}{2} \ln \frac{1}{\gamma}$, and the property (16) holds. Thus the "weak contraction" result of convergence (described in section 6.2) applies and convergence occurs.

FUTURE WORK

This work proves the convergence to the optimal value as the resolution tends to the limit, but does not provide us with the rate of convergence. Our future work will focus on defining upper bounds of the approximation error, especially for variable resolution discretizations, and we will also consider the stochastic case.

ACKNOWLEDGMENTS

This research was sponsored by DASSAULT-AVIATION and CMU.

References

[AMS97] C. G. Atkeson, A. W. Moore, and S. A. Schaal. Locally Weighted Learning. *AI Review*, 11:11–73, April 1997.

[Bar94] Guy Barles. *Solutions de viscosité des équations de Hamilton-Jacobi*, volume 17 of *Mathématiques et Applications*. Springer-Verlag, 1994.

[BS91] Guy Barles and P.E. Souganidis. Convergence of approximation schemes for fully nonlinear second order equations. *Asymptotic Analysis*, 4:271–283, 1991.

[Dav96] Scott Davies. Multidimensional triangulation and interpolation for reinforcement learning. *Advances in Neural Information Processing Systems*, 8, 1996.

[FS93] Wendell H. Fleming and H. Mete Soner. *Controlled Markov Processes and Viscosity Solutions*. Applications of Mathematics. Springer-Verlag, 1993.

[Gor95] G. Gordon. Stable function approximation in dynamic programming. *International Conference on Machine Learning*, 1995.

[Kus90] Harold J. Kushner. Numerical methods for stochastic control problems in continuous time. *SIAM J. Control and Optimization*, 28:999–1048, 1990.

[Mun97] Rémi Munos. A convergent reinforcement learning algorithm in the continuous case based on a finite difference method. *International Joint Conference on Artificial Intelligence*, 1997.

[Mun98] Rémi Munos. A general convergence theorem for reinforcement learning in the continuous case. *European Conference on Machine Learning*, 1998.

[Omo87] S. M. Omohundro. Efficient Algorithms with Neural Network Behaviour. *Journal of Complex Systems*, 1(2):273–347, 1987.

Risk Sensitive Reinforcement Learning

Ralph Neuneier
Siemens AG, Corporate Technology
D-81730 München, Germany
Ralph.Neuneier@mchp.siemens.de

Oliver Mihatsch
Siemens AG, Corporate Technology
D-81730 München, Germany
Oliver.Mihatsch@mchp.siemens.de

Abstract

As already known, the expected return of a policy in Markov Decision Problems is not always the most suitable optimality criterion. For many applications control strategies have to meet various constraints like avoiding very bad states (risk-avoiding) or generating high profit within a short time (risk-seeking) although this might probably cause significant costs. We propose a modified Q-learning algorithm which uses a single continuous parameter $\kappa \in [-1, 1]$ to determine in which sense the resulting policy is optimal. For $\kappa = 0$, the policy is optimal with respect to the usual expected return criterion, while $\kappa \to 1$ generates a solution which is optimal in worst case. Analogous, the closer κ is to -1 the more risk seeking the policy becomes. In contrast to other related approaches in the field of MDPs we do not have to transform the cost model or to increase the state space in order to take risk into account. Our new approach is evaluated by computing optimal investment strategies for an artificial stock market.

1 WHY IT SOMETIMES PAYS TO ACT CAUTIOUSLY

Reinforcement learning (RL) deals with the computation of favorable control policies in sequential decision task. Its theoretical framework of Markov Decision Problems (MDPs) evaluates and compares policies by their expected (sometimes discounted or averaged) sum of the immediate returns or costs per time step (Bertsekas & Tsitsiklis, 1996). But there are numerous applications which require a more sophisticated control scheme: e. g. a policy should take into account that bad outcomes or states may be possible even if they are very rare because they are so disastrous, that they should be certainly avoided.

An obvious example is the field of finance where the main question is how to invest resources among various opportunities (e.g. assets like stocks, bonds, etc.) to achieve remarkable returns while simultaneously controlling the risk exposure of the investments due to changing markets or economic conditions. Many traders try to achieve this by a Markovitz-like portfolio management which distributes capital according to return and risk estimates of the assets. A new approach using reinforcement learning techniques which additionally integrates trading costs and other market imperfections has been proposed in Neuneier, 1998. Here, these algorithms are naturally extended such that an explicit risk control is now possible. The investor can decide how much risk she/he is willing to accept and then compute an optimal risk-averse investment strategy. Similar trade-off scenarios can be formulated in robotics, traffic control and further application areas.

The fact that the popular expected value criterion is not always suitable has been already known in the field of AI (Koenig & Simmons, 1994), control theory and reinforcement learning (Heger, 1994 and Szepesvári, 1997). Several techniques have been proposed to handle this problem. The most obvious way is to transform the sum of returns $\sum_t r_t$ using an appropriate utility function U which reflects the desired properties of the solution. Unfortunately, interesting nonlinear utility functions incorporating the variance of the return, such as $U(\sum_t r_t) = \sum_t r_t - \lambda(\sum_t r_t - E(\sum_t r_t))^2$, lead to non-Markovian decision problems. The popular class of exponential utility functions $U(\sum_t r_t) = \exp(\lambda \sum_t r_t)$ preserves the Markov property but requires time dependent policies even for discounted infinite horizon MDPs. Furthermore, it is not possible to formulate a corresponding model-free learning algorithm. A further alternative changes the state space model by including past returns as an additional state element at the cost of a higher dimensionality of the MDP. Furthermore, it is not always clear in which way the states should be augmented. One may also transform the cost model, i.e. by punishing large losses stronger than minor costs. While requiring a significant amount of prior knowledge, this also increases the complexity of the MDP.

In contrast to these approaches we modify the popular Q-learning algorithm by introducing a control parameter which determines in which sense the resulting policy is optimal. Intuitively and loosely speaking, our algorithm simulates the learning behavior of an optimistic (pessimistic) person by overweighting (underweighting) experiences which are more positive (negative) than expected. This main idea will be made more precise in section 2 and mathematically thoroughly analyzed in section 3. Using artificial data, we demonstrate some properties of the new algorithm by constructing an optimal risk-avoiding investment strategy (section 4).

2 RISK SENSITIVE Q-LEARNING

For brevity we restrict ourselves to the subclass of infinite horizon discounted Markov decision problems (MDP). Furthermore, we assume the immediate rewards being deterministic functions of the current state and control action. Let $S = \{1, \ldots, n\}$ be the finite state space and U be the finite action space. Transition probabilities and immediate rewards are denoted by $p_{ij}(u)$ and $g_i(u)$, respectively. γ denotes the discount factor. Let Π be the set of all deterministic policies mapping states to control actions.

A commonly used objective is to learn a policy π that

$$\text{maximizes} \left(\overline{Q}^\pi(i, u) := g_i(u) + E\left\{ \sum_{k=1}^{\infty} \gamma^k g_{i_k}(\pi(i_k)) \right\} \right) \quad (1)$$

quantifying the expected reward if one executes control action u in state i and follows the policy π thereafter. It is a well-known result that the optimal Q-values $\overline{Q}^*(i, u) := max_{\pi \in \Pi} \overline{Q}^\pi(i, u)$ satisfy the following optimality equation

$$\overline{Q}^*(i, u) = g_i(u) + \gamma \sum_{j \in S} p_{ij}(u) \max_{u' \in U} \overline{Q}^*(j, u') \quad \forall i \in S, u \in U. \quad (2)$$

Any policy $\overline{\pi}$ with $\overline{\pi}(i) = \arg\max_{u \in U} \overline{Q}^*(i, u)$ is optimal with respect to the expected reward criterion.

The Q-function $\overline{Q}^\pi$ averages over the outcome of all possible trajectories (series of states) of the Markov process generated by following the policy π. However, the outcome of a specific realization of the Markov process may deviate significantly from this mean value. The expected reward criterion does not consider any risk, although the cases where the discounted reward falls considerably below the mean value is of a living interest for many applications. Therefore, depending on the application at hand the expected reward approach is not always appropriate. Alternatively, Heger (1994) and Littman & Szepesvári (1996) present a performance criterion that exclusively focuses on risk avoiding policies:

$$\text{maximize} \left(\underline{Q}^\pi(i,u) := g_i(u) + \inf_{\substack{i_1,i_2,\ldots \\ p(i_1,i_2,\ldots)>0}} \left\{ \sum_{k=1}^\infty \gamma^k g_{i_k}(\pi(i_k)) \right\} \right). \quad (3)$$

The Q-function $\underline{Q}^\pi(i,u)$ denotes the worst possible outcome if one executes control action u in state i and follows the policy π thereafter. The corresponding optimality equation for $\underline{Q}^*(i,u) := \max_{\pi \in \Pi} \underline{Q}^\pi(i,u)$ is given by

$$\underline{Q}^*(i,u) = g_i(u) + \gamma \min_{\substack{j \in S \\ p_{ij}(u)>0}} \max_{u' \in U} \underline{Q}^*(j,u'). \quad (4)$$

Any policy $\underline{\pi}$ satisfying $\underline{\pi}(i) = \arg\max_{u \in U} \underline{Q}^*(i,u)$ is optimal with respect to this minimal reward criterion. In most real world applications this approach is too restrictive because it takes very rare events (that in practice never happen) fully into account. This usually leads to policies with a lower average performance than the application requires. An investment manager, for instance, which acts with respect to this very pessimistic objective function will not invest at all.

To handle the trade-off between a sufficient average performance and a risk avoiding (risk seeking) behavior, we propose a family of new optimality equations parameterized by a meta-parameter κ ($-1 < \kappa < 1$):

$$0 = \sum_{j \in S} p_{ij}(u) \mathcal{X}^\kappa \left(g_i(u) + \gamma \max_{u' \in U} Q_\kappa(j,u') - Q_\kappa(i,u) \right) \quad \forall i \in S, u \in U \quad (5)$$

where $\mathcal{X}^\kappa(x) := (1 - \kappa \operatorname{sign}(x))x$. (In the next section we will show that a unique solution Q_κ of the above equation (5) exists.) Obviously, for $\kappa = 0$ we recover equation (2), the optimality equation for the expected reward criterion. If we choose κ to be positive ($0 < \kappa < 1$) then we overweight negative temporal differences

$$g_i(u) + \gamma \max_{u' \in U} Q_\kappa(j,u') - Q_\kappa(i,u) < 0 \quad (6)$$

with respect to positive ones. Loosely speaking, we overweight transitions to states where the future return is lower than the average one. On the other hand, we underweight transitions to states that promise a higher return than in the average. Thus, an agent that behaves according to the policy $\pi_\kappa(i) := \arg\max_{u \in U} Q_\kappa(i,u)$ is risk avoiding if $\kappa > 0$. In the limit $\kappa \to 1$ the policy π_κ approaches the optimal worst-case policy $\underline{\pi}$, as we will show in the following section. (To get an intuition about this, the reader may easily check that the optimal worst-case Q-value $\underline{Q}^*$ fulfills the modified optimality equation (5) for $\kappa = 1$.) Similarly, the policy π_κ becomes risk seeking if we choose κ to be negative.

It is straightforward to formulate a risk sensitive Q-learning algorithm that bases on the modified optimality equation (5). Let $\hat{Q}_\kappa(i,u;w)$ be a parametric approximation of the Q-function $Q_\kappa(i,u)$. The states and actions encountered at time step k during simulation are denoted by i_k and u_k respectively. At each time step apply the following update rule:

$$\begin{aligned} d^{(k)} &= g_{i_k}(u_k) + \gamma \max_{u' \in U} \hat{Q}_\kappa(i_{k+1}, u'; w^{(k)}) - \hat{Q}_\kappa(i_k, u_k; w^{(k)}), \\ w^{(k+1)} &= w^{(k)} + \alpha_\kappa^{(k)} \mathcal{X}^\kappa(d^{(k)}) \nabla_w \hat{Q}_\kappa(i_k, u_k; w^{(k)}), \end{aligned} \quad (7)$$

where $\alpha_\kappa^{(k)}$ denotes a stepsize sequence. The following section analyzes the properties of the new optimality equations and the corresponding Q-learning algorithm.

3 PROPERTIES OF THE RISK SENSITIVE Q-FUNCTION

Due to space limitations we are not able to give detailed proofs of our results. Instead, we focus on interpreting their practical consequences. The proofs will be published elsewhere.

Before formulating the mathematical results, we introduce some notation to make the exposition more concise. Using an arbitrary stepsize $0 < \alpha < 1$, we define the value iteration operator corresponding to our modified optimality equation (5) as

$$\mathcal{T}_{\alpha,\kappa}[Q](i,u) := Q(i,u) + \alpha \sum_{j \in S} p_{ij}(u) \mathcal{X}^\kappa \left(g_i(u) + \gamma \max_{u' \in U} Q(j,u') - Q(i,u) \right). \tag{8}$$

The operator $\mathcal{T}_{\alpha,\kappa}$ acts on the space of Q-functions. For every Q-function Q and every state-action pair (i,u) we define $N_\kappa[Q](i,u)$ to be the set of all successor states j for which $\max_{u' \in U} Q(j,u')$ attains its minimum:

$$N_\kappa[Q](i,u) := \left\{ j \in S | p_{ij}(u) > 0 \text{ and } \max_{u' \in U} Q(j,u') = \min_{\substack{j' \in S \\ p_{ij'}(u) > 0}} \max_{u' \in U} Q(j',u') \right\}. \tag{9}$$

Let $p_\kappa[Q](i,u) := \sum_{j \in N_\kappa[Q](i,u)} p_{ij}(u)$ be the probability of transitions to such successor states.

We have the following lemma ensuring the contraction property of $\mathcal{T}_{\alpha,\kappa}$.

Lemma 1 (Contraction Property) *Let* $|Q| = \max_{i \in S, u \in U} Q(i,u)$ *and* $0 < \alpha < 1$, $0 < \gamma < 1$. *Then*

$$|\mathcal{T}_{\alpha,\kappa}[Q_1] - \mathcal{T}_{\alpha,\kappa}[Q_2]| \leq (1 - \alpha(1-|\kappa|)(1-\gamma)) |Q_1 - Q_2| \quad \forall Q_1, Q_2. \tag{10}$$

The operator $\mathcal{T}_{\alpha,\kappa}$ *is contracting, because* $0 < (1 - \alpha(1-|\kappa|)(1-\gamma)) < 1$.

The lemma has several important consequences.

1. The risk sensitive optimality equation (5), i.e. $\mathcal{T}_{\alpha,\kappa}[Q] = Q$ has a unique solution Q_κ for all $-1 < \kappa < 1$.

2. The value iteration procedure $Q_{\text{new}} := \mathcal{T}_{\alpha,\kappa}[Q]$ converges towards Q_κ.

3. The existing convergence results for traditional Q-learning (Bertsekas & Tsitsiklis 1997, Tsitsiklis & Van Roy 1997) remain also valid in the risk sensitive case $\kappa \neq 0$. Particularly, risk sensitive Q-learning (7) converges with probability one in the case of lookup table representations as well as in the case of optimal stopping problems combined with linear representations.

4. The speed of convergence for both, risk sensitive value iteration and Q-learning becomes worse if $|\kappa| \to 1$. We can remedy this to some extent if we increase the stepsize α appropriately.

Let π_κ be a greedy policy with respect to the unique solution Q_κ of our modified optimality equation; that is $\pi_\kappa(i) = \arg\max_{u \in U} Q_\kappa(i,u)$. The following theorem examines the performance of π_κ for the risk avoiding case $\kappa \geq 0$. It gives us a feeling about the expected outcome $\overline{Q}^{\pi_\kappa}$ and the worst possible outcome $\underline{Q}^{\pi_\kappa}$ of policy π_κ for different values of κ. The theorem clarifies the limiting behavior of π_κ if $\kappa \to 1$.

Risk Sensitive Reinforcement Learning

Theorem 2 *Let $0 \leq \kappa < 1$. The following inequalities hold componentwise, i. e. for each pair $(i, u) \in S \times U$.*

$$0 \leq \overline{Q}^* - \overline{Q}^{\pi_\kappa} \leq 2\kappa \frac{\gamma}{1-\gamma}(\overline{Q}^* - \underline{Q}^*) \tag{11}$$

$$0 \leq p_\kappa[Q_\kappa](\underline{Q}^* - \underline{Q}^{\pi_\kappa}) \leq \frac{(1-\kappa)}{2\kappa} \frac{\gamma}{1-\gamma}(\overline{Q}^* - \underline{Q}^*) \tag{12}$$

Moreover, $\lim_{\kappa \to 0} \overline{Q}^{\pi_\kappa} = \overline{Q}^*$ and $\lim_{\kappa \to 1} \underline{Q}^{\pi_\kappa} = \underline{Q}^*$.

The difference $\overline{Q}^* - \underline{Q}^*$ between the optimal expected reward and the optimal worst case reward is crucial in the above inequalities. It measures the amount of risk being inherent in our MDP at hand. Besides the value of κ, this quantity essentially influences the difference between the performance of the policy π_κ and the optimal performance with respect to both, the expected reward and the worst case criterion. The second inequality (12) states that the performance of policy π_κ in the worst case sense tends to the optimal worst case performance if $\kappa \to 1$. The "speed of convergence" is influenced by the quantity $p_\kappa[Q_\kappa]$, i. e. the probability that a worst case transition really occurs. (Note that $p_\kappa[Q_\kappa]$ is bounded from below.) A higher probability $p_\kappa[Q_\kappa]$ of worst case transitions implies a stronger risk avoiding attitude of the policy π_κ.

4 EXPERIMENTS: RISK-AVERSE INVESTMENT DECISIONS

Our algorithm is now tested on the task of constructing an optimal investment policy for an artificial stock price analogous to the empirical analysis in Neuneier, 1998. The task, illustrated as a MDP in fig. 1, is to decide at each time step (e. g. each day or after each mayor event on the market) whether to buy the stock and therefore speculating on increasing stock prices or to keep the capital in cash which avoids potential losses due to decreasing stock prices.

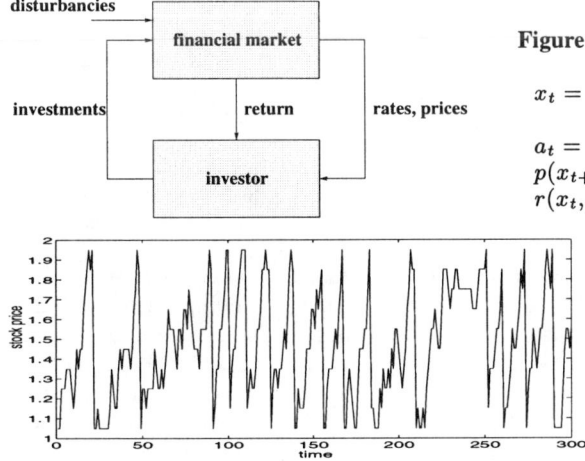

Figure 1. The Markov Decision Problem:

$x_t = (\$_t, K_t)'$ state: market $\$_t$ and portfolio K_t
$a_t = \mu(x_t)$ policy μ, actions
$p(x_{t+1}|x_t)$ transition probabilities
$r(x_t, a_t, \$_{t+1})$ return function

Figure 2. A realization of the artificial stock price for 300 time steps. It is obvious that the price follows an increasing trend but with higher values a sudden drop to low values becomes more and more probable.

It is assumed, that the investor is not able to influence the market by the investment decisions. This leads to a MDP with some of the state elements being uncontrollable and results in two computationally import implications: first, one can simulate the investments by historical data without investing (and potentially losing) real money. Second, one can formulate a very efficient (memory saving) and more robust Q-learning algorithms. Due to space restriction we skip a detailed description of these algorithms and refer the interested reader to Neuneier, 1998.

The artificial stock price is in the range of $[1, 2]$. The transition probabilities are chosen such that the stock market simulates a situation where the price follows an increasing trend but with higher values a drop to very low values becomes more and more probable (fig. 2).

The state vector consists of the current stock price and the current investment, i.e. the amount of money invested in stocks or cash. Changing the investment from cash to stocks results in some transaction costs consisting of variable and fixed terms. These costs are essential to define the investment problem as a MDP because they couple the actions made at different time steps. Otherwise we could solve the problem by a pure prediction of the next stock price. The function which quantifies the immediate return for each time step is defined as follows: if the capital is invested in cash, then there is nothing to earn even if the stock price increases, if the investor has bought stocks the return is equal the relative change of the stock price weighted by the invested amount of capital minus the transaction costs which apply if one changed from cash to stocks.

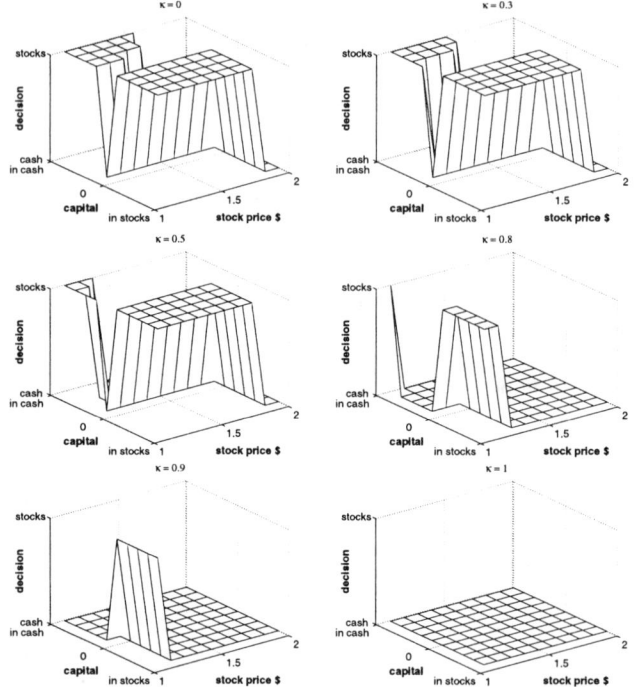

Figure 3. Left: Risk neutral policy, $\kappa = 0$. Right: A small bias of $\kappa = 0.3$ against risk changes the policy if one is not invested (transaction costs apply in this case).

Figure 4. Left: $\kappa = 0.5$ yields a stronger risk averse attitude. Right: With $\kappa = 0.8$ the policy becomes also more cautious if already invested in stocks.

Figure 5. Left: $\kappa = 0.9$ leads to a policy which invests in stocks in only 5 cases. Right: The worst case solution never invests because there is always a positive probability for decreasing stock prices.

As a reinforcement learning method, Q-learning has to interact with the environment (here the stock market) to learn optimal investment behavior. Thus, a training set of 2000 data points is generated. The training phase is divided into epochs which consists of as many trials as data in the training set exist. At every trial the algorithm selects randomly a stock price from the data set, chooses a random investment state and updates the tabulated Q-values according to the procedure given in Neuneier, 1998. The only difference of our new risk averse Q-learning is that negative experiences, i.e. smaller returns than in the mean, are overweighted in comparison to positive experiences using the κ-factor of eq. (7). Using different κ values from 0 (recovering the original Q-learning procedure) to 1 (leading to worst case Q-learning) we plot the resulting policies as mappings from the state space to control actions in figures 3 to 5. Obviously, with increasing κ the investor acts more and more cautiously because there are less states associated with an investment decision for stocks. In the extreme case of $\kappa = 1$, there is no stock investment at all in order to avoid any loss. The policy is not useful in practice. This supports our introductory comments that worst case Q-learning is not appropriate in many tasks.

Risk Sensitive Reinforcement Learning

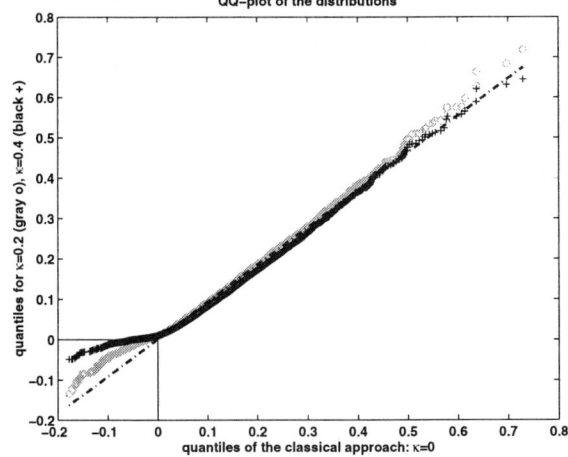

Figure 6. The quantiles of the distributions of the discounted sum of returns for $\kappa = 0.2$ (o) and $\kappa = 0.4$ (+) are plotted against the quantiles for the classical risk neutral approach $\kappa = 0$. The distributions only differ significantly for negative accumulated returns (left tail of the distributions).

For further analysis, we specify a risky start state i_0 for which a sudden drop of the stock price in the near future is very probable. Starting at i_0 we compute the cumulated discounted rewards of 10000 different trajectories following the policies π_0, $\pi_{0.2}$ and $\pi_{0.4}$ which have been generated using $\kappa = 0$ (risk neutral), $\kappa = 0.2$ and $\kappa = 0.4$. The resulting three data sets are compared using a quantile-quantile plot whose purpose is to determine whether the samples come from the same distribution type. If they do so, the plot will be linear. Fig. 6 clearly shows that for higher κ-values the left tail of the distribution (negative returns) bends up indicating a fewer number of losses. On the other hand there is no significant difference for positive quantiles. In contrast to naive utility functions which penalizes high variance in general, our risk sensitive Q-learning asymmetrically reduces the probability for losses which may be more suitable for many applications.

5 CONCLUSION

We have formulated a new Q-learning algorithm which can be continuously tuned towards risk seeking or risk avoiding policies. Thus, it is possible to construct control strategies which are more suitable for the problem at hand by only small modifications of Q-learning algorithm. The advantage of our approch in comparison to already known solutions is, that we have neither to change the cost nor the state model. We can prove that our algorithm converges under the usual assumptions. Future work will focus on the connections between our approach and the utility theoretic point of view.

References

D. P. Bertsekas, J. N. Tsitsiklis (1996) *Neuro-Dynamic Programming*. Athena Scientific.
M. Heger (1994) Consideration of Risk and Reinforcement Learning, in Machine Learning, proceedings of the 11th International Conference, Morgan Kaufmann Publishers.
S. Koenig, R. G. Simmons (1994) Risk-Sensitive Planning with Probabilistic Decision Graphs. Proc. of the Fourth Int. Conf. on Principles of Knowledge Representation and Reasoning (KR).
M. L. Littman, Cs. Szepesvári (1996), A generalized reinforcement-learning model: Convergence and applications. In International Conference of Machine Learning '96. Bari.
R. Neuneier (1998) Enhancing Q-learning for Optimal Asset Allocation, in *Advances in Neural Information Processing Systems 10*, Cambridge, MA: MIT Press.
M. L. Puterman (1994), *Markov Decision Processes*, John Wiley & Sons.
Cs. Szepesvári (1997) Non-Markovian Policies in Sequential Decision Problems, Acta Cybernetica.
J. N. Tsitsiklis, B. Van Roy (1997) Approximate Solutions to Optimal Stopping Problems, in *Advances in Neural Information Processing Systems 9*, Cambridge, MA: MIT Press.

Coordinate Transformation Learning of Hand Position Feedback Controller by Using Change of Position Error Norm

Eimei Oyama*
Mechanical Eng. Lab.
Namiki 1-2, Tsukuba Science City
Ibaraki 305-8564 Japan

Susumu Tachi
The University of Tokyo
Hongo 7-3-1, Bunkyo-ku
Tokyo 113-0033 Japan

Abstract

In order to grasp an object, we need to solve the inverse kinematics problem, i.e., the coordinate transformation from the visual coordinates to the joint angle vector coordinates of the arm. Although several models of coordinate transformation learning have been proposed, they suffer from a number of drawbacks. In human motion control, the learning of the hand position error feedback controller in the inverse kinematics solver is important. This paper proposes a novel model of the coordinate transformation learning of the human visual feedback controller that uses the change of the joint angle vector and the corresponding change of the square of the hand position error norm. The feasibility of the proposed model is illustrated using numerical simulations.

1 INTRODUCTION

The task of calculating every joint angle that would result in a specific hand position is called the inverse kinematics problem. An important topic in neuroscience is the study of the learning mechanisms involved in the human inverse kinematics solver.

We questioned five pediatricians about the motor function of infants suffering from serious upper limb disabilities. The doctors stated that the infants still were able to touch and stroke an object without hindrance. In one case, an infant without a thumb had a major kinematically influential surgical operation, transplanting an index finger as a thumb. After the operation, the child was able to learn how to use the index finger like a thumb [1]. In order to explain the human motor learning

---

*Phone:+81-298-58-7298, Fax:+81-298-58-7201, e-mail:eimei@mel.go.jp

capability, we believe that the coordinate transformation learning of the feedback controller is a necessary component.

Although a number of learning models of the inverse kinematics solver have been proposed, a definitive learning model has not yet been obtained. This is from the point of view of the structural complexity of the learning model and the biological plausibility of employed hypothesis. The *Direct Inverse Modeling* employed by many researchers [2] requires the complex switching of the input signal of the inverse model. When the hand position control is performed, the input of the inverse model is the desired hand position, velocity, or acceleration. When the inverse model learning is performed, the input is the observed hand position, velocity, or acceleration. Although the desired signal and the observed signal could coincide, the characteristics of the two signals are very different. Currently, no research has succeesfully modeled the switching system. Furthermore, that learning model is not "goal-directed"; i.e., there is no direct way to find an action that corresponds to a particular desired result. The *Forward and Inverse Modeling* proposed by Jordan [3] requires the back-propagation signal, a technique does not have a biological basis. That model also requires the complex switching of the desired output signal for the forward model. When the forward model learning is performed, the desired output is the observed hand position. When the inverse kinematics solver learning is performed, the desired output is the desired hand position. The *Feedback Error Learning* proposed by Kawato [4] requires a pre-existing accurate feedback controller.

It is necessary to obtain a learning model that possesses a number of characteristics: (1) it can explain the human learning function; (2) it has a simple structure; and (3) it is biologically plausible. This paper presents a learning model of coordinate transformation function of the hand position feedback controller. This model uses the joint angle vector change and the corresponding change of square of the hand position error norm.

2 BACKGROUND

2.1 Discrete Time First Order Model of Hand Position Controller

Let $\boldsymbol{\theta} \in \mathbf{R}^m$ be the joint angle vector and $\boldsymbol{x} \in \mathbf{R}^n$ be the hand position/orientation vector given by the vision system. The relationship between $\boldsymbol{x}$ and $\boldsymbol{\theta}$ is expressed as $\boldsymbol{x} = \boldsymbol{f}(\boldsymbol{\theta})$ where $\boldsymbol{f}$ is a C^1 class function. The Jacobian of the hand position vector is expressed as $\boldsymbol{J}(\boldsymbol{\theta}) = \partial \boldsymbol{f}(\boldsymbol{\theta})/\partial \boldsymbol{\theta}$. Let $\boldsymbol{x}_d$ be the desired hand position and $\boldsymbol{e} = \boldsymbol{x}_d - \boldsymbol{x} = \boldsymbol{x}_d - \boldsymbol{f}(\boldsymbol{\theta})$ be the hand position error vector. In this paper, an inverse kinematics problem is assumed to be a least squares minimization problem that calculates $\boldsymbol{\theta}$ in order to minimize the square of the hand position error norm $S(\boldsymbol{x}_d, \boldsymbol{\theta}) = |\boldsymbol{e}|^2/2 = |\boldsymbol{x}_d - \boldsymbol{f}(\boldsymbol{\theta})|^2/2$.

First, the feed-forward controller in the human inverse kinematics solver is disregarded and the following first order control system, consisting of a learning feedback controller, is considered:

$$\boldsymbol{\theta}(k+1) = \boldsymbol{\theta}(k) + \boldsymbol{\Delta\theta}(k) \quad (1)$$

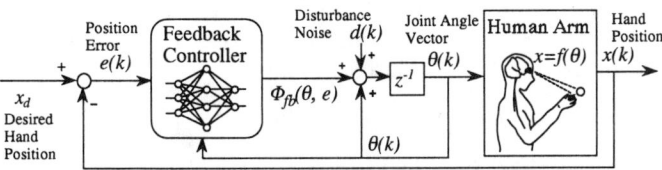

Figure 1: Configuration of 1-st Order Model of Hand Position Controller

$$\Delta\boldsymbol{\theta}(k) = \boldsymbol{\Phi}_{fb}(\boldsymbol{\theta}(k), \boldsymbol{e}(k)) + \boldsymbol{d}(k) \tag{2}$$
$$\boldsymbol{e}(k) = \boldsymbol{x}_d - \boldsymbol{f}(\boldsymbol{\theta}(k)) \tag{3}$$

where $\boldsymbol{d}(k)$ is assumed to be a disturbance noise from all components except the hand position control system. Figure 1 shows the configuration of the control system. In this figure, z^{-1} is the operator that indicates a delay in the discrete time signal by a sampling interval of Δt. Although the human hand position control system includes higher order complex dynamics terms which are ignored in Equation (2), McRuer's experimental model of human compensation control suggests that the term that converts the hand position error to the hand velocity is a major term in the human control system [5]. We consider Equation (2) to be a good approximate model for the analysis of human coordinates transformation learning.

The learner $\boldsymbol{\Phi}_{fb}(\boldsymbol{\theta}, \boldsymbol{e}) \in \mathbf{R}^m$, which provides the hand position error feedback, is modeled using the artificial neural network. In this paper, the hand position error feedback controller learning by observing output $\boldsymbol{x}(k)$ is considered without any prior knowledge of the function $\boldsymbol{f}(\boldsymbol{\theta})$.

2.2 Learning Model of the Neural Network

Let $\boldsymbol{\Phi}'_{fb}(\boldsymbol{\theta}, \boldsymbol{e})$ be the desired output of the learner $\boldsymbol{\Phi}_{fb}(\boldsymbol{\theta}, \boldsymbol{e})$. $\boldsymbol{\Phi}'_{fb}(\boldsymbol{\theta}, \boldsymbol{e})$ functions as a teacher for $\boldsymbol{\Phi}_{fb}(\boldsymbol{\theta}, \boldsymbol{e})$. Let $\boldsymbol{\Phi}^+_{fb}(\boldsymbol{\theta}, \boldsymbol{e})$ be the updated output of $\boldsymbol{\Phi}_{fb}(\boldsymbol{\theta}, \boldsymbol{e})$ by the learning. Let $E[t(\boldsymbol{\theta}, \boldsymbol{e})|\boldsymbol{\theta}, \boldsymbol{e}]$ be the expected value of a scalar, a vector, or a matrix function $t(\boldsymbol{\theta}, \boldsymbol{e})$ when the input vector $(\boldsymbol{\theta}, \boldsymbol{e})$ is given. We assume that $\boldsymbol{\Phi}_{fb}(\boldsymbol{\theta}, \boldsymbol{e})$ is an ideal learner which is capable of realizing the mean of the desired output signal, completely. $\boldsymbol{\Phi}^+{}_{fb}(\boldsymbol{\theta}, \boldsymbol{e})$ can be expressed as follows:

$$\boldsymbol{\Phi}^+_{fb}(\boldsymbol{\theta}, \boldsymbol{e}) \approx E[\boldsymbol{\Phi}'_{fb}(\boldsymbol{\theta}, \boldsymbol{e})|\boldsymbol{\theta}, \boldsymbol{e}] = \boldsymbol{\Phi}_{fb}(\boldsymbol{\theta}, \boldsymbol{e}) + E[\Delta\boldsymbol{\Phi}_{fb}(\boldsymbol{\theta}, \boldsymbol{e})|\boldsymbol{\theta}, \boldsymbol{e}] \tag{4}$$

$$\Delta\boldsymbol{\Phi}_{fb}(\boldsymbol{\theta}, \boldsymbol{e}) = \boldsymbol{\Phi}'_{fb}(\boldsymbol{\theta}, \boldsymbol{e}) - \boldsymbol{\Phi}_{fb}(\boldsymbol{\theta}, \boldsymbol{e}) \tag{5}$$

When the expected value of $\Delta\boldsymbol{\Phi}_{fb}(\boldsymbol{\theta}, \boldsymbol{e})$ is expressed as:

$$E[\Delta\boldsymbol{\Phi}_{fb}(\boldsymbol{\theta}, \boldsymbol{e})|\boldsymbol{\theta}, \boldsymbol{e}] \approx \boldsymbol{G}_{fb}\boldsymbol{e} - \boldsymbol{R}_{fb}\boldsymbol{\Phi}_{fb}(\boldsymbol{\theta}, \boldsymbol{e}), \tag{6}$$

$\boldsymbol{R}_{fb} \in \mathbf{R}^{m \times m}$ is a positive definite matrix, and the inequality

$$\left|\frac{\partial \boldsymbol{\Phi}^+_{fb}(\boldsymbol{\theta}, \boldsymbol{e})}{\partial \boldsymbol{\Phi}_{fb}(\boldsymbol{\theta}, \boldsymbol{e})}\right| = \left|\frac{\partial(\boldsymbol{G}_{fb}\boldsymbol{e} - (\boldsymbol{R}_{fb} - \boldsymbol{I})\boldsymbol{\Phi}_{fb}(\boldsymbol{\theta}, \boldsymbol{e}))}{\partial \boldsymbol{\Phi}_{fb}(\boldsymbol{\theta}, \boldsymbol{e})}\right| < 1 \tag{7}$$

is satisfied, the final learning result can be expressed as:

$$\boldsymbol{\Phi}_{fb}(\boldsymbol{\theta}, \boldsymbol{e}) \approx \boldsymbol{R}^{-1}_{fb}\boldsymbol{G}_{fb}\boldsymbol{e} \tag{8}$$

by the iteration of the update of $\boldsymbol{\Phi}_{fb}(\boldsymbol{\theta}, \boldsymbol{e})$ expressed in Equation (4).

3 USE OF CHANGE OF POSITION ERROR NORM

3.1 A Novel Learning Model of Feedback Controller

The change of the square of the hand position error norm $\Delta S = S(\boldsymbol{x}_d, \boldsymbol{\theta} + \Delta\boldsymbol{\theta}) - S(\boldsymbol{x}_d, \boldsymbol{\theta})$ reflects whether or not the change of the joint angle vector $\Delta\boldsymbol{\theta}$ is in proper direction. The propose novel learning model can be expressed as follows:

$$\boldsymbol{\Phi}'_{fb}(\boldsymbol{\theta}, \boldsymbol{e}) = -\alpha \Delta S \Delta\boldsymbol{\theta} \tag{9}$$

where α is a small positive real number. We now consider a large number of trials of Equation (2) with a large variety of initial status $\boldsymbol{\theta}(0)$ with learnings conducted at the point of the input space of the feedback controller $(\boldsymbol{\theta}, \boldsymbol{e}) = (\boldsymbol{\theta}(k-1), \boldsymbol{e}(k-1))$ at time k. ΔS and $\Delta\boldsymbol{\theta}$ can be calculated as follows.

$$\Delta S = S(k) - S(k-1) = \frac{1}{2}(|\boldsymbol{e}(k)|^2 - |\boldsymbol{e}(k-1)|^2) \tag{10}$$

$$\Delta\boldsymbol{\theta} = \Delta\boldsymbol{\theta}(k-1) \tag{11}$$

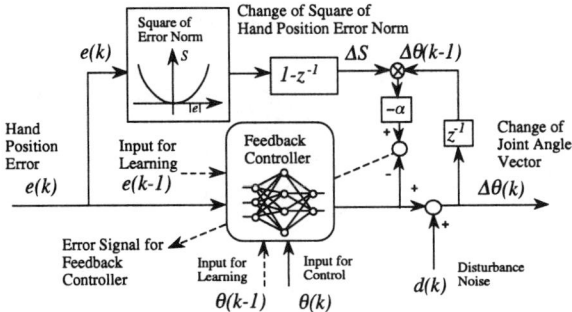

Figure 2: Configuration of Learning Model of Feedback Controller

Figure 2 shows the conceptual diagram of the proposed learning model.

Let $p(q|\theta, e)$ be the probability density function of a vector q at at the point (θ, e) in the input space of $\Phi_{fb}(\theta, e)$. In order to simplify the analysis of the proposed learning model, $d(k)$ is assumed to satisfy the following equation:

$$p(d|\theta, e) = p(-d|\theta, e) \tag{12}$$

When $\Delta\theta$ is small enough, the result of the learning using Equation (9) can be expressed as:

$$\Phi_{fb}(\theta, e) \approx \alpha(\frac{\alpha}{2}R_\theta J^T(\theta)J(\theta) + I)^{-1}R_\theta J^T(\theta)e \tag{13}$$

$$R_\theta = E[\Delta\theta\Delta\theta^T|\theta, e] \tag{14}$$

where $J^T(\theta)e$ is a vector in the steepest descent direction of $S(x_d, \theta)$. When $d(k)$ is a non-zero vector, R_θ is a positive definite symmetric matrix and $(\frac{\alpha}{2}R_\theta J^T J + I)^{-1}$ is a positive definite matrix. When α is appropriate, $\Phi_{fb}(\theta, e)$ as expressed in Equation (13) can provide appropriate output error feedback control. The derivation of the above result will be illustrated in Section 3.2. A partially modified steepest descent direction can be obtained without using the forward model or the back-propagation signal, as Jordan's forward modeling [3].

Let R_d be the covariance matrix of the disturbance noise $d(k)$. When α is infinitesimal, $R_\theta \approx R_d$ is established and an approximate solution $\Phi_{fb}(\theta, e) \approx \alpha R_d J^T(\theta)e$ is obtained.

3.2 Derivation of Learning Result

The change of the square of the hand position error norm $\Delta S(x_d, \theta)$ by $\Delta\theta$ can be determined as:

$$\Delta S(x_d, \theta) = \frac{\partial S(x_d, \theta)}{\partial \theta}\Delta\theta + \frac{1}{2}\Delta\theta^T H(x_d, \theta)\Delta\theta + O(\Delta\theta^3) \tag{15}$$

$$= -e^T(J(\theta) + \frac{1}{2}\frac{\partial J(\theta)}{\partial \theta} \otimes \Delta\theta)\Delta\theta + \frac{1}{2}\Delta\theta^T J^T(\theta)J(\theta)\Delta\theta + O(\Delta\theta^3)$$

where $\otimes$ is a 2-operand operator that indicates the Croneker's product. $H(x_d, \theta) \in \mathbf{R}^{m \times m}$ is the Hessian of $S(x_d, \theta)$. $O(\Delta\theta^3)$ is the sum of third and higher order terms of $\Delta\theta$ in each equation. When $\Delta\theta$ is small enough, the following approximate equations are obtained:

$$\Delta x \approx J(\theta)\Delta\theta \approx J(\theta + \frac{1}{2}\Delta\theta)\Delta\theta \approx (J(\theta) + \frac{1}{2}\frac{\partial J(\theta)}{\partial \theta} \otimes \Delta\theta)\Delta\theta \tag{16}$$

Therefore, ΔS can be approximated as follows:

$$\Delta S \approx -e^T J(\theta)\Delta\theta + \frac{1}{2}|\Delta x|^2 \tag{17}$$

Since $e^T J \Delta\theta \Delta\theta = \Delta\theta \Delta\theta^T J^T e$ and $|\Delta x|^2 \Delta\theta = \Delta\theta \Delta\theta^T J^T J \Delta\theta$ are determined, $\Delta S \Delta\theta$ can be approximated as:

$$\Delta S \Delta\theta \approx -\Delta\theta \Delta\theta^T J^T(\theta) e + \frac{1}{2} \Delta\theta \Delta\theta^T J^T(\theta) J(\theta) \Delta\theta \qquad (18)$$

Considering $\Delta\theta_{nfb}$ defined as $\Delta\theta_{nfb} = \Delta\theta - \Phi_{fb}(\theta, e)$, the expected value of the product of $\Delta\theta$ and ΔS at the point (θ, e) in the input space of $\Phi_{fb}(\theta, e)$ can be approximated as follows:

$$E[\Delta S \Delta\theta | \theta, e] \approx -R_\theta J^T e + \frac{1}{2} R_\theta J^T J \Phi_{fb}(\theta, e) \qquad (19)$$
$$+ \frac{1}{2} E[\Delta\theta \Delta\theta^T J^T J \Delta\theta_{nfb} | \theta, e]$$

When the arm is controlled according to Equation (2), $\Delta\theta_{nfb}$ is the disturbance noise $d(k)$. Since $d(k)$ satisfies Equation (12), the following equation is established.

$$E[\Delta\theta \Delta\theta^T J^T J \Delta\theta_{nfb} | \theta, e] = 0 \qquad (20)$$

Therefore, the expected value of $\Delta\Phi_{fb}(\theta, e)$ can be expressed as;

$$E[\Delta\Phi_{fb}(\theta, e) | \theta, e] \approx \alpha R_\theta J^T e - (\frac{\alpha}{2} R_\theta J^T J + I) \Phi_{fb}(\theta, e) \qquad (21)$$

When α is small enough, the condition described in Equation (7) is established. The learning result expressed as Equation (13) is obtained as described in Section 2.2.

It should be noted that the learning algorithm expressed in Equation (9) is applicable not only to $S(x_d, \theta)$, but also to general penalty functions of hand position error norm $|e|$. The proposed learning model synthesizes a direction that decreases $S(x_d, \theta)$ by summing after weighting $\Delta\theta$ based on the increase or decrease of $S(x_d, \theta)$.

The feedback controller defined in Equation (13) requires a number of iterations to find a correct inverse kinematics solution, as the coordinates transformation function of the controller is incomplete. However, by using Kawato's feedback error learning [4], the second feedback controller; the feed-forward controller; or the inverse kinematics model that has a complete coordinate transformation function can be obtained as shown in Section 4.

4 TRACKING CONTROL SYSTEM LEARNING

In this section, we will consider the case where x_d changes as $x_d(k)(k = 1, 2, \ldots)$. The hybrid controller that includes the learning feed-forward controller $\Phi_{ff}(\theta(k), \Delta x_d(k)) \in \mathbf{R}^m$ that transforms the change of the desired hand position $\Delta x_d(k) = x_d(k+1) - x_d(k)$ to the joint angle vector space is considered:

$$\Delta\theta(k) = \Phi_{ff}(\theta(k), \Delta x_d(k)) + \Phi_{fb}(\theta(k), e(k)) + d(k) \qquad (22)$$
$$e(k) = x_d(k) - x(k) \qquad (23)$$

The configuration of the hybrid controller is illustrated in Figure 3.
By using the modified change of the square of the error norm expressed as:

$$\Delta S = \frac{1}{2}(|x_d(k-1) - x(k)|^2 - |e(k-1)|^2) \qquad (24)$$

and $\Delta\theta(k)$ as defined in Equation (22), the feedback controller learning rule defined in Equation (9) is useful for the tracking control system. A sample holder for memorizing $x_d(k-1)$ is necessary for the calculation of ΔS. When the distribution

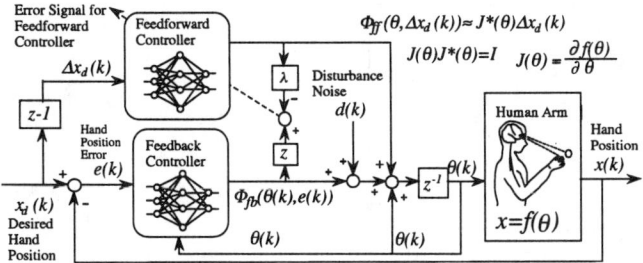

Figure 3: Configuration of Hybrid Controller

of $\Delta x_d(k)$ satisfies Equation (20), Equation (13) still holds. When $\Delta x_d(k)$ has no correlation with $d(k)$ and $\Delta x_d(k)$ satisfies $p(\Delta x_d|\theta,e) = p(-\Delta x_d|\theta,e)$, Equation (20) is approximately established after the feed-forward controller learning.

Using $\Delta \theta(k)$ defined in Equation (2) and $e(k)$ defined in Equation (23), ΔS defined in Equation (10) can be useful for the calculation of $\Phi'_{fb}(\theta, e)$. Although the learning calculation becomes simpler, the learning speed becomes much lower.

Let $\Phi'_{ff}(\theta(k), \Delta x_d(k))$ be the desired output of $\Phi_{ff}(\theta(k), \Delta x_d(k))$. According to Kawato's feedback error learning [4], we use $\Phi'_{ff}(\theta(k), \Delta x_d(k))$ expressed as:

$$\Phi'_{ff}(\theta(k), \Delta x_d(k)) = (1-\lambda)\Phi_{ff}(\theta(k), \Delta x_d(k)) + \Phi_{fb}(\theta(k+1), e(k+1)) \quad (25)$$

where λ is a small, positive, real number for stabilizing the learning process and ensuring that equation $\Phi_{ff}(\theta, 0) \approx 0$ holds. If λ is small enough, the learning feed-forward controller will fulfill the equation:

$$J\Phi_{ff}(\theta, \Delta x_d) \approx \Delta x_d \quad (26)$$

5 NUMERICAL SIMULATION

Numerical simulation experiments were performed in order to evaluate the performance of the proposed model. The inverse kinematics of a 3 DOF arm moving on a 2 DOF plane were considered. The relationship between the joint angle vector $\theta = (\theta_1, \theta_2, \theta_3)^T$ and the hand position vector $x = (x, y)^T$ was defined as:

$$x = x_0 + L_1 \cos(\theta_1) + L_2 \cos(\theta_1 + \theta_2) + L_3 \cos(\theta_1 + \theta_2 + \theta_3) \quad (27)$$

$$y = y_0 + L_1 \sin(\theta_1) + L_2 \sin(\theta_1 + \theta_2) + L_3 \sin(\theta_1 + \theta_2 + \theta_3) \quad (28)$$

The range for θ_1 was $(-30°, 120°)$; the range for θ_2 was $(0°, 120°)$; and the range for θ_3 was $(-75°, 75°)$. L_1 was 0.30 m, L_2 was 0.25 m and L_3 was 0.15 m.

Random straight lines were generated as desired trajectories for the hand. The tracking control trials expressed as Equation (22) with the learning of the feedback controller and the feed-forward controller were performed. The standard deviation of each component of d was 0.01. Learnings based on Equations (9), (22), (24), and (25) were conducted 20 times in one tracking trial. 1,000 tracking trials were conducted to estimate the RMS(Root Mean Square) of $e(k)$.

In order to accelerate the learning, α in Equation (9) was modified as $\alpha = 0.5/(|\Delta x|^2 + 0.1|\Delta \theta|^2)$. λ in Equation (25) was set to 0.001.

Two neural networks with 4 layers were used for the simulation. The first layer had 5 neurons and the forth layer had 3 neurons. The other layers had 15 neurons each. The first layer and the forth layer consisted of linear neurons. The initial values of weights of the neural networks were generated by using uniform random numbers. The back-propagation method without optimized learning coefficients was utilized for the learning.

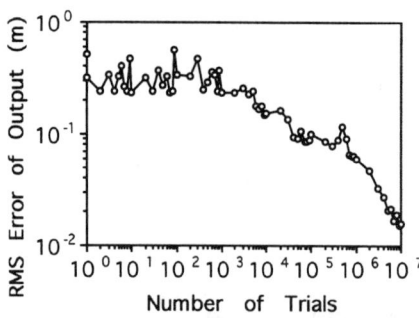
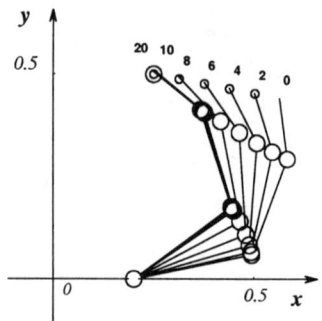

Figure 4: Learning Process of Controller   Figure 5: One Example of Tracking Control

Figure 4 shows the progress of the proposed learning model. It can be seen that the RMS error decreases and the precision of the solver becomes higher as the number of trials increases. The RMS error became 9.31×10^{-3}m after 2×10^7 learning trials. Figure 5 illustrates the hand position control by the inverse kinematics solver after 2×10^7 learning trials. The number near the end point of the arm indicates the value of k. The center of the small circle in Figure 5 indicates the desired hand position. The center of the large circle indicates the final desired hand position. Through learning, a precise inverse kinematics solver can be obtained. However, for RMS error to fall below 0.02, trials must be repeated more than 10^6 times. In such cases, more efficient learner or a learning rule is necessary.

6 CONCLUSION

A learning model of coordinate transformation of the hand position feedback controller was proposed in this paper. Although the proposed learning model may take a long time to learn, it is capable of learning a correct inverse kinematics solver without using a forward model, a back-propagation signal, or a pre-existing feedback controller.

We believe that the slow learning speed can be improved by using neural networks that have a structure suitable for the coordinate transformation. A major limitation of the proposed model is the structure of the learning rule, since the learning rule requires the calculation of the product of the change of the error penalty function and the change of the joint angle vector. However, the existence of such structure in the nervous system is unknown. An advanced learning model which can be directly compared with the physiological and psychological experimental results is necessary.

References

[1] T. Ogino and S. Ishii,"Long-term Results after Pollicization for Congenital Hand Deformities," Hand Surgery, 2, 2,pp.79-85,1997

[2] F. H. Guenther and D. M. Barreca," Neural models for flexible control of redundant systems," in P. Morasso and V. Sanguineti (Eds.), Self-organization, Computational Maps, and Motor Control. Amsterdam: Elsevier, pp.383-421,1997

[3] M. I. Jordan, "Supervised Learning and Systems with Excess Degrees of Freedom," COINS Technical Report,88-27,pp.1-41,1988

[4] M. Kawato, K. Furukawa and R. Suzuki, "A Hierarchical Neural-network Model for Control and Learning of Voluntary Movement," Biological Cybernetics, 57, pp.169-185, 1987

[5] D.T. McRuer and H. R. Jex,"A Review of Quasi-Linear Pilot Models," IEEE Trans. on Human Factors in Electronics, HFE-8, 3, pp.38-51, 1963

Learning Macro-Actions in Reinforcement Learning

Jette Randløv
Niels Bohr Inst., Blegdamsvej 17,
University of Copenhagen,
DK-2100 Copenhagen Ø, Denmark
randlov@nbi.dk

Abstract

We present a method for automatically constructing macro-actions from scratch from primitive actions during the reinforcement learning process. The overall idea is to reinforce the tendency to perform action b after action a if such a pattern of actions has been rewarded. We test the method on a bicycle task, the car-on-the-hill task, the race-track task and some grid-world tasks. For the bicycle and race-track tasks the use of macro-actions approximately halves the learning time, while for one of the grid-world tasks the learning time is reduced by a factor of 5. The method did not work for the car-on-the-hill task for reasons we discuss in the conclusion.

1 INTRODUCTION

A macro-action is a sequence of actions chosen from the primitive actions of the problem.[1] Lumping actions together as macros can be of great help for solving large problems (Korf, 1985a,b; Gullapalli, 1992) and can sometimes greatly speed up learning (Iba, 1989; McGovern, Sutton & Fagg, 1997; McGovern & Sutton, 1998; Sutton, Precup & Singh, 1998; Sutton, Singh, Precup & Ravindran, 1999). Macro-actions might be essential for scaling up reinforcement learning to very large problems. Construction of macro-actions by hand requires insight into the problem at hand. It would be more elegant and useful if the agent itself could decide what actions to lump together (Iba, 1989; McGovern & Sutton, 1998; Sutton, Precup & Singh, 1998; Hauskrecht et al., 1998). (Iba, 1989; McGovern & Sutton, 1998; Sutton, Precup & Singh, 1998; Hauskrecht et al., 1998).

---

[1]This is a special case of definitions of macro-actions seen elsewhere. Some researchers take macro-actions to consist of a policy, terminal conditions and an input set (Precup & Sutton, 1998; Sutton, Precup & Singh, 1998; Sutton, Singh, Precup & Ravindran, 1999) while others define it as a local policy (Hauskrecht et al., 1998).

2 ACTION-TO-ACTION MAPPING

In reinforcement learning we want to learn a mapping from states to actions, $s \rightarrow a$ that maximizes the total expected reward (Sutton & Barto, 1998). Sometimes it might be of use to learn a mapping from actions to actions as well. We believe that acting according to an action-to-action mapping can be useful for three reasons:

1. During the early stages of learning the agent will enter areas of the state space it has never visited before. If the agent acts according to an action-to-action mapping it might be guided through such areas where there is yet no clear choice of action otherwise. In other words it is much more likely that an action-to-action mapping could guide the agent to perform almost optimally in states never visited than a random policy.

2. In some situations, for instance in an emergency, it can be useful to perform a certain open-loop sequence of actions, without being guided by state information. Consider for instance an agent learning to balance on a bicycle (Randløv & Alstrøm, 1998). If the bicycle is in an unbalanced state, the agent must forget about the position of the bicycle and carry out a sequence of actions to balance the bicycle again. Some of the state information—the position of the bicycle relative to some goal—does not matter, and might actually distract the agent, while the history of the most recent actions might contain just the needed information to pick the next action.

3. An action-to-action mapping might lead the agent to explore the relevant areas of the state space in an efficient way instead of just hitting them by chance.

We therefore expect that learning an action-to-action mapping in addition to a state-action mapping can lead to faster overall learning. Even though the system has the Markov property, it may be useful to remember a bit of the action history. We want the agent to perform a sequence of actions while being aware of the development of the states, but not only being controlled by the states.

Many people have tried to deal with imperfect state information by adding memory of previous states and actions to the information the agent receives (Andreae & Cashin, 1969; McCallum, 1995; Hansen, Barto & Zilberstein, 1997; Burgard et al., 1998). In this work we are not specially concerned with non-Markov problems. However the results in this paper suggest that some methods for partially observable MDP could be applied to MDPs and result in faster learning.

The difficult part is how to combine the suggestion made by the action-to-action mapping with the conventional state-to-action mapping. Obviously we do not want to learn the mapping $(s_t, a_{t-1}) \rightarrow a_t$ on tabular form, since that would destroy the possibility of using the action-to-action mapping generalisation over the state space.

In our approach we decided to learn two value mappings. The mapping Q_s is the conventional Q-value normally used for state-to-action mapping, while the mapping Q_a represents the value belonging to the action-to-action mapping. When making a choice, we add the Q-values of the suggestions made by the two mappings, normalize and use the new values to pick an action in the usual way:

$$\tilde{Q}(s_t, a_{t-1}, a_t) = \frac{Q_s(s_t, a_t) + \beta \, Q_a(a_{t-1}, a_t)}{1 + \beta}.$$

Here $\tilde{Q}$ is the Q-value that we actually use to pick the next action. The parameter β determines the influence of the action-to-action mapping. For $\beta = 0$ we are back with the usual Q-values. The idea is to reinforce the tendency to perform action b after action a if such a pattern of actions is rewarded. In this way the agent forms habits or macro-actions and it will sometimes act according to them.

3 RESULTS

How do we implement an action-to-action mapping and the $\tilde{Q}$-values? Many algorithms have been developed to find near optimal state-to-action mappings on a trial-and-error basis. An example of such a algorithm is Sarsa(λ), developed by Rummery and Niranjan (Rummery & Niranjan, 1994; Rummery, 1995). We use Sarsa(λ) with replacing eligibility traces (Singh & Sutton, 1996) and table look-up. Eligibility traces are attached to the Q_a-values—one for each action-action pair.[2] During learning the Q_s and Q_a-values are both adjusted according to the overall TD error $\delta_t = r_{t+1} + \gamma \tilde{Q}_t(s_{t+1}, a_{t+1}) - \tilde{Q}_t(s_t, a_t)$. The update for the Q_a-values has the form $\Delta Q_a(a_{t-1}, a_t) = \beta \, \delta \, e(a_{t-1}, a_t)$. For description of

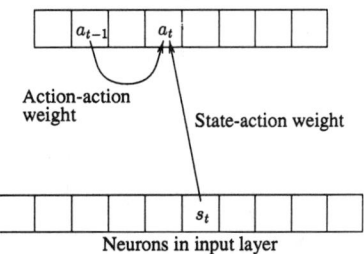

Figure 1: One can think of the action-to-action mapping in terms of weights between output neurons in a network calculating the Q-value.

the Sarsa(λ)-algorithm see Rummery (1995) or Sutton & Barto (1998). Figure 1 shows the idea in terms of a neural network with no hidden layers. The new Q_a-values correspond to weights from output neurons to output neurons.

3.1 THE BICYCLE

We first tested the new $\tilde{Q}$-values on a bicycle system. To solve this problem the agent has to learn to balance a bicycle for 1000 seconds and thereby ride 2.8 km. At each time step the agent receives information about the state of the bicycle: the angle and angular velocity of the handlebars, the angle, angular velocity and angular acceleration of the angle of the bicycle from vertical.

The agent chooses two basic actions: the torque that should be applied to the handle bars, and how much the centre of mass should be displaced from the bicycle's plan—a total of 9 possible actions (Randløv & Alstrøm, 1998). The reward at each time step is 0 unless the bicycle has fallen, in which case it is -1. The agent uses $\alpha = 0.5$, $\gamma = 0.99$ and $\lambda = 0.95$. For further description and the equations for the system we refer the reader to the original paper. Figure 2 shows how the learning time varies with the value of β. The error bars show the standard error in all graphs. For small values of β (≈ 0.03) the agent learns the task faster than with usual Sarsa(λ) ($\beta = 0$). As expected, large values of β slow down learning.

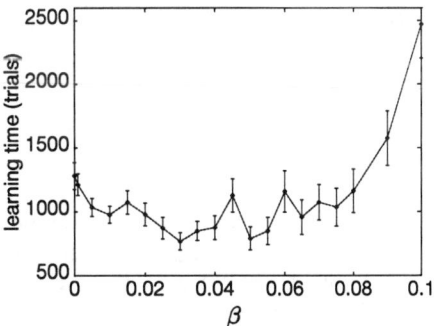

Figure 2: Learning time as a function of the parameter β for the bicycle experiment. Each point is an average of 200 runs.

3.2 THE CAR ON THE HILL

The second example is Boyan and Moore's mountain-car task (Boyan & Moore, 1995; Singh & Sutton, 1996; Sutton, 1996). Consider driving an under-powered car up a steep mountain road. The problem is that gravity is stronger than the car's engine, and the car cannot accelerate up the slope. The agent must first move the car away from the goal and

---

[2] If one action is taken in a state, we allow the traces for the other actions to continue decaying instead of cutting them to 0, contrary to Singh and Sutton (Singh & Sutton, 1996).

up the opposite slope, and then apply full throttle and build up enough momentum to reach the goal. The reward at each time step is -1 until the agent reaches the goal, where it receives reward 0. The agent must choose one of three possible actions at each time step: full thrust forward, no thrust, or full thrust backwards. Refer to Singh & Sutton (1996) for the equations of the task.

We used one of the Sarsa-agents with five 9×9 CMAC tilings that have been thoroughly examined by Singh & Sutton (1996) . The agent's parameters are $\lambda = 0.9$, $\alpha = 0.7$, $\gamma = 1$, and a greedy selection of actions. (These are the best values found by Singh and Sutton.) As in Singh and Sutton's treatment of the problem, all agents were tried for 20 trials, where a trial is one run from a randomly selected starting state to the goal. All the agents used the same set of starting states. The performance measure is the average trial time over the first 20 trials. Figure 3 shows results for two of our simulations. Obviously the action-to-action weights are of no use to the agent, since the lowest point is at $\beta = 0$.

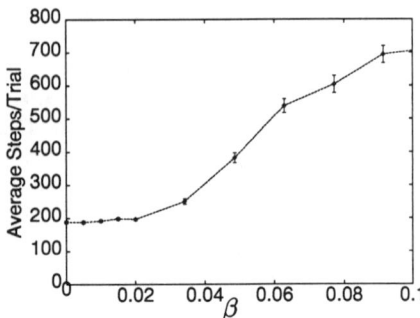

Figure 3: Average trial time of the 20 trials as a function of the parameter β for the car on the hill. Each point is an average of 200 runs.

3.3 THE RACE TRACK PROBLEM

In the race track problem, which originally was presented by Barto, Bradtke & Singh (1995), the agent controls a car in a race track. The agent must guide the car from the start line to the finish line in the least number of steps possible. The exact position on the start line is randomly selected. The state is given by the position and velocity (p_x, p_y, v_x, v_y) (all integer values). The total number of reachable

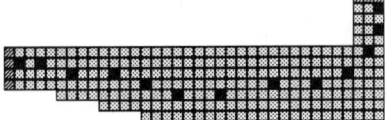

Figure 4: An example of a near-optimal path for the race-track problem. Starting line to the left and finish line at the upper right.

states is 9115 for the track shown in Fig. 4. At each step, the car can accelerate with $a \in \{-1, 0 +1\}$ in both dimensions. Thus, the agent has 9 possible combinations of actions to choose from. Figure 4 shows positions on a near-optimal path. The agent receives a reward of -1 for each step it makes without reaching the goal, and -2 for hitting the boundary of the track. Besides the punishment for hitting the boundary of the track, and the fact that the agent's choice of action is always carried out, the problem is as stated in Barto, Bradtke & Singh (1995) and Rummery (1995). The agent's parameters are $\alpha = 0.5$, $\lambda = 0.8$ and $\gamma = 0.98$.

The learning process is divided into epochs consisting of 10 trials each. We consider the task learned if the agent has navigated the car from start to goal in an average of less than 20 time steps for one full epoch. The learning time is defined as the number of the first epoch for which the criterion is met. This learning criterion emphasizes stable learning—the agent needs to be able to solve the problem several times in a row.

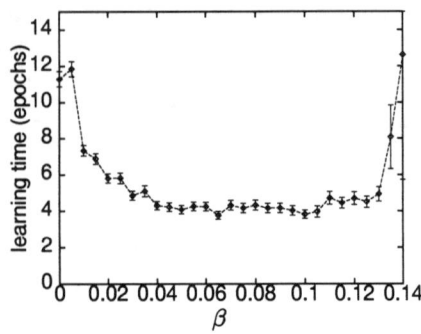

Figure 5: Learning time as a function of the parameter β for the race track. Each point is an average of 200 runs.

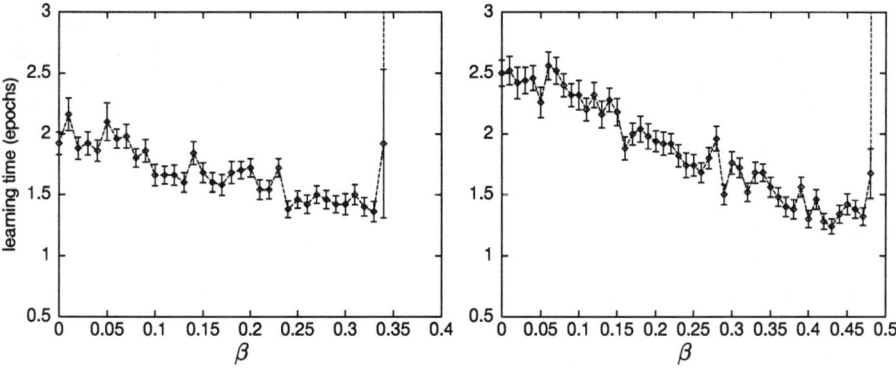

Figure 6: Learning time as a function of the parameter β for grid-world tasks: A 3-dimensional grid-world with 216 states (left) and a 4-dimensional grid-world with 256 states (right). All points are averages of 50 runs.

Figure 5 shows how the learning time varies with the value of β. For a large range of small values of β we see a considerable reduction in learning time from 11.5 epochs to 4.2 epochs. As before, large values of β slow down learning.

3.4 GRID-WORLD TASKS

We tried the new method on a set of grid-world problems in 3, 4 and 5 dimensions. In all the problems the starting point is located at $(1, 1, \ldots)$. For 3 dimensions the goal is located at $(4, 6, 4)$, in 4 dimensions at $(2, 4, 2, 4)$ and in 5 dimensions at $(2, 4, 2, 4, 2)$.

For a d-dimensional problem, the agent has $2d$ actions to choose from. Action $2i - 1$ is to move by -1 in the ith dimension, and action $2i$ is to move by $+1$ in the ith dimension. The agent receives a reward of -0.1 for each step it makes without reaching the goal, and $+1$ for reaching the goal. If the agent tries to step outside the boundary of the world it maintains its position. The 3-dimensional problem takes place in a $6 \times 6 \times 6$ grid-world, while the 4- and 5-dimensional worlds have each dimension of size 4. Again, the learning process is divided into epochs consisting of 10 trials each. The task is considered learned if the agent has navigated from start to goal in an average of less than some fixed number (15 for 3 dimensions, 19 for 4 and 50 for 5 dimensions) for one full epoch. The agent uses $\alpha = 0.5$, $\lambda = 0.9$ and $\gamma = 0.98$.

Figures 6 and 7 show our results for the grid-world tasks. The learning time is reduced a lot. The usefullness of our new method seems to improve with the number of actions: the more actions the better it works.

Figure 8 shows one of the more clear (but not untypical) set of values for the action-to-action weights for the 3-dimensional

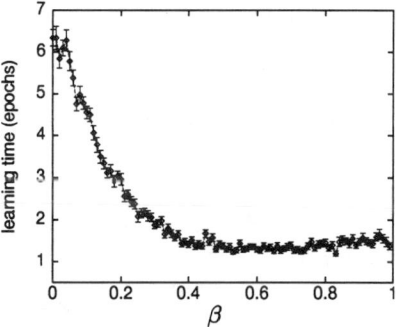

Figure 7: Learning time as a function of the parameter β for a 5-dimensional grid-world with 1024 states. All points are averages of 50 runs.

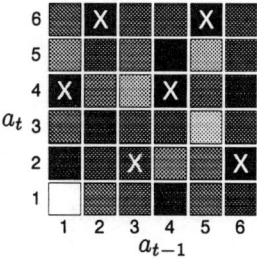

Figure 8: The values of the action-to-action weights; the darker the square the stronger the relationship.

problem. Recommended actions are marked with a white 'X'. The agent has learned two macro-actions. If the agent has performed action number 4 it will continue to perform action 4 all other things being equal. The other macro-action consists of cycling between action 2 and 6. This is a reasonable choice, as one route to the goal consists of performing the actions (44444) and then (262626).

3.5 A TASK WITH MANY ACTIONS

Finally we tried a problem with a large number of actions. The world is a 10 times 10 meter square. Instead of picking a dimension to advance in, the agent chooses a direction. The angular space consists of 36 parts of 10°. The exact position of the agent is discreetized in boxes of 0.1 times 0.1 meter. The goal is a square centered at $(9.5, 7.5)$ with sides measuring 0.4 m. The agent moves 0.3 m per time step, and receives a reward of $+1$ for reaching the goal and -0.1 otherwise. The task is considered learned if the agent has navigated from start to goal in an average of less than 200 time steps for one full epoch (10 trials).

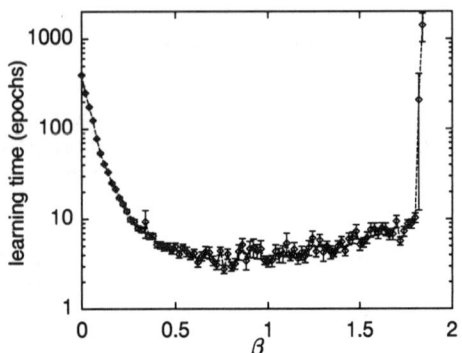

Figure 9: Learning time as a function of the parameter β. All points are averages of 50 runs. Note the logarithmic scale.

Figure 9 shows the learning curve. The learning time is reduced by a factor of 147 from 397 (± 7) to 2.7 (± 0.2). The only real difference compared to the grid-world problems is the number of actions. The results therefore indicate that the larger the number of actions the better the method works.

4 CONCLUSION AND DISCUSSION

We presented a new method for calculating Q-values that mix the conventional Q-values for the state-to-action mapping with Q-values for an action-to-action mapping. We tested the method on a number of problems and found that for all problems except one, the method reduces the total learning time. Furthermore, the agent found macros and learned them. A value function based on values from both state-action and action-action pairs is not guaranteed to converge. Indeed for large values of β the method seems unstable, with large variances in the learning time. A good strategy could be to start with a high initial β and gradually decrease the value. The empirical results indicate that the usefulness of the method depends on the number of actions: the more actions the better it works. This is also intuitively reasonable, as the information content of the knowledge that a particular action was performed is higher if the agent has more actions to choose from.

Acknowledgment

The author wishes to thank Andrew G. Barto, Preben Alstrøm, Doina Precup and Amy McGovern for useful comments and suggestions on earlier drafts of this paper and Richard Sutton and Matthew Schlesinger for helpful discussion. Also a lot of thanks to David Cohen for his patience with later than last-minute corrections.

References

Andreae, J. H. & Cashin, P. M. (1969). A learning machine with monologue. *International Journal of Man-Machine Studies, 1*, 1–20.

Barto, A. G., Bradtke, S. J. & Singh, S. (1995). Learning to act using real-time dynamic programming. *Artificial Intelligence, 72*, 81–138.

Boyan, J. A. & Moore, A. W. (1995). Generalization in reinforcement learning: Safely approximating the value function. In *NIPS 7*. (pp. 369–376). The MIT Press.

Burgard, W., Cremers, A. B., Fox, D., Haehnel, D., Lakemeyer, G., Schulz, D., Steiner, W. & Thrun, S. (1998). The interactive museum tour-guide robot. In *Fifteenth National Conference on Artificial Intelligence*.

Gullapalli, V. (1992). *Reinforcement Learning and Its Application to Control*. PhD thesis, University of Massachusetts. COINS Technical Report 92-10.

Hansen, E., Barto, A, & Zilberstein, S. (1997) Reinforcement learning for mixed open-loop and closed-loop control. In *NIPS 9*. The MIT Press.

Hauskrecht, M., Meuleau, N., Boutilier, C., Kaelbling, L. P. & Dean, T. (1998). Hierarchical solution of markov decision processes using macro-actions. In *Proceedings of the Fourteenth International Conference on Uncertainty In Artificial Intelligence*.

Iba, G. A. (1989). A heuristic approach to the discovery of macro-operators. *Machine Learning, 3*.

Korf, R. E. (1985a). Learning to solve problems by searching for macro-operators. *Research Notes in Artificial Intelligence, 5*.

Korf, R. E. (1985b). Macro-operators: A weak method for learning. *Artificial Intelligence, 26*, 35–77.

McCallum, R. A. (1995). *Reinforcement Learning with Selective Perception and Hidden State*. PhD thesis, University of Rochester.

McGovern, A. & Sutton, R. S. (1998). Macro-actions in reinforcement learning: An empirical analysis. Technical Report 98-70, University of Massachusetts.

McGovern, A., Sutton, R. S. & Fagg, A. H. (1997). Roles of macro-actions in accelerating reinforcement learning. In *1997 Grace Hopper Celebration of Women in Computing*.

Precup, D. & Sutton, R. S. (1998). Multi-time models for temporally abstract planning. In *NIPS 10*. The MIT Press.

Randløv, J. & Alstrøm, P. (1998). Learning to drive a bicycle using reinforcement learning and shaping. In *Proceedings of the 15th International Conference on Machine Learning*.

Rummery, G. A. (1995). *Problem Solving with Reinforcement Learning*. PhD thesis, Cambridge University Engineering Department.

Rummery, G. A. & Niranjan, M. (1994). On-line Q-learning using connectionist systems. Technical Report CUED/F-INFENG/TR 166, Engineering Department, Cambridge University.

Singh, S. P. & Sutton, R. S. (1996). Reinforcement learning with replacing eligibility traces. *Machine Learning, 22*, 123–158.

Sutton, R. S. (1996). Generalization in reinforcement learning: Successful examples using sparse coarse coding. In *NIPS 8*. (pp. 1038–1044). The MIT Press.

Sutton, R. S. & Barto, A. G. (1998). *Introduction to Reinforcement Learning*. MIT Press/Bradford Books.

Sutton, R. S., Precup, D. & Singh, S. (1998). Between MDPs and semi-MDPs: Learning, planning, and representing knowledge at multiple temporal scales. Technical Report UM-CS-1998-074, Department of Computer Science, UMass.

Sutton, R. S., Singh, S., Precup, D. & Ravindran, B. (1999). Improved switching among temporally abstract actions. In *NIPS 11*. The MIT Press.

Reinforcement Learning based on On-line EM Algorithm

Masa-aki Sato †
†ATR Human Information Processing Research Laboratories
Seika, Kyoto 619-0288, Japan   masaaki@hip.atr.co.jp

Shin Ishii ‡†
‡Nara Institute of Science and Technology
Ikoma, Nara 630-0101, Japan   ishii@is.aist-nara.ac.jp

Abstract

In this article, we propose a new reinforcement learning (RL) method based on an actor-critic architecture. The actor and the critic are approximated by Normalized Gaussian Networks (NGnet), which are networks of local linear regression units. The NGnet is trained by the on-line EM algorithm proposed in our previous paper. We apply our RL method to the task of swinging-up and stabilizing a single pendulum and the task of balancing a double pendulum near the upright position. The experimental results show that our RL method can be applied to optimal control problems having continuous state/action spaces and that the method achieves good control with a small number of trial-and-errors.

1 INTRODUCTION

Reinforcement learning (RL) methods (Barto et al., 1990) have been successfully applied to various Markov decision problems having finite state/action spaces, such as the backgammon game (Tesauro, 1992) and a complex task in a dynamic environment (Lin, 1992). On the other hand, applications to continuous state/action problems (Werbos, 1990; Doya, 1996; Sofge & White, 1992) are much more difficult than the finite state/action cases. Good function approximation methods and fast learning algorithms are crucial for successful applications.

In this article, we propose a new RL method that has the above-mentioned two features. This method is based on an actor-critic architecture (Barto et al., 1983), although the detailed implementations of the actor and the critic are quite different from those in the original actor-critic model. The actor and the critic in our method estimate a policy and a Q-function, respectively, and are approximated by Normalized Gaussian Networks (NGnet) (Moody & Darken, 1989). The NGnet is a network of local linear regression units. The model softly partitions the input space by using normalized Gaussian functions, and each local unit linearly approximates the output within its partition. As pointed out by Sutton (1996), local models such as the NGnet are more suitable than global models such as multi-layered perceptrons, for avoiding serious learning interference in on-line RL processes. The NGnet is trained by the on-line EM algorithm proposed in our previous paper (Sato & Ishii, 1998). It was shown that this on-line EM algorithm is faster than a gradient descent algorithm. In the on-line EM algorithm, the positions of the local units can be adjusted according to the input and output data distribution. Moreover, unit creation and unit deletion are performed according to the data distribution. Therefore, the model can be adapted to dynamic environments in which the input and output data distribution changes with time (Sato & Ishii, 1998).

We have applied the new RL method to optimal control problems for deterministic nonlinear dynamical systems. The first experiment is the task of swinging-up and stabilizing a single pendulum with a limited torque (Doya, 1996). The second experiment is the task of balancing a double pendulum where a torque is applied only to the first pendulum. Our RL method based on the on-line EM algorithm demonstrated good performances in these experiments.

2 NGNET AND ON-LINE EM ALGORITHM

In this section, we review the on-line EM algorithm for the NGnet proposed in our previous paper (Sato & Ishii, 1998). The NGnet (Moody & Darken, 1989), which transforms an N-dimensional input vector x to a D-dimensional output vector y, is defined by the following equations.

$$y = \sum_{i=1}^{M} \left(\frac{G_i(x)}{\sum_{j=1}^{M} G_j(x)} \right) (W_i x + b_i) \tag{1a}$$

$$G_i(x) \equiv (2\pi)^{-N/2} |\Sigma_i|^{-1/2} \exp\left[-\frac{1}{2}(x - \mu_i)' \Sigma_i^{-1} (x - \mu_i)\right]. \tag{1b}$$

M denotes the number of units, and the prime (') denotes a transpose. $G_i(x)$ is an N-dimensional Gaussian function, which has an N-dimensional center μ_i and an $(N \times N)$-dimensional covariance matrix Σ_i. W_i and b_i are a $(D \times N)$-dimensional linear regression matrix and a D-dimensional bias vector, respectively. Subsequently, we use notations $\tilde{W}_i \equiv (W_i, b_i)$ and $\tilde{x}' \equiv (x', 1)$.

The NGnet can be interpreted as a stochastic model, in which a pair of an input and an output, (x, y), is a stochastic event. For each event, a unit index $i \in \{1, ..., M\}$ is assumed to be selected, which is regarded as a hidden variable. The stochastic model is defined by the probability distribution for a triplet (x, y, i), which is called a complete event:

$$P(x, y, i | \theta) = (2\pi)^{-(D+N)/2} \sigma_i^{-D} |\Sigma_i|^{-1/2} M^{-1} \tag{2}$$

$$\times \exp\left[-\frac{1}{2}(x - \mu_i)' \Sigma_i^{-1} (x - \mu_i) - \frac{1}{2\sigma_i^2}(y - \tilde{W}_i \tilde{x})^2\right].$$

Here, $\theta \equiv \{\mu_i, \Sigma_i, \sigma_i^2, \tilde{W}_i \mid i = 1, ..., M\}$ is a set of model parameters. We can easily prove that the expectation value of the output y for a given input x, i.e., $E[y|x] \equiv$

$\int y P(y|x,\theta) dy$, is identical to equation (1). Namely, the probability distribution (2) provides a stochastic model for the NGnet.

From a set of T events (observed data) $(X, Y) \equiv \{(x(t), y(t)) \mid t = 1, ..., T\}$, the model parameter θ of the stochastic model (2) can be determined by the maximum likelihood estimation method, in particular, by the EM algorithm (Dempster et al., 1977). The EM algorithm repeats the following E- and M-steps.

E (Estimation) step: Let $\bar\theta$ be the present estimator. By using $\bar\theta$, the posterior probability that the i-th unit is selected for $(x(t), y(t))$ is given as

$$P(i|x(t), y(t), \bar\theta) = P(x(t), y(t), i|\bar\theta) / \sum_{j=1}^{M} P(x(t), y(t), j|\bar\theta). \tag{3}$$

M (Maximization) step: Using the posterior probability (3), the expected log-likelihood $L(\theta|\bar\theta, X, Y)$ for the complete events is defined by

$$L(\theta|\bar\theta, X, Y) = \sum_{t=1}^{T} \sum_{i=1}^{M} P(i|x(t), y(t), \bar\theta) \log P(x(t), y(t), i|\theta). \tag{4}$$

Since an increase of $L(\theta|\bar\theta, X, Y)$ implies an increase of the log-likelihood for the observed data (X, Y) (Dempster et al., 1977), $L(\theta|\bar\theta, X, Y)$ is maximized with respect to θ. A solution of the necessity condition $\partial L/\partial \theta = 0$ is given by (Xu et al., 1995)

$$\mu_i = \langle x \rangle_i(T) / \langle 1 \rangle_i(T) \tag{5a}$$

$$\Sigma_i^{-1} = [\langle xx' \rangle_i(T) / \langle 1 \rangle_i(T) - \mu_i(T)\mu_i'(T)]^{-1} \tag{5b}$$

$$\tilde W_i = \langle y\tilde x' \rangle_i(T)[\langle \tilde x \tilde x' \rangle_i(T)]^{-1} \tag{5c}$$

$$\sigma_i^2 = \frac{1}{D} \left[\langle |y|^2| \rangle_i(T) - \text{Tr}\left(\tilde W_i \langle \tilde x y' \rangle_i(T)\right) \right] / \langle 1 \rangle_i(T), \tag{5d}$$

where $\langle \cdot \rangle_i$ denotes a weighted mean with respect to the posterior probability (3) and it is defined by

$$\langle f(x,y) \rangle_i(T) \equiv \frac{1}{T} \sum_{t=1}^{T} f(x(t), y(t)) P(i|x(t), y(t), \bar\theta). \tag{6}$$

The EM algorithm introduced above is based on batch learning (Xu et al., 1995), namely, the parameters are updated after seeing all of the observed data. We introduce here an on-line version (Sato & Ishii, 1998) of the EM algorithm. Let $\theta(t)$ be the estimator after the t-th observed data $(x(t), y(t))$. In this on-line EM algorithm, the weighted mean (6) is replaced by

$$\ll f(x,y) \gg_i (T) \equiv \eta(T) \sum_{t=1}^{T} (\prod_{s=t+1}^{T} \lambda(s)) f(x(t), y(t)) P(i|x(t), y(t), \theta(t-1)). \tag{7}$$

The parameter $\lambda(t) \in [0, 1]$ is a discount factor, which is introduced for forgetting the effect of earlier inaccurate estimator. $\eta(T) \equiv (\sum_{t=1}^{T} (\prod_{s=t+1}^{T} \lambda(s)))^{-1}$ is a normalization coefficient and it is iteratively calculated by $\eta(t) = (1 + \lambda(t)/\eta(t-1))^{-1}$. The modified weighted mean $\ll \cdot \gg_i$ can be obtained by the step-wise equation:

$$\ll f(x,y) \gg_i (t) = \ll f(x,y) \gg_i (t-1) \tag{8}$$
$$+ \eta(t) \left[f(x(t), y(t)) P_i(t) - \ll f(x,y) \gg_i (t-1) \right],$$

where $P_i(t) \equiv P(i|x(t), y(t), \theta(t-1))$. Using the modified weighted mean, the new parameters are obtained by the following equations.

$$\tilde{\Lambda}_i(t) = \frac{1}{1-\eta(t)} \left[\tilde{\Lambda}_i(t-1) - \frac{P_i(t)\tilde{\Lambda}_i(t-1)\tilde{x}(t)\tilde{x}'(t)\tilde{\Lambda}_i(t-1)}{(1/\eta(t)-1) + P_i(t)\tilde{x}'(t)\tilde{\Lambda}_i(t-1)\tilde{x}(t)} \right] \quad (9a)$$

$$\mu_i(t) = \ll x \gg_i (t) / \ll 1 \gg_i (t) \quad (9b)$$

$$\tilde{W}_i(t) = \tilde{W}_i(t-1) + \eta(t)P_i(t)(y(t) - \tilde{W}_i(t-1)\tilde{x}(t))\tilde{x}'(t)\tilde{\Lambda}_i(t) \quad (9c)$$

$$\sigma_i^2(t) = \frac{1}{D} \left[\ll |y|^2 \gg_i (t) - \text{Tr}\left(\tilde{W}_i(t) \ll \tilde{x}y' \gg_i (t)\right) \right] / \ll 1 \gg_i (t), \quad (9d)$$

where $\tilde{\Lambda}_i(t) \equiv [\ll \tilde{x}\tilde{x}' \gg_i]^{-1}$. $\Sigma_i^{-1}(t)$ can be obtained from the following relation with $\tilde{\Lambda}_i(t)$.

$$\tilde{\Lambda}_i(t) \ll 1 \gg_i (t) = \begin{pmatrix} \Sigma_i^{-1}(t) & -\Sigma_i^{-1}(t)\mu_i(t) \\ -\mu_i'(t)\Sigma_i^{-1}(t) & 1 + \mu_i'(t)\Sigma_i^{-1}(t)\mu_i(t) \end{pmatrix}. \quad (10)$$

It can be proved that this on-line EM algorithm is equivalent to the stochastic approximation for finding the maximum likelihood estimator, if the time course of the discount factor $\lambda(t)$ is given by

$$\lambda(t) \stackrel{t \to \infty}{\longrightarrow} 1 - (1-a)/(at+b), \quad (11)$$

where a $(1 > a > 0)$ and b are constants (Sato & Ishii, 1998).

We also employ dynamic unit manipulation mechanisms in order to efficiently allocate the units (Sato & Ishii, 1998). The probability $P(x(t), y(t), i \mid \theta(t-1))$ indicates how probable the i-th unit produces the datum $(x(t), y(t))$ with the present parameter $\theta(t-1)$. If the probability for every unit is less than some threshold value, a new unit is produced to account for the new datum. The weighted mean $\ll 1 \gg_i (t)$ indicates how much the i-th unit has been used to account for the data until t. If the mean becomes less than some threshold value, this unit is deleted.

In order to deal with a singular input distribution, a regularization for $\Sigma_i^{-1}(t)$ is introduced as follows.

$$\Sigma_i^{-1}(t) = [(\ll xx' \gg_i (t) - \mu_i(t)\mu_i'(t) \ll 1 \gg_i (t) \quad (12a)$$
$$+ \alpha \ll \Delta_i^2 \gg_i (t)I_N) / \ll 1 \gg_i (t)]^{-1}$$

$$\ll \Delta_i^2 \gg_i (t) = (\ll |x|^2 \gg_i (t) - |\mu_i(t)|^2 \ll 1 \gg_i (t))/N, \quad (12b)$$

where I_N is the $(N \times N)$-dimensional identity matrix and α is a small constant. The corresponding $\tilde{\Lambda}_i(t)$ can be calculated in an on-line manner using a similar equation to (9a) (Sato & Ishii, 1998).

3 REINFORCEMENT LEARNING

In this section, we propose a new RL method based on the on-line EM algorithm described in the previous section. In the following, we consider optimal control problems for deterministic nonlinear dynamical systems having continuous state/action spaces. It is assumed that there is no knowledge of the controlled system. An actor-critic architecture (Barto et al.,1983) is used for the learning system. In the original actor-critic model, the actor and the critic approximated the probability of each action and the value function, respectively, and were trained by using the TD-error. The actor and the critic in our RL method are different from those in the original model as explained later.

For the current state, $x_c(t)$, of the controlled system, the actor outputs a control signal (action) $u(t)$, which is given by the policy function $\Omega(\cdot)$, i.e., $u(t) = \Omega(x_c(t))$. The controlled system changes its state to $x_c(t+1)$ after receiving the control signal $u(t)$. Subsequently, a reward $r(x_c(t), u(t))$ is given to the learning system. The objective of the learning system is to find the optimal policy function that maximizes the discounted future return defined by

$$V(x_c) \equiv \sum_{t=0}^{\infty} \gamma^t r(x_c(t), \Omega(x_c(t)))\Big|_{x_c(0)=x_c}, \tag{13}$$

where $0 < \gamma < 1$ is a discount factor. $V(x_c)$, which is called the value function, is defined for the current policy function $\Omega(\cdot)$ employed by the actor. The Q-function is defined by

$$Q(x_c, u) = \gamma V(x_c(t+1)) + r(x_c, u), \tag{14}$$

where $x_c(t) = x_c$ and $u(t) = u$ are assumed. The value function can be obtained from the Q-function:

$$V(x_c) = Q(x_c, \Omega(x_c)). \tag{15}$$

The Q-function should satisfy the consistency condition

$$Q(x_c(t), u(t)) = \gamma Q(x_c(t+1), \Omega(x_c(t+1))) + r(x_c(t), u(t)). \tag{16}$$

In our RL method, the policy function and the Q-function are approximated by the NGnets, which are called the actor-network and the critic-network, respectively. In the learning phase, a stochastic actor is necessary in order to explore a better policy. For this purpose, we employ a stochastic model defined by (2), corresponding to the actor-network. A stochastic action is generated in the following way. A unit index i is selected randomly according to the conditional probability $P(i|x_c)$ for a given state x_c. Subsequently, an action u is generated randomly according to the conditional probability $P(u|x_c, i)$ for a given x_c and the selected i. The value function can be defined for either the stochastic policy or the deterministic policy. Since the controlled system is deterministic, we use the value function defined for the deterministic policy which is given by the actor-network.

The learning process proceeds as follows. For the current state $x_c(t)$, a stochastic action $u(t)$ is generated by the stochastic model corresponding to the current actor-network. At the next time step, the learning system gets the next state $x_c(t+1)$ and the reward $r(x_c(t), u(t))$. The critic-network is trained by the on-line EM algorithm. The input to the critic-network is $(x_c(t), u(t))$. The target output is given by the right hand side of (16), where the Q-function and the deterministic policy function $\Omega(\cdot)$ are calculated using the current critic-network and the current actor-network, respectively. The actor-network is also trained by the on-line EM algorithm. The input to the actor-network is $x_c(t)$. The target output is given by using the gradient of the critic-network (Sofge & White, 1992):

$$u_{target} = \Omega(x_c(t)) + \epsilon \frac{\partial Q}{\partial u}(x_c(t), \Omega(x_c(t))), \tag{17}$$

where the Q-function and the deterministic policy function $\Omega(\cdot)$ are calculated using the modified critic-network and the current actor-network, respectively. ϵ is a small constant. This target output gives a better action, which increases the Q-function value for the current state $x_c(t)$, than the current deterministic action $\Omega(x_c(t))$.

In the above learning scheme, the critic-network and the actor-network are updated concurrently. One can consider another learning scheme. In this scheme, the learning system tries to control the controlled system for a given period of time by using the fixed actor-network. In this period, the critic-network is trained to estimate the

Q-function for the fixed actor-network. The state trajectory in this period is saved. At the next stage, the actor-network is trained along the saved trajectory using the critic-network modified in the first stage.

4 EXPERIMENTS

The first experiment is the task of swinging-up and stabilizing a single pendulum with a limited torque (Doya, 1996). The state of the pendulum is represented by $x_c \equiv (\phi, \dot\phi)$, where ϕ and $\dot\phi$ denote the angle from the upright position and the angular velocity of the pendulum, respectively. The reward $r(x_c(t), u(t))$ is assumed to be given by $\tilde r(x_c(t+1))$, where

$$\tilde r(x_c) = \exp(-(\dot\phi)^2/(2\nu_1^2) - \phi^2/(2\nu_2^2)). \tag{18}$$

ν_1 and ν_2 are constants. The reward (18) encourages the pendulum to stay high. After releasing the pendulum from a vicinity of the upright position, the control and the learning process of the actor-critic network is conducted for 7 seconds. This is a single episode. The reinforcement learning is done by repeating these episodes. After 40 episodes, the system is able to make the pendulum achieve an upright position from almost every initial state. Even from a low initial position, the system swings the pendulum several times and stabilizes it at the upright position. Figure 1 shows a control process, i.e., stroboscopic time-series of the pendulum, using the deterministic policy after training. According to our previous experiment, in which both of the actor- and critic- networks are the NGnets with fixed centers trained by the gradient descent algorithm, a good control was obtained after about 2000 episodes. Therefore, our new RL method is able to obtain a good control much faster than that based on the gradient descent algorithm.

The second experiment is the task of balancing a double pendulum near the upright position. A torque is applied only to the first pendulum. The state of the pendulum is represented by $x_c \equiv (\dot\phi_1, \dot\phi_2, \phi_1, \phi_2)$, where ϕ_1 and ϕ_2 are the first pendulum's angle from the upright direction and the second pendulum's angle from the first pendulum's direction, respectively. $\dot\phi_1(\dot\phi_2)$ is the angular velocity of the first (second) pendulum. The reward is given by the height of the second pendulum's end from the lowest position. After 40 episodes, the system is able to stabilize the double pendulum. Figure 2 shows the control process using the deterministic policy after training. The upper two figures show stroboscopic time-series of the pendulum. The dashed, dotted, and solid lines in the bottom figure denote ϕ_1/π, ϕ_2/π, and the control signal u produced by the actor-network, respectively. After a transient period, the pendulum is successfully controlled to stay near the upright position.

The numbers of units in the actor- (critic-) networks after training are 50 (109) and 96 (121) for the single and double pendulum cases, respectively. The RL method using center-fixed NGnets trained by the gradient descent algorithm employed 441 ($= 21^2$) actor units and 18,081 ($= 21^2 \times 41$) critic units, for the single pendulum task. For the double pendulum task, this scheme did not work even when 14,641 ($= 11^4$) actor units and 161,051 ($= 11^4 \times 11$) critic units were prepared. The numbers of units in the NGnets trained by the on-line EM algorithm scale moderately as the input dimension increases.

5 CONCLUSION

In this article, we proposed a new RL method based on the on-line EM algorithm. We showed that our RL method can be applied to the task of swinging-up and stabilizing a single pendulum and the task of balancing a double pendulum near the upright position. The number of trial-and-errors needed to achieve good control was found to be very small in the two tasks. In order to apply a RL method to continuous state/action problems, good function approximation methods and fast learning algorithms are crucial. The experimental results showed that our RL method has both features.

References

Barto, A. G., Sutton, R. S., & Anderson, C. W. (1983). *IEEE Transactions on Systems, Man, and Cybernetics*, **13**, 834-846.

Barto, A. G., Sutton, R. S., & Watkins, C. J. C. H. (1990). *Learning and Computational Neuroscience: Foundations of Adaptive Networks* (pp. 539-602), MIT Press.

Dempster, A. P., Laird, N. M., & Rubin, D. B. (1977). *Journal of Royal Statistical Society B*, **39**, 1-22.

Doya, K. (1996). *Advances in Neural Information Processing Systems 8* (pp. 1073-1079), MIT Press.

Lin, L. J. (1992). *Machine Learning*, **8**, 293-321.

Moody, J., & Darken, C. J. (1989). *Neural Computation*, **1**, 281-294.

Sato, M., & Ishii, S. (1998). *ATR Technical Report*, **TR-H-243**, ATR.

Sofge, D. A., & White, D. A. (1992). *Handbook of Intelligent Control* (pp. 259-282), Van Nostrand Reinhold.

Sutton, R. S. (1996). *Advances in Neural Information Processing Systems 8* (pp. 1038-1044), MIT Press.

Tesauro, G. J. (1992). *Machine Learning*, **8**, 257-278.

Werbos, P. J. (1990). *Neural Networks for Control* (pp. 67-95), MIT Press.

Xu, L., Jordan, M. I., & Hinton, G. E. (1995). *Advances in Neural Information Processing Systems 7* (pp. 633-640), MIT Press.

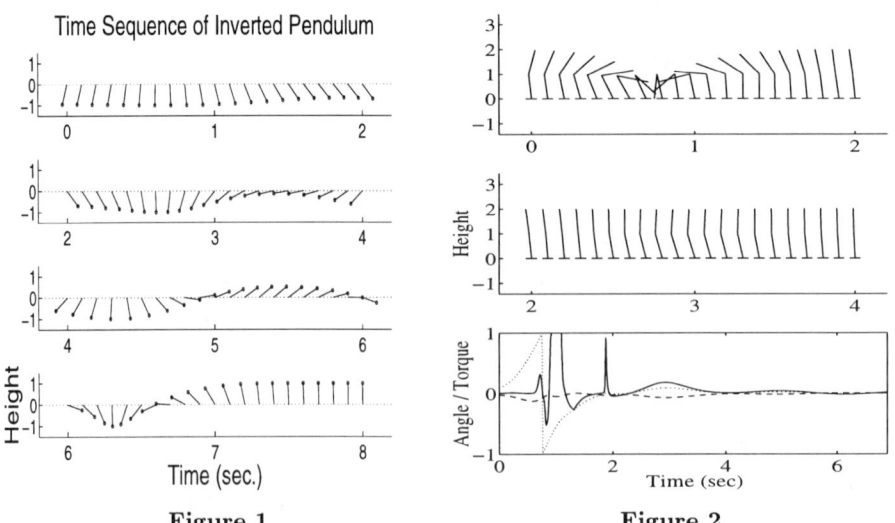

Figure 1   Figure 2

A Reinforcement Learning Algorithm in Partially Observable Environments Using Short-Term Memory

Nobuo Suematsu and Akira Hayashi
Faculty of Computer Sciences
Hiroshima City University
3-4-1 Ozuka-higashi, Asaminami-ku, Hiroshima 731-3194 Japan
{suematsu,akira}@im.hiroshima-cu.ac.jp

Abstract

We describe a Reinforcement Learning algorithm for partially observable environments using short-term memory, which we call BLHT. Since BLHT learns a stochastic model based on Bayesian Learning, the overfitting problem is reasonably solved. Moreover, BLHT has an efficient implementation. This paper shows that the model learned by BLHT converges to one which provides the most accurate predictions of percepts and rewards, given short-term memory.

1 INTRODUCTION

Research on Reinforcement Learning (RL) problem for partially observable environments is gaining more attention recently. This is mainly because the assumption that perfect and complete perception of the state of the environment is available for the learning agent, which many previous RL algorithms require, is not valid for many realistic environments.

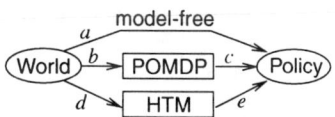

Figure 1: Three approaches

One of the approaches to the problem is the model-free approach (Singh et al. 1995; Jaakkola et al. 1995) (arrow a in the Fig.1) which gives up state estimation and uses *memory-less* policies. We can not expect the approach to find a really effective policy when it is necessary to accumulate information to estimate the state. Model based approaches are superior in these environments.

A popular model based approach is via a Partially Observable Markov Decision Process (POMDP) model which represents the decision process of the agent. In Fig.1 the approach is described by the route from "World" to "Policy" through "POMDP". The approach has two serious difficulties. One is in the learning of POMDPs (arrow b in Fig.1). Abe and

Warmuth (1992) shows that learning of probabilistic automata is NP-hard, which means that learning of POMDPs is also NP-hard. The other difficulty is in finding the optimal policy of a given POMDP model (arrow c in Fig.1). Its PSAPCE-hardness is shown in Papadimitriou and Tsitsiklis (1987). Accordingly, the methods based on this approach (Chrisman 1992; McCallum 1993), will not scale well to large problems.

The approach using short-term memory is computationally more tractable. Of course we can construct environments in which long-term memory is essential. However, in many environments, because of their stochasticity, the significance of the past information decreases exponentially fast as the time goes. In such environments, memories of moderate length will work fine.

McCallum (1995) proposes "utile suffix memory" (USM) algorithm. USM uses a tree structure to represent short-term memories with variable length. USM's model learning is based on a statistical test, which requires time and space proportional to the learning steps. This makes it difficult to adapt USM to the environments which require long learning steps. USM suffers from the overfitting problem which is a difficult problem faced by most of model based learning methods. USM may overfit or underfit up to the significance level used for the statistical test and we can not know its proper level in advance.

In this paper, we introduce an algorithm called BLHT (Suematsu et al. 1997), in which the environment is modeled as a *history tree model* (HTM), a stochastic model with variable memory length. Although BLHT shares the tree structured representation of short-term memory with USM, the computational time required by BLHT is constant in each step and BLHT copes with environments which require large learning steps. In addition, because BLHT is based on Bayesian Learning, the overfitting problem is solved reasonably in it. A similar version of HTMs was introduced and has been used for learning of Hidden Markov Models in Ron et al. (1994). In their learning method, a tree is grown in a similar way with USM. If we try to adapt it to our RL problem, it will face the same problems with USM.

This paper shows that the HTM learned by BLHT converges to the optimal one in the sense that it provides the most accurate predictions of percepts and rewards, given short-term memory. BLHT can learn a HTM in an efficient way (arrow d in Fig.1). And since HTMs compose a subset of Markov Decision Processes (MDPs), it can be efficiently solved by Dynamic Programming (DP) techniques (arrow e in Fig.1). So, we can see BLHT as an approach to follow an easy way from "World" to "Policy" which goes around "POMDP".

2 THE POMDP MODEL

The decision process of an agent in a partially observable environment can be formulated as a POMDP. Let the finite set of states of the environment be $\mathcal{S}$, the finite set of agent's actions be $\mathcal{A}$, and the finite set of all possible percepts be $\mathcal{I}$. Let us denote the probability of and the reward for making transition from state s to s' using action a by $p_{s'|sa}$ and $w_{sas'}$ respectively. We also denote the probability of obtaining percept i after a transition from s to s' using action a by $o_{i|sas'}$. Then, a POMDP model is specified by $\langle \mathcal{S}, \mathcal{A}, \mathcal{I}, \mathcal{P}, \mathcal{O}, \mathcal{W}, \boldsymbol{x}_0 \rangle$, where $\mathcal{P} = \{p_{s'|sa} \mid s, s' \in \mathcal{S}, a \in \mathcal{A}\}$, $\mathcal{O} = \{o_{i|sas'} | s, s' \in \mathcal{S}, a \in \mathcal{A}, i \in \mathcal{I}\}$, $\mathcal{W} = \{w_{sas'} | s, s' \in \mathcal{S}, a \in \mathcal{A}\}$, and $\boldsymbol{x}_0 = (x^0_{s_1}, \ldots, x^0_{s_{|\mathcal{S}|-1}})$ is the probability distribution of the initial state.

We denote the history of actions and percepts of the agent till time t, $(\ldots, a_{t-2}, i_{t-1}, a_{t-1}, i_t)$ by D_t. If the POMDP model, $M = \langle \mathcal{S}, \mathcal{A}, \mathcal{I}, \mathcal{P}, \mathcal{O}, \mathcal{W}, \boldsymbol{x}_i \rangle$ is given, one can compute the belief state, $\boldsymbol{x}_t = (x^t_{s_1}, \ldots, x^t_{s_{|\mathcal{S}|-1}})$ from D_t, which is the state estimation at time t. We denote the mapping from histories to belief states defined by POMDP model M by $\boldsymbol{X}_M(\cdot)$, that is, $\boldsymbol{x}_t = \boldsymbol{X}_M(D_t)$. The belief state $\boldsymbol{x}_t$ is the most precise state estimation and it is known to be the sufficient statistics for the optimal policy in POMDPs (Bertsekas 1987). It is also known that the stochastic process $\{\boldsymbol{x}_t, t \geq 0\}$ is an MDP in the continuous space, $\mathcal{X} \equiv \{(x_1, dots, x_{|\mathcal{S}|-1}) \mid x_1, \ldots, x_{|\mathcal{S}|-1} \geq 0, \sum_{j=1}^{|\mathcal{S}|-1} x_j \leq 1\}$.

3 BAYESIAN LEARNING OF HISTORY TREE MODELS (BLHT)

In this section, we summarize our RL algorithm for partially observable environments, which we call BLHT (Suematsu et al. 1997).

3.1 HISTORY TREE MODELS

BLHT is Bayesian Learning on a hypothesis space which is composed of predictive models, which we call History Tree Models (HTMs). Given short-term memory, a HTM provides the probability disctribution of the next percept and the expected immediate reward for each action. A HTM is represented by a tree structure called a history tree and parameters given for each leaf of the tree.

A history tree h associates history D_t with a leaf as follows. Starting from the root of h, we check the most recent percept, i_t and follow the appropriate branch and then we check the action a_{t-1} and follow the appropriate branch. This procedure is repeated till we reach a leaf. We denote the reached leaf by $\lambda_h(D_t)$ and the set of leaves of h by $\mathcal{L}_h$.

Each leaf $l \in \mathcal{L}_h$ has parameters $\theta_{i|la}$ and ω_{la}. $\theta_{i|la}$ denotes the probability of observing i at time $t+1$ when $\lambda_h(D_t) = l$ and the last action a_t was a. ω_{la} denotes the expected immediate reward for performing a when $\lambda_h(D_t) = l$. Let $\Theta_h = \{\theta_{i|la} \mid i \in \mathcal{I}, l \in \mathcal{L}_h, a \in \mathcal{A}\}$.

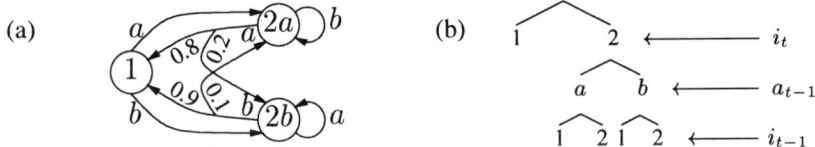

Figure 2: (a) A three-state environment, in which the agent receives percept 1 in state 1 and percept 2 in states $2a$ and $2b$. (b) A history tree which can represent the environment.

Fig. 2 shows a three-state environment (a) and a history tree which can represent the environment (b). We can construct a HTM which is equivalent with the environment by setting appropriate parameters in each leaf of the history tree.

3.2 BAYESIAN LEARNING

BLHT is designed as Bayesian Learning on the hypothesis space, $\mathcal{H}$, which is a set of history trees. First we show the posterior probability of a history tree $h \in \mathcal{H}$ given history D_t. To derive the posterior probability we set the prior density of Θ_h as

$$\rho(\Theta_h|h) = \prod_{l \in \mathcal{L}_h} \prod_{a \in \mathcal{A}} K_{la} \prod_{i \in \mathcal{I}} \theta_{i|la}^{\alpha_{i|la}-1},$$

where K_{la} is the normalization constant and $\alpha_{i|la}$ is a hyper parameter to specify the prior density. Then we can have the posterior probability of h,

$$P(h|D_t, \mathcal{H}) = c_t P(h|\mathcal{H}) \prod_{l \in \mathcal{L}_h} \prod_{a \in \mathcal{A}} K_{la} \frac{\prod_{i \in \mathcal{I}} \Gamma(N_{i|la}^t + \alpha_{i|la})}{\Gamma(N_{la}^t + \alpha_{la})}, \quad (1)$$

where c_t is the normalization constant, $\Gamma(\cdot)$ is the gamma function, $N_{i|la}^t$ is the number of times i is observed after executing a when $\lambda_h(D_{t'}) = l$ in the history D_t, $N_{la}^t = \sum_{i \in \mathcal{I}} N_{i|la}^t$, and $\alpha_{la} = \sum_{i \in \mathcal{I}} \alpha_{i|la}$.

Next, we show the estimates of the parameters. We use the average of $\theta_{i|la}$ with its posterior density as the estimate, $\hat{\theta}^t_{i|la}$, which is expressed as

$$\hat{\theta}^t_{i|la} = \frac{N^t_{i|la} + \alpha_{i|la}}{N^t_{la} + \alpha_{la}}.$$

ω_{la} is estimated just by accumulating rewards received after executing a when $\lambda_h(D_t) = l$, and dividing it by the number of times a was performed when $\lambda_h(D_t) = l$, N^t_{la}. That is,

$$\hat{\omega}^t_{la} = \frac{1}{N^t_{la}} \sum_{k=1}^{N^t_{la}} r_{t_k+1},$$

where t_k is the k-th occurrence of execution of a when $\lambda_h(D_t) = l$.

3.3 LEARNING ALGORITHM

In principle, by evaluating Eq.(1) for all $h \in \mathcal{H}$, we can extract the MAP model. However, it is often impractical, because a proper hypothesis space $\mathcal{H}$ is very large when the agent has little prior knowledge concerning the environment. Fortunately, we can design an efficient learning algorithm by assuming that the hypothesis space, $\mathcal{H}$, is the set of pruned trees of a large history tree $h_\mathcal{H}$ and the ratio of prior probabilities of a history tree h and h' obtained by pruning off subtree Δh from h is given by a known function $q(\Delta h)$[1].

We define function $g(h|D_t, \mathcal{H})$ by taking logarithm of the R.H.S. of Eq.(1) without the normalization constant, which can be rewritten as

$$g(h|D_t, \mathcal{H}) = \log P(h|\mathcal{H}) + \sum_{l \in \mathcal{L}_h} \Lambda^t_l, \qquad (2)$$

where

$$\Lambda^t_l = \sum_{a \in \mathcal{A}} \log \left[K_{la} \frac{\prod_{i \in \mathcal{I}} \Gamma(N^t_{i|la} + \alpha_{i|la})}{\Gamma(N^t_{la} + \alpha_{la})} \right]. \qquad (3)$$

Then, we can extract the MAP model by finding the history tree which maximizes g. Eq.(2) shows that $g(h|D_t, \mathcal{H})$ can be evaluated by summing up Λ^t_l over $\mathcal{L}_h$. Accordingly, we can implement an efficient algorithm using the tree $h_\mathcal{H}$ whose each (internal or leaf) node l stores Λ_l, $N_{i|la}$, $\alpha_{i|la}$, and ω_{la}.

Suppose that the agent observed i_{t+1} when the last action was a_t. Then, from Eq.(3),

$$\Lambda^{t+1}_l = \begin{cases} \Lambda^t_l + \log \frac{N^t_{i_{t+1}|la_t} + \alpha_{i_{t+1}|la_t}}{N^t_{la_t} + \alpha_{la_t}} & \text{for } l \in \mathcal{N}_{D_t} \\ \Lambda^t_l & \text{otherwise} \end{cases}, \qquad (4)$$

where $\mathcal{N}_{D_t}$ is the set of nodes on the path from the root to leaf $\lambda_{h_\mathcal{H}}(D_t)$. Thus, $h_\mathcal{H}$ is updated just by evaluating Eq(4), adding 1 to $N_{i|la}$, and recalculating ω_{la} in nodes of $\mathcal{N}_{D_t}$.

After $h_\mathcal{H}$ is updated, we can extract the MAP model using the procedure "Find-MAP-Subtree" shown in Fig. 3(a). We show the learning algorithm in Fig.3(b), in which the MAP model is extracted and policy π is updated only when a given condition is satisfied.

4 LIMIT THEOREMS

In this section, we describe limit theorems of BLHT. Throughout the section, we assume that policy π is used while learning and the stochastic process $\{(s_t, a_t, i_{t+1}), t \geq 0\}$ is ergodic under π.

First we show a theorem which ensures that the history tree model learned by BLHT does not miss any relevant memories (see Suematsu et al. (1997) for the proof).

---

[1] The condition is satisfied, for example, when $P(h|\mathcal{H}) \propto \gamma^{|h|}$ where $0 < \gamma \leq 1$ and $|h|$ denotes the size of h.

An RL Algorithm in Partially Observable Environments Using Memory

Find-MAP-Subtree(node l)
1: $\Delta h \leftarrow \emptyset, \Lambda \leftarrow 0$
2: $\mathcal{C} \leftarrow$ {all child nodes of node l}
3: if $|\mathcal{C}| = 0$ then return $\{l, \Lambda_l\}$
4: for each $c \in \mathcal{C}$ do
5: $\quad \{\Delta h_c, \Lambda_c\} \leftarrow$ Find-MAP-Subtree(c)
6: $\quad \Delta h \leftarrow \Delta h \cup \Delta h_c$
7: $\quad \Lambda \leftarrow \Lambda + \Lambda_c$
8: end
9: $\Delta g \leftarrow \log q(\Delta h) + \Lambda - \Lambda_l$
10: if $\Delta g > 0$ then return $\{\Delta h, \Lambda\}$
11: else return $\{l, \Lambda_l\}$
(a)

Main-Loop(condition C)
1: $t \leftarrow 0, D_t \leftarrow ()$
2: $\pi \leftarrow$ "policy selecting action at random"
3: $a_t \leftarrow \pi(D_t)$ or exploratory action
4: perform a_t and receive i_{t+1} and r_{t+1}
5: update $h_{\mathcal{H}}$.
6: if (condition C is satisfied) do
7: $\quad h \leftarrow$ Find-MAP-Subtree(Root($h_{\mathcal{H}}$))
8: $\quad \pi \leftarrow$ Dynamic-Programming(h)
9: end
10: $D_{t+1} \leftarrow (D_t, a_t, i_{t+1}), \quad t \leftarrow t+1$
11: goto 3
(b)

Figure 3: The procedure to find MAP subtree (a) and the main loop (b).

Theorem 1 *For any $h \in \mathcal{H}$,*

$$\lim_{t \to \infty} \frac{1}{t} g(h|D_t, \mathcal{H}) = -H_h(I|L, A),$$

where $H_h(I|L, A)$ is the conditional entropy of i_{t+1} given $l_t = \lambda_h(D_t)$ and a_t defined by

$$H_h(I|L, A) \equiv E_\pi \left\{ \sum_{i \in \mathcal{I}} -P_\pi(i_{t+1} = i \mid l_t, a_t) \log P_\pi(i_{t+1} = i \mid l_t, a_t) \right\},$$

where $P_\pi(\cdot)$ and $E_\pi(\cdot)$ denotes probability and expected value under π respectively.

Let the history tree shown in Fig.2(b) be h^* and a history tree obtained by pruning a subtree of h^* be h^-. Then, for the environment shown in Fig.2(a) $H_{h^-}(I|L, A) > H_{h^*}(I|L, A)$, because h^- misses some relevant memories and it makes the conditional entropy increase. Since BLHT learns the history tree which maximizes $g(h|D_t, \mathcal{H})$ (minimizes $H_h(I|L, A)$), the learned history tree does not miss any relevant memory.

Next we show a limit theorem concerning the estimates of the parameters. We denote the true POMDP model by $M = \langle \mathcal{S}, \mathcal{A}, \mathcal{I}, \mathcal{P}, \mathcal{O}, \mathcal{W}, \boldsymbol{x}_i \rangle$ and define the following parameters,

$$\sigma_{i|sa} \equiv P(i_{t+1} = i \mid s_t = s, a_t = a) = \sum_{s' \in \mathcal{S}} p_{s'|sa} o_{i|sas'}$$

$$\mu_{sa} \equiv E(r_{t+1}|s_t = s, a_t = a) = \sum_{s' \in \mathcal{S}} w_{sas'} p_{s'|sa}.$$

Then, the following theorem holds.

Theorem 2 *For any leaf $l \in \mathcal{L}_h, a \in \mathcal{A}, i \in \mathcal{I}$*

$$\lim_{t \to \infty} \hat{\theta}^t_{i|la} = \sum_{s \in \mathcal{S}} \sigma_{i|sa} y^\pi_{s|la}, \tag{5}$$

$$\lim_{t \to \infty} \hat{\omega}^t_{la} = \sum_{s \in \mathcal{S}} \mu_{sa} y^\pi_{s|la}, \tag{6}$$

where $y^\pi_{s|la} \equiv P_\pi(s_t = s|\lambda_h(D_t) = l, a_t = a)$.

Outline of proof : Using the Ergodic Theorem, We have

$$\lim_{t \to \infty} \hat{\theta}^t_{i|la} = P_\pi(i_{t+1} = i|\lambda_h(D_t) = l, a_t = a).$$

By expanding R.H.S of the above equation using the chain rule, we can derive Eq.(5). Eq.(6) can be derived in a similar way. ∎

To explain what Theorem 2 means clearly, we show the relationship between $y^\pi_{s|la}$ and the belief state x_t.

$$P_\pi(s_t = s|\lambda_h(D_t) = l, a_t = a, x_0 = x_i)$$
$$= \sum_{D \in \mathcal{D}^t_l} P(s_t = s|D_t = D, a_t = a, x_0 = x_i) P_\pi(D_t = D|l_t = l, a_t = a, x_0 = x_i)$$
$$= \int_{\mathcal{X}} \sum_{D \in \mathcal{D}^t_l} \mathbb{1}_{\mathcal{D}^t_x}(D)\{X_M(D)\}_s P_\pi(D_t = D|l_t = l, a_t = a, x_0 = x_i) dx$$
$$= \int_{\mathcal{X}} x_s P_\pi(x_t = x|l_t = l, a_t = a, x_0 = x_i) dx,$$

where $\mathcal{D}^t_l \equiv \{D_t|\lambda_h(D_t) = l\}$, $\mathbb{1}_B(\cdot)$ is the indicator function of a set B, $\mathcal{D}^t_x \equiv \{D_t|X_M(D_t) = x\}$, and $dx = dx_1 \cdots dx_{|S|-1}$. Under the ergodic assumption, by taking $\lim_{t \to \infty}$ of the above equation, we have

$$y^\pi_{la} = \int_{\mathcal{X}} x \Phi^\pi_{la}(x) dx \quad (7)$$

where $y^\pi_{la} = (y^\pi_{s_1|la}, \ldots, y^\pi_{s_{|S|-1}|la})$ and $\Phi^\pi_{la}(x) = P_\pi(x_t = x|\lambda_h(D_t) = l, a_t = a)$.

We see from Eq.(7) that y^π_{la} is the average of belief state x_t with conditional density Φ^π_{la}, that is, the belief states distributed according to Φ^π_{la} are represented by y^π_{la}. When short-term memory of l gives the dominant information of D_t, Φ^π_{la} is concentrated and y^π_{la} is a reasonable approximation of the belief states. An extreme of the case is when Φ^π_{la} is non-zero only at a point in $\mathcal{X}$. Then $y^\pi_{la} = x_t$ when $\lambda_h(D_t) = l$.

Please note that given short-term memory represented by l and a, y^π_{la} is the most accurate state estimation. Consequently, Theorem 1 and 2 ensure that learned HTM converges to the model which provides the most accurate predictions of percepts and rewards among $\mathcal{H}$. This fact provides a solid basis for BLHT, and we believe BLHT can be compared favorably with other methods using short-term memory. Of course, Theorem 1 and 2 also say that BLHT will find the optimal policy if the environment is Markovian or semi-Markovian whose order is small enough for the equivalent model to be contained in $\mathcal{H}$.

5 EXPERIMENT

We made experiments in various environments. In this paper, we show one of them to demonstrate the effectiveness of BLHT. The environment we used is the grid world shown in Fig.4(a). The agent has four actions to change its location to one of the four neighboring grids, which will fail with probability 0.2. On failure, the agent does not change the location with probability 0.1 or goes to one of the two grids which are perpendicular to the direction the agent is trying to go with probability 0.1. The agent can detect merely the existence of the four surrounding walls. The agent receives a reward of 10 when he reaches the goal which is the grid marked with "G" and - 1 when he tries to go to a grid occupied by an obstacle. At the goal, any action will relocate the agent to one of the starting states which are marked with "S" at random. In order to achieve high performance in the environment, the agent has to select different actions for an identical immediate percept, because many of the states are aliased (i.e. they look identical by the immediate percepts). The environment has 50 states, which is among the largest problems shown in the literature of the model based RL techniques for partially observable environments.

Fig.4(b) shows the learning curve which is obtained by averaging over 10 independent runs. While learning, the agent updated the policy every 10 trials (10 visits to the goal) and the policy was evaluated through a run of 100,000 steps. Actions were selected using the policy or at random and the probability of selecting at random was decreased exponentially as the time goes. We used the tree which has homogeneous depth of 5 as $h_\mathcal{H}$. In Fig.4(b), the horizontal broken line indicates the average reward for the MDP model obtained by assuming perfect and complete perception. It gives an upper bound for the original problem, and it will be higher than the optimal one for the original problem. The learning curve shown there is close to the upper bound in the later stage.

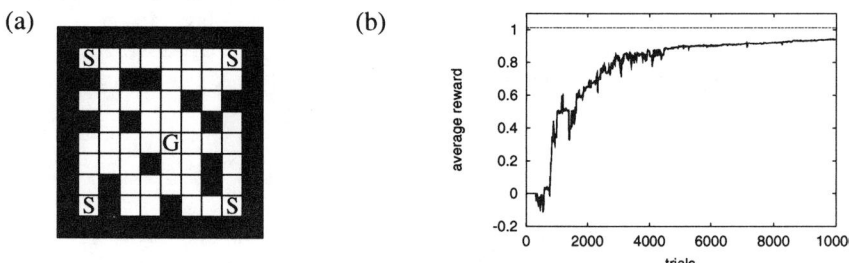

Figure 4: The grid world (a) and the learning curve (b).

6 SUMMARY

This paper has described a RL algorithm for partially observable environments using short-term memory, which we call BLHT. We have proved that the model learned by BLHT converges to the optimal model in given hypothesis space, $\mathcal{H}$, which provides the most accurate predictions of percepts and rewards, given short-term memory. We believe this fact provides a solid basis for BLHT, and BLHT can be compared favorably with other methods using short-term memory.

References

Abe, N. and M. K. Warmuth (1992). On the computational compleixy of apporximating distributions by probabilistic automata. *Machine Learning*, 9:205–260.

Bertsekas, D. P. (1987). *Dyanamic Programming*. Prentice-Hall.

Chrisman, L. (1992). Reinforcemnt learning with perceptual aliasing: The perceptual distinctions approach. In *Proc. the 10th National Conference on Artificial Intelligence*.

Jaakkola, T., S. P. Singh, and M. I. Jordan (1995). Reinforcement learning algorithm for parially observable markov decision problems. In *Advances in Neural Information Processing Systems 7*, pp. 345–352.

McCallum, R. A. (1993). Overcoming incomplete perception with utile distiction memory. In *Proc. the 10th International Conference on Machine Learning*.

McCallum, R. A. (1995). Instance-based utile distinctions for reinforcement learning with hidden state. In *Proc. the 12th International Conference on Machine Learning*.

Papadimitriou, C. H. and J. N. Tsitsiklis (1987). The complexity of markov decision processes. *Mathematics of Operations Research*, 12(3):441–450.

Ron, D., Y. Singer, and N. Tishby (1994). Learning probabilistic automata with variable memory length. In *Proc. of Computational Learning Theory*, pp. 35–46.

Singh, S. P., T. Jaakkola, and M. I. Jordan (1995). Learning without state-estimation in partially observable markov decision processes. In *Proc. the 12th International Conference on Machine Learning*, pp. 284–292.

Suematsu, N., A. Hayashi, and S. Li (1997). A Bayesian approch to model learning in non-markovian environments. In *Proc. the 14th International Conference on Machine Learning*, pp. 349–357.

Improved Switching
among Temporally Abstract Actions

Richard S. Sutton Satinder Singh
AT&T Labs
Florham Park, NJ 07932
{sutton,baveja}@research.att.com

Doina Precup Balaraman Ravindran
University of Massachusetts
Amherst, MA 01003-4610
{dprecup,ravi}@cs.umass.edu

Abstract

In robotics and other control applications it is commonplace to have a pre-existing set of controllers for solving subtasks, perhaps hand-crafted or previously learned or planned, and still face a difficult problem of how to choose and switch among the controllers to solve an overall task as well as possible. In this paper we present a framework based on Markov decision processes and semi-Markov decision processes for phrasing this problem, a basic theorem regarding the improvement in performance that can be obtained by switching flexibly between given controllers, and example applications of the theorem. In particular, we show how an agent can plan with these high-level controllers and then use the results of such planning to find an even better plan, by modifying the existing controllers, with negligible additional cost and no re-planning. In one of our examples, the complexity of the problem is reduced from 24 billion state-action pairs to less than a million state-controller pairs.

In many applications, solutions to parts of a task are known, either because they were hand-crafted by people or because they were previously learned or planned. For example, in robotics applications, there may exist controllers for moving joints to positions, picking up objects, controlling eye movements, or navigating along hallways. More generally, an intelligent system may have available to it several temporally extended courses of action to choose from. In such cases, a key challenge is to take full advantage of the existing temporally extended actions, to choose or switch among them effectively, and to plan at their level rather than at the level of individual actions.

Recently, several researchers have begun to address these challenges within the framework of reinforcement learning and Markov decision processes (e.g., Singh, 1992; Kaelbling, 1993; Dayan & Hinton, 1993; Thrun and Schwartz, 1995; Sutton, 1995; Dietterich, 1998; Parr & Russell, 1998; McGovern, Sutton & Fagg, 1997). Common to much of this recent work is the modeling of a temporally extended action as a policy (controller) and a condition for terminating, which we together refer to as an *option* (Sutton, Precup & Singh, 1998). In this paper we consider the problem of effectively combining given options into one overall policy, generalizing prior work by Kaelbling (1993). Sections 1–3 introduce the framework; our new results are in Sections 4 and 5.

1 Reinforcement Learning (MDP) Framework

In a *Markov decision process (MDP)*, an agent interacts with an environment at some discrete, lowest-level time scale $t = 0, 1, 2, \ldots$ On each time step, the agent perceives the state of the environment, $s_t \in \mathcal{S}$, and on that basis chooses a *primitive* action, $a_t \in \mathcal{A}$. In response to each action, a_t, the environment produces one step later a numerical reward, r_{t+1}, and a next state, s_{t+1}. The *one-step model* of the environment consists of the one-step state-transition probabilities and the one-step expected rewards,

$$p^a_{ss'} = \Pr\{s_{t+1} = s' \mid s_t = s, a_t = a\} \quad \text{and} \quad r^a_s = E\{r_{t+1} \mid s_t = s, a_t = a\},$$

for all $s, s' \in \mathcal{S}$ and $a \in \mathcal{A}$. The agent's objective is to learn an *optimal Markov policy*, a mapping from states to probabilities of taking each available primitive action, $\pi : \mathcal{S} \times \mathcal{A} \to [0, 1]$, that maximizes the expected discounted future reward from each state s:

$$V^\pi(s) = E\left\{r_{t+1} + \gamma r_{t+2} + \cdots \mid s_t = s, \pi\right\} = \sum_{a \in \mathcal{A}_s} \pi(s, a)[r^a_s + \gamma \sum_{s'} p^a_{ss'} V^\pi(s')],$$

where $\pi(s, a)$ is the probability with which the policy π chooses action $a \in \mathcal{A}_s$ in state s, and $\gamma \in [0, 1]$ is a *discount-rate* parameter. $V^\pi(s)$ is called the *value* of state s under policy π, and V^π is called the *state-value function* for π. The *optimal* state-value function gives the value of a state under an optimal policy: $V^*(s) = \max_\pi V^\pi(s) = \max_{a \in \mathcal{A}_s}[r^a_s + \gamma \sum_{s'} p^a_{ss'} V^*(s')]$. Given V^*, an optimal policy is easily formed by choosing in each state s any action that achieves the maximum in this equation. A parallel set of value functions, denoted Q^π and Q^*, and Bellman equations can be defined for state-action pairs, rather than for states. Planning in reinforcement learning refers to the use of models of the environment to compute value functions and thereby to optimize or improve policies.

2 Options

We use the term *options* for our generalization of primitive actions to include temporally extended courses of action. Let $h_{t,T} = s_t, a_t, r_{t+1}, s_{t+1}, a_{t+1}, \ldots, r_T, s_T$ be the history sequence from time $t \leq T$ to time T, and let Ω denote the set of all possible histories in the given MDP. Options consist of three components: an initiation set $\mathcal{I} \subseteq \mathcal{S}$, a policy $\pi : \Omega \times \mathcal{A} \to [0, 1]$, and a termination condition $\beta : \Omega \to [0, 1]$. An option $o = \langle \mathcal{I}, \pi, \beta \rangle$ can be taken in state s if and only if $s \in \mathcal{I}$. If o is taken in state s_t, the next action a_t is selected according to $\pi(s_t, \cdot)$. The environment then makes a transition to s_{t+1}, where o terminates with probability $\beta(h_{t,t+1})$, or else continues, determining a_{t+1} according to $\pi(h_{t,t+1}, \cdot)$, and transitioning to state s_{t+2}, where o terminates with probability $\beta(h_{t,t+2})$ etc. We call the general options defined above *semi-Markov* because π and β depend on the history sequence; in *Markov* options π and β depend only on the current state. Semi-Markov options allow "timeouts", i.e., termination after some period of time has elapsed, and other extensions which cannot be handled by Markov options.

The initiation set and termination condition of an option together limit the states over which the option's policy must be defined. For example, a hand-crafted policy π for a mobile robot to dock with its battery charger might be defined only for states $\mathcal{I}$ in which the battery charger is within sight. The termination condition β would be defined to be 1 outside of $\mathcal{I}$ and when the robot is successfully docked.

We can now define *policies over options*. Let the set of options available in state s be denoted $\mathcal{O}_s$; the set of all options is denoted $\mathcal{O} = \bigcup_{s \in \mathcal{S}} \mathcal{O}_s$. When initiated in a state s_t, the Markov policy over options $\mu : \mathcal{S} \times \mathcal{O} \to [0, 1]$ selects an option $o \in \mathcal{O}_{s_t}$ according to the probability distribution $\mu(s_t, \cdot)$. The option o is then taken in s_t, determining actions until it terminates in s_{t+k}, at which point a new option is selected, according to $\mu(s_{t+k}, \cdot)$, and so on. In this way a policy over options, μ, determines a (non-stationary) policy over actions, or *flat policy*, $\pi = f(\mu)$. We define the value of a state s under a general flat policy π as the expected return if the policy is started in s:

$$V^\pi(s) \stackrel{\text{def}}{=} E\left\{r_{t+1} + \gamma r_{t+2} + \cdots \mid \mathcal{E}(\pi, s, t)\right\},$$

where $\mathcal{E}(\pi, s, t)$ denotes the event of π being initiated in s at time t. The value of a state under a general policy (i.e., a policy over options) μ can then be defined as the value of the state under the corresponding flat policy: $V^\mu(s) \stackrel{\text{def}}{=} V^{f(\mu)}(s)$. An analogous definition can be used for the *option-value* function, $Q^\mu(s, o)$. For semi-Markov options it is useful to define $Q^\mu(h, o)$ as the expected discounted future reward after having followed option o through history h.

3 SMDP Planning

Options are closely related to the actions in a special kind of decision problem known as a *semi-Markov decision process*, or *SMDP* (Puterman, 1994; see also Singh, 1992; Bradtke & Duff, 1995; Mahadevan et. al., 1997; Parr & Russell, 1998). In fact, any MDP with a fixed set of options *is* an SMDP. Accordingly, the theory of SMDPs provides an important basis for a theory of options. In this section, we review the standard SMDP framework for planning, which will provide the basis for our extension.

Planning with options requires a model of their consequences. The form of this model is given by prior work with SMDPs. The reward part of the model of o for state $s \in \mathcal{S}$ is the total reward received along the way:

$$r_s^o = E\left\{r_{t+1} + \gamma r_{t+2} + \cdots + \gamma^{k-1} r_{t+k} \mid \mathcal{E}(o, s, t)\right\},$$

where $\mathcal{E}(o, s, t)$ denotes the event of o being initiated in state s at time t. The state-prediction part of the model is

$$p_{ss'}^o = \sum_{k=1}^{\infty} p(s', k)\gamma^k, E\{\gamma^k \delta_{s' s_{t+k}} \mid \mathcal{E}(o, s, t)\},$$

for all $s' \in \mathcal{S}$, where $p(s', k)$ is the probability that the option terminates in s' after k steps. We call this kind of model a *multi-time model* because it describes the outcome of an option not at a single time but at potentially many different times, appropriately combined.

Using multi-time models we can write Bellman equations for general policies and options. For any general Markov policy μ, its value functions satisfy the equations:

$$V^\mu(s) = \sum_{o \in \mathcal{O}_s} \mu(s, o) \left[r_s^o + \sum_{s'} p_{ss'}^o V^\mu(s')\right] \quad \text{and} \quad Q^\mu(s, o) = r_s^o + \sum_{s'} p_{ss'}^o V^\mu(s').$$

Let us denote a restricted set of options by $\mathcal{O}$ and the set of all policies selecting only from options in $\mathcal{O}$ by $\Pi(\mathcal{O})$. Then the optimal value function given that we can select only from $\mathcal{O}$ is $V_\mathcal{O}^*(s) = \max_{o \in \mathcal{O}_s} [r_s^o + \sum_{s'} p_{ss'}^o V_\mathcal{O}^*(s')]$. A corresponding *optimal policy*, denoted $\mu_\mathcal{O}^*$, is any policy that achieves $V_\mathcal{O}^*$, i.e., for which $V^{\mu_\mathcal{O}^*}(s) = V_\mathcal{O}^*(s)$ in all states $s \in \mathcal{S}$. If $V_\mathcal{O}^*$ and the models of the options are known, then $\mu_\mathcal{O}^*$ can be formed by choosing in any proportion among the maximizing options in the equation above for $V_\mathcal{O}^*$.

It is straightforward to extend MDP planning methods to SMDPs. For example, *synchronous value iteration* with options initializes an approximate value function $V_0(s)$ arbitrarily and then updates it by:

$$V_{k+1}(s) \leftarrow \max_{o \in \mathcal{O}_s}[r_s^o + \sum_{s' \in \mathcal{S}} p_{ss'}^o V_k(s')], \quad \forall s \in \mathcal{S}.$$

Note that this algorithm reduces to conventional value iteration in the special case in which $\mathcal{O} = \mathcal{A}$. Standard results from SMDP theory guarantee that such processes converge for general semi-Markov options: $\lim_{k\to\infty} V_k(s) = V_\mathcal{O}^*(s)$ for all $s \in \mathcal{S}$, $o \in \mathcal{O}$, and for all $\mathcal{O}$. The policies found using temporally abstract options are approximate in the sense that they achieve only $V_\mathcal{O}^*$, which is typically less than the maximum possible, V^*.

4 Interrupting Options

We are now ready to present the main new insight and result of this paper. SMDP methods apply to options, but only when they are treated as opaque indivisible units. Once an option has been selected, such methods require that its policy be followed until the option terminates. More interesting and potentially more powerful methods are possible by looking inside options and by altering their internal structure (e.g. Sutton, Precup & Singh, 1998).

In particular, suppose we have determined the option-value function $Q^\mu(s, o)$ for some policy μ and for all state–options pairs s, o that could be encountered while following μ. This function tells us how well we do while following μ committing irrevocably to each option, but it can also be used to re-evaluate our commitment on each step. Suppose at time t we are in the midst of executing option o. If o is Markov in s, then we can compare the value of continuing with o, which is $Q^\mu(s_t, o)$, to the value of interrupting o and selecting a new option according to μ, which is $V^\mu(s) = \sum_{o'} \mu(s, o') Q^\mu(s, o')$. If the latter is more highly valued, then why not interrupt o and allow the switch? This new way of behaving is indeed better, as shown below.

We can characterize the new way of behaving as following a policy μ' that is the same as the original one, but over new options, i.e. $\mu'(s, o') = \mu(s, o)$, for all $s \in \mathcal{S}$. Each new option o' is the same as the corresponding old option o except that it terminates whenever switching seems better than continuing according to Q^μ. We call such a μ' an *interrupted policy* of μ. We will now state a general theorem, which extends the case described above, in that options may be semi-Markov (instead of Markov) and interruption is optional at each state where it could be done. The latter extension lifts the requirement that Q^μ be completely known, since the interruption can be restricted to states for which this information is available.

Theorem 1 (Interruption) *For any MDP, any set of options $\mathcal{O}$, and any Markov policy $\mu : \mathcal{S} \times \mathcal{O} \to [0, 1]$, define a new set of options, $\mathcal{O}'$, with a one-to-one mapping between the two option sets as follows: for every $o = \langle \mathcal{I}, \pi, \beta \rangle \in \mathcal{O}$ we define a corresponding $o' = \langle \mathcal{I}, \pi, \beta' \rangle \in \mathcal{O}'$, where $\beta' = \beta$ except that for any history h in which $Q^\mu(h, o) < V^\mu(s)$, where s is the final state of h, we may choose to set $\beta'(h) = 1$. Any histories whose termination conditions are changed in this way are called interrupted histories. Let μ' be the policy over o' corresponding to μ: $\mu'(s, o') = \mu(s, o)$, where o is the option in $\mathcal{O}$ corresponding to o', for all $s \in \mathcal{S}$. Then*

1. $V^{\mu'}(s) \geq V^\mu(s)$ for all $s \in \mathcal{S}$.
2. *If from state $s \in \mathcal{S}$ there is a non-zero probability of encountering an interrupted history upon initiating μ' in s, then $V^{\mu'}(s) > V^\mu(s)$.*

Proof: The idea is to show that, for an arbitrary start state s, executing the option given by the termination improved policy μ' and then following policy μ thereafter is no worse than always following policy μ. In other words, we show that the following inequality holds:

$$\sum_{o'} \mu'(s, o')[r_s^{o'} + \sum_{s'} p_{ss'}^{o'} V^\mu(s')] \geq V^\mu(s) = \sum_o \mu(s, o)[r_s^o + \sum_{s'} p_{ss'}^o V^\mu(s')]. \quad (1)$$

If this is true, then we can use it to expand the left-hand side, repeatedly replacing every occurrence of $V^\mu(x)$ on the left by the corresponding $\sum_{o'} \mu'(x, o')[r_x^{o'} + \sum_{x'} p_{xx'}^{o'} V^\mu(x')]$. In the limit, the left-hand side becomes $V^{\mu'}$, proving that $V^{\mu'} \geq V^\mu$. Since $\mu'(s, o') = \mu(s, o)$ $\forall s \in \mathcal{S}$, we need to show that

$$r_s^{o'} + \sum_{s'} p_{ss'}^{o'} V^\mu(s') \geq r_s^o + \sum_{s'} p_{ss'}^o V^\mu(s'). \quad (2)$$

Let Γ denote the set of all interrupted histories: $\Gamma = \{h \in \Omega : \beta(h) \neq \beta'(h)\}$. Then, the left hand side of (2) can be re-written as

$$E\left\{r + \gamma^k V^\mu(s') \,\Big|\, \mathcal{E}(o',s), h_{ss'} \notin \Gamma\right\} + E\left\{r + \gamma^k V^\mu(s') \,\Big|\, \mathcal{E}(o',s), h_{ss'} \in \Gamma\right\},$$

where s', r, and k are the next state, cumulative reward, and number of elapsed steps following option o from s ($h_{ss'}$ is the history from s to s'). Trajectories that end because of encountering a history $h_{ss'} \notin \Gamma$ never encounter a history in Γ, and therefore also occur with the same probability and expected reward upon executing option o in state s. Therefore, we can re-write the right hand side of (2) as $E\left\{r + \gamma^k V^\mu(s') \,\Big|\, \mathcal{E}(o',s), h_{ss'} \notin \Gamma\right\} +$

$$E\left\{\beta(s')[r + \gamma^k V^\mu(s')] + (1 - \beta(s'))[r + \gamma^k Q^\mu(h_{ss'}, o)] \,\Big|\, \mathcal{E}(o',s), h_{ss'} \in \Gamma\right\}.$$

This proves (1) because for all $h_{ss'} \in \Gamma$, $Q_\mathcal{O}^\mu(h_{ss'}, o) \leq V^\mu(s')$. Note that strict inequality holds in (2) if $Q_\mathcal{O}^\mu(h_{ss'}, o) < V^\mu(s')$ for at least one history $h_{ss'} \in \Gamma$ that ends a trajectory generated by o' with non-zero probability.[1]   ◇

As one application of this result, consider the case in which μ is an optimal policy for a given set of Markov options $\mathcal{O}$. The interruption theorem gives us a way of improving over $\mu_\mathcal{O}^*$ with just the cost of checking (on each time step) if a better option exists, which is negligible compared to the combinatorial process of computing $Q_\mathcal{O}^*$ or $V_\mathcal{O}^*$. Kaelbling (1993) and Dietterich (1998) demonstrated a similar performance improvement by interrupting temporally extended actions in a different setting.

5 Illustration

Figure 1 shows a simple example of the gain that can be obtained by interrupting options. The task is to navigate from a start location to a goal location within a continuous two-dimensional state space. The actions are movements of length 0.01 in any direction from the current state. Rather than work with these low-level actions, infinite in number, we introduce seven landmark locations in the space. For each landmark we define a controller that takes us to the landmark in a direct path. Each controller is only applicable within a limited range of states, in this case within a certain distance of the corresponding landmark. Each controller then defines an option: the circular region around the controller's landmark is the option's initiation set, the controller itself is the policy, and the arrival at the target landmark is the termination condition. We denote the set of seven landmark options by $\mathcal{O}$. Any action within 0.01 of the goal location transitions to the terminal state, $\gamma = 1$, and the reward is -1 on all transitions, which makes this a minimum-time task.

One of the landmarks coincides with the goal, so it is possible to reach the goal while picking only from $\mathcal{O}$. The optimal policy within $\Pi(\mathcal{O})$ runs from landmark to landmark, as shown by the thin line in Figure 1. This is the optimal solution to the SMDP defined by $\mathcal{O}$ and is indeed the best that one can do while picking only from these options. But of course one can do better if the options are not followed all the way to each landmark. The trajectory shown by the thick line in Figure 1 cuts the corners and is shorter. This is the interrupted policy with respect to the SMDP-optimal policy. The interrupted policy takes 474 steps from start to goal which, while not as good as the optimal policy (425 steps), is much better than the SMDP-optimal policy, which takes 600 steps. The state-value functions, $V^{\mu_\mathcal{O}^*}$ and $V^{\mu'}$ for the two policies are also shown in Figure 1.

Figure 2 presents a more complex, mission planning task. A mission is a flight from base to observe as many of a given set of sites as possible and to return to base without running out of fuel. The local weather at each site flips from cloudy to clear according to independent

---

[1] We note that the same proof would also apply for switching to other options (not selected by μ) if they improved over continuing with o. That result would be more general and closer to conventional policy improvement. We prefer the result given here because it emphasizes its primary application.

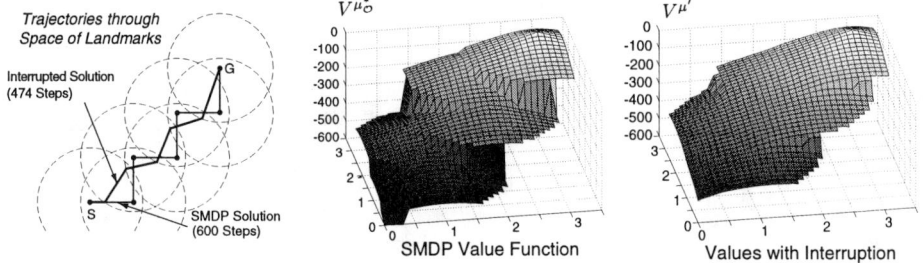

Figure 1: Using interruption to improve navigation with landmark-directed controllers. The task (left) is to navigate from S to G in minimum time using options based on controllers that run each to one of seven landmarks (the black dots). The circles show the region around each landmark within which the controllers operate. The thin line shows the optimal behavior that uses only these controllers run to termination, and the thick line shows the corresponding interrupted behavior, which cuts the corners. The right panels show the state-value functions for the SMDP-optimal and interrupted policies.

Poisson processes. If the sky at a given site is cloudy when the plane gets there, no observation is made and the reward is 0. If the sky is clear, the plane gets a reward, according to the importance of the site. The positions, rewards, and mean time between two weather changes for each site are given in Figure 2. The plane has a limited amount of fuel, and it consumes one unit of fuel during each time tick. If the fuel runs out before reaching the base, the plane crashes and receives a reward of -100.

The primitive actions are tiny movements in any direction (there is no inertia). The state of the system is described by several variables: the current position of the plane, the fuel level, the sites that have been observed so far, and the current weather at each of the remaining sites. The state-action space has approximately 24.3 billion elements (assuming 100 discretization levels of the continuous variables) and is intractable by normal dynamic programming methods. We introduced options that can take the plane to each of the sites (including the base), from any position in the state space. The resulting SMDP has only 874,800 elements and it is feasible to exactly determine $V^*_{\mathcal{O}}(s')$ for all sites s'. From this solution and the model of the options, we can determine $Q^*_{\mathcal{O}}(s, o) = r^o_s + \sum_{s'} p^o_{ss'} V^*_{\mathcal{O}}(s')$ for any option o and any state s in the whole space.

We performed asynchronous value iteration using the options in order to compute the optimal option-value function, and then used the interruption approach based on the values computed. The policies obtained by both approaches were compared to the results of a static planner, which exhaustively searches for the best tour assuming the weather does not change, and then re-plans whenever the weather does change. The graph in Figure 2 shows the reward obtained by each of these methods, averaged over 100 independent simulated missions. The policy obtained by interruption performs significantly better than the SMDP policy, which in turn is significantly better than the static planner.[2]

6 Closing

This paper has developed a natural, even obvious, observation—that one can do better by continually re-evaluating one's commitment to courses of action than one can by committing irrevocably to them. Our contribution has been to formulate this observation precisely enough to prove it and to demonstrate it empirically. Our final example suggests that this technique can be used in applications far too large to be solved at the level of primitive actions. Note that this was achieved using exact methods, without function approximators to represent the value function. With function approximators and other reinforcement learning techniques, it should be possible to address problems that are substantially larger still.

---

[2]In preliminary experiments, we also used interruption on a crudely learned estimate of $Q^*_{\mathcal{O}}$. The performance of the interrupted solution was very close to the result reported here.

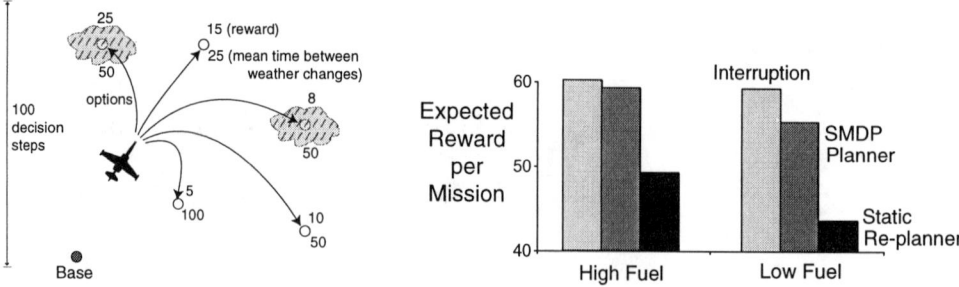

Figure 2: The mission planning task and the performance of policies constructed by SMDP methods, interruption of the SMDP policy, and an optimal static re-planner that does not take into account possible changes in weather conditions.

Acknowledgments

The authors gratefully acknowledge the substantial help they have received from many colleagues, including especially Amy McGovern, Andrew Barto, Ron Parr, Tom Dietterich, Andrew Fagg, Leo Zelevinsky and Manfred Huber. We also thank Paul Cohen, Robbie Moll, Mance Harmon, Sascha Engelbrecht, and Ted Perkins for helpful reactions and constructive criticism. This work was supported by NSF grant ECS-9511805 and grant AFOSR-F49620-96-1-0254, both to Andrew Barto and Richard Sutton. Satinder Singh was supported by NSF grant IIS-9711753.

References

Bradtke, S. J. & Duff, M. O. (1995). Reinforcement learning methods for continuous-time Markov decision problems. In *NIPS 7* (393–500). MIT Press.

Dayan, P. & Hinton, G. E. (1993). Feudal reinforcement learning. In *NIPS 5* (271–278). MIT Press.

Dietterich, T. G. (1998). The MAXQ method for hierarchical reinforcement learning. In *Proceedings of the Fifteenth International Conference on Machine Learning*. Morgan Kaufmann.

Kaelbling, L. P. (1993). Hierarchical learning in stochastic domains: Preliminary results. In *Proceedings of the Tenth International Conference on Machine Learning* (167–173). Morgan Kaufmann.

Mahadevan, S., Marchallek, N., Das, T. K. & Gosavi, A. (1997). Self-improving factory simulation using continuous-time average-reward reinforcement learning. In *Proceedings of the Fourteenth International Conference on Machine Learning* (202–210). Morgan Kaufmann.

McGovern, A., Sutton, R. S., & Fagg, A. H. (1997). Roles of macro-actions in accelerating reinforcement learning. In *Grace Hopper Celebration of Women in Computing* (13–17).

Parr, R. & Russell, S. (1998). Reinforcement learning with hierarchies of machines. In *NIPS 10*. MIT Press.

Puterman, M. L. (1994). *Markov Decision Processes: Discrete Stochastic Dynamic Programming*. Wiley.

Singh, S. P. (1992). Reinforcement learning with a hierarchy of abstract models. In *Proceedings of the Tenth National Conference on Artificial Intelligence* (202–207). MIT/AAAI Press.

Sutton, R. S. (1995). TD models: Modeling the world as a mixture of time scales. In *Proceedings of the Twelfth International Conference on Machine Learning* (531–539). Morgan Kaufmann.

Sutton, R. S., Precup, D. & Singh, S. (1998). Intra-option learning about temporally abstract actions. In *Proceedings of the Fifteenth International Conference on Machine Learning*. Morgan Kaufman.

Sutton, R. S., Precup, D. & Singh, S. (1998). Between MDPs and Semi-MDPs: learning, planning, and representing knowledge at multiple temporal scales. TR 98-74, Department of Comp. Sci., University of Massachusetts, Amherst.

Thrun, S. & Schwartz, A. (1995). Finding structure in reinforcement learning. In *NIPS 7* (385–392). MIT Press.

Experimental Results on Learning Stochastic Memoryless Policies for Partially Observable Markov Decision Processes

John K. Williams
Department of Mathematics
University of Colorado
Boulder, CO 80309-0395
jkwillia@euclid.colorado.edu

Satinder Singh
AT&T Labs-Research
180 Park Avenue
Florham Park, NJ 07932
baveja@research.att.com

Abstract

Partially Observable Markov Decision Processes (POMDPs) constitute an important class of reinforcement learning problems which present unique theoretical and computational difficulties. In the absence of the Markov property, popular reinforcement learning algorithms such as Q-learning may no longer be effective, and memory-based methods which remove partial observability via state-estimation are notoriously expensive. An alternative approach is to seek a stochastic memoryless policy which for each observation of the environment prescribes a probability distribution over available actions that maximizes the average reward per timestep. A reinforcement learning algorithm which learns a locally optimal stochastic memoryless policy has been proposed by Jaakkola, Singh and Jordan, but not empirically verified. We present a variation of this algorithm, discuss its implementation, and demonstrate its viability using four test problems.

1 INTRODUCTION

Reinforcement learning techniques have proven quite effective in solving Markov Decision Processes (MDPs), control problems in which the exact state of the environment is available to the learner and the expected result of an action depends only on the present state [10]. Algorithms such as Q-learning learn optimal deterministic policies for MDPs—rules which for every state prescribe an action that maximizes the expected future reward. In many important problems, however, the exact state of the environment is either inherently unknowable or prohibitively expensive to obtain, and only a limited, possibly stochastic observation of the environment is available. Such

Partially Observable Markov Decision Processes (POMDPs) [3,6] are often much more difficult than MDPs to solve [4]. Distinct sequences of observations and actions preceding a given observation in a POMDP may lead to different probabilities of occupying the underlying exact states of the MDP. If the efficacy of an action depends on the hidden exact state of the environment, an optimal choice may require knowing the past history as well as the current observation, and the problem is no longer Markov. In light of this difficulty, one approach to solving POMDPs is to explore the environment while building up a memory of past observations, actions and rewards which allows estimation of the current hidden state [1]. Such methods produce deterministic policies, but they are computationally expensive and may not scale well with problem size. Furthermore, policies that require state-estimation using memory may be complicated to implement.

Memoryless policies are particularly appropriate for problems in which the state is expensive to obtain or inherently difficult to estimate, and they have the advantage of being extremely simple to act upon. For a POMDP, the optimal memoryless policy is generally a stochastic policy—one which for each observation of the environment prescribes a probability distribution over the available actions. In fact, examples of POMDPs can be constructed for which a stochastic policy is arbitrarily better than the optimal deterministic policy [9]. An algorithm proposed by Jaakkola, Singh and Jordan (JSJ) [2], which we investigate here, learns memoryless stochastic policies for POMDPs.

2 POMDPs AND DIFFERENTIAL-REWARD Q-VALUES

We assume that the environment has discrete states $S = \{s^1, s^2, .. s^N\}$, and the learner chooses actions from a set $\mathcal{A}$. State transitions depend only on the current state s and the action a taken (the Markov property); they occur with probabilities $P^a(s,s')$ and result in expected rewards $R^a(s,s')$. In a POMDP, the learner cannot sense exactly the state s of the environment, but rather perceives only an observation—or "message"—from a set $\mathcal{M} = \{m^1, m^2, .. m^M\}$ according to a conditional probability distribution $P(m|s)$. The learner will in general not know the size of the underlying state space, its transition probabilities, reward function, or the conditional distributions of the messages.

In MDPs, there always exists a policy which simultaneously maximizes the expected future reward for all states, but this is not the case for POMDPs [9]. An appropriate alternative measure of the merit of a stochastic POMDP policy $\pi(a|m)$ is the asymptotic average reward per timestep, R^π, that it achieves. In seeking an optimal stochastic policy, the JSJ algorithm makes use of Q-values determined by the infinite-horizon differential reward for each observation-action pair (m,a). In particular, if r_t denotes the reward obtained at time t, we may define the differential-reward Q-values by

$$Q^\pi(s,a) = \sum_{t=1}^{\infty} E_\pi[r_t - R^\pi \mid s_1 = s, a_1 = a]; \quad Q^\pi(m,a) = E_s[Q^\pi(s,a) \mid M(s) = m] \quad (1)$$

where M is the observation operator. Note that $E[r_t] \to R^\pi$ as $t \to \infty$, so the summand converges to zero. The value functions $V^\pi(s)$ and $V^\pi(m)$ may be defined similarly.

3 POLICY IMPROVEMENT

The JSJ algorithm consists of a method for evaluating Q^π and V^π and a mechanism for using them to improve the current policy. Roughly speaking, if $Q^\pi(m,a) > V^\pi(m)$, then action a realized a higher differential reward than the average for observation m, and assigning it a slightly greater probability will increase the average reward per timestep, R^π. We interpret the quantities $\Delta_m(a) = Q^\pi(m,a) - V^\pi(m)$ as comprising a "gradient" of R^π in policy space. Their projections onto the probability simplexes may then be written as $\delta_m = \Delta_m - \langle \Delta_m, \mathbf{1} \rangle \mathbf{1}/|\mathcal{A}|$, where $\mathbf{1}$ is the one-vector $(1,1,\ldots,1)$, $\langle\,,\,\rangle$ is the inner product, and $|\mathcal{A}|$ is the number of actions, or

$$\delta_m(a) = \Delta_m(a) - \frac{1}{|A|}\sum_{a' \in A}\Delta_m(a') = Q^\pi(m,a) - \frac{1}{|A|}\sum_{a' \in A}Q^\pi(m,a'). \tag{2}$$

For sufficiently small ε_m, an improved policy $\pi'(a|m)$ may be obtained by the increments

$$\pi'(a|m) = \pi(a|m) + \varepsilon_m\,\delta_m(a). \tag{3}$$

In practice, we also enforce $\pi'(a|m) \geq P_{min}$ for all a and m to guarantee continued exploration. The original JSJ algorithm prescribed using $\Delta_m(a)$ in place of $\delta_m(a)$ in equation (3), followed by renormalization [2]. Our method has the advantage that a given value of Δ yields the same increment regardless of the current value of the policy, and it ensures that the step is in the correct direction. We also do not require the differential-reward value estimate, V^π.

4 Q-EVALUATION

As the POMDP is simulated under a fixed stochastic policy π, every occurrence of an observation-action pair (m,a) begins a sequence of rewards which can be used to estimate $Q^\pi(m,a)$. Exploiting the fact that the $Q^\pi(m,a)$ are defined as sums, the JSJ Q-evaluation method recursively averages the estimates from all such sequences using a so-called "every-visit" Monte-Carlo method. In order to reduce the bias and variance caused by the dependence of the evaluation sequences, a factor β is used to discount their shared "tails". Specifically, at time t the learner makes observation m_t, takes action a_t, and obtains reward r_t. The number of visits $K(m_t,a_t)$ is incremented, the tail discount rate $\gamma(m,a) = 1-K(m,a)^{-1/4}$, and the following updates are performed (the indicator function $\chi_t(m,a)$ is 1 if $(m,a) = (m_t,a_t)$ and 0 otherwise).

$$\beta(m,a) = \left[1 - \frac{\chi_t(m,a)}{K(m,a)}\right]\gamma(m,a)\beta(m,a) + \frac{\chi_t(m,a)}{K(m,a)} \quad \text{(tail discount factor)} \tag{4}$$

$$Q(m,a) = \left[1 - \frac{\chi_t(m,a)}{K(m,a)}\right]Q(m,a) + \beta(m,a)\,[r_t - R] \quad (Q^\pi\text{-estimate}) \tag{5}$$

$$C(m,a) = \left[1 - \frac{\chi_t(m,a)}{K(m,a)}\right]C(m,a) + \beta(m,a) \quad \text{(cumulative discount effect)} \tag{6}$$

$$R = (1 - 1/t)R + (1/t)r_t \quad (R^\pi\text{-estimate}) \tag{7}$$

$$Q(m,a) = Q(m,a) - C(m,a)\,[R - R_{old}]; \quad R_{old} = R \quad (Q^\pi\text{-estimate correction}) \tag{8}$$

Other schedules for $\gamma(m,a)$ are possible—see [2]—and the correction provided by (8) need not be performed at every step, but can be delayed until the Q^π-estimate is needed.

This evaluation method can be used as given for a policy-iteration type algorithm in which independent T-step evaluations of Q^π are interspersed with policy improvements as prescribed in section 3. However, an online version of the algorithm which performs policy improvement after every step requires that old experience be gradually "forgotten" so that the Q^π-estimate can respond to more recent experience. To achieve this, we multiply the previous estimates of β, Q, and C at each timestep by a "decay" factor α, $0 < \alpha < 1$, before they are updated via equations (4)–(6), and replace equation (7) by

$$R = \alpha(1 - 1/t)R + [1 - \alpha(1 - 1/t)]r_t. \tag{9}$$

An alternative method, which also works reasonably well, is to multiply K and t by α at each timestep instead.

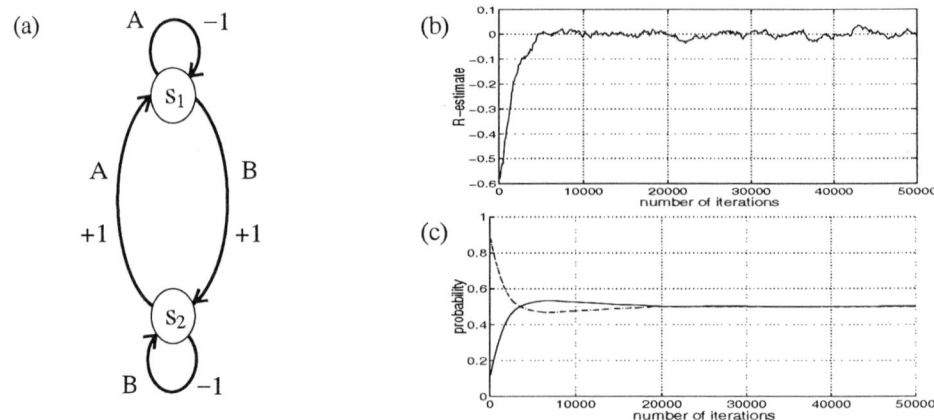

Figure 1: (a) Schematic of confounded two-state POMDP, (b) evolution of the R^π-estimate, and (c) evolution of $\pi(A)$ *(solid)* and $\pi(B)$ *(dashed)* for $\varepsilon = 0.0002$, $\alpha = 0.9995$.

5 EMPIRICAL RESULTS

We present only results from single runs of our online algorithm, including the modified JSJ policy improvement and Q-evaluation procedures described above. Results from the policy iteration version are qualitatively similar, and statistics performed on multiple runs verify that those shown are representative of the algorithm's behavior. To simplify the presentation, we fix a constant learning rate, ε, and decay factor, α, for each problem, and we use $P_{min} = 0.02$ throughout. Note, however, that appropriate schedules or online heuristics for decreasing ε and P_{min} while increasing α would improve performance and are necessary to ensure convergence. Except for the first problem, we choose the initial policy π to be uniform. In the last two problems, values of $\pi(a|m) < 0.03$ are rounded down to zero, with renormalization, before the learned policy is evaluated.

5.1 CONFOUNDED TWO-STATE PROBLEM

The two-state MDP diagrammed in Figure 1(a) becomes a POMDP when the two states are confounded into a single observation. The learner may take action A or B, and receives a reward of either +1 or −1; the state transition is deterministic, as indicated in the diagram. Note that either stationary deterministic policy results in $R^\pi = -1$, whereas the optimal stochastic policy assigns each action the probability 1/2, resulting in $R^\pi = 0$.

The evolution of the R^π-estimate and policy, starting from the initial policy $\pi(A) = 0.1$ and $\pi(B) = 0.9$, is shown in Figure 1. Clearly the learned policy approaches the optimal stochastic policy $\pi = (1/2, 1/2)$.

5.2 MATRIX GAME: SCISSORS-PAPER-STONE-GLASS-WATER

Scissors-Paper-Stone-Glass-Water (SPSGW), an extension of the well-known Scissors-Paper-Stone, is a symmetric zero-sum matrix game in which the learner selects a row i, the opponent selects a column j, and the learner's payoff is determined by the matrix entry $M(i,j)$. A game-theoretic solution is a stochastic (or "mixed") policy which guarantees the learner an expected payoff of at least zero. It can be shown using linear programming that the unique optimal strategy for SPSGW, yielding $R^\pi = 0$, is to play stone and water with probability 1/3, and to play scissors, paper, and glass with probability 1/9 [7]. Any stationary deterministic policy results in $R^\pi = -1$, since the opponent eventually learns to anticipate the learner's choice and exploit it.

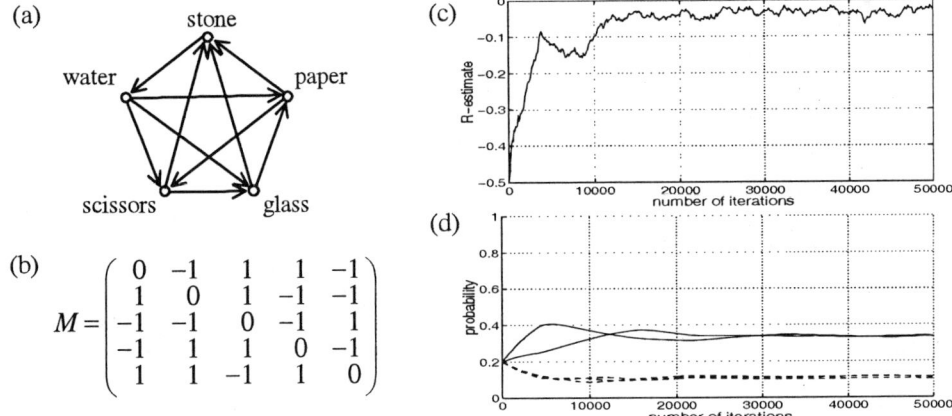

Figure 2: (a) Diagram of Scissors-Paper-Stone-Glass-Water, (b) the payoff matrix, (c) evolution of the R^π-estimate, and (d) evolution of π(stone) and π(water) *(solid)* and π(scissors), π(paper), and π(glass) *(dashed)* for $\varepsilon = 0.00005$, $\alpha = 0.9995$.

In formulating SPSGW as a POMDP, it is necessary to include in the state sufficient information to allow the opponent to exploit any sub-optimal strategy. We thus choose as states the learner's past action frequencies, multiplied at each timestep by the decay factor, α. There is only one observation, and the learner acts by selecting the "row" scissors, paper, stone, glass or water, producing a deterministic state transition. The simulated opponent plays the column which maximizes its expected payoff against the estimate of the learner's strategy obtained from the state. The learner's reward is then obtained from the appropriate entry of the payoff matrix.

The policy $\pi = (0.1124, 0.1033, 0.3350, 0.1117, 0.3376)$ learned after 50,000 iterations (see Figure 2) is very close to the optimal policy $\pi = (1/9, 1/9, 1/3, 1/9, 1/3)$.

5.3 PARR AND RUSSELL'S GRID WORLD

Parr and Russell's grid world [8] consists of 11 states in a 4x3 grid with a single obstacle as shown in Figure 3(a). The learner senses only walls to its immediate east or west and whether it is in the goal state (upper right corner) or penalty state (directly below the goal), resulting in the 6 possible observations (0–3, G and P) indicated in the diagram. The available actions are to move N, E, S, or W, but there is a probability 0.1 of slipping to either side and only 0.8 of moving in the desired direction; a movement into a wall results in bouncing back to the original state. The learner receives a reward of +1 for a transition into the goal state, −1 for a transition into the penalty state, and −0.04 for all other transitions. The goal and penalty states are connected to a cost-free absorbing state; when the learner reaches either of them it is teleported immediately to a new start state chosen with uniform probability.

The results are shown in Figure 3. A separate 10^6-step evaluation of the final learned policy resulted in $R^\pi = 0.047$. In contrast, the optimal deterministic policy indicated by arrows in Figure 3(a) yields $R^\pi = 0.024$ [5], while Parr and Russell's memory-based SPOVA-RL algorithm achieved $R^\pi = 0.12$ after learning for 400,000 iterations [8].

5.4 MULTI-SERVER QUEUE

At each timestep, an arriving job having type 1, 2, or 3 with probability 1/2, 1/3 or 1/6, respectively, must be assigned to server A, B or C; see Figure 4(a). Each server is optimized for a particular job type which it can complete in an expected time of 2.6

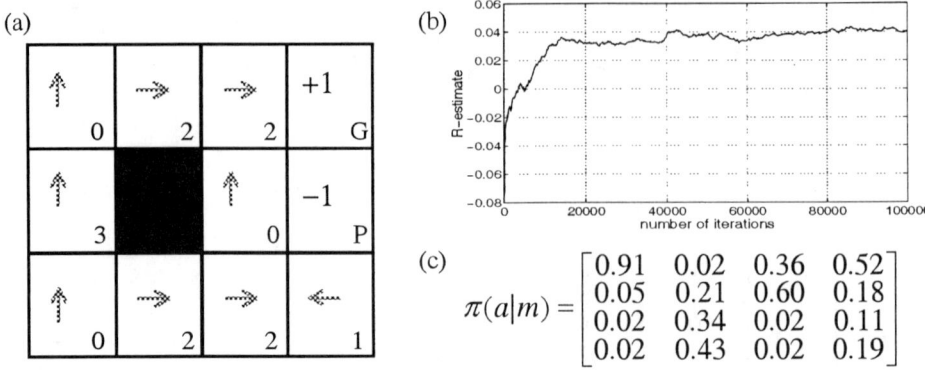

Figure 3: (a) Parr and Russell's grid world, with observations shown in lower right corners and the optimal deterministic memoryless policy represented by arrows, (b) evolution of the R^π-estimate, and (c) the resulting learned policy (observations 0–3 across columns, actions N, E, S, W down rows) for $\varepsilon = 0.02$, $\alpha = 0.9999$.

timesteps, while the other job types require 50% longer. All jobs in a server's queue are handled in parallel, up to a capacity of 10 for each server; they finish with probability $1/f$ at each timestep, where f is the product of the expected time for the job and the number of jobs in the server's queue. The states for this POMDP are all combinations of waiting jobs and server occupancies of the three job types, but the learner's observation is restricted to the type of the waiting job. The state transition is obtained by removing all jobs which have finished and adding the waiting job to the chosen server if it has space available. The reward is +1 if the job is successfully placed, or 0 if it is dropped.

The results are shown in Figure 4. A separate 10^6-step evaluation of the learned policy obtained $R^\pi = 0.95$, corresponding to 95% success in placing jobs. In contrast, the optimal deterministic policy, which assigns each job to the server optimized for it, attained only 87% success. Thus the learned policy more than halves the drop rate!

6 CONCLUSION

Our online version of an algorithm proposed by Jaakkola, Singh and Jordan efficiently learns a stochastic memoryless policy which is either provably optimal or at least superior to any deterministic memoryless policy for each of four test problems. Many enhancements are possible, including appropriate learning schedules to improve performance and ensure convergence, estimation of the time between observation-action visits to obtain better discount rates γ and thereby enhance Q^π-estimate bias and variance reduction (see [2]), and multiple starts or simulated annealing to avoid local minima. In addition, observations could be extended to include some past history when appropriate.

Most POMDP algorithms use memory and attempt to learn an optimal deterministic policy based on belief states. The stochastic memoryless policies learned by the JSJ algorithm may not always be as good, but they are simpler to act upon and can adapt smoothly in non-stationary environments. Moreover, because it searches the space of stochastic policies, the JSJ algorithm has the potential to find the optimal memoryless policy. These considerations, along with the success of our simple implementation, suggest that this algorithm may be a viable candidate for solving real-world POMDPs, including distributed control or network admission and routing problems in which the numbers of states are enormous and complete state information may be difficult to obtain or estimate in a timely manner.

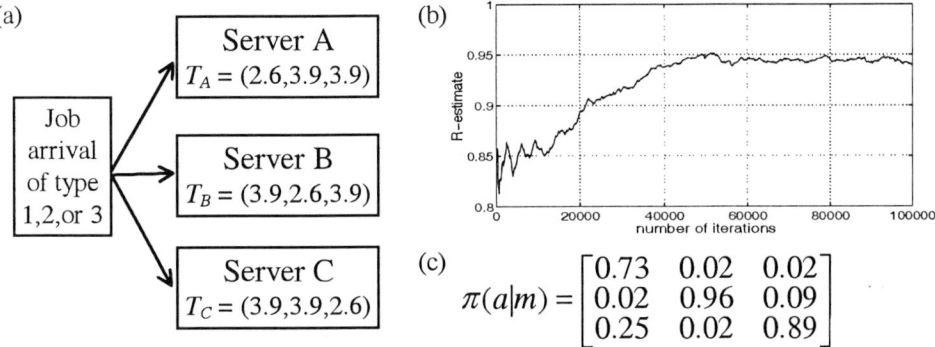

Figure 4: (a) Schematic of the multi-server queue, (b) evolution of the R^π-estimate, and (c) the resulting learned policy (observations 1, 2, 3 across columns, actions A, B, C down rows) for $\varepsilon = 0.005$, $\alpha = 0.9999$.

Acknowledgements

We would like to thank Mike Mozer and Tim Brown for helpful discussions. Satinder Singh was funded by NSF grant IIS-9711753.

References

[1] Chrisman, L. (1992). Reinforcement learning with perceptual aliasing: The perceptual distinctions approach. In *Proceedings of the Tenth National Conference on Artificial Intelligence*.

[2] Jaakkola, T., Singh, S. P., and Jordan, M. I. (1995). Reinforcement learning algorithm for partially observable Markov decision problems. In *Advances in Neural Information Processing Systems 7*.

[3] Littman, M., Cassandra, A., and Kaelbling, L. (1995). Learning policies for partially observable environments: Scaling up. In *Proceedings of the Twelfth International Conference on Machine Learning*.

[4] Littman, M. L. (1994). Memoryless policies: Theoretical limitations and practical results. *Proceedings of the Third International Conference on Simulation of Adaptive Behavior: From Animals to Animats*.

[5] Loch, J., and Singh, S. P. (1998). Using eligibility traces to find the best memoryless policy in partially observable Markov decision processes. In *Machine Learning: Proceedings of the Fifteenth International Conference*.

[6] Lovejoy, W. S. (1991). A survey of algorithmic methods for partially observable Markov decision processes. In *Annals of Operations Research*, 28.

[7] Morris, P. (1994). *Introduction to Game Theory*. Springer-Verlag, New York.

[8] Parr, R. and Russell, S. (1995). Approximating optimal policies for partially observable stochastic domains. In *Proceedings of the International Joint Conference on Artificial Intelligence*.

[9] Singh, S. P., Jaakkola, T., and Jordan, M. I. (1994). Learning without state-estimation in partially observable Markovian decision processes. In *Machine Learning: Proceedings of the Eleventh International Conference*.

[10] Sutton, R. S. and Barto, A. G. (1998). *Reinforcement Learning: An Introduction*. MIT Press.

Index of Authors

Abbott, L. F., 69, 90
Abramowicz, Halina, 868
Adams, Nicholas J., 634
Adorján, Peter, 76
Al-Ansari, Mohammad A., 961
Amari, Shun-ichi, 239
Atiya, Amir, 522
Attias, Hagai, 361
Austin, Jim, 713

Baird, Leemon, 968
Baluja, Shumeet, 847, 854
Baraduc, Pierre, 83
Barber, David, 183
Bartlett, Peter, 190, 288, 330
Barto, Andrew G., 1017
Baxter, Jonathan, 288
Becker, Suzanna, 17
Beckmann, C. F., 337
Bennett, Kristin, 368
Bersini, Hugues, 375
Bhushan, Nikhil, 3
Birattari, Mauro, 375
Bishop, Christopher M., 382
Blake, Andrew, 389
Bollmann-Sdorra, Peter, 438
Bontempi, Gianluca, 375
Borger, Julia, 931
Bottou, Leon, 571
Boyen, Xavier, 396
Brabant, Georg, 931
Brand, Matthew, 723
Braun, Jochen, 789
Briegel, Thomas, 403
Brown, Lyndon J., 975
Brown, Timothy X, 982
Buhmann, Joachim M., 452
Burnod, Yves, 83
Busey, Thomas A., 24

Campbell, Colin, 204
Canu, Stéphane, 445
Cauwenberghs, Gert, 657, 678
Chance, Frances S., 90
Chechik, Gal, 97
Chen, Ke, 10
Cho, Jung-Wook, 664
Christianson, G. Bjorn, 17
Cichocki, Andrzej, 648
Coggins, Richard J., 671
Coolen, A. C. C., 197, 211, 316, 337
Cornford, Dan, 861
Cottrell, Garrison W., 24

Coughlan, James M., 641, 761
Courchesne, Eric, 118
Cristianini, Nello, 204
Cross, Andrew D. J., 896

Düring, A., 211
Dailey, Matthew N., 24
Darrell, Trevor, 768
Davidowitz, Hanan, 146
Dayan, Peter, 174, 274
Demiriz, Ayhan, 368
Deneve, Sophie, 104
de Freitas, João F. G., 410
Dhawan, Atam P., 627
Doucet, Arnaud, 410
Douglas, Rodney, 706
Dror, Gideon, 868

Edwards, R. Timothy, 678
Etienne-Cummings, Ralph, 685

Ferrari-Trecate, Giancarlo, 218
Forsyth, David, 782
Frank, Jeremy, 952
Freeman, William T., 775
Frieß, Thilo T., 585
Friedman, Nir, 417

Gao, Fangyu, 620
Gat, Itay, 111
Gdalyahu, Yoram, 424, 838
Gee, Andrew, 410
Gentile, Claudio, 225
Gerstner, Wulfram, 125
Ghahramani, Zoubin, 431, 599
Ghani, Mohammed Abdel, 685
Gonye, Gregory E., 975
Graepel, Thore, 438
Grandvalet, Yves, 445
Granger, Eric, 875
Grossberg, Stephen, 875
Gruev, Viktor, 685
Grzeszczuk, Radek, 882
Guigon, Emmanuel, 83

Haffner, Patrick, 571
Hancock, Edwin R., 896
Hansen, Volker, 945
Harris, John G., 692
Haruno, Masahiko, 31
Haussler, David, 487

Hayashi, Akira, 989, 1059
Held, Marcus, 452
Herbrich, Ralf, 438
Herschkowitz, Didier, 232
Higgins, Charles M., 699
Hinton, Geoffrey, 599, 882
Hochreiter, Sepp, 459
Hofmann, Thomas, 466
Hogden, John E., 744
Hollmen, Jaakko, 889
Horn, David, 868
Hornik, Kurt, 267
Hoyer, Patrik, 473
Huet, Benoit, 896
Hyvarinen, Aapo, 473

Ikeda, Shiro, 239
Ioffe, Sergey, 782
Isard, Michael, 389
Isbell, Jr., Charles Lee, 480
Ishii, Shin, 1052
Itti, Laurent, 789

Jaakkola, Tommi, 487
Jabri, Marwan A., 671
Jacobs, David W., 838
Jebara, Tony, 494, 910
Jordan, Michael, 466
Jung, Tzyy-Ping, 118

Kégl, Balázs, 501
Kabashima, Yoshiyuki, 246
Karakoulas, Grigoris, 253
Kawato, Mitsuo, 31
Kearns, Michael, 260, 996
Kempter, Richard, 125
Kennedy, John, 713
Klein, Barbara, 620
Klein, Ronald, 620
Koch, Christof, 132, 160, 699, 789
Koenig, Sven, 1003
Koller, Daphne, 396
Krzyzak, Adam, 501

Latham, Peter E., 104
Lee, Dale K., 789
Lee, Daniel D., 515
Lee, Soo-Young, 664
Lee, Te-Won, 508
Leen, Todd K., 824
Leisch, Friedrich, 267
Lewicki, Michael S., 508, 730
Le Cun, Yann, 571
Li, Zhaoping, 274, 796
Lin, Xiwu, 620
Linder, Tamás, 501
Lippman, Andrew, 606

Liu, Zili, 45
Loch, John, 1010
Love, Bradley C., 38

Müller, Klaus-R., 536, 564
Maass, Wolfgang, 281
Magdon-Ismail, Malik, 522
Maiorov, Vitaly, 190, 295
Makeig, Scott, 118
Manwani, Amit, 132
Marrs, Alan D., 529
Mason, Llew, 288
McGovern, Amy, 903
Meilijson, Isaac, 97
Meir, Ron, 190, 295
Mihatsch, Oliver, 1031
Mika, Sebastian, 536
Moghaddam, Baback, 910
Moll, Robert, 1017
Moody, John, 917
Moore, Andrew W., 543, 968, 1024
Moss, Eliot, 903
Mozer, Michael C., 52
Munos, Remi, 1024
Murray-Smith, Roderick, 945

Nabney, Ian T., 861
Nadal, Jean-Pierre, 232
Nakahara, Hiroyuki, 239
Nakano, Ryohei, 599
Nelson, Sacha B., 90
Neukirchen, Christoph, 737
Neuneier, Ralph, 1031
Niranjan, Mahesan, 410
Nix, David A., 744
North, Ben, 389

Obermayer, Klaus, 76, 139, 438
Oja, Erkki, 473
Oliver, Nuria, 924
Onoda, Takashi, 564
Opper, Manfred, 218, 302, 309
Oyama, Eimei, 1038

Pasztor, Egon C., 775
Pavel, Misha, 824
Pelillo, Marcello, 550
Pentland, Alex, 494, 910, 924
Perkins, Theodore J., 1017
Phillips, P. Jonathon, 803
Piepenbrock, Christian, 139
Pineda, Fernando J., 678
Platt, John, 557
Pouget, Alexandre, 104
Prank, Klaus, 931
Precup, Doina, 1066
Principe, Jose C., 692

Index of Authors

Pu, Chiang-Jung, 692
Puzicha, Jan, 452, 466

Rätsch, Gunnar, 536, 564
Rae, H. C., 316
Rahim, Mazin, 751
Randløv, Jette, 1045
Rao, Rajesh P. N., 810
Ravindran, B., 1066
Rigoll, Gerhard, 737
Rinberg, Dmitry, 146
Rosario, Barbara, 924
Rosenholtz, Ruth, 817
Roweis, Sam T., 431
Rubin, Mark A., 875
Ruderman, Daniel L., 810
Ruppin, Eytan, 97

Saad, David, 197, 246
Saffell, Matthew, 917
Sajda, Paul, 938
Sakurai, Akito, 323
Sato, Masa-aki, 1052
Saul, Lawrence, 260, 751
Schöfl, Christof, 931
Schölkopf, Bernhard, 330, 536, 585
Schmidhuber, Juergen, 459
Scholz, Matthias, 536
Schwaber, James S., 975
Schwartz, Odelia, 153
Sejnowski, Terrence J., 118, 508, 730
Shadmehr, Reza, 3
Sharma, Ravi K., 824
Shawe-Taylor, John, 204, 253
Sherrington, D., 211
Simard, Patrice Y., 571
Simoncelli, Eero P., 153
Singer, Yoram, 417, 578
Singh, Satinder, 982, 996, 1066, 1073
Skantzos, N. S., 337
Smola, Alex, 330
Smola, Alex J., 536, 585
Sollich, Peter, 316, 344
Sompolinsky, Haim, 167, 515
Song, Sen, 69
Sontag, Eduardo D., 281
Spence, Clay D., 938
Stemmler, Martin, 160
Stocker, Alan, 706
Streilein, William W., 875
Suematsu, Nobuo, 989, 1059
Sutton, Richard S., 1017, 1066

Tachi, Susumu, 1038
Tanaka, Toshiyuki, 351
Tenenbaum, Joshua B., 59
Terzopoulos, Demetri, 882
Thornber, Karvel K., 831

Tipping, Michael E., 592
Tishby, Naftali, 111, 146
Tong, Hui, 982
Townsend, Jeanne, 118
Trapletti, Adrian, 267
Tresp, Volker, 403, 889
Turner, Kagan, 952

Ueda, Naonori, 599

van Hemmen, J. Leo, 125
Vasconcelos, Nuno, 606
Viola, Paul, 480
Vivarelli, Francesco, 302, 613
von zur Mühlen, Alexander, 931

Wahba, Grace, 620
Wang, DeLiang L., 10
Wang, Raymond J. W., 671
Warmuth, Manfred K., 225, 578
Waskiewicz, James, 657
Webb, Andrew R., 529
Weinshall, Daphna, 45, 424, 838
Werman, Michael, 424
Westerfield, Marissa, 118
Wheeler, Kevin R., 627
Wiegerinck, Wim, 183
Williams, Christopher K. I., 218, 613, 634, 861
Williams, John K., 1073
Williams, Lance R., 831
Williams, Ronald J., 961
Williamson, Matthew M., 945
Williamson, Robert, 330
Winther, Ole, 309
Wolpert, Daniel M., 31
Wolpert, David, 952

Xiang, Dong, 620

Yoon, Hyoungsoo, 167
Yuille, A.L., 641, 761

Zeger, Kenneth, 501
Zemel, Richard S., 174
Zhang, Liqing, 648
Zhou, Ping, 713

Keyword Index

ε-insensitive loss, 330
2D optical flow, 706

A*, 641
absolute shrinkage, 445
acoustic classification, 678
acoustic transients, 678
active noise canceling, 664
actor-critic architecture, 1052
AdaBoost, 564
adaptation, 3
adaptive classification, 671
adaptive partitioning, 961
adaptive search, 1003
additive modeling, 445
admission control, 982
analog computing, 281
analog neuro-chip, 664
analog noise, 281
analog VLSI, 657, 671, 692
analogy, 38
Angiotensin II, 975
annealing, 466
approximate E-step, 403
approximate interpolation, 522
approximation by neural networks, 295
approximation function, 1024
arcing, 564
arithmetic, 17
arm movements, 3, 83
articulated figures, 768
artifact removal, 118
ARTMAP-FD, 875
associative memories, 97
associative multiplication, 17
associative networks, 17
asymmetric networks, 274
asynchronous dynamic programming, 1003
atmospheric fronts, 861
attentional modulation, 789
attractor neural networks, 97
automatic speech recognition, 751
autonavigation, 685
autoregressive neural networks, 267
average margin, 225
average reward, 1073
aVLSI implementation, 706

backpropagation, 882
bandwidth selection, 375
baroreflex, 975
Bayes networks, 183, 260, 361, 775

Bayesian framework, 302, 309
Bayesian inference, 59, 382, 410
Bayesian integration, 924
Bayesian learning, 232, 810, 1059
Bayesian modeling, 723, 910
Bayesian prediction, 417
Bayesian statistics, 246, 861
behavior/gesture recognition, 924
belief networks, 183, 260, 361, 775
belief propagation, 246
benchmarks, 713
Bhattacharyya distance, 896
bias-variance tradeoff, 606, 620
binary correlation matrix memory, 713
bio-control, 975
biometrics, 803
biosequence analysis, 487
blended memories, 24
blind separation of sources, 508, 648, 931
Boltzmann machines, 183, 351
boosting, 253, 288
boundary segmentation, 657
bounding for maximization, 494
Brownian motion, 831

calcium spikes, 931
categorization, 59
cellular neural networks, 657
CEM algorithm, 494
centroid localization, 685
channel noise, 132
character recognition, 847
classification, 309, 438, 564, 838
classifier systems, 989
closure, 831
clustering, 232, 368, 452, 543, 838
coding, 246
cognitive architecture, 38
collective intelligence, 952
combinatorial optimization, 1017
combined classifiers, 288
competition and coexistence, 337
competitive networks, 139
complex cells, 90
complexity analysis, 1003
complexity control, 204
compression, 536, 723
computational complexity, 281
computer graphics, 768, 882
computer vision, 389, 466, 768, 782
computer-aided diagnosis, 938
concept learning, 59
condensing, 838

conjunction search, 796
constrained optimization, 557
constraint solving, 706
constructing macro-actions, 1045
context, 938
continuous state/action spaces, 1052
contrast adaptation, 76
convergence, 522, 968, 1024
convergence rates, 501, 641
convolutions, 571
cooperative activity, 111
coordinate transformation, 1038
coring, 473
correlated noise, 167
correlation-based learning, 125, 139
cortical amplifiers, 90
cortical circuits, 90, 104
cortical maps, 139
cortical modeling, 153
cosine tuning, 83
covariance function, 344
cross-validation, 627
curse of dimensionality, 961

data mining, 543, 592, 896
de-noising, 473, 536, 627
degrees of freedom, 382
dendritic integration, 132
density estimation, 174, 522, 606, 723, 910
dependency tree, 854
desynchronization, 10
deterministic anealing, 606
developmental model, 139
dial-a-ride problem, 1017
differential geometry, 487
differential Sharpe ratio, 917
diffusion, 831
digit recognition, 847
directed graphs, 382
discontinuities, 861
discrete data, 466
discriminative training, 494
distribution function, 522
divergence, 225
dynamic Bayesian networks, 396
dynamic binding, 38
dynamic programming, 1024, 1031
dynamic stability, 274
dynamic trees, 634
dynamical models, 389
dynamical systems, 104, 160, 267, 431, 550, 882

ecological vision, 153
EEG, 118
effective dimensionality, 382
efficient coding, 730
egomotion, 699
eigen-analysis, 613

eigenfaces, 910
eigenvalue decomposition, 344
electrocardiogram, 671
eligibility traces, 1010
EM algorithm, 239, 389, 396, 431, 466, 494, 508, 543, 578, 599, 606, 723, 854, 889, 1052
energy minimization, 706
ensembles, 288
entropy minimization, 723
ERP, 118
error models, 330
event-related potentials, 118
evolutionary game theory, 550
excitatory-inhibitory networks, 274
expectation maximization, 239, 389, 396, 403, 431, 466, 494, 508, 543, 578, 599, 606, 723, 854, 889, 1052
exploration, 1003
extended Kalman smoothing, 403, 431

face orientation, 854
face recognition, 24, 803, 910
facial morphs, 24
factor analysis, 239, 599
familiarity discrimination, 875
fast synaptic depression, 76
fat-shattering dimension, 253
feature extraction, 459, 473, 501, 515, 536, 571
feedback controller learning, 1038
feedforward neural networks, 190, 323, 868
FERET, 803
finance, 410
finite-dimensional approximation, 218
firing rate representation, 160
Fisher information, 167, 232
Fisher scoring, 403
fixed architecture, 868
FMS, 459
focal-plane image processing, 657
focus of expansion, 699
forward models, 3, 31, 882, 1038
fraud detection, 744, 889
fuzzy ARTMAP, 875

gain control, 153
game theory, 961
Gaussian mixtures, 578, 599, 945
Gaussian processes, 218, 302, 309, 344, 487, 515, 613, 861
generalization, 45, 59, 197, 218, 253, 288, 302, 316, 344, 737
generalized EM, 403
generative models, 174, 810
genetic algorithms, 989
Gibbs learning, 232
gradient descent, 968
graph matching, 550, 896

Keyword Index

graph theory, 424
graphical models, 183, 487, 889, 924

Hamilton-Jacobi-Bellman equation, 1024
hard margins, 564
hardware implementation, 664, 713
Hebbian learning, 69, 125
Helmholtz machine, 239
hidden features, 613
hidden Markov models, 723, 737, 744, 751, 889, 924, 945
hierarchical priors, 417
hierarchical representations, 38, 52, 361, 606, 938, 1066
histogram data, 452
HMMs, 723, 737, 744, 751, 889, 924, 945
Hodgkin-Huxley, 160
hormonal stimulus, 931
human learning, 59
human vision, 45
hybrid SIR, 410
hypercolumn, 789

ICA, 118, 361, 459, 473, 508, 648, 931
illusory contour, 831
image coding, 508
image databases, 838, 910
image fusion, 824
image segmentation, 817
image statistics, 153
image transformations, 810
imbalanced datasets, 253
implantable defibrillator, 671
importance sampling, 424
in-plane rotation, 847
in-sample cross validation, 620
incremental algorithms, 295, 875
independent component analysis, 118, 361, 459, 473, 508, 648, 931
independent components, 153, 480
indirect algorithms, 996
infomax, 76
information geometry, 351
information retrieval, 466, 480
information theory, 111, 132
input generalization, 989
inside/outside relations, 10
instruction scheduling, 903
integer programming, 368
integrated processes, 267
interleaving planning and plan-execution, 1003
intracellular calcium, 931
intracortical interaction, 796
invariance, 810
inverse models, 3, 31, 1038
isometric embedding, 438

junction trees, 889

k-means, 838
k-NN pattern classification, 713
Kalman filtering, 410, 431, 648
kd-trees, 543
kernel density estimation, 24
kernel methods, 204, 302, 309, 585
kernel PCA, 536
kernel regression, 445
kernel-adatron, 204
Kullback-Leibler divergence, 183, 351, 620

language recognition, 281
large datasets, 543
large deviation theory, 260
large margins, 564
LASSO, 445
latent-variable models, 515, 529, 592, 723
lateral connections, 139
lazy learning, 375
learning, 389, 501, 723, 782, 1045, 1066
learning curves, 218, 302, 344
learning dynamics, 197, 316, 882
learning macro-actions, 1045
learning real-time heuristic search, 1003
learning windows, 125
LEGION, 10
LIDAR range-finder, 945
Lie groups, 810
lifting, 627
linear cables, 132
linear programming, 585
linear response, 351
local model-selection, 375
local PCA, 824
local regression, 375
local search, 1017
long-term depression, 69
long-term potentiation, 69
low-level vision, 775

macro-actions, 1045, 1066
mammograms, 938
manifold learning, 768
MAP estimation, 723, 896
margins, 253, 288
Markov chain Monte Carlo, 382, 634
Markov chains, 267
Markov decision processes, 996, 1031, 1059, 1066
Markov models, 389
Markov processes on curves, 751
mathematical psychological models, 24
maximum clique, 550
maximum conditional likelihood, 494
maximum entropy learning, 761
maximum likelihood, 104, 494, 508, 592
maximum margin, 557
mean field approximations, 183, 309, 351
medical images, 938

memory, 24
memory-based learning, 375, 952
memoryless policies, 1073
microcalcification, 938
micropower, 671
minimax learning, 761
mistake bound, 225
mixed-mode VLSI, 678
mixture models, 382, 452, 466, 494, 508, 543, 599
mixture of modes, 403
model learning, 1059
model selection, 204, 1059
modularity, 31
Monte Carlo, 410, 1073
motion discrimination, 45
motion estimation, 174, 775
motion perception, 45
motor control, 3, 31
motor cortex, 83
motor learning, 3
multi-criteria, 982
multi-unit recording, 111
multidimensional scaling, 438
multinomial distribution, 417
multiple models, 31
multiplicative update algorithms, 578
multiresolution, 938
mutual information, 160, 232

nearest neighbors, 838, 875
network routing, 952
neural coding, 132
neural development, 160
neural networks, 968
neural population, 167
neuromorphic engineering, 657, 692
neuronal regulation, 97
noise robustness, 281
non-Hebbian learning, 160
non-linear control, 975
non-metric similarity, 838
non-stationarity modelling, 508
nonlinear dynamics, 3
nonlinear PCA, 536
nonlinear state space model, 403
normalization, 153
normalized Gaussian networks, 1052
novelty detection, 875
numerical methods, 557
numerical representation, 17

object manipulation, 31
object recognition, 606, 782
object-based attention, 52
obstacle avoidance, 685
ocular dominance, 139
on-chip learning, 664
on-line algorithms, 225

on-line EM algorithm, 1052
on-line learning, 197, 316, 396, 578
optical flow, 699
optimal control, 1024, 1052, 1073
optimal memoryless policies, 1010
optimization, 288, 641
orientation discrimination, 847, 854
orientation selective circuit, 274
oscillations, 274
oscillatory correlation, 10

pairwise clustering, 424
parameter estimation, 232, 578, 723
parameter priors, 723, 945
part-whole relationships, 52
parti-game, 961
partial observability, 1073
partially observable Markov decision processes,
    968, 989, 1010, 1059, 1073
particle detectors, 868
pattern recognition, 868
pattern vision, 789
PCA, 382, 459, 515, 803, 910
penalized likelihood estimation, 620
perceptual learning, 45
phase diagrams, 337
phase space, 761
physics-based animation, 882
PI control, 975
piecewise-polynomial activation function, 323
planning, 1066
Plefka expansion, 351
Poisson processes, 125
polynomial activation, 190
polynomial approximation, 571
POMDPs, 968, 989, 1010, 1059, 1073
pop-out, 796, 817
population coding, 104, 146, 167, 174
population vector, 83
practical application, 664
pre-attentive segmentation, 796
prediction, 253
primary visual cortex, 76, 90
principal component analysis, 382, 459, 515, 803,
    910
principal curves, 501, 536
prior knowledge, 585
priors selection, 924
probabilistic clustering, 452
probabilistic filtering, 396
probabilistic fusion, 824
probabilistic graphical models, 396
probabilistic inference, 592, 723
probabilistic modeling, 361, 854, 945
projected Bayes regression, 218
proximity data, 438, 452
pseudo-Euclidean space, 438
psychophysics, 789

Keyword Index

Q-learning, 917, 996, 1031
quad-trees, 571
quadratic programming, 550
quality of service, 982
quantization, 571, 713

radar identification, 875
radial basis functions, 431, 529, 768
randomized trace estimates, 620
re-sampling methods, 529
real-time recurrent learning, 917
recurrent neural networks, 76, 90, 104, 211, 337, 706, 882, 952
recursive least-squares, 375
regime-switching model, 889
regression, 302, 330, 494, 585
regular languages, 281
regularity detection, 52
regularization, 459, 585, 737
reinforcement learning, 903, 917, 952, 961, 968, 982, 989, 996, 1003, 1010, 1017, 1024, 1031, 1045, 1052, 1059, 1066
reproducing kernel Hilbert space, 620
revenue maximization, 982
ridge regression, 445
risk-sensitive control, 1031
robot docking, 945
robotic agents, 1010
rollout, 903
rotation invariance, 847
run-length encoding, 571

saliency, 817
sampling methods, 410
SARSA algorithm, 1010, 1045
scale invariance, 831
search asymmetry, 796
selective amplification, 274
self motion, 699
self-organizing networks, 83, 97, 139
semi-Markov decision processes, 1066
semi-supervised learning, 368
semiparametric models, 585
sensitivity analysis, 917
sensor fusion, 824
sensorimotor learning, 1038
sensorimotor mapping, 83
sequence processing, 744
sequence storage, 211
sequential learning, 410
sequential minimal optimization, 557
shape from shading, 775
shape recognition, 896
shift invariance, 730
short-range interactions, 789
short-term memory, 1059
shortest path algorithms, 952
shrinkage, 473

signal detection, 132
signal processing, 146
signal transduction models, 975
similarity, 487
simulated annealing, 634
single-trial ERP, 118
singular points, 699
size-weight illusion, 31
slow synaptic plasticity, 76
SMO, 557
smoothing, 606
soft classification, 620
soft margins, 564
sound localization, 692
sound processing, 692
sparse coding, 459, 473, 730
spatial models, 861
speech processing, 730, 744
speech production, 744
speech recognition, 737, 744
spike coding, 125, 160
spike sorting, 146
spike timing, 69
spiral problem, 10
spline smoothing, 445
split and merge operations, 599
state space approaches, 648
stationarity, 267
statistical image processing, 817
statistical learning theory, 368
statistical mechanics, 183, 309
statistical physics, 246
stimulus representations, 24
stochastic algorithms, 522
stochastic completion field, 831
stochastic policies, 1073
stochastic systems, 281, 396
storage capacity, 211
structural risk minimization, 438
structure discovery, 723
structure formation, 125
subset selection, 445
supervised learning, 494, 838
support vector machines, 204, 253, 330, 368, 438, 487, 536, 557, 564, 585, 803
symmetric networks, 274
synaptic modification, 97
synaptic noise, 132
synaptic plasticity, 69
synaptic pruning, 97
synchrony and asynchrony, 10, 38
synergy, 111
synthetic agents, 924
system identification, 431

TAP approach, 246, 351
task difficulty, 45
telecommunication, 889
telecommunication networks, 982

template correlation, 678
temporal abstraction, 1066
temporal coding, 69
texture, 452, 817
time delays, 10
time series, 267, 396, 431, 723
trading system optimization, 917
tragedy of the commons, 952
transduction, 368
transfer, 45
tree-structured belief network, 634
triangle inequality, 838
TSBN, 634
tuning curves, 167

uncertain position, 938
unequal loss, 253
uniform convergence, 996
unlabeled data, 368, 854
unsupervised classification, 508
unsupervised learning, 52, 232, 459, 466, 515, 723, 810
upper and lower bounds, 295

V1, 796
value functions, 1017
value iteration, 996
Vapnik-Chernovenkis bounds, 190, 204, 323
variability, 69
variable resolution, 961
variational methods, 183, 260, 361, 592
vector quantization, 501, 671
verification, 803
video fusion, 824
vision, 838
vision chips, 685, 699
visual attention, 789, 817
visual correspondence, 768
visual cortex, 831
visual feedback control, 1038
visual perception, 10
visual recognition, 810
visual responses, 90
visual scene analysis, 52, 775
visual search, 641, 796, 817
visual surveillance, 723, 924
visualization, 452, 592

Wake-Sleep algorithm, 239
wavelet regression, 627
wavelets, 473, 627
wind fields, 861
worst-case control, 1031